Laxton's
NRM Building Price Book

2022 edition

Author: V B Johnson LLP

Publishers: Laxton's Publishing Limited

Laxton's NRM Building Price Book – 2022

Published by
Laxton's Publishing Limited
34 Dulverton Drive
Furzton
Milton Keynes
Buckinghamshire MK4 1DF

First published 2021

ISBN... 978-0-9954965-9-0

INTRODUCTION

Laxton's 2022 pricing data is prepared from "first principles" with the results indicating labour allowances and the cost of materials required for each item of work.

Laxton's 2022 has up-to-date prices in an easy to follow and comprehensive format. The main contents page and the index section enable quick identification of specific items. There is also a contents list to the Existing Site/Buildings/Services section to assist those pricing alteration works and an index to Products and Services.

Covid-19 continues to have a significant impact on the construction industry, with supply chains disrupted and a shortage of materials and labour. It is thought Brexit is also responsible for the lack of labour and delays of materials from abroad and it is not known when this will settle. There is no consistency in price changes, with most products increasing, some more than 100%.

Products that are no longer in great demand, or have been replaced by an alternative, are subject to higher prices, for example cast iron and clay pipes. Alternative materials should be considered to offset these increases in cost. Many products come and go each year and Laxton's endeavours to ensure that new products, changes in name and specification are included. However, the range of new products coming to the market is wide and users are welcome to make suggestions for items that they consider should be included.

The information detailed will be of interest, and may be used by, Cost Estimators, Quantity Surveyors, Contractors, Sub-contractors, Self Builders, Architects, Developers, Students, Government and Local and Public Health Authorities as well as anyone interested in the cost of building works.

Users should understand the limitations of any price book or pricing structure and should familiarise themselves with the introductory sections including "How to Use", "Essential Information", "Regional Variations" and the "Preliminaries Section". When pricing major quantities of an item, a firm price should be obtained from a supplier.

The Price Book is structured generally in accordance with the RICS New Rules of Measurement (NRM2: Detailed measurement for building works – first edition). The detailed rates can easily be applied to items measured in accordance with the Standard Method of Measurement of Building Works (SMM7). The New Rules of Measurement (NRM2) are published by the RICS and became operative on 1st January 2013 within the United Kingdom.

The user is urged to read the relevant sections of NRM2 to ensure understanding of the measurement rules, definition rules and coverage rules to be observed. Certain work items are deemed to be included in the measured items (and prices) without mention, and care should be taken to ascertain precisely the extent of these items by reference to the Coverage Rules in NRM2. It is worth noting that the items deemed included vary to SMM7.

Uniclass table J is based on the Common Arrangement and is used for organising information in specifications and bills of quantities and for classifying information on particular types of construction operations and is reflected herein.

The "Build-up" of the "All-in" labour rates has been calculated to include the basic Labour Rates and National Insurance contributions and is illustrated in the Preliminaries/General Conditions pages. All-in labour rates are shown at the head of each page in each of the Work sections. The National Agreed Wage award included in this edition is applicable from 28th June 2021. The plumbing and electrical wage rates included herein come into effect on 3rd January 2022. CIJC announced a pay freeze for June 2020 Wage Award as did JIB for January 2021

Material prices used are those current during September and October 2021.

The internet has made it possible to easily obtain competitive prices and check that quotations received are competitive even where large quantities are required so it is still worthwhile searching the internet for pricing information. The prices used have been obtained from a mixture of online prices, quotations from suppliers and suppliers price lists with an allowance for delivery costs included.

The analysis of materials included has shown that an item may consist of a number of different materials which have different waste factors. The waste % indicated within the book is for the predominant material.

The Basic Prices of Materials sections are linked to the built up prices in the delivered to site column of the priced sections.

The Composite Prices section has prices linked to those included in the detailed priced sections and is useful for those who wish to produce a quick estimate as a guide perhaps for budget purposes. Care must be taken to include items not described.

The Approximate Estimating section has been costed to enable complete buildings to be priced following the format of the Standard Form of Cost Analysis as published by BCIS. The section gives examples of a detailed analysis for a detached house and an office block together with alternative composite prices enabling quick and comprehensive estimates to be produced and amended as detail design continues. Users should note that alternative forms of construction, as well as compliance with the latest Building Regulations and the requirements to achieve reductions in carbon emissions, will need to be incorporated in any cost estimate. This section has been tailored to the needs of the Contractor and Quantity Surveyor for approximate estimating data in detail but in a simpler format than can be obtained from other sources. Descriptions in the approximate estimating section have been abbreviated and care must be taken to understand the extent of works included. Allowances should be added for any changes from the norm.

Regional Variations in construction costs occur and allowances should be made for the location where the works are to be carried out. Not all materials incur regional variations, such as ironmongery, with some resources being subject to greater regional variation than others although differences in delivery costs will need to be considered. Further information is included in the Essential Information chapter. The prices in this book are based on national average prices of 1.00.

The Landfill Tax (Qualifying Material) Order 1996 and 2011 gives a lower rate for inactive (or inert) waste for materials listed (eg rocks or soil) and a standard rate for other waste.
Rates are:-

	Standard Rate	Lower Rate
01.04.12 to 31.03.13 –	£64.00 per tonne	2.50
01.04.13 to 31.03.14 –	£72.00 per tonne	2.50
01.04.14 to 31.03.15 –	£80.00 per tonne	2.50
01.04.15 to 31.03.16 –	£82.60 per tonne	2.60
01.04.16 to 31.03.18 –	£84.40 per tonne	2.65
01.04.18 to 31.03.19 –	£88.95 per tonne	2.80
01.04.19 to 31.03.20 –	£91.35 per tonne	2.90
01.04.20 to 31.03.21 -	£94.15 per tonne	3.00
From 01.04.21 to	£96.70 per tonne	3.10

Users of Laxton's should note that the Landfill Tax has been included within Disposal items with alternatives for Inert, Active and Contaminated materials. In this edition the standard rate of tax included is £96.70 per tonne and lower rate of £3.10.

The Construction (Design and Management) Regulations 2015 must be observed and it is a criminal offence not to observe the regulations. The CDM regulations place specific requirements upon Clients, Principal Designers, Designers, Principal Contractors, Contractors and Workers.

INTRODUCTION

The Aggregates Levy is charged at a single flat rate of £2.00 per tonne and less on smaller amounts. The levy applies to any sand, gravel or crushed rock commercially extracted in the UK or its territorial waters or imported into the UK. The levy will not apply to coal, clay, soil, slate, metals and metal ores, gemstones or semi precious stones, industrial minerals and recycled aggregates.

The London Congestion Charge, Low Emission Zones, other local congestion charges and toll road costs are not included within the rates. Where applicable, due allowances should be made to preliminaries and rates as these costs could be considerable.

For Example: London Low Emission Zone currently charges £300 a day for lorries and heavier vehicles which don't meet Euro IV (typically those registered before 1st October 2006). There are also charges for smaller vehicles with over 1.205 tonnes unladen weight. Further information can be found at www.tfl.gov.uk.

The Company Information Section contains details of internet links to many company and useful websites and will enable the reader to find further information on materials, products and services and where to source, search or obtain further details. Brands and Trade Names are listed with associated suppliers to assist searching for that elusive supplier.

Every endeavour has been made to ensure the accuracy of the information provided but the Author, Publishers or Editors of Laxton's cannot accept liability for any loss occasioned by the use of the information given.

Further information is added to the website on an on-going basis and users may wish to check latest developments on a regular basis.

The contents list and comprehensive index should be used to assist in locating specific items and subjects.

The Editors wish to thank the Professional Bodies, Trade Organisations and firms who have kindly given help and provided information for this edition. For addresses, websites and details see company information section.

ACO Technologies plc
Akzo Nobel Decorative Coatings Ltd
Alumasc Interior Building Products
Ancon Building Products
Angle Ring Co. Ltd
Ariel Plastics
BES Ltd
Birtley Group
Blucher UK Ltd
Boddingtons Ltd
BRC Ltd
Bridgman & Bridgman LLP
Broxap Ltd
British Sisalkraft Ltd
Builder Depot
Building and Engineering Services Association (was HVCA)
C & W Berry Ltd
Cannock Gates Ltd
Carter Concrete Ltd
Celuform Ltd
CECA - Civil Engineering Contractors Association.
Chiltern Timber
Clay Pipe Development Association Ltd
Construction Employers Federation
Drainage Superstore
Durable Ltd
E H Smith (Builders Merchants) Ltd
ECA - Electrical Contractors' Association
Federation of Master Builders
Fixatrad Ltd
Forterra
Fosroc Ltd
Glassolutions
Go Glass
Grass Concrete Ltd
Halfen Ltd
Hanson
Heidelberg Cement Group
Hepworth Building Products Ltd
H.S.S. Hire Shops
Ibstock Brick Ltd
Jackson Fencing Ltd
Jeld-wen UK Ltd
Joint Industry Board for the Electrical Contracting Industry
Keyline Builders Merchants Ltd
Keller
Kee Safety Ltd
Kingston Craftsmen Structural Timber Engineering Ltd
Kirkstone
Lawsons Ltd
London Concrete
Marley Eternit
Marshalls plc
Mastic Asphalt Council Ltd
Milton Precast Ltd.
National Domelight Company
National Federation of Terrazzo, Marble and Mosaic Specialists
Orbital Fasteners
Painting & Decorating Association
Parker Steel
PFC Corofil
Polypipe Terrain Ltd
Promat UK Limited
Rackham Housefloors Ltd
Ramsay & Sons (Forfar) Ltd
R.C. Cutting & Co Ltd t/a Cuttings
Ready Mix Concrete
Rentokil Initial plc
Robbins Timber
Rockwool Ltd
Roof-maker
Roofing Superstore
Royal Institute of British Architects
Royal Institution of Chartered Surveyors
Saint-Gobain Construction Products Ltd t/a British Gypsum
Saint-Gobain Ltd
Screwfix
Sealmaster
Security Direct UK
SIG Roofing Supplies
SL Hardwoods Ltd
SKANSKA UK plc.
Smyth Composites Limited
Speedy Plant Hire Ltd
Stoakes Systems Ltd
Stowell Concrete Ltd
Swann Group Ltd
Swish Building Products Ltd
Syston Rolling Shutters Ltd
T&S Architectural
Tarkett
Tarmac Ltd.
Tata Steel
Thorn Lighting Ltd.
Timloc Building Products
Toolstation
Townscape Products Ltd
Travis Perkins
Tremco Illbruck Ltd
Unite the Union
VB Johnson LLP
Velux Co.Ltd
Wavin Ltd
Zarges (UK) Ltd

and many more

HOW TO USE AND ESSENTIAL INFORMATION

Laxton's NRM Pricing Book is divided into 4 main sections;

SECTIONS

1 **INTRODUCTION AND PRELIMINARIES**

Important information to be used in conjunction with the price book, including How to Use, Allowances to be made for Regional Factors and Tender Values, and Preliminary items.

2 **MEASURED RATES**

Measured rates are given for all descriptions of building work generally in accordance with NRM2 (New Rules of Measurement: Detailed measurement for building works - first edition). A complete breakdown is shown for all measured items, under 10 headings. This approach provides the reader with the price build-up at a glance enabling adjustments to be made easily. Net and gross rates are given for each item.

Details of Basic Prices of Materials, Composite Prices for Approximate Estimating and examples of a cost plan for an Office Development and a Detached House are included.

Prices reflect national average costs and represent target costs that should be achievable on projects in excess of £100,000. Estimators and purchasers should prepare material schedules and obtain quotations as appropriate to check that prices are achieved or improved and relevant adjustments made to the rates.

3 **GENERAL INFORMATION**

A useful reference section covering: Standard Rates of Wages, Builders' and Contractors' Plant, Guide Prices to Building Types, National Working Rule Agreement, Daywork Charges, Construction (Design and Management) Regulations 2015, Fees, Tables and Memoranda and Metric and Imperial Systems.

4 **BRANDS AND TRADE NAMES - COMPANY INFORMATION – PRODUCTS AND SERVICES**

A unique list of Brands and Trade Names, with names and addresses given in the adjacent Company Information Section. Every company listed has been written to and amendments received entered within the database. The majority of the companies now have websites and links to these can be found on our website at **www.laxton-s.co.uk**, which is a useful route should you wish to make frequent searches for company websites. Simply add our website to your list of favourites.

The Product and Services section provides details of manufacturers and suppliers. These lists are useful for locating a particular branded item. There is an index at the end of the section to assist with identification.

RATES GENERALLY

Rates given are within the context of a complete contract of construction where all trades work are involved. When pricing sub-contract work careful consideration must be given to the special circumstances pertaining to the pricing of such work and the very different labour outputs that can be achieved by specialists.

The comprehensive index will take the reader straight to any particular measured item.

Users should understand the limitations of any pricing structure and should familiarise themselves with NRM2 and the information within.

SCHEDULES OF RATES

In the event that Laxton's is to be used as a Schedule of Rates the employer should at tender stage clearly indicate whether rates are to be adjusted for regional factors, tender values and for overheads and profit.

It is suggested that the employer should state that works are to be valued in accordance with Laxton's NRM Price Book 2021 Net Rate column with the addition of a percentage to be stated by the contractor to include for regional factor adjustment, tender value adjustment, overheads, profit and preliminary items not covered elsewhere. A procedure for adjustment of fluctuations should be stated (e.g. by the use of indices) and dates applicable.

Contractors must recognise that the net rates indicated within Laxton's works sections are national average costs. For large or small items of work, works in listed buildings, work of high quality or with difficult access, rates are likely to require adjustment. Minor items of maintenance works may require considerable adjustment.

PRICING AND FORMAT

Materials

The delivered to site price is given together with a percentage allowance for waste on site, where appropriate, the resultant materials cost being shown in the shaded column. The prices used are those included in the Basic Prices of Materials section. Note that where small quantities are required additional delivery charges may be incurred or allowances should be included in preliminaries for collection costs.

Labour

Hours for Craft Operative and Labourer (general building operatives) are given, these being applied to the labour rates shown in the top left-hand shaded panel, the resultant total labour cost being shown in the shaded column.

The "Build-up" of the "All-in" labour rates has been calculated to include the basic labour rates and National Insurance contributions. The national agreed wage award included in Laxton's 2022 was applicable from 28th June 2021. The plumbing and electrical wage rates included are current from 3rdh January 2022. Note: CIJC froze the national wage award rates for 2020 as did JIB for Plumbers and Electricians in 2021

Sundries

These are incidental costs not included in the main materials or labour cost columns.

Mechanical Plant

Items of Mechanical Plant not included in Preliminaries/General conditions have been allowed for in the measured rates all as NRM2.

Plant and Transport costs are indicated separately in the measured rates for items where these are a major factor and material costs are insignificant as in the case of some groundwork items.

Rates

Net rates shown in the shaded column are exclusive of overheads and profit.

Gross rates are inclusive of 10% Main Contractor's overheads and profit. Readers can, of course, adjust the rates for any other percentages that they may wish to apply.

PERCENTAGE ADJUSTMENTS FOR TENDER VALUES

Care must be taken when applying percentage additions and omissions to Laxton's prices and it should be noted that discounts cannot be achieved on some items of work, whilst considerable discounts can be achieved on other items, however as an overall guide to pricing works of lower or larger values and for cost planning or budgetary purposes, the following adjustments may be applied to overall contract values

Contract value

£ 20,000 to £ 50,000 .... add 10.0%
£ 50,000 to £ 100,000 .... add 5.0%
£ 100,000 to £ 500,000 .... rates as shown
£ 500,000 to £ 1,000,000 .... deduct 5.0%
£ 1,000,000 to £10,000,000 .... deduct 10.0%

MINOR WORKS, RENOVATION WORKS AND WORK IN EXISTING UNOCCUPIED PREMISES

The rates may be used for orders of lower value, renovation works and works in existing unoccupied premises however due allowances must be added for disproportionate waste factors, preparation works, difficulty of access and any double handling and additional preliminary items.

WORKING IN OCCUPIED PREMISES

Nearly all work of this nature is more costly in execution in that it has to be organised to suit the specific working conditions due to occupation and allowances should be made for the following:

(a) Reduction in output arising there from.

(b) Moving tradesmen on and off site as the progress of the contract demands.

(c) Suppression of noise and dust.

As a guide, the extra labour involved in carrying out work in occupied premises could add between 50% and 100% to the labour cost of the same work in unoccupied premises.

REGIONAL VARIATIONS

The cost of a building is affected by its location. Many localised variables combine to produce a unique cost, including market factors such as demand and supply of labour and materials, workload, taxation and grants. The physical characteristics of a particular site, its size, accessibility and topography also contribute. Not even identical buildings built at the same time but in different localities will obtain identical tenders.

While all these factors are particular to a time and place, certain areas of the country tend to have different tender levels than others.

Laxton's NRM Building Price Book is based upon national average prices.

The following Location Factors have been extracted from National Statistics for 'Regional factors for the public sector building (non-housing) tender price index' as at 2nd[nd] Quarter 2014.

Great Britain –

North -	0.94
Wales -	0.98
Midlands -	0.94
East -	1.05
South West -	1.04
South East -	1.07
London –	1.09
Scotland -	0.94

The regions chosen are administrative areas and are not significant cost boundaries as far as the building industry is concerned. It should be stressed that even within counties or large conurbations great variations in tender levels are evident and that in many cases these will outweigh the effect of general regional factors.

The Office for National Statistics are no longer producing these regional factor indexes. Construction Output Price Indices have replaced the previous system but at the time of writing these didn't reflect different regions, only general inflation rates.

Further information on the effect of location factors may be derived from the BCIS Tender Price Index.

USE OF FACTORS AND ADJUSTMENTS

Regional factors and tender value adjustments should only be applied to adjust overall pricing or total contract values. They should not be applied to individual rates or trades. Users will need to allow for individual local fluctuations in prices by obtaining quotations from suppliers for specific items.

VALUE ADDED TAX

Prices throughout exclude Value Added Tax.

Note:

Current VAT rate is 20% (since 4th January 2011)

From 1st March 2021, the domestic VAT reverse charge must be used for most supplies of building and construction services.

CONTENTS

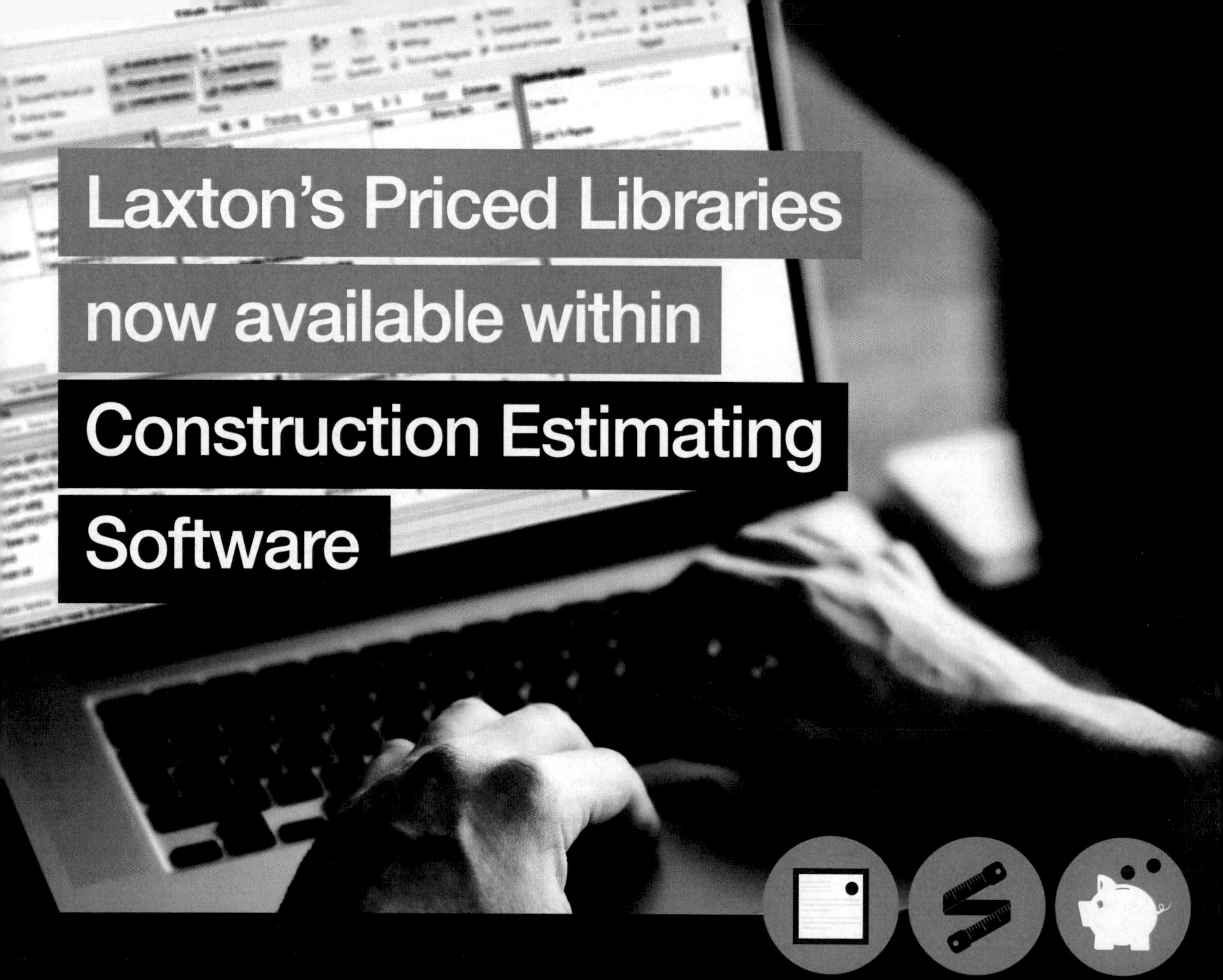

INDEX

C

C (Cont'd)

D

E

F

INDEX

R (Cont'd)

S

GENERALLY

The prices throughout this section offer in a convenient form the means of arriving at approximate rates for the various operations commonly met in connection with normal types of buildings. The basis on which the rates are estimated is given below and should be examined and understood before making any adjustments necessary to adapt the prices to a specific contract or to rates of wages other than those given.

The basic rates of wages used throughout are those which come into force on 28th June 2021. The next pay increase is due in June 2022. Note: From 1st January 2017 Industry Holiday entitlement increased to 30 days (8 bank holidays plus 22 days holiday).

BASIC RATES OF WAGES – BUILDING WORKERS

ALL-IN LABOUR RATES

Effective Dates of rates used:

Wages	June 28th, 2021
National Insurances	April 6th, 2021
Holidays entitlement	January 1st 2017
Workplace Pension	April 6th, 2019

For earlier effective dates of the above see Standard Rates of Wages Section

BUILDING

Calculation of labour rates used throughout the book:-

			Craft Operative £		General Building Operative £
Guaranteed minimum weekly earnings			506.61		381.03
	39 hours at		12.99		9.77
Working hours (includes inclement weather allowance)	2,015 hours at	£12.99	26,174.85	£9.77	19,686.55
Productivity Payments			2,617.49		1,968.66
Non-Productive Overtime	131 hours at	£12.99	1,701.69	£9.77	1,279.87
Sick Pay as WR.20 (3 days unpaid, 3 days paid).			138.38		138.38
Holidays with Pay (Template)	234 hours at	£12.99	3,099.66	£9.77	2,286.18
			33,672.07		25,359.64
National Insurance (Earnings threshold 52 weeks at £169.01)	- 13.8%	of £24,831.55	3,426.75	of £16,519.12	2,279.64
Training (CITB Levy)	0.35%		117.85		88.76
Death benefit	52 weeks at	£1.49	77.48		77.48
Retirement Benefit	3%		1,010.16		760.79
			38,304.31		28,566.31
Severance Pay (Including loss of production during notice period, absenteeism and turnover of labour)	1.5%		574.56		428.49
			38,878.87		28,994.80
Employers Liability and Third Party Insurance	2.5%		971.97		724.87
Trade Supervision	3%		1,166.37		869.84
Cost per annum			41,017.21		30,589.51
Cost per hour	1,965 working hours		£ 20.87		£ 15.57

Calculation of other skill rates as above would be as follows:-

Skilled Operative Rate:-		
	Skill Rate 1.	£19.84
	Skill Rate 2.	£19.09
	Skill Rate 3.	£17.83
	Skill Rate 4.	£16.82

Note: Public Holidays included within Holidays with Pay

Calculation of Hours Worked used above.

Summer: based on average 45 hours per week working			Hours
	40 weeks		1800
Less Holidays:			
Summer	2 weeks		(90)
Other (Five days)	1 week		(45)
	37 weeks	at 45 hours	1665
Less Bank Holidays (Good Friday, Easter Monday, May, Spring and Summer Bank holidays) 5 days at 8 hours.			(40)
			1625

Winter: based on average 43 hours per week working		Hours
	12 weeks	516
Less Holidays: Winter (includes Christmas, Boxing and New Years days)	2 weeks	(86)
	10 weeks at 43 hours	430
Less Sick leave	5 days at 8 hours	(40)
		390
Add Summer Hours		1625
Total Hours		2015
(Less Inclement Weather time)		50
Total Actual Hours Worked		**1965**

BASIC RATES OF WAGES (Cont'd)

Calculation of Non-Productive Overtime hours included above

Based on a 45 hour working week in Summer and a 43 hour working week in Winter, the calculation is as follows:-

				Hours
Summer	6 hours overtime per week at time and a half	=	3 hours x 37 weeks	111
Winter	4 hours overtime per week at time and a half	=	2 hours x 10 weeks	20
	Non-Productive hours per annum			131

Holidays with Pay as per W.R. 18

Bank Holidays	63 hours	(8 days)
Winter, Spring, and Summer Holidays	171 hours	(22 days)
	234 hours	(30 days)

Note The rule changed in January 2017 to become:-
The holiday year runs from the 1st January for each year with an annual (52 weeks) entitlement of 22 days of Industry plus 8 days of Public/Bank holidays. The above calculations reflect this.

PLUMBING

The rates of wages used in the Plumbing and Mechanical Engineering Installations Section are those approved by The Joint Industry Board for Plumbing and Mechanical Engineering Services in England and Wales.

The All-in Labour rate calculations are as follows:

Effective dates of rates used:

Wages..	January 3rd 2022
National Insurance..............................	April 6th 2021
Holiday and Welfare contributions..........	January 1st 2019

			Trained Plumber £		Advanced Plumber £		Technical Plumber £
45.6 weeks at 37.5 hours	1710 hours	at £13.96	23,871.60	at £16.26	27,804.60	at £18.06	30,882.60
Welding Supplement (Gas or Arc)	1710 hours		-	at £0.36	615.60	at £0.36	615.60
Travel time			-		-		-
			23,871.60		28,420.20		31,498.20
Allowance for Incentive Pay	15%		3,580.74		4,263.03		4,724.73
		(a)	27,452.34		32,683.23		36,222.93
Holiday Pay	240 hours	at £13.96	3,350.40	at £16.29	3,988.80	at £18.06	4,420.80
Welfare Benefit Credits	64 No	at £2.60	171.60	at £3.15	207.90	at £3.55	234.30
			30,974.34		36,879.93		40,878.03
National Insurance	13.8% of	22,133.82	3,054.47	28,039.41	3,869.44	32,037.51	4,421.18
(Earnings Threshold 52 weeks at £169.01 = £8,788.52)							
less rebate on earnings LEL to UEL	3.50% of	22,133.82	- 774.68	28,039.41	- 981.38	32,037.51	-1,121.31
Pension Contribution	7.50% of (a)		2,058.93		2,451.24		2,716.72
			35,313.06		42,219.23		46,894.62
Redundancy Payments	1.5%		529.70		633.29		703.42
Employer's Liability Insurance	2.5%		882.83		1,055.48		1,172.37
Fares	say 4720 miles @ 45p a mile		2,124.00		2,124.00		2,124.00
Cost per annum			38,849.57		46,032.00		50,894.41
Cost per hour	1710 hours		22.72		26.92		29.76
Inclement Weather time	1%		0.23		0.27		0.30
			£ 22.95		£ 27.19		£ 30.06

The Plumber's all-in wage rate used throughout the book is an average of 1 Trained, 3 Advanced and 1 Technical Plumbers rates giving an average rate of **£ 26.91** per hour.

Note : 1. Travel time – Discontinued for distances up to 20 miles
2. Tool Allowance – Discontinued

BASIC RATES OF WAGES (Cont'd)

ELECTRICAL

The rates of wages used in the Electrical Engineering Installation Section are those approved by the Joint Industry Board for the Electrical Contracting Industry. www.jib.org.uk

The All-in Labour rate calculations using Job reporting operatives with own transport is as follows:

Effective dates of rates used:

Wages.. January 3rd 2022
National Insurance..................... April 6th 2021

Job reporting; own transport	days	wks	hrs	Approved Electrician + 50p rate		Approved Electrician rate		Electrician rate		Electrical / Site Technician rate	
HOURS WORKED (LESS 1 WK SICK)		44	45	18.20	36,036.00	17.70	35,046.00	16.32	32,313.60	19.94	39,481.20
SICK PAY	2			136.50	273.00	132.75	265.50	122.40	244.80	145.88	299.10
NPOT		44	3.75	18.20	3,003.00	17.70	2,920.50	16.32	2,692.80	19.94	3,290.10
INCENTIVE PAYMENT	15%				5,405.40		5,256.90		4,847.04		5,922.18
TRAVEL TIME– up to 15 miles - Nil					0.00		0.00		0.00		0.00
BANK HOLIDAYS	8		7.5	18.20	1,092.00	17.70	1,062.00	16.32	979.20	19.94	1,196.40
HOLIDAYS	24		7.5	18.20	3,276.00	17.70	3,186.00	16.32	2,937.60	19.94	3,589.20
	sub total A				49,085.40		47,736.90		44,015.04		53,778.18
PENSION CONTRIBUTION		52		57.65	2,997.80	57.65	2,997.80	53.90	2,802.80	63.52	3,303.04
					52,083.20		50,734.70		46,817.84		57,081.22
NATIONAL INS				13.80%	7,187.48	13.80%	7,001.39	13.80%	6,460.86	13.80%	7,877.21
(Lower earnings allowance)		52		£170.01	-1,219.99	£170.01	-1,219.99	£170.01	-1,219.99	£170.01	-1,219.99
	sub total B				58,050.69		56,516.10		52,058.71		63,738.44
TRAINING	2.5% of A			2.50%	1,227.14	2.50%	1,193.42	2.50%	1,110.38	2.50%	1,344.45
TRAVEL ALLOWANCE– up to 15 miles - Nil					0.00		0.00		0.00		0.00
			sub total		59,277.83		57,709.52		53,159.09		65,082.89
SEVERANCE PAY	2%			2.00%	1,185.56	2.00%	1,154.19	2.00%	1,063.18	2.00%	1,301.66
			sub total		60,463.39		58,863.71		54,222.27		66,384.55
EMP. LIAB & 3rd PARTY				2.50%	1,511.58	2.50%	1,471.59	2.50%	1,355.56	2.50%	1,659.61
COST PER YEAR					61,974.97		60,335.30		55,577.83		68,044.16

GANG RATE						INDIVIDUAL RATES
TECH.	68,044.16	x	1	NON PRODUCTIVE	68,044.16	**£ 34.37**
APPROVED ELEC. +	61,974.97	x	1	100% PRODUCTIVE	61,974.97	**£ 31.30**
APPROVED ELEC.	60,335.30	x	2	100% PRODUCTIVE	120,670.60	**£ 30.47**
ELEC.	55,577.83	x	4	100% PRODUCTIVE	222,311.32	**£ 28.07**
					461,976.93	
AVERAGE MAN HOURS	44	x	45 =	1980 hrs		
AVERAGE COST PER MAN		7	Men working	**£ 34.13** Per hour		

Note:

Based on National JIB rates

a Basic week= 37.5hrs
b Hours to be worked before overtime paid= 37.5 hrs
c The above JIB hourly rates are from the 03/01/2022.
d Hours remain at 45 as this seems to be the minimum paid in the industry at this time

The Electricians all in wage rate used throughout the book is an average of 1 Approved Electrician plus, 2 Approved Electricians and 4 Electricians giving an average rate of **£ 34.13** per hour.

BASIC RATES OF WAGES (Cont'd)
ELECTRICAL (Cont'd)

JIB Categories for Operatives Hourly Pay

All-in wage costs

1. **Shop Employed Operative**
   - payable to an operative who is required to start and finish at the shop:

-	Technician	£ 30.69
-	Approved Electrician Plus	£ 27.69
-	Approved Electrician	£ 26.86
-	Electrician	£ 24.46

- Average Cost per Man - £ 30.00
(as above with Technician Non-Productive)

2. **Job Employed Operative (transport provided)**
   - payable to an operative who is required to start and finish at normal starting and finishing times on jobs, travelling in their own time in transport provided by the employer. The operative shall also be entitled to payment for travel time, where eligible as detailed in the appropriate scale:

-	Technician	£ 32.71
-	Approved Electrician Plus	£ 29.74
-	Approved Electrician	£ 28.92
-	Electrician	£ 26.45

- Average Cost per Man - £ 32.30
(as above with Technician Non-Productive)

3. **Job Employed Operative - (own transport)**
   as used in the example on previous page
   - payable to an operative who is required to start and finish at normal starting and finishing times on jobs, travelling in their own time by their own means; the operative shall be entitled to payment for travel time and travel allowance where eligible, as detailed in the appropriate scale.

Note: For basic London rates within the M25 see the Wages section at the rear of this book.

SITE PRELIMINARIES

GENERAL NOTES

The calculation of the costs to be included for Site Preliminaries requires careful consideration of the specific conditions relating to the particular project. No pre-conceived percentage addition can be adopted with any degree of accuracy. The cost of Site Preliminaries is dependent on the type of contract under consideration, its value, its planned programme time, its location and also on the anticipated requirements for the administration and management of the actual site. Alteration works may require consideration of special supervision, whether water and power are available locally, additional allowances for transport and time required to obtain and dispose of small quantities, any requirements relating to working in occupied premises, are the measured rates adequate for the project under consideration.

Two factors which must be established prior to commencement of the detailed calculations are (i) the value of the main contractor's work (from which is derived the value of the contractor's labour force) and (ii) the programme time for completion of the Works. If the latter is not stated in the contract conditions, it must be decided by the contractor. If it is stated in the contract conditions, it must be checked and confirmed by the contractor as being reasonable.

All figures quoted are exclusive of VAT and due allowances should be made and identified on all quotations as appropriate

NOTES ON SITE PRELIMINARIES

Section 1.1 – Employers requirements

Section 1.1.1 - Site accommodation

Site accommodation for the employer and the employer's representatives where separate from main contractor's site accommodation such as may be required for the Architect, Clerk of Works or Resident Engineer.

Attendance on site

Provision of chainmen and any special attendance required by the Clerk of Works or employer's representatives.

Section 1.1.2 - Site records

Operation and maintenance manuals and compilation of health and safety file

Section 1.1.2 - Completion and post-completion requirements

Handover requirements, to include training of building user's staff, provision of spare parts tools and portable indicating instruments, operation and maintenance of building engineering services installations, mechanical plant and equipment and the like and landscape management services

Section 1.2 - Main Contractor's cost items

Section 1.2.1 - Management and Staff

Project-specific management and staff

The numbers, types and grades of Site Staff to be included are matters for judgement by the Contractor.

A selection from the following list will provide the range of staff required to administer a normal building project:

Project manager/director	Supervisor
Contracts Administrator	Planner
Construction manager/Site Agent	General Foreman
Engineer	Administrator/Receptionist
Storeman	Cashier/Wages Clerk
Materials Purchasing Clerk	Plant Clerk
Quantity Surveyor	Resources Manager
Productivity Controller	Health and Safety Officer
Plant Fitter	Administrative Manager

Allowance for Trades Supervision has been made in the Gross Wage build up.

On small contracts, individual staff members may combine the duties of several of the foregoing grades. On larger contracts more than one member may be required for certain duties. For example, two or more Engineers may be required in the initial stages for setting out the Works and for checking the frame construction.

Part 4 of CDM 2015 contains the duties to control specific worksite health and safety risks and is equivalent to the duties contained in the old Construction (Health, Safety and Welfare) Regulations 1996. The regulations apply to the health, safety and welfare of workers on construction sites - the associated costs of which are not specifically identified in this section and acquaintance with these regulations is necessary.

Visiting management and staff

As noted above staff to be included is a matter of judgement.

Extraordinary support costs

Legal advice, recruitment, team building, associated transport and other extraordinary support costs.

Special Conditions of Contract

These can refer to any particular point required by the Employer, and a careful perusal of the Conditions and the Preambles to the Bills of Quantities or Specification is necessary to ensure that no requirement is overlooked. Typical items are: the suppression of noisy mechanical equipment; regulations dealing with the restricted use of tower cranes; or limitations to ground disturbance during piling operations

Travelling Time and Fares

Payments for travelling time and fares can be a major expense and since all contracts, and particularly the JCT Conditions of Contract, place on the Contractor the onus of including in the tender sum the cost of importing labour, investigation should be made into the prevailing conditions regarding the availability of local labour. When all enquiries have been made, the calculations of anticipated expenditure must be based on the Contractor's judgement of the labour position. Rates of payment for travelling time and fares are laid down in the relevant national and local Working Rule Agreements.

Defects

Allowance for the cost of labour and materials in rectifying minor defects prior to handover of the Works and during the Defects Liability Period.

Section 1.2.2 – Site establishment

Site accommodation

The size of the office required to accommodate the contractor's site staff will depend on the number of staff envisaged. An allowance of $10m^2$ per staff member plus 25% for circulation space and toilets is normal.

The overall cost will vary according to the contract period if the hutting is to be hired. Otherwise a use and waste allowance can be made if the hutting is supplied from the contractors own resources. The cost should include for erection, maintenance, adaptations/alterations during the works and eventual dismantling and, in the case of contracts extending over several years, for labour and materials in repairs and redecoration.

In works of renovation and rehabilitation, office accommodation and space for storage of materials is often available in the existing premises. Otherwise a simple lock up hut is all that is normally required for small works contracts.

Accommodation priced in this Section could include offices, stores, welfare facilities, site toilets, canteen, drying rooms and sanitary facilities, first aid cabin, plant fitters sheds, reinforcement bending sheds, etc.

Consideration should also be given to any off-site rented temporary accommodation, maintenance and associated costs.

Storage of Materials

Consideration should be given to the provision of the following items:

Cement storage shed.
Aggregate storage bins.
Use and waste of tarpaulins and plastic sheeting.
Lockups and toolboxes for tradesmen's tools.

Temporary works in connection with site establishment

Allowance should be made for foundations to site accommodation, temporary drainage, temporary services, intruder alarms, heating, lighting, furniture, equipment and any attendance required.

NOTES ON SITE PRELIMINARIES (Cont'd)
Section 1.2 - Main Contractor's cost items (Cont'd)
Section 1.2.2 – Site establishment (Cont'd)

Temporary Roads

This section includes providing access to the site for heavy excavating equipment and for site roads and hard-standings constructed in ash, hardcore or timber sleepers. Allowance should be made for drainage, maintenance over the contract period and for eventual breaking up and removal. Crossovers, planked footways and any automatic stop/go lights required should be included. If the base courses of permanent roads can be utilised as temporary roads, an allowance should be made for making good the base prior to final surfacing.

Allow also for any cleaning and maintenance which may be required on public or private roads, especially if surplus excavated material has to be carted off site.

Furniture and equipment

General office furniture, including canteen equipment, floor coverings, maintenance and removal.

IT systems

Computer hardware, software and consumables. Line rental, website and internet services, support and maintenance.

Consumables and services

Office consumables including stationery, postage, tea, coffee, water bottles and the like.

Brought-in services

Catering, maintenance, printing, off-site parking etc.

Sundries

Signboards and notices

General Attendance on Nominated Subcontractors

General Attendance on Nominated Subcontractors by the Main Contractor is deemed to include: the use of the Contractor's temporary roads, pavings and paths; standing scaffolding not required to be altered or retained; standing power-operated hoisting plant; the provision of temporary lighting and water supplies; clearing away rubbish; provision of space for the subcontractor's own offices; the storage of his plant and materials; and the use of mess-rooms, sanitary accommodation and welfare facilities provided by the Contractor for his own use.

The estimated cost of such attendance is generally added by the Contractor in the Bills of Quantities as a percentage of the Prime Cost Sum shown for each Nominated Subcontractor.

Alternatively it can be included as a lump sum according to the Contractor's experience and judgement. The actual percentage can vary from as little as 0.1%, up to 2.5% or more, depending on the anticipated or known requirements of the Nominated Subcontractor.

Section 1.2.3 – Temporary services

Water Company charges

Charges made by various Water Companies for the provision of water and drainage differ considerably throughout the country and the actual rate to be paid should be ascertained regionally. Some water companies meter the water required for building purposes. Charges to be considered include:

Infrastructure charges

Water	£342.00
Waste-water	£573.00

Water connection charges

Boundary Box	£502.00
Temporary Building Supply	£964.00

Off site connections

Single/double connection charge up to 5 metres	£1,044.00
Single/double connection charge over 5 metres	£1,300.00
4 port manifold connection (up to 5m)	£2,556.00
6 port manifold connection charge (over 5m)	£3,941.00

Additional charges for excavation – per linear metre

Part made roads and footpaths	£123.19
Highway/carriage	£140.51
Verge, unmade and open ground	£67.94
Use duct supplied by developer or lay additional pipes in same trench	£33.60

Design deposit

1 to 100 properties	£1,654.80
101 to 200 properties	£1,893.60
Additional site visit	£286.80

Additional Costs

To all above fees, additional costs must be added including the cost of all temporary plumbing required on the site such as trenching and builder's work in connection, distribution piping, standpipes, hoses and tanks, alterations, repairs and removals.

Any reinstatement costs would also need to be added.

Volume Charges per cubic metre (average rate)

Water Supply	£1.60
Wastewater Services	£1.57

Drainage charges

Fees for new sewer connection – vetting and administration: -

Direct Connection -- public sewer via lateral drain	£328.00
Indirect connection to public sewer	£116.00
Adoption of a lateral drain	£289.00
Building near to public sewer	£414.00 per agreement
Highway drainage connection by Highway Authority	£390.00 per street

Note: New Build Standards and Mandatory Adoption

Section 42 of the Flood and Water Management Act 2010 introduced mandatory adoption and new build standards for new sewers and lateral drains. Upon implementation of Section 42, it will not be possible to apply for a sewer connection unless there is an adoption agreement in place for all of the new sewers and lateral drains on the site.

Temporary gas supply

Include for connection, distribution, charges and bottled gas.

Temporary electricity supply

Lighting

This item provides for any lighting required inside the buildings during construction or for external floodlighting installed during the winter months to maintain progress. To the cost of wiring, lights and other equipment, should be added the charge for electricity and electrician's time for the installation and removal of the system.

On small works contracts the contractor, by agreement with the client, may be permitted to use existing services. A nominal amount should be included for the use of electricity and any temporary lighting required.

Temporary telecommunication systems

This item provides for line connections and rental, equipment, maintenance and support.

NOTES ON SITE PRELIMINARIES (Cont'd)
Section 1.2 - Main Contractor's cost items (Cont'd)
Section 1.2.3 – Temporary services (Cont'd)

Temporary drainage

Pumping of ground water - Provision for the pumping of ground water (as opposed to water from normal rainfall) is entirely dependent upon the conditions applying to the particular site in question. Under the JCT Standard Form of Contract this is usually covered by a Provisional or Prime Cost Sum, but in contracts where the onus is placed on the contractor it is important that a visit to the site of the proposed works, should be paid during the tendering period, to ascertain as far as possible the nature of the ground and the likelihood of encountering water. Internet research should also be carried out of historical flooding. When, as a result of investigations, it is decided that pumping will be necessary, say during excavation of foundations and until the foundation walls have reached a certain height, the calculations will be based upon the length of time it is thought necessary to keep pumps working.

A typical build-up of cost is as follows:

Assuming one 75mm pump will be kept running continuously for six weeks and for three weeks a second 75mm pump will be required during working hours with a standby pump of 50mm diameter available for emergencies:

(a)	Hire of 75mm pump & hose 6 weeks at £192.00	1,15.00
	Operator's time attending, fuelling, etc. –	
	28 hours at £16.82 per hour = £470.96 x 6 weeks....	2,825.76
	Hire of extra hose 6 weeks at £22.00	132.00
(b)	Hire of 75mm pump & hose 3 weeks at £192.00	576.00
	Operator's time attending, fuelling, etc. –	
	12 hours at £16.82 per hour = £201.84 x 3 weeks....	606.52
	Hire of extra hose 3 weeks at £22.00	66.00
(c)	Standby pump 6 weeks at £125.00	750.00
	Total cost of pumping	£6,107.28

Section 1.2.4 - Security

Security of Site - Allow for the provision of a watchman if required, or for periodic visits by a security organisation; electronic surveillance, and protection of scaffolds, security equipment, hoardings, fences and gates. Some allowance may also be required in particular localities for loss of materials due to theft.

Section 1.2.5 – Safety and environmental protection

Safety programme

Personal protective equipment (PPE), including for employer and consultants

Protective helmets, boots, goggles and protective clothing for operatives; wet weather clothing, drying sheds; provision of site toilets and items of a similar nature.

The requirement to provide welfare facilities on construction sites is defined in the Construction (Design and Management) Regulations 2015 and applies to the health, safety and welfare of workers on construction sites – See Section 1.2.2 above.

Barriers and safety scaffolding

Guard rails, barriers, debris netting etc (see also section 1.2.8 scaffolding)

Environmental protection measures

Control of pollution and noise, management and reporting

Other safety measures

Provision for winter working.

This can range from heating aggregates in the stockpiles to the provision of polythene sheeting to protect the operatives and/or the Works during construction

Section 1.2.6 – Control and protection

Surveys, inspections and monitoring

Setting out

Setting out equipment including the use of theodolites, levels or other items and provision of pegs, paint, etc.

Protection of Works

The protection of completed work during the contract period is usually priced in the relevant bill rates. Types of work requiring special protection include expensive stonework or precast concrete features, stair treads, floor finishes, wall linings, high class joinery and glazing to windows. Glass breakage during unloading or after fixing should be included.

Samples

Sample panels.

Environmental control of building

Dry out building

Allowance should be made in this Section for drying out the building by the use of blow heaters or, if permitted, by the provision of fuel to the heating system as installed.

Section 1.2.7 - Mechanical Plant

This section comprises the cost of all mechanical plant which has not been priced in the Bills of Quantities. It includes site transport, Tower Cranes, Mobile Cranes, Goods and Passenger hoists, pumping plant for dewatering, small plan and tools.

The apportioning of the cost of tower cranes and hoists to separate items of the Bills of Quantities is made difficult and unreliable by the fact that very often they deal with various materials in differing trades. As such, the correct time allocation to the individual trades is virtually impossible. Moreover, although not always working to capacity, they cannot be removed from site entirely and a certain proportion of their time is wasted in standing idle. It is therefore normal practice to view the contract as a whole, decide the overall period for which the particular tower crane or hoist will be required, and include the whole cost in the Preliminaries.

Site Transport

Include for all requisite site transport not priced in the rates, such as site lorries, dumpers, vans, forklift trucks, tractors and trailers. The cost of transporting mechanical plant, scaffolding and temporary accommodation, is also included in this section. The cost of double handling materials during unloading may also be considered for inclusion in this section.

Tower Cranes

There is a large variety of cranes available in the market and the most suitable crane for each particular contract must be selected. The transport of the crane from the plant yard to the site can be a costly item, and the installation of track, the erection, testing and final dismantling of the crane can, on occasion, constitute a greater expenditure than the hire charge for the crane.

Mobile Tower Crane - A typical build up of cost of mobile tower crane is as follows:

Installation			£
	Prepare ground and lay crane track		6,300
	Supply of track materials...		3,600
	Transport erect & dismantle....................................		17,800
			27,700
Running Costs per week		£	
	Crane hire & driver	2,700	
	Running costs, electricity	200	
	Banksman..	675	
		3,575	
	x 30 weeks		107,250
			£134,950

Static Tower Crane - A typical build up of cost of small static tower crane is as follows:

Installation			£
	Transport, erect & dismantle....................................		12,100
	Expendable base and foundation............................		15,400
			27,500
Running Costs per week		£	
	Crane hire & driver......................................	2,700	
	Running costs, electricity	80	
	Banksman..	675	
		3,455	
	x 17 weeks		58,735
			£86,235

PRELIMINARIES

NOTES ON SITE PRELIMINARIES (Cont'd)
Section 1.2 - Main Contractor's cost items (Cont'd)
Section 1.2.7 - Mechanical Plant (Cont'd)

Mobile Cranes

A mobile crane may be required during the frame construction for lifting heavy items such as precast concrete floors or cladding units. The weekly hire rates will vary according to the lifting capacity of the crane required but a typical build up of cost is as follows:

	£
Crane hire & driver	2,100
Banksman	675
	2,775
x 4 weeks	11,100
Transporting to and from site	525
	£11,625

Hoists

Provision of hoist, base, erection, testing, operator, maintenance and removal

Access plant

Fork lifts, scissor lifts, platforms etc

Concrete Plant

Mixers, batching etc

Other plant

Small plant and tools

Small plant and tools comprise ladders, wheelbarrows, trestles, picks, shovels, spades, sledgehammers, cold chisels and similar items. The cost of these minor items is usually allowed for by an addition to the overall cost of labour of between 1% and 2%.

Section 1.2.8 – Temporary works

Access scaffolding

The cost of scaffolding varies not only with the superficial area of the structure but also with the length of time the scaffolding is required to stand and the nature of the building. When calculating the cost, the girth of the building should be multiplied by the height and the area priced at the appropriate rate as shown below, to which should be added the additional charge for standing time exceeding the basic 12 weeks as shown. Provision must also be made for any internal scaffolding required to lift and stair wells and for fixing suspended ceilings. Debris netting along with boards and ladder access are included with the rates.

Erected

Scaffolding for brickwork		Putlog	Independent
		£	£
Average 6m high	m²	10.20	15.90
Average 12m high	m²	11.50	16.70
Average 18m high	m²	12.60	20.50
Add for each additional week	m²	0.85	0.95

Hire Charges

Mobile towers for one week

Height	2.20m	4.20m	6.20m	8.20m
	£	£	£	£
	91.00	172.00	254.00	334.00

Support Scaffolding

Hire Charges

		£
Scaffolding for suspended ceilings for one week	m²	9.90
Lift shaft tower to 20m high for one week	item	680.00

Hoardings, fans and fencing

The nature of these items is completely dependent upon the site, type of contract, and the frontage of the building area on the public highway and therefore it is difficult to offer any general method of calculating the anticipated cost. Consideration must be given to the means of stabilizing hoardings on sites where basements or other deep excavations come right up to the line of the hoarding, and gates must be sited to give easy access from the road. Gantries may require artificial lighting throughout their length in certain conditions, particularly in narrow streets in city centres. Any police requirements for offloading materials must be ascertained. Allowance must also be made for giving notices and paying any licence fees required by Local Authorities.

Hire Charges

	£
Mesh fence 2m high per week – minimum 13 weeks	3.00 per m

Section 1.2.9 – Site records

Photography, works records, manuals, as built drawings, CDM and Health and Safety File

Section 1.2.10 – Completion and post-completion requirements

Testing, commissioning, handover and post completion services

Section 1.2.11 – Cleaning

Site tidy

Includes for keeping the site tidy throughout the construction period, clearing out after subcontract trades and the final cleaning up on completion of the Works prior to handover.

Rubbish disposal

Waste management including removal of rubbish during construction and clearing out after subcontract trades. Consideration should be given to recycling / sorting facilities.

Maintenance of roads, paths and pavings

Maintenance of public, private and temporary roads, paths and pavings.

Building clean

Final builder's clean

Section 1.2.12 – Fees and charges

Rates and Taxes on temporary buildings. The charges made by the Local Authority for rates on site accommodation should be ascertained locally.

Section 1.2.13 – Site services

Temporary non specific works

Section 1.2.14 – Insurance, bonds, guarantees and warranties

Works Insurance

The Contract Bills of Quantities will normally state whether Fire Insurance is the responsibility of the Contractor or of the Employer. Rates of insurance vary according to the nature of the work but are usually in the range £0.10% to £0.30% of the total value to be insured.

The total insurable value should include for full reinstatement of any damage caused, all cost escalation, any demolition of damaged work required and an appropriate percentage addition for professional fees.

Note: allowance should be made for Terrorism insurance if required.

Bonds

Sureties or bonds. The cost of any surety or performance bond for due completion of the Works required by the Contract Documents. Rates for this vary depending on the financial status of the Contractor.

SPECIMEN SITE PRELIMINARIES

The examples of the build up of Site Preliminaries which follow are based on alternative building contract values of £100,000 and £1,500,000 (excluding Preliminaries) made up as follows:

	£250,000 project	£1,500,000 project
	Minor Works	Major Works
	£	£
Specialist Subcontractors	-	300,000
Named/Specialist Suppliers	-	100,000
Provisional Sums	30,000	100,000
Main Contractors Labour	60,000	300,000
Main Contractors Materials	80,000	300,000
Subcontractors	80,000	400,000
	£250,000	£1,500,000

The Contract Periods have been programmed as 20 weeks (Minor Works) and 40 weeks (Major Works).

Section 1.1 – Employers requirements

Attendance on site

	Minor Works	Major Works
Chainman attending Engineer	-	500
Carried to Summary		£ 500

Section 1.2 - Main Contractor's cost items

Section 1.2.1 - Management and Staff

	Minor Works			Major Works		
	Per Week £	No. of Weeks	£	Per Week £	No. of Weeks	£
Project Manager/Site Agent	-	-	-	1330	24	31,920
General Foreman	1070 x 40%	20	8,560	1070	20	21,400
Site Engineer	-	-	-	1175	4	4,700
Wages Clerk/Productivity Controller	-	-	-	660	20	13,200
Secretary/Telephonist	-	-	-	530	20	10,600
		£	8,560		£	81,820

Travelling Time and Fares

		Minor Works		Major Works	
Main Contractor's Labour	300,000				
Labour in Preliminaries	40,000				
	£340,000				
Average £500 per week = 680 man/weeks in contract.					
680 man/weeks x 50% of men local		-		-	
x 20% of men receive £15.00 per week		-		2,040	
x 20% of men receive £20.00 per week		-		2,720	
x 10% of men receive £25.00 per week		-		1,700	
Travelling time and fares:					
Allow 40 man weeks at average £25.00 per week		1,000	1,000	-	6,460

Defects

	Minor Works		Major Works	
Defects Liability period:				
Allow 2 tradesmen and 2 labourers for 1 week	-		2,800	
Materials	-		1,000	
Handover and defects liability:				
Labour	570		-	
Materials	200	770	-	3,800
Carried to Summary		£10,330		£92,080

Section 1.2.2 - Site Accommodation

	Minor Works		Major Works	
	£	£	£	£
Contractors Office: 50m² at £45.00 per m²		-		2,250
Office furniture and equipment		300		475
Clerk of Works Office: 15m² at £45.00 per m²		-		675
Stores: 30m² at £25.00 per m²		-		750
Canteen/Drying Room: 50m² at £45.00 per m²		-		2,250
Canteen equipment		-		440
Cabins or site huts		-		300
Lockups and toolboxes		-		140
Office: Use of existing accommodation. Allow for making good on completion		180		-
Stores: Use existing. Allow for shelving and lockups for materials storage		250		-
Contractors signboards		-		275
Labour attendance in offices		-		1,200

Temporary Roads and Hardstandings

	Minor Works		Major Works	
Temporary Roads and Hardstandings:				
Hardcore road: 100 m² at £13.00 per m²	-		1,350	
Hardstandings: 100 m² at £13.00 per m²	-		1,350	
Temporary Roads - allow for access to site	540	540	-	2,700
Carried to Summary		£ 1,270		£11,455

SPECIMEN SITE PRELIMINARIES (Cont'd)

Section 1.2.3 – Temporary services

	Minor Works £	£	Major Works £	£
Water				
Site Water connection	220		965	
Water Company charges	250		2,700	
Service piping: 100m at £6.00 per m	-		650	
Stand pipes: £30 a week	-		1,280	
Hoses tanks and sundry materials	120	590	250	5,845
Power and Lighting				
Connection to mains	-		600	
Distribution unit, cables, floodlights, lamps, plugs and sundry materials	-		1,600	
Electrician in attendance	-		1,680	
Cost of electricity: 40 weeks at £28 per week	-		1,120	
Heating and lighting offices: 40 weeks at £25.00 per week	-		1,000	
Power and lighting: 20 weeks at £24.00 per week	480	480	-	6,000
Telephone and Administration				
Installation	-		240	
Rental	-		360	
Calls: 40 weeks at £25 per week	-		1,000	
Telephones: 20 weeks at £22.00 per week	440	440	-	1,600
Carried to Summary		£1,510		£13,445

Section 1.2.4 – Security

	Minor Works £	£	Major Works £	£
Weekend site supervision: 40 weeks at average £52 per week	-		2,080	
Security: allow for loss of materials	400	400	-	2,080
Carried to Summary		£ 400		£2,080

Section 1.2.5 - Safety and environmental protection

	Minor Works £	£	Major Works £	£
Site Latrines: 2 no. at £750.00	-		1,500	
Latrine materials: 40 weeks at £7.00 per week	-		280	
Latrine materials 20 weeks at £3.00 per week	60		-	
Sewer connection	-		420	
Drainage; installation and removal	-		700	
First Aid	35		270	
Protective clothing	250		1,800	
CDM	230		800	
Winter working	-	575	1,250	7,020
Carried to Summary		£ 575		£7,020

Section 1.2.6 – Control and protection

	Minor Works £	£	Major Works £	£
Samples				
Sample panels	-		350	
Testing concrete cubes	-		400	
Drying Out				
Heaters and Fuel	150	150	600	1,350
Carried to Summary		£ 150		£1,350

Section 1.2.7 – Mechanical plant

	Minor Works £	£	Major Works £	£
Transport				
Site tractor and trailer	-		750	
Site van and driver	-		1,200	
Transport Plant to Site:				
Machine excavator	-		370	
Mechanical equipment including concrete mixers, hoists, and pumps	-		470	
Site offices and storage hutting	-		380	
Scaffolding	-		380	
Sundries	-		400	
Double handling materials on site	500		-	
Transport scaffolding and small plant to site	300	800	-	3,950

SPECIMEN SITE PRELIMINARIES (Cont'd)

Section 1.2.7 – Mechanical plant (Cont'd)

	Minor Works £	Minor Works £		Major Works £	Major Works £
Mechanical Plant					
Hoists: Assuming a 400kg hoist is required for 12 weeks:			per week		
Hire of hoist per week	-		520		
Fuel, oil and grease	-		40		
Operator (part-time)	-		190		
	-		750		
x 12 hoist weeks				9,000	
Scaffold Hoist: Allow 6 weeks at £148 per week	888			-	
Pumping and Dewatering. It is assumed that a Provisional Sum is included in the Bills of Quantities: A typical build up is shown in the notes....................				-	
Pumps: Allow 50mm pump at £115 per week x 2 weeks	230	1,118		-	9,000
Small Plant and Tools					
Labour value £300,000 x 1.5%	-			4,500	
Labour value £ 60,000 x 1.5%	900	900		-	4,500
Carried to Summary		£2,818			£17,450

Section 1.2.8 – Temporary works

	Minor Works £	Minor Works £	Major Works £	Major Works £
Scaffolding				
Assuming a three storey office building 60m x 10m x 10m high in traditional brick construction:				
External putlog scaffolding				
1400m² at £10.20 per m²	-		14,280	
Mobile tower 8 weeks at £210 each including erection and dismantling	-		1,680	
Internal scaffolding for suspended ceilings				
1800m² at £9.90 per m²......................................	-		17,820	
Mobile towers				
6 weeks at £205 each including erection and dismantling.	1,230	1,230	-	33,780
Hoardings, Fans, Fencing etc				
Hoarding 2m high: 100m at £44 per metre	-		4,400	
Gate	-	-	240	4,640
Carried to summary		£1,230		£38,420

Note;- Where quotations are used for scaffolding, plant and the like allowances must be made for additional hire and changes to anticipated requirements; scaffolding is notorious for costing more than anticipated with actual cost often being more than double the original quotation used at tender stage.

Section 1.2.11 – Cleaning

	Minor Works £	Minor Works £	Major Works £	Major Works £
Rubbish Disposal and Cleaning Site				
Site clearance during construction: 20 weeks at average £60 per week	1,200		-	
Site clearance during construction: 40 weeks at average £100 per week	-		4,000	
Final cleaning	240	1,440	470	4,470
Carried to summary		£1,440		£4,470

Section 1.2.12 – Fees and charges

	Minor Works £	Major Works £
Rates and Taxes on temporary buildings...	250	1,200
Carried to summary	250	1,200

SPECIMEN SITE PRELIMINARIES (Cont'd)

Section 1.2.14 – Insurance, bonds, guarantees and warranties

	Minor Works £	Minor Works £		Major Works £	Major Works £
Insurance of works					
Contract Sum say	250,000			1,500,000	
Allow for part demolition and clearing up	3,200			25,000	
	253,200			1,525,000	
Increased costs over contract period: say 2%	5,064			-	
Increased costs over contract period: say 5%	-			76,250	
	258,264			1,601,250	
Increased costs over reconstruction period: say 2%	5,165			-	
Increased costs over reconstruction period: say 5%	-			80,063	
	263,429			1,681,313	
Professional fees: 15%	39,514			252,197	
	£302,943			£ 1,933,510	
Cost of Insurance: £0.35%		1,060	£0.25%		4,834
Carried to summary		£ 1,060			£4,834

SITE PRELIMINARIES - SUMMARY

NRM Section		Minor Works £	Minor Works £		Major Works £	Major Works £
1.1.1	Employers requirements	-	-		500	500
1.2.1	Management and staff	10,330	10,330		92,080	92,080
1.2.2	Site accommodation	1,270	1,270		11,455	11,455
1.2.3	Temporary services					
	Water	5920			5,845	
	Power and lighting	480			6,000	
	Telephone and administration	440	1,510		1,600	13,445
1.2.4	Security	400	400		2,080	2,080
1.2.5	Safety and environmental protection	575	575		7,020	7,020
1.2.6	Control and protection					
	Samples and drying out	150	150		1,350	1,350
1.2.7	Mechanical Plant					
	Transport	800			3,950	
	Mechanical Plant	1,118			9,000	
	Small Plant and Tools	900	2,818		4,500	17,450
1.2.8	Temporary works					
	Scaffolding	1,230			33,780	
	Hoardings	-	1,230		4,640	38,420
1.2.11	Cleaning					
	Rubbish Disposal and Cleaning Site	1,440	1,440		4,470	4,470
1.2.12	Fees and charges					
	Rates and taxes	250	250		1,200	1,200
1.2.14	Insurance, bonds, guarantees and warranties					
	Insurance of Works	1,060	1,060		4,834	4,834
			£21,033			£194,304
	Overheads and Profit: 12.5%		£2,629	7.5%		£14,573
	Total of Site Preliminaries		**£ 23,662**			**£ 208,877**

SPECIMEN SITE PRELIMINARIES (Cont'd)

FIRM PRICE ADDITION (Major Works)

The amount to be added for a firm price tender is dependent upon the overall contract period of the project, the known or anticipated dates of wage awards and the estimated percentage amount of the award. Separate calculations must be carried out for any anticipated labour cost increases, materials increase, plant increases, staff salary awards and the increased costs required by direct subcontractors, if any. The total of these represents the addition to be made for a firm price tender.

A typical calculation is as follows:

	£	£
Labour:		
Assume a 3% wage award half way through the 40 week contract period		
The value of labour affected by the award is calculated as £155,000		
The firm price addition is 3% on £155,000		4,650
Materials:		
The value of materials affected by the award is estimated as £180,000		
Firm price addition for materials: allow average 2% on £180,000		3,600
Plant: Required mainly at the start of project: allow		700
Staff: Allow 3% increase on £25,000		750
Subcontractors:		
Net value affected by increased costs, say £160,000		
Allow labour 4% on £75,000	3,000	
Allow materials 2% on £85,000	1,700	4,700
Net addition for firm price:		£14,400

FIRM PRICE ADDITION (Minor Works)

Firm Price: Most small works contracts are based on firm price tenders. This is due in the main to the relatively short contract periods normally involved. It is therefore the usual practice to make a lump sum allowance in the Preliminaries for any anticipated cost increases in labour and materials. (or maybe ignored altogether should the contractor consider adequate provision is included within the rates)

	£
Allowance for firm price........	500
Net addition for firm price:	£ 500

LANDFILL TAX

The Landfill Tax is included as indicated within the Disposal items of the Groundworks Section in this edition.

The two rates of Tax applicable from 1st April 2021 and as used in this edition are:-

£3.10 per tonne for inactive waste.
£96.70 per tonne for all other waste.

Additional allowances should also be added for contaminated waste and specific quotations obtained as required.

The cost of excavation will be affected by the nature of the soil and its subsequent bulking factor in handling and disposal.

A typical conversion rate is 2.10 tonnes per cubic metre. This could result in an addition of £6.51 per cubic metre for inactive waste and £203.07 per cubic metre for all other waste to basic disposal costs.

Allowances for disposal and Landfill tax must be added to all items of demolitions, alterations and rubbish disposal as appropriate.

Recycling of redundant building materials is now essential, not only on environmental grounds but also to achieve savings in costs.

AGGREGATES LEVY (Major and Minor Works)

The Aggregates Levy came into effect on 1st April 2002. It applies to any sand, gravel or crushed rock commercially exploited in the UK or its territorial waters, or imported into the UK.

The levy does not apply to coal, clay and slate, metals and metal ores, gemstones or semi-precious stones, industrial minerals and recycled aggregates.

The levy has been charged at a single flat rate of £2.00 per tonne. (£5m³ approx) from 1 April 2009. The effect of this levy on building materials has generally been included within the rates.

There is one rate per whole tonne. This is apportioned on amounts less than one tonne. So, for example, the levy due on half a tonne from 1 April 2009 is £1.00.

Date	£ per tonne
01.04.02 to 31.03.08 (inclusive)	£1.60
01.04.08 to 31.03.09 (inclusive)	£1.95
From 01.04.09	£2.00

Further details of the Aggregates Levy may be obtained from the www.hmrc.gov.uk website

This page left blank intentionally

Laxton's NRM Building Price Book

2022 edition

WORK SECTIONS

-

MEASURED RATES

The Measured rates in the following guide give an indication of prices applied to works in the range of £100,000 to £500,000 based on National Average Prices

RATES GENERALLY

Rates given are within the context of a complete contract of construction where all trades work is involved.

PERCENTAGE ADJUSTMENTS FOR TENDER VALUES

As a guide to pricing works of lower or larger values and for cost planning or budgetary purposes, the following adjustments may be applied to overall contract values

Contract value

£20,000	to	£50,000	add 10.0%
£50,000	to	£100,000	add 5.0%
£100,000	to	£500,000..................	rates as shown
£500,000	to	£1,000,000	deduct 5.0%
£1,000,000	to	£10,000,000..................	deduct 10.0%

MINOR WORKS, RENOVATION WORKS AND WORK IN EXISTING UNOCCUPIED PREMISES

The rates may be used for orders of lower value, renovation works and works in existing unoccupied premises however due allowances must be added for disproportionate waste factors, preparation works, difficulty of access and any double handling and additional preliminary items.

REGIONAL VARIATIONS

The cost of a building is affected by its location; Laxton's NRM Building Price Book is based upon national average prices.

The following Location Factors have been extracted from National Statistics for 'Regional factors for the public sector building (non-housing) tender price index' as at 2nd Quarter 2014.

Great Britain –

North -	0.94
Wales -	0.98
Midlands -	0.94
East -	1.05
South West -	1.04
South East -	1.07
London –	1.09
Scotland -	0.94

USE OF FACTORS AND ADJUSTMENTS

Regional factors and tender value adjustments should only be applied to adjust overall pricing or total contract values. They should not be applied to individual rates or trades. Users will need to allow for individual local fluctuations in prices by obtaining quotations from suppliers for specific items.

VALUE ADDED TAX

Prices throughout exclude Value Added Tax.

Labour hourly rates: (except Specialists) Craft Operatives 20.87 Labourer 15.57 Rates are national average prices. Refer to REGIONAL VARIATIONS for indicative levels of overall pricing in regions	MATERIALS			LABOUR				RATES		
	Del to Site £	Waste %	Material Cost £	Craft Optve Hrs	Lab Hrs	Labour Cost £	Sunds £	Nett Rate £	Unit	Gross rate (10%) £
DEMOLITIONS										
Pulling down outbuildings										
Demolishing individual structures										
timber outbuilding; 2.50 x 2.00 x 3.00m maximum high	-	-	-	-	11.00	171.27	98.17	269.45	nr	296.39
outbuilding with half brick walls, one brick piers and felt covered timber roof; 2.50 x 2.00 x 3.00m maximum high	-	-	-	-	22.00	342.54	196.35	538.89	nr	592.78
greenhouse with half brick dwarf walls and timber framing to upper walls and roof; 3.00 x 2.00 x 3.00m maximum high	-	-	-	-	18.00	280.26	168.30	448.56	nr	493.42
Demolishing individual structures; setting aside materials for re-use										
metal framed greenhouse; 3.00 x 2.00 x 3.00m maximum high	-	-	-	4.00	7.00	192.47	-	192.47	nr	211.72
prefabricated concrete garage; 5.40 x 2.60 x 2.40m maximum high	-	-	-	6.00	11.00	296.49	-	296.49	nr	326.14
Demolishing individual structures; making good structures										
timber framed lean-to outbuilding and remove flashings and make good facing brick wall at ridge and vertical abutments 3.00 x 1.90 x 2.40m maximum high	-	-	-	1.50	12.00	218.15	103.95	322.09	nr	354.30
Unit rates for pricing the above and similar work										
pull down building; 3.00 x 1.90 x 2.40m maximum high	-	-	-	-	10.00	155.70	98.17	253.88	nr	279.26
remove flashing	-	-	-	-	0.12	1.87	0.56	2.43	m	2.67
make good facing brick wall at ridge	-	-	-	0.20	0.20	7.29	0.51	7.80	m	8.58
make good facing brick wall at vertical abutment	-	-	-	0.17	0.17	6.19	0.51	6.71	m	7.38
make good rendered wall at ridge	-	-	-	0.20	0.20	7.29	1.19	8.48	m	9.32
make good rendered wall at vertical abutment	-	-	-	0.20	0.20	7.29	1.19	8.48	m	9.32
Demolishing individual structures; making good structures										
lean-to outbuilding with half brick walls and slate covered timber roof and remove flashings, hack off plaster to house wall and make good with rendering to match existing 1.50 x 1.00 x 2.00m maximum high	-	-	-	4.00	12.50	278.11	66.07	344.17	nr	378.59
Unit rates for pricing the above and similar work										
pull down building with half brick walls; 1.50 x 1.00 x 2.00m maximum high	-	-	-	-	5.30	82.52	44.88	127.40	nr	140.14
pull down building with one brick walls; 1.50 x 1.00 x 2.00m maximum high	-	-	-	-	10.00	155.70	84.15	239.85	nr	263.83
hack off plaster or rendering and make good to match existing brick facings	-	-	-	1.00	2.00	52.01	1.68	53.69	m²	59.06
hack off plaster or rendering and make good to match existing rendering	-	-	-	1.30	2.30	62.94	6.78	69.72	m²	76.70
Removal of old work										
Demolishing parts of structures										
in-situ plain concrete bed										
75mm thick	-	-	-	-	0.90	14.01	4.21	18.22	m²	20.04
100mm thick	-	-	-	-	1.20	18.68	5.61	24.29	m²	26.72
150mm thick	-	-	-	-	1.80	28.03	8.41	36.44	m²	40.09
200mm thick	-	-	-	-	2.40	37.37	11.22	48.59	m²	53.45
in-situ reinforced concrete flat roof										
100mm thick	-	-	-	-	1.90	29.58	5.61	35.19	m²	38.71
150mm thick	-	-	-	-	2.85	44.37	8.41	52.79	m²	58.07
200mm thick	-	-	-	-	3.80	59.17	11.22	70.39	m²	77.42
225mm thick	-	-	-	-	4.28	66.64	12.62	79.26	m²	87.19
in-situ reinforced concrete upper floor										
100mm thick	-	-	-	-	1.90	29.58	5.61	35.19	m²	38.71
150mm thick	-	-	-	-	2.85	44.37	8.41	52.79	m²	58.07
200mm thick	-	-	-	-	3.80	59.17	11.22	70.39	m²	77.42
225mm thick	-	-	-	-	4.28	66.64	12.62	79.26	m²	87.19
in-situ reinforced concrete beam	-	-	-	-	19.00	295.83	56.10	351.93	m³	387.12
in-situ reinforced concrete column	-	-	-	-	18.00	280.26	56.10	336.36	m³	370.00
in-situ reinforced concrete wall										
100mm thick	-	-	-	-	1.80	28.03	5.61	33.64	m²	37.00
150mm thick	-	-	-	-	2.70	42.04	8.41	50.45	m²	55.50
200mm thick	-	-	-	-	3.60	56.05	11.22	67.27	m²	74.00
225mm thick	-	-	-	-	4.05	63.06	12.62	75.68	m²	83.25
in-situ reinforced concrete casing to beam	-	-	-	-	16.00	249.12	56.10	305.22	m³	335.74
in-situ reinforced concrete casing to column	-	-	-	-	15.25	237.44	56.10	293.54	m³	322.90
brick internal walls in lime mortar										
102mm thick	-	-	-	-	0.63	9.81	5.73	15.53	m²	17.09
215mm thick	-	-	-	-	1.30	20.24	12.06	32.30	m²	35.53
327mm thick	-	-	-	-	2.00	31.14	18.35	49.49	m²	54.44
brick internal walls in cement mortar										
102mm thick	-	-	-	-	0.95	14.79	5.73	20.52	m²	22.57
215mm thick	-	-	-	-	1.94	30.21	12.06	42.27	m²	46.49
327mm thick	-	-	-	-	2.98	46.40	18.35	64.75	m²	71.22
reinforced brick internal walls in cement lime mortar										
102mm thick	-	-	-	-	0.95	14.79	5.73	20.52	m²	22.57
215mm thick	-	-	-	-	1.94	30.21	12.06	42.27	m²	46.49
hollow clay block internal walls in cement-lime mortar										
50mm thick	-	-	-	-	0.30	4.67	2.81	7.48	m²	8.22
75mm thick	-	-	-	-	0.40	6.23	4.21	10.44	m²	11.48
100mm thick	-	-	-	-	0.52	8.10	5.61	13.71	m²	15.08

Labour hourly rates: (except Specialists) Craft Operatives 20.87 Labourer 15.57 Rates are national average prices. Refer to REGIONAL VARIATIONS for indicative levels of overall pricing in regions	MATERIALS			LABOUR				RATES		
	Del to Site £	Waste %	Material Cost £	Craft Optve Hrs	Lab Hrs	Labour Cost £	Sunds £	Nett Rate £	Unit	Gross rate (10%) £
DEMOLITIONS (Cont'd)										
Removal of old work (Cont'd)										
Demolishing parts of structures (Cont'd)										
hollow clay block internal walls in cement mortar										
50mm thick	-	-	-	-	0.32	4.98	2.81	7.79	m²	8.57
75mm thick	-	-	-	-	0.43	6.70	4.21	10.90	m²	11.99
100mm thick	-	-	-	-	0.57	8.87	5.61	14.48	m²	15.93
concrete block internal walls in cement lime mortar										
75mm thick	-	-	-	-	0.35	5.45	4.21	9.66	m²	10.62
100mm thick	-	-	-	-	0.53	8.25	5.61	13.86	m²	15.25
190mm thick	-	-	-	-	0.70	10.90	10.66	21.56	m²	23.71
215mm thick	-	-	-	-	1.41	21.95	12.06	34.02	m²	37.42
concrete block internal walls in cement mortar										
75mm thick	-	-	-	-	0.56	8.72	4.21	12.93	m²	14.22
100mm thick	-	-	-	-	0.73	11.37	5.61	16.98	m²	18.67
190mm thick	-	-	-	-	0.91	14.17	10.66	24.83	m²	27.31
215mm thick	-	-	-	-	1.67	26.00	12.06	38.06	m²	41.87
if internal walls plastered, add per side	-	-	-	-	0.12	1.87	1.12	2.99	m²	3.29
if internal walls rendered, add per side	-	-	-	-	0.18	2.80	1.12	3.92	m²	4.32
brick external walls in lime mortar										
102mm thick	-	-	-	-	0.48	7.47	5.73	13.20	m²	14.52
215mm thick	-	-	-	-	0.98	15.26	12.06	27.32	m²	30.05
327mm thick	-	-	-	-	1.51	23.51	18.35	41.86	m²	46.04
brick external walls in cement mortar										
102mm thick	-	-	-	-	0.63	9.81	5.73	15.53	m²	17.09
215mm thick	-	-	-	-	1.30	20.24	12.06	32.30	m²	35.53
327mm thick	-	-	-	-	2.00	31.14	18.35	49.49	m²	54.44
reinforced brick external walls in cement lime mortar										
102mm thick	-	-	-	-	0.63	9.81	5.73	15.53	m²	17.09
215mm thick	-	-	-	-	1.30	20.24	12.06	32.30	m²	35.53
if external walls plastered, add per side	-	-	-	-	0.09	1.40	1.12	2.52	m²	2.78
if external walls rendered or rough cast, add per side	-	-	-	-	0.12	1.87	1.12	2.99	m²	3.29
clean old bricks in lime mortar and stack for re-use, per thousand	-	-	-	-	15.00	233.55	-	233.55	nr	256.90
clean old bricks in cement mortar and stack for re-use, per thousand	-	-	-	-	25.00	389.25	-	389.25	nr	428.17
rough rubble walling, in lime mortar; 600mm thick	-	-	-	-	3.75	58.39	33.66	92.05	m²	101.25
random rubble walling, in lime mortar; 350mm thick	-	-	-	-	2.20	34.25	19.64	53.89	m²	59.28
random rubble walling, in lime mortar; 500mm thick	-	-	-	-	3.10	48.27	28.05	76.32	m²	83.95
dressed stone walling, in gauged mortar; 100mm thick	-	-	-	2.00	2.30	77.55	5.61	83.16	m²	91.48
dressed stone walling, in gauged mortar; 200mm thick	-	-	-	3.90	4.50	151.46	11.22	162.68	m²	178.95
stone copings; 300 x 50mm	-	-	-	0.20	0.26	8.22	0.84	9.06	m	9.97
stone copings; 375 x 100mm	-	-	-	0.40	0.52	16.44	2.11	18.56	m	20.41
stone staircases	-	-	-	-	15.00	233.55	56.10	289.65	m³	318.61
stone steps	-	-	-	-	14.75	229.66	56.10	285.76	m³	314.33
structural timbers										
50 x 75mm	-	-	-	-	0.13	2.02	0.21	2.24	m	2.46
50 x 100mm	-	-	-	-	0.15	2.34	0.28	2.62	m	2.88
50 x 150mm	-	-	-	-	0.18	2.80	0.43	3.23	m	3.55
50 x 225mm	-	-	-	-	0.24	3.74	0.63	4.36	m	4.80
75 x 100mm	-	-	-	-	0.18	2.80	0.43	3.23	m	3.55
75 x 150mm	-	-	-	-	0.20	3.11	0.63	3.74	m	4.12
75 x 225mm	-	-	-	-	0.31	4.83	0.94	5.77	m	6.34
steelwork										
steel beams, joists and lintels; not exceeding 10 kg/m	-	-	-	50.00	50.00	1822.00	56.10	1878.10	t	2065.91
steel beams, joists and lintels 10 - 20 kg/m	-	-	-	46.00	46.00	1676.24	56.10	1732.34	t	1905.57
steel beams, joists and lintels 20 - 50 kg/m	-	-	-	40.00	40.00	1457.60	56.10	1513.70	t	1665.07
steel columns and stanchions; not exceeding 10 kg/m	-	-	-	60.00	60.00	2186.40	56.10	2242.50	t	2466.75
steel columns and stanchions; 10 - 20 kg/m	-	-	-	56.00	56.00	2040.64	56.10	2096.74	t	2306.41
steel columns and stanchions; 20 - 50 kg/m	-	-	-	50.00	50.00	1822.00	56.10	1878.10	t	2065.91
steel purlins and rails; not exceeding 10 kg/m	-	-	-	50.00	50.00	1822.00	56.10	1878.10	t	2065.91
steel purlins and rails; 10 - 20 kg/m	-	-	-	50.00	50.00	1822.00	56.10	1878.10	t	2065.91
SHORING, FAÇADE RETENTION AND TEMPORARY WORKS										
Temporary support of structures, roads and the like										
Provide and erect timber raking shore complete with sole piece, cleats, needles and 25mm brace boarding										
two 150 x 150mm rakers (total length 8.00m) and 50 x 175mm wall piece	214.67	10.00	236.13	4.00	4.00	145.76	32.21	414.10	nr	455.51
weekly cost of maintaining last	-	-	-	1.00	1.00	36.44	1.62	38.06	nr	41.86
three 225 x 225mm rakers (total length 21.00m) and 50 x 250mm wall piece	576.95	10.00	634.65	23.20	23.20	845.41	140.04	1620.09	nr	1782.10
weekly cost of maintaining last	-	-	-	1.50	1.50	54.66	6.91	61.57	nr	67.73
Provide and erect timber flying shore of 100 x 150mm main member, 50 x 175mm wall pieces and 50 x 100mm straining pieces and 75 x 100mm struts, distance between wall faces										
4.00m	273.20	10.00	300.51	15.00	15.00	546.60	6.91	854.03	nr	939.43
weekly cost of maintaining last	-	-	-	2.50	2.50	91.10	1.62	92.72	nr	101.99
5.00m	314.85	10.00	346.34	17.80	17.80	648.63	8.05	1003.02	nr	1103.32
weekly cost of maintaining last	-	-	-	3.00	3.00	109.32	1.85	111.17	nr	122.28
6.00m	349.49	10.00	384.44	5.10	20.60	427.18	8.93	820.54	nr	902.60
weekly cost of maintaining last	-	-	-	3.50	3.50	127.54	2.11	129.65	nr	142.62

ALTERATIONS, REPAIRS AND CONSERVATION

Section Contents
The main headings in this section are:-

Labour hourly rates: (except Specialists) Craft Operatives 20.87 Labourer 15.57 Rates are national average prices. Refer to REGIONAL VARIATIONS for indicative levels of overall pricing in regions	MATERIALS			LABOUR				RATES		
	Del to Site £	Waste %	Material Cost £	Craft Optve Hrs	Lab Hrs	Labour Cost £	Sunds £	Nett Rate £	Unit	Gross rate (10%) £
ALTERATION WORK TO EXISTING BUILDINGS										
The following items are usually specified as spot items where all work in all trades is included in one item; to assist in adapting these items for varying circumstances, unit rates have been given for the component operation where possible while these items may not be in accordance with NRM2 either by description or measurement, it is felt that the pricing information given will be of value to the reader										
Works of alteration; strutting for forming openings										
Strutting generally										
the cost of strutting in connection with forming openings is to be added to the cost of forming openings; the following are examples of costs for strutting for various sizes and locations of openings. Costs are based on three uses of timber										
Strutting for forming small openings in internal load bearing walls										
opening size 900 x 2000mm	17.63	5.00	18.51	2.00	0.33	46.88	1.09	66.48	nr	73.13
opening size 2000 x 2300mm	29.52	5.00	31.00	5.00	0.83	117.27	2.36	150.63	nr	165.69
Strutting for forming openings in external one brick walls										
opening size 900 x 2000mm	17.63	5.00	18.51	3.00	0.50	70.40	1.88	90.79	nr	99.87
opening size 1500 x 1200mm	20.33	5.00	21.35	3.00	0.50	70.40	1.88	93.62	nr	102.98
Strutting for forming openings in external 280mm brick cavity walls										
opening size 900 x 2000mm	18.13	5.00	19.03	4.00	0.66	93.76	2.11	114.90	nr	126.39
opening size 1500 x 1200mm	27.06	5.00	28.42	4.00	0.66	93.76	2.11	124.28	nr	136.71

Labour hourly rates: (except Specialists) Craft Operatives 20.87 Labourer 15.57 Rates are national average prices. Refer to REGIONAL VARIATIONS for indicative levels of overall pricing in regions	MATERIALS			LABOUR				RATES		
	Del to Site £	Waste %	Material Cost £	Craft Optve Hrs	Lab Hrs	Labour Cost £	Sunds £	Nett Rate £	Unit	Gross rate (10%) £
ALTERATION WORK TO EXISTING BUILDINGS (Cont'd)										
Works of alteration; strutting for forming openings (Cont'd)										
Strutting for forming large openings in internal load bearing walls on the ground floor of an average two storey building with timber floors and pitched roof; with load bearing surface 450mm below ground floor; including cutting holes and making good										
opening size 3700 x 2300mm	260.10	5.00	273.10	20.00	20.00	728.80	25.01	1026.92	nr	1129.61
Unit rates for pricing the above and similar work										
plates, struts, braces or wedges in supports to floor and roof	5.69	5.00	5.97	0.28	0.28	10.20	0.36	16.54	m	18.19
dead shore and needle, sole plates, braces and wedges including cutting holes and making good	131.23	5.00	137.79	10.00	10.00	364.40	12.46	514.65	nr	566.12
Strutting for forming large openings in external one brick walls on the ground floor of an average two storey building as described above										
opening size 6000 x 2500mm	497.24	5.00	522.11	40.00	40.00	1457.60	49.62	2029.32	nr	2232.26
Unit rates for pricing the above and similar work										
strutting to window opening over new opening	29.22	5.00	30.68	2.00	2.00	72.88	2.46	106.02	nr	116.62
plates, struts, braces or wedges in supports to floor and roof	4.53	5.00	4.76	0.28	0.28	10.20	0.36	15.32	m	16.85
dead shore and needle, sole plates, braces and wedges including cutting holes and making good	182.32	5.00	191.44	15.70	15.70	572.11	19.55	783.10	nr	861.41
set of two raking shores with 50mm wall piece, wedges and dogs	84.42	5.00	88.64	4.00	4.00	145.76	4.93	239.33	nr	263.26
Strutting for forming large openings in external 280mm brick cavity walls on the ground floor of an average two storey building as above described										
opening size 6000 x 2500mm	502.90	5.00	528.04	43.90	43.90	1599.72	54.55	2182.31	nr	2400.54
Unit rates for pricing the above and similar work										
strutting to window opening over new opening	59.46	5.00	62.43	4.00	4.00	145.76	4.93	213.13	nr	234.44
plates, struts, braces and wedges in supports to floor and roof	4.53	5.00	4.76	0.28	0.28	10.20	0.36	15.32	m	16.85
dead shore and needle, sole plates, braces and wedges including cutting holes and making good	195.24	5.00	205.00	16.70	16.70	608.55	20.84	834.39	nr	917.83
set of two raking shores with 50mm wall piece, wedges and dogs	84.42	5.00	88.64	4.00	4.00	145.76	4.93	239.33	nr	263.26
Works of alteration; work to chimney stacks										
Seal and ventilate top of flue - remove chimney pot and flaunching and provide 50mm precast concrete, BS 8500, designed mix C20, 20mm aggregate, weathered and throated capping and bed in cement mortar (1:3) to seal top of stack; cut opening through brick side of stack and build in 225 x 225mm clay air brick to ventilate flue and make good facings										
stack size 600 x 600mm with one flue	51.85	10.00	55.59	4.90	4.90	178.56	7.13	241.27	nr	265.40
stack size 825 x 600mm with two flues	80.38	10.00	85.51	9.00	9.00	327.96	13.13	426.61	nr	469.27
stack size 1050 x 600mm with three flues	108.91	10.00	115.44	13.10	13.10	477.36	18.00	610.81	nr	671.89
Renew defective chimney pot - remove chimney pot and provide new clay chimney pot set and flaunched in cement mortar (1:3)										
150mm diameter x 600mm high	62.91	-	62.91	2.50	2.50	91.10	6.45	160.46	nr	176.51
Rebuild defective chimney stack - pull down defective stack to below roof level for a height of 2.00m; prepare for raising and rebuild in common brickwork faced with picked stock facings in gauged mortar (1:2:9) pointed to match existing; parge and core flues; provide No. 4 lead flashings and soakers; provide 150mm diameter clay chimney pots 600mm high set and flaunched in cement mortar (1:3); make good roof tiling and all other work disturbed										
600 x 600mm with one flue	421.98	10.00	457.89	35.30	37.55	1321.36	97.35	1876.60	nr	2064.26
825 x 600mm with two flues	570.62	10.00	615.10	47.15	47.90	1729.82	135.30	2480.22	nr	2728.24
Remove defective chimney stack - pull down stack to below roof level; remove all flashings and soakers; piece in 50 x 100mm rafters; extend roof tiling with machine made plain tiles to 100mm gauge nailed every fourth course with galvanised nails to and with 25 x 19mm battens; bond new tiling to existing										
850 x 600mm for a height of 2.00m	47.01	10.00	51.71	26.00	22.30	889.83	59.40	1000.94	nr	1101.04
Works of alteration; work to chimney breasts and fireplaces										
Take out fireplace and fill in opening - remove fire surround, fire back and hearth; hack up screed to hearth and extend 25mm tongued and grooved softwood floor boarding over hearth on and with bearers; fill in opening where fireplace removed with 75mm concrete blocks in gauged mortar (1:2:9) bonded to existing at jambs and wedged and pinned up to soffits; form 225 x 225mm opening and provide and build in 225 x 225mm fibrous plaster louvered air vent; plaster filling with 12mm two coat lightweight plaster on 12mm (average) dubbing plaster; extend 19 x 100mm softwood chamfered skirting over filling and join with existing; make good all new finishings to existing										
fireplace opening 570 x 685mm, hearth 1030 x 405mm	47.66	-	47.66	8.00	7.45	282.96	16.99	347.61	nr	382.37
fireplace opening 800 x 760mm, hearth 1260 x 405mm	58.27	-	58.27	9.65	8.95	340.75	19.80	418.82	nr	460.70

Labour hourly rates: (except Specialists) Craft Operatives 20.87 Labourer 15.57 Rates are national average prices. Refer to REGIONAL VARIATIONS for indicative levels of overall pricing in regions	MATERIALS			LABOUR				RATES		
	Del to Site £	Waste %	Material Cost £	Craft Optve Hrs	Lab Hrs	Labour Cost £	Sunds £	Nett Rate £	Unit	Gross rate (10%) £
ALTERATION WORK TO EXISTING BUILDINGS (Cont'd)										
Works of alteration; work to chimney breasts and fireplaces (Cont'd)										
Remove chimney breast - pull down chimney breast for full height from ground to roof level (two storeys) including removing two fire surrounds and hearths complete; make out brickwork where flues removed and make out brickwork where breasts removed; extend 50 x 175mm floor joists and 25mm tongued and grooved softwood floor boarding (ground and first floors); extend 50 x 100mm ceiling joists (first floor); plaster walls with 12mm two coat lightweight plaster on 12mm (average) plaster dubbing; extend ceiling plaster with expanded metal lathing and 19mm three coat lightweight plaster; run 19 x 100mm softwood chamfered skirting to walls to join with existing; make good all new finishings up to existing										
chimney breast 2.00m wide and 7.50m high including gathering in roof space	196.52	-	196.52	62.00	84.00	2601.82	237.60	3035.94	nr	3339.53
Works of alteration; form dormer in roof										
Form opening through existing roof and covering for and construct dormer window; remove covering, cut out rafters, insert 75 x 100mm rafters trimmers; construct dormer cheeks of 50 x 100mm framing covered with 19mm tongue and grooved boarding and three layer fibre based felt roofing; construct flat dormer roof of 50 x 100mm joists covered with 19mm plywood on firrings and three layer fibre based felt roofing dressed under existing rood covering; form No. 4 lead secret gutter at cheeks with tilting fillets and insert No. 4 lead apron at sill dressed over existing roof coverings; make good existing roof covering all round, insulate cheeks and roof with 100mm glass fibre insulation quilt and line internally with 12.5mm plasterboard with filled and scrimmed joints finished with 5mm setting coat of plaster and painted one thinned and two coats of emulsion paint; run 25 x 150mm fascia at edge of roof on three sides and finish edge of roof covering with and seal to anodised aluminium alloy edge trim; knot, prime, stop and paint two undercoats and one gloss finishing coat on fascia complete with pre-finished softwood casement window, double glazed with clear glass										
Flat roofed dormer with softwood window in plain tile roof; size 631 x 1050mm; type LEW110C	545.25	10.00	584.24	47.25	22.00	1328.65	28.55	1941.43	nr	2135.58
Dormer with softwood window in plain tile roof; size 1200 x 1050mm; type LEW210CC	774.00	10.00	822.37	53.30	23.00	1470.48	31.84	2324.69	nr	2557.16
Dormer with softwood window in slated roof; size 630 x 1050mm; type LEW110C	640.68	10.00	692.07	60.25	23.50	1623.31	31.35	2346.73	nr	2581.41
Dormer with softwood window type in slated roof; size 1200 x 1050mm; type LEW210CC	907.95	10.00	973.60	66.80	26.00	1798.94	34.32	2806.85	nr	3087.54
Works of alteration; form trap door in ceiling										
Form new trap door in ceiling with 100mm deep joists and lath and plaster finish; cut away and trim ceiling joists around opening and insert new trimming and trimmer joists; provide 32x 127mm softwood lining with 15 x 25mm stop and 20 x 70mm architrave; provide and place in position 18mm blockboard trap door, lipped all round; make good existing ceiling plaster around openings										
600 x 900mm	79.24	-	79.24	21.85	5.60	543.20	15.01	637.45	nr	701.20
Unit rates for pricing the above and similar work										
cut away plastered plasterboard ceiling	-	-	-	1.50	0.33	36.44	1.40	37.85	m²	41.63
cut away lath and plaster ceiling	-	-	-	2.00	0.41	48.12	1.68	49.81	m²	54.79
cut away and trim existing 100mm deep joists around opening										
664 x 964mm	-	-	-	0.95	0.16	22.32	1.17	23.49	nr	25.84
964 x 1444mm	-	-	-	1.90	0.33	44.79	2.36	47.15	nr	51.87
cut away and trim existing 150mm deep joists around opening										
664 x 964mm	-	-	-	1.43	0.24	33.58	1.80	35.38	nr	38.92
964 x 1444mm	-	-	-	2.86	0.48	67.16	3.53	70.69	nr	77.76
softwood trimming or trimmer joists										
75 x 100mm	4.19	10.00	4.61	0.95	0.16	22.32	0.59	27.52	m	30.27
75 x 150mm	6.20	10.00	6.82	1.00	0.17	23.52	0.64	30.98	m	34.08
softwood lining										
38 x 125mm	3.03	15.00	3.48	1.50	0.25	35.20	0.18	38.86	m	42.75
38 x 150mm	3.63	15.00	4.17	1.60	0.27	37.60	0.13	41.90	m	46.09
15 x 25mm softwood stop	0.53	10.00	0.58	0.33	0.05	7.67	0.08	8.33	m	9.16
19 x 50mm softwood twice rounded architrave to Patt. 18	0.68	10.00	0.75	0.33	0.05	7.67	0.08	8.50	m	9.35
18mm blockboard trap door lipped all round										
600 x 900mm	21.23	10.00	23.35	2.00	0.33	46.88	0.28	70.51	nr	77.56
900 x 1280mm	44.22	10.00	48.64	3.00	0.50	70.40	0.50	119.53	nr	131.49
75mm steel butt hinge to softwood	0.10	2.50	0.11	0.33	0.05	7.74	0.16	8.02	nr	8.82
make good plastered plasterboard ceiling around opening	-	-	-	0.75	0.75	27.33	2.03	29.36	m	32.30
make good lath and plaster ceiling around opening	-	-	-	0.83	0.83	30.25	2.49	32.74	m	36.01
Removing; fittings and fixtures										
Removing fittings and fixtures										
cupboard with doors, frames, architraves, etc	-	-	-	-	0.59	9.19	1.72	10.90	m²	11.99
worktop with legs and bearers	-	-	-	-	0.56	8.72	2.29	11.01	m²	12.11
shelving exceeding 300mm wide with bearers and brackets	-	-	-	-	0.45	7.01	1.45	8.46	m²	9.30
shelving not exceeding 300mm wide with bearers and brackets	-	-	-	-	0.20	3.11	0.46	3.58	m	3.93
draining board and bearers										
500 x 600mm	-	-	-	-	0.28	4.36	0.87	5.23	nr	5.76
600 x 900mm	-	-	-	-	0.37	5.76	1.55	7.31	nr	8.04
wall cupboard unit										
510 x 305 x 305mm	-	-	-	-	0.47	7.32	1.39	8.70	nr	9.57
510 x 305 x 610mm	-	-	-	-	0.65	10.12	2.69	12.81	nr	14.09

Labour hourly rates: (except Specialists) Craft Operatives 20.87 Labourer 15.57 Rates are national average prices. Refer to REGIONAL VARIATIONS for indicative levels of overall pricing in regions	MATERIALS			LABOUR				RATES		
	Del to Site £	Waste %	Material Cost £	Craft Optve Hrs	Lab Hrs	Labour Cost £	Sunds £	Nett Rate £	Unit	Gross rate (10%) £
ALTERATION WORK TO EXISTING BUILDINGS (Cont'd)										
Removing; fittings and fixtures (Cont'd)										
Removing fittings and fixtures (Cont'd)										
wall cupboard unit (Cont'd)										
1020 x 305 x 610mm	-	-	-	-	0.94	14.64	5.46	20.10	nr	22.11
1220 x 305 x 610mm	-	-	-	-	1.15	17.91	6.50	24.41	nr	26.85
floor cupboard unit										
510 x 510 x 915mm	-	-	-	-	0.92	14.32	6.83	21.16	nr	23.27
610 x 510 x 915mm	-	-	-	-	1.21	18.84	8.15	26.99	nr	29.69
1020 x 510 x 915mm	-	-	-	-	1.65	25.69	13.66	39.35	nr	43.29
1220 x 510 x 915mm	-	-	-	-	1.93	30.05	16.37	46.42	nr	51.06
sink base unit										
585 x 510 x 895mm	-	-	-	-	0.92	14.32	7.71	22.03	nr	24.23
1070 x 510 x 895mm	-	-	-	-	1.65	25.69	14.02	39.72	nr	43.69
tall cupboard unit										
510 x 510 x 1505mm	-	-	-	-	1.56	24.29	11.25	35.54	nr	39.10
610 x 510 x 1505mm	-	-	-	-	1.77	27.56	13.45	41.01	nr	45.11
bath panel and bearers	-	-	-	-	0.47	7.32	1.45	8.77	nr	9.65
steel or concrete clothes line post with concrete base	-	-	-	-	0.50	7.78	2.87	10.66	nr	11.72

This section continues on the next page

Labour hourly rates: (except Specialists) Craft Operatives 26.39 Labourer 15.57 Rates are national average prices. Refer to REGIONAL VARIATIONS for indicative levels of overall pricing in regions	MATERIALS			LABOUR				RATES		
	Del to Site £	Waste %	Material Cost £	Craft Optve Hrs	Lab Hrs	Labour Cost £	Sunds £	Nett Rate £	Unit	Gross rate (10%) £
ALTERATION WORK TO EXISTING BUILDINGS (Cont'd)										
Removing; plumbing items or installations										
Removing plumbing items or installations										
cast iron rainwater gutters										
100mm	-	-	-	0.20	-	5.28	0.28	5.56	m	6.11
cast iron rainwater pipes										
75mm	-	-	-	0.25	-	6.60	0.31	6.91	m	7.60
cast iron rainwater pipes										
100mm	-	-	-	0.25	-	6.60	0.53	7.13	m	7.84
cast iron rainwater head	-	-	-	0.30	-	7.92	0.87	8.79	nr	9.67
cast iron soil and vent pipe with caulked joints										
50mm	-	-	-	0.35	-	9.24	0.16	9.40	m	10.34
75mm	-	-	-	0.35	-	9.24	0.31	9.55	m	10.51
100mm	-	-	-	0.35	-	9.24	0.53	9.76	m	10.74
150mm	-	-	-	0.50	-	13.19	1.25	14.45	m	15.89
asbestos cement soil and vent pipe										
100mm	-	-	-	0.25	-	6.60	0.53	7.13	m	7.84
150mm	-	-	-	0.25	-	6.60	1.25	7.85	m	8.64
p.v.c. soil and vent pipe										
100mm	-	-	-	0.25	-	6.60	0.53	7.13	m	7.84
150mm	-	-	-	0.25	-	6.60	1.25	7.85	m	8.64
lead soil and vent pipe										
100mm	-	-	-	0.35	-	9.24	0.53	9.76	m	10.74
150mm	-	-	-	0.35	-	9.24	1.25	10.49	m	11.54
sanitary fittings										
w.c. suites	-	-	-	1.55	-	40.90	5.38	46.28	nr	50.91
lavatory basins	-	-	-	1.35	-	35.63	3.23	38.86	nr	42.75
baths	-	-	-	1.55	-	40.90	10.77	51.68	nr	56.85
glazed ware sinks	-	-	-	1.35	-	35.63	5.38	41.01	nr	45.11
stainless steel sinks	-	-	-	1.35	-	35.63	3.23	38.86	nr	42.75
stainless steel sinks with single drainer	-	-	-	1.35	-	35.63	4.32	39.95	nr	43.94
stainless steel sinks with double drainer	-	-	-	1.35	-	35.63	5.38	41.01	nr	45.11
hot and cold water, waste pipes, etc. 8 - 25mm diameter										
copper	-	-	-	0.15	-	3.96	0.07	4.02	m	4.43
lead	-	-	-	0.15	-	3.96	0.07	4.02	m	4.43
polythene or p.v.c.	-	-	-	0.15	-	3.96	0.07	4.02	m	4.43
stainless steel	-	-	-	0.25	-	6.60	0.07	6.66	m	7.33
steel	-	-	-	0.25	-	6.60	0.07	6.66	m	7.33
hot and cold water, waste pipes, etc. 32 - 50mm diameter										
copper	-	-	-	0.20	-	5.28	0.16	5.44	m	5.99
lead	-	-	-	0.20	-	5.28	0.16	5.44	m	5.99
polythene or p.v.c.	-	-	-	0.20	-	5.28	0.16	5.44	m	5.99
stainless steel	-	-	-	0.30	-	7.92	0.16	8.08	m	8.89
steel	-	-	-	0.30	-	7.92	0.16	8.08	m	8.89
fittings										
cold water cisterns up to 454 litres capacity	-	-	-	2.00	-	52.78	24.45	77.23	nr	84.96
hot water tanks or cylinders up to 227 litre capacity	-	-	-	2.00	-	52.78	12.21	64.99	nr	71.49
solid fuel boilers up to 66000 BTU output	-	-	-	3.75	-	98.96	-	98.96	nr	108.86
gas or oil fired boilers up to 66000 BTU output	-	-	-	3.75	-	98.96	-	98.96	nr	108.86
wall mounted water heaters	-	-	-	2.00	-	52.78	-	52.78	nr	58.06
wall type radiators; up to 914mm long, up to 610mm high	-	-	-	1.00	-	26.39	1.09	27.48	nr	30.23
wall type radiators; up to 914mm long, 610 - 914mm high	-	-	-	1.35	-	35.63	2.16	37.79	nr	41.57
wall type radiators; 914 - 1829mm long, up to 610mm high	-	-	-	1.55	-	40.90	3.30	44.20	nr	48.62
wall type radiators; 914 - 1829mm long, 610 - 914mm high	-	-	-	1.95	-	51.46	4.32	55.78	nr	61.36
column type radiators; up to 914mm long, up to 610mm high	-	-	-	1.00	-	26.39	5.66	32.05	nr	35.25
column type radiators; up to 914mm long, 610 - 914mm high	-	-	-	1.35	-	35.63	11.30	46.93	nr	51.62
column type radiators; 914 - 1829mm long, up to 610mm high	-	-	-	1.55	-	40.90	16.96	57.87	nr	63.65
column type radiators; 914 - 1829mm long, 610 - 914mm high	-	-	-	1.95	-	51.46	22.60	74.07	nr	81.47
insulation from										
pipes; 8 - 25mm diameter	-	-	-	0.10	-	2.64	0.16	2.80	m	3.08
pipes; 32 - 50mm diameter	-	-	-	0.13	-	3.43	0.31	3.74	m	4.12
water tank or calorifier from tanks; up to 227 litres	-	-	-	0.50	-	13.19	12.21	25.40	nr	27.95
water tank or calorifier from tanks; 227 - 454 litres	-	-	-	0.75	-	19.79	24.45	44.25	nr	48.67
Removing plumbing and electrical installations; setting aside for re-use										
cast iron soil and vent pipe with caulked joints										
50mm	-	-	-	0.55	-	14.51	-	14.51	m	15.97
75mm	-	-	-	0.60	-	15.83	-	15.83	m	17.42
100mm	-	-	-	0.80	-	21.11	-	21.11	m	23.22
150mm	-	-	-	1.00	-	26.39	-	26.39	m	29.03

This section continues on the next page

Labour hourly rates: (except Specialists) Craft Operatives 34.13 Labourer 15.57 Rates are national average prices. Refer to REGIONAL VARIATIONS for indicative levels of overall pricing in regions	MATERIALS			LABOUR				RATES		
	Del to Site £	Waste %	Material Cost £	Craft Optve Hrs	Lab Hrs	Labour Cost £	Sunds £	Nett Rate £	Unit	Gross rate (10%) £
ALTERATION WORK TO EXISTING BUILDINGS (Cont'd)										
Removing; electrical items or installations										
Removing electrical items or installations										
wall mounted electric fire	-	-	-	2.00	-	68.26	2.87	71.13	nr	78.24
night storage heater; 1.5 kW	-	-	-	2.50	-	85.33	8.61	93.94	nr	103.33
night storage heater; 2 KW	-	-	-	2.50	-	85.33	11.48	96.81	nr	106.49
night storage heater; 3 KW	-	-	-	2.50	-	85.33	17.23	102.55	nr	112.81
Removing electrical items or installations; extending and making good finishings										
lighting points	-	-	-	1.25	-	42.66	2.34	45.01	nr	49.51
flush type switches	-	-	-	1.25	-	42.66	2.34	45.01	nr	49.51
surface mounted type switches	-	-	-	1.00	-	34.13	1.88	36.01	nr	39.61
flush type socket outlets	-	-	-	1.25	-	42.66	2.34	45.01	nr	49.51
surface mounted type socket outlets	-	-	-	1.00	-	34.13	1.88	36.01	nr	39.61
flush type fitting points	-	-	-	1.25	-	42.66	2.34	45.01	nr	49.51
surface mounted type fitting points	-	-	-	1.00	-	34.13	1.88	36.01	nr	39.61
surface mounted p.v.c. insulated and sheathed cables	-	-	-	0.04	-	1.37	0.10	1.46	m	1.61
surface mounted mineral insulated copper sheathed cables	-	-	-	0.10	-	3.41	0.20	3.61	m	3.97
conduits up to 25mm diameter with junction boxes	-	-	-	0.15	-	5.12	0.28	5.40	m	5.94
surface mounted cable trunking up to 100 x 100mm	-	-	-	0.55	-	18.77	1.02	19.79	m	21.77

This section continues on the next page

Labour hourly rates: (except Specialists) Craft Operatives 20.87 Labourer 15.57 Rates are national average prices. Refer to REGIONAL VARIATIONS for indicative levels of overall pricing in regions	MATERIALS			LABOUR				RATES		
	Del to Site £	Waste %	Material Cost £	Craft Optve Hrs	Lab Hrs	Labour Cost £	Sunds £	Nett Rate £	Unit	Gross rate (10%) £
ALTERATION WORK TO EXISTING BUILDINGS (Cont'd)										
Removing; finishes										
Removing finishings										
cement and sand to floors	-	-	-	-	0.86	13.39	2.87	16.26	m²	17.89
granolithic to floors	-	-	-	-	0.92	14.32	2.87	17.20	m²	18.91
granolithic to treads and risers	-	-	-	-	1.43	22.27	2.87	25.14	m²	27.65
plastic or similar tiles to floors	-	-	-	-	0.20	3.11	0.30	3.41	m²	3.75
plastic or similar tiles to floors; cleaning off for new	-	-	-	-	0.47	7.32	0.30	7.61	m²	8.38
plastic or similar tiles to floors and screed under	-	-	-	-	1.05	16.35	3.17	19.52	m²	21.47
linoleum and underlay to floors	-	-	-	-	0.07	1.09	2.87	3.96	m²	4.36
ceramic or quarry tiles to floors	-	-	-	-	1.21	18.84	1.72	20.56	m²	22.61
ceramic or quarry tiles to floors and screed under	-	-	-	-	2.39	37.21	4.59	41.80	m²	45.98
extra; cleaning and keying surface of concrete under	-	-	-	-	0.53	8.25	0.07	8.32	m²	9.15
asphalt to floors on loose underlay	-	-	-	-	0.35	5.45	1.15	6.60	m²	7.26
asphalt to floors keyed to concrete or screed	-	-	-	-	0.76	11.83	1.15	12.99	m²	14.29
granolithic skirtings	-	-	-	-	0.33	5.14	0.30	5.44	m	5.98
plastic or similar skirtings; cleaning off for new	-	-	-	-	0.13	2.02	0.07	2.09	m	2.30
timber skirtings	-	-	-	-	0.12	1.87	0.30	2.17	m	2.38
ceramic or quarry tile skirtings	-	-	-	-	0.43	6.70	0.33	7.03	m	7.73
plaster to walls	-	-	-	-	0.60	9.34	1.15	10.50	m²	11.55
rendering to walls	-	-	-	-	0.87	13.55	1.15	14.70	m²	16.17
rough cast to walls	-	-	-	-	0.90	14.01	1.45	15.47	m²	17.01
match boarding linings to walls with battens	-	-	-	-	0.38	5.92	1.72	7.63	m²	8.40
plywood or similar sheet linings to walls with battens	-	-	-	-	0.31	4.83	1.72	6.54	m²	7.20
insulating board linings to walls with battens	-	-	-	-	0.31	4.83	1.72	6.54	m²	7.20
plasterboard to walls	-	-	-	-	0.31	4.83	0.87	5.70	m²	6.27
plasterboard dry linings to walls	-	-	-	-	0.50	7.78	0.87	8.66	m²	9.53
plasterboard and skim to walls	-	-	-	-	0.60	9.34	1.15	10.50	m²	11.55
lath and plaster to walls	-	-	-	-	0.44	6.85	1.45	8.30	m²	9.13
metal lath and plaster to walls	-	-	-	-	0.33	5.14	1.45	6.59	m²	7.25
ceramic tiles to walls	-	-	-	-	0.75	11.68	0.87	12.55	m²	13.81
ceramic tiles to walls and backing under	-	-	-	-	1.11	17.28	1.45	18.73	m²	20.61
asphalt coverings to walls keyed to concrete or brickwork	-	-	-	-	0.66	10.28	1.15	11.43	m²	12.57
plaster to ceilings	-	-	-	-	0.74	11.52	1.15	12.68	m²	13.94
match boarding linings to ceilings with battens	-	-	-	-	0.54	8.41	1.72	10.12	m²	11.14
plywood or similar sheet linings to ceilings with battens	-	-	-	-	0.38	5.92	1.72	7.63	m²	8.40
insulating board linings to ceilings with battens	-	-	-	-	0.26	4.05	1.72	5.76	m²	6.34
plasterboard to ceilings	-	-	-	-	0.33	5.14	0.87	6.01	m²	6.61
plasterboard and skim to ceilings	-	-	-	-	0.40	6.23	1.15	7.38	m²	8.12
lath and plaster to ceilings	-	-	-	-	0.59	9.19	1.45	10.64	m²	11.70
metal lath and plaster to ceilings	-	-	-	-	0.47	7.32	1.45	8.77	m²	9.65
Extending and making good finishings										
plaster cornices; up to 100mm girth on face	0.92	10.00	1.01	0.78	0.78	28.42	0.12	29.55	m	32.51
plaster cornices; 100 - 200mm girth on face	1.51	10.00	1.66	0.88	0.88	32.07	0.30	34.02	m	37.43
plaster cornices; 200 - 300mm girth on face	2.66	10.00	2.93	0.97	0.97	35.35	0.87	39.15	m	43.06
plaster ceiling roses; up to 300mm diameter	0.46	10.00	0.51	0.41	0.41	14.94	0.23	15.68	nr	17.25
plaster ceiling roses; 300 - 450mm diameter	0.92	10.00	1.01	0.64	0.64	23.32	0.46	24.80	nr	27.28
plaster ceiling roses; 450 - 600mm diameter	1.81	10.00	1.99	0.90	0.90	32.80	0.91	35.69	nr	39.26
Carefully handling and disposing toxic or other special waste by approved method										
asbestos cement sheet linings to walls	-	-	-	2.00	2.00	72.88	4.59	77.47	m²	85.21
asbestos cement sheet linings to ceilings	-	-	-	3.00	3.00	109.32	4.59	113.91	m²	125.30
Removing; roof coverings										
Removing coverings										
felt to roofs	-	-	-	-	0.28	4.36	1.15	5.51	m²	6.07
felt skirtings to roofs	-	-	-	-	0.33	5.14	0.12	5.25	m	5.78
asphalt to roofs	-	-	-	-	0.35	5.45	1.45	6.90	m²	7.59
asphalt skirtings to roofs; on expanded metal reinforcement	-	-	-	-	0.20	3.11	0.23	3.35	m	3.68
asphalt skirtings to roofs; keyed to concrete, brickwork, etc.	-	-	-	-	0.30	4.67	0.23	4.90	m	5.39
asphalt coverings to roofs; on expanded metal reinforcement; per 100mm of width	-	-	-	-	0.13	2.02	0.18	2.21	m	2.43
asphalt coverings to roofs; keyed to concrete, brickwork, etc.; per 100mm of width	-	-	-	-	0.20	3.11	0.18	3.30	m	3.63
slate to roofs	-	-	-	-	0.34	5.29	1.15	6.45	m²	7.09
tiles to roofs	-	-	-	-	0.31	4.83	1.72	6.54	m²	7.20
extra; removing battens	-	-	-	-	0.28	4.36	1.15	5.51	m²	6.07
extra; removing counter battens	-	-	-	-	0.10	1.56	0.23	1.79	m²	1.97
extra; removing underfelt	-	-	-	-	0.20	3.11	0.46	3.58	m²	3.93
lead to roofs	-	-	-	-	0.48	7.47	1.15	8.63	m²	9.49
lead flashings to roofs; per 25mm of girth	-	-	-	-	0.05	0.78	0.07	0.84	m	0.93
zinc to roofs	-	-	-	-	0.34	5.29	1.15	6.45	m²	7.09
zinc flashings to roofs; per 25mm of girth	-	-	-	-	0.03	0.47	0.07	0.53	m	0.59
copper to roofs	-	-	-	-	0.34	5.29	1.15	6.45	m²	7.09
copper flashings to roofs; per 25mm of girth	-	-	-	-	0.03	0.47	0.07	0.53	m	0.59
corrugated metal sheeting to roofs	-	-	-	-	0.31	4.83	1.72	6.54	m²	7.20
corrugated translucent sheeting to roofs	-	-	-	-	0.31	4.83	1.72	6.54	m²	7.20
board roof decking	-	-	-	-	0.31	4.83	1.72	6.54	m²	7.20
woodwool roof decking	-	-	-	-	0.39	6.07	1.72	7.79	m²	8.57
Removing coverings; setting aside for re-use										
slate to roofs	-	-	-	-	0.60	9.34	-	9.34	m²	10.28
tiles to roofs	-	-	-	-	0.60	9.34	-	9.34	m²	10.28
clean and stack 405 x 205mm slates; per 100	-	-	-	-	1.50	23.35	-	23.35	nr	25.69
clean and stack 510 x 255mm slates; per 100	-	-	-	-	1.89	29.43	-	29.43	nr	32.37
clean and stack 610 x 305mm slates; per 100	-	-	-	-	2.24	34.88	-	34.88	nr	38.36
clean and stack concrete tiles; per 100	-	-	-	-	2.24	34.88	-	34.88	nr	38.36
clean and stack plain tiles; per 100	-	-	-	-	1.50	23.35	-	23.35	nr	25.69

Labour hourly rates: (except Specialists) Craft Operatives 20.87 Labourer 15.57 Rates are national average prices. Refer to REGIONAL VARIATIONS for indicative levels of overall pricing in regions	MATERIALS			LABOUR				RATES		
	Del to Site £	Waste %	Material Cost £	Craft Optve Hrs	Lab Hrs	Labour Cost £	Sunds £	Nett Rate £	Unit	Gross rate (10%) £
ALTERATION WORK TO EXISTING BUILDINGS (Cont'd)										
Removing; roof coverings (Cont'd)										
Removing coverings; carefully handling and disposing toxic or other special waste by approved method										
asbestos cement sheeting to roofs	-	-	-	2.00	2.00	72.88	4.59	77.47	m²	85.21
asbestos cement roof decking	-	-	-	2.00	2.00	72.88	4.59	77.47	m²	85.21
Removing; wall cladding										
Removing cladding										
corrugated metal sheeting to walls	-	-	-	-	0.25	3.89	1.72	5.61	m²	6.17
corrugated translucent sheeting to walls	-	-	-	-	0.25	3.89	1.72	5.61	m²	6.17
Timber weather boarding	-	-	-	-	0.31	4.83	1.72	6.54	m²	7.20
Removing coverings; carefully handling and disposing toxic or other special waste by approved method										
asbestos cement sheeting to walls	-	-	-	1.75	1.75	63.77	4.59	68.36	m²	75.19
Removing; woodwork										
Removing										
stud partitions plastered both sides	-	-	-	-	0.66	10.28	4.32	14.60	m²	16.06
roof boarding	-	-	-	-	0.19	2.96	1.45	4.41	m²	4.85
roof boarding; prepare joists for new	-	-	-	-	0.45	7.01	1.45	8.46	m²	9.30
gutter boarding and the like	-	-	-	-	0.19	2.96	1.45	4.41	m²	4.85
weather boarding and battens	-	-	-	-	0.24	3.74	1.72	5.45	m²	6.00
tilting fillets, angle fillets and the like	-	-	-	-	0.09	1.40	0.12	1.52	m	1.67
fascia boards 150 mm wide	-	-	-	-	0.10	1.56	0.23	1.79	m	1.97
barge boards 200mm wide	-	-	-	-	0.10	1.56	0.30	1.85	m	2.04
soffit boards 300mm wide	-	-	-	-	0.10	1.56	0.46	2.02	m	2.22
floor boarding	-	-	-	-	0.33	5.14	1.45	6.59	m²	7.25
handrails and brackets	-	-	-	-	0.10	1.56	0.91	2.46	m	2.71
balustrades complete down to and with cappings to aprons or strings	-	-	-	0.58	0.10	13.66	2.29	15.96	m	17.55
newel posts; cut off flush with landing or string	-	-	-	0.48	0.08	11.26	0.58	11.84	nr	13.02
ends of treads projecting beyond face of cut outer string including scotia under; make good treads where balusters removed	-	-	-	0.90	0.15	21.12	1.72	22.83	m	25.12
dado or picture rails with grounds	-	-	-	-	0.10	1.56	0.23	1.79	m	1.97
architrave	-	-	-	-	0.06	0.93	0.23	1.17	m	1.28
window boards and bearers	-	-	-	-	0.12	1.87	0.46	2.33	m	2.56
Removing; setting aside for reuse										
handrails and brackets	-	-	-	0.25	0.04	5.84	-	5.84	m	6.42
Removing; windows and doors										
Removing										
metal windows with internal and external sills; in conjunction with demolition										
997 x 923mm	-	-	-	-	0.40	6.23	2.76	8.98	nr	9.88
1486 x 923mm	-	-	-	-	0.50	7.78	3.96	11.74	nr	12.92
1486 x 1513mm	-	-	-	-	0.60	9.34	6.50	15.84	nr	17.43
1994 x 1513mm	-	-	-	-	0.70	10.90	8.68	19.58	nr	21.54
metal windows with internal and external sills; preparatory to filling openings; cut out lugs										
997 x 923mm	-	-	-	-	1.30	20.24	2.76	23.00	nr	25.30
1486 x 923mm	-	-	-	-	1.60	24.91	3.96	28.87	nr	31.76
1486 x 1513mm	-	-	-	-	2.00	31.14	6.50	37.64	nr	41.41
1994 x 1513mm	-	-	-	-	2.30	35.81	8.68	44.49	nr	48.94
wood single or multi-light casements and frames with internal and external sills; in conjunction with demolition										
440 x 920mm	-	-	-	-	0.28	4.36	1.78	6.14	nr	6.76
1225 x 1070mm	-	-	-	-	0.29	4.52	5.63	10.14	nr	11.16
2395 x 1225mm	-	-	-	-	0.30	4.67	12.64	17.31	nr	19.04
wood single or multi-light casements and frames with internal and external sills; preparatory to filling openings; cut out fixing cramps										
440 x 920mm	-	-	-	-	1.25	19.46	1.78	21.24	nr	23.37
1225 x 1070mm	-	-	-	-	1.70	26.47	5.63	32.10	nr	35.31
2395 x 1225mm	-	-	-	-	2.52	39.24	12.64	51.88	nr	57.06
wood cased frames and sashes with internal and external sills complete with accessories and weights; in conjunction with demolition										
610 x 1225mm	-	-	-	-	0.61	9.50	4.32	13.82	nr	15.20
915 x 1525mm	-	-	-	-	0.66	10.28	8.04	18.31	nr	20.14
1370 x 1525mm	-	-	-	-	0.75	11.68	12.00	23.67	nr	26.04
wood cased frames and sashes with internal and external sills complete with accessories and weights; preparatory to filling openings; cut out fixing cramps										
610 x 1225mm	-	-	-	-	1.79	27.87	4.32	32.19	nr	35.41
915 x 1525mm	-	-	-	-	2.56	39.86	8.04	47.89	nr	52.68
1370 x 1525mm	-	-	-	-	4.11	63.99	12.00	75.99	nr	83.59
wood doors										
single internal doors	-	-	-	-	0.23	3.58	3.45	7.03	nr	7.73
single internal doors and frames; in conjunction with demolition	-	-	-	-	0.18	2.80	7.76	10.56	nr	11.61
single internal doors and frames; preparatory to filling openings; cut out fixing cramps	-	-	-	-	1.00	15.57	7.76	23.33	nr	25.66
double internal doors	-	-	-	-	0.47	7.32	6.90	14.21	nr	15.64
double internal doors and frames; in conjunction with demolition	-	-	-	-	0.19	2.96	11.78	14.74	nr	16.21
double internal doors and frames; preparatory to filling openings; cut out fixing cramps	-	-	-	-	1.20	18.68	11.78	30.47	nr	33.51
single external doors	-	-	-	-	0.25	3.89	5.74	9.63	nr	10.60
single external doors and frames; in conjunction with demolition	-	-	-	-	0.18	2.80	10.33	13.13	nr	14.44
single external doors and frames; preparatory to filling openings; cut out fixing cramps	-	-	-	-	1.00	15.57	10.33	25.90	nr	28.49

Labour hourly rates: (except Specialists) Craft Operatives 20.87 Labourer 15.57 Rates are national average prices. Refer to REGIONAL VARIATIONS for indicative levels of overall pricing in regions	MATERIALS			LABOUR				RATES		
	Del to Site £	Waste %	Material Cost £	Craft Optve Hrs	Lab Hrs	Labour Cost £	Sunds £	Nett Rate £	Unit	Gross rate (10%) £
ALTERATION WORK TO EXISTING BUILDINGS (Cont'd)										
Removing; windows and doors (Cont'd)										
Removing (Cont'd)										
wood doors (Cont'd)										
double external doors	-	-	-	-	0.47	7.32	6.90	14.21	nr	15.64
double external doors and frames; in conjunction with demolition	-	-	-	-	0.19	2.96	11.78	14.74	nr	16.21
double external doors and frames; preparatory to filling openings; cut out fixing cramps	-	-	-	-	1.20	18.68	11.78	30.47	nr	33.51
single door frames; in conjunction with demolition	-	-	-	-	0.17	2.65	4.32	6.97	nr	7.67
single door frames; preparatory to filling openings; cut out fixing cramps	-	-	-	-	0.77	11.99	4.32	16.31	nr	17.94
double door frames; in conjunction with demolition	-	-	-	-	0.18	2.80	4.88	7.69	nr	8.46
double door frames; preparatory to filling openings; cut out fixing cramps	-	-	-	-	0.82	12.77	4.88	17.65	nr	19.42
Removing; setting aside for reuse										
metal windows with internal and external sills; in conjunction with demolition										
997 x 923mm	-	-	-	0.70	0.50	22.39	-	22.39	nr	24.63
1486 x 923mm	-	-	-	0.85	0.65	27.86	-	27.86	nr	30.65
1486 x 1513mm	-	-	-	0.90	0.75	30.46	-	30.46	nr	33.51
1994 x 1513mm	-	-	-	1.00	0.85	34.10	-	34.10	nr	37.51
metal windows with internal and external sills; preparatory to filling openings; cut out lugs										
997 x 923mm	-	-	-	0.70	1.40	36.41	-	36.41	nr	40.05
1486 x 923mm	-	-	-	0.85	1.75	44.99	-	44.99	nr	49.49
1486 x 1513mm	-	-	-	0.90	2.15	52.26	-	52.26	nr	57.48
1994 x 1513mm	-	-	-	1.00	2.45	59.02	-	59.02	nr	64.92
wood single or multi-light casements and frames with internal and external sills; in conjunction with demolition										
440 x 920mm	-	-	-	0.50	0.36	16.04	-	16.04	nr	17.64
1225 x 1070mm	-	-	-	0.83	0.43	24.02	-	24.02	nr	26.42
2395 x 1225mm	-	-	-	1.00	0.46	28.03	-	28.03	nr	30.84
wood single or multi-light casements and frames with internal and external sills; preparatory to filling openings; cut out fixing cramps										
440 x 920mm	-	-	-	0.50	1.33	31.14	-	31.14	nr	34.26
1225 x 1070mm	-	-	-	0.83	1.84	45.97	-	45.97	nr	50.57
2395 x 1225mm	-	-	-	1.00	2.68	62.60	-	62.60	nr	68.86
wood cased frames and sashes with internal and external sills complete with accessories and weights; in conjunction with demolition										
610 x 1225mm	-	-	-	0.97	0.78	32.39	-	32.39	nr	35.63
915 x 1525mm	-	-	-	1.63	0.93	48.50	-	48.50	nr	53.35
1370 x 1525mm	-	-	-	1.94	1.07	57.15	-	57.15	nr	62.86
wood cased frames and sashes with internal and external sills complete with accessories and weights; preparatory to filling openings; cut out fixing cramps										
610 x 1225mm	-	-	-	0.97	1.96	50.76	-	50.76	nr	55.84
915 x 1525mm	-	-	-	1.63	2.83	78.08	-	78.08	nr	85.89
1370 x 1525mm	-	-	-	1.94	4.43	109.46	-	109.46	nr	120.41
note: the above rates assume that windows and sashes will be re-glazed when re-used										
wood doors										
single internal doors	-	-	-	0.50	0.31	15.26	-	15.26	nr	16.79
single internal doors and frames; in conjunction with demolition	-	-	-	1.00	0.34	26.16	-	26.16	nr	28.78
single internal doors and frames; preparatory to filling openings; cut out fixing cramps	-	-	-	1.00	1.16	38.93	-	38.93	nr	42.82
double internal doors	-	-	-	1.00	0.63	30.68	-	30.68	nr	33.75
double internal doors and frames; in conjunction with demolition	-	-	-	1.47	0.43	37.37	-	37.37	nr	41.11
double internal doors and frames; preparatory to filling openings; cut out fixing cramps	-	-	-	1.47	1.45	53.26	-	53.26	nr	58.58
single external doors	-	-	-	0.50	0.33	15.57	-	15.57	nr	17.13
single external doors and frames; in conjunction with demolition	-	-	-	1.00	0.34	26.16	-	26.16	nr	28.78
single external doors and frames; preparatory to filling openings; cut out fixing cramps	-	-	-	1.00	1.16	38.93	-	38.93	nr	42.82
double external doors	-	-	-	1.00	0.63	30.68	-	30.68	nr	33.75
double external doors and frames; in conjunction with demolition	-	-	-	1.47	0.44	37.53	-	37.53	nr	41.28
double external doors and frames; preparatory to filling openings; cut out fixing cramps	-	-	-	1.47	1.45	53.26	-	53.26	nr	58.58
single door frames; in conjunction with demolition	-	-	-	0.50	0.25	14.33	-	14.33	nr	15.76
single door frames; preparatory to filling openings; cut out fixing cramps	-	-	-	0.50	0.85	23.67	-	23.67	nr	26.04
double door frames; in conjunction with demolition	-	-	-	0.50	0.26	14.48	-	14.48	nr	15.93
double door frames; preparatory to filling openings; cut out fixing cramps	-	-	-	0.50	0.90	24.45	-	24.45	nr	26.89
Removing; ironmongery										
Removing door ironmongery (piecing in doors and frames included elsewhere)										
butt hinges	-	-	-	-	0.06	0.93	0.02	0.95	nr	1.05
tee hinges up to 300mm	-	-	-	-	0.20	3.11	0.02	3.13	nr	3.44
floor spring hinges and top centres	-	-	-	-	0.92	14.32	0.33	14.65	nr	16.12
barrel bolts up to 200mm	-	-	-	-	0.13	2.02	0.02	2.04	nr	2.24
flush bolts up to 200mm	-	-	-	-	0.17	2.65	0.02	2.66	nr	2.93
indicating bolts	-	-	-	-	0.23	3.58	0.02	3.60	nr	3.96
double panic bolts	-	-	-	-	0.69	10.74	0.18	10.92	nr	12.02
single panic bolts	-	-	-	-	0.58	9.03	0.12	9.15	nr	10.06
Norfolk or Suffolk latches	-	-	-	-	0.23	3.58	0.02	3.60	nr	3.96
cylinder rim night latches	-	-	-	-	0.23	3.58	0.02	3.60	nr	3.96
rim locks or latches and furniture	-	-	-	-	0.23	3.58	0.02	3.60	nr	3.96

ALTERATIONS, REPAIRS AND CONSERVATION

Labour hourly rates: (except Specialists) Craft Operatives 20.87 Labourer 15.57 Rates are national average prices. Refer to REGIONAL VARIATIONS for indicative levels of overall pricing in regions	MATERIALS			LABOUR				RATES		
	Del to Site £	Waste %	Material Cost £	Craft Optve Hrs	Lab Hrs	Labour Cost £	Sunds £	Nett Rate £	Unit	Gross rate (10%) £
ALTERATION WORK TO EXISTING BUILDINGS (Cont'd)										
Removing; ironmongery (Cont'd)										
Removing door ironmongery (piecing in doors and frames included elsewhere) (Cont'd)										
mortice dead locks	-	-	-	-	0.17	2.65	0.02	2.66	nr	2.93
mortice locks or latches and furniture	-	-	-	-	0.29	4.52	0.02	4.53	nr	4.98
Bales catches	-	-	-	-	0.12	1.87	0.02	1.88	nr	2.07
overhead door closers, surface fixed	-	-	-	-	0.29	4.52	0.18	4.70	nr	5.17
pull handles	-	-	-	-	0.12	1.87	0.02	1.88	nr	2.07
push plates	-	-	-	-	0.12	1.87	0.02	1.88	nr	2.07
kicking plates	-	-	-	-	0.17	2.65	0.07	2.71	nr	2.98
letter plates	-	-	-	-	0.12	1.87	0.02	1.88	nr	2.07
Removing window ironmongery										
sash centres	-	-	-	-	0.12	1.87	0.02	1.88	nr	2.07
sash fasteners	-	-	-	-	0.17	2.65	0.02	2.66	nr	2.93
sash lifts	-	-	-	-	0.07	1.09	0.02	1.11	nr	1.22
sash screws	-	-	-	-	0.17	2.65	0.02	2.66	nr	2.93
casement fasteners	-	-	-	-	0.12	1.87	0.02	1.88	nr	2.07
casement stays	-	-	-	-	0.12	1.87	0.02	1.88	nr	2.07
quadrant stays	-	-	-	-	0.12	1.87	0.02	1.88	nr	2.07
fanlight catches	-	-	-	-	0.13	2.02	0.02	2.04	nr	2.24
curtain tracks	-	-	-	-	0.15	2.34	0.12	2.45	m	2.70
Removing sundry ironmongery										
hat and coat hooks	-	-	-	-	0.07	1.09	0.02	1.11	nr	1.22
cabin hooks and eyes	-	-	-	-	0.12	1.87	0.02	1.88	nr	2.07
shelf brackets	-	-	-	-	0.07	1.09	0.07	1.16	nr	1.27
toilet roll holders	-	-	-	-	0.09	1.40	0.07	1.47	nr	1.61
towel rollers	-	-	-	-	0.12	1.87	0.12	1.98	nr	2.18
Removing; metalwork										
Removing										
balustrades 1067mm high	-	-	-	-	0.81	12.61	1.49	14.10	m	15.51
wire mesh screens with timber or metal beads screwed on										
generally	-	-	-	-	0.62	9.65	1.45	11.11	m²	12.22
225 x 225mm	-	-	-	-	0.20	3.11	0.12	3.23	nr	3.55
305 x 305mm	-	-	-	-	0.22	3.43	0.18	3.61	nr	3.97
guard bars of vertical bars at 100mm centres welded to horizontal fixing bars at 450mm centres, fixed with bolts	-	-	-	-	0.62	9.65	1.45	11.11	m²	12.22
guard bars of vertical bars at 100mm centres welded to horizontal fixing bars at 450mm centres, fixed with screws	-	-	-	-	0.39	6.07	1.45	7.52	m²	8.28
extra; piecing in softwood after removal of bolts	-	-	-	0.25	0.04	5.84	0.15	5.99	nr	6.59
small bracket	-	-	-	-	0.18	2.80	0.12	2.92	nr	3.21
Removing; making good finishings										
balustrades 1067mm high; making good mortices in treads	-	-	-	0.97	0.97	35.35	1.88	37.23	m	40.95
guard bars of vertical bars at 100mm centres welded to horizontal fixing bars at 450mm centres fixed in mortices; making good concrete or brickwork and plaster	-	-	-	0.60	1.42	34.63	1.96	36.59	m²	40.25
small bracket built or cast in; making good concrete or brickwork and plaster	-	-	-	0.25	0.25	9.11	0.78	9.89	nr	10.87
Removing; manholes										
Removing										
remove cover and frame; break up brick sides and concrete bottom; fill in void with hardcore										
overall size 914 x 1067mm and 600mm deep to invert	5.53	30.00	7.19	-	10.00	155.70	5.74	168.63	nr	185.49
overall size 914 x 1219mm and 900mm deep to invert	11.06	30.00	14.38	-	11.50	179.05	6.32	199.75	nr	219.73
manhole covers and frames; clean off brickwork	-	-	-	-	0.50	7.78	1.02	8.81	nr	9.69
fresh air inlets; clean out pipe socket	-	-	-	-	0.50	7.78	0.33	8.11	nr	8.93
Removing; fencing										
Removing										
chestnut pale fencing with posts										
610mm high	-	-	-	-	0.30	4.67	0.91	5.58	m	6.14
914mm high	-	-	-	-	0.34	5.29	1.39	6.68	m	7.35
1219mm high	-	-	-	-	0.38	5.92	1.85	7.76	m	8.54
close boarded fencing with posts										
1219mm high	-	-	-	-	0.68	10.59	2.11	12.70	m	13.97
1524mm high	-	-	-	-	0.81	12.61	2.64	15.25	m	16.78
1829mm high	-	-	-	-	0.91	14.17	3.17	17.34	m	19.07
chain link fencing with posts										
914mm high	-	-	-	-	0.29	4.52	1.02	5.54	m	6.09
1219mm high	-	-	-	-	0.34	5.29	4.26	9.55	m	10.51
1524mm high	-	-	-	-	0.38	5.92	1.72	7.63	m	8.40
1829mm high	-	-	-	-	0.42	6.54	2.11	8.65	m	9.52
timber gate and posts	-	-	-	-	0.98	15.26	4.32	19.58	nr	21.54
Cutting or forming openings/recesses/chases etc; openings through concrete										
Form opening for door frame through 150mm reinforced concrete wall plastered both sides and with skirting both sides; take off skirtings, cut opening through wall, square up reveals, make good existing plaster up to new frame both sides and form fitted ends on existing skirtings up to new frame; extend cement and sand floor screed and vinyl floor covering through opening and make good up to existing										
838 x 2032mm	22.62	-	22.62	22.50	28.00	905.54	49.83	977.98	nr	1075.78

Labour hourly rates: (except Specialists) Craft Operatives 20.87 Labourer 15.57 Rates are national average prices. Refer to REGIONAL VARIATIONS for indicative levels of overall pricing in regions	MATERIALS			LABOUR				RATES		
	Del to Site £	Waste %	Material Cost £	Craft Optve Hrs	Lab Hrs	Labour Cost £	Sunds £	Nett Rate £	Unit	Gross rate (10%) £
ALTERATION WORK TO EXISTING BUILDINGS (Cont'd)										
Cutting or forming openings/recesses/chases etc; openings through concrete (Cont'd)										
Unit rates for pricing the above and similar work										
cut opening through wall										
100mm thick	-	-	-	-	5.30	82.52	11.73	94.25	m²	103.68
150mm thick	-	-	-	-	7.90	123.00	17.54	140.54	m²	154.60
200mm thick	-	-	-	-	10.50	163.49	23.35	186.83	m²	205.52
make good fair face around opening	-	-	-	-	0.80	12.46	0.82	13.28	m	14.61
square up reveals to opening										
100mm wide	-	-	-	0.75	0.75	27.33	2.05	29.38	m	32.31
150mm wide	-	-	-	1.07	1.07	38.99	2.89	41.88	m	46.07
200mm wide	-	-	-	1.38	1.38	50.29	4.59	54.87	m	60.36
make good existing plaster up to new frame	0.85	10.00	0.94	0.55	0.55	20.04	-	20.98	m	23.08
13mm two coat hardwall plaster to reveal not exceeding 300mm wide	1.71	10.00	1.88	0.64	0.64	23.32	-	25.20	m	27.72
take off old skirting	-	-	-	0.22	-	4.59	0.16	4.76	m	5.23
form fitted end on existing skirting up to new frame	-	-	-	0.38	-	7.93	-	7.93	nr	8.72
short length of old skirting up to 100mm long with mitre with existing one end	-	-	-	0.58	-	12.10	0.07	12.17	nr	13.39
short length of old skirting up to 200mm long with mitres with existing both ends	-	-	-	1.15	-	24.00	0.10	24.10	nr	26.51
38mm cement and sand (1:3) screeded bed in opening	6.43	5.00	6.75	1.54	1.54	56.12	-	62.87	m²	69.16
vinyl or similar floor covering to match existing, fixed with adhesive, not exceeding 300mm wide	5.99	10.00	6.58	0.15	0.15	5.47	0.31	12.36	m	13.60
iroko threshold; twice oiled; plugged and screwed										
15 x 100mm	9.85	10.00	10.84	0.90	-	18.78	0.08	29.70	m	32.67
15 x 150mm	13.93	10.00	15.32	1.20	-	25.04	0.10	40.47	m	44.51
15 x 200mm	19.82	10.00	21.80	1.55	-	32.35	0.15	54.30	m	59.73
Form opening for staircase through 150mm reinforced concrete suspended floor plastered on soffit and with screed and vinyl floor covering on top; take up floor covering and screed, cut opening through floor, square up edges of slab, make good ceiling plaster up to lining and make good screed and floor covering to lining										
900 x 2134mm	88.95	-	88.95	19.00	39.00	1003.76	64.35	1157.06	nr	1272.76
Unit rates for pricing the above and similar work										
take up vinyl or similar floor covering	-	-	-	-	0.55	8.56	0.23	8.79	m²	9.67
hack up screed	-	-	-	-	1.50	23.35	2.13	25.48	m²	28.03
cut opening through slab; 150mm thick	-	-	-	-	7.90	123.00	17.54	140.54	m²	154.60
cut opening through slab; 200mm thick	-	-	-	-	10.50	163.49	23.35	186.83	m²	205.52
make good fair face around opening	-	-	-	-	0.80	12.46	0.78	13.23	m	14.55
square up edges of slab; 150mm thick	-	-	-	1.07	1.07	38.99	3.05	42.04	m	46.25
square up edges of slab; 200mm thick	-	-	-	1.38	1.38	50.29	4.08	54.36	m	59.80
make good existing plaster up to new lining	0.85	10.00	0.94	0.55	0.55	20.04	-	20.98	m	23.08
make good existing 38mm floor screed up to new lining	1.01	5.00	1.06	0.45	0.45	16.40	-	17.46	m	19.21
make good existing vinyl or similar floor covering up to new lining	7.98	10.00	8.78	0.67	0.67	24.41	0.50	33.69	m	37.06
Cutting or forming openings/recesses/chases etc; openings through brickwork or blockwork										
Form openings for door frames through 100mm block partition plastered both sides and with skirting both sides; take off skirtings, cut opening through partition, insert 100 x 140mm prestressed precast concrete lintel and wedge and pin up over, quoin up jambs, extend plaster to faces of lintel and make good junction with existing plaster; make good existing plaster up to new frame both sides and form fitted ends on existing skirtings up to new frame; extend softwood board flooring through opening on and with bearers and make good up to existing										
838 x 2032mm	26.11	-	26.11	20.00	17.20	685.20	20.95	732.27	nr	805.50
Unit rates for pricing the above and similar work										
cut opening through 75mm block partition plastered both sides	-	-	-	1.10	1.30	43.20	6.45	49.65	m²	54.61
cut opening through 100mm block partition plastered both sides	-	-	-	1.30	1.56	51.42	7.57	58.99	m²	64.89
make good fair face around opening	-	-	-	0.25	0.25	9.11	0.16	9.27	m	10.20
prestressed precast concrete lintel; 65 x 140 x 1200mm	11.45	2.50	11.74	0.80	0.80	29.15	0.41	41.30	nr	45.43
prestressed precast concrete lintel; 100 x 140 x 1200mm	16.04	2.50	16.44	1.00	1.00	36.44	0.54	53.43	nr	58.77
wedge and pin up over lintel; 75mm wide	-	-	-	0.50	0.50	18.22	1.02	19.24	m	21.17
wedge and pin up over lintel; 100mm wide	-	-	-	0.66	0.66	24.05	1.35	25.40	m	27.94
quoin up 75mm wide jambs	-	-	-	0.52	0.52	18.95	1.02	19.97	m	21.97
quoin up 100mm wide jambs	-	-	-	0.68	0.68	24.78	1.35	26.13	m	28.75
extend 13mm hardwall plaster to face of lintel	5.72	10.00	6.29	2.13	2.13	77.62	0.10	84.00	m²	92.40
make good existing plaster up to new frame	0.85	10.00	0.94	0.55	0.55	20.04	-	20.98	m	23.08
take off old skirting	-	-	-	0.22	-	4.59	0.16	4.76	m	5.23
form fitted end on existing skirting up to new frame	-	-	-	0.38	-	7.93	-	7.93	nr	8.72
38mm cement and sand (1:3) screeded bed in opening	6.43	5.00	6.75	1.54	1.54	56.12	-	62.87	m²	69.16
extend 25mm softwood board flooring through opening on and with bearers	42.29	20.00	48.12	16.20	2.70	380.13	0.89	429.15	m²	472.06
iroko threshold; twice oiled; plugged and screwed										
19 x 75mm	7.82	10.00	8.60	0.80	-	16.70	0.12	25.41	m	27.95
19 x 100mm	9.85	10.00	10.84	0.90	-	18.78	0.13	29.75	m	32.73
Form openings for door frames through one brick wall plastered one side and with external rendering other side; take off skirting, cut opening through wall, insert 215 x 140mm prestressed precast concrete lintel and wedge and pin up over; quoin up jambs; extend plaster to face of lintel and make good junction with existing plaster; make good existing plaster up to new frame one side; extend external rendering to face of lintel and to reveals and make good up to existing rendering and new frame the other side; form fitted ends on existing skirting up to new frame										
914 x 2082mm	47.87	-	47.87	28.00	25.40	979.84	46.36	1074.07	nr	1181.48

ALTERATIONS, REPAIRS AND CONSERVATION

Labour hourly rates: (except Specialists) Craft Operatives 20.87 Labourer 15.57 Rates are national average prices. Refer to REGIONAL VARIATIONS for indicative levels of overall pricing in regions	MATERIALS			LABOUR				RATES		
	Del to Site £	Waste %	Material Cost £	Craft Optve Hrs	Lab Hrs	Labour Cost £	Sunds £	Nett Rate £	Unit	Gross rate (10%) £
ALTERATION WORK TO EXISTING BUILDINGS (Cont'd)										
Cutting or forming openings/recesses/chases etc; openings through brickwork or blockwork (Cont'd)										
Unit rates for pricing the above and similar work										
cut opening through half brick wall	-	-	-	1.95	2.40	78.06	7.85	85.92	m²	94.51
cut opening through one brick wall	-	-	-	3.80	4.70	152.49	14.87	167.35	m²	184.09
make good fair face around opening	-	-	-	0.50	0.50	18.22	1.02	19.24	m	21.17
make good facings to match existing around opening	2.17	10.00	2.39	0.50	0.50	18.22	1.02	21.63	m	23.79
prestressed precast concrete lintel; 100 x 140 x 1200mm	16.04	2.50	16.44	1.00	1.00	36.44	0.59	53.48	nr	58.82
prestressed precast concrete lintel; 215 x 140 x 1200mm	41.41	2.50	42.45	1.50	1.50	54.66	1.22	98.33	nr	108.16
wedge and pin up over lintel; 102mm wide	-	-	-	0.66	0.66	24.05	1.35	25.40	m	27.94
wedge and pin up over lintel; 215mm wide	-	-	-	1.00	1.00	36.44	2.89	39.33	m	43.26
quoin up half brick jambs	-	-	-	0.70	0.70	25.51	1.35	26.86	m	29.55
quoin up one brick jambs	-	-	-	1.27	1.27	46.28	2.89	49.17	m	54.08
facings to match existing to margin	2.17	10.00	2.39	0.67	0.67	24.41	1.35	28.15	m	30.97
make good existing plaster up to new frame	0.85	10.00	0.94	0.55	0.55	20.04	-	20.98	m	23.08
13mm two coat hardwall plaster to reveal not exceeding 300mm wide	1.71	10.00	1.88	0.78	0.78	28.42	0.03	30.33	m	33.37
make good existing external rendering up to new frame	0.29	10.00	0.31	0.47	0.47	17.13	-	17.44	m	19.18
13mm two coat cement and sand (1:3) external rendering to reveal not exceeding 300mm wide	0.57	10.00	0.63	0.74	0.74	26.97	0.03	27.63	m	30.39
take off old skirting	-	-	-	0.23	-	4.80	0.15	4.95	m	5.44
short length of old skirting up to 100mm long with mitre with existing one end	-	-	-	0.58	-	12.10	0.07	12.17	nr	13.39
short length of old skirting up to 300mm long with mitres with existing both ends	-	-	-	1.15	-	24.00	0.08	24.08	nr	26.49
38mm cement and sand (1:3) screeded bed in opening	6.43	5.00	6.75	1.54	1.54	56.12	-	62.87	m²	69.16
extend 25mm softwood board flooring through opening on and with bearers	8.45	15.00	9.46	3.65	0.61	85.67	0.23	95.36	nr	104.90
iroko threshold, twice oiled, plugged and screwed										
15 x 113mm	10.87	10.00	11.96	0.90	-	18.78	0.08	30.82	m	33.90
15 x 225mm	21.28	10.00	23.41	1.65	-	34.44	0.15	57.99	m	63.79
Form opening for window through 275mm hollow wall with two half brick skins, plastered one side and faced with picked stock facings the other; cut opening through wall, insert galvanised steel lintel; insert damp proof course and cavity gutter; quoin up jambs, close cavity at jambs with brickwork bonded to existing and with vertical damp proof course and close cavity at sill with one course of slates; face margin externally to match existing and extend plaster to face of lintel and to reveals and make good up to existing plaster and new frame										
900 x 900mm	70.25	-	70.25	15.90	16.80	593.41	24.09	687.75	nr	756.53
Unit rates for pricing the above and similar work										
cut opening through wall with two half brick skins	-	-	-	3.90	4.80	156.13	13.46	169.59	m²	186.55
cut opening through wall with one half brick and one 100mm block skins	-	-	-	3.25	3.96	129.48	13.46	142.95	m²	157.24
galvanised steel lintel, Birtley CB70; 120mm deep x 1200mm long	31.54	2.50	32.33	2.10	2.10	76.52	1.35	110.21	nr	121.23
close cavity at jambs with blockwork bonded to existing and with 112.5mm wide Hyload pitch polymer damp proof course	3.09	10.00	3.40	0.50	0.50	18.22	0.35	21.97	m	24.17
close cavity at jambs with brickwork bonded to existing and with 112.5mm wide Hyload pitch polymer damp proof course	2.95	10.00	3.25	0.70	0.70	25.51	1.35	30.11	m	33.12
close cavity at jambs with slates in cement mortar (1:3) set vertically	4.08	10.00	4.49	0.44	0.44	16.03	0.35	20.87	m	22.95
close cavity at sill with one course of slates in cement mortar (1:3)	4.08	10.00	4.49	0.44	0.44	16.03	0.35	20.87	m	22.95
polythene DPC damp proof course and cavity tray; BS 6515; width exceeding 300mm	0.79	10.00	0.87	0.80	0.80	29.15	0.35	30.37	m²	33.41
prestressed precast concrete lintel; 140 x 215 x 1200mm long	41.41	2.50	42.45	1.50	1.50	54.66	0.99	98.10	nr	107.90
mild steel angle arch bar, primed; 75 x 75 x 6mm	15.75	5.00	16.54	0.50	0.50	18.22	1.02	35.78	m	39.36
take out three courses of facing bricks and build brick-on-end flat arch in picked stock facing bricks	8.26	10.00	9.09	1.00	1.00	36.44	2.99	48.52	m	53.37
For unit rates for finishes, quoining up jambs, etc see previous items										
Form opening for window where door removed, with window head at same level as old door head, through one brick wall plastered one side and faced the other with picked stock facings; remove old lintel and flat arch, cut away for and insert 102 x 225mm precast concrete lintel and wedge and pin up over; build brick-on-end flat arch in facing bricks on 76 x 76 x 6mm mild steel angle arch bar and point to match existing; cut away jambs of old door opening to extend width; quoin up jambs and face margins externally to match existing; fill in lower part of old opening with brickwork in gauged mortar (1:2:9), bond to existing and face externally and point to match existing										
1200 x 900mm; old door opening 914 x 2082mm; extend plaster to face of lintel, reveals and filling and make good up to existing plaster and new frame; extend skirting one side and make good junction with existing	151.96	-	151.96	22.00	21.50	793.90	41.25	987.11	nr	1085.82
Unit rates for pricing the above and similar work										
take out old lintel	-	-	-	1.00	1.30	41.11	5.61	46.72	m	51.39
cut away one brick wall to increase width of opening	-	-	-	3.80	4.70	152.49	14.02	166.51	m²	183.16
cut away 275mm hollow wall of two half brick skins to increase width of opening	-	-	-	3.90	4.80	156.13	14.02	170.15	m²	187.17
For other unit rates for pricing the above and similar work see previous items and items in "Filling openings in Brickwork and Blockwork" section										

Labour hourly rates: (except Specialists) Craft Operatives 20.87 Labourer 15.57 Rates are national average prices. Refer to REGIONAL VARIATIONS for indicative levels of overall pricing in regions	MATERIALS			LABOUR				RATES		
	Del to Site £	Waste %	Material Cost £	Craft Optve Hrs	Lab Hrs	Labour Cost £	Sunds £	Nett Rate £	Unit	Gross rate (10%) £
ALTERATION WORK TO EXISTING BUILDINGS (Cont'd)										
Cutting or forming openings/recesses/chases etc; openings through brickwork or blockwork (Cont'd)										
Form opening for door frame where old window removed, with door head at same level as old window head, through one brick wall plastered one side and faced the other with picked stock facings; remove old lintel and flat arch, cut away for and insert 102 x 225mm precast concrete lintel and wedge and pin up over; build brick-on-end flat arch in facing bricks on 76 x 76 x 6mm mild steel angle arch bar and point, fill old opening at sides of new opening to reduce width with brickwork in gauged mortar (1:2:9), bond to existing, wedge and pin up at soffit, face externally and to margins and point to match existing; take off skirtings, cut away wall below sill of old opening, quion up jambs and face margins externally										
914 x 2082mm, old window opening 1200 x 900mm; extend plaster to face of lintel and filling and make good up to existing plaster and new frame; form fitted ends on existing skirting up to new frame	91.90	-	91.90	24.00	23.80	871.45	47.02	1010.37	nr	1111.41
For unit rates for pricing the above and similar work see previous items and items in "Filling openings in Brickwork and Blockwork" section										
Cutting or forming openings/recesses/chases etc; openings through rubble walling										
Form opening for door frame through 600mm rough rubble wall faced both sides; cut opening through wall, insert 600 x 150mm precast concrete lintel finished fair on all exposed faces and wedge and pin up over; quoin and face up jambs and extend softwood board flooring through opening on and with bearers and make good up to existing										
838 x 2032mm	98.36	-	98.36	41.30	43.70	1542.34	100.81	1741.52	nr	1915.67
Unit rates for pricing the above and similar work										
cut opening through 350mm random rubble wall	-	-	-	6.00	7.00	234.21	19.64	253.85	m²	279.23
cut opening through 600mm rough rubble wall	-	-	-	10.00	12.00	395.54	33.66	429.20	m²	472.12
wedge and pin up over lintel; 350mm wide	-	-	-	2.00	2.00	72.88	3.40	76.28	m	83.91
wedge and pin up over lintel; 600mm wide	-	-	-	3.00	3.00	109.32	5.96	115.28	m	126.80
quoin up; 350mm wide jambs	-	-	-	2.00	2.00	72.88	3.40	76.28	m	83.91
quoin up; 600mm wide jambs	-	-	-	3.00	3.00	109.32	5.96	115.28	m	126.80
extend 25mm softwood board flooring through opening on and with bearers	21.13	15.00	23.65	9.70	1.60	227.35	0.64	251.64	nr	276.81
Cutting or forming openings/recesses/chases etc; openings through stone faced walls										
Form opening for window through wall of half brick backing, plastered, and 100mm stone facing; cut opening through wall, insert 100 x 140mm prestressed precast concrete lintel and wedge and pin up over and build in 76 x 76 x 6mm mild steel angle arch bar to support stone facing, clean soffit of stone and point; quoin up jambs and face up and point externally; extend plaster to face of lintel and to reveals and make good up to existing plaster and new frame										
900 x 900mm	34.63	-	34.63	19.20	19.80	708.99	31.18	774.80	nr	852.28
Unit rates for pricing the above and similar work										
cut opening through wall	-	-	-	5.15	5.85	198.57	13.46	212.03	m²	233.23
prestressed precast concrete lintel; 100 x 140 x 1200mm	16.04	2.50	16.44	1.05	1.05	38.26	0.51	55.22	nr	60.74
mild steel angle arch bar, primed; 75 x 75 x 6mm	15.75	5.00	16.54	0.50	0.50	18.22	1.02	35.78	m	39.36
quoin up jambs	-	-	-	0.70	0.70	25.51	1.53	27.04	m	29.75
face stone jambs and point	-	-	-	2.10	2.10	76.52	4.26	80.78	m	88.86
clean stone head and point	-	-	-	2.10	2.10	76.52	0.51	77.04	m	84.74
For unit rates for finishes, etc. see previous items										
Cutting or forming openings/recesses/chases etc; openings through stud partitions										
Form opening for door frame through lath and plaster finished 50 x 100mm stud partition; take off skirtings, cut away plaster, cut away and trim studding around opening and insert new studding at head and jambs of opening; make good existing lath and plaster up to new frame both sides and form fitted ends on existing skirtings up to new frame; extend softwood board flooring through opening on and with bearers and make good up to existing										
838 x 2032mm	27.24	-	27.24	18.10	6.10	472.72	26.57	526.53	nr	579.18
Unit rates for pricing the above and similar work										
cut away plastered plasterboard	-	-	-	1.00	0.25	24.76	1.40	26.17	m²	28.78
cut away lath and plaster	-	-	-	1.10	0.26	27.01	1.68	28.69	m²	31.56
cut away and trim existing 75mm studding around opening										
838 x 2032mm	-	-	-	2.05	0.36	48.39	3.60	51.99	nr	57.18
914 x 2032mm	-	-	-	2.05	0.36	48.39	3.60	51.99	nr	57.18
cut away and trim existing 100mm studding around opening										
838 x 2032mm	-	-	-	2.55	0.45	60.23	4.70	64.93	nr	71.42
914 x 2032mm	-	-	-	2.55	0.45	60.23	4.70	64.93	nr	71.42
softwood studding; 50 x 75mm	1.97	10.00	2.17	0.50	0.08	11.68	0.18	14.03	m	15.43
softwood studding; 50 x 100mm	2.59	10.00	2.84	0.60	0.10	14.08	0.20	17.12	m	18.83
make good plastered plasterboard around opening	-	-	-	0.75	0.75	27.33	2.03	29.36	m	32.30
make good lath and plaster around opening	-	-	-	0.83	0.83	30.25	2.49	32.74	m	36.01
take off skirting	-	-	-	0.21	-	4.38	0.30	4.68	m	5.15
form fitted end on existing skirting	-	-	-	0.57	-	11.90	-	11.90	nr	13.09

Labour hourly rates: (except Specialists) Craft Operatives 20.87 Labourer 15.57 Rates are national average prices. Refer to REGIONAL VARIATIONS for indicative levels of overall pricing in regions	MATERIALS			LABOUR				RATES		
	Del to Site £	Waste %	Material Cost £	Craft Optve Hrs	Lab Hrs	Labour Cost £	Sunds £	Nett Rate £	Unit	Gross rate (10%) £
ALTERATION WORK TO EXISTING BUILDINGS (Cont'd)										
Cutting or forming openings/recesses/chases etc; openings through stud partitions (Cont'd)										
Unit rates for pricing the above and similar work (Cont'd)										
cut away and trim existing 100mm studding around opening (Cont'd)										
extend 25mm softwood tongued and grooved board flooring through opening on and with bearers	4.23	20.00	4.81	1.50	0.25	35.20	0.10	40.11	nr	44.12
Filling in openings/recesses etc; filling holes in concrete										
Fill holes in concrete structure where pipes removed with concrete to BS 8500, designed mix C20, 20mm aggregate; formwork										
wall; thickness 100mm; pipe diameter										
50mm	-	-	-	0.60	0.30	17.19	2.52	19.72	nr	21.69
100mm	-	-	-	0.78	0.39	22.35	3.33	25.68	nr	28.25
150mm	-	-	-	0.98	0.49	28.08	4.01	32.09	nr	35.30
wall; thickness 200mm; pipe diameter										
50mm	-	-	-	0.78	0.39	22.35	3.33	25.68	nr	28.25
100mm	-	-	-	0.98	0.49	28.08	4.01	32.09	nr	35.30
150mm	-	-	-	1.00	0.77	32.86	5.15	38.01	nr	41.81
floor; thickness 200mm; pipe diameter										
50mm	-	-	-	0.74	0.37	21.20	3.02	24.22	nr	26.65
100mm	-	-	-	0.93	0.46	26.57	3.86	30.43	nr	33.48
150mm	-	-	-	0.95	0.48	27.30	4.88	32.18	nr	35.40
Make good fair face to filling and surrounding work										
to one side of wall; pipe diameter										
50mm	-	-	-	0.10	0.10	3.64	0.35	3.99	nr	4.39
100mm	-	-	-	0.20	0.20	7.29	0.53	7.82	nr	8.60
150mm	-	-	-	0.25	0.25	9.11	0.64	9.75	nr	10.73
to soffit of floor; pipe diameter										
50mm	-	-	-	0.10	0.10	3.64	0.35	3.99	nr	4.39
100mm	-	-	-	0.20	0.20	7.29	0.53	7.82	nr	8.60
150mm	-	-	-	0.25	0.25	9.11	0.64	9.75	nr	10.73
Make good plaster to filling and surrounding work										
to one side of wall; pipe diameter										
50mm	-	-	-	0.19	0.19	6.92	0.35	7.27	nr	8.00
100mm	-	-	-	0.36	0.36	13.12	0.53	13.65	nr	15.01
150mm	-	-	-	0.45	0.45	16.40	0.64	17.04	nr	18.75
to soffit of floor; pipe diameter										
50mm	-	-	-	0.20	0.20	7.29	0.35	7.63	nr	8.40
100mm	-	-	-	0.40	0.40	14.58	0.53	15.10	nr	16.61
150mm	-	-	-	0.50	0.50	18.22	0.64	18.86	nr	20.75
Make good floor screed and surrounding work; pipe diameter										
50mm	-	-	-	0.19	0.19	6.92	0.15	7.07	nr	7.78
100mm	-	-	-	0.36	0.36	13.12	0.31	13.43	nr	14.78
150mm	-	-	-	0.45	0.45	16.40	0.43	16.83	nr	18.51
Make good vinyl or similar floor covering and surrounding work; pipe diameter										
50mm	-	-	-	0.50	0.50	18.22	2.57	20.79	nr	22.87
100mm	-	-	-	1.00	1.00	36.44	3.45	39.89	nr	43.88
150mm	-	-	-	1.20	1.20	43.73	4.83	48.56	nr	53.42
Fill holes in concrete structure where metal sections removed with concrete to BS 8500, designed mix C20, 20mm aggregate; formwork										
wall; thickness 100mm; section not exceeding 250mm deep	-	-	-	0.60	0.60	21.86	3.07	24.93	nr	27.43
wall; thickness 200mm; section not exceeding 250mm deep	-	-	-	0.75	0.75	27.33	4.47	31.80	nr	34.98
wall; thickness 100mm; section 250 - 500mm deep	-	-	-	0.75	0.75	27.33	4.47	31.80	nr	34.98
wall; thickness 200mm; section 250 - 500mm deep	-	-	-	0.90	0.90	32.80	5.40	38.19	nr	42.01
Make good fair face to filling and surrounding work										
to one side of wall; section not exceeding 250mm deep	-	-	-	0.22	0.22	8.02	0.30	8.31	nr	9.15
to one side of wall; section 250 - 500mm deep	-	-	-	0.26	0.26	9.47	0.46	9.94	nr	10.93
Make good plaster to filling and surrounding work										
to one side of wall; section not exceeding 250mm deep	-	-	-	0.35	0.35	12.75	0.81	13.56	nr	14.92
to one side of wall; section 250 - 500mm deep	-	-	-	0.43	0.43	15.67	1.22	16.89	nr	18.58
Filling in openings/recesses etc; filling openings in concrete										
Fill opening where door removed in 150mm reinforced concrete wall with concrete reinforced with 12mm mild steel bars at 300mm centres both ways tied to existing structure; hack off plaster to reveals, hack up floor covering and screed in opening, prepare edges of opening to form joint with filling, drill edges of opening and tie in new reinforcement, plaster filling both sides and extended skirting both sides; making good junction of new and existing plaster and skirtings and make good floor screed and vinyl covering up to filling both sides										
838 x 2032mm	149.03	-	149.03	22.50	34.50	1006.74	15.89	1171.66	nr	1288.83
Unit rates for pricing the above and similar work										
hack off plaster to reveal; not exceeding 100mm wide	-	-	-	-	0.24	3.74	0.12	3.85	m	4.24
hack off plaster to reveal; 100 - 200mm wide	-	-	-	-	0.33	5.14	0.23	5.37	m	5.91
take up vinyl or similar floor covering and screed	-	-	-	-	2.00	31.14	2.36	33.50	m²	36.85
prepare edge of opening wide to form joint with filling; 100mm wide	-	-	-	0.25	0.25	9.11	-	9.11	m	10.02
prepare edge of opening wide to form joint with filling; 200mm wide	-	-	-	0.35	0.35	12.75	-	12.75	m	14.03
concrete to BS 8500, design mix C 16/20 - 20 N/mm²; 20mm aggregate in walls; 150 - 450m thick	97.76	5.00	102.65	-	12.00	186.84	0.68	290.16	m³	319.18

Labour hourly rates: (except Specialists) Craft Operatives 20.87 Labourer 15.57 Rates are national average prices. Refer to REGIONAL VARIATIONS for indicative levels of overall pricing in regions	MATERIALS			LABOUR				RATES		
	Del to Site £	Waste %	Material Cost £	Craft Optve Hrs	Lab Hrs	Labour Cost £	Sunds £	Nett Rate £	Unit	Gross rate (10%) £
ALTERATION WORK TO EXISTING BUILDINGS (Cont'd)										
Filling in openings/recesses etc; filling openings in concrete (Cont'd)										
Unit rates for pricing the above and similar work (Cont'd)										
concrete to BS 8500, design mix C 16/20 - 20 N/mm²; 20mm aggregate in walls; not exceeding 150mm thick	97.76	5.00	102.65	-	12.00	186.84	0.68	290.16	m³	319.18
12mm mild steel bar reinforcement; straight	1330.00	10.00	1463.00	85.00	-	1773.95	7.44	3244.39	t	3568.83
drill edge of opening and tie in new reinforcement	-	-	-	-	1.00	15.57	0.68	16.25	m	17.87
formwork and basic finish to wall, per side	10.98	10.00	12.08	2.50	2.50	91.10	1.62	104.80	m²	115.28
formwork and fine formed finish to wall, per side	10.98	10.00	12.08	2.75	2.75	100.21	1.81	114.10	m²	125.51
junction between new and existing fair face	-	-	-	-	0.30	4.67	-	4.67	m	5.14
13mm two coat hardwall plaster over 300mm wide	5.72	10.00	6.29	1.30	1.30	47.37	-	53.66	m²	59.02
25 x 100mm softwood chamfered skirting, primed all round	1.61	10.00	1.77	0.56	0.09	13.09	0.18	15.04	m	16.55
junction with existing	-	-	-	0.50	0.08	11.68	-	11.68	nr	12.85
make good floor screed and vinyl or similar floor covering up to filling not exceeding 300mm wide	7.85	5.00	8.55	1.12	1.12	40.81	0.53	49.89	m	54.87
Fill opening where staircase removed in 150mm reinforced concrete floor with concrete reinforced with 12mm mild steel bars at 225mm centres both ways tied to existing structure; remove timber lining, prepare edges of opening to form joint with filling, drill edges of opening tie in new reinforcement, plaster filling on soffit and extend cement and sand screed and vinyl floor covering to match existing; make good junction of new and existing plaster and vinyl floor covering										
900 x 2134mm	168.68	-	168.68	14.75	22.30	655.04	13.20	836.93	nr	920.62
Unit rates for pricing the above and similar work										
take off timber lining	-	-	-	-	0.24	3.74	0.16	3.90	m	4.29
prepare edge of opening to form joint with filling; 150mm wide	-	-	-	0.30	0.30	10.93	-	10.93	m	12.03
prepare edge of opening to form joint with filling; 200mm wide	-	-	-	0.35	0.35	12.75	-	12.75	m	14.03
concrete to BS 8500, design mix C 16/20 - 20 N/mm²; 20mm aggregate in slabs; 150 - 450mm thick	97.76	5.00	102.65	-	12.00	186.84	0.68	290.16	m³	319.18
concrete to BS 8500, design mix C 16/20 - 20 N/mm²; 20mm aggregate in slabs; not exceeding 150mm thick	97.76	5.00	102.65	-	12.00	186.84	0.68	290.16	m³	319.18
12mm mild steel bar reinforcement; straight	1330.00	10.00	1463.00	85.00	-	1773.95	7.44	3244.39	t	3568.83
drill edge of opening and tie in new reinforcement	-	-	-	-	1.00	15.57	0.68	16.25	m	17.87
formwork and basic finish to soffit; slab thickness not exceeding 200mm; height to soffit 1.50 - 3.00m	15.58	10.00	17.13	2.25	2.25	81.99	1.60	100.73	m²	110.80
formwork and basic finish to soffit; slab thickness 200 - 300mm; height to soffit 1.50 - 3.00m	17.14	10.00	18.85	2.50	2.50	91.10	1.81	111.76	m²	122.94
formwork and fine formed finish to soffit; slab thickness not exceeding 200mm; height to soffit 1.50 - 3.00m	15.58	10.00	17.13	2.50	2.50	91.10	1.85	110.08	m²	121.09
formwork and fine formed finish to soffit; slab thickness 200 - 300mm; height to soffit 1.50 - 3.00m	17.14	10.00	18.85	2.75	2.75	100.21	1.91	120.97	m²	133.07
junction between new and existing fair face	-	-	-	-	0.30	4.67	-	4.67	m	5.14
10mm two coat lightweight plaster over 300mm wide	5.72	10.00	6.29	1.30	1.30	47.37	-	53.66	m²	59.02
38mm cement and sand (1:3) trowelled bed	6.43	5.00	6.75	0.63	0.63	22.96	-	29.71	m²	32.68
vinyl or similar floor covering to match existing fixed with adhesive exceeding 300mm wide	19.95	10.00	21.95	1.25	0.50	33.87	0.92	56.74	m²	62.42
Filling openings/recesses etc; filling openings in brickwork or blockwork										
Fill opening where door removed in 100mm block wall with concrete blocks in gauged mortar (1:2:9); provide 50mm preservative treated softwood sole plate on timber floor in opening, bond to blockwork at jambs and wedge and pin up at head; plaster filling both sides and extend skirting both sides; make good junction of new and existing plaster and skirtings										
838 x 2032mm	68.52	-	68.52	14.10	8.15	421.16	13.99	503.67	nr	554.04
Unit rates for pricing the above and similar work										
blockwork in filling; 75mm	11.80	10.00	12.98	1.00	1.25	40.33	1.86	55.18	m²	60.69
blockwork in filling; 100mm	15.50	10.00	17.05	1.20	1.50	48.40	2.56	68.01	m²	74.81
blockwork in filling and fair face and flush smooth pointing one side; 75mm	11.80	10.00	12.98	1.25	1.50	49.44	2.21	64.63	m²	71.10
blockwork in filling and fair face and flush smooth pointing one side; 100mm	15.50	10.00	17.05	1.45	1.75	57.51	2.72	77.28	m²	85.01
preservative treated softwood sole plate										
50 x 75mm	1.97	10.00	2.17	0.30	0.05	7.04	0.35	9.55	m	10.51
50 x 100mm	2.59	10.00	2.84	0.33	0.06	7.82	0.46	11.13	m	12.24
Hyload pitch polymer damp proof course, width not exceeding 225mm	6.79	10.00	7.47	0.80	0.80	29.15	0.68	37.30	m²	41.03
wedge and pin up at head; 75mm wide	-	-	-	0.10	0.10	3.64	0.68	4.32	m	4.75
wedge and pin up at head; 100mm wide	-	-	-	0.12	0.12	4.37	1.02	5.40	m	5.94
cut pockets and bond to existing blockwork at jambs; 75mm filling to existing blockwork at jambs	-	-	-	0.40	0.40	14.58	1.19	15.76	m	17.34
cut pockets and bond to existing blockwork at jambs; 100mm filling	-	-	-	0.50	0.50	18.22	1.68	19.90	m	21.89
12mm (average) cement and sand dubbing over 300mm wide on filling	2.03	5.00	2.13	0.54	0.54	19.68	-	21.80	m²	23.98
13mm two coat lightweight plaster over 300mm wide on filling	5.72	10.00	6.29	1.27	1.27	46.28	0.03	52.60	m²	57.86
19 x 100mm softwood chamfered skirting, primed all round	1.24	10.00	1.36	0.50	0.08	11.68	0.18	13.23	m	14.55
junction with existing	-	-	-	0.50	0.08	11.68	-	11.68	nr	12.85
make good vinyl or similar floor covering up to filling	6.64	10.00	7.31	0.50	0.50	18.22	0.23	25.76	m	28.33
Fill opening where door removed in half brick wall with brickwork in gauged mortar (1:2:9); provide lead cored damp proof course in opening, lapped with existing, bond to existing brickwork at jambs and wedge and pin up at head; plaster filling both sides and extend skirting both sides; make good junction of new and existing plaster and skirtings										
838 x 2032mm	72.67	-	72.67	15.70	12.75	526.18	17.16	616.01	nr	677.61

Labour hourly rates: (except Specialists) Craft Operatives 20.87 Labourer 15.57 Rates are national average prices. Refer to REGIONAL VARIATIONS for indicative levels of overall pricing in regions	MATERIALS			LABOUR				RATES		
	Del to Site £	Waste %	Material Cost £	Craft Optve Hrs	Lab Hrs	Labour Cost £	Sunds £	Nett Rate £	Unit	Gross rate (10%) £
ALTERATION WORK TO EXISTING BUILDINGS (Cont'd)										
Filling openings/recesses etc; filling openings in brickwork or blockwork (Cont'd)										
Unit rates for pricing the above and similar work										
half brick filling in common bricks	18.72	10.00	20.59	2.00	2.00	72.88	4.26	97.73	m²	107.50
half brick filling in common bricks fair faced and flush pointed one side	18.72	10.00	20.59	2.33	2.33	84.91	4.59	110.08	m²	121.09
50 x 100mm softwood sole plate	2.59	10.00	2.84	0.33	0.06	7.82	0.41	11.08	m	12.19
Hyload pitch polymer damp proof course, width not exceeding 225mm	6.79	10.00	7.47	0.80	0.80	29.15	0.68	37.30	m²	41.03
wedge and pin up at head 102mm wide	-	-	-	0.12	0.12	4.37	1.02	5.40	m	5.94
cut pockets and bond half brick filling to existing brickwork at jambs	-	-	-	0.50	0.50	18.22	1.70	19.92	m	21.91
For unit rates for finishes, etc see previous items										
Fill opening where door removed in one brick external wall with brickwork in gauged mortar (1:2:9) faced externally with picked stock facings pointed to match existing; remove old lintel and arch, provide lead cored damp proof course in opening lapped with existing, bond to existing brickwork at jambs and wedge and pin up at head; plaster filling one side and extend skirting; make good junction of new and existing plaster and skirting										
914 x 2082mm	238.45	-	238.45	19.65	18.85	703.59	42.40	984.45	nr	1082.89
Unit rates for pricing the above and similar work										
remove old lintel and arch	-	-	-	1.46	1.64	56.01	3.37	59.37	m	65.31
one brick filling in common bricks	37.44	10.00	41.18	4.00	4.00	145.76	10.20	197.14	m²	216.86
one brick filling in common bricks faced one side with picked stock facings and point to match existing	65.16	10.00	71.68	5.00	5.00	182.20	10.20	264.07	m²	290.48
one brick filling in common bricks fair faced and flush smooth pointing one side	37.44	10.00	41.18	4.33	4.33	157.79	10.20	209.17	m²	230.08
two course slate damp proof course, width not exceeding 225mm	32.64	10.00	35.90	1.02	1.02	37.17	1.19	74.26	m²	81.69
Hyload pitch polymer damp proof course, BS 6398, Class F, width not exceeding 225mm	6.79	10.00	7.47	0.80	0.80	29.15	0.51	37.14	m²	40.85
wedge and pin up at head 215mm wide	-	-	-	0.20	0.20	7.29	2.38	9.66	m	10.63
cut pockets and bond one brick filling to existing brickwork at jambs	-	-	-	1.00	1.00	36.44	3.91	40.35	m	44.39
12mm cement and sand (1:3) two coat external rendering over 300mm wide on filling	2.03	5.00	2.13	1.25	1.25	45.55	0.07	47.74	m²	52.52
For unit rates for internal finishes, etc. see previous items										
Fill opening where door removed in 275mm external hollow wall with inner skin in common bricks and outer skin in picked stock facings pointed to match existing, in gauged mortar (1:2:9); remove old lintel and arch, provide lead cored combined damp proof course and cavity gutter lapped with existing; form cavity with ties; bond to existing brickwork at jambs and wedge and pin up at head; plaster filling one side and extend skirting; make good junction of new and existing plaster and skirting										
914 x 2082mm	150.60	-	150.60	19.90	19.10	712.70	43.31	906.61	nr	997.27
Unit rates for pricing the above and similar work										
half brick filling in common bricks	18.72	10.00	20.59	2.00	2.00	72.88	4.26	97.73	m²	107.50
half brick filling in common bricks and fair face and flush smooth pointing one side	18.72	10.00	20.59	2.33	2.33	84.91	4.59	110.08	m²	121.09
half brick filling in picked stock facings and point to match existing	37.20	10.00	40.92	2.95	2.95	107.50	4.59	153.01	m²	168.31
form 50mm wide cavity with stainless steel housing type 4 wall ties built in	0.82	10.00	0.90	0.20	0.20	7.29	-	8.19	m²	9.01
Hyload "Original", pitch polymer damp proof course and cavity tray, width exceeding 225mm	6.79	10.00	7.47	0.80	0.80	29.15	0.51	37.14	m²	40.85
wedge and pin up at head 102mm wide	-	-	-	0.12	0.12	4.37	1.02	5.40	m	5.94
cut pockets and bond half brick wall in common bricks to existing brickwork at jambs	-	-	-	0.50	0.50	18.22	1.70	19.92	m	21.91
cut pockets and bond half brick wall in facing bricks to existing brickwork at jambs and make good facings	-	-	-	0.60	0.60	21.86	3.56	25.43	m	27.97
For unit rates for internal finishes, etc. see previous items										
Filling in openings/recesses etc; filling openings in rubble walling										
Fill opening where window removed in 600mm rough rubble wall with rubble walling in lime mortar (1:3) pointed to match existing; bond to existing walling at jambs and wedge and pin up at head; plaster filling one side and make good junction of new and existing plaster										
900 x 900mm	135.57	-	135.57	12.00	12.00	437.28	26.23	599.08	nr	658.99
Unit rates for pricing the above and similar work										
rough rubble walling in filling										
600mm thick	132.34	10.00	145.57	6.00	6.00	218.64	20.39	384.60	m²	423.06
random rubble walling in filling										
300mm thick	103.95	10.00	114.35	5.80	5.80	211.35	10.20	335.89	m²	369.48
500mm thick	111.64	10.00	122.80	10.90	10.90	397.20	16.99	536.99	m²	590.69
wedge and pin up at head										
300mm wide	-	-	-	0.28	0.28	10.20	3.40	13.60	m	14.96
500mm wide	-	-	-	0.47	0.47	17.13	5.78	22.90	m	25.19
600mm wide	-	-	-	0.56	0.56	20.41	6.80	27.20	m	29.92

Labour hourly rates: (except Specialists) Craft Operatives 20.87 Labourer 15.57 Rates are national average prices. Refer to REGIONAL VARIATIONS for indicative levels of overall pricing in regions	MATERIALS			LABOUR				RATES		
	Del to Site £	Waste %	Material Cost £	Craft Optve Hrs	Lab Hrs	Labour Cost £	Sunds £	Nett Rate £	Unit	Gross rate (10%) £
ALTERATION WORK TO EXISTING BUILDINGS (Cont'd)										
Filling in openings/recesses etc; filling openings in rubble walling (Cont'd)										
Unit rates for pricing the above and similar work (Cont'd)										
cut pockets and bond walling to existing at jambs										
300mm	7.80	10.00	8.58	0.83	0.83	30.25	1.02	39.84	m	43.83
500mm	8.37	10.00	9.21	1.38	1.38	50.29	1.53	61.03	m	67.14
600mm	9.93	10.00	10.92	1.75	1.75	63.77	1.86	76.55	m	84.21
Filling openings/recesses etc; filling openings in stud partitions										
Fill opening where door removed in stud partition with 50 x 100mm studding and sole plate, covered on both sides with 9.5mm plasterboard baseboard with 5mm one coat board finish plaster; extend skirting on both sides; make good junction of new and existing plaster and skirtings										
838 x 2032mm	54.48	-	54.48	16.00	5.36	417.38	4.95	476.80	nr	524.48
Unit rates for pricing the above and similar work										
softwood sole plate; 50 x 75mm	1.97	10.00	2.17	0.50	0.08	11.68	0.18	14.03	m	15.43
softwood sole plate; 50 x 100mm	2.59	10.00	2.84	0.60	0.10	14.08	0.23	17.15	m	18.87
softwood studding; 50 x 75mm	1.97	10.00	2.17	0.50	0.08	11.68	0.18	14.03	m	15.43
softwood studding; 50 x 100mm	2.59	10.00	2.84	0.60	0.10	14.08	0.23	17.15	m	18.87
9.5mm plasterboard baseboard to filling	4.10	10.00	4.51	0.50	0.10	11.99	0.46	16.96	m²	18.66
9.5mm plasterboard baseboard to filling including packing out not exceeding 10mm	4.10	10.00	4.51	1.00	0.17	23.52	0.61	28.64	m²	31.50
5mm one coat board finish plaster on plasterboard to filling	1.33	10.00	1.47	0.91	0.91	33.16	0.05	34.68	m²	38.14
10mm two coat hardwall plaster on plasterboard to filling	2.22	10.00	2.45	1.27	1.27	46.28	0.05	48.77	m²	53.65
softwood chamfered skirting, primed all round; 19 x 100mm	1.24	10.00	1.36	0.54	0.09	12.67	0.30	14.33	m	15.77
junction with existing; 19 x 100mm	-	-	-	0.57	-	11.90	-	11.90	nr	13.09
softwood chamfered skirting, primed all round; 25 x 150mm	2.56	10.00	2.82	0.55	0.09	12.88	0.40	16.09	m	17.70
junction with existing; 25 x 150mm	-	-	-	0.57	-	11.90	-	11.90	nr	13.09
For unit rates for internal finishes, etc. see previous items										
Removing existing and replacing; masonry										
Cut out decayed bricks and replace with new bricks in gauged mortar (1:2:9) and make good surrounding work										
Fair faced common bricks										
singly	0.31	10.00	0.34	0.17	0.17	6.19	0.23	6.77	nr	7.45
small patches	18.72	10.00	20.59	5.80	5.80	211.35	9.87	241.81	m²	265.99
Picked stock facing bricks										
singly	0.62	10.00	0.68	0.17	0.17	6.19	0.23	7.11	nr	7.82
small patches	37.20	10.00	40.92	5.80	5.80	211.35	9.87	262.14	m²	288.35
Cut out defective wall and re-build in gauged mortar (1:2:9) and tooth and bond to surrounding work (25% new bricks allowed)										
Half brick wall; stretcher bond										
common bricks	4.68	10.00	5.15	4.00	4.00	145.76	5.66	156.57	m²	172.22
One brick wall; English bond										
common bricks	9.36	10.00	10.30	7.90	7.90	287.88	12.16	310.33	m²	341.37
common bricks faced one side with picked stock facings	16.29	10.00	17.92	8.30	8.30	302.45	12.16	332.53	m²	365.78
picked stock facing bricks faced both sides	18.60	10.00	20.46	8.80	8.80	320.67	12.16	353.29	m²	388.62
One brick wall; Flemish bond										
common bricks	9.36	10.00	10.30	7.90	7.90	287.88	5.66	303.83	m²	334.21
common bricks faced one side with picked stock facings	16.29	10.00	17.92	8.30	8.30	302.45	12.16	332.53	m²	365.78
picked stock facing bricks faced both sides	18.60	10.00	20.46	8.80	8.80	320.67	12.16	353.29	m²	388.62
275mm hollow wall; skins in stretcher bond										
two half brick skins in common bricks	9.36	10.00	10.30	8.16	8.16	297.35	12.39	320.04	m²	352.04
one half brick skin in common bricks and one half brick skin in picked stock facings	13.98	10.00	15.38	8.60	8.60	313.38	12.39	341.15	m²	375.27
one 100mm skin in concrete blocks and one half brick skin in picked stock facings	13.18	10.00	14.49	8.26	8.26	300.99	11.58	327.07	m²	359.78
Cut out crack in brickwork and stitch across with new bricks in gauged mortar(1:2:9); average 450mm wide										
Half brick wall										
common bricks	8.11	10.00	8.92	1.90	1.90	69.24	5.49	83.65	m	92.02
common bricks fair faced one side	8.11	10.00	8.92	2.30	2.30	83.81	5.49	98.23	m	108.05
picked stock facing bricks faced both sides	16.12	10.00	17.73	2.40	2.40	87.46	5.49	110.68	m	121.75
One brick wall										
common bricks	16.22	10.00	17.85	3.90	3.90	142.12	11.83	171.79	m	188.97
common bricks fair faced one side	16.22	10.00	17.85	4.40	4.40	160.34	11.83	190.01	m	209.01
common bricks faced one side with picked stock facings	28.24	10.00	31.06	4.60	4.60	167.62	11.83	210.51	m	231.57
picked stock facing bricks faced both sides	32.24	10.00	35.46	4.70	4.70	171.27	11.83	218.56	m	240.42
Cut out defective arch; re-build in picked stock facing bricks in gauged mortar (1:2:9) including centering										
Brick-on-edge flat arch										
102mm on soffit	4.34	10.00	4.77	1.00	1.00	36.44	1.39	42.60	m	46.86
215mm on soffit	8.26	10.00	9.09	0.95	0.95	34.62	2.43	46.13	m	50.75
Brick-on-end flat arch										
102mm on soffit	8.26	10.00	9.09	0.95	0.95	34.62	2.43	46.13	m	50.75
215mm on soffit	16.53	10.00	18.18	1.90	1.90	69.24	4.85	92.27	m	101.50
Segmental arch in two half brick rings										
102mm on soffit	8.26	10.00	9.09	2.90	2.90	105.68	2.43	117.19	m	128.91
215mm on soffit	16.53	10.00	18.18	2.90	2.90	105.68	4.85	128.71	m	141.58
Semi-circular arch in two half brick rings										
102mm on soffit	8.26	10.00	9.09	2.90	2.90	105.68	2.43	117.19	m	128.91
215mm on soffit	16.53	10.00	18.18	2.90	2.90	105.68	4.85	128.71	m	141.58

Labour hourly rates: (except Specialists) Craft Operatives 20.87 Labourer 15.57 Rates are national average prices. Refer to REGIONAL VARIATIONS for indicative levels of overall pricing in regions	MATERIALS			LABOUR				RATES		
	Del to Site £	Waste %	Material Cost £	Craft Optve Hrs	Lab Hrs	Labour Cost £	Sunds £	Nett Rate £	Unit	Gross rate (10%) £
ALTERATION WORK TO EXISTING BUILDINGS (Cont'd)										
Removing existing and replacing; masonry (Cont'd)										
Cut out defective external sill and re-build										
Shaped brick-on-edge sill in picked stock facing bricks in gauged mortar (1:2:9)										
225mm wide	8.26	10.00	9.09	1.00	1.00	36.44	3.38	48.91	m	53.80
Roofing tile sill set weathering and projecting in cement mortar (1:3)										
two courses	8.04	10.00	8.84	1.20	1.20	43.73	1.75	54.32	m	59.75
Take down defective brick-on-edge coping and re-build in picked stock facing bricks in gauged mortar (1:2:9)										
Coping										
to one brick wall	8.26	10.00	9.09	0.60	0.60	21.86	3.38	34.34	m	37.77
Coping with cement fillets both sides										
to one brick wall; with oversailing course	12.40	10.00	13.64	0.67	0.67	24.41	5.08	43.14	m	47.45
to one brick wall; with single course tile creasing	12.28	10.00	13.51	1.09	1.09	39.72	4.26	57.49	m	63.24
to one brick wall; with double course tile creasing	16.30	10.00	17.94	1.38	1.38	50.29	6.01	74.23	m	81.65
Cut out defective air brick and replace with new; bed and point in gauged mortar (1:2:9)										
Cast iron, light, square hole										
225 x 75mm	14.17	-	14.17	0.45	0.45	16.40	0.26	30.83	nr	33.91
225 x 150mm	25.83	-	25.83	0.45	0.45	16.40	0.43	42.66	nr	46.93
Terra cotta										
215 x 65mm	4.17	-	4.17	0.45	0.45	16.40	0.26	20.83	nr	22.92
215 x 140mm	6.18	-	6.18	0.45	0.45	16.40	0.43	23.01	nr	25.31
Air bricks in old walls										
Cut opening through old one brick wall, render all round in cement mortar (1:3); build in clay air brick externally and fibrous plaster ventilator internally and make good facings and plaster										
215 x 140mm	7.68	-	7.68	1.75	1.75	63.77	0.91	72.36	nr	79.59
225 x 225mm	16.59	-	16.59	2.33	2.33	84.91	1.14	102.63	nr	112.89
Cut opening through old 275mm hollow brick wall and seal cavity with slates; build in clay air brick externally and fibrous plaster ventilator internally and make good facings and plaster										
215 x 140mm	11.76	10.00	12.17	2.14	2.14	77.98	0.91	91.06	nr	100.16
225 x 225mm	20.67	10.00	21.08	2.81	2.81	102.40	1.14	124.61	nr	137.07
Removing existing and replacing; concrete										
Re-bed loose copings										
Take off loose concrete coping and clean and remove old bedding mortar										
re-bed, joint and point in cement mortar (1:3)	-	-	-	1.00	1.00	36.44	1.65	38.09	m	41.90
Repairing cracks in concrete										
Repair cracks; clean out all dust and debris and fill with mortar mixed with a bonding agent										
up to 5mm wide	-	-	-	0.50	0.50	18.22	0.79	19.01	m	20.91
Repair cracks; cutting out to form groove, treat with bonding agent and fill with fine concrete mixed with a bonding agent										
25 x 25mm deep	-	-	-	0.50	0.50	18.22	1.44	19.66	m	21.62
40 x 40mm deep	-	-	-	0.60	0.60	21.86	3.40	25.26	m	27.79
Breaking up and reinstatement of concrete floors for excavations										
Break up concrete bed and 150mm hardcore bed under for a width of 760mm for excavation of trench and reinstate with new hardcore and in-situ concrete, BS 8500, design mix C20P; 20mm aggregate; make good up to new wall and existing concrete bed both sides										
with 100mm plain concrete bed	14.80	7.50	16.80	-	2.70	42.04	10.66	69.50	m	76.45
with 150mm plain concrete bed	20.24	7.50	22.64	-	5.00	77.85	12.90	113.39	m	124.73
with 100mm concrete bed reinforced with steel fabric to BS 4483, Reference A193	18.83	7.50	21.23	-	4.05	63.06	10.66	94.94	m	104.44
with 150mm concrete bed reinforced with steel fabric to BS 4483, Reference A193	24.26	7.50	27.07	-	7.33	114.13	12.90	154.10	m	169.51
Removing existing and replacing; stone										
Note										
restoration and repair of stonework is work for a specialist; prices should be obtained for specific projects. Some firms that specialise in this class of work are included within the Products and Services pages at the end of the book										
Repairs in Portland stone work and set in gauged mortar (1:2:9) and point to match existing										
Cut out decayed stones in facings of walls, piers or the like, prepare for and set new 75mm thick stone facings										
single stone	436.80	-	436.80	15.00	15.00	546.60	11.14	994.54	m²	1093.99
areas of two or more adjacent stones	436.80	-	436.80	12.00	12.00	437.28	11.14	885.22	m²	973.74
Take out decayed stone sill, prepare for and set new sunk weathered and throated sill										
175 x 100mm	229.32	-	229.32	1.80	1.80	65.59	1.50	296.41	m	326.05
250 x 125mm	312.31	-	312.31	2.50	2.50	91.10	2.54	405.95	m	446.55
Take out sections of decayed stone coping, prepare for and set new weathered and twice throated coping										
300 x 75mm	278.46	-	278.46	1.40	1.40	51.02	1.88	331.36	m	364.49
300 x 100mm	316.68	-	316.68	1.70	1.70	61.95	2.49	381.12	m	419.23

Labour hourly rates: (except Specialists) Craft Operatives 20.87 Labourer 15.57 Rates are national average prices. Refer to REGIONAL VARIATIONS for indicative levels of overall pricing in regions	MATERIALS			LABOUR				RATES		
	Del to Site £	Waste %	Material Cost £	Craft Optve Hrs	Lab Hrs	Labour Cost £	Sunds £	Nett Rate £	Unit	Gross rate (10%) £
ALTERATION WORK TO EXISTING BUILDINGS (Cont'd)										
Removing existing and replacing; stone (Cont'd)										
Repairs in York stone work and set in gauged mortar (1:2:9) and point to match existing										
Cut out decayed stones in facings of walls, piers or the like, prepare for and set new 75mm thick stone facings										
single stone	242.00	-	242.00	17.00	17.00	619.48	11.14	872.62	m²	959.88
areas of two or more adjacent stones	242.00	-	242.00	13.75	13.75	501.05	11.14	754.19	m²	829.61
Take out decayed stone sill, prepare for and set new sunk weathered and throated sill										
175 x 100mm	86.84	-	86.84	1.80	1.80	65.59	1.88	154.32	m	169.75
250 x 125mm	134.43	-	134.43	2.50	2.50	91.10	2.49	228.02	m	250.82
Take out sections of decayed stone coping, prepare for and set new weathered and twice throated coping										
300 x 75mm	95.17	-	95.17	1.40	1.40	51.02	1.88	148.07	m	162.88
300 x 100mm	111.83	-	111.83	1.70	1.70	61.95	2.49	176.27	m	193.89
Rake out decayed mortar joints and re-point in gauged mortar (1:2:9)										
Re-point rubble walling										
coursed	-	-	-	1.25	1.25	45.55	1.85	47.40	m²	52.14
uncoursed	-	-	-	1.32	1.32	48.10	1.85	49.95	m²	54.94
squared	-	-	-	1.25	1.25	45.55	1.85	47.40	m²	52.14
Re-point stonework										
ashlar	-	-	-	1.20	1.20	43.73	1.85	45.58	m²	50.13
coursed block	-	-	-	1.20	1.20	43.73	1.85	45.58	m²	50.13
Removing existing and replacing; timber										
Cut out rotten or infected structural timber members including cutting away wall, etc. and shoring up adjacent work and replace with new pressure impregnated timber										
Plates and bed in cement mortar (1:3)										
50 x 75mm	1.97	10.00	2.17	0.30	0.30	10.93	0.28	13.38	m	14.72
75 x 100mm	4.19	10.00	4.61	0.50	0.50	18.22	0.54	23.37	m	25.71
Floor or roof joists										
50 x 175mm	4.53	10.00	4.98	0.57	0.57	20.77	0.63	26.38	m	29.02
50 x 225mm	5.83	10.00	6.41	0.67	0.67	24.41	0.81	31.64	m	34.80
75 x 175mm	7.23	10.00	7.95	0.79	0.79	28.79	0.96	37.70	m	41.47
Rafters										
38 x 100mm	2.20	10.00	2.42	0.35	0.35	12.75	0.28	15.45	m	17.00
50 x 100mm	2.59	10.00	2.84	0.38	0.38	13.85	0.36	17.05	m	18.76
Ceiling joists and collars										
50 x 100mm	2.59	10.00	2.84	0.38	0.38	13.85	0.36	17.05	m	18.76
50 x 150mm	3.88	10.00	4.27	0.52	0.52	18.95	0.54	23.76	m	26.14
Purlins, ceiling beams and struts										
75 x 100mm	4.19	10.00	4.61	0.55	0.55	20.04	0.54	25.20	m	27.72
100 x 225mm	18.27	10.00	20.10	1.23	1.23	44.82	1.63	66.55	m	73.21
Roof trusses										
75 x 100mm	4.19	10.00	4.61	0.92	0.92	33.52	0.54	38.68	m	42.55
75 x 150mm	6.20	10.00	6.82	1.37	1.37	49.92	0.81	57.55	m	63.31
Hangers in roof										
25 x 75mm	0.95	10.00	1.04	0.30	0.30	10.93	0.15	12.13	m	13.34
38 x 100mm	2.20	10.00	2.42	0.45	0.45	16.40	0.28	19.10	m	21.01
Cut out rotten or infected timber and prepare timber under to receive new										
Roof boarding; provide new 25mm pressure impregnated softwood boarding										
flat boarding; areas not exceeding 0.50m²	19.91	10.00	21.90	1.96	1.96	71.42	1.80	95.13	m²	104.64
flat boarding; areas 0.50 - 5.00m²	19.91	10.00	21.90	1.63	1.63	59.40	1.80	83.10	m²	91.41
sloping boarding; areas not exceeding 0.50m²	19.91	10.00	21.90	2.34	2.34	85.27	1.80	108.97	m²	119.87
sloping boarding; areas 0.50 - 5.00m²	19.91	10.00	21.90	1.89	1.89	68.87	1.80	92.57	m²	101.83
Gutter boarding and bearers; provide new 25mm pressure impregnated softwood boarding and 50 x 50mm bearers										
over 300mm wide	25.15	10.00	27.67	2.06	2.06	75.07	2.16	104.90	m²	115.39
200mm	6.60	10.00	7.26	0.55	0.55	20.04	0.73	28.03	m	30.83
225mm	7.10	10.00	7.81	0.62	0.62	22.59	0.79	31.20	m	34.31
Gutter sides; provide new 19mm pressure impregnated softwood boarding										
150mm	1.98	15.00	2.28	0.46	0.46	16.76	0.20	19.24	m	21.16
200mm	4.03	15.00	4.63	0.50	0.50	18.22	0.28	23.14	m	25.45
225mm	4.66	15.00	5.36	0.57	0.57	20.77	0.31	26.44	m	29.08
Eaves or verge soffit and bearers and provide new 25mm pressure impregnated softwood boarding and 25 x 50mm bearers										
over 300mm wide	21.33	15.00	24.46	2.10	2.10	76.52	2.16	103.15	m²	113.46
225mm	5.37	15.00	6.10	0.67	0.67	24.41	0.79	31.31	m	34.44
Fascia; provide new pressure impregnated softwood										
25 x 150mm	2.52	15.00	2.90	0.46	0.46	16.76	0.28	19.94	m	21.94
25 x 200mm	3.44	15.00	3.96	0.51	0.51	18.58	0.36	22.90	m	25.19
Barge board; provide new pressure impregnated softwood										
25 x 225mm	3.95	15.00	4.54	0.55	0.55	20.04	0.41	25.00	m	27.50
25 x 250mm	4.17	15.00	4.80	0.57	0.57	20.77	0.46	26.03	m	28.63
Take up floor boarding, remove all nails and clean joists under, re-lay boarding, clear away and replace damaged boards and sand surface (20% new softwood boards allowed)										
Square edged boarding										
25mm	3.21	15.00	3.70	1.73	1.73	63.04	0.73	67.46	m²	74.21
38mm	5.07	15.00	5.83	1.76	1.76	64.13	0.91	70.88	m²	77.96
Tongued and grooved boarding										
25mm	3.22	20.00	3.86	1.87	1.87	68.14	0.73	72.73	m²	80.00
32mm	5.67	20.00	6.80	1.89	1.89	68.87	0.91	76.58	m²	84.24

ALTERATIONS, REPAIRS AND CONSERVATION

Labour hourly rates: (except Specialists) Craft Operatives 20.87 Labourer 15.57 Rates are national average prices. Refer to REGIONAL VARIATIONS for indicative levels of overall pricing in regions	MATERIALS			LABOUR				RATES		
	Del to Site £	Waste %	Material Cost £	Craft Optve Hrs	Lab Hrs	Labour Cost £	Sunds £	Nett Rate £	Unit	Gross rate (10%) £
ALTERATION WORK TO EXISTING BUILDINGS (Cont'd)										
Removing existing and replacing; timber (Cont'd)										
Take up floor boarding, remove all nails and clean joists under, re-lay boarding, destroy and replace infected boards with new pressure impregnated boards and sand surface (20% new softwood boards allowed)										
Square edged boarding										
25mm	3.98	15.00	4.58	1.81	1.81	65.96	0.73	71.26	m²	78.39
38mm	5.59	15.00	6.43	1.83	1.83	66.69	0.91	74.02	m²	81.42
Tongued and grooved boarding										
25mm	3.50	20.00	4.20	1.94	1.94	70.69	0.73	75.62	m²	83.18
32mm	6.04	20.00	7.25	1.95	1.95	71.06	0.91	79.22	m²	87.14
Take up worn or damaged floor boarding, remove all nails and clean joists under and replace with new softwood boarding										
Square edged boarding										
25mm in areas not exceeding 0.50m²	16.07	15.00	18.48	1.90	1.90	69.24	1.80	89.51	m²	98.47
38mm in areas not exceeding 0.50m²	25.36	15.00	29.17	1.94	1.94	70.69	2.29	102.16	m²	112.37
25mm in areas 0.50 - 3.00m²	16.07	15.00	18.48	1.57	1.57	57.21	1.80	77.49	m²	85.24
38mm in areas 0.50 - 3.00m²	25.36	15.00	29.17	1.61	1.61	58.67	2.29	90.13	m²	99.14
Tongued and grooved boarding										
25mm in areas not exceeding 0.50m²	16.09	20.00	19.30	2.00	2.00	72.88	1.80	93.98	m²	103.38
32mm in areas not exceeding 0.50m²	28.33	20.00	34.00	2.06	2.06	75.07	2.29	111.36	m²	122.50
25mm in areas 0.50 - 3.00m²	16.09	20.00	19.30	1.82	1.82	66.32	1.80	87.42	m²	96.17
32mm in areas 0.50 - 3.00m²	28.33	20.00	34.00	1.87	1.87	68.14	2.29	104.44	m²	114.88
Punch down all nails, remove all tacks, etc. and fill nail holes										
Surface of existing flooring										
generally	-	-	-	0.50	0.10	11.99	0.05	12.04	m²	13.25
generally and machine sand in addition	-	-	-	1.00	0.30	25.54	1.95	27.49	m²	30.24
Note										
removal of old floor coverings included elsewhere										
Easing and overhauling doors										
Ease and adjust door and oil ironmongery										
762 x 1981mm	-	-	-	0.33	0.06	7.82	0.03	7.85	nr	8.64
914 x 2134mm	-	-	-	0.39	0.06	9.07	0.03	9.11	nr	10.02
Take off door, shave 12mm off bottom edge and re-hang										
762 x 1981mm	-	-	-	0.66	0.11	15.49	-	15.49	nr	17.04
914 x 2134mm	-	-	-	0.79	0.13	18.51	-	18.51	nr	20.36
Adapting doors										
Take off door and re-hang on opposite hand, piece out as necessary and oil ironmongery										
762 x 1981mm	-	-	-	2.50	0.25	56.07	0.16	56.23	nr	61.86
914 x 2134mm	-	-	-	2.65	0.44	62.16	0.16	62.32	nr	68.55
Refixing removed doors and frames										
Doors										
762 x 1981mm	-	-	-	2.00	0.34	47.03	0.23	47.26	nr	51.99
914 x 2134mm	-	-	-	2.25	0.38	52.87	0.23	53.11	nr	58.42
Doors and frames; oil existing ironmongery										
762 x 1981mm	-	-	-	4.00	0.66	93.76	0.58	94.33	nr	103.77
914 x 2134mm	-	-	-	4.50	0.75	105.59	0.58	106.17	nr	116.79
Repairing doors and frames										
Piece in door where ironmongery removed										
rim lock	-	-	-	1.00	0.15	23.21	0.26	23.47	nr	25.82
rim lock or latch and furniture	-	-	-	1.50	0.25	35.20	0.64	35.84	nr	39.43
mortice lock	-	-	-	1.50	0.25	35.20	0.64	35.84	nr	39.43
mortice lock or latch and furniture	-	-	-	2.00	0.32	46.72	0.76	47.48	nr	52.23
butt hinge	-	-	-	0.50	0.08	11.68	0.36	12.04	nr	13.25
Piece in frame where ironmongery removed										
lock or latch keep	-	-	-	0.50	0.08	11.68	0.36	12.04	nr	13.25
butt hinge	-	-	-	0.50	0.08	11.68	0.36	12.04	nr	13.25
Take off door, dismantle as necessary, cramp and re-wedge with new glued wedges, pin and re-hang										
panelled; 762 x 1981mm	-	-	-	5.00	0.84	117.43	0.26	117.69	nr	129.46
panelled; 914 x 2134mm	-	-	-	6.00	1.00	140.79	0.26	141.05	nr	155.16
glazed panelled; 762 x 1981mm	-	-	-	5.50	0.90	128.80	0.26	129.06	nr	141.97
glazed panelled; 914 x 2134mm	-	-	-	6.50	1.08	152.47	0.26	152.73	nr	168.01
Take off softwood panelled door 762 x 1981mm, dismantle as necessary and replace the following damaged members and re-hang										
top rail; 38 x 125mm	2.31	10.00	2.54	2.15	0.36	50.48	0.74	53.76	nr	59.13
hanging stile; 38 x 125mm	6.00	10.00	6.60	2.36	0.39	55.33	1.88	63.81	nr	70.19
locking stile; 38 x 125mm	6.00	10.00	6.60	2.36	0.39	55.33	1.88	63.81	nr	70.19
middle rail; 38 x 200mm	3.70	10.00	4.07	4.23	0.71	99.33	1.22	104.62	nr	115.08
bottom rail; 38 x 200mm	3.70	10.00	4.07	2.20	0.37	51.67	1.22	56.96	nr	62.66
Take off ash panelled door 762 x 1981mm, dismantle as necessary and replace the following damaged members and re-hang										
top rail; 38 x 125mm	12.37	10.00	13.61	5.20	0.87	122.07	0.74	136.42	nr	150.07
top rail; 38 x 150mm	14.85	10.00	16.34	5.20	0.87	122.07	0.74	139.15	nr	153.06
hanging stile; 38 x 125mm	32.17	10.00	35.39	5.36	0.89	125.72	1.88	162.99	nr	179.29
locking stile; 38 x 125mm	32.17	10.00	35.39	5.36	0.89	125.72	1.88	162.99	nr	179.29
middle rail; 38 x 150mm	14.85	10.00	16.34	10.40	1.73	243.98	1.22	261.54	nr	287.70
middle rail; 38 x 200mm	19.80	10.00	21.78	10.40	1.73	243.98	1.22	266.98	nr	293.68
bottom rail; 38 x 175mm	14.85	10.00	16.34	5.30	0.88	124.31	1.22	141.87	nr	156.06
bottom rail; 38 x 200mm	19.80	10.00	21.78	5.30	0.88	124.31	1.22	147.31	nr	162.04
Take off damaged softwood stop and replace with new										
12 x 38mm	0.53	10.00	0.58	0.35	0.06	8.24	0.16	8.99	m	9.89
25 (fin) x 50mm glue and screw on	0.83	10.00	0.91	0.45	0.08	10.64	0.20	11.75	m	12.92

Labour hourly rates: (except Specialists) Craft Operatives 20.87 Labourer 15.57 Rates are national average prices. Refer to REGIONAL VARIATIONS for indicative levels of overall pricing in regions	MATERIALS			LABOUR				RATES		
	Del to Site £	Waste %	Material Cost £	Craft Optve Hrs	Lab Hrs	Labour Cost £	Sunds £	Nett Rate £	Unit	Gross rate (10%) £
ALTERATION WORK TO EXISTING BUILDINGS (Cont'd)										
Removing existing and replacing; timber (Cont'd)										
Repairing doors and frames (Cont'd)										
Take off damaged ash stop and replace with new										
12 x 38mm	3.72	10.00	4.09	0.45	0.08	10.64	0.16	14.89	m	16.38
25 (fin) x 50mm glue and screw on	4.12	10.00	4.53	0.69	0.12	16.27	0.20	21.00	m	23.10
Flush facing old doors										
Take off panelled door, remove ironmongery, cover both sides with 3.2mm hardboard; refix ironmongery, adjust stops and re-hang										
762 x 1981mm	13.79	10.00	15.17	3.10	0.50	72.48	0.41	88.07	nr	96.87
838 x 1981mm	13.79	10.00	15.17	3.15	0.51	73.68	0.41	89.27	nr	98.19
Take off panelled door, remove ironmongery, cover one side with 3.2mm hardboard and other side with 6mm fire resistant sheeting screwed on; refix ironmongery, adjust stops and re-hang										
762 x 1981mm	85.35	10.00	93.88	4.00	0.67	93.91	1.35	189.15	nr	208.06
838 x 1981mm	85.35	10.00	93.88	4.05	0.68	95.11	1.35	190.35	nr	209.38
Take off panelled door, remove ironmongery, cover one side with 3.2mm hardboard, fill panels on other side with 6mm fire resistant sheeting and cover with 6mm fire resistant sheeting screwed on; refix ironmongery, adjust stops and re-hang										
762 x 1981mm	124.57	10.00	137.03	5.00	0.83	117.27	1.73	256.03	nr	281.64
838 x 1981mm	124.57	10.00	137.03	5.05	0.84	118.47	1.73	257.23	nr	282.96
Take off flush door, remove ironmongery, cover one side with 6mm fire resistant sheeting screwed on; refix ironmongery and re-hang										
762 x 1981mm	78.45	10.00	86.29	2.50	0.42	58.71	0.87	145.88	nr	160.47
838 x 1981mm	78.45	10.00	86.29	2.50	0.43	58.87	0.87	146.04	nr	160.64
Easing and overhauling windows										
Ease and adjust and oil ironmongery										
casement opening light	-	-	-	0.41	0.07	9.65	0.03	9.68	nr	10.65
double hung sash and renew sash lines with Flax cord	0.84	10.00	0.92	1.64	0.27	38.43	0.08	39.44	nr	43.38
Refixing removed windows										
Windows										
casement opening light and oil ironmongery	-	-	-	1.03	0.17	24.14	0.07	24.21	nr	26.63
double hung sash and provide new Flax cord	0.84	10.00	0.92	1.70	0.28	39.84	0.08	40.84	nr	44.93
Single or multi-light timber casements and frames										
440 x 920mm	-	-	-	4.00	0.66	93.76	0.07	93.82	nr	103.20
1225 x 1070mm	-	-	-	6.00	1.00	140.79	0.08	140.87	nr	154.96
2395 x 1225mm	-	-	-	8.00	1.33	187.67	0.10	187.77	nr	206.54
Repairing windows										
Remove damaged members of cased frame and replace with new softwood										
parting bead	0.91	10.00	1.01	1.16	0.19	27.17	0.08	28.26	m	31.08
pulley stile	4.45	10.00	4.90	1.68	0.28	39.42	0.23	44.55	m	49.01
stop bead	1.77	10.00	1.94	0.62	0.10	14.50	0.08	16.52	m	18.18
Take out sash not exceeding 50mm thick, dismantle as necessary, replace the following damaged members in softwood and re-hang with new Flax sash cord										
glazing bar	3.79	10.00	4.17	3.14	0.52	73.63	0.08	77.88	m	85.67
stile	12.25	10.00	13.47	3.03	0.50	71.02	0.15	84.64	m	93.10
rail	7.81	10.00	8.59	2.80	0.45	65.44	0.41	74.44	m	81.89
Take out casement opening light not exceeding 50mm thick, dismantle as necessary, replace the following damaged members in softwood and re-hang										
glazing bar	2.95	10.00	3.25	1.97	0.32	46.10	0.08	49.42	m	54.37
hanging stile	11.41	10.00	12.55	1.85	0.30	43.28	0.16	55.99	m	61.59
shutting stile	11.41	10.00	12.55	1.85	0.30	43.28	0.16	55.99	m	61.59
rail	6.97	10.00	7.67	1.61	0.27	37.80	0.43	45.90	m	50.49
Take out sash, cramp and re-wedge with new glued wedges, pin and re-hang										
sliding sash	-	-	-	5.65	0.95	132.71	1.44	134.14	nr	147.56
opening casement light	-	-	-	5.00	0.85	117.58	1.44	119.02	nr	130.92
Repair corner of sash with 100 x 100mm angle repair plate let in flush	0.35	-	0.35	1.00	0.17	23.52	0.28	24.15	nr	26.56
Carefully rake out and dry crack in sill and fill with two part wood repair system	-	-	-	0.50	0.08	11.68	2.47	14.16	m	15.57
Repairs to softwood skirtings, picture rails, architraves, etc.										
Take off and refix										
skirting	-	-	-	0.40	0.07	9.44	0.07	9.50	m	10.45
dado or picture rail	-	-	-	0.35	0.06	8.24	0.05	8.29	m	9.12
architrave	-	-	-	0.26	0.05	6.20	0.05	6.25	m	6.88
Cut out damaged section and piece in new										
square skirting; 19 x 100mm	1.24	10.00	1.36	0.69	0.11	16.11	0.33	17.81	m	19.59
square skirting; 25 x 150mm	2.33	10.00	2.56	0.71	0.12	16.69	0.40	19.65	m	21.61
moulded skirting; 19 x 125mm	1.55	10.00	1.71	0.70	0.11	16.32	0.38	18.41	m	20.25
moulded dado or picture rail; 25 x 50mm	1.26	10.00	1.39	0.74	0.12	17.31	0.16	18.86	m	20.75
moulded or splayed architrave; 25 x 50mm	1.26	10.00	1.39	0.51	0.09	12.05	0.20	13.63	m	14.99
moulded or splayed architrave; 38 x 75mm	2.57	10.00	2.83	0.52	0.09	12.25	0.38	15.46	m	17.01
Cut out rotten or infected skirting and grounds and replace with new treated softwood										
square skirting; 19 x 100mm	1.34	10.00	1.47	1.00	0.17	23.52	0.45	25.44	m	27.98
square skirting; 25 x 150mm	2.52	10.00	2.77	1.07	0.18	25.13	0.61	28.52	m	31.37
moulded skirting; 19 x 125mm	1.67	10.00	1.84	1.03	0.17	24.14	0.51	26.49	m	29.14
Repairs to staircase members in softwood										
Cut out damaged members of staircase and piece in new										
tread; 32 x 275mm	8.13	10.00	8.94	4.33	0.72	101.58	0.76	111.28	m	122.40
tread; 38 x 275mm	8.18	10.00	8.99	4.85	0.81	113.83	0.87	123.70	m	136.07

Labour hourly rates: (except Specialists) Craft Operatives 20.87 Labourer 15.57 Rates are national average prices. Refer to REGIONAL VARIATIONS for indicative levels of overall pricing in regions	MATERIALS			LABOUR				RATES		
	Del to Site £	Waste %	Material Cost £	Craft Optve Hrs	Lab Hrs	Labour Cost £	Sunds £	Nett Rate £	Unit	Gross rate (10%) £
ALTERATION WORK TO EXISTING BUILDINGS (Cont'd)										
Removing existing and replacing; timber (Cont'd)										
Repairs to staircase members in softwood (Cont'd)										
Cut out damaged members of staircase and piece in new (Cont'd)										
riser; 19 x 200mm	3.60	10.00	3.96	2.25	0.38	52.87	0.30	57.14	m	62.85
riser; 25 x 200mm	3.74	10.00	4.11	3.03	0.51	71.18	0.45	75.74	m	83.31
Cut back old tread for a width of 125mm and provide and fix new nosing with glued and dowelled joints to tread										
with rounded nosing; 32mm	2.69	10.00	2.95	2.16	0.36	50.68	1.25	54.89	m	60.38
with rounded nosing; 38mm	2.69	10.00	2.95	2.55	0.43	59.91	1.40	64.27	m	70.70
with moulded nosing; 32mm	2.69	10.00	2.95	2.54	0.42	59.55	1.25	63.76	m	70.13
with moulded nosing; 38mm	2.69	10.00	2.95	3.06	0.51	71.80	1.49	76.24	m	83.87
Replace missing square bar baluster 914mm high; clean out old mortices										
25 x 25mm	0.65	-	0.65	0.56	0.09	13.09	-	13.73	nr	15.11
38 x 38mm	1.07	-	1.07	0.75	0.13	17.68	-	18.75	nr	20.62
Cut out damaged square bar baluster 914mm high and piece in new										
25 x 25mm	0.65	-	0.65	0.75	0.03	16.12	0.05	16.82	nr	18.50
38 x 38mm	1.07	-	1.07	0.91	0.15	21.33	0.08	22.48	nr	24.73
Cut out damaged handrail and piece in new										
50mm mopstick	1.89	10.00	2.08	1.95	0.33	45.83	5.28	53.19	m	58.51
75 x 100mm moulded	6.85	10.00	7.54	3.97	0.66	93.13	5.73	106.39	m	117.03
Refixing removed handrail										
to new balustrade	-	-	-	0.69	0.12	16.27	-	16.27	m	17.90
Repairs to staircase members in oak										
Cut out damaged members of staircase and piece in new										
tread; 22 x 270mm	43.28	10.00	47.61	6.09	1.02	142.98	0.76	191.35	m	210.49
tread; 38 x 275mm	61.12	10.00	67.24	7.18	1.20	168.53	0.87	236.64	m	260.31
riser; 19 x 200mm	27.32	10.00	30.05	3.34	0.56	78.43	0.30	108.77	m	119.65
riser; 25 x 200mm	30.07	10.00	33.08	4.56	0.76	107.00	0.48	140.56	m	154.62
Cut back old tread for a width of 125mm and provide and fix new nosing with glued and dowelled joints to tread										
with rounded nosing; 22mm	5.95	10.00	6.55	2.23	0.37	52.30	1.25	60.10	m	66.11
with rounded nosing; 38mm	33.82	10.00	37.20	2.92	0.49	68.57	1.49	107.26	m	117.98
with moulded nosing; 32mm	31.22	10.00	34.34	3.20	0.53	75.04	1.25	110.63	m	121.69
with moulded nosing; 38mm	35.12	10.00	38.63	3.95	0.66	92.71	1.49	132.82	m	146.11
Replace missing square bar baluster 914mm high; clean out old mortices										
25 x 25mm	7.16	-	7.16	0.94	0.16	22.11	-	29.27	nr	32.20
38 x 38mm	7.89	-	7.89	0.99	0.17	23.31	-	31.20	nr	34.32
Cut out damaged square bar baluster 914mm high and piece in new										
25 x 25mm	7.16	-	7.16	1.21	0.20	28.37	0.05	35.58	nr	39.13
38 x 38mm	7.89	-	7.89	1.32	0.22	30.97	0.08	38.95	nr	42.84
Cut out damaged handrail and piece in new										
44mm mopstick	15.84	10.00	17.42	3.64	0.61	85.46	5.28	108.17	m	118.99
75 x 100mm moulded	105.05	10.00	115.56	5.50	0.92	129.11	5.73	250.39	m	275.43
Refixing removed handrail										
to new balustrade	-	-	-	1.35	0.23	31.76	-	31.76	m	34.93
Remove broken ironmongery and fix only new to softwood										
Door ironmongery										
75mm butt hinges	-	-	-	0.23	0.04	5.42	0.02	5.44	nr	5.98
100mm butt hinges	-	-	-	0.23	0.04	5.42	0.02	5.44	nr	5.98
tee hinges up to 300mm	-	-	-	0.62	0.10	14.50	0.02	14.51	nr	15.96
single action floor spring hinges	-	-	-	3.00	0.50	70.40	2.14	72.54	nr	79.79
barrel bolt up to 300mm	-	-	-	0.41	0.07	9.65	0.02	9.66	nr	10.63
lock or latch furniture	-	-	-	0.44	0.07	10.27	0.02	10.29	nr	11.32
rim lock	-	-	-	0.80	0.13	18.72	0.02	18.74	nr	20.61
rim latch	-	-	-	0.80	0.13	18.72	0.02	18.74	nr	20.61
mortice lock	-	-	-	1.22	0.20	28.58	0.02	28.59	nr	31.45
mortice latch	-	-	-	1.08	0.18	25.34	0.02	25.36	nr	27.89
pull handle	-	-	-	0.40	0.07	9.44	0.05	9.49	nr	10.44
Window ironmongery										
sash fastener	-	-	-	1.09	0.18	25.55	0.02	25.57	nr	28.12
sash lift	-	-	-	0.23	0.04	5.42	0.02	5.44	nr	5.98
casement stay	-	-	-	0.40	0.07	9.44	0.02	9.45	nr	10.40
casement fastener	-	-	-	0.40	0.07	9.44	0.02	9.45	nr	10.40
Sundry ironmongery										
hat and coat hook	-	-	-	0.29	0.05	6.83	0.02	6.85	nr	7.53
toilet roll holder	-	-	-	0.29	0.05	6.83	0.02	6.85	nr	7.53
Remove broken ironmongery and fix only new to hardwood										
Door ironmongery										
75mm butt hinges	-	-	-	0.30	0.05	7.04	0.02	7.06	nr	7.76
100mm butt hinges	-	-	-	0.30	0.05	7.04	0.02	7.06	nr	7.76
tee hinges up to 300mm	-	-	-	0.86	0.14	20.13	0.02	20.14	nr	22.16
single action floor spring hinges	-	-	-	4.20	0.70	98.55	2.14	100.70	nr	110.77
barrel bolt up to 300mm	-	-	-	0.60	0.10	14.08	0.02	14.10	nr	15.51
lock or latch furniture	-	-	-	0.61	0.10	14.29	0.02	14.30	nr	15.73
rim lock	-	-	-	1.15	0.19	26.96	0.02	26.98	nr	29.67
rim latch	-	-	-	1.15	0.19	26.96	0.02	26.98	nr	29.67
mortice lock	-	-	-	1.77	0.30	41.61	0.02	41.63	nr	45.79
mortice latch	-	-	-	1.58	0.26	37.02	0.02	37.04	nr	40.74
pull handle	-	-	-	0.57	0.10	13.45	0.05	13.50	nr	14.85
Window ironmongery										
sash fastener	-	-	-	1.57	0.26	36.81	0.02	36.83	nr	40.51
sash lift	-	-	-	0.31	0.05	7.25	0.02	7.26	nr	7.99
casement stay	-	-	-	0.56	0.09	13.09	0.02	13.11	nr	14.42
casement fastener	-	-	-	0.56	0.09	13.09	0.02	13.11	nr	14.42

Labour hourly rates: (except Specialists) Craft Operatives 20.87 Labourer 15.57 Rates are national average prices. Refer to REGIONAL VARIATIONS for indicative levels of overall pricing in regions	MATERIALS			LABOUR				RATES		
	Del to Site £	Waste %	Material Cost £	Craft Optve Hrs	Lab Hrs	Labour Cost £	Sunds £	Nett Rate £	Unit	Gross rate (10%) £
ALTERATION WORK TO EXISTING BUILDINGS (Cont'd)										
Removing existing and replacing; timber (Cont'd)										
Remove broken ironmongery and fix only new to hardwood (Cont'd)										
Sundry ironmongery										
hat and coat hook	-	-	-	0.42	0.07	9.86	0.02	9.87	nr	10.86
toilet roll holder	-	-	-	0.42	0.07	9.86	0.02	9.87	nr	10.86
Removing existing and replacing; metal										
Replace defective arch bar										
Take out defective arch bar including cutting away brickwork as necessary, replace with new mild steel arch bar primed all round and make good all work disturbed										
flat arch bar; 30 x 6mm	3.52	-	3.52	1.03	1.03	37.53	1.17	42.22	m	46.44
flat arch bar; 50 x 6mm	5.57	-	5.57	1.12	1.12	40.81	1.72	48.10	m	52.91
angle arch bar; 50 x 50 x 6mm	9.62	-	9.62	1.27	1.27	46.28	3.05	58.95	m	64.85
angle arch bar; 75 x 50 x 6mm	11.76	-	11.76	1.44	1.44	52.47	3.84	68.08	m	74.89
Replace defective baluster										
Cut out defective baluster, clean core and bottom rails, provide new mild steel baluster and weld on										
12mm diameter x 686mm long	3.78	-	3.78	0.92	0.92	33.52	2.44	39.75	nr	43.73
12mm diameter x 762mm long	4.20	-	4.20	0.94	0.94	34.25	2.44	40.90	nr	44.99
12 x 23 x 686mm long	3.78	-	3.78	0.94	0.94	34.25	2.89	40.93	nr	45.02
12 x 12 x 762mm long	4.20	-	4.20	0.95	0.95	34.62	2.89	41.71	nr	45.88
Repair damaged weld										
Clean off damaged weld including removing remains of weld and cleaning off surrounding paint back to bright metal and re-weld connection between 10mm rail and										
13mm diameter rod	-	-	-	0.50	0.50	18.22	3.60	21.82	nr	24.00
13 x 13mm bar	-	-	-	0.53	0.53	19.31	4.27	23.59	nr	25.95
25 x 25mm bar	-	-	-	0.60	0.60	21.86	5.36	27.23	nr	29.95
Removing existing and replacing; corrugated fibre cement roofing repairs										
Remove damaged sheets and provide and fix new with screws and washers to timber purlins and ease and adjust edges of adjoining sheets as necessary										
one sheet; 2450mm long Profile 3 natural grey	27.65	10.00	30.42	1.23	1.23	44.82	3.28	78.52	nr	86.37
one sheet; 2450mm long Profile 3 standard colour	33.18	10.00	36.50	1.23	1.23	44.82	3.28	84.60	nr	93.06
one sheet; 1825mm long Profile 6 natural grey	16.50	10.00	18.15	1.78	1.78	64.86	4.85	87.86	nr	96.65
one sheet; 1825mm long Profile 6 standard colour	23.72	10.00	26.09	1.78	1.78	64.86	4.85	95.81	nr	105.39
over one sheet; Profile 3 natural grey	17.39	10.00	19.13	0.89	0.89	32.43	3.10	54.66	m²	60.13
over one sheet; Profile 3 standard colour	20.87	10.00	22.95	0.89	0.89	32.43	3.10	58.49	m²	64.34
over one sheet; Profile 6 natural grey	9.04	10.00	9.95	0.89	0.89	32.43	4.57	46.95	m²	51.64
over one sheet; Profile 6 standard colour	12.96	10.00	14.26	0.89	0.89	32.43	4.57	51.26	m²	56.39
Remove damaged sheets and provide and fix new with hook bolts and washers to steel purlins and ease and adjust edges of adjoining sheets as necessary										
one sheet; 2450mm long Profile 3 natural grey	27.65	10.00	30.42	1.37	1.37	49.92	3.28	83.62	nr	91.98
one sheet; 2450mm long Profile 3 standard colour	33.18	10.00	36.50	1.37	1.37	49.92	3.28	89.70	nr	98.67
one sheet; 1825mm long Profile 6 natural grey	16.50	10.00	18.15	1.98	1.98	72.15	4.85	95.15	nr	104.67
one sheet; 1825mm long Profile 6 standard colour	23.72	10.00	26.09	1.98	1.98	72.15	4.85	103.09	nr	113.40
over one sheet; Profile 3 natural grey	17.39	10.00	19.13	1.03	1.03	37.53	3.10	59.76	m²	65.74
over one sheet; Profile 3 standard colour	20.87	10.00	22.95	1.03	1.03	37.53	3.10	63.59	m²	69.95
over one sheet; Profile 6 natural grey	9.04	10.00	9.95	1.03	1.03	37.53	4.57	52.05	m²	57.25
over one sheet; Profile 6 standard colour	12.96	10.00	14.26	1.03	1.03	37.53	4.57	56.36	m²	62.00
Removing existing and replacing; felt roofing repairs for roofs covered with bituminous felt roofing, BS EN 13707										
Sweep clean, cut out defective layer, re-bond adjacent felt and cover with one layer of felt bonded in hot bitumen; patches not exceeding 1.00m²										
fibre based roofing felt type 1B	1.73	15.00	1.99	0.88	0.88	32.07	3.93	37.99	m²	41.79
for each defective underlayer cut out and replaced, add	1.73	15.00	1.99	0.88	0.88	32.07	3.93	37.99	m²	41.79
fibre based mineral surfaced roofing felt type 1E	4.41	15.00	5.07	1.05	1.05	38.26	3.93	47.25	m²	51.98
polyester based roofing felt type 5B	3.67	15.00	4.22	1.02	1.02	37.17	3.93	45.31	m²	49.85
for each defective underlayer cut out and replaced, add	3.67	15.00	4.22	1.02	1.02	37.17	3.93	45.31	m²	49.85
high performance polyester based mineral surfaced roofing felt type 5E	3.67	15.00	4.22	1.13	1.13	41.18	3.93	49.32	m²	54.25
Sweep clean, cut out defective layer, re-bond adjacent felt and cover with one layer of felt bonded in hot bitumen; patches 1.00 - 3.00m²										
fibre based roofing felt type 1B	1.73	15.00	1.99	0.43	0.43	15.67	3.93	21.59	m²	23.75
for each defective underlayer cut out and replaced, add	1.73	15.00	1.99	0.43	0.43	15.67	3.93	21.59	m²	23.75
fibre based mineral surfaced roofing felt type 1E	4.41	15.00	5.07	0.56	0.56	20.41	3.93	29.40	m²	32.34
polyester based roofing felt type 5B	3.67	15.00	4.22	0.53	0.53	19.31	3.93	27.46	m²	30.20
for each defective underlayer cut out and replaced, add	3.67	15.00	4.22	0.53	0.53	19.31	3.93	27.46	m²	30.20
polyester based mineral surfaced roofing felt type 5E	3.67	15.00	4.22	0.65	0.65	23.69	3.93	31.83	m²	35.01
Sweep clean surface of existing roof, prime with hot bitumen and dress with										
13mm layer of limestone or granite chippings	1.78	10.00	1.96	-	0.23	3.58	2.19	7.73	m²	8.51
13mm layer of pea shingle	1.06	10.00	1.16	-	0.36	5.61	2.19	8.96	m²	9.86
extra; removing existing chippings or shingle	-	-	-	-	0.24	3.74	0.66	4.40	m²	4.84

Labour hourly rates: (except Specialists) Craft Operatives 26.39 Labourer 15.57 Rates are national average prices. Refer to REGIONAL VARIATIONS for indicative levels of overall pricing in regions	MATERIALS			LABOUR				RATES		
	Del to Site £	Waste %	Material Cost £	Craft Optve Hrs	Lab Hrs	Labour Cost £	Sunds £	Nett Rate £	Unit	Gross rate (10%) £
ALTERATION WORK TO EXISTING BUILDINGS (Cont'd)										
Removing existing and replacing; lead flashings, etc.; replace with new lead										
Remove flashing and provide new code Nr4 lead; wedge into groove										
150mm girth	7.40	5.00	7.77	1.06	-	27.97	0.43	36.17	m	39.79
240mm girth	11.60	5.00	12.18	1.49	-	39.32	0.43	51.93	m	57.12
300mm girth	14.80	5.00	15.54	1.82	-	48.03	0.43	64.00	m	70.40
Remove stepped flashing and provide new code Nr 4 lead; wedge into groove										
180mm girth	10.40	5.00	10.92	1.54	-	40.64	0.43	51.99	m	57.19
240mm girth	11.60	5.00	12.18	1.94	-	51.20	0.43	63.81	m	70.19
300mm girth	14.80	5.00	15.54	2.34	-	61.75	0.43	77.72	m	85.49
Remove apron flashing and provide new code Nr 5 lead; wedge into groove										
150mm girth	9.20	5.00	9.66	1.06	-	27.97	0.43	38.06	m	41.87
300mm girth	18.40	5.00	19.32	1.82	-	48.03	0.43	67.78	m	74.56
450mm girth	27.60	5.00	28.98	2.58	-	68.09	0.66	97.73	m	107.50
Remove lining to valley gutter and provide new code Nr 5 lead										
240mm girth	14.60	5.00	15.33	1.49	-	39.32	-	54.65	m	60.12
300mm girth	18.40	5.00	19.32	1.82	-	48.03	-	67.35	m	74.08
450mm girth	27.60	5.00	28.98	2.58	-	68.09	-	97.07	m	106.77
Remove gutter lining and provide new code Nr 6 lead										
360mm girth	26.00	5.00	27.30	2.12	-	55.95	-	83.25	m	91.57
390mm girth	28.20	5.00	29.61	2.43	-	64.13	-	93.74	m	103.11
450mm girth	32.60	5.00	34.23	2.58	-	68.09	-	102.32	m	112.55
Removing existing and replacing; zinc flashings, etc.; replace with 0.8mm zinc										
Remove flashing and provide new; wedge into groove										
150mm girth	9.75	5.00	10.24	1.12	-	29.56	0.30	40.09	m	44.10
240mm girth	15.60	5.00	16.38	1.60	-	42.22	0.30	58.90	m	64.79
300mm girth	19.50	5.00	20.47	1.94	-	51.20	0.43	72.10	m	79.31
Remove stepped flashing and provide new; wedge into groove										
180mm girth	11.70	5.00	12.28	1.65	-	43.54	0.30	56.13	m	61.74
240mm girth	15.60	5.00	16.38	2.08	-	54.89	0.30	71.57	m	78.73
300mm girth	19.50	5.00	20.47	2.52	-	66.50	0.43	87.41	m	96.15
Remove apron flashing and provide new; wedge into groove										
150mm girth	9.75	5.00	10.24	1.12	-	29.56	0.30	40.09	m	44.10
300mm girth	19.50	5.00	20.47	1.94	-	51.20	0.43	72.10	m	79.31
450mm girth	29.25	5.00	30.71	2.76	-	72.84	0.53	104.08	m	114.48
Remove lining to valley gutter and provide new										
240mm girth	15.60	5.00	16.38	1.60	-	42.22	-	58.60	m	64.46
300mm girth	19.50	5.00	20.47	1.94	-	51.20	-	71.67	m	78.84
450mm girth	29.25	5.00	30.71	2.76	-	72.84	-	103.55	m	113.90
Remove gutter lining and provide new										
360mm girth	23.40	5.00	24.57	2.27	-	59.91	-	84.48	m	92.92
420mm girth	27.30	5.00	28.66	2.61	-	68.88	-	97.54	m	107.30
450mm girth	29.25	5.00	30.71	2.76	-	72.84	-	103.55	m	113.90
Removing existing and replacing; copper flashings, etc.; replace with 0.70mm copper										
Remove flashing and provide new; wedge into groove										
150mm girth	18.60	5.00	19.53	1.06	-	27.97	0.59	48.10	m	52.91
240mm girth	29.76	5.00	31.25	1.49	-	39.32	0.59	71.16	m	78.28
300mm girth	37.20	5.00	39.06	1.82	-	48.03	0.59	87.68	m	96.45
Remove stepped flashing and provide new; wedge into groove										
180mm girth	22.32	5.00	23.44	1.54	-	40.64	0.59	64.67	m	71.14
240mm girth	29.76	5.00	31.25	1.94	-	51.20	0.59	83.04	m	91.34
300mm girth	37.20	5.00	39.06	2.34	-	61.75	0.59	101.41	m	111.55
Remove apron flashing and provide new; wedge into groove										
150mm girth	18.60	5.00	19.53	1.06	-	27.97	0.59	48.10	m	52.91
300mm girth	37.20	5.00	39.06	1.82	-	48.03	0.59	87.68	m	96.45
450mm girth	55.80	5.00	58.59	2.58	-	68.09	0.89	127.57	m	140.32
Remove lining to valley gutter and provide new										
240mm girth	29.76	5.00	31.25	1.49	-	39.32	-	70.57	m	77.63
300mm girth	37.20	5.00	39.06	1.82	-	48.03	-	87.09	m	95.80
450mm girth	55.80	5.00	58.59	2.58	-	68.09	-	126.68	m	139.34
Remove gutter lining and provide new										
360mm girth	44.64	5.00	46.87	2.12	-	55.95	-	102.82	m	113.10
420mm girth	52.08	5.00	54.68	2.43	-	64.13	-	118.81	m	130.69
450mm girth	55.80	5.00	58.59	2.58	-	68.09	-	126.68	m	139.34
Removing existing and replacing; aluminium flashings etc; replace with 0.60mm aluminium										
Remove flashings and provide new; wedge into groove										
150mm girth	2.88	5.00	3.03	1.06	-	27.97	0.26	31.27	m	34.39
240mm girth	4.62	5.00	4.85	1.49	-	39.32	0.26	44.43	m	48.88
300mm girth	5.77	5.00	6.06	1.82	-	48.03	0.26	54.35	m	59.79
Remove stepped flashing and provide new; wedge into groove										
180mm girth	3.46	5.00	3.64	1.54	-	40.64	0.26	44.54	m	48.99
240mm girth	4.62	5.00	4.85	1.94	-	51.20	0.26	56.31	m	61.94

Labour hourly rates: (except Specialists) Craft Operatives 26.39 Labourer 15.57 Rates are national average prices. Refer to REGIONAL VARIATIONS for indicative levels of overall pricing in regions	MATERIALS			LABOUR				RATES		
	Del to Site £	Waste %	Material Cost £	Craft Optve Hrs	Lab Hrs	Labour Cost £	Sunds £	Nett Rate £	Unit	Gross rate (10%) £
ALTERATION WORK TO EXISTING BUILDINGS (Cont'd)										
Removing existing and replacing; aluminium flashings etc; replace with 0.60mm aluminium (Cont'd)										
Remove stepped flashing and provide new; wedge into groove (Cont'd)										
300mm girth	5.77	5.00	6.06	2.34	-	61.75	0.26	68.08	m	74.88
Remove apron flashing and provide new; wedge into groove										
150mm girth	2.88	5.00	3.03	1.06	-	27.97	0.26	31.27	m	34.39
300mm girth	5.77	5.00	6.06	1.82	-	48.03	0.26	54.35	m	59.79
450mm girth	8.65	5.00	9.09	2.56	-	67.56	4.95	81.60	m	89.75
Remove lining to valley gutter and provide new										
240mm girth	4.62	5.00	4.85	1.49	-	39.32	-	44.17	m	48.58
300mm girth	5.77	5.00	6.06	1.82	-	48.03	-	54.09	m	59.50
450mm girth	8.65	5.00	9.09	2.58	-	68.09	-	77.17	m	84.89
Remove gutter lining and provide new										
360mm girth	6.92	5.00	7.27	2.12	-	55.95	-	63.22	m	69.54
420mm girth	8.08	5.00	8.48	2.43	-	64.13	-	72.61	m	79.87
450mm girth	8.65	5.00	9.09	2.58	-	68.09	-	77.17	m	84.89

This section continues on the next page

Labour hourly rates: (except Specialists) Craft Operatives 20.87 Labourer 15.57 Rates are national average prices. Refer to REGIONAL VARIATIONS for indicative levels of overall pricing in regions	MATERIALS			LABOUR				RATES		
	Del to Site £	Waste %	Material Cost £	Craft Optve Hrs	Lab Hrs	Labour Cost £	Sunds £	Nett Rate £	Unit	Gross rate (10%) £
ALTERATION WORK TO EXISTING BUILDINGS (Cont'd)										
Removing existing and replacing; wall and ceiling finishings										
Cut out damaged two coat plaster to wall in patches and make out in new plaster to match existing										
under 1.00m²	5.27	10.00	5.79	2.13	2.13	77.62	0.85	84.26	m²	92.69
1.00 - 2.00m²	5.27	10.00	5.79	1.76	1.76	64.13	0.85	70.78	m²	77.86
2.00 - 4.00m²	5.27	10.00	5.79	1.39	1.39	50.65	0.85	57.30	m²	63.03
Cut out damaged three coat plaster to wall in patches and make out in new plaster to match existing										
under 1.00m²	6.83	10.00	7.52	2.50	2.50	91.10	1.31	99.93	m²	109.92
1.00 - 2.00m²	6.83	10.00	7.52	2.06	2.06	75.07	1.31	83.89	m²	92.28
2.00 - 4.00m²	6.83	10.00	7.52	1.62	1.62	59.03	1.31	67.86	m²	74.65
Cut out damaged two coat rendering to wall in patches and make out in new rendering to match existing										
under 1.00m²	1.85	10.00	2.04	1.93	1.93	70.33	0.85	73.22	m²	80.54
1.00 - 2.00m²	1.85	10.00	2.04	1.60	1.60	58.30	0.85	61.20	m²	67.32
2.00 - 4.00m²	1.85	10.00	2.04	1.26	1.26	45.91	0.85	48.81	m²	53.69
Cut out damaged three coat rendering to wall in patches and make out in new rendering to match existing										
under 1.00m²	2.85	10.00	3.14	2.28	2.28	83.08	1.31	87.53	m²	96.29
1.00 - 2.00m²	2.85	10.00	3.14	1.87	1.87	68.14	1.31	72.59	m²	79.85
2.00 - 4.00m²	2.85	10.00	3.14	1.47	1.47	53.57	1.31	58.02	m²	63.82
Cut out damaged two coat plaster to ceiling in patches and make out in new plaster to match existing										
under 1.00m²	5.27	10.00	5.79	2.38	2.38	86.73	0.85	93.37	m²	102.71
1.00 - 2.00m²	5.27	10.00	5.79	1.96	1.96	71.42	0.85	78.07	m²	85.87
2.00 - 4.00m²	5.27	10.00	5.79	1.54	1.54	56.12	0.85	62.76	m²	69.04
Cut out damaged three coat plaster to ceiling in patches and make out in new plaster to match existing										
under 1.00m²	6.83	10.00	7.52	2.79	2.79	101.67	1.31	110.49	m²	121.54
1.00 - 2.00m²	6.83	10.00	7.52	2.30	2.30	83.81	1.31	92.64	m²	101.90
2.00 - 4.00m²	6.83	10.00	7.52	1.81	1.81	65.96	1.31	74.78	m²	82.26
Cut out damaged 9.5mm plasterboard and two coat plaster to wall in patches and make out in new plasterboard and plaster to match existing										
under 1.00m²	9.30	10.00	10.23	2.23	2.23	81.26	1.46	92.95	m²	102.25
1.00 - 2.00m²	9.30	10.00	10.23	1.78	1.78	64.86	1.46	76.55	m²	84.21
2.00 - 4.00m²	9.30	10.00	10.23	1.36	1.36	49.56	1.46	61.25	m²	67.37
Cut out damaged 12.5mm plasterboard and two coat plaster to wall in patches and make out in new plasterboard and plaster to match existing										
under 1.00m²	9.33	10.00	10.26	2.28	2.28	83.08	1.62	94.97	m²	104.47
1.00 - 2.00m²	9.33	10.00	10.26	1.83	1.83	66.69	1.62	78.57	m²	86.43
2.00 - 4.00m²	9.33	10.00	10.26	1.38	1.38	50.29	1.63	62.18	m²	68.40
Cut out damaged 9.5mm plasterboard and two coat plaster to ceiling in patches and make out in new plasterboard and plaster to match existing										
under 1.00m²	9.30	10.00	10.23	2.54	2.54	92.56	1.46	104.25	m²	114.67
1.00 - 2.00m²	9.30	10.00	10.23	2.03	2.03	73.97	1.46	85.66	m²	94.23
2.00 - 4.00m²	9.30	10.00	10.23	1.55	1.55	56.48	1.46	68.17	m²	74.99
Cut out damaged 12.5mm plasterboard and two coat plaster to ceiling in patches and make out in new plasterboard and plaster to match existing										
under 1.00m²	9.33	10.00	10.26	2.56	2.56	93.29	1.62	105.17	m²	115.69
1.00 - 2.00m²	9.33	10.00	10.26	2.06	2.06	75.07	1.62	86.95	m²	95.65
2.00 - 4.00m²	9.33	10.00	10.26	1.57	1.57	57.21	1.62	69.10	m²	76.01
Cut out damaged lath and plaster to wall in patches and make out with new metal lathing and three coat plaster to match existing										
under 1.00m²	13.32	10.00	14.66	2.53	2.53	92.19	1.62	108.47	m²	119.32
1.00 - 2.00m²	13.32	10.00	14.66	2.14	2.14	77.98	1.62	94.26	m²	103.69
2.00 - 4.00m²	13.32	10.00	14.66	1.73	1.73	63.04	1.62	79.32	m²	87.25
Cut out damaged lath and plaster to ceiling in patches and make out with new metal lathing and three coat plaster to match existing										
under 1.00m²	13.32	10.00	14.66	2.87	2.87	104.58	1.62	120.86	m²	132.95
1.00 - 2.00m²	13.32	10.00	14.66	2.43	2.43	88.55	1.62	104.83	m²	115.31
2.00 - 4.00m²	13.32	10.00	14.66	1.95	1.95	71.06	1.62	87.34	m²	96.07
Cut out crack in plaster, form dovetailed key and make good with plaster										
not exceeding 50mm wide	0.34	10.00	0.38	0.20	0.20	7.29	0.05	7.71	m	8.48
Make good plaster where the following removed										
small pipe	-	-	-	0.16	0.16	5.83	0.05	5.88	nr	6.47
small steel section	-	-	-	0.21	0.21	7.65	0.07	7.72	nr	8.49
Cut out damaged plaster moulding or cornice and make out with new to match existing										
up to 100mm girth on face	2.56	10.00	2.81	1.25	0.63	35.90	0.34	39.06	m	42.96
100 - 150mm girth on face	4.26	10.00	4.69	1.86	0.93	53.30	0.67	58.66	m	64.53
150 - 200mm girth on face	8.53	10.00	9.38	2.25	1.13	64.55	1.21	75.15	m	82.66
Remove damaged fibrous plaster louvered ventilator, replace with new and make good										
229 x 75mm	1.00	5.00	1.05	0.50	0.50	18.22	0.16	19.43	nr	21.38
229 x 150mm	1.50	-	1.50	0.60	0.60	21.86	0.28	23.64	nr	26.01

Labour hourly rates: (except Specialists) Craft Operatives 20.87 Labourer 15.57 Rates are national average prices. Refer to REGIONAL VARIATIONS for indicative levels of overall pricing in regions	MATERIALS			LABOUR				RATES		
	Del to Site £	Waste %	Material Cost £	Craft Optve Hrs	Lab Hrs	Labour Cost £	Sunds £	Nett Rate £	Unit	Gross rate (10%) £
ALTERATION WORK TO EXISTING BUILDINGS (Cont'd)										
Removing existing and replacing; wall and ceiling finishings (Cont'd)										
Take out damaged 152 x 152 x 5.5mm white glazed wall tiles and renew to match existing										
isolated tile	25.00	5.00	26.25	0.32	0.32	11.66	0.10	38.01	nr	41.81
patch of 5 tiles	125.00	5.00	131.25	0.60	0.60	21.86	0.49	153.61	nr	168.97
patch 0.50 - 1.00m²	1100.00	5.00	1155.00	2.32	2.32	84.54	3.85	1243.39	m²	1367.73
patch 1.00 - 2.00m²	1100.00	5.00	1155.00	1.66	1.66	60.49	3.85	1219.34	m²	1341.28
Removing existing and replacing; floor finishings										
Take out damaged 150 x 150 x 12.5mm clay floor tiles and renew to match existing										
isolated tile	0.56	5.00	0.59	0.32	0.21	9.95	0.10	10.63	nr	11.70
patch of 5 tiles	2.79	5.00	2.93	0.65	0.45	20.57	0.49	23.99	nr	26.39
patch 0.50 - 1.00m²	25.11	5.00	26.37	2.40	1.61	75.16	3.85	105.38	m²	115.91
patch 1.00 - 2.00m²	25.11	5.00	26.37	1.90	1.27	59.43	3.85	89.65	m²	98.61
Cut out damaged 25mm granolithic paving in patches and make out in new granolithic to match existing										
under 1.00m²	4.18	5.00	4.39	1.50	1.50	54.66	1.80	60.85	m²	66.94
1.00 - 2.00m²	4.18	5.00	4.39	1.25	1.25	45.55	1.80	51.74	m²	56.92
2.00 - 4.00m²	4.18	5.00	4.39	1.07	1.07	38.99	1.80	45.18	m²	49.70
Cut out damaged 32mm granolithic paving in patches and make out in new granolithic to match existing										
under 1.00m²	5.35	5.00	5.62	1.68	1.68	61.22	2.12	68.95	m²	75.85
1.00 - 2.00m²	5.35	5.00	5.62	1.38	1.38	50.29	2.12	58.02	m²	63.82
2.00 - 4.00m²	5.35	5.00	5.62	1.15	1.15	41.91	2.12	49.64	m²	54.60
Cut out damaged 38mm granolithic paving in patches and make out in new granolithic to match existing										
under 1.00m²	6.35	5.00	6.67	1.80	1.80	65.59	2.49	74.76	m²	82.23
1.00 - 2.00m²	6.35	5.00	6.67	1.50	1.50	54.66	2.49	63.83	m²	70.21
2.00 - 4.00m²	6.35	5.00	6.67	1.25	1.25	45.55	2.49	54.72	m²	60.19
Cut out damaged 50mm granolithic paving in patches and make out in new granolithic to match existing										
under 1.00m²	8.36	5.00	8.78	2.12	2.12	77.25	3.03	89.07	m²	97.97
1.00 - 2.00m²	8.36	5.00	8.78	1.73	1.73	63.04	3.03	74.86	m²	82.34
2.00 - 4.00m²	8.36	5.00	8.78	1.45	1.45	52.84	3.03	64.65	m²	71.12
Cut out damaged granolithic paving to tread 275mm wide and make out in new granolithic to match existing										
25mm thick	1.17	5.00	1.23	0.44	0.44	16.03	0.51	17.77	m	19.55
32mm thick	1.51	5.00	1.58	0.48	0.48	17.49	0.57	19.65	m	21.61
38mm thick	1.67	5.00	1.76	0.50	0.50	18.22	0.67	20.65	m	22.71
50mm thick	2.34	5.00	2.46	0.59	0.59	21.50	0.84	24.79	m	27.27
Cut out damaged granolithic covering to plain riser 175mm wide and make out in new granolithic to match existing										
13mm thick	0.33	5.00	0.35	0.80	0.80	29.15	4.62	34.13	m	37.54
19mm thick	0.50	5.00	0.53	0.84	0.84	30.61	4.66	35.79	m	39.37
25mm thick	0.67	5.00	0.70	0.88	0.88	32.07	4.71	37.48	m	41.22
32mm thick	1.00	5.00	1.05	0.93	0.93	33.89	4.74	39.68	m	43.65
Cut out damaged granolithic covering to undercut riser 175mm wide and make out in new granolithic to match existing										
13mm thick	0.33	5.00	0.35	0.87	0.87	31.70	4.62	36.68	m	40.35
19mm thick	0.50	5.00	0.53	0.93	0.93	33.89	4.66	39.07	m	42.98
25mm thick	0.67	5.00	0.70	0.98	0.98	35.71	4.71	41.12	m	45.23
32mm thick	1.00	5.00	1.05	1.04	1.04	37.90	4.74	43.69	m	48.06
Cut out damaged granolithic skirting 150mm wide and make out in new granolithic to match existing										
13mm thick	0.33	5.00	0.35	0.72	0.72	26.24	3.95	30.54	m	33.59
19mm thick	0.50	5.00	0.53	0.76	0.76	27.69	4.00	32.22	m	35.45
25mm thick	0.67	5.00	0.70	0.80	0.80	29.15	4.03	33.89	m	37.28
32mm thick	0.84	5.00	0.88	0.82	0.82	29.88	4.08	34.84	m	38.33
Cut out crack in granolithic paving not exceeding 50mm wide, form dovetailed key and make good to match existing										
25mm thick	0.17	5.00	0.18	0.60	0.60	21.86	0.08	22.12	m	24.33
32mm thick	0.33	5.00	0.35	0.66	0.66	24.05	0.10	24.50	m	26.95
38mm thick	0.33	5.00	0.35	0.69	0.69	25.14	0.13	25.63	m	28.19
50mm thick	0.50	5.00	0.53	0.79	0.79	28.79	0.15	29.46	m	32.41

This section continues on the next page

Labour hourly rates: (except Specialists) Craft Operatives 26.39 Labourer 15.57 Rates are national average prices. Refer to REGIONAL VARIATIONS for indicative levels of overall pricing in regions	MATERIALS			LABOUR				RATES		
	Del to Site £	Waste %	Material Cost £	Craft Optve Hrs	Lab Hrs	Labour Cost £	Sunds £	Nett Rate £	Unit	Gross rate (10%) £
ALTERATION WORK TO EXISTING BUILDINGS (Cont'd)										
Removing existing and replacing; balloon gratings										
Remove remains of old balloon grating and provide new plastic grating in outlet or end of pipe										
50mm diameter	3.61	2.00	3.68	0.50	-	13.19	-	16.88	nr	18.56
82mm diameter	4.54	2.00	4.63	0.50	-	13.19	-	17.83	nr	19.61
110mm diameter	12.01	2.00	12.25	0.50	-	13.19	-	25.45	nr	27.99
Removing existing and replacing; stopcocks, valves, etc.										
Turn off water supply, drain down as necessary, take out old valves and re-new with joints to copper										
brass stopcock; 13mm	4.03	2.00	4.11	2.00	-	52.78	-	56.89	nr	62.58
brass bib cock; 13mm	27.23	2.00	27.78	2.00	-	52.78	-	80.56	nr	88.61
drain tap (BS 2879) Type B; 13mm	0.86	2.00	0.88	2.00	-	52.78	-	53.66	nr	59.02
high pressure ball valve (BS 1212) piston type with copper ball; 13mm	14.46	2.00	14.75	2.00	-	52.78	-	67.53	nr	74.28
high pressure ball valve (BS 1212) piston type with plastic ball; 13mm	7.46	2.00	7.61	2.00	-	52.78	-	60.39	nr	66.43
low pressure ball valve (BS 1212) piston type with copper ball; 13mm	14.46	2.00	14.75	2.00	-	52.78	-	67.53	nr	74.28
low pressure ball valve (BS 1212) piston type with plastic ball; 13mm	7.46	2.00	7.61	2.00	-	52.78	-	60.39	nr	66.43
high pressure ball valve (BS 1212) piston type with copper ball; 19mm	20.16	2.00	20.56	2.50	-	65.97	-	86.53	nr	95.19
high pressure ball valve (BS 1212) piston type with plastic ball; 19mm	11.02	2.00	11.24	2.50	-	65.97	-	77.21	nr	84.94
Removing existing and replacing; traps										
Take out old plastic trap and replace with new 76mm seal trap (BS EN 274) with "O"" ring joint outlet										
P trap; 32mm diameter	6.07	2.00	6.19	1.25	-	32.99	-	39.18	nr	43.10
P trap; 40mm diameter	6.72	2.00	6.85	1.50	-	39.58	-	46.44	nr	51.08
S trap; 32mm diameter	7.06	2.00	7.20	1.25	-	32.99	-	40.19	nr	44.21
S trap; 40mm diameter	7.44	2.00	7.59	1.50	-	39.58	-	47.17	nr	51.89
bath trap with overflow connection; 40mm diameter	8.62	2.00	8.79	1.75	-	46.18	-	54.97	nr	60.47
Take out old copper trap and replace with new 76mm seal two piece trap with compression joint										
P trap; 35mm diameter	39.36	2.00	40.15	1.25	-	32.99	-	73.13	nr	80.45
P trap; 42mm diameter	40.94	2.00	41.76	1.50	-	39.58	-	81.34	nr	89.48
S trap; 35mm diameter	121.17	2.00	123.59	1.25	-	32.99	-	156.58	nr	172.24
S trap; 42mm diameter	145.02	2.00	147.92	1.50	-	39.58	-	187.51	nr	206.26
bath trap with male iron overflow connection; 42mm diameter	230.35	2.00	234.96	1.75	-	46.18	-	281.14	nr	309.25
Removing existing and replacing; preparation of pipe for insertion of new pipe or fitting										
Cut into cast iron pipe and take out a length up to 1.00m for insertion of new pipe or fitting										
50mm diameter	-	-	-	3.70	-	97.64	-	97.64	nr	107.41
64 and 76mm diameter	-	-	-	4.30	-	113.48	-	113.48	nr	124.82
89 and 102mm diameter	-	-	-	4.90	-	129.31	-	129.31	nr	142.24
Cut into cast iron pipe with caulked joint and take out a length up to 1.00m for insertion of new pipe or fitting										
50mm diameter	-	-	-	3.70	-	97.64	-	97.64	nr	107.41
64 and 76mm diameter	-	-	-	4.30	-	113.48	-	113.48	nr	124.82
89 and 102mm diameter	-	-	-	4.90	-	129.31	-	129.31	nr	142.24
Cut into asbestos cement pipe and take out a length up to 1.00m for insertion of new pipe or fitting										
50mm diameter	-	-	-	3.15	-	83.13	-	83.13	nr	91.44
64 and 76mm diameter	-	-	-	3.75	-	98.96	-	98.96	nr	108.86
89 and 102mm diameter	-	-	-	4.35	-	114.80	-	114.80	nr	126.28
Cut into polythene or p.v.c. pipe and take out a length up to 1.00m for insertion of new pipe or fitting										
up to 25mm diameter	-	-	-	2.50	-	65.97	-	65.97	nr	72.57
32 - 50mm diameter	-	-	-	3.15	-	83.13	-	83.13	nr	91.44
64 and 76mm diameter	-	-	-	3.75	-	98.96	-	98.96	nr	108.86
89 and 102mm diameter	-	-	-	4.40	-	116.12	-	116.12	nr	127.73
Cut into steel pipe and take out a length up to 1.00m for insertion of new pipe or fitting										
up to 25mm diameter	-	-	-	3.05	-	80.49	-	80.49	nr	88.54
32 - 50mm diameter	-	-	-	3.70	-	97.64	-	97.64	nr	107.41
64 and 76mm diameter	-	-	-	4.30	-	113.48	-	113.48	nr	124.82
89 and 102mm diameter	-	-	-	4.90	-	129.31	-	129.31	nr	142.24
Cut into stainless steel pipe and take out a length up to 1.00m for insertion of new pipe or fitting										
up to 25mm diameter	-	-	-	2.90	-	76.53	-	76.53	nr	84.18
32 - 50mm diameter	-	-	-	3.50	-	92.36	-	92.36	nr	101.60
64 and 76mm diameter	-	-	-	4.10	-	108.20	-	108.20	nr	119.02
89 and 102mm diameter	-	-	-	4.75	-	125.35	-	125.35	nr	137.89
Cut into copper pipe and take out a length up to 1.00m for insertion of new pipe or fitting										
up to 25mm diameter	-	-	-	2.90	-	76.53	-	76.53	nr	84.18
32 - 50mm diameter	-	-	-	3.50	-	92.36	-	92.36	nr	101.60
64 and 76mm diameter	-	-	-	4.10	-	108.20	-	108.20	nr	119.02
89 and 102mm diameter	-	-	-	4.75	-	125.35	-	125.35	nr	137.89

Labour hourly rates: (except Specialists) Craft Operatives 26.39 Labourer 15.57 Rates are national average prices. Refer to REGIONAL VARIATIONS for indicative levels of overall pricing in regions	MATERIALS			LABOUR				RATES		
	Del to Site £	Waste %	Material Cost £	Craft Optve Hrs	Lab Hrs	Labour Cost £	Sunds £	Nett Rate £	Unit	Gross rate (10%) £
ALTERATION WORK TO EXISTING BUILDINGS (Cont'd)										
Removing existing and replacing; preparation of pipe for insertion of new pipe or fitting (Cont'd)										
Cut into lead pipe and take out a length up to 1.00m for insertion of new pipe or fitting										
up to 25mm diameter	-	-	-	3.05	-	80.49	-	80.49	nr	88.54
32 - 50mm diameter	-	-	-	3.70	-	97.64	-	97.64	nr	107.41
64 and 76mm diameter	-	-	-	4.30	-	113.48	-	113.48	nr	124.82
89 and 102mm diameter	-	-	-	4.90	-	129.31	-	129.31	nr	142.24
Removing existing and replacing; sanitary fittings										
Disconnect trap, valves and services pipes, remove old fitting and provide and fix new including re-connecting trap, valves and services pipes										
stainless steel sink with single drainer with 38mm chromium plated waste outlet, plug, chain and stay; 500 x 965mm	81.43	5.00	85.50	6.00	-	158.34	-	243.84	nr	268.23
stainless steel sink with double drainer with 38mm chromium plated waste outlet, overflow plug, chain and stay; 600 x 1500mm	177.27	5.00	186.13	6.50	-	171.54	-	357.67	nr	393.43
pressed steel vitreous enamelled rectangular top bath with cradles and with 38mm chromium plated waste outlet, plug, chain and stay and 32mm chromium plated overflow and including removing old cast iron bath; 1700mm	137.27	5.00	144.14	8.00	-	211.12	-	355.26	nr	390.78
Take off old W.C. seat and provide and fix new ring pattern black plastic seat and cover	13.61	5.00	14.29	1.50	-	39.58	-	53.88	nr	59.26
Disconnect supply pipe, overflow and flush pipe and take out old W.C. cistern and provide and fix new 9 litre black plastic W.C. cistern with cover and connect pipe and ball valve										
low level	83.33	5.00	87.50	5.00	-	131.95	-	219.45	nr	241.39
high level	119.95	5.00	125.95	5.00	-	131.95	-	257.90	nr	283.69
Disconnect flush pipe, take off seat and remove old W.C. pan, provide and fix new white china pan, connect flush pipe, form cement joint with drain and refix old seat										
S or P trap pan	58.29	5.00	61.21	5.00	-	131.95	-	193.16	nr	212.47
Disconnect and remove old high level W.C. suite complete and provide and fix new suite with P or S trap pan, plastic ring seat and cover, plastic flush pipe or bend, 9 litre plastic W.C. cistern with cover, chain and pull or lever handle and 13mm low pressure ball valve; adapt supply pipe and overflow as necessary and connect to new suite and cement joint to drain										
new high level suite	237.48	5.00	249.35	8.50	-	224.32	-	473.66	nr	521.03
new low level suite (vitreous china cistern)	141.64	5.00	148.72	9.00	-	237.51	-	386.23	nr	424.86
Disconnect and remove old low level W.C. suite complete and provide and fix new suite with P or S trap pan, plastic ring seat and cover, plastic flush bend, 9 litre vitreous china W.C. cistern with cover, lever handle and 13mm low pressure ball valve with plastic ball; re-connect supply pipe and overflow and cement joint to drain										
new low level suite	141.64	5.00	148.72	8.50	-	224.32	-	373.04	nr	410.34
Removing existing and replacing; water tanks										
Disconnect all pipework, set aside ball valve and take out cold water storage cistern in roof space; replace with new GRP water storage tank (BS EN 13280); reconnect all pipework and ball valve; remove metal filings and clean inside of tank										
size 915 x 610 x 580mm (227 litre); 250 litres	377.00	2.00	384.54	9.00	-	237.51	0.82	622.88	nr	685.16

This section continues on the next page

Labour hourly rates: (except Specialists) Craft Operatives 34.13 Labourer 15.57 Rates are national average prices. Refer to REGIONAL VARIATIONS for indicative levels of overall pricing in regions	MATERIALS			LABOUR				RATES		
	Del to Site £	Waste %	Material Cost £	Craft Optve Hrs	Lab Hrs	Labour Cost £	Sunds £	Nett Rate £	Unit	Gross rate (10%) £
ALTERATION WORK TO EXISTING BUILDINGS (Cont'd)										
Removing existing and replacing; electrical installations										
Note the following approximate estimates of costs are dependent on the number and position of the points. Lamps and fittings together with cutting and making good are excluded										
Removing existing and replacing; strip out and re-wire complete										
Provide new lamp holders, flush switches, flush socket outlets, fitting outlets and consumer unit with circuit breakers; a three bedroom house with fourteen lighting points and associated switches, nineteen 13 amp socket outlets, four 13 amp fitting outlets, one 30 amp cooker control panel, three earth bonding points and one fifteen way consumer unit										
PVC cables in existing conduit	421.86	2.50	452.44	126.38	-	4313.35	110.31	4876.11	nr	5363.72
PVC cables and conduit	470.11	2.50	503.90	178.42	-	6089.47	110.31	6703.69	nr	7374.06
Removing existing and replacing; strip out and re-wire with PVC insulated and sheathed cable in existing conduit										
Point to junction box, re-using existing lamp holder, socket outlet etc										
5 amp socket outlet	2.96	15.00	3.40	3.93	-	134.13	-	137.53	nr	151.29
13 amp socket or fitting outlet	4.32	15.00	4.97	3.31	-	112.97	-	117.94	nr	129.74
lighting point or switch	1.54	15.00	1.77	2.92	-	99.66	-	101.43	nr	111.58
Removing existing and replacing; strip out and re-wire with PVC insulated and sheathed cable and new conduit										
Point to junction box, re-using existing lamp holder, socket outlet etc										
5 amp socket outlet	4.89	15.00	5.50	5.56	-	189.76	-	195.26	nr	214.79
13 amp socket outlet	6.36	15.00	7.18	4.68	-	159.73	-	166.91	nr	183.60
lighting point or switch	3.37	15.00	3.76	4.13	-	140.96	-	144.72	nr	159.19
Removing existing and replacing; luminaires and accessories										
Take out damaged and renew										
flourescent or LED lamp fitting 1500mm, batten type, single tube and replace with LED equivalent	26.82	-	26.82	0.56	-	19.11	0.41	46.35	nr	50.98
flourescent or LED lamp fitting 1500mm, batten type, twin tube and replace with LED equivalent	45.18	-	45.18	0.56	-	19.11	0.41	64.71	nr	71.18
lamp holder, batten type	4.09	2.50	4.19	0.56	-	19.11	0.41	23.72	nr	26.09
lamp holder, pendant type with rose	1.88	2.50	1.93	1.06	-	36.18	0.41	38.52	nr	42.37
switch, flush type	1.05	2.50	1.08	0.75	-	25.60	0.74	27.42	nr	30.16
switch, surface mounted type	1.78	2.50	1.83	0.75	-	25.60	0.74	28.17	nr	30.98
13 amp socket outlet, flush type	3.14	2.50	3.22	0.75	-	25.60	0.74	29.56	nr	32.52
13 amp socket outlet, surface mounted type	4.78	2.50	4.90	0.88	-	30.03	0.74	35.68	nr	39.25
5 amp socket outlet, flush type	5.24	2.50	5.37	0.70	-	23.89	0.74	30.01	nr	33.01
5 amp socket outlet, surface mounted type	3.99	2.50	4.09	0.88	-	30.03	0.74	34.87	nr	38.36

This section continues on the next page

Labour hourly rates: (except Specialists) Craft Operatives 20.87 Labourer 15.57 Rates are national average prices. Refer to REGIONAL VARIATIONS for indicative levels of overall pricing in regions	MATERIALS			LABOUR				RATES		
	Del to Site £	Waste %	Material Cost £	Craft Optve Hrs	Lab Hrs	Labour Cost £	Sunds £	Nett Rate £	Unit	Gross rate (10%) £
ALTERATION WORK TO EXISTING BUILDINGS (Cont'd)										
Removing existing and replacing; work to existing drains										
Break up concrete paving for excavating drain trench and reinstate - break up 100mm concrete paving and 150mm hardcore bed under for excavation of drain trench and reinstate with new hardcore and concrete, BS 8500, design C20P; 20mm aggregate and make good up to existing paving both sides										
400mm wide	7.79	30.00	8.84	-	3.27	50.91	5.61	65.37	m	71.90
Take up flag paving for excavating drain trench and reinstate - carefully take up 50mm precast concrete flag paving and set aside for re-use and break up 150mm hardcore bed under for excavation of drain trench and reinstate with new hardcore and re-lay salvaged flag paving on and with 25mm sand bed and grout in lime sand (1:3) and make good up to existing paving on both sides										
400mm wide	3.25	30.00	4.20	1.47	1.47	53.57	5.16	62.93	m	69.22
Insert new junction in existing drain - excavate for and trace and expose existing drain, break into glazed vitrified clay drain and insert junction with 100mm branch, short length of new pipe and double collar and joint to existing drain; support earthwork, make good concrete bed and haunching and backfill										
existing 100mm diameter drain, invert depth										
600mm	51.72	5.00	54.31	3.00	12.00	249.45	14.27	318.03	nr	349.83
750mm	51.72	5.00	54.31	3.00	14.25	284.48	15.43	354.22	nr	389.64
900mm	51.72	5.00	54.31	3.00	16.50	319.52	16.91	390.73	nr	429.81
existing 150mm diameter drain invert depth										
750mm	82.07	5.00	86.18	4.50	15.75	339.14	17.82	443.14	nr	487.45
900mm	82.07	5.00	86.18	4.50	18.00	374.18	20.21	480.57	nr	528.62
1050mm	82.07	5.00	86.18	4.50	20.25	409.21	22.11	517.50	nr	569.24
1200mm	82.07	5.00	86.18	4.50	22.50	444.24	24.17	554.59	nr	610.05
Repair defective drain - excavate for and trace and expose existing drain, break out fractured glazed vitrified clay drain pipe, replace with new pipe and double collars and joint to existing drain; support earthwork, make good concrete bed and haunching and backfill										
existing 100mm diameter drain; single pipe length; invert depth										
450mm	32.51	5.00	34.14	3.00	11.50	241.66	10.81	286.61	nr	315.27
600mm	32.51	5.00	34.14	3.00	13.50	272.80	13.03	319.98	nr	351.97
750mm	32.51	5.00	34.14	3.00	16.00	311.73	15.92	361.79	nr	397.97
add for each additional pipe length; invert depth										
450mm	21.42	5.00	22.49	2.00	6.75	146.84	10.31	179.64	nr	197.61
600mm	21.42	5.00	22.49	2.00	7.60	160.07	12.46	195.02	nr	214.52
750mm	21.42	5.00	22.49	2.00	8.80	178.76	14.93	216.18	nr	237.80
Removing existing and replacing; work to existing manholes										
Raise top of existing manhole - take off cover and frame and set aside for re-use, prepare level bed on existing one brick sides of manhole internal size 610 x 457mm and raise with Class B engineering brickwork in cement mortar (1:3) finished with a fair face and flush pointed; refix salvaged cover and frame, bed frame in cement mortar and cover in grease and sand										
raising 150mm high	21.06	10.00	23.17	5.30	5.30	193.13	5.23	221.53	nr	243.68
raising 225mm high	31.59	10.00	34.75	6.75	6.75	245.97	7.76	288.47	nr	317.32
raising 300mm high	42.12	10.00	46.33	8.50	8.50	309.74	9.93	366.01	nr	402.61
Insert new branch bend in bottom of existing manhole - break into bottom and one brick side of manhole, insert new glazed vitrified clay three quarter section branch bend to discharge over existing main channel, build in end of new drain and make good benching and side of manhole to match existing										
100mm diameter branch bend	42.82	10.00	47.11	5.75	5.75	209.53	3.75	260.38	nr	286.42
Extend existing manhole - take off cover and frame and set aside; break up one brick end wall of 457mm wide (internal) manhole and excavate for and extend manhole 225mm; support earthwork, level and compact bottom, part backfill and remove surplus spoil from site; extend bottom with 150mm concrete, BS 8500, ordinary prescribed mix C15P, 20mmaggregate bed; extend one brick sides and end with Class B engineering brickwork in cement mortar (1:3) fair faced and flush pointed and bond to existing; extend 100mm main channel and insert 100mm three quarter section branch channel bend; extend benching and build in end of new 100mm drain to one brick side, corbel over end of manhole										
manholes of the following invert depths; refix salvaged cover and frame, bed frame in cement mortar and cover in grease and sand										
450mm	64.29	10.00	70.72	17.60	17.90	646.02	14.45	731.19	nr	804.31
600mm	69.65	10.00	76.61	19.80	20.20	727.74	18.58	822.93	nr	905.23
750mm	77.15	10.00	84.86	22.00	22.50	809.47	22.70	917.03	nr	1008.74
900mm	85.72	10.00	94.29	24.20	24.80	891.19	26.83	1012.31	nr	1113.54
Removing existing and replacing; softwood fencing										
Remove defective timber fence post and replace with new 102 x 102mm post; letting post 450mm into ground; backfilling around in concrete mix C20P; 20mm aggregate; securing ends of existing arris rails and gravel boards to new post										
to suit fencing; 914mm high	20.82	7.50	21.30	2.04	2.04	74.34	0.68	96.31	nr	105.94
to suit fencing; 1219mm high	23.69	7.50	24.17	2.06	2.06	75.07	0.78	100.02	nr	110.02
to suit fencing; 1524mm high	26.57	7.50	27.05	2.08	2.08	75.80	0.91	103.75	nr	114.13
to suit fencing; 1829mm high	29.44	7.50	29.92	2.10	2.10	76.52	1.06	107.50	nr	118.25

Labour hourly rates: (except Specialists) Craft Operatives 20.87 Labourer 15.57 Rates are national average prices. Refer to REGIONAL VARIATIONS for indicative levels of overall pricing in regions	MATERIALS			LABOUR				RATES		
	Del to Site £	Waste %	Material Cost £	Craft Optve Hrs	Lab Hrs	Labour Cost £	Sunds £	Nett Rate £	Unit	Gross rate (10%) £
ALTERATION WORK TO EXISTING BUILDINGS (Cont'd)										
Removing existing and replacing; softwood fencing (Cont'd)										
Remove defective pale from palisade fence and replace with new 19 x 75mm pointed pale; fixing with galvanised nails										
764mm long	1.50	-	1.50	0.55	0.09	12.88	0.30	14.68	nr	16.14
1069mm long	1.80	-	1.80	0.56	0.09	13.09	0.36	15.25	nr	16.78
1374mm long	2.25	-	2.25	0.58	0.10	13.66	0.41	16.32	nr	17.96
Remove defective pales from close boarded fence and replace with new 100mm wide feather edged pales; fixing with galvanised nails										
singly	1.90	-	1.90	0.25	0.04	5.84	0.35	8.09	m	8.90
areas up to 1.00m²	12.50	20.00	15.00	1.32	0.22	30.97	2.89	48.86	m²	53.75
areas over 1.00m²	12.50	20.00	15.00	0.98	0.16	22.94	2.89	40.83	m²	44.91
Remove defective gravel board and centre stump and replace with new 25 x 150mm gravel board and 50 x 50mm centre stump; fixing with galvanised nails										
securing to fence posts	5.48	5.00	5.75	0.53	0.09	12.46	0.35	18.56	m	20.41
Removing existing and replacing; oak fencing										
Remove defective timber fence post and replace with new post; letting post 450mm into ground; backfilling around in concrete mix C20P; 20mm aggregate; securing ends of existing arris rails and gravel boards to new post										
to suit fencing; 914mm high	18.92	7.50	19.41	2.17	2.17	79.07	0.68	99.16	nr	109.07
to suit fencing; 1219mm high	20.42	7.50	20.91	2.21	2.21	80.53	0.78	102.21	nr	112.43
to suit fencing; 1524mm high	22.42	7.50	22.91	2.25	2.25	81.99	0.91	105.80	nr	116.38
to suit fencing; 1829mm high	25.42	7.50	25.91	2.29	2.29	83.45	1.06	110.41	nr	121.45
Remove defective pale from palisade fence and replace with new 19 x 75mm pointed pale; fixing with galvanised nails										
764mm long	2.50	-	2.50	0.70	0.12	16.48	0.30	19.27	nr	21.20
1069mm long	2.85	-	2.85	0.76	0.13	17.89	0.36	21.10	nr	23.21
1374mm long	3.45	-	3.45	0.83	0.14	19.50	0.41	23.36	nr	25.70
Remove defective pales from close boarded fence and replace with new 100mm wide feather edged pales; fixing with galvanised nails										
singly	4.49	-	4.49	0.27	0.05	6.41	0.35	11.25	m	12.37
areas up to 1.00m²	32.00	20.00	38.40	2.56	0.43	60.12	2.89	101.41	m²	111.55
areas over 1.00m²	32.00	20.00	38.40	2.07	0.35	48.65	2.89	89.94	m²	98.93
Remove defective gravel board and centre stump and replace with new 25 x 150mm gravel board and 50 x 50mm centre stump; fixing with galvanised nails										
securing to fence posts	7.00	5.00	7.35	1.10	0.18	25.76	0.35	33.45	m	36.80
Repairs to posts										
100 x 100mm precast concrete spur 1219mm long; setting into ground; backfilling around in concrete mix C20P; 20mm aggregate										
bolting to existing timber post	12.90	7.50	13.39	0.76	0.76	27.69	2.74	43.82	nr	48.20
Removing existing and replacing; precast concrete flag paving										
Take up uneven paving and set aside for re-use; level up and consolidate existing hardcore and relay salvaged paving										
bedding on 25mm sand bed; grouting in lime mortar (1:3)	0.89	33.00	1.15	0.67	0.93	28.46	0.20	29.81	m²	32.79
Removing existing and replacing; Yorkstone paving										
Take up old paving; re-square; relay random in random sizes										
bedding, jointing and pointing in cement mortar (1:3)	5.15	10.00	5.66	1.10	1.10	40.08	1.49	47.23	m²	51.96
Removing existing and replacing; granite sett paving										
Take up, clean and stack										
old paving	-	-	-	-	0.90	14.01	-	14.01	m²	15.41
Take up old paving, clean and re-lay										
bedding and grouting in cement mortar (1:3)	-	-	-	1.65	2.55	74.14	1.98	76.12	m²	83.73
Clean out joints of old paving and re-grout										
in cement mortar (1:3)	-	-	-	-	0.55	8.56	0.86	9.42	m²	10.36
Removing existing and replacing; bitumen paving										
Cut out damaged 50mm paving to footpath										
and fill with bitumen macadam under 1.00m²	51.96	10.00	57.16	1.65	2.55	74.14	1.98	133.28	m²	146.60
Cut out damaged 75mm paving to road										
fill with macadam and seal all around with hot bitumen under 1.00m²	77.94	10.00	85.73	1.65	2.55	74.14	-	159.87	m²	175.86
Preparing existing structures for connection or attachment of new works; Hacking surfaces										
of concrete as key for new finishings										
ceiling	-	-	-	-	0.67	10.43	0.07	10.50	m²	11.55
floor	-	-	-	-	0.53	8.25	0.07	8.32	m²	9.15
wall	-	-	-	-	0.53	8.25	0.07	8.32	m²	9.15
of brick wall and raking out joints as key for new finishings										
wall	-	-	-	-	0.60	9.34	0.07	9.41	m²	10.35

Labour hourly rates: (except Specialists) Craft Operatives 20.87 Labourer 15.57 Rates are national average prices. Refer to REGIONAL VARIATIONS for indicative levels of overall pricing in regions	MATERIALS			LABOUR				RATES		
	Del to Site £	Waste %	Material Cost £	Craft Optve Hrs	Lab Hrs	Labour Cost £	Sunds £	Nett Rate £	Unit	Gross rate (10%) £
ALTERATION WORK TO EXISTING BUILDINGS (Cont'd)										
Repointing joints										
Rake out joints of old brickwork 20mm deep and re-point in cement mortar (1:3)										
For turned in edge of lead flashing										
flush pointing; horizontal	-	-	-	0.50	0.50	18.22	0.40	18.62	m	20.48
flush pointing; stepped	-	-	-	0.85	0.85	30.97	0.56	31.53	m	34.69
weathered pointing; horizontal	-	-	-	0.55	0.55	20.04	0.40	20.44	m	22.48
weathered pointing; stepped	-	-	-	0.90	0.90	32.80	0.56	33.36	m	36.69
ironed in pointing; horizontal	-	-	-	0.55	0.55	20.04	0.40	20.44	m	22.48
ironed in pointing; stepped	-	-	-	0.90	0.90	32.80	0.56	33.36	m	36.69
Repointing										
Rake out joints of old brickwork 20mm deep and re-point in cement-lime mortar(1:1:6)										
Generally; English bond										
flush pointing	-	-	-	1.00	0.66	31.15	1.14	32.28	m²	35.51
weathered pointing	-	-	-	1.00	0.66	31.15	1.14	32.28	m²	35.51
ironed in pointing	-	-	-	1.20	0.80	37.50	1.14	38.64	m²	42.50
Generally; Flemish bond										
flush pointing	-	-	-	1.00	0.66	31.15	1.14	32.28	m²	35.51
weathered pointing	-	-	-	1.00	0.66	31.15	1.14	32.28	m²	35.51
ironed in pointing	-	-	-	1.20	0.80	37.50	1.14	38.64	m²	42.50
Isolated areas not exceeding 1.00m²; English bond										
flush pointing	-	-	-	1.50	1.00	46.88	1.14	48.01	m²	52.81
weathered pointing	-	-	-	1.50	1.00	46.88	1.14	48.01	m²	52.81
ironed in pointing	-	-	-	1.80	1.20	56.25	1.14	57.39	m²	63.13
Isolated areas not exceeding 1.00m²; Flemish bond										
flush pointing	-	-	-	1.50	1.00	46.88	1.14	48.01	m²	52.81
weathered pointing	-	-	-	1.50	1.00	46.88	1.14	48.01	m²	52.81
ironed in pointing	-	-	-	1.80	1.20	56.25	1.14	57.39	m²	63.13
For using coloured mortar										
add	-	-	-	-	-	-	0.82	0.82	m²	0.91
Rake out joints of old brickwork 20mm deep and re-point in cement mortar (1:3)										
Generally; English bond										
flush pointing	-	-	-	1.20	0.80	37.50	1.14	38.64	m²	42.50
weathered pointing	-	-	-	1.20	0.80	37.50	1.14	38.64	m²	42.50
Generally; Flemish bond										
flush pointing	-	-	-	1.20	0.80	37.50	1.14	38.64	m²	42.50
weathered pointing	-	-	-	1.20	0.80	37.50	1.14	38.64	m²	42.50
Isolated areas not exceeding 1.00m²; English bond										
flush pointing	-	-	-	1.80	1.20	56.25	1.14	57.39	m²	63.13
weathered pointing	-	-	-	1.80	1.20	56.25	1.14	57.39	m²	63.13
Isolated areas not exceeding 1.00m²; Flemish bond										
flush pointing	-	-	-	1.80	1.20	56.25	1.14	57.39	m²	63.13
weathered pointing	-	-	-	1.80	1.20	56.25	1.14	57.39	m²	63.13
REPAIRS/CLEANING/RENOVATING AND CONSERVING										
Repairing; asphalt work										
Cut out crack in old covering and make good with new material to match existing										
Floor or tanking										
in two coats, horizontal; 20mm thick	-	-	-	0.66	0.66	24.05	0.82	24.88	m	27.36
in three coats, horizontal; 30mm thick	-	-	-	0.90	0.90	32.80	1.24	34.03	m	37.44
in three coats, vertical; 30mm thick	-	-	-	1.19	1.19	43.36	1.24	44.60	m	49.06
Cut out detached blister in old covering and make good with new material to match existing										
Floor or tanking										
in two coats, horizontal; 20mm thick	-	-	-	0.30	0.30	10.93	0.41	11.34	nr	12.48
in three coats, horizontal; 30mm thick	-	-	-	0.35	0.35	12.75	0.58	13.33	nr	14.66
in three coats, vertical; 30mm thick	-	-	-	0.48	0.48	17.49	0.58	18.07	nr	19.88
Roof covering										
in two coats; 20mm thick	-	-	-	0.30	0.30	10.93	0.41	11.34	nr	12.48
Cut out crack in old covering and make good with new material to match existing										
Roof covering										
in two coats; 20mm thick	-	-	-	0.66	0.66	24.05	0.82	24.88	m	27.36
Repairing slate roofing; repairs to roofs covered with 610 x 300mm slates										
Remove damaged slates and replace with new; sloping or vertical										
one slate	12.45	5.00	13.07	0.32	0.32	11.66	0.15	24.88	nr	27.37
patch of 10 slates	124.50	5.00	130.72	1.10	1.10	40.08	1.15	171.96	nr	189.16
patch of slates 1.00 - 3.00m²	152.51	5.00	160.14	1.25	1.25	45.55	1.25	206.94	m²	227.64
Examine battens, remove defective and provide 20% new										
19 x 38mm	0.58	10.00	0.64	0.09	0.09	3.28	0.08	4.01	m²	4.41
25 x 50mm	1.01	10.00	1.11	0.09	0.09	3.28	0.12	4.51	m²	4.96
Re-cover roof with slates previously removed and stacked and fix with slate nails										
with 75mm lap	-	-	-	0.77	0.77	28.06	0.15	28.21	m²	31.03
extra for providing 20% new slates	30.50	5.00	32.03	-	-	-	0.30	32.32	m²	35.56
Remove double course at eaves and										
refix	-	-	-	0.24	0.24	8.75	0.51	9.26	m	10.18
extra for providing 20% new slates	10.58	5.00	11.11	-	-	-	0.15	11.26	m	12.39

Labour hourly rates: (except Specialists) Craft Operatives 20.87 Labourer 15.57 Rates are national average prices. Refer to REGIONAL VARIATIONS for indicative levels of overall pricing in regions	MATERIALS			LABOUR				RATES		
	Del to Site £	Waste %	Material Cost £	Craft Optve Hrs	Lab Hrs	Labour Cost £	Sunds £	Nett Rate £	Unit	Gross rate (10%) £
REPAIRS/CLEANING/RENOVATING AND CONSERVING (Cont'd)										
Repairing slate roofing; repairs to roofs covered with 610 x 300mm slates (Cont'd)										
Remove double course at verge and replace with new slates and bed and point in mortar	46.56	5.00	48.89	0.29	0.29	10.57	0.96	60.42	m	66.46
Repairing slate roofing; repairs to roofs covered with 510 x 250mm slates										
Remove damaged slates and replace with new; sloping or vertical										
one slate	5.19	5.00	5.45	0.32	0.32	11.66	0.15	17.26	nr	18.98
patch of 10 slates	51.90	5.00	54.49	1.00	1.00	36.44	0.97	91.91	nr	101.10
patch of slates 1.00 - 3.00m²	93.42	5.00	98.09	1.49	1.49	54.30	1.24	153.62	m²	168.99
Examine battens, remove defective and provide 20% new										
19 x 38mm	0.72	10.00	0.79	0.11	0.11	4.01	0.12	4.91	m²	5.40
25 x 50mm	1.24	10.00	1.37	0.11	0.11	4.01	0.15	5.52	m²	6.08
Re-cover roof with slates previously removed and stacked and fix with slate nails										
with 75mm lap	-	-	-	1.00	1.00	36.44	0.21	36.65	m²	40.32
extra for providing 20% new slates	18.68	5.00	19.62	-	-	-	0.30	19.92	m²	21.91
Remove double course at eaves and										
refix	-	-	-	0.25	0.25	9.11	0.87	9.98	m	10.98
extra for providing 20% new slates	5.81	5.00	6.10	-	-	-	0.13	6.24	m	6.86
Remove double course at verge and replace with new slates and bed and point in mortar	23.87	5.00	25.07	0.29	0.29	10.57	0.94	36.58	m	40.23
Repairing slate roofing; repairs to roofs covered with 405 x 200mm slates										
Remove damaged slates and replace with new; sloping or vertical										
one slate	2.61	5.00	2.74	0.32	0.32	11.66	0.13	14.53	nr	15.99
patch of 10 slates	26.10	5.00	27.40	0.90	0.90	32.80	0.84	61.04	nr	67.15
patch of slates 1.00 - 3.00m²	78.30	5.00	82.21	2.07	2.07	75.43	1.37	159.02	m²	174.92
Examine battens, remove defective and provide 20% new										
19 x 38mm	0.96	10.00	1.06	0.13	0.13	4.74	0.13	5.92	m²	6.52
25 x 50mm	1.66	10.00	1.83	0.13	0.13	4.74	0.15	6.71	m²	7.38
Re-cover roof with slates previously removed and stacked and fix with slate nails										
with 75mm lap	-	-	-	1.14	1.14	41.54	0.31	41.86	m²	46.04
extra for providing 20% new slates	15.66	5.00	16.44	-	-	-	0.30	16.74	m²	18.41
Remove double course at eaves and										
refix	-	-	-	0.26	0.26	9.47	0.86	10.33	m	11.37
extra for providing 20% new slates	3.55	5.00	3.73	-	-	-	0.13	3.86	m	4.24
Remove double course at verge and replace with new slates and bed and point in mortar	15.22	5.00	15.98	0.30	0.30	10.93	1.04	27.95	m	30.74
Repairing tile roofing; repairs to roofs covered with machine made clay plain tiles laid to 100mm gauge										
Remove damaged tiles and replace with new, sloping or vertical										
one tile	0.49	10.00	0.54	0.32	0.32	11.66	0.05	12.25	nr	13.47
patch of 10 tiles	4.90	10.00	5.39	0.90	0.90	32.80	0.41	38.60	nr	42.46
patch of tiles 1.00 - 3.00m²	29.89	10.00	32.88	1.72	1.72	62.68	2.64	98.20	m²	108.02
Examine battens, remove defective and provide 20% new										
19 x 25mm	2.13	10.00	2.34	0.13	0.13	4.74	0.13	7.21	m²	7.93
19 x 38mm	1.56	10.00	1.72	0.14	0.14	5.10	0.15	6.97	m²	7.66
19 x 50mm	3.60	10.00	3.96	0.14	0.14	5.10	0.18	9.25	m²	10.17
Remove defective and provide twin ply polypropylene underlay; 150 laps; fixing with galvanised steel clout nails										
horizontal or vertical	0.74	15.00	0.86	0.25	0.25	9.11	0.08	10.05	m²	11.05
Re-cover roof with tiles previously removed and stacked										
nail every fourth course with galvanised nails	-	-	-	1.00	1.00	36.44	0.28	36.72	m²	40.39
extra for nailing every course	-	-	-	0.20	0.20	7.29	0.74	8.03	m²	8.83
extra for providing 20% new tiles	5.98	10.00	6.58	-	-	-	0.30	6.87	m²	7.56
Repairing tile roofing; repairs to roofs covered with machine made clay plain tiles laid to 90mm gauge										
Remove damaged tiles and replace with new, sloping or vertical										
one tile	0.49	10.00	0.54	0.32	0.32	11.66	0.05	12.25	nr	13.47
patch of 10 tiles	4.90	10.00	5.39	0.90	0.90	32.80	0.41	38.60	nr	42.46
patch of tiles 1.00 - 3.00m²	33.32	10.00	36.65	2.05	2.05	74.70	2.94	114.29	m²	125.72
Examine battens, remove defective and provide 20% new										
19 x 25mm	2.37	10.00	2.60	0.14	0.14	5.10	0.15	7.85	m²	8.64
19 x 38mm	1.73	10.00	1.90	0.15	0.15	5.47	0.18	7.55	m²	8.30
19 x 50mm	4.00	10.00	4.40	0.15	0.15	5.47	0.20	10.07	m²	11.08
Re-cover roof with tiles previously removed and stacked										
nail every fourth course with galvanised nails	-	-	-	1.15	1.15	41.91	0.31	42.22	m²	46.44
extra for nailing every course	-	-	-	0.23	0.23	8.38	0.78	9.16	m²	10.07
extra for providing 20% new tiles	6.66	10.00	7.33	-	-	-	0.30	7.63	m²	8.39

Labour hourly rates: (except Specialists) Craft Operatives 20.87 Labourer 15.57 Rates are national average prices. Refer to REGIONAL VARIATIONS for indicative levels of overall pricing in regions	MATERIALS			LABOUR				RATES		
	Del to Site £	Waste %	Material Cost £	Craft Optve Hrs	Lab Hrs	Labour Cost £	Sunds £	Nett Rate £	Unit	Gross rate (10%) £
REPAIRS/CLEANING/RENOVATING AND CONSERVING (Cont'd)										
Repairing tile roofing; repairs to roofs covered with hand made clay plain tiles laid to 100mm gauge										
Remove damaged tiles and replace with new, sloping or vertical										
one tile	1.31	10.00	1.44	0.32	0.32	11.66	0.05	13.15	nr	14.47
patch of 10 tiles	13.10	10.00	14.41	0.90	0.90	32.80	0.41	47.62	nr	52.38
patch of tiles 1.00 - 3.00m²	79.91	10.00	87.90	1.72	1.72	62.68	2.64	153.22	m²	168.54
Examine battens, remove defective and provide 20% new										
19 x 25mm	2.13	10.00	2.34	0.13	0.13	4.74	0.13	7.21	m²	7.93
19 x 38mm	1.56	10.00	1.72	0.14	0.14	5.10	0.15	6.97	m²	7.66
19 x 50mm	3.60	10.00	3.96	0.14	0.14	5.10	0.18	9.25	m²	10.17
Remove defective and provide twin ply polypropylene; 150 laps; fixing with galvanised steel clout nails										
horizontal or vertical	0.74	15.00	0.86	0.25	0.25	9.11	0.08	10.05	m²	11.05
Re-cover roof with tiles previously removed and stacked										
nail every fourth course with galvanised nails	-	-	-	1.00	1.00	36.44	0.28	36.72	m²	40.39
extra for nailing every course	-	-	-	0.20	0.20	7.29	0.74	8.03	m²	8.83
extra for providing 20% new tiles	15.98	10.00	17.58	-	-	-	0.30	17.88	m²	19.66
Repairing tile roofing; repairs to roofs covered with hand made clay plain tiles laid to 90mm gauge										
Remove damaged tiles and replace with new, sloping or vertical										
one tile	1.31	10.00	1.44	0.32	0.32	11.66	0.05	13.15	nr	14.47
patch of 10 tiles	13.10	10.00	14.41	0.90	0.90	32.80	0.41	47.62	nr	52.38
patch of tiles 1.00 - 3.00m²	89.08	10.00	97.99	2.05	2.05	74.70	2.94	175.63	m²	193.19
Examine battens, remove defective and provide 20% new										
19 x 25mm	2.37	10.00	2.60	0.14	0.14	5.10	0.15	7.85	m²	8.64
19 x 38mm	1.73	10.00	1.90	0.15	0.15	5.47	0.18	7.55	m²	8.30
19 x 50mm	4.00	10.00	4.40	0.15	0.15	5.47	0.20	10.07	m²	11.08
Remove defective and provide twin ply polypropylene; 150 laps; fixing with galvanised steel clout nails										
horizontal or vertical	0.74	15.00	0.86	0.25	0.25	9.11	0.08	10.05	m²	11.05
Re-cover roof with tiles previously removed and stacked										
nail every fourth course with galvanised nails	-	-	-	1.15	1.15	41.91	0.31	42.22	m²	46.44
extra for nailing every course	-	-	-	0.23	0.23	8.38	0.78	9.16	m²	10.07
extra for providing 20% new tiles	17.82	10.00	19.60	-	-	-	0.30	19.89	m²	21.88
Repairing tile roofing; repairs to roofs covered with concrete granular faced plain tiles laid to 100mm gauge										
Remove damaged tiles and replace with new, sloping or vertical										
one tile	0.42	10.00	0.46	0.32	0.32	11.66	0.05	12.17	nr	13.39
patch of 10 tiles	4.20	10.00	4.62	0.90	0.90	32.80	0.41	37.83	nr	41.61
patch of tiles 1.00 - 3.00m²	25.62	10.00	28.18	1.72	1.72	62.68	2.64	93.50	m²	102.85
Examine battens, remove defective and provide 20% new										
19 x 25mm	2.13	10.00	2.34	0.13	0.13	4.74	0.13	7.21	m²	7.93
19 x 38mm	1.56	10.00	1.72	0.14	0.14	5.10	0.15	6.97	m²	7.66
19 x 50mm	3.60	10.00	3.96	0.14	0.14	5.10	0.18	9.25	m²	10.17
Remove defective and provide twin ply polypropylene; 150 laps; fixing with galvanised steel clout nails										
horizontal or vertical	0.74	15.00	0.86	0.25	0.25	9.11	0.08	10.05	m²	11.05
Re-cover roof with tiles previously removed and stacked										
nail every fourth course with galvanised nails	-	-	-	1.00	1.00	36.44	0.28	36.72	m²	40.39
extra for nailing every course	-	-	-	0.20	0.20	7.29	0.74	8.03	m²	8.83
extra for providing 20% new tiles	5.12	10.00	5.64	-	-	-	0.30	5.93	m²	6.53
Repairing tile roofing; repairs to roofs covered with 381 x 227mm concrete interlocking tiles laid to 75mm laps										
Remove damaged tiles and replace with new, sloping or vertical										
one tile	0.84	10.00	0.92	0.32	0.32	11.66	0.12	12.70	nr	13.97
patch of 10 tiles	8.40	10.00	9.24	0.90	0.90	32.80	1.20	43.24	nr	47.56
patch of tiles 1.00 - 3.00m²	14.28	10.00	15.71	0.85	0.85	30.97	1.91	48.60	m²	53.46
Examine battens, remove defective and provide 20% new										
19 x 25mm	0.77	10.00	0.84	0.05	0.05	1.82	0.12	2.78	m²	3.06
19 x 38mm	0.56	10.00	0.62	0.06	0.06	2.19	0.12	2.92	m²	3.21
19 x 50mm	1.30	10.00	1.43	0.07	0.07	2.55	0.13	4.11	m²	4.52
Re-cover roof with tiles previously removed and stacked										
nail every fourth course with galvanised nails	-	-	-	0.50	0.50	18.22	0.03	18.25	m²	20.08
extra for nailing every course	-	-	-	0.05	0.05	1.82	0.10	1.92	m²	2.11
extra for providing 20% new tiles	3.36	10.00	3.70	-	-	-	0.36	4.06	m²	4.46
Repairing tile roofing; repairs generally										
Remove damaged clay tiles and provide new machine made tiles										
half round ridge or hip and bed in mortar	19.07	5.00	20.03	0.60	0.60	21.86	1.80	43.69	m	48.06
bonnet hip	46.24	5.00	48.55	0.75	0.75	27.33	0.50	76.38	m	84.01
trough valley	46.24	5.00	48.55	0.75	0.75	27.33	0.50	76.38	m	84.01
vertical angle	52.02	5.00	54.62	0.75	0.75	27.33	0.50	82.45	m	90.69
Remove double course and replace with new machine made clay tiles and bed and point in mortar										
at eaves	5.88	10.00	6.47	0.23	0.23	8.38	0.74	15.59	m	17.15
at verge	14.70	10.00	16.17	0.38	0.38	13.85	2.29	32.31	m	35.54

ALTERATIONS, REPAIRS AND CONSERVATION

Labour hourly rates: (except Specialists) Craft Operatives 20.87 Labourer 15.57 Rates are national average prices. Refer to REGIONAL VARIATIONS for indicative levels of overall pricing in regions	MATERIALS			LABOUR				RATES		
	Del to Site £	Waste %	Material Cost £	Craft Optve Hrs	Lab Hrs	Labour Cost £	Sunds £	Nett Rate £	Unit	Gross rate (10%) £
REPAIRS/CLEANING/RENOVATING AND CONSERVING (Cont'd)										
Repairing tile roofing; repairs generally (Cont'd)										
Rake out defective pointing and re-point in cement mortar (1:3)										
ridge or hip tiles	-	-	-	0.34	0.34	12.39	0.28	12.67	m	13.94
Hack off defective cement mortar fillet and renew in cement mortar (1:3)	-	-	-	0.34	0.34	12.39	0.56	12.95	m	14.25
Remove defective hip hook and replace with new	1.02	5.00	1.07	0.34	0.34	12.39	0.12	13.58	nr	14.93
Remove damaged clay tiles and provide new hand made tiles										
half round ridge or hip and bed in mortar	26.15	5.00	27.46	0.60	0.60	21.86	1.80	51.12	m	56.23
bonnet hip	107.60	5.00	112.98	0.75	0.75	27.33	0.50	140.80	m	154.89
trough valley	63.40	5.00	66.57	0.75	0.75	27.33	0.50	94.39	m	103.83
vertical angle	76.28	5.00	80.09	0.75	0.75	27.33	0.50	107.91	m	118.71
Remove double course and replace with hand made new clay tiles and bed and point in mortar										
at eaves	10.80	10.00	11.88	0.23	0.23	8.38	0.74	21.00	m	23.10
at verge	31.10	10.00	34.21	0.38	0.38	13.85	2.29	50.35	m	55.39
Rake out defective pointing and re-point in cement mortar (1:3)										
ridge or hip tiles	-	-	-	0.34	0.34	12.39	0.28	12.67	m	13.94
Hack off defective cement mortar fillet and renew in cement mortar (1:3)	-	-	-	0.34	0.34	12.39	0.56	12.95	m	14.25
Remove defective hip hook and replace with new	1.02	5.00	1.07	0.34	0.34	12.39	0.12	13.58	nr	14.93
Remove damaged clay tiles and provide new concrete tiles										
half round ridge or hip and bed in mortar	18.02	5.00	18.92	0.60	0.60	21.86	1.80	42.59	m	46.84
bonnet hip	41.76	5.00	43.85	0.75	0.75	27.33	0.50	71.67	m	78.84
trough valley	42.24	5.00	44.35	0.75	0.75	27.33	0.50	72.18	m	79.39
vertical angle	48.06	5.00	50.46	0.75	0.75	27.33	0.50	78.29	m	86.12
Remove double course and replace with new concrete tiles and bed and point in mortar										
at eaves	5.46	10.00	6.01	0.23	0.23	8.38	0.74	15.13	m	16.64
at verge	13.95	10.00	15.35	0.38	0.38	13.85	2.29	31.49	m	34.63
Rake out defective pointing and re-point in cement mortar (1:3)										
ridge or hip tiles	-	-	-	0.34	0.34	12.39	0.28	12.67	m	13.94
Hack off defective cement mortar fillet and renew in cement mortar (1:3)	-	-	-	0.34	0.34	12.39	0.56	12.95	m	14.25
Remove defective hip hook and replace with new	1.02	5.00	1.07	0.34	0.34	12.39	0.12	13.58	nr	14.93
Repairing liquid bitumen; proofing (black) brush applied on old roof covering including cleaning old covering										
Corrugated asbestos roofing										
one coat	1.08	10.00	1.18	-	0.21	3.27	-	4.45	m²	4.90
two coats	2.15	10.00	2.37	-	0.25	3.89	-	6.26	m²	6.88
Felt roofing										
one coat	1.08	10.00	1.18	-	0.17	2.65	-	3.83	m²	4.21
two coats	2.15	10.00	2.37	-	0.21	3.27	-	5.63	m²	6.20
For top coat in green in lieu black										
add	2.04	10.00	2.24	-	-	-	-	2.24	m²	2.47

This section continues on the next page

Labour hourly rates: (except Specialists) Craft Operatives 26.39 Labourer 15.57 Rates are national average prices. Refer to REGIONAL VARIATIONS for indicative levels of overall pricing in regions	MATERIALS			LABOUR				RATES		
	Del to Site £	Waste %	Material Cost £	Craft Optve Hrs	Lab Hrs	Labour Cost £	Sunds £	Nett Rate £	Unit	Gross rate (10%) £
REPAIRS/CLEANING/RENOVATING AND CONSERVING (Cont'd)										
Repairing; lead roofing										
Repair crack clean out and fill with copper bit solder	-	-	-	0.80	-	21.11	0.50	21.61	m	23.77
Turn back flashing and re-dress	-	-	-	0.48	-	12.67	-	12.67	m	13.93

This section continues on the next page

Labour hourly rates: (except Specialists) Craft Operatives 20.87 Labourer 15.57 Rates are national average prices. Refer to REGIONAL VARIATIONS for indicative levels of overall pricing in regions	MATERIALS			LABOUR				RATES		
	Del to Site £	Waste %	Material Cost £	Craft Optve Hrs	Lab Hrs	Labour Cost £	Sunds £	Nett Rate £	Unit	Gross rate (10%) £
REPAIRS/CLEANING/RENOVATING AND CONSERVING (Cont'd)										
Repairing; resecure glass										
Remove decayed putties, paint one coat on edge of rebate and re-putty										
wood window	0.19	10.00	0.21	0.69	-	14.40	0.03	14.65	m	16.11
metal window	0.19	10.00	0.21	0.76	-	15.86	0.03	16.11	m	17.72
Remove beads, remove decayed bedding materials, paint one coat on edge of rebate, re-bed glass and re-fix beads										
wood window	0.19	10.00	0.21	1.22	-	25.46	0.03	25.71	m	28.28
metal window	0.19	10.00	0.21	1.32	-	27.55	0.03	27.79	m	30.57

This section continues on the next page

Labour hourly rates: (except Specialists) Craft Operatives 26.39 Labourer 15.57 Rates are national average prices. Refer to REGIONAL VARIATIONS for indicative levels of overall pricing in regions	MATERIALS			LABOUR				RATES		
	Del to Site £	Waste %	Material Cost £	Craft Optve Hrs	Lab Hrs	Labour Cost £	Sunds £	Nett Rate £	Unit	Gross rate (10%) £
REPAIRS/CLEANING/RENOVATING AND CONSERVING (Cont'd)										
Repairing; rainwater goods										
Clean out and make good loose fixings										
eaves gutter	-	-	-	0.40	-	10.56	-	10.56	m	11.61
rainwater pipe	-	-	-	0.40	-	10.56	-	10.56	m	11.61
rainwater head	-	-	-	0.75	-	19.79	-	19.79	nr	21.77
Clean out defective joint to existing eaves gutter and re-make joint with jointing compound and new bolt	0.11	-	0.11	0.75	-	19.79	-	19.90	nr	21.89
Repairing; stopcocks, valves, etc.										
Turn off water supply drain down as necessary and re-new washer to the following up to 19mm										
main stopcock	0.18	-	0.18	2.00	-	52.78	-	52.96	nr	58.26
service stopcock	0.18	-	0.18	2.00	-	52.78	-	52.96	nr	58.26
bib or pillar cock	0.18	-	0.18	2.00	-	52.78	-	52.96	nr	58.26
supatap	0.18	-	0.18	2.00	-	52.78	-	52.96	nr	58.26
draining tap	0.18	-	0.18	2.00	-	52.78	-	52.96	nr	58.26
Repairing; removal of traps, valves, etc., for re-use										
Take out the following, including unscrewing or uncoupling, for re-use and including draining down as necessary										
trap; up to 25mm diameter	-	-	-	0.70	-	18.47	-	18.47	nr	20.32
trap; 32 - 50mm diameter	-	-	-	0.85	-	22.43	-	22.43	nr	24.67
stop valve; up to 25mm diameter	-	-	-	2.00	-	52.78	-	52.78	nr	58.06
stop valve; 32 - 50mm diameter	-	-	-	2.25	-	59.38	-	59.38	nr	65.32
radiator valve; up to 25mm diameter	-	-	-	2.00	-	52.78	-	52.78	nr	58.06
radiator valve; 32 - 50mm diameter	-	-	-	2.25	-	59.38	-	59.38	nr	65.32
tap; up to 25mm diameter	-	-	-	2.00	-	52.78	-	52.78	nr	58.06
tap; 32 - 50mm diameter	-	-	-	2.25	-	59.38	-	59.38	nr	65.32
extra; burning out one soldered joint up to 25mm diameter	-	-	-	0.50	-	13.19	-	13.19	nr	14.51
extra; burning out one soldered joint 32 - 50mm diameter	-	-	-	0.80	-	21.11	-	21.11	nr	23.22

This section continues on the next page

Labour hourly rates: (except Specialists) Craft Operatives 20.87 Labourer 15.57 Rates are national average prices. Refer to REGIONAL VARIATIONS for indicative levels of overall pricing in regions	MATERIALS			LABOUR				RATES		
	Del to Site £	Waste %	Material Cost £	Craft Optve Hrs	Lab Hrs	Labour Cost £	Sunds £	Nett Rate £	Unit	Gross rate (10%) £
REPAIRS/CLEANING/RENOVATING AND CONSERVING (Cont'd)										
Damp-proof course renewal/insertion										
Insert damp proof course in old wall by cutting out one course of brickwork in alternate lengths not exceeding 1.00m and replace old bricks with 50mm bricks in cement mortar (1:3)										
Hyload, pitch polymer in										
one brick wall	1.53	10.00	1.68	3.00	3.00	109.32	9.12	120.13	m	132.14
one and a half brick wall	2.30	10.00	2.53	4.00	4.00	145.76	13.71	162.00	m	178.20
254mm hollow wall	1.53	10.00	1.68	3.50	3.50	127.54	9.12	138.35	m	152.18
Two courses slates in cement mortar (1:3) in										
one brick wall	8.16	10.00	8.98	3.00	3.00	109.32	9.12	127.42	m	140.16
one and a half brick wall	12.24	10.00	13.46	4.00	4.00	145.76	13.71	172.94	m	190.23
254mm hollow wall	8.16	10.00	8.98	3.50	3.50	127.54	9.12	145.64	m	160.20
Insert damp proof course in old wall by hand sawing in 600mm lengths										
Hyload, pitch polymer in										
one brick wall	1.53	10.00	1.68	2.50	2.50	91.10	13.65	106.43	m	117.07
one and a half brick wall	2.30	10.00	2.53	3.50	3.50	127.54	20.48	150.54	m	165.60
254mm hollow wall	1.53	10.00	1.68	3.00	3.00	109.32	13.65	124.65	m	137.11
Two courses slates in cement mortar (1:3) in										
one brick wall	8.16	10.00	8.98	2.50	2.50	91.10	13.65	113.72	m	125.09
one and a half brick wall	12.24	10.00	13.46	3.50	3.50	127.54	20.48	161.48	m	177.63
254mm hollow wall	4.08	10.00	4.49	3.00	3.00	109.32	13.65	127.45	m	140.20
Insert damp proof course in old wall by machine sawing in 600mm lengths										
Hyload, pitch polymer in										
one brick wall	1.53	10.00	1.68	2.00	2.00	72.88	18.12	92.68	m	101.95
one and a half brick wall	2.30	10.00	2.53	3.00	3.00	109.32	27.16	139.01	m	152.91
254mm hollow wall	1.53	10.00	1.68	2.50	2.50	91.10	18.12	110.90	m	121.99
Two courses slates in cement mortar (1:3) in										
one brick wall	8.16	10.00	8.98	2.00	2.00	72.88	18.12	99.97	m	109.97
one and a half brick wall	12.24	10.00	13.46	3.00	3.00	109.32	27.16	149.94	m	164.94
254mm hollow wall	4.08	10.00	4.49	2.50	2.50	91.10	18.12	113.71	m	125.08
Insert cavity tray in old wall by cutting out by hand in short lengths; insert individual trays and make good with picked stock facing bricks in gauged mortar (1:2:9) including pinning up with slates										
Type E Cavitray by Cavity Trays Ltd in										
half brick skin of cavity wall	12.63	10.00	13.89	1.75	1.75	63.77	11.58	89.25	m	98.17
external angle	8.25	10.00	9.07	1.00	1.00	36.44	10.64	56.16	nr	61.77
internal angle	8.25	10.00	9.07	1.25	1.25	45.55	10.64	65.27	nr	71.79
Type X Cavitray by Cavity Trays Ltd; to suit 40 degree pitched roof complete with attached code 4 lead flashing and dress over tiles in										
half brick skin of cavity wall	61.88	10.00	68.07	4.25	4.25	154.87	23.18	246.12	m	270.73
ridge tray	14.24	10.00	15.66	1.00	1.00	36.44	5.40	57.50	nr	63.25
catchment tray; short	6.94	10.00	7.63	0.50	0.50	18.22	2.84	28.69	nr	31.56
corner catchment tray	14.87	10.00	16.36	1.00	1.00	36.44	5.40	58.19	nr	64.01
Damp proofing old brick wall by silicone injection method (excluding removal and reinstatement of plaster, etc.)										
Damp proofing										
one brick wall	1.92	-	1.92	1.00	1.00	36.44	1.24	39.60	m	43.56
one and a half brick wall	2.88	-	2.88	1.50	1.50	54.66	1.85	59.39	m	65.33
254mm hollow wall	1.92	-	1.92	1.35	1.35	49.19	1.24	52.35	m	57.59
Cleaning surfaces										
Thoroughly clean existing concrete surfaces prior to applying damp proof membrane										
floors	-	-	-	-	0.19	2.96	0.03	2.99	m²	3.29
walls	-	-	-	-	0.21	3.27	0.03	3.30	m²	3.63
Thoroughly clean existing concrete surfaces, fill in nail holes and small surface imperfections and leave smooth										
walls	-	-	-	0.35	0.20	10.42	0.07	10.48	m²	11.53
soffits	-	-	-	0.50	0.29	14.95	0.07	15.02	m²	16.52
Thoroughly clean existing brick or block surfaces prior to applying damp proof membrane										
walls	-	-	-	-	0.25	3.89	-	3.89	m²	4.28
Clean out air brick										
225 x 150mm	-	-	-	-	0.20	3.11	-	3.11	nr	3.43
DECONTAMINATION										
Infestation removal/eradication; protective treatment of existing timbers										
Treat with two coats of spray applied preservative										
boarding	0.72	10.00	0.80	-	0.15	2.34	0.07	3.20	m²	3.52
structural timbers	1.09	10.00	1.20	-	0.20	3.11	0.08	4.39	m²	4.83
Treat with two coats of brush applied preservative										
boarding	1.09	10.00	1.20	-	0.26	4.05	0.05	5.29	m²	5.82
structural timbers	1.67	10.00	1.83	-	0.80	12.46	0.08	14.37	m²	15.81

Labour hourly rates: (except Specialists) Craft Operatives 20.87 Labourer 15.57 Rates are national average prices. Refer to REGIONAL VARIATIONS for indicative levels of overall pricing in regions	MATERIALS			LABOUR				RATES		
	Del to Site £	Waste %	Material Cost £	Craft Optve Hrs	Lab Hrs	Labour Cost £	Sunds £	Nett Rate £	Unit	Gross rate (10%) £
DECONTAMINATION (Cont'd)										
Infestation removal/eradication; insecticide treatment of existing timbers										
Treat worm infected timbers with spray applied proprietary insecticide										
boarding	1.09	10.00	1.20	-	0.24	3.74	0.08	5.02	m²	5.52
structural timbers	1.45	10.00	1.59	-	0.28	4.36	0.10	6.05	m²	6.66
joinery timbers	1.45	10.00	1.59	-	0.32	4.98	0.10	6.68	m²	7.34
Treat worm infected timbers with brush applied proprietary insecticide										
boarding	1.45	10.00	1.59	-	0.36	5.61	0.05	7.25	m²	7.97
structural timbers	1.74	10.00	1.91	-	0.42	6.54	0.08	8.54	m²	9.39
joinery timbers	1.74	10.00	1.91	-	0.48	7.47	0.08	9.47	m²	10.42
Infestation removal/eradication; treatment of wall surfaces										
Treat surfaces of concrete and brickwork adjoining areas where infected timbers removed										
with a blow lamp	-	-	-	-	0.25	3.89	0.05	3.94	m²	4.34
TEMPORARY WORKS										
Temporary weatherproof coverings										
Providing and erecting and clearing away on completion; for scaffold tube framework see preliminaries										
flexible reinforced plastic sheeting	0.67	10.00	0.73	0.10	0.25	5.98	1.06	7.77	m²	8.55
tarpaulins	1.12	10.00	1.24	0.10	0.25	5.98	1.06	8.27	m²	9.10
Temporary internal screens										
Providing and erecting and clearing away on completion; temporary screen of 50 x 50mm softwood framing and cover with										
reinforced building paper	3.94	10.00	4.33	0.43	0.30	13.65	0.36	18.34	m²	20.17
heavy duty polythene sheeting	4.63	10.00	5.09	0.43	0.30	13.65	0.33	19.07	m²	20.97
3mm hardboard	7.98	10.00	8.77	0.53	0.32	16.04	0.54	25.36	m²	27.90
Providing and erecting and clearing away on completion; temporary dustproof screen of 50 x 75mm softwood framing securely fixed to walls, floor and ceiling, the joints and edges of lining sealed with masking tape and cover with										
3mm hardboard lining one side	9.76	10.00	10.73	1.10	0.18	25.76	0.73	37.22	m²	40.94
3mm hardboard lining both sides	14.20	10.00	15.62	1.30	0.22	30.56	0.91	47.08	m²	51.79
6mm plywood lining one side	10.65	10.00	11.72	1.15	0.19	26.96	0.81	39.49	m²	43.44
6mm plywood lining both sides	15.99	10.00	17.59	1.40	0.23	32.80	1.27	51.66	m²	56.82
providing 35mm hardboard faced flush door size 838 x 1981mm in dustproof screen with 25 x 87mm softwood frame, 18 x 25mm softwood stop, pair of 100mm butts, pull handle and ball catch	116.79	10.00	128.47	1.50	0.25	35.20	4.59	168.25	nr	185.08
Temporary dustproof corridors										
Note for prices of walls and doors, see dustproof screens above										
Providing and erecting and clearing away on completion; ceiling of 50 x 75mm softwood joists at 450mm centres, the joints and edges sealed with masking tape and cover with										
3mm hardboard lining to soffit	10.74	10.00	11.82	1.10	0.18	25.76	0.73	38.30	m²	42.13
6mm plywood lining to soffit	11.64	10.00	12.80	1.15	0.19	26.96	0.91	40.67	m²	44.74
Temporary timber balustrades										
Providing and erecting and clearing away on completion; temporary softwood balustrade consisting of 50 x 75mm plate, 50 x 50mm standards at 900mm centres, four 25 x 150mm intermediate rails and 50 x 50mm handrail										
1150mm high	10.23	10.00	11.25	1.00	0.26	24.92	2.08	38.25	m	42.07
Temporary steel balustrades										
Providing and erecting and clearing away on completion; temporary steel balustrade constructed of 50mm diameter galvanised scaffold tubing and fittings with standards at 900mm centres intermediate rail, handrail, plastic mesh infill and with plates on ends of standards fixed to floor										
1150mm high	34.02	-	34.02	0.18	0.90	17.77	0.50	52.28	m	57.51
weekly cost of hire and maintenance	7.50	-	7.50	0.02	0.10	1.97	0.07	9.54	m	10.49
Temporary fillings to openings in external walls										
Providing and erecting and clearing away on completion; temporary filling to window or door opening of 50 x 100mm softwood framing and cover with										
corrugated iron sheeting	10.36	10.00	11.40	0.45	0.45	16.40	2.16	29.96	m²	32.95
25mm softwood boarding	17.23	10.00	18.95	0.60	0.60	21.86	2.52	43.34	m²	47.68
12mm external quality plywood	16.26	10.00	17.88	0.50	0.50	18.22	1.63	37.74	m²	41.51

This page left blank intentionally

Labour hourly rates: (except Specialists) Craft Operatives 20.87 Labourer 15.57 Rates are national average prices. Refer to REGIONAL VARIATIONS for indicative levels of overall pricing in regions	PLANT AND TRANSPORT			LABOUR				RATES		
	Plant Cost £	Trans Cost £	P and T Cost £	Craft Optve Hrs	Lab Hrs	Labour Cost £	Sunds £	Nett Rate £	Unit	Gross rate (10%) £
SITE CLEARANCE/PREPARATION										
Removing trees										
Removing trees; filling voids left by removal of roots with selected material arising from excavation										
girth 0.60 - 1.50m	224.84	-	224.84	-	11.00	171.27	-	396.11	nr	435.73
girth 1.50 - 3.00m	415.10	-	415.10	-	23.00	358.11	-	773.21	nr	850.53
girth exceeding 3.00m	605.35	-	605.35	-	35.00	544.95	-	1150.30	nr	1265.33
Site clearance										
Clearing site vegetation; filling voids left by removal of roots with selected material arising from excavation										
bushes, scrub, undergrowth, hedges, trees and tree stumps not exceeding 600mm girth.	1.41	-	1.41	-	-	-	-	1.41	m²	1.55
Site preparation										
Lifting turf for preservation										
stacking on site average 100m distant for future use; watering	-	-	-	-	0.60	9.34	-	9.34	m²	10.28
Remove top soil for preservation - by machine; (depositing on site measured separately)										
average 150mm deep	0.97	-	0.97	-	-	-	-	0.97	m²	1.07
Remove top soil for preservation - by hand; (depositing on site measured separately)										
average 150mm deep	-	-	-	-	0.33	5.14	-	5.14	m²	5.65
Breaking out existing hard pavings; extra over any types of excavating irrespective of depth - by machine										
concrete, 150mm thick	3.15	-	3.15	-	-	-	-	3.15	m²	3.47
reinforced concrete, 200mm thick	5.25	-	5.25	-	-	-	-	5.25	m²	5.78
coated macadam or asphalt, 75mm thick	0.63	-	0.63	-	-	-	-	0.63	m²	0.69
Breaking out existing hard pavings; extra over any types of excavating irrespective of depth - by hand										
concrete, 150mm thick	-	-	-	-	1.65	25.69	-	25.69	m²	28.26
reinforced concrete, 200mm thick	-	-	-	-	3.30	51.38	-	51.38	m²	56.52
coated macadam or asphalt, 75mm thick	-	-	-	-	0.30	4.67	-	4.67	m²	5.14
EXCAVATIONS										
Excavating - by machine										
Bulk excavation; to reduce levels maximum depth not exceeding										
0.25m	7.51	-	7.51	-	-	-	-	7.51	m³	8.26
1.00m	3.94	-	3.94	-	-	-	-	3.94	m³	4.34
2.00m	4.53	-	4.53	-	-	-	-	4.53	m³	4.98
4.00m	3.37	-	3.37	-	-	-	-	3.37	m³	3.70
6.00m	4.13	-	4.13	-	-	-	-	4.13	m³	4.55
Bulk excavation; basements and the like maximum depth not exceeding										
0.25m	7.51	-	7.51	-	0.45	7.01	-	14.51	m³	15.96
1.00m	4.74	-	4.74	-	0.50	7.78	-	12.52	m³	13.78
2.00m	5.53	-	5.53	-	0.55	8.56	-	14.10	m³	15.51
4.00m	5.19	-	5.19	-	0.70	10.90	-	16.09	m³	17.70
6.00m	7.28	-	7.28	-	0.85	13.23	-	20.52	m³	22.57
Foundation excavation; trenches width not exceeding 0.30m maximum depth not exceeding										
0.25m	19.37	-	19.37	-	2.00	31.14	-	50.51	m³	55.56
1.00m	20.06	-	20.06	-	2.10	32.70	-	52.76	m³	58.04
Foundation excavation; trenches width exceeding 0.30m maximum depth not exceeding										
0.25m	19.34	-	19.34	-	0.65	10.12	-	29.46	m³	32.40
1.00m	16.57	-	16.57	-	0.70	10.90	-	27.47	m³	30.22
2.00m	16.57	-	16.57	-	0.80	12.46	-	29.03	m³	31.93
4.00m	12.98	-	12.98	-	1.00	15.57	-	28.55	m³	31.40
6.00m	12.98	-	12.98	-	1.20	18.68	-	31.66	m³	34.83
commencing 1.50m below existing ground level, maximum depth not exceeding										
0.25m	16.60	-	16.60	-	1.00	15.57	-	32.17	m³	35.39
1.00m	16.60	-	16.60	-	1.05	16.35	-	32.95	m³	36.25
2.00m	10.92	-	10.92	-	1.30	20.24	-	31.17	m³	34.28
commencing 3.00m below existing ground level, maximum depth not exceeding										
0.25m	10.92	-	10.92	-	1.45	22.58	-	33.50	m³	36.85
1.00m	12.98	-	12.98	-	1.55	24.13	-	37.11	m³	40.82
2.00m	12.98	-	12.98	-	1.75	27.25	-	40.22	m³	44.25

Labour hourly rates: (except Specialists) Craft Operatives 20.87 Labourer 15.57 Rates are national average prices. Refer to REGIONAL VARIATIONS for indicative levels of overall pricing in regions	PLANT AND TRANSPORT			LABOUR				RATES		
	Plant Cost £	Trans Cost £	P and T Cost £	Craft Optve Hrs	Lab Hrs	Labour Cost £	Sunds £	Nett Rate £	Unit	Gross rate (10%) £
EXCAVATIONS (Cont'd)										
Excavating - by machine (Cont'd)										
Foundation excavation; pile caps and ground beams between piles maximum depth not exceeding										
0.25m	20.10	-	20.10	-	0.95	14.79	-	34.89	m³	38.38
1.00m	19.72	-	19.72	-	1.00	15.57	-	35.29	m³	38.82
2.00m	19.72	-	19.72	-	1.15	17.91	-	37.62	m³	41.38
Foundation excavation; pits maximum depth not exceeding										
0.25m	16.95	-	16.95	-	0.95	14.79	-	31.74	m³	34.92
1.00m	20.89	-	20.89	-	1.00	15.57	-	36.46	m³	40.11
2.00m.	20.89	-	20.89	-	1.15	17.91	-	38.80	m³	42.68
4.00m	15.57	-	15.57	-	1.45	22.58	-	38.15	m³	41.96
Extra over any types of excavating irrespective of depth										
excavating below ground water level	17.16	-	17.16	-	-	-	-	17.16	m³	18.87
excavating in unstable ground; running silt, running sand or liquid mud	29.78	-	29.78	-	-	-	-	29.78	m³	32.76
excavating below ground water level in running silt, running sand or liquid mud	40.96	-	40.96	-	-	-	-	40.96	m³	45.05
excavating in heavy soil or clay	3.81	-	3.81	-	-	-	-	3.81	m³	4.19
excavating in gravel	5.95	-	5.95	-	-	-	-	5.95	m³	6.54
excavating in brash, loose rock or chalk	7.13	-	7.13	-	-	-	-	7.13	m³	7.84
Extra over any types of excavating irrespective of depth										
Breaking out existing materials										
sandstone	17.86	-	17.86	-	-	-	-	17.86	m³	19.65
hard rock	26.90	-	26.90	-	-	-	-	26.90	m³	29.59
concrete	23.12	-	23.12	-	-	-	-	23.12	m³	25.43
reinforced concrete	33.62	-	33.62	-	-	-	-	33.62	m³	36.98
brickwork, blockwork or stonework	12.82	-	12.82	-	-	-	-	12.82	m³	14.10
Breaking out existing materials; drain and concrete bed under										
100mm diameter	2.10	-	2.10	-	-	-	-	2.10	m	2.31
150mm diameter	2.52	-	2.52	-	-	-	-	2.52	m	2.77
225mm diameter	2.94	-	2.94	-	-	-	-	2.94	m	3.24
Excavating - by hand										
Bulk excavation; to reduce levels maximum depth not exceeding										
0.25m	-	-	-	-	2.75	42.82	-	42.82	m³	47.10
1.00m	-	-	-	-	2.90	45.15	-	45.15	m³	49.67
2.00m	-	-	-	-	3.30	51.38	-	51.38	m³	56.52
4.00m	-	-	-	-	4.30	66.95	-	66.95	m³	73.65
6.00m	-	-	-	-	5.35	83.30	-	83.30	m³	91.63
Bulk excavation; basements and the like maximum depth not exceeding										
0.25m.	-	-	-	-	2.85	44.37	-	44.37	m³	48.81
1.00m	-	-	-	-	3.05	47.49	-	47.49	m³	52.24
2.00m	-	-	-	-	3.40	52.94	-	52.94	m³	58.23
4.00m	-	-	-	-	4.40	68.51	-	68.51	m³	75.36
6.00m	-	-	-	-	5.35	83.30	-	83.30	m³	91.63
Foundation excavation; trenches width not exceeding 0.30m maximum depth not exceeding										
0.25m	-	-	-	-	4.70	73.18	-	73.18	m³	80.50
1.00m	-	-	-	-	4.95	77.07	-	77.07	m³	84.78
Foundation excavation; trenches width exceeding 0.30m maximum depth not exceeding										
0.25m	-	-	-	-	3.14	48.89	-	48.89	m³	53.78
1.00m	-	-	-	-	3.30	51.38	-	51.38	m³	56.52
2.00m	-	-	-	-	3.85	59.94	-	59.94	m³	65.94
4.00m	-	-	-	-	4.80	74.74	-	74.74	m³	82.21
6.00m	-	-	-	-	6.05	94.20	-	94.20	m³	103.62
commencing 1.50m below existing ground level, maximum depth not exceeding										
0.25m	-	-	-	-	4.70	73.18	-	73.18	m³	80.50
1.00m	-	-	-	-	4.95	77.07	-	77.07	m³	84.78
2.00m	-	-	-	-	6.20	96.53	-	96.53	m³	106.19
commencing 3.00m below existing ground level, maximum depth not exceeding										
0.25m	-	-	-	-	7.00	108.99	-	108.99	m³	119.89
1.00m.	-	-	-	-	7.30	113.66	-	113.66	m³	125.03
2.00m	-	-	-	-	8.40	130.79	-	130.79	m³	143.87
Foundation excavation; pile caps and ground beams between piles maximum depth not exceeding										
0.25m.	-	-	-	-	3.70	57.61	-	57.61	m³	63.37
1.00m	-	-	-	-	3.85	59.94	-	59.94	m³	65.94
2.00m	-	-	-	-	4.40	68.51	-	68.51	m³	75.36
Foundation excavation; pits maximum depth not exceeding										
0.25m	-	-	-	-	3.70	57.61	-	57.61	m³	63.37
1.00m	-	-	-	-	3.85	59.94	-	59.94	m³	65.94
2.00m	-	-	-	-	4.40	68.51	-	68.51	m³	75.36
4.00m	-	-	-	-	5.60	87.19	-	87.19	m³	95.91
Extra over any types of excavating irrespective of depth										
excavating below ground water level	-	-	-	-	1.65	25.69	-	25.69	m³	28.26
excavating in running silt, running sand or liquid mud	-	-	-	-	4.95	77.07	-	77.07	m³	84.78
excavating below ground water level in running silt, running sand or liquid mud	-	-	-	-	6.60	102.76	-	102.76	m³	113.04

EXCAVATION AND FILLING

Labour hourly rates: (except Specialists) Craft Operatives 20.87 Labourer 15.57 Rates are national average prices. Refer to REGIONAL VARIATIONS for indicative levels of overall pricing in regions	PLANT AND TRANSPORT			LABOUR				RATES		
	Plant Cost £	Trans Cost £	P and T Cost £	Craft Optve Hrs	Lab Hrs	Labour Cost £	Sunds £	Nett Rate £	Unit	Gross rate (10%) £
EXCAVATIONS (Cont'd)										
Excavating - by hand (Cont'd)										
Extra over any types of excavating irrespective of depth (Cont'd)										
excavating in heavy soil or clay	-	-	-	-	0.70	10.90	-	10.90	m³	11.99
excavating in gravel	-	-	-	-	1.80	28.03	-	28.03	m³	30.83
excavating in brash, loose rock or chalk	-	-	-	-	3.70	57.61	-	57.61	m³	63.37
Breaking out existing materials; extra over any types of excavating irrespective of depth										
sandstone	-	-	-	-	7.30	113.66	-	113.66	m³	125.03
hard rock	-	-	-	-	14.70	228.88	-	228.88	m³	251.77
concrete	-	-	-	-	11.00	171.27	-	171.27	m³	188.40
reinforced concrete	-	-	-	-	16.50	256.90	-	256.90	m³	282.60
brickwork, blockwork or stonework	-	-	-	-	7.70	119.89	-	119.89	m³	131.88
drain and concrete bed under										
100mm diameter	-	-	-	-	0.90	14.01	-	14.01	m	15.41
150mm diameter	-	-	-	-	1.10	17.13	-	17.13	m	18.84
225mm diameter	-	-	-	-	1.25	19.46	-	19.46	m	21.41
Excavating inside existing building - by hand										
Bulk excavation; to reduce levels maximum depth not exceeding										
0.25m	-	-	-	-	3.85	59.94	-	59.94	m³	65.94
1.00m	-	-	-	-	4.10	63.84	-	63.84	m³	70.22
2.00m	-	-	-	-	4.65	72.40	-	72.40	m³	79.64
4.00m	-	-	-	-	6.00	93.42	-	93.42	m³	102.76
Foundation excavation; trenches width not exceeding 0.30m maximum depth not exceeding										
0.25m	-	-	-	-	6.65	103.54	-	103.54	m³	113.89
1.00m	-	-	-	-	7.00	108.99	-	108.99	m³	119.89
Foundation excavation; trenches width exceeding 0.30m maximum depth not exceeding										
0.25m	-	-	-	-	4.45	69.29	-	69.29	m³	76.22
1.00m	-	-	-	-	4.70	73.18	-	73.18	m³	80.50
2.00m	-	-	-	-	5.50	85.63	-	85.63	m³	94.20
4.00m	-	-	-	-	6.80	105.88	-	105.88	m³	116.46
Foundation excavation; pits maximum depth not exceeding										
0.25m	-	-	-	-	5.20	80.96	-	80.96	m³	89.06
1.00m	-	-	-	-	5.40	84.08	-	84.08	m³	92.49
2.00m	-	-	-	-	6.20	96.53	-	96.53	m³	106.19
4.00m	-	-	-	-	7.85	122.22	-	122.22	m³	134.45
Extra over any types of excavating irrespective of depth										
excavating below ground water level	-	-	-	-	2.35	36.59	-	36.59	m³	40.25
Breaking out existing materials; extra over any types of excavating irrespective of depth										
concrete	-	-	-	-	12.00	186.84	-	186.84	m³	205.52
reinforced concrete	-	-	-	-	17.30	269.36	-	269.36	m³	296.30
brickwork, blockwork or stonework	-	-	-	-	7.80	121.45	-	121.45	m³	133.59
drain and concrete bed under										
100mm diameter	-	-	-	-	1.25	19.46	-	19.46	m	21.41
150mm diameter	-	-	-	-	1.50	23.35	-	23.35	m	25.69
Breaking out existing hard pavings; extra over any types of excavating irrespective of depth										
concrete 150mm thick	-	-	-	-	1.65	25.69	-	25.69	m²	28.26
reinforced concrete 200mm thick	-	-	-	-	3.30	51.38	-	51.38	m²	56.52

This section continues on the next page

Labour hourly rates: (except Specialists) Craft Operatives 20.87 Labourer 15.57 Rates are national average prices. Refer to REGIONAL VARIATIONS for indicative levels of overall pricing in regions	MATERIALS			LABOUR				RATES		
	Del to Site £	Waste %	Material Cost £	Craft Optve Hrs	Lab Hrs	Labour Cost £	Sunds £	Nett Rate £	Unit	Gross rate (10%) £
EXCAVATIONS (Cont'd)										
Earthwork support										
Note Not withstanding the requirements of NRM, rates for earthwork support are given below; appropriate allowances should be added to items of excavtion where earthwork support is deemed to be included										
Earthwork support distance between opposing faces not exceeding 2.00m; maximum depth not exceeding										
1.00m	1.16	-	1.16	-	0.21	3.27	0.05	4.48	m²	4.93
2.00m	1.46	-	1.46	-	0.26	4.05	0.07	5.57	m²	6.13
4.00m	1.66	-	1.66	-	0.32	4.98	0.08	6.72	m²	7.39
6.00m	1.88	-	1.88	-	0.37	5.76	0.08	7.72	m²	8.49
distance between opposing faces 2.00 - 4.00m; maximum depth not exceeding										
1.00m.	1.26	-	1.26	-	0.22	3.43	0.07	4.75	m²	5.23
2.00m	1.54	-	1.54	-	0.27	4.20	0.07	5.81	m²	6.40
4.00m	1.83	-	1.83	-	0.34	5.29	0.08	7.21	m²	7.93
6.00m	2.06	-	2.06	-	0.39	6.07	0.10	8.23	m²	9.06
distance between opposing faces exceeding 4.00m; maximum depth not exceeding										
1.00m	1.43	-	1.43	-	0.23	3.58	0.07	5.08	m²	5.59
2.00m	1.67	-	1.67	-	0.29	4.52	0.08	6.27	m²	6.89
4.00m	1.98	-	1.98	-	0.35	5.45	0.10	7.53	m²	8.28
6.00m	2.22	-	2.22	-	0.41	6.38	0.10	8.71	m²	9.58
Earthwork support; unstable ground distance between opposing faces not exceeding 2.00m; maximum depth not exceeding										
1.00m.	1.98	-	1.98	-	0.35	5.45	0.10	7.53	m²	8.28
2.00m	2.37	-	2.37	-	0.44	6.85	0.12	9.34	m²	10.27
4.00m	2.74	-	2.74	-	0.53	8.25	0.13	11.13	m²	12.24
6.00m	3.13	-	3.13	-	0.62	9.65	0.15	12.93	m²	14.22
distance between opposing faces 2.00 - 4.00m; maximum depth not exceeding										
1.00m	2.17	-	2.17	-	0.37	5.76	0.10	8.03	m²	8.84
2.00m	2.60	-	2.60	-	0.45	7.01	0.12	9.72	m²	10.69
4.00m	3.03	-	3.03	-	0.56	8.72	0.13	11.88	m²	13.07
6.00m	3.47	-	3.47	-	0.65	10.12	0.15	13.74	m²	15.12
distance between opposing faces exceeding 4.00m; maximum depth not exceeding										
1.00m	2.37	-	2.37	-	0.37	5.76	0.12	8.25	m²	9.07
2.00m	2.79	-	2.79	-	0.49	7.63	0.13	10.55	m²	11.61
4.00m	3.32	-	3.32	-	0.58	9.03	0.15	12.50	m²	13.75
6.00m	3.77	-	3.77	-	0.68	10.59	0.16	14.52	m²	15.97
Earthwork support; next to roadways distance between opposing faces not exceeding 2.00m; maximum depth not exceeding										
1.00m	2.30	-	2.30	-	0.42	6.54	0.10	8.94	m²	9.83
2.00m	2.79	-	2.79	-	0.53	8.25	0.13	11.18	m²	12.29
4.00m	3.32	-	3.32	-	0.63	9.81	0.15	13.28	m²	14.61
6.00m	3.77	-	3.77	-	0.74	11.52	0.16	15.46	m²	17.00
distance between opposing faces 2.00 - 4.00m; maximum depth not exceeding										
1.00m	2.60	-	2.60	-	0.44	6.85	0.12	9.56	m²	10.52
2.00m	3.10	-	3.10	-	0.55	8.56	0.15	11.81	m²	13.00
4.00m	3.66	-	3.66	-	0.67	10.43	0.16	14.25	m²	15.68
6.00m.	4.13	-	4.13	-	0.78	12.14	0.20	16.47	m²	18.12
distance between opposing faces exceeding 4.00m; maximum depth not exceeding										
1.00m	2.79	-	2.79	-	0.46	7.16	0.13	10.09	m²	11.10
2.00m	3.39	-	3.39	-	0.59	9.19	0.15	12.72	m²	13.99
4.00m	3.95	-	3.95	-	0.69	10.74	0.18	14.88	m²	16.37
6.00m	4.52	-	4.52	-	0.82	12.77	0.21	17.50	m²	19.26
Earthwork support; left in distance between opposing faces not exceeding 2.00m; maximum depth not exceeding										
1.00m	4.18	-	4.18	-	0.17	2.65	0.10	6.92	m²	7.61
2.00m	4.18	-	4.18	-	0.21	3.27	0.12	7.56	m²	8.32
4.00m	4.18	-	4.18	-	0.25	3.89	0.13	8.20	m²	9.02
6.00m	4.18	-	4.18	-	0.29	4.52	0.15	8.84	m²	9.72
distance between opposing faces 2.00 - 4.00m; maximum depth not exceeding										
1.00m	4.18	-	4.18	-	0.18	2.80	0.10	7.08	m²	7.79
2.00m	4.18	-	4.18	-	0.22	3.43	0.13	7.73	m²	8.51
4.00m	4.18	-	4.18	-	0.27	4.20	0.15	8.53	m²	9.38
6.00m	4.18	-	4.18	-	0.32	4.98	0.18	9.34	m²	10.27
distance between opposing faces exceeding 4.00m; maximum depth not exceeding										
1.00m	5.56	-	5.56	-	0.19	2.96	0.12	8.63	m²	9.50
2.00m	5.56	-	5.56	-	0.23	3.58	0.13	9.27	m²	10.20
4.00m	5.56	-	5.56	-	0.27	4.20	0.16	9.93	m²	10.92
6.00m	5.56	-	5.56	-	0.33	5.14	0.18	10.88	m²	11.97
Earthwork support; next to roadways; left in distance between opposing faces not exceeding 2.00m; maximum depth not exceeding										
1.00m	13.90	-	13.90	-	0.34	5.29	0.18	19.38	m²	21.32
2.00m	13.90	-	13.90	-	0.42	6.54	0.23	20.67	m²	22.74
4.00m	13.90	-	13.90	-	0.51	7.94	0.26	22.11	m²	24.32

EXCAVATION AND FILLING

Labour hourly rates: (except Specialists) Craft Operatives 20.87 Labourer 15.57 Rates are national average prices. Refer to REGIONAL VARIATIONS for indicative levels of overall pricing in regions	MATERIALS			LABOUR				RATES		
	Del to Site £	Waste %	Material Cost £	Craft Optve Hrs	Lab Hrs	Labour Cost £	Sunds £	Nett Rate £	Unit	Gross rate (10%) £
EXCAVATIONS (Cont'd)										
Earthwork support (Cont'd)										
Earthwork support; next to roadways; left in (Cont'd)										
distance between opposing faces not exceeding 2.00m; maximum depth not exceeding (Cont'd)										
6.00m	13.90	-	13.90	-	0.59	9.19	0.30	23.39	m²	25.72
distance between opposing faces 2.00 - 4.00m; maximum depth not exceeding										
1.00m	16.68	-	16.68	-	0.36	5.61	0.21	22.50	m²	24.75
2.00m	16.68	-	16.68	-	0.44	6.85	0.26	23.80	m²	26.18
4.00m	16.68	-	16.68	-	0.54	8.41	0.33	25.42	m²	27.96
6.00m	16.68	-	16.68	-	0.62	9.65	0.36	26.70	m²	29.37
distance between opposing faces exceeding 4.00m; maximum depth not exceeding										
1.00m	20.86	-	20.86	-	0.37	5.76	0.25	26.87	m²	29.55
2.00m	20.86	-	20.86	-	0.47	7.32	0.28	28.46	m²	31.30
4.00m	20.86	-	20.86	-	0.56	8.72	0.35	29.93	m²	32.92
6.00m	20.86	-	20.86	-	0.65	10.12	0.41	31.39	m²	34.53
Earthwork support; unstable ground; left in										
distance between opposing faces not exceeding 2.00m; maximum depth not exceeding										
1.00m	9.74	-	9.74	-	0.27	4.20	0.16	14.11	m²	15.52
2.00m	9.74	-	9.74	-	0.36	5.61	0.20	15.54	m²	17.09
4.00m	9.74	-	9.74	-	0.42	6.54	0.21	16.49	m²	18.14
6.00m	9.74	-	9.74	-	0.49	7.63	0.25	17.61	m²	19.38
distance between opposing faces 2.00 - 4.00m; maximum depth not exceeding										
1.00m	11.12	-	11.12	-	0.29	4.52	0.18	15.82	m²	17.40
2.00m	11.12	-	11.12	-	0.36	5.61	0.21	16.94	m²	18.64
4.00m	11.12	-	11.12	-	0.44	6.85	0.25	18.22	m²	20.04
6.00m	11.12	-	11.12	-	0.53	8.25	0.28	19.65	m²	21.62
distance between opposing faces exceeding 4.00m; maximum depth not exceeding										
1.00m	13.90	-	13.90	-	0.32	4.98	0.20	19.08	m²	20.99
2.00m	13.90	-	13.90	-	0.40	6.23	0.23	20.36	m²	22.40
4.00m	13.90	-	13.90	-	0.46	7.16	0.26	21.33	m²	23.46
6.00m	13.90	-	13.90	-	0.55	8.56	0.30	22.76	m²	25.04
Earthwork support; inside existing building										
distance between opposing faces not exceeding 2.00m; maximum depth not exceeding										
1.00m	1.21	-	1.21	-	0.23	3.58	0.05	4.84	m²	5.33
2.00m	1.51	-	1.51	-	0.29	4.52	0.07	6.09	m²	6.70
4.00m	1.85	-	1.85	-	0.32	4.98	0.08	6.92	m²	7.61
distance between opposing faces 2.00 - 4.00m; maximum depth not exceeding										
1.00m	1.33	-	1.33	-	0.24	3.74	0.07	5.14	m²	5.65
2.00m	1.66	-	1.66	-	0.30	4.67	0.08	6.41	m²	7.05
4.00m	1.88	-	1.88	-	0.37	5.76	0.08	7.72	m²	8.49
distance between opposing faces exceeding 4.00m; maximum depth not exceeding										
1.00m	1.50	-	1.50	-	0.25	3.89	0.07	5.45	m²	6.00
2.00m	1.79	-	1.79	-	0.33	5.14	0.08	7.01	m²	7.71
4.00m	2.06	-	2.06	-	0.38	5.92	0.10	8.08	m²	8.89
Earthwork support; unstable ground; inside existing building										
distance between opposing faces not exceeding 2.00m; maximum depth not exceeding										
1.00m.	2.06	-	2.06	-	0.38	5.92	0.10	8.08	m²	8.89
2.00m	2.50	-	2.50	-	0.48	7.47	0.12	10.09	m²	11.09
4.00m	2.89	-	2.89	-	0.58	9.03	0.13	12.05	m²	13.26
distance between opposing faces 2.00 - 4.00m; maximum depth not exceeding										
1.00m	2.27	-	2.27	-	0.41	6.38	0.10	8.76	m²	9.63
2.00m	2.72	-	2.72	-	0.49	7.63	0.12	10.46	m²	11.51
4.00m	3.19	-	3.19	-	0.61	9.50	0.15	12.83	m²	14.12
distance between opposing faces exceeding 4.00m; maximum depth not exceeding										
1.00m	2.50	-	2.50	-	0.43	6.70	0.10	9.29	m²	10.22
2.00m	2.94	-	2.94	-	0.55	8.56	0.13	11.64	m²	12.80
4.00m	3.47	-	3.47	-	0.64	9.96	0.15	13.59	m²	14.94

This section continues on the next page

Labour hourly rates: (except Specialists) Craft Operatives 20.87 Labourer 15.57 Rates are national average prices. Refer to REGIONAL VARIATIONS for indicative levels of overall pricing in regions	PLANT AND TRANSPORT			LABOUR				RATES		
	Plant Cost £	Trans Cost £	P and T Cost £	Craft Optve Hrs	Lab Hrs	Labour Cost £	Sunds £	Nett Rate £	Unit	Gross rate (10%) £
DISPOSAL										
Disposal - by machine										
Disposal of preserved top soil										
depositing on site in temporary spoil heaps where directed										
25m	-	4.46	4.46	-	0.12	1.87	-	6.33	m³	6.96
50m	-	4.65	4.65	-	0.12	1.87	-	6.52	m³	7.18
100m	-	5.09	5.09	-	0.12	1.87	-	6.95	m³	7.65
Disposal of excavated material										
depositing on site in temporary spoil heaps where directed										
25m	-	4.46	4.46	-	0.12	1.87	-	6.33	m³	6.96
50m	-	4.65	4.65	-	0.12	1.87	-	6.52	m³	7.18
100m	-	5.09	5.09	-	0.12	1.87	-	6.95	m³	7.65
400m	-	6.02	6.02	-	0.12	1.87	-	7.89	m³	8.68
800m	-	7.82	7.82	-	0.12	1.87	-	9.69	m³	10.66
1200m	-	8.35	8.35	-	0.12	1.87	-	10.22	m³	11.24
1600m	-	8.85	8.85	-	0.12	1.87	-	10.72	m³	11.79
extra for each additional 1600m	-	1.37	1.37	-	-	-	-	1.37	m³	1.51
removing from site to tip a) Inert	-	38.12	38.12	-	-	-	-	38.12	m³	41.94
removing from site to tip b) Active	-	78.79	78.79	-	-	-	-	78.79	m³	86.67
removing from site to tip c) Contaminated (Guide price - always seek a quotation for specialist disposal costs.)	-	228.74	228.74	-	-	-	-	228.74	m³	251.61
Disposal - by hand										
Disposal of preserved top soil										
depositing on site in temporary spoil heaps where directed										
25m	-	-	-	-	1.40	21.80	-	21.80	m³	23.98
50m	-	-	-	-	1.65	25.69	-	25.69	m³	28.26
100m	-	-	-	-	2.20	34.25	-	34.25	m³	37.68
Disposal of excavated material										
depositing on site in temporary spoil heaps where directed										
25m	-	-	-	-	1.40	21.80	-	21.80	m³	23.98
50m	-	-	-	-	1.65	25.69	-	25.69	m³	28.26
100m	-	-	-	-	2.20	34.25	-	34.25	m³	37.68
400m	-	6.02	6.02	-	1.72	26.78	-	32.80	m³	36.08
800m	-	7.82	7.82	-	1.72	26.78	-	34.60	m³	38.06
1200m	-	8.35	8.35	-	1.72	26.78	-	35.13	m³	38.64
1600m	-	8.85	8.85	-	1.72	26.78	-	35.63	m³	39.20
extra for each additional 1600m	-	1.37	1.37	-	-	-	-	1.37	m³	1.50
removing from site to tip a) Inert	-	38.12	38.12	-	1.50	23.35	-	61.48	m³	67.63
removing from site to tip b) Active	-	78.79	78.79	-	1.50	23.35	-	102.14	m³	112.36
removing from site to tip c) Contaminated (Guide price - always seek a quotation for specialist disposal costs.)	-	228.74	228.74	-	1.50	23.35	-	252.09	m³	277.30
Disposal inside existing building - by hand										
Disposal of excavated material										
depositing on site in temporary spoil heaps where directed										
25m	-	-	-	-	1.95	30.36	-	30.36	m³	33.40
50m	-	-	-	-	2.15	33.48	-	33.48	m³	36.82
removing from site to tip a) Inert	-	38.12	38.12	-	2.50	38.92	-	77.05	m³	84.75
removing from site to tip b) Active	-	78.79	78.79	-	2.50	38.92	-	117.71	m³	129.48
removing from site to tip c) Contaminated (Guide price - always seek a quotation for specialist disposal costs.)	-	228.74	228.74	-	2.50	38.92	-	267.66	m³	294.43
FILLINGS										
Notes										
Not withstanding the requirements of NRM rates for filling for thicknesses not exceeding 500mm thick are given in m²										
Not withstanding the requirements of NRM rates for trimming vertical or battered sides are given below; appropriate allowances should be added to items of filling where trimming vertical or battered sides is deemed to be included; compacting layers and surfaces generally are included in the rates										
Not withstanding the requirements of NRM where rates for surface treatments are given below; appropriate allowances should be added to items of filling where surface treatments is deemed to be included										
Excavated material arising from excavation - by machine										
Filling to excavation										
average thickness exceeding 500mm	-	-	-	-	-	-	4.52	4.52	m³	4.97
Selected excavated material obtained from on site spoil heaps 25m distant - by machine										
Filling to make up levels; depositing in layers 150mm maximum thickness										
finished thickness 250mm	-	-	-	-	-	-	2.06	2.06	m²	2.27
average thickness exceeding 500mm	-	-	-	-	-	-	5.63	5.63	m³	6.19
Trimming										
sides of cuttings; vertical or battered	-	-	-	-	-	-	0.94	0.94	m²	1.03
sides of embankments; vertical or battered	-	-	-	-	-	-	0.94	0.94	m²	1.03

Labour hourly rates: (except Specialists) Craft Operatives 20.87 Labourer 15.57 Rates are national average prices. Refer to REGIONAL VARIATIONS for indicative levels of overall pricing in regions	PLANT AND TRANSPORT			LABOUR				RATES		
	Plant Cost £	Trans Cost £	P and T Cost £	Craft Optve Hrs	Lab Hrs	Labour Cost £	Sunds £	Nett Rate £	Unit	Gross rate (10%) £
FILLINGS (Cont'd)										
Selected excavated material obtained from on site spoil heaps 50m distant - by machine										
Filling to make up levels; depositing in layers 150mm maximum thickness										
finished thickness 250mm	-	-	-	-	-	-	2.31	2.31	m²	2.54
average thickness exceeding 500mm	-	-	-	-	-	-	6.91	6.91	m³	7.60
Trimming										
sides of cuttings; vertical or battered	-	-	-	-	-	-	0.94	0.94	m²	1.03
sides of embankments; vertical or battered	-	-	-	-	-	-	0.94	0.94	m²	1.03
Preserved topsoil obtained from on site spoil heaps not exceeding 100m distant - by machine										
Filling to make up levels										
finished thickness 250mm	-	-	-	-	-	-	2.71	2.71	m²	2.98

This section continues on the next page

Labour hourly rates: (except Specialists) Craft Operatives 20.87 Labourer 15.57 Rates are national average prices. Refer to REGIONAL VARIATIONS for indicative levels of overall pricing in regions	MATERIALS			LABOUR				RATES		
	Del to Site £	Waste %	Material Cost £	Craft Optve Hrs	Lab Hrs	Labour Cost £	Sunds £	Nett Rate £	Unit	Gross rate (10%) £
FILLINGS (Cont'd)										
Imported topsoil; wheeling not exceeding 50m - by machine										
Filling to make up levels										
finished thickness 250mm	8.16	10.00	8.98	-	-	-	3.30	12.28	m²	13.50
Hard, dry, broken brick or stone to be obtained off site; wheeling not exceeding 25m - by machine										
Filling to make up levels; depositing in layers 150mm maximum thickness										
finished thickness 250mm	10.80	25.00	13.50	-	-	-	1.42	14.92	m²	16.41
average thickness exceeding 500mm	43.20	25.00	54.00	-	-	-	4.67	58.67	m³	64.54
Surface packing to filling										
to vertical or battered faces	-	-	-	-	-	-	0.94	0.94	m²	1.03
Compacting with 680 kg vibratory roller										
filling; blinding with sand, ashes or similar fine material	0.45	33.00	0.59	-	0.05	0.78	0.35	1.72	m²	1.89
Compacting with 6 - 8 tonnes smooth wheeled roller										
filling; blinding with sand, ashes or similar fine material	0.45	33.00	0.59	-	0.05	0.78	0.68	2.05	m²	2.25
Hard, dry, broken brick or stone to be obtained off site; wheeling not exceeding 50m - by machine										
Filling to make up levels; depositing in layers 150mm maximum thickness										
finished thickness 250mm	10.80	25.00	13.50	-	-	-	1.65	15.15	m²	16.67
average thickness exceeding 500mm	43.20	25.00	54.00	-	-	-	5.63	59.63	m³	65.59
Surface packing to filling										
to vertical or battered faces	-	-	-	-	-	-	0.94	0.94	m²	1.03
Compacting with 680 kg vibratory roller										
filling; blinding with sand, ashes or similar fine material	0.45	33.00	0.59	-	0.05	0.78	0.35	1.72	m²	1.89
Compacting with 6 - 8 tonnes smooth wheeled roller										
filling; blinding with sand, ashes or similar fine material	0.45	33.00	0.59	-	0.05	0.78	0.68	2.05	m²	2.25
MOT Type 1 to be obtained off site; wheeling not exceeding 25m - by machine										
Filling to make up levels; depositing in layers 150mm maximum thickness										
finished thickness 250mm	11.52	25.00	14.40	-	-	-	1.42	15.82	m²	17.40
average thickness exceeding 500mm	46.08	25.00	57.60	-	-	-	4.67	62.27	m³	68.50
Surface packing to filling										
to vertical or battered faces	-	-	-	-	-	-	0.94	0.94	m²	1.03
Compacting with 680 kg vibratory roller										
filling; blinding with sand, ashes or similar fine material	0.45	33.00	0.59	-	0.05	0.78	0.35	1.72	m²	1.89
Compacting with 6 - 8 tonnes smooth wheeled roller										
filling; blinding with sand, ashes or similar fine material	0.45	33.00	0.59	-	0.05	0.78	0.68	2.05	m²	2.25
MOT Type 1 to be obtained off site; wheeling not exceeding 50m - by machine										
Filling to make up levels; depositing in layers 150mm maximum thickness										
finished thickness 250mm	11.52	25.00	14.40	-	-	-	1.65	16.05	m²	17.66
average thickness exceeding 500mm	46.08	25.00	57.60	-	-	-	5.63	63.23	m³	69.55
Surface packing to filling										
to vertical or battered faces	-	-	-	-	-	-	0.94	0.94	m²	1.03
Compacting with 680 kg vibratory roller										
filling; blinding with sand, ashes or similar fine material	0.45	33.00	0.59	-	0.05	0.78	0.35	1.72	m²	1.89
Compacting with 6 - 8 tonnes smooth wheeled roller										
filling; blinding with sand, ashes or similar fine material	0.45	33.00	0.59	-	0.05	0.78	0.68	2.05	m²	2.25
MOT Type 2 to be obtained off site; wheeling not exceeding 25m - by machine										
Filling to make up levels; depositing in layers 150mm maximum thickness										
finished thickness 250mm	11.52	25.00	14.40	-	-	-	1.42	15.82	m²	17.40
average thickness exceeding 500mm	46.08	25.00	57.60	-	-	-	4.67	62.27	m³	68.50
Surface packing to filling										
to vertical or battered faces	-	-	-	-	-	-	0.94	0.94	m²	1.03
Compacting with 680 kg vibratory roller										
filling; blinding with sand, ashes or similar fine material	0.45	33.00	0.59	-	0.05	0.78	0.35	1.72	m²	1.89
Compacting with 6 - 8 tonnes smooth wheeled roller										
filling; blinding with sand, ashes or similar fine material	0.45	33.00	0.59	-	0.05	0.78	0.68	2.05	m²	2.25
MOT Type 2 to be obtained off site; wheeling not exceeding 50m - by machine										
Filling to make up levels; depositing in layers 150mm maximum thickness										
finished thickness 250mm	11.52	25.00	14.40	-	-	-	1.65	16.05	m²	17.66
average thickness exceeding 500mm	46.08	25.00	57.60	-	-	-	5.63	63.23	m³	69.55

Labour hourly rates: (except Specialists) Craft Operatives 20.87 Labourer 15.57 Rates are national average prices. Refer to REGIONAL VARIATIONS for indicative levels of overall pricing in regions	MATERIALS			LABOUR				RATES		
	Del to Site £	Waste %	Material Cost £	Craft Optve Hrs	Lab Hrs	Labour Cost £	Sunds £	Nett Rate £	Unit	Gross rate (10%) £
FILLINGS (Cont'd)										
MOT Type 2 to be obtained off site; wheeling not exceeding 50m - by machine (Cont'd)										
Surface packing to filling										
to vertical or battered faces	-	-	-	-	-	-	0.94	0.94	m²	1.03
Compacting with 680 kg vibratory roller										
filling; blinding with sand, ashes or similar fine material	0.45	33.00	0.59	-	0.05	0.78	0.35	1.72	m²	1.89
Compacting with 6 - 8 tonnes smooth wheeled roller										
filling; blinding with sand, ashes or similar fine material	0.45	33.00	0.59	-	0.05	0.78	0.68	2.05	m²	2.25
Sand to be obtained off site; wheeling not exceeding 25m - by machine										
Filling to make up levels; depositing in layers 150mm maximum thickness										
finished thickness 250mm	7.44	33.00	9.90	-	-	-	2.06	11.96	m²	13.15
average thickness exceeding 500mm	29.76	33.00	39.58	-	-	-	5.61	45.19	m³	49.71
Sand to be obtained off site; wheeling not exceeding 50m - by machine										
Filling to make up levels; depositing in layers 150mm maximum thickness										
finished thickness 250mm	7.44	33.00	9.90	-	-	-	2.31	12.21	m²	13.43
average thickness exceeding 500mm	29.76	33.00	39.58	-	-	-	6.53	46.11	m³	50.73
Hoggin to be obtained off site; wheeling not exceeding 25m - by machine										
Filling to make up levels; depositing in layers 150mm maximum thickness										
finished thickness 250mm	11.52	33.00	15.32	-	-	-	1.81	17.14	m²	18.85
average thickness exceeding 500mm	46.08	33.00	61.29	-	-	-	4.67	65.96	m³	72.55
Hoggin to be obtained off site; wheeling not exceeding 50m - by machine										
Filling to make up levels; depositing in layers 150mm maximum thickness										
finished thickness 250mm	11.52	33.00	15.32	-	-	-	2.06	17.38	m²	19.12
average thickness exceeding 500mm	46.08	33.00	61.29	-	-	-	5.61	66.90	m³	73.59
Excavated material arising from excavation - by hand										
Filling to excavation										
average thickness exceeding 500mm	-	-	-	-	1.44	22.42	-	22.42	m³	24.66
Selected excavated material obtained from on site spoil heaps 25m distant - by hand										
Filling to make up levels; depositing in layers 150mm maximum thickness										
finished thickness 250mm	-	-	-	-	0.50	7.78	-	7.78	m²	8.56
average thickness exceeding 500mm	-	-	-	-	1.60	24.91	-	24.91	m³	27.40
Trimming										
sides of cuttings; vertical or battered	-	-	-	-	0.22	3.43	-	3.43	m²	3.77
sides of embankments; vertical or battered	-	-	-	-	0.22	3.43	-	3.43	m²	3.77
Selected excavated material obtained from on site spoil heaps 50m distant - by hand										
Filling to make up levels; depositing in layers 150mm maximum thickness										
finished thickness 250mm	-	-	-	-	0.80	12.46	-	12.46	m²	13.70
average thickness exceeding 500mm	-	-	-	-	1.95	30.36	-	30.36	m³	33.40
Trimming										
sides of cuttings; vertical or battered	-	-	-	-	0.22	3.43	-	3.43	m²	3.77
sides of embankments; vertical or battered	-	-	-	-	0.22	3.43	-	3.43	m²	3.77
Preserved topsoil obtained from on site spoil heaps not exceeding 100m distant - by hand										
Filling to make up levels										
finished thickness 250mm	-	-	-	-	1.10	17.13	-	17.13	m²	18.84
Filling to external planters										
finished thickness 250mm	-	-	-	-	1.40	21.80	-	21.80	m²	23.98
Imported topsoil; wheeling not exceeding 50m - by hand										
Filling to make up levels										
finished thickness 250mm	8.16	10.00	8.98	-	1.00	15.57	-	24.55	m²	27.00
Filling to external planters										
finished thickness 250mm	8.16	10.00	8.98	-	1.25	19.46	-	28.44	m²	31.28
Hard, dry, broken brick or stone to be obtained off site; wheeling not exceeding 25m - by hand										
Filling to make up levels; depositing in layers 150mm maximum thickness										
finished thickness 250mm	10.80	25.00	13.50	-	0.65	10.12	-	23.62	m²	25.98

Labour hourly rates: (except Specialists) Craft Operatives 20.87 Labourer 15.57 Rates are national average prices. Refer to REGIONAL VARIATIONS for indicative levels of overall pricing in regions	MATERIALS			LABOUR				RATES		
	Del to Site £	Waste %	Material Cost £	Craft Optve Hrs	Lab Hrs	Labour Cost £	Sunds £	Nett Rate £	Unit	Gross rate (10%) £
FILLINGS (Cont'd)										
Hard, dry, broken brick or stone to be obtained off site; wheeling not exceeding 25m - by hand (Cont'd)										
Filling to make up levels; depositing in layers 150mm maximum thickness (Cont'd)										
average thickness exceeding 500mm	43.20	25.00	54.00	-	1.31	20.40	-	74.40	m³	81.84
Surface packing to filling										
to vertical or battered faces	-	-	-	-	0.22	3.43	-	3.43	m²	3.77
Compacting with 680 kg vibratory roller										
filling; blinding with sand, ashes or similar fine material	0.45	33.00	0.59	-	0.05	0.78	0.35	1.72	m²	1.89
Compacting with 6 - 8 tonnes smooth wheeled roller										
filling; blinding with sand, ashes or similar fine material	0.45	33.00	0.59	-	0.05	0.78	0.68	2.05	m²	2.25
Hard, dry, broken brick or stone to be obtained off site; wheeling not exceeding 50m - by hand										
Filling to make up levels; depositing in layers 150mm maximum thickness										
finished thickness 250mm	10.80	25.00	13.50	-	0.75	11.68	-	25.18	m²	27.70
average thickness exceeding 500mm	43.20	25.00	54.00	-	1.58	24.60	-	78.60	m³	86.46
Surface packing to filling										
to vertical or battered faces	-	-	-	-	0.22	3.43	-	3.43	m²	3.77
Compacting with 680 kg vibratory roller										
filling; blinding with sand, ashes or similar fine material	0.45	33.00	0.59	-	0.05	0.78	0.35	1.72	m²	1.89
Compacting with 6 - 8 tonnes smooth wheeled roller										
filling; blinding with sand, ashes or similar fine material	0.45	33.00	0.59	-	0.05	0.78	0.68	2.05	m²	2.25
MOT Type 1 to be obtained off site; wheeling not exceeding 25m - by hand										
Filling to make up levels; depositing in layers 150mm maximum thickness										
finished thickness 250mm	11.52	25.00	14.40	-	0.65	10.12	-	24.52	m²	26.97
average thickness exceeding 500mm	46.08	25.00	57.60	-	1.31	20.40	-	78.00	m³	85.80
Surface packing to filling										
to vertical or battered faces	-	-	-	-	0.22	3.43	-	3.43	m²	3.77
Compacting with 680 kg vibratory roller										
filling; blinding with sand, ashes or similar fine material	0.45	33.00	0.59	-	0.05	0.78	0.35	1.72	m²	1.89
Compacting with 6 - 8 tonnes smooth wheeled roller										
filling; blinding with sand, ashes or similar fine material	0.45	33.00	0.59	-	0.05	0.78	0.68	2.05	m²	2.25
MOT Type 1 to be obtained off site; wheeling not exceeding 50m - by hand										
Filling to make up levels; depositing in layers 150mm maximum thickness										
finished thickness 250mm	11.52	25.00	14.40	-	0.75	11.68	-	26.08	m²	28.69
average thickness exceeding 500mm	46.08	25.00	57.60	-	1.58	24.60	-	82.20	m³	90.42
Surface packing to filling										
to vertical or battered faces	-	-	-	-	0.22	3.43	-	3.43	m²	3.77
Compacting with 680 kg vibratory roller										
filling; blinding with sand, ashes or similar fine material	0.45	33.00	0.59	-	0.05	0.78	0.35	1.72	m²	1.89
Compacting with 6 - 8 tonnes smooth wheeled roller										
filling; blinding with sand, ashes or similar fine material	0.45	33.00	0.59	-	0.05	0.78	0.68	2.05	m²	2.25
MOT Type 2 to be obtained off site; wheeling not exceeding 25m - by hand										
Filling to make up levels; depositing in layers 150mm maximum thickness										
finished thickness 250mm	11.52	25.00	14.40	-	0.65	10.12	-	24.52	m²	26.97
average thickness exceeding 500mm	46.08	25.00	57.60	-	1.31	20.40	-	78.00	m³	85.80
Surface packing to filling										
to vertical or battered faces	-	-	-	-	0.22	3.43	-	3.43	m²	3.77
Compacting with 680 kg vibratory roller										
filling; blinding with sand, ashes or similar fine material	0.45	33.00	0.59	-	0.05	0.78	0.35	1.72	m²	1.89
Compacting with 6 - 8 tonnes smooth wheeled roller										
filling; blinding with sand, ashes or similar fine material	0.45	33.00	0.59	-	0.05	0.78	0.68	2.05	m²	2.25
MOT Type 2 to be obtained off site; wheeling not exceeding 50m - by hand										
Filling to make up levels; depositing in layers 150mm maximum thickness										
finished thickness 250mm	11.52	25.00	14.40	-	0.75	11.68	-	26.08	m²	28.69
average thickness exceeding 500mm	46.08	25.00	57.60	-	1.58	24.60	-	82.20	m³	90.42
Surface packing to filling										
to vertical or battered faces	-	-	-	-	0.22	3.43	-	3.43	m²	3.77
Compacting with 680 kg vibratory roller										
filling; blinding with sand, ashes or similar fine material	0.45	33.00	0.59	-	0.05	0.78	0.35	1.72	m²	1.89

Labour hourly rates: (except Specialists) Craft Operatives 20.87 Labourer 15.57 Rates are national average prices. Refer to REGIONAL VARIATIONS for indicative levels of overall pricing in regions	MATERIALS			LABOUR				RATES		
	Del to Site £	Waste %	Material Cost £	Craft Optve Hrs	Lab Hrs	Labour Cost £	Sunds £	Nett Rate £	Unit	Gross rate (10%) £
FILLINGS (Cont'd)										
MOT Type 2 to be obtained off site; wheeling not exceeding 50m - by hand (Cont'd)										
Compacting with 6 - 8 tonnes smooth wheeled roller										
filling; blinding with sand, ashes or similar fine material	0.45	33.00	0.59	-	0.05	0.78	0.68	2.05	m²	2.25
Sand to be obtained off site; wheeling not exceeding 25m - by hand										
Filling to make up levels; depositing in layers 150mm maximum thickness										
finished thickness 250mm	7.44	33.00	9.90	-	0.75	11.68	-	21.57	m²	23.73
average thickness exceeding 500mm	29.76	33.00	39.58	-	1.58	24.60	-	64.18	m³	70.60
Sand to be obtained off site; wheeling not exceeding 50m - by hand										
Filling to make up levels; depositing in layers 150mm maximum thickness										
finished thickness 250mm	7.44	33.00	9.90	-	0.80	12.46	-	22.35	m²	24.59
average thickness exceeding 500mm	29.76	33.00	39.58	-	1.84	28.65	-	68.23	m³	75.05
Hoggin to be obtained off site; wheeling not exceeding 25m - by hand										
Filling to make up levels; depositing in layers 150mm maximum thickness										
finished thickness 250mm	11.52	33.00	15.32	-	0.65	10.12	-	25.44	m²	27.99
average thickness exceeding 500mm	46.08	33.00	61.29	-	1.30	20.24	-	81.53	m³	89.68
Hoggin to be obtained off site; wheeling not exceeding 50m - by hand										
Filling to make up levels; depositing in layers 150mm maximum thickness										
finished thickness 250mm	11.52	33.00	15.32	-	0.70	10.90	-	26.22	m²	28.84
average thickness exceeding 500mm	46.08	33.00	61.29	-	1.55	24.13	-	85.42	m³	93.96
Excavated material arising from excavation; work inside existing building - by hand										
Filling to excavation										
average thickness exceeding 500mm	-	-	-	-	2.80	43.60	-	43.60	m³	47.96
Selected excavated material obtained from on site spoil heaps 25m distant; work inside existing building - by hand										
Filling to make up levels; depositing in layers 150mm maximum thickness										
finished thickness 250mm	-	-	-	-	0.82	12.77	-	12.77	m²	14.04
average thickness exceeding 500mm	-	-	-	-	3.08	47.96	-	47.96	m³	52.75
Selected excavated material obtained from on site spoil heaps 50m distant; work inside existing building - by hand										
Filling to make up levels; depositing in layers 150mm maximum thickness										
finished thickness 250mm	-	-	-	-	1.15	17.91	-	17.91	m²	19.70
average thickness exceeding 500mm	-	-	-	-	3.36	52.32	-	52.32	m³	57.55
Hard, dry, broken brick or stone to be obtained off site; wheeling not exceeding 25m; work inside existing building - by hand										
Filling to make up levels; depositing in layers 150mm maximum thickness										
finished thickness 250mm	10.80	25.00	13.50	-	1.00	15.57	-	29.07	m²	31.98
average thickness exceeding 500mm	43.20	25.00	54.00	-	2.81	43.75	-	97.75	m³	107.53
Surface packing to filling										
to vertical or battered faces	-	-	-	-	0.22	3.43	-	3.43	m²	3.77
Compacting										
filling; blinding with sand, ashes or similar fine material	0.45	33.00	0.59	-	0.05	0.78	0.35	1.72	m²	1.89
Hard, dry, broken brick or stone to be obtained off site; wheeling not exceeding 50m; work inside existing building - by hand										
Filling to make up levels; depositing in layers 150mm maximum thickness										
finished thickness 250mm	10.80	25.00	13.50	-	1.07	16.66	-	30.16	m²	33.18
average thickness exceeding 500mm	43.20	25.00	54.00	-	2.99	46.55	-	100.55	m³	110.61
Surface packing to filling										
to vertical or battered faces	-	-	-	-	0.22	3.43	-	3.43	m²	3.77
Compacting										
filling; blinding with sand, ashes or similar fine material	0.45	33.00	0.59	-	0.05	0.78	0.35	1.72	m²	1.89
Sand to be obtained off site; wheeling not exceeding 25m; work inside existing building - by hand										
Filling to make up levels; depositing in layers 150mm maximum thickness										
finished thickness 250mm	7.44	33.00	9.90	-	1.07	16.66	-	26.56	m²	29.21

Labour hourly rates: (except Specialists) Craft Operatives 20.87 Labourer 15.57 Rates are national average prices. Refer to REGIONAL VARIATIONS for indicative levels of overall pricing in regions	MATERIALS			LABOUR				RATES		
	Del to Site £	Waste %	Material Cost £	Craft Optve Hrs	Lab Hrs	Labour Cost £	Sunds £	Nett Rate £	Unit	Gross rate (10%) £
FILLINGS (Cont'd)										
Sand to be obtained off site; wheeling not exceeding 25m; work inside existing building - by hand (Cont'd)										
Filling to make up levels; depositing in layers 150mm maximum thickness (Cont'd)										
average thickness exceeding 500mm	29.76	33.00	39.58	-	2.99	46.55	-	86.14	m³	94.75
Sand to be obtained off site; wheeling not exceeding 50m; work inside existing building - by hand										
Filling to make up levels; depositing in layers 150mm maximum thickness										
finished thickness 250mm	7.44	33.00	9.90	-	1.13	17.59	-	27.49	m²	30.24
average thickness exceeding 500mm	29.76	33.00	39.58	-	3.26	50.76	-	90.34	m³	99.37
MEMBRANES										
Waterproof building paper										
laying on hardcore to receive concrete										
Grade B1F	0.34	25.00	0.42	-	0.06	0.93	-	1.36	m²	1.49
Grade B2	2.20	25.00	2.75	-	0.06	0.93	-	3.68	m²	4.05
Polythene sheeting										
laying on hardcore to receive concrete										
300mu	0.31	20.00	0.38	-	0.06	0.93	-	1.31	m²	1.44
Claymaster low density expanded polystyrene permanent formwork; fixing with Clayfix hooks - 3/m²										
To underside of foundations; horizontal; laid on earth or hardcore; 75mm thick										
over 500mm wide	6.49	5.00	6.81	-	0.05	0.78	-	7.59	m²	8.35
To underside of foundations; horizontal; laid on earth or hardcore; 100mm thick										
over 500mm wide	9.48	5.00	9.95	-	0.07	1.09	-	11.04	m²	12.14
To underside of foundations; horizontal; laid on earth or hardcore; 150mm thick										
over 500mm wide	13.81	5.00	14.50	-	0.08	1.25	-	15.75	m²	17.32
Sides of foundations; vertical 75mm thick										
height not exceeding 250mm	1.62	5.00	1.70	-	0.02	0.31	0.35	2.36	m	2.60
height 250-500mm	3.24	5.00	3.41	-	0.08	1.25	0.35	5.00	m	5.50
height exceeding 500mm	6.49	5.00	6.81	-	0.07	1.09	1.04	8.94	m²	9.84
Sides of foundations; vertical 100mm thick										
height not exceeding 250mm	2.37	5.00	2.49	-	0.03	0.47	0.35	3.30	m	3.63
height 250-500mm	4.74	5.00	4.97	-	0.05	0.78	0.35	6.10	m	6.71
height exceeding 500mm	9.48	5.00	9.95	-	0.09	1.40	1.04	12.39	m²	13.63
Sides of foundations; vertical 150mm thick										
height not exceeding 250mm	3.45	5.00	3.63	-	0.03	0.47	0.35	4.44	m	4.88
height 250-500mm	6.91	5.00	7.25	-	0.07	1.09	0.35	8.69	m	9.56
height exceeding 500mm	13.81	5.00	14.50	-	0.11	1.71	1.04	17.26	m²	18.98

Labour hourly rates: (except Specialists) Craft Operatives 20.87 Labourer 15.57 Rates are national average prices. Refer to REGIONAL VARIATIONS for indicative levels of overall pricing in regions	MATERIALS			LABOUR				RATES		
	Del to Site £	Waste %	Material Cost £	Craft Optve Hrs	Lab Hrs	Labour Cost £	Sunds £	Nett Rate £	Unit	Gross rate (10%) £
BORED PILING										
Prices include for a 21 N/mm² concrete mix, nominal reinforcement and a minimum number of 50 piles on any one contract. The working loads sizes and lengths given below will depend on the nature of the soils in which the piles will be founded as well as structure to be supported (KELLER GROUND ENGINEERING)										
On/Off site charge										
in addition to the following prices add approximately	-	-	Specialist	-	-	Specialist	-	9321.62	sum	10253.79
Short auger piles										
up to 6m long; 450mm nominal diameter; 8 tonnes normal working load	-	-	Specialist	-	-	Specialist	-	54.59	m	60.04
up to 6m long; 610mm nominal diameter; 30 tonnes normal working load	-	-	Specialist	-	-	Specialist	-	82.57	m	90.83
Bored cast in-situ piles										
up to 15m long; 450mm nominal diameter; 40 tonnes normal working load	-	-	Specialist	-	-	Specialist	-	50.37	m	55.41
up to 15m long; 610mm nominal diameter; 120 tonnes normal working load	-	-	Specialist	-	-	Specialist	-	78.38	m	86.22
Auger piles										
up to 20m long; 450mm nominal diameter	-	-	Specialist	-	-	Specialist	-	51.09	m	56.20
up to 30m long; 1200mm nominal diameter	-	-	Specialist	-	-	Specialist	-	253.34	m	278.68
Large diameter auger piles (plain shaft)										
up to 20m long; 610mm nominal diameter; 150 tonnes normal working load	-	-	Specialist	-	-	Specialist	-	77.73	m	85.51
up to 30m long; 1525mm nominal diameter; 600 tonnes normal working load	-	-	Specialist	-	-	Specialist	-	394.13	m	433.54
Large diameter auger piles (belled base)										
up to 20m long; 610mm nominal diameter; 150 tonnes normal working load	-	-	Specialist	-	-	Specialist	-	106.39	m	117.03
up to 30m long; 1525mm nominal diameter; 1000 tonnes normal working load	-	-	Specialist	-	-	Specialist	-	506.84	m	557.53
Boring through obstructions, rock like formations, etc; undertaken on a time basis at a rate per piling rig per hour										
Cutting off tops of piles; including preparation and integration of reinforcement into pile cap or ground beam and disposal										
450-610mm nominal diameter	-	-	Specialist	-	-	Specialist	-	18.71	m	20.58
610-1525mm nominal diameter	-	-	Specialist	-	-	Specialist	-	72.02	m	79.22
DRIVEN PILING										
Mild steel Universal Bearing Piles "H" section, to BS EN 10025 Grade S275 and high yield steel Grade S275JR in lengths 9 - 15m supplied, handled, pitched and driven vertically with landbased plant (KELLER GROUND ENGINEERING)										
Note; the following prices are based on quantities of 25 - 150 tonnes										
On/Off site charge										
in addition to the following prices, add approximately	-	-	Specialist	-	-	Specialist	-	7902.90	sum	8693.19
Mild steel piles										
203 x 203 x 45 kg/m, SWL 40 tonnes	-	-	Specialist	-	-	Specialist	-	76.42	m	84.07
203 x 203 x 54 kg/m, SWL 50 tonnes	-	-	Specialist	-	-	Specialist	-	86.20	m	94.82
254 x 254 x 63 kg/m, SWL 60 tonnes	-	-	Specialist	-	-	Specialist	-	97.44	m	107.18
254 x 254 x 71 kg/m, SWL 70 tonnes	-	-	Specialist	-	-	Specialist	-	104.93	m	115.42
305 x 305 x 79 kg/m, SWL 75 tonnes	-	-	Specialist	-	-	Specialist	-	123.57	m	135.93
254 x 254 x 85 kg/m, SWL 80 tonnes	-	-	Specialist	-	-	Specialist	-	127.18	m	139.89
305 x 305 x 88 kg/m, SWL 85 tonnes	-	-	Specialist	-	-	Specialist	-	133.98	m	147.38
305 x 305 x 95 kg/m, SWL 90 tonnes	-	-	Specialist	-	-	Specialist	-	142.46	m	156.70
356 x 368 x 109 kg/m, SWL 105 tonnes	-	-	Specialist	-	-	Specialist	-	170.69	m	187.76
305 x 305 x 110 kg/m, SWL 105 tonnes	-	-	Specialist	-	-	Specialist	-	160.57	m	176.63
305 x 305 x 126 kg/m, SWL 120 tonnes	-	-	Specialist	-	-	Specialist	-	183.18	m	201.50
305 x 305 x 149 kg/m, SWL 140 tonnes	-	-	Specialist	-	-	Specialist	-	202.16	m	222.38
356 x 368 x 133 kg/m, SWL 130 tonnes	-	-	Specialist	-	-	Specialist	-	211.60	m	232.76
356 x 368 x 152 kg/m, SWL 140 tonnes	-	-	Specialist	-	-	Specialist	-	224.57	m	247.03
356 x 368 x 174 kg/m, SWL 165 tonnes	-	-	Specialist	-	-	Specialist	-	258.26	m	284.09
305 x 305 x 186 kg/m, SWL 175 tonnes	-	-	Specialist	-	-	Specialist	-	280.80	m	308.89
305 x 305 x 223 kg/m, SWL 210 tonnes	-	-	Specialist	-	-	Specialist	-	307.32	m	338.05
Extra for high yield steel										
add	-	-	Specialist	-	-	Specialist	-	84.12	t	92.54
For quiet piling, add										
to terminal charge, lump sum	-	-	Specialist	-	-	Specialist	-	1678.18	sum	1846.00
plus for all piles	-	-	Specialist	-	-	Specialist	-	4.07	m	4.47

Labour hourly rates: (except Specialists)
Craft Operatives 20.87 Labourer 15.57
Rates are national average prices.
Refer to REGIONAL VARIATIONS for indicative levels of overall pricing in regions

	MATERIALS			LABOUR				RATES		
	Del to Site £	Waste %	Material Cost £	Craft Optve Hrs	Lab Hrs	Labour Cost £	Sunds £	Nett Rate £	Unit	Gross rate (10%) £
INTERLOCKING PILING										
Mild steel sheet piling to BS EN 10025 Grade S275 or high yield steel Grade S275JR in lengths 4.5-15m supplied, handled, pitched and driven by land based plant in one visit (KELLER GROUND ENGINEERING)										
On/Off site charge										
in addition to the following prices, add approximately	-	-	Specialist	-	-	Specialist	-	7537.45	sum	8291.19
Mild steel sheet piling										
Larssen 6W										
section	-	-	Specialist	-	-	Specialist	-	165.66	m²	182.23
extra for high yield steel	-	-	Specialist	-	-	Specialist	-	9.07	m²	9.97
extra for one coat L.B.V.(Lowca Varnish to BS 1070 Type 2)										
before driving	-	-	Specialist	-	-	Specialist	-	6.62	m²	7.29
extra for corners	-	-	Specialist	-	-	Specialist	-	66.21	m	72.84
extra for junctions	-	-	Specialist	-	-	Specialist	-	90.29	m	99.32
Frodingham 1N and Larssen 9W										
section	-	-	Specialist	-	-	Specialist	-	182.98	m²	201.27
extra for high yield steel	-	-	Specialist	-	-	Specialist	-	7.54	m²	8.29
extra for one coat L.B.V.(Lowca Varnish to BS 1070 Type 2)										
before driving	-	-	Specialist	-	-	Specialist	-	6.62	m²	7.29
extra for corners	-	-	Specialist	-	-	Specialist	-	66.21	m	72.84
extra for junctions	-	-	Specialist	-	-	Specialist	-	90.29	m	99.32
Frodingham 2N and Larssen 12W										
section	-	-	Specialist	-	-	Specialist	-	203.67	m²	224.04
extra for high yield steel	-	-	Specialist	-	-	Specialist	-	9.64	m²	10.60
extra for one coat L.B.V.(Lowca Varnish to BS 1070 Type 2)										
before driving	-	-	Specialist	-	-	Specialist	-	6.62	m²	7.29
extra for corners	-	-	Specialist	-	-	Specialist	-	66.21	m	72.84
extra for junctions	-	-	Specialist	-	-	Specialist	-	90.29	m	99.32
Frodingham 1BXN										
section	-	-	Specialist	-	-	Specialist	-	225.74	m²	248.31
extra for high yield steel	-	-	Specialist	-	-	Specialist	-	14.94	m²	16.43
extra for one coat L.B.V.(Lowca Varnish to BS 1070 Type 2)										
before driving	-	-	Specialist	-	-	Specialist	-	6.03	m²	6.63
extra for corners	-	-	Specialist	-	-	Specialist	-	72.25	m	79.47
extra for junctions	-	-	Specialist	-	-	Specialist	-	90.29	m	99.32
Frodingham 3N and Larssen 16W										
section	-	-	Specialist	-	-	Specialist	-	227.75	m²	250.52
extra for high yield steel	-	-	Specialist	-	-	Specialist	-	12.36	m²	13.59
extra for one coat L.B.V.(Lowca Varnish to BS 1070 Type 2)										
before driving	-	-	Specialist	-	-	Specialist	-	6.03	m²	6.63
extra for corners	-	-	Specialist	-	-	Specialist	-	72.25	m	79.47
extra for junctions	-	-	Specialist	-	-	Specialist	-	90.29	m	99.32
Larssen Section 20W										
section	-	-	Specialist	-	-	Specialist	-	257.69	m²	283.46
extra for high yield steel	-	-	Specialist	-	-	Specialist	-	13.54	m²	14.90
extra for one coat L.B.V.(Lowca Varnish to BS 1070 Type 2)										
before driving	-	-	Specialist	-	-	Specialist	-	6.78	m²	7.46
extra for corners	-	-	Specialist	-	-	Specialist	-	78.25	m	86.08
extra for junctions	-	-	Specialist	-	-	Specialist	-	105.32	m	115.85
Frodingham 4N and Larssen 25W										
section	-	-	Specialist	-	-	Specialist	-	285.35	m²	313.88
extra for high yield steel	-	-	Specialist	-	-	Specialist	-	14.75	m²	16.23
extra for one coat L.B.V.(Lowca Varnish to BS 1070 Type 2)										
before driving	-	-	Specialist	-	-	Specialist	-	7.54	m²	8.29
extra for corners	-	-	Specialist	-	-	Specialist	-	84.26	m	92.69
extra for junctions	-	-	Specialist	-	-	Specialist	-	105.32	m	115.85
Larssen 32W										
section	-	-	Specialist	-	-	Specialist	-	336.90	m²	370.59
extra for high yield steel	-	-	Specialist	-	-	Specialist	-	16.40	m²	18.04
extra for one coat L.B.V.(Lowca Varnish to BS 1070 Type 2)										
before driving	-	-	Specialist	-	-	Specialist	-	8.13	m²	8.94
extra for corners	-	-	Specialist	-	-	Specialist	-	90.29	m	99.32
extra for junctions	-	-	Specialist	-	-	Specialist	-	111.46	m	122.61
Frodingham 5										
section	-	-	Specialist	-	-	Specialist	-	380.18	m²	418.20
extra for high yield steel	-	-	Specialist	-	-	Specialist	-	21.68	m²	23.84
extra for one coat L.B.V.(Lowca Varnish to BS 1070 Type 2)										
before driving	-	-	Specialist	-	-	Specialist	-	14.14	m²	15.55
extra for corners	-	-	Specialist	-	-	Specialist	-	90.29	m	99.32
extra for junctions	-	-	Specialist	-	-	Specialist	-	120.39	m	132.43
For quiet piling, add										
lump sum	-	-	Specialist	-	-	Specialist	-	1530.33	sum	1683.36
plus for all sections, from	-	-	Specialist	-	-	Specialist	-	6.99	m²	7.69
to	-	-	Specialist	-	-	Specialist	-	11.67	m²	12.84

Labour hourly rates: (except Specialists) Craft Operatives 20.87 Labourer 15.57 Rates are national average prices. Refer to REGIONAL VARIATIONS for indicative levels of overall pricing in regions	MATERIALS			LABOUR				RATES		
	Del to Site £	Waste %	Material Cost £	Craft Optve Hrs	Lab Hrs	Labour Cost £	Sunds £	Nett Rate £	Unit	Gross rate (10%) £
UNDERPINNING										
Information										
The work of underpinning in this section comprises work to be carried out in short lengths; prices are exclusive of shoring and other temporary supports										
Excavating										
Preliminary trenches maximum depth not exceeding										
1.00m	-	-	-	-	5.00	77.85	-	77.85	m³	85.64
2.00m	-	-	-	-	6.00	93.42	-	93.42	m³	102.76
4.00m	-	-	-	-	7.00	108.99	-	108.99	m³	119.89
Underpinning pits maximum depth not exceeding										
1.00m	-	-	-	-	5.85	91.08	-	91.08	m³	100.19
2.00m	-	-	-	-	7.30	113.66	-	113.66	m³	125.03
4.00m	-	-	-	-	8.80	137.02	-	137.02	m³	150.72
Earthwork support										
preliminary trenches; distance between opposing faces not exceeding 2.00m; maximum depth not exceeding										
1.00m	1.67	-	1.67	-	0.53	8.25	0.03	9.95	m²	10.95
2.00m	2.10	-	2.10	-	0.67	10.43	0.05	12.58	m²	13.84
4.00m	2.40	-	2.40	-	0.72	11.21	0.05	13.66	m²	15.02
preliminary trenches; distance between opposing faces 2.00 - 4.00m; maximum depth not exceeding										
1.00m	1.82	-	1.82	-	0.55	8.56	0.03	10.41	m²	11.45
2.00m	2.30	-	2.30	-	0.70	10.90	0.05	13.25	m²	14.57
4.00m	2.52	-	2.52	-	0.84	13.08	0.07	15.67	m²	17.23
underpinning pits; distance between opposing faces not exceeding 2.00m; maximum depth not exceeding										
1.00m	1.96	-	1.96	-	0.61	9.50	0.03	11.50	m²	12.65
2.00m	2.43	-	2.43	-	0.77	11.99	0.05	14.47	m²	15.92
4.00m	2.73	-	2.73	-	0.83	12.92	0.07	15.72	m²	17.29
underpinning pits; distance between opposing faces 2.00 - 4.00m; maximum depth not exceeding										
1.00m	2.08	-	2.08	-	0.64	9.96	0.03	12.07	m²	13.28
2.00m	2.63	-	2.63	-	0.80	12.46	0.05	15.14	m²	16.65
4.00m	3.03	-	3.03	-	0.95	14.79	0.07	17.89	m²	19.67
Cutting away existing projecting foundations										
masonry; maximum width 103mm; maximum depth 150mm	-	-	-	-	0.90	14.01	-	14.01	m	15.41
masonry; maximum width 154mm; maximum depth 225mm	-	-	-	-	1.07	16.66	-	16.66	m	18.33
concrete; maximum width 253mm; maximum depth 190mm	-	-	-	-	1.29	20.09	-	20.09	m	22.09
concrete; maximum width 304mm; maximum depth 300mm	-	-	-	-	1.52	23.67	-	23.67	m	26.03
Preparing the underside of the existing work to receive the pinning up of the new work										
350mm wide	-	-	-	-	0.45	7.01	-	7.01	m	7.71
500mm wide	-	-	-	-	0.56	8.72	-	8.72	m	9.59
1000mm wide	-	-	-	-	1.13	17.59	-	17.59	m	19.35
Compacting bottoms of excavations	-	-	-	-	0.45	7.01	-	7.01	m²	7.71
Disposal of excavated material removing from site to tip (including tipping charges but excluding landfill tax)	-	-	-	-	3.38	52.63	19.31	71.93	m³	79.12
Excavated material arising from excavations										
Filling to excavations average thickness exceeding 0.25m	-	-	-	-	2.25	35.03	-	35.03	m³	38.54
Compacting filling	-	-	-	-	0.23	3.58	-	3.58	m²	3.94
Plain in-situ concrete; BS 8500, ordinary prescribed mix ST3, 20mm aggregate										
Foundations; poured on or against earth or unblinded hardcore generally	101.40	7.50	109.01	-	5.34	83.14	-	192.15	m³	211.36
Plain in-situ concrete; BS 8500, ordinary prescribed mix ST4, 20mm aggregate										
Foundations; poured on or against earth or unblinded hardcore generally	105.04	7.50	112.92	-	5.34	83.14	-	196.06	m³	215.67
Formwork and basic finish										
Sides of foundations; plain vertical										
height exceeding 1.00m	13.04	10.00	14.34	3.94	0.79	94.53	2.54	111.41	m²	122.55
height not exceeding 250mm	4.56	10.00	5.02	1.19	0.25	28.73	0.76	34.51	m	37.96

Labour hourly rates: (except Specialists) Craft Operatives 20.87 Labourer 15.57 Rates are national average prices. Refer to REGIONAL VARIATIONS for indicative levels of overall pricing in regions	MATERIALS			LABOUR				RATES		
	Del to Site	Waste	Material Cost	Craft Optve	Lab	Labour Cost	Sunds	Nett Rate	Unit	Gross rate (10%)
	£	%	£	Hrs	Hrs	£	£	£		£
UNDERPINNING (Cont'd)										
Formwork and basic finish (Cont'd)										
Sides of foundations; plain vertical (Cont'd)										
height 250 - 500mm	7.17	10.00	7.89	2.16	0.43	51.77	1.40	61.06	m	67.17
height 0.50m - 1.00m	14.34	10.00	15.78	4.03	0.81	96.72	2.57	115.07	m	126.57
Common bricks, BS EN 772, Category M, 215 x 102.5 x 65mm, compressive strength not less than 5.2 N/mm²; in cement mortar (1:3)										
Walls; vertical										
215mm thick; English bond	37.11	5.00	38.97	4.70	5.00	175.94	11.02	225.93	m²	248.52
327mm thick; English bond	55.83	5.00	58.62	5.70	6.15	214.71	17.32	290.66	m²	319.72
440mm thick; English bond	74.23	5.00	77.94	6.30	6.90	238.91	23.61	340.46	m²	374.51
Bonding to existing including extra material										
thickness of new work 215mm	4.05	5.00	4.26	1.32	1.32	48.10	1.19	53.55	m	58.90
thickness of new work 327mm	6.24	5.00	6.55	1.90	1.90	69.24	1.78	77.57	m	85.32
thickness of new work 440mm	8.11	5.00	8.51	2.50	2.50	91.10	2.38	101.99	m	112.19
Second Hard Stock bricks, BS EN 772, Category M, 215 x 102.5 x 65mm, in cement mortar (1:3)										
Walls; vertical										
215mm thick; English bond	73.78	5.00	77.47	4.70	5.00	175.94	11.02	264.43	m²	290.87
327mm thick; English bond	110.98	5.00	116.53	5.70	6.15	214.71	17.32	348.57	m²	383.43
440mm thick; English bond	147.56	5.00	154.94	6.30	6.90	238.91	23.61	417.46	m²	459.21
Bonding to existing including extra material										
thickness of new work 215mm	8.06	5.00	8.46	1.90	1.90	69.24	1.19	78.89	m	86.78
thickness of new work 327mm	12.40	5.00	13.02	1.90	1.90	69.24	1.78	84.04	m	92.44
thickness of new work 440mm	16.12	5.00	16.93	2.50	2.50	91.10	2.38	110.40	m	121.44
Engineering bricks, BS EN 772, Category F, 215 x 102.5 x 65mm, class A; in cement mortar (1:3)										
Walls; vertical										
215mm thick; English bond	125.63	5.00	131.91	5.20	5.50	194.16	11.02	337.09	m²	370.80
327mm thick; English bond	188.97	5.00	198.42	6.30	6.75	236.58	17.32	452.33	m²	497.56
440mm thick; English bond	251.26	5.00	263.83	6.95	7.55	262.60	23.61	550.04	m²	605.04
Bonding to existing including extra material										
thickness of new work 215mm	13.72	5.00	14.41	1.45	1.45	52.84	1.19	68.44	m	75.28
thickness of new work 327mm	21.11	5.00	22.17	2.10	2.10	76.52	1.78	100.48	m	110.52
thickness of new work 440mm	27.45	5.00	28.82	2.75	2.75	100.21	2.38	131.41	m	144.55
Engineering bricks, BS EN 772, Category F, 215 x 102.5 x 65mm, Class B; in cement mortar (1:3)										
Walls; vertical										
215mm thick; English bond	46.41	5.00	48.73	5.20	5.50	194.16	11.02	253.91	m²	279.30
327mm thick; English bond	69.81	5.00	73.30	6.30	6.75	236.58	17.32	327.20	m²	359.92
440mm thick; English bond	92.82	5.00	97.46	6.95	7.55	262.60	23.61	383.67	m²	422.04
Bonding to existing including extra material										
thickness of new work 215mm	5.07	5.00	5.32	1.45	1.45	52.84	1.19	59.35	m	65.28
thickness of new work 327mm	7.80	5.00	8.19	2.10	2.10	76.52	1.78	86.50	m	95.15
thickness of new work 440mm	10.14	5.00	10.65	2.75	2.75	100.21	2.38	113.23	m	124.56
Sundry items										
Wedging and pinning up to underside of existing construction with two courses slates in cement mortar (1:3)										
215mm walls	5.94	15.00	6.83	0.60	0.60	21.86	0.31	29.00	m	31.90
327mm walls	8.90	15.00	10.24	0.87	0.87	31.70	0.38	42.32	m	46.55
440mm walls	11.95	15.00	13.75	1.14	1.14	41.54	0.41	55.70	m	61.27

DIAPHRAGM WALLS AND EMBEDDED RETAINING WALLS

Labour hourly rates: (except Specialists) Craft Operatives 20.87 Labourer 15.57 Rates are national average prices. Refer to REGIONAL VARIATIONS for indicative levels of overall pricing in regions	MATERIALS			LABOUR				RATES		
	Del to Site £	Waste %	Material Cost £	Craft Optve Hrs	Lab Hrs	Labour Cost £	Sunds £	Nett Rate £	Unit	Gross rate (10%) £
WALLS										
Embedded retaining walls; contiguous panel construction; panel lengths not exceeding 5m. Note:- the following prices are indicative only: firm quotations should always be obtained (CEMENTATION FOUNDATIONS SKANSKA LIMITED)										
On/Off site charge										
in addition to the following prices, add for bringing plant to site, erecting and dismantling, maintaining and removing from site, approximately	-	-	Specialist	-	-	Specialist	-	154175.10	sum	169592.60
Excavation and Bentonite slurry and disposal										
600mm thick wall; maximum depth										
5m	-	-	Specialist	-	-	Specialist	-	463.67	m³	510.03
10m	-	-	Specialist	-	-	Specialist	-	463.67	m³	510.03
15m	-	-	Specialist	-	-	Specialist	-	463.67	m³	510.03
20m	-	-	Specialist	-	-	Specialist	-	463.67	m³	510.03
800mm thick wall; maximum depth										
5m	-	-	Specialist	-	-	Specialist	-	386.01	m³	424.61
10m	-	-	Specialist	-	-	Specialist	-	386.01	m³	424.61
15m	-	-	Specialist	-	-	Specialist	-	386.01	m³	424.61
20m	-	-	Specialist	-	-	Specialist	-	386.01	m³	424.61
1000mm thick wall; maximum depth										
5m	-	-	Specialist	-	-	Specialist	-	308.35	m³	339.19
10m	-	-	Specialist	-	-	Specialist	-	308.35	m³	339.19
15m	-	-	Specialist	-	-	Specialist	-	308.35	m³	339.19
20m	-	-	Specialist	-	-	Specialist	-	308.35	m³	339.19
Excavating through obstructions, rock like formations, etc undertaken on a time basis at a rate per rig per hour	-	-	Specialist	-	-	Specialist	-	899.93	hr	989.92
Reinforced concrete; BS 8500, designed mix C25, 20mm aggregate, minimum cement content 400 kg/m³										
600mm thick wall	-	-	Specialist	-	-	Specialist	-	191.86	m³	211.05
800mm thick wall	-	-	Specialist	-	-	Specialist	-	191.86	m³	211.05
1000mm thick wall	-	-	Specialist	-	-	Specialist	-	191.86	m³	211.05
Reinforced in-situ concrete; sulphate resisting; BS 8500, designed mix C25, 20mm aggregate, minimum cement content 400 kg/m³										
600mm thick wall	-	-	Specialist	-	-	Specialist	-	219.27	m³	241.20
800mm thick wall	-	-	Specialist	-	-	Specialist	-	219.27	m³	241.20
1000mm thick wall	-	-	Specialist	-	-	Specialist	-	219.27	m³	241.20
Reinforcement bars; BS 4449 hot rolled plain round mild steel; including hooks tying wire, and spacers and chairs which are at the discretion of the Contractor										
16mm; straight	-	-	Specialist	-	-	Specialist	-	1375.01	t	1512.51
20mm; straight	-	-	Specialist	-	-	Specialist	-	1375.01	t	1512.51
25mm; straight	-	-	Specialist	-	-	Specialist	-	1375.01	t	1512.51
32mm; straight	-	-	Specialist	-	-	Specialist	-	1375.01	t	1512.51
40mm; straight	-	-	Specialist	-	-	Specialist	-	1375.01	t	1512.51
16mm; bent	-	-	Specialist	-	-	Specialist	-	1375.01	t	1512.51
20mm; bent	-	-	Specialist	-	-	Specialist	-	1375.01	t	1512.51
25mm; bent	-	-	Specialist	-	-	Specialist	-	1375.01	t	1512.51
32mm; bent	-	-	Specialist	-	-	Specialist	-	1372.85	t	1510.13
40mm; bent	-	-	Specialist	-	-	Specialist	-	1372.85	t	1510.13
Reinforcement bars; BS 4449 hot rolled deformed high yield steel; including hooks tying wire, and spacers and chairs which are at the discretion of the Contractor										
16mm; straight	-	-	Specialist	-	-	Specialist	-	1372.85	t	1510.13
20mm; straight	-	-	Specialist	-	-	Specialist	-	1372.85	t	1510.13
25mm; straight	-	-	Specialist	-	-	Specialist	-	1372.85	t	1510.13
32mm; straight	-	-	Specialist	-	-	Specialist	-	1372.85	t	1510.13
40mm; straight	-	-	Specialist	-	-	Specialist	-	1372.85	t	1510.13
16mm; bent	-	-	Specialist	-	-	Specialist	-	1372.85	t	1510.13
20mm; bent	-	-	Specialist	-	-	Specialist	-	1372.85	t	1510.13
25mm; bent	-	-	Specialist	-	-	Specialist	-	1372.85	t	1510.13
32mm; bent	-	-	Specialist	-	-	Specialist	-	1372.85	t	1510.13
40mm; bent	-	-	Specialist	-	-	Specialist	-	1372.85	t	1510.13
Guide walls; excavation, disposal and support; reinforced in-situ concrete; BS 8500, designed mix C25, 20mm aggregate, minimum cement content 290 kg/m³; reinforced with one layer fabric BS 4483 reference A252, 3.95 kg/m² including laps, tying wire, all cutting and bending, and spacers and chairs which are at the discretion of the Contractor; formwork both sides										
600mm apart; propped top and bottom at 2000mm centres; both sides, 1000mm high	-	-	Specialist	-	-	Specialist	-	475.09	m	522.60
800mm apart; propped top and bottom at 2000mm centres; both sides, 1000mm high	-	-	Specialist	-	-	Specialist	-	475.09	m	522.60
1000mm apart; propped top and bottom at 2000mm centres; both sides, 1000mm high	-	-	Specialist	-	-	Specialist	-	475.09	m	522.60

Labour hourly rates: (except Specialists) Craft Operatives 20.87 Labourer 15.57 Rates are national average prices. Refer to REGIONAL VARIATIONS for indicative levels of overall pricing in regions	MATERIALS			LABOUR				RATES		
	Del to Site £	Waste %	Material Cost £	Craft Optve Hrs	Lab Hrs	Labour Cost £	Sunds £	Nett Rate £	Unit	Gross rate (10%) £
WALLS (Cont'd)										
Embedded retaining walls; contiguous panel construction; panel lengths not exceeding 5m. Note:- the following prices are indicative only: firm quotations should always be obtained (CEMENTATION FOUNDATIONS SKANSKA LIMITED) (Cont'd)										
Guide walls; excavation, disposal and support; reinforced in-situ concrete; BS 8500, designed mix C25, 20mm aggregate, minimum cement content 290 kg/m³; reinforced with one layer fabric BS 4483 reference A252, 3.95 kg/m² including laps, tying wire, all cutting and bending, and spacers and chairs which are at the discretion of the Contractor; formwork both sides (Cont'd)										
600mm apart; propped top and bottom at 2000mm centres; both sides, 1500mm high	-	-	Specialist	-	-	Specialist	-	730.90	m	803.99
800mm apart; propped top and bottom at 2000mm centres; both sides, 1500mm high	-	-	Specialist	-	-	Specialist	-	730.90	m	803.99
1000mm apart; propped top and bottom at 2000mm centres; both sides, 1500mm high	-	-	Specialist	-	-	Specialist	-	730.90	m	803.99

Labour hourly rates: (except Specialists) Craft Operatives 20.87 Labourer 15.57 Rates are national average prices. Refer to REGIONAL VARIATIONS for indicative levels of overall pricing in regions	MATERIALS			LABOUR				RATES		
	Del to Site £	Waste %	Material Cost £	Craft Optve Hrs	Lab Hrs	Labour Cost £	Sunds £	Nett Rate £	Unit	Gross rate (10%) £
CRIB WALLS										
Retaining Walls										
Betoflor precast concrete landscape retaining walls including soil filling to pockets but excluding excavation, concrete foundations, stone backfill to rear of wall and planting which are all deemed measured separately										
Betoplus interlocking units 500mm long x 250mm wide x 200mm modular deep in wall 250mm wide										
Natural blocks										
....	69.00	5.00	72.45	-	5.00	77.85	-	150.30	m²	165.33
Extra over for colours	10.00	5.00	10.50	-	0.50	7.78	-	18.28	m²	20.11
Betoatlas interlocking units 250mm long x 500mm wide x 200mm modular deep in wall 500mm wide										
Natural blocks										
....	119.00	5.00	124.95	-	7.00	108.99	-	233.94	m²	257.33
Extra over for colours	12.00	5.00	12.60	-	0.10	1.56	-	14.16	m²	15.57
Betonap 100/50 woven mesh geotextile as reinforcement to backfill	5.96	5.00	6.26	-	0.30	4.67	-	10.93	m²	12.02
For Betoplus or Betoatlas										
graded stone filling behind blocks	50.02	5.00	52.52	-	4.00	62.28	-	114.80	m³	126.28
concrete haunching to base of blocks	7.86	5.00	8.26	-	0.45	7.01	-	15.26	m	16.79

This page left blank intentionally

Labour hourly rates: (except Specialists) Craft Operatives 20.87 Labourer 15.57 Rates are national average prices. Refer to REGIONAL VARIATIONS for indicative levels of overall pricing in regions	MATERIALS			LABOUR				RATES		
	Del to Site £	Waste %	Material Cost £	Craft Optve Hrs	Lab Hrs	Labour Cost £	Sunds £	Nett Rate £	Unit	Gross rate (10%) £
IN-SITU CONCRETE; PLAIN IN-SITU CONCRETE; READY MIXED										
Plain in-situ mass concrete; BS 8500; ordinary prescribed mix ST3, 20mm aggregate										
In filling voids	101.40	7.50	109.01	-	2.30	35.81	-	144.82	m³	159.30
In trench filling	101.40	7.50	109.01	-	2.30	35.81	-	144.82	m³	159.30
Poured on or against earth or unblinded hardcore										
In filling voids	101.40	7.50	109.01	-	2.30	35.81	-	144.82	m³	159.30
In trench filling	101.40	7.50	109.01	-	2.30	35.81	-	144.82	m³	159.30
Plain in-situ concrete in horizontal work; BS 8500; ordinary prescribed mix ST3, 20mm aggregate										
In blinding	101.40	7.50	109.01	-	2.30	35.81	-	144.82	m³	159.30
thickness not exceeding 300mm	101.40	7.50	109.01	-	3.10	48.27	-	157.27	m³	173.00
In structures	101.40	7.50	109.01	-	3.30	51.38	-	160.39	m³	176.42
thickness not exceeding 300mm	101.40	7.50	109.01	-	3.60	56.05	-	165.06	m³	181.56
Poured on or against earth or unblinded hardcore										
In blinding	101.40	7.50	109.01	-	2.30	35.81	-	144.82	m³	159.30
thickness not exceeding 300mm	101.40	7.50	109.01	-	3.10	48.27	-	157.27	m³	173.00
In structures	101.40	7.50	109.01	-	3.30	51.38	-	160.39	m³	176.42
thickness not exceeding 300mm	101.40	7.50	109.01	-	3.60	56.05	-	165.06	m³	181.56
Plain in-situ concrete in sloping work less than 15o; BS 8500; ordinary prescribed mix ST3, 20mm aggregate										
In blinding	101.40	7.50	109.01	-	2.30	35.81	-	144.82	m³	159.30
thickness not exceeding 300mm	101.40	7.50	109.01	-	3.10	48.27	-	157.27	m³	173.00
In structures	101.40	7.50	109.01	-	3.30	51.38	-	160.39	m³	176.42
thickness not exceeding 300mm	101.40	7.50	109.01	-	3.60	56.05	-	165.06	m³	181.56
In staircases	101.40	7.50	109.01	-	3.30	51.38	-	160.39	m³	176.42
thickness not exceeding 300mm	101.40	7.50	109.01	-	5.50	85.63	-	194.64	m³	214.10
Poured on or against earth or unblinded hardcore										
In blinding	101.40	7.50	109.01	-	2.30	35.81	-	144.82	m³	159.30
thickness not exceeding 300mm	101.40	7.50	109.01	-	3.10	48.27	-	157.27	m³	173.00
In structures	101.40	7.50	109.01	-	3.30	51.38	-	160.39	m³	176.42
thickness not exceeding 300mm	101.40	7.50	109.01	-	3.60	56.05	-	165.06	m³	181.56
In staircases	101.40	7.50	109.01	-	3.30	51.38	-	160.39	m³	176.42
thickness not exceeding 300mm	101.40	7.50	109.01	-	5.50	85.63	-	194.64	m³	214.10
Plain in-situ concrete in sloping work greater than 15o; BS 8500; ordinary prescribed mix ST3, 20mm aggregate										
In blinding	101.40	7.50	109.01	-	2.30	35.81	-	144.82	m³	159.30
thickness not exceeding 300mm	101.40	7.50	109.01	-	3.10	48.27	-	157.27	m³	173.00
In structures	101.40	7.50	109.01	-	3.30	51.38	-	160.39	m³	176.42
thickness not exceeding 300mm	101.40	7.50	109.01	-	3.60	56.05	-	165.06	m³	181.56
In staircases	101.40	7.50	109.01	-	3.30	51.38	-	160.39	m³	176.42
thickness not exceeding 300mm	101.40	7.50	109.01	-	5.50	85.63	-	194.64	m³	214.10
Poured on or against earth or unblinded hardcore										
In blinding	101.40	7.50	109.01	-	2.30	35.81	-	144.82	m³	159.30
thickness not exceeding 300mm	101.40	7.50	109.01	-	3.10	48.27	-	157.27	m³	173.00
In structures	101.40	7.50	109.01	-	3.30	51.38	-	160.39	m³	176.42
thickness not exceeding 300mm	101.40	7.50	109.01	-	3.60	56.05	-	165.06	m³	181.56
In staircases	101.40	7.50	109.01	-	3.30	51.38	-	160.39	m³	176.42
thickness not exceeding 300mm	101.40	7.50	109.01	-	5.50	85.63	-	194.64	m³	214.10
Plain in-situ concrete in vertical work; BS 8500; ordinary prescribed mix ST3, 20mm aggregate										
In structures	101.40	7.50	109.01	-	3.30	51.38	-	160.39	m³	176.42
thickness not exceeding 300mm	101.40	5.00	106.47	-	5.50	85.63	-	192.10	m³	211.32
Plain sundry in-situ concrete work; BS 8500; ordinary prescribed mix ST3, 20mm aggregate										
Horizontal	101.40	7.50	109.01	-	2.30	35.81	-	144.82	m³	159.30
width or thickness not exceeding 300mm	101.40	5.00	106.47	-	5.50	85.63	-	192.10	m³	211.32
Sloping	101.40	7.50	109.01	-	2.30	35.81	-	144.82	m³	159.30
width or thickness not exceeding 300mm	101.40	5.00	106.47	-	5.50	85.63	-	192.10	m³	211.32
Vertical	101.40	7.50	109.01	-	3.30	51.38	-	160.39	m³	176.42
width or thickness not exceeding 300mm	101.40	5.00	106.47	-	5.50	85.63	-	192.10	m³	211.32
Plain in-situ mass concrete; BS 8500; ordinary prescribed mix ST4, 20mm aggregate										
In filling voids	105.04	7.50	112.92	-	2.30	35.81	-	148.73	m³	163.60
In trench filling	105.04	7.50	112.92	-	2.30	35.81	-	148.73	m³	163.60
Poured on or against earth or unblinded hardcore										
In filling voids	105.04	7.50	112.92	-	2.30	35.81	-	148.73	m³	163.60
In trench filling	105.04	7.50	112.92	-	2.30	35.81	-	148.73	m³	163.60

Labour hourly rates: (except Specialists) Craft Operatives 20.87 Labourer 15.57 Rates are national average prices. Refer to REGIONAL VARIATIONS for indicative levels of overall pricing in regions	MATERIALS			LABOUR				RATES		
	Del to Site £	Waste %	Material Cost £	Craft Optve Hrs	Lab Hrs	Labour Cost £	Sunds £	Nett Rate £	Unit	Gross rate (10%) £
IN-SITU CONCRETE; PLAIN IN-SITU CONCRETE; READY MIXED (Cont'd)										
Plain in-situ concrete in horizontal work; BS 8500; ordinary prescribed mix ST4, 20mm aggregate										
In blinding	105.04	7.50	112.92	-	2.30	35.81	-	148.73	m³	163.60
thickness not exceeding 300mm	105.04	7.50	112.92	-	3.10	48.27	-	161.19	m³	177.30
In structures	105.04	7.50	112.92	-	3.30	51.38	-	164.30	m³	180.73
thickness not exceeding 300mm	105.04	7.50	112.92	-	3.60	56.05	-	168.97	m³	185.87
Poured on or against earth or unblinded hardcore										
In blinding	105.04	7.50	112.92	-	2.30	35.81	-	148.73	m³	163.60
thickness not exceeding 300mm	105.04	7.50	112.92	-	3.10	48.27	-	161.19	m³	177.30
In structures	105.04	7.50	112.92	-	3.30	51.38	-	164.30	m³	180.73
thickness not exceeding 300mm	105.04	7.50	112.92	-	3.60	56.05	-	168.97	m³	185.87
Plain in-situ concrete in sloping work less than 15o; BS 8500; ordinary prescribed mix ST4, 20mm aggregate										
In blinding	105.04	7.50	112.92	-	2.30	35.81	-	148.73	m³	163.60
thickness not exceeding 300mm	105.04	7.50	112.92	-	3.10	48.27	-	161.19	m³	177.30
In structures	105.04	7.50	112.92	-	3.30	51.38	-	164.30	m³	180.73
thickness not exceeding 300mm	105.04	7.50	112.92	-	3.60	56.05	-	168.97	m³	185.87
In staircases	105.04	7.50	112.92	-	3.30	51.38	-	164.30	m³	180.73
thickness not exceeding 300mm	105.04	7.50	112.92	-	5.50	85.63	-	198.55	m³	218.41
Poured on or against earth or unblinded hardcore										
In blinding	105.04	7.50	112.92	-	2.30	35.81	-	148.73	m³	163.60
thickness not exceeding 300mm	105.04	7.50	112.92	-	3.10	48.27	-	161.19	m³	177.30
In structures	105.04	7.50	112.92	-	3.30	51.38	-	164.30	m³	180.73
thickness not exceeding 300mm	105.04	7.50	112.92	-	3.60	56.05	-	168.97	m³	185.87
In staircases	105.04	7.50	112.92	-	3.30	51.38	-	164.30	m³	180.73
thickness not exceeding 300mm	105.04	7.50	112.92	-	5.50	85.63	-	198.55	m³	218.41
Plain in-situ concrete in sloping work greater than 15o; BS 8500; ordinary prescribed mix ST4, 20mm aggregate										
In blinding	105.04	7.50	112.92	-	2.30	35.81	-	148.73	m³	163.60
thickness not exceeding 300mm	105.04	7.50	112.92	-	3.10	48.27	-	161.19	m³	177.30
In structures	105.04	7.50	112.92	-	3.30	51.38	-	164.30	m³	180.73
thickness not exceeding 300mm	105.04	7.50	112.92	-	3.60	56.05	-	168.97	m³	185.87
In staircases	105.04	7.50	112.92	-	3.30	51.38	-	164.30	m³	180.73
thickness not exceeding 300mm	105.04	7.50	112.92	-	5.50	85.63	-	198.55	m³	218.41
Poured on or against earth or unblinded hardcore										
In blinding	105.04	7.50	112.92	-	2.30	35.81	-	148.73	m³	163.60
thickness not exceeding 300mm	105.04	7.50	112.92	-	3.10	48.27	-	161.19	m³	177.30
In structures	105.04	7.50	112.92	-	3.30	51.38	-	164.30	m³	180.73
thickness not exceeding 300mm	105.04	7.50	112.92	-	3.60	56.05	-	168.97	m³	185.87
In staircases	105.04	7.50	112.92	-	3.30	51.38	-	164.30	m³	180.73
thickness not exceeding 300mm	105.04	7.50	112.92	-	5.50	85.63	-	198.55	m³	218.41
Plain in-situ concrete in vertical work; BS 8500; ordinary prescribed mix ST4, 20mm aggregate										
In structures	105.04	7.50	112.92	-	3.30	51.38	-	164.30	m³	180.73
thickness not exceeding 300mm	110.24	5.00	115.75	-	5.50	85.63	-	201.39	m³	221.53
Plain sundry in-situ concrete work; BS 8500; ordinary prescribed mix ST4, 20mm aggregate										
Horizontal	105.04	7.50	112.92	-	3.10	48.27	-	161.19	m³	177.30
width or thickness not exceeding 300mm	110.24	5.00	115.75	-	5.50	85.63	-	201.39	m³	221.53
Sloping	105.04	7.50	112.92	-	3.10	48.27	-	161.19	m³	177.30
width or thickness not exceeding 300mm	110.24	5.00	115.75	-	5.50	85.63	-	201.39	m³	221.53
Vertical	105.04	7.50	112.92	-	3.30	51.38	-	164.30	m³	180.73
width or thickness not exceeding 300mm	110.24	5.00	115.75	-	5.50	85.63	-	201.39	m³	221.53
Plain in-situ mass concrete; BS 8500; ordinary prescribed mix ST5, 20mm aggregate										
In filling voids	110.24	7.50	118.51	-	2.30	35.81	-	154.32	m³	169.75
In trench filling	110.24	7.50	118.51	-	2.30	35.81	-	154.32	m³	169.75
Poured on or against earth or unblinded hardcore										
In filling voids	110.24	7.50	118.51	-	2.30	35.81	-	154.32	m³	169.75
In trench filling	110.24	7.50	118.51	-	2.30	35.81	-	154.32	m³	169.75
Plain in-situ concrete in horizontal work; BS 8500; ordinary prescribed mix ST5, 20mm aggregate										
In blinding	110.24	7.50	118.51	-	2.30	35.81	-	154.32	m³	169.75
thickness not exceeding 300mm	110.24	7.50	118.51	-	3.10	48.27	-	166.78	m³	183.45
In structures	110.24	7.50	118.51	-	3.30	51.38	-	169.89	m³	186.88
thickness not exceeding 300mm	110.24	7.50	118.51	-	3.60	56.05	-	174.56	m³	192.02
Poured on or against earth or unblinded hardcore										
In blinding	110.24	7.50	118.51	-	2.30	35.81	-	154.32	m³	169.75
thickness not exceeding 300mm	110.24	7.50	118.51	-	3.10	48.27	-	166.78	m³	183.45
In structures	110.24	7.50	118.51	-	3.30	51.38	-	169.89	m³	186.88
thickness not exceeding 300mm	110.24	7.50	118.51	-	3.60	56.05	-	174.56	m³	192.02
Plain in-situ concrete in sloping work less than 15o; BS 8500; ordinary prescribed mix ST5, 20mm aggregate										
In blinding	110.24	7.50	118.51	-	2.30	35.81	-	154.32	m³	169.75
thickness not exceeding 300mm	110.24	7.50	118.51	-	3.10	48.27	-	166.78	m³	183.45
In structures	110.24	7.50	118.51	-	3.30	51.38	-	169.89	m³	186.88
thickness not exceeding 300mm	110.24	7.50	118.51	-	3.60	56.05	-	174.56	m³	192.02
In staircases	110.24	7.50	118.51	-	3.30	51.38	-	169.89	m³	186.88
thickness not exceeding 300mm	110.24	7.50	118.51	-	5.50	85.63	-	204.14	m³	224.56
Poured on or against earth or unblinded hardcore										
In blinding	110.24	7.50	118.51	-	2.30	35.81	-	154.32	m³	169.75

Labour hourly rates: (except Specialists) Craft Operatives 20.87 Labourer 15.57 Rates are national average prices. Refer to REGIONAL VARIATIONS for indicative levels of overall pricing in regions	MATERIALS			LABOUR				RATES		
	Del to Site £	Waste %	Material Cost £	Craft Optve Hrs	Lab Hrs	Labour Cost £	Sunds £	Nett Rate £	Unit	Gross rate (10%) £
IN-SITU CONCRETE; PLAIN IN-SITU CONCRETE; READY MIXED (Cont'd)										
Plain in-situ concrete in sloping work less than 15o; BS 8500; ordinary prescribed mix ST5, 20mm aggregate (Cont'd)										
Poured on or against earth or unblinded hardcore (Cont'd)										
thickness not exceeding 300mm	110.24	7.50	118.51	-	3.10	48.27	-	166.78	m³	183.45
In structures	110.24	7.50	118.51	-	3.30	51.38	-	169.89	m³	186.88
thickness not exceeding 300mm	110.24	7.50	118.51	-	3.60	56.05	-	174.56	m³	192.02
In staircases	110.24	7.50	118.51	-	3.30	51.38	-	169.89	m³	186.88
thickness not exceeding 300mm	110.24	7.50	118.51	-	5.50	85.63	-	204.14	m³	224.56
Plain in-situ concrete in sloping work greater than 15o; BS 8500; ordinary prescribed mix ST5, 20mm aggregate										
In blinding	110.24	7.50	118.51	-	2.30	35.81	-	154.32	m³	169.75
thickness not exceeding 300mm	110.24	7.50	118.51	-	3.10	48.27	-	166.78	m³	183.45
In structures	110.24	7.50	118.51	-	3.30	51.38	-	169.89	m³	186.88
thickness not exceeding 300mm	110.24	7.50	118.51	-	3.60	56.05	-	174.56	m³	192.02
In staircases	110.24	7.50	118.51	-	3.30	51.38	-	169.89	m³	186.88
thickness not exceeding 300mm	110.24	7.50	118.51	-	5.50	85.63	-	204.14	m³	224.56
Poured on or against earth or unblinded hardcore										
In blinding	110.24	7.50	118.51	-	2.30	35.81	-	154.32	m³	169.75
thickness not exceeding 300mm	110.24	7.50	118.51	-	3.10	48.27	-	166.78	m³	183.45
In structures	110.24	7.50	118.51	-	3.30	51.38	-	169.89	m³	186.88
thickness not exceeding 300mm	110.24	7.50	118.51	-	3.60	56.05	-	174.56	m³	192.02
In staircases	110.24	7.50	118.51	-	3.30	51.38	-	169.89	m³	186.88
thickness not exceeding 300mm	110.24	7.50	118.51	-	5.50	85.63	-	204.14	m³	224.56
Plain in-situ concrete in vertical work; BS 8500; ordinary prescribed mix ST5, 20mm aggregate										
In structures	110.24	7.50	118.51	-	3.30	51.38	-	169.89	m³	186.88
thickness not exceeding 300mm	110.24	5.00	115.75	-	5.50	85.63	-	201.39	m³	221.53
Plain sundry in-situ concrete work; BS 8500; ordinary prescribed mix ST5, 20mm aggregate										
Horizontal	110.24	7.50	118.51	-	3.10	48.27	-	166.78	m³	183.45
width or thickness not exceeding 300mm	110.24	5.00	115.75	-	5.50	85.63	-	201.39	m³	221.53
Sloping	110.24	7.50	118.51	-	3.10	48.27	-	166.78	m³	183.45
width or thickness not exceeding 300mm	110.24	5.00	115.75	-	5.50	85.63	-	201.39	m³	221.53
Vertical	110.24	7.50	118.51	-	3.30	51.38	-	169.89	m³	186.88
width or thickness not exceeding 300mm	110.24	5.00	115.75	-	5.50	85.63	-	201.39	m³	221.53
IN-SITU CONCRETE; REINFORCED IN-SITU CONCRETE; READY MIXED										
Reinforced in-situ mass concrete; BS 8500; designed mix C12/15, 20mm aggregate, minimum cement content 220 kg/m³; vibrated										
In filling voids	93.60	5.00	98.28	-	2.60	40.48	0.82	139.59	m³	153.55
In trench filling	93.60	5.00	98.28	-	2.60	40.48	0.82	139.59	m³	153.55
Poured on or against earth or unblinded hardcore										
In filling voids	93.60	5.00	98.28	-	2.60	40.48	0.82	139.59	m³	153.55
In trench filling	93.60	5.00	98.28	-	2.60	40.48	0.82	139.59	m³	153.55
Reinforced in-situ concrete in horizontal work; BS 8500; designed mix C12/15, 20mm aggregate, minimum cement content 220 kg/m³; vibrated										
In blinding	93.60	5.00	98.28	-	2.60	40.48	0.82	139.59	m³	153.55
thickness not exceeding 300mm	93.60	5.00	98.28	-	3.50	54.49	0.82	153.60	m³	168.96
In structures	93.60	5.00	98.28	-	3.60	56.05	0.82	155.16	m³	170.67
thickness not exceeding 300mm	93.60	5.00	98.28	-	3.90	60.72	0.82	159.83	m³	175.81
Poured on or against earth or unblinded hardcore										
In blinding	93.60	5.00	98.28	-	2.60	40.48	0.82	139.59	m³	153.55
thickness not exceeding 300mm	93.60	5.00	98.28	-	3.50	54.49	0.82	153.60	m³	168.96
In structures	93.60	5.00	98.28	-	3.60	56.05	0.82	155.16	m³	170.67
thickness not exceeding 300mm	93.60	5.00	98.28	-	3.90	60.72	0.82	159.83	m³	175.81
Reinforced in-situ concrete in sloping work less than 15o; BS 8500; designed mix C12/15, 20mm aggregate, minimum cement content 220 kg/m³; vibrated										
In blinding	93.60	5.00	98.28	-	2.60	40.48	0.82	139.59	m³	153.55
thickness not exceeding 300mm	93.60	5.00	98.28	-	3.50	54.49	0.82	153.60	m³	168.96
In structures	93.60	5.00	98.28	-	3.60	56.05	0.82	155.16	m³	170.67
thickness not exceeding 300mm	93.60	5.00	98.28	-	3.90	60.72	0.82	159.83	m³	175.81
In staircases	93.60	5.00	98.28	-	3.60	56.05	0.82	155.16	m³	170.67
thickness not exceeding 300mm	93.60	2.50	95.94	-	5.50	85.63	0.82	182.40	m³	200.64
Poured on or against earth or unblinded hardcore										
In blinding	93.60	5.00	98.28	-	2.60	40.48	0.82	139.59	m³	153.55
thickness not exceeding 300mm	93.60	5.00	98.28	-	3.50	54.49	0.82	153.60	m³	168.96
In structures	93.60	5.00	98.28	-	3.60	56.05	0.82	155.16	m³	170.67
thickness not exceeding 300mm	93.60	5.00	98.28	-	3.90	60.72	0.82	159.83	m³	175.81
In staircases	93.60	5.00	98.28	-	3.60	56.05	0.82	155.16	m³	170.67
thickness not exceeding 300mm	93.60	2.50	95.94	-	5.50	85.63	0.82	182.40	m³	200.64
Reinforced in-situ concrete in sloping work greater than 15o; BS 8500; designed mix C12/15, 20mm aggregate, minimum cement content 220 kg/m³; vibrated										
In blinding	93.60	5.00	98.28	-	2.60	40.48	0.82	139.59	m³	153.55
thickness not exceeding 300mm	93.60	5.00	98.28	-	3.50	54.49	0.82	153.60	m³	168.96
In structures	93.60	5.00	98.28	-	3.60	56.05	0.82	155.16	m³	170.67
thickness not exceeding 300mm	93.60	5.00	98.28	-	3.90	60.72	0.82	159.83	m³	175.81
In staircases	93.60	5.00	98.28	-	3.60	56.05	0.82	155.16	m³	170.67

Labour hourly rates: (except Specialists) Craft Operatives 20.87 Labourer 15.57 Rates are national average prices. Refer to REGIONAL VARIATIONS for indicative levels of overall pricing in regions	MATERIALS			LABOUR				RATES		
	Del to Site £	Waste %	Material Cost £	Craft Optve Hrs	Lab Hrs	Labour Cost £	Sunds £	Nett Rate £	Unit	Gross rate (10%) £
IN-SITU CONCRETE; REINFORCED IN-SITU CONCRETE; READY MIXED (Cont'd)										
Reinforced in-situ concrete in sloping work greater than 15o; BS 8500; designed mix C12/15, 20mm aggregate, minimum cement content 220 kg/m³; vibrated (Cont'd)										
thickness not exceeding 300mm	93.60	2.50	95.94	-	5.50	85.63	0.82	182.40	m³	200.64
Poured on or against earth or unblinded hardcore										
In blinding	93.60	5.00	98.28	-	2.60	40.48	0.82	139.59	m³	153.55
thickness not exceeding 300mm	93.60	5.00	98.28	-	3.50	54.49	0.82	153.60	m³	168.96
In structures	93.60	5.00	98.28	-	3.60	56.05	0.82	155.16	m³	170.67
thickness not exceeding 300mm	93.60	5.00	98.28	-	3.90	60.72	0.82	159.83	m³	175.81
In staircases	93.60	5.00	98.28	-	3.60	56.05	0.82	155.16	m³	170.67
thickness not exceeding 300mm	93.60	2.50	95.94	-	5.50	85.63	0.82	182.40	m³	200.64
Reinforced in-situ concrete in vertical work; BS 8500; designed mix C12/15, 20mm aggregate, minimum cement content 220 kg/m³; vibrated										
In structures	93.60	5.00	98.28	-	3.60	56.05	0.82	155.16	m³	170.67
thickness not exceeding 300mm	93.60	2.50	95.94	-	5.00	77.85	0.82	174.61	m³	192.08
Reinforced sundry in-situ concrete work; BS 8500; designed mix C12/15, 20mm aggregate, minimum cement content 220 kg/m³; vibrated										
Horizontal	93.60	5.00	98.28	-	2.60	40.48	0.82	139.59	m³	153.55
width or thickness not exceeding 300mm	93.60	5.00	98.28	-	3.50	54.49	0.82	153.60	m³	168.96
Sloping	93.60	5.00	98.28	-	2.60	40.48	0.82	139.59	m³	153.55
width or thickness not exceeding 300mm	93.60	5.00	98.28	-	3.50	54.49	0.82	153.60	m³	168.96
Vertical	93.60	5.00	98.28	-	3.60	56.05	0.82	155.16	m³	170.67
width or thickness not exceeding 300mm	93.60	2.50	95.94	-	5.50	85.63	0.82	182.40	m³	200.64
Reinforced in-situ mass concrete; BS 8500; designed mix C16/20, 20mm aggregate, minimum cement content 240 kg/m³; vibrated										
In filling voids	97.76	5.00	102.65	-	2.60	40.48	0.82	143.96	m³	158.35
In trench filling	97.76	5.00	102.65	-	2.60	40.48	0.82	143.96	m³	158.35
Poured on or against earth or unblinded hardcore										
In filling voids	97.76	5.00	102.65	-	2.60	40.48	0.82	143.96	m³	158.35
In trench filling	97.76	5.00	102.65	-	2.60	40.48	0.82	143.96	m³	158.35
Reinforced in-situ concrete in horizontal work; BS 8500; designed mix C16/20, 20mm aggregate, minimum cement content 240 kg/m³; vibrated										
In blinding	97.76	5.00	102.65	-	2.60	40.48	0.82	143.96	m³	158.35
thickness not exceeding 300mm	97.76	5.00	102.65	-	3.50	54.49	0.82	157.97	m³	173.76
In structures	97.76	5.00	102.65	-	3.60	56.05	0.82	159.52	m³	175.48
thickness not exceeding 300mm	97.76	5.00	102.65	-	3.90	60.72	0.82	164.20	m³	180.62
Poured on or against earth or unblinded hardcore										
In blinding	97.76	5.00	102.65	-	2.60	40.48	0.82	143.96	m³	158.35
thickness not exceeding 300mm	97.76	5.00	102.65	-	3.50	54.49	0.82	157.97	m³	173.76
In structures	97.76	5.00	102.65	-	3.60	56.05	0.82	159.52	m³	175.48
thickness not exceeding 300mm	97.76	5.00	102.65	-	3.90	60.72	0.82	164.20	m³	180.62
Reinforced in-situ concrete in sloping work less than 15o; BS 8500; designed mix C16/20, 20mm aggregate, minimum cement content 240 kg/m³; vibrated										
In blinding	97.76	5.00	102.65	-	2.60	40.48	0.82	143.96	m³	158.35
thickness not exceeding 300mm	97.76	5.00	102.65	-	3.50	54.49	0.82	157.97	m³	173.76
In structures	97.76	5.00	102.65	-	3.60	56.05	0.82	159.52	m³	175.48
thickness not exceeding 300mm	97.76	5.00	102.65	-	3.90	60.72	0.82	164.20	m³	180.62
In staircases	97.76	5.00	102.65	-	3.60	56.05	0.82	159.52	m³	175.48
thickness not exceeding 300mm	97.76	2.50	100.20	-	5.50	85.63	0.82	186.66	m³	205.33
Poured on or against earth or unblinded hardcore										
In blinding	97.76	5.00	102.65	-	2.60	40.48	0.82	143.96	m³	158.35
thickness not exceeding 300mm	97.76	5.00	102.65	-	3.50	54.49	0.82	157.97	m³	173.76
In structures	97.76	5.00	102.65	-	3.60	56.05	0.82	159.52	m³	175.48
thickness not exceeding 300mm	97.76	5.00	102.65	-	3.90	60.72	0.82	164.20	m³	180.62
In staircases	97.76	5.00	102.65	-	3.60	56.05	0.82	159.52	m³	175.48
thickness not exceeding 300mm	97.76	2.50	100.20	-	5.50	85.63	0.82	186.66	m³	205.33
Reinforced in-situ concrete in sloping work greater than 15o; BS 8500; designed mix C16/20, 20mm aggregate, minimum cement content 240 kg/m³; vibrated										
In blinding	97.76	5.00	102.65	-	2.60	40.48	0.82	143.96	m³	158.35
thickness not exceeding 300mm	97.76	5.00	102.65	-	3.50	54.49	0.82	157.97	m³	173.76
In structures	97.76	5.00	102.65	-	3.60	56.05	0.82	159.52	m³	175.48
thickness not exceeding 300mm	97.76	5.00	102.65	-	3.90	60.72	0.82	164.20	m³	180.62
In staircases	97.76	5.00	102.65	-	3.60	56.05	0.82	159.52	m³	175.48
thickness not exceeding 300mm	97.76	2.50	100.20	-	5.50	85.63	0.82	186.66	m³	205.33
Poured on or against earth or unblinded hardcore										
In blinding	97.76	5.00	102.65	-	2.60	40.48	0.82	143.96	m³	158.35
thickness not exceeding 300mm	97.76	5.00	102.65	-	3.50	54.49	0.82	157.97	m³	173.76
In structures	97.76	5.00	102.65	-	3.60	56.05	0.82	159.52	m³	175.48
thickness not exceeding 300mm	97.76	5.00	102.65	-	3.90	60.72	0.82	164.20	m³	180.62
In staircases	97.76	5.00	102.65	-	3.60	56.05	0.82	159.52	m³	175.48
thickness not exceeding 300mm	97.76	2.50	100.20	-	5.50	85.63	0.82	186.66	m³	205.33
Reinforced in-situ concrete in vertical work; BS 8500; designed mix C16/20, 20mm aggregate, minimum cement content 240 kg/m³; vibrated										
In structures	97.76	5.00	102.65	-	3.60	56.05	0.82	159.52	m³	175.48
thickness not exceeding 300mm	97.76	2.50	100.20	-	5.00	77.85	0.82	178.88	m³	196.77

Labour hourly rates: (except Specialists) Craft Operatives 20.87 Labourer 15.57 Rates are national average prices. Refer to REGIONAL VARIATIONS for indicative levels of overall pricing in regions	MATERIALS			LABOUR				RATES		
	Del to Site £	Waste %	Material Cost £	Craft Optve Hrs	Lab Hrs	Labour Cost £	Sunds £	Nett Rate £	Unit	Gross rate (10%) £
IN-SITU CONCRETE; REINFORCED IN-SITU CONCRETE; READY MIXED (Cont'd)										
Reinforced sundry in-situ concrete work; BS 8500; designed mix C16/20, 20mm aggregate, minimum cement content 240 kg/m^3; vibrated										
Horizontal	97.76	5.00	102.65	-	2.60	40.48	0.82	143.96	m^3	158.35
width or thickness not exceeding 300mm	97.76	5.00	102.65	-	3.50	54.49	0.82	157.97	m^3	173.76
Sloping	97.76	5.00	102.65	-	2.60	40.48	0.82	143.96	m^3	158.35
width or thickness not exceeding 300mm	97.76	5.00	102.65	-	3.50	54.49	0.82	157.97	m^3	173.76
Vertical	97.76	5.00	102.65	-	3.60	56.05	0.82	159.52	m^3	175.48
width or thickness not exceeding 300mm	97.76	2.50	100.20	-	5.50	85.63	0.82	186.66	m^3	205.33
Reinforced in-situ mass concrete; BS 8500; designed mix C20/25, 20mm aggregate, minimum cement content 290 kg/m^3; vibrated										
In filling voids	101.92	5.00	107.02	-	2.60	40.48	0.82	148.32	m^3	163.16
In trench filling	101.92	5.00	107.02	-	2.60	40.48	0.82	148.32	m^3	163.16
Poured on or against earth or unblinded hardcore										
In filling voids	101.92	5.00	107.02	-	2.60	40.48	0.82	148.32	m^3	163.16
In trench filling	101.92	5.00	107.02	-	2.60	40.48	0.82	148.32	m^3	163.16
Reinforced in-situ concrete in horizontal work; BS 8500; designed mix C20/25, 20mm aggregate, minimum cement content 290 kg/m^3; vibrated										
In blinding	101.92	5.00	107.02	-	2.60	40.48	0.82	148.32	m^3	163.16
thickness not exceeding 300mm	101.92	5.00	107.02	-	3.50	54.49	0.82	162.34	m^3	178.57
In structures	101.92	5.00	107.02	-	3.60	56.05	0.82	163.89	m^3	180.28
thickness not exceeding 300mm	101.92	5.00	107.02	-	3.90	60.72	0.82	168.56	m^3	185.42
Poured on or against earth or unblinded hardcore										
In blinding	101.92	5.00	107.02	-	2.60	40.48	0.82	148.32	m^3	163.16
thickness not exceeding 300mm	101.92	5.00	107.02	-	3.50	54.49	0.82	162.34	m^3	178.57
In structures	101.92	5.00	107.02	-	3.60	56.05	0.82	163.89	m^3	180.28
thickness not exceeding 300mm	101.92	5.00	107.02	-	3.90	60.72	0.82	168.56	m^3	185.42
Reinforced in-situ concrete in sloping work less than 15o; BS 8500; designed mix C20/25, 20mm aggregate, minimum cement content 290 kg/m^3; vibrated										
In blinding	101.92	5.00	107.02	-	2.60	40.48	0.82	148.32	m^3	163.16
thickness not exceeding 300mm	101.92	5.00	107.02	-	3.50	54.49	0.82	162.34	m^3	178.57
In structures	101.92	5.00	107.02	-	3.60	56.05	0.82	163.89	m^3	180.28
thickness not exceeding 300mm	101.92	5.00	107.02	-	3.90	60.72	0.82	168.56	m^3	185.42
In staircases	101.92	5.00	107.02	-	3.60	56.05	0.82	163.89	m^3	180.28
thickness not exceeding 300mm	101.92	2.50	104.47	-	5.50	85.63	0.82	190.93	m^3	210.02
Poured on or against earth or unblinded hardcore										
In blinding	101.92	5.00	107.02	-	2.60	40.48	0.82	148.32	m^3	163.16
thickness not exceeding 300mm	101.92	5.00	107.02	-	3.50	54.49	0.82	162.34	m^3	178.57
In structures	101.92	5.00	107.02	-	3.60	56.05	0.82	163.89	m^3	180.28
thickness not exceeding 300mm	101.92	5.00	107.02	-	3.90	60.72	0.82	168.56	m^3	185.42
In staircases	101.92	5.00	107.02	-	3.60	56.05	0.82	163.89	m^3	180.28
thickness not exceeding 300mm	101.92	2.50	104.47	-	5.50	85.63	0.82	190.93	m^3	210.02
Reinforced in-situ concrete in sloping work greater than 15o; BS 8500; designed mix C20/25, 20mm aggregate, minimum cement content 290 kg/m^3; vibrated										
In blinding	101.92	5.00	107.02	-	2.60	40.48	0.82	148.32	m^3	163.16
thickness not exceeding 300mm	101.92	5.00	107.02	-	3.50	54.49	0.82	162.34	m^3	178.57
In structures	101.92	5.00	107.02	-	3.60	56.05	0.82	163.89	m^3	180.28
thickness not exceeding 300mm	101.92	5.00	107.02	-	3.90	60.72	0.82	168.56	m^3	185.42
In staircases	101.92	5.00	107.02	-	3.60	56.05	0.82	163.89	m^3	180.28
thickness not exceeding 300mm	101.92	2.50	104.47	-	5.50	85.63	0.82	190.93	m^3	210.02
Poured on or against earth or unblinded hardcore										
In blinding	101.92	5.00	107.02	-	2.60	40.48	0.82	148.32	m^3	163.16
thickness not exceeding 300mm	101.92	5.00	107.02	-	3.50	54.49	0.82	162.34	m^3	178.57
In structures	101.92	5.00	107.02	-	3.60	56.05	0.82	163.89	m^3	180.28
thickness not exceeding 300mm	101.92	5.00	107.02	-	3.90	60.72	0.82	168.56	m^3	185.42
In staircases	101.92	5.00	107.02	-	3.60	56.05	0.82	163.89	m^3	180.28
thickness not exceeding 300mm	101.92	2.50	104.47	-	5.50	85.63	0.82	190.93	m^3	210.02
Reinforced in-situ concrete in vertical work; BS 8500; designed mix C20/25, 20mm aggregate, minimum cement content 290 kg/m^3; vibrated										
In structures	101.92	5.00	107.02	-	3.60	56.05	0.82	163.89	m^3	180.28
thickness not exceeding 300mm	101.92	2.50	104.47	-	5.00	77.85	0.82	183.14	m^3	201.46
Reinforced sundry in-situ concrete work; BS 8500; designed mix C20/25, 20mm aggregate, minimum cement content 290 kg/m^3; vibrated										
Horizontal	101.92	5.00	107.02	-	2.60	40.48	0.82	148.32	m^3	163.16
width or thickness not exceeding 300mm	101.92	5.00	107.02	-	3.50	54.49	0.82	162.34	m^3	178.57
Sloping	101.92	5.00	107.02	-	2.60	40.48	0.82	148.32	m^3	163.16
width or thickness not exceeding 300mm	101.92	5.00	107.02	-	3.50	54.49	0.82	162.34	m^3	178.57
Vertical	101.92	5.00	107.02	-	3.60	56.05	0.82	163.89	m^3	180.28
width or thickness not exceeding 300mm	101.92	2.50	104.47	-	5.50	85.63	0.82	190.93	m^3	210.02
Reinforced in-situ mass concrete; BS 8500; designed mix C25/30, 20mm aggregate, minimum cement content 290 kg/m^3; vibrated										
In filling voids	106.08	5.00	111.38	-	2.60	40.48	0.82	152.69	m^3	167.96
In trench filling	106.08	5.00	111.38	-	2.60	40.48	0.82	152.69	m^3	167.96
Poured on or against earth or unblinded hardcore										
In filling voids	106.08	5.00	111.38	-	2.60	40.48	0.82	152.69	m^3	167.96

Labour hourly rates: (except Specialists) Craft Operatives 20.87 Labourer 15.57 Rates are national average prices. Refer to REGIONAL VARIATIONS for indicative levels of overall pricing in regions	MATERIALS			LABOUR				RATES		
	Del to Site	Waste	Material Cost	Craft Optve	Lab	Labour Cost	Sunds	Nett Rate		Gross rate (10%)
	£	%	£	Hrs	Hrs	£	£	£	Unit	£
IN-SITU CONCRETE; REINFORCED IN-SITU CONCRETE; READY MIXED (Cont'd)										
Reinforced in-situ mass concrete; BS 8500; designed mix C25/30, 20mm aggregate, minimum cement content 290 kg/m³; vibrated (Cont'd)										
Poured on or against earth or unblinded hardcore (Cont'd)										
In trench filling	106.08	5.00	111.38	-	2.60	40.48	0.82	152.69	m³	167.96
Reinforced in-situ concrete in horizontal work; BS 8500; designed mix C25/30, 20mm aggregate, minimum cement content 290 kg/m³; vibrated										
In blinding	106.08	5.00	111.38	-	2.60	40.48	0.82	152.69	m³	167.96
thickness not exceeding 300mm	106.08	5.00	111.38	-	3.50	54.49	0.82	166.70	m³	183.37
In structures	106.08	5.00	111.38	-	3.60	56.05	0.82	168.26	m³	185.09
thickness not exceeding 300mm	106.08	5.00	111.38	-	3.90	60.72	0.82	172.93	m³	190.23
Poured on or against earth or unblinded hardcore										
In blinding	106.08	5.00	111.38	-	2.60	40.48	0.82	152.69	m³	167.96
thickness not exceeding 300mm	106.08	5.00	111.38	-	3.50	54.49	0.82	166.70	m³	183.37
In structures	106.08	5.00	111.38	-	3.60	56.05	0.82	168.26	m³	185.09
thickness not exceeding 300mm	106.08	5.00	111.38	-	3.90	60.72	0.82	172.93	m³	190.23
Reinforced in-situ concrete in sloping work less than 15o; BS 8500; designed mix C25/30, 20mm aggregate, minimum cement content 290 kg/m³; vibrated										
In blinding	106.08	5.00	111.38	-	2.60	40.48	0.82	152.69	m³	167.96
thickness not exceeding 300mm	106.08	5.00	111.38	-	3.50	54.49	0.82	166.70	m³	183.37
In structures	106.08	5.00	111.38	-	3.60	56.05	0.82	168.26	m³	185.09
thickness not exceeding 300mm	106.08	5.00	111.38	-	3.90	60.72	0.82	172.93	m³	190.23
In staircases	106.08	2.50	108.73	-	3.60	56.05	0.82	165.61	m³	182.17
thickness not exceeding 300mm	106.08	2.50	108.73	-	5.50	85.63	0.82	195.19	m³	214.71
Poured on or against earth or unblinded hardcore										
In blinding	106.08	5.00	111.38	-	2.60	40.48	0.82	152.69	m³	167.96
thickness not exceeding 300mm	106.08	5.00	111.38	-	3.50	54.49	0.82	166.70	m³	183.37
In structures	106.08	5.00	111.38	-	3.60	56.05	0.82	168.26	m³	185.09
thickness not exceeding 300mm	106.08	5.00	111.38	-	3.90	60.72	0.82	172.93	m³	190.23
In staircases	106.08	5.00	111.38	-	3.60	56.05	0.82	168.26	m³	185.09
thickness not exceeding 300mm	106.08	2.50	108.73	-	5.50	85.63	0.82	195.19	m³	214.71
Reinforced in-situ concrete in sloping work greater than 15o; BS 8500; designed mix C25/30, 20mm aggregate, minimum cement content 290 kg/m³; vibrated										
In blinding	106.08	5.00	111.38	-	2.60	40.48	0.82	152.69	m³	167.96
thickness not exceeding 300mm	106.08	5.00	111.38	-	3.50	54.49	0.82	166.70	m³	183.37
In structures	106.08	5.00	111.38	-	3.60	56.05	0.82	168.26	m³	185.09
thickness not exceeding 300mm	106.08	5.00	111.38	-	3.90	60.72	0.82	172.93	m³	190.23
In staircases	106.08	5.00	111.38	-	3.60	56.05	0.82	168.26	m³	185.09
thickness not exceeding 300mm	106.08	2.50	108.73	-	5.50	85.63	0.82	195.19	m³	214.71
Poured on or against earth or unblinded hardcore										
In blinding	106.08	5.00	111.38	-	2.60	40.48	0.82	152.69	m³	167.96
thickness not exceeding 300mm	106.08	5.00	111.38	-	3.50	54.49	0.82	166.70	m³	183.37
In structures	106.08	5.00	111.38	-	3.60	56.05	0.82	168.26	m³	185.09
thickness not exceeding 300mm	106.08	5.00	111.38	-	3.90	60.72	0.82	172.93	m³	190.23
In staircases	106.08	5.00	111.38	-	3.60	56.05	0.82	168.26	m³	185.09
thickness not exceeding 300mm	106.08	2.50	108.73	-	5.50	85.63	0.82	195.19	m³	214.71
Reinforced in-situ concrete in vertical work; BS 8500; designed mix C25/30, 20mm aggregate, minimum cement content 290 kg/m³; vibrated										
In structures	106.08	5.00	111.38	-	3.60	56.05	0.82	168.26	m³	185.09
thickness not exceeding 300mm	106.08	2.50	108.73	-	5.00	77.85	0.82	187.41	m³	206.15
Reinforced sundry in-situ concrete work; BS 8500; designed mix C25/30, 20mm aggregate, minimum cement content 290 kg/m³; vibrated										
Horizontal	106.08	5.00	111.38	-	2.60	40.48	0.82	152.69	m³	167.96
width or thickness not exceeding 300mm	106.08	5.00	111.38	-	3.50	54.49	0.82	166.70	m³	183.37
Sloping	106.08	5.00	111.38	-	2.60	40.48	0.82	152.69	m³	167.96
width or thickness not exceeding 300mm	106.08	5.00	111.38	-	3.50	54.49	0.82	166.70	m³	183.37
Vertical	106.08	5.00	111.38	-	3.60	56.05	0.82	168.26	m³	185.09
width or thickness not exceeding 300mm	106.08	5.00	111.38	-	5.50	85.63	0.82	197.84	m³	217.63
IN-SITU CONCRETE; PLAIN IN-SITU CONCRETE; SITE MIXED										
Plain in-situ mass concrete; mix 1:6, all in aggregate										
In filling voids	144.57	7.50	155.42	-	3.40	52.94	2.97	211.32	m³	232.46
In trench filling	144.57	7.50	155.42	-	3.40	52.94	2.97	211.32	m³	232.46
Poured on or against earth or unblinded hardcore										
In filling voids	144.57	7.50	155.42	-	3.40	52.94	2.97	211.32	m³	232.46
In trench filling	144.57	7.50	155.42	-	3.40	52.94	2.97	211.32	m³	232.46
Plain in-situ concrete in horizontal work; mix 1:6, all in aggregate										
In blinding	144.57	7.50	155.42	-	3.40	52.94	2.97	211.32	m³	232.46
thickness not exceeding 300mm	144.57	7.50	155.42	-	4.45	69.29	2.97	227.67	m³	250.44
In structures	144.57	7.50	155.42	-	4.40	68.51	2.97	226.89	m³	249.58
thickness not exceeding 300mm	144.57	7.50	155.42	-	4.70	73.18	2.97	231.56	m³	254.72
Poured on or against earth or unblinded hardcore										
In blinding	144.57	7.50	155.42	-	3.40	52.94	2.97	211.32	m³	232.46
thickness not exceeding 300mm	144.57	7.50	155.42	-	4.45	69.29	2.97	227.67	m³	250.44
In structures	144.57	7.50	155.42	-	4.40	68.51	2.97	226.89	m³	249.58
thickness not exceeding 300mm	144.57	7.50	155.42	-	4.70	73.18	2.97	231.56	m³	254.72

Labour hourly rates: (except Specialists) Craft Operatives 20.87 Labourer 15.57 Rates are national average prices. Refer to REGIONAL VARIATIONS for indicative levels of overall pricing in regions	MATERIALS			LABOUR				RATES		
	Del to Site £	Waste %	Material Cost £	Craft Optve Hrs	Lab Hrs	Labour Cost £	Sunds £	Nett Rate £	Unit	Gross rate (10%) £
IN-SITU CONCRETE; PLAIN IN-SITU CONCRETE; SITE MIXED (Cont'd)										
Plain in-situ concrete in sloping work less than 15o; mix 1:6, all in aggregate										
In blinding	144.57	7.50	155.42	-	3.40	52.94	2.97	211.32	m³	232.46
thickness not exceeding 300mm	144.57	7.50	155.42	-	4.45	69.29	2.97	227.67	m³	250.44
In structures	144.57	7.50	155.42	-	4.40	68.51	2.97	226.89	m³	249.58
thickness not exceeding 300mm	144.57	7.50	155.42	-	4.70	73.18	2.97	231.56	m³	254.72
Poured on or against earth or unblinded hardcore										
In blinding	144.57	7.50	155.42	-	3.40	52.94	2.97	211.32	m³	232.46
thickness not exceeding 300mm	144.57	7.50	155.42	-	4.45	69.29	2.97	227.67	m³	250.44
In structures	144.57	7.50	155.42	-	4.40	68.51	2.97	226.89	m³	249.58
thickness not exceeding 300mm	144.57	7.50	155.42	-	4.70	73.18	2.97	231.56	m³	254.72
Plain in-situ concrete in sloping work greater than 15o; mix 1:6, all in aggregate										
In blinding	144.57	7.50	155.42	-	3.40	52.94	2.97	211.32	m³	232.46
thickness not exceeding 300mm	144.57	7.50	155.42	-	4.45	69.29	2.97	227.67	m³	250.44
In structures	144.57	7.50	155.42	-	4.40	68.51	2.97	226.89	m³	249.58
thickness not exceeding 300mm	144.57	7.50	155.42	-	4.70	73.18	2.97	231.56	m³	254.72
Poured on or against earth or unblinded hardcore										
In blinding	144.57	7.50	155.42	-	3.40	52.94	2.97	211.32	m³	232.46
thickness not exceeding 300mm	144.57	7.50	155.42	-	4.45	69.29	2.97	227.67	m³	250.44
In structures	636.12	7.50	683.83	-	4.40	68.51	2.97	755.31	m³	830.84
thickness not exceeding 300mm	144.57	7.50	155.42	-	4.70	73.18	2.97	231.56	m³	254.72
Plain in-situ concrete in vertical work; mix 1:6, all in aggregate										
In structures	144.57	7.50	155.42	-	4.40	68.51	2.97	226.89	m³	249.58
thickness not exceeding 300mm	144.57	7.50	155.42	-	6.60	102.76	2.97	261.15	m³	287.26
Plain sundry in-situ concrete work; mix 1:6, all in aggregate										
Horizontal	144.57	7.50	155.42	-	3.40	52.94	2.97	211.32	m³	232.46
width or thickness not exceeding 300mm	144.57	7.50	155.42	-	4.45	69.29	2.97	227.67	m³	250.44
Sloping	144.57	7.50	155.42	-	3.40	52.94	2.97	211.32	m³	232.46
width or thickness not exceeding 300mm	144.57	7.50	155.42	-	4.45	69.29	2.97	227.67	m³	250.44
Plain in-situ mass concrete; mix 1:8, all in aggregate										
In filling voids	136.60	7.50	146.85	-	3.40	52.94	2.97	202.76	m³	223.03
In trench filling	136.60	7.50	146.85	-	3.40	52.94	2.97	202.76	m³	223.03
Poured on or against earth or unblinded hardcore										
In filling voids	136.60	7.50	146.85	-	3.40	52.94	2.97	202.76	m³	223.03
In trench filling	136.60	7.50	146.85	-	3.40	52.94	2.97	202.76	m³	223.03
Plain in-situ concrete in horizontal work; mix 1:8, all in aggregate										
In blinding	136.60	7.50	146.85	-	3.40	52.94	2.97	202.76	m³	223.03
thickness not exceeding 300mm	136.60	7.50	146.85	-	3.40	52.94	2.97	202.76	m³	223.03
In structures	136.60	7.50	146.85	-	4.40	68.51	2.97	218.33	m³	240.16
thickness not exceeding 300mm	136.60	7.50	146.85	-	4.70	73.18	2.97	223.00	m³	245.30
Poured on or against earth or unblinded hardcore										
In blinding	136.60	7.50	146.85	-	3.40	52.94	2.97	202.76	m³	223.03
thickness not exceeding 300mm	136.60	7.50	146.85	-	4.25	66.17	2.97	215.99	m³	237.59
In structures	136.60	7.50	146.85	-	4.40	68.51	2.97	218.33	m³	240.16
thickness not exceeding 300mm	136.60	7.50	146.85	-	4.70	73.18	2.97	223.00	m³	245.30
Plain in-situ concrete in sloping work less than 15o; mix 1:8, all in aggregate										
In blinding	136.60	7.50	146.85	-	3.40	52.94	2.97	202.76	m³	223.03
thickness not exceeding 300mm	136.60	7.50	146.85	-	4.25	66.17	2.97	215.99	m³	237.59
In structures	136.60	7.50	146.85	-	4.40	68.51	2.97	218.33	m³	240.16
thickness not exceeding 300mm	136.60	7.50	146.85	-	4.70	73.18	2.97	223.00	m³	245.30
Poured on or against earth or unblinded hardcore										
In blinding	136.60	7.50	146.85	-	3.40	52.94	2.97	202.76	m³	223.03
thickness not exceeding 300mm	136.60	7.50	146.85	-	4.25	66.17	2.97	215.99	m³	237.59
In structures	136.60	7.50	146.85	-	4.40	68.51	2.97	218.33	m³	240.16
thickness not exceeding 300mm	136.60	7.50	146.85	-	4.70	73.18	2.97	223.00	m³	245.30
Plain in-situ concrete in sloping work greater than 15o; mix 1:8, all in aggregate										
In blinding	136.60	7.50	146.85	-	3.40	52.94	2.97	202.76	m³	223.03
thickness not exceeding 300mm	136.60	7.50	146.85	-	4.25	66.17	2.97	215.99	m³	237.59
In structures	136.60	7.50	146.85	-	4.40	68.51	2.97	218.33	m³	240.16
thickness not exceeding 300mm	136.60	7.50	146.85	-	4.70	73.18	2.97	223.00	m³	245.30
Poured on or against earth or unblinded hardcore										
In blinding	136.60	7.50	146.85	-	3.40	52.94	2.97	202.76	m³	223.03
thickness not exceeding 300mm	136.60	7.50	146.85	-	4.25	66.17	2.97	215.99	m³	237.59
In structures	136.60	7.50	146.85	-	4.40	68.51	2.97	218.33	m³	240.16
thickness not exceeding 300mm	136.60	7.50	146.85	-	4.70	73.18	2.97	223.00	m³	245.30
Plain in-situ concrete in vertical work; mix 1:8, all in aggregate										
In structures	136.60	7.50	146.85	-	4.40	68.51	2.97	218.33	m³	240.16
thickness not exceeding 300mm	136.60	7.50	146.85	-	6.60	102.76	2.97	252.58	m³	277.84
Plain sundry in-situ concrete work; mix 1:8, all in aggregate										
Horizontal	136.60	7.50	146.85	-	3.40	52.94	2.97	202.76	m³	223.03
width or thickness not exceeding 300mm	136.60	7.50	146.85	-	4.25	66.17	2.97	215.99	m³	237.59
Sloping	136.60	7.50	146.85	-	3.40	52.94	2.97	202.76	m³	223.03
width or thickness not exceeding 300mm	136.60	7.50	146.85	-	4.25	66.17	2.97	215.99	m³	237.59
Plain in-situ mass concrete; mix 1:12, all in aggregate										
In filling voids	131.67	7.50	141.55	-	3.40	52.94	2.97	197.46	m³	217.20

Labour hourly rates: (except Specialists) Craft Operatives 20.87 Labourer 15.57 Rates are national average prices. Refer to REGIONAL VARIATIONS for indicative levels of overall pricing in regions	MATERIALS			LABOUR				RATES		
	Del to Site £	Waste %	Material Cost £	Craft Optve Hrs	Lab Hrs	Labour Cost £	Sunds £	Nett Rate £	Unit	Gross rate (10%) £
IN-SITU CONCRETE; PLAIN IN-SITU CONCRETE; SITE MIXED (Cont'd)										
Plain in-situ mass concrete; mix 1:12, all in aggregate (Cont'd)										
In trench filling	131.67	7.50	141.55	-	3.40	52.94	2.97	197.46	m³	217.20
Poured on or against earth or unblinded hardcore										
In filling voids	131.67	7.50	141.55	-	3.40	52.94	2.97	197.46	m³	217.20
In trench filling	131.67	7.50	141.55	-	3.40	52.94	2.97	197.46	m³	217.20
Plain in-situ concrete in horizontal work; mix 1:12, all in aggregate										
In blinding	131.67	7.50	141.55	-	3.40	52.94	2.97	197.46	m³	217.20
thickness not exceeding 300mm	131.67	7.50	141.55	-	4.25	66.17	2.97	210.69	m³	231.76
In structures	131.67	7.50	141.55	-	4.40	68.51	2.97	213.03	m³	234.33
thickness not exceeding 300mm	131.67	7.50	141.55	-	4.70	73.18	2.97	217.70	m³	239.47
Poured on or against earth or unblinded hardcore										
In blinding	131.67	7.50	141.55	-	3.40	52.94	2.97	197.46	m³	217.20
thickness not exceeding 300mm	131.67	7.50	141.55	-	4.25	66.17	2.97	210.69	m³	231.76
In structures	131.67	7.50	141.55	-	4.40	68.51	2.97	213.03	m³	234.33
thickness not exceeding 300mm	131.67	7.50	141.55	-	4.70	73.18	2.97	217.70	m³	239.47
Plain in-situ concrete in sloping work less than 15o; mix 1:12, all in aggregate										
In blinding	131.67	7.50	141.55	-	3.40	52.94	2.97	197.46	m³	217.20
thickness not exceeding 300mm	131.67	7.50	141.55	-	4.25	66.17	2.97	210.69	m³	231.76
In structures	131.67	7.50	141.55	-	4.40	68.51	2.97	213.03	m³	234.33
thickness not exceeding 300mm	131.67	7.50	141.55	-	4.70	73.18	2.97	217.70	m³	239.47
Poured on or against earth or unblinded hardcore										
In blinding	131.67	7.50	141.55	-	3.40	52.94	2.97	197.46	m³	217.20
thickness not exceeding 300mm	131.67	7.50	141.55	-	4.25	66.17	2.97	210.69	m³	231.76
In structures	131.67	7.50	141.55	-	4.40	68.51	2.97	213.03	m³	234.33
thickness not exceeding 300mm	131.67	7.50	141.55	-	4.70	73.18	2.97	217.70	m³	239.47
Plain in-situ concrete in sloping work greater than 15o; mix 1:12, all in aggregate										
In blinding	131.67	7.50	141.55	-	3.40	52.94	2.97	197.46	m³	217.20
thickness not exceeding 300mm	131.67	7.50	141.55	-	4.25	66.17	2.97	210.69	m³	231.76
In structures	131.67	7.50	141.55	-	4.40	68.51	2.97	213.03	m³	234.33
thickness not exceeding 300mm	131.67	7.50	141.55	-	4.70	73.18	2.97	217.70	m³	239.47
Poured on or against earth or unblinded hardcore										
In blinding	131.67	7.50	141.55	-	3.40	52.94	2.97	197.46	m³	217.20
thickness not exceeding 300mm	131.67	7.50	141.55	-	4.25	66.17	2.97	210.69	m³	231.76
In structures	131.67	7.50	141.55	-	4.40	68.51	2.97	213.03	m³	234.33
thickness not exceeding 300mm	131.67	7.50	141.55	-	4.70	73.18	2.97	217.70	m³	239.47
Plain in-situ concrete in vertical work; mix 1:12, all in aggregate										
In structures	131.67	7.50	141.55	-	4.40	68.51	2.97	213.03	m³	234.33
thickness not exceeding 300mm	131.67	7.50	141.55	-	6.60	102.76	2.97	247.28	m³	272.01
Plain sundry in-situ concrete work; mix 1:12, all in aggregate										
Horizontal	131.67	7.50	141.55	-	3.40	52.94	2.97	197.46	m³	217.20
width or thickness not exceeding 300mm	131.67	7.50	141.55	-	4.25	66.17	2.97	210.69	m³	231.76
Sloping	131.67	7.50	141.55	-	3.40	52.94	2.97	197.46	m³	217.20
width or thickness not exceeding 300mm	131.67	7.50	141.55	-	4.25	66.17	2.97	210.69	m³	231.76
Plain in-situ mass concrete; BS 8500; ordinary prescribed mix C15P, 20mm aggregate										
In filling voids	141.64	7.50	152.27	-	3.40	52.94	2.97	208.17	m³	228.99
In trench filling	141.64	7.50	152.27	-	3.40	52.94	2.97	208.17	m³	228.99
Poured on or against earth or unblinded hardcore										
In filling voids	141.64	7.50	152.27	-	3.40	52.94	2.97	208.17	m³	228.99
In trench filling	141.64	7.50	152.27	-	3.40	52.94	2.97	208.17	m³	228.99
Plain in-situ concrete in horizontal work; BS 8500; ordinary prescribed mix C15P, 20mm aggregate										
In blinding	141.64	7.50	152.27	-	3.40	52.94	2.97	208.17	m³	228.99
thickness not exceeding 300mm	141.64	7.50	152.27	-	3.40	52.94	2.97	208.17	m³	228.99
In structures	141.64	7.50	152.27	-	4.40	68.51	2.97	223.74	m³	246.12
thickness not exceeding 300mm	141.64	7.50	152.27	-	4.70	73.18	2.97	228.42	m³	251.26
Poured on or against earth or unblinded hardcore										
In blinding	141.64	7.50	152.27	-	3.40	52.94	2.97	208.17	m³	228.99
thickness not exceeding 300mm	141.64	7.50	152.27	-	4.25	66.17	2.97	221.41	m³	243.55
In structures	141.64	7.50	152.27	-	4.40	68.51	2.97	223.74	m³	246.12
thickness not exceeding 300mm	141.64	7.50	152.27	-	4.70	73.18	2.97	228.42	m³	251.26
Plain in-situ concrete in sloping work less than 15o; BS 8500; ordinary prescribed mix C15P, 20mm aggregate										
In blinding	141.64	7.50	152.27	-	3.40	52.94	2.97	208.17	m³	228.99
thickness not exceeding 300mm	141.64	7.50	152.27	-	4.25	66.17	2.97	221.41	m³	243.55
In structures	141.64	7.50	152.27	-	4.40	68.51	2.97	223.74	m³	246.12
thickness not exceeding 300mm	141.64	7.50	152.27	-	4.70	73.18	2.97	228.42	m³	251.26
Poured on or against earth or unblinded hardcore										
In blinding	141.64	7.50	152.27	-	3.40	52.94	2.97	208.17	m³	228.99
thickness not exceeding 300mm	141.64	7.50	152.27	-	4.25	66.17	2.97	221.41	m³	243.55
In structures	141.64	7.50	152.27	-	4.40	68.51	2.97	223.74	m³	246.12
thickness not exceeding 300mm	141.64	7.50	152.27	-	4.70	73.18	2.97	228.42	m³	251.26
Plain in-situ concrete in sloping work greater than 15o; BS 8500; ordinary prescribed mix C15P, 20mm aggregate										
In blinding	141.64	7.50	152.27	-	3.40	52.94	2.97	208.17	m³	228.99

Labour hourly rates: (except Specialists) Craft Operatives 20.87 Labourer 15.57 Rates are national average prices. Refer to REGIONAL VARIATIONS for indicative levels of overall pricing in regions	MATERIALS			LABOUR				RATES		
	Del to Site £	Waste %	Material Cost £	Craft Optve Hrs	Lab Hrs	Labour Cost £	Sunds £	Nett Rate £	Unit	Gross rate (10%) £
IN-SITU CONCRETE; PLAIN IN-SITU CONCRETE; SITE MIXED (Cont'd)										
Plain in-situ concrete in sloping work greater than 15o; BS 8500; ordinary prescribed mix C15P, 20mm aggregate (Cont'd)										
thickness not exceeding 300mm	141.64	7.50	152.27	-	4.25	66.17	2.97	221.41	m³	243.55
In structures	141.64	7.50	152.27	-	4.40	68.51	2.97	223.74	m³	246.12
thickness not exceeding 300mm	141.64	7.50	152.27	-	4.70	73.18	2.97	228.42	m³	251.26
Poured on or against earth or unblinded hardcore										
In blinding	141.64	7.50	152.27	-	3.40	52.94	2.97	208.17	m³	228.99
thickness not exceeding 300mm	141.64	7.50	152.27	-	4.25	66.17	2.97	221.41	m³	243.55
In structures	141.64	7.50	152.27	-	4.40	68.51	2.97	223.74	m³	246.12
thickness not exceeding 300mm	141.64	7.50	152.27	-	4.70	73.18	2.97	228.42	m³	251.26
Plain in-situ concrete in vertical work; BS 8500; ordinary prescribed mix C15P, 20mm aggregate										
In structures	141.64	7.50	152.27	-	4.40	68.51	2.97	223.74	m³	246.12
thickness not exceeding 300mm	141.64	7.50	152.27	-	6.60	102.76	2.97	258.00	m³	283.80
Plain sundry in-situ concrete work; BS 8500; ordinary prescribed mix C15P, 20mm aggregate										
Horizontal	141.64	7.50	152.27	-	3.40	52.94	2.97	208.17	m³	228.99
width or thickness not exceeding 300mm	141.64	7.50	152.27	-	4.25	66.17	2.97	221.41	m³	243.55
Sloping	141.64	7.50	152.27	-	3.40	52.94	2.97	208.17	m³	228.99
width or thickness not exceeding 300mm	141.64	7.50	152.27	-	4.25	66.17	2.97	221.41	m³	243.55
Plain in-situ mass concrete; BS 8500; ordinary prescribed mix C20P, 20mm aggregate										
In filling voids	142.96	7.50	153.68	-	3.40	52.94	2.97	209.59	m³	230.55
In trench filling	142.96	7.50	153.68	-	3.40	52.94	2.97	209.59	m³	230.55
Poured on or against earth or unblinded hardcore										
In filling voids	142.96	7.50	153.68	-	3.40	52.94	2.97	209.59	m³	230.55
In trench filling	142.96	7.50	153.68	-	3.40	52.94	2.97	209.59	m³	230.55
Plain in-situ concrete in horizontal work; BS 8500; ordinary prescribed mix C20P, 20mm aggregate										
In blinding	142.96	7.50	153.68	-	3.40	52.94	2.97	209.59	m³	230.55
thickness not exceeding 300mm	142.96	7.50	153.68	-	4.25	66.17	2.97	222.82	m³	245.11
In structures	142.96	7.50	153.68	-	4.40	68.51	2.97	225.16	m³	247.68
thickness not exceeding 300mm	142.96	7.50	153.68	-	4.70	73.18	2.97	229.83	m³	252.81
Poured on or against earth or unblinded hardcore										
In blinding	142.96	7.50	153.68	-	3.40	52.94	2.97	209.59	m³	230.55
thickness not exceeding 300mm	142.96	7.50	153.68	-	4.25	66.17	2.97	222.82	m³	245.11
In structures	142.96	7.50	153.68	-	4.40	68.51	2.97	225.16	m³	247.68
thickness not exceeding 300mm	142.96	7.50	153.68	-	4.70	73.18	2.97	229.83	m³	252.81
Plain in-situ concrete in sloping work less than 15o; BS 8500; ordinary prescribed mix C20P, 20mm aggregate										
In blinding	142.96	7.50	153.68	-	3.40	52.94	2.97	209.59	m³	230.55
thickness not exceeding 300mm	142.96	7.50	153.68	-	4.25	66.17	2.97	222.82	m³	245.11
In structures	142.96	7.50	153.68	-	4.40	68.51	2.97	225.16	m³	247.68
thickness not exceeding 300mm	142.96	7.50	153.68	-	4.70	73.18	2.97	229.83	m³	252.81
Poured on or against earth or unblinded hardcore										
In blinding	142.96	7.50	153.68	-	3.40	52.94	2.97	209.59	m³	230.55
thickness not exceeding 300mm	142.96	7.50	153.68	-	4.25	66.17	2.97	222.82	m³	245.11
In structures	142.96	7.50	153.68	-	4.40	68.51	2.97	225.16	m³	247.68
thickness not exceeding 300mm	142.96	7.50	153.68	-	4.70	73.18	2.97	229.83	m³	252.81
Plain in-situ concrete in sloping work greater than 15o; BS 8500; ordinary prescribed mix C20P, 20mm aggregate										
In blinding	142.96	7.50	153.68	-	3.40	52.94	2.97	209.59	m³	230.55
thickness not exceeding 300mm	142.96	7.50	153.68	-	4.25	66.17	2.97	222.82	m³	245.11
In structures	142.96	7.50	153.68	-	4.40	68.51	2.97	225.16	m³	247.68
thickness not exceeding 300mm	142.96	7.50	153.68	-	4.70	73.18	2.97	229.83	m³	252.81
Poured on or against earth or unblinded hardcore										
In blinding	142.96	7.50	153.68	-	3.40	52.94	2.97	209.59	m³	230.55
thickness not exceeding 300mm	142.96	7.50	153.68	-	4.25	66.17	2.97	222.82	m³	245.11
In structures	142.96	7.50	153.68	-	4.40	68.51	2.97	225.16	m³	247.68
thickness not exceeding 300mm	142.96	7.50	153.68	-	4.70	73.18	2.97	229.83	m³	252.81
Plain in-situ concrete in vertical work; BS 8500; ordinary prescribed mix C20P, 20mm aggregate										
In structures	142.96	7.50	153.68	-	4.40	68.51	2.97	225.16	m³	247.68
thickness not exceeding 300mm	142.96	7.50	153.68	-	6.60	102.76	2.97	259.41	m³	285.36
Plain sundry in-situ concrete work; BS 8500; ordinary prescribed mix C20P, 20mm aggregate										
Horizontal	142.96	7.50	153.68	-	3.40	52.94	2.97	209.59	m³	230.55
width or thickness not exceeding 300mm	142.96	7.50	153.68	-	4.25	66.17	2.97	222.82	m³	245.11
Sloping	142.96	7.50	153.68	-	3.40	52.94	2.97	209.59	m³	230.55
width or thickness not exceeding 300mm	142.96	7.50	153.68	-	4.25	66.17	2.97	222.82	m³	245.11
Plain in-situ mass concrete; BS 8500; ordinary prescribed mix C25P, 20mm aggregate										
In filling voids	151.34	7.50	162.69	-	3.40	52.94	2.97	218.60	m³	240.46
In trench filling	151.34	7.50	162.69	-	3.40	52.94	2.97	218.60	m³	240.46
Poured on or against earth or unblinded hardcore										
In filling voids	151.34	7.50	162.69	-	3.40	52.94	2.97	218.60	m³	240.46
In trench filling	151.34	7.50	162.69	-	3.40	52.94	2.97	218.60	m³	240.46

Labour hourly rates: (except Specialists) Craft Operatives 20.87 Labourer 15.57 Rates are national average prices. Refer to REGIONAL VARIATIONS for indicative levels of overall pricing in regions	MATERIALS			LABOUR				RATES		
	Del to Site £	Waste %	Material Cost £	Craft Optve Hrs	Lab Hrs	Labour Cost £	Sunds £	Nett Rate £	Unit	Gross rate (10%) £
IN-SITU CONCRETE; PLAIN IN-SITU CONCRETE; SITE MIXED (Cont'd)										
Plain in-situ concrete in horizontal work; BS 8500; ordinary prescribed mix C25P, 20mm aggregate										
In blinding	151.34	7.50	162.69	-	3.40	52.94	2.97	218.60	m³	240.46
thickness not exceeding 300mm	151.34	7.50	162.69	-	4.25	66.17	2.97	231.84	m³	255.02
In structures	151.34	7.50	162.69	-	4.40	68.51	2.97	234.17	m³	257.59
thickness not exceeding 300mm	151.34	7.50	162.69	-	4.70	73.18	2.97	238.84	m³	262.73
Poured on or against earth or unblinded hardcore										
In blinding	151.34	7.50	162.69	-	3.40	52.94	2.97	218.60	m³	240.46
thickness not exceeding 300mm	151.34	7.50	162.69	-	4.25	66.17	2.97	231.84	m³	255.02
In structures	151.34	7.50	162.69	-	4.40	68.51	2.97	234.17	m³	257.59
thickness not exceeding 300mm	151.34	7.50	162.69	-	4.70	73.18	2.97	238.84	m³	262.73
Plain in-situ concrete in sloping work less than 15o; BS 8500; ordinary prescribed mix C25P, 20mm aggregate										
In blinding	151.34	7.50	162.69	-	3.40	52.94	2.97	218.60	m³	240.46
thickness not exceeding 300mm	151.34	7.50	162.69	-	4.25	66.17	2.97	231.84	m³	255.02
In structures	151.34	7.50	162.69	-	4.40	68.51	2.97	234.17	m³	257.59
thickness not exceeding 300mm	151.34	7.50	162.69	-	4.70	73.18	2.97	238.84	m³	262.73
Poured on or against earth or unblinded hardcore										
In blinding	151.34	7.50	162.69	-	3.40	52.94	2.97	218.60	m³	240.46
thickness not exceeding 300mm	151.34	7.50	162.69	-	4.25	66.17	2.97	231.84	m³	255.02
In structures	151.34	7.50	162.69	-	4.40	68.51	2.97	234.17	m³	257.59
thickness not exceeding 300mm	151.34	7.50	162.69	-	4.70	73.18	2.97	238.84	m³	262.73
Plain in-situ concrete in sloping work greater than 15o; BS 8500; ordinary prescribed mix C25P, 20mm aggregate										
In blinding	151.34	7.50	162.69	-	3.40	52.94	2.97	218.60	m³	240.46
thickness not exceeding 300mm	151.34	7.50	162.69	-	4.25	66.17	2.97	231.84	m³	255.02
In structures	151.34	7.50	162.69	-	4.40	68.51	2.97	234.17	m³	257.59
thickness not exceeding 300mm	151.34	7.50	162.69	-	4.70	73.18	2.97	238.84	m³	262.73
Poured on or against earth or unblinded hardcore										
In blinding	151.34	7.50	162.69	-	3.40	52.94	2.97	218.60	m³	240.46
thickness not exceeding 300mm	151.34	7.50	162.69	-	4.25	66.17	2.97	231.84	m³	255.02
In structures	151.34	7.50	162.69	-	4.40	68.51	2.97	234.17	m³	257.59
thickness not exceeding 300mm	151.34	7.50	162.69	-	4.70	73.18	2.97	238.84	m³	262.73
Plain in-situ concrete in vertical work; BS 8500; ordinary prescribed mix C25P, 20mm aggregate										
In structures	151.34	7.50	162.69	-	4.40	68.51	2.97	234.17	m³	257.59
thickness not exceeding 300mm	151.34	7.50	162.69	-	6.60	102.76	2.97	268.43	m³	295.27
Plain sundry in-situ concrete work; BS 8500; ordinary prescribed mix C25P, 20mm aggregate										
Horizontal	151.34	7.50	162.69	-	3.40	52.94	2.97	218.60	m³	240.46
width or thickness not exceeding 300mm	151.34	7.50	162.69	-	4.25	66.17	2.97	231.84	m³	255.02
Sloping	151.34	7.50	162.69	-	3.40	52.94	2.97	218.60	m³	240.46
width or thickness not exceeding 300mm	151.34	7.50	162.69	-	4.25	66.17	2.97	231.84	m³	255.02
IN-SITU CONCRETE; REINFORCED IN-SITU CONCRETE; SITE MIXED										
The foregoing concrete is based on the use of Portland cement. For other cements and waterproofers ADD as follows										
Concrete 1:6										
rapid hardening cement	79.48	-	79.48	-	-	-	-	79.48	m³	87.42
sulphate resisting cement	15.35	-	15.35	-	-	-	-	15.35	m³	16.89
waterproofing liquid	5.17	-	5.17	-	-	-	-	5.17	m³	5.68
Concrete 1:8										
rapid hardening cement	63.17	-	63.17	-	-	-	-	63.17	m³	69.49
sulphate resisting cement	12.20	-	12.20	-	-	-	-	12.20	m³	13.42
waterproofing liquid	4.11	-	4.11	-	-	-	-	4.11	m³	4.52
Concrete 1:12										
rapid hardening cement	43.81	-	43.81	-	-	-	-	43.81	m³	48.20
sulphate resisting cement	8.46	-	8.46	-	-	-	-	8.46	m³	9.31
waterproofing liquid	2.85	-	2.85	-	-	-	-	2.85	m³	3.13
Concrete ST3 and C15										
rapid hardening cement	71.33	-	71.33	-	-	-	-	71.33	m³	78.46
sulphate resisting cement	13.78	-	13.78	-	-	-	-	13.78	m³	15.15
waterproofing liquid	4.64	-	4.64	-	-	-	-	4.64	m³	5.10
Concrete ST4 and C20										
rapid hardening cement	81.51	-	81.51	-	-	-	-	81.51	m³	89.67
sulphate resisting cement	15.74	-	15.74	-	-	-	-	15.74	m³	17.32
waterproofing liquid	5.30	-	5.30	-	-	-	-	5.30	m³	5.83
Concrete ST5 and C25										
rapid hardening cement	91.70	-	91.70	-	-	-	-	91.70	m³	100.87
sulphate resisting cement	17.71	-	17.71	-	-	-	-	17.71	m³	19.48
waterproofing liquid	5.96	-	5.96	-	-	-	-	5.96	m³	6.56
Reinforced in-situ lightweight concrete in horizontal work; 20.5 N/mm²; vibrated										
In structures	149.06	2.50	152.78	-	4.40	68.51	3.79	225.09	m³	247.60
thickness not exceeding 300mm	149.06	2.50	152.78	-	5.60	87.19	3.79	243.77	m³	268.15
Reinforced in-situ lightweight concrete in sloping work less than 15o; 20.5 N/mm²; vibrated										
In structures	149.06	2.50	152.78	-	4.40	68.51	3.79	225.09	m³	247.60
thickness not exceeding 300mm	149.06	2.50	152.78	-	5.60	87.19	3.79	243.77	m³	268.15

Labour hourly rates: (except Specialists) Craft Operatives 20.87 Labourer 15.57 Rates are national average prices. Refer to REGIONAL VARIATIONS for indicative levels of overall pricing in regions	MATERIALS			LABOUR				RATES		
	Del to Site £	Waste %	Material Cost £	Craft Optve Hrs	Lab Hrs	Labour Cost £	Sunds £	Nett Rate £	Unit	Gross rate (10%) £
IN-SITU CONCRETE; REINFORCED IN-SITU CONCRETE; SITE MIXED (Cont'd)										
Reinforced in-situ lightweight concrete in sloping work greater than 15o; 20.5 N/mm²; vibrated										
In structures	149.06	2.50	152.78	-	4.40	68.51	3.79	225.09	m³	247.60
thickness not exceeding 300mm	149.06	2.50	152.78	-	5.60	87.19	3.79	243.77	m³	268.15
Reinforced in-situ lightweight concrete in vertical work; 20.5 N/mm²; vibrated										
In structures	149.06	2.50	152.78	-	4.85	75.51	3.79	232.09	m³	255.30
thickness not exceeding 300mm	149.06	2.50	152.78	-	5.60	87.19	3.79	243.77	m³	268.15
Reinforced sundry in-situ lightweight concrete work; 20.5 N/mm²; vibrated										
Horizontal	149.06	2.50	152.78	-	4.40	68.51	3.79	225.09	m³	247.60
width or thickness not exceeding 300mm	149.06	2.50	152.78	-	5.60	87.19	3.79	243.77	m³	268.15
Sloping	149.06	2.50	152.78	-	4.40	68.51	3.79	225.09	m³	247.60
width or thickness not exceeding 300mm	149.06	2.50	152.78	-	5.60	87.19	3.79	243.77	m³	268.15
Reinforced in-situ lightweight concrete; 26.0 N/mm²; vibrated										
In structures	153.83	2.50	157.67	-	4.40	68.51	3.79	229.98	m³	252.97
thickness not exceeding 300mm	153.83	2.50	157.67	-	5.60	87.19	3.79	248.66	m³	273.53
Reinforced in-situ lightweight concrete in sloping work less than 15o; 26.0 N/mm²; vibrated										
In structures	153.83	2.50	157.67	-	4.40	68.51	3.79	229.98	m³	252.97
thickness not exceeding 300mm	153.83	2.50	157.67	-	5.60	87.19	3.79	248.66	m³	273.53
Reinforced in-situ lightweight concrete in sloping work greater than 15o; 26.0 N/mm²; vibrated										
In structures	153.83	2.50	157.67	-	4.40	68.51	3.79	229.98	m³	252.97
thickness not exceeding 300mm	153.83	2.50	157.67	-	5.60	87.19	3.79	248.66	m³	273.53
Reinforced in-situ lightweight concrete in vertical work; 26.0 N/mm²; vibrated										
In structures	153.83	2.50	157.67	-	4.85	75.51	3.79	236.98	m³	260.68
thickness not exceeding 300mm	153.83	2.50	157.67	-	5.60	87.19	3.79	248.66	m³	273.53
Reinforced sundry in-situ lightweight concrete work; 26.0 N/mm²; vibrated										
Horizontal	153.83	2.50	157.67	-	4.40	68.51	3.79	229.98	m³	252.97
width or thickness not exceeding 300mm	153.83	2.50	157.67	-	5.60	87.19	3.79	248.66	m³	273.53
Sloping	153.83	2.50	157.67	-	4.40	68.51	3.79	229.98	m³	252.97
width or thickness not exceeding 300mm	153.83	2.50	157.67	-	5.60	87.19	3.79	248.66	m³	273.53
Reinforced in-situ lightweight concrete; 41.5 N/mm²; vibrated										
In structures	153.83	2.50	157.67	-	4.40	68.51	3.79	229.98	m³	252.97
thickness not exceeding 300mm	153.83	2.50	157.67	-	5.60	87.19	3.79	248.66	m³	273.53
Reinforced in-situ lightweight concrete in sloping work less than 15o; 41.5 N/mm²; vibrated										
In structures	157.08	2.50	161.01	-	4.40	68.51	3.79	233.31	m³	256.65
thickness not exceeding 300mm	157.08	2.50	161.01	-	5.60	87.19	3.79	252.00	m³	277.20
Reinforced in-situ lightweight concrete in sloping work greater than 15o; 41.5 N/mm²; vibrated										
In structures	157.08	2.50	161.01	-	4.40	68.51	3.79	233.31	m³	256.65
thickness not exceeding 300mm	157.08	2.50	161.01	-	5.60	87.19	3.79	252.00	m³	277.20
Reinforced in-situ lightweight concrete in vertical work; 41.5 N/mm²; vibrated										
In structures	157.08	2.50	161.01	-	4.85	75.51	3.79	240.32	m³	264.35
thickness not exceeding 300mm	157.08	2.50	161.01	-	5.60	87.19	3.79	252.00	m³	277.20
Reinforced sundry in-situ lightweight concrete work; 41.5 N/mm²; vibrated										
Horizontal	157.08	2.50	161.01	-	4.40	68.51	3.79	233.31	m³	256.65
width or thickness not exceeding 300mm	157.08	2.50	161.01	-	5.60	87.19	3.79	252.00	m³	277.20
Sloping	157.08	2.50	161.01	-	4.40	68.51	3.79	233.31	m³	256.65
width or thickness not exceeding 300mm	157.08	2.50	161.01	-	5.60	87.19	3.79	252.00	m³	277.20
SURFACE FINISHES TO INSITU CONCRETE										
Trowelling										
Trowelling										
to top surfaces	-	-	-	-	0.36	5.61	-	5.61	m²	6.17
to top surfaces to falls	-	-	-	-	0.39	6.07	-	6.07	m²	6.68
Power floating										
Vacuum dewatering; power floating and power trowelling										
to top surfaces	-	-	-	-	0.22	3.43	0.36	3.79	m²	4.17
Hacking										
Hacking; by hand										
to top surfaces	-	-	-	-	0.55	8.56	-	8.56	m²	9.42
to faces	-	-	-	-	0.60	9.34	-	9.34	m²	10.28
to soffits	-	-	-	-	0.72	11.21	-	11.21	m²	12.33
Hacking; by machine										
to top surfaces	-	-	-	-	0.22	3.43	0.38	3.80	m²	4.19
to faces	-	-	-	-	0.24	3.74	0.38	4.12	m²	4.53
to soffits	-	-	-	-	0.28	4.36	0.38	4.74	m²	5.21

Labour hourly rates: (except Specialists) Craft Operatives 20.87 Labourer 15.57 Rates are national average prices. Refer to REGIONAL VARIATIONS for indicative levels of overall pricing in regions	MATERIALS			LABOUR				RATES		
	Del to Site £	Waste %	Material Cost £	Craft Optve Hrs	Lab Hrs	Labour Cost £	Sunds £	Nett Rate £	Unit	Gross rate (10%) £
SURFACE FINISHES TO INSITU CONCRETE (Cont'd)										
Other surface treatments										
Tamping unset concrete										
to top surfaces	-	-	-	-	0.22	3.43	0.48	3.90	m²	4.29
to top surfaces to falls	-	-	-	-	0.45	7.01	0.63	7.63	m²	8.40
Bush hammering										
to top surfaces	-	-	-	1.43	-	29.84	1.07	30.92	m²	34.01
to faces	-	-	-	1.60	-	33.39	1.24	34.63	m²	38.09
to soffits	-	-	-	2.20	-	45.91	1.42	47.33	m²	52.07
Polythene sheeting laying as temporary protection to surface of concrete (use and waste)										
125mu	0.41	20.00	0.49	-	0.03	0.47	-	0.96	m²	1.05
FORMWORK										
Plain formwork; Sides of foundations and bases										
plain vertical										
height not exceeding 250mm	1.60	12.50	1.80	0.53	0.11	12.77	0.36	14.94	m	16.43
height 250 - 500mm	2.82	12.50	3.17	0.96	0.19	22.99	0.68	26.84	m	29.52
height exceeding 500mm	5.15	12.50	5.79	1.75	0.35	41.97	1.17	48.93	m²	53.83
plain vertical; left in										
height not exceeding 250mm	7.12	-	7.12	0.30	0.06	7.20	0.25	14.56	m	16.02
height 250 - 500mm	13.15	-	13.15	0.55	0.11	13.19	0.40	26.74	m	29.41
height exceeding 500mm	23.88	-	23.88	1.00	0.20	23.98	0.71	48.58	m²	53.43
Plain formwork; Edges of horizontal work										
plain vertical										
height not exceeding 250mm	1.60	12.50	1.80	0.53	0.11	12.77	0.36	14.94	m	16.43
height 250 - 500mm	2.81	12.50	3.17	0.96	0.19	22.99	0.68	26.84	m	29.52
height exceeding 500mm	5.15	12.50	5.79	1.75	0.35	41.97	1.17	48.93	m²	53.83
plain vertical; curved 10m radius										
height not exceeding 250mm	2.90	12.50	3.26	1.00	0.20	23.98	0.71	27.95	m	30.75
plain vertical; curved 1m radius										
height not exceeding 250mm	4.90	12.50	5.51	1.65	0.33	39.57	1.12	46.21	m	50.83
plain vertical; curved 20m radius										
height not exceeding 250mm	2.18	12.50	2.45	0.74	0.15	17.78	0.46	20.69	m	22.76
plain vertical; left in										
height not exceeding 250mm	7.12	-	7.12	0.30	0.06	7.20	0.25	14.56	m	16.02
height 250 - 500mm	13.15	-	13.15	0.55	0.11	13.19	0.40	26.74	m	29.41
height exceeding 500mm	23.88	-	23.88	1.00	0.20	23.98	0.68	48.54	m²	53.40
Plain formwork; Soffits of horizontal work										
horizontal										
concrete thickness not exceeding 300mm; height to soffit										
not exceeding 3.00m	15.58	10.00	17.13	1.65	0.33	39.57	1.85	58.56	m²	64.41
3.00 - 4.50m	15.58	10.00	17.13	1.87	0.38	44.94	2.43	64.50	m²	70.95
4.50 - 6.00m	15.58	10.00	17.13	2.09	0.43	50.31	2.97	70.42	m²	77.46
concrete thickness 300 - 450mm; height to soffit										
not exceeding 3.00m	19.19	10.00	21.11	1.82	0.38	43.90	2.03	67.04	m²	73.75
3.00 - 4.50m	19.19	10.00	21.11	2.06	0.42	49.53	2.67	73.32	m²	80.65
4.50 - 6.00m	19.19	10.00	21.11	2.30	0.47	55.32	3.30	79.73	m²	87.70
Soffits of landings; horizontal										
concrete thickness not exceeding 300mm; height to soffit										
not exceeding 1.50m	17.13	10.00	18.84	1.98	0.40	47.55	1.81	68.21	m²	75.03
1.50 - 3.00m	17.13	10.00	18.84	2.22	0.45	53.34	2.49	74.67	m²	82.14
3.00 - 4.50m	17.13	10.00	18.84	2.46	0.51	59.28	3.10	81.23	m²	89.35
Soffits of landings; horizontal; left in										
concrete thickness not exceeding 300mm; height to soffit										
not exceeding 3.00m	47.23	-	47.23	1.10	0.22	26.38	1.32	74.93	m²	82.43
3.00 - 4.50m	51.95	-	51.95	1.21	0.24	28.99	1.49	82.43	m²	90.67
Soffits of landings; horizontal; with frequent uses of prefabricated panels										
concrete thickness not exceeding 300mm; height to soffit										
not exceeding 3.00m	4.62	15.00	5.32	1.65	0.33	39.57	1.80	46.69	m²	51.36
3.00 - 4.50m	4.62	15.00	5.32	1.87	0.38	44.94	2.43	52.68	m²	57.95
4.50 - 6.00m	4.62	15.00	5.32	2.09	0.43	50.31	2.97	58.60	m²	64.46
concrete thickness 300 - 450mm; height to soffit										
not exceeding 3.00m	5.57	15.00	6.41	1.82	0.36	43.59	1.98	51.97	m²	57.17
3.00 - 4.50m	5.57	15.00	6.41	2.06	0.42	49.53	2.67	58.61	m²	64.47
4.50 - 6.00m	5.57	15.00	6.41	3.00	0.47	69.93	3.30	79.63	m²	87.60
Plain formwork; Sides and soffits of isolated beams										
rectangular; height to soffit										
1.50 - 3.00m	11.41	10.00	12.55	2.35	0.47	56.36	1.45	70.37	m²	77.40
3.00 - 4.50m	11.41	10.00	12.55	2.35	0.47	56.36	1.77	70.68	m²	77.75
Plain formwork; Sides and soffits of attached beams										
rectangular; height to soffit										
not exceeding 3.00m	10.88	10.00	11.97	2.25	0.45	53.96	1.45	67.39	m²	74.13
3.00 - 4.50m	10.88	10.00	11.97	2.25	0.45	53.96	1.77	67.70	m²	74.47
Note										
not withstanding the requirements of NRM works to 500mm high are shown in lineal metres.										

Labour hourly rates: (except Specialists) Craft Operatives 20.87 Labourer 15.57 Rates are national average prices. Refer to REGIONAL VARIATIONS for indicative levels of overall pricing in regions	MATERIALS			LABOUR				RATES		
	Del to Site £	Waste %	Material Cost £	Craft Optve Hrs	Lab Hrs	Labour Cost £	Sunds £	Nett Rate £	Unit	Gross rate (10%) £
FORMWORK (Cont'd)										
Plain formwork; Sides of upstand beams										
rectangular; height to soffit										
not exceeding 3.00m										
height not exceeding 250mm	2.29	12.50	2.58	0.75	0.15	17.99	0.46	21.03	m	23.13
height 250 - 500mm	2.68	12.50	3.01	0.88	0.18	21.17	0.61	24.79	m	27.27
height exceeding 500mm	5.15	12.50	5.79	1.75	0.35	41.97	1.17	48.93	m²	53.83
3.00 - 4.50m										
height not exceeding 250mm	2.29	12.50	2.58	0.83	0.17	19.97	0.54	23.09	m	25.40
height 250 - 500mm	2.68	12.50	3.01	0.97	0.20	23.36	0.74	27.11	m	29.82
height exceeding 500mm	5.15	12.50	5.79	1.93	0.39	46.35	1.40	53.54	m²	58.90
Plain formwork; Sides of isolated columns										
Columns										
rectangular, height not exceeding 3.00m above floor level	7.51	10.00	8.27	2.25	0.45	53.96	1.37	63.60	m²	69.96
rectangular, height exceeding 3.00m above floor level	7.51	10.00	8.27	2.30	0.45	55.01	1.65	64.92	m²	71.42
Column casings										
rectangular, height not exceeding 3.00m above floor level	8.09	10.00	8.90	2.25	0.45	53.96	1.37	64.23	m²	70.65
rectangular, height exceeding 3.00m above floor level	8.09	10.00	8.90	2.30	0.45	55.01	1.65	65.56	m²	72.11
Plain formwork; Sides of attached columns										
Columns										
rectangular, height not exceeding 3.00m above floor level	7.56	10.00	8.31	2.30	0.46	55.16	1.37	64.85	m²	71.33
rectangular, height exceeding 3.00m above floor level	6.89	10.00	7.58	2.40	0.46	57.25	1.65	66.48	m²	73.12
Column casings										
rectangular, height not exceeding 3.00m above floor level	7.51	10.00	8.27	2.30	0.46	55.16	1.37	64.80	m²	71.28
rectangular, height exceeding 3.00m above floor level	7.51	10.00	8.27	2.40	0.46	57.25	1.65	67.17	m²	73.88
Plain formwork; Faces of walls and other vertical work										
plain	12.61	15.00	14.51	1.60	0.32	38.37	1.52	54.40	m²	59.84
plain; height exceeding 5.00m above floor level	11.63	15.00	13.38	1.60	0.32	38.37	1.70	53.45	m²	58.80
interrupted	11.63	15.00	13.38	1.75	0.35	41.97	1.67	57.02	m²	62.72
interrupted; height exceeding 5.00m above floor level	12.42	15.00	14.28	1.75	0.35	41.97	1.85	58.10	m²	63.91
Walls; vertical; curved 1m radius										
plain	25.80	15.00	29.67	4.00	0.80	95.94	3.78	129.39	m²	142.33
Walls; vertical; curved 10m radius										
plain	15.52	15.00	17.85	2.40	0.48	57.56	2.31	77.72	m²	85.49
Walls; vertical; curved 20m radius										
plain	11.61	15.00	13.35	1.80	0.36	43.17	1.70	58.23	m²	64.05
Walls; battered one face										
plain	12.36	15.00	14.22	1.92	0.38	45.99	1.85	62.05	m²	68.26
Plain formwork; Extra over										
Openings in walls for doors or the like; wall thickness not exceeding 250mm										
not exceeding 5m²	27.46	15.00	31.58	4.77	0.99	114.96	4.16	150.70	nr	165.77
5m² to 10m²	39.66	15.00	45.61	6.89	1.43	166.06	6.01	217.68	nr	239.45
Plain formwork; Wall ends, soffits and steps in walls										
Wall ends, soffits and steps in walls; plain										
width not exceeding 250mm	3.05	15.00	3.51	0.53	0.11	12.77	0.46	16.74	m	18.42
Plain formwork; Soffits of sloping work										
sloping one way not exceeding 15 degrees										
concrete thickness not exceeding 300mm; height to soffit										
not exceeding 3.00m	19.22	10.00	21.15	1.82	0.38	43.90	2.03	67.08	m²	73.78
3.00 - 4.50m	19.22	10.00	21.15	2.06	0.42	49.53	2.67	73.35	m²	80.69
4.50 - 6.00m	19.22	10.00	21.15	2.30	0.47	55.32	3.30	79.76	m²	87.74
sloping exceeding 15 degrees										
concrete thickness not exceeding 300mm; height to soffit										
not exceeding 3.00m	22.08	10.00	24.29	2.00	0.42	48.28	2.23	74.79	m²	82.27
3.00 - 4.50m	22.08	10.00	24.29	2.27	0.47	54.69	2.94	81.92	m²	90.11
4.50 - 6.00m	22.08	10.00	24.29	2.53	0.52	60.90	3.63	88.81	m²	97.70
Plain formwork; Staircase strings, risers and the like										
Stairflights; 1000mm wide; 155mm thick waist; 178mm risers; includes formwork to soffits, risers and strings										
strings 300mm wide	23.25	10.00	25.57	6.05	1.21	145.10	3.43	174.11	m	191.52
string 300mm wide; junction with wall	23.25	10.00	25.57	6.05	1.21	145.10	3.43	174.11	m	191.52
Stairflights; 1500mm wide; 180mm thick waist; 178mm risers; includes formwork to soffits, risers and strings										
strings 325mm wide	29.10	10.00	32.01	7.56	1.51	181.29	4.29	217.59	m	239.35
string 325mm wide; junction with wall	29.10	10.00	32.01	7.56	1.51	181.29	4.29	217.59	m	239.35
Stairflights; 1000mm wide; 155mm thick waist; 178mm undercut risers; includes formwork to soffits, risers and strings										
strings 300mm wide	23.25	10.00	25.57	6.05	1.21	145.10	3.43	174.11	m	191.52
string 300mm wide; junction with wall	23.25	10.00	25.57	6.05	1.21	145.10	3.43	174.11	m	191.52
Stairflights; 1500mm wide; 180mm thick waist; 178mm undercut risers; includes formwork to soffits, risers and strings										
strings 325mm wide	29.08	10.00	31.99	7.56	1.51	181.29	4.29	217.57	m	239.33
string 325mm wide; junction with wall	29.08	10.00	31.99	7.56	1.51	181.29	4.29	217.57	m	239.33

Labour hourly rates: (except Specialists)
Craft Operatives 20.87 Labourer 15.57
Rates are national average prices.
Refer to REGIONAL VARIATIONS for indicative levels of overall pricing in regions

	MATERIALS			LABOUR				RATES		
	Del to Site £	Waste %	Material Cost £	Craft Optve Hrs	Lab Hrs	Labour Cost £	Sunds £	Nett Rate £	Unit	Gross rate (10%) £
FORMWORK (Cont'd)										
Plain formwork; Sloping top surfaces										
Top formwork										
sloping exceeding 15 degrees	5.64	10.00	6.21	1.50	0.30	35.98	0.94	43.12	m²	47.43
Plain formwork; Steps in top surfaces										
plain vertical										
height not exceeding 250mm	2.29	12.50	2.58	0.75	0.15	17.99	0.46	21.03	m	23.13
height 250 - 500mm	2.68	12.50	3.01	0.88	0.18	21.17	0.61	24.79	m	27.27
Wall kickers										
Plain										
straight	1.50	15.00	1.73	0.25	0.05	6.00	0.30	8.02	m	8.82
curved 2m radius	3.68	15.00	4.24	0.66	0.15	16.11	0.59	20.94	m	23.03
curved 10m radius	2.24	15.00	2.57	0.40	0.08	9.59	0.38	12.54	m	13.80
curved 20m radius	1.64	15.00	1.88	0.30	0.06	7.20	0.33	9.41	m	10.35
Suspended										
straight	1.62	15.00	1.86	0.28	0.06	6.78	0.31	8.96	m	9.85
curved 2m radius	4.08	15.00	4.69	0.73	0.17	17.88	0.64	23.21	m	25.54
curved 10m radius	2.40	15.00	2.76	0.44	0.09	10.58	0.41	13.76	m	15.14
curved 20m radius	1.86	15.00	2.14	0.33	0.07	7.98	0.36	10.48	m	11.53
Special finish formwork										
Extra over a basic finish for a fine formed finish										
slabs	-	-	-	-	0.35	5.45	-	5.45	m²	5.99
walls	-	-	-	-	0.35	5.45	-	5.45	m²	5.99
beams	-	-	-	-	0.35	5.45	-	5.45	m²	5.99
columns	-	-	-	-	0.35	5.45	-	5.45	m²	5.99
Formwork and basic finish; coating with retarding agent; Sides of foundations and bases										
plain vertical										
height not exceeding 250mm	1.68	12.50	1.89	0.53	0.14	13.24	0.36	15.49	m	17.04
height 250 - 500mm	3.17	12.50	3.57	0.96	0.28	24.39	0.68	28.64	m	31.51
height exceeding 500mm	6.13	12.50	6.90	1.75	0.59	45.71	1.17	53.78	m²	59.15
Formwork and basic finish; coating with retarding agent; Edges of horizontal work										
plain vertical										
height not exceeding 250mm	1.68	12.50	1.89	0.53	0.14	13.24	0.36	15.49	m	17.04
height 250 - 500mm	3.17	12.50	3.57	0.96	0.28	24.39	0.68	28.64	m	31.51
height exceeding 500mm	6.16	12.50	6.93	1.75	0.59	45.71	1.17	53.81	m²	59.20
plain vertical; curved 10m radius										
height not exceeding 250mm	4.94	12.50	5.55	1.65	0.36	40.04	1.12	46.72	m	51.39
plain vertical; curved 1m radius										
height not exceeding 250mm	2.99	12.50	3.36	1.00	0.23	24.45	0.71	28.52	m	31.38
plain vertical; curved 20m radius										
height not exceeding 250mm	2.27	12.50	2.55	0.74	0.18	18.25	0.45	21.24	m	23.37
Formwork and basic finish; coating with retarding agent; Soffits of horizontal work										
horizontal										
slab thickness not exceeding 300mm; height to soffit										
not exceeding 3.00m	16.41	10.00	18.05	1.65	0.57	43.31	1.80	63.16	m²	69.47
3.00 - 4.50m	16.41	10.00	18.05	1.87	0.62	48.68	2.43	69.15	m²	76.07
4.50 - 6.00m	16.41	10.00	18.05	2.09	0.67	54.05	2.97	75.07	m²	82.57
slab thickness 300 - 450mm; height to soffit										
not exceeding 3.00m	19.75	10.00	21.72	1.82	0.63	47.79	1.98	71.49	m²	78.64
3.00 - 4.50m	19.75	10.00	21.72	2.06	0.68	53.58	2.67	77.97	m²	85.77
4.50 - 6.00m	19.75	10.00	21.72	2.30	0.74	59.52	3.30	84.54	m²	93.00
horizontal; with frequent uses of prefabricated panels										
slab thickness not exceeding 300mm; height to soffit										
not exceeding 3.00m	5.63	15.00	6.47	1.65	0.78	46.58	1.80	54.85	m²	60.34
3.00 - 4.50m	5.63	15.00	6.47	1.87	0.83	51.95	2.43	60.85	m²	66.93
4.50 - 6.00m	5.63	15.00	6.47	2.09	0.88	57.32	2.97	66.76	m²	73.44
slab thickness 300 - 450mm; height to soffit										
not exceeding 3.00m	7.37	15.00	8.48	1.82	0.86	51.37	1.98	61.83	m²	68.02
3.00 - 4.50m	7.37	15.00	8.48	2.06	0.91	57.16	2.67	68.31	m²	75.14
4.50 - 6.00m	7.37	15.00	8.48	2.30	0.97	63.10	3.27	74.85	m²	82.34
Soffits of landings; horizontal										
slab thickness not exceeding 300mm; height to soffit										
not exceeding 1.50m	18.05	15.00	20.75	2.00	0.66	52.02	1.81	74.58	m²	82.04
1.50 - 3.00m	18.05	15.00	20.75	2.22	0.72	57.54	2.49	80.79	m²	88.87
3.00 - 4.50m	18.05	15.00	20.75	2.46	0.77	63.33	2.82	86.90	m²	95.59
Formwork and basic finish; coating with retarding agent; Sides and soffits of isolated beams										
regular shaped; rectangular; height to soffit										
not exceeding - 3.00m	12.38	10.00	13.62	2.35	0.71	60.10	1.45	75.17	m²	82.69
3.00 - 4.50m	12.38	10.00	13.62	2.35	0.71	60.10	1.77	75.48	m²	83.03
Formwork and basic finish; coating with retarding agent; Sides and soffits of attached beams										
regular shaped; rectangular; height to soffit										
not exceeding - 3.00m	11.92	10.00	13.11	2.25	0.69	57.70	1.45	72.26	m²	79.49
3.00 - 4.50m	11.92	10.00	13.11	2.25	0.69	57.70	1.77	72.58	m²	79.83

Labour hourly rates: (except Specialists) Craft Operatives 20.87 Labourer 15.57 Rates are national average prices. Refer to REGIONAL VARIATIONS for indicative levels of overall pricing in regions	MATERIALS			LABOUR				RATES		
	Del to Site £	Waste %	Material Cost £	Craft Optve Hrs	Lab Hrs	Labour Cost £	Sunds £	Nett Rate £	Unit	Gross rate (10%) £
FORMWORK (Cont'd)										
Formwork and basic finish; coating with retarding agent; Sides of isolated columns										
Columns										
rectangular, height not exceeding 3.00m above floor level	8.70	10.00	9.57	2.25	0.70	57.86	1.37	68.80	m²	75.68
rectangular, height exceeding 3.00m above floor level	8.70	10.00	9.57	2.48	0.70	62.66	1.65	73.88	m²	81.27
Column casings										
regular shaped; rectangular	8.70	10.00	9.57	2.38	0.69	60.41	1.37	71.35	m²	78.49
regular shaped; rectangular, height exceeding 3.00m above floor level	8.70	10.00	9.57	2.48	0.69	62.50	1.65	73.72	m²	81.09
Formwork and basic finish; coating with retarding agent; Sides of attached columns										
Columns										
rectangular, height not exceeding 3.00m above floor level	8.70	10.00	9.57	2.30	0.70	58.90	1.37	69.84	m²	76.82
rectangular, height exceeding 3.00m above floor level	8.70	10.00	9.57	2.43	0.70	61.61	1.65	72.83	m²	80.12
Column casings										
regular shaped; rectangular	8.70	10.00	9.57	2.30	0.70	58.90	1.65	70.12	m²	77.13
regular shaped; rectangular, height exceeding 3.00m above floor level	8.70	10.00	9.57	2.40	0.70	60.99	1.37	71.93	m²	79.12
Formwork and basic finish; coating with retarding agent; Faces of walls and other vertical work										
plain	11.51	15.00	13.24	1.60	0.56	42.11	1.52	56.87	m²	62.55
plain; height exceeding 3.00m above floor level	12.69	15.00	14.60	1.60	0.56	42.11	1.70	58.41	m²	64.25
interrupted	12.42	15.00	14.28	1.75	0.59	45.71	1.67	61.66	m²	67.82
interrupted; height exceeding 3.00m above floor level	13.29	15.00	15.29	1.75	0.59	45.71	1.85	62.84	m²	69.13
Walls; vertical; curved 1m radius										
plain	26.58	15.00	30.57	4.00	1.04	99.67	3.78	134.02	m²	147.43
Walls; vertical; curved 10m radius										
plain	16.55	15.00	19.03	2.40	0.72	61.30	2.31	82.64	m²	90.90
Walls; vertical; curved 20m radius										
plain	12.67	15.00	14.57	1.80	0.60	46.91	1.70	63.18	m²	69.50
Walls; battered										
plain	13.41	15.00	15.42	1.92	0.62	49.72	1.85	66.99	m²	73.69
Formwork and basic finish; coating with retarding agent; Extra over										
Openings in walls; wall thickness not exceeding 250mm										
not exceeding 5m2	30.85	15.00	35.48	4.77	12.24	290.13	4.16	329.76	m	362.74
5m2 to 10m2	44.56	15.00	51.25	6.89	2.21	178.20	6.01	235.46	m	259.00
Formwork and basic finish; coating with retarding agent; Wall ends, soffits and steps in walls										
Plain										
width not exceeding 250mm	3.43	15.00	3.94	0.53	0.17	13.71	0.46	18.11	m	19.92
Formwork and basic finish; coating with retarding agent; Soffits of sloping work										
Sloping one way not exceeding 15 degrees										
slab thickness not exceeding 300mm; height to soffit										
not exceeding 3.00m	19.81	15.00	22.78	1.82	0.63	47.79	1.98	72.55	m²	79.80
3.00 - 4.50m	19.81	15.00	22.78	2.06	0.68	53.58	2.67	79.03	m²	86.93
4.50 - 6.00m	19.81	15.00	22.78	2.30	0.74	59.52	3.30	85.60	m²	94.16
Soffits of slabs; sloping exceeding 15 degrees										
slab thickness not exceeding 300mm; height to soffit										
not exceeding 3.00m	20.64	15.00	23.73	1.90	0.65	49.77	2.31	75.81	m²	83.40
3.00 - 4.50m	20.64	15.00	23.73	2.15	0.71	55.93	2.94	82.59	m²	90.85
4.50 - 6.00m	20.64	15.00	23.73	2.40	0.76	61.92	3.60	89.25	m²	98.17
Formwork and basic finish; coating with retarding agent; Staircase strings, risers and the like										
Stairflights; 1000mm wide; 155mm thick waist; 178mm risers; includes formwork to soffits, risers and strings										
strings 300mm wide	25.26	10.00	27.78	6.05	1.74	153.36	3.43	184.57	m	203.03
string 300mm wide; junction with wall	25.26	10.00	27.78	6.05	1.74	153.36	3.43	184.57	m	203.03
Stairflights; 1500mm wide; 180mm thick waist; 178mm risers; includes formwork to soffits, risers and strings										
strings 325mm wide	31.57	10.00	34.73	7.56	2.17	191.56	4.29	230.58	m	253.64
string 325mm wide; junction with wall	31.57	10.00	34.73	7.56	2.17	191.56	4.29	230.58	m	253.64
Stairflights; 1000mm wide; 155mm thick waist; 178mm undercut risers; includes formwork to soffits, risers and strings										
strings 300mm wide	25.26	10.00	27.78	6.05	1.74	153.36	3.43	184.57	m	203.03
string 300mm wide; junction with wall	25.26	10.00	27.78	6.05	1.74	153.36	3.43	184.57	m	203.03
Stairflights; 1500mm wide; 180mm thick waist; 178mm undercut risers; includes formwork to soffits, risers and strings										
strings 325mm wide	31.57	10.00	34.73	7.56	2.17	191.56	4.29	230.58	m	253.64
string 325mm wide; junction with wall	31.57	10.00	34.73	7.56	2.17	191.56	4.29	230.58	m	253.64
Formwork and basic finish; coating with retarding agent; Sloping top surfaces										
Top formwork										
sloping exceeding 15 degrees	6.82	15.00	7.84	1.50	0.54	39.71	0.94	48.50	m²	53.34

Labour hourly rates: (except Specialists) Craft Operatives 20.87 Labourer 15.57 Rates are national average prices. Refer to REGIONAL VARIATIONS for indicative levels of overall pricing in regions	MATERIALS			LABOUR				RATES		
	Del to Site £	Waste %	Material Cost £	Craft Optve Hrs	Lab Hrs	Labour Cost £	Sunds £	Nett Rate £	Unit	Gross rate (10%) £
FORMWORK (Cont'd)										
Formwork and basic finish; coating with retarding agent; Steps in top surfaces										
plain vertical										
height not exceeding 250mm	2.47	12.50	2.78	0.75	0.18	18.46	0.45	21.68	m	23.85
height 250 - 500mm	3.04	12.50	3.42	0.88	0.27	22.57	0.59	26.58	m	29.24
Wall kickers										
Plain										
straight	1.61	15.00	1.85	0.25	0.09	6.62	0.30	8.77	m	9.65
curved 2m radius	3.80	15.00	4.36	0.66	0.17	16.42	0.59	21.38	m	23.52
curved 10m radius	2.35	15.00	2.70	0.40	0.12	10.22	0.38	13.30	m	14.63
curved 20m radius	1.83	15.00	2.11	0.30	0.10	7.82	0.33	10.25	m	11.28
Suspended										
straight	1.82	15.00	2.09	0.28	0.10	7.40	0.33	9.82	m	10.80
curved 2m radius	4.17	15.00	4.79	0.73	0.19	18.19	0.66	23.64	m	26.01
curved 10m radius	2.60	15.00	2.99	0.44	0.13	11.21	0.41	14.61	m	16.07
curved 20m radius	1.98	15.00	2.28	0.33	0.11	8.60	0.36	11.24	m	12.37
Special finish formwork										
Extra over a basic finish for a fine formed finish										
slabs	-	-	-	-	0.35	5.45	-	5.45	m²	5.99
walls	-	-	-	-	0.35	5.45	-	5.45	m²	5.99
beams	-	-	-	-	0.35	5.45	-	5.45	m²	5.99
columns	-	-	-	-	0.35	5.45	-	5.45	m²	5.99
Soffits of horizontal work; Expamet Hy-rib permanent shuttering and reinforcement										
Reference 2611, 4.23 kg/m²; to soffits of slabs; horizontal; one rib side laps; 150mm end laps										
slab thickness 75mm; strutting and supports at 750mm centres; height to soffit										
not exceeding 3.00m	20.52	7.50	22.06	1.19	0.30	29.51	1.77	53.33	m²	58.67
3.00 - 4.50m	20.52	7.50	22.06	1.37	0.34	33.89	2.18	58.12	m²	63.94
slab thickness 100mm; strutting and supports at 650mm centres; height to soffit										
not exceeding 3.00m	20.52	7.50	22.06	1.21	0.30	29.92	2.00	53.98	m²	59.38
3.00 - 4.50m	20.52	7.50	22.06	1.39	0.35	34.46	2.69	59.21	m²	65.13
slab thickness 125mm; strutting and supports at 550mm centres; height to soffit										
not exceeding 3.00m	20.52	7.50	22.06	1.23	0.31	30.50	2.24	54.80	m²	60.28
3.00 - 4.50m	20.52	7.50	22.06	1.41	0.35	34.88	3.25	60.19	m²	66.21
slab thickness 150mm; strutting and supports at 450mm centres; height to soffit										
not exceeding 3.00m	20.52	7.50	22.06	1.25	0.31	30.91	2.52	55.50	m²	61.05
3.00 - 4.50m	20.52	7.50	22.06	1.44	0.36	35.66	3.78	61.50	m²	67.65
Reference 2411, 6.35 kg/m²; to soffits of slabs; horizontal; one rib side laps; 150mm end laps										
slab thickness 75mm; strutting and supports at 850mm centres; height to soffit										
not exceeding 3.00m	37.54	7.50	40.35	1.22	0.31	30.29	1.77	72.41	m²	79.65
3.00 - 4.50m	37.54	7.50	40.35	1.40	0.35	34.67	2.18	77.20	m²	84.92
slab thickness 100mm; strutting and supports at 750mm centres; height to soffit										
not exceeding 3.00m	37.54	7.50	40.35	1.24	0.31	30.71	2.00	73.06	m²	80.36
3.00 - 4.50m	37.54	7.50	40.35	1.43	0.36	35.45	2.69	78.49	m²	86.34
slab thickness 125mm; strutting and supports at 650mm centres; height to soffit										
not exceeding 3.00m	37.54	7.50	40.35	1.25	0.32	31.07	2.24	73.67	m²	81.03
3.00 - 4.50m	37.54	7.50	40.35	1.45	0.36	35.87	3.25	79.47	m²	87.42
slab thickness 150mm; strutting and supports at 550mm centres; height to soffit										
not exceeding 3.00m	37.54	7.50	40.35	1.28	0.32	31.70	2.52	74.57	m²	82.03
3.00 - 4.50m	37.54	7.50	40.35	1.47	0.37	36.44	3.78	80.57	m²	88.63
slab thickness 175mm; strutting and supports at 450mm centres; height to soffit										
not exceeding 3.00m	37.54	7.50	40.35	1.31	0.33	32.48	2.90	75.74	m²	83.31
3.00 - 4.50m	37.54	7.50	40.35	1.51	0.38	37.43	4.50	82.29	m²	90.52
slab thickness 200mm; strutting and supports at 350mm centres; height to soffit										
not exceeding 3.00m	37.54	7.50	40.35	1.34	0.34	33.26	3.27	76.88	m²	84.57
3.00 - 4.50m	37.54	7.50	40.35	1.54	0.39	38.21	5.25	83.81	m²	92.19
Reference 2611, 4.23 kg/m²; to soffits of arched slabs; one rib side laps										
900mm span; 75mm rise; height to soffit										
not exceeding 3.00m	20.52	7.50	22.06	1.31	0.33	32.48	1.30	55.84	m²	61.43
1200mm span; 75mm rise; one row strutting and supports per span; height to soffit										
not exceeding 3.00m	20.52	7.50	22.06	1.31	0.33	32.48	1.77	56.30	m²	61.93
3.00 - 4.50m	20.52	7.50	22.06	1.49	0.37	36.86	2.18	61.10	m²	67.21
Reference 2411, 6.35 kg/m²; to soffits of arched slabs; one rib side laps										
1500mm span; 100mm rise; two rows strutting and supports per span; height to soffit										
not exceeding 3.00m	37.54	7.50	40.35	1.62	0.40	40.04	3.76	84.15	m²	92.57
3.00 - 4.50m	37.54	7.50	40.35	1.84	0.46	45.56	5.03	90.95	m²	100.04

Labour hourly rates: (except Specialists) Craft Operatives 20.87 Labourer 15.57 Rates are national average prices. Refer to REGIONAL VARIATIONS for indicative levels of overall pricing in regions	MATERIALS			LABOUR				RATES		
	Del to Site £	Waste %	Material Cost £	Craft Optve Hrs	Lab Hrs	Labour Cost £	Sunds £	Nett Rate £	Unit	Gross rate (10%) £
FORMWORK (Cont'd)										
Soffits of horizontal work; Expamet Hy-rib permanent shuttering and reinforcement (Cont'd)										
Reference 2411, 6.35 kg/m²; to soffits of arched slabs; one rib side laps (Cont'd)										
1800mm span; 150mm rise; two rows strutting and supports per span; height to soffit										
not exceeding 3.00m	37.54	7.50	40.35	1.62	0.40	40.04	3.76	84.15	m²	92.57
3.00 - 4.50m	37.54	7.50	40.35	1.84	0.46	45.56	5.03	90.95	m²	100.04
REINFORCEMENT										
Mild steel bars; Reinforcement bars; BS 4449, hot rolled plain round mild steel including hooks and tying wire, and spacers and chairs which are at the discretion of the Contractor										
Straight										
6mm	1731.03	7.50	1860.86	51.00	5.00	1142.22	44.35	3047.43	t	3352.18
8mm	1630.77	7.50	1753.08	44.00	5.00	996.13	39.27	2788.48	t	3067.32
10mm	1497.73	7.50	1610.06	36.00	5.00	829.17	31.88	2471.10	t	2718.22
12mm	1266.67	7.50	1361.67	31.00	5.00	724.82	27.26	2113.75	t	2325.12
16mm	1269.23	7.50	1364.42	24.00	5.00	578.73	22.42	1965.57	t	2162.13
20mm	1211.11	7.50	1301.94	20.00	5.00	495.25	12.25	1809.45	t	1990.39
25mm	1175.89	7.50	1264.08	20.00	5.00	495.25	12.25	1771.58	t	1948.74
32mm	1107.97	7.50	1191.07	20.00	5.00	495.25	12.25	1698.57	t	1868.43
Bent										
6mm	1731.03	7.50	1860.86	51.00	5.00	1142.22	44.35	3047.43	t	3352.18
8mm	1630.77	7.50	1753.08	44.00	5.00	996.13	39.27	2788.48	t	3067.32
10mm	1497.73	7.50	1610.06	36.00	5.00	829.17	31.88	2471.10	t	2718.22
12mm	1266.67	7.50	1361.67	31.00	5.00	724.82	27.26	2113.75	t	2325.12
16mm	1269.23	7.50	1364.42	24.00	5.00	578.73	22.42	1965.57	t	2162.13
20mm	1211.11	7.50	1301.94	20.00	5.00	495.25	12.25	1809.45	t	1990.39
25mm	1175.89	7.50	1264.08	20.00	5.00	495.25	12.25	1771.58	t	1948.74
32mm	1107.97	7.50	1191.07	20.00	5.00	495.25	12.25	1698.57	t	1868.43
Links										
6mm	1731.03	7.50	1860.86	66.00	5.00	1455.27	44.35	3360.48	t	3696.53
8mm	1630.77	7.50	1753.08	66.00	5.00	1455.27	39.27	3247.62	t	3572.38
High yield steel bars; Reinforcement bars; BS 4449, hot rolled deformed high yield steel including hooks and tying wire, and spacers and chairs which are at the discretion of the Contractor										
Straight										
6mm	1630.14	7.50	1752.40	51.00	5.00	1142.22	44.35	2938.97	t	3232.87
8mm	1623.08	7.50	1744.81	44.00	5.00	996.13	39.27	2780.21	t	3058.23
10mm	1428.10	7.50	1535.21	36.00	5.00	829.17	31.88	2396.25	t	2635.88
12mm	1420.51	7.50	1527.05	31.00	5.00	724.82	27.26	2279.13	t	2507.04
16mm	1253.14	7.50	1347.13	24.00	5.00	578.73	22.42	1948.27	t	2143.10
20mm	1187.65	7.50	1276.73	20.00	5.00	495.25	12.25	1784.23	t	1962.66
25mm	919.85	7.50	988.84	20.00	5.00	495.25	12.25	1496.34	t	1645.98
32mm	918.64	7.50	987.54	20.00	5.00	495.25	12.25	1495.05	t	1644.55
Bent										
6mm	1630.14	7.50	1752.40	51.00	5.00	1142.22	44.35	2938.97	t	3232.87
8mm	1623.08	7.50	1744.81	44.00	5.00	996.13	39.27	2780.21	t	3058.23
10mm	1428.10	7.50	1535.21	36.00	5.00	829.17	31.88	2396.25	t	2635.88
12mm	1420.51	7.50	1527.05	31.00	5.00	724.82	27.26	2279.13	t	2507.04
16mm	1253.14	7.50	1347.13	24.00	5.00	578.73	22.42	1948.27	t	2143.10
20mm	1187.65	7.50	1276.73	20.00	5.00	495.25	12.25	1784.23	t	1962.66
25mm	919.85	7.50	988.84	20.00	5.00	495.25	12.25	1496.34	t	1645.98
32mm	918.64	7.50	987.54	20.00	5.00	495.25	12.25	1495.05	t	1644.55
Links										
6mm	1630.14	7.50	1752.40	66.00	5.00	1455.27	44.35	3252.02	t	3577.22
8mm	1623.08	7.50	1744.81	66.00	5.00	1455.27	39.27	3239.35	t	3563.28
Mild steel bars - Take delivery, cut bend and fix; Take delivery, cut, bend and fix reinforcing rods; including hooks and tying wire, and spacers and chairs which are at the discretion of the Contractor										
Straight										
6mm	-	-	-	55.00	5.00	1225.70	44.35	1270.05	t	1397.06
8mm	-	-	-	48.00	5.00	1079.61	39.27	1118.88	t	1230.77
10mm	-	-	-	40.00	5.00	912.65	31.88	944.53	t	1038.98
12mm	-	-	-	34.00	5.00	787.43	27.26	814.69	t	896.16
16mm	-	-	-	26.00	5.00	620.47	22.42	642.89	t	707.18
20mm	-	-	-	22.00	5.00	536.99	12.25	549.24	t	604.17
25mm	-	-	-	22.00	5.00	536.99	12.25	549.24	t	604.17
32mm	-	-	-	22.00	5.00	536.99	12.25	549.24	t	604.17
Bent										
6mm	-	-	-	75.00	5.00	1643.10	44.35	1687.45	t	1856.20
8mm	-	-	-	66.00	5.00	1455.27	39.27	1494.54	t	1643.99
10mm	-	-	-	55.00	5.00	1225.70	31.88	1257.58	t	1383.34
12mm	-	-	-	47.00	5.00	1058.74	27.26	1086.00	t	1194.60
16mm	-	-	-	37.00	5.00	850.04	22.42	872.46	t	959.70
20mm	-	-	-	31.00	5.00	724.82	12.25	737.07	t	810.78
25mm	-	-	-	29.00	5.00	683.08	12.25	695.33	t	764.87
32mm	-	-	-	29.00	5.00	683.08	12.25	695.33	t	764.87
Links										
6mm	-	-	-	99.00	5.00	2143.98	44.35	2188.33	t	2407.17

Labour hourly rates: (except Specialists) Craft Operatives 20.87 Labourer 15.57 Rates are national average prices. Refer to REGIONAL VARIATIONS for indicative levels of overall pricing in regions	MATERIALS			LABOUR				RATES		
	Del to Site £	Waste %	Material Cost £	Craft Optve Hrs	Lab Hrs	Labour Cost £	Sunds £	Nett Rate £	Unit	Gross rate (10%) £
REINFORCEMENT (Cont'd)										
Mild steel bars - Take delivery, cut bend and fix; Take delivery, cut, bend and fix reinforcing rods; including hooks and tying wire, and spacers and chairs which are at the discretion of the Contractor (Cont'd)										
Links (Cont'd)										
8mm	-	-	-	99.00	5.00	2143.98	39.27	2183.25	t	2401.58
Mild steel bars - Take delivery and fix; Take delivery and fix reinforcing rods supplied cut to length and bent; including tying wire, and spacers and chairs which are at the discretion of the Contractor										
Straight										
6mm	-	-	-	51.00	5.00	1142.22	44.35	1186.57	t	1305.23
8mm	-	-	-	44.00	5.00	996.13	39.27	1035.40	t	1138.94
10mm	-	-	-	36.00	5.00	829.17	31.88	861.05	t	947.15
12mm	-	-	-	31.00	5.00	724.82	27.26	752.08	t	827.29
16mm	-	-	-	24.00	5.00	578.73	22.42	601.15	t	661.26
20mm	-	-	-	20.00	5.00	495.25	12.25	507.50	t	558.25
25mm	-	-	-	20.00	5.00	495.25	12.25	507.50	t	558.25
32mm	-	-	-	20.00	5.00	495.25	12.25	507.50	t	558.25
Bent										
6mm	-	-	-	51.00	5.00	1142.22	44.35	1186.57	t	1305.23
8mm	-	-	-	44.00	5.00	996.13	39.27	1035.40	t	1138.94
10mm	-	-	-	36.00	5.00	829.17	31.88	861.05	t	947.15
12mm	-	-	-	31.00	5.00	724.82	27.26	752.08	t	827.29
16mm	-	-	-	24.00	5.00	578.73	22.42	601.15	t	661.26
20mm	-	-	-	20.00	5.00	495.25	12.25	507.50	t	558.25
25mm	-	-	-	20.00	5.00	495.25	12.25	507.50	t	558.25
Links										
6mm	-	-	-	66.00	5.00	1455.27	44.35	1499.62	t	1649.58
8mm	-	-	-	66.00	5.00	1455.27	39.27	1494.54	t	1643.99
High yield stainless steel bars; Reinforcement bars; high yield stainless steel BS 6744, Type 2 (minimum yield stress 460 N/mm²); including hooks and tying wire, and spacers and chairs which are at the discretion of the Contractor										
Straight										
8mm	4800.00	7.50	5160.00	83.00	10.00	1887.91	152.46	7200.37	t	7920.41
10mm	4506.02	7.50	4843.98	69.00	10.00	1595.73	110.00	6549.71	t	7204.68
12mm	4545.46	7.50	4886.36	60.00	10.00	1407.90	104.06	6398.32	t	7038.16
16mm	4429.63	7.50	4761.85	50.00	10.00	1199.20	89.54	6050.59	t	6655.65
20mm	4525.61	7.50	4865.03	41.00	10.00	1011.37	66.55	5942.95	t	6537.25
25mm	4340.62	7.50	4666.17	33.00	10.00	844.41	48.40	5558.98	t	6114.88
Bent										
8mm	4800.00	7.50	5160.00	83.00	10.00	1887.91	152.46	7200.37	t	7920.41
10mm	4506.02	7.50	4843.98	69.00	10.00	1595.73	110.00	6549.71	t	7204.68
12mm	4545.46	7.50	4886.36	60.00	10.00	1407.90	104.06	6398.32	t	7038.16
16mm	4429.63	7.50	4761.85	50.00	10.00	1199.20	89.54	6050.59	t	6655.65
20mm	4525.61	7.50	4865.03	41.00	10.00	1011.37	66.55	5942.95	t	6537.25
25mm	4340.62	7.50	4666.17	33.00	10.00	844.41	48.40	5558.98	t	6114.88
Links										
6mm	5311.77	7.50	5710.16	130.00	10.00	2868.80	152.46	8731.42	t	9604.56
8mm	4800.00	7.50	5160.00	115.00	10.00	2555.75	110.00	7825.75	t	8608.33
Mesh; Reinforcement fabric; BS 4483, hard drawn plain round steel; welded; including laps, tying wire, all cutting and bending, and spacers and chairs which are at the discretion of the Contractor										
Reference A98; 1.54 kg/m²; 200mm side laps; 200mm end laps										
generally	3.79	17.50	4.46	0.07	0.01	1.62	0.09	6.16	m²	6.78
strips in one width										
750mm wide	3.79	17.50	4.46	0.11	0.01	2.45	0.09	7.00	m²	7.69
900mm wide	3.79	17.50	4.46	0.10	0.01	2.24	0.09	6.79	m²	7.46
1050mm wide	3.79	17.50	4.46	0.09	0.01	2.03	0.09	6.58	m²	7.24
1200mm wide	3.79	17.50	4.46	0.08	0.01	1.83	0.09	6.37	m²	7.01
Reference A142; 2.22kg/m²; 200mm side laps; 200mm end laps										
generally	3.78	17.50	4.44	0.08	0.02	1.98	0.13	6.56	m²	7.21
strips in one width										
750mm wide	3.78	17.50	4.44	0.12	0.02	2.82	0.13	7.39	m²	8.13
900mm wide	3.78	17.50	4.44	0.11	0.02	2.61	0.13	7.18	m²	7.90
1050mm wide	3.78	17.50	4.44	0.10	0.02	2.40	0.13	6.97	m²	7.67
1200mm wide	3.78	17.50	4.44	0.10	0.02	2.40	0.13	6.97	m²	7.67
Reference A193; 3.02kg/m²; 200mm side laps; 200mm end laps										
generally	5.29	17.50	6.22	0.08	0.02	1.98	0.18	8.38	m²	9.22
strips in one width										
750mm wide	5.29	17.50	6.22	0.12	0.02	2.82	0.18	9.21	m²	10.13
900mm wide	5.29	17.50	6.22	0.11	0.02	2.61	0.18	9.00	m²	9.90
1050mm wide	5.29	17.50	6.22	0.10	0.02	2.40	0.18	8.79	m²	9.67
1200mm wide	5.29	17.50	6.22	0.10	0.02	2.40	0.18	8.79	m²	9.67
Reference A252; 3.95kg/m²; 200mm side laps; 200mm end laps										
generally	6.81	17.50	8.00	0.09	0.02	2.19	0.22	10.41	m²	11.45
strips in one width										
750mm wide	6.81	17.50	8.00	0.14	0.02	3.23	0.22	11.45	m²	12.60
900mm wide	6.81	17.50	8.00	0.13	0.02	3.02	0.22	11.24	m²	12.37
1050mm wide	6.81	17.50	8.00	0.12	0.02	2.82	0.22	11.03	m²	12.14

Labour hourly rates: (except Specialists) Craft Operatives 20.87 Labourer 15.57 Rates are national average prices. Refer to REGIONAL VARIATIONS for indicative levels of overall pricing in regions	MATERIALS			LABOUR				RATES		
	Del to Site £	Waste %	Material Cost £	Craft Optve Hrs	Lab Hrs	Labour Cost £	Sunds £	Nett Rate £	Unit	Gross rate (10%) £
REINFORCEMENT (Cont'd)										
Mesh; Reinforcement fabric; BS 4483, hard drawn plain round steel; welded; including laps, tying wire, all cutting and bending, and spacers and chairs which are at the discretion of the Contractor (Cont'd)										
Reference A252; 3.95kg/m²; 200mm side laps; 200mm end laps (Cont'd)										
strips in one width (Cont'd)										
1200mm wide	6.81	17.50	8.00	0.11	0.02	2.61	0.22	10.82	m²	11.91
Reference A393; 6.16 kg/m²; 200mm side laps; 200mm end laps										
generally	10.91	17.50	12.82	0.10	0.02	2.40	0.33	15.55	m²	17.10
strips in one width										
750mm wide	10.91	17.50	12.82	0.15	0.02	3.44	0.33	16.59	m²	18.25
900mm wide	10.91	17.50	12.82	0.14	0.02	3.23	0.33	16.38	m²	18.02
1050mm wide	10.91	17.50	12.82	0.13	0.02	3.02	0.33	16.17	m²	17.79
1200mm wide	10.91	17.50	12.82	0.12	0.02	2.82	0.33	15.96	m²	17.56
Reference B1131; 10.90 kg/m²; 100mm side laps; 200mm end laps										
generally	20.29	17.50	23.84	0.14	0.03	3.39	0.59	27.82	m²	30.61
strips in one width										
750mm wide	20.29	17.50	23.84	0.21	0.03	4.85	0.59	29.29	m²	32.21
900mm wide	20.29	17.50	23.84	0.20	0.03	4.64	0.59	29.08	m²	31.98
1050mm wide	20.29	17.50	23.84	0.18	0.03	4.22	0.59	28.66	m²	31.53
1200mm wide	20.29	17.50	23.84	0.17	0.03	4.02	0.59	28.45	m²	31.30
Reference B196; 3.05 kg/m²; 100mm side laps; 200mm end laps										
generally	6.17	17.50	7.25	0.08	0.02	1.98	0.33	9.56	m²	10.52
strips in one width										
750mm wide	6.17	17.50	7.25	0.12	0.02	2.82	0.33	10.40	m²	11.44
900mm wide	6.17	17.50	7.25	0.11	0.02	2.61	0.33	10.19	m²	11.21
1050mm wide	6.17	17.50	7.25	0.10	0.02	2.40	0.33	9.98	m²	10.98
1200mm wide	6.17	17.50	7.25	0.10	0.02	2.40	0.33	9.98	m²	10.98
Reference B283; 3.73 kg/m²; 100mm side laps; 200mm end laps										
generally	6.98	17.50	8.20	0.08	0.02	1.98	0.20	10.38	m²	11.42
strips in one width										
750mm wide	6.98	17.50	8.20	0.12	0.02	2.82	0.20	11.22	m²	12.34
900mm wide	6.98	17.50	8.20	0.11	0.02	2.61	0.20	11.01	m²	12.11
1050mm wide	6.98	17.50	8.20	0.10	0.02	2.40	0.20	10.80	m²	11.88
1200mm wide	6.98	17.50	8.20	0.10	0.02	2.40	0.20	10.80	m²	11.88
Reference B385; 4.53 kg/m²; 100mm side laps; 200mm end laps										
generally	9.54	17.50	11.21	0.09	0.02	2.19	0.24	13.65	m²	15.01
strips in one width										
750mm wide	9.54	17.50	11.21	0.14	0.02	3.23	0.24	14.69	m²	16.16
900mm wide	9.54	17.50	11.21	0.13	0.02	3.02	0.24	14.48	m²	15.93
1050mm wide	9.54	17.50	11.21	0.12	0.02	2.82	0.24	14.27	m²	15.70
1200mm wide	9.54	17.50	11.21	0.11	0.02	2.61	0.24	14.06	m²	15.47
Reference B503; 5.93 kg/m²; 100mm side laps; 200mm end laps										
generally	11.04	17.50	12.97	0.10	0.02	2.40	0.33	15.70	m²	17.27
strips in one width										
750mm wide	11.04	17.50	12.97	0.15	0.02	3.44	0.33	16.74	m²	18.42
900mm wide	11.04	17.50	12.97	0.14	0.02	3.23	0.33	16.53	m²	18.19
1050mm wide	11.04	17.50	12.97	0.13	0.02	3.02	0.33	16.32	m²	17.96
1200mm wide	11.04	17.50	12.97	0.12	0.02	2.82	0.33	16.12	m²	17.73
Reference B785; 8.14 kg/m²; 100mm side laps; 200mm end laps										
generally	15.42	17.50	18.12	0.11	0.03	2.76	0.44	21.32	m²	23.45
strips in one width										
750mm wide	15.42	17.50	18.12	0.16	0.03	3.81	0.44	22.37	m²	24.60
900mm wide	15.42	17.50	18.12	0.15	0.03	3.60	0.44	22.16	m²	24.37
1050mm wide	15.42	17.50	18.12	0.14	0.03	3.39	0.44	21.95	m²	24.14
1200mm wide	15.42	17.50	18.12	0.13	0.03	3.18	0.44	21.74	m²	23.91
Reference C283; 2.61 kg/m²; 100mm side laps; 400mm end laps										
generally	6.68	17.50	7.85	0.08	0.02	1.98	0.15	9.98	m²	10.98
strips in one width										
750mm wide	6.68	17.50	7.85	0.12	0.02	2.82	0.15	10.82	m²	11.90
900mm wide	6.68	17.50	7.85	0.11	0.02	2.61	0.15	10.61	m²	11.67
1050mm wide	6.68	17.50	7.85	0.10	0.02	2.40	0.15	10.40	m²	11.44
1200mm wide	6.68	17.50	7.85	0.10	0.02	2.40	0.15	10.40	m²	11.44
Reference C385; 3.41 kg/m²; 100mm side laps; 400mm end laps										
generally	8.08	17.50	9.50	0.08	0.02	1.98	0.20	11.68	m²	12.84
strips in one width										
750mm wide	8.08	17.50	9.50	0.12	0.02	2.82	0.20	12.51	m²	13.76
900mm wide	8.08	17.50	9.50	0.11	0.02	2.61	0.20	12.30	m²	13.53
1050mm wide	8.08	17.50	9.50	0.10	0.02	2.40	0.20	12.09	m²	13.30
1200mm wide	8.08	17.50	9.50	0.10	0.02	2.40	0.20	12.09	m²	13.30
Reference C503; 4.34 kg/m²; 100mm side laps; 400mm end laps										
generally	9.04	17.50	10.62	0.09	0.02	2.19	0.24	13.05	m²	14.36
strips in one width										
750mm wide	9.04	17.50	10.62	0.14	0.02	3.23	0.24	14.09	m²	15.50
900mm wide	9.04	17.50	10.62	0.13	0.02	3.02	0.24	13.88	m²	15.27
1050mm wide	9.04	17.50	10.62	0.12	0.02	2.82	0.24	13.68	m²	15.04
1200mm wide	9.04	17.50	10.62	0.11	0.02	2.61	0.24	13.47	m²	14.81
Reference C636; 5.55 kg/m²; 100mm side laps; 400mm end laps										
generally	11.81	17.50	13.88	0.10	0.02	2.40	0.31	16.58	m²	18.24
strips in one width										
750mm wide	11.81	17.50	13.88	0.15	0.02	3.44	0.31	17.63	m²	19.39
900mm wide	11.81	17.50	13.88	0.14	0.02	3.23	0.31	17.42	m²	19.16
1050mm wide	11.81	17.50	13.88	0.13	0.02	3.02	0.31	17.21	m²	18.93

Labour hourly rates: (except Specialists) Craft Operatives 20.87 Labourer 15.57 Rates are national average prices. Refer to REGIONAL VARIATIONS for indicative levels of overall pricing in regions	MATERIALS			LABOUR				RATES		
	Del to Site £	Waste %	Material Cost £	Craft Optve Hrs	Lab Hrs	Labour Cost £	Sunds £	Nett Rate £	Unit	Gross rate (10%) £
REINFORCEMENT (Cont'd)										
Mesh; Reinforcement fabric; BS 4483, hard drawn plain round steel; welded; including laps, tying wire, all cutting and bending, and spacers and chairs which are at the discretion of the Contractor (Cont'd)										
Reference C636; 5.55 kg/m²; 100mm side laps; 400mm end laps (Cont'd)										
strips in one width (Cont'd)										
1200mm wide	11.81	17.50	13.88	0.12	0.02	2.82	0.31	17.00	m²	18.70
Reference C785; 6.72 kg/m²; 100mm side laps; 400mm end laps										
generally	13.94	17.50	16.38	0.10	0.02	2.40	0.37	19.16	m²	21.07
strips in one width										
750mm wide	13.94	17.50	16.38	0.15	0.02	3.44	0.37	20.20	m²	22.22
900mm wide	13.94	17.50	16.38	0.14	0.02	3.23	0.37	19.99	m²	21.99
1050mm wide	13.94	17.50	16.38	0.13	0.02	3.02	0.37	19.78	m²	21.76
1200mm wide	13.94	17.50	16.38	0.12	0.02	2.82	0.37	19.57	m²	21.53
Reference D49; 0.77 kg/m²; 100mm side laps; 100mm end laps										
bent	6.93	17.50	8.15	0.04	0.01	0.99	0.13	9.27	m²	10.19
Reference D98; 1.54 kg/m²; 200mm side laps; 200mm end laps										
bent	5.34	17.50	6.27	0.04	0.01	0.99	0.13	7.39	m²	8.13
Expamet flattened security mesh expanded steel reinforcement (uncoated); including laps										
Reference HD1; 150mm side laps; 150mm end laps										
generally	10.56	17.50	12.41	0.12	0.02	2.82	0.44	15.66	m²	17.23
JOINTS IN CONCRETE										
Formed joints										
Incorporating 10mm thick Korkpak; Grace Construction Products Limited - Servicised; formwork; reinforcement laid continuously across joint										
in concrete, depth not exceeding 150mm; horizontal	6.04	5.00	6.34	-	0.08	1.25	7.74	15.33	m	16.86
in concrete, depth 150 - 300mm; horizontal	12.08	5.00	12.69	-	0.09	1.40	13.55	27.63	m	30.40
in concrete, depth 300 - 450mm; horizontal	18.12	5.00	19.03	-	0.10	1.56	19.70	40.29	m	44.31
Incorporating 13mm thick Korkpak; Grace Construction Products Limited - Servicised; formwork; reinforcement laid continuously across joint										
in concrete, depth not exceeding 150mm; horizontal	7.93	5.00	8.33	-	0.08	1.25	7.74	17.31	m	19.05
in concrete, depth 150 - 300mm; horizontal	15.87	5.00	16.66	-	0.09	1.40	13.55	31.61	m	34.77
in concrete, depth 300 - 450mm; horizontal	23.80	5.00	24.99	-	0.10	1.56	19.70	46.25	m	50.87
Incorporating 20mm thick Korkpak; Grace Construction Products Limited - Servicised; formwork; reinforcement laid continuously across joint										
in concrete, depth not exceeding 150mm; horizontal	11.04	5.00	11.59	-	0.08	1.25	7.74	20.58	m	22.64
in concrete, depth 150 - 300mm; horizontal	22.08	5.00	23.19	-	0.09	1.40	13.55	38.14	m	41.95
in concrete, depth 300 - 450mm; horizontal	33.13	5.00	34.78	-	0.10	1.56	19.70	56.04	m	61.64
Incorporating 195mm wide "Serviseal 195"; external face type p.v.c waterstop, Grace Construction Products Limited - Servicised; heat welded joints; formwork; reinforcement laid continuously across joint										
in concrete, depth not exceeding 150mm; horizontal	22.50	10.00	24.75	-	0.44	6.85	7.74	39.34	m	43.27
in concrete, depth 150 - 300mm; horizontal	22.50	10.00	24.75	-	0.44	6.85	13.55	45.15	m	49.66
in concrete, depth 300 - 450mm; horizontal	22.50	10.00	24.75	-	0.44	6.85	19.70	51.30	m	56.43
vertical L piece	62.14	10.00	68.36	-	0.22	3.43	-	71.78	nr	78.96
flat L piece	34.61	10.00	38.08	-	0.22	3.43	-	41.50	nr	45.65
flat T piece	59.33	10.00	65.27	-	0.28	4.36	-	69.62	nr	76.59
flat X piece	89.53	10.00	98.48	-	0.33	5.14	-	103.62	nr	113.98
in concrete, width not exceeding 150mm; vertical	22.50	10.00	24.75	-	0.55	8.56	7.74	41.05	m	45.16
in concrete, width 150 - 300mm; vertical	22.50	10.00	24.75	-	0.55	8.56	13.55	46.86	m	51.55
in concrete, width 300 - 450mm; vertical	22.50	10.00	24.75	-	0.55	8.56	19.70	53.01	m	58.32
flat L piece	34.61	10.00	38.08	-	0.22	3.43	-	41.50	nr	45.65
flat T piece	59.33	10.00	65.27	-	0.28	4.36	-	69.62	nr	76.59
flat X piece	89.53	10.00	98.48	-	0.33	5.14	-	103.62	nr	113.98
Incorporating 240mm wide "Serviseal 240"; heavy duty section external face type p.v.c. waterstop, Grace Construction Products Limited - Servicised; heat welded joints; formwork; reinforcement laid continuously across joint										
in concrete, depth not exceeding 150mm; horizontal	46.67	10.00	51.33	-	0.50	7.78	7.74	66.86	m	73.54
in concrete, depth 150 - 300mm; horizontal	46.67	10.00	51.33	-	0.50	7.78	13.55	72.67	m	79.93
in concrete, depth 300 - 450mm; horizontal	46.67	10.00	51.33	-	0.50	7.78	19.70	78.82	m	86.70
vertical L piece	73.76	10.00	81.14	-	0.22	3.43	-	84.56	nr	93.02
flat L piece	44.58	10.00	49.04	-	0.22	3.43	-	52.46	nr	57.71
flat T piece	75.35	10.00	82.88	-	0.28	4.36	-	87.24	nr	95.96
flat X piece	112.20	10.00	123.42	-	0.33	5.14	-	128.56	nr	141.42
in concrete, width not exceeding 150mm; vertical	46.67	10.00	51.33	-	0.61	9.50	7.74	68.57	m	75.43
in concrete, width 150 - 300mm; vertical	46.67	10.00	51.33	-	0.61	9.50	13.55	74.38	m	81.82
in concrete, width 300 - 450mm; vertical	46.67	10.00	51.33	-	0.61	9.50	19.70	80.53	m	88.59
flat L piece	44.58	10.00	49.04	-	0.22	3.43	-	52.46	nr	57.71
flat T piece	75.35	10.00	82.88	-	0.28	4.36	-	87.24	nr	95.96
flat X piece	112.20	10.00	123.42	-	0.33	5.14	-	128.56	nr	141.42
Incorporating 320mm wide "Serviseal K 320"; external face type p.v.c. kicker joint waterstop, Grace Construction Products Limited - Servicised; heat welded joints; formwork; reinforcement laid continuously across joint										
in concrete, depth not exceeding 150mm; vertical	46.40	10.00	51.04	-	0.66	10.28	7.74	69.05	m	75.96

Labour hourly rates: (except Specialists) Craft Operatives 20.87 Labourer 15.57 Rates are national average prices. Refer to REGIONAL VARIATIONS for indicative levels of overall pricing in regions	MATERIALS			LABOUR				RATES		
	Del to Site £	Waste %	Material Cost £	Craft Optve Hrs	Lab Hrs	Labour Cost £	Sunds £	Nett Rate £	Unit	Gross rate (10%) £
JOINTS IN CONCRETE (Cont'd)										
Formed joints (Cont'd)										
Incorporating 320mm wide "Serviseal K 320"; external face type p.v.c. kicker joint waterstop, Grace Construction Products Limited - Servicised; heat welded joints; formwork; reinforcement laid continuously across joint (Cont'd)										
in concrete, depth 150 - 300mm; vertical	46.40	10.00	51.04	-	0.66	10.28	13.55	74.86	m	82.35
in concrete, depth 300 - 450mm; vertical	46.40	10.00	51.04	-	0.66	10.28	19.70	81.01	m	89.12
vertical L piece	113.71	10.00	125.08	-	0.28	4.36	-	129.44	nr	142.38
flat L piece	100.36	10.00	110.39	-	0.28	4.36	-	114.75	nr	126.23
flat T piece	146.90	10.00	161.59	-	0.33	5.14	-	166.73	nr	183.40
flat X piece	182.98	10.00	201.27	-	0.39	6.07	-	207.35	nr	228.08
Incorporating 210mm wide "PVC Edgetie 210"; centre bulb type internally placed p.v.c. waterstop, Grace Construction Products Limited - Servicised; heat welded joints; formwork; reinforcement laid continuously across joint										
in concrete, depth not exceeding 150mm; horizontal	14.48	10.00	15.93	-	0.44	6.85	7.74	30.52	m	33.58
in concrete, depth 150 - 300mm; horizontal	14.48	10.00	15.93	-	0.44	6.85	13.55	36.33	m	39.96
in concrete, depth 300 - 450mm; horizontal	14.48	10.00	15.93	-	0.44	6.85	19.70	42.49	m	46.73
flat L piece	31.47	10.00	34.61	-	0.22	3.43	-	38.04	nr	41.84
flat T piece	41.71	10.00	45.88	-	0.28	4.36	-	50.24	nr	55.26
flat X piece	63.04	10.00	69.34	-	0.33	5.14	-	74.48	nr	81.93
in concrete, width not exceeding 150mm; vertical	14.48	10.00	15.93	-	0.55	8.56	7.74	32.24	m	35.46
in concrete, width 150 - 300mm; vertical	14.48	10.00	15.93	-	0.55	8.56	13.55	38.04	m	41.85
in concrete, width 300 - 450mm; vertical	14.48	10.00	15.93	-	0.55	8.56	19.70	44.20	m	48.62
vertical L piece	40.31	10.00	44.34	-	0.22	3.43	-	47.77	nr	52.55
flat L piece	31.47	10.00	34.61	-	0.22	3.43	-	38.04	nr	41.84
vertical T piece	63.45	10.00	69.80	-	0.28	4.36	-	74.15	nr	81.57
flat T piece	41.71	10.00	45.88	-	0.28	4.36	-	50.24	nr	55.26
flat X piece	63.04	10.00	69.34	-	0.33	5.14	-	74.48	nr	81.93
Incorporating 260mm wide "PVC Edgetie 260"; centre bulb type internally placed p.v.c. waterstop, Grace Construction Products Limited - Servicised; heat welded joints; formwork; reinforcement laid continuously across joint										
in concrete, depth not exceeding 150mm; horizontal	19.44	10.00	21.38	-	0.50	7.78	7.74	36.90	m	40.59
in concrete, depth 150 - 300mm; horizontal	19.44	10.00	21.38	-	0.50	7.78	13.55	42.71	m	46.98
in concrete, depth 300 - 450mm; horizontal	19.44	10.00	21.38	-	0.50	7.78	19.70	48.87	m	53.75
flat L piece	39.49	10.00	43.44	-	0.22	3.43	-	46.86	nr	51.55
flat T piece	54.40	10.00	59.84	-	0.28	4.36	-	64.20	nr	70.62
flat X piece	76.41	10.00	84.05	-	0.35	5.45	-	89.50	nr	98.45
in concrete, width not exceeding 150mm; vertical	19.44	10.00	21.38	-	0.61	9.50	7.74	38.62	m	42.48
in concrete, width 150 - 300mm; vertical	19.44	10.00	21.38	-	0.61	9.50	13.55	44.42	m	48.87
in concrete, width 300 - 450mm; vertical	19.44	10.00	21.38	-	0.61	9.50	19.70	50.58	m	55.64
vertical L piece	55.53	10.00	61.08	-	0.22	3.43	-	64.51	nr	70.96
flat L piece	39.49	10.00	43.44	-	0.22	3.43	-	46.86	nr	51.55
vertical T piece	75.79	10.00	83.37	-	0.28	4.36	-	87.73	nr	96.50
flat T piece	54.40	10.00	59.84	-	0.28	4.36	-	64.20	nr	70.62
flat X piece	76.41	10.00	84.05	-	0.33	5.14	-	89.19	nr	98.10
Incorporating 10 x 150mm wide PVC "Servitite"; bulb type internally placed waterstop; Grace Construction Products Limited - Servicised; heat welded joints fixed with "Secura" clips; formwork; reinforcement laid continuously across joint										
in concrete, depth not exceeding 150mm; horizontal	27.17	10.00	29.89	-	0.50	7.78	7.74	45.41	m	49.95
in concrete, depth 150 - 300mm; horizontal	27.17	10.00	29.89	-	0.50	7.78	13.55	51.22	m	56.34
in concrete, depth 300 - 450mm; horizontal	27.17	10.00	29.89	-	0.50	7.78	19.70	57.37	m	63.11
flat L piece	43.31	10.00	47.65	-	0.22	3.43	-	51.07	nr	56.18
flat T piece	62.42	10.00	68.66	-	0.28	4.36	-	73.02	nr	80.32
flat X piece	76.52	10.00	84.17	-	0.35	5.45	-	89.62	nr	98.59
in concrete, width not exceeding 150mm; vertical	27.17	10.00	29.89	-	0.61	9.50	7.74	47.12	m	51.83
in concrete, width 150 - 300mm; vertical	27.17	10.00	29.89	-	0.61	9.50	13.55	52.93	m	58.22
in concrete, width 300 - 450mm; vertical	27.17	10.00	29.89	-	0.61	9.50	19.70	59.08	m	64.99
vertical L piece	43.09	10.00	47.40	-	0.22	3.43	-	50.83	nr	55.91
flat L piece	43.31	10.00	47.65	-	0.22	3.43	-	51.07	nr	56.18
vertical T piece	72.41	10.00	79.65	-	0.28	4.36	-	84.01	nr	92.42
flat T piece	62.42	10.00	68.66	-	0.28	4.36	-	73.02	nr	80.32
flat X piece	76.52	10.00	84.17	-	0.33	5.14	-	89.31	nr	98.24
Incorporating 10 x 230mm wide PVC "Servitite"; bulb type internally placed waterstop; Grace Construction Products Limited - Servicised; heat welded joints fixed with "Secura" clips; formwork; reinforcement laid continuously across joint										
in concrete, depth not exceeding 150mm; horizontal	40.20	10.00	44.22	-	0.50	7.78	7.74	59.74	m	65.72
in concrete, depth 150 - 300mm; horizontal	40.20	10.00	44.22	-	0.50	7.78	13.55	65.55	m	72.11
in concrete, depth 300 - 450mm; horizontal	40.20	10.00	44.22	-	0.50	7.78	19.70	71.71	m	78.88
flat L piece	51.79	10.00	56.96	-	0.22	3.43	-	60.39	nr	66.43
flat T piece	75.10	10.00	82.61	-	0.28	4.36	-	86.97	nr	95.67
flat X piece	94.04	10.00	103.45	-	0.35	5.45	-	108.90	nr	119.79
in concrete, width not exceeding 150mm; vertical	40.20	10.00	44.22	-	0.61	9.50	7.74	61.46	m	67.60
in concrete, width 150 - 300mm; vertical	40.20	10.00	44.22	-	0.61	9.50	13.55	67.26	m	73.99
in concrete, width 300 - 450mm; vertical	40.20	10.00	44.22	-	0.61	9.50	19.70	73.42	m	80.76
vertical L piece	63.56	10.00	69.91	-	0.22	3.43	-	73.34	nr	80.67
flat L piece	51.79	10.00	56.96	-	0.22	3.43	-	60.39	nr	66.43
vertical T piece	76.52	10.00	84.17	-	0.28	4.36	-	88.53	nr	97.39
flat T piece	75.10	10.00	82.61	-	0.28	4.36	-	86.97	nr	95.67
flat X piece	94.04	10.00	103.45	-	0.33	5.14	-	108.59	nr	119.45
Incorporating 10 x 305mm wide PVC "Servitite"; bulb type internally placed waterstop; Grace Construction Products Limited - Servicised; heat welded joints fixed with "Secura" clips; formwork; reinforcement laid continuously across joint										
in concrete, depth not exceeding 150mm; horizontal	69.20	10.00	76.12	-	0.50	7.78	7.74	91.64	m	100.81

Labour hourly rates: (except Specialists) Craft Operatives 20.87 Labourer 15.57 Rates are national average prices. Refer to REGIONAL VARIATIONS for indicative levels of overall pricing in regions	MATERIALS			LABOUR				RATES		
	Del to Site £	Waste %	Material Cost £	Craft Optve Hrs	Lab Hrs	Labour Cost £	Sunds £	Nett Rate £	Unit	Gross rate (10%) £
JOINTS IN CONCRETE (Cont'd)										
Formed joints (Cont'd)										
Incorporating 10 x 305mm wide PVC "Servitite"; bulb type internally placed waterstop; Grace Construction Products Limited - Servicised; heat welded joints fixed with "Secura" clips; formwork; reinforcement laid continuously across joint (Cont'd)										
in concrete, depth 150 - 300mm; horizontal	69.20	10.00	76.12	-	0.50	7.78	13.55	97.45	m	107.20
in concrete, depth 300 - 450mm; horizontal	69.20	10.00	76.12	-	0.50	7.78	19.70	103.61	m	113.97
flat L piece	88.86	10.00	97.75	-	0.22	3.43	-	101.17	nr	111.29
flat T piece	124.85	10.00	137.34	-	0.28	4.36	-	141.70	nr	155.87
flat X piece	170.10	10.00	187.12	-	0.35	5.45	-	192.56	nr	211.82
in concrete, width not exceeding 150mm; vertical	69.20	10.00	76.12	-	0.61	9.50	7.74	93.36	m	102.69
in concrete, width 150 - 300mm; vertical	69.20	10.00	76.12	-	0.61	9.50	13.55	99.16	m	109.08
in concrete, width 300 - 450mm; vertical	69.20	10.00	76.12	-	0.61	9.50	19.70	105.32	m	115.85
vertical L piece	97.77	10.00	107.55	-	0.22	3.43	-	110.97	nr	122.07
flat L piece	88.86	10.00	97.75	-	0.22	3.43	-	101.17	nr	111.29
vertical T piece	152.40	10.00	167.64	-	0.28	4.36	-	172.00	nr	189.20
flat T piece	124.85	10.00	137.34	-	0.28	4.36	-	141.70	nr	155.87
flat X piece	170.10	10.00	187.12	-	0.33	5.14	-	192.25	nr	211.48
Incorporating 445mm wide Reference 2411, 6.34 kg/m² Expamet Hy-rib permanent shuttering and reinforcement; 150mm end laps; temporary supports; formwork laid continuously across joint										
in concrete, depth not exceeding 150mm; horizontal	5.63	7.50	6.05	0.25	0.07	6.31	8.33	20.69	m	22.76
in concrete, depth 150 - 300mm; horizontal	11.26	7.50	12.11	0.25	0.07	6.31	14.57	32.98	m	36.28
in concrete, width not exceeding 150mm; vertical	5.63	7.50	6.05	0.39	0.10	9.70	8.33	24.08	m	26.49
in concrete, width 150 - 300mm; vertical	11.26	7.50	12.11	0.39	0.10	9.70	14.57	36.37	m	40.01
Incorporating 445mm wide Reference 2611, 4.86 kg/m² Expamet Hy-rib permanent shuttering and reinforcement; 150mm end laps; temporary supports; formwork laid continuously across joint										
in concrete, depth not exceeding 150mm; horizontal	3.08	7.50	3.31	0.25	0.07	6.31	8.33	17.95	m	19.74
in concrete, depth 150 - 300mm; horizontal	6.16	7.50	6.62	0.25	0.07	6.31	14.57	27.50	m	30.24
in concrete, width not exceeding 150mm; vertical	3.08	7.50	3.31	0.39	0.10	9.70	8.33	21.34	m	23.47
in concrete, width 150 - 300mm; vertical	6.16	7.50	6.62	0.39	0.10	9.70	14.57	30.88	m	33.97
Incorporating 445mm wide Reference 2811, 3.39 kg/m² Expamet Hy-rib permanent shuttering and reinforcement; 150mm end laps; temporary supports; formwork laid continuously across joint										
in concrete, depth not exceeding 150mm; horizontal	6.12	7.50	6.57	0.25	0.07	6.31	8.33	21.21	m	23.34
in concrete, depth 150 - 300mm; horizontal	12.23	7.50	13.15	0.25	0.07	6.31	14.57	34.03	m	37.43
in concrete, width not exceeding 150mm; vertical	6.12	7.50	6.57	0.39	0.10	9.70	8.33	24.60	m	27.06
in concrete, width 150 - 300mm; vertical	12.23	7.50	13.15	0.39	0.10	9.70	14.57	37.41	m	41.16
Sealant to joint; Grace Construction Products Limited - Servicised. Servijoint ONE DW (one-part sealant); including preparation, cleaning and priming										
10 x 25mm; horizontal	7.24	5.00	7.60	-	0.15	2.34	-	9.94	m	10.93
13 x 25mm; horizontal	9.17	5.00	9.63	-	0.20	3.11	-	12.74	m	14.02
19 x 25mm; horizontal	13.31	5.00	13.97	-	0.25	3.89	-	17.86	m	19.65
Sealant to joint; Grace Construction Products Limited - Servicised. "Paraseal" pouring grade 2 part grey polysulphide sealant; including preparation, cleaners, primers and sealant										
10 x 25mm; horizontal	4.43	5.00	4.65	-	0.11	1.71	-	6.36	m	6.99
13 x 25mm; horizontal	5.75	5.00	6.04	-	0.12	1.87	-	7.91	m	8.70
19 x 25mm; horizontal	8.41	5.00	8.83	-	0.13	2.02	-	10.85	m	11.94
ACCESSORIES CAST IN TO IN-SITU CONCRETE										
Cast in accessories										
12mm diameter x 400mm long	1.93	10.00	2.12	-	0.08	1.25	-	3.37	nr	3.71
12mm diameter x 600mm long	2.17	10.00	2.39	-	0.12	1.87	-	4.26	nr	4.68
Galvanised expanded metal tie										
300 x 50mm; bending and temporarily fixing to formwork	1.06	10.00	1.16	-	0.13	2.02	-	3.19	nr	3.51
Galvanised steel dovetailed masonry slots with 3mm thick twisted tie to suit 50mm cavity										
100mm long; temporarily fixing to formwork	1.05	10.00	1.15	0.11	-	2.30	-	3.45	nr	3.79
Stainless steel channel with anchors at 250mm centres										
28 x 15mm; temporarily fixing to formwork	15.42	5.00	16.20	0.28	-	5.84	-	22.04	m	24.24
28 x 15 x 150mm long; temporarily fixing to formwork	2.59	5.00	2.72	0.12	-	2.50	-	5.23	nr	5.75
M10 bolt 50mm long with `T' head nut and washers	5.32	5.00	5.59	0.05	-	1.04	-	6.63	nr	7.29
fishtailed tie to suit 50mm cavity	2.14	5.00	2.25	0.06	-	1.25	-	3.50	nr	3.85
Stainless steel angle drilled at 450mm centres										
70 x 90 x 5mm	39.60	5.00	41.58	0.80	-	16.70	-	58.28	m	64.10
Copper dovetailed masonry slots with 3mm thick twisted tie to suit 50mm cavity										
100mm long; temporarily fixing to formwork	11.16	10.00	12.28	0.11	-	2.30	-	14.57	nr	16.03
Bolt boxes; The Expanded Metal Co. Ltd										
reference 220 for use with poured concrete; 75mm diameter										
150mm long	3.84	10.00	4.22	0.28	-	5.84	0.94	11.01	nr	12.11
225mm long	5.67	10.00	6.23	0.33	-	6.89	0.94	14.06	nr	15.47
300mm long	7.49	10.00	8.24	0.39	-	8.14	0.94	17.32	nr	19.06
reference 220 for use with poured concrete; 100mm diameter										
375mm long	11.58	10.00	12.73	0.44	-	9.18	0.94	22.86	nr	25.14
450mm long	13.40	10.00	14.74	0.50	-	10.44	0.94	26.12	nr	28.73
600mm long	17.06	10.00	18.77	0.55	-	11.48	0.94	31.18	nr	34.30
reference 220 for use with vibrated concrete; wrap with single layer of thin polythene sheet; 75mm diameter										
150mm long	3.91	10.00	4.31	0.28	-	5.84	1.14	11.29	nr	12.42

Labour hourly rates: (except Specialists) Craft Operatives 20.87 Labourer 15.57 Rates are national average prices. Refer to REGIONAL VARIATIONS for indicative levels of overall pricing in regions	MATERIALS			LABOUR				RATES		
	Del to Site £	Waste %	Material Cost £	Craft Optve Hrs	Lab Hrs	Labour Cost £	Sunds £	Nett Rate £	Unit	Gross rate (10%) £
ACCESSORIES CAST IN TO IN-SITU CONCRETE (Cont'd)										
Cast in accessories (Cont'd)										
Bolt boxes; The Expanded Metal Co. Ltd (Cont'd)										
reference 220 for use with vibrated concrete; wrap with single layer of thin polythene sheet; 75mm diameter (Cont'd)										
225mm long	5.78	10.00	6.36	0.33	-	6.89	1.14	14.38	nr	15.82
300mm long	7.64	10.00	8.41	0.39	-	8.14	1.14	17.69	nr	19.45
reference 220 for use with vibrated concrete; wrap with single layer of thin polythene sheet; 100mm diameter										
375mm long	11.81	10.00	12.99	0.44	-	9.18	1.14	23.31	nr	25.64
450mm long	13.67	10.00	15.04	0.50	-	10.44	1.14	26.61	nr	29.27
600mm long	17.40	10.00	19.14	0.55	-	11.48	1.14	31.76	nr	34.93
Bolt cones; waxed cardboard										
for use with poured concrete										
229mm	0.70	10.00	0.77	0.28	-	5.84	0.94	7.55	nr	8.31
305mm	0.99	10.00	1.09	0.33	-	6.89	0.94	8.92	nr	9.81
380mm	1.47	10.00	1.62	0.39	-	8.14	0.94	10.70	nr	11.77
457mm	1.90	10.00	2.09	0.44	-	9.18	0.94	12.21	nr	13.43
534mm	2.65	10.00	2.92	0.50	-	10.44	0.94	14.29	nr	15.72
610mm	2.90	10.00	3.19	0.55	-	11.48	0.94	15.61	nr	17.17
762mm	4.92	10.00	5.41	0.59	-	12.31	0.94	18.67	nr	20.53
Steel rag bolts										
M 10 x 100mm long	0.26	5.00	0.27	0.10	-	2.09	-	2.36	nr	2.59
M 10 x 160mm long	0.79	5.00	0.83	0.12	-	2.50	-	3.33	nr	3.67
M 12 x 100mm long	0.43	5.00	0.45	0.10	-	2.09	-	2.54	nr	2.79
M 12 x 160mm long	0.57	5.00	0.60	0.12	-	2.50	-	3.11	nr	3.42
M 12 x 200mm long	0.70	5.00	0.73	0.14	-	2.92	-	3.66	nr	4.02
M 16 x 120mm long	0.89	5.00	0.94	0.10	-	2.09	-	3.03	nr	3.33
M 16 x 160mm long	1.22	5.00	1.28	0.12	-	2.50	-	3.78	nr	4.16
M 16 x 200mm long	1.27	5.00	1.33	0.14	-	2.92	-	4.25	nr	4.68
M 16 x 300mm long	2.40	5.00	2.52	0.16	-	3.34	-	5.86	nr	6.45
M 20 x 450mm long	5.53	5.00	5.81	0.20	-	4.17	-	9.98	nr	10.98
M 24 x 450mm long	8.08	5.00	8.48	0.25	-	5.22	-	13.70	nr	15.07
IN-SITU CONCRETE SUNDRIES										
Grouting; Cement and sand (1; 3)										
Grouting.										
stanchion bases.	4.28	10.00	4.71	-	0.45	7.01	1.73	13.45	nr	14.79

This page left blank intentionally

Labour hourly rates: (except Specialists) Craft Operatives 20.87 Labourer 15.57 Rates are national average prices. Refer to REGIONAL VARIATIONS for indicative levels of overall pricing in regions	MATERIALS			LABOUR				RATES		
	Del to Site £	Waste %	Material Cost £	Craft Optve Hrs	Lab Hrs	Labour Cost £	Sunds £	Nett Rate £	Unit	Gross rate (10%) £
PRECAST/COMPOSITE CONCRETE DECKING & FLOORING										
Composite concrete work; Prestressed concrete beams and 100mm building blocks; hoist bed and grout										
155mm thick floors										
beams at 510mm centres	30.35	2.50	31.11	-	1.15	17.91	0.74	49.76	m²	54.73
beams at 510mm and 285mm centres	38.10	2.50	39.05	-	1.05	16.35	0.74	56.14	m²	61.76
double beams at 624mm centres	45.85	2.50	47.00	-	1.00	15.57	0.74	63.31	m²	69.64
beams at 285mm centres	45.85	2.50	47.00	-	1.15	17.91	0.74	65.64	m²	72.21
double beams at 399mm centres	73.92	2.50	75.77	-	1.05	16.35	0.74	92.86	m²	102.15
beams at 114mm centres with concrete between	90.68	2.50	92.94	-	1.00	15.57	0.74	109.25	m²	120.18
225mm thick floors										
beams at 530mm centres	35.82	2.50	36.72	-	1.15	17.91	0.74	55.36	m²	60.90
beams at 305mm centres	57.18	2.50	58.61	-	1.05	16.35	0.74	75.70	m²	83.27
beams at 140mm centres with concrete between	115.83	2.50	118.73	-	1.00	15.57	0.74	135.04	m²	148.55
Passive fall arrest provision										
Add to the foregoing rates for providing safety decking, airbags or netting as appropriate to the works										
total area less than 100 m²	10.22	2.50	10.47	-	-	-	-	10.47	m²	11.52
total area over 100m²	10.14	2.50	10.39	-	-	-	-	10.39	m²	11.43

This page left blank intentionally

Labour hourly rates: (except Specialists) Craft Operatives 20.87 Labourer 15.57 Rates are national average prices. Refer to REGIONAL VARIATIONS for indicative levels of overall pricing in regions	MATERIALS			LABOUR				RATES		
	Del to Site £	Waste %	Material Cost £	Craft Optve Hrs	Lab Hrs	Labour Cost £	Sunds £	Nett Rate £	Unit	Gross rate (10%) £
PRECAST CONCRETE SLABS										
Precast concrete goods; Precast concrete hollowcore floors and hoist bed and grout										
150 mm thick planks 750 wide										
span between supports 7.6m; UDL not exceeding 2KN/m²	78.44	2.50	80.40	-	-	-	-	80.40	m²	88.44
span between supports 6.6m; UDL not exceeding 4KN/m²	78.44	2.50	80.40	-	-	-	-	80.40	m²	88.44
span between supports 5.9m; UDL not exceeding 6KN/m²	78.44	2.50	80.40	-	-	-	-	80.40	m²	88.44
span between supports 5.4m; UDL not exceeding 8KN/m²	78.44	2.50	80.40	-	-	-	-	80.40	m²	88.44
span between supports 5.0m; UDL not exceeding 10KN/m²	78.44	2.50	80.40	-	-	-	-	80.40	m²	88.44
200 mm thick planks 750 wide										
span between supports 9.3m; UDL not exceeding 2KN/m²	85.86	2.50	88.01	-	-	-	-	88.01	m²	96.81
span between supports 8.1m; UDL not exceeding 4KN/m²	85.86	2.50	88.01	-	-	-	-	88.01	m²	96.81
span between supports 7.3m; UDL not exceeding 6KN/m²	85.86	2.50	88.01	-	-	-	-	88.01	m²	96.81
span between supports 6.7m; UDL not exceeding 8KN/m²	85.86	2.50	88.01	-	-	-	-	88.01	m²	96.81
span between supports 6.2m; UDL not exceeding 10KN/m²	85.86	2.50	88.01	-	-	-	-	88.01	m²	96.81
250 mm thick planks 750 wide										
span between supports 10.6m; UDL not exceeding 2KN/m²	93.68	2.50	96.03	-	-	-	-	96.03	m²	105.63
span between supports 9.3m; UDL not exceeding 4KN/m²	93.68	2.50	96.03	-	-	-	-	96.03	m²	105.63
span between supports 8.5m; UDL not exceeding 6KN/m²	93.68	2.50	96.03	-	-	-	-	96.03	m²	105.63
span between supports 7.8m; UDL not exceeding 8KN/m²	93.68	2.50	96.03	-	-	-	-	96.03	m²	105.63
span between supports 7.2m; UDL not exceeding 10KN/m²	93.68	2.50	96.03	-	-	-	-	96.03	m²	105.63
300 mm thick planks 750 wide										
span between supports 11.5m; UDL not exceeding 2KN/m²	101.46	2.50	103.99	-	-	-	-	103.99	m²	114.39
span between supports 10.3m; UDL not exceeding 4KN/m²	101.46	2.50	103.99	-	-	-	-	103.99	m²	114.39
span between supports 9.4m; UDL not exceeding 6KN/m²	101.46	2.50	103.99	-	-	-	-	103.99	m²	114.39
span between supports 8.7m; UDL not exceeding 8KN/m²	101.46	2.50	103.99	-	-	-	-	103.99	m²	114.39
span between supports 8.1m; UDL not exceeding 10KN/m²	101.46	2.50	103.99	-	-	-	-	103.99	m²	114.39
Passive fall arrest provision										
Add to the foregoing rates for providing safety decking, airbags or netting as appropriate to the works										
total area less than 100 m²	10.22	2.50	10.47	-	-	-	-	10.47	m²	11.52
total area over 100m²	10.14	2.50	10.39	-	-	-	-	10.39	m²	11.43

PRECAST CONCRETE

This page left blank intentionally

Labour hourly rates: (except Specialists) Craft Operatives 20.87 Labourer 15.57 Rates are national average prices. Refer to REGIONAL VARIATIONS for indicative levels of overall pricing in regions	MATERIALS			LABOUR				RATES		
	Del to Site £	Waste %	Material Cost £	Craft Optve Hrs	Lab Hrs	Labour Cost £	Sunds £	Nett Rate £	Unit	Gross rate (10%) £
BRICK/BLOCK WALLING										
Walls; brickwork; Common bricks, BS EN 772, Category M, 215 x 102.5 x 65mm, compressive strength 20.5 N/mm²; in cement-lime mortar (1:2:9)										
Walls										
102mm thick; stretcher bond	18.40	5.00	19.32	1.45	1.10	47.39	4.04	70.75	m²	77.83
215mm thick; English bond	37.11	5.00	38.97	2.35	1.85	77.85	9.44	126.26	m²	138.88
327mm thick; English bond	55.83	5.00	58.62	2.85	2.30	95.29	14.83	168.74	m²	185.61
Skins of hollow walls										
102mm thick; stretcher bond	18.40	5.00	19.32	1.45	1.10	47.39	4.04	70.75	m²	77.83
215mm thick; English bond	37.11	5.00	38.97	2.35	1.85	77.85	9.44	126.26	m²	138.88
Walls; building against concrete (ties measured separately); vertical										
102mm thick; stretcher bond	18.40	5.00	19.32	1.60	1.20	52.08	4.04	75.44	m²	82.98
Walls; building against old brickwork; tie new to old with 200mm stainless steel housing type 4 wall ties - 6/m²; vertical										
102mm thick; stretcher bond	20.02	10.00	21.10	1.60	1.20	52.08	4.04	77.22	m²	84.94
215mm thick; English bond	38.73	10.00	40.75	2.65	2.05	87.22	9.44	137.41	m²	151.15
Walls; bonding to stonework; including extra material; vertical										
102mm thick; stretcher bond	19.44	5.00	20.41	1.60	1.20	52.08	4.04	76.53	m²	84.18
215mm thick; English bond	39.19	5.00	41.15	2.65	2.05	87.22	9.44	137.81	m²	151.60
327mm thick; English bond	57.91	5.00	60.80	3.15	2.50	104.67	14.83	180.30	m²	198.33
440mm thick; English bond	76.31	5.00	80.12	3.70	3.00	123.93	20.23	224.28	m²	246.71
Walls; bonding to old brickwork; cutting pockets; including extra material; vertical										
102mm thick; stretcher bond	19.44	5.00	20.41	3.65	2.55	115.88	4.04	140.33	m²	154.37
215mm thick; English bond	39.19	5.00	41.15	4.60	3.30	147.38	9.44	197.97	m²	217.77
Walls; curved 2m radius; including extra material; vertical										
102mm thick; stretcher bond	18.40	5.00	19.32	2.85	2.05	91.40	4.04	114.76	m²	126.24
215mm thick; English bond	37.11	5.00	38.97	5.20	3.75	166.91	9.44	215.32	m²	236.85
327mm thick; English bond	55.83	5.00	58.62	7.10	5.10	227.58	14.83	301.03	m²	331.14
Walls; curved 6m radius; including extra material; vertical										
102mm thick; stretcher bond	18.40	5.00	19.32	2.15	1.55	69.00	4.04	92.37	m²	101.60
215mm thick; English bond	37.11	5.00	38.97	3.75	2.80	121.86	9.44	170.27	m²	187.29
327mm thick; English bond	55.83	5.00	58.62	4.95	3.70	160.92	14.83	234.37	m²	257.80
Skins of hollow walls; curved 2m radius; including extra material; vertical										
102mm thick; stretcher bond	18.40	5.00	19.32	2.85	2.05	91.40	4.04	114.76	m²	126.24
215mm thick; English bond	37.11	5.00	38.97	5.20	3.75	166.91	9.44	215.32	m²	236.85
Skins of hollow walls; curved 6m radius; including extra material; vertical										
102mm thick; stretcher bond	18.40	5.00	19.32	2.15	1.55	69.00	4.04	92.37	m²	101.60
215mm thick; English bond	37.11	5.00	38.97	3.75	2.80	121.86	9.44	170.27	m²	187.29
Isolated piers										
215mm thick; English bond	37.11	5.00	38.97	4.70	3.40	151.03	9.44	199.43	m²	219.38
327mm thick; English bond	55.83	5.00	58.62	5.70	4.20	184.35	14.83	257.80	m²	283.58
440mm thick; English bond	74.23	5.00	77.94	6.60	4.95	214.81	20.23	312.98	m²	344.28
Chimney stacks										
440mm thick; English bond	74.23	5.00	77.94	6.60	5.45	222.60	20.23	320.77	m²	352.84
890mm thick; English bond	148.45	5.00	155.88	10.40	8.80	354.06	40.46	550.40	m²	605.44
Projections										
215mm wide x 112mm projection	4.16	5.00	4.37	0.30	0.23	9.84	1.07	15.28	m	16.81
215mm wide x 215mm projection	8.31	5.00	8.73	0.50	0.39	16.51	2.16	27.40	m	30.14
327mm wide x 112mm projection	6.24	5.00	6.55	0.45	0.35	14.84	1.62	23.01	m	25.31
327mm wide x 215mm projection	12.47	5.00	13.10	0.75	0.59	24.84	3.23	41.17	m	45.29
Projections; horizontal										
215mm wide x 112mm projection	4.16	5.00	4.37	0.30	0.23	9.84	1.07	15.28	m	16.81
215mm wide x 215mm projection	8.31	5.00	8.73	0.50	0.39	16.51	2.16	27.40	m	30.14
327mm wide x 112mm projection	6.24	5.00	6.55	0.45	0.35	14.84	1.62	23.01	m	25.31
327mm wide x 215mm projection	12.47	5.00	13.10	0.75	0.59	24.84	3.23	41.17	m	45.29
Projections; bonding to old brickwork; cutting pockets; including extra material; vertical										
215mm wide x 112mm projection	6.93	5.00	7.27	0.93	0.65	29.53	1.80	38.60	m	42.46
215mm wide x 215mm projection	11.08	5.00	11.64	1.13	0.81	36.19	2.87	50.70	m	55.77
327mm wide x 112mm projection	10.39	5.00	10.91	1.40	0.98	44.48	2.69	58.08	m	63.89
327mm wide x 215mm projection	15.24	5.00	16.01	1.70	1.22	54.47	3.96	74.44	m	81.89
Projections; bonding to old brickwork; cutting pockets; including extra material; horizontal										
215mm wide x 112mm projection	6.93	5.00	7.27	0.93	0.65	29.53	1.80	38.60	m	42.46
215mm wide x 215mm projection	11.08	5.00	11.64	1.13	0.81	36.19	2.87	50.70	m	55.77
327mm wide x 112mm projection	10.39	5.00	10.91	1.40	0.98	44.48	2.69	58.08	m	63.89

Labour hourly rates: (except Specialists) Craft Operatives 20.87 Labourer 15.57 Rates are national average prices. Refer to REGIONAL VARIATIONS for indicative levels of overall pricing in regions	MATERIALS			LABOUR				RATES		
	Del to Site £	Waste %	Material Cost £	Craft Optve Hrs	Lab Hrs	Labour Cost £	Sunds £	Nett Rate £	Unit	Gross rate (10%) £
BRICK/BLOCK WALLING (Cont'd)										
Walls; brickwork; Common bricks, BS EN 772, Category M, 215 x 102.5 x 65mm, compressive strength 20.5 N/mm²; in cement-lime mortar (1:2:9) (Cont'd)										
Projections; bonding to old brickwork; cutting pockets; including extra material; horizontal (Cont'd)										
327mm wide x 215mm projection	15.24	5.00	16.01	1.70	1.22	54.47	3.96	74.44	m	81.89
Arches including centering; flat										
112mm high on face; 215mm thick; width of exposed soffit 215mm; bricks-on-edge	4.16	5.00	4.37	1.50	1.00	46.88	1.07	52.31	m	57.54
215mm high on face; 112mm thick; width of exposed soffit 112mm; bricks-on-end	4.16	5.00	4.37	1.45	1.00	45.83	1.07	51.27	m	56.40
Arches including centering; semi-circular										
112mm high on face; 215mm thick; width of exposed soffit 215mm; bricks-on-edge	6.53	5.00	6.85	2.15	1.35	65.89	1.70	74.44	m	81.89
215mm high on face; 215mm thick; width of exposed soffit 215mm; bricks-on-edge	13.06	5.00	13.71	2.95	1.95	91.93	3.38	109.02	m	119.92
Closing cavities										
50mm wide with brickwork 102mm thick	2.03	5.00	2.13	0.40	0.27	12.55	0.53	15.21	m	16.73
75mm wide with brickwork 102mm thick	2.03	5.00	2.13	0.40	0.27	12.55	0.53	15.21	m	16.73
Closing cavities; horizontal										
50mm wide with slates	6.20	5.00	6.51	0.66	0.44	20.62	0.53	27.66	m	30.43
75mm wide with slates	6.20	5.00	6.51	0.66	0.44	20.62	0.53	27.66	m	30.43
50mm wide with brickwork 102mm thick	2.03	5.00	2.13	0.40	0.27	12.55	0.53	15.21	m	16.73
75mm wide with brickwork 102mm thick	2.03	5.00	2.13	0.40	0.27	12.55	0.53	15.21	m	16.73
Bonding ends to existing common brickwork; cutting pockets; extra material										
walls; bonding every third course										
102mm thick	1.38	5.00	1.45	0.37	0.25	11.61	0.36	13.43	m	14.77
215mm thick	2.77	5.00	2.91	0.66	0.44	20.62	0.73	24.26	m	26.68
327mm thick	4.16	5.00	4.37	0.95	0.63	29.64	1.07	35.07	m	38.58
Walls; brickwork; Second hard stock bricks, BS EN 772, Category M, 215 x 102.5 x 65mm; in cement-lime mortar (1:2:9)										
Walls										
102mm thick; stretcher bond	36.58	5.00	38.41	1.45	1.10	47.39	4.04	89.84	m²	98.82
215mm thick; English bond	73.78	5.00	77.47	2.35	1.85	77.85	9.44	164.76	m²	181.23
327mm thick; English bond	110.98	5.00	116.53	2.85	2.30	95.29	14.83	226.65	m²	249.32
Skins of hollow walls										
102mm thick; stretcher bond	36.58	5.00	38.41	1.45	1.10	47.39	4.04	89.84	m²	98.82
215mm thick; English bond	73.78	5.00	77.47	2.35	1.85	77.85	9.44	164.76	m²	181.23
Walls; building against concrete (ties measured separately); vertical										
102mm thick; stretcher bond	36.58	5.00	38.41	1.60	1.20	52.08	4.04	94.53	m²	103.98
Walls; building against old brickwork; tie new to old with 200mm stainless steel housing type 4 wall ties - 6/m²; vertical										
102mm thick; stretcher bond	38.20	10.00	40.19	1.60	1.20	52.08	4.04	96.31	m²	105.94
215mm thick; English bond	75.40	10.00	79.25	2.65	2.05	87.22	9.44	175.91	m²	193.50
Walls; bonding to stonework; including extra material; vertical										
102mm thick; stretcher bond	38.64	5.00	40.58	1.60	1.20	52.08	4.27	96.93	m²	106.62
215mm thick; English bond	77.92	5.00	81.81	2.65	2.05	87.22	9.98	179.02	m²	196.92
327mm thick; English bond	115.12	5.00	120.87	3.15	2.50	104.67	15.38	240.91	m²	265.01
440mm thick; English bond	151.70	5.00	159.28	3.70	3.00	123.93	20.79	304.00	m²	334.40
Walls; bonding to old brickwork; cutting pockets; including extra material; vertical										
102mm thick; stretcher bond	38.64	5.00	40.58	3.65	2.55	115.88	4.27	160.73	m²	176.80
215mm thick; English bond	77.92	5.00	81.81	4.60	3.30	147.38	9.98	239.18	m²	263.09
Walls; curved 2m radius; including extra material; vertical										
102mm thick; stretcher bond	36.58	5.00	38.41	2.85	2.05	91.40	4.04	133.85	m²	147.23
215mm thick; English bond	73.78	5.00	77.47	5.20	3.75	166.91	9.44	253.82	m²	279.20
327mm thick; English bond	110.98	5.00	116.53	7.10	5.10	227.58	14.83	358.95	m²	394.84
Walls; curved 6m radius; including extra material; vertical										
102mm thick; stretcher bond	36.58	5.00	38.41	2.15	1.55	69.00	4.04	111.46	m²	122.60
215mm thick; English bond	73.78	5.00	77.47	3.75	2.80	121.86	9.44	208.77	m²	229.64
327mm thick; English bond	110.98	5.00	116.53	4.95	3.70	160.92	14.83	292.28	m²	321.51
Skins of hollow walls; curved 2m radius; including extra material; vertical										
102mm thick; stretcher bond	36.58	5.00	38.41	2.85	2.05	91.40	4.04	133.85	m²	147.23
215mm thick; English bond	73.78	5.00	77.47	5.20	3.75	166.91	9.44	253.82	m²	279.20
Skins of hollow walls; curved 6m radius; including extra material; vertical										
102mm thick; stretcher bond	36.58	5.00	38.41	2.15	1.55	69.00	4.04	111.46	m²	122.60
215mm thick; English bond	73.78	5.00	77.47	3.75	2.80	121.86	9.44	208.77	m²	229.64
Isolated piers										
215mm thick; English bond	73.78	5.00	77.47	4.70	3.40	151.03	9.44	237.93	m²	261.73
327mm thick; English bond	110.98	5.00	116.53	5.70	4.20	184.35	14.83	315.72	m²	347.29
440mm thick; English bond	147.56	5.00	154.94	6.60	4.95	214.81	20.23	389.98	m²	428.98
Chimney stacks										
440mm thick; English bond	147.56	5.00	154.94	6.60	5.45	222.60	20.23	397.77	m²	437.54
890mm thick; English bond	295.12	5.00	309.88	10.40	8.80	354.06	40.46	704.40	m²	774.84

Labour hourly rates: (except Specialists) Craft Operatives 20.87 Labourer 15.57 Rates are national average prices. Refer to REGIONAL VARIATIONS for indicative levels of overall pricing in regions	MATERIALS			LABOUR				RATES		
	Del to Site £	Waste %	Material Cost £	Craft Optve Hrs	Lab Hrs	Labour Cost £	Sunds £	Nett Rate £	Unit	Gross rate (10%) £
BRICK/BLOCK WALLING (Cont'd)										
Walls; brickwork; Second hard stock bricks, BS EN 772, Category M, 215 x 102.5 x 65mm; in cement-lime mortar (1:2:9) (Cont'd)										
Projections										
215mm wide x 112mm projection	8.26	5.00	8.68	0.30	0.23	9.84	1.07	19.59	m	21.55
215mm wide x 215mm projection	16.53	5.00	17.36	0.50	0.39	16.51	2.16	36.02	m	39.63
327mm wide x 112mm projection	12.40	5.00	13.02	0.45	0.35	14.84	1.62	29.48	m	32.43
327mm wide x 215mm projection	24.80	5.00	26.04	0.75	0.59	24.84	3.23	54.11	m	59.52
Projections; horizontal										
215mm wide x 112mm projection	8.26	5.00	8.68	0.30	0.23	9.84	1.07	19.59	m	21.55
215mm wide x 215mm projection	16.53	5.00	17.36	0.50	0.39	16.51	2.16	36.02	m	39.63
327mm wide x 112mm projection	12.40	5.00	13.02	0.45	0.35	14.84	1.62	29.48	m	32.43
327mm wide x 215mm projection	24.80	5.00	26.04	0.75	0.59	24.84	3.23	54.11	m	59.52
Projections; bonding to old brickwork; cutting pockets; including extra material; vertical										
215mm wide x 112mm projection	13.77	5.00	14.46	0.93	0.65	29.53	1.80	45.79	m	50.37
215mm wide x 215mm projection	22.03	5.00	23.14	1.13	0.81	36.19	2.87	62.20	m	68.42
327mm wide x 112mm projection	20.66	5.00	21.70	1.40	0.98	44.48	2.69	68.86	m	75.75
327mm wide x 215mm projection	30.31	5.00	31.82	1.70	1.22	54.47	3.96	90.26	m	99.28
Projections; bonding to old brickwork; cutting pockets; including extra material; horizontal										
215mm wide x 112mm projection	13.77	5.00	14.46	0.93	0.65	29.53	1.80	45.79	m	50.37
215mm wide x 215mm projection	22.03	5.00	23.14	1.13	0.81	36.19	2.87	62.20	m	68.42
327mm wide x 112mm projection	20.66	5.00	21.70	1.40	0.98	44.48	2.69	68.86	m	75.75
327mm wide x 215mm projection	30.31	5.00	31.82	1.70	1.22	54.47	3.96	90.26	m	99.28
Arches including centering; flat										
112mm high on face; 215mm thick; width of exposed soffit 215mm; bricks-on-edge	8.26	5.00	8.68	1.50	1.00	46.88	1.07	56.63	m	62.29
215mm high on face; 112mm thick; width of exposed soffit 112mm; bricks-on-end	8.26	5.00	8.68	1.45	1.00	45.83	1.07	55.58	m	61.14
Arches including centering; semi-circular										
112mm high on face; 215mm thick; width of exposed soffit 215mm; bricks-on-edge	12.98	5.00	13.63	2.15	1.35	65.89	1.70	81.21	m	89.34
215mm high on face; 215mm thick; width of exposed soffit 215mm; bricks-on-edge	25.96	5.00	27.26	2.95	1.95	91.93	3.38	122.57	m	134.82
Closing cavities										
50mm wide with brickwork 102mm thick	4.03	5.00	4.23	0.40	0.27	12.55	0.53	17.31	m	19.04
75mm wide with brickwork 102mm thick	4.03	5.00	4.23	0.40	0.27	12.55	0.53	17.31	m	19.04
Closing cavities; horizontal										
50mm wide with slates	6.20	5.00	6.51	0.66	0.44	20.62	0.53	27.66	m	30.43
75mm wide with slates	6.20	5.00	6.51	0.66	0.44	20.62	0.53	27.66	m	30.43
50mm wide with brickwork 102mm thick	4.03	5.00	4.23	0.40	0.27	12.55	0.53	17.31	m	19.04
75mm wide with brickwork 102mm thick	4.03	5.00	4.23	0.40	0.27	12.55	0.53	17.31	m	19.04
Bonding ends to existing common brickwork; cutting pockets; extra material										
walls; bonding every third course										
102mm thick	2.75	5.00	2.89	0.37	0.25	11.61	0.36	14.87	m	16.35
215mm thick	5.51	5.00	5.78	0.66	0.44	20.62	0.73	27.13	m	29.85
327mm thick	8.26	5.00	8.68	0.95	0.63	29.64	1.07	39.39	m	43.32
Walls; brickwork; Engineering bricks, BS EN 772, Category F, 215 x 102.5 x 65mm, Class B; in cement-lime mortar (1:2:9)										
Walls										
102mm thick; stretcher bond	23.01	5.00	24.16	1.60	1.20	52.08	4.04	80.28	m²	88.31
215mm thick; English bond	46.41	5.00	48.73	2.60	2.05	86.18	9.44	144.35	m²	158.78
327mm thick; English bond	69.81	5.00	73.30	3.15	2.55	105.44	14.83	193.58	m²	212.94
Skins of hollow walls										
102mm thick; stretcher bond	23.01	5.00	24.16	1.60	1.20	52.08	4.04	80.28	m²	88.31
215mm thick; English bond	46.41	5.00	48.73	2.60	2.05	86.18	9.44	144.35	m²	158.78
Walls; building against concrete (ties measured separately); vertical										
102mm thick; stretcher bond	23.01	5.00	24.16	1.75	1.30	56.76	4.04	84.97	m²	93.46
Walls; building against old brickwork; tie new to old with 200mm stainless steel housing type 4 wall ties - 6/m²; vertical										
102mm thick; stretcher bond	24.63	10.00	25.94	1.75	1.30	56.76	4.04	86.75	m²	95.42
215mm thick; English bond	48.03	10.00	50.51	2.90	2.25	95.56	9.44	155.51	m²	171.06
Walls; bonding to stonework; including extra material; vertical										
102mm thick; stretcher bond	24.31	5.00	25.52	1.75	1.30	56.76	4.27	86.56	m²	95.22
215mm thick; English bond	49.01	5.00	51.46	2.90	2.25	95.56	9.98	157.00	m²	172.70
327mm thick; English bond	72.41	5.00	76.03	3.45	2.75	114.82	15.38	206.23	m²	226.85
440mm thick; English bond	95.42	5.00	100.19	4.05	3.30	135.90	20.79	256.89	m²	282.58
Walls; bonding to old brickwork; cutting pockets; including extra material; vertical										
102mm thick; stretcher bond	24.31	5.00	25.52	4.00	2.80	127.08	4.27	156.87	m²	172.56
215mm thick; English bond	49.01	5.00	51.46	5.05	3.65	162.22	9.98	223.67	m²	246.04
Walls; curved 2m radius; including extra material; vertical										
102mm thick; stretcher bond	23.01	5.00	24.16	3.15	2.25	100.77	4.04	128.98	m²	141.87
215mm thick; English bond	46.41	5.00	48.73	5.70	4.10	182.80	9.44	240.96	m²	265.06
327mm thick; English bond	69.81	5.00	73.30	7.80	5.60	249.98	14.83	338.11	m²	371.92
Walls; curved 6m radius; including extra material; vertical										
102mm thick; stretcher bond	23.01	5.00	24.16	2.35	1.70	75.51	4.04	103.72	m²	114.09

Labour hourly rates: (except Specialists) Craft Operatives 20.87 Labourer 15.57 Rates are national average prices. Refer to REGIONAL VARIATIONS for indicative levels of overall pricing in regions	MATERIALS			LABOUR				RATES		
	Del to Site £	Waste %	Material Cost £	Craft Optve Hrs	Lab Hrs	Labour Cost £	Sunds £	Nett Rate £	Unit	Gross rate (10%) £
BRICK/BLOCK WALLING (Cont'd)										
Walls; brickwork; Engineering bricks, BS EN 772, Category F, 215 x 102.5 x 65mm, Class B; in cement-lime mortar (1:2:9) (Cont'd)										
Walls; curved 6m radius; including extra material; vertical (Cont'd)										
215mm thick; English bond	46.41	5.00	48.73	4.10	3.10	133.83	9.44	192.00	m²	211.20
327mm thick; English bond	69.81	5.00	73.30	5.45	4.05	176.80	14.83	264.93	m²	291.43
Skins of hollow walls; curved 2m radius; including extra material; vertical										
102mm thick; stretcher bond	23.01	5.00	24.16	3.15	2.25	100.77	4.04	128.98	m²	141.87
215mm thick; English bond	46.41	5.00	48.73	5.70	4.10	182.80	9.44	240.96	m²	265.06
Skins of hollow walls; curved 6m radius; including extra material; vertical										
102mm thick; stretcher bond	23.01	5.00	24.16	2.35	1.70	75.51	4.04	103.72	m²	114.09
215mm thick; English bond	46.41	5.00	48.73	4.10	3.10	133.83	9.44	192.00	m²	211.20
Isolated piers										
215mm thick; English bond	46.41	5.00	48.73	5.15	3.75	165.87	9.44	224.04	m²	246.44
327mm thick; English bond	69.81	5.00	73.30	6.25	4.60	202.06	14.83	290.19	m²	319.21
440mm thick; English bond	92.82	5.00	97.46	7.25	5.45	236.16	20.23	353.85	m²	389.24
Chimney stacks										
440mm thick; English bond	92.82	5.00	97.46	7.25	5.45	236.16	20.23	353.85	m²	389.24
890mm thick; English bond	185.64	5.00	194.92	11.45	8.80	375.98	40.46	611.36	m²	672.49
Projections										
215mm wide x 112mm projection	5.20	5.00	5.46	0.33	0.25	10.78	1.07	17.31	m	19.04
215mm wide x 215mm projection	10.40	5.00	10.92	0.55	0.42	18.02	2.16	31.10	m	34.21
327mm wide x 112mm projection	7.80	5.00	8.19	0.50	0.38	16.35	1.62	26.16	m	28.77
327mm wide x 215mm projection	15.60	5.00	16.38	0.83	0.63	27.13	3.23	46.75	m	51.42
Projections; horizontal										
215mm wide x 112mm projection	5.20	5.00	5.46	0.33	0.25	10.78	1.07	17.31	m	19.04
215mm wide x 215mm projection	10.40	5.00	10.92	0.55	0.42	18.02	2.16	31.10	m	34.21
327mm wide x 112mm projection	7.80	5.00	8.19	0.50	0.38	16.35	1.62	26.16	m	28.77
327mm wide x 215mm projection	15.60	5.00	16.38	0.83	0.63	27.13	3.23	46.75	m	51.42
Projections; bonding to old brickwork; cutting pockets; including extra material; vertical										
215mm wide x 112mm projection	8.66	5.00	9.09	1.02	0.72	32.50	1.80	43.39	m	47.73
215mm wide x 215mm projection	13.86	5.00	14.55	1.24	0.89	39.74	2.87	57.16	m	62.88
327mm wide x 112mm projection	13.00	5.00	13.65	1.54	1.08	48.96	2.69	65.29	m	71.82
327mm wide x 215mm projection	19.06	5.00	20.02	1.87	1.34	59.89	3.96	83.87	m	92.25
Projections; bonding to old brickwork; cutting pockets; including extra material; horizontal										
215mm wide x 112mm projection	8.66	5.00	9.09	1.02	0.72	32.50	1.80	43.39	m	47.73
215mm wide x 215mm projection	13.86	5.00	14.55	1.24	0.89	39.74	2.87	57.16	m	62.88
327mm wide x 112mm projection	13.00	5.00	13.65	1.54	1.08	48.96	2.69	65.29	m	71.82
327mm wide x 215mm projection	19.06	5.00	20.02	1.87	1.34	59.89	3.96	83.87	m	92.25
Arches including centering; flat										
112mm high on face; 215mm thick; width of exposed soffit 215mm; bricks-on-edge	5.20	5.00	5.46	1.60	1.05	49.74	1.07	56.27	m	61.90
215mm high on face; 112mm thick; width of exposed soffit 112mm; bricks-on-end	5.20	5.00	5.46	1.55	1.10	49.48	1.07	56.01	m	61.61
Arches including centering; semi-circular										
112mm high on face; 215mm thick; width of exposed soffit 215mm; bricks-on-edge	8.16	5.00	8.57	2.25	1.40	68.76	1.70	79.03	m	86.93
215mm high on face; 215mm thick; width of exposed soffit 215mm; bricks-on-edge	16.33	5.00	17.15	3.10	2.05	96.62	3.38	117.14	m	128.86
Closing cavities										
50mm wide with brickwork 102mm thick	2.53	5.00	2.66	0.44	0.30	13.85	0.53	17.04	m	18.75
75mm wide with brickwork 102mm thick	2.53	5.00	2.66	0.44	0.30	13.85	0.53	17.04	m	18.75
Closing cavities; horizontal										
50mm wide with slates	6.20	5.00	6.51	0.66	0.44	20.62	0.53	27.66	m	30.43
75mm wide with slates	6.20	5.00	6.51	0.66	0.44	20.62	0.53	27.66	m	30.43
50mm wide with brickwork 102mm thick	2.53	5.00	2.66	0.44	0.30	13.85	0.53	17.04	m	18.75
75mm wide with brickwork 102mm thick	2.53	5.00	2.66	0.44	0.30	13.85	0.53	17.04	m	18.75
Bonding ends to existing common brickwork; cutting pockets; extra material										
walls; bonding every third course										
102mm thick	1.73	5.00	1.82	0.41	0.28	12.92	0.36	15.10	m	16.61
215mm thick	3.46	5.00	3.64	0.73	0.48	22.71	0.73	27.07	m	29.78
327mm thick	5.20	5.00	5.46	1.05	0.69	32.66	1.07	39.19	m	43.11
Walls; brickwork; Engineering bricks, BS EN 772, Category F, 215 x 102.5 x 65mm, Class A; in cement-lime mortar (1:2:9)										
Walls										
102mm thick; stretcher bond	62.29	5.00	65.40	1.60	1.20	52.08	4.04	121.52	m²	133.67
215mm thick; English bond	125.63	5.00	131.91	2.60	2.05	86.18	9.44	227.53	m²	250.28
327mm thick; English bond	188.97	5.00	198.42	3.15	2.55	105.44	14.83	318.70	m²	350.57
Skins of hollow walls										
102mm thick; stretcher bond	62.29	5.00	65.40	1.60	1.20	52.08	4.04	121.52	m²	133.67
215mm thick; English bond	125.63	5.00	131.91	2.60	2.05	86.18	9.44	227.53	m²	250.28
Walls; building against concrete (ties measured separately); vertical										
102mm thick; stretcher bond	62.29	5.00	65.40	1.75	1.30	56.76	4.04	126.21	m²	138.83

Labour hourly rates: (except Specialists) Craft Operatives 20.87 Labourer 15.57 Rates are national average prices. Refer to REGIONAL VARIATIONS for indicative levels of overall pricing in regions	MATERIALS			LABOUR				RATES		
	Del to Site £	Waste %	Material Cost £	Craft Optve Hrs	Lab Hrs	Labour Cost £	Sunds £	Nett Rate £	Unit	Gross rate (10%) £
BRICK/BLOCK WALLING (Cont'd)										
Walls; brickwork; Engineering bricks, BS EN 772, Category F, 215 x 102.5 x 65mm, Class A; in cement-lime mortar (1:2:9) (Cont'd)										
Walls; building against old brickwork; tie new to old with 200mm stainless steel housing type 4 wall ties - 6/m²; vertical										
102mm thick; stretcher bond	63.91	10.00	67.18	1.75	1.30	56.76	4.04	127.99	m²	140.79
215mm thick; English bond	127.25	10.00	133.69	2.90	2.25	95.56	9.44	238.69	m²	262.56
Walls; bonding to stonework; including extra material; vertical										
102mm thick; stretcher bond	65.80	5.00	69.09	1.75	1.30	56.76	4.27	130.13	m²	143.14
215mm thick; English bond	132.67	5.00	139.31	2.90	2.25	95.56	9.98	244.84	m²	269.33
327mm thick; English bond	196.02	5.00	205.82	3.45	2.75	114.82	15.38	336.01	m²	369.62
440mm thick; English bond	258.30	5.00	271.22	4.05	3.30	135.90	20.79	427.91	m²	470.71
Walls; bonding to old brickwork; cutting pockets; including extra material; vertical										
102mm thick; stretcher bond	65.80	5.00	69.09	4.00	2.80	127.08	4.27	200.44	m²	220.49
215mm thick; English bond	132.67	5.00	139.31	5.05	3.65	162.22	9.98	311.51	m²	342.66
Walls; curved 2m radius; including extra material; vertical										
102mm thick; stretcher bond	62.29	5.00	65.40	3.15	2.25	100.77	4.04	170.22	m²	187.24
215mm thick; English bond	125.63	5.00	131.91	5.70	4.10	182.80	9.44	324.15	m²	356.56
327mm thick; English bond	188.97	5.00	198.42	7.80	5.60	249.98	14.83	463.24	m²	509.56
Walls; curved 6m radius; including extra material; vertical										
102mm thick; stretcher bond	62.29	5.00	65.40	2.35	1.70	75.51	4.04	144.96	m²	159.45
215mm thick; English bond	125.63	5.00	131.91	4.10	3.10	133.83	9.44	275.18	m²	302.70
327mm thick; English bond	188.97	5.00	198.42	5.45	4.05	176.80	14.83	390.06	m²	429.06
Skins of hollow walls; curved 2m radius; including extra material; vertical										
102mm thick; stretcher bond	62.29	5.00	65.40	3.15	2.25	100.77	4.04	170.22	m²	187.24
215mm thick; English bond	125.63	5.00	131.91	5.70	4.10	182.80	9.44	324.15	m²	356.56
327mm thick; English bond	188.97	5.00	198.42	7.80	5.60	249.98	14.83	463.24	m²	509.56
Skins of hollow walls; curved 6m radius; including extra material; vertical										
102mm thick; stretcher bond	62.29	5.00	65.40	2.35	1.70	75.51	4.04	144.96	m²	159.45
215mm thick; English bond	125.63	5.00	131.91	4.10	3.10	133.83	9.44	275.18	m²	302.70
Isolated piers										
215mm thick; English bond	125.63	5.00	131.91	5.15	3.75	165.87	9.44	307.22	m²	337.94
327mm thick; English bond	188.97	5.00	198.42	6.25	4.60	202.06	14.83	415.32	m²	456.85
440mm thick; English bond	251.26	5.00	263.83	7.25	5.45	236.16	20.23	520.22	m²	572.24
Chimney stacks										
440mm thick; English bond	251.26	5.00	263.83	7.25	5.45	236.16	20.23	520.22	m²	572.24
890mm thick; English bond	502.53	5.00	527.65	11.45	8.80	375.98	40.46	944.09	m²	1038.50
Projections										
215mm wide x 112mm projection	14.07	5.00	14.78	0.33	0.25	10.78	1.07	26.63	m	29.29
215mm wide x 215mm projection	28.15	5.00	29.55	0.55	0.42	18.02	2.16	49.73	m	54.71
327mm wide x 112mm projection	21.11	5.00	22.17	0.50	0.38	16.35	1.62	40.14	m	44.15
327mm wide x 215mm projection	42.23	5.00	44.34	0.83	0.63	27.13	3.23	74.71	m	82.18
Projections; horizontal										
215mm wide x 112mm projection	14.07	5.00	14.78	0.33	0.25	10.78	1.07	26.63	m	29.29
215mm wide x 215mm projection	28.15	5.00	29.55	0.55	0.42	18.02	2.16	49.73	m	54.71
327mm wide x 112mm projection	21.11	5.00	22.17	0.50	0.38	16.35	1.62	40.14	m	44.15
327mm wide x 215mm projection	42.23	5.00	44.34	0.83	0.63	27.13	3.23	74.71	m	82.18
Projections; bonding to old brickwork; cutting pockets; including extra material; vertical										
215mm wide x 112mm projection	23.45	5.00	24.62	1.02	0.72	32.50	1.80	58.92	m	64.81
215mm wide x 215mm projection	37.52	5.00	39.40	1.24	0.89	39.74	2.87	82.00	m	90.20
327mm wide x 112mm projection	35.19	5.00	36.95	1.54	1.08	48.96	2.69	88.59	m	97.45
327mm wide x 215mm projection	51.60	5.00	54.18	1.87	1.34	59.89	3.96	118.03	m	129.84
Projections; bonding to old brickwork; cutting pockets; including extra material; horizontal										
215mm wide x 112mm projection	23.45	5.00	24.62	1.02	0.72	32.50	1.80	58.92	m	64.81
215mm wide x 215mm projection	37.52	5.00	39.40	1.24	0.89	39.74	2.87	82.00	m	90.20
327mm wide x 112mm projection	35.19	5.00	36.95	1.54	1.08	48.96	2.69	88.59	m	97.45
327mm wide x 215mm projection	51.60	5.00	54.18	1.87	1.34	59.89	3.96	118.03	m	129.84
Arches including centering; flat										
112mm high on face; 215mm thick; width of exposed soffit 215mm; bricks-on-edge	14.07	5.00	14.78	1.60	1.05	49.74	1.07	65.59	m	72.15
215mm high on face; 112mm thick; width of exposed soffit 112mm; bricks-on-end	14.07	5.00	14.78	1.55	1.10	49.48	1.07	65.32	m	71.86
Arches including centering; semi-circular										
112mm high on face; 215mm thick; width of exposed soffit 215mm; bricks-on-edge	22.10	5.00	23.20	2.25	1.40	68.76	1.70	93.66	m	103.02
215mm high on face; 215mm thick; width of exposed soffit 215mm; bricks-on-edge	44.20	5.00	46.41	3.10	2.05	96.62	3.38	146.41	m	161.05
Closing cavities										
50mm wide with brickwork 102mm thick	6.86	5.00	7.21	0.44	0.30	13.85	0.53	21.59	m	23.75
75mm wide with brickwork 102mm thick	6.86	5.00	7.21	0.44	0.30	13.85	0.53	21.59	m	23.75
Closing cavities; horizontal										
50mm wide with slates	6.20	5.00	6.51	0.66	0.44	20.62	0.53	27.66	m	30.43
75mm wide with slates	6.20	5.00	6.51	0.66	0.44	20.62	0.53	27.66	m	30.43
50mm wide with brickwork 102mm thick	6.86	5.00	7.21	0.44	0.30	13.85	0.53	21.59	m	23.75
75mm wide with brickwork 102mm thick	6.86	5.00	7.21	0.44	0.30	13.85	0.53	21.59	m	23.75

Labour hourly rates: (except Specialists) Craft Operatives 20.87 Labourer 15.57 Rates are national average prices. Refer to REGIONAL VARIATIONS for indicative levels of overall pricing in regions	MATERIALS			LABOUR				RATES		
	Del to Site £	Waste %	Material Cost £	Craft Optve Hrs	Lab Hrs	Labour Cost £	Sunds £	Nett Rate £	Unit	Gross rate (10%) £
BRICK/BLOCK WALLING (Cont'd)										
Walls; brickwork; Engineering bricks, BS EN 772, Category F, 215 x 102.5 x 65mm, Class A; in cement-lime mortar (1:2:9) (Cont'd)										
Bonding ends to existing common brickwork; cutting pockets; extra material										
walls; bonding every third course										
102mm thick	4.69	5.00	4.92	0.41	0.28	12.92	0.36	18.20	m	20.02
215mm thick	9.37	5.00	9.84	0.73	0.48	22.71	0.73	33.28	m	36.61
327mm thick	14.07	5.00	14.78	1.05	0.69	32.66	1.07	48.51	m	53.36
For other mortar mixes, ADD or DEDUCT as follows:										
For each half brick thickness										
1:1:6 cement-lime mortar	-	-	-	-	-	-	0.59	0.59	m²	0.65
1:4 cement mortar	-	-	-	-	-	-	0.18	0.18	m²	0.20
1:3 cement mortar	-	-	-	-	-	-	0.25	0.25	m²	0.27
For using Sulphate Resisting cement in lieu of Portland cement, ADD as follows										
For each half brick thickness										
1:2:9 cement-lime mortar	-	-	-	-	-	-	0.16	0.16	m²	0.18
1:1:6 cement-lime mortar	-	-	-	-	-	-	0.23	0.23	m²	0.25
1:4 cement mortar	-	-	-	-	-	-	0.38	0.38	m²	0.42
1:3 cement mortar	-	-	-	-	-	-	0.48	0.48	m²	0.53
Walls; brickwork; Staffordshire Blue Brindle wirecut bricks, BS EN 772, Category F, 215 x 102.5 x 65mm; in cement mortar (1:3)										
Walls										
215mm thick; English bond	116.62	5.00	122.45	2.60	2.05	86.18	10.02	218.65	m²	240.51
Walls; brickwork; Staffordshire Blue pressed bricks, BS EN 772, Category F, 215 x 102.5 x 65mm; in cement mortar (1:3)										
Walls										
215mm thick; English bond	226.10	5.00	237.40	2.60	2.05	86.18	10.02	333.60	m²	366.96
Walls; brickwork; Composite walling of Staffordshire Blue Brindle bricks, BS EN 772, Category F, 215 x 102.5 x 65mm; in cement mortar (1:3); wirecut bricks backing; pressed bricks facing; weather struck pointing as work proceeds										
Walls										
English bond; facework one side	197.52	5.00	207.40	2.90	2.25	95.56	10.02	312.97	m²	344.26
Flemish bond; facework one side	188.32	5.00	197.74	2.90	2.25	95.56	10.02	303.31	m²	333.64
Walls; brickwork; Common bricks, BS EN 772, Category M, 215 x 102.5 x 65mm, compressive strength 20.5 N/mm²; in cement-lime mortar (1:2:9); flush smooth pointing as work proceeds										
Walls										
stretcher bond; facework one side										
102mm thick	18.40	5.00	19.32	1.75	1.30	56.76	4.04	80.13	m²	88.14
stretcher bond; facework both sides										
102mm thick	18.40	5.00	19.32	2.05	1.50	66.14	4.04	89.50	m²	98.45
English bond; facework one side										
215mm thick	37.11	5.00	38.97	2.65	2.05	87.22	9.44	135.63	m²	149.19
English bond; facework both sides										
215mm thick	37.11	5.00	38.97	2.95	2.25	96.60	9.44	145.01	m²	159.51
Skins of hollow walls										
stretcher bond; facework one side										
102mm thick	18.40	5.00	19.32	1.75	1.30	56.76	4.04	80.13	m²	88.14
Walls; brickwork; Engineering bricks, BS EN 772, Category F, 215 x 102.5 x 65mm, Class B; in cement-lime mortar (1:2:9); flush smooth pointing as work proceeds										
Walls										
stretcher bond; facework one side										
102mm thick	23.01	5.00	24.16	1.90	1.40	61.45	4.04	89.65	m²	98.62
stretcher bond; facework both sides										
102mm thick	23.01	5.00	24.16	2.20	1.60	70.83	4.04	99.03	m²	108.93
English bond; facework one side										
215mm thick	46.41	5.00	48.73	2.90	2.25	95.56	9.44	153.72	m²	169.10
English bond; facework both sides										
215mm thick	46.41	5.00	48.73	3.20	2.45	104.93	9.44	163.10	m²	179.41
Skins of hollow walls										
stretcher bond; facework one side										
102mm thick	23.01	5.00	24.16	1.90	1.40	61.45	4.04	89.65	m²	98.62
Walls; brickwork; Engineering bricks, BS EN 772, Category F, 215 x 102.5 x 65mm, Class A; in cement-lime mortar (1:2:9); flush smooth pointing as work proceeds										
Walls										
stretcher bond; facework one side										
102mm thick	62.29	5.00	65.40	1.90	1.40	61.45	4.04	130.90	m²	143.99
stretcher bond; facework both sides										
102mm thick	62.29	5.00	65.40	2.20	1.60	70.83	4.04	140.27	m²	154.30
English bond; facework one side										
215mm thick	125.63	5.00	131.91	2.90	2.25	95.56	9.44	236.91	m²	260.60

Labour hourly rates: (except Specialists) Craft Operatives 20.87 Labourer 15.57 Rates are national average prices. Refer to REGIONAL VARIATIONS for indicative levels of overall pricing in regions	MATERIALS			LABOUR				RATES		
	Del to Site £	Waste %	Material Cost £	Craft Optve Hrs	Lab Hrs	Labour Cost £	Sunds £	Nett Rate £	Unit	Gross rate (10%) £
BRICK/BLOCK WALLING (Cont'd)										
Walls; brickwork; Engineering bricks, BS EN 772, Category F, 215 x 102.5 x 65mm, Class A; in cement-lime mortar (1:2:9); flush smooth pointing as work proceeds (Cont'd)										
Walls (Cont'd)										
English bond; facework both sides										
215mm thick	125.63	5.00	131.91	3.20	2.45	104.93	9.44	246.28	m²	270.91
Skins of hollow walls										
stretcher bond; facework one side										
102mm thick	62.29	5.00	65.40	1.90	1.40	61.45	4.04	130.90	m²	143.99
Walls; brickwork; Facing bricks, second hard stocks, BS EN 772, Category M, 215 x 102.5 x 65mm; in cement-lime mortar (1:2:9); flush smooth pointing as work proceeds										
Walls										
stretcher bond; facework one side										
102mm thick	36.58	5.00	38.41	1.75	1.30	56.76	4.04	99.22	m²	109.14
stretcher bond; facework both sides										
102mm thick	36.58	5.00	38.41	2.05	1.50	66.14	4.04	108.59	m²	119.45
English bond; facework one side										
215mm thick	73.78	5.00	77.47	2.65	2.05	87.22	9.44	174.13	m²	191.54
English bond; facework both sides										
215mm thick	73.78	5.00	77.47	2.95	2.25	96.60	9.44	183.51	m²	201.86
Skins of hollow walls										
stretcher bond; facework one side										
102mm thick	36.58	5.00	38.41	1.75	1.30	56.76	4.04	99.22	m²	109.14
Walls; brickwork; Facing bricks p.c. £200.00 per 1000, 215 x 102.5 x 65mm; in cement-lime mortar (1:2:9); flush smooth pointing as work proceeds										
Walls										
stretcher bond; facework one side										
102mm thick	11.80	5.00	12.39	1.75	1.30	56.76	4.04	73.20	m²	80.52
stretcher bond; facework both sides										
102mm thick	11.80	5.00	12.39	2.05	1.50	66.14	4.04	82.57	m²	90.83
English bond; facework both sides										
215mm thick	23.80	5.00	24.99	2.65	2.05	87.22	9.44	121.65	m²	133.82
Flemish bond; facework both sides										
215mm thick	23.80	5.00	24.99	2.95	2.25	96.60	9.44	131.03	m²	144.13
Skins of hollow walls										
stretcher bond; facework one side										
102mm thick	11.80	5.00	12.39	1.75	1.30	56.76	4.04	73.20	m²	80.52
extra; special bricks; vertical angles; squint; BS 4729, type AN.1.1. (p.c. £200.00 per 100)	26.66	5.00	27.99	0.25	0.15	7.55	-	35.55	m	39.10
extra; special bricks; intersections; birdsmouth; BS 4729, type AN.4.1. (p.c. £200.00 per 100)	26.66	5.00	27.99	0.25	0.15	7.55	-	35.55	m	39.10
Walls; building overhand										
stretcher bond; facework one side										
102mm thick	11.80	5.00	12.39	2.15	1.55	69.00	4.04	85.44	m²	93.98
stretcher bond; facework both sides										
102mm thick	11.80	5.00	12.39	2.45	1.75	78.38	4.04	94.81	m²	104.29
English bond; facework both sides										
215mm thick	23.80	5.00	24.99	3.05	2.30	99.46	9.44	133.89	m²	147.28
Flemish bond; facework both sides										
215mm thick	23.80	5.00	24.99	3.35	2.50	108.84	9.44	143.27	m²	157.59
Skins of hollow walls; building overhand										
stretcher bond; facework one side										
102mm thick	11.80	5.00	12.39	2.15	1.55	69.00	4.04	85.44	m²	93.98
Arches including centering; flat										
112mm high on face; 215mm thick; width of exposed soffit 112mm; bricks-on-edge	2.67	5.00	2.80	1.05	0.80	34.37	1.07	38.24	m	42.07
112mm high on face; 215mm thick; width of exposed soffit 215mm; bricks-on-edge	2.67	5.00	2.80	1.50	1.00	46.88	1.07	50.75	m	55.82
215mm high on face; 112mm thick; width of exposed soffit 112mm; bricks-on-end	2.67	5.00	2.80	1.45	1.00	45.83	1.07	49.70	m	54.67
Arches including centering; segmental										
215mm high on face; 215mm thick; width of exposed soffit 112mm; bricks-on-edge	5.33	5.00	5.60	2.40	1.65	75.78	2.16	83.54	m	91.89
215mm high on face; 215mm thick; width of exposed soffit 215mm; bricks-on-edge	5.33	5.00	5.60	2.95	1.95	91.93	2.16	99.69	m	109.66
Arches including centering; semi-circular										
215mm high on face; 215mm thick; width of exposed soffit 112mm; bricks-on-edge	5.33	5.00	5.60	2.40	1.65	75.78	2.16	83.54	m	91.89
215mm high on face; 215mm thick; width of exposed soffit 215mm; bricks-on-edge	5.33	5.00	5.60	2.95	1.95	91.93	2.16	99.69	m	109.66
Facework copings; bricks-on-edge; pointing top and each side										
215 x 102.5mm; horizontal	2.67	5.00	2.80	0.70	0.50	22.39	1.07	26.27	m	28.89
215 x 102.5mm; with oversailing course and cement fillets both sides; horizontal	2.67	5.00	2.80	1.10	0.75	34.63	1.07	38.51	m	42.36
327 x 102.5mm; horizontal	4.00	5.00	4.20	1.05	0.75	33.59	1.62	39.41	m	43.35
327 x 102.5mm; with oversailing course and cement fillets both sides; horizontal	4.00	5.00	4.20	1.50	1.05	47.65	1.62	53.47	m	58.82
extra; galvanised safety frame cramp at angle or end	0.32	5.00	0.34	0.04	0.03	1.30	-	1.64	nr	1.81

MASONRY

Labour hourly rates: (except Specialists) Craft Operatives 20.87 Labourer 15.57 Rates are national average prices. Refer to REGIONAL VARIATIONS for indicative levels of overall pricing in regions	MATERIALS			LABOUR				RATES		
	Del to Site £	Waste %	Material Cost £	Craft Optve Hrs	Lab Hrs	Labour Cost £	Sunds £	Nett Rate £	Unit	Gross rate (10%) £
BRICK/BLOCK WALLING (Cont'd)										
Walls; brickwork; Facing bricks p.c. £250.00 per 1000, 215 x 102.5 x 65mm; in cement-lime mortar (1:2:9); flush smooth pointing as work proceeds										
Walls										
stretcher bond; facework one side										
102mm thick	14.75	5.00	15.49	1.75	1.30	56.76	4.04	76.29	m²	83.92
stretcher bond; facework both sides										
102mm thick	14.75	5.00	15.49	2.05	1.50	66.14	4.04	85.67	m²	94.24
English bond; facework both sides										
215mm thick	29.75	5.00	31.24	2.65	2.05	87.22	9.44	127.90	m²	140.69
Flemish bond; facework both sides										
215mm thick	29.75	5.00	31.24	2.95	2.25	96.60	9.44	137.27	m²	151.00
Skins of hollow walls										
stretcher bond; facework one side										
102mm thick	14.75	5.00	15.49	1.75	1.30	56.76	4.04	76.29	m²	83.92
extra; special bricks; vertical angles; squint; BS 4729, type AN.1.1. (p.c. £250.00 per 100)	33.33	5.00	34.99	0.25	0.15	7.55	-	42.54	m	46.80
extra; special bricks; intersections; birdsmouth; BS 4729, type AN.4.1. (p.c. £250.00 per 100)	33.33	5.00	34.99	0.25	0.15	7.55	-	42.54	m	46.80
Walls; building overhand										
stretcher bond; facework one side										
102mm thick	14.75	5.00	15.49	2.15	1.55	69.00	4.04	88.53	m²	97.39
stretcher bond; facework both sides										
102mm thick	14.75	5.00	15.49	2.45	1.75	78.38	4.04	97.91	m²	107.70
English bond; facework both sides										
215mm thick	29.75	5.00	31.24	3.05	2.30	99.46	9.44	140.14	m²	154.15
Flemish bond; facework both sides										
215mm thick	29.75	5.00	31.24	3.35	2.50	108.84	9.44	149.51	m²	164.47
Skins of hollow walls; building overhand										
stretcher bond; facework one side										
102mm thick	14.75	5.00	15.49	2.15	1.55	69.00	4.04	88.53	m²	97.39
Arches including centering; flat										
112mm high on face; 215mm thick; width of exposed soffit 112mm; bricks-on-edge	3.33	5.00	3.50	1.05	0.80	34.37	1.07	38.94	m	42.84
112mm high on face; 215mm thick; width of exposed soffit 215mm; bricks-on-edge	3.33	5.00	3.50	1.50	1.00	46.88	1.07	51.45	m	56.59
215mm high on face; 112mm thick; width of exposed soffit 112mm; bricks-on-end	3.33	5.00	3.50	1.45	1.00	45.83	1.07	50.40	m	55.44
Arches including centering; segmental										
215mm high on face; 215mm thick; width of exposed soffit 112mm; bricks-on-edge	6.66	5.00	7.00	2.40	1.65	75.78	2.16	84.94	m	93.43
215mm high on face; 215mm thick; width of exposed soffit 215mm; bricks-on-edge	6.66	5.00	7.00	2.95	1.95	91.93	2.16	101.09	m	111.20
Arches including centering; semi-circular										
215mm high on face; 215mm thick; width of exposed soffit 112mm; bricks-on-edge	6.66	5.00	7.00	2.40	1.65	75.78	2.16	84.94	m	93.43
215mm high on face; 215mm thick; width of exposed soffit 215mm; bricks-on-edge	6.66	5.00	7.00	2.95	1.95	91.93	2.16	101.09	m	111.20
Facework copings; bricks-on-edge; pointing top and each side										
215 x 102.5mm; horizontal	3.33	5.00	3.50	0.70	0.50	22.39	1.07	26.97	m	29.66
215 x 102.5mm; with oversailing course and cement fillets both sides; horizontal	3.33	5.00	3.50	1.10	0.75	34.63	1.07	39.21	m	43.13
327 x 102.5mm; horizontal	5.00	5.00	5.25	1.05	0.75	33.59	1.62	40.46	m	44.50
327 x 102.5mm; with oversailing course and cement fillets both sides; horizontal	5.00	5.00	5.25	1.50	1.05	47.65	1.62	54.52	m	59.97
extra; galvanised safety frame cramp at angle or end	0.32	5.00	0.34	0.04	0.03	1.30	-	1.64	nr	1.81
Walls; brickwork; Facing bricks p.c. £300.00 per 1000, 215 x 102.5 x 65mm; in cement-lime mortar (1:2:9); flush smooth pointing as work proceeds										
Walls										
stretcher bond; facework one side										
102mm thick	17.70	5.00	18.58	1.75	1.30	56.76	4.04	79.39	m²	87.33
stretcher bond; facework both sides										
102mm thick	17.70	5.00	18.58	2.05	1.50	66.14	4.04	88.77	m²	97.64
English bond; facework both sides										
215mm thick	35.70	5.00	37.49	2.65	2.05	87.22	9.44	134.15	m²	147.56
Flemish bond; facework both sides										
215mm thick	35.70	5.00	37.49	2.95	2.25	96.60	9.44	143.52	m²	157.87
Skins of hollow walls										
stretcher bond; facework one side										
102mm thick	17.70	5.00	18.58	1.75	1.30	56.76	4.04	79.39	m²	87.33
extra; special bricks; vertical angles; squint; BS 4729, type AN.1.1. (p.c. £300.00 per 100)	39.99	5.00	41.99	0.25	0.15	7.55	-	49.54	m	54.50
extra; special bricks; intersections; birdsmouth; BS 4729, type AN.4.1. (p.c. £300.00 per 100)	39.99	5.00	41.99	0.25	0.15	7.55	-	49.54	m	54.50
Walls; building overhand										
stretcher bond; facework one side										
102mm thick	17.70	5.00	18.58	2.15	1.55	69.00	4.04	91.63	m²	100.79
stretcher bond; facework both sides										
102mm thick	17.70	5.00	18.58	2.45	1.75	78.38	4.04	101.01	m²	111.11
English bond; facework both sides										
215mm thick	35.70	5.00	37.49	3.05	2.30	99.46	9.44	146.39	m²	161.03
Flemish bond; facework both sides										
215mm thick	35.70	5.00	37.49	3.35	2.50	108.84	9.44	155.76	m²	171.34

Labour hourly rates: (except Specialists) Craft Operatives 20.87 Labourer 15.57 Rates are national average prices. Refer to REGIONAL VARIATIONS for indicative levels of overall pricing in regions	MATERIALS			LABOUR				RATES		
	Del to Site £	Waste %	Material Cost £	Craft Optve Hrs	Lab Hrs	Labour Cost £	Sunds £	Nett Rate £	Unit	Gross rate (10%) £
BRICK/BLOCK WALLING (Cont'd)										
Walls; brickwork; Facing bricks p.c. £300.00 per 1000, 215 x 102.5 x 65mm; in cement-lime mortar (1:2:9); flush smooth pointing as work proceeds (Cont'd)										
Skins of hollow walls; building overhand										
stretcher bond; facework one side										
102mm thick	17.70	5.00	18.58	2.15	1.55	69.00	4.04	91.63	m²	100.79
Arches including centering; flat										
112mm high on face; 215mm thick; width of exposed soffit 112mm; bricks-on-edge	4.00	5.00	4.20	1.05	0.80	34.37	1.07	39.64	m	43.61
112mm high on face; 215mm thick; width of exposed soffit 215mm; bricks-on-edge	4.00	5.00	4.20	1.50	1.00	46.88	1.07	52.15	m	57.36
215mm high on face; 112mm thick; width of exposed soffit 112mm; bricks-on-end	4.00	5.00	4.20	1.45	1.00	45.83	1.07	51.10	m	56.21
Arches including centering; segmental										
215mm high on face; 215mm thick; width of exposed soffit 112mm; bricks-on-edge	8.00	5.00	8.40	2.40	1.65	75.78	2.16	86.34	m	94.97
215mm high on face; 215mm thick; width of exposed soffit 215mm; bricks-on-edge	8.00	5.00	8.40	2.95	1.95	91.93	2.16	102.49	m	112.74
Arches including centering; semi-circular										
215mm high on face; 215mm thick; width of exposed soffit 112mm; bricks-on-edge	8.00	5.00	8.40	2.40	1.65	75.78	2.16	86.34	m	94.97
215mm high on face; 215mm thick; width of exposed soffit 215mm; bricks-on-edge	8.00	5.00	8.40	2.95	1.95	91.93	2.16	102.49	m	112.74
Facework copings; bricks-on-edge; pointing top and each side										
215 x 102.5mm; horizontal	4.00	5.00	4.20	0.70	0.50	22.39	1.07	27.67	m	30.43
215 x 102.5mm; with oversailing course and cement fillets both sides; horizontal	4.00	5.00	4.20	1.10	0.75	34.63	1.07	39.91	m	43.90
327 x 102.5mm; horizontal	6.00	5.00	6.30	1.05	0.75	33.59	1.62	41.51	m	45.66
327 x 102.5mm; with oversailing course and cement fillets both sides; horizontal	6.00	5.00	6.30	1.50	1.05	47.65	1.62	55.57	m	61.13
extra; galvanised safety frame cramp at angle or end	0.32	5.00	0.34	0.04	0.03	1.30	-	1.64	nr	1.81
Walls; brickwork; Facing bricks p.c. £350.00 per 1000, 215 x 102.5 x 65mm; in cement-lime mortar (1:2:9); flush smooth pointing as work proceeds										
Walls										
stretcher bond; facework one side										
102mm thick	20.65	5.00	21.68	1.75	1.30	56.76	4.04	82.49	m²	90.74
stretcher bond; facework both sides										
102mm thick	20.65	5.00	21.68	2.05	1.50	66.14	4.04	91.86	m²	101.05
English bond; facework both sides										
215mm thick	41.65	5.00	43.73	2.65	2.05	87.22	9.44	140.39	m²	154.43
Flemish bond; facework both sides										
215mm thick	41.65	5.00	43.73	2.95	2.25	96.60	9.44	149.77	m²	164.75
Skins of hollow walls										
stretcher bond; facework one side										
102mm thick	20.65	5.00	21.68	1.75	1.30	56.76	4.04	82.49	m²	90.74
extra; special bricks; vertical angles; squint; BS 4729, type AN.1.1. (p.c. £350.00 per 100)	46.65	5.00	48.99	0.25	0.15	7.55	-	56.54	m	62.19
extra; special bricks; intersections; birdsmouth; BS 4729, type AN.4.1. (p.c. £350.00 per 100)	46.65	5.00	48.99	0.25	0.15	7.55	-	56.54	m	62.19
Walls; building overhand										
stretcher bond; facework one side										
102mm thick	20.65	5.00	21.68	2.15	1.55	69.00	4.04	94.73	m²	104.20
stretcher bond; facework both sides										
102mm thick	20.65	5.00	21.68	2.45	1.75	78.38	4.04	104.10	m²	114.51
English bond; facework both sides										
215mm thick	41.65	5.00	43.73	3.05	2.30	99.46	9.44	152.63	m²	167.90
Flemish bond; facework both sides										
215mm thick	41.65	5.00	43.73	3.35	2.50	108.84	9.44	162.01	m²	178.21
Arches including centering; flat										
112mm high on face; 215mm thick; width of exposed soffit 112mm; bricks-on-edge	4.67	5.00	4.90	1.05	0.80	34.37	1.07	40.34	m	44.37
112mm high on face; 215mm thick; width of exposed soffit 215mm; bricks-on-edge	4.67	5.00	4.90	1.50	1.00	46.88	1.07	52.85	m	58.13
215mm high on face; 112mm thick; width of exposed soffit 112mm; bricks-on-end	4.67	5.00	4.90	1.45	1.00	45.83	1.07	51.80	m	56.98
Arches including centering; segmental										
215mm high on face; 215mm thick; width of exposed soffit 112mm; bricks-on-edge	9.33	5.00	9.80	2.40	1.65	75.78	2.16	87.74	m	96.51
215mm high on face; 215mm thick; width of exposed soffit 215mm; bricks-on-edge	9.33	5.00	9.80	2.95	1.95	91.93	2.16	103.89	m	114.28
Arches including centering; semi-circular										
215mm high on face; 215mm thick; width of exposed soffit 112mm; bricks-on-edge	9.33	5.00	9.80	2.40	1.65	75.78	2.16	87.74	m	96.51
215mm high on face; 215mm thick; width of exposed soffit 215mm; bricks-on-edge	9.33	5.00	9.80	2.95	1.95	91.93	2.16	103.89	m	114.28
Facework copings; bricks-on-edge; pointing top and each side										
215 x 102.5mm; horizontal	4.67	5.00	4.90	0.70	0.50	22.39	1.07	28.37	m	31.20
215 x 102.5mm; with oversailing course and cement fillets both sides; horizontal	4.67	5.00	4.90	1.10	0.75	34.63	1.07	40.61	m	44.67
327 x 102.5mm; horizontal	7.00	5.00	7.35	1.05	0.75	33.59	1.62	42.56	m	46.81
327 x 102.5mm; with oversailing course and cement fillets both sides; horizontal	7.00	5.00	7.35	1.50	1.05	47.65	1.62	56.62	m	62.28

Labour hourly rates: (except Specialists) Craft Operatives 20.87 Labourer 15.57 Rates are national average prices. Refer to REGIONAL VARIATIONS for indicative levels of overall pricing in regions	MATERIALS			LABOUR				RATES		
	Del to Site £	Waste %	Material Cost £	Craft Optve Hrs	Lab Hrs	Labour Cost £	Sunds £	Nett Rate £	Unit	Gross rate (10%) £
BRICK/BLOCK WALLING (Cont'd)										
Walls; brickwork; Facing bricks p.c. £350.00 per 1000, 215 x 102.5 x 65mm; in cement-lime mortar (1:2:9); flush smooth pointing as work proceeds (Cont'd)										
Facework copings; bricks-on-edge; pointing top and each side (Cont'd)										
extra; galvanised safety frame cramp at angle or end	0.32	5.00	0.34	0.04	0.03	1.30	-	1.64	nr	1.81
Walls; brickwork										
Facing bricks p.c. £400.00 per 1000, 215 x 102.5 x 65mm; in cement-lime mortar (1:2:9); flush smooth pointing as work proceeds										
Walls										
stretcher bond; facework one side 102mm thick	23.60	5.00	24.78	1.75	1.30	56.76	4.04	85.59	m²	94.14
stretcher bond; facework both sides 102mm thick	23.60	5.00	24.78	2.05	1.50	66.14	4.04	94.96	m²	104.46
English bond; facework both sides 215mm thick	47.60	5.00	49.98	2.65	2.05	87.22	9.44	146.64	m²	161.31
Flemish bond; facework both sides 215mm thick	47.60	5.00	49.98	2.95	2.25	96.60	9.44	156.02	m²	171.62
Skins of hollow walls										
stretcher bond; facework one side 102mm thick	23.60	5.00	24.78	1.75	1.30	56.76	4.04	85.59	m²	94.14
extra; special bricks; vertical angles; squint; BS 4729, type AN.1.1. (p.c. £400.00 per 100)	53.32	5.00	55.99	0.25	0.15	7.55	-	63.54	m	69.89
extra; special bricks; intersections; birdsmouth; BS 4729, type AN.4.1. (p.c. £400.00 per 100)	53.32	5.00	55.99	0.25	0.15	7.55	-	63.54	m	69.89
Walls; building overhand										
stretcher bond; facework one side 102mm thick	23.60	5.00	24.78	2.15	1.55	69.00	4.04	97.83	m²	107.61
stretcher bond; facework both sides 102mm thick	23.60	5.00	24.78	2.45	1.75	78.38	4.04	107.20	m²	117.92
English bond; facework both sides 215mm thick	47.60	5.00	49.98	3.05	2.30	99.46	9.44	158.88	m²	174.77
Flemish bond; facework both sides 215mm thick	47.60	5.00	49.98	3.35	2.50	108.84	9.44	168.26	m²	185.08
Skins of hollow walls; building overhand										
stretcher bond; facework one side 102mm thick	23.60	5.00	24.78	2.15	1.55	69.00	4.04	97.83	m²	107.61
Arches including centering; flat										
112mm high on face; 215mm thick; width of exposed soffit 112mm; bricks-on-edge	5.33	5.00	5.60	1.05	0.80	34.37	1.07	41.04	m	45.14
112mm high on face; 215mm thick; width of exposed soffit 215mm; bricks-on-edge	5.33	5.00	5.60	1.50	1.00	46.88	1.07	53.55	m	58.90
215mm high on face; 112mm thick; width of exposed soffit 112mm; bricks-on-end	5.33	5.00	5.60	1.45	1.00	45.83	1.07	52.50	m	57.75
Arches including centering; segmental										
215mm high on face; 215mm thick; width of exposed soffit 112mm; bricks-on-edge	10.66	5.00	11.20	2.40	1.65	75.78	2.16	89.14	m	98.05
215mm high on face; 215mm thick; width of exposed soffit 215mm; bricks-on-edge	10.66	5.00	11.20	2.95	1.95	91.93	2.16	105.29	m	115.82
Arches including centering; semi-circular										
215mm high on face; 215mm thick; width of exposed soffit 112mm; bricks-on-edge	10.66	5.00	11.20	2.40	1.65	75.78	2.16	89.14	m	98.05
215mm high on face; 215mm thick; width of exposed soffit 215mm; bricks-on-edge	10.66	5.00	11.20	2.95	1.95	91.93	2.16	105.29	m	115.82
Facework copings; bricks-on-edge; pointing top and each side										
215 x 102.5mm; horizontal	5.33	5.00	5.60	0.70	0.50	22.39	1.07	29.07	m	31.97
215 x 102.5mm; with oversailing course and cement fillets both sides; horizontal	5.33	5.00	5.60	1.10	0.75	34.63	1.07	41.31	m	45.44
327 x 102.5mm; horizontal	8.00	5.00	8.40	1.05	0.75	33.59	1.62	43.61	m	47.97
327 x 102.5mm; with oversailing course and cement fillets both sides; horizontal	8.00	5.00	8.40	1.50	1.05	47.65	1.62	57.67	m	63.44
extra; galvanised safety frame cramp at angle or end	0.32	5.00	0.34	0.04	0.03	1.30	-	1.64	nr	1.81
Walls; brickwork										
Facing bricks p.c. £500.00 per 1000, 215 x 102.5 x 65mm; in cement-lime mortar (1:2:9); flush smooth pointing as work proceeds										
Walls										
stretcher bond; facework one side 102mm thick	29.50	5.00	30.97	1.75	1.30	56.76	4.04	91.78	m²	100.96
stretcher bond; facework both sides 102mm thick	29.50	5.00	30.97	2.05	1.50	66.14	4.04	101.16	m²	111.27
English bond; facework both sides 215mm thick	59.50	5.00	62.47	2.65	2.05	87.22	9.44	159.14	m²	175.05
Flemish bond; facework both sides 215mm thick	59.50	5.00	62.47	2.95	2.25	96.60	9.44	168.51	m²	185.36
Skins of hollow walls										
stretcher bond; facework one side 102mm thick	29.50	5.00	30.97	1.75	1.30	56.76	4.04	91.78	m²	100.96
extra; special bricks; vertical angles; squint; BS 4729, type AN.1.1. (p.c. £500.00 per 100)	66.65	5.00	69.98	0.25	0.15	7.55	-	77.54	m	85.29

Labour hourly rates: (except Specialists) Craft Operatives 20.87 Labourer 15.57 Rates are national average prices. Refer to REGIONAL VARIATIONS for indicative levels of overall pricing in regions	MATERIALS			LABOUR				RATES		
	Del to Site £	Waste %	Material Cost £	Craft Optve Hrs	Lab Hrs	Labour Cost £	Sunds £	Nett Rate £	Unit	Gross rate (10%) £
BRICK/BLOCK WALLING (Cont'd)										
Facing bricks p.c. £500.00 per 1000, 215 x 102.5 x 65mm; in cement-lime mortar (1:2:9); flush smooth pointing as work proceeds (Cont'd)										
Skins of hollow walls (Cont'd)										
stretcher bond; facework one side (Cont'd)										
extra; special bricks; intersections; birdsmouth; BS 4729, type AN.4.1. (p.c. £500.00 per 100)	66.65	5.00	69.98	0.25	0.15	7.55	-	77.54	m	85.29
Walls; building overhand										
stretcher bond; facework one side										
102mm thick	29.50	5.00	30.97	2.15	1.55	69.00	4.04	104.02	m²	114.42
stretcher bond; facework both sides										
102mm thick	29.50	5.00	30.97	2.45	1.75	78.38	4.04	113.40	m²	124.74
English bond; facework both sides										
215mm thick	59.50	5.00	62.47	3.05	2.30	99.46	9.44	171.38	m²	188.52
Flemish bond; facework both sides										
215mm thick	59.50	5.00	62.47	3.35	2.50	108.84	9.44	180.75	m²	198.83
Skins of hollow walls; building overhand										
stretcher bond; facework one side										
102mm thick	29.50	5.00	30.97	2.15	1.55	69.00	4.04	104.02	m²	114.42
Arches including centering; flat										
112mm high on face; 215mm thick; width of exposed soffit 112mm; bricks-on-edge	6.66	5.00	7.00	1.05	0.80	34.37	1.07	42.44	m	46.68
112mm high on face; 215mm thick; width of exposed soffit 215mm; bricks-on-edge	6.66	5.00	7.00	1.50	1.00	46.88	1.07	54.95	m	60.44
215mm high on face; 112mm thick; width of exposed soffit 112mm; bricks-on-end	6.66	5.00	7.00	1.45	1.00	45.83	1.07	53.90	m	59.29
Arches including centering; segmental										
215mm high on face; 215mm thick; width of exposed soffit 112mm; bricks-on-edge	13.33	5.00	14.00	2.40	1.65	75.78	2.16	91.94	m	101.13
215mm high on face; 215mm thick; width of exposed soffit 215mm; bricks-on-edge	13.33	5.00	14.00	2.95	1.95	91.93	2.16	108.09	m	118.89
Arches including centering; semi-circular										
215mm high on face; 215mm thick; width of exposed soffit 112mm; bricks-on-edge	13.33	5.00	14.00	2.40	1.65	75.78	2.16	91.94	m	101.13
215mm high on face; 215mm thick; width of exposed soffit 215mm; bricks-on-edge	13.33	5.00	14.00	2.95	1.95	91.93	2.16	108.09	m	118.89
Facework copings; bricks-on-edge; pointing top and each side										
215 x 102.5mm; horizontal	6.66	5.00	7.00	0.70	0.50	22.39	1.07	30.46	m	33.51
215 x 102.5mm; with oversailing course and cement fillets both sides; horizontal	6.66	5.00	7.00	1.10	0.75	34.63	1.07	42.71	m	46.98
327 x 102.5mm; horizontal	10.00	5.00	10.50	1.05	0.75	33.59	1.62	45.71	m	50.28
327 x 102.5mm; with oversailing course and cement fillets both sides; horizontal	10.00	5.00	10.50	1.50	1.05	47.65	1.62	59.77	m	65.75
extra; galvanised safety frame cramp at angle or end	0.32	5.00	0.34	0.04	0.03	1.30	-	1.64	nr	1.81
Walls; brickwork										
Facing bricks p.c. £600.00 per 1000, 215 x 102.5 x 65mm; in cement-lime mortar (1:2:9); flush smooth pointing as work proceeds										
Walls										
stretcher bond; facework one side										
102mm thick	35.40	5.00	37.17	1.75	1.30	56.76	4.04	97.98	m²	107.77
stretcher bond; facework both sides										
102mm thick	35.40	5.00	37.17	2.05	1.50	66.14	4.04	107.35	m²	118.09
English bond; facework both sides										
215mm thick	71.40	5.00	74.97	2.65	2.05	87.22	9.44	171.63	m²	188.80
Flemish bond; facework both sides										
215mm thick	71.40	5.00	74.97	2.95	2.25	96.60	9.44	181.01	m²	199.11
Skins of hollow walls										
stretcher bond; facework one side										
102mm thick	35.40	5.00	37.17	1.75	1.30	56.76	4.04	97.98	m²	107.77
extra; special bricks; vertical angles; squint; BS 4729, type AN.1.1. (p.c. £600.00 per 100)	79.98	5.00	83.98	0.25	0.15	7.55	-	91.53	m	100.69
extra; special bricks; intersections; birdsmouth; BS 4729, type AN.4.1. (p.c. £600.00 per 100)	79.98	5.00	83.98	0.25	0.15	7.55	-	91.53	m	100.69
Walls; building overhand										
stretcher bond; facework one side										
102mm thick	35.40	5.00	37.17	2.15	1.55	69.00	4.04	110.22	m²	121.24
stretcher bond; facework both sides										
102mm thick	35.40	5.00	37.17	2.45	1.75	78.38	4.04	119.59	m²	131.55
English bond; facework both sides										
215mm thick	71.40	5.00	74.97	3.05	2.30	99.46	9.44	183.87	m²	202.26
Flemish bond; facework both sides										
215mm thick	71.40	5.00	74.97	3.35	2.50	108.84	9.44	193.25	m²	212.57
Skins of hollow walls; building overhand										
stretcher bond; facework one side										
102mm thick	35.40	5.00	37.17	2.15	1.55	69.00	4.04	110.22	m²	121.24
Arches including centering; flat										
112mm high on face; 215mm thick; width of exposed soffit 112mm; bricks-on-edge	8.00	5.00	8.40	1.05	0.80	34.37	1.07	43.84	m	48.22
112mm high on face; 215mm thick; width of exposed soffit 215mm; bricks-on-edge	8.00	5.00	8.40	1.50	1.00	46.88	1.07	56.35	m	61.98

Labour hourly rates: (except Specialists) Craft Operatives 20.87 Labourer 15.57 Rates are national average prices. Refer to REGIONAL VARIATIONS for indicative levels of overall pricing in regions	MATERIALS			LABOUR				RATES		
	Del to Site £	Waste %	Material Cost £	Craft Optve Hrs	Lab Hrs	Labour Cost £	Sunds £	Nett Rate £	Unit	Gross rate (10%) £
BRICK/BLOCK WALLING (Cont'd)										
Facing bricks p.c. £600.00 per 1000, 215 x 102.5 x 65mm; in cement-lime mortar (1:2:9); flush smooth pointing as work proceeds (Cont'd)										
Arches including centering; flat (Cont'd)										
215mm high on face; 112mm thick; width of exposed soffit 112mm; bricks-on-end	8.00	5.00	8.40	1.45	1.00	45.83	1.07	55.30	m	60.83
Arches including centering; segmental										
215mm high on face; 215mm thick; width of exposed soffit 112mm; bricks-on-edge	16.00	5.00	16.80	2.40	1.65	75.78	2.16	94.74	m	104.21
215mm high on face; 215mm thick; width of exposed soffit 215mm; bricks-on-edge	16.00	5.00	16.80	2.95	1.95	91.93	2.16	110.89	m	121.97
Arches including centering; semi-circular										
215mm high on face; 215mm thick; width of exposed soffit 112mm; bricks-on-edge	16.00	5.00	16.80	2.40	1.65	75.78	2.16	94.74	m	104.21
215mm high on face; 215mm thick; width of exposed soffit 215mm; bricks-on-edge	16.00	5.00	16.80	2.95	1.95	91.93	2.16	110.89	m	121.97
Facework copings; bricks-on-edge; pointing top and each side										
215 x 102.5mm; horizontal	8.00	5.00	8.40	0.70	0.50	22.39	1.07	31.86	m	35.05
215 x 102.5mm; with oversailing course and cement fillets both sides; horizontal	8.00	5.00	8.40	1.10	0.75	34.63	1.07	44.10	m	48.52
327 x 102.5mm; horizontal	12.00	5.00	12.60	1.05	0.75	33.59	1.62	47.81	m	52.59
327 x 102.5mm; with oversailing course and cement fillets both sides; horizontal	12.00	5.00	12.60	1.50	1.05	47.65	1.62	61.87	m	68.06
extra; galvanised safety frame cramp at angle or end	0.32	5.00	0.34	0.04	0.03	1.30	-	1.64	nr	1.81
Walls; brickwork										
Facing bricks p.c. £700.00 per 1000, 215 x 102.5 x 65mm; in cement-lime mortar (1:2:9); flush smooth pointing as work proceeds										
Walls										
stretcher bond; facework one side 102mm thick	41.30	5.00	43.36	1.75	1.30	56.76	4.04	104.17	m²	114.59
stretcher bond; facework both sides 102mm thick	41.30	5.00	43.36	2.05	1.50	66.14	4.04	113.55	m²	124.90
English bond; facework both sides 215mm thick	83.30	5.00	87.46	2.65	2.05	87.22	9.44	184.13	m²	202.54
Flemish bond; facework both sides 215mm thick	83.30	5.00	87.46	2.95	2.25	96.60	9.44	193.50	m²	212.85
Skins of hollow walls										
stretcher bond; facework one side 102mm thick	41.30	5.00	43.36	1.75	1.30	56.76	4.04	104.17	m²	114.59
extra; special bricks; vertical angles; squint; BS 4729, type AN.1.1. (p.c. £700.00 per 100)	93.31	5.00	97.98	0.25	0.15	7.55	-	105.53	m	116.08
extra; special bricks; intersections; birdsmouth; BS 4729, type AN.4.1. (p.c. £700.00 per 100)	93.31	5.00	97.98	0.25	0.15	7.55	-	105.53	m	116.08
Walls; building overhand										
stretcher bond; facework one side 102mm thick	41.30	5.00	43.36	2.15	1.55	69.00	4.04	116.41	m²	128.05
stretcher bond; facework both sides 102mm thick	41.30	5.00	43.36	2.45	1.75	78.38	4.04	125.79	m²	138.37
English bond; facework both sides 215mm thick	83.30	5.00	87.46	3.05	2.30	99.46	9.44	196.37	m²	216.00
Flemish bond; facework both sides 215mm thick	83.30	5.00	87.46	3.35	2.50	108.84	9.44	205.74	m²	226.32
Skins of hollow walls; building overhand										
stretcher bond; facework one side 102mm thick	41.30	5.00	43.36	2.15	1.55	69.00	4.04	116.41	m²	128.05
Arches including centering; flat										
112mm high on face; 215mm thick; width of exposed soffit 112mm; bricks-on-edge	9.33	5.00	9.80	1.05	0.80	34.37	1.07	45.24	m	49.76
112mm high on face; 215mm thick; width of exposed soffit 215mm; bricks-on-edge	9.33	5.00	9.80	1.50	1.00	46.88	1.07	57.75	m	63.52
215mm high on face; 112mm thick; width of exposed soffit 112mm; bricks-on-end	9.33	5.00	9.80	1.45	1.00	45.83	1.07	56.70	m	62.37
Arches including centering; segmental										
215mm high on face; 215mm thick; width of exposed soffit 112mm; bricks-on-edge	18.66	5.00	19.60	2.40	1.65	75.78	2.16	97.54	m	107.29
215mm high on face; 215mm thick; width of exposed soffit 215mm; bricks-on-edge	18.66	5.00	19.60	2.95	1.95	91.93	2.16	113.68	m	125.05
Arches including centering; semi-circular										
215mm high on face; 215mm thick; width of exposed soffit 112mm; bricks-on-edge	18.66	5.00	19.60	2.40	1.65	75.78	2.16	97.54	m	107.29
215mm high on face; 215mm thick; width of exposed soffit 215mm; bricks-on-edge	18.66	5.00	19.60	2.95	1.95	91.93	2.16	113.68	m	125.05
Facework copings; bricks-on-edge; pointing top and each side										
215 x 102.5mm; horizontal	9.33	5.00	9.80	0.70	0.50	22.39	1.07	33.26	m	36.59
215 x 102.5mm; with oversailing course and cement fillets both sides; horizontal	9.33	5.00	9.80	1.10	0.75	34.63	1.07	45.50	m	50.06
327 x 102.5mm; horizontal	14.00	5.00	14.70	1.05	0.75	33.59	1.62	49.91	m	54.90
327 x 102.5mm; with oversailing course and cement fillets both sides; horizontal	14.00	5.00	14.70	1.50	1.05	47.65	1.62	63.97	m	70.37
extra; galvanised safety frame cramp at angle or end	0.32	5.00	0.34	0.04	0.03	1.30	-	1.64	nr	1.81

Labour hourly rates: (except Specialists) Craft Operatives 20.87 Labourer 15.57 Rates are national average prices. Refer to REGIONAL VARIATIONS for indicative levels of overall pricing in regions	MATERIALS			LABOUR				RATES		
	Del to Site £	Waste %	Material Cost £	Craft Optve Hrs	Lab Hrs	Labour Cost £	Sunds £	Nett Rate £	Unit	Gross rate (10%) £
BRICK/BLOCK WALLING (Cont'd)										
Walls; brickwork										
Facing bricks p.c. £800.00 per 1000, 215 x 102.5 x 65mm; in cement-lime mortar (1:2:9); flush smooth pointing as work proceeds										
Walls										
stretcher bond; facework one side 102mm thick	47.20	5.00	49.56	1.75	1.30	56.76	4.04	110.37	m²	121.40
stretcher bond; facework both sides 102mm thick	47.20	5.00	49.56	2.05	1.50	66.14	4.04	119.74	m²	131.72
English bond; facework both sides 215mm thick	95.20	5.00	99.96	2.65	2.05	87.22	9.44	196.62	m²	216.28
Flemish bond; facework both sides 215mm thick	95.20	5.00	99.96	2.95	2.25	96.60	9.44	206.00	m²	226.60
Skins of hollow walls										
stretcher bond; facework one side 102mm thick	47.20	5.00	49.56	1.75	1.30	56.76	4.04	110.37	m²	121.40
extra; special bricks; vertical angles; squint; BS 4729, type AN.1.1. (p.c. £800.00 per 100)	106.64	5.00	111.97	0.25	0.15	7.55	-	119.52	m	131.48
extra; special bricks; intersections; birdsmouth; BS 4729, type AN.4.1. (p.c. £800.00 per 100)	106.64	5.00	111.97	0.25	0.15	7.55	-	119.52	m	131.48
Walls; building overhand										
stretcher bond; facework one side 102mm thick	47.20	5.00	49.56	2.15	1.55	69.00	4.04	122.61	m²	134.87
stretcher bond; facework both sides 102mm thick	47.20	5.00	49.56	2.45	1.75	78.38	4.04	131.98	m²	145.18
English bond; facework both sides 215mm thick	95.20	5.00	99.96	3.05	2.30	99.46	9.44	208.86	m²	229.75
Flemish bond; facework both sides 215mm thick	95.20	5.00	99.96	3.35	2.50	108.84	9.44	218.24	m²	240.06
Skins of hollow walls; building overhand										
stretcher bond; facework one side 102mm thick	47.20	5.00	49.56	2.15	1.55	69.00	4.04	122.61	m²	134.87
Arches including centering; flat										
112mm high on face; 215mm thick; width of exposed soffit 112mm; bricks-on-edge	10.66	5.00	11.20	1.05	0.80	34.37	1.07	46.64	m	51.30
112mm high on face; 215mm thick; width of exposed soffit 215mm; bricks-on-edge	10.66	5.00	11.20	1.50	1.00	46.88	1.07	59.14	m	65.06
215mm high on face; 112mm thick; width of exposed soffit 112mm; bricks-on-end	10.66	5.00	11.20	1.45	1.00	45.83	1.07	58.10	m	63.91
Arches including centering; segmental										
215mm high on face; 215mm thick; width of exposed soffit 112mm; bricks-on-edge	21.33	5.00	22.39	2.40	1.65	75.78	2.16	100.33	m	110.37
215mm high on face; 215mm thick; width of exposed soffit 215mm; bricks-on-edge	21.33	5.00	22.39	2.95	1.95	91.93	2.16	116.48	m	128.13
Arches including centering; semi-circular										
215mm high on face; 215mm thick; width of exposed soffit 112mm; bricks-on-edge	21.33	5.00	22.39	2.40	1.65	75.78	2.16	100.33	m	110.37
215mm high on face; 215mm thick; width of exposed soffit 215mm; bricks-on-edge	21.33	5.00	22.39	2.95	1.95	91.93	2.16	116.48	m	128.13
Facework copings; bricks-on-edge; pointing top and each side										
215 x 102.5mm; horizontal	10.66	5.00	11.20	0.70	0.50	22.39	1.07	34.66	m	38.13
215 x 102.5mm; with oversailing course and cement fillets both sides; horizontal	10.66	5.00	11.20	1.10	0.75	34.63	1.07	46.90	m	51.59
327 x 102.5mm; horizontal	16.00	5.00	16.80	1.05	0.75	33.59	1.62	52.01	m	57.21
327 x 102.5mm; with oversailing course and cement fillets both sides; horizontal	16.00	5.00	16.80	1.50	1.05	47.65	1.62	66.07	m	72.68
extra; galvanised safety frame cramp at angle or end	0.32	5.00	0.34	0.04	0.03	1.30	-	1.64	nr	1.81
Walls; brickwork										
Facing bricks p.c. £900.00 per 1000, 215 x 102.5 x 65mm; in cement-lime mortar (1:2:9); flush smooth pointing as work proceeds										
Walls										
stretcher bond; facework one side 102mm thick	53.10	5.00	55.75	1.75	1.30	56.76	4.04	116.56	m²	128.22
stretcher bond; facework both sides 102mm thick	53.10	5.00	55.75	2.05	1.50	66.14	4.04	125.94	m²	138.53
English bond; facework both sides 215mm thick	107.10	5.00	112.45	2.65	2.05	87.22	9.44	209.12	m²	230.03
Flemish bond; facework both sides 215mm thick	107.10	5.00	112.45	2.95	2.25	96.60	9.44	218.49	m²	240.34
Skins of hollow walls										
stretcher bond; facework one side 102mm thick	53.10	5.00	55.75	1.75	1.30	56.76	4.04	116.56	m²	128.22
extra; special bricks; vertical angles; squint; BS 4729, type AN.1.1. (p.c. £900.00 per 100)	119.97	5.00	125.97	0.25	0.15	7.55	-	133.52	m	146.87
extra; special bricks; intersections; birdsmouth; BS 4729, type AN.4.1. (p.c. £900.00 per 100)	119.97	5.00	125.97	0.25	0.15	7.55	-	133.52	m	146.87
Walls; building overhand										
stretcher bond; facework one side 102mm thick	53.10	5.00	55.75	2.15	1.55	69.00	4.04	128.80	m²	141.68
stretcher bond; facework both sides 102mm thick	53.10	5.00	55.75	2.45	1.75	78.38	4.04	138.18	m²	151.99

Labour hourly rates: (except Specialists) Craft Operatives 20.87 Labourer 15.57 Rates are national average prices. Refer to REGIONAL VARIATIONS for indicative levels of overall pricing in regions	MATERIALS			LABOUR				RATES		
	Del to Site £	Waste %	Material Cost £	Craft Optve Hrs	Lab Hrs	Labour Cost £	Sunds £	Nett Rate £	Unit	Gross rate (10%) £
BRICK/BLOCK WALLING (Cont'd)										
Facing bricks p.c. £900.00 per 1000, 215 x 102.5 x 65mm; in cement-lime mortar (1:2:9); flush smooth pointing as work proceeds (Cont'd)										
Walls; building overhand (Cont'd)										
English bond; facework both sides										
215mm thick	107.10	5.00	112.45	3.05	2.30	99.46	9.44	221.36	m²	243.49
Flemish bond; facework both sides										
215mm thick	107.10	5.00	112.45	3.35	2.50	108.84	9.44	230.73	m²	253.81
Skins of hollow walls; building overhand										
stretcher bond; facework one side										
102mm thick	53.10	5.00	55.75	2.15	1.55	69.00	4.04	128.80	m²	141.68
Arches including centering; flat										
112mm high on face; 215mm thick; width of exposed soffit 112mm; bricks-on-edge	12.00	5.00	12.60	1.05	0.80	34.37	1.07	48.04	m	52.84
112mm high on face; 215mm thick; width of exposed soffit 215mm; bricks-on-edge	12.00	5.00	12.60	1.50	1.00	46.88	1.07	60.54	m	66.60
215mm high on face; 112mm thick; width of exposed soffit 112mm; bricks-on-end	12.00	5.00	12.60	1.45	1.00	45.83	1.07	59.50	m	65.45
Arches including centering; segmental										
215mm high on face; 215mm thick; width of exposed soffit 112mm; bricks-on-edge	23.99	5.00	25.19	2.40	1.65	75.78	2.16	103.13	m	113.45
215mm high on face; 215mm thick; width of exposed soffit 215mm; bricks-on-edge	23.99	5.00	25.19	2.95	1.95	91.93	2.16	119.28	m	131.21
Arches including centering; semi-circular										
215mm high on face; 215mm thick; width of exposed soffit 112mm; bricks-on-edge	23.99	5.00	25.19	2.40	1.65	75.78	2.16	103.13	m	113.45
215mm high on face; 215mm thick; width of exposed soffit 215mm; bricks-on-edge	23.99	5.00	25.19	2.95	1.95	91.93	2.16	119.28	m	131.21
Facework copings; bricks-on-edge; pointing top and each side										
215 x 102.5mm; horizontal	12.00	5.00	12.60	0.70	0.50	22.39	1.07	36.06	m	39.67
215 x 102.5mm; with oversailing course and cement fillets both sides; horizontal	12.00	5.00	12.60	1.10	0.75	34.63	1.07	48.30	m	53.13
327 x 102.5mm; horizontal	18.00	5.00	18.90	1.05	0.75	33.59	1.62	54.11	m	59.52
327 x 102.5mm; with oversailing course and cement fillets both sides; horizontal	18.00	5.00	18.90	1.50	1.05	47.65	1.62	68.17	m	74.99
extra; galvanised safety frame cramp at angle or end	0.32	5.00	0.34	0.04	0.03	1.30	-	1.64	nr	1.81
Walls; brickwork; Composite walling of bricks 215 x 102.5x 65mm; in cement-lime mortar (1:2:9); common bricks BS EN 772 Category M backing, compressive strength 20.5 N/mm²; facing bricks p.c. £200.00 per 1000; flush smooth pointing as work proceeds										
Walls										
English bond; facework one side										
215mm thick	26.84	5.00	28.19	2.65	2.05	87.22	9.44	124.85	m²	137.33
327mm thick	45.24	5.00	47.51	3.15	2.50	104.67	14.83	167.01	m²	183.71
Flemish bond; facework one side										
215mm thick	27.96	5.00	29.36	2.65	2.05	87.22	9.44	126.02	m²	138.63
327mm thick	46.36	5.00	48.68	3.15	2.50	104.67	14.83	168.18	m²	185.00
Walls; building overhand										
English bond; facework one side										
215mm thick	26.84	5.00	28.19	3.05	2.35	100.24	9.44	137.87	m²	151.65
327mm thick	45.24	5.00	47.51	3.55	2.80	117.68	14.83	180.03	m²	198.03
Flemish bond; facework one side										
215mm thick	27.96	5.00	29.36	3.05	2.35	100.24	9.44	139.04	m²	152.95
327mm thick	46.36	5.00	48.68	3.55	2.80	117.68	14.83	181.20	m²	199.32
Walls; brickwork; Composite walling of bricks 215 x 102.5 x 65mm; in cement-lime mortar (1:2:9); common bricks BS EN 772 Category M backing, compressive strength 20.5 N/mm²; facing bricks p.c. £250.00 per 1000; flush smooth pointing as work proceeds										
Walls										
English bond; facework one side										
215mm thick	31.29	5.00	32.86	2.65	2.05	87.22	9.44	129.52	m²	142.47
327mm thick	49.69	5.00	52.18	3.15	2.50	104.67	14.83	171.68	m²	188.85
Flemish bond; facework one side										
215mm thick	31.91	5.00	33.51	2.65	2.05	87.22	9.44	130.17	m²	143.19
327mm thick	50.31	5.00	52.83	3.15	2.50	104.67	14.83	172.33	m²	189.56
Walls; building overhand										
English bond; facework one side										
215mm thick	31.29	5.00	32.86	3.05	2.35	100.24	9.44	142.54	m²	156.79
327mm thick	49.69	5.00	52.18	3.55	2.80	117.68	14.83	184.70	m²	203.17
Flemish bond; facework one side										
215mm thick	31.91	5.00	33.51	3.05	2.35	100.24	9.44	143.19	m²	157.51
327mm thick	50.31	5.00	52.83	3.55	2.80	117.68	14.83	185.35	m²	203.88
Walls; brickwork; Composite walling of bricks 215 x 102.5 x 65mm; in cement-lime mortar (1:2:9); common bricks BS EN 772 Category M backing, compressive strength 20.5 N/mm²; facing bricks p.c. £300.00 per 1000; flush smooth pointing as work proceeds										
Walls										
English bond; facework one side										
215mm thick	35.74	5.00	37.53	2.65	2.05	87.22	9.44	134.19	m²	147.61

Labour hourly rates: (except Specialists) Craft Operatives 20.87 Labourer 15.57 Rates are national average prices. Refer to REGIONAL VARIATIONS for indicative levels of overall pricing in regions	MATERIALS			LABOUR				RATES		
	Del to Site £	Waste %	Material Cost £	Craft Optve Hrs	Lab Hrs	Labour Cost £	Sunds £	Nett Rate £	Unit	Gross rate (10%) £
BRICK/BLOCK WALLING (Cont'd)										
Walls; brickwork; Composite walling of bricks 215 x 102.5 x 65mm; in cement-lime mortar (1:2:9); common bricks BS EN 772 Category M backing, compressive strength 20.5 N/mm²; facing bricks p.c. £300.00 per 1000; flush smooth pointing as work proceeds (Cont'd)										
Walls (Cont'd)										
English bond; facework one side (Cont'd)										
327mm thick	54.15	5.00	56.85	3.15	2.50	104.67	14.83	176.35	m²	193.99
Flemish bond; facework one side										
215mm thick	35.86	5.00	37.66	2.65	2.05	87.22	9.44	134.32	m²	147.75
327mm thick	54.26	5.00	56.98	3.15	2.50	104.67	14.83	176.48	m²	194.12
Walls; building overhand										
English bond; facework one side										
215mm thick	35.74	5.00	37.53	3.05	2.35	100.24	9.44	147.21	m²	161.93
327mm thick	54.15	5.00	56.85	3.55	2.80	117.68	14.83	189.37	m²	208.31
Flemish bond; facework one side										
215mm thick	35.86	5.00	37.66	3.05	2.35	100.24	9.44	147.34	m²	162.07
327mm thick	54.26	5.00	56.98	3.55	2.80	117.68	14.83	189.49	m²	208.44
Walls; brickwork; Composite walling of bricks 215 x 102.5 x 65mm; in cement-lime mortar (1:2:9); common bricks BS EN 772 Category M backing, compressive strength 20.5 N/mm²; facing bricks p.c. £350.00 per 1000; flush smooth pointing as work proceeds										
Walls										
English bond; facework one side										
215mm thick	40.19	5.00	42.20	2.65	2.05	87.22	9.44	138.87	m²	152.75
327mm thick	58.59	5.00	61.52	3.15	2.50	104.67	14.83	181.02	m²	199.13
Flemish bond; facework one side										
215mm thick	39.81	5.00	41.80	2.65	2.05	87.22	9.44	138.47	m²	152.31
327mm thick	58.21	5.00	61.12	3.15	2.50	104.67	14.83	180.62	m²	198.69
Walls; building overhand										
English bond; facework one side										
215mm thick	40.19	5.00	42.20	3.05	2.35	100.24	9.44	151.89	m²	167.07
327mm thick	58.59	5.00	61.52	3.55	2.80	117.68	14.83	194.04	m²	213.45
Flemish bond; facework one side										
215mm thick	39.81	5.00	41.80	3.05	2.35	100.24	9.44	151.48	m²	166.63
327mm thick	58.21	5.00	61.12	3.55	2.80	117.68	14.83	193.64	m²	213.01
Walls; brickwork										
Composite walling of bricks 215 x 102.5x 65mm; in cement-lime mortar (1:2:9); common bricks BS EN 772 Category M backing, compressive strength 20.5 N/mm²; facing bricks p.c. £400.00 per 1000; flush smooth pointing as work proceeds										
Walls										
English bond; facework one side										
215mm thick	44.64	5.00	46.88	2.65	2.05	87.22	9.44	143.54	m²	157.89
327mm thick	63.05	5.00	66.20	3.15	2.50	104.67	14.83	185.70	m²	204.27
Flemish bond; facework one side										
215mm thick	43.76	5.00	45.95	2.65	2.05	87.22	9.44	142.61	m²	156.87
327mm thick	62.16	5.00	65.27	3.15	2.50	104.67	14.83	184.77	m²	203.25
Walls; building overhand										
English bond; facework one side										
215mm thick	44.64	5.00	46.88	3.05	2.35	100.24	9.44	156.56	m²	172.21
327mm thick	63.05	5.00	66.20	3.55	2.80	117.68	14.83	198.72	m²	218.59
Flemish bond; facework one side										
215mm thick	43.76	5.00	45.95	3.05	2.35	100.24	9.44	155.63	m²	171.20
327mm thick	62.16	5.00	65.27	3.55	2.80	117.68	14.83	197.79	m²	217.57
Walls; brickwork										
Composite walling of bricks 215 x 102.5x 65mm; in cement-lime mortar (1:2:9); common bricks BS EN 772 Category M backing, compressive strength 20.5 N/mm²; facing bricks p.c. £500.00 per 1000; flush smooth pointing as work proceeds										
Walls										
English bond; facework one side										
215mm thick	53.54	5.00	56.22	2.65	2.05	87.22	9.44	152.88	m²	168.17
327mm thick	71.94	5.00	75.54	3.15	2.50	104.67	14.83	195.04	m²	214.55
Flemish bond; facework one side										
215mm thick	51.66	5.00	54.25	2.65	2.05	87.22	9.44	150.91	m²	166.00
327mm thick	70.06	5.00	73.57	3.15	2.50	104.67	14.83	193.07	m²	212.37
Walls; building overhand										
English bond; facework one side										
215mm thick	53.54	5.00	56.22	3.05	2.35	100.24	9.44	165.90	m²	182.49
327mm thick	71.94	5.00	75.54	3.55	2.80	117.68	14.83	208.06	m²	228.87
Flemish bond; facework one side										
215mm thick	51.66	5.00	54.25	3.05	2.35	100.24	9.44	163.93	m²	180.32
327mm thick	70.06	5.00	73.57	3.55	2.80	117.68	14.83	206.08	m²	226.69

Labour hourly rates: (except Specialists) Craft Operatives 20.87 Labourer 15.57 Rates are national average prices. Refer to REGIONAL VARIATIONS for indicative levels of overall pricing in regions	MATERIALS			LABOUR				RATES		
	Del to Site £	Waste %	Material Cost £	Craft Optve Hrs	Lab Hrs	Labour Cost £	Sunds £	Nett Rate £	Unit	Gross rate (10%) £
BRICK/BLOCK WALLING (Cont'd)										
Walls; brickwork										
Composite walling of bricks 215 x 102.5x 65mm; in cement-lime mortar (1:2:9); common bricks BS EN 772 Category M backing, compressive strength 20.5 N/mm²; facing bricks p.c. £600.00 per 1000; flush smooth pointing as work proceeds										
Walls										
English bond; facework one side										
215mm thick	62.44	5.00	65.57	2.65	2.05	87.22	9.44	162.23	m²	178.45
327mm thick	80.85	5.00	84.89	3.15	2.50	104.67	14.83	204.39	m²	224.82
Flemish bond; facework one side										
215mm thick	59.56	5.00	62.54	2.65	2.05	87.22	9.44	159.20	m²	175.12
327mm thick	77.96	5.00	81.86	3.15	2.50	104.67	14.83	201.36	m²	221.50
Walls; building overhand										
English bond; facework one side										
215mm thick	62.44	5.00	65.57	3.05	2.35	100.24	9.44	175.25	m²	192.77
327mm thick	80.85	5.00	84.89	3.55	2.80	117.68	14.83	217.41	m²	239.15
Flemish bond; facework one side										
215mm thick	59.56	5.00	62.54	3.05	2.35	100.24	9.44	172.22	m²	189.44
327mm thick	77.96	5.00	81.86	3.55	2.80	117.68	14.83	214.38	m²	235.82
Walls; brickwork										
Composite walling of bricks 215 x 102.5x 65mm; in cement-lime mortar (1:2:9); common bricks BS EN 772 Category M backing, compressive strength 20.5 N/mm²; facing bricks p.c. £700.00 per 1000; flush smooth pointing as work proceeds										
Walls										
English bond; facework one side										
215mm thick	71.34	5.00	74.91	2.65	2.05	87.22	9.44	171.57	m²	188.73
327mm thick	89.74	5.00	94.23	3.15	2.50	104.67	14.83	213.73	m²	235.10
Flemish bond; facework one side										
215mm thick	67.46	5.00	70.84	2.65	2.05	87.22	9.44	167.50	m²	184.25
327mm thick	85.86	5.00	90.16	3.15	2.50	104.67	14.83	209.66	m²	230.62
Walls; building overhand										
English bond; facework one side										
215mm thick	71.34	5.00	74.91	3.05	2.35	100.24	9.44	184.59	m²	203.05
327mm thick	89.74	5.00	94.23	3.55	2.80	117.68	14.83	226.75	m²	249.43
Flemish bond; facework one side										
215mm thick	67.46	5.00	70.84	3.05	2.35	100.24	9.44	180.52	m²	198.57
327mm thick	85.86	5.00	90.16	3.55	2.80	117.68	14.83	222.67	m²	244.94
Walls; brickwork										
Composite walling of bricks 215 x 102.5x 65mm; in cement-lime mortar (1:2:9); common bricks BS EN 772 Category M backing, compressive strength 20.5 N/mm²; facing bricks p.c. £800.00 per 1000; flush smooth pointing as work proceeds										
Walls										
English bond; facework one side										
215mm thick	80.24	5.00	84.26	2.65	2.05	87.22	9.44	180.92	m²	199.01
327mm thick	98.65	5.00	103.58	3.15	2.50	104.67	14.83	223.08	m²	245.38
Flemish bond; facework one side										
215mm thick	75.36	5.00	79.13	2.65	2.05	87.22	9.44	175.79	m²	193.37
327mm thick	93.76	5.00	98.45	3.15	2.50	104.67	14.83	217.95	m²	239.75
Walls; building overhand										
English bond; facework one side										
215mm thick	80.24	5.00	84.26	3.05	2.35	100.24	9.44	193.94	m²	213.33
327mm thick	98.65	5.00	103.58	3.55	2.80	117.68	14.83	236.10	m²	259.70
Flemish bond; facework one side										
215mm thick	75.36	5.00	79.13	3.05	2.35	100.24	9.44	188.81	m²	207.69
327mm thick	93.76	5.00	98.45	3.55	2.80	117.68	14.83	230.97	m²	254.07
Walls; brickwork										
Composite walling of bricks 215 x 102.5x 65mm; in cement-lime mortar (1:2:9); common bricks BS EN 772 Category M backing, compressive strength 20.5 N/mm²; facing bricks p.c. £900.00 per 1000; flush smooth pointing as work proceeds										
Walls										
English bond; facework one side										
215mm thick	89.14	5.00	93.60	2.65	2.05	87.22	9.44	190.26	m²	209.29
327mm thick	107.54	5.00	112.92	3.15	2.50	104.67	14.83	232.42	m²	255.66
Flemish bond; facework one side										
215mm thick	83.26	5.00	87.43	2.65	2.05	87.22	9.44	184.09	m²	202.50
327mm thick	101.66	5.00	106.75	3.15	2.50	104.67	14.83	226.25	m²	248.87
Walls; building overhand										
English bond; facework one side										
215mm thick	89.14	5.00	93.60	3.05	2.35	100.24	9.44	203.28	m²	223.61
327mm thick	107.54	5.00	112.92	3.55	2.80	117.68	14.83	245.44	m²	269.98
Flemish bond; facework one side										
215mm thick	83.26	5.00	87.43	3.05	2.35	100.24	9.44	197.11	m²	216.82
327mm thick	101.66	5.00	106.75	3.55	2.80	117.68	14.83	239.26	m²	263.19

Labour hourly rates: (except Specialists) Craft Operatives 20.87 Labourer 15.57 Rates are national average prices. Refer to REGIONAL VARIATIONS for indicative levels of overall pricing in regions	MATERIALS			LABOUR				RATES		
	Del to Site £	Waste %	Material Cost £	Craft Optve Hrs	Lab Hrs	Labour Cost £	Sunds £	Nett Rate £	Unit	Gross rate (10%) £
BRICK/BLOCK WALLING (Cont'd)										
For each £10.00 difference in cost of 1000 facing bricks, add or deduct the following										
Wall; in facing bricks										
102mm thick; English bond; facework one side	0.90	5.00	0.94	-	-	-	-	0.94	m²	1.04
215mm thick; facework both sides	1.20	5.00	1.26	-	-	-	-	1.26	m²	1.39
Composite wall; common brick backing; facing bricks facework										
215mm thick; English bond; facework one side	0.90	5.00	0.94	-	-	-	-	0.94	m²	1.04
215mm thick; Flemish bond; facework one side	0.80	5.00	0.84	-	-	-	-	0.84	m²	0.92
Extra over flush smooth pointing for the following types of pointing										
Pointing; as work proceeds										
ironing in joints	-	-	-	0.03	0.02	0.94	-	0.94	m²	1.03
weathered pointing	-	-	-	0.03	0.02	0.94	-	0.94	m²	1.03
recessed pointing	-	-	-	0.04	0.03	1.30	-	1.30	m²	1.43
Raking out joints and pointing; on completion										
flush smooth pointing with cement-lime mortar (1:2:9)	-	-	-	0.75	0.50	23.44	0.26	23.70	m²	26.07
flush smooth pointing with coloured cement-lime mortar (1:2:9)	-	-	-	0.75	0.50	23.44	0.36	23.80	m²	26.18
weathered pointing with cement-lime mortar (1:2:9)	-	-	-	0.83	0.55	25.89	0.26	26.15	m²	28.76
weathered pointing with coloured cement-lime mortar (1:2:9)	-	-	-	0.83	0.55	25.89	0.36	26.25	m²	28.87
Extra over cement-lime mortar (1:2:9) for bedding and pointing for using coloured cement-lime mortar (1:2:9) for the following										
Wall										
102mm thick; pointing both sides	-	-	-	-	-	-	1.37	1.37	m²	1.51
215mm thick; pointing both sides	-	-	-	-	-	-	3.18	3.18	m²	3.50
Walls; Blockwork; Aerated concrete blocks, Thermalite, 440 x 215mm, Shield blocks (4.0 N/mm²); in cement-lime mortar (1:1:6)										
Walls										
75mm thick; stretcher bond	11.80	5.00	12.39	0.60	0.50	20.31	1.24	33.93	m²	37.33
100mm thick; stretcher bond	13.10	5.00	13.76	0.80	0.65	26.82	1.55	42.12	m²	46.33
140mm thick; stretcher bond	25.15	5.00	26.41	0.90	0.75	30.46	2.33	59.19	m²	65.11
150mm thick; stretcher bond	24.10	5.00	25.30	0.92	0.78	31.35	2.72	59.37	m²	65.31
215mm thick; stretcher bond	31.60	5.00	33.18	1.00	0.85	34.10	3.22	70.50	m²	77.55
Skins of hollow walls										
75mm thick; stretcher bond	11.80	5.00	12.39	0.60	0.50	20.31	1.24	33.93	m²	37.33
100mm thick; stretcher bond	13.10	5.00	13.76	0.80	0.65	26.82	1.55	42.12	m²	46.33
140mm thick; stretcher bond	25.15	5.00	26.41	0.90	0.75	30.46	2.33	59.19	m²	65.11
150mm thick; stretcher bond	24.10	5.00	25.30	0.92	0.78	31.35	2.72	59.37	m²	65.31
215mm thick; stretcher bond	31.60	5.00	33.18	1.00	0.85	34.10	3.22	70.50	m²	77.55
Closing cavities; vertical										
50mm wide with blockwork 100mm thick	3.28	5.00	3.44	0.20	0.10	5.73	0.33	9.50	m	10.45
75mm wide with blockwork 100mm thick	3.28	5.00	3.44	0.20	0.10	5.73	0.33	9.50	m	10.45
Closing cavities; horizontal										
50mm wide with blockwork 100mm thick	3.28	5.00	3.44	0.20	0.10	5.73	0.33	9.50	m	10.45
75mm wide with blockwork 100mm thick	3.28	5.00	3.44	0.20	0.10	5.73	0.33	9.50	m	10.45
Bonding ends to common brickwork; forming pockets; extra material										
walls; bonding every third course										
75mm	2.95	5.00	3.10	0.15	0.10	4.69	-	7.79	m	8.56
100mm	3.28	5.00	3.44	0.25	0.20	8.33	-	11.77	m	12.95
140mm	6.29	5.00	6.60	0.35	0.25	11.20	-	17.80	m	19.58
150mm	6.03	5.00	6.33	0.38	0.28	12.29	-	18.62	m	20.48
215mm	7.90	5.00	8.30	0.45	0.35	14.84	-	23.14	m	25.45
Bonding ends to existing common brickwork; cutting pockets; extra material										
walls; bonding every third course										
75mm	2.95	5.00	3.10	0.30	0.20	9.38	-	12.47	m	13.72
100mm	3.28	5.00	3.44	0.50	0.40	16.66	-	20.10	m	22.11
140mm	6.29	5.00	6.60	0.70	0.50	22.39	-	29.00	m	31.90
150mm	6.03	5.00	6.33	0.75	0.55	24.22	-	30.54	m	33.60
215mm	7.90	5.00	8.30	0.90	0.70	29.68	-	37.98	m	41.77
Bonding ends to existing concrete blockwork; cutting pockets; extra material										
walls; bonding every third course										
75mm	2.95	5.00	3.10	0.25	0.20	8.33	-	11.43	m	12.57
100mm	3.28	5.00	3.44	0.40	0.30	13.02	-	16.46	m	18.10
140mm	6.29	5.00	6.60	0.55	0.40	17.71	-	24.31	m	26.74
150mm	6.03	5.00	6.33	0.60	0.45	19.53	-	25.85	m	28.44
215mm	7.90	5.00	8.30	0.75	0.60	24.99	-	33.29	m	36.62
Walls; Blockwork; Aerated concrete blocks, Thermalite, 440 x 215mm, Turbo blocks (2.8 N/mm²); in cement-lime mortar (1:1:6)										
Walls										
100mm thick; stretcher bond	14.00	5.00	14.70	0.80	0.65	26.82	1.55	43.07	m²	47.37
150mm thick; stretcher bond	17.84	5.00	18.73	0.90	0.75	30.46	2.33	51.52	m²	56.67
215mm thick; stretcher bond	26.20	5.00	27.51	1.00	0.85	34.10	3.86	65.48	m²	72.02
265mm thick; stretcher bond	38.67	5.00	40.60	1.00	0.90	34.88	3.86	79.35	m²	87.28

Labour hourly rates: (except Specialists) Craft Operatives 20.87 Labourer 15.57 Rates are national average prices. Refer to REGIONAL VARIATIONS for indicative levels of overall pricing in regions	MATERIALS			LABOUR				RATES		
	Del to Site £	Waste %	Material Cost £	Craft Optve Hrs	Lab Hrs	Labour Cost £	Sunds £	Nett Rate £	Unit	Gross rate (10%) £
BRICK/BLOCK WALLING (Cont'd)										
Walls; Blockwork; Aerated concrete blocks, Thermalite, 440 x 215mm, Turbo blocks (2.8 N/mm²); in cement-lime mortar (1:1:6) (Cont'd)										
Skins of hollow walls										
100mm thick; stretcher bond	14.00	5.00	14.70	0.80	0.65	26.82	1.55	43.07	m²	47.37
150mm thick; stretcher bond	17.84	5.00	18.73	0.90	0.75	30.46	2.33	51.52	m²	56.67
215mm thick; stretcher bond	26.20	5.00	27.51	1.00	0.85	34.10	3.86	65.48	m²	72.02
265mm thick; stretcher bond	38.67	5.00	40.60	1.00	0.90	34.88	3.86	79.35	m²	87.28
Closing cavities										
50mm wide with blockwork 100mm thick	3.50	5.00	3.67	0.20	0.10	5.73	0.33	9.74	m	10.71
75mm wide with blockwork 100mm thick	3.50	5.00	3.67	0.20	0.10	5.73	0.33	9.74	m	10.71
Closing cavities; horizontal										
50mm wide with blockwork 100mm thick	3.50	5.00	3.67	0.20	0.10	5.73	0.33	9.74	m	10.71
75mm wide with blockwork 100mm thick	3.50	5.00	3.67	0.20	0.10	5.73	0.33	9.74	m	10.71
Walls; Blockwork; Aerated concrete blocks, Thermalite, 440 x 215mm, Turbo blocks (2.8 N/mm²); in thin joint mortar										
Walls										
100mm thick; stretcher bond	19.77	5.00	20.76	0.64	0.52	21.45	0.78	42.99	m²	47.29
150mm thick; stretcher bond	26.50	5.00	27.83	0.72	0.60	24.37	1.16	53.36	m²	58.69
215mm thick; stretcher bond	38.61	5.00	40.54	0.80	0.68	27.28	1.93	69.76	m²	76.73
Skins of hollow walls										
100mm thick; stretcher bond	21.08	5.00	22.13	0.80	0.65	26.82	1.15	50.10	m²	55.11
150mm thick; stretcher bond	26.50	5.00	27.83	0.72	0.60	24.37	1.16	53.36	m²	58.69
215mm thick; stretcher bond	38.61	5.00	40.54	0.80	0.68	27.28	1.93	69.76	m²	76.73
Closing cavities										
50mm wide with blockwork 100mm thick	3.97	5.00	4.17	0.20	0.10	5.73	0.16	10.07	m	11.07
75mm wide with blockwork 100mm thick	3.97	5.00	4.17	0.20	0.10	5.73	0.16	10.07	m	11.07
Closing cavities; horizontal										
50mm wide with blockwork 100mm thick	3.97	5.00	4.17	0.20	0.10	5.73	0.16	10.07	m	11.07
75mm wide with blockwork 100mm thick	3.97	5.00	4.17	0.20	0.10	5.73	0.16	10.07	m	11.07
Walls; Blockwork; Aerated concrete blocks, Thermalite, 440 x 215mm, Party wall blocks (4.0 N/mm²); in cement-lime mortar (1:1:6)										
Walls										
215mm thick; stretcher bond	31.60	5.00	33.18	1.00	0.85	34.10	3.86	71.15	m²	78.26
Walls; Blockwork; Aerated concrete blocks, Thermalite, 440 x 215mm, Hi-Strength 7 blocks (7.0 N/mm²); in cement-lime mortar (1:1:6)										
Walls										
100mm thick; stretcher bond	20.40	5.00	21.42	0.80	0.65	26.82	1.55	49.79	m²	54.77
140mm thick; stretcher bond	27.90	5.00	29.29	0.90	0.75	30.46	2.33	62.08	m²	68.29
150mm thick; stretcher bond	30.39	5.00	31.91	0.90	0.75	30.46	2.33	64.70	m²	71.17
200mm thick; stretcher bond	42.83	5.00	44.97	1.00	0.85	34.10	3.09	82.16	m²	90.38
215mm thick; stretcher bond	42.80	5.00	44.94	1.00	0.85	34.10	3.86	82.91	m²	91.20
Skins of hollow walls										
100mm thick; stretcher bond	20.40	5.00	21.42	0.80	0.65	26.82	1.55	49.79	m²	54.77
140mm thick; stretcher bond	27.90	5.00	29.29	0.90	0.75	30.46	2.33	62.08	m²	68.29
150mm thick; stretcher bond	30.39	5.00	31.91	0.90	0.75	30.46	2.33	64.70	m²	71.17
200mm thick; stretcher bond	42.83	5.00	44.97	1.00	0.85	34.10	3.09	82.16	m²	90.38
215mm thick; stretcher bond	42.80	5.00	44.94	1.00	0.85	34.10	3.86	82.91	m²	91.20
Closing cavities										
50mm wide with blockwork 100mm thick	5.10	5.00	5.35	0.20	0.10	5.73	0.33	11.42	m	12.56
75mm wide with blockwork 100mm thick	5.10	5.00	5.35	0.20	0.10	5.73	0.33	11.42	m	12.56
Closing cavities; horizontal										
50mm wide with blockwork 100mm thick	5.10	5.00	5.35	0.20	0.10	5.73	0.33	11.42	m	12.56
75mm wide with blockwork 100mm thick	5.10	5.00	5.35	0.20	0.10	5.73	0.33	11.42	m	12.56
Walls; Blockwork; Aerated concrete blocks, Thermalite, 440 x 215mm, Trenchblocks (4.0 N/mm²); in cement mortar (1:4)										
Walls										
300mm thick; stretcher bond	44.00	5.00	46.20	1.65	1.25	53.90	3.86	103.96	m²	114.35
355mm thick; stretcher bond	61.70	5.00	64.78	1.95	1.50	64.05	4.49	133.32	m²	146.66
Walls; Blockwork; Tarmac Topblock, medium density concrete block, Hemelite, 440 x 215mm, solid Standard blocks (3.5 N/mm²); in cement-lime mortar (1:1:6)										
Walls										
100mm thick; stretcher bond	11.10	5.00	11.65	0.90	0.75	30.46	1.55	43.67	m²	48.03
140mm thick; stretcher bond	16.18	5.00	16.99	1.00	0.85	34.10	2.33	53.42	m²	58.76
Skins of hollow walls										
100mm thick; stretcher bond	11.10	5.00	11.65	0.90	0.75	30.46	1.55	43.67	m²	48.03
140mm thick; stretcher bond	16.18	5.00	16.99	1.00	0.85	34.10	2.33	53.42	m²	58.76
Closing cavities										
50mm wide with blockwork 100mm thick	2.78	5.00	2.91	0.20	0.10	5.73	0.33	8.97	m	9.87
75mm wide with blockwork 100mm thick	2.78	5.00	2.91	0.20	0.10	5.73	0.33	8.97	m	9.87
Closing cavities; horizontal										
50mm wide with blockwork 100mm thick	2.78	5.00	2.91	0.20	0.10	5.73	0.33	8.97	m	9.87
75mm wide with blockwork 100mm thick	2.78	5.00	2.91	0.20	0.10	5.73	0.33	8.97	m	9.87

Labour hourly rates: (except Specialists) Craft Operatives 20.87 Labourer 15.57 Rates are national average prices. Refer to REGIONAL VARIATIONS for indicative levels of overall pricing in regions	MATERIALS			LABOUR				RATES		
	Del to Site £	Waste %	Material Cost £	Craft Optve Hrs	Lab Hrs	Labour Cost £	Sunds £	Nett Rate £	Unit	Gross rate (10%) £
BRICK/BLOCK WALLING (Cont'd)										
Walls; Blockwork; Tarmac Topblock, medium density concrete block, Hemelite, 440 x 215mm, solid Standard blocks (3.5 N/mm²); in cement-lime mortar (1:1:6) (Cont'd)										
Bonding ends to common brickwork; forming pockets; extra material										
walls; bonding every third course										
100mm	2.78	5.00	2.91	0.30	0.25	10.15	-	13.07	m	14.37
140mm	4.04	5.00	4.25	0.40	0.30	13.02	-	17.27	m	18.99
Bonding ends to existing common brickwork; cutting pockets; extra material										
walls; bonding every third course										
100mm	2.78	5.00	2.91	0.60	0.50	20.31	-	23.22	m	25.54
140mm	4.04	5.00	4.25	0.80	0.60	26.04	-	30.28	m	33.31
Bonding ends to existing concrete blockwork; cutting pockets; extra material										
walls; bonding every third course										
100mm	2.78	5.00	2.91	0.45	0.35	14.84	-	17.75	m	19.53
140mm	4.04	5.00	4.25	0.60	0.45	19.53	-	23.78	m	26.15
Walls; Blockwork; Tarmac Topblock, medium density concrete block, Hemelite, 440 x 215mm, solid Standard blocks (7.0 N/mm²); in cement-lime mortar (1:1:6)										
Walls										
100mm thick; stretcher bond	14.40	5.00	15.12	0.90	0.75	30.46	1.55	47.13	m²	51.84
140mm thick; stretcher bond	15.00	5.00	15.75	1.00	0.85	34.10	2.33	52.18	m²	57.40
Skins of hollow walls										
100mm thick; stretcher bond	14.40	5.00	15.12	0.90	0.75	30.46	1.55	47.13	m²	51.84
140mm thick; stretcher bond	15.00	5.00	15.75	1.00	0.85	34.10	2.33	52.18	m²	57.40
Closing cavities										
50mm wide with blockwork 100mm thick	3.60	5.00	3.78	0.20	0.10	5.73	0.33	9.84	m	10.83
75mm wide with blockwork 100mm thick	3.60	5.00	3.78	0.20	0.10	5.73	0.33	9.84	m	10.83
Closing cavities; horizontal										
50mm wide with blockwork 100mm thick	3.60	5.00	3.78	0.20	0.10	5.73	0.33	9.84	m	10.83
75mm wide with blockwork 100mm thick	3.60	5.00	3.78	0.20	0.10	5.73	0.33	9.84	m	10.83
Walls; Blockwork; Tarmac Topblock, fair face concrete blocks, Lignacite, 440 x 215mm, solid Standard blocks (7.0 N/mm²); in cement-lime mortar (1:1:6)										
Walls										
100mm thick; stretcher bond	16.42	5.00	17.24	0.95	0.80	32.28	1.55	51.07	m²	56.18
140mm thick; stretcher bond	23.85	5.00	25.04	1.10	0.90	36.97	2.33	64.34	m²	70.77
190mm thick; stretcher bond	51.66	5.00	54.24	1.15	0.95	38.79	3.09	96.12	m²	105.73
Skins of hollow walls										
100mm thick; stretcher bond	16.42	5.00	17.24	0.95	0.80	32.28	1.55	51.07	m²	56.18
140mm thick; stretcher bond	23.85	5.00	25.04	1.10	0.90	36.97	2.33	64.34	m²	70.77
190mm thick; stretcher bond	51.66	5.00	54.24	1.15	0.95	38.79	3.09	96.12	m²	105.73
Closing cavities										
50mm wide with blockwork 100mm thick	4.10	5.00	4.31	0.20	0.10	5.73	0.33	10.37	m	11.41
75mm wide with blockwork 100mm thick	4.10	5.00	4.31	0.20	0.10	5.73	0.33	10.37	m	11.41
Closing cavities; horizontal										
50mm wide with blockwork 100mm thick	4.10	5.00	4.31	0.20	0.10	5.73	0.33	10.37	m	11.41
75mm wide with blockwork 100mm thick	4.10	5.00	4.31	0.20	0.10	5.73	0.33	10.37	m	11.41
Walls; Blockwork; Tarmac Topblock, dense concrete blocks, Topcrete, 440 x 215mm, solid '7' blocks (7.0 N/mm²); in cement-lime mortar (1:1:6)										
Walls										
90mm thick; stretcher bond	23.84	5.00	25.04	1.15	0.95	38.79	1.55	65.38	m²	71.92
100mm thick; stretcher bond	14.00	5.00	14.70	1.20	1.00	40.61	1.55	56.87	m²	62.55
140mm thick; stretcher bond	35.44	5.00	37.21	1.30	1.10	44.26	2.33	83.80	m²	92.18
190mm thick; stretcher bond	47.69	5.00	50.07	1.40	1.15	47.12	3.09	100.28	m²	110.31
215mm thick; stretcher bond	53.68	5.00	56.36	1.50	1.20	49.99	3.86	110.21	m²	121.23
Skins of hollow walls										
90mm thick; stretcher bond	23.84	5.00	25.04	1.15	0.95	38.79	1.55	65.38	m²	71.92
100mm thick; stretcher bond	14.00	5.00	14.70	1.20	1.00	40.61	1.55	56.87	m²	62.55
140mm thick; stretcher bond	35.44	5.00	37.21	1.30	1.10	44.26	2.33	83.80	m²	92.18
190mm thick; stretcher bond	47.69	5.00	50.07	1.40	1.15	47.12	3.09	100.28	m²	110.31
215mm thick; stretcher bond	53.68	5.00	56.36	1.50	1.20	49.99	3.86	110.21	m²	121.23
Closing cavities										
50mm wide with blockwork 100mm thick	3.50	5.00	3.67	0.20	0.10	5.73	0.33	9.74	m	10.71
75mm wide with blockwork 100mm thick	3.50	5.00	3.67	0.20	0.10	5.73	0.33	9.74	m	10.71
Closing cavities; horizontal										
50mm wide with blockwork 100mm thick	3.50	5.00	3.67	0.20	0.10	5.73	0.33	9.74	m	10.71
75mm wide with blockwork 100mm thick	3.50	5.00	3.67	0.20	0.10	5.73	0.33	9.74	m	10.71
Walls; Blockwork; Tarmac Topblock, dense concrete blocks, Topcrete, 440 x 215mm, cellular Standard blocks (7.0 N/mm²); in cement-lime mortar (1:1:6)										
Walls										
100mm thick; stretcher bond	10.25	5.00	10.76	1.20	1.00	40.61	1.55	52.93	m²	58.22
140mm thick; stretcher bond	12.75	5.00	13.39	1.30	1.10	44.26	2.33	59.97	m²	65.97

Labour hourly rates: (except Specialists) Craft Operatives 20.87 Labourer 15.57 Rates are national average prices. Refer to REGIONAL VARIATIONS for indicative levels of overall pricing in regions	MATERIALS			LABOUR				RATES		
	Del to Site £	Waste %	Material Cost £	Craft Optve Hrs	Lab Hrs	Labour Cost £	Sunds £	Nett Rate £	Unit	Gross rate (10%) £
BRICK/BLOCK WALLING (Cont'd)										
Walls; Blockwork; Tarmac Topblock, dense concrete blocks, Topcrete, 440 x 215mm, cellular Standard blocks (7.0 N/mm²); in cement-lime mortar (1:1:6) (Cont'd)										
Skins of hollow walls										
100mm thick; stretcher bond	10.25	5.00	10.76	1.20	1.00	40.61	1.55	52.93	m²	58.22
140mm thick; stretcher bond	12.75	5.00	13.39	1.30	1.10	44.26	2.33	59.97	m²	65.97
Walls; Blockwork; Tarmac Topblock, dense concrete blocks, Topcrete, 440 x 215mm hollow standard blocks (7.0 N/mm²); in cement-lime mortar (1:1:6)										
Walls										
215mm thick; stretcher bond	23.00	5.00	24.15	1.50	0.81	43.92	3.86	71.93	m²	79.12
Walls; Blockwork; Tarmac Topblock, fair face concrete blocks, Lignacite, 440 x 215mm, solid Standard blocks (7.0 N/mm²); in cement-lime mortar (1:1:6); flush smooth pointing as work proceeds										
Walls										
stretcher bond; facework one side										
100mm thick	16.42	5.00	17.24	1.15	0.95	38.79	1.55	57.58	m²	63.34
140mm thick	23.85	5.00	25.04	1.30	1.05	43.48	2.33	70.85	m²	77.93
190mm thick	51.66	5.00	54.24	1.35	1.10	45.30	3.09	102.63	m²	112.89
stretcher bond; facework both sides										
100mm thick	16.42	5.00	17.24	1.35	1.10	45.30	1.55	64.09	m²	70.50
140mm thick	23.85	5.00	25.04	1.50	1.20	49.99	2.33	77.36	m²	85.09
190mm thick	51.66	5.00	54.24	1.55	1.25	51.81	3.09	109.14	m²	120.05
Skins of hollow walls										
stretcher bond; facework one side										
100mm thick	16.42	5.00	17.24	1.15	0.95	38.79	1.55	57.58	m²	63.34
140mm thick	23.85	5.00	25.04	1.30	1.05	43.48	2.33	70.85	m²	77.93
190mm thick	51.66	5.00	54.24	1.35	1.10	45.30	3.09	102.63	m²	112.89
Flue linings; Firebricks, 215 x 102.5 x 65mm; in fire cement										
bonding to surrounding brickwork with headers -4/m²										
112mm thick; stretcher bond	87.91	5.00	92.31	1.90	1.40	61.45	11.06	164.81	m²	181.29
built clear of main brickwork but with one header in each course set projecting to contact main work										
112mm thick; stretcher bond	87.91	5.00	92.31	1.90	1.40	61.45	11.06	164.81	m²	181.29
112mm thick; stretcher bond; in segmental top to flue	87.91	5.00	92.31	2.50	1.80	80.20	11.06	183.56	m²	201.92
Clay flue linings										
Clay flue linings, BS EN 1457; rebated joints; jointed in cement mortar (1:3)										
150mm diameter, class A1	46.77	5.00	49.11	0.45	0.35	14.84	0.48	64.43	m	70.87
terminal Type 6F	66.23	5.00	69.54	0.45	0.35	14.84	0.25	84.63	nr	93.09
185mm diameter, class A1	34.66	5.00	36.40	0.50	0.40	16.66	0.63	53.69	m	59.06
terminal Type 6F	81.83	5.00	85.92	0.50	0.40	16.66	0.28	102.86	nr	113.15
225mm diameter, class A1	73.41	5.00	77.08	0.55	0.45	18.49	0.68	96.24	m	105.86
terminal Type 6F	104.29	5.00	109.50	0.55	0.45	18.49	0.36	128.35	nr	141.19
Extra over walls for perimeters and abutments; Precast concrete copings BS 5642 Part 2; bedding in cement-lime mortar (1:1:6)										
Copings; figure 1; horizontal										
75 x 200mm; splayed; rebated joints	29.52	2.50	30.25	0.25	0.13	7.24	0.26	37.76	m	41.54
extra; stopped ends	2.95	-	2.95	-	-	-	-	2.95	nr	3.25
extra; internal angles	5.38	-	5.38	-	-	-	-	5.38	nr	5.92
100 x 300mm; splayed; rebated joints	45.83	2.50	46.98	0.50	0.25	14.33	0.41	61.72	m	67.89
extra; stopped ends	4.58	-	4.58	-	-	-	-	4.58	nr	5.04
extra; internal angles	9.48	-	9.48	-	-	-	-	9.48	nr	10.43
75 x 200mm; saddleback; rebated joints	28.47	2.50	29.18	0.25	0.13	7.24	0.26	36.68	m	40.35
extra; hipped ends	2.85	-	2.85	-	-	-	-	2.85	nr	3.13
extra; internal angles	8.81	-	8.81	-	-	-	-	8.81	nr	9.69
100 x 300mm; saddleback; rebated joints	37.15	2.50	38.08	0.50	0.25	14.33	0.41	52.82	m	58.10
extra; hipped ends	3.71	-	3.71	-	-	-	-	3.71	nr	4.09
extra; internal angles	11.77	-	11.77	-	-	-	-	11.77	nr	12.95
Extra over walls for perimeters and abutments; Restraint channels										
Ancon 25/14 restraint system Channel; fixing to steelwork with M8 screws complete with plate washer at 450mm centres; incorporating ties at 450mm centres										
100mm long SD25 ties	6.44	5.00	6.76	0.50	0.25	14.33	1.04	22.13	m	24.34
125mm long SD25 ties	8.20	5.00	8.61	0.50	0.25	14.33	1.22	24.16	m	26.57
150mm long SD25 ties	10.24	5.00	10.75	0.50	0.25	14.33	1.39	26.47	m	29.11
Extra over walls for perimeters and abutments; Wall profiles										
Stainless steel Simpson 'Strong Tie' wall extension profiles; plugging and screwing to brickwork and building ties in to joints of new walls										
60 - 250mm wall thickness; Ref. C2K	3.00	5.00	3.15	0.30	-	6.26	-	9.41	m	10.35
Extra over walls for opening perimeters; Slate and tile sills										
Clay plain roofing tiles, red, BS EN 1304, machine made, 265 x 165 x 13mm; in cement-lime mortar										
one course 150mm wide; set weathering	1.96	5.00	2.06	0.45	0.30	14.06	0.36	16.48	m	18.13

Labour hourly rates: (except Specialists) Craft Operatives 20.87 Labourer 15.57 Rates are national average prices. Refer to REGIONAL VARIATIONS for indicative levels of overall pricing in regions	MATERIALS			LABOUR				RATES		
	Del to Site £	Waste %	Material Cost £	Craft Optve Hrs	Lab Hrs	Labour Cost £	Sunds £	Nett Rate £	Unit	Gross rate (10%) £
BRICK/BLOCK WALLING (Cont'd)										
Extra over walls for opening perimeters; Slate and tile sills (Cont'd)										
Clay plain roofing tiles, red, BS EN 1304, machine made, 265 x 165 x 13mm; in cement-lime mortar (Cont'd)										
two courses 150mm wide; set weathering	3.92	5.00	4.12	0.75	0.50	23.44	0.71	28.26	m	31.09
Extra over walls for opening perimeters; Precast concrete sills; BS 5642 Part 1; bedding in cement lime mortar (1:1:6)										
Sills; figure 2 or figure 4										
50 x 150mm splayed and grooved										
300mm	73.33	2.50	75.17	0.15	0.15	5.47	0.18	80.81	nr	88.90
400mm	73.33	2.50	75.17	0.20	0.20	7.29	0.21	82.67	nr	90.94
700mm	73.33	2.50	75.17	0.30	0.30	10.93	0.31	86.41	nr	95.05
1300mm	102.67	2.50	105.23	0.50	0.50	18.22	0.46	123.92	nr	136.31
extra for stooled end	15.83	-	15.83	-	-	-	-	15.83	nr	17.42
100 x 150mm splayed and grooved										
300mm	66.00	2.50	67.65	0.20	0.20	7.29	0.18	75.12	nr	82.63
400mm	66.00	2.50	67.65	0.25	0.25	9.11	0.21	76.97	nr	84.67
700mm	66.00	2.50	67.65	0.40	0.40	14.58	0.31	82.54	nr	90.79
1300mm	115.50	2.50	118.39	0.60	0.60	21.86	0.46	140.71	nr	154.78
extra for stooled end	22.00	-	22.00	-	-	-	-	22.00	nr	24.20
Extra over walls for opening perimeters; Cavity Closers										
Fire rated cavity closers by Cavity Trays Ltd built into masonry										
Cavi Type V; Cavicloser vertical	6.94	5.00	7.29	0.33	0.16	9.38	-	16.67	m	18.34
Cavi Type V; Cavicloser horizontal	6.94	5.00	7.29	0.33	0.16	9.38	-	16.67	m	18.34
Fire rated Cavicheck fire integrity stop by Cavity Trays Ltd built into masonry										
Cavi 240 type CFIS; Cavicheck vertical	3.68	5.00	3.87	0.33	0.16	9.38	-	13.25	m	14.57
Cavi 240 type CFIS; Cavicheck horizontal	3.68	5.00	3.87	0.33	0.16	9.38	-	13.25	m	14.57
Fire rated party wall integrity barrier by Cavity Trays Ltd built into masonry										
Cavi 240 type PWIB; Party wall integrity barrier vertical	9.48	5.00	9.95	0.33	0.16	9.38	-	19.33	m	21.26
Cavi 240 type PWIB; Party wall integrity barrier horizontal	9.48	5.00	9.95	0.33	0.16	9.38	-	19.33	m	21.26
Thermabate insulated cavity closers; fixing to timber with nails										
Thermabate 50; vertical	5.19	5.00	5.45	0.33	0.16	9.38	-	14.83	m	16.32
Thermabate 75; vertical	5.67	5.00	5.95	0.33	0.16	9.38	-	15.33	m	16.86
Thermabate 100; vertical	5.95	5.00	6.25	0.33	0.16	9.38	-	15.63	m	17.19
Thermabate 125; vertical	8.22	5.00	8.63	0.33	0.16	9.38	-	18.01	m	19.81
Thermabate 150; vertical	9.02	5.00	9.47	0.33	0.16	9.38	-	18.85	m	20.74
Thermabate 50; horizontal	5.19	5.00	5.45	0.33	0.16	9.38	-	14.83	m	16.32
Thermabate 75; horizontal	5.67	5.00	5.95	0.33	0.16	9.38	-	15.33	m	16.86
Thermabate 100; horizontal	5.95	5.00	6.25	0.33	0.16	9.38	-	15.63	m	17.19
Thermabate 125; horizontal	8.22	5.00	8.63	0.33	0.16	9.38	-	18.01	m	19.81
Thermabate 150; horizontal	9.02	5.00	9.47	0.33	0.16	9.38	-	18.85	m	20.74
Thermabate insulated cavity closers; fixing to masonry with PVC-U ties at 225mm centres										
Thermabate 50; vertical	5.19	5.00	5.45	0.33	0.16	9.38	-	14.83	m	16.32
Thermabate 75; vertical	5.67	5.00	5.95	0.33	0.16	9.38	-	15.33	m	16.86
Thermabate 100; vertical	5.95	5.00	6.25	0.33	0.16	9.38	-	15.63	m	17.19
Thermabate 50; horizontal	5.19	5.00	5.45	0.33	0.16	9.38	-	14.83	m	16.32
Thermabate 75; horizontal	5.67	5.00	5.95	0.33	0.16	9.38	-	15.33	m	16.86
Thermabate 100; horizontal	5.95	5.00	6.25	0.33	0.16	9.38	-	15.63	m	17.19
Extra over walls for opening perimeters; Lintels; concrete										
Precast prestressed concrete lintels; roughcast; bedding in cement-lime mortar (1:1:6)										
100 x 65mm										
900mm long	5.23	2.50	5.36	0.24	0.12	6.88	0.40	12.63	nr	13.90
1050mm long	6.06	2.50	6.21	0.27	0.14	7.81	0.43	14.46	nr	15.90
1200mm long	6.96	2.50	7.13	0.31	0.16	8.96	0.51	16.61	nr	18.27
1500mm long	8.58	2.50	8.79	0.38	0.19	10.89	0.61	20.29	nr	22.32
1800mm long	10.29	2.50	10.55	0.44	0.22	12.61	0.68	23.83	nr	26.22
2100mm long	12.04	2.50	12.34	0.50	0.25	14.33	0.78	27.44	nr	30.19
2400mm long	13.76	2.50	14.10	0.55	0.28	15.84	0.89	30.83	nr	33.92
2700mm long	15.47	2.50	15.85	0.60	0.30	17.19	0.96	34.00	nr	37.40
3000mm long	17.21	2.50	17.64	0.66	0.33	18.91	1.07	37.63	nr	41.39
150 x 65mm										
900mm long	8.57	2.50	8.78	0.25	0.13	7.24	0.40	16.42	nr	18.06
1050mm long	9.95	2.50	10.20	0.28	0.14	8.02	0.46	18.68	nr	20.55
1200mm long	11.45	2.50	11.74	0.32	0.16	9.17	0.51	21.42	nr	23.56
1500mm long	13.63	2.50	13.97	0.39	0.20	11.25	0.63	25.85	nr	28.43
1800mm long	16.50	2.50	16.91	0.45	0.23	12.97	0.69	30.58	nr	33.64
2100mm long	18.86	2.50	19.33	0.51	0.26	14.69	0.82	34.85	nr	38.33
2400mm long	21.85	2.50	22.40	0.57	0.29	16.41	0.89	39.70	nr	43.67
2700mm long	24.32	2.50	24.93	0.62	0.31	17.77	0.94	43.64	nr	48.00
3000mm long	27.14	2.50	27.82	0.68	0.34	19.49	1.11	48.41	nr	53.25
215 x 65mm										
900mm long	14.51	2.50	14.87	0.26	0.13	7.45	0.40	22.72	nr	24.99
1050mm long	15.55	2.50	15.94	0.29	0.15	8.39	0.46	24.79	nr	27.27
1200mm long	17.20	2.50	17.63	0.33	0.17	9.53	0.51	27.68	nr	30.44
1500mm long	21.08	2.50	21.61	0.40	0.20	11.46	0.63	33.70	nr	37.07
1800mm long	25.28	2.50	25.91	0.46	0.23	13.18	0.69	39.79	nr	43.76
2100mm long	30.95	2.50	31.72	0.52	0.26	14.90	0.82	47.45	nr	52.19
2400mm long	32.93	2.50	33.75	0.58	0.29	16.62	0.94	51.31	nr	56.45
2700mm long	39.50	2.50	40.49	0.63	0.32	18.13	1.06	59.67	nr	65.64
3000mm long	43.90	2.50	45.00	0.69	0.35	19.85	1.11	65.95	nr	72.55

Labour hourly rates: (except Specialists) Craft Operatives 20.87 Labourer 15.57 Rates are national average prices. Refer to REGIONAL VARIATIONS for indicative levels of overall pricing in regions	MATERIALS			LABOUR				RATES		
	Del to Site £	Waste %	Material Cost £	Craft Optve Hrs	Lab Hrs	Labour Cost £	Sunds £	Nett Rate £	Unit	Gross rate (10%) £
BRICK/BLOCK WALLING (Cont'd)										
Extra over walls for opening perimeters; Lintels; concrete (Cont'd)										
Precast prestressed concrete lintels; roughcast; bedding in cement-lime mortar (1:1:6) (Cont'd)										
255 x 65mm										
900mm long	17.61	2.50	18.05	0.26	0.13	7.45	0.45	25.95	nr	28.54
1050mm long	21.48	2.50	22.01	0.30	0.15	8.60	0.48	31.09	nr	34.20
1200mm long	23.50	2.50	24.09	0.33	0.17	9.53	0.54	34.17	nr	37.58
1500mm long	29.36	2.50	30.09	0.40	0.20	11.46	0.63	42.18	nr	46.40
1800mm long	35.22	2.50	36.10	0.47	0.24	13.55	0.74	50.39	nr	55.43
2100mm long	41.11	2.50	42.14	0.53	0.27	15.27	0.86	58.26	nr	64.09
2400mm long	46.97	2.50	48.14	0.60	0.30	17.19	0.92	66.26	nr	72.89
2700mm long	52.85	2.50	54.17	0.64	0.32	18.34	1.06	73.57	nr	80.92
3000mm long	58.72	2.50	60.19	0.70	0.35	20.06	1.11	81.35	nr	89.49
215 x 100mm										
1500mm long	41.40	2.50	42.44	0.40	0.20	11.46	0.63	54.52	nr	59.98
1800mm long	49.46	2.50	50.70	0.47	0.24	13.55	0.74	64.98	nr	71.48
2100mm long	58.66	2.50	60.13	0.53	0.27	15.27	0.86	76.25	nr	83.87
2400mm long	66.73	2.50	68.40	0.60	0.30	17.19	0.92	86.52	nr	95.17
2700mm long	74.80	2.50	76.67	0.64	0.32	18.34	1.06	96.07	nr	105.67
3000mm long	84.02	2.50	86.12	0.70	0.35	20.06	1.11	107.28	nr	118.01
100 x 140mm										
900mm long	13.05	2.50	13.38	0.26	0.13	7.45	0.40	21.22	nr	23.35
1050mm long	15.87	2.50	16.27	0.29	0.15	8.39	0.46	25.12	nr	27.63
1200mm long	16.04	2.50	16.44	0.33	0.17	9.53	0.54	26.52	nr	29.17
1500mm long	20.66	2.50	21.18	0.40	0.20	11.46	0.63	33.27	nr	36.59
1800mm long	25.28	2.50	25.91	0.46	0.23	13.18	0.74	39.84	nr	43.82
2100mm long	26.20	2.50	26.85	0.52	0.26	14.90	0.82	42.58	nr	46.84
2400mm long	33.11	2.50	33.94	0.58	0.29	16.62	0.94	51.50	nr	56.65
2700mm long	37.67	2.50	38.61	0.63	0.32	18.13	1.06	57.80	nr	63.58
3000mm long	42.56	2.50	43.62	0.69	0.35	19.85	1.11	64.58	nr	71.04
215 x 140mm										
1200mm long	41.41	2.50	42.45	0.33	0.17	9.53	0.54	52.52	nr	57.78
1500mm long	51.78	2.50	53.07	0.40	0.20	11.46	0.63	65.16	nr	71.68
1800mm long	62.12	2.50	63.67	0.46	0.23	13.18	0.74	77.60	nr	85.36
2100mm long	72.49	2.50	74.30	0.52	0.26	14.90	0.82	90.03	nr	99.03
2400mm long	82.85	2.50	84.92	0.58	0.29	16.62	0.94	102.48	nr	112.73
2700mm long	94.38	2.50	96.74	0.63	0.32	18.13	1.06	115.93	nr	127.52
3000mm long	104.72	2.50	107.34	0.69	0.35	19.85	1.11	128.29	nr	141.12
Extra over walls for opening perimeters; Lintels; steel										
Galvanised steel lintels; SUPERGALV (BIRTLEY) lintels reference CB 50; bedding in cement-lime mortar (1:1:6)										
125mm deep x 750mm long	20.49	2.50	21.00	0.28	0.28	10.20	-	31.21	nr	34.33
125mm deep x 1200mm long	31.76	2.50	32.55	0.38	0.38	13.85	-	46.40	nr	51.04
125mm deep x 1350mm long	38.13	2.50	39.08	0.41	0.41	14.94	-	54.02	nr	59.43
125mm deep x 1500mm long	41.68	2.50	42.72	0.44	0.44	16.03	-	58.76	nr	64.63
125mm deep x 1650mm long	48.03	2.50	49.23	0.47	0.47	17.13	-	66.36	nr	72.99
165mm deep x 1800mm long	51.42	2.50	52.71	0.50	0.50	18.22	-	70.93	nr	78.02
165mm deep x 1950mm long	57.04	2.50	58.47	0.53	0.53	19.31	-	77.78	nr	85.56
165mm deep x 2100mm long	59.06	2.50	60.54	0.56	0.56	20.41	-	80.94	nr	89.04
165mm deep x 2250mm long	68.42	2.50	70.13	0.60	0.60	21.86	-	91.99	nr	101.19
165mm deep x 2400mm long	71.58	2.50	73.37	0.63	0.63	22.96	-	96.33	nr	105.96
215mm deep x 2550mm long	81.57	2.50	83.61	0.67	0.67	24.41	-	108.02	nr	118.83
215mm deep x 2850mm long	111.29	2.50	114.07	0.71	0.71	25.87	-	139.94	nr	153.94
215mm deep x 3000mm long	117.08	2.50	120.01	0.75	0.75	27.33	-	147.34	nr	162.07
215mm deep x 3300mm long	136.46	2.50	139.87	0.81	0.81	29.52	-	169.39	nr	186.33
215mm deep x 3600mm long	154.68	2.50	158.55	0.88	0.88	32.07	-	190.61	nr	209.68
215mm deep x 3900mm long	190.81	2.50	195.58	0.94	0.94	34.25	-	229.83	nr	252.82
Galvanised steel lintels; SUPERGALV (BIRTLEY) lintels reference AT 50.; bedding in cement-lime mortar (1:1:6)										
165mm deep x 750mm long	34.36	2.50	35.22	0.28	0.28	10.20	-	45.42	nr	49.96
165mm deep x 1050mm long	47.67	2.50	48.86	0.34	0.34	12.39	-	61.25	nr	67.38
165mm deep x 1200mm long	54.88	2.50	56.25	0.38	0.38	13.85	-	70.10	nr	77.11
165mm deep x 1350mm long	61.73	2.50	63.27	0.41	0.41	14.94	-	78.21	nr	86.04
165mm deep x 1500mm long	67.36	2.50	69.04	0.44	0.44	16.03	-	85.08	nr	93.59
215mm deep x 1650mm long	76.75	2.50	78.67	0.47	0.47	17.13	-	95.80	nr	105.38
215mm deep x 1800mm long	84.20	2.50	86.30	0.50	0.50	18.22	-	104.52	nr	114.98
215mm deep x 2100mm long	99.55	2.50	102.04	0.56	0.56	20.41	-	122.45	nr	134.69
215mm deep x 2250mm long	111.99	2.50	114.79	0.60	0.60	21.86	-	136.65	nr	150.32
215mm deep x 2400mm long	119.45	2.50	122.44	0.63	0.63	22.96	-	145.39	nr	159.93
215mm deep x 2550mm long	126.92	2.50	130.09	0.67	0.67	24.41	-	154.51	nr	169.96
215mm deep x 2700mm long	134.39	2.50	137.75	0.71	0.71	25.87	-	163.62	nr	179.98
215mm deep x 3000mm long	144.79	2.50	148.41	0.78	0.78	28.42	-	176.83	nr	194.52
Galvanised steel lintels; SUPERGALV (BIRTLEY) lintels reference CB 70; bedding in cement-lime mortar (1:1:6)										
120mm deep x 750mm long	19.85	2.50	20.35	0.29	0.29	10.57	-	30.91	nr	34.01
120mm deep x 1200mm long	31.54	2.50	32.33	0.40	0.40	14.58	-	46.90	nr	51.59
120mm deep x 1350mm long	37.05	2.50	37.98	0.43	0.43	15.67	-	53.65	nr	59.01
120mm deep x 1500mm long	41.15	2.50	42.18	0.46	0.46	16.76	-	58.94	nr	64.84
120mm deep x 1650mm long	46.62	2.50	47.79	0.49	0.49	17.86	-	65.64	nr	72.21
160mm deep x 1800mm long	50.61	2.50	51.88	0.53	0.53	19.31	-	71.19	nr	78.31
160mm deep x 1950mm long	56.52	2.50	57.93	0.56	0.56	20.41	-	78.34	nr	86.17
160mm deep x 2100mm long	59.05	2.50	60.53	0.59	0.59	21.50	-	82.03	nr	90.23
215mm deep x 2250mm long	67.85	2.50	69.55	0.63	0.63	22.96	-	92.50	nr	101.75
215mm deep x 2400mm long	72.36	2.50	74.17	0.66	0.66	24.05	-	98.22	nr	108.04
215mm deep x 2550mm long	83.17	2.50	85.25	0.70	0.70	25.51	-	110.76	nr	121.83
215mm deep x 2850mm long	109.87	2.50	112.62	0.75	0.75	27.33	-	139.95	nr	153.94
215mm deep x 3000mm long	118.02	2.50	120.97	0.79	0.79	28.79	-	149.76	nr	164.73

Labour hourly rates: (except Specialists) Craft Operatives 20.87 Labourer 15.57 Rates are national average prices. Refer to REGIONAL VARIATIONS for indicative levels of overall pricing in regions	MATERIALS			LABOUR				RATES		
	Del to Site £	Waste %	Material Cost £	Craft Optve Hrs	Lab Hrs	Labour Cost £	Sunds £	Nett Rate £	Unit	Gross rate (10%) £
BRICK/BLOCK WALLING (Cont'd)										
Extra over walls for opening perimeters; Lintels; steel (Cont'd)										
Galvanised steel lintels; SUPERGALV (BIRTLEY) lintels reference CB 70; bedding in cement-lime mortar (1:1:6) (Cont'd)										
215mm deep x 3300mm long	136.47	2.50	139.88	0.85	0.85	30.97	-	170.86	nr	187.94
215mm deep x 3600mm long	150.01	2.50	153.76	0.92	0.92	33.52	-	187.29	nr	206.01
215mm deep x 3900mm long	183.15	2.50	187.73	0.99	0.99	36.08	-	223.80	nr	246.18
Galvanised steel lintels; SUPERGALV (BIRTLEY) lintels reference AT 70.; bedding in cement-lime mortar (1:1:6)										
160mm deep x 750mm long	32.22	2.50	33.03	0.29	0.29	10.57	-	43.59	nr	47.95
160mm deep x 1050mm long	45.13	2.50	46.26	0.36	0.36	13.12	-	59.38	nr	65.31
160mm deep x 1200mm long	50.17	2.50	51.42	0.40	0.40	14.58	-	66.00	nr	72.60
160mm deep x 1350mm long	56.62	2.50	58.04	0.43	0.43	15.67	-	73.70	nr	81.08
160mm deep x 1500mm long	65.76	2.50	67.40	0.46	0.46	16.76	-	84.17	nr	92.58
215mm deep x 1650mm long	71.31	2.50	73.09	0.49	0.49	17.86	-	90.95	nr	100.04
215mm deep x 1800mm long	77.79	2.50	79.73	0.53	0.53	19.31	-	99.05	nr	108.95
215mm deep x 2100mm long	95.47	2.50	97.86	0.59	0.59	21.50	-	119.36	nr	131.29
215mm deep x 2250mm long	107.41	2.50	110.10	0.63	0.63	22.96	-	133.05	nr	146.36
215mm deep x 2400mm long	114.57	2.50	117.43	0.66	0.66	24.05	-	141.48	nr	155.63
215mm deep x 2550mm long	121.73	2.50	124.77	0.70	0.70	25.51	-	150.28	nr	165.31
215mm deep x 3300mm long	146.47	2.50	150.14	0.82	0.82	29.88	-	180.02	nr	198.02
Galvanised steel lintels; SUPERGALV (BIRTLEY) lintels reference CB 50/130; bedding in cement-lime mortar (1:1:6)										
120mm deep x 750mm long	20.58	2.50	21.09	0.31	0.31	11.30	-	32.39	nr	35.63
120mm deep x 1200mm long	32.71	2.50	33.53	0.42	0.42	15.30	-	48.83	nr	53.72
120mm deep x 1350mm long	37.47	2.50	38.41	0.45	0.45	16.40	-	54.80	nr	60.29
120mm deep x 1500mm long	41.45	2.50	42.49	0.48	0.48	17.49	-	59.98	nr	65.98
120mm deep x 1650mm long	48.22	2.50	49.43	0.52	0.52	18.95	-	68.37	nr	75.21
165mm deep x 1800mm long	51.94	2.50	53.24	0.55	0.55	20.04	-	73.28	nr	80.61
165mm deep x 1950mm long	57.31	2.50	58.74	0.58	0.58	21.14	-	79.88	nr	87.87
165mm deep x 2100mm long	61.91	2.50	63.46	0.62	0.62	22.59	-	86.05	nr	94.66
165mm deep x 2250mm long	70.95	2.50	72.72	0.66	0.66	24.05	-	96.77	nr	106.45
165mm deep x 2400mm long	75.70	2.50	77.59	0.69	0.69	25.14	-	102.74	nr	113.01
215mm deep x 2550mm long	85.78	2.50	87.92	0.74	0.74	26.97	-	114.89	nr	126.38
215mm deep x 2850mm long	120.88	2.50	123.90	0.78	0.78	28.42	-	152.33	nr	167.56
215mm deep x 3000mm long	124.96	2.50	128.08	0.83	0.83	30.25	-	158.33	nr	174.16
215mm deep x 3300mm long	139.56	2.50	143.05	0.89	0.89	32.43	-	175.48	nr	193.03
215mm deep x 3600mm long	153.68	2.50	157.52	0.97	0.97	35.35	-	192.87	nr	212.16
215mm deep x 3900mm long	225.21	2.50	230.84	1.03	1.03	37.53	-	268.37	nr	295.21
Galvanised steel lintels; SUPERGALV (BIRTLEY) lintels reference HS 50; bedding in cement-lime mortar (1:1:6)										
160mm deep x 750mm long	34.74	2.50	35.61	0.31	0.31	11.30	-	46.90	nr	51.60
160mm deep x 1200mm long	55.38	2.50	56.76	0.42	0.42	15.30	-	72.07	nr	79.28
160mm deep x 1350mm long	62.73	2.50	64.30	0.45	0.45	16.40	-	80.70	nr	88.77
160mm deep x 1500mm long	68.68	2.50	70.40	0.48	0.48	17.49	-	87.89	nr	96.68
215mm deep x 1650mm long	76.00	2.50	77.90	0.52	0.52	18.95	-	96.85	nr	106.53
215mm deep x 1800mm long	79.19	2.50	81.17	0.55	0.55	20.04	-	101.21	nr	111.33
215mm deep x 1950mm long	89.62	2.50	91.86	0.58	0.58	21.14	-	113.00	nr	124.30
215mm deep x 2250mm long	108.31	2.50	111.02	0.66	0.66	24.05	-	135.07	nr	148.57
215mm deep x 2400mm long	116.50	2.50	119.41	0.69	0.69	25.14	-	144.56	nr	159.01
215mm deep x 2550mm long	121.11	2.50	124.14	0.74	0.74	26.97	-	151.10	nr	166.21
215mm deep x 2700mm long	133.80	2.50	137.15	0.80	0.80	29.15	-	166.30	nr	182.93
215mm deep x 3000mm long	154.69	2.50	158.56	0.83	0.83	30.25	-	188.80	nr	207.68
215mm deep x 3300mm long	178.18	2.50	182.63	0.86	0.86	31.34	-	213.97	nr	235.37
215mm deep x 3600mm long	194.02	2.50	198.87	0.97	0.97	35.35	-	234.22	nr	257.64
225mm deep x 3900mm long	223.37	2.50	228.95	1.03	1.03	37.53	-	266.49	nr	293.14
225mm deep x 4200mm long	246.90	2.50	253.07	1.09	1.09	39.72	-	292.79	nr	322.07
Galvanised steel lintels; SUPERGALV (BIRTLEY) lintels reference CB 70/130; bedding in cement-lime mortar (1:1:6)										
115mm deep x 750mm long	24.91	2.50	25.53	0.31	0.31	11.30	-	36.83	nr	40.51
115mm deep x 1200mm long	41.04	2.50	42.07	0.42	0.42	15.30	-	57.37	nr	63.11
115mm deep x 1350mm long	47.23	2.50	48.41	0.45	0.45	16.40	-	64.81	nr	71.29
115mm deep x 1500mm long	51.82	2.50	53.12	0.48	0.48	17.49	-	70.61	nr	77.67
115mm deep x 1650mm long	63.91	2.50	65.51	0.52	0.52	18.95	-	84.46	nr	92.90
155mm deep x 1800mm long	71.29	2.50	73.07	0.55	0.55	20.04	-	93.11	nr	102.43
155mm deep x 1950mm long	77.24	2.50	79.17	0.58	0.58	21.14	-	100.31	nr	110.34
155mm deep x 2100mm long	82.10	2.50	84.15	0.62	0.62	22.59	-	106.75	nr	117.42
155mm deep x 2250mm long	111.06	2.50	113.84	0.66	0.66	24.05	-	137.89	nr	151.68
155mm deep x 2400mm long	118.46	2.50	121.42	0.69	0.69	25.14	-	146.57	nr	161.22
210mm deep x 2550mm long	131.30	2.50	134.58	0.74	0.74	26.97	-	161.55	nr	177.70
210mm deep x 2850mm long	175.09	2.50	179.47	0.78	0.78	28.42	-	207.89	nr	228.68
210mm deep x 3000mm long	195.52	2.50	200.41	0.83	0.83	30.25	-	230.65	nr	253.72
210mm deep x 3300mm long	215.06	2.50	220.44	0.89	0.89	32.43	-	252.87	nr	278.15
210mm deep x 3600mm long	234.59	2.50	240.45	0.95	0.95	34.62	-	275.07	nr	302.58
210mm deep x 3900mm long	270.21	2.50	276.97	1.03	1.03	37.53	-	314.50	nr	345.95
Galvanised steel lintels; SUPERGALV (BIRTLEY) lintels reference CB 90; bedding in cement-lime mortar (1:1:6)										
750mm long	21.15	2.50	21.68	0.33	0.33	12.03	-	33.70	nr	37.07
1200mm long	32.78	2.50	33.60	0.44	0.44	16.03	-	49.63	nr	54.60
1350mm long	38.37	2.50	39.33	0.47	0.47	17.13	-	56.46	nr	62.10
1500mm long	40.87	2.50	41.89	0.50	0.50	18.22	-	60.11	nr	66.12
1650mm long	47.52	2.50	48.71	0.55	0.55	20.04	-	68.75	nr	75.62
1800mm long	50.36	2.50	51.62	0.57	0.57	20.77	-	72.39	nr	79.63
1950mm long	60.82	2.50	62.34	0.60	0.60	21.86	-	84.20	nr	92.62
2100mm long	60.83	2.50	62.35	0.65	0.65	23.69	-	86.04	nr	94.64
2250mm long	74.15	2.50	76.00	0.69	0.69	25.14	-	101.15	nr	111.26
2400mm long	78.40	2.50	80.36	0.72	0.72	26.24	-	106.60	nr	117.26
2550mm long	87.19	2.50	89.37	0.78	0.78	28.42	-	117.79	nr	129.57
2850mm long	112.97	2.50	115.79	0.81	0.81	29.52	-	145.31	nr	159.84

Labour hourly rates: (except Specialists) Craft Operatives 20.87 Labourer 15.57 Rates are national average prices. Refer to REGIONAL VARIATIONS for indicative levels of overall pricing in regions	MATERIALS			LABOUR				RATES		
	Del to Site £	Waste %	Material Cost £	Craft Optve Hrs	Lab Hrs	Labour Cost £	Sunds £	Nett Rate £	Unit	Gross rate (10%) £
BRICK/BLOCK WALLING (Cont'd)										
Extra over walls for opening perimeters; Lintels; steel (Cont'd)										
Galvanised steel lintels; SUPERGALV (BIRTLEY) lintels reference CB 90; bedding in cement-lime mortar (1:1:6) (Cont'd)										
3000mm long	117.36	2.50	120.29	0.87	0.87	31.70	-	152.00	nr	167.20
3300mm long	133.72	2.50	137.06	0.93	0.93	33.89	-	170.95	nr	188.05
3600mm long	152.81	2.50	156.63	0.98	0.98	35.71	-	192.34	nr	211.58
3900mm long	190.43	2.50	195.19	1.07	1.07	38.99	-	234.18	nr	257.60
Galvanised steel lintels; SUPERGALV (BIRTLEY) lintels reference CB 90/130; bedding in cement-lime mortar (1:1:6)										
750mm long	29.50	2.50	30.24	0.35	0.35	12.75	-	42.99	nr	47.29
1200mm long	47.14	2.50	48.32	0.46	0.46	16.76	-	65.08	nr	71.59
1350mm long	53.03	2.50	54.36	0.49	0.49	17.86	-	72.21	nr	79.43
1500mm long	56.88	2.50	58.30	0.52	0.52	18.95	-	77.25	nr	84.98
1650mm long	65.89	2.50	67.54	0.57	0.57	20.77	-	88.31	nr	97.14
1800mm long	71.87	2.50	73.67	0.59	0.59	21.50	-	95.17	nr	104.68
1950mm long	84.83	2.50	86.95	0.62	0.62	22.59	-	109.54	nr	120.50
2100mm long	86.47	2.50	88.63	0.68	0.68	24.78	-	113.41	nr	124.75
2250mm long	112.69	2.50	115.51	0.72	0.72	26.24	-	141.74	nr	155.92
2400mm long	120.57	2.50	123.58	0.75	0.75	27.33	-	150.91	nr	166.01
2550mm long	123.49	2.50	126.58	0.82	0.82	29.88	-	156.46	nr	172.10
2850mm long	197.33	2.50	202.26	0.86	0.86	31.34	-	233.60	nr	256.96
3000mm long	198.51	2.50	203.47	0.90	0.90	32.80	-	236.27	nr	259.90
3300mm long	223.11	2.50	228.69	0.96	0.96	34.98	-	263.67	nr	290.04
3600mm long	234.84	2.50	240.71	1.01	1.01	36.80	-	277.52	nr	305.27
3900mm long	273.54	2.50	280.38	1.10	1.10	40.08	-	320.46	nr	352.51
Galvanised steel lintels; SUPERGALV (BIRTLEY) lintels reference HS 90; bedding in cement-lime mortar (1:1:6)										
750mm long	38.22	2.50	39.18	0.33	0.33	12.03	-	51.20	nr	56.32
1200mm long	61.12	2.50	62.65	0.44	0.44	16.03	-	78.68	nr	86.55
1350mm long	67.38	2.50	69.06	0.47	0.47	17.13	-	86.19	nr	94.81
1500mm long	75.67	2.50	77.56	0.50	0.50	18.22	-	95.78	nr	105.36
1650mm long	80.67	2.50	82.69	0.55	0.55	20.04	-	102.73	nr	113.00
1800mm long	90.03	2.50	92.28	0.57	0.57	20.77	-	113.05	nr	124.36
1950mm long	99.88	2.50	102.38	0.60	0.60	21.86	-	124.24	nr	136.67
2100mm long	108.63	2.50	111.35	0.68	0.68	24.78	-	136.12	nr	149.74
2250mm long	115.05	2.50	117.93	0.72	0.72	26.24	-	144.16	nr	158.58
2400mm long	128.58	2.50	131.79	0.77	0.77	28.06	-	159.85	nr	175.84
2550mm long	149.09	2.50	152.82	0.82	0.82	29.88	-	182.70	nr	200.97
2700mm long	160.37	2.50	164.38	0.84	0.84	30.61	-	194.99	nr	214.49
2850mm long	168.98	2.50	173.20	0.86	0.86	31.34	-	204.54	nr	225.00
3000mm long	181.09	2.50	185.62	0.90	0.90	32.80	-	218.41	nr	240.25
3300mm long	207.54	2.50	212.73	0.93	0.93	33.89	-	246.62	nr	271.28
3600mm long	226.43	2.50	232.09	0.99	0.99	36.08	-	268.17	nr	294.98
3900mm long	252.53	2.50	258.84	1.07	1.07	38.99	-	297.83	nr	327.62
4200mm long	289.55	2.50	296.79	1.12	1.12	40.81	-	337.60	nr	371.36
4500mm long	324.87	2.50	332.99	1.18	1.18	43.00	-	375.99	nr	413.59
4800mm long	346.95	2.50	355.62	1.24	1.24	45.19	-	400.81	nr	440.89
Galvanised steel lintels; SUPERGALV (BIRTLEY) lintels reference HS 90/130; bedding in cement-lime mortar (1:1:6)										
750mm long	42.38	2.50	43.44	0.35	0.35	12.75	-	56.19	nr	61.81
1200mm long	70.16	2.50	71.91	0.46	0.46	16.76	-	88.68	nr	97.54
1350mm long	79.90	2.50	81.90	0.49	0.49	17.86	-	99.75	nr	109.73
1500mm long	97.39	2.50	99.82	0.52	0.52	18.95	-	118.77	nr	130.65
1650mm long	112.30	2.50	115.11	0.57	0.57	20.77	-	135.88	nr	149.47
1800mm long	122.49	2.50	125.55	0.59	0.59	21.50	-	147.05	nr	161.76
1950mm long	135.32	2.50	138.70	0.62	0.62	22.59	-	161.30	nr	177.43
2100mm long	145.74	2.50	149.38	0.68	0.68	24.78	-	174.16	nr	191.58
2250mm long	159.60	2.50	163.59	0.75	0.75	27.33	-	190.92	nr	210.01
2400mm long	170.24	2.50	174.50	0.82	0.82	29.88	-	204.38	nr	224.81
2550mm long	180.88	2.50	185.40	0.84	0.84	30.61	-	216.01	nr	237.61
2700mm long	194.08	2.50	198.93	0.86	0.86	31.34	-	230.27	nr	253.30
2850mm long	202.77	2.50	207.84	0.90	0.90	32.80	-	240.64	nr	264.70
3000mm long	220.62	2.50	226.14	0.92	0.92	33.52	-	259.66	nr	285.63
3300mm long	245.91	2.50	252.06	0.96	0.96	34.98	-	287.04	nr	315.74
3600mm long	280.86	2.50	287.88	1.01	1.01	36.80	-	324.69	nr	357.15
Galvanised steel lintels; SUPERGALV (BIRTLEY) lintels reference CB 110; bedding in cement-lime mortar (1:1:6)										
750mm long	25.31	2.50	25.94	0.37	0.37	13.48	-	39.43	nr	43.37
1200mm long	40.50	2.50	41.51	0.48	0.48	17.49	-	59.00	nr	64.90
1350mm long	45.59	2.50	46.73	0.51	0.51	18.58	-	65.31	nr	71.85
1500mm long	50.65	2.50	51.92	0.54	0.54	19.68	-	71.59	nr	78.75
1650mm long	65.26	2.50	66.89	0.59	0.59	21.50	-	88.39	nr	97.23
1800mm long	71.20	2.50	72.98	0.61	0.61	22.23	-	95.21	nr	104.73
1950mm long	91.04	2.50	93.32	0.64	0.64	23.32	-	116.64	nr	128.30
2100mm long	98.05	2.50	100.50	0.70	0.70	25.51	-	126.01	nr	138.61
2250mm long	142.95	2.50	146.52	0.75	0.75	27.33	-	173.85	nr	191.24
2400mm long	152.48	2.50	156.29	0.82	0.82	29.88	-	186.17	nr	204.79
2550mm long	162.02	2.50	166.07	0.84	0.84	30.61	-	196.68	nr	216.35
2700mm long	171.55	2.50	175.84	0.86	0.86	31.34	-	207.18	nr	227.89
2850mm long	181.08	2.50	185.61	0.89	0.89	32.43	-	218.04	nr	239.84
3000mm long	190.60	2.50	195.37	0.93	0.93	33.89	-	229.25	nr	252.18
3300mm long	223.44	2.50	229.03	0.99	0.99	36.08	-	265.10	nr	291.61
Galvanised steel lintels; SUPERGALV (BIRTLEY) lintels reference HS 110; bedding in cement-lime mortar (1:1:6)										
750mm long	38.51	2.50	39.47	0.37	0.37	13.48	-	52.96	nr	58.25
1200mm long	66.28	2.50	67.94	0.48	0.48	17.49	-	85.43	nr	93.97
1350mm long	74.57	2.50	76.43	0.51	0.51	18.58	-	95.02	nr	104.52
1500mm long	82.86	2.50	84.93	0.54	0.54	19.68	-	104.61	nr	115.07

Labour hourly rates: (except Specialists) Craft Operatives 20.87 Labourer 15.57 Rates are national average prices. Refer to REGIONAL VARIATIONS for indicative levels of overall pricing in regions	MATERIALS			LABOUR				RATES		
	Del to Site £	Waste %	Material Cost £	Craft Optve Hrs	Lab Hrs	Labour Cost £	Sunds £	Nett Rate £	Unit	Gross rate (10%) £
BRICK/BLOCK WALLING (Cont'd)										
Extra over walls for opening perimeters; Lintels; steel (Cont'd)										
Galvanised steel lintels; SUPERGALV (BIRTLEY) lintels reference HS 110; bedding in cement-lime mortar (1:1:6) (Cont'd)										
1650mm long	91.14	2.50	93.42	0.59	0.59	21.50	-	114.92	nr	126.41
1800mm long	99.42	2.50	101.91	0.61	0.61	22.23	-	124.13	nr	136.55
1950mm long	119.71	2.50	122.70	0.64	0.64	23.32	-	146.02	nr	160.63
2100mm long	128.92	2.50	132.14	0.70	0.70	25.51	-	157.65	nr	173.42
2250mm long	128.92	2.50	132.14	0.75	0.75	27.33	-	159.47	nr	175.42
2400mm long	147.34	2.50	151.02	0.82	0.82	29.88	-	180.90	nr	198.99
2550mm long	174.54	2.50	178.90	0.84	0.84	30.61	-	209.51	nr	230.46
2700mm long	184.81	2.50	189.43	0.86	0.86	31.34	-	220.77	nr	242.85
2850mm long	195.09	2.50	199.97	0.89	0.89	32.43	-	232.40	nr	255.64
3000mm long	205.34	2.50	210.47	0.93	0.93	33.89	-	244.36	nr	268.80
3300mm long	244.63	2.50	250.75	0.99	0.99	36.08	-	286.82	nr	315.50
3600mm long	274.37	2.50	281.23	1.07	1.07	38.99	-	320.22	nr	352.24
3900mm long	306.20	2.50	313.86	1.12	1.12	40.81	-	354.67	nr	390.13
4200mm long	341.32	2.50	349.85	1.18	1.18	43.00	-	392.85	nr	432.14
4500mm long	372.30	2.50	381.61	1.24	1.24	45.19	-	426.79	nr	469.47
4800mm long	389.80	2.50	399.54	1.28	1.28	46.64	-	446.19	nr	490.81
Galvanised steel lintels; SUPERGALV (BIRTLEY) lintels reference CB 125; bedding in cement-lime mortar (1:1:6)										
750mm long	36.73	2.50	37.65	0.39	0.39	14.21	-	51.86	nr	57.05
1200mm long	58.31	2.50	59.77	0.50	0.50	18.22	-	77.99	nr	85.79
1350mm long	65.50	2.50	67.14	0.53	0.53	19.31	-	86.45	nr	95.10
1500mm long	72.73	2.50	74.55	0.56	0.56	20.41	-	94.95	nr	104.45
1650mm long	79.91	2.50	81.91	0.61	0.61	22.23	-	104.14	nr	114.55
1800mm long	87.10	2.50	89.28	0.64	0.64	23.32	-	112.60	nr	123.86
1950mm long	97.45	2.50	99.89	0.70	0.70	25.51	-	125.39	nr	137.93
2100mm long	104.88	2.50	107.50	0.73	0.73	26.60	-	134.10	nr	147.51
2250mm long	130.08	2.50	133.33	0.82	0.82	29.88	-	163.21	nr	179.53
2400mm long	138.69	2.50	142.16	0.84	0.84	30.61	-	172.77	nr	190.04
2550mm long	147.28	2.50	150.96	0.86	0.86	31.34	-	182.30	nr	200.53
2700mm long	155.93	2.50	159.83	0.89	0.89	32.43	-	192.26	nr	211.49
2850mm long	179.03	2.50	183.51	0.93	0.93	33.89	-	217.39	nr	239.13
3000mm long	188.77	2.50	193.49	0.96	0.96	34.98	-	228.47	nr	251.32
3300mm long	207.17	2.50	212.35	1.02	1.02	37.17	-	249.52	nr	274.47
Galvanised steel lintels; SUPERGALV (BIRTLEY) lintels reference HS 125; bedding in cement-lime mortar (1:1:6)										
750mm long	46.95	2.50	48.12	0.39	0.39	14.21	-	62.34	nr	68.57
1200mm long	75.12	2.50	77.00	0.50	0.50	18.22	-	95.22	nr	104.74
1350mm long	84.51	2.50	86.62	0.53	0.53	19.31	-	105.94	nr	116.53
1500mm long	93.90	2.50	96.25	0.56	0.56	20.41	-	116.65	nr	128.32
1650mm long	103.29	2.50	105.87	0.61	0.61	22.23	-	128.10	nr	140.91
1800mm long	112.68	2.50	115.50	0.64	0.64	23.32	-	138.82	nr	152.70
1950mm long	122.07	2.50	125.12	0.70	0.70	25.51	-	150.63	nr	165.69
2100mm long	131.46	2.50	134.75	0.73	0.73	26.60	-	161.35	nr	177.48
2250mm long	158.46	2.50	162.42	0.82	0.82	29.88	-	192.30	nr	211.53
2400mm long	169.02	2.50	173.25	0.84	0.84	30.61	-	203.86	nr	224.24
2550mm long	179.59	2.50	184.08	0.86	0.86	31.34	-	215.42	nr	236.96
2700mm long	190.16	2.50	194.91	0.89	0.89	32.43	-	227.35	nr	250.08
2850mm long	200.71	2.50	205.73	0.93	0.93	33.89	-	239.62	nr	263.58
3000mm long	211.28	2.50	216.56	0.96	0.96	34.98	-	251.54	nr	276.70
3300mm long	279.41	2.50	286.40	1.02	1.02	37.17	-	323.56	nr	355.92
3600mm long	304.81	2.50	312.43	1.12	1.12	40.81	-	353.24	nr	388.57
3900mm long	330.21	2.50	338.47	1.18	1.18	43.00	-	381.46	nr	419.61
4200mm long	355.61	2.50	364.50	1.24	1.24	45.19	-	409.69	nr	450.65
4500mm long	387.36	2.50	397.04	1.28	1.28	46.64	-	443.69	nr	488.06
4800mm long	406.41	2.50	416.57	1.32	1.32	48.10	-	464.67	nr	511.14
Galvanised steel lintels; SUPERGALV (BIRTLEY) lintels reference TF 50; bedding in cement-lime mortar (1:1:6)										
750mm long	9.01	2.50	9.24	0.29	0.29	10.57	-	19.80	nr	21.78
900mm long	10.69	2.50	10.96	0.33	0.33	12.03	-	22.98	nr	25.28
1050mm long	12.55	2.50	12.86	0.37	0.37	13.48	-	26.35	nr	28.98
1200mm long	14.36	2.50	14.72	0.40	0.40	14.58	-	29.29	nr	32.22
1350mm long	17.12	2.50	17.55	0.43	0.43	15.67	-	33.22	nr	36.54
1500mm long	18.71	2.50	19.18	0.46	0.46	16.76	-	35.94	nr	39.53
1650mm long	22.82	2.50	23.39	0.49	0.49	17.86	-	41.25	nr	45.37
1800mm long	24.84	2.50	25.46	0.53	0.53	19.31	-	44.77	nr	49.25
1950mm long	28.21	2.50	28.92	0.56	0.56	20.41	-	49.32	nr	54.25
2100mm long	30.91	2.50	31.68	0.59	0.59	21.50	-	53.18	nr	58.50
2250mm long	37.81	2.50	38.76	0.63	0.63	22.96	-	61.71	nr	67.88
2400mm long	41.34	2.50	42.37	0.66	0.66	24.05	-	66.42	nr	73.07
2550mm long	47.48	2.50	48.67	0.70	0.70	25.51	-	74.17	nr	81.59
2700mm long	50.25	2.50	51.51	0.73	0.73	26.60	-	78.11	nr	85.92
2850mm long	63.67	2.50	65.26	0.75	0.75	27.33	-	92.59	nr	101.85
3000mm long	68.04	2.50	69.74	0.79	0.79	28.79	-	98.53	nr	108.38
3300mm long	76.07	2.50	77.97	0.85	0.85	30.97	-	108.95	nr	119.84
3600mm long	105.82	2.50	108.47	0.92	0.92	33.52	-	141.99	nr	156.19
3900mm long	118.59	2.50	121.55	0.99	0.99	36.08	-	157.63	nr	173.39
Galvanised steel lintels; SUPERGALV (BIRTLEY) lintels reference TF 50HD; bedding in cement-lime mortar (1:1:6)										
750mm long	23.71	2.50	24.30	0.31	0.31	11.30	-	35.60	nr	39.16
900mm long	28.45	2.50	29.16	0.36	0.36	13.12	-	42.28	nr	46.51
1050mm long	34.06	2.50	34.91	0.40	0.40	14.58	-	49.49	nr	54.44
1200mm long	38.94	2.50	39.91	0.42	0.42	15.30	-	55.22	nr	60.74
1350mm long	43.80	2.50	44.89	0.45	0.45	16.40	-	61.29	nr	67.42
1500mm long	42.03	2.50	43.08	0.48	0.48	17.49	-	60.57	nr	66.63
1650mm long	53.54	2.50	54.88	0.52	0.52	18.95	-	73.83	nr	81.21

Labour hourly rates: (except Specialists) Craft Operatives 20.87 Labourer 15.57 Rates are national average prices. Refer to REGIONAL VARIATIONS for indicative levels of overall pricing in regions	MATERIALS			LABOUR				RATES		
	Del to Site £	Waste %	Material Cost £	Craft Optve Hrs	Lab Hrs	Labour Cost £	Sunds £	Nett Rate £	Unit	Gross rate (10%) £
BRICK/BLOCK WALLING (Cont'd)										
Extra over walls for opening perimeters; Lintels; steel (Cont'd)										
Galvanised steel lintels; SUPERGALV (BIRTLEY) lintels reference TF 50HD; bedding in cement-lime mortar (1:1:6) (Cont'd)										
1800mm long	58.39	2.50	59.85	0.55	0.55	20.04	-	79.89	nr	87.88
1950mm long	63.25	2.50	64.83	0.58	0.58	21.14	-	85.97	nr	94.56
2100mm long	68.11	2.50	69.81	0.62	0.62	22.59	-	92.41	nr	101.65
2250mm long	73.00	2.50	74.82	0.66	0.66	24.05	-	98.88	nr	108.76
2400mm long	77.86	2.50	79.81	0.69	0.69	25.14	-	104.95	nr	115.45
2550mm long	82.73	2.50	84.80	0.74	0.74	26.97	-	111.76	nr	122.94
2700mm long	87.59	2.50	89.78	0.76	0.76	27.69	-	117.47	nr	129.22
2850mm long	92.46	2.50	94.77	0.78	0.78	28.42	-	123.19	nr	135.51
3000mm long	97.33	2.50	99.76	0.83	0.83	30.25	-	130.01	nr	143.01
3300mm long	107.05	2.50	109.73	0.89	0.89	32.43	-	142.16	nr	156.37
3600mm long	129.50	2.50	132.74	0.95	0.95	34.62	-	167.36	nr	184.09
3900mm long	139.64	2.50	143.13	1.03	1.03	37.53	-	180.66	nr	198.73
4200mm long	146.64	2.50	150.31	1.07	1.07	38.99	-	189.30	nr	208.23
4500mm long	157.39	2.50	161.32	1.12	1.12	40.81	-	202.14	nr	222.35
4800mm long	167.99	2.50	172.19	1.18	1.18	43.00	-	215.19	nr	236.71
Galvanised steel lintels; SUPERGALV (BIRTLEY) lintels reference SB 100; bedding in cement-lime mortar (1:1:6)										
75mm deep x 750mm long	13.64	2.50	13.98	0.45	0.45	16.40	-	30.38	nr	33.42
75mm deep x 900mm long	15.93	2.50	16.33	0.48	0.48	17.49	-	33.82	nr	37.20
75mm deep x 1050mm long	18.87	2.50	19.34	0.51	0.51	18.58	-	37.93	nr	41.72
75mm deep x 1200mm long	20.97	2.50	21.49	0.54	0.54	19.68	-	41.17	nr	45.29
75mm deep x 1500mm long	26.26	2.50	26.92	0.60	0.60	21.86	-	48.78	nr	53.66
140mm deep x 1800mm long	40.18	2.50	41.18	0.65	0.65	23.69	-	64.87	nr	71.36
140mm deep x 1950mm long	45.72	2.50	46.86	0.69	0.69	25.14	-	72.01	nr	79.21
140mm deep x 2100mm long	48.55	2.50	49.76	0.73	0.73	26.60	-	76.36	nr	84.00
140mm deep x 2250mm long	52.23	2.50	53.54	0.77	0.77	28.06	-	81.59	nr	89.75
140mm deep x 2400mm long	56.29	2.50	57.70	0.82	0.82	29.88	-	87.58	nr	96.34
140mm deep x 2550mm long	60.73	2.50	62.25	0.87	0.87	31.70	-	93.95	nr	103.35
140mm deep x 2700mm long	64.54	2.50	66.15	0.92	0.92	33.52	-	99.68	nr	109.65
215mm deep x 2850mm long	97.64	2.50	100.08	0.93	0.93	33.89	-	133.97	nr	147.37
215mm deep x 3000mm long	103.49	2.50	106.08	0.95	0.95	34.62	-	140.70	nr	154.76
215mm deep x 3300mm long	114.35	2.50	117.21	0.97	0.97	35.35	-	152.56	nr	167.81
215mm deep x 3600mm long	125.14	2.50	128.27	0.99	0.99	36.08	-	164.34	nr	180.78
215mm deep x 3900mm long	162.03	2.50	166.08	1.03	1.03	37.53	-	203.61	nr	223.98
215mm deep x 4200mm long	178.48	2.50	182.94	1.09	1.09	39.72	-	222.66	nr	244.93
215mm deep x 4500mm long	199.69	2.50	204.68	1.16	1.16	42.27	-	246.95	nr	271.65
215mm deep x 4800mm long	218.97	2.50	224.44	1.24	1.24	45.19	-	269.63	nr	296.59
Galvanised steel lintels; SUPERGALV (BIRTLEY) lintels reference SB 140; bedding in cement-lime mortar (1:1:6)										
140mm deep x 750mm long	17.24	2.50	17.67	0.45	0.45	16.40	-	34.07	nr	37.48
140mm deep x 900mm long	20.80	2.50	21.32	0.48	0.48	17.49	-	38.81	nr	42.69
140mm deep x 1050mm long	24.52	2.50	25.13	0.51	0.51	18.58	-	43.72	nr	48.09
140mm deep x 1200mm long	28.05	2.50	28.75	0.54	0.54	19.68	-	48.43	nr	53.27
140mm deep x 1350mm long	31.82	2.50	32.62	0.57	0.57	20.77	-	53.39	nr	58.72
140mm deep x 1500mm long	36.14	2.50	37.04	0.60	0.60	21.86	-	58.91	nr	64.80
140mm deep x 1650mm long	43.40	2.50	44.49	0.62	0.62	22.59	-	67.08	nr	73.79
140mm deep x 1800mm long	47.18	2.50	48.36	0.65	0.65	23.69	-	72.05	nr	79.25
140mm deep x 1950mm long	45.99	2.50	47.14	0.69	0.69	25.14	-	72.28	nr	79.51
140mm deep x 2100mm long	58.13	2.50	59.58	0.73	0.73	26.60	-	86.18	nr	94.80
140mm deep x 2250mm long	64.10	2.50	65.70	0.77	0.77	28.06	-	93.76	nr	103.14
140mm deep x 2400mm long	67.31	2.50	68.99	0.82	0.82	29.88	-	98.87	nr	108.76
140mm deep x 2550mm long	71.33	2.50	73.11	0.87	0.87	31.70	-	104.82	nr	115.30
140mm deep x 2700mm long	75.51	2.50	77.40	0.92	0.92	33.52	-	110.92	nr	122.01
215mm deep x 2850mm long	109.47	2.50	112.21	0.95	0.95	34.62	-	146.82	nr	161.51
215mm deep x 3000mm long	113.96	2.50	116.81	0.97	0.97	35.35	-	152.16	nr	167.37
215mm deep x 3300mm long	128.50	2.50	131.71	0.99	0.99	36.08	-	167.79	nr	184.57
215mm deep x 3600mm long	138.07	2.50	141.52	1.03	1.03	37.53	-	179.05	nr	196.96
215mm deep x 3900mm long	177.89	2.50	182.34	1.09	1.09	39.72	-	222.06	nr	244.26
215mm deep x 4200mm long	193.29	2.50	198.12	1.16	1.16	42.27	-	240.39	nr	264.43
215mm deep x 4500mm long	222.87	2.50	228.44	1.24	1.24	45.19	-	273.63	nr	300.99
215mm deep x 4800mm long	238.88	2.50	244.85	1.32	1.32	48.10	-	292.95	nr	322.25
Galvanised steel lintels; SUPERGALV (BIRTLEY) lintels reference SBL 200; bedding in cement-lime mortar (1:1:6)										
142mm deep x 750mm long	23.84	2.50	24.44	0.45	0.45	16.40	-	40.83	nr	44.92
142mm deep x 900mm long	29.49	2.50	30.23	0.48	0.48	17.49	-	47.72	nr	52.49
142mm deep x 1050mm long	33.20	2.50	34.03	0.51	0.51	18.58	-	52.61	nr	57.88
142mm deep x 1200mm long	40.30	2.50	41.31	0.54	0.54	19.68	-	60.99	nr	67.08
142mm deep x 1350mm long	42.42	2.50	43.48	0.60	0.60	21.86	-	65.34	nr	71.88
142mm deep x 1500mm long	49.39	2.50	50.62	0.65	0.65	23.69	-	74.31	nr	81.74
142mm deep x 1650mm long	54.26	2.50	55.62	0.67	0.67	24.41	-	80.03	nr	88.03
142mm deep x 1800mm long	61.13	2.50	62.66	0.72	0.72	26.24	-	88.90	nr	97.78
142mm deep x 1950mm long	64.75	2.50	66.37	0.76	0.76	27.69	-	94.06	nr	103.47
142mm deep x 2100mm long	71.55	2.50	73.34	0.80	0.77	28.68	-	102.02	nr	112.23
142mm deep x 2250mm long	79.47	2.50	81.46	0.77	0.80	28.53	-	109.98	nr	120.98
142mm deep x 2400mm long	86.19	2.50	88.34	0.82	0.82	29.88	-	118.23	nr	130.05
142mm deep x 2550mm long	93.30	2.50	95.63	0.87	0.87	31.70	-	127.34	nr	140.07
142mm deep x 2700mm long	100.66	2.50	103.18	0.92	0.92	33.52	-	136.70	nr	150.37
218mm deep x 2850mm long	132.77	2.50	136.09	0.93	0.93	33.89	-	169.98	nr	186.98
218mm deep x 3000mm long	140.82	2.50	144.34	0.95	0.95	34.62	-	178.96	nr	196.85
Galvanised steel lintels; SUPERGALV (BIRTLEY) internal door lintels reference INT 100; bedding in cement-lime mortar (1:1:6)										
100mm wide, 900mm long	5.05	2.50	5.18	0.33	0.33	12.03	-	17.20	nr	18.92
100mm wide, 1050mm long	5.79	2.50	5.93	0.36	0.36	13.12	-	19.05	nr	20.96
100mm wide, 1200mm long	6.52	2.50	6.68	0.38	0.38	13.85	-	20.53	nr	22.58

Labour hourly rates: (except Specialists) Craft Operatives 20.87 Labourer 15.57 Rates are national average prices. Refer to REGIONAL VARIATIONS for indicative levels of overall pricing in regions	MATERIALS			LABOUR				RATES		
	Del to Site £	Waste %	Material Cost £	Craft Optve Hrs	Lab Hrs	Labour Cost £	Sunds £	Nett Rate £	Unit	Gross rate (10%) £
BRICK/BLOCK WALLING (Cont'd)										
Special purpose blocks or stones; Precast concrete padstones; BS 8500, designed mix C25, 20mm aggregate, minimum cement content 360 kg/m³; vibrated; reinforced at contractor's discretion; bedding in cement-lime mortar (1:1:6)										
Padstones										
215 x 140 x 102mm	9.16	2.50	9.39	0.06	0.03	1.72	0.18	11.29	nr	12.42
215 x 215 x 102mm	15.26	2.50	15.64	0.06	0.03	1.72	0.18	17.54	nr	19.30
215 x 215 x 140mm	17.81	2.50	18.26	0.08	0.04	2.29	0.18	20.73	nr	22.80
330 x 215 x 102mm	27.74	2.50	28.43	0.11	0.05	3.07	0.20	31.70	nr	34.87
440 x 215 x 102mm	19.42	2.50	19.91	0.17	0.08	4.79	0.23	24.93	nr	27.42
440 x 215 x 140mm	23.73	2.50	24.32	0.17	0.08	4.79	0.23	29.35	nr	32.28
440 x 440 x 140mm	47.46	2.50	48.65	0.20	0.10	5.73	0.26	54.64	nr	60.11
600 x 140 x 102mm	21.45	2.50	21.99	0.20	0.10	5.73	0.26	27.98	nr	30.78
Forming cavity										
Cavity with 200mm stainless steel housing type 4 wall ties, -4/m² built in width of cavity 50mm	1.08	10.00	1.19	0.10	0.07	3.18	-	4.36	m²	4.80
Cavity with 225mm stainless steel housing type 4 wall ties, -4/m² built in width of cavity 100mm	1.08	10.00	1.19	0.10	0.07	3.18	-	4.36	m²	4.80
Cavity with 250mm stainless steel housing type 4 wall ties, -4/m² built in width of cavity 150mm	1.08	10.00	1.19	0.10	0.07	3.18	-	4.36	m²	4.80
Forming cavity - insulation full fill to cavity										
Cavity with 200mm stainless steel housing type 4 wall ties -4/m² built in; 50mm fibreglass resin bonded slab cavity insulation width of cavity 50mm	3.59	10.00	3.95	0.35	0.25	11.20	1.78	16.92	m²	18.62
Cavity with 203mm stainless steel vertical twisted wall ties -4/m² built in; 50mm fibreglass resin bonded slab cavity insulation width of cavity 50mm	4.44	10.00	4.89	0.35	0.25	11.20	1.78	17.87	m²	19.65
Cavity with 200mm stainless steel housing type 4 wall ties -4/m² built in; 75mm fibreglass resin bonded slab cavity insulation width of cavity 75mm	4.27	10.00	4.70	0.40	0.25	12.24	1.78	18.72	m²	20.59
Cavity with stainless steel vertical twisted wall ties -4/m² built in; 75mm fibreglass resin bonded slab cavity insulation width of cavity 75mm	5.13	10.00	5.64	0.40	0.25	12.24	1.78	19.66	m²	21.63
Cavity with 225mm stainless steel housing type 4 wall ties -4/m² built in; 100mm fibreglass resin bonded slab cavity insulation width of cavity 100mm	3.89	10.00	4.28	0.40	0.25	12.24	1.78	18.30	m²	20.13
Cavity with stainless steel vertical twisted wall ties -4/m² built in; 100mm fibreglass resin bonded slab cavity insulation width of cavity 100mm	5.47	10.00	6.01	0.40	0.25	12.24	1.78	20.04	m²	22.04
Cavity with stainless steel vertical twisted wall ties -4/m² built in; 75mm Dritherm 32 fibreglass cavity insulation width of cavity 75mm	9.11	10.00	10.02	0.40	0.25	12.24	1.78	24.04	m²	26.45
Cavity with stainless steel vertical twisted wall ties -4/m² built in;100mm Dritherm 32 fibreglass cavity insulation width of cavity 100mm	10.96	10.00	12.05	0.40	0.25	12.24	1.78	26.08	m²	28.68
Cavity with 225mm Staifix RT2 stainless steel wall ties -4/m² built in; 75mm CavityTherm Thin-R CT/PIR full fill insulation width of cavity 75mm	27.56	10.00	30.32	0.40	0.25	12.24	1.78	44.34	m²	48.77
Cavity with 225mm Staifix RT2 stainless steel wall ties -4/m² built in; 90mm CavityTherm Thin-R CT/PIR full fill insulation width of cavity 90mm	31.96	10.00	35.15	0.40	0.25	12.24	1.78	49.17	m²	54.09
Cavity with 225mm Staifix RT2 stainless steel wall ties - 4/m² built in; 100mm CavityTherm Thin-R CT/PIR full fill insulation width of cavity 100mm	36.33	10.00	39.96	0.40	0.25	12.24	1.78	53.99	m²	59.38
Cavity with 250mm Staifix RT2 stainless steel wall ties - 4/m² built in; 125mm CavityTherm Thin-R CT/PIR full fill insulation width of cavity 125mm	43.63	10.00	47.99	0.40	0.25	12.24	1.78	62.01	m²	68.21
Cavity with 275mm Staifix RT2 stainless steel wall ties - 4/m² built in; 150mm CavityTherm Thin-R CT/PIR full fill insulation width of cavity 150mm	52.64	10.00	57.91	0.40	0.25	12.24	1.78	71.93	m²	79.12
Forming cavity - insulation part-fill to cavity										
Cavity with 200mm Staifix RT2 stainless steel wall ties -4/m² built in; 25mm Celotex CW4025 cavity insulation boards width of cavity 50mm	10.29	10.00	11.32	0.35	0.35	12.75	1.78	25.86	m²	28.44
Cavity with 225mm Staifix RT2 stainless steel wall ties - 4/m² built in; 40mm Celotex CW4040 cavity insulation boards width of cavity 75mm	8.63	10.00	9.49	0.40	0.35	13.80	1.78	25.07	m²	27.58
Cavity with 255mm Staifix TJ2 stainless steel thin joint wall ties - 4/m² built in; 50mm Celotex CW4050 cavity insulation boards width of cavity 80mm	12.87	10.00	14.16	0.40	0.35	13.80	1.78	29.74	m²	32.71
Cavity with 225mm Staifix RT2 stainless steel wall ties - 4/m² built in; 75mm Celotex CW4075 cavity insulation boards width of cavity 100mm	14.02	10.00	15.42	0.45	0.40	15.62	1.78	32.82	m²	36.10

Labour hourly rates: (except Specialists) Craft Operatives 20.87 Labourer 15.57 Rates are national average prices. Refer to REGIONAL VARIATIONS for indicative levels of overall pricing in regions	MATERIALS			LABOUR				RATES		
	Del to Site £	Waste %	Material Cost £	Craft Optve Hrs	Lab Hrs	Labour Cost £	Sunds £	Nett Rate £	Unit	Gross rate (10%) £
BRICK/BLOCK WALLING (Cont'd)										
Forming cavity - insulation part-fill to cavity (Cont'd)										
Cavity with 250mm Staifix RT2 stainless steel wall ties -4/m² built in; 100mm Celotex CW4100 cavity insulation boards										
width of cavity 125mm	17.89	10.00	19.68	0.45	0.40	15.62	1.78	37.08	m²	40.79
Cavity with 225mm Staifix RT2 stainless steel wall ties -4/m² built in; 40mm Xtratherm Thin-R XT/CW partial fill insulation										
width of cavity 90mm	12.77	10.00	14.05	0.45	0.40	15.62	1.78	31.45	m²	34.60
Cavity with 225mm Staifix RT2 stainless steel wall ties -4/m² built in; 45mm Xtratherm Thin-R XT/CW partial fill insulation										
width of cavity 95mm	11.00	10.00	12.10	0.45	0.40	15.62	1.78	29.50	m²	32.45
Cavity with 225mm Staifix RT2 stainless steel wall ties -4/m² built in; 50mm Xtratherm Thin-R XT/CW partial fill insulation										
width of cavity 100mm	11.57	10.00	12.73	0.45	0.40	15.62	1.78	30.13	m²	33.14
Damp proof courses										
BS 6515 Polythene; 100mm laps; bedding in cement mortar (1:3); no allowance made for laps										
100mm wide; vertical	0.07	5.00	0.08	0.10	-	2.09	-	2.16	m	2.38
225mm wide; vertical	0.17	5.00	0.17	0.15	-	3.13	-	3.30	m	3.64
width exceeding 300mm; vertical	0.72	5.00	0.76	0.45	-	9.39	-	10.15	m²	11.16
100mm wide; horizontal	0.07	5.00	0.08	0.06	-	1.25	-	1.33	m	1.46
225mm wide; horizontal	0.17	5.00	0.17	0.09	-	1.88	-	2.05	m	2.26
width exceeding 300mm; horizontal	0.72	5.00	0.76	0.30	-	6.26	-	7.02	m²	7.72
cavity trays; 275mm wide; horizontal	0.22	5.00	0.23	0.17	-	3.55	-	3.77	m	4.15
cavity trays; width exceeding 300mm; horizontal	0.72	5.00	0.76	0.50	-	10.44	-	11.19	m²	12.31
Hyload, pitch polymer; 100mm laps; bedding in cement lime mortar (1:1:6); no allowance made for laps										
100mm wide; vertical	0.62	5.00	0.65	0.10	-	2.09	-	2.73	m	3.01
225mm wide; vertical	1.39	5.00	1.46	0.15	-	3.13	-	4.59	m	5.05
width exceeding 300mm; vertical	6.18	5.00	6.49	0.45	-	9.39	-	15.88	m²	17.47
100mm wide; horizontal	0.62	5.00	0.65	0.06	-	1.25	-	1.90	m	2.09
225mm wide; horizontal	1.39	5.00	1.46	0.09	-	1.88	-	3.34	m	3.67
width exceeding 300mm; horizontal	6.18	5.00	6.49	0.30	-	6.26	-	12.75	m²	14.02
Synthaprufe bituminous latex emulsion; two coats brushed on; blinded with sand										
225mm wide	1.29	5.00	1.35	-	0.15	2.34	0.12	3.80	m	4.18
width exceeding 300mm; vertical	4.28	5.00	4.50	-	0.30	4.67	0.23	9.40	m²	10.34
Synthaprufe bituminous latex emulsion; three coats brushed on; blinded with sand										
225mm wide	1.77	5.00	1.86	-	0.20	3.11	0.12	5.09	m	5.60
width exceeding 300mm; vertical	6.44	5.00	6.76	-	0.42	6.54	0.26	13.56	m²	14.92
Bituminous emulsion; two coats brushed on										
225mm wide	1.40	5.00	1.47	-	0.12	1.87	0.12	3.46	m	3.80
width exceeding 300mm; vertical	4.68	5.00	4.92	-	0.26	4.05	0.23	9.20	m²	10.11
Bituminous emulsion; three coats brushed on										
225mm wide	1.87	5.00	1.97	-	0.18	2.80	0.12	4.88	m	5.37
width exceeding 300mm; vertical	6.51	5.00	6.83	-	0.36	5.61	0.26	12.70	m²	13.97
One course slates in cement mortar (1:3)										
112mm wide; vertical	1.78	15.00	2.05	0.20	0.14	6.35	-	8.41	m	9.25
225mm wide; vertical	3.57	15.00	4.11	0.40	0.27	12.55	-	16.66	m	18.32
width exceeding 300mm; vertical	12.24	15.00	14.08	1.20	0.80	37.50	-	51.58	m²	56.73
112mm wide; horizontal	1.78	15.00	2.05	0.12	0.10	4.17	-	6.22	m	6.84
225mm wide; horizontal	3.57	15.00	4.11	0.25	0.20	8.33	-	12.44	m	13.68
width exceeding 300mm; horizontal	12.24	15.00	14.08	0.70	0.50	22.39	-	36.47	m²	40.12
Two courses slates in cement mortar (1:3)										
112mm wide; vertical	3.57	15.00	4.11	0.33	0.22	10.31	-	14.42	m	15.86
225mm wide; vertical	7.14	15.00	8.21	0.66	0.42	20.31	-	28.52	m	31.38
width exceeding 300mm; vertical	24.48	15.00	28.15	2.00	1.35	62.76	-	90.91	m²	100.00
112mm wide; horizontal	3.57	15.00	4.11	0.20	0.13	6.20	-	10.30	m	11.33
225mm wide; horizontal	7.14	15.00	8.21	0.40	0.26	12.40	-	20.61	m	22.67
width exceeding 300mm; horizontal	24.48	15.00	28.15	1.20	0.80	37.50	-	65.65	m²	72.22
Cavity trays										
Type G Cavitray by Cavity Trays Ltd in										
half brick skin of cavity wall	10.91	5.00	11.46	0.20	-	4.17	-	15.63	m	17.19
external angle	5.39	5.00	5.66	0.10	-	2.09	-	7.75	nr	8.52
internal angle	5.39	5.00	5.66	0.10	-	2.09	-	7.75	nr	8.52
Type X Cavitray by Cavity Trays Ltd to suit 40 degree pitched roof complete with attached code 4 lead flashing and dress over tiles in										
half brick skin of cavity wall	61.88	5.00	64.97	0.20	-	4.17	-	69.15	m	76.06
ridge tray	14.24	5.00	14.95	0.10	-	2.09	-	17.04	nr	18.74
catchment tray; long	9.70	5.00	10.18	0.10	-	2.09	-	12.27	nr	13.50
corner catchment angle tray	14.87	5.00	15.61	0.10	-	2.09	-	17.70	nr	19.47
Type W Cavity weep/ventilator by Cavity Trays Ltd in										
half brick skin of cavity wall	0.71	5.00	0.75	0.10	-	2.09	-	2.83	nr	3.12
extension duct	1.13	5.00	1.19	0.10	-	2.09	-	3.27	nr	3.60
Joint reinforcement										
Expamet grade 304/S15 Exmet reinforcement, stainless steel; 150mm laps										
65mm wide	1.11	5.00	1.17	0.04	0.02	1.15	0.05	2.36	m	2.60
115mm wide	2.93	5.00	3.08	0.05	0.03	1.51	0.05	4.64	m	5.10

Labour hourly rates: (except Specialists) Craft Operatives 20.87 Labourer 15.57 Rates are national average prices. Refer to REGIONAL VARIATIONS for indicative levels of overall pricing in regions	MATERIALS			LABOUR				RATES		
	Del to Site £	Waste %	Material Cost £	Craft Optve Hrs	Lab Hrs	Labour Cost £	Sunds £	Nett Rate £	Unit	Gross rate (10%) £
BRICK/BLOCK WALLING (Cont'd)										
Joint reinforcement (Cont'd)										
Expamet grade 304/S15 Exmet reinforcement, stainless steel; 150mm laps (Cont'd)										
175mm wide	2.84	5.00	2.99	0.06	0.03	1.72	0.07	4.77	m	5.25
225mm wide	4.80	5.00	5.04	0.07	0.04	2.08	0.08	7.21	m	7.93
305mm wide	4.75	5.00	4.99	0.07	0.04	2.08	0.08	7.16	m	7.87
Brickforce, galvanised steel; 150mm laps										
60mm wide ref GBF30W60	0.64	5.00	0.67	0.04	0.02	1.15	0.05	1.87	m	2.05
60mm wide ref GBF35W60	0.95	5.00	1.00	0.04	0.02	1.15	0.05	2.19	m	2.41
60mm wide ref GBF40W60	1.22	5.00	1.28	0.04	0.02	1.15	0.05	2.48	m	2.72
60mm wide ref GBF45W60	1.51	5.00	1.58	0.04	0.02	1.15	0.05	2.78	m	3.06
60mm wide ref GBF50W60	1.71	5.00	1.80	0.04	0.02	1.15	0.05	2.99	m	3.29
100mm wide ref GBF30W100	1.78	5.00	1.87	0.05	0.03	1.33	0.05	3.24	m	3.57
100mm wide ref GBF35W100	2.55	5.00	2.68	0.05	0.03	1.33	0.05	4.05	m	4.46
100mm wide ref GBF40W100	3.28	5.00	3.45	0.05	0.03	1.33	0.05	4.82	m	5.31
100mm wide ref GBF45W100	3.83	5.00	4.02	0.05	0.03	1.33	0.05	5.40	m	5.94
100mm wide ref GBF50W100	5.44	5.00	5.71	0.05	0.03	1.33	0.05	7.09	m	7.80
150mm wide ref GBF30W150	0.87	5.00	0.91	0.05	0.03	1.51	0.05	2.47	m	2.72
150mm wide ref GBF35W150	1.18	5.00	1.24	0.05	0.03	1.51	0.05	2.80	m	3.08
150mm wide ref GBF40W150	1.51	5.00	1.58	0.05	0.03	1.51	0.05	3.14	m	3.46
150mm wide ref GBF45W150	1.84	5.00	1.93	0.05	0.03	1.51	0.05	3.49	m	3.84
150mm wide ref GBF50W150	2.26	5.00	2.37	0.05	0.03	1.51	0.05	3.93	m	4.33
175mm wide ref GBF30W175	0.89	5.00	0.94	0.05	0.04	1.69	0.05	2.68	m	2.95
175mm wide ref GBF35W175	1.18	5.00	1.24	0.05	0.04	1.69	0.05	2.98	m	3.28
175mm wide ref GBF40W175	1.56	5.00	1.63	0.05	0.04	1.69	0.05	3.38	m	3.71
175mm wide ref GBF45W175	1.88	5.00	1.98	0.05	0.04	1.69	0.05	3.72	m	4.09
175mm wide ref GBF50W175	2.59	5.00	2.72	0.05	0.04	1.69	0.05	4.46	m	4.91
Brickforce, stainless steel; 150mm laps										
60mm wide ref SBF30W60	1.63	5.00	1.72	0.04	0.02	1.15	0.05	2.91	m	3.20
60mm wide ref SBF35W60	2.35	5.00	2.47	0.04	0.02	1.15	0.05	3.67	m	4.03
60mm wide ref SBF40W60	2.98	5.00	3.13	0.04	0.02	1.15	0.05	4.33	m	4.76
60mm wide ref SBF45W60	3.75	5.00	3.94	0.04	0.02	1.15	0.05	5.13	m	5.65
60mm wide ref SBF50W60	5.34	5.00	5.61	0.04	0.02	1.15	0.05	6.80	m	7.48
100mm wide ref SBF30W100	1.78	5.00	1.87	0.05	0.03	1.33	0.05	3.24	m	3.57
100mm wide ref SBF35W100	2.55	5.00	2.68	0.05	0.03	1.33	0.05	4.05	m	4.46
100mm wide ref SBF40W100	3.28	5.00	3.45	0.05	0.03	1.33	0.05	4.82	m	5.31
100mm wide ref SBF45W100	3.83	5.00	4.02	0.05	0.03	1.33	0.05	5.40	m	5.94
100mm wide ref SBF50W100	5.44	5.00	5.71	0.05	0.03	1.33	0.05	7.09	m	7.80
150mm wide ref SBF30W150	1.94	5.00	2.03	0.05	0.03	1.41	0.05	3.49	m	3.84
150mm wide ref SBF35W150	2.74	5.00	2.88	0.05	0.03	1.41	0.05	4.34	m	4.77
150mm wide ref SBF40W150	3.45	5.00	3.63	0.05	0.03	1.41	0.05	5.08	m	5.59
150mm wide ref SBF45W150	3.98	5.00	4.18	0.05	0.03	1.41	0.05	5.64	m	6.20
150mm wide ref SBF50W150	5.57	5.00	5.85	0.05	0.03	1.41	0.05	7.30	m	8.03
175mm wide ref SBF30W175	2.07	5.00	2.17	0.05	0.03	1.51	0.05	3.73	m	4.10
175mm wide ref SBF35W175	2.94	5.00	3.08	0.05	0.03	1.51	0.05	4.64	m	5.11
175mm wide ref SBF40W175	3.66	5.00	3.84	0.05	0.03	1.51	0.05	5.40	m	5.94
175mm wide ref SBF45W175	4.14	5.00	4.34	0.05	0.03	1.51	0.05	5.90	m	6.49
175mm wide ref SBF50W175	5.67	5.00	5.96	0.05	0.03	1.51	0.05	7.52	m	8.27
Pointing; Pointing in flashings										
Cement mortar (1:3)										
horizontal	-	-	-	0.40	-	8.35	0.36	8.71	m	9.58
horizontal; in old wall	-	-	-	0.45	-	9.39	0.36	9.75	m	10.73
stepped	-	-	-	0.65	-	13.57	0.58	14.14	m	15.56
stepped; in old wall	-	-	-	0.70	-	14.61	0.58	15.19	m	16.71
Joints										
Expansion joints in facing brickwork 15mm wide; vertical; filling with Servicised Ltd, Aerofill 1 filler, Vertiseal compound pointing one side; including preparation, cleaners, primers and sealers										
102mm thick wall	6.81	7.50	7.32	0.09	0.18	4.68	-	12.00	m	13.20
215mm thick wall	9.88	7.50	10.62	0.10	0.20	5.20	-	15.82	m	17.40
Expansion joints in blockwork 15mm wide; vertical; filling with Servicised Ltd, Aerofill 1 filler, Vertiseal compound pointing one side; including preparation, cleaners, primers and sealers										
100mm thick wall	6.81	7.50	7.32	0.09	0.18	4.68	-	12.00	m	13.20
Expansion joints in glass blockwork 10mm wide; vertical; in filling with compressible material, polysulphide sealant both sides including preparation, cleaners, primers and sealers										
80mm thick wall	8.15	7.50	8.76	0.09	0.18	4.68	-	13.44	m	14.79
Wedging and pinning										
Two courses slates in cement mortar (1:3)										
width of wall 215mm	6.12	15.00	7.04	0.50	0.25	14.33	0.21	21.58	m	23.74
Creasing										
Nibless creasing tiles, red, machine made, 265 x 165 x 10mm; in cement-lime mortar (1:1:6)										
one course 253mm wide	5.44	5.00	5.71	0.50	0.35	15.88	0.38	21.97	m	24.17
one course 365mm wide	8.82	5.00	9.26	0.70	0.55	23.17	0.54	32.98	m	36.28
two courses 253mm wide	10.88	5.00	11.42	0.85	0.55	26.30	0.78	38.50	m	42.35
two courses 365mm wide	17.64	5.00	18.52	1.15	0.85	37.24	1.09	56.85	m	62.53

Labour hourly rates: (except Specialists) Craft Operatives 20.87 Labourer 15.57 Rates are national average prices. Refer to REGIONAL VARIATIONS for indicative levels of overall pricing in regions	MATERIALS			LABOUR				RATES		
	Del to Site £	Waste %	Material Cost £	Craft Optve Hrs	Lab Hrs	Labour Cost £	Sunds £	Nett Rate £	Unit	Gross rate (10%) £
BRICK/BLOCK WALLING (Cont'd)										
Proprietary and individual spot items; Chimney pots										
Clay chimney pots; set and flaunched in cement mortar (1:3)										
tapered roll top; 600mm high	62.91	5.00	66.05	0.75	0.63	25.46	0.63	92.14	nr	101.36
tapered roll top; 750mm high	82.32	5.00	86.43	0.88	0.75	30.04	0.79	117.27	nr	128.99
tapered roll top; 900mm high	100.89	5.00	105.94	1.00	0.93	35.35	0.94	142.23	nr	156.45
Proprietary and individual spot items; Air bricks										
Clay air bricks, BS 493, square hole pattern; opening with slate lintel over										
common brick wall 102mm thick; opening size										
215 x 65mm	4.17	-	4.17	0.20	0.10	5.73	0.94	10.84	nr	11.93
215 x 140mm	6.18	-	6.18	0.25	0.13	7.24	0.99	14.41	nr	15.85
215 x 215mm	14.53	-	14.53	0.30	0.15	8.60	1.09	24.22	nr	26.64
common brick wall 215mm thick; opening size										
215 x 65mm	4.17	-	4.17	0.30	0.15	8.60	1.78	14.55	nr	16.00
215 x 140mm	6.18	-	6.18	0.38	0.19	10.89	1.86	18.93	nr	20.83
215 x 215mm	14.53	-	14.53	0.45	0.23	12.97	2.00	29.50	nr	32.45
common brick wall 215mm thick; facework one side; opening size										
215 x 65mm	4.17	-	4.17	0.40	0.20	11.46	1.78	17.41	nr	19.16
215 x 140mm	6.18	-	6.18	0.50	0.25	14.33	1.86	22.37	nr	24.61
215 x 215mm	14.53	-	14.53	0.60	0.30	17.19	2.00	33.72	nr	37.09
common brick wall 327mm thick; facework one side; opening size										
215 x 65mm	4.17	-	4.17	0.60	0.30	17.19	2.87	24.23	nr	26.66
215 x 140mm	6.18	-	6.18	0.70	0.35	20.06	3.02	29.26	nr	32.18
215 x 215mm	14.53	-	14.53	0.80	0.40	22.92	3.12	40.57	nr	44.63
common brick wall 440mm thick; facework one side; opening size										
215 x 65mm	4.17	-	4.17	0.80	0.40	22.92	3.83	30.92	nr	34.01
215 x 140mm	6.18	-	6.18	0.90	0.45	25.79	3.96	35.93	nr	39.52
215 x 215mm	14.53	-	14.53	1.00	0.50	28.66	4.09	47.28	nr	52.00
cavity wall 252mm thick with 102mm facing brick outer skin, 100mm block inner skin and 50mm cavity; sealing cavity with slates in cement mortar (1:3); rendering all round with cement mortar (1:3); opening size										
215 x 65mm	4.17	-	4.17	0.60	0.30	17.19	3.45	24.81	nr	27.29
215 x 140mm	6.18	-	6.18	0.70	0.35	20.06	4.24	30.48	nr	33.53
215 x 215mm	14.53	-	14.53	0.80	0.40	22.92	4.97	42.42	nr	46.66
Proprietary and individual spot items; Fires and fire parts										
Solid one piece or two piece firebacks; BS 1251; bed and joint in fire cement; concrete filling at back										
fire size 400mm	71.44	2.50	73.23	1.00	0.67	31.30	1.78	106.31	nr	116.94
fire size 450mm	78.13	2.50	80.09	1.10	0.73	34.32	1.98	116.39	nr	128.03
Frets and stools; black vitreous enamelled; place in position										
fire size 400mm	40.17	-	40.17	0.33	0.22	10.31	-	50.48	nr	55.53
fire size 450mm	52.88	-	52.88	0.36	0.24	11.25	-	64.12	nr	70.54
Frets and stools; lustre finish; place in position										
fire size 400mm	47.82	-	47.82	0.33	0.22	10.31	-	58.13	nr	63.94
fire size 450mm	71.43	-	71.43	0.36	0.24	11.25	-	82.68	nr	90.94
Threefold brick sets										
fire size 400mm	26.04	2.50	26.69	1.00	0.67	31.30	1.78	59.78	nr	65.75
fire size 450mm	28.29	2.50	29.00	1.00	0.67	31.30	1.98	62.28	nr	68.51
Proprietary and individual spot items; Gas flue blocks										
Dunbrik concrete gas flue blocks; bedding and jointing in flue joint silicone sealant										
recess block reference 1RM, 460 x 140 x 222mm	9.21	5.00	9.67	0.30	-	6.26	1.98	17.91	nr	19.70
deep and wide recess block reference MS, 554 x 272 x 222mm	14.07	5.00	14.77	0.35	-	7.30	2.14	24.22	nr	26.65
gather block reference 1GM, 460 x 140 x 222mm	14.69	5.00	15.42	0.45	-	9.39	1.98	26.80	nr	29.48
deep and wide gather block reference MG, 554 x 272 x 222mm	26.31	5.00	27.63	0.50	-	10.44	2.14	40.21	nr	44.23
Dense backup block 100mm reference MD100, 525 x 100 x 215	8.06	5.00	8.46	0.20	-	4.17	0.99	13.63	nr	14.99
straight flue block reference 2M, 320 x 140 x 225mm	7.37	5.00	7.74	0.25	-	5.22	1.90	14.85	nr	16.34
straight flue block reference 2M/150, 320 x 140 x 150mm	5.57	5.00	5.85	0.25	-	5.22	1.90	12.96	nr	14.26
straight flue block reference 2M/75, 320 x 140 x 75mm	5.57	5.00	5.85	0.30	-	6.26	1.90	14.01	nr	15.41
95mm lateral offset block reference 3ME, 340 x 140 x 225mm	8.28	5.00	8.69	0.37	-	7.72	1.98	18.40	nr	20.24
125mm backset block reference 2BM, 245 x 265 x 260mm	25.73	5.00	27.02	0.35	-	7.30	1.98	36.30	nr	39.93
Top exit transfer block reference 4M, 265 x 200 x 160mm	16.55	5.00	17.38	0.35	-	7.30	1.90	26.58	nr	29.24
Side exit transfer block reference 5M, 340 x 140 x 225mm	24.20	5.00	25.41	0.40	-	8.35	1.98	35.74	nr	39.31
Proprietary and individual spot items; Arch bars										
Steel flat arch bar										
30 x 6mm	5.05	-	5.05	0.70	-	14.61	-	19.66	m	21.62
50 x 6mm	6.00	-	6.00	0.70	-	14.61	-	20.61	m	22.67
Steel angle arch bar										
50 x 50 x 6mm	9.89	-	9.89	0.70	-	14.61	-	24.50	m	26.95
75 x 50 x 6mm	17.33	-	17.33	0.80	-	16.70	-	34.02	m	37.42
Proprietary and individual spot items; Building in										
Building in metal windows; building in lugs; bedding in cement mortar (1:3), pointing with Secomastic standard mastic one side										
200mm high; lugs to brick jambs; plugging and screwing to brick sill and concrete head										
500mm wide	-	-	-	0.53	0.22	14.49	1.53	16.02	nr	17.62
600mm wide	-	-	-	0.58	0.24	15.84	1.91	17.76	nr	19.53
900mm wide	-	-	-	0.74	0.29	19.96	2.62	22.58	nr	24.84
1200mm wide	-	-	-	0.90	0.34	24.08	3.38	27.46	nr	30.21
1500mm wide	-	-	-	1.06	0.39	28.19	4.09	32.29	nr	35.52

MASONRY

Labour hourly rates: (except Specialists) Craft Operatives 20.87 Labourer 15.57 Rates are national average prices. Refer to REGIONAL VARIATIONS for indicative levels of overall pricing in regions	MATERIALS			LABOUR				RATES		
	Del to Site £	Waste %	Material Cost £	Craft Optve Hrs	Lab Hrs	Labour Cost £	Sunds £	Nett Rate £	Unit	Gross rate (10%) £
BRICK/BLOCK WALLING (Cont'd)										
Proprietary and individual spot items; Building in (Cont'd)										
Building in metal windows; building in lugs; bedding in cement mortar (1:3), pointing with Secomastic standard mastic one side (Cont'd)										
200mm high; lugs to brick jambs; plugging and screwing to brick sill and concrete head (Cont'd)										
1800mm wide	-	-	-	1.22	0.44	32.31	4.80	37.11	nr	40.83
500mm high; lugs to brick jambs; plugging and screwing to brick sill and concrete head										
500mm wide	-	-	-	0.64	0.25	17.25	2.38	19.63	nr	21.59
600mm wide	-	-	-	0.69	0.27	18.60	2.61	21.21	nr	23.33
900mm wide	-	-	-	0.85	0.32	22.72	3.32	26.04	nr	28.64
1200mm wide	-	-	-	1.02	0.37	27.05	4.04	31.09	nr	34.20
1500mm wide	-	-	-	1.18	0.43	31.32	4.80	36.12	nr	39.74
1800mm wide	-	-	-	1.34	0.48	35.44	5.46	40.90	nr	44.99
700mm high; lugs to brick jambs; plugging and screwing to brick sill and concrete head										
500mm wide	-	-	-	0.75	0.28	20.01	2.84	22.85	nr	25.14
600mm wide	-	-	-	0.80	0.30	21.37	3.09	24.45	nr	26.90
900mm wide	-	-	-	0.97	0.35	25.69	3.83	29.52	nr	32.47
1200mm wide	-	-	-	1.13	0.41	29.97	4.54	34.50	nr	37.95
1500mm wide	-	-	-	1.30	0.46	34.29	5.25	39.54	nr	43.49
1800mm wide	-	-	-	1.46	0.52	38.57	5.94	44.51	nr	48.96
900mm high; lugs to brick jambs; plugging and screwing to brick sill and concrete head										
500mm wide	-	-	-	0.85	0.30	22.41	3.28	25.69	nr	28.26
600mm wide	-	-	-	0.91	0.32	23.97	3.46	27.44	nr	30.18
900mm wide	-	-	-	1.08	0.38	28.46	4.26	32.71	nr	35.98
1200mm wide	-	-	-	1.25	0.44	32.94	4.97	37.90	nr	41.70
1500mm wide	-	-	-	1.42	0.50	37.42	5.69	43.11	nr	47.42
1800mm wide	-	-	-	1.58	0.55	41.54	6.37	47.91	nr	52.70
1100mm high; lugs to brick jambs; plugging and screwing to brick sill and concrete head										
500mm wide	-	-	-	0.96	0.33	25.17	3.81	28.98	nr	31.88
600mm wide	-	-	-	1.02	0.35	26.74	3.98	30.71	nr	33.78
900mm wide	-	-	-	1.19	0.41	31.22	4.72	35.94	nr	39.53
1200mm wide	-	-	-	1.36	0.47	35.70	5.44	41.15	nr	45.26
1500mm wide	-	-	-	1.54	0.53	40.39	6.17	46.56	nr	51.22
1800mm wide	-	-	-	1.71	0.59	44.87	6.90	51.77	nr	56.95
1300mm high; lugs to brick jambs; plugging and screwing to brick sill and concrete head										
500mm wide	-	-	-	1.07	0.36	27.94	4.21	32.14	nr	35.36
600mm wide	-	-	-	1.12	0.38	29.29	4.45	33.75	nr	37.12
900mm wide	-	-	-	1.30	0.44	33.98	5.18	39.16	nr	43.08
1200mm wide	-	-	-	1.48	0.50	38.67	5.91	44.58	nr	49.04
1500mm wide	-	-	-	1.65	0.57	43.31	6.65	49.96	nr	54.96
1800mm wide	-	-	-	1.83	0.63	48.00	7.36	55.36	nr	60.90
1500mm high; lugs to brick jambs; plugging and screwing to brick sill and concrete head										
500mm wide	-	-	-	1.18	0.39	30.70	4.70	35.40	nr	38.94
600mm wide	-	-	-	1.23	0.41	32.05	4.90	36.95	nr	40.65
900mm wide	-	-	-	1.42	0.47	36.95	5.64	42.60	nr	46.86
1200mm wide	-	-	-	1.59	0.54	41.59	6.35	47.94	nr	52.74
1500mm wide	-	-	-	1.77	0.60	46.28	7.05	53.33	nr	58.66
1800mm wide	-	-	-	1.95	0.67	51.13	7.82	58.95	nr	64.84
2100mm high; lugs to brick jambs; plugging and screwing to brick sill and concrete head										
500mm wide	-	-	-	1.39	0.44	35.86	6.07	41.93	nr	46.13
600mm wide	-	-	-	1.45	0.46	37.42	6.32	43.74	nr	48.12
900mm wide	-	-	-	1.64	0.53	42.48	7.03	49.51	nr	54.46
1200mm wide	-	-	-	1.82	0.60	47.33	7.82	55.15	nr	60.66
1500mm wide	-	-	-	2.01	0.67	52.38	8.48	60.86	nr	66.95
1800mm wide	-	-	-	2.19	0.74	57.23	9.24	66.47	nr	73.11
Building in factory glazed metal windows; screwing with galvanised screws; bedding in cement mortar (1:3), pointing with Secomastic standard mastic one side										
300mm high; plugging and screwing lugs to brick jambs and sill and concrete head										
600mm wide	-	-	-	0.70	0.30	19.28	2.13	21.41	nr	23.55
900mm wide	-	-	-	0.84	0.34	22.82	2.87	25.70	nr	28.27
1200mm wide	-	-	-	0.98	0.38	26.37	3.58	29.95	nr	32.94
1500mm wide	-	-	-	1.12	0.41	29.76	4.31	34.06	nr	37.47
1800mm wide	-	-	-	1.26	0.45	33.30	5.00	38.30	nr	42.13
2400mm wide	-	-	-	1.54	0.53	40.39	6.47	46.86	nr	51.55
3000mm wide	-	-	-	1.82	0.60	47.33	7.89	55.21	nr	60.73
700mm high; plugging and screwing lugs to brick jambs and sill and concrete head										
600mm wide	-	-	-	0.96	0.40	26.26	3.09	29.35	nr	32.28
900mm wide	-	-	-	1.17	0.48	31.89	3.83	35.72	nr	39.29
1200mm wide	-	-	-	1.37	0.57	37.47	4.59	42.05	nr	46.26
1500mm wide	-	-	-	1.58	0.64	42.94	5.25	48.19	nr	53.01
1800mm wide	-	-	-	1.79	0.73	48.72	5.94	54.66	nr	60.13
2400mm wide	-	-	-	2.21	0.90	60.14	7.41	67.54	nr	74.30
3000mm wide	-	-	-	2.62	1.06	71.18	8.88	80.06	nr	88.07
900mm high; plugging and screwing lugs to brick jambs and sill and concrete head										
600mm wide	-	-	-	1.09	0.45	29.75	3.55	33.30	nr	36.63
900mm wide	-	-	-	1.33	0.55	36.32	4.26	40.58	nr	44.64
1200mm wide	-	-	-	1.57	0.66	43.04	4.97	48.01	nr	52.81
1500mm wide	-	-	-	1.81	0.76	49.61	5.69	55.30	nr	60.83

Labour hourly rates: (except Specialists) Craft Operatives 20.87 Labourer 15.57 Rates are national average prices. Refer to REGIONAL VARIATIONS for indicative levels of overall pricing in regions	MATERIALS			LABOUR				RATES		
	Del to Site £	Waste %	Material Cost £	Craft Optve Hrs	Lab Hrs	Labour Cost £	Sunds £	Nett Rate £	Unit	Gross rate (10%) £
BRICK/BLOCK WALLING (Cont'd)										
Proprietary and individual spot items; Building in (Cont'd)										
Building in factory glazed metal windows; screwing with galvanised screws; bedding in cement mortar (1:3), pointing with Secomastic standard mastic one side (Cont'd)										
900mm high; plugging and screwing lugs to brick jambs and sill and concrete head (Cont'd)										
1800mm wide	-	-	-	2.06	0.87	56.54	6.37	62.91	nr	69.20
2400mm wide	-	-	-	2.54	1.08	69.83	7.85	77.68	nr	85.45
3000mm wide	-	-	-	3.02	1.29	83.11	9.31	92.42	nr	101.66
1100mm high; plugging and screwing lugs to brick jambs and sill and concrete head										
600mm wide	-	-	-	1.22	0.50	33.25	3.99	37.24	nr	40.96
900mm wide	-	-	-	1.49	0.62	40.75	4.72	45.47	nr	50.02
1200mm wide	-	-	-	1.77	0.75	48.62	5.43	54.05	nr	59.45
1500mm wide	-	-	-	2.04	0.88	56.28	6.17	62.45	nr	68.69
1800mm wide	-	-	-	2.32	1.01	64.14	6.90	71.04	nr	78.15
2400mm wide	-	-	-	2.87	1.27	79.67	8.32	87.99	nr	96.79
3000mm wide	-	-	-	3.42	1.52	95.04	9.78	104.83	nr	115.31
1300mm high; plugging and screwing lugs to brick jambs and sill and concrete head										
600mm wide	-	-	-	1.34	0.54	36.37	4.72	41.09	nr	45.20
900mm wide	-	-	-	1.66	0.70	45.54	5.18	50.72	nr	55.80
1200mm wide	-	-	-	1.96	0.85	54.14	5.92	60.06	nr	66.07
1500mm wide	-	-	-	2.28	0.99	63.00	6.65	69.65	nr	76.61
1800mm wide	-	-	-	2.59	1.15	71.96	7.36	79.32	nr	87.25
2400mm wide	-	-	-	3.21	1.45	89.57	8.74	98.31	nr	108.15
3000mm wide	-	-	-	3.83	1.75	107.18	10.18	117.36	nr	129.10
1500mm high; plugging and screwing lugs to brick jambs and sill and concrete head										
600mm wide	-	-	-	1.47	0.59	39.87	4.90	44.77	nr	49.24
900mm wide	-	-	-	1.82	0.77	49.97	5.64	55.62	nr	61.18
1200mm wide	-	-	-	2.16	0.94	59.72	6.35	66.07	nr	72.67
1500mm wide	-	-	-	2.51	1.11	69.67	7.11	76.78	nr	84.46
1800mm wide	-	-	-	2.85	1.29	79.56	7.82	87.39	nr	96.12
2400mm wide	-	-	-	3.54	1.64	99.41	9.26	108.67	nr	119.54
3000mm wide	-	-	-	4.23	1.98	119.11	10.68	129.78	nr	142.76
2100mm high; plugging and screwing lugs to brick jambs and sill and concrete head										
600mm wide	-	-	-	1.86	0.74	50.34	6.32	56.66	nr	62.33
900mm wide	-	-	-	2.31	0.98	63.47	7.03	70.50	nr	77.55
1200mm wide	-	-	-	2.75	1.22	76.39	7.80	84.19	nr	92.61
1500mm wide	-	-	-	3.20	1.46	89.52	8.48	98.00	nr	107.80
1800mm wide	-	-	-	3.65	1.71	102.80	9.19	111.99	nr	123.19
2400mm wide	-	-	-	4.54	2.19	128.85	10.64	139.49	nr	153.44
3000mm wide	-	-	-	5.43	2.67	154.90	12.06	166.96	nr	183.65
Building in wood windows; building in lugs; bedding in cement mortar (1:3), pointing with Secomastic standard mastic one side										
768mm high; lugs to brick jambs										
438mm wide	-	-	-	1.43	0.09	31.25	2.87	34.12	nr	37.53
641mm wide	-	-	-	1.64	0.09	35.63	3.38	39.01	nr	42.91
1225mm wide	-	-	-	2.24	0.10	48.31	4.82	53.12	nr	58.44
1809mm wide	-	-	-	2.86	0.11	61.40	6.29	67.69	nr	74.46
2394mm wide	-	-	-	3.46	0.12	74.08	7.76	81.83	nr	90.02
920mm high; lugs to brick jambs										
438mm wide	-	-	-	1.61	0.09	35.00	3.20	38.20	nr	42.02
641mm wide	-	-	-	1.82	0.10	39.54	3.68	43.22	nr	47.54
1225mm wide	-	-	-	2.45	0.11	52.84	5.18	58.03	nr	63.83
1809mm wide	-	-	-	3.07	0.13	66.10	6.65	72.74	nr	80.02
2394mm wide	-	-	-	3.70	0.14	79.40	8.09	87.48	nr	96.23
1073mm high; lugs to brick jambs										
438mm wide	-	-	-	1.80	0.10	39.12	3.58	42.70	nr	46.97
641mm wide	-	-	-	2.01	0.11	43.66	4.09	47.75	nr	52.53
1225mm wide	-	-	-	2.66	0.12	57.38	5.56	62.94	nr	69.24
1809mm wide	-	-	-	3.30	0.14	71.05	6.98	78.03	nr	85.83
2394mm wide	-	-	-	3.95	0.16	84.93	8.46	93.39	nr	102.73
1225mm high; lugs to brick jambs										
438mm wide	-	-	-	1.98	0.10	42.88	3.96	46.84	nr	51.52
641mm wide	-	-	-	2.20	0.11	47.63	4.42	52.05	nr	57.25
1225mm wide	-	-	-	2.87	0.13	61.92	5.91	67.83	nr	74.61
1809mm wide	-	-	-	3.52	0.16	75.95	7.29	83.25	nr	91.57
2394mm wide	-	-	-	4.19	0.18	90.25	8.78	99.03	nr	108.93
1378mm high; lugs to brick jambs										
438mm wide	-	-	-	2.16	0.10	46.64	4.29	50.93	nr	56.02
641mm wide	-	-	-	2.39	0.11	51.59	4.80	56.39	nr	62.03
1225mm wide	-	-	-	3.07	0.14	66.25	6.27	72.52	nr	79.77
1809mm wide	-	-	-	3.75	0.17	80.91	7.71	88.61	nr	97.48
2394mm wide	-	-	-	4.43	0.20	95.57	9.17	104.74	nr	115.22
Building in fireplace interior with slabbed tile surround and loose hearth tiles for 400mm opening; bed and joint interior in fire cement and fill with concrete at back; plug and screw on surround lugs; bed hearth tiles in cement mortar (1:3) and point in										
with firebrick back	-	-	-	5.00	3.50	158.85	7.29	166.14	nr	182.75
with back boiler unit and self contained flue	-	-	-	6.00	4.00	187.50	8.78	196.28	nr	215.91

Labour hourly rates: (except Specialists) Craft Operatives 20.87 Labourer 15.57 Rates are national average prices. Refer to REGIONAL VARIATIONS for indicative levels of overall pricing in regions	MATERIALS			LABOUR				RATES		
	Del to Site £	Waste %	Material Cost £	Craft Optve Hrs	Lab Hrs	Labour Cost £	Sunds £	Nett Rate £	Unit	Gross rate (10%) £
GLASS BLOCK WALLING										
Walls; Glass blockwork; Hollow glass blocks, white, cross ribbed, in cement mortar (1:3); continuous joints; flat recessed pointing as work proceeds										
Screens or panels; facework both sides										
190 x 190mm blocks; vertical; 80mm thick	56.25	10.00	61.88	3.00	3.00	109.32	82.12	253.32	m²	278.65
240 x 240mm blocks; vertical; 80mm thick	104.00	10.00	114.40	2.50	2.50	91.10	66.10	271.60	m²	298.76
NATURAL STONE RUBBLE WALLING AND DRESSINGS										
Walls; Natural stone; Stone rubble work; random stones of Yorkshire limestone; bedding and jointing in lime mortar (1:3); uncoursed										
Walls; tapering both sides; including extra material										
500mm thick	59.70	15.00	68.65	3.75	3.75	136.65	13.61	218.92	m²	240.81
600mm thick	69.65	15.00	80.10	4.50	4.50	163.98	16.33	260.41	m²	286.45
Walls; Stone rubble work; squared rubble face stones of Yorkshire limestone; bedding and jointing in lime mortar (1:3); irregular coursed; courses average 150mm high										
Walls; vertical; face stones 100 - 150mm on bed; bonding to brickwork; including extra material; scappled or axed face; weather struck pointing as work proceeds										
150mm thick; faced one side	73.50	15.00	84.53	3.00	3.00	109.32	4.54	198.38	m²	218.22
Walls; vertical; face stones 100 - 150mm on bed; bonding to brickwork; including extra material; hammer dressed face; weather struck pointing as work proceeds										
150mm thick; faced one side	73.50	15.00	84.53	3.30	3.30	120.25	4.54	209.31	m²	230.25
Walls; vertical; face stones 100 - 150mm on bed; bonding to brickwork; including extra material; rock worked face; pointing with a parallel joint as work proceeds										
150mm thick; faced one side	73.50	15.00	84.53	3.60	3.60	131.18	4.54	220.25	m²	242.27
Walls; Stone rubble work; squared rubble face stones of Yorkshire limestone; bedding and jointing in lime mortar (1:3); regular coursed; courses average 150mm high										
Walls; vertical; face stones 100 - 150mm on bed; bonding to brickwork; including extra material; scappled or axed face; weather struck pointing as work proceeds										
150mm thick; faced one side	78.75	15.00	90.56	3.20	3.20	116.61	4.54	211.71	m²	232.88
Walls; vertical; face stones 100 - 150mm on bed; bonding to brickwork; including extra material; hammer dressed face; weather struck pointing as work proceeds										
150mm thick; faced one side	78.75	15.00	90.56	3.50	3.50	127.54	4.54	222.64	m²	244.90
Walls; vertical; face stones 100 - 150mm on bed; bonding to brickwork; including extra material; rock worked face; pointing with a parallel joint as work proceeds										
150mm thick; faced one side	78.75	15.00	90.56	3.80	3.80	138.47	4.54	233.57	m²	256.93
Walls; Stone rubble work; random rubble backing and squared rubble face stones of Yorkshire limestone; bedding and jointing in lime mortar (1:3); irregular coursed; courses average 150mm high										
Walls; vertical; face stones 100 - 150mm on bed; scappled or axed face; weather struck pointing as work proceeds										
350mm thick; faced one side	94.50	15.00	108.67	4.00	4.00	145.76	9.49	263.92	m²	290.31
500mm thick; faced one side	111.64	15.00	128.39	4.75	4.75	173.09	13.61	315.09	m²	346.60
Walls; vertical; face stones 100 - 150mm on bed; hammer dressed face; weather struck pointing as work proceeds										
350mm thick; faced one side	94.50	15.00	108.67	4.30	4.30	156.69	9.49	274.85	m²	302.34
500mm thick; faced one side	111.64	15.00	128.39	5.05	5.05	184.02	13.61	326.02	m²	358.62
Walls; vertical; face stones 100 - 150mm on bed; rock worked face; pointing with a parallel joint as work proceeds										
350mm thick; faced one side	94.50	15.00	108.67	4.60	4.60	167.62	9.49	285.79	m²	314.37
500mm thick; faced one side	111.64	15.00	128.39	5.35	5.35	194.95	13.61	336.95	m²	370.65
Grooves										
12 x 25mm	-	-	-	0.25	-	5.22	-	5.22	m	5.74
12 x 38mm	-	-	-	0.30	-	6.26	-	6.26	m	6.89
Arches; relieving										
225mm high on face, 180mm wide on soffit	124.95	5.00	131.20	1.50	0.75	42.98	1.07	175.25	m	192.78
225mm high on face, 250mm wide on soffit	171.15	5.00	179.71	2.00	1.00	57.31	1.49	238.50	m	262.35
Special purpose blocks or stones; Quoin stones										
scappled or axed face; attached; faced two adjacent faces										
250 x 200 x 350mm	37.04	5.00	38.90	0.50	0.25	14.33	0.46	53.69	nr	59.05
250 x 200 x 500mm	54.41	5.00	57.13	0.80	0.40	22.92	0.66	80.71	nr	88.78
250 x 250 x 350mm	48.62	5.00	51.05	0.65	0.35	19.02	0.58	70.64	nr	77.71
250 x 250 x 500mm	68.30	5.00	71.71	0.90	0.45	25.79	0.82	98.33	nr	108.16
380 x 200 x 350mm	57.88	5.00	60.78	0.80	0.40	22.92	0.74	84.44	nr	92.89
380 x 200 x 500mm	81.03	5.00	85.09	1.00	0.50	28.66	0.99	114.73	nr	126.20
rock worked face; attached; faced two adjacent faces										
250 x 200 x 350mm	37.04	5.00	38.90	0.55	0.25	15.37	0.46	54.73	nr	60.20
250 x 200 x 500mm	54.41	5.00	57.13	0.85	0.40	23.97	0.66	81.76	nr	89.93
250 x 250 x 350mm	48.62	5.00	51.05	0.70	0.35	20.06	0.58	71.69	nr	78.86
250 x 250 x 500mm	68.30	5.00	71.71	0.95	0.45	26.83	0.82	99.37	nr	109.31

Labour hourly rates: (except Specialists) Craft Operatives 20.87 Labourer 15.57 Rates are national average prices. Refer to REGIONAL VARIATIONS for indicative levels of overall pricing in regions	MATERIALS			LABOUR				RATES		
	Del to Site £	Waste %	Material Cost £	Craft Optve Hrs	Lab Hrs	Labour Cost £	Sunds £	Nett Rate £	Unit	Gross rate (10%) £
NATURAL STONE RUBBLE WALLING AND DRESSINGS (Cont'd)										
Walls; Stone rubble work; random rubble backing and squared rubble face stones of Yorkshire limestone; bedding and jointing in lime mortar (1:3); irregular coursed; courses average 150mm high (Cont'd)										
Special purpose blocks or stones; Quoin stones (Cont'd)										
rock worked face; attached; faced two adjacent faces (Cont'd)										
380 x 200 x 350mm	57.88	5.00	60.78	0.85	0.40	23.97	0.74	85.49	nr	94.03
380 x 200 x 500mm	81.03	5.00	85.09	1.10	0.50	30.74	0.99	116.82	nr	128.50
plain faced; attached; faced two adjacent faces										
215 x 215 x 100mm	25.00	5.00	26.25	0.50	0.25	14.33	0.46	41.04	nr	45.14
340 x 215 x 100mm	28.50	5.00	29.92	0.50	0.25	14.33	0.46	44.71	nr	49.19
440 x 215 x 100mm	29.50	5.00	30.97	0.70	0.35	20.06	0.58	51.61	nr	56.77
285 x 285 x 100mm	28.50	5.00	29.92	0.70	0.35	20.06	0.58	50.56	nr	55.62
340 x 285 x 100mm	30.50	5.00	32.02	0.70	0.35	20.06	0.58	52.66	nr	57.93
440 x 285 x 100mm	32.50	5.00	34.12	0.85	0.40	23.97	0.74	58.84	nr	64.72
Stone rubble work; random rubble backing and squared rubble face stones of Yorkshire limestone; bedding and jointing in lime mortar (1:3); regular coursed; courses average 150mm high										
Walls; vertical; face stones 100 - 150mm on bed; scappled or axed face; weather struck pointing as work proceeds										
350mm thick; faced one side	103.95	15.00	119.54	4.20	4.20	153.05	9.49	282.08	m²	310.29
Walls; vertical; face stones 125 - 200mm on bed; scappled or axed face; weather struck pointing as work proceeds										
500mm thick; faced one side	124.38	15.00	143.03	4.95	4.95	180.38	13.61	337.02	m²	370.73
Walls; vertical; face stones 100 - 150mm on bed; hammer dressed face; weather struck pointing as work proceeds										
350mm thick; faced one side	103.95	15.00	119.54	4.50	4.50	163.98	9.49	293.01	m²	322.31
500mm thick; faced one side	124.38	15.00	143.03	5.25	5.25	191.31	13.61	347.95	m²	382.75
Walls; vertical; face stones 100 - 150mm on bed; rock worked face; pointing with a parallel joint as work proceeds										
350mm thick; faced one side	103.95	15.00	119.54	4.80	4.80	174.91	9.49	303.94	m²	334.34
500mm thick; faced one side	124.38	15.00	143.03	5.55	5.55	202.24	13.61	358.89	m²	394.78
NATURAL STONE ASHLAR WALLING AND DRESSINGS										
Walls; Natural stone										
Note										
stonework is work for a specialist; prices being obtained for specific projects. Some firms that specialise in this class of work are included within the list at the end of this section										
Natural stonework dressings; natural Dorset limestone; Portland Whitbed; bedding and jointing in mason's mortar (1:3:12); flush smooth pointing as work proceeds; slurrying with weak lime mortar and cleaning down on completion										
Walls; vertical; building against brickwork; BS EN 845 Fig 1 specification 3.5 wall ties - 4/m² built in										
50mm thick; plain and rubbed one side	191.10	2.50	195.88	4.00	2.60	123.96	9.07	328.91	m²	361.81
75mm thick; plain and rubbed one side	259.90	2.50	266.39	4.50	3.15	142.96	9.90	419.25	m²	461.18
100mm thick; plain and rubbed one side	343.98	2.50	352.58	5.00	3.70	161.96	10.72	525.26	m²	577.79
Natural stonework; natural Dorset limestone, Portland Whitbed; bedding and jointing in cement-lime mortar (1:2:9); flush smooth pointing as work proceeds; Bands										
Band courses; moulded; horizontal										
225 x 125mm	191.10	2.50	195.88	1.60	1.15	51.30	4.95	252.12	m	277.34
250 x 150mm	230.41	2.50	236.17	1.80	1.35	58.59	5.78	300.53	m	330.59
300 x 150mm	271.91	2.50	278.71	2.00	1.55	65.87	6.76	351.34	m	386.48
Natural stonework; natural Dorset limestone, Portland Whitbed; bedding and jointing in cement-lime mortar (1:2:9); flush smooth pointing as work proceeds; Extra over walls for perimeters and abutments										
Copings; horizontal										
plain and rubbed faces -2; weathered and rubbed faces -1; throats -2; cramped joints with stainless steel cramps										
300 x 50mm	132.13	2.50	135.44	0.75	0.50	23.44	6.93	165.80	m	182.38
300 x 75mm	155.06	2.50	158.94	0.90	0.70	29.68	7.76	196.38	m	216.02
375 x 100mm	214.03	2.50	219.38	1.35	1.00	43.74	9.32	272.45	m	299.69
Natural stonework; natural Dorset limestone, Portland Whitbed; bedding and jointing in cement-lime mortar (1:2:9); flush smooth pointing as work proceeds; Extra over walls for opening perimeters										
Lintels										
plain and rubbed faces -3; splayed and rubbed faces -1										
200 x 100mm	81.90	2.50	83.95	1.25	0.85	39.32	2.06	125.33	m	137.87
225 x 125mm	104.83	2.50	107.45	1.50	1.10	48.43	2.64	158.52	m	174.38
Sills										
plain and rubbed faces -3; sunk weathered and rubbed faces -1; grooves -1; throats -1										
200 x 75mm	110.29	2.50	113.05	1.00	0.65	30.99	3.13	147.17	m	161.89
250 x 75mm	132.13	2.50	135.44	1.20	0.80	37.50	3.63	176.57	m	194.22

Labour hourly rates: (except Specialists) Craft Operatives 20.87 Labourer 15.57 Rates are national average prices. Refer to REGIONAL VARIATIONS for indicative levels of overall pricing in regions	MATERIALS			LABOUR				RATES		
	Del to Site £	Waste %	Material Cost £	Craft Optve Hrs	Lab Hrs	Labour Cost £	Sunds £	Nett Rate £	Unit	Gross rate (10%) £
NATURAL STONE ASHLAR WALLING AND DRESSINGS (Cont'd)										
Natural stonework; natural Dorset limestone, Portland Whitbed; bedding and jointing in cement-lime mortar (1:2:9); flush smooth pointing as work proceeds; Extra over walls for opening perimeters (Cont'd)										
Sills (Cont'd) plain and rubbed faces -3; sunk weathered and rubbed faces -1; grooves -1; throats -1 (Cont'd)										
300 x 75mm	152.88	2.50	156.70	1.40	1.00	44.79	4.04	205.53	m	226.09
Jamb stones; attached plain and rubbed faces -3; splayed and rubbed faces -1; rebates -1; grooves -1										
175 x 75mm	84.08	2.50	86.19	1.00	0.65	30.99	2.72	119.90	m	131.89
200 x 100mm	92.82	2.50	95.14	1.25	1.00	41.66	3.55	140.35	m	154.38
Natural stonework, natural Yorkshire sandstone, Bolton Wood; bedding and jointing in cement-lime mortar (1:2:9); flush smooth pointing as work proceeds; Extra over walls for perimeters and abutments										
Copings; horizontal plain and rubbed faces -2; weathered and rubbed faces -2; throats -2; cramped joints with stainless steel cramps										
300 x 75mm	86.52	2.50	88.68	0.90	0.70	29.68	4.95	123.31	m	135.65
300 x 100mm	101.66	2.50	104.20	1.10	0.80	35.41	5.44	145.06	m	159.57
Kerbs; horizontal plain and sawn faces - 4										
150 x 150mm	54.08	2.50	55.43	0.85	0.65	27.86	1.81	85.10	m	93.61
225 x 150mm	80.03	2.50	82.03	1.20	1.00	40.61	2.72	125.37	m	137.91
Cover stones 75 x 300; rough edges -2; plain and sawn face -1	45.42	2.50	46.56	0.85	0.65	27.86	3.63	78.05	m	85.85
Templates 150 x 300; rough edges -2; plain and sawn face -1	101.66	2.50	104.20	1.50	1.20	49.99	4.54	158.73	m	174.60
Steps; plain plain and rubbed top and front										
225 x 75mm	41.10	2.50	42.12	0.75	0.55	24.22	3.63	69.97	m	76.97
225 x 150mm	80.03	2.50	82.03	1.30	1.00	42.70	4.54	129.27	m	142.20
300 x 150mm	107.07	2.50	109.74	1.60	1.30	53.63	5.44	168.82	m	185.70
Natural stonework, natural Yorkshire sandstone, Bolton Wood; bedding and jointing in cement-lime mortar (1:2:9); flush smooth pointing as work proceeds; Extra over walls for opening perimeters										
Sills plain and rubbed faces -3; sunk weathered and rubbed faces -1; throats -1										
175 x 100mm	78.95	2.50	80.92	1.25	0.85	39.32	2.06	122.31	m	134.54
250 x 125mm	122.21	2.50	125.27	1.40	1.00	44.79	2.72	172.78	m	190.05
Natural stonework, natural Yorkshire sandstone, Bolton Wood; bedding and jointing in cement-lime mortar (1:2:9); flush smooth pointing as work proceeds; Special purpose blocks or stones										
Landings 75 x 900 x 900mm; sawn edges -4; plain and rubbed face -1	144.92	2.50	148.54	2.00	1.75	68.99	5.44	222.98	nr	245.27
ARTIFICIAL/CAST STONE WALLING AND DRESSINGS										
Walls; Cast stone; Reconstructed stone blocks, Marshalls Marshalite; coursed random length; pitched pace buff walling blocks; in cement-lime mortar (1:1:6); flat recessed pointing as work proceeds										
Walls										
90mm thick; alternate courses 102mm and 140mm high blocks; stretcher bond; facework one side	54.10	5.00	56.80	1.90	1.40	61.45	2.33	120.58	m²	132.64
90mm thick; one course 102mm high blocks and two courses 140mm high blocks; stretcher bond; facework one side	54.10	5.00	56.80	1.90	1.40	61.45	2.33	120.58	m²	132.64
Walls; Cast stone; Cast stonework dressings; simulated Dorset limestone; Portland Whitbed; bedding and jointing in cement-lime mortar (1:2:9); flush smooth pointing as work proceeds										
Walls; vertical; building against brickwork; BS EN 845 Fig 1 specification 3.5 wall ties -4/m² built in										
100mm thick; plain and rubbed one side	100.33	5.00	105.34	4.00	2.50	122.40	9.07	236.82	m²	260.51
Fair raking cutting 100 thick	20.07	5.00	21.07	1.00	0.50	28.66	-	49.72	m	54.70
Bands; Band courses; plain; horizontal										
225 x 125mm	45.52	5.00	47.80	1.40	1.00	44.79	2.23	94.82	m	104.30
extra; external return	31.52	5.00	33.09	-	-	-	-	33.09	nr	36.40
250 x 150mm	59.53	5.00	62.51	1.50	1.10	48.43	2.72	113.66	m	125.03
extra; external return	31.52	5.00	33.09	-	-	-	-	33.09	nr	36.40
300 x 150mm	66.53	5.00	69.86	1.60	1.20	52.08	3.13	125.07	m	137.58
extra; external return	31.52	5.00	33.09	-	-	-	-	33.09	nr	36.40

Labour hourly rates: (except Specialists) Craft Operatives 20.87 Labourer 15.57 Rates are national average prices. Refer to REGIONAL VARIATIONS for indicative levels of overall pricing in regions	MATERIALS			LABOUR				RATES		
	Del to Site £	Waste %	Material Cost £	Craft Optve Hrs	Lab Hrs	Labour Cost £	Sunds £	Nett Rate £	Unit	Gross rate (10%) £
ARTIFICIAL/CAST STONE WALLING AND DRESSINGS (Cont'd)										
Extra over walls for perimeters and abutments										
Copings; horizontal										
plain and rubbed faces -2; weathered and rubbed faces -2; throats -2; cramped joints with stainless steel cramps										
300 x 50mm	35.02	5.00	36.77	0.50	0.30	15.11	4.12	56.00	m	61.60
extra; internal angles	31.52	5.00	33.09	-	-	-	-	33.09	nr	36.40
extra; external angles	31.52	5.00	33.09	-	-	-	-	33.09	nr	36.40
300 x 75mm	41.38	5.00	43.45	0.60	0.35	17.97	4.54	65.96	m	72.56
extra; internal angles	31.52	5.00	33.09	-	-	-	-	33.09	nr	36.40
extra; external angles	31.52	5.00	33.09	-	-	-	-	33.09	nr	36.40
375 x 100mm	55.35	5.00	58.12	0.75	0.50	23.44	5.44	87.00	m	95.70
extra; internal angles	28.65	5.00	30.08	-	-	-	-	30.08	nr	33.09
extra; external angles	28.65	5.00	30.08	-	-	-	-	30.08	nr	33.09
Extra over walls for opening perimeters; Cast stonework; simulated Dorset limestone; Portland Whitbed; bedding and jointing in cement-lime mortar (1:2:9); flush smooth pointing as work proceeds										
Lintels										
plain and rubbed faces -3; splayed and rubbed faces -1										
200 x 100mm	51.50	5.00	54.07	1.00	0.60	30.21	1.32	85.61	m	94.17
225 x 125mm	58.40	5.00	61.32	1.25	0.75	37.76	1.81	100.90	m	110.99
Sills; plain and rubbed faces -3; sunk weathered and rubbed faces -1; grooves -1; throats -1										
200 x 75mm										
Sill	58.98	5.00	61.93	0.90	0.50	26.57	1.81	90.31	m	99.34
extra; stoolings	10.51	5.00	11.03	-	-	-	-	11.03	nr	12.13
250 x 75mm										
Sill	45.52	5.00	47.80	1.00	0.60	30.21	2.23	80.24	m	88.26
extra; stoolings	10.51	5.00	11.03	-	-	-	-	11.03	nr	12.13
300 x 75mm										
Sill	54.28	5.00	56.99	1.25	0.75	37.76	2.72	97.48	m	107.23
extra; stoolings	10.51	5.00	11.03	-	-	-	-	11.03	nr	12.13
Jamb stones; attached										
plain and rubbed faces -3; splayed and rubbed faces -1; rebates -1; grooves -1										
175 x 75mm	45.52	5.00	47.80	0.90	0.50	26.57	1.40	75.77	m	83.35
200 x 100mm	57.78	5.00	60.67	1.00	0.60	30.21	2.72	93.60	m	102.96
Steps; plain										
300 x 150mm; plain and rubbed tread and riser	58.89	5.00	61.84	1.25	0.90	40.10	3.63	105.57	m	116.13
Steps; spandril										
250mm wide tread; 180mm high riser; plain and rubbed tread and riser; carborundum finish to tread	81.18	5.00	85.24	2.00	1.25	61.20	2.72	149.16	m	164.08
Special purpose blocks or stones										
Landings										
150 x 900 x 900mm; plain and rubbed top surface	144.85	5.00	152.09	1.50	1.00	46.88	3.63	202.60	nr	222.85

Labour hourly rates: (except Specialists) Craft Operatives 20.87 Labourer 15.57 Rates are national average prices. Refer to REGIONAL VARIATIONS for indicative levels of overall pricing in regions	MATERIALS			LABOUR				RATES		
	Del to Site £	Waste %	Material Cost £	Craft Optve Hrs	Lab Hrs	Labour Cost £	Sunds £	Nett Rate £	Unit	Gross rate (10%) £
STRUCTURAL STEELWORK										
Framed members, framing and fabrication										
Prices generally for fabricated steelwork										
Note prices can vary considerably dependent upon the character of the work; the following are average prices for work fabricated and delivered to site										
Framing, fabrication; including shop and site black bolts, nuts and washers for structural framing to structural framing connections										
Weldable steel, BS EN 10025 : 1993 Grade S275JR, hot rolled sections BS 4-1 (Euronorm 54); welded fabrication in accordance with BS EN 1994-1										
Columns; length over 1.00 but not exceeding 9.00m										
weight less than 25 Kg/m	945.00	-	945.00	-	-	-	-	945.00	t	1039.50
weight 25-50 Kg/m	945.00	-	945.00	-	-	-	-	945.00	t	1039.50
weight 50-100 Kg/m	920.00	-	920.00	-	-	-	-	920.00	t	1012.00
weight exceeding 100 Kg/m	940.00	-	940.00	-	-	-	-	940.00	t	1034.00
Beams; length over 1.00 but not exceeding 9.00m										
weight less than 25 Kg/m	1020.00	-	1020.00	-	-	-	-	1020.00	t	1122.00
weight 25-50 Kg/m	1010.00	-	1010.00	-	-	-	-	1010.00	t	1111.00
weight 50-100 Kg/m	1100.00	-	1100.00	-	-	-	-	1100.00	t	1210.00
weight exceeding 100 Kg/m	1120.00	-	1120.00	-	-	-	-	1120.00	t	1232.00
Beams, castellated; length over 1.00 but not exceeding 9.00m										
weight less than 25 Kg/m	1820.00	-	1820.00	-	-	-	-	1820.00	t	2002.00
weight 25-50 Kg/m	1820.00	-	1820.00	-	-	-	-	1820.00	t	2002.00
weight 50-100 Kg/m	1820.00	-	1820.00	-	-	-	-	1820.00	t	2002.00
weight exceeding 100 Kg/m	1820.00	-	1820.00	-	-	-	-	1820.00	t	2002.00
Beams, curved; length over 1.00 but not exceeding 9.00m										
weight less than 25 Kg/m	2190.00	-	2190.00	-	-	-	-	2190.00	t	2409.00
weight 25-50 Kg/m	2190.00	-	2190.00	-	-	-	-	2190.00	t	2409.00
weight 50-100 Kg/m	2190.00	-	2190.00	-	-	-	-	2190.00	t	2409.00
weight exceeding 100 Kg/m	2190.00	-	2190.00	-	-	-	-	2190.00	t	2409.00
Bracings, tubular; length over 1.00 but not exceeding 9.00m										
weight less than 25 Kg/m	1660.00	-	1660.00	-	-	-	-	1660.00	t	1826.00
weight 25-50 Kg/m	1660.00	-	1660.00	-	-	-	-	1660.00	t	1826.00
weight 50-100 Kg/m	1660.00	-	1660.00	-	-	-	-	1660.00	t	1826.00
weight exceeding 100 Kg/m	1660.00	-	1660.00	-	-	-	-	1660.00	t	1826.00
Purlins and cladding rails; length over 1.00 but not exceeding 9.00m										
weight less than 25 Kg/m	1660.00	-	1660.00	-	-	-	-	1660.00	t	1826.00
weight 25-50 Kg/m	1660.00	-	1660.00	-	-	-	-	1660.00	t	1826.00
weight 50-100 Kg/m	1660.00	-	1660.00	-	-	-	-	1660.00	t	1826.00
weight exceeding 100 Kg/m	1660.00	-	1660.00	-	-	-	-	1660.00	t	1826.00
Trusses; length over 1.00 but not exceeding 9.00m										
portal frames	1530.00	-	1530.00	-	-	-	-	1530.00	t	1683.00
trusses 12m to 18m span	2130.00	-	2130.00	-	-	-	-	2130.00	t	2343.00
trusses 6m to 12m span	2180.00	-	2180.00	-	-	-	-	2180.00	t	2398.00
trusses up to 6m span	2320.00	-	2320.00	-	-	-	-	2320.00	t	2552.00
Weldable steel BS EN 10210 : 1994 Grade S275JRH, hot rolled sections BS EN 10210-2 (Euronorm 57); welded fabrication in accordance with BS EN 1994-1										
column, square hollow section; length over 1.00 but not exceeding 9.00m										
weight less than 25 Kg/m	1300.00	-	1300.00	-	-	-	-	1300.00	t	1430.00
weight 25-50 Kg/m	1300.00	-	1300.00	-	-	-	-	1300.00	t	1430.00
weight 50-100 Kg/m	1300.00	-	1300.00	-	-	-	-	1300.00	t	1430.00
weight exceeding 100 Kg/m	1300.00	-	1300.00	-	-	-	-	1300.00	t	1430.00
column, rectangular hollow section; length over 1.00 but not exceeding 9.00m										
weight less than 25 Kg/m	1440.00	-	1440.00	-	-	-	-	1440.00	t	1584.00
weight 25-50 Kg/m	1440.00	-	1440.00	-	-	-	-	1440.00	t	1584.00
weight 50-100 Kg/m	1440.00	-	1440.00	-	-	-	-	1440.00	t	1584.00
weight exceeding 100 Kg/m	1440.00	-	1440.00	-	-	-	-	1440.00	t	1584.00
Framed members, permanent erection on site										
Note the following prices for erection include for the site to be reasonably clear, ease of access and the erection carried out during normal working hours										
Permanent erection of fabricated steelwork on site with bolted connections; weldable steel, BS EN 10025 : 1993 Grade S275JR, hot rolled sections BS 4-1 (Euronorm 54); welded fabrication in accordance with BS 5950-1										
framing	-	-	-	23.00	-	480.01	-	480.01	t	528.01
Columns; length over 1.00 but not exceeding 9.00m										
weight less than 25 Kg/m	-	-	-	23.00	-	480.01	-	480.01	t	528.01

Labour hourly rates: (except Specialists) Craft Operatives 20.87 Labourer 15.57 Rates are national average prices. Refer to REGIONAL VARIATIONS for indicative levels of overall pricing in regions	MATERIALS			LABOUR				RATES		
	Del to Site £	Waste %	Material Cost £	Craft Optve Hrs	Lab Hrs	Labour Cost £	Sunds £	Nett Rate £	Unit	Gross rate (10%) £
STRUCTURAL STEELWORK (Cont'd)										
Framed members, permanent erection on site (Cont'd)										
Permanent erection of fabricated steelwork on site with bolted connections; weldable steel, BS EN 10025 : 1993 Grade S275JR, hot rolled sections BS 4-1 (Euronorm 54); welded fabrication in accordance with BS 5950-1 (Cont'd)										
Columns; length over 1.00 but not exceeding 9.00m (Cont'd)										
weight 25-50 Kg/m	-	-	-	23.00	-	480.01	-	480.01	t	528.01
weight 50-100 Kg/m	-	-	-	23.00	-	480.01	-	480.01	t	528.01
weight exceeding 100 Kg/m	-	-	-	23.00	-	480.01	-	480.01	t	528.01
Beams; length over 1.00 but not exceeding 9.00m										
weight less than 25 Kg/m	-	-	-	23.00	-	480.01	-	480.01	t	528.01
weight 25-50 Kg/m	-	-	-	23.00	-	480.01	-	480.01	t	528.01
weight 50-100 Kg/m	-	-	-	23.00	-	480.01	-	480.01	t	528.01
weight exceeding 100 Kg/m	-	-	-	23.00	-	480.01	-	480.01	t	528.01
Beams, castellated; length over 1.00 but not exceeding 9.00m										
weight less than 25 Kg/m	-	-	-	23.00	-	480.01	-	480.01	t	528.01
weight 25-50 Kg/m	-	-	-	23.00	-	480.01	-	480.01	t	528.01
weight 50-100 Kg/m	-	-	-	23.00	-	480.01	-	480.01	t	528.01
weight exceeding 100 Kg/m	-	-	-	23.00	-	480.01	-	480.01	t	528.01
Beams, curved; length over 1.00 but not exceeding 9.00m										
weight less than 25 Kg/m	-	-	-	23.00	-	480.01	-	480.01	t	528.01
weight 25-50 Kg/m	-	-	-	23.00	-	480.01	-	480.01	t	528.01
weight 50-100 Kg/m	-	-	-	23.00	-	480.01	-	480.01	t	528.01
weight exceeding 100 Kg/m	-	-	-	23.00	-	480.01	-	480.01	t	528.01
Bracings, tubular; length over 1.00 but not exceeding 9.00m										
weight less than 25 Kg/m	-	-	-	23.00	-	480.01	-	480.01	t	528.01
weight 25-50 Kg/m	-	-	-	23.00	-	480.01	-	480.01	t	528.01
weight 50-100 Kg/m	-	-	-	23.00	-	480.01	-	480.01	t	528.01
weight exceeding 100 Kg/m	-	-	-	23.00	-	480.01	-	480.01	t	528.01
Purlins and cladding rails; length over 1.00 but not exceeding 9.00m										
weight less than 25 Kg/m	-	-	-	23.00	-	480.01	-	480.01	t	528.01
weight 25-50 Kg/m	-	-	-	23.00	-	480.01	-	480.01	t	528.01
weight 50-100 Kg/m	-	-	-	23.00	-	480.01	-	480.01	t	528.01
weight exceeding 100 Kg/m	-	-	-	23.00	-	480.01	-	480.01	t	528.01
Trusses; length over 1.00 but not exceeding 9.00m										
portal frames	-	-	-	23.00	-	480.01	-	480.01	t	528.01
trusses 12m to 18m span	-	-	-	23.00	-	480.01	-	480.01	t	528.01
trusses 6m to 12m span	-	-	-	23.00	-	480.01	-	480.01	t	528.01
trusses up to 6m span	-	-	-	23.00	-	480.01	-	480.01	t	528.01
Weldable steel BS EN 10210 : 1994 Grade S275JOH, hot rolled sections BS EN 10210-2 (Euronorm 57); welded fabrication in accordance with BS 5950-1										
column, square hollow section; length over 1.00 but not exceeding 9.00m										
weight less than 25 Kg/m	-	-	-	23.00	-	480.01	-	480.01	t	528.01
weight 25-50 Kg/m	-	-	-	23.00	-	480.01	-	480.01	t	528.01
weight 50-100 Kg/m	-	-	-	23.00	-	480.01	-	480.01	t	528.01
weight exceeding 100 Kg/m	-	-	-	23.00	-	480.01	-	480.01	t	528.01
column, rectangular hollow section; length over 1.00 but not exceeding 9.00m										
weight less than 25 Kg/m	-	-	-	23.00	-	480.01	-	480.01	t	528.01
weight 25-50 Kg/m	-	-	-	23.00	-	480.01	-	480.01	t	528.01
weight 50-100 Kg/m	-	-	-	23.00	-	480.01	-	480.01	t	528.01
weight exceeding 100 Kg/m	-	-	-	23.00	-	480.01	-	480.01	t	528.01
Isolated structural members, fabrication										
Weldable steel, BS EN 10149 : 1996 Grade S275, hot rolled sections; various dimensions										
plain member; beam										
weight less than 25 Kg/m	1400.00	-	1400.00	-	-	-	-	1400.00	t	1540.00
weight 25-50 Kg/m	1400.00	-	1400.00	-	-	-	-	1400.00	t	1540.00
weight 50-100 Kg/m	1400.00	-	1400.00	-	-	-	-	1400.00	t	1540.00
weight exceeding 100 Kg/m	1400.00	-	1400.00	-	-	-	-	1400.00	t	1540.00
Steel Metsec short span lattice joists primed at works; treated timber inserts in top and bottom chords; full depth end seatings for bolting to supporting structure										
200mm deep, 8.2 kg/m	30.97	2.50	31.74	-	-	-	-	31.74	m	34.91
250mm deep, 8.5 kg/m	30.97	2.50	31.74	-	-	-	-	31.74	m	34.91
300mm deep, 10.7 kg/m	34.06	2.50	34.91	-	-	-	-	34.91	m	38.41
350mm deep, 11.6 kg/m	37.16	2.50	38.09	-	-	-	-	38.09	m	41.90
350mm deep, 12.8 kg/m	52.64	2.50	53.96	-	-	-	-	53.96	m	59.35
Steel Metsec short span lattice joists primed at works; treated timber inserts in top and bottom chords; full depth end seatings for bolting to supporting structure										
200mm deep, 8.2 kg/m	30.97	2.50	31.74	-	-	-	-	31.74	m	34.91
250mm deep, 8.5 kg/m	30.97	2.50	31.74	-	-	-	-	31.74	m	34.91
300mm deep, 10.7 kg/m	34.06	2.50	34.91	-	-	-	-	34.91	m	38.41
350mm deep, 11.6 kg/m	37.16	2.50	38.09	-	-	-	-	38.09	m	41.90
350mm deep, 12.8 kg/m	52.64	2.50	53.96	-	-	-	-	53.96	m	59.35
Steel Metsec intermediate span lattice joists primed at works; treated timber inserts in top and bottom chords; full depth end seatings for bolting to supporting structure										
450mm deep, 12.2 kg/m	55.74	2.50	57.13	-	-	-	-	57.13	m	62.85
500mm deep, 15.8 kg/m	58.84	2.50	60.31	-	-	-	-	60.31	m	66.34
550mm deep, 19.4 kg/m	61.93	2.50	63.48	-	-	-	-	63.48	m	69.83
600mm deep, 22.5 kg/m	86.71	2.50	88.87	-	-	-	-	88.87	m	97.76
650mm deep, 29.7 kg/m	89.80	2.50	92.05	-	-	-	-	92.05	m	101.25

Labour hourly rates: (except Specialists) Craft Operatives 20.87 Labourer 15.57 Rates are national average prices. Refer to REGIONAL VARIATIONS for indicative levels of overall pricing in regions	MATERIALS			LABOUR				RATES		
	Del to Site £	Waste %	Material Cost £	Craft Optve Hrs	Lab Hrs	Labour Cost £	Sunds £	Nett Rate £	Unit	Gross rate (10%) £
STRUCTURAL STEELWORK (Cont'd)										
Isolated structural members, fabrication (Cont'd)										
Steel Metsec intermediate span lattice joists primed at works; treated timber inserts in top and bottom chords; full depth end seatings for bolting to supporting structure										
450mm deep, 12.2 kg/m	55.74	2.50	57.13	-	-	-	-	57.13	m	62.85
500mm deep, 15.8 kg/m	58.84	2.50	60.31	-	-	-	-	60.31	m	66.34
550mm deep, 19.4 kg/m	61.93	2.50	63.48	-	-	-	-	63.48	m	69.83
600mm deep, 22.5 kg/m	86.71	2.50	88.87	-	-	-	-	88.87	m	97.76
650mm deep, 29.7 kg/m	89.80	2.50	92.05	-	-	-	-	92.05	m	101.25
Steel Metsec long span lattice joists primed at works; treated timber inserts in top and bottom chords; full depth end seatings for bolting to supporting structure										
700mm deep, 39.2 kg/m	114.57	2.50	117.44	-	-	-	-	117.44	m	129.18
800mm deep, 44.1 kg/m	117.67	2.50	120.61	-	-	-	-	120.61	m	132.68
900mm deep, 45.3 kg/m	148.64	2.50	152.35	-	-	-	-	152.35	m	167.59
1000mm deep, 46.1 kg/m	151.74	2.50	155.53	-	-	-	-	155.53	m	171.08
1500mm deep, 54.2 kg/m	161.02	2.50	165.05	-	-	-	-	165.05	m	181.55
Steel Metsec long span lattice joists primed at works; treated timber inserts in top and bottom chords; full depth end seatings for bolting to supporting structure										
700mm deep, 39.2 kg/m	114.57	2.50	117.44	-	-	-	-	117.44	m	129.18
800mm deep, 44.1 kg/m	117.67	2.50	120.61	-	-	-	-	120.61	m	132.68
900mm deep, 45.3 kg/m	148.64	2.50	152.35	-	-	-	-	152.35	m	167.59
1000mm deep, 46.1 kg/m	151.74	2.50	155.53	-	-	-	-	155.53	m	171.08
1500mm deep, 54.2 kg/m	161.02	2.50	165.05	-	-	-	-	165.05	m	181.55
Isolated structural members, permanent erection on site										
Weldable steel, BS EN 10149 : 1996 Grade S275, hot rolled sections; various dimensions										
plain member; beam										
weight less than 25 Kg/m	-	-	-	44.12	-	920.78	-	920.78	t	1012.86
weight 25-50 Kg/m	-	-	-	41.18	-	859.43	-	859.43	t	945.37
weight 50-100 Kg/m	-	-	-	41.18	-	859.43	-	859.43	t	945.37
weight exceeding 100 Kg/m	-	-	-	36.75	-	766.97	-	766.97	t	843.67
Steel Metsec short span lattice joists primed at works; treated timber inserts in top and bottom chords; full depth end seatings for bolting to supporting structure; hoist and fix 3.00m above ground level										
Reference MB22 - 220mm deep, 10 kg/m	-	-	-	0.66	0.08	15.02	-	15.02	m	16.52
Reference MB27 - 270mm deep, 10 kg/m	-	-	-	0.68	0.09	15.59	-	15.59	m	17.15
Reference MB30 - 300mm deep, 11 kg/m	-	-	-	0.75	0.09	17.05	-	17.05	m	18.76
Reference MB35 - 350mm deep, 12 kg/m	-	-	-	0.81	0.10	18.46	-	18.46	m	20.31
Reference MD35 - 350mm deep, 17 kg/m	-	-	-	0.90	0.11	20.50	-	20.50	m	22.55
Steel Metsec short span lattice joists primed at works; treated timber inserts in top and bottom chords; full depth end seatings for bolting to supporting structure; hoist and fix 6.00m above ground level										
Reference MB22 - 220mm deep, 10 kg/m	-	-	-	0.72	0.09	16.43	-	16.43	m	18.07
Reference MB27 - 270mm deep, 10 kg/m	-	-	-	0.75	0.09	17.05	-	17.05	m	18.76
Reference MB30 - 300mm deep, 11 kg/m	-	-	-	0.82	0.10	18.67	-	18.67	m	20.54
Reference MB35 - 350mm deep, 12 kg/m	-	-	-	0.89	0.11	20.29	-	20.29	m	22.32
Reference MD35 - 350mm deep, 17 kg/m	-	-	-	0.98	0.12	22.32	-	22.32	m	24.55
Steel Metsec intermediate span lattice joists primed at works; treated timber inserts in top and bottom chords; full depth end seatings for bolting to supporting structure; hoist and fix 3.00m above ground level										
Reference MD45 - 450mm deep, 18 kg/m	-	-	-	0.85	0.11	19.45	-	19.45	m	21.40
Reference MD50 - 500mm deep, 19 kg/m	-	-	-	1.03	0.13	23.52	-	23.52	m	25.87
Reference MD55 - 550mm deep, 20 kg/m	-	-	-	1.26	0.16	28.79	-	28.79	m	31.67
Reference MG60W - 600mm deep, 28 kg/m	-	-	-	1.35	0.17	30.82	-	30.82	m	33.90
Reference MG65W - 650mm deep, 29 kg/m	-	-	-	1.78	0.22	40.57	-	40.57	m	44.63
Steel Metsec intermediate span lattice joists primed at works; treated timber inserts in top and bottom chords; full depth end seatings for bolting to supporting structure; hoist and fix 6.00m above ground level										
Reference MD45 - 450mm deep, 18 kg/m	-	-	-	0.94	0.12	21.49	-	21.49	m	23.63
Reference MD50 - 500mm deep, 19 kg/m	-	-	-	1.13	0.14	25.76	-	25.76	m	28.34
Reference MD55 - 550mm deep, 20 kg/m	-	-	-	1.39	0.17	31.66	-	31.66	m	34.82
Reference MG60W - 600mm deep, 28 kg/m	-	-	-	1.49	0.19	34.05	-	34.05	m	37.46
Reference MG65W - 650mm deep, 29 kg/m	-	-	-	1.96	0.25	44.80	-	44.80	m	49.28
Steel Metsec long span lattice joists primed at works; treated timber inserts in top and bottom chords; full depth end seatings for bolting to supporting structure; hoist and fix 3.00m above ground level										
Reference MJ70W - 700mm deep, 39 kg/m	-	-	-	1.96	0.25	44.80	-	44.80	m	49.28
Reference MJ80W - 800mm deep, 38 kg/m	-	-	-	2.21	0.28	50.48	-	50.48	m	55.53
Reference ML90W - 900mm deep, 48 kg/m	-	-	-	2.27	0.28	51.73	-	51.73	m	56.91
Reference ML100W - 1000mm deep, 48 kg/m	-	-	-	2.31	0.29	52.73	-	52.73	m	58.00
Reference MML150W - 1500mm deep, 52 kg/m	-	-	-	2.40	0.30	54.76	-	54.76	m	60.23
Steel Metsec long span lattice joists primed at works; treated timber inserts in top and bottom chords; full depth end seatings for bolting to supporting structure; hoist and fix 6.00m above ground level										
Reference MJ70W - 700mm deep, 39 kg/m	-	-	-	2.16	0.27	49.28	-	49.28	m	54.21
Reference MJ80W - 800mm deep, 38 kg/m	-	-	-	2.43	0.30	55.39	-	55.39	m	60.92

Labour hourly rates: (except Specialists) Craft Operatives 20.87 Labourer 15.57 Rates are national average prices. Refer to REGIONAL VARIATIONS for indicative levels of overall pricing in regions	MATERIALS			LABOUR				RATES		
	Del to Site £	Waste %	Material Cost £	Craft Optve Hrs	Lab Hrs	Labour Cost £	Sunds £	Nett Rate £	Unit	Gross rate (10%) £
STRUCTURAL STEELWORK (Cont'd)										
Isolated structural members, permanent erection on site (Cont'd)										
Steel Metsec long span lattice joists primed at works; treated timber inserts in top and bottom chords; full depth end seatings for bolting to supporting structure; hoist and fix 6.00m above ground level (Cont'd)										
Reference ML90W - 900mm deep, 48 kg/m	-	-	-	2.50	0.31	57.00	-	57.00	m	62.70
Reference ML100W - 1000mm deep, 48 kg/m	-	-	-	2.54	0.32	57.99	-	57.99	m	63.79
Reference MML150W - 1500mm deep, 52 kg/m	-	-	-	2.64	0.33	60.23	-	60.23	m	66.26
Allowance for fittings										
To framed members										
Components for jointing members including brackets, supports and the like	945.00	-	945.00	23.00	-	480.01	-	1425.01	t	1567.51
To isolated members										
Components for jointing members including brackets, supports and the like	1400.00	-	1400.00	44.12	-	920.78	-	2320.78	t	2552.86
Cold rolled purlins, cladding rails and the like; Zed purlins and cladding rails; Metsec, galvanised steel										
Purlins and cladding rails; sleeved system (section only); fixing to cleats on frame members at 6000mm centres; hoist and fix 3.00m above ground level; fixing with bolts										
reference 14214; 3.03 kg/m	31.68	2.50	32.47	0.20	0.03	4.64	-	37.11	m	40.82
reference 14216; 3.47 kg/m	35.76	2.50	36.66	0.20	0.03	4.64	-	41.30	m	45.43
reference 17214; 3.66 kg/m	37.47	2.50	38.40	0.25	0.03	5.68	-	44.09	m	48.49
reference 17216; 4.11 kg/m	42.59	2.50	43.65	0.25	0.03	5.68	-	49.34	m	54.27
reference 20216; 4.49 kg/m	46.49	2.50	47.65	0.30	0.04	6.88	-	54.54	m	59.99
reference 20218; 5.03 kg/m	52.45	2.50	53.76	0.30	0.04	6.88	-	60.64	m	66.71
reference 20220; 5.57 kg/m	57.81	2.50	59.26	0.30	0.04	6.88	-	66.14	m	72.75
reference 23218; 5.73 kg/m	59.51	2.50	61.00	0.33	0.04	7.51	-	68.51	m	75.36
reference 23220; 6.34 kg/m	66.00	2.50	67.65	0.33	0.04	7.51	-	75.16	m	82.68
Purlins and cladding rails; sleeved system (section only); fixing to cleats on frame members at 6000mm centres; hoist and fix 6.00m above ground level; fixing with bolts										
reference 14214; 3.03 kg/m	31.68	2.50	32.47	0.22	0.03	5.06	-	37.53	m	41.28
reference 14216; 3.47 kg/m	35.76	2.50	36.66	0.22	0.03	5.06	-	41.71	m	45.88
reference 17214; 3.66 kg/m	37.47	2.50	38.40	0.28	0.04	6.47	-	44.87	m	49.35
reference 17216; 4.11 kg/m	42.59	2.50	43.65	0.28	0.04	6.47	-	50.12	m	55.13
reference 20216; 4.49 kg/m	46.49	2.50	47.65	0.33	0.04	7.51	-	55.16	m	60.68
reference 20218; 5.03 kg/m	52.45	2.50	53.76	0.33	0.04	7.51	-	61.27	m	67.39
reference 20220; 5.57 kg/m	57.81	2.50	59.26	0.33	0.04	7.51	-	66.77	m	73.44
reference 23218; 5.73 kg/m	59.51	2.50	61.00	0.36	0.05	8.29	-	69.29	m	76.22
reference 23220; 6.34 kg/m	66.00	2.50	67.65	0.36	0.05	8.29	-	75.94	m	83.54
Purlins and cladding rails; Side rail sleeved system (section only); fixing to cleats on stanchions at 6000mm centres; hoist and fix 3.00m above ground level; fixing with bolts										
reference 14214; 3.03 kg/m	30.75	2.50	31.52	0.20	0.03	4.64	-	36.16	m	39.78
reference 14216; 3.47 kg/m	34.72	2.50	35.59	0.20	0.03	4.64	-	40.23	m	44.25
reference 17215; 3.85 kg/m	36.37	2.50	37.28	0.25	0.03	5.68	-	42.97	m	47.26
reference 17216; 4.11 kg/m	41.35	2.50	42.38	0.25	0.03	5.68	-	48.07	m	52.87
reference 20216; 4.49 kg/m	45.14	2.50	46.26	0.30	0.04	6.88	-	53.15	m	58.46
reference 20218; 5.03 kg/m	50.92	2.50	52.19	0.30	0.04	6.88	-	59.07	m	64.98
reference 20220; 5.57 kg/m	56.13	2.50	57.53	0.30	0.04	6.88	-	64.41	m	70.85
reference 23218; 5.73 kg/m	57.78	2.50	59.22	0.33	0.04	7.51	-	66.73	m	73.41
reference 23223; 7.26 kg/m	64.08	2.50	65.68	0.33	0.04	7.51	-	73.19	m	80.51
Purlins and cladding rails; Side rail sleeved system (section only); fixing to cleats on stanchions at 6000mm centres; hoist and fix 6.00m above ground level; fixing with bolts										
reference 14214; 3.03 kg/m	30.75	2.50	31.52	0.22	0.03	5.06	-	36.58	m	40.24
reference 14216; 3.47 kg/m	34.72	2.50	35.59	0.22	0.03	5.06	-	40.65	m	44.71
reference 17215; 3.85 kg/m	36.37	2.50	37.28	0.28	0.04	6.47	-	43.75	m	48.12
reference 17216; 4.11 kg/m	41.35	2.50	42.38	0.28	0.04	6.47	-	48.85	m	53.73
reference 20216; 4.49 kg/m	45.14	2.50	46.26	0.33	0.04	7.51	-	53.77	m	59.15
reference 20218; 5.03 kg/m	50.92	2.50	52.19	0.33	0.04	7.51	-	59.70	m	65.67
reference 20220; 5.57 kg/m	56.13	2.50	57.53	0.33	0.04	7.51	-	65.04	m	71.54
reference 23218; 5.73 kg/m	57.78	2.50	59.22	0.36	0.05	8.29	-	67.52	m	74.27
reference 23223; 7.26 kg/m	64.08	2.50	65.68	0.36	0.05	8.29	-	73.97	m	81.37
Sag rods; Round-lok anti-sag rods; to purlins										
purlins at 1150mm centres	10.83	2.50	11.10	0.25	0.03	5.68	-	16.78	nr	18.46
purlins at 1350mm centres	12.56	2.50	12.88	0.25	0.03	5.68	-	18.56	nr	20.42
purlins at 1550mm centres	14.19	2.50	14.55	0.33	0.04	7.51	-	22.06	nr	24.26
purlins at 1700mm centres	16.00	2.50	16.40	0.33	0.04	7.51	-	23.91	nr	26.30
purlins at 1950mm centres	16.48	2.50	16.89	0.33	0.04	7.51	-	24.40	nr	26.84
Other; Black metal purlin cleats; weld on										
Reference 142 for 142mm deep purlins	10.74	2.50	11.01	-	-	-	-	11.01	nr	12.11
Reference 172 for 172mm deep purlins	12.69	2.50	13.01	-	-	-	-	13.01	nr	14.31
Reference 202 for 202mm deep purlins	13.35	2.50	13.68	-	-	-	-	13.68	nr	15.05
Reference 232 for 232mm deep purlins	14.70	2.50	15.06	-	-	-	-	15.06	nr	16.57
Reference 262 for 262mm deep purlins	16.08	2.50	16.48	-	-	-	-	16.48	nr	18.13
Other; Black metal side rail cleats; weld on										
Reference 142 for 142mm wide rails	10.74	2.50	11.01	-	-	-	-	11.01	nr	12.11
Reference 172 for 172mm wide rails	12.69	2.50	13.01	-	-	-	-	13.01	nr	14.31
Reference 202 for 202mm wide rails	13.35	2.50	13.68	-	-	-	-	13.68	nr	15.05
Reference 232 for 232mm wide rails	14.70	2.50	15.06	-	-	-	-	15.06	nr	16.57

Labour hourly rates: (except Specialists) Craft Operatives 20.87 Labourer 15.57 Rates are national average prices. Refer to REGIONAL VARIATIONS for indicative levels of overall pricing in regions	MATERIALS			LABOUR				RATES		
	Del to Site £	Waste %	Material Cost £	Craft Optve Hrs	Lab Hrs	Labour Cost £	Sunds £	Nett Rate £	Unit	Gross rate (10%) £
STRUCTURAL STEELWORK (Cont'd)										
Cold rolled purlins, cladding rails and the like; Zed purlins and cladding rails; Metsec, galvanised steel (Cont'd)										
Other; Galvanised side rail supports; 122-262 series; weld on										
rail 1000mm long	31.61	2.50	32.40	0.35	0.04	7.93	-	40.33	nr	44.36
rail 1400mm long	34.49	2.50	35.35	0.35	0.04	7.93	-	43.27	nr	47.60
rail 1600mm long	38.25	2.50	39.21	0.45	0.06	10.33	-	49.53	nr	54.49
rail 1800mm long	46.06	2.50	47.21	0.45	0.06	10.33	-	57.54	nr	63.29
Other; Diagonal tie wire ropes (assembled with end brackets); bolt on										
1700mm long	61.66	2.50	63.20	0.30	0.04	6.88	-	70.09	nr	77.10
2200mm long	68.99	2.50	70.72	0.30	0.04	6.88	-	77.60	nr	85.36
2600mm long	76.32	2.50	78.23	0.40	0.05	9.13	-	87.36	nr	96.10
3600mm long	94.24	2.50	96.59	0.40	0.05	9.13	-	105.72	nr	116.29
Metal decking; Galvanised steel troughed decking; 0.7mm thick metal, 35mm overall depth; natural soffit and top surface; 150mm end laps and one corrugation side laps										
Decking; fixed to steel rails at 1200mm centres with self tapping screws; drilling holes										
sloping; 10 degrees pitch	-	-	Specialist	-	-	Specialist	-	53.23	m²	58.56
Extra over decking for										
raking cutting	-	-	Specialist	-	-	Specialist	-	8.99	m	9.89
holes 50mm diameter; formed on site	-	-	Specialist	-	-	Specialist	-	24.85	nr	27.33
Metal decking; Galvanised steel troughed decking; 0.7mm thick metal, 48mm overall depth; natural soffit and top surface; 150mm end laps and one corrugation side laps										
Decking; fixed to steel rails at 1500mm centres with self tapping screws; drilling holes										
sloping; 10 degrees pitch	-	-	Specialist	-	-	Specialist	-	53.23	m²	58.56
Extra over decking for										
raking cutting	-	-	Specialist	-	-	Specialist	-	8.99	m	9.89
holes 50mm diameter; formed on site	-	-	Specialist	-	-	Specialist	-	24.85	nr	27.33
Metal decking; Galvanised steel troughed decking; 0.7mm thick metal, 63mm overall depth; natural soffit and top surface; 150mm end laps and one corrugation side laps										
Decking; fixed to steel rails at 2000mm centres with self tapping screws; drilling holes										
sloping; 10 degrees pitch	-	-	Specialist	-	-	Specialist	-	56.84	m²	62.52
Extra over decking for										
raking cutting	-	-	Specialist	-	-	Specialist	-	8.99	m	9.89
holes 50mm diameter; formed on site	-	-	Specialist	-	-	Specialist	-	24.85	nr	27.33
Metal decking; Galvanised steel troughed decking; 0.7mm thick metal, 100mm overall depth; natural soffit and top surface; 150mm end laps and one corrugation side laps										
Decking; fixed to steel rails at 3500mm centres with self tapping screws; drilling holes										
sloping; 10 degrees pitch	-	-	Specialist	-	-	Specialist	-	60.12	m²	66.13
Extra over decking for										
raking cutting	-	-	Specialist	-	-	Specialist	-	8.99	m	9.89
holes 50mm diameter; formed on site	-	-	Specialist	-	-	Specialist	-	24.85	nr	27.33
Metal decking; Galvanised steel troughed decking; 0.9mm thick metal, 35mm overall depth; natural soffit and top surface; 150mm end laps and one corrugation side laps										
Decking; fixed to steel rails at 1500mm centres with self tapping screws; drilling holes										
sloping; 10 degrees pitch	-	-	Specialist	-	-	Specialist	-	59.87	m²	65.86
Extra over decking for										
raking cutting	-	-	Specialist	-	-	Specialist	-	8.99	m	9.89
holes 50mm diameter; formed on site	-	-	Specialist	-	-	Specialist	-	24.85	nr	27.33
Metal decking; Galvanised steel troughed decking; 0.9mm thick metal, 48mm overall depth; natural soffit and top surface; 150mm end laps and one corrugation side laps										
Decking; fixing to steel rails at 2000mm centres with self tapping screws; drilling holes										
sloping; 10 degrees pitch	-	-	Specialist	-	-	Specialist	-	59.92	m²	65.91
Extra over decking for										
raking cutting	-	-	Specialist	-	-	Specialist	-	8.99	m	9.89
holes 50mm diameter; formed on site	-	-	Specialist	-	-	Specialist	-	24.85	nr	27.33
Metal decking; Galvanised steel troughed decking; 0.9mm thick metal, 63mm overall depth; natural soffit and top surface; 150mm end laps and one corrugation side laps										
Decking; fixing to steel rails at 2500mm centres with self tapping screws; drilling holes										
sloping; 10 degrees pitch	-	-	Specialist	-	-	Specialist	-	64.11	m²	70.52
Extra over decking for										
raking cutting	-	-	Specialist	-	-	Specialist	-	8.99	m	9.89
holes 50mm diameter; formed on site	-	-	Specialist	-	-	Specialist	-	24.85	nr	27.33

Labour hourly rates: (except Specialists) Craft Operatives 20.87 Labourer 15.57 Rates are national average prices. Refer to REGIONAL VARIATIONS for indicative levels of overall pricing in regions	MATERIALS			LABOUR				RATES		
	Del to Site £	Waste %	Material Cost £	Craft Optve Hrs	Lab Hrs	Labour Cost £	Sunds £	Nett Rate £	Unit	Gross rate (10%) £
STRUCTURAL STEELWORK (Cont'd)										
Metal decking; Galvanised steel troughed decking; 0.9mm thick metal, 100mm overall depth; natural soffit and top surface; 150mm end laps and one corrugation side laps										
Decking; fixing to steel rails at 4000mm centres with self tapping screws; drilling holes										
sloping; 10 degrees pitch	-	-	Specialist	-	-	Specialist	-	67.21	m²	73.93
Extra over decking for										
raking cutting	-	-	Specialist	-	-	Specialist	-	8.99	m	9.89
holes 50mm diameter; formed on site	-	-	Specialist	-	-	Specialist	-	24.85	nr	27.33
Metal decking; Galvanised steel troughed decking; 1.2mm thick metal, 35mm overall depth; natural soffit and top surface; 150mm end laps and one corrugation side laps										
Decking; fixing to steel rails at 2000mm centres with self tapping screws; drilling holes										
sloping; 10 degrees pitch	-	-	Specialist	-	-	Specialist	-	67.40	m²	74.14
Extra over decking for										
raking cutting	-	-	Specialist	-	-	Specialist	-	8.99	m	9.89
holes 50mm diameter; formed on site	-	-	Specialist	-	-	Specialist	-	24.85	nr	27.33
Metal decking; Galvanised steel troughed decking; 1.2mm thick metal, 48mm overall depth; natural soffit and top surface; 150mm end laps and one corrugation side laps										
Decking; fixing to steel rails at 2500mm centres with self tapping screws; drilling holes										
sloping; 10 degrees pitch	-	-	Specialist	-	-	Specialist	-	67.40	m²	74.14
Extra over decking for										
raking cutting	-	-	Specialist	-	-	Specialist	-	8.99	m	9.89
holes 50mm diameter; formed on site	-	-	Specialist	-	-	Specialist	-	24.85	nr	27.33
Metal decking; Galvanised steel troughed decking; 1.2mm thick metal, 63mm overall depth; natural soffit and top surface; 150mm end laps and one corrugation side laps										
Decking; fixing to steel rails at 3000mm centres with self tapping screws; drilling holes										
sloping; 10 degrees pitch	-	-	Specialist	-	-	Specialist	-	71.22	m²	78.34
Extra over decking for										
raking cutting	-	-	Specialist	-	-	Specialist	-	8.99	m	9.89
holes 50mm diameter; formed on site	-	-	Specialist	-	-	Specialist	-	24.85	nr	27.33
Metal decking; Galvanised steel troughed decking; 1.2mm thick metal, 100mm overall depth; natural soffit and top surface; 150mm end laps and one corrugation side laps										
Decking; fixing to steel rails at 4500mm centres with self tapping screws; drilling holes										
sloping; 10 degrees pitch	-	-	Specialist	-	-	Specialist	-	77.14	m²	84.86
Extra over decking for										
raking cutting	-	-	Specialist	-	-	Specialist	-	8.99	m	9.89
holes 50mm diameter; formed on site	-	-	Specialist	-	-	Specialist	-	24.85	nr	27.33
Holding down bolts or assemblies; mild steel; supply only										
rag or indented bolts; M 10 with nuts and washers										
100mm long	1.48	5.00	1.55	-	-	-	-	1.55	nr	1.71
160mm long	1.54	5.00	1.62	-	-	-	-	1.62	nr	1.78
rag or indented bolts; M 12 with nuts and washers										
100mm long	1.60	5.00	1.68	-	-	-	-	1.68	nr	1.85
160mm long	1.76	5.00	1.85	-	-	-	-	1.85	nr	2.03
200mm long	1.98	5.00	2.08	-	-	-	-	2.08	nr	2.29
rag or indented bolts; M 16 with nuts and washers										
120mm long	2.29	5.00	2.40	-	-	-	-	2.40	nr	2.64
160mm long	2.62	5.00	2.75	-	-	-	-	2.75	nr	3.03
200mm long	3.06	5.00	3.21	-	-	-	-	3.21	nr	3.53
holding down bolt assembly; M 20 bolt with 100 x 100 x 10mm plate washer tack welded to head; with nuts and washers										
300mm long	2.70	5.00	2.84	-	-	-	-	2.84	nr	3.12
350mm long	3.36	5.00	3.53	-	-	-	-	3.53	nr	3.88
450mm long	4.21	5.00	4.42	-	-	-	-	4.42	nr	4.86
Special bolts; Black bolts; BS 4190 grade 4.6; galvanised										
M 8; with nuts and washers										
50mm long	0.15	5.00	0.16	0.07	-	1.46	-	1.62	nr	1.78
60mm long	0.17	5.00	0.18	0.07	-	1.46	-	1.64	nr	1.80
70mm long	0.18	5.00	0.19	0.08	-	1.67	-	1.86	nr	2.04
80mm long	0.20	5.00	0.21	0.08	-	1.67	-	1.88	nr	2.07
M 10; with nuts and washers										
40mm long	0.29	5.00	0.31	0.07	-	1.46	-	1.77	nr	1.94
50mm long	0.33	5.00	0.35	0.07	-	1.46	-	1.81	nr	1.99
60mm long	0.37	5.00	0.39	0.07	-	1.46	-	1.85	nr	2.03
70mm long	0.41	5.00	0.43	0.08	-	1.67	-	2.10	nr	2.31
80mm long	0.44	5.00	0.47	0.08	-	1.67	-	2.14	nr	2.35
90mm long	0.49	5.00	0.51	0.08	-	1.67	-	2.18	nr	2.40
100mm long	0.53	5.00	0.55	0.08	-	1.67	-	2.22	nr	2.45
120mm long	0.62	5.00	0.65	0.09	-	1.88	-	2.53	nr	2.78
140mm long	0.71	5.00	0.75	0.10	-	2.09	-	2.83	nr	3.12
150mm long	0.75	5.00	0.79	0.12	-	2.50	-	3.30	nr	3.63

Labour hourly rates: (except Specialists) Craft Operatives 20.87 Labourer 15.57 Rates are national average prices. Refer to REGIONAL VARIATIONS for indicative levels of overall pricing in regions	MATERIALS			LABOUR				RATES		
	Del to Site £	Waste %	Material Cost £	Craft Optve Hrs	Lab Hrs	Labour Cost £	Sunds £	Nett Rate £	Unit	Gross rate (10%) £
STRUCTURAL STEELWORK (Cont'd)										
Special bolts; Black bolts; BS 4190 grade 4.6; galvanised (Cont'd)										
M 12; with nuts and washers										
40mm long	0.26	5.00	0.28	0.08	-	1.67	-	1.94	nr	2.14
50mm long	0.36	5.00	0.38	0.08	-	1.67	-	2.05	nr	2.25
60mm long	0.42	5.00	0.44	0.08	-	1.67	-	2.11	nr	2.32
70mm long	0.62	5.00	0.65	0.08	-	1.67	-	2.32	nr	2.55
80mm long	0.68	5.00	0.71	0.08	-	1.67	-	2.38	nr	2.62
90mm long	0.73	5.00	0.77	0.08	-	1.67	-	2.44	nr	2.68
100mm long	0.79	5.00	0.83	0.09	-	1.88	-	2.71	nr	2.98
120mm long	0.90	5.00	0.95	0.09	-	1.88	-	2.83	nr	3.11
140mm long	1.02	5.00	1.07	0.12	-	2.50	-	3.57	nr	3.93
150mm long	1.07	5.00	1.13	0.12	-	2.50	-	3.63	nr	3.99
160mm long	1.13	5.00	1.19	0.12	-	2.50	-	3.69	nr	4.06
180mm long	1.24	5.00	1.31	0.13	-	2.71	-	4.02	nr	4.42
200mm long	1.36	5.00	1.43	0.14	-	2.92	-	4.35	nr	4.78
220mm long	2.24	5.00	2.35	0.15	-	3.13	-	5.48	nr	6.03
240mm long	2.48	5.00	2.61	0.16	-	3.34	-	5.95	nr	6.54
260mm long	2.24	5.00	2.35	0.17	-	3.55	-	5.90	nr	6.49
300mm long	3.94	5.00	4.14	0.20	-	4.17	-	8.31	nr	9.14
M 16; with nuts and washers										
50mm long	0.67	5.00	0.70	0.08	-	1.67	-	2.37	nr	2.61
60mm long	0.73	5.00	0.76	0.08	-	1.67	-	2.43	nr	2.68
70mm long	0.87	5.00	0.91	0.08	-	1.67	-	2.58	nr	2.84
80mm long	0.95	5.00	1.00	0.09	-	1.88	-	2.88	nr	3.17
90mm long	1.09	5.00	1.15	0.09	-	1.88	-	3.02	nr	3.33
100mm long	1.33	5.00	1.39	0.10	-	2.09	-	3.48	nr	3.83
120mm long	1.59	5.00	1.67	0.10	-	2.09	-	3.76	nr	4.13
140mm long	1.72	5.00	1.81	0.12	-	2.50	-	4.31	nr	4.74
150mm long	1.82	5.00	1.91	0.13	-	2.71	-	4.62	nr	5.08
160mm long	1.70	5.00	1.78	0.14	-	2.92	-	4.70	nr	5.17
180mm long	2.22	5.00	2.33	0.14	-	2.92	-	5.25	nr	5.78
200mm long	2.46	5.00	2.58	0.15	-	3.13	-	5.71	nr	6.28
220mm long	3.00	5.00	3.15	0.15	-	3.13	-	6.28	nr	6.91
M 20; with nuts and washers										
60mm long	1.13	5.00	1.19	0.08	-	1.67	-	2.86	nr	3.15
70mm long	1.22	5.00	1.29	0.08	-	1.67	-	2.95	nr	3.25
80mm long	1.28	5.00	1.35	0.09	-	1.88	-	3.22	nr	3.55
90mm long	1.63	5.00	1.71	0.10	-	2.09	-	3.80	nr	4.18
100mm long	1.45	5.00	1.52	0.10	-	2.09	-	3.61	nr	3.97
140mm long	2.60	5.00	2.73	0.13	-	2.71	-	5.44	nr	5.99
150mm long	2.98	5.00	3.13	0.14	-	2.92	-	6.06	nr	6.66
180mm long	3.63	5.00	3.81	0.15	-	3.13	-	6.94	nr	7.64
200mm long	4.11	5.00	4.32	0.16	-	3.34	-	7.65	nr	8.42
220mm long	4.80	5.00	5.04	0.17	-	3.55	-	8.59	nr	9.45
240mm long	5.56	5.00	5.83	0.18	-	3.76	-	9.59	nr	10.55
260mm long	6.02	5.00	6.32	0.20	-	4.17	-	10.49	nr	11.54
300mm long	6.83	5.00	7.18	0.23	-	4.80	-	11.98	nr	13.17
M 24; with nuts and washers										
70mm long	2.67	5.00	2.80	0.10	-	2.09	-	4.89	nr	5.38
80mm long	1.37	5.00	1.44	0.10	-	2.09	-	3.52	nr	3.87
90mm long	1.63	5.00	1.71	0.12	-	2.50	-	4.22	nr	4.64
100mm long	1.67	5.00	1.76	0.12	-	2.50	-	4.26	nr	4.69
130mm long	3.99	5.00	4.19	0.13	-	2.71	-	6.90	nr	7.60
150mm long	4.71	5.00	4.94	0.15	-	3.13	-	8.07	nr	8.88
180mm long	5.41	5.00	5.68	0.15	-	3.13	-	8.81	nr	9.69
200mm long	5.83	5.00	6.12	0.16	-	3.34	-	9.46	nr	10.41
M 30; with nuts and washers										
110mm long	6.33	5.00	6.65	0.17	-	3.55	-	10.20	nr	11.22
140mm long	6.71	5.00	7.04	0.18	-	3.76	-	10.80	nr	11.88
200mm long	8.53	5.00	8.96	0.21	-	4.38	-	13.34	nr	14.67
Special bolts; High strength friction grip bolts; BS 14399 Part 1 - general grade										
M 16; with nuts and washers										
50mm long	0.90	5.00	0.94	0.09	-	1.88	-	2.82	nr	3.11
60mm long	1.08	5.00	1.13	0.09	-	1.88	-	3.01	nr	3.31
75mm long	1.44	5.00	1.51	0.10	-	2.09	-	3.60	nr	3.96
80mm long	1.44	5.00	1.51	0.10	-	2.09	-	3.60	nr	3.96
90mm long	1.62	5.00	1.70	0.12	-	2.50	-	4.21	nr	4.63
M 20; with nuts and washers										
60mm long	1.62	5.00	1.70	0.09	-	1.88	-	3.58	nr	3.94
70mm long	1.89	5.00	1.98	0.10	-	2.09	-	4.07	nr	4.48
80mm long	2.16	5.00	2.27	0.10	-	2.09	-	4.36	nr	4.79
90mm long	2.43	5.00	2.55	0.12	-	2.50	-	5.06	nr	5.56
M 24; with nuts and washers										
65mm long	2.34	5.00	2.46	0.13	-	2.71	-	5.17	nr	5.69
80mm long	2.88	5.00	3.02	0.13	-	2.71	-	5.74	nr	6.31
90mm long	3.24	5.00	3.40	0.14	-	2.92	-	6.32	nr	6.96
100mm long	3.60	5.00	3.78	0.14	-	2.92	-	6.70	nr	7.37
120mm long	3.96	5.00	4.16	0.16	-	3.34	-	7.50	nr	8.25
140mm long	4.68	5.00	4.91	0.17	-	3.55	-	8.46	nr	9.31
Surface treatment; Off site at works										
Note notwithstanding the requirement of NRM to measure painting on structural steelwork in m², painting off site has been given in tonnes of structural steelwork in accordance with normal steelwork contractors practice										
Blast cleaning										
surfaces of steelwork	-	-	Specialist	-	-	Specialist	-	124.97	t	137.47

Labour hourly rates: (except Specialists) Craft Operatives 20.87 Labourer 15.57 Rates are national average prices. Refer to REGIONAL VARIATIONS for indicative levels of overall pricing in regions	MATERIALS			LABOUR				RATES		
	Del to Site £	Waste %	Material Cost £	Craft Optve Hrs	Lab Hrs	Labour Cost £	Sunds £	Nett Rate £	Unit	Gross rate (10%) £
STRUCTURAL STEELWORK (Cont'd)										
Surface treatment; Off site at works (Cont'd)										
One coat micaceous oxide primer, 75 microns										
surfaces of steelwork	-	-	Specialist	-	-	Specialist	-	139.58	t	153.54
Two coats micaceous oxide primer, 150 microns										
surfaces of steelwork	-	-	Specialist	-	-	Specialist	-	259.68	t	285.65
STRUCTURAL ALUMINIUM WORK										
Metal decking; Aluminium troughed decking; 0.9mm thick metal 35mm overall depth; natural soffit and top surface; 150mm end laps and one corrugation side laps										
Decking; fixing to steel rails at 900mm centres with self tapping screws; drilling holes										
sloping; 10 degrees pitch	-	-	Specialist	-	-	Specialist	-	67.31	m²	74.04
Extra over decking for										
raking cutting	-	-	Specialist	-	-	Specialist	-	8.99	m	9.89
holes 50mm diameter; formed on site	-	-	Specialist	-	-	Specialist	-	24.85	nr	27.33
Metal decking; Aluminium troughed decking; 0.9mm thick metal, 48mm overall depth; natural soffit and top surface; 150mm end laps and one corrugation side laps										
Decking; fixing to steel rails at 1200mm centres with self tapping screws; drilling holes										
sloping; 10 degrees pitch	-	-	Specialist	-	-	Specialist	-	67.31	m²	74.04
Extra over decking for										
raking cutting	-	-	Specialist	-	-	Specialist	-	8.99	m	9.89
holes 50mm diameter; formed on site	-	-	Specialist	-	-	Specialist	-	24.85	nr	27.33
Metal decking; Aluminium troughed decking; 0.9mm thick metal, 63mm overall depth; natural soffit and top surface; 150mm end laps and one corrugation side laps										
Decking; fixing to steel rails at 1500mm centres with self tapping screws; drilling holes										
sloping; 10 degrees pitch	-	-	Specialist	-	-	Specialist	-	72.14	m²	79.36
Extra over decking for										
raking cutting	-	-	Specialist	-	-	Specialist	-	8.99	m	9.89
holes 50mm diameter; formed on site	-	-	Specialist	-	-	Specialist	-	24.85	nr	27.33
Metal decking; Aluminium troughed decking; 0.9mm thick metal, 100mm overall depth; natural soffit and top surface; 150mm end laps and one corrugation side laps										
Decking; fixing to steel rails at 2900mm centres with self tapping screws; drilling holes										
sloping; 10 degrees pitch	-	-	Specialist	-	-	Specialist	-	77.30	m²	85.03
Extra over decking for										
raking cutting	-	-	Specialist	-	-	Specialist	-	8.99	m	9.89
holes 50mm diameter; formed on site	-	-	Specialist	-	-	Specialist	-	24.85	nr	27.33
Metal decking; Aluminium troughed decking; 1.2mm thick metal, 35mm overall depth; natural soffit and top surface; 150mm end laps and one corrugation side laps										
Decking; fixing to steel rails at 1200mm centres with self tapping screws; drilling holes										
sloping; 10 degrees pitch	-	-	Specialist	-	-	Specialist	-	74.46	m²	81.91
Extra over decking for										
raking cutting	-	-	Specialist	-	-	Specialist	-	8.99	m	9.89
holes 50mm diameter; formed on site	-	-	Specialist	-	-	Specialist	-	24.85	nr	27.33
Metal decking; Aluminium troughed decking; 1.2mm thick metal, 48mm overall depth; natural soffit and top surface; 150mm end laps and one corrugation side laps										
Decking; fixing to steel rails at 1700mm centres with self tapping screws; drilling holes										
sloping; 10 degrees pitch	-	-	Specialist	-	-	Specialist	-	74.46	m²	81.91
Extra over decking for										
raking cutting	-	-	Specialist	-	-	Specialist	-	8.99	m	9.89
holes 50mm diameter; formed on site	-	-	Specialist	-	-	Specialist	-	24.85	nr	27.33
Metal decking; Aluminium troughed decking; 1.2mm thick metal, 63mm overall depth; natural soffit and top surface; 150mm end laps and one corrugation side laps										
Decking; fixing to steel rails at 2000mm centres with self tapping screws; drilling holes										
sloping; 10 degrees pitch	-	-	Specialist	-	-	Specialist	-	80.13	m²	88.14
Extra over decking for										
raking cutting	-	-	Specialist	-	-	Specialist	-	8.99	m	9.89
holes 50mm diameter; formed on site	-	-	Specialist	-	-	Specialist	-	24.85	nr	27.33

Labour hourly rates: (except Specialists) Craft Operatives 20.87 Labourer 15.57 Rates are national average prices. Refer to REGIONAL VARIATIONS for indicative levels of overall pricing in regions	MATERIALS			LABOUR				RATES		
	Del to Site £	Waste %	Material Cost £	Craft Optve Hrs	Lab Hrs	Labour Cost £	Sunds £	Nett Rate £	Unit	Gross rate (10%) £
STRUCTURAL ALUMINIUM WORK (Cont'd)										
Metal decking; Aluminium troughed decking; 1.2mm thick metal, 100mm overall depth; natural soffit and top surface; 150mm end laps and one corrugation side laps										
Decking; fixing to steel rails at 3000mm centres with self tapping screws; drilling holes										
sloping; 10 degrees pitch	-	-	Specialist	-	-	Specialist	-	86.68	m²	95.35
Extra over decking for										
raking cutting	-	-	Specialist	-	-	Specialist	-	8.99	m	9.89
holes 50mm diameter; formed on site	-	-	Specialist	-	-	Specialist	-	24.85	nr	27.33

This page left blank intentionally

Labour hourly rates: (except Specialists) Craft Operatives 20.87 Labourer 15.57 Rates are national average prices. Refer to REGIONAL VARIATIONS for indicative levels of overall pricing in regions	MATERIALS			LABOUR				RATES		
	Del to Site £	Waste %	Material Cost £	Craft Optve Hrs	Lab Hrs	Labour Cost £	Sunds £	Nett Rate £	Unit	Gross rate (10%) £
TIMBER FRAMING										
Engineered or prefabricated members/items										
Roof trusses; Trussed Rafters; softwood, sawn, impregnated; plated joints										
22.5 degree Standard duo pitch; 450mm overhangs; fixing with clips (included elsewhere); span over wall plates										
5000mm	35.87	2.50	36.77	1.10	0.14	25.14	9.07	70.98	nr	78.08
6000mm	42.56	2.50	43.62	1.20	0.15	27.38	9.90	80.90	nr	88.99
7000mm	47.58	2.50	48.77	1.30	0.16	29.62	10.72	89.11	nr	98.02
8000mm	59.28	2.50	60.77	1.40	0.17	31.86	11.55	104.18	nr	114.60
9000mm	75.51	2.50	77.40	1.50	0.19	34.26	12.38	124.03	nr	136.44
10000mm	90.56	2.50	92.82	1.60	0.20	36.51	13.20	142.53	nr	156.78
35 degree Standard duo pitch; 450mm overhangs; fixing with clips (included elsewhere); span over wall plates										
5000mm	38.94	2.50	39.91	1.10	0.14	25.14	9.07	74.12	nr	81.53
6000mm	45.63	2.50	46.77	1.20	0.15	27.38	9.90	84.05	nr	92.45
7000mm	50.64	2.50	51.91	1.30	0.16	29.62	10.72	92.26	nr	101.48
8000mm	72.18	2.50	73.99	1.40	0.17	31.86	11.55	117.40	nr	129.14
9000mm	80.54	2.50	82.56	1.50	0.19	34.26	12.38	129.20	nr	142.12
45 degree Standard duo pitch; 450mm overhangs; fixing with clips (included elsewhere); span over wall plates										
5000mm	43.37	2.50	44.46	1.10	0.14	25.14	9.07	78.67	nr	86.53
6000mm	56.75	2.50	58.17	1.20	0.15	27.38	9.90	95.45	nr	104.99
7000mm	71.80	2.50	73.60	1.30	0.16	29.62	10.72	113.94	nr	125.34
8000mm	103.65	2.50	106.24	1.40	0.17	31.86	11.55	149.66	nr	164.62
9000mm	118.70	2.50	121.67	1.50	0.19	34.26	12.38	168.31	nr	185.14
22.5 degree Bobtail duo pitch; 450mm overhangs; fixing with clips (included elsewhere); span over wall plates										
4000mm	40.47	2.50	41.48	1.00	0.13	22.89	8.25	72.63	nr	79.89
5000mm	48.83	2.50	50.06	1.10	0.14	25.14	9.07	84.27	nr	92.69
6000mm	60.54	2.50	62.05	1.20	0.15	27.38	9.90	99.33	nr	109.27
7000mm	73.92	2.50	75.77	1.30	0.16	29.62	10.72	116.11	nr	127.73
8000mm	85.63	2.50	87.77	1.40	0.17	31.86	11.55	131.18	nr	144.30
9000mm	97.33	2.50	99.77	1.50	0.19	34.26	12.38	146.40	nr	161.04
35 degree Bobtail duo pitch; 450mm overhangs; fixing with clips (included elsewhere); span over wall plates										
4000mm	40.90	2.50	41.93	1.00	0.13	22.89	8.25	73.07	nr	80.38
5000mm	54.28	2.50	55.64	1.10	0.14	25.14	9.07	89.85	nr	98.84
6000mm	62.64	2.50	64.21	1.20	0.15	27.38	9.90	101.49	nr	111.64
7000mm	72.68	2.50	74.49	1.30	0.16	29.62	10.72	114.84	nr	126.33
8000mm	87.73	2.50	89.92	1.40	0.17	31.86	11.55	133.34	nr	146.67
9000mm	99.43	2.50	101.92	1.50	0.19	34.26	12.38	148.56	nr	163.42
45 degree Bobtail duo pitch; 450mm overhangs; fixing with clips (included elsewhere); span over wall plates										
4000mm	36.47	2.50	37.38	1.00	0.13	22.89	8.25	68.53	nr	75.38
5000mm	53.19	2.50	54.52	1.10	0.14	25.14	9.07	88.73	nr	97.61
6000mm	69.92	2.50	71.66	1.20	0.15	27.38	9.90	108.94	nr	119.84
7000mm	89.98	2.50	92.23	1.30	0.16	29.62	10.72	132.58	nr	145.84
8000mm	120.09	2.50	123.09	1.40	0.17	31.86	11.55	166.50	nr	183.15
9000mm	128.45	2.50	131.66	1.50	0.19	34.26	12.38	178.30	nr	196.13
22.5 degree Monopitch; 450mm overhangs; fixing with clips (included elsewhere); span over wall plates										
2000mm	23.25	2.50	23.83	0.80	0.10	18.25	6.60	48.68	nr	53.55
3000mm	27.43	2.50	28.12	0.90	0.11	20.50	7.42	56.04	nr	61.64
4000mm	35.79	2.50	36.69	1.00	0.13	22.89	8.25	67.83	nr	74.62
5000mm	44.15	2.50	45.26	1.10	0.14	25.14	9.07	79.47	nr	87.42
6000mm	57.53	2.50	58.97	1.20	0.15	27.38	9.90	96.25	nr	105.88
35 degree Monopitch; 450mm overhangs; fixing with clips (included elsewhere); span over wall plates										
2000mm	28.90	2.50	29.62	0.80	0.10	18.25	6.60	54.48	nr	59.92
3000mm	37.26	2.50	38.19	0.90	0.11	20.50	7.42	66.12	nr	72.73
4000mm	43.95	2.50	45.05	1.00	0.13	22.89	8.25	76.19	nr	83.81
5000mm	53.99	2.50	55.34	1.10	0.14	25.14	9.07	89.55	nr	98.50
6000mm	69.04	2.50	70.76	1.20	0.15	27.38	9.90	108.04	nr	118.85
45 degree Monopitch; 450mm overhangs; fixing with clips (included elsewhere); span over wall plates										
2000mm	23.45	2.50	24.03	0.80	0.10	18.25	6.60	48.89	nr	53.78
3000mm	35.15	2.50	36.03	0.90	0.11	20.50	7.42	63.95	nr	70.35
4000mm	45.19	2.50	46.32	1.00	0.13	22.89	8.25	77.46	nr	85.21
22.5 degree duo pitch Girder Truss; fixing with clips (included elsewhere); span over wall plates										
5000mm	135.38	2.50	138.76	1.10	0.14	25.14	9.07	172.97	nr	190.27
6000mm	153.77	2.50	157.62	1.20	0.15	27.38	9.90	194.90	nr	214.39
7000mm	170.50	2.50	174.76	1.30	0.16	29.62	10.72	215.11	nr	236.62
8000mm	203.94	2.50	209.04	1.40	0.17	31.86	11.55	252.46	nr	277.70
9000mm	220.67	2.50	226.18	1.50	0.19	34.26	12.38	272.82	nr	300.10
10000mm	287.56	2.50	294.75	1.60	0.20	36.51	13.20	344.45	nr	378.90
35 degree duo pitch Girder Truss; fixing with clips (included elsewhere); span over wall plates										
5000mm	135.83	2.50	139.22	1.10	0.14	25.14	9.07	173.43	nr	190.78
6000mm	152.55	2.50	156.36	1.20	0.15	27.38	9.90	193.64	nr	213.01

Labour hourly rates: (except Specialists) Craft Operatives 20.87 Labourer 15.57 Rates are national average prices. Refer to REGIONAL VARIATIONS for indicative levels of overall pricing in regions	MATERIALS			LABOUR				RATES		
	Del to Site £	Waste %	Material Cost £	Craft Optve Hrs	Lab Hrs	Labour Cost £	Sunds £	Nett Rate £	Unit	Gross rate (10%) £
TIMBER FRAMING (Cont'd)										
Engineered or prefabricated members/items (Cont'd)										
Roof trusses; Trussed Rafters; softwood, sawn, impregnated; plated joints (Cont'd)										
35 degree duo pitch Girder Truss; fixing with clips (included elsewhere); span over wall plates (Cont'd)										
7000mm	172.62	2.50	176.93	1.30	0.16	29.62	10.72	217.28	nr	239.01
8000mm	206.06	2.50	211.22	1.40	0.17	31.86	11.55	254.63	nr	280.09
9000mm	236.17	2.50	242.07	1.50	0.19	34.26	12.38	288.71	nr	317.58
10000mm	286.34	2.50	293.49	1.60	0.20	36.51	13.20	343.20	nr	377.52
45 degree duo pitch Girder Truss; fixing with clips (included elsewhere); span over wall plates										
5000mm	108.87	2.50	111.59	1.10	0.14	25.14	9.07	145.80	nr	160.38
6000mm	159.04	2.50	163.02	1.20	0.15	27.38	9.90	200.30	nr	220.33
7000mm	205.87	2.50	211.01	1.30	0.16	29.62	10.72	251.36	nr	276.49
8000mm	242.66	2.50	248.72	1.40	0.17	31.86	11.55	292.14	nr	321.35
9000mm	287.81	2.50	295.00	1.50	0.19	34.26	12.38	341.64	nr	375.81
22.5 degree pitch gable ladder; 450mm overhang; span over wall plate										
5000mm	49.34	2.50	50.57	1.10	0.14	25.14	9.07	84.78	nr	93.26
6000mm	52.68	2.50	54.00	1.20	0.15	27.38	9.90	91.28	nr	100.41
7000mm	57.70	2.50	59.14	1.30	0.16	29.62	10.72	99.49	nr	109.44
8000mm	66.06	2.50	67.71	1.40	0.17	31.86	11.55	111.13	nr	122.24
9000mm	69.41	2.50	71.14	1.50	0.19	34.26	12.38	117.78	nr	129.56
10000mm	75.04	2.50	76.91	1.60	0.20	36.51	13.20	126.62	nr	139.28
35 degree pitch gable ladder; 450mm overhang; span over wall plate										
5000mm	43.47	2.50	44.56	1.10	0.14	25.14	9.07	78.77	nr	86.64
6000mm	58.52	2.50	59.98	1.20	0.15	27.38	9.90	97.26	nr	106.99
7000mm	73.10	2.50	74.93	1.30	0.16	29.62	10.72	115.28	nr	126.80
8000mm	89.82	2.50	92.07	1.40	0.17	31.86	11.55	135.49	nr	149.03
9000mm	103.20	2.50	105.78	1.50	0.19	34.26	12.38	152.42	nr	167.66
10000mm	116.58	2.50	119.50	1.60	0.20	36.51	13.20	169.20	nr	186.12
45 degree pitch gable ladder; 450mm overhang; span over wall plate										
5000mm	65.17	2.50	66.80	1.10	0.14	25.14	9.07	101.01	nr	111.11
6000mm	80.22	2.50	82.23	1.20	0.15	27.38	9.90	119.51	nr	131.46
7000mm	93.60	2.50	95.94	1.30	0.16	29.62	10.72	136.29	nr	149.92
8000mm	103.91	2.50	106.51	1.40	0.17	31.86	11.55	149.92	nr	164.92
9000mm	117.29	2.50	120.22	1.50	0.19	34.26	12.38	166.86	nr	183.55
10000mm	129.00	2.50	132.22	1.60	0.20	36.51	13.20	181.93	nr	200.12
TIMBER FIRST FIXINGS										
Stress grading softwood										
General Structural (GS) grade included in rates										
Special Structural (SS) grade add 10% to materials prices										
Flame proofing treatment to softwood										
For timbers treated with proofing process to Class 1 add 100% to materials prices										
Primary or structural timbers; Softwood, sawn, BS 4978, GS grade; carcassing										
Rafters and associated roof timbers										
25 x 75mm	0.95	15.00	1.09	0.14	0.02	3.23	0.03	4.36	m	4.79
25 x 125mm	1.77	15.00	2.04	0.16	0.02	3.65	0.05	5.74	m	6.31
32 x 175mm	3.76	15.00	4.32	0.22	0.03	5.06	0.07	9.45	m	10.39
32 x 225mm	4.84	15.00	5.57	0.25	0.03	5.68	0.07	11.32	m	12.45
38 x 75mm	1.65	15.00	1.90	0.15	0.02	3.44	0.03	5.37	m	5.91
38 x 100mm	2.20	15.00	2.53	0.18	0.02	4.07	0.05	6.65	m	7.31
50 x 75mm	1.97	15.00	2.27	0.18	0.02	4.07	0.05	6.38	m	7.02
50 x 100mm	2.59	15.00	2.97	0.20	0.03	4.64	0.05	7.66	m	8.43
50 x 125mm	3.24	15.00	3.73	0.23	0.03	5.27	0.07	9.06	m	9.97
50 x 150mm	3.88	15.00	4.46	0.26	0.03	5.89	0.07	10.42	m	11.46
50 x 225mm	5.83	15.00	6.70	0.36	0.05	8.29	0.10	15.10	m	16.60
50 x 250mm	9.87	15.00	11.35	0.40	0.05	9.13	0.10	20.58	m	22.63
75 x 100mm	4.19	15.00	4.82	0.26	0.03	5.89	0.07	10.78	m	11.86
75 x 150mm	6.20	15.00	7.13	0.35	0.05	8.08	0.10	15.31	m	16.84
100 x 150mm	12.18	15.00	14.01	0.45	0.06	10.33	0.12	24.45	m	26.89
100 x 225mm	18.27	15.00	21.01	0.60	0.08	13.77	0.16	34.94	m	38.44
Wall plates										
38 x 75mm	1.65	15.00	1.90	0.18	0.02	4.07	0.05	6.02	m	6.62
38 x 100mm	2.20	15.00	2.53	0.21	0.03	4.85	0.05	7.43	m	8.17
50 x 75mm	1.97	15.00	2.27	0.21	0.03	4.85	0.05	7.16	m	7.88
50 x 100mm	2.59	15.00	2.97	0.24	0.03	5.48	0.07	8.51	m	9.37
75 x 150mm	4.19	15.00	4.82	0.40	0.05	9.13	0.10	14.04	m	15.45
38 x 75mm; fixing by bolting	1.65	15.00	1.90	0.22	0.03	5.06	-	6.96	m	7.65
38 x 100mm; fixing by bolting	2.20	15.00	2.53	0.25	0.03	5.68	-	8.21	m	9.04
50 x 75mm; fixing by bolting	1.97	15.00	2.27	0.25	0.03	5.68	-	7.95	m	8.75
50 x 100mm; fixing by bolting	2.59	15.00	2.97	0.29	0.04	6.68	-	9.65	m	10.61
75 x 150mm; fixing by bolting	6.20	15.00	7.13	0.48	0.06	10.95	-	18.08	m	19.89
Roof joists; flat										
50 x 175mm	4.53	15.00	5.21	0.24	0.03	5.48	0.07	10.75	m	11.83
50 x 200mm	5.18	15.00	5.96	0.27	0.04	6.26	0.07	12.28	m	13.51
50 x 225mm	5.83	15.00	6.70	0.29	0.04	6.68	0.08	13.46	m	14.81
50 x 250mm	9.87	15.00	11.35	0.32	0.04	7.30	0.08	18.73	m	20.61

Labour hourly rates: (except Specialists)
Craft Operatives 20.87 Labourer 15.57
Rates are national average prices.
Refer to REGIONAL VARIATIONS for indicative levels of overall pricing in regions

	MATERIALS			LABOUR				RATES		
	Del to Site £	Waste %	Material Cost £	Craft Optve Hrs	Lab Hrs	Labour Cost £	Sunds £	Nett Rate £	Unit	Gross rate (10%) £
TIMBER FIRST FIXINGS (Cont'd)										
Primary or structural timbers; Softwood, sawn, BS 4978, GS grade; carcassing (Cont'd)										
Roof joists; flat (Cont'd)										
75 x 175mm	7.23	15.00	8.31	0.33	0.04	7.51	0.08	15.91	m	17.50
75 x 200mm	8.27	15.00	9.51	0.35	0.05	8.08	0.10	17.69	m	19.46
75 x 225mm	9.30	15.00	10.69	0.40	0.05	9.13	0.10	19.92	m	21.91
75 x 250mm	15.75	15.00	18.11	0.45	0.06	10.33	0.12	28.55	m	31.41
Floor joists										
38 x 75mm	1.65	15.00	1.90	0.12	0.01	2.66	0.03	4.59	m	5.05
38 x 100mm	2.20	15.00	2.53	0.14	0.02	3.23	0.03	5.80	m	6.38
50 x 75mm	1.97	15.00	2.27	0.14	0.02	3.23	0.03	5.53	m	6.08
50 x 100mm	2.59	15.00	2.97	0.16	0.02	3.65	0.05	6.67	m	7.34
50 x 150mm	3.88	15.00	4.46	0.20	0.03	4.56	0.06	9.08	m	9.99
50 x 175mm	4.53	15.00	5.21	0.24	0.03	5.48	0.07	10.75	m	11.83
50 x 200mm	5.18	15.00	5.96	0.27	0.04	6.26	0.07	12.28	m	13.51
50 x 225mm	5.83	15.00	6.70	0.29	0.04	6.68	0.08	13.46	m	14.81
50 x 250mm	9.87	15.00	11.35	0.32	0.04	7.30	0.08	18.73	m	20.61
75 x 150mm	6.20	15.00	7.13	0.29	0.04	6.68	0.08	13.89	m	15.28
75 x 175mm	7.23	15.00	8.31	0.33	0.04	7.51	0.08	15.91	m	17.50
75 x 200mm	8.27	15.00	9.51	0.35	0.05	8.08	0.10	17.69	m	19.46
75 x 225mm	9.30	15.00	10.69	0.40	0.05	9.13	0.10	19.92	m	21.91
75 x 250mm	15.75	15.00	18.11	0.45	0.06	10.33	0.12	28.55	m	31.41
Partition and wall members										
38 x 75mm	1.65	15.00	1.90	0.18	0.02	4.07	0.05	6.02	m	6.62
38 x 100mm	2.20	15.00	2.53	0.21	0.03	4.85	0.05	7.43	m	8.17
50 x 75mm	1.97	15.00	2.27	0.21	0.03	4.85	0.05	7.16	m	7.88
50 x 100mm	2.59	15.00	2.97	0.24	0.03	5.48	0.07	8.51	m	9.37
75 x 100mm	4.19	15.00	4.82	0.30	0.04	6.88	0.08	11.78	m	12.96
38 x 75mm; fixing to masonry	1.65	15.00	1.90	0.36	0.04	8.14	0.10	10.13	m	11.15
38 x 100mm; fixing to masonry	2.20	15.00	2.53	0.39	0.05	8.92	0.10	11.55	m	12.70
50 x 75mm; fixing to masonry	1.97	15.00	2.27	0.39	0.05	8.92	0.10	11.28	m	12.41
50 x 100mm; fixing to masonry	2.59	15.00	2.97	0.43	0.05	9.75	0.12	12.84	m	14.12
75 x 100mm; fixing to masonry	4.19	15.00	4.82	0.50	0.06	11.37	0.13	16.32	m	17.95
Strutting; herringbone; depth of joist 175mm										
50 x 50mm	2.36	15.00	2.71	0.65	0.08	14.81	0.18	17.70	m	19.47
Strutting; herringbone; depth of joist 200mm										
50 x 50mm	2.75	15.00	3.16	0.65	0.08	14.81	0.18	18.16	m	19.97
Strutting; herringbone; depth of joist 225mm										
50 x 50mm	3.14	15.00	3.62	0.65	0.08	14.81	0.18	18.61	m	20.47
Strutting; herringbone; depth of joist 250mm										
50 x 50mm	3.54	15.00	4.07	0.65	0.08	14.81	0.18	19.06	m	20.97
Strutting; block; depth of joist 100mm										
50 x 100mm	2.59	15.00	2.97	0.65	0.08	14.81	0.18	17.97	m	19.76
Strutting; block; depth of joist 150mm										
50 x 150mm	3.88	15.00	4.46	0.65	0.08	14.81	0.18	19.45	m	21.40
Strutting; block; depth of joist 175mm										
50 x 175mm	4.53	15.00	5.21	0.70	0.09	16.01	0.18	21.40	m	23.54
Strutting; block; depth of joist 200mm										
50 x 200mm	5.18	15.00	5.96	0.70	0.09	16.01	0.18	22.15	m	24.36
Strutting; block; depth of joist 225mm										
50 x 225mm	5.83	15.00	6.70	0.75	0.09	17.05	0.20	23.96	m	26.35
Strutting; block; depth of joist 250mm										
50 x 250mm	9.87	15.00	11.35	0.75	0.09	17.05	0.20	28.60	m	31.46
Noggins to joists										
50 x 50mm	1.31	15.00	1.51	0.28	0.04	6.47	0.08	8.06	m	8.86
50 x 75mm	1.97	15.00	2.27	0.33	0.04	7.51	0.08	9.86	m	10.84
wrought surfaces										
plain; 50mm wide	-	-	-	0.15	-	3.13	-	3.13	m	3.44
plain; 75mm wide	-	-	-	0.20	-	4.17	-	4.17	m	4.59
plain; 100mm wide	-	-	-	0.25	-	5.22	-	5.22	m	5.74
plain; 150mm wide	-	-	-	0.30	-	6.26	-	6.26	m	6.89
plain; 200mm wide	-	-	-	0.35	-	7.30	-	7.30	m	8.03
Primary or structural timbers; Softwood, sawn, BS 4978, GS grade; carcassing; impregnated										
Rafters and associated roof timbers										
25 x 75mm	1.04	15.00	1.20	0.14	0.02	3.23	0.03	4.46	m	4.91
25 x 125mm	2.39	15.00	2.75	0.16	0.02	3.65	0.05	6.45	m	7.09
32 x 175mm	4.09	15.00	4.70	0.22	0.03	5.06	0.07	9.83	m	10.81
32 x 225mm	5.27	15.00	6.06	0.25	0.03	5.68	0.07	11.81	m	12.99
38 x 75mm	1.79	15.00	2.06	0.15	0.02	3.44	0.03	5.53	m	6.09
38 x 100mm	2.62	15.00	3.01	0.18	0.02	4.07	0.05	7.13	m	7.84
50 x 75mm	2.15	15.00	2.47	0.18	0.02	4.07	0.05	6.59	m	7.25
50 x 100mm	2.83	15.00	3.25	0.20	0.03	4.64	0.05	7.94	m	8.74
50 x 125mm	3.76	15.00	4.32	0.23	0.03	5.27	0.07	9.65	m	10.62
50 x 150mm	4.23	15.00	4.86	0.26	0.03	5.89	0.07	10.82	m	11.90
50 x 225mm	6.36	15.00	7.31	0.36	0.05	8.29	0.10	15.70	m	17.28
50 x 250mm	10.46	15.00	12.03	0.40	0.05	9.13	0.10	21.25	m	23.38
75 x 100mm	4.57	15.00	5.26	0.26	0.03	5.89	0.07	11.22	m	12.34
75 x 150mm	6.76	15.00	7.77	0.35	0.05	8.08	0.10	15.96	m	17.55
100 x 150mm	12.93	15.00	14.87	0.45	0.06	10.33	0.12	25.31	m	27.84
100 x 225mm	19.40	15.00	22.31	0.60	0.08	13.77	0.16	36.24	m	39.87

Labour hourly rates: (except Specialists) Craft Operatives 20.87 Labourer 15.57 Rates are national average prices. Refer to REGIONAL VARIATIONS for indicative levels of overall pricing in regions	MATERIALS			LABOUR				RATES		
	Del to Site £	Waste %	Material Cost £	Craft Optve Hrs	Lab Hrs	Labour Cost £	Sunds £	Nett Rate £	Unit	Gross rate (10%) £
TIMBER FIRST FIXINGS (Cont'd)										
Primary or structural timbers; Softwood, sawn, BS 4978, GS grade; carcassing; impregnated (Cont'd)										
Wall plates										
38 x 75mm	1.79	15.00	2.06	0.18	0.02	4.07	0.05	6.18	m	6.79
38 x 100mm	2.62	15.00	3.01	0.21	0.03	4.85	0.05	7.91	m	8.70
50 x 75mm	2.15	15.00	2.47	0.21	0.03	4.85	0.05	7.37	m	8.11
50 x 100mm	2.83	15.00	3.25	0.24	0.03	5.48	0.07	8.80	m	9.67
75 x 150mm	4.57	15.00	5.26	0.40	0.05	9.13	0.10	14.48	m	15.93
38 x 75mm; fixing by bolting	1.79	15.00	2.06	0.22	0.03	5.06	-	7.12	m	7.83
38 x 100mm; fixing by bolting	2.62	15.00	3.01	0.25	0.03	5.68	-	8.69	m	9.56
50 x 75mm; fixing by bolting	2.15	15.00	2.47	0.25	0.03	5.68	-	8.16	m	8.97
50 x 100mm; fixing by bolting	2.83	15.00	3.25	0.29	0.04	6.68	-	9.93	m	10.92
75 x 150mm; fixing by bolting	4.57	15.00	5.26	0.48	0.06	10.95	-	16.21	m	17.83
Roof joists; flat										
50 x 100mm	2.83	15.00	3.25	0.20	0.03	4.56	0.07	7.88	m	8.67
50 x 175mm	4.94	15.00	5.68	0.24	0.03	5.48	0.07	11.22	m	12.35
50 x 200mm	5.65	15.00	6.50	0.27	0.04	6.26	0.07	12.82	m	14.10
50 x 225mm	6.36	15.00	7.31	0.29	0.04	6.68	0.08	14.07	m	15.48
50 x 250mm	10.46	15.00	12.03	0.32	0.04	7.30	0.08	19.41	m	21.35
75 x 175mm	7.89	15.00	9.07	0.33	0.04	7.51	0.08	16.67	m	18.33
75 x 200mm	9.02	15.00	10.37	0.35	0.05	8.08	0.10	18.56	m	20.41
75 x 225mm	10.14	15.00	11.66	0.40	0.05	9.13	0.10	20.89	m	22.98
75 x 250mm	16.69	15.00	19.19	0.45	0.06	10.33	0.12	29.63	m	32.60
Floor joists										
38 x 75mm	1.79	15.00	2.06	0.12	0.01	2.66	0.03	4.75	m	5.23
38 x 100mm	2.62	15.00	3.01	0.14	0.02	3.23	0.03	6.28	m	6.90
50 x 75mm	2.15	15.00	2.47	0.14	0.02	3.23	0.03	5.74	m	6.31
50 x 100mm	2.83	15.00	3.25	0.16	0.02	3.65	0.05	6.95	m	7.65
50 x 150mm	4.23	15.00	4.86	0.20	0.03	4.56	0.06	9.48	m	10.43
50 x 175mm	4.94	15.00	5.68	0.24	0.03	5.48	0.07	11.22	m	12.35
50 x 200mm	5.65	15.00	6.50	0.27	0.04	6.26	0.07	12.82	m	14.10
50 x 225mm	6.36	15.00	7.31	0.29	0.04	6.68	0.08	14.07	m	15.48
50 x 250mm	10.46	15.00	12.03	0.32	0.04	7.30	0.08	19.41	m	21.35
75 x 150mm	6.76	15.00	7.77	0.29	0.04	6.68	0.08	14.53	m	15.98
75 x 175mm	7.89	15.00	9.07	0.33	0.04	7.51	0.08	16.67	m	18.33
75 x 200mm	9.02	15.00	10.37	0.35	0.05	8.08	0.10	18.56	m	20.41
75 x 225mm	10.14	15.00	11.66	0.40	0.05	9.13	0.10	20.89	m	22.98
75 x 250mm	16.69	15.00	19.19	0.45	0.06	10.33	0.12	29.63	m	32.60
Partition and wall members										
38 x 75mm	1.79	15.00	2.06	0.18	0.02	4.07	0.05	6.18	m	6.79
38 x 100mm	2.62	15.00	3.01	0.21	0.03	4.85	0.05	7.91	m	8.70
50 x 75mm	2.15	15.00	2.47	0.21	0.03	4.85	0.05	7.37	m	8.11
50 x 100mm	2.83	15.00	3.25	0.24	0.03	5.48	0.07	8.80	m	9.67
75 x 100mm	4.57	15.00	5.26	0.30	0.04	6.88	0.08	12.22	m	13.45
38 x 75mm; fixing to masonry	1.79	15.00	2.06	0.36	0.04	8.14	0.10	10.29	m	11.32
38 x 100mm; fixing to masonry	2.62	15.00	3.01	0.39	0.05	8.92	0.10	12.03	m	13.23
50 x 75mm; fixing to masonry	2.15	15.00	2.47	0.39	0.05	8.92	0.10	11.49	m	12.64
50 x 100mm; fixing to masonry	2.83	15.00	3.25	0.43	0.05	9.75	0.12	13.12	m	14.43
75 x 100mm; fixing to masonry	4.57	15.00	5.26	0.50	0.06	11.37	0.13	16.76	m	18.43
Strutting; herringbone; depth of joist 175mm										
50 x 50mm	2.57	15.00	2.96	0.65	0.08	14.81	0.18	17.95	m	19.75
Strutting; herringbone; depth of joist 200mm										
50 x 50mm	3.00	15.00	3.45	0.65	0.08	14.81	0.18	18.44	m	20.29
Strutting; herringbone; depth of joist 225mm										
50 x 50mm	3.43	15.00	3.94	0.65	0.08	14.81	0.18	18.94	m	20.83
Strutting; herringbone; depth of joist 250mm										
50 x 50mm	3.86	15.00	4.44	0.65	0.08	14.81	0.18	19.43	m	21.37
Strutting; block; depth of joist 100mm										
50 x 100mm	2.83	15.00	3.25	0.65	0.08	14.81	0.18	18.25	m	20.07
Strutting; block; depth of joist 150mm										
50 x 150mm	4.23	15.00	4.86	0.65	0.08	14.81	0.18	19.86	m	21.84
Strutting; block; depth of joist 175mm										
50 x 175mm	4.94	15.00	5.68	0.70	0.09	16.01	0.18	21.87	m	24.06
Strutting; block; depth of joist 200mm										
50 x 200mm	5.65	15.00	6.50	0.70	0.09	16.01	0.18	22.69	m	24.96
Strutting; block; depth of joist 225mm										
50 x 225mm	6.36	15.00	7.31	0.75	0.09	17.05	0.20	24.57	m	27.02
Strutting; block; depth of joist 250mm										
50 x 250mm	10.46	15.00	12.03	0.75	0.09	17.05	0.20	29.28	m	32.21
Noggins to joists										
50 x 50mm	1.43	15.00	1.64	0.28	0.04	6.47	0.08	8.19	m	9.01
50 x 75mm	2.15	15.00	2.47	0.33	0.04	7.51	0.08	10.06	m	11.07
wrought surfaces										
plain; 50mm wide	-	-	-	0.15	-	3.13	-	3.13	m	3.44
plain; 75mm wide	-	-	-	0.20	-	4.17	-	4.17	m	4.59
plain; 100mm wide	-	-	-	0.25	-	5.22	-	5.22	m	5.74
plain; 150mm wide	-	-	-	0.30	-	6.26	-	6.26	m	6.89
plain; 200mm wide	-	-	-	0.35	-	7.30	-	7.30	m	8.03

Labour hourly rates: (except Specialists) Craft Operatives 20.87 Labourer 15.57 Rates are national average prices. Refer to REGIONAL VARIATIONS for indicative levels of overall pricing in regions	MATERIALS			LABOUR				RATES		
	Del to Site £	Waste %	Material Cost £	Craft Optve Hrs	Lab Hrs	Labour Cost £	Sunds £	Nett Rate £	Unit	Gross rate (10%) £
TIMBER FIRST FIXINGS (Cont'd)										
Primary or structural timbers; Oak; sawn carcassing										
Rafters and associated roof timbers										
25 x 75mm	4.13	10.00	4.54	0.25	0.03	5.68	0.07	10.29	m	11.32
25 x 125mm	6.88	10.00	7.57	0.28	0.04	6.47	0.08	14.12	m	15.53
32 x 175mm	9.49	10.00	10.44	0.39	0.05	8.92	0.10	19.46	m	21.41
32 x 225mm	11.10	10.00	12.21	0.44	0.06	10.12	0.12	22.44	m	24.68
38 x 75mm	4.39	10.00	4.83	0.26	0.03	5.89	0.07	10.79	m	11.87
38 x 100mm	5.86	10.00	6.44	0.32	0.04	7.30	0.08	13.83	m	15.21
50 x 75mm	5.78	10.00	6.36	0.32	0.04	7.30	0.08	13.74	m	15.12
50 x 100mm	7.71	10.00	8.48	0.35	0.04	7.93	0.10	16.50	m	18.15
50 x 125mm	9.63	10.00	10.60	0.40	0.05	9.13	0.10	19.82	m	21.80
50 x 150mm	11.56	10.00	12.71	0.46	0.06	10.53	0.13	23.38	m	25.72
50 x 225mm	17.34	10.00	19.07	0.63	0.08	14.39	0.16	33.63	m	36.99
50 x 250mm	19.26	10.00	21.19	0.70	0.09	16.01	0.18	37.38	m	41.12
75 x 100mm	18.50	10.00	20.35	0.46	0.06	10.53	0.13	31.01	m	34.12
75 x 150mm	27.75	10.00	30.52	0.61	0.08	13.98	0.16	44.66	m	49.13
Wall plates										
38 x 75mm	4.39	10.00	4.83	0.32	0.04	7.30	0.08	12.21	m	13.44
38 x 100mm	5.86	10.00	6.44	0.37	0.05	8.50	0.10	15.04	m	16.55
50 x 75mm	5.78	10.00	6.36	0.37	0.05	8.50	0.10	14.96	m	16.45
50 x 100mm	7.71	10.00	8.48	0.42	0.05	9.54	0.12	18.14	m	19.95
75 x 150mm	18.50	10.00	20.35	0.52	0.06	11.79	0.13	32.27	m	35.49
38 x 75mm; fixing by bolting	4.39	10.00	4.83	0.38	0.05	8.71	-	13.54	m	14.89
38 x 100mm; fixing by bolting	5.86	10.00	6.44	0.44	0.05	9.96	-	16.40	m	18.04
50 x 75mm; fixing by bolting	5.78	10.00	6.36	0.44	0.06	10.12	-	16.48	m	18.12
50 x 100mm; fixing by bolting	7.71	10.00	8.48	0.50	0.06	11.37	-	19.85	m	21.83
75 x 150mm; fixing by bolting	18.50	10.00	20.35	0.62	0.07	14.03	-	34.38	m	37.81
Roof joists; flat										
50 x 175mm	13.49	10.00	14.83	0.42	0.05	9.54	0.12	24.49	m	26.94
50 x 200mm	15.41	10.00	16.95	0.47	0.06	10.74	0.13	27.83	m	30.61
50 x 225mm	17.34	10.00	19.07	0.51	0.06	11.58	0.13	30.78	m	33.86
50 x 250mm	19.26	10.00	21.19	0.56	0.07	12.78	0.15	34.12	m	37.53
75 x 175mm	32.37	10.00	35.61	0.58	0.07	13.19	0.15	48.95	m	53.85
75 x 200mm	37.00	10.00	40.70	0.61	0.08	13.98	0.16	54.84	m	60.32
75 x 225mm	41.62	10.00	45.78	0.70	0.09	16.01	0.18	61.97	m	68.17
75 x 250mm	46.25	10.00	50.87	0.79	0.10	18.04	0.21	69.13	m	76.04
100 x 150mm	45.39	10.00	49.93	0.61	0.08	13.98	0.16	64.07	m	70.48
100 x 225mm	68.08	10.00	74.89	0.90	0.13	20.81	0.28	95.98	m	105.58
Floor joists										
38 x 75mm	4.39	10.00	4.83	0.21	0.03	4.85	0.05	9.73	m	10.70
38 x 100mm	5.86	10.00	6.44	0.24	0.03	5.48	0.07	11.98	m	13.18
50 x 75mm	5.78	10.00	6.36	0.24	0.03	5.48	0.07	11.90	m	13.09
50 x 100mm	7.71	10.00	8.48	0.28	0.04	6.47	0.08	15.03	m	16.53
50 x 175mm	13.49	10.00	14.83	0.42	0.05	9.54	0.12	24.49	m	26.94
50 x 200mm	15.41	10.00	16.95	0.47	0.06	10.74	0.13	27.83	m	30.61
50 x 225mm	17.34	10.00	19.07	0.51	0.06	11.58	0.13	30.78	m	33.86
50 x 250mm	19.26	10.00	21.19	0.56	0.07	12.78	0.15	34.12	m	37.53
75 x 150mm	27.75	10.00	30.52	0.51	0.06	11.58	0.13	42.23	m	46.46
75 x 175mm	32.37	10.00	35.61	0.58	0.07	13.19	0.15	48.95	m	53.85
75 x 200mm	37.00	10.00	40.70	0.61	0.08	13.98	0.16	54.84	m	60.32
75 x 225mm	41.62	10.00	45.78	0.70	0.09	16.01	0.18	61.97	m	68.17
75 x 250mm	46.25	10.00	50.87	0.79	0.10	18.04	0.21	69.13	m	76.04
Partition and wall members										
38 x 75mm	4.39	10.00	4.83	0.32	0.04	7.30	0.08	12.21	m	13.44
38 x 100mm	5.86	10.00	6.44	0.37	0.05	8.50	0.10	15.04	m	16.55
50 x 75mm	5.78	10.00	6.36	0.37	0.05	8.50	0.10	14.96	m	16.45
50 x 100mm	7.71	10.00	8.48	0.42	0.05	9.54	0.12	18.14	m	19.95
75 x 100mm	18.50	10.00	20.35	0.52	0.06	11.79	0.13	32.27	m	35.49
38 x 75mm; fixing to masonry	4.39	10.00	4.83	0.53	0.07	12.15	0.15	17.13	m	18.84
38 x 100mm; fixing to masonry	5.86	10.00	6.44	0.59	0.07	13.40	0.16	20.01	m	22.01
50 x 75mm; fixing to masonry	5.78	10.00	6.36	0.59	0.07	13.40	0.16	19.93	m	21.92
50 x 100mm; fixing to masonry	7.71	10.00	8.48	0.65	0.08	14.81	0.18	23.47	m	25.82
75 x 100mm; fixing to masonry	18.50	10.00	20.35	0.78	0.10	17.84	0.21	38.40	m	42.24
Strutting; herringbone; depth of joist 175mm										
50 x 50mm	6.94	10.00	7.63	1.10	0.14	25.14	0.30	33.06	m	36.37
Strutting; herringbone; depth of joist 200mm										
50 x 50mm	8.09	10.00	8.90	1.10	0.14	25.14	0.30	34.33	m	37.77
Strutting; herringbone; depth of joist 225mm										
50 x 50mm	9.25	10.00	10.17	1.10	0.14	25.14	0.30	35.61	m	39.17
Strutting; herringbone; depth of joist 250mm										
50 x 50mm	10.40	10.00	11.44	1.10	0.14	25.14	0.30	36.88	m	40.56
Strutting; block; depth of joist 150mm										
50 x 150mm	11.56	10.00	12.71	1.10	0.14	25.14	0.30	38.15	m	41.96
Strutting; block; depth of joist 175mm										
50 x 175mm	13.49	10.00	14.83	1.20	0.15	27.38	0.33	42.54	m	46.80
Strutting; block; depth of joist 200mm										
50 x 200mm	15.41	10.00	16.95	1.20	0.15	27.38	0.33	44.66	m	49.13
Strutting; block; depth of joist 225mm										
50 x 225mm	17.34	10.00	19.07	1.30	0.16	29.62	0.35	49.04	m	53.95
Strutting; block; depth of joist 250mm										
50 x 250mm	19.26	10.00	21.19	1.30	0.16	29.62	0.35	51.16	m	56.28

Labour hourly rates: (except Specialists) Craft Operatives 20.87 Labourer 15.57 Rates are national average prices. Refer to REGIONAL VARIATIONS for indicative levels of overall pricing in regions	MATERIALS			LABOUR				RATES		
	Del to Site £	Waste %	Material Cost £	Craft Optve Hrs	Lab Hrs	Labour Cost £	Sunds £	Nett Rate £	Unit	Gross rate (10%) £
TIMBER FIRST FIXINGS (Cont'd)										
Primary or structural timbers; Oak; sawn carcassing (Cont'd)										
Noggins to joists										
50 x 50mm	3.85	10.00	4.24	0.50	0.06	11.37	0.13	15.74	m	17.31
50 x 75mm	5.78	10.00	6.36	0.60	0.08	13.77	0.16	20.29	m	22.32
wrought surfaces										
plain; 50mm wide	-	-	-	0.30	-	6.26	-	6.26	m	6.89
plain; 75mm wide	-	-	-	0.40	-	8.35	-	8.35	m	9.18
plain; 100mm wide	-	-	-	0.50	-	10.44	-	10.44	m	11.48
plain; 150mm wide	-	-	-	0.60	-	12.52	-	12.52	m	13.77
plain; 200mm wide	-	-	-	0.70	-	14.61	-	14.61	m	16.07
Beams; laminated beams; softwood, wrought, GS grade										
Glued laminated beams										
65 x 150 x 4000mm	40.95	2.50	41.97	0.60	0.07	13.61	6.27	61.86	nr	68.04
65 x 175 x 4000mm	48.30	2.50	49.51	0.80	0.10	18.25	7.01	74.77	nr	82.25
65 x 200 x 4000mm	54.60	2.50	55.96	0.90	0.11	20.50	7.84	84.30	nr	92.73
65 x 225 x 4000mm	61.95	2.50	63.50	1.10	0.14	25.14	9.73	98.37	nr	108.21
65 x 250 x 4000mm	68.25	2.50	69.96	1.20	0.15	27.38	10.56	107.90	nr	118.69
65 x 250 x 6000mm	102.90	2.50	105.47	1.30	0.16	29.62	11.47	146.56	nr	161.22
65 x 275 x 4000mm	75.60	2.50	77.49	1.30	0.16	29.62	11.47	118.58	nr	130.44
65 x 275 x 6000mm	112.35	2.50	115.16	1.40	0.18	32.02	12.29	159.47	nr	175.42
65 x 300 x 4000mm	81.90	2.50	83.95	1.40	0.18	32.02	12.29	128.26	nr	141.09
65 x 300 x 6000mm	122.85	2.50	125.92	1.50	0.19	34.26	13.28	173.47	nr	190.81
65 x 325 x 4000mm	89.25	2.50	91.48	1.60	0.20	36.51	14.11	142.09	nr	156.30
65 x 325 x 6000mm	133.35	2.50	136.68	1.70	0.21	38.75	15.01	190.45	nr	209.49
65 x 325 x 8000mm	266.70	2.50	273.37	1.80	0.22	40.99	15.84	330.20	nr	363.22
90 x 150 x 4000mm	56.70	2.50	58.12	0.90	0.11	20.50	7.84	86.45	nr	95.10
90 x 175 x 4000mm	66.15	2.50	67.80	1.10	0.14	25.14	9.73	102.68	nr	112.94
90 x 200 x 4000mm	75.60	2.50	77.49	1.20	0.15	27.38	10.56	115.43	nr	126.97
90 x 225 x 4000mm	85.05	2.50	87.18	1.30	0.16	29.62	11.47	128.27	nr	141.09
90 x 250 x 4000mm	94.50	2.50	96.86	1.40	0.18	32.02	12.29	141.18	nr	155.29
90 x 250 x 6000mm	141.75	2.50	145.29	1.50	0.19	34.26	13.28	192.84	nr	212.12
90 x 275 x 4000mm	103.95	2.50	106.55	1.50	0.19	34.26	13.28	154.09	nr	169.50
90 x 275 x 6000mm	156.45	2.50	160.36	1.60	0.20	36.51	14.11	210.97	nr	232.07
90 x 300 x 4000mm	113.40	2.50	116.24	1.70	0.21	38.75	15.01	170.00	nr	187.00
90 x 300 x 6000mm	170.10	2.50	174.35	1.80	0.22	40.99	15.84	231.18	nr	254.30
90 x 325 x 4000mm	122.85	2.50	125.92	1.80	0.22	40.99	15.84	182.75	nr	201.03
90 x 325 x 6000mm	184.80	2.50	189.42	1.90	0.24	43.39	16.83	249.64	nr	274.60
90 x 325 x 8000mm	368.55	2.50	377.76	2.00	0.25	45.63	17.57	440.97	nr	485.07
90 x 350 x 4000mm	132.30	2.50	135.61	1.90	0.24	43.39	16.83	195.83	nr	215.41
90 x 350 x 6000mm	198.45	2.50	203.41	2.00	0.25	45.63	17.57	266.62	nr	293.28
90 x 350 x 8000mm	396.90	2.50	406.82	2.10	0.26	47.88	18.48	473.18	nr	520.50
90 x 375 x 4000mm	141.75	2.50	145.29	2.00	0.25	45.63	17.57	208.50	nr	229.35
90 x 375 x 6000mm	213.15	2.50	218.48	2.10	0.26	47.88	18.48	284.83	nr	313.32
90 x 375 x 8000mm	425.25	2.50	435.88	2.20	0.28	50.27	19.31	505.46	nr	556.01
90 x 375 x 10000mm	531.30	2.50	544.58	2.30	0.29	52.52	20.21	617.31	nr	679.04
90 x 400 x 4000mm	151.20	2.50	154.98	2.20	0.28	50.27	19.31	224.56	nr	247.01
90 x 400 x 6000mm	226.80	2.50	232.47	2.30	0.29	52.52	20.21	305.20	nr	335.72
90 x 400 x 8000mm	453.60	2.50	464.94	2.40	0.30	54.76	21.12	540.82	nr	594.90
90 x 400 x 10000mm	567.00	2.50	581.17	2.50	0.31	57.00	22.03	660.20	nr	726.22
90 x 425 x 6000mm	240.45	2.50	246.46	2.40	0.30	54.76	21.12	322.34	nr	354.57
90 x 425 x 8000mm	481.95	2.50	494.00	2.50	0.31	57.00	22.03	573.03	nr	630.33
90 x 425 x 10000mm	602.70	2.50	617.77	2.60	0.33	59.40	22.85	700.02	nr	770.02
90 x 425 x 12000mm	723.45	2.50	741.54	2.70	0.34	61.64	23.76	826.94	nr	909.63
90 x 450 x 6000mm	255.15	2.50	261.53	2.50	0.31	57.00	22.03	340.56	nr	374.61
90 x 450 x 8000mm	510.30	2.50	523.06	2.60	0.33	59.40	22.85	605.31	nr	665.84
90 x 450 x 10000mm	638.40	2.50	654.36	2.70	0.34	61.64	23.76	739.76	nr	813.74
90 x 450 x 12000mm	765.45	2.50	784.59	2.80	0.35	63.89	24.67	873.14	nr	960.45
115 x 250 x 4000mm	120.75	2.50	123.77	1.70	0.21	38.75	15.01	177.53	nr	195.29
115 x 250 x 6000mm	181.65	2.50	186.19	1.80	0.22	40.99	15.84	243.02	nr	267.32
115 x 275 x 4000mm	133.35	2.50	136.68	1.80	0.22	40.99	15.84	193.52	nr	212.87
115 x 275 x 6000mm	199.50	2.50	204.49	1.90	0.24	43.39	16.83	264.71	nr	291.18
115 x 300 x 4000mm	144.90	2.50	148.52	1.90	0.24	43.39	16.83	208.74	nr	229.62
115 x 300 x 6000mm	217.35	2.50	222.78	2.00	0.25	45.63	17.57	285.99	nr	314.59
115 x 325 x 4000mm	157.50	2.50	161.44	2.00	0.25	45.63	17.57	224.64	nr	247.11
115 x 325 x 6000mm	235.20	2.50	241.08	2.10	0.26	47.88	18.48	307.44	nr	338.18
115 x 325 x 8000mm	471.45	2.50	483.24	2.20	0.28	50.27	19.31	552.81	nr	608.10
115 x 350 x 4000mm	169.05	2.50	173.28	2.20	0.28	50.27	19.31	242.85	nr	267.14
115 x 350 x 6000mm	254.10	2.50	260.45	2.30	0.29	52.52	20.21	333.18	nr	366.50
115 x 350 x 8000mm	507.15	2.50	519.83	2.40	0.30	54.76	21.12	595.71	nr	655.28
115 x 375 x 4000mm	181.65	2.50	186.19	2.30	0.29	52.52	20.21	258.92	nr	284.81
115 x 375 x 6000mm	271.95	2.50	278.75	2.40	0.30	54.76	21.12	354.63	nr	390.09
115 x 375 x 8000mm	543.90	2.50	557.50	2.50	0.31	57.00	22.03	636.53	nr	700.18
115 x 400 x 4000mm	193.20	2.50	198.03	2.40	0.30	54.76	21.12	273.91	nr	301.30
115 x 400 x 6000mm	289.80	2.50	297.04	2.50	0.31	57.00	22.03	376.07	nr	413.68
115 x 400 x 8000mm	579.60	2.50	594.09	2.60	0.33	59.40	22.85	676.34	nr	743.98
115 x 400 x 10000mm	724.50	2.50	742.61	2.70	0.34	61.64	23.76	828.02	nr	910.82
115 x 425 x 6000mm	307.65	2.50	315.34	2.60	0.33	59.40	22.85	397.59	nr	437.35
115 x 425 x 8000mm	616.35	2.50	631.76	2.70	0.34	61.64	23.76	717.16	nr	788.88
115 x 425 x 10000mm	769.65	2.50	788.89	2.80	0.35	63.89	24.67	877.44	nr	965.19
115 x 425 x 12000mm	924.00	2.50	947.10	2.90	0.36	66.13	25.57	1038.80	nr	1142.68
115 x 450 x 6000mm	326.55	2.50	334.71	2.80	0.35	63.89	24.67	423.27	nr	465.59
115 x 450 x 8000mm	652.05	2.50	668.35	2.90	0.36	66.13	25.57	760.05	nr	836.06
115 x 450 x 10000mm	814.80	2.50	835.17	3.00	0.38	68.53	26.40	930.10	nr	1023.11
115 x 450 x 12000mm	978.60	2.50	1003.06	3.10	0.39	70.77	27.31	1101.14	nr	1211.26
115 x 475 x 6000mm	344.40	2.50	353.01	2.90	0.36	66.13	25.57	444.71	nr	489.18
115 x 475 x 8000mm	688.80	2.50	706.02	3.00	0.38	68.53	26.40	800.95	nr	881.04
115 x 475 x 10000mm	859.95	2.50	881.45	3.10	0.39	70.77	27.31	979.53	nr	1077.48
115 x 475 x 12000mm	1032.15	2.50	1057.95	3.20	0.40	73.01	28.22	1159.18	nr	1275.10
115 x 475 x 14000mm	1204.35	2.50	1234.46	3.30	0.41	75.25	29.04	1338.75	nr	1472.63

Labour hourly rates: (except Specialists) Craft Operatives 20.87 Labourer 15.57 Rates are national average prices. Refer to REGIONAL VARIATIONS for indicative levels of overall pricing in regions	MATERIALS			LABOUR				RATES		
	Del to Site £	Waste %	Material Cost £	Craft Optve Hrs	Lab Hrs	Labour Cost £	Sunds £	Nett Rate £	Unit	Gross rate (10%) £
TIMBER FIRST FIXINGS (Cont'd)										
Beams; laminated beams; softwood, wrought, GS grade (Cont'd)										
Glued laminated beams (Cont'd)										
115 x 500 x 6000mm	362.25	2.50	371.31	3.00	0.38	68.53	26.40	466.23	nr	512.86
115 x 500 x 8000mm	724.50	2.50	742.61	3.10	0.39	70.77	27.31	840.69	nr	924.76
115 x 500 x 10000mm	906.15	2.50	928.80	3.20	0.40	73.01	28.22	1030.03	nr	1133.03
115 x 500 x 12000mm	1086.75	2.50	1113.92	3.30	0.41	75.25	29.04	1218.21	nr	1340.03
115 x 500 x 14000mm	1268.40	2.50	1300.11	3.40	0.42	77.50	29.86	1407.47	nr	1548.22
140 x 350 x 4000mm	205.80	2.50	210.94	2.40	0.30	54.76	21.12	286.82	nr	315.51
140 x 350 x 6000mm	308.70	2.50	316.42	2.50	0.31	57.00	22.03	395.45	nr	434.99
140 x 350 x 8000mm	617.40	2.50	632.84	2.60	0.33	59.40	22.85	715.09	nr	786.60
140 x 375 x 4000mm	220.50	2.50	226.01	2.50	0.31	57.00	22.03	305.04	nr	335.55
140 x 375 x 6000mm	330.75	2.50	339.02	2.60	0.33	59.40	22.85	421.27	nr	463.40
140 x 375 x 8000mm	661.50	2.50	678.04	2.70	0.34	61.64	23.76	763.44	nr	839.78
140 x 375 x 10000mm	827.40	2.50	848.09	2.80	0.35	63.89	24.67	936.64	nr	1030.30
140 x 400 x 6000mm	352.80	2.50	361.62	2.80	0.35	63.89	24.67	450.17	nr	495.19
140 x 400 x 8000mm	705.60	2.50	723.24	2.90	0.36	66.13	25.57	814.94	nr	896.44
140 x 400 x 10000mm	882.00	2.50	904.05	3.00	0.38	68.53	26.40	998.98	nr	1098.87
140 x 425 x 6000mm	374.85	2.50	384.22	2.90	0.36	66.13	25.57	475.92	nr	523.52
140 x 425 x 8000mm	749.70	2.50	768.44	3.00	0.38	68.53	26.40	863.37	nr	949.71
140 x 425 x 10000mm	937.65	2.50	961.09	3.10	0.39	70.77	27.31	1059.17	nr	1165.08
140 x 425 x 12000mm	1124.55	2.50	1152.66	3.20	0.40	73.01	28.22	1253.89	nr	1379.28
140 x 450 x 6000mm	396.90	2.50	406.82	3.00	0.38	68.53	26.40	501.75	nr	551.92
140 x 450 x 8000mm	793.80	2.50	813.64	3.10	0.39	70.77	27.31	911.72	nr	1002.89
140 x 450 x 10000mm	992.25	2.50	1017.06	3.20	0.40	73.01	28.22	1118.28	nr	1230.11
140 x 450 x 12000mm	1190.70	2.50	1220.47	3.30	0.41	75.25	29.04	1324.76	nr	1457.24
140 x 475 x 6000mm	418.95	2.50	429.42	3.10	0.39	70.77	27.31	527.50	nr	580.25
140 x 475 x 8000mm	837.90	2.50	858.85	3.20	0.40	73.01	28.22	960.07	nr	1056.08
140 x 475 x 10000mm	1047.90	2.50	1074.10	3.30	0.41	75.25	29.04	1178.39	nr	1296.23
140 x 475 x 12000mm	1256.85	2.50	1288.27	3.40	0.42	77.50	29.86	1395.63	nr	1535.20
140 x 475 x 14000mm	1466.85	2.50	1503.52	3.50	0.44	79.90	30.77	1614.19	nr	1775.61
165 x 425 x 6000mm	442.05	2.50	453.10	3.10	0.39	70.77	27.31	551.18	nr	606.30
165 x 425 x 8000mm	884.10	2.50	906.20	3.20	0.40	73.01	28.22	1007.43	nr	1108.17
165 x 425 x 10000mm	1104.60	2.50	1132.21	3.30	0.41	75.25	29.04	1236.51	nr	1360.16
165 x 425 x 12000mm	1325.10	2.50	1358.23	3.40	0.42	77.50	29.86	1465.59	nr	1612.15
165 x 450 x 6000mm	468.30	2.50	480.01	3.20	0.40	73.01	28.22	581.23	nr	639.36
165 x 450 x 8000mm	935.55	2.50	958.94	3.30	0.41	75.25	29.04	1063.23	nr	1169.56
165 x 450 x 10000mm	1169.70	2.50	1198.94	3.40	0.42	77.50	29.86	1306.30	nr	1436.94
165 x 450 x 12000mm	1403.85	2.50	1438.95	3.50	0.44	79.90	30.77	1549.61	nr	1704.58
165 x 475 x 6000mm	517.00	2.50	529.92	3.40	0.42	77.50	29.86	637.29	nr	701.02
165 x 475 x 8000mm	1035.10	2.50	1060.98	3.50	0.44	79.90	30.77	1171.65	nr	1288.81
165 x 475 x 10000mm	1293.60	2.50	1325.94	3.60	0.45	82.14	31.68	1439.76	nr	1583.73
165 x 475 x 12000mm	1552.10	2.50	1590.90	3.70	0.46	84.38	32.59	1707.87	nr	1878.66
165 x 475 x 14000mm	1810.60	2.50	1855.86	3.80	0.48	86.78	33.41	1976.06	nr	2173.66
190 x 475 x 6000mm	569.10	2.50	583.33	3.60	0.45	82.14	31.68	697.15	nr	766.86
190 x 475 x 8000mm	1137.15	2.50	1165.58	3.70	0.46	84.38	32.59	1282.55	nr	1410.80
190 x 475 x 10000mm	1421.70	2.50	1457.24	3.80	0.48	86.78	33.41	1577.43	nr	1735.18
190 x 475 x 12000mm	1706.25	2.50	1748.91	3.90	0.49	89.02	34.32	1872.25	nr	2059.47
190 x 475 x 14000mm	1989.75	2.50	2039.49	4.00	0.50	91.26	35.23	2165.99	nr	2382.58
Softwood, sawn; supports										
Butt jointed supports										
width exceeding 600mm; 19 x 38mm at 300mm centres; fixing to masonry	1.91	15.00	2.19	1.00	0.13	22.89	0.26	25.35	m²	27.89
width exceeding 600mm; 25 x 50mm at 300mm centres; fixing to masonry	2.36	15.00	2.72	1.10	0.14	25.14	0.30	28.15	m²	30.97
Framed supports										
width exceeding 600mm; 38 x 50mm members at 400mm centres one way; 38 x 50mm subsidiary members at 400mm centres one way	5.35	15.00	6.15	1.00	0.13	22.89	0.26	29.31	m²	32.24
width exceeding 600mm; 38 x 50mm members at 500mm centres one way; 38 x 50mm subsidiary members at 400mm centres one way	4.82	15.00	5.54	0.80	0.10	18.25	0.21	24.00	m²	26.41
width exceeding 600mm; 50 x 50mm members at 400mm centres one way; 50 x 50mm subsidiary members at 400mm centres one way	6.55	15.00	7.53	1.10	0.14	25.14	0.30	32.97	m²	36.26
width exceeding 600mm; 50 x 50mm members at 500mm centres one way; 50 x 50mm subsidiary members at 400mm centres one way	5.89	15.00	6.78	0.90	0.11	20.50	0.25	27.52	m²	30.27
width exceeding 600mm; 19 x 38mm members at 300mm centres one way; 19 x 38mm subsidiary members at 300mm centres one way; fixing to masonry	3.82	15.00	4.39	2.25	0.28	51.32	0.59	56.30	m²	61.93
width exceeding 600mm; 25 x 50mm members at 300mm centres one way; 25 x 50mm subsidiary members at 300mm centres one way; fixing to masonry	4.73	15.00	5.44	2.35	0.29	53.56	0.63	59.62	m²	65.59
width 300mm; 38 x 50mm members longitudinally; 38 x 50mm subsidiary members at 400mm centres laterally	5.35	15.00	6.15	0.40	0.05	9.13	0.10	15.38	m	16.92
width 300mm; 50 x 50mm members longitudinally; 50 x 50mm subsidiary members at 400mm centres laterally	6.55	15.00	7.53	0.45	0.06	10.33	0.12	17.97	m	19.77
Individual supports										
6 x 38mm	0.25	10.00	0.28	0.08	0.01	1.83	0.02	2.12	m	2.33
12 x 38mm	0.51	10.00	0.56	0.08	0.01	1.83	0.02	2.40	m	2.64
16 x 22mm	0.32	15.00	0.37	0.08	0.01	1.83	0.02	2.21	m	2.43
16 x 38mm	0.51	15.00	0.59	0.08	0.01	1.83	0.02	2.43	m	2.67
16 x 50mm	0.68	15.00	0.78	0.09	0.01	2.03	0.02	2.83	m	3.12
16 x 75mm	1.02	15.00	1.17	0.10	0.01	2.24	0.03	3.45	m	3.79
19 x 38mm	0.57	15.00	0.66	0.09	0.01	2.03	0.02	2.71	m	2.98
19 x 50mm	0.71	15.00	0.82	0.10	0.01	2.24	0.03	3.09	m	3.40
19 x 75mm	0.95	15.00	1.09	0.10	0.01	2.24	0.03	3.37	m	3.71

Labour hourly rates: (except Specialists) Craft Operatives 20.87 Labourer 15.57 Rates are national average prices. Refer to REGIONAL VARIATIONS for indicative levels of overall pricing in regions	MATERIALS			LABOUR				RATES		
	Del to Site £	Waste %	Material Cost £	Craft Optve Hrs	Lab Hrs	Labour Cost £	Sunds £	Nett Rate £	Unit	Gross rate (10%) £
TIMBER FIRST FIXINGS (Cont'd)										
Softwood, sawn; supports (Cont'd)										
Individual supports (Cont'd)										
19 x 100mm	1.01	15.00	1.16	0.11	0.01	2.45	0.03	3.64	m	4.01
19 x 150mm	2.12	15.00	2.44	0.12	0.02	2.82	0.03	5.29	m	5.82
25 x 50mm	0.71	15.00	0.82	0.10	0.01	2.24	0.03	3.09	m	3.40
25 x 100mm	1.01	15.00	1.16	0.12	0.02	2.82	0.03	4.01	m	4.41
25 x 150mm	2.12	15.00	2.44	0.18	0.03	4.22	0.05	6.71	m	7.38
25 x 175mm	2.47	15.00	2.84	0.21	0.03	4.85	0.07	7.76	m	8.53
25 x 200mm	2.83	15.00	3.25	0.19	0.02	4.28	0.05	7.58	m	8.34
38 x 50mm	1.07	15.00	1.23	0.11	0.01	2.45	0.03	3.71	m	4.09
50 x 50mm	1.31	15.00	1.51	0.12	0.02	2.82	0.03	4.36	m	4.79
50 x 150mm	3.88	15.00	4.46	0.17	0.02	3.86	0.05	8.37	m	9.21
50 x 300mm	11.63	15.00	13.37	0.23	0.03	5.27	0.07	18.71	m	20.58
75 x 75mm	3.18	15.00	3.66	0.17	0.02	3.86	0.05	7.57	m	8.32
75 x 100mm	4.19	15.00	4.82	0.18	0.02	4.07	0.05	8.94	m	9.83
75 x 150mm	6.20	15.00	7.13	0.21	0.03	4.85	0.07	12.05	m	13.25
100 x 100mm	9.00	15.00	10.35	0.19	0.02	4.28	0.05	14.68	m	16.14
100 x 150mm	12.18	15.00	14.01	0.23	0.03	5.27	0.07	19.34	m	21.27
100 x 200mm	16.24	15.00	18.68	0.26	0.04	6.05	0.08	24.81	m	27.29
100 x 300mm	24.75	15.00	28.46	0.40	0.05	9.13	0.13	37.72	m	41.49
150 x 150mm	17.78	15.00	20.45	0.30	0.04	6.88	0.10	27.43	m	30.18
6 x 38mm; fixing to masonry	0.25	10.00	0.28	0.23	0.03	5.27	0.07	5.61	m	6.18
12 x 38mm; fixing to masonry	0.51	10.00	0.56	0.23	0.03	5.27	0.07	5.89	m	6.48
19 x 38mm; fixing to masonry	0.57	15.00	0.66	0.24	0.03	5.48	0.07	6.20	m	6.82
25 x 50mm; fixing to masonry	0.71	15.00	0.82	0.25	0.03	5.68	0.07	6.57	m	7.22
38 x 50mm; fixing to masonry	1.07	15.00	1.23	0.27	0.03	6.10	0.07	7.40	m	8.14
50 x 50mm; fixing to masonry	1.31	15.00	1.51	0.28	0.04	6.47	0.08	8.06	m	8.86
Softwood, sawn, impregnated; supports										
Butt jointed supports										
width exceeding 600mm; 50mm wide x 25mm average depth at 450mm centres	2.89	10.00	3.17	0.30	0.04	6.88	0.08	10.14	m²	11.15
width exceeding 600mm; 50mm wide x 25mm average depth at 600mm centres	2.16	10.00	2.37	0.23	0.03	5.27	0.07	7.71	m²	8.48
width exceeding 600mm; 50mm wide x 50mm average depth at 450mm centres	4.57	10.00	5.03	0.36	0.05	8.29	0.10	13.42	m²	14.76
width exceeding 600mm; 50mm wide x 50mm average depth at 600mm centres	3.42	10.00	3.76	0.27	0.03	6.10	0.07	9.93	m²	10.92
width exceeding 600mm; 50mm wide x 63mm average depth at 450mm centres	8.61	10.00	9.47	0.40	0.05	9.13	0.10	18.70	m²	20.57
width exceeding 600mm; 50mm wide x 63mm average depth at 600mm centres	6.44	10.00	7.08	0.30	0.04	6.88	0.08	14.05	m²	15.45
width exceeding 600mm; 50mm wide x 75mm average depth at 450mm centres	9.39	10.00	10.33	0.43	0.05	9.75	0.12	20.20	m²	22.21
width exceeding 600mm; 50mm wide x 75mm average depth at 600mm centres	7.02	10.00	7.72	0.33	0.04	7.51	0.08	15.31	m²	16.85
width exceeding 600mm; 19 x 38mm at 300mm centres; fixing to masonry	1.91	15.00	2.19	1.00	0.13	22.89	0.26	25.35	m²	27.89
width exceeding 600mm; 25 x 50mm at 300mm centres; fixing to masonry	2.57	15.00	2.95	1.10	0.14	25.14	0.30	28.39	m²	31.22
Framed supports										
width exceeding 600mm; 38 x 50mm members at 400mm centres one way; 38 x 50mm subsidiary members at 400mm centres one way	5.86	15.00	6.73	1.00	0.13	22.89	0.26	29.89	m²	32.88
width exceeding 600mm; 38 x 50mm members at 500mm centres one way; 38 x 50mm subsidiary members at 400mm centres one way	5.27	15.00	6.06	0.80	0.10	18.25	0.21	24.53	m²	26.98
width exceeding 600mm; 50 x 50mm members at 400mm centres one way; 50 x 50mm subsidiary members at 400mm centres one way	7.14	15.00	8.22	1.10	0.14	25.14	0.30	33.65	m²	37.02
width exceeding 600mm; 50 x 50mm members at 500mm centres one way; 50 x 50mm subsidiary members at 400mm centres one way	6.43	15.00	7.40	0.90	0.11	20.50	0.25	28.14	m²	30.95
width exceeding 600mm; 19 x 38mm members at 300mm centres one way; 19 x 38mm subsidiary members at 300mm centres one way; fixing to masonry	3.82	15.00	4.39	2.25	0.28	51.32	0.59	56.30	m²	61.93
width exceeding 600mm; 25 x 50mm members at 300mm centres one way; 25 x 50mm subsidiary members at 300mm centres one way; fixing to masonry	5.13	15.00	5.91	2.35	0.29	53.56	0.63	60.09	m²	66.10
width 300mm; 38 x 50mm members longitudinally; 38 x 50mm subsidiary members at 400mm centres laterally	5.86	15.00	6.73	0.40	0.05	9.13	0.10	15.96	m	17.55
width 300mm; 50 x 50mm members longitudinally; 50 x 50mm subsidiary members at 400mm centres laterally	7.14	15.00	8.22	0.45	0.06	10.33	0.12	18.66	m	20.52
Individual supports										
16 x 16mm	0.34	15.00	0.39	0.08	0.01	1.83	0.02	2.23	m	2.46
16 x 38mm	0.56	15.00	0.64	0.08	0.01	1.83	0.02	2.48	m	2.73
16 x 50mm	1.07	15.00	1.23	0.09	0.01	2.03	0.02	3.28	m	3.61
16 x 75mm	0.24	15.00	0.28	0.10	0.01	2.24	0.03	2.56	m	2.81
19 x 38mm	0.57	15.00	0.66	0.09	0.01	2.03	0.02	2.71	m	2.98
19 x 50mm	0.83	15.00	0.96	0.10	0.01	2.24	0.03	3.23	m	3.56
19 x 75mm	0.91	15.00	1.04	0.10	0.01	2.24	0.03	3.32	m	3.65
19 x 100mm	1.21	15.00	1.39	0.11	0.01	2.45	0.03	3.88	m	4.26
19 x 150mm	1.73	15.00	1.99	0.12	0.02	2.82	0.03	4.84	m	5.33
25 x 50mm	0.77	15.00	0.89	0.10	0.01	2.24	0.03	3.16	m	3.48
25 x 100mm	1.40	15.00	1.61	0.12	0.02	2.82	0.03	4.46	m	4.90
25 x 150mm	2.02	15.00	2.32	0.18	0.03	4.22	0.05	6.60	m	7.26
25 x 175mm	2.69	15.00	3.09	0.21	0.03	4.85	0.07	8.01	m	8.81
25 x 200mm	3.08	15.00	3.54	0.19	0.02	4.28	0.05	7.87	m	8.65
38 x 50mm	1.17	15.00	1.35	0.11	0.01	2.45	0.03	3.83	m	4.21

Labour hourly rates: (except Specialists) Craft Operatives 20.87 Labourer 15.57 Rates are national average prices. Refer to REGIONAL VARIATIONS for indicative levels of overall pricing in regions	MATERIALS			LABOUR				RATES		
	Del to Site £	Waste %	Material Cost £	Craft Optve Hrs	Lab Hrs	Labour Cost £	Sunds £	Nett Rate £	Unit	Gross rate (10%) £
TIMBER FIRST FIXINGS (Cont'd)										
Softwood, sawn, impregnated; supports (Cont'd)										
Individual supports (Cont'd)										
50 x 50mm	1.43	15.00	1.64	0.12	0.02	2.82	0.03	4.49	m	4.94
50 x 150mm	4.23	15.00	4.86	0.17	0.02	3.86	0.05	8.77	m	9.65
50 x 300mm	12.34	15.00	14.19	0.23	0.03	5.27	0.07	19.52	m	21.48
75 x 75mm	3.46	15.00	3.98	0.17	0.02	3.86	0.05	7.89	m	8.68
75 x 100mm	4.57	15.00	5.26	0.18	0.02	4.07	0.05	9.37	m	10.31
75 x 150mm	6.76	15.00	7.77	0.21	0.03	4.85	0.07	12.69	m	13.96
100 x 100mm	5.25	15.00	6.04	0.19	0.02	4.28	0.05	10.36	m	11.40
100 x 150mm	12.93	15.00	14.87	0.23	0.03	5.27	0.07	20.20	m	22.22
100 x 200mm	17.24	15.00	19.83	0.26	0.04	6.05	0.08	25.96	m	28.55
100 x 300mm	26.25	15.00	30.19	0.40	0.05	9.13	0.13	39.45	m	43.39
150 x 150mm	12.15	15.00	13.98	0.30	0.04	6.88	0.10	20.96	m	23.05
16 x 38mm; fixing to masonry	0.56	15.00	0.64	0.23	0.03	5.27	0.07	5.97	m	6.57
19 x 38mm; fixing to masonry	0.57	15.00	0.66	0.24	0.03	5.48	0.07	6.20	m	6.82
25 x 50mm; fixing to masonry	0.77	15.00	0.89	0.25	0.03	5.68	0.07	6.64	m	7.30
38 x 50mm; fixing to masonry	1.17	15.00	1.35	0.27	0.03	6.10	0.07	7.51	m	8.27
50 x 50mm; fixing to masonry	1.43	15.00	1.64	0.28	0.04	6.47	0.08	8.19	m	9.01
25 x 25mm; 1 labours	0.55	10.00	0.60	0.11	0.01	2.45	0.03	3.08	m	3.39
25 x 25mm; 2 labours	0.67	10.00	0.73	0.11	0.01	2.45	0.03	3.22	m	3.54
25 x 38mm; 1 labours	0.65	10.00	0.71	0.11	0.01	2.45	0.03	3.20	m	3.52
25 x 38mm; 2 labours	0.77	10.00	0.84	0.11	0.01	2.45	0.03	3.33	m	3.66
triangular; extreme dimensions										
25 x 25mm	0.43	10.00	0.47	0.11	0.01	2.45	0.03	2.95	m	3.25
38 x 75mm	1.22	10.00	1.35	0.13	0.02	3.02	0.03	4.40	m	4.84
50 x 75mm	1.26	10.00	1.39	0.15	0.02	3.44	0.03	4.86	m	5.35
50 x 100mm	1.62	10.00	1.78	0.17	0.02	3.86	0.05	5.69	m	6.26
75 x 100mm	4.57	10.00	5.03	0.19	0.02	4.28	0.05	9.35	m	10.29
rounded roll for lead										
50 x 50mm	1.80	10.00	1.98	0.22	0.03	5.06	0.07	7.10	m	7.81
50 x 75mm	2.70	10.00	2.97	0.25	0.03	5.68	0.07	8.72	m	9.59
rounded roll for lead; birdsmouthed on to ridge or hip										
50 x 50mm	1.80	10.00	1.98	0.38	0.05	8.71	0.10	10.79	m	11.87
50 x 75mm	2.70	10.00	2.97	0.41	0.05	9.34	0.12	12.42	m	13.66
rounded roll for zinc										
32 x 44mm	1.80	10.00	1.98	0.16	0.02	3.65	0.05	5.68	m	6.25
Softwood, wrought; supports										
Butt jointed supports										
width exceeding 600mm; 19 x 38mm at 600mm centres; fixing to masonry	2.13	10.00	2.34	1.00	0.13	22.89	0.26	25.50	m²	28.05
width exceeding 600mm; 25 x 50mm at 600mm centres; fixing to masonry	2.76	10.00	3.04	1.10	0.14	25.14	0.30	28.47	m²	31.32
width exceeding 600mm; 19 x 38mm at 600mm centres; fixing to masonry with screws	2.24	10.00	2.46	1.40	0.16	31.71	0.08	34.25	m²	37.68
width exceeding 600mm; 25 x 50mm at 600mm centres; fixing to masonry with screws	2.91	10.00	3.19	1.50	0.21	34.57	0.08	37.85	m²	41.63
width exceeding 600mm; 19 x 38mm at 600mm centres; fixing to masonry with screws	2.31	10.00	2.53	1.80	0.20	40.68	0.16	43.37	m²	47.71
width exceeding 600mm; 25 x 50mm at 600mm centres; plugged and screwed to masonry	2.97	10.00	3.26	1.90	0.21	42.92	0.20	46.38	m²	51.02
Framed supports										
width exceeding 600mm; 38 x 50mm members at 400mm centres one way; 38 x 50mm subsidiary members at 400mm centres one way	6.20	10.00	6.82	1.00	0.13	22.89	0.26	29.98	m²	32.98
width exceeding 600mm; 38 x 50mm members at 500mm centres one way; 38 x 50mm subsidiary members at 400mm centres one way	5.58	10.00	6.14	0.80	0.10	18.25	0.21	24.61	m²	27.07
width exceeding 600mm; 50 x 50mm members at 400mm centres one way; 50 x 50mm subsidiary members at 400mm centres one way	8.05	10.00	8.86	1.10	0.14	25.14	0.30	34.29	m²	37.72
width exceeding 600mm; 50 x 50mm members at 500mm centres one way; 50 x 50mm subsidiary members at 400mm centres one way	7.24	10.00	7.97	0.90	0.11	20.50	0.25	28.71	m²	31.58
width exceeding 600mm; 19 x 38mm members at 600mm centres one way; 19 x 38mm subsidiary members at 600mm centres one way; fixing to masonry	4.26	10.00	4.69	2.25	0.28	51.32	0.59	56.60	m²	62.26
width exceeding 600mm; 25 x 50mm members at 600mm centres one way; 25 x 50mm subsidiary members at 600mm centres one way; fixing to masonry	5.53	10.00	6.08	2.35	0.29	53.56	0.63	60.27	m²	66.29
width not exceeding 600mm; 38 x 50mm members longitudinally; 38 x 50mm subsidiary members at 400mm centres laterally	6.20	10.00	6.82	0.40	0.05	9.13	0.10	16.05	m	17.65
width not exceeding 600mm; 50 x 50mm members longitudinally; 50 x 50mm subsidiary members at 400mm centres laterally	8.05	10.00	8.86	0.45	0.06	10.33	0.12	19.30	m	21.23
Individual supports										
6 x 38mm	0.26	10.00	0.29	0.08	0.01	1.83	0.02	2.13	m	2.35
12 x 38mm	0.53	10.00	0.58	0.08	0.01	1.83	0.02	2.42	m	2.67
19 x 38mm	0.64	10.00	0.70	0.09	0.01	2.03	0.02	2.75	m	3.03
25 x 50mm	0.83	10.00	0.91	0.10	0.01	2.24	0.03	3.19	m	3.51
38 x 50mm	1.24	10.00	1.36	0.11	0.01	2.45	0.03	3.85	m	4.23
50 x 50mm	1.61	10.00	1.77	0.12	0.02	2.82	0.03	4.62	m	5.08
50 x 75mm	2.42	10.00	2.66	0.14	0.02	3.23	0.03	5.93	m	6.52
50 x 100mm	3.15	10.00	3.47	0.15	0.02	3.44	0.05	6.96	m	7.65
50 x 150mm	4.73	10.00	5.20	0.17	0.02	3.86	0.05	9.11	m	10.02
50 x 200mm	6.35	10.00	6.99	0.20	0.02	4.49	0.05	11.52	m	12.67
50 x 300mm	10.88	10.00	11.97	0.23	0.03	5.27	0.07	17.30	m	19.03
75 x 75mm	3.63	10.00	3.99	0.17	0.02	3.86	0.05	7.90	m	8.69
75 x 100mm	4.87	10.00	5.36	0.18	0.02	4.07	0.05	9.47	m	10.42
75 x 150mm	7.09	10.00	7.80	0.21	0.03	4.85	0.07	12.71	m	13.99

Labour hourly rates: (except Specialists) Craft Operatives 20.87 Labourer 15.57 Rates are national average prices. Refer to REGIONAL VARIATIONS for indicative levels of overall pricing in regions	MATERIALS			LABOUR				RATES		
	Del to Site £	Waste %	Material Cost £	Craft Optve Hrs	Lab Hrs	Labour Cost £	Sunds £	Nett Rate £	Unit	Gross rate (10%) £
TIMBER FIRST FIXINGS (Cont'd)										
Softwood, wrought; supports (Cont'd)										
Individual supports (Cont'd)										
100 x 100mm	9.20	10.00	10.12	0.19	0.02	4.28	0.05	14.45	m	15.89
100 x 150mm	12.75	10.00	14.03	0.23	0.03	5.27	0.07	19.36	m	21.29
150 x 150mm	19.04	10.00	20.94	0.30	0.04	6.88	0.10	27.93	m	30.72
6 x 38mm; fixing to masonry	0.26	10.00	0.29	0.23	0.03	5.27	0.07	5.62	m	6.19
12 x 38mm; fixing to masonry	0.53	10.00	0.58	0.23	0.03	5.27	0.07	5.92	m	6.51
19 x 38mm; fixing to masonry	0.64	10.00	0.70	0.24	0.03	5.48	0.07	6.25	m	6.87
25 x 50mm; fixing to masonry	0.83	10.00	0.91	0.25	0.03	5.68	0.07	6.66	m	7.33
38 x 50mm; fixing to masonry	1.24	10.00	1.36	0.27	0.03	6.10	0.07	7.53	m	8.29
50 x 50mm; fixing to masonry	1.61	10.00	1.77	0.28	0.04	6.47	0.08	8.32	m	9.15
6 x 38mm, fixing with screws	0.29	10.00	0.32	0.23	0.01	4.96	0.02	5.30	m	5.82
12 x 38mm, fixing with screws	0.56	10.00	0.62	0.23	0.01	4.96	0.02	5.59	m	6.15
19 x 38mm, fixing with screws	0.67	10.00	0.73	0.20	0.01	4.33	0.02	5.08	m	5.59
25 x 50mm, fixing with screws	0.87	10.00	0.95	0.20	0.01	4.33	0.03	5.31	m	5.84
38 x 50mm, fixing with screws	1.29	10.00	1.42	0.21	0.01	4.54	0.03	5.99	m	6.59
50 x 50mm, fixing with screws	1.76	10.00	1.93	0.27	0.02	5.95	0.03	7.91	m	8.70
50 x 75mm, fixing with screws	2.57	10.00	2.82	0.28	0.02	6.16	0.03	9.01	m	9.91
50 x 100mm, fixing with screws	3.30	10.00	3.63	0.30	0.02	6.57	0.03	10.23	m	11.26
50 x 150mm, fixing with screws	4.96	10.00	5.45	0.40	0.02	8.66	0.05	14.15	m	15.57
50 x 200mm, fixing with screws	6.58	10.00	7.23	0.42	0.02	9.08	0.05	16.35	m	17.99
50 x 300mm, fixing with screws	11.19	10.00	12.29	0.53	0.03	11.53	0.07	23.89	m	26.27
6 x 38mm; plug and screwing to masonry	0.32	10.00	0.35	0.38	0.03	8.40	0.07	8.81	m	9.69
12 x 38mm; plug and screwing to masonry	0.59	10.00	0.64	0.38	0.03	8.40	0.07	9.11	m	10.02
19 x 38mm; plug and screwing to masonry	0.68	10.00	0.75	0.29	0.03	6.52	0.07	7.34	m	8.07
25 x 50mm; plug and screwing to masonry	0.88	10.00	0.97	0.30	0.03	6.73	0.07	7.76	m	8.54
38 x 50mm; plug and screwing to masonry	1.36	10.00	1.49	0.39	0.03	8.61	0.07	10.16	m	11.18
50 x 50mm; plug and screwing to masonry	1.83	10.00	2.01	0.42	0.04	9.39	0.08	11.48	m	12.62
50 x 75mm; plug and screwing to masonry	2.64	10.00	2.90	0.44	0.04	9.81	0.08	12.79	m	14.06
50 x 100mm; plug and screwing to masonry	3.37	10.00	3.70	0.46	0.04	10.22	0.08	14.01	m	15.41
50 x 150mm; plug and screwing to masonry	5.07	10.00	5.56	0.79	0.04	17.11	0.99	23.66	m	26.02
50 x 200mm; plug and screwing to masonry	6.69	10.00	7.34	0.81	0.04	17.53	0.12	24.98	m	27.48
TIMBER, METAL AND PLASTIC BOARDING, SHEETING, DECKING, CASINGS AND LININGS										
Softwood, sawn; fixing to timber - boarded flooring										
Boarding to floors, square edges; 19mm thick, 75mm wide boards width exceeding 600mm	12.67	7.50	13.62	0.60	0.08	13.77	0.16	27.55	m²	30.30
Boarding to floors, square edges; 25mm thick, 125mm wide boards width exceeding 600mm	14.16	7.50	15.22	0.55	0.07	12.57	0.15	27.94	m²	30.73
Boarding to floors, square edges; 32mm thick, 150mm wide boards width exceeding 600mm	21.47	7.50	23.08	0.55	0.07	12.57	0.15	35.79	m²	39.37
Softwood, wrought; fixing to timber - boarded flooring										
Boarding to floors, square edges; 19mm thick, 75mm wide boards width exceeding 600mm	12.93	7.50	13.90	0.70	0.09	16.01	0.18	30.09	m²	33.10
Boarding to floors, square edges; 25mm thick, 125mm wide boards width exceeding 600mm	16.83	7.50	18.10	0.65	0.08	14.81	0.18	33.09	m²	36.40
Boarding to floors, square edges; 32mm thick, 150mm wide boards width exceeding 600mm	24.20	7.50	26.02	0.65	0.08	14.81	0.18	41.01	m²	45.11
Boarding to floors, tongued and grooved joints; 19mm thick, 75mm wide boards width exceeding 600mm	13.09	7.50	14.07	0.80	0.10	18.25	0.21	32.54	m²	35.79
Boarding to floors, tongued and grooved joints; 25mm thick, 125mm wide boards width exceeding 600mm	18.36	7.50	19.74	0.75	0.10	17.21	0.20	37.15	m²	40.86
Boarding to floors, tongued and grooved joints; 32mm thick, 150mm wide boards width exceeding 600mm	29.07	7.50	31.25	0.75	0.10	17.21	0.20	48.66	m²	53.52
Abutments										
19mm thick softwood boarding										
raking cutting	1.29	7.50	1.39	0.06	-	1.25	-	2.64	m	2.91
curved cutting	1.94	7.50	2.09	0.09	-	1.88	-	3.96	m	4.36
25mm thick softwood boarding										
raking cutting	1.68	7.50	1.81	0.06	-	1.25	-	3.06	m	3.37
curved cutting	2.52	7.50	2.71	0.09	-	1.88	-	4.59	m	5.05
32mm thick softwood boarding										
raking cutting	2.42	7.50	2.60	0.06	-	1.25	-	3.85	m	4.24
curved cutting	3.63	7.50	3.90	0.09	-	1.88	-	5.78	m	6.36
Surface treatment of existing wood flooring; Sanding and sealing existing wood flooring										
Machine sanding width exceeding 600mm	-	-	-	0.50	-	10.44	1.10	11.54	m²	12.69
Prepare, one priming coat and one finish coat of seal width exceeding 600mm	-	-	-	0.16	-	3.34	0.55	3.89	m²	4.28

Labour hourly rates: (except Specialists) Craft Operatives 20.87 Labourer 15.57 Rates are national average prices. Refer to REGIONAL VARIATIONS for indicative levels of overall pricing in regions	MATERIALS			LABOUR				RATES		
	Del to Site £	Waste %	Material Cost £	Craft Optve Hrs	Lab Hrs	Labour Cost £	Sunds £	Nett Rate £	Unit	Gross rate (10%) £
TIMBER, METAL AND PLASTIC BOARDING, SHEETING, DECKING, CASINGS AND LININGS (Cont'd)										
Softwood, sawn, impregnated; fixing to timber; roof boarding										
Boarding to roofs, butt joints; 19mm thick, 75mm wide boards; external										
width exceeding 600mm	14.85	7.50	15.96	0.60	0.07	13.61	0.16	29.74	m²	32.72
width exceeding 600mm; sloping	14.85	7.50	15.96	0.70	0.09	16.01	0.18	32.16	m²	35.37
Boarding to roofs, butt joints; 25mm thick, 125mm wide boards; external										
width exceeding 600mm	15.43	7.50	16.59	0.55	0.07	12.57	0.15	29.31	m²	32.24
width exceeding 600mm; sloping	15.43	7.50	16.59	0.65	0.08	14.81	0.18	31.58	m²	34.74
Softwood, wrought, impregnated; fixing to timber; roof boarding										
Boarding to roofs, tongued and grooved joints; 19mm thick, 75mm wide boards external										
width exceeding 600mm	21.80	7.50	23.43	0.80	0.10	18.25	0.21	41.90	m²	46.09
extra; cross rebated and rounded drip; 50mm wide	2.47	10.00	2.72	0.20	0.03	4.64	0.05	7.41	m	8.15
extra; dovetailed cesspool 225 x 225 x 150mm	4.35	10.00	4.78	1.40	0.17	31.86	0.38	37.03	nr	40.73
extra; dovetailed cesspool 300 x 300 x 150mm	5.78	10.00	6.36	1.60	0.20	36.51	0.43	43.29	nr	47.62
width exceeding 600mm; sloping	21.80	7.50	23.43	0.90	0.11	20.50	0.25	44.18	m²	48.60
Boarding to roofs, tongued and grooved joints; 25mm thick, 125mm wide boards external										
width exceeding 600mm	21.79	7.50	23.43	0.75	0.09	17.05	0.20	40.68	m²	44.75
extra; cross rebated and rounded drip; 50mm wide	2.25	10.00	2.48	0.20	0.03	4.64	0.05	7.17	m	7.88
extra; dovetailed cesspool 225 x 225 x 150mm	4.80	10.00	5.28	1.50	0.19	34.26	0.40	39.94	nr	43.93
extra; dovetailed cesspool 300 x 300 x 150mm	6.24	10.00	6.86	1.70	0.21	38.75	0.46	46.07	nr	50.68
width exceeding 600mm; sloping	21.79	7.50	23.43	0.85	0.11	19.45	0.23	43.11	m²	47.42
Abutments										
19mm thick softwood boarding										
raking cutting	2.97	7.50	3.19	0.35	-	7.30	-	10.50	m	11.55
curved cutting	4.46	7.50	4.79	0.55	-	11.48	-	16.27	m	17.89
rebates	-	-	-	0.18	-	3.76	-	3.76	m	4.13
grooves	-	-	-	0.18	-	3.76	-	3.76	m	4.13
chamfers	-	-	-	0.13	-	2.71	-	2.71	m	2.98
25mm thick softwood boarding										
raking cutting	2.78	7.50	2.99	0.45	-	9.39	-	12.38	m	13.62
curved cutting	4.17	7.50	4.48	0.65	-	13.57	-	18.04	m	19.85
rebates	-	-	-	0.18	-	3.76	-	3.76	m	4.13
grooves	-	-	-	0.18	-	3.76	-	3.76	m	4.13
chamfers	-	-	-	0.13	-	2.71	-	2.71	m	2.98
Douglas Fir plywood, unsanded select sheathing quality, WBP bonded; tongued and grooved joints long edges										
15mm thick sheeting to floors width exceeding 600mm	18.67	7.50	20.08	0.29	0.04	6.68	0.16	26.92	m²	29.61
18mm thick sheeting to floors width exceeding 600mm	15.75	7.50	16.93	0.30	0.04	6.88	0.16	23.98	m²	26.38
Birch faced plywood, BB quality, WBP bonded; tongued and grooved joints all edges										
12mm thick sheeting to floors width exceeding 600mm	13.46	7.50	14.47	0.27	0.04	6.26	0.16	20.89	m²	22.98
15mm thick sheeting to floors width exceeding 600mm	15.60	7.50	16.77	0.29	0.04	6.68	0.16	23.61	m²	25.98
18mm thick sheeting to floors width exceeding 600mm	18.29	7.50	19.66	0.30	0.04	6.88	0.16	26.71	m²	29.38
Wood particle board (chipboard), BS EN 312, type P4 load bearing flooring, square edges; butt joints										
18mm thick sheeting to floors width exceeding 600mm	6.85	7.50	7.36	0.30	0.04	6.88	0.16	14.41	m²	15.85
22mm thick sheeting to floors width exceeding 600mm	8.69	7.50	9.34	0.30	0.04	6.88	0.16	16.39	m²	18.03
Wood particle board (chipboard), BS EN 312, type P5 load bearing moisture resistant flooring, square edges; butt joints										
18mm thick sheeting to floors width exceeding 600mm	6.08	7.50	6.53	0.30	0.04	6.88	0.16	13.58	m²	14.94
22mm thick sheeting to floors width exceeding 600mm	7.50	7.50	8.06	0.30	0.04	6.88	0.16	15.11	m²	16.62
Wood particle board (chipboard), BS EN 312, type P6 heavyduty load bearing flooring, square edges; butt joints										
18mm thick sheeting to floors width exceeding 600mm	9.62	7.50	10.35	0.30	0.04	6.88	0.16	17.40	m²	19.14
22mm thick sheeting to floors width exceeding 600mm	11.88	7.50	12.77	0.30	0.04	6.88	0.16	19.82	m²	21.80
38mm thick sheeting to floors width exceeding 600mm	16.32	7.50	17.54	0.40	0.10	9.91	0.25	27.70	m²	30.46

CARPENTRY

Labour hourly rates: (except Specialists) Craft Operatives 20.87 Labourer 15.57 Rates are national average prices. Refer to REGIONAL VARIATIONS for indicative levels of overall pricing in regions	MATERIALS			LABOUR				RATES		
	Del to Site £	Waste %	Material Cost £	Craft Optve Hrs	Lab Hrs	Labour Cost £	Sunds £	Nett Rate £	Unit	Gross rate (10%) £
TIMBER, METAL AND PLASTIC BOARDING, SHEETING, DECKING, CASINGS AND LININGS (Cont'd)										
Wood particle board (chipboard), BS EN 312, type P4 load bearing flooring; tongued and grooved joints										
18mm thick sheeting to floors										
width exceeding 600mm	6.08	7.50	6.53	0.30	0.04	6.88	0.16	13.58	m²	14.94
22mm thick sheeting to floors										
width exceeding 600mm	7.50	7.50	8.06	0.30	0.04	6.88	0.16	15.11	m²	16.62
Wood particle board (chipboard), BS EN 312, type P5 load bearing moisture resistant flooring; tongued and grooved joints										
18mm thick sheeting to floors										
width exceeding 600mm	8.33	7.50	8.96	0.30	0.04	6.88	0.16	16.01	m²	17.61
22mm thick sheeting to floors										
width exceeding 600mm	11.11	7.50	11.94	0.30	0.04	6.88	0.16	18.99	m²	20.89
Abutments										
12mm thick plywood linings										
raking cutting	1.35	7.50	1.45	0.03	-	0.63	-	2.07	m	2.28
curved cutting	2.02	7.50	2.17	0.05	-	1.04	-	3.21	m	3.53
15mm thick plywood linings										
raking cutting	1.56	7.50	1.68	0.04	-	0.83	-	2.51	m	2.76
curved cutting	2.34	7.50	2.52	0.06	-	1.25	-	3.77	m	4.15
18mm thick plywood linings										
raking cutting	1.83	7.50	1.97	0.04	-	0.83	-	2.80	m	3.08
curved cutting	2.74	7.50	2.95	0.06	-	1.25	-	4.20	m	4.62
18mm thick wood particle board (chipboard) linings										
raking cutting	0.68	7.50	0.74	0.03	-	0.63	-	1.36	m	1.50
curved cutting	1.03	7.50	1.10	0.05	-	1.04	-	2.15	m	2.36
22mm thick wood particle board (particle board (chipboard)) linings										
raking cutting	0.87	7.50	0.93	0.04	-	0.83	-	1.77	m	1.95
curved cutting	1.30	7.50	1.40	0.06	-	1.25	-	2.65	m	2.92
Floating insulated floors; Wood particle board (chipboard), BS EN 312, type P4 load bearing flooring; glued tongued and grooved joints										
18mm thick sheeting laid loose over insulation										
width exceeding 600mm	6.08	7.50	6.53	0.30	0.04	6.88	0.16	13.58	m²	14.94
22mm thick sheeting to floors										
width exceeding 600mm	7.50	7.50	8.06	0.30	0.04	6.88	0.16	15.11	m²	16.62
Floating insulated floors; Wood particle board (chipboard), BS EN 312, type P5 load bearing moisture resistant flooring; glued tongued and grooved joints										
18mm thick sheeting laid loose over insulation										
width exceeding 600mm	8.33	7.50	8.96	0.30	0.04	6.88	0.16	16.01	m²	17.61
22mm thick sheeting to floors										
width exceeding 600mm	11.11	7.50	11.94	0.30	0.04	6.88	0.16	18.99	m²	20.89
Sound insulated floors; Foam backed softwood battens covered with tongued and grooved particle board (chipboard) or plywood panels										
19mm particle board (chipboard) panels to level sub-floors										
width exceeding 600mm; battens at 450mm centres; elevation										
42mm	11.98	10.00	12.89	0.27	0.03	6.10	0.43	19.42	m²	21.36
82mm	12.51	10.00	13.44	0.27	0.03	6.10	0.46	20.01	m²	22.01
width exceeding 600mm; battens at 600mm centres; elevation										
42mm	10.49	10.00	11.32	0.27	0.03	6.10	0.36	17.79	m²	19.57
82mm	10.89	10.00	11.74	0.27	0.03	6.10	0.38	18.22	m²	20.04
18mm particle board (chipboard) panels with improved moisture resistance to level sub-floors										
width exceeding 600mm; battens at 450mm centres; elevation										
42mm	14.24	10.00	15.37	0.27	0.03	6.10	0.43	21.90	m²	24.09
82mm	14.77	10.00	15.93	0.27	0.03	6.10	0.46	22.49	m²	24.74
width exceeding 600mm; battens at 600mm centres; elevation										
42mm	12.75	10.00	13.80	0.27	0.03	6.10	0.36	20.27	m²	22.30
82mm	13.15	10.00	14.22	0.27	0.03	6.10	0.38	20.70	m²	22.77
18mm plywood panels to level sub-floors										
width exceeding 600mm; battens at 450mm centres; elevation										
42mm	21.66	10.00	23.53	0.27	0.03	6.10	0.43	30.06	m²	33.07
82mm	22.19	10.00	24.09	0.27	0.03	6.10	0.46	30.65	m²	33.72
Fibreboards and hardboards; Standard hardboard, BS EN 622; butt joints										
3.2mm thick linings to walls										
width exceeding 600mm	1.57	5.00	1.65	0.33	0.04	7.51	0.54	9.70	m²	10.67
300mm wide	0.47	10.00	0.52	0.20	0.01	4.33	0.33	5.18	m	5.69
4.8mm thick linings to walls										
width exceeding 600mm	5.52	5.00	5.80	0.34	0.04	7.72	0.56	14.08	m²	15.49
300mm wide	1.66	10.00	1.82	0.20	0.01	4.33	0.33	6.48	m	7.13

Labour hourly rates: (except Specialists) Craft Operatives 20.87 Labourer 15.57 Rates are national average prices. Refer to REGIONAL VARIATIONS for indicative levels of overall pricing in regions	MATERIALS			LABOUR				RATES		
	Del to Site £	Waste %	Material Cost £	Craft Optve Hrs	Lab Hrs	Labour Cost £	Sunds £	Nett Rate £	Unit	Gross rate (10%) £
TIMBER, METAL AND PLASTIC BOARDING, SHEETING, DECKING, CASINGS AND LININGS (Cont'd)										
Fibreboards and hardboards; Standard hardboard, BS EN 622; butt joints (Cont'd)										
6.4mm thick linings to walls										
width exceeding 600mm	7.37	5.00	7.74	0.35	0.04	7.93	0.58	16.24	m²	17.87
300mm wide	2.21	10.00	2.43	0.21	0.01	4.54	0.35	7.32	m	8.05
3.2mm thick sheeting to floors										
width exceeding 600mm	1.57	5.00	1.65	0.17	0.02	3.86	0.28	5.79	m²	6.36
3.2mm thick linings to ceilings										
width exceeding 600mm	1.57	5.00	1.65	0.41	0.05	9.34	0.68	11.66	m²	12.82
300mm wide	0.47	10.00	0.52	0.25	0.02	5.53	0.41	6.46	m	7.10
4.8mm thick linings to ceilings										
width exceeding 600mm	5.52	5.00	5.80	0.43	0.05	9.75	0.71	16.26	m²	17.89
300mm wide	1.66	10.00	1.82	0.26	0.02	5.74	0.43	7.99	m	8.79
6.4mm thick linings to ceilings										
width exceeding 600mm	7.37	5.00	7.74	0.44	0.05	9.96	0.73	18.42	m²	20.27
300mm wide	2.21	10.00	2.43	0.26	0.02	5.74	0.43	8.60	m	9.46
Fibreboards and hardboards; Tempered hardboard, BS EN 622; butt joints										
3.2mm thick linings to walls										
width exceeding 600mm	3.43	5.00	3.60	0.33	0.04	7.51	0.54	11.66	m²	12.82
300mm wide	1.03	10.00	1.13	0.20	0.01	4.33	0.33	5.79	m	6.37
4.8mm thick linings to walls										
width exceeding 600mm	4.83	5.00	5.07	0.34	0.04	7.72	0.56	13.35	m²	14.69
300mm wide	1.45	10.00	1.59	0.20	0.01	4.33	0.33	6.25	m	6.88
6.4mm thick linings to walls										
width exceeding 600mm	6.81	5.00	7.15	0.35	0.04	7.93	0.58	15.66	m²	17.23
300mm wide	2.04	10.00	2.25	0.21	0.01	4.54	0.35	7.13	m	7.85
3.2mm thick linings to ceilings										
width exceeding 600mm	3.43	5.00	3.60	0.41	0.05	9.34	0.68	13.62	m²	14.98
300mm wide	1.03	10.00	1.13	0.25	0.02	5.53	0.41	7.07	m	7.78
4.8mm thick linings to ceilings										
width exceeding 600mm	4.83	5.00	5.07	0.43	0.05	9.75	0.71	15.54	m²	17.09
300mm wide	1.45	10.00	1.59	0.26	0.02	5.74	0.43	7.76	m	8.54
6.4mm thick linings to ceilings										
width exceeding 600mm	6.81	5.00	7.15	0.44	0.05	9.96	0.73	17.84	m²	19.63
300mm wide	2.04	10.00	2.25	0.26	0.02	5.74	0.43	8.42	m	9.26
Fibreboards and hardboards; Flame retardant hardboard, BS EN 622 tested to BS 476 Part 7 Class 1; butt joints										
3.2mm thick linings to walls										
width exceeding 600mm	12.99	5.00	13.64	0.33	0.04	7.51	0.54	21.70	m²	23.87
300mm wide	3.90	10.00	4.29	0.20	0.01	4.33	0.33	8.95	m	9.84
4.8mm thick linings to walls										
width exceeding 600mm	17.35	5.00	18.22	0.34	0.04	7.72	0.56	26.50	m²	29.15
300mm wide	5.21	10.00	5.73	0.20	0.01	4.33	0.33	10.39	m	11.42
6.4mm thick linings to walls										
width exceeding 600mm	23.53	5.00	24.71	0.35	0.04	7.93	0.58	33.21	m²	36.53
300mm wide	7.06	10.00	7.76	0.21	0.01	4.54	0.35	12.65	m	13.91
3.2mm thick linings to ceilings										
width exceeding 600mm	12.99	5.00	13.64	0.41	0.05	9.34	0.68	23.66	m²	26.02
300mm wide	3.90	10.00	4.29	0.25	0.02	5.53	0.41	10.23	m	11.25
4.8mm thick linings to ceilings										
width exceeding 600mm	17.35	5.00	18.22	0.43	0.05	9.75	0.71	28.68	m²	31.55
300mm wide	5.21	10.00	5.73	0.26	0.02	5.74	0.43	11.89	m	13.08
6.4mm thick linings to ceilings										
width exceeding 600mm	23.53	5.00	24.71	0.44	0.06	10.12	0.73	35.55	m²	39.10
300mm wide	7.06	10.00	7.76	0.26	0.02	5.74	0.43	13.93	m	15.32
Fibreboards and hardboards; Medium density fibreboard, BS EN 622, type MDF; butt joints										
9mm thick linings to walls										
width exceeding 600mm	4.46	5.00	4.69	0.35	0.04	7.93	0.58	13.19	m²	14.51
300mm wide	1.34	10.00	1.47	0.21	0.01	4.54	0.35	6.36	m	6.99
12mm thick linings to walls										
width exceeding 600mm	5.79	5.00	6.08	0.38	0.05	8.71	0.63	15.41	m²	16.96
300mm wide	1.74	10.00	1.91	0.23	0.02	5.11	0.38	7.40	m	8.14
18mm thick linings to walls										
width exceeding 600mm	9.66	5.00	10.15	0.41	0.05	9.34	0.68	20.16	m²	22.17
300mm wide	2.90	10.00	3.19	0.24	0.02	5.32	0.40	8.91	m	9.80
25mm thick linings to walls										
width exceeding 600mm	10.22	5.00	10.73	0.44	0.06	10.12	0.73	21.57	m²	23.73
300mm wide	3.07	10.00	3.37	0.26	0.02	5.74	0.43	9.54	m	10.49
9mm thick linings to ceilings										
width exceeding 600mm	4.46	5.00	4.69	0.44	0.06	10.12	0.73	15.53	m²	17.08
300mm wide	1.34	10.00	1.47	0.26	0.02	5.74	0.43	7.64	m	8.40

Labour hourly rates: (except Specialists) Craft Operatives 20.87 Labourer 15.57 Rates are national average prices. Refer to REGIONAL VARIATIONS for indicative levels of overall pricing in regions	MATERIALS			LABOUR				RATES		
	Del to Site £	Waste %	Material Cost £	Craft Optve Hrs	Lab Hrs	Labour Cost £	Sunds £	Nett Rate £	Unit	Gross rate (10%) £
TIMBER, METAL AND PLASTIC BOARDING, SHEETING, DECKING, CASINGS AND LININGS (Cont'd)										
Fibreboards and hardboards; Medium density fibreboard, BS EN 622, type MDF; butt joints (Cont'd)										
12mm thick linings to ceilings										
width exceeding 600mm	5.79	5.00	6.08	0.48	0.06	10.95	0.79	17.82	m²	19.60
300mm wide	1.74	10.00	1.91	0.29	0.02	6.36	0.48	8.75	m	9.63
18mm thick linings to ceilings										
width exceeding 600mm	9.66	5.00	10.15	0.52	0.07	11.94	0.86	22.95	m²	25.24
300mm wide	2.90	10.00	3.19	0.31	0.02	6.78	0.51	10.48	m	11.53
25mm thick linings to ceilings										
width exceeding 600mm	10.22	5.00	10.73	0.56	0.07	12.78	0.92	24.43	m²	26.87
300mm wide	3.07	10.00	3.37	0.34	0.02	7.41	0.56	11.34	m	12.47
Fibreboards and hardboards; Insulating softboard, BS EN 622; butt joints										
13mm thick linings to walls										
width exceeding 600mm	2.92	5.00	3.06	0.38	0.05	8.71	0.63	12.40	m²	13.64
300mm wide	0.88	10.00	0.96	0.23	0.02	5.11	0.38	6.45	m	7.10
13mm thick linings to ceilings										
width exceeding 600mm	2.92	5.00	3.06	0.48	0.06	10.95	0.79	14.81	m²	16.29
300mm wide	0.88	10.00	0.96	0.29	0.02	6.36	0.48	7.81	m	8.59
Roof boarding; Plywood BS EN 636, II/III grade, WBP bonded; butt joints										
18mm thick sheeting to roofs; external										
width exceeding 600mm	13.07	10.00	14.37	0.30	0.04	6.88	0.08	21.34	m²	23.47
extra; cesspool 225 x 225 x 150mm	2.61	10.00	2.87	1.40	0.18	32.02	0.38	35.27	nr	38.80
extra; cesspool 300 x 300 x 150mm	3.59	10.00	3.95	1.50	0.19	34.26	0.40	38.61	nr	42.47
width exceeding 600mm; sloping	13.07	10.00	14.37	0.40	0.05	9.13	0.10	23.60	m²	25.96
Abutments										
raking cutting	1.31	10.00	1.44	0.30	-	6.26	-	7.70	m	8.47
curved cutting	1.96	10.00	2.16	0.45	-	9.39	-	11.55	m	12.70
rebates	-	-	-	0.18	-	3.76	-	3.76	m	4.13
grooves	-	-	-	0.18	-	3.76	-	3.76	m	4.13
chamfers	-	-	-	0.13	-	2.71	-	2.71	m	2.98
24mm thick sheeting to roofs; external										
width exceeding 600mm	18.08	10.00	19.89	0.35	0.04	7.93	0.08	27.90	m²	30.69
extra; cesspool 225 x 225 x 150mm	3.62	10.00	3.98	1.50	0.19	34.26	0.40	38.64	nr	42.50
extra; cesspool 300 x 300 x 150mm	4.97	10.00	5.47	1.60	0.20	36.51	0.43	42.40	nr	46.64
width exceeding 600mm; sloping	18.08	10.00	19.89	0.45	0.06	10.33	0.12	30.33	m²	33.36
Abutments										
raking cutting	1.81	10.00	1.99	0.40	-	8.35	-	10.34	m	11.37
curved cutting	2.71	10.00	2.98	0.60	-	12.52	-	15.51	m	17.06
rebates	-	-	-	0.18	-	3.76	-	3.76	m	4.13
grooves	-	-	-	0.18	-	3.76	-	3.76	m	4.13
chamfers	-	-	-	0.13	-	2.71	-	2.71	m	2.98
Roof boarding; Wood particle board (chipboard), BS EN 312, type 1 standard; butt joints										
12mm thick sheeting to roofs; external										
width exceeding 600mm	3.66	10.00	4.03	0.25	0.03	5.68	0.07	9.78	m²	10.76
extra; cesspool 225 x 225 x 150mm	0.73	10.00	0.81	1.30	0.16	29.62	0.35	30.77	nr	33.85
extra; cesspool 300 x 300 x 150mm	1.01	10.00	1.11	1.40	0.18	32.02	0.38	33.51	nr	36.86
width exceeding 600mm; sloping	3.66	10.00	4.03	0.35	0.04	7.93	0.10	12.06	m²	13.26
Abutments										
raking cutting	0.37	10.00	0.40	0.25	-	5.22	-	5.62	m	6.18
curved cutting	0.55	10.00	0.60	0.35	-	7.30	-	7.91	m	8.70
rebates	-	-	-	0.18	-	3.76	-	3.76	m	4.13
grooves	-	-	-	0.18	-	3.76	-	3.76	m	4.13
chamfers	-	-	-	0.13	-	2.71	-	2.71	m	2.98
18mm thick sheeting to roofs; external										
width exceeding 600mm	4.92	10.00	5.41	0.30	0.04	6.88	0.08	12.37	m²	13.61
extra; cesspool 225 x 225 x 150mm	0.98	10.00	1.08	1.40	0.18	32.02	0.38	33.48	nr	36.83
extra; cesspool 300 x 300 x 150mm	1.35	10.00	1.49	1.50	0.19	34.26	0.40	36.15	nr	39.76
width exceeding 600mm; sloping	4.92	10.00	5.41	0.40	0.05	9.13	0.10	14.63	m²	16.10
Abutments										
raking cutting	0.49	10.00	0.54	0.30	-	6.26	-	6.80	m	7.48
curved cutting	0.74	10.00	0.81	0.45	-	9.39	-	10.20	m	11.22
rebates	-	-	-	0.18	-	3.76	-	3.76	m	4.13
grooves	-	-	-	0.18	-	3.76	-	3.76	m	4.13
chamfers	-	-	-	0.13	-	2.71	-	2.71	m	2.98
Softwood, wrought, impregnated; gutter boarding										
Gutter boards including sides, tongued and grooved joints										
width exceeding 600mm; 19mm thick	13.89	10.00	15.28	2.00	0.25	45.63	0.53	61.44	m²	67.58
width exceeding 600mm; 25mm thick	17.51	10.00	19.26	2.25	0.28	51.32	0.59	71.17	m²	78.28
width not exceeding 600mm; 19mm thick										
150mm wide	2.08	10.00	2.29	0.30	0.04	6.88	0.08	9.26	m	10.18
225mm wide	3.13	10.00	3.44	0.40	0.05	9.13	0.10	12.66	m	13.93
width not exceeding 600mm; 25mm thick										
150mm wide	2.63	10.00	2.89	0.33	0.04	7.51	0.08	10.48	m	11.53
225mm wide	3.94	10.00	4.33	0.44	0.05	9.96	0.12	14.41	m	15.85
cesspool 225 x 225 x 150mm deep	3.24	10.00	3.56	1.50	0.19	34.26	0.40	38.22	nr	42.04

Labour hourly rates: (except Specialists) Craft Operatives 20.87 Labourer 15.57 Rates are national average prices. Refer to REGIONAL VARIATIONS for indicative levels of overall pricing in regions	MATERIALS			LABOUR				RATES		
	Del to Site £	Waste %	Material Cost £	Craft Optve Hrs	Lab Hrs	Labour Cost £	Sunds £	Nett Rate £	Unit	Gross rate (10%) £
TIMBER, METAL AND PLASTIC BOARDING, SHEETING, DECKING, CASINGS AND LININGS (Cont'd)										
Softwood, wrought, impregnated; gutter boarding (Cont'd)										
Chimney gutter boards, butt joints										
width not exceeding 600mm; 25mm thick x 100mm average wide	1.75	10.00	1.93	0.50	0.06	11.37	0.13	13.43	m	14.77
gusset end	0.69	10.00	0.76	0.35	0.04	7.93	0.10	8.79	nr	9.66
width not exceeding 600mm; 25mm thick x 175mm average wide	3.06	10.00	3.37	0.65	0.08	14.81	0.18	18.36	m	20.20
gusset end	0.96	10.00	1.05	0.40	0.05	9.13	0.10	10.28	nr	11.30
Lier boards; tongued and grooved joints										
width exceeding 600mm; 19mm thick	13.89	10.00	15.28	0.90	0.11	20.50	0.25	36.02	m²	39.62
width exceeding 600mm; 25mm thick	17.51	10.00	19.26	1.00	0.12	22.74	0.26	42.26	m²	46.48
Valley sole boards; butt joints										
width not exceeding 600mm; 25mm thick										
100mm wide	1.75	10.00	1.93	0.45	0.06	10.33	0.12	12.37	m	13.60
150mm wide	2.63	10.00	2.89	0.50	0.06	11.37	0.13	14.39	m	15.83
Plywood BS EN 636, II/III grade, WBP bonded, butt joints; gutter boarding										
Gutter boards including sides, butt joints										
width exceeding 600mm; 18mm thick	14.04	10.00	15.45	1.50	0.19	34.26	0.40	50.11	m²	55.12
width exceeding 600mm; 25mm thick	19.67	10.00	21.64	1.65	0.21	37.71	0.45	59.79	m²	65.77
width not exceeding 600mm; 18mm thick										
150mm wide	2.11	10.00	2.32	0.20	0.03	4.64	0.05	7.01	m	7.71
225mm wide	3.16	10.00	3.48	0.22	0.03	5.06	0.07	8.60	m	9.46
width not exceeding 600mm; 25mm thick										
150mm wide	2.95	10.00	3.25	0.23	0.03	5.27	0.07	8.58	m	9.44
225mm wide	4.43	10.00	4.87	0.25	0.03	5.68	0.07	10.62	m	11.68
cesspool 225 x 225 x 150mm deep	3.64	10.00	4.00	1.50	0.19	34.26	0.40	38.66	nr	42.53
Softwood, wrought, impregnated; eaves and verge boarding										
Fascia and barge boards										
width not exceeding 600mm; 25mm thick										
150mm wide	2.63	10.00	2.89	0.22	0.03	5.06	0.07	8.01	m	8.81
200mm wide	3.50	10.00	3.85	0.23	0.03	5.27	0.07	9.18	m	10.10
Fascia and barge boards, tongued, grooved and veed joints										
width not exceeding 600mm; 25mm thick										
225mm wide	3.94	10.00	4.33	0.30	0.04	6.88	0.08	11.30	m	12.43
250mm wide	4.38	10.00	4.81	0.32	0.04	7.30	0.08	12.20	m	13.42
Eaves or verge soffit boards										
width exceeding 600mm; 25mm thick	17.51	10.00	19.26	1.00	0.12	22.74	0.26	42.26	m²	46.48
width not exceeding 600mm; 25mm thick										
225mm wide	3.94	10.00	4.33	0.30	0.04	6.88	0.08	11.30	m	12.43
Plywood BS EN 636, II/III grade, WBP bonded, butt joints; eaves and verge boarding										
Fascia and barge boards										
width not exceeding 600mm; 18mm thick										
150mm wide	2.11	10.00	2.32	0.22	0.03	5.06	0.07	7.44	m	8.19
225mm wide	3.16	10.00	3.48	0.23	0.03	5.27	0.07	8.81	m	9.69
250mm wide	3.51	10.00	3.86	0.24	0.03	5.48	0.07	9.40	m	10.34
Eaves or verge soffit boards										
width exceeding 600mm; 18mm thick	14.04	10.00	15.45	0.75	0.09	17.05	0.20	32.70	m²	35.97
width not exceeding 600mm; 18mm thick										
225mm wide	3.16	10.00	3.48	0.25	0.03	5.68	0.07	9.23	m	10.15
Fascia and bargeboards; PVC										
Fascia; 9mm thick; mahogany woodgrain square edge with return leg; fixing to timber with Polytop screws										
175mm wide	6.46	5.00	6.79	0.20	0.03	4.64	0.79	12.22	m	13.44
225mm wide	7.79	5.00	8.18	0.20	0.03	4.64	0.79	13.61	m	14.97
400mm wide	17.74	5.00	18.62	0.25	0.04	5.76	1.58	25.97	m	28.57
Fascia; 22mm thick; white solid bullnose with soffit groove; fixing to timber with Polytop screws										
150mm wide	7.70	5.00	8.08	0.20	0.03	4.64	0.79	13.52	m	14.87
200mm wide	10.80	5.00	11.34	0.20	0.03	4.64	0.79	16.78	m	18.45
250mm wide	13.00	5.00	13.65	0.20	0.03	4.64	1.58	19.88	m	21.86
Fascia; 10mm thick; white square edge board; fixing to timber with Polytop screws										
100mm wide	2.22	5.00	2.33	0.30	0.04	6.88	0.79	10.01	m	11.01
150mm wide	3.11	5.00	3.27	0.30	0.04	6.88	0.79	10.94	m	12.04
225mm wide	4.77	5.00	5.01	0.30	0.04	6.88	0.79	12.69	m	13.96
Multi purpose 9mm thick; white pre-vented soffit board; fixing to timber with Polytop screws										
150mm wide	4.15	5.00	4.36	0.40	0.06	9.28	0.79	14.43	m	15.87
225mm wide	5.15	5.00	5.41	0.40	0.06	9.28	1.58	16.28	m	17.90
300mm wide	6.60	5.00	6.93	0.60	0.08	13.77	2.38	23.07	m	25.38
Multi purpose 10mm thick soffit board; fixing to timber with Polytop screws										
100mm wide	2.22	5.00	2.33	0.40	0.06	9.28	0.79	12.41	m	13.65
175mm wide	3.45	5.00	3.62	0.40	0.06	9.28	0.79	13.70	m	15.07
200mm wide	3.49	5.00	3.67	0.40	0.06	9.28	1.58	14.54	m	15.99
300mm wide	6.21	5.00	6.52	0.60	0.08	13.77	2.38	22.66	m	24.93

Labour hourly rates: (except Specialists) Craft Operatives 20.87 Labourer 15.57 Rates are national average prices. Refer to REGIONAL VARIATIONS for indicative levels of overall pricing in regions	MATERIALS			LABOUR				RATES		
	Del to Site £	Waste %	Material Cost £	Craft Optve Hrs	Lab Hrs	Labour Cost £	Sunds £	Nett Rate £	Unit	Gross rate (10%) £
METAL AND PLASTIC ACCESSORIES										
Metal fixings, fastenings and fittings										
Steel; tie rods and straps										
19mm diameter; threaded										
Tie rod	7.68	2.50	7.87	0.25	0.03	5.68	-	13.56	m	14.91
extra; for nut and washer	0.55	2.50	0.56	0.20	0.03	4.64	-	5.20	nr	5.73
25mm diameter; threaded										
Tie rod	11.52	2.50	11.81	0.30	0.04	6.88	-	18.69	m	20.56
extra; for nut and washer	1.04	2.50	1.07	0.30	0.04	6.88	-	7.95	nr	8.74
Straps; 3 x 38; holes -4; fixing with bolts (bolts included elsewhere)										
500mm long	0.81	2.50	0.83	0.13	0.02	3.02	-	3.85	nr	4.24
750mm long	1.56	2.50	1.60	0.19	0.02	4.28	-	5.88	nr	6.46
1000mm long	1.90	2.50	1.95	0.25	0.03	5.68	-	7.63	nr	8.40
Straps; 6 x 50; holes -4; fixing with bolts (bolts included elsewhere)										
500mm long	1.67	2.50	1.71	0.16	0.02	3.65	-	5.36	nr	5.90
750mm long	3.28	2.50	3.36	0.23	0.03	5.27	-	8.63	nr	9.49
1000mm long	4.08	2.50	4.18	0.30	0.04	6.88	-	11.07	nr	12.17
Steel; galvanised; straps										
Straps and clips; Expamet Bat; light duty strapping; fixing with nails										
600mm long	1.36	5.00	1.43	0.15	0.02	3.44	0.03	4.90	nr	5.39
800mm long	1.94	5.00	2.04	0.17	0.02	3.86	0.05	5.95	nr	6.54
1000mm long	2.24	5.00	2.35	0.18	0.02	4.07	0.05	6.47	nr	7.12
1200mm long	2.29	5.00	2.40	0.19	0.02	4.28	0.05	6.73	nr	7.40
1600mm long	3.86	5.00	4.06	0.20	0.02	4.49	0.05	8.59	nr	9.45
Straps and clips; Expamet Bat; light duty strapping; twists -1; fixing with nails										
600mm long	1.36	5.00	1.43	0.15	0.02	3.44	0.03	4.90	nr	5.39
800mm long	1.94	5.00	2.04	0.17	0.02	3.86	0.05	5.95	nr	6.54
1000mm long	2.24	5.00	2.35	0.18	0.02	4.07	0.05	6.47	nr	7.12
1200mm long	2.29	5.00	2.40	0.19	0.02	4.28	0.05	6.73	nr	7.40
1600mm long	3.22	5.00	3.38	0.20	0.02	4.49	0.05	7.92	nr	8.71
Straps and clips; Expamet Bat; heavy duty strapping; bends -1; nailing one end (building in included elsewhere)										
600mm long	2.04	5.00	2.14	0.08	0.02	1.98	0.03	4.16	nr	4.57
800mm long	2.48	5.00	2.60	0.08	0.02	1.98	0.03	4.62	nr	5.08
1000mm long	3.48	5.00	3.65	0.09	0.02	2.19	0.03	5.88	nr	6.46
1200mm long	4.02	5.00	4.22	0.09	0.02	2.19	0.03	6.44	nr	7.09
1600mm long	5.23	5.00	5.49	0.10	0.02	2.40	0.03	7.92	nr	8.72
Straps and clips; Expamet Bat; heavy duty strapping; bends -1; twists -1; nailing one end (building in included elsewhere)										
600mm long	2.04	5.00	2.14	0.08	0.02	1.98	0.03	4.16	nr	4.57
800mm long	2.48	5.00	2.60	0.08	0.02	1.98	0.03	4.62	nr	5.08
1000mm long	3.48	5.00	3.65	0.09	0.02	2.19	0.03	5.88	nr	6.46
1200mm long	4.02	5.00	4.22	0.09	0.02	2.19	0.03	6.44	nr	7.09
1600mm long	5.23	5.00	5.49	0.10	0.02	2.40	0.03	7.92	nr	8.72
truss clips; fixing with nails										
for 38mm thick members	0.31	5.00	0.33	0.20	0.02	4.49	0.05	4.86	nr	5.35
for 50mm thick members	0.40	5.00	0.42	0.20	0.02	4.49	0.05	4.95	nr	5.45
Steel; galvanised; shoes										
Post shoe fixing with bolts to concrete										
to suit 100 x 100 post	5.25	5.00	5.51	0.40	0.04	8.97	1.15	15.64	nr	17.20
to suit 150 x 150 post	6.04	5.00	6.34	0.44	0.05	9.96	0.12	16.42	nr	18.06
Bolts; steel; black, BS 4190 grade 4.6										
M 8; with nuts and washers										
30mm long	0.11	5.00	0.12	0.07	0.01	1.62	-	1.73	nr	1.91
40mm long	0.11	5.00	0.12	0.08	0.01	1.83	-	1.94	nr	2.14
50mm long	0.14	5.00	0.14	0.08	0.01	1.83	-	1.97	nr	2.17
60mm long	0.14	5.00	0.14	0.08	0.01	1.83	-	1.97	nr	2.16
70mm long	0.13	5.00	0.14	0.10	0.01	2.24	-	2.38	nr	2.62
80mm long	0.14	5.00	0.15	0.10	0.01	2.24	-	2.39	nr	2.63
90mm long	0.14	5.00	0.15	0.10	0.01	2.24	-	2.39	nr	2.63
100mm long	0.21	5.00	0.22	0.10	0.01	2.24	-	2.46	nr	2.70
120mm long	0.23	5.00	0.24	0.10	0.01	2.24	-	2.48	nr	2.73
M 10; with nuts and washers										
40mm long	0.16	5.00	0.17	0.08	0.01	1.83	-	1.99	nr	2.19
50mm long	0.20	5.00	0.21	0.08	0.01	1.83	-	2.03	nr	2.24
60mm long	0.21	5.00	0.22	0.08	0.01	1.83	-	2.05	nr	2.25
70mm long	0.25	5.00	0.27	0.08	0.01	1.83	-	2.09	nr	2.30
80mm long	0.25	5.00	0.26	0.10	0.01	2.24	-	2.51	nr	2.76
90mm long	0.26	5.00	0.28	0.10	0.01	2.24	-	2.52	nr	2.77
100mm long	0.35	5.00	0.37	0.10	0.01	2.24	-	2.61	nr	2.87
120mm long	0.34	5.00	0.36	0.10	0.01	2.24	-	2.60	nr	2.86
140mm long	0.40	5.00	0.42	0.11	0.02	2.61	-	3.02	nr	3.33
150mm long	0.48	5.00	0.50	0.12	0.02	2.82	-	3.32	nr	3.65
M 12; with nuts and washers										
40mm long	0.27	5.00	0.29	0.10	0.01	2.24	-	2.53	nr	2.78
50mm long	0.27	5.00	0.28	0.10	0.01	2.24	-	2.53	nr	2.78
60mm long	0.31	5.00	0.33	0.10	0.01	2.24	-	2.57	nr	2.83
70mm long	0.35	5.00	0.37	0.10	0.01	2.24	-	2.61	nr	2.87
80mm long	0.39	5.00	0.41	0.10	0.01	2.24	-	2.65	nr	2.92
90mm long	0.42	5.00	0.44	0.10	0.01	2.24	-	2.68	nr	2.95
100mm long	0.43	5.00	0.45	0.11	0.01	2.45	-	2.90	nr	3.19
120mm long	0.45	5.00	0.47	0.13	0.02	3.02	-	3.50	nr	3.85
140mm long	0.56	5.00	0.59	0.12	0.02	2.82	-	3.41	nr	3.75
150mm long	0.71	5.00	0.74	0.13	0.02	3.02	-	3.77	nr	4.15
160mm long	0.56	5.00	0.58	0.13	0.02	3.02	-	3.61	nr	3.97
180mm long	0.58	5.00	0.61	0.14	0.02	3.23	-	3.85	nr	4.23

Labour hourly rates: (except Specialists) Craft Operatives 20.87 Labourer 15.57 Rates are national average prices. Refer to REGIONAL VARIATIONS for indicative levels of overall pricing in regions	MATERIALS			LABOUR				RATES		
	Del to Site £	Waste %	Material Cost £	Craft Optve Hrs	Lab Hrs	Labour Cost £	Sunds £	Nett Rate £	Unit	Gross rate (10%) £
METAL AND PLASTIC ACCESSORIES (Cont'd)										
Metal fixings, fastenings and fittings (Cont'd)										
Bolts; steel; black, BS 4190 grade 4.6 (Cont'd)										
M 12; with nuts and washers (Cont'd)										
200mm long	0.67	5.00	0.70	0.17	0.02	3.86	-	4.56	nr	5.02
220mm long	1.12	5.00	1.18	0.17	0.02	3.86	-	5.04	nr	5.54
240mm long	1.10	5.00	1.15	0.17	0.02	3.86	-	5.01	nr	5.52
250mm long	1.25	5.00	1.32	0.18	0.02	4.07	-	5.38	nr	5.92
M 16; with nuts and washers										
50mm long	0.54	5.00	0.57	0.10	0.01	2.24	-	2.81	nr	3.09
60mm long	0.50	5.00	0.52	0.10	0.01	2.24	-	2.77	nr	3.04
70mm long	0.65	5.00	0.69	0.10	0.01	2.24	-	2.93	nr	3.22
80mm long	0.62	5.00	0.65	0.10	0.01	2.24	-	2.89	nr	3.18
90mm long	0.77	5.00	0.81	0.10	0.01	2.24	-	3.05	nr	3.36
100mm long	0.88	5.00	0.93	0.11	0.01	2.45	-	3.38	nr	3.72
120mm long	1.03	5.00	1.08	0.13	0.02	3.02	-	4.11	nr	4.52
140mm long	1.01	5.00	1.06	0.12	0.02	2.82	-	3.88	nr	4.27
150mm long	1.10	5.00	1.15	0.13	0.02	3.02	-	4.18	nr	4.59
160mm long	1.04	5.00	1.10	0.14	0.02	3.23	-	4.33	nr	4.76
180mm long	1.12	5.00	1.17	0.16	0.02	3.65	-	4.82	nr	5.30
200mm long	1.41	5.00	1.48	0.17	0.02	3.86	-	5.34	nr	5.88
220mm long	1.59	5.00	1.67	0.17	0.02	3.86	-	5.53	nr	6.08
300mm long	2.51	5.00	2.64	0.18	0.02	4.07	-	6.71	nr	7.38
M 20; with nuts and washers										
60mm long	0.89	5.00	0.94	0.10	0.01	2.24	-	3.18	nr	3.50
70mm long	0.95	5.00	0.99	0.10	0.01	2.24	-	3.24	nr	3.56
80mm long	1.11	5.00	1.17	0.10	0.01	2.24	-	3.41	nr	3.75
90mm long	1.40	5.00	1.47	0.11	0.01	2.45	-	3.92	nr	4.31
100mm long	1.17	5.00	1.23	0.12	0.02	2.82	-	4.04	nr	4.45
120mm long	1.46	5.00	1.53	0.14	0.02	3.23	-	4.76	nr	5.24
140mm long	1.62	5.00	1.70	0.13	0.02	3.02	-	4.73	nr	5.20
150mm long	1.50	5.00	1.58	0.14	0.02	3.23	-	4.81	nr	5.29
160mm long	2.02	5.00	2.12	0.17	0.02	3.86	-	5.98	nr	6.57
180mm long	2.19	5.00	2.30	0.17	0.02	3.86	-	6.15	nr	6.77
200mm long	2.37	5.00	2.49	0.16	0.02	3.65	-	6.14	nr	6.75
220mm long	2.08	5.00	2.18	0.17	0.02	3.86	-	6.04	nr	6.65
240mm long	2.40	5.00	2.52	0.18	0.02	4.07	-	6.59	nr	7.25
260mm long	3.27	5.00	3.44	0.20	0.02	4.49	-	7.92	nr	8.71
280mm long	3.68	5.00	3.87	0.21	0.02	4.69	-	8.56	nr	9.42
300mm long	3.97	5.00	4.16	0.23	0.02	5.11	-	9.28	nr	10.20
M 24; with nuts and washers										
70mm long	1.63	5.00	1.71	0.10	0.01	2.24	-	3.95	nr	4.35
80mm long	1.86	5.00	1.96	0.11	0.01	2.45	-	4.41	nr	4.85
90mm long	1.75	5.00	1.84	0.12	0.01	2.66	-	4.50	nr	4.95
100mm long	2.39	5.00	2.51	0.12	0.02	2.82	-	5.33	nr	5.86
120mm long	2.15	5.00	2.26	0.12	0.02	2.82	-	5.08	nr	5.58
140mm long	3.10	5.00	3.26	0.13	0.02	3.02	-	6.28	nr	6.91
150mm long	2.93	5.00	3.08	0.15	0.02	3.44	-	6.52	nr	7.17
160mm long	2.99	5.00	3.14	0.15	0.02	3.44	-	6.58	nr	7.24
180mm long	3.33	5.00	3.50	0.15	0.02	3.44	-	6.94	nr	7.63
200mm long	3.75	5.00	3.94	0.16	0.02	3.65	-	7.59	nr	8.35
220mm long	3.77	5.00	3.96	0.17	0.02	3.86	-	7.82	nr	8.60
240mm long	3.69	5.00	3.87	0.18	0.02	4.07	-	7.94	nr	8.73
260mm long	4.93	5.00	5.18	0.21	0.02	4.69	-	9.87	nr	10.86
280mm long	4.33	5.00	4.55	0.23	0.02	5.11	-	9.66	nr	10.63
300mm long	5.65	5.00	5.93	0.25	0.02	5.53	-	11.46	nr	12.61
M 12; with nuts and 38 x 38 x 3mm square plate washers										
100mm long	0.43	5.00	0.45	0.11	0.01	2.45	-	2.90	nr	3.19
120mm long	0.36	5.00	0.38	0.13	0.02	3.02	-	3.40	nr	3.74
160mm long	0.53	5.00	0.56	0.13	0.02	3.02	-	3.58	nr	3.94
180mm long	0.69	5.00	0.72	0.14	0.02	3.23	-	3.95	nr	4.35
200mm long	0.84	5.00	0.88	0.17	0.02	3.86	-	4.74	nr	5.21
M 12; with nuts and 50 x 50 x 3mm square plate washers										
100mm long	0.40	5.00	0.42	0.11	0.01	2.45	-	2.88	nr	3.16
120mm long	0.43	5.00	0.45	0.13	0.02	3.02	-	3.47	nr	3.82
160mm long	0.60	5.00	0.63	0.13	0.02	3.02	-	3.66	nr	4.02
180mm long	0.76	5.00	0.79	0.14	0.02	3.23	-	4.03	nr	4.43
200mm long	0.91	5.00	0.95	0.17	0.02	3.86	-	4.81	nr	5.29
Bolts; zinc plated, BS 4933 Grade 4.6, cup head, square neck										
M 6; with nuts and washers										
25mm long	0.04	5.00	0.04	0.08	0.01	1.83	-	1.86	nr	2.05
50mm long	0.04	5.00	0.05	0.08	0.01	1.83	-	1.87	nr	2.06
75mm long	0.06	5.00	0.06	0.10	0.01	2.24	-	2.31	nr	2.54
100mm long	0.07	5.00	0.08	0.10	0.01	2.24	-	2.32	nr	2.55
150mm long	0.10	5.00	0.11	0.11	0.01	2.45	-	2.56	nr	2.81
M 8; with nuts and washers										
25mm long	0.09	5.00	0.10	0.08	0.01	1.83	-	1.92	nr	2.11
50mm long	0.11	5.00	0.12	0.08	0.01	1.83	-	1.94	nr	2.14
75mm long	0.13	5.00	0.14	0.10	0.01	2.24	-	2.38	nr	2.62
100mm long	0.15	5.00	0.16	0.10	0.01	2.24	-	2.40	nr	2.64
150mm long	0.20	5.00	0.21	0.11	0.01	2.45	-	2.66	nr	2.93
M 10; with nuts and washers										
50mm long	0.22	5.00	0.24	0.08	0.01	1.83	-	2.06	nr	2.27
75mm long	0.26	5.00	0.28	0.10	0.01	2.24	-	2.52	nr	2.77
100mm long	0.37	5.00	0.39	0.10	0.01	2.24	-	2.63	nr	2.90
150mm long	0.37	5.00	0.39	0.12	0.02	2.82	-	3.20	nr	3.52
M 12; with nuts and washers										
50mm long	0.40	5.00	0.42	0.10	0.01	2.24	-	2.66	nr	2.93
75mm long	0.47	5.00	0.49	0.10	0.01	2.24	-	2.73	nr	3.01
100mm long	0.47	5.00	0.49	0.11	0.01	2.45	-	2.95	nr	3.24
150mm long	0.57	5.00	0.60	0.13	0.02	3.02	-	3.62	nr	3.99

Labour hourly rates: (except Specialists) Craft Operatives 20.87 Labourer 15.57 Rates are national average prices. Refer to REGIONAL VARIATIONS for indicative levels of overall pricing in regions	MATERIALS			LABOUR				RATES		
	Del to Site £	Waste %	Material Cost £	Craft Optve Hrs	Lab Hrs	Labour Cost £	Sunds £	Nett Rate £	Unit	Gross rate (10%) £
METAL AND PLASTIC ACCESSORIES (Cont'd)										
Metal fixings, fastenings and fittings (Cont'd)										
Bolts; steel; galvanised; BS 4190 grade 4.6, hexagon head										
M 12; with nuts and washers										
100mm long	0.23	5.00	0.24	0.11	0.01	2.45	-	2.69	nr	2.96
120mm long	0.25	5.00	0.26	0.13	0.02	3.02	-	3.29	nr	3.62
160mm long	0.43	5.00	0.45	0.13	0.02	3.02	-	3.47	nr	3.82
180mm long	0.58	5.00	0.61	0.14	0.02	3.23	-	3.84	nr	4.23
200mm long	0.95	5.00	1.00	0.17	0.02	3.86	-	4.86	nr	5.35
M 16; with nuts and washers										
100mm long	0.42	5.00	0.44	0.11	0.01	2.45	-	2.89	nr	3.18
120mm long	0.77	5.00	0.81	0.13	0.02	3.02	-	3.83	nr	4.21
160mm long	1.05	5.00	1.10	0.14	0.02	3.23	-	4.33	nr	4.77
180mm long	1.49	5.00	1.56	0.16	0.02	3.65	-	5.21	nr	5.73
200mm long	1.57	5.00	1.65	0.17	0.02	3.86	-	5.50	nr	6.06
M 20; with nuts and washers										
100mm long	0.71	5.00	0.74	0.12	0.02	2.82	-	3.56	nr	3.91
120mm long	0.91	5.00	0.95	0.11	0.01	2.45	-	3.40	nr	3.74
160mm long	1.31	5.00	1.38	0.17	0.02	3.86	-	5.24	nr	5.76
180mm long	1.33	5.00	1.40	0.17	0.02	3.86	-	5.26	nr	5.78
200mm long	1.64	5.00	1.72	0.17	0.02	3.86	-	5.58	nr	6.13
M 12; with nuts and 38 x 38 x 3mm square plate washers										
100mm long	0.26	5.00	0.28	0.11	0.01	2.45	-	2.73	nr	3.00
120mm long	0.29	5.00	0.30	0.13	0.02	3.02	-	3.33	nr	3.66
160mm long	0.46	5.00	0.49	0.13	0.02	3.02	-	3.51	nr	3.86
180mm long	0.62	5.00	0.65	0.14	0.02	3.23	-	3.88	nr	4.27
200mm long	0.99	5.00	1.04	0.17	0.02	3.86	-	4.90	nr	5.39
M 12; with nuts and 50 x 50 x 3mm square plate washers										
100mm long	0.30	5.00	0.31	0.11	0.01	2.45	-	2.77	nr	3.04
120mm long	0.32	5.00	0.34	0.13	0.02	3.02	-	3.36	nr	3.70
160mm long	0.50	5.00	0.52	0.13	0.02	3.02	-	3.55	nr	3.90
180mm long	0.65	5.00	0.68	0.14	0.02	3.23	-	3.92	nr	4.31
200mm long	1.02	5.00	1.08	0.17	0.02	3.86	-	4.94	nr	5.43
Bolts; expanding; bolt projecting Rawlbolts; drilling masonry										
with nuts and washers; reference										
44 - 505 (M6 10P)	0.40	5.00	0.42	0.24	0.03	5.48	-	5.90	nr	6.49
44 - 510 (M6 25P)	0.48	5.00	0.50	0.24	0.03	5.48	-	5.98	nr	6.57
44 - 515 (M6 60P)	0.42	5.00	0.45	0.24	0.03	5.48	-	5.92	nr	6.51
44 - 555 (M8 10P)	0.56	5.00	0.59	0.26	0.03	5.89	-	6.48	nr	7.13
44 - 560 (M8 25P)	0.84	5.00	0.88	0.26	0.03	5.89	-	6.77	nr	7.45
44 - 565 (M8 60P)	0.89	5.00	0.94	0.26	0.03	5.89	-	6.83	nr	7.51
44 - 565 (M8 60P)	0.96	5.00	1.01	0.30	0.04	6.88	-	7.89	nr	8.68
44 - 610 (M10 30P)	0.99	5.00	1.04	0.30	0.04	6.88	-	7.93	nr	8.72
44 - 615 (M10 60P)	1.05	5.00	1.11	0.30	0.04	6.88	-	7.99	nr	8.79
44 - 655 (M12 15P)	1.48	5.00	1.55	0.32	0.04	7.30	-	8.85	nr	9.73
44 - 660 (M12 30P)	2.03	5.00	2.13	0.32	0.04	7.30	-	9.43	nr	10.37
44 - 665 (M12 75P)	1.56	5.00	1.64	0.32	0.04	7.30	-	8.94	nr	9.84
44 - 705 (M16 15P)	3.83	5.00	4.02	0.36	0.05	8.29	-	12.31	nr	13.54
44 - 710 (M16 35P)	3.70	5.00	3.88	0.36	0.05	8.29	-	12.17	nr	13.39
44 - 715 (M16 75P)	4.41	5.00	4.63	0.36	0.05	8.29	-	12.92	nr	14.22
44 - 755 (M20 15P)	12.07	5.00	12.68	0.40	0.05	9.13	-	21.80	nr	23.98
44 - 760 (M20 30P)	12.65	5.00	13.28	0.40	0.05	9.13	-	22.41	nr	24.65
44 - 765 (M20 100P)	14.16	5.00	14.87	0.40	0.05	9.13	-	24.00	nr	26.40
Bolts; expanding; Sleeve Anchor (Rawlok); bolt projecting type; drilling masonry										
with nuts and washers; reference										
69 - 506 M5; 56 long; (Max fixture thickness 25mm)	0.09	5.00	0.10	0.19	0.02	4.28	-	4.37	nr	4.81
69 - 508; M6; 40 long; (Max fixture thickness 10mm)	0.10	5.00	0.11	0.22	0.03	5.06	-	5.17	nr	5.68
69 - 510; M6; 65 long; (Max fixture thickness 35mm)	0.14	5.00	0.15	0.22	0.03	5.06	-	5.21	nr	5.73
69 - 514; M8; 50 long; (Max fixture thickness 10mm)	0.21	5.00	0.22	0.24	0.03	5.48	-	5.70	nr	6.27
69 - 516; M8; 75 long; (Max fixture thickness 36mm)	0.26	5.00	0.28	0.24	0.03	5.48	-	5.75	nr	6.33
69 - 518; M8; 95 long; (Max fixture thickness 55mm)	0.31	5.00	0.33	0.24	0.03	5.48	-	5.80	nr	6.39
69 - 520; M10; 60 long; (Max fixture thickness 10mm)	0.32	5.00	0.33	0.26	0.03	5.89	-	6.23	nr	6.85
69 - 524; M10; 100 long; (Max fixture thickness 50mm)	0.47	5.00	0.50	0.26	0.03	5.89	-	6.39	nr	7.03
69 - 525; M10; 130 long; (Max fixture thickness 80mm)	0.61	5.00	0.64	0.26	0.03	5.89	-	6.53	nr	7.18
69 - 528; M12; 110 long; (Max fixture thickness 55mm)	0.79	5.00	0.83	0.30	0.04	6.88	-	7.72	nr	8.49
69 - 530; M12; 145 long; (Max fixture thickness 85mm)	1.02	5.00	1.08	0.30	0.04	6.88	-	7.96	nr	8.75
Bolts; expanding; loose bolt Rawlbolts; drilling masonry										
with washers; reference										
44 - 015 (M6 10L)	0.71	5.00	0.75	0.24	0.03	5.48	-	6.22	nr	6.85
44 - 020 (M6 25L)	0.71	5.00	0.75	0.24	0.03	5.48	-	6.22	nr	6.85
44 - 025 (M6 40L)	0.78	5.00	0.82	0.24	0.03	5.48	-	6.29	nr	6.92
44 - 055 (M8 10L)	0.74	5.00	0.78	0.26	0.03	5.89	-	6.67	nr	7.34
44 - 060 (M8 25L)	0.84	5.00	0.88	0.26	0.03	5.89	-	6.77	nr	7.45
44 - 065 (M8 40L)	0.89	5.00	0.94	0.26	0.03	5.89	-	6.83	nr	7.51
44 - 105 (M10 10L)	0.89	5.00	0.94	0.30	0.04	6.88	-	7.82	nr	8.60
44 - 110 (M10 25L)	0.99	5.00	1.04	0.30	0.04	6.88	-	7.92	nr	8.72
44 - 115 (M10 50L)	1.01	5.00	1.07	0.30	0.04	6.88	-	7.95	nr	8.74
44 - 120 (M10 75L)	1.09	5.00	1.14	0.30	0.04	6.88	-	8.03	nr	8.83
44 - 155 (M12 10L)	1.61	5.00	1.69	0.32	0.04	7.30	-	8.99	nr	9.89
44 - 160 (M12 25L)	1.66	5.00	1.75	0.32	0.04	7.30	-	9.05	nr	9.95
44 - 165 (M12 40L)	1.66	5.00	1.75	0.32	0.04	7.30	-	9.05	nr	9.95
44 - 170 (M12 60L)	2.11	5.00	2.21	0.32	0.04	7.30	-	9.51	nr	10.46
44 - 205 (M16 15L)	3.58	5.00	3.76	0.36	0.05	8.29	-	12.05	nr	13.26
44 - 210 (M16 30L)	3.73	5.00	3.92	0.36	0.05	8.29	-	12.21	nr	13.43
44 - 215 (M16 60L)	4.43	5.00	4.65	0.36	0.05	8.29	-	12.95	nr	14.24
44 - 255 (M20 60L)	22.87	5.00	24.01	0.40	0.05	9.13	-	33.14	nr	36.45
44 - 260 (M20 100L)	22.87	5.00	24.01	0.40	0.05	9.13	-	33.14	nr	36.45
44 - 310 (M24 150L)	27.98	5.00	29.38	0.45	0.05	10.17	-	39.55	nr	43.51

Labour hourly rates: (except Specialists) Craft Operatives 20.87 Labourer 15.57 Rates are national average prices. Refer to REGIONAL VARIATIONS for indicative levels of overall pricing in regions	MATERIALS			LABOUR				RATES		
	Del to Site £	Waste %	Material Cost £	Craft Optve Hrs	Lab Hrs	Labour Cost £	Sunds £	Nett Rate £	Unit	Gross rate (10%) £
METAL AND PLASTIC ACCESSORIES (Cont'd)										
Metal fixings, fastenings and fittings (Cont'd)										
Bolts; safety anchors										
Bolts; safety anchors; Spit Triga high performance safety anchors; bolt head version; drilling masonry										
with washers, reference										
M10; 105mm long, ref 050689 (Max fixture thickness 20mm)....	3.44	5.00	3.61	0.30	0.03	6.73	-	10.34	nr	11.37
M12; 120mm long, ref 050697 (Max fixture thickness 25mm)....	5.78	5.00	6.07	0.32	0.03	7.15	-	13.22	nr	14.54
M16; 145mm long, ref 050705 (Max fixture thickness 25mm)....	13.12	5.00	13.78	0.36	0.04	8.14	-	21.91	nr	24.10
M20; 170mm long, ref 050711 (Max fixture thickness 25mm)....	18.03	5.00	18.93	0.40	0.04	8.97	-	27.90	nr	30.69
Bolts; safety anchors; Spit Fix high performance through bolt BZP anchors; drilling masonry										
with nuts and washers, reference										
M6; 55mm long; Ref 050520 (Max fixture thickness 20mm).......	0.25	5.00	0.26	0.22	0.03	5.06	-	5.32	nr	5.86
M6; 85mm long; Ref 050530 (Max fixture thickness 50mm).......	0.27	5.00	0.28	0.22	0.03	5.06	-	5.34	nr	5.87
M8; 55mm long; Ref 050535 (Max fixture thickness 5mm)........	0.27	5.00	0.28	0.24	0.03	5.48	-	5.76	nr	6.33
M8; 90mm long; Ref 056420 (Max fixture thickness 40mm).......	0.31	5.00	0.33	0.24	0.03	5.48	-	5.80	nr	6.38
M8; 130mm long; Ref 056430 (Max fixture thickness 80mm).....	0.38	5.00	0.40	0.24	0.03	5.48	-	5.87	nr	6.46
M10; 75mm long; Ref 056530 (Max fixture thickness 15mm).....	0.40	5.00	0.42	0.26	0.03	5.89	-	6.31	nr	6.94
M10; 96mm long; Ref 056540 (Max fixture thickness 36mm).....	0.44	5.00	0.46	0.26	0.03	5.89	-	6.35	nr	6.99
M12; 100mm long; Ref 055335 (Max fixture thickness 25mm)...	0.59	5.00	0.62	0.30	0.03	6.73	-	7.35	nr	8.08
M12; 140mm long; Ref 056590 (Max fixture thickness 65mm)...	0.71	5.00	0.75	0.30	0.03	6.73	-	7.48	nr	8.23
M12; 180mm long; Ref 056650 (Max fixture thickness 105mm)	0.91	5.00	0.96	0.30	0.03	6.73	-	7.69	nr	8.45
M12; 220mm long; Ref 056660 (Max fixture thickness 145mm).	1.69	5.00	1.78	0.30	0.03	6.73	-	8.51	nr	9.36
M16; 125mm long; Ref 056700 (Max fixture thickness 30mm)...	1.21	5.00	1.27	0.32	0.03	7.15	-	8.41	nr	9.25
M16; 170mm long; Ref 056710 (Max fixture thickness 75mm)...	1.66	5.00	1.74	0.32	0.03	7.15	-	8.88	nr	9.77
M20; 160mm long; Ref 056730(Max fixture thickness 50mm)....	3.45	5.00	3.62	0.36	0.04	8.14	-	11.76	nr	12.93
M20; 215mm long; Ref 056740 (Max fixture thickness 105mm).	5.18	5.00	5.44	0.36	0.04	8.14	-	13.58	nr	14.94
Bolts; expanding; steel; plated; hook Rawlbolts; drilling masonry										
with nuts and washers; reference										
44 - 401 (M6H)	0.94	5.00	0.99	0.24	0.03	5.48	-	6.46	nr	7.11
44 - 406 (M8H)	1.11	5.00	1.17	0.26	0.03	5.89	-	7.06	nr	7.77
44 - 411 (M10H)	1.29	5.00	1.35	0.30	0.04	6.88	-	8.24	nr	9.06
44 - 416 (M12H)	2.62	5.00	2.75	0.32	0.04	7.30	-	10.06	nr	11.06
Bolts; expanding; steel; plated; eye Rawlbolts; drilling masonry										
with nuts and washers; reference										
44 - 432 (M6)	0.94	5.00	0.99	0.24	0.03	5.48	-	6.46	nr	7.11
44 - 437 (M8)	1.05	5.00	1.10	0.26	0.03	5.89	-	6.99	nr	7.69
44 - 442 (M10)	1.24	5.00	1.30	0.30	0.04	6.88	-	8.18	nr	9.00
44 - 447 (M12)	2.55	5.00	2.68	0.32	0.04	7.30	-	9.98	nr	10.98
Bolts; expanding; bolt projecting Rawl Throughbolts; drilling masonry										
with nuts and washers; reference										
R-XPT-06065/5 (M6 x 65mm)	0.23	5.00	0.24	0.22	0.03	5.06	-	5.30	nr	5.83
R-XPT-06085/25 (M6 x 85mm)	0.24	5.00	0.25	0.22	0.03	5.06	-	5.31	nr	5.84
R-XPT-08065/15 (M8 x 65mm)	0.23	5.00	0.24	0.24	0.03	5.48	-	5.72	nr	6.29
R-XPT-08085/20 (M8 x 85mm)	0.23	5.00	0.24	0.24	0.03	5.48	-	5.72	nr	6.29
R-XPT-08095/30 (M8 x 95mm)	0.26	5.00	0.28	0.24	0.03	5.48	-	5.75	nr	6.33
R-XPT-08115/50 (M8 x 115mm)	0.29	5.00	0.31	0.24	0.03	5.48	-	5.78	nr	6.36
R-XPT-10065/5 (M10 x 65mm)	0.33	5.00	0.35	0.26	0.03	5.89	-	6.24	nr	6.86
R-XPT-10080/10 (M10 x 80mm)	0.33	5.00	0.35	0.26	0.03	5.89	-	6.24	nr	6.86
R-XPT-10095/25 (M10 x 95mm)	0.36	5.00	0.38	0.26	0.03	5.89	-	6.27	nr	6.90
R-XPT-10140/70 (M10 x 140mm)	0.40	5.00	0.42	0.26	0.03	5.89	-	6.32	nr	6.95
R-XPT-12080/5 (M12 x 80mm)	0.41	5.00	0.43	0.30	0.04	6.88	-	7.31	nr	8.04
R-XPT-12100/5 (M12 x 100mm)	0.44	5.00	0.46	0.30	0.04	6.88	-	7.34	nr	8.08
R-XPT-12125/30 (M12 x 125mm)	0.50	5.00	0.52	0.30	0.04	6.88	-	7.40	nr	8.14
R-XPT-12140/45 (M12 x 140mm)	0.50	5.00	0.53	0.30	0.04	6.88	-	7.41	nr	8.15
R-XPT-12150/55 (M12 x 150mm)	0.57	5.00	0.59	0.30	0.04	6.88	-	7.48	nr	8.23
R-XPT-16105/10 (M16 x 105mm)	0.79	5.00	0.83	0.32	0.04	7.30	-	8.13	nr	8.94
R-XPT-16150/30 (M16 x 150mm)	0.93	5.00	0.98	0.32	0.04	7.30	-	8.28	nr	9.11
R-XPT-16180/60 (M16 x 180mm)	1.02	5.00	1.07	0.32	0.04	7.30	-	8.37	nr	9.21
R-XPT-16220/100 (M16 x 220mm)	1.36	5.00	1.43	0.32	0.04	7.30	-	8.73	nr	9.60
R-XPT-20125/5 (M20 x 125mm)	1.62	5.00	1.70	0.36	0.05	8.29	-	9.99	nr	10.99
R-XPT-20160/20 (M20 x 160mm)	1.84	5.00	1.93	0.36	0.05	8.29	-	10.22	nr	11.24
R-XPT-20200/60 (M20 x 200mm)	1.94	5.00	2.04	0.36	0.05	8.29	-	10.33	nr	11.36
R-XPT-20300/160 (M20 x 300mm)	2.98	5.00	3.13	0.36	0.05	8.29	-	11.42	nr	12.56
R-XPT-24180/20 (M24 x 180mm)	7.26	5.00	7.62	0.40	0.05	9.13	-	16.75	nr	18.42
R-XPT-24260/100 (M24 x 260mm)	9.91	5.00	10.40	0.40	0.05	9.13	-	19.53	nr	21.48
Bolts; expanding; Stainless steel grade 316; bolt projecting Rawl Throughbolts; drilling masonry										
with nuts and washers; reference										
R-XPTA-406050/10 (M6 x 50mm)	0.49	5.00	0.51	0.22	0.03	5.06	-	5.57	nr	6.13
R-XPTA-408075/10 (M8 x 75mm)	0.76	5.00	0.80	0.24	0.03	5.48	-	6.27	nr	6.90
R-XPTA-408095/30 (M8 x 95mm)	0.92	5.00	0.97	0.24	0.03	5.48	-	6.44	nr	7.09
R-XPTA-410080/10 (M10 x 80mm)	1.20	5.00	1.26	0.26	0.03	5.89	-	7.15	nr	7.87
R-XPTA-410115/45 (M10 x 115mm)	1.39	5.00	1.46	0.26	0.03	5.89	-	7.36	nr	8.09
R-XPTA-410130/60 (M10 x 130mm)	1.50	5.00	1.57	0.26	0.03	5.89	-	7.47	nr	8.21
R-XPTA-412100/5 (M12 x 100mm)	1.85	5.00	1.94	0.30	0.04	6.88	-	8.82	nr	9.70
R-XPTA-412125/30 (M12 x 125mm)	2.23	5.00	2.34	0.30	0.04	6.88	-	9.23	nr	10.15
R-XPTA-412150/55 (M12 x 150mm)	2.40	5.00	2.52	0.30	0.04	6.88	-	9.40	nr	10.35
R-XPTA-416180/60 (M16 x 180mm)	6.86	5.00	7.20	0.32	0.04	7.30	-	14.51	nr	15.96
R-XPTA-416220/100 (M16 x 220mm)	10.30	5.00	10.82	0.32	0.04	7.30	-	18.12	nr	19.93
R-XPTA-420160/20 (M20 x 160mm)	11.80	5.00	12.39	0.36	0.05	8.29	-	20.68	nr	22.75
R-XPTA-420300/160 (M20 x 300mm)	21.43	5.00	22.50	0.36	0.05	8.29	-	30.79	nr	33.87
R-XPTA-424260/100 (M24 x 260mm)	37.47	5.00	39.35	0.40	0.05	9.13	-	48.47	nr	53.32

Labour hourly rates: (except Specialists) Craft Operatives 20.87 Labourer 15.57 Rates are national average prices. Refer to REGIONAL VARIATIONS for indicative levels of overall pricing in regions	MATERIALS			LABOUR				RATES		
	Del to Site £	Waste %	Material Cost £	Craft Optve Hrs	Lab Hrs	Labour Cost £	Sunds £	Nett Rate £	Unit	Gross rate (10%) £
METAL AND PLASTIC ACCESSORIES (Cont'd)										
Metal fixings, fastenings and fittings (Cont'd)										
Chemical anchors										
Chemical anchors; Kemfix capsules and standard studs; drilling masonry										
capsule reference 60-428; stud reference 60-708; with nuts and washers (M8 x 110mm)	0.95	5.00	1.00	0.29	0.04	6.68	-	7.67	nr	8.44
capsule reference 60-430; stud reference 60-710; with nuts and washers (M10 x 130mm)	1.15	5.00	1.20	0.32	0.04	7.30	-	8.51	nr	9.36
capsule reference 60-432; stud reference 60-712; with nuts and washers (M12 x 160mm)	1.48	5.00	1.55	0.36	0.05	8.29	-	9.84	nr	10.83
Chemical anchors; Kemfix capsules and stainless steel studs; drilling masonry										
capsule reference 60-428; stud reference R-STUDS-08110-A4; with nuts and washers (M8 x 110mm)	1.95	5.00	2.05	0.29	0.04	6.68	-	8.73	nr	9.60
capsule reference 60-430; stud reference R-STUDS-10130-A4; with nuts and washers (M10 x 130mm)	2.54	5.00	2.67	0.32	0.04	7.30	-	9.97	nr	10.97
capsule reference 60-432; stud reference R-STUDS-12160-A4; with nuts and washers (M12 x 160mm)	4.37	5.00	4.59	0.36	0.05	8.29	-	12.88	nr	14.17
capsule reference 60-436; stud reference R-STUDS-16190-A4; with nuts and washers (M16 x 190mm)	8.83	5.00	9.27	0.40	0.05	9.13	-	18.40	nr	20.24
capsule reference 60-442; stud reference R-STUDS-20260-A4; with nuts and washers (M20 x 260mm)	19.25	5.00	20.21	0.42	0.05	9.54	-	29.75	nr	32.73
capsule reference 60-446; stud reference R-STUDS-24300-A4; with nuts and washers (M24 x 295mm)	30.25	5.00	31.77	0.46	0.06	10.53	-	42.30	nr	46.53
Chemical anchors; Kemfix capsules and standard internal threaded sockets; drilling masonry										
capsule reference 60-428; socket reference 60-623 (M8 x 90mm)	1.36	5.00	1.43	0.36	0.05	8.29	-	9.72	nr	10.69
capsule reference 60-430; socket reference 60-626 (M10 x 100mm)	1.85	5.00	1.94	0.40	0.05	9.13	-	11.06	nr	12.17
capsule reference 60-432; socket reference 60-628 (M12 x 80mm)	1.94	5.00	2.03	0.42	0.05	9.54	-	11.58	nr	12.73
capsule reference 60-436; socket reference 60-630 (M16 x 95mm)	3.32	5.00	3.49	0.46	0.06	10.53	-	14.02	nr	15.43
Chemical anchors; Kemfix capsules and stainless steel internal threaded sockets; drilling masonry										
capsule reference 60-428; socket reference 60-988 (M8 x 90mm)	2.75	5.00	2.89	0.36	0.05	8.29	-	11.18	nr	12.30
capsule reference 60-430; socket reference 60-992 (M10 x 100mm)	3.42	5.00	3.60	0.40	0.05	9.13	-	12.72	nr	13.99
capsule reference 60-432; socket reference 60-993 (M12 x 100mm)	4.74	5.00	4.98	0.42	0.05	9.54	-	14.53	nr	15.98
capsule reference 60-436; socket reference 60-995 (M16 x 125mm)	7.46	5.00	7.83	0.46	0.06	10.53	-	18.37	nr	20.20
Chemical anchors in low density material; Kemfix capsules, mesh sleeves and standard studs; drilling masonry										
capsule reference 60-428; sleeve reference 60-805; stud reference 60-708; with nuts and washers (M8 x 110mm)	2.34	5.00	2.46	0.25	0.03	5.68	-	8.14	nr	8.96
capsule reference 60-430; sleeve reference 60-809; stud reference 60-710; with nuts and washers (M10 x 130mm)	2.71	5.00	2.84	0.32	0.04	7.30	-	10.14	nr	11.16
capsule reference 60-432; sleeve reference 60-115; stud reference 60-712; with nuts and washers (M12 x 160mm)	3.10	5.00	3.25	0.36	0.05	8.29	-	11.54	nr	12.70
capsule reference 60-436; sleeve reference 60-117; stud reference 60-716; with nuts and washers (M16 x 190mm)	3.66	5.00	3.84	0.42	0.05	9.54	-	13.39	nr	14.73
Chemical anchors in low density material; Kemfix capsules, mesh sleeves and stainless steel studs; drilling masonry										
capsule reference 60-428; sleeve reference 60-805; stud reference RSTUDS-08110-A4; with nuts and washers (M8 x 110mm)	3.35	5.00	3.51	0.29	0.04	6.68	-	10.19	nr	11.21
capsule reference 60-430; sleeve reference 60-809; stud reference RSTUDS-10130-A4; with nuts and washers (M10 x 130mm)	4.11	5.00	4.31	0.32	0.04	7.30	-	11.61	nr	12.77
capsule reference 60-432; sleeve reference 60-115; stud reference RSTUDS-12160-A4; with nuts and washers (M12 x 160mm)	5.99	5.00	6.29	0.36	0.05	8.29	-	14.58	nr	16.04
capsule reference 60-436; sleeve reference 60-117; stud reference RSTUDS-16190-A4; with nuts and washers (M16 x 190mm)	10.46	5.00	10.98	0.42	0.05	9.54	-	20.52	nr	22.58
Chemical anchors in low density material; Kemfix capsules, mesh sleeves and standard internal threaded sockets; drilling masonry										
capsule reference 60-428; sleeve reference 60-805; socket reference 60-623 (M8 x 90mm)	2.75	5.00	2.89	0.29	0.04	6.68	-	9.56	nr	10.52
capsule reference 60-430; sleeve reference 60-809; socket reference 60-626 (M10 x 100mm)	3.41	5.00	3.58	0.32	0.04	7.30	-	10.88	nr	11.97
capsule reference 60-432; sleeve reference 60-113; socket reference 60-674 (M12 x 100mm)	3.56	5.00	3.73	0.36	0.05	8.29	-	12.03	nr	13.23
capsule reference 60-436; sleeve reference 60-117; socket reference 60-676 (M16 x 125mm)	4.95	5.00	5.20	0.40	0.05	9.13	-	14.33	nr	15.76
Chemical anchors in low density material; Kemfix capsules, mesh sleeves and stainless steel internal threaded sockets; drilling masonry										
capsule reference 60-428; sleeve reference 60-805; socket reference 60-988 (M8 x 90mm)	4.14	5.00	4.35	0.29	0.04	6.68	-	11.03	nr	12.13
capsule reference 60-430; sleeve reference 60-809; socket reference 60-992 (M10 x 100mm)	4.98	5.00	5.23	0.32	0.04	7.30	-	12.53	nr	13.79
capsule reference 60-436; sleeve reference 60-117; socket reference 60-995 (M16 x 125mm)	9.09	5.00	9.54	0.40	0.05	9.13	-	18.67	nr	20.54
Spit Maxima high performance chemical anchors; capsules and zinc coated steel studs; drilling masonry										
capsule reference M8; stud reference SM8; with nuts and washers	1.83	5.00	1.92	0.28	0.03	6.31	-	8.23	nr	9.06

Labour hourly rates: (except Specialists) Craft Operatives 20.87 Labourer 15.57 Rates are national average prices. Refer to REGIONAL VARIATIONS for indicative levels of overall pricing in regions	MATERIALS			LABOUR				RATES		
	Del to Site £	Waste %	Material Cost £	Craft Optve Hrs	Lab Hrs	Labour Cost £	Sunds £	Nett Rate £	Unit	Gross rate (10%) £
METAL AND PLASTIC ACCESSORIES (Cont'd)										
Metal fixings, fastenings and fittings (Cont'd)										
Chemical anchors (Cont'd)										
Spit Maxima high performance chemical anchors; capsules and zinc coated steel studs; drilling masonry (Cont'd)										
capsule reference M10; stud reference SM10; with nuts and washers	2.19	5.00	2.30	0.31	0.04	7.09	-	9.40	nr	10.33
capsule reference M12; stud reference SM12; with nuts and washers	2.74	5.00	2.87	0.35	0.03	7.77	-	10.65	nr	11.71
capsule reference M16; stud reference SM16; with nuts and washers	4.26	5.00	4.47	0.38	0.03	8.40	-	12.87	nr	14.15
capsule reference M20; stud reference SM20; with nuts and washers	7.78	5.00	8.17	0.40	0.04	8.97	-	17.14	nr	18.85
capsule reference M24; stud reference SM24; with nuts and washers	14.22	5.00	14.93	0.44	0.04	9.81	-	24.74	nr	27.21
Spit Maxima high performance chemical anchors; capsules and stainless steel studs Grade 316 (A4); drilling masonry										
capsule reference M8 stud reference SM8i; with nuts and washers	3.41	5.00	3.58	0.28	0.03	6.31	-	9.89	nr	10.88
capsule reference M10; stud reference SM10i; with nuts and washers	5.07	5.00	5.32	0.31	0.03	6.94	-	12.26	nr	13.49
capsule reference M12; stud reference SM12i; with nuts and washers	8.10	5.00	8.50	0.35	0.03	7.77	-	16.27	nr	17.90
capsule reference M16; stud reference SM16i; with nuts and washers	13.72	5.00	14.40	0.38	0.03	8.40	-	22.80	nr	25.08
capsule reference M20; stud reference SM20i; with nuts and washers	28.86	5.00	30.30	0.40	0.04	8.97	-	39.27	nr	43.20
capsule reference M24; stud reference SM24i; with nuts and washers	60.08	5.00	63.09	0.44	0.04	9.81	-	72.89	nr	80.18
Holding down bolts or assemblies; mild steel										
rag or indented bolts; M 10 with nuts and washers										
100mm long	1.48	5.00	1.55	0.10	-	2.09	-	3.64	nr	4.01
160mm long	1.54	5.00	1.62	0.11	-	2.30	-	3.91	nr	4.30
rag or indented bolts; M 12 with nuts and washers										
100mm long	1.60	5.00	1.68	0.10	-	2.09	-	3.77	nr	4.14
160mm long	1.76	5.00	1.85	0.13	-	2.71	-	4.56	nr	5.02
200mm long	1.98	5.00	2.08	0.14	-	2.92	-	5.00	nr	5.50
rag or indented bolts; M 16 with nuts and washers										
120mm long	2.29	5.00	2.40	0.11	-	2.30	-	4.70	nr	5.17
160mm long	2.62	5.00	2.75	0.14	-	2.92	-	5.67	nr	6.24
200mm long	3.06	5.00	3.21	0.16	-	3.34	-	6.55	nr	7.21
holding down bolt assembly; M 20 bolt with 100 x 100 x 10mm plate washer tack welded to head; with nuts and washers										
300mm long	2.70	5.00	2.84	0.28	-	5.84	-	8.68	nr	9.55
350mm long	3.36	5.00	3.53	0.32	-	6.68	-	10.21	nr	11.23
450mm long	4.21	5.00	4.42	0.55	-	11.48	-	15.90	nr	17.49
High strength friction grip bolts; BS 14399 Part 1 - general grade										
M 16; with nuts and washers										
50mm long	0.90	5.00	0.94	0.09	-	1.88	-	2.82	nr	3.11
60mm long	1.08	5.00	1.13	0.09	-	1.88	-	3.01	nr	3.31
75mm long	1.44	5.00	1.51	0.10	-	2.09	-	3.60	nr	3.96
80mm long	1.44	5.00	1.51	0.10	-	2.09	-	3.60	nr	3.96
90mm long	1.62	5.00	1.70	0.12	-	2.50	-	4.21	nr	4.63
M 20; with nuts and washers										
60mm long	1.62	5.00	1.70	0.09	-	1.88	-	3.58	nr	3.94
70mm long	1.89	5.00	1.98	0.10	-	2.09	-	4.07	nr	4.48
80mm long	2.16	5.00	2.27	0.10	-	2.09	-	4.36	nr	4.79
90mm long	2.43	5.00	2.55	0.12	-	2.50	-	5.06	nr	5.56
M 24; with nuts and washers										
65mm long	2.34	5.00	2.46	0.13	-	2.71	-	5.17	nr	5.69
80mm long	2.88	5.00	3.02	0.13	-	2.71	-	5.74	nr	6.31
90mm long	3.24	5.00	3.40	0.14	-	2.92	-	6.32	nr	6.96
100mm long	3.60	5.00	3.78	0.14	-	2.92	-	6.70	nr	7.37
110mm long	3.96	5.00	4.16	0.16	-	3.34	-	7.50	nr	8.25
130mm long	4.68	5.00	4.91	0.17	-	3.55	-	8.46	nr	9.31
M 30; with nuts and washers										
80mm long	4.68	5.00	4.91	0.15	-	3.13	-	8.04	nr	8.85
100mm long	5.40	5.00	5.67	0.17	-	3.55	-	9.22	nr	10.14
Steel; galvanised; joist hangers										
Joist hangers; BAT Building Products Ltd; (building in where required included elsewhere)										
SPH type S, for 47 x 100mm joist	1.86	2.50	1.91	-	-	-	-	1.91	nr	2.10
SPH type S, for 47 x 125mm joist	1.92	2.50	1.97	-	-	-	-	1.97	nr	2.16
SPH type S, for 47 x 150mm joist	1.51	2.50	1.55	-	-	-	-	1.55	nr	1.70
SPH type S, for 47 x 175mm joist	1.59	2.50	1.63	-	-	-	-	1.63	nr	1.79
SPH type S, for 47 x 200mm joist	1.78	2.50	1.82	-	-	-	-	1.82	nr	2.01
SPH type S, for 47 x 225mm joist	1.88	2.50	1.93	-	-	-	-	1.93	nr	2.12
SPH type S, for 47 x 250mm joist	3.03	2.50	3.11	-	-	-	-	3.11	nr	3.42
SPH type S, for 75 x 100mm joist	3.20	2.50	3.28	-	-	-	-	3.28	nr	3.61
SPH type S, for 75 x 125mm joist	3.31	2.50	3.39	-	-	-	-	3.39	nr	3.73
SPH type S, for 75 x 150mm joist	3.74	2.50	3.83	-	-	-	-	3.83	nr	4.22
SPH type S, for 75 x 175mm joist	3.52	2.50	3.61	-	-	-	-	3.61	nr	3.97
SPH type S, for 75 x 200mm joist	3.76	2.50	3.85	-	-	-	-	3.85	nr	4.24
SPH type S, for 75 x 225mm joist	4.02	2.50	4.12	-	-	-	-	4.12	nr	4.53
SPH type S, for 75 x 250mm joist	4.28	2.50	4.39	-	-	-	-	4.39	nr	4.83
SPH type S, for 100 x 100mm joist	4.33	2.50	4.44	-	-	-	-	4.44	nr	4.88
SPH type S, for 100 x 125mm joist	4.55	2.50	4.66	-	-	-	-	4.66	nr	5.13
SPH type S, for 100 x 150mm joist	4.77	2.50	4.89	-	-	-	-	4.89	nr	5.38
SPH type S, for 100 x 175mm joist	5.17	2.50	5.30	-	-	-	-	5.30	nr	5.83
SPH type S, for 100 x 200mm joist	4.97	2.50	5.09	-	-	-	-	5.09	nr	5.60

Labour hourly rates: (except Specialists) Craft Operatives 20.87 Labourer 15.57 Rates are national average prices. Refer to REGIONAL VARIATIONS for indicative levels of overall pricing in regions	MATERIALS			LABOUR				RATES		
	Del to Site £	Waste %	Material Cost £	Craft Optve Hrs	Lab Hrs	Labour Cost £	Sunds £	Nett Rate £	Unit	Gross rate (10%) £
METAL AND PLASTIC ACCESSORIES (Cont'd)										
Metal fixings, fastenings and fittings (Cont'd)										
Steel; galvanised; joist hangers (Cont'd)										
Joist hangers; BAT Building Products Ltd; (building in where required included elsewhere) (Cont'd)										
SPH type S, for 100 x 225mm joist	5.25	2.50	5.38	-	-	-	-	5.38	nr	5.92
SPH type S, for 100 x 250mm joist	5.56	2.50	5.70	-	-	-	-	5.70	nr	6.27
SPH type R, for 50 x 100mm joist	6.46	2.50	6.62	-	-	-	-	6.62	nr	7.28
SPH type R, for 50 x 125mm joist	6.71	2.50	6.88	-	-	-	-	6.88	nr	7.57
SPH type R, for 50 x 150mm joist	6.43	2.50	6.59	-	-	-	-	6.59	nr	7.25
SPH type R, for 50 x 175mm joist	6.19	2.50	6.35	-	-	-	-	6.35	nr	6.98
SPH type R, for 50 x 200mm joist	8.13	2.50	8.33	-	-	-	-	8.33	nr	9.17
SPH type R, for 50 x 225mm joist	8.87	2.50	9.09	-	-	-	-	9.09	nr	10.00
SPH type R, for 50 x 250mm joist	10.57	2.50	10.83	-	-	-	-	10.83	nr	11.92
SPH type R, for 63 x 100mm joist	9.53	2.50	9.77	-	-	-	-	9.77	nr	10.75
SPH type R, for 63 x 125mm joist	9.76	2.50	10.00	-	-	-	-	10.00	nr	11.00
SPH type R, for 63 x 150mm joist	10.20	2.50	10.45	-	-	-	-	10.45	nr	11.50
SPH type R, for 63 x 175mm joist	10.49	2.50	10.76	-	-	-	-	10.76	nr	11.83
SPH type R, for 63 x 200mm joist	10.72	2.50	10.98	-	-	-	-	10.98	nr	12.08
SPH type R, for 63 x 225mm joist	9.06	2.50	9.29	-	-	-	-	9.29	nr	10.22
SPH type R, for 63 x 250mm joist	12.19	2.50	12.50	-	-	-	-	12.50	nr	13.75
SPH type ST for 50 x 100mm joist	12.80	2.50	13.12	-	-	-	-	13.12	nr	14.43
SPH type ST for 50 x 125mm joist	12.89	2.50	13.21	-	-	-	-	13.21	nr	14.53
SPH type ST for 50 x 150mm joist	12.15	2.50	12.45	-	-	-	-	12.45	nr	13.70
SPH type ST for 50 x 175mm joist	12.74	2.50	13.06	-	-	-	-	13.06	nr	14.36
SPH type ST for 50 x 200mm joist	13.27	2.50	13.60	-	-	-	-	13.60	nr	14.96
SPH type ST for 50 x 225mm joist	12.93	2.50	13.26	-	-	-	-	13.26	nr	14.58
SPH type ST for 50 x 250mm joist	19.11	2.50	19.59	-	-	-	-	19.59	nr	21.55
Speedy Minor type for the following size joists; fixing with nails										
38 x 100mm	0.57	2.50	0.58	0.15	0.02	3.44	0.03	4.06	nr	4.47
50 x 100mm	0.50	2.50	0.51	0.15	0.02	3.44	0.03	3.99	nr	4.39
Speedy short leg type for the following size joists fixing with nails										
38 x 175mm	1.67	2.50	1.71	0.15	0.02	3.44	0.03	5.19	nr	5.71
50 x 175mm	1.47	2.50	1.51	0.15	0.02	3.44	0.03	4.98	nr	5.48
Speedy Standard Leg type for the following size joists; fixing with nails										
38 x 100mm	0.84	2.50	0.86	0.15	0.02	3.44	0.03	4.34	nr	4.77
50 x 175mm	0.84	2.50	0.86	0.15	0.02	3.44	0.03	4.34	nr	4.77
63 x 225mm	0.88	2.50	0.90	0.15	0.02	3.44	0.03	4.38	nr	4.81
75 x 225mm	0.88	2.50	0.90	0.17	0.02	3.86	0.05	4.81	nr	5.29
100 x 225mm	0.92	2.50	0.94	0.17	0.02	3.86	0.05	4.85	nr	5.34
Steel; galvanised; joist struts										
Herringbone joist struts; BAT Building Products Ltd; to suit joists at the following centres; fixing with nails										
400mm	0.59	5.00	0.62	0.25	0.03	5.68	0.07	6.37	m	7.01
450mm	0.67	5.00	0.70	0.25	0.03	5.68	0.07	6.45	m	7.10
600mm	0.74	5.00	0.78	0.20	0.03	4.64	0.07	5.48	m	6.03
Steel; galvanised; truss plates and framing anchors										
Truss plates; BAT Building Products Ltd; fixing with nails										
51 x 114mm	0.36	5.00	0.37	0.35	0.04	7.93	0.10	8.40	nr	9.24
76 x 254mm	1.24	5.00	1.30	1.00	0.13	22.89	0.26	24.46	nr	26.91
114 x 152mm	1.00	5.00	1.05	1.00	0.13	22.89	0.26	24.21	nr	26.63
114 x 254mm	1.82	5.00	1.91	1.50	0.19	34.26	0.40	36.57	nr	40.23
152 x 152mm	1.21	5.00	1.27	1.60	0.20	36.51	0.43	38.20	nr	42.02
Framing anchors; BAT Building Products Ltd.										
type A; fixing with nails	0.91	5.00	0.96	0.20	0.02	4.49	0.05	5.49	nr	6.04
type B; fixing with nails	0.91	5.00	0.96	0.20	0.02	4.49	0.05	5.49	nr	6.04
type C; fixing with nails	0.33	5.00	0.35	0.20	0.02	4.49	0.05	4.88	nr	5.37
Steel timber connectors; BS EN 912										
split ring connectors table 1										
63mm diameter	2.68	5.00	2.82	0.08	0.01	1.83	-	4.64	nr	5.11
100 mm diameter	11.86	5.00	12.45	0.08	0.01	1.83	-	14.28	nr	15.71
shear plate connectors, table 2										
67mm diameter	2.65	5.00	2.78	0.08	0.01	1.83	-	4.61	nr	5.07
single sided round toothed-plate connectors, table 4										
38mm diameter	0.48	5.00	0.50	0.08	0.01	1.83	-	2.33	nr	2.56
50mm diameter	0.38	5.00	0.40	0.08	0.01	1.83	-	2.22	nr	2.45
63mm diameter	0.68	5.00	0.71	0.08	0.01	1.83	-	2.54	nr	2.79
75mm diameter	0.83	5.00	0.87	0.08	0.01	1.83	-	2.70	nr	2.97
double sided round toothed-plate connector, table 4										
38mm diameter	0.53	5.00	0.56	0.08	0.01	1.83	-	2.38	nr	2.62
50mm diameter	0.43	5.00	0.45	0.08	0.01	1.83	-	2.28	nr	2.50
63mm diameter	0.80	5.00	0.84	0.08	0.01	1.83	-	2.67	nr	2.93
75mm diameter	0.86	5.00	0.90	0.08	0.01	1.83	-	2.73	nr	3.00

Labour hourly rates: (except Specialists) Craft Operatives 20.87 Labourer 15.57 Rates are national average prices. Refer to REGIONAL VARIATIONS for indicative levels of overall pricing in regions	MATERIALS			LABOUR				RATES		
	Del to Site £	Waste %	Material Cost £	Craft Optve Hrs	Lab Hrs	Labour Cost £	Sunds £	Nett Rate £	Unit	Gross rate (10%) £
BITUMINOUS FELTS										
Roofing; felt BS EN 13707, comprising 1 layer perfored underlay, 1 layer sanded underlay, 1 layer mineral surface top sheet										
Roof coverings; exceeding 500mm wide; layers of felt -3; bonding with hot bitumen compound to timber base										
pitch 7.5 degrees from horizontal	21.28	15.00	24.91	0.46	0.06	10.53	-	35.45	m²	38.99
pitch 40 degrees from horizontal	21.28	15.00	24.91	0.76	0.09	17.26	-	42.18	m²	46.39
pitch 75 degrees from horizontal	21.28	15.00	24.91	0.92	0.12	21.07	-	45.98	m²	50.58
Roof coverings; exceeding 500mm wide; layers of felt -3; bonding with hot bitumen compound to cement and sand or concrete base										
pitch 7.5 degrees from horizontal	21.28	15.00	24.91	0.46	0.06	10.53	-	35.45	m²	38.99
pitch 40 degrees from horizontal	21.28	15.00	24.91	0.76	0.09	17.26	-	42.18	m²	46.39
pitch 75 degrees from horizontal	21.28	15.00	24.91	0.92	0.12	21.07	-	45.98	m²	50.58
Eaves trim; extruded aluminium alloy										
butt joints over matching sleeve pieces 200mm long; fixing to timber base with aluminium alloy screws; bedding in mastic										
45mm wide x 45mm face depth	3.23	5.00	3.39	0.40	-	8.35	2.36	14.10	m	15.51
50mm wide x 50mm face depth	3.91	5.00	4.10	0.40	-	8.35	2.39	14.84	m	16.33
50mm wide x 100mm face depth	5.34	5.00	5.61	0.40	-	8.35	2.47	16.43	m	18.07
60mm wide x 45mm face depth	4.09	5.00	4.30	0.40	-	8.35	2.47	15.12	m	16.64
60mm wide x 64mm face depth	4.60	5.00	4.83	0.40	-	8.35	2.61	15.79	m	17.37
75mm wide x 75mm face depth	5.37	5.00	5.64	0.40	-	8.35	2.47	16.46	m	18.11
80mm wide x 64mm face depth	5.26	5.00	5.53	0.40	-	8.35	2.61	16.48	m	18.13
80mm wide x 110mm face depth	7.19	5.00	7.55	0.40	-	8.35	2.67	18.57	m	20.43
100mm wide x 75mm face depth	6.23	5.00	6.54	0.40	-	8.35	2.72	17.62	m	19.38
110mm wide x 64mm face depth	6.04	5.00	6.34	0.40	-	8.35	2.77	17.46	m	19.21
150mm wide x 64mm face depth	10.69	5.00	11.23	0.50	-	10.44	2.92	24.58	m	27.04
Eaves trim; glass fibre reinforced										
butt joints; fixing to timber base with stainless steel screws; bedding in mastic										
90mm face	4.55	5.00	4.78	0.40	-	8.35	3.00	16.13	m	17.74
120mm face	4.68	5.00	4.92	0.50	-	10.44	3.55	18.90	m	20.79
Upstands; skirtings; layers of felt - 3; bonding with hot bitumen compound to brickwork base										
girth O - 200mm	4.26	15.00	4.98	0.28	0.03	6.31	-	11.29	m	12.42
girth 200 - 400mm	8.51	15.00	9.97	0.46	0.06	10.53	-	20.50	m	22.55
Collars around pipes; standard and the like; layers of felt -1; bonding with hot bitumen compound to metal base										
50mm diameter x 150mm long; hole in 3 layer covering	1.73	15.00	2.00	0.17	0.02	3.86	-	5.86	nr	6.44
100mm diameter x 150mm long; hole in 3 layer covering	2.25	15.00	2.61	0.22	0.03	5.06	-	7.67	nr	8.44
Roof ventilators										
plastic; setting in position	8.48	2.50	8.69	0.85	-	17.74	0.91	27.34	nr	30.07
aluminium; setting in position	10.39	2.50	10.65	0.85	-	17.74	0.91	29.30	nr	32.23
Roofing; BS EN 13707, all layers type 3B -1.8 kg/m², 75mm laps; fully bonding layers with hot bitumen bonding compound										
Roof coverings; exceeding 500mm wide; layers of felt -2; bonding with hot bitumen compound to timber base										
pitch 7.5 degrees from horizontal	9.50	15.00	11.22	0.38	0.05	8.71	-	19.93	m²	21.92
pitch 40 degrees from horizontal	9.50	15.00	11.22	0.63	0.08	14.39	-	25.62	m²	28.18
pitch 75 degrees from horizontal	9.50	15.00	11.22	0.76	0.09	17.26	-	28.48	m²	31.33
Roof coverings; exceeding 500mm wide; layers of felt -2; bonding with hot bitumen compound to cement and sand or concrete base										
pitch 7.5 degrees from horizontal	9.50	15.00	11.22	0.38	0.05	8.71	-	19.93	m²	21.92
pitch 40 degrees from horizontal	9.50	15.00	11.22	0.63	0.08	14.39	-	25.62	m²	28.18
pitch 75 degrees from horizontal	9.50	15.00	11.22	0.76	0.09	17.26	-	28.48	m²	31.33
Roof coverings; exceeding 500mm wide; layers of felt -3; bonding with hot bitumen compound to timber base										
pitch 7.5 degrees from horizontal	14.25	15.00	16.83	0.55	0.07	12.57	-	29.40	m²	32.34
pitch 40 degrees from horizontal	14.25	15.00	16.83	0.92	0.12	21.07	-	37.90	m²	41.69
pitch 75 degrees from horizontal	14.25	15.00	16.83	1.10	0.14	25.14	-	41.97	m²	46.17
Roof coverings; exceeding 500mm wide; layers of felt -3; bonding with hot bitumen compound to cement and sand or concrete base										
pitch 7.5 degrees from horizontal	14.25	15.00	16.83	0.55	0.07	12.57	-	29.40	m²	32.34
pitch 40 degrees from horizontal	14.25	15.00	16.83	0.92	0.12	21.07	-	37.90	m²	41.69
pitch 75 degrees from horizontal	14.25	15.00	16.83	1.10	0.14	25.14	-	41.97	m²	46.17

Labour hourly rates: (except Specialists) Craft Operatives 20.87 Labourer 15.57 Rates are national average prices. Refer to REGIONAL VARIATIONS for indicative levels of overall pricing in regions	MATERIALS			LABOUR				RATES		
	Del to Site £	Waste %	Material Cost £	Craft Optve Hrs	Lab Hrs	Labour Cost £	Sunds £	Nett Rate £	Unit	Gross rate (10%) £
BITUMINOUS FELTS (Cont'd)										
Roofing; felt BS EN 13707, bottom and intermediate layers type 3B -1.8 kg/m², top layer green mineral surface 3.8 kg/m², 75mm laps; fully bonding layers with hot bitumen bonding compound										
Roof coverings; exceeding 500mm wide; layers of felt -2; bonding with hot bitumen compound to timber base										
pitch 7.5 degrees from horizontal	12.13	15.00	14.25	0.38	0.05	8.71	-	22.95	m²	25.25
pitch 40 degrees from horizontal	12.13	15.00	14.25	0.63	0.08	14.39	-	28.64	m²	31.50
pitch 75 degrees from horizontal	12.13	15.00	14.25	0.76	0.09	17.26	-	31.51	m²	34.66
Roof coverings; exceeding 500mm wide; layers of felt -2; bonding with hot bitumen compound to cement and sand or concrete base										
pitch 7.5 degrees from horizontal	12.13	15.00	14.25	0.38	0.05	8.71	-	22.95	m²	25.25
pitch 40 degrees from horizontal	12.13	15.00	14.25	0.63	0.08	14.39	-	28.64	m²	31.50
pitch 75 degrees from horizontal	12.13	15.00	14.25	0.76	0.09	17.26	-	31.51	m²	34.66
Roof coverings; exceeding 500mm wide; layers of felt -3; bonding with hot bitumen compound to timber base										
pitch 7.5 degrees from horizontal	16.88	15.00	19.86	0.55	0.07	12.57	-	32.43	m²	35.67
pitch 40 degrees from horizontal	16.88	15.00	19.86	0.92	0.12	21.07	-	40.93	m²	45.02
pitch 75 degrees from horizontal	16.88	15.00	19.86	1.10	0.14	25.14	-	44.99	m²	49.49
Roof coverings; exceeding 500mm wide; layers of felt -3; bonding with hot bitumen compound to cement and sand or concrete base										
pitch 7.5 degrees from horizontal	16.88	15.00	19.86	0.55	0.07	12.57	-	32.43	m²	35.67
pitch 40 degrees from horizontal	16.88	15.00	19.86	0.92	0.12	21.07	-	40.93	m²	45.02
pitch 75 degrees from horizontal	16.88	15.00	19.86	1.10	0.14	25.14	-	44.99	m²	49.49
Upstands; skirtings; layers of felt - 3; bonding with hot bitumen compound to brickwork base										
girth O - 200mm	3.38	15.00	3.97	0.28	0.03	6.31	-	10.28	m	11.31
girth 200 - 400mm	6.75	15.00	7.94	0.46	0.06	10.53	-	18.48	m	20.32
Collars around pipes; standard and the like; layers of felt -1; bonding with hot bitumen compound to metal base										
50mm diameter x 150mm long; hole in 3 layer covering	1.32	15.00	1.53	0.17	0.02	3.86	-	5.39	nr	5.93
100mm diameter x 150mm long; hole in 3 layer covering	1.77	15.00	2.06	0.22	0.03	5.06	-	7.11	nr	7.82
Roofing; sheet, IKO Ruberoid Building Products hot bonded system, bottom layer perforated slate underlay (formerly type 3G); intermediate layer glass fibre underlay (formerly lype 3B); top layer glass fibre SBS mineral surfaced cap sheet, 50mm side laps, 75mm end laps; partially bonding bottom layer, fully bonding other layers in hot bonding bitumen										
Roof coverings; exceeding 500mm wide; layers of sheet -3; bonding with hot bitumen compound to timber base										
pitch not exceeding 5.0 degrees from horizontal	27.21	15.00	32.03	0.55	0.28	15.84	-	47.87	m²	52.65
Roof coverings; exceeding 500mm wide; layers of sheet -3; bonding with hot bitumen compound to cement and sand or concrete base										
pitch not exceeding 5.0 degrees from horizontal	27.21	15.00	32.03	0.55	0.28	15.84	-	47.87	m²	52.65
Roof coverings; exceeding 500mm wide; layers of sheet -3; bonding with hot bitumen compound to metal base										
pitch not exceeding 5.0 degrees from horizontal	27.21	15.00	32.03	0.55	0.28	15.84	-	47.87	m²	52.65
Upstands; skirtings; layers of sheet -2; bonding with hot bitumen compound to brickwork base										
girth O - 200mm	16.80	15.00	20.05	0.28	0.05	6.62	-	26.67	m	29.34
girth 200 - 400mm	18.96	15.00	22.54	0.46	0.06	10.53	-	33.07	m	36.38
Roofing; sheet, IKO Ruberoid Building Products hot bonded system, bottom layer perforated slate underlay (formerly type 3G); intermediate layer glass fibre underlay (formerly lype 3B); top layer glass fibre SBS mineral surfaced cap sheet, 50mm side laps, 75mm end laps; partially bonding bottom layer, fully bonding other layers in hot bonding bitumen; 25mm Kingspan Thermaroof TR27 on a vapour control layer										
Roof coverings; exceeding 500mm wide; layers of sheet -3; bonding with hot bitumen compound to timber base										
pitch not exceeding 5.0 degrees from horizontal	39.94	15.00	46.66	1.12	0.36	28.98	1.83	77.47	m²	85.22
Roof coverings; exceeding 500mm wide; layers of sheet -3; bonding with hot bitumen compound to cement and sand or concrete base										
pitch not exceeding 5.0 degrees from horizontal	39.94	15.00	46.66	1.18	0.36	30.23	1.83	78.73	m²	86.60
Roof coverings; exceeding 500mm wide; layers of sheet -3; bonding with hot bitumen compound to metal base										
pitch not exceeding 5.0 degrees from horizontal	39.94	15.00	46.66	1.16	0.36	29.81	1.83	78.31	m²	86.14
Roofing; sheet, IKO Ruberoid Building Products hot bonded system, bottom layer perforated slate underlay (formerly type 3G); intermediate layer glass fibre underlay (formerly lype 3B); top layer glass fibre SBS mineral surfaced cap sheet, 50mm side laps, 75mm end laps; partially bonding bottom layer, fully bonding other layers in hot bonding bitumen; 50mm Kingspan Thermaroof TR27										
Roof coverings; exceeding 500mm wide; layers of sheet -3; bonding with hot bitumen compound to timber base										
pitch not exceeding 5.0 degrees from horizontal	43.78	15.00	51.08	1.20	0.36	30.65	1.83	83.56	m²	91.91

Labour hourly rates: (except Specialists) Craft Operatives 20.87 Labourer 15.57 Rates are national average prices. Refer to REGIONAL VARIATIONS for indicative levels of overall pricing in regions	MATERIALS			LABOUR				RATES		
	Del to Site £	Waste %	Material Cost £	Craft Optve Hrs	Lab Hrs	Labour Cost £	Sunds £	Nett Rate £	Unit	Gross rate (10%) £
BITUMINOUS FELTS (Cont'd)										
Roofing; sheet, IKO Ruberoid Building Products hot bonded system, bottom layer perforated slate underlay (formerly type 3G); intermediate layer glass fibre underlay (formerly lype 3B); top layer glass fibre SBS mineral surfaced cap sheet, 50mm side laps, 75mm end laps; partially bonding bottom layer, fully bonding other layers in hot bonding bitumen; 50mm Kingspan Thermaroof TR27 (Cont'd)										
Roof coverings; exceeding 500mm wide; layers of sheet -3; bonding with hot bitumen compound to cement and sand or concrete base										
pitch not exceeding 5.0 degrees from horizontal	43.78	15.00	51.08	1.26	0.36	31.90	1.83	84.81	m²	93.29
Roof coverings; exceeding 500mm wide; layers of sheet -3; bonding with hot bitumen compound to metal base										
pitch not exceeding 5.0 degrees from horizontal	43.78	15.00	51.08	1.24	0.36	31.48	1.83	84.39	m²	92.83
Roofing; sheet, IKO Ruberoid Building Products hot bonded system, bottom layer perforated slate underlay (formerly type 3G); intermediate layer glass fibre underlay (formerly lype 3B); top layer glass fibre SBS mineral surfaced cap sheet, 50mm side laps, 75mm end laps; partially bonding bottom layer, fully bonding other layers in hot bonding bitumen; 100mm Kingspan Thermaboard TR27 Board										
Roof coverings; exceeding 500mm wide; layers of sheet -3; bonding with hot bitumen compound to timber base										
pitch not exceeding 5.0 degrees from horizontal	61.65	15.00	71.63	1.34	0.40	34.19	1.83	107.65	m²	118.42
Roof coverings; exceeding 500mm wide; layers of sheet -3; bonding with hot bitumen compound to cement and sand or concrete base										
pitch not exceeding 5.0 degrees from horizontal	61.65	15.00	71.63	1.36	0.40	34.61	1.83	108.07	m²	118.88
Roof coverings; exceeding 500mm wide; layers of sheet -3; bonding with hot bitumen compound to metal base										
pitch not exceeding 5.0 degrees from horizontal	61.65	15.00	71.63	1.34	0.40	34.19	1.83	107.65	m²	118.42
Roofing; sheet, IKO Ruberoid Building Products Torch-on system, bottom layer Universal T-O Underlay; top layer Permatorch T-O slate surfaced cap sheet, 75mm side and end laps; fully bonding both layers (by torching)										
Roof coverings; exceeding 500mm wide; layers of sheet -3; bonding to timber base										
pitch not exceeding 5.0 degrees from horizontal	8.16	15.00	9.39	0.55	0.28	15.84	4.74	29.96	m²	32.95
Roof coverings; exceeding 500mm wide; layers of sheet -3; bonding to cement and sand or concrete base										
pitch not exceeding 5.0 degrees from horizontal	8.16	15.00	9.39	0.55	0.28	15.84	4.74	29.96	m²	32.95
Roof coverings; exceeding 500mm wide; layers of sheet -3; bonding to metal base										
pitch not exceeding 5.0 degrees from horizontal	8.16	15.00	9.39	0.59	0.28	16.67	4.74	30.79	m²	33.87
Upstands; skirtings; layers of sheet -2; bonding with hot bitumen compound to brickwork base										
girth 0 - 200mm	1.63	15.00	1.88	0.28	0.05	6.62	0.96	9.46	m	10.40
girth 200 - 400mm	3.26	15.00	3.75	0.46	0.06	10.53	1.91	16.20	m	17.82
Roofing; sheet, IKO Ruberoid Building Products Torch-on system, bottom layer Universal T-O Underlay; top layer Permatorch T-O slate surfaced cap sheet, 75mm side and end laps; fully bonding both layers (by torching), 25mm Kingspan Thermaroof TR27 insulation with bitumen primed surface										
Roof coverings; exceeding 500mm wide; layers of sheet -3; bonding to timber base										
pitch not exceeding 5.0 degrees from horizontal	20.89	15.00	24.02	1.12	0.36	28.98	4.74	57.73	m²	63.51
Roof coverings; exceeding 500mm wide; layers of sheet -3; bonding to cement and sand or concrete base										
pitch not exceeding 5.0 degrees from horizontal	20.89	15.00	24.02	1.12	0.36	28.98	4.74	57.73	m²	63.51
Roof coverings; exceeding 500mm wide; layers of sheet -3; bonding to metal base										
pitch not exceeding 5.0 degrees from horizontal	20.89	15.00	24.02	1.17	0.36	30.02	4.74	58.78	m²	64.66
Roofing; sheet, IKO Ruberoid Building Products Torch-on system, bottom layer Universal T-O Underlay; top layer Permatorch T-O slate surfaced cap sheet, 75mm side and end laps; fully bonding both layers (by torching), 50mm Kingspan Thermaroof TR27 insulation with bitumen primed surface; Superbar vapour control layer										
Roof coverings; exceeding 500mm wide; layers of sheet -3; bonding to timber base										
pitch not exceeding 5.0 degrees from horizontal	24.73	15.00	28.43	1.20	0.36	30.65	4.74	63.82	m²	70.20

Labour hourly rates: (except Specialists) Craft Operatives 20.87 Labourer 15.57 Rates are national average prices. Refer to REGIONAL VARIATIONS for indicative levels of overall pricing in regions	MATERIALS			LABOUR				RATES		
	Del to Site £	Waste %	Material Cost £	Craft Optve Hrs	Lab Hrs	Labour Cost £	Sunds £	Nett Rate £	Unit	Gross rate (10%) £
BITUMINOUS FELTS (Cont'd)										
Roofing; sheet, IKO Ruberoid Building Products Torch-on system, bottom layer Universal T-O Underlay; top layer Permatorch T-O slate surfaced cap sheet, 75mm side and end laps; fully bonding both layers (by torching), 100mm Kingspan Thermaroof TR27 insulation with bitumen primed surface; Superbar vapour control layer										
Roof coverings; exceeding 500mm wide; layers of sheet -3; bonding to timber base										
pitch not exceeding 5.0 degrees from horizontal	42.60	15.00	48.98	1.20	0.36	30.65	4.74	84.37	m²	92.81
Roofing; sheet, IKO Ruberoid Building Products Torch-on system, bottom layer Universal T-O Underlay; top layer Permatorch T-O slate surfaced cap sheet, 75mm side and end laps; fully bonding both layers (by torching), 120mm Kingspan Thermaroof TR27 insulation with bitumen primed surface; Superbar vapour control layer										
Roof coverings; exceeding 500mm wide; layers of sheet -3; bonding to timber base										
pitch not exceeding 5.0 degrees from horizontal	50.19	15.00	57.72	1.20	0.36	30.65	4.74	93.10	m²	102.41
Roofing; sheet, IKO Ruberoid Building Products Torch-on system, bottom layer Universal T-O Underlay; top layer Permatorch T-O slate surfaced cap sheet, 75mm side and end laps; fully bonding both layers (by torching), 70mm Xtratherm Flat Roof FR-MG insulation with bitumen primed surface; Superbar vapour control layer										
Roof coverings; exceeding 500mm wide; layers of sheet -3; bonding to timber base										
pitch not exceeding 5.0 degrees from horizontal	29.62	15.00	34.07	1.20	0.36	30.65	4.74	69.45	m²	76.40
Roofing; sheet, IKO Ruberoid Building Products Torch-on system, bottom layer Universal T-O Underlay; top layer Permatorch T-O slate surfaced cap sheet, 75mm side and end laps; fully bonding both layers (by torching), 90mm Xtratherm Flat Roof FR-MG insulation with bitumen primed surface; Superbar vapour control layer										
Roof coverings; exceeding 500mm wide; layers of sheet -3; bonding to timber base										
pitch not exceeding 5.0 degrees from horizontal	37.05	15.00	42.61	1.20	0.36	30.65	4.74	77.99	m²	85.79
Roofing; sheet, IKO Ruberoid Building Products Torch-on system, bottom layer Universal T-O Underlay; top layer Permatorch T-O slate surfaced cap sheet, 75mm side and end laps; fully bonding both layers (by torching), 100mm Xtratherm Flat Roof FR-MG insulation with bitumen primed surface; Superbar vapour control layer										
Roof coverings; exceeding 500mm wide; layers of sheet -3; bonding to timber base										
pitch not exceeding 5.0 degrees from horizontal	40.07	15.00	46.08	1.20	0.36	30.65	4.74	81.47	m²	89.61
Roofing; sheet, IKO Ruberoid Building Products Torch-on system, bottom layer Universal T-O Underlay; top layer Permatorch T-O slate surfaced cap sheet, 75mm side and end laps; fully bonding both layers (by torching), 120mm Xtratherm Flat Roof FR-MG insulation with bitumen primed surface; Superbar vapour control layer										
Roof coverings; exceeding 500mm wide; layers of sheet -3; bonding to timber base										
pitch not exceeding 5.0 degrees from horizontal	46.12	15.00	53.04	1.20	0.36	30.65	4.74	88.42	m²	97.26
Roofing; sheet, IKO Ruberoid Building Products Torch-on system, bottom layer Universal T-O Underlay; top layer Permatorch T-O slate surfaced cap sheet, 75mm side and end laps; fully bonding both layers (by torching), 150mm Xtratherm Flat Roof FR-MG insulation with bitumen primed surface; Superbar vapour control layer										
Roof coverings; exceeding 500mm wide; layers of sheet -3; bonding to timber base										
pitch not exceeding 5.0 degrees from horizontal	78.85	15.00	90.67	1.20	0.36	30.65	4.74	126.06	m²	138.66
PLASTIC SHEETS										
Sarnafil polymeric waterproofing membrane ref: S327-12EL; Sarnabar mechanically fastened system; 85mm thick; Sarnatherm S CFC & HCFC free (0.25 U-value) rigid urethane insulation board mechanically fastened; Sarnavap 1000E vapour control layer loose laid all laps sealed										
Roof Coverings; exceeding 500mm wide										
Pitch not exceeding 5 degrees; to metal decking or the like	-	-	Specialist	-	-	Specialist	-	91.54	m²	100.69
Sarnafil polymeric waterproofing membrane ref: G410-12ELF fleece backed membrane; fully adhered system; 90mm thick Sarnatherm G CFC & HCFC free (0.25 U-value) insulation board bedded in hot bitumen; BS EN 13707 type 5U felt vapour control layer bonded in hot bitumen; prime concrete with spirit bitumen priming solution										
Roof Coverings; exceeding 500mm wide										
Pitch not exceeding 5 degrees; to concrete base or the like	-	-	Specialist	-	-	Specialist	-	117.03	m²	128.74

Labour hourly rates: (except Specialists) Craft Operatives 20.87 Labourer 15.57 Rates are national average prices. Refer to REGIONAL VARIATIONS for indicative levels of overall pricing in regions	MATERIALS			LABOUR				RATES		
	Del to Site £	Waste %	Material Cost £	Craft Optve Hrs	Lab Hrs	Labour Cost £	Sunds £	Nett Rate £	Unit	Gross rate (10%) £
PLASTIC SHEETS (Cont'd)										
Sarnafil polymeric waterproofing membrane ref: G410-12ELF fleece backed membrane; fully adhered system; 90mm thick Sarnatherm G CFC & HCFC free (0.25 U-value) insulation board bedded in hot bitumen; BS EN 13707 type 5U felt vapour control layer bonded in hot bitumen; prime concrete with spirit bitumen priming solution (Cont'd)										
Eaves Detail; Sarnametal drip edge to gutter; standard Sarnafil detail 1.3										
not exceeding 200 girth	-	-	Specialist	-	-	Specialist	-	34.62	m	38.08
Upstands; skirting to brickwork with galvanised steel counter flashing to top edge; standard Sarnafil detail 2.3										
not exceeding 200 girth	-	-	Specialist	-	-	Specialist	-	51.77	m	56.95
200 - 400 girth	-	-	Specialist	-	-	Specialist	-	55.23	m	60.75
400 - 600 girth	-	-	Specialist	-	-	Specialist	-	62.60	m	68.86
Skirting/Upstands; Skirting to brickwork with Sarnametal Raglet to chase; standard Sarnafil detail 2.8										
not exceeding 200 girth	-	-	Specialist	-	-	Specialist	-	72.09	m	79.30
200 - 400 girth	-	-	Specialist	-	-	Specialist	-	75.55	m	83.11
400 - 600 girth	-	-	Specialist	-	-	Specialist	-	82.95	m	91.25
Coverings to Kerb; Parapet Flashing; Sarnatrim 50 deep on face 100 fixing arm; standard Sarnafil detail 1.1										
not exceeding 200 girth	-	-	Specialist	-	-	Specialist	-	63.51	m	69.86
200 - 400 girth	-	-	Specialist	-	-	Specialist	-	66.96	m	73.66
400 - 600 girth	-	-	Specialist	-	-	Specialist	-	74.35	m	81.78
Outlets and Dishing to Gullies										
fix Sarnadrain pvc rainwater outlet; 110 diameter; weld membrane to same; fit plastic leafguard	-	-	-	-	-	-	1.83	192.26	nr	211.48
Collars around Pipe Standards and The Like										
50 diameter x 150 high	-	-	Specialist	-	-	Specialist	-	59.69	nr	65.66
100 diameter x 150 high	-	-	Specialist	-	-	Specialist	-	59.69	nr	65.66
Glass Reinforced Plastic (GRP) Roofing; roofing resin, top coat and 450 gsm glass fabric										
Roof coverings; exceeding 500mm wide; to WBP or OSB3 base										
Pitch 7.5 degrees from horizontal	13.39	15.00	15.40	0.55	0.07	12.57	-	27.97	m²	30.76
Pitch 40 degrees from horizontal	13.39	15.00	15.40	0.92	0.12	21.07	-	36.47	m²	40.12
Pitch 75 degrees from horizontal	13.39	15.00	15.40	1.10	0.14	25.14	-	40.54	m²	44.59
Upstands; skirtings; roofing resin, top coat and 450 gsm glass fabric										
girth O - 150mm	2.98	15.00	3.42	0.28	0.03	6.31	-	9.73	m	10.71
girth 150 - 300mm	5.95	15.00	6.85	0.46	0.06	10.53	-	17.38	m	19.12
Collars around pipes; standard and the like; roofing resin, top coat and 450 gsm glass fabric										
50mm diameter x 150mm long; hole in 3 layer covering	2.66	15.00	3.06	0.17	0.02	3.86	-	6.92	nr	7.62
100mm diameter x 150mm long; hole in 3 layer covering	4.12	15.00	4.74	0.22	0.03	5.06	-	9.80	nr	10.78
Glass Reinforced Plastic (GRP) Roofing; roofing resin, top coat and 450 gsm glass fabric; on 18mm plywood, 100mm Kingspan Thermaroof TR27 insulation, 1000 gauge vapour control layer on 18mm plywood deck										
Roof coverings; exceeding 500mm wide; fixed to timber joists										
pitch not exceeding 5.0 degrees from horizontal	75.24	15.00	85.07	1.20	0.36	30.65	4.74	120.45	m²	132.50
Glass Reinforced Plastic (GRP) Roofing; roofing resin, top coat and 450 gsm glass fabric; on 18mm plywood, 120mm Kingspan Thermaroof TR27 insulation, 1000 gauge vapour control layer on 18mm plywood deck										
Roof coverings; exceeding 500mm wide; fixed to timber joists										
pitch not exceeding 5.0 degrees from horizontal	82.84	15.00	93.80	1.20	0.36	30.65	4.74	129.19	m²	142.11
Glass Reinforced Plastic (GRP) Roofing; roofing resin, top coat and 450 gsm glass fabric; on 18mm plywood, 100mm Xtratherm Flat Roof FR-BGM insulation, 1000 gauge vapour control layer on 18mm plywood deck										
Roof coverings; exceeding 500mm wide; layers of sheet -3; bonding to timber base										
pitch not exceeding 5.0 degrees from horizontal	72.66	15.00	82.10	1.20	0.36	30.65	4.74	117.48	m²	129.23
Glass Reinforced Plastic (GRP) Roofing; roofing resin, top coat and 450 gsm glass fabric; on 18mm plywood, 150mm Xtratherm Flat Roof FR-BGM insulation, 1000 gauge vapour control layer on 18mm plywood deck										
Roof coverings; exceeding 500mm wide; layers of sheet -3; bonding to timber base										
pitch not exceeding 5.0 degrees from horizontal	88.26	15.00	100.03	1.20	0.36	30.65	4.74	135.42	m²	148.96

Labour hourly rates: (except Specialists) Craft Operatives 26.39 Labourer 15.57 Rates are national average prices. Refer to REGIONAL VARIATIONS for indicative levels of overall pricing in regions	MATERIALS			LABOUR				RATES		
	Del to Site £	Waste %	Material Cost £	Craft Optve Hrs	Lab Hrs	Labour Cost £	Sunds £	Nett Rate £	Unit	Gross rate (10%) £
SHEET METALS; LEAD										
Sheet lead										
Technical data										
Code 3, 1.32mm thick, 14.97 kg/m², colour code green										
Code 4, 1.80mm thick, 20.41 kg/m², colour code blue										
Code 5, 2.24mm thick, 25.40 kg/m², colour code red										
Code 6, 2.65mm thick, 30.05 kg/m², colour code black										
Code 7, 3.15mm thick, 35.72 kg/m², colour code white										
Code 8, 3.55mm thick, 40.26 kg/m², colour code orange										
Milled lead sheet, BS EN 12588										
Nr 3 roof coverings; exceeding 500mm wide; fixing to timber with milled lead cleats and galvanised screws; sloping										
pitch 7.5 degrees from horizontal	36.00	5.00	37.80	4.40	-	116.12	0.41	154.33	m²	169.76
pitch 40 degrees from horizontal	36.00	5.00	37.80	5.05	-	133.27	0.41	171.48	m²	188.63
pitch 75 degrees from horizontal	36.00	5.00	37.80	5.70	-	150.42	0.41	188.64	m²	207.50
Nr 4 roof coverings; exceeding 500mm wide; fixing to timber with milled lead cleats and galvanised screws; sloping										
pitch 7.5 degrees from horizontal	49.00	5.00	51.45	5.05	-	133.27	0.50	185.21	m²	203.74
pitch 40 degrees from horizontal	49.00	5.00	51.45	5.70	-	150.42	0.50	202.37	m²	222.60
pitch 75 degrees from horizontal	49.00	5.00	51.45	6.35	-	167.58	0.50	219.52	m²	241.47
Nr 5 roof coverings; exceeding 500mm wide; fixing to timber with milled lead cleats and galvanised screws; sloping										
pitch 7.5 degrees from horizontal	61.00	5.00	64.05	5.70	-	150.42	0.59	215.07	m²	236.57
pitch 40 degrees from horizontal	61.00	5.00	64.05	6.35	-	167.58	0.59	232.22	m²	255.44
pitch 75 degrees from horizontal	61.00	5.00	64.05	6.95	-	183.41	0.59	248.05	m²	272.86
Extra										
oil patination to surfaces	0.13	10.00	0.15	0.23	-	6.07	-	6.22	m²	6.84
Nr 3 wall coverings; exceeding 500mm wide; fixing to timber with milled lead cleats and galvanised screws										
vertical	36.00	5.00	37.80	8.00	-	211.12	0.41	249.33	m²	274.27
Nr 4 wall coverings; exceeding 500mm wide; fixing to timber with milled lead cleats and galvanised screws										
vertical	49.00	5.00	51.45	8.65	-	228.27	0.50	280.22	m²	308.24
Nr 5 wall coverings; exceeding 500mm wide; fixing to timber with milled lead cleats and galvanised screws										
vertical	61.00	5.00	64.05	9.25	-	244.11	0.59	308.75	m²	339.63
Extra for forming										
Nr 3 edges										
welted	-	-	-	0.20	-	5.28	-	5.28	m	5.81
beaded	-	-	-	0.20	-	5.28	-	5.28	m	5.81
Nr 4 edges										
welted	-	-	-	0.20	-	5.28	-	5.28	m	5.81
beaded	-	-	-	0.20	-	5.28	-	5.28	m	5.81
Nr 5 edges										
welted	-	-	-	0.20	-	5.28	-	5.28	m	5.81
beaded	-	-	-	0.20	-	5.28	-	5.28	m	5.81
Nr 3 seams										
leadburned	2.01	-	2.01	0.23	-	6.07	-	8.08	m	8.89
Nr 4 seams										
leadburned	2.68	-	2.68	0.23	-	6.07	-	8.75	m	9.62
Nr 5 seams										
leadburned	3.35	-	3.35	0.23	-	6.07	-	9.42	m	10.36
Nr 3 dressings										
corrugated roofing; fibre cement; down corrugations	-	-	-	0.29	-	7.65	-	7.65	m	8.42
corrugated roofing; fibre cement; across corrugations	-	-	-	0.29	-	7.65	-	7.65	m	8.42
glass and glazing bars; timber	-	-	-	0.29	-	7.65	-	7.65	m	8.42
Nr 4 dressings										
corrugated roofing; fibre cement; down corrugations	-	-	-	0.29	-	7.65	-	7.65	m	8.42
corrugated roofing; fibre cement; across corrugations	-	-	-	0.29	-	7.65	-	7.65	m	8.42
glass and glazing bars; timber	-	-	-	0.29	-	7.65	-	7.65	m	8.42
Nr 5 dressings										
corrugated roofing; fibre cement; down corrugations	-	-	-	0.29	-	7.65	-	7.65	m	8.42
corrugated roofing; fibre cement; across corrugations	-	-	-	0.29	-	7.65	-	7.65	m	8.42
glass and glazing bars; timber	-	-	-	0.29	-	7.65	-	7.65	m	8.42
Flashings; horizontal										
Nr 3; 150mm lapped joints; fixing to masonry with milled lead clips and lead wedges										
150mm girth	5.40	5.00	5.67	0.46	-	12.14	0.41	18.22	m	20.04
240mm girth	8.60	5.00	9.03	0.74	-	19.53	0.41	28.97	m	31.87
300mm girth	10.80	5.00	11.34	0.92	-	24.28	0.41	36.03	m	39.63
Nr 4; 150mm lapped joints; fixing to masonry with milled lead clips and lead wedges										
150mm girth	7.40	5.00	7.77	0.50	-	13.19	0.50	21.46	m	23.61
240mm girth	11.60	5.00	12.18	0.82	-	21.64	0.50	34.31	m	37.75
300mm girth	14.80	5.00	15.54	1.02	-	26.92	0.50	42.95	m	47.25
Nr 5; 150mm lapped joints; fixing to masonry with milled lead clips and lead wedges										
150mm girth	9.20	5.00	9.66	0.58	-	15.31	0.59	25.56	m	28.12

Labour hourly rates: (except Specialists) Craft Operatives 26.39 Labourer 15.57 Rates are national average prices. Refer to REGIONAL VARIATIONS for indicative levels of overall pricing in regions	MATERIALS			LABOUR				RATES		
	Del to Site £	Waste %	Material Cost £	Craft Optve Hrs	Lab Hrs	Labour Cost £	Sunds £	Nett Rate £	Unit	Gross rate (10%) £
SHEET METALS; LEAD (Cont'd)										
Milled lead sheet, BS EN 12588 (Cont'd)										
Flashings; horizontal (Cont'd)										
Nr 5; 150mm lapped joints; fixing to masonry with milled lead clips and lead wedges (Cont'd)										
240mm girth	14.60	5.00	15.33	0.92	-	24.28	0.59	40.20	m	44.22
300mm girth	18.40	5.00	19.32	1.15	-	30.35	0.59	50.26	m	55.29
Nr 3; 150mm lapped joints; fixing to timber with copper nails										
150mm girth	5.40	5.00	5.67	0.46	-	12.14	0.48	18.29	m	20.12
240mm girth	8.60	5.00	9.03	0.74	-	19.53	0.48	29.04	m	31.94
300mm girth	10.80	5.00	11.34	0.92	-	24.28	0.48	36.10	m	39.71
Nr 4; 150mm lapped joints; fixing to timber with copper nails										
150mm girth	7.40	5.00	7.77	0.50	-	13.19	0.48	21.44	m	23.59
240mm girth	11.60	5.00	12.18	0.82	-	21.64	0.48	34.30	m	37.73
300mm girth	14.80	5.00	15.54	1.02	-	26.92	0.48	42.94	m	47.23
Nr 5; 150mm lapped joints; fixing to timber with copper nails										
150mm girth	9.20	5.00	9.66	0.58	-	15.31	0.48	25.44	m	27.99
240mm girth	14.60	5.00	15.33	0.92	-	24.28	0.48	40.09	m	44.10
300mm girth	18.40	5.00	19.32	1.15	-	30.35	0.48	50.15	m	55.16
Flashings; stepped										
Nr 3; 150mm lapped joints; fixing to masonry with milled lead clips and lead wedges										
210mm girth	7.60	5.00	7.98	0.74	-	19.53	0.58	28.09	m	30.89
240mm girth	8.60	5.00	9.03	0.98	-	25.86	0.58	35.47	m	39.02
300mm girth	10.80	5.00	11.34	1.24	-	32.72	0.58	44.64	m	49.11
Nr 4; 150mm lapped joints; fixing to masonry with milled lead clips and lead wedges										
180mm girth	10.40	5.00	10.92	0.82	-	21.64	0.76	33.32	m	36.65
240mm girth	11.60	5.00	12.18	1.10	-	29.03	0.76	41.97	m	46.16
300mm girth	14.80	5.00	15.54	1.36	-	35.89	0.76	52.19	m	57.41
Nr 5; 150mm lapped joints; fixing to masonry with milled lead clips and lead wedges										
180mm girth	12.80	5.00	13.44	0.92	-	24.28	0.91	38.63	m	42.49
240mm girth	14.60	5.00	15.33	1.22	-	32.20	0.91	48.43	m	53.28
300mm girth	18.40	5.00	19.32	1.52	-	40.11	0.91	60.34	m	66.37
Aprons; horizontal										
Nr 3; 150mm lapped joints; fixing to masonry with milled lead clips and lead wedges										
150mm girth	5.40	5.00	5.67	0.46	-	12.14	0.41	18.22	m	20.04
240mm girth	8.60	5.00	9.03	0.74	-	19.53	0.41	28.97	m	31.87
300mm girth	10.80	5.00	11.34	0.92	-	24.28	0.41	36.03	m	39.63
450mm girth	16.20	5.00	17.01	1.38	-	36.42	0.58	54.01	m	59.41
Nr 4; 150mm lapped joints; fixing to masonry with milled lead clips and lead wedges										
150mm girth	7.40	5.00	7.77	0.50	-	13.19	0.50	21.46	m	23.61
240mm girth	11.60	5.00	12.18	0.82	-	21.64	0.50	34.31	m	37.75
300mm girth	14.80	5.00	15.54	1.02	-	26.92	0.50	42.95	m	47.25
450mm girth	22.00	5.00	23.10	1.52	-	40.11	0.76	63.97	m	70.37
Nr 5; 150mm lapped joints; fixing to masonry with milled lead clips and lead wedges										
150mm girth	9.20	5.00	9.66	0.58	-	15.31	0.59	25.56	m	28.12
240mm girth	14.60	5.00	15.33	0.92	-	24.28	0.59	40.20	m	44.22
300mm girth	18.40	5.00	19.32	1.15	-	30.35	0.59	50.26	m	55.29
450mm girth	27.60	5.00	28.98	1.72	-	45.39	0.91	75.28	m	82.81
Hips; sloping; dressing over slating and tiling										
Nr 3; 150mm lapped joints; fixing to timber with milled lead clips										
240mm girth	8.60	5.00	9.03	0.74	-	19.53	0.41	28.97	m	31.87
300mm girth	10.80	5.00	11.34	0.92	-	24.28	0.41	36.03	m	39.63
450mm girth	16.20	5.00	17.01	1.38	-	36.42	0.58	54.01	m	59.41
Nr 4; 150mm lapped joints; fixing to timber with milled lead clips										
240mm girth	11.60	5.00	12.18	0.82	-	21.64	0.50	34.31	m	37.75
300mm girth	14.80	5.00	15.54	1.02	-	26.92	0.50	42.95	m	47.25
450mm girth	22.00	5.00	23.10	1.52	-	40.11	0.76	63.97	m	70.37
Nr 5; 150mm lapped joints; fixing to timber with milled lead clips										
240mm girth	14.60	5.00	15.33	0.92	-	24.28	0.59	40.20	m	44.22
300mm girth	18.40	5.00	19.32	1.15	-	30.35	0.59	50.26	m	55.29
450mm girth	27.60	5.00	28.98	1.72	-	45.39	0.91	75.28	m	82.81
Kerbs; horizontal										
Nr 3; 150mm lapped joints; fixing to timber with copper nails										
240mm girth	8.60	5.00	9.03	0.74	-	19.53	0.41	28.97	m	31.87
300mm girth	10.80	5.00	11.34	0.92	-	24.28	0.41	36.03	m	39.63
450mm girth	16.20	5.00	17.01	1.38	-	36.42	0.58	54.01	m	59.41
Nr 4; 150mm lapped joints; fixing to timber with copper nails										
240mm girth	11.60	5.00	12.18	0.82	-	21.64	0.50	34.31	m	37.75
300mm girth	14.80	5.00	15.54	1.02	-	26.92	0.50	42.95	m	47.25
450mm girth	22.00	5.00	23.10	1.52	-	40.11	0.76	63.97	m	70.37
Nr 5; 150mm lapped joints; fixing to timber with copper nails										
240mm girth	14.60	5.00	15.33	0.92	-	24.28	0.59	40.20	m	44.22
300mm girth	18.40	5.00	19.32	1.15	-	30.35	0.59	50.26	m	55.29
450mm girth	27.60	5.00	28.98	1.72	-	45.39	0.91	75.28	m	82.81

Labour hourly rates: (except Specialists) Craft Operatives 26.39 Labourer 15.57 Rates are national average prices. Refer to REGIONAL VARIATIONS for indicative levels of overall pricing in regions	MATERIALS			LABOUR				RATES		
	Del to Site £	Waste %	Material Cost £	Craft Optve Hrs	Lab Hrs	Labour Cost £	Sunds £	Nett Rate £	Unit	Gross rate (10%) £
SHEET METALS; LEAD (Cont'd)										
Milled lead sheet, BS EN 12588 (Cont'd)										
Ridges; horizontal; dressing over slating and tiling										
Nr 3; 150mm lapped joints; fixing to timber with milled lead clips										
240mm girth	8.60	5.00	9.03	0.74	-	19.53	0.41	28.97	m	31.87
300mm girth	10.80	5.00	11.34	0.92	-	24.28	0.41	36.03	m	39.63
450mm girth	16.20	5.00	17.01	1.38	-	36.42	0.58	54.01	m	59.41
Nr 4; 150mm lapped joints; fixing to timber with milled lead clips										
240mm girth	11.60	5.00	12.18	0.82	-	21.64	0.50	34.31	m	37.75
300mm girth	14.80	5.00	15.54	1.02	-	26.92	0.50	42.95	m	47.25
450mm girth	22.00	5.00	23.10	1.52	-	40.11	0.76	63.97	m	70.37
Nr 5; 150mm lapped joints; fixing to timber with milled lead clips										
240mm girth	14.60	5.00	15.33	0.92	-	24.28	0.59	40.20	m	44.22
300mm girth	18.40	5.00	19.32	1.15	-	30.35	0.59	50.26	m	55.29
450mm girth	27.60	5.00	28.98	1.72	-	45.39	0.91	75.28	m	82.81
Cavity gutters										
Nr 3; 150mm lapped joints; bedding in cement mortar (1:3)										
225mm girth	8.20	5.00	8.61	0.74	-	19.53	0.76	28.90	m	31.79
360mm girth	13.00	5.00	13.65	1.10	-	29.03	1.14	43.82	m	48.20
Valleys; sloping										
Nr 3; dressing over tilting fillets -1; 150mm lapped joints; fixing to timber with copper nails										
240mm girth	8.60	5.00	9.03	0.74	-	19.53	0.41	28.97	m	31.87
300mm girth	10.80	5.00	11.34	0.92	-	24.28	0.41	36.03	m	39.63
450mm girth	16.20	5.00	17.01	1.38	-	36.42	0.58	54.01	m	59.41
Nr 4; dressing over tilting fillets -1; 150mm lapped joints; fixing to timber with copper nails										
240mm girth	11.60	5.00	12.18	0.82	-	21.64	0.50	34.31	m	37.75
300mm girth	14.80	5.00	15.54	1.02	-	26.92	0.50	42.95	m	47.25
450mm girth	22.00	5.00	23.10	1.52	-	40.11	0.76	63.97	m	70.37
Nr 5; dressing over tilting fillets -1; 150mm lapped joints; fixing to timber with copper nails										
240mm girth	14.60	5.00	15.33	0.92	-	24.28	0.59	40.20	m	44.22
300mm girth	18.40	5.00	19.32	1.15	-	30.35	0.59	50.26	m	55.29
450mm girth	27.60	5.00	28.98	1.72	-	45.39	0.91	75.28	m	82.81
Spot items										
Nr 3 collars around pipes, standards and the like; 150mm long; soldered joints to metal covering										
50mm diameter	30.13	5.00	31.63	1.00	-	26.39	-	58.02	nr	63.83
100mm diameter	30.13	5.00	31.63	1.15	-	30.35	-	61.98	nr	68.18
Nr 4 collars around pipes, standards and the like; 150mm long; soldered joints to metal covering										
50mm diameter	32.52	5.00	34.15	1.15	-	30.35	-	64.50	nr	70.95
100mm diameter	32.52	5.00	34.15	1.15	-	30.35	-	64.50	nr	70.95
Nr 5 collars around pipes, standards and the like; 150mm long; soldered joints to metal covering										
50mm diameter	40.84	5.00	42.88	1.15	-	30.35	-	73.23	nr	80.55
100mm diameter	40.84	5.00	42.88	1.15	-	30.35	-	73.23	nr	80.55
Nr 3 dots										
cast lead	2.41	5.00	2.53	0.77	-	20.32	-	22.85	nr	25.14
soldered	23.43	5.00	24.60	0.86	-	22.70	-	47.30	nr	52.03
Nr 4 dots										
cast lead	3.21	5.00	3.37	0.77	-	20.32	-	23.69	nr	26.06
soldered	23.43	5.00	24.60	0.86	-	22.70	-	47.30	nr	52.03
Nr 5 dots										
cast lead	4.42	5.00	4.64	0.77	-	20.32	-	24.96	nr	27.46
soldered	23.43	5.00	24.60	0.86	-	22.70	-	47.30	nr	52.03
Fittings										
Nr 3 soakers and slates; handed to others for fixing										
180 x 180mm	1.08	5.00	1.13	0.23	-	6.07	-	7.20	nr	7.92
180 x 300mm	1.94	5.00	2.04	0.23	-	6.07	-	8.11	nr	8.92
450 x 450mm	7.29	5.00	7.65	0.23	-	6.07	-	13.72	nr	15.10
Nr 4 soakers and slates; handed to others for fixing										
180 x 180mm	1.47	5.00	1.54	0.23	-	6.07	-	7.61	nr	8.37
180 x 300mm	2.65	5.00	2.78	0.23	-	6.07	-	8.85	nr	9.73
450 x 450mm	9.92	5.00	10.42	0.23	-	6.07	-	16.49	nr	18.14
Nr 5 soakers and slates; handed to others for fixing										
180 x 180mm	1.83	5.00	1.92	0.23	-	6.07	-	7.99	nr	8.79
180 x 300mm	3.29	5.00	3.46	0.23	-	6.07	-	9.53	nr	10.48
450 x 450mm	12.35	5.00	12.97	0.23	-	6.07	-	19.04	nr	20.94
SHEET METALS; ALUMINIUM										
Aluminium sheet, BS EN 485 grade S1BO, commercial purity										
0.60mm thick roof coverings; exceeding 500mm wide; fixing to timber with aluminium cleats and aluminium alloy screws; sloping										
pitch 7.5 degrees from horizontal	19.23	5.00	20.19	5.05	-	133.27	0.23	153.69	m²	169.06
pitch 40 degrees from horizontal	19.23	5.00	20.19	5.70	-	150.42	0.23	170.85	m²	187.93
pitch 75 degrees from horizontal	19.23	5.00	20.19	6.35	-	167.58	0.23	188.00	m²	206.80

Labour hourly rates: (except Specialists) Craft Operatives 26.39 Labourer 15.57 Rates are national average prices. Refer to REGIONAL VARIATIONS for indicative levels of overall pricing in regions	MATERIALS			LABOUR				RATES		
	Del to Site £	Waste %	Material Cost £	Craft Optve Hrs	Lab Hrs	Labour Cost £	Sunds £	Nett Rate £	Unit	Gross rate (10%) £
SHEET METALS; ALUMINIUM (Cont'd)										
Aluminium sheet, BS EN 485 grade S1BO, commercial purity (Cont'd)										
0.60mm thick edges										
welted	-	-	-	0.20	-	5.28	-	5.28	m	5.81
beaded	-	-	-	0.20	-	5.28	-	5.28	m	5.81
Flashings; horizontal										
0.60mm thick; 150mm lapped joints; fixing to masonry with aluminium clips and wedges										
150mm girth	2.88	5.00	3.03	0.51	-	13.46	0.23	16.72	m	18.39
240mm girth	4.62	5.00	4.85	0.82	-	21.64	0.23	26.72	m	29.39
300mm girth	5.77	5.00	6.06	1.02	-	26.92	0.23	33.21	m	36.53
Flashings; stepped										
0.60mm thick; 150mm lapped joints; fixing to masonry with aluminium clips and wedges										
180mm girth	3.46	5.00	3.64	0.82	-	21.64	0.35	25.62	m	28.18
240mm girth	4.62	5.00	4.85	1.09	-	28.77	0.35	33.96	m	37.35
300mm girth	5.77	5.00	6.06	1.37	-	36.15	0.35	42.56	m	46.82
Aprons; horizontal										
0.60mm thick; 150mm lapped joints; fixing to masonry with aluminium clips and wedges										
150mm girth	2.88	5.00	3.03	0.51	-	13.46	0.23	16.72	m	18.39
180mm girth	3.46	5.00	3.64	0.82	-	21.64	0.23	25.51	m	28.06
240mm girth	4.62	5.00	4.85	1.02	-	26.92	0.23	32.00	m	35.20
450mm girth	8.65	5.00	9.09	1.53	-	40.38	0.35	49.81	m	54.79
Hips; sloping										
0.60mm thick; 150mm lapped joints; fixing to timber with aluminium clips										
240mm girth	4.62	5.00	4.85	0.82	-	21.64	0.23	26.72	m	29.39
300mm girth	5.77	5.00	6.06	1.02	-	26.92	0.23	33.21	m	36.53
450mm girth	8.65	5.00	9.09	1.53	-	40.38	0.35	49.81	m	54.79
Kerbs; horizontal										
0.60mm thick; 150mm lapped joints; fixing to timber with aluminium clips										
240mm girth	4.62	5.00	4.85	0.82	-	21.64	0.23	26.72	m	29.39
300mm girth	5.77	5.00	6.06	1.02	-	26.92	0.23	33.21	m	36.53
450mm girth	8.65	5.00	9.09	1.53	-	40.38	0.35	49.81	m	54.79
Ridges; horizontal										
0.60mm thick; 150mm lapped joints; fixing to timber with aluminium clips										
240mm girth	4.62	5.00	4.85	0.82	-	21.64	0.23	26.72	m	29.39
300mm girth	5.77	5.00	6.06	1.02	-	26.92	0.23	33.21	m	36.53
450mm girth	8.65	5.00	9.09	1.53	-	40.38	0.35	49.81	m	54.79
Valleys; sloping										
0.60mm thick; 150mm lapped joints; fixing to timber with aluminium clips										
240mm girth	4.62	5.00	4.85	0.82	-	21.64	0.23	26.72	m	29.39
300mm girth	5.77	5.00	6.06	1.02	-	26.92	0.23	33.21	m	36.53
450mm girth	8.65	5.00	9.09	1.53	-	40.38	0.35	49.81	m	54.79
0.60mm thick soakers and slates handed to others for fixing										
180 x 180mm	3.46	5.00	3.64	0.23	-	6.07	-	9.70	nr	10.68
180 x 300mm	5.77	5.00	6.06	0.23	-	6.07	-	12.13	nr	13.34
SHEET METALS; COPPER										
Copper sheet; BS EN 1172										
0.60mm thick roof coverings; exceeding 500mm wide; fixing to timber with copper cleats and copper nails; sloping										
pitch 7.5 degrees from horizontal	102.00	5.00	107.10	5.05	-	133.27	0.68	241.05	m²	265.15
pitch 40 degrees from horizontal	102.00	5.00	107.10	5.70	-	150.42	0.68	258.20	m²	284.02
pitch 75 degrees from horizontal	102.00	5.00	107.10	6.35	-	167.58	0.68	275.35	m²	302.89
0.70mm thick roof coverings; exceeding 500mm wide; fixing to timber with copper cleats and copper nails; sloping										
pitch 7.5 degrees from horizontal	124.00	5.00	130.20	5.70	-	150.42	0.86	281.48	m²	309.63
pitch 40 degrees from horizontal	124.00	5.00	130.20	6.35	-	167.58	0.86	298.63	m²	328.50
pitch 75 degrees from horizontal	124.00	5.00	130.20	6.95	-	183.41	0.86	314.47	m²	345.92
Extra for forming										
0.60mm thick edges										
welted	-	-	-	0.17	-	4.49	-	4.49	m	4.93
beaded	-	-	-	0.17	-	4.49	-	4.49	m	4.93
0.70mm thick edges										
welted	-	-	-	0.17	-	4.49	-	4.49	m	4.93
beaded	-	-	-	0.17	-	4.49	-	4.49	m	4.93
Flashings; horizontal										
0.70mm thick; 150mm lapped joints; fixing to masonry with copper clips and wedges										
150mm girth	18.60	5.00	19.53	0.51	-	13.46	0.68	33.67	m	37.03

Labour hourly rates: (except Specialists) Craft Operatives 26.39 Labourer 15.57 Rates are national average prices. Refer to REGIONAL VARIATIONS for indicative levels of overall pricing in regions	MATERIALS			LABOUR				RATES		
	Del to Site £	Waste %	Material Cost £	Craft Optve Hrs	Lab Hrs	Labour Cost £	Sunds £	Nett Rate £	Unit	Gross rate (10%) £
SHEET METALS; COPPER (Cont'd)										
Copper sheet; BS EN 1172 (Cont'd)										
Flashings; horizontal (Cont'd)										
0.70mm thick; 150mm lapped joints; fixing to masonry with copper clips and wedges (Cont'd)										
240mm girth	29.76	5.00	31.25	0.82	-	21.64	0.68	53.56	m	58.92
300mm girth	37.20	5.00	39.06	1.02	-	26.92	0.68	66.65	m	73.32
Flashings; stepped										
0.70mm thick; 150mm lapped joints; fixing to masonry with copper clips and wedges										
180mm girth	22.32	5.00	23.44	0.82	-	21.64	1.02	46.10	m	50.71
240mm girth	29.76	5.00	31.25	1.09	-	28.77	1.02	61.04	m	67.14
300mm girth	37.20	5.00	39.06	1.37	-	36.15	1.02	76.24	m	83.86
Aprons; horizontal										
0.70mm thick; 150mm lapped joints; fixing to timber with copper clips										
150mm girth	18.60	5.00	19.53	0.51	-	13.46	0.68	33.67	m	37.03
240mm girth	29.76	5.00	31.25	0.82	-	21.64	0.68	53.56	m	58.92
300mm girth	37.20	5.00	39.06	1.02	-	26.92	0.68	66.65	m	73.32
450mm girth	55.80	5.00	58.59	1.53	-	40.38	1.02	99.99	m	109.99
Hips; sloping										
0.70mm thick; 150mm lapped joints; fixing to timber with copper clips										
240mm girth	29.76	5.00	31.25	0.71	-	18.74	0.59	50.58	m	55.64
300mm girth	37.20	5.00	39.06	1.02	-	26.92	0.68	66.65	m	73.32
450mm girth	55.80	5.00	58.59	1.53	-	40.38	1.02	99.99	m	109.99
Kerbs; horizontal										
0.70mm thick; 150mm lapped joints; fixing to timber with copper clips										
240mm girth	29.76	5.00	31.25	0.82	-	21.64	0.68	53.56	m	58.92
300mm girth	37.20	5.00	39.06	1.02	-	26.92	0.68	66.65	m	73.32
450mm girth	55.80	5.00	58.59	1.53	-	40.38	1.02	99.99	m	109.99
Ridges; horizontal										
0.70mm thick; 150mm lapped joints; fixing to timber with copper clips										
240mm girth	29.76	5.00	31.25	0.82	-	21.64	0.68	53.56	m	58.92
300mm girth	37.20	5.00	39.06	1.02	-	26.92	0.68	66.65	m	73.32
450mm girth	55.80	5.00	58.59	1.53	-	40.38	1.02	99.99	m	109.99
Valleys; sloping										
0.70mm thick; 150mm lapped joints; fixing to timber with copper clips										
240mm girth	29.76	5.00	31.25	0.82	-	21.64	0.68	53.56	m	58.92
300mm girth	37.20	5.00	39.06	1.02	-	26.92	0.68	66.65	m	73.32
450mm girth	55.80	5.00	58.59	1.53	-	40.38	1.02	99.99	m	109.99
SHEET METALS; ZINC										
Zinc alloy sheet; BS EN 988										
0.8mm thick roof coverings; exceeding 500mm wide; roll cap; fixing to timber with zinc clips; sloping										
pitch 7.5 degrees from horizontal	65.00	5.00	68.25	5.70	-	150.42	0.33	219.00	m²	240.90
pitch 40 degrees from horizontal	65.00	5.00	68.25	6.35	-	167.58	0.33	236.16	m²	259.77
pitch 75 degrees from horizontal	65.00	5.00	68.25	6.95	-	183.41	0.33	251.99	m²	277.19
Extra for forming										
0.65mm thick edges										
welted	-	-	-	0.20	-	5.28	-	5.28	m	5.81
beaded	-	-	-	0.20	-	5.28	-	5.28	m	5.81
0.8mm thick edges										
welted	-	-	-	0.20	-	5.28	-	5.28	m	5.81
beaded	-	-	-	0.20	-	5.28	-	5.28	m	5.81
Flashings; horizontal										
0.8mm thick; 150mm lapped joints; fixing to masonry with zinc clips and wedges										
150mm girth	9.75	5.00	10.24	0.51	-	13.46	0.25	23.94	m	26.34
240mm girth	15.60	5.00	16.38	0.82	-	21.64	0.25	38.27	m	42.09
300mm girth	19.50	5.00	20.47	1.02	-	26.92	0.25	47.64	m	52.40
Flashings; stepped										
0.8mm thick; 150mm lapped joints; fixing to masonry with zinc clips and wedges										
180mm girth	11.70	5.00	12.28	0.71	-	18.74	0.33	31.35	m	34.49
240mm girth	15.60	5.00	16.38	1.09	-	28.77	0.38	45.52	m	50.08
300mm girth	19.50	5.00	20.47	1.37	-	36.15	0.38	57.01	m	62.71
Aprons; horizontal										
0.8mm thick; 150mm lapped joints; fixing to masonry with zinc clips and wedges										
150mm girth	9.75	5.00	10.24	0.92	-	24.28	0.51	35.03	m	38.53
240mm girth	15.60	5.00	16.38	0.82	-	21.64	0.25	38.27	m	42.09
300mm girth	19.50	5.00	20.47	1.02	-	26.92	0.25	47.64	m	52.40
450mm girth	29.25	5.00	30.71	1.53	-	40.38	0.38	71.47	m	78.62

Labour hourly rates: (except Specialists) Craft Operatives 26.39 Labourer 15.57 Rates are national average prices. Refer to REGIONAL VARIATIONS for indicative levels of overall pricing in regions	MATERIALS			LABOUR				RATES		
	Del to Site £	Waste %	Material Cost £	Craft Optve Hrs	Lab Hrs	Labour Cost £	Sunds £	Nett Rate £	Unit	Gross rate (10%) £
SHEET METALS; ZINC (Cont'd)										
Zinc alloy sheet; BS EN 988 (Cont'd)										
Hips; sloping										
0.8mm thick; 150mm lapped joints; fixing to timber with zinc clips										
240mm girth	15.60	5.00	16.38	0.82	-	21.64	0.25	38.27	m	42.09
300mm girth	19.50	5.00	20.47	1.02	-	26.92	0.25	47.64	m	52.40
450mm girth	29.25	5.00	30.71	1.53	-	40.38	0.38	71.47	m	78.62
Kerbs; horizontal										
0.8mm thick; 150mm lapped joints; fixing to timber with zinc clips										
240mm girth	15.60	5.00	16.38	0.82	-	21.64	0.25	38.27	m	42.09
300mm girth	19.50	5.00	20.47	1.02	-	26.92	0.25	47.64	m	52.40
450mm girth	29.25	5.00	30.71	1.53	-	40.38	0.38	71.47	m	78.62
Ridges; horizontal										
0.8mm thick; 150mm lapped joints; fixing to timber with zinc clips										
240mm girth	15.60	5.00	16.38	0.82	-	21.64	0.25	38.27	m	42.09
300mm girth	19.50	5.00	20.47	1.02	-	26.92	0.25	47.64	m	52.40
450mm girth	29.25	5.00	30.71	1.53	-	40.38	0.38	71.47	m	78.62
Valleys; sloping										
0.8mm thick; 150mm lapped joints; fixing to timber with zinc clips										
240mm girth	15.60	5.00	16.38	0.82	-	21.64	0.25	38.27	m	42.09
300mm girth	19.50	5.00	20.47	1.02	-	26.92	0.25	47.64	m	52.40
450mm girth	29.25	5.00	30.71	1.53	-	40.38	0.38	71.47	m	78.62
Fittings										
0.8mm thick soakers and slates -; handed to others for fixing										
180 x 180mm	2.11	5.00	2.21	0.23	-	6.07	-	8.28	nr	9.11
180 x 300mm	3.51	5.00	3.69	0.23	-	6.07	-	9.76	nr	10.73
450 x 450mm	13.16	5.00	13.82	0.23	-	6.07	-	19.89	nr	21.88
0.8mm thick collars around pipes, standards and the like; 150mm long; soldered joints to metal covering										
50mm diameter	14.62	5.00	15.36	1.00	-	26.39	-	41.75	nr	45.92
100mm diameter	19.50	5.00	20.47	1.00	-	26.39	-	46.86	nr	51.55

This page left blank intentionally

TILE AND SLATE ROOF AND WALL COVERINGS

Labour hourly rates: (except Specialists) Craft Operatives 20.87 Labourer 15.57 Rates are national average prices. Refer to REGIONAL VARIATIONS for indicative levels of overall pricing in regions	MATERIALS			LABOUR				RATES		
	Del to Site £	Waste %	Material Cost £	Craft Optve Hrs	Lab Hrs	Labour Cost £	Sunds £	Nett Rate £	Unit	Gross rate (10%) £
PLAIN TILING										
Quantities required for 1m² of tiling										
Plain tiles to 65mm lap tiles, 60nr battens, 10m										
Plain tiles to 85mm lap tiles, 70nr battens, 11m										
Roof coverings; clayware Machine made plain tiles BS EN 1304, red, 265 x 165mm; fixing every fourth course with two galvanised nails per tile to 65mm lap; 38 x 19mm pressure impregnated softwood battens fixed with galvanised nails; twin-ply underlay 145gsm with polypropylene; 150mm laps; fixing with galvanised steel clout nails										
Pitched 50 degrees from horizontal										
generally	37.88	5.00	40.23	0.72	0.36	20.63	2.57	63.43	m²	69.78
holes	-	-	-	0.58	0.29	16.62	-	16.62	nr	18.28
Boundary work										
abutments; square	2.94	5.00	3.09	0.28	0.14	8.02	-	11.11	m	12.22
abutments; raking	5.14	5.00	5.40	0.42	0.21	12.04	-	17.44	m	19.18
double course at top edges with clips and nailing each tile with two aluminium nails	2.94	5.00	3.09	0.34	0.17	9.74	6.29	19.12	m	21.03
double course at eaves; Machine made eaves tile	2.94	5.00	3.09	0.35	0.18	10.11	0.91	14.10	m	15.51
Machine made ridge tiles, half round; in 300mm effective lengths; butt jointed; bedding and pointing in coloured cement-lime mortar (1:1:6)	19.25	5.00	20.21	0.35	0.18	10.11	0.69	31.01	m	34.11
verges; bed and point in coloured cement-lime mortar (1:1:6)	2.94	5.00	3.09	0.40	0.20	11.46	0.69	15.24	m	16.77
verges; single extra undercloak course plain tiles; bed and point in coloured cement-lime mortar (1:1:6)	5.88	5.00	6.17	0.58	0.29	16.62	0.69	23.49	m	25.84
Machine made valley tiles; angular	41.04	5.00	43.09	0.55	0.28	15.76	0.69	59.54	m	65.50
Machine made hip tiles, half round; in 300mm effective lengths; butt jointed; bedding and pointing in coloured cement-lime mortar (1:1:6)	19.25	5.00	20.21	0.35	0.18	10.11	0.69	31.01	m	34.11
Machine made hip tiles; arris; bedding and pointing in cement mortar	41.04	5.00	43.09	0.55	0.28	15.76	0.69	59.54	m	65.50
Machine made hip tiles; bonnet pattern; bedding and pointing in coloured cement-lime mortar (1:1:6)	41.04	5.00	43.09	0.55	0.28	15.76	0.69	59.54	m	65.50
Roof coverings; clayware Machine made plain tiles BS EN 1304, red, 265 x 165mm; fixing every fourth course with two galvanised nails per tile to 65mm lap; 50 x 19mm pressure impregnated softwood battens fixed with galvanised nails; twin-ply underlay 145gsm with polypropylene; 150mm laps; fixing with galvanised steel clout nails										
Pitched 50 degrees from horizontal										
generally	48.10	5.00	51.47	0.70	0.35	20.06	2.57	74.10	m²	81.51
Roof coverings; clayware Machine made plain tiles BS EN 1304, red, 265 x 165mm; fixing every course with two galvanised nails per tile to 65mm lap; 38 x 19mm pressure impregnated softwood battens fixed with galvanised nails; twin-ply underlay 145gsm with polypropylene; 150mm laps; fixing with galvanised steel clout nails										
Pitched 50 degrees from horizontal										
generally	37.88	5.00	40.23	0.85	0.43	24.43	4.95	69.61	m²	76.57
Roof coverings; clayware Machine made plain tiles BS EN 1304, red, 265 x 165mm; fixing every fourth course with two copper nails per tile to 65mm lap; 38 x19mm pressure impregnated softwood battens fixed with galvanised nails; twin-ply underlay 145gsm with polypropylene; 150mm laps; fixing with galvanised steel clout nails										
Pitched 50 degrees from horizontal										
generally	37.88	5.00	40.23	0.70	0.35	20.06	3.96	64.25	m²	70.67
Roof coverings; clayware Machine made plain tiles BS EN 1304, red, 265 x 165mm; fixing every course with two copper nails per tile to 65mm lap; 38 x 19mm pressure impregnated softwood battens fixed with galvanised nails; twin-ply underlay 145gsm with polypropylene; 150mm laps; fixing with galvanised steel clout nails										
Pitched 50 degrees from horizontal										
generally	37.88	5.00	40.23	0.85	0.43	24.43	9.07	73.74	m²	81.11

Labour hourly rates: (except Specialists) Craft Operatives 20.87 Labourer 15.57 Rates are national average prices. Refer to REGIONAL VARIATIONS for indicative levels of overall pricing in regions	MATERIALS			LABOUR				RATES		
	Del to Site £	Waste %	Material Cost £	Craft Optve Hrs	Lab Hrs	Labour Cost £	Sunds £	Nett Rate £	Unit	Gross rate (10%) £
PLAIN TILING (Cont'd)										
Roof coverings; clayware Machine made plain tiles BS EN 1304, red, 265 x 165mm; fixing every fourth course with two galvanised nails per tile to 85mm lap; 38 x 19mm pressure impregnated softwood battens fixed with galvanised nails; twin-ply underlay 145gsm with polypropylene; 150mm laps; fixing with galvanised steel clout nails										
Pitched 40 degrees from horizontal										
generally	43.56	5.00	46.23	0.80	0.40	22.92	2.57	71.73	m²	78.90
Wall coverings; clayware Machine made plain tiles BS EN 1304, red, 265 x 165mm; fixing every course with two galvanised nails per tile to 35mm lap; 38 x 19mm pressure impregnated softwood battens fixed with galvanised nails; twin-ply underlay 145gsm with polypropylene; 150mm laps; fixing with galvanised steel clout nails										
Vertical										
generally	32.94	5.00	35.00	0.85	0.43	24.43	3.76	63.19	m²	69.51
holes	-	-	-	0.87	0.44	24.93	-	24.93	nr	27.42
Boundary work										
abutments; square	2.94	5.00	3.09	0.42	0.21	12.04	-	15.12	m	16.63
abutments; raking	5.14	5.00	5.40	0.63	0.31	18.05	-	23.45	m	25.80
double course at eaves; Machine made eaves tile	2.94	5.00	3.09	0.52	0.27	15.16	0.91	19.16	m	21.07
verges; bed and point in coloured cement-lime mortar (1:1:6)	2.94	5.00	3.09	0.60	0.30	17.19	0.69	20.97	m	23.07
verges; single extra undercloak course plain tiles; bed and point in coloured cement-lime mortar (1:1:6)	5.88	5.00	6.17	0.87	0.44	24.93	0.69	31.80	m	34.98
vertical angle tiles; machine made	50.29	10.00	55.31	0.87	0.44	24.93	0.69	80.94	m	89.03
Roof coverings; clayware Hand made plain tiles BS EN 1304, red, 265 x 165mm; fixing every fourth course with two galvanised nails per tile to 65mm lap; 38 x 19mm pressure impregnated softwood battens fixed with galvanised nails; twin-ply underlay 145gsm with polypropylene; 150mm laps; fixing with galvanised steel clout nails										
Pitched 50 degrees from horizontal										
generally	8.55	5.00	9.44	0.72	0.36	20.63	2.57	32.65	m²	35.91
holes	-	-	-	0.58	0.29	16.62	-	16.62	nr	18.28
Boundary work										
abutments; square	7.93	5.00	8.32	0.28	0.14	8.02	-	16.35	m	17.98
abutments; raking	10.57	5.00	11.10	0.42	0.21	12.04	-	23.13	m	25.45
double course at top edges with clips and nailing each tile with two aluminium nails	7.86	5.00	8.25	0.34	0.17	9.74	6.29	24.28	m	26.71
double course at eaves; Hand made eaves tile	7.86	5.00	8.25	0.35	0.18	10.11	0.91	19.27	m	21.19
Hand made ridge tiles, half round; in 300mm effective lengths; butt jointed; bedding and pointing in coloured cement-lime mortar (1:1:6)	26.39	5.00	27.71	0.35	0.18	10.11	0.69	38.51	m	42.36
verges; bed and point in coloured cement-lime mortar (1:1:6)	7.93	5.00	8.32	0.40	0.20	11.46	0.69	20.48	m	22.53
verges; single extra undercloak course plain tiles; bed and point in coloured cement-lime mortar (1:1:6)	7.93	5.00	8.33	0.58	0.29	16.62	0.69	25.64	m	28.21
Hand made valley tiles; angular; bedding and pointing in cement mortar	56.27	5.00	59.08	0.55	0.28	15.76	0.69	75.53	m	83.09
Hand made hip tiles, half round; in 300mm effective lengths; butt jointed; bedding and pointing in coloured cement-lime mortar (1:1:6)	26.39	5.00	27.71	0.35	0.18	10.11	0.69	38.51	m	42.36
Hand made hip tiles; angular	56.27	5.00	59.08	0.55	0.28	15.76	0.69	75.53	m	83.09
Hand made hip tiles; bonnet pattern; bedding and pointing in coloured cement-lime mortar (1:1:6)	95.49	5.00	100.27	0.55	0.28	15.76	0.69	116.72	m	128.40
Roof coverings; clayware Hand made plain tiles BS EN 1304, red, 265 x 165mm; fixing every fourth course with two galvanised nails per tile to 85mm lap; 38 x 19mm pressure impregnated softwood battens fixed with galvanised nails; twin-ply underlay 145gsm with polypropylene; 150mm laps; fixing with galvanised steel clout nails										
Pitched 40 degrees from horizontal										
generally	9.35	5.00	10.31	0.80	0.40	22.92	2.52	35.76	m²	39.34
Fittings										
Hip irons										
galvanised mild steel; 32 x 3 x 380mm girth; scrolled; fixing with galvanised steel screws to timber	1.02	5.00	1.07	0.12	0.06	3.44	-	4.51	nr	4.96
Lead soakers										
fixing only	-	-	-	0.35	0.18	10.11	-	10.11	nr	11.12
Wall coverings; clayware hand made plain tiles BS EN 1304, red, 265 x 165mm; fixing every course with two galvanised nails per tile to 35mm lap; 38 x 19mm pressure impregnated softwood battens fixed with galvanised nails; twin-ply underlay 145gsm with polypropylene; 150mm laps; fixing with galvanised steel clout nails										
Vertical										
generally	32.94	5.00	35.00	0.85	0.43	24.43	3.76	63.19	m²	69.51
holes	-	-	-	0.87	0.44	24.93	-	24.93	nr	27.42
Boundary work										
abutments; square	7.93	5.00	8.32	0.42	0.21	12.04	-	20.36	m	22.39
abutments; raking	10.57	5.00	11.10	0.63	0.31	18.05	-	29.15	m	32.07
double course at eaves; Hand made eaves tile	7.86	5.00	8.25	0.52	0.27	15.16	0.91	24.32	m	26.75
verges; bed and point in coloured cement-lime mortar (1:1:6)	7.93	5.00	8.32	0.60	0.30	17.19	0.69	26.21	m	28.83

Labour hourly rates: (except Specialists) Craft Operatives 20.87 Labourer 15.57 Rates are national average prices. Refer to REGIONAL VARIATIONS for indicative levels of overall pricing in regions	MATERIALS			LABOUR				RATES		
	Del to Site £	Waste %	Material Cost £	Craft Optve Hrs	Lab Hrs	Labour Cost £	Sunds £	Nett Rate £	Unit	Gross rate (10%) £
PLAIN TILING (Cont'd)										
Wall coverings; clayware hand made plain tiles BS EN 1304, red, 265 x 165mm; fixing every course with two galvanised nails per tile to 35mm lap; 38 x 19mm pressure impregnated softwood battens fixed with galvanised nails; twin-ply underlay 145gsm with polypropylene; 150mm laps; fixing with galvanised steel clout nails (Cont'd)										
Vertical (Cont'd)										
Boundary work (Cont'd)										
verges; single extra undercloak course plain tiles; bed and point in coloured cement-lime mortar (1:1:6)	7.93	5.00	8.33	0.87	0.44	24.93	0.69	33.95	m	37.35
vertical angle tiles; hand made	73.73	10.00	81.11	0.87	0.44	24.93	0.69	106.73	m	117.40
Roof coverings; Redland Plain granular faced tiles, 268 x 165mm; fixing every fifth course with two aluminium nails to each tile to 65mm lap; 38 x 19mm pressure impregnated softwood battens fixed with galvanised nails; twin-ply underlay 145gsm with polypropylene; 150mm laps; fixing with galvanised steel clout nails										
Pitched 40 degrees from horizontal										
generally	36.53	5.00	38.95	0.70	0.35	20.06	1.90	60.91	m²	67.00
holes	-	-	-	0.58	0.29	16.62	-	16.62	nr	18.28
Boundary work										
abutments; square	2.49	5.00	2.61	0.28	0.14	8.02	-	10.64	m	11.70
abutments; raking	4.37	5.00	4.59	0.42	0.21	12.04	-	16.62	m	18.29
double course at top edges with clips and nailing each tile with two aluminium nails	2.55	5.00	2.67	0.34	0.17	9.74	6.29	18.70	m	20.57
double course at eaves and nailing each tile with two aluminium nails	2.52	5.00	2.65	0.35	0.18	10.11	0.84	13.59	m	14.95
ridge or hip tiles, Plain angle; butt jointed; bedding and pointing in tinted cement mortar (1:3)	15.15	5.00	15.91	0.35	0.18	10.11	0.69	26.71	m	29.38
ridge or hip tiles, half round; butt jointed; bedding and pointing in tinted cement mortar (1:3)	17.80	5.00	18.69	0.35	0.18	10.11	0.69	29.49	m	32.44
verges; Redland Dry Verge system with plain tiles and tile-and-a-half tiles in alternate courses, clips and aluminium nails	18.36	5.00	19.28	0.28	0.14	8.02	1.78	29.08	m	31.99
verges; plain tile undercloak; tiles and undercloak bedded and pointed in tinted cement mortar (1:3) and with plain tiles and tile-and-a-half tiles in alternate courses and aluminium nails	5.01	5.00	5.26	0.28	0.14	8.02	0.74	14.03	m	15.43
valley tiles, Plain valley tiles; bedding and pointing in cement mortar	37.49	5.00	39.36	0.55	0.28	15.76	0.69	55.82	m	61.40
hip tiles; angular; bedding and pointing in cement mortar	35.36	5.00	37.13	0.55	0.28	15.76	0.69	53.58	m	58.94
hip tiles; bonnet; bedding and pointing in coloured cement-lime mortar (1:1:6)	37.06	5.00	38.92	0.55	0.28	15.76	0.69	55.37	m	60.91
Roof coverings; Redland Plain granular faced tiles, 268 x 165mm; fixing every fifth course with two aluminium nails to each tile to 65mm lap; 50 x 25mm pressure impregnated softwood battens fixed with galvanised nails; twin-ply underlay 145gsm with polypropylene; 150mm laps; fixing with galvanised steel clout nails										
Pitched 40 degrees from horizontal										
generally	36.53	5.00	38.95	0.70	0.35	20.06	1.90	60.91	m²	67.00
Boundary work										
abutments; square	2.49	5.00	2.61	0.28	0.15	8.18	-	10.79	m	11.87
abutments; raking	4.37	5.00	4.59	0.43	0.21	12.24	-	16.83	m	18.52
abutments; curved to 3000mm radius	6.66	5.00	6.99	0.56	0.28	16.05	-	23.04	m	25.34
Roof coverings; Redland Plain granular faced tiles, 268 x 165mm; fixing each tile with two aluminium nails to 35mm lap; 38 x 19mm pressure impregnated softwood battens fixed with galvanised nails; twin-ply underlay 145gsm with polypropylene; 150mm laps; fixing with galvanised steel clout nails										
Vertical										
generally	29.30	5.00	31.17	0.83	0.42	23.86	3.76	58.80	m²	64.68
holes	-	-	-	0.87	0.44	24.93	-	24.93	nr	27.42
Boundary work										
abutments; square	2.49	5.00	2.61	0.42	0.21	12.04	-	14.65	m	16.11
abutments; raking	4.37	5.00	4.59	0.63	0.31	18.05	-	22.64	m	24.91
double course at eaves; Machine made eaves tile	2.52	5.00	2.65	0.52	0.27	15.16	0.91	18.71	m	20.59
verges; bed and point in coloured cement-lime mortar (1:1:6)	2.49	5.00	2.61	0.60	0.30	17.19	0.69	20.50	m	22.55
verges; single extra undercloak course plain tiles; bed and point in coloured cement-lime mortar (1:1:6)	5.01	5.00	5.26	0.87	0.44	24.93	0.69	30.88	m	33.97
vertical angle tiles	35.24	5.00	37.01	0.87	0.44	24.93	0.69	62.63	m	68.89
Roof coverings; Plain through coloured tiles, 268 x 165mm; fixing every fifth course with two aluminium nails to each tile to 65mm lap; 38 x 19mm pressure impregnated softwood battens fixed with galvanised nails; twin-ply underlay 145gsm with polypropylene; 150mm laps; fixing with galvanised steel clout nails										
Pitched 40 degrees from horizontal										
generally	33.68	5.00	35.82	0.70	0.35	20.06	1.90	57.77	m²	63.55
Boundary work										
double course at top edges with clips and nailing each tile with two aluminium nails	2.52	5.00	2.65	0.34	0.17	9.74	6.29	18.68	m	20.54
double course at eaves and nailing each tile with two aluminium nails	2.52	5.00	2.65	0.34	0.17	9.74	0.84	13.23	m	14.55
ridge or hip tiles, Plain angle; butt jointed; bedding and pointing in tinted cement mortar (1:3)	15.15	5.00	15.91	0.35	0.18	10.11	0.69	26.71	m	29.38

Labour hourly rates: (except Specialists) Craft Operatives 20.87 Labourer 15.57 Rates are national average prices. Refer to REGIONAL VARIATIONS for indicative levels of overall pricing in regions	MATERIALS			LABOUR				RATES		
	Del to Site £	Waste %	Material Cost £	Craft Optve Hrs	Lab Hrs	Labour Cost £	Sunds £	Nett Rate £	Unit	Gross rate (10%) £
PLAIN TILING (Cont'd)										
Roof coverings; Plain through coloured tiles, 268 x 165mm; fixing every fifth course with two aluminium nails to each tile to 65mm lap; 38 x 19mm pressure impregnated softwood battens fixed with galvanised nails; twin-ply underlay 145gsm with polypropylene; 150mm laps; fixing with galvanised steel clout nails (Cont'd)										
Pitched 40 degrees from horizontal (Cont'd)										
Boundary work (Cont'd)										
ridge or hip tiles, half round; butt jointed; bedding and pointing in tinted cement mortar (1:3)	17.78	5.00	18.67	0.35	0.18	10.11	0.69	29.47	m	32.42
verges; Redland Dry Verge system with plain tiles and tile-and-a-half tiles in alternate courses, clips and aluminium nails	18.36	5.00	19.28	0.28	0.14	8.02	1.78	29.08	m	31.99
verges; plain tile undercloak; tiles and undercloak bedded and pointed in tinted cement mortar (1:3) and with plain tiles and tile-and-a-half tiles in alternate courses and aluminium nails	5.01	5.00	5.26	0.28	0.14	8.02	0.74	14.03	m	15.43
valley tiles, Plain valley tiles; bedding and pointing in cement mortar	37.49	5.00	39.36	0.55	0.28	15.76	0.69	55.82	m	61.40
Roof coverings; Redland Heathland plain granular faced tiles, 268 x 165mm; fixing every fifth course with two aluminium nails to each tile to 65mm lap; 38 x 19mm pressure impregnated softwood battens fixed with galvanised nails; twin-ply underlay 145gsm with polypropylene; 150mm laps; fixing with galvanised steel clout nails										
Pitched 40 degrees from horizontal										
generally	39.15	5.00	41.56	0.70	0.35	20.06	1.90	63.52	m²	69.87
Boundary work										
double course at top edges with clips and nailing each tile with two aluminium nails	3.07	5.00	3.22	0.34	0.17	9.74	6.29	19.25	m	21.17
double course at eaves and nailing each tile with two aluminium nails	3.07	5.00	3.22	0.34	0.17	9.74	0.84	13.80	m	15.19
ridge or hip tiles, Redland Plain angle; butt jointed; bedding and pointing in tinted cement mortar (1:3)	15.15	5.00	15.91	0.35	0.18	10.11	0.69	26.71	m	29.38
ridge or hip tiles, Redland half round; butt jointed; bedding and pointing in tinted cement mortar (1:3)	17.78	5.00	18.67	0.35	0.18	10.11	0.69	29.47	m	32.42
verges; Redland Dry Verge system with plain tiles and tile-and-a-half tiles in alternate courses, clips and aluminium nails	17.40	5.00	18.27	0.28	0.14	8.02	1.78	28.08	m	30.89
verges; plain tile undercloak; tiles and undercloak bedded and pointed in tinted cement mortar (1:3) and with plain tiles and tile-and-a-half tiles in alternate courses and aluminium nails	3.07	5.00	3.22	0.28	0.14	8.02	0.74	11.99	m	13.19
valley tiles, Redland Plain valley tiles	20.71	5.00	21.75	0.35	0.18	10.11	0.69	32.55	m	35.80
Roof coverings; Redland Heathland plain through coloured tiles, 268 x 165mm; fixing every fifth course with two aluminium nails to each tile to 65mm lap; 38 x 19mm pressure impregnated softwood battens fixed with galvanised nails; twin-ply underlay 145gsm with polypropylene 150mm laps; fixing with galvanised steel clout nails										
Pitched 40 degrees from horizontal										
generally	39.15	5.00	41.56	0.70	0.35	20.06	1.90	63.52	m²	69.87
Boundary work										
double course at top edges with clips and nailing each tile with two aluminium nails	3.00	5.00	3.15	0.34	0.17	9.74	6.29	19.18	m	21.10
double course at eaves and nailing each tile with two aluminium nails	3.00	5.00	3.15	0.34	0.17	9.74	0.84	13.73	m	15.11
ridge or hip tiles, Plain angle; butt jointed; bedding and pointing in tinted cement mortar (1:3)	15.15	5.00	15.91	0.35	0.18	10.11	0.69	26.71	m	29.38
ridge or hip tiles, half round; butt jointed; bedding and pointing in tinted cement mortar (1:3)	26.67	5.00	28.01	0.35	0.18	10.11	0.69	38.81	m	42.69
verges; Dry Verge system with plain tiles and tile-and-a-half tiles in alternate courses, clips and aluminium nails	18.90	5.00	19.84	0.28	0.14	8.02	1.78	29.65	m	32.62
verges; plain tile undercloak; tiles and undercloak bedded and pointed in tinted cement mortar (1:3) and with plain tiles and tile-and-a-half tiles in alternate courses and aluminium nails	6.10	5.00	6.40	0.28	0.14	8.02	0.74	15.17	m	16.68
valley tiles, Plain valley tiles; bedding and pointing in cement mortar	44.16	5.00	46.37	0.55	0.28	15.76	0.69	62.82	m	69.11
hip tiles; arris; bedding and pointing in cement mortar	44.16	5.00	46.37	0.55	0.28	15.76	0.69	62.82	m	69.11
hip tiles; bonnet; bedding and pointing in coloured cement-lime mortar (1:1:6)	44.16	5.00	46.37	0.55	0.28	15.76	0.69	62.82	m	69.11
Fittings										
Ventilator tiles										
Ridge Vent ridge ventilation terminal 450mm long for										
half round ridge	63.33	5.00	66.50	1.45	0.73	41.63	1.09	109.21	nr	120.13
universal angle ridge	63.33	5.00	66.50	1.45	0.73	41.63	1.09	109.21	nr	120.13
ThruVent ventilator tiles for										
Stonewold slates	70.00	5.00	73.50	0.50	0.25	14.33	0.36	88.19	nr	97.01
Regent tiles	70.00	5.00	73.50	0.50	0.25	14.33	0.36	88.19	nr	97.01
Grovebury double pantiles	70.00	5.00	73.50	0.50	0.25	14.33	0.36	88.19	nr	97.01
Fenland pantiles	70.00	5.00	73.50	0.50	0.25	14.33	0.36	88.19	nr	97.01
Redland 49 tiles	70.00	5.00	73.50	0.50	0.25	14.33	0.36	88.19	nr	97.01
Renown tiles	70.00	5.00	73.50	0.50	0.25	14.33	0.36	88.19	nr	97.01
Redland 50 double roman tiles	70.00	5.00	73.50	0.50	0.25	14.33	0.36	88.19	nr	97.01
Redland plain tiles	104.90	5.00	110.14	0.56	0.28	16.05	0.41	126.60	nr	139.26
Eaves ventilation										
Insulation Interupter and roof space ventilator										
Felt support eaves ventilator tray fixing with aluminium nails	1.11	5.00	1.17	0.25	0.12	7.16	0.05	8.38	m	9.22
Over fascia ventilator										
10mm	2.57	5.00	2.70	0.30	0.15	8.60	0.05	11.34	m	12.48

Labour hourly rates: (except Specialists) Craft Operatives 20.87 Labourer 15.57 Rates are national average prices. Refer to REGIONAL VARIATIONS for indicative levels of overall pricing in regions	MATERIALS			LABOUR				RATES		
	Del to Site £	Waste %	Material Cost £	Craft Optve Hrs	Lab Hrs	Labour Cost £	Sunds £	Nett Rate £	Unit	Gross rate (10%) £
PLAIN TILING (Cont'd)										
Fittings (Cont'd)										
Eaves ventilation (Cont'd)										
Over fascia ventilator (Cont'd)										
25mm	12.13	5.00	12.74	0.30	0.15	8.60	0.05	21.38	m	23.52
Gas terminals										
Gas Flue ridge terminal, 450mm long with sealing gasket and fixing brackets										
half round ridge	140.58	5.00	147.61	1.68	0.84	48.14	1.09	196.84	nr	216.52
universal angle ridge	140.58	5.00	147.61	1.68	0.84	48.14	1.09	196.84	nr	216.52
Gas Flue ridge terminal, 450mm long with sealing gasket and fixing brackets with adaptor for										
half round ridge	180.35	5.00	189.37	1.68	0.84	48.14	1.09	238.60	nr	262.46
universal angle ridge	180.35	5.00	189.37	1.68	2.84	79.28	1.09	269.74	nr	296.71
extra for extension adaptor and gasket	180.35	5.00	189.37	0.35	0.17	9.95	0.41	199.73	nr	219.70
Hip irons										
galvanised mild steel; 32 x 3 x 380mm girth; scrolled; fixing with galvanised steel screws to timber	1.02	5.00	1.07	0.11	0.06	3.23	-	4.30	nr	4.73
Lead soakers										
fixing only	-	-	-	0.34	0.17	9.74	-	9.74	nr	10.72
INTERLOCKING TILING										
Roof coverings; Redland Stonewold II through coloured slates, 430 x 380mm; fixing every fourth course with galvanised nails to 75mm lap; 38 x 19mm pressure impregnated softwood battens fixed with galvanised nails; twin-ply underlay 145gsm with polypropylene; 150mm laps; fixing with galvanised steel clout nails										
Pitched 40 degrees from horizontal										
generally	49.41	5.00	52.06	0.48	0.24	13.75	1.34	67.15	m²	73.87
Boundary work										
abutments; square	4.64	5.00	4.87	0.12	0.06	3.44	-	8.31	m	9.14
abutments; raking	6.96	5.00	7.31	0.17	0.09	4.95	-	12.26	m	13.48
abutments; curved to 3000mm radius	9.28	5.00	9.74	0.23	0.12	6.67	-	16.41	m	18.05
supplementary fixing eaves course with one clip per slate	0.45	5.00	0.47	0.03	0.02	0.94	-	1.41	m	1.55
ridge or hip tiles, Redland third round; butt jointed; bedding and pointing in tinted cement mortar (1:3)	10.47	5.00	10.99	0.23	0.12	6.67	0.69	18.35	m	20.18
ridge or hip tiles, Redland half round; butt jointed; bedding and pointing in tinted cement mortar (1:3)	10.51	5.00	11.04	0.23	0.12	6.67	0.69	18.40	m	20.24
ridge tiles, Redland universal angle; butt jointed; bedding and pointing in tinted cement mortar (1:3)	10.47	5.00	10.99	0.23	0.12	6.67	0.69	18.35	m	20.18
ridge tiles, Redland universal half round type Monopitch; butt jointed; fixing with aluminium nails and bedding and pointing in tinted cement mortar (1:3)	15.04	5.00	15.79	0.23	0.12	6.67	0.69	23.15	m	25.47
ridge tiles, Redland Dry Ridge system with half round ridge tiles; fixing with stainless steel batten straps and ring shanked fixing nails with neoprene washers and sleeves; polypropylene ridge seals and uPVC profile filler units	25.55	5.00	26.83	0.45	0.23	12.97	-	39.80	m	43.78
ridge tiles, Redland Dry Ridge system with universal angle ridge tiles; fixing with stainless steel batten straps and ring shanked fixing nails with neoprene washers and sleeves; polypropylene ridge seals and uPVC profile filler units	25.51	5.00	26.78	0.45	0.23	12.97	-	39.75	m	43.73
ridge tiles, Redland Dry Vent Ridge system with half round ridge tiles; fixing with stainless steel batten straps and ring shanked nails with neoprene washers and sleeves; polypropylene ridge seals, PVC air flow control units and uPVC ventilated profile filler units	17.78	5.00	18.67	0.45	0.23	12.97	-	31.64	m	34.81
ridge tiles, Redland Dry Vent Ridge system with Universal angle ridge tiles; fixing with stainless steel batten straps and ring shanked nails with neoprene washers and sleeves; polypropylene ridge seals, PVC air flow control units and uPVC ventilated profile filler units	17.74	5.00	18.62	0.45	0.23	12.97	-	31.60	m	34.75
verges; Redland Dry Verge system with half slates, full slates and clips	41.33	5.00	43.40	0.28	0.14	8.02	3.17	54.59	m	60.05
verges; Redland Dry Verge system with half slates, verge slates and clips	43.03	5.00	45.18	0.28	0.14	8.02	3.17	56.37	m	62.01
verges; 150 x 6mm fibre cement undercloak, slates and undercloak bedded and pointed in tinted cement mortar (1:3) and with half slates, full slates and clips	77.77	5.00	81.66	0.23	0.12	6.67	3.75	92.07	m	101.28
verges; 150 x 6mm fibre cement undercloak, slates and undercloak bedded and pointed in tinted cement mortar (1:3) and with half slates, verge slates and clips	28.79	5.00	30.23	0.23	0.12	6.67	3.75	40.65	m	44.71
valley tiles, Redland Universal valley troughs; laid with 100mm laps	75.93	5.00	79.73	0.56	0.28	16.05	0.69	96.47	m	106.11
Roof coverings; Redland Stonewold II through coloured slates, 430 x 380mm; fixing every fourth course with galvanised nails to 75mm lap; 38 x 25mm pressure impregnated softwood battens fixed with galvanised nails; twin-ply underlay 145gsm with polypropylene; 150mm laps; fixing with galvanised steel clout nails										
Pitched 40 degrees from horizontal										
generally	50.16	5.00	52.89	0.47	0.24	13.55	1.34	67.77	m²	74.54

TILE AND SLATE ROOF AND WALL COVERINGS

Labour hourly rates: (except Specialists) Craft Operatives 20.87 Labourer 15.57 Rates are national average prices. Refer to REGIONAL VARIATIONS for indicative levels of overall pricing in regions	MATERIALS			LABOUR				RATES		
	Del to Site	Waste	Material Cost	Craft Optve	Lab	Labour Cost	Sunds	Nett Rate		Gross rate (10%)
	£	%	£	Hrs	Hrs	£	£	£	Unit	£
INTERLOCKING TILING (Cont'd)										
Roof coverings; Redland Stonewold II through coloured slates, 430 x 380mm; fixing each course with galvanised nails to 75mm; 38 x 25mm pressure impregnated softwood battens fixed with galvanised nails; twin-ply underlay 145gsm with polypropylene; 150mm laps; fixing with galvanised steel clout nails										
Pitched 40 degrees from horizontal										
generally	50.16	5.00	52.89	0.52	0.26	14.90	3.86	71.65	m²	78.81
Roof coverings; Redland Stonewold II through coloured slates, 430 x 380mm; fixing every fourth course with galvanised nails to 75mm lap; 38 x 25mm pressure impregnated softwood battens fixed with galvanised nails; underlay, BS EN 13707 type 1F aluminium foil surfaced reinforced bitumen felt; 150mm laps; fixing with galvanised steel clout nails										
Pitched 40 degrees from horizontal										
generally	50.16	5.00	52.89	0.48	0.24	13.75	1.34	67.98	m²	74.77
Roof coverings; Redland Stonewold II through coloured slates, 430 x 380mm; fixing every fourth course with galvanised nails to 75mm lap; 38 x 25mm pressure impregnated softwood battens fixed with galvanised nails; underlay, BS EN 13707 type 1F reinforced bitumen felt with 50mm glass fibre insulation bonded on; 150mm laps; fixing with galvanised steel clout nails										
Pitched 40 degrees from horizontal										
generally	50.16	5.00	52.89	0.58	0.29	16.62	1.34	70.84	m²	77.93
Roof coverings; Redland Regent granular faced tiles, 418 x 332mm; fixing every fourth course with galvanised nails to 75mm lap; 38 x 25mm pressure impregnated softwood battens fixed with galvanised nails; twin-ply underlay 145gsm with polypropylene; 150mm laps; fixing with galvanised steel clout nails										
Pitched 40 degrees from horizontal										
generally	15.15	5.00	16.13	0.47	0.24	13.55	1.50	31.18	m²	34.30
Boundary work										
reform eaves filler unit and eaves clip to each eaves tile	0.45	5.00	0.47	0.07	0.04	2.08	1.17	3.73	m	4.10
ridge or hip tiles, Redland third round; butt jointed; bedding and pointing in tinted cement mortar (1:3); dentil slips in pan of each tile set in bedding	10.01	5.00	10.51	0.34	0.17	9.74	2.69	22.94	m	25.24
ridge or hip tiles, Redland half round; butt jointed; bedding and pointing in tinted cement mortar (1:3); dentil slips in pan of each tile set in bedding	10.05	5.00	10.56	0.34	0.17	9.74	2.69	22.99	m	25.29
ridge tiles, Redland universal half round type Monopitch; butt jointed; fixing with aluminium nails and bedding and pointing in tinted cement mortar (1:3); dentil slips in pan of each tile set in bedding	15.04	5.00	15.79	0.34	0.17	9.74	2.69	28.22	m	31.05
verges; cloaked verge tiles and aluminium nails	17.52	5.00	18.40	0.17	0.09	4.95	0.12	23.46	m	25.81
verges; half tiles, cloaked verge tiles and aluminium nails	19.87	5.00	20.86	0.23	0.12	6.67	0.20	27.73	m	30.50
verges; 150 x 6mm fibre cement undercloak; tiles and undercloak bedded and pointed in tinted cement mortar (1:3) and with standard tiles and clips	15.34	5.00	16.11	0.23	0.12	6.67	3.75	26.52	m	29.17
verges; 150 x 6mm fibre cement undercloak; tiles and undercloak bedded and pointed in tinted cement mortar (1:3) and with verge tiles and clips	15.34	5.00	16.11	0.23	0.12	6.67	3.75	26.52	m	29.17
verges; 150 x 6mm fibre cement undercloak; tiles and undercloak bedded and pointed in tinted cement mortar (1:3) and with half tiles, standard tiles and clips	32.86	5.00	34.50	0.23	0.12	6.67	3.75	44.92	m	49.41
verges; 150 x 6mm fibre cement undercloak; tiles and undercloak bedded and pointed in tinted cement mortar (1:3) and with half tiles, verge tiles and clips	32.86	5.00	34.50	0.23	0.12	6.67	3.75	44.92	m	49.41
valley tiles, Redland universal valley troughs; laid with 100mm laps	75.93	5.00	79.73	0.34	0.17	9.74	0.69	90.16	m	99.18
Roof coverings; Redland Regent granular faced tiles, 418 x 332mm; fixing every fourth course with aluminium nails to 75mm lap; 38 x 25mm pressure impregnated softwood battens fixed with galvanised nails; twin-ply underlay 145gsm with polypropylene; 150mm laps; fixing with galvanised steel clout nails										
Pitched 40 degrees from horizontal										
generally	15.15	5.00	16.13	0.47	0.24	13.55	1.77	31.44	m²	34.59
Roof coverings; Redland Regent granular faced tiles, 418 x 332mm; fixing every fourth course with galvanised nails to 100mm lap; 38 x 25mm pressure impregnated softwood battens fixed with galvanised nails; twin-ply underlay 145gsm with polypropylene; 150mm laps; fixing with galvanised steel clout nails										
Pitched 40 degrees from horizontal										
generally	16.09	5.00	17.12	0.47	0.24	13.55	1.07	31.74	m²	34.91
Boundary work										
abutments; square	1.23	5.00	1.29	0.11	0.06	3.23	-	4.52	m	4.98
abutments; raking	1.84	5.00	1.93	0.17	0.09	4.95	-	6.88	m	7.57
abutments; curved to 3000mm radius	2.46	5.00	2.59	0.23	0.12	6.67	-	9.26	m	10.18

Labour hourly rates: (except Specialists) Craft Operatives 20.87 Labourer 15.57 Rates are national average prices. Refer to REGIONAL VARIATIONS for indicative levels of overall pricing in regions	MATERIALS			LABOUR				RATES		
	Del to Site £	Waste %	Material Cost £	Craft Optve Hrs	Lab Hrs	Labour Cost £	Sunds £	Nett Rate £	Unit	Gross rate (10%) £
INTERLOCKING TILING (Cont'd)										
Roof coverings; Redland Regent through coloured tiles, 418 x 332mm; fixing every fourth course with galvanised nails to 75mm lap; 38 x 25mm pressure impregnated softwood battens fixed with galvanised nails; twin-ply underlay 145gsm with polypropylene; 150mm laps; fixing with galvanised steel clout nails										
Pitched 40 degrees from horizontal										
generally	15.15	5.00	16.13	0.47	0.24	13.55	1.50	31.18	m²	34.30
Boundary work										
reform eaves filler unit and eaves clip to each eaves tile	0.45	5.00	0.47	0.07	0.04	2.08	1.17	3.73	m	4.10
verges; cloaked verge tiles and aluminium nails	17.52	5.00	18.40	0.17	0.09	4.95	0.12	23.46	m	25.81
verges; 150 x 6mm fibre cement undercloak; tiles and undercloak bedded and pointed in tinted cement mortar (1:3) and with standard tiles and clips	15.34	5.00	16.11	0.23	0.12	6.67	3.75	26.52	m	29.17
verges; 150 x 6mm fibre cement undercloak; tiles and undercloak bedded and pointed in tinted cement mortar (1:3) and with verge tiles and clips	15.34	5.00	16.11	0.23	0.12	6.67	3.75	26.52	m	29.17
verges; 150 x 6mm fibre cement undercloak; tiles and undercloak bedded and pointed in tinted cement mortar (1:3) and with half tiles, standard tiles and clips	32.86	5.00	34.50	0.23	0.12	6.67	3.75	44.92	m	49.41
verges; 150 x 6mm fibre cement undercloak; tiles and undercloak bedded and pointed in tinted cement mortar (1:3) and with half tiles, verge tiles and clips	32.86	5.00	34.50	0.23	0.12	6.67	3.75	44.92	m	49.41
valley tiles, Redland universal valley troughs; laid with 100mm laps	75.93	5.00	79.73	0.34	0.17	9.74	0.69	90.16	m	99.18
Roof coverings; Redland Regent through coloured tiles, 418 x 332mm; fixing every fourth course with galvanised nails to 100mm lap; 38 x 25mm pressure impregnated softwood battens fixed with galvanised nails; twin-ply underlay 145gsm with polypropylene; 150mm laps; fixing with galvanised steel clout nails										
Pitched 40 degrees from horizontal										
generally	16.09	5.00	17.12	0.47	0.24	13.55	1.50	32.16	m²	35.38
Boundary work										
abutments; square	1.23	5.00	1.29	0.11	0.06	3.23	-	4.52	m	4.98
abutments; raking	1.84	5.00	1.93	0.17	0.09	4.95	-	6.88	m	7.57
abutments; curved to 3000mm radius	2.46	5.00	2.59	0.23	0.12	6.67	-	9.26	m	10.18
Roof coverings; Redland Grovebury granular faced double pantiles, 418 x 332mm; fixing every fourth course with galvanised nails to 75mm lap; 38 x 22mm pressure impregnated softwood battens fixed with galvanised nails; twin-ply underlay 145gsm with polypropylene; 150mm laps; fixing with galvanised steel clout nails										
Pitched 40 degrees from horizontal										
generally	14.53	5.00	15.48	0.47	0.24	13.55	1.50	30.53	m²	33.58
Boundary work										
reform eaves filler unit and eaves clip to each eaves tile	0.45	5.00	0.47	0.07	0.04	2.08	1.17	3.73	m	4.10
ridge or hip tiles, Redland third round; butt jointed; bedding and pointing in tinted cement mortar (1:3)	10.01	5.00	10.51	0.34	0.17	9.74	3.75	24.00	m	26.40
ridge or hip tiles, Redland half round; butt jointed; bedding and pointing in tinted cement mortar (1:3)	10.05	5.00	10.56	0.34	0.17	9.74	3.75	24.04	m	26.45
verges; cloaked verge tiles and aluminium nails	17.52	5.00	18.40	0.17	0.09	4.95	0.12	23.46	m	25.81
verges; half tiles, cloaked verge tiles and aluminium nails	19.74	5.00	20.73	0.23	0.12	6.67	0.18	27.58	m	30.33
verges; 150 x 6mm fibre cement undercloak; tiles and undercloak bedded and pointed in tinted cement mortar (1:3) and with standard tiles and clips	15.15	5.00	15.91	0.23	0.12	6.67	3.75	26.32	m	28.95
verges; 150 x 6mm fibre cement undercloak; tiles and undercloak bedded and pointed in tinted cement mortar (1:3) and with treble roll verge tiles and clips	15.15	5.00	15.91	0.23	0.12	6.67	3.75	26.32	m	28.95
valley tiles, Redland Universal valley troughs; laid with 100mm laps	75.93	5.00	79.73	0.34	0.17	9.74	0.69	90.16	m	99.18
Roof coverings; Redland Grovebury through coloured double pantiles, 418 x 332mm; fixing every fourth course with galvanised nails to 75mm lap; 38 x 22mm pressure impregnated softwood battens fixed with galvanised nails; twin-ply underlay 145gsm with polypropylene; 150mm laps; fixing with galvanised steel clout nails										
Pitched 40 degrees from horizontal										
generally	14.53	5.00	15.48	0.47	0.24	13.55	1.50	30.53	m²	33.58
Boundary work										
reform eaves filler unit and eaves clip to each eaves tile	0.45	5.00	0.47	0.07	0.04	2.08	1.17	3.73	m	4.10
ridge or hip tiles, Redland third round; butt jointed; bedding and pointing in tinted cement mortar (1:3)	10.01	5.00	10.51	0.34	0.17	9.74	0.69	20.95	m	23.04
ridge or hip tiles, Redland half round; butt jointed; bedding and pointing in tinted cement mortar (1:3)	10.05	5.00	10.56	0.34	0.17	9.74	0.69	20.99	m	23.09
verges; cloaked verge tiles and aluminium nails	17.52	5.00	18.40	0.17	0.09	4.95	0.12	23.46	m	25.81
verges; half tiles, cloaked verge tiles and aluminium nails	19.74	5.00	20.73	0.23	0.12	6.67	0.18	27.58	m	30.33
verges; 150 x 6mm fibre cement undercloak; tiles and undercloak bedded and pointed in tinted cement mortar (1:3) and with standard tiles and clips	15.15	5.00	15.91	0.23	0.12	6.67	3.75	26.32	m	28.95
verges; 150 x 6mm fibre cement undercloak; tiles and undercloak bedded and pointed in tinted cement mortar (1:3) and with treble roll verge tiles and clips	15.15	5.00	15.91	0.23	0.12	6.67	3.75	26.32	m	28.95
valley tiles, Redland Universal valley troughs; laid with 100mm laps	75.93	5.00	79.73	0.34	0.17	9.74	0.69	90.16	m	99.18

TILE AND SLATE ROOF AND WALL COVERINGS

Labour hourly rates: (except Specialists) Craft Operatives 20.87 Labourer 15.57 Rates are national average prices. Refer to REGIONAL VARIATIONS for indicative levels of overall pricing in regions	MATERIALS			LABOUR				RATES		
	Del to Site £	Waste %	Material Cost £	Craft Optve Hrs	Lab Hrs	Labour Cost £	Sunds £	Nett Rate £	Unit	Gross rate (10%) £
INTERLOCKING TILING (Cont'd)										
Roof coverings; Redland Fenland through coloured pantiles, 381 x 227mm; fixing every fourth course with galvanised nails to 75mm lap; 38 x 25mm pressure impregnated softwood battens fixed with galvanised nails; twin-ply underlay 145gsm with polypropylene; 150mm laps; fixing with galvanised steel clout nails										
Pitched 40 degrees from horizontal										
generally	18.49	5.00	19.69	0.61	0.31	17.56	2.18	39.42	m²	43.36
Boundary work										
abutments; square	1.37	5.00	1.44	0.11	0.06	3.23	-	4.67	m	5.13
abutments; raking	2.05	5.00	2.15	0.17	0.09	4.95	-	7.10	m	7.81
abutments; curved to 3000mm radius	2.74	5.00	2.88	0.23	0.12	6.67	-	9.54	m	10.50
reform eaves filler unit and aluminium nails to each eaves tile	0.45	5.00	0.47	0.07	0.04	2.08	1.17	3.73	m	4.10
ridge or hip tiles, Redland third round; butt jointed; bedding and pointing in tinted cement mortar (1:3)	10.47	5.00	10.99	0.34	0.17	9.74	0.69	21.42	m	23.57
ridge or hip tiles, Redland half round; butt jointed; bedding and pointing in tinted cement mortar (1:3)	10.51	5.00	11.04	0.34	0.17	9.74	0.69	21.47	m	23.62
verges; plain tile undercloak; tiles and undercloak bedded and pointed in tinted cement mortar (1:3) and with standard tiles and aluminium nails	2.52	5.00	2.65	0.11	0.06	3.23	0.74	6.62	m	7.28
verges; plain tile undercloak; tiles and undercloak bedded and pointed in tinted cement mortar (1:3) and with standard tiles and clips	2.52	5.00	2.65	0.11	0.06	3.23	5.69	11.57	m	12.73
verges; 150 x 6mm fibre cement undercloak; tiles and undercloak bedded and pointed in tinted cement mortar (1:3) and with standard tiles and aluminium nails	14.34	5.00	15.06	0.17	0.09	4.95	0.79	20.80	m	22.88
verges; 150 x 6mm fibre cement undercloak; tiles and undercloak bedded and pointed in tinted cement mortar (1:3) and with standard tiles and clips	14.34	5.00	15.06	0.17	0.09	4.95	5.69	25.70	m	28.27
valley tiles, Redland Universal valley troughs; laid with 100mm laps	75.93	5.00	79.73	0.34	0.17	9.74	0.69	90.16	m	99.18
Roof coverings; Redland Fenland through coloured pantiles, 381 x 227mm; fixing every fourth course with aluminium nails to 75mm lap; 38 x 25mm pressure impregnated softwood battens fixed with galvanised nails; twin-ply underlay 145gsm with polypropylene; 150mm laps; fixing with galvanised steel clout nails										
Pitched 40 degrees from horizontal										
generally	18.49	5.00	19.69	0.61	0.31	17.56	2.18	39.42	m²	43.36
Roof coverings; Redland Fenland through coloured pantiles, 381 x 227mm; fixing every fourth course with galvanised nails to 100mm lap; 38 x 25mm pressure impregnated softwood battens fixed with galvanised nails; twin-ply underlay 145gsm with polypropylene; 150mm laps; fixing with galvanised steel clout nails										
Pitched 40 degrees from horizontal										
generally	19.75	5.00	21.01	0.66	0.33	18.91	2.33	42.25	m²	46.47
Roof coverings; Redland 49 granular faced tiles, 381 x 227mm; fixing every fourth course with galvanised nails to 75mm lap; 38 x 25mm pressure impregnated softwood battens fixed with galvanised nails; twin-ply underlay 145gsm with polypropylene; 150mm laps; fixing with galvanised steel clout nails										
Pitched 40 degrees from horizontal										
generally	17.40	5.00	18.50	0.61	0.31	17.56	2.18	38.23	m²	42.05
Boundary work										
supplementary fixing eaves course with one aluminium nail per tile	-	-	-	0.02	0.01	0.57	0.05	0.62	m	0.68
ridge or hip tiles, Redland third round; butt jointed; bedding and pointing in tinted cement mortar (1:3)	10.47	5.00	10.99	0.34	0.17	9.74	0.69	21.42	m	23.57
ridge or hip tiles, Redland half round; butt jointed; bedding and pointing in tinted cement mortar (1:3)	10.51	5.00	11.04	0.34	0.17	9.74	0.69	21.47	m	23.62
verges; Redland Dry Verge system with standard tiles and clips	26.87	5.00	28.22	0.28	0.14	8.02	3.17	39.41	m	43.35
verges; Redland Dry Verge system with verge tiles and clips	26.87	5.00	28.22	0.28	0.14	8.02	3.17	39.41	m	43.35
verges; plain tile undercloak; tiles and undercloak bedded and pointed in tinted cement mortar (1:3) and with standard tiles and aluminium nails	2.51	5.00	2.64	0.11	0.06	3.23	0.79	6.66	m	7.32
verges; plain tile undercloak; tiles and undercloak bedded and pointed in tinted cement mortar (1:3) and with verge tiles and aluminium nails	2.51	5.00	2.64	0.11	0.06	3.23	0.79	6.66	m	7.32
verges; 150 x 6mm fibre cement undercloak; tiles and undercloak bedded and pointed in tinted cement mortar (1:3) and with standard tiles and aluminium nails	14.33	5.00	15.05	0.17	0.09	4.95	0.79	20.79	m	22.87
verges; 150 x 6mm fibre cement undercloak; tiles and undercloak bedded and pointed in tinted cement mortar (1:3) and with verge tiles and aluminium nails	14.33	5.00	15.05	0.17	0.09	4.95	0.79	20.79	m	22.87
valley tiles, Redland Universal valley troughs; laid with 100mm laps	75.93	5.00	79.73	0.34	0.17	9.74	0.69	90.16	m	99.18
Roof coverings; Redland 49 granular faced tiles, 381 x 227mm; fixing every fourth course with galvanised nails to 100mm lap; 38 x 25mm pressure impregnated softwood battens fixed with galvanised nails; twin-ply underlay 145gsm with polypropylene; 150mm laps; fixing with galvanised steel clout nails										
Pitched 40 degrees from horizontal										
generally	18.66	5.00	19.81	0.66	0.33	18.91	2.33	41.05	m²	45.16

Labour hourly rates: (except Specialists) Craft Operatives 20.87 Labourer 15.57 Rates are national average prices. Refer to REGIONAL VARIATIONS for indicative levels of overall pricing in regions	MATERIALS			LABOUR				RATES		
	Del to Site £	Waste %	Material Cost £	Craft Optve Hrs	Lab Hrs	Labour Cost £	Sunds £	Nett Rate £	Unit	Gross rate (10%) £
INTERLOCKING TILING (Cont'd)										
Roof coverings; Redland 49 granular faced tiles, 381 x 227mm; fixing every fourth course with galvanised nails to 100mm lap; 38 x 25mm pressure impregnated softwood battens fixed with galvanised nails; twin-ply underlay 145gsm with polypropylene; 150mm laps; fixing with galvanised steel clout nails (Cont'd)										
Pitched 40 degrees from horizontal (Cont'd)										
Boundary work										
abutments; square	1.49	5.00	1.56	0.11	0.06	3.23	-	4.79	m	5.27
abutments; raking	2.23	5.00	2.35	0.17	0.09	4.95	-	7.29	m	8.02
abutments; curved to 3000mm radius	2.36	5.00	2.48	0.23	0.12	6.67	-	9.15	m	10.06
Roof coverings; Redland 49 through coloured tiles, 381 x 227mm; fixing every fourth course with galvanised nails to 75mm lap; 38 x 25mm pressure impregnated softwood battens fixed with galvanised nails; twin-ply underlay 145gsm with polypropylene; 150mm laps; fixing with galvanised steel clout nails										
Pitched 40 degrees from horizontal										
generally	17.40	5.00	18.50	0.61	0.31	17.56	2.18	38.23	m²	42.05
Boundary work										
abutments; square	1.36	5.00	1.43	0.11	0.06	3.23	-	4.66	m	5.13
abutments; raking	2.05	5.00	2.15	0.17	0.09	4.95	-	7.10	m	7.81
abutments; curved to 3000mm radius	2.76	5.00	2.90	0.23	0.12	6.67	-	9.57	m	10.52
supplementary fixing eaves course with one aluminium nail per tile	-	-	-	0.02	0.01	0.57	0.05	0.62	m	0.68
ridge or hip tiles, Redland third round; butt jointed; bedding and pointing in tinted cement mortar (1:3)	10.47	5.00	10.99	0.34	0.17	9.74	0.69	21.42	m	23.57
ridge or hip tiles, Redland half round; butt jointed; bedding and pointing in tinted cement mortar (1:3)	10.51	5.00	11.04	0.34	0.17	9.74	0.69	21.47	m	23.62
verges; Redland Dry Verge system with standard tiles and clips	26.87	5.00	28.22	0.28	0.14	8.02	3.17	39.41	m	43.35
verges; Redland Dry Verge system with verge tiles and clips	26.87	5.00	28.22	0.28	0.14	8.02	3.17	39.41	m	43.35
verges; plain tile undercloak; tiles and undercloak bedded and pointed in tinted cement mortar (1:3) and with standard tiles and aluminium nails	2.51	5.00	2.64	0.11	0.06	3.23	0.79	6.66	m	7.32
verges; plain tile undercloak; tiles and undercloak bedded and pointed in tinted cement mortar (1:3) and with verge tiles and aluminium nails	2.51	5.00	2.64	0.11	0.06	3.23	0.79	6.66	m	7.32
verges; 150 x 6mm fibre cement undercloak; tiles and undercloak bedded and pointed in tinted cement mortar (1:3) and with standard tiles and aluminium nails	14.33	5.00	15.05	0.17	0.09	4.95	0.79	20.79	m	22.87
verges; 150 x 6mm fibre cement undercloak; tiles and undercloak bedded and pointed in tinted cement mortar (1:3) and with verge tiles and aluminium nails	14.33	5.00	15.05	0.17	0.09	4.95	0.79	20.79	m	22.87
valley tiles, Redland Universal valley troughs; laid with 100mm laps	75.93	5.00	79.73	0.34	0.17	9.74	0.69	90.16	m	99.18
Roof coverings; Redland 49 through coloured tiles, 381 x 227mm; fixing every fourth course with galvanised nails to 100mm lap; 38 x 25mm pressure impregnated softwood battens fixed with galvanised nails; twin-ply underlay 145gsm with polypropylene; 150mm laps; fixing with galvanised steel clout nails										
Pitched 40 degrees from horizontal										
generally	18.66	5.00	19.81	0.66	0.33	18.91	2.33	41.05	m²	45.16
Roof coverings; Redland Renown granular faced tiles, 418 x 330mm; fixing every fourth course with galvanised nails to 75mm lap; 38 x 25mm pressure impregnated softwood battens fixed with galvanised nails; twin-ply underlay 145gsm with polypropylene; 150mm laps; fixing with galvanised steel clout nails										
Pitched 40 degrees from horizontal										
generally	14.25	5.00	15.19	0.47	0.24	13.55	0.94	29.67	m²	32.64
Boundary work										
abutments; square	1.05	5.00	1.10	0.11	0.06	3.23	-	4.33	m	4.76
abutments; raking	1.58	5.00	1.66	0.17	0.09	4.95	-	6.61	m	7.27
abutments; curved to 3000mm radius	2.10	5.00	2.20	0.23	0.12	6.67	-	8.87	m	9.76
reform eaves filler unit and aluminium nails to each eaves tile	0.45	5.00	0.47	0.07	0.04	2.08	1.17	3.73	m	4.10
ridge or hip tiles, Redland third round; butt jointed; bedding and pointing in tinted cement mortar (1:3)	10.47	5.00	10.99	0.34	0.17	9.74	0.69	21.42	m	23.57
ridge or hip tiles, Redland half round; butt jointed; bedding and pointing in tinted cement mortar (1:3)	10.51	5.00	11.04	0.34	0.17	9.74	0.69	21.47	m	23.62
verges; cloaked verge tiles and aluminium nails	3.57	5.00	3.75	0.17	0.09	4.95	0.18	8.88	m	9.76
verges; half tiles, cloaked verge tiles and aluminium nails	20.76	5.00	21.80	0.17	0.09	4.95	0.79	27.54	m	30.30
verges; plain tile undercloak; tiles and undercloak bedded and pointed in tinted cement mortar (1:3) and with standard tiles and aluminium nails	3.24	5.00	3.40	0.11	0.06	3.23	0.79	7.43	m	8.17
verges; plain tile undercloak; tiles and undercloak bedded and pointed in tinted cement mortar (1:3) and with verge tiles and aluminium nails	3.24	5.00	3.40	0.11	0.06	3.23	0.79	7.43	m	8.17
verges; 150 x 6mm fibre cement undercloak; tiles and undercloak bedded and pointed in tinted cement mortar (1:3) and with standard tiles and aluminium nails	15.06	5.00	15.82	0.17	0.09	4.95	0.79	21.56	m	23.71
verges; 150 x 6mm fibre cement undercloak; tiles and undercloak bedded and pointed in tinted cement mortar (1:3) and with verge tiles and aluminium nails	15.06	5.00	15.82	0.17	0.09	4.95	0.79	21.56	m	23.71
valley tiles, Redland Universal valley troughs; laid with 100mm laps	58.21	5.00	61.12	0.34	0.17	9.74	0.69	71.56	m	78.72

TILE AND SLATE ROOF AND WALL COVERINGS

Labour hourly rates: (except Specialists) Craft Operatives 20.87 Labourer 15.57 Rates are national average prices. Refer to REGIONAL VARIATIONS for indicative levels of overall pricing in regions	MATERIALS			LABOUR				RATES		
	Del to Site £	Waste %	Material Cost £	Craft Optve Hrs	Lab Hrs	Labour Cost £	Sunds £	Nett Rate £	Unit	Gross rate (10%) £
INTERLOCKING TILING (Cont'd)										
Roof coverings; Redland 50 double roman tiles, 418 x 330mm; fixing every fourth course with galvanised nails to 75mm lap; 38 x 25mm pressure impregnated softwood battens fixed with galvanised nails; twin-ply underlay 145gsm with polypropylene; 150mm laps; fixing with galvanised steel clout nails										
Pitched 40 degrees from horizontal										
generally	14.53	5.00	15.48	0.47	0.24	13.55	1.14	30.17	m²	33.18
Boundary work										
reform eaves filler unit and aluminium nails to each eaves tile	0.45	5.00	0.47	0.07	0.04	2.08	1.17	3.73	m	4.10
ridge or hip tiles, Redland third round; butt jointed; bedding and pointing in tinted cement mortar (1:3)	10.47	5.00	10.99	0.34	0.17	9.74	0.69	21.42	m	23.57
ridge or hip tiles, Redland half round; butt jointed; bedding and pointing in tinted cement mortar (1:3)	10.51	5.00	11.04	0.34	0.17	9.74	0.69	21.47	m	23.62
verges; cloaked verge tiles and aluminium nails	20.85	5.00	21.89	0.17	0.09	4.95	0.12	26.96	m	29.65
verges; half tiles, cloaked verge tiles and aluminium nails	19.74	5.00	20.73	0.23	0.12	6.67	0.12	27.51	m	30.26
verges; plain tile undercloak; tiles and undercloak bedded and pointed in tinted cement mortar (1:3) and with standard tiles and aluminium nails	3.33	5.00	3.50	0.11	0.06	3.23	0.79	7.52	m	8.27
verges; plain tile undercloak; tiles and undercloak bedded and pointed in tinted cement mortar (1:3) and with treble roll verge tiles and aluminium nails	3.33	5.00	3.50	0.11	0.06	3.23	0.79	7.52	m	8.27
verges; 150 x 6mm fibre cement undercloak; tiles and undercloak bedded and pointed in tinted cement mortar (1:3) and with standard tiles and aluminium nails	15.15	5.00	15.91	0.17	0.09	4.95	0.79	21.65	m	23.81
verges; 150 x 6mm fibre cement undercloak; tiles and undercloak bedded and pointed in tinted cement mortar (1:3) and with treble roll verge tiles and aluminium nails	15.15	5.00	15.91	0.17	0.09	4.95	0.79	21.65	m	23.81
valley tiles, Redland Universal valley troughs; laid with 100mm laps	75.93	5.00	79.73	0.34	0.17	9.74	0.69	90.16	m	99.18
Roof coverings; Redland 50 through coloured double roman tiles, 418 x 330mm; fixing every fourth course with galvanised nails to 75mm lap; 38 x 25mm pressure impregnated softwood battens fixed with galvanised nails; twin-ply underlay 145gsm with polypropylene; 150mm laps; fixing with galvanised steel clout nails										
Pitched 40 degrees from horizontal										
generally	14.53	5.00	15.48	0.47	0.24	13.55	1.14	30.17	m²	33.18
Boundary work										
reform eaves filler unit and aluminium nails to each eaves tile	0.45	5.00	0.47	0.07	0.04	2.08	1.17	3.73	m	4.10
ridge or hip tiles, Redland third round; butt jointed; bedding and pointing in tinted cement mortar (1:3)	10.47	5.00	10.99	0.34	0.17	9.74	0.69	21.42	m	23.57
ridge or hip tiles, Redland half round; butt jointed; bedding and pointing in tinted cement mortar (1:3)	10.51	5.00	11.04	0.34	0.17	9.74	0.69	21.47	m	23.62
verges; cloaked verge tiles and aluminium nails	20.85	5.00	21.89	0.17	0.09	4.95	0.12	26.96	m	29.65
verges; half tiles, cloaked verge tiles and aluminium nails	20.85	5.00	21.89	0.17	0.09	4.95	0.12	26.96	m	29.65
verges; plain tile undercloak; tiles and undercloak bedded and pointed in tinted cement mortar (1:3) and with standard tiles and aluminium nails	3.33	5.00	3.50	0.11	0.06	3.23	0.79	7.52	m	8.27
verges; plain tile undercloak; tiles and undercloak bedded and pointed in tinted cement mortar (1:3) and with treble roll verge tiles and aluminium nails	3.33	5.00	3.50	0.11	0.06	3.23	0.79	7.52	m	8.27
verges; 150 x 6mm fibre cement undercloak; tiles and undercloak bedded and pointed in tinted cement mortar (1:3) and with standard tiles and aluminium nails	15.15	5.00	15.91	0.17	0.09	4.95	0.79	21.65	m	23.81
verges; 150 x 6mm fibre cement undercloak; tiles and undercloak bedded and pointed in tinted cement mortar (1:3) and with treble roll verge tiles and aluminium nails	15.15	5.00	15.91	0.17	0.09	4.95	0.79	21.65	m	23.81
valley tiles, Redland Universal valley troughs; laid with 100mm laps	75.93	5.00	79.73	0.34	0.17	9.74	0.69	90.16	m	99.18
Fittings										
Ventilator tiles										
Ridge Vent ridge ventilation terminal 450mm long for										
half round ridge	72.71	5.00	76.35	1.45	0.73	41.63	1.09	119.06	nr	130.97
universal angle ridge	72.71	5.00	76.35	1.45	0.73	41.63	1.09	119.06	nr	130.97
Thruvent tiles for										
Stonewold slates	75.60	5.00	79.38	0.56	0.28	16.05	0.41	95.84	nr	105.42
Regent tiles	70.00	5.00	73.50	0.56	0.28	16.05	0.41	89.96	nr	98.96
Grovebury double pantiles	70.00	5.00	73.50	0.56	0.28	16.05	0.41	89.96	nr	98.96
Fenland pantiles	70.00	5.00	73.50	0.56	0.28	16.05	0.41	89.96	nr	98.96
Redland 49 tiles	70.00	5.00	73.50	0.56	0.28	16.05	0.41	89.96	nr	98.96
Renown tiles	70.00	5.00	73.50	0.56	0.28	16.05	0.41	89.96	nr	98.96
Redland 50 double roman tiles	70.00	5.00	73.50	0.56	0.28	16.05	0.41	89.96	nr	98.96
Red line ventilation tile complete with underlay seal and fixing clips for										
Stonewold slates	80.13	5.00	84.14	1.12	0.56	32.09	0.41	116.64	nr	128.31
Regent tiles	80.13	5.00	84.14	1.12	0.56	32.09	0.41	116.64	nr	128.31
Grovebury double pantiles	80.13	5.00	84.14	1.12	0.56	32.09	0.41	116.64	nr	128.31
Renown tiles	80.13	5.00	84.14	1.12	0.56	32.09	0.41	116.64	nr	128.31
Redland 50 double roman tiles	80.13	5.00	84.14	1.12	0.56	32.09	0.41	116.64	nr	128.31
Eaves ventilation										
Insulation Interupter and roof space ventilator										
Felt support eaves ventilator tray fixing with aluminium nails	1.11	5.00	1.17	0.25	0.12	7.16	0.05	8.38	m	9.22
Over fascia ventilator										
10mm	2.57	5.00	2.70	0.30	0.15	8.60	0.05	11.34	m	12.48
25mm	12.13	5.00	12.74	0.30	0.15	8.60	0.05	21.38	m	23.52

Labour hourly rates: (except Specialists) Craft Operatives 20.87 Labourer 15.57 Rates are national average prices. Refer to REGIONAL VARIATIONS for indicative levels of overall pricing in regions	MATERIALS			LABOUR				RATES		
	Del to Site £	Waste %	Material Cost £	Craft Optve Hrs	Lab Hrs	Labour Cost £	Sunds £	Nett Rate £	Unit	Gross rate (10%) £
INTERLOCKING TILING (Cont'd)										
Fittings (Cont'd)										
Gas terminals										
Gas Flue ridge terminal, 450mm long with sealing gasket and fixing brackets										
half round ridge	140.58	5.00	147.61	1.69	0.84	48.35	1.09	197.05	nr	216.75
extra for 150mm extension adaptor	39.77	5.00	41.76	0.34	0.17	9.74	0.41	51.91	nr	57.11
Hip irons										
galvanised mild steel; 32 x 3 x 380mm girth; scrolled; fixing with galvanised steel screws to timber	1.02	5.00	1.07	0.11	0.06	3.23	-	4.30	nr	4.73
Lead soakers										
fixing only	-	-	-	0.34	0.17	9.74	-	9.74	nr	10.72
FIBRE CEMENT SLATING										
Quantities required for 1m² of slating										
Slates to 70mm lap										
400 x 240mm, 25.3nr										
Slates to 102mm lap										
600 x 300mm, 13nr										
500 x 250mm, 19.5nr										
400 x 200mm, 32nr										
Roof coverings; asbestos-free cement slates, 600 x 300mm; centre fixing with copper nails and copper disc rivets to 102mm lap; 38 x 19mm pressure impregnated softwood battens fixed with galvanised nails; twin-ply underlay 145gsm with polypropylene; 150mm laps; fixing with galvanised steel clout nails										
Pitched 30 degrees from horizontal										
generally	16.28	5.00	17.31	0.60	0.30	17.19	2.64	37.15	m²	40.86
holes	-	-	-	0.58	0.29	16.62	-	16.62	nr	18.28
Boundary work										
abutments; square	1.25	5.00	1.31	0.23	0.12	6.67	-	7.98	m	8.78
abutments; raking	1.87	5.00	1.97	0.28	0.14	8.02	-	9.99	m	10.99
abutments; curved to 3000mm radius	2.50	5.00	2.62	0.35	0.18	10.11	-	12.73	m	14.00
double course at eaves	3.36	5.00	3.53	0.17	0.09	4.95	1.20	9.68	m	10.65
verges; slate undercloak and point in cement mortar (1:3)	1.92	5.00	2.02	0.09	0.05	2.66	0.99	5.66	m	6.23
ridges or hips; asbestos free cement; fixing with nails	22.76	5.00	23.90	0.23	0.12	6.67	0.69	31.26	m	34.38
Roof coverings; asbestos-free cement slates, 600 x 300mm; centre fixing with copper nails and copper disc rivets to 102mm lap; 50 x 25mm pressure impregnated softwood battens fixed with galvanised nails; twin-ply underlay 145gsm with polypropylene; 150mm laps; fixing with galvanised steel clout nails										
Pitched 30 degrees from horizontal										
generally	18.56	5.00	19.82	0.64	0.32	18.34	2.64	40.80	m²	44.88
Roof coverings; asbestos-free cement slates, 600 x 300mm; centre fixing with copper nails and copper disc rivets to 102mm lap (close boarding on rafters included elsewhere); twin-ply underlay 145gsm with polypropylene; 150mm laps; fixing with galvanised steel clout nails										
Pitched 30 degrees from horizontal										
generally	13.16	5.00	13.88	0.48	0.24	13.75	1.93	29.57	m²	32.52
Roof coverings; asbestos-free cement slates, 500 x 250mm; centre fixing with copper nails and copper disc rivets to 102mm lap; 38 x 19mm pressure impregnated softwood battens fixed with galvanised nails; twin-ply underlay 145gsm with polypropylene; 150mm laps; fixing with galvanised steel clout nails										
Pitched 30 degrees from horizontal										
generally	25.05	5.00	26.57	0.67	0.34	19.28	3.60	49.44	m²	54.38
holes	-	-	-	0.58	0.29	16.62	-	16.62	nr	18.28
Boundary work										
abutments; square	2.05	5.00	2.15	0.23	0.12	6.67	-	8.82	m	9.70
abutments; raking	3.08	5.00	3.23	0.35	0.18	10.11	-	13.34	m	14.67
abutments; curved to 3000mm radius	4.09	5.00	4.30	0.46	0.23	13.18	-	17.48	m	19.23
double course at eaves	4.20	5.00	4.41	0.21	0.11	6.10	1.29	11.79	m	12.97
ridges or hips; asbestos free cement; fixing with nails	22.76	5.00	23.90	0.23	0.12	6.67	0.69	31.26	m	34.38
verges; slate undercloak and point in cement mortar (1:3)	2.62	5.00	2.76	0.12	0.06	3.44	1.06	7.25	m	7.98
Roof coverings; asbestos-free cement slates, 500 x 250mm; centre fixing with copper nails and copper disc rivets to 102mm lap; 50 x 25mm pressure impregnated softwood battens fixed with galvanised nails; twin-ply underlay 145gsm with polypropylene; 150mm laps; fixing with galvanised steel clout nails										
Pitched 30 degrees from horizontal										
generally	27.90	5.00	29.70	0.72	0.36	20.63	3.60	53.93	m²	59.32

TILE AND SLATE ROOF AND WALL COVERINGS

Labour hourly rates: (except Specialists) Craft Operatives 20.87 Labourer 15.57 Rates are national average prices. Refer to REGIONAL VARIATIONS for indicative levels of overall pricing in regions	MATERIALS			LABOUR				RATES		
	Del to Site £	Waste %	Material Cost £	Craft Optve Hrs	Lab Hrs	Labour Cost £	Sunds £	Nett Rate £	Unit	Gross rate (10%) £
FIBRE CEMENT SLATING (Cont'd)										
Roof coverings; asbestos-free cement slates, 400 x 200mm; centre fixing with copper nails and copper disc rivets to 102mm lap; 38 x 19mm pressure impregnated softwood battens fixed with galvanised nails; twin-ply underlay 145gsm with polypropylene; 150mm laps; fixing with galvanised steel clout nails										
Pitched 30 degrees from horizontal										
generally	31.92	5.00	33.81	0.71	0.36	20.42	5.46	59.70	m²	65.67
holes	-	-	-	0.58	0.29	16.62	-	16.62	nr	18.28
Boundary work										
abutments; square	2.66	5.00	2.79	0.29	0.15	8.39	-	11.18	m	12.29
abutments; raking	3.98	5.00	4.18	0.44	0.22	12.61	-	16.79	m	18.47
abutments; curved to 3000mm radius	5.31	5.00	5.58	0.58	0.29	16.62	-	22.20	m	24.42
double course at eaves	4.15	5.00	4.36	0.23	0.97	19.90	1.44	25.70	m	28.27
ridges or hips; asbestos free cement; fixing with nails	22.76	5.00	23.90	0.23	0.12	6.67	0.69	31.26	m	34.38
verges; slate undercloak and point in cement mortar (1:3)	2.49	5.00	2.61	0.14	0.07	4.01	1.12	7.75	m	8.52
Roof coverings; asbestos-free cement slates, 400 x 200mm; centre fixing with copper nails and copper disc rivets to 102mm lap; 50 x 25mm pressure impregnated softwood battens fixed with galvanised nails; twin-ply underlay 145gsm with polypropylene; 150mm laps; fixing with galvanised steel clout nails										
Pitched 30 degrees from horizontal										
generally	35.34	5.00	37.58	0.80	0.40	22.92	5.46	65.96	m²	72.56
Fittings										
Hip irons										
galvanised mild steel; 32 x 3 x 380mm girth; scrolled; fixing with galvanised steel screws to timber	1.02	5.00	1.07	0.11	0.06	3.23	-	4.30	nr	4.73
Lead soakers										
fixing only	-	-	-	0.34	0.17	9.74	-	9.74	nr	10.72
NATURAL SLATING										
Quantities required for 1m² of slating										
Slates to 75mm lap 600 x 300mm, 12.65nr 500 x 250mm, 18.9nr 400 x 200mm, 31nr										
Roof coverings; blue/grey slates, 600 x 300mm, 6.5mm thick; fixing with slate nails to 75mm lap; 38 x 19mm pressure impregnated softwood battens fixed with galvanised nails; twin-ply underlay 145gsm with polypropylene; 150mm laps; fixing with galvanised steel clout nails										
Pitched 30 degrees from horizontal										
generally	161.29	5.00	169.58	0.58	0.29	16.62	0.92	187.12	m²	205.83
holes	-	-	-	0.58	0.29	16.62	-	16.62	nr	18.28
Boundary work										
abutments; square	15.31	5.00	16.08	0.17	0.09	4.95	-	21.03	m	23.13
abutments; raking	23.03	5.00	24.18	0.26	0.13	7.45	-	31.63	m	34.80
double course at eaves	43.58	5.00	45.75	0.16	0.08	4.58	0.82	51.16	m	56.28
verges; slate undercloak and point in cement mortar (1:3)	24.90	5.00	26.14	0.09	0.05	2.66	0.76	29.56	m	32.52
Roof coverings; blue/grey slates, 600 x 300mm, 6.5mm thick; fixing with aluminium nails to 75mm lap; 38 x 19mm pressure impregnated softwood battens fixed with galvanised nails; twin-ply underlay 145gsm with polypropylene; 150mm laps; fixing with galvanised steel clout nails										
Pitched 30 degrees from horizontal										
generally	161.29	5.00	169.58	0.58	0.29	16.62	1.83	188.03	m²	206.83
Roof coverings; blue/grey slates, 600 x 300mm, 6.5mm thick; fixing with copper nails to 75mm laps; 38 x 19mm pressure impregnated softwood battens fixed with galvanised nails; twin-ply underlay 145gsm with polypropylene; 150mm laps; fixing with galvanised steel clout nails										
Pitched 30 degrees from horizontal										
generally	161.29	5.00	169.58	0.58	0.29	16.62	2.28	188.47	m²	207.32
Roof coverings; blue/grey slates, 600 x 300mm, 6.5mm thick; fixing with slate nails to 75mm lap; 50 x 25mm pressure impregnated softwood battens fixed with galvanised nails; twin-ply underlay 145gsm with polypropylene; 150mm laps; fixing with galvanised steel clout nails										
Pitched 30 degrees from horizontal										
generally	163.57	5.00	172.08	0.62	0.31	17.77	0.92	190.77	m²	209.85

Labour hourly rates: (except Specialists) Craft Operatives 20.87 Labourer 15.57 Rates are national average prices. Refer to REGIONAL VARIATIONS for indicative levels of overall pricing in regions	MATERIALS			LABOUR				RATES		
	Del to Site £	Waste %	Material Cost £	Craft Optve Hrs	Lab Hrs	Labour Cost £	Sunds £	Nett Rate £	Unit	Gross rate (10%) £
NATURAL SLATING (Cont'd)										
Roof coverings; blue/grey slates, 600 x 300mm, 6.5mm thick; fixing with slate nails to 75mm lap; 50 x 25mm pressure impregnated softwood counterbattens at 1067mm centres and 38 x 19mm pressure impregnated softwood battens fixed with galvanised nails; twin-ply underlay 145gsm with polypropylene; 150mm laps; fixing with galvanised steel clout nails										
Pitched 30 degrees from horizontal										
generally	163.57	5.00	172.08	0.62	0.31	17.77	1.88	191.73	m²	210.90
Roof coverings; blue/grey slates, 500 x 250mm, 6.5mm thick; fixing with slate nails to 75mm lap; 38 x 19mm pressure impregnated softwood battens fixed with galvanised nails; twin-ply underlay 145gsm with polypropylene; 150mm laps; fixing with galvanised steel clout nails										
Pitched 30 degrees from horizontal										
generally	102.67	5.00	108.06	0.67	0.34	19.28	1.37	128.71	m²	141.58
holes	-	-	-	0.58	0.29	16.62	-	16.62	nr	18.28
Boundary work										
abutments; square	9.45	5.00	9.92	0.23	0.12	6.67	-	16.59	m	18.25
abutments; raking	14.17	5.00	14.88	0.35	0.18	10.11	-	24.98	m	27.48
double course at eaves	20.76	5.00	21.80	0.20	0.10	5.73	1.32	28.85	m	31.73
verges; slate undercloak and point in cement mortar (1:3)	12.98	5.00	13.62	0.12	0.06	3.44	0.78	17.84	m	19.62
Roof coverings; blue/grey slates, 500 x 250mm, 6.5mm thick; fixing with aluminium nails to 75mm lap; 38 x 19mm pressure impregnated softwood battens fixed with galvanised nails; twin-ply underlay 145gsm with polypropylene; 150mm laps; fixing with galvanised steel clout nails										
Pitched 30 degrees from horizontal										
generally	102.67	5.00	108.06	0.67	0.34	19.28	2.72	130.06	m²	143.07
Roof coverings; blue/grey slates, 500 x 250mm, 6.5mm thick; fixing with copper nails to 75mm lap; 38 x 19mm pressure impregnated softwood battens fixed with galvanised nails; twin-ply underlay 145gsm with polypropylene; 150mm laps; fixing with galvanised steel clout nails										
Pitched 30 degrees from horizontal										
generally	102.67	5.00	108.06	0.67	0.34	19.28	3.40	130.74	m²	143.81
Roof coverings; blue/grey slates, 500 x 250mm, 6.5mm thick; fixing with slate nails to 75mm lap; 50 x 25mm pressure impregnated softwood battens fixed with galvanised nails; twin-ply underlay 145gsm with polypropylene; 150mm laps; fixing with galvanised steel clout nails										
Pitched 30 degrees from horizontal										
generally	105.52	5.00	111.20	0.72	0.36	20.63	1.37	133.20	m²	146.52
Roof coverings; blue/grey slates, 400 x 200mm, 6.5mm thick; fixing with slate nails to 75mm lap; 38 x 19mm pressure impregnated softwood battens fixed with galvanised nails; twin-ply underlay 145gsm with polypropylene; 150mm laps; fixing with galvanised steel clout nails										
Pitched 30 degrees from horizontal										
generally	86.27	5.00	90.88	0.80	0.40	22.92	2.28	116.08	m²	127.69
holes	-	-	-	0.58	0.29	16.62	-	16.62	nr	18.28
Boundary work										
abutments; square	7.83	5.00	8.22	0.29	0.15	8.39	-	16.61	m	18.27
abutments; raking	11.74	5.00	12.33	0.44	0.22	12.61	-	24.94	m	27.43
double course at eaves	15.66	5.00	16.44	0.23	0.12	6.67	0.68	23.79	m	26.17
verges; slate undercloak and point in cement mortar (1:3)	7.83	5.00	8.22	0.14	0.07	4.01	0.79	13.03	m	14.33
Roof coverings; blue/grey slates, 400 x 200mm, 6.5mm thick; fixing with aluminium nails to 75mm lap; 38 x 19mm pressure impregnated softwood battens fixed with galvanised nails; twin-ply underlay 145gsm with polypropylene; 150mm laps; fixing with galvanised steel clout nails										
Pitched 30 degrees from horizontal										
generally	86.27	5.00	90.88	0.80	0.40	22.92	4.50	118.31	m²	130.14
Roof coverings; blue/grey slates, 400 x200mm, 6.5mm thick; fixing with copper nails to 75mmlap; 38 x 19mm pressure impregnated softwood battens fixed with galvanised nails; twin-ply underlay 145gsm with polypropylene; 150mm laps; fixing with galvanised steel clout nails										
Pitched 30 degrees from horizontal										
generally	86.27	5.00	90.88	0.80	0.40	22.92	5.63	119.43	m²	131.37
Roof coverings; blue/grey slates, 400 x 200mm, 6.5mm thick; fixing with slate nails to 75mm lap; 50 x 25mm pressure impregnated softwood battens fixed with galvanised nails; twin-ply underlay 145gsm with polypropylene; 150mm laps; fixing with galvanised steel clout nails										
Pitched 30 degrees from horizontal										
generally	89.69	5.00	94.64	0.87	0.44	25.01	2.28	121.93	m²	134.12

Labour hourly rates: (except Specialists) Craft Operatives 20.87 Labourer 15.57 Rates are national average prices. Refer to REGIONAL VARIATIONS for indicative levels of overall pricing in regions	MATERIALS			LABOUR				RATES		
	Del to Site	Waste	Material Cost	Craft Optve	Lab	Labour Cost	Sunds	Nett Rate		Gross rate (10%)
	£	%	£	Hrs	Hrs	£	£	£	Unit	£
NATURAL SLATING (Cont'd)										
Roof coverings; green slates, best random fixed in diminishing courses with alloy nails to 75mm lap; 38 x 19mm pressure impregnated softwood battens fixed with galvanised nails; twin-ply underlay 145gsm with polypropylene; 150mm laps; fixing with galvanised steel clout nails										
Pitched 30 degrees from horizontal										
generally	85.11	5.00	89.66	0.86	0.43	24.64	3.35	117.66	m²	129.42
Boundary work										
abutments; square	7.97	5.00	8.37	0.23	0.12	6.67	-	15.04	m	16.55
abutments; raking	11.96	5.00	12.56	0.35	0.18	10.11	-	22.67	m	24.93
double course at eaves	17.40	5.00	18.27	0.23	0.12	6.67	1.67	26.60	m	29.27
verges; slate undercloak and point in cement mortar (1:3)	11.60	5.00	12.18	0.23	0.12	6.67	1.02	19.87	m	21.86
hips, valleys and angles; close mitred	13.05	5.00	13.70	0.40	0.20	11.46	1.07	26.24	m	28.86
Fittings										
Hip irons										
galvanised mild steel; 32 x 3 x 380mm girth; scrolled; fixing with galvanised steel screws to timber	1.02	5.00	1.07	0.11	0.06	3.23	-	4.30	nr	4.73
Lead soakers										
fixing only	-	-	-	0.34	0.17	9.74	-	9.74	nr	10.72
NATURAL OR ARTIFICIAL STONE SLATING										
Roof coverings; Redland Cambrian interlocking slates, 300 x 336mm; fixing every slate with two stainless steel nails and one stainless steel clip to 50mm laps; 38 x 19mm pressure impregnated softwood battens fixed with galvanised nails; twin-ply underlay 145gsm with polypropylene; 150mm laps; fixing with galvanised steel clout nails										
Pitched 40 degrees from horizontal										
generally	34.45	5.00	36.40	0.54	0.27	15.47	3.23	55.11	m²	60.62
Boundary work										
abutments; square	3.06	5.00	3.21	0.11	0.06	3.23	-	6.44	m	7.09
abutments; raking	4.60	5.00	4.83	0.17	0.09	4.95	-	9.78	m	10.76
abutments; curved to 3000mm radius	6.12	5.00	6.42	0.23	0.12	6.67	-	13.09	m	14.40
supplementary fixing at eaves with stainless steel eaves clip to each slate	1.40	5.00	1.47	0.05	0.03	1.51	-	2.98	m	3.27
ridge or hip tiles, Redland third round; butt jointed; bedding and pointing in tinted cement mortar (1:3)	32.36	5.00	33.98	0.23	0.12	6.67	0.69	41.34	m	45.47
ridge or hip tiles, Redland half round; butt jointed; bedding and pointing in tinted cement mortar (1:3)	10.51	5.00	11.04	0.23	0.12	6.67	0.69	18.40	m	20.24
ridge or hip tiles, Redland universal angle; butt jointed; bedding and pointing in tinted cement mortar (1:3)	23.26	5.00	24.42	0.23	0.12	6.67	0.69	31.78	m	34.96
ridge tiles, Redland Dry Ridge system with half round ridge tiles; fixing with stainless steel batten straps and ring shanked fixing nails with neoprene washers and sleeves; polypropylene ridge seals and uPVC profile filler units	26.93	5.00	28.28	0.45	0.23	12.97	-	41.25	m	45.37
ridge tiles, Redland Dry Ridge system with universal angle ridge tiles; fixing with stainless steel batten straps and ring shanked fixing nails with neoprene washers and sleeves; polypropylene ridge seals and uPVC profile filler units	26.93	5.00	28.28	0.45	0.23	12.97	-	41.25	m	45.37
ridge tiles, Redland Dry Vent Ridge system with half round ridge tiles; fixing with stainless steel batten straps and ring shanked nails with neoprene washers and sleeves; polypropylene ridge seals, PVC air flow control units and uPVC ventilated profile filler units	26.93	5.00	28.28	0.45	0.23	12.97	-	41.25	m	45.37
ridge tiles, Redland Dry Vent Ridge system with Universal angle ridge tiles; fixing with stainless steel batten straps and ring shanked nails with neoprene washers and sleeves; polypropylene ridge seals, PVC air flow control units and uPVC ventilated profile filler units	26.93	5.00	28.28	0.45	0.23	12.97	-	41.25	m	45.37
Monoridge filler units in conjunction with top tile, bed tile in nonsetting mastic sealant and screw on through filler unit with screws, washers and caps	30.86	5.00	32.40	0.20	0.12	6.04	-	38.44	m	42.29
verges; 150 x 6mm fibre cement undercloak; slates and undercloak bedded and pointed in tinted cement mortar (1:3) with full slates and a half slates in alternate courses and stainless steel verge clips	8.95	5.00	9.40	0.23	0.12	6.67	3.75	19.81	m	21.79
verges; 150 x 6mm fibre cement undercloak; slates and undercloak bedded and pointed in tinted cement mortar (1:3) with verge slates and slate and a half verge slates in alternate courses and stainless steel verge clips	8.95	5.00	9.40	0.23	0.12	6.67	3.75	19.81	m	21.79
valley tiles, Redland Universal valley troughs; laid with 100mm laps	75.93	5.00	79.73	0.50	0.28	14.79	0.69	95.21	m	104.74
Roof coverings; Redland Cambrian interlocking slates, 300 x 336mm; fixing every slate with two stainless steel nails and one stainless steel clip to 90mm lap; 38 x 25mm pressure impregnated softwood battens fixed with galvanised nails; twin-ply underlay 145gsm with polypropylene; 150mm laps; fixing with galvanised steel clout nails										
Pitched 40 degrees from horizontal										
generally	41.15	5.00	43.47	0.62	0.31	17.77	4.17	65.41	m²	71.95
Boundary work										
abutments; square	3.66	5.00	3.84	0.11	0.06	3.23	-	7.07	m	7.78
abutments; raking	5.47	5.00	5.75	0.17	0.09	4.95	-	10.70	m	11.77
abutments; curved to 3000mm radius	7.31	5.00	7.68	0.23	0.12	6.67	-	14.35	m	15.78

Labour hourly rates: (except Specialists) Craft Operatives 20.87 Labourer 15.57 Rates are national average prices. Refer to REGIONAL VARIATIONS for indicative levels of overall pricing in regions	MATERIALS			LABOUR				RATES		
	Del to Site £	Waste %	Material Cost £	Craft Optve Hrs	Lab Hrs	Labour Cost £	Sunds £	Nett Rate £	Unit	Gross rate (10%) £
NATURAL OR ARTIFICIAL STONE SLATING (Cont'd)										
Fittings										
Ventilator tiles										
Ridge Vent ridge ventilation terminal 450mm long for										
half round ridge	72.71	5.00	76.35	1.45	0.73	41.63	-	117.97	nr	129.77
universal angle ridge	72.71	5.00	76.35	1.45	0.73	41.63	-	117.97	nr	129.77
Redland Cambrian Thruvent interlocking slate complete with weather cap, underlay seal and fixing clips										
slate	75.60	5.00	79.38	0.56	0.28	16.05	-	95.43	nr	104.97
Hip irons										
galvanised mild steel; 32 x 3 x 380mm girth; scrolled; fixing with galvanised steel screws to timber	1.02	5.00	1.07	0.11	0.06	3.23	-	4.30	nr	4.73
Lead soakers										
fixing only	-	-	-	0.34	0.17	9.74	-	9.74	nr	10.72
Fittings										
Timloc uPVC eaves ventilators; reference 1121 fixing with nails to timber at 400mm centres										
330mm wide	0.84	5.00	0.88	0.28	0.14	8.02	0.50	9.40	m	10.34
Timloc uPVC eaves ventilators; reference 1131 fixing with nails to timber at 600mm centres										
330mm wide	1.10	5.00	1.16	0.22	0.11	6.30	0.50	7.96	m	8.75
Timlock uPVC soffit ventilators; reference 1137, 10mm airflow; fixing with screws to timber										
type C	1.02	5.00	1.08	0.17	0.06	4.48	0.20	5.76	m	6.33
Timlock uPVC soffit ventilators; reference 1138, 10mm airflow; fixing with screws to timber										
type C	1.99	5.00	2.09	0.18	0.07	4.85	0.20	7.13	m	7.84
Timlock uPVC Mark 2 eaves ventilators; reference 1122; fitting between trusses at 600mm centres										
300mm girth	3.33	5.00	3.50	0.22	0.11	6.30	0.50	10.30	m	11.33
Timlock polypropylene over-fascia ventilators; reference 3011; fixing with screws to timber										
to top of fascia	2.68	5.00	2.81	0.22	0.11	6.30	0.30	9.42	m	10.36
TIMBER OR BITUMINOUS FELT SHINGLES										
Roof coverings; Western Red Cedar Shingles; fixing every course with silicon bronze annular ring nails to 25mm lap; 38 x 19mm pressure impregnated softwood battens fixed with galvanised nails; twin-ply underlay 145gsm with polypropylene; 150mm laps; fixing with galvanised steel clout nails										
Pitched 45 degrees from horizontal										
generally	53.73	5.00	56.79	0.55	0.55	20.04	-	76.84	m²	84.52
Boundary work										
abutments; square	20.83	5.00	21.88	0.60	0.60	21.86	-	43.74	m	48.11
abutments; raking	20.83	5.00	21.88	1.00	1.00	36.44	-	58.32	m	64.15
abutments; curved to 3000mm radius	20.83	5.00	21.88	1.50	1.50	54.66	-	76.54	m	84.19
eaves course	15.63	5.00	16.41	0.40	0.40	14.58	-	30.98	m	34.08
verges	20.83	5.00	21.88	0.60	0.60	21.86	-	43.74	m	48.11
top cutting to ridge or hip per single side	20.83	5.00	21.88	0.60	0.60	21.86	-	43.74	m	48.11
cutting to valleys and gutters	20.83	5.00	21.88	1.00	1.00	36.44	-	58.32	m	64.15

This page left blank intentionally

Labour hourly rates: (except Specialists) Craft Operatives 20.87 Labourer 15.57 Rates are national average prices. Refer to REGIONAL VARIATIONS for indicative levels of overall pricing in regions	MATERIALS			LABOUR				RATES		
	Del to Site £	Waste %	Material Cost £	Craft Optve Hrs	Lab Hrs	Labour Cost £	Sunds £	Nett Rate £	Unit	Gross rate (10%) £
MASTIC ASPHALT ROOFING										
Roofing; BS 6925 (limestone aggregate); sand rubbing; BS EN 13707 type 4A sheathing felt isolating membrane, butt joints										
Roofing 20mm thick; coats of asphalt -2; to concrete base; pitch not exceeding 6 degrees from horizontal										
width exceeding 500mm	-	-	Specialist	-	-	Specialist	-	47.81	m²	52.59
extra; solid water check roll	-	-	Specialist	-	-	Specialist	-	26.75	m	29.42
Roofing 20mm thick; coats of asphalt -2; to concrete base; pitch 30 degrees from horizontal										
width exceeding 500mm	-	-	Specialist	-	-	Specialist	-	76.64	m²	84.30
Roofing 20mm thick; coats of asphalt -2; to concrete base; pitch 45 degrees from horizontal										
width exceeding 500mm	-	-	Specialist	-	-	Specialist	-	99.91	m²	109.90
Paint two coats of Solar reflective roof paint on surfaces of asphalt										
width exceeding 500mm	-	-	Specialist	-	-	Specialist	-	12.81	m²	14.09
Skirtings 13mm thick; coats of asphalt -2; to brickwork base										
girth not exceeding 150mm	-	-	Specialist	-	-	Specialist	-	31.49	m	34.63
Coverings to kerbs 20mm thick; coats of asphalt -2; to concrete base										
girth 600mm	-	-	Specialist	-	-	Specialist	-	65.15	m	71.66
Jointing new roofing to existing										
20mm thick	-	-	Specialist	-	-	Specialist	-	40.14	m	44.15
Edge trim; aluminium; silver anodized										
priming with bituminous primer; butt joints with internal jointing sleeves; fixing with aluminium alloy screws to timber; working two coat asphalt into grooves -1										
45mm wide x 45mm face depth	3.23	5.00	3.39	0.40	-	8.35	2.81	14.55	m	16.00
50mm wide x 50mm face depth	3.91	5.00	4.10	0.40	-	8.35	2.84	15.29	m	16.82
50mm wide x 100mm face depth	5.34	5.00	5.61	0.40	-	8.35	2.92	16.88	m	18.56
60mm wide x 45mm face depth	4.09	5.00	4.30	0.40	-	8.35	2.92	15.57	m	17.13
60mm wide x 64mm face depth	4.60	5.00	4.83	0.40	-	8.35	3.05	16.23	m	17.86
75mm wide x 75mm face depth	5.37	5.00	5.64	0.40	-	8.35	2.97	16.96	m	18.66
80mm wide x 64mm face depth	5.26	5.00	5.53	0.40	-	8.35	3.05	16.93	m	18.62
80mm wide x 110mm face depth	7.19	5.00	7.55	0.50	-	10.44	3.25	21.24	m	23.36
100mm wide x 75mm face depth	6.23	5.00	6.54	0.50	-	10.44	3.33	20.31	m	22.34
110mm wide x 64mm face depth	6.04	5.00	6.34	0.50	-	10.44	3.33	20.11	m	22.12
150mm wide x 64mm face depth	10.69	5.00	11.23	0.50	-	10.44	3.45	25.11	m	27.62
Edge trim; glass fibre reinforced										
butt joints; fixing with stainless steel screws to timber; working two coat asphalt into grooves -1	4.55	5.00	4.78	0.30	-	6.26	2.46	13.50	m	14.85
Roof Ventilators										
plastic; setting in position	8.48	2.50	8.69	0.75	-	15.65	0.81	25.15	nr	27.67
aluminium; setting in position	10.39	2.50	10.65	0.75	-	15.65	0.81	27.11	nr	29.82
Roofing; BS 6925 (limestone aggregate); covering with 13mm white spar chippings in hot bitumen; BS EN 13707 type 4A sheathing felt isolating membrane; butt joints										
Roofing 20mm thick; coats of asphalt -2; to concrete base; pitch not exceeding 6 degrees from horizontal										
width not exceeding 500mm	-	-	Specialist	-	-	Specialist	-	51.32	m²	56.45
Roofing 20mm thick; coats of asphalt -2; to concrete base; pitch 30 degrees from horizontal										
width not exceeding 500mm	-	-	Specialist	-	-	Specialist	-	76.91	m²	84.61
ASPHALT TANKING OR DAMP PROOFING										
Tanking and damp proofing BS 6925 (limestone aggregate)										
Tanking and damp proofing 13mm thick; coats of asphalt -1; to concrete base; horizontal										
work subsequently covered										
width not exceeding 500mm	-	-	Specialist	-	-	Specialist	-	19.43	m	21.37
width exceeding 500mm	-	-	Specialist	-	-	Specialist	-	30.56	m²	33.62
Tanking and damp proofing 20mm thick; coats of asphalt -2; to concrete base; horizontal										
work subsequently covered										
width not exceeding 500mm	-	-	Specialist	-	-	Specialist	-	24.43	m	26.87
width exceeding 500mm	-	-	Specialist	-	-	Specialist	-	44.42	m²	48.86
Tanking and damp proofing 30mm thick; coats of asphalt -3; to concrete base; horizontal										
work subsequently covered										
width not exceeding 500mm	-	-	Specialist	-	-	Specialist	-	34.89	m	38.38
width exceeding 500mm	-	-	Specialist	-	-	Specialist	-	63.38	m²	69.72

Labour hourly rates: (except Specialists) Craft Operatives 20.87 Labourer 15.57 Rates are national average prices. Refer to REGIONAL VARIATIONS for indicative levels of overall pricing in regions	MATERIALS			LABOUR				RATES		
	Del to Site £	Waste %	Material Cost £	Craft Optve Hrs	Lab Hrs	Labour Cost £	Sunds £	Nett Rate £	Unit	Gross rate (10%) £
ASPHALT TANKING OR DAMP PROOFING (Cont'd)										
Tanking and damp proofing BS 6925 (limestone aggregate) (Cont'd)										
Tanking and damp proofing 20mm thick; coats of asphalt -2; to concrete base; vertical										
work subsequently covered										
width not exceeding 500mm	-	-	Specialist	-	-	Specialist	-	55.73	m	61.31
width exceeding 500mm	-	-	Specialist	-	-	Specialist	-	101.34	m²	111.47
Tanking and damp proofing 20mm thick; coats of asphalt -3; to concrete base; vertical										
work subsequently covered										
width not exceeding 500mm	-	-	Specialist	-	-	Specialist	-	77.06	m	84.77
width exceeding 500mm	-	-	Specialist	-	-	Specialist	-	140.13	m²	154.14
Internal angle fillets to concrete base; priming base with bitumen two coats; work subsequently covered	-	-	Specialist	-	-	Specialist	-	14.62	m	16.09
APPLIED LIQUID TANKING OR DAMP PROOFING										
Synthaprufe bituminous emulsion; blinding with sand										
Coverings, coats -2; to concrete base; horizontal										
width not exceeding 500mm	3.82	10.00	4.21	-	0.13	2.02	0.12	6.35	m	6.98
width exceeding 500mm	7.65	10.00	8.41	-	0.20	3.11	0.21	11.74	m²	12.91
Coverings, coats -3; to concrete base; horizontal										
width not exceeding 500mm	5.71	10.00	6.28	-	0.18	2.80	0.12	9.20	m	10.12
width exceeding 500mm	11.41	10.00	12.56	-	0.28	4.36	0.21	17.13	m²	18.84
Coverings; coats -2; to concrete base; vertical										
width not exceeding 500mm	3.82	10.00	4.21	-	0.20	3.11	0.12	7.44	m	8.18
width exceeding 500mm	7.65	10.00	8.41	-	0.30	4.67	0.21	13.30	m²	14.63
Coverings; coats -3; to concrete base; vertical										
width not exceeding 500mm	5.71	10.00	6.28	-	0.28	4.36	0.12	10.75	m	11.83
width exceeding 500mm	11.41	10.00	12.56	-	0.42	6.54	0.21	19.31	m²	21.24
Bituminous emulsion										
Coverings, coats -2; to concrete base; horizontal										
width not exceeding 500mm	1.33	10.00	1.47	-	0.12	1.95	0.12	3.53	m	3.88
width exceeding 500mm	2.67	10.00	2.93	-	0.20	3.11	0.23	6.28	m²	6.91
Coverings, coats -3; to concrete base; horizontal										
width not exceeding 500mm	1.87	10.00	2.05	-	0.18	2.80	0.12	4.97	m	5.47
width exceeding 500mm	3.73	10.00	4.11	-	0.28	4.36	0.23	8.70	m²	9.57
Coverings; coats -2; to concrete base; vertical										
width not exceeding 500mm	1.33	10.00	1.47	-	0.19	2.96	0.12	4.54	m	4.99
width exceeding 500mm	2.67	10.00	2.93	-	0.30	4.67	0.23	7.83	m²	8.62
Coverings; coats -3; to concrete base; vertical										
width not exceeding 500mm	1.87	10.00	2.05	-	0.27	4.20	0.12	6.37	m	7.01
width exceeding 500mm	3.73	10.00	4.11	-	0.42	6.54	0.23	10.88	m²	11.96
R.I.W. liquid asphaltic composition										
Coverings, coats -2; to concrete base; horizontal										
width not exceeding 500mm	8.06	10.00	8.86	-	0.15	2.34	0.12	11.31	m	12.44
width exceeding 500mm	16.11	10.00	17.72	-	0.23	3.58	0.23	21.54	m²	23.69
Coverings, coats -3; to concrete base; horizontal										
width not exceeding 500mm	12.18	10.00	13.39	-	0.21	3.27	0.12	16.78	m	18.46
width exceeding 500mm	24.26	10.00	26.69	-	0.32	4.98	0.23	31.90	m²	35.09
Coverings; coats -2; to concrete base; vertical										
width not exceeding 500mm	8.06	10.00	8.86	-	0.23	3.58	0.12	12.56	m	13.81
width exceeding 500mm	16.11	10.00	17.72	-	0.35	5.45	0.23	23.40	m²	25.75
Coverings; coats -3; to concrete base; vertical										
width not exceeding 500mm	12.18	10.00	13.39	-	0.32	4.98	0.12	18.49	m	20.34
width exceeding 500mm	24.26	10.00	26.69	-	0.48	7.47	0.23	34.39	m²	37.83
FLEXIBLE SHEET TANKING OR DAMP PROOFING										
Polythene sheeting; 100mm welted laps										
Tanking and damp proofing; 125mu										
horizontal; on concrete base	0.45	20.00	0.54	-	0.06	0.93	-	1.47	m²	1.62
vertical; on concrete base	0.45	20.00	0.54	-	0.09	1.40	-	1.94	m²	2.13
Tanking and damp proofing; 250mu										
horizontal; on concrete base	0.30	20.00	0.36	-	0.09	1.40	-	1.76	m²	1.94
vertical; on concrete base	0.30	20.00	0.36	-	0.14	2.18	-	2.54	m²	2.80
Tanking and damp proofing; 300mu										
horizontal; on concrete base	0.31	20.00	0.38	-	0.11	1.71	-	2.09	m²	2.30
vertical; on concrete base	0.31	20.00	0.38	-	0.17	2.65	-	3.02	m²	3.33
Bituthene 4000 self adhesive damp proof membrane; 25mm lapped joints										
Tanking and damp proofing										
horizontal; on concrete base	8.59	20.00	10.31	-	0.18	2.80	-	13.12	m²	14.43
vertical; on concrete base	8.59	20.00	10.31	-	0.27	4.20	-	14.52	m²	15.97

Labour hourly rates: (except Specialists) Craft Operatives 20.87 Labourer 15.57 Rates are national average prices. Refer to REGIONAL VARIATIONS for indicative levels of overall pricing in regions	MATERIALS			LABOUR				RATES		
	Del to Site £	Waste %	Material Cost £	Craft Optve Hrs	Lab Hrs	Labour Cost £	Sunds £	Nett Rate £	Unit	Gross rate (10%) £
FLEXIBLE SHEET TANKING OR DAMP PROOFING (Cont'd)										
Bituthene 500X self adhesive damp proof membrane; 75mm lapped joints										
Tanking and damp proofing										
horizontal; on concrete base	9.41	20.00	11.30	-	0.23	3.58	-	14.88	m²	16.36
vertical; on concrete base; priming with Servicised B primer	9.41	20.00	11.30	-	0.35	5.45	0.43	17.17	m²	18.89
British Sisalkraft Ltd 728 damp proof membrane; 150mm laps sealed with tape										
Tanking and damp proofing										
horizontal; on concrete base	2.20	25.00	2.75	-	0.08	1.25	0.18	4.18	m²	4.59
Visqueen 1200 super damp proof membrane; 150mm laps sealed with tape and mastic										
Tanking and damp proofing										
horizontal; on concrete base	0.39	20.00	0.47	-	0.08	1.25	0.18	1.90	m²	2.09

This page left blank intentionally

Labour hourly rates: (except Specialists) Craft Operatives 20.87 Labourer 15.57 Rates are national average prices. Refer to REGIONAL VARIATIONS for indicative levels of overall pricing in regions	MATERIALS			LABOUR				RATES		
	Del to Site £	Waste %	Material Cost £	Craft Optve Hrs	Lab Hrs	Labour Cost £	Sunds £	Nett Rate £	Unit	Gross rate (10%) £
METAL FRAMED SYSTEMS TO WALLS AND CEILINGS; UNDER PURLIN/INSIDE RAIL PANEL LININGS										
Gypliner metal grid fixing system; square edge sheeting of one layer 12.5mm thick Gyproc wallboard, BS EN 520, butt joints; screwing to mild steel grid.										
12.5mm thick linings to walls										
width exceeding 300mm	14.60	5.00	15.34	0.80	0.40	22.92	0.44	38.71	m²	42.58
width not exceeding 300mm	19.25	5.00	20.22	0.48	0.12	11.89	0.44	32.54	m	35.80
12.5mm thick linings to ceilings										
width exceeding 300mm	14.42	5.00	15.16	1.00	0.50	28.66	0.44	44.26	m²	48.68
width not exceeding 300mm	12.62	5.00	13.25	0.60	0.15	14.86	0.44	28.54	m	31.40
METAL FRAMED SYSTEMS TO WALLS AND CEILINGS										
Metal stud partitions; proprietary partitions; Gyproc Gypwall metal stud; tapered edge sheeting of one layer 12.5mm thick Gyproc wallboard for direct decoration, BS EN 520, butt joints; applying continuous beads of Gyproc acoustical sealant to perimeters of construction both sides, fixing with Pozidriv head screws to steel frame comprising 50mm head and floor channels, 48mm vertical studs at 600mm centres; butt joints filled with joint filler tape and joint finish, spot filling; fixing to masonry with cartridge fired nails										
Height 2100 - 2400mm, 75mm thick boarded both sides	65.39	5.00	68.67	2.50	1.25	71.64	-	140.31	m	154.34
Metal stud partitions; proprietary partitions; Gyproc Gypwall metal stud; tapered edge sheeting of two layers 12.5mm thick Gyproc wallboard for direct decoration, BS EN 520, butt joints; applying continuous beads of Gyproc acoustical sealant to perimeters of construction both sides, fixing with Pozidriv head screws to steel frame comprising 50mm head and floor channels, 48mm vertical studs at 600mm centres; butt joints filled with joint filler tape and joint finish, spot filling; fixing to masonry with cartridge fired nails										
Height 2100 - 2400mm, 100mm thick boarded both sides	111.63	5.00	117.22	2.80	1.40	80.23	-	197.45	m	217.20
Height 2400 - 2700mm, 100mm thick boarded both sides	124.08	5.00	130.29	3.15	1.58	90.34	-	220.63	m	242.69
Height 2700 - 3000mm, 100mm thick boarded both sides	136.52	5.00	143.36	3.50	1.75	100.29	-	243.65	m	268.01
Angles to partitions; fixing end studs together through partition; extending sheeting to one side across end of partition; joints filled with joint filler tape and joint finish										
Plain										
75mm thick partitions	2.31	10.00	2.46	0.10	-	2.09	-	4.55	m	5.01
100mm thick partitions	2.55	10.00	2.72	0.10	-	2.09	-	4.81	m	5.29

This page left blank intentionally

Labour hourly rates: (except Specialists) Craft Operatives 20.87 Labourer 15.57 Rates are national average prices. Refer to REGIONAL VARIATIONS for indicative levels of overall pricing in regions	MATERIALS			LABOUR				RATES		
	Del to Site £	Waste %	Material Cost £	Craft Optve Hrs	Lab Hrs	Labour Cost £	Sunds £	Nett Rate £	Unit	Gross rate (10%) £
PATENT GLAZING, CURTAIN WALLING & RAINSCREEN CLADDING										
Patent glazing with aluminium alloy bars 2000mm long with aluminium wings and seatings for glass, spaced at approximately 600mm centres, glazed with BS 952 Georgian wired cast, 7mm thick										
Walls; vertical surfaces; exceeding 600 wide										
single tier	175.53	5.00	184.31	1.70	1.70	61.95	4.26	250.51	m²	275.56
multi-tier	186.35	5.00	195.67	1.95	1.95	71.06	4.26	270.98	m²	298.08
Roof areas; exceeding 600 wide										
single tier	158.91	5.00	166.86	1.68	1.68	61.22	4.26	232.33	m²	255.57
multi-tier	169.61	5.00	178.09	1.95	1.95	71.06	4.26	253.40	m²	278.74
Patent glazing with aluminium alloy bars 2000mm long with aluminium wings and seatings for glass, spaced at approximately 600mm centres, glazed with BS 952 Georgian wired polished, 6mm thick										
Walls; vertical surfaces; exceeding 600 wide										
single tier	254.96	5.00	267.71	1.90	1.90	69.24	4.26	341.20	m²	375.32
multi-tier	270.40	5.00	283.92	2.20	2.20	80.17	4.26	368.34	m²	405.18
Roof areas; exceeding 600 wide										
single tier	238.30	5.00	250.22	1.90	1.90	69.24	4.26	323.71	m²	356.08
multi-tier	255.20	5.00	267.96	2.20	2.20	80.17	4.26	352.38	m²	387.62
Patent glazing with aluminium alloy bars 3000mm long with aluminium wings and seatings for glass, spaced at approximately 600mm centres, glazed with BS 952 Georgian wired cast, 7mm thick										
Walls; vertical surfaces; exceeding 600 wide										
single tier	201.78	5.00	211.87	1.70	1.70	61.95	4.26	278.07	m²	305.88
multi-tier	214.57	5.00	225.29	1.95	1.95	71.06	4.26	300.61	m²	330.67
Roof areas; exceeding 600 wide										
single tier	186.61	5.00	195.94	1.70	1.70	61.95	4.26	262.15	m²	288.36
multi-tier	197.82	5.00	207.72	1.95	1.95	71.06	4.26	283.03	m²	311.33
Patent glazing with aluminium alloy bars 3000mm long with aluminium wings and seatings for glass, spaced at approximately 600mm centres, glazed with BS 952 Georgian wired polished, 6mm thick										
Walls; vertical surfaces; exceeding 600 wide										
single tier	280.49	5.00	294.52	1.90	1.90	69.24	4.26	368.01	m²	404.81
multi-tier	179.55	5.00	188.52	2.20	2.20	80.17	4.26	272.95	m²	300.24
Roof areas; exceeding 600 wide										
single tier	264.30	5.00	277.51	1.90	1.90	69.24	4.26	351.00	m²	386.10
multi-tier	283.14	5.00	297.30	2.20	2.20	80.17	4.26	381.72	m²	419.89
Extra over patent glazing in roof areas with aluminium alloy bars 2000mm long with aluminium wings and seatings for glass, spaced at approximately 600mm centres, glazed with BS 952 Georgian wired polished, 6mm thick										
Opening lights including opening gear										
600 x 600mm	320.76	5.00	336.79	5.00	5.00	182.20	-	518.99	nr	570.89
600 x 900mm	386.25	5.00	405.56	6.30	6.30	229.57	-	635.14	nr	698.65
Extra over patent glazing in roof areas with aluminium alloy bars 2000mm long with aluminium wings and seatings for glass, spaced at approximately 600mm centres, glazed with BS 952 Georgian wired cast, 7mm thick										
Opening lights including opening gear										
600 x 600mm	320.14	5.00	336.15	4.60	4.60	167.62	-	503.77	nr	554.15
600 x 900mm	386.24	5.00	405.55	5.75	5.75	209.53	-	615.08	nr	676.59
Extra over patent glazing in vertical surfaces with aluminium alloy bars 3000mm long with aluminium wings and seatings for glass, spaced at approximately 600mm centres, glazed with BS 952 Georgian wired cast, 7mm thick										
Opening lights including opening gear										
600 x 600mm	461.65	5.00	484.73	2.30	2.30	83.81	-	568.55	nr	625.40
600 x 900mm	558.59	5.00	586.52	3.50	3.50	127.54	-	714.06	nr	785.46

Labour hourly rates: (except Specialists) Craft Operatives 20.87 Labourer 15.57 Rates are national average prices. Refer to REGIONAL VARIATIONS for indicative levels of overall pricing in regions	MATERIALS			LABOUR				RATES		
	Del to Site £	Waste %	Material Cost £	Craft Optve Hrs	Lab Hrs	Labour Cost £	Sunds £	Nett Rate £	Unit	Gross rate (10%) £
PATENT GLAZING, CURTAIN WALLING & RAINSCREEN CLADDING (Cont'd)										
Extra over patent glazing to vertical surfaces with aluminium alloy bars 3000mm long with aluminium wings and seatings for glass, spaced at approximately 600mm centres, glazed with BS 952 Georgian wired polished, 6mm thick										
Opening lights including opening gear										
600 x 600mm	461.70	5.00	484.79	2.55	2.55	92.92	-	577.71	nr	635.48
600 x 900mm	558.68	5.00	586.62	3.75	3.75	136.65	-	723.27	nr	795.59
WEATHERBOARDING										
Softwood, wrought, impregnated										
Boarding to walls, shiplapped joints; 19mm thick, 125mm wide boards										
width exceeding 600mm; fixing to timber	13.69	10.00	15.06	0.90	0.11	20.50	0.25	35.80	m²	39.38
Boarding to walls, shiplapped joints; 25mm thick, 150mm wide boards										
width exceeding 600mm; fixing to timber	19.93	10.00	21.92	0.90	0.11	20.50	0.25	42.66	m²	46.93
Western Red Cedar										
Boarding to walls, shiplapped joints; 19mm thick, 150mm wide boards										
width exceeding 600mm; fixing to timber	74.80	10.00	82.28	0.90	0.12	20.65	0.25	103.18	m²	113.50
Boarding to walls, shiplapped joints; 25mm thick, 150mm wide boards										
width exceeding 600mm; fixing to timber	60.44	10.00	66.49	0.95	0.12	21.69	0.25	88.43	m²	97.27
Abutments										
19mm thick softwood boarding										
raking cutting	1.37	10.00	1.51	0.07	-	1.46	-	2.97	m	3.26
curved cutting	2.05	10.00	2.26	0.10	-	2.09	-	4.35	m	4.78
25mm thick softwood boarding										
raking cutting	1.99	10.00	2.19	0.08	-	1.67	-	3.86	m	4.25
curved cutting	2.99	10.00	3.29	0.12	-	2.50	-	5.79	m	6.37
19mm thick Western Red Cedar boarding										
raking cutting	7.48	10.00	8.23	0.09	-	1.88	-	10.11	m	11.12
curved cutting	11.22	10.00	12.34	0.13	-	2.71	-	15.06	m	16.56
25mm thick Western Red Cedar boarding										
raking cutting	6.04	10.00	6.65	0.10	-	2.09	-	8.74	m	9.61
curved cutting	9.07	10.00	9.97	0.15	-	3.13	-	13.10	m	14.41
PROFILED SHEET CLADDING OR ROOFING; FIBRE CEMENT										
Roof coverings; corrugated reinforced cement Profile 3 sheeting, standard grey colour; lapped one and a half corrugations at sides and 150mm at ends										
Coverings; fixing to timber joists at 900mm general spacing with galvanised mild steel drive screws and washers; drilling holes										
width exceeding 600mm; pitch 30 degrees from horizontal	18.64	15.00	21.43	0.28	0.28	10.20	0.79	32.43	m²	35.67
Coverings; fixing to steel purlins at 900mm general spacing with galvanised hook bolts and washers; drilling holes										
width exceeding 600mm; pitch 30 degrees from horizontal	18.64	15.00	21.43	0.38	0.38	13.85	1.62	36.90	m²	40.59
Extra for										
Holes										
for pipes, standards or the like	-	-	-	0.58	-	12.10	-	12.10	nr	13.32
Boundary work										
Ridges										
two piece plain angular adjustable ridge tiles	17.03	10.00	18.73	0.23	0.23	8.38	-	27.11	m	29.82
Bottom edges; Aprons/sills										
apron flashings	24.64	10.00	27.10	0.15	0.15	5.47	-	32.57	m	35.83
Eaves										
eaves filler pieces	2.25	10.00	2.48	0.12	0.12	4.37	-	6.85	m	7.53
Verge barge boards										
standard barge boards	11.35	10.00	12.49	0.12	0.12	4.37	-	16.86	m	18.55
Finials										
standard ridge cap finials	18.57	10.00	20.43	0.17	0.17	6.19	-	26.62	nr	29.28
Cutting										
raking	3.73	15.00	4.29	0.28	0.28	10.20	-	14.49	m	15.94
Roof coverings; corrugated reinforced cement Profile 3 sheeting, standard coloured; lapped one and a half corrugations at sides and 150mm at ends										
Coverings; fixing to timber joists at 900mm general spacing with galvanised mild steel drive screws and washers; drilling holes										
width exceeding 600mm; pitch 30 degrees from horizontal	22.83	15.00	26.26	0.28	0.28	10.20	1.06	37.51	m²	41.27
Coverings; fixing to steel purlins at 900mm general spacing with galvanised hook bolts and washers; drilling holes										
width exceeding 600mm; pitch 30 degrees from horizontal	22.83	15.00	26.26	0.38	0.38	13.85	2.08	42.18	m²	46.40
Extra for										
Holes										
for pipes, standards or the like	-	-	-	0.58	-	12.10	-	12.10	nr	13.32

Labour hourly rates: (except Specialists) Craft Operatives 20.87 Labourer 15.57 Rates are national average prices. Refer to REGIONAL VARIATIONS for indicative levels of overall pricing in regions	MATERIALS			LABOUR				RATES		
	Del to Site £	Waste %	Material Cost £	Craft Optve Hrs	Lab Hrs	Labour Cost £	Sunds £	Nett Rate £	Unit	Gross rate (10%) £
PROFILED SHEET CLADDING OR ROOFING; FIBRE CEMENT (Cont'd)										
Roof coverings; corrugated reinforced cement Profile 3 sheeting, standard coloured; lapped one and a half corrugations at sides and 150mm at ends (Cont'd)										
Boundary work Ridges two piece plain angular adjustable ridge tiles	24.30	10.00	26.73	0.23	0.23	8.38	-	35.11	m	38.62
Bottom edges; Aprons/sills apron flashings	21.32	10.00	23.46	0.15	0.15	5.47	-	28.92	m	31.81
Eaves eaves filler pieces	2.25	10.00	2.48	0.12	0.12	4.37	-	6.85	m	7.53
Barge boards standard barge boards	16.35	10.00	17.98	0.12	0.12	4.37	-	22.36	m	24.59
Finials standard ridge cap finials	29.74	10.00	32.71	0.17	0.17	6.19	-	38.91	nr	42.80
Cutting raking	4.57	15.00	5.25	0.28	0.28	10.20	-	15.45	m	17.00
Roof coverings; corrugated reinforced cement Profile 6 sheeting, standard grey colour; lapped half a corrugation at sides and 150mm at ends										
Coverings; fixing to timber joists at 900mm general spacing with galvanised mild steel drive screws and washers; drilling holes; exceeding 600 wide pitch 30 degrees from horizontal	9.17	15.00	10.54	0.28	0.28	10.20	0.86	21.60	m²	23.76
Coverings; fixing to steel purlins at 900mm general spacing with galvanised hook bolts and washers; drilling holes; exceeding 600 wide pitch 30 degrees from horizontal	9.17	15.00	10.54	0.38	0.38	13.85	1.68	26.07	m²	28.68
Extra for Holes for pipes, standards or the like	-	-	-	0.58	-	12.10	-	12.10	nr	13.32
Boundary work Ridges two piece plain angular adjustable ridge tiles	12.78	10.00	14.06	0.23	0.23	8.38	-	22.44	m	24.68
Bottom edges; Aprons/sills apron flashings	16.68	10.00	18.35	0.15	0.15	5.47	-	23.81	m	26.20
Eaves eaves filler pieces	2.25	10.00	2.48	0.12	0.12	4.37	-	6.85	m	7.53
Barge boards standard barge boards	11.35	10.00	12.49	0.12	0.12	4.37	-	16.86	m	18.55
Finials standard ridge cap finials	16.27	10.00	17.90	0.17	0.17	6.19	-	24.09	nr	26.50
Cutting raking	1.83	15.00	2.11	0.28	0.28	10.20	-	12.31	m	13.54
Roof coverings; corrugated reinforced cement Profile 6 sheeting, standard coloured; lapped half a corrugation at sides and 150mm at ends										
Coverings; fixing to timber joists at 900mm general spacing with galvanised mild steel drive screws and washers; drilling holes; exceeding 600 wide pitch 30 degrees from horizontal	12.79	15.00	14.71	0.28	0.28	10.20	1.04	25.95	m²	28.55
Coverings; fixing to steel purlins at 900mm general spacing with galvanised hook bolts and washers; drilling holes; exceeding 600 wide pitch 30 degrees from horizontal	12.79	15.00	14.71	0.38	0.38	13.85	2.08	30.64	m²	33.70
Extra for Holes for pipes, standards or the like	-	-	-	0.58	-	12.10	-	12.10	nr	13.32
Boundary work Ridges two piece plain angular adjustable ridge tiles	17.90	10.00	19.69	0.23	0.23	8.38	-	28.07	m	30.88
Bottom edges; Aprons/sills apron flashings	16.87	10.00	18.56	0.15	0.15	5.47	-	24.02	m	26.43
Eaves eaves filler pieces	2.25	10.00	2.48	0.12	0.12	4.37	-	6.85	m	7.53
Barge boards standard barge boards	16.90	10.00	18.59	0.12	0.12	4.37	-	22.97	m	25.26
Finials standard ridge cap finials	21.90	10.00	24.09	0.17	0.17	6.19	-	30.28	nr	33.31
Cutting raking	2.56	15.00	2.94	0.28	0.28	10.20	-	13.15	m	14.46
PROFILED SHEET CLADDING OR ROOFING; METAL										
Wall cladding; PVC colour coated both sides galvanised steel profiled sheeting 0.50mm thick and with sheets secured at seams and laps										
Coverings; fixing to steel rails at 900mm general spacing with galvanised hook bolts and washers; drilling holes; exceeding 600 wide pitch 90 degrees from horizontal	11.75	5.00	12.34	0.40	0.40	14.58	1.95	28.86	m²	31.75
Angles; internal vertical corner flashings	6.58	5.00	6.91	0.17	0.17	6.19	-	13.11	m	14.42

Labour hourly rates: (except Specialists) Craft Operatives 20.87 Labourer 15.57 Rates are national average prices. Refer to REGIONAL VARIATIONS for indicative levels of overall pricing in regions	MATERIALS			LABOUR				RATES		
	Del to Site £	Waste %	Material Cost £	Craft Optve Hrs	Lab Hrs	Labour Cost £	Sunds £	Nett Rate £	Unit	Gross rate (10%) £
PROFILED SHEET CLADDING OR ROOFING; METAL (Cont'd)										
Wall cladding; PVC colour coated both sides galvanised steel profiled sheeting 0.50mm thick and with sheets secured at seams and laps (Cont'd)										
Angles; external										
vertical corner flashings	6.58	5.00	6.91	0.17	0.17	6.19	-	13.11	m	14.42
Filler blocks										
PVC	1.44	5.00	1.51	0.12	0.12	4.37	-	5.88	m	6.47
Cutting										
raking	2.35	5.00	2.47	0.28	0.28	10.20	-	12.67	m	13.94
Wall cladding; PVC colour coated both sides galvanised steel profiled sheeting 0.70mm thick and with sheets secured at seams and laps										
Coverings; fixing to steel rails at 900mm general spacing with galvanised hook bolts and washers; drilling holes; exceeding 600 wide										
pitch 90 degrees from horizontal	15.25	5.00	16.01	0.40	0.40	14.58	1.95	32.54	m²	35.79
Angles; internal										
vertical corner flashings	6.58	5.00	6.91	0.17	0.17	6.19	-	13.11	m	14.42
Angles; external										
vertical corner flashings	6.58	5.00	6.91	0.17	0.17	6.19	-	13.11	m	14.42
Filler blocks										
PVC	1.44	5.00	1.51	0.12	0.12	4.37	-	5.88	m	6.47
Cutting										
raking	3.05	5.00	3.20	0.28	0.28	10.20	-	13.41	m	14.75
Roof coverings; PVC colour coated both sides galvanised steel profiled sheeting 0.70mm thick and with sheets secured at seams and laps										
Coverings; fixing to steel purlins at 900mm general spacing with galvanised hook bolts and washers; drilling holes; exceeding 600 wide										
pitch 30 degrees from horizontal	15.25	5.00	16.01	0.35	0.35	12.75	2.01	30.78	m²	33.86
Boundary work										
Ridges										
ridge cappings	6.58	5.00	6.91	0.17	0.17	6.19	-	13.11	m	14.42
Flashings										
gable flashings	7.35	5.00	7.72	0.17	0.17	6.19	-	13.91	m	15.30
eaves flashings	7.35	5.00	7.72	0.17	0.17	6.19	-	13.91	m	15.30
Filler blocks										
PVC	1.44	5.00	1.51	0.12	0.12	4.37	-	5.88	m	6.47
Cutting										
raking	3.05	5.00	3.20	0.28	0.28	10.20	-	13.41	m	14.75
PROFILED SHEET CLADDING OR ROOFING; PLASTICS										
Roof coverings; standard corrugated glass fibre reinforced translucent sheeting; lapped one and a half corrugations at sides and 150mm at ends										
Coverings; fixing to timber joists at 900mm general spacing with galvanised mild steel drive screws and washers; drilling holes; exceeding 600 wide										
pitch 30 degrees from horizontal	15.34	5.00	16.11	0.28	0.28	10.20	0.54	26.86	m²	29.54
Coverings; fixing to steel purlins at 900mm general spacing with galvanised hook bolts and washers; drilling holes; exceeding 600 wide										
pitch 30 degrees from horizontal	15.34	5.00	16.11	0.35	0.35	12.75	0.68	29.54	m²	32.49
Cutting										
raking	3.07	5.00	3.22	0.28	0.28	10.20	-	13.43	m	14.77
Roof coverings; fire resisting corrugated glass fibre reinforced translucent sheeting; lapped one and a half corrugations at sides and 150mm at ends										
Coverings; fixing to timber joists at 900mm general spacing with galvanised mild steel drive screws and washers; drilling holes; exceeding 600 wide										
pitch 30 degrees from horizontal	26.81	5.00	28.15	0.28	0.28	10.20	0.54	38.90	m²	42.78
Coverings; fixing to steel purlins at 900mm general spacing with galvanised hook bolts and washers; drilling holes; exceeding 600 wide										
pitch 30 degrees from horizontal	26.81	5.00	28.15	0.35	0.35	12.75	0.87	41.78	m²	45.95
Cutting										
raking	5.36	5.00	5.63	0.28	0.28	10.20	-	15.83	m	17.42
Roof coverings; standard vinyl corrugated sheeting; lapped one and a half corrugations at sides and 150mm at ends										
Coverings; fixing to timber joists at 900mm general spacing with galvanised mild steel drive screws and washers; drilling holes; exceeding 600 wide										
pitch 30 degrees from horizontal	8.16	5.00	8.57	0.28	0.28	10.20	0.87	19.65	m²	21.61

Labour hourly rates: (except Specialists) Craft Operatives 20.87 Labourer 15.57 Rates are national average prices. Refer to REGIONAL VARIATIONS for indicative levels of overall pricing in regions	MATERIALS			LABOUR				RATES		
	Del to Site £	Waste %	Material Cost £	Craft Optve Hrs	Lab Hrs	Labour Cost £	Sunds £	Nett Rate £	Unit	Gross rate (10%) £
PROFILED SHEET CLADDING OR ROOFING; PLASTICS (Cont'd)										
Roof coverings; standard vinyl corrugated sheeting; lapped one and a half corrugations at sides and 150mm at ends (Cont'd)										
Coverings; fixing to steel purlins at 900mm general spacing with galvanised hook bolts and washers; drilling holes; exceeding 600 wide										
pitch 30 degrees from horizontal	8.16	5.00	8.57	0.35	0.35	12.75	0.87	22.20	m²	24.42
Cutting										
raking	1.63	5.00	1.71	0.28	0.28	10.20	-	11.92	m	13.11
Wall cladding; Swish Products high impact rigid uPVC profiled sections; colour white; secured with starter sections and clips										
Coverings with shiplap profile code C002 giving 150mm cover; fixing to timber; exceeding 600 wide										
vertical cladding										
sections applied horizontally	64.60	5.00	67.83	0.42	0.42	15.30	3.25	86.39	m²	95.02
sections applied vertically	64.60	5.00	67.83	0.42	0.42	15.30	3.25	86.39	m²	95.02
Coverings with open V profile code C003 giving 150mm cover; fixing to timber; exceeding 600 wide										
vertical cladding										
sections applied horizontally	64.60	5.00	67.83	0.45	0.45	16.40	4.64	88.86	m²	97.75
sections applied vertically	64.60	5.00	67.83	0.45	0.45	16.40	4.64	88.86	m²	97.75
Coverings with open V profile code C269 giving 100mm cover; fixing to timber; exceeding 600 wide										
vertical cladding										
sections applied horizontally	72.96	5.00	76.61	0.38	0.38	13.85	3.25	93.71	m²	103.08
sections applied vertically	72.96	5.00	76.61	0.38	0.38	13.85	3.25	93.71	m²	103.08
Vertical angles										
section C030 for vertically applied section	8.85	5.00	9.29	0.11	0.11	4.01	0.26	13.56	m	14.92
PANEL OR SLAB CLADDING OR ROOFING										
Blue/grey slate facings; natural riven finish; bedding, jointing and pointing in gauged mortar (1:2:9)										
450 x 600 x 20mm units to walls on brickwork or blockwork base plain, width exceeding 600mm	74.00	2.50	75.85	2.00	2.00	72.88	0.84	149.57	m²	164.53
450 x 600 x 30mm units to walls on brickwork or blockwork base plain, width exceeding 600mm	95.00	2.50	97.38	2.60	2.60	94.74	0.94	193.06	m²	212.37
450 x 600 x 40mm units to walls on brickwork or blockwork base plain, width exceeding 600mm	115.00	2.50	117.88	2.90	2.90	105.68	1.30	224.85	m²	247.34
450 x 600 x 50mm units to walls on brickwork or blockwork base plain, width exceeding 600mm	140.00	2.50	143.50	3.45	3.45	125.72	1.60	270.82	m²	297.90

This page left blank intentionally

Labour hourly rates: (except Specialists)
Craft Operatives 20.87 Labourer 15.57
Rates are national average prices.
Refer to REGIONAL VARIATIONS for indicative levels of overall pricing in regions

	MATERIALS			LABOUR				RATES		
	Del to Site £	Waste %	Material Cost £	Craft Optve Hrs	Lab Hrs	Labour Cost £	Sunds £	Nett Rate £	Unit	Gross rate (10%) £
UNFRAMED ISOLATED TRIMS, SKIRTINGS AND SUNDRY ITEMS										
Softwood, wrought - skirtings, architraves, picture rails and cover fillets										
Skirtings, picture rails, architraves and the like; (finished sizes)										
19 x 100mm	1.24	10.00	1.36	0.25	0.03	5.68	0.06	7.11	m	7.82
19 x 150mm	1.86	10.00	2.05	0.28	0.04	6.47	0.08	8.59	m	9.45
25 x 100mm	1.61	10.00	1.77	0.27	0.03	6.10	0.06	7.93	m	8.73
25 x 150mm	2.33	10.00	2.56	0.31	0.04	7.09	0.08	9.73	m	10.70
19 x 50mm chamfered and rounded	0.68	10.00	0.75	0.25	0.03	5.68	0.06	6.49	m	7.14
19 x 75mm chamfered and rounded	1.02	10.00	1.12	0.28	0.04	6.47	0.08	7.66	m	8.43
19 x 100mm chamfered and rounded	1.24	10.00	1.36	0.27	0.03	6.10	0.06	7.53	m	8.28
32 x 100mm chamfered and rounded	3.50	10.00	3.85	0.31	0.04	7.09	0.08	11.02	m	12.12
15 x 50mm; mouldings -1	1.53	10.00	1.68	0.21	0.03	4.85	0.06	6.59	m	7.25
15 x 100mm; mouldings -1	2.13	10.00	2.34	0.25	0.03	5.68	0.06	8.09	m	8.90
19 x 75mm; mouldings -1	1.02	10.00	1.12	0.22	0.03	5.06	0.06	6.24	m	6.86
19 x 125mm; mouldings -1	1.55	10.00	1.71	0.27	0.03	6.10	0.06	7.87	m	8.65
25 x 50mm; mouldings -1	1.26	10.00	1.39	0.22	0.03	5.06	0.06	6.50	m	7.15
25 x 63mm; mouldings -1	1.34	10.00	1.47	0.24	0.03	5.48	0.06	7.01	m	7.71
25 x 75mm; mouldings -1	1.34	10.00	1.47	0.25	0.03	5.68	0.06	7.22	m	7.94
32 x 100mm; mouldings -1	4.28	10.00	4.71	0.30	0.04	6.88	0.08	11.67	m	12.84
38 x 75mm; mouldings -1	2.57	10.00	2.83	0.28	0.04	6.47	0.08	9.37	m	10.31
Cover fillets, stops, trims, beads, nosings and the like; (finished sizes)										
12 x 50mm; mouldings -1	0.99	10.00	1.09	0.21	0.03	4.85	0.06	6.00	m	6.60
19 x 19mm; mouldings -1	0.99	10.00	1.09	0.19	0.02	4.28	0.05	5.41	m	5.95
19 x 50mm; mouldings -1	0.99	10.00	1.09	0.22	0.03	5.06	0.06	6.21	m	6.83
25 x 25mm; mouldings -1	1.19	10.00	1.31	0.21	0.03	4.85	0.06	6.22	m	6.84
25 x 38mm; mouldings -1	1.38	10.00	1.52	0.22	0.03	5.06	0.06	6.64	m	7.30
19 x 19mm; chamfers -1	0.99	10.00	1.09	0.19	0.02	4.28	0.05	5.41	m	5.95
25 x 25mm; chamfers -1	0.99	10.00	1.09	0.21	0.03	4.85	0.06	6.00	m	6.60
25 x 38mm; chamfers -1	1.38	10.00	1.52	0.22	0.03	5.06	0.06	6.64	m	7.30
Oak, wrought - skirtings, architraves, picture rails and cover fillets										
Skirtings, picture rails, architraves and the like; (finished sizes)										
Plain										
19 x 100mm	6.90	10.00	7.59	0.42	0.05	9.54	0.15	17.28	m	19.01
19 x 150mm	10.46	10.00	11.50	0.48	0.06	10.95	0.15	22.61	m	24.87
25 x 100mm	10.49	10.00	11.54	0.46	0.06	10.53	0.15	22.23	m	24.45
25 x 150mm	13.88	10.00	15.26	0.48	0.06	10.95	0.15	26.36	m	29.00
extra; ends	1.00	10.00	1.10	0.05	0.01	1.20	0.01	2.31	nr	2.55
extra; angles	2.00	-	2.00	0.10	0.01	2.24	0.01	4.26	nr	4.68
extra; mitres	2.00	-	2.00	0.10	0.01	2.24	0.03	4.27	nr	4.70
extra; intersections	2.00	-	2.00	0.10	0.01	2.24	0.03	4.27	nr	4.70
splays - 1										
25 x 50mm	6.50	10.00	7.15	0.37	0.05	8.50	0.15	15.80	m	17.38
25 x 63mm	7.79	10.00	8.57	0.41	0.05	9.34	0.15	18.06	m	19.86
25 x 75mm	9.10	10.00	10.01	0.42	0.05	9.54	0.15	19.70	m	21.67
32 x 100mm	12.69	10.00	13.96	0.48	0.06	10.95	0.15	25.06	m	27.57
38 x 75mm	15.71	10.00	17.28	0.48	0.06	10.95	0.15	28.38	m	31.22
extra; ends	1.33	-	1.33	0.05	0.01	1.20	0.01	2.54	nr	2.80
extra; angles	2.26	-	2.26	0.10	0.01	2.24	0.03	4.53	nr	4.99
extra; mitres	2.26	-	2.26	0.10	0.01	2.24	0.03	4.53	nr	4.99
extra; intersections	2.26	-	2.26	0.10	0.01	2.24	0.03	4.53	nr	4.99
mouldings -1										
15 x 50mm	5.28	10.00	5.80	0.36	0.05	8.29	0.15	14.24	m	15.67
15 x 125mm	11.29	10.00	12.42	0.42	0.05	9.54	0.15	22.12	m	24.33
19 x 50mm	5.28	10.00	5.80	0.37	0.05	8.50	0.15	14.45	m	15.90
19 x 125mm	11.29	10.00	12.42	0.46	0.06	10.53	0.15	23.11	m	25.42
25 x 50mm	6.50	10.00	7.15	0.37	0.05	8.50	0.15	15.80	m	17.38
25 x 63mm	7.79	10.00	8.57	0.41	0.05	9.34	0.15	18.06	m	19.86
25 x 75mm	9.10	10.00	10.01	0.42	0.05	9.54	0.15	19.70	m	21.67
32 x 100mm	12.69	10.00	13.96	0.48	0.06	10.95	0.15	25.06	m	27.57
38 x 75mm	15.71	10.00	17.28	0.48	0.06	10.95	0.15	28.38	m	31.22
extra; ends	1.51	-	1.51	0.05	0.01	1.20	0.01	2.72	nr	2.99
extra; angles	2.56	-	2.56	0.10	0.01	2.24	0.03	4.83	nr	5.32
extra; mitres	2.56	-	2.56	0.10	0.01	2.24	0.03	4.83	nr	5.32
extra; intersections	2.56	-	2.56	0.10	0.01	2.24	0.03	4.83	nr	5.32
chamfers -1										
15 x 125mm	11.29	10.00	12.42	0.42	0.05	9.54	0.15	22.12	m	24.33
19 x 125mm	11.29	10.00	12.42	0.46	0.06	10.53	0.15	23.11	m	25.42
25 x 75mm	9.10	10.00	10.01	0.42	0.05	9.54	0.15	19.70	m	21.67
25 x 100mm	10.74	10.00	11.82	0.44	0.06	10.12	0.15	22.08	m	24.29

Labour hourly rates: (except Specialists) Craft Operatives 20.87 Labourer 15.57 Rates are national average prices. Refer to REGIONAL VARIATIONS for indicative levels of overall pricing in regions	MATERIALS			LABOUR				RATES		
	Del to Site £	Waste %	Material Cost £	Craft Optve Hrs	Lab Hrs	Labour Cost £	Sunds £	Nett Rate £	Unit	Gross rate (10%) £
UNFRAMED ISOLATED TRIMS, SKIRTINGS AND SUNDRY ITEMS (Cont'd)										
Ash, wrought - skirtings, architraves, picture rails and cover fillets										
Cover fillets, stops, trims, beads, nosings and the like; (finished sizes)										
12 x 50mm; mouldings -1	5.69	10.00	6.26	0.36	0.05	8.29	0.12	14.67	m	16.14
19 x 19mm; mouldings -1	3.33	10.00	3.67	0.32	0.04	7.30	0.12	11.09	m	12.20
19 x 50mm; mouldings -1	5.69	10.00	6.26	0.37	0.05	8.50	0.12	14.88	m	16.37
25 x 25mm; mouldings -1	4.29	10.00	4.72	0.36	0.05	8.29	0.12	13.13	m	14.44
25 x 38mm; mouldings -1	6.78	10.00	7.46	0.37	0.05	8.50	0.12	16.08	m	17.69
19 x 19mm; chamfers -1	3.33	10.00	3.67	0.32	0.04	7.30	0.12	11.09	m	12.20
25 x 25mm; chamfers -1	4.29	10.00	4.72	0.36	0.05	8.29	0.12	13.13	m	14.44
25 x 38mm; chamfers -1	6.78	10.00	7.46	0.37	0.05	8.50	0.12	16.08	m	17.69
Medium density fibreboard, skirtings, architraves, picture rails and cover fillets										
Skirtings, picture rails, architraves and the like; (finished sizes)										
18 x 44mm; chamfered	1.33	10.00	1.47	0.28	0.04	6.47	0.09	8.02	m	8.82
18 x 94mm; chamfered	2.37	10.00	2.61	0.29	0.04	6.68	0.09	9.37	m	10.31
18 x 144mm; chamfered	3.56	10.00	3.91	0.31	0.04	7.09	0.09	11.09	m	12.20
18 x 44mm; moulded	1.33	10.00	1.47	0.29	0.04	6.68	0.09	8.23	m	9.05
18 x 68mm; moulded	1.78	10.00	1.96	0.29	0.04	6.68	0.09	8.72	m	9.59
18 x 94mm; moulded	2.37	10.00	2.61	0.30	0.04	6.88	0.09	9.58	m	10.54
18 x 144mm; moulded	3.56	10.00	3.91	0.32	0.04	7.30	0.09	11.30	m	12.43
18 x 219mm; moulded	6.55	10.00	7.20	0.35	0.04	7.93	0.09	15.22	m	16.74
Cover fillets, stops, trims, beads, nosings and the like; (finished sizes)										
18 x 58mm Dado rail	1.85	10.00	2.04	0.33	0.02	7.20	0.09	9.33	m	10.26
25 x 70mm Dado rail	2.74	10.00	3.01	0.35	0.02	7.62	0.09	10.72	m	11.79
Softwood; wrought cover fillets and mouldings										
Cover strips, mouldings and the like; (finished sizes)										
12 x 32mm; mouldings -1	0.99	10.00	1.09	0.19	0.02	4.28	0.05	5.41	m	5.95
12 x 50mm; mouldings -1	0.99	10.00	1.09	0.21	0.03	4.85	0.06	6.00	m	6.60
19 x 19mm; mouldings -1	0.99	10.00	1.09	0.19	0.02	4.28	0.05	5.41	m	5.95
19 x 50mm; mouldings -1	0.99	10.00	1.09	0.22	0.03	5.06	0.06	6.21	m	6.83
25 x 25mm; mouldings -1	1.19	10.00	1.31	0.21	0.03	4.85	0.06	6.22	m	6.84
25 x 38mm; mouldings -1	1.38	10.00	1.52	0.22	0.03	5.06	0.06	6.64	m	7.30
Oak; cover fillets and mouldings										
Cover strips, mouldings and the like; (finished sizes)										
12 x 34mm; mouldings -1	3.87	10.00	4.25	0.32	0.04	7.30	0.10	11.66	m	12.83
12 x 50mm; mouldings -1	5.28	10.00	5.80	0.36	0.05	8.29	0.12	14.21	m	15.64
19 x 19mm; mouldings -1	3.18	10.00	3.50	0.32	0.04	7.30	0.12	10.92	m	12.01
19 x 50mm; mouldings -1	5.28	10.00	5.80	0.37	0.05	8.50	0.12	14.42	m	15.87
25 x 38mm; mouldings -1	6.16	10.00	6.77	0.37	0.05	8.50	0.12	15.39	m	16.93
Maple; cover fillets and mouldings										
Cover strips, mouldings and the like; (finished sizes)										
12 x 34mm; mouldings -1	4.85	10.00	5.34	0.32	0.04	7.30	0.10	12.75	m	14.02
12 x 50mm; mouldings -1	6.12	10.00	6.73	0.36	0.05	8.29	0.12	15.14	m	16.66
19 x 19mm; mouldings -1	3.62	10.00	3.99	0.32	0.04	7.30	0.12	11.41	m	12.55
19 x 50mm; mouldings -1	7.47	10.00	8.21	0.37	0.05	8.50	0.12	16.83	m	18.52
25 x 38mm; mouldings -1	7.56	10.00	8.32	0.37	0.05	8.50	0.12	16.94	m	18.63
Softwood, wrought - cappings										
Cover fillets, stops, trims, beads, nosings and the like; (finished sizes)										
25 x 50mm; level; rebates -1; mouldings -1	2.55	10.00	2.81	0.22	0.03	5.06	0.06	7.92	m	8.72
50 x 75mm; level; rebates -1; mouldings -1	5.74	10.00	6.31	0.31	0.04	7.09	0.08	13.48	m	14.83
50 x 100mm; level; rebates -1; mouldings -1	8.74	10.00	9.61	0.34	0.04	7.72	0.08	17.41	m	19.15
25 x 50mm; ramped; rebates -1; mouldings -1	2.55	10.00	2.81	0.33	0.04	7.51	0.08	10.39	m	11.43
50 x 75mm; ramped; rebates -1; mouldings -1	5.74	10.00	6.31	0.46	0.06	10.53	0.12	16.97	m	18.67
50 x 100mm; ramped; rebates -1; mouldings -1	8.74	10.00	9.61	0.51	0.06	11.58	0.12	21.31	m	23.44
Ash, wrought - cappings										
Cover fillets, stops, trims, beads, nosings and the like; (finished sizes)										
25 x 50mm; level; rebates -1; mouldings -1										
straight lengths	6.90	10.00	7.59	0.37	0.05	8.50	0.09	16.18	m	17.80
50 x 75mm; level; rebates -1; mouldings -1										
straight lengths	16.53	10.00	18.18	0.53	0.07	12.15	0.14	30.47	m	33.52
extra; ends	2.75	-	2.75	0.08	0.01	1.83	0.01	4.59	nr	5.05
extra; angles	4.12	-	4.12	0.13	0.02	3.02	0.03	7.18	nr	7.90
extra; mitres	4.12	-	4.12	0.13	0.02	3.02	0.03	7.18	nr	7.90
extra; rounded corners not exceeding 300mm girth	4.12	-	4.12	0.53	0.07	12.15	0.14	16.41	nr	18.05
50 x 100mm; level; rebates -1; mouldings -1										
straight lengths	21.05	10.00	23.15	0.58	0.07	13.19	0.14	36.48	m	40.13
extra; ends	3.44	-	3.44	0.09	0.01	2.03	0.01	5.49	nr	6.04
extra; angles	5.50	-	5.50	0.14	0.02	3.23	0.03	8.76	nr	9.64
extra; mitres	5.50	-	5.50	0.14	0.02	3.23	0.03	8.76	nr	9.64
extra; rounded corners not exceeding 300mm girth	5.50	-	5.50	0.58	0.07	13.19	0.14	18.83	nr	20.71
25 x 50mm; ramped; rebates -1; mouldings -1										
straight lengths	6.90	10.00	7.59	0.55	0.07	12.57	0.14	20.29	m	22.32
50 x 75mm; ramped; rebates -1; mouldings -1										
straight lengths	16.53	10.00	18.18	0.80	0.10	18.25	0.19	36.63	m	40.29
extra; ends	2.75	-	2.75	0.12	0.02	2.82	0.03	5.60	nr	6.16
extra; angles	4.12	-	4.12	0.20	0.03	4.64	0.05	8.81	nr	9.69

Labour hourly rates: (except Specialists) Craft Operatives 20.87 Labourer 15.57 Rates are national average prices. Refer to REGIONAL VARIATIONS for indicative levels of overall pricing in regions	MATERIALS			LABOUR				RATES		
	Del to Site £	Waste %	Material Cost £	Craft Optve Hrs	Lab Hrs	Labour Cost £	Sunds £	Nett Rate £	Unit	Gross rate (10%) £
UNFRAMED ISOLATED TRIMS, SKIRTINGS AND SUNDRY ITEMS (Cont'd)										
Ash, wrought - cappings (Cont'd)										
Cover fillets, stops, trims, beads, nosings and the like; (finished sizes) (Cont'd)										
50 x 75mm; ramped; rebates -1; mouldings -1 (Cont'd)										
extra; mitres	4.12	-	4.12	0.20	0.03	4.64	0.05	8.81	nr	9.69
extra; rounded corners not exceeding 300mm girth	4.12	-	4.12	0.80	0.10	18.25	0.19	22.57	nr	24.83
50 x 100mm; ramped; rebates -1; mouldings -1										
straight lengths	21.05	10.00	23.15	0.90	0.11	20.50	0.22	43.87	m	48.26
extra; ends	3.44	-	3.44	0.13	0.02	3.02	0.03	6.49	nr	7.14
extra; angles	5.50	-	5.50	0.22	0.03	5.06	0.06	10.62	nr	11.68
extra; mitres	5.50	-	5.50	0.22	0.03	5.06	0.06	10.62	nr	11.68
extra; rounded corners not exceeding 300mm girth	5.50	-	5.50	0.90	0.11	20.50	0.22	26.22	nr	28.84
Oak; wrought - cappings										
Cover fillets, stops, trims, beads, nosings and the like; (finished sizes)										
25 x 50mm; level; rebates -1; mouldings -1										
straight lengths	6.80	10.00	7.48	0.33	0.04	7.51	0.08	15.06	m	16.57
50 x 75mm; level; rebates -1; mouldings -1										
straight lengths	27.88	10.00	30.67	0.46	0.06	10.53	0.12	41.32	m	45.45
extra; ends	2.75	-	2.75	0.07	0.01	1.62	0.01	4.38	nr	4.82
extra; angles	4.13	-	4.13	0.12	0.02	2.82	0.03	6.98	nr	7.67
extra; mitres	4.13	-	4.13	0.12	0.02	2.82	0.03	6.98	nr	7.67
extra; rounded corners not exceeding 300mm girth	4.13	-	4.13	0.46	0.06	10.53	0.12	14.78	nr	16.26
50 x 100mm; level; rebates -1; mouldings -1										
straight lengths	32.73	10.00	36.00	0.50	0.06	11.37	0.12	47.49	m	52.24
extra; ends	2.75	-	2.75	0.08	0.01	1.83	0.01	4.59	nr	5.05
extra; angles	4.13	-	4.13	0.13	0.02	3.02	0.03	7.18	nr	7.90
extra; mitres	4.13	-	4.13	0.13	0.02	3.02	0.03	7.18	nr	7.90
extra; rounded corners not exceeding 300mm girth	4.13	-	4.13	0.50	0.06	11.37	0.12	15.62	nr	17.18
25 x 50mm; ramped; rebates -1; mouldings -1										
straight lengths	6.80	10.00	7.48	0.50	0.06	11.37	0.12	18.97	m	20.87
50 x 75mm; ramped; rebates -1; mouldings -1										
straight lengths	27.88	10.00	30.67	0.70	0.09	16.01	0.17	46.84	m	51.53
extra; ends	2.75	10.00	3.03	0.10	0.01	2.24	0.03	5.30	nr	5.83
extra; angles	4.13	-	4.13	0.17	0.02	3.86	0.05	8.03	nr	8.84
extra; mitres	4.13	-	4.13	0.17	0.02	3.86	0.05	8.03	nr	8.84
extra; rounded corners not exceeding 300mm girth	4.13	-	4.13	0.70	0.09	16.01	0.17	20.31	nr	22.34
50 x 100mm; ramped; rebates -1; mouldings -1										
straight lengths	32.73	10.00	36.00	0.75	0.09	17.05	0.18	53.24	m	58.56
extra; ends	2.75	-	2.75	0.11	0.01	2.45	0.03	5.23	nr	5.75
extra; angles	4.13	-	4.13	0.19	0.02	4.28	0.05	8.45	nr	9.30
extra; mitres	4.13	-	4.13	0.19	0.02	4.28	0.05	8.45	nr	9.30
extra; rounded corners not exceeding 300mm girth	4.13	-	4.13	0.75	0.09	17.05	0.18	21.36	nr	23.50
Softwood, wrought - isolated shelves and worktops										
Cover fillets, stops, trims, beads, nosings and the like; (finished sizes)										
19 x 12mm	0.78	10.00	0.86	0.18	0.02	4.07	0.05	4.97	m	5.47
19 x 16mm	0.78	10.00	0.86	0.19	0.02	4.28	0.05	5.18	m	5.70
19 x 18mm	0.78	10.00	0.86	0.19	0.02	4.28	0.05	5.18	m	5.70
19 x 22mm	0.78	10.00	0.86	0.20	0.03	4.64	0.05	5.54	m	6.10
19 x 25mm	0.78	10.00	0.86	0.20	0.03	4.64	0.05	5.54	m	6.10
Isolated shelves and worktops										
25 x 150mm	3.09	10.00	3.40	0.20	0.03	4.64	0.05	8.09	m	8.89
25 x 225mm	4.77	10.00	5.25	0.25	0.03	5.68	0.06	10.99	m	12.09
25 x 300mm	10.69	10.00	11.76	0.30	0.04	6.88	0.08	18.72	m	20.59
32 x 150mm	4.11	10.00	4.52	0.22	0.03	5.06	0.06	9.64	m	10.60
32 x 225mm	5.58	10.00	6.14	0.27	0.03	6.10	0.06	12.30	m	13.53
32 x 300mm	18.00	10.00	19.80	0.33	0.04	7.51	0.08	27.38	m	30.12
25 x 450mm; cross tongued	13.54	2.50	13.88	0.35	0.04	7.93	0.09	21.90	m	24.09
25 x 600mm; cross tongued	25.38	2.50	26.01	0.45	0.06	10.33	0.10	36.45	m	40.09
32 x 450mm; cross tongued	15.16	2.50	15.54	0.40	0.06	9.28	0.10	24.93	m	27.42
32 x 600mm; cross tongued	40.00	2.50	41.00	0.50	0.06	11.37	0.12	52.49	m	57.74
38 x 450mm; cross tongued	19.38	2.50	19.86	0.45	0.06	10.33	0.10	30.30	m	33.32
38 x 600mm; cross tongued	35.24	2.50	36.12	0.55	0.07	12.57	0.14	48.82	m	53.71
25 x 450mm overall; 25 x 50mm slats spaced 25mm apart	6.72	10.00	7.39	1.00	0.13	22.89	0.24	30.53	m	33.58
25 x 450mm overall; 25 x 50mm slats spaced 32mm apart	6.72	10.00	7.39	0.90	0.11	20.50	0.22	28.11	m	30.92
25 x 600mm overall; 25 x 50mm slats spaced 25mm apart	8.64	10.00	9.50	1.25	0.16	28.58	0.30	38.38	m	42.22
25 x 600mm overall; 25 x 50mm slats spaced 32mm apart	7.68	10.00	8.45	1.15	0.14	26.18	0.28	34.91	m	38.40
25 x 900mm overall; 25 x 50mm slats spaced 25mm apart	12.48	10.00	13.73	1.90	0.24	43.39	0.47	57.58	m	63.34
25 x 900mm overall; 25 x 50mm slats spaced 32mm apart	11.52	10.00	12.67	1.80	0.23	41.15	0.44	54.25	m	59.68
Oak, wrought - isolated shelves and worktops										
Cover fillets, stops, trims, beads, nosings and the like; (finished sizes)										
19 x 12mm	3.28	10.00	3.61	0.31	0.04	7.09	0.08	10.78	m	11.85
19 x 16mm	3.88	10.00	4.27	0.33	0.04	7.51	0.08	11.85	m	13.04
19 x 18mm	3.88	10.00	4.27	0.33	0.04	7.51	0.08	11.85	m	13.04
19 x 22mm	3.88	10.00	4.27	0.35	0.04	7.93	0.09	12.29	m	13.51
19 x 25mm	3.88	10.00	4.27	0.35	0.04	7.93	0.09	12.29	m	13.51
Isolated shelves and worktops										
25 x 150mm	21.35	10.00	23.49	0.35	0.04	7.93	0.09	31.50	m	34.65
25 x 225mm	41.16	10.00	45.28	0.44	0.06	10.12	0.10	55.50	m	61.05
25 x 300mm; cross tongued	60.03	10.00	66.03	0.53	0.07	12.15	0.14	78.32	m	86.15
32 x 150mm	31.26	10.00	34.39	0.38	0.05	8.71	0.09	43.19	m	47.50
32 x 225mm	46.14	10.00	50.75	0.47	0.06	10.74	0.12	61.62	m	67.78

Labour hourly rates: (except Specialists) Craft Operatives 20.87 Labourer 15.57 Rates are national average prices. Refer to REGIONAL VARIATIONS for indicative levels of overall pricing in regions	MATERIALS			LABOUR				RATES		
	Del to Site £	Waste %	Material Cost £	Craft Optve Hrs	Lab Hrs	Labour Cost £	Sunds £	Nett Rate £	Unit	Gross rate (10%) £
UNFRAMED ISOLATED TRIMS, SKIRTINGS AND SUNDRY ITEMS (Cont'd)										
Oak, wrought - isolated shelves and worktops (Cont'd)										
Isolated shelves and worktops (Cont'd)										
32 x 300mm; cross tongued	68.52	10.00	75.37	0.56	0.07	12.78	0.14	88.28	m	97.11
25 x 450mm; cross tongued	88.32	2.50	90.53	0.60	0.08	13.77	0.15	104.45	m	114.89
25 x 600mm; cross tongued	126.06	2.50	129.21	0.80	0.10	18.25	0.19	147.66	m	162.43
32 x 450mm; cross tongued	98.28	2.50	100.74	0.70	0.09	16.01	0.17	116.91	m	128.60
32 x 600mm; cross tongued	135.54	2.50	138.93	0.90	0.11	20.50	0.22	159.65	m	175.61
38 x 450mm; cross tongued	122.76	2.50	125.83	0.80	0.10	18.25	0.19	144.28	m	158.70
38 x 600mm; cross tongued	168.18	2.50	172.38	1.00	0.13	22.89	0.24	195.52	m	215.07
Plywood BS EN 636, II/III face grade, INT bonded; butt joints - isolated shelves and worktops										
Cover fillets, stops, trims, beads, nosings and the like										
50 x 6.5mm	0.43	20.00	0.52	0.16	0.02	3.65	0.08	4.25	m	4.67
50 x 12mm	0.36	20.00	0.43	0.16	0.02	3.65	0.08	4.16	m	4.57
50 x 15mm	0.38	20.00	0.45	0.17	0.02	3.86	0.08	4.39	m	4.83
50 x 19mm	0.45	20.00	0.54	0.18	0.02	4.07	0.08	4.68	m	5.15
100 x 6.5mm	0.87	20.00	1.04	0.16	0.02	3.65	0.08	4.77	m	5.24
100 x 12mm	0.72	20.00	0.86	0.17	0.02	3.86	0.08	4.80	m	5.28
100 x 15mm	0.76	20.00	0.91	0.18	0.02	4.07	0.08	5.05	m	5.56
100 x 19mm	0.90	20.00	1.08	0.19	0.02	4.28	0.08	5.43	m	5.97
Isolated shelves and worktops										
6.5 x 150mm	1.30	20.00	1.56	0.18	0.02	4.07	0.08	5.71	m	6.28
6.5 x 225mm	1.95	20.00	2.34	0.23	0.02	5.11	0.08	7.53	m	8.28
6.5 x 300mm	2.60	20.00	3.12	0.28	0.04	6.47	0.08	9.67	m	10.63
6.5 x 450mm	3.91	20.00	4.69	0.33	0.04	7.51	0.08	12.27	m	13.50
6.5 x 600mm	5.21	20.00	6.25	0.38	0.05	8.71	0.08	15.03	m	16.54
12 x 150mm	1.08	20.00	1.29	0.19	0.02	4.28	0.08	5.64	m	6.21
12 x 225mm	1.62	20.00	1.94	0.24	0.03	5.48	0.08	7.49	m	8.24
12 x 300mm	2.15	20.00	2.58	0.29	0.04	6.68	0.08	9.33	m	10.27
12 x 450mm	3.23	20.00	3.88	0.34	0.04	7.72	0.08	11.67	m	12.84
12 x 600mm	4.31	20.00	5.17	0.39	0.05	8.92	0.08	14.16	m	15.58
15 x 150mm	1.14	20.00	1.36	0.23	0.03	5.27	0.08	6.71	m	7.38
15 x 225mm	1.70	20.00	2.04	0.25	0.03	5.68	0.08	7.80	m	8.58
15 x 300mm	2.27	20.00	2.73	0.30	0.04	6.88	0.08	9.69	m	10.65
15 x 450mm	3.41	20.00	4.09	0.35	0.04	7.93	0.08	12.09	m	13.30
15 x 600mm	4.54	20.00	5.45	0.40	0.05	9.13	0.08	14.65	m	16.12
19 x 150mm	1.35	20.00	1.62	0.20	0.03	4.64	0.08	6.33	m	6.97
19 x 225mm	2.02	20.00	2.43	0.25	0.03	5.68	0.08	8.19	m	9.01
19 x 300mm	2.70	20.00	3.24	0.30	0.04	6.88	0.08	10.20	m	11.21
19 x 450mm	4.05	20.00	4.85	0.35	0.04	7.93	0.08	12.86	m	14.14
19 x 600mm	5.39	20.00	6.47	0.40	0.05	9.13	0.08	15.67	m	17.24
Blockboard, 2/2 grade, INT bonded, butt joints - isolated shelves and worktops										
Isolated shelves and worktops										
18 x 150mm	1.88	20.00	2.26	0.23	0.03	5.27	0.14	7.66	m	8.43
18 x 225mm	2.82	20.00	3.39	0.29	0.04	6.68	0.14	10.20	m	11.22
18 x 300mm	3.77	20.00	4.52	0.34	0.04	7.72	0.14	12.37	m	13.61
18 x 450mm	5.65	20.00	6.78	0.40	0.05	9.13	0.14	16.04	m	17.64
18 x 600mm	7.53	20.00	9.04	0.46	0.06	10.53	0.14	19.71	m	21.68
Wood chipboard BS EN 312, type I standard; butt joints - isolated shelves and worktops										
Isolated shelves and worktops										
12 x 150mm	0.55	20.00	0.66	0.19	0.02	4.28	0.08	5.01	m	5.51
12 x 225mm	0.82	20.00	0.99	0.24	0.03	5.48	0.08	6.54	m	7.19
12 x 300mm	1.10	20.00	1.32	0.29	0.04	6.68	0.08	8.07	m	8.88
12 x 450mm	1.65	20.00	1.98	0.34	0.04	7.72	0.08	9.77	m	10.75
12 x 600mm	2.20	20.00	2.64	0.39	0.05	8.92	0.08	11.63	m	12.79
18 x 150mm	0.74	20.00	0.88	0.20	0.03	4.64	0.08	5.60	m	6.16
18 x 225mm	1.11	20.00	1.33	0.25	0.03	5.68	0.08	7.09	m	7.80
18 x 300mm	1.48	20.00	1.77	0.30	0.04	6.88	0.08	8.73	m	9.60
18 x 450mm	2.21	20.00	2.65	0.35	0.04	7.93	0.08	10.66	m	11.72
18 x 600mm	2.95	20.00	3.54	0.40	0.05	9.13	0.08	12.74	m	14.02
25 x 150mm	1.15	20.00	1.38	0.20	0.03	4.64	0.08	6.10	m	6.71
25 x 225mm	1.73	20.00	2.07	0.25	0.03	5.68	0.08	7.83	m	8.62
25 x 300mm	2.30	20.00	2.76	0.30	0.04	6.88	0.08	9.72	m	10.69
25 x 450mm	3.45	20.00	4.15	0.35	0.04	7.93	0.08	12.15	m	13.36
25 x 600mm	4.61	20.00	5.53	0.40	0.05	9.13	0.08	14.73	m	16.20
Blockboard, 2/2 grade, INT bonded, faced with 1.5mm laminated plastic sheet, BS EN 438, classified HGS, with 1.2mm laminated plastic sheet balance veneer; butt joints										
Isolated shelves and worktops										
18 x 150mm	1.88	20.00	2.26	0.40	0.05	9.13	0.14	11.52	m	12.67
18 x 225mm	2.82	20.00	3.39	0.50	0.06	11.37	0.14	14.89	m	16.38
18 x 300mm	3.77	20.00	4.52	0.60	0.08	13.77	0.14	18.42	m	20.26
18 x 450mm	5.65	20.00	6.78	0.70	0.09	16.01	0.14	22.92	m	25.22
18 x 600mm	7.53	20.00	9.04	0.80	0.10	18.25	0.14	27.42	m	30.17
Softwood, wrought - window boards										
Cover fillets, stops, trims, beads, nosings and the like; (finished sizes)										
mouldings -1; tongued on										
25 x 50mm	2.55	10.00	2.81	0.25	0.03	5.68	0.06	8.55	m	9.40
25 x 75mm	4.05	10.00	4.46	0.26	0.03	5.89	0.06	10.41	m	11.45

Labour hourly rates: (except Specialists) Craft Operatives 20.87 Labourer 15.57 Rates are national average prices. Refer to REGIONAL VARIATIONS for indicative levels of overall pricing in regions	MATERIALS			LABOUR				RATES		
	Del to Site £	Waste %	Material Cost £	Craft Optve Hrs	Lab Hrs	Labour Cost £	Sunds £	Nett Rate £	Unit	Gross rate (10%) £
UNFRAMED ISOLATED TRIMS, SKIRTINGS AND SUNDRY ITEMS (Cont'd)										
Softwood, wrought - window boards (Cont'd)										
Cover fillets, stops, trims, beads, nosings and the like; (finished sizes) (Cont'd)										
mouldings -1; tongued on (Cont'd)										
32 x 50mm	4.50	10.00	4.95	0.28	0.04	6.47	0.08	11.49	m	12.64
32 x 75mm	4.58	10.00	5.04	0.29	0.04	6.68	0.08	11.79	m	12.97
rounded edges -1; tongued on										
25 x 50mm	2.55	10.00	2.81	0.25	0.03	5.68	0.06	8.55	m	9.40
25 x 75mm	4.05	10.00	4.46	0.26	0.03	5.89	0.06	10.41	m	11.45
32 x 50mm	4.50	10.00	4.95	0.28	0.04	6.47	0.08	11.49	m	12.64
32 x 75mm	4.58	10.00	5.04	0.29	0.04	6.68	0.08	11.79	m	12.97
Window boards										
25 x 150mm; mouldings -1	6.94	10.00	7.63	0.30	0.04	6.88	0.08	14.59	m	16.05
32 x 150mm; mouldings -1	8.91	10.00	9.80	0.33	0.04	7.51	0.08	17.39	m	19.12
25 x 150mm; rounded edges -1	6.94	10.00	7.63	0.30	0.04	6.88	0.08	14.59	m	16.05
32 x 150mm; rounded edges -1	8.91	10.00	9.80	0.33	0.04	7.51	0.08	17.39	m	19.12
Teak, wrought - window boards										
Cover fillets, stops, trims, beads, nosings and the like; (finished sizes)										
mouldings -1; tongued on										
25 x 50mm	28.30	10.00	31.13	0.38	0.05	8.71	0.09	39.92	m	43.92
25 x 75mm	42.46	10.00	46.70	0.40	0.05	9.13	0.09	55.92	m	61.51
38 x 50mm	43.02	10.00	47.32	0.42	0.05	9.54	0.10	56.97	m	62.67
38 x 75mm	64.52	10.00	70.98	0.44	0.06	10.12	0.10	81.20	m	89.32
rounded edges -1; tongued on										
25 x 50mm	28.30	10.00	31.13	0.38	0.05	8.71	0.09	39.92	m	43.92
25 x 75mm	42.46	10.00	46.70	0.40	0.05	9.13	0.09	55.92	m	61.51
38 x 50mm	43.02	10.00	47.32	0.42	0.05	9.54	0.10	56.97	m	62.67
38 x 75mm	64.52	10.00	70.98	0.44	0.06	10.12	0.10	81.20	m	89.32
Window boards										
25 x 150mm; mouldings -1	84.90	10.00	93.39	0.52	0.07	11.94	0.14	105.47	m	116.01
38 x 150mm; mouldings -1	129.05	10.00	141.95	0.58	0.07	13.19	0.14	155.28	m	170.81
25 x 150mm; rounded edges -1	84.90	10.00	93.39	0.52	0.07	11.94	0.14	105.47	m	116.01
38 x 150mm; rounded edges -1	129.05	10.00	141.95	0.58	0.07	13.19	0.14	155.28	m	170.81
Sapele; wrought - window boards										
Cover fillets, stops, trims, beads, nosings and the like; (finished sizes)										
mouldings -1; tongued on										
25 x 50mm	5.41	10.00	5.95	0.37	0.05	8.50	0.09	14.54	m	16.00
25 x 75mm	7.61	10.00	8.37	0.39	0.05	8.92	0.09	17.38	m	19.12
32 x 50mm	6.64	10.00	7.30	0.41	0.05	9.34	0.10	16.74	m	18.42
32 x 75mm	9.46	10.00	10.41	0.43	0.05	9.75	0.10	20.26	m	22.29
rounded edges -1; tongued on										
25 x 50mm	5.41	10.00	5.95	0.37	0.05	8.50	0.09	14.54	m	16.00
25 x 75mm	7.61	10.00	8.37	0.39	0.05	8.92	0.09	17.38	m	19.12
32 x 50mm	6.64	10.00	7.30	0.41	0.05	9.34	0.10	16.74	m	18.42
32 x 75mm	9.46	10.00	10.41	0.43	0.05	9.75	0.10	20.26	m	22.29
Window boards										
25 x 150mm; mouldings -1	14.22	10.00	15.64	0.45	0.06	10.33	0.10	26.07	m	28.68
32 x 150mm; mouldings -1	17.92	10.00	19.71	0.50	0.06	11.37	0.12	31.20	m	34.32
25 x 150mm; rounded edges -1	14.22	10.00	15.64	0.45	0.06	10.33	0.10	26.07	m	28.68
32 x 150mm; rounded edges -1	17.92	10.00	19.71	0.50	0.06	11.37	0.12	31.20	m	34.32
Moisture resistant medium density fibreboard - MDF, BS EN 622										
Window boards										
25 x 200mm; nosed and tongued	7.86	10.00	8.65	0.30	0.04	6.88	0.08	15.60	m	17.17
25 x 244mm; nosed and tongued	9.58	10.00	10.53	0.32	0.04	7.30	0.08	17.91	m	19.70
Duct fronts; plywood BS EN 636, II/III grade, MR bonded; butt joints; fixing to timber with screws, countersinking										
12mm thick linings to walls										
width exceeding 300mm	14.87	20.00	17.84	1.00	0.13	22.89	0.26	41.00	m²	45.10
width exceeding 300mm; fixing to timber with brass screws and cups	14.87	20.00	17.84	1.50	0.19	34.26	0.96	53.06	m²	58.37
Blockboard, 2/2 grade, MR bonded; butt joints										
18mm thick linings to walls										
width exceeding 300mm	9.72	20.00	11.66	1.20	0.15	27.38	0.33	39.37	m²	43.31
width exceeding 300mm; fixing to timber with brass screws and cups	9.72	20.00	11.66	1.75	0.22	39.95	1.02	52.63	m²	57.90
Extra over plywood BS EN 636, II/III grade, MR bonded; butt joints; 12mm thick linings to walls; width exceeding 300mm										
Access panels										
300 x 600mm	-	-	-	0.50	0.05	11.21	0.13	11.35	nr	12.48
600 x 600mm	-	-	-	0.65	0.07	14.66	0.16	14.82	nr	16.30
600 x 900mm	-	-	-	0.80	0.08	17.94	0.21	18.16	nr	19.97
Extra over blockboard, 2/2 grade, MR bonded, butt joints; 18mm thick linings to walls; width exceeding 300mm										
Access panels										
300 x 600mm	-	-	-	0.60	0.07	13.61	0.16	13.78	nr	15.15

Labour hourly rates: (except Specialists) Craft Operatives 20.87 Labourer 15.57 Rates are national average prices. Refer to REGIONAL VARIATIONS for indicative levels of overall pricing in regions	MATERIALS			LABOUR				RATES		
	Del to Site £	Waste %	Material Cost £	Craft Optve Hrs	Lab Hrs	Labour Cost £	Sunds £	Nett Rate £	Unit	Gross rate (10%) £
UNFRAMED ISOLATED TRIMS, SKIRTINGS AND SUNDRY ITEMS (Cont'd)										
Extra over blockboard, 2/2 grade, MR bonded, butt joints; 18mm thick linings to walls; width exceeding 300mm (Cont'd)										
Access panels (Cont'd)										
600 x 600mm	-	-	-	0.80	0.08	17.94	0.21	18.16	nr	19.97
600 x 900mm	-	-	-	1.10	0.11	24.67	0.30	24.97	nr	27.46
Pipe casings; standard hardboard, BS EN 622, type SHA; butt joints										
3mm thick linings to pipe ducts and casings										
width exceeding 300mm	1.57	20.00	1.88	0.80	0.10	18.25	0.21	20.35	m²	22.38
width not exceeding 300mm	0.47	20.00	0.56	0.25	0.03	5.68	0.07	6.31	m	6.95
Plywood BS EN 636, II/III grade, MR bonded; butt joints; fixing to timber with screws, countersinking										
12mm thick linings to pipe ducts and casings										
width exceeding 300mm	14.87	20.00	17.84	1.50	0.19	34.26	0.40	52.50	m²	57.75
width not exceeding 300mm	4.46	20.00	5.35	0.50	0.06	11.37	0.13	16.85	m	18.54
Pendock Profiles Ltd preformed plywood casings; white melamine finish; butt joints; fixing to timber with polytop white screws, countersinking										
5mm thick skirting casings; horizontal										
reference TK45110										
45 x 110mm casings	11.90	20.00	14.28	0.40	0.05	9.13	0.33	23.74	m	26.12
extra; internal corner	5.84	2.50	5.99	0.25	0.03	5.68	0.33	12.00	nr	13.20
extra; external corner	6.48	2.50	6.64	0.25	0.03	5.68	0.33	12.66	nr	13.92
extra; stop end	2.77	2.50	2.84	0.15	0.02	3.44	0.16	6.45	nr	7.09
reference TK45150										
45 x 150mm casings	12.48	20.00	14.98	0.42	0.05	9.54	0.33	24.85	m	27.33
extra; internal corner	6.78	2.50	6.95	0.25	0.03	5.68	0.33	12.96	nr	14.26
extra; external corner	7.00	2.50	7.17	0.25	0.03	5.68	0.33	13.19	nr	14.51
extra; stop end	2.97	2.50	3.04	0.15	0.02	3.44	0.16	6.65	nr	7.32
reference TK45190										
45 x 190mm casings	14.03	20.00	16.84	0.44	0.05	9.96	0.33	27.13	m	29.84
extra; internal corner	7.12	2.50	7.30	0.25	0.03	5.68	0.33	13.31	nr	14.64
extra; external corner	7.62	2.50	7.81	0.25	0.03	5.68	0.33	13.83	nr	15.21
extra; stop end	3.33	2.50	3.41	0.15	0.02	3.44	0.16	7.02	nr	7.72
5mm thick casings; vertical										
reference TK45135										
45 x 135mm casings	16.56	20.00	19.87	0.40	0.05	9.13	0.33	29.33	m	32.26
reference TK45220										
45 x 220mm casings	25.94	20.00	31.13	0.44	0.05	9.96	0.33	41.42	m	45.57
reference TK45300										
45 x 300mm casings	29.12	20.00	34.94	0.46	0.05	10.38	0.33	45.65	m	50.22
5mm thick casings; horizontal										
reference MX 1010										
100 x 100mm casings	16.03	20.00	19.24	0.42	0.05	9.54	0.33	29.11	m	32.02
extra; internal corner	28.88	3.00	29.75	0.25	0.03	5.68	0.33	35.76	nr	39.34
extra; external corner	26.66	3.00	27.46	0.25	0.03	5.68	0.33	33.47	nr	36.82
extra; stop end	3.85	2.50	3.95	0.15	0.02	3.44	0.16	7.55	nr	8.31
8mm thick casings; horizontal										
reference MX 1515										
150 x 150mm casings	25.62	20.00	30.74	0.45	0.06	10.33	0.33	41.39	m	45.53
extra; internal corner	29.78	2.50	30.52	0.25	0.03	5.68	0.33	36.54	nr	40.19
extra; external corner	31.12	2.50	31.90	0.25	0.03	5.68	0.33	37.91	nr	41.70
extra; stop end	3.93	2.50	4.03	0.15	0.02	3.44	0.16	7.64	nr	8.40
reference MX 1520										
200 x 150mm casings	28.48	20.00	34.18	0.46	0.06	10.53	0.33	45.04	m	49.54
extra; internal corner	39.40	3.00	40.58	0.25	0.03	5.68	0.33	46.60	nr	51.26
extra; external corner	32.92	3.00	33.91	0.25	0.03	5.68	0.33	39.92	nr	43.91
extra; stop end	4.43	2.50	4.54	0.15	0.02	3.44	0.16	8.15	nr	8.96
reference MX 2020										
200 x 200mm casings	32.38	20.00	38.85	0.47	0.06	10.74	0.33	49.92	m	54.92
extra; internal corner	37.56	2.50	38.50	0.25	0.03	5.68	0.33	44.51	nr	48.96
extra; external corner	36.28	2.50	37.19	0.25	0.03	5.68	0.33	43.20	nr	47.52
extra; stop end	6.44	2.50	6.60	0.15	0.02	3.44	0.16	10.21	nr	11.23
reference MX 2030										
200 x 300mm casings	42.50	20.00	51.00	0.48	0.06	10.95	0.33	62.29	m	68.52
extra; internal corner	40.42	3.00	41.63	0.25	0.03	5.68	0.33	47.65	nr	52.41
extra; external corner	39.54	3.00	40.73	0.25	0.03	5.68	0.33	46.74	nr	51.41
extra; stop end	7.25	2.50	7.43	0.15	0.02	3.44	0.16	11.04	nr	12.14
reference MX 1530										
300 x 150mm casings	41.81	20.00	50.17	0.50	0.06	11.37	0.33	61.87	m	68.06
extra; internal corner	43.68	3.00	44.99	0.25	0.03	5.68	0.33	51.00	nr	56.11
extra; external corner	34.28	3.00	35.31	0.25	0.03	5.68	0.33	41.32	nr	45.46
extra; stop end	7.26	3.00	7.48	0.15	0.02	3.44	0.16	11.09	nr	12.20
reference MX 3030										
300 x 300mm casings	43.56	20.00	52.27	0.50	0.06	11.37	0.33	63.97	m	70.36
extra; internal corner	42.82	2.50	43.89	0.25	0.03	5.68	0.33	49.91	nr	54.90
extra; external corner	40.80	2.50	41.82	0.25	0.03	5.68	0.33	47.83	nr	52.62
extra; stop end	8.63	2.50	8.85	0.15	0.02	3.44	0.16	12.45	nr	13.70

Labour hourly rates: (except Specialists) Craft Operatives 20.87 Labourer 15.57 Rates are national average prices. Refer to REGIONAL VARIATIONS for indicative levels of overall pricing in regions	MATERIALS			LABOUR				RATES		
	Del to Site £	Waste %	Material Cost £	Craft Optve Hrs	Lab Hrs	Labour Cost £	Sunds £	Nett Rate £	Unit	Gross rate (10%) £
UNFRAMED ISOLATED TRIMS, SKIRTINGS AND SUNDRY ITEMS (Cont'd)										
Laminated plastic sheet, BS EN 438 classification HGP										
Cover fillets, stops, trims, beads, nosings and the like; fixing with adhesive										
0.7 x 16mm	0.36	20.00	0.43	0.20	0.03	4.64	0.09	5.16	m	5.68
0.7 x 18mm	0.41	20.00	0.49	0.21	0.03	4.85	0.10	5.44	m	5.98
0.7 x 22mm	0.50	20.00	0.59	0.23	0.03	5.27	0.12	5.98	m	6.58
0.7 x 25mm	0.56	20.00	0.67	0.25	0.03	5.68	0.14	6.49	m	7.14
0.7 x 75mm	1.69	20.00	2.02	0.30	0.04	6.88	0.42	9.33	m	10.26
Isolated shelves and worktops; fixing with adhesive										
0.7 x 150mm	3.37	20.00	4.05	0.35	0.04	7.93	0.84	12.81	m	14.10
0.7 x 225mm	5.06	20.00	6.07	0.40	0.05	9.13	1.26	16.46	m	18.10
0.7 x 300mm	6.75	20.00	8.10	0.45	0.06	10.33	1.68	20.10	m	22.11
0.7 x 450mm	10.12	20.00	12.14	0.53	0.07	12.15	2.54	26.83	m	29.51
0.7 x 600mm	13.49	20.00	16.19	0.60	0.08	13.77	3.38	33.33	m	36.67
FLOOR, WALL AND CEILING BOARDING, SHEETING, PANELLING, LININGS AND CASINGS										
Strip flooring; hardwood, wrought, selected for transparent finish; sanded, two coats sealer finish										
Boarding to floors, tongued and grooved joints; 22mm thick, 75mm wide boards; fixing on and with 25 x 50mm impregnated softwood battens to masonry										
width exceeding 300mm; secret fixing to timber	126.89	7.50	136.35	1.25	0.15	28.42	0.33	165.10	m²	181.61
Boarding to floors, tongued and grooved joints; 12mm thick, 75mm wide boards; overlay										
width exceeding 300mm; secret fixing to timber	76.67	7.50	82.41	1.00	0.13	22.89	0.26	105.57	m²	116.13
Semi-sprung floors; foam backed softwood battens covered with hardwood tongued and grooved strip flooring										
22mm Standard Beech strip flooring to level sub-floors										
width exceeding 600mm; battens at approximately 400mm centres; elevation										
75mm	-	-	Specialist	-	-	Specialist	-	79.69	m²	87.66
22mm "Sylva Squash" Beech strip flooring to level sub-floors										
width exceeding 600mm; battens at approximately 430mm centres; elevation										
75mm	-	-	Specialist	-	-	Specialist	-	85.21	m²	93.73
20mm Prime Maple strip flooring to level sub-floors										
width exceeding 600mm; battens at approximately 600mm centres; elevation										
75mm	-	-	Specialist	-	-	Specialist	-	64.84	m²	71.32
20mm First Grade Maple strip flooring to level sub-floors										
width exceeding 600mm; battens at approximately 600mm centres; elevation										
75mm	-	-	Specialist	-	-	Specialist	-	70.39	m²	77.43
Softwood, wrought; fixing to timber; wall boarding										
Boarding to walls, tongued, grooved and veed joints; 19mm thick, 100mm wide boards										
width exceeding 600mm	14.20	10.00	15.63	1.00	0.13	22.89	0.26	38.78	m²	42.66
Boarding to walls, tongued, grooved and veed joints; 19mm thick, 150mm wide boards										
width exceeding 600mm	14.73	10.00	16.21	0.70	0.09	16.01	0.18	32.40	m²	35.64
Boarding to walls, tongued, grooved and veed joints; 25mm thick, 100mm wide boards										
width exceeding 600mm	18.41	10.00	20.25	1.05	0.13	23.94	0.28	44.47	m²	48.91
Boarding to walls, tongued, grooved and veed joints; 25mm thick, 150mm wide boards										
width exceeding 600mm	19.25	10.00	21.17	0.75	0.09	17.05	0.20	38.42	m²	42.27
Boarding to ceilings, tongued, grooved and veed joints; 19mm thick, 100mm wide boards										
width exceeding 600mm	14.20	10.00	15.63	1.50	0.19	34.26	0.40	50.28	m²	55.31
Boarding to ceilings, tongued, grooved and veed joints; 19mm thick, 150mm wide boards										
width exceeding 600mm	14.73	10.00	16.21	1.00	0.13	22.89	0.26	39.36	m²	43.30
Boarding to ceilings, tongued, grooved and veed joints; 25mm thick, 100mm wide boards										
width exceeding 600mm	18.41	10.00	20.25	1.55	0.19	35.31	0.41	55.97	m²	61.57
Boarding to ceilings, tongued, grooved and veed joints; 25mm thick, 150mm wide boards										
width exceeding 600mm	19.25	10.00	21.17	1.05	0.13	23.94	0.28	45.39	m²	49.93
Western Red Cedar, wrought; fixing to timber; wall boarding										
Boarding to walls, tongued, grooved and veed joints; 19mm thick, 100mm wide boards										
width exceeding 600mm	101.74	10.00	111.92	1.05	0.13	23.94	0.28	136.14	m²	149.75
Boarding to walls, tongued, grooved and veed joints; 19mm thick, 150mm wide boards										
width exceeding 600mm	103.63	10.00	113.99	0.75	0.10	17.21	0.20	131.40	m²	144.54

Labour hourly rates: (except Specialists) Craft Operatives 20.87 Labourer 15.57 Rates are national average prices. Refer to REGIONAL VARIATIONS for indicative levels of overall pricing in regions	MATERIALS			LABOUR				RATES		
	Del to Site £	Waste %	Material Cost £	Craft Optve Hrs	Lab Hrs	Labour Cost £	Sunds £	Nett Rate £	Unit	Gross rate (10%) £
FLOOR, WALL AND CEILING BOARDING, SHEETING, PANELLING, LININGS AND CASINGS (Cont'd)										
Western Red Cedar, wrought; fixing to timber; wall boarding (Cont'd)										
Boarding to walls, tongued, grooved and veed joints; 25mm thick, 100mm wide boards										
width exceeding 600mm	138.37	10.00	152.21	1.10	0.14	25.14	0.30	177.64	m²	195.41
Boarding to walls, tongued, grooved and veed joints; 25mm thick, 150mm wide boards										
width exceeding 600mm	126.59	10.00	139.25	0.80	0.10	18.25	0.21	157.72	m²	173.49
Knotty Pine, wrought, selected for transparent finish; fixing to timber; wall boarding										
Boarding to walls, tongued, grooved and veed joints; 19mm thick, 100mm wide boards										
width exceeding 600mm	44.25	10.00	48.68	1.30	0.16	29.62	0.35	78.65	m²	86.51
Boarding to walls, tongued, grooved and veed joints; 19mm thick, 150mm wide boards										
width exceeding 600mm	50.74	10.00	55.81	0.90	0.11	20.50	0.25	76.55	m²	84.21
Boarding to walls, tongued, grooved and veed joints; 25mm thick, 100mm wide boards										
width exceeding 600mm	64.09	10.00	70.50	1.35	0.17	30.82	0.36	101.68	m²	111.85
Boarding to walls, tongued, grooved and veed joints; 25mm thick, 150mm wide boards										
width exceeding 600mm	58.75	10.00	64.62	0.95	0.12	21.69	0.25	86.57	m²	95.22
Boarding to ceilings, tongued, grooved and veed joints; 19mm thick, 100mm wide boards										
width exceeding 600mm	44.25	10.00	48.68	1.85	0.23	42.19	0.50	91.37	m²	100.50
Boarding to ceilings, tongued, grooved and veed joints; 19mm thick, 150mm wide boards										
width exceeding 600mm	50.74	10.00	55.81	1.35	0.17	30.82	0.36	87.00	m²	95.69
Boarding to ceilings, tongued, grooved and veed joints; 25mm thick, 100mm wide boards										
width exceeding 600mm	64.09	10.00	70.50	1.90	0.24	43.39	0.51	114.40	m²	125.84
Boarding to ceilings, tongued, grooved and veed joints; 25mm thick, 150mm wide boards										
width exceeding 600mm	58.75	10.00	64.62	1.40	0.18	32.02	0.38	97.02	m²	106.73
Sapele, wrought, selected for transparent finish; fixing to timber; wall boarding										
Boarding to walls, tongued, grooved and veed joints; 19mm thick, 100mm wide boards										
width exceeding 600mm	114.27	10.00	125.69	1.45	0.18	33.06	0.40	159.15	m²	175.07
Boarding to walls, tongued, grooved and veed joints; 19mm thick, 150mm wide boards										
width exceeding 600mm	96.60	10.00	106.26	1.00	0.12	22.74	0.26	129.26	m²	142.19
Boarding to walls, tongued, grooved and veed joints; 25mm thick, 100mm wide boards										
width exceeding 600mm	154.70	10.00	170.17	1.50	0.19	34.26	0.40	204.83	m²	225.31
Boarding to walls, tongued, grooved and veed joints; 25mm thick, 150mm wide boards										
width exceeding 600mm	131.71	10.00	144.88	1.05	0.13	23.94	0.28	169.10	m²	186.01
Boarding to ceilings, tongued, grooved and veed joints; 19mm thick, 100mm wide boards										
width exceeding 600mm	114.27	10.00	125.69	2.00	0.25	45.63	0.54	171.87	m²	189.06
Boarding to ceilings, tongued, grooved and veed joints; 19mm thick, 150mm wide boards										
width exceeding 600mm	96.60	10.00	106.26	1.50	0.19	34.26	0.40	140.92	m²	155.01
Boarding to ceilings, tongued, grooved and veed joints; 25mm thick, 100mm wide boards										
width exceeding 600mm	154.70	10.00	170.17	2.05	0.26	46.83	0.54	217.55	m²	239.30
Boarding to ceilings, tongued, grooved and veed joints; 25mm thick, 150mm wide boards										
width exceeding 600mm	131.71	10.00	144.88	1.55	0.19	35.31	0.41	180.60	m²	198.66
Abutments										
19mm thick softwood boarding										
raking cutting	1.42	10.00	1.56	0.06	-	1.25	-	2.81	m	3.10
curved cutting	2.13	10.00	2.34	0.09	-	1.88	-	4.22	m	4.64
25mm thick softwood boarding										
raking cutting	1.84	10.00	2.02	0.07	-	1.46	-	3.49	m	3.83
curved cutting	2.76	10.00	3.04	0.10	-	2.09	-	5.12	m	5.64
19mm thick Western Red Cedar boarding										
raking cutting	10.17	10.00	11.19	0.07	-	1.46	-	12.65	m	13.92
curved cutting	15.26	10.00	16.79	0.10	-	2.09	-	18.87	m	20.76
25mm thick Western Red Cedar boarding										
raking cutting	13.84	10.00	15.22	0.08	-	1.67	-	16.89	m	18.58
curved cutting	20.76	10.00	22.83	0.11	-	2.30	-	25.13	m	27.64

Labour hourly rates: (except Specialists) Craft Operatives 20.87 Labourer 15.57 Rates are national average prices. Refer to REGIONAL VARIATIONS for indicative levels of overall pricing in regions	MATERIALS			LABOUR				RATES		
	Del to Site £	Waste %	Material Cost £	Craft Optve Hrs	Lab Hrs	Labour Cost £	Sunds £	Nett Rate £	Unit	Gross rate (10%) £
FLOOR, WALL AND CEILING BOARDING, SHEETING, PANELLING, LININGS AND CASINGS (Cont'd)										
Abutments (Cont'd)										
19 mm thick hardwood boarding										
raking cutting	11.43	10.00	12.57	0.14	-	2.92	-	15.49	m	17.04
curved cutting	17.14	10.00	18.85	0.21	-	4.38	-	23.24	m	25.56
25 mm thick hardwood boarding										
raking cutting	15.47	10.00	17.02	0.16	-	3.34	-	20.36	m	22.39
curved cutting	23.20	10.00	25.53	0.24	-	5.01	-	30.53	m	33.59
Finished angles										
External; 19mm thick softwood boarding tongued and mitred	-	-	-	0.67	-	13.98	-	13.98	m	15.38
External; 25mm thick softwood boarding tongued and mitred	-	-	-	0.70	-	14.61	-	14.61	m	16.07
External; 19mm thick hardwood boarding tongued and mitred	-	-	-	0.95	-	19.83	-	19.83	m	21.81
External; 25mm thick hardwood boarding tongued and mitred	-	-	-	1.00	-	20.87	-	20.87	m	22.96
Solid wood panelling; softwood, wrot - wall panelling										
19mm thick panelled linings to walls; square framed; including grounds										
width exceeding 600mm	35.21	2.50	36.09	1.60	0.20	36.51	0.45	73.04	m²	80.34
width exceeding 600mm; fixing to masonry with screws	35.21	2.50	36.09	2.60	0.32	59.24	0.73	96.06	m²	105.66
25mm thick panelled linings to walls; square framed; including grounds										
width exceeding 600mm	52.84	2.50	54.16	1.70	0.21	38.75	0.48	93.39	m²	102.73
width exceeding 600mm; fixing to masonry with screws	52.84	2.50	54.16	2.70	0.34	61.64	0.78	116.58	m²	128.24
19mm thick panelled linings to walls; square framed; obstructed by integral services; including grounds										
width exceeding 600mm	35.21	2.50	36.09	2.10	0.26	47.88	0.59	84.56	m²	93.01
width exceeding 600mm; fixing to masonry with screws	35.21	2.50	36.09	3.10	0.39	70.77	0.87	107.73	m²	118.50
25mm thick panelled linings to walls; square framed; obstructed by integral services; including grounds										
width exceeding 600mm	52.84	2.50	54.16	2.20	0.27	50.12	0.63	104.91	m²	115.40
width exceeding 600mm; fixing to masonry with screws	52.84	2.50	54.16	3.20	0.40	73.01	0.91	128.08	m²	140.89
19mm thick panelled linings to walls; moulded; including grounds										
width exceeding 600mm	38.73	2.50	39.70	1.70	0.21	38.75	0.48	78.92	m²	86.82
width exceeding 600mm; fixing to masonry with screws	38.73	2.50	39.70	2.70	0.34	61.64	0.78	102.11	m²	112.33
25mm thick panelled linings to walls; moulded; including grounds										
width exceeding 600mm	58.12	2.50	59.58	1.80	0.22	40.99	0.50	101.06	m²	111.17
width exceeding 600mm; fixing to masonry with screws	58.12	2.50	59.58	2.80	0.35	63.89	0.79	124.25	m²	136.68
19mm thick panelled linings to walls; moulded; obstructed by integral services; including grounds										
width exceeding 600mm	38.73	2.50	39.70	2.20	0.27	50.12	0.63	90.44	m²	99.49
width exceeding 600mm; fixing to masonry with screws	38.73	2.50	39.70	3.20	0.40	73.01	0.91	113.62	m²	124.98
25mm thick panelled linings to walls; moulded; obstructed by integral services; including grounds										
width exceeding 600mm	58.12	2.50	59.58	2.30	0.29	52.52	0.64	112.74	m²	124.01
width exceeding 600mm; fixing to masonry with screws	58.12	2.50	59.58	3.30	0.41	75.25	0.94	135.77	m²	149.35
Solid wood panelling; Oak, wrot, selected for transparent finish - wall panelling										
19mm thick panelled linings to walls; square framed; including grounds										
width exceeding 600mm	93.19	2.50	95.52	2.25	0.28	51.32	0.64	147.49	m²	162.23
width exceeding 600mm; fixing to masonry with screws	93.19	2.50	95.52	3.25	0.41	74.21	0.92	170.66	m²	187.73
25mm thick panelled linings to walls; square framed; including grounds										
width exceeding 600mm	159.76	2.50	163.76	2.35	0.29	53.56	0.66	217.98	m²	239.77
width exceeding 600mm; fixing to masonry with screws	159.76	2.50	163.76	3.35	0.42	76.45	0.96	241.17	m²	265.28
19mm thick panelled linings to walls; square framed; obstructed by integral services; including grounds										
width exceeding 600mm	93.19	2.50	95.52	2.75	0.34	62.69	0.78	158.99	m²	174.89
width exceeding 600mm; fixing to masonry with screws	93.19	2.50	95.52	3.75	0.47	85.58	1.06	182.16	m²	200.38
25mm thick panelled linings to walls; square framed; obstructed by integral services; including grounds										
width exceeding 600mm	159.76	2.50	163.76	2.85	0.36	65.08	0.79	229.63	m²	252.60
width exceeding 600mm; fixing to masonry with screws	159.76	2.50	163.76	3.85	0.48	87.82	1.09	252.67	m²	277.94
19mm thick panelled linings to walls; moulded; including grounds										
width exceeding 600mm	102.51	2.50	105.08	2.40	0.30	54.76	0.68	160.51	m²	176.56
width exceeding 600mm; fixing to masonry with screws	102.51	2.50	105.08	3.40	0.42	77.50	0.96	183.53	m²	201.89
25mm thick panelled linings to walls; moulded; including grounds										
width exceeding 600mm	175.74	2.50	180.13	2.50	0.31	57.00	0.71	237.84	m²	261.63
width exceeding 600mm; fixing to masonry with screws	175.74	2.50	180.13	3.50	0.44	79.90	0.99	261.02	m²	287.12
19mm thick panelled linings to walls; moulded; obstructed by integral services; including grounds										
width exceeding 600mm	102.51	2.50	105.08	2.90	0.36	66.13	0.81	172.01	m²	189.22
width exceeding 600mm; fixing to masonry with screws	102.51	2.50	105.08	3.90	0.49	89.02	1.09	195.19	m²	214.71

Labour hourly rates: (except Specialists) Craft Operatives 20.87 Labourer 15.57 Rates are national average prices. Refer to REGIONAL VARIATIONS for indicative levels of overall pricing in regions	MATERIALS			LABOUR				RATES		
	Del to Site £	Waste %	Material Cost £	Craft Optve Hrs	Lab Hrs	Labour Cost £	Sunds £	Nett Rate £	Unit	Gross rate (10%) £
FLOOR, WALL AND CEILING BOARDING, SHEETING, PANELLING, LININGS AND CASINGS (Cont'd)										
Solid wood panelling; Oak, wrot, selected for transparent finish - wall panelling (Cont'd)										
25mm thick panelled linings to walls; moulded; obstructed by integral services; including grounds										
width exceeding 600mm	175.74	2.50	180.13	3.00	0.37	68.37	0.84	249.35	m²	274.28
width exceeding 600mm; fixing to masonry with screws	175.74	2.50	180.13	4.00	0.50	91.26	1.12	272.52	m²	299.77
Solid wood panelling; Sapele, wrot, selected for transparent finish - wall panelling										
19mm thick panelled linings to walls; square framed; including grounds										
width exceeding 600mm	87.83	2.50	90.02	2.05	0.26	46.83	0.58	137.43	m²	151.18
width exceeding 600mm; fixing to masonry with screws	87.83	2.50	90.02	3.05	0.38	69.57	0.87	160.47	m²	176.52
25mm thick panelled linings to walls; square framed; including grounds										
width exceeding 600mm	119.75	2.50	122.74	2.15	0.27	49.07	0.61	172.43	m²	189.67
width exceeding 600mm; fixing to masonry with screws	119.75	2.50	122.74	3.15	0.39	71.81	0.89	195.44	m²	214.99
19mm thick panelled linings to walls; square framed; obstructed by integral services; including grounds										
width exceeding 600mm	87.83	2.50	90.02	2.55	0.32	58.20	0.73	148.95	m²	163.85
width exceeding 600mm; fixing to masonry with screws	87.83	2.50	90.02	3.55	0.44	80.94	1.01	171.97	m²	189.17
25mm thick panelled linings to walls; square framed; obstructed by integral services; including grounds										
width exceeding 600mm	119.75	2.50	122.74	2.65	0.33	60.44	0.74	183.93	m²	202.32
width exceeding 600mm; fixing to masonry with screws	119.75	2.50	122.74	3.65	0.46	83.34	1.02	207.10	m²	227.81
19mm thick panelled linings to walls; moulded; including grounds										
width exceeding 600mm	96.61	2.50	99.03	2.15	0.27	49.07	0.61	148.71	m²	163.58
width exceeding 600mm; fixing to masonry with screws	96.61	2.50	99.03	3.15	0.39	71.81	0.89	171.73	m²	188.90
25mm thick panelled linings to walls; moulded; including grounds										
width exceeding 600mm	131.72	2.50	135.02	2.30	0.29	52.52	0.64	188.17	m²	206.99
width exceeding 600mm; fixing to masonry with screws	131.72	2.50	135.02	3.30	0.41	75.25	0.94	211.21	m²	232.33
19mm thick panelled linings to walls; moulded; obstructed by integral services; including grounds										
width exceeding 600mm	96.61	2.50	99.03	2.65	0.33	60.44	0.74	160.21	m²	176.23
width exceeding 600mm; fixing to masonry with screws	96.61	2.50	99.03	3.65	0.46	83.34	1.02	183.39	m²	201.73
25mm thick panelled linings to walls; moulded; obstructed by integral services; including grounds										
width exceeding 600mm	131.72	2.50	135.02	2.80	0.35	63.89	0.79	199.69	m²	219.66
width exceeding 600mm; fixing to masonry with screws	131.72	2.50	135.02	3.80	0.47	86.62	1.07	222.71	m²	244.98
Veneered plywood panelling; pre-finished, decorative veneers; butt joints - wall panelling. Note. prices are for panelling with Afrormosia, Ash, Beech, Cherry, Elm, Oak, Knotted Pine, Sapele or Teak faced veneers										
4mm thick linings to walls										
width exceeding 600mm	11.74	15.00	13.50	0.80	0.10	18.25	0.21	31.97	m²	35.17
width exceeding 600mm; fixing to timber with adhesive	11.74	15.00	13.50	0.95	0.12	21.69	3.30	38.50	m²	42.35
width exceeding 600mm; fixing to plaster with adhesive	11.74	15.00	13.50	0.90	0.11	20.50	3.30	37.30	m²	41.03
Veneered plywood panelling; flame retardant, pre-finished, decorative, veneers not matched; random V-grooves on face; butt joints - wall panelling. Note. prices are for panelling with Afrormosia, Ash, Beech, Cherry, Elm, Oak, Knotted Pine, Sapele or Teak faced veneers										
6mm thick linings to walls										
width exceeding 600mm	41.17	15.00	47.35	0.80	0.10	18.25	0.21	65.82	m²	72.40
width exceeding 600mm; fixing to timber with adhesive	41.17	15.00	47.35	0.95	0.12	21.69	3.30	72.35	m²	79.58
width exceeding 600mm; fixing to plaster with adhesive	41.17	15.00	47.35	0.90	0.11	20.50	3.30	71.15	m²	78.26
Veneered blockboard panelling; decorative veneers; butt joints - wall panelling; Oak faced										
18mm thick linings to walls fixed to timber										
width exceeding 600mm	24.83	10.00	27.32	0.80	0.10	18.25	0.21	45.78	m²	50.36
Veneered medium density fibre board panelling; decorative veneers; butt joints - wall panelling; Pine faced one side										
6mm thick linings to walls fixed to timber										
width exceeding 600mm	20.30	10.00	22.33	0.80	0.10	18.25	0.21	40.80	m²	44.88
19mm thick linings to walls fixed to timber										
width exceeding 600mm	23.49	10.00	25.84	1.00	0.20	23.98	0.33	50.15	m²	55.17
Veneered medium density fibre board panelling; butt joints - wall panelling; Oak faced one side										
6mm thick linings to walls fixed to timber										
width exceeding 600mm	11.49	10.00	12.64	0.80	0.10	18.25	0.21	31.11	m²	34.22
13mm thick linings to walls fixed to timber										
width exceeding 600mm	13.41	10.00	14.75	0.90	0.15	21.12	0.26	36.13	m²	39.74
19mm thick linings to walls fixed to timber										
width exceeding 600mm	14.60	10.00	16.06	0.80	0.10	18.25	0.21	34.52	m²	37.98

Labour hourly rates: (except Specialists) Craft Operatives 20.87 Labourer 15.57 Rates are national average prices. Refer to REGIONAL VARIATIONS for indicative levels of overall pricing in regions	MATERIALS			LABOUR				RATES		
	Del to Site £	Waste %	Material Cost £	Craft Optve Hrs	Lab Hrs	Labour Cost £	Sunds £	Nett Rate £	Unit	Gross rate (10%) £
FLOOR, WALL AND CEILING BOARDING, SHEETING, PANELLING, LININGS AND CASINGS (Cont'd)										
Veneered medium density fibre board panelling; butt joints - wall panelling; Maple faced one side										
19mm thick linings to walls fixed to timber										
width exceeding 600mm	28.52	10.00	31.38	0.80	0.10	18.25	0.21	49.84	m²	54.83
IRONMONGERY										
Fix only ironmongery (prime cost sum for supply included elsewhere)										
To softwood										
butt hinges; 50mm	-	-	-	0.17	-	3.55	-	3.55	nr	3.90
butt hinges; 100mm	-	-	-	0.17	-	3.55	-	3.55	nr	3.90
rising hinges; 100mm	-	-	-	0.30	-	6.26	-	6.26	nr	6.89
tee hinges; 150mm	-	-	-	0.45	-	9.39	-	9.39	nr	10.33
tee hinges; 300mm	-	-	-	0.55	-	11.48	-	11.48	nr	12.63
tee hinges; 450mm	-	-	-	0.65	-	13.57	-	13.57	nr	14.92
hook and band hinges; 300mm	-	-	-	0.90	-	18.78	-	18.78	nr	20.66
hook and band hinges; 450mm	-	-	-	1.10	-	22.96	-	22.96	nr	25.25
hook and band hinges; 900mm	-	-	-	1.65	-	34.44	-	34.44	nr	37.88
collinge hinges; 600mm	-	-	-	1.00	-	20.87	-	20.87	nr	22.96
collinge hinges; 750mm	-	-	-	1.25	-	26.09	-	26.09	nr	28.70
collinge hinges; 900mm	-	-	-	1.55	-	32.35	-	32.35	nr	35.58
single action floor springs and top centres	-	-	-	2.75	-	57.39	-	57.39	nr	63.13
double action floor springs and top centres	-	-	-	3.30	-	68.87	-	68.87	nr	75.76
coil springs	-	-	-	0.30	-	6.26	-	6.26	nr	6.89
overhead door closers	-	-	-	1.65	-	34.44	-	34.44	nr	37.88
concealed overhead door closers	-	-	-	2.75	-	57.39	-	57.39	nr	63.13
Perko door closers	-	-	-	1.65	-	34.44	-	34.44	nr	37.88
door selectors	-	-	-	2.20	0.28	50.27	-	50.27	nr	55.30
cabin hooks	-	-	-	0.25	-	5.22	-	5.22	nr	5.74
fanlight catches	-	-	-	0.40	-	8.35	-	8.35	nr	9.18
roller catches	-	-	-	0.40	-	8.35	-	8.35	nr	9.18
casement fasteners	-	-	-	0.40	-	8.35	-	8.35	nr	9.18
sash fasteners	-	-	-	1.10	-	22.96	-	22.96	nr	25.25
sash screws	-	-	-	0.55	-	11.48	-	11.48	nr	12.63
mortice latches	-	-	-	0.70	-	14.61	-	14.61	nr	16.07
night latches	-	-	-	1.10	-	22.96	-	22.96	nr	25.25
Norfolk latches	-	-	-	0.90	-	18.78	-	18.78	nr	20.66
rim latches	-	-	-	0.95	-	19.83	-	19.83	nr	21.81
Suffolk latches	-	-	-	0.90	-	18.78	-	18.78	nr	20.66
budget locks	-	-	-	0.75	-	15.65	-	15.65	nr	17.22
cylinder locks	-	-	-	1.10	-	22.96	-	22.96	nr	25.25
dead locks	-	-	-	0.90	-	18.78	-	18.78	nr	20.66
mortice locks	-	-	-	1.10	-	22.96	-	22.96	nr	25.25
rim locks	-	-	-	0.90	-	18.78	-	18.78	nr	20.66
automatic coin collecting locks	-	-	-	2.20	-	45.91	-	45.91	nr	50.51
casement stays	-	-	-	0.30	-	6.26	-	6.26	nr	6.89
quadrant stays	-	-	-	0.30	-	6.26	-	6.26	nr	6.89
barrel bolts; 150mm	-	-	-	0.35	-	7.30	-	7.30	nr	8.03
barrel bolts; 250mm	-	-	-	0.45	-	9.39	-	9.39	nr	10.33
door bolts; 150mm	-	-	-	0.35	-	7.30	-	7.30	nr	8.03
door bolts; 250mm	-	-	-	0.45	-	9.39	-	9.39	nr	10.33
monkey tail bolts; 300mm	-	-	-	0.40	-	8.35	-	8.35	nr	9.18
monkey tail bolts; 450mm	-	-	-	0.45	-	9.39	-	9.39	nr	10.33
monkey tail bolts; 600mm	-	-	-	0.55	-	11.48	-	11.48	nr	12.63
flush bolts; 200mm	-	-	-	0.75	-	15.65	-	15.65	nr	17.22
flush bolts; 450mm	-	-	-	1.10	-	22.96	-	22.96	nr	25.25
indicating bolts	-	-	-	1.10	-	22.96	-	22.96	nr	25.25
panic bolts; to single door	-	-	-	1.65	-	34.44	-	34.44	nr	37.88
panic bolts; to double doors	-	-	-	2.20	-	45.91	-	45.91	nr	50.51
knobs	-	-	-	0.25	-	5.22	-	5.22	nr	5.74
lever handles	-	-	-	0.25	-	5.22	-	5.22	nr	5.74
sash lifts	-	-	-	0.20	-	4.17	-	4.17	nr	4.59
pull handles; 150mm	-	-	-	0.20	-	4.17	-	4.17	nr	4.59
pull handles; 225mm	-	-	-	0.25	-	5.22	-	5.22	nr	5.74
pull handles; 300mm	-	-	-	0.30	-	6.26	-	6.26	nr	6.89
back plates	-	-	-	0.30	-	6.26	-	6.26	nr	6.89
escutcheon plates	-	-	-	0.25	-	5.22	-	5.22	nr	5.74
kicking plates	-	-	-	0.55	-	11.48	-	11.48	nr	12.63
letter plates	-	-	-	1.65	-	34.44	-	34.44	nr	37.88
push plates; 225mm	-	-	-	0.25	-	5.22	-	5.22	nr	5.74
push plates; 300mm	-	-	-	0.30	-	6.26	-	6.26	nr	6.89
shelf brackets	-	-	-	0.30	-	6.26	-	6.26	nr	6.89
sash cleats	-	-	-	0.25	-	5.22	-	5.22	nr	5.74
To softwood and brickwork										
cabin hooks	-	-	-	0.30	-	6.26	-	6.26	nr	6.89
To hardwood or the like										
butt hinges; 50mm	-	-	-	0.25	-	5.22	-	5.22	nr	5.74
butt hinges; 100mm	-	-	-	0.25	-	5.22	-	5.22	nr	5.74
rising hinges; 100mm	-	-	-	0.40	-	8.35	-	8.35	nr	9.18
tee hinges; 150mm	-	-	-	0.60	-	12.52	-	12.52	nr	13.77
tee hinges; 300mm	-	-	-	0.75	-	15.65	-	15.65	nr	17.22
tee hinges; 450mm	-	-	-	0.90	-	18.78	-	18.78	nr	20.66
hook and band hinges; 300mm	-	-	-	1.20	-	25.04	-	25.04	nr	27.55
hook and band hinges; 450mm	-	-	-	1.55	-	32.35	-	32.35	nr	35.58
hook and band hinges; 900mm	-	-	-	2.20	-	45.91	-	45.91	nr	50.51
collinge hinges; 600mm	-	-	-	1.45	-	30.26	-	30.26	nr	33.29
collinge hinges; 750mm	-	-	-	1.85	-	38.61	-	38.61	nr	42.47

Labour hourly rates: (except Specialists) Craft Operatives 20.87 Labourer 15.57 Rates are national average prices. Refer to REGIONAL VARIATIONS for indicative levels of overall pricing in regions	MATERIALS			LABOUR				RATES		
	Del to Site £	Waste %	Material Cost £	Craft Optve Hrs	Lab Hrs	Labour Cost £	Sunds £	Nett Rate £	Unit	Gross rate (10%) £
IRONMONGERY (Cont'd)										
Fix only ironmongery (prime cost sum for supply included elsewhere) (Cont'd)										
To hardwood or the like (Cont'd)										
collinge hinges; 900mm	-	-	-	2.25	-	46.96	-	46.96	nr	51.65
single action floor springs and top centres	-	-	-	4.10	-	85.57	-	85.57	nr	94.12
double action floor springs and top centres	-	-	-	4.90	-	102.26	-	102.26	nr	112.49
coil springs	-	-	-	0.45	-	9.39	-	9.39	nr	10.33
overhead door closers	-	-	-	2.45	-	51.13	-	51.13	nr	56.24
concealed overhead door closers	-	-	-	4.10	-	85.57	-	85.57	nr	94.12
Perko door closers	-	-	-	2.45	-	51.13	-	51.13	nr	56.24
door selectors	-	-	-	3.30	0.40	75.10	-	75.10	nr	82.61
cabin hooks	-	-	-	0.35	-	7.30	-	7.30	nr	8.03
fanlight catches	-	-	-	0.55	-	11.48	-	11.48	nr	12.63
roller catches	-	-	-	0.55	-	11.48	-	11.48	nr	12.63
casement fasteners	-	-	-	0.55	-	11.48	-	11.48	nr	12.63
sash fasteners	-	-	-	1.65	-	34.44	-	34.44	nr	37.88
sash screws	-	-	-	0.80	-	16.70	-	16.70	nr	18.37
mortice latches	-	-	-	1.10	-	22.96	-	22.96	nr	25.25
night latches	-	-	-	1.65	-	34.44	-	34.44	nr	37.88
Norfolk latches	-	-	-	1.30	-	27.13	-	27.13	nr	29.84
rim latches	-	-	-	0.80	-	16.70	-	16.70	nr	18.37
Suffolk latches	-	-	-	1.30	-	27.13	-	27.13	nr	29.84
budget locks	-	-	-	1.10	-	22.96	-	22.96	nr	25.25
cylinder locks	-	-	-	1.65	-	34.44	-	34.44	nr	37.88
dead locks	-	-	-	1.30	-	27.13	-	27.13	nr	29.84
mortice locks	-	-	-	1.65	-	34.44	-	34.44	nr	37.88
rim locks	-	-	-	1.30	-	27.13	-	27.13	nr	29.84
automatic coin collecting locks	-	-	-	3.30	-	68.87	-	68.87	nr	75.76
casement stays	-	-	-	0.40	-	8.35	-	8.35	nr	9.18
quadrant stays	-	-	-	0.40	-	8.35	-	8.35	nr	9.18
barrel bolts; 150mm	-	-	-	0.45	-	9.39	-	9.39	nr	10.33
barrel bolts; 250mm	-	-	-	0.60	-	12.52	-	12.52	nr	13.77
door bolts; 150mm	-	-	-	0.45	-	9.39	-	9.39	nr	10.33
door bolts; 250mm	-	-	-	0.60	-	12.52	-	12.52	nr	13.77
monkey tail bolts; 300mm	-	-	-	0.55	-	11.48	-	11.48	nr	12.63
monkey tail bolts; 450mm	-	-	-	0.65	-	13.57	-	13.57	nr	14.92
monkey tail bolts; 600mm	-	-	-	0.75	-	15.65	-	15.65	nr	17.22
flush bolts; 200mm	-	-	-	1.10	-	22.96	-	22.96	nr	25.25
flush bolts; 450mm	-	-	-	1.65	-	34.44	-	34.44	nr	37.88
indicating bolts	-	-	-	1.65	-	34.44	-	34.44	nr	37.88
panic bolts; to single door	-	-	-	2.45	-	51.13	-	51.13	nr	56.24
panic bolts; to double doors	-	-	-	3.30	-	68.87	-	68.87	nr	75.76
knobs	-	-	-	0.35	-	7.30	-	7.30	nr	8.03
lever handles	-	-	-	0.35	-	7.30	-	7.30	nr	8.03
sash lifts	-	-	-	0.35	-	7.30	-	7.30	nr	8.03
pull handles; 150mm	-	-	-	0.30	-	6.26	-	6.26	nr	6.89
pull handles; 225mm	-	-	-	0.35	-	7.30	-	7.30	nr	8.03
pull handles; 300mm	-	-	-	0.40	-	8.35	-	8.35	nr	9.18
back plates	-	-	-	0.40	-	8.35	-	8.35	nr	9.18
escutcheon plates	-	-	-	0.35	-	7.30	-	7.30	nr	8.03
kicking plates	-	-	-	0.80	-	16.70	-	16.70	nr	18.37
letter plates	-	-	-	2.45	-	51.13	-	51.13	nr	56.24
push plates; 225mm	-	-	-	0.35	-	7.30	-	7.30	nr	8.03
push plates; 300mm	-	-	-	0.40	-	8.35	-	8.35	nr	9.18
shelf brackets	-	-	-	0.45	-	9.39	-	9.39	nr	10.33
sash cleats	-	-	-	0.35	-	7.30	-	7.30	nr	8.03
To hardwood and brickwork										
cabin hooks	-	-	-	0.40	-	8.35	-	8.35	nr	9.18
Water bars; steel; galvanised										
Water bars; to concrete										
flat section; setting in groove in mastic										
25 x 3 x 900mm long	4.45	5.00	4.68	0.75	0.09	17.05	0.68	22.41	nr	24.65
40 x 3 x 900mm long	5.27	5.00	5.54	0.75	0.09	17.05	0.82	23.42	nr	25.76
75 x 6 x 900mm long	18.17	5.00	19.08	0.75	0.09	17.05	0.82	36.96	nr	40.65
100 x 6 x 900mm long	28.50	5.00	29.92	0.75	0.09	17.05	0.82	47.80	nr	52.58
150 x 6 x 900mm long	30.27	5.00	31.79	0.75	0.09	17.05	0.82	49.67	nr	54.63
Water bars; to hardwood										
flat section; setting in groove in mastic										
25 x 3 x 900mm long	4.45	5.00	4.68	0.65	0.08	14.81	0.68	20.16	nr	22.18
40 x 3 x 900mm long	5.27	5.00	5.54	0.65	0.08	14.81	0.82	21.17	nr	23.29
75 x 6 x 900mm long	18.17	5.00	19.08	0.65	0.08	14.81	0.82	34.71	nr	38.18
100 x 6 x 900mm long	28.50	5.00	29.92	0.65	0.08	14.81	0.82	45.56	nr	50.12
150 x 6 x 900mm long	30.27	5.00	31.79	0.65	0.08	14.81	0.82	47.42	nr	52.17
Sliding door gear, P.C Henderson Ltd.										
To softwood, interior straight sliding door gear sets for commercial and domestic doors										
Senator single door										
Door set comprising track, hangers, end stops and bottom guide; for doors 20 - 35mm thick, maximum weight 25kg maximum 900mm wide	42.47	2.50	43.53	1.65	-	34.44	-	77.97	nr	85.76
aluminium track 1800mm long; 21A/1800	25.67	2.50	26.31	0.70	-	14.61	-	40.92	nr	45.01
door stop; white nylon; 28P	1.67	2.50	1.71	0.11	-	2.30	-	4.01	nr	4.41
door guide; 162	3.94	2.50	4.04	0.40	-	8.35	-	12.39	nr	13.63
Phantom single door										
Door set comprising top assembly, hangers, adjustable nylon guide and door stops; for doors 30 - 50mm thick, maximum weight 45kg, 610 - 915mm wide	71.62	2.50	73.41	1.95	-	40.70	-	114.11	nr	125.52

Labour hourly rates: (except Specialists) Craft Operatives 20.87 Labourer 15.57 Rates are national average prices. Refer to REGIONAL VARIATIONS for indicative levels of overall pricing in regions	MATERIALS			LABOUR				RATES		
	Del to Site £	Waste %	Material Cost £	Craft Optve Hrs	Lab Hrs	Labour Cost £	Sunds £	Nett Rate £	Unit	Gross rate (10%) £
IRONMONGERY (Cont'd)										
Sliding door gear, P.C Henderson Ltd. (Cont'd)										
To softwood, interior straight sliding door gear sets for commercial and domestic doors (Cont'd)										
Phantom single door (Cont'd)										
track 1525mm long; 171	27.11	2.50	27.79	0.70	-	14.61	-	42.40	nr	46.64
door stop; white nylon; rubber buffer; 110N	1.93	2.50	1.98	0.11	-	2.30	-	4.27	nr	4.70
door guide; 162	3.94	2.50	4.04	0.40	-	8.35	-	12.39	nr	13.63
Marathon 55 Junior door										
Nr J2 single door set comprising top assembly, hangers, end stops, inverted guide channel and nylon guide; for doors 32 - 50mm thick, maximum weight, 55kg, 400 - 750mm wide; forming groove for guide channel	61.73	2.50	63.27	2.65	-	55.31	-	118.58	nr	130.44
Nr J3 single door set comprising top assembly, hangers, end stops, inverted guide channel and nylon guide; for doors 32 - 50mm thick, maximum weight, 55kg, 750 - 900mm wide; forming groove for guide channel	65.15	2.50	66.78	2.85	-	59.48	-	126.26	nr	138.88
Nr J4 single door set comprising top assembly, hangers, end stops, inverted guide channel and nylon guide; for doors 32 - 50mm thick, maximum weight, 55kg, 900 - 1050mm wide; forming groove for guide channel	70.52	2.50	72.28	3.10	-	64.70	-	136.98	nr	150.68
Nr J5 single door set comprising top assembly, hangers, end stops, inverted guide channel and nylon guide; for doors 32 - 50mm thick, maximum weight, 55kg, 1050 - 1200mm wide; forming groove for guide channel	79.72	2.50	81.71	3.30	-	68.87	-	150.58	nr	165.64
Nr J6 single door set comprising top assembly, hangers, end stops, inverted guide channel and nylon guide; for doors 32 - 50mm thick, maximum weight, 55kg, 1200 - 1500mm wide; forming groove for guide channel	132.25	2.50	135.56	3.50	-	73.05	-	208.60	nr	229.46
steel guide channel 1800mm long; 93S/1800	15.65	2.50	16.04	0.70	-	14.61	-	30.65	nr	33.72
nylon top plate; 43	6.03	2.50	6.18	0.11	-	2.30	-	8.48	nr	9.32
Marathon 90 Senior door										
Nr S3 single door set comprising top assembly, hangers, end stops, inverted guide channel and nylon guide; for doors 32 - 50mm thick maximum weight 90kg, 750 - 900mm wide; forming groove for guide channel	87.41	2.50	89.60	3.10	-	64.70	-	154.29	nr	169.72
Nr S4 single door set comprising top assembly, hangers, end stops, inverted guide channel and nylon guide; for doors 32 - 50mm thick maximum weight 90kg, 900 - 1050mm wide; forming groove for guide channel	97.07	2.50	99.50	3.30	-	68.87	-	168.37	nr	185.20
Nr S5 single door set comprising top assembly, hangers, end stops, inverted guide channel and nylon guide; for doors 32 - 50mm thick maximum weight 90kg, 1050 - 1200mm wide; forming groove for guide channel	107.10	2.50	109.78	3.50	-	73.05	-	182.82	nr	201.10
Nr S6 single door set comprising top assembly, hangers, end stops, inverted guide channel and nylon guide; for doors 32 - 50mm thick maximum weight 90kg, 1200 - 1500mm wide; forming groove for guide channel	171.68	2.50	175.97	3.65	-	76.18	-	252.15	nr	277.36
steel guide channel 2400mm long; 93S/2400	20.83	2.50	21.35	0.70	-	14.61	-	35.96	nr	39.56
nylon guide 102N/93	2.89	2.50	2.96	0.11	-	2.30	-	5.26	nr	5.78
To softwood, interior straight sliding door gear sets for wardrobe and cupboard doors										
Single Top door										
;	24.91	2.50	25.53	1.40	-	29.22	-	54.75	nr	60.23
Nr ST15 single door set comprising track, hangers, guides and safety stop; for door 16 - 35mm thick, maximum weight 25kg, maximum 900mm wide; one door to 750mm wide opening	28.28	2.50	28.99	1.50	-	31.31	-	60.29	nr	66.32
Nr ST18 single door set comprising track, hangers, guides and safety stop; for door 16 - 35mm thick, maximum weight 25kg, maximum 900mm wide; one door to 900mm wide opening	32.02	2.50	32.82	1.60	-	33.39	-	66.21	nr	72.83
Double Top door										
Nr W12 bi-passing door set comprising double track section, hangers, guides and safety stop; for doors 16 - 35mm thick, maximum weight 25kg, maximum 900mm wide; two doors in 1200mm wide opening	43.10	2.50	44.18	2.20	-	45.91	-	90.09	nr	99.10
Nr W15 bi-passing door set comprising double track section, hangers, guides and safety stop; for doors 16 - 35mm thick, maximum weight 25kg, maximum 900mm wide; two doors in 1500mm wide opening	48.03	2.50	49.23	2.30	-	48.00	-	97.23	nr	106.95
Nr W18 bi-passing door set comprising double track section, hangers, guides and safety stop; for doors 16 - 35mm thick, maximum weight 25kg, maximum 900mm wide; two doors in 1800mm wide opening	53.27	2.50	54.60	2.40	-	50.09	-	104.69	nr	115.16
Nr W24 bi-passing door set comprising double track section, hangers, guides and safety stop; for doors 16 - 35mm thick, maximum weight 25kg, maximum 900mm wide; three doors in 2400mm wide opening	69.89	2.50	71.64	2.65	-	55.31	-	126.94	nr	139.64
Bifold door										
Nr B10-2 folding door set comprising top guide track, top and bottom pivots; top guide and hinges; for doors 20 - 35mm thick; maximum weight 14kg each leaf, maximum 530mm wide; two doors in 1000mm wide opening	39.62	2.50	40.61	3.30	-	68.87	-	109.48	nr	120.43
Nr B15-4 folding door set comprising top guide track, top and bottom pivots, top guide and hinges; for doors 20 - 35mm thick, maximum weight 14kg each leaf, maximum 530mm wide; four doors in 1500mm wide opening with aligner	68.40	2.50	70.11	6.60	-	137.74	-	207.85	nr	228.64
Nr B20-4 folding door set comprising top guide track, top and bottom pivots, top guide and hinges; for doors 20 - 35mm thick, maximum weight 14kg each leaf, maximum 530mm wide; four doors in 2000mm wide opening with aligner	73.60	2.50	75.44	7.15	-	149.22	-	224.66	nr	247.13

Labour hourly rates: (except Specialists) Craft Operatives 20.87 Labourer 15.57 Rates are national average prices. Refer to REGIONAL VARIATIONS for indicative levels of overall pricing in regions	MATERIALS			LABOUR				RATES		
	Del to Site £	Waste %	Material Cost £	Craft Optve Hrs	Lab Hrs	Labour Cost £	Sunds £	Nett Rate £	Unit	Gross rate (10%) £
IRONMONGERY (Cont'd)										
Sliding door gear, P.C Henderson Ltd. (Cont'd)										
To softwood interior straight sliding door gear sets for built in cupboard doors										
Slipper door										
Nr SS4 double passing door set comprising two top tracks, sliders, safety stop, flush pulls and guides; for doors 16 - 30mm thick, maximum weight 9kg, maximum 900mm wide; two doors in 1200mm wide opening	30.41	2.50	31.17	2.05	-	42.78	-	73.95	nr	81.35
Nr SS5 double passing door set comprising two top tracks, sliders, safety stop, flush pulls and guides; for doors 16 - 30mm thick, maximum weight 9kg, maximum 900mm wide; two doors in 1500mm wide opening	35.76	2.50	36.65	2.20	-	45.91	-	82.57	nr	90.82
Nr SS6 double passing door set comprising two top tracks, sliders, safety stop, flush pulls and guides; for doors 16 - 30mm thick, maximum weight 9kg, maximum 900mm wide; two doors in 1800mm wide opening	39.91	2.50	40.91	2.35	-	49.04	-	89.95	nr	98.95
To softwood, interior straight sliding door gear sets for cupboards, book cases and cabinet work										
Loretto door										
Nr D4 bi-passing door set comprising two top guide channels, two bottom rails, nylon guides and bottom rollers; for doors 20 - 45mm thick; maximum weight 23kg, maximum 900mm wide; two doors in 1200mm wide opening; forming grooves for top guide channels and bottom rails; forming sinkings for bottom rollers	51.49	2.50	52.78	2.75	-	57.39	-	110.17	nr	121.19
Nr D5 bi-passing door set comprising two top guide channels, two bottom rails, nylon guides and bottom rollers; for doors 20 - 45mm thick; maximum weight 23kg, maximum 900mm wide; two doors in 1500mm wide opening; forming grooves for top guide channels and bottom rails; forming sinkings for bottom rollers	57.26	2.50	58.69	2.85	-	59.48	-	118.17	nr	129.99
Nr D6 bi-passing door set comprising two top guide channels, two bottom rails, nylon guides and bottom rollers; for doors 20 - 45mm thick; maximum weight 23kg, maximum 900mm wide; two doors in 1800mm wide opening; forming grooves for top guide channels and bottom rails; forming sinkings for bottom rollers	64.76	2.50	66.38	3.00	-	62.61	-	128.99	nr	141.89
extra for mortice fixed bottom rollers (pair)	12.83	2.50	13.15	0.40	-	8.35	-	21.50	nr	23.65
extra for flush pull	18.67	2.50	19.14	0.30	-	6.26	-	25.40	nr	27.94
To softwood, interior straight room divider gear sets										
Husky 50 door										
Nr H50/15 steel track sliding door gear; 1500mm track length	56.31	2.50	57.72	6.40	-	133.57	-	191.29	nr	210.41
To softwood interior straight sliding door gear sets for glass panels										
Zenith door										
Nr Z12 double passing door set comprising double top guide, bottom rail, glass rail with rubber glazing strip, end caps and bottom rollers; for panels 6mm thick, maximum weight 16kg or 1m² per panel; two panels nr 1200mm wide opening	79.26	2.50	81.24	1.65	-	34.44	-	115.68	nr	127.24
Nr Z15 double passing door set comprising double top guide, bottom rail, glass rail with rubber glazing strip, end caps and bottom rollers; for panels 6mm thick, maximum weight 16kg or 1m² per panel; two panels nr 1500mm wide opening	90.03	2.50	92.28	1.80	-	37.57	-	129.85	nr	142.83
Z18 double passing door set comprising double top guide, bottom rail, glass rail with rubber glazing strip, end caps and bottom rollers; for panels 6mm thick, maximum weight 16kg or 1m² per panel; two panels nr 1800mm wide opening	100.77	2.50	103.29	2.00	-	41.74	-	145.03	nr	159.53
extra for finger pull	5.33	2.50	5.46	0.45	-	9.39	-	14.85	nr	16.34
extra for cylinder lock	20.95	2.50	21.47	1.10	-	22.96	-	44.43	nr	48.87
extra for glazing strip	2.84	2.50	2.91	0.35	-	7.30	-	10.22	m	11.24
Hinges; standard quality										
To softwood										
backflap hinges; steel										
25mm	0.30	2.50	0.30	0.15	-	3.13	-	3.43	nr	3.78
38mm	0.49	2.50	0.50	0.17	-	3.55	-	4.05	nr	4.45
50mm	0.90	2.50	0.92	0.17	-	3.55	-	4.47	nr	4.91
63mm	1.81	2.50	1.85	0.17	-	3.55	-	5.40	nr	5.94
75mm	2.73	2.50	2.80	0.17	-	3.55	-	6.35	nr	6.98
butt hinges; steel; light medium pattern										
38mm	0.15	2.50	0.15	0.17	-	3.55	-	3.70	nr	4.07
50mm	0.19	2.50	0.19	0.17	-	3.55	-	3.74	nr	4.11
63mm	0.24	2.50	0.25	0.17	-	3.55	-	3.80	nr	4.18
75mm	0.10	2.50	0.11	0.17	-	3.55	-	3.65	nr	4.02
100mm	0.25	2.50	0.26	0.17	-	3.55	-	3.81	nr	4.19
butt hinges; steel; strong pattern										
75mm	0.59	2.50	0.61	0.17	-	3.55	-	4.16	nr	4.57
100mm	0.74	2.50	0.76	0.17	-	3.55	-	4.31	nr	4.74
butt hinges; steel; electro brass finish; washered; No.1838										
75mm	0.54	-	0.54	0.17	-	3.55	-	4.09	nr	4.49
butt hinges; cast iron; light										
50mm	1.41	2.50	1.45	0.17	-	3.55	-	5.00	nr	5.49
63mm	1.32	2.50	1.35	0.17	-	3.55	-	4.90	nr	5.39
75mm	1.94	2.50	1.99	0.17	-	3.55	-	5.54	nr	6.09
100mm	3.13	2.50	3.21	0.17	-	3.55	-	6.76	nr	7.43
butt hinges; brass, brass pin										
38mm	1.12	2.50	1.15	0.17	-	3.55	-	4.70	nr	5.17
50mm	0.26	2.50	0.26	0.17	-	3.55	-	3.81	nr	4.19
63mm	1.25	2.50	1.28	0.17	-	3.55	-	4.83	nr	5.31
75mm	0.28	2.50	0.29	0.17	-	3.55	-	3.84	nr	4.22

Labour hourly rates: (except Specialists) Craft Operatives 20.87 Labourer 15.57 Rates are national average prices. Refer to REGIONAL VARIATIONS for indicative levels of overall pricing in regions	MATERIALS			LABOUR				RATES		
	Del to Site £	Waste %	Material Cost £	Craft Optve Hrs	Lab Hrs	Labour Cost £	Sunds £	Nett Rate £	Unit	Gross rate (10%) £
IRONMONGERY (Cont'd)										
Hinges; standard quality (Cont'd)										
To softwood (Cont'd)										
butt hinges; brass, brass pin (Cont'd)										
100mm	0.70	2.50	0.72	0.17	-	3.55	-	4.27	nr	4.69
butt hinges; brass, steel washers, steel pin										
75mm	3.16	2.50	3.24	0.17	-	3.55	-	6.79	nr	7.47
100mm	3.60	2.50	3.69	0.17	-	3.55	-	7.24	nr	7.96
butt hinges; brass, B.M.A., steel washers, steel pin										
75mm	6.73	2.50	6.90	0.17	-	3.55	-	10.45	nr	11.49
100mm	10.61	2.50	10.88	0.17	-	3.55	-	14.43	nr	15.87
butt hinges; brass, chromium plated, double phosphor bronze washers, steel pin										
75mm	5.90	2.50	6.05	0.17	-	3.55	-	9.60	nr	10.55
100mm	5.35	2.50	5.48	0.17	-	3.55	-	9.03	nr	9.93
butt hinges; aluminium, stainless steel pin; nylon washers										
75mm	6.19	2.50	6.34	0.17	-	3.55	-	9.89	nr	10.88
100mm	3.59	2.50	3.68	0.17	-	3.55	-	7.23	nr	7.95
rising hinges; steel										
75mm	1.57	2.50	1.61	0.30	-	6.26	-	7.87	nr	8.66
100mm	1.99	2.50	2.03	0.30	-	6.26	-	8.30	nr	9.13
spring hinges; steel, lacquered; single action										
100mm	8.71	2.50	8.93	0.57	-	11.90	-	20.82	nr	22.90
125mm	14.15	2.50	14.51	0.62	-	12.94	-	27.45	nr	30.19
150mm	15.74	2.50	16.13	0.67	-	13.98	-	30.12	nr	33.13
spring hinges; steel, lacquered; double action										
75mm	7.42	2.50	7.61	0.67	-	13.98	-	21.59	nr	23.75
100mm	8.71	2.50	8.93	0.67	-	13.98	-	22.91	nr	25.20
125mm	14.15	2.50	14.51	0.77	-	16.07	-	30.58	nr	33.64
150mm	15.74	2.50	16.13	0.77	-	16.07	-	32.20	nr	35.42
tee hinges; japanned; light										
150mm	0.71	2.50	0.73	0.45	-	9.39	-	10.12	nr	11.13
230mm	1.03	2.50	1.06	0.50	-	10.44	-	11.49	nr	12.64
300mm	1.35	2.50	1.39	0.55	-	11.48	-	12.87	nr	14.15
tee hinges; japanned; medium										
375mm	2.73	2.50	2.80	0.60	-	12.52	-	15.32	nr	16.85
450mm	3.46	2.50	3.54	0.65	-	13.57	-	17.11	nr	18.82
tee hinges; galvanised; heavy										
230mm	2.73	2.50	2.80	0.55	-	11.48	-	14.28	nr	15.70
300mm	3.18	2.50	3.26	0.60	-	12.52	-	15.78	nr	17.36
375mm	5.02	2.50	5.15	0.65	-	13.57	-	18.71	nr	20.58
450mm	6.85	2.50	7.03	0.70	-	14.61	-	21.63	nr	23.80
600mm	10.06	2.50	10.31	0.75	-	15.65	-	25.96	nr	28.56
hook and band hinges; on plate; heavy; black										
300mm	6.02	2.50	6.17	0.90	-	18.78	-	24.95	nr	27.45
450mm	8.73	2.50	8.95	1.10	-	22.96	-	31.90	nr	35.09
610mm	11.10	2.50	11.38	1.30	-	27.13	-	38.51	nr	42.36
910mm	18.32	2.50	18.77	1.65	-	34.44	-	53.21	nr	58.53
collinge hinges; cup for wood; best quality										
610mm	120.00	2.50	123.00	1.00	-	20.87	-	143.87	nr	158.26
762mm	155.00	2.50	158.88	1.25	-	26.09	-	184.96	nr	203.46
914mm	185.00	2.50	189.62	1.55	-	32.35	-	221.97	nr	244.17
parliament hinges; steel; 100mm	1.63	2.50	1.67	0.30	-	6.26	-	7.93	nr	8.72
cellar flap hinges; wrought, welded, plain joint; 450mm	10.12	2.50	10.38	0.55	-	11.48	-	21.86	nr	24.04
To hardwood or the like										
backflap hinges; steel										
25mm	0.30	2.50	0.30	0.25	-	5.22	-	5.52	nr	6.07
38mm	0.49	2.50	0.50	0.25	-	5.22	-	5.72	nr	6.29
50mm	0.90	2.50	0.92	0.25	-	5.22	-	6.14	nr	6.75
63mm	1.81	2.50	1.85	0.25	-	5.22	-	7.07	nr	7.78
75mm	2.73	2.50	2.80	0.25	-	5.22	-	8.01	nr	8.82
butt hinges; steel; light medium pattern										
38mm	0.15	2.50	0.15	0.25	-	5.22	-	5.37	nr	5.91
50mm	0.19	2.50	0.19	0.25	-	5.22	-	5.41	nr	5.95
63mm	0.24	2.50	0.25	0.25	-	5.22	-	5.47	nr	6.01
75mm	0.10	2.50	0.11	0.25	-	5.22	-	5.32	nr	5.86
100mm	0.25	2.50	0.26	0.25	-	5.22	-	5.48	nr	6.03
butt hinges; steel; strong pattern										
75mm	0.59	2.50	0.61	0.25	-	5.22	-	5.83	nr	6.41
100mm	0.74	2.50	0.76	0.25	-	5.22	-	5.97	nr	6.57
butt hinges; cast iron; light										
50mm	1.41	2.50	1.45	0.25	-	5.22	-	6.66	nr	7.33
63mm	1.32	2.50	1.35	0.25	-	5.22	-	6.57	nr	7.23
75mm	1.94	2.50	1.99	0.25	-	5.22	-	7.21	nr	7.93
100mm	3.13	2.50	3.21	0.25	-	5.22	-	8.43	nr	9.27
butt hinges; brass, brass pin										
38mm	1.12	2.50	1.15	0.25	-	5.22	-	6.37	nr	7.01
50mm	0.26	2.50	0.26	0.25	-	5.22	-	5.48	nr	6.03
63mm	1.25	2.50	1.28	0.25	-	5.22	-	6.50	nr	7.15
75mm	0.28	2.50	0.29	0.25	-	5.22	-	5.51	nr	6.06
100mm	0.70	2.50	0.72	0.25	-	5.22	-	5.94	nr	6.53
butt hinges; brass, steel washers, steel pin										
75mm	3.16	2.50	3.24	0.25	-	5.22	-	8.46	nr	9.31
100mm	3.60	2.50	3.69	0.25	-	5.22	-	8.91	nr	9.80
butt hinges; brass, B.M.A., steel washers, steel pin										
75mm	6.73	2.50	6.90	0.25	-	5.22	-	12.12	nr	13.33
100mm	10.61	2.50	10.88	0.25	-	5.22	-	16.10	nr	17.71
butt hinges; brass, chromium plated, double phosphor washers, steel pin										
75mm	5.90	2.50	6.05	0.25	-	5.22	-	11.27	nr	12.39
100mm	5.35	2.50	5.48	0.25	-	5.22	-	10.70	nr	11.77

Labour hourly rates: (except Specialists) Craft Operatives 20.87 Labourer 15.57 Rates are national average prices. Refer to REGIONAL VARIATIONS for indicative levels of overall pricing in regions	MATERIALS			LABOUR				RATES		
	Del to Site £	Waste %	Material Cost £	Craft Optve Hrs	Lab Hrs	Labour Cost £	Sunds £	Nett Rate £	Unit	Gross rate (10%) £
IRONMONGERY (Cont'd)										
Hinges; standard quality (Cont'd)										
To hardwood or the like (Cont'd)										
butt hinges; aluminium, aluminium pin; nylon washers										
75mm	6.19	2.50	6.34	0.25	-	5.22	-	11.56	nr	12.72
100mm	3.59	2.50	3.68	0.25	-	5.22	-	8.90	nr	9.79
rising hinges; steel										
75mm	1.57	2.50	1.61	0.40	-	8.35	-	9.96	nr	10.95
100mm	1.99	2.50	2.03	0.40	-	8.35	-	10.38	nr	11.42
spring hinges; steel, lacquered; single action										
100mm	8.71	2.50	8.93	0.85	-	17.74	-	26.67	nr	29.33
125mm	14.15	2.50	14.51	0.90	-	18.78	-	33.29	nr	36.62
150mm	15.74	2.50	16.13	0.95	-	19.83	-	35.96	nr	39.55
spring hinges; steel, lacquered; double action										
75mm	7.42	2.50	7.61	0.90	-	18.78	-	26.39	nr	29.03
100mm	8.71	2.50	8.93	0.95	-	19.83	-	28.75	nr	31.63
125mm	14.15	2.50	14.51	1.05	-	21.91	-	36.42	nr	40.06
150mm	15.74	2.50	16.13	1.10	-	22.96	-	39.09	nr	43.00
tee hinges; japanned; light										
150mm	0.71	2.50	0.73	0.60	-	12.52	-	13.25	nr	14.57
230mm	1.03	2.50	1.06	0.65	-	13.57	-	14.62	nr	16.09
300mm	1.35	2.50	1.39	0.75	-	15.65	-	17.04	nr	18.74
tee hinges; japanned; medium										
375mm	2.73	2.50	2.80	0.80	-	16.70	-	19.49	nr	21.44
450mm	3.46	2.50	3.54	0.90	-	18.78	-	22.33	nr	24.56
tee hinges; galvanised; heavy										
230mm	2.73	2.50	2.80	0.75	-	15.65	-	18.45	nr	20.29
300mm	3.18	2.50	3.26	0.80	-	16.70	-	19.96	nr	21.95
375mm	5.02	2.50	5.15	0.85	-	17.74	-	22.89	nr	25.17
450mm	6.85	2.50	7.03	0.90	-	18.78	-	25.81	nr	28.39
600mm	10.06	2.50	10.31	1.00	-	20.87	-	31.18	nr	34.30
hook and band hinges; on plate; heavy										
300mm	6.02	2.50	6.17	1.20	-	25.04	-	31.22	nr	34.34
450mm	8.73	2.50	8.95	1.55	-	32.35	-	41.30	nr	45.43
610mm	11.10	2.50	11.38	1.90	-	39.65	-	51.03	nr	56.14
914mm	18.32	2.50	18.77	2.20	-	45.91	-	64.69	nr	71.16
collinge hinges; cup for wood; best quality										
610mm	120.00	2.50	123.00	1.45	-	30.26	-	153.26	nr	168.59
762mm	155.00	2.50	158.88	1.85	-	38.61	-	197.48	nr	217.23
914mm	185.00	2.50	189.62	2.25	-	46.96	-	236.58	nr	260.24
parliament hinges; steel; 100mm	1.63	2.50	1.67	0.40	-	8.35	-	10.02	nr	11.02
cellar flap hinges; wrought, welded, plain joint; 450mm	10.12	2.50	10.38	0.85	-	17.74	-	28.12	nr	30.93
Floor springs; standard quality										
To softwood										
single action floor springs and top centres; stainless steel cover	213.15	2.50	218.48	2.75	-	57.39	-	275.87	nr	303.46
single action floor springs and top centres; stainless steel cover; hold open	213.15	2.50	218.48	2.75	-	57.39	-	275.87	nr	303.46
double action floor springs and top centres; stainless steel cover.	202.10	2.50	207.15	3.30	-	68.87	-	276.02	nr	303.63
double action floor springs and top centres; stainless steel cover; hold open	202.10	2.50	207.15	3.30	-	68.87	-	276.02	nr	303.63
To hardwood or the like										
single action floor springs and top centres; stainless steel cover	213.15	2.50	218.48	4.10	-	85.57	-	304.05	nr	334.45
single action floor springs and top centres; stainless steel cover; hold open	213.15	2.50	218.48	4.10	-	85.57	-	304.05	nr	334.45
double action floor springs and top centres; stainless steel cover.	202.10	2.50	207.15	4.90	-	102.26	-	309.42	nr	340.36
double action floor springs and top centres; stainless steel cover; hold open	202.10	2.50	207.15	4.90	-	102.26	-	309.42	nr	340.36
Door closers; standard quality										
To softwood										
coil door springs; japanned	3.35	2.50	3.43	0.30	-	6.26	-	9.69	nr	10.66
overhead door closers; liquid check and spring; "Briton" 2003 series; silver; light doors	50.03	2.50	51.28	1.65	-	34.44	-	85.71	nr	94.28
overhead door closers; liquid check and spring; "Briton" 2003V series; silver; medium doors	52.45	2.50	53.76	1.65	-	34.44	-	88.20	nr	97.02
overhead door closers; liquid check and spring; "Briton" 2004 series; silver; heavy doors	70.00	2.50	71.75	1.65	-	34.44	-	106.19	nr	116.80
concealed overhead door closers; liquid check and spring; medium doors	123.90	2.50	127.00	2.75	-	57.39	-	184.39	nr	202.83
Perko door closers; brass plate	18.30	2.50	18.76	1.65	-	34.44	-	53.19	nr	58.51
To hardwood or the like										
coil door springs; japanned	3.35	2.50	3.43	0.45	-	9.39	-	12.83	nr	14.11
overhead door closers; liquid check and spring; "Briton" 2003 series; silver; light doors	50.03	2.50	51.28	2.45	-	51.13	-	102.41	nr	112.65
overhead door closers; liquid check and spring; "Briton" 2003V series; silver; medium doors	52.45	2.50	53.76	2.45	-	51.13	-	104.89	nr	115.38
overhead door closers; liquid check and spring; "Briton" 2004 series; silver; heavy doors	70.00	2.50	71.75	2.45	-	51.13	-	122.88	nr	135.17
concealed overhead door closers; liquid check and spring; medium doors	123.90	2.50	127.00	4.10	-	85.57	-	212.56	nr	233.82
Perko door closers; brass plate	18.30	2.50	18.76	2.45	-	51.13	-	69.89	nr	76.88
Door selectors; standard quality										
To softwood or the like										
Roller arm door selectors; polished nickel finish	32.45	2.50	33.26	2.20	0.28	50.27	-	83.53	nr	91.89
To hardwood or the like										
Roller arm door selectors; polished nickel finish	32.45	2.50	33.26	3.30	0.41	75.25	-	108.52	nr	119.37

Labour hourly rates: (except Specialists) Craft Operatives 20.87 Labourer 15.57 Rates are national average prices. Refer to REGIONAL VARIATIONS for indicative levels of overall pricing in regions	MATERIALS			LABOUR				RATES		
	Del to Site £	Waste %	Material Cost £	Craft Optve Hrs	Lab Hrs	Labour Cost £	Sunds £	Nett Rate £	Unit	Gross rate (10%) £
IRONMONGERY (Cont'd)										
Locks and latches; standard quality										
To softwood										
magnetic catches; 2Kg pull	0.24	2.50	0.25	0.25	-	5.22	-	5.46	nr	6.01
magnetic catches; 3-5Kg pull	0.24	2.50	0.25	0.25	-	5.22	-	5.46	nr	6.01
magnetic catches; 6Kg pull	0.47	2.50	0.48	0.25	-	5.22	-	5.70	nr	6.27
roller catches; mortice; nylon; 18mm	2.62	2.50	2.69	0.40	-	8.35	-	11.03	nr	12.14
roller catches; mortice; nylon; 27mm	5.00	2.50	5.12	0.40	-	8.35	-	13.47	nr	14.82
roller catches; surface, adjustable; nylon; 16mm	0.34	2.50	0.35	0.30	-	6.26	-	6.61	nr	7.27
roller catches; mortice, adjustable; satin chrome plated; 25 x 22 x 10mm	1.49	2.50	1.53	0.45	-	9.39	-	10.92	nr	12.01
roller catches; double ball; brass; 50 x 8mm	0.41	2.50	0.42	0.35	-	7.30	-	7.72	nr	8.50
mortice latches; tubular; stamped steel case; 75mm	0.80	2.50	0.82	0.60	-	12.52	-	13.34	nr	14.68
mortice latches; upright; stamped steel case; 75mm	4.09	2.50	4.19	0.70	-	14.61	-	18.80	nr	20.68
mortice night latches; "Union" L2C24; to suit Euro profile cylinder; key operated outside, handle inside, 83mm black coated steel case; stainless steel finish	16.91	2.50	17.33	0.80	-	16.70	-	34.03	nr	37.43
mortice sashlocks; "Union" L2244; Euro sashlock case; key to throw deadbolt; withdraw latch via handle; 109mm high, 25mm wide, 67mm deep red coated steel case; security box striking plate; satin chrome finish	41.72	2.50	42.76	0.80	-	16.70	-	59.46	nr	65.40
cylinder rim night latches; "Legge" 707; silver grey finish	23.88	2.50	24.48	1.10	-	22.96	-	47.43	nr	52.18
cylinder rim night latches; "Union" 1022; silver case; chromium plated cylinder	23.01	2.50	23.59	1.10	-	22.96	-	46.54	nr	51.20
cylinder rim night latches; "Yale" 88; grey case; chromium plated cylinder	17.89	2.50	18.34	1.10	-	22.96	-	41.29	nr	45.42
Suffolk latches; epoxy black; size Nr 2 - 2mm gauge; 190 x 45mm plate	4.54	2.50	4.66	0.90	-	18.78	-	23.44	nr	25.78
Suffolk latches; galvanised; size Nr 2 - 2mm gauge; 190 x 45mm plate	5.09	2.50	5.22	0.90	-	18.78	-	24.00	nr	26.40
Suffolk latches; galvanised; size Nr 3; 2.5mm gauge; 204 x 45mm plate	7.74	2.50	7.94	0.90	-	18.78	-	26.72	nr	29.39
Suffolk latches; galvanised; size Nr 4; 2.5mm gauge; 230 x 45mm plate	9.16	2.50	9.39	0.90	-	18.78	-	28.17	nr	30.99
cupboard locks; 1 lever; brass; 63mm	10.20	2.50	10.45	0.80	-	16.70	-	27.15	nr	29.87
cupboard locks; 2 lever; brass; 50mm	18.26	2.50	18.72	0.80	-	16.70	-	35.41	nr	38.95
cupboard locks; 2 lever; brass; 63mm	19.50	2.50	19.99	0.80	-	16.70	-	36.68	nr	40.35
cupboard locks; 4 lever; brass; 63mm	22.05	2.50	22.60	0.80	-	16.70	-	39.30	nr	43.23
rim dead locks; japanned case; 102 x 76mm	6.25	2.50	6.41	0.90	-	18.78	-	25.19	nr	27.71
rim dead locks; japanned case; 140 x 76mm	7.25	2.50	7.43	0.90	-	18.78	-	26.21	nr	28.84
rim dead locks; japanned case; 152 x 102mm	8.97	2.50	9.19	0.90	-	18.78	-	27.97	nr	30.77
mortice dead locks; japanned case; 75mm	5.55	2.50	5.69	0.90	-	18.78	-	24.47	nr	26.92
mortice locks; three levers	5.55	2.50	5.69	1.10	-	22.96	-	28.65	nr	31.51
mortice locks; five levers	8.65	2.50	8.87	1.10	-	22.96	-	31.82	nr	35.01
rim locks; japanned case; 102 x 76mm	6.25	2.50	6.41	0.90	-	18.78	-	25.19	nr	27.71
rim locks; japanned case; 152 x 102mm	8.15	2.50	8.35	0.90	-	18.78	-	27.14	nr	29.85
rim lock; black enamel case; strong pattern; 152 x 103mm	23.30	2.50	23.88	0.90	-	18.78	-	42.67	nr	46.93
padlocks, "Squire", 25mm solid brass body; hardened steel shackle; LN2	5.80	2.50	5.95	-	-	-	-	5.95	nr	6.54
padlocks, "Squire", 40mm solid brass body; hardened steel shackle; LN4	3.00	2.50	3.07	-	-	-	-	3.07	nr	3.38
padlocks, "Squire", 50mm solid brass body; hardened steel shackle; LN5	13.28	2.50	13.61	-	-	-	-	13.61	nr	14.97
padlocks; "Squire", weather resistant 40mm combination padlock; die cast alloy body; 4 wheel; closed shackle; CP40CS	12.59	2.50	12.90	-	-	-	-	12.90	nr	14.20
padlocks; "Squire", 4 levers; galvanised case; 220 Old English	6.83	2.50	7.00	-	-	-	-	7.00	nr	7.70
padlocks; "Squire Warrior" 45mm padlock; armoured steel body; 8mm hardened steel shackle	17.95	2.50	18.40	-	-	-	-	18.40	nr	20.24
padlocks; "Squire Stronghold" pattern; 50mm; SS50S	36.51	2.50	37.42	-	-	-	-	37.42	nr	41.17
hasps and locks; "Squire Stronghold"; 150mm overall width; HLS50S; hardened steel; Electrophoretic finish	102.22	3.00	105.29	0.50	-	10.44	-	115.72	nr	127.29
hasps and staples; japanned wire; light; 75mm	0.51	2.50	0.52	0.35	-	7.30	-	7.83	nr	8.61
hasps and staples; japanned wire; light; 100mm	0.97	2.50	0.99	0.35	-	7.30	-	8.30	nr	9.13
hasps and staples; galvanised safety; 75mm	2.34	2.50	2.40	0.35	-	7.30	-	9.71	nr	10.68
hasps and staples; galvanised medium; 200mm	6.37	2.50	6.53	0.35	-	7.30	-	13.83	nr	15.21
hasps and staples; galvanised heavy; 200mm	8.21	2.50	8.41	0.35	-	7.30	-	15.72	nr	17.29
locking bars; heavy duty; japanned; 250mm	9.85	2.50	10.10	0.50	-	10.44	-	20.53	nr	22.59
locking bars; heavy duty; japanned; 300mm	13.63	2.50	13.97	0.50	-	10.44	-	24.40	nr	26.84
locking bars; heavy duty; japanned; 400mm	23.42	2.50	24.01	0.50	-	10.44	-	34.44	nr	37.88
To hardwood or the like										
magnetic catches; 2Kg pull	0.24	2.50	0.25	0.35	-	7.30	-	7.55	nr	8.31
magnetic catches; 3-5Kg pull	0.24	2.50	0.25	0.35	-	7.30	-	7.55	nr	8.31
magnetic catches; 6Kg pull	0.47	2.50	0.48	0.35	-	7.30	-	7.79	nr	8.56
roller catches; mortice; nylon; 18mm	2.62	2.50	2.69	0.55	-	11.48	-	14.17	nr	15.58
roller catches; mortice; nylon; 27mm	5.00	2.50	5.12	0.55	-	11.48	-	16.60	nr	18.26
roller catches; surface, adjustable; nylon; 16mm	0.34	2.50	0.35	0.45	-	9.39	-	9.74	nr	10.72
roller catches; mortice, adjustable; satin chrome plated; 25 x 22 x 10mm	1.49	2.50	1.53	0.65	-	13.57	-	15.09	nr	16.60
roller catches; double ball; brass; 50 x 8mm	0.41	2.50	0.42	0.50	-	10.44	-	10.86	nr	11.94
mortice latches; tubular; stamped steel case; 75mm	0.80	2.50	0.82	1.00	-	20.87	-	21.69	nr	23.86
mortice latches; upright; stamped steel case; 75mm	4.09	2.50	4.19	1.10	-	22.96	-	27.15	nr	29.87
mortice night latches; "Union" L2C24; to suit Euro profile cylinder; key operated outside, handle inside, 83mm black coated steel case; stainless steel finish	16.91	2.50	17.33	1.20	-	25.04	-	42.38	nr	46.61
mortice sashlocks; "Union" L2244; Euro sashlock case; key to throw deadbolt; withdraw latch via handle; 109mm high, 25mm wide, 67mm deep red coated steel case; security box striking plate; satin chrome finish	41.72	2.50	42.76	1.20	-	25.04	-	67.81	nr	74.59
cylinder rim night latches; "Legge" 707; silver grey finish	23.88	2.50	24.48	1.65	-	34.44	-	58.91	nr	64.80
cylinder rim night latches; "Union" 1022; silver case; chromium plated cylinder	23.01	2.50	23.59	1.65	-	34.44	-	58.02	nr	63.82

Labour hourly rates: (except Specialists) Craft Operatives 20.87 Labourer 15.57 Rates are national average prices. Refer to REGIONAL VARIATIONS for indicative levels of overall pricing in regions	MATERIALS			LABOUR				RATES		
	Del to Site £	Waste %	Material Cost £	Craft Optve Hrs	Lab Hrs	Labour Cost £	Sunds £	Nett Rate £	Unit	Gross rate (10%) £
IRONMONGERY (Cont'd)										
Locks and latches; standard quality (Cont'd)										
To hardwood or the like (Cont'd)										
cylinder rim night latches; "Yale" 88; grey case; chromium plated cylinder	17.89	2.50	18.34	1.65	-	34.44	-	52.77	nr	58.05
Suffolk latches; epoxy black; size Nr 2 - 2mm gauge; 190 x 45mm plate	4.54	2.50	4.66	1.30	-	27.13	-	31.79	nr	34.97
Suffolk latches; galvanised; size Nr 2 - 2mm gauge; 190 x 45mm plate	5.09	2.50	5.22	1.30	-	27.13	-	32.35	nr	35.59
Suffolk latches; galvanised; size Nr 3; 2.5mm gauge; 204 x 45mm plate	7.74	2.50	7.94	1.30	-	27.13	-	35.07	nr	38.57
Suffolk latches; galvanised; size Nr 4; 2.5mm gauge; 230 x 45mm plate	9.16	2.50	9.39	1.30	-	27.13	-	36.52	nr	40.17
cupboard locks; 1 lever; brass; 63mm	10.20	2.50	10.45	1.20	-	25.04	-	35.50	nr	39.05
cupboard locks; 2 lever; brass; 50mm	18.26	2.50	18.72	1.20	-	25.04	-	43.76	nr	48.14
cupboard locks; 2 lever; brass; 63mm	19.50	2.50	19.99	1.20	-	25.04	-	45.03	nr	49.53
cupboard locks; 4 lever; brass; 63mm	22.05	2.50	22.60	1.20	-	25.04	-	47.65	nr	52.41
rim dead locks; japanned case; 76mm	6.25	2.50	6.41	1.30	-	27.13	-	33.54	nr	36.89
rim dead locks; japanned case; 102 x 76mm	7.25	2.50	7.43	1.30	-	27.13	-	34.56	nr	38.02
rim dead locks; japanned case; 140 x 76mm	8.97	2.50	9.19	1.30	-	27.13	-	36.32	nr	39.95
rim dead locks; japanned case; 152 x 102mm	5.55	2.50	5.69	1.30	-	27.13	-	32.82	nr	36.10
mortice locks; three levers	5.55	2.50	5.69	1.65	-	34.44	-	40.12	nr	44.14
mortice locks; five levers	8.65	2.50	8.87	1.65	-	34.44	-	43.30	nr	47.63
rim locks; japanned case; 102 x 76mm	6.25	2.50	6.41	1.30	-	27.13	-	33.54	nr	36.89
rim locks; japanned case; 152 x 102mm	8.15	2.50	8.35	1.30	-	27.13	-	35.48	nr	39.03
rim locks; black enamel case; strong pattern; 152 x 103mm	23.30	2.50	23.88	1.30	-	27.13	-	51.01	nr	56.11
padlocks, "Squire", 25mm solid brass body; hardened steel shackle; LN2	5.80	2.50	5.95	-	-	-	-	5.95	nr	6.54
padlocks, "Squire", 40mm solid brass body; hardened steel shackle; LN4	3.00	2.50	3.07	-	-	-	-	3.07	nr	3.38
padlocks, "Squire", 50mm solid brass body; hardened steel shackle; LN5	13.28	2.50	13.61	-	-	-	-	13.61	nr	14.97
padlocks; "Squire", weather resistant 40mm combination padlock; die cast alloy body; 4 wheel; closed shackle; CP40CS	12.59	2.50	12.90	-	-	-	-	12.90	nr	14.20
padlocks; "Squire", 4 levers; galvanised case; 220 Old English	6.83	2.50	7.00	-	-	-	-	7.00	nr	7.70
padlocks; "Squire Warrior" 45mm padlock; armoured steel body; 8mm hardened steel shackle	17.95	2.50	18.40	-	-	-	-	18.40	nr	20.24
padlocks; "Squire Stronghold"; 50mm; SS50S	36.51	2.50	37.42	-	-	-	-	37.42	nr	41.17
hasps and locks; "Squire Stronghold"; 150mm overall width; HLS50S; hardened steel; Electrophoretic finish	102.22	3.00	105.29	0.65	-	13.57	-	118.85	nr	130.74
hasps and staples; japanned wire; light; 75mm	0.51	2.50	0.52	0.50	-	10.44	-	10.96	nr	12.05
hasps and staples; japanned wire; light; 100mm	0.97	2.50	0.99	0.55	-	11.48	-	12.47	nr	13.72
hasps and staples; galvanised safety; 75mm	2.34	2.50	2.40	0.55	-	11.48	-	13.88	nr	15.27
hasps and staples; galvanised medium; 200mm	6.37	2.50	6.53	0.55	-	11.48	-	18.00	nr	19.81
hasps and staples; galvanised heavy; 200mm	8.21	2.50	8.41	0.55	-	11.48	-	19.89	nr	21.88
locking bars; heavy duty; japanned; 250mm	9.85	2.50	10.10	0.65	-	13.57	-	23.66	nr	26.03
locking bars; heavy duty; japanned; 300mm	13.63	2.50	13.97	0.65	-	13.57	-	27.53	nr	30.29
locking bars; heavy duty; japanned; 400mm	23.42	2.50	24.01	0.65	-	13.57	-	37.57	nr	41.33
Bolts; standard quality										
To softwood										
barrel bolts; japanned, steel barrel; medium										
100mm	0.70	2.50	0.72	0.30	-	6.26	-	6.98	nr	7.68
150mm	1.48	2.50	1.52	0.35	-	7.30	-	8.82	nr	9.71
barrel bolts; galvanised, steel barrel; medium										
150mm	2.91	2.50	2.98	0.35	-	7.30	-	10.29	nr	11.31
barrel bolts; japanned, steel barrel; heavy										
100mm	9.16	2.50	9.39	0.30	-	6.26	-	15.65	nr	17.21
150mm	9.99	2.50	10.24	0.35	-	7.30	-	17.55	nr	19.30
200mm	4.83	2.50	4.95	0.40	-	8.35	-	13.30	nr	14.63
250mm	10.71	2.50	10.98	0.45	-	9.39	-	20.37	nr	22.40
300mm	11.54	2.50	11.83	0.50	-	10.44	-	22.27	nr	24.49
barrel bolts; extruded brass, round brass shoot; 25mm wide										
75mm	2.29	2.50	2.35	0.30	-	6.26	-	8.61	nr	9.47
100mm	2.60	2.50	2.66	0.30	-	6.26	-	8.93	nr	9.82
150mm	3.64	2.50	3.73	0.35	-	7.30	-	11.04	nr	12.14
barrel bolts; extruded brass; B.M.A., round brass shoot; 25mm wide										
75mm	20.49	2.50	21.00	0.30	-	6.26	-	27.27	nr	29.99
100mm	21.39	2.50	21.93	0.30	-	6.26	-	28.19	nr	31.01
150mm	22.97	2.50	23.54	0.35	-	7.30	-	30.85	nr	33.93
barrel bolts; extruded brass, chromium plated, round brass shoot; 25mm wide										
75mm	2.55	2.50	2.61	0.30	-	6.26	-	8.87	nr	9.76
100mm	2.97	2.50	3.04	0.30	-	6.26	-	9.31	nr	10.24
150mm	4.23	2.50	4.34	0.35	-	7.30	-	11.64	nr	12.80
barrel bolts; extruded aluminium, S.A.A., round aluminium shoot; 25mm wide										
75mm	0.95	2.50	0.97	0.30	-	6.26	-	7.23	nr	7.96
100mm	1.26	2.50	1.29	0.30	-	6.26	-	7.55	nr	8.31
150mm	1.63	2.50	1.67	0.35	-	7.30	-	8.98	nr	9.87
monkey tail bolts										
japanned; 300mm	8.21	2.50	8.41	0.40	-	8.35	-	16.76	nr	18.44
japanned; 450mm	10.96	2.50	11.23	0.45	-	9.39	-	20.62	nr	22.69
japanned; 610mm	15.54	2.50	15.93	0.55	-	11.48	-	27.41	nr	30.15
flush bolts; brass										
100mm	6.19	2.50	6.34	0.55	-	11.48	-	17.82	nr	19.61
150mm	8.70	2.50	8.92	0.65	-	13.57	-	22.48	nr	24.73
200mm	10.46	2.50	10.72	0.75	-	15.65	-	26.37	nr	29.01
flush bolts; S.C.P.										
100mm	6.96	2.50	7.13	0.55	-	11.48	-	18.61	nr	20.47
150mm	6.96	2.50	7.13	0.65	-	13.57	-	20.70	nr	22.77

Labour hourly rates: (except Specialists) Craft Operatives 20.87 Labourer 15.57 Rates are national average prices. Refer to REGIONAL VARIATIONS for indicative levels of overall pricing in regions	MATERIALS			LABOUR				RATES		
	Del to Site £	Waste %	Material Cost £	Craft Optve Hrs	Lab Hrs	Labour Cost £	Sunds £	Nett Rate £	Unit	Gross rate (10%) £
IRONMONGERY (Cont'd)										
Bolts; standard quality (Cont'd)										
To softwood (Cont'd)										
flush bolts; S.C.P. (Cont'd)										
200mm	10.46	2.50	10.72	0.75	-	15.65	-	26.37	nr	29.01
lever action flush bolts; brass										
150mm	8.54	2.50	8.76	0.65	-	13.57	-	22.32	nr	24.55
200mm	12.21	2.50	12.51	0.75	-	15.65	-	28.17	nr	30.98
lever action flush bolts; chrome										
150mm	8.70	2.50	8.92	0.65	-	13.57	-	22.48	nr	24.73
200mm	10.46	2.50	10.72	0.75	-	15.65	-	26.37	nr	29.01
necked bolts; extruded brass, round brass shoot; 25mm wide										
75mm	2.40	2.50	2.46	0.30	-	6.26	-	8.72	nr	9.59
100mm	2.80	2.50	2.87	0.30	-	6.26	-	9.13	nr	10.04
150mm	3.95	2.50	4.05	0.35	-	7.30	-	11.35	nr	12.49
necked bolts; extruded aluminium, S.A.A., round aluminium shoot; 25mm wide										
75mm	0.95	2.50	0.97	0.30	-	6.26	-	7.23	nr	7.96
100mm	1.41	2.50	1.45	0.30	-	6.26	-	7.71	nr	8.48
150mm	1.78	2.50	1.82	0.35	-	7.30	-	9.13	nr	10.04
indicating bolts; S.A.A.	3.45	2.50	3.54	1.10	-	22.96	-	26.49	nr	29.14
indicating bolts; B.M.A.	55.85	2.50	57.25	1.10	-	22.96	-	80.20	nr	88.22
panic latches; to single door; iron, bronzed or silver	43.60	2.50	44.69	1.65	-	34.44	-	79.13	nr	87.04
panic bolts; to single door; aluminium box, steel shoots and cross rail, anodised silver	47.80	2.50	48.99	1.65	-	34.44	-	83.43	nr	91.77
panic latches; to double doors; iron bronzed or silver	87.20	2.50	89.38	2.20	-	45.91	-	135.29	nr	148.82
panic bolts; to double doors; aluminium box, steel shoots and cross rail, anodised silver	96.05	2.50	98.45	2.20	-	45.91	-	144.37	nr	158.80
padlock bolts; Brenton; galvanised; heavy										
150mm	4.25	2.50	4.36	0.35	-	7.30	-	11.66	nr	12.83
200mm	4.90	2.50	5.02	0.35	-	7.30	-	12.33	nr	13.56
250mm	5.41	2.50	5.54	0.50	-	10.44	-	15.98	nr	17.58
290mm	11.81	2.50	12.10	0.50	-	10.44	-	22.54	nr	24.79
To hardwood or the like										
barrel bolts; japanned, steel barrel; medium										
100mm	0.70	2.50	0.72	0.40	-	8.35	-	9.07	nr	9.97
150mm	1.48	2.50	1.52	0.45	-	9.39	-	10.91	nr	12.00
barrel bolts; galvanised, steel barrel; medium										
150mm	2.91	2.50	2.98	0.45	-	9.39	-	12.37	nr	13.61
barrel bolts; japanned, steel barrel; heavy										
100mm	9.16	2.50	9.39	0.40	-	8.35	-	17.73	nr	19.51
150mm	9.99	2.50	10.24	0.45	-	9.39	-	19.63	nr	21.60
200mm	4.83	2.50	4.95	0.55	-	11.48	-	16.43	nr	18.08
250mm	10.71	2.50	10.98	0.60	-	12.52	-	23.50	nr	25.85
300mm	11.54	2.50	11.83	0.70	-	14.61	-	26.44	nr	29.08
barrel bolts; extruded brass, round brass shoot; 25mm wide										
75mm	2.29	2.50	2.35	0.40	-	8.35	-	10.70	nr	11.76
100mm	2.60	2.50	2.66	0.40	-	8.35	-	11.01	nr	12.11
150mm	3.64	2.50	3.73	0.45	-	9.39	-	13.12	nr	14.43
barrel bolts; extruded brass; B.M.A., round brass shoot; 25mm wide										
75mm	20.49	2.50	21.00	0.40	-	8.35	-	29.35	nr	32.29
100mm	21.39	2.50	21.93	0.40	-	8.35	-	30.27	nr	33.30
150mm	22.97	2.50	23.54	0.45	-	9.39	-	32.93	nr	36.23
barrel bolts; extruded brass, chromium plated, round brass shoot; 25mm wide										
75mm	2.55	2.50	2.61	0.40	-	8.35	-	10.96	nr	12.06
100mm	2.97	2.50	3.04	0.40	-	8.35	-	11.39	nr	12.53
150mm	4.23	2.50	4.34	0.45	-	9.39	-	13.73	nr	15.10
barrel bolts; extruded aluminium, S.A.A., round aluminium shoot; 25mm wide										
75mm	0.95	2.50	0.97	0.40	-	8.35	-	9.32	nr	10.25
100mm	1.26	2.50	1.29	0.40	-	8.35	-	9.64	nr	10.60
150mm	1.63	2.50	1.67	0.45	-	9.39	-	11.06	nr	12.17
monkey tail bolts										
japanned; 300mm	8.21	2.50	8.41	0.55	-	11.48	-	19.89	nr	21.88
japanned; 450mm	10.96	2.50	11.23	0.65	-	13.57	-	24.80	nr	27.28
japanned; 610mm	15.54	2.50	15.93	0.75	-	15.65	-	31.58	nr	34.74
flush bolts; brass										
100mm	6.19	2.50	6.34	0.90	-	18.78	-	25.13	nr	27.64
150mm	8.70	2.50	8.92	1.00	-	20.87	-	29.79	nr	32.77
200mm	10.46	2.50	10.72	1.10	-	22.96	-	33.68	nr	37.04
flush bolts; S.C.P.										
100mm	6.96	2.50	7.13	0.90	-	18.78	-	25.91	nr	28.51
150mm	6.96	2.50	7.13	1.00	-	20.87	-	28.00	nr	30.80
200mm	10.46	2.50	10.72	1.10	-	22.96	-	33.68	nr	37.04
lever action flush bolts; brass										
150mm	8.54	2.50	8.76	1.00	-	20.87	-	29.63	nr	32.59
200mm	12.21	2.50	12.51	1.10	-	22.96	-	35.47	nr	39.02
lever action flush bolts; chrome										
150mm	8.70	2.50	8.92	1.00	-	20.87	-	29.79	nr	32.77
200mm	10.46	2.50	10.72	1.10	-	22.96	-	33.68	nr	37.04
necked bolts; extruded brass, round brass shoot; 25mm wide										
75mm	2.40	2.50	2.46	0.40	-	8.35	-	10.81	nr	11.89
100mm	2.80	2.50	2.87	0.40	-	8.35	-	11.22	nr	12.34
150mm	3.95	2.50	4.05	0.45	-	9.39	-	13.44	nr	14.78
necked bolts; extruded aluminium, S.A.A., round aluminium shoot; 25mm wide										
75mm	0.95	2.50	0.97	0.40	-	8.35	-	9.32	nr	10.25
100mm	1.41	2.50	1.45	0.40	-	8.35	-	9.79	nr	10.77
150mm	1.78	2.50	1.82	0.45	-	9.39	-	11.22	nr	12.34

Labour hourly rates: (except Specialists) Craft Operatives 20.87 Labourer 15.57 Rates are national average prices. Refer to REGIONAL VARIATIONS for indicative levels of overall pricing in regions	MATERIALS			LABOUR				RATES		
	Del to Site £	Waste %	Material Cost £	Craft Optve Hrs	Lab Hrs	Labour Cost £	Sunds £	Nett Rate £	Unit	Gross rate (10%) £
IRONMONGERY (Cont'd)										
Bolts; standard quality (Cont'd)										
To hardwood or the like (Cont'd)										
indicating bolts										
S.A.A.	3.45	2.50	3.54	1.65	-	34.44	-	37.97	nr	41.77
B.M.A.	55.85	2.50	57.25	1.65	-	34.44	-	91.68	nr	100.85
panic bolts / latches										
to single door; iron, bronzed or silver	43.60	2.50	44.69	2.45	-	51.13	-	95.82	nr	105.40
to single door; aluminium box, steel shoots and cross rail, anodised silver	47.80	2.50	48.99	2.45	-	51.13	-	100.13	nr	110.14
to double doors; iron bronzed or silver	87.20	2.50	89.38	3.30	-	68.87	-	158.25	nr	174.08
to double doors; aluminium box, steel shoots and cross rail, anodised silver	96.05	2.50	98.45	3.30	-	68.87	-	167.32	nr	184.05
padlock bolts; Brenton; galvanised; heavy										
150mm	4.25	2.50	4.36	0.50	-	10.44	-	14.79	nr	16.27
200mm	4.90	2.50	5.02	0.50	-	10.44	-	15.46	nr	17.00
250mm	5.41	2.50	5.54	0.75	-	15.65	-	21.20	nr	23.32
290mm	11.81	2.50	12.10	0.75	-	15.65	-	27.76	nr	30.53
Door handles; standard quality										
To softwood										
lever handles; spring action; B.M.A., best quality; 41 x 150mm	71.39	2.50	73.18	0.25	-	5.22	-	78.40	nr	86.24
lever handles; spring action; chromium plated, housing quality; 41 x 150mm	3.33	2.50	3.41	0.25	-	5.22	-	8.63	nr	9.49
lever handles; spring action; chromium plated, best quality; 41 x 150mm	53.68	2.50	55.02	0.25	-	5.22	-	60.24	nr	66.26
lever handles; spring action; S.A.A. housing quality; 41 x 150mm	2.87	2.50	2.94	0.25	-	5.22	-	8.15	nr	8.97
lever handles; spring action; S.A.A., best quality; 41 x 150mm	24.59	2.50	25.20	0.25	-	5.22	-	30.42	nr	33.46
lever handles; spring action; plastic/nylon, housing quality; 41 x 150mm	24.22	2.50	24.83	0.25	-	5.22	-	30.04	nr	33.05
pull handles; B.M.A.; 150mm	10.56	2.50	10.82	0.20	-	4.17	-	15.00	nr	16.50
pull handles; B.M.A.; 200mm	26.13	2.50	26.78	0.25	-	5.22	-	32.00	nr	35.20
pull handles; B.M.A.; 300mm	42.90	2.50	43.97	0.30	-	6.26	-	50.23	nr	55.26
pull handles; S.A.A.; 150mm	1.65	2.50	1.69	0.20	-	4.17	-	5.87	nr	6.45
pull handles; S.A.A.; 225mm	4.04	2.50	4.14	0.25	-	5.22	-	9.36	nr	10.29
pull handles; S.A.A.; 300mm	6.51	2.50	6.67	0.30	-	6.26	-	12.93	nr	14.23
pull handles on 63 x 325mm plate, lettered; polished aluminium	20.29	2.50	20.80	0.45	-	9.39	-	30.19	nr	33.21
pull handles on 75 x 375mm plate, lettered; stainless steel	32.95	2.50	33.77	0.45	-	9.39	-	43.17	nr	47.48
To hardwood or the like										
lever handles; spring action; B.M.A., best quality; 41 x 150mm	71.39	2.50	73.18	0.35	-	7.30	-	80.48	nr	88.53
lever handles; spring action; chromium plated, housing quality; 41 x 150mm	3.33	2.50	3.41	0.35	-	7.30	-	10.71	nr	11.78
lever handles; spring action; chromium plated, best quality; 41 x 150mm	53.68	2.50	55.02	0.35	-	7.30	-	62.33	nr	68.56
lever handles; spring action; S.A.A. housing quality; 41 x 150mm	2.87	2.50	2.94	0.35	-	7.30	-	10.24	nr	11.27
lever handles; spring action; S.A.A., best quality; 41 x 150mm	24.59	2.50	25.20	0.35	-	7.30	-	32.51	nr	35.76
lever handles; spring action; plastic/nylon, housing quality; 41 x 150mm	24.22	2.50	24.83	0.35	-	7.30	-	32.13	nr	35.34
pull handles; B.M.A.; 150mm	10.56	2.50	10.82	0.30	-	6.26	-	17.09	nr	18.79
pull handles; B.M.A.; 200mm	26.13	2.50	26.78	0.35	-	7.30	-	34.09	nr	37.50
pull handles; B.M.A.; 300mm	42.90	2.50	43.97	0.40	-	8.35	-	52.32	nr	57.55
pull handles; S.A.A.; 150mm	1.65	2.50	1.69	0.30	-	6.26	-	7.95	nr	8.75
pull handles; S.A.A.; 225mm	4.04	2.50	4.14	0.35	-	7.30	-	11.45	nr	12.59
pull handles; S.A.A.; 300mm	6.51	2.50	6.67	0.40	-	8.35	-	15.02	nr	16.52
pull handles on 63 x 325mm plate, lettered; polished aluminium	20.29	2.50	20.80	0.65	-	13.57	-	34.36	nr	37.80
pull handles on 75 x 375mm plate, lettered; stainless steel	32.95	2.50	33.77	0.65	-	13.57	-	47.34	nr	52.07
Door furniture; standard quality										
To softwood										
knobs; bronze; surface fixing	8.29	2.50	8.50	0.25	-	5.22	-	13.72	nr	15.09
knobs; polished chrome; surface fixing	5.93	2.50	6.07	0.25	-	5.22	-	11.29	nr	12.42
knobs; bronze; secret fixing	13.05	2.50	13.38	0.35	-	7.30	-	20.68	nr	22.75
knobs; polished chrome; secret fixing	11.35	2.50	11.64	0.35	-	7.30	-	18.94	nr	20.84
kicking plate; SAA; 750 x 150	4.44	2.50	4.55	0.55	-	11.48	-	16.03	nr	17.63
kicking plate; SAA; 825 x 150	5.33	2.50	5.46	0.55	-	11.48	-	16.94	nr	18.64
push plate; SAA; 300 x 75	1.04	2.50	1.07	0.30	-	6.26	-	7.33	nr	8.06
sign plate; SAA; black engraved 300 x 75	3.00	2.50	3.07	0.30	-	6.26	-	9.34	nr	10.27
To hardwood or the like										
knobs; bronze; surface fixing	8.29	2.50	8.50	0.35	-	7.30	-	15.80	nr	17.38
knobs; polished chrome; surface fixing	5.93	2.50	6.07	0.35	-	7.30	-	13.38	nr	14.72
knobs; bronze; secret fixing	13.05	2.50	13.38	0.50	-	10.44	-	23.82	nr	26.20
knobs; polished chrome; secret fixing	11.35	2.50	11.64	0.50	-	10.44	-	22.07	nr	24.28
kicking plate; SAA; 750 x 150	4.44	2.50	4.55	0.80	-	16.70	-	21.25	nr	23.37
kicking plate; SAA; 825 x 150	5.33	2.50	5.46	0.80	-	16.70	-	22.16	nr	24.38
push plate; SAA; 300 x 75	1.04	2.50	1.07	0.40	-	8.35	-	9.41	nr	10.36
sign plate; SAA; black engraved 300 x 75	3.00	2.50	3.07	0.40	-	8.35	-	11.42	nr	12.57
Window furniture; standard quality										
To softwood										
fanlight catches; brass	8.63	2.50	8.85	0.40	-	8.35	-	17.19	nr	18.91
fanlight catches; bronze	10.60	2.50	10.86	0.40	-	8.35	-	19.21	nr	21.13
fanlight catches; chromium plated	9.69	2.50	9.93	0.40	-	8.35	-	18.28	nr	20.11
casement fasteners; wedge plate; black malleable iron	3.61	2.50	3.70	0.40	-	8.35	-	12.05	nr	13.25
casement fasteners; wedge plate; brass	11.52	2.50	11.81	0.40	-	8.35	-	20.16	nr	22.17
casement fasteners; wedge plate; chromium plated	6.91	2.50	7.08	0.40	-	8.35	-	15.43	nr	16.97
casement fasteners; wedge plate; S.A.A.	1.90	2.50	1.95	0.40	-	8.35	-	10.30	nr	11.33
sash fasteners; brass	5.43	2.50	5.57	1.10	-	22.96	-	28.52	nr	31.38
sash fasteners; bronze finish	7.14	2.50	7.32	1.10	-	22.96	-	30.28	nr	33.30
sash fasteners; chromium plated	4.27	2.50	4.38	1.10	-	22.96	-	27.33	nr	30.07

Labour hourly rates: (except Specialists) Craft Operatives 20.87 Labourer 15.57 Rates are national average prices. Refer to REGIONAL VARIATIONS for indicative levels of overall pricing in regions	MATERIALS			LABOUR				RATES		
	Del to Site £	Waste %	Material Cost £	Craft Optve Hrs	Lab Hrs	Labour Cost £	Sunds £	Nett Rate £	Unit	Gross rate (10%) £
IRONMONGERY (Cont'd)										
Window furniture; standard quality (Cont'd)										
To softwood (Cont'd)										
casement stays; two pins; black malleable iron										
200mm	3.61	2.50	3.70	0.40	-	8.35	-	12.05	nr	13.25
250mm	3.79	2.50	3.88	0.40	-	8.35	-	12.23	nr	13.46
300mm	3.90	2.50	4.00	0.40	-	8.35	-	12.35	nr	13.58
casement stays; two pins; B.M.A.										
200mm	11.68	2.50	11.97	0.40	-	8.35	-	20.32	nr	22.35
250mm	11.77	2.50	12.06	0.40	-	8.35	-	20.41	nr	22.45
300mm	12.56	2.50	12.87	0.40	-	8.35	-	21.22	nr	23.34
casement stays; two pins; chromium plated										
200mm	7.91	2.50	8.11	0.40	-	8.35	-	16.46	nr	18.10
250mm	7.28	2.50	7.46	0.40	-	8.35	-	15.81	nr	17.39
300mm	8.16	2.50	8.36	0.40	-	8.35	-	16.71	nr	18.38
casement stays; two pins; S.A.A.										
200mm	1.63	2.50	1.67	0.40	-	8.35	-	10.02	nr	11.02
250mm	1.70	2.50	1.74	0.40	-	8.35	-	10.09	nr	11.10
300mm	1.78	2.50	1.82	0.40	-	8.35	-	10.17	nr	11.19
sash lifts										
polished brass; 50mm	2.19	2.50	2.24	0.25	-	5.22	-	7.46	nr	8.21
bronze; 50mm	4.75	2.50	4.87	0.25	-	5.22	-	10.09	nr	11.09
chromium plated; 50mm	1.98	2.50	2.03	0.25	-	5.22	-	7.25	nr	7.97
flush lifts										
brass; 75mm	4.21	2.50	4.32	0.55	-	11.48	-	15.79	nr	17.37
bronze; 75mm	31.62	2.50	32.42	0.55	-	11.48	-	43.89	nr	48.28
chromium plated; 75mm	4.57	2.50	4.68	0.55	-	11.48	-	16.16	nr	17.78
sash cleat hooks										
polished brass; 76mm	2.65	2.50	2.72	0.25	-	5.22	-	7.93	nr	8.73
B.M.A.; 76mm	12.61	2.50	12.92	0.25	-	5.22	-	18.14	nr	19.95
chromium plated; 76mm	2.85	2.50	2.92	0.25	-	5.22	-	8.14	nr	8.95
sash pulleys										
frame and wheel	1.53	2.50	1.57	0.55	-	11.48	-	13.05	nr	14.35
To hardwood or the like										
fanlight catches; brass	8.63	2.50	8.85	0.55	-	11.48	-	20.32	nr	22.36
fanlight catches; bronze	10.60	2.50	10.86	0.55	-	11.48	-	22.34	nr	24.58
fanlight catches; chromium plated	9.69	2.50	9.93	0.55	-	11.48	-	21.41	nr	23.55
casement fasteners; wedge plate; black malleable iron	3.61	2.50	3.70	0.55	-	11.48	-	15.18	nr	16.70
casement fasteners; wedge plate; brass	11.52	2.50	11.81	0.55	-	11.48	-	23.29	nr	25.62
casement fasteners; wedge plate; chromium plated	6.91	2.50	7.08	0.55	-	11.48	-	18.56	nr	20.42
casement fasteners; wedge plate; S.A.A.	1.90	2.50	1.95	0.55	-	11.48	-	13.43	nr	14.77
sash fasteners; brass	5.43	2.50	5.57	1.65	-	34.44	-	40.00	nr	44.00
sash fasteners; bronze finish	7.14	2.50	7.32	1.65	-	34.44	-	41.75	nr	45.93
sash fasteners; chromium plated	4.27	2.50	4.38	1.65	-	34.44	-	38.81	nr	42.69
casement stays; two pins; black malleable iron										
200mm	3.61	2.50	3.70	0.55	-	11.48	-	15.18	nr	16.70
250mm	3.79	2.50	3.88	0.55	-	11.48	-	15.36	nr	16.90
300mm	3.90	2.50	4.00	0.55	-	11.48	-	15.48	nr	17.02
casement stays; two pins; B.M.A.										
200mm	11.68	2.50	11.97	0.55	-	11.48	-	23.45	nr	25.80
250mm	11.77	2.50	12.06	0.55	-	11.48	-	23.54	nr	25.90
300mm	12.56	2.50	12.87	0.55	-	11.48	-	24.35	nr	26.79
casement stays; two pins; chromium plated										
200mm	7.91	2.50	8.11	0.55	-	11.48	-	19.59	nr	21.54
250mm	7.28	2.50	7.46	0.55	-	11.48	-	18.94	nr	20.83
300mm	8.16	2.50	8.36	0.55	-	11.48	-	19.84	nr	21.83
casement stays; two pins; S.A.A.										
200mm	1.63	2.50	1.67	0.55	-	11.48	-	13.15	nr	14.46
250mm	1.70	2.50	1.74	0.55	-	11.48	-	13.22	nr	14.54
300mm	1.78	2.50	1.82	0.55	-	11.48	-	13.30	nr	14.63
sash lifts										
polished brass; 50mm	2.19	2.50	2.24	0.35	-	7.30	-	9.55	nr	10.50
bronze; 50mm	4.75	2.50	4.87	0.35	-	7.30	-	12.17	nr	13.39
chromium plated; 50mm	1.98	2.50	2.03	0.35	-	7.30	-	9.33	nr	10.27
flush lifts										
brass; 75mm	4.21	2.50	4.32	0.80	-	16.70	-	21.01	nr	23.11
bronze; 75mm	31.62	2.50	32.42	0.80	-	16.70	-	49.11	nr	54.02
chromium plated; 75mm	4.57	2.50	4.68	0.80	-	16.70	-	21.38	nr	23.52
sash cleat hooks										
polished brass; 76mm	2.65	2.50	2.72	0.35	-	7.30	-	10.02	nr	11.02
B.M.A.; 76mm	12.61	2.50	12.92	0.35	-	7.30	-	20.23	nr	22.25
chromium plated; 76mm	2.85	2.50	2.92	0.35	-	7.30	-	10.23	nr	11.25
sash pulleys										
frame and wheel	1.53	2.50	1.57	0.80	-	16.70	-	18.27	nr	20.09
Window furniture; trickle vents - to softwood or the like										
Frame vent; PVCu white										
265mm long	3.99	2.50	4.09	0.22	0.03	5.06	0.25	9.41	nr	10.35
366mm long	4.56	2.50	4.67	0.33	0.04	7.51	0.30	12.48	nr	13.73
Canopy grille; PVCu white										
364mm long	3.42	2.50	3.50	0.22	0.03	5.06	0.12	8.68	nr	9.55
Canopy grille; aluminium with epoxy paint finish										
440mm long	4.16	2.50	4.26	0.33	0.03	7.35	0.18	11.80	nr	12.98
Window furniture; trickle vents - to hardwood or the like										
Frame vent; PVCu white										
265mm long	3.99	2.50	4.09	0.33	0.05	7.67	0.25	12.01	nr	13.21
366mm long	4.56	2.50	4.67	0.50	0.07	11.52	0.30	16.50	nr	18.15

Labour hourly rates: (except Specialists) Craft Operatives 20.87 Labourer 15.57 Rates are national average prices. Refer to REGIONAL VARIATIONS for indicative levels of overall pricing in regions	MATERIALS			LABOUR				RATES		
	Del to Site £	Waste %	Material Cost £	Craft Optve Hrs	Lab Hrs	Labour Cost £	Sunds £	Nett Rate £	Unit	Gross rate (10%) £
IRONMONGERY (Cont'd)										
Window furniture; trickle vents - to hardwood or the like (Cont'd)										
Canopy grille; PVCu white										
364mm long	3.42	2.50	3.50	0.33	0.05	7.67	0.12	11.29	nr	12.42
Canopy grille; aluminium with epoxy paint finish										
440mm long	4.16	2.50	4.26	0.50	0.07	11.52	0.18	15.97	nr	17.56
Letter plates; standard quality										
To softwood										
plain; polished brass; 356mm wide	28.95	2.50	29.67	1.65	-	34.44	-	64.11	nr	70.52
telescopic; anodised silver flap; 300mm wide	4.75	2.50	4.87	1.65	-	34.44	-	39.30	nr	43.23
interior; gravity flap; polished brass; 280mm wide	7.50	2.50	7.69	1.65	-	34.44	-	42.12	nr	46.34
interior; gravity flap; chromium plated; 280mm wide	10.65	2.50	10.92	1.65	-	34.44	-	45.35	nr	49.89
interior; gravity flap, satin nickel; 280mm wide	11.35	2.50	11.63	1.75	-	36.52	-	48.16	nr	52.97
postal knockers; polished brass; frame 254 x 79mm; opening 185 x 43m	23.35	2.50	23.93	1.75	-	36.52	-	60.46	nr	66.50
To hardwood or the like										
plain; polished brass; 356mm wide	28.95	2.50	29.67	2.50	-	52.18	-	81.85	nr	90.03
telescopic; anodised silver flap; 300mm wide	4.75	2.50	4.87	2.50	-	52.18	-	57.04	nr	62.75
interior; gravity flap; polished brass; 280mm wide	7.50	2.50	7.69	2.50	-	52.18	-	59.86	nr	65.85
interior; gravity flap; chromium plated; 280mm wide	10.65	2.50	10.92	2.50	-	52.18	-	63.09	nr	69.40
interior; gravity flap, satin nickel; 280mm wide	11.35	2.50	11.63	2.65	-	55.31	-	66.94	nr	73.63
postal knockers; polished brass; frame 254 x 79mm; opening 185 x 43m	23.35	2.50	23.93	2.65	-	55.31	-	79.24	nr	87.16
Security locks; standard quality										
To hardwood or the like										
window catches; locking; polished brass	4.80	2.50	4.92	1.20	-	25.04	-	29.96	nr	32.96
dual screws; brass	1.66	2.50	1.71	1.00	-	20.87	-	22.58	nr	24.83
window stops; locking; brass	1.58	2.50	1.62	1.00	-	20.87	-	22.49	nr	24.74
mortice latches; locking	3.90	2.50	4.00	3.50	-	73.05	-	77.04	nr	84.75
double cylinder automatic deadlatches; high security; Brass finish	39.90	2.50	40.90	3.50	-	73.05	-	113.94	nr	125.34
double cylinder automatic deadlatches; standard security; chromium plated	23.30	2.50	23.88	3.50	-	73.05	-	96.93	nr	106.62
mortice deadlocks; Union 3G115PB	35.84	2.50	36.74	3.50	-	73.05	-	109.78	nr	120.76
5 lever high security sashlock; Union 2201	22.34	2.50	22.90	3.50	-	73.05	-	95.95	nr	105.54
metal window locks; brass; Yale 8K118	4.88	2.50	5.00	1.50	-	31.31	-	36.30	nr	39.93
security door chains; steel chain; brass plated	4.90	2.50	5.02	0.60	-	12.52	-	17.54	nr	19.30
security door chains; steel chain; chromium plated	4.90	2.50	5.02	0.60	-	12.52	-	17.54	nr	19.30
security mortice rackbolts; loose keys; brass; 60mm long	2.44	2.50	2.50	1.20	-	25.04	-	27.55	nr	30.30
security hinge bolts; Satin Chrome	2.05	2.50	2.10	1.80	-	37.57	-	39.67	nr	43.63
door viewers; chromium plated	3.25	2.50	3.33	1.50	-	31.31	-	34.64	nr	38.10
Shelf brackets; standard quality										
To softwood										
shelf brackets; white finished										
100 x 75mm	0.29	2.50	0.30	0.25	-	5.22	-	5.52	nr	6.07
150 x 125mm	0.42	2.50	0.43	0.25	-	5.22	-	5.64	nr	6.21
200 x 150mm	0.52	2.50	0.53	0.25	-	5.22	-	5.75	nr	6.33
250 x 200mm	12.48	2.50	12.79	0.25	-	5.22	-	18.01	nr	19.81
350 x 300mm	0.96	2.50	0.98	0.25	-	5.22	-	6.20	nr	6.82
Cabin hooks; standard quality										
To softwood										
cabin hooks and eyes; black japanned										
100mm	0.69	2.50	0.71	0.25	-	5.22	-	5.93	nr	6.52
150mm	0.47	2.50	0.48	0.25	-	5.22	-	5.70	nr	6.27
200mm	1.20	2.50	1.23	0.25	-	5.22	-	6.45	nr	7.09
250mm	4.61	2.50	4.73	0.25	-	5.22	-	9.94	nr	10.94
cabin hooks and eyes; polished brass										
100mm	3.20	2.50	3.28	0.25	-	5.22	-	8.50	nr	9.35
200mm	6.58	2.50	6.74	0.25	-	5.22	-	11.96	nr	13.16
To hardwood or the like										
cabin hooks and eyes; black japanned										
100mm	0.69	2.50	0.71	0.35	-	7.30	-	8.01	nr	8.82
150mm	0.47	2.50	0.48	0.35	-	7.30	-	7.78	nr	8.56
200mm	1.20	2.50	1.23	0.35	-	7.30	-	8.53	nr	9.39
250mm	4.61	2.50	4.73	0.35	-	7.30	-	12.03	nr	13.23
cabin hooks and eyes; polished brass										
100mm	3.20	2.50	3.28	0.35	-	7.30	-	10.58	nr	11.64
200mm	6.58	2.50	6.74	0.35	-	7.30	-	14.05	nr	15.45
To softwood and brickwork										
cabin hooks and eyes; black japanned										
100mm	0.69	2.50	0.71	0.30	-	6.26	-	6.97	nr	7.67
150mm	0.47	2.50	0.48	0.30	-	6.26	-	6.74	nr	7.41
200mm	1.20	2.50	1.23	0.30	-	6.26	-	7.49	nr	8.24
250mm	4.61	2.50	4.73	0.30	-	6.26	-	10.99	nr	12.08
cabin hooks and eyes; polished brass										
100mm	3.20	2.50	3.28	0.30	-	6.26	-	9.54	nr	10.50
200mm	6.58	2.50	6.74	0.30	-	6.26	-	13.01	nr	14.31
To hardwood and brickwork										
cabin hooks and eyes; black japanned										
100mm	0.69	2.50	0.71	0.40	-	8.35	-	9.06	nr	9.96
150mm	0.47	2.50	0.48	0.40	-	8.35	-	8.83	nr	9.71
200mm	1.20	2.50	1.23	0.40	-	8.35	-	9.58	nr	10.54
250mm	4.61	2.50	4.73	0.40	-	8.35	-	13.07	nr	14.38

Labour hourly rates: (except Specialists) Craft Operatives 20.87 Labourer 15.57 Rates are national average prices. Refer to REGIONAL VARIATIONS for indicative levels of overall pricing in regions	MATERIALS			LABOUR				RATES		
	Del to Site £	Waste %	Material Cost £	Craft Optve Hrs	Lab Hrs	Labour Cost £	Sunds £	Nett Rate £	Unit	Gross rate (10%) £
IRONMONGERY (Cont'd)										
Cabin hooks; standard quality (Cont'd)										
To hardwood and brickwork (Cont'd)										
cabin hooks and eyes; polished brass										
100mm	3.20	2.50	3.28	0.40	-	8.35	-	11.63	nr	12.79
200mm	6.58	2.50	6.74	0.40	-	8.35	-	15.09	nr	16.60
Draught seals and strips; standard quality										
To softwood										
draught excluders; plastic foam, self-adhesive										
900mm long	0.11	10.00	0.12	0.15	-	3.13	-	3.25	nr	3.58
2000mm long	0.39	10.00	0.43	0.30	-	6.26	-	6.69	nr	7.36
draught excluders; aluminium section, rubber tubing										
900mm long	0.38	10.00	0.42	0.17	0.02	3.86	-	4.28	nr	4.71
2000mm long	0.85	10.00	0.94	0.35	0.04	7.93	-	8.87	nr	9.75
draught excluders; aluminium section, vinyl seal										
900mm long	13.73	10.00	15.10	0.17	0.02	3.86	-	18.96	nr	20.86
2000mm long	24.65	10.00	27.11	0.35	0.04	7.93	-	35.04	nr	38.55
draught excluders; plastic moulding, nylon brush										
900mm long	1.08	10.00	1.18	0.17	0.02	3.86	-	5.04	nr	5.55
draught excluders; aluminium base, nylon brush										
900mm long	1.49	10.00	1.64	0.25	0.03	5.68	-	7.33	nr	8.06
draught excluders; aluminium threshold, 2 part Stormguard										
914mm long	16.66	10.00	18.32	0.30	0.04	6.88	-	25.21	nr	27.73
Draught seals and strips; Sealmaster Ltd										
Threshold seals										
reference BDA; fixing to masonry with screws	25.84	2.50	26.49	0.45	0.06	10.33	0.33	37.15	m	40.86
reference BDB; fixing to masonry with screws	33.14	2.50	33.97	0.45	0.06	10.33	0.45	44.74	m	49.22
reference WTSHED WEABRD 1000MM AA; fixing to timber with screws	56.36	2.50	57.77	0.70	0.10	16.17	0.52	74.46	m	81.91
surface mounted stop strip with blade; fixing to timber with screws	20.80	2.50	21.32	0.33	0.05	7.67	0.33	29.32	m	32.25
Drawer pulls; standard quality										
To softwood										
drawer pulls; brass; 100mm	2.40	2.50	2.46	0.20	-	4.17	-	6.63	nr	7.30
drawer pulls; chromium plated; 100mm	5.96	2.50	6.11	0.20	-	4.17	-	10.28	nr	11.31
To hardwood or the like										
drawer pulls; brass; 100mm	2.40	2.50	2.46	0.30	-	6.26	-	8.72	nr	9.59
drawer pulls; chromium plated; 100mm	5.96	2.50	6.11	0.30	-	6.26	-	12.37	nr	13.60
Hooks; standard quality										
To softwood										
cup hooks; polished brass; 25mm	0.07	2.50	0.07	0.07	-	1.46	-	1.53	nr	1.68
hat and coat hooks; brass	1.65	2.50	1.69	0.30	-	6.26	-	7.95	nr	8.75
hat and coat hooks; chromium plated	1.65	2.50	1.69	0.30	-	6.26	-	7.95	nr	8.75
hat and coat hooks; S.A.A.	0.65	2.50	0.67	0.30	-	6.26	-	6.93	nr	7.62
To hardwood or the like										
cup hooks; polished brass; 25mm	0.07	2.50	0.07	0.10	-	2.09	-	2.16	nr	2.37
hat and coat hooks; brass	1.65	2.50	1.69	0.45	-	9.39	-	11.08	nr	12.19
hat and coat hooks; chromium plated	1.65	2.50	1.69	0.45	-	9.39	-	11.08	nr	12.19
hat and coat hooks; S.A.A.	0.65	2.50	0.67	0.45	-	9.39	-	10.06	nr	11.06

This page left blank intentionally

Labour hourly rates: (except Specialists) Craft Operatives 20.87 Labourer 15.57 Rates are national average prices. Refer to REGIONAL VARIATIONS for indicative levels of overall pricing in regions	MATERIALS			LABOUR				RATES		
	Del to Site £	Waste %	Material Cost £	Craft Optve Hrs	Lab Hrs	Labour Cost £	Sunds £	Nett Rate £	Unit	Gross rate (10%) £
TIMBER WINDOWS AND SHOP FRONTS										
Windows in softwood, base coat stained by manufacturer; Bedding in cement mortar (1:3); pointing with Silicone standard mastic one side										
Jeld-Wen Ltd. Softwood Stormsure windows plain casement non bar type side hung; factory double glazed; weatherstripping, hinges; fasteners										
630 x 750mm overall; LEW107C	249.99	2.50	256.41	2.45	0.95	65.96	2.67	325.05	nr	357.55
630 x 900mm overall; LEW109C	265.58	2.50	272.41	2.81	1.10	75.81	2.67	350.89	nr	385.98
630 x 1050mm overall; LEW110C	273.99	2.50	281.05	3.12	1.22	84.21	2.67	367.94	nr	404.73
630 x 1200mm overall; LEW112C	291.91	2.50	299.43	3.38	1.32	91.13	2.67	393.24	nr	432.57
630 x 1350mm overall; LEW113C	307.45	2.50	315.39	3.69	1.45	99.63	2.67	417.69	nr	459.46
1200 x 750mm overall; LEW207CC	426.76	2.50	437.68	3.38	1.30	90.78	2.67	531.13	nr	584.24
1200 x 900mm overall; LEW209CC	448.95	2.50	460.43	3.74	1.45	100.63	2.67	563.73	nr	620.11
1200 x 1050mm overall; LEW210CC	472.07	2.50	484.15	3.95	1.52	106.10	2.67	592.92	nr	652.22
1200 x 1200mm overall; LEW212CC	385.00	2.50	394.92	4.26	1.65	114.60	2.67	512.19	nr	563.41
1200 x 1350mm overall; LEW213CC	535.43	2.50	549.14	4.57	1.77	122.93	2.67	674.74	nr	742.22
1770 x 750mm overall; LEW307CC	543.84	2.50	557.75	4.38	1.65	117.10	2.67	677.52	nr	745.27
1770 x 900mm overall; LEW309CC	437.95	2.50	449.24	4.62	1.77	123.94	2.67	575.84	nr	633.43
1770 x 1050mm overall; LEW310CC	471.02	2.50	483.15	4.83	1.85	129.56	2.67	615.38	nr	676.92
1770 x 1200mm overall; LEW312CC	469.82	2.50	481.93	5.19	2.00	139.41	2.67	624.02	nr	686.42
1770 x 1350mm overall; LEW313CC	683.16	2.50	700.62	5.55	2.15	149.26	2.67	852.56	nr	937.81
2339 x 900mm overall; LEW409CMC	696.62	2.50	714.44	5.60	2.15	150.26	2.67	867.38	nr	954.11
2339 x 1050mm overall; LEW410CMC	735.08	2.50	753.88	5.96	2.30	160.11	2.67	916.66	nr	1008.33
2339 x 1200mm overall; LEW412CMC	775.21	2.50	795.03	6.23	2.42	167.62	2.67	965.32	nr	1061.85
2339 x 1350mm overall; LEW413CMC	829.11	2.50	850.30	6.58	2.55	176.94	2.67	1029.92	nr	1132.91
Jeld-Wen Ltd. Softwood Stormsure unglazed window casements; glazing beads; weatherstripping, hinges; fasteners										
630 x 750mm overall; W107C	159.38	2.50	163.54	2.35	0.90	63.10	2.67	229.31	nr	252.24
630 x 900mm overall; W109V	171.39	2.50	175.87	2.51	0.95	67.22	2.67	245.76	nr	270.34
630 x 1050mm overall; W110V	174.97	2.50	179.55	2.87	1.10	77.07	2.67	259.29	nr	285.22
630 x 1200mm overall; W112C	179.29	2.50	184.00	3.18	1.22	85.40	2.67	272.08	nr	299.29
910 x 750mm overall; W2N07C	196.97	2.50	202.15	2.82	1.07	75.43	2.67	280.25	nr	308.27
915 x 1045mm overall; W2N10C	212.75	2.50	218.30	3.39	1.30	90.91	2.67	311.88	nr	343.07
915 x 1200mm overall; W2N12C	222.75	2.50	228.60	3.65	1.40	97.89	2.67	329.16	nr	362.08
915 x 750mm overall; W2N07CC	243.99	2.50	250.30	2.82	1.07	75.43	2.67	328.40	nr	361.24
915 x 1050mm overall; W2N10CC	266.45	2.50	273.35	3.39	1.30	90.91	2.67	366.93	nr	403.62
915 x 1200mm overall; W2N12CC	279.35	2.50	286.60	3.65	1.40	97.89	2.67	387.16	nr	425.88
1200 x 900mm overall; W209CV	250.57	2.50	257.10	3.44	1.30	92.03	2.67	351.81	nr	386.99
1200 x 1050mm overall; W210CC	295.26	2.50	302.92	3.80	1.45	101.88	2.67	407.47	nr	448.22
1200 x 1200mm overall; W212CC	308.16	2.50	316.17	4.01	1.52	107.36	2.67	426.19	nr	468.81
1340 x 900mm overall; W3N09CC	314.69	2.50	322.87	4.28	1.60	114.24	2.67	439.78	nr	483.76
1340 x 1200mm overall; W3N12CC	343.00	2.50	351.91	4.32	1.65	115.85	2.67	470.44	nr	517.48
1770 x 1050mm overall; W310CC	359.48	2.50	368.82	4.43	1.65	118.10	2.67	489.59	nr	538.55
1770 x 1200mm overall; W312CVC	374.46	2.50	384.19	4.74	1.77	126.44	2.67	513.31	nr	564.64
2340 x 900mm overall; W409CMC	375.93	2.50	385.72	4.95	1.85	132.07	2.67	520.46	nr	572.51
2340 x 1050mm overall; W410CMC	391.70	2.50	401.90	5.31	2.00	141.92	2.67	546.49	nr	601.14
Windows in hardwood, base coat stained by manufacturer; Bedding in cement mortar (1:3); pointing with Silicone standard mastic one side										
Jeld-Wen Ltd. Oak Stormsure windows; plain side hung casement; factory double glazed; weatherstripping, hinges; fasteners; factory finished stain by manufacturer										
630 x 750mm overall; OLEW107C	608.12	2.50	623.50	3.02	1.22	82.02	2.67	708.19	nr	779.01
630 x 900mm overall; OLEW109C	637.25	2.50	653.37	3.26	1.32	88.63	2.67	744.68	nr	819.15
630 x 1050mm overall; OLEW110C	666.39	2.50	683.26	3.22	1.32	87.75	2.67	773.69	nr	851.06
630 x 1200mm overall; OLEW112CH	695.53	2.50	713.14	3.48	1.37	94.00	2.67	809.82	nr	890.80
630 x 1350mm overall; OLEW113C	724.67	2.50	743.03	3.54	1.37	95.25	2.67	840.95	nr	925.05
1200 x 750mm overall; OLEW207C	967.66	2.50	992.09	3.38	1.30	90.78	2.67	1085.55	nr	1194.10
1200 x 900mm overall; OLEW209C	996.79	2.50	1021.97	3.64	1.40	97.76	2.67	1122.41	nr	1234.65
1200 x 1050mm overall; OLEW210C	1025.93	2.50	1051.86	3.95	1.52	106.10	2.67	1160.64	nr	1276.70
1200 x 1200mm overall; OLEW212C	1055.06	2.50	1081.74	4.30	1.65	115.35	2.67	1199.76	nr	1319.74
1200 x 1350mm overall; OLEW213C	1084.20	2.50	1111.62	4.57	1.77	122.93	2.67	1237.23	nr	1360.95
1770 x 750mm overall; OLEW307CC	1472.40	2.50	1509.53	4.31	1.65	115.60	2.67	1627.80	nr	1790.58
1770 x 900mm overall; OLEW309CC	1504.42	2.50	1542.36	4.62	1.77	123.94	2.67	1668.97	nr	1835.87
1770 x 1050mm overall; OLEW310CC	1536.44	2.50	1575.20	4.83	1.85	129.56	2.67	1707.44	nr	1878.18
1770 x 1200mm overall; OLEW312CC	1568.45	2.50	1608.03	5.19	2.00	139.41	2.67	1750.12	nr	1925.13
1770 x 1350mm overall; OLEW313CC	1600.47	2.50	1640.87	5.55	2.15	149.26	2.67	1792.80	nr	1972.08
2339 x 900mm overall; OLEW409CMC	1682.42	2.50	1724.89	5.80	2.25	156.00	2.67	1883.55	nr	2071.91
2339 x 1050mm overall; OLEW410CMC	1754.73	2.50	1799.02	5.96	2.30	160.11	2.67	1961.80	nr	2157.99
2339 x 1200mm overall; OLEW412CMC	1827.04	2.50	1873.15	6.27	2.42	168.45	2.67	2044.28	nr	2248.70
2339 x 1350mm overall; OLEW413CMC	1899.33	2.50	1947.28	6.53	2.52	175.43	2.67	2125.38	nr	2337.92
Jeld-Wen Ltd. Oak Stormsure windows; plain side hung casement with vents; factory double glazed; weatherstripping, hinges; fasteners; factory finished stain by manufacturer										
630 x 750mm overall; OLEW107V	551.55	2.50	565.51	2.50	0.95	67.01	2.67	635.19	nr	698.71
630 x 900mm overall; OLEW109V	587.87	2.50	602.76	3.26	1.08	84.89	2.67	690.32	nr	759.36
630 x 1050mm overall; OLEW110V	624.20	2.50	640.02	3.12	1.22	84.15	2.67	726.84	nr	799.53

Labour hourly rates: (except Specialists) Craft Operatives 20.87 Labourer 15.57 Rates are national average prices. Refer to REGIONAL VARIATIONS for indicative levels of overall pricing in regions	MATERIALS			LABOUR				RATES		
	Del to Site £	Waste %	Material Cost £	Craft Optve Hrs	Lab Hrs	Labour Cost £	Sunds £	Nett Rate £	Unit	Gross rate (10%) £
TIMBER WINDOWS AND SHOP FRONTS (Cont'd)										
Windows in hardwood, base coat stained by manufacturer; Bedding in cement mortar (1:3); pointing with Silicone standard mastic one side (Cont'd)										
Jeld-Wen Ltd. Oak Stormsure windows; plain side hung casement with vents; factory double glazed; weatherstripping, hinges; fasteners; factory finished stain by manufacturer (Cont'd)										
630 x 1200mm overall; OLEW112V	660.53	2.50	677.28	3.33	1.30	89.78	2.67	769.73	nr	846.70
630 x 1350mm overall; OLEW113V	696.87	2.50	714.53	3.79	1.50	102.49	2.67	819.70	nr	901.67
915 x 900mm overall; OLEW2N09W	722.20	2.50	740.48	2.53	1.40	74.52	2.67	817.67	nr	899.44
915 x 1350mm overall; OLEW2N13W	794.09	2.50	814.23	4.06	1.57	109.09	2.67	925.99	nr	1018.59
915 x 750mm overall; OLEW2N07CV	850.56	2.50	872.04	3.12	1.22	84.03	2.67	958.74	nr	1054.61
915 x 900mm overall; OLEW2N09CV	886.83	2.50	909.23	3.33	1.30	89.65	2.67	1001.56	nr	1101.71
915 x 1050mm overall; OLEW2N10CV	924.97	2.50	948.33	3.64	1.42	97.99	2.67	1049.00	nr	1153.90
915 x 1200mm overall; OLEW2N12CV	970.51	2.50	995.03	3.80	1.47	102.11	2.67	1099.82	nr	1209.80
1200 x 900mm overall; OLEW209T	965.86	2.50	990.27	3.79	1.47	101.99	2.67	1094.93	nr	1204.42
1200 x 1050mm overall; OLEW210T	1008.66	2.50	1034.16	3.95	1.52	106.10	2.67	1142.94	nr	1257.23
1200 x 1200mm overall; OLEW212T	1055.81	2.50	1082.51	4.26	1.65	114.60	2.67	1199.78	nr	1319.75
1200 x 1350mm overall; OLEW213T	1103.50	2.50	1131.40	4.62	1.80	124.45	2.67	1258.52	nr	1384.37
1200 x 1500mm overall; OLEW215T	1183.72	2.50	1213.65	4.68	1.80	125.70	2.67	1342.02	nr	1476.22
1770 x 1050mm overall; OLEW310CVC	1470.58	2.50	1507.70	4.93	1.90	132.43	2.67	1642.80	nr	1807.08
1770 x 1200mm overall; OLEW312CVC	1547.05	2.50	1586.10	5.29	2.05	142.28	2.67	1731.05	nr	1904.15
1770 x 1350mm overall; OLEW313CVC	1639.67	2.50	1681.05	5.55	2.15	149.26	2.67	1832.98	nr	2016.28
1770 x 1500mm overall; OLEW315CVC	1762.31	2.50	1806.77	5.81	2.25	156.25	2.67	1965.69	nr	2162.26
Jeld-Wen Ltd. Oak Stormsure windows - horizontal glazing bar type; factory glazed 24mm low E glass; weatherstripping, hinges; fasteners; base coat stain by manufacturer										
625 x 595mm overall; OLEW106A	484.59	2.50	496.90	2.76	1.08	74.46	2.67	574.03	nr	631.43
625 x 745mm overall; OLEW107A	522.08	2.50	535.34	2.92	1.02	76.86	2.67	614.88	nr	676.37
625 x 1195mm overall; OLEW112A	614.38	2.50	629.96	3.38	1.32	91.13	2.67	723.77	nr	796.15
910 x 595mm overall; OLEW2N06A	613.26	2.50	628.84	3.49	1.35	93.90	2.67	725.41	nr	797.95
910 x 895mm overall; OLEW2N09A	694.57	2.50	712.20	3.64	1.40	97.76	2.67	812.64	nr	893.90
910 x 1045mm overall; OLEW2N10A	724.53	2.50	742.93	8.00	1.45	189.54	2.67	935.14	nr	1028.65
910 x 1195mm overall; OLEW2N12A	760.73	2.50	780.05	4.11	1.58	110.38	2.67	893.10	nr	982.40
1195 x 595mm overall; OLEW206A	708.13	2.50	726.16	3.92	1.45	104.39	2.67	833.22	nr	916.54
1195 x 895mm overall; OLEW209A	796.03	2.50	816.28	4.23	1.50	111.59	2.67	930.55	nr	1023.60
1195 x 1045mm overall; OLEW210A	829.11	2.50	850.20	4.44	1.75	119.87	2.67	972.74	nr	1070.02
1195 x 1195mm overall; OLEW212A	868.42	2.50	890.52	4.70	1.72	124.83	2.67	1018.02	nr	1119.82
1765 x 745mm overall; OLEW307AE	971.64	2.50	996.35	4.91	1.98	133.22	2.67	1132.24	nr	1245.47
1765 x 1045mm overall; OLEW310AE	1071.79	2.50	1099.02	5.32	2.08	143.33	2.67	1245.03	nr	1369.53
1765 x 1195mm overall; OLEW312AE	1125.16	2.50	1153.75	5.73	2.12	152.51	2.67	1308.93	nr	1439.82
Purpose made windows										
Note										
Notwithstanding the requirements of the NRM purpose made windows are shown here in square metres and excludes bedding and pointing										
Purpose made windows in softwood, wrought										
38mm moulded casements or fanlights										
in one pane	194.68	2.50	199.55	1.50	0.19	34.26	0.40	234.21	m²	257.63
divided into panes 0.10 - 0.50m²	306.51	2.50	314.17	1.50	0.19	34.26	0.40	348.83	m²	383.72
divided into panes not exceeding 0.10m²	355.24	2.50	364.12	1.50	0.19	34.26	0.40	398.78	m²	438.66
50mm moulded casements or fanlights										
in one pane	233.62	2.50	239.46	1.60	0.20	36.51	0.43	276.39	m²	304.03
divided into panes 0.10 - 0.50m²	367.81	2.50	377.01	1.60	0.20	36.51	0.43	413.94	m²	455.34
divided into panes not exceeding 0.10m²	426.29	2.50	436.95	1.60	0.20	36.51	0.43	473.88	m²	521.27
38mm moulded casements with semi-circular heads (measured square)										
in one pane	344.68	2.50	353.30	1.65	0.21	37.71	0.45	391.45	m²	430.59
divided into panes 0.10 - 0.50m²	456.51	2.50	467.92	1.65	0.21	37.71	0.45	506.07	m²	556.68
divided into panes not exceeding 0.10m²	505.24	2.50	517.87	1.65	0.21	37.71	0.45	556.02	m²	611.62
50mm moulded casements with semi-circular heads (measured square)										
in one pane	393.62	2.50	403.46	1.75	0.22	39.95	0.46	443.87	m²	488.25
divided into panes 0.10 - 0.50m²	527.81	2.50	541.01	1.75	0.22	39.95	0.46	581.42	m²	639.56
divided into panes not exceeding 0.10m²	586.29	2.50	600.95	1.75	0.22	39.95	0.46	641.36	m²	705.49
38mm bullseye casements										
457mm diameter in one pane	275.74	2.50	282.64	1.00	0.12	22.74	0.26	305.64	nr	336.20
762mm diameter in one pane	344.68	2.50	353.30	1.50	0.19	34.26	0.40	387.96	nr	426.75
50mm bullseye casements										
457mm diameter in one pane	314.89	2.50	322.77	1.10	0.14	25.14	0.30	348.20	nr	383.02
762mm diameter in one pane	393.62	2.50	403.46	1.65	0.21	37.71	0.45	441.61	nr	485.77
Labours										
check throated edge	1.00	2.50	1.02	-	-	-	-	1.02	m	1.13
rebated and splayed bottom rail	1.00	2.50	1.02	-	-	-	-	1.02	m	1.13
rebated and beaded meeting stile	1.30	2.50	1.33	-	-	-	-	1.33	m	1.47
fitting and hanging casement or fanlight on butts (included elsewhere)										
38mm	-	-	-	0.67	0.08	15.23	-	15.23	nr	16.75
50mm	-	-	-	0.74	0.09	16.85	-	16.85	nr	18.53
fitting and hanging casement or fanlight on sash centres (included elsewhere)										
38mm	-	-	-	1.50	0.19	34.26	-	34.26	nr	37.69
50mm	-	-	-	1.65	0.21	37.71	-	37.71	nr	41.48

Labour hourly rates: (except Specialists) Craft Operatives 20.87 Labourer 15.57 Rates are national average prices. Refer to REGIONAL VARIATIONS for indicative levels of overall pricing in regions	MATERIALS			LABOUR				RATES		
	Del to Site £	Waste %	Material Cost £	Craft Optve Hrs	Lab Hrs	Labour Cost £	Sunds £	Nett Rate £	Unit	Gross rate (10%) £
TIMBER WINDOWS AND SHOP FRONTS (Cont'd)										
Purpose made windows in Sapele, wrought										
38mm moulded casements or fanlights										
in one pane	256.53	2.50	262.94	2.25	0.28	51.32	0.61	314.87	m²	346.36
divided into panes 0.10 - 0.50m²	300.80	2.50	308.32	2.25	0.28	51.32	0.61	360.25	m²	396.27
divided into panes not exceeding 0.10m²	430.88	2.50	441.65	2.25	0.28	51.32	0.61	493.58	m²	542.94
50mm moulded casements or fanlights										
in one pane	307.84	2.50	315.53	2.40	0.30	54.76	0.64	370.93	m²	408.03
divided into panes 0.10 - 0.50m²	360.96	2.50	369.98	2.40	0.30	54.76	0.64	425.39	m²	467.93
divided into panes not exceeding 0.10m²	517.06	2.50	529.98	2.40	0.30	54.76	0.64	585.38	m²	643.92
38mm moulded casements with semi-circular heads (measured square)										
in one pane	406.53	2.50	416.69	2.45	0.31	55.96	0.66	473.31	m²	520.64
divided into panes 0.10 - 0.50m²	450.80	2.50	462.07	2.45	0.31	55.96	0.66	518.69	m²	570.56
divided into panes not exceeding 0.10m²	580.88	2.50	595.40	2.45	0.31	55.96	0.66	652.02	m²	717.22
50mm moulded casements with semi-circular heads (measured square)										
in one pane	467.84	2.50	479.53	2.60	0.32	59.24	0.69	539.47	m²	593.42
divided into panes 0.10 - 0.50m²	520.96	2.50	533.98	2.60	0.32	59.24	0.69	593.92	m²	653.31
divided into panes not exceeding 0.10m²	677.06	2.50	693.98	2.60	0.32	59.24	0.69	753.92	m²	829.31
38mm bullseye casements										
457mm diameter in one pane	325.22	2.50	333.35	1.50	0.19	34.26	0.40	368.01	nr	404.82
762mm diameter in one pane	406.53	2.50	416.69	2.25	0.28	51.32	0.61	468.62	nr	515.48
50mm bullseye casements										
457mm diameter in one pane	374.27	2.50	383.63	1.65	0.21	37.71	0.45	421.78	nr	463.95
762mm diameter in one pane	467.84	2.50	479.53	2.45	0.31	55.96	0.66	536.15	nr	589.77
Labours										
check throated edge	1.70	2.50	1.74	-	-	-	-	1.74	m	1.92
rebated and splayed bottom rail	1.70	2.50	1.74	-	-	-	-	1.74	m	1.92
rebated and beaded meeting stile	2.15	2.50	2.20	-	-	-	-	2.20	m	2.42
fitting and hanging casement or fanlight on butts (included elsewhere)										
38mm	-	-	-	1.00	0.12	22.74	-	22.74	nr	25.01
50mm	-	-	-	1.10	0.14	25.14	-	25.14	nr	27.65
fitting and hanging casement or fanlight on sash centres (included elsewhere)										
38mm	-	-	-	2.25	0.28	51.32	-	51.32	nr	56.45
50mm	-	-	-	2.45	0.31	55.96	-	55.96	nr	61.55
Purpose made windows in European Oak, wrought										
38mm moulded casements or fanlights										
in one pane	398.00	2.50	407.95	3.00	0.37	68.37	0.81	477.13	m²	524.84
divided into panes 0.10 - 0.50m²	465.90	2.50	477.55	3.00	0.37	68.37	0.81	546.73	m²	601.40
divided into panes not exceeding 0.10m²	606.93	2.50	622.10	3.00	0.37	68.37	0.81	691.28	m²	760.41
50mm moulded casements or fanlights										
in one pane	477.60	2.50	489.54	3.20	0.40	73.01	0.86	563.41	m²	619.75
divided into panes 0.10 - 0.50m²	559.08	2.50	573.06	3.20	0.40	73.01	0.86	646.93	m²	711.62
divided into panes not exceeding 0.10m²	728.32	2.50	746.52	3.20	0.40	73.01	0.86	820.39	m²	902.43
38mm moulded casements with semi-circular heads (measured square)										
in one pane	548.00	2.50	561.70	3.30	0.41	75.25	0.89	637.85	m²	701.63
divided into panes 0.10 - 0.50m²	615.90	2.50	631.30	3.30	0.41	75.25	0.89	707.44	m²	778.19
divided into panes not exceeding 0.10m²	756.93	2.50	775.85	3.30	0.41	75.25	0.89	852.00	m²	937.20
50mm moulded casements with semi-circular heads (measured square)										
in one pane	637.60	2.50	653.54	3.50	0.44	79.90	0.94	734.38	m²	807.81
divided into panes 0.10 - 0.50m²	719.08	2.50	737.06	3.50	0.44	79.90	0.94	817.89	m²	899.68
divided into panes not exceeding 0.10m²	888.32	2.50	910.52	3.50	0.44	79.90	0.94	991.36	m²	1090.50
38mm bullseye casements										
457mm diameter in one pane	438.40	2.50	449.36	2.00	0.25	45.63	0.54	495.54	nr	545.09
762mm diameter in one pane	548.00	2.50	561.70	3.00	0.37	68.37	0.81	630.88	nr	693.97
50mm bullseye casements										
457mm diameter in one pane	510.08	2.50	522.83	2.20	0.27	50.12	0.59	573.54	nr	630.90
762mm diameter in one pane	637.60	2.50	653.54	3.30	0.41	75.25	0.89	729.69	nr	802.65
Labours										
check throated edge	2.00	2.50	2.05	-	-	-	-	2.05	m	2.26
rebated and splayed bottom rail	2.00	2.50	2.05	-	-	-	-	2.05	m	2.26
rebated and beaded meeting stile	2.70	2.50	2.77	-	-	-	-	2.77	m	3.04
fitting and hanging casement or fanlight on butts (included elsewhere)										
38mm	-	-	-	1.30	0.16	29.62	-	29.62	nr	32.58
50mm	-	-	-	1.45	0.18	33.06	-	33.06	nr	36.37
fitting and hanging casement or fanlight on sash centres (included elsewhere)										
38mm	-	-	-	3.00	0.37	68.37	-	68.37	nr	75.21
50mm	-	-	-	3.30	0.41	75.25	-	75.25	nr	82.78

Labour hourly rates: (except Specialists) Craft Operatives 20.87 Labourer 15.57 Rates are national average prices. Refer to REGIONAL VARIATIONS for indicative levels of overall pricing in regions	MATERIALS			LABOUR				RATES		
	Del to Site £	Waste %	Material Cost £	Craft Optve Hrs	Lab Hrs	Labour Cost £	Sunds £	Nett Rate £	Unit	Gross rate (10%) £
TIMBER WINDOWS AND SHOP FRONTS (Cont'd)										
Sash windows in softwood, wrought, preservative treated; pre-finished white by manufacturer; Bedding in cement mortar (1:3); pointing with Silicone standard mastic one side										
Jeld-wen softwood sliding sash windows; non-bar; factory double glazed; trickle vents; 168mm cill; weather stripping; pre-tensioned balances; chrome fittings; fully finished in white										
630 x 1045mm overall	728.97	2.50	747.43	4.57	1.90	124.92	2.56	874.91	nr	962.40
630 x 1345mm overall	875.94	2.50	898.12	5.04	2.07	137.37	2.56	1038.05	nr	1141.85
855 x 1345mm overall	981.26	2.50	1006.06	5.01	2.07	136.75	2.56	1145.37	nr	1259.90
1080 x 1045mm overall	945.30	2.50	969.20	5.01	2.07	136.75	2.56	1108.50	nr	1219.35
1080 x 1345mm overall	1089.88	2.50	1117.43	5.48	2.25	149.36	2.56	1269.35	nr	1396.28
1080 x 1645mm overall	1234.46	2.50	1265.66	5.90	2.40	160.46	2.56	1428.68	nr	1571.55
Jeld-wen softwood sliding sash windows; all-bar (Georgian); factory double glazed; trickle vents; 168mm cill; weatherstripping; pre-tensioned balances; chrome fittings; fully finished in white; fixing to masonry with galvanised steel cramps -4 nr, 25 x 3 x 150mm girth, flat section, holes -2										
855 x 1045mm overall	720.22	2.50	738.46	3.49	1.30	93.04	2.56	834.06	nr	917.46
855 x 1345mm overall	836.05	2.50	857.23	3.89	1.50	104.50	2.56	964.28	nr	1060.71
1080 x 1345mm overall	922.92	2.50	946.30	4.38	1.70	117.84	2.56	1066.69	nr	1173.36
Sash windows; purpose made										
Note										
Notwithstanding the requirements of the NRM purpose made windows are shown here in square metres and excludes bedding and pointing										
Sash windows; purpose made; mainly in softwood, wrought										
Cased frames; 25mm inside and outside linings; 32mm pulley stiles and head; 10mm beads, back linings, etc; 76mm oak sunk weathered and throated sills; 50mm moulded sashes										
in one pane	616.91	2.50	632.33	2.75	0.34	62.69	0.74	695.76	m²	765.33
divided into panes 0.50 - 1.00m²	645.95	2.50	662.09	2.75	0.34	62.69	0.74	725.52	m²	798.07
divided into panes 0.10 - 0.50m²	704.03	2.50	721.63	2.75	0.34	62.69	0.74	785.05	m²	863.56
divided into panes not exceeding 0.10m²	733.07	2.50	751.39	2.75	0.34	62.69	0.74	814.82	m²	896.30
extra; windows in three lights with boxed mullions	152.00	2.50	155.80	0.75	0.09	17.05	0.20	173.05	nr	190.36
extra; windows with moulded horns	16.00	2.50	16.40	-	-	-	-	16.40	nr	18.04
extra; deep bottom rails and draught beads	10.00	2.50	10.25	-	-	-	-	10.25	m	11.27
Labours										
throats	1.00	2.50	1.02	-	-	-	-	1.02	m	1.13
grooves for jamb linings	1.00	2.50	1.02	-	-	-	-	1.02	m	1.13
fitting and hanging sashes in double hung windows; providing brass faced steel pulleys, best flax cords and steel weights										
38mm thick weighing 14 lbs per sash	13.95	2.50	14.30	1.40	0.17	31.86	-	46.16	nr	50.78
50mm thick weighing 20 lbs per sash	21.42	2.50	21.96	1.40	0.17	31.86	-	53.82	nr	59.20
Note										
for small frames and sashes, i.e. 1.25m² and under, add 20% to the foregoing prices										
Sash windows; purpose made; in Meranti, wrought										
Cased frames; 25mm inside and outside linings; 32mm pulley stiles and head; 10mm beads, back linings, etc; 76mm oak sunk weathered and throated sills; 50mm moulded sashes										
in one pane	715.61	2.50	733.50	4.80	0.60	109.52	1.29	844.31	m²	928.74
divided into panes 0.50 - 1.00m²	749.29	2.50	768.03	4.80	0.60	109.52	1.29	878.83	m²	966.72
divided into panes 0.10 - 0.50m²	816.67	2.50	837.09	4.80	0.60	109.52	1.29	947.89	m²	1042.68
divided into panes not exceeding 0.10m²	850.35	2.50	871.61	4.80	0.60	109.52	1.29	982.42	m²	1080.66
extra; windows in three lights with boxed mullions	177.00	2.50	181.43	1.30	0.16	29.62	0.35	211.39	nr	232.53
extra; windows with moulded horns	22.00	2.50	22.55	-	-	-	-	22.55	nr	24.81
extra; deep bottom rails and draught beads	12.00	2.50	12.30	-	-	-	-	12.30	m	13.53
Labours										
throats	2.00	2.50	2.05	-	-	-	-	2.05	m	2.26
grooves for jamb linings	2.00	2.50	2.05	-	-	-	-	2.05	m	2.26
fitting and hanging sashes in double hung windows; providing brass faced steel pulleys, best flax cords and steel weights										
38mm thick weighing 14 lbs per sash	13.95	2.50	14.30	2.50	0.31	57.00	-	71.30	nr	78.43
50mm thick weighing 20 lbs per sash	21.42	2.50	21.96	2.50	0.31	57.00	-	78.96	nr	86.85
Note										
for small frames and sashes, i.e. 1.25m² and under, add 20% to the foregoing prices										
Sash windows; purpose made; in Accoya, wrought										
Cased frames; 25mm inside and outside linings; 32mm pulley stiles and head; 10mm beads, back linings, etc; 76mm oak sunk weathered and throated sills; 50mm moulded sashes										
in one pane	1042.57	2.50	1068.63	5.50	0.69	125.53	1.49	1195.65	m²	1315.21
divided into panes 0.50 - 1.00m²	1091.65	2.50	1118.94	5.50	0.69	125.53	1.49	1245.95	m²	1370.54
divided into panes 0.10 - 0.50m²	1189.80	2.50	1219.55	5.50	0.69	125.53	1.49	1346.56	m²	1481.21
divided into panes not exceeding 0.10m²	1238.88	2.50	1269.85	5.50	0.69	125.53	1.49	1396.87	m²	1536.55
extra; windows in three lights with boxed mullions	258.00	2.50	264.45	1.55	0.19	35.31	0.41	300.17	nr	330.19
extra; windows with moulded horns	24.00	2.50	24.60	-	-	-	-	24.60	nr	27.06
extra; deep bottom rails and draught beads	14.00	2.50	14.35	-	-	-	-	14.35	m	15.78
Labours										
throats	2.00	2.50	2.05	-	-	-	-	2.05	m	2.26
grooves for jamb linings	2.00	2.50	2.05	-	-	-	-	2.05	m	2.26

Labour hourly rates: (except Specialists) Craft Operatives 20.87 Labourer 15.57 Rates are national average prices. Refer to REGIONAL VARIATIONS for indicative levels of overall pricing in regions	MATERIALS			LABOUR				RATES		
	Del to Site £	Waste %	Material Cost £	Craft Optve Hrs	Lab Hrs	Labour Cost £	Sunds £	Nett Rate £	Unit	Gross rate (10%) £
TIMBER WINDOWS AND SHOP FRONTS (Cont'd)										
Sash windows; purpose made; in Accoya, wrought (Cont'd)										
Labours (Cont'd)										
fitting and hanging sashes in double hung windows; providing brass faced steel pulleys, best flax cords and steel weights										
38mm thick weighing 14 lbs per sash	13.95	2.50	14.30	2.80	0.35	63.89	-	78.18	nr	86.00
50mm thick weighing 20 lbs per sash	21.42	2.50	21.96	2.80	0.35	63.89	-	85.84	nr	94.43
Note										
for small frames and sashes, i.e. 1.25m² and under, add 20% to the foregoing prices										
Note										
Bedding in cement mortar (1:3); pointing with Silicone standard mastic one side' is included with standard windows as noted above; adjustment will need to be made for two part polysuphide pointing and bedding and pointing to purpose made frames										
Bedding and pointing frames										
Bedding in cement mortar (1:3); pointing with Silicone standard mastic one side										
wood frames	1.19	5.00	1.28	0.20	-	4.17	-	5.46	m	6.00
Bedding in cement mortar (1:3); pointing with coloured two part polysulphide mastic one side										
wood frames	1.72	5.00	1.86	0.20	-	4.17	-	6.04	m	6.64
TIMBER ROOFLIGHTS, SKYLIGHTS AND LANTERNLIGHTS										
Skylights in softwood, wrought										
Chamfered, straight bar										
38mm	199.42	2.50	204.40	1.50	0.19	34.26	0.40	239.06	m²	262.97
50mm	230.81	2.50	236.58	1.75	0.22	39.95	0.46	276.99	m²	304.69
63mm	243.12	2.50	249.19	2.00	0.25	45.63	0.54	295.37	m²	324.91
Moulded, straight bar										
38mm	210.04	2.50	215.29	1.50	0.19	34.26	0.40	249.95	m²	274.94
50mm	241.39	2.50	247.42	1.75	0.22	39.95	0.46	287.83	m²	316.61
63mm	273.12	2.50	279.95	2.00	0.25	45.63	0.54	326.13	m²	358.74
Skylights in Oak, wrought										
Chamfered, straight bar										
38mm	555.86	2.50	569.76	2.30	0.29	52.52	0.61	622.88	m²	685.17
50mm	644.34	2.50	660.45	2.70	0.34	61.64	0.73	722.81	m²	795.10
63mm	730.89	2.50	749.16	3.10	0.39	70.77	0.82	820.76	m²	902.83
Moulded, straight bar										
38mm	586.64	2.50	601.30	2.30	0.29	52.52	0.61	654.43	m²	719.87
50mm	673.19	2.50	690.02	2.70	0.34	61.64	0.73	752.39	m²	827.63
63mm	761.66	2.50	780.71	3.10	0.39	70.77	0.82	852.30	m²	937.53
Skylight kerbs in softwood, wrought										
Kerbs; dovetailed at angles										
38 x 225mm	14.17	2.50	14.52	0.31	0.04	7.09	0.08	21.70	m	23.86
50 x 225mm	16.97	2.50	17.40	0.35	0.04	7.93	0.08	25.41	m	27.95
38 x 225mm; chamfers -1 nr	14.85	2.50	15.22	0.31	0.04	7.09	0.08	22.40	m	24.64
50 x 225mm; chamfers -1 nr	17.68	2.50	18.12	0.35	0.04	7.93	0.08	26.13	m	28.75
Kerbs; in two thicknesses to circular skylights										
38 x 225mm	42.41	2.50	43.47	0.47	0.06	10.74	0.13	54.35	m	59.78
50 x 225mm	50.84	2.50	52.11	0.53	0.07	12.15	0.13	64.39	m	70.83
38 x 225mm; chamfers -1 nr	43.87	2.50	44.97	0.47	0.06	10.74	0.13	55.84	m	61.43
50 x 225mm; chamfers -1 nr	52.33	2.50	53.63	0.53	0.07	12.15	0.13	65.92	m	72.51
Skylight kerbs in Oak, wrought										
Kerbs; dovetailed at angles										
38 x 225mm	67.88	2.50	69.58	0.62	0.08	14.19	0.16	83.93	m	92.32
50 x 225mm	81.46	2.50	83.50	0.69	0.08	15.65	0.18	99.32	m	109.26
38 x 225mm; chamfers -1 nr	71.27	2.50	73.05	0.62	0.08	14.19	0.16	87.40	m	96.15
50 x 225mm; chamfers -1 nr	84.84	2.50	86.96	0.69	0.08	15.65	0.18	102.79	m	113.07
Kerbs; in two thicknesses to circular skylights										
38 x 225mm	203.65	2.50	208.74	0.94	0.12	21.49	0.25	230.48	m	253.53
50 x 225mm	243.94	2.50	250.04	1.06	0.13	24.15	0.28	274.47	m	301.92
38 x 225mm; chamfers -1 nr	210.83	2.50	216.10	0.94	0.12	21.49	0.25	237.83	m	261.62
50 x 225mm; chamfers -1 nr	250.57	2.50	256.83	1.06	0.13	24.15	0.28	281.26	m	309.38
Roof windows in Nordic red pine, wrought, treated, including flashings for slate up to 8mm thick or tiles up to 45mm in profile										
Velux roof windows GGL/GPL 3066 Pine Range, factory glazed clear 'Extra Low Energy 66' triple glazed sealed unit; laminated inner; enhanced strength outer pane; fixing to timber with screws; dressing flashings										
550 x 780mm overall, CK02 GGL Centre Pivot	343.80	2.50	352.39	4.50	2.25	128.95	-	481.34	nr	529.48
550 x 980mm overall, CK04 GGL Centre Pivot	355.41	2.50	364.29	5.25	2.62	150.36	-	514.66	nr	566.12
660 x 1180mm overall, FK06 GGL Centre Pivot	392.23	2.50	402.03	5.25	2.62	150.36	-	552.39	nr	607.63
780 x 980mm overall, MK04 GGL Centre Pivot	377.23	2.50	386.66	5.00	2.50	143.28	-	529.93	nr	582.92
780 x 1180mm overall, MK06 GGL Centre Pivot	406.66	2.50	416.83	5.00	2.50	143.28	-	560.10	nr	616.11
780 x 1400mm overall, MK08 GGL Centre Pivot	453.00	2.50	464.32	5.50	2.75	157.60	-	621.93	nr	684.12
940 x 1600mm overall, PK10 GGL Centre Pivot	504.75	2.50	517.37	5.50	2.75	157.60	-	674.97	nr	742.47
1140 x 1180mm overall, SK06 GGL Centre Pivot	494.58	2.50	506.95	6.00	3.00	171.93	-	678.88	nr	746.77

Labour hourly rates: (except Specialists) Craft Operatives 20.87 Labourer 15.57 Rates are national average prices. Refer to REGIONAL VARIATIONS for indicative levels of overall pricing in regions	MATERIALS			LABOUR				RATES		
	Del to Site £	Waste %	Material Cost £	Craft Optve Hrs	Lab Hrs	Labour Cost £	Sunds £	Nett Rate £	Unit	Gross rate (10%) £
TIMBER ROOFLIGHTS, SKYLIGHTS AND LANTERNLIGHTS (Cont'd)										
Roof windows in Nordic red pine, wrought, treated, including flashings for slate up to 8mm thick or tiles up to 45mm in profile (Cont'd)										
Velux roof windows GGL/GPL 3066 Pine Range, factory glazed clear 'Extra Low Energy 66' triple glazed sealed unit; laminated inner; enhanced strength outer pane; fixing to timber with screws; dressing flashings (Cont'd)										
1340 x 980mm overall, UK04 GGL Centre Pivot	483.08	2.50	495.16	6.00	3.00	171.93	-	667.09	nr	733.80
550 x 980mm overall, CK04 GPL Top Hung	428.23	2.50	438.94	5.75	2.87	164.69	-	603.63	nr	663.99
660 x 1180mm overall, FK06 GPL Top Hung	477.20	2.50	489.13	5.75	2.87	164.69	-	653.82	nr	719.20
780 x 980mm overall, MK04 GPL Top Hung	456.48	2.50	467.90	5.75	2.87	164.69	-	632.58	nr	695.84
780 x 1180mm overall, MK06 GPL Top Hung	496.62	2.50	509.04	6.50	3.25	186.26	-	695.30	nr	764.83
780 x 1400mm overall, MK08 GPL Top Hung	534.80	2.50	548.17	6.50	3.25	186.26	-	734.43	nr	807.87
1140 x 1180mm overall, SK06 GPL Top Hung	613.83	2.50	629.17	6.50	3.25	186.26	-	815.43	nr	896.97
Velux roof windows GGL/GPL 3070 Pine Range, factory glazed clear 'Safety 70' double glazed sealed unit; laminated inner; toughened outer pane; fixing to timber with screws; dressing flashings										
550 x 780mm overall, CK02 GGL Centre Pivot	235.32	2.50	241.20	4.50	2.25	128.95	-	370.15	nr	407.16
550 x 980mm overall, CK04 GGL Centre Pivot	256.92	2.50	263.35	5.25	2.62	150.36	-	413.71	nr	455.08
660 x 1180mm overall, FK06 GGL Centre Pivot	293.10	2.50	300.43	5.25	2.62	150.36	-	450.79	nr	495.87
780 x 980mm overall, MK04 GGL Centre Pivot	308.30	2.50	316.00	5.00	2.50	143.28	-	459.28	nr	505.21
780 x 1180mm overall, MK06 GGL Centre Pivot	343.90	2.50	352.49	5.00	2.50	143.28	-	495.77	nr	545.35
780 x 1400mm overall, MK08 GGL Centre Pivot	378.43	2.50	387.89	5.50	2.75	157.60	-	545.50	nr	600.05
940 x 1600mm overall, PK10 GGL Centre Pivot	447.62	2.50	458.81	5.50	2.75	157.60	-	616.41	nr	678.05
1140 x 1180mm overall, SK06 GGL Centre Pivot	437.47	2.50	448.40	6.00	3.00	171.93	-	620.33	nr	682.37
1340 x 980mm overall, UK04 GGL Centre Pivot	425.97	2.50	436.62	6.00	3.00	171.93	-	608.55	nr	669.40
550 x 980mm overall, CK04 GPL Top Hung	310.42	2.50	318.19	5.75	2.87	164.69	-	482.87	nr	531.16
660 x 1180mm overall, FK06 GPL Top Hung	359.38	2.50	368.36	5.75	2.87	164.69	-	533.05	nr	586.35
780 x 980mm overall, MK04 GPL Top Hung	338.68	2.50	347.14	5.75	2.87	164.69	-	511.83	nr	563.01
780 x 1180mm overall, MK06 GPL Top Hung	378.82	2.50	388.29	6.50	3.25	186.26	-	574.54	nr	632.00
780 x 1400mm overall, MK08 GPL Top Hung	416.98	2.50	427.41	6.50	3.25	186.26	-	613.67	nr	675.03
1140 x 1180mm overall, SK06 GPL Top Hung	496.02	2.50	508.42	6.50	3.25	186.26	-	694.67	nr	764.14
Velux roof windows GGL 3060 Pine Range, factory glazed 'Comfort 60' clear double glazed sealed unit; 6.4mm laminated inner; toughened outer pane coated; plus enhanced noise-reduction glazing; fixing to timber with screws; dressing flashings										
550 x 780mm overall, CK02 GGL Centre Pivot	235.32	2.50	241.20	4.50	2.25	128.95	-	370.15	nr	407.16
550 x 980mm overall, CK04 GGL Centre Pivot	256.92	2.50	263.35	5.25	2.62	150.36	-	413.71	nr	455.08
660 x 1180mm overall, FK06 GGL Centre Pivot	293.10	2.50	300.43	5.25	2.62	150.36	-	450.79	nr	495.87
780 x 980mm overall, MK04 GGL Centre Pivot	268.47	2.50	275.18	5.00	2.50	143.28	-	418.45	nr	460.30
780 x 1180mm overall, MK06 GGL Centre Pivot	307.20	2.50	314.88	5.00	2.50	143.28	-	458.15	nr	503.97
780 x 1400mm overall, MK08 GGL Centre Pivot	317.75	2.50	325.69	5.50	2.75	157.60	-	483.30	nr	531.63
940 x 1600mm overall, PK10 GGL Centre Pivot	386.93	2.50	396.61	5.50	2.75	157.60	-	554.21	nr	609.63
1140 x 1180mm overall, SK06 GGL Centre Pivot	376.77	2.50	386.19	6.00	3.00	171.93	-	558.12	nr	613.94
1340 x 980mm overall, UK04 GGL Centre Pivot	365.28	2.50	374.41	6.00	3.00	171.93	-	546.34	nr	600.97
Velux roof windows GGL 307021U Pine Electric Range, factory glazed clear 'Safety 70' double glazed sealed unit; laminated inner; toughened outer pane; fixing to timber with screws; dressing flashings										
550 x 780mm overall, CK02 GGL Centre Pivot	450.90	2.50	462.17	4.60	2.30	131.81	-	593.99	nr	653.38
550 x 980mm overall, CK04 GGL Centre Pivot	462.51	2.50	474.07	5.35	2.67	153.23	-	627.30	nr	690.03
660 x 1180mm overall, FK06 GGL Centre Pivot	499.33	2.50	511.81	5.35	2.67	153.23	-	665.03	nr	731.54
780 x 980mm overall, MK04 GGL Centre Pivot	484.33	2.50	496.43	5.35	2.55	151.36	-	647.79	nr	712.57
780 x 1180mm overall, MK06 GGL Centre Pivot	513.76	2.50	526.60	5.10	2.55	146.14	-	672.74	nr	740.02
780 x 1400mm overall, MK08 GGL Centre Pivot	542.65	2.50	556.22	5.60	2.80	160.47	-	716.68	nr	788.35
940 x 1600mm overall, PK10 GGL Centre Pivot	611.85	2.50	627.15	5.60	2.80	160.47	-	787.61	nr	866.38
1140 x 1180mm overall, SK06 GGL Centre Pivot	601.68	2.50	616.73	6.10	3.05	174.80	-	791.52	nr	870.67
1340 x 980mm overall, UK04 GGL Centre Pivot	590.18	2.50	604.94	6.10	3.05	174.80	-	779.73	nr	857.71
Roof windows in pine with white polyurethane finish, including flashings for slate up to 8mm thick or tiles up to 45mm in profile										
Velux roof windows GGU/GPU 0066 White Polyurethane Range, factory glazed clear 'Extra Low Energy 66' triple glazed sealed unit; laminated inner; enhanced strength outer pane; fixing to timber with screws; dressing flashings										
550 x 780mm overall, CK02 GGU Centre Pivot	389.50	2.50	399.24	4.50	2.25	128.95	-	528.18	nr	581.00
550 x 980mm overall, CK04 GGU Centre Pivot	403.25	2.50	413.33	5.25	2.62	150.36	-	563.69	nr	620.06
660 x 1180mm overall, FK06 GGU Centre Pivot	424.35	2.50	434.96	5.25	2.62	150.36	-	585.32	nr	643.85
780 x 980mm overall, MK04 GGU Centre Pivot	429.35	2.50	440.08	5.00	2.50	143.28	-	583.36	nr	641.69
780 x 1180mm overall, MK06 GGU Centre Pivot	465.92	2.50	477.57	5.00	2.50	143.28	-	620.85	nr	682.93
780 x 1400mm overall, MK08 GGU Centre Pivot	501.25	2.50	513.78	5.50	2.75	157.60	-	671.38	nr	738.52
1140 x 1180mm overall, SK06 GGU Centre Pivot	572.42	2.50	586.73	6.00	3.00	171.93	-	758.66	nr	834.52
660 x 1180mm overall, FK06 GPU Top Hung	530.75	2.50	544.02	5.75	2.87	164.69	-	708.71	nr	779.58
780 x 1180mm overall, MK06 GPU Top Hung	553.03	2.50	566.86	6.50	3.25	186.26	-	753.12	nr	828.43
780 x 1400mm overall, MK08 GPU Top Hung	597.62	2.50	612.57	6.50	3.25	186.26	-	798.82	nr	878.71
1140 x 1180mm overall, SK06 GPU Top Hung	688.80	2.50	706.02	6.50	3.25	186.26	-	892.28	nr	981.51
Velux roof windows GGU 007030 White Polyurethane Range, Solar powered via solar technology with no requirement for an external power supply, factory glazed 'Safety 70' clear double glazed sealed unit; laminated inner; toughened outer pane; fixing to timber with screws; dressing flashings										
550 x 780mm overall, CK02 GGU Centre Pivot	525.87	2.50	539.01	4.50	2.25	128.95	-	667.96	nr	734.76
550 x 980mm overall, CK04 GGU Centre Pivot	539.62	2.50	553.11	5.25	2.62	150.36	-	703.47	nr	773.82
660 x 1180mm overall, FK06 GGU Centre Pivot	584.30	2.50	598.91	5.25	2.62	150.36	-	749.27	nr	824.20
780 x 980mm overall, MK04 GGU Centre Pivot	565.72	2.50	579.87	5.00	2.50	143.28	-	723.14	nr	795.46

Labour hourly rates: (except Specialists) Craft Operatives 20.87 Labourer 15.57 Rates are national average prices. Refer to REGIONAL VARIATIONS for indicative levels of overall pricing in regions	MATERIALS			LABOUR				RATES		
	Del to Site £	Waste %	Material Cost £	Craft Optve Hrs	Lab Hrs	Labour Cost £	Sunds £	Nett Rate £	Unit	Gross rate (10%) £
TIMBER ROOFLIGHTS, SKYLIGHTS AND LANTERNLIGHTS (Cont'd)										
Roof windows in pine with white polyurethane finish, including flashings for slate up to 8mm thick or tiles up to 45mm in profile (Cont'd)										
Velux roof windows GGU 007030 White Polyurethane Range, Solar powered via solar technology with no requirement for an external power supply, factory glazed 'Safety 70' clear double glazed sealed unit; laminated inner; toughened outer pane; fixing to timber with screws; dressing flashings (Cont'd)										
780 x 1180mm overall, MK06 GGU Centre Pivot	602.30	2.50	617.36	5.00	2.50	143.28	-	760.63	nr	836.70
780 x 1400mm overall, MK08 GGU Centre Pivot	637.62	2.50	653.56	5.50	2.75	157.60	-	811.16	nr	892.28
1140 x 1180mm overall, SK06 GGU Centre Pivot	708.78	2.50	726.50	6.00	3.00	171.93	-	898.43	nr	988.28
Velux roof windows GGU/GPU 0070 White Polyurethane Range, factory double glazed sealed unit; laminated inner; toughened outer pane coated; fixing to timber with screws; dressing flashings										
550 x 780mm overall, CK02 GGU Centre Pivot	271.68	2.50	278.48	4.50	2.25	128.95	-	407.42	nr	448.17
550 x 980mm overall, CK04 GGU Centre Pivot	280.85	2.50	287.87	5.25	2.62	150.36	-	438.23	nr	482.06
660 x 1180mm overall, FK06 GGU Centre Pivot	330.11	2.50	338.36	5.25	2.62	150.36	-	488.72	nr	537.59
780 x 980mm overall, MK04 GGU Centre Pivot	311.55	2.50	319.34	5.00	2.50	143.28	-	462.61	nr	508.88
780 x 1180mm overall, MK06 GGU Centre Pivot	348.12	2.50	356.82	5.00	2.50	143.28	-	500.09	nr	550.10
780 x 1400mm overall, MK08 GGU Centre Pivot	383.42	2.50	393.01	5.50	2.75	157.60	-	550.61	nr	605.67
1140 x 1180mm overall, SK06 GGU Centre Pivot	454.60	2.50	465.96	6.00	3.00	171.93	-	637.90	nr	701.68
660 x 1180mm overall, FK06 GPU Top Hung	414.36	2.50	424.72	5.72	2.87	164.06	-	588.78	nr	647.66
780 x 1180mm overall, MK06 GPU Top Hung	434.51	2.50	445.37	6.50	3.25	186.26	-	631.63	nr	694.79
780 x 1400mm overall, MK08 GPU Top Hung	458.40	2.50	469.86	6.50	3.25	186.26	-	656.12	nr	721.73
1140 x 1180mm overall, SK06 GPU Top Hung	454.60	2.50	465.96	6.50	3.25	186.26	-	652.22	nr	717.44
Velux roof windows GGU 007021U Integra White Polyurethane Electric Range, factory glazed 'Safety 70' clear double glazed sealed unit; laminated inner; toughened outer pane; fixing to timber with screws; dressing flashings										
550 x 780mm overall, CK02 GGU Centre Pivot	496.60	2.50	509.02	4.60	2.30	131.81	-	640.83	nr	704.91
550 x 980mm overall, CK04 GGU Centre Pivot	510.35	2.50	523.11	5.35	2.67	153.23	-	676.34	nr	743.97
660 x 1180mm overall, FK06 GGU Centre Pivot	555.02	2.50	568.89	5.35	2.67	153.23	-	722.12	nr	794.33
780 x 980mm overall, MK04 GGU Centre Pivot	536.45	2.50	549.86	5.10	2.55	146.14	-	696.00	nr	765.60
780 x 1180mm overall, MK06 GGU Centre Pivot	573.03	2.50	587.35	5.10	2.55	146.14	-	733.49	nr	806.84
780 x 1400mm overall, MK08 GGU Centre Pivot	608.35	2.50	623.56	5.60	2.80	160.47	-	784.03	nr	862.43
1140 x 1180mm overall, SK06 GGU Centre Pivot	679.52	2.50	696.50	6.10	3.05	174.80	-	871.30	nr	958.43
METAL WINDOWS AND SHOP FRONTS										
Windows in galvanised steel; Bedding in cement mortar (1:3); pointing with Silicone standard mastic one side										
Crittall Windows Ltd. Duralife Homelight; weatherstripping; fixing to masonry with lugs										
fixed lights										
508 x 292mm, NG5	39.23	2.50	40.31	0.93	0.25	23.30	-	63.61	nr	69.97
508 x 923mm, NC5	54.58	2.50	56.13	1.55	0.35	37.84	-	93.97	nr	103.36
508 x 1218mm, ND5	62.53	2.50	64.31	1.92	0.41	46.45	-	110.76	nr	121.84
997 x 628mm, NE13	71.42	2.50	73.41	1.77	0.40	43.17	-	116.58	nr	128.24
997 x 923mm, NC13	83.38	2.50	85.70	2.01	0.44	48.76	-	134.46	nr	147.91
997 x 1218mm, ND13	92.53	2.50	95.11	2.39	0.51	57.74	-	152.85	nr	168.14
1486 x 628mm, NE14	85.89	2.50	88.30	2.35	0.53	57.21	-	145.51	nr	160.06
1486 x 923mm, NC14	96.62	2.50	99.34	2.59	0.58	63.17	-	162.51	nr	178.76
1486 x 1218mm, ND14	109.29	2.50	112.36	2.98	0.66	72.51	-	184.87	nr	203.36
top hung lights										
508 x 292mm, NG1	127.14	2.50	130.42	0.93	0.25	23.30	-	153.72	nr	169.09
508 x 457mm, NH1	138.83	2.50	142.42	1.13	0.25	27.39	-	169.81	nr	186.79
508 x 628mm, NE1	149.58	2.50	153.46	1.31	0.29	31.94	-	185.40	nr	203.94
997 x 628mm, NE13E	209.94	2.50	215.39	1.77	0.32	41.92	-	257.31	nr	283.04
997 x 923mm, NC13C	226.35	2.50	232.25	2.01	0.40	48.13	-	280.39	nr	308.43
bottom hung lights										
508 x 628mm, NL1	194.17	2.50	199.17	1.31	0.32	32.41	-	231.58	nr	254.73
side hung lights										
508 x 628mm, NES1	162.64	2.50	166.85	1.31	0.32	32.41	-	199.25	nr	219.18
508 x 923mm, NC1	175.26	2.50	179.82	1.55	0.35	37.84	-	217.66	nr	239.42
508 x 1067mm, NC01	185.92	2.50	190.76	1.73	0.38	42.02	-	232.79	nr	256.06
508 x 1218mm, ND1	198.00	2.50	203.17	1.92	0.41	46.45	-	249.62	nr	274.58
mixed lights										
279 x 923mm, NC6F	134.61	2.50	138.12	1.46	0.35	35.94	-	174.06	nr	191.47
508 x 923mm, NC5F	155.45	2.50	159.51	1.55	0.35	37.84	-	197.35	nr	217.09
508 x 1067mm, NC05F	159.41	2.50	163.59	1.73	0.38	42.02	-	205.61	nr	226.17
997 x 292mm, NG2	157.00	2.50	161.09	1.37	0.33	33.65	-	194.74	nr	214.21
997 x 457mm, NH2	171.74	2.50	176.21	1.56	0.37	38.36	-	214.57	nr	236.03
997 x 628mm, NE2	186.68	2.50	191.55	1.77	0.40	43.17	-	234.71	nr	258.19
997 x 628mm, NES2	220.78	2.50	226.51	1.77	0.40	43.17	-	269.67	nr	296.64
997 x 923mm, NC2	241.46	2.50	247.74	2.01	0.44	48.76	-	296.50	nr	326.15
997 x 923mm, NC2F	319.02	2.50	327.23	2.01	0.44	48.76	-	375.99	nr	413.59
997 x 1067mm, NC02	262.55	2.50	269.37	2.20	0.47	53.15	-	322.52	nr	354.77
997 x 1067mm, NC02F	347.83	2.50	356.78	2.20	0.47	53.15	-	409.93	nr	450.93
997 x 1218mm, ND2	279.76	2.50	287.03	2.39	0.51	57.74	-	344.77	nr	379.25
997 x 1218mm, ND2F	351.98	2.50	361.05	2.39	0.51	57.74	-	418.79	nr	460.67
997 x 1513mm, NDV2FSB	405.55	2.50	416.00	2.63	0.58	64.00	-	480.00	nr	528.00
1486 x 628mm, NE3	235.31	2.50	241.46	2.35	0.51	56.90	-	298.36	nr	328.19
1486 x 923mm, NC4	397.48	2.50	407.72	2.59	0.58	63.17	-	470.88	nr	517.97
1486 x 923mm, NC4F	485.27	2.50	497.70	2.59	0.58	63.17	-	560.87	nr	616.95
1486 x 1067mm, NC04	428.01	2.50	439.03	2.65	0.58	64.36	-	503.39	nr	553.73
1486 x 1067mm, NC04F	512.95	2.50	526.09	2.79	0.61	67.75	-	593.84	nr	653.22
1486 x 1218mm, ND4	456.63	2.50	468.38	2.98	0.66	72.51	-	540.89	nr	594.98
1486 x 1218mm, ND4F	541.65	2.50	555.53	2.98	0.66	72.51	-	628.04	nr	690.85

Labour hourly rates: (except Specialists) Craft Operatives 20.87 Labourer 15.57 Rates are national average prices. Refer to REGIONAL VARIATIONS for indicative levels of overall pricing in regions	MATERIALS			LABOUR				RATES		
	Del to Site £	Waste %	Material Cost £	Craft Optve Hrs	Lab Hrs	Labour Cost £	Sunds £	Nett Rate £	Unit	Gross rate (10%) £
METAL WINDOWS AND SHOP FRONTS (Cont'd)										
Windows in galvanised steel; Bedding in cement mortar (1:3); pointing with Silicone standard mastic one side (Cont'd)										
Crittall Windows Ltd. Duralife Homelight; weatherstripping; fixing to masonry with lugs (Cont'd)										
mixed lights (Cont'd)										
1486 x 1513mm, NDV4FSB	625.99	2.50	642.01	3.24	0.69	78.36	-	720.38	nr	792.41
1994 x 923mm, NC11F	527.01	2.50	540.55	3.18	0.69	77.05	-	617.60	nr	679.36
1994 x 1218mm, ND11F	570.48	2.50	585.14	3.59	0.81	87.43	-	672.57	nr	739.83
1994 x 1513mm, NDV11FSB	666.16	2.50	683.25	3.87	0.86	94.22	-	777.47	nr	855.22
Extra for mullions										
292mm high	21.73	2.50	22.27	0.20	0.10	5.73	-	28.00	nr	30.80
457mm high	30.38	2.50	31.14	0.30	0.15	8.60	-	39.74	nr	43.71
628mm high	39.24	2.50	40.22	0.40	0.20	11.46	-	51.68	nr	56.85
923mm high	54.56	2.50	55.92	0.50	0.25	14.33	-	70.25	nr	77.27
1067mm high	63.17	2.50	64.75	0.60	0.30	17.19	-	81.94	nr	90.14
1218mm high	71.09	2.50	72.86	0.80	0.40	22.92	-	95.79	nr	105.37
1513mm high	86.38	2.50	88.54	1.00	0.50	28.66	-	117.20	nr	128.92
Extra for transoms										
279mm wide	22.53	2.50	23.10	0.20	0.10	5.73	-	28.83	nr	31.71
508mm wide	34.72	2.50	35.59	0.30	0.15	8.60	-	44.19	nr	48.61
997mm wide	90.55	2.50	92.82	0.60	0.30	17.19	-	110.01	nr	121.01
1143mm wide	100.58	2.50	103.09	1.00	0.50	28.66	-	131.75	nr	144.92
Ectra for Controlair Ventilators, permanent, mill finish										
508mm wide	58.00	2.50	59.45	-	-	-	-	59.45	nr	65.39
997mm wide	77.90	2.50	79.84	-	-	-	-	79.84	nr	87.83
1486mm wide	175.47	2.50	179.85	-	-	-	-	179.85	nr	197.84
Extra for Controlair Ventilators, permanent, mill finish, flyscreen										
508mm wide	68.94	2.50	70.66	-	-	-	-	70.66	nr	77.73
997mm wide	98.21	2.50	100.67	-	-	-	-	100.67	nr	110.73
1486mm wide	203.11	2.50	208.18	-	-	-	-	208.18	nr	229.00
Extra for Controlair Ventilators, adjustable										
508mm wide 1-LT	69.13	2.50	70.86	-	-	-	-	70.86	nr	77.94
997mm wide 2-LT	87.40	2.50	89.59	-	-	-	-	89.59	nr	98.55
Extra for Controlair Ventilators, adjustable, flyscreen										
508mm wide 1-LT	79.64	2.50	81.63	-	-	-	-	81.63	nr	89.79
997mm wide 2-LT	107.73	2.50	110.42	-	-	-	-	110.42	nr	121.46
Extra for locks with Parkes locking handles for										
side hung lights	71.72	2.50	73.52	-	-	-	-	73.52	nr	80.87
horizontally pivoted lights	71.72	2.50	73.52	-	-	-	-	73.52	nr	80.87
Windows in galvanised steel; polyester powder coated; white matt; Bedding in cement mortar (1:3); pointing with Silicone standard mastic one side										
Crittall Windows Ltd. Duralife Homelight; weatherstripping; fixing to masonry with lugs										
fixed lights										
508 x 292mm, NG5	45.71	2.50	46.96	0.93	0.25	23.30	-	70.26	nr	77.28
508 x 923mm, NC5	63.43	2.50	65.19	1.55	0.35	37.84	-	103.03	nr	113.34
508 x 1218mm, ND5	72.66	2.50	74.69	1.92	0.41	46.45	-	121.15	nr	133.26
997 x 628mm, NE13	83.17	2.50	85.45	1.77	0.40	43.17	-	128.62	nr	141.48
997 x 923mm, NC13	97.40	2.50	100.08	2.01	0.44	48.76	-	148.83	nr	163.72
997 x 1218mm, ND13	112.89	2.50	115.99	2.39	0.51	57.74	-	173.72	nr	191.10
1486 x 628mm, NE14	100.20	2.50	102.97	2.35	0.53	57.21	-	160.19	nr	176.20
1486 x 923mm, NC14	112.37	2.50	115.48	2.59	0.58	63.17	-	178.65	nr	196.51
1486 x 1218mm, ND14	127.12	2.50	130.63	2.98	0.66	72.51	-	203.14	nr	223.46
top hung lights										
508 x 292mm, NG1	141.42	2.50	145.05	0.93	0.25	23.30	-	168.35	nr	185.19
508 x 457mm, NH1	158.30	2.50	162.37	1.13	0.25	27.39	-	189.77	nr	208.74
508 x 628mm, NE1	170.09	2.50	174.48	1.31	0.29	31.94	-	206.42	nr	227.06
997 x 628mm, NE13E	236.06	2.50	242.17	1.77	0.32	41.92	-	284.09	nr	312.50
997 x 923mm, NC13C	256.55	2.50	263.20	2.01	0.40	48.13	-	311.34	nr	342.47
bottom hung lights										
508 x 628mm, NL1	240.13	2.50	246.28	1.31	0.32	32.41	-	278.68	nr	306.55
side hung lights										
508 x 628mm, NES1	182.62	2.50	187.33	1.31	0.32	32.41	-	219.73	nr	241.70
508 x 923mm, NC1	196.92	2.50	202.02	1.55	0.35	37.84	-	239.86	nr	263.85
508 x 1067mm, NC01	208.88	2.50	214.30	1.73	0.38	42.02	-	256.32	nr	281.95
508 x 1218mm, ND1	222.77	2.50	228.55	1.92	0.41	46.45	-	275.01	nr	302.51
mixed lights										
279 x 923mm, NC6F	153.91	2.50	157.90	1.46	0.35	35.94	-	193.84	nr	213.23
508 x 923mm, NC5F	174.28	2.50	178.81	1.55	0.35	37.84	-	216.65	nr	238.32
508 x 1067mm, NC05F	178.86	2.50	183.52	1.73	0.38	42.02	-	225.54	nr	248.10
997 x 292mm, NG2	184.52	2.50	189.29	1.37	0.33	33.65	-	222.94	nr	245.23
997 x 457mm, NH2	194.50	2.50	199.55	1.56	0.37	38.36	-	237.91	nr	261.70
997 x 628mm, NE2	214.40	2.50	219.97	1.77	0.40	43.17	-	263.13	nr	289.45
997 x 628mm, NES2	249.10	2.50	255.53	1.77	0.40	43.17	-	298.70	nr	328.57
997 x 923mm, NC2	272.04	2.50	279.08	2.01	0.44	48.76	-	327.84	nr	360.62
997 x 923mm, NC2F	356.19	2.50	365.33	2.01	0.44	48.76	-	414.09	nr	455.50
997 x 1067mm, NC02	294.36	2.50	301.98	2.20	0.47	53.15	-	355.12	nr	390.64
997 x 1067mm, NC02F	388.64	2.50	398.61	2.20	0.47	53.15	-	451.76	nr	496.94
997 x 1218mm, ND2	318.06	2.50	326.29	2.39	0.51	57.74	-	384.02	nr	422.43
997 x 1218mm, ND2F	393.19	2.50	403.29	2.39	0.51	57.74	-	461.03	nr	507.13
997 x 1513mm, NDV2FSB	455.91	2.50	467.62	2.63	0.58	64.00	-	531.63	nr	584.79
1486 x 628mm, NE3	278.67	2.50	285.90	2.35	0.51	56.90	-	342.81	nr	377.09
1486 x 923mm, NC4	443.72	2.50	455.11	2.59	0.58	63.17	-	518.28	nr	570.10
1486 x 923mm, NC4F	541.16	2.50	554.99	2.59	0.58	63.17	-	618.16	nr	679.98
1486 x 1067mm, NC04	500.35	2.50	513.18	2.79	0.58	67.28	-	580.46	nr	638.51
1486 x 1067mm, NC04F	578.14	2.50	592.91	2.79	0.61	67.75	-	660.66	nr	726.73
1486 x 1218mm, ND4	539.48	2.50	553.31	2.98	0.66	72.51	-	625.82	nr	688.40
1486 x 1218mm, ND4F	609.57	2.50	625.14	2.98	0.66	72.51	-	697.65	nr	767.42
1486 x 1513mm, NDV4FSB	741.52	2.50	760.44	3.24	0.69	78.36	-	838.80	nr	922.68

Labour hourly rates: (except Specialists) Craft Operatives 20.87 Labourer 15.57 Rates are national average prices. Refer to REGIONAL VARIATIONS for indicative levels of overall pricing in regions	MATERIALS			LABOUR				RATES		
	Del to Site £	Waste %	Material Cost £	Craft Optve Hrs	Lab Hrs	Labour Cost £	Sunds £	Nett Rate £	Unit	Gross rate (10%) £
METAL WINDOWS AND SHOP FRONTS (Cont'd)										
Windows in galvanised steel; polyester powder coated; white matt; Bedding in cement mortar (1:3); pointing with Silicone standard mastic one side (Cont'd)										
Crittall Windows Ltd. Duralife Homelight; weatherstripping; fixing to masonry with lugs (Cont'd)										
mixed lights (Cont'd)										
1994 x 923mm, NC11F	592.54	2.50	607.72	3.18	0.69	77.05	-	684.77	nr	753.24
1994 x 1218mm, ND11F	643.67	2.50	660.16	3.60	0.81	87.64	-	747.80	nr	822.58
1994 x 1513mm, NDV11FSB	748.33	2.50	767.47	3.87	0.86	94.22	-	861.69	nr	947.86
Extra for mullions										
292mm high	26.47	2.50	27.13	0.20	0.10	5.73	-	32.86	nr	36.15
457mm high	35.15	2.50	36.03	0.30	0.15	8.60	-	44.62	nr	49.09
628mm high	44.32	2.50	45.43	0.40	0.20	11.46	-	56.89	nr	62.58
923mm high	59.79	2.50	61.28	0.50	0.25	14.33	-	75.61	nr	83.17
1067mm high	68.75	2.50	70.46	0.60	0.30	17.19	-	87.66	nr	96.42
1218mm high	76.64	2.50	78.55	0.80	0.40	22.92	-	101.48	nr	111.63
1513mm high	92.24	2.50	94.54	1.00	0.50	28.66	-	123.20	nr	135.52
Extra for transoms										
279mm wide	28.11	2.50	28.81	0.20	0.10	5.73	-	34.54	nr	37.99
508mm wide	40.68	2.50	41.70	0.30	0.15	8.60	-	50.30	nr	55.33
997mm wide	110.87	2.50	113.64	0.60	0.30	17.19	-	130.84	nr	143.92
1143mm wide	121.43	2.50	124.46	1.00	0.50	28.66	-	153.12	nr	168.43
Extra for Controlair Ventilators, permanent, mill finish										
508mm wide	58.00	2.50	59.45	-	-	-	-	59.45	nr	65.39
997mm wide	77.90	2.50	79.84	-	-	-	-	79.84	nr	87.83
1486mm wide	175.47	2.50	179.85	-	-	-	-	179.85	nr	197.84
Extra for Controlair Ventilators, permanent, mill finish, flyscreen										
508mm wide	68.94	2.50	70.66	-	-	-	-	70.66	nr	77.73
997mm wide	98.21	2.50	100.67	-	-	-	-	100.67	nr	110.73
1486mm wide	203.11	2.50	208.18	-	-	-	-	208.18	nr	229.00
Extra for Controlair Ventilators, adjustable										
508mm wide 1-LT	69.13	2.50	70.86	-	-	-	-	70.86	nr	77.94
997mm wide 2-LT	87.40	2.50	89.59	-	-	-	-	89.59	nr	98.55
Extra for Controlair Ventilators, adjustable, flyscreen										
508mm wide 1-LT	79.64	2.50	81.63	-	-	-	-	81.63	nr	89.79
997mm wide 2-LT	107.73	2.50	110.42	-	-	-	-	110.42	nr	121.46
Extra for locks with Parkes locking handles for										
side hung lights	71.72	2.50	73.52	-	-	-	-	73.52	nr	80.87
horizontally pivoted lights	71.72	2.50	73.52	-	-	-	-	73.52	nr	80.87
Windows in aluminium; polyester powder finish; white matt; Bedding in cement mortar (1:3); pointing with Silicone standard mastic one side										
Casement range; factory Low E double glazed; fixing to masonry with lugs										
fixed lights										
600 x 400mm	225.71	2.50	231.48	1.21	0.35	30.70	-	262.18	nr	288.40
600 x 800mm	250.00	2.50	256.42	1.81	0.46	44.94	-	301.36	nr	331.50
600 x 1000mm	265.48	2.50	272.31	2.04	0.58	51.61	-	323.92	nr	356.31
600 x 1200mm	284.29	2.50	291.62	2.41	0.68	60.88	-	352.50	nr	387.75
600 x 1600mm	330.24	2.50	338.77	2.57	0.68	64.22	-	402.99	nr	443.29
800 x 400mm	249.52	2.50	255.91	1.45	0.39	36.33	-	292.25	nr	321.47
800 x 800mm	273.81	2.50	280.85	2.17	0.63	55.10	-	335.95	nr	369.55
800 x 1000mm	277.62	2.50	284.78	2.43	0.71	61.77	-	346.55	nr	381.21
800 x 1200mm	273.09	2.50	280.17	2.89	0.89	74.17	-	354.34	nr	389.78
800 x 1600mm	342.38	2.50	351.24	3.05	0.89	77.51	-	428.75	nr	471.62
1200 x 400mm	272.14	2.50	279.14	1.77	0.44	43.79	-	322.94	nr	355.23
1200 x 800mm	296.43	2.50	304.09	2.61	0.76	66.30	-	370.39	nr	407.43
1200 x 1000mm	311.90	2.50	319.98	2.92	0.86	74.33	-	394.31	nr	433.74
1200 x 1200mm	330.71	2.50	339.28	3.44	1.91	101.53	-	440.81	nr	484.89
1200 x 1600mm	376.67	2.50	386.43	3.60	1.91	104.87	-	491.30	nr	540.43
1400 x 800mm	315.24	2.50	323.39	2.96	1.71	88.40	-	411.79	nr	452.97
1400 x 1000mm	330.71	2.50	339.28	3.31	1.85	97.88	-	437.16	nr	480.88
1400 x 1400mm	368.33	2.50	377.89	4.01	2.12	116.70	-	494.59	nr	544.05
1400 x 1600mm	395.48	2.50	405.74	4.09	2.12	118.37	-	524.10	nr	576.51
top hung casement										
600 x 800mm	417.33	2.50	427.94	1.81	0.52	45.87	-	473.81	nr	521.19
600 x 1000mm	435.81	2.50	446.90	2.04	0.58	51.61	-	498.51	nr	548.36
600 x 1200mm	458.29	2.50	469.97	2.41	0.68	60.88	-	530.85	nr	583.94
800 x 800mm	431.81	2.50	442.80	2.17	0.63	55.10	-	497.90	nr	547.69
800 x 1000mm	450.29	2.50	461.77	2.43	0.71	61.77	-	523.54	nr	575.89
800 x 1200mm	472.76	2.50	484.83	2.89	0.89	74.17	-	559.00	nr	614.90
top hung fanlights										
600 x 400mm	361.38	2.50	370.54	1.21	0.35	30.70	-	401.24	nr	441.37
800 x 600mm	383.33	2.50	393.09	1.53	0.39	38.00	-	431.09	nr	474.20
1200 x 600mm	424.29	2.50	435.12	1.85	0.44	45.46	-	480.58	nr	528.63
Casement range; factory Low E double glazed, one pane obscure glass; fixing to masonry with lugs										
fixed lights										
600 x 400mm	275.74	2.50	282.76	1.21	0.35	30.70	-	313.46	nr	344.81
600 x 800mm	305.25	2.50	313.06	1.81	0.46	44.94	-	358.00	nr	393.80
600 x 1000mm	324.09	2.50	332.39	2.04	0.58	51.61	-	384.00	nr	422.40
600 x 1200mm	347.01	2.50	355.90	1.69	0.68	45.86	-	401.76	nr	441.94
600 x 1600mm	403.04	2.50	413.39	2.57	0.68	64.22	-	477.61	nr	525.37
800 x 400mm	304.78	2.50	312.55	1.45	0.39	36.33	-	348.88	nr	383.77
800 x 800mm	334.29	2.50	342.85	2.17	0.63	55.10	-	397.94	nr	437.74
800 x 1000mm	338.85	2.50	347.54	2.43	0.71	61.77	-	409.31	nr	450.24
1200 x 400mm	332.25	2.50	340.75	1.77	0.44	43.79	-	384.55	nr	423.00
1200 x 800mm	361.76	2.50	371.05	2.61	0.76	66.30	-	437.36	nr	481.09

Labour hourly rates: (except Specialists) Craft Operatives 20.87 Labourer 15.57 Rates are national average prices. Refer to REGIONAL VARIATIONS for indicative levels of overall pricing in regions	MATERIALS			LABOUR				RATES		
	Del to Site £	Waste %	Material Cost £	Craft Optve Hrs	Lab Hrs	Labour Cost £	Sunds £	Nett Rate £	Unit	Gross rate (10%) £
METAL WINDOWS AND SHOP FRONTS (Cont'd)										
Windows in aluminium; polyester powder finish; white matt; Bedding in cement mortar (1:3); pointing with Silicone standard mastic one side (Cont'd)										
Casement range; factory Low E double glazed, one pane obscure glass; fixing to masonry with lugs (Cont'd)										
top hung casement										
600 x 800mm	425.61	2.50	436.43	1.81	0.52	45.87	-	482.30	nr	530.53
600 x 1000mm	444.45	2.50	455.76	2.04	0.58	51.61	-	507.37	nr	558.10
600 x 1200mm	467.37	2.50	479.27	2.41	0.68	60.88	-	540.16	nr	594.17
800 x 800mm	440.37	2.50	451.58	2.17	0.63	55.10	-	506.67	nr	557.34
800 x 1000mm	459.21	2.50	470.91	2.43	0.71	61.77	-	532.68	nr	585.95
800 x 1200mm	482.12	2.50	494.42	2.89	0.89	74.17	-	568.60	nr	625.45
top hung fanlights										
600 x400mm	368.56	2.50	377.90	0.81	0.35	22.35	-	400.25	nr	440.28
800 x 600mm	390.93	2.50	400.88	1.53	0.39	38.00	-	438.88	nr	482.77
1200 x 600mm	432.69	2.50	443.73	1.85	0.44	45.46	-	489.19	nr	538.11
Sliding windows in aluminium; polyester powder finish; white matt; Bedding in cement mortar (1:3); pointing with Silicone standard mastic one side										
Factory double glazed, 24mm - 4/16/4 units with clear 'Low E' glass; fixing to masonry with lugs										
vertical sliders										
600 x 800mm	557.80	2.50	571.92	1.81	0.52	45.87	-	617.80	nr	679.58
600 x 1000mm	545.51	2.50	559.35	2.04	0.58	51.61	-	610.95	nr	672.05
600 x 1200mm	638.73	2.50	654.92	2.26	0.62	56.82	-	711.74	nr	782.92
800 x 800mm	788.90	2.50	808.82	2.17	0.63	55.10	-	863.92	nr	950.31
800 x 1000mm	919.71	2.50	942.93	2.43	0.71	61.77	-	1004.69	nr	1105.16
800 x 1200mm	1028.36	2.50	1054.31	2.71	0.81	69.17	-	1123.48	nr	1235.83
1200 x 800mm	1644.29	2.50	1685.65	2.84	0.86	72.66	-	1758.31	nr	1934.14
1200 x 1000mm	1749.76	2.50	1793.78	3.13	0.98	80.58	-	1874.36	nr	2061.79
1200 x 1200mm	1898.71	2.50	1946.47	3.44	1.08	88.61	-	2035.08	nr	2238.59
1400 x 800mm	2080.64	2.50	2132.93	3.50	1.14	90.79	-	2223.72	nr	2446.09
1400 x 1000mm	2216.86	2.50	2272.58	3.85	1.28	100.28	-	2372.86	nr	2610.14
1400 x 1200mm	2319.14	2.50	2377.44	3.93	1.11	99.30	-	2476.74	nr	2724.42
horizontal sliders										
1200 x 800mm	522.71	2.50	536.03	2.61	0.76	66.30	-	602.33	nr	662.56
1200 x 1000mm	551.03	2.50	565.08	2.92	0.86	74.33	-	639.41	nr	703.35
1200 x 1400mm	621.49	2.50	637.35	3.29	0.98	83.92	-	721.27	nr	793.40
1400 x 800mm	549.27	2.50	563.28	2.96	0.87	75.32	-	638.60	nr	702.46
1400 x 1000mm	586.02	2.50	600.97	3.31	1.01	84.81	-	685.77	nr	754.35
1400 x 1400mm	649.96	2.50	666.56	3.74	1.14	95.80	-	762.37	nr	838.60
1400 x 1600mm	683.30	2.50	700.76	4.09	1.28	105.29	-	806.04	nr	886.65
1600 x 800mm	583.09	2.50	597.97	3.33	1.00	85.07	-	683.04	nr	751.34
1600 x 1000mm	619.77	2.50	635.59	3.71	1.16	95.49	-	731.08	nr	804.19
1600 x 1600mm	722.06	2.50	740.51	4.56	1.48	118.21	-	858.72	nr	944.59
Window sills in galvanised pressed steel BS 6510; fixing to metal										
for opening										
508mm wide; AWA	24.24	2.50	24.85	0.50	0.25	14.33	-	39.17	nr	43.09
508mm wide; AWB	26.82	2.50	27.49	0.50	0.25	14.33	-	41.82	nr	46.00
508mm wide; PS	27.79	2.50	28.49	0.50	0.25	14.33	-	42.82	nr	47.10
508mm wide; RPS	27.79	2.50	28.49	0.50	0.25	14.33	-	42.82	nr	47.10
628mm wide; AWA	26.93	2.50	27.61	0.60	0.30	17.19	-	44.80	nr	49.28
628mm wide; AWB	29.28	2.50	30.01	0.60	0.30	17.19	-	47.20	nr	51.92
628mm wide; PS	33.05	2.50	33.87	0.60	0.30	17.19	-	51.07	nr	56.17
628mm wide; RPS	33.05	2.50	33.87	0.60	0.30	17.19	-	51.07	nr	56.17
997mm wide; AWA	37.84	2.50	38.79	0.70	0.35	20.06	-	58.85	nr	64.73
997mm wide; AWB	42.68	2.50	43.74	0.70	0.35	20.06	-	63.80	nr	70.18
997mm wide; PS	38.18	2.50	39.14	0.70	0.35	20.06	-	59.20	nr	65.12
997mm wide; RPS	39.36	2.50	40.35	0.70	0.35	20.06	-	60.41	nr	66.45
1237mm wide; AWA	42.69	2.50	43.75	0.80	0.40	22.92	-	66.68	nr	73.35
1237mm wide; AWB	44.07	2.50	45.17	0.80	0.40	22.92	-	68.09	nr	74.90
1237mm wide; PS	39.82	2.50	40.82	0.80	0.40	22.92	-	63.74	nr	70.11
1237mm wide; RPS	41.29	2.50	42.32	0.80	0.40	22.92	-	65.24	nr	71.77
1486mm wide; AWA	47.74	2.50	48.93	0.90	0.45	25.79	-	74.72	nr	82.20
1486mm wide; AWB	49.25	2.50	50.48	0.90	0.45	25.79	-	76.27	nr	83.90
1486mm wide; PS	44.12	2.50	45.23	0.90	0.45	25.79	-	71.02	nr	78.12
1486mm wide; RPS	45.86	2.50	47.01	0.90	0.45	25.79	-	72.80	nr	80.08
1846mm wide; AWA	51.13	2.50	52.41	1.00	0.50	28.66	-	81.06	nr	89.17
1846mm wide; AWB	53.10	2.50	54.42	1.00	0.50	28.66	-	83.08	nr	91.39
1846mm wide; PS	46.60	2.50	47.76	1.00	0.50	28.66	-	76.42	nr	84.06
1846mm wide; RPS	48.75	2.50	49.97	1.00	0.50	28.66	-	78.62	nr	86.48
METAL ROOFLIGHTS, SKYLIGHTS AND LANTERNLIGHTS										
Rooflights										
Pyramid rooflight; mainly in aluminium; powder coat finish; non-ventilating base frame; fixing to masonry with screws										
Double glazed factory unit with toughened clear glass										
600 x 600mm	744.00	2.50	762.60	2.00	1.00	57.31	-	819.91	nr	901.90
600 x 900mm	820.00	2.50	840.50	2.30	1.15	65.91	-	906.41	nr	997.05
900 x 900mm	941.00	2.50	964.52	2.30	1.15	65.91	-	1030.43	nr	1133.47
900 x 1200mm	1028.00	2.50	1053.70	2.50	1.25	71.64	-	1125.34	nr	1237.87
1200 x 1200mm	1184.00	2.50	1213.60	2.80	1.40	80.23	-	1293.83	nr	1423.22
Fixed flat rooflight; mainly in aluminium; powder coat finish; non-ventilating base frame; fixing to masonry with screws										
Double glazed factory unit with toughened clear glass										
600 x 600mm	375.00	2.50	384.38	2.00	1.00	57.31	-	441.68	nr	485.85
600 x 1200mm	625.00	2.50	640.62	2.30	1.15	65.91	-	706.53	nr	777.18

Labour hourly rates: (except Specialists) Craft Operatives 20.87 Labourer 15.57 Rates are national average prices. Refer to REGIONAL VARIATIONS for indicative levels of overall pricing in regions	MATERIALS			LABOUR				RATES		
	Del to Site £	Waste %	Material Cost £	Craft Optve Hrs	Lab Hrs	Labour Cost £	Sunds £	Nett Rate £	Unit	Gross rate (10%) £
METAL ROOFLIGHTS, SKYLIGHTS AND LANTERNLIGHTS (Cont'd)										
Rooflights (Cont'd)										
Fixed flat rooflight; mainly in aluminium; powder coat finish; non-ventilating base frame; fixing to masonry with screws (Cont'd)										
Double glazed factory unit with toughened clear glass (Cont'd)										
800 x 800mm	575.00	2.50	589.38	2.30	1.15	65.91	-	655.28	nr	720.81
1000 x 1000mm	600.00	2.50	615.00	2.50	1.25	71.64	-	686.64	nr	755.30
1000 x 1500mm	750.00	2.50	768.75	2.80	1.40	80.23	-	848.98	nr	933.88
Triple glazed factory unit with toughened clear glass										
600 x 600mm	528.00	2.50	541.20	2.00	1.00	57.31	-	598.51	nr	658.36
600 x 900mm	668.00	2.50	684.70	2.30	1.15	65.91	-	750.61	nr	825.67
900 x 900mm	805.00	2.50	825.12	2.30	1.15	65.91	-	891.03	nr	980.13
900 x 1200mm	907.00	2.50	929.67	2.50	1.25	71.64	-	1001.31	nr	1101.44
1200 x 1200mm	1197.00	2.50	1226.92	2.80	1.40	80.23	-	1307.16	nr	1437.88
METAL SCREENS, BORROWED LIGHTS AND FRAMES										
Screens in mild steel										
Screens; 6 x 50 x 50mm angle framing to perimeter; 75 x 75 x 3mm mesh infill; welded connections										
2000 x 2000mm overall; fixing to masonry with screws	412.02	5.00	432.62	6.00	3.00	171.93	-	604.55	nr	665.01
3000 x 2000mm overall; fixing to masonry with screws	523.25	5.00	549.41	8.00	4.00	229.24	-	778.65	nr	856.51
Screens; 6 x 50 x 50mm angle framing to perimeter; 75 x 75 x 5mm mesh infill; welded connections										
2000 x 2000mm overall; fixing to masonry with screws	438.14	5.00	460.05	6.00	3.00	171.93	-	631.98	nr	695.17
Screens; 6 x 50 x 75mm angle framing to perimeter; 75 x 75 x 3mm mesh infill; welded connections										
3000 x 2000mm overall; fixing to masonry with screws	643.72	5.00	675.91	8.00	4.00	229.24	-	905.15	nr	995.66
Screens; 6 x 50 x 50mm angle framing to perimeter; 6 x 51 x 102mm tee mullion; 75 x 75 x 3mm mesh infill; welded connections										
2000 x 4000mm overall; mullions -1 nr; fixing to masonry with screws	1060.71	5.00	1113.75	8.00	4.00	229.24	-	1342.99	nr	1477.29
Screens; 38.1 x 38.1 x 3.2mm hollow section framing to perimeter; 75 x 75 x 3mm mesh infill; welded connections										
2000 x 2000mm overall; fixing to masonry with screws	543.32	5.00	570.48	6.00	3.00	171.93	-	742.41	nr	816.65
Screens; 38.1 x 38.1 x 3.2mm hollow section framing to perimeter; 75 x 75 x 5mm mesh infill; welded connections										
2000 x 2000mm overall; fixing to masonry with screws	582.12	5.00	611.23	6.00	3.00	171.93	-	783.16	nr	861.47
Screens; 76.2 x 38.1 x 4mm hollow section framing to perimeter; 75 x 75 x 3mm mesh infill; welded connections										
2000 x 2000mm overall; fixing to masonry with screws	609.87	5.00	640.37	6.00	3.00	171.93	-	812.30	nr	893.53
Grilles in mild steel										
Grilles; 13 x 51mm flat bar framing to perimeter; 13mm diameter vertical infill bars at 150mm centres; welded connections										
1000 x 1000mm overall; fixing to masonry with screws	413.06	5.00	433.71	6.00	3.00	171.93	-	605.64	nr	666.20
2000 x 1000mm overall; fixing to masonry with screws	557.88	5.00	585.77	8.00	4.00	229.24	-	815.01	nr	896.51
Grilles; 13 x 51mm flat bar framing to perimeter; 13mm diameter vertical infill bars at 300mm centres; welded connections										
1000 x 1000mm overall; fixing to masonry with screws	392.27	5.00	411.88	4.00	2.00	114.62	-	526.50	nr	579.15
Grilles; 13 x 51mm flat bar framing to perimeter; 18mm diameter vertical infill bars at 150mm centres; welded connections										
1000 x 1000mm overall; fixing to masonry with screws	426.43	5.00	447.75	4.00	2.00	114.62	-	562.37	nr	618.61
Glazing frames in mild steel										
Glazing frames; 13 x 38 x 3mm angle framing to perimeter; welded connections; 13 x 13mm glazing beads, fixed with screws										
500 x 500mm overall; fixing to timber with screws	243.62	5.00	255.80	3.00	1.50	85.97	-	341.76	nr	375.94
Glazing frames; 15 x 21 x 3mm angle framing to perimeter; welded connections; 13 x 13mm glazing beads, fixed with screws										
500 x 1000mm overall; fixing to timber with screws	393.90	5.00	413.60	3.00	1.50	85.97	-	499.56	nr	549.52
Glazing frames; 18 x 25 x 3mm angle framing to perimeter; welded connections; 9 x 25mm glazing beads, fixed with screws										
1000 x 1000mm overall; fixing to timber with screws	473.65	5.00	497.33	4.00	2.00	114.62	-	611.95	nr	673.15
Glazing frames; 18 x 25 x 3mm angle framing to perimeter; welded connections; 13 x 13mm glazing beads, fixed with screws										
1000 x 1000mm overall; fixing to timber with screws	510.57	5.00	536.10	4.00	2.00	114.62	-	650.72	nr	715.79
Glazing frames; 18 x 38 x 3mm angle framing to perimeter; welded connections; 9 x 25mm glazing beads, fixed with screws										
1000 x 1000mm overall; fixing to timber with screws	636.02	5.00	667.82	3.00	1.50	85.97	-	753.78	nr	829.16
Glazing frames; 18 x 25 x 3mm angle framing to perimeter; welded connections; 15 x 15 x 3mm channel glazing beads; fixed with screws										
1000 x 1000mm overall; fixing to timber with screws	520.51	5.00	546.54	3.00	1.50	85.97	-	632.50	nr	695.75
Glazing frames; 18 x 38 x 3mm angle framing to perimeter; welded connections; 15 x 15 x 3mm channel glazing beads; fixed with screws										
1000 x 1000mm overall; fixing to timber with screws	636.02	5.00	667.82	3.00	1.50	85.97	-	753.78	nr	829.16

Labour hourly rates: (except Specialists)
Craft Operatives 20.87 Labourer 15.57
Rates are national average prices.
Refer to REGIONAL VARIATIONS for indicative levels of overall pricing in regions

	MATERIALS			LABOUR				RATES		
	Del to Site £	Waste %	Material Cost £	Craft Optve Hrs	Lab Hrs	Labour Cost £	Sunds £	Nett Rate £	Unit	Gross rate (10%) £
METAL SCREENS, BORROWED LIGHTS AND FRAMES (Cont'd)										
Glazing frames in aluminium										
Glazing frames; 13 x 38 x 3mm angle framing to perimeter; welded connections; 13 x 13mm glazing beads, fixed with screws										
500 x 500mm overall; fixing to timber with screws	437.68	5.00	459.57	3.00	1.50	85.97	-	545.53	nr	600.09
Glazing frames; 15 x 21 x 3mm angle framing to perimeter; welded connections; 13 x 13mm glazing beads, fixed with screws										
500 x 1000mm overall; fixing to timber with screws	442.40	5.00	464.52	3.00	1.50	85.97	-	550.49	nr	605.54
Glazing frames; 18 x 25 x 3mm angle framing to perimeter; welded connections; 9 x 25mm glazing beads, fixed with screws										
1000 x 1000mm overall; fixing to timber with screws	474.34	5.00	498.06	4.00	2.00	114.62	-	612.68	nr	673.95
Glazing frames; 18 x 25 x 3mm angle framing to perimeter; welded connections; 13 x 13mm glazing beads, fixed with screws										
1000 x 1000mm overall; fixing to timber with screws	481.42	5.00	505.49	4.00	2.00	114.62	-	620.11	nr	682.12
Glazing frames; 18 x 38 x 3mm angle framing to perimeter; welded connections; 9 x 25mm glazing beads, fixed with screws										
1000 x 1000mm overall; fixing to timber with screws	543.20	5.00	570.36	4.00	2.00	114.62	-	684.98	nr	753.48
Glazing frames; 18 x 25 x 3mm angle framing to perimeter; welded connections; 15 x 15 x 3mm channel glazing beads; fixed with screws										
1000 x 1000mm overall; fixing to timber with screws	496.23	5.00	521.04	4.00	2.00	114.62	-	635.66	nr	699.22
Glazing frames; 18 x 38 x 3mm angle framing to perimeter; welded connections; 15 x 15 x 3mm channel glazing beads; fixed with screws										
1000 x 1000mm overall; fixing to timber with screws	565.56	5.00	593.84	4.00	2.00	114.62	-	708.46	nr	779.31
Note										
Bedding in cement mortar (1:3); pointing with Silicone standard mastic one side' is included with standard windows as noted above; adjustment will need to be made for two part polysuphide pointing and bedding and pointing to purpose made frames, grilles, screens and the like										
Bedding and pointing frames										
Pointing with Silicone										
standard metal frames one side	1.08	10.00	1.19	0.14	-	2.92	-	4.11	m	4.53
Bedding in cement mortar (1:3); pointing with Silicone standard mastic one side										
metal frames	1.41	5.00	1.52	0.20	-	4.17	-	5.69	m	6.26
PLASTIC WINDOWS AND SHOP FRONTS										
Windows in uPVC; white; Bedding in cement mortar (1:3); pointing with Silicone standard mastic one side										
Windows; factory glazed 24mm double glazed units; hinges; fastenings										
fixed light; fixing to masonry with cleats and screws; overall size										
600 x 600mm	74.09	2.50	76.09	3.08	1.30	84.52	2.56	163.17	nr	179.48
600 x 900mm	80.53	2.50	82.73	3.85	1.62	105.57	2.56	190.86	nr	209.95
600 x 1050mm	83.75	2.50	86.05	4.21	1.77	115.42	2.56	204.03	nr	224.43
600 x 1200mm	86.97	2.50	89.36	4.62	1.95	126.78	2.56	218.70	nr	240.57
600 x 1500mm toughened glass	107.80	2.50	110.76	5.39	2.27	147.83	2.56	261.15	nr	287.26
750 x 600mm	77.31	2.50	79.41	3.49	1.47	95.72	2.56	177.70	nr	195.47
750 x 900mm	85.18	2.50	87.51	4.26	1.80	116.93	2.56	207.00	nr	227.70
750 x 1050mm	89.82	2.50	92.28	4.62	1.95	126.78	2.56	221.62	nr	243.79
750 x 1200mm	93.04	2.50	95.61	4.98	2.10	136.63	2.56	234.80	nr	258.28
750 x 1500mm; toughened glass	118.91	2.50	122.16	5.75	2.42	157.68	2.56	282.40	nr	310.64
900 x 600mm	80.53	2.50	82.73	3.85	1.62	105.57	2.56	190.86	nr	209.95
900 x 900mm	89.82	2.50	92.28	4.62	1.95	126.78	2.56	221.62	nr	243.79
900 x 1050mm	94.47	2.50	97.08	4.88	2.05	133.76	2.56	233.40	nr	256.74
900 x 1200mm	99.12	2.50	101.86	5.39	2.27	147.83	2.56	252.25	nr	277.47
900 x 1500mm toughened glass	128.58	2.50	132.10	6.11	2.57	167.53	2.56	302.19	nr	332.40
1200 x 600mm	86.97	2.50	89.36	4.37	1.82	119.54	2.56	211.46	nr	232.61
1200 x 900mm	99.12	2.50	101.86	5.14	2.15	140.75	2.56	245.16	nr	269.68
1200 x 1050mm	103.77	2.50	106.64	5.50	2.30	150.60	2.56	259.79	nr	285.77
1200 x 1200mm	109.84	2.50	112.89	5.96	2.50	163.31	2.56	278.76	nr	306.63
1200 x 1500mm toughened glass	149.36	2.50	153.43	6.78	2.85	185.87	2.56	341.86	nr	376.04
fixed light with fixed light; fixing to masonry with cleats and screws; overall size										
600 x 1000mm	119.52	2.50	122.71	4.84	2.00	132.15	2.56	257.42	nr	283.16
600 x 1500mm toughened glass	144.98	2.50	148.87	5.39	2.27	147.83	2.56	299.26	nr	329.18
600 x 1800mm toughened glass	170.02	2.50	174.57	5.81	2.42	158.93	2.56	336.06	nr	369.67
600 x 2100mm toughened glass	180.76	2.50	185.61	6.23	2.57	170.04	2.56	358.21	nr	394.03
750 x 1350mm	133.43	2.50	137.03	5.39	2.27	147.83	2.56	287.42	nr	316.16
750 x 1500mm toughened glass	154.66	2.50	158.80	5.75	2.42	157.68	2.56	319.04	nr	350.95
750 x 1800mm toughened glass	181.85	2.50	186.71	6.17	2.57	168.78	2.56	358.05	nr	393.86
750 x 2100mm toughened glass	194.74	2.50	199.97	6.64	2.75	181.39	2.56	383.92	nr	422.31
900 x 1350mm	138.09	2.50	141.82	5.75	2.42	157.68	2.56	302.06	nr	332.26
900 x 1500mm toughened glass	164.33	2.50	168.74	6.11	2.57	167.53	2.56	338.83	nr	372.71
900 x 1800mm toughened glass	193.67	2.50	198.85	6.48	2.70	177.28	2.56	378.68	nr	416.55
900 x 2100mm toughened glass	207.29	2.50	212.85	7.00	2.90	191.24	2.56	406.65	nr	447.31
1200 x 1350mm	151.67	2.50	155.78	6.42	2.70	176.02	2.56	334.36	nr	367.80
1200 x 1500mm toughened glass	186.55	2.50	191.55	6.78	2.85	185.87	2.56	379.98	nr	417.98
1200 x 1800mm toughened glass	218.76	2.50	224.60	7.25	3.02	198.33	2.56	425.49	nr	468.04
1200 x 2100mm toughened glass	236.68	2.50	243.00	7.67	3.17	209.43	2.56	454.99	nr	500.49

Labour hourly rates: (except Specialists) Craft Operatives 20.87 Labourer 15.57 Rates are national average prices. Refer to REGIONAL VARIATIONS for indicative levels of overall pricing in regions	MATERIALS			LABOUR				RATES		
	Del to Site £	Waste %	Material Cost £	Craft Optve Hrs	Lab Hrs	Labour Cost £	Sunds £	Nett Rate £	Unit	Gross rate (10%) £
PLASTIC WINDOWS AND SHOP FRONTS (Cont'd)										
Windows in uPVC; white; Bedding in cement mortar (1:3); pointing with Silicone standard mastic one side (Cont'd)										
Windows; factory glazed 24mm double glazed units; hinges; fastenings (Cont'd)										
overall, tilt/turn; fixing to masonry with cleats and screws; overall size										
600 x 650mm	141.05	2.50	144.72	3.08	1.30	84.52	2.56	231.80	nr	254.98
600 x 900mm	191.18	2.50	196.15	3.85	1.62	105.57	2.56	304.28	nr	334.71
600 x 1050mm	167.26	2.50	171.65	4.21	1.80	115.89	2.56	290.09	nr	319.10
600 x 1200mm	171.81	2.50	176.32	4.62	1.95	126.78	2.56	305.66	nr	336.23
750 x 650mm	144.19	2.50	147.97	3.49	1.47	95.72	2.56	246.25	nr	270.87
750 x 900mm	165.86	2.50	170.21	4.26	1.80	116.93	2.56	289.70	nr	318.67
750 x 1050mm	174.60	2.50	179.18	4.62	1.95	126.78	2.56	308.52	nr	339.37
750 x 1200mm	179.14	2.50	183.86	4.98	2.10	136.63	2.56	323.05	nr	355.36
750 x 1350mm	200.45	2.50	205.72	5.39	2.27	147.83	2.56	356.11	nr	391.72
750 x 1500mm toughened glass	224.39	2.50	230.28	5.75	2.42	157.68	2.56	390.52	nr	429.57
900 x 900mm	182.98	2.50	187.77	4.62	1.95	126.78	2.56	317.11	nr	348.82
900 x 1050mm	193.11	2.50	198.18	4.88	2.05	133.76	2.56	334.50	nr	367.96
900 x 1200mm	197.66	2.50	202.86	5.39	2.27	147.83	2.56	353.25	nr	388.58
900 x 1350mm	220.36	2.50	226.15	5.75	2.42	157.68	2.56	386.39	nr	425.02
900 x 1500mm toughened glass	253.78	2.50	260.43	6.11	2.57	167.53	2.56	430.52	nr	473.57
tilt/turn sash with fixed side light; fixing to masonry with cleats and screws; overall size										
900 x 1350mm	249.69	2.50	256.21	5.75	2.42	157.68	2.56	416.45	nr	458.09
900 x 1500mm toughened glass	278.62	2.50	285.89	6.11	2.57	167.53	2.56	455.98	nr	501.57
900 x 2100mm toughened glass	320.81	2.50	329.21	7.00	2.90	191.24	2.56	523.01	nr	575.31
1200 x 1350mm	261.57	2.50	268.43	6.42	2.70	176.02	2.56	447.01	nr	491.71
1200 x 1500mm toughened glass	299.11	2.50	306.92	6.78	2.85	185.87	2.56	495.35	nr	544.89
1200 x 2100mm toughened glass	348.36	2.50	357.48	7.67	3.17	209.43	2.56	569.46	nr	626.41
1500 x 900mm	244.69	2.50	251.12	6.18	3.09	177.09	2.56	430.77	nr	473.84
1500 x 1200mm	280.59	2.50	287.97	7.05	3.53	202.02	2.56	492.55	nr	541.80
1500 x 1350mm	292.01	2.50	299.68	7.30	3.65	209.18	2.56	511.42	nr	562.56
1500 x 1500mm toughened glass	336.85	2.50	345.67	7.92	3.96	226.95	2.56	575.18	nr	632.69
1800 x 900mm	270.31	2.50	277.40	6.38	2.65	174.41	2.56	454.37	nr	499.81
1800 x 1050mm	284.62	2.50	292.10	6.79	2.82	185.61	2.56	480.27	nr	528.29
1800 x 1200mm	308.72	2.50	316.81	7.25	3.02	198.33	2.56	517.70	nr	569.47
1800 x 1350mm	320.25	2.50	328.65	6.50	3.25	186.26	2.56	517.46	nr	569.21
1800 x 1500mm toughened glass	373.59	2.50	383.34	8.12	3.40	222.40	2.56	608.30	nr	669.13
tilt/turn sash with centre fixed light; fixing to masonry with cleats and screws; overall size										
2400 x 1200mm	438.63	2.50	450.04	8.74	3.65	239.23	2.56	691.84	nr	761.02
2400 x 1350mm	457.15	2.50	469.04	9.20	3.85	251.95	2.56	723.55	nr	795.90
2400 x 1500mm toughened glass	529.06	2.50	542.78	9.56	4.00	261.80	2.56	807.13	nr	887.84
Windows; factory glazed 40mm triple glazed units; hinges; fastenings										
fixed light; fixing to masonry with cleats and screws; overall size										
600 x 600mm	159.45	2.50	163.58	3.08	1.30	84.52	2.56	250.66	nr	275.73
600 x 1200mm	237.68	2.50	243.84	4.62	1.95	126.78	2.56	373.18	nr	410.50
600 x 1500mm toughened glass	294.03	2.50	301.64	5.39	2.27	147.83	2.56	452.03	nr	497.24
800 x 600mm	187.95	2.50	192.82	3.49	1.47	95.72	2.56	291.10	nr	320.21
800 x 1500mm toughened glass	361.62	2.50	370.94	5.75	2.42	157.68	2.56	531.18	nr	584.29
900 x 600mm	202.38	2.50	207.63	3.85	1.62	105.57	2.56	315.76	nr	347.33
900 x 1500mm toughened glass	397.83	2.50	408.08	6.11	2.57	167.53	2.56	578.17	nr	635.98
1200 x 600mm	243.80	2.50	250.11	4.37	1.82	119.54	2.56	372.21	nr	409.43
1200 x 1200mm	392.71	2.50	402.83	5.96	2.50	163.31	2.56	568.70	nr	625.57
1200 x 1500mm toughened glass	500.12	2.50	512.96	6.78	2.85	185.87	2.56	701.39	nr	771.53
fixed light with opening top light; fixing to masonry with cleats and screws; overall size										
600 x 900mm	277.35	2.50	284.47	3.85	1.62	105.57	2.56	392.60	nr	431.86
600 x 1400mm	339.74	2.50	348.48	5.00	2.15	137.83	2.56	488.87	nr	537.75
600 x 1500mm toughened glass	372.06	2.50	381.62	5.39	2.27	147.83	2.56	532.01	nr	585.21
800 x 900mm	315.35	2.50	323.44	4.26	1.80	116.93	2.56	442.93	nr	487.22
800 x 1500mm toughened glass	438.12	2.50	449.35	5.75	2.27	155.35	2.56	607.25	nr	667.98
900 x 900mm	334.53	2.50	343.11	4.62	1.95	126.78	2.56	472.45	nr	519.70
900 x 1500mm toughened glass	474.33	2.50	486.49	6.11	2.57	167.53	2.56	656.58	nr	722.24
1200 x 900mm	408.53	2.50	419.00	5.14	2.15	140.75	2.56	562.31	nr	618.54
1200 x 1500mm toughened glass	590.39	2.50	605.48	6.78	2.85	185.87	2.56	793.91	nr	873.31
Note Bedding in cement mortar (1:3); pointing with Silicone standard mastic one side' is included with standard windows as noted above; adjustment will need to be made for two part polysuphide pointing and bedding and pointing to purpose made frames										
Bedding and pointing frames										
Pointing with Silicone standard mastic plastics frames one side	1.95	10.00	2.15	0.14	-	2.92	-	5.07	m	5.57
Bedding in cement mortar (1:3); pointing with Silicone standard mastic one side plastics frames	2.82	5.00	3.07	0.20	-	4.17	-	7.24	m	7.97

Labour hourly rates: (except Specialists) Craft Operatives 20.87 Labourer 15.57 Rates are national average prices. Refer to REGIONAL VARIATIONS for indicative levels of overall pricing in regions	MATERIALS			LABOUR				RATES		
	Del to Site £	Waste %	Material Cost £	Craft Optve Hrs	Lab Hrs	Labour Cost £	Sunds £	Nett Rate £	Unit	Gross rate (10%) £
PLASTIC ROOFLIGHTS, SKYLIGHTS AND LANTERNLIGHTS										
Roof domelights; polycarbonate; triple glazed										
Rooflights, 'Thermadome' from the National Domelight Company; triple skin UV protected polycarbonate domes with 150mm high insulated kerb										
un-ventilated upstand pvc kerb; fixing to masonry with screws; roof opening size										
600 x 600mm	208.33	2.50	213.54	1.80	0.90	51.58	-	265.12	nr	291.63
600 x 900mm	250.00	2.50	256.25	2.00	1.00	57.31	-	313.56	nr	344.92
900 x 900mm	323.33	2.50	331.42	2.00	1.00	57.31	-	388.73	nr	427.60
900 x 1200mm	380.83	2.50	390.35	2.20	1.10	63.04	-	453.39	nr	498.73
1200 x 1200mm	455.00	2.50	466.38	2.50	1.25	71.64	-	538.01	nr	591.81
ventilated upstand pvc kerb with manually controllable rotating vents; fixing to masonry with screws; roof opening size										
600 x 600mm	230.83	2.50	236.60	1.80	0.90	51.58	-	288.18	nr	317.00
600 x 900mm	272.50	2.50	279.31	2.00	1.00	57.31	-	336.62	nr	370.28
900 x 900mm	345.83	2.50	354.48	2.00	1.00	57.31	-	411.79	nr	452.97
900 x 1200mm	403.33	2.50	413.42	2.20	1.10	63.04	-	476.46	nr	524.10
1200 x 1200mm	480.00	2.50	492.00	2.50	1.25	71.64	-	563.64	nr	620.00
hinged rooflight for ventilation; upstand pvc kerb; winding rod; fixing to masonry with screws; roof opening size										
600 x 600mm	292.50	2.50	299.81	1.80	0.90	51.58	-	351.39	nr	386.53
600 x 900mm	335.83	2.50	344.23	2.00	1.00	57.31	-	401.54	nr	441.69
900 x 900mm	420.00	2.50	430.50	2.00	1.00	57.31	-	487.81	nr	536.59
900 x 1200mm	480.83	2.50	492.85	2.20	1.10	63.04	-	555.89	nr	611.48
1200 x 1200mm	565.00	2.50	579.12	2.50	1.25	71.64	-	650.76	nr	715.84

DOORS, SHUTTERS AND HATCHES

Labour hourly rates: (except Specialists) Craft Operatives 20.87 Labourer 15.57 Rates are national average prices. Refer to REGIONAL VARIATIONS for indicative levels of overall pricing in regions	MATERIALS			LABOUR				RATES		
	Del to Site £	Waste %	Material Cost £	Craft Optve Hrs	Lab Hrs	Labour Cost £	Sunds £	Nett Rate £	Unit	Gross rate (10%) £
TIMBER DOORS AND FRAMES										
Door sets mainly in softwood, wrought										
Door sets; 28mm thick jambs, head and transome with 12mm thick stop to suit 100mm thick wall; 14mm thick hardwood threshold; honeycomb core plywood faced flush door lipped two long edges; 6mm plywood transome panel fixed with pinned beads; 65mm snap in hinges; 57mm backset mortice latch; fixing frame to masonry with screws										
526 x 2040 x 40mm flush door -1 nr; basic dimensions										
600 x 2100mm	159.32	2.50	163.31	1.25	0.16	28.58	-	191.89	nr	211.07
600 x 2400mm	194.81	2.50	199.68	1.35	0.17	30.82	-	230.50	nr	253.55
626 x 2040 x 40mm flush door -1 nr; basic dimensions										
700 x 2100mm	159.32	2.50	163.31	1.25	0.16	28.58	-	191.89	nr	211.07
700 x 2400mm	194.81	2.50	199.68	1.35	0.17	30.82	-	230.50	nr	253.55
726 x 2040 x 40mm flush door -1 nr; basic dimensions										
800 x 2100mm	159.32	2.50	163.31	1.25	0.16	28.58	-	191.89	nr	211.07
800 x 2400mm	194.81	2.50	199.68	1.35	0.17	30.82	-	230.50	nr	253.55
826 x 2040 x 40mm flush door -1 nr; basic dimensions										
900 x 2100mm	166.26	2.50	170.42	1.25	0.16	28.58	-	199.00	nr	218.89
900 x 2400mm	198.96	2.50	203.93	1.35	0.17	30.82	-	234.76	nr	258.23
Doors in softwood, wrought										
Internal panelled doors; SA; Magnet Trade; pre-glazed										
762 x 1981 x 34mm (f sizes)	107.40	2.50	110.08	1.20	0.16	27.54	-	137.62	nr	151.38
Doors in softwood, wrought, preservative treated										
External ledged and braced doors										
686 x 1981 x 44mm (f sizes)	53.00	2.50	54.32	1.10	0.14	25.14	-	79.46	nr	87.41
762 x 1981 x 44mm (f sizes)	53.00	2.50	54.32	1.30	0.16	29.62	-	83.95	nr	92.34
838 x 1981 x 44mm (f sizes)	53.00	2.50	54.32	1.50	0.19	34.26	-	88.59	nr	97.45
External framed, ledged and braced doors; YX										
686 x 1981 x 44mm (f sizes)	72.30	2.50	74.11	1.10	0.14	25.14	-	99.24	nr	109.17
762 x 1981 x 44mm (f sizes)	72.30	2.50	74.11	1.30	0.16	29.62	-	103.73	nr	114.10
813 x 2032 x 44mm (f sizes)	72.30	2.50	74.11	1.50	0.19	34.26	-	108.37	nr	119.21
838 x 1981 x 44mm (f sizes)	72.30	2.50	74.11	1.50	0.19	34.26	-	108.37	nr	119.21
External panelled doors; KXT CDS										
762 x 1981 x 44mm (f sizes)	121.90	2.50	124.95	1.30	0.16	29.62	-	154.57	nr	170.03
External panelled doors; 2XG										
762 x 1981 x 44mm (f sizes)	100.70	2.50	103.22	1.30	0.16	29.62	-	132.84	nr	146.12
813 x 2032 x 44mm (f sizes)	100.70	2.50	103.22	1.50	0.19	34.26	-	137.48	nr	151.23
838 x 1981 x 44mm (f sizes)	100.70	2.50	103.22	1.50	0.19	34.26	-	137.48	nr	151.23
Garage doors; MFL, pair, side hung										
1981 x 2134 x 44mm (f sizes) overall	264.16	2.50	270.76	3.50	0.44	79.90	-	350.66	nr	385.73
2134 x 2134 x 44mm (f sizes) overall	279.16	2.50	286.14	3.65	0.46	83.34	-	369.48	nr	406.42
Garage doors; 301, pair, pre-glazed obscure, side hung										
1981 x 2134 x 44mm (f sizes) overall	307.49	2.50	315.18	3.50	0.44	79.90	-	395.07	nr	434.58
2134 x 2134 x 44mm (f sizes) overall	316.66	2.50	324.58	3.65	0.46	83.34	-	407.91	nr	448.71
Doors in Hardwood (solid, laminated or veneered), wrought										
External panelled doors; Carolina M & T; unglazed; Magnet Trade										
813 x 2032 x 44mm (f sizes)	180.10	2.50	184.60	1.50	0.19	34.26	-	218.87	nr	240.75
838 x 1981 x 44mm (f sizes)	180.10	2.50	184.60	1.50	0.19	34.26	-	218.87	nr	240.75
External panelled doors; Carolina M & T; pre-glazed obscure toughened glass; Magnet Trade										
813 x 2032 x 44mm (f sizes)	258.30	2.50	264.76	2.30	0.29	52.52	-	317.27	nr	349.00
838 x 1981 x 44mm (f sizes)	258.30	2.50	264.76	2.30	0.29	52.52	-	317.27	nr	349.00
External panelled doors; Stable; 9 pane; Meratini veneered; upper door pre-glazed with clear toughened glass; Magnet Trade										
762 x 1981 x 44mm (f sizes)	171.00	2.50	175.27	3.20	0.40	73.01	-	248.29	nr	273.12
838 x 1981 x 44mm (f sizes)	171.00	2.50	175.27	3.50	0.44	79.90	-	255.17	nr	280.69
External panelled doors; Stable; 1 pane; Meratini veneered; upper door pre-glazed with clear toughened glass; Magnet Trade										
762 x 1981 x 44mm (f sizes)	258.30	2.50	264.76	3.20	0.40	73.01	-	337.77	nr	371.55
838 x 1981 x 44mm (f sizes)	258.30	2.50	264.76	3.50	0.44	79.90	-	344.65	nr	379.12
External panelled doors; 2 panel; 2XG; pre-glazed with clear toughened double glazed units; Magnet Trade										
838 x 1981 x 44mm (f sizes)	252.30	2.50	258.61	2.30	0.29	52.52	-	311.12	nr	342.24
External panelled doors; Newbury oak veneered; preglazed obscure; Magnet Trade										
762 x 1981 x 44mm (f sizes)	356.70	2.50	365.62	2.10	0.26	47.88	-	413.49	nr	454.84
813 x 2032 x 44mm (f sizes)	356.70	2.50	365.62	2.30	0.29	52.52	-	418.13	nr	459.95

Labour hourly rates: (except Specialists) Craft Operatives 20.87 Labourer 15.57 Rates are national average prices. Refer to REGIONAL VARIATIONS for indicative levels of overall pricing in regions	MATERIALS			LABOUR				RATES		
	Del to Site £	Waste %	Material Cost £	Craft Optve Hrs	Lab Hrs	Labour Cost £	Sunds £	Nett Rate £	Unit	Gross rate (10%) £
TIMBER DOORS AND FRAMES (Cont'd)										
Doors in Hardwood (solid, laminated or veneered), wrought (Cont'd)										
External panelled doors; Goodwood oak veneered; preglazed obscure; Magnet Trade										
838 x 1981 x 44mm (f sizes)	356.70	2.50	365.62	2.30	0.29	52.52	-	418.13	nr	459.95
External panelled doors; Colonial 6 panel meranti veneer; Magnet Trade										
762 x 1981 x 44mm (f sizes)	180.10	2.50	184.60	2.10	0.26	47.88	-	232.48	nr	255.73
838 x 1981 x 44mm (f sizes)	180.10	2.50	184.60	2.30	0.29	52.52	-	237.12	nr	260.83
External panelled doors; Malton 2 panel meranti veneer, pre-glazed with clear toughened glass; Magnet Trade										
762 x 1981 x 44mm (f sizes)	290.10	2.50	297.35	2.10	0.26	47.88	-	345.23	nr	379.75
838 x 1981 x 44mm (f sizes)	290.10	2.50	297.35	2.30	0.29	52.52	-	349.87	nr	384.86
Internal panelled doors; Regency 6 panel; prefinished oak										
762 x 1981 x 35mm (f sizes)	150.25	2.50	154.01	2.10	0.26	47.88	-	201.88	nr	222.07
Internal panelled doors; Regency 6 panel; prefinished oak; FD30 fire door										
762 x 1981 x 44mm (f sizes)	244.90	2.50	251.02	2.10	0.26	47.88	-	298.90	nr	328.79
Internal panelled doors; Mexicana oak										
762 x 1981 x 35mm (f sizes)	117.20	2.50	120.13	2.10	0.26	47.88	-	168.01	nr	184.81
Internal panelled doors; Mexicana oak FD30 fire door										
762 x 1981 x 44mm (f sizes)	168.50	2.50	172.71	2.10	0.26	47.88	-	220.59	nr	242.65
Internal panelled doors; Mexicana Pattern 10 oak; Magnet Trade										
762 x 1981 x 35mm (f sizes)	133.50	2.50	136.84	2.10	0.26	47.88	-	184.71	nr	203.18
Hollwcore doors with moulded panel facings										
Internal panelled doors; 6 panel; Magnet Trade										
610 x 1981 x 35mm (f sizes)	43.80	2.50	44.89	1.60	0.20	36.51	-	81.40	nr	89.54
686 x 1981 x 35mm (f sizes)	43.80	2.50	44.89	1.70	0.21	38.75	-	83.64	nr	92.01
762 x 1981 x 35mm (f sizes)	43.80	2.50	44.89	1.90	0.24	43.39	-	88.28	nr	97.11
826 x 2040 x 35mm (f sizes)	43.80	2.50	44.89	1.90	0.24	43.39	-	88.28	nr	97.11
Internal panelled doors; 4 Panel Grained; Magnet Trade										
686 x 1981 x 35mm (f sizes)	28.80	2.50	29.52	1.70	0.21	38.75	-	68.27	nr	75.10
762 x 1981 x 35mm (f sizes)	28.80	2.50	29.52	1.90	0.24	43.39	-	72.91	nr	80.20
838 x 1981 x 35mm (f sizes)	28.80	2.50	29.52	1.90	0.24	43.39	-	72.91	nr	80.20
Flush doors										
Internal; Magnaseal; Magnet Trade										
610 x 1981 x 35mm	34.90	2.50	35.77	1.80	0.23	41.15	-	76.92	nr	84.61
686 x 1981 x 35mm	34.90	2.50	35.77	1.70	0.21	38.75	-	74.52	nr	81.97
762 x 1981 x 35mm	34.90	2.50	35.77	1.90	0.24	43.39	-	79.16	nr	87.08
838 x 1981 x 35mm	34.90	2.50	35.77	2.20	0.28	50.27	-	86.05	nr	94.65
Internal; veneered paintgrade facings; Magnet Trade										
381 x 1981 x 35mm	42.40	2.50	43.46	1.10	0.14	25.14	-	68.60	nr	75.46
457 x 1981 x 35mm	42.40	2.50	43.46	1.20	0.15	27.38	-	70.84	nr	77.92
533 x 1981 x 35mm	42.40	2.50	43.46	1.30	0.16	29.62	-	73.08	nr	80.39
610 x 1981 x 35mm	42.40	2.50	43.46	1.40	0.18	32.02	-	75.48	nr	83.03
686 x 1981 x 35mm	42.40	2.50	43.46	1.50	0.19	34.26	-	77.72	nr	85.50
711 x 1981 x 35mm	42.40	2.50	43.46	1.60	0.20	36.51	-	79.97	nr	87.96
762 x 1981 x 35mm	42.40	2.50	43.46	1.70	0.21	38.75	-	82.21	nr	90.43
813 x 2032 x 35mm	42.40	2.50	43.46	1.90	0.24	43.39	-	86.85	nr	95.53
838 x 1981 x 35mm	42.40	2.50	43.46	1.90	0.24	43.39	-	86.85	nr	95.53
Internal; Ash prefinished; Magnet Trade										
686 x 1981 x 35mm	106.20	2.50	108.85	1.70	0.21	38.75	-	147.60	nr	162.36
762 x 1981 x 35mm	106.20	2.50	108.85	2.10	0.26	47.88	-	156.73	nr	172.40
838 x 1981 x 35mm	106.20	2.50	108.85	2.10	0.26	47.88	-	156.73	nr	172.40
External; FD30, veneered paintgrade facings; Magnet Trade										
762 x 1981 x 44mm	87.00	2.50	89.17	1.80	0.23	41.15	-	130.32	nr	143.35
838 x 1981 x 44mm	87.00	2.50	89.17	2.00	0.25	45.63	-	134.81	nr	148.29
Internal; fire resisting; 4 Panel smooth; FD30; Magnet Trade										
838 x 1981 x 44mm	96.40	2.50	98.81	2.20	0.28	50.27	-	149.08	nr	163.99
Internal; fire resisting; veneered paintgrade facings; FD30; Magnet Trade										
686 x 1981 x 44mm	60.70	2.50	62.22	1.70	0.21	38.75	-	100.97	nr	111.06
762 x 1981 x 44mm	60.70	2.50	62.22	1.90	0.24	43.39	-	105.61	nr	116.17
813 x 2032 x 44mm	60.70	2.50	62.22	2.20	0.28	50.27	-	112.49	nr	123.74
838 x 1981 x 44mm	60.70	2.50	62.22	2.20	0.28	50.27	-	112.49	nr	123.74
Internal; fire resisting; veneered paintgrade facings; GO; FD30; Magnet Trade										
762 x 1981 x 44mm; pre-glazed clear wired glass aperture 450 x 450mm	168.10	2.50	172.30	1.90	0.24	43.39	-	215.69	nr	237.26
813 x 2032 x 44mm; pre-glazed clear wired glass aperture 450 x 450mm	168.10	2.50	172.30	2.20	0.29	50.43	-	222.73	nr	245.00
838 x 1981 x 44mm; pre-glazed clear wired glass aperture 450 x 450mm	168.10	2.50	172.30	2.20	0.29	50.43	-	222.73	nr	245.00
External; fire resisting; veneered paintgrade facings; FD30; Magnet Trade										
762 x 1981 x 44mm	87.00	2.50	89.17	1.90	0.24	43.39	-	132.56	nr	145.82
838 x 1981 x 44mm	87.00	2.50	89.17	2.30	0.29	52.52	-	141.69	nr	155.86

Labour hourly rates: (except Specialists) Craft Operatives 20.87 Labourer 15.57 Rates are national average prices. Refer to REGIONAL VARIATIONS for indicative levels of overall pricing in regions	MATERIALS			LABOUR				RATES		
	Del to Site £	Waste %	Material Cost £	Craft Optve Hrs	Lab Hrs	Labour Cost £	Sunds £	Nett Rate £	Unit	Gross rate (10%) £
TIMBER DOORS AND FRAMES (Cont'd)										
Flush doors (Cont'd)										
External; fire resisting; Hardwood lipped; solid core; FD60; Magnet Trade										
762 x 1981 x 44mm	145.90	2.50	149.55	2.50	0.50	59.96	-	209.51	nr	230.46
838 x 1981 x 44mm	145.90	2.50	149.55	2.70	0.55	64.91	-	214.46	nr	235.91
Panelled doors in softwood, wrought										
35mm square framed (or chamfered or moulded one or both sides)										
two panel	48.17	2.50	49.38	0.85	0.11	19.45	-	68.83	m²	75.71
four panel	48.17	2.50	49.38	0.85	0.11	19.45	-	68.83	m²	75.71
six panel	48.17	2.50	49.38	0.85	0.11	19.45	-	68.83	m²	75.71
add if upper panels open moulded in small squares for glass	43.19	2.50	44.27	-	-	-	-	44.27	m²	48.70
44mm square framed (or chamfered or moulded one or both sides)										
two panel	88.60	2.50	90.81	1.00	0.11	22.58	-	113.39	m²	124.73
four panel	88.60	2.50	90.81	1.00	0.11	22.58	-	113.39	m²	124.73
six panel	88.60	2.50	90.81	1.00	0.11	22.58	-	113.39	m²	124.73
add if upper panels open moulded in small squares for glass	43.19	2.50	44.27	-	-	-	-	44.27	m²	48.70
Panelled doors in Oak, wrought										
35mm square framed (or chamfered or moulded one or both sides)										
two panel	93.03	2.50	95.35	1.50	0.19	34.26	-	129.62	m²	142.58
four panel	93.03	2.50	95.35	1.50	0.19	34.26	-	129.62	m²	142.58
six panel	93.03	2.50	95.35	1.50	0.19	34.26	-	129.62	m²	142.58
add if upper panels open moulded in small squares for glass	43.19	2.50	44.27	-	-	-	-	44.27	m²	48.70
44mm square framed (or chamfered or moulded one or both sides)										
two panel	199.35	2.50	204.34	1.75	0.22	39.95	-	244.29	m²	268.72
four panel	199.35	2.50	204.34	1.75	0.22	39.95	-	244.29	m²	268.72
six panel	199.35	2.50	204.34	1.75	0.22	39.95	-	244.29	m²	268.72
add if upper panels open moulded in small squares for glass	43.19	2.50	44.27	-	-	-	-	44.27	m²	48.70
Panelled doors in Sapele, wrought										
38mm square framed (or chamfered or moulded one or both sides)										
two panel	310.30	2.50	318.06	1.25	0.16	28.58	-	346.64	m²	381.30
four panel	334.55	2.50	342.92	1.25	0.16	28.58	-	371.50	m²	408.65
six panel	358.80	2.50	367.77	1.25	0.16	28.58	-	396.35	m²	435.99
add if upper panels open moulded in small squares for glass	58.19	2.50	59.64	-	-	-	-	59.64	m²	65.60
50mm square framed (or chamfered or moulded one or both sides)										
two panel	334.55	2.50	342.92	1.50	0.19	34.26	-	377.18	m²	414.90
four panel	358.80	2.50	367.77	1.50	0.19	34.26	-	402.04	m²	442.24
six panel	383.05	2.50	392.63	1.50	0.19	34.26	-	426.89	m²	469.58
add if upper panels open moulded in small squares for glass	43.19	2.50	44.27	-	-	-	-	44.27	m²	48.70
Garage doors in softwood, wrought										
Side hung; framed, tongued and grooved boarded										
2134 x 1981 x 44mm overall, pair	264.16	2.50	270.76	4.10	0.51	93.51	-	364.27	nr	400.70
2134 x 2134 x 44mm overall, pair	279.16	2.50	286.14	4.25	0.53	96.95	-	383.09	nr	421.40
Up and over; framed, tongued and grooved boarded; up and over door gear										
2134 x 1981 x 44mm	755.00	2.50	773.88	8.00	1.00	182.53	-	956.41	nr	1052.05
Garage doors in Western Red Cedar, wrought										
Side hung; framed, tongued and grooved boarded										
2134 x 1981 x 44mm overall, pair	683.33	2.50	700.42	4.50	0.56	102.63	-	803.05	nr	883.36
2134 x 2134 x 44mm overall, pair	683.33	2.50	700.42	4.75	0.59	108.32	-	808.74	nr	889.61
Up and over; framed, tongued and grooved boarded; up and over door gear										
2134 x 1981 x 44mm	844.77	2.50	865.89	8.40	1.05	191.66	-	1057.55	nr	1163.30
Garage doors in Oak, wrought										
Side hung; framed, tongued and grooved boarded										
2134 x 1981 x 44mm overall, pair	1709.78	2.50	1752.53	7.15	0.90	163.23	-	1915.76	nr	2107.33
2134 x 2134 x 44mm overall, pair	1804.78	2.50	1849.90	7.40	0.95	169.23	-	2019.13	nr	2221.04
Up and over; framed, tongued and grooved boarded; up and over door gear										
2134 x 1981 x 44mm	1793.75	2.50	1838.59	12.00	1.50	273.80	-	2112.39	nr	2323.63
Folding patio doors white aluminium outside; Oak inside										
Triple glazed with Low E argon filled units, Magnet Trade, doors and frames fully finished, fixing frame to masonry with screws										
2090 x 1790mm overall	3403.00	2.50	3488.07	11.00	1.50	252.93	-	3741.00	nr	4115.10
2090 x 2390mm overall	3812.00	2.50	3907.30	12.00	1.50	273.80	-	4181.09	nr	4599.20
2090 X 3590mm overall	5649.00	2.50	5790.23	12.50	2.00	292.02	-	6082.24	nr	6690.46
Door frames in softwood, wrought										
Note										
Notwithstanding the requirements of the NRM frames shown in metres exclude bedding and pointing										
38 x 75mm jambs	3.85	2.50	3.95	0.18	0.02	4.07	0.05	8.06	m	8.87
38 x 100mm jambs	4.80	2.50	4.92	0.18	0.02	4.07	0.05	9.04	m	9.94
50 x 75mm jambs	4.75	2.50	4.87	0.20	0.03	4.64	0.05	9.56	m	10.52
50 x 100mm jambs	6.00	2.50	6.15	0.20	0.03	4.64	0.05	10.84	m	11.92
50 x 125mm jambs	7.25	2.50	7.43	0.20	0.03	4.64	0.05	12.12	m	13.33
63 x 100mm jambs	7.30	2.50	7.48	0.20	0.03	4.64	0.05	12.17	m	13.39

Labour hourly rates: (except Specialists) Craft Operatives 20.87 Labourer 15.57 Rates are national average prices. Refer to REGIONAL VARIATIONS for indicative levels of overall pricing in regions	MATERIALS			LABOUR				RATES		
	Del to Site £	Waste %	Material Cost £	Craft Optve Hrs	Lab Hrs	Labour Cost £	Sunds £	Nett Rate £	Unit	Gross rate (10%) £
TIMBER DOORS AND FRAMES (Cont'd)										
Door frames in softwood, wrought (Cont'd)										
Note (Cont'd)										
Notwithstanding the requirements of the NRM frames shown in metres exclude bedding and pointing (Cont'd)										
75 x 100mm jambs	8.50	2.50	8.71	0.22	0.03	5.06	0.07	13.84	m	15.22
75 x 113mm jambs	9.48	2.50	9.72	0.22	0.03	5.06	0.07	14.84	m	16.33
100 x 100mm jambs	11.00	2.50	11.27	0.25	0.03	5.68	0.07	17.03	m	18.73
100 x 113mm jambs	12.30	2.50	12.61	0.27	0.03	6.10	0.07	18.78	m	20.65
100 x 125mm jambs	13.50	2.50	13.84	0.27	0.03	6.10	0.07	20.01	m	22.01
113 x 113mm jambs	13.77	2.50	14.11	0.27	0.03	6.10	0.07	20.28	m	22.31
113 x 125mm jambs	15.13	2.50	15.51	0.30	0.04	6.88	0.08	22.47	m	24.72
113 x 150mm jambs	17.95	2.50	18.40	0.30	0.04	6.88	0.08	25.37	m	27.90
38 x 75mm jambs; labours -1	3.85	2.50	3.95	0.18	0.02	4.07	0.05	8.06	m	8.87
38 x 75mm jambs; labours -2	4.85	2.50	4.97	0.18	0.02	4.07	0.05	9.09	m	10.00
38 x 75mm jambs; labours -3	5.85	2.50	6.00	0.18	0.02	4.07	0.05	10.11	m	11.13
38 x 75mm jambs; labours -4	6.85	2.50	7.02	0.18	0.02	4.07	0.05	11.14	m	12.25
38 x 75mm heads	3.85	2.50	3.95	0.18	0.02	4.07	0.05	8.06	m	8.87
38 x 100mm heads	4.80	2.50	4.92	0.18	0.02	4.07	0.05	9.04	m	9.94
50 x 75mm heads	4.75	2.50	4.87	0.20	0.03	4.64	0.05	9.56	m	10.52
50 x 100mm heads	6.00	2.50	6.15	0.20	0.03	4.64	0.05	10.84	m	11.92
50 x 125mm heads	7.25	2.50	7.43	0.20	0.03	4.64	0.05	12.12	m	13.33
63 x 100mm heads	7.30	2.50	7.48	0.20	0.03	4.64	0.05	12.17	m	13.39
75 x 100mm heads	8.50	2.50	8.71	0.22	0.03	5.06	0.07	13.84	m	15.22
75 x 113mm heads	9.48	2.50	9.72	0.22	0.03	5.06	0.07	14.84	m	16.33
100 x 100mm heads	11.00	2.50	11.27	0.25	0.03	5.68	0.07	17.03	m	18.73
100 x 113mm heads	12.30	2.50	12.61	0.27	0.03	6.10	0.07	18.78	m	20.65
100 x 125mm heads	13.50	2.50	13.84	0.27	0.03	6.10	0.07	20.01	m	22.01
113 x 113mm heads	13.77	2.50	14.11	0.27	0.03	6.10	0.07	20.28	m	22.31
113 x 125mm heads	15.13	2.50	15.51	0.30	0.04	6.88	0.08	22.47	m	24.72
113 x 150mm heads	17.95	2.50	18.40	0.30	0.04	6.88	0.08	25.37	m	27.90
38 x 75mm heads; labours -1	3.85	2.50	3.95	0.18	0.02	4.07	0.05	8.06	m	8.87
38 x 75mm heads; labours -2	4.85	2.50	4.97	0.18	0.02	4.07	0.05	9.09	m	10.00
38 x 75mm heads; labours -3	5.85	2.50	6.00	0.18	0.02	4.07	0.05	10.11	m	11.13
38 x 75mm heads; labours -4	6.85	2.50	7.02	0.18	0.02	4.07	0.05	11.14	m	12.25
63 x 125mm sills	8.88	2.50	9.10	0.23	0.03	5.27	0.07	14.44	m	15.88
75 x 125mm sills	10.38	2.50	10.64	0.24	0.03	5.48	0.07	16.18	m	17.80
75 x 150mm sills	12.25	2.50	12.56	0.25	0.03	5.68	0.07	18.31	m	20.14
63 x 125mm sills; labours -1	8.88	2.50	9.10	0.23	0.03	5.27	0.07	14.44	m	15.88
63 x 125mm sills; labours -2	9.88	2.50	10.13	0.23	0.03	5.27	0.07	15.46	m	17.01
63 x 125mm sills; labours -3	10.88	2.50	11.15	0.23	0.03	5.27	0.07	16.49	m	18.13
63 x 125mm sills; labours -4	11.88	2.50	12.18	0.23	0.03	5.27	0.07	17.51	m	19.26
63 x 100mm mullions	8.30	2.50	8.51	0.05	0.01	1.20	-	9.71	m	10.68
75 x 100mm mullions	9.50	2.50	9.74	0.05	0.01	1.20	-	10.94	m	12.03
75 x 113mm mullions	10.48	2.50	10.74	0.05	0.01	1.20	-	11.94	m	13.14
100 x 100mm mullions	12.00	2.50	12.30	0.05	0.01	1.20	-	13.50	m	14.85
100 x 125mm mullions	13.30	2.50	13.63	0.05	0.01	1.20	-	14.83	m	16.31
63 x 100mm mullions; labours -1	8.30	2.50	8.51	0.05	0.01	1.20	-	9.71	m	10.68
63 x 100mm mullions; labours -2	8.30	2.50	8.51	0.05	0.01	1.20	-	9.71	m	10.68
63 x 100mm mullions; labours -3	9.30	2.50	9.53	0.05	0.01	1.20	-	10.73	m	11.80
63 x 100mm mullions; labours -4	10.30	2.50	10.56	0.05	0.01	1.20	-	11.76	m	12.93
63 x 100mm transoms	8.30	2.50	8.51	0.05	0.01	1.20	-	9.71	m	10.68
75 x 100mm transoms	9.50	2.50	9.74	0.05	0.01	1.20	-	10.94	m	12.03
75 x 113mm transoms	10.48	2.50	10.74	0.05	0.01	1.20	-	11.94	m	13.14
100 x 100mm transoms	12.00	2.50	12.30	0.05	0.01	1.20	-	13.50	m	14.85
100 x 125mm transoms	13.30	2.50	13.63	0.05	0.01	1.20	-	14.83	m	16.31
63 x 100mm transoms; labours -1	8.30	2.50	8.51	0.05	0.01	1.20	-	9.71	m	10.68
63 x 100mm transoms; labours -2	8.30	2.50	8.51	0.05	0.01	1.20	-	9.71	m	10.68
63 x 100mm transoms; labours -3	9.30	2.50	9.53	0.05	0.01	1.20	-	10.73	m	11.80
63 x 100mm transoms; labours -4	10.30	2.50	10.56	0.05	0.01	1.20	-	11.76	m	12.93
Internal door frame sets; supplied unassembled										
38 x 63mm jambs and head; stops (supplied loose); assembling										
for 686 x 1981mm doors	16.60	2.50	17.01	1.00	0.13	22.89	0.26	40.17	nr	44.19
for 762 x 1981mm doors	16.60	2.50	17.01	1.00	0.13	22.89	0.26	40.17	nr	44.19
38 x 75mm jambs and head; stops (supplied loose); assembling										
for 686 x 1981mm doors	17.90	2.50	18.35	1.00	0.13	22.89	0.26	41.51	nr	45.66
for 762 x 1981mm doors	17.90	2.50	18.35	1.00	0.13	22.89	0.26	41.51	nr	45.66
50 x 100mm jambs and head; stops (supplied loose); assembling										
for 686 x 1981mm doors	24.50	2.50	25.11	1.00	0.13	22.89	0.26	48.27	nr	53.10
for 762 x 1981mm doors	24.50	2.50	25.11	1.00	0.13	22.89	0.26	48.27	nr	53.10
50 x 113mm jambs and head; stops (supplied loose); assembling										
for 686 x 1981mm doors	27.00	2.50	27.67	1.00	0.13	22.89	0.26	50.83	nr	55.92
for 762 x 1981mm doors	27.00	2.50	27.67	1.00	0.13	22.89	0.26	50.83	nr	55.92
External door frame sets; one coat external primer before delivery to site; Bedding in cement mortar (1:3); pointing with Silicone standard mastic one side										
63 x 75mm jambs and head; rebates -1										
for 762 x 1981 x 50mm doors	44.60	2.50	46.01	1.95	0.13	42.62	0.26	88.89	nr	97.78
for 838 x 1981 x 50mm doors	44.69	2.50	46.11	1.96	0.13	42.93	0.26	89.30	nr	98.23
63 x 88mm jambs and head; rebates -1										
for 762 x 1981 x 50mm doors	49.49	2.50	51.02	1.95	0.13	42.62	0.26	93.90	nr	103.29
for 838 x 1981 x 50mm doors	49.58	2.50	51.12	1.96	0.13	42.93	0.26	94.31	nr	103.74
63 x 75mm jambs and head, rebates -1 nr; hardwood sill										
for 762 x 1981 x 50mm doors	57.15	2.50	58.92	2.35	0.16	51.47	0.33	110.72	nr	121.79
for 838 x 1981 x 50mm doors	57.33	2.50	59.11	2.38	0.16	52.12	0.33	111.56	nr	122.72
63 x 88mm jambs and head, rebates -1 nr; hardwood sill										
for 762 x 1981 x 50mm doors	61.62	2.50	63.50	2.35	0.16	51.47	0.33	115.30	nr	126.83
for 838 x 1981 x 50mm doors	61.80	2.50	63.69	2.38	0.16	52.12	0.33	116.14	nr	127.76
for 1168 x 1981 x 50mm doors	64.62	2.50	66.63	2.76	0.19	60.56	0.40	127.59	nr	140.34

Labour hourly rates: (except Specialists) Craft Operatives 20.87 Labourer 15.57 Rates are national average prices. Refer to REGIONAL VARIATIONS for indicative levels of overall pricing in regions	MATERIALS			LABOUR				RATES		
	Del to Site £	Waste %	Material Cost £	Craft Optve Hrs	Lab Hrs	Labour Cost £	Sunds £	Nett Rate £	Unit	Gross rate (10%) £
TIMBER DOORS AND FRAMES (Cont'd)										
Door frames in softwood, wrought (Cont'd)										
External garage door frame sets; one coat external primer before delivery to site; supplied unassembled; Bedding in cement mortar (1:3); pointing with Silicone standard mastic one side										
75 x 100mm jambs and head; assembling										
for 2134 x 1981mm side hung doors	126.41	2.50	129.95	3.47	0.28	76.76	0.61	207.31	nr	228.05
for 2134 x 2134mm side hung doors	126.77	2.50	130.34	3.53	0.28	78.03	0.61	208.98	nr	229.88
75 x 75mm jambs and head; assembling										
for 2134 x 1981mm up and over doors	105.57	2.50	108.59	3.47	0.28	76.76	0.61	185.96	nr	204.56
Door frames in Teak, wrought, selected for transparent finish										
Note										
Notwithstanding the requirements of the NRM frames shown in metres exclude bedding and pointing										
38 x 75mm jambs	53.77	2.50	55.11	0.31	0.04	7.09	0.08	62.29	m	68.52
38 x 100mm jambs	71.69	2.50	73.48	0.31	0.04	7.09	0.08	80.66	m	88.72
50 x 75mm jambs	70.75	2.50	72.52	0.35	0.04	7.93	0.10	80.55	m	88.60
50 x 100mm jambs	94.33	2.50	96.69	0.35	0.04	7.93	0.10	104.71	m	115.19
50 x 125mm jambs	117.92	2.50	120.87	0.35	0.04	7.93	0.10	128.89	m	141.78
63 x 100mm jambs	118.86	2.50	121.83	0.35	0.04	7.93	0.10	129.86	m	142.84
75 x 100mm jambs	141.50	2.50	145.04	0.38	0.05	8.71	0.10	153.85	m	169.23
75 x 113mm jambs	176.88	2.50	181.30	0.38	0.05	8.71	0.10	190.11	m	209.12
100 x 100mm jambs	188.37	2.50	193.08	0.44	0.05	9.96	0.12	203.16	m	223.47
100 x 113mm jambs	212.25	2.50	217.56	0.47	0.06	10.74	0.13	228.43	m	251.27
100 x 125mm jambs	237.62	2.50	243.56	0.47	0.06	10.74	0.13	254.44	m	279.88
113 x 113mm jambs	257.50	2.50	263.94	0.47	0.06	10.74	0.13	274.81	m	302.29
113 x 125mm jambs	267.44	2.50	274.13	0.52	0.07	11.94	0.15	286.22	m	314.84
113 x 150mm jambs	318.38	2.50	326.34	0.52	0.07	11.94	0.15	338.43	m	372.27
38 x 75mm jambs; labours -1	57.77	2.50	59.21	0.31	0.04	7.09	0.08	66.39	m	73.03
38 x 75mm jambs; labours -2	61.77	2.50	63.31	0.31	0.04	7.09	0.08	70.49	m	77.54
38 x 75mm jambs; labours -3	65.77	2.50	67.41	0.31	0.04	7.09	0.08	74.59	m	82.05
38 x 75mm jambs; labours -4	69.77	2.50	71.51	0.31	0.04	7.09	0.08	78.69	m	86.56
38 x 75mm heads	53.77	2.50	55.11	0.31	0.04	7.09	0.08	62.29	m	68.52
38 x 100mm heads	71.69	2.50	73.48	0.31	0.04	7.09	0.08	80.66	m	88.72
50 x 75mm heads	70.75	2.50	72.52	0.31	0.04	7.09	0.08	79.69	m	87.66
50 x 100mm heads	94.33	2.50	96.69	0.35	0.04	7.93	0.10	104.71	m	115.19
50 x 125mm heads	117.92	2.50	120.87	0.35	0.04	7.93	0.10	128.89	m	141.78
63 x 100mm heads	118.86	2.50	121.83	0.35	0.04	7.93	0.10	129.86	m	142.84
75 x 100mm heads	141.50	2.50	145.04	0.38	0.05	8.71	0.10	153.85	m	169.23
75 x 113mm heads	176.88	2.50	181.30	0.38	0.05	8.71	0.10	190.11	m	209.12
100 x 100mm heads	188.37	2.50	193.08	0.44	0.05	9.96	0.12	203.16	m	223.47
100 x 113mm heads	212.25	2.50	217.56	0.47	0.06	10.74	0.13	228.43	m	251.27
100 x 125mm heads	237.62	2.50	243.56	0.47	0.06	10.74	0.13	254.44	m	279.88
113 x 113mm heads	257.50	2.50	263.94	0.47	0.06	10.74	0.13	274.81	m	302.29
113 x 125mm heads	267.44	2.50	274.13	0.52	0.07	11.94	0.15	286.22	m	314.84
113 x 150mm heads	318.38	2.50	326.34	0.52	0.07	11.94	0.15	338.43	m	372.27
38 x 75mm heads; labours -1	57.77	2.50	59.21	0.31	0.04	7.09	0.08	66.39	m	73.03
38 x 75mm heads; labours -2	61.77	2.50	63.31	0.31	0.04	7.09	0.08	70.49	m	77.54
38 x 75mm heads; labours -3	65.77	2.50	67.41	0.31	0.04	7.09	0.08	74.59	m	82.05
38 x 75mm heads; labours -4	69.77	2.50	71.51	0.31	0.04	7.09	0.08	78.69	m	86.56
63 x 125mm sills	148.58	2.50	152.29	0.40	0.05	9.13	0.10	161.52	m	177.67
75 x 125mm sills	176.88	2.50	181.30	0.44	0.06	10.12	0.12	191.53	m	210.69
75 x 150mm sills	212.25	2.50	217.56	0.45	0.06	10.33	0.12	228.00	m	250.80
63 x 125mm sills; labours -1	152.58	2.50	156.39	0.40	0.05	9.13	0.10	165.62	m	182.18
63 x 125mm sills; labours -2	156.58	2.50	160.49	0.40	0.05	9.13	0.10	169.72	m	186.69
63 x 125mm sills; labours -3	160.58	2.50	164.59	0.40	0.05	9.13	0.10	173.82	m	191.20
63 x 125mm sills; labours -4	164.58	2.50	168.69	0.40	0.05	9.13	0.10	177.92	m	195.71
63 x 100mm mullions	118.86	2.50	121.83	0.05	0.01	1.20	-	123.03	m	135.33
75 x 100mm mullions	141.50	2.50	145.04	0.05	0.01	1.20	-	146.24	m	160.86
75 x 113mm mullions	176.88	2.50	181.30	0.05	0.01	1.20	-	182.50	m	200.75
100 x 100mm mullions	188.37	2.50	193.08	0.05	0.01	1.20	-	194.28	m	213.71
100 x 125mm mullions	237.62	2.50	243.56	0.05	0.01	1.20	-	244.76	m	269.24
63 x 100mm mullions; labours -1	122.86	2.50	125.93	0.05	0.01	1.20	-	127.13	m	139.84
63 x 100mm mullions; labours -2	126.86	2.50	130.03	0.05	0.01	1.20	-	131.23	m	144.35
63 x 100mm mullions; labours -3	130.86	2.50	134.13	0.05	0.01	1.20	-	135.33	m	148.86
63 x 100mm mullions; labours -4	134.86	2.50	138.23	0.05	0.01	1.20	-	139.43	m	153.37
63 x 100mm transoms	118.86	2.50	121.83	0.05	0.01	1.20	-	123.03	m	135.33
75 x 100mm transoms	141.50	2.50	145.04	0.05	0.01	1.20	-	146.24	m	160.86
75 x 113mm transoms	176.88	2.50	181.30	0.05	0.01	1.20	-	182.50	m	200.75
100 x 100mm transoms	188.37	2.50	193.08	0.05	0.01	1.20	-	194.28	m	213.71
100 x 125mm transoms	237.62	2.50	243.56	0.05	0.01	1.20	-	244.76	m	269.24
63 x 100mm transoms; labours -1	122.86	2.50	125.93	0.05	0.01	1.20	-	127.13	m	139.84
63 x 100mm transoms; labours -2	126.86	2.50	130.03	0.05	0.01	1.20	-	131.23	m	144.35
63 x 100mm transoms; labours -3	130.86	2.50	134.13	0.05	0.01	1.20	-	135.33	m	148.86
63 x 100mm transoms; labours -4	134.86	2.50	138.23	0.05	0.01	1.20	-	139.43	m	153.37
Door frames in Sapele, wrought, selected for transparent finish										
Note										
Notwithstanding the requirements of the NRM frames shown in metres exclude bedding and pointing										
38 x 75mm jambs	12.25	2.50	12.56	0.27	0.03	6.10	0.07	18.72	m	20.60
38 x 100mm jambs	15.67	2.50	16.06	0.27	0.03	6.10	0.07	22.23	m	24.45
50 x 75mm jambs	15.49	2.50	15.88	0.30	0.04	6.88	0.08	22.84	m	25.13
50 x 100mm jambs	19.98	2.50	20.48	0.30	0.04	6.88	0.08	27.45	m	30.19
50 x 125mm jambs	24.92	2.50	25.54	0.30	0.04	6.88	0.08	32.51	m	35.76
63 x 100mm jambs	27.78	2.50	28.47	0.30	0.04	6.88	0.08	35.44	m	38.98
75 x 100mm jambs	30.97	2.50	31.74	0.33	0.04	7.51	0.08	39.34	m	43.27
75 x 113mm jambs	37.72	2.50	38.66	0.33	0.04	7.51	0.08	46.26	m	50.88
100 x 100mm jambs	39.87	2.50	40.87	0.37	0.05	8.50	0.10	49.47	m	54.41

Labour hourly rates: (except Specialists) Craft Operatives 20.87 Labourer 15.57 Rates are national average prices. Refer to REGIONAL VARIATIONS for indicative levels of overall pricing in regions	MATERIALS			LABOUR				RATES		
	Del to Site £	Waste %	Material Cost £	Craft Optve Hrs	Lab Hrs	Labour Cost £	Sunds £	Nett Rate £	Unit	Gross rate (10%) £
TIMBER DOORS AND FRAMES (Cont'd)										
Door frames in Sapele, wrought, selected for transparent finish (Cont'd)										
Note (Cont'd)										
Notwithstanding the requirements of the NRM frames shown in metres exclude bedding and pointing (Cont'd)										
100 x 113mm jambs	45.05	2.50	46.18	0.40	0.05	9.13	0.12	55.42	m	60.96
100 x 125mm jambs	49.84	2.50	51.09	0.40	0.05	9.13	0.12	60.33	m	66.36
113 x 113mm jambs	50.91	2.50	52.18	0.40	0.05	9.13	0.12	61.42	m	67.57
113 x 125mm jambs	56.20	2.50	57.60	0.45	0.06	10.33	0.12	68.05	m	74.85
113 x 150mm jambs	67.58	2.50	69.27	0.45	0.06	10.33	0.12	79.71	m	87.68
38 x 75mm jambs; labours -1	16.25	2.50	16.66	0.27	0.03	6.10	0.07	22.82	m	25.11
38 x 75mm jambs; labours -2	20.25	2.50	20.76	0.27	0.03	6.10	0.07	26.92	m	29.62
38 x 75mm jambs; labours -3	24.25	2.50	24.86	0.27	0.03	6.10	0.07	31.02	m	34.13
38 x 75mm jambs; labours -4	28.25	2.50	28.96	0.27	0.03	6.10	0.07	35.12	m	38.64
38 x 75mm heads	12.25	2.50	12.56	0.27	0.03	6.10	0.07	18.72	m	20.60
38 x 100mm heads	15.67	2.50	16.06	0.27	0.03	6.10	0.07	22.23	m	24.45
50 x 75mm heads	15.49	2.50	15.88	0.30	0.04	6.88	0.08	22.84	m	25.13
50 x 100mm heads	19.98	2.50	20.48	0.30	0.04	6.88	0.08	27.45	m	30.19
50 x 125mm heads	24.92	2.50	25.54	0.30	0.04	6.88	0.08	32.51	m	35.76
63 x 100mm heads	27.78	2.50	28.47	0.30	0.04	6.88	0.08	35.44	m	38.98
75 x 100mm heads	30.97	2.50	31.74	0.33	0.04	7.51	0.08	39.34	m	43.27
75 x 113mm heads	37.72	2.50	38.66	0.33	0.04	7.51	0.08	46.26	m	50.88
100 x 100mm heads	39.87	2.50	40.87	0.37	0.05	8.50	0.10	49.47	m	54.41
100 x 113mm heads	45.05	2.50	46.18	0.40	0.05	9.13	0.12	55.42	m	60.96
100 x 125mm heads	49.84	2.50	51.09	0.40	0.05	9.13	0.12	60.33	m	66.36
113 x 113mm heads	50.91	2.50	52.18	0.40	0.05	9.13	0.12	61.42	m	67.57
113 x 125mm heads	56.20	2.50	57.60	0.45	0.06	10.33	0.12	68.05	m	74.85
113 x 150mm heads	67.58	2.50	69.27	0.45	0.06	10.33	0.12	79.71	m	87.68
38 x 75mm heads; labours -1	16.25	2.50	16.66	0.27	0.03	6.10	0.07	22.82	m	25.11
38 x 75mm heads; labours -2	20.25	2.50	20.76	0.27	0.03	6.10	0.07	26.92	m	29.62
38 x 75mm heads; labours -3	24.25	2.50	24.86	0.27	0.03	6.10	0.07	31.02	m	34.13
38 x 75mm heads; labours -4	28.25	2.50	28.96	0.27	0.03	6.10	0.07	35.12	m	38.64
63 x 125mm sills	32.73	2.50	33.55	0.35	0.04	7.93	0.10	41.57	m	45.73
75 x 125mm sills	38.71	2.50	39.68	0.37	0.05	8.50	0.10	48.28	m	53.10
75 x 150mm sills	46.18	2.50	47.33	0.37	0.05	8.50	0.10	55.93	m	61.53
63 x 125mm sills; labours -1	36.73	2.50	37.65	0.35	0.04	7.93	0.10	45.67	m	50.24
63 x 125mm sills; labours -2	40.73	2.50	41.75	0.35	0.04	7.93	0.10	49.77	m	54.75
63 x 125mm sills; labours -3	44.73	2.50	45.85	0.35	0.04	7.93	0.10	53.87	m	59.26
63 x 125mm sills; labours -4	48.73	2.50	49.95	0.35	0.04	7.93	0.10	57.97	m	63.77
63 x 100mm mullions	27.78	2.50	28.47	0.05	0.01	1.20	-	29.67	m	32.64
75 x 100mm mullions	32.56	2.50	33.37	0.05	0.01	1.20	-	34.57	m	38.03
75 x 113mm mullions	36.45	2.50	37.37	0.05	0.01	1.20	-	38.56	m	42.42
100 x 100mm mullions	42.53	2.50	43.59	0.05	0.01	1.20	-	44.79	m	49.27
100 x 125mm mullions	52.49	2.50	53.81	0.05	0.01	1.20	-	55.01	m	60.51
63 x 100mm mullions; labours -1	31.78	2.50	32.57	0.05	0.01	1.20	-	33.77	m	37.15
63 x 100mm mullions; labours -2	35.78	2.50	36.67	0.05	0.01	1.20	-	37.87	m	41.66
63 x 100mm mullions; labours -3	39.78	2.50	40.77	0.05	0.01	1.20	-	41.97	m	46.17
63 x 100mm mullions; labours -4	43.78	2.50	44.87	0.05	0.01	1.20	-	46.07	m	50.68
63 x 100mm transoms	27.78	2.50	28.47	0.05	0.01	1.20	-	29.67	m	32.64
75 x 100mm transoms	32.56	2.50	33.37	0.05	0.01	1.20	-	34.57	m	38.03
75 x 113mm transoms	36.45	2.50	37.37	0.05	0.01	1.20	-	38.56	m	42.42
100 x 100mm transoms	42.53	2.50	43.59	0.05	0.01	1.20	-	44.79	m	49.27
100 x 125mm transoms	52.49	2.50	53.81	0.05	0.01	1.20	-	55.01	m	60.51
63 x 100mm transoms; labours -1	31.78	2.50	32.57	0.05	0.01	1.20	-	33.77	m	37.15
63 x 100mm transoms; labours -2	35.78	2.50	36.67	0.05	0.01	1.20	-	37.87	m	41.66
63 x 100mm transoms; labours -3	39.78	2.50	40.77	0.05	0.01	1.20	-	41.97	m	46.17
63 x 100mm transoms; labours -4	43.78	2.50	44.87	0.05	0.01	1.20	-	46.07	m	50.68
Door linings in softwood, wrought										
linings; fixing to masonry with screws										
32 x 113mm	3.93	2.50	4.03	0.40	0.05	9.13	0.12	13.27	m	14.60
32 x 150mm	4.70	2.50	4.81	0.40	0.05	9.13	0.12	14.06	m	15.46
32 x 225mm	7.84	2.50	8.04	0.60	0.07	13.61	0.16	21.81	m	24.00
32 x 330mm	12.32	2.50	12.63	0.60	0.07	13.61	0.16	26.40	m	29.04
38 x 113mm	5.01	2.50	5.13	0.40	0.05	9.13	0.12	14.38	m	15.81
38 x 150mm	4.70	2.50	4.81	0.40	0.05	9.13	0.12	14.06	m	15.46
38 x 225mm	7.84	2.50	8.04	0.60	0.07	13.61	0.16	21.81	m	24.00
38 x 330mm	14.63	2.50	14.99	0.60	0.07	13.61	0.16	28.77	m	31.65
linings										
32 x 113mm; labours -1	4.31	2.50	4.42	0.20	0.02	4.49	0.07	8.97	m	9.87
32 x 113mm; labours -2	5.67	2.50	5.82	0.20	0.02	4.49	0.07	10.37	m	11.40
32 x 113mm; labours -3	7.68	2.50	7.88	0.20	0.02	4.49	0.07	12.43	m	13.67
32 x 113mm; labours -4	8.53	2.50	8.75	0.20	0.02	4.49	0.07	13.30	m	14.63
38 x 113mm; labours -1	6.71	2.50	6.88	0.20	0.02	4.49	0.07	11.43	m	12.57
38 x 113mm; labours -2	7.56	2.50	7.75	0.20	0.02	4.49	0.07	12.30	m	13.53
38 x 113mm; labours -3	8.41	2.50	8.62	0.20	0.02	4.49	0.07	13.17	m	14.49
38 x 113mm; labours -4	9.26	2.50	9.49	0.20	0.02	4.49	0.07	14.04	m	15.45
Internal door lining sets; supplied unassembled; fixing to masonry with screws										
35 x 94mm rebated linings; assembling										
for 610 x 1981mm doors	15.85	2.50	16.25	2.00	0.25	45.63	0.53	62.41	nr	68.65
for 686 x 1981mm doors	15.85	2.50	16.25	2.00	0.25	45.63	0.53	62.41	nr	68.65
for 762 x 1981mm doors	15.85	2.50	16.25	2.00	0.25	45.63	0.53	62.41	nr	68.65
35 x 144mm rebated linings; assembling										
for 610 x 1981mm doors	25.77	2.50	26.41	2.00	0.25	45.63	0.53	72.57	nr	79.83
for 686 x 1981mm doors	25.77	2.50	26.41	2.00	0.25	45.63	0.53	72.57	nr	79.83
for 762 x 1981mm doors	25.77	2.50	26.41	2.00	0.25	45.63	0.53	72.57	nr	79.83
Door linings in Oak, wrought, selected for transparent finish										
linings; fixing to masonry with screws										
32 x 113mm	33.34	2.50	34.17	0.60	0.08	13.77	0.16	48.11	m	52.92

Labour hourly rates: (except Specialists) Craft Operatives 20.87 Labourer 15.57 Rates are national average prices. Refer to REGIONAL VARIATIONS for indicative levels of overall pricing in regions	MATERIALS			LABOUR				RATES		
	Del to Site £	Waste %	Material Cost £	Craft Optve Hrs	Lab Hrs	Labour Cost £	Sunds £	Nett Rate £	Unit	Gross rate (10%) £
TIMBER DOORS AND FRAMES (Cont'd)										
Door linings in Oak, wrought, selected for transparent finish (Cont'd)										
linings; fixing to masonry with screws (Cont'd)										
32 x 150mm	45.79	2.50	46.94	0.60	0.08	13.77	0.16	60.87	m	66.96
32 x 225mm	81.61	2.50	83.65	0.90	0.11	20.50	0.25	104.39	m	114.83
32 x 330mm	91.59	2.50	93.88	0.90	0.11	20.50	0.25	114.62	m	126.08
38 x 113mm	50.82	2.50	52.09	0.60	0.08	13.77	0.16	66.02	m	72.63
38 x 150mm	60.98	2.50	62.51	0.60	0.08	13.77	0.16	76.44	m	84.09
38 x 225mm	110.13	2.50	112.89	0.90	0.11	20.50	0.25	133.63	m	146.99
38 x 330mm	121.97	2.50	125.02	0.90	0.11	20.50	0.25	145.76	m	160.34
linings										
32 x 113mm; labours -1	35.54	2.50	36.43	0.30	0.04	6.88	0.10	43.41	m	47.75
32 x 113mm; labours -2	37.74	2.50	38.68	0.30	0.04	6.88	0.10	45.67	m	50.23
32 x 113mm; labours -3	39.94	2.50	40.94	0.30	0.04	6.88	0.10	47.92	m	52.71
32 x 113mm; labours -4	42.14	2.50	43.19	0.30	0.04	6.88	0.10	50.18	m	55.20
38 x 113mm; labours -1	53.02	2.50	54.35	0.30	0.04	6.88	0.10	61.33	m	67.46
38 x 113mm; labours -2	55.22	2.50	56.60	0.30	0.04	6.88	0.10	63.58	m	69.94
38 x 113mm; labours -3	57.42	2.50	58.86	0.30	0.04	6.88	0.10	65.84	m	72.42
38 x 113mm; labours -4	59.62	2.50	61.11	0.30	0.04	6.88	0.10	68.09	m	74.90
Door linings in Sapele, wrought, selected for transparent finish										
linings; fixing to masonry with screws										
32 x 113mm	22.77	2.50	23.34	0.55	0.07	12.57	0.15	36.06	m	39.66
32 x 150mm	27.33	2.50	28.02	0.55	0.07	12.57	0.15	40.74	m	44.81
32 x 225mm	40.99	2.50	42.02	0.80	0.08	17.94	0.23	60.19	m	66.21
32 x 330mm	63.76	2.50	65.36	0.80	0.08	17.94	0.23	83.53	m	91.88
38 x 113mm	26.67	2.50	27.33	0.55	0.07	12.57	0.15	40.05	m	44.05
38 x 150mm	31.86	2.50	32.66	0.55	0.07	12.57	0.15	45.38	m	49.92
38 x 225mm	46.83	2.50	48.00	0.80	0.08	17.94	0.23	66.17	m	72.79
38 x 330mm	75.45	2.50	77.34	0.80	0.08	17.94	0.23	95.51	m	105.06
linings										
32 x 113mm; labours -1	23.17	2.50	23.75	0.27	0.03	6.10	0.07	29.92	m	32.91
32 x 113mm; labours -2	23.42	2.50	24.01	0.27	0.03	6.10	0.07	30.18	m	33.19
32 x 113mm; labours -3	23.67	2.50	24.26	0.27	0.03	6.10	0.07	30.43	m	33.48
32 x 113mm; labours -4	23.94	2.50	24.54	0.27	0.03	6.10	0.07	30.71	m	33.78
38 x 113mm; labours -1	27.07	2.50	27.74	0.27	0.03	6.10	0.07	33.91	m	37.30
38 x 113mm; labours -2	27.33	2.50	28.02	0.27	0.03	6.10	0.07	34.19	m	37.61
38 x 113mm; labours -3	27.58	2.50	28.27	0.27	0.03	6.10	0.07	34.44	m	37.89
38 x 113mm; labours -4	27.85	2.50	28.55	0.27	0.03	6.10	0.07	34.72	m	38.19
TIMBER SHUTTERS AND HATCHES										
Trap doors in softwood, wrought										
19mm matchboarding on 25 x 75mm ledges										
457 x 610mm	42.84	2.50	43.91	0.18	0.02	4.07	-	47.98	nr	52.78
610 x 610mm	52.98	2.50	54.31	0.19	0.02	4.28	-	58.59	nr	64.44
762 x 610mm	65.33	2.50	66.97	0.20	0.02	4.49	-	71.45	nr	78.60
Trap doors in B.C. Pine, wrought										
19mm matchboarding on 25 x 75mm ledges										
457 x 610mm	53.06	2.50	54.39	0.18	0.02	4.07	-	58.46	nr	64.30
610 x 610mm	75.01	2.50	76.89	0.19	0.02	4.28	-	81.16	nr	89.28
762 x 610mm	95.89	2.50	98.28	0.20	0.02	4.49	-	102.77	nr	113.05
METAL DOORS AND FRAMES										
Doors and sidelights in galvanised steel; door sets										
Steel security door with multi-point locking system; weatherstripping; fixing to masonry with lugs; Bedding in cement mortar (1:3); pointing with Silicone standard mastic one side										
850 x 2075mm door	321.71	2.50	330.10	4.03	1.45	106.62	-	436.72	nr	480.39
1025 x 2075mm door	322.27	2.50	330.71	4.32	1.60	115.09	-	445.80	nr	490.38
850 x 2075mm door with 176 x 786mm vision panel	446.71	2.50	458.22	4.03	1.45	106.62	-	564.84	nr	621.33
1025 x 2075mm door with 176 x 786mm vision panel	447.27	2.50	458.83	4.32	1.60	115.09	-	573.92	nr	631.31
Doors and sidelights in galvanised steel; polyester powder coated; white matt; door sets										
Steel security door with multi-point locking system; weatherstripping; fixing to masonry with lugs; Bedding in cement mortar (1:3); pointing with Silicone standard mastic one side										
850 x 2075mm door	421.71	2.50	432.60	4.03	1.45	106.62	-	539.22	nr	593.14
1025 x 2075mm door	422.27	2.50	433.21	4.32	1.60	115.09	-	548.30	nr	603.13
850 x 2075mm door with 176 x 786mm vision panel	546.71	2.50	560.72	4.03	1.45	106.62	-	667.34	nr	734.08
1025 x 2075mm door with 176 x 786mm vision panel	547.27	2.50	561.33	4.32	1.60	115.09	-	676.42	nr	744.06
Garage doors; Cardale Gemini II in galvanised steel; Plastisol finish by manufacturer										
Overhead garage doors; tensioning device Tracked spring counterbalanced										
fixing to timber with screws; for opening size										
2134 x 1981mm	490.83	2.50	503.10	4.00	4.00	145.76	-	648.86	nr	713.75
2134 x 2134mm	490.83	2.50	503.10	4.00	4.00	145.76	-	648.86	nr	713.75
Overhead garage doors; counterbalanced by springs										
4267 x 1981mm	1033.33	2.50	1059.17	6.00	6.00	218.64	-	1277.81	nr	1405.59
4267 x 2134mm	1033.33	2.50	1059.17	6.00	6.00	218.64	-	1277.81	nr	1405.59

Labour hourly rates: (except Specialists) Craft Operatives 20.87 Labourer 15.57 Rates are national average prices. Refer to REGIONAL VARIATIONS for indicative levels of overall pricing in regions	MATERIALS			LABOUR				RATES		
	Del to Site £	Waste %	Material Cost £	Craft Optve Hrs	Lab Hrs	Labour Cost £	Sunds £	Nett Rate £	Unit	Gross rate (10%) £
METAL SHUTTERS AND HATCHES										
Roller shutters in steel, galvanised										
Note roller shutters are always purpose made to order and the following prices are indicative only. Firm quotations should always be obtained, bedding and pointing is excluded.										
Crank handle operation 4572 x 3658mm overall; fixing to masonry with screws	1901.00	2.50	1948.52	16.00	16.00	583.04	-	2531.56	nr	2784.72
Endless hand chain operation 5486 x 4267mm overall; fixing to masonry with screws	2595.00	2.50	2659.88	20.00	20.00	728.80	-	3388.67	nr	3727.54
Electric motor operation 6096 x 6096mm overall; fixing to masonry with screws	4302.00	2.50	4409.55	30.00	30.00	1093.20	-	5502.75	nr	6053.02
Roller shutters in aluminium										
Endless hand chain operation 3553 x 3048mm overall; fixing to masonry with screws	1734.00	2.50	1777.35	20.00	20.00	728.80	-	2506.15	nr	2756.77
Note Bedding in cement mortar (1:3); pointing with Silicone standard mastic one side' is included with standard door sets as noted above; adjustment will need to be made for two part polysuphide pointing and bedding and pointing to purpose made frames etc										
Bedding and pointing frames										
Pointing with Silicone standard mastic metal frames one side	1.30	10.00	1.43	0.12	0.06	3.44	-	4.87	m	5.36
Bedding in cement mortar (1:3); pointing with Silicone standard mastic one side metal frames one side	1.62	5.00	1.76	0.20	0.10	5.73	-	7.49	m	8.24
PLASTIC DOORS & FRAMES										
Flexible doors mainly in plastics and rubber										
Standard doors; 43mm diameter steel tube frame; top and bottom plates with pivoting arrangements and spring unit; 8mm rubber panel doors with triangular perspex window in each leaf fixing to masonry; for opening size										
1800 x 2100mm	1285.40	2.50	1317.53	4.00	4.00	145.76	-	1463.29	nr	1609.62
2440 x 2400mm	1991.35	2.50	2041.13	5.00	5.00	182.20	-	2223.33	nr	2445.66
Standard doors; 43mm diameter steel tube frame; top and bottom plates with pivoting arrangements and spring unit; 12mm rubber panel doors with triangular perspex window in each leaf fixing to masonry; for opening size										
1800 x 2100mm	1131.75	2.50	1160.05	4.00	4.00	145.76	-	1305.81	nr	1436.39
2440 x 2400mm	1753.31	2.50	1797.14	5.00	5.00	182.20	-	1979.34	nr	2177.28
Standard doors; 43mm diameter steel tube frame; top and bottom plates with pivoting arrangements and spring unit; 6mm clear flexible panel doors fixing to masonry; for opening size										
1800 x 2100mm	1104.90	2.50	1132.52	3.85	3.85	140.29	-	1272.81	nr	1400.09
2440 x 2400mm	1497.75	2.50	1535.19	4.40	4.40	160.34	-	1695.53	nr	1865.08
Note Bedding in cement mortar (1:3); pointing with Silicone standard mastic one side' is included with external door sets a snoted above; adjustment will need to be made for two part polysuphide pointing and bedding and pointing to purpose made external frames										
Bedding and pointing frames										
Bedding in cement mortar (1:3); pointing one side wood frames	0.54	5.00	0.57	0.14	-	2.92	-	3.49	m	3.84
Bedding in cement mortar (1:3); pointing each side wood frames	0.72	5.00	0.76	0.20	-	4.17	-	4.93	m	5.42
Bedding in cement mortar (1:3); pointing with Silicone standard mastic one side wood frames one side	12.51	5.00	13.49	0.20	-	4.17	-	17.66	m	19.43
Flexible strip curtains mainly in pvc										
Strip curtains; 200mm wide x 2.0mm thick clear pvc strip curtains, suspended from hanging rail; fixing to masonry double maximum overlap; for opening size										
1800 x 2100mm	187.12	2.50	191.79	2.00	2.00	72.88	-	264.67	nr	291.14
2100 x 2440mm	234.91	2.50	240.78	2.30	2.30	83.81	-	324.59	nr	357.05
single minimum overlap; for opening size										
1800 x 2100mm	136.85	2.50	140.27	1.80	1.80	65.59	-	205.86	nr	226.45
2100 x 2440mm	162.69	2.50	166.76	2.10	2.10	76.52	-	243.28	nr	267.61
Strip curtains; 300mm wide x 3mm thick clear pvc strip curtains, suspended from hanging rail; fixing to masonry double maximum overlap; for opening size										
2440 x 2740mm	331.86	2.50	340.15	2.64	2.64	96.20	-	436.36	nr	479.99
2740 x 2900mm	380.73	2.50	390.25	2.94	2.94	107.13	-	497.38	nr	547.12
single minimum overlap; for opening size										
2440 x 2740mm	257.89	2.50	264.34	2.44	2.44	88.91	-	353.25	nr	388.58
2740 x 2900mm	284.77	2.50	291.89	2.74	2.74	99.85	-	391.73	nr	430.90

Labour hourly rates: (except Specialists) Craft Operatives 20.87 Labourer 15.57 Rates are national average prices. Refer to REGIONAL VARIATIONS for indicative levels of overall pricing in regions	MATERIALS			LABOUR				RATES		
	Del to Site £	Waste %	Material Cost £	Craft Optve Hrs	Lab Hrs	Labour Cost £	Sunds £	Nett Rate £	Unit	Gross rate (10%) £
PLASTIC DOORS & FRAMES (Cont'd)										
Flexible strip curtains mainly in pvc (Cont'd)										
Strip curtains; 400mm wide x 4.0mm thick clear pvc strip curtains, suspended from hanging rail; fixing to masonry										
double maximum overlap; for opening size										
2440 x 2740mm	425.92	2.50	436.56	2.90	2.90	105.68	-	542.24	nr	596.47
2740 x 2900mm	473.42	2.50	485.25	3.23	3.23	117.70	-	602.95	nr	663.25
single minimum overlap; for opening size										
2440 x 2740mm	302.10	2.50	309.65	2.68	2.68	97.66	-	407.31	nr	448.04
2740 x 2900mm	344.51	2.50	353.12	3.01	3.01	109.68	-	462.81	nr	509.09
Patio doors in uPVC; white										
Double glazed clear toughened glass, one opening leaf, fixing frame to masonry with screws; Bedding in cement mortar (1:3); pointing with silicone standard mastic one side										
1500 x 2020mm overall, including cill and vent	538.62	2.50	552.53	13.43	1.50	303.68	-	856.21	nr	941.83
1790 x 2090mm overall, including cill and vent	569.79	2.50	584.51	13.55	1.50	306.19	-	890.70	nr	979.77
2390 x 2090mm overall, including cill and vent	624.35	2.50	640.51	13.79	1.50	311.19	-	951.71	nr	1046.88
French doors in uPVC; white										
Double glazed clear toughened glass, pair opening doors; Bedding in cement mortar (1:3); pointing with silicone standard mastic one side										
1490 x 2090mm overall, including cill and vent	593.53	2.50	608.82	13.43	1.50	303.68	-	912.50	nr	1003.75
1790 x 2090mm overall, including cill and vent	617.66	2.50	633.58	13.55	1.50	306.19	-	939.77	nr	1033.74
2090 x 2090mm overall, including cill; side panel and vent	766.63	2.50	786.32	15.67	2.00	358.21	-	1144.53	nr	1258.99
2400 x 2090mm overall; including cill, pair of side panels and vent	887.11	2.50	909.85	15.79	2.00	360.72	-	1270.57	nr	1397.62
PLASTIC SHUTTERS AND HATCHES										
Loft hatch door and frame: insulated white plastic; hinged; lock										
Sets										
686 x 856 overall fitting	24.99	2.50	25.62	1.00	0.15	23.21	-	48.82	nr	53.70
GLASS DOORS										
Glass doors; glass, BS 952, toughened clear, polished plate; fittings finish BMA, satin chrome or polished chrome; prices include the provision of floor springs but exclude handles										
8mm thick										
750mm wide x 2150mm high	433.00	-	433.00	9.00	9.00	327.96	-	760.96	nr	837.06
762mm wide x 2134mm high	433.00	-	433.00	9.00	9.00	327.96	-	760.96	nr	837.06
800mm wide x 2150mm high	447.00	-	447.00	9.00	9.00	327.96	-	774.96	nr	852.46
838mm wide x 2134mm high	447.00	-	447.00	9.00	9.00	327.96	-	774.96	nr	852.46
850mm wide x 2150mm high	458.00	-	458.00	9.00	9.00	327.96	-	785.96	nr	864.56
900mm wide x 2150mm high	458.00	-	458.00	9.00	9.00	327.96	-	785.96	nr	864.56
914mm wide x 2134mm high	732.00	-	732.00	9.00	9.00	327.96	-	1059.96	nr	1165.96
950mm wide x 2150mm high	732.00	-	732.00	10.00	10.00	364.40	-	1096.40	nr	1206.04
1000mm wide x 2150mm high	732.00	-	732.00	10.00	10.00	364.40	-	1096.40	nr	1206.04
1100mm wide x 2150mm high	732.00	-	732.00	11.00	11.00	400.84	-	1132.84	nr	1246.12
1200mm wide x 2150mm high	732.00	-	732.00	11.00	11.00	400.84	-	1132.84	nr	1246.12
12mm thick										
750mm wide x 2150mm high	475.80	-	475.80	9.00	9.00	327.96	-	803.76	nr	884.14
762mm wide x 2134mm high	475.80	-	475.80	9.00	9.00	327.96	-	803.76	nr	884.14
800mm wide x 2150mm high	490.07	-	490.07	9.00	9.00	327.96	-	818.03	nr	899.83
838mm wide x 2134mm high	499.00	-	499.00	9.00	9.00	327.96	-	826.96	nr	909.66
850mm wide x 2150mm high	504.34	-	504.34	9.00	9.00	327.96	-	832.30	nr	915.53
900mm wide x 2150mm high	518.60	-	518.60	9.00	9.00	327.96	-	846.56	nr	931.22
914mm wide x 2134mm high	783.22	-	783.22	9.00	9.00	327.96	-	1111.18	nr	1222.30
950mm wide x 2150mm high	795.78	-	795.78	10.00	10.00	364.40	-	1160.18	nr	1276.20
1000mm wide x 2150mm high	810.04	-	810.04	10.00	10.00	364.40	-	1174.44	nr	1291.88
1100mm wide x 2150mm high	838.58	-	838.58	11.00	11.00	400.84	-	1239.42	nr	1363.36
1200mm wide x 2150mm high	867.11	-	867.11	11.00	11.00	400.84	-	1267.95	nr	1394.74
ASSOCIATED IRONMONGERY										
Intumescent strips and smoke seals										
white self adhesive										
10 x 4mm intumescent strip, half hour application; setting into groove in timber frame or door	0.61	10.00	0.68	0.15	-	3.13	-	3.81	m	4.19
20 x 4mm intumescent strip, one hour application; setting into groove in timber frame or door	1.09	10.00	1.20	0.15	-	3.13	-	4.33	m	4.76
15 x 4mm intumescent strip with integral cold smoke seal, half hour application; setting into groove in timber frame or door	0.95	10.00	1.04	0.15	-	3.13	-	4.17	m	4.59
20 x 4mm intumescent strip with integral cold smoke seal, one hour application; setting into groove in timber frame or door	1.19	10.00	1.30	0.15	-	3.13	-	4.44	m	4.88
12 x 3mm intumescent strip, half hour application; fixing to both sides of glass behind glazing beads	0.80	10.00	0.88	0.30	-	6.26	-	7.14	m	7.85
Lorient Polyproducts Ltd; System 36 Plus										
15 x 12mm glazing channel to suit 9-11mm glass; fitting over the edge of the pane	7.24	10.00	7.97	0.15	-	3.13	-	11.10	m	12.21
Lorient Polyproducts Ltd; System 90 Plus										
27 x 27mm glazing channel reference LG2727; fitting over the edge of the pane	9.47	10.00	10.42	0.15	-	3.13	-	13.55	m	14.90
intumescent lining reference LX5402 to suit 54mm thick doors; fixing to timber with adhesive	8.94	10.00	9.83	0.30	-	6.26	-	16.09	m	17.70

Labour hourly rates: (except Specialists) Craft Operatives 20.87 Labourer 15.57 Rates are national average prices. Refer to REGIONAL VARIATIONS for indicative levels of overall pricing in regions	MATERIALS			LABOUR				RATES		
	Del to Site £	Waste %	Material Cost £	Craft Optve Hrs	Lab Hrs	Labour Cost £	Sunds £	Nett Rate £	Unit	Gross rate (10%) £
ASSOCIATED IRONMONGERY (Cont'd)										
Intumescent strips and smoke seals (Cont'd)										
Mann McGowan Fabrications Ltd										
Pyroglaze 30 half hour application; fixing to both sides of glass behind glazing beads	1.29	10.00	1.41	0.35	-	7.30	-	8.72	m	9.59
Pyroglaze 60 one hour application; fixing to both sides of glass behind glazing beads	4.81	10.00	5.30	0.35	-	7.30	-	12.60	m	13.86

STAIRS, WALKWAYS AND BALUSTRADES

Labour hourly rates: (except Specialists) Craft Operatives 20.87 Labourer 15.57 Rates are national average prices. Refer to REGIONAL VARIATIONS for indicative levels of overall pricing in regions	MATERIALS			LABOUR				RATES		
	Del to Site £	Waste %	Material Cost £	Craft Optve Hrs	Lab Hrs	Labour Cost £	Sunds £	Nett Rate £	Unit	Gross rate (10%) £
TIMBER STAIRCASES										
Stairs in softwood, wrought										
Straight flight staircase and balustrade; 22mm MDF treads; 22mm MDF risers, glued; wedged and blocked; 32mm strings; 75 x 75mm newels; square balusters; 38 x 75mm hardwood handrail										
855mm wide x 2600mm rise overall; balustrade to one side; fixing to masonry with screws	584.58	2.50	599.19	15.00	1.90	342.63	3.96	945.78	nr	1040.36
855mm wide x 2600mm rise overall with 3 nr winders at bottom; balustrade to one side; fixing to masonry with screws	727.73	2.50	745.93	20.00	2.50	456.33	5.36	1207.61	nr	1328.38
855mm wide x 2600mm rise overall with 3 nr winders at top; balustrade to one side; fixing to masonry with screws	754.16	2.50	773.02	20.00	2.50	456.33	5.36	1234.70	nr	1358.17
Balustrades in softwood, wrought										
Isolated balustrades; 32 x 32mm square balusters at 150mm centres; housed construction (handrail included elsewhere)										
914mm high; fixing to timber with screws	8.97	2.50	9.19	0.80	0.10	18.25	0.21	27.66	m	30.43
Isolated balustrades; 41 x 41mm square balusters at 150mm centres; housed construction (handrail included elsewhere)										
914mm high; fixing to timber with screws	10.40	2.50	10.66	1.15	0.14	26.18	0.31	37.16	m	40.87
Isolated balustrades; 41 x 41mm Edwardian moulded balusters at 150mm centres; housed construction (handrail included elsewhere)										
914mm high; fixing to timber with screws	13.27	2.50	13.61	1.30	0.16	29.62	0.35	43.57	m	47.93
Isolated balustrades; 32 x 32mm square balusters at 150mm centres; moulded baserail and handrail; housed construction										
914mm high; fixing to timber with screws	22.59	2.50	23.16	1.20	0.15	27.38	0.33	50.87	m	55.96
extra; ramps	53.77	2.50	55.11	1.10	0.14	25.14	0.30	80.55	nr	88.60
extra; wreaths	107.53	2.50	110.22	2.15	0.27	49.07	0.58	159.87	nr	175.85
extra; bends	53.77	2.50	55.11	0.70	0.09	16.01	0.18	71.31	nr	78.44
Isolated balustrades; 41 x 41mm square balusters at 150mm centres; moulded baserail and handrail; housed construction										
914mm high; fixing to timber with screws	24.07	2.50	24.67	1.55	0.19	35.31	0.41	60.39	m	66.42
extra; ramps	53.77	2.50	55.11	1.10	0.14	25.14	0.30	80.55	nr	88.60
extra; wreaths	107.53	2.50	110.22	2.15	0.27	49.07	0.58	159.87	nr	175.85
extra; bends	53.77	2.50	55.11	0.70	0.09	16.01	0.18	71.31	nr	78.44
Isolated balustrades; 41 x 41mm moulded balusters at 150mm centres; moulded baserail and handrail; housed construction										
914mm high; fixing to timber with screws	27.01	2.50	27.68	1.75	0.22	39.95	0.46	68.09	m	74.90
extra; ramps	53.77	2.50	55.11	1.10	0.14	25.14	0.30	80.55	nr	88.60
extra; wreaths	107.52	2.50	110.20	2.15	0.27	49.07	0.58	159.86	nr	175.84
extra; bends	53.77	2.50	55.11	0.70	0.09	16.01	0.18	71.31	nr	78.44
Balustrades in European Oak, wrought, selected for transparent finish										
Isolated balustrades; 41 x 41mm square balusters at 150mm centres; moulded baserail and handrail; housed construction										
914mm high; fixing to timber with screws	86.82	2.50	88.99	2.60	0.26	58.31	0.68	147.98	m	162.77
extra; ramps	129.37	2.50	132.61	1.80	0.23	41.15	0.48	174.23	nr	191.66
extra; wreaths	258.62	2.50	265.08	3.60	0.45	82.14	0.97	348.19	nr	383.01
extra; bends	129.37	2.50	132.61	1.30	0.16	29.62	0.35	162.58	nr	178.83
Isolated balustrades; 50 x 50mm moulded balusters at 150mm centres; moulded baserail and handrail handrail; housed construction										
914mm high; fixing to timber with screws	106.28	2.50	108.93	3.00	0.38	68.53	0.81	178.27	m	196.09
extra; ramps	129.37	2.50	132.61	1.80	0.23	41.15	0.48	174.23	nr	191.66
extra; wreaths	258.62	2.50	265.08	3.60	0.45	82.14	0.97	348.19	nr	383.01
extra; bends	129.37	2.50	132.61	1.30	0.16	29.62	0.35	162.58	nr	178.83
Handrails in softwood, wrought										
Associated handrails										
44mm mopstick; fixing through metal backgrounds with screws										
handrail	4.75	5.00	4.99	0.40	0.05	9.13	0.10	14.21	m	15.63
extra; ramps	49.93	5.00	52.43	1.20	0.15	27.38	0.33	80.14	nr	88.15
extra; wreaths	99.85	5.00	104.84	2.40	0.30	54.76	0.64	160.24	nr	176.27
extra; bends	49.93	5.00	52.43	1.20	0.15	27.38	0.33	80.14	nr	88.15
94 x 34mm; Pigs Ear wall rails; fixing with screws										
handrail	6.18	5.00	6.49	0.50	0.06	11.37	0.13	17.99	m	19.79
extra; ramps	73.95	5.00	77.65	1.45	0.18	33.06	0.40	111.11	nr	122.22
extra; wreaths	147.92	5.00	155.32	2.90	0.36	66.13	0.78	222.22	nr	244.44
extra; bends	73.95	5.00	77.65	1.45	0.18	33.06	0.40	111.11	nr	122.22

Labour hourly rates: (except Specialists) Craft Operatives 20.87 Labourer 15.57 Rates are national average prices. Refer to REGIONAL VARIATIONS for indicative levels of overall pricing in regions	MATERIALS			LABOUR				RATES		
	Del to Site £	Waste %	Material Cost £	Craft Optve Hrs	Lab Hrs	Labour Cost £	Sunds £	Nett Rate £	Unit	Gross rate (10%) £
TIMBER STAIRCASES (Cont'd)										
Handrails in African Mahogany, wrought, selected for transparent finish										
Associated handrails										
50mm mopstick; fixing through metal backgrounds with screws										
handrail	21.52	5.00	22.60	0.60	0.08	13.77	0.16	36.53	m	40.18
extra; ramps	56.74	5.00	59.58	1.80	0.23	41.15	0.48	101.20	nr	111.32
extra; wreaths	113.46	5.00	119.13	3.60	0.45	82.14	0.97	202.24	nr	222.47
extra; bends	56.74	5.00	59.58	1.80	0.23	41.15	0.48	101.20	nr	111.32
75 x 100mm; moulded; fixing through metal backgrounds with screws										
handrail	52.53	5.00	55.16	0.70	0.09	16.01	0.18	71.35	m	78.48
extra; ramps	84.05	5.00	88.25	2.15	0.27	49.07	0.58	137.90	nr	151.69
extra; wreaths	168.08	5.00	176.48	4.30	0.54	98.15	1.15	275.79	nr	303.37
extra; bends	84.05	5.00	88.25	2.15	0.27	49.07	0.58	137.90	nr	151.69
Handrails in European Oak, wrought, selected for transparent finish										
Associated handrails										
44mm mopstick; fixing through metal backgrounds with screws										
handrail	19.04	5.00	19.99	0.60	0.08	13.77	0.16	33.92	m	37.31
extra; ramps	72.80	5.00	76.44	1.80	0.23	41.15	0.48	118.06	nr	129.87
extra; wreaths	145.57	5.00	152.85	3.60	0.45	82.14	0.97	235.96	nr	259.55
extra; bends	72.80	5.00	76.44	1.80	0.23	41.15	0.48	118.06	nr	129.87
94 x 34mm; Pigs Ear wall rail; fixing with screws										
handrail	26.18	5.00	27.49	0.70	0.09	16.01	0.18	43.68	m	48.05
extra; ramps	84.05	5.00	88.25	2.15	0.27	49.07	0.58	137.90	nr	151.69
extra; wreaths	168.08	5.00	176.48	4.30	0.54	98.15	1.15	275.79	nr	303.37
extra; bends	84.05	5.00	88.25	2.15	0.26	48.92	0.58	137.75	nr	151.52
METAL STAIRCASES										
Staircases in steel										
Straight flight staircases; 180 x 10mm flat stringers, shaped ends to top and bottom; 6 x 250mm on plain raised pattern plate treads, with 50 x 50 x 6mm shelf angles and 40 x 40 x 6mm stiffening bars, bolted to stringers; welded, cleated and bolted connections										
770mm wide x 3000mm going x 2600mm rise overall; fixing to masonry with 4 nr Rawlbolts	-	-	Specialist	-	-	Specialist	-	2945.75	nr	3240.32
920mm wide x 3000mm going x 2600mm rise overall; fixing to masonry with 4 nr Rawlbolts	-	-	Specialist	-	-	Specialist	-	3116.16	nr	3427.78
Straight flight staircases, 180 x 10mm flat stringers, shaped ends to top and bottom; 6 x 250mm tray treads, with three 6mm diameter reinforcing bars welded to inside, and 50 x 50 x 6mm shelf angles, bolted to stringers; welded, cleated and bolted connections										
770mm wide x 3000mm going x 2600mm rise overall; fixing to masonry with 4 nr Rawlbolts	-	-	Specialist	-	-	Specialist	-	2791.56	nr	3070.72
920mm wide x 3000mm going x 2600mm rise overall; fixing to masonry with 4 nr Rawlbolts	-	-	Specialist	-	-	Specialist	-	2888.94	nr	3177.83
Straight flight staircases; 178 x 76mm channel stringers, shaped ends to top and bottom; 6 x 250mm on plain raised pattern plate treads, with 50 x 50 x 6mm shelf angles and 40 x 40 x 6mm stiffening bars, bolted to stringers; welded, cleated and bolted connections										
770mm wide x 3000mm going x 2600mm rise overall; fixing to masonry with 4 nr Rawlbolts	-	-	Specialist	-	-	Specialist	-	3189.20	nr	3508.11
920mm wide x 3000mm going x 2600mm rise overall; fixing to masonry with 4 nr Rawlbolts	-	-	Specialist	-	-	Specialist	-	3635.52	nr	3999.07
Straight flight staircases and balustrades; 180 x 10mm flat stringers, shaped ends to top and bottom; 6 x 250mm on plain raised pattern plate treads with 50 x 50 x 6mm shelf angles and 40 x 40 x 6mm stiffening bars, bolted to stringers; 915mm high balustrade to both sides consisting of 25mm diameter solid bar handrail and 32mm diameter solid bar standards at 250mm centres with base plate welded on and bolted to face of stringer, and ball type joints at intersections; welded, cleated and bolted connections										
770mm wide x 3000mm going x 2600mm rise overall; fixing to masonry with 4 nr Rawlbolts	-	-	Specialist	-	-	Specialist	-	4284.72	nr	4713.19
Straight flight staircases and balustrades; 180 x 10mm flat stringers, shaped ends to top and bottom; 6 x 250mm on plain raised pattern plate treads with 50 x 50 x 6mm shelf angles and 40 x 40 x 6mm stiffening bars, bolted to stringers; 915mm high balustrade to both sides consisting of 25mm diameter solid bar handrail and 32mm diameter solid bar standards at 250mm centres with base plate welded on and bolted to top of stringer, and ball type joints at intersections; welded, cleated and bolted connections										
770mm wide x 3000mm going x 2600mm rise overall; fixing to masonry with 4 nr Rawlbolts	-	-	Specialist	-	-	Specialist	-	4284.72	nr	4713.19

Labour hourly rates: (except Specialists) Craft Operatives 20.87 Labourer 15.57 Rates are national average prices. Refer to REGIONAL VARIATIONS for indicative levels of overall pricing in regions	MATERIALS			LABOUR				RATES		
	Del to Site £	Waste %	Material Cost £	Craft Optve Hrs	Lab Hrs	Labour Cost £	Sunds £	Nett Rate £	Unit	Gross rate (10%) £
METAL STAIRCASES (Cont'd)										
Staircases in steel (Cont'd)										
Straight flight staircases and balustrades; 180 x 10mm flat stringers, shaped ends to top and bottom; 6 x 250mm on plain raised pattern plate treads with 50 x 50 x 6mm shelf angles and 40 x 40 x 6mm stiffening bars, bolted to stringers; 915mm high balustrade to one side consisting of 25mm diameter solid bar handrail and 32mm diameter solid bar standards at 250mm centres with base plate welded on and bolted to face of stringer, and ball type joints at intersections; welded, cleated and bolted connections										
770mm wide x 3000mm going x 2600mm rise overall; fixing to masonry with 4 nr Rawlbolts	-	-	Specialist	-	-	Specialist	-	3992.58	nr	4391.84
Straight flight staircases and balustrades; 180 x 10mm flat stringers, shaped ends to top and bottom; 6 x 250mm on plain raised pattern plate treads with 50 x 50 x 6mm shelf angles and 40 x 40 x 6mm stiffening bars, bolted to stringers; 915mm high balustrade to one side consisting of 25mm diameter solid bar handrail and 32mm diameter solid bar standards at 250mm centres with base plate welded on and bolted to top of stringer, and ball type joints at intersections; welded, cleated and bolted connections										
770mm wide x 3000mm going x 2600mm rise overall; fixing to masonry with 4 nr Rawlbolts	-	-	Specialist	-	-	Specialist	-	3992.58	nr	4391.84
Straight flight staircases and balustrades; 180 x 10mm flat stringers, shaped ends to top and bottom; 6 x 250mm on plain raised pattern plate treads with 50 x 50 x 6mm shelf angles and 40 x 40 x 6mm stiffening bars, bolted to stringers; 1070mm high balustrade to both sides consisting of 25mm diameter solid bar handrail and 32mm diameter solid bar standards at 250mm centres with base plate welded on and bolted to top of stringer, and ball type joints at intersections; welded, cleated and bolted connections										
770mm wide x 3000mm going x 2600mm rise overall; fixing to masonry with 4 nr Rawlbolts	-	-	Specialist	-	-	Specialist	-	4325.29	nr	4757.82
Straight flight staircases and balustrades; 180 x 10mm flat stringers, shaped ends to top and bottom; 6 x 250mm on plain raised pattern plate treads with 50 x 50 x 6mm shelf angles and 40 x 40 x 6mm stiffening bars, bolted to stringers; 1070mm high balustrade to one side consisting of 25mm diameter solid bar handrail and 32mm diameter solid bar standards at 250mm centres with base plate welded on and bolted to top of stringer, and ball type joints at intersections; welded, cleated and bolted connections										
770mm wide x 3000mm going x 2600mm rise overall; fixing to masonry with 4 nr Rawlbolts	-	-	Specialist	-	-	Specialist	-	4033.16	nr	4436.47
Straight flight staircases and balustrades; 180 x 10mm flat stringers, shaped ends to top and bottom; 6 x 250mm on plain raised pattern plate treads with 50 x 50 x 6mm shelf angles and 40 x 40 x 6mm stiffening bars, bolted to stringers; 915mm high balustrade to one side consisting of 25mm diameter solid bar handrail and intermediate rail, and 32mm diameter solid bar standards at 250mm centres with base plate welded on and bolted to top of stringer, and ball type joints at intersections										
770mm wide x 3000mm going x 2600mm rise overall; fixing to masonry with 4 nr Rawlbolts	-	-	Specialist	-	-	Specialist	-	4000.70	nr	4400.76
Straight flight staircases and balustrades; 180 x 10mm flat stringers, shaped ends to top and bottom; 6 x 250mm on plain raised pattern plate treads with 50 x 50 x 6mm shelf angles and 40 x 40 x 6mm stiffening bars, bolted to stringers; 1070mm high balustrade to one side consisting of 25mm diameter solid bar handrail and intermediate rail, and 32mm diameter solid bar standards at 250mm centres with base plate welded on and bolted to top of stringer, and ball type joints at intersections										
770mm wide x 3000mm going x 2600mm rise overall; fixing to masonry with 4 nr Rawlbolts	-	-	Specialist	-	-	Specialist	-	4033.16	nr	4436.47
Quarter landing staircases, in two flights; 180 x 10mm flat stringers, shaped ends to top and bottom; 6 x 250mm on plain raised pattern plate treads, with 50 x 50 x 6mm shelf angles and 40 x 40 x 6mm stiffening bars, bolted to stringers; 6mm on plain raised pattern plate landing, welded on; 100 x 8mm flat kicking plates welded on; welded, cleated and bolted connections										
770mm wide x 2000mm going first flight excluding landing x 1000mm going second flight excluding landing x 2600mm rise overall; 770 x 770mm landing overall; fixing to masonry with 4 nr Rawlbolts	-	-	Specialist	-	-	Specialist	-	6443.31	nr	7087.64
920mm wide x 2000mm going first flight excluding landing x 1000mm going second flight excluding landing x 2600mm rise overall; 920 x 920mm landing overall; fixing to masonry with 4 nr Rawlbolts	-	-	Specialist	-	-	Specialist	-	6767.91	nr	7444.70

Labour hourly rates: (except Specialists) Craft Operatives 20.87 Labourer 15.57 Rates are national average prices. Refer to REGIONAL VARIATIONS for indicative levels of overall pricing in regions	MATERIALS			LABOUR				RATES		
	Del to Site £	Waste %	Material Cost £	Craft Optve Hrs	Lab Hrs	Labour Cost £	Sunds £	Nett Rate £	Unit	Gross rate (10%) £
METAL STAIRCASES (Cont'd)										
Staircases in steel (Cont'd)										
Half landing staircases, in two flights; 180 x 10mm flat stringers, shaped ends to top and bottom; 6 x 250mm on plain raised pattern plate treads, with 50 x 50 x 6mm shelf angles and 40 x 40 x 6mm stiffening bars, bolted to stringers; 6mm on plain raised pattern plate landing, welded on; 100 x 8mm flat kicking plates welded on; welded, cleated and bolted connections										
770mm wide x 2000mm going first flight excluding landing x 1000mm going second flight excluding landing x 2600mm rise overall; 770 x 1640mm landing overall; fixing to masonry with 4 nr Rawlbolts	-	-	Specialist	-	-	Specialist	-	7222.35	nr	7944.59
920mm wide x 2000mm going first flight excluding landing x 1000mm going second flight excluding landing x 2600mm rise overall; 920 x 1940mm landing overall; fixing to masonry with 4 nr Rawlbolts	-	-	Specialist	-	-	Specialist	-	8196.15	nr	9015.77
Balustrades in steel										
Isolated balustrades; 6 x 38mm flat core rail; 13mm diameter balusters at 250mm centres; welded fabrication ground to smooth finish; casting into mortices in concrete; wedging in position; temporary wedges										
838mm high; level										
balustrade	181.36	2.50	185.89	1.00	0.50	28.66	-	214.55	m	236.00
extra; ramps	32.15	2.50	32.96	1.00	0.50	28.66	-	61.61	nr	67.78
extra; wreaths	53.53	2.50	54.87	2.00	1.00	57.31	-	112.18	nr	123.39
extra; bends	29.19	2.50	29.92	1.00	0.50	28.66	-	58.57	nr	64.43
838mm high; raking										
balustrade	188.39	2.50	193.10	1.25	0.65	36.21	-	229.31	m	252.24
914mm high; level										
balustrade	184.31	2.50	188.92	1.00	0.50	28.66	-	217.57	m	239.33
extra; ramps	32.69	2.50	33.50	1.00	0.50	28.66	-	62.16	nr	68.37
extra; wreaths	54.63	2.50	55.99	2.00	1.00	57.31	-	113.30	nr	124.63
extra; bends	29.81	2.50	30.56	1.00	0.50	28.66	-	59.21	nr	65.13
914mm high; raking										
balustrade	215.87	2.50	221.26	1.25	0.65	36.21	-	257.47	m	283.22
Isolated balustrades; 6 x 38mm flat core rail; 13 x 13mm balusters at 250mm centres; welded fabrication ground to smooth finish; casting into mortices in concrete; wedging in position; temporary wedges										
838mm high; level	190.48	2.50	195.24	1.00	0.50	28.66	-	223.89	m	246.28
838mm high; raking	196.93	2.50	201.86	1.00	0.50	28.66	-	230.51	m	253.56
914mm high; level	206.91	2.50	212.09	1.00	0.50	28.66	-	240.74	m	264.82
914mm high; raking	220.74	2.50	226.25	1.00	0.50	28.66	-	254.91	m	280.40
Isolated balustrades; 13 x 51mm rounded handrail; 13mm diameter balusters at 250mm centres; welded fabrication ground to smooth finish; casting into mortices in concrete; wedging in position; temporary wedges										
838mm high; level										
balustrade	220.54	2.50	226.06	1.00	0.50	28.66	-	254.71	m	280.18
extra; ramps	35.32	2.50	36.21	1.00	0.50	28.66	-	64.86	nr	71.35
extra; wreaths	58.77	2.50	60.24	2.00	1.00	57.31	-	117.55	nr	129.30
extra; bends	31.86	2.50	32.66	1.00	0.50	28.66	-	61.31	nr	67.44
838mm high; raking										
balustrade	224.57	2.50	230.19	1.00	0.50	28.66	-	258.84	m	284.73
914mm high; level										
balustrade	234.17	2.50	240.03	1.00	0.50	28.66	-	268.68	m	295.55
extra; ramps	35.32	2.50	36.21	1.00	0.50	28.66	-	64.86	nr	71.35
extra; wreaths	58.77	2.50	60.24	2.00	1.00	57.31	-	117.55	nr	129.30
extra; bends	31.86	2.50	32.66	1.00	0.50	28.66	-	61.31	nr	67.44
914mm high; raking										
balustrade	243.86	2.50	249.96	1.00	0.50	28.66	-	278.62	m	306.48
Isolated balustrades; 6 x 38mm flat core rail; 10 x 51mm flat bottom rail; 13mm diameter infill balusters at 250mm centres; 25 x 25mm standards at 3000mm centres; welded fabrication ground to smooth finish; casting into mortices in concrete; wedging in position; temporary wedges										
838mm high; level										
balustrade	243.77	2.50	249.86	1.00	0.50	28.66	-	278.52	m	306.37
extra; ramps	60.45	2.50	61.96	1.00	0.50	28.66	-	90.62	nr	99.68
extra; wreaths	75.49	2.50	77.38	2.00	1.00	57.31	-	134.69	nr	148.16
extra; bends	53.53	2.50	54.87	1.00	0.50	28.66	-	83.52	nr	91.87
838mm high; raking										
balustrade	252.12	2.50	258.42	1.00	0.50	28.66	-	287.08	m	315.78
914mm high; level										
balustrade	267.76	2.50	274.46	1.00	0.50	28.66	-	303.11	m	333.42
extra; ramps	60.45	2.50	61.96	1.00	0.50	28.66	-	90.62	nr	99.68
extra; wreaths	75.49	2.50	77.38	2.00	1.00	57.31	-	134.69	nr	148.16
extra; bends	53.53	2.50	54.87	1.00	0.50	28.66	-	83.52	nr	91.87
Balustrades in steel tubing, BS EN 10255;, medium grade; galvanised after fabrication										
Isolated balustrades; 40mm diameter handrails; 40mm diameter standards at 1500mm centres; welded fabrication ground to smooth finish; casting into mortices in concrete; wedging in position; temporary wedges										
838mm high; level	113.92	2.50	116.77	0.75	0.40	21.88	-	138.65	m	152.51
838mm high; raking	122.08	2.50	125.13	0.75	0.40	21.88	-	147.01	m	161.71
914mm high; level	121.98	2.50	125.03	0.75	0.40	21.88	-	146.91	m	161.60

Labour hourly rates: (except Specialists) Craft Operatives 20.87 Labourer 15.57 Rates are national average prices. Refer to REGIONAL VARIATIONS for indicative levels of overall pricing in regions	MATERIALS			LABOUR				RATES		
	Del to Site £	Waste %	Material Cost £	Craft Optve Hrs	Lab Hrs	Labour Cost £	Sunds £	Nett Rate £	Unit	Gross rate (10%) £
METAL STAIRCASES (Cont'd)										
Balustrades in steel tubing, BS EN 10255;, medium grade; galvanised after fabrication (Cont'd)										
Isolated balustrades; 40mm diameter handrails; 40mm diameter standards at 1500mm centres; welded fabrication ground to smooth finish; casting into mortices in concrete; wedging in position; temporary wedges (Cont'd)										
914mm high; raking	130.14	2.50	133.39	0.75	0.40	21.88	-	155.27	m	170.80
Isolated balustrades; 40mm diameter handrails; 40mm diameter standards at 1500mm centres, with 6 x 75mm diameter fixing plates welded on to end, holes -3 nr; welded fabrication ground to smooth finish; fixing to masonry with Rawlbolts										
838mm high; level	130.04	2.50	133.29	1.00	0.50	28.66	-	161.95	m	178.14
838mm high; raking	138.39	2.50	141.85	1.00	0.50	28.66	-	170.51	m	187.56
914mm high; level	154.85	2.50	158.72	1.00	0.50	28.66	-	187.38	m	206.11
914mm high; raking	170.93	2.50	175.21	1.00	0.50	28.66	-	203.86	m	224.25
Spiral staircases in steel										
Domestic spiral staircases powder coated grey before delivery to site; comprising tread modules complete with centre column, tread support, metal tread, tread baluster, handrail section, PVC handrail cover, landing platform and with attachment brackets for fixing to floor and newel extending from centre column; assembling and bolting together										
1600mm diameter; for floor to floor height units between 2400mm and 2640mm; fixing base and ground plates to timber										
Spiral staircase	1264.17	2.50	1295.77	30.00	15.00	859.65	-	2155.42	nr	2370.97
extra; additional tread modules, 180 - 220mm per rise	150.00	2.50	153.75	1.50	0.75	42.98	-	196.73	nr	216.41
extra; riser bars; set of 11nr.	160.00	2.50	164.00	8.80	4.40	252.16	-	416.16	nr	457.78
extra; riser bars; single	16.00	2.50	16.40	0.80	0.40	22.92	-	39.32	nr	43.26
stairwell balustrading to match staircase including PVC handrail cover	150.00	2.50	153.75	1.75	0.90	50.54	-	204.29	m	224.71
Exterior spiral staircases; galvanised; comprising profiled perforated treads complete with centre core, spacers, baluster bar and section of handrail, tread riser bars and standard landing with balustrade one side, bars at 115mm centres; assembling and bolting together										
1600mm diameter; ground to first floor assembly, with base and ground plates; for floor to floor heights between 2520mm and 2860mm; fixing base plates and landing to masonry with expanding bolts										
Spiral staircase	1422.50	2.50	1458.06	40.00	20.00	1146.20	-	2604.26	nr	2864.69
extra; single tread modules maximum 220mm per rise	183.33	2.50	187.91	1.50	0.75	42.98	-	230.90	nr	253.99
extra; two tread modules maximum 220mm per rise with post extension	366.17	2.50	375.32	3.00	1.50	85.97	-	461.29	nr	507.42
extra; three tread modules maximum 220mm per rise with post extension	550.00	2.50	563.75	4.00	2.00	114.62	-	678.37	nr	746.21
Ladders in steel										
Vertical ladders; 65 x 10mm flat stringers; 65 x 10 x 250mm girth stringer brackets, bent once, bolted to stringers; 20mm diameter solid bar rungs welded to stringers; fixing to masonry with expanding bolts										
395mm wide x 3000mm long overall; brackets -6 nr; rungs -7 nr	409.66	2.50	419.90	10.00	10.00	364.40	-	784.30	nr	862.73
395mm wide x 5000mm long overall; brackets -8 nr; rungs -14 nr	590.23	2.50	604.98	12.00	12.00	437.28	-	1042.26	nr	1146.49
470mm wide x 3000mm long overall; brackets -6 nr; rungs -7 nr	499.42	2.50	511.91	10.00	10.00	364.40	-	876.31	nr	963.94
470mm wide x 5000mm long overall; brackets -8 nr; rungs -14 nr	875.62	2.50	897.51	12.00	12.00	437.28	-	1334.79	nr	1468.27
395mm wide x 3000mm long overall, stringers rising and returning 900mm above top fixing points; brackets -6 nr; rungs -7 nr	499.42	2.50	511.91	10.00	10.00	364.40	-	876.31	nr	963.94
395mm wide x 5000mm long overall, stringers rising and returning 900mm above top fixing points; brackets -8 nr; rungs -14 nr	875.62	2.50	897.51	12.00	12.00	437.28	-	1334.79	nr	1468.27
470mm wide x 3000mm long overall, stringers rising and returning 900mm above top fixing points; brackets -6 nr; rungs -7 nr	738.04	2.50	756.50	10.00	10.00	364.40	-	1120.90	nr	1232.99
470mm wide x 5000mm long overall, stringers rising and returning 900mm above top fixing points; brackets -8 nr; rungs -14 nr	1063.71	2.50	1090.30	12.00	12.00	437.28	-	1527.58	nr	1680.34
Vertical ladders; 65 x 10mm flat stringers; 65 x 10 x 250mm girth stringer brackets, bent once, bolted to stringers; 20mm diameter solid bar rungs welded to stringers; 65 x 10mm flat back hoops 900mm diameter, welded to stringers										
395mm wide x 3000mm long overall; brackets -6 nr; rungs -7 nr; hoops -7 nr	933.99	2.50	957.34	15.00	15.00	546.60	-	1503.94	nr	1654.33
395mm wide x 5000mm long overall; brackets -8 nr; rungs -14 nr; hoops -14 nr	1168.54	2.50	1197.75	20.00	20.00	728.80	-	1926.55	nr	2119.21
470mm wide x 3000mm long overall; brackets -6 nr; rungs -7 nr; hoops -7 nr	1031.73	2.50	1057.53	15.00	15.00	546.60	-	1604.13	nr	1764.54
470mm wide x 5000mm long overall; brackets -8 nr; rungs -14 nr; hoops -14 nr	1318.48	2.50	1351.45	20.00	20.00	728.80	-	2080.25	nr	2288.27
395mm wide x 3000mm long overall, stringers rising and returning 900mm above top fixing points; brackets -6 nr; rungs -7 nr; hoops -7 nr	1018.31	2.50	1043.77	15.00	15.00	546.60	-	1590.37	nr	1749.41
395mm wide x 5000mm long overall, stringers rising and returning 900mm above top fixing points; brackets -8 nr; rungs -14 nr; hoops -14 nr	1264.78	2.50	1296.40	20.00	20.00	728.80	-	2025.20	nr	2227.72

Labour hourly rates: (except Specialists) Craft Operatives 20.87 Labourer 15.57 Rates are national average prices. Refer to REGIONAL VARIATIONS for indicative levels of overall pricing in regions	MATERIALS			LABOUR				RATES		
	Del to Site £	Waste %	Material Cost £	Craft Optve Hrs	Lab Hrs	Labour Cost £	Sunds £	Nett Rate £	Unit	Gross rate (10%) £
METAL STAIRCASES (Cont'd)										
Ladders in steel (Cont'd)										
Vertical ladders; 65 x 10mm flat stringers; 65 x 10 x 250mm girth stringer brackets, bent once, bolted to stringers; 20mm diameter solid bar rungs welded to stringers; 65 x 10mm flat back hoops 900mm diameter, welded to stringers (Cont'd)										
470mm wide x 3000mm long overall, stringers rising and returning 900mm above top fixing points; brackets -6 nr; rungs -7 nr; hoops -7 nr	1154.52	2.50	1183.38	15.00	15.00	546.60	-	1729.98	nr	1902.98
470mm wide x 5000mm long overall, stringers rising and returning 900mm above top fixing points; brackets -8 nr; rungs -14 nr; hoops -14 nr	1504.76	2.50	1542.38	20.00	20.00	728.80	-	2271.18	nr	2498.30
Ship type ladders; 75 x 10mm flat stringers, shaped and cleated ends to tops and bottoms; 65 x 10 x 350mm girth stringer brackets, bent once, bolted to stringers; 8 x 75mm on plain raised pattern plate treads with 50 x 50 x 6mm shelf angles, bolted to stringers; 25mm diameter solid bar handrails to both sides, with flattened ends bolted to stringers; 32mm diameter x 175mm long solid bar standards with three way ball type joint at intersection with handrail, and flattened ends bolted to stringers; fixing to masonry with expanding bolts										
420mm wide x 3000mm long overall, handrails rising and returning 900mm above top of stringers; brackets -4 nr; treads -12 nr; standards -6 nr	890.03	2.50	912.28	10.00	10.00	364.40	-	1276.68	nr	1404.35
420mm wide x 5000mm long overall, handrails rising and returning 900mm above top of stringers; brackets -4 nr; treads -21 nr; standards -10 nr	1259.73	2.50	1291.23	12.00	12.00	437.28	-	1728.51	nr	1901.36
470mm wide x 3000mm long overall, handrails rising and returning 900mm above top of stringers; brackets -4 nr; treads -12 nr; standards -6 nr	1033.80	2.50	1059.64	10.00	10.00	364.40	-	1424.04	nr	1566.45
470mm wide x 5000mm long overall, handrails rising and returning 900mm above top of stringers; brackets -4 nr; treads -21 nr; standards -10 nr	1396.66	2.50	1431.58	12.00	12.00	437.28	-	1868.86	nr	2055.74
Ship type ladders; 75 x 10mm flat stringers, shaped and cleated ends to tops and bottoms; 65 x 10 x 350mm girth stringer brackets, bent once, bolted to stringers; 8 x 75mm on plain raised pattern plate treads with 50 x 50 x 6mm shelf angles, bolted to stringers; 25mm diameter solid bar handrails to both sides, with flattened ends bolted to stringers; 32mm diameter x 330mm long solid bar standards with three way ball type joint at intersection with handrail, and flattened ends bolted to stringers; fixing to masonry with expanding bolts										
420mm wide x 3000mm long overall, handrails rising and returning 900mm above top of stringers; brackets -4 nr; treads -12 nr; standards -6 nr	890.03	2.50	912.28	10.00	10.00	364.40	-	1276.68	nr	1404.35
420mm wide x 5000mm long overall, handrails rising and returning 900mm above top of stringers; brackets -4 nr; treads -21 nr; standards -10 nr	1280.27	2.50	1312.28	12.00	12.00	437.28	-	1749.56	nr	1924.51
470mm wide x 3000mm long overall, handrails rising and returning 900mm above top of stringers; brackets -4 nr; treads -12 nr; standards -6 nr	1109.12	2.50	1136.85	10.00	10.00	364.40	-	1501.25	nr	1651.37
470mm wide x 5000mm long overall, handrails rising and returning 900mm above top of stringers; brackets -4 nr; treads -21 nr; standards -10 nr	1417.21	2.50	1452.64	12.00	12.00	437.28	-	1889.92	nr	2078.91

Labour hourly rates: (except Specialists) Craft Operatives 20.87 Labourer 15.57 Rates are national average prices. Refer to REGIONAL VARIATIONS for indicative levels of overall pricing in regions	MATERIALS			LABOUR				RATES		
	Del to Site £	Waste %	Material Cost £	Craft Optve Hrs	Lab Hrs	Labour Cost £	Sunds £	Nett Rate £	Unit	Gross rate (10%) £
GENERAL METALWORK										
Wire mesh; galvanised wire netting, BS EN 10223-2; Butt joints										
13mm mesh x Nr 19 gauge; across members at 450mm centres										
soffit	3.92	5.00	4.12	-	0.14	2.18	0.05	6.34	m²	6.98
vertical	3.92	5.00	4.12	-	0.10	1.56	0.05	5.72	m²	6.29
25mm mesh x Nr 19 gauge; across members at 450mm centres										
soffit	2.45	5.00	2.58	-	0.14	2.18	0.05	4.80	m²	5.28
vertical	2.45	5.00	2.58	-	0.10	1.56	0.05	4.18	m²	4.60
50mm mesh x Nr 19 gauge; across members at 450mm centres										
soffit	3.01	5.00	3.16	-	0.14	2.18	0.05	5.38	m²	5.92
vertical	3.01	5.00	3.16	-	0.10	1.56	0.05	4.76	m²	5.24

This page left blank intentionally

Labour hourly rates: (except Specialists) Craft Operatives 20.87 Labourer 15.57 Rates are national average prices. Refer to REGIONAL VARIATIONS for indicative levels of overall pricing in regions	MATERIALS			LABOUR				RATES		
	Del to Site £	Waste %	Material Cost £	Craft Optve Hrs	Lab Hrs	Labour Cost £	Sunds £	Nett Rate £	Unit	Gross rate (10%) £
GLASS										
Glass; BS 952, clear float										
3mm thick to wood rebates with putty										
not exceeding 0.15m²	61.39	5.00	64.46	0.96	0.10	21.59	0.53	86.58	m²	95.24
0.15 - 4.00m²	61.39	5.00	64.46	0.48	0.05	10.80	0.26	75.52	m²	83.08
4mm thick to wood rebates with putty										
not exceeding 0.15m²	31.51	5.00	33.09	0.96	0.10	21.59	0.53	55.21	m²	60.73
0.15 - 4.00m²	31.51	5.00	33.09	0.48	0.05	10.80	0.26	44.15	m²	48.56
6mm thick to wood rebates with putty										
not exceeding 0.15m²	51.86	5.00	54.45	1.08	0.10	24.10	0.53	79.08	m²	86.99
0.15 - 4.00m²	51.86	5.00	54.45	0.54	0.05	12.05	0.26	66.77	m²	73.44
3mm thick to wood rebates with bradded wood beads (included elsewhere) and putty										
not exceeding 0.15m²	61.39	5.00	64.46	1.20	0.10	26.60	0.53	91.59	m²	100.75
0.15 - 4.00m²	61.39	5.00	64.46	0.60	0.05	13.30	0.26	78.03	m²	85.83
4mm thick to wood rebates with bradded wood beads (included elsewhere) and putty										
not exceeding 0.15m²	31.51	5.00	33.09	1.20	0.10	26.60	0.53	60.21	m²	66.24
0.15 - 4.00m²	31.51	5.00	33.09	0.60	0.05	13.30	0.26	46.65	m²	51.31
6mm thick to wood rebates with bradded wood beads (included elsewhere) and putty										
not exceeding 0.15m²	51.86	5.00	54.45	1.32	0.10	29.11	0.53	84.09	m²	92.50
0.15 - 4.00m²	51.86	5.00	54.45	0.66	0.05	14.55	0.26	69.27	m²	76.20
3mm thick to wood rebates with screwed wood beads and glazing strip (included elsewhere)										
not exceeding 0.15m²	61.39	5.00	64.46	1.68	0.10	36.62	0.53	101.61	m²	111.77
0.15 - 4.00m²	61.39	5.00	64.46	0.84	0.05	18.31	0.26	83.04	m²	91.34
4mm thick to wood rebates with screwed wood beads and glazing strip (included elsewhere)										
not exceeding 0.15m²	31.51	5.00	33.09	1.68	0.10	36.62	0.53	70.23	m²	77.26
0.15 - 4.00m²	31.51	5.00	33.09	0.84	0.05	18.31	0.26	51.66	m²	56.82
6mm thick to wood rebates with screwed wood beads and glazing strip (included elsewhere)										
not exceeding 0.15m²	51.86	5.00	54.45	1.80	0.10	39.12	0.53	94.10	m²	103.51
0.15 - 4.00m²	51.86	5.00	54.45	0.90	0.05	19.56	0.26	74.28	m²	81.71
3mm thick to metal rebates with metal casement glazing compound										
not exceeding 0.15m²	61.39	5.00	64.46	1.08	0.10	24.10	0.61	89.17	m²	98.09
0.15 - 4.00m²	61.39	5.00	64.46	0.54	0.05	12.05	0.30	76.81	m²	84.49
4mm thick to metal rebates with metal casement glazing compound										
not exceeding 0.15m²	31.51	5.00	33.09	1.08	0.10	24.10	0.61	57.79	m²	63.57
0.15 - 4.00m²	31.51	5.00	33.09	0.54	0.05	12.05	0.30	45.43	m²	49.97
6mm thick to metal rebates with metal casement glazing compound										
not exceeding 0.15m²	51.86	5.00	54.45	1.20	0.10	26.60	0.61	81.66	m²	89.83
0.15 - 4.00m²	51.86	5.00	54.45	0.60	0.05	13.30	0.30	68.05	m²	74.86
3mm thick to metal rebates with clipped metal beads and gaskets (included elsewhere)										
not exceeding 0.15m²	61.39	5.00	64.46	1.44	0.10	31.61	0.53	96.60	m²	106.26
0.15 - 4.00m²	61.39	5.00	64.46	0.72	0.05	15.80	0.26	80.53	m²	88.58
4mm thick to metal rebates with clipped metal beads and gaskets (included elsewhere)										
not exceeding 0.15m²	31.51	5.00	33.09	1.44	0.10	31.61	0.53	65.22	m²	71.75
0.15 - 4.00m²	31.51	5.00	33.09	0.72	0.05	15.80	0.26	49.15	m²	54.07
6mm thick to metal rebates with clipped metal beads and gaskets (included elsewhere)										
not exceeding 0.15m²	51.86	5.00	54.45	1.56	0.10	34.11	0.53	89.10	m²	98.00
0.15 - 4.00m²	51.86	5.00	54.45	0.78	0.05	17.06	0.26	71.77	m²	78.95
Glass; BS 952, rough cast										
6mm thick to wood rebates with putty										
not exceeding 0.15m²	49.46	5.00	51.93	1.08	0.10	24.10	0.53	76.56	m²	84.21
0.15 - 4.00m²	49.46	5.00	51.93	0.54	0.05	12.05	0.26	64.25	m²	70.67
6mm thick to wood rebates with bradded wood beads (included elsewhere) and putty										
not exceeding 0.15m²	49.46	5.00	51.93	1.32	0.10	29.11	0.53	81.57	m²	89.72
0.15 - 4.00m²	49.46	5.00	51.93	0.66	0.05	14.55	0.26	66.75	m²	73.42

Labour hourly rates: (except Specialists) Craft Operatives 20.87 Labourer 15.57 Rates are national average prices. Refer to REGIONAL VARIATIONS for indicative levels of overall pricing in regions	MATERIALS			LABOUR				RATES		
	Del to Site £	Waste %	Material Cost £	Craft Optve Hrs	Lab Hrs	Labour Cost £	Sunds £	Nett Rate £	Unit	Gross rate (10%) £
GLASS (Cont'd)										
Glass; BS 952, rough cast (Cont'd)										
6mm thick to wood rebates with screwed wood beads and glazing strip (included elsewhere)										
not exceeding 0.15m²	49.46	5.00	51.93	1.80	0.10	39.12	0.53	91.58	m²	100.74
0.15 - 4.00m²	49.46	5.00	51.93	0.90	0.05	19.56	0.26	71.76	m²	78.93
6mm thick to metal rebates with metal casement glazing compound										
not exceeding 0.15m²	49.46	5.00	51.93	1.20	0.10	26.60	0.61	79.14	m²	87.06
0.15 - 4.00m²	49.46	5.00	51.93	0.60	0.05	13.30	0.30	65.53	m²	72.08
6mm thick to metal rebates with clipped metal beads and gaskets (included elsewhere)										
not exceeding 0.15m²	49.46	5.00	51.93	1.56	0.10	34.11	0.61	86.66	m²	95.32
0.15 - 4.00m²	49.46	5.00	51.93	0.78	0.05	17.06	0.30	69.29	m²	76.22
Glass; BS 952, Pyroshield clear										
6mm thick to wood rebates with screwed beads and intumescent glazing strip (included elsewhere)										
not exceeding 0.15m²	100.18	5.00	105.19	2.16	0.10	46.64	-	151.82	m²	167.00
not exceeding 0.15m²; aligning panes with adjacent panes	100.18	8.50	108.69	2.40	0.10	51.65	-	160.34	m²	176.37
0.15 - 4.00m²	100.18	5.00	105.19	1.08	0.05	23.32	-	128.50	m²	141.35
0.15 - 4.00m²; aligning panes with adjacent panes	100.18	8.50	108.69	1.20	0.05	25.82	-	134.51	m²	147.97
6mm thick to wood rebates with screwed beads and Pyroglazing strip (included elsewhere)										
not exceeding 0.15m²	100.18	5.00	105.19	2.16	0.10	46.64	-	151.82	m²	167.00
not exceeding 0.15m²; aligning panes with adjacent panes	100.18	8.50	108.69	2.40	0.10	51.65	-	160.34	m²	176.37
0.15 - 4.00m²	100.18	5.00	105.19	1.08	0.05	23.32	-	128.50	m²	141.35
0.15 - 4.00m²; aligning panes with adjacent panes	100.18	8.50	108.69	1.20	0.05	25.82	-	134.51	m²	147.97
6mm thick to wood rebates with screwed beads and Lorient System 90 (included elsewhere)										
not exceeding 0.15m²	100.18	5.00	105.19	2.40	0.10	51.65	-	156.83	m²	172.51
not exceeding 0.15m²; aligning panes with adjacent panes	100.18	8.50	108.69	2.64	0.10	56.65	-	165.35	m²	181.88
0.15 - 4.00m²	100.18	5.00	105.19	1.20	0.05	25.82	-	131.01	m²	144.11
0.15 - 4.00m²; aligning panes with adjacent panes	100.18	8.50	108.69	1.32	0.05	28.33	-	137.02	m²	150.72
6mm thick to metal rebates with screwed metal beads and mild steel flat strips (included elsewhere)										
not exceeding 0.15m²	100.18	5.00	105.19	2.16	0.10	46.64	-	151.82	m²	167.00
not exceeding 0.15m²; aligning panes with adjacent panes	100.18	8.50	108.69	2.40	0.10	51.65	-	160.34	m²	176.37
0.15 - 4.00m²	100.18	5.00	105.19	1.08	0.05	23.32	-	128.50	m²	141.35
0.15 - 4.00m²; aligning panes with adjacent panes	100.18	8.50	108.69	1.20	0.05	25.82	-	134.51	m²	147.97
Glass; BS 952, Pyroshield safety clear										
6mm thick to wood rebates with screwed beads and intumescent glazing strip (included elsewhere)										
not exceeding 0.15m²	117.56	5.00	123.43	2.16	0.10	46.64	-	170.07	m²	187.08
not exceeding 0.15m²; aligning panes with adjacent panes	117.56	8.50	127.55	2.40	0.10	51.65	-	179.19	m²	197.11
0.15 - 4.00m²	117.56	5.00	123.43	1.08	0.05	23.32	-	146.75	m²	161.43
0.15 - 4.00m²; aligning panes with adjacent panes	117.56	8.50	127.55	1.20	0.05	25.82	-	153.37	m²	168.71
6mm thick to wood rebates with screwed beads and Pyroglazing strip (included elsewhere)										
not exceeding 0.15m²	117.56	5.00	123.43	2.16	0.10	46.64	-	170.07	m²	187.08
not exceeding 0.15m²; aligning panes with adjacent panes	117.56	8.50	127.55	2.40	0.10	51.65	-	179.19	m²	197.11
0.15 - 4.00m²	117.56	5.00	123.43	1.08	0.05	23.32	-	146.75	m²	161.43
0.15 - 4.00m²; aligning panes with adjacent panes	117.56	8.50	127.55	1.20	0.05	25.82	-	153.37	m²	168.71
6mm thick to wood rebates with screwed beads and Lorient System 90 (included elsewhere)										
not exceeding 0.15m²	117.56	5.00	123.43	2.40	0.10	51.65	-	175.08	m²	192.59
not exceeding 0.15m²; aligning panes with adjacent panes	117.56	8.50	127.55	2.64	0.10	56.65	-	184.20	m²	202.62
0.15 - 4.00m²	117.56	5.00	123.43	1.20	0.05	25.82	-	149.26	m²	164.18
0.15 - 4.00m²; aligning panes with adjacent panes	117.56	8.50	127.55	1.32	0.05	28.33	-	155.88	m²	171.46
6mm thick to metal rebates with screwed metal beads and mild steel flat strips (included elsewhere)										
not exceeding 0.15m²	117.56	5.00	123.43	2.16	0.10	46.64	-	170.07	m²	187.08
not exceeding 0.15m²; aligning panes with adjacent panes	117.56	8.50	127.55	2.40	0.10	51.65	-	179.19	m²	197.11
0.15 - 4.00m²	117.56	5.00	123.43	1.08	0.05	23.32	-	146.75	m²	161.43
0.15 - 4.00m²; aligning panes with adjacent panes	117.56	8.50	127.55	1.20	0.05	25.82	-	153.37	m²	168.71
Glass; BS 952, Pyroshield texture										
7mm thick to wood rebates with screwed beads and intumescent glazing strip (included elsewhere)										
not exceeding 0.15m²	47.93	5.00	50.32	2.16	0.10	46.64	-	96.96	m²	106.66
not exceeding 0.15m²; aligning panes with adjacent panes	47.93	8.50	52.00	2.40	0.10	51.65	-	103.65	m²	114.01
0.15 - 4.00m²	47.93	5.00	50.32	1.08	0.05	23.32	-	73.64	m²	81.01
0.15 - 4.00m²; aligning panes with adjacent panes	47.93	8.50	52.00	1.20	0.05	25.82	-	77.82	m²	85.61
7mm thick to wood rebates with screwed beads and Pyroglazing strip (included elsewhere)										
not exceeding 0.15m²	47.93	5.00	50.32	2.16	0.10	46.64	-	96.96	m²	106.66
not exceeding 0.15m²; aligning panes with adjacent panes	47.93	8.50	52.00	2.40	0.10	51.65	-	103.65	m²	114.01
0.15 - 4.00m²	47.93	5.00	50.32	1.08	0.05	23.32	-	73.64	m²	81.01
0.15 - 4.00m²; aligning panes with adjacent panes	47.93	8.50	52.00	1.20	0.05	25.82	-	77.82	m²	85.61
7mm thick to wood rebates with screwed beads and Lorient System 90 (included elsewhere)										
not exceeding 0.15m²	47.93	5.00	50.32	2.40	0.10	51.65	-	101.97	m²	112.17
not exceeding 0.15m²; aligning panes with adjacent panes	47.93	8.50	52.00	2.64	0.10	56.65	-	108.65	m²	119.52

Labour hourly rates: (except Specialists) Craft Operatives 20.87 Labourer 15.57 Rates are national average prices. Refer to REGIONAL VARIATIONS for indicative levels of overall pricing in regions	MATERIALS			LABOUR				RATES		
	Del to Site £	Waste %	Material Cost £	Craft Optve Hrs	Lab Hrs	Labour Cost £	Sunds £	Nett Rate £	Unit	Gross rate (10%) £
GLASS (Cont'd)										
Glass; BS 952, Pyroshield texture (Cont'd)										
7mm thick to wood rebates with screwed beads and Lorient System 90 (included elsewhere) (Cont'd)										
0.15 - 4.00m²	47.93	5.00	50.32	1.20	0.05	25.82	-	76.15	m²	83.76
0.15 - 4.00m²; aligning panes with adjacent panes	47.93	8.50	52.00	1.32	0.05	28.33	-	80.33	m²	88.36
7mm thick to metal rebates with screwed metal beads and mild steel flat strips (included elsewhere)										
not exceeding 0.15m²	47.93	5.00	50.32	2.16	0.10	46.64	-	96.96	m²	106.66
not exceeding 0.15m²; aligning panes with adjacent panes	47.93	8.50	52.00	2.40	0.10	51.65	-	103.65	m²	114.01
0.15 - 4.00m²	47.93	5.00	50.32	1.08	0.05	23.32	-	73.64	m²	81.01
0.15 - 4.00m²; aligning panes with adjacent panes	47.93	8.50	52.00	1.20	0.05	25.82	-	77.82	m²	85.61
Glass; BS 952, Pyroshield safety texture										
7mm thick to wood rebates with screwed beads and intumescent glazing strip (included elsewhere)										
not exceeding 0.15m²	61.57	5.00	64.65	2.16	0.10	46.64	-	111.28	m²	122.41
not exceeding 0.15m²; aligning panes with adjacent panes	61.57	8.50	66.80	2.40	0.10	51.65	-	118.45	m²	130.29
0.15 - 4.00m²	61.57	5.00	64.65	1.08	0.05	23.32	-	87.96	m²	96.76
0.15 - 4.00m²; aligning panes with adjacent panes	61.57	8.50	66.80	1.20	0.05	25.82	-	92.62	m²	101.88
7mm thick to wood rebates with screwed beads and Pyroglazing strip (included elsewhere)										
not exceeding 0.15m²	61.57	5.00	64.65	2.16	0.10	46.64	-	111.28	m²	122.41
not exceeding 0.15m²; aligning panes with adjacent panes	61.57	8.50	66.80	2.40	0.10	51.65	-	118.45	m²	130.29
0.15 - 4.00m²	61.57	5.00	64.65	1.08	0.05	23.32	-	87.96	m²	96.76
0.15 - 4.00m²; aligning panes with adjacent panes	61.57	8.50	66.80	1.20	0.05	25.82	-	92.62	m²	101.88
7mm thick to wood rebates with screwed beads and Lorient System 90 (included elsewhere)										
not exceeding 0.15m²	61.57	5.00	64.65	2.40	0.10	51.65	-	116.29	m²	127.92
not exceeding 0.15m²; aligning panes with adjacent panes	61.57	8.50	66.80	2.64	0.10	56.65	-	123.45	m²	135.80
0.15 - 4.00m²	61.57	5.00	64.65	1.20	0.05	25.82	-	90.47	m²	99.51
0.15 - 4.00m²; aligning panes with adjacent panes	61.57	8.50	66.80	1.32	0.05	28.33	-	95.13	m²	104.64
7mm thick to metal rebates with screwed metal beads and mild steel flat strips (included elsewhere)										
not exceeding 0.15m²	61.57	5.00	64.65	2.16	0.10	46.64	-	111.28	m²	122.41
not exceeding 0.15m²; aligning panes with adjacent panes	61.57	8.50	66.80	2.40	0.10	51.65	-	118.45	m²	130.29
0.15 - 4.00m²	61.57	5.00	64.65	1.08	0.05	23.32	-	87.96	m²	96.76
0.15 - 4.00m²; aligning panes with adjacent panes	61.57	8.50	66.80	1.20	0.05	25.82	-	92.62	m²	101.88
Glass; BS 952, white patterned										
4mm thick to wood rebates with putty										
not exceeding 0.15m²	37.40	5.00	39.27	0.96	0.10	21.59	0.53	61.39	m²	67.53
0.15 - 4.00m²	37.40	5.00	39.27	0.48	0.05	10.80	0.26	50.33	m²	55.36
6mm thick to wood rebates with putty										
not exceeding 0.15m²	68.20	5.00	71.61	1.08	0.10	24.10	0.53	96.23	m²	105.86
0.15 - 4.00m²	68.20	5.00	71.61	0.54	0.05	12.05	0.26	83.92	m²	92.31
4mm thick to wood rebates with bradded wood beads (included elsewhere) and putty										
not exceeding 0.15m²	37.40	5.00	39.27	1.20	0.10	26.60	0.53	66.40	m²	73.04
0.15 - 4.00m²	37.40	5.00	39.27	0.60	0.05	13.30	0.26	52.83	m²	58.12
6mm thick to wood rebates with bradded wood beads (included elsewhere) and putty										
not exceeding 0.15m²	68.20	5.00	71.61	1.32	0.10	29.11	0.53	101.24	m²	111.37
0.15 - 4.00m²	68.20	5.00	71.61	0.66	0.05	14.55	0.26	86.43	m²	95.07
4mm thick to wood rebates with screwed wood beads and glazing strip (included elsewhere)										
not exceeding 0.15m²	37.40	5.00	39.27	1.68	0.10	36.62	0.53	76.42	m²	84.06
0.15 - 4.00m²	37.40	5.00	39.27	0.84	0.05	18.31	0.26	57.84	m²	63.63
6mm thick to wood rebates with screwed wood beads and glazing strip (included elsewhere)										
not exceeding 0.15m²	68.20	5.00	71.61	1.80	0.10	39.12	0.53	111.26	m²	122.39
0.15 - 4.00m²	68.20	5.00	71.61	0.90	0.05	19.56	0.26	91.44	m²	100.58
4mm thick to metal rebates with metal casement glazing compound										
not exceeding 0.15m²	37.40	5.00	39.27	1.08	0.10	24.10	0.61	63.98	m²	70.37
0.15 - 4.00m²	37.40	5.00	39.27	0.54	0.05	12.05	0.30	51.62	m²	56.78
6mm thick to metal rebates with metal casement glazing compound										
not exceeding 0.15m²	68.20	5.00	71.61	1.20	0.10	26.60	0.61	98.82	m²	108.70
0.15 - 4.00m²	68.20	5.00	71.61	0.60	0.05	13.30	0.30	85.21	m²	93.73
4mm thick to metal rebates with clipped metal beads and gaskets (included elsewhere)										
not exceeding 0.15m²	37.40	5.00	39.27	1.44	0.10	31.61	0.53	71.41	m²	78.55
0.15 - 4.00m²	37.40	5.00	39.27	0.72	0.05	15.80	0.26	55.34	m²	60.87
6mm thick to metal rebates with clipped metal beads and gaskets (included elsewhere)										
not exceeding 0.15m²	68.20	5.00	71.61	1.56	0.10	34.11	0.53	106.25	m²	116.88
0.15 - 4.00m²	68.20	5.00	71.61	0.78	0.05	17.06	0.26	88.93	m²	97.82
Glass; BS 952, tinted patterned										
4mm thick to wood rebates with putty										
not exceeding 0.15m²	44.00	5.00	46.20	0.96	0.10	21.59	0.53	68.32	m²	75.15

Labour hourly rates: (except Specialists) Craft Operatives 20.87 Labourer 15.57 Rates are national average prices. Refer to REGIONAL VARIATIONS for indicative levels of overall pricing in regions	MATERIALS			LABOUR				RATES		
	Del to Site £	Waste %	Material Cost £	Craft Optve Hrs	Lab Hrs	Labour Cost £	Sunds £	Nett Rate £	Unit	Gross rate (10%) £
GLASS (Cont'd)										
Glass; BS 952, tinted patterned (Cont'd)										
4mm thick to wood rebates with putty (Cont'd)										
0.15 - 4.00m²	44.00	5.00	46.20	0.48	0.05	10.80	0.26	57.26	m²	62.99
6mm thick to wood rebates with putty										
not exceeding 0.15m²	78.65	5.00	82.58	1.08	0.10	24.10	0.53	107.21	m²	117.93
0.15 - 4.00m²	78.65	5.00	82.58	0.54	0.05	12.05	0.26	94.89	m²	104.38
4mm thick to wood rebates with bradded wood beads (included elsewhere) and putty										
not exceeding 0.15m²	44.00	5.00	46.20	1.20	0.10	26.60	0.53	73.33	m²	80.66
0.15 - 4.00m²	44.00	5.00	46.20	0.60	0.05	13.30	0.26	59.76	m²	65.74
6mm thick to wood rebates with bradded wood beads (included elsewhere) and putty										
not exceeding 0.15m²	78.65	5.00	82.58	1.32	0.10	29.11	0.53	112.22	m²	123.44
0.15 - 4.00m²	78.65	5.00	82.58	0.66	0.05	14.55	0.26	97.40	m²	107.14
4mm thick to wood rebates with screwed wood beads and glazing strip (included elsewhere)										
not exceeding 0.15m²	44.00	5.00	46.20	1.68	0.10	36.62	0.53	83.35	m²	91.68
0.15 - 4.00m²	44.00	5.00	46.20	0.84	0.05	18.31	0.26	64.77	m²	71.25
6mm thick to wood rebates with screwed wood beads and glazing strip (included elsewhere)										
not exceeding 0.15m²	78.65	5.00	82.58	1.80	0.10	39.12	0.53	122.23	m²	134.46
0.15 - 4.00m²	78.65	5.00	82.58	0.90	0.05	19.56	0.26	102.41	m²	112.65
4mm thick to metal rebates with metal casement glazing compound										
not exceeding 0.15m²	44.00	5.00	46.20	1.08	0.10	24.10	0.59	70.89	m²	77.98
0.15 - 4.00m²	44.00	5.00	46.20	0.54	0.05	12.05	0.30	58.55	m²	64.40
6mm thick to metal rebates with metal casement glazing compound										
not exceeding 0.15m²	78.65	5.00	82.58	1.20	0.10	26.60	0.59	109.78	m²	120.76
0.15 - 4.00m²	78.65	5.00	82.58	0.60	0.05	13.30	0.30	96.18	m²	105.80
4mm thick to metal rebates with clipped metal beads and gaskets (included elsewhere)										
not exceeding 0.15m²	44.00	5.00	46.20	1.44	0.10	31.61	0.53	78.34	m²	86.17
0.15 - 4.00m²	44.00	5.00	46.20	0.72	0.05	15.80	0.26	62.27	m²	68.50
6mm thick to metal rebates with clipped metal beads and gaskets (included elsewhere)										
not exceeding 0.15m²	78.65	5.00	82.58	1.56	0.10	34.11	0.53	117.22	m²	128.95
0.15 - 4.00m²	78.65	5.00	82.58	0.78	0.05	17.06	0.26	99.90	m²	109.89
Patterns available										
4mm Bronze tint										
Autumn; Cotswold; Everglade; Sycamore										
Patterns available; 4mm Bronze tint; Autumn; Cotswold; Everglade; Sycamore										
4mm white										
Arctic										
Patterns available; 4mm White; Artic; Autumn; Cotswold; Driftwood; Everglade; Flemish; Linkon; Mayflower; Reeded; Stippolyte										
6mm white										
Deep Flemish										
Patterns available; 6mm White; Deep Flemish										
4 and 6mm white										
Autumn; Cotswold; Driftwood; Everglade; Flemish; Linkon; Mayflower; Reeded; Stippolyte										
Patterns available; 6mm Bronze tint; Autumn; Cotswold; Everglade										
Glass; BS 952, antisun float; grey										
4mm thick to wood rebates with putty										
not exceeding 2400 x 1200mm	73.85	5.00	77.55	0.72	0.12	16.89	0.38	94.82	m²	104.30
6mm thick to wood rebates with putty										
not exceeding 5950 x 3150mm	106.52	5.00	111.85	0.78	0.12	18.15	0.38	130.38	m²	143.41
10mm thick to wood rebates with putty										
not exceeding 5950 x 3150mm	190.46	5.00	199.98	1.80	0.12	39.43	0.48	239.89	m²	263.88
12mm thick to wood rebates with putty										
not exceeding 5950 x 3150mm	263.88	5.00	277.07	2.40	0.12	51.96	0.59	329.62	m²	362.58
4mm thick to wood rebates with bradded wood beads (included elsewhere) and putty										
not exceeding 2400 x 1200mm	73.85	5.00	77.55	0.84	0.12	19.40	0.38	97.33	m²	107.06
6mm thick to wood rebates with bradded wood beads (included elsewhere) and putty										
not exceeding 5950 x 3150mm	106.52	5.00	111.85	0.90	0.12	20.65	0.38	132.88	m²	146.17
10mm thick to wood rebates with bradded wood beads (included elsewhere) and putty										
not exceeding 5950 x 3150mm	190.46	5.00	199.98	1.92	0.12	41.94	0.48	242.40	m²	266.64

Labour hourly rates: (except Specialists) Craft Operatives 20.87 Labourer 15.57 Rates are national average prices. Refer to REGIONAL VARIATIONS for indicative levels of overall pricing in regions	MATERIALS			LABOUR				RATES		
	Del to Site £	Waste %	Material Cost £	Craft Optve Hrs	Lab Hrs	Labour Cost £	Sunds £	Nett Rate £	Unit	Gross rate (10%) £
GLASS (Cont'd)										
Glass; BS 952, antisun float; grey (Cont'd)										
12mm thick to wood rebates with bradded wood beads (included elsewhere) and putty not exceeding 5950 x 3150mm	263.88	5.00	277.07	2.52	0.12	54.46	0.59	332.12	m²	365.34
4mm thick to wood rebates with screwed wood beads and glazing strip (included elsewhere) not exceeding 2400 x 1200mm	73.85	5.00	77.55	1.08	0.12	24.41	-	101.95	m²	112.15
6mm thick to wood rebates with screwed wood beads and glazing strip (included elsewhere) not exceeding 5950 x 3150mm	106.52	5.00	111.85	1.14	0.12	25.66	-	137.51	m²	151.26
10mm thick to wood rebates with screwed wood beads and glazing strip (included elsewhere) not exceeding 5950 x 3150mm	190.46	5.00	199.98	2.04	0.12	44.44	-	244.42	m²	268.86
12mm thick to wood rebates with screwed wood beads and glazing strip (included elsewhere) not exceeding 5950 x 3150mm	263.88	5.00	277.07	2.64	0.12	56.97	-	334.03	m²	367.44
Glass; BS 952, antisun float; bronze										
4mm thick to wood rebates with putty not exceeding 2400 x 1200mm	73.85	5.00	77.55	0.72	0.12	16.89	0.38	94.82	m²	104.30
6mm thick to wood rebates with putty not exceeding 5950 x 3150mm	106.52	5.00	111.85	0.78	0.12	18.15	0.38	130.38	m²	143.41
10mm thick to wood rebates with putty not exceeding 5950 x 3150mm	190.46	5.00	199.98	1.80	0.12	39.43	0.48	239.89	m²	263.88
12mm thick to wood rebates with putty not exceeding 5950 x 3150mm	262.89	5.00	276.04	2.40	0.12	51.96	0.59	328.59	m²	361.45
4mm thick to wood rebates with bradded wood beads (included elsewhere) and putty not exceeding 2400 x 1200mm	73.85	5.00	77.55	0.84	0.12	19.40	0.38	97.33	m²	107.06
6mm thick to wood rebates with bradded wood beads (included elsewhere) and putty not exceeding 5950 x 3150mm	106.52	5.00	111.85	0.90	0.12	20.65	0.38	132.88	m²	146.17
10mm thick to wood rebates with bradded wood beads (included elsewhere) and putty not exceeding 5950 x 3150mm	190.46	5.00	199.98	1.92	0.12	41.94	0.48	242.40	m²	266.64
12mm thick to wood rebates with bradded wood beads (included elsewhere) and putty not exceeding 5950 x 3150mm	262.89	5.00	276.04	2.52	0.12	54.46	0.59	331.09	m²	364.20
4mm thick to wood rebates with screwed wood beads and glazing strip (included elsewhere) not exceeding 2400 x 1200mm	73.85	5.00	77.55	1.08	0.12	24.41	-	101.95	m²	112.15
6mm thick to wood rebates with screwed wood beads and glazing strip (included elsewhere) not exceeding 5950 x 3150mm	106.52	5.00	111.85	1.14	0.12	25.66	-	137.51	m²	151.26
10mm thick to wood rebates with screwed wood beads and glazing strip (included elsewhere) not exceeding 5950 x 3150mm	190.46	5.00	199.98	2.04	0.12	44.44	-	244.42	m²	268.86
12mm thick to wood rebates with screwed wood beads and glazing strip (included elsewhere) not exceeding 5950 x 3150mm	262.89	5.00	276.04	2.64	0.12	56.97	-	333.00	m²	366.31
Glass; BS 952, antisun float; green										
6mm thick to wood rebates with putty not exceeding 3150 x 2050mm	136.55	5.00	143.38	0.78	0.12	18.15	0.38	161.91	m²	178.10
6mm thick to wood rebates with bradded wood beads (included elsewhere) and putty not exceeding 3150 x 2050mm	136.55	5.00	143.38	0.90	0.12	20.65	0.38	164.41	m²	180.85
6mm thick to wood rebates with screwed wood beads and glazing strip (included elsewhere) not exceeding 3150 x 2050mm	136.55	5.00	143.38	1.14	0.12	25.66	-	169.04	m²	185.94
Glass; BS 952, clear float										
10mm thick to wood rebates with screwed wood beads and glazing strip (included elsewhere) not exceeding 5950 x 3150mm	122.76	5.00	128.90	2.70	0.12	58.22	-	187.12	m²	205.83
12mm thick to wood rebates with screwed wood beads and glazing strip (included elsewhere) not exceeding 5950 x 3150mm	171.60	5.00	180.18	3.30	0.12	70.74	-	250.92	m²	276.01
15mm thick to wood rebates with screwed wood beads and glazing strip (included elsewhere) not exceeding 2950 x 2000mm	226.80	5.00	238.14	4.20	0.12	89.52	-	327.66	m²	360.43
19mm thick to wood rebates with screwed wood beads and glazing strip (included elsewhere) not exceeding 2950 x 2000mm	307.32	5.00	322.69	4.80	0.12	102.04	-	424.73	m²	467.20

Labour hourly rates: (except Specialists) Craft Operatives 20.87 Labourer 15.57 Rates are national average prices. Refer to REGIONAL VARIATIONS for indicative levels of overall pricing in regions	MATERIALS			LABOUR				RATES		
	Del to Site £	Waste %	Material Cost £	Craft Optve Hrs	Lab Hrs	Labour Cost £	Sunds £	Nett Rate £	Unit	Gross rate (10%) £
GLASS (Cont'd)										
Glass; BS 952, clear float (Cont'd)										
25mm thick to wood rebates with screwed wood beads and glazing strip (included elsewhere) not exceeding 2950 x 2000mm	482.20	5.00	506.31	5.40	0.12	114.57	-	620.88	m²	682.96
Glass; BS 952, toughened clear float										
4mm thick to metal rebates with screwed metal beads and gaskets (included elsewhere) not exceeding 2400 x 1300mm	44.00	5.00	46.20	0.72	0.12	16.89	-	63.09	m²	69.40
5mm thick to metal rebates with screwed metal beads and gaskets (included elsewhere) not exceeding 2500 x 1520mm	56.55	5.00	59.38	0.72	0.12	16.89	-	76.27	m²	83.90
6mm thick to metal rebates with screwed metal beads and gaskets (included elsewhere) not exceeding 2500 x 1520mm	66.00	5.00	69.30	0.78	0.12	18.15	-	87.45	m²	96.19
10mm thick to metal rebates with screwed metal beads and gaskets (included elsewhere) not exceeding 2500 x 1520mm	78.00	5.00	81.90	1.80	0.12	39.43	-	121.33	m²	133.47
12mm thick to metal rebates with screwed metal beads and gaskets (included elsewhere) not exceeding 2500 x 1520mm	85.00	5.00	89.25	2.40	0.12	51.96	-	141.21	m²	155.33
Glass; BS 952, toughened white patterned										
4mm thick to metal rebates with screwed metal beads and gaskets (included elsewhere) not exceeding 2100 x 1300mm	67.10	5.00	70.45	0.72	0.12	16.89	-	87.35	m²	96.08
6mm thick to metal rebates with screwed metal beads and gaskets (included elsewhere) not exceeding 2100 x 1300mm	84.70	5.00	88.93	0.78	0.12	18.15	-	107.08	m²	117.79
Patterns available										
4mm tinted Everglade Paterns available; 4mm Tinted; Everglade; Autumn; Cotswold										
4mm white Reeded Paterns available; 4mm White; Reeded; Autumn; Cotswold; Driftwood; Everglade; Flemish; Linkon; Mayflower; Stippolyte; Sycamore										
4mm tinted Autumn; Cotswold Paterns available; 6mm Tinted; Everglade; Autumn; Cotswold										
4 and 6mm white Autumn; Cotswold; Driftwood; Everglade; Flemish; Linkon; Mayflower; Stippolyte; Sycamore Paterns available; 6mm White; Autumn; Cotswold; Driftwood; Everglade; Flemish; Linkon; Mayflower; Stippolyte; Sycamore										
Glass; BS 952, toughened antisun float; grey										
4mm thick to metal rebates with screwed metal beads and gaskets (included elsewhere) not exceeding 2100 x 1250mm	108.28	5.00	113.69	0.72	0.12	16.89	-	130.58	m²	143.64
6mm thick to metal rebates with screwed metal beads and gaskets (included elsewhere) not exceeding 2500 x 1520mm	112.88	5.00	118.52	0.78	0.12	18.15	-	136.67	m²	150.34
10mm thick to metal rebates with screwed metal beads and gaskets (included elsewhere) not exceeding 2500 x 1520mm	223.41	5.00	234.58	1.80	0.12	39.43	-	274.02	m²	301.42
12mm thick to metal rebates with screwed metal beads and gaskets (included elsewhere) not exceeding 2500 x 1520mm	293.98	5.00	308.68	2.40	0.12	51.96	-	360.64	m²	396.70
Glass; BS 952, toughened antisun float; bronze										
4mm thick to metal rebates with screwed metal beads and gaskets (included elsewhere) not exceeding 2100 x 1250mm	108.19	5.00	113.60	0.72	0.12	16.89	-	130.49	m²	143.54
6mm thick to metal rebates with screwed metal beads and gaskets (included elsewhere) not exceeding 2500 x 1520mm	112.88	5.00	118.52	0.78	0.12	18.15	-	136.67	m²	150.34
10mm thick to metal rebates with screwed metal beads and gaskets (included elsewhere) not exceeding 2500 x 1520mm	224.91	5.00	236.15	1.80	0.12	39.43	-	275.59	m²	303.15
12mm thick to metal rebates with screwed metal beads and gaskets (included elsewhere) not exceeding 2500 x 1520mm	293.98	5.00	308.68	2.40	0.12	51.96	-	360.64	m²	396.70

Labour hourly rates: (except Specialists) Craft Operatives 20.87 Labourer 15.57 Rates are national average prices. Refer to REGIONAL VARIATIONS for indicative levels of overall pricing in regions	MATERIALS			LABOUR				RATES		
	Del to Site £	Waste %	Material Cost £	Craft Optve Hrs	Lab Hrs	Labour Cost £	Sunds £	Nett Rate £	Unit	Gross rate (10%) £
GLASS (Cont'd)										
Glass; BS 952, laminated safety, clear float										
6.4mm thick to metal rebates with screwed metal beads and gaskets (included elsewhere)										
not exceeding 3210 x 2000mm	56.00	5.00	58.80	2.40	0.12	51.96	-	110.76	m²	121.83
8.8mm thick to metal rebates with screwed metal beads and gaskets (included elsewhere)										
not exceeding 3210 x 2000mm	114.00	5.00	119.70	2.80	0.12	60.30	-	180.00	m²	198.00
10.8mm thick to metal rebates with screwed metal beads and gaskets (included elsewhere)										
not exceeding 3210 x 2000mm	123.00	5.00	129.15	3.20	0.12	68.65	-	197.80	m²	217.58
Glass; BS 952, laminated anti-bandit, clear float										
9.5mm thick to metal rebates with screwed metal beads and gaskets (included elsewhere)										
not exceeding 3600 x 2500mm	155.00	5.00	162.75	3.30	0.12	70.74	-	233.49	m²	256.84
13.5mm thick to metal rebates with screwed metal beads and gaskets (included elsewhere)										
not exceeding 3180 x 2000mm	180.00	5.00	189.00	3.90	0.12	83.26	-	272.26	m²	299.49
not exceeding 4500 x 2500mm	20.74	5.00	21.78	3.90	0.12	83.26	-	105.04	m²	115.54
Sealed glazed units; factory made double glazed hermetically sealed units										
Two panes BS 952, clear float 4mm thick; to metal rebates with screwed metal beads and gaskets (included elsewhere)										
521mm wide x 421mm high	10.45	5.00	10.97	1.15	-	24.00	-	34.97	nr	38.47
521mm wide x 621mm high	13.52	5.00	14.20	1.45	-	30.26	-	44.46	nr	48.90
740mm wide x 740mm high	22.89	5.00	24.03	2.00	-	41.74	-	65.77	nr	72.35
848mm wide x 848mm high	30.06	5.00	31.56	2.30	-	48.00	-	79.56	nr	87.52
1048mm wide x 1048mm high	45.91	5.00	48.21	2.90	-	60.52	-	108.73	nr	119.60
1148mm wide x 1248mm high	59.89	5.00	62.88	3.45	-	72.00	-	134.89	nr	148.37
Two panes BS 952, clear float 5 or 6mm thick; to metal rebates with screwed metal beads and gaskets (included elsewhere)										
521mm wide x 421mm high	19.25	5.00	20.21	1.25	-	26.09	-	46.30	nr	50.93
521mm wide x 621mm high	24.93	5.00	26.18	1.60	-	33.39	-	59.57	nr	65.53
740mm wide x 740mm high	42.17	5.00	44.28	2.20	-	45.91	-	90.19	nr	99.21
848mm wide x 848mm high	55.37	5.00	58.14	2.50	-	52.18	-	110.31	nr	121.34
1048mm wide x 1048mm high	68.43	5.00	71.85	3.20	-	66.78	-	138.64	nr	152.50
1148mm wide x 1248mm high	110.32	5.00	115.83	3.80	-	79.31	-	195.14	nr	214.66
Inner pane BS 952, clear float 4mm thick; outer pane BS 952, white patterned 4mm thick; to metal rebates with screwed metal beads and gaskets (included elsewhere)										
521mm wide x 421mm high	12.65	5.00	13.28	1.15	-	24.00	-	37.28	nr	41.01
521mm wide x 621mm high	16.37	5.00	17.19	1.45	-	30.26	-	47.45	nr	52.20
740mm wide x 740mm high	27.71	5.00	29.10	2.00	-	41.74	-	70.84	nr	77.92
848mm wide x 848mm high	36.39	5.00	38.21	2.30	-	48.00	-	86.21	nr	94.83
1048mm wide x 1048mm high	44.97	5.00	47.22	2.90	-	60.52	-	107.74	nr	118.52
1148mm wide x 1248mm high	72.49	5.00	76.11	3.45	-	72.00	-	148.12	nr	162.93
Inner pane BS 952, clear float 4mm thick; outer pane BS 952, white patterned 6mm thick; to metal rebates with screwed metal beads and gaskets (included elsewhere)										
521mm wide x 421mm high	21.45	5.00	22.52	1.25	-	26.09	-	48.61	nr	53.47
521mm wide x 621mm high	27.76	5.00	29.15	1.60	-	33.39	-	62.54	nr	68.80
740mm wide x 740mm high	46.98	5.00	49.33	2.20	-	45.91	-	95.24	nr	104.77
848mm wide x 848mm high	61.70	5.00	64.78	2.50	-	52.18	-	116.96	nr	128.65
1048mm wide x 1048mm high	76.25	5.00	80.06	3.20	-	66.78	-	146.85	nr	161.53
1148mm wide x 1248mm high	122.93	5.00	129.07	3.80	-	79.31	-	208.38	nr	229.21
Inner pane BS 952, clear float 4mm thick; outer pane BS 952, Antisun toughened 6mm thick; to metal rebates with screwed metal beads and gaskets (included elsewhere)										
521mm wide x 421mm high	23.10	5.00	24.25	1.25	-	26.09	-	50.34	nr	55.38
521mm wide x 621mm high	29.90	5.00	31.39	1.60	-	33.39	-	64.79	nr	71.27
740mm wide x 740mm high	50.60	5.00	53.13	2.20	-	45.91	-	99.04	nr	108.95
848mm wide x 848mm high	66.45	5.00	69.77	2.50	-	52.18	-	121.95	nr	134.14
1048mm wide x 1048mm high	82.12	5.00	86.23	3.20	-	66.78	-	153.01	nr	168.31
1148mm wide x 1248mm high	132.38	5.00	139.00	3.80	-	79.31	-	218.30	nr	240.14
Drilling										
Hole through sheet or float glass; not exceeding 6mm thick										
6 - 15mm diameter	4.54	-	4.54	-	-	-	-	4.54	nr	5.00
16 - 38mm diameter	6.42	-	6.42	-	-	-	-	6.42	nr	7.06
exceeding 38mm diameter	12.95	-	12.95	-	-	-	-	12.95	nr	14.25
Hole through sheet or float glass; not exceeding 10mm thick										
6 - 15mm diameter	5.89	-	5.89	-	-	-	-	5.89	nr	6.47
16 - 38mm diameter	9.07	-	9.07	-	-	-	-	9.07	nr	9.98
exceeding 38mm diameter	15.73	-	15.73	-	-	-	-	15.73	nr	17.30
Hole through sheet or float glass; not exceeding 12mm thick										
6 - 15mm diameter	7.29	-	7.29	-	-	-	-	7.29	nr	8.02
16 - 38mm diameter	10.31	-	10.31	-	-	-	-	10.31	nr	11.34
exceeding 38mm diameter	18.66	-	18.66	-	-	-	-	18.66	nr	20.52
Hole through sheet or float glass; not exceeding 19mm thick										
6 - 15mm diameter	9.11	-	9.11	-	-	-	-	9.11	nr	10.03
16 - 38mm diameter	12.95	-	12.95	-	-	-	-	12.95	nr	14.25
exceeding 38mm diameter	23.03	-	23.03	-	-	-	-	23.03	nr	25.34

Labour hourly rates: (except Specialists) Craft Operatives 20.87 Labourer 15.57 Rates are national average prices. Refer to REGIONAL VARIATIONS for indicative levels of overall pricing in regions	MATERIALS			LABOUR				RATES		
	Del to Site £	Waste %	Material Cost £	Craft Optve Hrs	Lab Hrs	Labour Cost £	Sunds £	Nett Rate £	Unit	Gross rate (10%) £
GLASS (Cont'd)										
Drilling (Cont'd)										
Hole through sheet or float glass; not exceeding 25mm thick										
6 - 15mm diameter	11.46	-	11.46	-	-	-	-	11.46	nr	12.60
16 - 38mm diameter	16.24	-	16.24	-	-	-	-	16.24	nr	17.86
exceeding 38mm diameter	28.62	-	28.62	-	-	-	-	28.62	nr	31.48
For wired and laminated glass add 50%										
For countersunk holes add 33 1/3%										
Bedding edges of panes										
Wash leather strips										
to edges of 3mm thick glass or the like	0.13	5.00	0.14	0.06	-	1.25	-	1.39	m	1.53
to edges of 6mm thick glass or the like	0.27	5.00	0.28	0.07	-	1.46	-	1.74	m	1.92
Butyl rubber glazing strips										
to edges of 3mm thick glass or the like	0.40	5.00	0.41	0.06	-	1.25	-	1.67	m	1.83
to edges of 6mm thick glass or the like	0.79	5.00	0.83	0.07	-	1.46	-	2.29	m	2.52
POLYCARBONATE										
UVA stabilised polycarbonate sheet latex paper masked both sides										
3mm thick to metal rebates with screwed metal beads and gaskets (included elsewhere) standard grade	53.43	5.00	56.10	1.20	0.12	26.91	-	83.02	m²	91.32
4mm thick to metal rebates with screwed metal beads and gaskets (included elsewhere) standard grade	71.25	5.00	74.82	1.20	0.12	26.91	-	101.73	m²	111.90
5mm thick to metal rebates with screwed metal beads and gaskets (included elsewhere) standard grade	89.06	5.00	93.52	1.20	0.12	26.91	-	120.43	m²	132.47
6mm thick to metal rebates with screwed metal beads and gaskets (included elsewhere) standard grade	106.88	5.00	112.22	1.38	0.12	30.67	-	142.89	m²	157.18
8mm thick to metal rebates with screwed metal beads and gaskets (included elsewhere) standard grade	142.50	5.00	149.62	1.62	0.12	35.68	-	185.30	m²	203.83
9.5mm thick to metal rebates with screwed metal beads and gaskets (included elsewhere) standard grade	163.70	5.00	171.88	1.80	0.12	39.43	-	211.32	m²	232.45
3mm thick to metal rebates with screwed metal beads and gaskets (included elsewhere) abrasion resistant hard coated grade	105.45	5.00	110.72	1.20	0.12	26.91	-	137.64	m²	151.40
4mm thick to metal rebates with screwed metal beads and gaskets (included elsewhere) abrasion resistant hard coated grade	146.97	5.00	154.32	1.20	0.12	26.91	-	181.23	m²	199.35
5mm thick to metal rebates with screwed metal beads and gaskets (included elsewhere) abrasion resistant hard coated grade	179.61	5.00	188.59	1.20	0.12	26.91	-	215.50	m²	237.06
6mm thick to metal rebates with screwed metal beads and gaskets (included elsewhere) abrasion resistant hard coated grade	206.88	5.00	217.23	1.38	0.12	30.67	-	247.90	m²	272.69
8mm thick to metal rebates with screwed metal beads and gaskets (included elsewhere) abrasion resistant hard coated grade	249.94	5.00	262.43	1.62	0.12	35.68	-	298.11	m²	327.92
9.5mm thick to metal rebates with screwed metal beads and gaskets (included elsewhere) abrasion resistant hard coated grade	349.83	5.00	367.32	1.80	0.12	39.43	-	406.75	m²	447.43
GLASS REINFORCED PLASTIC										
GRP vandal resistant glazing; Georgian, clear, smooth both faces or crinkle one face										
3mm thick to wood rebates with screwed wood beads (included elsewhere) and putty										
general purpose grade	42.82	5.00	44.97	1.15	0.12	25.87	0.25	71.08	m²	78.19
fire retardant grade, class 2	49.26	5.00	51.72	1.15	0.12	25.87	0.25	77.84	m²	85.62
fire retardant grade, class 0	66.39	5.00	69.71	1.15	0.12	25.87	0.25	95.82	m²	105.40
4mm thick to wood rebates with screwed wood beads (included elsewhere) and putty										
general purpose grade	47.71	5.00	50.09	1.15	0.12	25.87	0.25	76.21	m²	83.83
fire retardant grade, class 2	54.87	5.00	57.62	1.15	0.12	25.87	0.25	83.73	m²	92.11
fire retardant grade, class 0	73.95	5.00	77.65	1.15	0.12	25.87	0.25	103.76	m²	114.14
6mm thick to wood rebates with screwed wood beads (included elsewhere) and putty										
general purpose grade	67.29	5.00	70.65	1.30	0.12	29.00	0.25	99.90	m²	109.89
fire retardant grade, class 2	70.35	5.00	73.87	1.30	0.12	29.00	0.25	103.12	m²	113.43
fire retardant grade, class 0	94.83	5.00	99.57	1.30	0.12	29.00	0.25	128.82	m²	141.70

Labour hourly rates: (except Specialists) Craft Operatives 20.87 Labourer 15.57 Rates are national average prices. Refer to REGIONAL VARIATIONS for indicative levels of overall pricing in regions	MATERIALS			LABOUR				RATES		
	Del to Site £	Waste %	Material Cost £	Craft Optve Hrs	Lab Hrs	Labour Cost £	Sunds £	Nett Rate £	Unit	Gross rate (10%) £
GLASS REINFORCED PLASTIC (Cont'd)										
GRP vandal resistant glazing; Georgian, clear, smooth both faces or crinkle one face (Cont'd)										
3mm thick to metal rebates with screwed metal beads and gaskets (included elsewhere)										
general purpose grade	42.82	5.00	44.97	1.15	0.12	25.87	-	70.83	m²	77.92
fire retardant grade, class 2	49.26	5.00	51.72	1.15	0.12	25.87	-	77.59	m²	85.35
fire retardant grade, class 0	66.39	5.00	69.71	1.15	0.12	25.87	-	95.57	m²	105.13
4mm thick to metal rebates with screwed metal beads and gaskets (included elsewhere)										
general purpose grade	47.71	5.00	50.09	1.15	0.12	25.87	-	75.96	m²	83.56
fire retardant grade, class 2	54.87	5.00	57.62	1.15	0.12	25.87	-	83.48	m²	91.83
fire retardant grade, class 0	73.95	5.00	77.65	1.15	0.12	25.87	-	103.52	m²	113.87
6mm thick to metal rebates with screwed metal beads and gaskets (included elsewhere)										
general purpose grade	67.29	5.00	70.65	1.30	0.12	29.00	-	99.65	m²	109.61
fire retardant grade, class 2	70.35	5.00	73.87	1.30	0.12	29.00	-	102.87	m²	113.16
fire retardant grade, class 0	94.83	5.00	99.57	1.30	0.12	29.00	-	128.57	m²	141.43
GRP Vandal resistant glazing; plain, opaque colours or clear, smooth both faces or crinkle one face										
3mm thick to wood rebates with screwed wood beads (included elsewhere) and putty										
general purpose grade	41.38	5.00	43.44	1.15	0.12	25.87	0.25	69.56	m²	76.52
fire retardant grade, class 2	47.57	5.00	49.95	1.15	0.12	25.87	0.25	76.07	m²	83.67
fire retardant grade, class 0	64.12	5.00	67.33	1.15	0.12	25.87	0.25	93.44	m²	102.79
4mm thick to wood rebates with screwed wood beads (included elsewhere) and putty										
general purpose grade	46.74	5.00	49.08	1.15	0.12	25.87	0.25	75.19	m²	82.71
fire retardant grade, class 2	53.74	5.00	56.43	1.15	0.12	25.87	0.25	82.54	m²	90.80
fire retardant grade, class 0	72.43	5.00	76.06	1.15	0.12	25.87	0.25	102.17	m²	112.39
6mm thick to wood rebates with screwed wood beads (included elsewhere) and putty										
general purpose grade	68.34	5.00	71.75	1.30	0.12	29.00	0.25	101.00	m²	111.10
fire retardant grade, class 2	71.43	5.00	75.01	1.30	0.12	29.00	0.25	104.25	m²	114.68
fire retardant grade, class 0	96.28	5.00	101.09	1.30	0.12	29.00	0.25	130.34	m²	143.37
3mm thick to metal rebates with screwed metal beads and gaskets (included elsewhere)										
general purpose grade	41.38	5.00	43.44	1.15	0.12	25.87	-	69.31	m²	76.24
fire retardant grade, class 2	47.57	5.00	49.95	1.15	0.12	25.87	-	75.82	m²	83.40
fire retardant grade, class 0	64.12	5.00	67.33	1.15	0.12	25.87	-	93.19	m²	102.51
4mm thick to metal rebates with screwed metal beads and gaskets (included elsewhere)										
general purpose grade	46.74	5.00	49.08	1.15	0.12	25.87	-	74.95	m²	82.44
fire retardant grade, class 2	53.74	5.00	56.43	1.15	0.12	25.87	-	82.29	m²	90.52
fire retardant grade, class 0	72.43	5.00	76.06	1.15	0.12	25.87	-	101.93	m²	112.12
6mm thick to metal rebates with screwed metal beads and gaskets (included elsewhere)										
general purpose grade	68.34	5.00	71.75	1.30	0.12	29.00	-	100.75	m²	110.83
fire retardant grade, class 2	71.43	5.00	75.01	1.30	0.12	29.00	-	104.01	m²	114.41
fire retardant grade, class 0	96.28	5.00	101.09	1.30	0.12	29.00	-	130.09	m²	143.10
GRP Vandal resistant glazing; diamond, clear, smooth both faces or crinkle one face										
3mm thick to wood rebates with screwed wood beads (included elsewhere) and putty										
general purpose grade	42.82	5.00	44.97	1.15	0.12	25.87	0.25	71.08	m²	78.19
fire retardant grade, class 2	49.26	5.00	51.72	1.15	0.12	25.87	0.25	77.84	m²	85.62
fire retardant grade, class 0	66.39	5.00	69.71	1.15	0.12	25.87	0.25	95.82	m²	105.40
4mm thick to wood rebates with screwed wood beads (included elsewhere) and putty										
general purpose grade	48.99	5.00	51.44	1.15	0.12	25.87	0.25	77.56	m²	85.31
fire retardant grade, class 2	56.34	5.00	59.15	1.15	0.12	25.87	0.25	85.27	m²	93.80
fire retardant grade, class 0	75.93	5.00	79.73	1.15	0.12	25.87	0.25	105.85	m²	116.43
6mm thick to wood rebates with screwed wood beads (included elsewhere) and putty										
general purpose grade	67.80	5.00	71.19	1.30	0.12	29.00	0.25	100.44	m²	110.48
fire retardant grade, class 2	77.98	5.00	81.88	1.30	0.12	29.00	0.25	111.13	m²	122.24
fire retardant grade, class 0	105.09	5.00	110.35	1.30	0.12	29.00	0.25	139.60	m²	153.56
3mm thick to metal rebates with screwed metal beads and gaskets (included elsewhere)										
general purpose grade	42.82	5.00	44.97	1.15	0.12	25.87	-	70.83	m²	77.92
fire retardant grade, class 2	49.26	5.00	51.72	1.15	0.12	25.87	-	77.59	m²	85.35
fire retardant grade, class 0	66.39	5.00	69.71	1.15	0.12	25.87	-	95.57	m²	105.13
4mm thick to metal rebates with screwed metal beads and gaskets (included elsewhere)										
general purpose grade	48.99	5.00	51.44	1.15	0.12	25.87	-	77.31	m²	85.04
fire retardant grade, class 2	56.34	5.00	59.15	1.15	0.12	25.87	-	85.02	m²	93.53
fire retardant grade, class 0	75.93	5.00	79.73	1.15	0.12	25.87	-	105.60	m²	116.16
6mm thick to metal rebates with screwed metal beads and gaskets (included elsewhere)										
general purpose grade	67.80	5.00	71.19	1.30	0.12	29.00	-	100.19	m²	110.21
fire retardant grade, class 2	77.98	5.00	81.88	1.30	0.12	29.00	-	110.88	m²	121.97

Labour hourly rates: (except Specialists) Craft Operatives 20.87 Labourer 15.57 Rates are national average prices. Refer to REGIONAL VARIATIONS for indicative levels of overall pricing in regions	MATERIALS			LABOUR				RATES		
	Del to Site £	Waste %	Material Cost £	Craft Optve Hrs	Lab Hrs	Labour Cost £	Sunds £	Nett Rate £	Unit	Gross rate (10%) £
GLASS REINFORCED PLASTIC (Cont'd)										
GRP Vandal resistant glazing; diamond, clear, smooth both faces or crinkle one face (Cont'd)										
6mm thick to metal rebates with screwed metal beads and gaskets (included elsewhere) (Cont'd)										
fire retardant grade, class 0	105.09	5.00	110.35	1.30	0.12	29.00	-	139.35	m²	153.28
POLYESTER WINDOW FILMS										
Polyester window films; Durable Berkeley Company Ltd.										
3M Scotchshield Safety films; applying to glass										
type SH4CLL, optically clear	-	-	Specialist	-	-	Specialist	-	46.94	m²	51.63
type SH4S1L, combination solar/safety	-	-	Specialist	-	-	Specialist	-	56.32	m²	61.95
3M Scotchtint Solar Control films; applying to glass										
type P18, silver	-	-	Specialist	-	-	Specialist	-	51.63	m²	56.79
type RE15S1X, external	-	-	Specialist	-	-	Specialist	-	65.70	m²	72.27
type RE35NEARL, neutral	-	-	Specialist	-	-	Specialist	-	51.63	m²	56.79
3M Scotchtint Plus All Seasons insulating films; applying to glass										
type LE20 S1AR (silver)	-	-	Specialist	-	-	Specialist	-	65.70	m²	72.27
type LE35 AMARL (bronze)	-	-	Specialist	-	-	Specialist	-	65.70	m²	72.27
type LE50 AMARL (bronze)	-	-	Specialist	-	-	Specialist	-	65.70	m²	72.27
MIRRORS										
BS 952, clear float, SG, silvered and protected with copper backing										
6mm thick; fixing to masonry with brass screws, chromium plated dome covers, rubber sleeves and washers										
holes 6mm diameter -4; edges polished										
254 x 400mm	48.92	5.00	51.37	0.50	-	10.44	0.68	62.48	nr	68.73
300 x 460mm	49.81	5.00	52.30	0.50	-	10.44	0.68	63.41	nr	69.75
360 x 500mm	52.62	5.00	55.26	0.50	-	10.44	0.68	66.37	nr	73.00
460 x 560mm	59.31	5.00	62.28	0.65	-	13.57	0.68	76.52	nr	84.17
460 x 600mm	60.98	5.00	64.03	0.65	-	13.57	0.68	78.27	nr	86.10
460 x 900mm	72.15	5.00	75.76	0.70	-	14.61	0.68	91.05	nr	100.15
500 x 680mm	65.99	5.00	69.29	0.65	-	13.57	0.68	83.53	nr	91.89
600 x 900mm	82.42	5.00	86.55	0.75	-	15.65	0.68	102.87	nr	113.16
holes 6mm diameter -4; edges bevelled										
254 x 400mm	55.15	5.00	57.91	0.50	-	10.44	0.68	69.02	nr	75.92
300 x 460mm	57.09	5.00	59.94	0.50	-	10.44	0.68	71.06	nr	78.16
360 x 500mm	60.87	5.00	63.91	0.50	-	10.44	0.68	75.02	nr	82.53
460 x 560mm	69.08	5.00	72.54	0.65	-	13.57	0.68	86.78	nr	95.46
460 x 600mm	71.14	5.00	74.70	0.65	-	13.57	0.68	88.94	nr	97.83
460 x 900mm	85.19	5.00	89.45	0.70	-	14.61	0.68	104.73	nr	115.21
500 x 680mm	77.30	5.00	81.16	0.65	-	13.57	0.68	95.41	nr	104.95
600 x 900mm	96.79	5.00	101.63	0.75	-	15.65	0.68	117.96	nr	129.76
HACKING OUT EXISTING GLASS										
Hacking out existing glass; preparing for re-glazing										
Float glass										
wood rebates	-	-	-	0.44	0.44	16.03	0.28	16.31	m	17.95
wood rebates and screwed wood beads; storing beads for re-use	-	-	-	0.52	0.52	18.95	0.28	19.23	m	21.15
metal rebates	-	-	-	0.46	0.46	16.76	0.28	17.04	m	18.75
metal rebates and screwed metal beads; storing beads for re-use	-	-	-	0.55	0.55	20.04	0.28	20.32	m	22.35
Float glass behind guard bars in position										
wood rebates and screwed wood beads; storing beads for re-use	-	-	-	0.85	0.85	30.97	0.28	31.25	m	34.38
metal rebates and screwed metal beads; storing beads for re-use	-	-	-	0.90	0.90	32.80	0.28	33.08	m	36.38

Labour hourly rates: (except Specialists) Craft Operatives 20.87 Labourer 15.57 Rates are national average prices. Refer to REGIONAL VARIATIONS for indicative levels of overall pricing in regions	MATERIALS			LABOUR				RATES		
	Del to Site £	Waste %	Material Cost £	Craft Optve Hrs	Lab Hrs	Labour Cost £	Sunds £	Nett Rate £	Unit	Gross rate (10%) £
IN-SITU, TILED, BLOCK, MOSAIC, SHEET, APPLIED LIQUID OR PLANTED FINISHES										
Screeds, beds and toppings; Mortar, cement and sand (1:3) - screeds										
19mm work to floors on concrete base; one coat; screeded										
level and to falls only not exceeding 15 degrees from horizontal	3.00	5.00	3.14	0.24	0.15	7.34	-	10.48	m²	11.53
to falls and crossfalls and to slopes not exceeding 15 degrees from horizontal	3.00	5.00	3.14	0.34	0.15	9.43	-	12.57	m²	13.82
25mm work to floors on concrete base; one coat; screeded										
level and to falls only not exceeding 15 degrees from horizontal	3.86	5.00	4.03	0.26	0.16	7.92	-	11.95	m²	13.15
to falls and crossfalls and to slopes not exceeding 15 degrees from horizontal	3.86	5.00	4.03	0.36	0.16	10.00	-	14.04	m²	15.44
32mm work to floors on concrete base; one coat; screeded										
level and to falls only not exceeding 15 degrees from horizontal	4.85	5.00	5.08	0.29	0.18	8.85	-	13.94	m²	15.33
to falls and crossfalls and to slopes not exceeding 15 degrees from horizontal	4.85	5.00	5.08	0.39	0.18	10.94	-	16.02	m²	17.63
38mm work to floors on concrete base; one coat; screeded										
level and to falls only not exceeding 15 degrees from horizontal	5.71	5.00	5.98	0.31	0.19	9.43	-	15.41	m²	16.95
to falls and crossfalls and to slopes not exceeding 15 degrees from horizontal	5.71	5.00	5.98	0.41	0.19	11.52	-	17.50	m²	19.24
50mm work to floors on concrete base; one coat; screeded										
level and to falls only not exceeding 15 degrees from horizontal	7.42	5.00	7.78	0.36	0.21	10.78	-	18.56	m²	20.42
to falls and crossfalls and to slopes not exceeding 15 degrees from horizontal	7.42	5.00	7.78	0.46	0.21	12.87	-	20.65	m²	22.71
19mm work to floors on concrete base; one coat; troweled										
level and to falls only not exceeding 15 degrees from horizontal	3.00	5.00	3.14	0.36	0.15	9.85	-	12.98	m²	14.28
to falls and crossfalls and to slopes not exceeding 15 degrees from horizontal	3.00	5.00	3.14	0.46	0.15	11.94	-	15.07	m²	16.58
25mm work to floors on concrete base; one coat; troweled										
level and to falls only not exceeding 15 degrees from horizontal	3.86	5.00	4.03	0.38	0.16	10.42	-	14.46	m²	15.90
to falls and crossfalls and to slopes not exceeding 15 degrees from horizontal	3.86	5.00	4.03	0.48	0.16	12.51	-	16.54	m²	18.20
32mm work to floors on concrete base; one coat; troweled										
level and to falls only not exceeding 15 degrees from horizontal	4.85	5.00	5.08	0.41	0.18	11.36	-	16.44	m²	18.09
to falls and crossfalls and to slopes not exceeding 15 degrees from horizontal	4.85	5.00	5.08	0.51	0.18	13.45	-	18.53	m²	20.38
38mm work to floors on concrete base; one coat; troweled										
level and to falls only not exceeding 15 degrees from horizontal	5.71	5.00	5.98	0.43	0.19	11.93	-	17.91	m²	19.70
to falls and crossfalls and to slopes not exceeding 15 degrees from horizontal	5.71	5.00	5.98	0.53	0.19	14.02	-	20.00	m²	22.00
50mm work to floors on concrete base; one coat; troweled										
level and to falls only not exceeding 15 degrees from horizontal	7.42	5.00	7.78	0.48	0.21	13.29	-	21.06	m²	23.17
to falls and crossfalls and to slopes not exceeding 15 degrees from horizontal	7.42	5.00	7.78	0.58	0.21	15.37	-	23.15	m²	25.47
19mm work to floors on concrete base; one coat; floated										
level and to falls only not exceeding 15 degrees from horizontal	3.00	5.00	3.14	0.34	0.15	9.43	-	12.57	m²	13.82
to falls and crossfalls and to slopes not exceeding 15 degrees from horizontal	3.00	5.00	3.14	0.44	0.15	11.52	-	14.65	m²	16.12
25mm work to floors on concrete base; one coat; floated										
level and to falls only not exceeding 15 degrees from horizontal	3.86	5.00	4.03	0.36	0.16	10.00	-	14.04	m²	15.44
to falls and crossfalls and to slopes not exceeding 15 degrees from horizontal	3.86	5.00	4.03	0.46	0.16	12.09	-	16.13	m²	17.74
32mm work to floors on concrete base; one coat; floated										
level and to falls only not exceeding 15 degrees from horizontal	4.85	5.00	5.08	0.39	0.18	10.94	-	16.02	m²	17.63
to falls and crossfalls and to slopes not exceeding 15 degrees from horizontal	4.85	5.00	5.08	0.49	0.18	13.03	-	18.11	m²	19.92
38mm work to floors on concrete base; one coat; floated										
level and to falls only not exceeding 15 degrees from horizontal	5.71	5.00	5.98	0.41	0.19	11.52	-	17.50	m²	19.24
to falls and crossfalls and to slopes not exceeding 15 degrees from horizontal	5.71	5.00	5.98	0.51	0.19	13.60	-	19.58	m²	21.54
50mm work to floors on concrete base; one coat; floated										
level and to falls only not exceeding 15 degrees from horizontal	7.42	5.00	7.78	0.46	0.21	12.87	-	20.65	m²	22.71
to falls and crossfalls and to slopes not exceeding 15 degrees from horizontal	7.42	5.00	7.78	0.56	0.21	14.96	-	22.73	m²	25.01
13mm work to walls on brickwork or blockwork base; one coat; screeded										
width exceeding 600mm	1.85	5.00	1.95	0.40	0.20	11.46	-	13.41	m²	14.75
width; 300mm	0.57	10.00	0.63	0.24	0.06	5.94	-	6.57	m	7.23

Labour hourly rates: (except Specialists) Craft Operatives 20.87 Labourer 15.57 Rates are national average prices. Refer to REGIONAL VARIATIONS for indicative levels of overall pricing in regions	MATERIALS			LABOUR				RATES		
	Del to Site £	Waste %	Material Cost £	Craft Optve Hrs	Lab Hrs	Labour Cost £	Sunds £	Nett Rate £	Unit	Gross rate (10%) £
IN-SITU, TILED, BLOCK, MOSAIC, SHEET, APPLIED LIQUID OR PLANTED FINISHES (Cont'd)										
Screeds, beds and toppings; Mortar, cement and sand (1:3) - screeds (Cont'd)										
13mm work to walls on brickwork or blockwork base; one coat; troweled										
width exceeding 600mm	1.85	5.00	1.95	0.52	0.20	13.97	-	15.91	m²	17.50
width: 300mm	0.57	10.00	0.63	0.31	0.06	7.40	-	8.03	m	8.83
13mm work to walls on brickwork or blockwork base; one coat; floated										
width exceeding 600mm	1.85	5.00	1.95	0.50	0.20	13.55	-	15.50	m²	17.05
width: 300mm	0.57	10.00	0.63	0.30	0.06	7.20	-	7.82	m	8.60
Screeds, beds and toppings; Mortar, cement and sand (1:3) - paving										
25mm work to floors on concrete base; one coat; troweled										
level and to falls only not exceeding 15 degrees from horizontal	3.86	5.00	4.03	0.38	0.16	10.42	-	14.46	m²	15.90
to falls and crossfalls and to slopes not exceeding 15 degrees from horizontal	3.86	5.00	4.03	0.48	0.16	12.51	-	16.54	m²	18.20
to slopes exceeding 15 degrees from horizontal	3.86	5.00	4.03	0.53	0.16	13.55	-	17.59	m²	19.34
32mm work to floors on concrete base; one coat; troweled										
level and to falls only not exceeding 15 degrees from horizontal	4.85	5.00	5.08	0.41	0.18	11.36	-	16.44	m²	18.09
to falls and crossfalls and to slopes not exceeding 15 degrees from horizontal	4.85	5.00	5.08	0.51	0.18	13.45	-	18.53	m²	20.38
to slopes exceeding 15 degrees from horizontal	4.85	5.00	5.08	0.56	0.18	14.49	-	19.57	m²	21.53
38mm work to floors on concrete base; one coat; troweled										
level and to falls only not exceeding 15 degrees from horizontal	5.71	5.00	5.98	0.43	0.19	11.93	-	17.91	m²	19.70
to falls and crossfalls and to slopes not exceeding 15 degrees from horizontal	5.71	5.00	5.98	0.53	0.19	14.02	-	20.00	m²	22.00
to slopes exceeding 15 degrees from horizontal	5.71	5.00	5.98	0.58	0.19	15.06	-	21.04	m²	23.15
50mm work to floors on concrete base; one coat; troweled										
level and to falls only not exceeding 15 degrees from horizontal	7.42	5.00	7.78	0.48	0.21	13.29	-	21.06	m²	23.17
to falls and crossfalls and to slopes not exceeding 15 degrees from horizontal	7.42	5.00	7.78	0.58	0.21	15.37	-	23.15	m²	25.47
to slopes exceeding 15 degrees from horizontal	7.42	5.00	7.78	0.63	0.21	16.42	-	24.20	m²	26.61
19mm work to treads on concrete base; screeded width 275mm	1.21	10.00	1.33	0.15	0.04	3.75	-	5.08	m	5.59
25mm work to treads on concrete base; screeded width 275mm	1.50	10.00	1.64	0.16	0.04	3.96	-	5.60	m	6.16
32mm work to treads on concrete base; screeded width 275mm	1.93	10.00	2.11	0.18	0.05	4.54	-	6.65	m	7.31
38mm work to treads on concrete base; screeded width 275mm	2.35	10.00	2.58	0.20	0.05	4.95	-	7.53	m	8.29
19mm work to treads on concrete base; floated width 275mm	1.21	10.00	1.33	0.20	0.04	4.80	-	6.12	m	6.74
25mm work to treads on concrete base; floated width 275mm	1.50	10.00	1.64	0.21	0.04	5.01	-	6.65	m	7.31
32mm work to treads on concrete base; floated width 275mm	1.93	10.00	2.11	0.23	0.05	5.58	-	7.69	m	8.46
38mm work to treads on concrete base; floated width 275mm	2.35	10.00	2.58	0.25	0.05	6.00	-	8.58	m	9.44
19mm work to treads on concrete base; troweled width 275mm	1.21	10.00	1.33	0.25	0.04	5.84	-	7.17	m	7.88
25mm work to treads on concrete base; troweled width 275mm	1.50	10.00	1.64	0.26	0.04	6.05	-	7.69	m	8.46
32mm work to treads on concrete base; troweled width 275mm	1.93	10.00	2.11	0.28	0.05	6.62	-	8.73	m	9.61
38mm work to treads on concrete base; troweled width 275mm	2.35	10.00	2.58	0.30	0.05	7.04	-	9.62	m	10.58
19mm work to plain risers on concrete base; keyed height 175mm	0.71	10.00	0.78	0.30	0.03	6.73	-	7.51	m	8.26
25mm work to plain risers on concrete base; keyed height 175mm	1.00	10.00	1.10	0.35	0.03	7.77	-	8.87	m	9.76
32mm work to plain risers on concrete base; keyed height 175mm	1.14	10.00	1.25	0.40	0.03	8.82	-	10.07	m	11.08
19mm work to plain risers on concrete base; troweled height 175mm	0.71	10.00	0.78	0.50	0.03	10.90	-	11.69	m	12.86
25mm work to plain risers on concrete base; troweled height 175mm	1.00	10.00	1.10	0.55	0.03	11.95	-	13.04	m	14.35
32mm work to plain risers on concrete base; troweled height 175mm	1.14	10.00	1.25	0.60	0.03	12.99	-	14.24	m	15.67
19mm work to undercut risers on concrete base; keyed height 175mm	0.71	10.00	0.78	0.35	0.03	7.77	-	8.56	m	9.41
25mm work to undercut risers on concrete base; keyed height 175mm	1.00	10.00	1.10	0.40	0.03	8.82	-	9.91	m	10.90

Labour hourly rates: (except Specialists) Craft Operatives 20.87 Labourer 15.57 Rates are national average prices. Refer to REGIONAL VARIATIONS for indicative levels of overall pricing in regions	MATERIALS			LABOUR				RATES		
	Del to Site £	Waste %	Material Cost £	Craft Optve Hrs	Lab Hrs	Labour Cost £	Sunds £	Nett Rate £	Unit	Gross rate (10%) £
IN-SITU, TILED, BLOCK, MOSAIC, SHEET, APPLIED LIQUID OR PLANTED FINISHES (Cont'd)										
Screeds, beds and toppings; Mortar, cement and sand (1:3) - paving (Cont'd)										
32mm work to undercut risers on concrete base; keyed										
height 175mm	1.14	10.00	1.25	0.45	0.03	9.86	-	11.11	m	12.22
19mm work to undercut risers on concrete base; troweled										
height 175mm	0.71	10.00	0.78	0.55	0.03	11.95	-	12.73	m	14.00
25mm work to undercut risers on concrete base; troweled										
height 175mm	1.00	10.00	1.10	0.60	0.03	12.99	-	14.09	m	15.50
32mm work to undercut risers on concrete base; troweled										
height 175mm	1.14	10.00	1.25	0.65	0.03	14.03	-	15.29	m	16.82
19mm work to skirtings on brickwork or blockwork base										
height 100mm	0.43	10.00	0.47	0.70	0.05	15.39	-	15.86	m	17.44
height 150mm	0.57	10.00	0.63	0.80	0.05	17.47	-	18.10	m	19.91
25mm work to skirtings on brickwork or blockwork base										
height 100mm	0.57	10.00	0.63	0.75	0.05	16.43	-	17.06	m	18.76
height 150mm	0.86	10.00	0.94	0.85	0.05	18.52	-	19.46	m	21.41
If paving oil proofed, add										
25mm work	0.18	10.00	0.20	-	0.03	0.47	-	0.67	m²	0.73
32mm work	0.23	10.00	0.25	-	0.03	0.47	-	0.72	m²	0.79
38mm work	0.27	10.00	0.30	-	0.04	0.62	-	0.92	m²	1.02
50mm work	0.36	10.00	0.40	-	0.05	0.78	-	1.17	m²	1.29
Screeds, beds and toppings; Granolithic screed; steel troweled										
25mm work to floors on concrete base; one coat										
level and to falls only not exceeding 15 degrees from horizontal	4.76	5.00	4.97	0.42	0.18	11.57	-	16.54	m²	18.19
to falls and crossfalls and to slopes not exceeding 15 degrees from horizontal	4.76	5.00	4.97	0.52	0.18	13.66	-	18.63	m²	20.49
to slopes exceeding 15 degrees from horizontal	4.76	5.00	4.97	0.57	0.18	14.70	-	19.67	m²	21.64
32mm work to floors on concrete base; one coat										
level and to falls only not exceeding 15 degrees from horizontal	5.93	5.00	6.20	0.45	0.20	12.51	-	18.71	m²	20.58
to falls and crossfalls and to slopes not exceeding 15 degrees from horizontal	5.93	5.00	6.20	0.55	0.20	14.59	-	20.79	m²	22.87
to slopes exceeding 15 degrees from horizontal	5.93	5.00	6.20	0.61	0.20	15.84	-	22.04	m²	24.25
38mm work to floors on concrete base; one coat										
level and to falls only not exceeding 15 degrees from horizontal	6.94	5.00	7.25	0.48	0.21	13.29	-	20.54	m²	22.59
to falls and crossfalls and to slopes not exceeding 15 degrees from horizontal	6.94	5.00	7.25	0.58	0.21	15.37	-	22.63	m²	24.89
to slopes exceeding 15 degrees from horizontal	6.94	5.00	7.25	0.63	0.21	16.42	-	23.67	m²	26.04
50mm work to floors on concrete base; one coat										
level and to falls only not exceeding 15 degrees from horizontal	8.94	5.00	9.36	0.54	0.24	15.01	-	24.37	m²	26.80
to falls and crossfalls and to slopes not exceeding 15 degrees from horizontal	8.94	5.00	9.36	0.64	0.24	17.09	-	26.45	m²	29.10
to slopes exceeding 15 degrees from horizontal	8.94	5.00	9.36	0.69	0.24	18.14	-	27.50	m²	30.25
25mm work to treads on concrete base										
width 275mm	1.82	10.00	1.98	0.25	0.05	6.00	-	7.98	m	8.78
32mm work to treads on concrete base										
width 275mm	2.32	10.00	2.54	0.30	0.06	7.20	-	9.73	m	10.71
38mm work to treads on concrete base										
width 275mm	2.82	10.00	3.09	0.35	0.06	8.24	-	11.33	m	12.46
50mm work to treads on concrete base										
width 275mm	3.66	10.00	4.01	0.40	0.07	9.44	-	13.45	m	14.79
13mm work to plain risers on concrete base										
height 175mm	0.50	10.00	0.55	0.50	0.05	11.21	-	11.77	m	12.94
19mm work to plain risers on concrete base										
height 175mm	0.84	10.00	0.92	0.55	0.05	12.26	-	13.18	m	14.49
25mm work to plain risers on concrete base										
height 175mm	1.17	10.00	1.29	0.60	0.05	13.30	-	14.59	m	16.05
32mm work to plain risers on concrete base										
height 175mm	1.34	10.00	1.47	0.65	0.05	14.34	-	15.82	m	17.40
13mm work to undercut risers on concrete base										
height 175mm	0.50	10.00	0.55	0.55	0.05	12.26	-	12.81	m	14.09
19mm work to undercut risers on concrete base										
height 175mm	0.84	10.00	0.92	0.60	0.05	13.30	-	14.22	m	15.64
25mm work to undercut risers on concrete base										
height 175mm	1.17	10.00	1.29	0.65	0.05	14.34	-	15.63	m	17.19
32mm work to undercut risers on concrete base										
height 175mm	1.34	10.00	1.47	0.70	0.05	15.39	-	16.86	m	18.55
13mm work to strings on concrete base										
height 300mm	1.00	10.00	1.10	0.70	0.05	15.39	-	16.49	m	18.14
19mm work to strings on concrete base										
height 300mm	1.51	10.00	1.66	0.75	0.05	16.43	-	18.09	m	19.90
25mm work to strings on concrete base										
height 300mm	1.84	10.00	2.02	0.80	0.05	17.47	-	19.50	m	21.45

Labour hourly rates: (except Specialists) Craft Operatives 20.87 Labourer 15.57 Rates are national average prices. Refer to REGIONAL VARIATIONS for indicative levels of overall pricing in regions	MATERIALS			LABOUR				RATES		
	Del to Site £	Waste %	Material Cost £	Craft Optve Hrs	Lab Hrs	Labour Cost £	Sunds £	Nett Rate £	Unit	Gross rate (10%) £
IN-SITU, TILED, BLOCK, MOSAIC, SHEET, APPLIED LIQUID OR PLANTED FINISHES (Cont'd)										
Screeds, beds and toppings; Granolithic screed; steel troweled (Cont'd)										
32mm work to strings on concrete base										
height 300mm	2.34	10.00	2.58	0.85	0.06	18.67	-	21.25	m	23.37
13mm work to strings on brickwork or blockwork base										
height 275mm	0.84	10.00	0.92	0.65	0.05	14.34	-	15.26	m	16.79
19mm work to strings on brickwork or blockwork base										
height 275mm	1.34	10.00	1.47	0.70	0.05	15.39	-	16.86	m	18.55
25mm work to strings on brickwork or blockwork base										
height 275mm	1.67	10.00	1.84	0.75	0.05	16.43	-	18.27	m	20.10
32mm work to strings on brickwork or blockwork base										
height 275mm	2.17	10.00	2.39	0.80	0.06	17.63	-	20.02	m	22.02
13mm work to aprons on concrete base										
height 150mm	0.50	10.00	0.55	0.50	0.05	11.21	-	11.77	m	12.94
19mm work to aprons on concrete base										
height 150mm	0.67	10.00	0.74	0.55	0.05	12.26	-	12.99	m	14.29
25mm work to aprons on concrete base										
height 150mm	1.00	10.00	1.10	0.60	0.05	13.30	-	14.40	m	15.84
32mm work to aprons on concrete base										
height 150mm	1.17	10.00	1.29	0.65	0.05	14.34	-	15.63	m	17.19
13mm work to skirtings on concrete base										
height 150mm	0.50	10.00	0.55	0.75	0.05	16.43	-	16.98	m	18.68
19mm work to skirtings on concrete base										
height 150mm	0.67	10.00	0.74	0.80	0.05	17.47	-	18.21	m	20.03
25mm work to skirtings on concrete base										
height 150mm	1.00	10.00	1.10	0.85	0.05	18.52	-	19.62	m	21.58
32mm work to skirtings on concrete base										
height 150mm	1.17	10.00	1.29	0.90	0.05	19.56	-	20.85	m	22.93
25mm linings to channels on concrete base										
150mm girth on face; to falls	1.08	10.00	1.18	0.20	0.05	4.95	-	6.13	m	6.74
225mm girth on face; to falls	1.48	10.00	1.62	0.25	0.05	6.00	-	7.61	m	8.37
32mm linings to channels on concrete base										
150mm girth on face; to falls	1.24	10.00	1.36	0.23	0.05	5.58	-	6.94	m	7.63
225mm girth on face; to falls	1.98	10.00	2.17	0.28	0.05	6.62	-	8.79	m	9.67
38mm linings to channels on concrete base										
150mm girth on face; to falls	1.58	10.00	1.73	0.25	0.05	6.00	-	7.72	m	8.50
225mm girth on face; to falls	2.32	10.00	2.54	0.30	0.05	7.04	-	9.58	m	10.53
50mm linings to channels on concrete base										
150mm girth on face; to falls	1.91	10.00	2.10	0.30	0.05	7.04	-	9.14	m	10.05
225mm girth on face; to falls	2.99	10.00	3.27	0.35	0.05	8.08	-	11.36	m	12.49
Rounded angles and intersections										
10 - 100mm radius	-	-	-	0.18	-	3.76	-	3.76	m	4.13
If paving tinted, add according to tint										
25mm work	1.95	10.00	2.14	-	0.03	0.47	-	2.61	m²	2.87
32mm work	2.50	10.00	2.75	-	0.03	0.47	-	3.21	m²	3.53
38mm work	2.96	10.00	3.26	-	0.04	0.62	-	3.88	m²	4.27
50mm work	3.90	10.00	4.29	-	0.05	0.78	-	5.07	m²	5.58
If carborundum troweled into surface										
add	2.42	10.00	2.66	0.08	0.04	2.29	-	4.95	m²	5.45
Screeds, beds and toppings; Surface hardeners on paving										
Proprietary surface hardener (Epoxy Resin Based)										
two coats	21.00	10.00	23.10	-	0.20	3.11	-	26.21	m²	28.83
three coats	28.77	10.00	31.64	-	0.25	3.89	-	35.54	m²	39.09
Polyurethane floor sealer										
two coats	4.99	10.00	5.49	-	0.20	3.11	-	8.60	m²	9.46
three coats	6.44	10.00	7.08	-	0.25	3.89	-	10.97	m²	12.07
Nitoflor Lithurin concrete surface dressing										
one coat	0.76	10.00	0.84	-	0.17	2.65	-	3.49	m²	3.84
two coats	1.53	10.00	1.68	-	0.24	3.74	-	5.42	m²	5.96
If on old floors										
add for cleaning and degreasing	0.95	5.00	0.99	-	0.35	5.45	-	6.44	m²	7.09
Screeds, beds and toppings; Vermiculite screed consisting of cement and Vermiculite aggregate finished with 20mm cement and sand (1:4) screeded bed										
45mm work to roofs on concrete base; two coats										
to falls and crossfalls and to slopes not exceeding 15 degrees from horizontal	7.93	5.00	8.31	0.45	0.48	16.87	-	25.18	m²	27.70
60mm work to roofs on concrete base; two coats										
to falls and crossfalls and to slopes not exceeding 15 degrees from horizontal	11.06	5.00	11.60	0.48	0.51	17.96	-	29.55	m²	32.51

Labour hourly rates: (except Specialists) Craft Operatives 20.87 Labourer 15.57 Rates are national average prices. Refer to REGIONAL VARIATIONS for indicative levels of overall pricing in regions	MATERIALS			LABOUR				RATES		
	Del to Site £	Waste %	Material Cost £	Craft Optve Hrs	Lab Hrs	Labour Cost £	Sunds £	Nett Rate £	Unit	Gross rate (10%) £
IN-SITU, TILED, BLOCK, MOSAIC, SHEET, APPLIED LIQUID OR PLANTED FINISHES (Cont'd)										
Screeds, beds and toppings; Vermiculite screed consisting of cement and Vermiculite aggregate finished with 20mm cement and sand (1:4) screeded bed (Cont'd)										
70mm work to roofs on concrete base; two coats										
to falls and crossfalls and to slopes not exceeding 15 degrees from horizontal	13.14	5.00	13.78	0.51	0.54	19.05	-	32.84	m²	36.12
80mm work to roofs on concrete base; two coats										
to falls and crossfalls and to slopes not exceeding 15 degrees from horizontal	15.23	5.00	15.97	0.53	0.56	19.78	-	35.75	m²	39.33
Screeds, beds and toppings; Lightweight concrete screed consisting of cement and lightweight aggregate, medium grade, 10 - 5 gauge, 800 kg/m³ (1:10) finished with 15mm cement and sand (1:4) troweled bed										
50mm work to roofs on concrete base; two coats										
to falls and crossfalls and to slopes not exceeding 15 degrees from horizontal	8.13	5.00	8.52	0.60	0.51	20.46	-	28.99	m²	31.89
75mm work to roofs on concrete base; two coats										
to falls and crossfalls and to slopes not exceeding 15 degrees from horizontal	12.43	5.00	13.04	0.65	0.56	22.28	-	35.32	m²	38.86
100mm work to roofs on concrete base; two coats										
to falls and crossfalls and to slopes not exceeding 15 degrees from horizontal	16.73	5.00	17.55	0.70	0.61	24.11	-	41.66	m²	45.83
Screeds, beds and toppings; Division strips										
Aluminium dividing strips; setting in bed										
5 x 25mm; flat section	4.76	5.00	5.00	0.15	-	3.13	-	8.13	m	8.94
Brass dividing strips; setting in bed										
5 x 25mm; flat section	24.89	5.00	26.13	0.15	-	3.13	-	29.26	m	32.19
Screeds, beds and toppings; Screed reinforcement										
Reinforcement; galvanised wire netting, BS EN 10223-2, 13mm mesh, 19 gauge wire; 150mm laps; placing in position										
floors	3.92	5.00	4.12	0.05	-	1.04	-	5.16	m²	5.68
Reinforcement; galvanised wire netting, BS EN 10223-2, 25mm mesh, 19 gauge wire; 150mm laps; placing in position										
floors	2.45	5.00	2.58	0.05	-	1.04	-	3.62	m²	3.98
Reinforcement; galvanised wire netting, BS EN 10223-2, 50mm mesh, 19 gauge wire; 150mm laps; placing in position										
floors	3.01	5.00	3.16	0.05	-	1.04	-	4.20	m²	4.62
Screeds, beds and toppings; Mastic asphalt flooring/floor underlays										
Paving; BS 6925 (limestone aggregate), brown, smooth floated finish										
Flooring and underlay 15mm thick; coats of asphalt - 1; to concrete base; flat										
width not exceeding 150mm	-	-	Specialist	-	-	Specialist	-	43.02	m²	47.33
width 150 - 225mm	-	-	Specialist	-	-	Specialist	-	36.06	m²	39.66
width 225 - 300mm	-	-	Specialist	-	-	Specialist	-	28.52	m²	31.37
width 300 - 600mm	-	-	Specialist	-	-	Specialist	-	23.77	m²	26.14
width exceeding 600mm	-	-	Specialist	-	-	Specialist	-	21.55	m²	23.71
Skirtings 15mm thick; coats of asphalt - 1; no underlay; to brickwork base										
girth not exceeding 150mm	-	-	Specialist	-	-	Specialist	-	13.85	m	15.23
Paving; BS 6925 (limestone aggregate), red, smooth floated finish										
Flooring and underlay 15mm thick; coats of asphalt - 1; to concrete base; flat										
width not exceeding 150mm	-	-	Specialist	-	-	Specialist	-	43.43	m²	47.78
width 150 - 225mm	-	-	Specialist	-	-	Specialist	-	38.84	m²	42.73
width 225 - 300mm	-	-	Specialist	-	-	Specialist	-	31.06	m²	34.16
width 300 - 600mm	-	-	Specialist	-	-	Specialist	-	24.01	m²	26.41
width exceeding 600mm	-	-	Specialist	-	-	Specialist	-	23.03	m²	25.33
Skirtings 15mm thick; coats of asphalt - 1; no underlay; to brickwork base										
girth not exceeding 150mm	-	-	Specialist	-	-	Specialist	-	15.41	m	16.95
Screeds, beds and toppings; Trowelled bitumen/resin/rubber-latex flooring										
One coat levelling screeds										
3mm work to floors on concrete base; one coat										
level and to falls only not exceeding 15 degrees from horizontal	2.73	5.00	2.87	0.40	0.05	9.13	-	11.99	m²	13.19
3mm work to floors on existing timber boarded base; one coat										
level and to falls only not exceeding 15 degrees from horizontal	2.73	5.00	2.87	0.50	0.06	11.37	-	14.24	m²	15.66
Screeds, beds and toppings; Plasterboard; baseboard underlay										
Baseboarding; Gyproc Handiboard; 5mm joints, filled with plaster and scrimmed; fixing with Galvanised nails, 30mm long at 400mm centres										
9.5mm work to walls on timber base										
width exceeding 600mm	4.34	5.00	4.54	0.29	0.15	8.39	-	12.93	m²	14.23
width; 300mm	1.37	10.00	1.49	0.17	0.05	4.33	-	5.82	m	6.40

Labour hourly rates: (except Specialists) Craft Operatives 20.87 Labourer 15.57 Rates are national average prices. Refer to REGIONAL VARIATIONS for indicative levels of overall pricing in regions	MATERIALS			LABOUR				RATES		
	Del to Site £	Waste %	Material Cost £	Craft Optve Hrs	Lab Hrs	Labour Cost £	Sunds £	Nett Rate £	Unit	Gross rate (10%) £
IN-SITU, TILED, BLOCK, MOSAIC, SHEET, APPLIED LIQUID OR PLANTED FINISHES (Cont'd)										
Screeds, beds and toppings; Plasterboard; baseboard underlay (Cont'd)										
Baseboarding; Gyproc Handiboard; 5mm joints, filled with plaster and scrimmed; fixing with Galvanised nails, 30mm long at 400mm centres (Cont'd)										
9.5mm work to isolated columns on timber base										
width exceeding 600mm	4.34	5.00	4.54	0.44	0.15	11.52	-	16.06	m²	17.67
width; 300mm	1.46	10.00	1.58	0.26	0.05	6.20	-	7.79	m	8.56
9.5mm work to ceilings on timber base										
width exceeding 600mm	4.34	5.00	4.54	0.35	0.15	9.64	-	14.18	m²	15.60
width; 300mm	1.46	10.00	1.58	0.21	0.05	5.16	-	6.74	m	7.42
9.5mm work to isolated beams on timber base										
width exceeding 600mm	4.34	5.00	4.54	0.44	0.15	11.52	-	16.06	m²	17.67
width; 300mm	1.46	10.00	1.58	0.26	0.05	6.20	-	7.79	m	8.56
Baseboarding; Gyproc Handiboard; 5mm joints, filled with plaster and scrimmed; fixing with adhesive dabs										
9.5mm work to walls on masonry base										
width exceeding 600mm	4.27	5.00	4.47	0.29	0.15	8.39	-	12.86	m²	14.15
width; 300mm	1.33	10.00	1.45	0.17	0.05	4.33	-	5.78	m	6.35
Baseboarding; Gyproc Handiboard; 3mm joints, filled with plaster; fixing with Galvanised nails, 30mm long at 400mm centres										
12.5mm work to walls on timber base										
width exceeding 600mm	9.65	5.00	10.12	0.35	0.18	10.11	-	20.23	m²	22.25
width; 300mm	2.96	10.00	3.25	0.21	0.05	5.16	-	8.41	m	9.25
12.5mm work to isolated columns on timber base										
width exceeding 600mm	9.65	5.00	10.12	0.53	0.18	13.86	-	23.99	m²	26.39
width; 300mm	2.96	10.00	3.25	0.32	0.05	7.46	-	10.70	m	11.77
12.5mm work to ceilings on timber base										
width exceeding 600mm	9.55	5.00	10.02	0.42	0.18	11.57	-	21.59	m²	23.75
width; 300mm	2.96	10.00	3.25	0.25	0.05	6.00	-	9.24	m	10.17
12.5mm work to isolated beams on timber base										
width exceeding 600mm	9.65	5.00	10.12	0.53	0.18	13.86	-	23.99	m²	26.39
width; 300mm	2.96	10.00	3.25	0.32	0.05	7.46	-	10.70	m	11.77
Baseboarding; Gyproc plank, square edge; 5mm joints, filled with plaster and scrimmed										
19mm work to walls on timber base										
width exceeding 600mm	9.08	5.00	9.52	0.47	0.24	13.55	-	23.07	m²	25.37
width; 300mm	2.82	10.00	3.09	0.28	0.07	6.93	-	10.02	m	11.02
19mm work to isolated columns on timber base										
width exceeding 600mm	9.08	5.00	9.52	0.71	0.24	18.55	-	28.08	m²	30.88
width; 300mm	2.82	10.00	3.09	0.43	0.07	10.06	-	13.15	m	14.46
19mm work to ceilings on timber base										
width exceeding 600mm	9.08	5.00	9.52	0.56	0.24	15.42	-	24.94	m²	27.44
width; 300mm	2.82	10.00	3.09	0.34	0.07	8.19	-	11.27	m	12.40
19mm work to isolated beams on timber base										
width exceeding 600mm	9.08	5.00	9.52	0.71	0.24	18.55	-	28.08	m²	30.88
width; 300mm	2.82	10.00	3.09	0.43	0.07	10.06	-	13.15	m	14.46
Baseboarding; Gyproc square edge wallboard; 3mm joints filled with plaster and scrimmed; fixing with Galvanised nails, 30mm long at 400mm centres										
9.5mm work to walls on timber base										
width exceeding 600mm	2.29	5.00	2.39	0.29	0.15	8.39	-	10.78	m²	11.86
width; 300mm	0.76	10.00	0.82	0.17	0.05	4.33	-	5.14	m	5.66
12.5mm work to walls on timber base										
width exceeding 600mm	2.32	5.00	2.43	0.35	0.18	10.11	-	12.53	m²	13.79
width; 300mm	0.76	10.00	0.83	0.21	0.05	5.16	-	5.99	m	6.59
15mm work to walls on timber base										
width exceeding 600mm	3.78	5.00	3.96	0.41	0.21	11.83	-	15.78	m²	17.36
width; 300mm	1.20	10.00	1.31	0.25	0.06	6.15	-	7.46	m	8.21
9.5mm work to isolated columns on timber base										
width exceeding 600mm	2.29	5.00	2.39	0.44	0.15	11.52	-	13.91	m²	15.30
width; 300mm	0.76	10.00	0.82	0.26	0.05	6.20	-	7.02	m	7.72
12.5mm work to isolated columns on timber base										
width exceeding 600mm	2.32	5.00	2.43	0.53	0.18	13.86	-	16.29	m²	17.92
width; 300mm	0.76	10.00	0.83	0.32	0.05	7.46	-	8.28	m	9.11
15mm work to isolated columns on timber base										
width exceeding 600mm	3.78	5.00	3.96	0.62	0.21	16.21	-	20.17	m²	22.18
width; 300mm	1.20	10.00	1.31	0.37	0.06	8.66	-	9.97	m	10.96
9.5mm work to ceilings on timber base										
width exceeding 600mm	2.29	5.00	2.39	0.35	0.15	9.64	-	12.03	m²	13.24
width; 300mm	0.76	10.00	0.82	0.21	0.05	5.16	-	5.98	m	6.58
12.5mm work to ceilings on timber base										
width exceeding 600mm	2.32	5.00	2.43	0.42	0.18	11.57	-	13.99	m²	15.39
width; 300mm	0.76	10.00	0.83	0.25	0.05	6.00	-	6.82	m	7.51
15mm work to ceilings on timber base										
width exceeding 600mm	3.78	5.00	3.96	0.49	0.25	14.12	-	18.08	m²	19.88
width; 300mm	1.20	10.00	1.31	0.29	0.08	7.30	-	8.61	m	9.47
9.5mm work to isolated beams on timber base										
width exceeding 600mm	2.29	5.00	2.39	0.44	0.15	11.52	-	13.91	m²	15.30
width; 300mm	0.76	10.00	0.82	0.26	0.05	6.20	-	7.02	m	7.72
12.5mm work to isolated beams on timber base										
width exceeding 600mm	2.32	5.00	2.43	0.53	0.18	13.86	-	16.29	m²	17.92
width; 300mm	0.76	10.00	0.83	0.32	0.05	7.46	-	8.28	m	9.11
15mm work to isolated beams on timber base										
width exceeding 600mm	3.78	5.00	3.96	0.62	0.21	16.21	-	20.17	m²	22.18
width; 300mm	1.20	10.00	1.31	0.37	0.06	8.66	-	9.97	m	10.96

FLOOR, WALL, CEILING AND ROOF FINISHINGS

Labour hourly rates: (except Specialists) Craft Operatives 20.87 Labourer 15.57 Rates are national average prices. Refer to REGIONAL VARIATIONS for indicative levels of overall pricing in regions	MATERIALS			LABOUR				RATES		
	Del to Site £	Waste %	Material Cost £	Craft Optve Hrs	Lab Hrs	Labour Cost £	Sunds £	Nett Rate £	Unit	Gross rate (10%) £
IN-SITU, TILED, BLOCK, MOSAIC, SHEET, APPLIED LIQUID OR PLANTED FINISHES (Cont'd)										
Screeds, beds and toppings; Plasterboard; baseboard underlay (Cont'd)										
Baseboarding; Gyproc square edge vapourcheck wallboard; 3mm joints filled with plaster and scrimmed; fixing with Galvanised nails, 30mm long at 400mm centres										
9.5mm work to walls on timber base										
width exceeding 600mm	3.65	5.00	3.82	0.29	0.15	8.39	-	12.21	m²	13.43
width; 300mm	1.16	10.00	1.27	0.17	0.05	4.33	-	5.59	m	6.15
12.5mm work to walls on timber base										
width exceeding 600mm	2.98	5.00	3.12	0.35	0.18	10.11	-	13.23	m²	14.55
width; 300mm	0.96	10.00	1.05	0.21	0.05	5.16	-	6.21	m	6.83
15mm work to walls on timber base										
width exceeding 600mm	3.78	5.00	3.96	0.41	0.21	11.83	-	15.78	m²	17.36
width; 300mm	1.20	10.00	1.31	0.25	0.06	6.15	-	7.46	m	8.21
9.5mm work to isolated columns on timber base										
width exceeding 600mm	3.65	5.00	3.82	0.44	0.15	11.52	-	15.34	m²	16.87
width; 300mm	1.16	10.00	1.27	0.26	0.05	6.20	-	7.47	m	8.22
12.5mm work to isolated columns on timber base										
width exceeding 600mm	2.98	5.00	3.12	0.53	0.18	13.86	-	16.98	m²	18.68
width; 300mm	0.96	10.00	1.05	0.32	0.05	7.46	-	8.50	m	9.35
15mm work to isolated columns on timber base										
width exceeding 600mm	3.78	5.00	3.96	0.62	0.21	16.21	-	20.17	m²	22.18
width; 300mm	1.20	10.00	1.31	0.37	0.06	8.66	-	9.97	m	10.96
9.5mm work to ceilings on timber base										
width exceeding 600mm	3.65	5.00	3.82	0.35	0.15	9.64	-	13.46	m²	14.80
width; 300mm	1.16	10.00	1.27	0.21	0.05	5.16	-	6.43	m	7.07
12.5mm work to ceilings on timber base										
width exceeding 600mm	2.98	5.00	3.12	0.42	0.18	11.57	-	14.69	m²	16.16
width; 300mm	0.96	10.00	1.05	0.25	0.05	6.00	-	7.04	m	7.75
15mm work to ceilings on timber base										
width exceeding 600mm	3.78	5.00	3.96	0.49	0.25	14.12	-	18.08	m²	19.88
width; 300mm	1.20	10.00	1.31	0.29	0.08	7.30	-	8.61	m	9.47
9.5mm work to isolated beams on timber base										
width exceeding 600mm	3.65	5.00	3.82	0.44	0.15	11.52	-	15.34	m²	16.87
width; 300mm	1.16	10.00	1.27	0.26	0.05	6.20	-	7.47	m	8.22
12.5mm work to isolated beams on timber base										
width exceeding 600mm	2.98	5.00	3.12	0.53	0.18	13.86	-	16.98	m²	18.68
width; 300mm	0.96	10.00	1.05	0.32	0.05	7.46	-	8.50	m	9.35
15mm work to isolated beams on timber base										
width exceeding 600mm	3.78	5.00	3.96	0.62	0.21	16.21	-	20.17	m²	22.18
width; 300mm	1.20	10.00	1.31	0.37	0.06	8.66	-	9.97	m	10.96
Baseboarding; Gyproc tapered edge Moisture Resistant wallboard; 3mm joints filled with plaster and scrimmed; fixing with Galvanised nails, 30mm long at 400mm centres										
12.5mm work to walls on timber base										
width exceeding 600mm	4.91	5.00	5.15	0.35	0.18	10.11	-	15.25	m²	16.78
width; 300mm	1.54	10.00	1.68	0.21	0.05	5.16	-	6.84	m	7.53
15mm work to walls on timber base										
width exceeding 600mm	5.69	5.00	5.96	0.41	0.21	11.83	-	17.79	m²	19.57
width; 300mm	1.77	10.00	1.94	0.25	0.06	6.15	-	8.09	m	8.90
12.5mm work to isolated columns on timber base										
width exceeding 600mm	4.91	5.00	5.15	0.53	0.18	13.86	-	19.01	m²	20.91
width; 300mm	1.54	10.00	1.68	0.32	0.05	7.46	-	9.14	m	10.05
15mm work to isolated columns on timber base										
width exceeding 600mm	5.69	5.00	5.96	0.62	0.21	16.21	-	22.17	m²	24.39
width; 300mm	1.77	10.00	1.94	0.37	0.06	8.66	-	10.60	m	11.65
12.5mm work to ceilings on timber base										
width exceeding 600mm	4.91	5.00	5.15	0.42	0.18	11.57	-	16.71	m²	18.38
width; 300mm	1.54	10.00	1.68	0.25	0.05	6.00	-	7.68	m	8.45
15mm work to ceilings on timber base										
width exceeding 600mm	5.69	5.00	5.96	0.49	0.25	14.12	-	20.08	m²	22.09
width; 300mm	1.77	10.00	1.94	0.29	0.08	7.30	-	9.24	m	10.16
12.5mm work to isolated beams on timber base										
width exceeding 600mm	4.91	5.00	5.15	0.53	0.18	13.86	-	19.01	m²	20.91
width; 300mm	1.54	10.00	1.68	0.32	0.05	7.46	-	9.14	m	10.05
15mm work to isolated beams on timber base										
width exceeding 600mm	5.69	5.00	5.96	0.62	0.21	16.21	-	22.17	m²	24.39
width; 300mm	1.77	10.00	1.94	0.37	0.06	8.66	-	10.60	m	11.65
Baseboarding; Gyproc tapered edge Fireline wallboard; 3mm joints filled with plaster and scrimmed; fixing with Galvanised nails, 30mm long at 400mm centres										
12.5mm work to walls on timber base										
width exceeding 600mm	3.49	5.00	3.65	0.35	0.18	10.11	-	13.76	m²	15.13
width; 300mm	1.11	10.00	1.21	0.21	0.05	5.16	-	6.37	m	7.01
15mm work to walls on timber base										
width exceeding 600mm	5.29	5.00	5.55	0.41	0.21	11.83	-	17.37	m²	19.11
width; 300mm	1.66	10.00	1.81	0.25	0.06	6.15	-	7.96	m	8.76
12.5mm work to isolated columns on timber base										
width exceeding 600mm	3.49	5.00	3.65	0.53	0.18	13.86	-	17.51	m²	19.27
width; 300mm	1.11	10.00	1.21	0.32	0.05	7.46	-	8.67	m	9.54
15mm work to isolated columns on timber base										
width exceeding 600mm	5.29	5.00	5.55	0.62	0.21	16.21	-	21.76	m²	23.93
width; 300mm	1.66	10.00	1.81	0.37	0.06	8.66	-	10.46	m	11.51
12.5mm work to ceilings on timber base										
width exceeding 600mm	3.49	5.00	3.65	0.42	0.18	11.57	-	15.22	m²	16.74
width; 300mm	1.11	10.00	1.21	0.25	0.05	6.00	-	7.21	m	7.93
15mm work to ceilings on timber base										
width exceeding 600mm	5.29	5.00	5.55	0.49	0.25	14.12	-	19.67	m²	21.63
width; 300mm	1.66	10.00	1.81	0.29	0.08	7.30	-	9.11	m	10.02

Labour hourly rates: (except Specialists) Craft Operatives 20.87 Labourer 15.57 Rates are national average prices. Refer to REGIONAL VARIATIONS for indicative levels of overall pricing in regions	MATERIALS			LABOUR				RATES		
	Del to Site £	Waste %	Material Cost £	Craft Optve Hrs	Lab Hrs	Labour Cost £	Sunds £	Nett Rate £	Unit	Gross rate (10%) £
IN-SITU, TILED, BLOCK, MOSAIC, SHEET, APPLIED LIQUID OR PLANTED FINISHES (Cont'd)										
Screeds, beds and toppings; Plasterboard; baseboard underlay (Cont'd)										
Baseboarding; Gyproc tapered edge Fireline wallboard; 3mm joints filled with plaster and scrimmed; fixing with Galvanised nails, 30mm long at 400mm centres (Cont'd)										
12.5mm work to isolated beams on timber base										
width exceeding 600mm	3.49	5.00	3.65	0.53	0.18	13.86	-	17.51	m²	19.27
width; 300mm	1.11	10.00	1.21	0.32	0.05	7.46	-	8.67	m	9.54
15mm work to isolated beams on timber base										
width exceeding 600mm	5.29	5.00	5.55	0.62	0.21	16.21	-	21.76	m²	23.93
width; 300mm	1.66	10.00	1.81	0.37	0.06	8.66	-	10.46	m	11.51
Baseboarding; Gyproc tapered edge Soundbloc wallboard; 3mm joints filled with plaster and scrimmed; fixing with Galvanised nails, 30mm long at 400mm centres										
12.5mm work to walls on timber base										
width exceeding 600mm	3.62	5.00	3.80	0.35	0.18	10.11	-	13.90	m²	15.29
width; 300mm	1.16	10.00	1.26	0.21	0.05	5.16	-	6.42	m	7.06
15mm work to walls on timber base										
width exceeding 600mm	5.06	5.00	5.31	0.41	0.21	11.83	-	17.13	m²	18.85
width; 300mm	1.59	10.00	1.73	0.25	0.06	6.15	-	7.88	m	8.67
12.5mm work to isolated columns on timber base										
width exceeding 600mm	3.62	5.00	3.80	0.53	0.18	13.86	-	17.66	m²	19.43
width; 300mm	1.16	10.00	1.26	0.32	0.05	7.46	-	8.72	m	9.59
15mm work to isolated columns on timber base										
width exceeding 600mm	5.06	5.00	5.31	0.62	0.21	16.21	-	21.51	m²	23.67
width; 300mm	1.59	10.00	1.73	0.37	0.06	8.66	-	10.39	m	11.43
12.5mm work to ceilings on timber base										
width exceeding 600mm	3.62	5.00	3.80	0.42	0.18	11.57	-	15.36	m²	16.90
width; 300mm	1.16	10.00	1.26	0.25	0.05	6.00	-	7.25	m	7.98
15mm work to ceilings on timber base										
width exceeding 600mm	5.06	5.00	5.31	0.49	0.25	14.12	-	19.42	m²	21.37
width; 300mm	1.59	10.00	1.73	0.29	0.08	7.30	-	9.03	m	9.93
12.5mm work to isolated beams on timber base										
width exceeding 600mm	3.62	5.00	3.80	0.53	0.18	13.86	-	17.66	m²	19.43
width; 300mm	1.16	10.00	1.26	0.32	0.05	7.46	-	8.72	m	9.59
15mm work to isolated beams on timber base										
width exceeding 600mm	5.06	5.00	5.31	0.62	0.21	16.21	-	21.51	m²	23.67
width; 300mm	1.59	10.00	1.73	0.37	0.06	8.66	-	10.39	m	11.43
Baseboarding; two layers 9.5mm Gyproc square edge wallboard; second layer with 3mm joints filled with plaster and scrimmed; fixing with Galvanised nails, 30mm long at 400mm centres										
19mm work to walls on timber base										
width exceeding 600mm	4.65	5.00	4.86	0.60	0.30	17.19	-	22.05	m²	24.26
width; 300mm	1.56	10.00	1.68	0.36	0.09	8.91	-	10.60	m	11.66
19mm work to isolated columns on timber base										
width exceeding 600mm	4.65	5.00	4.86	0.80	0.30	21.37	-	26.23	m²	28.85
width; 300mm	1.56	10.00	1.68	0.48	0.09	11.42	-	13.10	m	14.41
19mm work to ceilings on timber base										
width exceeding 600mm	4.65	5.00	4.86	0.72	0.30	19.70	-	24.56	m²	27.01
width; 300mm	1.56	10.00	1.68	0.43	0.09	10.38	-	12.06	m	13.26
19mm work to isolated beams on timber base										
width exceeding 600mm	4.65	5.00	4.86	0.80	0.30	21.37	-	26.23	m²	28.85
width; 300mm	1.56	10.00	1.68	0.48	0.09	11.42	-	13.10	m	14.41
Baseboarding; one layer 9.5mm and one layer 12.5mm Gyproc square edge wallboard; second layer with 3mm joints filled with plaster and scrimmed; fixing with Galvanised nails, 30mm long at 400mm centres										
22mm work to walls on timber base										
width exceeding 600mm	4.68	5.00	4.89	0.65	0.33	18.70	-	23.60	m²	25.96
width; 300mm	1.57	10.00	1.69	0.39	0.10	9.70	-	11.39	m	12.53
22mm work to isolated columns on timber base										
width exceeding 600mm	4.68	5.00	4.89	0.98	0.33	25.59	-	30.48	m²	33.53
width; 300mm	1.57	10.00	1.69	0.59	0.10	13.87	-	15.56	m	17.12
22mm work to ceilings on timber base										
width exceeding 600mm	4.68	5.00	4.89	0.78	0.33	21.42	-	26.31	m²	28.94
width; 300mm	1.57	10.00	1.69	0.47	0.10	11.37	-	13.06	m	14.37
22mm work to isolated beams on timber base										
width exceeding 600mm	4.68	5.00	4.89	0.98	0.33	25.59	-	30.48	m²	33.53
width; 300mm	1.57	10.00	1.69	0.59	0.10	13.87	-	15.56	m	17.12
Baseboarding; two layers 12.5mm Gyproc square edge wallboard; second layer with 3mm joints filled with plaster and scrimmed; fixing with Galvanised nails, 30mm long at 400mm centres										
25mm work to walls on timber base										
width exceeding 600mm	4.72	5.00	4.93	0.70	0.35	20.06	-	24.98	m²	27.48
width; 300mm	1.58	10.00	1.70	0.42	0.11	10.48	-	12.18	m	13.40
25mm work to isolated columns on timber base										
width exceeding 600mm	4.72	5.00	4.93	1.05	0.35	27.36	-	32.29	m²	35.52
width; 300mm	1.58	10.00	1.70	0.64	0.11	15.07	-	16.77	m	18.45
25mm work to ceilings on timber base										
width exceeding 600mm	4.72	5.00	4.93	0.84	0.35	22.98	-	27.91	m²	30.70
width; 300mm	1.58	10.00	1.70	0.50	0.11	12.15	-	13.85	m	15.24
25mm work to isolated beams on timber base										
width exceeding 600mm	4.72	5.00	4.93	1.05	0.35	27.36	-	32.29	m²	35.52
width; 300mm	1.58	10.00	1.70	0.64	0.11	15.07	-	16.77	m	18.45

Labour hourly rates: (except Specialists) Craft Operatives 20.87 Labourer 15.57 Rates are national average prices. Refer to REGIONAL VARIATIONS for indicative levels of overall pricing in regions	MATERIALS			LABOUR				RATES		
	Del to Site	Waste	Material Cost	Craft Optve	Lab	Labour Cost	Sunds	Nett Rate		Gross rate (10%)
	£	%	£	Hrs	Hrs	£	£	£	Unit	£
IN-SITU, TILED, BLOCK, MOSAIC, SHEET, APPLIED LIQUID OR PLANTED FINISHES (Cont'd)										
Screeds, beds and toppings; Plasterboard; baseboard underlay (Cont'd)										
Baseboarding; two layers 15mm Gyproc square edge wallboard; second layer with 3mm joints filled with plaster and scrimmed; fixing with Galvanised nails, 30mm long at 400mm centres										
30mm work to walls on timber base										
width exceeding 600mm	7.63	5.00	7.99	0.75	0.38	21.57	-	29.56	m²	32.51
width; 300mm	2.45	10.00	2.67	0.45	0.11	11.10	-	13.77	m	15.15
30mm work to isolated columns on timber base										
width exceeding 600mm	7.63	5.00	7.99	1.13	0.38	29.50	-	37.49	m²	41.24
width; 300mm	2.45	10.00	2.67	0.68	0.11	15.90	-	18.57	m	20.43
30mm work to ceilings on timber base										
width exceeding 600mm	7.63	5.00	7.99	0.90	0.38	24.70	-	32.69	m²	35.96
width; 300mm	2.45	10.00	2.67	0.54	0.11	12.98	-	15.65	m	17.21
30mm work to isolated beams on timber base										
width exceeding 600mm	7.63	5.00	7.99	1.13	0.38	29.50	-	37.49	m²	41.24
width; 300mm	2.45	10.00	2.67	0.68	0.11	15.90	-	18.57	m	20.43
Baseboarding; two layers; first layer 9.5mm Gyproc vapourcheck wallboard, second layer 9.5mm Gyproc wallboard both layers with square edge boards; second layer with 3mm joints filled with plaster and scrimmed; fixing with Galvanised nails, 30mm long at 400mm centres										
19mm work to walls on timber base										
width exceeding 600mm	6.01	5.00	6.29	0.60	0.30	17.19	-	23.48	m²	25.83
width; 300mm	1.97	10.00	2.13	0.36	0.09	8.91	-	11.05	m	12.15
19mm work to isolated columns on timber base										
width exceeding 600mm	6.01	5.00	6.29	0.80	0.30	21.37	-	27.65	m²	30.42
width; 300mm	1.97	10.00	2.13	0.48	0.09	11.42	-	13.55	m	14.91
19mm work to ceilings on timber base										
width exceeding 600mm	6.01	5.00	6.29	0.72	0.30	19.70	-	25.98	m²	28.58
width; 300mm	1.97	10.00	2.13	0.43	0.09	10.38	-	12.51	m	13.76
19mm work to isolated beams on timber base										
width exceeding 600mm	6.01	5.00	6.29	0.80	0.30	21.37	-	27.65	m²	30.42
width; 300mm	1.97	10.00	2.13	0.48	0.09	11.42	-	13.55	m	14.91
Baseboarding; two layers; first layer 12.5mm Gyproc vapourcheck wallboard, second layer 9.5mm Gyproc wallboard, both layers with square edge boards; second layer with 3mm joints filled with plaster and scrimmed; fixing with Galvanised nails, 30mm long at 400mm centres										
22mm work to walls on timber base										
width exceeding 600mm	5.34	5.00	5.59	0.65	0.33	18.70	-	24.29	m²	26.72
width; 300mm	1.77	10.00	1.91	0.39	0.10	9.70	-	11.61	m	12.77
22mm work to isolated columns on timber base										
width exceeding 600mm	5.34	5.00	5.59	0.98	0.33	25.59	-	31.18	m²	34.29
width; 300mm	1.77	10.00	1.91	0.59	0.10	13.87	-	15.78	m	17.36
22mm work to ceilings on timber base										
width exceeding 600mm	5.34	5.00	5.59	0.78	0.33	21.42	-	27.00	m²	29.70
width; 300mm	1.77	10.00	1.91	0.47	0.10	11.37	-	13.28	m	14.60
22mm work to isolated beams on timber base										
width exceeding 600mm	5.34	5.00	5.59	0.98	0.33	25.59	-	31.18	m²	34.29
width; 300mm	1.77	10.00	1.91	0.59	0.10	13.87	-	15.78	m	17.36
Baseboarding; two layers; first layer 12.5mm Gyproc vapourcheck wallboard, second layer 12.5mm Gyproc wallboard, both layers with square edge boards; second layer with 3mm joints filled with plaster and scrimmed; fixing with Galvanised nails, 30mm long at 400mm centres										
25mm work to walls on timber base										
width exceeding 600mm	5.38	5.00	5.62	0.70	0.35	20.06	-	25.68	m²	28.24
width; 300mm	1.78	10.00	1.92	0.42	0.11	10.48	-	12.40	m	13.64
25mm work to isolated columns on timber base										
width exceeding 600mm	5.38	5.00	5.62	1.05	0.35	27.36	-	32.98	m²	36.28
width; 300mm	1.78	10.00	1.92	0.64	0.11	15.07	-	16.99	m	18.69
25mm work to ceilings on timber base										
width exceeding 600mm	5.38	5.00	5.62	0.84	0.35	22.98	-	28.60	m²	31.46
width; 300mm	1.78	10.00	1.92	0.50	0.11	12.15	-	14.07	m	15.48
25mm work to isolated beams on timber base										
width exceeding 600mm	5.38	5.00	5.62	1.05	0.35	27.36	-	32.98	m²	36.28
width; 300mm	1.78	10.00	1.92	0.64	0.11	15.07	-	16.99	m	18.69
Baseboarding; two layers; first layer 15mm Gyproc vapourcheck wallboard, second layer 15mm Gyproc wallboard, both layers with square edge boards; second layer with 3mm joints filled with plaster and scrimmed; fixing with Galvanised nails, 30mm long at 400mm centres										
30mm work to walls on timber base										
width exceeding 600mm	7.63	5.00	7.99	0.75	0.38	21.57	-	29.56	m²	32.51
width; 300mm	2.45	10.00	2.67	0.45	0.11	11.10	-	13.77	m	15.15
30mm work to isolated columns on timber base										
width exceeding 600mm	7.63	5.00	7.99	1.13	0.38	29.50	-	37.49	m²	41.24
width; 300mm	2.45	10.00	2.67	0.68	0.11	15.90	-	18.57	m	20.43
30mm work to ceilings on timber base										
width exceeding 600mm	7.63	5.00	7.99	0.90	0.38	24.70	-	32.69	m²	35.96
width; 300mm	2.45	10.00	2.67	0.54	0.11	12.98	-	15.65	m	17.21
30mm work to isolated beams on timber base										
width exceeding 600mm	7.63	5.00	7.99	1.13	0.38	29.50	-	37.49	m²	41.24
width; 300mm	2.45	10.00	2.67	0.68	0.11	15.90	-	18.57	m	20.43

FLOOR, WALL, CEILING AND ROOF FINISHINGS

Labour hourly rates: (except Specialists) Craft Operatives 20.87 Labourer 15.57 Rates are national average prices. Refer to REGIONAL VARIATIONS for indicative levels of overall pricing in regions	MATERIALS			LABOUR				RATES		
	Del to Site £	Waste %	Material Cost £	Craft Optve Hrs	Lab Hrs	Labour Cost £	Sunds £	Nett Rate £	Unit	Gross rate (10%) £
IN-SITU, TILED, BLOCK, MOSAIC, SHEET, APPLIED LIQUID OR PLANTED FINISHES (Cont'd)										
Screeds, beds and toppings; damp wall treatment: Newlath underlay; fixing with masonry nails.										
Work to walls on brickwork or blockwork base										
width exceeding 600mm	7.64	5.00	7.99	0.40	0.20	11.46	-	19.45	m²	21.40
width; 300mm	2.29	10.00	2.50	0.24	0.06	5.94	-	8.44	m	9.29
Finish to floors; clay floor quarries, BS EN ISO 10545, terracotta; 3mm joints, symmetrical layout; bedding in 10mm cement mortar (1:3); pointing in cement mortar (1:3); on cement and sand base										
150 x 150 x 12.5mm units to floors level or to falls only not exceeding 15 degrees from horizontal										
plain	26.15	5.00	27.46	0.80	0.50	24.48	-	51.94	m²	57.13
150 x 150 x 20mm units to floors level or to falls only not exceeding 15 degrees from horizontal										
plain	36.77	5.00	38.61	1.00	0.60	30.21	-	68.82	m²	75.70
225 x 225 x 25mm units to floors level or to falls only not exceeding 15 degrees from horizontal										
plain	20.87	5.00	21.92	0.70	0.45	21.62	-	43.53	m²	47.88
150 x 150 x 12.5mm units to floors to falls and crossfalls and to slopes not exceeding 15 degrees from horizontal										
plain	26.15	5.00	27.46	0.88	0.50	26.15	-	53.61	m²	58.97
150 x 150 x 20mm units to floors to falls and crossfalls and to slopes not exceeding 15 degrees from horizontal										
plain	36.77	5.00	38.61	1.10	0.60	32.30	-	70.91	m²	78.00
225 x 225 x 25mm units to floors to falls and crossfalls and to slopes not exceeding 15 degrees from horizontal										
plain	20.87	5.00	21.92	0.75	0.45	22.66	-	44.57	m²	49.03
Extra for pointing with tinted mortar										
150 x 150 x 12.5mm tiles	0.55	10.00	0.60	0.10	-	2.09	-	2.69	m²	2.96
150 x 150 x 20mm tiles	0.55	10.00	0.60	0.10	-	2.09	-	2.69	m²	2.96
225 x 225 x 25mm tiles	0.55	10.00	0.60	0.07	-	1.46	-	2.06	m²	2.27
150 x 150 x 12.5mm units to skirtings on brickwork or blockwork base										
height 150mm; square top edge	4.34	10.00	4.75	0.30	0.08	7.51	-	12.26	m	13.48
height 150mm; rounded top edge	12.68	10.00	13.92	0.30	0.08	7.51	-	21.43	m	23.57
150 x 150 x 20mm units to skirtings on brickwork or blockwork base										
height 150mm; square top edge	7.19	10.00	7.89	0.38	0.09	9.33	-	17.22	m	18.95
Finish to floors; clay floor quarries, BS EN ISO 10545, blended; 3mm joints symmetrical layout; bedding in 10mm cement mortar (1:3); pointing in cement mortar (1:3); on cement and sand base										
150 x 150 x 12.5mm units to floors level or to falls only not exceeding 15 degrees from horizontal										
plain	26.15	5.00	27.46	0.80	0.50	24.48	-	51.94	m²	57.13
150 x 150 x 20mm units to floors level or to falls only not exceeding 15 degrees from horizontal										
plain	36.77	5.00	38.61	1.00	0.60	30.21	-	68.82	m²	75.70
225 x 225 x 25mm units to floors level or to falls only not exceeding 15 degrees from horizontal										
plain	20.87	5.00	21.92	0.70	0.45	21.62	-	43.53	m²	47.88
150 x 150 x 12.5mm units to floors to falls and crossfalls and to slopes not exceeding 15 degrees from horizontal										
plain	26.15	5.00	27.46	0.88	0.50	26.15	-	53.61	m²	58.97
150 x 150 x 20mm units to floors to falls and crossfalls and to slopes not exceeding 15 degrees from horizontal										
plain	36.77	5.00	38.61	1.10	0.60	32.30	-	70.91	m²	78.00
225 x 225 x 25mm units to floors to falls and crossfalls and to slopes not exceeding 15 degrees from horizontal										
plain	20.87	5.00	21.92	0.75	0.45	22.66	-	44.57	m²	49.03
Extra for pointing with tinted mortar										
150 x 150 x 12.5mm tiles	0.55	10.00	0.60	0.10	-	2.09	-	2.69	m²	2.96
150 x 150 x 20mm tiles	0.55	10.00	0.60	0.10	-	2.09	-	2.69	m²	2.96
225 x 225 x 25mm tiles	0.55	10.00	0.60	0.07	-	1.46	-	2.06	m²	2.27
150 x 150 x 12.5mm units to skirtings on brickwork or blockwork base										
height 150mm; square top edge	4.34	10.00	4.75	0.30	0.08	7.51	-	12.26	m	13.48
height 150mm; rounded top edge	12.68	10.00	13.92	0.30	0.08	7.51	-	21.43	m	23.57
150 x 150 x 20mm units to skirtings on brickwork or blockwork base										
height 150mm; square top edge	7.19	10.00	7.89	0.38	0.09	9.33	-	17.22	m	18.95
height 150mm; rounded top edge	7.19	10.00	7.89	0.38	0.09	9.33	-	17.22	m	18.95

Labour hourly rates: (except Specialists) Craft Operatives 20.87 Labourer 15.57 Rates are national average prices. Refer to REGIONAL VARIATIONS for indicative levels of overall pricing in regions	MATERIALS			LABOUR				RATES		
	Del to Site £	Waste %	Material Cost £	Craft Optve Hrs	Lab Hrs	Labour Cost £	Sunds £	Nett Rate £	Unit	Gross rate (10%) £
IN-SITU, TILED, BLOCK, MOSAIC, SHEET, APPLIED LIQUID OR PLANTED FINISHES (Cont'd)										
Finish to floors; ceramic floor tiles pc £20.00 per m²; 3mm joints, symmetrical layout; bedding in 10mm cement mortar (1:3); pointing in cement mortar (1:3); on cement and sand base										
100 x 100mm units to floors level or to falls only not exceeding 15 degrees from horizontal plain	22.14	5.00	23.25	1.60	0.90	47.41	-	70.65	m²	77.72
150 x 150mm units to floors level or to falls only not exceeding 15 degrees from horizontal plain	22.14	5.00	23.25	0.90	0.55	27.35	-	50.59	m²	55.65
450 x 450mm units to floors level or to falls only not exceeding 15 degrees from horizontal plain	22.14	5.00	23.25	0.80	0.45	23.70	-	46.95	m²	51.64
600 x 600mm units to floors level or to falls only not exceeding 15 degrees from horizontal plain	22.14	10.00	24.25	1.20	0.80	37.50	-	61.75	m²	67.92
100 x 100mm units to floors to falls and crossfalls and to slopes not exceeding 15 degrees from horizontal plain	22.14	5.00	23.25	1.76	0.90	50.74	-	73.99	m²	81.39
150 x 150mm units to floors to falls and crossfalls and to slopes not exceeding 15 degrees from horizontal plain	22.14	5.00	23.25	0.99	0.55	29.22	-	52.47	m²	57.72
450 x 450mm units to floors to falls and crossfalls and to slopes not exceeding 15 degrees from horizontal plain	22.14	5.00	23.25	0.89	0.45	25.58	-	48.83	m²	53.71
600 x 600mm units to floors to falls and crossfalls and to slopes not exceeding 15 degrees from horizontal plain	22.14	10.00	24.25	1.33	0.80	40.21	-	64.46	m²	70.91
Extra for pointing with tinted mortar										
100 x 100mm tiles	0.55	10.00	0.60	0.15	-	3.13	-	3.73	m²	4.11
150 x 150mm tiles	0.55	10.00	0.60	0.10	-	2.09	-	2.69	m²	2.96
450 x 450mm tiles	0.55	10.00	0.60	0.09	-	1.88	-	2.48	m²	2.73
600 x 600mm tiles	0.55	10.00	0.60	0.08	-	1.67	-	2.27	m²	2.50
100 x 100mm units to skirtings on brickwork or blockwork base height 100mm; square top edge	2.29	10.00	2.50	0.36	0.09	8.91	-	11.41	m	12.56
150 x 150mm units to skirtings on brickwork or blockwork base height 150mm; square top edge	3.47	10.00	3.79	0.33	0.08	8.13	-	11.93	m	13.12
Finish to floors; ceramic floor tiles pc £30.00 per m²; 3mm joints, symmetrical layout; bedding in 10mm cement mortar (1:3); pointing in cement mortar (1:3); on cement and sand base										
100 x 100mm units to floors level or to falls only not exceeding 15 degrees from horizontal plain	32.14	5.00	33.75	1.60	0.90	47.41	-	81.15	m²	89.27
150 x 150mm units to floors level or to falls only not exceeding 15 degrees from horizontal plain	32.14	5.00	33.75	0.90	0.55	27.35	-	61.09	m²	67.20
450 x 450mm units to floors level or to falls only not exceeding 15 degrees from horizontal plain	32.14	5.00	33.75	0.80	0.45	23.70	-	57.45	m²	63.19
600 x 600mm units to floors level or to falls only not exceeding 15 degrees from horizontal plain	32.14	10.00	35.25	1.20	0.80	37.50	-	72.75	m²	80.02
100 x 100mm units to floors to falls and crossfalls and to slopes not exceeding 15 degrees from horizontal plain	32.14	5.00	33.75	1.76	0.90	50.74	-	84.49	m²	92.94
150 x 150mm units to floors to falls and crossfalls and to slopes not exceeding 15 degrees from horizontal plain	32.14	5.00	33.75	0.99	0.55	29.22	-	62.97	m²	69.27
450 x 450mm units to floors to falls and crossfalls and to slopes not exceeding 15 degrees from horizontal plain	32.14	5.00	33.75	0.89	0.45	25.58	-	59.33	m²	65.26
600 x 600mm units to floors to falls and crossfalls and to slopes not exceeding 15 degrees from horizontal plain	32.14	10.00	35.25	1.33	0.80	40.21	-	75.46	m²	83.01
Extra for pointing with tinted mortar										
100 x 100mm tiles	0.55	10.00	0.60	0.15	-	3.13	-	3.73	m²	4.11
150 x 150mm tiles	0.55	10.00	0.60	0.10	-	2.09	-	2.69	m²	2.96
450 x 450mm tiles	0.55	10.00	0.60	0.09	-	1.88	-	2.48	m²	2.73
600 x 600mm tiles	0.55	10.00	0.60	0.08	-	1.67	-	2.27	m²	2.50
100 x 100mm units to skirtings on brickwork or blockwork base height 100mm; square top edge	3.29	10.00	3.60	0.36	0.09	8.91	-	12.51	m	13.77
150 x 150mm units to skirtings on brickwork or blockwork base height 150mm; square top edge	4.99	10.00	5.47	0.33	0.08	8.13	-	13.60	m	14.96

FLOOR, WALL, CEILING AND ROOF FINISHINGS

Labour hourly rates: (except Specialists) Craft Operatives 20.87 Labourer 15.57 Rates are national average prices. Refer to REGIONAL VARIATIONS for indicative levels of overall pricing in regions	MATERIALS			LABOUR				RATES		
	Del to Site £	Waste %	Material Cost £	Craft Optve Hrs	Lab Hrs	Labour Cost £	Sunds £	Nett Rate £	Unit	Gross rate (10%) £
IN-SITU, TILED, BLOCK, MOSAIC, SHEET, APPLIED LIQUID OR PLANTED FINISHES (Cont'd)										
Finish to floors; ceramic floor tiles pc £40.00 per m²; 3mm joints, symmetrical layout; bedding in 10mm cement mortar (1:3); pointing in cement mortar (1:3); on cement and sand base										
100 x 100mm units to floors level or to falls only not exceeding 15 degrees from horizontal										
plain	42.14	5.00	44.25	1.60	0.90	47.41	-	91.65	m²	100.82
150 x 150mm units to floors level or to falls only not exceeding 15 degrees from horizontal										
plain	42.14	5.00	44.25	0.90	0.55	27.35	-	71.59	m²	78.75
450 x 450mm units to floors level or to falls only not exceeding 15 degrees from horizontal										
plain	42.14	5.00	44.25	0.80	0.45	23.70	-	67.95	m²	74.74
600 x 600mm units to floors level or to falls only not exceeding 15 degrees from horizontal										
plain	42.14	10.00	46.25	1.20	0.80	37.50	-	83.75	m²	92.12
100 x 100mm units to floors to falls and crossfalls and to slopes not exceeding 15 degrees from horizontal										
plain	42.14	5.00	44.25	1.76	0.90	50.74	-	94.99	m²	104.49
150 x 150mm units to floors to falls and crossfalls and to slopes not exceeding 15 degrees from horizontal										
plain	42.14	5.00	44.25	0.99	0.55	29.22	-	73.47	m²	80.82
450 x 450mm units to floors to falls and crossfalls and to slopes not exceeding 15 degrees from horizontal										
plain	42.14	5.00	44.25	0.89	0.45	25.58	-	69.83	m²	76.81
600 x 600mm units to floors to falls and crossfalls and to slopes not exceeding 15 degrees from horizontal										
plain	42.14	10.00	46.25	1.33	0.80	40.21	-	86.46	m²	95.11
Extra for pointing with tinted mortar										
100 x 100mm tiles	0.55	10.00	0.60	0.15	-	3.13	-	3.73	m²	4.11
150 x 150mm tiles	0.55	10.00	0.60	0.10	-	2.09	-	2.69	m²	2.96
450 x 450mm tiles	0.55	10.00	0.60	0.09	-	1.88	-	2.48	m²	2.73
600 x 600mm tiles	0.55	10.00	0.60	0.08	-	1.67	-	2.27	m²	2.50
100 x 100mm units to skirtings on brickwork or blockwork base										
height 100mm; square top edge	4.29	10.00	4.70	0.36	0.09	8.91	-	13.61	m	14.98
150 x 150mm units to skirtings on brickwork or blockwork base										
height 150mm; square top edge	6.51	10.00	7.14	0.33	0.08	8.13	-	15.27	m	16.80
Finish to floors; terrazzo tiles, BS EN 13748, aggregate size random, ground, grouted and polished, standard colour range; 3mm joints, symmetrical layout; bedding in 40mm cement mortar (1:3); grouting with white cement; in-situ margins										
300 x 300 x 28mm units to floors on concrete base; level or to falls only not exceeding 15 degrees from horizontal										
plain	78.54	5.00	82.55	1.10	0.65	33.08	-	115.62	m²	127.19
305 x 305 x 28mm units to treads on concrete base										
width 292mm; rounded nosing	43.31	5.00	45.51	0.75	0.19	18.61	-	64.12	m	70.53
305 x 305 x 28mm units to plain risers on concrete base										
height 165mm	13.71	5.00	14.41	0.50	0.11	12.15	-	26.56	m	29.22
Finish to floors and walls; terrazzo, white cement and white marble chippings (2:5); polished; on cement and sand base										
16mm work to floors; one coat; floated										
level and to falls only not exceeding 15 degrees from horizontal; laid in bays, average size 610 x 610mm	20.51	5.00	21.53	2.25	1.13	64.55	-	86.08	m²	94.69
6mm work to walls										
width exceeding 600mm	7.69	5.00	8.07	3.60	1.80	103.16	-	111.23	m²	122.36
width 300mm	3.85	10.00	4.23	2.16	0.54	53.49	-	57.72	m	63.49
16mm work to treads; one coat										
width 279mm	8.97	5.00	9.42	3.00	0.32	67.59	-	77.01	m	84.71
extra; two line carborundum non-slip inlay	23.15	5.00	24.31	0.25	-	5.22	-	29.53	m	32.48
16mm work to undercut risers; one coat										
height 178mm	5.13	5.00	5.38	2.00	0.20	44.85	-	50.24	m	55.26
6mm work to strings; one coat										
height 150mm	1.28	5.00	1.35	1.80	0.27	41.77	-	43.12	m	47.43
height 200mm	2.56	5.00	2.69	2.50	0.36	57.78	-	60.47	m	66.52
6mm work to skirtings										
height 75mm	1.28	5.00	1.35	1.25	0.14	28.27	-	29.61	m	32.57
height 75mm; curved to 3000mm radius	1.28	5.00	1.35	1.67	0.14	37.03	-	38.38	m	42.22
16mm work to skirtings on brickwork or blockwork base										
height 150mm	5.13	5.00	5.38	1.60	0.27	37.60	-	42.98	m	47.28
height 150mm; curved to 3000mm radius	5.13	5.00	5.38	2.13	0.27	48.66	-	54.04	m	59.44
Rounded angles and intersections										
10 - 100mm radius	-	-	-	0.18	-	3.76	-	3.76	m	4.13

Labour hourly rates: (except Specialists) Craft Operatives 20.87 Labourer 15.57 Rates are national average prices. Refer to REGIONAL VARIATIONS for indicative levels of overall pricing in regions	MATERIALS			LABOUR				RATES		
	Del to Site £	Waste %	Material Cost £	Craft Optve Hrs	Lab Hrs	Labour Cost £	Sunds £	Nett Rate £	Unit	Gross rate (10%) £
IN-SITU, TILED, BLOCK, MOSAIC, SHEET, APPLIED LIQUID OR PLANTED FINISHES (Cont'd)										
Finish to floors and walls; terrazzo, white cement and white marble chippings (2:5); polished; on cement and sand base (Cont'd)										
Coves										
25mm girth	-	-	-	0.40	-	8.35	-	8.35	m	9.18
40mm girth	-	-	-	0.60	-	12.52	-	12.52	m	13.77
Finish to floors; dividing strips										
Plastic dividing strips; setting in bed and finishing										
6 x 16mm; flat section	3.14	-	3.14	0.25	-	5.22	-	8.36	m	9.19
Finish to floors; Maple wood blocks, tongued and grooved joints; symmetrical herringbone pattern layout, two block plain borders; fixing with adhesive; sanding, one coat sealer										
70 x 230 x 20mm units to floors on cement and sand base; level or to falls only not exceeding 15 degrees from horizontal										
plain	52.81	5.00	55.45	1.50	1.25	50.77	-	106.22	m²	116.84
Finish to floors; Merbau wood blocks, tongued and grooved joints; symmetrical herringbone pattern layout, two block plain borders; fixing with adhesive; sanding, one coat sealer										
70 x 230 x 20mm units to floors on cement and sand base; level or to falls only not exceeding 15 degrees from horizontal										
plain	46.81	5.00	49.15	1.50	1.25	50.77	-	99.92	m²	109.91
Finish to floors; Oak wood blocks, tongued and grooved joints; symmetrical herringbone pattern layout, two block plain borders; fixing with adhesive; sanding, one coat sealer										
70 x 230 x 20mm units to floors on cement and sand base; level or to falls only not exceeding 15 degrees from horizontal										
plain	38.47	5.00	40.39	1.50	1.25	50.77	-	91.16	m²	100.28
Finish to floors; rubber floor tiles; butt joints, symmetrical layout; fixing with adhesive; on cement and sand base										
610 x 610 x 2.5mm units to floors level or to falls only not exceeding 15 degrees from horizontal										
width exceeding 600mm	38.53	5.00	40.60	0.35	0.23	10.89	-	51.49	m²	56.64
width 300mm	12.00	10.00	13.20	0.21	0.07	5.47	-	18.67	m	20.54
500 x 500 x 2.6mm units to floors level or to falls only not exceeding 15 degrees from horizontal										
width exceeding 600mm	28.74	5.00	30.33	0.35	0.23	10.89	-	41.21	m²	45.33
width 300mm	9.06	10.00	9.97	0.21	0.07	5.47	-	15.44	m	16.99
Finish to floors; smooth finish rubber matting; butt joints; fixing with adhesive; on cement and sand base										
3mm work to floors level or to falls only not exceeding 15 degrees from horizontal										
width exceeding 600mm	16.23	5.00	17.19	0.20	0.15	6.51	-	23.70	m²	26.07
width 300mm	5.31	10.00	5.84	0.12	0.05	3.28	-	9.13	m	10.04
4mm work to floors level or to falls only not exceeding 15 degrees from horizontal										
width exceeding 600mm	16.93	5.00	17.92	0.20	0.15	6.51	-	24.43	m²	26.88
width 300mm	5.52	10.00	6.07	0.12	0.05	3.28	-	9.36	m	10.29
6mm work to floors level or to falls only not exceeding 15 degrees from horizontal										
width exceeding 600mm	30.02	5.00	31.67	0.20	0.15	6.51	-	38.18	m²	42.00
width 300mm	9.45	10.00	10.39	0.12	0.05	3.28	-	13.68	m	15.05
Finish to floors; PVC floor tiles, BS EN ISO 10595; butt joints, symmetrical layout; fixing with adhesive; two coats sealer; on cement and sand base										
300 x 300 x 2mm units to floors level or to falls only not exceeding 15 degrees from horizontal										
width exceeding 600mm	8.60	5.00	9.11	0.45	0.23	12.97	-	22.09	m²	24.30
width 300mm	2.83	10.00	3.11	0.27	0.07	6.72	-	9.84	m	10.82
300 x 300 x 3.2mm units to floors level or to falls only not exceeding 15 degrees from horizontal										
width exceeding 600mm	12.45	5.00	13.16	0.45	0.23	12.97	-	26.13	m²	28.74
width 300mm	3.98	10.00	4.38	0.27	0.07	6.72	-	11.11	m	12.22
Finish to floors; fully flexible PVC heavy duty floor tiles, BS EN ISO 10581; butt joints, symmetrical layout; fixing with adhesive; two coats sealer; on cement and sand base										
610 x 610 x 2mm units to floors level or to falls only not exceeding 15 degrees from horizontal										
width exceeding 600mm	10.60	5.00	11.21	0.45	0.23	12.97	-	24.19	m²	26.61
width 300mm	3.43	10.00	3.77	0.27	0.07	6.72	-	10.50	m	11.55
610 x 610 x 2.5mm units to floors level or to falls only not exceeding 15 degrees from horizontal										
width exceeding 600mm	14.15	5.00	14.94	0.45	0.23	12.97	-	27.91	m²	30.71
width 300mm	4.49	10.00	4.94	0.27	0.07	6.72	-	11.67	m	12.84

Labour hourly rates: (except Specialists) Craft Operatives 20.87 Labourer 15.57 Rates are national average prices. Refer to REGIONAL VARIATIONS for indicative levels of overall pricing in regions	MATERIALS			LABOUR				RATES		
	Del to Site £	Waste %	Material Cost £	Craft Optve Hrs	Lab Hrs	Labour Cost £	Sunds £	Nett Rate £	Unit	Gross rate (10%) £
IN-SITU, TILED, BLOCK, MOSAIC, SHEET, APPLIED LIQUID OR PLANTED FINISHES (Cont'd)										
Finish to floors; fully flexible PVC heavy duty sheet, BS EN ISO 10581; butt joints; welded; fixing with adhesive; two coats sealer; on cement and sand base										
2mm work to floors level or to falls only not exceeding 15 degrees from horizontal										
width exceeding 600mm	10.10	5.00	10.69	0.30	0.15	8.60	-	19.29	m²	21.21
width 300mm	3.28	10.00	3.61	0.18	0.05	4.54	-	8.14	m	8.96
3.2mm work to floors level or to falls only not exceeding 15 degrees from horizontal										
width exceeding 600mm	11.60	5.00	12.26	0.30	0.15	8.60	-	20.86	m²	22.95
width 300mm	3.73	10.00	4.10	0.18	0.05	4.54	-	8.64	m	9.50
Finish to floors; PVC coved skirting; fixing with adhesive										
Skirtings on plaster base										
height 100mm - Set in	4.18	5.00	4.40	0.20	0.01	4.33	-	8.73	m	9.61
height 100mm - Sit on	4.18	5.00	4.40	0.20	0.02	4.49	-	8.89	m	9.78
Finish to floors; luxury vinyl, Karndean or similar; butt joints, symmetrical layout; fixing with adhesive; on cement and sand base										
400 x 400 x 3mm luxury vinyl tiles p.c. £35 per m²; floors level or to falls only not exceeding 15 degrees from horizontal										
width exceeding 400mm	36.65	5.00	38.57	0.45	0.23	12.97	-	51.54	m²	56.69
width less than 400mm	14.74	5.00	15.52	0.27	0.07	6.72	-	22.24	m	24.47
Finish to floors; luxury vinyl, Karndean or similar; butt joints, symmetrical layout; fixing with adhesive; on cement and sand base										
450 x 450 x 3mm luxury vinyl tiles p.c. £40 per m²; floors level or to falls only not exceeding 15 degrees from horizontal										
width exceeding 450mm	41.65	5.00	43.82	0.45	0.23	12.97	-	56.79	m²	62.47
width less than 450mm	18.74	5.00	19.72	0.27	0.07	6.72	-	26.44	m	29.09
Finish to floors; cork tiles, BS 8203; butt joints; symmetrical layout; fixing with adhesive; two coats seal; on cement and sand base										
300 x 300 x 3.2mm units to floors level or to falls only not exceeding 15 degrees from horizontal										
width exceeding 600mm	22.97	5.00	24.46	0.75	0.23	19.23	-	43.70	m²	48.07
width 300mm	7.30	10.00	8.03	0.45	0.07	10.48	-	18.51	m	20.36
300 x 300 x 4.7mm units to floors level or to falls only not exceeding 15 degrees from horizontal										
width exceeding 600mm	28.50	5.00	30.27	0.75	0.23	19.23	-	49.51	m²	54.46
width 300mm	8.99	10.00	9.88	0.45	0.07	10.48	-	20.36	m	22.40
Finish to floors; linoleum tiles, BS EN ISO 24011; butt joints, symmetrical layout; fixing with adhesive; on cement and sand base										
330 x 330 x 2mm units to floors level or to falls only not exceeding 15 degrees from horizontal										
width exceeding 600mm	17.60	5.00	18.56	0.35	0.23	10.89	-	29.45	m²	32.39
width 300mm	5.53	5.00	5.84	0.21	0.07	5.47	-	11.32	m	12.45
500 x 500 x 2.5mm units to floors level or to falls only not exceeding 15 degrees from horizontal										
width exceeding 600mm	19.60	5.00	20.66	0.35	0.23	10.89	-	31.55	m²	34.70
width 300mm	6.13	5.00	6.47	0.21	0.07	5.47	-	11.95	m	13.14
Finish to floors; linoleum sheet, BS EN ISO 24011; butt joints, laying loose; on cement and sand base										
2.5mm work to floors level or to falls only not exceeding 15 degrees from horizontal										
width exceeding 600mm	15.80	5.00	16.59	0.15	0.13	5.15	-	21.74	m²	23.92
width 300mm	4.74	10.00	5.21	0.09	0.04	2.50	-	7.72	m	8.49
3.2mm work to floors level or to falls only not exceeding 15 degrees from horizontal										
width exceeding 600mm	17.80	5.00	18.69	0.15	0.13	5.15	-	23.84	m²	26.23
width 300mm	5.34	10.00	5.87	0.09	0.04	2.50	-	8.38	m	9.21
Finish to floors; carpet tiles; heavy ribbed, polypropylene/nylon fibre bonded; butt joints, symmetrical layout; fixing with adhesive; on cement and sand base										
500 x 500 units to floors; level or to falls only not exceeding 15 degrees from horizontal										
heavy contract grade										
width exceeding 600mm	14.09	5.00	14.81	0.35	0.23	10.89	-	25.70	m²	28.27
Finish to floors; carpet tiles; looped pile, polypropylene; butt joints, symmetrical layout; fixing with adhesive; on cement and sand base										
500 x 500 units to floors; level or to falls only not exceeding 15 degrees from horizontal										
general contract grade										
width exceeding 600mm	16.89	5.00	17.75	0.35	0.23	10.89	-	28.64	m²	31.50

Labour hourly rates: (except Specialists) Craft Operatives 20.87 Labourer 15.57 Rates are national average prices. Refer to REGIONAL VARIATIONS for indicative levels of overall pricing in regions	MATERIALS			LABOUR				RATES		
	Del to Site £	Waste %	Material Cost £	Craft Optve Hrs	Lab Hrs	Labour Cost £	Sunds £	Nett Rate £	Unit	Gross rate (10%) £
IN-SITU, TILED, BLOCK, MOSAIC, SHEET, APPLIED LIQUID OR PLANTED FINISHES (Cont'd)										
Finish to floors; carpet tiles; hard twist cut pile, polypropylene; butt joints, symmetrical layout; fixing with adhesive; on cement and sand base										
500 x 500 units to floors; level or to falls only not exceeding 15 degrees from horizontal										
heavy contract grade										
width exceeding 600mm	19.09	5.00	20.06	0.35	0.23	10.89	-	30.95	m²	34.04
Finish to floors; fitted carpeting; fibre bonded polypropylene/nylon; fixing with adhesive; on cement and sand base										
Work to floors; level or to falls only not exceeding 15 degrees from horizontal										
heavy contract grade										
width exceeding 600mm	11.74	5.00	12.34	0.30	0.20	9.38	-	21.72	m²	23.89
Finish to floors; fitted carpeting; ribbed fibre bonded polypropylene/nylon; fixing with adhesive; on cement and sand base										
Work to floors; level or to falls only not exceeding 15 degrees from horizontal										
heavy contract grade										
width exceeding 600mm	12.29	5.00	12.92	0.30	0.20	9.38	-	22.29	m²	24.52
Finish to floors; underlay to carpeting; Tredaire Brio 8mm; fixing with tacks; on timber base										
Work to floors; level or to falls only not exceeding 15 degrees from horizontal										
width exceeding 300mm	1.90	5.00	1.99	0.15	0.08	4.38	0.25	6.62	m²	7.28
Finish to floors; fitted carpeting; Tufted wool/nylon; fixing with tackless grippers; on timber base										
Work to floors; level or to falls only not exceeding 15 degrees from horizontal										
width exceeding 300mm	26.60	5.00	27.93	0.30	0.20	9.38	0.25	37.55	m²	41.31
Finish to floors; fitted carpeting; Axminster wool/nylon; fixing with tackless grippers; on timber base										
Work to floors; level or to falls only not exceeding 15 degrees from horizontal										
width exceeding 300mm	45.00	5.00	47.25	0.30	0.20	9.38	0.25	56.87	m²	62.56
Finish to floors; fitted carpeting; Wilton wool/nylon; fixing with tackless grippers; on timber base										
Work to floors; level or to falls only not exceeding 15 degrees from horizontal										
width exceeding 300mm	31.66	5.00	33.24	0.30	0.20	9.38	0.25	42.86	m²	47.15
Raised access floors; Microfloor "Bonded 600" light grade full access system; 600 x 600mm high density particle board panels, BS EN 312 and DIN EU 312; 100 x 100mm precast lightweight concrete pedestals at 600mm centres fixed to sub-floor with epoxy resin adhesive										
Thickness of panel 30mm										
finished floor height										
50mm	-	-	Specialist	-	-	Specialist	-	31.23	m²	34.35
75mm	-	-	Specialist	-	-	Specialist	-	31.45	m²	34.60
100mm	-	-	Specialist	-	-	Specialist	-	31.84	m²	35.03
125mm	-	-	Specialist	-	-	Specialist	-	32.18	m²	35.40
150mm	-	-	Specialist	-	-	Specialist	-	32.83	m²	36.12
175mm	-	-	Specialist	-	-	Specialist	-	33.35	m²	36.69
200mm	-	-	Specialist	-	-	Specialist	-	33.64	m²	37.01
Raised access floors; Microfloor "Bonded 600" medium grade full access system; 600 x 600mm high density particle board panels, BS EN 312 and DIN EU 312; 100 x 100mm precast lightweight concrete pedestals at 600mm centres fixed to sub-floor with epoxy resin adhesive										
Thickness of panel 38mm										
finished floor height										
50mm	-	-	Specialist	-	-	Specialist	-	35.51	m²	39.06
75mm	-	-	Specialist	-	-	Specialist	-	35.51	m²	39.06
100mm	-	-	Specialist	-	-	Specialist	-	36.19	m²	39.81
125mm	-	-	Specialist	-	-	Specialist	-	36.50	m²	40.15
150mm	-	-	Specialist	-	-	Specialist	-	37.69	m²	41.45
175mm	-	-	Specialist	-	-	Specialist	-	37.99	m²	41.79
200mm	-	-	Specialist	-	-	Specialist	-	38.29	m²	42.12
Raised access floors; Microfloor "Bonded 600" office loadings grade full access system; 600 x 600mm high density particle board panels, BS EN 634 and DIN EU 312; 100 x 100mm precast lightweight concrete pedestals at 600mm centres fixed to sub-floor with epoxy resin adhesive										
Thickness of panel 30mm										
finished floor height										
50mm	-	-	Specialist	-	-	Specialist	-	24.31	m²	26.74

Labour hourly rates: (except Specialists) Craft Operatives 20.87 Labourer 15.57 Rates are national average prices. Refer to REGIONAL VARIATIONS for indicative levels of overall pricing in regions	MATERIALS			LABOUR				RATES		
	Del to Site £	Waste %	Material Cost £	Craft Optve Hrs	Lab Hrs	Labour Cost £	Sunds £	Nett Rate £	Unit	Gross rate (10%) £
IN-SITU, TILED, BLOCK, MOSAIC, SHEET, APPLIED LIQUID OR PLANTED FINISHES (Cont'd)										
Raised access floors; Microfloor "Bonded 600" office loadings grade full access system; 600 x 600mm high density particle board panels, BS EN 634 and DIN EU 312; 100 x 100mm precast lightweight concrete pedestals at 600mm centres fixed to sub-floor with epoxy resin adhesive (Cont'd)										
Thickness of panel 30mm (Cont'd)										
finished floor height (Cont'd)										
75mm	-	-	Specialist	-	-	Specialist	-	24.46	m²	26.90
100mm	-	-	Specialist	-	-	Specialist	-	24.99	m²	27.49
125mm	-	-	Specialist	-	-	Specialist	-	25.30	m²	27.83
150mm	-	-	Specialist	-	-	Specialist	-	25.92	m²	28.51
175mm	-	-	Specialist	-	-	Specialist	-	26.50	m²	29.15
200mm	-	-	Specialist	-	-	Specialist	-	26.78	m²	29.46
Finish to roofs; extensive green roof; Sedum roof										
Sedum standard grade mat laid over Substrate E BB; filter fleece; 20mm HD Polyethylene drainage board; 3.6mm protection matt										
level and to falls not exceeding 15º from horizontal										
width exceeding 600mm; 130mm overall thickness; 80mm substrate	42.35	10.00	46.59	0.56	0.56	20.41	-	66.99	m²	73.69
width exceeding 600mm; 150mm overall thickness; 100mm substrate	43.95	10.00	48.35	0.59	0.59	21.50	-	69.85	m²	76.83
Finish to roofs; extensive green roof; Wild flower roof										
Wild flower mat laid over Substrate E BB; 1.1mm filter fleece; 40mm drainage board; 3.6mm protection matt										
level and to falls not exceeding 15º from horizontal										
width exceeding 600mm; 170mm overall thickness; 100mm substrate	47.17	10.00	51.89	0.60	0.60	21.86	-	73.75	m²	81.13
width exceeding 600mm; 190mm overall thickness; 120mm substrate	49.92	10.00	54.92	0.64	0.64	23.32	-	78.24	m²	86.06
Finish to roofs; extensive green roof; Biodiverse roof										
20nr plug plants; Substrate E BB; 1.1mm filter fleece; 40mm drainage board; 3.6mm protection matt										
level and to falls not exceeding 15º from horizontal										
width exceeding 600mm; 150mm overall thickness; 100mm substrate	37.77	10.00	41.55	0.49	0.49	17.86	-	59.41	m²	65.35
width exceeding 600mm; 150mm overall thickness; 120mm substrate	40.52	10.00	44.58	0.52	0.52	18.95	-	63.53	m²	69.88
Finish to roofs; extensive green roof; Seeded roof										
Seeds; Substrate E BB; filter fleece; 40mm drainage board; protection matt										
level and to falls not exceeding 15º from horizontal										
width exceeding 600mm; 150mm overall thickness; 100mm substrate	29.42	10.00	32.37	0.32	0.32	11.66	-	44.03	m²	48.43
width exceeding 600mm; 170mm overall thickness; 120mm substrate	32.17	10.00	35.39	0.36	0.36	13.12	-	48.51	m²	53.36
Finish to roofs; extensive green roof; Vegetation barrier										
20-40mm screened pebbles										
level and to falls not exceeding 15º from horizontal										
width exceeding 600mm; 80mm overall thickness	18.70	10.00	20.57	0.26	0.26	9.47	-	30.04	m²	33.05
width 300mm; 80mm overall thickness	5.61	10.00	6.17	0.10	0.10	3.64	-	9.82	m	10.80
Finish to roofs; extensive green roof; Edge trim										
80mm high; aluminium										
level and to falls not exceeding 15º from horizontal										
fixed to waterproofing layer	15.36	10.00	16.90	0.10	0.10	3.64	-	20.54	m	22.60
Finish to Walls, isolated columns, ceilings and isolated beams; Portland cement work										
Plain face, first and finishing coats cement and sand (1:3), total 13mm thick; wood floated										
13mm work to walls on brickwork or blockwork base										
width exceeding 600mm	1.85	5.00	1.95	0.60	0.30	17.19	-	19.14	m²	21.05
width exceeding 600mm; dubbing average 6mm thick	2.71	5.00	2.85	0.84	0.44	24.38	-	27.23	m²	29.95
width exceeding 600mm; dubbing average 12mm thick	3.57	5.00	3.74	0.88	0.58	27.40	-	31.14	m²	34.25
width exceeding 600mm; dubbing average 19mm thick	4.56	5.00	4.79	0.92	0.74	30.72	-	35.51	m²	39.07
width exceeding 600mm; curved to 3000mm radius	1.85	5.00	1.95	0.80	0.30	21.37	-	23.31	m²	25.64
width 300mm	0.57	10.00	0.63	0.36	0.09	8.91	-	9.54	m	10.50
width 300mm; dubbing average 6mm thick	0.86	10.00	0.94	0.53	0.17	13.71	-	14.65	m	16.11
width 300mm; dubbing average 12mm thick	1.14	10.00	1.25	0.53	0.17	13.71	-	14.96	m	16.46
width 300mm; dubbing average 19mm thick	1.43	10.00	1.57	0.55	0.22	14.90	-	16.47	m	18.12
width 300mm; curved to 3000mm radius	0.57	10.00	0.63	0.48	0.09	11.42	-	12.05	m	13.25
Work forming flush skirting; 13mm thick										
height 150mm	0.29	50.00	0.43	0.60	0.05	13.30	-	13.73	m	15.10
height 225mm	0.43	50.00	0.64	0.65	0.07	14.66	-	15.30	m	16.83
height 150mm; curved to 3000mm radius	0.29	50.00	0.43	0.80	0.05	17.47	-	17.90	m	19.69
height 225mm; curved to 3000mm radius	0.43	50.00	0.64	0.86	0.07	19.04	-	19.68	m	21.65
Work forming projecting skirting; 13mm projection										
height 150mm	0.29	50.00	0.43	0.90	0.05	19.56	-	19.99	m	21.99
height 225mm	0.43	50.00	0.64	0.98	0.07	21.54	-	22.18	m	24.40
height 150mm; curved to 3000mm radius	0.29	50.00	0.43	1.20	0.05	25.82	-	26.25	m	28.88
height 225mm; curved to 3000mm radius	0.43	50.00	0.64	1.29	0.07	28.01	-	28.65	m	31.52

Labour hourly rates: (except Specialists) Craft Operatives 20.87 Labourer 15.57 Rates are national average prices. Refer to REGIONAL VARIATIONS for indicative levels of overall pricing in regions	MATERIALS			LABOUR				RATES		
	Del to Site £	Waste %	Material Cost £	Craft Optve Hrs	Lab Hrs	Labour Cost £	Sunds £	Nett Rate £	Unit	Gross rate (10%) £
IN-SITU, TILED, BLOCK, MOSAIC, SHEET, APPLIED LIQUID OR PLANTED FINISHES (Cont'd)										
Finish to Walls, isolated columns, ceilings and isolated beams; Portland cement work (Cont'd)										
Plain face, first and finishing coats cement and sand (1:3), total 13mm thick; wood floated (Cont'd)										
Rounded angles										
radius 10 - 100mm	-	-	-	0.30	-	6.26	-	6.26	m	6.89
If plain face waterproofed										
add	0.09	10.00	0.10	-	0.02	0.31	-	0.42	m²	0.46
Finish to Walls, isolated columns, ceilings and isolated beams; Rough cast										
Render and dry dash; first and finishing coats cement and sand (1:3), total 15mm thick; wood floated; dry dash of pea shingle; external; 15mm work to walls on brickwork or blockwork base										
width exceeding 600mm										
flat	2.44	5.00	2.58	0.85	0.43	24.43	-	27.02	m²	29.72
extra; spatterdash coat	1.52	10.00	1.67	0.23	0.12	6.67	-	8.34	m²	9.18
curved to 3000mm radius	2.44	5.00	2.58	1.15	0.43	30.70	-	33.28	m²	36.60
width 300mm										
flat	0.56	10.00	0.61	0.51	0.13	12.67	-	13.28	m	14.61
extra; spatterdash coat	0.04	10.00	0.05	0.14	0.04	3.54	-	3.59	m	3.95
curved to 3000mm radius	0.56	10.00	0.61	0.69	0.13	16.42	-	17.04	m	18.74
Render and wet dash; first and finishing coats cement and sand (1:3), total 15mm thick; wood floated; wet dash of crushed stone or shingle and cement slurry; 15mm work to walls on brickwork or blockwork base										
width exceeding 600mm										
flat	3.59	5.00	3.84	0.95	0.48	27.30	-	31.14	m²	34.25
extra; spatterdash coat	0.78	10.00	0.86	0.28	0.14	8.02	-	8.89	m²	9.78
curved to 3000mm radius	3.59	5.00	3.84	1.24	0.48	33.35	-	37.19	m²	40.91
width 300mm										
flat	1.21	10.00	1.33	0.57	0.14	14.08	-	15.41	m	16.95
extra; spatterdash coat	0.37	10.00	0.41	0.17	0.04	4.17	-	4.58	m	5.04
curved to 3000mm radius	2.16	10.00	2.38	0.74	0.14	17.62	-	20.00	m	22.00
Finish to Walls, isolated columns, ceilings and isolated beams; Tyrolean finish										
Render and Tyrolean finish; first and finishing coats cement and sand (1:3), total 15mm thick; wood floated; Tyrolean finish of "Cullamix" mixture applied by machine										
15mm work to walls on brickwork or blockwork base										
width exceeding 600mm	3.60	5.00	3.78	1.05	0.30	26.58	-	32.66	m²	35.93
width 300mm	1.20	10.00	1.32	0.63	0.09	14.55	-	17.25	m	18.97
Finish to Walls, isolated columns, ceilings and isolated beams; Hardwall plastering										
Plaster, BS EN 13279, Part 1, Class B; finishing coat of board finish, 3mm thick; steel troweled										
3mm work to walls on concrete or plasterboard base										
width exceeding 600mm	0.89	5.00	0.93	0.25	0.13	7.24	0.02	8.19	m²	9.01
width exceeding 600mm; curved to 3000mm radius	0.89	5.00	0.93	0.33	0.13	8.91	0.02	9.86	m²	10.85
width 300mm	0.44	10.00	0.49	0.15	0.04	3.75	0.01	4.25	m	4.67
width 300mm; curved to 3000mm radius	0.44	10.00	0.49	0.20	0.04	4.80	0.01	5.29	m	5.82
3mm work to isolated columns on concrete or plasterboard base										
width exceeding 600mm	0.89	5.00	0.93	0.38	0.13	9.95	0.02	10.91	m²	12.00
width 300mm	0.44	10.00	0.49	0.23	0.04	5.42	0.01	5.92	m	6.51
3mm work to ceilings on concrete or plasterboard base										
width exceeding 600mm	0.89	5.00	0.93	0.30	0.13	8.29	0.02	9.24	m²	10.16
width exceeding 600mm; 3.50 - 5.00m above floor	0.89	5.00	0.93	0.33	0.13	8.91	0.02	9.86	m²	10.85
width 300mm	0.44	10.00	0.49	0.18	0.04	4.38	0.01	4.87	m	5.36
width 300mm; 3.50 - 5.00m above floor	0.44	10.00	0.49	0.20	0.04	4.80	0.01	5.29	m	5.82
3mm work to isolated beams on concrete or plasterboard base										
width exceeding 600mm	0.89	5.00	0.93	0.38	0.13	9.95	0.02	10.91	m²	12.00
width 300mm	0.44	10.00	0.49	0.23	0.04	5.42	0.01	5.92	m	6.51
Plaster; first coat of hardwall, 11mm thick; finishing coat of multi-finish 2mm thick; steel troweled										
13mm work to walls on brickwork or blockwork base										
width exceeding 600mm	3.55	5.00	3.73	0.45	0.23	12.97	0.07	16.77	m²	18.45
width exceeding 600mm; curved to 3000mm radius	3.55	5.00	3.73	0.60	0.23	16.10	0.07	19.90	m²	21.89
width 300mm	1.61	10.00	1.77	0.27	0.07	6.72	0.02	8.51	m	9.37
width 300mm; curved to 3000mm radius	1.61	10.00	1.77	0.36	0.07	8.60	0.02	10.39	m	11.43
13mm work to isolated columns on concrete base										
width exceeding 600mm	3.55	5.00	3.73	0.68	0.23	17.77	0.07	21.57	m²	23.73
width 300mm	1.61	10.00	1.77	0.41	0.07	9.65	0.02	11.44	m	12.58
13mm work to ceilings on concrete base										
width exceeding 600mm	3.55	5.00	3.73	0.54	0.23	14.85	0.07	18.65	m²	20.52
width exceeding 600mm; 3.50 - 5.00m above floor	3.55	5.00	3.73	0.59	0.23	15.89	0.07	19.70	m²	21.67
width 300mm	1.61	10.00	1.77	0.32	0.07	7.77	0.02	9.56	m	10.51
width 300mm; 3.50 - 5.00m above floor	1.61	10.00	1.77	0.35	0.07	8.39	0.02	10.18	m	11.20
13mm work to isolated beams on concrete base										
width exceeding 600mm	3.55	5.00	3.73	0.68	0.23	17.77	0.07	21.57	m²	23.73
width 300mm	1.61	10.00	1.77	0.41	0.07	9.65	0.02	11.44	m	12.58
Rounded angles										
radius 10 - 100mm	-	-	-	0.24	-	5.01	-	5.01	m	5.51

FLOOR, WALL, CEILING AND ROOF FINISHINGS

Labour hourly rates: (except Specialists) Craft Operatives 20.87 Labourer 15.57 Rates are national average prices. Refer to REGIONAL VARIATIONS for indicative levels of overall pricing in regions	MATERIALS			LABOUR				RATES		
	Del to Site £	Waste %	Material Cost £	Craft Optve Hrs	Lab Hrs	Labour Cost £	Sunds £	Nett Rate £	Unit	Gross rate (10%) £
IN-SITU, TILED, BLOCK, MOSAIC, SHEET, APPLIED LIQUID OR PLANTED FINISHES (Cont'd)										
Finish to Walls, isolated columns, ceilings and isolated beams; Hardwall plastering (Cont'd)										
Plaster; Thistle Universal one coat plaster, 13mm thick; steel troweled; Note: the thickness is from the face of the metal lathing										
13mm work to walls on metal lathing base										
width exceeding 600mm	3.07	5.00	3.23	0.35	0.18	10.11	0.08	13.42	m²	14.76
width exceeding 600mm; curved to 3000mm radius	3.07	5.00	3.23	0.47	0.18	12.61	0.08	15.92	m²	17.51
width 300mm	0.03	10.00	0.04	0.21	0.05	5.16	0.03	5.22	m	5.75
width 300mm; curved to 3000mm radius	0.03	10.00	0.04	0.28	0.05	6.62	0.03	6.68	m	7.35
13mm work to isolated columns on metal lathing base										
width exceeding 600mm	3.07	5.00	3.23	0.53	0.18	13.86	0.08	17.17	m²	18.89
width 300mm	0.03	10.00	0.04	0.32	0.05	7.46	0.03	7.52	m	8.27
13mm work to ceilings on metal lathing base										
width exceeding 600mm	3.07	5.00	3.23	0.42	0.18	11.57	0.08	14.88	m²	16.36
width exceeding 600mm; 3.50 - 5.00m above floor	3.07	5.00	3.23	0.46	0.18	12.40	0.08	15.71	m²	17.28
width 300mm	0.03	10.00	0.04	0.25	0.05	6.00	0.03	6.06	m	6.66
width 300mm; 3.50 - 5.00m above floor	0.03	10.00	0.04	0.28	0.05	6.62	0.03	6.68	m	7.35
13mm work to isolated beams on metal lathing base										
width exceeding 600mm	3.07	5.00	3.23	0.53	0.18	13.86	0.08	17.17	m²	18.89
width 300mm	0.03	10.00	0.04	0.32	0.05	7.46	0.03	7.52	m	8.27
Rounded angles										
radius 10 - 100mm	-	-	-	0.18	-	3.76	-	3.76	m	4.13
Finish to Walls, isolated columns, ceilings and isolated beams; lightweight plastering										
Plaster, Thistle; pre-mixed; floating coat of browning, 11mm thick; finishing coat of multi-finish, 2mm thick; steel troweled										
13mm work to walls on brickwork or blockwork base										
width exceeding 600mm	3.21	5.00	3.37	0.40	0.20	11.46	0.05	14.89	m²	16.37
width exceeding 600mm; curved to 3000mm radius	3.21	5.00	3.37	0.53	0.20	14.18	0.05	17.60	m²	19.36
width exceeding 600mm; dubbing average 6mm thick	4.77	5.00	5.01	0.63	0.38	19.06	0.08	24.15	m²	26.57
width exceeding 600mm; dubbing average 6mm thick; curved to 3000mm radius	4.77	5.00	5.01	0.84	0.38	23.45	0.08	28.54	m²	31.39
width exceeding 600mm; dubbing average 12mm thick	5.94	5.00	6.24	0.63	0.38	19.06	0.11	25.41	m²	27.95
width exceeding 600mm; dubbing average 12mm thick; curved to 3000mm radius	5.94	5.00	6.24	0.84	0.38	23.45	0.11	29.79	m²	32.77
width exceeding 600mm; dubbing average 19mm thick	7.50	5.00	7.87	0.65	0.49	21.19	0.11	29.17	m²	32.09
width exceeding 600mm; dubbing average 19mm thick; curved to 3000mm radius	7.89	5.00	8.28	0.87	0.49	25.79	0.11	34.18	m²	37.59
width 300mm	1.41	5.00	1.49	0.24	0.06	5.94	0.02	7.45	m	8.20
width 300mm; curved to 3000mm radius	1.41	5.00	1.49	0.32	0.06	7.61	0.02	9.12	m	10.03
width 300mm; dubbing average 6mm thick	2.19	5.00	2.31	0.36	0.09	8.91	0.02	11.25	m	12.37
width 300mm; dubbing average 6mm thick; curved to 3000mm radius	2.19	5.00	2.31	0.48	0.09	11.42	0.02	13.75	m	15.13
width 300mm; dubbing average 12mm thick	2.58	5.00	2.72	0.38	0.09	9.33	0.03	12.08	m	13.29
width 300mm; dubbing average 12mm thick; curved to 3000mm radius	2.58	5.00	2.72	0.51	0.09	12.05	0.03	14.80	m	16.28
width 300mm; dubbing average 19mm thick	3.36	5.00	3.54	0.39	0.15	10.47	0.03	14.05	m	15.45
width 300mm; dubbing average 19mm thick; curved to 3000mm radius	3.36	5.00	3.54	0.52	0.15	13.19	0.03	16.76	m	18.43
Rounded angles										
radius 10 - 100mm	-	-	-	0.24	-	5.01	-	5.01	m	5.51
Plaster, Thistle; pre-mixed; floating coat of bonding 8mm thick; finishing coat of multi-finish, 2mm thick; steel troweled										
10mm work to walls on concrete or plasterboard base										
width exceeding 600mm	2.73	5.00	2.86	0.40	0.20	11.46	0.05	14.38	m²	15.82
width exceeding 600mm; curved to 3000mm radius	2.73	5.00	2.86	0.53	0.20	14.18	0.05	17.09	m²	18.80
width 300mm	1.20	10.00	1.32	0.24	0.06	5.94	0.02	7.28	m	8.01
width 300mm; curved to 3000mm radius	1.20	10.00	1.32	0.32	0.06	7.61	0.02	8.95	m	9.85
10mm work to isolated columns on concrete or plasterboard base										
width exceeding 600mm	2.73	5.00	2.86	0.60	0.20	15.64	0.05	18.55	m²	20.41
width 300mm	1.20	10.00	1.32	0.36	0.06	8.45	0.02	9.79	m	10.77
10mm work to ceilings on concrete or plasterboard base										
width exceeding 600mm	2.73	5.00	2.86	0.48	0.20	13.13	0.05	16.05	m²	17.65
width exceeding 600mm; 3.50 - 5.00m above floor	2.73	5.00	2.86	0.52	0.20	13.97	0.05	16.88	m²	18.57
width 300mm	1.20	10.00	1.32	0.29	0.06	6.99	0.02	8.33	m	9.16
width 300mm; 3.50 - 5.00m above floor	1.20	10.00	1.32	0.31	0.06	7.40	0.02	8.74	m	9.62
10mm work to isolated beams on concrete or plasterboard base										
width exceeding 600mm	2.73	5.00	2.86	0.60	0.20	15.64	0.05	18.55	m²	20.41
width 300mm	1.20	10.00	1.32	0.36	0.06	8.45	0.02	9.79	m	10.77
Rounded angles										
radius 10 - 100mm	-	-	-	0.24	-	5.01	-	5.01	m	5.51
Plaster, Thistle; pre-mixed; floating coat of bonding 11mm thick; finishing coat of multi-finish, 2mm thick; steel troweled										
13mm work to ceilings on precast concrete beam and infill blocks base										
width exceeding 600mm	3.69	5.00	3.87	0.48	0.20	13.13	0.08	17.09	m²	18.80
width 300mm	1.84	10.00	2.03	0.29	0.06	6.99	0.03	9.04	m	9.95
Plaster, Thistle; tough coat, 11mm thick; finish 2mm thick steel troweled; Note: the thickness is from the face of the metal lathing										
13mm work to walls on metal lathing base										
width exceeding 600mm	3.56	5.00	3.73	0.55	0.28	15.84	0.05	19.63	m²	21.59
width exceeding 600mm; curved to 3000mm radius	3.56	5.00	3.73	0.73	0.28	19.59	0.05	23.38	m²	25.72
width 300mm	1.56	10.00	1.71	0.33	0.08	8.13	0.02	9.86	m	10.85
width 300mm; curved to 3000mm radius	1.56	10.00	1.71	0.44	0.08	10.43	0.02	12.16	m	13.38
13mm work to isolated columns on metal lathing base										
width exceeding 600mm	3.56	5.00	3.73	0.83	0.28	21.68	0.05	25.47	m²	28.02
width 300mm	1.56	10.00	1.71	0.50	0.08	11.68	0.02	13.41	m	14.75

Labour hourly rates: (except Specialists) Craft Operatives 20.87 Labourer 15.57 Rates are national average prices. Refer to REGIONAL VARIATIONS for indicative levels of overall pricing in regions	MATERIALS			LABOUR				RATES		
	Del to Site £	Waste %	Material Cost £	Craft Optve Hrs	Lab Hrs	Labour Cost £	Sunds £	Nett Rate £	Unit	Gross rate (10%) £
IN-SITU, TILED, BLOCK, MOSAIC, SHEET, APPLIED LIQUID OR PLANTED FINISHES (Cont'd)										
Finish to Walls, isolated columns, ceilings and isolated beams; lightweight plastering (Cont'd)										
Plaster, Thistle; tough coat, 11mm thick; finish 2mm thick steel troweled; Note: the thickness is from the face of the metal lathing (Cont'd)										
13mm work to ceilings on metal lathing base										
width exceeding 600mm	3.56	5.00	3.73	0.66	0.28	18.13	0.05	21.92	m²	24.12
width exceeding 600mm; 3.50 - 5.00m above floor	3.56	5.00	3.73	0.72	0.28	19.39	0.05	23.18	m²	25.49
width 300mm	1.56	10.00	1.71	0.40	0.08	9.59	0.02	11.33	m	12.46
width 300mm; 3.50 - 5.00m above floor	1.56	10.00	1.71	0.43	0.08	10.22	0.02	11.95	m	13.15
13mm work to isolated beams on metal lathing base										
width exceeding 600mm	3.56	5.00	3.73	0.83	0.28	21.68	0.05	25.47	m²	28.02
width 300mm	1.56	10.00	1.71	0.50	0.08	11.68	0.02	13.41	m	14.75
Rounded angles										
radius 10 - 100mm	-	-	-	0.30	-	6.26	-	6.26	m	6.89
Finish to Walls, isolated columns, ceilings and isolated beams; applied liquid bonding fluid										
Prepare and apply bonding fluid to receive plaster or cement rendering										
Work to walls on existing cement and sand base										
width exceeding 300mm	0.45	10.00	0.50	0.20	-	4.17	-	4.67	m²	5.14
Work to walls on existing glazed tiling base										
width exceeding 300mm	0.34	10.00	0.37	0.15	-	3.13	-	3.50	m²	3.86
Work to walls on existing painted surface										
width exceeding 300mm	0.41	10.00	0.45	0.18	-	3.76	-	4.21	m²	4.63
Work to walls on existing concrete base										
width exceeding 300mm	0.45	10.00	0.50	0.20	-	4.17	-	4.67	m²	5.14
Work to ceilings on existing cement and sand base										
width exceeding 300mm	0.45	10.00	0.50	0.24	-	5.01	-	5.51	m²	6.06
Work to ceilings on existing painted surface										
width exceeding 300mm	0.41	10.00	0.45	0.22	-	4.59	-	5.04	m²	5.54
Work to ceilings on existing concrete base										
width exceeding 300mm	0.45	10.00	0.50	0.24	-	5.01	-	5.51	m²	6.06
Finish to Walls, isolated columns, ceilings and isolated beams; dry lining plasterboard										
Linings; tapered edge sheeting of one layer 9.5mm thick Gyproc wall board for direct decoration, BS EN 520, butt joints; fixing with galvanised nails to timber base; butt joints filled with joint filler tape and joint finish, spot filling										
Walls										
over 600mm wide	4.37	5.00	4.58	0.40	0.20	11.46	-	16.05	m²	17.65
Columns; 4nr faces										
total girth 600 - 1200mm	5.37	10.00	5.87	0.88	0.21	21.64	-	27.51	m	30.26
total girth 1200 - 1800mm	7.98	10.00	8.73	1.31	0.32	32.32	-	41.05	m	45.16
Ceilings										
generally	4.39	5.00	4.60	0.40	0.18	11.15	-	15.75	m²	17.32
Beams; isolated; 3nr faces										
total girth 600 - 1200mm	5.30	10.00	5.80	0.88	0.21	21.64	-	27.43	m	30.17
Reveals and soffits of openings and recesses										
width 300mm	1.38	10.00	1.51	0.21	0.05	5.16	-	6.67	m	7.34
Finish to Walls, isolated columns, ceilings and isolated beams; linings; tapered edge sheeting of one layer 12.5mm thick Gyproc wallboard for direct decoration, BS EN 520 butt joints; fixing with galvanised nails to timber base; butt joints filled with joint filler tape and joint finish, spot filling										
Walls										
over 600mm wide	9.69	5.00	10.16	0.47	0.24	13.55	-	23.71	m²	26.08
Columns; 4nr faces										
total girth 600 - 1200mm	11.75	10.00	12.89	1.02	0.24	25.02	-	37.91	m	41.70
total girth 1200 - 1800mm	17.54	10.00	19.25	1.53	0.36	37.54	-	56.79	m	62.47
Ceilings										
generally	9.70	5.00	10.18	0.46	0.20	12.71	-	22.89	m²	25.18
Beams; isolated; 3nr faces										
total girth 600 - 1200mm	11.67	10.00	12.81	1.02	0.24	25.02	-	37.83	m	41.62
Reveals and soffits of openings and recesses										
width 300mm	2.97	10.00	3.26	0.21	0.06	5.32	-	8.58	m	9.44
Finish to Walls, isolated columns, ceilings and isolated beams; linings; tapered edge sheeting of one layer 15mm thick Gyproc wall board for direct decoration, BS EN 520, butt joints; fixing with galvanised nails to timber base; butt joints filled with joint filler tape and joint finish, spot filling										
Walls										
over 600mm wide	3.81	5.00	4.00	0.54	0.28	15.63	-	19.62	m²	21.59
Columns; 4nr faces										
total girth 600 - 1200mm	4.70	10.00	5.13	1.16	0.27	28.41	-	33.55	m	36.90
total girth 1200 - 1800mm	6.97	10.00	7.62	1.74	0.41	42.70	-	50.32	m	55.35
Ceilings										
generally	3.83	5.00	4.01	0.52	0.22	14.28	-	18.29	m²	20.12
Beams; isolated; 3nr faces										
total girth 600 - 1200mm	4.62	10.00	5.06	1.16	0.27	28.41	-	33.47	m	36.82
Reveals and soffits of openings and recesses										
width 300mm	1.21	10.00	1.32	0.22	0.06	5.53	-	6.85	m	7.53

Labour hourly rates: (except Specialists) Craft Operatives 20.87 Labourer 15.57 Rates are national average prices. Refer to REGIONAL VARIATIONS for indicative levels of overall pricing in regions	MATERIALS			LABOUR				RATES		
	Del to Site £	Waste %	Material Cost £	Craft Optve Hrs	Lab Hrs	Labour Cost £	Sunds £	Nett Rate £	Unit	Gross rate (10%) £
IN-SITU, TILED, BLOCK, MOSAIC, SHEET, APPLIED LIQUID OR PLANTED FINISHES (Cont'd)										
Finish to Walls, isolated columns, ceilings and isolated beams; linings; tapered edge sheeting of one layer 12.5mm thick Gyproc vapourcheck wallboard for direct decoration, BS EN 520, butt joints; fixing with galvanised nails to timber base; butt joints filled with joint filler tape and joint finish, spot filling										
Walls										
over 600mm wide	3.02	5.00	3.16	0.47	0.24	13.55	-	16.70	m²	18.37
Columns; 4nr faces										
total girth 600 - 1200mm	2.95	10.00	3.21	1.02	0.24	25.02	-	28.23	m	31.06
total girth 1200 - 1800mm	4.35	10.00	4.74	1.53	0.36	37.54	-	42.27	m	46.50
Ceilings										
generally	3.03	5.00	3.17	0.46	0.20	12.71	-	15.89	m²	17.47
Beams; isolated; 3nr faces										
total girth 600 - 1200mm	2.87	10.00	3.13	1.02	0.24	25.02	-	28.16	m	30.97
Reveals and soffits of openings and recesses										
width 300mm	0.78	10.00	0.84	0.21	0.06	5.32	-	6.16	m	6.78
Finish to Walls, isolated columns, ceilings and isolated beams; linings; tapered edge sheeting of one layer 15mm thick Gyproc vapourcheck wallboard for direct decoration, BS EN 520, butt joints; fixing with galvanised nails to timber base; butt joints filled with joint filler tape and joint finish, spot filling										
Walls										
over 600mm wide	3.81	5.00	4.00	0.54	0.28	15.63	-	19.62	m²	21.59
Columns; 4nr faces										
total girth 600 - 1200mm	4.70	10.00	5.13	1.16	0.27	28.41	-	33.55	m	36.90
total girth 1200 - 1800mm	6.97	10.00	7.62	1.74	0.41	42.70	-	50.32	m	55.35
Ceilings										
generally	3.83	5.00	4.01	0.52	0.22	14.28	-	18.29	m²	20.12
Beams; isolated; 3nr faces										
total girth 600 - 1200mm	4.62	10.00	5.06	1.16	0.27	28.41	-	33.47	m	36.82
Reveals and soffits of openings and recesses										
width 300mm	1.21	10.00	1.32	0.22	0.06	5.53	-	6.85	m	7.53
Finish to Walls, isolated columns, ceilings and isolated beams; linings; tapered edge sheeting of one layer 19mm thick Gyproc plank for direct decoration, BS EN 520, butt joints; fixing with galvanised nails to timber base; butt joints filled with joint filler tape and joint finish, spot filling										
Walls										
over 600mm wide	9.15	5.00	9.60	0.60	0.30	17.19	-	26.79	m²	29.47
Columns; 4nr faces										
total girth 600 - 1200mm	11.06	10.00	12.12	1.50	0.30	35.98	-	48.10	m	52.91
total girth 1200 - 1800mm	16.52	10.00	18.11	2.25	0.45	53.96	-	72.07	m	79.28
Ceilings										
generally	9.17	5.00	9.61	0.60	0.25	16.41	-	26.02	m²	28.63
Beams; isolated; 3nr faces										
total girth 600 - 1200mm	10.99	10.00	12.05	1.50	0.30	35.98	-	48.02	m	52.82
Reveals and soffits of openings and recesses										
width 300mm	2.80	10.00	3.07	0.30	0.08	7.51	-	10.58	m	11.63
Finish to Walls, isolated columns, ceilings and isolated beams; linings; two layers of Gypsum wallboard, first layer square edge sheeting 9.5mm thick, second layer tapered edge sheeting 9.5mm thick for direct decoration, BS EN 520, butt joints; fixing with galvanised nails to timber base; butt joints of second layer filled with joint filler tape and joint finish, spot filling										
Walls										
over 600mm wide	8.79	5.00	9.20	0.70	0.35	20.06	-	29.26	m²	32.19
Columns; 4nr faces										
total girth 600 - 1200mm	10.67	10.00	11.66	1.62	0.36	39.41	-	51.08	m	56.18
total girth 1200 - 1800mm	15.93	10.00	17.41	2.43	0.54	59.12	-	76.54	m	84.19
Ceilings										
generally	8.80	5.00	9.22	0.70	0.30	19.28	-	28.50	m²	31.35
Beams; isolated; 3nr faces										
total girth 600 - 1200mm	5.68	10.00	6.17	1.62	0.36	39.41	-	45.59	m	50.15
Reveals and soffits of openings and recesses										
width 300mm	2.71	10.00	2.96	0.33	0.09	8.29	-	11.24	m	12.37
Finish to Walls, isolated columns, ceilings and isolated beams; linings; two layers of Gypsum wallboard, first layer square edge sheeting 9.5mm thick, second layer tapered edge sheeting 12.5mm thick for direct decoration, BS EN 520, butt joints; fixing with galvanised nails to timber base; butt joints of second layer filled with joint filler tape and joint finish, spot filling										
Walls										
over 600mm wide	14.10	5.00	14.78	0.84	0.40	23.76	-	38.54	m²	42.39
Columns; 4nr faces										
total girth 600 - 1200mm	17.04	10.00	18.43	1.78	0.39	43.22	-	61.65	m	67.81
total girth 1200 - 1800mm	25.49	10.00	27.57	2.66	0.59	64.70	-	92.27	m	101.49
Ceilings										
generally	14.11	5.00	14.79	0.76	0.33	21.00	-	35.79	m²	39.37
Beams; isolated; 3nr faces										
total girth 600 - 1200mm	16.97	10.00	18.35	1.78	0.39	43.22	-	61.57	m	67.73
Reveals and soffits of openings and recesses										
width 300mm	4.30	10.00	4.65	0.36	0.10	9.07	-	13.72	m	15.09

Labour hourly rates: (except Specialists) Craft Operatives 20.87 Labourer 15.57 Rates are national average prices. Refer to REGIONAL VARIATIONS for indicative levels of overall pricing in regions	MATERIALS			LABOUR				RATES		
	Del to Site £	Waste %	Material Cost £	Craft Optve Hrs	Lab Hrs	Labour Cost £	Sunds £	Nett Rate £	Unit	Gross rate (10%) £
IN-SITU, TILED, BLOCK, MOSAIC, SHEET, APPLIED LIQUID OR PLANTED FINISHES (Cont'd)										
Finish to Walls, isolated columns, ceilings and isolated beams; linings; two layers of Gypsum wallboard, first layer square edge sheeting 12.5mm thick, second layer tapered edge sheeting 12.5mm thick for direct decoration, BS EN 520, butt joints; fixing with galvanised nails to timber base; butt joints of second layer filled with joint filler tape and joint finish, spot filling										
Walls										
over 600mm wide	19.41	5.00	20.36	0.82	0.43	23.81	-	44.17	m²	48.58
Columns; 4nr faces										
total girth 600 - 1200mm	23.42	10.00	25.69	1.92	0.42	46.61	-	72.30	m	79.53
total girth 1200 - 1800mm	35.05	10.00	38.45	2.88	0.63	69.91	-	108.37	m	119.21
Ceilings										
generally	19.43	5.00	20.37	0.82	0.35	22.56	-	42.94	m²	47.23
Beams; isolated; 3nr faces										
total girth 600 - 1200mm	23.34	10.00	25.61	1.92	0.42	46.61	-	72.22	m	79.44
Reveals and soffits of openings and recesses										
width 300mm	5.89	10.00	6.46	0.39	0.11	9.85	-	16.31	m	17.95
Finish to Walls, isolated columns, ceilings and isolated beams; linings; two layers of Gypsum wallboard, first layer square edge sheeting 15mm thick, second layer tapered edge sheeting 15mm thick for direct decoration, BS EN 520, butt joints; fixing with galvanised nails to timber base; butt joints of second layer filled with joint filler tape and joint finish, spot filling										
Walls										
over 600mm wide	7.67	5.00	8.03	0.90	0.46	25.95	-	33.97	m²	37.37
Columns; 4nr faces										
total girth 600 - 1200mm	9.32	10.00	10.18	1.68	0.45	42.07	-	52.25	m	57.48
total girth 1200 - 1800mm	13.91	10.00	15.20	2.52	0.68	63.18	-	78.38	m	86.21
Ceilings										
generally	7.68	5.00	8.04	0.86	0.38	23.86	-	31.91	m²	35.10
Beams; isolated; 3nr faces										
total girth 600 - 1200mm	9.25	10.00	10.11	1.68	0.45	42.07	-	52.17	m	57.39
Reveals and soffits of openings and recesses										
width 300mm	2.37	10.00	2.59	0.45	0.11	11.10	-	13.69	m	15.06
Finish to Walls, isolated columns, ceilings and isolated beams; linings; two layers of Gypsum wallboard, first layer vapourcheck square edge sheeting 12.5mm thick, second layer tapered edge sheeting 12.5mm thick for direct decoration, BS EN 520, butt joints; fixing with galvanised nails to timber base; butt joints of second layer filled with joint filler tape and joint finish, spot filling										
Walls										
over 600mm wide	12.74	5.00	13.35	0.85	0.43	24.43	-	37.79	m²	41.57
Columns; 4nr faces										
total girth 600 - 1200mm	15.41	10.00	16.72	1.92	0.42	46.61	-	63.33	m	69.66
total girth 1200 - 1800mm	23.05	10.00	25.00	2.88	0.63	69.91	-	94.91	m	104.40
Ceilings										
generally	12.76	5.00	13.37	0.82	0.35	22.56	-	35.93	m²	39.53
Beams; isolated; 3nr faces										
total girth 600 - 1200mm	15.34	10.00	16.64	1.92	0.42	46.61	-	63.25	m	69.57
Reveals and soffits of openings and recesses										
width 300mm	3.89	10.00	4.22	0.39	0.11	9.85	-	14.07	m	15.48
Finish to Walls, isolated columns, ceilings and isolated beams; linings; two layers of Gypsum wallboard, first layer vapourcheck square edge sheeting 15mm thick, second layer tapered edge sheeting 15mm thick for direct decoration, BS EN 520, butt joints; fixing with galvanised nails to timber base; butt joints of second layer filled with joint filler tape and joint finish, spot filling										
Walls										
over 600mm wide	7.67	5.00	8.03	0.90	0.46	25.95	-	33.97	m²	37.37
Columns; 4nr faces										
total girth 600 - 1200mm	9.32	10.00	9.97	1.68	0.45	42.07	-	52.04	m	57.24
total girth 1200 - 1800mm	13.91	10.00	14.88	2.52	0.68	63.18	-	78.06	m	85.86
Ceilings										
generally	7.68	5.00	8.04	0.86	0.38	23.86	-	31.91	m²	35.10
Beams; isolated; 3nr faces										
total girth 600 - 1200mm	9.25	10.00	9.89	1.68	0.45	42.07	-	51.96	m	57.16
Reveals and soffits of openings and recesses										
width 300mm	2.37	10.00	2.53	0.45	0.11	11.10	-	13.64	m	15.00
Finish to Walls, isolated columns, ceilings and isolated beams; linings; tapered edge sheeting of one layer 12.5mm thick Gyproc wallboard for direct decoration, BS EN 520 butt joints; fixing with Drywall screws to and including Gypframe MF suspended ceiling system to timber joists; butt joints filled with joint filler tape and joint finish, spot filling										
Ceilings										
generally	25.12	5.00	26.38	0.60	0.26	16.57	-	42.95	m²	47.24

Labour hourly rates: (except Specialists) Craft Operatives 20.87 Labourer 15.57 Rates are national average prices. Refer to REGIONAL VARIATIONS for indicative levels of overall pricing in regions	MATERIALS			LABOUR				RATES		
	Del to Site £	Waste %	Material Cost £	Craft Optve Hrs	Lab Hrs	Labour Cost £	Sunds £	Nett Rate £	Unit	Gross rate (10%) £
IN-SITU, TILED, BLOCK, MOSAIC, SHEET, APPLIED LIQUID OR PLANTED FINISHES (Cont'd)										
Finish to Walls, isolated columns, ceilings and isolated beams; linings; tapered edge sheeting of one layer 15mm thick Gyproc wall board for direct decoration, BS EN 520, butt joints; fixing with Drywall screws to and including Gypframe MF suspended ceiling system to timber joists; butt joints filled with joint filler tape and joint finish, spot filling										
Ceilings										
generally	19.46	5.00	20.43	0.66	0.28	18.13	-	38.56	m²	42.42
Finish to Walls, isolated columns, ceilings and isolated beams; linings; tapered edge sheeting of one layer 12.5mm thick Gyproc vapourcheck wallboard for direct decoration, BS EN 520, butt joints; fixing with Drywall screws to and including Gypframe MF suspended ceiling system to timber joists; butt joints filled with joint filler tape and joint finish, spot filling										
Ceilings										
generally	18.66	5.00	19.59	0.60	0.26	16.57	-	36.16	m²	39.77
Finish to Walls, isolated columns, ceilings and isolated beams; linings; tapered edge sheeting of one layer 15mm thick Gyproc vapourcheck wallboard for direct decoration, BS EN 520, butt joints; fixing with Drywall screws to and including Gypframe MF suspended ceiling system to timber joists; butt joints filled with joint filler tape and joint finish, spot filling										
Ceilings										
generally	19.46	5.00	20.43	0.66	0.28	18.13	-	38.56	m²	42.42
Finish to Walls, isolated columns, ceilings and isolated beams; linings; tapered edge sheeting of one layer 19mm thick Gyproc plank for direct decoration, BS EN 520, butt joints; fixing with Drywall screws to and including Gypframe MF suspended ceiling system to timber joists; butt joints filled with joint filler tape and joint finish, spot filling										
Ceilings										
generally	24.80	5.00	26.03	0.74	0.31	20.27	-	46.30	m²	50.93
Finish to Walls, isolated columns, ceilings and isolated beams; linings; two layers of Gypsum wallboard, first layer square edge sheeting 12.5mm thick, second layer tapered edge sheeting 12.5mm thick for direct decoration, BS EN 520, butt joints; fixing with Drywall screws to and including Gypframe MF suspended ceiling system to timber joists; butt joints of second layer filled with joint filler tape and joint finish, spot filling										
Ceilings										
generally	35.06	5.00	36.79	0.96	0.41	26.42	-	63.21	m²	69.53
Finish to Walls, isolated columns, ceilings and isolated beams; linings; two layers of Gypsum wallboard, first layer square edge sheeting 15mm thick, second layer tapered edge sheeting 15mm thick for direct decoration, BS EN 520, butt joints; fixing with Drywall screws to and including Gypframe MF suspended ceiling system to timber joists; butt joints of second layer filled with joint filler tape and joint finish, spot filling										
Ceilings										
generally	23.32	5.00	24.46	1.00	0.44	27.72	-	52.18	m²	57.40
Finish to Walls, isolated columns, ceilings and isolated beams; linings; two layers of Gypsum wallboard, first layer vapourcheck square edge sheeting 12.5mm thick, second layer tapered edge sheeting 12.5mm thick for direct decoration, BS EN 520, butt joints; fixing with Drywall screws to and including Gypframe MF suspended ceiling system to timber joists; butt joints of second layer filled with joint filler tape and joint finish, spot filling										
Ceilings										
generally	28.39	5.00	29.79	0.96	0.41	26.42	-	56.20	m²	61.83
Finish to Walls, isolated columns, ceilings and isolated beams; linings; two layers of Gypsum wallboard, first layer vapourcheck square edge sheeting 15mm thick, second layer tapered edge sheeting 15mm thick for direct decoration, BS EN 520, butt joints; fixing with Drywall screws to and including Gypframe MF suspended ceiling system to timber joists; butt joints of second layer filled with joint filler tape and joint finish, spot filling										
Ceilings										
generally	23.32	5.00	24.46	1.00	0.44	27.72	-	52.18	m²	57.40
Finish to Walls, isolated columns, ceilings and isolated beams; extra for 50mm acoustic insulation laid over plasterboard on metal framing to include acoustic hangers and mastic seal to perimeters										
Ceilings										
generally	8.93	5.00	9.38	0.10	0.05	2.87	-	12.24	m²	13.47

Labour hourly rates: (except Specialists) Craft Operatives 20.87 Labourer 15.57 Rates are national average prices. Refer to REGIONAL VARIATIONS for indicative levels of overall pricing in regions	MATERIALS			LABOUR				RATES		
	Del to Site £	Waste %	Material Cost £	Craft Optve Hrs	Lab Hrs	Labour Cost £	Sunds £	Nett Rate £	Unit	Gross rate (10%) £
IN-SITU, TILED, BLOCK, MOSAIC, SHEET, APPLIED LIQUID OR PLANTED FINISHES (Cont'd)										
Finish to Walls, isolated columns, ceilings and isolated beams; linings; tapered edged sheeting of one layer 22mm thick Gyproc Thermaline BASIC board vapour check grade for direct decoration, butt joints; fixing with galvanised nails to timber base; butt joints filled with joint filler tape and joint finish, spot filling										
Walls over 600mm wide	7.53	5.00	7.90	0.72	0.38	20.94	-	28.84	m²	31.72
Ceilings generally	7.55	5.00	7.91	0.72	0.30	19.70	-	27.61	m²	30.37
Reveals and soffits of openings and recesses width 300mm	2.33	10.00	2.55	0.36	0.09	8.91	-	11.46	m	12.61
Finish to Walls, isolated columns, ceilings and isolated beams; linings; tapered edged sheeting of one layer 30mm thick Gyproc thermaline BASIC grade for direct decoration, butt joints; fixing with galvanised nails to timber base; butt joints filled with joint filler tape and joint finish, spot filling										
Walls over 600mm wide	10.22	5.00	10.72	0.85	0.43	24.43	-	35.15	m²	38.66
Ceilings generally	10.23	5.00	10.73	0.84	0.36	23.14	-	33.87	m²	37.25
Reveals and soffits of openings and recesses width 300mm	3.13	10.00	3.43	0.42	0.11	10.48	-	13.91	m	15.30
Finish to Walls, isolated columns, ceilings and isolated beams; linings; tapered edged sheeting of one layer 40mm thick Gyproc Thermaline BASIC grade for direct decoration, butt joints; fixing with galvanised nails to timber base; butt joints filled with joint filler tape and joint finish, spot filling										
Walls over 600mm wide	9.99	5.00	10.47	0.96	0.49	27.66	-	38.14	m²	41.95
Ceilings generally	10.00	5.00	10.49	0.96	0.42	26.57	-	37.06	m²	40.77
Reveals and soffits of openings and recesses width 300mm	3.06	10.00	3.36	0.48	0.12	11.89	-	15.24	m	16.77
Finish to Walls, isolated columns, ceilings and isolated beams; linings; tapered edged sheeting of one layer 50mm thick Gyproc Thermaline SUPER grade for direct decoration, butt joints; fixing with galvanised nails to timber base; butt joints filled with joint filler tape and joint finish, spot filling										
Walls over 600mm wide	21.76	5.00	22.84	1.10	0.56	31.68	-	54.51	m²	59.96
Ceilings generally	21.78	5.00	22.85	1.08	0.48	30.01	-	52.86	m²	58.15
Reveals and soffits of openings and recesses width 300mm	6.60	10.00	7.24	0.54	0.14	13.45	-	20.69	m	22.76
Finish to Walls, isolated columns, ceilings and isolated beams; linings; tapered edged sheeting of one layer 60mm thick Gyproc Thermaline SUPER grade for direct decoration, butt joints; fixing with galvanised nails to timber base; butt joints filled with joint filler tape and joint finish, spot filling										
Walls over 600mm wide	24.66	10.00	27.10	1.10	0.56	31.68	-	58.77	m²	64.65
Ceilings generally	24.68	10.00	27.11	1.08	0.48	30.01	-	57.12	m²	62.84
Reveals and soffits of openings and recesses width 300mm	24.47	10.00	26.90	0.54	0.14	13.45	-	40.35	m	44.39
Finish to Walls, isolated columns, ceilings and isolated beams; linings; tapered edged sheeting of one layer 70mm thick Gyproc Thermaline SUPER grade for direct decoration, butt joints; fixing with galvanised nails to timber base; butt joints filled with joint filler tape and joint finish, spot filling										
Walls over 600mm wide	27.63	10.00	30.36	1.10	0.56	31.68	-	62.03	m²	68.24
Ceilings generally	27.64	10.00	30.37	1.08	0.48	30.01	-	60.38	m²	66.42
Reveals and soffits of openings and recesses width 300mm	27.43	10.00	30.16	0.54	0.14	13.45	-	43.61	m	47.97
Finish to walls; ceramic tiles pc £15.00/m²; 2mm joints, symmetrical layout; bedding in 10mm cement mortar (1:3); pointing with neat white cement; on brickwork or blockwork base										
100 x 100mm units to walls plain, width exceeding 300mm	16.62	5.00	17.46	1.30	0.75	38.81	-	56.27	m²	61.89
plain, width 300mm	5.46	10.00	5.99	0.78	0.47	23.60	-	29.59	m	32.54
150 x 150mm units to walls plain, width exceeding 300mm	16.54	5.00	17.37	1.00	0.60	30.21	-	47.59	m²	52.34
plain, width 300mm	5.10	10.00	5.59	0.60	0.36	18.13	-	23.72	m	26.09
300 x 300mm units to walls plain, width exceeding 300mm	16.54	5.00	17.37	0.90	0.55	27.35	-	44.72	m²	49.19
plain, width 300mm	4.98	10.00	5.45	0.58	0.32	17.09	-	22.54	m	24.79
600 x 600mm units to walls plain, width exceeding 300mm	16.56	10.00	18.15	1.20	0.70	35.94	-	54.09	m²	59.50

Labour hourly rates: (except Specialists) Craft Operatives 20.87 Labourer 15.57 Rates are national average prices. Refer to REGIONAL VARIATIONS for indicative levels of overall pricing in regions	MATERIALS			LABOUR				RATES		
	Del to Site £	Waste %	Material Cost £	Craft Optve Hrs	Lab Hrs	Labour Cost £	Sunds £	Nett Rate £	Unit	Gross rate (10%) £
IN-SITU, TILED, BLOCK, MOSAIC, SHEET, APPLIED LIQUID OR PLANTED FINISHES (Cont'd)										
Finish to walls; ceramic tile cills, pc £15.00/m²; 2mm joints, symmetrical layout; bedding in 10mm cement mortar (1:3); pointing with neat white cement; on brickwork or blockwork base - cills										
100 x 100mm units to cills on brickwork or blockwork base										
width 150mm; rounded angle	5.00	5.00	5.26	0.39	0.11	9.85	-	15.11	m	16.62
width 225mm; rounded angle	6.82	5.00	7.16	0.54	0.17	13.92	-	21.08	m	23.19
width 300mm; rounded angle	7.95	5.00	8.35	0.69	0.23	17.98	-	26.33	m	28.97
150 x 150mm units to cills on brickwork or blockwork base										
width 150mm; rounded angle	5.63	5.00	5.91	0.33	0.09	8.29	-	14.20	m	15.62
width 225mm; rounded angle	6.93	5.00	7.27	0.44	0.14	11.36	-	18.64	m	20.50
width 300mm; rounded angle	8.36	5.00	8.79	0.55	0.18	14.28	-	23.07	m	25.37
Finish to walls; ceramic tiles pc £15.00/m²; 2mm joints; symmetrical layout; fixing with thin bed adhesive; pointing with neat white cement; on plaster base										
100 x 100mm units to walls										
plain, width exceeding 300mm	17.39	5.00	18.38	1.30	0.75	38.81	-	57.19	m²	62.91
plain, width 300mm	6.03	10.00	6.63	0.78	0.47	23.60	-	30.23	m	33.25
150 x 150mm units to walls										
plain, width exceeding 300mm	17.31	5.00	18.30	1.00	0.60	30.21	-	48.51	m²	53.36
plain, width 300mm	5.66	10.00	6.23	0.60	0.36	18.13	-	24.36	m	26.79
300 x 300mm units to walls										
plain, width exceeding 300mm	17.31	5.00	18.30	0.90	0.55	27.35	-	45.64	m²	50.21
plain, width 300mm	5.54	10.00	6.09	0.58	0.32	17.09	-	23.18	m	25.50
600 x 600mm units to walls										
plain, width exceeding 300mm	17.33	10.00	19.07	1.20	0.70	35.94	-	55.01	m²	60.51
Finish to walls; ceramic tiles pc £15.00/m²; 2mm joints, symmetrical layout; fixing with thick bed adhesive; pointing with neat white cement; on cement and sand base										
100 x 100mm units to walls										
plain, width exceeding 300mm	18.50	5.00	19.60	1.30	0.75	38.81	-	58.41	m²	64.25
plain, width 300mm	6.52	10.00	7.17	0.78	0.47	23.60	-	30.77	m	33.85
150 x 150mm units to walls										
plain, width exceeding 300mm	18.42	5.00	19.51	1.00	0.60	30.21	-	49.72	m²	54.70
plain, width 300mm	6.16	10.00	6.77	0.60	0.36	18.13	-	24.90	m	27.39
300 x 300mm units to walls										
plain, width exceeding 300mm	18.42	5.00	19.51	0.90	0.55	27.35	-	46.86	m²	51.54
plain, width 300mm	6.03	10.00	6.64	0.58	0.32	17.09	-	23.72	m	26.10
600 x 600mm units to walls										
plain, width exceeding 300mm	18.44	10.00	20.28	1.20	0.70	35.94	-	56.23	m²	61.85
Finish to walls; ceramic tiles pc £25.00/m²; 2mm joints, symmetrical layout; bedding in 10mm cement mortar (1:3); pointing with neat white cement; on brickwork or blockwork base										
100 x 100mm units to walls										
plain, width exceeding 300mm	26.62	5.00	27.96	1.30	0.75	38.81	-	66.77	m²	73.44
plain, width 300mm	8.76	10.00	9.62	0.78	0.47	23.60	-	33.22	m	36.54
150 x 150mm units to walls										
plain, width exceeding 300mm	26.54	5.00	27.87	1.00	0.60	30.21	-	58.09	m²	63.89
plain, width 300mm	8.18	10.00	8.98	0.60	0.36	18.13	-	27.10	m	29.81
300 x 300mm units to walls										
plain, width exceeding 300mm	26.54	5.00	27.87	0.90	0.55	27.35	-	55.22	m²	60.74
plain, width 300mm	7.98	10.00	8.75	0.58	0.32	17.09	-	25.84	m	28.42
600 x 600mm units to walls										
plain, width exceeding 300mm	26.56	10.00	29.15	1.20	0.70	35.94	-	65.09	m²	71.60
Finish to walls; ceramic tiles pc £25.00/m²; 2mm joints; symmetrical layout; fixing with thin bed adhesive; pointing with neat white cement; on plaster base										
100 x 100mm units to walls										
plain, width exceeding 300mm	27.39	5.00	28.88	1.30	0.75	38.81	-	67.69	m²	74.46
plain, width 300mm	9.33	10.00	10.26	0.78	0.47	23.60	-	33.86	m	37.24
150 x 150mm units to walls										
plain, width exceeding 300mm	27.31	5.00	28.80	1.00	0.60	30.21	-	59.01	m²	64.91
plain, width 300mm	8.74	10.00	9.62	0.60	0.36	18.13	-	27.74	m	30.52
300 x 300mm units to walls										
plain, width exceeding 300mm	27.31	5.00	28.80	0.90	0.55	27.35	-	56.14	m²	61.76
plain, width 300mm	8.54	10.00	9.39	0.58	0.32	17.09	-	26.48	m	29.13
600 x 600mm units to walls										
plain, width exceeding 300mm	27.33	10.00	30.07	1.20	0.70	35.94	-	66.01	m²	72.61
Finish to walls; ceramic tiles pc £25.00/m²; 2mm joints, symmetrical layout; fixing with thick bed adhesive; pointing with neat white cement; on cement and sand base										
100 x 100mm units to walls										
plain, width exceeding 300mm	28.50	5.00	30.10	1.30	0.75	38.81	-	68.91	m²	75.80

Labour hourly rates: (except Specialists) Craft Operatives 20.87 Labourer 15.57 Rates are national average prices. Refer to REGIONAL VARIATIONS for indicative levels of overall pricing in regions	MATERIALS			LABOUR				RATES		
	Del to Site £	Waste %	Material Cost £	Craft Optve Hrs	Lab Hrs	Labour Cost £	Sunds £	Nett Rate £	Unit	Gross rate (10%) £
IN-SITU, TILED, BLOCK, MOSAIC, SHEET, APPLIED LIQUID OR PLANTED FINISHES (Cont'd)										
Finish to walls; ceramic tiles pc £25.00/m²; 2mm joints, symmetrical layout; fixing with thick bed adhesive; pointing with neat white cement; on cement and sand base (Cont'd)										
100 x 100mm units to walls (Cont'd)										
plain, width 300mm	9.82	10.00	10.80	0.78	0.47	23.60	-	34.40	m	37.84
150 x 150mm units to walls										
plain, width exceeding 300mm	28.42	5.00	30.01	1.00	0.60	30.21	-	60.22	m²	66.25
plain, width 300mm	9.24	10.00	10.16	0.60	0.36	18.13	-	28.29	m	31.12
300 x 300mm units to walls										
plain, width exceeding 300mm	28.42	5.00	30.01	0.90	0.55	27.35	-	57.36	m²	63.09
plain, width 300mm	9.03	10.00	9.94	0.58	0.32	17.09	-	27.02	m	29.73
600 x 600mm units to walls										
plain, width exceeding 300mm	28.44	10.00	31.28	1.20	0.70	35.94	-	67.23	m²	73.95
Finish to walls; ceramic tiles pc £35.00/m²; 2mm joints, symmetrical layout; bedding in 10mm cement mortar (1:3); pointing with neat white cement; on brickwork or blockwork base										
100 x 100mm units to walls										
plain, width exceeding 300mm	36.62	5.00	38.46	1.30	0.75	38.81	-	77.27	m²	84.99
plain, width 300mm	12.06	10.00	13.25	0.78	0.47	23.60	-	36.85	m	40.53
150 x 150mm units to walls										
plain, width exceeding 300mm	36.54	5.00	38.37	1.00	0.60	30.21	-	68.59	m²	75.44
plain, width 300mm	11.26	10.00	12.37	0.60	0.36	18.13	-	30.49	m	33.54
300 x 300mm units to walls										
plain, width exceeding 300mm	26.54	5.00	27.87	0.90	0.55	27.35	-	55.22	m²	60.74
plain, width 300mm	10.98	10.00	12.05	0.58	0.32	17.09	-	29.14	m	32.05
600 x 600mm units to walls										
plain, width exceeding 300mm	36.56	10.00	40.15	1.20	0.70	35.94	-	76.09	m²	83.70
Finish to walls; ceramic tiles pc £35.00/m²; 2mm joints; symmetrical layout; fixing with thin bed adhesive; pointing with neat white cement; on plaster base										
100 x 100mm units to walls										
plain, width exceeding 300mm	37.39	5.00	39.38	1.30	0.75	38.81	-	78.19	m²	86.01
plain, width 300mm	12.63	10.00	13.89	0.78	0.47	23.60	-	37.49	m	41.23
150 x 150mm units to walls										
plain, width exceeding 300mm	37.31	5.00	39.30	1.00	0.60	30.21	-	69.51	m²	76.46
plain, width 300mm	11.82	10.00	13.01	0.60	0.36	18.13	-	31.13	m	34.25
300 x 300mm units to walls										
plain, width exceeding 300mm	37.31	5.00	39.30	0.90	0.55	27.35	-	66.64	m²	73.31
plain, width 300mm	11.54	10.00	12.69	0.58	0.32	17.09	-	29.78	m	32.76
600 x 600mm units to walls										
plain, width exceeding 300mm	37.33	10.00	41.07	1.20	0.70	35.94	-	77.01	m²	84.71
Finish to walls; ceramic tiles pc £35.00/m²; 2mm joints, symmetrical layout; fixing with thick bed adhesive; pointing with neat white cement; on cement and sand base										
100 x 100mm units to walls										
plain, width exceeding 300mm	38.50	5.00	40.60	1.30	0.75	38.81	-	79.41	m²	87.35
plain, width 300mm	13.12	10.00	14.43	0.78	0.47	23.60	-	38.03	m	41.83
150 x 150mm units to walls										
plain, width exceeding 300mm	38.42	5.00	40.51	1.00	0.60	30.21	-	70.72	m²	77.80
plain, width 300mm	12.32	10.00	13.55	0.60	0.36	18.13	-	31.68	m	34.84
300 x 300mm units to walls										
plain, width exceeding 300mm	38.42	5.00	40.51	0.90	0.55	27.35	-	67.86	m²	74.64
plain, width 300mm	12.03	10.00	13.24	0.58	0.32	17.09	-	30.32	m	33.36
600 x 600mm units to walls										
plain, width exceeding 300mm	38.44	10.00	42.28	1.20	0.70	35.94	-	78.23	m²	86.05
Finish to walls; extra over ceramic tiles, pc £15.00/m²; 2mm joints, symmetrical layout; bedding or fixing in any material to general surfaces on any base										
Special tiles										
rounded edge	5.50	5.00	5.78	-	-	-	-	5.78	m	6.35
external angle	11.00	5.00	11.55	-	-	-	-	11.55	m	12.70
internal angle to skirting	-	-	-	0.07	-	1.46	-	1.46	nr	1.61
external angle to skirting	-	-	-	0.07	-	1.46	-	1.46	nr	1.61
internal angle	-	-	-	0.10	-	2.09	-	2.09	m	2.30
Finish to walls; extra over ceramic tiles, pc £25.00/m²; 2mm joints, symmetrical layout; bedding or fixing in any material to general surfaces on any base										
Special tiles										
rounded edge	7.70	5.00	8.09	-	-	-	-	8.09	m	8.89
external angle	15.40	5.00	16.17	-	-	-	-	16.17	m	17.79
internal angle to skirting	-	-	-	0.07	-	1.46	-	1.46	nr	1.61
external angle to skirting	-	-	-	0.07	-	1.46	-	1.46	nr	1.61
internal angle	-	-	-	0.10	-	2.09	-	2.09	m	2.30

Labour hourly rates: (except Specialists) Craft Operatives 20.87 Labourer 15.57 Rates are national average prices. Refer to REGIONAL VARIATIONS for indicative levels of overall pricing in regions	MATERIALS			LABOUR				RATES		
	Del to Site £	Waste %	Material Cost £	Craft Optve Hrs	Lab Hrs	Labour Cost £	Sunds £	Nett Rate £	Unit	Gross rate (10%) £
IN-SITU, TILED, BLOCK, MOSAIC, SHEET, APPLIED LIQUID OR PLANTED FINISHES (Cont'd)										
Finish to walls; extra over ceramic tiles, pc £35.00/m²; 2mm joints, symmetrical layout; bedding or fixing in any material to general surfaces on any base										
Special tiles										
rounded edge	9.90	5.00	10.39	-	-	-	-	10.39	m	11.43
external angle	19.80	5.00	20.79	-	-	-	-	20.79	m	22.87
internal angle to skirting	-	-	-	0.07	-	1.46	-	1.46	nr	1.61
external angle to skirting	-	-	-	0.07	-	1.46	-	1.46	nr	1.61
internal angle	-	-	-	0.10	-	2.09	-	2.09	m	2.30
Finish to walls; clay quarry tile cills, BS EN ISO 10545, terracotta; 3mm joints, symmetrical layout; bedding in 10mm cement mortar (1:3); pointing in cement mortar (1:3); on cement and sand base - cills										
152 x 152 x 12.5mm units to cills on brickwork or blockwork base										
width 152mm; rounded angle	12.68	10.00	13.92	0.30	0.08	7.51	-	21.43	m	23.57
width 225mm; rounded angle	14.92	5.00	16.28	0.40	0.12	10.22	-	26.49	m	29.14
width 300mm; rounded angle	17.16	5.00	18.63	0.51	0.17	13.29	-	31.92	m	35.11
Coves; plasterboard										
Gyproc cove; fixing with adhesive										
100mm girth										
straight lengths	1.59	10.00	1.75	0.18	0.09	5.16	-	6.90	m	7.60
extra; ends	-	-	-	0.06	-	1.25	-	1.25	nr	1.38
extra; internal angles	-	-	-	0.30	-	6.26	-	6.26	nr	6.89
extra; external angles	-	-	-	0.30	-	6.26	-	6.26	nr	6.89
127mm girth										
straight lengths	1.82	10.00	2.00	0.18	0.09	5.16	-	7.16	m	7.88
extra; ends	-	-	-	0.06	-	1.25	-	1.25	nr	1.38
extra; internal angles	-	-	-	0.30	-	6.26	-	6.26	nr	6.89
extra; external angles	-	-	-	0.30	-	6.26	-	6.26	nr	6.89
Gyproc cove; fixing with nails to timber										
90mm girth										
straight lengths	1.42	10.00	1.56	0.12	0.06	3.44	0.10	5.10	m	5.61
extra; ends	-	-	-	0.06	-	1.25	-	1.25	nr	1.38
extra; internal angles	-	-	-	0.30	-	6.26	-	6.26	nr	6.89
extra; external angles	-	-	-	0.30	-	6.26	-	6.26	nr	6.89
127mm girth										
straight lengths	1.65	10.00	1.82	0.12	0.06	3.44	0.10	5.35	m	5.89
extra; ends	-	-	-	0.06	-	1.25	-	1.25	nr	1.38
extra; internal angles	-	-	-	0.30	-	6.26	-	6.26	nr	6.89
extra; external angles	-	-	-	0.30	-	6.26	-	6.26	nr	6.89
Finish to walls; movement joints										
6mm x 6mm silicon sealant gun applied	0.38	5.00	0.40	0.15	0.08	4.38	-	4.77	m	5.25
Beads and stops; for plaster and renders										
galvanised steel angle beads										
fixing to brickwork or blockwork with masonry nails										
Standard	0.41	10.00	0.45	0.10	-	2.09	-	2.54	m	2.79
3mm for Thin Coat	0.43	10.00	0.48	0.10	-	2.09	-	2.56	m	2.82
6mm for Thin Coat	0.43	10.00	0.48	0.10	-	2.09	-	2.56	m	2.82
galvanised steel stop beads										
fixing to brickwork or blockwork with masonry nails										
3mm for Thin Coat	0.66	10.00	0.72	0.10	-	2.09	-	2.81	m	3.09
6mm for Thin Coat	0.72	10.00	0.79	0.10	-	2.09	-	2.88	m	3.17
10mm	0.65	10.00	0.71	0.10	-	2.09	-	2.80	m	3.08
13mm	0.65	10.00	0.71	0.10	-	2.09	-	2.80	m	3.08
16mm	0.77	10.00	0.85	0.10	-	2.09	-	2.94	m	3.23
19mm	0.77	10.00	0.85	0.10	-	2.09	-	2.94	m	3.23
galvanised steel plasterboard edging beads										
fixing to timber with galvanised nails, 30mm long at 400mm centres										
10mm	12.69	10.00	12.77	0.10	-	2.09	-	14.86	m	16.34
13mm	12.69	10.00	12.77	0.10	-	2.09	-	14.86	m	16.34
Beads and stops; external; for plaster and renders										
Stainless steel stop beads										
fixing to brickwork or blockwork with masonry nails										
16-20mm	2.31	10.00	2.54	0.10	-	2.09	-	4.63	m	5.09
Stainless steel angle beads										
fixing to brickwork or blockwork with masonry nails										
16-20mm	3.01	10.00	3.31	0.10	-	2.09	-	5.39	m	5.93
Nosings										
Heavy duty aluminium alloy stair nosings with anti-slip inserts; 46mm wide with single line insert; fixing to timber with screws										
11.5mm drop	8.16	5.00	8.57	0.40	-	8.35	0.09	17.01	m	18.71
22mm drop	9.49	5.00	9.97	0.40	-	8.35	0.09	18.40	m	20.24
25mm drop	12.49	5.00	13.11	0.40	-	8.35	0.09	21.55	m	23.70
32mm drop	11.55	5.00	12.13	0.40	-	8.35	0.09	20.57	m	22.62
38mm drop	12.60	5.00	13.24	0.40	-	8.35	0.09	21.67	m	23.84
46mm drop	15.65	5.00	16.43	0.40	-	8.35	0.09	24.87	m	27.35

Labour hourly rates: (except Specialists) Craft Operatives 20.87 Labourer 15.57 Rates are national average prices. Refer to REGIONAL VARIATIONS for indicative levels of overall pricing in regions	MATERIALS			LABOUR				RATES		
	Del to Site £	Waste %	Material Cost £	Craft Optve Hrs	Lab Hrs	Labour Cost £	Sunds £	Nett Rate £	Unit	Gross rate (10%) £
IN-SITU, TILED, BLOCK, MOSAIC, SHEET, APPLIED LIQUID OR PLANTED FINISHES (Cont'd)										
Nosings (Cont'd)										
Heavy duty aluminium alloy stair nosings with anti-slip inserts; 80mm wide with two line inserts; fixing to timber with screws										
22mm drop	15.52	5.00	16.30	0.55	-	11.48	0.13	27.91	m	30.70
25mm drop	16.54	5.00	17.37	0.55	-	11.48	0.13	28.98	m	31.87
32mm drop	18.24	5.00	19.15	0.55	-	11.48	0.13	30.76	m	33.84
51mm drop	19.03	5.00	19.99	0.55	-	11.48	0.13	31.60	m	34.75
63mm drop	20.75	5.00	21.78	0.55	-	11.48	0.13	33.39	m	36.73
Heavy duty aluminium alloy stair nosings with anti-slip inserts; 46mm wide with single line insert; fixing to masonry with screws										
11.5mm drop	8.16	5.00	8.57	0.65	-	13.57	0.13	22.27	m	24.49
22mm drop	9.49	5.00	9.97	0.65	-	13.57	0.13	23.66	m	26.03
25mm drop	12.49	5.00	13.11	0.65	-	13.57	0.13	26.81	m	29.49
32mm drop	11.55	5.00	12.13	0.65	-	13.57	0.13	25.83	m	28.41
38mm drop	12.60	5.00	13.24	0.65	-	13.57	0.13	26.93	m	29.63
46mm drop	15.65	5.00	16.43	0.65	-	13.57	0.13	30.13	m	33.14
Heavy duty aluminium alloy stair nosings with anti-slip inserts; 80mm wide with two line inserts; fixing to masonry with screws										
22mm drop	15.52	5.00	16.30	0.80	-	16.70	0.20	33.19	m	36.51
25mm drop	16.54	5.00	17.37	0.80	-	16.70	0.20	34.26	m	37.69
32mm drop	18.24	5.00	19.15	0.80	-	16.70	0.20	36.04	m	39.65
51mm drop	19.03	5.00	19.99	0.80	-	16.70	0.20	36.88	m	40.57
63mm drop	20.75	5.00	21.78	0.80	-	16.70	0.20	38.68	m	42.54
Aluminium stair nosings with anti-slip inserts; 46mm wide with single line insert; fixing to timber with screws										
22mm drop	7.07	5.00	7.42	0.40	-	8.35	0.09	15.86	m	17.44
33mm drop	10.66	5.00	11.20	0.40	-	8.35	0.09	19.63	m	21.59
Aluminium stair nosings with anti-slip inserts; 66mm wide with single line insert; fixing to timber with screws										
22mm drop	11.49	5.00	12.06	0.45	-	9.39	0.13	21.58	m	23.74
25mm drop	10.75	5.00	11.28	0.45	-	9.39	0.13	20.81	m	22.89
32mm drop	13.98	5.00	14.68	0.45	-	9.39	0.13	24.20	m	26.62
Aluminium stair nosings with anti-slip inserts; 80mm wide with two line inserts; fixing to timber with screws										
22mm drop	13.18	5.00	13.84	0.55	-	11.48	0.13	25.45	m	28.00
28mm drop	14.89	5.00	15.63	0.55	-	11.48	0.13	27.24	m	29.97
51mm drop	18.87	5.00	19.81	0.55	-	11.48	0.13	31.42	m	34.56
Aluminium alloy stair nosings with anti-slip inserts; 46mm wide with single line insert; fixing to masonry with screws										
22mm drop	7.07	5.00	7.42	0.65	-	13.57	0.13	21.12	m	23.23
32mm drop	10.66	5.00	11.20	0.65	-	13.57	0.13	24.89	m	27.38
Aluminium alloy stair nosings with anti-slip inserts; 66mm wide with single line insert; fixing to masonry with screws										
22mm drop	11.49	5.00	12.06	0.70	-	14.61	0.20	26.87	m	29.55
25mm drop	10.75	5.00	11.28	0.70	-	14.61	0.20	26.09	m	28.70
32mm drop	13.98	5.00	14.68	0.70	-	14.61	0.20	29.48	m	32.43
Aluminium alloy stair nosings with anti-slip inserts; 80mm wide with two line inserts; fixing to masonry with screws										
22mm drop	13.18	5.00	13.84	0.80	-	16.70	0.20	30.73	m	33.81
28mm drop	14.89	5.00	15.63	0.80	-	16.70	0.20	32.52	m	35.78
51mm drop	18.87	5.00	19.81	0.80	-	16.70	0.20	36.71	m	40.38
Aluminium alloy carpet nosings with anti-slip inserts; with single line insert; fixing to timber with screws										
65mm wide x 24mm drop	18.69	5.00	19.63	0.45	-	9.39	0.13	29.15	m	32.06
116mm wide overall with carpet gripper x 42mm drop	26.70	5.00	28.04	0.50	-	10.44	0.20	38.67	m	42.53
Aluminium alloy carpet nosings with anti-slip inserts; with two line inserts; fixing to timber with screws										
80mm wide x 31mm drop	21.36	5.00	22.43	0.55	-	11.48	0.13	34.04	m	37.45
Aluminium alloy carpet nosings with anti-slip inserts; with single line insert; fixing to masonry with screws										
65mm wide x 24mm drop	18.69	5.00	19.63	0.70	-	14.61	0.20	34.43	m	37.88
116mm wide overall with carpet gripper x 42mm drop	26.70	5.00	28.04	0.75	-	15.65	0.26	43.95	m	48.35
Aluminium alloy carpet nosings with anti-slip inserts; with two line inserts; fixing to masonry with screws										
80mm wide x 31mm drop	21.36	5.00	22.43	0.80	-	16.70	0.20	39.33	m	43.26
Metal mesh lathing; anti-crack strips										
Lathing; BB galvanised expanded metal lath, 9mm mesh X 0.500mm thick x 0.89kg/m²; butt joints fixing with nails										
100mm wide to walls; one edge to timber; one edge to brickwork or blockwork	0.65	5.00	0.68	0.10	-	2.09	0.08	2.85	m	3.14
100mm wide to walls; one edge to timber; one edge to concrete	0.65	5.00	0.68	0.12	-	2.50	0.10	3.28	m	3.61
100mm wide to walls; one edge to brickwork or blockwork; one edge to concrete	0.65	5.00	0.68	0.14	-	2.92	0.11	3.72	m	4.09
Lathing; BB galvanised expanded metal lath, 9mm mesh x 0.725mm thick x 1.11 kg/m²; butt joints; fixing with nails										
100mm wide to walls; one edge to timber; one edge to brickwork or blockwork	0.89	5.00	0.93	0.10	-	2.09	0.08	3.10	m	3.41
100mm wide to walls; one edge to timber; one edge to concrete	0.89	5.00	0.93	0.12	-	2.50	0.10	3.54	m	3.89
100mm wide to walls; one edge to brickwork or blockwork; one edge to concrete	0.89	5.00	0.93	0.14	-	2.92	0.11	3.97	m	4.37

Labour hourly rates: (except Specialists) Craft Operatives 20.87 Labourer 15.57 Rates are national average prices. Refer to REGIONAL VARIATIONS for indicative levels of overall pricing in regions	MATERIALS			LABOUR				RATES		
	Del to Site £	Waste %	Material Cost £	Craft Optve Hrs	Lab Hrs	Labour Cost £	Sunds £	Nett Rate £	Unit	Gross rate (10%) £
IN-SITU, TILED, BLOCK, MOSAIC, SHEET, APPLIED LIQUID OR PLANTED FINISHES (Cont'd)										
Metal mesh lathing; BB galvanised expanded metal lath, 9mm mesh x 0.500mm thick x 0.89 kg/m²; butt joints; fixing with galvanised staples for plastered coatings										
Work to walls										
width exceeding 600mm	6.49	5.00	6.82	0.15	0.08	4.38	0.12	11.32	m²	12.45
width 300mm	2.27	10.00	2.50	0.09	0.02	2.19	0.07	4.76	m	5.24
Work to isolated columns										
width exceeding 600mm	6.49	5.00	6.82	0.23	0.08	6.05	0.19	13.05	m²	14.36
width 300mm	2.27	10.00	2.50	0.14	0.02	3.23	0.11	5.85	m	6.43
Work to ceilings										
width exceeding 600mm	6.49	5.00	6.82	0.18	0.08	5.00	0.15	11.97	m²	13.16
width 300mm	2.27	10.00	2.50	0.11	0.02	2.61	0.09	5.20	m	5.72
Work to isolated beams										
width exceeding 600mm	6.49	5.00	6.82	0.23	0.08	6.05	0.19	13.05	m²	14.36
width 300mm	2.27	10.00	2.50	0.14	0.02	3.23	0.11	5.85	m	6.43
Metal mesh lathing; BB galvanised expanded metal lath 9mm mesh x 0.725mm thick x 1.11 kg/m²; butt joints; fixing with galvanised staples for plastered coatings										
Work to walls										
width exceeding 600mm	8.90	5.00	9.34	0.15	0.08	4.38	0.11	13.83	m²	15.22
width 300mm	3.11	10.00	3.43	0.09	0.02	2.19	0.11	5.73	m	6.30
Work to isolated columns										
width exceeding 600mm	8.90	5.00	9.34	0.23	0.08	6.05	0.11	15.50	m²	17.05
width 300mm	3.11	10.00	3.43	0.14	0.02	3.23	0.11	6.77	m	7.45
Work to ceilings										
width exceeding 600mm	8.90	5.00	9.34	0.18	0.08	5.00	0.11	14.46	m²	15.90
width 300mm	3.11	10.00	3.43	0.11	0.02	2.61	0.11	6.15	m	6.76
Work to isolated beams										
width exceeding 600mm	8.90	5.00	9.34	0.23	0.08	6.05	0.11	15.50	m²	17.05
width 300mm	3.11	10.00	3.43	0.14	0.02	3.23	0.11	6.77	m	7.45
Metal mesh lathing; galvanised expanded metal lath 9mm mesh x 1.61 kg/m²; butt joints; fixing with galvanised staples										
Work to walls										
width exceeding 600mm	12.91	5.00	13.55	0.15	0.08	4.38	0.11	18.04	m²	19.85
width 300mm	4.52	10.00	4.97	0.09	0.02	2.19	0.11	7.27	m	8.00
Work to isolated columns										
width exceeding 600mm	12.91	5.00	13.55	0.23	0.08	6.05	0.11	19.71	m²	21.69
width 300mm	4.52	10.00	4.97	0.14	0.02	3.23	0.11	8.32	m	9.15
Work to ceilings										
width exceeding 600mm	12.91	5.00	13.55	0.18	0.08	5.00	0.11	18.67	m²	20.54
width 300mm	4.52	10.00	4.97	0.11	0.02	2.61	0.11	7.69	m	8.46
Work to isolated beams										
width exceeding 600mm	12.91	5.00	13.55	0.23	0.08	6.05	0.11	19.71	m²	21.69
width 300mm	4.52	10.00	4.97	0.14	0.02	3.23	0.11	8.32	m	9.15
Metal mesh lathing; Expamet galvanised Rib-Lath, 0.300mm thick x 1.16 kg/m²; butt joints; fixing with galvanised staples										
Work to walls										
width exceeding 600mm	9.78	5.00	10.27	0.15	0.08	4.38	0.11	14.76	m²	16.23
width 300mm	3.39	10.00	3.73	0.09	0.02	2.19	0.11	6.04	m	6.64
Work to isolated columns										
width exceeding 600mm	9.78	5.00	10.27	0.23	0.08	6.05	0.11	16.43	m²	18.07
width 300mm	3.39	10.00	3.73	0.14	0.02	3.23	0.11	7.08	m	7.79
Work to ceilings										
width exceeding 600mm	9.78	5.00	10.27	0.18	0.08	5.00	0.11	15.38	m²	16.92
width 300mm	3.39	10.00	3.73	0.11	0.02	2.61	0.11	6.46	m	7.10
Work to isolated beams										
width exceeding 600mm	9.78	5.00	10.27	0.23	0.08	6.05	0.11	16.43	m²	18.07
width 300mm	3.39	10.00	3.73	0.14	0.02	3.23	0.11	7.08	m	7.79
Metal mesh lathing; Expamet galvanised Rib-Lath, 0.500mm thick x 1.86 kg/m²; butt joints; fixing with galvanised staples										
Work to walls										
width exceeding 600mm	12.34	5.00	12.95	0.15	0.08	4.38	0.11	17.44	m²	19.19
width 300mm	4.32	10.00	4.75	0.09	0.02	2.19	0.11	7.05	m	7.76
Work to isolated columns										
width exceeding 600mm	12.34	5.00	12.95	0.23	0.08	6.05	0.11	19.11	m²	21.02
width 300mm	4.32	10.00	4.75	0.14	0.02	3.23	0.11	8.10	m	8.91
Work to ceilings										
width exceeding 600mm	12.34	5.00	12.95	0.18	0.08	5.00	0.11	18.07	m²	19.88
width 300mm	4.32	10.00	4.75	0.11	0.02	2.61	0.11	7.47	m	8.22
Work to isolated beams										
width exceeding 600mm	12.34	5.00	12.95	0.23	0.08	6.05	0.11	19.11	m²	21.02
width 300mm	4.32	10.00	4.75	0.14	0.02	3.23	0.11	8.10	m	8.91

Labour hourly rates: (except Specialists) Craft Operatives 20.87 Labourer 15.57 Rates are national average prices. Refer to REGIONAL VARIATIONS for indicative levels of overall pricing in regions	MATERIALS			LABOUR				RATES		
	Del to Site £	Waste %	Material Cost £	Craft Optve Hrs	Lab Hrs	Labour Cost £	Sunds £	Nett Rate £	Unit	Gross rate (10%) £
IN-SITU, TILED, BLOCK, MOSAIC, SHEET, APPLIED LIQUID OR PLANTED FINISHES (Cont'd)										
Metal mesh lathing; Expamet stainless steel Rib-Lath, 1.48 kg/m²; butt joints; fixing with stainless steel staples										
Work to walls										
width exceeding 600mm	15.65	5.00	16.44	0.15	0.08	4.38	0.11	20.93	m²	23.02
width 300mm	5.48	10.00	6.03	0.09	0.02	2.19	0.11	8.33	m	9.16
Work to isolated columns										
width exceeding 600mm	15.65	5.00	16.44	0.23	0.08	6.05	0.11	22.60	m²	24.86
width 300mm	5.48	10.00	6.03	0.14	0.02	3.23	0.11	9.37	m	10.31
Work to ceilings										
width exceeding 600mm	15.65	5.00	16.44	0.18	0.08	5.00	0.11	21.55	m²	23.71
width 300mm	5.48	10.00	6.03	0.11	0.02	2.61	0.11	8.75	m	9.62
Work to isolated beams										
width exceeding 600mm	15.65	5.00	16.44	0.23	0.08	6.05	0.11	22.60	m²	24.86
width 300mm	5.48	10.00	6.03	0.14	0.02	3.23	0.11	9.37	m	10.31
Metal mesh lathing; stainless steel expanded metal lath 1.11kg/m² for render; butt joints; fixing with galvanised staples										
Work to walls										
width exceeding 600mm	13.42	5.00	14.09	0.15	0.08	4.38	0.11	18.58	m²	20.44
width 300mm	4.70	10.00	5.17	0.09	0.02	2.19	0.11	7.47	m	8.22
Work to isolated columns										
width exceeding 600mm	13.42	5.00	14.09	0.23	0.08	6.05	0.11	20.25	m²	22.27
width 300mm	4.70	10.00	5.17	0.14	0.02	3.23	0.11	8.51	m	9.36
Work to ceilings										
width exceeding 600mm	13.42	5.00	14.09	0.18	0.08	5.00	0.11	19.20	m²	21.13
width 300mm	4.70	10.00	5.17	0.11	0.02	2.61	0.11	7.89	m	8.68
Work to isolated beams										
width exceeding 600mm	13.42	5.00	14.09	0.23	0.08	6.05	0.11	20.25	m²	22.27
width 300mm	4.70	10.00	5.17	0.14	0.02	3.23	0.11	8.51	m	9.36
Metal mesh lathing; galvanised Red-rib lath, 0.500mm thick x 1.91kg/m², butt joints; fixing with galvanised staples										
Work to walls										
width exceeding 600mm	49.61	5.00	52.09	0.15	0.08	4.38	0.11	56.58	m²	62.24
width 300mm	17.36	10.00	19.10	0.09	0.02	2.19	0.11	21.40	m	23.55
Work to isolated columns										
width exceeding 600mm	49.61	5.00	52.09	0.23	0.08	6.05	0.11	58.25	m²	64.08
width 300mm	17.36	10.00	19.10	0.14	0.02	3.23	0.11	22.45	m	24.69
Work to ceilings										
width exceeding 600mm	49.61	5.00	52.09	0.18	0.08	5.00	0.11	57.21	m²	62.93
width 300mm	17.36	10.00	19.10	0.11	0.02	2.61	0.11	21.82	m	24.00
Work to isolated beams										
width exceeding 600mm	49.61	5.00	52.09	0.23	0.08	6.05	0.11	58.25	m²	64.08
width 300mm	17.36	10.00	19.10	0.14	0.02	3.23	0.11	22.45	m	24.69
Metal mesh lathing; extra cost of fixing lathing to brickwork, blockwork or concrete with cartridge fired nails in lieu of to timber with staples										
Work to walls										
width exceeding 600mm	-	-	-	0.10	-	2.09	0.25	2.33	m²	2.57
width 300mm	-	-	-	0.06	-	1.25	0.15	1.40	m	1.54
Metal mesh lathing; extra cost of fixing lathing to steel with tying wire in lieu of to timber with staples										
Work to walls										
width exceeding 600mm	-	-	-	0.15	-	3.13	0.37	3.50	m²	3.85
width 300mm	-	-	-	0.09	-	1.88	0.22	2.10	m	2.31
Work to ceilings										
width exceeding 600mm	-	-	-	0.15	-	3.13	0.37	3.50	m²	3.85
width 300mm	-	-	-	0.09	-	1.88	0.22	2.10	m	2.31
Work to isolated beams										
width exceeding 600mm	-	-	-	0.15	-	3.13	0.37	3.50	m²	3.85
width 300mm	-	-	-	0.09	-	1.88	0.22	2.10	m	2.31
Work to isolated columns										
width exceeding 600mm	-	-	-	0.15	-	3.13	0.37	3.50	m²	3.85
width 300mm	-	-	-	0.09	-	1.88	0.22	2.10	m	2.31
Metal mesh lathing; Expamet galvanised arch formers and fix to brickwork or blockwork with galvanised nails, 30mm long at 400mm centres										
Arch corners										
372mm radius	12.31	5.00	12.92	0.33	0.17	9.53	2.26	24.72	nr	27.19
452mm radius	13.43	5.00	14.10	0.33	0.17	9.53	2.76	26.40	nr	29.04
602mm radius	16.22	5.00	17.03	0.33	0.17	9.53	3.44	30.01	nr	33.01
752mm radius	21.91	5.00	23.01	0.33	0.17	9.53	4.53	37.07	nr	40.77
Semi-circular arches										
372mm radius	33.50	5.00	35.17	0.67	0.34	19.28	4.51	58.96	nr	64.86
397mm radius	35.06	5.00	36.81	0.67	0.34	19.28	4.63	60.72	nr	66.79

Labour hourly rates: (except Specialists) Craft Operatives 20.87 Labourer 15.57 Rates are national average prices. Refer to REGIONAL VARIATIONS for indicative levels of overall pricing in regions	MATERIALS			LABOUR				RATES		
	Del to Site £	Waste %	Material Cost £	Craft Optve Hrs	Lab Hrs	Labour Cost £	Sunds £	Nett Rate £	Unit	Gross rate (10%) £
IN-SITU, TILED, BLOCK, MOSAIC, SHEET, APPLIED LIQUID OR PLANTED FINISHES (Cont'd)										
Metal mesh lathing; Expamet galvanised arch formers and fix to brickwork or blockwork with galvanised nails, 30mm long at 400mm centres (Cont'd)										
Semi-circular arches (Cont'd)										
412mm radius	35.74	5.00	37.52	0.67	0.34	19.28	4.79	61.59	nr	67.75
452mm radius	40.11	5.00	42.12	0.67	0.34	19.28	5.54	66.94	nr	73.63
602mm radius	56.66	5.00	59.49	0.67	0.34	19.28	6.98	85.75	nr	94.32
752mm radius	84.71	5.00	88.95	0.67	0.34	19.28	9.61	117.84	nr	129.62
Elliptical arches										
1220mm wide x 340mm rise	41.71	5.00	43.79	0.67	0.34	19.28	8.69	71.76	nr	78.94
1370mm wide x 360mm rise	52.30	5.00	54.91	0.67	0.34	19.28	8.86	83.05	nr	91.35
1520mm wide x 380mm rise	52.97	5.00	55.61	0.67	0.34	19.28	9.77	84.66	nr	93.12
1830mm wide x 410mm rise	58.91	5.00	61.86	1.00	0.50	28.66	10.38	100.89	nr	110.98
2130mm wide x 430mm rise	65.54	5.00	68.82	1.00	0.50	28.66	11.18	108.65	nr	119.52
2440mm wide x 440mm rise	76.49	5.00	80.32	1.00	0.50	28.66	11.40	120.37	nr	132.41
3050mm wide x 520mm rise	87.49	5.00	91.86	1.00	0.50	28.66	11.87	132.38	nr	145.62
Spandrel arches										
760mm wide x 180mm radius x 220mm rise	40.04	5.00	42.04	0.67	0.34	19.28	5.87	67.19	nr	73.91
910mm wide x 180mm radius x 240mm rise	43.14	5.00	45.30	0.67	0.34	19.28	6.22	70.79	nr	77.87
1220mm wide x 230mm radius x 290mm rise	53.92	5.00	56.62	0.67	0.34	19.28	8.00	83.90	nr	92.29
1520mm wide x 230mm radius x 330mm rise	55.01	5.00	57.76	0.67	0.34	19.28	8.90	85.93	nr	94.52
1830mm wide x 230mm radius x 360mm rise	66.85	5.00	70.19	0.67	0.34	19.28	9.00	98.46	nr	108.31
2130mm wide x 230mm radius x 370mm rise	74.80	5.00	78.54	0.67	0.34	19.28	10.66	108.48	nr	119.32
2440mm wide x 230mm radius x 390mm rise	89.10	5.00	93.55	1.33	0.67	38.19	11.32	143.06	nr	157.36
3050mm wide x 230mm radius x 440mm rise	95.31	5.00	100.07	1.33	0.67	38.19	11.95	150.21	nr	165.23
Bulls-eyes										
222mm radius	28.17	5.00	29.58	0.17	0.09	4.95	5.65	40.18	nr	44.20
Soffit strips										
155mm wide	3.99	5.00	4.19	0.09	0.05	2.66	0.57	7.42	m	8.16
Make-up pieces										
600mm long	13.67	5.00	14.35	0.17	0.09	4.95	1.37	20.67	nr	22.74
Metal mesh lathing; Expamet galvanised circular window formers and fix to brickwork or blockwork with galvanised nails, 30mm long at 400mm centres										
Circular windows										
594mm diameter	26.34	5.00	27.66	1.33	0.67	38.19	4.92	70.77	nr	77.84
Accessories; Plaster ventilators										
Fibrous plaster ventilator; fixing in plastered wall										
Plain										
229 x 79mm	1.00	5.00	1.05	0.15	-	3.13	-	4.18	nr	4.60
229 x 152mm	1.50	5.00	1.57	0.18	-	3.76	-	5.33	nr	5.86
229 x 229mm	2.06	5.00	2.16	0.20	-	4.17	-	6.33	nr	6.97
Flyproof										
229 x 79mm	0.53	5.00	0.56	0.20	-	4.17	-	4.73	nr	5.21
229 x 152mm	0.68	5.00	0.72	0.23	-	4.80	-	5.52	nr	6.07
229 x 229mm	0.93	5.00	0.98	0.25	-	5.22	-	6.20	nr	6.82

Labour hourly rates: (except Specialists) Craft Operatives 20.87 Labourer 15.57 Rates are national average prices. Refer to REGIONAL VARIATIONS for indicative levels of overall pricing in regions	MATERIALS			LABOUR				RATES		
	Del to Site £	Waste %	Material Cost £	Craft Optve Hrs	Lab Hrs	Labour Cost £	Sunds £	Nett Rate £	Unit	Gross rate (10%) £
PAINTING & CLEAR FINISHINGS; EMULSION PAINTING										
Mist coat, one full coat emulsion paint										
Concrete general surfaces										
girth exceeding 300mm	0.21	10.00	0.23	0.15	-	3.13	0.17	3.53	m²	3.88
Concrete general surfaces 3.50 - 5.00m above floor										
girth exceeding 300mm	0.21	10.00	0.23	0.17	-	3.55	0.19	3.97	m²	4.37
Plaster general surfaces										
girth exceeding 300mm	0.17	10.00	0.19	0.13	-	2.71	0.14	3.04	m²	3.35
isolated surfaces, girth not exceeding 300mm	0.51	10.00	0.56	0.07	-	1.46	0.08	2.10	m	2.31
Plaster general surfaces 3.50 - 5.00m above floor										
girth exceeding 300mm	0.17	10.00	0.19	0.15	-	3.13	0.17	3.48	m²	3.83
Plasterboard general surfaces										
girth exceeding 300mm	0.17	10.00	0.19	0.13	-	2.71	0.14	3.04	m²	3.35
Plasterboard general surfaces 3.50 - 5.00m above floor										
girth exceeding 300mm	0.17	10.00	0.19	0.15	-	3.13	0.17	3.48	m²	3.83
Brickwork general surfaces										
girth exceeding 300mm	0.21	10.00	0.23	0.17	-	3.55	0.19	3.97	m²	4.37
Paper covered general surfaces										
girth exceeding 300mm	0.17	10.00	0.19	0.14	-	2.92	0.15	3.26	m²	3.59
Paper covered general surfaces 3.50 - 5.00m above floor										
girth exceeding 300mm	0.17	10.00	0.19	0.16	-	3.34	0.18	3.70	m²	4.07
Mist coat, two full coats emulsion paint										
Concrete general surfaces										
girth exceeding 300mm	0.36	10.00	0.39	0.21	-	4.38	0.23	5.01	m²	5.51
Concrete general surfaces 3.50 - 5.00m above floor										
girth exceeding 300mm	0.36	10.00	0.39	0.24	-	5.01	0.26	5.67	m²	6.23
Plaster general surfaces										
girth exceeding 300mm	0.29	10.00	0.32	0.19	-	3.97	0.21	4.49	m²	4.94
isolated surfaces, girth not exceeding 300mm	0.09	10.00	0.09	0.10	-	2.09	0.11	2.29	m	2.52
Plaster general surfaces 3.50 - 5.00m above floor										
girth exceeding 300mm	0.29	10.00	0.32	0.22	-	4.59	0.24	5.15	m²	5.67
Plasterboard general surfaces										
girth exceeding 300mm	0.29	10.00	0.32	0.19	-	3.97	0.21	4.49	m²	4.94
Plasterboard general surfaces 3.50 - 5.00m above floor										
girth exceeding 300mm	0.29	10.00	0.32	0.22	-	4.59	0.24	5.15	m²	5.67
Brickwork general surfaces										
girth exceeding 300mm	0.36	10.00	0.39	0.24	-	5.01	0.26	5.67	m²	6.23
Paper covered general surfaces										
girth exceeding 300mm	0.29	10.00	0.32	0.20	-	4.17	0.22	4.71	m²	5.18
Paper covered general surfaces 3.50 - 5.00m above floor										
girth exceeding 300mm	0.29	10.00	0.32	0.30	-	6.26	0.33	6.91	m²	7.60
PAINTING & CLEAR FINISHINGS; CEMENT PAINTING										
One coat waterproof cement paint; external work										
Cement rendered general surfaces										
girth exceeding 300mm	0.60	10.00	0.66	0.11	-	2.30	0.12	3.08	m²	3.39
isolated surfaces, girth not exceeding 300mm	0.60	10.00	0.66	0.04	-	0.83	0.04	1.54	m	1.70
Concrete general surfaces										
girth exceeding 300mm	0.60	10.00	0.66	0.11	-	2.30	0.12	3.08	m²	3.39
Brickwork general surfaces										
girth exceeding 300mm	0.70	10.00	0.77	0.13	-	2.71	0.14	3.63	m²	3.99
Rough cast general surfaces										
girth exceeding 300mm	0.80	10.00	0.88	0.17	-	3.55	0.19	4.61	m²	5.07
Two coats waterproof cement paint; external work										
Cement rendered general surfaces										
girth exceeding 300mm	1.59	10.00	1.75	0.22	-	4.59	0.24	6.58	m²	7.24
isolated surfaces, girth not exceeding 300mm	0.48	10.00	0.53	0.08	-	1.67	0.09	2.29	m	2.52
Concrete general surfaces										
girth exceeding 300mm	1.21	10.00	1.33	0.22	-	4.59	0.24	6.16	m²	6.78
Brickwork general surfaces										
girth exceeding 300mm	1.40	10.00	1.54	0.24	-	5.01	0.26	6.81	m²	7.49

Labour hourly rates: (except Specialists) Craft Operatives 20.87 Labourer 15.57 Rates are national average prices. Refer to REGIONAL VARIATIONS for indicative levels of overall pricing in regions	MATERIALS			LABOUR				RATES		
	Del to Site £	Waste %	Material Cost £	Craft Optve Hrs	Lab Hrs	Labour Cost £	Sunds £	Nett Rate £	Unit	Gross rate (10%) £
PAINTING & CLEAR FINISHINGS; CEMENT PAINTING (Cont'd)										
Two coats waterproof cement paint; external work (Cont'd)										
Rough cast general surfaces										
girth exceeding 300mm	1.59	10.00	1.75	0.33	-	6.89	0.36	9.00	m²	9.90
One coat sealer, one coat waterproof cement paint; external work										
Cement rendered general surfaces										
girth exceeding 300mm	2.67	10.00	2.93	0.18	-	3.76	0.20	6.89	m²	7.58
isolated surfaces, girth not exceeding 300mm	0.78	10.00	0.85	0.06	-	1.25	0.07	2.17	m	2.39
Concrete general surfaces										
girth exceeding 300mm	2.47	10.00	2.72	0.18	-	3.76	0.20	6.68	m²	7.34
Brickwork general surfaces										
girth exceeding 300mm	2.57	10.00	2.83	0.21	-	4.38	0.23	7.44	m²	8.19
Rough cast general surfaces										
girth exceeding 300mm	2.67	10.00	2.93	0.27	-	5.63	0.30	8.87	m²	9.75
Two coats sealer, one coat waterproof cement paint; external work										
Cement rendered general surfaces										
girth exceeding 300mm	3.96	10.00	4.36	0.34	-	7.10	0.37	11.83	m²	13.01
isolated surfaces, girth not exceeding 300mm	1.18	10.00	1.29	0.11	-	2.30	0.12	3.71	m	4.08
Concrete general surfaces										
girth exceeding 300mm	3.37	10.00	3.70	0.34	-	7.10	0.37	11.17	m²	12.29
Brickwork general surfaces										
girth exceeding 300mm	3.86	10.00	4.25	0.39	-	8.14	0.43	12.82	m²	14.10
Rough cast general surfaces										
girth exceeding 300mm	3.96	10.00	4.36	0.51	-	10.64	0.56	15.56	m²	17.12
One coat textured masonry paint; external work										
Cement rendered general surfaces										
girth exceeding 300mm	0.56	10.00	0.61	0.11	-	2.30	0.12	3.03	m²	3.33
isolated surfaces, girth not exceeding 300mm	0.22	10.00	0.25	0.04	-	0.83	0.04	1.12	m	1.24
Concrete general surfaces										
girth exceeding 300mm	0.78	10.00	0.86	0.11	-	2.30	0.12	3.28	m²	3.60
Brickwork general surfaces										
girth exceeding 300mm	1.40	10.00	1.54	0.13	-	2.71	0.14	4.39	m²	4.83
Rough cast general surfaces										
girth exceeding 300mm	1.84	10.00	2.03	0.17	-	3.55	0.19	5.76	m²	6.34
Two coats textured masonry paint; external work										
Cement rendered general surfaces										
girth exceeding 300mm	1.56	10.00	1.72	0.22	-	4.59	0.24	6.55	m²	7.21
isolated surfaces, girth not exceeding 300mm	0.45	10.00	0.49	0.08	-	1.67	0.09	2.25	m	2.47
Concrete general surfaces										
girth exceeding 300mm	1.56	10.00	1.72	0.22	-	4.59	0.24	6.55	m²	7.21
Brickwork general surfaces										
girth exceeding 300mm	2.79	10.00	3.07	0.24	-	5.01	0.26	8.34	m²	9.18
Rough cast general surfaces										
girth exceeding 300mm	3.68	10.00	4.05	0.33	-	6.89	0.36	11.30	m²	12.43
One coat stabilizing solution, one coat textured masonry paint; external work										
Cement rendered general surfaces										
girth exceeding 300mm	1.18	10.00	1.30	0.18	-	3.76	0.20	5.25	m²	5.78
isolated surfaces, girth not exceeding 300mm	0.34	10.00	0.38	0.06	-	1.25	0.07	1.70	m	1.87
Concrete general surfaces										
girth exceeding 300mm	1.18	10.00	1.30	0.18	-	3.76	0.20	5.25	m²	5.78
Brickwork general surfaces										
girth exceeding 300mm	1.79	10.00	1.97	0.21	-	4.38	0.23	6.59	m²	7.25
Rough cast general surfaces										
girth exceeding 300mm	2.24	10.00	2.47	0.27	-	5.63	0.30	8.40	m²	9.24
One coat stabilizing solution, two coats textured masonry paint; external work										
Cement rendered general surfaces										
girth exceeding 300mm	1.96	10.00	2.16	0.34	-	7.10	0.37	9.63	m²	10.59
isolated surfaces, girth not exceeding 300mm	0.57	10.00	0.62	0.11	-	2.30	0.12	3.04	m	3.34
Concrete general surfaces										
girth exceeding 300mm	1.96	10.00	2.16	0.34	-	7.10	0.37	9.63	m²	10.59
Brickwork general surfaces										
girth exceeding 300mm	3.19	10.00	3.51	0.39	-	8.14	0.43	12.08	m²	13.29
Rough cast general surfaces										
girth exceeding 300mm	4.08	10.00	4.49	0.51	-	10.64	0.56	15.70	m²	17.27

Labour hourly rates: (except Specialists) Craft Operatives 20.87 Labourer 15.57 Rates are national average prices. Refer to REGIONAL VARIATIONS for indicative levels of overall pricing in regions	MATERIALS			LABOUR				RATES		
	Del to Site £	Waste %	Material Cost £	Craft Optve Hrs	Lab Hrs	Labour Cost £	Sunds £	Nett Rate £	Unit	Gross rate (10%) £
PAINTING & CLEAR FINISHINGS; PRESERVATIVE TREATMENT										
One coat creosote BS 144; external work (sawn timber)										
Wood general surfaces										
girth exceeding 300mm	0.45	10.00	0.50	0.10	-	2.09	0.11	2.69	m²	2.96
isolated surfaces, girth not exceeding 300mm	0.14	10.00	0.15	0.04	-	0.83	0.04	1.03	m	1.13
Two coats creosote BS 144; external work (sawn timber)										
Wood general surfaces										
girth exceeding 300mm	0.92	10.00	1.01	0.20	-	4.17	0.22	5.40	m²	5.94
isolated surfaces, girth not exceeding 300mm	0.27	10.00	0.30	0.07	-	1.46	0.08	1.84	m	2.02
One coat wood preservative, internal work (sawn timber)										
Wood general surfaces										
girth exceeding 300mm	0.53	10.00	0.59	0.11	-	2.30	0.12	3.00	m²	3.30
isolated surfaces, girth not exceeding 300mm	0.17	10.00	0.18	0.04	-	0.83	0.04	1.06	m	1.17
One coat wood preservative, internal work (wrought timber)										
Wood general surfaces										
girth exceeding 300mm	0.45	10.00	0.49	0.09	-	1.88	0.10	2.47	m²	2.71
isolated surfaces, girth not exceeding 300mm	0.13	10.00	0.15	0.03	-	0.63	0.03	0.81	m	0.89
One coat wood preservative, external work (sawn timber)										
Wood general surfaces										
girth exceeding 300mm	0.53	10.00	0.59	0.10	-	2.09	0.11	2.78	m²	3.06
isolated surfaces, girth not exceeding 300mm	0.17	10.00	0.18	0.04	-	0.83	0.04	1.06	m	1.17
One coat wood preservative, external work (wrought timber)										
Wood general surfaces										
girth exceeding 300mm	0.45	10.00	0.49	0.08	-	1.67	0.09	2.25	m²	2.47
isolated surfaces, girth not exceeding 300mm	0.13	10.00	0.15	0.02	-	0.42	0.02	0.59	m	0.64
Two coats wood preservative, internal work (sawn timber)										
Wood general surfaces										
girth exceeding 300mm	1.07	10.00	1.17	0.22	-	4.59	0.24	6.01	m²	6.61
isolated surfaces, girth not exceeding 300mm	0.33	10.00	0.37	0.08	-	1.67	0.09	2.12	m	2.34
Two coats wood preservative, internal work (wrought timber)										
Wood general surfaces										
girth exceeding 300mm	0.89	10.00	0.97	0.18	-	3.76	0.20	4.93	m²	5.42
isolated surfaces, girth not exceeding 300mm	0.27	10.00	0.29	0.05	-	1.04	0.05	1.39	m	1.53
Two coats wood preservative, external work (sawn timber)										
Wood general surfaces										
girth exceeding 300mm	1.07	10.00	1.17	0.20	-	4.17	0.22	5.57	m²	6.12
isolated surfaces, girth not exceeding 300mm	0.33	10.00	0.37	0.07	-	1.46	0.08	1.90	m	2.09
Two coats wood preservative, external work (wrought timber)										
Wood general surfaces										
girth exceeding 300mm	0.89	10.00	0.97	0.16	-	3.34	0.18	4.49	m²	4.94
isolated surfaces, girth not exceeding 300mm	0.27	10.00	0.29	0.05	-	1.04	0.05	1.39	m	1.53
Two coats Sadolins High Performance Extra Durable Varnish										
Wood general surfaces										
girth exceeding 300mm	3.53	10.00	3.89	0.30	-	6.26	0.33	10.48	m²	11.53
isolated surfaces, girth not exceeding 300mm	1.06	10.00	1.17	0.11	-	2.30	0.12	3.58	m	3.94
Wood glazed doors										
girth exceeding 300mm; panes, area not exceeding 0.10m²	2.02	10.00	2.22	0.98	-	20.45	1.08	23.75	m²	26.13
girth exceeding 300mm; panes, area 0.10 - 0.50m²	1.43	10.00	1.57	0.71	-	14.82	0.78	17.17	m²	18.89
girth exceeding 300mm; panes, area 0.50 - 1.00m²	1.26	10.00	1.39	0.60	-	12.52	0.66	14.57	m²	16.03
girth exceeding 300mm; panes, area exceeding 1.00m²	1.26	10.00	1.39	0.52	-	10.85	0.57	12.81	m²	14.09
Wood partially glazed doors										
girth exceeding 300mm; panes, area 0.50 - 1.00m²	1.94	10.00	2.13	0.60	-	12.52	0.66	15.31	m²	16.84
girth exceeding 300mm; panes, area exceeding 1.00m²	1.94	10.00	2.13	0.58	-	12.10	0.64	14.87	m²	16.36
Wood windows and screens										
girth exceeding 300mm; panes, area not exceeding 0.10m²	2.02	10.00	2.22	1.09	-	22.75	1.20	26.17	m²	28.79
girth exceeding 300mm; panes, area 0.10 - 0.50m²	1.43	10.00	1.57	0.78	-	16.28	0.86	18.71	m²	20.58
girth exceeding 300mm; panes, area 0.50 - 1.00m²	1.26	10.00	1.39	0.66	-	13.77	0.75	15.91	m²	17.50
girth exceeding 300mm; panes, area exceeding 1.00m²	1.26	10.00	1.39	0.58	-	12.10	0.64	14.13	m²	15.54
One coat Sadolins Classic; two coats Sadolins Extra Woodstain; external work										
Wood general surfaces										
girth exceeding 300mm	3.21	10.00	3.53	0.55	-	11.48	0.61	15.61	m²	17.18
isolated surfaces, girth not exceeding 300mm	0.95	10.00	1.04	0.19	-	3.97	0.21	5.22	m	5.74
Wood glazed doors										
girth exceeding 300mm; panes, area not exceeding 0.10m²	1.76	10.00	1.93	0.86	-	17.95	0.95	20.83	m²	22.91
girth exceeding 300mm; panes, area 0.10 - 0.50m²	1.26	10.00	1.39	0.62	-	12.94	0.68	15.01	m²	16.51
girth exceeding 300mm; panes, area 0.50 - 1.00m²	1.14	10.00	1.25	0.52	-	10.85	0.57	12.68	m²	13.95
girth exceeding 300mm; panes, area exceeding 1.00m²	1.14	10.00	1.25	0.46	-	9.60	0.51	11.36	m²	12.50
Wood partially glazed doors										
girth exceeding 300mm; panes, area 0.50 - 1.00m²	1.76	10.00	1.93	0.52	-	10.85	0.57	13.36	m²	14.69
girth exceeding 300mm; panes, area exceeding 1.00m²	1.76	10.00	1.93	0.50	-	10.44	0.55	12.92	m²	14.21

Labour hourly rates: (except Specialists) Craft Operatives 20.87 Labourer 15.57 Rates are national average prices. Refer to REGIONAL VARIATIONS for indicative levels of overall pricing in regions	MATERIALS			LABOUR				RATES		
	Del to Site £	Waste %	Material Cost £	Craft Optve Hrs	Lab Hrs	Labour Cost £	Sunds £	Nett Rate £	Unit	Gross rate (10%) £
PAINTING & CLEAR FINISHINGS; PRESERVATIVE TREATMENT (Cont'd)										
One coat Sadolins Classic; two coats Sadolins Extra Woodstain; external work (Cont'd)										
Wood windows and screens										
girth exceeding 300mm; panes, area not exceeding 0.10m²	1.76	10.00	1.93	0.98	-	20.45	1.08	23.46	m²	25.81
girth exceeding 300mm; panes, area 0.10 - 0.50m²	1.26	10.00	1.39	0.72	-	15.03	0.79	17.21	m²	18.93
girth exceeding 300mm; panes, area 0.50 - 1.00m²	1.14	10.00	1.25	0.61	-	12.73	0.67	14.65	m²	16.12
girth exceeding 300mm; panes, area exceeding 1.00m²	1.14	10.00	1.25	0.54	-	11.27	0.59	13.12	m²	14.43
Wood railings fences and gates; open type										
girth exceeding 300mm	2.46	10.00	2.70	0.55	-	11.48	0.61	14.78	m²	16.26
isolated surfaces, girth not exceeding 300mm	0.95	10.00	1.04	0.19	-	3.97	0.21	5.22	m	5.74
Wood railings fences and gates; close type										
girth exceeding 300mm	3.21	10.00	3.53	0.55	-	11.48	0.61	15.61	m²	17.18
PAINTING & CLEAR FINISHINGS; OIL PAINTING WALLS AND CEILINGS										
One coat primer, one undercoat, one coat full gloss finish										
Concrete general surfaces										
girth exceeding 300mm	2.54	10.00	2.79	0.33	-	6.89	0.36	10.04	m²	11.05
Concrete general surfaces 3.50 - 5.00m above floor										
girth exceeding 300mm	2.54	10.00	2.79	0.36	-	7.51	0.40	10.70	m²	11.77
Brickwork general surfaces										
girth exceeding 300mm	3.01	10.00	3.31	0.37	-	7.72	0.41	11.44	m²	12.58
Plasterboard general surfaces										
girth exceeding 300mm	2.32	10.00	2.55	0.30	-	6.26	0.33	9.14	m²	10.06
Plasterboard general surfaces 3.50 - 5.00m above floor										
girth exceeding 300mm	2.32	10.00	2.55	0.33	-	6.89	0.36	9.80	m²	10.78
Plaster general surfaces										
girth exceeding 300mm	2.32	10.00	2.55	0.30	-	6.26	0.33	9.14	m²	10.06
isolated surfaces, girth not exceeding 300mm	5.03	10.00	5.53	0.13	-	2.71	0.14	8.39	m	9.23
Plaster general surfaces 3.50 - 5.00m above floor										
girth exceeding 300mm	2.32	10.00	2.55	0.33	-	6.89	0.36	9.80	m²	10.78
One coat primer, two undercoats, one coat full gloss finish										
Concrete general surfaces										
girth exceeding 300mm	2.88	10.00	3.17	0.44	-	9.18	0.48	12.83	m²	14.12
Concrete general surfaces 3.50 - 5.00m above floor										
girth exceeding 300mm	2.88	10.00	3.17	0.48	-	10.02	0.53	13.71	m²	15.08
Brickwork general surfaces										
girth exceeding 300mm	3.51	10.00	3.86	0.50	-	10.44	0.55	14.84	m²	16.32
Plasterboard general surfaces										
girth exceeding 300mm	2.91	10.00	3.21	0.40	-	8.35	0.44	11.99	m²	13.19
Plasterboard general surfaces 3.50 - 5.00m above floor										
girth exceeding 300mm	2.66	10.00	2.93	0.44	-	9.18	0.48	12.59	m²	13.85
Plaster general surfaces										
girth exceeding 300mm	2.66	10.00	2.93	0.40	-	8.35	0.44	11.72	m²	12.89
isolated surfaces, girth not exceeding 300mm	0.82	10.00	0.90	0.18	-	3.76	0.20	4.85	m	5.34
Plaster general surfaces 3.50 - 5.00m above floor										
girth exceeding 300mm	2.66	10.00	2.93	0.44	-	9.18	0.48	12.59	m²	13.85
One coat primer, one undercoat, one coat eggshell finish										
Concrete general surfaces										
girth exceeding 300mm	2.61	10.00	2.87	0.33	-	6.89	0.36	10.12	m²	11.13
Concrete general surfaces 3.50 - 5.00m above floor										
girth exceeding 300mm	2.61	10.00	2.87	0.36	-	7.51	0.40	10.78	m²	11.86
Brickwork general surfaces										
girth exceeding 300mm	3.22	10.00	3.55	0.37	-	7.72	0.41	11.68	m²	12.84
Plasterboard general surfaces										
girth exceeding 300mm	2.39	10.00	2.62	0.30	-	6.26	0.33	9.21	m²	10.14
Plasterboard general surfaces 3.50 - 5.00m above floor										
girth exceeding 300mm	2.39	10.00	2.62	0.33	-	6.89	0.36	9.87	m²	10.86
Plaster general surfaces										
girth exceeding 300mm	2.39	10.00	2.62	0.30	-	6.26	0.33	9.21	m²	10.14
isolated surfaces, girth not exceeding 300mm	5.05	10.00	5.56	0.13	-	2.71	0.14	8.41	m	9.25
Plaster general surfaces 3.50 - 5.00m above floor										
girth exceeding 300mm	2.39	10.00	2.62	0.33	-	6.89	0.36	9.87	m²	10.86
One coat primer, two undercoats, one coat eggshell finish										
Concrete general surfaces										
girth exceeding 300mm	2.95	10.00	3.24	0.44	-	9.18	0.48	12.91	m²	14.20
Concrete general surfaces 3.50 - 5.00m above floor										
girth exceeding 300mm	2.95	10.00	3.24	0.48	-	10.02	0.53	13.79	m²	15.17
Brickwork general surfaces										
girth exceeding 300mm	3.59	10.00	3.95	0.50	-	10.44	0.55	14.94	m²	16.43

Labour hourly rates: (except Specialists) Craft Operatives 20.87 Labourer 15.57 Rates are national average prices. Refer to REGIONAL VARIATIONS for indicative levels of overall pricing in regions	MATERIALS			LABOUR				RATES		
	Del to Site £	Waste %	Material Cost £	Craft Optve Hrs	Lab Hrs	Labour Cost £	Sunds £	Nett Rate £	Unit	Gross rate (10%) £
PAINTING & CLEAR FINISHINGS; OIL PAINTING WALLS AND CEILINGS (Cont'd)										
One coat primer, two undercoats, one coat eggshell finish (Cont'd)										
Plasterboard general surfaces										
girth exceeding 300mm	2.73	10.00	3.00	0.40	-	8.35	0.44	11.79	m²	12.97
Plasterboard general surfaces 3.50 - 5.00m above floor										
girth exceeding 300mm	2.73	10.00	3.00	0.44	-	9.18	0.48	12.67	m²	13.93
Plaster general surfaces										
girth exceeding 300mm	2.73	10.00	3.00	0.40	-	8.35	0.44	11.79	m²	12.97
isolated surfaces, girth not exceeding 300mm	0.84	10.00	0.92	0.18	-	3.76	0.20	4.88	m	5.36
Plaster general surfaces 3.50 - 5.00m above floor										
girth exceeding 300mm	2.73	10.00	3.00	0.44	-	9.18	0.08	12.26	m²	13.48
PAINTING & CLEAR FINISHINGS; SPRAY PAINTING										
Spray one coat primer, one undercoat, one coat full gloss finish										
Concrete general surfaces										
girth exceeding 300mm	2.76	10.00	3.03	0.26	-	5.43	0.29	8.74	m²	9.62
Brickwork general surfaces										
girth exceeding 300mm	3.39	10.00	3.73	0.30	-	6.26	0.33	10.32	m²	11.35
Plaster general surfaces										
girth exceeding 300mm	2.54	10.00	2.79	0.24	-	5.01	0.26	8.06	m²	8.87
Spray one coat primer, two undercoats, one coat full gloss finish										
Concrete general surfaces										
girth exceeding 300mm	3.15	10.00	3.46	0.31	-	6.47	0.34	10.28	m²	11.30
Brickwork general surfaces										
girth exceeding 300mm	3.91	10.00	4.30	0.35	-	7.30	0.39	11.99	m²	13.19
Plaster general surfaces										
girth exceeding 300mm	2.93	10.00	3.22	0.28	-	5.84	0.31	9.38	m²	10.31
Spray one coat primer, one basecoat, one coat multicolour finish										
Concrete general surfaces										
girth exceeding 300mm	2.13	10.00	2.35	0.39	-	8.14	0.43	10.92	m²	12.01
Brickwork general surfaces										
girth exceeding 300mm	2.60	10.00	2.86	0.41	-	8.56	0.45	11.87	m²	13.06
Plaster general surfaces										
girth exceeding 300mm	1.95	10.00	2.14	0.37	-	7.72	0.41	10.27	m²	11.30
PAINTING & CLEAR FINISHINGS; ACRYLATED RUBBER PAINTING										
One coat primer, two coats acrylated rubber paint										
Concrete general surfaces										
girth exceeding 300mm	6.97	10.00	7.66	0.33	-	6.89	0.36	14.91	m²	16.40
Brickwork general surfaces										
girth exceeding 300mm	8.31	10.00	9.14	0.35	-	7.30	0.39	16.83	m²	18.52
Plasterboard general surfaces										
girth exceeding 300mm	6.25	10.00	6.88	0.32	-	6.68	0.35	13.91	m²	15.30
Plaster general surfaces										
girth exceeding 300mm	6.25	10.00	6.88	0.32	-	6.68	0.35	13.91	m²	15.30
isolated surfaces, girth not exceeding 300mm	1.82	10.00	2.00	0.14	-	2.92	0.15	5.08	m	5.59
PAINTING & CLEAR FINISHINGS; PLASTIC FINISH										
Textured plastic coating - Stippled finish										
Concrete general surfaces										
girth exceeding 300mm	0.89	10.00	0.98	0.25	-	5.22	0.28	6.48	m²	7.12
Concrete general surfaces 3.50 - 5.00m above floor										
girth exceeding 300mm	0.89	10.00	0.98	0.28	-	5.84	0.31	7.13	m²	7.85
Brickwork general surfaces										
girth exceeding 300mm	1.07	10.00	1.17	0.30	-	6.26	0.33	7.76	m²	8.54
Plasterboard general surfaces										
girth exceeding 300mm	0.80	10.00	0.88	0.20	-	4.17	0.22	5.27	m²	5.80
Plasterboard general surfaces 3.50 - 5.00m above floor										
girth exceeding 300mm	0.80	10.00	0.88	0.22	-	4.59	0.24	5.71	m²	6.28
Plaster general surfaces										
girth exceeding 300mm	0.80	10.00	0.88	0.20	-	4.17	0.22	5.27	m²	5.80
Plaster general surfaces 3.50 - 5.00m above floor										
girth exceeding 300mm	0.80	10.00	0.88	0.22	-	4.59	0.24	5.71	m²	6.28
Textured plastic coating - Combed Finish										
Concrete general surfaces										
girth exceeding 300mm	1.07	10.00	1.17	0.30	-	6.26	0.33	7.76	m²	8.54

Labour hourly rates: (except Specialists) Craft Operatives 20.87 Labourer 15.57 Rates are national average prices. Refer to REGIONAL VARIATIONS for indicative levels of overall pricing in regions	MATERIALS			LABOUR				RATES		
	Del to Site £	Waste %	Material Cost £	Craft Optve Hrs	Lab Hrs	Labour Cost £	Sunds £	Nett Rate £	Unit	Gross rate (10%) £
PAINTING & CLEAR FINISHINGS; PLASTIC FINISH (Cont'd)										
Textured plastic coating - Combed Finish (Cont'd)										
Concrete general surfaces 3.50 - 5.00m above floor										
girth exceeding 300mm	1.07	10.00	1.17	0.33	-	6.89	0.36	8.42	m²	9.27
Brickwork general surfaces										
girth exceeding 300mm	1.28	10.00	1.41	0.35	-	7.30	0.39	9.10	m²	10.01
Plasterboard general surfaces										
girth exceeding 300mm	0.96	10.00	1.06	0.25	-	5.22	0.28	6.55	m²	7.20
Plasterboard general surfaces 3.50 - 5.00m above floor										
girth exceeding 300mm	0.96	10.00	1.06	0.27	-	5.63	0.30	6.99	m²	7.69
Plaster general surfaces										
girth exceeding 300mm	0.96	10.00	1.06	0.25	-	5.22	0.28	6.55	m²	7.20
Plaster general surfaces 3.50 - 5.00m above floor										
girth exceeding 300mm	0.96	10.00	1.06	0.27	-	5.63	0.30	6.99	m²	7.69
PAINTING & CLEAR FINISHINGS; OIL PAINTING METALWORK										
One undercoat, one coat full gloss finish on ready primed metal surfaces										
Iron or steel structural work										
girth exceeding 300mm	0.75	10.00	0.83	0.31	-	6.47	0.34	7.64	m²	8.40
isolated surfaces, girth not exceeding 300mm	0.23	10.00	0.25	0.13	-	2.71	0.14	3.11	m	3.42
Iron or steel structural members of roof trusses, lattice girders, purlins and the like										
girth exceeding 300mm	0.75	10.00	0.83	0.40	-	8.35	0.44	9.62	m²	10.58
isolated surfaces, girth not exceeding 300mm	0.23	10.00	0.25	0.13	-	2.71	0.14	3.11	m	3.42
Two undercoats, one coat full gloss finish on ready primed metal surfaces										
Iron or steel structural work										
girth exceeding 300mm	1.09	10.00	1.20	0.46	-	9.60	0.51	11.31	m²	12.44
isolated surfaces, girth not exceeding 300mm	0.34	10.00	0.37	0.15	-	3.13	0.17	3.67	m	4.03
Iron or steel structural members of roof trusses, lattice girders, purlins and the like										
girth exceeding 300mm	1.09	10.00	1.20	0.59	-	12.31	0.65	14.17	m²	15.58
isolated surfaces, girth not exceeding 300mm	0.34	10.00	0.37	0.20	-	4.17	0.22	4.76	m	5.24
One coat primer, one undercoat, one coat full gloss finish on metal surfaces										
Iron or steel general surfaces										
girth exceeding 300mm	1.96	10.00	2.16	0.43	-	8.97	0.47	11.61	m²	12.77
isolated surfaces, girth not exceeding 300mm	0.62	10.00	0.68	0.14	-	2.92	0.15	3.75	m	4.13
Galvanised glazed doors, windows or screens										
girth exceeding 300mm; panes, area not exceeding 0.10m²	1.06	10.00	1.17	0.79	-	16.49	0.87	18.53	m²	20.38
girth exceeding 300mm; panes, area 0.10 - 0.50m²	0.78	10.00	0.86	0.56	-	11.69	0.62	13.17	m²	14.48
girth exceeding 300mm; panes, area 0.50 - 1.00m²	0.67	10.00	0.74	0.47	-	9.81	0.52	11.06	m²	12.17
girth exceeding 300mm; panes, area exceeding 1.00m²	0.67	10.00	0.74	0.43	-	8.97	0.47	10.19	m²	11.20
Iron or steel structural work										
girth exceeding 300mm	1.96	10.00	2.16	0.46	-	9.60	0.51	12.26	m²	13.49
isolated surfaces, girth not exceeding 300mm	0.62	10.00	0.68	0.20	-	4.17	0.22	5.07	m	5.58
Iron or steel structural members of roof trusses, lattice girders, purlins and the like										
girth exceeding 300mm	1.96	10.00	2.16	0.59	-	12.31	0.65	15.12	m²	16.63
isolated surfaces, girth not exceeding 300mm	0.62	10.00	0.68	0.20	-	4.17	0.22	5.07	m	5.58
Iron or steel services										
girth exceeding 300mm	1.96	10.00	2.16	0.59	-	12.31	0.65	15.12	m²	16.63
isolated surfaces, girth not exceeding 300mm	0.62	10.00	0.68	0.20	-	4.17	0.22	5.07	m	5.58
isolated areas not exceeding 0.50m² irrespective of girth	1.01	10.00	1.11	0.59	-	12.31	0.65	14.07	nr	15.48
Copper services										
girth exceeding 300mm	1.96	10.00	2.16	0.59	-	12.31	0.65	15.12	m²	16.63
isolated surfaces, girth not exceeding 300mm	0.62	10.00	0.68	0.20	-	4.17	0.22	5.07	m	5.58
Galvanised services										
girth exceeding 300mm	1.96	10.00	2.16	0.59	-	12.31	0.65	15.12	m²	16.63
isolated surfaces, girth not exceeding 300mm	0.62	10.00	0.68	0.20	-	4.17	0.22	5.07	m	5.58
One coat primer, one undercoat, one coat full gloss finish on metal surfaces; external work										
Iron or steel general surfaces										
girth exceeding 300mm	1.96	10.00	2.16	0.46	-	9.60	0.51	12.26	m²	13.49
isolated surfaces, girth not exceeding 300mm	0.62	10.00	0.68	0.18	-	3.76	0.20	4.63	m	5.10
Galvanised glazed doors, windows or screens										
girth exceeding 300mm; panes, area not exceeding 0.10m²	1.06	10.00	1.17	0.83	-	17.32	0.91	19.41	m²	21.35
girth exceeding 300mm; panes, area 0.10 - 0.50m²	0.78	10.00	0.86	0.59	-	12.31	0.65	13.82	m²	15.21
girth exceeding 300mm; panes, area 0.50 - 1.00m²	0.67	10.00	0.74	0.51	-	10.64	0.56	11.94	m²	13.14
girth exceeding 300mm; panes, area exceeding 1.00m²	0.67	10.00	0.74	0.46	-	9.60	0.51	10.84	m²	11.93
Iron or steel structural work										
girth exceeding 300mm	1.96	10.00	2.16	0.46	-	9.60	0.51	12.26	m²	13.49
isolated surfaces, girth not exceeding 300mm	0.62	10.00	0.68	0.20	-	4.17	0.22	5.07	m	5.58

Labour hourly rates: (except Specialists) Craft Operatives 20.87 Labourer 15.57 Rates are national average prices. Refer to REGIONAL VARIATIONS for indicative levels of overall pricing in regions	MATERIALS			LABOUR				RATES		
	Del to Site £	Waste %	Material Cost £	Craft Optve Hrs	Lab Hrs	Labour Cost £	Sunds £	Nett Rate £	Unit	Gross rate (10%) £
PAINTING & CLEAR FINISHINGS; OIL PAINTING METALWORK (Cont'd)										
One coat primer, one undercoat, one coat full gloss finish on metal surfaces; external work (Cont'd)										
Iron or steel structural members of roof trusses, lattice girders, purlins and the like										
girth exceeding 300mm	1.96	10.00	2.16	0.59	-	12.31	0.65	15.12	m²	16.63
isolated surfaces, girth not exceeding 300mm	0.62	10.00	0.68	0.20	-	4.17	0.22	5.07	m	5.58
Iron or steel railings, fences and gates; plain open type										
girth exceeding 300mm	1.51	10.00	1.66	0.43	-	8.97	0.47	11.11	m²	12.22
isolated surfaces, girth not exceeding 300mm	0.62	10.00	0.68	0.14	-	2.92	0.15	3.75	m	4.13
Iron or steel railings, fences and gates; close type										
girth exceeding 300mm	1.96	10.00	2.16	0.36	-	7.51	0.40	10.07	m²	11.07
Iron or steel railings, fences and gates; ornamental type										
girth exceeding 300mm	1.51	10.00	1.66	0.73	-	15.24	0.80	17.70	m²	19.47
Iron or steel eaves gutters										
girth exceeding 300mm	1.96	10.00	2.16	0.50	-	10.44	0.55	13.14	m²	14.46
isolated surfaces, girth not exceeding 300mm	0.62	10.00	0.68	0.17	-	3.55	0.19	4.41	m	4.85
Galvanised eaves gutters										
girth exceeding 300mm	1.96	10.00	2.16	0.50	-	10.44	0.55	13.14	m²	14.46
isolated surfaces, girth not exceeding 300mm	0.62	10.00	0.68	0.17	-	3.55	0.19	4.41	m	4.85
Iron or steel services										
girth exceeding 300mm	1.96	10.00	2.16	0.59	-	12.31	0.65	15.12	m²	16.63
isolated surfaces, girth not exceeding 300mm	0.62	10.00	0.68	0.20	-	4.17	0.22	5.07	m	5.58
isolated areas not exceeding 0.50m² irrespective of girth	1.01	10.00	1.11	0.59	-	12.31	0.65	14.07	nr	15.48
Copper services										
girth exceeding 300mm	1.96	10.00	2.16	0.59	-	12.31	0.65	15.12	m²	16.63
isolated surfaces, girth not exceeding 300mm	0.62	10.00	0.68	0.20	-	4.17	0.22	5.07	m	5.58
Galvanised services										
girth exceeding 300mm	1.96	10.00	2.16	0.59	-	12.31	0.65	15.12	m²	16.63
isolated surfaces, girth not exceeding 300mm	0.62	10.00	0.68	0.20	-	4.17	0.22	5.07	m	5.58
One coat primer, two undercoats, one coat full gloss finish on metal surfaces										
Iron or steel general surfaces										
girth exceeding 300mm	2.30	10.00	2.53	0.57	-	11.90	0.63	15.06	m²	16.56
isolated surfaces, girth not exceeding 300mm	0.72	10.00	0.79	0.19	-	3.97	0.21	4.97	m	5.46
Galvanised glazed doors, windows or screens										
girth exceeding 300mm; panes, area not exceeding 0.10m²	1.25	10.00	1.37	1.06	-	22.12	1.17	24.66	m²	27.13
girth exceeding 300mm; panes, area 0.10 - 0.50m²	0.92	10.00	1.01	0.75	-	15.65	0.83	17.48	m²	19.23
girth exceeding 300mm; panes, area 0.50 - 1.00m²	0.78	10.00	0.85	0.63	-	13.15	0.69	14.69	m²	16.16
girth exceeding 300mm; panes, area exceeding 1.00m²	0.78	10.00	0.85	0.57	-	11.90	0.63	13.38	m²	14.71
Iron or steel structural work										
girth exceeding 300mm	2.30	10.00	2.53	0.62	-	12.94	0.68	16.15	m²	17.77
isolated surfaces, girth not exceeding 300mm	0.72	10.00	0.79	0.24	-	5.01	0.26	6.07	m	6.67
Iron or steel structural members of roof trusses, lattice girders, purlins and the like										
girth exceeding 300mm	2.30	10.00	2.53	0.79	-	16.49	0.87	19.89	m²	21.88
isolated surfaces, girth not exceeding 300mm	0.72	10.00	0.79	0.24	-	5.01	0.26	6.07	m	6.67
Iron or steel services										
girth exceeding 300mm	2.30	10.00	2.53	0.69	-	14.40	0.76	17.69	m²	19.46
isolated surfaces, girth not exceeding 300mm	0.72	10.00	0.79	0.23	-	4.80	0.25	5.85	m	6.43
isolated areas not exceeding 0.50m² irrespective of girth	1.17	10.00	1.28	0.69	-	14.40	0.76	16.44	nr	18.09
Copper services										
girth exceeding 300mm	2.30	10.00	2.53	0.69	-	14.40	0.76	17.69	m²	19.46
isolated surfaces, girth not exceeding 300mm	0.72	10.00	0.79	0.23	-	4.80	0.25	5.85	m	6.43
Galvanised services										
girth exceeding 300mm	2.30	10.00	2.53	0.69	-	14.40	0.76	17.69	m²	19.46
isolated surfaces, girth not exceeding 300mm	0.72	10.00	0.79	0.23	-	4.80	0.25	5.85	m	6.43
One coat primer, two undercoats, one coat full gloss finish on metal surfaces; external work										
Iron or steel general surfaces										
girth exceeding 300mm	2.30	10.00	2.53	0.62	-	12.94	0.68	16.15	m²	17.77
isolated surfaces, girth not exceeding 300mm	0.72	10.00	0.79	0.21	-	4.38	0.23	5.41	m	5.95
Galvanised glazed doors, windows or screens										
girth exceeding 300mm; panes, area not exceeding 0.10m²	1.25	10.00	1.37	1.10	-	22.96	1.21	25.54	m²	28.09
girth exceeding 300mm; panes, area 0.10 - 0.50m²	0.92	10.00	1.01	0.79	-	16.49	0.87	18.36	m²	20.20
girth exceeding 300mm; panes, area 0.50 - 1.00m²	0.78	10.00	0.85	0.67	-	13.98	0.74	15.57	m²	17.13
girth exceeding 300mm; panes, area exceeding 1.00m²	0.78	10.00	0.85	0.62	-	12.94	0.68	14.48	m²	15.92
Iron or steel structural work										
girth exceeding 300mm	2.30	10.00	2.53	0.62	-	12.94	0.68	16.15	m²	17.77
isolated surfaces, girth not exceeding 300mm	0.72	10.00	0.79	0.24	-	5.01	0.26	6.07	m	6.67
Iron or steel structural members of roof trusses, lattice girders, purlins and the like										
girth exceeding 300mm	2.30	10.00	2.53	0.79	-	16.49	0.87	19.89	m²	21.88
isolated surfaces, girth not exceeding 300mm	0.72	10.00	0.79	0.24	-	5.01	0.26	6.07	m	6.67
Iron or steel railings, fences and gates; plain open type										
girth exceeding 300mm	1.78	10.00	1.95	0.57	-	11.90	0.63	14.48	m²	15.92

Labour hourly rates: (except Specialists) Craft Operatives 20.87 Labourer 15.57 Rates are national average prices. Refer to REGIONAL VARIATIONS for indicative levels of overall pricing in regions	MATERIALS			LABOUR				RATES		
	Del to Site £	Waste %	Material Cost £	Craft Optve Hrs	Lab Hrs	Labour Cost £	Sunds £	Nett Rate £	Unit	Gross rate (10%) £
PAINTING & CLEAR FINISHINGS; OIL PAINTING METALWORK (Cont'd)										
One coat primer, two undercoats, one coat full gloss finish on metal surfaces; external work (Cont'd)										
Iron or steel railings, fences and gates; plain open type (Cont'd)										
isolated surfaces, girth not exceeding 300mm	0.72	10.00	0.79	0.19	-	3.97	0.21	4.97	m	5.46
Iron or steel railings, fences and gates; close type										
girth exceeding 300mm	2.30	10.00	2.53	0.48	-	10.02	0.53	13.08	m²	14.39
Iron or steel railings, fences and gates; ornamental type										
girth exceeding 300mm	1.78	10.00	1.95	0.97	-	20.24	1.07	23.26	m²	25.59
Iron or steel eaves gutters										
girth exceeding 300mm	2.30	10.00	2.53	0.66	-	13.77	0.73	17.03	m²	18.74
isolated surfaces, girth not exceeding 300mm	0.72	10.00	0.79	0.22	-	4.59	0.24	5.63	m	6.19
Galvanised eaves gutters										
girth exceeding 300mm	2.30	10.00	2.53	0.66	-	13.77	0.73	17.03	m²	18.74
isolated surfaces, girth not exceeding 300mm	0.72	10.00	0.79	0.22	-	4.59	0.24	5.63	m	6.19
Iron or steel services										
girth exceeding 300mm	2.30	10.00	2.53	0.69	-	14.40	0.76	17.69	m²	19.46
isolated surfaces, girth not exceeding 300mm	0.72	10.00	0.79	0.23	-	4.80	0.25	5.85	m	6.43
isolated areas not exceeding 0.50m² irrespective of girth	1.19	10.00	1.31	0.69	-	14.40	0.76	16.47	nr	18.12
Copper services										
girth exceeding 300mm	2.30	10.00	2.53	0.69	-	14.40	0.76	17.69	m²	19.46
isolated surfaces, girth not exceeding 300mm	0.72	10.00	0.79	0.23	-	4.80	0.25	5.85	m	6.43
Galvanised services										
girth exceeding 300mm	2.30	10.00	2.53	0.69	-	14.40	0.76	17.69	m²	19.46
isolated surfaces, girth not exceeding 300mm	0.72	10.00	0.79	0.23	-	4.80	0.25	5.85	m	6.43
One coat primer, one undercoat, two coats full gloss finish on metal surfaces										
Iron or steel general surfaces										
girth exceeding 300mm	2.37	10.00	2.61	0.57	-	11.90	0.63	15.13	m²	16.65
isolated surfaces, girth not exceeding 300mm	0.74	10.00	0.82	0.19	-	3.97	0.21	4.99	m	5.49
Galvanised glazed doors, windows or screens										
girth exceeding 300mm; panes, area not exceeding 0.10m²	1.29	10.00	1.42	1.06	-	22.12	1.17	24.70	m²	27.17
girth exceeding 300mm; panes, area 0.10 - 0.50m²	0.94	10.00	1.04	0.75	-	15.65	0.83	17.51	m²	19.27
girth exceeding 300mm; panes, area 0.50 - 1.00m²	0.80	10.00	0.88	0.63	-	13.15	0.69	14.72	m²	16.19
girth exceeding 300mm; panes, area exceeding 1.00m²	0.80	10.00	0.88	0.57	-	11.90	0.63	13.40	m²	14.74
Iron or steel structural work										
girth exceeding 300mm	2.37	10.00	2.61	0.62	-	12.94	0.68	16.23	m²	17.86
isolated surfaces, girth not exceeding 300mm	0.74	10.00	0.82	0.24	-	5.01	0.26	6.09	m	6.70
Iron or steel structural members of roof trusses, lattice girders, purlins and the like										
girth exceeding 300mm	2.37	10.00	2.61	0.79	-	16.49	0.87	19.97	m²	21.96
isolated surfaces, girth not exceeding 300mm	0.74	10.00	0.82	0.24	-	5.01	0.26	6.09	m	6.70
Iron or steel services										
girth exceeding 300mm	2.37	10.00	2.61	0.69	-	14.40	0.76	17.77	m²	19.55
isolated surfaces, girth not exceeding 300mm	0.74	10.00	0.82	0.23	-	4.80	0.25	5.87	m	6.46
isolated areas not exceeding 0.50m² irrespective of girth	1.23	10.00	1.35	0.69	-	14.40	0.76	16.51	nr	18.17
Copper services										
girth exceeding 300mm	2.37	10.00	2.61	0.69	-	14.40	0.76	17.77	m²	19.55
isolated surfaces, girth not exceeding 300mm	0.74	10.00	0.82	0.23	-	4.80	0.25	5.87	m	6.46
Galvanised services										
girth exceeding 300mm	2.37	10.00	2.61	0.69	-	14.40	0.76	17.77	m²	19.55
isolated surfaces, girth not exceeding 300mm	0.74	10.00	0.82	0.23	-	4.80	0.25	5.87	m	6.46
One coat primer, one undercoat, two coats full gloss finish on metal surfaces; external work										
Iron or steel general surfaces										
girth exceeding 300mm	2.37	10.00	2.61	0.62	-	12.94	0.68	16.23	m²	17.86
isolated surfaces, girth not exceeding 300mm	0.74	10.00	0.82	0.21	-	4.38	0.23	5.43	m	5.97
Galvanised glazed doors, windows or screens										
girth exceeding 300mm; panes, area not exceeding 0.10m²	1.29	10.00	1.42	1.10	-	22.96	1.21	25.58	m²	28.14
girth exceeding 300mm; panes, area 0.10 - 0.50m²	0.94	10.00	1.04	0.79	-	16.49	0.87	18.39	m²	20.23
girth exceeding 300mm; panes, area 0.50 - 1.00m²	0.80	10.00	0.88	0.67	-	13.98	0.74	15.60	m²	17.16
girth exceeding 300mm; panes, area exceeding 1.00m²	0.80	10.00	0.88	0.62	-	12.94	0.68	14.50	m²	15.95
Iron or steel structural work										
girth exceeding 300mm	2.37	10.00	2.61	0.62	-	12.94	0.68	16.23	m²	17.86
isolated surfaces, girth not exceeding 300mm	0.74	10.00	0.82	0.62	-	12.94	0.68	14.44	m²	15.88
Iron or steel structural members of roof trusses, lattice girders, purlins and the like										
girth exceeding 300mm	2.37	10.00	2.61	0.62	-	12.94	0.68	16.23	m²	17.86
isolated surfaces, girth not exceeding 300mm	0.74	10.00	0.82	0.24	-	5.01	0.26	6.09	m	6.70
Iron or steel railings, fences and gates; plain open type										
girth exceeding 300mm	1.83	10.00	2.01	0.57	-	11.90	0.63	14.54	m²	15.99
isolated surfaces, girth not exceeding 300mm	0.74	10.00	0.82	0.19	-	3.97	0.21	4.99	m	5.49
Iron or steel railings, fences and gates; close type										
girth exceeding 300mm	2.37	10.00	2.61	0.48	-	10.02	0.53	13.16	m²	14.47
Iron or steel railings, fences and gates; ornamental type										
girth exceeding 300mm	1.83	10.00	2.01	0.97	-	20.24	1.07	23.32	m²	25.66

Labour hourly rates: (except Specialists) Craft Operatives 20.87 Labourer 15.57 Rates are national average prices. Refer to REGIONAL VARIATIONS for indicative levels of overall pricing in regions	MATERIALS			LABOUR				RATES		
	Del to Site £	Waste %	Material Cost £	Craft Optve Hrs	Lab Hrs	Labour Cost £	Sunds £	Nett Rate £	Unit	Gross rate (10%) £
PAINTING & CLEAR FINISHINGS; OIL PAINTING METALWORK (Cont'd)										
One coat primer, one undercoat, two coats full gloss finish on metal surfaces; external work (Cont'd)										
Iron or steel eaves gutters										
girth exceeding 300mm	2.37	10.00	2.61	0.66	-	13.77	0.73	17.11	m²	18.82
isolated surfaces, girth not exceeding 300mm	0.74	10.00	0.82	0.22	-	4.59	0.24	5.65	m	6.22
Galvanised eaves gutters										
girth exceeding 300mm	2.37	10.00	2.61	0.66	-	13.77	0.73	17.11	m²	18.82
isolated surfaces, girth not exceeding 300mm	0.74	10.00	0.82	0.22	-	4.59	0.24	5.65	m	6.22
Iron or steel services										
girth exceeding 300mm	2.37	10.00	2.61	0.69	-	14.40	0.76	17.77	m²	19.55
isolated surfaces, girth not exceeding 300mm	0.74	10.00	0.82	0.23	-	4.80	0.25	5.87	m	6.46
isolated areas not exceeding 0.50m² irrespective of girth	1.23	10.00	1.35	0.69	-	14.40	0.76	16.51	nr	18.17
Copper services										
girth exceeding 300mm	2.37	10.00	2.61	0.69	-	14.40	0.76	17.77	m²	19.55
isolated surfaces, girth not exceeding 300mm	0.74	10.00	0.82	0.23	-	4.80	0.25	5.87	m	6.46
Galvanised services										
girth exceeding 300mm	2.37	10.00	2.61	0.69	-	14.40	0.76	17.77	m²	19.55
isolated surfaces, girth not exceeding 300mm	0.74	10.00	0.82	0.23	-	4.80	0.25	5.87	m	6.46
PAINTING & CLEAR FINISHINGS; METALLIC PAINTING										
One coat aluminium or silver metallic paint										
Iron or steel radiators; panel type										
girth exceeding 300mm	0.85	10.00	0.94	0.15	-	3.13	0.17	4.23	m²	4.65
Iron or steel radiators; column type										
girth exceeding 300mm	0.85	10.00	0.94	0.22	-	4.59	0.24	5.77	m²	6.35
Iron or steel services										
isolated surfaces, girth not exceeding 300mm	0.26	10.00	0.29	0.06	-	1.25	0.07	1.61	m	1.77
Copper services										
isolated surfaces, girth not exceeding 300mm	0.26	10.00	0.29	0.06	-	1.25	0.07	1.61	m	1.77
Galvanised services										
isolated surfaces, girth not exceeding 300mm	0.26	10.00	0.29	0.06	-	1.25	0.07	1.61	m	1.77
Two coats aluminium or silver metallic paint										
Iron or steel radiators; panel type										
girth exceeding 300mm	1.70	10.00	1.87	0.31	-	6.47	0.34	8.68	m²	9.55
Iron or steel radiators; column type										
girth exceeding 300mm	1.70	10.00	1.87	0.44	-	9.18	0.48	11.54	m²	12.69
Iron or steel services										
isolated surfaces, girth not exceeding 300mm	0.52	10.00	0.58	0.11	-	2.30	0.12	2.99	m	3.29
Copper services										
isolated surfaces, girth not exceeding 300mm	0.52	10.00	0.58	0.11	-	2.30	0.12	2.99	m	3.29
Galvanised services										
isolated surfaces, girth not exceeding 300mm	0.52	10.00	0.58	0.11	-	2.30	0.12	2.99	m	3.29
One coat gold or bronze metallic paint										
Iron or steel radiators; panel type										
girth exceeding 300mm	1.70	10.00	1.87	0.15	-	3.13	0.17	5.16	m²	5.68
Iron or steel radiators; column type										
girth exceeding 300mm	1.70	10.00	1.87	0.22	-	4.59	0.24	6.70	m²	7.37
Iron or steel services										
isolated surfaces, girth not exceeding 300mm	0.50	10.00	0.55	0.06	-	1.25	0.07	1.87	m	2.05
Copper services										
isolated surfaces, girth not exceeding 300mm	0.50	10.00	0.55	0.06	-	1.25	0.07	1.87	m	2.05
Galvanised services										
isolated surfaces, girth not exceeding 300mm	0.50	10.00	0.55	0.06	-	1.25	0.07	1.87	m	2.05
Two coats gold or bronze metallic paint										
Iron or steel radiators; panel type										
girth exceeding 300mm	3.39	10.00	3.73	0.31	-	6.47	0.34	10.54	m²	11.59
Iron or steel radiators; column type										
girth exceeding 300mm	3.39	10.00	3.73	0.44	-	9.18	0.48	13.40	m²	14.74
Iron or steel services										
isolated surfaces, girth not exceeding 300mm	1.00	10.00	1.10	0.11	-	2.30	0.12	3.51	m	3.87
Copper services										
isolated surfaces, girth not exceeding 300mm	1.00	10.00	1.10	0.11	-	2.30	0.12	3.51	m	3.87
Galvanised services										
isolated surfaces, girth not exceeding 300mm	1.00	10.00	1.10	0.11	-	2.30	0.12	3.51	m	3.87
PAINTING & CLEAR FINISHINGS; BITUMINOUS PAINT										
One coat black bitumen paint; external work										
Iron or steel general surfaces										
girth exceeding 300mm	0.42	10.00	0.46	0.14	-	2.92	0.15	3.54	m²	3.89

Labour hourly rates: (except Specialists) Craft Operatives 20.87 Labourer 15.57 Rates are national average prices. Refer to REGIONAL VARIATIONS for indicative levels of overall pricing in regions	MATERIALS			LABOUR				RATES		
	Del to Site £	Waste %	Material Cost £	Craft Optve Hrs	Lab Hrs	Labour Cost £	Sunds £	Nett Rate £	Unit	Gross rate (10%) £
PAINTING & CLEAR FINISHINGS; BITUMINOUS PAINT (Cont'd)										
One coat black bitumen paint; external work (Cont'd)										
Iron or steel eaves gutters										
girth exceeding 300mm	0.42	10.00	0.46	0.15	-	3.13	0.17	3.76	m²	4.14
Iron or steel services										
girth exceeding 300mm	0.42	10.00	0.46	0.17	-	3.55	0.19	4.20	m²	4.62
isolated surfaces, girth not exceeding 300mm	0.13	10.00	0.15	0.06	-	1.25	0.07	1.47	m	1.61
Two coats black bitumen paint; external work										
Iron or steel general surfaces										
girth exceeding 300mm	0.84	10.00	0.93	0.29	-	6.05	0.32	7.30	m²	8.03
Iron or steel eaves gutters										
girth exceeding 300mm	0.84	10.00	0.93	0.31	-	6.47	0.34	7.74	m²	8.51
isolated surfaces, girth not exceeding 300mm	0.25	10.00	0.27	0.10	-	2.09	0.11	2.47	m	2.72
Iron or steel services										
girth exceeding 300mm	0.84	10.00	0.93	0.33	-	6.89	0.36	8.18	m²	9.00
isolated surfaces, girth not exceeding 300mm	0.25	10.00	0.27	0.10	-	2.09	0.11	2.47	m	2.72
PAINTING & CLEAR FINISHINGS; OIL PAINTING WOODWORK										
One coat primer; carried out on site before fixing members										
Wood general surfaces										
girth exceeding 300mm	0.63	10.00	0.69	0.18	-	3.76	0.20	4.64	m²	5.11
isolated surfaces, girth not exceeding 300mm	0.18	10.00	0.20	0.07	-	1.46	0.08	1.73	m	1.91
One undercoat, one coat full gloss finish on ready primed wood surfaces										
Wood general surfaces										
girth exceeding 300mm	0.75	10.00	0.83	0.35	-	7.30	0.39	8.52	m²	9.37
isolated surfaces, girth not exceeding 300mm	0.23	10.00	0.25	0.12	-	2.50	0.13	2.89	m	3.18
Wood glazed doors										
girth exceeding 300mm; panes, area not exceeding 0.10m²	0.41	10.00	0.45	0.59	-	12.31	0.65	13.41	m²	14.75
girth exceeding 300mm; panes, area 0.10 - 0.50m²	0.29	10.00	0.32	0.42	-	8.77	0.46	9.55	m²	10.50
girth exceeding 300mm; panes, area 0.50 - 1.00m²	0.29	10.00	0.32	0.35	-	7.30	0.39	8.01	m²	8.81
girth exceeding 300mm; panes, area exceeding 1.00m²	0.29	10.00	0.32	0.32	-	6.68	0.35	7.35	m²	8.08
Wood partially glazed doors										
girth exceeding 300mm; panes, area not exceeding 0.10m²	0.58	10.00	0.64	0.47	-	9.81	0.52	10.96	m²	12.06
girth exceeding 300mm; panes, area 0.10 - 0.50m²	0.46	10.00	0.51	0.39	-	8.14	0.43	9.08	m²	9.99
girth exceeding 300mm; panes, area 0.50 - 1.00m²	0.41	10.00	0.45	0.35	-	7.30	0.39	8.14	m²	8.95
girth exceeding 300mm; panes, area exceeding 1.00m²	0.41	10.00	0.45	0.34	-	7.10	0.37	7.92	m²	8.71
Wood windows and screens										
girth exceeding 300mm; panes, area not exceeding 0.10m²	0.58	10.00	0.64	0.65	-	13.57	0.72	14.92	m²	16.41
girth exceeding 300mm; panes, area 0.10 - 0.50m²	0.46	10.00	0.51	0.46	-	9.60	0.51	10.62	m²	11.68
girth exceeding 300mm; panes, area 0.50 - 1.00m²	0.41	10.00	0.45	0.39	-	8.14	0.43	9.01	m²	9.92
girth exceeding 300mm; panes, area exceeding 1.00m²	0.41	10.00	0.45	0.35	-	7.30	0.39	8.14	m²	8.95
One undercoat, one coat full gloss finish on ready primed wood surfaces; external work										
Wood general surfaces										
girth exceeding 300mm	0.75	10.00	0.83	0.37	-	7.72	0.41	8.96	m²	9.85
isolated surfaces, girth not exceeding 300mm	0.23	10.00	0.25	0.13	-	2.71	0.14	3.11	m	3.42
Wood glazed doors										
girth exceeding 300mm; panes, area not exceeding 0.10m²	0.41	10.00	0.45	0.59	-	12.31	0.65	13.41	m²	14.75
girth exceeding 300mm; panes, area 0.10 - 0.50m²	0.29	10.00	0.32	0.42	-	8.77	0.46	9.55	m²	10.50
girth exceeding 300mm; panes, area 0.50 - 1.00m²	0.29	10.00	0.32	0.35	-	7.30	0.39	8.01	m²	8.81
girth exceeding 300mm; panes, area exceeding 1.00m²	0.29	10.00	0.32	0.32	-	6.68	0.35	7.35	m²	8.08
Wood partially glazed doors										
girth exceeding 300mm; panes, area not exceeding 0.10m²	0.58	10.00	0.64	0.47	-	9.81	0.52	10.96	m²	12.06
girth exceeding 300mm; panes, area 0.10 - 0.50m²	0.46	10.00	0.51	0.39	-	8.14	0.43	9.08	m²	9.99
girth exceeding 300mm; panes, area 0.50 - 1.00m²	0.41	10.00	0.45	0.35	-	7.30	0.39	8.14	m²	8.95
girth exceeding 300mm; panes, area exceeding 1.00m²	0.41	10.00	0.45	0.34	-	7.10	0.37	7.92	m²	8.71
Wood windows and screens										
girth exceeding 300mm; panes, area not exceeding 0.10m²	0.58	10.00	0.64	0.67	-	13.98	0.74	15.36	m²	16.89
girth exceeding 300mm; panes, area 0.10 - 0.50m²	0.46	10.00	0.51	0.48	-	10.02	0.53	11.06	m²	12.16
girth exceeding 300mm; panes, area 0.50 - 1.00m²	0.41	10.00	0.45	0.41	-	8.56	0.45	9.45	m²	10.40
girth exceeding 300mm; panes, area exceeding 1.00m²	0.41	10.00	0.45	0.37	-	7.72	0.41	8.57	m²	9.43
Wood railings fences and gates; open type										
girth exceeding 300mm	0.58	10.00	0.64	0.28	-	5.84	0.31	6.79	m²	7.47
isolated surfaces, girth not exceeding 300mm	0.23	10.00	0.25	0.09	-	1.88	0.10	2.23	m	2.46
Wood railings fences and gates; close type										
girth exceeding 300mm	0.75	10.00	0.83	0.24	-	5.01	0.26	6.10	m²	6.71
Two undercoats, one coat full gloss finish on ready primed wood surfaces										
Wood general surfaces										
girth exceeding 300mm	1.09	10.00	1.20	0.51	-	10.64	0.56	12.41	m²	13.65
isolated surfaces, girth not exceeding 300mm	0.34	10.00	0.37	0.17	-	3.55	0.19	4.11	m	4.52
Wood glazed doors										
girth exceeding 300mm; panes, area not exceeding 0.10m²	0.59	10.00	0.65	0.84	-	17.53	0.92	19.10	m²	21.01
girth exceeding 300mm; panes, area 0.10 - 0.50m²	0.42	10.00	0.46	0.61	-	12.73	0.67	13.86	m²	15.25
girth exceeding 300mm; panes, area 0.50 - 1.00m²	0.42	10.00	0.46	0.51	-	10.64	0.56	11.67	m²	12.83

Labour hourly rates: (except Specialists) Craft Operatives 20.87 Labourer 15.57 Rates are national average prices. Refer to REGIONAL VARIATIONS for indicative levels of overall pricing in regions	MATERIALS			LABOUR				RATES		
	Del to Site £	Waste %	Material Cost £	Craft Optve Hrs	Lab Hrs	Labour Cost £	Sunds £	Nett Rate £	Unit	Gross rate (10%) £
PAINTING & CLEAR FINISHINGS; OIL PAINTING WOODWORK (Cont'd)										
Two undercoats, one coat full gloss finish on ready primed wood surfaces (Cont'd)										
Wood glazed doors (Cont'd)										
girth exceeding 300mm; panes, area exceeding 1.00m²	0.42	10.00	0.46	0.45	-	9.39	0.50	10.35	m²	11.38
Wood partially glazed doors										
girth exceeding 300mm; panes, area not exceeding 0.10m²	0.84	10.00	0.93	0.67	-	13.98	0.74	15.65	m²	17.21
girth exceeding 300mm; panes, area 0.10 - 0.50m²	0.67	10.00	0.74	0.56	-	11.69	0.62	13.04	m²	14.35
girth exceeding 300mm; panes, area 0.50 - 1.00m²	0.59	10.00	0.65	0.51	-	10.64	0.56	11.85	m²	13.04
girth exceeding 300mm; panes, area exceeding 1.00m²	0.59	10.00	0.65	0.48	-	10.02	0.53	11.19	m²	12.31
Wood windows and screens										
girth exceeding 300mm; panes, area not exceeding 0.10m²	0.84	10.00	0.93	0.92	-	19.20	1.01	21.14	m²	23.25
girth exceeding 300mm; panes, area 0.10 - 0.50m²	0.67	10.00	0.74	0.67	-	13.98	0.74	15.46	m²	17.01
girth exceeding 300mm; panes, area 0.50 - 1.00m²	0.59	10.00	0.65	0.56	-	11.69	0.62	12.95	m²	14.25
girth exceeding 300mm; panes, area exceeding 1.00m²	0.59	10.00	0.65	0.50	-	10.44	0.55	11.63	m²	12.80
Two undercoats, one coat full gloss finish on ready primed wood surfaces; external work										
Wood general surfaces										
girth exceeding 300mm	1.09	10.00	1.20	0.54	-	11.27	0.59	13.07	m²	14.37
isolated surfaces, girth not exceeding 300mm	0.34	10.00	0.37	0.19	-	3.97	0.21	4.54	m	5.00
Wood glazed doors										
girth exceeding 300mm; panes, area not exceeding 0.10m²	0.59	10.00	0.65	0.84	-	17.53	0.92	19.10	m²	21.01
girth exceeding 300mm; panes, area 0.10 - 0.50m²	0.42	10.00	0.46	0.61	-	12.73	0.67	13.86	m²	15.25
girth exceeding 300mm; panes, area 0.50 - 1.00m²	0.42	10.00	0.46	0.51	-	10.64	0.56	11.67	m²	12.83
girth exceeding 300mm; panes, area exceeding 1.00m²	0.42	10.00	0.46	0.45	-	9.39	0.50	10.35	m²	11.38
Wood partially glazed doors										
girth exceeding 300mm; panes, area not exceeding 0.10m²	0.84	10.00	0.93	0.67	-	13.98	0.74	15.65	m²	17.21
girth exceeding 300mm; panes, area 0.10 - 0.50m²	0.67	10.00	0.74	0.56	-	11.69	0.62	13.04	m²	14.35
girth exceeding 300mm; panes, area 0.50 - 1.00m²	0.59	10.00	0.65	0.51	-	10.64	0.56	11.85	m²	13.04
girth exceeding 300mm; panes, area exceeding 1.00m²	0.59	10.00	0.65	0.48	-	10.02	0.53	11.19	m²	12.31
Wood windows and screens										
girth exceeding 300mm; panes, area not exceeding 0.10m²	0.84	10.00	0.93	0.96	-	20.04	1.06	22.02	m²	24.22
girth exceeding 300mm; panes, area 0.10 - 0.50m²	0.67	10.00	0.74	0.70	-	14.61	0.77	16.12	m²	17.73
girth exceeding 300mm; panes, area 0.50 - 1.00m²	0.59	10.00	0.65	0.59	-	12.31	0.65	13.61	m²	14.97
girth exceeding 300mm; panes, area exceeding 1.00m²	0.59	10.00	0.65	0.53	-	11.06	0.58	12.29	m²	13.52
Wood railings fences and gates; open type										
girth exceeding 300mm	0.84	10.00	0.93	0.42	-	8.77	0.46	10.15	m²	11.17
isolated surfaces, girth not exceeding 300mm	0.34	10.00	0.37	0.14	-	2.92	0.15	3.45	m	3.79
Wood railings fences and gates; close type										
girth exceeding 300mm	1.09	10.00	1.20	0.36	-	7.51	0.40	9.11	m²	10.02
One coat primer, one undercoat, one coat full gloss finish on wood surfaces										
Wood general surfaces										
girth exceeding 300mm	1.38	10.00	1.52	0.51	-	10.64	0.56	12.72	m²	13.99
isolated surfaces, girth not exceeding 300mm	0.41	10.00	0.45	0.17	-	3.55	0.19	4.19	m	4.61
Wood glazed doors										
girth exceeding 300mm; panes, area not exceeding 0.10m²	0.76	10.00	0.84	0.84	-	17.53	0.92	19.29	m²	21.22
girth exceeding 300mm; panes, area 0.10 - 0.50m²	0.56	10.00	0.61	0.61	-	12.73	0.67	14.02	m²	15.42
girth exceeding 300mm; panes, area 0.50 - 1.00m²	0.51	10.00	0.56	0.51	-	10.64	0.56	11.77	m²	12.95
girth exceeding 300mm; panes, area exceeding 1.00m²	0.51	10.00	0.56	0.45	-	9.39	0.50	10.45	m²	11.50
Wood partially glazed doors										
girth exceeding 300mm; panes, area not exceeding 0.10m²	1.07	10.00	1.18	0.67	-	13.98	0.74	15.90	m²	17.49
girth exceeding 300mm; panes, area 0.10 - 0.50m²	0.82	10.00	0.90	0.56	-	11.69	0.62	13.21	m²	14.53
girth exceeding 300mm; panes, area 0.50 - 1.00m²	0.76	10.00	0.84	0.51	-	10.64	0.56	12.04	m²	13.25
girth exceeding 300mm; panes, area exceeding 1.00m²	0.76	10.00	0.84	0.48	-	10.02	0.53	11.39	m²	12.52
Wood windows and screens										
girth exceeding 300mm; panes, area not exceeding 0.10m²	1.07	10.00	1.18	0.92	-	19.20	1.01	21.39	m²	23.53
girth exceeding 300mm; panes, area 0.10 - 0.50m²	0.82	10.00	0.90	0.67	-	13.98	0.74	15.62	m²	17.19
girth exceeding 300mm; panes, area 0.50 - 1.00m²	0.76	10.00	0.84	0.56	-	11.69	0.62	13.14	m²	14.46
girth exceeding 300mm; panes, area exceeding 1.00m²	0.76	10.00	0.84	0.50	-	10.44	0.55	11.82	m²	13.01
One coat primer, one undercoat, one coat full gloss finish on wood surfaces; external work										
Wood general surfaces										
girth exceeding 300mm	1.38	10.00	1.52	0.54	-	11.27	0.59	13.38	m²	14.72
isolated surfaces, girth not exceeding 300mm	0.41	10.00	0.45	0.19	-	3.97	0.21	4.63	m	5.09
Wood glazed doors										
girth exceeding 300mm; panes, area not exceeding 0.10m²	0.76	10.00	0.84	0.84	-	17.53	0.92	19.29	m²	21.22
girth exceeding 300mm; panes, area 0.10 - 0.50m²	0.56	10.00	0.61	0.61	-	12.73	0.67	14.02	m²	15.42
girth exceeding 300mm; panes, area 0.50 - 1.00m²	0.51	10.00	0.56	0.51	-	10.64	0.09	11.30	m²	12.43
girth exceeding 300mm; panes, area exceeding 1.00m²	0.51	10.00	0.56	0.45	-	9.39	0.50	10.45	m²	11.50
Wood partially glazed doors										
girth exceeding 300mm; panes, area not exceeding 0.10m²	1.07	10.00	1.18	0.67	-	13.98	0.74	15.90	m²	17.49
girth exceeding 300mm; panes, area 0.10 - 0.50m²	0.82	10.00	0.90	0.56	-	11.69	0.62	13.21	m²	14.53
girth exceeding 300mm; panes, area 0.50 - 1.00m²	0.76	10.00	0.84	0.51	-	10.64	0.56	12.04	m²	13.25
girth exceeding 300mm; panes, area exceeding 1.00m²	0.76	10.00	0.84	0.48	-	10.02	0.53	11.39	m²	12.52
Wood windows and screens										
girth exceeding 300mm; panes, area not exceeding 0.10m²	1.07	10.00	1.18	0.96	-	20.04	1.06	22.27	m²	24.50
girth exceeding 300mm; panes, area 0.10 - 0.50m²	0.82	10.00	0.90	0.70	-	14.61	0.77	16.28	m²	17.91

Labour hourly rates: (except Specialists) Craft Operatives 20.87 Labourer 15.57 Rates are national average prices. Refer to REGIONAL VARIATIONS for indicative levels of overall pricing in regions	MATERIALS			LABOUR				RATES		
	Del to Site £	Waste %	Material Cost £	Craft Optve Hrs	Lab Hrs	Labour Cost £	Sunds £	Nett Rate £	Unit	Gross rate (10%) £
PAINTING & CLEAR FINISHINGS; OIL PAINTING WOODWORK (Cont'd)										
One coat primer, one undercoat, one coat full gloss finish on wood surfaces; external work (Cont'd)										
Wood windows and screens (Cont'd)										
girth exceeding 300mm; panes, area 0.50 - 1.00m²	0.76	10.00	0.84	0.59	-	12.31	0.65	13.80	m²	15.18
girth exceeding 300mm; panes, area exceeding 1.00m²	0.76	10.00	0.84	0.53	-	11.06	0.58	12.48	m²	13.73
Wood railings fences and gates; open type										
girth exceeding 300mm	1.07	10.00	1.18	0.42	-	8.77	0.46	10.41	m²	11.45
isolated surfaces, girth not exceeding 300mm	0.41	10.00	0.45	0.14	-	2.92	0.15	3.53	m	3.88
Wood railings fences and gates; close type										
girth exceeding 300mm	1.38	10.00	1.52	0.36	-	7.51	0.40	9.43	m²	10.37
One coat primer, two undercoats, one coat full gloss finish on wood surfaces										
Wood general surfaces										
girth exceeding 300mm	1.72	10.00	1.89	0.66	-	13.77	0.73	16.39	m²	18.03
isolated surfaces, girth not exceeding 300mm	0.52	10.00	0.57	0.22	-	4.59	0.24	5.40	m	5.94
Wood glazed doors										
girth exceeding 300mm; panes, area not exceeding 0.10m²	0.95	10.00	1.04	1.10	-	22.96	1.21	25.21	m²	27.73
girth exceeding 300mm; panes, area 0.10 - 0.50m²	0.69	10.00	0.76	0.79	-	16.49	0.87	18.11	m²	19.93
girth exceeding 300mm; panes, area 0.50 - 1.00m²	0.64	10.00	0.71	0.66	-	13.77	0.73	15.21	m²	16.73
girth exceeding 300mm; panes, area exceeding 1.00m²	0.64	10.00	0.71	0.59	-	12.31	0.65	13.67	m²	15.04
Wood partially glazed doors										
girth exceeding 300mm; panes, area not exceeding 0.10m²	1.33	10.00	1.47	0.88	-	18.37	0.97	20.80	m²	22.88
girth exceeding 300mm; panes, area 0.10 - 0.50m²	1.03	10.00	1.13	0.73	-	15.24	0.80	17.17	m²	18.89
girth exceeding 300mm; panes, area 0.50 - 1.00m²	0.95	10.00	1.04	0.66	-	13.77	0.73	15.54	m²	17.10
girth exceeding 300mm; panes, area exceeding 1.00m²	0.95	10.00	1.04	0.63	-	13.15	0.69	14.88	m²	16.37
Wood windows and screens										
girth exceeding 300mm; panes, area not exceeding 0.10m²	1.33	10.00	1.47	1.21	-	25.25	1.33	28.05	m²	30.86
girth exceeding 300mm; panes, area 0.10 - 0.50m²	1.03	10.00	1.13	0.87	-	18.16	0.96	20.25	m²	22.27
girth exceeding 300mm; panes, area 0.50 - 1.00m²	0.95	10.00	1.04	0.73	-	15.24	0.80	17.08	m²	18.79
girth exceeding 300mm; panes, area exceeding 1.00m²	0.95	10.00	1.04	0.65	-	13.57	0.72	15.32	m²	16.85
One coat primer, two undercoats, one coat full gloss finish on wood surfaces; external work										
Wood general surfaces										
girth exceeding 300mm	1.72	10.00	1.89	0.70	-	14.61	0.77	17.27	m²	19.00
isolated surfaces, girth not exceeding 300mm	0.52	10.00	0.57	0.24	-	5.01	0.26	5.84	m²	6.42
Wood glazed doors										
girth exceeding 300mm; panes, area not exceeding 0.10m²	0.95	10.00	1.04	1.10	-	22.96	1.21	25.21	m²	27.73
girth exceeding 300mm; panes, area 0.10 - 0.50m²	0.69	10.00	0.76	0.79	-	16.49	0.87	18.11	m²	19.93
girth exceeding 300mm; panes, area 0.50 - 1.00m²	0.64	10.00	0.71	0.66	-	13.77	0.73	15.21	m²	16.73
girth exceeding 300mm; panes, area exceeding 1.00m²	0.64	10.00	0.71	0.59	-	12.31	0.65	13.67	m²	15.04
Wood partially glazed doors										
girth exceeding 300mm; panes, area not exceeding 0.10m²	1.33	10.00	1.47	0.88	-	18.37	0.97	20.80	m²	22.88
girth exceeding 300mm; panes, area 0.10 - 0.50m²	1.03	10.00	1.13	0.73	-	15.24	0.80	17.17	m²	18.89
girth exceeding 300mm; panes, area 0.50 - 1.00m²	0.95	10.00	1.04	0.66	-	13.77	0.73	15.54	m²	17.10
girth exceeding 300mm; panes, area exceeding 1.00m²	0.95	10.00	1.04	0.63	-	13.15	0.69	14.88	m²	16.37
Wood windows and screens										
girth exceeding 300mm; panes, area not exceeding 0.10m²	1.33	10.00	1.47	1.25	-	26.09	1.38	28.93	m²	31.82
girth exceeding 300mm; panes, area 0.10 - 0.50m²	1.03	10.00	1.13	0.91	-	18.99	1.00	21.13	m²	23.24
girth exceeding 300mm; panes, area 0.50 - 1.00m²	0.95	10.00	1.04	0.77	-	16.07	0.85	17.96	m²	19.75
girth exceeding 300mm; panes, area exceeding 1.00m²	0.95	10.00	1.04	0.69	-	14.40	0.76	16.20	m²	17.82
Wood railings fences and gates; open type										
girth exceeding 300mm	1.33	10.00	1.47	0.55	-	11.48	0.61	13.55	m²	14.91
isolated surfaces, girth not exceeding 300mm	0.52	10.00	0.57	0.19	-	3.97	0.21	4.74	m	5.22
Wood railings fences and gates; close type										
girth exceeding 300mm	1.72	10.00	1.89	0.48	-	10.02	0.53	12.44	m²	13.68
One coat primer, one undercoat, two coats full gloss finish on wood surfaces										
Wood general surfaces										
girth exceeding 300mm	1.79	10.00	1.97	0.66	-	13.77	0.73	16.47	m²	18.12
isolated surfaces, girth not exceeding 300mm	0.54	10.00	0.59	0.22	-	4.59	0.24	5.42	m	5.97
Wood glazed doors										
girth exceeding 300mm; panes, area not exceeding 0.10m²	0.98	10.00	1.08	1.10	-	22.96	1.21	25.25	m²	27.78
girth exceeding 300mm; panes, area 0.10 - 0.50m²	0.72	10.00	0.79	0.79	-	16.49	0.87	18.14	m²	19.96
girth exceeding 300mm; panes, area 0.50 - 1.00m²	0.67	10.00	0.74	0.66	-	13.77	0.73	15.24	m²	16.76
girth exceeding 300mm; panes, area exceeding 1.00m²	0.67	10.00	0.74	0.59	-	12.31	0.65	13.70	m²	15.07
Wood partially glazed doors										
girth exceeding 300mm; panes, area not exceeding 0.10m²	1.39	10.00	1.53	0.88	-	18.37	0.97	20.86	m²	22.95
girth exceeding 300mm; panes, area 0.10 - 0.50m²	1.07	10.00	1.18	0.73	-	15.24	0.80	17.22	m²	18.94
girth exceeding 300mm; panes, area 0.50 - 1.00m²	0.98	10.00	1.08	0.66	-	13.77	0.73	15.58	m²	17.14
girth exceeding 300mm; panes, area exceeding 1.00m²	0.98	10.00	1.08	0.63	-	13.15	0.69	14.92	m²	16.42
Wood windows and screens										
girth exceeding 300mm; panes, area not exceeding 0.10m²	1.39	10.00	1.53	1.21	-	25.25	1.33	28.11	m²	30.92
girth exceeding 300mm; panes, area 0.10 - 0.50m²	1.07	10.00	1.18	0.87	-	18.16	0.96	20.30	m²	22.33
girth exceeding 300mm; panes, area 0.50 - 1.00m²	0.98	10.00	1.08	0.73	-	15.24	0.80	17.12	m²	18.83
girth exceeding 300mm; panes, area exceeding 1.00m²	0.98	10.00	1.08	0.65	-	13.57	0.72	15.36	m²	16.90

Labour hourly rates: (except Specialists) Craft Operatives 20.87 Labourer 15.57 Rates are national average prices. Refer to REGIONAL VARIATIONS for indicative levels of overall pricing in regions	MATERIALS			LABOUR				RATES		
	Del to Site £	Waste %	Material Cost £	Craft Optve Hrs	Lab Hrs	Labour Cost £	Sunds £	Nett Rate £	Unit	Gross rate (10%) £
PAINTING & CLEAR FINISHINGS; OIL PAINTING WOODWORK (Cont'd)										
One coat primer, one undercoat, two coats full gloss finish wood surfaces; external work										
Wood general surfaces										
girth exceeding 300mm	1.79	10.00	1.97	0.70	-	14.61	0.77	17.35	m²	19.08
isolated surfaces, girth not exceeding 300mm	0.54	10.00	0.59	0.24	-	5.01	0.26	5.86	m	6.45
Wood glazed doors										
girth exceeding 300mm; panes, area not exceeding 0.10m²	0.98	10.00	1.08	1.10	-	22.96	1.21	25.25	m²	27.78
girth exceeding 300mm; panes, area 0.10 - 0.50m²	0.72	10.00	0.79	0.79	-	16.49	0.87	18.14	m²	19.96
girth exceeding 300mm; panes, area 0.50 - 1.00m²	0.67	10.00	0.74	0.66	-	13.77	0.73	15.24	m²	16.76
girth exceeding 300mm; panes, area exceeding 1.00m²	0.67	10.00	0.74	0.59	-	12.31	0.65	13.70	m²	15.07
Wood partially glazed doors										
girth exceeding 300mm; panes, area not exceeding 0.10m²	1.39	10.00	1.53	0.88	-	18.37	0.97	20.86	m²	22.95
girth exceeding 300mm; panes, area 0.10 - 0.50m²	1.07	10.00	1.18	0.73	-	15.24	0.80	17.22	m²	18.94
girth exceeding 300mm; panes, area 0.50 - 1.00m²	0.98	10.00	1.08	0.66	-	13.77	0.73	15.58	m²	17.14
girth exceeding 300mm; panes, area exceeding 1.00m²	0.98	10.00	1.08	0.63	-	13.15	0.69	14.92	m²	16.42
Wood windows and screens										
girth exceeding 300mm; panes, area not exceeding 0.10m²	1.39	10.00	1.53	1.25	-	26.09	1.38	28.99	m²	31.89
girth exceeding 300mm; panes, area 0.10 - 0.50m²	1.07	10.00	1.18	0.91	-	18.99	1.00	21.17	m²	23.29
girth exceeding 300mm; panes, area 0.50 - 1.00m²	0.98	10.00	1.08	0.77	-	16.07	0.85	18.00	m²	19.80
girth exceeding 300mm; panes, area exceeding 1.00m²	0.98	10.00	1.08	0.69	-	14.40	0.76	16.24	m²	17.87
Wood railings fences and gates; open type										
girth exceeding 300mm	1.39	10.00	1.53	0.55	-	11.48	0.61	13.61	m²	14.97
isolated surfaces, girth not exceeding 300mm	0.54	10.00	0.59	0.19	-	3.97	0.21	4.77	m	5.24
Wood railings fences and gates; close type										
girth exceeding 300mm	1.79	10.00	1.97	0.48	-	10.02	0.53	12.52	m²	13.77
PAINTING & CLEAR FINISHINGS; WATER BASED PAINTING WOODWORK										
One undercoat, one coat water based gloss finish on ready primed wood surfaces										
Wood general surfaces										
girth exceeding 300mm	1.28	10.00	1.41	0.35	-	7.30	0.39	9.10	m²	10.01
isolated surfaces, girth not exceeding 300mm	0.39	10.00	0.43	0.12	-	2.50	0.13	3.07	m	3.38
Wood glazed doors										
girth exceeding 300mm; panes, area not exceeding 0.10m²	0.69	10.00	0.76	0.59	-	12.31	0.65	13.72	m²	15.09
girth exceeding 300mm; panes, area 0.10 - 0.50m²	0.49	10.00	0.54	0.42	-	8.77	0.46	9.77	m²	10.75
girth exceeding 300mm; panes, area 0.50 - 1.00m²	0.49	10.00	0.54	0.35	-	7.30	0.39	8.23	m²	9.06
girth exceeding 300mm; panes, area exceeding 1.00m²	0.49	10.00	0.54	0.32	-	6.68	0.35	7.57	m²	8.33
Two undercoats, one coat water based gloss finish on ready primed wood surfaces										
Wood general surfaces										
girth exceeding 300mm	1.93	10.00	2.13	0.51	-	10.64	0.56	13.33	m²	14.66
isolated surfaces, girth not exceeding 300mm	0.59	10.00	0.65	0.17	-	3.55	0.19	4.39	m	4.83
Wood glazed doors										
girth exceeding 300mm; panes, area not exceeding 0.10m²	1.04	10.00	1.15	0.84	-	17.53	0.92	19.60	m²	21.56
girth exceeding 300mm; panes, area 0.10 - 0.50m²	0.74	10.00	0.82	0.61	-	12.73	0.67	14.22	m²	15.64
girth exceeding 300mm; panes, area 0.50 - 1.00m²	0.74	10.00	0.82	0.51	-	10.64	0.56	12.02	m²	13.22
girth exceeding 300mm; panes, area exceeding 1.00m²	0.74	10.00	0.82	0.45	-	9.39	0.50	10.70	m²	11.77
One coat primer, one undercoat, one coat water based gloss finish on wood surfaces										
Wood general surfaces										
girth exceeding 300mm	1.91	10.00	2.10	0.51	-	10.64	0.56	13.31	m²	14.64
isolated surfaces, girth not exceeding 300mm	0.57	10.00	0.63	0.17	-	3.55	0.19	4.37	m	4.80
Wood glazed doors										
girth exceeding 300mm; panes, area not exceeding 0.10m²	1.05	10.00	1.15	0.84	-	17.53	0.92	19.61	m²	21.57
girth exceeding 300mm; panes, area 0.10 - 0.50m²	0.76	10.00	0.84	0.61	-	12.73	0.67	14.24	m²	15.66
girth exceeding 300mm; panes, area 0.50 - 1.00m²	0.72	10.00	0.79	0.51	-	10.64	0.56	11.99	m²	13.19
girth exceeding 300mm; panes, area exceeding 1.00m²	0.72	10.00	0.79	0.45	-	9.39	0.50	10.68	m²	11.74
One coat primer, two undercoats, one coat water based gloss finish on wood surfaces										
Wood general surfaces										
girth exceeding 300mm	2.56	10.00	2.82	0.66	-	13.77	0.73	17.32	m²	19.05
isolated surfaces, girth not exceeding 300mm	0.77	10.00	0.85	0.22	-	4.59	0.24	5.68	m	6.25
Wood glazed doors										
girth exceeding 300mm; panes, area not exceeding 0.10m²	1.40	10.00	1.54	1.10	-	22.96	1.21	25.71	m²	28.28
girth exceeding 300mm; panes, area 0.10 - 0.50m²	1.01	10.00	1.11	0.79	-	16.49	0.87	18.47	m²	20.32
girth exceeding 300mm; panes, area 0.50 - 1.00m²	0.97	10.00	1.06	0.66	-	13.77	0.73	15.56	m²	17.12
girth exceeding 300mm; panes, area exceeding 1.00m²	0.97	10.00	1.06	0.59	-	12.31	0.65	14.03	m²	15.43
One coat primer, one undercoat, two coats water based gloss finish on wood surfaces										
Wood general surfaces										
girth exceeding 300mm	2.54	10.00	2.80	0.66	-	13.77	0.73	17.30	m²	19.03
isolated surfaces, girth not exceeding 300mm	0.77	10.00	0.85	0.22	-	4.59	0.24	5.68	m	6.25
Wood glazed doors										
girth exceeding 300mm; panes, area not exceeding 0.10m²	1.39	10.00	1.53	1.10	-	22.96	1.21	25.70	m²	28.27
girth exceeding 300mm; panes, area 0.10 - 0.50m²	1.01	10.00	1.11	0.79	-	16.49	0.87	18.46	m²	20.31

Labour hourly rates: (except Specialists) Craft Operatives 20.87 Labourer 15.57 Rates are national average prices. Refer to REGIONAL VARIATIONS for indicative levels of overall pricing in regions	MATERIALS			LABOUR				RATES		
	Del to Site £	Waste %	Material Cost £	Craft Optve Hrs	Lab Hrs	Labour Cost £	Sunds £	Nett Rate £	Unit	Gross rate (10%) £
PAINTING & CLEAR FINISHINGS; WATER BASED PAINTING WOODWORK (Cont'd)										
One coat primer, one undercoat, two coats water based gloss finish on wood surfaces (Cont'd)										
Wood glazed doors (Cont'd)										
girth exceeding 300mm; panes, area 0.50 - 1.00m²	0.96	10.00	1.06	0.66	-	13.77	0.73	15.56	m²	17.11
girth exceeding 300mm; panes, area exceeding 1.00m²	0.96	10.00	1.06	0.59	-	12.31	0.65	14.02	m²	15.42
PAINTING & CLEAR FINISHINGS; POLYURETHANE LACQUER										
Two coats polyurethane lacquer										
Wood general surfaces										
girth exceeding 300mm	1.04	10.00	1.14	0.44	-	9.18	0.48	10.81	m²	11.89
isolated surfaces, girth not exceeding 300mm	0.31	10.00	0.34	0.14	-	2.92	0.15	3.42	m	3.76
Wood glazed doors										
girth exceeding 300mm; panes, area not exceeding 0.10m²	0.59	10.00	0.65	0.74	-	15.44	0.81	16.90	m²	18.59
girth exceeding 300mm; panes, area 0.10 - 0.50m²	0.41	10.00	0.46	0.53	-	11.06	0.58	12.10	m²	13.31
girth exceeding 300mm; panes, area 0.50 - 1.00m²	0.38	10.00	0.42	0.44	-	9.18	0.48	10.09	m²	11.09
girth exceeding 300mm; panes, area exceeding 1.00m²	0.38	10.00	0.42	0.40	-	8.35	0.44	9.21	m²	10.13
Wood partially glazed doors										
girth exceeding 300mm; panes, area not exceeding 0.10m²	0.83	10.00	0.91	0.59	-	12.31	0.65	13.87	m²	15.26
girth exceeding 300mm; panes, area 0.10 - 0.50m²	0.62	10.00	0.68	0.48	-	10.02	0.53	11.23	m²	12.35
girth exceeding 300mm; panes, area 0.50 - 1.00m²	0.59	10.00	0.65	0.44	-	9.18	0.48	10.31	m²	11.34
girth exceeding 300mm; panes, area exceeding 1.00m²	0.59	10.00	0.65	0.42	-	8.77	0.46	9.87	m²	10.86
Wood windows and screens										
girth exceeding 300mm; panes, area not exceeding 0.10m²	0.83	10.00	0.91	0.81	-	16.90	0.89	18.71	m²	20.58
girth exceeding 300mm; panes, area 0.10 - 0.50m²	0.62	10.00	0.68	0.58	-	12.10	0.64	13.43	m²	14.77
girth exceeding 300mm; panes, area 0.50 - 1.00m²	0.59	10.00	0.65	0.48	-	10.02	0.53	11.19	m²	12.31
girth exceeding 300mm; panes, area exceeding 1.00m²	0.59	10.00	0.65	0.44	-	9.18	0.48	10.31	m²	11.34
Two coats polyurethane lacquer; external work										
Wood general surfaces										
girth exceeding 300mm	1.04	10.00	1.14	0.46	-	9.60	0.51	11.25	m²	12.37
isolated surfaces, girth not exceeding 300mm	0.31	10.00	0.34	0.15	-	3.13	0.17	3.64	m	4.00
Wood glazed doors										
girth exceeding 300mm; panes, area not exceeding 0.10m²	0.59	10.00	0.65	0.74	-	15.44	0.81	16.90	m²	18.59
girth exceeding 300mm; panes, area 0.10 - 0.50m²	0.41	10.00	0.46	0.53	-	11.06	0.58	12.10	m²	13.31
girth exceeding 300mm; panes, area 0.50 - 1.00m²	0.38	10.00	0.42	0.44	-	9.18	0.48	10.09	m²	11.09
girth exceeding 300mm; panes, area exceeding 1.00m²	0.38	10.00	0.42	0.40	-	8.35	0.44	9.21	m²	10.13
Wood partially glazed doors										
girth exceeding 300mm; panes, area not exceeding 0.10m²	0.83	10.00	0.91	0.59	-	12.31	0.65	13.87	m²	15.26
girth exceeding 300mm; panes, area 0.10 - 0.50m²	0.62	10.00	0.68	0.48	-	10.02	0.53	11.23	m²	12.35
girth exceeding 300mm; panes, area 0.50 - 1.00m²	0.59	10.00	0.65	0.44	-	9.18	0.48	10.31	m²	11.34
girth exceeding 300mm; panes, area exceeding 1.00m²	0.59	10.00	0.65	0.42	-	8.77	0.46	9.87	m²	10.86
Wood windows and screens										
girth exceeding 300mm; panes, area not exceeding 0.10m²	0.83	10.00	0.91	0.84	-	17.53	0.92	19.37	m²	21.30
girth exceeding 300mm; panes, area 0.10 - 0.50m²	0.62	10.00	0.68	0.61	-	12.73	0.67	14.09	m²	15.49
girth exceeding 300mm; panes, area 0.50 - 1.00m²	0.59	10.00	0.65	0.51	-	10.64	0.56	11.85	m²	13.04
girth exceeding 300mm; panes, area exceeding 1.00m²	0.59	10.00	0.65	0.46	-	9.60	0.51	10.75	m²	11.83
Three coats polyurethane lacquer										
Wood general surfaces										
girth exceeding 300mm	1.52	10.00	1.67	0.52	-	10.85	0.57	13.10	m²	14.41
isolated surfaces, girth not exceeding 300mm	0.45	10.00	0.49	0.18	-	3.76	0.20	4.45	m	4.89
Wood glazed doors										
girth exceeding 300mm; panes, area not exceeding 0.10m²	0.86	10.00	0.95	0.86	-	17.95	0.95	19.84	m²	21.83
girth exceeding 300mm; panes, area 0.10 - 0.50m²	0.62	10.00	0.68	0.62	-	12.94	0.68	14.31	m²	15.74
girth exceeding 300mm; panes, area 0.50 - 1.00m²	0.55	10.00	0.61	0.52	-	10.85	0.57	12.03	m²	13.24
girth exceeding 300mm; panes, area exceeding 1.00m²	0.55	10.00	0.61	0.46	-	9.60	0.51	10.71	m²	11.79
Wood partially glazed doors										
girth exceeding 300mm; panes, area not exceeding 0.10m²	1.21	10.00	1.33	0.69	-	14.40	0.76	16.49	m²	18.14
girth exceeding 300mm; panes, area 0.10 - 0.50m²	0.90	10.00	0.99	0.63	-	13.15	0.69	14.83	m²	16.31
girth exceeding 300mm; panes, area 0.50 - 1.00m²	0.83	10.00	0.91	0.52	-	10.85	0.57	12.34	m²	13.57
girth exceeding 300mm; panes, area exceeding 1.00m²	0.83	10.00	0.91	0.50	-	10.44	0.55	11.90	m²	13.09
Wood windows and screens										
girth exceeding 300mm; panes, area not exceeding 0.10m²	0.86	10.00	0.95	0.95	-	19.83	1.05	21.82	m²	24.00
girth exceeding 300mm; panes, area 0.10 - 0.50m²	0.62	10.00	0.68	0.68	-	14.19	0.75	15.62	m²	17.19
girth exceeding 300mm; panes, area 0.50 - 1.00m²	0.55	10.00	0.61	0.57	-	11.90	0.63	13.13	m²	14.44
girth exceeding 300mm; panes, area exceeding 1.00m²	0.55	10.00	0.61	0.51	-	10.64	0.56	11.81	m²	12.99
Three coats polyurethane lacquer; external work										
Wood general surfaces										
girth exceeding 300mm	1.52	10.00	1.67	0.55	-	11.48	0.61	13.76	m²	15.13
isolated surfaces, girth not exceeding 300mm	0.45	10.00	0.49	0.19	-	3.97	0.21	4.67	m	5.14
Wood glazed doors										
girth exceeding 300mm; panes, area not exceeding 0.10m²	0.86	10.00	0.95	0.86	-	17.95	0.95	19.84	m²	21.83
girth exceeding 300mm; panes, area 0.10 - 0.50m²	0.62	10.00	0.68	0.62	-	12.94	0.68	14.31	m²	15.74
girth exceeding 300mm; panes, area 0.50 - 1.00m²	0.55	10.00	0.61	0.52	-	10.85	0.57	12.03	m²	13.24
girth exceeding 300mm; panes, area exceeding 1.00m²	0.55	10.00	0.61	0.46	-	9.60	0.51	10.71	m²	11.79
Wood partially glazed doors										
girth exceeding 300mm; panes, area not exceeding 0.10m²	1.21	10.00	1.33	0.69	-	14.40	0.76	16.49	m²	18.14
girth exceeding 300mm; panes, area 0.10 - 0.50m²	0.90	10.00	0.99	0.63	-	13.15	0.69	14.83	m²	16.31
girth exceeding 300mm; panes, area 0.50 - 1.00m²	0.83	10.00	0.91	0.52	-	10.85	0.57	12.34	m²	13.57

Labour hourly rates: (except Specialists) Craft Operatives 20.87 Labourer 15.57 Rates are national average prices. Refer to REGIONAL VARIATIONS for indicative levels of overall pricing in regions	MATERIALS			LABOUR				RATES		
	Del to Site £	Waste %	Material Cost £	Craft Optve Hrs	Lab Hrs	Labour Cost £	Sunds £	Nett Rate £	Unit	Gross rate (10%) £
PAINTING & CLEAR FINISHINGS; POLYURETHANE LACQUER (Cont'd)										
Three coats polyurethane lacquer; external work (Cont'd)										
Wood partially glazed doors (Cont'd)										
girth exceeding 300mm; panes, area exceeding 1.00m²	0.83	10.00	0.91	0.50	-	10.44	0.55	11.90	m²	13.09
Wood windows and screens										
girth exceeding 300mm; panes, area not exceeding 0.10m²	0.86	10.00	0.95	0.98	-	20.45	1.08	22.48	m²	24.73
girth exceeding 300mm; panes, area 0.10 - 0.50m²	0.62	10.00	0.68	0.72	-	15.03	0.79	16.50	m²	18.15
girth exceeding 300mm; panes, area 0.50 - 1.00m²	0.55	10.00	0.61	0.61	-	12.73	0.67	14.01	m²	15.41
girth exceeding 300mm; panes, area exceeding 1.00m²	0.55	10.00	0.61	0.54	-	11.27	0.59	12.47	m²	13.72
PAINTING & CLEAR FINISHINGS; FIRE RETARDANT PAINTS AND VARNISHES										
Two coats fire retardant paint										
Wood general surfaces										
girth exceeding 300mm	6.93	10.00	7.62	0.40	-	8.35	0.44	16.41	m²	18.05
isolated surfaces, girth not exceeding 300mm	2.10	10.00	2.31	0.13	-	2.71	0.14	5.17	m	5.68
Two coats fire retardant varnish, one overcoat varnish										
Wood general surfaces										
girth exceeding 300mm	11.20	10.00	12.32	0.54	-	11.27	0.59	24.18	m²	26.60
isolated surfaces, girth not exceeding 300mm	3.42	10.00	3.76	0.18	-	3.76	0.20	7.72	m	8.49
PAINTING & CLEAR FINISHINGS; OILING HARDWOOD										
Two coats raw linseed oil										
Wood general surfaces										
girth exceeding 300mm	1.85	10.00	2.04	0.44	-	9.18	0.48	11.70	m²	12.87
isolated surfaces, girth not exceeding 300mm	0.55	10.00	0.61	0.15	-	3.13	0.17	3.90	m	4.29
PAINTING & CLEAR FINISHINGS; FRENCH AND WAX POLISHING										
Stain; two coats white polish										
Wood general surfaces										
girth exceeding 300mm	6.35	10.00	6.98	0.56	-	11.69	0.62	19.29	m²	21.22
isolated surfaces, girth not exceeding 300mm	2.00	10.00	2.20	0.19	-	3.97	0.21	6.38	m	7.02
Open grain French polish										
Wood general surfaces										
girth exceeding 300mm	6.93	10.00	7.63	2.64	-	55.10	2.90	65.63	m²	72.19
isolated surfaces, girth not exceeding 300mm	2.19	10.00	2.41	0.88	-	18.37	0.97	21.74	m	23.91
Stain; body in; fully French polish										
Wood general surfaces										
girth exceeding 300mm	11.06	10.00	12.16	3.96	-	82.65	4.36	99.16	m²	109.08
isolated surfaces, girth not exceeding 300mm	3.49	10.00	3.84	1.32	-	27.55	1.45	32.84	m	36.12
PAINTING & CLEAR FINISHINGS; ROAD MARKINGS										
One coat solvent based road marking paint; external work										
Concrete general surfaces										
isolated surfaces, 50mm wide	0.17	5.00	0.18	0.10	-	2.09	0.11	2.38	m	2.62
isolated surfaces, 100mm wide	0.34	5.00	0.36	0.12	-	2.50	0.13	3.00	m	3.30
Two coats solvent based road marking paint; external work										
Concrete general surfaces										
isolated surfaces, 50mm wide	0.34	5.00	0.36	0.15	-	3.13	0.17	3.66	m	4.02
isolated surfaces, 100mm wide	0.69	5.00	0.72	0.18	-	3.76	0.20	4.68	m	5.15
Prime and apply non-reflective self adhesive road marking tape; external work										
Concrete general surfaces										
isolated surfaces, 50mm wide	1.38	5.00	1.45	0.10	-	2.09	0.11	3.65	m	4.01
isolated surfaces, 100mm wide	1.51	5.00	1.58	0.13	-	2.71	0.14	4.44	m	4.88
Prime and apply reflective self adhesive road marking tape; external work										
Concrete general surfaces										
isolated surfaces, 50mm wide	2.25	5.00	2.36	0.10	-	2.09	0.11	4.56	m	5.01
isolated surfaces, 100mm wide	1.86	5.00	1.95	0.13	-	2.71	0.14	4.80	m	5.29
PAINTING & CLEAR FINISHINGS; REDECORATIONS: EMULSION PAINTING										
Generally										
Note: the following rates include for the cost of all preparatory work, e.g. washing down, etc.										
Two coats emulsion paint, existing emulsion painted surfaces										
Concrete general surfaces										
girth exceeding 300mm	0.29	10.00	0.32	0.32	-	6.68	0.35	7.35	m²	8.08
Plaster general surfaces										
girth exceeding 300mm	0.23	10.00	0.25	0.28	-	5.84	0.31	6.41	m²	7.05

Labour hourly rates: (except Specialists) Craft Operatives 20.87 Labourer 15.57 Rates are national average prices. Refer to REGIONAL VARIATIONS for indicative levels of overall pricing in regions	MATERIALS			LABOUR				RATES		
	Del to Site £	Waste %	Material Cost £	Craft Optve Hrs	Lab Hrs	Labour Cost £	Sunds £	Nett Rate £	Unit	Gross rate (10%) £
PAINTING & CLEAR FINISHINGS; REDECORATIONS: EMULSION PAINTING (Cont'd)										
Two coats emulsion paint, existing emulsion painted surfaces (Cont'd)										
Plasterboard general surfaces girth exceeding 300mm	0.23	10.00	0.25	0.29	-	6.05	0.32	6.62	m²	7.29
Brickwork general surfaces girth exceeding 300mm	0.29	10.00	0.32	0.32	-	6.68	0.35	7.35	m²	8.08
Paper covered general surfaces girth exceeding 300mm	0.23	10.00	0.25	0.30	-	6.26	0.33	6.84	m²	7.53
Two full coats emulsion paint, existing washable distempered surfaces										
Concrete general surfaces girth exceeding 300mm	0.29	10.00	0.32	0.33	-	6.89	0.36	7.57	m²	8.33
Plaster general surfaces girth exceeding 300mm	0.23	10.00	0.25	0.29	-	6.05	0.32	6.62	m²	7.29
Plasterboard general surfaces girth exceeding 300mm	0.23	10.00	0.25	0.30	-	6.26	0.33	6.84	m²	7.53
Brickwork general surfaces girth exceeding 300mm	0.29	10.00	0.32	0.33	-	6.89	0.36	7.57	m²	8.33
Paper covered general surfaces girth exceeding 300mm	0.23	10.00	0.25	0.30	-	6.26	0.33	6.84	m²	7.53
Two full coats emulsion paint, existing textured plastic coating surfaces										
Concrete general surfaces girth exceeding 300mm	0.29	10.00	0.32	0.36	-	7.51	0.40	8.23	m²	9.05
Plaster general surfaces girth exceeding 300mm	0.23	10.00	0.25	0.32	-	6.68	0.35	7.28	m²	8.01
Plasterboard general surfaces girth exceeding 300mm	0.23	10.00	0.25	0.33	-	6.89	0.36	7.50	m²	8.25
Brickwork general surfaces girth exceeding 300mm	0.30	10.00	0.33	0.36	-	7.51	0.40	8.24	m²	9.06
Paper covered general surfaces girth exceeding 300mm	0.23	10.00	0.25	0.33	-	6.89	0.36	7.50	m²	8.25
Mist coat, two full coats emulsion paint, existing non-washable distempered surfaces										
Concrete general surfaces girth exceeding 300mm	0.36	10.00	0.39	0.38	-	7.93	0.42	8.74	m²	9.62
Plaster general surfaces girth exceeding 300mm	0.29	10.00	0.32	0.34	-	7.10	0.37	7.79	m²	8.57
Plasterboard general surfaces girth exceeding 300mm	0.29	10.00	0.32	0.35	-	7.30	0.39	8.01	m²	8.81
Brickwork general surfaces girth exceeding 300mm	0.36	10.00	0.39	0.38	-	7.93	0.42	8.74	m²	9.62
Paper covered general surfaces girth exceeding 300mm	0.29	10.00	0.32	0.35	-	7.30	0.39	8.01	m²	8.81
Two full coats emulsion paint, existing gloss painted surfaces										
Concrete general surfaces girth exceeding 300mm	0.29	10.00	0.32	0.33	-	6.89	0.36	7.57	m²	8.33
Plaster general surfaces girth exceeding 300mm	0.23	10.00	0.25	0.29	-	6.05	0.32	6.62	m²	7.29
Plasterboard general surfaces girth exceeding 300mm	0.23	10.00	0.25	0.30	-	6.26	0.33	6.84	m²	7.53
Brickwork general surfaces girth exceeding 300mm	0.30	10.00	0.33	0.33	-	6.89	0.36	7.58	m²	8.34
Paper covered general surfaces girth exceeding 300mm	0.23	10.00	0.25	0.30	-	6.26	0.33	6.84	m²	7.53
PAINTING & CLEAR FINISHINGS; REDECORATIONS: CEMENT PAINTING										
Generally										
Note: the following rates include for the cost of all preparatory work, e.g. washing down, etc.										
One coat sealer, one coat waterproof cement paint; external work										
Cement rendered general surfaces girth exceeding 300mm	2.67	10.00	2.93	0.36	-	7.51	0.40	10.84	m²	11.93
Concrete general surfaces girth exceeding 300mm	2.47	10.00	2.72	0.43	-	8.97	0.47	12.17	m²	13.39

Labour hourly rates: (except Specialists) Craft Operatives 20.87 Labourer 15.57 Rates are national average prices. Refer to REGIONAL VARIATIONS for indicative levels of overall pricing in regions	MATERIALS			LABOUR				RATES		
	Del to Site £	Waste %	Material Cost £	Craft Optve Hrs	Lab Hrs	Labour Cost £	Sunds £	Nett Rate £	Unit	Gross rate (10%) £
PAINTING & CLEAR FINISHINGS; REDECORATIONS: CEMENT PAINTING (Cont'd)										
One coat sealer, one coat waterproof cement paint; external work (Cont'd)										
Brickwork general surfaces girth exceeding 300mm	2.57	10.00	2.83	0.43	-	8.97	0.47	12.28	m²	13.50
Rough cast general surfaces girth exceeding 300mm	2.67	10.00	2.93	0.52	-	10.85	0.57	14.36	m²	15.80
Two coats sealer, one coat waterproof cement paint; external work										
Cement rendered general surfaces girth exceeding 300mm	3.96	10.00	4.36	0.47	-	9.81	0.52	14.68	m²	16.15
Concrete general surfaces girth exceeding 300mm	3.37	10.00	3.70	0.58	-	12.10	0.64	16.45	m²	18.09
Brickwork general surfaces girth exceeding 300mm	3.86	10.00	4.25	0.58	-	12.10	0.64	16.99	m²	18.69
Rough cast general surfaces girth exceeding 300mm	3.96	10.00	4.36	0.70	-	14.61	0.77	19.74	m²	21.71
One coat waterproof cement paint existing cement painted surfaces; external work										
Cement rendered general surfaces girth exceeding 300mm	0.60	10.00	0.66	0.27	-	5.63	0.30	6.60	m²	7.25
Concrete general surfaces girth exceeding 300mm	0.60	10.00	0.66	0.34	-	7.10	0.37	8.13	m²	8.95
Brickwork general surfaces girth exceeding 300mm	0.70	10.00	0.77	0.34	-	7.10	0.37	8.24	m²	9.06
Rough cast general surfaces girth exceeding 300mm	0.80	10.00	0.88	0.44	-	9.18	0.48	10.54	m²	11.60
Two coats waterproof cement paint existing cement painted surfaces; external work										
Cement rendered general surfaces girth exceeding 300mm	1.59	10.00	1.75	0.38	-	7.93	0.42	10.10	m²	11.11
Concrete general surfaces girth exceeding 300mm	1.21	10.00	1.33	0.49	-	10.23	0.54	12.09	m²	13.30
Brickwork general surfaces girth exceeding 300mm	1.40	10.00	1.54	0.49	-	10.23	0.54	12.30	m²	13.53
Rough cast general surfaces girth exceeding 300mm	1.59	10.00	1.75	0.60	-	12.52	0.66	14.93	m²	16.43
One coat stabilizing solution, one coat textured masonry paint, existing undecorated surfaces; external work										
Cement rendered general surfaces girth exceeding 300mm	0.96	10.00	1.05	0.35	-	7.30	0.39	8.74	m²	9.62
Concrete general surfaces girth exceeding 300mm	1.18	10.00	1.30	0.42	-	8.77	0.46	10.53	m²	11.58
Brickwork general surfaces girth exceeding 300mm	1.79	10.00	1.97	0.42	-	8.77	0.46	11.20	m²	12.32
Rough cast general surfaces girth exceeding 300mm	2.24	10.00	2.47	0.52	-	10.85	0.57	13.89	m²	15.28
One coat stabilizing solution, two coats textured masonry paint, existing undecorated surfaces; external work										
Cement rendered general surfaces girth exceeding 300mm	1.96	10.00	2.16	0.47	-	9.81	0.52	12.48	m²	13.73
Concrete general surfaces girth exceeding 300mm	1.96	10.00	2.16	0.57	-	11.90	0.63	14.68	m²	16.15
Brickwork general surfaces girth exceeding 300mm	3.19	10.00	3.51	0.57	-	11.90	0.63	16.03	m²	17.64
Rough cast general surfaces girth exceeding 300mm	4.08	10.00	4.49	0.70	-	14.61	0.77	19.87	m²	21.86
One coat textured masonry paint, existing cement painted surfaces; external work										
Cement rendered general surfaces girth exceeding 300mm	0.56	10.00	0.61	0.26	-	5.43	0.29	6.33	m²	6.96
Concrete general surfaces girth exceeding 300mm	0.78	10.00	0.86	0.33	-	6.89	0.36	8.11	m²	8.92
Brickwork general surfaces girth exceeding 300mm	1.40	10.00	1.54	0.33	-	6.89	0.36	8.79	m²	9.66
Rough cast general surfaces girth exceeding 300mm	1.84	10.00	2.03	0.43	-	8.97	0.47	11.47	m²	12.62

Labour hourly rates: (except Specialists) Craft Operatives 20.87 Labourer 15.57 Rates are national average prices. Refer to REGIONAL VARIATIONS for indicative levels of overall pricing in regions	MATERIALS			LABOUR				RATES		
	Del to Site £	Waste %	Material Cost £	Craft Optve Hrs	Lab Hrs	Labour Cost £	Sunds £	Nett Rate £	Unit	Gross rate (10%) £
PAINTING & CLEAR FINISHINGS; REDECORATIONS: CEMENT PAINTING (Cont'd)										
Two coats textured masonry paint, existing cement painted surfaces; external work										
Cement rendered general surfaces girth exceeding 300mm	1.56	10.00	1.72	0.39	-	8.14	0.43	10.29	m²	11.32
Concrete general surfaces girth exceeding 300mm	1.56	10.00	1.72	0.48	-	10.02	0.53	12.26	m²	13.49
Brickwork general surfaces girth exceeding 300mm	2.79	10.00	3.07	0.48	-	10.02	0.53	13.62	m²	14.98
Rough cast general surfaces girth exceeding 300mm	3.68	10.00	4.05	0.62	-	12.94	0.68	17.67	m²	19.44
PAINTING & CLEAR FINISHINGS; REDECORATIONS: OIL PAINTING WALLS AND CEILINGS										
Generally										
Note: the following rates include for the cost of all preparatory work, e.g. washing down, etc.										
One undercoat, one coat full gloss finish, existing gloss painted surfaces										
Concrete general surfaces girth exceeding 300mm	0.78	10.00	0.86	0.38	-	7.93	0.42	9.21	m²	10.13
Brickwork general surfaces girth exceeding 300mm	0.85	10.00	0.93	0.39	-	8.14	0.43	9.50	m²	10.45
Plasterboard general surfaces girth exceeding 300mm	0.72	10.00	0.79	0.35	-	7.30	0.39	8.48	m²	9.33
Plaster general surfaces girth exceeding 300mm	0.72	10.00	0.79	0.34	-	7.10	0.37	8.26	m²	9.09
One undercoat, one coat eggshell finish, existing gloss painted surfaces										
Concrete general surfaces girth exceeding 300mm	0.85	10.00	0.93	0.38	-	7.93	0.42	9.28	m²	10.21
Brickwork general surfaces girth exceeding 300mm	1.07	10.00	1.17	0.39	-	8.14	0.43	9.74	m²	10.71
Plasterboard general surfaces girth exceeding 300mm	0.79	10.00	0.86	0.35	-	7.30	0.39	8.55	m²	9.41
Plaster general surfaces girth exceeding 300mm	0.79	10.00	0.86	0.34	-	7.10	0.37	8.33	m²	9.17
Two undercoats, one coat full gloss finish, existing gloss painted surfaces										
Concrete general surfaces girth exceeding 300mm	1.12	10.00	1.23	0.48	-	10.02	0.53	11.78	m²	12.96
Brickwork general surfaces girth exceeding 300mm	1.35	10.00	1.48	0.48	-	10.02	0.53	12.03	m²	13.23
Plasterboard general surfaces girth exceeding 300mm	1.06	10.00	1.17	0.45	-	9.39	0.50	11.05	m²	12.16
Plaster general surfaces girth exceeding 300mm	1.06	10.00	1.17	0.44	-	9.18	0.48	10.84	m²	11.92
Two undercoats, one coat eggshell finish, existing gloss painted surfaces										
Concrete general surfaces girth exceeding 300mm	1.19	10.00	1.31	0.48	-	10.02	0.53	11.86	m²	13.04
Brickwork general surfaces girth exceeding 300mm	1.43	10.00	1.58	0.48	-	10.02	0.53	12.12	m²	13.33
Plasterboard general surfaces girth exceeding 300mm	1.13	10.00	1.24	0.45	-	9.39	0.50	11.13	m²	12.24
Plaster general surfaces girth exceeding 300mm	1.13	10.00	1.24	0.44	-	9.18	0.48	10.91	m²	12.00
One coat primer, one undercoat, one coat full gloss finish, existing washable distempered or emulsion painted surfaces										
Concrete general surfaces girth exceeding 300mm	1.99	10.00	2.19	0.48	-	10.02	0.53	12.73	m²	14.01
Brickwork general surfaces girth exceeding 300mm	2.33	10.00	2.56	0.48	-	10.02	0.53	13.11	m²	14.42
Plasterboard general surfaces girth exceeding 300mm	1.82	10.00	2.00	0.45	-	9.39	0.50	11.89	m²	13.08
Plaster general surfaces girth exceeding 300mm	1.82	10.00	2.00	0.44	-	9.18	0.48	11.67	m²	12.84

Labour hourly rates: (except Specialists) Craft Operatives 20.87 Labourer 15.57 Rates are national average prices. Refer to REGIONAL VARIATIONS for indicative levels of overall pricing in regions	MATERIALS			LABOUR				RATES		
	Del to Site £	Waste %	Material Cost £	Craft Optve Hrs	Lab Hrs	Labour Cost £	Sunds £	Nett Rate £	Unit	Gross rate (10%) £
PAINTING & CLEAR FINISHINGS; REDECORATIONS: OIL PAINTING WALLS AND CEILINGS (Cont'd)										
One coat primer, one undercoat, one coat eggshell finish, existing washable distempered or emulsion painted surfaces										
Concrete general surfaces girth exceeding 300mm	2.06	10.00	2.26	0.48	-	10.02	0.53	12.81	m²	14.09
Brickwork general surfaces girth exceeding 300mm	2.55	10.00	2.80	0.48	-	10.02	0.53	13.35	m²	14.68
Plasterboard general surfaces girth exceeding 300mm	1.89	10.00	2.07	0.45	-	9.39	0.50	11.96	m²	13.16
Plaster general surfaces girth exceeding 300mm	1.89	10.00	2.07	0.44	-	9.18	0.48	11.74	m²	12.91
One coat primer, two undercoats, one coat full gloss finish, existing washable distempered or emulsion painted surfaces										
Concrete general surfaces girth exceeding 300mm	2.33	10.00	2.56	0.58	-	12.10	0.64	15.30	m²	16.84
Brickwork general surfaces girth exceeding 300mm	2.83	10.00	3.11	0.59	-	12.31	0.65	16.08	m²	17.68
Plasterboard general surfaces girth exceeding 300mm	2.16	10.00	2.38	0.55	-	11.48	0.61	14.46	m²	15.91
Plaster general surfaces girth exceeding 300mm	2.16	10.00	2.38	0.54	-	11.27	0.59	14.24	m²	15.67
One coat primer, two undercoats, one coat eggshell finish, existing washable distempered or emulsion painted surfaces										
Concrete general surfaces girth exceeding 300mm	2.40	10.00	2.64	0.58	-	12.10	0.64	15.38	m²	16.92
Brickwork general surfaces girth exceeding 300mm	2.92	10.00	3.21	0.59	-	12.31	0.65	16.17	m²	17.79
Plasterboard general surfaces girth exceeding 300mm	2.23	10.00	2.45	0.55	-	11.48	0.61	14.53	m²	15.99
Plaster general surfaces girth exceeding 300mm	2.23	10.00	2.45	0.54	-	11.27	0.59	14.31	m²	15.74
One coat primer, one undercoat, one coat full gloss finish, existing non-washable distempered surfaces										
Concrete general surfaces girth exceeding 300mm	1.99	10.00	2.19	0.48	-	10.02	0.53	12.73	m²	14.01
Brickwork general surfaces girth exceeding 300mm	2.33	10.00	2.56	0.48	-	10.02	0.53	13.11	m²	14.42
Plasterboard general surfaces girth exceeding 300mm	1.82	10.00	2.00	0.45	-	9.39	0.50	11.89	m²	13.08
Plaster general surfaces girth exceeding 300mm	1.82	10.00	2.00	0.44	-	9.18	0.48	11.67	m²	12.84
One coat primer, one undercoat, one coat eggshell finish, existing non-washable distempered surfaces										
Concrete general surfaces girth exceeding 300mm	2.06	10.00	2.26	0.48	-	10.02	0.53	12.81	m²	14.09
Brickwork general surfaces girth exceeding 300mm	2.55	10.00	2.80	0.48	-	10.02	0.53	13.35	m²	14.68
Plasterboard general surfaces girth exceeding 300mm	1.89	10.00	2.07	0.45	-	9.39	0.50	11.96	m²	13.16
Plaster general surfaces girth exceeding 300mm	1.89	10.00	2.07	0.44	-	9.18	0.48	11.74	m²	12.91
One coat primer, two undercoats, one coat full gloss finish, existing non-washable distempered surfaces										
Concrete general surfaces girth exceeding 300mm	2.33	10.00	2.56	0.58	-	12.10	0.64	15.30	m²	16.84
Brickwork general surfaces girth exceeding 300mm	2.83	10.00	3.11	0.59	-	12.31	0.65	16.08	m²	17.68
Plasterboard general surfaces girth exceeding 300mm	2.16	10.00	2.38	0.55	-	11.48	0.61	14.46	m²	15.91
Plaster general surfaces girth exceeding 300mm	2.16	10.00	2.38	0.54	-	11.27	0.59	14.24	m²	15.67
One coat primer, two undercoats, one coat eggshell finish, existing non-washable distempered surfaces										
Concrete general surfaces girth exceeding 300mm	2.40	10.00	2.64	0.58	-	12.10	0.64	15.38	m²	16.92
Brickwork general surfaces girth exceeding 300mm	2.92	10.00	3.21	0.59	-	12.31	0.65	16.17	m²	17.79
Plasterboard general surfaces girth exceeding 300mm	2.23	10.00	2.45	0.55	-	11.48	0.61	14.53	m²	15.99

Labour hourly rates: (except Specialists) Craft Operatives 20.87 Labourer 15.57 Rates are national average prices. Refer to REGIONAL VARIATIONS for indicative levels of overall pricing in regions	MATERIALS			LABOUR				RATES		
	Del to Site £	Waste %	Material Cost £	Craft Optve Hrs	Lab Hrs	Labour Cost £	Sunds £	Nett Rate £	Unit	Gross rate (10%) £
PAINTING & CLEAR FINISHINGS; REDECORATIONS: OIL PAINTING WALLS AND CEILINGS (Cont'd)										
One coat primer, two undercoats, one coat eggshell finish, existing non-washable distempered surfaces (Cont'd)										
Plaster general surfaces girth exceeding 300mm	2.23	10.00	2.45	0.54	-	11.27	0.59	14.31	m²	15.74
PAINTING & CLEAR FINISHINGS; REDECORATIONS: PLASTIC FINISH										
Generally										
Note: the following rates include for the cost of all preparatory work, e.g. washing down, etc.										
Textured plastic coating - stippled finish, existing washable distempered or emulsion painted surfaces										
Concrete general surfaces girth exceeding 300mm	0.89	10.00	0.98	0.40	-	8.35	0.44	9.77	m²	10.75
Brickwork general surfaces girth exceeding 300mm	1.07	10.00	1.17	0.45	-	9.39	0.50	11.06	m²	12.17
Plasterboard general surfaces girth exceeding 300mm	0.80	10.00	0.88	0.34	-	7.10	0.37	8.35	m²	9.18
Plaster general surfaces girth exceeding 300mm	0.80	10.00	0.88	0.34	-	7.10	0.37	8.35	m²	9.18
Textured plastic coating - combed finish, existing washable distempered or emulsion painted surfaces										
Concrete general surfaces girth exceeding 300mm	1.07	10.00	1.17	0.45	-	9.39	0.50	11.06	m²	12.17
Brickwork general surfaces girth exceeding 300mm	1.28	10.00	1.41	0.50	-	10.44	0.55	12.39	m²	13.63
Plasterboard general surfaces girth exceeding 300mm	0.96	10.00	1.06	0.40	-	8.35	0.44	9.84	m²	10.83
Plaster general surfaces girth exceeding 300mm	0.96	10.00	1.06	0.40	-	8.35	0.44	9.84	m²	10.83
Textured plastic coating - stippled finish, existing non-washable distempered surfaces										
Concrete general surfaces girth exceeding 300mm	0.89	10.00	0.98	0.45	-	9.39	0.50	10.87	m²	11.96
Brickwork general surfaces girth exceeding 300mm	1.07	10.00	1.17	0.50	-	10.44	0.55	12.16	m²	13.37
Plasterboard general surfaces girth exceeding 300mm	0.80	10.00	0.88	0.40	-	8.35	0.44	9.67	m²	10.63
Plaster general surfaces girth exceeding 300mm	0.80	10.00	0.88	0.40	-	8.35	0.44	9.67	m²	10.63
Textured plastic coating - combed finish, existing non-washable distempered surfaces										
Concrete general surfaces girth exceeding 300mm	1.07	10.00	1.17	0.50	-	10.44	0.55	12.16	m²	13.37
Brickwork general surfaces girth exceeding 300mm	1.28	10.00	1.41	0.56	-	11.69	0.62	13.71	m²	15.08
Plasterboard general surfaces girth exceeding 300mm	0.96	10.00	1.06	0.45	-	9.39	0.50	10.94	m²	12.04
Plaster general surfaces girth exceeding 300mm	0.96	10.00	1.06	0.45	-	9.39	0.50	10.94	m²	12.04
PAINTING & CLEAR FINISHINGS; REDECORATIONS: CLEAN OUT GUTTERS										
Generally										
Note: the following rates include for the cost of all preparatory work, e.g. washing down, etc.										
Clean out gutters prior to repainting, staunch joints with red lead, bituminous compound or mastic										
Iron or steel eaves gutters generally	-	-	-	0.06	-	1.25	0.10	1.35	m	1.49
PAINTING & CLEAR FINISHINGS; REDECORATIONS: OIL PAINTING METALWORK										
Generally										
Note: the following rates include for the cost of all preparatory work, e.g. washing down, etc.										

Labour hourly rates: (except Specialists) Craft Operatives 20.87 Labourer 15.57 Rates are national average prices. Refer to REGIONAL VARIATIONS for indicative levels of overall pricing in regions	MATERIALS			LABOUR				RATES		
	Del to Site £	Waste %	Material Cost £	Craft Optve Hrs	Lab Hrs	Labour Cost £	Sunds £	Nett Rate £	Unit	Gross rate (10%) £
PAINTING & CLEAR FINISHINGS; REDECORATIONS: OIL PAINTING METALWORK (Cont'd)										
One undercoat, one coat full gloss finish, existing gloss painted metal surfaces										
Iron or steel general surfaces										
girth exceeding 300mm	0.75	10.00	0.83	0.47	-	9.81	0.52	11.15	m²	12.27
isolated surfaces, girth not exceeding 300mm	0.23	10.00	0.25	0.16	-	3.34	0.18	3.77	m	4.15
Galvanised glazed doors, windows or screens										
girth exceeding 300mm; panes, area not exceeding 0.10m²	0.41	10.00	0.45	0.88	-	18.37	0.97	19.78	m²	21.76
girth exceeding 300mm; panes, area 0.10 - 0.50m²	0.29	10.00	0.32	0.64	-	13.36	0.70	14.38	m²	15.82
girth exceeding 300mm; panes, area 0.50 - 1.00m²	0.23	10.00	0.25	0.53	-	11.06	0.58	11.90	m²	13.09
girth exceeding 300mm; panes, area exceeding 1.00m²	0.23	10.00	0.25	0.46	-	9.60	0.51	10.36	m²	11.40
Iron or steel structural work										
girth exceeding 300mm	0.75	10.00	0.83	0.52	-	10.85	0.57	12.25	m²	13.48
isolated surfaces, girth not exceeding 300mm	0.23	10.00	0.25	0.21	-	4.38	0.23	4.87	m	5.36
Iron or steel structural members of roof trusses, lattice girders, purlins and the like										
girth exceeding 300mm	0.75	10.00	0.83	0.65	-	13.57	0.72	15.11	m²	16.62
isolated surfaces, girth not exceeding 300mm	0.23	10.00	0.25	0.22	-	4.59	0.24	5.09	m	5.60
Iron or steel services										
girth exceeding 300mm	0.75	10.00	0.83	0.65	-	13.57	0.72	15.11	m²	16.62
isolated surfaces, girth not exceeding 300mm	0.23	10.00	0.25	0.22	-	4.59	0.24	5.09	m	5.60
isolated areas not exceeding 0.50m² irrespective of girth	0.41	10.00	0.45	0.65	-	13.57	0.72	14.73	nr	16.20
Copper services										
girth exceeding 300mm	0.75	10.00	0.83	0.65	-	13.57	0.72	15.11	m²	16.62
isolated surfaces, girth not exceeding 300mm	0.23	10.00	0.25	0.22	-	4.59	0.24	5.09	m	5.60
Galvanised services										
girth exceeding 300mm	0.75	10.00	0.83	0.65	-	13.57	0.72	15.11	m²	16.62
isolated surfaces, girth not exceeding 300mm	0.23	10.00	0.25	0.22	-	4.59	0.24	5.09	m	5.60
One undercoat, one coat full gloss finish, existing gloss painted metal surfaces; external work										
Iron or steel general surfaces										
girth exceeding 300mm	0.75	10.00	0.83	0.50	-	10.44	0.55	11.81	m²	12.99
isolated surfaces, girth not exceeding 300mm	0.23	10.00	0.25	0.17	-	3.55	0.19	3.99	m	4.39
Galvanised glazed doors, windows or screens										
girth exceeding 300mm; panes, area not exceeding 0.10m²	0.41	10.00	0.45	0.90	-	18.78	0.99	20.22	m²	22.24
girth exceeding 300mm; panes, area 0.10 - 0.50m²	0.29	10.00	0.32	0.67	-	13.98	0.74	15.04	m²	16.54
girth exceeding 300mm; panes, area 0.50 - 1.00m²	0.23	10.00	0.25	0.55	-	11.48	0.61	12.34	m²	13.57
girth exceeding 300mm; panes, area exceeding 1.00m²	0.23	10.00	0.25	0.49	-	10.23	0.54	11.02	m²	12.12
Iron or steel structural work										
girth exceeding 300mm	0.75	10.00	0.83	0.52	-	10.85	0.57	12.25	m²	13.48
isolated surfaces, girth not exceeding 300mm	0.23	10.00	0.25	0.21	-	4.38	0.23	4.87	m	5.36
Iron or steel structural members of roof trusses, lattice girders, purlins and the like										
girth exceeding 300mm	0.75	10.00	0.83	0.65	-	13.57	0.72	15.11	m²	16.62
isolated surfaces, girth not exceeding 300mm	0.23	10.00	0.25	0.22	-	4.59	0.24	5.09	m	5.60
Iron or steel railings, fences and gates; plain open type										
girth exceeding 300mm	0.58	10.00	0.64	0.49	-	10.23	0.54	11.40	m²	12.54
isolated surfaces, girth not exceeding 300mm	0.23	10.00	0.25	0.16	-	3.34	0.18	3.77	m	4.15
Iron or steel railings, fences and gates; close type										
girth exceeding 300mm	0.75	10.00	0.83	0.45	-	9.39	0.50	10.71	m²	11.79
Iron or steel railings, fences and gates; ornamental type										
girth exceeding 300mm	0.58	10.00	0.64	0.90	-	18.78	0.99	20.41	m²	22.45
Iron or steel eaves gutters										
girth exceeding 300mm	0.75	10.00	0.83	0.53	-	11.06	0.58	12.47	m²	13.72
isolated surfaces, girth not exceeding 300mm	0.23	10.00	0.25	0.17	-	3.55	0.19	3.99	m	4.39
Galvanised eaves gutters										
girth exceeding 300mm	0.75	10.00	0.83	0.53	-	11.06	0.58	12.47	m²	13.72
isolated surfaces, girth not exceeding 300mm	0.23	10.00	0.25	0.17	-	3.55	0.19	3.99	m	4.39
Iron or steel services										
girth exceeding 300mm	0.75	10.00	0.83	0.65	-	13.57	0.72	15.11	m²	16.62
isolated surfaces, girth not exceeding 300mm	0.23	10.00	0.25	0.22	-	4.59	0.24	5.09	m	5.60
isolated areas not exceeding 0.50m² irrespective of girth	0.41	10.00	0.45	0.65	-	13.57	0.72	14.73	nr	16.20
Copper services										
girth exceeding 300mm	0.75	10.00	0.83	0.65	-	13.57	0.72	15.11	m²	16.62
isolated surfaces, girth not exceeding 300mm	0.23	10.00	0.25	0.22	-	4.59	0.24	5.09	m	5.60
Galvanised services										
girth exceeding 300mm	0.75	10.00	0.83	0.65	-	13.57	0.72	15.11	m²	16.62
isolated surfaces, girth not exceeding 300mm	0.23	10.00	0.25	0.22	-	4.59	0.24	5.09	m	5.60
Two coats full gloss finish, existing gloss painted metal surfaces										
Iron or steel general surfaces										
girth exceeding 300mm	0.82	10.00	0.91	0.47	-	9.81	0.52	11.23	m²	12.35
isolated surfaces, girth not exceeding 300mm	0.25	10.00	0.28	0.16	-	3.34	0.18	3.79	m	4.17
Galvanised glazed doors, windows or screens										
girth exceeding 300mm; panes, area not exceeding 0.10m²	0.44	10.00	0.49	0.88	-	18.37	0.97	19.82	m²	21.80
girth exceeding 300mm; panes, area 0.10 - 0.50m²	0.32	10.00	0.35	0.64	-	13.36	0.70	14.41	m²	15.85

DECORATION

Labour hourly rates: (except Specialists) Craft Operatives 20.87 Labourer 15.57 Rates are national average prices. Refer to REGIONAL VARIATIONS for indicative levels of overall pricing in regions	MATERIALS			LABOUR				RATES		
	Del to Site £	Waste %	Material Cost £	Craft Optve Hrs	Lab Hrs	Labour Cost £	Sunds £	Nett Rate £	Unit	Gross rate (10%) £
PAINTING & CLEAR FINISHINGS; REDECORATIONS: OIL PAINTING METALWORK (Cont'd)										
Two coats full gloss finish, existing gloss painted metal surfaces (Cont'd)										
Galvanised glazed doors, windows or screens (Cont'd)										
girth exceeding 300mm; panes, area 0.50 - 1.00m²	0.25	10.00	0.28	0.53	-	11.06	0.58	11.92	m²	13.11
girth exceeding 300mm; panes, area exceeding 1.00m²	0.25	10.00	0.28	0.46	-	9.60	0.51	10.38	m²	11.42
Iron or steel structural work										
girth exceeding 300mm	0.82	10.00	0.91	0.52	-	10.85	0.57	12.33	m²	13.56
isolated surfaces, girth not exceeding 300mm	0.25	10.00	0.28	0.21	-	4.38	0.23	4.89	m	5.38
Iron or steel structural members of roof trusses, lattice girders, purlins and the like										
girth exceeding 300mm	0.82	10.00	0.91	0.65	-	13.57	0.72	15.19	m²	16.70
isolated surfaces, girth not exceeding 300mm	0.25	10.00	0.28	0.22	-	4.59	0.24	5.11	m	5.62
Iron or steel services										
girth exceeding 300mm	0.82	10.00	0.91	0.65	-	13.57	0.72	15.19	m²	16.70
isolated surfaces, girth not exceeding 300mm	0.25	10.00	0.28	0.22	-	4.59	0.24	5.11	m	5.62
isolated areas not exceeding 0.50m² irrespective of girth	0.41	10.00	0.45	0.65	-	13.57	0.72	14.73	nr	16.21
Copper services										
girth exceeding 300mm	0.82	10.00	0.91	0.65	-	13.57	0.72	15.19	m²	16.70
isolated surfaces, girth not exceeding 300mm	0.25	10.00	0.28	0.22	-	4.59	0.24	5.11	m	5.62
Galvanised services										
girth exceeding 300mm	0.82	10.00	0.91	0.65	-	13.57	0.72	15.19	m²	16.70
isolated surfaces, girth not exceeding 300mm	0.25	10.00	0.28	0.22	-	4.59	0.24	5.11	m	5.62
Two coats full gloss finish, existing gloss painted metal surfaces; external work										
Iron or steel general surfaces										
girth exceeding 300mm	0.82	10.00	0.91	0.50	-	10.44	0.55	11.89	m²	13.08
isolated surfaces, girth not exceeding 300mm	0.25	10.00	0.28	0.17	-	3.55	0.19	4.01	m	4.41
Galvanised glazed doors, windows or screens										
girth exceeding 300mm; panes, area not exceeding 0.10m²	0.44	10.00	0.49	0.90	-	18.78	0.99	20.26	m²	22.29
girth exceeding 300mm; panes, area 0.10 - 0.50m²	0.32	10.00	0.35	0.67	-	13.98	0.74	15.07	m²	16.57
girth exceeding 300mm; panes, area 0.50 - 1.00m²	0.25	10.00	0.28	0.55	-	11.48	0.61	12.36	m	13.60
girth exceeding 300mm; panes, area exceeding 1.00m²	0.25	10.00	0.28	0.49	-	10.23	0.54	11.04	m²	12.15
Iron or steel structural work										
girth exceeding 300mm	0.82	10.00	0.91	0.52	-	10.85	0.57	12.33	m²	13.56
isolated surfaces, girth not exceeding 300mm	0.25	10.00	0.28	0.21	-	4.38	0.23	4.89	m	5.38
Iron or steel structural members of roof trusses, lattice girders, purlins and the like										
girth exceeding 300mm	0.82	10.00	0.91	0.65	-	13.57	0.72	15.19	m²	16.70
isolated surfaces, girth not exceeding 300mm	0.25	10.00	0.28	0.22	-	4.59	0.24	5.11	m	5.62
Iron or steel railings, fences and gates; plain open type										
girth exceeding 300mm	0.63	10.00	0.70	0.49	-	10.23	0.54	11.46	m²	12.61
isolated surfaces, girth not exceeding 300mm	0.25	10.00	0.28	0.16	-	3.34	0.18	3.79	m	4.17
Iron or steel railings, fences and gates; close type										
girth exceeding 300mm	0.82	10.00	0.91	0.45	-	9.39	0.50	10.79	m²	11.87
Iron or steel railings, fences and gates; ornamental type										
girth exceeding 300mm	0.63	10.00	0.70	0.82	-	17.11	0.90	18.71	m²	20.58
Iron or steel eaves gutters										
girth exceeding 300mm	0.82	10.00	0.91	0.53	-	11.06	0.58	12.55	m²	13.80
isolated surfaces, girth not exceeding 300mm	0.25	10.00	0.28	0.17	-	3.55	0.19	4.01	m	4.41
Galvanised eaves gutters										
girth exceeding 300mm	0.82	10.00	0.91	0.53	-	11.06	0.58	12.55	m²	13.80
isolated surfaces, girth not exceeding 300mm	0.25	10.00	0.28	0.17	-	3.55	0.19	4.01	m	4.41
Iron or steel services										
girth exceeding 300mm	0.82	10.00	0.91	0.65	-	13.57	0.72	15.19	m²	16.70
isolated surfaces, girth not exceeding 300mm	0.25	10.00	0.28	0.22	-	4.59	0.24	5.11	m	5.62
isolated areas not exceeding 0.50m² irrespective of girth	0.41	10.00	0.45	0.65	-	13.57	0.72	14.73	nr	16.21
Copper services										
girth exceeding 300mm	0.82	10.00	0.91	0.65	-	13.57	0.72	15.19	m²	16.70
isolated surfaces, girth not exceeding 300mm	0.25	10.00	0.28	0.22	-	4.59	0.24	5.11	m	5.62
Galvanised services										
girth exceeding 300mm	0.82	10.00	0.91	0.65	-	13.57	0.72	15.19	m²	16.70
isolated surfaces, girth not exceeding 300mm	0.25	10.00	0.28	0.22	-	4.59	0.24	5.11	m	5.62
Two undercoats, one coat full gloss finish, existing gloss painted metal surfaces										
Iron or steel general surfaces										
girth exceeding 300mm	1.09	10.00	1.20	0.62	-	12.94	0.68	14.82	m²	16.31
isolated surfaces, girth not exceeding 300mm	0.34	10.00	0.37	0.21	-	4.38	0.23	4.98	m	5.48
Galvanised glazed doors, windows or screens										
girth exceeding 300mm; panes, area not exceeding 0.10m²	0.59	10.00	0.65	1.15	-	24.00	1.26	25.91	m²	28.50
girth exceeding 300mm; panes, area 0.10 - 0.50m²	0.42	10.00	0.46	0.83	-	17.32	0.91	18.70	m²	20.57
girth exceeding 300mm; panes, area 0.50 - 1.00m²	0.34	10.00	0.37	0.69	-	14.40	0.76	15.53	m²	17.08
girth exceeding 300mm; panes, area exceeding 1.00m²	0.34	10.00	0.37	0.61	-	12.73	0.67	13.77	m²	15.15
Iron or steel structural work										
girth exceeding 300mm	1.09	10.00	1.20	0.67	-	13.98	0.74	15.92	m²	17.52
isolated surfaces, girth not exceeding 300mm	0.34	10.00	0.37	0.27	-	5.63	0.30	6.30	m	6.93

Labour hourly rates: (except Specialists) Craft Operatives 20.87 Labourer 15.57 Rates are national average prices. Refer to REGIONAL VARIATIONS for indicative levels of overall pricing in regions	MATERIALS			LABOUR				RATES		
	Del to Site £	Waste %	Material Cost £	Craft Optve Hrs	Lab Hrs	Labour Cost £	Sunds £	Nett Rate £	Unit	Gross rate (10%) £
PAINTING & CLEAR FINISHINGS; REDECORATIONS: OIL PAINTING METALWORK (Cont'd)										
Two undercoats, one coat full gloss finish, existing gloss painted metal surfaces (Cont'd)										
Iron or steel structural members of roof trusses, lattice girders, purlins and the like										
girth exceeding 300mm	1.09	10.00	1.20	0.84	-	17.53	0.92	19.66	m²	21.62
isolated surfaces, girth not exceeding 300mm	0.34	10.00	0.37	0.28	-	5.84	0.31	6.52	m	7.17
Iron or steel services										
girth exceeding 300mm	1.09	10.00	1.20	0.84	-	17.53	0.92	19.66	m²	21.62
isolated surfaces, girth not exceeding 300mm	0.34	10.00	0.37	0.28	-	5.84	0.31	6.52	m	7.17
isolated areas not exceeding 0.50m² irrespective of girth	0.56	10.00	0.62	0.84	-	17.53	0.92	19.07	nr	20.98
Copper services										
girth exceeding 300mm	1.09	10.00	1.20	0.84	-	17.53	0.92	19.66	m²	21.62
isolated surfaces, girth not exceeding 300mm	0.34	10.00	0.37	0.28	-	5.84	0.31	6.52	m	7.17
Galvanised services										
girth exceeding 300mm	1.09	10.00	1.20	0.84	-	17.53	0.92	19.66	m²	21.62
isolated surfaces, girth not exceeding 300mm	0.34	10.00	0.37	0.28	-	5.84	0.31	6.52	m	7.17
Two undercoats, one coat full gloss finish, existing gloss painted metal surfaces; external work										
Iron or steel general surfaces										
girth exceeding 300mm	1.09	10.00	1.20	0.65	-	13.57	0.72	15.48	m²	17.03
isolated surfaces, girth not exceeding 300mm	0.34	10.00	0.37	0.22	-	4.59	0.24	5.20	m	5.72
Galvanised glazed doors, windows or screens										
girth exceeding 300mm; panes, area not exceeding 0.10m²	0.59	10.00	0.65	1.18	-	24.63	1.30	26.57	m²	29.23
girth exceeding 300mm; panes, area 0.10 - 0.50m²	0.42	10.00	0.46	0.86	-	17.95	0.95	19.36	m²	21.29
girth exceeding 300mm; panes, area 0.50 - 1.00m²	0.34	10.00	0.37	0.72	-	15.03	0.79	16.19	m²	17.81
girth exceeding 300mm; panes, area exceeding 1.00m²	0.34	10.00	0.37	0.64	-	13.36	0.70	14.43	m²	15.87
Iron or steel structural work										
girth exceeding 300mm	1.09	10.00	1.20	0.67	-	13.98	0.74	15.92	m²	17.52
isolated surfaces, girth not exceeding 300mm	0.34	10.00	0.37	0.27	-	5.63	0.30	6.30	m	6.93
Iron or steel structural members of roof trusses, lattice girders, purlins and the like										
girth exceeding 300mm	1.09	10.00	1.20	0.84	-	17.53	0.92	19.66	m²	21.62
isolated surfaces, girth not exceeding 300mm	0.34	10.00	0.37	0.28	-	5.84	0.31	6.52	m	7.17
Iron or steel railings, fences and gates; plain open type										
girth exceeding 300mm	0.84	10.00	0.93	0.63	-	13.15	0.69	14.77	m²	16.24
isolated surfaces, girth not exceeding 300mm	0.34	10.00	0.37	0.21	-	4.38	0.23	4.98	m	5.48
Iron or steel railings, fences and gates; close type										
girth exceeding 300mm	1.09	10.00	1.20	0.57	-	11.90	0.63	13.73	m²	15.10
Iron or steel railings, fences and gates; ornamental type										
girth exceeding 300mm	0.84	10.00	0.93	1.06	-	22.12	1.17	24.21	m²	26.64
Iron or steel eaves gutters										
girth exceeding 300mm	1.09	10.00	1.20	0.68	-	14.19	0.75	16.14	m²	17.76
isolated surfaces, girth not exceeding 300mm	0.34	10.00	0.37	0.23	-	4.80	0.25	5.42	m	5.97
Galvanised eaves gutters										
girth exceeding 300mm	1.09	10.00	1.20	0.68	-	14.19	0.75	16.14	m²	17.76
isolated surfaces, girth not exceeding 300mm	0.34	10.00	0.37	0.23	-	4.80	0.25	5.42	m	5.97
Iron or steel services										
girth exceeding 300mm	1.09	10.00	1.20	0.84	-	17.53	0.92	19.66	m²	21.62
isolated surfaces, girth not exceeding 300mm	0.34	10.00	0.37	0.28	-	5.84	0.31	6.52	m	7.17
isolated areas not exceeding 0.50m² irrespective of girth	0.56	10.00	0.62	0.84	-	17.53	0.92	19.07	nr	20.98
Copper services										
girth exceeding 300mm	1.09	10.00	1.20	0.84	-	17.53	0.92	19.66	m²	21.62
isolated surfaces, girth not exceeding 300mm	0.34	10.00	0.37	0.28	-	5.84	0.31	6.52	m	7.17
Galvanised services										
girth exceeding 300mm	1.09	10.00	1.20	0.84	-	17.53	0.92	19.66	m²	21.62
isolated surfaces, girth not exceeding 300mm	0.34	10.00	0.37	0.28	-	5.84	0.31	6.52	m	7.17
One undercoat, two coats full gloss finish, existing gloss painted metal surfaces										
Iron or steel general surfaces										
girth exceeding 300mm	1.16	10.00	1.28	0.62	-	12.94	0.68	14.90	m²	16.39
isolated surfaces, girth not exceeding 300mm	0.36	10.00	0.39	0.21	-	4.38	0.23	5.01	m	5.51
Galvanised glazed doors, windows or screens										
girth exceeding 300mm; panes, area not exceeding 0.10m²	0.63	10.00	0.69	1.16	-	24.21	1.28	26.17	m²	28.79
girth exceeding 300mm; panes, area 0.10 - 0.50m²	0.45	10.00	0.49	0.83	-	17.32	0.91	18.73	m²	20.60
girth exceeding 300mm; panes, area 0.50 - 1.00m²	0.36	10.00	0.39	0.69	-	14.40	0.76	15.55	m²	17.11
girth exceeding 300mm; panes, area exceeding 1.00m²	0.36	10.00	0.39	0.61	-	12.73	0.67	13.80	m²	15.18
Iron or steel structural work										
girth exceeding 300mm	1.16	10.00	1.28	0.67	-	13.98	0.74	16.00	m²	17.60
isolated surfaces, girth not exceeding 300mm	0.36	10.00	0.39	0.27	-	5.63	0.30	6.33	m	6.96
Iron or steel structural members of roof trusses, lattice girders, purlins and the like										
girth exceeding 300mm	1.16	10.00	1.28	0.84	-	17.53	0.92	19.74	m²	21.71
isolated surfaces, girth not exceeding 300mm	0.36	10.00	0.39	0.28	-	5.84	0.31	6.55	m	7.20
Iron or steel services										
girth exceeding 300mm	1.16	10.00	1.28	0.84	-	17.53	0.92	19.74	m²	21.71

Labour hourly rates: (except Specialists) Craft Operatives 20.87 Labourer 15.57 Rates are national average prices. Refer to REGIONAL VARIATIONS for indicative levels of overall pricing in regions	MATERIALS			LABOUR				RATES		
	Del to Site £	Waste %	Material Cost £	Craft Optve Hrs	Lab Hrs	Labour Cost £	Sunds £	Nett Rate £	Unit	Gross rate (10%) £
PAINTING & CLEAR FINISHINGS; REDECORATIONS: OIL PAINTING METALWORK (Cont'd)										
One undercoat, two coats full gloss finish, existing gloss painted metal surfaces (Cont'd)										
Iron or steel services (Cont'd)										
isolated surfaces, girth not exceeding 300mm	0.36	10.00	0.39	0.28	-	5.84	0.31	6.55	m	7.20
isolated areas not exceeding 0.50m² irrespective of girth	0.63	10.00	0.69	0.84	-	17.53	0.92	19.14	nr	21.06
Copper services										
girth exceeding 300mm	1.16	10.00	1.28	0.84	-	17.53	0.92	19.74	m²	21.71
isolated surfaces, girth not exceeding 300mm	0.36	10.00	0.39	0.28	-	5.84	0.31	6.55	m	7.20
Galvanised services										
girth exceeding 300mm	1.16	10.00	1.28	0.84	-	17.53	0.92	19.74	m²	21.71
isolated surfaces, girth not exceeding 300mm	0.36	10.00	0.39	0.28	-	5.84	0.31	6.55	m	7.20
One undercoat, two coats full gloss finish, existing gloss painted metal surfaces; external work										
Iron or steel general surfaces										
girth exceeding 300mm	1.16	10.00	1.28	0.65	-	13.57	0.72	15.56	m²	17.12
isolated surfaces, girth not exceeding 300mm	0.36	10.00	0.39	0.22	-	4.59	0.24	5.23	m	5.75
Galvanised glazed doors, windows or screens										
girth exceeding 300mm; panes, area not exceeding 0.10m²	0.63	10.00	0.69	1.18	-	24.63	1.30	26.61	m²	29.28
girth exceeding 300mm; panes, area 0.10 - 0.50m²	0.45	10.00	0.49	0.86	-	17.95	0.95	19.39	m²	21.33
girth exceeding 300mm; panes, area 0.50 - 1.00m²	0.36	10.00	0.39	0.72	-	15.03	0.79	16.21	m²	17.83
girth exceeding 300mm; panes, area exceeding 1.00m²	0.36	10.00	0.39	0.64	-	13.36	0.70	14.45	m²	15.90
Iron or steel structural work										
girth exceeding 300mm	1.16	10.00	1.28	0.67	-	13.98	0.74	16.00	m²	17.60
isolated surfaces, girth not exceeding 300mm	0.36	10.00	0.39	0.27	-	5.63	0.30	6.33	m	6.96
Iron or steel structural members of roof trusses, lattice girders, purlins and the like										
girth exceeding 300mm	1.16	10.00	1.28	0.84	-	17.53	0.92	19.74	m²	21.71
isolated surfaces, girth not exceeding 300mm	0.36	10.00	0.39	0.28	-	5.84	0.31	6.55	m	7.20
Iron or steel railings, fences and gates; plain open type										
girth exceeding 300mm	0.90	10.00	0.99	0.64	-	13.36	0.70	15.05	m²	16.55
isolated surfaces, girth not exceeding 300mm	0.36	10.00	0.39	0.21	-	4.38	0.23	5.01	m	5.51
Iron or steel railings, fences and gates; close type										
girth exceeding 300mm	1.16	10.00	1.28	0.57	-	11.90	0.63	13.80	m²	15.18
Iron or steel railings, fences and gates; ornamental type										
girth exceeding 300mm	0.90	10.00	0.99	1.06	-	22.12	1.17	24.27	m²	26.70
Iron or steel eaves gutters										
girth exceeding 300mm	1.16	10.00	1.28	0.68	-	14.19	0.75	16.22	m²	17.84
isolated surfaces, girth not exceeding 300mm	0.36	10.00	0.39	0.23	-	4.80	0.25	5.45	m	5.99
Galvanised eaves gutters										
girth exceeding 300mm	1.16	10.00	1.28	0.68	-	14.19	0.75	16.22	m²	17.84
isolated surfaces, girth not exceeding 300mm	0.36	10.00	0.39	0.23	-	4.80	0.25	5.45	m	5.99
Iron or steel services										
girth exceeding 300mm	1.16	10.00	1.28	0.84	-	17.53	0.92	19.74	m²	21.71
isolated surfaces, girth not exceeding 300mm	0.36	10.00	0.39	0.28	-	5.84	0.31	6.55	m	7.20
isolated areas not exceeding 0.50m² irrespective of girth	0.63	10.00	0.69	0.84	-	17.53	0.92	19.14	nr	21.06
Copper services										
girth exceeding 300mm	1.16	10.00	1.28	0.84	-	17.53	0.92	19.74	m²	21.71
isolated surfaces, girth not exceeding 300mm	0.36	10.00	0.39	0.28	-	5.84	0.31	6.55	m	7.20
Galvanised services										
girth exceeding 300mm	1.16	10.00	1.28	0.84	-	17.53	0.92	19.74	m²	21.71
isolated surfaces, girth not exceeding 300mm	0.36	10.00	0.39	0.28	-	5.84	0.31	6.55	m	7.20
PAINTING & CLEAR FINISHINGS; REDECORATIONS: OIL PAINTING WOODWORK										
Generally										
Note: the following rates include for the cost of all preparatory work, e.g. washing down, etc.										
One undercoat, one coat full gloss finish, existing gloss painted wood surfaces										
Wood general surfaces										
girth exceeding 300mm	0.75	10.00	0.83	0.45	-	9.39	0.50	10.71	m²	11.79
isolated surfaces, girth not exceeding 300mm	0.23	10.00	0.25	0.15	-	3.13	0.17	3.55	m	3.91
Wood glazed doors										
girth exceeding 300mm; panes, area not exceeding 0.10m²	0.41	10.00	0.45	0.79	-	16.49	0.87	17.80	m²	19.58
girth exceeding 300mm; panes, area 0.10 - 0.50m²	0.29	10.00	0.32	0.57	-	11.90	0.63	12.84	m²	14.13
girth exceeding 300mm; panes, area 0.50 - 1.00m²	0.29	10.00	0.32	0.48	-	10.02	0.53	10.86	m²	11.95
girth exceeding 300mm; panes, area exceeding 1.00m²	0.29	10.00	0.32	0.41	-	8.56	0.45	9.33	m²	10.26
Wood partially glazed doors										
girth exceeding 300mm; panes, area not exceeding 0.10m²	0.58	10.00	0.64	0.67	-	13.98	0.74	15.36	m²	16.89
girth exceeding 300mm; panes, area 0.10 - 0.50m²	0.46	10.00	0.51	0.54	-	11.27	0.59	12.37	m²	13.61
girth exceeding 300mm; panes, area 0.50 - 1.00m²	0.41	10.00	0.45	0.48	-	10.02	0.53	10.99	m²	12.09
girth exceeding 300mm; panes, area exceeding 1.00m²	0.41	10.00	0.45	0.43	-	8.97	0.47	9.89	m²	10.88
Wood windows and screens										
girth exceeding 300mm; panes, area not exceeding 0.10m²	0.58	10.00	0.64	0.85	-	17.74	0.94	19.31	m²	21.24
girth exceeding 300mm; panes, area 0.10 - 0.50m²	0.46	10.00	0.51	0.61	-	12.73	0.67	13.91	m²	15.30

Labour hourly rates: (except Specialists) Craft Operatives 20.87 Labourer 15.57 Rates are national average prices. Refer to REGIONAL VARIATIONS for indicative levels of overall pricing in regions	MATERIALS			LABOUR				RATES		
	Del to Site £	Waste %	Material Cost £	Craft Optve Hrs	Lab Hrs	Labour Cost £	Sunds £	Nett Rate £	Unit	Gross rate (10%) £
PAINTING & CLEAR FINISHINGS; REDECORATIONS: OIL PAINTING WOODWORK (Cont'd)										
One undercoat, one coat full gloss finish, existing gloss painted wood surfaces (Cont'd)										
Wood windows and screens (Cont'd)										
girth exceeding 300mm; panes, area 0.50 - 1.00m²	0.41	10.00	0.45	0.52	-	10.85	0.57	11.87	m²	13.06
girth exceeding 300mm; panes, area exceeding 1.00m²	0.41	10.00	0.45	0.44	-	9.18	0.48	10.11	m²	11.12
One undercoat, one coat full gloss finish, existing gloss painted wood surfaces; external work										
Wood general surfaces										
girth exceeding 300mm	0.75	10.00	0.83	0.48	-	10.02	0.53	11.37	m²	12.51
isolated surfaces, girth not exceeding 300mm	0.23	10.00	0.25	0.16	-	3.34	0.18	3.77	m	4.15
Wood glazed doors										
girth exceeding 300mm; panes, area not exceeding 0.10m²	0.41	10.00	0.45	0.81	-	16.90	0.89	18.24	m²	20.07
girth exceeding 300mm; panes, area 0.10 - 0.50m²	0.29	10.00	0.32	0.59	-	12.31	0.65	13.28	m²	14.61
girth exceeding 300mm; panes, area 0.50 - 1.00m²	0.29	10.00	0.32	0.49	-	10.23	0.54	11.08	m²	12.19
girth exceeding 300mm; panes, area exceeding 1.00m²	0.29	10.00	0.32	0.42	-	8.77	0.46	9.55	m²	10.50
Wood partially glazed doors										
girth exceeding 300mm; panes, area not exceeding 0.10m²	0.58	10.00	0.64	0.69	-	14.40	0.76	15.80	m²	17.38
girth exceeding 300mm; panes, area 0.10 - 0.50m²	0.46	10.00	0.51	0.56	-	11.69	0.62	12.81	m²	14.09
girth exceeding 300mm; panes, area 0.50 - 1.00m²	0.41	10.00	0.45	0.49	-	10.23	0.54	11.21	m²	12.33
girth exceeding 300mm; panes, area exceeding 1.00m²	0.41	10.00	0.45	0.44	-	9.18	0.48	10.11	m²	11.12
Wood windows and screens										
girth exceeding 300mm; panes, area not exceeding 0.10m²	0.58	10.00	0.64	0.89	-	18.57	0.98	20.19	m²	22.21
girth exceeding 300mm; panes, area 0.10 - 0.50m²	0.46	10.00	0.51	0.65	-	13.57	0.72	14.79	m²	16.27
girth exceeding 300mm; panes, area 0.50 - 1.00m²	0.41	10.00	0.45	0.55	-	11.48	0.61	12.53	m²	13.78
girth exceeding 300mm; panes, area exceeding 1.00m²	0.41	10.00	0.45	0.47	-	9.81	0.52	10.77	m²	11.85
Wood railings fences and gates; open type										
girth exceeding 300mm	0.58	10.00	0.64	0.41	-	8.56	0.45	9.64	m²	10.61
isolated surfaces, girth not exceeding 300mm	0.23	10.00	0.25	0.13	-	2.71	0.14	3.11	m	3.42
Wood railings fences and gates; close type										
girth exceeding 300mm	0.75	10.00	0.83	0.37	-	7.72	0.41	8.96	m²	9.85
Two coats full gloss finish, existing gloss painted wood surfaces										
Wood general surfaces										
girth exceeding 300mm	0.82	10.00	0.91	0.45	-	9.39	0.50	10.79	m²	11.87
isolated surfaces, girth not exceeding 300mm	0.25	10.00	0.28	0.15	-	3.13	0.17	3.57	m	3.93
Wood glazed doors										
girth exceeding 300mm; panes, area not exceeding 0.10m²	0.44	10.00	0.49	0.79	-	16.49	0.87	17.84	m²	19.63
girth exceeding 300mm; panes, area 0.10 - 0.50m²	0.32	10.00	0.35	0.57	-	11.90	0.63	12.87	m²	14.16
girth exceeding 300mm; panes, area 0.50 - 1.00m²	0.32	10.00	0.35	0.48	-	10.02	0.53	10.89	m²	11.98
girth exceeding 300mm; panes, area exceeding 1.00m²	0.32	10.00	0.35	0.41	-	8.56	0.45	9.36	m²	10.29
Wood partially glazed doors										
girth exceeding 300mm; panes, area not exceeding 0.10m²	0.63	10.00	0.70	0.67	-	13.98	0.74	15.42	m²	16.96
girth exceeding 300mm; panes, area 0.10 - 0.50m²	0.51	10.00	0.56	0.54	-	11.27	0.59	12.42	m²	13.66
girth exceeding 300mm; panes, area 0.50 - 1.00m²	0.44	10.00	0.49	0.48	-	10.02	0.53	11.03	m²	12.14
girth exceeding 300mm; panes, area exceeding 1.00m²	0.44	10.00	0.49	0.43	-	8.97	0.47	9.93	m²	10.93
Wood windows and screens										
girth exceeding 300mm; panes, area not exceeding 0.10m²	0.63	10.00	0.70	0.85	-	17.74	0.94	19.37	m²	21.31
girth exceeding 300mm; panes, area 0.10 - 0.50m²	0.51	10.00	0.56	0.61	-	12.73	0.67	13.96	m²	15.35
girth exceeding 300mm; panes, area 0.50 - 1.00m²	0.44	10.00	0.49	0.52	-	10.85	0.57	11.91	m²	13.10
girth exceeding 300mm; panes, area exceeding 1.00m²	0.44	10.00	0.49	0.44	-	9.18	0.48	10.15	m²	11.17
Two coats full gloss finish, existing gloss painted wood surfaces; external work										
Wood general surfaces										
girth exceeding 300mm	0.82	10.00	0.91	0.48	-	10.02	0.53	11.45	m²	12.60
isolated surfaces, girth not exceeding 300mm	0.25	10.00	0.28	0.16	-	3.34	0.18	3.79	m	4.17
Wood glazed doors										
girth exceeding 300mm; panes, area not exceeding 0.10m²	0.44	10.00	0.49	0.81	-	16.90	0.89	18.28	m²	20.11
girth exceeding 300mm; panes, area 0.10 - 0.50m²	0.32	10.00	0.35	0.59	-	12.31	0.65	13.31	m²	14.64
girth exceeding 300mm; panes, area 0.50 - 1.00m²	0.32	10.00	0.35	0.49	-	10.23	0.54	11.11	m²	12.22
girth exceeding 300mm; panes, area exceeding 1.00m²	0.32	10.00	0.35	0.42	-	8.77	0.46	9.58	m²	10.53
Wood partially glazed doors										
girth exceeding 300mm; panes, area not exceeding 0.10m²	0.63	10.00	0.70	0.69	-	14.40	0.76	15.86	m²	17.44
girth exceeding 300mm; panes, area 0.10 - 0.50m²	0.51	10.00	0.56	0.56	-	11.69	0.62	12.86	m²	14.15
girth exceeding 300mm; panes, area 0.50 - 1.00m²	0.44	10.00	0.49	0.49	-	10.23	0.54	11.25	m²	12.38
girth exceeding 300mm; panes, area exceeding 1.00m²	0.44	10.00	0.49	0.44	-	9.18	0.48	10.15	m²	11.17
Wood windows and screens										
girth exceeding 300mm; panes, area not exceeding 0.10m²	0.63	10.00	0.70	0.89	-	18.57	0.98	20.25	m²	22.27
girth exceeding 300mm; panes, area 0.10 - 0.50m²	0.51	10.00	0.56	0.65	-	13.57	0.72	14.84	m²	16.32
girth exceeding 300mm; panes, area 0.50 - 1.00m²	0.44	10.00	0.49	0.55	-	11.48	0.61	12.57	m²	13.83
girth exceeding 300mm; panes, area exceeding 1.00m²	0.44	10.00	0.49	0.47	-	9.81	0.52	10.81	m²	11.89
Wood railings fences and gates; open type										
girth exceeding 300mm	0.63	10.00	0.70	0.41	-	8.56	0.45	9.70	m²	10.67
isolated surfaces, girth not exceeding 300mm	0.25	10.00	0.28	0.13	-	2.71	0.14	3.13	m	3.45
Wood railings fences and gates; close type										
girth exceeding 300mm	0.82	10.00	0.91	0.37	-	7.72	0.41	9.03	m²	9.94

Labour hourly rates: (except Specialists) Craft Operatives 20.87 Labourer 15.57 Rates are national average prices. Refer to REGIONAL VARIATIONS for indicative levels of overall pricing in regions	MATERIALS			LABOUR				RATES		
	Del to Site £	Waste %	Material Cost £	Craft Optve Hrs	Lab Hrs	Labour Cost £	Sunds £	Nett Rate £	Unit	Gross rate (10%) £
PAINTING & CLEAR FINISHINGS; REDECORATIONS: OIL PAINTING WOODWORK (Cont'd)										
Two undercoats, one coat full gloss finish, existing gloss painted wood surfaces										
Wood general surfaces										
girth exceeding 300mm	1.09	10.00	1.20	0.61	-	12.73	0.67	14.60	m²	16.07
isolated surfaces, girth not exceeding 300mm	0.34	10.00	0.37	0.20	-	4.17	0.22	4.76	m	5.24
Wood glazed doors										
girth exceeding 300mm; panes, area not exceeding 0.10m²	0.59	10.00	0.65	1.04	-	21.70	1.14	23.50	m²	25.85
girth exceeding 300mm; panes, area 0.10 - 0.50m²	0.42	10.00	0.46	0.76	-	15.86	0.84	17.16	m²	18.88
girth exceeding 300mm; panes, area 0.50 - 1.00m²	0.42	10.00	0.46	0.64	-	13.36	0.70	14.52	m²	15.98
girth exceeding 300mm; panes, area exceeding 1.00m²	0.42	10.00	0.46	0.54	-	11.27	0.59	12.33	m²	13.56
Wood partially glazed doors										
girth exceeding 300mm; panes, area not exceeding 0.10m²	0.84	10.00	0.93	0.87	-	18.16	0.96	20.04	m²	22.04
girth exceeding 300mm; panes, area 0.10 - 0.50m²	0.67	10.00	0.74	0.71	-	14.82	0.78	16.34	m²	17.97
girth exceeding 300mm; panes, area 0.50 - 1.00m²	0.59	10.00	0.65	0.64	-	13.36	0.70	14.71	m²	16.18
girth exceeding 300mm; panes, area exceeding 1.00m²	0.59	10.00	0.65	0.57	-	11.90	0.63	13.17	m²	14.49
Wood windows and screens										
girth exceeding 300mm; panes, area not exceeding 0.10m²	0.84	10.00	0.93	1.12	-	23.37	1.23	25.53	m²	28.09
girth exceeding 300mm; panes, area 0.10 - 0.50m²	0.67	10.00	0.74	0.82	-	17.11	0.90	18.76	m²	20.63
girth exceeding 300mm; panes, area 0.50 - 1.00m²	0.59	10.00	0.65	0.69	-	14.40	0.76	15.81	m²	17.39
girth exceeding 300mm; panes, area exceeding 1.00m²	0.59	10.00	0.65	0.59	-	12.31	0.65	13.61	m²	14.97
Two undercoats, one coat full gloss finish, existing gloss painted wood surfaces; external work										
Wood general surfaces										
girth exceeding 300mm	1.09	10.00	1.20	0.65	-	13.57	0.72	15.48	m²	17.03
isolated surfaces, girth not exceeding 300mm	0.34	10.00	0.37	0.22	-	4.59	0.24	5.20	m	5.72
Wood glazed doors										
girth exceeding 300mm; panes, area not exceeding 0.10m²	0.59	10.00	0.65	1.26	-	26.30	1.39	28.33	m²	31.16
girth exceeding 300mm; panes, area 0.10 - 0.50m²	0.42	10.00	0.46	0.78	-	16.28	0.86	17.60	m²	19.36
girth exceeding 300mm; panes, area 0.50 - 1.00m²	0.42	10.00	0.46	0.65	-	13.57	0.72	14.74	m²	16.22
girth exceeding 300mm; panes, area exceeding 1.00m²	0.42	10.00	0.46	0.55	-	11.48	0.61	12.55	m²	13.80
Wood partially glazed doors										
girth exceeding 300mm; panes, area not exceeding 0.10m²	0.84	10.00	0.93	0.89	-	18.57	0.98	20.48	m²	22.53
girth exceeding 300mm; panes, area 0.10 - 0.50m²	0.67	10.00	0.74	0.73	-	15.24	0.80	16.78	m²	18.46
girth exceeding 300mm; panes, area 0.50 - 1.00m²	0.59	10.00	0.65	0.65	-	13.57	0.72	14.93	m²	16.42
girth exceeding 300mm; panes, area exceeding 1.00m²	0.59	10.00	0.65	0.58	-	12.10	0.64	13.39	m²	14.73
Wood windows and screens										
girth exceeding 300mm; panes, area not exceeding 0.10m²	0.84	10.00	0.93	1.18	-	24.63	1.30	26.85	m²	29.54
girth exceeding 300mm; panes, area 0.10 - 0.50m²	0.67	10.00	0.74	0.87	-	18.16	0.96	19.85	m²	21.84
girth exceeding 300mm; panes, area 0.50 - 1.00m²	0.59	10.00	0.65	0.73	-	15.24	0.80	16.69	m²	18.35
girth exceeding 300mm; panes, area exceeding 1.00m²	0.59	10.00	0.65	0.63	-	13.15	0.69	14.49	m²	15.94
Wood railings fences and gates; open type										
girth exceeding 300mm	0.84	10.00	0.93	0.55	-	11.48	0.61	13.01	m²	14.31
isolated surfaces, girth not exceeding 300mm	0.34	10.00	0.37	0.18	-	3.76	0.20	4.32	m	4.76
Wood railings fences and gates; close type										
girth exceeding 300mm	1.09	10.00	1.20	0.49	-	10.23	0.54	11.97	m²	13.17
One undercoat, two coats full gloss finish, existing gloss painted wood surfaces										
Wood general surfaces										
girth exceeding 300mm	1.16	10.00	1.28	0.61	-	12.73	0.67	14.68	m²	16.15
isolated surfaces, girth not exceeding 300mm	0.36	10.00	0.39	0.20	-	4.17	0.22	4.79	m	5.27
Wood glazed doors										
girth exceeding 300mm; panes, area not exceeding 0.10m²	0.63	10.00	0.69	1.04	-	21.70	1.14	23.54	m²	25.89
girth exceeding 300mm; panes, area 0.10 - 0.50m²	0.45	10.00	0.49	0.76	-	15.86	0.84	17.19	m²	18.91
girth exceeding 300mm; panes, area 0.50 - 1.00m²	0.45	10.00	0.49	0.64	-	13.36	0.70	14.55	m²	16.01
girth exceeding 300mm; panes, area exceeding 1.00m²	0.45	10.00	0.49	0.54	-	11.27	0.59	12.36	m²	13.59
Wood partially glazed doors										
girth exceeding 300mm; panes, area not exceeding 0.10m²	0.90	10.00	0.99	0.87	-	18.16	0.96	20.10	m²	22.11
girth exceeding 300mm; panes, area 0.10 - 0.50m²	0.72	10.00	0.79	0.71	-	14.82	0.78	16.39	m²	18.03
girth exceeding 300mm; panes, area 0.50 - 1.00m²	0.63	10.00	0.69	0.64	-	13.36	0.70	14.75	m²	16.23
girth exceeding 300mm; panes, area exceeding 1.00m²	0.63	10.00	0.69	0.57	-	11.90	0.63	13.21	m²	14.53
Wood windows and screens										
girth exceeding 300mm; panes, area not exceeding 0.10m²	0.90	10.00	0.99	1.12	-	23.37	1.23	25.59	m²	28.15
girth exceeding 300mm; panes, area 0.10 - 0.50m²	0.72	10.00	0.79	0.82	-	17.11	0.90	18.80	m²	20.68
girth exceeding 300mm; panes, area 0.50 - 1.00m²	0.63	10.00	0.69	0.69	-	14.40	0.76	15.85	m²	17.43
girth exceeding 300mm; panes, area exceeding 1.00m²	0.63	10.00	0.69	0.59	-	12.31	0.65	13.65	m²	15.02
One undercoat, two coats full gloss finish, existing gloss painted wood surfaces; external work										
Wood general surfaces										
girth exceeding 300mm	1.16	10.00	1.28	0.65	-	13.57	0.72	15.56	m²	17.12
isolated surfaces, girth not exceeding 300mm	0.36	10.00	0.39	0.22	-	4.59	0.24	5.23	m	5.75
Wood glazed doors										
girth exceeding 300mm; panes, area not exceeding 0.10m²	0.63	10.00	0.69	1.06	-	22.12	1.17	23.98	m²	26.38
girth exceeding 300mm; panes, area 0.10 - 0.50m²	0.45	10.00	0.49	0.78	-	16.28	0.86	17.63	m²	19.39
girth exceeding 300mm; panes, area 0.50 - 1.00m²	0.45	10.00	0.49	0.65	-	13.57	0.72	14.77	m²	16.25
girth exceeding 300mm; panes, area exceeding 1.00m²	0.45	10.00	0.49	0.55	-	11.48	0.61	12.58	m²	13.83
Wood partially glazed doors										
girth exceeding 300mm; panes, area not exceeding 0.10m²	0.90	10.00	0.99	0.89	-	18.57	0.98	20.54	m²	22.59

Labour hourly rates: (except Specialists) Craft Operatives 20.87 Labourer 15.57 Rates are national average prices. Refer to REGIONAL VARIATIONS for indicative levels of overall pricing in regions	MATERIALS			LABOUR				RATES		
	Del to Site £	Waste %	Material Cost £	Craft Optve Hrs	Lab Hrs	Labour Cost £	Sunds £	Nett Rate £	Unit	Gross rate (10%) £
PAINTING & CLEAR FINISHINGS; REDECORATIONS: OIL PAINTING WOODWORK (Cont'd)										
One undercoat, two coats full gloss finish, existing gloss painted wood surfaces; external work (Cont'd)										
Wood partially glazed doors (Cont'd)										
girth exceeding 300mm; panes, area 0.10 - 0.50m²	0.72	10.00	0.79	0.73	-	15.24	0.80	16.83	m²	18.51
girth exceeding 300mm; panes, area 0.50 - 1.00m²	0.63	10.00	0.69	0.65	-	13.57	0.72	14.97	m²	16.47
girth exceeding 300mm; panes, area exceeding 1.00m²	0.63	10.00	0.69	0.58	-	12.10	0.64	13.43	m²	14.78
Wood windows and screens										
girth exceeding 300mm; panes, area not exceeding 0.10m²	0.90	10.00	0.99	1.18	-	24.63	1.30	26.91	m²	29.60
girth exceeding 300mm; panes, area 0.10 - 0.50m²	0.72	10.00	0.79	0.87	-	18.16	0.96	19.90	m²	21.89
girth exceeding 300mm; panes, area 0.50 - 1.00m²	0.63	10.00	0.69	0.73	-	15.24	0.80	16.73	m²	18.40
girth exceeding 300mm; panes, area exceeding 1.00m²	0.63	10.00	0.69	0.63	-	13.15	0.69	14.53	m²	15.98
Wood railings fences and gates; open type										
girth exceeding 300mm	0.90	10.00	0.99	0.55	-	11.48	0.61	13.07	m²	14.38
isolated surfaces, girth not exceeding 300mm	0.36	10.00	0.39	0.18	-	3.76	0.20	4.35	m	4.78
Wood railings fences and gates; close type										
girth exceeding 300mm	1.16	10.00	1.28	0.49	-	10.23	0.54	12.05	m²	13.25
Burn off, one coat primer, one undercoat, one coat full gloss finish, existing painted wood surfaces										
Wood general surfaces										
girth exceeding 300mm	1.38	10.00	1.52	0.90	-	18.78	1.98	22.28	m²	24.51
isolated surfaces, girth not exceeding 300mm	0.41	10.00	0.45	0.26	-	5.43	0.57	6.45	m	7.09
Wood glazed doors										
girth exceeding 300mm; panes, area not exceeding 0.10m²	0.76	10.00	0.84	1.50	-	31.31	3.30	35.44	m²	38.99
girth exceeding 300mm; panes, area 0.10 - 0.50m²	0.56	10.00	0.61	1.08	-	22.54	2.38	25.53	m²	28.08
girth exceeding 300mm; panes, area 0.50 - 1.00m²	0.51	10.00	0.56	0.90	-	18.78	1.98	21.33	m²	23.46
girth exceeding 300mm; panes, area exceeding 1.00m²	0.51	10.00	0.56	0.80	-	16.70	1.76	19.02	m²	20.92
Wood partially glazed doors										
girth exceeding 300mm; panes, area not exceeding 0.10m²	1.07	10.00	1.18	1.20	-	25.04	2.64	28.86	m²	31.75
girth exceeding 300mm; panes, area 0.10 - 0.50m²	0.82	10.00	0.90	0.99	-	20.66	2.18	23.74	m²	26.12
girth exceeding 300mm; panes, area 0.50 - 1.00m²	0.76	10.00	0.84	0.90	-	18.78	1.98	21.60	m²	23.76
girth exceeding 300mm; panes, area exceeding 1.00m²	0.76	10.00	0.84	0.86	-	17.95	1.89	20.68	m²	22.75
Wood windows and screens										
girth exceeding 300mm; panes, area not exceeding 0.10m²	1.07	10.00	1.18	1.65	-	34.44	3.63	39.24	m²	43.17
girth exceeding 300mm; panes, area 0.10 - 0.50m²	0.82	10.00	0.90	1.18	-	24.63	2.60	28.13	m²	30.94
girth exceeding 300mm; panes, area 0.50 - 1.00m²	0.76	10.00	0.84	0.99	-	20.66	2.18	23.68	m²	26.05
girth exceeding 300mm; panes, area exceeding 1.00m²	0.76	10.00	0.84	0.88	-	18.37	1.94	21.14	m²	23.26
Burn off, one coat primer, one undercoat, one coat full gloss finish, existing painted wood surfaces; external work										
Wood general surfaces										
girth exceeding 300mm	1.38	10.00	1.52	0.95	-	19.83	2.09	23.43	m²	25.78
isolated surfaces, girth not exceeding 300mm	0.41	10.00	0.45	0.29	-	6.05	0.64	7.14	m	7.86
Wood glazed doors										
girth exceeding 300mm; panes, area not exceeding 0.10m²	0.76	10.00	0.84	1.50	-	31.31	3.30	35.44	m²	38.99
girth exceeding 300mm; panes, area 0.10 - 0.50m²	0.56	10.00	0.61	1.08	-	22.54	2.38	25.53	m²	28.08
girth exceeding 300mm; panes, area 0.50 - 1.00m²	0.51	10.00	0.56	0.90	-	18.78	1.98	21.33	m²	23.46
girth exceeding 300mm; panes, area exceeding 1.00m²	0.51	10.00	0.56	0.80	-	16.70	1.76	19.02	m²	20.92
Wood partially glazed doors										
girth exceeding 300mm; panes, area not exceeding 0.10m²	1.07	10.00	1.18	1.20	-	25.04	2.64	28.86	m²	31.75
girth exceeding 300mm; panes, area 0.10 - 0.50m²	0.82	10.00	0.90	0.99	-	20.66	2.18	23.74	m²	26.12
girth exceeding 300mm; panes, area 0.50 - 1.00m²	0.76	10.00	0.84	0.90	-	18.78	1.98	21.60	m²	23.76
girth exceeding 300mm; panes, area exceeding 1.00m²	0.76	10.00	0.84	0.86	-	17.95	1.89	20.68	m²	22.75
Wood windows and screens										
girth exceeding 300mm; panes, area not exceeding 0.10m²	1.07	10.00	1.18	1.69	-	35.27	3.72	40.17	m²	44.18
girth exceeding 300mm; panes, area 0.10 - 0.50m²	0.82	10.00	0.90	1.22	-	25.46	2.68	29.05	m²	31.95
girth exceeding 300mm; panes, area 0.50 - 1.00m²	0.76	10.00	0.84	1.03	-	21.50	2.27	24.60	m²	27.06
girth exceeding 300mm; panes, area exceeding 1.00m²	0.76	10.00	0.84	0.92	-	19.20	2.02	22.06	m²	24.27
Wood railings fences and gates; open type										
girth exceeding 300mm	1.07	10.00	1.18	0.81	-	16.90	1.78	19.87	m²	21.85
isolated surfaces, girth not exceeding 300mm	0.41	10.00	0.45	0.24	-	5.01	0.53	5.99	m	6.59
Wood railings fences and gates; close type										
girth exceeding 300mm	1.38	10.00	1.52	0.76	-	15.86	1.67	19.05	m²	20.96
Burn off, one coat primer, two undercoats, one coat full gloss finish, existing painted wood surfaces										
Wood general surfaces										
girth exceeding 300mm	1.72	10.00	1.89	1.06	-	22.12	2.33	26.35	m²	28.98
isolated surfaces, girth not exceeding 300mm	0.52	10.00	0.57	0.32	-	6.68	0.70	7.95	m	8.74
Wood glazed doors										
girth exceeding 300mm; panes, area not exceeding 0.10m²	0.95	10.00	1.04	1.76	-	36.73	3.87	41.64	m²	45.81
girth exceeding 300mm; panes, area 0.10 - 0.50m²	0.69	10.00	0.76	1.27	-	26.50	2.79	30.06	m²	33.06
girth exceeding 300mm; panes, area 0.50 - 1.00m²	0.64	10.00	0.71	1.06	-	22.12	2.33	25.16	m²	27.68
girth exceeding 300mm; panes, area exceeding 1.00m²	0.64	10.00	0.71	0.95	-	19.83	2.09	22.63	m²	24.89
Wood partially glazed doors										
girth exceeding 300mm; panes, area not exceeding 0.10m²	1.33	10.00	1.47	1.41	-	29.43	3.10	34.00	m²	37.40
girth exceeding 300mm; panes, area 0.10 - 0.50m²	1.03	10.00	1.13	1.17	-	24.42	2.57	28.13	m²	30.94
girth exceeding 300mm; panes, area 0.50 - 1.00m²	0.95	10.00	1.04	1.06	-	22.12	2.33	25.50	m²	28.05
girth exceeding 300mm; panes, area exceeding 1.00m²	0.95	10.00	1.04	1.00	-	20.87	2.20	24.11	m²	26.52

Labour hourly rates: (except Specialists) Craft Operatives 20.87 Labourer 15.57 Rates are national average prices. Refer to REGIONAL VARIATIONS for indicative levels of overall pricing in regions	MATERIALS			LABOUR				RATES		
	Del to Site £	Waste %	Material Cost £	Craft Optve Hrs	Lab Hrs	Labour Cost £	Sunds £	Nett Rate £	Unit	Gross rate (10%) £
PAINTING & CLEAR FINISHINGS; REDECORATIONS: OIL PAINTING WOODWORK (Cont'd)										
Burn off, one coat primer, two undercoats, one coat full gloss finish, existing painted wood surfaces (Cont'd)										
Wood windows and screens										
girth exceeding 300mm; panes, area not exceeding 0.10m²	1.33	10.00	1.47	1.94	-	40.49	4.27	46.22	m²	50.85
girth exceeding 300mm; panes, area 0.10 - 0.50m²	1.03	10.00	1.13	1.40	-	29.22	3.08	33.43	m²	36.78
girth exceeding 300mm; panes, area 0.50 - 1.00m²	0.95	10.00	1.04	1.17	-	24.42	2.57	28.03	m²	30.84
girth exceeding 300mm; panes, area exceeding 1.00m²	0.95	10.00	1.04	1.03	-	21.50	2.27	24.80	m²	27.28
Burn off, one coat primer, two undercoats, one coat full gloss finish, existing painted wood surfaces; external work										
Wood general surfaces										
girth exceeding 300mm	1.72	10.00	1.89	1.11	-	23.17	2.44	27.50	m²	30.25
isolated surfaces, girth not exceeding 300mm	0.52	10.00	0.57	0.35	-	7.30	0.77	8.64	m	9.51
Wood glazed doors										
girth exceeding 300mm; panes, area not exceeding 0.10m²	0.95	10.00	1.04	1.76	-	36.73	3.87	41.64	m²	45.81
girth exceeding 300mm; panes, area 0.10 - 0.50m²	0.69	10.00	0.76	1.27	-	26.50	2.79	30.06	m²	33.06
girth exceeding 300mm; panes, area 0.50 - 1.00m²	0.64	10.00	0.71	1.06	-	22.12	2.33	25.16	m²	27.68
girth exceeding 300mm; panes, area exceeding 1.00m²	0.64	10.00	0.71	0.95	-	19.83	2.09	22.63	m²	24.89
Wood partially glazed doors										
girth exceeding 300mm; panes, area not exceeding 0.10m²	1.33	10.00	1.47	1.41	-	29.43	3.10	34.00	m²	37.40
girth exceeding 300mm; panes, area 0.10 - 0.50m²	1.03	10.00	1.13	1.17	-	24.42	2.57	28.13	m²	30.94
girth exceeding 300mm; panes, area 0.50 - 1.00m²	0.95	10.00	1.04	1.06	-	22.12	2.33	25.50	m²	28.05
girth exceeding 300mm; panes, area exceeding 1.00m²	0.95	10.00	1.04	1.00	-	20.87	2.20	24.11	m²	26.52
Wood windows and screens										
girth exceeding 300mm; panes, area not exceeding 0.10m²	1.33	10.00	1.47	1.99	-	41.53	4.38	47.38	m²	52.11
girth exceeding 300mm; panes, area 0.10 - 0.50m²	1.03	10.00	1.13	1.45	-	30.26	3.19	34.59	m²	38.04
girth exceeding 300mm; panes, area 0.50 - 1.00m²	0.95	10.00	1.04	1.22	-	25.46	2.68	29.19	m²	32.11
girth exceeding 300mm; panes, area exceeding 1.00m²	0.95	10.00	1.04	1.09	-	22.75	2.40	26.19	m²	28.81
Wood railings fences and gates; open type										
girth exceeding 300mm	1.33	10.00	1.47	0.95	-	19.83	2.09	23.38	m²	25.72
isolated surfaces, girth not exceeding 300mm	0.52	10.00	0.57	0.29	-	6.05	0.64	7.26	m	7.98
Wood railings fences and gates; close type										
girth exceeding 300mm	1.72	10.00	1.89	0.88	-	18.37	1.94	22.19	m²	24.41
Burn off, one coat primer, one undercoat, two coats full gloss finish, existing painted wood surfaces										
Wood general surfaces										
girth exceeding 300mm	1.79	10.00	1.97	1.06	-	22.12	2.33	26.42	m²	29.07
isolated surfaces, girth not exceeding 300mm	0.54	10.00	0.59	0.32	-	6.68	0.70	7.97	m	8.77
Wood glazed doors										
girth exceeding 300mm; panes, area not exceeding 0.10m²	0.98	10.00	1.08	1.76	-	36.73	3.87	41.69	m²	45.86
girth exceeding 300mm; panes, area 0.10 - 0.50m²	0.72	10.00	0.79	1.27	-	26.50	2.79	30.09	m²	33.10
girth exceeding 300mm; panes, area 0.50 - 1.00m²	0.67	10.00	0.74	1.06	-	22.12	2.33	25.19	m²	27.71
girth exceeding 300mm; panes, area exceeding 1.00m²	0.67	10.00	0.74	0.95	-	19.83	2.09	22.66	m²	24.92
Wood partially glazed doors										
girth exceeding 300mm; panes, area not exceeding 0.10m²	1.39	10.00	1.53	1.41	-	29.43	3.10	34.06	m²	37.46
girth exceeding 300mm; panes, area 0.10 - 0.50m²	1.07	10.00	1.18	1.17	-	24.42	2.57	28.17	m²	30.99
girth exceeding 300mm; panes, area 0.50 - 1.00m²	0.98	10.00	1.08	1.06	-	22.12	2.33	25.54	m²	28.09
girth exceeding 300mm; panes, area exceeding 1.00m²	0.98	10.00	1.08	1.00	-	20.87	2.20	24.15	m²	26.57
Wood windows and screens										
girth exceeding 300mm; panes, area not exceeding 0.10m²	1.39	10.00	1.53	1.94	-	40.49	4.27	46.28	m²	50.91
girth exceeding 300mm; panes, area 0.10 - 0.50m²	1.07	10.00	1.18	1.40	-	29.22	3.08	33.48	m²	36.83
girth exceeding 300mm; panes, area 0.50 - 1.00m²	0.98	10.00	1.08	1.17	-	24.42	2.57	28.08	m²	30.88
girth exceeding 300mm; panes, area exceeding 1.00m²	0.98	10.00	1.08	1.03	-	21.50	2.27	24.85	m²	27.33
Burn off, one coat primer, one undercoat, two coats full gloss finish, existing painted wood surfaces; external work										
Wood general surfaces										
girth exceeding 300mm	1.79	10.00	1.97	1.11	-	23.17	2.44	27.58	m²	30.34
isolated surfaces, girth not exceeding 300mm	0.54	10.00	0.59	0.35	-	7.30	0.77	8.67	m	9.53
Wood glazed doors										
girth exceeding 300mm; panes, area not exceeding 0.10m²	0.98	10.00	1.08	1.76	-	36.73	3.87	41.69	m²	45.86
girth exceeding 300mm; panes, area 0.10 - 0.50m²	0.72	10.00	0.79	1.27	-	26.50	2.79	30.09	m²	33.10
girth exceeding 300mm; panes, area 0.50 - 1.00m²	0.67	10.00	0.74	1.06	-	22.12	2.33	25.19	m²	27.71
girth exceeding 300mm; panes, area exceeding 1.00m²	0.67	10.00	0.74	0.95	-	19.83	2.09	22.66	m²	24.92
Wood partially glazed doors										
girth exceeding 300mm; panes, area not exceeding 0.10m²	1.39	10.00	1.53	1.41	-	29.43	3.10	34.06	m²	37.46
girth exceeding 300mm; panes, area 0.10 - 0.50m²	1.07	10.00	1.18	1.17	-	24.42	2.57	28.17	m²	30.99
girth exceeding 300mm; panes, area 0.50 - 1.00m²	0.98	10.00	1.08	1.06	-	22.12	2.33	25.54	m²	28.09
girth exceeding 300mm; panes, area exceeding 1.00m²	0.98	10.00	1.08	1.00	-	20.87	2.20	24.15	m²	26.57
Wood windows and screens										
girth exceeding 300mm; panes, area not exceeding 0.10m²	1.39	10.00	1.53	1.99	-	41.53	4.38	47.44	m²	52.18
girth exceeding 300mm; panes, area 0.10 - 0.50m²	1.07	10.00	1.18	1.45	-	30.26	3.19	34.63	m²	38.10
girth exceeding 300mm; panes, area 0.50 - 1.00m²	0.98	10.00	1.08	1.22	-	25.46	2.68	29.23	m²	32.15
girth exceeding 300mm; panes, area exceeding 1.00m²	0.98	10.00	1.08	1.09	-	22.75	2.40	26.23	m²	28.85
Wood railings fences and gates; open type										
girth exceeding 300mm	1.39	10.00	1.53	0.95	-	19.83	2.09	23.44	m²	25.79
isolated surfaces, girth not exceeding 300mm	0.54	10.00	0.59	0.29	-	6.05	0.64	7.28	m	8.01
Wood railings fences and gates; close type										
girth exceeding 300mm	1.79	10.00	1.97	0.88	-	18.37	1.94	22.27	m²	24.50

Labour hourly rates: (except Specialists) Craft Operatives 20.87 Labourer 15.57 Rates are national average prices. Refer to REGIONAL VARIATIONS for indicative levels of overall pricing in regions	MATERIALS			LABOUR				RATES		
	Del to Site £	Waste %	Material Cost £	Craft Optve Hrs	Lab Hrs	Labour Cost £	Sunds £	Nett Rate £	Unit	Gross rate (10%) £
PAINTING & CLEAR FINISHINGS; REDECORATIONS: POLYURETHANE LACQUER										
Generally										
Note: the following rates include for the cost of all preparatory work, e.g. washing down, etc.										
Two coats polyurethane lacquer, existing lacquered surfaces										
Wood general surfaces										
girth exceeding 300mm	1.04	10.00	1.14	0.54	-	11.27	0.59	13.00	m²	14.31
isolated surfaces, girth not exceeding 300mm	0.31	10.00	0.34	0.18	-	3.76	0.20	4.30	m	4.73
Wood glazed doors										
girth exceeding 300mm; panes, area not exceeding 0.10m²	0.59	10.00	0.65	0.92	-	19.20	1.01	20.86	m²	22.94
girth exceeding 300mm; panes, area 0.10 - 0.50m²	0.41	10.00	0.46	0.67	-	13.98	0.74	15.18	m²	16.69
girth exceeding 300mm; panes, area 0.50 - 1.00m²	0.38	10.00	0.42	0.55	-	11.48	0.61	12.50	m²	13.75
girth exceeding 300mm; panes, area exceeding 1.00m²	0.38	10.00	0.42	0.48	-	10.02	0.53	10.96	m²	12.06
Wood partially glazed doors										
girth exceeding 300mm; panes, area not exceeding 0.10m²	0.83	10.00	0.91	0.77	-	16.07	0.85	17.83	m²	19.61
girth exceeding 300mm; panes, area 0.10 - 0.50m²	0.62	10.00	0.68	0.62	-	12.94	0.68	14.31	m²	15.74
girth exceeding 300mm; panes, area 0.50 - 1.00m²	0.59	10.00	0.65	0.55	-	11.48	0.61	12.73	m²	14.00
girth exceeding 300mm; panes, area exceeding 1.00m²	0.59	10.00	0.65	0.50	-	10.44	0.55	11.63	m²	12.79
Wood windows and screens										
girth exceeding 300mm; panes, area not exceeding 0.10m²	0.83	10.00	0.91	0.99	-	20.66	1.09	22.66	m²	24.93
girth exceeding 300mm; panes, area 0.10 - 0.50m²	0.62	10.00	0.68	0.65	-	13.57	0.72	14.96	m²	16.46
girth exceeding 300mm; panes, area 0.50 - 1.00m²	0.59	10.00	0.65	0.59	-	12.31	0.65	13.61	m²	14.97
girth exceeding 300mm; panes, area exceeding 1.00m²	0.59	10.00	0.65	0.52	-	10.85	0.57	12.07	m²	13.28
Two coats polyurethane lacquer, existing lacquered surfaces; external work										
Wood general surfaces										
girth exceeding 300mm	1.04	10.00	1.14	0.57	-	11.90	0.63	13.66	m²	15.03
isolated surfaces, girth not exceeding 300mm	0.31	10.00	0.34	0.19	-	3.97	0.21	4.52	m	4.97
Wood glazed doors										
girth exceeding 300mm; panes, area not exceeding 0.10m²	0.59	10.00	0.65	0.94	-	19.62	1.03	21.30	m²	23.43
girth exceeding 300mm; panes, area 0.10 - 0.50m²	0.41	10.00	0.46	0.68	-	14.19	0.75	15.40	m²	16.94
girth exceeding 300mm; panes, area 0.50 - 1.00m²	0.38	10.00	0.42	0.56	-	11.69	0.62	12.72	m²	13.99
girth exceeding 300mm; panes, area exceeding 1.00m²	0.38	10.00	0.42	0.49	-	10.23	0.54	11.18	m²	12.30
Wood partially glazed doors										
girth exceeding 300mm; panes, area not exceeding 0.10m²	0.83	10.00	0.91	0.79	-	16.49	0.87	18.27	m²	20.10
girth exceeding 300mm; panes, area 0.10 - 0.50m²	0.62	10.00	0.68	0.63	-	13.15	0.69	14.53	m²	15.98
girth exceeding 300mm; panes, area 0.50 - 1.00m²	0.59	10.00	0.65	0.56	-	11.69	0.62	12.95	m²	14.24
girth exceeding 300mm; panes, area exceeding 1.00m²	0.59	10.00	0.65	0.51	-	10.64	0.56	11.85	m²	13.04
Wood windows and screens										
girth exceeding 300mm; panes, area not exceeding 0.10m²	0.83	10.00	0.91	1.04	-	21.70	1.14	23.76	m²	26.14
girth exceeding 300mm; panes, area 0.10 - 0.50m²	0.62	10.00	0.68	0.76	-	15.86	0.84	17.38	m²	19.12
girth exceeding 300mm; panes, area 0.50 - 1.00m²	0.59	10.00	0.65	0.63	-	13.15	0.69	14.49	m²	15.94
girth exceeding 300mm; panes, area exceeding 1.00m²	0.59	10.00	0.65	0.55	-	11.48	0.61	12.73	m²	14.00
Three coats polyurethane lacquer, existing lacquered surfaces										
Wood general surfaces										
girth exceeding 300mm	1.52	10.00	1.67	0.62	-	12.94	0.68	15.29	m²	16.82
isolated surfaces, girth not exceeding 300mm	0.45	10.00	0.49	0.21	-	4.38	0.23	5.11	m	5.62
Wood glazed doors										
girth exceeding 300mm; panes, area not exceeding 0.10m²	0.86	10.00	0.95	1.04	-	21.70	1.14	23.80	m²	26.18
girth exceeding 300mm; panes, area 0.10 - 0.50m²	0.62	10.00	0.68	0.76	-	15.86	0.84	17.38	m²	19.12
girth exceeding 300mm; panes, area 0.50 - 1.00m²	0.55	10.00	0.61	0.63	-	13.15	0.69	14.45	m²	15.89
girth exceeding 300mm; panes, area exceeding 1.00m²	0.55	10.00	0.61	0.54	-	11.27	0.59	12.47	m²	13.72
Wood partially glazed doors										
girth exceeding 300mm; panes, area not exceeding 0.10m²	1.21	10.00	1.33	0.87	-	18.16	0.96	20.44	m²	22.49
girth exceeding 300mm; panes, area 0.10 - 0.50m²	0.90	10.00	0.99	0.77	-	16.07	0.85	17.91	m²	19.70
girth exceeding 300mm; panes, area 0.50 - 1.00m²	0.83	10.00	0.91	0.63	-	13.15	0.69	14.75	m²	16.23
girth exceeding 300mm; panes, area exceeding 1.00m²	0.83	10.00	0.91	0.58	-	12.10	0.64	13.66	m²	15.02
Wood windows and screens										
girth exceeding 300mm; panes, area not exceeding 0.10m²	0.86	10.00	0.95	1.13	-	23.58	1.24	25.78	m²	28.35
girth exceeding 300mm; panes, area 0.10 - 0.50m²	0.62	10.00	0.68	0.82	-	17.11	0.90	18.70	m²	20.57
girth exceeding 300mm; panes, area 0.50 - 1.00m²	0.55	10.00	0.61	0.68	-	14.19	0.75	15.55	m²	17.10
girth exceeding 300mm; panes, area exceeding 1.00m²	0.55	10.00	0.61	0.59	-	12.31	0.65	13.57	m²	14.93
Three coats polyurethane lacquer, existing lacquered surfaces; external work										
Wood general surfaces										
girth exceeding 300mm	1.52	10.00	1.67	0.66	-	13.77	0.73	16.17	m²	17.79
isolated surfaces, girth not exceeding 300mm	0.45	10.00	0.49	0.22	-	4.59	0.24	5.33	m	5.86
Wood glazed doors										
girth exceeding 300mm; panes, area not exceeding 0.10m²	0.86	10.00	0.95	1.06	-	22.12	1.17	24.24	m²	26.66
girth exceeding 300mm; panes, area 0.10 - 0.50m²	0.62	10.00	0.68	0.77	-	16.07	0.85	17.60	m²	19.36
girth exceeding 300mm; panes, area 0.50 - 1.00m²	0.55	10.00	0.61	0.64	-	13.36	0.70	14.67	m²	16.14
girth exceeding 300mm; panes, area exceeding 1.00m²	0.55	10.00	0.61	0.54	-	11.27	0.59	12.47	m²	13.72
Wood partially glazed doors										
girth exceeding 300mm; panes, area not exceeding 0.10m²	1.21	10.00	1.33	0.89	-	18.57	0.98	20.88	m²	22.97
girth exceeding 300mm; panes, area 0.10 - 0.50m²	0.90	10.00	0.99	0.78	-	16.28	0.86	18.13	m²	19.94
girth exceeding 300mm; panes, area 0.50 - 1.00m²	0.83	10.00	0.91	0.64	-	13.36	0.70	14.97	m²	16.47
girth exceeding 300mm; panes, area exceeding 1.00m²	0.83	10.00	0.91	0.59	-	12.31	0.65	13.87	m²	15.26

Labour hourly rates: (except Specialists) Craft Operatives 20.87 Labourer 15.57 Rates are national average prices. Refer to REGIONAL VARIATIONS for indicative levels of overall pricing in regions	MATERIALS			LABOUR				RATES		
	Del to Site £	Waste %	Material Cost £	Craft Optve Hrs	Lab Hrs	Labour Cost £	Sunds £	Nett Rate £	Unit	Gross rate (10%) £
PAINTING & CLEAR FINISHINGS; REDECORATIONS: POLYURETHANE LACQUER (Cont'd)										
Three coats polyurethane lacquer, existing lacquered surfaces; external work (Cont'd)										
Wood windows and screens										
girth exceeding 300mm; panes, area not exceeding 0.10m²	0.86	10.00	0.95	1.18	-	24.63	1.30	26.88	m²	29.56
girth exceeding 300mm; panes, area 0.10 - 0.50m²	0.62	10.00	0.68	0.87	-	18.16	0.96	19.80	m²	21.78
girth exceeding 300mm; panes, area 0.50 - 1.00m²	0.55	10.00	0.61	0.73	-	15.24	0.80	16.65	m²	18.31
girth exceeding 300mm; panes, area exceeding 1.00m²	0.55	10.00	0.61	0.63	-	13.15	0.69	14.45	m²	15.89
PAINTING & CLEAR FINISHINGS; REDECORATIONS: FRENCH AND WAX POLISHING										
Generally										
Note: the following rates include for the cost of all preparatory work, e.g. washing down, etc.										
Stain; two coats white polish										
Wood general surfaces										
girth exceeding 300mm	6.33	10.00	6.96	0.40	-	8.35	0.44	15.75	m²	17.32
isolated surfaces, girth not exceeding 300mm	1.99	10.00	2.19	0.14	-	2.92	0.15	5.27	m	5.80
Strip old polish, oil, two coats wax polish, existing polished surfaces										
Wood general surfaces										
girth exceeding 300mm	6.33	10.00	6.96	1.23	-	25.67	1.35	33.98	m²	37.38
isolated surfaces, girth not exceeding 300mm	1.99	10.00	2.19	0.37	-	7.72	0.41	10.32	m	11.35
Strip old polish, oil, stain, two coats wax polish, existing polished surfaces										
Wood general surfaces										
girth exceeding 300mm	6.33	10.00	6.96	1.35	-	28.17	1.49	36.62	m²	40.28
isolated surfaces, girth not exceeding 300mm	1.99	10.00	2.19	0.42	-	8.77	0.46	11.42	m	12.56
Open grain French polish existing polished surfaces										
Wood general surfaces										
girth exceeding 300mm	6.93	10.00	7.63	2.64	-	55.10	2.90	65.63	m²	72.19
isolated surfaces, girth not exceeding 300mm	2.19	10.00	2.41	0.88	-	18.37	0.97	21.74	m	23.91
Fully French polish existing polished surfaces										
Wood general surfaces										
girth exceeding 300mm	11.06	10.00	12.16	1.54	-	32.14	1.69	46.00	m²	50.60
isolated surfaces, girth not exceeding 300mm	3.49	10.00	3.84	0.52	-	10.85	0.57	15.26	m	16.79
Strip old polish, oil, open grain French polish, existing polished surfaces										
Wood general surfaces										
girth exceeding 300mm	6.93	10.00	7.63	3.43	-	71.58	3.77	82.98	m²	91.28
isolated surfaces, girth not exceeding 300mm	2.19	10.00	2.41	1.14	-	23.79	1.25	27.45	m	30.20
Strip old polish, oil, stain, open grain French polish, existing polished surfaces										
Wood general surfaces										
girth exceeding 300mm	6.93	10.00	7.63	3.55	-	74.09	3.90	85.62	m²	94.18
isolated surfaces, girth not exceeding 300mm	2.19	10.00	2.41	1.19	-	24.84	1.31	28.55	m	31.41
Strip old polish, oil, body in, fully French polish existing polished surfaces										
Wood general surfaces										
girth exceeding 300mm	11.06	10.00	12.16	4.63	-	96.63	5.09	113.88	m²	125.27
isolated surfaces, girth not exceeding 300mm	3.49	10.00	3.84	1.54	-	32.14	1.69	37.67	m	41.44
Strip old polish, oil, stain, body in, fully French polish, existing polished surfaces										
Wood general surfaces										
girth exceeding 300mm	11.06	10.00	12.16	4.74	-	98.92	5.21	116.30	m²	127.93
isolated surfaces, girth not exceeding 300mm	3.49	10.00	3.84	1.58	-	32.97	1.74	38.55	m	42.41
PAINTING & CLEAR FINISHINGS; REDECORATIONS: WATER REPELLENT										
One coat solvent based water repellent, existing surfaces										
Cement rendered general surfaces										
girth exceeding 300mm	0.16	5.00	0.16	0.12	-	2.50	0.13	2.80	m²	3.08
Stone general surfaces										
girth exceeding 300mm	0.19	5.00	0.20	0.13	-	2.71	0.14	3.06	m²	3.36
Brickwork general surfaces										
girth exceeding 300mm	0.19	5.00	0.20	0.13	-	2.71	0.14	3.06	m²	3.36
PAINTING & CLEAR FINISHINGS; REDECORATIONS: REMOVAL OF MOULD GROWTH										
Apply fungicide to existing decorated and infected surfaces										
Cement rendered general surfaces										
girth exceeding 300mm	0.17	5.00	0.18	0.22	-	4.59	0.24	5.01	m²	5.52

Labour hourly rates: (except Specialists) Craft Operatives 20.87 Labourer 15.57 Rates are national average prices. Refer to REGIONAL VARIATIONS for indicative levels of overall pricing in regions	MATERIALS			LABOUR				RATES		
	Del to Site £	Waste %	Material Cost £	Craft Optve Hrs	Lab Hrs	Labour Cost £	Sunds £	Nett Rate £	Unit	Gross rate (10%) £
PAINTING & CLEAR FINISHINGS; REDECORATIONS: REMOVAL OF MOULD GROWTH (Cont'd)										
Apply fungicide to existing decorated and infected surfaces (Cont'd)										
Concrete general surfaces girth exceeding 300mm	0.21	5.00	0.22	0.22	-	4.59	0.24	5.05	m²	5.56
Plaster general surfaces girth exceeding 300mm	0.15	5.00	0.16	0.22	-	4.59	0.24	4.99	m²	5.49
Brickwork general surfaces girth exceeding 300mm	0.21	5.00	0.22	0.24	-	5.01	0.26	5.49	m²	6.04
Apply fungicide to existing decorated and infected surfaces; external work										
Cement rendered general surfaces girth exceeding 300mm	0.17	5.00	0.18	0.24	-	5.01	0.26	5.45	m²	6.00
Concrete general surfaces girth exceeding 300mm	0.21	5.00	0.22	0.24	-	5.01	0.26	5.49	m²	6.04
Plaster general surfaces girth exceeding 300mm	0.15	5.00	0.16	0.24	-	5.01	0.26	5.43	m²	5.98
Brickwork general surfaces girth exceeding 300mm	0.21	5.00	0.22	0.26	-	5.43	0.29	5.93	m²	6.53
DECORATIVE PAPERS OR FABRICS										
Lining paper (prime cost sum for supply and allowance for waste included elsewhere); sizing; applying adhesive; hanging; butt joints										
Plaster walls and columns exceeding 0.50m²	0.05	10.00	0.05	0.13	-	2.71	0.14	2.91	m²	3.20
Plaster ceilings and beams exceeding 0.50m²	0.05	10.00	0.05	0.14	-	2.92	0.15	3.13	m²	3.44
Pulp paper (prime cost sum for supply and allowance for waste included elsewhere); sizing; applying adhesive; hanging; butt joints										
Plaster walls and columns exceeding 0.50m²	0.05	10.00	0.05	0.31	-	6.47	0.34	6.87	m²	7.55
Plaster ceilings and beams exceeding 0.50m²	0.05	10.00	0.05	0.34	-	7.10	0.37	7.52	m²	8.28
Washable paper (prime cost sum for supply and allowance for waste included elsewhere); sizing; applying adhesive; hanging; butt joints										
Plaster walls and columns exceeding 0.50m²	0.07	10.00	0.07	0.24	-	5.01	0.26	5.35	m²	5.88
Plaster ceilings and beams exceeding 0.50m²	0.07	10.00	0.07	0.26	-	5.43	0.29	5.78	m²	6.36
Vinyl coated paper (prime cost sum for supply and allowance for waste included elsewhere); sizing; applying adhesive; hanging; butt joints										
Plaster walls and columns exceeding 0.50m²	0.07	10.00	0.07	0.24	-	5.01	0.26	5.35	m²	5.88
Plaster ceilings and beams exceeding 0.50m²	0.07	10.00	0.07	0.26	-	5.43	0.29	5.78	m²	6.36
Embossed or textured paper (prime cost sum for supply and allowance for waste included elsewhere); sizing; applying adhesive; hanging; butt joints										
Plaster walls and columns exceeding 0.50m²	0.07	10.00	0.07	0.24	-	5.01	0.26	5.35	m²	5.88
Plaster ceilings and beams exceeding 0.50m²	0.13	10.00	0.15	0.26	-	5.43	0.29	5.86	m²	6.45
Woodchip paper (prime cost sum for supply and allowance for waste included elsewhere); sizing; applying adhesive; hanging; butt joints										
Plaster walls and columns exceeding 0.50m²	0.05	10.00	0.05	0.24	-	5.01	0.26	5.33	m²	5.86
Plaster ceilings and beams exceeding 0.50m²	0.05	10.00	0.05	0.26	-	5.43	0.29	5.77	m²	6.34
Paper border strips (prime cost sum for supply and allowance for waste included elsewhere); sizing; applying adhesive; hanging; butt joints										
Border strips										
25mm wide to papered walls and columns	0.01	10.00	0.01	0.09	-	1.88	0.10	1.98	m	2.18
75mm wide to papered walls and columns	0.02	10.00	0.02	0.10	-	2.09	0.11	2.22	m	2.44

Labour hourly rates: (except Specialists) Craft Operatives 20.87 Labourer 15.57 Rates are national average prices. Refer to REGIONAL VARIATIONS for indicative levels of overall pricing in regions	MATERIALS			LABOUR				RATES		
	Del to Site	Waste	Material Cost	Craft Optve	Lab	Labour Cost	Sunds	Nett Rate		Gross rate (10%)
	£	%	£	Hrs	Hrs	£	£	£	Unit	£
DECORATIVE PAPERS OR FABRICS (Cont'd)										
Lining paper; 1000g; sizing; applying adhesive; hanging; butt joints										
Plaster walls and columns exceeding 0.50m²	0.43	12.00	0.48	0.13	-	2.71	0.14	3.34	m²	3.67
Plaster ceilings and beams exceeding 0.50m²	0.43	12.00	0.48	0.14	-	2.92	0.15	3.56	m²	3.92
Pulp paper pc £4.00 roll; sizing; applying adhesive; hanging; butt joints										
Plaster walls and columns exceeding 0.50m²	0.85	30.00	1.09	0.24	-	5.01	0.26	6.37	m²	7.00
Plaster ceilings and beams exceeding 0.50m²	0.85	25.00	1.05	0.26	-	5.43	0.29	6.77	m²	7.44
Pulp paper (24" drop pattern match) pc £6.00 roll; sizing; applying adhesive; hanging; butt joints										
Plaster walls and columns exceeding 0.50m²	1.25	40.00	1.74	0.31	-	6.47	0.34	8.55	m²	9.40
Plaster ceilings and beams exceeding 0.50m²	1.25	35.00	1.68	0.33	-	6.89	0.36	8.93	m²	9.82
Washable paper pc £6.00 roll; sizing; applying adhesive; hanging; butt joints										
Plaster walls and columns exceeding 0.50m²	1.27	25.00	1.57	0.24	-	5.01	0.26	6.85	m²	7.53
Plaster ceilings and beams exceeding 0.50m²	1.27	20.00	1.51	0.26	-	5.43	0.29	7.22	m²	7.95
Vinyl coated paper pc £6.50 roll; sizing; applying adhesive; hanging; butt joints										
Plaster walls and columns exceeding 0.50m²	1.37	25.00	1.70	0.24	-	5.01	0.26	6.97	m²	7.67
Plaster ceilings and beams exceeding 0.50m²	1.37	20.00	1.63	0.26	-	5.43	0.29	7.34	m²	8.08
Vinyl coated paper pc £7.00 roll; sizing; applying adhesive; hanging; butt joints										
Plaster walls and columns exceeding 0.50m²	1.47	25.00	1.82	0.24	-	5.01	0.26	7.10	m²	7.80
Plaster ceilings and beams exceeding 0.50m²	1.47	20.00	1.75	0.26	-	5.43	0.29	7.46	m²	8.21
Embossed paper pc £6.00 roll; sizing; applying adhesive; hanging; butt joints										
Plaster walls and columns exceeding 0.50m²	1.33	25.00	1.65	0.24	-	5.01	0.26	6.92	m²	7.61
Plaster ceilings and beams exceeding 0.50m²	1.33	20.00	1.59	0.26	-	5.43	0.29	7.30	m²	8.03
Textured paper pc £6.50 roll; sizing; applying adhesive; hanging; butt joints										
Plaster walls and columns exceeding 0.50m²	1.40	25.00	1.74	0.24	-	5.01	0.24	6.99	m²	7.68
Plaster ceilings and beams exceeding 0.50m²	1.40	20.00	1.67	0.26	-	5.43	0.26	7.36	m²	8.10
Woodchip paper pc £4.00 roll; sizing; applying adhesive; hanging; butt joints										
Plaster walls and columns exceeding 0.50m²	0.85	25.00	1.05	0.24	-	5.01	0.24	6.31	m²	6.94
Plaster ceilings and beams exceeding 0.50m²	0.85	20.00	1.01	0.26	-	5.43	0.26	6.71	m²	7.38
Paper border strips pc £0.50m; applying adhesive; hanging; butt joints										
Border strips 25mm wide to papered walls and columns	0.51	10.00	0.56	0.09	-	1.88	0.10	2.53	m	2.79
Paper border strips pc £1.00m; applying adhesive; hanging; butt joints										
Border strips 75mm wide to papered walls and columns	1.02	10.00	1.12	0.10	-	2.09	0.11	3.32	m	3.65
Hessian wall covering (prime cost sum for supply and allowance for waste included elsewhere); sizing; applying adhesive; hanging; butt joints										
Plaster walls and columns exceeding 0.50m²	0.20	10.00	0.22	0.44	-	9.18	0.48	9.89	m²	10.88

Labour hourly rates: (except Specialists) Craft Operatives 20.87 Labourer 15.57 Rates are national average prices. Refer to REGIONAL VARIATIONS for indicative levels of overall pricing in regions	MATERIALS			LABOUR				RATES		
	Del to Site £	Waste %	Material Cost £	Craft Optve Hrs	Lab Hrs	Labour Cost £	Sunds £	Nett Rate £	Unit	Gross rate (10%) £
DECORATIVE PAPERS OR FABRICS (Cont'd)										
Textile hessian paper backed wall covering (prime cost sum for supply and allowance for waste included elsewhere); sizing; applying adhesive; hanging; butt joints										
Plaster walls and columns exceeding 0.50m²	0.20	10.00	0.22	0.36	-	7.51	0.40	8.13	m²	8.94
Hessian wall covering pc £4.50m²; sizing; applying adhesive; hanging; butt joints										
Plaster walls and columns exceeding 0.50m²	4.70	30.00	6.07	0.24	-	5.01	0.26	11.34	m²	12.48
Textile hessian paper backed wall covering pc £8.00m²; sizing; applying adhesive; hanging; butt joints										
Plaster walls and columns exceeding 0.50m²	8.20	25.00	10.22	0.36	-	7.51	0.40	18.13	m²	19.94
DECORATIVE PAPERS OR FABRICS; REDECORATIONS										
Stripping existing paper; lining paper (prime cost sum for supply and allowance for waste included elsewhere); sizing; applying adhesive hanging; butt joints										
Hard building board walls and columns exceeding 0.50m²	0.05	10.00	0.05	0.32	-	6.68	0.64	7.37	m²	8.11
Plaster walls and columns exceeding 0.50m²	0.05	10.00	0.05	0.28	-	5.84	0.62	6.51	m²	7.17
Hard building board ceilings and beams exceeding 0.50m²	0.05	10.00	0.05	0.35	-	7.30	0.77	8.13	m²	8.94
Plaster ceilings and beams exceeding 0.50m²	0.05	10.00	0.05	0.30	-	6.26	0.66	6.98	m²	7.67
Stripping existing paper; lining paper and cross lining (prime cost sum for supply and allowance for waste included elsewhere); sizing; applying adhesive; hanging; butt joints										
Hard building board walls and columns exceeding 0.50m²	0.10	10.00	0.11	0.45	-	9.39	0.99	10.49	m²	11.54
Plaster walls and columns exceeding 0.50m²	0.10	10.00	0.11	0.41	-	8.56	0.90	9.57	m²	10.53
Hard building board ceilings and beams exceeding 0.50m²	0.10	10.00	0.11	0.50	-	10.44	1.10	11.65	m²	12.81
Plaster ceilings and beams exceeding 0.50m²	0.10	10.00	0.11	0.44	-	9.18	0.97	10.26	m²	11.29
Stripping existing paper; pulp paper (prime cost sum for supply and allowance for waste included elsewhere); applying adhesive; hanging; butt joints										
Hard building board walls and columns exceeding 0.50m²	0.05	10.00	0.05	0.43	-	8.97	0.95	9.98	m²	10.97
Plaster walls and columns exceeding 0.50m²	0.05	10.00	0.05	0.39	-	8.14	0.86	9.05	m²	9.96
Hard building board ceilings and beams exceeding 0.50m²	0.05	10.00	0.05	0.47	-	9.81	1.03	10.90	m²	11.99
Plaster ceilings and beams exceeding 0.50m²	0.05	10.00	0.05	0.42	-	8.77	0.92	9.74	m²	10.72
Stripping existing washable or vinyl coated paper; washable paper (prime cost sum for supply and allowance for waste included elsewhere); applying adhesive; hanging; butt joints										
Hard building board walls and columns exceeding 0.50m²	0.07	10.00	0.07	0.44	-	9.18	0.97	10.22	m²	11.25
Plaster walls and columns exceeding 0.50m²	0.07	10.00	0.07	0.40	-	8.35	0.88	9.30	m²	10.23
Hard building board ceilings and beams exceeding 0.50m²	0.07	10.00	0.07	0.48	-	10.02	1.06	11.15	m²	12.26
Plaster ceilings and beams exceeding 0.50m²	0.07	10.00	0.07	0.43	-	8.97	0.95	9.99	m²	10.99
Stripping existing washable or vinyl coated paper; vinyl coated paper (prime cost sum for supply and allowance for waste included elsewhere); sizing; applying adhesive; hanging; butt joints										
Hard building board walls and columns exceeding 0.50m²	0.07	10.00	0.07	0.44	-	9.18	0.97	10.22	m²	11.25
Plaster walls and columns exceeding 0.50m²	0.07	10.00	0.07	0.40	-	8.35	0.88	9.30	m²	10.23
Hard building board ceilings and beams exceeding 0.50m²	0.07	10.00	0.07	0.48	-	10.02	1.06	11.15	m²	12.26
Plaster ceilings and beams exceeding 0.50m²	0.07	10.00	0.07	0.43	-	8.97	0.95	9.99	m²	10.99

Labour hourly rates: (except Specialists) Craft Operatives 20.87 Labourer 15.57 Rates are national average prices. Refer to REGIONAL VARIATIONS for indicative levels of overall pricing in regions	MATERIALS			LABOUR				RATES		
	Del to Site £	Waste %	Material Cost £	Craft Optve Hrs	Lab Hrs	Labour Cost £	Sunds £	Nett Rate £	Unit	Gross rate (10%) £
DECORATIVE PAPERS OR FABRICS; REDECORATIONS (Cont'd)										
Stripping existing paper; embossed or textured paper; (prime cost sum for supply and allowance for waste included elsewhere); sizing; applying adhesive; hanging; butt joints										
Hard building board walls and columns exceeding 0.50m²	0.13	10.00	0.15	0.43	-	8.97	0.95	10.07	m²	11.07
Plaster walls and columns exceeding 0.50m²	0.13	10.00	0.15	0.39	-	8.14	0.86	9.14	m²	10.06
Hard building board ceilings and beams exceeding 0.50m²	0.13	10.00	0.15	0.47	-	9.81	1.03	10.99	m²	12.09
Plaster ceilings and beams exceeding 0.50m²	0.13	10.00	0.15	0.42	-	8.77	0.92	9.84	m²	10.82
Stripping existing paper; woodchip paper (prime cost sum for supply and allowance for waste included elsewhere); sizing; applying adhesive; hanging; butt joints										
Hard building board walls and columns exceeding 0.50m²	0.05	10.00	0.05	0.43	-	8.97	0.95	9.98	m²	10.97
Plaster walls and columns exceeding 0.50m²	0.05	10.00	0.05	0.39	-	8.14	0.86	9.05	m²	9.96
Hard building board ceilings and beams exceeding 0.50m²	0.05	10.00	0.05	0.47	-	9.81	1.03	10.90	m²	11.99
Plaster ceilings and beams exceeding 0.50m²	0.05	10.00	0.05	0.42	-	8.77	0.92	9.74	m²	10.72
Stripping existing varnished or painted paper; woodchip paper (prime cost sum for supply and allowance for waste included elsewhere); sizing; applying adhesive; hanging; butt joints										
Hard building board walls and columns exceeding 0.50m²	0.05	10.00	0.05	0.57	-	11.90	1.25	13.20	m²	14.53
Plaster walls and columns exceeding 0.50m²	0.05	10.00	0.05	0.53	-	11.06	1.17	12.28	m²	13.51
Hard building board ceilings and beams exceeding 0.50m²	0.05	10.00	0.05	0.63	-	13.15	1.39	14.59	m²	16.05
Plaster ceilings and beams exceeding 0.50m²	0.05	10.00	0.05	0.58	-	12.10	1.28	13.44	m²	14.78
Stripping existing paper; lining paper; sizing; applying adhesive; hanging; butt joints										
Hard building board walls and columns exceeding 0.50m²	0.43	12.00	0.48	0.32	-	6.68	1.30	8.46	m²	9.31
Plaster walls and columns exceeding 0.50m²	0.43	12.00	0.48	0.28	-	5.84	0.62	6.94	m²	7.64
Hard building board ceilings and beams exceeding 0.50m²	0.43	12.00	0.48	0.35	-	7.30	0.77	8.56	m²	9.41
Plaster ceilings and beams exceeding 0.50m²	0.43	12.00	0.48	0.30	-	6.26	0.66	7.41	m²	8.15
Stripping existing paper; lining paper; cross lining; sizing; applying adhesive; hanging; butt joints										
Hard building board walls and columns exceeding 0.50m²	0.87	12.00	0.97	0.45	-	9.39	0.99	11.35	m²	12.49
Plaster walls and columns exceeding 0.50m²	0.87	12.00	0.97	0.41	-	8.56	0.81	10.34	m²	11.37
Hard building board ceilings and beams exceeding 0.50m²	0.87	12.00	0.97	0.50	-	10.44	1.10	12.50	m²	13.75
Plaster ceilings and beams exceeding 0.50m²	0.87	12.00	0.97	0.44	-	9.18	0.97	11.12	m²	12.23
Stripping existing paper; pulp paper pc £4.00 roll; sizing; applying adhesive; hanging; butt joints										
Hard building board walls and columns exceeding 0.50m²	0.85	30.00	1.09	0.43	-	8.97	0.95	11.02	m²	12.12
Plaster walls and columns exceeding 0.50m²	0.85	30.00	1.09	0.39	-	8.14	0.86	10.09	m²	11.10
Hard building board ceilings and beams exceeding 0.50m²	0.85	25.00	1.05	0.47	-	9.81	1.03	11.90	m²	13.09
Plaster ceilings and beams exceeding 0.50m²	0.85	25.00	1.05	0.42	-	8.77	0.92	10.74	m²	11.82
Stripping existing paper; pulp paper with 24" drop pattern; pc £6.00 roll; sizing; applying adhesive; hanging; butt joints										
Hard building board walls and columns exceeding 0.50m²	1.25	40.00	1.74	0.50	-	10.44	1.10	13.27	m²	14.60

Labour hourly rates: (except Specialists) Craft Operatives 20.87 Labourer 15.57 Rates are national average prices. Refer to REGIONAL VARIATIONS for indicative levels of overall pricing in regions	MATERIALS			LABOUR				RATES		
	Del to Site £	Waste %	Material Cost £	Craft Optve Hrs	Lab Hrs	Labour Cost £	Sunds £	Nett Rate £	Unit	Gross rate (10%) £
DECORATIVE PAPERS OR FABRICS; REDECORATIONS (Cont'd)										
Stripping existing paper; pulp paper with 24" drop pattern; pc £6.00 roll; sizing; applying adhesive; hanging; butt joints (Cont'd)										
Plaster walls and columns exceeding 0.50m²	1.25	40.00	1.74	0.45	-	9.39	0.99	12.12	m²	13.33
Hard building board ceilings and beams exceeding 0.50m²	1.25	35.00	1.68	0.54	-	11.27	1.19	14.13	m²	15.55
Plaster ceilings and beams exceeding 0.50m²	1.25	35.00	1.68	0.48	-	10.02	1.06	12.75	m²	14.02
Stripping existing washable or vinyl coated paper; washable paper pc £6.00 roll; sizing; applying adhesive; hanging; butt joints										
Hard building board walls and columns exceeding 0.50m²	1.27	25.00	1.57	0.44	-	9.18	0.97	11.72	m²	12.90
Plaster walls and columns exceeding 0.50m²	1.27	25.00	1.57	0.40	-	8.35	0.88	10.80	m²	11.88
Hard building board ceilings and beams exceeding 0.50m²	1.27	20.00	1.51	0.48	-	10.02	1.06	12.59	m²	13.84
Plaster ceilings and beams exceeding 0.50m²	1.27	20.00	1.51	0.43	-	8.97	0.95	11.43	m²	12.58
Stripping existing washable or vinyl coated paper; vinyl coated paper pc £6.50 roll; sizing; applying adhesive; hanging; butt joints										
Hard building board walls and columns exceeding 0.50m²	1.37	25.00	1.70	0.44	-	9.18	0.97	11.85	m²	13.03
Plaster walls and columns exceeding 0.50m²	1.37	25.00	1.70	0.40	-	8.35	0.88	10.93	m²	12.02
Hard building board ceilings and beams exceeding 0.50m²	1.37	20.00	1.63	0.48	-	10.02	1.06	12.71	m²	13.98
Plaster ceilings and beams exceeding 0.50m²	1.37	20.00	1.63	0.43	-	8.97	0.95	11.55	m²	12.71
Stripping existing washable or vinyl coated paper; vinyl coated paper pc £8.00 roll; sizing; applying adhesive; hanging; butt joints										
Hard building board walls and columns exceeding 0.50m²	1.67	25.00	2.07	0.44	-	9.18	0.97	12.22	m²	13.45
Plaster walls and columns exceeding 0.50m²	1.67	25.00	2.07	0.40	-	8.35	0.88	11.30	m²	12.43
Hard building board ceilings and beams exceeding 0.50m²	1.67	20.00	1.99	0.48	-	10.02	1.06	13.07	m²	14.37
Plaster ceilings and beams exceeding 0.50m²	1.67	20.00	1.99	0.43	-	8.97	0.95	11.91	m²	13.10
Stripping existing washable or vinyl coated paper; vinyl coated paper pc £10.00 roll; sizing; applying adhesive; hanging; butt joints										
Hard building board walls and columns exceeding 0.50m²	2.47	25.00	3.07	0.44	-	9.18	0.97	13.22	m²	14.55
Plaster walls and columns exceeding 0.50m²	2.47	25.00	3.07	0.40	-	8.35	0.88	12.30	m²	13.53
Hard building board ceilings and beams exceeding 0.50m²	2.47	20.00	2.95	0.48	-	10.02	1.06	14.03	m²	15.43
Plaster ceilings and beams exceeding 0.50m²	2.47	20.00	2.95	0.43	-	8.97	0.95	12.87	m²	14.16
Stripping existing washable or vinyl coated paper; vinyl coated paper pc £12.00 roll; sizing; applying adhesive; hanging; butt joints										
Hard building board walls and columns exceeding 0.50m²	2.07	25.00	2.57	0.44	-	9.18	0.97	12.72	m²	14.00
Plaster walls and columns exceeding 0.50m²	2.07	25.00	2.57	0.40	-	8.35	0.88	11.80	m²	12.98
Hard building board ceilings and beams exceeding 0.50m²	2.07	20.00	2.47	0.48	-	10.02	1.06	13.55	m²	14.90
Plaster ceilings and beams exceeding 0.50m²	2.07	20.00	2.47	0.43	-	8.97	0.95	12.39	m²	13.63
Stripping existing paper; embossed paper pc £6.00 roll; sizing; applying adhesive; hanging; butt joints										
Hard building board walls and columns exceeding 0.50m²	1.33	25.00	1.65	0.43	-	8.97	0.95	11.57	m²	12.72

Labour hourly rates: (except Specialists) Craft Operatives 20.87 Labourer 15.57 Rates are national average prices. Refer to REGIONAL VARIATIONS for indicative levels of overall pricing in regions	MATERIALS			LABOUR				RATES		
	Del to Site £	Waste %	Material Cost £	Craft Optve Hrs	Lab Hrs	Labour Cost £	Sunds £	Nett Rate £	Unit	Gross rate (10%) £
DECORATIVE PAPERS OR FABRICS; REDECORATIONS (Cont'd)										
Stripping existing paper; embossed paper pc £6.00 roll; sizing; applying adhesive; hanging; butt joints (Cont'd)										
Plaster walls and columns exceeding 0.50m²	1.33	25.00	1.65	0.39	-	8.14	0.86	10.64	m²	11.71
Hard building board ceilings and beams exceeding 0.50m²	1.33	20.00	1.59	0.47	-	9.81	1.03	12.43	m²	13.67
Plaster ceilings and beams exceeding 0.50m²	1.33	20.00	1.59	0.42	-	8.77	0.92	11.28	m²	12.40
Stripping existing paper; textured paper pc £6.50 roll; sizing; applying adhesive; hanging; butt joints										
Hard building board walls and columns exceeding 0.50m²	1.40	25.00	1.74	0.43	-	8.97	0.95	11.66	m²	12.82
Plaster walls and columns exceeding 0.50m²	1.40	25.00	1.74	0.39	-	8.14	0.86	10.73	m²	11.81
Hard building board ceilings and beams exceeding 0.50m²	1.40	20.00	1.67	0.47	-	9.81	1.03	12.51	m²	13.76
Plaster ceilings and beams exceeding 0.50m²	1.40	20.00	1.67	0.42	-	8.77	0.92	11.36	m²	12.50
Stripping existing paper; woodchip paper pc £4.00 roll; sizing; applying adhesive; hanging; butt joints										
Hard building board walls and columns exceeding 0.50m²	0.85	25.00	1.05	0.43	-	8.97	0.95	10.98	m²	12.07
Plaster walls and columns exceeding 0.50m²	0.85	25.00	1.05	0.39	-	8.14	0.86	10.05	m²	11.06
Hard building board ceilings and beams exceeding 0.50m²	0.85	20.00	1.01	0.47	-	9.81	1.03	11.86	m²	13.04
Plaster ceilings and beams exceeding 0.50m²	0.85	20.00	1.01	0.42	-	8.77	0.92	10.70	m²	11.77
Washing down old distempered or painted surfaces; lining paper; sizing; applying adhesive; hanging; butt joints										
Hard building board walls and columns exceeding 0.50m²	0.43	12.00	0.48	0.22	-	4.59	0.24	5.32	m²	5.85
Plaster walls and columns exceeding 0.50m²	0.43	12.00	0.48	0.22	-	4.59	0.24	5.32	m²	5.85
Hard building board ceilings and beams exceeding 0.50m²	0.43	12.00	0.48	0.23	-	4.80	0.25	5.54	m²	6.09
Plaster ceilings and beams exceeding 0.50m²	0.43	12.00	0.48	0.23	-	4.80	0.25	5.54	m²	6.09
Lining papered walls and columns exceeding 0.50m²	0.43	12.00	0.48	0.22	-	4.59	0.24	5.32	m²	5.85
Lining papered ceilings and beams exceeding 0.50m²	0.43	12.00	0.48	0.23	-	4.80	0.25	5.54	m²	6.09
Washing down old distempered or painted surfaces; lining paper; cross lining; sizing; applying adhesive; hanging; butt joints										
Hard building board walls and columns exceeding 0.50m²	0.87	12.00	0.97	0.35	-	7.30	0.39	8.66	m²	9.52
Plaster walls and columns exceeding 0.50m²	0.87	12.00	0.97	0.35	-	7.30	0.39	8.66	m²	9.52
Hard building board ceilings and beams exceeding 0.50m²	0.87	12.00	0.97	0.37	-	7.72	0.41	9.10	m²	10.01
Plaster ceilings and beams exceeding 0.50m²	0.87	12.00	0.97	0.37	-	7.72	0.41	9.10	m²	10.01
Washing down old distempered or painted surfaces; pulp paper pc £4.00 roll; sizing; applying adhesive; hanging; butt joints										
Hard building board walls and columns exceeding 0.50m²	0.85	30.00	1.09	0.33	-	6.89	0.36	8.35	m²	9.18
Plaster walls and columns exceeding 0.50m²	0.85	30.00	1.09	0.33	-	6.89	0.36	8.35	m²	9.18
Hard building board ceilings and beams exceeding 0.50m²	0.85	25.00	1.05	0.35	-	7.30	0.39	8.74	m²	9.62
Plaster ceilings and beams exceeding 0.50m²	0.85	25.00	1.05	0.35	-	7.30	0.39	8.74	m²	9.62
Washing down old distempered or painted surfaces; pulp paper with 24" drop pattern; pc £6.00 roll; sizing; applying adhesive; hanging; butt joints										
Hard building board walls and columns exceeding 0.50m²	1.25	40.00	1.74	0.40	-	8.35	0.44	10.52	m²	11.58

Labour hourly rates: (except Specialists) Craft Operatives 20.87 Labourer 15.57 Rates are national average prices. Refer to REGIONAL VARIATIONS for indicative levels of overall pricing in regions	MATERIALS			LABOUR				RATES		
	Del to Site £	Waste %	Material Cost £	Craft Optve Hrs	Lab Hrs	Labour Cost £	Sunds £	Nett Rate £	Unit	Gross rate (10%) £
DECORATIVE PAPERS OR FABRICS; REDECORATIONS (Cont'd)										
Washing down old distempered or painted surfaces; pulp paper with 24" drop pattern; pc £6.00 roll; sizing; applying adhesive; hanging; butt joints (Cont'd)										
Plaster walls and columns exceeding 0.50m²	1.25	40.00	1.74	0.40	-	8.35	0.44	10.52	m²	11.58
Hard building board ceilings and beams exceeding 0.50m²	1.25	35.00	1.68	0.42	-	8.77	0.46	10.90	m²	11.99
Plaster ceilings and beams exceeding 0.50m²	1.25	35.00	1.68	0.42	-	8.77	0.46	10.90	m²	11.99
Washing down old distempered or painted surfaces; washable paper pc £6.00 roll; sizing; applying adhesive; hanging; butt joints										
Hard building board walls and columns exceeding 0.50m²	1.27	25.00	1.57	0.33	-	6.89	0.36	8.82	m²	9.70
Plaster walls and columns exceeding 0.50m²	1.27	25.00	1.57	0.33	-	6.89	0.36	8.82	m²	9.70
Hard building board ceilings and beams exceeding 0.50m²	1.27	20.00	1.51	0.35	-	7.30	0.39	9.20	m²	10.12
Plaster ceilings and beams exceeding 0.50m²	1.27	20.00	1.51	0.35	-	7.30	0.35	9.17	m²	10.09
Washing down old distempered or painted surfaces; vinyl coated paper pc £6.50 roll; sizing; applying adhesive; hanging; butt joints										
Hard building board walls and columns exceeding 0.50m²	1.37	25.00	1.70	0.33	-	6.89	0.36	8.95	m²	9.84
Plaster walls and columns exceeding 0.50m²	1.37	25.00	1.70	0.33	-	6.89	0.36	8.95	m²	9.84
Hard building board ceilings and beams exceeding 0.50m²	1.37	20.00	1.63	0.35	-	7.30	0.39	9.32	m²	10.25
Plaster ceilings and beams exceeding 0.50m²	1.37	20.00	1.63	0.35	-	7.30	0.39	9.32	m²	10.25
Washing down old distempered or painted surfaces; vinyl coated paper pc £7.00 roll; sizing; applying adhesive; hanging; butt joints										
Hard building board walls and columns exceeding 0.50m²	1.47	25.00	1.82	0.33	-	6.89	0.36	9.07	m²	9.98
Plaster walls and columns exceeding 0.50m²	1.47	25.00	1.82	0.33	-	6.89	0.36	9.07	m²	9.98
Hard building board ceilings and beams exceeding 0.50m²	1.47	20.00	1.75	0.35	-	7.30	0.39	9.44	m²	10.39
Plaster ceilings and beams exceeding 0.50m²	1.47	20.00	1.75	0.35	-	7.30	0.39	9.44	m²	10.39
Washing down old distempered or painted surfaces; embossed paper pc £6.00 roll; sizing; applying adhesive; hanging; butt joints										
Hard building board walls and columns exceeding 0.50m²	1.33	25.00	1.65	0.33	-	6.89	0.36	8.90	m²	9.79
Plaster walls and columns exceeding 0.50m²	1.33	25.00	1.65	0.33	-	6.89	0.36	8.90	m²	9.79
Hard building board ceilings and beams exceeding 0.50m²	1.33	20.00	1.59	0.35	-	7.30	0.39	9.28	m²	10.20
Plaster ceilings and beams exceeding 0.50m²	1.33	20.00	1.59	0.35	-	7.30	0.39	9.28	m²	10.20
Washing down old distempered or painted surfaces; textured paper pc £6.50 roll; sizing; applying adhesive; hanging; butt joints										
Hard building board walls and columns exceeding 0.50m²	1.40	25.00	1.74	0.33	-	6.89	0.36	8.99	m²	9.88
Plaster walls and columns exceeding 0.50m²	1.40	25.00	1.74	0.33	-	6.89	0.36	8.99	m²	9.88
Hard building board ceilings and beams exceeding 0.50m²	1.40	20.00	1.67	0.35	-	7.30	0.39	9.36	m²	10.30
Plaster ceilings and beams exceeding 0.50m²	1.40	20.00	1.67	0.35	-	7.30	0.39	9.36	m²	10.30
Washing down old distempered or painted surfaces; woodchip paper pc £4.00 roll; sizing; applying adhesive; hanging; butt joints										
Hard building board walls and columns exceeding 0.50m²	0.85	25.00	1.05	0.33	-	6.89	0.36	8.31	m²	9.14

Labour hourly rates: (except Specialists) Craft Operatives 20.87 Labourer 15.57 Rates are national average prices. Refer to REGIONAL VARIATIONS for indicative levels of overall pricing in regions	MATERIALS			LABOUR				RATES		
	Del to Site	Waste	Material Cost	Craft Optve	Lab	Labour Cost	Sunds	Nett Rate		Gross rate (10%)
	£	%	£	Hrs	Hrs	£	£	£	Unit	£
DECORATIVE PAPERS OR FABRICS; REDECORATIONS (Cont'd)										
Washing down old distempered or painted surfaces; woodchip paper pc £4.00 roll; sizing; applying adhesive; hanging; butt joints (Cont'd)										
Plaster walls and columns exceeding 0.50m²	0.85	25.00	1.05	0.33	-	6.89	0.36	8.31	m²	9.14
Hard building board ceilings and beams exceeding 0.50m²	0.85	20.00	1.01	0.35	-	7.30	0.39	8.70	m²	9.57
Plaster ceilings and beams exceeding 0.50m²	0.85	20.00	1.01	0.35	-	7.30	0.39	8.70	m²	9.57
Stripping existing paper; hessian wall covering (prime cost sum for supply and allowance for waste included elsewhere); sizing; applying adhesive; hanging; butt joints										
Hard building board walls and columns exceeding 0.50m²	0.20	10.00	0.22	0.63	-	13.15	1.39	14.75	m²	16.23
Plaster walls and columns exceeding 0.50m²	0.20	10.00	0.22	0.58	-	12.10	1.28	13.60	m²	14.96
Stripping existing paper; textile hessian paper backed wall covering (prime cost sum for supply and allowance for waste included elsewhere); sizing; applying adhesive; hanging; butt joints										
Hard building board walls and columns exceeding 0.50m²	0.20	10.00	0.22	0.55	-	11.48	1.21	12.91	m²	14.20
Plaster walls and columns exceeding 0.50m²	0.20	10.00	0.22	0.51	-	10.64	1.12	11.99	m²	13.18
Stripping existing hessian; hessian surfaced wall paper (prime cost sum for supply and allowance for waste included elsewhere); sizing; applying adhesive; hanging; butt joints										
Hard building board walls and columns exceeding 0.50m²	0.20	10.00	0.22	1.03	-	21.50	2.27	23.98	m²	26.38
Plaster walls and columns exceeding 0.50m²	0.20	10.00	0.22	0.99	-	20.66	2.18	23.06	m²	25.37
Stripping existing hessian; textile hessian paper backed wall covering (prime cost sum for supply and allowance for waste included elsewhere); sizing; applying adhesive; hanging; butt joints										
Hard building board walls and columns exceeding 0.50m²	0.20	10.00	0.22	0.96	-	20.04	2.11	22.37	m²	24.60
Plaster walls and columns exceeding 0.50m²	0.20	10.00	0.22	0.91	-	18.99	2.00	21.21	m²	23.34
Stripping existing hessian, paper backed; hessian surfaced wall paper (prime cost sum for supply and allowance for waste included elsewhere); sizing; applying adhesive; hanging; butt joints										
Hard building board walls and columns exceeding 0.50m²	0.20	10.00	0.22	0.63	-	13.15	1.28	14.64	m²	16.11
Plaster walls and columns exceeding 0.50m²	0.20	10.00	0.22	0.58	-	12.10	1.28	13.60	m²	14.96
Stripping existing hessian, paper backed; textile hessian paper backed wall covering (prime cost sum for supply and allowance for waste included elsewhere); sizing; applying adhesive; hanging; butt joints										
Hard building board walls and columns exceeding 0.50m²	0.20	10.00	0.22	0.55	-	11.48	1.21	12.91	m²	14.20
Plaster walls and columns exceeding 0.50m²	0.20	10.00	0.22	0.51	-	10.64	1.12	11.99	m²	13.18
Stripping existing paper; hessian surfaced wall paper pc £4.50m²; sizing; applying adhesive; hanging; butt joints										
Hard building board walls and columns exceeding 0.50m²	4.70	30.00	6.07	0.63	-	13.15	1.39	20.60	m²	22.66
Plaster walls and columns exceeding 0.50m²	4.70	30.00	6.07	0.58	-	12.10	1.28	19.45	m²	21.40
Stripping existing paper; textile hessian paper backed wall covering pc £8.0m²; sizing; applying adhesive; hanging; butt joints										
Hard building board walls and columns exceeding 0.50m²	8.20	25.00	10.22	0.55	-	11.48	1.21	22.91	m²	25.20
Plaster walls and columns exceeding 0.50m²	8.20	25.00	10.22	0.51	-	10.64	1.12	21.99	m²	24.18

Labour hourly rates: (except Specialists) Craft Operatives 20.87 Labourer 15.57 Rates are national average prices. Refer to REGIONAL VARIATIONS for indicative levels of overall pricing in regions	MATERIALS			LABOUR				RATES		
	Del to Site £	Waste %	Material Cost £	Craft Optve Hrs	Lab Hrs	Labour Cost £	Sunds £	Nett Rate £	Unit	Gross rate (10%) £
DECORATIVE PAPERS OR FABRICS; REDECORATIONS (Cont'd)										
Stripping existing hessian; hessian surfaced wall paper pc £4.50m²; sizing; applying adhesive; hanging; butt joints										
Hard building board walls and columns exceeding 0.50m²	4.70	30.00	6.07	1.03	-	21.50	2.27	29.83	m²	32.82
Plaster walls and columns exceeding 0.50m²	4.70	30.00	6.07	0.99	-	20.66	2.18	28.91	m²	31.80
Stripping existing hessian; textile hessian paper backed wall covering pc £8.00m²; sizing; applying adhesive; hanging; butt joints										
Hard building board walls and columns exceeding 0.50m²	8.20	25.00	10.22	0.96	-	20.04	2.11	32.37	m²	35.60
Plaster walls and columns exceeding 0.50m²	8.20	25.00	10.22	0.91	-	18.99	2.00	31.21	m²	34.34
Stripping existing hessian, paper backed; hessian surfaced wall paper pc £4.50m²; sizing; applying adhesive; hanging; butt joints										
Hard building board walls and columns exceeding 0.50m²	4.70	30.00	6.07	0.63	-	13.15	1.39	20.60	m²	22.66
Plaster walls and columns exceeding 0.50m²	4.70	30.00	6.07	0.58	-	12.10	1.17	19.34	m²	21.27
Stripping existing hessian, paper backed; textile hessian paper backed wall covering pc £8.00m²; sizing; applying adhesive; hanging; butt joints										
Hard building board walls and columns exceeding 0.50m²	8.20	25.00	10.22	0.55	-	11.48	1.10	22.80	m²	25.08
Plaster walls and columns exceeding 0.50m²	0.91	25.00	1.12	0.51	-	10.64	-	11.76	m²	12.94

DECORATION

This page left blank intentionally

Labour hourly rates: (except Specialists) Craft Operatives 20.87 Labourer 15.57 Rates are national average prices. Refer to REGIONAL VARIATIONS for indicative levels of overall pricing in regions	MATERIALS			LABOUR				RATES		
	Del to Site £	Waste %	Material Cost £	Craft Optve Hrs	Lab Hrs	Labour Cost £	Sunds £	Nett Rate £	Unit	Gross rate (10%) £
DEMOUNTABLE SUSPENDED CEILINGS										
Suspended ceilings; 1200 x 600mm bevelled, grooved and rebated plain mineral fibre tiles; laying in position in metal suspension system of main channel members on wire or rod hangers										
Depth of suspension 150 - 500mm										
15.8mm thick linings; fixing hangers to masonry	6.81	5.00	7.15	0.50	0.25	14.33	7.18	28.65	m²	31.52
15.8mm thick linings not exceeding 300mm wide; fixing hangers to masonry	2.04	10.00	2.25	0.30	0.08	7.43	4.29	13.96	m	15.36
Suspended ceilings; 600 x 600mm bevelled, grooved and rebated plain mineral fibre tiles; laying in position in metal suspension system of main channel members on wire or rod hangers										
Depth of suspension 150 - 500mm										
15.8mm thick linings; fixing hangers to masonry	6.60	5.00	6.93	0.60	0.30	17.19	4.37	28.49	m²	31.34
15.8mm thick linings not exceeding 300mm wide; fixing hangers to masonry	1.98	10.00	2.18	0.36	0.09	8.91	4.29	15.38	m	16.92
Suspended ceilings; 1200 x 600mm bevelled, grooved and rebated textured mineral fibre tiles; laying in position in metal suspension system of main channel members on wire or rod hangers										
Depth of suspension 150 - 500mm										
15.8mm thick linings; fixing hangers to masonry	11.94	5.00	12.54	0.50	0.25	14.33	7.18	34.05	m²	37.45
15.8mm thick linings not exceeding 300mm wide; fixing hangers to masonry	3.58	10.00	3.94	0.30	0.08	7.43	4.29	15.66	m	17.23
Suspended ceilings; 600 x 600mm bevelled, grooved and rebated regular drilled mineral fibre tiles; laying in position in metal suspension system of main channel members on wire or rod hangers										
Depth of suspension 150 - 500mm										
15.8mm thick linings; fixing hangers to masonry	12.50	5.00	13.12	0.60	0.30	17.19	4.37	34.69	m²	38.16
15.8mm thick linings not exceeding 300mm wide; fixing hangers to masonry	3.75	10.00	4.12	0.36	0.09	8.91	2.64	15.68	m	17.25
Suspended ceilings; 1200 x 600mm bevelled, grooved and rebated patterned tiles p.c. £20.00/m²; laying in position in metal suspension system of main channel members on wire or rod hangers										
Depth of suspension 150 - 500mm										
15.8mm thick linings; fixing hangers to masonry	20.00	5.00	21.00	0.50	0.25	14.33	7.18	42.51	m²	46.76
15.8mm thick linings not exceeding 300mm wide; fixing hangers to masonry	6.00	10.00	6.60	0.30	0.08	7.43	4.29	18.32	m	20.15
Suspended ceilings; 600 x 600mm bevelled, grooved and rebated patterned tiles p.c. £20.00/m²; laying in position in metal suspension system of main channel members on wire or rod hangers										
Depth of suspension 150 - 500mm										
15.8mm thick linings; fixing hangers to masonry	20.00	5.00	21.00	0.60	0.30	17.19	4.37	42.57	m²	46.82
15.8mm thick linings not exceeding 300mm wide; fixing hangers to masonry	6.00	10.00	6.60	0.36	0.09	8.91	2.64	18.15	m	19.97
Suspended ceiling; British Gypsum Ltd, 1200 x 600mm Vinyl faced tiles; laid into grid system										
Depth of suspension 150-500mm										
10mm thick linings; fixing hangers to masonry	9.17	5.00	9.63	0.60	0.11	14.23	7.18	31.04	m²	34.14
10mm thick linings not exceeding 300mm wide; fixing hangers to masonry	2.75	10.00	3.03	0.36	0.09	8.91	7.18	19.12	m	21.03
Edge trims										
Plain										
angle section; white stove enamelled aluminium; fixing to masonry with screws at 450mm centres	1.45	5.00	1.52	0.40	0.20	11.46	-	12.98	m	14.28

This page left blank intentionally

INSULATION, FIRE STOPPING AND FIRE PROTECTION

Labour hourly rates: (except Specialists) Craft Operatives 20.87 Labourer 15.57 Rates are national average prices. Refer to REGIONAL VARIATIONS for indicative levels of overall pricing in regions	MATERIALS			LABOUR				RATES		
	Del to Site £	Waste %	Material Cost £	Craft Optve Hrs	Lab Hrs	Labour Cost £	Sunds £	Nett Rate £	Unit	Gross rate (10%) £
BOARD, SHEET, QUILT, SPRAYED, LOOSE FILL OR FOAMED INSULATION AND FIRE PROTECTION INSTALLATIONS										
Boards; Masterboard Class O fire resisting boards; butt joints										
6mm thick linings to walls; plain areas; vertical										
width exceeding 300mm	19.84	5.00	20.83	0.45	0.06	10.33	0.74	31.90	m²	35.09
width not exceeding 300mm	5.95	10.00	6.55	0.27	0.02	5.95	0.45	12.94	m	14.23
9mm thick linings to walls; plain areas; vertical										
width exceeding 300mm	39.15	5.00	41.11	0.49	0.06	11.16	0.81	53.08	m²	58.39
width not exceeding 300mm	11.75	10.00	12.92	0.29	0.02	6.36	0.48	19.76	m	21.74
12mm thick linings to walls; plain areas; vertical										
width exceeding 300mm	51.65	5.00	54.23	0.53	0.07	12.15	0.87	67.26	m²	73.98
width not exceeding 300mm	15.49	10.00	17.04	0.32	0.02	6.99	0.53	24.56	m	27.02
6mm thick linings to ceilings; plain areas; soffit										
width exceeding 300mm	19.84	5.00	20.83	0.57	0.07	12.99	0.94	34.76	m²	38.23
width not exceeding 300mm	5.95	10.00	6.55	0.34	0.02	7.41	0.56	14.52	m	15.97
9mm thick linings to ceilings; plain areas; soffit										
width exceeding 300mm	39.15	5.00	41.11	0.61	0.08	13.98	1.01	56.09	m²	61.70
width not exceeding 300mm	11.75	10.00	12.92	0.37	0.02	8.03	0.61	21.56	m	23.72
12mm thick linings to ceilings; plain areas; soffit										
width exceeding 300mm	51.65	5.00	54.23	0.67	0.08	15.23	1.11	70.56	m²	77.62
width not exceeding 300mm	15.49	10.00	17.04	0.40	0.02	8.66	0.66	26.36	m	29.00
Boards; Supalux fire resisting boards; sanded; butt joints; fixing to timber with self tapping screws										
6mm thick linings to walls; plain areas; vertical										
width exceeding 300mm	26.33	5.00	27.64	0.45	0.06	10.33	0.74	38.71	m²	42.58
width not exceeding 300mm	7.90	10.00	8.69	0.27	0.02	5.95	0.45	15.08	m	16.59
9mm thick linings to walls; plain areas; vertical										
width exceeding 300mm	34.78	5.00	36.51	0.49	0.06	11.16	0.81	48.48	m²	53.33
width not exceeding 300mm	10.43	10.00	11.48	0.29	0.02	6.36	0.48	18.32	m	20.15
12mm thick linings to walls; plain areas; vertical										
width exceeding 300mm	45.20	5.00	47.46	0.53	0.07	12.15	0.87	60.48	m²	66.53
width not exceeding 300mm	13.56	10.00	14.92	0.32	0.02	6.99	0.53	22.43	m	24.68
15mm thick linings to walls; plain areas; vertical										
width exceeding 300mm	66.51	5.00	69.84	0.57	0.08	13.14	0.94	83.92	m²	92.31
width not exceeding 300mm	19.95	10.00	21.95	0.35	0.03	7.69	0.58	30.22	m	33.24
6mm thick linings to ceilings; plain areas; soffit										
width exceeding 300mm	26.33	5.00	27.64	0.57	0.07	12.99	0.94	41.57	m²	45.73
width not exceeding 300mm	7.90	10.00	8.69	0.34	0.02	7.41	0.56	16.66	m	18.32
9mm thick linings to ceilings; plain areas; soffit										
width exceeding 300mm	34.78	5.00	36.51	0.61	0.08	13.98	1.01	51.50	m²	56.65
width not exceeding 300mm	10.43	10.00	11.48	0.37	0.02	8.03	0.61	20.12	m	22.13
12mm thick linings to ceilings; plain areas; soffit										
width exceeding 300mm	45.20	5.00	47.46	0.67	0.08	15.23	1.11	63.79	m²	70.17
width not exceeding 300mm	13.56	10.00	14.92	0.40	0.02	8.66	0.66	24.23	m	26.66
15mm thick linings to ceilings; plain areas; soffit										
width exceeding 300mm	66.51	5.00	69.84	0.72	0.09	16.35	1.19	87.37	m²	96.11
width not exceeding 300mm	19.95	10.00	21.95	0.40	0.02	8.66	0.66	31.27	m	34.39
6mm thick casings to isolated beams or the like										
total girth not exceeding 600mm	26.33	10.00	28.96	1.13	0.14	25.76	1.86	56.59	m²	62.24
total girth 600 - 1200mm	26.33	5.00	27.64	0.68	0.09	15.59	1.12	44.36	m²	48.79
9mm thick casings to isolated beams or the like										
total girth not exceeding 600mm	34.78	10.00	38.25	1.21	0.15	27.59	2.00	67.84	m²	74.62
total girth 600 - 1200mm	34.78	5.00	36.51	0.74	0.09	16.85	1.22	54.58	m²	60.04
12mm thick casings to isolated beams or the like										
total girth not exceeding 600mm	45.20	10.00	49.72	1.33	0.17	30.40	2.19	82.32	m²	90.55
total girth 600 - 1200mm	45.20	5.00	47.46	0.80	0.10	18.25	1.32	67.03	m²	73.73
15mm thick casings to isolated beams or the like										
total girth not exceeding 600mm	66.51	10.00	73.16	1.45	0.19	33.22	2.39	108.77	m²	119.65
total girth 600 - 1200mm	66.51	5.00	69.84	0.85	0.12	19.61	1.40	90.85	m²	99.93
6mm thick casings to isolated columns or the like										
total girth 600 - 1200mm	26.33	10.00	28.96	1.13	0.14	25.76	1.86	56.59	m²	62.24
total girth 1200 - 1800mm	26.33	5.00	27.64	0.68	0.09	15.59	1.12	44.36	m²	48.79
9mm thick casings to isolated columns or the like										
total girth 600 - 1200mm	34.78	10.00	38.25	1.21	0.15	27.59	2.00	67.84	m²	74.62
total girth 1200 - 1800mm	34.78	5.00	36.51	0.74	0.09	16.85	1.22	54.58	m²	60.04
12mm thick casings to isolated columns or the like										
total girth 600 - 1200mm	45.20	10.00	49.72	1.33	0.17	30.40	2.19	82.32	m²	90.55

Labour hourly rates: (except Specialists) Craft Operatives 20.87 Labourer 15.57 Rates are national average prices. Refer to REGIONAL VARIATIONS for indicative levels of overall pricing in regions	MATERIALS			LABOUR				RATES		
	Del to Site £	Waste %	Material Cost £	Craft Optve Hrs	Lab Hrs	Labour Cost £	Sunds £	Nett Rate £	Unit	Gross rate (10%) £
BOARD, SHEET, QUILT, SPRAYED, LOOSE FILL OR FOAMED INSULATION AND FIRE PROTECTION INSTALLATIONS (Cont'd)										
Boards; Supalux fire resisting boards; sanded; butt joints; fixing to timber with self tapping screws (Cont'd)										
12mm thick casings to isolated columns or the like (Cont'd)										
total girth 1200 - 1800mm	45.20	5.00	47.46	0.80	0.10	18.25	1.32	67.03	m²	73.73
15mm thick casings to isolated columns or the like										
total girth 600 - 1200mm	66.51	10.00	73.16	1.45	0.19	33.22	2.39	108.77	m²	119.65
total girth 1200 - 1800mm	66.51	5.00	69.84	0.85	0.12	19.61	1.40	90.85	m²	99.93
9mm thick linings to pipe ducts and casings										
width exceeding 300mm	34.78	20.00	41.73	1.50	0.19	34.26	0.40	76.39	m²	84.03
width not exceeding 300mm	10.43	20.00	12.52	0.50	0.06	11.37	0.13	24.02	m	26.42
Boards; Promatect L500 fire resisting boards; butt joints; fixing to steel with self tapping screws, countersinking										
20mm thick casings to isolated beams or the like										
total girth not exceeding 600mm	67.01	10.00	73.71	1.50	0.19	34.26	2.47	110.45	m²	121.50
total girth 600 - 1200mm	67.01	5.00	70.36	0.90	0.11	20.50	1.49	92.34	m²	101.58
30mm thick casings to isolated beams or the like										
total girth not exceeding 600mm	106.77	10.00	117.45	1.65	0.21	37.71	2.72	157.88	m²	173.67
total girth 600 - 1200mm	106.77	5.00	112.11	1.00	0.13	22.89	1.65	136.66	m²	150.32
40mm thick casings to isolated beams or the like										
total girth not exceeding 600mm	164.77	10.00	181.24	1.80	0.23	41.15	2.97	225.36	m²	247.90
total girth 600 - 1200mm	164.77	5.00	173.00	1.08	0.14	24.72	1.78	199.51	m²	219.46
50mm thick casings to isolated beams or the like										
total girth not exceeding 600mm	227.15	10.00	249.87	1.95	0.24	44.43	3.22	297.52	m²	327.27
total girth 600 - 1200mm	227.15	5.00	238.51	1.17	0.15	26.75	1.93	267.19	m²	293.91
20mm thick casings to isolated columns or the like										
total girth 600 - 1200mm	67.01	10.00	73.71	1.50	0.19	34.26	2.47	110.45	m²	121.50
total girth 1200 - 1800mm	67.01	5.00	70.36	0.90	0.11	20.50	1.49	92.34	m²	101.58
30mm thick casings to isolated columns or the like										
total girth 600 - 1200mm	106.77	10.00	117.45	1.65	0.21	37.71	2.72	157.88	m²	173.67
total girth 1200 - 1800mm	106.77	5.00	112.11	1.00	0.13	22.89	1.65	136.66	m²	150.32
40mm thick casings to isolated columns or the like										
total girth 600 - 1200mm	164.77	10.00	181.24	1.80	0.23	41.15	2.97	225.36	m²	247.90
total girth 1200 - 1800mm	164.77	5.00	173.00	1.08	0.14	24.72	1.78	199.51	m²	219.46
50mm thick casings to isolated columns or the like										
total girth 600 - 1200mm	227.15	10.00	249.87	1.95	0.24	44.43	3.22	297.52	m²	327.27
total girth 1200 - 1800mm	227.15	5.00	238.51	1.17	0.15	26.75	1.93	267.19	m²	293.91
50 x 25mm x 07mm mild steel fixing angle										
fixing to masonry	2.74	5.00	2.88	0.40	0.05	9.13	0.66	12.67	m	13.93
fixing to steel	2.74	5.00	2.88	0.40	0.05	9.13	0.66	12.67	m	13.93
Boards; Vermiculite fire board; butt joints; fixing with screws; countersinking										
20mm thick casings to isolated beams or the like; including noggins										
total girth not exceeding 600mm	102.40	10.00	112.29	1.42	0.18	32.44	2.34	147.07	m²	161.78
total girth 600 - 1200mm	102.40	5.00	107.51	0.85	0.11	19.45	1.40	128.37	m²	141.21
25mm thick casings to isolated beams or the like; including noggins										
total girth not exceeding 600mm	56.76	10.00	62.05	1.58	0.20	36.09	2.61	100.75	m²	110.83
total girth 600 - 1200mm	56.76	5.00	59.60	0.95	0.12	21.69	1.57	82.86	m²	91.14
35mm thick casings to isolated beams or the like; including noggins										
total girth not exceeding 600mm	90.60	10.00	99.23	1.65	0.21	37.71	2.72	139.66	m²	153.62
total girth 600 - 1200mm	91.58	5.00	96.16	1.00	0.13	22.89	1.65	120.71	m²	132.78
20mm thick casings to isolated columns or the like										
total girth 600 - 1200mm	97.48	10.00	107.13	1.42	0.18	32.44	2.34	141.91	m²	156.10
total girth 1200 - 1800mm	97.48	5.00	102.35	0.85	0.11	19.45	1.40	123.21	m²	135.53
25mm thick casings to isolated columns or the like										
total girth 600 - 1200mm	51.84	10.00	56.89	1.58	0.20	36.09	2.61	95.59	m²	105.15
total girth 1200 - 1800mm	51.84	5.00	54.43	0.95	0.12	21.69	1.57	77.70	m²	85.47
35mm thick casings to isolated columns or the like										
total girth 600 - 1200mm	85.69	10.00	94.07	1.65	0.21	37.71	2.72	134.50	m²	147.95
total girth 1200 - 1800mm	85.69	5.00	89.97	1.00	0.13	22.89	1.65	114.51	m²	125.96
Boards; Celotex GA4000 series insulation board; butt joints										
50mm thick; plain areas										
horizontal	7.39	10.00	8.13	0.15	0.03	3.60	-	11.73	m²	12.90
70mm thick; plain areas										
horizontal	10.51	10.00	11.56	0.20	0.04	4.80	-	16.35	m²	17.99
80mm thick; plain areas										
horizontal	11.47	10.00	12.62	0.22	0.05	5.40	-	18.02	m²	19.82
100mm thick; plain areas										
horizontal	13.08	10.00	14.39	0.25	0.05	6.00	-	20.38	m²	22.42

Labour hourly rates: (except Specialists) Craft Operatives 20.87 Labourer 15.57 Rates are national average prices. Refer to REGIONAL VARIATIONS for indicative levels of overall pricing in regions	MATERIALS			LABOUR				RATES		
	Del to Site £	Waste %	Material Cost £	Craft Optve Hrs	Lab Hrs	Labour Cost £	Sunds £	Nett Rate £	Unit	Gross rate (10%) £
BOARD, SHEET, QUILT, SPRAYED, LOOSE FILL OR FOAMED INSULATION AND FIRE PROTECTION INSTALLATIONS (Cont'd)										
Sheets; Waterproof reinforced building paper; grade A1F; 150mm lapped joints										
Across members at 450mm centres vertical	1.36	5.00	1.42	0.17	0.02	3.86	0.03	5.31	m²	5.85
Sheets; Waterproof reinforced building paper; foil faced; 150mm lapped joints										
Across members at 450mm centres vertical	2.45	5.00	2.57	0.17	0.02	3.86	0.03	6.46	m²	7.11
Sheets; Waterproof reinforced building paper;BS 1521; grade A1F; polythene coated; 150mm lapped joints										
Across members at 450mm centres vertical	1.44	5.00	1.51	0.17	0.02	3.86	0.03	5.40	m²	5.94
Quilts; Novia Vapour Control Layer 1000 gauge; 150mm laps sealed with tape										
Across members at 450mm centres horizontal; fixing to timber with stainless steel staples	1.11	10.00	1.22	0.10	0.01	2.24	0.09	3.55	m²	3.90
Plain areas horizontal; laid loose	1.11	10.00	1.22	0.06	0.01	1.41	-	2.62	m²	2.89
Quilts; Mineral rockwool insulation quilt; butt joints										
100mm thick; across members at 450mm centres horizontal; laid loose	1.73	15.00	1.99	0.12	0.01	2.66	-	4.65	m²	5.12
Quilts; Glass fibre insulation quilt; butt joints										
100mm thick; across members at 450mm centres horizontal; laid loose	1.43	15.00	1.64	0.09	0.01	2.03	-	3.67	m²	4.04
200mm thick; across members at 450mm centres horizontal; laid loose	3.61	15.00	4.15	0.09	0.01	2.03	-	6.19	m²	6.80
300mm thick; across members at 450mm centres horizontal; laid loose	5.04	15.00	5.79	0.27	0.03	6.10	-	11.89	m²	13.08
400mm thick; across members at 450mm centres horizontal; laid loose	7.22	15.00	8.30	0.36	0.04	8.14	-	16.44	m²	18.08
100mm thick; between members at 450mm centres horizontal; laid loose	1.43	15.00	1.64	0.15	0.02	3.44	-	5.08	m²	5.59
200mm thick; between members at 450mm centres horizontal; laid loose	3.61	15.00	4.15	0.15	0.02	3.44	-	7.59	m²	8.35
Quilts; Sheeps wool insulation quilt; butt joints										
200mm thick; across members at 450mm centres horizontal; laid loose	15.75	10.00	17.32	0.09	0.01	2.03	-	19.36	m²	21.29
200mm thick; between members at 450mm centres horizontal; laid loose	15.75	10.00	17.32	0.15	0.02	3.44	-	20.77	m²	22.84
Quilts; Knauf 'Earthwool Loftroll 40'; butt joints										
100mm thick; between members at 450mm centres horizontal; laid loose	1.62	10.00	1.79	0.15	0.02	3.44	-	5.23	m²	5.75
150mm thick; between members at 450mm centres horizontal; laid loose	2.39	10.00	2.63	0.15	0.02	3.44	-	6.08	m²	6.68
200mm thick; between members at 450mm centres horizontal; laid loose	3.61	10.00	3.97	0.15	0.02	3.44	-	7.41	m²	8.15
200mm thick total - 100mm between members at 450mm centres; 100mm across members at 450mm centres horizontal; laid loose	3.25	10.00	3.57	0.24	0.03	5.48	-	9.05	m²	9.95
250mm thick total - 150mm between members at 450mm centres; 100mm across members at 450mm centres horizontal; laid loose	4.02	10.00	4.42	0.24	0.03	5.48	-	9.90	m²	10.89
300mm thick total - 150mm between members at 450mm centres; 150mm across members at 450mm centres horizontal; laid loose	4.79	10.00	5.27	0.24	0.03	5.48	-	10.74	m²	11.82
400mm thick total - 150mm between members at 450mm centres; 250mm across members at 450mm centres horizontal; laid loose	6.41	10.00	7.06	0.36	0.05	8.29	-	15.35	m²	16.88
Quilts; Rockwool Rollbatts; insulation quilt; butt joints										
100mm thick; between members at 450mm centres horizontal; laid loose	7.17	10.00	7.89	0.10	0.01	2.24	-	10.13	m²	11.15
150mm thick; between members at 450mm centres horizontal; laid loose	11.38	10.00	12.52	0.15	0.02	3.44	-	15.96	m²	17.56
200mm thick total; 100mm between members at 450mm centres; 100mm across members at 450mm centres horizontal; laid loose	14.34	10.00	15.78	0.20	0.03	4.64	-	20.42	m²	22.46

Labour hourly rates: (except Specialists) Craft Operatives 20.87 Labourer 15.57 Rates are national average prices. Refer to REGIONAL VARIATIONS for indicative levels of overall pricing in regions	MATERIALS			LABOUR				RATES		
	Del to Site £	Waste %	Material Cost £	Craft Optve Hrs	Lab Hrs	Labour Cost £	Sunds £	Nett Rate £	Unit	Gross rate (10%) £
BOARD, SHEET, QUILT, SPRAYED, LOOSE FILL OR FOAMED INSULATION AND FIRE PROTECTION INSTALLATIONS (Cont'd)										
Quilts; Rockwool Rollbatts; insulation quilt; butt joints (Cont'd)										
300mm thick total; 150mm between members at 450mm centres; 150mm across members at 450mm centres										
horizontal; laid loose	22.77	10.00	25.04	0.24	0.03	5.48	-	30.52	m²	33.57
400mm thick total; 150mm between members at 450mm centres; 250mm across members at 450mm centres										
horizontal; laid loose	29.94	10.00	32.93	0.36	0.05	8.29	-	41.23	m²	45.35
Quilts; Glass fibre medium density insulation board; butt joints										
50mm thick; plain areas										
horizontal; bedding in bitumen	2.35	10.00	2.58	0.20	0.02	4.49	2.25	9.32	m²	10.25
75mm thick; plain areas										
horizontal; bedding in bitumen	3.03	10.00	3.34	0.22	0.03	5.06	2.25	10.64	m²	11.71
100mm thick; plain areas										
horizontal; bedding in bitumen	3.37	10.00	3.71	0.25	0.03	5.68	2.25	11.64	m²	12.81
50mm thick; across members at 450mm centres										
vertical	2.35	10.00	2.58	0.20	0.02	4.49	0.05	7.11	m²	7.82
75mm thick; across members at 450mm centres										
vertical	3.03	10.00	3.34	0.22	0.03	5.06	0.05	8.44	m²	9.28
100mm thick; across members at 450mm centres										
vertical	3.37	10.00	3.71	0.25	0.03	5.68	0.05	9.44	m²	10.38
Quilts; Dow Construction Products; Styrofoam Floormate 300A; butt joints										
50mm thick; plain areas										
horizontal; laid loose	7.17	10.00	7.88	0.10	0.01	2.24	-	10.13	m²	11.14
100mm thick; plain areas										
horizontal; laid loose	14.33	10.00	15.77	0.15	0.02	3.44	-	19.21	m²	21.13
Quilts; Dow Construction Products; Styrofloor; butt joints										
43mm thick; plain areas										
horizontal; laid loose	21.28	10.00	23.41	0.15	0.03	3.60	-	27.01	m²	29.71
68mm thick; plain areas										
horizontal; laid loose	27.26	10.00	29.98	0.15	0.03	3.60	-	33.58	m²	36.94
93mm thick; plain areas										
horizontal; laid loose	33.16	10.00	36.48	0.20	0.04	4.80	-	41.27	m²	45.40
118mm thick; plain areas										
horizontal; laid loose	37.33	10.00	41.06	0.20	0.04	4.80	-	45.86	m²	50.44
168mm thick; plain areas										
horizontal; laid loose	50.87	10.00	55.95	0.20	0.03	4.64	-	60.60	m²	66.66
Quilts; Sempatap latex foam sheeting; butt joints										
10mm thick; plain areas										
soffit; fixing with adhesive	18.72	15.00	21.53	1.25	1.25	45.55	3.60	70.68	m²	77.75
vertical; fixing with adhesive	18.72	15.00	21.53	1.00	1.00	36.44	3.60	61.57	m²	67.72
Quilts; Sempafloor SBR latex foam sheeting with coated non woven polyester surface; butt joints										
4.5mm thick; plain areas										
horizontal; fixing with adhesive	17.04	15.00	19.60	0.75	0.75	27.33	3.08	50.00	m²	55.00
Quilts; Expanded polystyrene sheeting; butt joints										
10mm thick; plain areas										
horizontal; laid loose	1.00	5.00	1.05	0.09	0.05	2.66	-	3.71	m²	4.08
vertical; fixing with adhesive	1.00	5.00	1.05	0.27	0.14	7.81	1.65	10.51	m²	11.57
20mm thick; plain areas										
horizontal; laid loose	2.00	5.00	2.10	0.10	0.05	2.87	-	4.96	m²	5.46
vertical; fixing with adhesive	2.00	5.00	2.10	0.28	1.06	22.35	1.65	26.10	m²	28.71
30mm thick; plain areas										
horizontal; laid loose	3.00	5.00	3.15	0.12	0.06	3.44	-	6.59	m²	7.25
vertical; fixing with adhesive	3.00	5.00	3.15	0.30	0.15	8.60	1.65	13.40	m²	14.73
50mm thick; plain areas										
horizontal; laid loose	5.00	5.00	5.25	0.14	0.07	4.01	-	9.26	m²	10.19
vertical; fixing with adhesive	5.00	5.00	5.25	0.32	0.16	9.17	1.65	16.07	m²	17.67
80mm thick; plain areas										
horizontal; laid loose	8.57	5.00	9.00	0.18	0.09	5.16	-	14.16	m²	15.57
vertical; fixing with adhesive	8.57	5.00	9.00	0.36	0.18	10.32	1.65	20.96	m²	23.06
Quilts; Polypropylene Insulation support netting										
20mm mesh; across members at 450mm centres										
horizontal	0.17	5.00	0.17	0.05	0.12	2.91	0.05	3.13	m²	3.44
vertical	0.17	5.00	0.17	0.05	0.18	3.85	0.05	4.06	m²	4.47

FURNITURE, FITTINGS AND EQUIPMENT

Labour hourly rates: (except Specialists) Craft Operatives 20.87 Labourer 15.57 Rates are national average prices. Refer to REGIONAL VARIATIONS for indicative levels of overall pricing in regions	MATERIALS			LABOUR				RATES		
	Del to Site £	Waste %	Material Cost £	Craft Optve Hrs	Lab Hrs	Labour Cost £	Sunds £	Nett Rate £	Unit	Gross rate (10%) £
GENERAL FIXTURES, FURNISHINGS AND EQUIPMENT; CURTAIN TRACKS										
Fixing only curtain track										
Metal or plastic track with fittings										
fixing with screws to softwood	-	-	-	0.50	-	10.44	-	10.44	m	11.48
fixing with screws to hardwood	-	-	-	0.70	-	14.61	-	14.61	m	16.07
GENERAL FIXTURES, FURNISHINGS AND EQUIPMENT; BLINDS										
Internal blinds										
Venetian blinds; stove enamelled aluminium alloy slats 25mm wide; plain colours										
1200mm drop; fixing to timber with screws										
1000mm wide	32.33	2.50	33.13	1.00	0.13	22.89	0.26	56.29	nr	61.92
2000mm wide	53.94	2.50	55.29	1.50	0.19	34.26	0.40	89.95	nr	98.94
3000mm wide	70.64	2.50	72.41	2.00	0.25	45.63	0.54	118.59	nr	130.44
Venetian blinds; stove enamelled aluminium alloy slats 50mm wide; plain colours										
1200mm drop; fixing to timber with screws										
1000mm wide	44.53	2.50	45.65	1.15	0.14	26.18	0.31	72.14	nr	79.35
2000mm wide	66.78	2.50	68.45	1.70	0.21	38.75	0.46	107.66	nr	118.43
3000mm wide	86.09	2.50	88.24	2.25	0.28	51.32	0.61	140.17	nr	154.19
Venetian blinds; stove enamelled aluminium alloy slats 25mm wide; plain colours with wand control										
1200mm drop; fixing to timber with screws										
1000mm wide	88.30	2.50	90.51	1.00	0.13	22.89	0.26	113.67	nr	125.03
2000mm wide	128.37	2.50	131.58	1.50	0.19	34.26	0.40	166.24	nr	182.86
3000mm wide	163.22	2.50	167.30	2.00	0.25	45.63	0.54	213.47	nr	234.82
Venetian blinds; Wood slat; plain or wood effect colours; slats 50mm wide; cord control										
1200mm drop; fixing to timber with screws										
1000mm wide	39.01	2.50	39.98	1.15	0.14	26.18	0.31	66.48	nr	73.12
2000mm wide	73.14	2.50	74.97	1.70	0.21	38.75	0.46	114.18	nr	125.60
2590mm wide	95.90	2.50	98.30	2.25	0.28	51.32	0.61	150.23	nr	165.25
Roller blinds; sprung ratchet action or side chain control; flame retardent material										
1200mm drop; fixing to timber with screws										
1000mm wide	29.30	2.50	30.03	1.00	0.13	22.89	0.26	53.19	nr	58.51
2000mm wide	45.90	2.50	47.05	1.50	0.19	34.26	0.40	81.71	nr	89.88
3000mm wide	61.53	2.50	63.07	2.00	0.25	45.63	0.54	109.25	nr	120.17
Roller blinds; automatic sprung ratchet action or side chain operation; patterned fabric										
1200mm drop; fixing to timber with screws										
1000mm wide	48.83	2.50	50.05	1.00	0.13	22.89	0.26	73.20	nr	80.52
2000mm wide	79.34	2.50	81.33	1.50	0.19	34.26	0.40	115.98	nr	127.58
3000mm wide	105.28	2.50	107.92	2.00	0.25	45.63	0.54	154.09	nr	169.50
Roller blinds; sprung ratchet action or side chain operation; blackout material										
1200mm drop; fixing to timber with screws										
1000mm wide	24.42	2.50	25.04	1.15	0.14	26.18	0.31	51.53	nr	56.68
2000mm wide	39.07	2.50	40.04	1.70	0.21	38.75	0.46	79.25	nr	87.18
3000mm wide	46.89	2.50	48.06	2.25	0.28	51.32	0.61	99.99	nr	109.99
Roller blinds; 100% blackout; natural anodised box and channels										
1200mm drop; fixing to timber with screws										
1000mm wide	89.17	2.50	91.40	2.00	0.25	45.63	0.54	137.57	nr	151.33
1900mm wide	116.67	2.50	119.58	2.75	0.34	62.69	0.74	183.01	nr	201.31
Vertical louvre blinds; 89mm wide louvres in standard material										
1200mm drop; fixing to timber with screws										
1000mm wide	42.24	2.50	43.30	0.90	0.11	20.50	0.25	64.04	nr	70.45
2000mm wide	65.20	2.50	66.83	1.35	0.17	30.82	0.36	98.01	nr	107.82
3000mm wide	89.99	2.50	92.24	1.80	0.23	41.15	0.48	133.87	nr	147.25
Vertical louvre blinds; 127mm wide louvres in standard material										
1200mm drop; fixing to timber with screws										
1000mm wide	42.24	2.50	43.30	0.95	0.12	21.69	0.25	65.24	nr	71.76
2000mm wide	65.20	2.50	66.83	1.40	0.18	32.02	0.38	99.23	nr	109.15
3000mm wide	89.99	2.50	92.24	1.85	0.23	42.19	0.50	134.93	nr	148.42
External blinds; manually operated										
Venetian blinds; stove enamelled aluminium slats 80mm wide; natural anodised side guides; excluding boxing										
1200mm drop; fixing to timber with screws										
1000mm wide	-	-	Specialist	-	-	Specialist	-	404.44	nr	444.89
2000mm wide	-	-	Specialist	-	-	Specialist	-	601.94	nr	662.13

Labour hourly rates: (except Specialists) Craft Operatives 20.87 Labourer 15.57 Rates are national average prices. Refer to REGIONAL VARIATIONS for indicative levels of overall pricing in regions	MATERIALS			LABOUR				RATES		
	Del to Site £	Waste %	Material Cost £	Craft Optve Hrs	Lab Hrs	Labour Cost £	Sunds £	Nett Rate £	Unit	Gross rate (10%) £
GENERAL FIXTURES, FURNISHINGS AND EQUIPMENT; BLINDS (Cont'd)										
External blinds; manually operated (Cont'd)										
Venetian blinds; stove enamelled aluminium slats 80mm wide; natural anodised side guides; excluding boxing (Cont'd)										
1200mm drop; fixing to timber with screws (Cont'd)										
3000mm wide	-	-	Specialist	-	-	Specialist	-	810.75	nr	891.83
Queensland awnings; acrylic material; natural anodised arms and boxing										
1000mm projection										
2000mm long	-	-	Specialist	-	-	Specialist	-	948.06	nr	1042.86
3000mm long	-	-	Specialist	-	-	Specialist	-	1421.21	nr	1563.33
4000mm long	-	-	Specialist	-	-	Specialist	-	1896.11	nr	2085.72
Rollscreen vertical drop roller blinds; mesh material; natural anodised side guides and boxing										
1200mm drop; fixing to timber with screws										
1000mm wide	-	-	Specialist	-	-	Specialist	-	394.98	nr	434.47
2000mm wide	-	-	Specialist	-	-	Specialist	-	592.55	nr	651.80
3000mm wide	-	-	Specialist	-	-	Specialist	-	789.71	nr	868.68
Quandrant canopy; acrylic material; natural anodised frames										
1000mm projection										
2000mm long	-	-	Specialist	-	-	Specialist	-	522.93	nr	575.23
3000mm long	-	-	Specialist	-	-	Specialist	-	799.45	nr	879.40
4000mm long	-	-	Specialist	-	-	Specialist	-	1087.25	nr	1195.98
Foldaway awning; acrylic material; natural anodised arms and front rail										
2000mm projection										
2000mm long	-	-	Specialist	-	-	Specialist	-	848.37	nr	933.21
3000mm long	-	-	Specialist	-	-	Specialist	-	1245.25	nr	1369.78
4000mm long	-	-	Specialist	-	-	Specialist	-	1619.61	nr	1781.57
External blinds; electrically operated										
Venetian blinds; stove enamelled aluminium slats 80mm wide; natural anodised side guides; excluding boxing										
1200mm drop; fixing to timber with screws										
1000mm wide	-	-	Specialist	-	-	Specialist	-	929.24	nr	1022.16
2000mm wide	-	-	Specialist	-	-	Specialist	-	1136.17	nr	1249.79
3000mm wide	-	-	Specialist	-	-	Specialist	-	1331.81	nr	1464.99
Queensland awnings; acrylic material; natural anodised arms and boxing										
1000mm projection										
2000mm long	-	-	Specialist	-	-	Specialist	-	1087.25	nr	1195.98
3000mm long	-	-	Specialist	-	-	Specialist	-	1551.88	nr	1707.06
4000mm long	-	-	Specialist	-	-	Specialist	-	1975.12	nr	2172.63
Rollscreen vertical drop roller blinds; mesh material; natural anodised side guides and boxing										
1200mm drop; fixing to timber with screws										
1000mm wide	-	-	Specialist	-	-	Specialist	-	752.42	nr	827.67
2000mm wide	-	-	Specialist	-	-	Specialist	-	948.06	nr	1042.86
3000mm wide	-	-	Specialist	-	-	Specialist	-	1145.57	nr	1260.12
Quandrant canopy; acrylic material; natural anodised frames										
1000mm projection										
2000mm long	-	-	Specialist	-	-	Specialist	-	680.95	nr	749.04
3000mm long	-	-	Specialist	-	-	Specialist	-	948.06	nr	1042.86
4000mm long	-	-	Specialist	-	-	Specialist	-	1264.07	nr	1390.48
Foldaway awning; acrylic material; natural anodised arms and front rail										
2000mm projection										
2000mm long	-	-	Specialist	-	-	Specialist	-	1243.39	nr	1367.73
3000mm long	-	-	Specialist	-	-	Specialist	-	1629.00	nr	1791.90
4000mm long	-	-	Specialist	-	-	Specialist	-	2069.17	nr	2276.09
GENERAL FIXTURES, FURNISHINGS AND EQUIPMENT; STORAGE SYSTEMS										
Delta Plus' Office Shelving; Pure White steel boltless storage systems; steel shelves; RAJA Workplace; assembling										
Open shelving with six shelves; units 986mm wide x 1850mm high; placing in position										
300mm deep code WSR476; initial bay	222.00	2.50	227.55	1.00	0.50	28.66	-	256.20	nr	281.83
300mm deep code WSR461; extension bay	177.00	2.50	181.43	1.00	0.50	28.66	-	210.08	nr	231.09
extra; additional steel shelf 300 deep; code WSR175	22.20	2.50	22.76	0.20	0.10	5.73	-	28.49	nr	31.33
Extra Height open shelving with six shelves; units 986mm wide x 2530mm high; placing in position										
450mm deep code WSR830; initial bay	281.00	2.50	288.02	1.10	0.55	31.52	-	319.55	nr	351.50
450mm deep code WSR627; extension bay	229.00	2.50	234.72	1.10	0.55	31.52	-	266.25	nr	292.87
extra; additional steel shelf 450 deep; code WSR164	29.90	2.50	30.65	0.20	0.10	5.73	-	36.38	nr	40.02

Labour hourly rates: (except Specialists) Craft Operatives 20.87 Labourer 15.57 Rates are national average prices. Refer to REGIONAL VARIATIONS for indicative levels of overall pricing in regions	MATERIALS			LABOUR				RATES		
	Del to Site £	Waste %	Material Cost £	Craft Optve Hrs	Lab Hrs	Labour Cost £	Sunds £	Nett Rate £	Unit	Gross rate (10%) £
GENERAL FIXTURES, FURNISHINGS AND EQUIPMENT; SHELVING SYSTEMS										
Wide access boltless office shelving systems; upright frames connected with shelf beams; chipboard shelves; RAJA Workplace.; assembling										
Open shelving with four shelves; placing in position										
1220mm wide x 2135mm high x 610mm deep code WSR660	268.00	2.50	274.70	1.30	0.65	37.25	-	311.95	nr	343.15
1220mm wide x 2135mm high x 915mm deep code WSR886	296.00	2.50	303.40	1.40	0.70	40.12	-	343.52	nr	377.87
1220mm wide x 2135mm high x 1220mm deep code WSR1034	401.00	2.50	411.02	1.50	0.75	42.98	-	454.01	nr	499.41
2440mm wide x 2135mm high x 610mm deep code WSR1165	471.00	2.50	482.77	1.40	0.70	40.12	-	522.89	nr	575.18
2440mm wide x 2135mm high x 915mm deep code WSR1335	520.00	2.50	533.00	1.50	0.75	42.98	-	575.98	nr	633.58
2440mm wide x 2135mm high x 1220mm deep code WSR1408	609.00	2.50	624.22	1.60	0.80	45.85	-	670.07	nr	737.08
2440mm wide x 2745mm high x 610mm deep code WSR1189	488.00	2.50	500.20	1.50	0.75	42.98	-	543.18	nr	597.50
2440mm wide x 2745mm high x 915mm deep code WSR1352	533.00	2.50	546.33	1.60	0.80	45.85	-	592.17	nr	651.39
2440mm wide x 2745mm high x 1220mm deep code WSR1417	622.00	2.50	637.55	1.70	0.85	48.71	-	686.26	nr	754.89
GENERAL FIXTURES, FURNISHINGS AND EQUIPMENT; SHELVING SUPPORT SYSTEMS										
Twin slot shelf supports in steel with white enamelled finish										
Wall uprights										
430mm long; fixing to masonry with screws	1.28	2.50	1.31	0.25	-	5.22	-	6.53	nr	7.18
1000mm long; fixing to masonry with screws	2.61	2.50	2.68	0.45	-	9.39	-	12.07	nr	13.27
1600mm long; fixing to masonry with screws	3.86	2.50	3.96	0.55	-	11.48	-	15.44	nr	16.98
2400mm long; fixing to masonry with screws	5.86	2.50	6.01	0.70	-	14.61	-	20.62	nr	22.68
Straight brackets										
120mm long	0.75	2.50	0.77	0.05	-	1.04	-	1.81	nr	1.99
270mm long	1.22	2.50	1.25	0.05	-	1.04	-	2.29	nr	2.52
370mm long	1.58	2.50	1.62	0.07	-	1.46	-	3.08	nr	3.39
470mm long	2.61	2.50	2.68	0.07	-	1.46	-	4.14	nr	4.55
GENERAL FIXTURES, FURNISHINGS AND EQUIPMENT; MAT RIMS										
Matwells in Aluminium										
Mat frames; welded fabrication										
34 x 26 x 6mm angle section; angles mitred; plain lugs -4, welded on; mat space										
610 x 457mm	44.87	2.50	45.99	1.00	1.00	36.44	-	82.43	nr	90.67
762 x 457mm	49.41	2.50	50.65	1.25	1.25	45.55	-	96.20	nr	105.82
914 x 610mm	58.53	2.50	59.99	1.50	1.50	54.66	-	114.65	nr	126.12
Matwells in polished brass										
Mat frames; brazed fabrication										
38 x 38 x 6mm angle section; angles mitred; plain lugs -4, welded on; mat space										
610 x 457mm	200.51	2.50	205.53	1.25	1.25	45.55	-	251.08	nr	276.18
762 x 457mm	236.97	2.50	242.89	1.50	1.50	54.66	-	297.55	nr	327.31
914 x 610mm	309.88	2.50	317.62	1.75	1.75	63.77	-	381.39	nr	419.53
GENERAL FIXTURES, FURNISHINGS AND EQUIPMENT; CLOTHES LOCKERS										
Lockers; RAJA Workplace; coated steel carcase; laminate doors; with cam locks										
1 compartment; placing in position										
300 x 300 x 1800mm; code 935-009	205.03	2.50	210.16	-	0.60	9.34	-	219.50	nr	241.45
300 x 450 x 1800mm; code 935-010	214.31	2.50	219.67	-	0.65	10.12	-	229.79	nr	252.77
2 compartment; placing in position										
300 x 300 x 1800mm; code 935-003	239.43	2.50	245.42	-	0.60	9.34	-	254.76	nr	280.23
300 x 450 x 1800mm; code 935-012	248.74	2.50	254.96	-	0.65	10.12	-	265.08	nr	291.59
3 compartment; placing in position										
300 x 300 x 1800mm; code 935-005	272.85	2.50	279.67	-	0.60	9.34	-	289.01	nr	317.91
300 x 450 x 1800mm; code 935-014	283.25	2.50	290.33	-	0.65	10.12	-	300.45	nr	330.50
4 compartment; placing in position										
300 x 300 x 1800mm; code 935-007	306.79	2.50	314.46	-	0.60	9.34	-	323.80	nr	356.18
300 x 450 x 1800mm; code 935-016	318.29	2.50	326.25	-	0.65	10.12	-	336.37	nr	370.00
GENERAL FIXTURES, FURNISHINGS AND EQUIPMENT; CLOAK ROOM EQUIPMENT										
Static square tube double sided coat racks; RAJA Workplace; hardwood seats; in assembled units										
Racks 1500mm long x 1675mm high x 600mm deep; placing in position; 40mm square tube										
10 hooks and angle framed steel mesh single shoe tray, reference 456-102 and 456-109; placing in position	647.99	2.50	664.19	-	0.60	9.34	-	673.53	nr	740.88
10 hooks, reference 456-102; placing in position	522.00	2.50	535.05	-	0.60	9.34	-	544.39	nr	598.83
Static square tube single sided coat racks; RAJA Workplace; mobile; in assembled units										
Racks 1500mm long x 1825mm high x 600mm deep; placing in position; 40mm square tube										
15 hangers and top tray, reference 456-103	468.00	2.50	479.70	-	0.60	9.34	-	489.04	nr	537.95

Labour hourly rates: (except Specialists) Craft Operatives 20.87 Labourer 15.57 Rates are national average prices. Refer to REGIONAL VARIATIONS for indicative levels of overall pricing in regions	MATERIALS			LABOUR				RATES		
	Del to Site £	Waste %	Material Cost £	Craft Optve Hrs	Lab Hrs	Labour Cost £	Sunds £	Nett Rate £	Unit	Gross rate (10%) £
GENERAL FIXTURES, FURNISHINGS AND EQUIPMENT; CLOAK ROOM EQUIPMENT (Cont'd)										
Free-standing bench seats; RAJA Workplace; steel square tube framing; hardwood seats; placing in position										
Bench seat with shelf 1500mm long x 300mm deep and 450mm high; placing in position; 40mm square tube										
single sided 300mm deep, reference 787-009	245.00	2.50	251.12	-	0.70	10.90	-	262.02	nr	288.23
double sided 600mm deep reference 787-010	292.00	2.50	299.30	-	0.70	10.90	-	310.20	nr	341.22
Wall rack RAJA Workplace; hardwood										
1200mm long; fixing to masonry										
6 hooks, reference 787-020	55.95	2.50	57.35	-	0.68	10.65	-	68.00	nr	74.80
1800mm long; fixing to masonry										
8 hooks, reference 787-021	62.95	2.50	64.52	-	1.03	15.97	-	80.50	nr	88.55
GENERAL FIXTURES, FURNISHINGS AND EQUIPMENT; HAT AND COAT RAILS										
Hat and coat rails										
Rails in softwood, wrought										
25 x 75mm; chamfers -2	2.24	10.00	2.46	0.29	0.04	6.68	0.08	9.22	m	10.14
25 x 100mm; chamfers -2	2.94	10.00	3.23	0.29	0.04	6.68	0.08	9.99	m	10.99
25 x 75mm; chamfers -2; fixing to masonry with screws	2.24	10.00	2.46	0.57	0.07	12.99	0.15	15.60	m	17.16
25 x 100mm; chamfers -2; fixing to masonry with screws	2.94	10.00	3.23	0.57	0.07	12.99	0.15	16.37	m	18.01
Rails in Sapele, wrought, selected for transparent finish										
25 x 75mm; chamfers -2	10.42	10.00	11.46	0.57	0.07	12.99	0.15	24.59	m	27.05
25 x 100mm; chamfers -2	13.89	10.00	15.28	0.57	0.07	12.99	0.15	28.42	m	31.26
25 x 75mm; chamfers -2; fixing to masonry with screws, countersinking and pellating	10.42	10.00	11.46	1.15	0.14	26.18	0.31	37.95	m	41.75
25 x 100mm; chamfers -2; fixing to masonry with screws, countersinking and pellating	13.89	10.00	15.28	1.15	0.14	26.18	0.31	41.78	m	45.95
Hat and coat hooks										
polished brass finish	2.55	2.50	2.61	0.40	-	8.35	-	10.96	nr	12.06
chromium plated	2.22	2.50	2.28	0.40	-	8.35	-	10.62	nr	11.69
Aluminium finish	1.25	2.50	1.28	0.40	-	8.35	-	9.63	nr	10.59
RAJA Workplace; steel; coloured finish; reference 456-122	4.20	2.50	4.30	0.40	-	8.35	-	12.65	nr	13.92
KITCHEN FITTINGS										
Standard melamine finish on chipboard units, with backs; high gloss white finish doors - self assembly										
Wall units										
fixing to masonry with screws										
300 x 330 x 700mm	39.72	2.50	40.71	1.75	0.22	39.95	-	80.66	nr	88.73
400 x 330 x 700mm	45.03	2.50	46.16	1.75	0.22	39.95	-	86.10	nr	94.71
500 x 330 x 700mm	47.68	2.50	48.87	1.90	0.25	43.55	-	92.42	nr	101.66
600 x 330 x 700mm	49.35	2.50	50.58	1.95	0.25	44.59	-	95.17	nr	104.69
600 x 330 x 256mm cooker hood unit	42.36	2.50	43.42	1.90	0.25	43.55	-	86.96	nr	95.66
1000 x 330 x 700mm	68.79	2.50	70.51	2.35	0.30	53.72	-	124.23	nr	136.65
635 x 330 x 700mm corner wall unit	84.76	2.50	86.88	1.90	0.25	43.55	-	130.42	nr	143.47
Floor units; without drawers										
fixing to masonry with screws										
400 x 600 x 900mm	51.08	2.50	52.36	2.00	0.25	45.63	-	97.99	nr	107.79
500 x 600 x 900mm	52.08	2.50	53.38	2.20	0.28	50.27	-	103.66	nr	114.02
600 x 600 x 900mm	60.88	2.50	62.40	2.40	0.30	54.76	-	117.16	nr	128.88
1000 x 600 x 900mm	73.24	2.50	75.07	3.20	0.40	73.01	-	148.08	nr	162.89
1000 x 600 x 900mm corner unit	66.20	2.50	67.85	3.20	0.40	73.01	-	140.87	nr	154.95
Floor units; with three drawers										
fixing to masonry with screws										
600 x 600 x 900mm	109.40	2.50	112.14	2.40	0.30	54.76	-	166.89	nr	183.58
Sink units										
1000 x 600 x 900mm, without drawer; fixing to masonry with screws	73.24	2.50	75.07	3.20	0.40	73.01	-	148.08	nr	162.89
Store cupboards - larder or appliance										
fixing to masonry with screws										
600 x 600 x 2120mm no doors or fascias	54.05	2.50	55.40	3.60	0.45	82.14	-	137.54	nr	151.29
600 x 600 x 2120mm with two doors	144.92	2.50	148.54	3.80	0.45	86.31	-	234.86	nr	258.34
600 x 600 x 2120mm to suit double oven with fascia and two doors	130.76	2.50	134.03	4.00	0.50	91.26	-	225.29	nr	247.82
Pre-Assembled kitchen units, white melamine finish; Moores Jazz range; Moores Furniture Group										
Drawerline units; 600 deep; fixing to masonry with screws										
floor units										
300mm	128.70	2.50	131.92	1.25	0.20	29.20	-	161.12	nr	177.23
500mm	165.00	2.50	169.12	1.25	0.23	29.67	-	198.79	nr	218.67
600mm	179.30	2.50	183.78	1.25	0.23	29.67	-	213.45	nr	234.80
1000mm single drawer	228.80	2.50	234.52	1.75	0.33	41.66	-	276.18	nr	303.80
hob floor units										
1000mm dummy drawer	224.40	2.50	230.01	1.75	0.30	41.19	-	271.20	nr	298.32
sink units										
1000mm dummy drawer	224.40	2.50	230.01	1.75	0.30	41.19	-	271.20	nr	298.32
Doorline units; 600 deep; fixing to masonry with screws										
floor units										
500mm	157.30	2.50	161.23	2.50	0.35	57.62	-	218.86	nr	240.74

Labour hourly rates: (except Specialists) Craft Operatives 20.87 Labourer 15.57 Rates are national average prices. Refer to REGIONAL VARIATIONS for indicative levels of overall pricing in regions	MATERIALS			LABOUR				RATES		
	Del to Site £	Waste %	Material Cost £	Craft Optve Hrs	Lab Hrs	Labour Cost £	Sunds £	Nett Rate £	Unit	Gross rate (10%) £
KITCHEN FITTINGS (Cont'd)										
Pre-Assembled kitchen units, white melamine finish; Moores Jazz range; Moores Furniture Group (Cont'd)										
Drawer units; fixing to masonry with screws										
three drawer floor units										
500mm	379.50	2.50	388.99	1.25	0.30	30.76	-	419.75	nr	461.72
Wall units; fixing to masonry with screws										
standard units										
300mm	114.40	2.50	117.26	1.25	0.22	29.51	-	146.77	nr	161.45
500mm	136.40	2.50	139.81	1.25	0.23	29.67	-	169.48	nr	186.43
600mm	143.00	2.50	146.57	1.25	0.30	30.76	-	177.33	nr	195.07
1000mm	286.00	2.50	293.15	2.20	0.38	51.83	-	344.98	nr	379.48
standard corner units										
diagonal	436.70	2.50	447.62	2.20	0.38	51.83	-	499.45	nr	549.39
Ancillaries										
Base unit plinth										
15 x 166mm upstand	5.23	25.00	6.54	0.25	0.03	5.68	-	12.22	m	13.44
Laminate worktops; fixing with screws										
round front edge										
38mm worktops, round front edge; premium range	19.86	25.00	24.83	1.50	0.19	34.26	-	59.09	m	65.00
Worktop plinth										
12 x 70mm upstand	7.22	25.00	9.03	0.25	0.03	5.68	-	14.71	m	16.18
Cornice										
40 x 40mm	7.98	25.00	9.98	0.25	0.03	5.68	-	15.66	m	17.23
Pelmet										
40 x 40mm	7.98	25.00	9.98	0.25	0.03	5.68	-	15.66	m	17.23
Worktop trim										
colourfil	4.13	25.00	5.16	0.25	0.03	5.68	-	10.85	m	11.93

This section continues on the next page

Labour hourly rates: (except Specialists) Craft Operatives 26.39 Labourer 15.57 Rates are national average prices. Refer to REGIONAL VARIATIONS for indicative levels of overall pricing in regions	MATERIALS			LABOUR				RATES		
	Del to Site £	Waste %	Material Cost £	Craft Optve Hrs	Lab Hrs	Labour Cost £	Sunds £	Nett Rate £	Unit	Gross rate (10%) £
SANITARY APPLIANCES AND FITTINGS										
Attendance on sanitary fittings										
Note: Sanitary fittings are usually included as p.c. items or provisional sums, the following are the allowances for attendance by the main contractor i.e. unloading, storing and distributing fittings for fixing by the plumber and returning empty cases and packings										
Sinks, fireclay										
610 x 457 x 254mm	-	-	-	-	1.00	15.57	0.89	16.46	nr	18.11
762 x 508 x 254mm	-	-	-	-	1.25	19.46	1.12	20.58	nr	22.64
add if including tubular stands	-	-	-	-	0.75	11.68	0.74	12.42	nr	13.66
Wash basins, 559 x 406mm; earthenware or fireclay										
single	-	-	-	-	0.80	12.46	0.74	13.20	nr	14.52
range of 4 with cover overlaps between basins	-	-	-	-	2.50	38.92	2.01	40.94	nr	45.03
Combined sinks and drainers; stainless steel										
1067 x 533mm	-	-	-	-	1.40	21.80	1.32	23.12	nr	25.43
1600 x 610mm	-	-	-	-	1.70	26.47	1.57	28.04	nr	30.84
add if including tubular stands	-	-	-	-	0.75	11.68	0.74	12.42	nr	13.66
Combined sinks and drainers; porcelain enamel										
1067 x 533mm	-	-	-	-	1.40	21.80	1.32	23.12	nr	25.43
1600 x 610mm	-	-	-	-	1.70	26.47	1.57	28.04	nr	30.84
Baths excluding panels; pressed steel										
694 x 1688 x 570mm overall	-	-	-	-	2.50	38.92	1.95	40.87	nr	44.96
W.C. suites; china										
complete with WWP, flush pipe etc.	-	-	-	-	1.40	21.80	1.32	23.12	nr	25.43
Block pattern urinals; with glazed ends, back and channel in one piece with separate tread including flushing cistern etc.										
single stall	-	-	-	-	2.75	42.82	2.23	45.04	nr	49.55
range of four with loose overlaps	-	-	-	-	6.00	93.42	5.20	98.62	nr	108.48
Wall urinals, bowl type, with flushing cistern, etc.										
single	-	-	-	-	1.40	21.80	1.32	23.12	nr	25.43
range of 3 with two divisions	-	-	-	-	3.30	51.38	2.67	54.05	nr	59.46
Slab urinals with one return end, flushing cistern, sparge pipe, etc.										
1219mm long x 1067mm high	-	-	-	-	2.75	42.82	2.97	45.79	nr	50.37
1829mm long x 1067mm high	-	-	-	-	3.75	58.39	4.45	62.84	nr	69.13
Fix only appliances (prime cost sum for supply included elsewhere)										
Sink units, stainless steel; combined overflow and waste outlet, plug and chain; pair pillar taps										
fixing on base unit with metal clips										
1000 x 600mm	-	-	-	3.00	-	79.17	1.32	80.49	nr	88.54
1600 x 600mm	-	-	-	3.50	-	92.36	1.32	93.68	nr	103.05
Sinks; white glazed fireclay; waste outlet, plug, chain and stay; cantilever brackets; pair bib taps										
fixing brackets to masonry with screws; sealing at back with white sealant										
610 x 457 x 254mm	-	-	-	4.00	-	105.56	2.14	107.70	nr	118.48
762 x 508 x 254mm	-	-	-	4.00	-	105.56	2.14	107.70	nr	118.48
Sinks; white glazed fireclay; waste outlet, plug, chain and stay; legs and screw-to-wall bearers; pair bib taps										
fixing legs to masonry with screws; sealing at back with mastic sealant										
610 x 457 x 254mm	-	-	-	4.50	-	118.75	2.14	120.90	nr	132.99
762 x 508 x 254mm	-	-	-	4.50	-	118.75	2.14	120.90	nr	132.99
Wash basins; vitreous china; waste outlet, plug, chain and stay; screw to wall brackets; pair pillar taps										
560 x 406mm; fixing brackets to masonry with screws; sealing at back with mastic sealant	-	-	-	3.00	-	79.17	2.14	81.31	nr	89.45
range of four, each 559 x 406mm with overlap strips; fixing brackets to masonry with screws; sealing overlap strips and at back with mastic sealant	-	-	-	12.75	-	336.47	8.17	344.64	nr	379.10
Wash basins; vitreous china; waste outlet, plug, chain and stay; legs and screw-to-wall bearers										
560 x 406mm; fixing legs to masonry with screws; sealing at back with mastic sealant	-	-	-	3.50	-	92.36	2.14	94.51	nr	103.96
range of 4, each 559 x 406mm with overlap strips; fixing legs to masonry with screws; sealing overlap strips and at back with mastic sealant	-	-	-	13.75	-	362.86	8.17	371.03	nr	408.13
Baths; enamelled pressed steel; combined overflow and waste outlet, plug and chain; metal cradles; pair pillar taps										
700 x 1700 x 570mm overall; sealing at walls with mastic sealant	-	-	-	5.50	-	145.14	4.78	149.93	nr	164.92

Labour hourly rates: (except Specialists) Craft Operatives 26.39 Labourer 15.57 Rates are national average prices. Refer to REGIONAL VARIATIONS for indicative levels of overall pricing in regions	MATERIALS			LABOUR				RATES		
	Del to Site £	Waste %	Material Cost £	Craft Optve Hrs	Lab Hrs	Labour Cost £	Sunds £	Nett Rate £	Unit	Gross rate (10%) £
SANITARY APPLIANCES AND FITTINGS (Cont'd)										
Fix only appliances (prime cost sum for supply included elsewhere) (Cont'd)										
High level W.C. suites; vitreous china pan; plastics cistern with valveless fittings, ball valve, chain and pull handle; flush pipe; plastics seat and cover										
fixing pan and cistern brackets to masonry with screws; bedding pan in mastic; jointing pan to drain with cement mortar (1:2) and gaskin joint	-	-	-	4.50	-	118.75	2.89	121.64	nr	133.81
fixing pan and cistern brackets to masonry with screws; bedding pan in mastic; jointing pan to soil pipe with Multikwik connector	-	-	-	4.50	-	118.75	2.89	121.64	nr	133.81
Low level W.C. suites; vitreous china pan; plastics cistern with valveless fittings and ball valve; flush pipe; plastics seat and cover										
fixing pan and cistern brackets to masonry with screws; bedding pan in mastic; jointing pan to drain with cement mortar (1:2) and gaskin joint	-	-	-	4.50	-	118.75	2.89	121.64	nr	133.81
fixing pan and cistern brackets to masonry with screws; bedding pan in mastic; jointing pan to soil pipe with Multikwik connector	-	-	-	4.50	-	118.75	2.89	121.64	nr	133.81
Wall urinals; vitreous china bowl; automatic cistern; spreads and flush pipe; waste outlet										
single bowl; fixing bowl, cistern and pipe brackets to masonry with screws	-	-	-	4.50	-	118.75	2.23	120.98	nr	133.08
range of three bowls; fixing bowls, divisions, cistern and pipe brackets to masonry with screws	-	-	-	11.50	-	303.48	4.54	308.02	nr	338.82
Single stall urinals; white glazed fireclay in one piece; white glazed fireclay tread; plastics automatic cistern; spreader and flush pipe; waste outlet and domed grating										
bedding stall and tread in cement mortar (1:4) and jointing tread with waterproof jointing compound; fixing cistern and pipe brackets to masonry with screws	-	-	-	7.00	-	184.73	5.44	190.17	nr	209.19
Slab urinals; range of four; white glazed fireclay back, ends, divisions, channel and tread; automatic cistern; flush and sparge pipes; waste outlet and domed grating										
bedding back, ends, channel and tread in cement mortar (1:4) and jointing with waterproof jointing compound; fixing divisions, cistern and pipe brackets to masonry with screws	-	-	-	19.00	-	501.41	17.32	518.73	nr	570.61
Showers; white glazed fireclay tray 760 x 760 x 180mm; waste outlet; recessed valve and spray head										
bedding tray in cement mortar (1:4); fixing valve head to masonry with screws; sealing at walls with mastic sealant	-	-	-	4.75	-	125.35	7.01	132.36	nr	145.60
Shower curtains with rails, hooks, supports and fittings										
straight, 914mm long x 1829mm drop; fixing supports to masonry with screws	-	-	-	1.00	-	26.39	0.54	26.93	nr	29.63
angled, 1676mm girth x 1829mm drop; fixing supports to masonry with screws	-	-	-	1.50	-	39.58	0.74	40.33	nr	44.36
Supply and fix appliances - sinks										
Note: the following prices include joints to copper services and wastes but do not include traps										
Sink units; single bowl with single drainer and back ledge; stainless steel; BS EN 13310 Type A; 38mm waste, plug and chain to BS EN 274 Part 1 with combined overflow; pair 13mm pillar taps										
fixing on base unit with metal clips										
965 x 500mm	66.48	2.50	68.14	3.00	-	79.17	1.32	148.63	nr	163.50
965 x 500mm - bowl and a half	95.65	2.50	98.04	3.50	-	92.36	1.32	191.73	nr	210.90
Sink units; single bowl with double drainer and back ledge; stainless steel; BS EN 13310 Type B; 38mm waste, plug and chain to BS EN 274 Part 1 with combined overflow; pair 13mm pillar taps										
fixing on base unit with metal clips										
1500 x 600mm	162.32	2.50	166.37	3.00	-	79.17	1.73	247.28	nr	272.01
Sinks; white glazed fireclay; BS 1206 with weir overflow; 38mm slotted waste, chain, stay and plug to BS EN 274 Part 1; aluminium alloy cantilever brackets										
screwing chain stay; fixing brackets to masonry with screws; sealing at back with mastic sealant										
455 x 380 x 205mm	196.58	2.50	201.49	3.50	-	92.36	2.14	296.00	nr	325.60
610 x 455 x 255mm	217.81	2.50	223.26	3.50	-	92.36	2.14	317.77	nr	349.54
760 x 455 x 255mm	287.83	2.50	295.02	3.50	-	92.36	2.14	389.53	nr	428.48
Sinks; white glazed fireclay; BS 1206 with wier overflow; 38mm slotted waste, chain, stay and plug to BS EN 274 Part 1; painted legs and screw-to-wall bearers										
screwing chain stay; fixing legs to masonry with screws; sealing at back with mastic sealant										
455 x 380 x 205mm	214.11	2.50	219.46	3.50	-	92.36	2.14	313.97	nr	345.37
610 x 455 x 255mm	242.81	2.50	248.88	3.50	-	92.36	2.14	343.39	nr	377.73
760 x 455 x 255mm	312.83	2.50	320.65	3.50	-	92.36	2.14	415.16	nr	456.67

Labour hourly rates: (except Specialists) Craft Operatives 26.39 Labourer 15.57 Rates are national average prices. Refer to REGIONAL VARIATIONS for indicative levels of overall pricing in regions	MATERIALS			LABOUR				RATES		
	Del to Site £	Waste %	Material Cost £	Craft Optve Hrs	Lab Hrs	Labour Cost £	Sunds £	Nett Rate £	Unit	Gross rate (10%) £
SANITARY APPLIANCES AND FITTINGS (Cont'd)										
Supply and fix appliances - lavatory basins										
Wash basins; white vitreous china; BS 5506 Part 3; 32mm slotted waste, chain, stay and plug to BS EN 274 Part 1; painted legs and screw-to-wall bearers; pair 13mm taps										
fixing legs to masonry with screws; sealing at back with mastic sealant										
570 x 406mm	203.94	2.50	209.04	4.10	-	108.20	2.14	319.38	nr	351.32
Wash basins; white vitreous china; BS 5506 Part 3; 32mm slotted waste, chain, stay and plug to BS EN 274 Part 1; painted towel rail brackets; pair 13mm pillar taps										
fixing brackets to masonry with screws; sealing at back with mastic sealant										
570 x 406mm	122.65	2.50	125.72	4.00	-	105.56	2.14	233.42	nr	256.76
Wash basins, angle type; white vitreous china; BS 5506 Part 3; 32mm slotted waste, chain, stay and plug to BS EN 274 Part 1; concealed brackets; pair 13mm pillar taps										
fixing brackets to masonry with screws; sealing at back with mastic sealant										
450 x 385mm	83.04	2.50	85.12	4.00	-	105.56	2.14	192.82	nr	212.10
Wash basins with pedestal; white vitreous china; BS 5506 Part 3; 32mm slotted waste, chain, stay and plug to BS EN 274 Part 1; pair 13mm pillar taps										
fixing basin to masonry with screws; sealing at back with mastic sealant										
570 x 406mm	70.15	2.50	71.90	4.50	-	118.75	2.14	192.80	nr	212.08
Supply and fix appliances - baths										
Baths; white enamelled pressed steel; BS EN 232; 32mm overflow with front grid and 38mm waste, chain and plug to BS EN 274 Part 1 with combined overflow; metal cradles with adjustable feet; pair 19mm pillar taps										
sealing at walls with mastic sealant										
700 x 1700 x 570mm overall	137.27	2.50	140.71	5.50	-	145.14	4.78	290.64	nr	319.70
Baths; white acrylic; BS EN 198; 32mm overflow with front grid and 38mm waste, chain and plug to BS EN 274 Part 1 with combined overflow; adjustable feet and wall fixing brackets; pair 19mm pillar taps										
700 x 1700 x 570mm overall; fixing brackets to masonry with screws; sealing at walls with mastic sealant	145.61	2.50	149.25	5.00	-	131.95	4.78	285.98	nr	314.58
700 x 1500 x 570mm overall; fixing brackets to masonry with screws; sealing at walls with mastic sealant	137.27	2.50	140.71	5.00	-	131.95	4.78	277.44	nr	305.19
Baths; P shaped shower bath; white acrylic; BS EN 198; 32mm overflow with front grid and 38mm waste, chain and plug to BS EN 274 Part 1 with combined overflow; pair 19mm pillar taps										
900 max x 1700 x 570mm overall; fixing brackets to masonry with screws; sealing at walls with mastic sealant	195.61	2.50	200.50	5.50	-	145.14	5.11	350.76	nr	385.83
Supply and fix appliances - W.C. pans										
White vitreous china pans to BS EN 997										
pan with horizontal outlet; fixing pan to timber with screws; bedding pan in mastic; jointing pan to soil pipe with Multikwik connector	45.30	2.50	46.43	2.50	-	65.97	1.15	113.56	nr	124.92
pan with horizontal outlet; fixing pan to masonry with screws; bedding pan in mastic; jointing pan to soil pipe with Multikwik connector	45.30	2.50	46.43	3.00	-	79.17	1.65	127.25	nr	139.98
Plastics W.C. seats; BS 1254, type 1										
black; fixing to pan	27.94	2.50	28.64	0.30	-	7.92	-	36.56	nr	40.21
Plastics W.C. seats and covers; BS 1254, type 1										
black; fixing to pan	13.61	2.50	13.95	0.30	-	7.92	-	21.87	nr	24.05
coloured; fixing to pan	24.96	2.50	25.58	0.30	-	7.92	-	33.50	nr	36.85
white; fixing to pan	14.18	2.50	14.53	0.30	-	7.92	-	22.45	nr	24.70
Supply and fix appliances - cisterns										
9 litre black plastics cistern with valveless fittings, chain and pull handle to BS 1125; 13mm piston type high pressure ball valve to BS 1212 Part 1 with 127mm plastics float to BS 2456										
fixing cistern brackets to masonry with screws	107.84	2.50	110.54	1.00	-	26.39	0.54	137.47	nr	151.22
Plastics flush pipe to BS 1125; adjustable										
for back wall fixing	3.10	2.50	3.18	0.75	-	19.79	0.54	23.51	nr	25.87
for side wall fixing	5.04	2.50	5.17	0.75	-	19.79	0.54	25.50	nr	28.05
Supply and fix appliances - W.C. suites										
High level W.C. suites; white vitreous china pan to BS EN 997; white vitreous china cistern with valveless fittings, chain and pull handle and plastics flush pipe to BS 1125; 13mm piston type high pressure ball valve to BS 1212 Part 1 with 127mm plastics float to BS 2456; white plastic seat and cover										
pan with S or P trap conversion bend to BS 5627; fixing pan to timber with screws; fixing cistern brackets to masonry with screws; bedding pan in mastic; jointing pan to soil pipe with Multikwik connector	237.48	2.50	243.41	4.00	-	105.56	2.89	351.86	nr	387.05

Labour hourly rates: (except Specialists) Craft Operatives 26.39 Labourer 15.57 Rates are national average prices. Refer to REGIONAL VARIATIONS for indicative levels of overall pricing in regions	MATERIALS			LABOUR				RATES		
	Del to Site £	Waste %	Material Cost £	Craft Optve Hrs	Lab Hrs	Labour Cost £	Sunds £	Nett Rate £	Unit	Gross rate (10%) £
SANITARY APPLIANCES AND FITTINGS (Cont'd)										
Supply and fix appliances - W.C. suites (Cont'd)										
High level W.C. suites; white vitreous china pan to BS EN 997; white vitreous china cistern with valveless fittings, chain and pull handle and plastics flush pipe to BS 1125; 13mm piston type high pressure ball valve to BS 1212 Part 1 with 127mm plastics float to BS 2456; white plastic seat and cover (Cont'd)										
pan with S or P trap conversion bend to BS 5627; fixing pan and cistern brackets to masonry with screws; bedding pan in mastic; jointing pan to soil pipe with Multikwik connector	237.48	2.50	243.41	4.50	-	118.75	2.89	365.05	nr	401.56
Low level W.C. suites; white vitreous china pan to BS EN 997; 9 litre white vitreous china cistern with valveless fittings and plastics flush bend to BS 1125; 13mm piston type high pressure ball valve to BS 1212 Part 1 with 127mm plastics float to BS 2456; white plastics seat and cover to BS 1254 type 1										
pan with S or P trap conversion bend to BS 5627; fixing pan to timber with screws; fixing cistern brackets to masonry with screws; bedding pan in mastic; jointing pan to soil pipe with Multikwik connector	141.64	2.50	145.18	4.00	-	105.56	2.89	253.63	nr	278.99
pan with S or P trap conversion bend to BS 5627; fixing pan and cistern brackets to masonry with screws; bedding pan in mastic; jointing pan to soil pipe with Multikwik connector	141.64	2.50	145.18	4.50	-	118.75	2.89	266.83	nr	293.51
Supply and fix appliances - urinals										
Wall urinals; white vitreous china bowl to BS 5520; 4.5 litre white vitreous china automatic cistern to BS 1876; spreader and stainless steel flush pipe; 32mm plastics waste outlet										
fixing bowl, cistern and pipe brackets to masonry with screws	94.12	2.50	96.48	4.50	-	118.75	2.23	217.46	nr	239.21
Wall urinals; range of 2; white vitreous china bowls to BS 5520; white vitreous china divisions; 9 litre white plastics automatic cistern to BS 1876; stainless steel flush pipes and spreaders; 32mm plastics waste outlets										
fixing bowls, divisions, cistern and pipe brackets to masonry with screws	296.00	2.50	303.40	9.00	-	237.51	3.30	544.21	nr	598.63
Wall urinals; range of 3; white vitreous china bowls to BS 5520; white vitreous china divisions; 14 litre white plastics automatic cistern to BS 1876; stainless steel flush pipes and spreaders; 32mm plastics waste outlets										
fixing bowls, divisions, cistern and pipe brackets to masonry with screws	365.00	2.50	374.12	13.50	-	356.26	4.37	734.76	nr	808.24
1200mm long stainless steel wall hung trough urinal with plastic; white; automatic cistern to BS 1876; spreader and stainless steel flush pipe; waste outlet and domed grating										
fixing urinal cistern and pipe brackets to masonry with screws	305.00	2.50	312.62	5.00	-	131.95	5.44	450.02	nr	495.02
1800mm long stainless steel wall hung trough urinal with plastic; white; automatic cistern to BS 1876; spreader and stainless steel flush pipe; waste outlet and domed grating										
fixing urinal cistern and pipe brackets to masonry with screws	350.00	2.50	358.75	7.00	-	184.73	9.40	552.89	nr	608.17
2400mm long stainless steel wall hung trough urinal with plastic; white; automatic cistern to BS 1876; spreader and stainless steel flush pipe; waste outlet and domed grating										
fixing urinal cistern and pipe brackets to masonry with screws	465.00	2.50	476.62	10.00	-	263.90	13.20	753.72	nr	829.10
Supply and fix appliances - showers										
Showers; white glazed stone resin tray, 760 x 760 x 95mm; 38mm waste outlet; surface mechanical valve										
bedding tray in cement mortar (1:4); fixing valve and head to masonry with screws; sealing at walls with mastic sealant	143.25	2.50	146.83	4.75	-	125.35	7.01	279.20	nr	307.12
Showers; white glazed stone resin tray, 760 x 760 x 95mm; 38mm waste outlet; recessed thermostatic valve and swivel spray head										
bedding tray in cement mortar (1:4); fixing valve and head to masonry with screws; sealing at walls with mastic sealant	170.75	2.50	175.02	4.75	-	125.35	7.01	307.38	nr	338.12
Showers; white moulded acrylic tray with removable front and side panels, 760 x 760 x 260mm with adjustable metal cradle; 38mm waste outlet; surface fixing mechanical valve, flexible tube hand spray and slide bar										
fixing cradle, valve and slide bar to masonry with screws; sealing at walls with mastic sealant	178.25	2.50	182.71	4.75	-	125.35	4.70	312.76	nr	344.04
Showers; white moulded acrylic tray with removable front and side panels, 760 x 760 x 260mm with adjustable metal cradle; 38mm waste outlet; surface fixing thermostatic valve, flexible tube hand spray and slide bar										
fixing cradle, valve and slide bar to masonry with screws; sealing at walls with mastic sealant	205.75	2.50	210.89	4.75	-	125.35	4.70	340.95	nr	375.04
Shower curtains; nylon; anodised aluminium rail, glider hooks, end and suspension fittings										
straight, 914mm long x 1829mm drop	20.82	2.50	21.34	1.20	-	31.67	0.66	53.67	nr	59.04
angled, 1676mm girth x 1829mm drop	27.49	2.50	28.18	1.50	-	39.58	0.82	68.59	nr	75.45
Shower curtains; heavy duty plastic; anodised aluminium rail, glider hooks, end and suspension fitting; fixing supports to masonry with screws										
straight, 914mm long x 1829mm drop	16.66	2.50	17.08	1.20	-	31.67	0.66	49.40	nr	54.34

Labour hourly rates: (except Specialists) Craft Operatives 26.39 Labourer 15.57 Rates are national average prices. Refer to REGIONAL VARIATIONS for indicative levels of overall pricing in regions	MATERIALS			LABOUR				RATES		
	Del to Site £	Waste %	Material Cost £	Craft Optve Hrs	Lab Hrs	Labour Cost £	Sunds £	Nett Rate £	Unit	Gross rate (10%) £
SANITARY APPLIANCES AND FITTINGS (Cont'd)										
Supply and fix appliances - showers (Cont'd)										
Shower curtains; heavy duty plastic; anodised aluminium rail, glider hooks, end and suspension fitting; fixing supports to masonry with screws (Cont'd)										
angled, 1676mm girth x 1829mm drop	33.33	2.50	34.16	1.50	-	39.58	0.82	74.57	nr	82.03

This section continues on the next page

Labour hourly rates: (except Specialists) Craft Operatives 20.87 Labourer 15.57 Rates are national average prices. Refer to REGIONAL VARIATIONS for indicative levels of overall pricing in regions	MATERIALS			LABOUR				RATES		
	Del to Site £	Waste %	Material Cost £	Craft Optve Hrs	Lab Hrs	Labour Cost £	Sunds £	Nett Rate £	Unit	Gross rate (10%) £
SANITARY APPLIANCES AND FITTINGS (Cont'd)										
Supply and fix bath panels										
MDF with bearers										
Front panel; bearers fixed to masonry	64.49	2.50	66.57	1.20	0.15	27.38	0.35	94.30	nr	103.72
End panel; bearers fixed to masonry	32.85	2.50	33.95	0.70	0.08	15.85	0.18	49.98	nr	54.98
Bath angle strip	3.69	2.50	3.78	0.12	0.02	2.82	-	6.60	nr	7.26
Bath Panel Plastic with plinth										
Front panel and plinth fixed to masonry	12.50	2.50	12.81	0.70	0.08	15.85	0.18	28.85	nr	31.73
End panel and plinth fixed to masonry	10.00	2.50	10.25	0.70	0.08	15.85	0.12	26.22	nr	28.84
NOTICES AND SIGNS										
Signwriting in gloss paint; one coat										
Letters or numerals, Helvetica medium style, on painted or varnished surfaces										
50mm high										
standard	0.03	10.00	0.03	0.14	-	2.92	0.01	2.97	nr	3.26
extra; shading	0.03	10.00	0.03	0.08	-	1.67	0.01	1.72	nr	1.89
extra; outline	0.03	10.00	0.03	0.12	-	2.50	0.01	2.55	nr	2.81
100mm high										
standard	0.03	10.00	0.03	0.28	-	5.84	0.02	5.90	nr	6.49
extra; shading	0.03	10.00	0.03	0.16	-	3.34	0.01	3.39	nr	3.72
extra; outline	0.03	10.00	0.03	0.24	-	5.01	0.02	5.07	nr	5.57
150mm high										
standard	0.06	10.00	0.07	0.42	-	8.77	0.03	8.87	nr	9.75
extra; shading	0.03	10.00	0.03	0.24	-	5.01	0.02	5.07	nr	5.57
extra; outline	0.03	10.00	0.03	0.36	-	7.51	0.03	7.58	nr	8.34
200mm high										
standard	0.06	10.00	0.07	0.56	-	11.69	0.04	11.80	nr	12.98
extra; shading	0.03	10.00	0.03	0.32	-	6.68	0.02	6.74	nr	7.41
extra; outline	0.03	10.00	0.03	0.48	-	10.02	0.04	10.10	nr	11.11
300mm high										
standard	0.09	10.00	0.10	0.84	-	17.53	0.07	17.70	nr	19.47
extra; shading	0.06	10.00	0.07	0.48	-	10.02	0.04	10.13	nr	11.14
extra; outline	0.06	10.00	0.07	0.72	-	15.03	0.05	15.15	nr	16.67
stops	-	-	-	0.04	-	0.83	-	0.83	nr	0.92
Signwriting in gloss paint; two coats										
Letters or numerals, Helvetica medium style, on painted or varnished surfaces										
50mm high	0.03	10.00	0.03	0.25	-	5.22	0.02	5.27	nr	5.80
100mm high	0.06	10.00	0.07	0.50	-	10.44	0.04	10.55	nr	11.60
150mm high	0.06	10.00	0.07	0.75	-	15.65	0.05	15.78	nr	17.35
200mm high	0.09	10.00	0.10	1.00	-	20.87	0.08	21.05	nr	23.16
250mm high	0.09	10.00	0.10	1.25	-	26.09	0.10	26.29	nr	28.92
300mm high	0.13	10.00	0.14	1.50	-	31.31	0.12	31.57	nr	34.72
stops	-	-	-	0.07	-	1.46	0.01	1.47	nr	1.62

This page left blank intentionally

Labour hourly rates: (except Specialists) Craft Operatives 26.39 Labourer 15.57 Rates are national average prices. Refer to REGIONAL VARIATIONS for indicative levels of overall pricing in regions	MATERIALS			LABOUR				RATES		
	Del to Site £	Waste %	Material Cost £	Craft Optve Hrs	Lab Hrs	Labour Cost £	Sunds £	Nett Rate £	Unit	Gross rate (10%) £
RAINWATER INSTALLATIONS; PIPEWORK										
Cast iron pipes and fittings, BS 460 Type A sockets; dry joints										
Pipes; straight										
75mm; in or on supports (included elsewhere)										
pipe, plain	57.85	5.00	60.74	0.67	-	17.68	-	78.42	m	86.26
extra; shoes	43.72	2.00	44.59	0.84	-	22.17	-	66.76	nr	73.44
extra; bends	37.49	2.00	38.24	0.67	-	17.68	-	55.92	nr	61.51
extra; offset bends 75mm projection	47.22	2.00	48.16	0.67	-	17.68	-	65.85	nr	72.43
extra; offset bends 150mm projection	47.22	2.00	48.16	0.67	-	17.68	-	65.85	nr	72.43
extra; offset bends 230mm projection	54.91	2.00	56.01	0.67	-	17.68	-	73.69	nr	81.06
extra; offset bends 305mm projection	64.37	2.00	65.66	0.67	-	17.68	-	83.34	nr	91.67
extra; branches	65.62	2.00	66.93	0.67	-	17.68	-	84.61	nr	93.08
100mm; in or on supports (included elsewhere)										
pipe, plain	78.92	5.00	82.86	0.80	-	21.11	-	103.98	m	114.37
extra; shoes	58.87	2.00	60.05	1.00	-	26.39	-	86.44	nr	95.08
extra; bends	53.05	2.00	54.11	0.80	-	21.11	-	75.22	nr	82.75
extra; offset bends 75mm projection	89.09	2.00	90.87	0.80	-	21.11	-	111.98	nr	123.18
extra; offset bends 150mm projection	89.09	2.00	90.87	0.80	-	21.11	-	111.98	nr	123.18
extra; offset bends 230mm projection	107.90	2.00	110.06	0.80	-	21.11	-	131.17	nr	144.29
extra; offset bends 305mm projection	107.90	2.00	110.06	0.80	-	21.11	-	131.17	nr	144.29
extra; branches	77.91	2.00	79.47	0.80	-	21.11	-	100.58	nr	110.64
Cast iron pipes and fittings, BS 460 Type A sockets; ears cast on; dry joints										
Pipes; straight										
63mm; ears fixing to masonry with galvanised pipe nails and distance pieces										
pipe with ears cast on	62.20	5.00	65.32	0.57	-	15.04	-	80.36	m	88.40
extra; shoes	50.44	2.00	51.45	0.71	-	18.74	-	70.19	nr	77.20
extra; bends	30.86	2.00	31.48	0.57	-	15.04	-	46.52	nr	51.17
extra; offset bends 75mm projection	47.22	2.00	48.16	0.57	-	15.04	-	63.21	nr	69.53
extra; offset bends 150mm projection	47.22	2.00	48.16	0.57	-	15.04	-	63.21	nr	69.53
extra; offset bends 230mm projection	54.91	2.00	56.01	0.57	-	15.04	-	71.05	nr	78.16
extra; offset bends 305mm projection	64.37	2.00	65.66	0.57	-	15.04	-	80.70	nr	88.77
extra; branches	59.59	2.00	60.78	0.57	-	15.04	-	75.82	nr	83.41
75mm; ears fixing to masonry with galvanised pipe nails and distance pieces										
pipe with ears cast on	62.20	5.00	65.32	0.67	-	17.68	-	83.00	m	91.30
extra; shoes	50.44	2.00	51.45	0.84	-	22.17	-	73.62	nr	80.98
extra; bends	37.49	2.00	38.24	0.67	-	17.68	-	55.92	nr	61.51
extra; offset bends 75mm projection	47.22	2.00	48.16	0.67	-	17.68	-	65.85	nr	72.43
extra; offset bends 150mm projection	47.22	2.00	48.16	0.67	-	17.68	-	65.85	nr	72.43
extra; offset bends 230mm projection	54.91	2.00	56.01	0.67	-	17.68	-	73.69	nr	81.06
extra; offset bends 305mm projection	64.37	2.00	65.66	0.67	-	17.68	-	83.34	nr	91.67
extra; branches	65.62	2.00	66.93	0.67	-	17.68	-	84.61	nr	93.08
100mm; ears fixing to masonry with galvanised pipe nails and distance pieces										
pipe with ears cast on	83.34	5.00	87.51	0.80	-	21.11	-	108.63	m	119.49
extra; shoes	65.62	2.00	66.93	1.00	-	26.39	-	93.32	nr	102.65
extra; bends	53.05	2.00	54.11	0.80	-	21.11	-	75.22	nr	82.75
extra; offset bends 75mm projection	89.09	2.00	90.87	0.80	-	21.11	-	111.98	nr	123.18
extra; offset bends 150mm projection	89.09	2.00	90.87	0.80	-	21.11	-	111.98	nr	123.18
extra; offset bends 230mm projection	107.90	2.00	110.06	0.80	-	21.11	-	131.17	nr	144.29
extra; offset bends 305mm projection	107.90	2.00	110.06	0.80	-	21.11	-	131.17	nr	144.29
extra; branches	77.91	2.00	79.47	0.80	-	21.11	-	100.58	nr	110.64
Pipe supports										
Steel holderbats										
for 75mm pipes; fixing to masonry with galvanised screws	15.31	2.00	15.62	0.17	-	4.49	-	20.10	nr	22.11
for 100mm pipes; fixing to masonry with galvanised screws	15.76	2.00	16.08	0.17	-	4.49	-	20.57	nr	22.62
Cast Iron holderbats										
for 75mm pipes; fixing to masonry with galvanised screws	39.97	2.00	40.77	0.17	-	4.49	-	45.25	nr	49.78
for 100mm pipes; fixing to masonry with galvanised screws	44.67	2.00	45.56	0.17	-	4.49	-	50.05	nr	55.05
Cast iron rectangular pipes and fittings; ears cast on; dry joints										
Pipes; straight										
100 x 75mm; ears fixing to masonry with galvanised pipe nails and distance pieces										
pipe with ears cast on	117.94	5.00	123.85	1.00	-	26.39	-	150.24	m	165.26
extra; shoes (front)	140.71	2.00	143.52	1.00	-	26.39	-	169.91	nr	186.91
extra; bends (front)	91.62	2.00	93.45	0.75	-	19.79	-	113.24	nr	124.57
extra; offset bends (front) 150 projection	100.36	2.00	102.37	0.75	-	19.79	-	122.16	nr	134.38
extra; offset bends (front) 300 projection	150.04	2.00	153.04	0.75	-	19.79	-	172.83	nr	190.12

Labour hourly rates: (except Specialists) Craft Operatives 26.39 Labourer 15.57 Rates are national average prices. Refer to REGIONAL VARIATIONS for indicative levels of overall pricing in regions	MATERIALS			LABOUR				RATES		
	Del to Site £	Waste %	Material Cost £	Craft Optve Hrs	Lab Hrs	Labour Cost £	Sunds £	Nett Rate £	Unit	Gross rate (10%) £
RAINWATER INSTALLATIONS; PIPEWORK (Cont'd)										
Cast aluminium pipes and fittings Section B, ears cast on; dry joints										
Pipes; straight										
63mm; ears fixing to masonry with galvanised screws										
pipe with ears cast on	19.41	5.00	20.38	0.50	-	13.19	-	33.57	m	36.93
extra; shoes	24.24	2.00	24.72	0.63	-	16.63	-	41.35	nr	45.49
extra; bends	22.87	2.00	23.33	0.50	-	13.19	-	36.52	nr	40.17
extra; offset bends 75mm projection	31.72	2.00	32.35	0.50	-	13.19	-	45.55	nr	50.10
extra; offset bends 150mm projection	34.28	2.00	34.97	0.50	-	13.19	-	48.16	nr	52.98
extra; offset bends 225mm projection	46.01	2.00	46.93	0.50	-	13.19	-	60.12	nr	66.14
extra; offset bends 300mm projection	50.71	2.00	51.72	0.50	-	13.19	-	64.92	nr	71.41
75mm; ears fixing to masonry with galvanised pipe nails										
pipe with ears cast on	21.78	5.00	22.86	0.67	-	17.68	-	40.55	m	44.60
extra; shoes	27.21	2.00	27.75	0.84	-	22.17	-	49.92	nr	54.91
extra; bends	24.08	2.00	24.56	0.67	-	17.68	-	42.24	nr	46.46
extra; offset bends 76mm projection	35.88	2.00	36.60	0.67	-	17.68	-	54.28	nr	59.71
extra; offset bends 152mm projection	41.45	2.00	42.28	0.67	-	17.68	-	59.96	nr	65.96
extra; offset bends 228mm projection	52.58	2.00	53.63	0.67	-	17.68	-	71.31	nr	78.45
extra; offset bends 304mm projection	58.92	2.00	60.10	0.67	-	17.68	-	77.78	nr	85.56
100mm; ears fixing to masonry with galvanised pipe nails										
pipe with ears cast on	33.90	5.00	35.59	0.80	-	21.11	-	56.71	m	62.38
extra; shoes	36.92	2.00	37.66	1.00	-	26.39	-	64.05	nr	70.45
extra; bends	34.99	2.00	35.69	0.80	-	21.11	-	56.80	nr	62.48
extra; offset bends 76mm projection	44.17	2.00	45.05	0.80	-	21.11	-	66.16	nr	72.78
extra; offset bends 152mm projection	51.00	2.00	52.02	0.80	-	21.11	-	73.13	nr	80.45
extra; offset bends 228mm projection	63.46	2.00	64.73	0.80	-	21.11	-	85.84	nr	94.43
extra; offset bends 304mm projection	81.57	2.00	83.20	0.80	-	21.11	-	104.31	nr	114.74
PVC-U pipes and fittings; push fit joints; pipework and supports self coloured										
Pipes; straight										
68mm; in standard holderbats fixing to masonry with galvanised screws										
pipe, plain	4.99	5.00	5.21	0.40	-	10.56	-	15.76	m	17.34
extra; shoes	5.41	2.00	5.52	0.31	-	8.18	-	13.70	nr	15.07
extra; bends	5.03	2.00	5.13	0.25	-	6.60	-	11.73	nr	12.90
extra; offset bends (spigot)	7.12	2.00	7.26	0.25	-	6.60	-	13.86	nr	15.25
extra; offset bends (socket)	7.12	2.00	7.26	0.25	-	6.60	-	13.86	nr	15.25
extra; angled branches	15.65	2.00	15.96	0.25	-	6.60	-	22.56	nr	24.82
RAINWATER INSTALLATIONS; PIPEWORK ANCILLARIES										
Aluminium pipework ancillaries										
Rainwater heads; square type										
250 x 180 x 180mm; 63mm outlet spigot; dry joint to pipe; fixing to masonry with galvanised screws	36.42	1.00	36.79	0.50	-	13.19	-	49.99	nr	54.99
250 x 180 x 180mm; 75mm outlet spigot; dry joint to pipe; fixing to masonry with galvanised screws	38.16	1.00	38.55	0.67	-	17.68	-	56.23	nr	61.85
250 x 180 x 180mm; 100mm outlet spigot; dry joint to pipe; fixing to masonry with galvanised screws	62.76	1.00	63.40	0.80	-	21.11	-	84.51	nr	92.96
Cast iron pipework ancillaries										
Rainwater heads; BS 460 hopper type (flat pattern)										
210 x 160 x 185mm; 65mm outlet spigot; dry joint to pipe; fixing to masonry with galvanised screws	46.15	1.00	46.62	0.50	-	13.19	-	59.81	nr	65.79
210 x 160 x 185mm; 75mm outlet spigot; dry joint to pipe; fixing to masonry with galvanised screws	46.65	1.00	47.12	0.67	-	17.68	-	64.80	nr	71.28
250 x 180 x 175mm; 100mm outlet spigot; dry joint to pipe; fixing to masonry with galvanised screws	115.99	1.00	117.15	0.80	-	21.11	-	138.27	nr	152.09
Rainwater heads; BS 460 square type (flat pattern)										
250 x 180 x 175mm; 65mm outlet spigot; dry joint to pipe; fixing to masonry with galvanised screws	83.69	1.00	84.53	0.50	-	13.19	-	97.73	nr	107.50
250 x 180 x 175mm; 75mm outlet spigot; dry joint to pipe; fixing to masonry with galvanised screws	4.58	1.00	4.63	0.67	-	17.68	-	22.31	nr	24.54
250 x 180 x 175mm; 100mm outlet spigot; dry joint to pipe; fixing to masonry with galvanised screws	83.69	1.00	84.53	0.80	-	21.11	-	105.64	nr	116.21
Roof outlets; luting flange for asphalt										
flat grating; 100mm outlet spigot; coupling joint to cast iron pipe	85.84	1.00	86.70	1.00	-	26.39	-	113.09	nr	124.40
domical grating; 100mm outlet spigot; coupling joint to cast iron pipe	85.84	1.00	86.70	1.00	-	26.39	-	113.09	nr	124.40
Plastics pipework ancillaries self coloured black										
Rainwater heads; square type										
280 x 155 x 230mm; 68mm outlet spigot; push fit joint to plastics pipe; fixing to masonry with galvanised screws	23.02	1.00	23.25	0.50	-	13.19	-	36.44	nr	40.09
252 x 195 x 210mm; 110mm outlet spigot; push fit joint to plastics pipe; fixing to masonry with galvanised screws	37.11	1.00	37.48	0.80	-	21.11	-	58.59	nr	64.45
Plastics pipework ancillaries, self coloured grey										
Roof outlets; luting flange for asphalt										
domical grating; 75mm outlet spigot; push fit joint to plastics pipe	44.40	1.00	44.84	0.37	-	9.76	-	54.61	nr	60.07
domical grating; 100mm outlet spigot; push fit joint to plastics pipe	65.42	1.00	66.07	0.37	-	9.76	-	75.84	nr	83.42

Labour hourly rates: (except Specialists) Craft Operatives 26.39 Labourer 15.57 Rates are national average prices. Refer to REGIONAL VARIATIONS for indicative levels of overall pricing in regions	MATERIALS			LABOUR				RATES		
	Del to Site £	Waste %	Material Cost £	Craft Optve Hrs	Lab Hrs	Labour Cost £	Sunds £	Nett Rate £	Unit	Gross rate (10%) £
RAINWATER INSTALLATIONS; GUTTERS										
Cast iron half round gutters and fittings, BS 460; bolted and mastic joints										
Gutters										
100mm; in standard fascia brackets fixing to timber with galvanised screws										
straight lengths	35.10	5.00	36.76	0.50	-	13.19	-	49.95	m	54.95
extra; stopped ends	5.57	2.00	5.68	0.50	-	13.19	-	18.88	nr	20.76
extra; running outlets	23.94	2.00	24.42	0.50	-	13.19	-	37.61	nr	41.38
extra; stopped ends with outlet	23.94	2.00	24.42	0.50	-	13.19	-	37.61	nr	41.38
extra; angles	23.94	2.00	24.42	0.50	-	13.19	-	37.61	nr	41.38
114mm; in standard fascia brackets fixing to timber with galvanised screws										
straight lengths	36.39	5.00	38.11	0.50	-	13.19	-	51.30	m	56.43
extra; stopped ends	7.13	2.00	7.27	0.50	-	13.19	-	20.47	nr	22.51
extra; running outlets	25.50	2.00	26.01	0.50	-	13.19	-	39.21	nr	43.13
extra; stopped ends with outlet	25.50	2.00	26.01	0.50	-	13.19	-	39.21	nr	43.13
extra; angles	25.50	2.00	26.01	0.50	-	13.19	-	39.21	nr	43.13
125mm; in standard fascia brackets fixing to timber with galvanised screws										
straight lengths	42.21	5.00	44.22	0.57	-	15.04	-	59.26	m	65.18
extra; stopped ends	7.71	2.00	7.86	0.57	-	15.04	-	22.91	nr	25.20
extra; running outlets	29.77	2.00	30.37	0.57	-	15.04	-	45.41	nr	49.95
extra; stopped ends with outlet	29.77	2.00	30.37	0.57	-	15.04	-	45.41	nr	49.95
extra; angles	29.77	2.00	30.37	0.57	-	15.04	-	45.41	nr	49.95
150mm; in standard fascia brackets fixing to timber with galvanised screws										
straight lengths	62.94	5.00	65.96	0.75	-	19.79	-	85.75	m	94.33
extra; stopped ends	8.81	2.00	8.99	0.75	-	19.79	-	28.78	nr	31.66
extra; running outlets	48.44	2.00	49.41	0.75	-	19.79	-	69.20	nr	76.12
extra; stopped ends with outlet	48.44	2.00	49.41	0.75	-	19.79	-	69.20	nr	76.12
extra; angles	48.44	2.00	49.41	0.75	-	19.79	-	69.20	nr	76.12
Cast iron OGEE gutters and fittings, BS 460; bolted and mastic joints										
Gutters										
100mm; fixing to timber with galvanised screws										
straight lengths	35.33	5.00	37.10	0.50	-	13.19	-	50.30	m	55.33
extra; stopped ends	7.28	2.00	7.43	0.50	-	13.19	-	20.62	nr	22.68
extra; running outlets	25.00	2.00	25.50	0.50	-	13.19	-	38.69	nr	42.56
extra; angles	25.00	2.00	25.50	0.50	-	13.19	-	38.69	nr	42.56
114mm; fixing to timber with galvanised screws										
straight lengths	38.89	5.00	40.84	0.50	-	13.19	-	54.03	m	59.43
extra; stopped ends	9.23	2.00	9.41	0.50	-	13.19	-	22.61	nr	24.87
extra; running outlets	27.15	2.00	27.69	0.50	-	13.19	-	40.89	nr	44.98
extra; angles	27.15	2.00	27.69	0.50	-	13.19	-	40.89	nr	44.98
125mm; fixing to timber with galvanised screws										
straight lengths	40.79	5.00	42.83	0.57	-	15.04	-	57.87	m	63.66
extra; stopped ends	9.73	2.00	9.92	0.57	-	15.04	-	24.97	nr	27.46
extra; running outlets	29.63	2.00	30.22	0.57	-	15.04	-	45.26	nr	49.79
extra; angles	29.63	2.00	30.22	0.57	-	15.04	-	45.26	nr	49.79
Cast iron moulded (stock sections) gutters and fittings; bolted and mastic joints										
Gutters										
100 x 75mm; in standard fascia brackets fixing to timber with galvanised screws										
straight lengths	45.08	5.00	47.24	0.75	-	19.79	-	67.03	m	73.74
extra; stopped ends	13.93	2.00	14.21	0.75	-	19.79	-	34.00	nr	37.40
extra; running outlets	36.51	2.00	37.24	0.75	-	19.79	-	57.03	nr	62.74
extra; angles	36.51	2.00	37.24	0.75	-	19.79	-	57.03	nr	62.74
extra; clips	14.58	2.00	14.87	0.75	-	19.79	-	34.66	nr	38.13
125 x 100mm; in standard fascia brackets fixing to timber with galvanised screws										
straight lengths	55.62	5.00	58.29	1.00	-	26.39	-	84.68	m	93.15
extra; stopped ends	17.21	2.00	17.55	1.00	-	26.39	-	43.94	nr	48.34
extra; running outlets	52.50	2.00	53.55	1.00	-	26.39	-	79.94	nr	87.93
extra; angles	52.50	2.00	53.55	1.00	-	26.39	-	79.94	nr	87.93
extra; clips	18.15	2.00	18.51	1.00	-	26.39	-	44.90	nr	49.39
Cast iron box gutters and fittings; bolted and mastic joints										
Gutters										
100 x 75mm; in or on brackets										
straight lengths	60.45	5.00	63.34	0.75	-	19.79	-	83.13	m	91.45
extra; stopped ends	8.00	2.00	8.16	0.75	-	19.79	-	27.95	nr	30.75
extra; running outlets	29.21	2.00	29.79	0.75	-	19.79	-	49.59	nr	54.55
extra; angles	29.21	2.00	29.79	0.75	-	19.79	-	49.59	nr	54.55
extra; clips	10.37	2.00	10.58	0.75	-	19.79	-	30.37	nr	33.41
Cast aluminium half round gutters and fittings, Section A; bolted and mastic joints										
Gutters										
102mm; in standard fascia brackets fixing to timber with galvanised screws										
straight lengths	25.13	5.00	26.33	0.50	-	13.19	-	39.52	m	43.48
extra; stopped ends	6.04	2.00	6.16	0.50	-	13.19	-	19.36	nr	21.29
extra; running outlets	14.65	2.00	14.94	0.50	-	13.19	-	28.14	nr	30.95
extra; angles	15.57	2.00	15.88	0.50	-	13.19	-	29.08	nr	31.98

Labour hourly rates: (except Specialists) Craft Operatives 26.39 Labourer 15.57 Rates are national average prices. Refer to REGIONAL VARIATIONS for indicative levels of overall pricing in regions	MATERIALS			LABOUR				RATES		
	Del to Site £	Waste %	Material Cost £	Craft Optve Hrs	Lab Hrs	Labour Cost £	Sunds £	Nett Rate £	Unit	Gross rate (10%) £
RAINWATER INSTALLATIONS; GUTTERS (Cont'd)										
Cast aluminium half round gutters and fittings, Section A; bolted and mastic joints (Cont'd)										
Gutters (Cont'd)										
127mm; in standard fascia brackets fixing to timber with galvanised screws										
straight lengths	30.30	5.00	31.72	0.57	-	15.04	-	46.76	m	51.44
extra; stopped ends	6.72	2.00	6.85	0.57	-	15.04	-	21.90	nr	24.09
extra; running outlets	16.79	2.00	17.13	0.57	-	15.04	-	32.17	nr	35.38
extra; angles	17.03	2.00	17.37	0.57	-	15.04	-	32.41	nr	35.65
PVC-U half round gutters and fittings; push fit connector joints; gutterwork and supports self coloured grey										
Gutters										
112mm; in standard fascia brackets fixing to timber with galvanised screws										
straight lengths	4.53	2.00	4.62	0.33	-	8.71	-	13.33	m	14.66
extra; stopped ends	3.49	2.00	3.56	0.33	-	8.71	-	12.27	nr	13.50
extra; running outlets	5.34	2.00	5.45	0.33	-	8.71	-	14.16	nr	15.57
extra; angles	7.44	2.00	7.59	0.33	-	8.71	-	16.30	nr	17.93
FOUL DRAINAGE INSTALLATIONS; PIPEWORK										
Cast iron soil and waste pipes and fittings, BS 416; bolted and synthetic rubber gasket couplings										
Pipes										
75mm; in or on supports (included elsewhere)										
straight lengths	61.27	5.00	64.07	0.67	-	17.68	-	81.75	m	89.93
extra; pipes with inspection door bolted and sealed	146.97	2.00	149.91	0.67	-	17.68	-	167.59	nr	184.35
extra; short radius bends	106.97	2.00	109.11	0.67	-	17.68	-	126.79	nr	139.47
extra; short radius bends with inspection door bolted and sealed	172.85	2.00	176.31	0.67	-	17.68	-	193.99	nr	213.39
extra; offset bends 150mm projection	115.61	2.00	117.92	0.67	-	17.68	-	135.60	nr	149.16
extra; single angled branches	151.77	2.00	154.81	1.00	-	26.39	-	181.20	nr	199.31
extra; single angled branches with inspection door bolted and sealed	192.20	2.00	196.04	1.00	-	26.39	-	222.43	nr	244.68
extra; double angled branches	250.25	2.00	255.26	1.33	-	35.10	-	290.35	nr	319.39
boss pipes with one threaded boss	183.62	2.00	187.29	0.67	-	17.68	-	204.97	nr	225.47
100mm; in or on supports (included elsewhere)										
straight lengths	79.10	5.00	82.78	0.80	-	21.11	-	103.89	m	114.28
extra; pipes with inspection door bolted and sealed	158.61	2.00	161.78	0.80	-	21.11	-	182.89	nr	201.18
extra; short radius bends	122.36	2.00	124.81	0.80	-	21.11	-	145.92	nr	160.51
extra; short radius bends with inspection door bolted and sealed	192.30	2.00	196.15	0.80	-	21.11	-	217.26	nr	238.98
extra; offset bends 150mm projection	147.67	2.00	150.62	0.80	-	21.11	-	171.74	nr	188.91
extra; offset bends 300mm projection	164.14	2.00	167.42	0.80	-	21.11	-	188.53	nr	207.39
extra; single angled branches	196.42	2.00	200.35	1.20	-	31.67	-	232.02	nr	255.22
extra; single angled branches with inspection door bolted and sealed	224.94	2.00	229.44	1.20	-	31.67	-	261.11	nr	287.22
extra; double angled branches	300.93	2.00	306.95	1.60	-	42.22	-	349.17	nr	384.09
extra; double angled branches with inspection door bolted and sealed	323.58	2.00	330.05	1.60	-	42.22	-	372.28	nr	409.50
extra; single anti-syphon branches, angled branch	180.84	2.00	184.45	1.20	-	31.67	-	216.12	nr	237.74
extra; straight wc connectors	104.35	2.00	106.44	0.80	-	21.11	-	127.55	nr	140.30
extra; roof connectors	60.13	2.00	61.33	0.80	-	21.11	-	82.44	nr	90.69
boss pipes with one boss	196.00	2.00	199.92	0.80	-	21.11	-	221.03	nr	243.14
boss pipes with two bosses	204.96	2.00	209.06	0.80	-	21.11	-	230.17	nr	253.19
50mm; in standard wall fixing bracket (fixing included elsewhere)										
straight lengths	57.13	5.00	59.74	0.55	-	14.51	-	74.26	m	81.68
extra; short radius bends	94.81	2.00	96.71	0.55	-	14.51	-	111.22	nr	122.34
extra; short radius bends with inspection door bolted and sealed	160.78	2.00	164.00	0.55	-	14.51	-	178.51	nr	196.36
extra; single angled branches	142.03	2.00	144.87	0.82	-	21.64	-	166.51	nr	183.16
extra; single angled branches with inspection door bolted and sealed	183.39	2.00	187.06	0.82	-	21.64	-	208.70	nr	229.57
Cast iron lightweight soil and waste pipes and fittings										
Pipes										
50mm; in or on supports (included elsewhere)										
straight lengths	23.33	5.00	24.42	0.55	-	14.51	-	38.93	m	42.82
extra; short pipe with access door	54.33	2.00	55.42	0.55	-	14.51	-	69.93	nr	76.92
extra; bends	32.10	2.00	32.74	0.55	-	14.51	-	47.26	nr	51.98
extra; offset bend 130mm projection	52.10	2.00	53.14	0.55	-	14.51	-	67.66	nr	74.42
extra; single angled branch	50.11	2.00	51.11	0.82	-	21.64	-	72.75	nr	80.03
extra; plug	14.64	2.00	14.93	0.27	-	7.13	-	22.06	nr	24.26
extra; universal plug with one inlet	25.32	2.00	25.83	0.14	-	3.69	-	29.53	nr	32.48
extra; step coupling for connection to BS 416 pipe	16.75	2.00	17.08	0.40	-	10.56	-	27.64	nr	30.40
70mm; in or on supports (included elsewhere)										
straight lengths	26.77	5.00	28.01	0.67	-	17.68	-	45.69	m	50.26
extra; short pipe with access door	63.59	2.00	64.86	0.67	-	17.68	-	82.54	nr	90.80
extra; bends	37.10	2.00	37.84	0.67	-	17.68	-	55.52	nr	61.08
extra; offset bend 130mm projection	74.93	2.00	76.43	0.67	-	17.68	-	94.11	nr	103.53
extra; single angled branch	55.88	2.00	57.00	1.00	-	26.39	-	83.39	nr	91.73
extra; diminishing piece 70/50	40.42	2.00	41.23	0.67	-	17.68	-	58.91	nr	64.80
extra; plug	16.40	2.00	16.73	0.33	-	8.71	-	25.44	nr	27.98
extra; step coupling for connection to BS 416 pipe	19.04	2.00	19.42	0.50	-	13.19	-	32.62	nr	35.88
100mm; in or on supports (included elsewhere)										
straight lengths	32.26	5.00	33.74	0.80	-	21.11	-	54.85	m	60.33
extra; short pipe with access door	74.67	2.00	76.17	0.80	-	21.11	-	97.28	nr	107.01
extra; bends	49.05	2.00	50.03	0.80	-	21.11	-	71.14	nr	78.26
extra; long radius bend	94.30	2.00	96.18	0.80	-	21.11	-	117.29	nr	129.02

Labour hourly rates: (except Specialists) Craft Operatives 26.39 Labourer 15.57 Rates are national average prices. Refer to REGIONAL VARIATIONS for indicative levels of overall pricing in regions	MATERIALS			LABOUR				RATES		
	Del to Site £	Waste %	Material Cost £	Craft Optve Hrs	Lab Hrs	Labour Cost £	Sunds £	Nett Rate £	Unit	Gross rate (10%) £
FOUL DRAINAGE INSTALLATIONS; PIPEWORK (Cont'd)										
Cast iron lightweight soil and waste pipes and fittings (Cont'd)										
Pipes (Cont'd)										
100mm; in or on supports (included elsewhere) (Cont'd)										
extra; offset bend 75mm projection	72.39	2.00	73.84	0.80	-	21.11	-	94.95	nr	104.44
extra; offset bend 130mm projection	81.09	2.00	82.71	0.80	-	21.11	-	103.82	nr	114.21
extra; single angled branch	78.21	2.00	79.77	1.20	-	31.67	-	111.44	nr	122.58
extra; double angled branch	112.11	2.00	114.35	1.60	-	42.22	-	156.58	nr	172.24
extra; diminishing piece 100/50	50.52	2.00	51.53	0.80	-	21.11	-	72.65	nr	79.91
extra; diminishing piece 100/70	51.94	2.00	52.98	0.80	-	21.11	-	74.09	nr	81.50
extra; plug	21.90	2.00	22.34	0.40	-	10.56	-	32.89	nr	36.18
extra; universal plug with three inlets	50.37	2.00	51.38	0.40	-	10.56	-	61.93	nr	68.13
extra; step coupling for connection to BS 416 pipe	40.73	2.00	41.55	0.60	-	15.83	-	57.38	nr	63.12
extra; traditional joint connector	60.87	2.00	62.09	0.80	-	21.11	-	83.20	nr	91.52
extra; roof connector (asphalt)	81.09	2.00	82.71	0.80	-	21.11	-	103.82	nr	114.20
Pipe supports										
galvanised steel vertical bracket										
for 50mm pipes; for fixing bolt(fixing included elsewhere)	6.00	2.00	6.12	-	-	-	-	6.12	nr	6.73
for 70mm pipes; for fixing bolt(fixing included elsewhere)	6.92	2.00	7.06	-	-	-	-	7.06	nr	7.76
for 100mm pipes; for fixing bolt(fixing included elsewhere)	9.95	2.00	10.15	-	-	-	-	10.15	nr	11.16
MuPVC pipes and fittings, BS EN 1329-1 Section Three; solvent welded joints										
Pipes										
32mm; in standard plastics pipe brackets fixing to timber with screws										
straight lengths	2.93	10.00	3.18	0.33	-	8.71	-	11.89	m	13.08
extra; straight expansion couplings	0.78	2.00	0.80	0.25	-	6.60	-	7.39	nr	8.13
extra; connections to plastics pipe socket; socket adaptor; solvent welded joint	0.73	2.00	0.74	0.25	-	6.60	-	7.34	nr	8.08
extra; connections to plastics pipe boss; boss adaptor; solvent welded joint	0.73	2.00	0.74	0.25	-	6.60	-	7.34	nr	8.08
extra; fittings; one end	0.76	2.00	0.78	0.13	-	3.43	-	4.21	nr	4.63
extra; fittings; two ends	0.72	2.00	0.73	0.25	-	6.60	-	7.33	nr	8.07
extra; fittings; three ends	0.76	2.00	0.78	0.25	-	6.60	-	7.37	nr	8.11
40mm; in standard plastics pipe brackets fixing to timber with screws										
straight lengths	3.40	10.00	3.70	0.33	-	8.71	-	12.41	m	13.65
extra; straight expansion couplings	0.83	2.00	0.85	0.25	-	6.60	-	7.44	nr	8.19
extra; connections to plastics pipe socket; socket adaptor; solvent welded joint	0.72	2.00	0.73	0.25	-	6.60	-	7.33	nr	8.07
extra; connections to plastics pipe boss; boss adaptor; solvent welded joint	0.72	2.00	0.73	0.25	-	6.60	-	7.33	nr	8.07
extra; fittings; one end	0.76	2.00	0.78	0.13	-	3.43	-	4.21	nr	4.63
extra; fittings; two ends	0.72	2.00	0.73	0.25	-	6.60	-	7.33	nr	8.07
extra; fittings; three ends	0.76	2.00	0.78	0.25	-	6.60	-	7.37	nr	8.11
50mm; in standard plastics pipe brackets fixing to timber with screws										
straight lengths	4.41	10.00	4.80	0.40	-	10.56	-	15.35	m	16.89
extra; straight expansion couplings	1.40	2.00	1.43	0.33	-	8.71	-	10.14	nr	11.15
extra; connections to plastics pipe socket; socket adaptor; solvent welded joint	1.10	2.00	1.12	0.33	-	8.71	-	9.83	nr	10.81
extra; connections to plastics pipe boss; boss adaptor; solvent welded joint	1.10	2.00	1.12	0.33	-	8.71	-	9.83	nr	10.81
extra; fittings; one end	1.60	2.00	1.63	0.17	-	4.49	-	6.12	nr	6.73
extra; fittings; two ends	1.10	2.00	1.12	0.33	-	8.71	-	9.83	nr	10.81
extra; fittings; three ends	1.40	2.00	1.43	0.33	-	8.71	-	10.14	nr	11.15
32mm; in standard plastics pipe brackets fixing to masonry with screws										
straight lengths	2.94	10.00	3.19	0.39	-	10.29	-	13.49	m	14.84
40mm; in standard plastics pipe brackets fixing to masonry with screws										
straight lengths	3.41	10.00	3.72	0.39	-	10.29	-	14.01	m	15.41
50mm; in standard plastics pipe brackets fixing to masonry with screws										
straight lengths	4.43	10.00	4.81	0.46	-	12.14	-	16.95	m	18.65
Polypropylene pipes and fittings; butyl 'O' ring joints										
Pipes										
32mm; in standard plastics pipe brackets fixing to timber with screws										
straight lengths	1.54	10.00	1.63	0.33	-	8.71	-	10.34	m	11.37
extra; connections to plastics pipe socket; socket adaptor; solvent welded joint	2.01	2.00	2.05	0.25	-	6.60	-	8.65	nr	9.51
extra; connections to plastics pipe boss; boss adaptor; solvent welded joint	2.01	2.00	2.05	0.25	-	6.60	-	8.65	nr	9.51
extra; fittings; one end	0.99	2.00	1.01	0.13	-	3.43	-	4.44	nr	4.88
extra; fittings; two ends	0.88	2.00	0.90	0.25	-	6.60	-	7.50	nr	8.24
extra; fittings; three ends	1.15	2.00	1.17	0.25	-	6.60	-	7.77	nr	8.55
40mm; in standard plastics pipe brackets fixing to timber with screws										
straight lengths	1.72	10.00	1.82	0.33	-	8.71	-	10.53	m	11.59
extra; connections to plastics pipe socket; socket adaptor; solvent welded joint	2.01	2.00	2.05	0.33	-	8.71	-	10.76	nr	11.83
extra; connections to plastics pipe boss; boss adaptor; solvent welded joint	2.01	2.00	2.05	0.33	-	8.71	-	10.76	nr	11.83
extra; fittings; one end	0.99	2.00	1.01	0.17	-	4.49	-	5.50	nr	6.05
extra; fittings; two ends	0.88	2.00	0.90	0.33	-	8.71	-	9.61	nr	10.57
extra; fittings; three ends	1.23	2.00	1.25	0.33	-	8.71	-	9.96	nr	10.96

DRAINAGE ABOVE GROUND

Labour hourly rates: (except Specialists) Craft Operatives 26.39 Labourer 15.57 Rates are national average prices. Refer to REGIONAL VARIATIONS for indicative levels of overall pricing in regions	MATERIALS			LABOUR				RATES		
	Del to Site £	Waste %	Material Cost £	Craft Optve Hrs	Lab Hrs	Labour Cost £	Sunds £	Nett Rate £	Unit	Gross rate (10%) £
FOUL DRAINAGE INSTALLATIONS; PIPEWORK (Cont'd)										
Polypropylene pipes and fittings; butyl 'O' ring joints (Cont'd)										
Pipes (Cont'd)										
32mm; in standard plastics pipe brackets fixing to masonry with screws										
straight lengths	1.56	10.00	1.65	0.39	-	10.29	-	11.94	m	13.13
40mm; in standard plastics pipe brackets fixing to masonry with screws										
straight lengths	1.73	10.00	1.84	0.39	-	10.29	-	12.13	m	13.34
PVC-U pipes and fittings, BS 4514; rubber ring joints; pipework self coloured grey										
Pipes										
82mm; in or on supports (included elsewhere)										
straight lengths	14.00	5.00	14.59	0.44	-	11.61	-	26.20	m	28.82
extra; pipes with inspection door	36.81	2.00	37.55	0.33	-	8.71	-	46.26	nr	50.89
extra; short radius bends	25.81	2.00	26.33	0.33	-	8.71	-	35.03	nr	38.54
extra; single angled branches	36.81	2.00	37.55	0.33	-	8.71	-	46.26	nr	50.89
pipes with one boss socket	20.02	2.00	20.42	0.33	-	8.71	-	29.13	nr	32.04
110mm; in or on supports (included elsewhere)										
straight lengths	5.42	5.00	5.65	0.50	-	13.19	-	18.84	m	20.73
extra; pipes with inspection door	14.17	2.00	14.45	0.50	-	13.19	-	27.65	nr	30.41
extra; short radius bends	7.50	2.00	7.65	0.50	-	13.19	-	20.84	nr	22.93
extra; single angled branches	15.79	2.00	16.11	0.50	-	13.19	-	29.30	nr	32.23
extra; straight wc connectors	11.42	2.00	11.65	0.50	-	13.19	-	24.84	nr	27.33
pipes with one boss socket	9.38	2.00	9.57	0.50	-	13.19	-	22.76	nr	25.04
Air admittance valve	15.36	2.00	15.67	0.50	-	13.19	-	28.86	nr	31.75
160mm; in or on supports (included elsewhere)										
straight lengths	14.94	5.00	15.59	0.75	-	19.79	-	35.38	m	38.92
extra; pipes with inspection door	48.77	2.00	49.75	0.75	-	19.79	-	69.54	nr	76.49
extra; short radius bends	21.76	2.00	22.20	0.75	-	19.79	-	41.99	nr	46.19
extra; single angled branches	25.55	2.00	26.06	0.75	-	19.79	-	45.85	nr	50.44
pipes with one boss socket	19.99	2.00	20.39	0.75	-	19.79	-	40.18	nr	44.20
PVC-U pipes and fittings, BS 4514; solvent weld joints; pipework self coloured grey										
Pipes										
110mm; in or on supports (included elsewhere)										
straight lengths	5.42	5.00	5.65	0.53	-	13.99	-	19.64	m	21.60
extra; pipes with inspection door	14.17	2.00	14.45	0.53	-	13.99	-	28.44	nr	31.28
extra; short radius bends	7.50	2.00	7.65	0.53	-	13.99	-	21.64	nr	23.80
extra; single angled branches	15.79	2.00	16.11	0.53	-	13.99	-	30.09	nr	33.10
extra; straight wc connectors	11.42	2.00	11.65	0.53	-	13.99	-	25.63	nr	28.20
pipes with one boss socket	9.38	2.00	9.57	0.53	-	13.99	-	23.55	nr	25.91
Air admittance valve	12.58	2.00	12.83	0.53	-	13.99	-	26.82	nr	29.50
160mm; in or on supports (included elsewhere)										
straight lengths	14.94	5.00	15.59	0.80	-	21.11	-	36.70	m	40.37
extra; pipes with inspection door	48.77	2.00	49.75	0.80	-	21.11	-	70.86	nr	77.94
extra; short radius bends	21.76	2.00	22.20	0.80	-	21.11	-	43.31	nr	47.64
extra; single angled branches	25.55	2.00	26.06	0.80	-	21.11	-	47.17	nr	51.89
pipes with one boss socket	19.99	2.00	20.39	0.80	-	21.11	-	41.50	nr	45.65
Plastics pipework ancillaries, self coloured grey										
Weathering aprons										
fitted to 82mm pipes	6.99	2.00	7.13	0.33	-	8.71	-	15.84	nr	17.42
fitted to 110mm pipes	3.38	2.00	3.45	0.50	-	13.19	-	16.64	nr	18.31
Pipe supports for PVC-U soil and vent pipes, rubber ring joints; self coloured grey										
Plastics coated metal holderbats										
for 82mm pipes; for building in (fixing included elsewhere)	4.94	2.00	5.04	-	-	-	-	5.04	nr	5.54
for 110mm pipes; for building in (fixing included elsewhere)	6.15	2.00	6.28	-	-	-	-	6.28	nr	6.90
for 82mm pipes; fixing to timber with galvanised screws	4.00	2.00	4.08	0.17	-	4.49	-	8.57	nr	9.42
for 110mm pipes; fixing to timber with galvanised screws	5.87	2.00	5.99	0.17	-	4.49	-	10.48	nr	11.52
for 160mm pipes; fixing to timber with galvanised screws	9.38	2.00	9.57	0.17	-	4.49	-	14.06	nr	15.46
Pipe supports; solvent weld joints										
Plastic brackets										
for 110mm pipes; for building in (fixing included elsewhere)	7.09	2.00	7.23	-	-	-	-	7.23	nr	7.95
for 110mm pipes; fixing to timber with galvanised screws	2.39	2.00	2.44	0.25	-	6.60	-	9.03	nr	9.94
FOUL DRAINAGE INSTALLATIONS; PIPEWORK ANCILLARIES										
Balloon gratings										
Plastic balloon gratings										
fitted to 50mm pipes	2.78	3.00	2.86	0.10	-	2.64	-	5.50	nr	6.05
fitted to 82mm pipes	5.67	3.00	5.84	0.10	-	2.64	-	8.48	nr	9.33
fitted to 110mm pipes	3.38	3.00	3.48	0.10	-	2.64	-	6.12	nr	6.73
Plastics pipework ancillaries self coloured white										
Traps; BS EN 274										
P, two piece, 75mm seal, inlet with coupling nut, outlet with seal ring socket										
32mm outlet	6.07	2.00	6.19	0.33	-	8.71	-	14.90	nr	16.39
40mm outlet	6.72	2.00	6.85	0.33	-	8.71	-	15.56	nr	17.12
S, two piece, 75mm seal, inlet with coupling nut, outlet with seal ring socket										
32mm outlet	7.06	2.00	7.20	0.33	-	8.71	-	15.91	nr	17.50
40mm outlet	7.44	2.00	7.59	0.33	-	8.71	-	16.30	nr	17.93

Labour hourly rates: (except Specialists) Craft Operatives 26.39 Labourer 15.57 Rates are national average prices. Refer to REGIONAL VARIATIONS for indicative levels of overall pricing in regions	MATERIALS			LABOUR				RATES		
	Del to Site £	Waste %	Material Cost £	Craft Optve Hrs	Lab Hrs	Labour Cost £	Sunds £	Nett Rate £	Unit	Gross rate (10%) £
FOUL DRAINAGE INSTALLATIONS; PIPEWORK ANCILLARIES (Cont'd)										
Plastics pipework ancillaries self coloured white (Cont'd)										
Traps; BS EN 274 (Cont'd)										
P, two piece, 75mm seal, with flexible polypropylene pipe for overflow connection, inlet with coupling nut, outlet with seal ring socket										
40mm outlet	8.62	2.00	8.79	0.50	-	13.19	-	21.99	nr	24.19
Copper pipework ancillaries										
Traps; Section Two (Solid Drawn)										
P, two piece, 75mm seal, inlet with coupling nut, compression outlet										
35mm outlet	39.36	2.00	40.15	0.33	-	8.71	-	48.86	nr	53.74
42mm outlet	40.94	2.00	41.76	0.33	-	8.71	-	50.47	nr	55.51
54mm outlet	481.07	2.00	490.69	0.70	-	18.47	-	509.16	nr	560.08
S, two piece, 75mm seal, inlet with coupling nut, compression outlet										
35mm outlet	121.17	2.00	123.59	0.33	-	8.71	-	132.30	nr	145.53
42mm outlet	145.02	2.00	147.92	0.33	-	8.71	-	156.63	nr	172.29
54mm outlet	508.11	2.00	518.27	0.70	-	18.47	-	536.75	nr	590.42
bath, two piece, 75mm seal, overflow connection, cleaning eye and plug, inlet with coupling nut, compression outlet										
42mm outlet	230.35	2.00	234.96	0.50	-	13.19	-	248.15	nr	272.97

This page left blank intentionally

Labour hourly rates: (except Specialists) Craft Operatives 26.39 Labourer 15.57 Rates are national average prices. Refer to REGIONAL VARIATIONS for indicative levels of overall pricing in regions	PLANT AND TRANSPORT			LABOUR				RATES		
	Plant Cost £	Trans Cost £	P and T Cost £	Craft Optve Hrs	Lab Hrs	Labour Cost £	Sunds £	Nett Rate £	Unit	Gross rate (10%) £
DRAINAGE										
Note										
Notwithstanding the requirements of NRM2 excavation, disposal, beds, benching and surrounds have not been included with the items for drain runs and manholes and prices for specific drain runs and manholes etc should be calculated from the details below.										
STORM WATER AND FOUL DRAIN SYSTEMS; DRAIN RUNS										
Excavating trenches by machine to receive pipes not exceeding 200mm nominal size; disposing of surplus excavated material by removing from site										
Excavations commencing from natural ground level average depth										
500mm	2.56	6.86	9.42	-	0.23	3.58	1.12	14.12	m	15.53
750mm	4.10	6.86	10.97	-	0.34	5.29	1.68	17.94	m	19.74
1000mm	5.51	6.86	12.38	-	0.45	7.01	2.26	21.64	m	23.81
1250mm	7.06	6.86	13.92	-	0.61	9.50	2.82	26.24	m	28.87
1500mm	8.47	6.86	15.34	-	0.73	11.37	3.38	30.08	m	33.09
1750mm	10.02	6.86	16.88	-	0.86	13.39	3.94	34.22	m	37.64
2000mm	11.38	6.86	18.25	-	0.98	15.26	4.50	38.01	m	41.81
2250mm	14.50	6.86	21.37	-	1.69	26.31	5.08	52.76	m	58.04
2500mm	16.09	6.86	22.95	-	1.88	29.27	5.64	57.87	m	63.65
2750mm	17.81	6.86	24.67	-	2.06	32.07	6.20	62.95	m	69.25
3000mm	19.40	6.86	26.26	-	2.25	35.03	6.76	68.06	m	74.86
3250mm	21.12	6.86	27.98	-	2.44	37.99	7.33	73.30	m	80.63
3500mm	22.66	6.86	29.52	-	2.63	40.95	7.89	78.36	m	86.19
3750mm	24.38	6.86	31.24	-	2.82	43.91	8.46	83.61	m	91.98
4000mm	26.02	6.86	32.88	-	3.00	46.71	9.03	88.61	m	97.47
4250mm	27.69	6.86	34.55	-	4.25	66.17	9.59	110.31	m	121.34
4500mm	29.27	6.86	36.14	-	4.50	70.07	10.15	116.35	m	127.98
4750mm	31.00	6.86	37.86	-	4.75	73.96	10.71	122.53	m	134.78
5000mm	32.53	6.86	39.40	-	6.87	106.97	12.41	158.77	m	174.65
5250mm	34.26	6.86	41.12	-	6.56	102.14	11.85	155.11	m	170.62
5500mm	35.84	6.86	42.71	-	6.87	106.97	12.41	162.08	m	178.29
5750mm	37.57	6.86	44.43	-	7.18	111.79	12.97	169.19	m	186.11
6000mm	39.59	6.86	46.45	-	7.50	116.77	13.53	176.76	m	194.43
Excavating trenches by machine to receive pipes 225mm nominal size; disposing of surplus excavated material by removing from site										
Excavations commencing from natural ground level average depth										
500mm	2.74	7.24	9.99	-	0.24	3.74	1.12	14.85	m	16.33
750mm	4.29	7.24	11.54	-	0.36	5.61	1.68	18.82	m	20.71
1000mm	5.84	7.24	13.08	-	0.47	7.32	2.26	22.66	m	24.93
1250mm	7.37	7.24	14.61	-	0.64	9.96	2.82	27.40	m	30.14
1500mm	8.99	7.24	16.23	-	0.77	11.99	3.38	31.60	m	34.76
1750mm	10.54	7.24	17.78	-	0.90	14.01	3.94	35.73	m	39.31
2000mm	12.07	7.24	19.31	-	1.03	16.04	4.50	39.85	m	43.84
2250mm	15.27	7.24	22.52	-	1.77	27.56	5.08	55.16	m	60.67
2500mm	17.08	7.24	24.33	-	1.97	30.67	5.64	60.64	m	66.71
2750mm	18.80	7.24	26.05	-	2.16	33.63	6.20	65.88	m	72.47
3000mm	20.53	7.24	27.77	-	2.36	36.75	6.76	71.28	m	78.41
3250mm	22.25	7.24	29.49	-	2.56	39.86	7.33	76.68	m	84.35
3500mm	24.06	7.24	31.30	-	2.76	42.97	7.89	82.16	m	90.38
3750mm	25.78	7.24	33.02	-	2.96	46.09	8.46	87.58	m	96.33
4000mm	27.36	7.24	34.60	-	3.15	49.05	9.03	92.67	m	101.94
4250mm	29.23	7.24	36.47	-	4.46	69.44	9.59	115.50	m	127.05
4500mm	31.08	7.24	38.33	-	4.70	73.18	10.15	121.65	m	133.82
4750mm	32.76	7.24	40.00	-	4.98	77.54	10.71	128.25	m	141.07
5000mm	34.48	7.24	41.72	-	6.56	102.14	12.41	156.27	m	171.90
5250mm	36.20	7.24	43.45	-	6.89	107.28	11.85	162.57	m	178.83
5500mm	38.06	7.24	45.30	-	7.20	112.10	12.41	169.82	m	186.80
5750mm	39.73	7.24	46.98	-	7.54	117.40	12.97	177.35	m	195.08
6000mm	41.46	7.24	48.70	-	7.85	122.22	13.53	184.46	m	202.90
Excavating trenches by machine to receive pipes 300mm nominal size; disposing of surplus excavated material by removing from site										
Excavations commencing from natural ground level average depth										
500mm	3.02	8.01	11.03	-	0.25	3.89	1.12	16.04	m	17.64
750mm	4.81	8.01	12.81	-	0.37	5.76	1.68	20.26	m	22.28
1000mm	6.54	8.01	14.55	-	0.50	7.78	2.26	24.59	m	27.05
1250mm	8.33	8.01	16.33	-	0.67	10.43	2.82	29.59	m	32.54
1500mm	10.11	8.01	18.12	-	0.80	12.46	3.38	33.96	m	37.35
1750mm	11.85	8.01	19.85	-	0.95	14.79	3.94	38.59	m	42.45

Labour hourly rates: (except Specialists) Craft Operatives 26.39 Labourer 15.57 Rates are national average prices. Refer to REGIONAL VARIATIONS for indicative levels of overall pricing in regions	PLANT AND TRANSPORT			LABOUR				RATES		
	Plant Cost £	Trans Cost £	P and T Cost £	Craft Optve Hrs	Lab Hrs	Labour Cost £	Sunds £	Nett Rate £	Unit	Gross rate (10%) £
STORM WATER AND FOUL DRAIN SYSTEMS; DRAIN RUNS (Cont'd)										
Excavating trenches by machine to receive pipes 300mm nominal size; disposing of surplus excavated material by removing from site (Cont'd)										
Excavations commencing from natural ground level (Cont'd)										
average depth (Cont'd)										
2000mm	13.63	8.01	21.64	-	1.10	17.13	4.50	43.27	m	47.60
2250mm	17.26	8.01	25.26	-	1.86	28.96	5.08	59.30	m	65.24
2500mm	19.25	8.01	27.26	-	2.07	32.23	5.64	65.13	m	71.64
2750mm	21.25	8.01	29.25	-	2.25	35.03	6.20	70.49	m	77.54
3000mm	23.19	8.01	31.20	-	2.48	38.61	6.76	76.58	m	84.23
3250mm	25.19	8.01	33.19	-	2.68	41.73	7.33	82.25	m	90.47
3500mm	27.13	8.01	35.14	-	2.90	45.15	7.89	88.18	m	97.00
3750mm	29.13	8.01	37.13	-	3.10	48.27	8.46	93.87	m	103.25
4000mm	31.12	8.01	39.13	-	3.30	51.38	9.03	99.54	m	109.49
4250mm	33.07	8.01	41.07	-	4.68	72.87	9.59	123.53	m	135.88
4500mm	35.06	8.01	43.07	-	4.95	77.07	10.15	130.29	m	143.32
4750mm	37.01	8.01	45.02	-	5.23	81.43	10.71	137.16	m	150.87
5000mm	39.00	8.01	47.01	-	6.88	107.12	12.41	166.54	m	183.19
5250mm	41.00	8.01	49.01	-	7.22	112.42	11.85	173.27	m	190.59
5500mm	42.95	8.01	50.95	-	7.55	117.55	12.41	180.91	m	199.00
5750mm	44.94	8.01	52.95	-	7.90	123.00	12.97	188.92	m	207.81
6000mm	46.94	8.01	54.94	-	8.25	128.45	13.53	196.92	m	216.62
Excavating trenches by machine to receive pipes 400mm nominal size; disposing of surplus excavated material by removing from site										
Excavations commencing from natural ground level										
average depth										
2250mm	20.15	9.53	29.68	-	2.03	31.61	5.08	66.37	m	73.00
2500mm	22.36	9.53	31.90	-	2.26	35.19	5.64	72.73	m	80.00
2750mm	24.72	9.53	34.25	-	2.47	38.46	6.20	78.91	m	86.80
3000mm	26.99	9.53	36.52	-	2.70	42.04	6.76	85.32	m	93.85
3250mm	29.34	9.53	38.87	-	2.92	45.46	7.33	91.66	m	100.83
3500mm	31.61	9.53	41.14	-	3.16	49.20	7.89	98.23	m	108.05
3750mm	33.96	9.53	43.49	-	3.38	52.63	8.46	104.59	m	115.04
4000mm	36.23	9.53	45.76	-	3.60	56.05	9.03	110.84	m	121.92
4250mm	38.59	9.53	48.12	-	5.10	79.41	9.59	137.11	m	150.82
4500mm	40.80	9.53	50.33	-	5.40	84.08	10.15	144.56	m	159.02
4750mm	29.51	9.53	39.04	-	5.70	88.75	11.17	138.96	m	152.86
5000mm	45.43	9.53	54.96	-	7.50	116.77	12.41	184.14	m	202.55
5250mm	47.78	9.53	57.31	-	7.85	122.22	11.85	191.38	m	210.52
5500mm	50.05	9.53	59.58	-	8.25	128.45	12.41	200.44	m	220.48
5750mm	52.40	9.53	61.93	-	8.60	133.90	12.97	208.80	m	229.69
6000mm	37.11	9.53	46.64	-	9.00	140.13	14.12	200.89	m	220.98
Excavating trenches by machine to receive pipes 450mm nominal size; disposing of surplus excavated material by removing from site										
Excavations commencing from natural ground level										
average depth										
2250mm	21.55	9.91	31.46	-	2.11	32.85	5.08	69.39	m	76.33
2500mm	24.04	9.91	33.95	-	2.35	36.59	5.64	76.18	m	83.80
2750mm	26.39	9.91	36.30	-	2.58	40.17	6.20	82.68	m	90.95
3000mm	28.93	9.91	38.84	-	2.81	43.75	6.76	89.36	m	98.30
3250mm	29.76	9.91	39.68	-	3.05	47.49	7.33	94.49	m	103.94
3500mm	33.91	9.91	43.83	-	3.29	51.23	7.89	102.94	m	113.23
3750mm	36.27	9.91	46.18	-	3.52	54.81	8.46	109.45	m	120.40
4000mm	38.81	9.91	48.72	-	3.75	58.39	9.03	116.13	m	127.75
4250mm	41.30	9.91	51.21	-	5.30	82.52	9.59	143.32	m	157.65
4500mm	43.79	9.91	53.70	-	5.63	87.66	10.15	151.51	m	166.66
4750mm	46.15	9.91	56.06	-	5.95	92.64	10.71	159.41	m	175.35
5000mm	48.69	9.91	58.60	-	7.80	121.45	12.41	192.45	m	211.70
5250mm	51.18	9.91	61.09	-	8.20	127.67	11.85	200.61	m	220.67
5500mm	53.67	9.91	63.58	-	8.60	133.90	12.41	209.89	m	230.88
5750mm	56.02	9.91	65.93	-	8.95	139.35	12.97	218.25	m	240.08
6000mm	58.56	9.91	68.47	-	9.35	145.58	13.53	227.58	m	250.34
Excavating trenches by hand to receive pipes not exceeding 200mm nominal size; disposing of surplus excavated material on site										
Excavations commencing from natural ground level										
average depth										
500mm	-	-	-	-	1.15	17.91	1.12	19.03	m	20.93
750mm	-	-	-	-	2.05	31.92	1.68	33.60	m	36.96
1000mm	-	-	-	-	2.95	45.93	2.26	48.19	m	53.01
1250mm	-	-	-	-	3.85	59.94	2.82	62.77	m	69.04
1500mm	-	-	-	-	4.75	73.96	3.38	77.34	m	85.07
1750mm	-	-	-	-	5.65	87.97	3.94	91.91	m	101.11
2000mm	-	-	-	-	6.50	101.21	4.50	105.71	m	116.28
2250mm	-	-	-	-	7.65	119.11	5.08	124.19	m	136.61
2500mm	-	-	-	-	8.80	137.02	5.64	142.66	m	156.92
2750mm	-	-	-	-	9.95	154.92	6.20	161.13	m	177.24
3000mm	-	-	-	-	11.10	172.83	6.76	179.59	m	197.55
3250mm	-	-	-	-	12.25	190.73	7.33	198.06	m	217.86
3500mm	-	-	-	-	13.45	209.42	7.89	217.30	m	239.03
3750mm	-	-	-	-	14.60	227.32	8.46	235.79	m	259.37
4000mm	-	-	-	-	15.80	246.01	9.03	255.03	m	280.53

Labour hourly rates: (except Specialists) Craft Operatives 26.39 Labourer 15.57 Rates are national average prices. Refer to REGIONAL VARIATIONS for indicative levels of overall pricing in regions	PLANT AND TRANSPORT			LABOUR				RATES		
	Plant Cost £	Trans Cost £	P and T Cost £	Craft Optve Hrs	Lab Hrs	Labour Cost £	Sunds £	Nett Rate £	Unit	Gross rate (10%) £
STORM WATER AND FOUL DRAIN SYSTEMS; DRAIN RUNS (Cont'd)										
Excavating trenches by hand to receive pipes 225mm nominal size; disposing of surplus excavated material on site										
Excavations commencing from natural ground level average depth										
500mm	-	-	-	-	1.28	19.93	1.12	21.05	m	23.16
750mm	-	-	-	-	2.23	34.72	1.68	36.40	m	40.04
1000mm	-	-	-	-	3.18	49.51	2.26	51.77	m	56.95
1250mm	-	-	-	-	4.13	64.30	2.82	67.13	m	73.84
1500mm	-	-	-	-	5.08	79.10	3.38	82.48	m	90.73
1750mm	-	-	-	-	6.03	93.89	3.94	97.83	m	107.61
2000mm	-	-	-	-	6.95	108.21	4.50	112.72	m	123.99
2250mm	-	-	-	-	8.23	128.14	5.08	133.22	m	146.55
2500mm	-	-	-	-	9.45	147.14	5.64	152.78	m	168.06
2750mm	-	-	-	-	10.70	166.60	6.20	172.80	m	190.08
3000mm	-	-	-	-	11.95	186.06	6.76	192.83	m	212.11
3250mm	-	-	-	-	13.20	205.52	7.33	212.85	m	234.13
3500mm	-	-	-	-	14.45	224.99	7.89	232.87	m	256.16
3750mm	-	-	-	-	15.70	244.45	8.46	252.91	m	278.20
4000mm	-	-	-	-	17.00	264.69	9.03	273.72	m	301.09
Excavating trenches by hand to receive pipes 300mm nominal size; disposing of surplus material on site										
Excavations commencing from natural ground level average depth										
500mm	-	-	-	-	1.40	21.80	1.12	22.92	m	25.21
750mm	-	-	-	-	2.40	37.37	1.68	39.05	m	42.96
1000mm	-	-	-	-	3.40	52.94	2.26	55.20	m	60.72
1250mm	-	-	-	-	4.40	68.51	2.82	71.33	m	78.46
1500mm	-	-	-	-	5.40	84.08	3.38	87.46	m	96.21
1750mm	-	-	-	-	6.40	99.65	3.94	103.59	m	113.95
2000mm	-	-	-	-	7.40	115.22	4.50	119.72	m	131.69
2250mm	-	-	-	-	8.80	137.02	5.08	142.10	m	156.31
2500mm	-	-	-	-	10.10	157.26	5.64	162.90	m	179.19
2750mm	-	-	-	-	11.45	178.28	6.20	184.48	m	202.93
3000mm	-	-	-	-	12.75	198.52	6.76	205.28	m	225.81
3250mm	-	-	-	-	14.10	219.54	7.33	226.86	m	249.55
3500mm	-	-	-	-	15.45	240.56	7.89	248.44	m	273.29
3750mm	-	-	-	-	16.80	261.58	8.46	270.04	m	297.04
4000mm	-	-	-	-	18.15	282.60	9.03	291.62	m	320.78

This section continues on the next page

Labour hourly rates: (except Specialists) Craft Operatives 20.87 Labourer 15.57 Rates are national average prices. Refer to REGIONAL VARIATIONS for indicative levels of overall pricing in regions	MATERIALS			LABOUR				RATES		
	Del to Site £	Waste %	Material Cost £	Craft Optve Hrs	Lab Hrs	Labour Cost £	Sunds £	Nett Rate £	Unit	Gross rate (10%) £
STORM WATER AND FOUL DRAIN SYSTEMS; DRAIN RUNS (Cont'd)										
Beds, benchings and covers; Granular material, 10mm nominal size pea shingle, to be obtained off site										
Beds										
400 x 150mm	4.37	10.00	4.81	-	0.15	2.34	-	7.14	m	7.86
450 x 150mm	4.88	10.00	5.37	-	0.16	2.49	-	7.86	m	8.64
525 x 150mm	5.68	10.00	6.25	-	0.17	2.65	-	8.89	m	9.78
600 x 150mm	6.55	10.00	7.21	-	0.22	3.43	-	10.63	m	11.70
700 x 150mm	7.65	10.00	8.41	-	0.24	3.74	-	12.15	m	13.36
750 x 150mm	8.23	10.00	9.05	-	0.27	4.20	-	13.26	m	14.58
Beds and surrounds										
400 x 150mm bed; 150mm thick surround to 100mm internal diameter pipes -1	11.65	10.00	12.82	-	0.46	7.16	-	19.98	m	21.98
450 x 150mm bed; 150mm thick surround to 150mm internal diameter pipes -1	14.71	10.00	16.18	-	0.52	8.10	-	24.28	m	26.70
525 x 150mm bed; 150mm thick surround to 225mm internal diameter pipes -1	20.03	10.00	22.03	-	0.68	10.59	-	32.62	m	35.88
600 x 150mm bed; 150mm thick surround to 300mm internal diameter pipes -1	26.21	10.00	28.84	-	0.84	13.08	-	41.92	m	46.11
700 x 150mm bed; 150mm thick surround to 400mm internal diameter pipes -1	35.68	10.00	39.25	-	1.00	15.57	-	54.82	m	60.30
750 x 150mm bed; 150mm thick surround to 450mm internal diameter pipes -1	40.78	10.00	44.86	-	1.16	18.06	-	62.92	m	69.21
Beds and filling to half pipe depth										
400 x 150mm overall; to 100mm internal diameter pipes - 1	10.19	10.00	11.21	-	0.12	1.87	-	13.08	m	14.39
450 x 225mm overall; to 150mm internal diameter pipes - 1	12.23	10.00	13.46	-	0.20	3.11	-	16.57	m	18.23
525 x 263mm overall; to 225mm internal diameter pipes - 1	18.64	10.00	20.51	-	0.28	4.36	-	24.87	m	27.35
600 x 300mm overall; to 300mm internal diameter pipes -1	26.21	10.00	28.84	-	0.36	5.61	-	34.44	m	37.89
700 x 350mm overall; to 400mm internal diameter pipes -1	38.23	10.00	42.05	-	0.49	7.63	-	49.68	m	54.65
750 x 375mm overall; to 450mm internal diameter pipes -1	45.00	10.00	49.50	-	0.56	8.72	-	58.22	m	64.04
Beds, benchings and covers; sand; to be obtained off site										
Beds										
400 x 50mm	0.60	5.00	0.62	-	0.04	0.62	-	1.25	m	1.37
400 x 100mm	1.19	5.00	1.25	-	0.08	1.25	-	2.50	m	2.75
450 x 50mm	0.65	5.00	0.69	-	0.05	0.78	-	1.47	m	1.61
450 x 100mm	1.34	5.00	1.41	-	0.09	1.40	-	2.81	m	3.09
525 x 50mm	0.77	5.00	0.81	-	0.06	0.93	-	1.75	m	1.92
525 x 100mm	1.55	5.00	1.62	-	0.11	1.71	-	3.34	m	3.67
600 x 50mm	0.89	5.00	0.94	-	0.06	0.93	-	1.87	m	2.06
600 x 100mm	1.79	5.00	1.87	-	0.12	1.87	-	3.74	m	4.12
700 x 50mm	1.04	5.00	1.09	-	0.07	1.09	-	2.18	m	2.40
700 x 100mm	2.08	5.00	2.19	-	0.14	2.18	-	4.37	m	4.80
750 x 50mm	1.10	5.00	1.16	-	0.08	1.25	-	2.40	m	2.64
750 x 100mm	2.23	5.00	2.34	-	0.15	2.34	-	4.68	m	5.15
Beds, benchings and covers; plain in-situ concrete; BS 8500, ordinary prescribed mix, ST3, 20mm aggregate										
Beds										
400 x 100mm	4.06	5.00	4.26	-	0.18	2.80	2.94	10.00	m	11.00
400 x 150mm	6.08	5.00	6.39	-	0.27	4.20	4.41	15.00	m	16.50
450 x 100mm	4.56	5.00	4.79	-	0.20	3.11	2.94	10.85	m	11.93
450 x 150mm	6.79	5.00	7.13	-	0.30	4.67	4.41	16.21	m	17.84
525 x 100mm	5.27	5.00	5.54	-	0.24	3.74	2.94	12.21	m	13.43
525 x 150mm	7.91	5.00	8.30	-	0.35	5.45	4.41	18.16	m	19.98
600 x 100mm	6.08	5.00	6.39	-	0.27	4.20	2.94	13.53	m	14.89
600 x 150mm	9.13	5.00	9.58	-	0.38	5.92	4.41	19.91	m	21.90
700 x 100mm	7.10	5.00	7.45	-	0.32	4.98	2.94	15.38	m	16.91
700 x 150mm	10.65	5.00	11.18	-	0.47	7.32	4.41	22.91	m	25.20
750 x 100mm	7.61	5.00	7.99	-	0.34	5.29	2.94	16.22	m	17.84
750 x 150mm	11.36	5.00	11.92	-	0.51	7.94	4.41	24.28	m	26.70
Beds and surrounds										
400 x 100mm bed; 150mm thick surround to 100mm internal diameter pipes -1	14.20	5.00	14.91	-	0.72	11.21	5.76	31.88	m	35.06
400 x 150mm bed; 150mm thick surround to 100mm internal diameter pipes -1	16.22	5.00	17.04	-	0.81	12.61	6.47	36.11	m	39.72
450 x 100mm bed; 150mm thick surround to 150mm internal diameter pipes -1	18.25	5.00	19.16	-	0.91	14.17	6.47	39.80	m	43.78
450 x 150mm bed; 150mm thick surround to 150mm internal diameter pipes -1	20.48	5.00	21.51	-	1.01	15.73	7.18	44.42	m	48.86
525 x 100mm bed; 150mm thick surround to 225mm internal diameter pipes -1	25.25	5.00	26.51	-	1.24	19.31	7.18	53.00	m	58.30
525 x 150mm bed; 150mm thick surround to 225mm internal diameter pipes -1	27.89	5.00	29.28	-	1.36	21.18	8.27	58.72	m	64.59
600 x 100mm bed; 150mm thick surround to 300mm internal diameter pipes -1	33.46	5.00	35.14	-	1.62	25.22	8.64	69.00	m	75.90
600 x 150mm bed; 150mm thick surround to 300mm internal diameter pipes -1	36.50	5.00	38.33	-	1.76	27.40	9.35	75.08	m	82.59
700 x 100mm bed; 150mm thick surround to 400mm internal diameter pipes -1	46.14	5.00	48.44	-	2.21	34.41	10.06	92.92	m	102.21
700 x 150mm bed; 150mm thick surround to 400mm internal diameter pipes -1	49.69	5.00	52.17	-	2.36	36.75	10.80	99.72	m	109.69
750 x 100mm bed; 150mm thick surround to 450mm internal diameter pipes -1	53.24	5.00	55.90	-	2.53	39.39	10.80	106.09	m	116.70
750 x 150mm bed; 150mm thick surround to 450mm internal diameter pipes -1	56.99	5.00	59.84	-	2.70	42.04	11.51	113.38	m	124.72

Labour hourly rates: (except Specialists) Craft Operatives 20.87 Labourer 15.57 Rates are national average prices. Refer to REGIONAL VARIATIONS for indicative levels of overall pricing in regions	MATERIALS			LABOUR				RATES		
	Del to Site £	Waste %	Material Cost £	Craft Optve Hrs	Lab Hrs	Labour Cost £	Sunds £	Nett Rate £	Unit	Gross rate (10%) £
STORM WATER AND FOUL DRAIN SYSTEMS; DRAIN RUNS (Cont'd)										
Beds, benchings and covers; plain in-situ concrete; BS 8500, ordinary prescribed mix, ST3, 20mm aggregate (Cont'd)										
Beds and haunchings										
400 x 150mm; to 100mm internal diameter pipes - 1	7.81	5.00	8.20	-	0.40	6.23	4.32	18.75	m	20.62
450 x 150mm; to 150mm internal diameter pipes - 1	9.63	5.00	10.11	-	0.46	7.16	4.32	21.60	m	23.76
525 x 150mm; to 225mm internal diameter pipes - 1	12.47	5.00	13.10	-	0.62	9.65	4.32	27.07	m	29.78
600 x 150mm; to 300mm internal diameter pipes - 1	15.62	5.00	16.40	-	0.81	12.61	4.32	33.33	m	36.66
700 x 150mm; to 400mm internal diameter pipes - 1	20.18	5.00	21.19	-	1.10	17.13	4.32	42.63	m	46.90
750 x 150mm; to 450mm internal diameter pipes - 1	22.61	5.00	23.74	-	1.35	21.02	4.32	49.08	m	53.99
Vertical casings										
400 x 400mm to 100mm internal diameter pipes - 1	41.15	5.00	41.96	-	0.80	12.46	-	54.41	m	59.86
450 x 450mm to 150mm internal diameter pipes - 1	48.52	5.00	49.55	-	1.01	15.73	-	65.27	m	71.80
525 x 525mm to 225mm internal diameter pipes - 1	60.91	5.00	62.30	-	1.38	21.49	-	83.79	m	92.17
600 x 600mm to 300mm internal diameter pipes - 1	73.89	5.00	75.71	-	1.80	28.03	-	103.74	m	114.11
700 x 700mm to 400mm internal diameter pipes - 1	93.30	5.00	95.79	-	2.45	38.15	-	133.93	m	147.33
750 x 750mm to 450mm internal diameter pipes - 1	103.72	5.00	106.57	-	2.81	43.75	-	150.32	m	165.35
Drains; vitrified clay pipes and fittings, normal; flexible mechanical joints										
Pipework in trenches										
375mm										
straight lengths	233.20	5.00	244.86	0.55	0.18	14.28	-	259.14	m	285.06
extra; bends	582.02	5.00	611.12	0.39	-	8.14	-	619.26	nr	681.19
450mm										
straight lengths	771.25	5.00	809.81	0.70	0.20	17.72	-	827.54	m	910.29
extra; bends	866.89	5.00	910.23	0.70	-	14.61	-	924.84	nr	1017.33
Pipework in trenches; vertical										
375mm	233.20	5.00	244.86	0.60	0.18	15.32	-	260.18	m	286.20
450mm	771.25	5.00	809.81	0.77	0.20	19.18	-	829.00	m	911.90
Drains; vitrified clay pipes and fittings; sleeve joints, push-fit polypropylene standard ring flexible couplings; Hepworth Supersleeve										
Pipework in trenches										
100mm										
straight lengths	17.26	5.00	18.13	0.16	0.06	4.27	-	22.40	m	24.64
extra; bends	14.03	5.00	14.73	0.08	-	1.67	-	16.40	nr	18.04
extra; branches	30.30	5.00	31.81	0.16	-	3.34	-	35.15	nr	38.67
150mm										
straight lengths	31.05	5.00	32.60	0.18	0.08	5.00	-	37.60	m	41.37
extra; bends	32.31	5.00	33.93	0.09	-	1.88	-	35.80	nr	39.38
extra; branches	44.34	5.00	46.56	0.18	-	3.76	-	50.31	nr	55.34
Pipework in trenches; vertical										
100mm	17.26	5.00	18.13	0.18	0.06	4.69	-	22.82	m	25.10
150mm	31.05	5.00	32.60	0.20	0.08	5.42	-	38.02	m	41.82
Drains; vitrified clay pipes and fittings; sleeve joints, push-fit polypropylene neoprene ring flexible couplings; Hepworth Supersleeve										
Pipework in trenches										
100mm	11.07	5.00	11.62	0.16	0.06	4.27	-	15.90	m	17.49
150mm	26.43	5.00	27.75	0.18	0.08	5.00	-	32.75	m	36.02
Pipework in trenches; vertical										
100mm	11.07	5.00	11.62	0.18	0.06	4.69	-	16.31	m	17.94
150mm	26.43	5.00	27.75	0.20	0.08	5.42	-	33.17	m	36.48
Drains; vitrified clay pipes and fittings, BS EN 295, normal; cement mortar (1:3)										
Pipework in trenches										
100mm										
straight lengths	12.83	5.00	13.49	0.33	0.03	7.35	-	20.84	m	22.92
extra; double collars	17.82	5.00	18.73	0.10	-	2.09	-	20.81	nr	22.90
extra; bends	17.75	5.00	18.65	0.20	-	4.17	-	22.83	nr	25.11
extra; rest bends	48.27	5.00	50.70	0.20	-	4.17	-	54.87	nr	60.36
extra; branches	43.99	5.00	46.21	0.22	-	4.59	-	50.80	nr	55.88
150mm										
straight lengths	30.71	5.00	32.26	0.44	0.04	9.81	-	42.06	m	46.27
extra; double collars	32.30	5.00	33.93	0.15	-	3.13	-	37.06	nr	40.77
extra; bends	44.70	5.00	46.95	0.27	-	5.63	-	52.59	nr	57.85
extra; rest bends	51.96	5.00	54.57	0.27	-	5.63	-	60.21	nr	66.23
extra; branches	59.38	5.00	62.37	0.28	-	5.84	-	68.21	nr	75.03
225mm										
straight lengths	70.92	5.00	74.49	0.55	0.07	12.57	-	87.06	m	95.77
extra; double collars	29.61	5.00	31.11	0.23	-	4.80	-	35.91	nr	39.51
300mm										
straight lengths	102.51	5.00	107.66	0.80	0.10	18.25	-	125.91	m	138.50
Pipework in trenches; vertical										
100mm	12.83	5.00	13.49	0.50	0.03	10.90	-	24.39	m	26.83
150mm	30.71	5.00	32.26	0.48	0.04	10.64	-	42.90	m	47.19
225mm	70.92	5.00	74.49	0.60	0.07	13.61	-	88.11	m	96.92
300mm	102.51	5.00	107.66	0.88	0.10	19.92	-	127.58	m	140.34

Labour hourly rates: (except Specialists) Craft Operatives 20.87 Labourer 15.57 Rates are national average prices. Refer to REGIONAL VARIATIONS for indicative levels of overall pricing in regions	MATERIALS			LABOUR				RATES		
	Del to Site £	Waste %	Material Cost £	Craft Optve Hrs	Lab Hrs	Labour Cost £	Sunds £	Nett Rate £	Unit	Gross rate (10%) £
STORM WATER AND FOUL DRAIN SYSTEMS; DRAIN RUNS (Cont'd)										
Drains; Wavin; PVC-U pipes and fittings, BS EN 13598-1; ring seal joints										
Pipework in trenches										
110mm										
straight lengths, ref. 4D.076	4.19	5.00	4.40	0.14	0.02	3.23	-	7.64	m	8.40
extra; connections to cast iron and clay sockets, ref. 4D.107	19.10	5.00	20.06	0.08	-	1.67	-	21.72	nr	23.90
extra; 45 degree bends, ref. 4D.163	11.75	5.00	12.34	0.14	0.02	3.23	-	15.57	nr	17.13
extra; branches, ref. 4D.210	22.24	5.00	23.35	0.14	0.02	3.23	-	26.59	nr	29.24
extra; connections cast iron and clay spigot, ref. 4D.128	16.59	5.00	17.42	0.08	-	1.67	-	19.09	nr	21.00
160mm										
straight lengths, ref. 6D.076	18.53	5.00	19.45	0.20	0.03	4.64	-	24.09	m	26.50
extra; connections to cast iron and clay sockets, ref. 6D.107	30.90	5.00	32.44	0.10	-	2.09	-	34.53	nr	37.98
extra; 45 degree bends, ref. 6D.163	45.72	5.00	48.01	0.20	0.03	4.64	-	52.65	nr	57.91
extra; branches, ref. 6D.210	92.40	5.00	97.03	0.20	0.03	4.64	-	101.67	nr	111.83
extra; connections to cast iron and clay spigot, ref. 6D.128	41.38	5.00	43.45	0.10	-	2.09	-	45.53	nr	50.09
Pipework in trenches; vertical										
110mm, ref. 4D.076	4.19	5.00	4.40	0.28	0.02	6.16	-	10.56	m	11.61
160mm, ref. 6D.076	18.53	5.00	19.45	0.24	0.03	5.48	-	24.93	m	27.42
Drains; PVC-U solid wall concentric external rib-reinforced Wavin "Ultra-Rib" pipes and fittings with sealing rings to joints										
Pipework in trenches										
150mm										
straight lengths 6UR046	30.13	5.00	31.63	0.20	0.02	4.49	-	36.12	m	39.73
extra; bends 6UR563	31.05	5.00	32.60	0.20	-	4.17	-	36.78	nr	40.45
extra; branches 6UR213	162.14	5.00	170.25	0.20	-	4.17	-	174.43	nr	191.87
extra; connections to clayware pipe ends 6UR129	132.29	5.00	138.90	0.10	-	2.09	-	140.99	nr	155.09
225mm										
straight lengths 9UR046	111.98	5.00	117.58	0.30	0.03	6.73	-	124.31	m	136.74
extra; bends 9UR563	282.05	5.00	296.16	0.30	-	6.26	-	302.42	nr	332.66
extra; branches 9UR213	562.42	5.00	590.54	0.30	-	6.26	-	596.81	nr	656.49
300mm										
straight lengths 12UR043	121.50	5.00	127.58	0.38	0.05	8.71	-	136.29	m	149.92
extra; bends 12UR563	434.08	5.00	455.78	0.38	-	7.93	-	463.71	nr	510.09
extra; branches 12UR213	1101.32	5.00	1156.39	0.38	-	7.93	-	1164.32	nr	1280.75
extra; connections to clayware pipe ends 12UR112	612.30	5.00	642.91	0.15	-	3.13	-	646.05	nr	710.65
Pipework in trenches; vertical										
150mm	30.13	5.00	31.63	0.40	0.02	8.66	-	40.29	m	44.32
225mm	111.98	5.00	117.58	0.38	0.03	8.40	-	125.98	m	138.57
300mm	121.50	5.00	127.58	0.48	0.05	10.80	-	138.37	m	152.21
Drains; unreinforced concrete pipes and fittings BS 5911, Class H, flexible joints										
Pipework in trenches										
300mm										
straight lengths	30.43	5.00	31.96	0.59	0.24	16.05	-	59.74	m	65.72
extra; bends	271.73	5.00	285.32	0.30	0.12	8.13	-	299.32	nr	329.25
extra; 100mm branches	238.71	5.00	250.65	0.24	0.06	5.94	-	259.53	nr	285.48
extra; 150mm branches	238.71	5.00	250.65	0.40	0.11	10.06	-	266.09	nr	292.70
extra; 225mm branches	420.18	5.00	441.19	0.56	0.16	14.18	-	463.20	nr	509.51
extra; 300mm branches	482.63	5.00	506.76	0.72	0.22	18.45	-	535.97	nr	589.57
375mm										
straight lengths	37.67	5.00	39.55	0.72	0.30	19.70	-	73.92	m	81.32
extra; bends	336.33	5.00	353.15	0.36	0.15	9.85	-	370.33	nr	407.37
extra; 100mm branches	279.27	5.00	293.24	0.24	0.06	5.94	-	302.11	nr	332.32
extra; 150mm branches	279.27	5.00	293.24	0.40	0.11	10.06	-	308.68	nr	339.54
extra; 225mm branches	438.72	5.00	460.65	0.56	0.16	14.18	-	482.66	nr	530.92
extra; 300mm branches	499.23	5.00	524.19	0.72	0.22	18.45	-	553.41	nr	608.75
extra; 375mm branches	559.73	5.00	587.72	0.88	0.27	22.57	-	623.49	nr	685.84
450mm										
straight lengths	44.48	5.00	46.71	0.85	0.37	23.50	-	88.30	m	97.13
extra; bends	397.16	5.00	417.02	0.43	0.18	11.78	-	437.60	nr	481.36
extra; 100mm branches	422.26	5.00	443.37	0.24	0.06	5.94	-	452.25	nr	497.47
extra; 150mm branches	422.26	5.00	443.37	0.40	0.11	10.06	-	458.81	nr	504.69
extra; 225mm branches	562.76	5.00	590.90	0.56	0.16	14.18	-	612.90	nr	674.19
extra; 300mm branches	635.38	5.00	667.15	0.72	0.22	18.45	-	696.36	nr	766.00
extra; 375mm branches	708.00	5.00	743.40	0.88	0.27	22.57	-	779.17	nr	857.09
extra; 450mm branches	835.07	5.00	876.82	1.04	0.33	26.84	-	919.80	nr	1011.78
525mm										
straight lengths	58.36	5.00	61.27	0.98	0.43	27.15	-	109.45	m	120.40
extra; bends	521.03	5.00	547.08	0.49	0.22	13.65	-	571.49	nr	628.64
extra; 100mm branches	518.36	5.00	544.28	0.24	0.06	5.94	-	553.15	nr	608.47
extra; 150mm branches	518.36	5.00	544.28	0.40	0.11	10.06	-	559.72	nr	615.69
extra; 225mm branches	608.31	5.00	638.73	0.56	0.16	14.18	-	660.73	nr	726.80
extra; 300mm branches	684.35	5.00	718.57	0.72	0.22	18.45	-	747.78	nr	822.56
extra; 375mm branches	760.40	5.00	798.42	0.88	0.27	22.57	-	834.19	nr	917.61
extra; 450mm branches	893.46	5.00	938.13	1.04	0.33	26.84	-	981.12	nr	1079.23
600mm										
straight lengths	44.48	5.00	46.71	1.10	0.50	30.74	-	101.90	m	112.09
extra; bends	654.01	5.00	686.71	0.55	0.25	15.37	-	714.31	nr	785.74
extra; 100mm branches	651.08	5.00	683.64	0.24	0.06	5.94	-	692.51	nr	761.77
extra; 150mm branches	651.08	5.00	683.64	0.40	0.11	10.06	-	699.08	nr	768.98
extra; 225mm branches	609.97	5.00	640.47	0.56	0.16	14.18	-	662.47	nr	728.72
extra; 300mm branches	682.59	5.00	716.72	0.72	0.22	18.45	-	745.93	nr	820.52
extra; 375mm branches	755.19	5.00	792.95	0.88	0.27	22.57	-	828.72	nr	911.59
extra; 450mm branches	882.27	5.00	926.39	1.04	0.33	26.84	-	969.37	nr	1066.31

Labour hourly rates: (except Specialists) Craft Operatives 20.87 Labourer 15.57 Rates are national average prices. Refer to REGIONAL VARIATIONS for indicative levels of overall pricing in regions	MATERIALS			LABOUR				RATES		
	Del to Site £	Waste %	Material Cost £	Craft Optve Hrs	Lab Hrs	Labour Cost £	Sunds £	Nett Rate £	Unit	Gross rate (10%) £
STORM WATER AND FOUL DRAIN SYSTEMS; DRAIN RUNS (Cont'd)										
Drains; reinforced concrete pipes and fittings, BS 5911, Class H, flexible joints										
Pipework in trenches										
450mm										
straight lengths	59.72	5.00	62.70	0.85	0.37	23.50	-	104.30	m	114.73
extra; bends	922.94	5.00	969.09	0.43	0.18	11.78	-	989.67	nr	1088.64
extra; 100mm branches	257.56	5.00	270.43	0.24	0.06	5.94	-	279.31	nr	307.24
extra; 150mm branches	263.39	5.00	276.56	0.40	0.11	10.06	-	292.00	nr	321.21
extra; 225mm branches	272.24	5.00	285.85	0.56	0.16	14.18	-	307.86	nr	338.64
extra; 300mm branches	331.16	5.00	347.72	0.72	0.22	18.45	-	376.93	nr	414.63
extra; 375mm branches	375.37	5.00	394.14	0.88	0.27	22.57	-	429.91	nr	472.90
extra; 450mm branches	434.31	5.00	456.02	1.04	0.33	26.84	-	499.00	nr	548.91
525mm										
straight lengths	52.10	5.00	54.71	0.98	0.43	27.15	-	102.89	m	113.18
extra; bends	1128.05	5.00	1184.45	0.49	0.22	13.65	-	1208.86	nr	1329.75
extra; 100mm branches	290.19	5.00	304.70	0.24	0.06	5.94	-	313.57	nr	344.93
extra; 150mm branches	296.09	5.00	310.89	0.40	0.11	10.06	-	326.34	nr	358.97
extra; 225mm branches	304.92	5.00	320.17	0.56	0.16	14.18	-	342.17	nr	376.39
extra; 300mm branches	349.12	5.00	366.58	0.72	0.22	18.45	-	395.79	nr	435.37
extra; 375mm branches	408.06	5.00	428.47	0.88	0.27	22.57	-	464.24	nr	510.67
extra; 450mm branches	467.00	5.00	490.35	1.04	0.33	26.84	-	533.33	nr	586.67
600mm										
straight lengths	65.40	5.00	68.67	1.10	0.50	30.74	-	123.87	m	136.25
extra; bends	1230.57	5.00	1292.10	0.55	0.25	15.37	-	1319.70	nr	1451.67
extra; 100mm branches	263.08	5.00	276.23	0.24	0.06	5.94	-	285.11	nr	313.62
extra; 150mm branches	327.92	5.00	344.32	0.40	0.11	10.06	-	359.76	nr	395.73
extra; 225mm branches	336.75	5.00	353.59	0.56	0.16	14.18	-	375.59	nr	413.15
extra; 300mm branches	380.95	5.00	400.00	0.72	0.22	18.45	-	429.21	nr	472.14
extra; 375mm branches	439.89	5.00	461.89	0.88	0.27	22.57	-	497.66	nr	547.43
extra; 450mm branches	498.83	5.00	523.77	1.04	0.33	26.84	-	566.76	nr	623.43

This section continues
on the next page

DRAINAGE BELOW GROUND

Labour hourly rates: (except Specialists) Craft Operatives 26.39 Labourer 15.57 Rates are national average prices. Refer to REGIONAL VARIATIONS for indicative levels of overall pricing in regions	MATERIALS			LABOUR				RATES		
	Del to Site £	Waste %	Material Cost £	Craft Optve Hrs	Lab Hrs	Labour Cost £	Sunds £	Nett Rate £	Unit	Gross rate (10%) £
STORM WATER AND FOUL DRAIN SYSTEMS; DRAIN RUNS (Cont'd)										
Drains; cast iron pipes and cast iron fittings BS 437, coated; bolted cast iron coupling and synthetic rubber gasket joints										
Pipework in trenches										
100mm										
straight lengths	26.08	5.00	27.26	1.00	-	26.39	-	53.65	m	59.01
extra; connectors, large socket for clayware	38.47	2.00	39.24	1.00	-	26.39	-	65.63	nr	72.19
extra; bends	52.69	2.00	53.74	1.00	-	26.39	-	80.13	nr	88.15
extra; branches	63.77	2.00	65.05	1.50	-	39.58	-	104.63	nr	115.09
extra; branches with access	89.40	2.00	91.19	1.50	-	39.58	-	130.77	nr	143.85
150mm										
straight lengths	51.26	5.00	53.59	1.50	-	39.58	-	93.17	m	102.49
extra; connectors, large socket for clayware	73.47	2.00	74.94	1.50	-	39.58	-	114.53	nr	125.98
extra; diminishing pieces, reducing to 100mm	77.16	2.00	78.70	1.50	-	39.58	-	118.29	nr	130.12
extra; bends	109.53	2.00	111.72	1.50	-	39.58	-	151.31	nr	166.44
extra; branches	136.57	2.00	139.30	2.25	-	59.38	-	198.68	nr	218.55
extra; branches with access	178.62	2.00	182.19	2.25	-	59.38	-	241.57	nr	265.73
in runs not exceeding 3m										
100mm	34.44	5.00	35.78	1.50	-	39.58	-	75.37	m	82.91
150mm	67.63	5.00	70.28	2.25	-	59.38	-	129.66	m	142.63
Pipework in trenches; vertical										
100mm	34.44	5.00	35.78	1.20	-	31.67	-	67.45	m	74.20
150mm	67.63	5.00	70.28	1.80	-	47.50	-	117.78	m	129.56
Drains; stainless steel pipes and fittings; ring seal push fit joints (AISI 316)										
Pipework in trenches										
75mm										
straight lengths	24.17	5.00	25.37	0.60	-	15.83	-	41.21	m	45.33
extra; bends	20.83	2.00	21.25	0.60	-	15.83	-	37.08	nr	40.79
extra; branches	51.67	2.00	52.70	0.90	-	23.75	-	76.45	nr	84.10
110mm										
straight lengths	31.25	5.00	32.81	0.75	-	19.79	-	52.60	m	57.87
extra; diminishing pieces, reducing to 75mm	41.67	2.00	42.50	0.75	-	19.79	-	62.30	nr	68.53
extra; bends	24.58	2.00	25.07	0.75	-	19.79	-	44.86	nr	49.35
extra; branches	61.67	2.00	62.90	1.12	-	29.56	-	92.46	nr	101.71
in runs not exceeding 3m										
75mm	24.17	5.00	25.37	0.90	-	23.75	-	49.12	m	54.04
110mm	31.25	5.00	32.81	1.12	-	29.56	-	62.37	m	68.61
Pipework in trenches; vertical										
75mm	24.17	5.00	25.37	0.75	-	19.79	-	45.17	m	49.68
110mm	31.25	5.00	32.81	0.94	-	24.81	-	57.62	m	63.38

This section continues on the next page

Labour hourly rates: (except Specialists) Craft Operatives 20.87 Labourer 15.57 Rates are national average prices. Refer to REGIONAL VARIATIONS for indicative levels of overall pricing in regions	MATERIALS			LABOUR				RATES		
	Del to Site £	Waste %	Material Cost £	Craft Optve Hrs	Lab Hrs	Labour Cost £	Sunds £	Nett Rate £	Unit	Gross rate (10%) £
STORM WATER AND FOUL DRAIN SYSTEMS; ACCESSORIES										
Vitrified clay accessories										
Gullies; Supersleve; joint to pipe; bedding and surrounding in concrete to BS 8500, ordinary prescribed mix ST3, 20mm aggregate; Hepworth Building Products										
100mm outlet, reference SG2/1, trapped, square; 150 x 150 top..	149.41	5.00	156.88	0.60	0.08	13.77	-	170.65	nr	187.71
100mm outlet, reference SG1/1, trapped, reversible, round; 100mm trap; hopper reference SH1, 100mm outlet, 150 x 150mm rebated top	259.38	5.00	272.35	1.00	0.10	22.43	-	294.78	nr	324.25
100mm outlet, reference SG1/1, trapped, reversible, round; 100mm trap; hopper reference SH2, 100mm outlet, 100mm horizontal inlet, 150 x 150mm rebated top	263.76	5.00	276.95	1.15	0.10	25.56	-	302.51	nr	332.76
100mm outlet, reference SG1/1, trapped, reversible, round; 100mm trap; raising pieces - 1, reference RRS2/2, 100mm diameter, 225mm high; hopper reference SH1, 100mm outlet, 150 x 150mm rebated top	399.16	5.00	419.12	1.40	0.15	31.55	-	450.67	nr	495.74
100mm outlet, reference SG1/1, trapped, reversible, round; 100mm trap; raising pieces - 1, reference RRS2/2, 100mm diameter, 225mm high; hopper reference SH2, 100mm outlet, 100mm horizontal inlet, 150 x 150mm rebated top	440.31	5.00	462.33	1.45	0.16	32.75	-	495.08	nr	544.59
100mm outlet, reference RGP5, trapped, round; 225mm diameter x 600mm deep; perforated galvanised steel bucket reference IBP3	465.88	5.00	489.17	2.50	0.25	56.07	-	545.24	nr	599.77
100mm outlet, reference RGR1, trapped, round; 300mm diameter x 600mm deep	343.97	5.00	361.17	2.50	0.33	57.31	-	418.48	nr	460.33
150mm outlet, reference RGR2, trapped, round; 300mm diameter x 600mm deep	351.02	5.00	368.57	2.50	0.33	57.31	-	425.88	nr	468.47
150mm outlet, reference RGR3, trapped, round; 400mm diameter x 750mm deep	399.02	5.00	418.97	4.00	0.45	90.49	-	509.46	nr	560.40
150mm outlet, reference RGR4, trapped, round; 450mm diameter x 900mm deep	521.94	5.00	548.04	5.50	0.50	122.57	-	670.61	nr	737.67
100mm outlet, reference RGU1, trapped; internal size 600 x 450 x 600mm deep; perforated tray and galvanised cover and frame .	2451.74	5.00	2574.33	10.00	1.50	232.06	-	2806.38	nr	3087.02
Rainwater shoes; Supersleve; joint to pipe; bedding and surrounding in concrete to BS 8500, ordinary prescribed mix ST3, 20mm aggregate										
100mm outlet, reference RRW/S3/1 trapless, round; 100mm vertical inlet, 250 x 150mm rectangular access opening	124.65	5.00	130.88	0.50	0.05	11.21	-	142.10	nr	156.31
Unreinforced concrete accessories										
Gullies; BS 5911; joint to pipe; bedding and surrounding in concrete to BS 8500 ordinary prescribed mix ST3, 20mm aggregate										
150mm outlet, trapped, round; 375mm diameter x 750mm deep internally, stopper	95.56	5.00	100.34	3.30	0.50	76.66	-	177.00	nr	194.70
150mm outlet, trapped, round; 375mm diameter x 900mm deep internally, stopper	114.75	5.00	120.49	3.50	0.50	80.83	-	201.32	nr	221.45
150mm outlet, trapped, round; 450mm diameter x 750mm deep internally, stopper	98.56	5.00	103.49	3.50	0.60	82.39	-	185.88	nr	204.46
150mm outlet, trapped, round; 450mm diameter x 900mm deep internally, stopper	116.85	5.00	122.69	3.70	0.60	86.56	-	209.25	nr	230.18
150mm outlet, trapped, round; 450mm diameter x 1050mm deep internally, stopper	128.57	5.00	134.99	4.00	0.60	92.82	-	227.82	nr	250.60
150mm outlet, trapped, round; 450mm diameter x 1200mm deep internally, stopper	152.45	5.00	160.08	4.50	0.60	103.26	-	263.33	nr	289.67
PVC-U accessories										
Gullies; Osma; joint to pipe; bedding and surrounding in concrete to BS 8500, ordinary prescribed mix ST3, 20mm aggregate										
110mm outlet trap, base reference 4D500, outlet bend with access reference 4D.569, inlet raising piece 300mm long, plain hopper reference 4D503	125.96	5.00	132.26	1.00	0.20	23.98	-	156.24	nr	171.87
110mm outlet bottle gulley, reference 4D900 trapped, round; 200mm diameter top with grating reference 4D919	85.91	5.00	90.21	1.50	0.25	35.20	-	125.40	nr	137.94
Sealed rodding eyes; Osma; joint to pipe; surrounding in concrete to BS 8500; ordinary prescribed mix ST3, 20mm aggregate										
110mm outlet, reference 4D360, with square cover	58.95	5.00	61.90	1.80	0.45	44.57	-	106.47	nr	117.12
Cast iron accessories, painted black										
Gratings; Hepworth Building Products										
reference IG6C; 140mm diameter	12.07	-	12.07	-	0.03	0.47	-	12.54	nr	13.79
reference IG7C; 197mm diameter	18.43	-	18.43	-	0.03	0.47	-	18.90	nr	20.79
reference IG8C; 284mm diameter	40.21	-	40.21	-	0.03	0.47	-	40.68	nr	44.74
reference IG2C; 150 x 150mm	11.53	-	11.53	-	0.03	0.47	-	12.00	nr	13.20
reference IG3C; 225 x 225mm	35.88	-	35.88	-	0.03	0.47	-	36.35	nr	39.98
reference IG4C; 300 x 300mm	80.81	-	80.81	-	0.03	0.47	-	81.28	nr	89.40
Gratings and frames; bedding frames in cement mortar (1:3)										
225mm diameter	149.80	15.00	172.26	1.70	-	35.48	-	207.74	nr	228.52
150 x 150mm with lock and key	20.99	15.00	24.13	1.25	-	26.09	-	50.22	nr	55.24
230 x 230mm with lock and key	88.30	15.00	101.54	1.75	-	36.52	-	138.06	nr	151.87
300 x 300mm with lock and key	110.99	15.00	127.63	1.90	-	39.65	-	167.29	nr	184.01
Sealing plates and frames; bedding frames in cement mortar (1:3)										
197mm diameter	54.59	15.00	62.77	1.25	-	26.09	-	88.86	nr	97.75
273mm diameter	87.16	15.00	100.23	1.70	-	35.48	-	135.71	nr	149.28

DRAINAGE BELOW GROUND

Labour hourly rates: (except Specialists) Craft Operatives 20.87 Labourer 15.57 Rates are national average prices. Refer to REGIONAL VARIATIONS for indicative levels of overall pricing in regions	MATERIALS			LABOUR				RATES		
	Del to Site £	Waste %	Material Cost £	Craft Optve Hrs	Lab Hrs	Labour Cost £	Sunds £	Nett Rate £	Unit	Gross rate (10%) £
STORM WATER AND FOUL DRAIN SYSTEMS; ACCESSORIES (Cont'd)										
Cast iron accessories, painted black (Cont'd)										
Sealing plates and frames; bedding frames in cement mortar (1:3) (Cont'd)										
150 x 150mm	44.31	15.00	50.95	1.25	-	26.09	-	77.04	nr	84.74
225 x 225mm	84.99	15.00	97.73	1.75	-	36.52	-	134.26	nr	147.68
Alloy accessories										
Gratings										
140mm diameter	12.07	15.00	13.88	-	0.03	0.47	-	14.35	nr	15.78
197mm diameter	18.43	15.00	21.19	-	0.03	0.47	-	21.66	nr	23.83
284mm diameter	40.13	15.00	46.15	-	0.03	0.47	-	46.62	nr	51.28
150 x 150mm	11.53	15.00	13.26	-	0.03	0.47	-	13.73	nr	15.10
225 x 225mm	35.88	15.00	41.26	-	0.03	0.47	-	41.73	nr	45.90
300 x 300mm	80.81	15.00	92.93	-	0.03	0.47	-	93.40	nr	102.74
Gratings and frames; bedding frames in cement mortar (1:3)										
193mm diameter	75.12	15.00	86.38	1.25	-	26.09	-	112.47	nr	123.72
150 x 150mm with lock and key	48.43	15.00	55.69	1.25	-	26.09	-	81.78	nr	89.95
225 x 225mm with lock and key	88.30	15.00	101.54	1.75	-	36.52	-	138.06	nr	151.87
Sealing plates and frames; bedding frames in cement mortar (1:3)										
263mm diameter	87.16	15.00	100.23	1.70	-	35.48	-	135.71	nr	149.28
150 x 150mm	46.58	15.00	53.56	1.25	-	26.09	-	79.65	nr	87.61
Cast iron accessories, painted black										
Gratings and frames; bedding frames in cement mortar (1:3)										
Watergate C250; 370 x 305mm	280.17	15.00	322.19	1.00	-	20.87	-	343.06	nr	377.37
Watergate C250; 370 x 430mm	336.29	15.00	386.73	2.50	-	52.18	-	438.90	nr	482.79
Watergate C250; 510 x 360mm	165.61	15.00	190.45	3.33	-	69.50	-	259.94	nr	285.94
Waterflow C250; 325 x 312mm	170.73	15.00	196.33	4.25	-	88.70	-	285.03	nr	313.53
Waterflow C250; 325 x 437mm	150.22	15.00	172.75	2.75	-	57.39	-	230.14	nr	253.15
Precast polyester concrete ACO Drain surface drainage systems; ACO Technologies plc; bedding and haunching in concrete to BS 8500 ordinary prescribed mix ST5, 20mm aggregate										
Multidrain 100D Channel system with resin composite non rusting lockable grating										
constant depth or complete with 0.6% fall										
channel system	61.66	5.00	64.75	1.50	1.95	61.67	-	126.41	m	139.06
extra; Multidrain M100D end cap	16.92	5.00	17.77	-	0.20	3.11	-	20.88	nr	22.97
Raindrain recycled polymer concrete channel and galvanised steel grating										
invert depth 115mm										
channel system	12.26	5.00	12.88	1.40	1.65	54.91	-	67.79	m	74.56
extra; end cap	3.43	5.00	3.60	-	0.20	3.11	-	6.72	nr	7.39
extra; rodding access unit	76.04	5.00	79.84	-	0.50	7.78	-	87.63	nr	96.39
extra; universal Gully assembly complete with bucket	618.19	5.00	649.10	1.00	1.00	36.44	-	685.54	nr	754.09
KerbDrain Class D400 combined kerb drainage system 305mm x 150mm x 500mm										
drainage system	42.52	5.00	44.65	1.20	1.45	47.62	-	92.27	nr	101.50
extra; rodding access	98.37	5.00	103.29	-	0.50	7.78	-	111.07	nr	122.18
extra; Class D400 Gully	526.43	5.00	552.75	1.00	1.00	36.44	-	589.19	nr	648.10

This section continues on the next page

Labour hourly rates: (except Specialists) Craft Operatives 20.87 Labourer 15.57 Rates are national average prices. Refer to REGIONAL VARIATIONS for indicative levels of overall pricing in regions	PLANT AND TRANSPORT			LABOUR				RATES		
	Plant Cost £	Trans Cost £	P and T Cost £	Craft Optve Hrs	Lab Hrs	Labour Cost £	Sunds £	Nett Rate £	Unit	Gross rate (10%) £
STORM WATER AND FOUL DRAIN SYSTEMS; MANHOLES, INSPECTION CHAMBERS AND SOAKAWAYS										
Excavating - by machine										
Excavating pits commencing from natural ground level; maximum depth not exceeding										
0.25m	7.34	-	7.34	-	0.84	13.08	-	20.42	m³	22.46
1.00m	9.78	-	9.78	-	0.88	13.70	-	23.48	m³	25.83
2.00m	10.76	-	10.76	-	1.00	15.57	-	26.33	m³	28.96
4.00m	11.74	-	11.74	-	1.27	19.77	-	31.51	m³	34.66
Working space allowance to excavation pits	9.78	-	9.78	-	0.60	9.34	-	19.12	m²	21.04
Compacting bottoms of excavations	2.35	-	2.35	-	-	-	-	2.35	m²	2.59
Excavated material depositing on site in temporary spoil heaps where directed										
25m	3.91	-	3.91	-	-	-	-	3.91	m³	4.30
50m	4.89	-	4.89	-	-	-	-	4.89	m³	5.38
100m	5.87	-	5.87	-	-	-	-	5.87	m³	6.46
Excavating - by hand										
Excavating pits commencing from natural ground level; maximum depth not exceeding										
0.25m	-	-	-	-	3.35	52.16	-	52.16	m³	57.38
1.00m	-	-	-	-	3.50	54.49	-	54.49	m³	59.94
2.00m	-	-	-	-	4.00	62.28	-	62.28	m³	68.51
4.00m	-	-	-	-	5.10	79.41	-	79.41	m³	87.35
Working space allowance to excavation pits	-	-	-	-	3.12	48.58	-	48.58	m²	53.44
Compacting bottoms of excavations	-	-	-	-	0.12	1.87	-	1.87	m²	2.06
Excavated material depositing on site in temporary spoil heaps where directed										
25m	-	-	-	-	1.25	19.46	-	19.46	m³	21.41
50m	-	-	-	-	1.50	23.35	-	23.35	m³	25.69
100m	-	-	-	-	2.00	31.14	-	31.14	m³	34.25

This section continues on the next page

Labour hourly rates: (except Specialists) Craft Operatives 20.87 Labourer 15.57 Rates are national average prices. Refer to REGIONAL VARIATIONS for indicative levels of overall pricing in regions	MATERIALS			LABOUR				RATES		
	Del to Site	Waste	Material Cost	Craft Optve	Lab	Labour Cost	Sunds	Nett Rate		Gross rate (10%)
	£	%	£	Hrs	Hrs	£	£	£	Unit	£
STORM WATER AND FOUL DRAIN SYSTEMS; MANHOLES, INSPECTION CHAMBERS AND SOAKAWAYS (Cont'd)										
Earthwork support										
Earthwork support										
distance between opposing faces not exceeding 2.00m; maximum depth not exceeding										
1.00m	0.93	-	0.93	-	0.20	3.11	-	4.04	m²	4.44
2.00m	1.24	-	1.24	-	0.25	3.89	-	5.13	m²	5.64
4.00m	1.54	-	1.54	-	0.30	4.67	-	6.22	m²	6.84
distance between opposing faces 2.00 - 4.00m; maximum not exceeding										
1.00m	1.85	-	1.85	-	0.21	3.27	-	5.12	m²	5.64
2.00m	2.16	-	2.16	-	0.26	4.05	-	6.21	m²	6.83
4.00m	2.47	-	2.47	-	0.32	4.98	-	7.45	m²	8.20
Earthwork support; in unstable ground										
distance between opposing faces not exceeding 2.00m; maximum depth not exceeding										
1.00m	3.40	-	3.40	-	0.33	5.14	-	8.54	m²	9.39
2.00m	3.71	-	3.71	-	0.42	6.54	-	10.25	m²	11.27
4.00m	4.02	-	4.02	-	0.50	7.78	-	11.80	m²	12.98
distance between opposing faces 2.00 - 4.00m; maximum depth not exceeding										
1.00m	4.02	-	4.02	-	0.35	5.45	-	9.47	m²	10.41
2.00m	4.33	-	4.33	-	0.43	6.70	-	11.02	m²	12.12
4.00m	4.63	-	4.63	-	0.53	8.25	-	12.89	m²	14.17
Excavated material arising from excavations										
Filling to excavation										
average thickness exceeding 0.25m	-	-	-	-	1.33	20.71	-	20.71	m³	22.78
Excavated material obtained from on site spoil heaps 25m distant										
Filling to excavation										
average thickness not exceeding 0.25m	-	-	-	-	1.75	27.25	-	27.25	m³	29.97
average thickness exceeding 0.25m	-	-	-	-	1.50	23.35	-	23.35	m³	25.69
Excavated material obtained from on site spoil heaps 50m distant										
Filling to excavation										
average thickness not exceeding 0.25m	-	-	-	-	2.00	31.14	-	31.14	m³	34.25
average thickness exceeding 0.25m	-	-	-	-	1.85	28.80	-	28.80	m³	31.68
Excavated material obtained from on site spoil heaps 100m distant										
Filling to excavation										
average thickness not exceeding 0.25m	-	-	-	-	2.50	38.92	-	38.92	m³	42.82
average thickness exceeding 0.25m	-	-	-	-	2.25	35.03	-	35.03	m³	38.54
Hard, dry broken brick or stone, 100 - 75mm gauge, to be obtained off site										
Filling to excavation										
average thickness exceeding 0.25m	43.20	25.00	54.00	-	1.25	19.46	-	73.46	m³	80.81
Plain in-situ concrete; BS 8500, ordinary prescribed mix ST3, 20mm aggregate										
Beds; poured on or against earth or unblinded hardcore										
thickness 150 - 450mm	101.40	5.00	106.47	-	4.00	62.28	-	168.75	m³	185.62
thickness not exceeding 150mm	101.40	5.00	106.47	-	4.30	66.95	-	173.42	m³	190.76
Benching in bottoms; rendering with 13mm cement and sand (1:2) before final set										
600 x 450 x average 225mm; trowelling	8.30	5.00	8.93	-	0.54	8.41	-	17.34	nr	19.07
675 x 675 x average 225mm; trowelling	13.97	5.00	15.02	-	0.92	14.32	-	29.35	nr	32.28
800 x 675 x average 225mm; trowelling	16.61	5.00	17.86	-	1.10	17.13	-	34.99	nr	38.48
800 x 800 x average 300mm; trowelling	27.34	5.00	29.41	-	1.73	26.94	-	56.35	nr	61.98
1025 x 800 x average 300mm; trowelling	34.17	5.00	36.76	-	2.21	34.41	-	71.17	nr	78.29
Reinforced in-situ concrete; BS 8500, designed mix ST4, 20mm aggregate, minimum cement content 240 kg/m³; vibrated										
Slabs										
thickness 150 - 450mm	105.04	5.00	110.29	-	3.50	54.49	-	164.79	m³	181.27
thickness not exceeding 150mm	105.04	5.00	110.29	-	4.00	62.28	-	172.57	m³	189.83
Formwork and basic finish										
Edges of suspended slabs; plain vertical										
height not exceeding 250mm	1.10	12.50	1.24	0.75	0.15	17.99	-	19.23	m	21.15
Soffits of slabs; horizontal										
slab thickness not exceeding 200mm; height to soffit not exceeding 1.50m	15.58	10.00	17.13	2.20	0.42	52.45	-	69.59	m²	76.55
slab thickness not exceeding 200mm; height to soffit 1.50 - 3.00m	15.58	10.00	17.13	2.00	0.42	48.28	-	65.41	m²	71.96

Labour hourly rates: (except Specialists) Craft Operatives 20.87 Labourer 15.57 Rates are national average prices. Refer to REGIONAL VARIATIONS for indicative levels of overall pricing in regions	MATERIALS			LABOUR				RATES		
	Del to Site £	Waste %	Material Cost £	Craft Optve Hrs	Lab Hrs	Labour Cost £	Sunds £	Nett Rate £	Unit	Gross rate (10%) £
STORM WATER AND FOUL DRAIN SYSTEMS; MANHOLES, INSPECTION CHAMBERS AND SOAKAWAYS (Cont'd)										
Formwork and basic finish (Cont'd)										
Holes; rectangular										
girth 1.00 - 2.00m; depth not exceeding 250mm	2.20	12.50	2.48	0.50	0.05	11.21	-	13.69	nr	15.06
girth 2.00 - 3.00m; depth not exceeding 250mm	3.30	12.50	3.71	0.80	0.10	18.25	-	21.97	nr	24.16
Reinforcement fabric; BS 4483; hard drawn plain round steel, welded; including laps, tying wire, all cutting and bending and spacers and chairs which are at the discretion of the Contractor										
Reference A142, 2.22kg/m²; 200mm side laps; 200mm end laps generally	3.78	15.00	4.35	0.25	0.02	5.53	-	9.88	m²	10.86
Common bricks, BS EN 772, Category M, 215 x 102.5 x 65mm, compressive strength 20.5 N/mm²; in cement mortar (1:3)										
Walls; vertical										
102mm thick; stretcher bond	24.73	5.00	26.54	1.33	1.45	50.33	-	76.87	m²	84.56
215mm thick; English bond	49.15	5.00	52.74	2.30	2.54	87.55	-	140.29	m²	154.32
Milton Hall Second hard stock bricks, BS EN 772, Category M, 215 x 102.5 x 65mm; in cement mortar (1:3)										
Walls; vertical										
102mm thick; stretcher bond	43.52	5.00	46.27	1.33	1.45	50.33	-	96.60	m²	106.26
215mm thick; English bond	86.43	5.00	91.89	2.30	2.54	87.55	-	179.44	m²	197.38
Engineering bricks, Category F, BS EN 772, 215 x 102.5 x 65mm, class B; in cement mortar (1:3)										
Walls; vertical										
102mm thick; stretcher bond	29.49	5.00	31.54	1.33	1.45	50.33	-	81.87	m²	90.06
215mm thick; English bond	58.60	5.00	62.67	2.30	2.54	87.55	-	150.22	m²	165.24
Common bricks, BS EN 772, Category M, 215 x 102.5 x 65mm, compressive strength 20.5 N/mm²; in cement mortar (1:3); flush smooth pointing as work proceeds										
Walls; vertical										
102mm thick; stretcher bond; facework one side	24.73	5.00	26.54	1.53	1.65	57.62	-	84.16	m²	92.57
215mm thick; English bond; facework one side	49.15	5.00	52.74	2.50	2.74	94.84	-	147.58	m²	162.34
Milton Hall Second hard stock bricks, BS EN 772, Category M, 215 x 102.5 x 65mm; in cement mortar (1:3); flush smooth pointing as work proceeds										
Walls; vertical										
102mm thick; stretcher bond; facework one side	43.52	5.00	46.27	1.53	1.65	57.62	-	103.89	m²	114.28
215mm thick; English bond; facework one side	86.43	5.00	91.89	2.50	2.74	94.84	-	186.73	m²	205.40
Engineering bricks, BS EN 772, Category F, 215 x 102.5 x 65mm, class B; in cement mortar (1:3); flush smooth pointing as work proceeds										
Walls; vertical										
102mm thick; stretcher bond; facework one side	29.49	5.00	31.54	1.53	1.65	57.62	-	89.16	m²	98.08
215mm thick; English bond; facework one side	58.60	5.00	62.67	2.50	2.74	94.84	-	157.51	m²	173.26
Accessories/sundry items for brick/block/stone walling										
Building in ends of pipes; 100mm diameter making good fair face one side										
102mm brickwork	0.14	15.00	0.16	0.08	0.08	2.92	-	3.08	nr	3.39
215mm brickwork	0.29	15.00	0.33	0.13	0.13	4.74	-	5.07	nr	5.57
Building in ends of pipes; 150mm diameter making good fair face one side										
102mm brickwork	0.14	15.00	0.16	0.13	0.13	4.74	-	4.90	nr	5.39
215mm brickwork	0.29	15.00	0.33	0.20	0.20	7.29	-	7.62	nr	8.38
Building in ends of pipes; 225mm diameter making good fair face one side										
102mm brickwork	0.29	15.00	0.33	0.20	0.20	7.29	-	7.62	nr	8.38
215mm brickwork	0.57	15.00	0.66	0.25	0.25	9.11	-	9.77	nr	10.74
Building in ends of pipes; 300mm diameter making good fair face one side										
102mm brickwork	0.43	15.00	0.49	0.25	0.25	9.11	-	9.60	nr	10.56
215mm brickwork	0.86	15.00	0.98	0.33	0.33	12.03	-	13.01	nr	14.31
Mortar, cement and sand (1:3)										
13mm work to walls on brickwork base; one coat; trowelled width exceeding 300mm	1.85	15.00	2.13	0.40	0.40	14.58	-	16.71	m²	18.38
13mm work to floors on concrete base; one coat; trowelled level and to falls only not exceeding 15 degrees from horizontal	1.85	15.00	2.13	0.60	0.60	21.86	-	24.00	m²	26.40

Labour hourly rates: (except Specialists) Craft Operatives 20.87 Labourer 15.57 Rates are national average prices. Refer to REGIONAL VARIATIONS for indicative levels of overall pricing in regions	MATERIALS			LABOUR				RATES		
	Del to Site £	Waste %	Material Cost £	Craft Optve Hrs	Lab Hrs	Labour Cost £	Sunds £	Nett Rate £	Unit	Gross rate (10%) £
STORM WATER AND FOUL DRAIN SYSTEMS; MANHOLES, INSPECTION CHAMBERS AND SOAKAWAYS (Cont'd)										
Channels in bottoms; vitrified clay, BS 65, normal, glazed; cement mortar (1:3) joints; bedding in cement mortar (1:3)										
Half section										
straight; 600mm effective length										
100mm	11.82	5.00	12.45	0.30	0.03	6.73	-	19.18	nr	21.10
150mm	19.69	5.00	20.73	0.40	0.04	8.97	-	29.70	nr	32.67
straight; 1000mm effective length										
100mm	16.79	5.00	17.71	0.50	0.05	11.21	-	28.92	nr	31.82
150mm	29.14	5.00	30.71	0.67	0.07	15.07	-	45.78	nr	50.36
225mm	68.49	5.00	72.05	0.84	0.08	18.78	-	90.83	nr	99.91
300mm	142.97	5.00	150.29	1.25	0.15	28.42	-	178.71	nr	196.59
curved; 500mm effective length										
100mm	16.57	5.00	17.44	0.30	0.03	6.73	-	24.17	nr	26.58
150mm	28.48	5.00	29.96	0.40	0.25	12.24	-	42.20	nr	46.42
225mm	103.82	5.00	109.10	0.50	0.05	11.21	-	120.31	nr	132.34
300mm	211.04	5.00	221.70	0.75	0.09	17.05	-	238.76	nr	262.63
curved; 900mm effective length										
100mm	19.47	5.00	20.53	0.60	0.06	13.46	-	33.98	nr	37.38
150mm	27.59	5.00	29.09	0.80	0.08	17.94	-	47.03	nr	51.73
225mm	105.04	5.00	110.44	1.00	0.10	22.43	-	132.86	nr	146.15
300mm	177.87	5.00	186.93	1.50	0.18	34.11	-	221.04	nr	243.14
Three quarter section										
branch bends										
100mm	51.38	5.00	54.80	0.33	0.03	7.35	-	62.16	nr	68.37
150mm	76.46	5.00	81.43	0.50	0.05	11.21	-	92.64	nr	101.91
225mm	275.61	5.00	289.53	1.00	0.10	22.43	-	311.96	nr	343.15
Channels in bottoms; P.V.C.; 'O' ring joints; bedding in cement mortar (1:3)										
For 610mm clear opening										
straight										
110mm	49.47	5.00	52.38	0.40	0.03	8.82	-	61.19	nr	67.31
160mm	68.25	5.00	72.23	0.50	0.04	11.06	-	83.29	nr	91.62
short bend 3/4 section										
110mm	32.89	5.00	34.97	0.20	0.01	4.33	-	39.30	nr	43.22
160mm	54.84	5.00	58.16	0.30	0.02	6.57	-	64.73	nr	71.20
long radius bend										
110mm	70.11	5.00	74.47	0.33	0.02	7.20	-	81.67	nr	89.83
160mm	128.03	5.00	135.58	0.50	0.04	11.06	-	146.63	nr	161.30
Precast concrete; standard or stock pattern units; BS 5911; jointing and pointing in cement mortar (1:3)										
Chamber or shaft sections										
900mm internal diameter										
250mm high	46.40	5.00	48.74	0.58	1.16	30.17	-	78.91	nr	86.80
500mm high	69.30	5.00	72.78	0.67	1.34	34.85	-	107.63	nr	118.39
750mm high	69.30	5.00	72.78	0.87	1.74	45.25	-	118.03	nr	129.83
1000mm high	92.36	5.00	96.99	0.93	1.86	48.37	-	145.36	nr	159.90
1050mm internal diameter										
250mm high	58.85	5.00	61.83	0.81	1.62	42.13	-	103.96	nr	114.36
500mm high	93.10	5.00	97.78	0.87	1.74	45.25	-	143.03	nr	157.33
750mm high	103.50	5.00	108.70	0.93	1.86	48.37	-	157.07	nr	172.77
1000mm high	130.29	5.00	136.83	0.99	1.98	51.49	-	188.32	nr	207.15
1200mm internal diameter										
250mm high	69.33	5.00	72.84	0.99	1.98	51.49	-	124.33	nr	136.76
500mm high	108.89	5.00	114.36	1.04	2.08	54.09	-	168.45	nr	185.29
750mm high	119.29	5.00	125.28	1.22	2.44	63.45	-	188.73	nr	207.60
1000mm high	150.23	5.00	157.76	1.28	2.56	66.57	-	224.34	nr	246.77
1500mm internal diameter										
500mm high	161.78	5.00	169.93	1.24	2.45	64.03	-	233.95	nr	257.35
750mm high	171.18	5.00	179.78	1.52	3.04	79.06	-	258.83	nr	284.72
1000mm high	245.37	5.00	257.68	1.58	3.16	82.18	-	339.85	nr	373.84
1800mm internal diameter										
500mm high	253.77	5.00	266.53	1.44	2.78	73.34	-	339.87	nr	373.86
750mm high	264.03	5.00	277.29	1.82	3.64	94.66	-	371.95	nr	409.14
1000mm high	351.57	5.00	369.21	1.88	3.76	97.78	-	466.98	nr	513.68
2100mm internal diameter										
500mm high	458.46	5.00	481.46	1.64	3.13	82.96	-	564.42	nr	620.87
750mm high	467.85	5.00	491.32	2.12	4.24	110.26	-	601.58	nr	661.74
1000mm high	589.18	5.00	618.71	2.18	4.36	113.38	-	732.10	nr	805.30
2400mm internal diameter										
500mm high	575.05	5.00	603.90	1.84	3.48	92.58	-	696.48	nr	766.13
1000mm high	723.68	5.00	759.96	2.48	4.96	128.98	-	888.95	nr	977.84
2700mm internal diameter										
500mm high	647.67	5.00	680.17	2.09	3.81	102.94	-	783.11	nr	861.42
1000mm high	875.60	5.00	919.49	1.78	5.56	123.72	-	1043.21	nr	1147.53
3000mm internal diameter										
1000mm high	1203.35	5.00	1263.65	2.08	6.16	139.32	-	1402.97	nr	1543.27

Labour hourly rates: (except Specialists) Craft Operatives 20.87 Labourer 15.57 Rates are national average prices. Refer to REGIONAL VARIATIONS for indicative levels of overall pricing in regions	MATERIALS			LABOUR				RATES		
	Del to Site £	Waste %	Material Cost £	Craft Optve Hrs	Lab Hrs	Labour Cost £	Sunds £	Nett Rate £	Unit	Gross rate (10%) £
STORM WATER AND FOUL DRAIN SYSTEMS; MANHOLES, INSPECTION CHAMBERS AND SOAKAWAYS (Cont'd)										
Precast concrete; standard or stock pattern units; BS 5911; jointing and pointing in cement mortar (1:3) (Cont'd)										
Cutting holes										
cutting holes for pipes; 100mm diameter; making good; pointing..	41.00	10.00	41.03	-	0.08	1.25	-	42.28	nr	46.50
cutting holes for pipes; 150mm diameter; making good; pointing..	41.14	10.00	41.19	-	0.10	1.56	-	42.74	nr	47.02
cutting holes for pipes; 225mm diameter; making good; pointing..	70.36	10.00	70.43	-	0.12	1.87	-	72.30	nr	79.53
cutting holes for pipes; 300mm diameter; making good; pointing..	81.36	10.00	81.46	-	0.15	2.34	-	83.80	nr	92.18
Step irons										
galvanised malleable cast iron step irons BS EN 13101;, cast in..	15.94	5.00	16.74	-	0.15	2.34	-	19.07	nr	20.98
Cover slabs, heavy duty										
for chamber or shaft sections 900mm internal diameter, 125mm thick; access opening 600mm x 600mm	99.26	5.00	104.25	1.50	2.25	66.34	-	170.58	nr	187.64
for chamber or shaft sections 1050mm internal diameter, 125mm thick; access opening 600mm x 600mm	106.46	5.00	111.81	2.00	3.00	88.45	-	200.26	nr	220.28
for chamber or shaft sections 1200mm internal diameter, 125mm thick; access opening 600mm x 600mm	128.99	5.00	135.46	2.50	3.75	110.56	-	246.03	nr	270.63
for chamber or shaft sections 1350mm internal diameter, 125mm thick; access opening 600mm x 600mm	187.49	5.00	196.89	3.00	4.50	132.68	-	329.56	nr	362.52
for chamber or shaft sections 1500mm internal diameter, 150mm thick; access opening 600mm x 600mm	216.23	5.00	227.08	3.50	5.25	154.79	-	381.87	nr	420.06
for chamber or shaft sections 1800mm internal diameter, 150mm thick access opening 600mm x 600mm	377.43	5.00	396.34	4.00	6.00	176.90	-	573.24	nr	630.57
for chamber or shaft sections 2100mm internal diameter, 150mm thick access opening 600mm x 600mm	712.25	5.00	747.94	4.50	6.75	199.01	-	946.95	nr	1041.64
for chamber or shaft sections 2400mm internal diameter, 150mm thick access opening 600mm x 600mm	973.11	5.00	1021.84	5.00	7.50	221.12	-	1242.96	nr	1367.26
for chamber or shaft sections 2700mm internal diameter, 150mm thick access opening 600mm x 600mm	1497.60	5.00	1572.56	5.50	8.25	243.24	-	1815.80	nr	1997.38
for chamber or shaft sections 3000mm internal diameter, 150mm thick access opening 600mm x 600mm	1922.26	5.00	2018.45	6.00	9.00	265.35	-	2283.80	nr	2512.18
Precast concrete inspection chambers; BS 5911; jointing and pointing in cement mortar (1:3)										
Rectangular inspection chambers, internal size 450 x 600mm										
150mm high	15.14	5.00	15.92	0.65	0.45	20.57	-	36.49	nr	40.14
225mm high	18.69	5.00	19.65	0.75	0.53	23.90	-	43.55	nr	47.91
extra; galvanised malleable cast iron step irons BS EN 13101;, built in	15.94	5.00	16.74	-	-	-	-	16.74	nr	18.41
Rectangular inspection chambers, internal size 750 x 600mm										
150mm high	21.93	5.00	23.07	1.05	0.75	33.59	-	56.66	nr	62.32
225mm high	27.18	5.00	28.58	1.21	0.88	38.95	-	67.53	nr	74.29
extra; galvanised malleable cast iron step irons BS EN 13101;, built in	15.94	5.00	16.74	-	-	-	-	16.74	nr	18.41
Rectangular inspection chambers, internal size 1000 x 675mm										
150mm high	27.78	5.00	29.21	1.05	0.75	33.59	-	62.80	nr	69.08
Rectangular inspection chambers, internal size 1200 x 750mm										
150mm high	43.17	5.00	45.39	1.20	0.85	38.28	-	83.66	nr	92.03
225mm high	57.82	5.00	60.77	1.38	1.00	44.37	-	105.14	nr	115.65
Base units										
450 x 610mm internal size; 360mm deep	68.38	5.00	71.84	1.05	0.75	33.59	-	105.43	nr	115.97
760 x 610mm internal size; 360mm deep	82.81	5.00	87.01	1.05	0.75	33.59	-	120.60	nr	132.66
Cover slab with integral cover										
450 x 600mm internal size	45.03	5.00	47.32	1.05	0.75	33.59	-	80.91	nr	89.00
760 x 610mm internal size	60.22	5.00	63.29	1.05	0.75	33.59	-	96.88	nr	106.57
Osma; Shallow inspection chamber ref. 4D960 Polypropylene with preformed benching. Light duty single sealed cover and frame ref. 4D961 set in position, 250mm diameter; for 100mm diameter pipes, depth to invert										
Chamber or shaft sections and benching										
600mm	105.45	5.00	110.72	2.00	0.10	43.30	-	154.02	nr	169.42
Osma; universal inspection chamber; Polypropylene; 450mm diameter										
preformed chamber base benching, ref. 4D922; for 100mm pipes	97.20	5.00	102.06	1.10	0.10	24.51	-	126.57	nr	139.23
chamber shaft 185mm effective length, ref. 4D925	27.74	5.00	29.13	-	0.50	7.78	-	36.91	nr	40.61
chamber shaft 230mm effective length, ref. 4D975	27.74	5.00	29.13	-	0.50	7.78	-	36.91	nr	40.61
cast iron cover and frame; single seal light duty to suit, ref. 4D942	84.44	5.00	88.66	0.50	-	10.44	-	99.10	nr	109.01
polypropylene sealed cover and frame, ref. 4D969	49.87	5.00	52.36	0.50	-	10.44	-	62.80	nr	69.08

Labour hourly rates: (except Specialists) Craft Operatives 26.39 Labourer 15.57 Rates are national average prices. Refer to REGIONAL VARIATIONS for indicative levels of overall pricing in regions	MATERIALS			LABOUR				RATES		
	Del to Site £	Waste %	Material Cost £	Craft Optve Hrs	Lab Hrs	Labour Cost £	Sunds £	Nett Rate £	Unit	Gross rate (10%) £
STORM WATER AND FOUL DRAIN SYSTEMS; MANHOLES, INSPECTION CHAMBERS AND SOAKAWAYS (Cont'd)										
Coated cast iron bolted inspection chambers										
100mm diameter straight chamber; coupling joints; bedding in cement mortar (1:3)										
with one branch each side	307.17	2.00	313.33	3.25	-	85.77	-	399.10	nr	439.01
150 x 100mm diameter straight chamber; coupling joints; bedding in cement mortar (1:3)										
with one branch one side	397.83	2.00	405.81	3.25	-	85.77	-	491.58	nr	540.73
150mm diameter straight chamber; coupling joints; bedding in cement mortar (1:3)										
with one branch each side	504.98	2.00	515.10	4.50	-	118.75	-	633.86	nr	697.24

This section continues
on the next page

Labour hourly rates: (except Specialists) Craft Operatives 20.87 Labourer 15.57 Rates are national average prices. Refer to REGIONAL VARIATIONS for indicative levels of overall pricing in regions	MATERIALS			LABOUR				RATES		
	Del to Site £	Waste %	Material Cost £	Craft Optve Hrs	Lab Hrs	Labour Cost £	Sunds £	Nett Rate £	Unit	Gross rate (10%) £
STORM WATER AND FOUL DRAIN SYSTEMS; OTHER TANKS AND PITS										
Fibreglass settlement tanks; including cover and frame										
Settlement tank; fibreglass; set in position										
1000mm deep to invert of inlet, standard grade										
2700 litres capacity	700.00	-	700.00	0.90	1.80	46.81	-	746.81	nr	821.49
3750 litres capacity	894.00	-	894.00	1.00	2.00	52.01	-	946.01	nr	1040.61
4500 litres capacity	1024.00	-	1024.00	1.10	2.20	57.21	-	1081.21	nr	1189.33
7500 litres capacity	2417.00	-	2417.00	1.20	2.40	62.41	-	2479.41	nr	2727.35
9000 litres capacity	2857.00	-	2857.00	1.30	2.60	67.61	-	2924.61	nr	3217.07
1500mm deep to invert of inlet, heavy grade										
2700 litres capacity	775.00	-	775.00	0.90	1.80	46.81	-	821.81	nr	903.99
3750 litres capacity	969.00	-	969.00	1.00	2.00	52.01	-	1021.01	nr	1123.11
4500 litres capacity	1099.00	-	1099.00	1.10	2.20	57.21	-	1156.21	nr	1271.83
6000 litres capacity	1312.89	-	1312.89	1.15	2.30	59.81	-	1372.70	nr	1509.97
7500 litres capacity	2682.49	-	2682.49	1.20	2.40	62.41	-	2744.90	nr	3019.39
9000 litres capacity	3153.29	-	3153.29	1.30	2.60	67.61	-	3220.90	nr	3542.99
Fibreglass underground water tanks; including cover and frame										
Underground water tank; fibreglass; set in position										
2000 litres capacity	1310.00	-	1310.00	0.90	1.80	46.81	-	1356.81	nr	1492.49
3000 litres capacity	1400.00	-	1400.00	1.00	2.00	52.01	-	1452.01	nr	1597.21
4000 litres capacity	1555.00	-	1555.00	1.10	2.20	57.21	-	1612.21	nr	1773.43
5000 litres capacity	1625.00	-	1625.00	1.15	2.30	59.81	-	1684.81	nr	1853.29
6000 litres capacity	1775.00	-	1775.00	1.20	2.40	62.41	-	1837.41	nr	2021.15
8000 litres capacity	2825.00	-	2825.00	1.30	2.60	67.61	-	2892.61	nr	3181.87
10000 litres capacity	3115.00	-	3115.00	1.40	2.80	72.81	-	3187.81	nr	3506.60
STORM WATER AND FOUL DRAIN SYSTEMS; SUNDRIES										
Manhole step irons										
Step irons; BS EN 13101; malleable cast iron; galvanised; building in to joints										
figure 1 general purpose pattern; 110mm tail	4.97	-	4.97	0.25	-	5.22	-	10.19	nr	11.21
figure 1 general purpose pattern; 225mm tail	6.83	-	6.83	0.25	-	5.22	-	12.05	nr	13.25
Vitrified clay intercepting traps										
Intercepting traps; BS 65; joint to pipe; building into side of manhole; bedding and surrounding in concrete to BS 8500 ordinary prescribed mix C15P, 20mm aggregate										
cleaning arm and stopper										
100mm outlet, ref. KRI2/1	167.48	5.00	175.85	1.25	1.00	41.66	-	217.51	nr	239.26
150mm outlet, ref. KRI2/2	240.80	5.00	252.84	1.75	1.50	59.88	-	312.72	nr	343.99
225mm outlet, ref. KRI2/3	707.47	5.00	742.84	2.25	2.00	78.10	-	820.94	nr	903.03
Aluminium; fresh air inlets										
Air inlet valve, mica flap; set in cement mortar (1:3)										
100mm diameter	94.45	5.00	99.19	1.15	-	24.00	-	123.19	nr	135.51
STORM WATER AND FOUL DRAIN SYSTEMS; COVERS AND FRAMES										
Manhole covers - A15 light duty										
Access covers; ductile iron; BS EN 124; coated; bedding frame in cement mortar (1:3); bedding cover in grease and sand										
single seal; clear opening 450mm dia	22.47	2.50	23.39	0.65	0.65	23.69	-	47.07	nr	51.78
single seal; clear opening 450 x 450mm	33.91	2.50	35.11	0.65	0.65	23.69	-	58.80	nr	64.68
single seal; clear opening 600 x 450mm	35.89	2.50	37.14	0.75	0.75	27.33	-	64.47	nr	70.92
single seal; clear opening 600 x 600mm	39.90	2.50	41.25	1.25	1.25	45.55	-	86.80	nr	95.48
double seal; clear opening 450 x 450mm	29.04	2.50	30.12	1.30	1.30	47.37	-	77.50	nr	85.24
double seal; clear opening 600 x 450mm	28.70	2.50	29.77	1.45	1.45	52.84	-	82.61	nr	90.87
double seal; clear opening 600 x 600mm	41.91	2.50	43.31	1.60	1.60	58.30	-	101.62	nr	111.78
lifting keys	5.90	2.50	6.05	-	-	-	-	6.05	nr	6.65
Access covers; galvansied steel; bedding frame in cement mortar (1:3); bedding cover in grease and sand										
recessed; clear opening 600 x 450mm	56.76	2.50	58.54	1.15	1.15	41.91	-	100.44	nr	110.49
recessed; clear opening 600 x 600mm	68.82	2.50	71.07	1.45	1.45	52.84	-	123.91	nr	136.30
recessed; clear opening 750 x 600mm	125.36	2.50	129.03	1.60	1.60	58.30	-	187.33	nr	206.06
lifting keys	5.90	2.50	6.05	-	-	-	-	6.05	nr	6.65
Manhole covers - B125 medium duty										
Access covers; BS EN 124:1994; coated; bedding frame in cement mortar (1:3); bedding cover in grease and sand										
450mm diameter	40.93	2.50	42.31	1.43	1.43	52.11	-	94.42	nr	103.86
600 x 450mm	62.45	2.50	64.37	1.43	1.43	52.11	-	116.48	nr	128.13
600 x 600mm	86.64	2.50	89.34	1.80	1.80	65.59	-	154.93	nr	170.42
750 x 600mm	110.25	2.50	113.72	2.13	2.13	77.62	-	191.34	nr	210.47
900 x 600mm	198.93	2.50	204.79	2.43	2.43	88.55	-	293.34	nr	322.68
900 x 900mm	263.97	2.50	271.64	2.80	2.80	102.03	-	373.68	nr	411.04
lifting keys	5.26	2.50	5.39	-	-	-	-	5.39	nr	5.93

Labour hourly rates: (except Specialists) Craft Operatives 20.87 Labourer 15.57 Rates are national average prices. Refer to REGIONAL VARIATIONS for indicative levels of overall pricing in regions	MATERIALS			LABOUR				RATES		
	Del to Site £	Waste %	Material Cost £	Craft Optve Hrs	Lab Hrs	Labour Cost £	Sunds £	Nett Rate £	Unit	Gross rate (10%) £
STORM WATER AND FOUL DRAIN SYSTEMS; COVERS AND FRAMES (Cont'd)										
Manhole covers - D400 heavy duty										
Access covers; BS EN 124; coated; bedding frame in cement mortar (1:3); bedding cover in grease and sand										
600mm diameter	137.70	2.50	141.50	1.89	1.89	68.87	-	210.37	nr	231.41
600 x 600mm	156.20	2.50	160.64	1.89	1.89	68.87	-	229.52	nr	252.47
750 x 750mm	241.47	2.50	248.58	2.25	2.25	81.99	-	330.57	nr	363.63
900 x 900mm	432.60	2.50	444.84	2.60	2.60	94.74	-	539.58	nr	593.54
1000 x 1000mm	708.09	2.50	727.40	2.93	2.93	106.77	-	834.17	nr	917.58
lifting keys	6.96	2.50	7.13	-	-	-	-	7.13	nr	7.85
STORM WATER AND FOUL DRAIN SYSTEMS; WORK TO EXISTING DRAINS										
Work to disused drains										
Sealing end of disused drain with plain in-situ concrete										
100mm diameter	1.07	5.00	1.13	0.20	-	4.17	-	5.30	nr	5.83
150mm diameter	2.03	5.00	2.13	0.30	-	6.26	-	8.39	nr	9.23
225mm diameter	3.24	5.00	3.41	0.40	-	8.35	-	11.76	nr	12.93
LAND DRAINAGE										
Drains; clayware pipes, BS 1196; butt joints										
Pipework in trenches										
75mm	11.60	5.00	12.18	-	0.22	3.43	-	15.61	m	17.17
100mm	19.73	5.00	20.72	-	0.24	3.74	-	24.46	m	26.90
150mm	28.77	5.00	30.21	-	0.30	4.67	-	34.88	m	38.36
Drains; perforated plastic twinwall land drain pipes										
Pipework in trenches										
80mm	1.13	5.00	1.19	-	0.20	3.11	-	4.30	m	4.73
100mm	1.19	5.00	1.25	-	0.22	3.43	-	4.67	m	5.14
160mm	2.35	5.00	2.47	-	0.25	3.89	-	6.36	m	7.00
Drains; clayware perforated pipes, butt joints; 150mm hardcore to sides and top										
Pipework in trenches										
100mm	34.06	5.00	36.35	-	0.42	6.54	-	42.89	m	47.18
150mm	55.28	5.00	58.77	-	0.54	8.41	-	67.18	m	73.90
225mm	106.20	5.00	112.51	-	0.60	9.34	-	121.85	m	134.03

Labour hourly rates: (except Specialists) Craft Operatives 20.87 Labourer 15.57 Rates are national average prices. Refer to REGIONAL VARIATIONS for indicative levels of overall pricing in regions	MATERIALS			LABOUR				RATES		
	Del to Site £	Waste %	Material Cost £	Craft Optve Hrs	Lab Hrs	Labour Cost £	Sunds £	Nett Rate £	Unit	Gross rate (10%) £
SITE WORKS										
Note										
Notwithstanding the requirements of NRM2 excavation and disposal has not been included with the items and should be added as appropriate and as detailed below.										
ROAD AND PATH PAVINGS; GRANULAR SUB-BASES										
Hard, dry, broken brick or stone to be obtained off site; wheeling not exceeding 25m - by machine										
Filling to make up levels; depositing in layers 150mm maximum thickness										
average thickness not exceeding 0.25m	43.20	25.00	54.00	-	-	-	4.83	58.83	m³	64.72
average thickness exceeding 0.25m	43.20	25.00	54.00	-	-	-	4.01	58.01	m³	63.81
Surface packing to filling										
to vertical or battered faces	-	-	-	-	-	-	0.82	0.82	m²	0.91
Compacting with 680 kg vibratory roller										
filling; blinding with sand, ashes or similar fine material	0.45	33.00	0.59	-	0.05	0.78	0.30	1.67	m²	1.84
Compacting with 6 - 8 tonnes smooth wheeled roller										
filling; blinding with sand, ashes or similar fine material	0.45	33.00	0.59	-	0.05	0.78	0.58	1.95	m²	2.14
Hard, dry, broken brick or stone to be obtained off site; wheeling not exceeding 50m - by machine										
Filling to make up levels; depositing in layers 150mm maximum thickness										
average thickness not exceeding 0.25m	43.20	25.00	54.00	-	-	-	5.63	59.63	m³	65.59
average thickness exceeding 0.25m	43.20	25.00	54.00	-	-	-	4.83	58.83	m³	64.72
Surface packing to filling										
to vertical or battered faces	-	-	-	-	-	-	0.82	0.82	m²	0.91
Compacting with 680 kg vibratory roller										
filling; blinding with sand, ashes or similar fine material	0.45	33.00	0.59	-	0.05	0.78	0.30	1.67	m²	1.84
Compacting with 6 - 8 tonnes smooth wheeled roller										
filling; blinding with sand, ashes or similar fine material	0.45	33.00	0.59	-	0.05	0.78	0.53	1.90	m²	2.09
MOT Type 1 to be obtained off site; wheeling not exceeding 25m - by machine										
Filling to make up levels; depositing in layers 150mm maximum thickness										
average thickness not exceeding 0.25m	46.08	25.00	57.60	-	-	-	5.63	63.23	m³	69.55
average thickness exceeding 0.25m	46.08	25.00	57.60	-	-	-	4.67	62.27	m³	68.50
Surface packing to filling										
to vertical or battered faces	-	-	-	-	-	-	0.82	0.82	m²	0.91
Compacting with 680 kg vibratory roller										
filling; blinding with sand, ashes or similar fine material	0.45	33.00	0.59	-	0.05	0.78	0.30	1.67	m²	1.84
Compacting with 6 - 8 tonnes smooth wheeled roller										
filling; blinding with sand, ashes or similar fine material	0.45	33.00	0.59	-	0.05	0.78	0.58	1.95	m²	2.14
MOT Type 1 to be obtained off site; wheeling not exceeding 50m - by machine										
Filling to make up levels; depositing in layers 150mm maximum thickness										
average thickness not exceeding 0.25m	46.08	25.00	57.60	-	-	-	5.63	63.23	m³	69.55
average thickness exceeding 0.25m	46.08	25.00	57.60	-	-	-	4.83	62.43	m³	68.68
Surface packing to filling										
to vertical or battered faces	-	-	-	-	-	-	0.82	0.82	m²	0.91
Compacting with 680 kg vibratory roller										
filling; blinding with sand, ashes or similar fine material	0.45	33.00	0.59	-	0.05	0.78	0.30	1.67	m²	1.84
Compacting with 6 - 8 tonnes smooth wheeled roller										
filling; blinding with sand, ashes or similar fine material	0.45	33.00	0.59	-	0.05	0.78	0.58	1.95	m²	2.14
MOT Type 2 to be obtained off site; wheeling not exceeding 25m - by machine										
Filling to make up levels; depositing in layers 150mm maximum thickness										
average thickness not exceeding 0.25m	46.08	25.00	57.60	-	-	-	4.83	62.43	m³	68.68
average thickness exceeding 0.25m	46.08	25.00	57.60	-	-	-	4.01	61.61	m³	67.77
Surface packing to filling										
to vertical or battered faces	-	-	-	-	-	-	0.82	0.82	m²	0.91

Labour hourly rates: (except Specialists) Craft Operatives 20.87 Labourer 15.57 Rates are national average prices. Refer to REGIONAL VARIATIONS for indicative levels of overall pricing in regions	MATERIALS			LABOUR				RATES		
	Del to Site £	Waste %	Material Cost £	Craft Optve Hrs	Lab Hrs	Labour Cost £	Sunds £	Nett Rate £	Unit	Gross rate (10%) £
ROAD AND PATH PAVINGS; GRANULAR SUB-BASES (Cont'd)										
MOT Type 2 to be obtained off site; wheeling not exceeding 25m - by machine (Cont'd)										
Compacting with 680 kg vibratory roller										
filling; blinding with sand, ashes or similar fine material	0.45	33.00	0.59	-	0.05	0.78	0.30	1.67	m²	1.84
Compacting with 6 - 8 tonnes smooth wheeled roller										
filling; blinding with sand, ashes or similar fine material	0.45	33.00	0.59	-	0.05	0.78	0.58	1.95	m²	2.14
MOT Type 2 to be obtained off site; wheeling not exceeding 50m - by machine										
Filling to make up levels; depositing in layers 150mm maximum thickness										
average thickness not exceeding 0.25m	46.08	25.00	57.60	-	-	-	5.63	63.23	m³	69.55
average thickness exceeding 0.25m	46.08	25.00	57.60	-	-	-	4.83	62.43	m³	68.68
Surface packing to filling										
to vertical or battered faces	-	-	-	-	-	-	0.82	0.82	m²	0.91
Compacting with 680 kg vibratory roller										
filling; blinding with sand, ashes or similar fine material	0.45	33.00	0.59	-	0.05	0.78	0.30	1.67	m²	1.84
Compacting with 6 - 8 tonnes smooth wheeled roller										
filling; blinding with sand, ashes or similar fine material	0.45	33.00	0.59	-	0.05	0.78	0.58	1.95	m²	2.14
Sand to be obtained off site; wheeling not exceeding 25m - by machine										
Filling to make up levels; depositing in layers 150mm maximum thickness										
average thickness not exceeding 0.25m	29.76	33.00	39.58	-	-	-	5.11	44.70	m³	49.17
Compacting with 680 kg vibratory roller										
filling	-	-	-	-	-	-	0.30	0.30	m²	0.33
Compacting with 6 - 8 tonnes smooth wheeled roller										
filling	-	-	-	-	-	-	0.58	0.58	m²	0.64
Sand to be obtained off site; wheeling not exceeding 50m - by machine										
Filling to make up levels; depositing in layers 150mm maximum thickness										
average thickness not exceeding 0.25m	29.76	33.00	39.58	-	-	-	6.91	46.49	m³	51.14
Compacting with 680 kg vibratory roller										
filling	-	-	-	-	-	-	0.30	0.30	m²	0.33
Compacting with 6 - 8 tonnes smooth wheeled roller										
filling	-	-	-	-	-	-	0.58	0.58	m²	0.64
Hoggin to be obtained off site; wheeling not exceeding 25m - by machine										
Filling to make up levels; depositing in layers 150mm maximum thickness										
average thickness not exceeding 0.25m	46.08	33.00	61.29	-	-	-	5.61	66.90	m³	73.59
average thickness exceeding 0.25m	46.08	33.00	61.29	-	-	-	4.67	65.96	m³	72.55
Compacting with 680 kg vibratory roller										
filling	-	-	-	-	-	-	0.30	0.30	m²	0.33
Compacting with 6 - 8 tonnes smooth wheeled roller										
filling	-	-	-	-	-	-	0.58	0.58	m²	0.64
Hoggin to be obtained off site; wheeling not exceeding 50m - by machine										
Filling to make up levels; depositing in layers 150mm maximum thickness										
average thickness not exceeding 0.25m	46.08	33.00	61.29	-	-	-	4.83	66.12	m³	72.73
average thickness exceeding 0.25m	46.08	33.00	61.29	-	-	-	4.01	65.30	m³	71.83
Compacting with 680 kg vibratory roller										
filling	-	-	-	-	-	-	0.30	0.30	m²	0.33
Compacting with 6 - 8 tonnes smooth wheeled roller										
filling	-	-	-	-	-	-	0.58	0.58	m²	0.64
Hard, dry, broken brick or stone to be obtained off site; wheeling not exceeding 25m - by hand										
Filling to make up levels; depositing in layers 150mm maximum thickness										
average thickness not exceeding 0.25m	43.20	25.00	54.00	-	1.50	23.35	-	77.35	m³	85.09
average thickness exceeding 0.25m	43.20	25.00	54.00	-	1.25	19.46	-	73.46	m³	80.81
Compacting with 680 kg vibratory roller										
filling; blinding with sand, ashes or similar fine material	0.45	33.00	0.59	-	0.05	0.78	0.30	1.67	m²	1.84
Compacting with 6 - 8 tonnes smooth wheeled roller										
filling; blinding with sand, ashes or similar fine material	0.45	33.00	0.59	-	0.05	0.78	0.58	1.95	m²	2.14

Labour hourly rates: (except Specialists) Craft Operatives 20.87 Labourer 15.57 Rates are national average prices. Refer to REGIONAL VARIATIONS for indicative levels of overall pricing in regions	MATERIALS			LABOUR				RATES		
	Del to Site £	Waste %	Material Cost £	Craft Optve Hrs	Lab Hrs	Labour Cost £	Sunds £	Nett Rate £	Unit	Gross rate (10%) £
ROAD AND PATH PAVINGS; GRANULAR SUB-BASES (Cont'd)										
Hard, dry, broken brick or stone to be obtained off site; wheeling not exceeding 50m - by hand										
Filling to make up levels; depositing in layers 150mm maximum thickness										
average thickness not exceeding 0.25m	43.20	25.00	54.00	-	1.75	27.25	-	81.25	m³	89.37
average thickness exceeding 0.25m	43.20	25.00	54.00	-	1.50	23.35	-	77.35	m³	85.09
Compacting with 680 kg vibratory roller filling; blinding with sand, ashes or similar fine material	0.45	33.00	0.59	-	0.05	0.78	0.30	1.67	m²	1.84
Compacting with 6 - 8 tonnes smooth wheeled roller filling; blinding with sand, ashes or similar fine material	0.45	33.00	0.59	-	0.05	0.78	0.58	1.95	m²	2.14
MOT Type 1 to be obtained off site; wheeling not exceeding 25m - by hand										
Filling to make up levels; depositing in layers 150mm maximum thickness										
average thickness not exceeding 0.25m	46.08	25.00	57.60	-	1.50	23.35	-	80.96	m³	89.05
average thickness exceeding 0.25m	46.08	25.00	57.60	-	1.25	19.46	-	77.06	m³	84.77
Compacting with 680 kg vibratory roller filling; blinding with sand, ashes or similar fine material	0.45	33.00	0.59	-	0.05	0.78	0.30	1.67	m²	1.84
Compacting with 6 - 8 tonnes smooth wheeled roller filling; blinding with sand, ashes or similar fine material	0.45	33.00	0.59	-	0.05	0.78	0.58	1.95	m²	2.14
MOT Type 1 to be obtained off site; wheeling not exceeding 50m - by hand										
Filling to make up levels; depositing in layers 150mm maximum thickness										
average thickness not exceeding 0.25m	46.08	25.00	57.60	-	1.75	27.25	-	84.85	m³	93.33
average thickness exceeding 0.25m	46.08	25.00	57.60	-	1.50	23.35	-	80.96	m³	89.05
Compacting with 680 kg vibratory roller filling; blinding with sand, ashes or similar fine material	0.45	33.00	0.59	-	0.05	0.78	0.30	1.67	m²	1.84
Compacting with 6 - 8 tonnes smooth wheeled roller filling; blinding with sand, ashes or similar fine material	0.45	33.00	0.59	-	0.05	0.78	0.58	1.95	m²	2.14
MOT Type 2 to be obtained off site; wheeling not exceeding 25m - by hand										
Filling to make up levels; depositing in layers 150mm maximum thickness										
average thickness not exceeding 0.25m	46.08	25.00	57.60	-	1.50	23.35	-	80.96	m³	89.05
average thickness exceeding 0.25m	46.08	25.00	57.60	-	1.25	19.46	-	77.06	m³	84.77
Compacting with 680 kg vibratory roller filling; blinding with sand, ashes or similar fine material	0.45	33.00	0.59	-	0.05	0.78	0.30	1.67	m²	1.84
Compacting with 6 - 8 tonnes smooth wheeled roller filling; blinding with sand, ashes or similar fine material	0.45	33.00	0.59	-	0.05	0.78	0.58	1.95	m²	2.14
MOT Type 2 to be obtained off site; wheeling not exceeding 50m - by hand										
Filling to make up levels; depositing in layers 150mm maximum thickness										
average thickness not exceeding 0.25m	46.08	25.00	57.60	-	1.75	27.25	-	84.85	m³	93.33
average thickness exceeding 0.25m	46.08	25.00	57.60	-	1.50	23.35	-	80.96	m³	89.05
Compacting with 680 kg vibratory roller filling; blinding with sand, ashes or similar fine material	0.45	33.00	0.59	-	0.05	0.78	0.30	1.67	m²	1.84
Compacting with 6 - 8 tonnes smooth wheeled roller filling; blinding with sand, ashes or similar fine material	0.45	33.00	0.59	-	0.05	0.78	0.58	1.95	m²	2.14
Sand to be obtained off site; wheeling not exceeding 25m - by hand										
Filling to make up levels; depositing in layers 150mm maximum thickness										
average thickness not exceeding 0.25m	29.76	33.00	39.58	-	1.60	24.91	-	64.49	m³	70.94
Compacting with 680 kg vibratory roller filling	-	-	-	-	-	-	0.30	0.30	m²	0.33
Compacting with 6 - 8 tonnes smooth wheeled roller filling	-	-	-	-	-	-	0.58	0.58	m²	0.64
Sand to be obtained off site; wheeling not exceeding 50m - by hand										
Filling to make up levels; depositing in layers 150mm maximum thickness										
average thickness not exceeding 0.25m	29.76	33.00	39.58	-	1.85	28.80	-	68.39	m³	75.22
Compacting with 680 kg vibratory roller filling	-	-	-	-	-	-	0.30	0.30	m²	0.33
Compacting with 6 - 8 tonnes smooth wheeled roller filling	-	-	-	-	-	-	0.58	0.58	m²	0.64

Labour hourly rates: (except Specialists) Craft Operatives 20.87 Labourer 15.57 Rates are national average prices. Refer to REGIONAL VARIATIONS for indicative levels of overall pricing in regions	MATERIALS			LABOUR				RATES		
	Del to Site £	Waste %	Material Cost £	Craft Optve Hrs	Lab Hrs	Labour Cost £	Sunds £	Nett Rate £	Unit	Gross rate (10%) £
ROAD AND PATH PAVINGS; GRANULAR SUB-BASES (Cont'd)										
Hoggin to be obtained off site; wheeling not exceeding 25m - by hand										
Filling to make up levels; depositing in layers 150mm maximum thickness										
average thickness not exceeding 0.25m	46.08	33.00	61.29	-	1.50	23.35	-	84.64	m³	93.11
average thickness exceeding 0.25m	46.08	33.00	61.29	-	1.25	19.46	-	80.75	m³	88.82
Compacting with 680 kg vibratory roller										
filling	-	-	-	-	-	-	0.30	0.30	m²	0.33
Compacting with 6 - 8 tonnes smooth wheeled roller										
filling	-	-	-	-	-	-	0.58	0.58	m²	0.64
Hoggin to be obtained off site; wheeling not exceeding 50m - by hand										
Filling to make up levels; depositing in layers 150mm maximum thickness										
average thickness not exceeding 0.25m	46.08	33.00	61.29	-	1.75	27.25	-	88.53	m³	97.39
average thickness exceeding 0.25m	46.08	33.00	61.29	-	1.50	23.35	-	84.64	m³	93.11
Compacting with 680 kg vibratory roller										
filling	-	-	-	-	-	-	0.30	0.30	m²	0.33
Compacting with 6 - 8 tonnes smooth wheeled roller										
filling	-	-	-	-	-	-	0.58	0.58	m²	0.64
ROAD AND PATH PAVINGS; IN-SITU CONCRETE										
Plain in-situ concrete; mix 1:8, all in aggregate										
Beds; poured on or against earth or unblinded hardcore										
thickness not exceeding 150mm	136.60	7.50	146.85	-	4.68	72.87	2.97	222.69	m³	244.96
Plain in-situ concrete; mix 1:6; all in aggregate										
Beds; poured on or against earth or unblinded hardcore										
thickness 150 - 450mm	144.57	7.50	155.42	-	4.40	68.51	2.97	226.89	m³	249.58
thickness not exceeding 150mm	144.57	7.50	155.42	-	4.68	72.87	2.97	231.25	m³	254.38
Plain in-situ concrete; BS 8500, ordinary prescribed mix ST4, 20mm aggregate										
Beds										
thickness not exceeding 150mm	105.04	5.00	110.29	-	4.68	72.87	2.97	186.13	m³	204.74
Beds; poured on or against earth or unblinded hardcore										
thickness not exceeding 150mm	105.04	5.00	110.29	-	4.68	72.87	2.97	186.13	m³	204.74
Reinforced in-situ concrete; BS 8500, designed mix C20, 20mm aggregate, minimum cement content 240 kg/m³; vibrated										
Beds										
thickness 150 - 450mm	97.76	5.00	102.65	-	4.68	72.87	0.82	176.34	m³	193.97
thickness not exceeding 150mm	97.76	5.00	102.65	-	4.95	77.07	0.82	180.54	m³	198.60
Formwork and basic finish										
Edges of beds										
height not exceeding 250mm	1.60	12.50	1.80	0.58	0.12	13.97	0.40	16.17	m	17.79
height 250 - 500mm	2.81	12.50	3.17	1.06	0.21	25.39	0.74	29.30	m	32.23
Formwork steel forms										
Edges of beds										
height not exceeding 250mm	4.14	15.00	4.76	0.40	0.08	9.59	0.40	14.75	m	16.23
height 250 - 500mm	7.14	15.00	8.21	0.70	0.14	16.79	0.74	25.74	m	28.32
Reinforcement fabric; BS 4483, hard drawn plain round steel; welded; including laps, tying wire, all cutting and bending, and spacers and chairs which are at the discretion of the Contractor										
Reference C283, 2.61 kg/m²; 100mm side laps; 400mm end laps										
generally	6.68	17.50	7.85	0.06	0.02	1.56	0.12	9.53	m²	10.48
Reference C385, 3.41 kg/m²; 100mm side laps; 400mm end laps										
generally	8.08	17.50	9.50	0.06	0.02	1.56	0.15	11.21	m²	12.33
Reference C503, 4.34 kg/m²; 100mm side laps; 400mm end laps										
generally	9.04	17.50	10.62	0.07	0.02	1.77	0.18	12.57	m²	13.83
Reference C636, 5.55 kg/m²; 100mm side laps; 400mm end laps										
generally	11.81	17.50	13.88	0.07	0.02	1.77	0.23	15.88	m²	17.47
Reference C785, 6.72 kg/m²; 100mm side laps; 400mm end laps										
generally	13.94	17.50	16.38	0.08	0.02	1.98	0.28	18.64	m²	20.51
Formed joints										
Sealant to joint; Grace Construction Products. Servicised joints, Paraseal (two-part sealant) including preparation, cleaners and primers										
10 x 25mm	4.43	5.00	4.65	-	0.11	1.71	-	6.36	m	6.99
12.5 x 25mm	5.75	5.00	6.04	-	0.12	1.87	-	7.91	m	8.70

Labour hourly rates: (except Specialists) Craft Operatives 20.87 Labourer 15.57 Rates are national average prices. Refer to REGIONAL VARIATIONS for indicative levels of overall pricing in regions	MATERIALS			LABOUR				RATES		
	Del to Site £	Waste %	Material Cost £	Craft Optve Hrs	Lab Hrs	Labour Cost £	Sunds £	Nett Rate £	Unit	Gross rate (10%) £
ROAD AND PATH PAVINGS; IN-SITU CONCRETE (Cont'd)										
Worked finish on in-situ concrete										
Tamping by mechanical means										
level surfaces	-	-	-	-	0.16	2.49	0.48	2.97	m²	3.27
sloping surfaces	-	-	-	-	0.33	5.14	0.63	5.77	m²	6.34
surfaces to falls	-	-	-	-	0.44	6.85	0.63	7.48	m²	8.23
Trowelling										
level surfaces	-	-	-	-	0.36	5.61	-	5.61	m²	6.17
sloping surfaces	-	-	-	-	0.44	6.85	-	6.85	m²	7.54
surfaces to falls	-	-	-	-	0.55	8.56	-	8.56	m²	9.42
Rolling with an indenting roller										
level surfaces	-	-	-	-	0.11	1.71	0.46	2.17	m²	2.39
sloping surfaces	-	-	-	-	0.17	2.65	0.46	3.11	m²	3.42
surfaces to falls	-	-	-	-	0.33	5.14	0.59	5.73	m²	6.31
Accessories cast into in-situ concrete										
Mild steel dowels; half coated with bitumen										
16mm diameter x 400mm long	0.50	10.00	0.55	-	0.06	0.93	0.30	1.78	nr	1.95
20mm diameter x 500mm long; with plastic compression cap	0.95	10.00	1.04	-	0.08	1.25	0.30	2.58	nr	2.84
ROAD AND PATH PAVINGS; COATED MACADAM/ASPHALT										
Coated macadam, BS 594987; base course 28mm nominal size aggregate, 50mm thick; wearing course 6mm nominal size aggregate, 20mm thick; rolled with 3 - 4 tonne roller; external										
70mm roads on concrete base; to falls and crossfalls, and slopes not exceeding 15 degrees from horizontal generally	-	-	Specialist	-	-	Specialist	-	22.43	m²	24.67
70mm pavings on concrete base; to falls and crossfalls, and slopes not exceeding 15 degrees from horizontal generally	-	-	Specialist	-	-	Specialist	-	24.95	m²	27.44
Coated macadam, BS 594987; base course 28mm nominal size aggregate, 50mm thick; wearing course 6mm nominal size aggregate, 20mm thick; rolled with 3 - 4 tonne roller; dressing surface with coated grit brushed on and lightly rolled; external										
70mm roads on concrete base; to falls and crossfalls, and slopes not exceeding 15 degrees from horizontal generally	-	-	Specialist	-	-	Specialist	-	27.17	m²	29.89
70mm pavings on concrete base; to falls and crossfalls, and slopes not exceeding 15 degrees from horizontal generally	-	-	Specialist	-	-	Specialist	-	29.62	m²	32.58
Coated macadam, BS 594987; base course 40mm nominal size aggregate, 65mm thick; wearing course 10mm nominal size aggregate, 25mm thick; rolled with 6 - 8 tonne roller; external										
90mm roads on concrete base; to falls and crossfalls, and slopes not exceeding 15 degrees from horizontal generally	-	-	Specialist	-	-	Specialist	-	27.17	m²	29.89
90mm pavings on concrete base; to falls and crossfalls, and slopes not exceeding 15 degrees from horizontal generally	-	-	Specialist	-	-	Specialist	-	29.80	m²	32.78
Coated macadam, BS 594987; base course 40mm nominal size aggregate, 65mm thick; wearing course 10mm nominal size aggregate, 25mm thick; rolled with 6 - 8 tonne roller; dressing surface with coated grit brushed on and lightly rolled; external										
90mm roads on concrete base; to falls and crossfalls, and slopes not exceeding 15 degrees from horizontal generally	-	-	Specialist	-	-	Specialist	-	32.23	m²	35.46
90mm pavings on concrete base; to falls and crossfalls, and slopes not exceeding 15 degrees from horizontal generally	-	-	Specialist	-	-	Specialist	-	33.35	m²	36.69
Fine cold asphalt, BS 594987; single course 6mm nominal size aggregate; rolled with 3 - 4 tonne roller; external										
12mm roads on concrete base; to falls and crossfalls, and slopes not exceeding 15 degrees from horizontal generally	-	-	Specialist	-	-	Specialist	-	10.22	m²	11.25
19mm roads on concrete base; to falls and crossfalls, and slopes not exceeding 15 degrees from horizontal generally	-	-	Specialist	-	-	Specialist	-	11.85	m²	13.03
25mm roads on concrete base; to falls and crossfalls, and slopes not exceeding 15 degrees from horizontal generally	-	-	Specialist	-	-	Specialist	-	14.07	m²	15.48
12mm pavings on concrete base; to falls and crossfalls, and slopes not exceeding 15 degrees from horizontal generally	-	-	Specialist	-	-	Specialist	-	10.84	m²	11.93

Labour hourly rates: (except Specialists) Craft Operatives 20.87 Labourer 15.57 Rates are national average prices. Refer to REGIONAL VARIATIONS for indicative levels of overall pricing in regions	MATERIALS			LABOUR				RATES		
	Del to Site £	Waste %	Material Cost £	Craft Optve Hrs	Lab Hrs	Labour Cost £	Sunds £	Nett Rate £	Unit	Gross rate (10%) £
ROAD AND PATH PAVINGS; COATED MACADAM/ASPHALT (Cont'd)										
Fine cold asphalt, BS 594987; single course 6mm nominal size aggregate; rolled with 3 - 4 tonne roller; external (Cont'd)										
19mm pavings on concrete base; to falls and crossfalls, and slopes not exceeding 15 degrees from horizontal										
generally	-	-	Specialist	-	-	Specialist	-	13.60	m²	14.96
25mm pavings on concrete base; to falls and crossfalls, and slopes not exceeding 15 degrees from horizontal										
generally	-	-	Specialist	-	-	Specialist	-	15.56	m²	17.12
ROAD AND PATH PAVINGS; GRAVEL/HOGGIN/WOODCHIP										
Gravel paving; first layer MOT type 1 75mm thick; intermediate layer coarse gravel 75mm thick; wearing layer blinding gravel 38mm thick; well water and roll										
188mm roads on blinded hardcore base; to falls and crossfalls and slopes not exceeding 15 degrees from horizontal										
generally	14.01	10.00	15.93	-	0.44	6.85	-	23.61	m²	25.97
Gravel paving; single layer blinding gravel; well water and roll										
50mm pavings on blinded hardcore base; to falls and crossfalls and slopes not exceeding 15 degrees from horizontal										
generally	4.48	10.00	4.92	-	0.15	2.34	-	7.47	m²	8.21
Gravel paving; first layer sand 50mm thick; wearing layer blinding gravel 38mm thick; well water and roll										
88mm pavings on blinded hardcore base; to falls and crossfalls and slopes not exceeding 15 degrees from horizontal										
generally	6.01	10.00	6.61	-	0.26	4.05	-	10.86	m²	11.95

This section continues on the next page

Labour hourly rates: (except Specialists) Craft Operatives 20.87 Labourer 15.57 Rates are national average prices. Refer to REGIONAL VARIATIONS for indicative levels of overall pricing in regions	PLANT AND TRANSPORT			LABOUR				RATES		
	Plant Cost £	Trans Cost £	P and T Cost £	Craft Optve Hrs	Lab Hrs	Labour Cost £	Sunds £	Nett Rate £	Unit	Gross rate (10%) £
ROAD AND PATH PAVINGS; KERBS/EDGINGS/CHANNELS/PAVING ACCESSORIES										
Excavating - by machine										
Trenches width not exceeding 0.30m										
maximum depth not exceeding 0.25m	12.11	-	12.11	-	1.71	26.62	-	38.73	m³	42.60
maximum depth not exceeding 1.00m	12.60	-	12.60	-	1.80	28.03	-	40.63	m³	44.69
Extra over any types of excavating irrespective of depth										
excavating below ground water level	10.67	-	10.67	-	-	-	-	10.67	m³	11.74
excavating in running silt, running sand or liquid mud	18.33	-	18.33	-	-	-	-	18.33	m³	20.17
Breaking out existing materials; extra over any types of excavating irrespective of depth										
hard rock	23.28	-	23.28	-	-	-	-	23.28	m³	25.61
concrete	19.33	-	19.33	-	-	-	-	19.33	m³	21.27
reinforced concrete	29.04	-	29.04	-	-	-	-	29.04	m³	31.95
brickwork, blockwork or stonework	12.90	-	12.90	-	-	-	-	12.90	m³	14.19
100mm diameter drain and concrete bed under	1.82	-	1.82	-	-	-	-	1.82	m	2.00
Breaking out existing hard pavings; extra over any types of excavating irrespective of depth										
concrete 150mm thick	3.05	-	3.05	-	-	-	-	3.05	m²	3.35
reinforced concrete 200mm thick	6.12	-	6.12	-	-	-	-	6.12	m²	6.73
brickwork, blockwork or stonework 100mm thick	1.44	-	1.44	-	-	-	-	1.44	m²	1.58
coated macadam or asphalt 75mm thick	0.51	-	0.51	-	-	-	-	0.51	m²	0.57
Disposal of excavated material										
depositing on site in temporary spoil heaps where directed										
25m	-	4.46	4.46	-	0.12	1.87	-	6.33	m³	6.96
100m	-	5.09	5.09	-	0.12	1.87	-	6.95	m³	7.65
800m	-	7.82	7.82	-	0.12	1.87	-	9.69	m³	10.66
1600m	-	8.85	8.85	-	0.12	1.87	-	10.72	m³	11.79
extra for each additional 1600m	-	1.37	1.37	-	-	-	-	1.37	m³	1.51
removing from site to tip a) Inert	-	38.12	38.12	-	-	-	-	38.12	m³	41.94
removing from site to tip b) Active	-	78.79	78.79	-	-	-	-	78.79	m³	86.67
removing from site to tip c) Contaminated (Guide price - always seek a quotation for specialist disposal costs.)	-	228.74	228.74	-	-	-	-	228.74	m³	251.61
Disposal of preserved top soil										
depositing on site in temporary spoil heaps where directed										
25m	-	4.46	4.46	-	0.12	1.87	-	6.33	m³	6.96
50m	-	4.65	4.65	-	0.12	1.87	-	6.52	m³	7.18
100m	-	5.09	5.09	-	0.12	1.87	-	6.95	m³	7.65
Surface treatments										
Compacting										
bottoms of excavations	0.38	-	0.38	-	-	-	-	0.38	m²	0.42
Excavating - by hand										
Trenches width not exceeding 0.30m										
maximum depth not exceeding 0.25m	-	-	-	-	4.25	66.17	-	66.17	m³	72.79
maximum depth not exceeding 1.00m	-	-	-	-	4.50	70.07	-	70.07	m³	77.07
Extra over any types of excavating irrespective of depth										
excavating below ground water level	-	-	-	-	1.50	23.35	-	23.35	m³	25.69
excavating in running silt, running sand or liquid mud	-	-	-	-	4.50	70.07	-	70.07	m³	77.07
Breaking out existing materials; extra over any types of excavating irrespective of depth										
hard rock	-	-	-	-	10.00	155.70	-	155.70	m³	171.27
concrete	-	-	-	-	7.00	108.99	-	108.99	m³	119.89
reinforced concrete	-	-	-	-	12.00	186.84	-	186.84	m³	205.52
brickwork, blockwork or stonework	-	-	-	-	4.00	62.28	-	62.28	m³	68.51
100mm diameter drain and concrete bed under	-	-	-	-	1.00	15.57	-	15.57	m	17.13
Breaking out existing hard pavings; extra over any types of excavating irrespective of depth										
concrete 150mm thick	-	-	-	-	1.50	23.35	-	23.35	m²	25.69
reinforced concrete 200mm thick	-	-	-	-	2.00	31.14	-	31.14	m²	34.25
brickwork, blockwork or stonework 100mm thick	-	-	-	-	0.70	10.90	-	10.90	m²	11.99
coated macadam or asphalt 75mm thick	-	-	-	-	0.25	3.89	-	3.89	m²	4.28
Disposal of excavated material										
depositing on site in temporary spoil heaps where directed										
25m	-	-	-	-	1.25	19.46	-	19.46	m³	21.41
50m	-	-	-	-	1.50	23.35	-	23.35	m³	25.69
100m	-	-	-	-	2.00	31.14	-	31.14	m³	34.25
extra for removing beyond 100m and not exceeding 400m	-	-	-	-	1.55	24.13	3.60	27.73	m³	30.50
extra for removing beyond 100m and not exceeding 800m	-	-	-	-	1.55	24.13	4.69	28.82	m³	31.70
depositing on site in permanent spoil heaps average 25m distant	-	-	-	-	1.25	19.46	-	19.46	m³	21.41
removing from site to tip										
a) Inert	-	-	-	-	1.35	21.02	19.14	40.16	m³	44.18
b) Active	-	-	-	-	1.35	21.02	216.53	237.55	m³	261.31
c) Contaminated (guide price - always seek a quote for specialist disposal cost	-	-	-	-	1.35	21.02	257.32	278.34	m³	306.18

Labour hourly rates: (except Specialists) Craft Operatives 20.87 Labourer 15.57 Rates are national average prices. Refer to REGIONAL VARIATIONS for indicative levels of overall pricing in regions	PLANT AND TRANSPORT			LABOUR				RATES		
	Plant Cost £	Trans Cost £	P and T Cost £	Craft Optve Hrs	Lab Hrs	Labour Cost £	Sunds £	Nett Rate £	Unit	Gross rate (10%) £
ROAD AND PATH PAVINGS; KERBS/EDGINGS/CHANNELS/PAVING ACCESSORIES (Cont'd)										
Surface treatments										
Compacting										
bottoms of excavations	-	-	-	-	0.12	1.87	-	1.87	m²	2.06

This section continues on the next page

Labour hourly rates: (except Specialists) Craft Operatives 20.87 Labourer 15.57 Rates are national average prices. Refer to REGIONAL VARIATIONS for indicative levels of overall pricing in regions	MATERIALS			LABOUR				RATES		
	Del to Site £	Waste %	Material Cost £	Craft Optve Hrs	Lab Hrs	Labour Cost £	Sunds £	Nett Rate £	Unit	Gross rate (10%) £
ROAD AND PATH PAVINGS; KERBS/EDGINGS/CHANNELS/PAVING ACCESSORIES (Cont'd)										
Earthwork support										
Earthwork support										
maximum depth not exceeding 1.00m; distance between opposing faces not exceeding 2.00m	0.93	-	0.93	-	0.20	3.11	0.03	4.07	m²	4.48
Earthwork support; curved										
Maximum depth not exceeding 1.00m; distance between opposing faces not exceeding 2.00m	1.24	-	1.24	-	0.30	4.67	0.07	5.97	m²	6.57
Earthwork support; unstable ground										
maximum depth not exceeding 1.00m; distance between opposing faces not exceeding 2.00m	1.66	-	1.66	-	0.36	5.61	0.03	7.30	m²	8.03
Earthwork support; next to roadways										
maximum depth not exceeding 1.00m; distance between opposing faces not exceeding 2.00m	1.82	-	1.82	-	0.40	6.23	0.07	8.12	m²	8.93
Precast concrete; standard or stock pattern units; BS EN 1340 Part 1; bedding, jointing and pointing in cement mortar (1:3); on plain in-situ concrete foundation; BS 8500 ordinary prescribed mix ST4, 20mm aggregate										
Kerbs; concrete foundation and haunching; formwork										
125 x 255mm kerb; 400 x 200mm foundation	19.21	5.00	20.40	-	1.09	16.97	-	37.37	m	41.11
125 x 255mm kerb; 400 x 200mm foundation; curved 10.00m radius	30.55	5.00	32.32	-	1.16	18.06	-	50.38	m	55.41
150 x 305mm kerb; 400 x 200mm foundation	34.22	5.00	36.17	-	1.16	18.06	-	54.23	m	59.65
150 x 305mm kerb; 400 x 200mm foundation; curved 10.00m radius	49.41	5.00	52.12	-	1.26	19.62	-	71.74	m	78.91
Edgings; concrete foundation and haunching; formwork										
50 x 150mm edging; 300 x 150mm foundation	11.44	5.00	12.14	-	0.78	12.14	-	24.28	m	26.71
50 x 200mm edging; 300 x 150mm foundation	13.82	5.00	14.64	-	0.90	14.01	-	28.66	m	31.52
50 x 250mm edging; 300 x 150mm foundation	16.82	5.00	17.79	-	1.02	15.88	-	33.67	m	37.04
Channels; concrete foundation and haunching; formwork										
255 x 125mm channel; 450 x 150mm foundation	22.18	5.00	23.48	-	0.86	13.39	-	36.87	m	40.55
255 x 125mm channel; 450 x 150mm foundation; curved 10.00 radius	32.10	5.00	33.89	-	0.93	14.48	-	48.37	m	53.21
Quadrants; concrete foundation and haunching; formwork										
305 x 305 x 150mm quadrant; 500 x 500 x 150mm foundation	29.16	5.00	30.72	-	0.61	9.50	-	40.22	nr	44.24
305 x 305 x 255mm quadrant; 500 x 500 x 150mm foundation	29.16	5.00	30.72	-	0.69	10.74	-	41.47	nr	45.61
455 x 455 x 150mm quadrant; 650 x 650 x 150mm foundation	40.90	5.00	43.11	-	0.85	13.23	-	56.34	nr	61.97
455 x 455 x 255mm quadrant; 650 x 650 x 150mm foundation	40.90	5.00	43.11	-	0.94	14.64	-	57.74	nr	63.51
Granite; standard units; BS EN 1343; bedding jointing and pointing in cement mortar (1:3); on plain in-situ concrete foundation; BS 8500 ordinary prescribed mix ST4, 20mm aggregate										
Edge kerb; concrete foundation and haunching; formwork										
150 x 300mm; 300 x 200mm foundation	61.65	2.50	63.64	0.55	0.72	22.69	-	86.33	m	94.96
150 x 300mm; 300 x 200mm foundation; curved external radius exceeding 1000mm	77.30	2.50	79.84	0.88	0.72	29.58	-	109.42	m	120.36
200 x 300mm; 350 x 200mm foundation	81.65	2.50	84.19	0.66	0.80	26.23	-	110.42	m	121.47
200 x 300mm; 350 x 200mm foundation; curved external radius exceeding 1000mm	141.98	2.50	146.19	0.99	0.80	33.12	-	179.31	m	197.24
Flat kerb; concrete foundation and haunching; formwork										
300 x 150mm; 450 x 200mm foundation	64.80	2.50	67.03	0.55	0.80	23.93	-	90.96	m	100.06
300 x 150mm; 450 x 200mm foundation; curved external radius exceeding 1000mm	80.45	2.50	83.23	0.88	0.80	30.82	-	114.05	m	125.46
300 x 200mm; 450 x 200mm foundation	83.75	2.50	86.45	0.66	0.83	26.70	-	113.15	m	124.47
300 x 200mm; 450 x 200mm foundation; curved external radius exceeding 1000mm	144.08	2.50	148.45	0.99	0.83	33.58	-	182.03	m	200.24
ROAD AND PATH PAVINGS; INTERLOCKING BRICK AND BLOCKS, SLABS, BRICKS, BLOCKS, SETTS AND COBBLES										
York stone paving; 13mm thick bedding, jointing and pointing in cement mortar (1:3)										
Paving on blinded hardcore base										
50mm thick; to falls and crossfalls and to slopes not exceeding 15 degrees from horizontal	108.64	10.00	114.04	0.30	0.30	10.93	1.72	126.69	m²	139.36
75mm thick; to falls and crossfalls and to slopes not exceeding 15 degrees from horizontal	151.45	10.00	159.03	0.36	0.36	13.12	1.81	173.96	m²	191.36
extra; rubbed top surface	19.73	5.00	20.72	-	-	-	-	20.72	m²	22.79
Treads on concrete base										
50mm thick; 300mm wide	92.44	5.00	97.06	0.36	0.36	13.12	0.50	110.68	m	121.74

SITE WORKS

Labour hourly rates: (except Specialists) Craft Operatives 20.87 Labourer 15.57 Rates are national average prices. Refer to REGIONAL VARIATIONS for indicative levels of overall pricing in regions	MATERIALS			LABOUR				RATES		
	Del to Site £	Waste %	Material Cost £	Craft Optve Hrs	Lab Hrs	Labour Cost £	Sunds £	Nett Rate £	Unit	Gross rate (10%) £
ROAD AND PATH PAVINGS; INTERLOCKING BRICK AND BLOCKS, SLABS, BRICKS, BLOCKS, SETTS AND COBBLES (Cont'd)										
Precast concrete flags, BS EN 1339 Part 1, natural finish; 6mm joints, symmetrical layout; bedding in 13mm cement mortar (1:3); jointing and pointing with lime and sand (1:2)										
600 x 450 x 50mm units to pavings on sand, granular or blinded hardcore base										
50mm thick; to falls and crossfalls and to slopes not exceeding 15 degrees from horizontal	17.01	5.00	17.74	0.30	0.30	10.93	1.75	30.43	m²	33.47
600 x 600 x 50mm units to pavings on sand, granular or blinded hardcore base										
50mm thick; to falls and crossfalls and to slopes not exceeding 15 degrees from horizontal	14.76	5.00	15.39	0.28	0.28	10.20	1.65	27.24	m²	29.97
600 x 750 x 50mm units to pavings on sand, granular or blinded hardcore base										
50mm thick; to falls and crossfalls and to slopes not exceeding 15 degrees from horizontal	14.62	5.00	15.21	0.25	0.50	13.00	1.77	29.97	m²	32.97
600 x 900 x 50mm units to pavings on sand, granular or blinded hardcore base										
50mm thick; to falls and crossfalls and to slopes not exceeding 15 degrees from horizontal	13.27	5.00	13.79	0.23	0.46	11.96	1.78	27.53	m²	30.29
600 x 450 x 63mm units to pavings on sand, granular or blinded hardcore base										
63mm thick; to falls and crossfalls and to slopes not exceeding 15 degrees from horizontal	31.30	5.00	32.72	0.30	0.30	10.93	1.75	45.40	m²	49.95
600 x 600 x 63mm units to pavings on sand, granular or blinded hardcore base										
63mm thick; to falls and crossfalls and to slopes not exceeding 15 degrees from horizontal	24.20	5.00	25.27	0.28	0.28	10.20	1.65	37.12	m²	40.84
600 x 750 x 63mm units to pavings on sand, granular or blinded hardcore base										
63mm thick; to falls and crossfalls and to slopes not exceeding 15 degrees from horizontal	24.70	5.00	25.79	0.25	0.50	13.00	1.67	40.46	m²	44.50
600 x 900 x 63mm units to pavings on sand, granular or blinded hardcore base										
63mm thick; to falls and crossfalls and to slopes not exceeding 15 degrees from horizontal	21.25	5.00	22.17	0.23	0.46	11.96	1.68	35.81	m²	39.40
Precast concrete flags, BS EN 1339 Part 1, natural finish; 6mm joints, symmetrical layout; bedding in 13mm lime mortar (1:3); jointing and pointing with lime and sand (1:2)										
600 x 450 x 50mm units to pavings on sand, granular or blinded hardcore base										
50mm thick; to falls and crossfalls and to slopes not exceeding 15 degrees from horizontal	19.91	5.00	20.65	0.30	0.30	10.93	1.75	33.33	m²	36.66
600 x 600 x 50mm units to pavings on sand, granular or blinded hardcore base										
50mm thick; to falls and crossfalls and to slopes not exceeding 15 degrees from horizontal	17.67	5.00	18.29	0.28	0.28	10.20	1.65	30.15	m²	33.16
600 x 750 x 50mm units to pavings on sand, granular or blinded hardcore base										
50mm thick; to falls and crossfalls and to slopes not exceeding 15 degrees from horizontal	16.95	5.00	17.54	0.25	0.50	13.00	1.67	32.21	m²	35.43
600 x 900 x 50mm units to pavings on sand, granular or blinded hardcore base										
50mm thick; to falls and crossfalls and to slopes not exceeding 15 degrees from horizontal	15.60	5.00	16.12	0.23	0.46	11.96	1.75	29.83	m²	32.82
600 x 450 x 63mm units to pavings on sand, granular or blinded hardcore base										
63mm thick; to falls and crossfalls and to slopes not exceeding 15 degrees from horizontal	33.63	5.00	35.06	0.30	0.30	10.93	1.75	47.74	m²	52.51
600 x 600 x 63mm units to pavings on sand, granular or blinded hardcore base										
63mm thick; to falls and crossfalls and to slopes not exceeding 15 degrees from horizontal	26.54	5.00	27.60	0.28	0.28	10.20	1.65	39.46	m²	43.40
600 x 750 x 63mm units to pavings on sand, granular or blinded hardcore base										
63mm thick; to falls and crossfalls and to slopes not exceeding 15 degrees from horizontal	27.03	5.00	28.12	0.25	0.50	13.00	1.67	42.79	m²	47.07
600 x 900 x 63mm units to pavings on sand, granular or blinded hardcore base										
63mm thick; to falls and crossfalls and to slopes not exceeding 15 degrees from horizontal	23.58	5.00	24.50	0.23	0.46	11.96	1.68	38.15	m²	41.96

Labour hourly rates: (except Specialists) Craft Operatives 20.87 Labourer 15.57 Rates are national average prices. Refer to REGIONAL VARIATIONS for indicative levels of overall pricing in regions	MATERIALS			LABOUR				RATES		
	Del to Site £	Waste %	Material Cost £	Craft Optve Hrs	Lab Hrs	Labour Cost £	Sunds £	Nett Rate £	Unit	Gross rate (10%) £
ROAD AND PATH PAVINGS; INTERLOCKING BRICK AND BLOCKS, SLABS, BRICKS, BLOCKS, SETTS AND COBBLES (Cont'd)										
Precast concrete flags, BS EN 1339 Part 1, natural finish; 6mm joints, symmetrical layout; bedding in 25mm sand; jointing and pointing with lime and sand (1:2)										
600 x 450 x 50mm units to pavings on sand, granular or blinded hardcore base										
50mm thick; to falls and crossfalls and to slopes not exceeding 15 degrees from horizontal	15.66	5.00	16.39	0.30	0.30	10.93	1.75	29.07	m²	31.98
600 x 600 x 50mm units to pavings on sand, granular or blinded hardcore base										
50mm thick; to falls and crossfalls and to slopes not exceeding 15 degrees from horizontal	13.73	5.00	14.37	0.28	0.28	10.20	1.65	26.22	m²	28.84
600 x 750 x 50mm units to pavings on sand, granular or blinded hardcore base										
50mm thick; to falls and crossfalls and to slopes not exceeding 15 degrees from horizontal	12.70	5.00	13.28	0.25	0.50	13.00	1.67	27.95	m²	30.75
600 x 900 x 50mm units to pavings on sand, granular or blinded hardcore base										
50mm thick; to falls and crossfalls and to slopes not exceeding 15 degrees from horizontal	11.34	5.00	11.87	0.23	0.46	11.96	1.68	25.51	m²	28.06
Keyblok precast concrete paving blocks; Marshalls Driveline; in standard units; bedding on sand; covering with sand, compacting with plate vibrator, sweeping off surplus										
200 x 100mm units to pavings on 50mm sand base; natural colour										
symmetrical half bond layout; level and to falls only										
50mm thick	28.63	10.00	31.50	-	1.35	21.02	2.34	54.86	m²	60.35
laid in straight herringbone pattern; level and to falls only										
50mm thick	28.63	10.00	31.50	-	1.50	23.35	2.34	57.20	m²	62.91
Brick paving on concrete base; 13mm thick bedding, jointing and pointing in cement mortar (1:3)										
Paving to falls and crossfalls and to slopes not exceeding 15 degrees from horizontal										
25mm thick Brick paviors P.C. £400.00 per 1000	24.00	5.00	25.20	2.75	1.55	81.53	1.72	108.44	m²	119.29
65mm thick Facing bricks P.C. £500.00 per 1000	30.00	5.00	31.50	2.75	1.55	81.53	1.72	114.74	m²	126.22
50mm thick blue chequered paviors P.C. £700.00 per 1000	42.00	5.00	44.10	2.75	1.55	81.53	1.72	127.34	m²	140.08
50mm thick blue chequered paviors P.C. £800.00 per 1000	48.00	5.00	50.40	2.75	1.55	81.53	1.72	133.64	m²	147.01
Granite sett paving on concrete base; 13mm thick bedding and grouting in cement mortar (1:3)										
Paving to falls and crossfalls and to slopes not exceeding 15 degrees from horizontal										
100mm thick; new	97.99	2.50	100.32	1.80	2.20	71.82	3.81	175.95	m²	193.54
150mm thick; new	105.70	2.50	108.20	2.00	2.35	78.33	4.36	190.89	m²	209.98
100mm thick; reclaimed	135.28	2.50	138.55	1.65	2.00	65.58	3.27	207.40	m²	228.14
150mm thick; reclaimed	114.99	2.50	117.74	1.80	2.20	71.82	3.81	193.37	m²	212.71
200mm thick; reclaimed	269.70	2.50	276.30	2.00	2.35	78.33	4.36	358.99	m²	394.89
Cobble paving set in concrete bed (measured separately) tight butted, dry grouted with cement and sand (1:3) watered and brushed										
Paving level and to falls only										
plain	44.17	2.50	45.27	1.65	1.65	60.13	4.21	109.60	m²	120.57
set to pattern	44.17	2.50	45.27	2.00	2.00	72.88	4.21	122.36	m²	134.59
Crazy paving on blinded hardcore base, bedding in 38mm thick sand; pointing in cement mortar (1:4)										
Paving to falls and crossfalls and to slopes not exceeding 15 degrees from horizontal										
50mm thick precast concrete flag	12.47	2.50	12.78	0.40	0.40	14.58	3.55	30.91	m²	34.00
38-50mm thick York stone	26.00	2.50	26.65	0.60	0.60	21.86	5.11	53.63	m²	58.99
25-40mm thick Llandraw Sandstone	29.00	2.50	29.72	0.60	0.60	21.86	3.55	55.14	m²	60.65
Grass concrete paving; voids filled with vegetable soil and sown with grass seed										
Precast concrete perforated slabs										
100mm thick units on 25mm thick sand bed; level and to falls only	55.63	2.50	57.40	0.32	0.32	11.66	-	69.06	m²	75.97
HARD LANDSCAPING; SITE FURNITURE										
Plain ordinary portland cement precast concrete bollards; Broxap Ltd; setting in ground, excavating hole, removing surplus spoil, filling with concrete mix ST4; working around base										
200mm diameter										
600mm high above ground level; Smooth Grey	69.00	-	69.00	0.50	0.50	18.22	5.11	92.33	nr	101.57
225mm diameter tapering										
900mm high above ground level; Smooth Grey	82.00	-	82.00	0.90	0.90	32.80	5.11	119.91	nr	131.90

Labour hourly rates: (except Specialists) Craft Operatives 20.87 Labourer 15.57 Rates are national average prices. Refer to REGIONAL VARIATIONS for indicative levels of overall pricing in regions	MATERIALS			LABOUR				RATES		
	Del to Site £	Waste %	Material Cost £	Craft Optve Hrs	Lab Hrs	Labour Cost £	Sunds £	Nett Rate £	Unit	Gross rate (10%) £
HARD LANDSCAPING; SITE FURNITURE (Cont'd)										
Cast Iron litter bin with galvanised liner; Broxap Ltd; setting in position										
Round; heavy duty										
90 litres capacity; Medium	675.00	-	675.00	1.00	1.00	36.44	0.53	711.97	nr	783.16
150 litres capacity; Large	765.00	-	765.00	1.00	1.00	36.44	0.63	802.07	nr	882.27
Benches and seats; Steel framed with recycled plastic slats; Broxap Ltd; fixed or free-standing										
Bench; placing in position										
1800mm long seat; five plastic slats	328.00	-	328.00	0.50	0.50	18.22	-	346.22	nr	380.84
1800mm long bench; three plastic slats	229.00	-	229.00	0.50	0.50	18.22	-	247.22	nr	271.94
Steel cycle rack, Broxap Ltd; galvanised steel construction; free standing										
Single sided										
Fishpond rack for 6 cycles	516.00	-	516.00	1.00	0.25	24.76	-	540.76	nr	594.84
Double sided										
Fishpond rack for 11 cycles	661.00	-	661.00	1.50	0.40	37.53	-	698.53	nr	768.39
Steel front wheel cycle supports; Broxap Ltd; galvanised steel construction, pillar mounted; bolting base plate to concrete										
Stands at 800mm centres										
5 stands	250.00	-	250.00	4.00	1.00	99.05	-	349.05	nr	383.96
6 stands	313.00	-	313.00	6.00	1.50	148.58	-	461.58	nr	507.73
Galvanised Steel shelters, Broxap Ltd; box section framing; 4mm 'ClearView' roofing; cycle rack not included; assembling; bolting to concrete										
Horizontal loading, single sided; Lightwood										
4100mm long	2363.00	-	2363.00	8.00	2.00	198.10	-	2561.10	nr	2817.21
5000mm long	2802.00	-	2802.00	8.00	2.00	198.10	-	3000.10	nr	3300.11

Labour hourly rates: (except Specialists) Craft Operatives 20.87 Labourer 15.57 Rates are national average prices. Refer to REGIONAL VARIATIONS for indicative levels of overall pricing in regions	MATERIALS			LABOUR				RATES		
	Del to Site £	Waste %	Material Cost £	Craft Optve Hrs	Lab Hrs	Labour Cost £	Sunds £	Nett Rate £	Unit	Gross rate (10%) £
POST AND WIRE FENCING										
Fencing; strained wire; BS 1722-2; concrete posts and struts; 4.00mm diameter galvanised mild steel line wires; galvanised steel fittings and accessories; backfilling around posts in concrete mix ST4										
900mm high fencing; type SC90; wires -3; posts with rounded tops										
posts at 2743mm centres; 600mm into ground	7.61	2.50	7.73	-	0.75	11.68	-	19.41	m	21.35
extra; end posts with struts -1	49.07	2.50	50.17	-	1.00	15.57	-	65.74	nr	72.32
extra; angle posts with struts -2	78.58	2.50	80.36	-	1.50	23.35	-	103.71	nr	114.08
1050mm high fencing; type SC105A; wires-5; posts rounded tops										
posts at 2743mm centres; 600mm into ground	9.08	2.50	9.24	-	0.80	12.46	-	21.70	m	23.87
extra; end posts with struts -1	53.77	2.50	54.99	-	1.10	17.13	-	72.11	nr	79.33
extra; angle posts with struts -2	84.82	2.50	86.75	-	1.65	25.69	-	112.44	nr	123.69
CHAIN LINK FENCING										
Fencing; chain link; BS 1722-1; concrete posts; galvanised mesh, line and tying wires; galvanised steel fittings and accessories; backfilling around posts in concrete mix ST4										
900mm high fencing; type GLC 90; posts with rounded tops										
posts at 2743mm centres; 600mm into ground	12.64	5.00	13.14	-	1.00	15.57	-	28.71	m	31.58
extra; end posts with struts -1	48.26	5.00	50.42	-	1.20	18.68	-	69.11	nr	76.02
extra; angle posts with struts -2	74.95	5.00	78.32	-	1.60	24.91	-	103.23	nr	113.56
1200mm high fencing; type GLC 120; posts with rounded tops										
posts at 2743mm centres; 600mm into ground	15.54	5.00	16.19	-	1.10	17.13	-	33.31	m	36.65
extra; end posts with struts -1	54.98	5.00	57.48	-	1.40	21.80	-	79.27	nr	87.20
extra; angle posts with struts -2	87.24	5.00	91.23	-	1.80	28.03	-	119.25	nr	131.18
1500mm high fencing; posts with rounded tops										
posts at 2743mm centres; 600mm into ground	18.44	5.00	19.24	-	1.20	18.68	-	37.92	m	41.72
extra; end posts with struts -1	65.80	5.00	68.83	-	1.55	24.13	-	92.97	nr	102.26
extra; angle posts with struts -2	104.64	5.00	109.50	-	2.00	31.14	-	140.64	nr	154.70
1800mm high fencing; posts with rounded tops										
posts at 2743mm centres; 600mm into ground	21.63	5.00	22.58	-	1.45	22.58	-	45.16	m	49.68
extra; end posts with struts -1	76.02	5.00	79.57	-	1.65	25.69	-	105.26	nr	115.78
extra; angle posts with struts -2	120.20	5.00	125.83	-	2.15	33.48	-	159.31	nr	175.24
Fencing; chain link; BS 1722-1; concrete posts; plastics coated Grade A mesh, line and tying wire; galvanised steel fittings and accessories; backfilling around posts in concrete mix ST4										
900mm high fencing; type PLC 90A; posts with rounded tops										
posts at 2743mm centres; 600mm into ground	11.31	5.00	11.75	-	1.00	15.57	-	27.32	m	30.06
extra; end posts with struts -1	49.07	5.00	51.27	-	1.20	18.68	-	69.96	nr	76.95
extra; angle posts with struts -2	76.16	5.00	79.59	-	1.60	24.91	-	104.50	nr	114.95
1200mm high fencing; type PLC 120; posts with rounded tops										
posts at 2743mm centres; 600mm into ground	13.91	5.00	14.48	-	1.10	17.13	-	31.60	m	34.76
extra; end posts with struts -1	56.19	5.00	58.75	-	1.40	21.80	-	80.54	nr	88.60
extra; angle posts with struts -2	89.66	5.00	93.76	-	1.80	28.03	-	121.79	nr	133.97
1500mm high fencing; type PLC 140A; posts with rounded tops										
posts at 2743mm centres; 600mm into ground	17.27	5.00	18.01	-	1.20	18.68	-	36.69	m	40.36
extra; end posts with struts -1	67.01	5.00	70.10	-	1.55	24.13	-	94.24	nr	103.66
extra; angle posts with struts -2	107.06	5.00	112.03	-	2.00	31.14	-	143.17	nr	157.49
1800mm high fencing; type PLC 180; posts with rounded tops										
posts at 2743mm centres; 600mm into ground	19.10	5.00	19.93	-	1.45	22.58	-	42.51	m	46.76
extra; end posts with struts -1	77.23	5.00	80.84	-	1.65	25.69	-	106.53	nr	117.18
extra; angle posts with struts -2	122.62	5.00	128.37	-	2.15	33.48	-	161.85	nr	178.03
Fencing; chain link; BS 1722-1; rolled steel angle posts; galvanised mesh, line and tying wires; galvanised steel fittings and accessories; backfilling around posts in concrete mix ST4										
900mm high fencing; type GLS 90; posts with rounded tops										
posts at 2743mm centres; 600mm into ground	13.26	2.50	13.51	-	0.65	10.12	-	23.63	m	26.00
extra; end posts with struts -1	51.40	2.50	52.53	-	1.00	15.57	-	68.10	nr	74.91
extra; angle posts with struts -2	62.49	2.50	63.83	-	1.60	24.91	-	88.74	nr	97.61
1200mm high fencing; type GLS 120; posts with rounded tops										
posts at 2743mm centres; 600mm into ground	15.80	2.50	16.12	-	0.75	11.68	-	27.80	m	30.58
extra; end posts with struts -1	60.33	2.50	61.68	-	1.10	17.13	-	78.81	nr	86.69
extra; angle posts with struts -2	83.24	2.50	85.10	-	1.75	27.25	-	112.34	nr	123.58
1500mm high fencing; type GLS 140A; posts with rounded tops										
posts at 2743mm centres; 600mm into ground	17.04	2.50	17.39	-	0.80	12.46	-	29.85	m	32.83
extra; end posts with struts -1	65.29	2.50	66.77	-	1.50	23.35	-	90.13	nr	99.14
extra; angle posts with struts -2	90.49	2.50	92.53	-	1.90	29.58	-	122.11	nr	134.32

Labour hourly rates: (except Specialists) Craft Operatives 20.87 Labourer 15.57 Rates are national average prices. Refer to REGIONAL VARIATIONS for indicative levels of overall pricing in regions	MATERIALS			LABOUR				RATES		
	Del to Site £	Waste %	Material Cost £	Craft Optve Hrs	Lab Hrs	Labour Cost £	Sunds £	Nett Rate £	Unit	Gross rate (10%) £
CHAIN LINK FENCING (Cont'd)										
Fencing; chain link; BS 1722-1; rolled steel angle posts; galvanised mesh, line and tying wires; galvanised steel fittings and accessories; backfilling around posts in concrete mix ST4 (Cont'd)										
1800mm high fencing; type GLS 180; posts with rounded tops										
posts at 2743mm centres; 600mm into ground	20.47	2.50	20.90	-	1.00	15.57	-	36.47	m	40.12
extra; end posts with struts -1	77.43	2.50	79.22	-	1.60	24.91	-	104.13	nr	114.54
extra; angle posts with struts -2	106.75	2.50	109.19	-	2.10	32.70	-	141.89	nr	156.08
Fencing; chain link; BS 1722 Part 1; rolled steel angle posts; plastics coated Grade A mesh, line and tying wires; galvanised steel fittings and accessories; backfilling around posts in concrete mix ST4										
900mm high fencing; type PLS 90A; posts with rounded tops										
posts at 2743mm centres; 600mm into ground	12.19	5.00	12.65	-	0.65	10.12	-	22.77	m	25.05
extra; end posts with struts -1	51.40	5.00	53.67	-	1.00	15.57	-	69.24	nr	76.16
extra; angle posts with struts -2	62.49	5.00	65.16	-	1.60	24.91	-	90.07	nr	99.08
1200mm high fencing; type PLS 120; posts with rounded tops										
posts at 2743mm centres; 600mm into ground	14.43	5.00	14.99	-	0.75	11.68	-	26.67	m	29.34
extra; end posts with struts -1	60.33	5.00	63.04	-	1.10	17.13	-	80.17	nr	88.18
extra; angle posts with struts -2	83.24	5.00	86.95	-	1.75	27.25	-	114.20	nr	125.62
1500mm high fencing; type PLS 140A; posts with rounded tops										
posts at 2743mm centres; 600mm into ground	16.12	5.00	16.78	-	0.80	12.46	-	29.23	m	32.16
extra; end posts with struts -1	65.29	5.00	68.25	-	1.50	23.35	-	91.61	nr	100.77
extra; angle posts with struts -2	90.49	5.00	94.56	-	1.90	29.58	-	124.14	nr	136.56
1800mm high fencing; type PLS 180; posts with rounded tops										
posts at 2743mm centres; 600mm into ground	18.37	5.00	19.14	-	1.00	15.57	-	34.71	m	38.18
extra; end posts with struts -1	77.43	5.00	81.00	-	1.60	24.91	-	105.91	nr	116.50
extra; angle posts with struts -2	106.75	5.00	111.63	-	2.10	32.70	-	144.33	nr	158.76
CHESTNUT FENCING										
Fencing; cleft chestnut pale; BS 1722 Part 4; sweet chestnut posts and struts; galvanised accessories; backfilling around posts in concrete mix ST4										
900mm high fencing; type CW90										
posts at 2000mm centres; 600mm into ground	27.19	5.00	28.09	-	0.25	3.89	-	31.98	m	35.18
extra; end posts with struts - 1	48.81	5.00	50.32	-	0.30	4.67	-	54.99	nr	60.49
extra; angle posts with struts - 2	60.99	5.00	62.64	-	0.40	6.23	-	68.87	nr	75.76
1200mm high fencing; type CW 120										
posts at 2000mm centres; 600mm into ground	33.89	5.00	35.12	-	0.17	2.65	-	37.77	m	41.54
extra; end posts with struts - 1	50.16	5.00	51.74	-	0.45	7.01	-	58.74	nr	64.62
extra; angle posts with struts - 2	63.69	5.00	65.48	-	0.60	9.34	-	74.82	nr	82.30
1500mm high fencing; type CW 150										
posts at 2000mm centres; 600mm into ground	39.98	5.00	41.51	-	0.22	3.43	-	44.93	m	49.43
extra; end posts with struts - 1	52.72	5.00	54.42	-	0.50	7.78	-	62.20	nr	68.42
extra; angle posts with struts - 2	66.99	5.00	68.94	-	0.65	10.12	-	79.07	nr	86.97
BOARDED FENCING										
Fencing; close boarded; BS 1722 Part 5; sawn softwood posts, rails, pales, gravel boards and centre stumps, pressure impregnated with preservative; backfilling around posts in concrete mix ST4										
1200mm high fencing; type BW 120										
posts at 3000mm centres; 600mm into ground	44.23	5.00	45.82	1.25	-	26.09	-	71.91	m	79.10
1500mm high fencing; type BW 150										
posts at 3000mm centres; 600mm into ground	53.01	5.00	55.05	1.50	-	31.31	-	86.36	m	94.99
1800mm high fencing; type BW 180A										
posts at 3000mm centres; 750mm into ground	57.64	5.00	59.91	1.67	-	34.85	-	94.76	m	104.24
Fencing; wooden palisade; BS 1722-5; softwood posts, rails, pales and stumps; pressure impregnated with preservative; backfilling around posts in concrete mix ST4										
1050mm high fencing; type WPW 105; 75 x 19mm rectangular pales with pointed tops										
posts at 3000mm centres; 600mm into ground	39.23	5.00	40.58	1.00	-	20.87	-	61.45	m	67.60
1200mm high fencing; type WPW 120; 75 x 19mm rectangular pales with pointed tops										
posts at 3000mm centres; 600mm into ground	43.18	5.00	44.73	1.25	-	26.09	-	70.81	m	77.90
STEEL RAILINGS										
Ornamental steel railings; Cannock Gates (UK) Ltd.; primed at works; fixing in brick openings										
Clifton Railings										
457mm high for 914mm gap width	82.00	1.50	83.23	0.75	0.38	21.57	0.35	105.15	nr	115.66
457mm high for 1829mm gap width	105.00	1.50	106.57	1.00	0.50	28.66	0.35	135.58	nr	149.13
457mm high for 2743mm gap width	127.00	1.50	128.90	1.50	0.75	42.98	0.35	172.23	nr	189.46
610mm high for 914mm gap width	85.00	1.50	86.28	0.75	0.38	21.57	0.35	108.19	nr	119.01
610mm high for 1829mm gap width	111.00	1.50	112.67	1.00	0.50	28.66	0.35	141.67	nr	155.83
610mm high for 2743mm gap width	138.00	1.50	140.07	1.50	0.75	42.98	0.35	183.40	nr	201.74
914mm high for 914mm gap width	91.00	1.50	92.36	1.50	0.75	42.98	0.35	135.69	nr	149.26
914mm high for 1829mm gap width	125.00	1.50	126.88	0.75	0.38	21.57	0.35	148.79	nr	163.67

Labour hourly rates: (except Specialists) Craft Operatives 20.87 Labourer 15.57 Rates are national average prices. Refer to REGIONAL VARIATIONS for indicative levels of overall pricing in regions	MATERIALS			LABOUR				RATES		
	Del to Site £	Waste %	Material Cost £	Craft Optve Hrs	Lab Hrs	Labour Cost £	Sunds £	Nett Rate £	Unit	Gross rate (10%) £
STEEL RAILINGS (Cont'd)										
Ornamental steel railings; Cannock Gates (UK) Ltd.; primed at works; fixing in brick openings (Cont'd)										
Clifton Railings (Cont'd)										
914mm high for 2743mm gap width	153.00	1.50	155.29	1.50	0.75	42.98	0.43	198.71	nr	218.58
Winchester Railings										
457mm high for 914mm gap width	78.90	1.50	80.08	0.75	0.38	21.57	0.35	102.00	nr	112.20
457mm high for 1829mm gap width	100.00	1.50	101.50	1.00	0.50	28.66	0.35	130.50	nr	143.55
457mm high for 2743mm gap width	125.60	1.50	127.48	1.50	0.75	42.98	0.35	170.81	nr	187.89
610mm high for 914mm gap width	81.20	1.50	82.42	0.75	0.38	21.57	0.35	104.33	nr	114.77
610mm high for 1829mm gap width	103.40	1.50	104.95	1.00	0.50	28.66	0.35	133.95	nr	147.35
610mm high for 2743mm gap width	130.00	1.50	131.95	1.50	0.75	42.98	0.35	175.28	nr	192.81
914mm high for 914mm gap width	84.50	1.50	85.77	1.50	0.75	42.98	0.35	129.10	nr	142.01
914mm high for 1829mm gap width	105.60	1.50	107.18	0.75	0.38	21.57	0.35	129.10	nr	142.01
914mm high for 2743mm gap width	132.30	1.50	134.28	1.50	0.75	42.98	0.43	177.70	nr	195.47
Marlborough Railings										
457mm high for 914mm gap width	83.00	1.50	84.24	0.75	0.38	21.57	0.35	106.16	nr	116.78
457mm high for 1829mm gap width	109.00	1.50	110.64	1.00	0.50	28.66	0.35	139.64	nr	153.60
457mm high for 2743mm gap width	134.00	1.50	136.01	1.50	0.75	42.98	0.35	179.34	nr	197.27
610mm high for 914mm gap width	86.00	1.50	87.29	0.75	0.38	21.57	0.35	109.21	nr	120.13
610mm high for 1829mm gap width	114.00	1.50	115.71	1.00	0.50	28.66	0.35	144.71	nr	159.18
610mm high for 2743mm gap width	150.00	1.50	152.25	1.50	0.75	42.98	0.35	195.58	nr	215.14
914mm high for 914mm gap width	92.00	1.50	93.38	1.50	0.75	42.98	0.35	136.71	nr	150.38
914mm high for 1829mm gap width	128.00	1.50	129.92	0.75	0.38	21.57	0.35	151.84	nr	167.02
914mm high for 2743mm gap width	160.00	1.50	162.40	1.50	0.75	42.98	0.43	205.81	nr	226.39
Royale Talisman Railings										
457mm high for 914mm gap width	258.90	1.50	262.78	0.75	0.38	21.57	0.35	284.70	nr	313.17
457mm high for 1829mm gap width	478.90	1.50	486.08	1.00	0.50	28.66	0.35	515.09	nr	566.59
457mm high for 2743mm gap width	714.50	1.50	725.22	1.50	0.75	42.98	0.35	768.55	nr	845.40
610mm high for 914mm gap width	262.30	1.50	266.23	0.75	0.38	21.57	0.35	288.15	nr	316.97
610mm high for 1829mm gap width	497.80	1.50	505.27	1.00	0.50	28.66	0.35	534.27	nr	587.70
610mm high for 2743mm gap width	742.30	1.50	753.43	1.50	0.75	42.98	0.35	796.76	nr	876.44
914mm high for 914mm gap width	270.60	1.50	274.66	1.50	0.75	42.98	0.35	317.99	nr	349.79
914mm high for 1829mm gap width	493.40	1.50	500.80	0.75	0.38	21.57	0.35	522.72	nr	574.99
914mm high for 2743mm gap width	772.30	1.50	783.88	1.50	0.75	42.98	0.43	827.30	nr	910.03
GUARD RAILS										
Aluminium guard rail of tubing to BS EN 10255; medium grade with Kee Klamp fittings										
Rail or standard										
42mm diameter	15.53	5.00	16.31	0.25	-	5.22	0.50	22.02	m	24.22
extra; flanged end	7.55	5.00	7.93	-	-	-	-	7.93	nr	8.72
extra; bend No.15-7	8.68	5.00	9.12	0.15	-	3.13	-	12.25	nr	13.47
extra; three-way intersection No.20-7	13.09	5.00	13.75	0.15	-	3.13	-	16.88	nr	18.56
extra; three-way intersection No.25-7	12.50	5.00	13.12	0.15	-	3.13	-	16.26	nr	17.88
extra; four-way intersection No.21-7	10.23	5.00	10.74	0.15	-	3.13	-	13.88	nr	15.26
extra; four-way intersection No.26-7	9.66	5.00	10.14	0.15	-	3.13	-	13.27	nr	14.60
extra; five-way intersection No.35-7	13.98	5.00	14.68	0.15	-	3.13	-	17.81	nr	19.59
extra; five-way intersection No.40-7	20.81	5.00	21.85	0.15	-	3.13	-	24.98	nr	27.48
extra; floor plate No.61-7	11.06	5.00	11.61	0.15	-	3.13	-	14.74	nr	16.22
Infill panel fixed with clips										
50 x 50mm welded mesh	33.25	5.00	34.91	0.80	-	16.70	0.33	51.94	m²	57.13
PRECAST CONCRETE POSTS										
Precast concrete fence posts; BS 1722 excavating holes, backfilling around posts in concrete mix C20, disposing of surplus materials, earthwork support										
Fence posts for three wires, housing pattern										
100 x 100mm tapering intermediate post 1570mm long; 600mm into ground	18.02	2.50	18.38	0.25	0.25	9.11	-	27.49	nr	30.24
100 x 100mm square strainer post (end or intermediate) 1570mm long; 600mm into ground	20.48	2.50	20.90	0.25	0.25	9.11	-	30.01	nr	33.01
Clothes line post										
125 x 125mm tapering, 2670mm long	48.88	2.50	50.01	0.33	0.33	12.03	-	62.03	nr	68.23
Close boarded fence post										
94 x 100mm, 2745mm long	33.51	2.50	34.25	0.40	0.40	14.58	-	48.82	nr	53.71
Slotted fence post										
94 x 100mm, 2625mm long	22.08	2.50	22.54	0.40	0.40	14.58	-	37.11	nr	40.82
Chain link fence post for 1800mm high fencing										
125 x 75mm tapering intermediate post, 2620mm long	31.84	2.50	32.54	0.33	0.33	12.03	-	44.56	nr	49.02
125 x 125mm end post, 1 strut, 2620mm long	57.81	2.50	59.06	0.66	0.66	24.05	-	83.11	nr	91.42
125 x 125mm angle post, 2 strut, 2620mm long	76.82	2.50	78.45	0.99	0.99	36.08	-	114.53	nr	125.98
125 x 125mm gate post, 2620mm long	27.56	2.50	28.16	0.33	0.33	12.03	-	40.18	nr	44.20
150 x 150mm gate post, 2620mm long	59.31	2.50	60.70	0.33	0.33	12.03	-	72.72	nr	79.99
GATES										
Gates; impregnated wrought softwood; featheredge pales; including ring latch and heavy hinges										
Gates (posts included elsewhere)										
900 x 1200mm	66.79	2.50	68.46	0.50	0.50	18.22	0.28	86.96	nr	95.66
900 x 1500mm	75.79	2.50	77.69	0.50	0.50	18.22	0.28	96.19	nr	105.81

Labour hourly rates: (except Specialists) Craft Operatives 20.87 Labourer 15.57 Rates are national average prices. Refer to REGIONAL VARIATIONS for indicative levels of overall pricing in regions	MATERIALS			LABOUR				RATES		
	Del to Site £	Waste %	Material Cost £	Craft Optve Hrs	Lab Hrs	Labour Cost £	Sunds £	Nett Rate £	Unit	Gross rate (10%) £
GATES (Cont'd)										
Ornamental steel gates; Cannock Gates (UK) Ltd.; primed at works; fixing in brick openings										
Clifton, 914mm high										
single gate, for 762mm wide opening	73.00	1.50	74.10	1.50	0.75	42.98	0.45	117.52	nr	129.28
single gate, for 838mm wide opening	80.00	1.50	81.20	1.50	0.75	42.98	0.45	124.63	nr	137.09
single gate, for 914mm wide opening	81.00	1.50	82.21	1.50	0.75	42.98	0.45	125.64	nr	138.21
single gate, for 991mm wide opening	87.00	1.50	88.31	1.50	0.75	42.98	0.45	131.73	nr	144.91
single gate, for 1067mm wide opening	88.00	1.50	89.32	1.50	0.75	42.98	0.45	132.75	nr	146.02
double gate, for 2286mm wide opening	180.00	1.50	182.70	2.25	1.12	64.47	0.81	247.98	nr	272.78
double gate, for 2591mm wide opening	186.00	1.50	188.79	2.25	1.12	64.47	0.81	254.07	nr	279.48
double gate, for 2743mm wide opening	195.00	1.50	197.93	2.25	1.12	64.47	0.81	263.21	nr	289.53
double gate, for 3048mm wide opening	208.00	1.50	211.12	2.25	1.12	64.47	0.81	276.40	nr	304.04
double gate, for 3658mm wide opening	246.00	1.50	249.69	2.25	1.12	64.47	0.81	314.97	nr	346.47
Clifton Arch Top, 1219mm high										
single gate, for 762mm wide opening	87.00	1.50	88.31	1.50	0.75	42.98	0.81	132.10	nr	145.31
single gate, for 1067mm wide opening	109.00	1.50	110.64	2.25	1.12	64.47	0.81	175.92	nr	193.51
Clifton, 1829mm high										
single gate, for 762mm wide opening	112.00	1.50	113.68	1.50	0.75	42.98	0.45	157.11	nr	172.82
single gate, for 1067mm wide opening	142.00	1.50	144.13	1.50	0.75	42.98	0.45	187.56	nr	206.31
double gate, for 2286mm wide opening	318.00	1.50	322.77	2.25	2.25	81.99	0.81	405.57	nr	446.13
double gate, for 2743mm wide opening	372.00	1.50	377.58	2.25	2.25	81.99	0.81	460.38	nr	506.42
double gate, for 3048mm wide opening	409.00	1.50	415.13	2.25	2.25	81.99	0.81	497.93	nr	547.73
Winchester, 914mm high										
double gate, for 2438mm wide opening	196.70	1.50	199.65	2.25	1.12	64.47	0.81	264.93	nr	291.43
double gate, for 2743mm wide opening	205.60	1.50	208.68	2.25	1.12	64.47	0.81	273.97	nr	301.36
double gate, for 3048mm wide opening	216.70	1.50	219.95	2.25	1.12	64.47	0.81	285.23	nr	313.76
double gate, for 3658mm wide opening	250.00	1.50	253.75	2.25	1.12	64.47	0.81	319.03	nr	350.94
Winchester, 914mm high										
single gate, for 762mm wide opening	73.35	1.50	74.45	1.50	0.75	42.98	0.45	117.88	nr	129.67
single gate, for 1067mm wide opening	90.00	1.50	91.35	1.50	0.75	42.98	0.45	134.78	nr	148.26
Winchester, 1829mm high										
single gate, for 762mm wide opening	120.00	1.50	121.80	1.50	0.75	42.98	0.45	165.23	nr	181.75
single gate, for 1067mm wide opening	151.20	1.50	153.47	1.50	0.75	42.98	0.45	196.90	nr	216.59
double gate, for 2286mm wide opening	315.60	1.50	320.33	2.25	2.25	81.99	0.81	403.13	nr	443.45
double gate, for 2743mm wide opening	366.70	1.50	372.20	2.25	2.25	81.99	0.81	455.00	nr	500.50
double gate, for 3048mm wide opening	402.30	1.50	408.33	2.25	2.25	81.99	0.81	491.13	nr	540.25
Cromwell, 914mm high										
single gate, for 762mm wide opening	102.00	1.50	103.53	1.50	0.75	42.98	0.45	146.96	nr	161.65
single gate, for 1067mm wide opening	128.00	1.50	129.92	1.50	0.75	42.98	0.45	173.35	nr	190.68
double gate, for 2286mm wide opening	280.00	1.50	284.20	2.25	1.12	64.47	0.81	349.48	nr	384.43
double gate, for 2591mm wide opening	348.00	1.50	353.22	2.25	1.12	64.47	0.81	418.50	nr	460.35
double gate, for 2896mm wide opening	374.00	1.50	379.61	2.25	1.12	64.47	0.81	444.89	nr	489.38
double gate, for 3200mm wide opening	393.00	1.50	398.89	2.25	1.12	64.47	0.81	464.18	nr	510.60
double gate, for 3505mm wide opening	414.00	1.50	420.21	2.25	1.12	64.47	0.81	485.49	nr	534.04
double gate, for 3658mm wide opening	421.00	1.50	427.32	2.25	1.12	64.47	0.81	492.60	nr	541.86
Cromwell, 1219mm high										
single gate, for 762mm wide opening	116.00	1.50	117.74	1.50	0.75	42.98	0.45	161.17	nr	177.28
single gate, for 1067mm wide opening	128.00	1.50	129.92	1.50	0.75	42.98	0.45	173.35	nr	190.68
Marlborough, 914mm high										
single gate, for 762mm wide opening	80.00	1.50	81.20	1.50	0.75	42.98	0.45	124.63	nr	137.09
single gate, for 1067mm wide opening	103.00	1.50	104.54	1.50	0.75	42.98	0.45	147.97	nr	162.77
double gate, for 2286mm wide opening	195.00	1.50	197.93	2.25	1.12	64.47	0.81	263.21	nr	289.53
double gate, for 3658mm wide opening	278.00	1.50	282.17	2.25	1.12	64.47	0.81	347.45	nr	382.20
folding (4 piece) gate, for 2286mm wide opening	265.00	1.50	268.98	3.00	1.50	85.97	0.82	355.77	nr	391.34
folding (4 piece) gate, for 3658mm wide opening	345.00	1.50	350.17	3.00	1.50	85.97	0.82	436.97	nr	480.66
Marlborough, 1219mm high										
single gate, for 762mm wide opening	85.00	1.50	86.28	1.50	0.75	42.98	0.45	129.70	nr	142.67
single gate, for 1067mm wide opening	108.00	1.50	109.62	1.50	0.75	42.98	0.45	153.05	nr	168.35
double gate, for 2286mm wide opening	212.00	1.50	215.18	2.25	1.12	64.47	0.81	280.46	nr	308.51
double gate, for 3048mm wide opening	267.00	1.50	271.01	2.25	1.12	64.47	0.81	336.29	nr	369.92
Marlborough, 1829mm high										
single gate, for 762mm wide opening	119.00	1.50	120.78	1.50	0.75	42.98	0.45	164.21	nr	180.63
single gate, for 1067mm wide opening	154.00	1.50	156.31	1.50	0.75	42.98	0.45	199.74	nr	219.71
double gate, for 2286mm wide opening	413.00	1.50	419.20	3.00	3.00	109.32	0.99	529.51	nr	582.46
double gate, for 3658mm wide opening	615.00	1.50	624.22	3.30	3.00	115.58	1.65	741.46	nr	815.60
Royale Talisman, 1219mm high										
single gate, for 914mm wide opening	266.70	1.50	270.70	1.75	0.88	50.15	0.66	321.51	nr	353.66
single gate, for 1067mm wide opening	300.00	1.50	304.50	1.75	0.88	50.15	0.66	355.31	nr	390.84
double gate, for 2438mm wide opening	731.15	1.50	742.12	3.00	1.50	85.97	1.32	829.40	nr	912.34
double gate, for 3200mm wide opening	850.00	1.50	862.75	3.00	1.50	85.97	1.32	950.03	nr	1045.04
double gate, for 4267mm wide opening	1476.70	1.50	1498.85	3.60	1.80	103.16	1.32	1603.33	nr	1763.66
Royale Talisman, 1829mm high										
single gate, for 914mm wide opening	353.40	1.50	358.70	1.75	0.88	50.15	0.66	409.51	nr	450.46
single gate, for 1067mm wide opening	391.20	1.50	397.07	1.75	0.88	50.15	0.66	447.87	nr	492.66
arched double gate, for 2438m wide opening	933.40	1.50	947.40	3.00	3.00	109.32	1.32	1058.04	nr	1163.85
arched double gate, for 3200mm wide opening	1110.00	1.50	1126.65	3.00	3.00	109.32	1.32	1237.29	nr	1361.02
arched double gate, for 4267mm wide opening	1446.70	1.50	1468.40	3.50	3.50	127.54	1.32	1597.26	nr	1756.99
arched double gate, for 4877mm wide opening	1682.30	1.50	1707.53	3.50	3.50	127.54	1.32	1836.39	nr	2020.03
double gate, for 2438mm wide opening	888.90	1.50	902.23	3.00	3.00	109.32	1.32	1012.87	nr	1114.16
double gate, for 4877mm wide opening	1455.60	1.50	1477.43	3.50	3.50	127.54	1.32	1606.29	nr	1766.92

Labour hourly rates: (except Specialists) Craft Operatives 20.87 Labourer 15.57 Rates are national average prices. Refer to REGIONAL VARIATIONS for indicative levels of overall pricing in regions	MATERIALS			LABOUR				RATES		
	Del to Site £	Waste %	Material Cost £	Craft Optve Hrs	Lab Hrs	Labour Cost £	Sunds £	Nett Rate £	Unit	Gross rate (10%) £
GATES (Cont'd)										
Ornamental steel gates; Cannock Gates (UK) Ltd.; primed at works; fixing in brick openings (Cont'd)										
Extra cost of fixing gates to and including pair of steel gate posts; backfilling around posts in concrete mix ST4										
for single or double gates 914 high; posts section 'C', size 50 x 50mm	89.56	1.50	90.97	0.33	0.17	9.53	-	100.88	nr	110.97
for single or double gates 1220 high; posts section 'C', size 50 x 50mm	98.31	1.50	99.85	0.33	0.17	9.53	-	109.76	nr	120.74
for single or double gates 1830 high; posts section 'C', size 50 x 50mm	122.16	1.50	124.07	0.33	0.17	9.53	-	134.06	nr	147.47
for single or double gates 1220 high; posts section 'B', size 75 x 75mm	110.56	1.50	112.28	0.33	0.17	9.53	-	122.20	nr	134.42
for single or double gates 1830 high; posts section 'B', size 75 x 75m	122.16	1.50	124.07	0.33	0.17	9.53	-	134.06	nr	147.47
for single or double gates 1220 high; posts section 'A', size 100 x 100mm	132.66	1.50	134.73	0.33	0.17	9.53	-	144.72	nr	159.19
for single or double gates 1830 high; posts section 'A', size 100 x 100mm	150.52	1.50	152.87	0.33	0.17	9.53	-	162.97	nr	179.27
Gates in chain link fencing										
Gate with 40 x 40 x 5mm painted angle iron framing, braces and rails, infilled with 50mm x 10 1/2 G mesh										
1000 x 1800mm; galvanised mesh	355.83	1.50	361.16	6.00	6.00	218.64	-	579.80	nr	637.78
1000 x 1800mm; plastic coated mesh	355.83	1.50	361.16	6.00	6.00	218.64	-	579.80	nr	637.78
Gate post of 80 x 80 x 6mm painted angle iron; back-filling around posts in concrete mix C30										
to suit 1800mm high gate	80.06	1.50	81.19	1.50	1.50	54.66	-	135.85	nr	149.43

FENCING

This page left blank intentionally

Labour hourly rates: (except Specialists) Craft Operatives 20.87 Labourer 15.57 Rates are national average prices. Refer to REGIONAL VARIATIONS for indicative levels of overall pricing in regions	MATERIALS			LABOUR				RATES		
	Del to Site £	Waste %	Material Cost £	Craft Optve Hrs	Lab Hrs	Labour Cost £	Sunds £	Nett Rate £	Unit	Gross rate (10%) £
CULTIVATING										
Cultivating tilth										
Surfaces of natural ground digging over one spit deep; removing debris; weeding	-	-	-	-	0.25	3.89	-	3.89	m²	4.28
Surfaces of filling digging over one spit deep	-	-	-	-	0.30	4.67	-	4.67	m²	5.14
SURFACE APPLICATIONS										
Weedkillers										
Selective weedkiller and feed, 0.03 kg/m²; applying by spreader general surfaces	0.07	5.00	0.08	-	0.05	0.78	-	0.85	m²	0.94
Fertilizer										
Bone meal, 0.06 kg/m²; raking in general surfaces	0.04	5.00	0.04	-	0.05	0.78	-	0.82	m²	0.90
Pre-seeding fertilizer at the rate of 0.04 kg/m² general surfaces	0.17	5.00	0.18	-	0.05	0.78	-	0.96	m²	1.05
General grass fertilizer at the rate of 0.03 kg/m² general surfaces	0.03	5.00	0.03	-	0.05	0.78	-	0.81	m²	0.89
SEEDING										
Grass seed										
Grass seed, 0.035 kg/m², raking in; rolling; maintaining for 12 months after laying general surfaces	0.16	5.00	0.16	-	0.20	3.11	-	3.28	m²	3.61
Stone pick, roll and cut grass with a rotary cutter and remove arisings general surfaces	-	-	-	-	0.10	1.56	-	1.56	m²	1.71
TURFING										
Turf										
Take turf from stack, wheel not exceeding 100m, lay, roll and water, maintaining for 12 months after laying general surfaces	-	-	-	-	0.50	7.78	-	7.78	m²	8.56
Rolawn® Medallion turf; cultivated; lay, roll and water; maintaining for 12 months after laying general surfaces	4.20	5.00	4.41	-	0.50	7.78	-	12.19	m²	13.41
TREES, SHRUBS, HEDGE PLANT, PLANTS, BULBS, CORMS AND TUBERS										
Planting trees, shrubs and hedge plants										
Note; Not withstanding the requirements of NRM2 Tree stakes are measured separately as noted below, all other staking is deemed included.										
Excavate or form pit, hole or trench, dig over ground in bottom, spread and pack around roots with finely broken soil, refill with top soil with one third by volume of farmyard manure incorporated, water in, remove surplus excavated material and provide labelling										
small tree	1.10	-	1.10	-	0.85	13.23	0.64	14.97	nr	16.47
medium tree	3.74	-	3.74	-	1.65	25.69	0.92	30.35	nr	33.39
large tree	9.94	-	9.94	-	3.30	51.38	1.19	62.51	nr	68.77
shrub	2.22	-	2.22	-	0.55	8.56	0.26	11.05	nr	12.15
hedge plant	1.16	-	1.16	-	0.28	4.36	0.26	5.78	nr	6.36
60mm diameter treated softwood tree stake, pointed and driven into ground and with two PVC tree ties secured around tree and nailed to stake										
2100mm long	5.60	-	5.60	-	0.33	5.14	2.28	13.02	nr	14.32
2400mm long	6.25	-	6.25	-	0.33	5.14	2.28	13.67	nr	15.03
75mm diameter treated softwood tree stake, pointed and driven into ground and with two PVC tree ties secured around tree and nailed to stake 3000mm long	10.35	-	10.35	-	0.35	5.45	2.39	18.19	nr	20.01
BULBS, CORMS AND TUBERS										
Planting herbaceous plants, bulbs, corms and tubers										
Provide planting bed of screened and conditioned Rolawn® topsoil										
150mm thick	18.41	5.00	19.33	-	0.75	11.68	-	31.01	m²	34.11
225mm thick	27.62	5.00	29.00	-	1.12	17.44	-	46.44	m²	51.08

Labour hourly rates: (except Specialists) Craft Operatives 20.87 Labourer 15.57 Rates are national average prices. Refer to REGIONAL VARIATIONS for indicative levels of overall pricing in regions	MATERIALS			LABOUR				RATES		
	Del to Site £	Waste %	Material Cost £	Craft Optve Hrs	Lab Hrs	Labour Cost £	Sunds £	Nett Rate £	Unit	Gross rate (10%) £
BULBS, CORMS AND TUBERS (Cont'd)										
Planting herbaceous plants, bulbs, corms and tubers (Cont'd)										
Form hole and plant										
herbaceous plants	0.49	5.00	0.52	-	0.20	3.11	-	3.63	nr	3.99
bulbs, corms and tubers	0.25	5.00	0.26	-	0.10	1.56	-	1.81	nr	2.00
Mulching after planting										
25mm bark; Rolawn®	2.83	-	2.83	-	0.10	1.56	-	4.39	m²	4.83
75mm farmyard manure	6.25	-	6.25	-	0.11	1.71	-	7.96	m²	8.76
PLANT CONTAINERS										
Precast concrete plant containers; Broxap Ltd; setting in position										
Plant container (soil filling included elsewhere)										
1800 x 600 x 450mm high	871.00	-	871.00	0.70	0.70	25.51	0.50	897.00	nr	986.70
1400 x 700 x 600mm high	1300.00	-	1300.00	0.60	0.60	21.86	0.50	1322.36	nr	1454.59
1500 x 1300 x 580mm high	1480.00	-	1480.00	0.80	0.80	29.15	0.50	1509.65	nr	1660.61
Recycled plastic planter; Broxap Ltd; setting in position										
Plant container (soil filling included elsewhere)										
1200mm hexagonal x 622mm high	409.00	-	409.00	0.50	0.50	18.22	0.53	427.75	nr	470.52
900 x 900 x 900mm high	385.00	-	385.00	0.50	0.50	18.22	0.53	403.75	nr	444.12

Labour hourly rates: (except Specialists) Craft Operatives 26.39 Labourer 15.57 Rates are national average prices. Refer to REGIONAL VARIATIONS for indicative levels of overall pricing in regions	MATERIALS			LABOUR				RATES		
	Del to Site £	Waste %	Material Cost £	Craft Optve Hrs	Lab Hrs	Labour Cost £	Sunds £	Nett Rate £	Unit	Gross rate (10%) £
PRIMARY EQUIPMENT										
Gas fired boilers										
Gas fired condensing combination boilers for central heating and hot water; automatically controlled by thermostat with electrical control, gas governor and flame failure device										
wall mounted boiler; fanned flue; approximate output rating										
24 KW	671.40	1.00	678.11	8.50	-	224.32	-	902.43	nr	992.67
30 KW	730.97	1.00	738.28	9.00	-	237.51	-	975.79	nr	1073.37
35 KW	854.97	1.00	863.52	9.50	-	250.70	-	1114.22	nr	1225.64
Gas fired condensing system boilers for central heating and hot water; automatically controlled by thermostat with electrical control, gas governor and flame failure device										
floor standing boiler; fanned flue; output rating:										
18 KW	1024.08	1.00	1034.32	8.00	-	211.12	-	1245.44	nr	1369.99
24 KW	1530.90	1.00	1546.21	8.00	-	211.12	-	1757.33	nr	1933.06
30 KW	1741.44	1.00	1758.86	8.00	-	211.12	-	1969.98	nr	2166.97
wall mounted boiler; fanned flue; output rating:										
12 KW	835.82	1.00	844.18	7.50	-	197.92	-	1042.10	nr	1146.31
15 KW	877.48	1.00	886.26	7.50	-	197.92	-	1084.18	nr	1192.60
18 KW	923.32	1.00	932.55	7.50	-	197.92	-	1130.48	nr	1243.52
24 KW	985.82	1.00	995.68	7.50	-	197.92	-	1193.60	nr	1312.96
27 KW	949.60	1.00	959.10	8.00	-	211.12	-	1170.22	nr	1287.24
30 KW	953.32	1.00	962.85	8.50	-	224.32	-	1187.17	nr	1305.88
Oil fired boilers										
Oil fired boilers for central heating and hot water; automatically controlled by thermostat, with electrical control box										
free standing boiler; fan flue; approximate output rating										
12/18 KW	1260.42	1.00	1273.02	6.00	-	158.34	-	1431.36	nr	1574.50
25 KW	1591.97	1.00	1607.89	6.00	-	158.34	-	1766.23	nr	1942.85
32 KW	1753.97	1.00	1771.51	6.50	-	171.54	-	1943.04	nr	2137.35
46 KW	1976.62	1.00	1996.38	7.50	-	197.92	-	2194.31	nr	2413.74
Oil fired combination boilers for central heating and hot water; automatically controlled by thermostat, with electrical control box										
free standing boiler; fan flue; approximate output rating										
21 KW	2069.97	1.00	2090.67	6.00	-	158.34	-	2249.01	nr	2473.91
26 KW	2089.97	1.00	2110.87	6.50	-	171.54	-	2282.40	nr	2510.64
36 KW	2315.97	1.00	2339.13	7.00	-	184.73	-	2523.86	nr	2776.24
Coal fired boilers										
Solid fuel boilers for central heating and hot water; thermostatically controlled; with tools										
free standing boiler, gravity feed; approximate output rating										
13.2 KW	1650.00	1.00	1666.50	6.00	-	158.34	-	1824.84	nr	2007.32
17.6 KW	1978.00	1.00	1997.78	6.00	-	158.34	-	2156.12	nr	2371.73
23.5 KW	2150.00	1.00	2171.50	7.50	-	197.92	-	2369.43	nr	2606.37
GRP water storage tanks										
GRP Sarena mfg Ltd; pre insulated water storage tanks with cover; One piece storage tanks including cover; pre-insulated										
90 litres	264.00	2.00	269.28	1.75	-	46.18	-	315.46	nr	347.01
125 litres	251.00	2.00	256.02	1.75	-	46.18	-	302.20	nr	332.42
160 litres	302.00	2.00	308.04	2.00	-	52.78	-	360.82	nr	396.90
187 litres	316.00	2.00	322.32	2.00	-	52.78	-	375.10	nr	412.61
225 litres	338.00	2.00	344.76	2.25	-	59.38	-	404.14	nr	444.55
250 litres	377.00	2.00	384.54	2.75	-	72.57	-	457.11	nr	502.82
305 litres	433.00	2.00	441.66	3.00	-	79.17	-	520.83	nr	572.91
340 litres	442.00	2.00	450.84	3.25	-	85.77	-	536.61	nr	590.27
375 litres	505.00	2.00	515.10	3.50	-	92.36	-	607.46	nr	668.21
454 litres	493.00	2.00	502.86	4.00	-	105.56	-	608.42	nr	669.26
500 litres	522.00	2.00	532.44	4.25	-	112.16	-	644.60	nr	709.06
650 litres	616.00	2.00	628.32	4.50	-	118.75	-	747.08	nr	821.78
750 litres	682.00	2.00	695.64	4.75	-	125.35	-	820.99	nr	903.09
909 litres	734.00	2.00	748.68	5.50	-	145.14	-	893.83	nr	983.21
1000 litres	722.00	2.00	736.44	6.00	-	158.34	-	894.78	nr	984.26
1220 litres	984.00	2.00	1003.68	7.00	-	184.73	-	1188.41	nr	1307.25
1500 litres	1066.00	2.00	1087.32	8.00	-	211.12	-	1298.44	nr	1428.28
2000 litres	1272.00	2.00	1297.44	9.00	-	237.51	-	1534.95	nr	1688.44
2500 litres	1524.00	2.00	1554.48	10.00	-	263.90	-	1818.38	nr	2000.22
3000 litres	1853.00	2.00	1890.06	12.00	-	316.68	-	2206.74	nr	2427.41
5000 litres	2375.00	2.00	2422.50	14.00	-	369.46	-	2791.96	nr	3071.16
7500 litres	3986.00	2.00	4065.72	18.00	-	475.02	-	4540.74	nr	4994.81
drilled holes for 13mm pipes	-	-	-	0.20	-	5.28	-	5.28	nr	5.81
drilled holes for 19mm pipes	-	-	-	0.20	-	5.28	-	5.28	nr	5.81
drilled holes for 25mm pipes	-	-	-	0.25	-	6.60	-	6.60	nr	7.26
drilled holed for 32mm pipes	-	-	-	0.25	-	6.60	-	6.60	nr	7.26
drilled holes for 38mm pipes	-	-	-	0.33	-	8.71	-	8.71	nr	9.58
drilled holes for 51mm pipes	-	-	-	0.33	-	8.71	-	8.71	nr	9.58

Labour hourly rates: (except Specialists) Craft Operatives 26.39 Labourer 15.57 Rates are national average prices. Refer to REGIONAL VARIATIONS for indicative levels of overall pricing in regions	MATERIALS			LABOUR				RATES		
	Del to Site £	Waste %	Material Cost £	Craft Optve Hrs	Lab Hrs	Labour Cost £	Sunds £	Nett Rate £	Unit	Gross rate (10%) £
PRIMARY EQUIPMENT (Cont'd)										
Plastics water storage cisterns										
Rectangular cold water storage cisterns; plastics; BS 4213 with sealed lid and byelaw 30 kit										
18 litres	30.53	2.00	31.14	1.25	-	32.99	-	64.13	nr	70.54
114 litres	89.14	2.00	90.92	1.75	-	46.18	-	137.11	nr	150.82
190 litres	139.21	2.00	141.99	2.00	-	52.78	-	194.77	nr	214.25
227 litres	146.53	2.00	149.46	2.50	-	65.97	-	215.44	nr	236.98
drilled holes for 13mm pipes	-	-	-	0.13	-	3.43	-	3.43	nr	3.77
drilled holes for 19mm pipes	-	-	-	0.13	-	3.43	-	3.43	nr	3.77
drilled holes for 25mm pipes	-	-	-	0.17	-	4.49	-	4.49	nr	4.93
drilled holed for 32mm pipes	-	-	-	0.17	-	4.49	-	4.49	nr	4.93
drilled holes for 38mm pipes	-	-	-	0.22	-	5.81	-	5.81	nr	6.39
drilled holes for 51mm pipes	-	-	-	0.22	-	5.81	-	5.81	nr	6.39
Copper direct hot water cylinders; pre-insulated										
Direct hot water cylinders; copper cylinder, BS 1566 Grade 3										
120 litres; four bosses	156.49	2.00	159.62	2.00	-	52.78	-	212.40	nr	233.64
144 litres; four bosses	179.09	2.00	182.67	2.00	-	52.78	-	235.45	nr	259.00
166 litres; four bosses	283.24	2.00	288.90	2.00	-	52.78	-	341.68	nr	375.85
Stainless steel direct hot water cylinders; pre-insulated										
Direct hot water cylinders; stainless steel cylinder										
120 litres; four bosses	132.10	2.00	134.74	2.00	-	52.78	-	187.52	nr	206.27
140 litres; four bosses	188.82	2.00	192.60	2.00	-	52.78	-	245.38	nr	269.91
160 litres; four bosses	225.41	2.00	229.92	2.00	-	52.78	-	282.70	nr	310.97
210 litres; four bosses	302.43	2.00	308.48	2.00	-	52.78	-	361.26	nr	397.38
250 litres; four bosses	364.59	2.00	371.88	2.00	-	52.78	-	424.66	nr	467.13
Copper indirect hot water cylinders; pre-insulated										
Double feed indirect hot water cylinders; copper cylinder, BS 1566 Part 1 Grade 3										
114 litres; four bosses	176.76	2.00	180.30	2.00	-	52.78	-	233.08	nr	256.38
117 litres; four bosses	176.15	2.00	179.67	2.00	-	52.78	-	232.45	nr	255.70
140 litres; four bosses	200.11	2.00	204.11	2.00	-	52.78	-	256.89	nr	282.58
162 litres; four bosses	292.55	2.00	298.40	2.00	-	52.78	-	351.18	nr	386.29
Stainless steel indirect hot water cylinders; pre-insulated										
Double feed indirect hot water cylinders; stainless steel cylinder										
120 litres; four bosses	142.37	2.00	145.22	2.00	-	52.78	-	198.00	nr	217.80
140 litres; four bosses	164.41	2.00	167.70	2.00	-	52.78	-	220.48	nr	242.53
160 litres; four bosses	179.06	2.00	182.64	2.00	-	52.78	-	235.42	nr	258.96
210 litres; four bosses	335.04	2.00	341.74	2.00	-	52.78	-	394.52	nr	433.97
250 litres; four bosses	418.39	2.00	426.76	2.00	-	52.78	-	479.54	nr	527.49
Copper combination hot water storage units; pre-insulated										
Combination direct hot water storage units; copper unit, BS 3198 with lid										
450mm diameter x 1050mm high; 115 litres hot water; 45 litres cold water	241.67	2.00	246.50	3.00	-	79.17	-	325.67	nr	358.24
450mm diameter x 1200mm high; 115 litres hot water; 115 litres cold water	250.00	2.00	255.00	3.00	-	79.17	-	334.17	nr	367.59
Combination double feed indirect hot water storage units; copper unit, BS 3198 with lid										
450mm diameter x 1075mm high; 115 litres hot water; 20 litres cold water	283.24	2.00	288.90	3.00	-	79.17	-	368.07	nr	404.88
450mm diameter x 1200mm high; 120 litres hot water; 40 litres cold water	301.24	2.00	307.26	3.00	-	79.17	-	386.43	nr	425.08
Plastic single skin fuel oil storage tanks										
Oil storage tanks; Plastic single skin tank complete with watchman probe, transmitter and long life battery with gate valve and filter.										
1300 litres	545.77	-	545.77	3.50	-	92.36	-	638.14	nr	701.95
1800 litres	714.40	-	714.40	3.75	-	98.96	-	813.36	nr	894.70
2500 litres	941.45	-	941.45	4.00	-	105.56	-	1047.01	nr	1151.71
Oil storage tanks; Plastic Bunded tank complete with watchman probe, transmitter and long life battery, Bundman leak indicator. Bund drain off point with gate valve and filter.										
1300 litres	1240.00	-	1240.00	3.50	-	92.36	-	1332.36	nr	1465.60
1800 litres	1370.00	-	1370.00	3.75	-	98.96	-	1468.96	nr	1615.86
2500 litres	1695.00	-	1695.00	4.00	-	105.56	-	1800.56	nr	1980.62
Accelerator pumps										
Variable head accelerator pumps for forced central heating; small bore indirect systems										
BSP connections; with valves										
20mm	92.58	2.00	94.43	1.00	-	26.39	-	120.82	nr	132.90
25mm	112.48	2.00	114.73	1.00	-	26.39	-	141.12	nr	155.23
TERMINAL EQUIPMENT AND FITTINGS										
Radiators										
Pressed steel radiators single panel with convector; air cock, plain plug										
300mm high; fixing brackets to masonry with screws										
600mm long	14.82	1.00	14.97	3.75	-	98.96	-	113.93	nr	125.32
1200mm long	26.65	1.00	26.92	3.75	-	98.96	-	125.88	nr	138.47

Labour hourly rates: (except Specialists) Craft Operatives 26.39 Labourer 15.57 Rates are national average prices. Refer to REGIONAL VARIATIONS for indicative levels of overall pricing in regions	MATERIALS			LABOUR				RATES		
	Del to Site £	Waste %	Material Cost £	Craft Optve Hrs	Lab Hrs	Labour Cost £	Sunds £	Nett Rate £	Unit	Gross rate (10%) £
TERMINAL EQUIPMENT AND FITTINGS (Cont'd)										
Radiators (Cont'd)										
Pressed steel radiators single panel with convector; air cock, plain plug (Cont'd)										
500mm high; fixing brackets to masonry with screws										
600mm long	25.40	1.00	25.65	3.75	-	98.96	-	124.62	nr	137.08
800mm long	34.32	1.00	34.66	3.75	-	98.96	-	133.63	nr	146.99
1200mm long	57.65	1.00	58.23	3.75	-	98.96	-	157.19	nr	172.91
600mm high; fixing brackets to masonry with screws										
600mm long	24.24	1.00	24.48	3.75	-	98.96	-	123.44	nr	135.79
900mm long	39.40	1.00	39.79	3.75	-	98.96	-	138.76	nr	152.63
1200mm long	46.32	1.00	46.78	3.75	-	98.96	-	145.75	nr	160.32
1600mm long	85.58	1.00	86.44	3.75	-	98.96	-	185.40	nr	203.94
700mm high; fixing brackets to masonry with screws										
600mm long	34.41	1.00	34.75	3.75	-	98.96	-	133.72	nr	147.09
900mm long	50.00	1.00	50.50	3.75	-	98.96	-	149.46	nr	164.41
1100mm long	64.83	1.00	65.48	3.75	-	98.96	-	164.44	nr	180.88
1200mm long	53.61	1.00	54.14	3.75	-	98.96	-	153.11	nr	168.42
Pressed steel radiators; double panel with single convector; air cock, plain plug										
300mm high; fixing brackets to masonry with screws										
600mm long	25.32	1.00	25.57	3.75	-	98.96	-	124.54	nr	136.99
800mm long	27.49	1.00	27.76	3.75	-	98.96	-	126.73	nr	139.40
1200mm long	42.50	1.00	42.92	3.75	-	98.96	-	141.89	nr	156.08
500mm high; fixing brackets to masonry with screws										
600mm long	35.65	1.00	36.01	3.75	-	98.96	-	134.97	nr	148.47
800mm long	47.90	1.00	48.38	3.75	-	98.96	-	147.34	nr	162.08
1200mm long	81.65	1.00	82.47	3.75	-	98.96	-	181.43	nr	199.57
600mm high; fixing brackets to masonry with screws										
600mm long	42.40	1.00	42.82	3.75	-	98.96	-	141.79	nr	155.97
900mm long	71.32	1.00	72.03	3.75	-	98.96	-	171.00	nr	188.10
1200mm long	64.15	1.00	64.79	3.75	-	98.96	-	163.75	nr	180.13
1600mm long	108.66	1.00	109.75	3.75	-	98.96	-	208.71	nr	229.58
2400mm long	249.00	2.00	253.98	3.75	-	98.96	-	352.94	nr	388.24
700mm high; fixing brackets to masonry with screws										
700mm long	47.91	1.00	48.39	3.75	-	98.96	-	147.35	nr	162.09
900mm long	57.00	1.00	57.57	3.75	-	98.96	-	156.53	nr	172.19
1200mm long	74.41	1.00	75.15	3.75	-	98.96	-	174.12	nr	191.53
Pressed steel radiators; double panel with double convector; air cock, plain plug										
300mm high; fixing brackets to masonry with screws										
600mm long	25.32	1.00	25.57	3.75	-	98.96	-	124.54	nr	136.99
800mm long	27.49	1.00	27.76	3.75	-	98.96	-	126.73	nr	139.40
1200mm long	42.50	1.00	42.92	3.75	-	98.96	-	141.89	nr	156.08
500mm high; fixing brackets to masonry with screws										
600mm long	35.65	1.00	36.01	3.75	-	98.96	-	134.97	nr	148.47
800mm long	47.90	1.00	48.38	3.75	-	98.96	-	147.34	nr	162.08
1200mm long	81.65	1.00	82.47	3.75	-	98.96	-	181.43	nr	199.57
1600mm long	117.75	1.00	118.93	3.75	-	98.96	-	217.89	nr	239.68
2000mm long	167.48	1.00	169.15	3.75	-	98.96	-	268.11	nr	294.92
2400mm long	195.81	1.00	197.77	3.75	-	98.96	-	296.73	nr	326.40
600mm high; fixing brackets to masonry with screws										
600mm long	42.40	1.00	42.82	3.75	-	98.96	-	141.79	nr	155.97
900mm long	71.32	1.00	72.03	3.75	-	98.96	-	171.00	nr	188.10
1200mm long	64.15	1.00	64.79	3.75	-	98.96	-	163.75	nr	180.13
1600mm long	108.66	1.00	109.75	3.75	-	98.96	-	208.71	nr	229.58
2000mm long	189.14	1.00	191.03	3.75	-	98.96	-	290.00	nr	319.00
2400mm long	229.14	1.00	231.43	3.75	-	98.96	-	330.40	nr	363.44
700mm high; fixing brackets to masonry with screws										
700mm long	47.91	1.00	48.39	3.75	-	98.96	-	147.35	nr	162.09
900mm long	57.00	1.00	57.57	3.75	-	98.96	-	156.53	nr	172.19
1200mm long	74.41	1.00	75.15	3.75	-	98.96	-	174.12	nr	191.53
Brass valves for radiators; self colour										
Valves for radiators, BS 2767; wheel head and lock shield										
inlet for copper; angle pattern										
15mm	17.97	1.00	18.14	0.60	-	15.83	-	33.98	nr	37.38
22mm	34.69	1.00	35.04	0.80	-	21.11	-	56.15	nr	61.77
Brass valves for radiators; chromium plated										
Valves for radiators, BS 2767; wheel head										
inlet for copper; angle pattern										
15mm	7.40	2.00	7.54	0.30	-	7.92	-	15.46	nr	17.01
22mm	13.75	2.00	14.02	0.40	-	10.56	-	24.58	nr	27.04
inlet for copper; straight pattern										
15mm	7.40	2.00	7.54	0.30	-	7.92	-	15.46	nr	17.01
22mm	16.87	2.00	17.20	0.40	-	10.56	-	27.76	nr	30.54
Valves for radiators, BS 2767; lock shield										
inlet for copper; angle pattern										
15mm	4.86	2.00	4.96	0.30	-	7.92	-	12.87	nr	14.16
22mm	16.42	2.00	16.75	0.40	-	10.56	-	27.31	nr	30.04
inlet for copper; straight pattern										
15mm	4.86	2.00	4.96	0.30	-	7.92	-	12.87	nr	14.16
22mm	16.42	2.00	16.75	0.40	-	10.56	-	27.31	nr	30.04
Brass thermostatic valves for radiators; chromium plated										
Thermostatic valves for radiators, one piece; ABS plastics head										
inlet for copper; angle pattern										
15mm	6.94	2.00	7.08	0.30	-	7.92	-	15.00	nr	16.50

Labour hourly rates: (except Specialists) Craft Operatives 26.39 Labourer 15.57 Rates are national average prices. Refer to REGIONAL VARIATIONS for indicative levels of overall pricing in regions	MATERIALS			LABOUR				RATES		
	Del to Site £	Waste %	Material Cost £	Craft Optve Hrs	Lab Hrs	Labour Cost £	Sunds £	Nett Rate £	Unit	Gross rate (10%) £
TERMINAL EQUIPMENT AND FITTINGS (Cont'd)										
Brass thermostatic valves for radiators; chromium plated (Cont'd)										
Thermostatic valves for radiators, one piece; ABS plastics head (Cont'd)										
inlet for copper; straight pattern										
15mm	6.25	2.00	6.38	0.30	-	7.92	-	14.29	nr	15.72

This section continues on the next page

Labour hourly rates: (except Specialists) Craft Operatives 34.13 Labourer 15.57 Rates are national average prices. Refer to REGIONAL VARIATIONS for indicative levels of overall pricing in regions	MATERIALS			LABOUR				RATES		
	Del to Site £	Waste %	Material Cost £	Craft Optve Hrs	Lab Hrs	Labour Cost £	Sunds £	Nett Rate £	Unit	Gross rate (10%) £
TERMINAL EQUIPMENT AND FITTINGS (Cont'd)										
Extract fans										
Extract fans including shutter, window mounted										
Note: the following prices exclude cutting holes in glass										
102mm diameter, with incorporated pull cord switch	24.72	2.50	25.34	1.25	-	42.66	-	68.00	nr	74.80
102mm diameter - low voltage, with incorporated pull cord switch	67.56	2.50	69.25	1.25	-	42.66	-	111.91	nr	123.10
257mm diameter, with ceiling mounted switch	165.25	2.50	169.38	1.50	-	51.19	-	220.57	nr	242.63
324mm diameter, with ceiling mounted switch	212.76	2.50	218.08	1.50	-	51.19	-	269.27	nr	296.20
Extract fans including shutter, wall mounted with wall duct										
Note: the following prices exclude forming hole and making good										
102mm diameter, with incorporated pull cord switch	24.72	2.50	25.34	1.50	-	51.19	-	76.53	nr	84.19
102mm diameter - low voltage, with incorporated pull cord switch	67.56	2.50	69.25	1.50	-	51.19	-	120.44	nr	132.49
257mm diameter, with ceiling mounted switch	189.25	2.50	193.98	2.00	-	68.26	-	262.24	nr	288.46
324mm diameter, with ceiling mounted switch	233.55	2.50	239.39	2.00	-	68.26	-	307.65	nr	338.41
Extract fans including shutter, built in wall; controlled by a PIR switch unit										
290 x 321 mm	138.98	2.50	142.45	2.50	0.08	86.57	-	229.02	nr	251.93
409 x 433 mm	377.22	2.50	386.65	2.70	0.08	93.40	-	480.05	nr	528.05
473 x 476 mm	418.02	2.50	428.47	2.80	0.08	96.81	-	525.28	nr	577.81

This section continues on the next page

Labour hourly rates: (except Specialists) Craft Operatives 26.39 Labourer 15.57 Rates are national average prices. Refer to REGIONAL VARIATIONS for indicative levels of overall pricing in regions	MATERIALS			LABOUR				RATES		
	Del to Site £	Waste %	Material Cost £	Craft Optve Hrs	Lab Hrs	Labour Cost £	Sunds £	Nett Rate £	Unit	Gross rate (10%) £
PIPEWORK										
Steel pipes and fittings; screwed and PTFE tape joints; pipework black or red primer										
Pipes, straight in malleable iron pipe brackets fixing to timber with screws										
15mm: pipe and fittings										
15mm pipe	5.99	5.00	6.28	0.50	-	13.19	-	19.48	m	21.43
extra; made bends	-	-	-	0.17	-	4.49	-	4.49	nr	4.93
extra; connections to copper pipe ends; compression joint	1.21	2.00	1.24	0.10	-	2.64	-	3.88	nr	4.26
extra; fittings; one end	0.68	2.00	0.69	0.13	-	3.43	-	4.12	nr	4.54
extra; fittings; two ends	0.79	2.00	0.81	0.25	-	6.60	-	7.40	nr	8.14
extra; fittings; three ends	1.16	2.00	1.18	0.25	-	6.60	-	7.78	nr	8.56
20mm; pipe and fittings										
20mm pipe	6.71	5.00	7.04	0.57	-	15.04	-	22.08	m	24.29
extra; made bends	-	-	-	0.25	-	6.60	-	6.60	nr	7.26
extra; connections to copper pipe ends; compression joint	1.91	2.00	1.95	0.17	-	4.49	-	6.43	nr	7.08
extra; fittings; one end	0.69	2.00	0.70	0.17	-	4.49	-	5.19	nr	5.71
extra; fittings; two ends	0.99	2.00	1.01	0.33	-	8.71	-	9.72	nr	10.69
extra; fittings; three ends	1.35	2.00	1.38	0.33	-	8.71	-	10.09	nr	11.09
25mm; pipe and fittings										
25mm pipe	9.48	5.00	9.94	0.67	-	17.68	-	27.62	m	30.38
extra; made bends	-	-	-	0.33	-	8.71	-	8.71	nr	9.58
extra; connections to copper pipe ends; compression joint	3.70	2.00	3.77	0.25	-	6.60	-	10.37	nr	11.41
extra; fittings; one end	0.82	2.00	0.84	0.25	-	6.60	-	7.43	nr	8.18
extra; fittings; two ends	1.42	2.00	1.45	0.50	-	13.19	-	14.64	nr	16.11
extra; fittings; three ends	2.07	2.00	2.11	0.50	-	13.19	-	15.31	nr	16.84
32mm; pipe and fittings										
32mm pipe	10.71	5.00	11.23	0.80	-	21.11	-	32.34	m	35.58
extra; made bends	-	-	-	0.50	-	13.19	-	13.19	nr	14.51
extra; connections to copper pipe ends; compression joint	6.77	2.00	6.90	0.33	-	8.71	-	15.61	nr	17.17
extra; fittings; one end	1.57	2.00	1.60	0.33	-	8.71	-	10.31	nr	11.34
extra; fittings; two ends	2.59	2.00	2.64	0.67	-	17.68	-	20.32	nr	22.36
extra; fittings; three ends	3.45	2.00	3.52	0.67	-	17.68	-	21.20	nr	23.32
40mm; pipe and fittings										
40mm pipe	12.94	5.00	13.57	1.00	-	26.39	-	39.96	m	43.95
extra; made bends	-	-	-	0.67	-	17.68	-	17.68	nr	19.45
extra; connections to copper pipe ends; compression joint	9.64	2.00	9.83	0.50	-	13.19	-	23.02	nr	25.32
extra; fittings; one end	1.67	2.00	1.70	0.42	-	11.08	-	12.79	nr	14.07
extra; fittings; two ends	4.34	2.00	4.43	0.83	-	21.90	-	26.33	nr	28.96
extra; fittings; three ends	4.63	2.00	4.72	0.83	-	21.90	-	26.63	nr	29.29
50mm; pipe and fittings										
50mm pipe	19.10	5.00	20.02	1.33	-	35.10	-	55.12	m	60.63
extra; made bends	-	-	-	1.00	-	26.39	-	26.39	nr	29.03
extra; connections to copper pipe ends; compression joint	14.09	2.00	14.37	0.67	-	17.68	-	32.05	nr	35.26
extra; fittings; one end	2.45	2.00	2.50	0.50	-	13.19	-	15.69	nr	17.26
extra; fittings; two ends	5.79	2.00	5.91	1.00	-	26.39	-	32.30	nr	35.53
extra; fittings; three ends	6.99	2.00	7.13	1.00	-	26.39	-	33.52	nr	36.87
Pipes straight in malleable iron pipe brackets fixing to masonry with screws										
15mm	6.00	5.00	6.29	0.53	-	13.99	-	20.28	m	22.31
20mm	6.72	5.00	7.04	0.60	-	15.83	-	22.88	m	25.16
25mm	9.48	5.00	9.95	0.70	-	18.47	-	28.42	m	31.26
32mm	10.72	5.00	11.24	0.83	-	21.90	-	33.14	m	36.45
40mm	12.96	5.00	13.58	1.03	-	27.18	-	40.76	m	44.84
50mm	19.11	5.00	20.03	1.36	-	35.89	-	55.92	m	61.51
Pipes straight in malleable iron single rings, 165mm long screwed both ends steel rods and malleable iron backplates fixing to timber with screws										
15mm	6.50	5.00	6.82	0.60	-	15.83	-	22.66	m	24.92
20mm	7.24	5.00	7.59	0.67	-	17.68	-	25.27	m	27.80
25mm	9.98	5.00	10.47	0.77	-	20.32	-	30.79	m	33.86
32mm	11.08	5.00	11.62	0.90	-	23.75	-	35.37	m	38.91
40mm	13.18	5.00	13.82	1.10	-	29.03	-	42.84	m	47.13
50mm	18.64	5.00	19.53	1.43	-	37.74	-	57.27	m	63.00
Steel pipes and fittings; screwed and PTFE tape joints; galvanised										
Pipes, straight in malleable iron pipe brackets fixing to timber with screws										
15mm; pipe and fittings										
15mm pipe	5.72	5.00	6.00	0.50	-	13.19	-	19.20	m	21.12
extra; made bends	-	-	-	0.17	-	4.49	-	4.49	nr	4.93
extra; connections to copper pipe ends; compression joint	1.21	2.00	1.24	0.10	-	2.64	-	3.88	nr	4.26
extra; fittings; one end	0.68	2.00	0.69	0.13	-	3.43	-	4.12	nr	4.54
extra; fittings; two ends	0.79	2.00	0.81	0.25	-	6.60	-	7.40	nr	8.14
extra; fittings; three ends	1.16	2.00	1.18	0.25	-	6.60	-	7.78	nr	8.56
20mm; pipe and fittings										
20mm pipe	6.40	5.00	6.72	0.57	-	15.04	-	21.76	m	23.93
extra; made bends	-	-	-	0.25	-	6.60	-	6.60	nr	7.26
extra; connections to copper pipe ends; compression joint	1.91	2.00	1.95	0.17	-	4.49	-	6.43	nr	7.08
extra; fittings; one end	0.69	2.00	0.70	0.17	-	4.49	-	5.19	nr	5.71

Labour hourly rates: (except Specialists) Craft Operatives 26.39 Labourer 15.57 Rates are national average prices. Refer to REGIONAL VARIATIONS for indicative levels of overall pricing in regions	MATERIALS			LABOUR				RATES		
	Del to Site £	Waste %	Material Cost £	Craft Optve Hrs	Lab Hrs	Labour Cost £	Sunds £	Nett Rate £	Unit	Gross rate (10%) £
PIPEWORK (Cont'd)										
Steel pipes and fittings; screwed and PTFE tape joints; galvanised (Cont'd)										
Pipes, straight in malleable iron pipe brackets fixing to timber with screws (Cont'd)										
20mm; pipe and fittings (Cont'd)										
extra; fittings; two ends	0.99	2.00	1.01	0.33	-	8.71	-	9.72	nr	10.69
extra; fittings; three ends	1.35	2.00	1.38	0.33	-	8.71	-	10.09	nr	11.09
25mm; pipe and fittings										
25mm pipe	9.09	5.00	9.55	0.67	-	17.68	-	27.23	m	29.95
extra; made bends	-	-	-	0.33	-	8.71	-	8.71	nr	9.58
extra; connections to copper pipe ends; compression joint	3.70	2.00	3.77	0.25	-	6.60	-	10.37	nr	11.41
extra; fittings; one end	0.82	2.00	0.84	0.25	-	6.60	-	7.43	nr	8.18
extra; fittings; two ends	1.42	2.00	1.45	0.50	-	13.19	-	14.64	nr	16.11
extra; fittings; three ends	2.07	2.00	2.11	0.50	-	13.19	-	15.31	nr	16.84
32mm; pipe and fittings										
32mm pipe	10.15	5.00	10.66	0.80	-	21.11	-	31.77	m	34.94
extra; made bends	-	-	-	0.50	-	13.19	-	13.19	nr	14.51
extra; connections to copper pipe ends; compression joint	6.77	2.00	6.90	0.33	-	8.71	-	15.61	nr	17.17
extra; fittings; one end	1.57	2.00	1.60	0.33	-	8.71	-	10.31	nr	11.34
extra; fittings; two ends	2.59	2.00	2.64	0.67	-	17.68	-	20.32	nr	22.36
extra; fittings; three ends	3.45	2.00	3.52	0.67	-	17.68	-	21.20	nr	23.32
40mm; pipe and fittings										
40mm pipe	12.15	5.00	12.76	1.00	-	26.39	-	39.15	m	43.06
extra; made bends	-	-	-	0.67	-	17.68	-	17.68	nr	19.45
extra; connections to copper pipe ends; compression joint	9.64	2.00	9.83	0.50	-	13.19	-	23.02	nr	25.32
extra; fittings; one end	1.67	2.00	1.70	0.42	-	11.08	-	12.79	nr	14.07
extra; fittings; two ends	4.34	2.00	4.43	0.83	-	21.90	-	26.33	nr	28.96
extra; fittings; three ends	4.63	2.00	4.72	0.83	-	21.90	-	26.63	nr	29.29
50mm; pipe and fittings										
50mm pipe	17.91	5.00	18.80	1.33	-	35.10	-	53.90	m	59.29
extra; made bends	-	-	-	1.00	-	26.39	-	26.39	nr	29.03
extra; connections to copper pipe ends; compression joint	14.09	2.00	14.37	0.67	-	17.68	-	32.05	nr	35.26
extra; fittings; one end	2.45	2.00	2.50	0.50	-	13.19	-	15.69	nr	17.26
extra; fittings; two ends	5.79	2.00	5.91	1.00	-	26.39	-	32.30	nr	35.53
extra; fittings; three ends	6.99	2.00	7.13	1.00	-	26.39	-	33.52	nr	36.87
Pipes straight in malleable iron pipe brackets fixing to masonry with screws										
15mm	6.00	5.00	6.29	0.53	-	13.99	-	20.28	m	22.30
20mm	6.71	5.00	7.04	0.60	-	15.83	-	22.87	m	25.16
25mm	9.48	5.00	9.94	0.70	-	18.47	-	28.42	m	31.26
32mm	10.71	5.00	11.23	0.83	-	21.90	-	33.13	m	36.45
40mm	12.95	5.00	13.57	1.03	-	27.18	-	40.76	m	44.83
50mm	19.10	5.00	20.02	1.36	-	35.89	-	55.91	m	61.50
Pipes straight in malleable iron single rings, 165mm long screwed both ends steel tubes and malleable iron backplates fixing to timber with screws										
15mm	7.03	5.00	7.37	0.60	-	15.83	-	23.21	m	25.53
20mm	8.06	5.00	8.45	0.67	-	17.68	-	26.13	m	28.74
25mm	10.85	5.00	11.39	0.77	-	20.32	-	31.71	m	34.88
32mm	11.97	5.00	12.55	0.90	-	23.75	-	36.30	m	39.93
40mm	14.35	5.00	15.05	1.10	-	29.03	-	44.08	m	48.48
50mm	19.93	5.00	20.89	1.43	-	37.74	-	58.63	m	64.49
Stainless steel pipes, BS EN 10312 Part 2; C.P. copper fittings, capillary, BS EN 1254 Part 2										
Pipes, straight in C.P. pipe brackets fixing to timber with screws										
15mm; pipe and fittings										
15mm pipe	13.56	5.00	14.21	0.40	-	10.56	-	24.77	m	27.24
extra; fittings; one end	10.73	3.00	11.05	0.06	-	1.58	-	12.64	nr	13.90
extra; fittings; two ends	7.78	3.00	8.01	0.12	-	3.17	-	11.18	nr	12.30
extra; fittings; three ends	10.26	3.00	10.57	0.12	-	3.17	-	13.73	nr	15.11
22mm; pipe and fittings										
22mm pipe	12.82	5.00	13.45	0.43	-	11.35	-	24.80	m	27.28
extra; fittings; one end	13.51	3.00	13.92	0.10	-	2.64	-	16.55	nr	18.21
extra; fittings; two ends	9.55	3.00	9.84	0.20	-	5.28	-	15.11	nr	16.63
extra; fittings; three ends	12.79	3.00	13.17	0.20	-	5.28	-	18.45	nr	20.30
28mm; pipe and fittings										
28mm pipe	20.17	5.00	21.16	0.48	-	12.67	-	33.83	m	37.21
extra; fittings; one end	16.13	3.00	16.61	0.15	-	3.96	-	20.57	nr	22.63
extra; fittings; two ends	13.29	3.00	13.69	0.30	-	7.92	-	21.61	nr	23.77
extra; fittings; three ends	15.45	3.00	15.91	0.30	-	7.92	-	23.83	nr	26.21
35mm; pipe and fittings										
35mm pipe	23.79	5.00	24.93	0.60	-	15.83	-	40.76	m	44.84
extra; fittings; one end	20.55	3.00	21.17	0.20	-	5.28	-	26.44	nr	29.09
extra; fittings; two ends	20.16	3.00	20.76	0.40	-	10.56	-	31.32	nr	34.45
extra; fittings; three ends	28.15	3.00	28.99	0.40	-	10.56	-	39.55	nr	43.51
42mm; pipe and fittings										
42mm pipe	28.96	5.00	30.35	0.80	-	21.11	-	51.46	m	56.61
extra; fittings; one end	26.65	3.00	27.45	0.30	-	7.92	-	35.37	nr	38.90
extra; fittings; two ends	28.89	3.00	29.76	0.60	-	15.83	-	45.59	nr	50.15
extra; fittings; three ends	34.69	3.00	35.73	0.60	-	15.83	-	51.56	nr	56.72

Labour hourly rates: (except Specialists) Craft Operatives 26.39 Labourer 15.57 Rates are national average prices. Refer to REGIONAL VARIATIONS for indicative levels of overall pricing in regions	MATERIALS			LABOUR				RATES		
	Del to Site £	Waste %	Material Cost £	Craft Optve Hrs	Lab Hrs	Labour Cost £	Sunds £	Nett Rate £	Unit	Gross rate (10%) £
PIPEWORK (Cont'd)										
Stainless steel pipes, BS EN 10312 Part 2; C.P. copper fittings, capillary, BS EN 1254 Part 2 (Cont'd)										
Pipes straight in C.P. pipe brackets fixing to masonry with screws										
15mm	13.56	5.00	14.22	0.45	-	11.88	-	26.09	m	28.70
22mm	12.83	5.00	13.45	0.48	-	12.67	-	26.12	m	28.73
28mm	20.18	5.00	21.17	0.53	-	13.99	-	35.15	m	38.67
35mm	23.79	5.00	24.93	0.65	-	17.15	-	42.09	m	46.30
42mm	28.97	5.00	30.36	0.85	-	22.43	-	52.79	m	58.07
Stainless steel pipes, BS EN 10312 Part 2; C.P. copper alloy fittings, compression, BS EN 1254 Part 2, Type A										
Pipes, straight in C.P. pipe brackets fixing to timber with screws										
15mm; pipe and fittings										
15mm pipe	14.53	5.00	15.21	0.40	-	10.56	-	25.77	m	28.35
extra; fittings; one end	8.49	3.00	8.74	0.06	-	1.58	-	10.33	nr	11.36
extra; fittings; two ends	10.54	3.00	10.86	0.12	-	3.17	-	14.02	nr	15.43
extra; fittings; three ends	28.54	3.00	29.40	0.12	-	3.17	-	32.56	nr	35.82
22mm; pipe and fittings										
22mm pipe	16.09	5.00	16.81	0.43	-	11.35	-	28.16	m	30.98
extra; fittings; one end	14.44	3.00	14.87	0.10	-	2.64	-	17.51	nr	19.26
extra; fittings; two ends	33.07	3.00	34.06	0.20	-	5.28	-	39.34	nr	43.27
extra; fittings; three ends	56.48	3.00	58.17	0.20	-	5.28	-	63.45	nr	69.80
28mm; pipe and fittings										
28mm pipe	26.61	5.00	27.79	0.48	-	12.67	-	40.46	m	44.50
extra; fittings; one end	27.17	3.00	27.99	0.15	-	3.96	-	31.94	nr	35.14
extra; fittings; two ends	70.93	3.00	73.06	0.30	-	7.92	-	80.97	nr	89.07
extra; fittings; three ends	77.22	3.00	79.54	0.30	-	7.92	-	87.45	nr	96.20
35mm; pipe and fittings										
35mm pipe	31.62	5.00	32.99	0.60	-	15.83	-	48.83	m	53.71
extra; fittings; one end	39.53	3.00	40.71	0.20	-	5.28	-	45.99	nr	50.59
extra; fittings; two ends	109.92	3.00	113.22	0.40	-	10.56	-	123.77	nr	136.15
extra; fittings; three ends	172.73	3.00	177.91	0.40	-	10.56	-	188.47	nr	207.31
42mm; pipe and fittings										
42mm pipe	39.65	5.00	41.36	0.80	-	21.11	-	62.47	m	68.72
extra; fittings; one end	56.19	3.00	57.88	0.30	-	7.92	-	65.80	nr	72.38
extra; fittings; two ends	171.64	3.00	176.79	0.60	-	15.83	-	192.62	nr	211.89
extra; fittings; three ends	237.80	3.00	244.93	0.60	-	15.83	-	260.77	nr	286.84
Pipes straight in C.P. pipe brackets fixing to masonry with screws										
15mm	14.54	5.00	15.22	0.45	-	11.88	-	27.10	m	29.81
22mm	16.09	5.00	16.82	0.48	-	12.67	-	29.49	m	32.44
28mm	26.61	5.00	27.80	0.53	-	13.99	-	41.78	m	45.96
35mm	31.63	5.00	33.00	0.65	-	17.15	-	50.15	m	55.17
42mm	39.65	5.00	41.36	0.85	-	22.43	-	63.79	m	70.17
Copper pipes, BS EN 1057 Type X; copper fittings, capillary, BS EN 1254 Part 2										
Pipes, straight in copper spacing clips to timber with screws										
15mm; pipe and fitings										
15mm pipe	3.01	5.00	3.16	0.33	-	8.71	-	11.87	m	13.06
extra; made bends	-	-	-	0.08	-	2.11	-	2.11	nr	2.32
extra; connections to iron pipe ends; screwed joint	28.17	3.00	29.02	0.10	-	2.64	-	31.65	nr	34.82
extra; fittings; one end	0.11	3.00	0.11	0.05	-	1.32	-	1.43	nr	1.58
extra; fittings; two ends	0.15	3.00	0.15	0.10	-	2.64	-	2.79	nr	3.07
extra; fittings; three ends	0.30	3.00	0.31	0.10	-	2.64	-	2.95	nr	3.24
22mm; pipe and fittings										
22mm pipe	5.90	5.00	6.19	0.36	-	9.50	-	15.69	m	17.26
extra; made bends	-	-	-	0.13	-	3.43	-	3.43	nr	3.77
extra; connections to iron pipe ends; screwed joint	31.86	3.00	32.82	0.17	-	4.49	-	37.30	nr	41.03
extra; fittings; one end	0.28	3.00	0.29	0.09	-	2.38	-	2.66	nr	2.93
extra; fittings; two ends	0.42	3.00	0.43	0.17	-	4.49	-	4.92	nr	5.41
extra; fittings; three ends	0.79	3.00	0.81	0.17	-	4.49	-	5.30	nr	5.83
28mm; pipe and fittings										
28mm pipe	9.35	5.00	9.81	0.40	-	10.56	-	20.37	m	22.40
extra; made bends	-	-	-	0.17	-	4.49	-	4.49	nr	4.93
extra; connections to iron pipe ends; screwed joint	47.99	3.00	49.43	0.25	-	6.60	-	56.03	nr	61.63
extra; fittings; one end	0.75	3.00	0.77	0.13	-	3.43	-	4.20	nr	4.62
extra; fittings; two ends	1.32	3.00	1.36	0.25	-	6.60	-	7.96	nr	8.75
extra; fittings; three ends	2.03	3.00	2.09	0.25	-	6.60	-	8.69	nr	9.56
35mm; pipe and fittings										
35mm pipe	16.96	5.00	17.80	0.50	-	13.19	-	30.99	m	34.09
extra; made bends	-	-	-	0.25	-	6.60	-	6.60	nr	7.26
extra; connections to iron pipe ends; screwed joint	55.40	3.00	57.06	0.33	-	8.71	-	65.77	nr	72.35
extra; fittings; one end	1.44	3.00	1.48	0.17	-	4.49	-	5.97	nr	6.57
extra; fittings; two ends	3.22	3.00	3.32	0.33	-	8.71	-	12.03	nr	13.23
extra; fittings; three ends	5.65	3.00	5.82	0.33	-	8.71	-	14.53	nr	15.98
42mm; pipe and fittings										
42mm pipe	20.64	5.00	21.66	0.67	-	17.68	-	39.35	m	43.28
extra; made bends	-	-	-	0.33	-	8.71	-	8.71	nr	9.58
extra; connections to iron pipe ends; screwed joint	86.28	3.00	88.86	0.50	-	13.19	-	102.06	nr	112.27
extra; fittings; one end	2.29	3.00	2.36	0.25	-	6.60	-	8.96	nr	9.85

Labour hourly rates: (except Specialists) Craft Operatives 26.39 Labourer 15.57 Rates are national average prices. Refer to REGIONAL VARIATIONS for indicative levels of overall pricing in regions	MATERIALS			LABOUR				RATES		
	Del to Site £	Waste %	Material Cost £	Craft Optve Hrs	Lab Hrs	Labour Cost £	Sunds £	Nett Rate £	Unit	Gross rate (10%) £
PIPEWORK (Cont'd)										
Copper pipes, BS EN 1057 Type X; copper fittings, capillary, BS EN 1254 Part 2 (Cont'd)										
Pipes, straight in copper spacing clips to timber with screws (Cont'd)										
42mm; pipe and fittings (Cont'd)										
extra; fittings; two ends	4.93	3.00	5.08	0.50	-	13.19	-	18.27	nr	20.10
extra; fittings; three ends	8.34	3.00	8.59	0.50	-	13.19	-	21.79	nr	23.96
54mm; pipe and fittings										
54mm pipe	27.48	5.00	28.84	1.00	-	26.39	-	55.23	m	60.75
extra; made bends	-	-	-	0.50	-	13.19	-	13.19	nr	14.51
extra; connections to iron pipe ends; screwed joint	67.80	3.00	69.84	0.67	-	17.68	-	87.52	nr	96.27
extra; fittings; one end	4.20	3.00	4.33	0.33	-	8.71	-	13.03	nr	14.34
extra; fittings; two ends	7.84	3.00	8.08	0.67	-	17.68	-	25.76	nr	28.33
extra; fittings; three ends	14.25	3.00	14.68	0.67	-	17.68	-	32.36	nr	35.59
Pipes straight in copper spacing clips fixing to masonry with screws										
15mm	3.02	5.00	3.17	0.36	-	9.50	-	12.67	m	13.94
22mm	5.90	5.00	6.20	0.39	-	10.29	-	16.49	m	18.14
28mm	9.35	5.00	9.82	0.43	-	11.35	-	21.17	m	23.28
35mm	16.96	5.00	17.80	0.53	-	13.99	-	31.79	m	34.97
42mm	20.65	5.00	21.67	0.70	-	18.47	-	40.14	m	44.16
54mm	27.49	5.00	28.84	1.03	-	27.18	-	56.03	m	61.63
Pipes straight in pressed brass pipe brackets fixing to timber with screws										
15mm	3.24	5.00	3.40	0.33	-	8.71	-	12.11	m	13.32
22mm	6.41	5.00	6.73	0.36	-	9.50	-	16.23	m	17.85
28mm	10.23	5.00	10.73	0.40	-	10.56	-	21.29	m	23.42
35mm	17.60	5.00	18.47	0.50	-	13.19	-	31.66	m	34.83
42mm	21.48	5.00	22.54	0.67	-	17.68	-	40.22	m	44.24
54mm	28.51	5.00	29.92	1.00	-	26.39	-	56.31	m	61.95
Pipes straight in cast brass pipe brackets fixing to timber with screws										
15mm	3.30	5.00	3.46	0.33	-	8.71	-	12.17	m	13.39
22mm	6.33	5.00	6.65	0.36	-	9.50	-	16.15	m	17.76
28mm	9.91	5.00	10.40	0.40	-	10.56	-	20.95	m	23.05
35mm	18.32	5.00	19.23	0.50	-	13.19	-	32.43	m	35.67
42mm	22.22	5.00	23.32	0.67	-	17.68	-	41.00	m	45.10
54mm	29.36	5.00	30.82	1.00	-	26.39	-	57.21	m	62.93
Pipes straight In cast brass single rings and back plates fixing to timber with screws										
15mm	3.58	5.00	3.76	0.36	-	9.50	-	13.26	m	14.58
22mm	6.52	5.00	6.85	0.39	-	10.29	-	17.14	m	18.85
28mm	10.00	5.00	10.49	0.43	-	11.35	-	21.84	m	24.02
35mm	17.77	5.00	18.65	0.53	-	13.99	-	32.63	m	35.90
42mm	21.29	5.00	22.35	0.70	-	18.47	-	40.82	m	44.90
54mm	28.45	5.00	29.86	1.03	-	27.18	-	57.04	m	62.75
67mm	28.81	5.00	30.23	1.50	-	39.58	-	69.81	m	76.80
76mm	39.41	5.00	41.35	2.00	-	52.78	-	94.13	m	103.54
108mm	65.36	5.00	68.54	3.00	-	79.17	-	147.71	m	162.48
Copper pipes, BS EN 1057 Type X; copper alloy fittings, compression, BS EN 1254 Part 2, Type A										
Pipes, straight in C.P. pipe brackets fixing to timber with screws										
15mm; pipe and fittings										
15mm pipe	3.30	5.00	3.46	0.33	-	8.71	-	12.17	m	13.39
extra; made bends	-	-	-	0.08	-	2.11	-	2.11	nr	2.32
extra; connections to iron pipe ends; screwed joint	1.54	3.00	1.59	0.10	-	2.64	-	4.23	nr	4.65
extra; fittings; one end	0.49	3.00	0.50	0.05	-	1.32	-	1.82	nr	2.01
extra; fittings; two ends	0.74	3.00	0.76	0.10	-	2.64	-	3.40	nr	3.74
extra; fittings; three ends	1.05	3.00	1.08	0.10	-	2.64	-	3.72	nr	4.09
22mm; pipe and fittings										
22mm pipe	6.45	5.00	6.76	0.36	-	9.50	-	16.26	m	17.89
extra; made bends	-	-	-	0.13	-	3.43	-	3.43	nr	3.77
extra; connections to iron pipe ends; screwed joint	2.78	3.00	2.87	0.17	-	4.49	-	7.35	nr	8.09
extra; fittings; one end	0.87	3.00	0.90	0.09	-	2.38	-	3.27	nr	3.60
extra; fittings; two ends	1.34	3.00	1.38	0.17	-	4.49	-	5.87	nr	6.45
extra; fittings; three ends	1.72	3.00	1.77	0.17	-	4.49	-	6.26	nr	6.88
28mm; pipe and fittings										
28mm pipe	10.47	5.00	10.96	0.40	-	10.56	-	21.52	m	23.67
extra; made bends	-	-	-	0.17	-	4.49	-	4.49	nr	4.93
extra; connections to iron pipe ends; screwed joint	4.40	3.00	4.53	0.25	-	6.60	-	11.13	nr	12.24
extra; fittings; one end	2.28	3.00	2.35	0.13	-	3.43	-	5.78	nr	6.36
extra; fittings; two ends	4.13	3.00	4.25	0.25	-	6.60	-	10.85	nr	11.94
extra; fittings; three ends	6.03	3.00	6.21	0.25	-	6.60	-	12.81	nr	14.09
35mm; pipe and fittings										
35mm pipe	21.57	5.00	22.55	0.50	-	13.19	-	35.74	m	39.32
extra; made bends	-	-	-	0.25	-	6.60	-	6.60	nr	7.26
extra; connections to iron pipe ends; screwed joint	13.57	3.00	13.98	0.33	-	8.71	-	22.68	nr	24.95
extra; fittings; one end	4.00	3.00	4.12	0.17	-	4.49	-	8.61	nr	9.47

Labour hourly rates: (except Specialists) Craft Operatives 26.39 Labourer 15.57 Rates are national average prices. Refer to REGIONAL VARIATIONS for indicative levels of overall pricing in regions	MATERIALS			LABOUR				RATES		
	Del to Site	Waste	Material Cost	Craft Optve	Lab	Labour Cost	Sunds	Nett Rate		Gross rate (10%)
PIPEWORK (Cont'd)	£	%	£	Hrs	Hrs	£	£	£	Unit	£
Copper pipes, BS EN 1057 Type X; copper alloy fittings, compression, BS EN 1254 Part 2, Type A (Cont'd)										
Pipes, straight in C.P. pipe brackets fixing to timber with screws (Cont'd)										
35mm; pipe and fittings (Cont'd)										
extra; fittings; two ends	8.64	3.00	8.90	0.33	-	8.71	-	17.61	nr	19.37
extra; fittings; three ends	11.22	3.00	11.56	0.33	-	8.71	-	20.27	nr	22.29
42mm; pipe and fittings										
42mm pipe	26.44	5.00	27.64	0.67	-	17.68	-	45.32	m	49.85
extra; made bends	-	-	-	0.33	-	8.71	-	8.71	nr	9.58
extra; connections to iron pipe ends; screwed joint	17.10	3.00	17.62	0.50	-	13.19	-	30.81	nr	33.89
extra; fittings; one end	5.64	3.00	5.81	0.25	-	6.60	-	12.41	nr	13.65
extra; fittings; two ends	11.69	3.00	12.04	0.50	-	13.19	-	25.24	nr	27.76
extra; fittings; three ends	14.80	3.00	15.24	0.50	-	13.19	-	28.44	nr	31.28
54mm; pipe and fittings										
54mm pipe	36.00	5.00	37.61	1.00	-	26.39	-	64.00	m	70.40
extra; made bends	-	-	-	0.50	-	13.19	-	13.19	nr	14.51
extra; connections to iron pipe ends; screwed joint	27.15	3.00	27.96	0.67	-	17.68	-	45.64	nr	50.21
extra; fittings; one end	9.18	3.00	9.46	0.33	-	8.71	-	18.16	nr	19.98
extra; fittings; two ends	19.42	3.00	20.00	0.67	-	17.68	-	37.68	nr	41.45
extra; fittings; three ends	24.10	3.00	24.82	0.67	-	17.68	-	42.50	nr	46.75
Pipes; straight; in copper spacing clips fixing to masonry with screws										
15mm	3.31	5.00	3.47	0.36	-	9.50	-	12.97	m	14.26
22mm	6.46	5.00	6.77	0.39	-	10.29	-	17.06	m	18.77
28mm	10.47	5.00	10.97	0.43	-	11.35	-	22.32	m	24.55
35mm	21.57	5.00	22.55	0.53	-	13.99	-	36.54	m	40.19
42mm	26.45	5.00	27.65	0.70	-	18.47	-	46.12	m	50.73
54mm	36.01	5.00	37.62	1.03	-	27.18	-	64.80	m	71.28
Pipes straight in pressed brass pipe brackets fixing to timber with screws										
15mm	3.53	5.00	3.70	0.33	-	8.71	-	12.41	m	13.65
22mm	6.96	5.00	7.30	0.36	-	9.50	-	16.80	m	18.48
28mm	11.35	5.00	11.89	0.40	-	10.56	-	22.44	m	24.69
35mm	22.21	5.00	23.22	0.50	-	13.19	-	36.41	m	40.05
42mm	27.28	5.00	28.52	0.67	-	17.68	-	46.20	m	50.82
54mm	37.03	5.00	38.70	1.00	-	26.39	-	65.09	m	71.60
Pipes straight in cast brass pipe brackets fixing to timber with screws										
15mm	3.59	5.00	3.76	0.33	-	8.71	-	12.47	m	13.72
22mm	6.89	5.00	7.22	0.36	-	9.50	-	16.72	m	18.39
28mm	11.03	5.00	11.55	0.40	-	10.56	-	22.11	m	24.32
35mm	22.93	5.00	23.98	0.50	-	13.19	-	37.17	m	40.89
42mm	28.02	5.00	29.30	0.67	-	17.68	-	46.98	m	51.68
54mm	37.88	5.00	39.59	1.00	-	26.39	-	65.98	m	72.58
Pipes straight in cast brass single rings and back plates fixing to timber with screws										
15mm	3.87	5.00	4.05	0.33	-	8.71	-	12.76	m	14.04
22mm	7.08	5.00	7.42	0.36	-	9.50	-	16.92	m	18.61
28mm	11.12	5.00	11.65	0.40	-	10.56	-	22.20	m	24.42
35mm	22.38	5.00	23.40	0.50	-	13.19	-	36.59	m	40.25
42mm	27.09	5.00	28.32	0.67	-	17.68	-	46.00	m	50.60
54mm	36.97	5.00	38.64	1.00	-	26.39	-	65.03	m	71.53
67mm	111.68	5.00	115.58	1.50	-	39.58	-	155.17	m	170.69
76mm	175.05	5.00	181.05	2.00	-	52.78	-	233.83	m	257.21
108mm	271.12	5.00	280.47	3.00	-	79.17	-	359.64	m	395.60
Copper pipes, BS EN 1057 Type X; copper alloy fittings, compression, BS EN 1254 Part 2 Type B										
Pipes, straight in copper spacing clips to timber with screws										
15mm; pipe and fittings										
15mm pipe	4.69	5.00	4.89	0.33	-	8.71	-	13.60	m	14.95
extra; made bends	-	-	-	0.08	-	2.11	-	2.11	nr	2.32
extra; connections to iron pipe ends; screwed joint	4.30	3.00	4.43	0.13	-	3.43	-	7.86	nr	8.64
extra; fittings; one end	6.26	3.00	6.45	0.07	-	1.85	-	8.29	nr	9.12
extra; fittings; two ends	4.83	3.00	4.98	0.13	-	3.43	-	8.41	nr	9.25
extra; fittings; three ends	8.27	3.00	8.52	0.13	-	3.43	-	11.95	nr	13.14
22mm; pipe and fittings										
22mm pipe	8.50	5.00	8.88	0.36	-	9.50	-	18.38	m	20.21
extra; made bends	-	-	-	0.13	-	3.43	-	3.43	nr	3.77
extra; connections to iron pipe ends; screwed joint	7.61	3.00	7.83	0.21	-	5.54	-	13.38	nr	14.71
extra; fittings; one end	7.45	3.00	7.67	0.11	-	2.90	-	10.58	nr	11.63
extra; fittings; two ends	7.59	3.00	7.81	0.21	-	5.54	-	13.36	nr	14.69
extra; fittings; three ends	12.72	3.00	13.10	0.21	-	5.54	-	18.64	nr	20.51
28mm; pipe and fittings										
28mm pipe	17.21	5.00	17.91	0.40	-	10.56	-	28.47	m	31.31
extra; made bends	-	-	-	0.17	-	4.49	-	4.49	nr	4.93
extra; connections to iron pipe ends; screwed joint	14.37	3.00	14.80	0.31	-	8.18	-	22.98	nr	25.28
extra; fittings; one end	24.69	3.00	25.43	0.16	-	4.22	-	29.65	nr	32.62
extra; fittings; two ends	20.65	3.00	21.27	0.31	-	8.18	-	29.45	nr	32.40

Labour hourly rates: (except Specialists) Craft Operatives 26.39 Labourer 15.57 Rates are national average prices. Refer to REGIONAL VARIATIONS for indicative levels of overall pricing in regions	MATERIALS			LABOUR				RATES		
	Del to Site £	Waste %	Material Cost £	Craft Optve Hrs	Lab Hrs	Labour Cost £	Sunds £	Nett Rate £	Unit	Gross rate (10%) £
PIPEWORK (Cont'd)										
Copper pipes, BS EN 1057 Type X; copper alloy fittings, compression, BS EN 1254 Part 2 Type B (Cont'd)										
Pipes, straight in copper spacing clips to timber with screws (Cont'd)										
28mm; pipe and fittings (Cont'd)										
extra; fittings; three ends	32.93	3.00	33.92	0.31	-	8.18	-	42.10	nr	46.31
35mm; pipe and fittings										
35mm pipe	29.19	5.00	30.40	0.50	-	13.19	-	43.60	m	47.96
extra; made bends	-	-	-	0.25	-	6.60	-	6.60	nr	7.26
extra; connections to iron pipe ends; screwed joint	47.20	3.00	48.61	0.40	-	10.56	-	59.17	nr	65.09
extra; fittings; one end	27.22	3.00	28.04	0.20	-	5.28	-	33.32	nr	36.65
extra; fittings; two ends	42.12	3.00	43.39	0.40	-	10.56	-	53.94	nr	59.34
extra; fittings; three ends	60.29	3.00	62.10	0.40	-	10.56	-	72.66	nr	79.92
42mm; pipe and fittings										
42mm pipe	37.24	5.00	38.76	0.67	-	17.68	-	56.45	m	62.09
extra; made bends	-	-	-	0.33	-	8.71	-	8.71	nr	9.58
extra; connections to iron pipe ends; screwed joint	70.81	3.00	72.93	0.63	-	16.63	-	89.56	nr	98.52
extra; fittings; one end	45.35	3.00	46.71	0.32	-	8.44	-	55.16	nr	60.67
extra; fittings; two ends	46.22	3.00	47.60	0.63	-	16.63	-	64.23	nr	70.65
extra; fittings; three ends	93.20	3.00	95.99	0.63	-	16.63	-	112.62	nr	123.88
54mm; pipe and fittings										
54mm pipe	51.97	5.00	54.06	1.00	-	26.39	-	80.45	m	88.50
extra; made bends	-	-	-	0.50	-	13.19	-	13.19	nr	14.51
extra; connections to iron pipe ends; screwed joint	104.53	3.00	107.67	0.83	-	21.90	-	129.57	nr	142.53
extra; fittings; one end	104.40	3.00	107.54	0.42	-	11.08	-	118.62	nr	130.48
extra; fittings; two ends	98.66	3.00	101.62	0.83	-	21.90	-	123.53	nr	135.88
extra; fittings; three ends	155.86	3.00	160.54	0.83	-	21.90	-	182.44	nr	200.68
Pipes straight in copper spacing clips fixing to masonry with screws										
15mm	4.69	5.00	4.89	0.36	-	9.50	-	14.39	m	15.83
22mm	8.51	5.00	8.88	0.39	-	10.29	-	19.17	m	21.09
28mm	17.22	5.00	17.92	0.43	-	11.35	-	29.27	m	32.19
35mm	29.20	5.00	30.41	0.53	-	13.99	-	44.40	m	48.83
42mm	37.25	5.00	38.77	0.70	-	18.47	-	57.24	m	62.97
54mm	51.98	5.00	54.07	1.03	-	27.18	-	81.25	m	89.38
Pipes straight in pressed brass pipe brackets fixing to timber with screws										
15mm	4.91	5.00	5.12	0.36	-	9.50	-	14.62	m	16.09
22mm	9.01	5.00	9.41	0.39	-	10.29	-	19.70	m	21.67
28mm	18.09	5.00	18.83	0.43	-	11.35	-	30.18	m	33.20
35mm	29.83	5.00	31.07	0.53	-	13.99	-	45.06	m	49.57
42mm	38.08	5.00	39.64	0.70	-	18.47	-	58.11	m	63.93
54mm	53.00	5.00	55.15	1.03	-	27.18	-	82.33	m	90.56
Pipes straight in cast brass pipe brackets fixing to timber with screws										
15mm	4.97	5.00	5.19	0.36	-	9.50	-	14.69	m	16.15
22mm	8.94	5.00	9.33	0.39	-	10.29	-	19.62	m	21.59
28mm	17.77	5.00	18.50	0.43	-	11.35	-	29.85	m	32.83
35mm	30.56	5.00	31.83	0.53	-	13.99	-	45.82	m	50.40
42mm	38.82	5.00	40.42	0.70	-	18.47	-	58.90	m	64.79
54mm	53.85	5.00	56.04	1.03	-	27.18	-	83.22	m	91.54
Pipes straight in cast brass single rings and back plates fixing to timber with screws										
15mm	5.25	5.00	5.48	0.36	-	9.50	-	14.98	m	16.48
22mm	9.13	5.00	9.53	0.39	-	10.29	-	19.82	m	21.81
28mm	17.86	5.00	18.59	0.43	-	11.35	-	29.94	m	32.93
35mm	30.00	5.00	31.25	0.53	-	13.99	-	45.24	m	49.76
42mm	37.89	5.00	39.45	0.70	-	18.47	-	57.92	m	63.71
54mm	52.94	5.00	55.09	1.03	-	27.18	-	82.27	m	90.49
Copper pipes, BS EN 1057 Type Y; copper fittings, capillary, BS EN 1254 Part 2										
Pipes; straight; in trenches										
15mm; pipe and fittings										
15mm pipe	6.19	5.00	6.50	0.20	-	5.28	-	11.78	m	12.96
extra; made bends	-	-	-	0.10	-	2.64	-	2.64	nr	2.90
extra; connections to iron pipe ends; screwed joint	28.17	3.00	29.02	0.16	-	4.22	-	33.24	nr	36.56
extra; fittings; one end	0.11	3.00	0.11	0.08	-	2.11	-	2.22	nr	2.45
extra; fittings; two ends	0.15	3.00	0.15	0.16	-	4.22	-	4.38	nr	4.81
extra; fittings; three ends	0.30	3.00	0.31	0.16	-	4.22	-	4.53	nr	4.98
22mm; pipe and fittings										
22mm pipe	11.23	5.00	11.79	0.22	-	5.81	-	17.59	m	19.35
extra; made bends	-	-	-	0.16	-	4.22	-	4.22	nr	4.64
extra; connections to iron pipe ends; screwed joint	31.86	3.00	32.82	0.25	-	6.60	-	39.41	nr	43.35
extra; fittings; one end	0.28	3.00	0.29	0.13	-	3.43	-	3.72	nr	4.09
extra; fittings; two ends	0.42	3.00	0.43	0.25	-	6.60	-	7.03	nr	7.73
extra; fittings; three ends	0.79	3.00	0.81	0.25	-	6.60	-	7.41	nr	8.15

Labour hourly rates: (except Specialists) Craft Operatives 26.39 Labourer 15.57 Rates are national average prices. Refer to REGIONAL VARIATIONS for indicative levels of overall pricing in regions	MATERIALS			LABOUR				RATES		
	Del to Site £	Waste %	Material Cost £	Craft Optve Hrs	Lab Hrs	Labour Cost £	Sunds £	Nett Rate £	Unit	Gross rate (10%) £
PIPEWORK (Cont'd)										
Copper pipes, BS EN 1057 Type Y; non-dezinctifiable fittings; compression, BS EN 1254 Part 2, Type B										
Pipes; straight; in trenches										
15mm; pipe and fittings										
15mm pipe	6.36	5.00	6.67	0.20	-	5.28	-	11.95	m	13.14
extra; made bends	-	-	-	0.10	-	2.64	-	2.64	nr	2.90
extra; connections to iron pipe ends; screwed joint	2.07	3.00	2.13	0.16	-	4.22	-	6.36	nr	6.99
extra; fittings; one end	0.94	3.00	0.97	0.08	-	2.11	-	3.08	nr	3.39
extra; fittings; two ends	1.13	3.00	1.16	0.16	-	4.22	-	5.39	nr	5.92
extra; fittings; three ends	1.55	3.00	1.60	0.16	-	4.22	-	5.82	nr	6.40
22mm; pipe and fittings										
22mm pipe	11.48	5.00	12.04	0.22	-	5.81	-	17.85	m	19.64
extra; made bends	-	-	-	0.16	-	4.22	-	4.22	nr	4.64
extra; connections to iron pipe ends; screwed joint	2.91	3.00	3.00	0.25	-	6.60	-	9.60	nr	10.56
extra; fittings; one end	1.27	3.00	1.31	0.13	-	3.43	-	4.74	nr	5.21
extra; fittings; two ends	2.04	3.00	2.10	0.25	-	6.60	-	8.70	nr	9.57
extra; fittings; three ends	3.32	3.00	3.42	0.25	-	6.60	-	10.02	nr	11.02
28mm; pipe and fittings										
28mm pipe	14.83	5.00	15.56	0.24	-	6.33	-	21.89	m	24.08
extra; made bends	-	-	-	0.20	-	5.28	-	5.28	nr	5.81
extra; connections to iron pipe ends; screwed joint	4.49	3.00	4.63	0.37	-	9.76	-	14.39	nr	15.83
extra; fittings; one end	2.72	3.00	2.80	0.19	-	5.01	-	7.82	nr	8.60
extra; fittings; two ends	4.59	3.00	4.73	0.37	-	9.76	-	14.49	nr	15.94
extra; fittings; three ends	8.79	3.00	9.05	0.37	-	9.76	-	18.82	nr	20.70
42mm; pipe and fittings										
42mm pipe	23.18	5.00	24.32	0.35	-	9.24	-	33.56	m	36.92
extra; made bends	-	-	-	0.40	-	10.56	-	10.56	nr	11.61
extra; connections to iron pipe ends; screwed joint	9.59	3.00	9.88	0.76	-	20.06	-	29.94	nr	32.93
extra; fittings; one end	20.13	3.00	20.73	0.38	-	10.03	-	30.76	nr	33.84
extra; fittings; two ends	28.44	3.00	29.29	0.76	-	20.06	-	49.35	nr	54.28
extra; fittings; three ends	43.69	3.00	45.00	0.76	-	20.06	-	65.06	nr	71.56
Polybutylene pipes; Wavin Hepworth Hep2O flexible plumbing system BS 7291 Class H; polybutylene demountable fittings										
Pipes, flexible in pipe clips to timber with screws										
15mm; pipe and fittings										
15mm pipe	3.11	10.00	3.34	0.37	-	9.76	-	13.11	m	14.42
extra; connector to copper	5.23	2.00	5.33	0.10	-	2.64	-	7.97	nr	8.77
extra; fittings; one end	2.76	2.00	2.82	0.05	-	1.32	-	4.13	nr	4.55
extra; fittings; two ends	2.15	2.00	2.19	0.10	-	2.64	-	4.83	nr	5.32
extra; fittings; three ends	3.03	2.00	3.09	0.10	-	2.64	-	5.73	nr	6.30
22mm; pipe and fittings										
22mm pipe	4.43	10.00	4.81	0.43	-	11.35	-	16.16	m	17.78
extra; connector to copper	7.50	2.00	7.65	0.17	-	4.49	-	12.14	nr	13.35
extra; fittings; one end	3.48	2.00	3.55	0.09	-	2.38	-	5.92	nr	6.52
extra; fittings; two ends	3.17	2.00	3.23	0.17	-	4.49	-	7.72	nr	8.49
extra; fittings; three ends	4.14	2.00	4.22	0.17	-	4.49	-	8.71	nr	9.58
28mm; pipe and fittings										
28mm pipe	7.38	10.00	8.02	0.50	-	13.19	-	21.22	m	23.34
extra; fittings; one end	6.15	2.00	6.27	0.17	-	4.49	-	10.76	nr	11.84
extra; fittings; two ends	9.10	2.00	9.28	0.33	-	8.71	-	17.99	nr	19.79
extra; fittings; three ends	12.57	2.00	12.82	0.33	-	8.71	-	21.53	nr	23.68
Pipes flexible in pipe clips fixing to masonry with screws										
15mm	3.15	10.00	3.39	0.33	-	8.71	-	12.09	m	13.30
22mm	4.45	10.00	4.83	0.37	-	9.76	-	14.60	m	16.06
28mm	7.39	10.00	8.04	0.50	-	13.19	-	21.23	m	23.36
Polythene pipes, BS EN 12201 Blue; MDPE fittings, compression										
Pipes; straight; in trenches										
20mm; pipe and fittings										
20mm pipe	0.72	10.00	0.78	0.17	-	4.49	-	5.27	m	5.80
extra; connections to copper pipe ends; compression joint	4.49	3.00	4.62	0.16	-	4.22	-	8.85	nr	9.73
extra; fittings; one end	6.97	3.00	7.18	0.08	-	2.11	-	9.29	nr	10.22
extra; fittings; two ends	6.14	3.00	6.32	0.16	-	4.22	-	10.55	nr	11.60
extra; fittings; three ends	8.69	3.00	8.95	0.16	-	4.22	-	13.17	nr	14.49
25mm; pipe and fittings										
25mm pipe	0.90	10.00	0.98	0.20	-	5.28	-	6.26	m	6.88
extra; connections to copper pipe ends; compression joint	5.03	3.00	5.18	0.25	-	6.60	-	11.78	nr	12.96
extra; fittings; one end	8.28	3.00	8.53	0.13	-	3.43	-	11.96	nr	13.16
extra; fittings; two ends	9.04	3.00	9.31	0.25	-	6.60	-	15.91	nr	17.50
extra; fittings; three ends	13.44	3.00	13.84	0.25	-	6.60	-	20.44	nr	22.48
32mm; pipe and fittings										
32mm pipe	1.77	10.00	1.91	0.24	-	6.33	-	8.24	m	9.06
extra; connections to copper pipe ends; compression joint	14.26	3.00	14.69	0.37	-	9.76	-	24.45	nr	26.90
extra; fittings; one end	11.47	3.00	11.81	0.19	-	5.01	-	16.83	nr	18.51
extra; fittings; two ends	17.83	3.00	18.36	0.37	-	9.76	-	28.13	nr	30.94
extra; fittings; three ends	22.16	3.00	22.82	0.37	-	9.76	-	32.59	nr	35.85

Labour hourly rates: (except Specialists) Craft Operatives 26.39 Labourer 15.57 Rates are national average prices. Refer to REGIONAL VARIATIONS for indicative levels of overall pricing in regions	MATERIALS			LABOUR				RATES		
	Del to Site £	Waste %	Material Cost £	Craft Optve Hrs	Lab Hrs	Labour Cost £	Sunds £	Nett Rate £	Unit	Gross rate (10%) £
PIPEWORK (Cont'd)										
Polythene pipes, BS EN 12201 Blue; MDPE fittings, compression (Cont'd)										
Pipes; straight; in trenches (Cont'd)										
50mm; pipe and fittings										
50mm pipe	4.44	10.00	4.79	0.40	-	10.56	-	15.35	m	16.88
extra; fittings; two ends	39.25	3.00	40.43	0.60	-	15.83	-	56.26	nr	61.89
extra; fittings; three ends	49.66	3.00	51.15	0.60	-	15.83	-	66.98	nr	73.68
63mm; pipe and fittings										
63mm pipe	9.70	10.00	10.33	0.54	-	14.25	-	24.59	m	27.04
extra; fittings; two ends	52.01	3.00	53.57	1.00	-	26.39	-	79.96	nr	87.96
extra; fittings; three ends	74.10	3.00	76.32	1.00	-	26.39	-	102.71	nr	112.98
PVC-U pipes, BS 3505 Class E; fittings, solvent welded joints										
Pipes, straight in standard plastics pipe brackets fixing to timber with screws										
3/8" - 17.1mm diameter; pipe and fittings										
3/8" - 17.1mm diameter pipe	10.70	5.00	11.13	0.33	-	8.71	-	19.84	m	21.82
extra; connections to iron pipe ends; screwed joint	1.80	2.00	1.84	0.10	-	2.64	-	4.48	nr	4.93
extra; fittings; one end	0.60	2.00	0.61	0.05	-	1.32	-	1.93	nr	2.12
extra; fittings; two ends	0.79	2.00	0.81	0.10	-	2.64	-	3.44	nr	3.79
extra; fittings; three ends	0.85	2.00	0.87	0.10	-	2.64	-	3.51	nr	3.86
1/2" - 21.5mm diameter; pipe and fittings										
1/2" - 21.5mm diameter pipe	4.58	5.00	4.72	0.37	-	9.76	-	14.48	m	15.93
extra; connections to iron pipe ends; screwed joint	1.77	2.00	1.80	0.17	-	4.49	-	6.29	nr	6.92
extra; fittings; one end	0.66	2.00	0.67	0.09	-	2.38	-	3.05	nr	3.35
extra; fittings; two ends	0.98	2.00	1.00	0.17	-	4.49	-	5.49	nr	6.03
extra; fittings; three ends	1.04	2.00	1.06	0.17	-	4.49	-	5.55	nr	6.10
3/4" - 26.7mm diameter; pipe and fittings										
3/4" - 26.7mm diameter pipe	3.67	5.00	3.80	0.43	-	11.35	-	15.14	m	16.66
extra; connections to iron pipe ends; screwed joint	2.03	2.00	2.07	0.25	-	6.60	-	8.67	nr	9.53
extra; fittings; one end	0.79	2.00	0.81	0.13	-	3.43	-	4.24	nr	4.66
extra; fittings; two ends	1.08	2.00	1.10	0.25	-	6.60	-	7.70	nr	8.47
extra; fittings; three ends	1.36	2.00	1.39	0.25	-	6.60	-	7.98	nr	8.78
1" - 33.4mm diameter; pipe and fittings										
1" - 33.4mm diameter pipe	3.56	5.00	3.69	0.50	-	13.19	-	16.89	m	18.58
extra; connections to iron pipe ends; screwed joint	2.48	2.00	2.53	0.33	-	8.71	-	11.24	nr	12.37
extra; fittings; one end	0.87	2.00	0.89	0.17	-	4.49	-	5.37	nr	5.91
extra; fittings; two ends	1.51	2.00	1.54	0.33	-	8.71	-	10.25	nr	11.27
extra; fittings; three ends	1.98	2.00	2.02	0.33	-	8.71	-	10.73	nr	11.80
1 1/4" - 42.2mm diameter; pipe and fittings										
1 1/4" - 42.2mm diameter pipe	5.15	5.00	5.32	0.60	-	15.83	-	21.15	m	23.27
extra; connections to iron pipe ends; screwed joint	3.25	2.00	3.31	0.50	-	13.19	-	16.51	nr	18.16
extra; fittings; one end	1.36	2.00	1.39	0.25	-	6.60	-	7.98	nr	8.78
extra; fittings; two ends	2.61	2.00	2.66	0.50	-	13.19	-	15.86	nr	17.44
extra; fittings; three ends	2.81	2.00	2.87	0.50	-	13.19	-	16.06	nr	17.67
1 1/2" - 48.3mm diameter; pipe and fittings										
1 1/2" - 48.3mm diameter pipe	6.23	5.00	6.44	0.75	-	19.79	-	26.24	m	28.86
extra; connections to iron pipe ends; screwed joint	4.16	2.00	4.24	0.67	-	17.68	-	21.93	nr	24.12
extra; fittings; one end	2.19	2.00	2.23	0.33	-	8.71	-	10.94	nr	12.04
extra; fittings; two ends	3.36	2.00	3.43	0.67	-	17.68	-	21.11	nr	23.22
extra; fittings; three ends	4.02	2.00	4.10	0.67	-	17.68	-	21.78	nr	23.96
Pipes straight In standard plastics pipe brackets fixing to masonry with screws										
3/8" - 17.1mm diameter	10.76	5.00	11.19	0.39	-	10.29	-	21.48	m	23.63
1/2" - 21.5mm diameter	4.63	5.00	4.77	0.43	-	11.35	-	16.12	m	17.73
3/4" - 26.7mm diameter	3.70	5.00	3.82	0.49	-	12.93	-	16.76	m	18.43
1" - 33.4mm diameter	3.45	5.00	3.58	0.56	-	14.78	-	18.36	m	20.19
1 1/4" - 42.2mm diameter	5.17	5.00	5.34	0.66	-	17.42	-	22.76	m	25.03
1 1/2" - 48.3mm diameter	6.37	5.00	6.59	0.81	-	21.38	-	27.96	m	30.76
Pipes; straight; in trenches										
3/8" - 17.1mm diameter	6.54	5.00	6.86	0.17	-	4.49	-	11.35	m	12.48
1/2" - 21.5mm diameter	1.02	5.00	1.06	0.18	-	4.75	-	5.81	m	6.40
3/4" - 26.7mm diameter	1.41	5.00	1.48	0.20	-	5.28	-	6.75	m	7.43
1" - 33.4mm diameter	1.87	5.00	1.95	0.25	-	6.60	-	8.55	m	9.41
1 1/4" - 42.2mm diameter	2.36	5.00	2.47	0.29	-	7.65	-	10.12	m	11.14
1 1/2" - 48.3mm diameter	3.02	5.00	3.16	0.33	-	8.71	-	11.87	m	13.05
PVC-U pipes and fittings; solvent welded joints; pipework self coloured white										
Pipes, straight in standard plastics pipe brackets fixing to timber with screws										
21mm; pipe and fittings										
21mm pipe	1.32	5.00	1.36	0.25	-	6.60	-	7.96	m	8.76
extra; fittings; two ends	1.35	2.00	1.38	0.20	-	5.28	-	6.65	nr	7.32
extra; fittings; three ends	1.40	2.00	1.43	0.20	-	5.28	-	6.71	nr	7.38
extra; fittings; tank connector	2.82	2.00	2.88	0.20	-	5.28	-	8.15	nr	8.97

Labour hourly rates: (except Specialists) Craft Operatives 26.39 Labourer 15.57 Rates are national average prices. Refer to REGIONAL VARIATIONS for indicative levels of overall pricing in regions	MATERIALS			LABOUR				RATES		
	Del to Site £	Waste %	Material Cost £	Craft Optve Hrs	Lab Hrs	Labour Cost £	Sunds £	Nett Rate £	Unit	Gross rate (10%) £
PIPEWORK (Cont'd)										
Ductile iron pipes and fittings, Tyton socketed flexible joints										
Pipes; straight; in trenches										
100mm; pipe and fittings										
100mm pipe	21.96	5.00	23.05	1.00	-	26.39	-	49.44	m	54.39
extra; bends, 90 degree	39.26	2.00	40.05	1.00	-	26.39	-	66.44	nr	73.08
extra; duckfoot bends, 90 degree	101.38	2.00	103.41	1.00	-	26.39	-	129.80	nr	142.78
extra; tees	37.17	2.00	37.91	1.50	-	39.58	-	77.50	nr	85.25
extra; hydrant tees	87.40	2.00	89.15	1.50	-	39.58	-	128.74	nr	141.61
extra; branches, 45 degree	26.33	2.00	26.86	1.50	-	39.58	-	66.44	nr	73.09
extra; flanged sockets	50.41	2.00	51.41	1.00	-	26.39	-	77.80	nr	85.58
extra; flanged spigots	46.01	2.00	46.93	1.00	-	26.39	-	73.32	nr	80.65
150mm; pipe and fittings										
150mm pipe	43.20	5.00	45.36	1.50	-	39.58	-	84.95	m	93.44
extra; bends, 90 degree	109.36	2.00	111.55	1.50	-	39.58	-	151.13	nr	166.25
extra; duckfoot bends, 90 degree	165.88	2.00	169.20	1.50	-	39.58	-	208.79	nr	229.66
extra; tees	89.39	2.00	91.18	2.25	-	59.38	-	150.56	nr	165.61
extra; hydrant tees	158.68	2.00	161.85	2.25	-	59.38	-	221.23	nr	243.35
extra; branches, 45 degree	63.28	2.00	64.55	2.25	-	59.38	-	123.92	nr	136.32
extra; flanged sockets	76.80	2.00	78.34	1.50	-	39.58	-	117.92	nr	129.71
extra; flanged spigots	53.36	2.00	54.43	1.50	-	39.58	-	94.02	nr	103.42
Gas flue pipes comprising galvanised steel outer skin and aluminium inner skin with air space between, BS 715; socketed joints										
Pipes; straight										
100mm										
pipe, plain	36.87	5.00	38.71	0.80	-	21.11	-	59.83	m	65.81
extra; connections to appliance	7.57	2.00	7.72	0.60	-	15.83	-	23.56	nr	25.91
extra; adjustable pipes	29.04	2.00	29.62	0.60	-	15.83	-	45.45	nr	50.00
extra; terminals	25.21	2.00	25.71	0.60	-	15.83	-	41.55	nr	45.70
extra; elbows 0- 90 degrees	24.61	2.00	25.10	0.60	-	15.83	-	40.94	nr	45.03
extra; tees	54.61	2.00	55.70	0.60	-	15.83	-	71.54	nr	78.69
125mm										
pipe, plain	42.90	5.00	45.04	0.96	-	25.33	-	70.38	m	77.42
extra; connections to appliance	8.56	2.00	8.73	0.80	-	21.11	-	29.84	nr	32.83
extra; adjustable pipes	35.25	2.00	35.95	0.80	-	21.11	-	57.07	nr	62.77
extra; terminals	27.69	2.00	28.24	0.80	-	21.11	-	49.36	nr	54.29
extra; elbows 0- 90 degrees	26.89	2.00	27.43	0.80	-	21.11	-	48.54	nr	53.39
extra; tees	54.61	2.00	55.70	0.80	-	21.11	-	76.81	nr	84.50
150mm										
pipe, plain	55.58	5.00	58.36	1.20	-	31.67	-	90.03	m	99.03
extra; connections to appliance	9.29	2.00	9.48	1.20	-	31.67	-	41.14	nr	45.26
extra; adjustable pipes	39.19	2.00	39.97	1.20	-	31.67	-	71.64	nr	78.81
extra; terminals	39.55	2.00	40.34	1.20	-	31.67	-	72.01	nr	79.21
extra; elbows 0- 90 degrees	35.96	2.00	36.68	1.20	-	31.67	-	68.35	nr	75.18
extra; tees	56.75	2.00	57.88	1.20	-	31.67	-	89.55	nr	98.51
Flue supports; galvanised steel wall bands										
fixing to masonry with screws										
for 100mm pipes	12.05	2.00	12.29	0.20	-	5.28	-	17.57	nr	19.33
for 125mm pipes	12.81	2.00	13.07	0.20	-	5.28	-	18.34	nr	20.18
for 150mm pipes	16.26	2.00	16.59	0.20	-	5.28	-	21.86	nr	24.05
Fire stop spacers										
for 100mm pipes	4.69	2.00	4.78	0.30	-	7.92	-	12.70	nr	13.97
for 125mm pipes	4.69	2.00	4.78	0.40	-	10.56	-	15.34	nr	16.87
for 150mm pipes	5.39	2.00	5.50	0.60	-	15.83	-	21.33	nr	23.46
PIPE ANCILLARIES										
Brass stopcocks										
Stopcocks; crutch head; DZR; joints to polythene BS EN 12201 each end										
15mm	6.24	2.00	6.36	0.33	-	8.71	-	15.07	nr	16.58
22mm	7.68	2.00	7.83	0.33	-	8.71	-	16.54	nr	18.20
Stopcocks, crutch head; compression joints to copper (Type A) each end										
15mm	4.03	2.00	4.11	0.25	-	6.60	-	10.71	nr	11.78
22mm	5.67	2.00	5.78	0.33	-	8.71	-	14.49	nr	15.94
28mm	11.00	2.00	11.22	0.50	-	13.19	-	24.41	nr	26.86
Stopcocks, crutch head; DZR; compression joints to copper (Type A)										
each end										
15mm	6.62	2.00	6.75	0.25	-	6.60	-	13.35	nr	14.68
22mm	9.57	2.00	9.76	0.33	-	8.71	-	18.47	nr	20.32
28mm	16.56	2.00	16.89	0.50	-	13.19	-	30.09	nr	33.10
35mm	40.75	2.00	41.57	0.67	-	17.68	-	59.25	nr	65.17
42mm	50.05	2.00	51.05	0.75	-	19.79	-	70.85	nr	77.93
54mm	83.47	2.00	85.14	1.00	-	26.39	-	111.53	nr	122.68

Labour hourly rates: (except Specialists) Craft Operatives 26.39 Labourer 15.57 Rates are national average prices. Refer to REGIONAL VARIATIONS for indicative levels of overall pricing in regions	MATERIALS			LABOUR				RATES		
	Del to Site £	Waste %	Material Cost £	Craft Optve Hrs	Lab Hrs	Labour Cost £	Sunds £	Nett Rate £	Unit	Gross rate (10%) £
PIPE ANCILLARIES (Cont'd)										
Polybutylene stopcocks										
Stopcocks; fitted with Hep2O ends each end										
15mm	8.23	2.00	8.39	0.25	-	6.60	-	14.99	nr	16.49
22mm	9.83	2.00	10.03	0.33	-	8.71	-	18.74	nr	20.61
Copper alloy ball valves										
Lever ball valves; screwed and PTFE joints each end threaded internally										
15mm	3.10	2.00	3.16	0.25	-	6.60	-	9.76	nr	10.74
22mm	4.41	2.00	4.50	0.33	-	8.71	-	13.21	nr	14.53
28mm	8.12	2.00	8.28	0.50	-	13.19	-	21.48	nr	23.63
35mm	15.85	2.00	16.17	0.67	-	17.68	-	33.85	nr	37.23
42mm	22.87	2.00	23.33	0.75	-	19.79	-	43.12	nr	47.43
54mm	36.25	2.00	36.97	1.00	-	26.39	-	63.36	nr	69.70
Copper alloy gate valves										
Gate valves; BS EN 12288 series B; compression joints to copper (Type A) each end										
15mm	4.91	2.00	5.01	0.25	-	6.60	-	11.61	nr	12.77
22mm	5.61	2.00	5.72	0.33	-	8.71	-	14.43	nr	15.87
28mm	10.23	2.00	10.43	0.50	-	13.19	-	23.63	nr	25.99
35mm	18.07	2.00	18.43	0.67	-	17.68	-	36.11	nr	39.72
42mm	27.77	2.00	28.33	0.75	-	19.79	-	48.12	nr	52.93
54mm	51.66	2.00	52.69	1.00	-	26.39	-	79.08	nr	86.99
Gate valves; DZR; fitted with Hep2O ends each end										
15mm	6.29	2.00	6.42	0.25	-	6.60	-	13.01	nr	14.31
22mm	9.16	2.00	9.34	0.33	-	8.71	-	18.05	nr	19.86
Copper alloy body float valves										
Float operated valves for low pressure; BS 1212; copper float inlet threaded externally; fixing to steel										
13mm; part 1	14.46	2.00	14.75	0.33	-	8.71	-	23.46	nr	25.80
13mm; part 2	14.46	2.00	14.75	0.33	-	8.71	-	23.46	nr	25.80
Float operated valves for low pressure; BS 1212; plastics float inlet threaded externally; fixing to steel										
13mm; part 1	7.46	2.00	7.61	0.33	-	8.71	-	16.32	nr	17.95
13mm; part 2	7.46	2.00	7.61	0.33	-	8.71	-	16.32	nr	17.95
Float operated valves for high pressure; BS 1212; copper float inlet threaded externally; fixing to steel										
13mm; part 1	14.46	2.00	14.75	0.33	-	8.71	-	23.46	nr	25.80
13mm; part 2	13.04	2.00	13.30	0.33	-	8.71	-	22.01	nr	24.21
19mm; part 1	20.16	2.00	20.56	0.50	-	13.19	-	33.75	nr	37.13
25mm; part 1	54.23	2.00	55.31	1.00	-	26.39	-	81.70	nr	89.87
Float operated valves for high pressure; BS 1212; plastics float inlet threaded externally; fixing to steel										
13mm; part 1	7.46	2.00	7.61	0.33	-	8.71	-	16.32	nr	17.95
13mm; part 2	6.04	2.00	6.16	0.33	-	8.71	-	14.87	nr	16.36
19mm; part 1	11.02	2.00	11.24	0.50	-	13.19	-	24.43	nr	26.88
25mm; part 1	34.60	2.00	35.30	1.00	-	26.39	-	61.69	nr	67.85
Brass draining taps										
Drain cocks; square head Type 2										
15mm	1.00	2.00	1.02	0.10	-	2.64	-	3.66	nr	4.02
22mm	2.42	2.00	2.47	0.13	-	3.43	-	5.90	nr	6.49
INSULATION AND FIRE PROTECTION										
Thermal insulation; foil faced glass fibre preformed lagging, butt joints in the running length; secured with metal bands										
20mm thick insulation to copper pipework around one pipe										
15mm	3.00	3.00	3.09	0.20	-	5.28	-	8.37	m	9.20
22mm	3.17	3.00	3.26	0.22	-	5.81	-	9.07	m	9.97
28mm	3.38	3.00	3.48	0.25	-	6.60	-	10.07	m	11.08
35mm	3.67	3.00	3.78	0.30	-	7.92	-	11.69	m	12.86
42mm	4.04	3.00	4.16	0.33	-	8.71	-	12.87	m	14.16
48mm	4.38	3.00	4.51	0.36	-	9.50	-	14.01	m	15.41
54mm	4.71	3.00	4.85	0.40	-	10.56	-	15.41	m	16.95
64mm	6.25	3.00	6.44	0.43	-	11.35	-	17.79	m	19.56
76mm	6.96	3.00	7.17	0.48	-	12.67	-	19.83	m	21.82
25mm thick insulation to copper pipework around one pipe										
15mm	3.42	3.00	3.52	0.20	-	5.28	-	8.80	m	9.68
22mm	3.54	3.00	3.65	0.22	-	5.81	-	9.45	m	10.40
28mm	3.79	3.00	3.91	0.25	-	6.60	-	10.50	m	11.55

Labour hourly rates: (except Specialists) Craft Operatives 26.39 Labourer 15.57 Rates are national average prices. Refer to REGIONAL VARIATIONS for indicative levels of overall pricing in regions	MATERIALS			LABOUR				RATES		
	Del to Site £	Waste %	Material Cost £	Craft Optve Hrs	Lab Hrs	Labour Cost £	Sunds £	Nett Rate £	Unit	Gross rate (10%) £
INSULATION AND FIRE PROTECTION (Cont'd)										
Thermal insulation; foil faced glass fibre preformed lagging, butt joints in the running length; secured with metal bands (Cont'd)										
25mm thick insulation to copper pipework (Cont'd)										
around one pipe (Cont'd)										
35mm	4.21	3.00	4.33	0.30	-	7.92	-	12.25	m	13.48
42mm	4.58	3.00	4.72	0.33	-	8.71	-	13.43	m	14.77
48mm	4.92	3.00	5.06	0.36	-	9.50	-	14.56	m	16.02
54mm	5.33	3.00	5.49	0.40	-	10.56	-	16.05	m	17.65
64mm	5.92	3.00	6.09	0.43	-	11.35	-	17.44	m	19.19
76mm	6.62	3.00	6.82	0.48	-	12.67	-	19.49	m	21.44
108mm	9.25	3.00	9.53	0.53	-	13.99	-	23.51	m	25.87
Thermal insulation; foamed polyurethane preformed lagging, butt joints in the running length; secured with adhesive bands										
13mm thick insulation to copper pipework										
around one pipe										
15mm	0.65	3.00	0.67	0.17	-	4.49	-	5.16	m	5.67
22mm	0.82	3.00	0.85	0.18	-	4.75	-	5.60	m	6.16
28mm	0.98	3.00	1.00	0.20	-	5.28	-	6.28	m	6.91
35mm	1.17	3.00	1.21	0.22	-	5.81	-	7.02	m	7.72
42mm	1.33	3.00	1.36	0.25	-	6.60	-	7.96	m	8.76
54mm	1.92	3.00	1.98	0.33	-	8.71	-	10.69	m	11.76
INSULATION AND FIRE PROTECTION TO EQUIPMENT										
Thermal insulation; glass fibre filled insulating jacket in strips, pvc covering both sides; secured with metal straps and wire holder ring at top										
80mm thick insulation to equipment										
sides and tops of cylinders; overall size										
400mm diameter x 1050mm high	24.54	5.00	25.77	0.75	-	19.79	-	45.56	nr	50.12
450mm diameter x 900mm high	21.68	5.00	22.76	0.75	-	19.79	-	42.56	nr	46.81
450mm diameter x 1050mm high	24.54	5.00	25.77	0.75	-	19.79	-	45.56	nr	50.12
450mm diameter x 1200mm high	26.67	5.00	28.00	0.75	-	19.79	-	47.80	nr	52.58
HEATING/COOLING/REFRIGERATION SYSTEMS; LOW TEMPERATURE HOT WATER HEATING (SMALL SCALE)										
Central heating installations - indicative prices										
Note										
the following are indicative prices for installation in two storey three bedroomed dwellings with a floor area of approximately 85m²										
Installation; boiler, copper piping, pressed steel radiators, heated towel rail; providing hot water to sink, bath, lavatory basin; complete with all necessary pumps, controls etc										
solid fuel fired	-	-	Specialist	-	-	Specialist	-	6105.28	it	6715.80
gas fired	-	-	Specialist	-	-	Specialist	-	5736.50	it	6310.15
oil fired, including oil storage tank	-	-	Specialist	-	-	Specialist	-	7047.70	it	7752.47

MECHANICAL SERVICES

Labour hourly rates: (except Specialists) Craft Operatives 34.13 Labourer 15.57 Rates are national average prices. Refer to REGIONAL VARIATIONS for indicative levels of overall pricing in regions	MATERIALS			LABOUR				RATES		
	Del to Site £	Waste %	Material Cost £	Craft Optve Hrs	Lab Hrs	Labour Cost £	Sunds £	Nett Rate £	Unit	Gross rate (10%) £
PRIMARY EQUIPMENT										
Three phase Switchgear and Distribution boards										
Switch fuse, mild steel enclosure, fixed to masonry with screws; plugging										
32 amp; three pole and solid neutral, including fuses	148.98	2.50	152.70	2.20	-	75.09	0.82	228.62	nr	251.48
Distribution boards, TP & N, IP41 protection, fitted with 125A incomer switch, fixed to masonry with screws; plugging										
8 way times three phase board	160.20	2.50	164.21	5.95	-	203.07	0.82	368.10	nr	404.91
16 ways times three phase board	148.20	2.50	151.90	9.70	-	331.06	0.82	483.79	nr	532.17
Accessories for Distribution boards										
Type B single pole MCB 10KA	4.62	2.50	4.74	0.14	-	4.78	-	9.51	nr	10.47
Type B three pole MCB 10KA	19.62	2.50	20.11	0.15	-	5.12	-	25.23	nr	27.75
Type C single pole MCB 10KA	4.62	2.50	4.74	0.14	-	4.78	-	9.51	nr	10.47
Type C three pole MCB 10KA	19.62	2.50	20.11	0.15	-	5.12	-	25.23	nr	27.75
TERMINAL EQUIPMENT AND FITTINGS										
Accessories; white plastics, with boxes, fixing to masonry with screws; plugging										
Flush plate switches										
10 amp; one gang; one way; single pole	1.31	2.50	1.34	0.42	-	14.33	0.41	16.09	nr	17.70
10 amp; two gang; one way; single pole	2.27	2.50	2.32	0.43	-	14.68	0.41	17.41	nr	19.15
Surface plate switches										
10 amp; one gang; one way; single pole	4.76	2.50	4.88	0.42	-	14.33	0.41	19.62	nr	21.59
10 amp; two gang; one way; single pole	2.74	2.50	2.81	0.43	-	14.68	0.41	17.90	nr	19.69
Ceiling switches										
6 amp; one gang; one way; single pole	2.77	2.50	2.84	0.43	-	14.68	0.41	17.92	nr	19.72
Flush switched socket outlets										
13 amp; one gang	2.27	2.50	2.32	0.43	-	14.68	0.41	17.41	nr	19.15
13 amp; two gang	3.62	2.50	3.71	0.43	-	14.68	0.41	18.80	nr	20.68
Surface switched socket outlets										
13 amp; one gang	2.75	2.50	2.82	0.43	-	14.68	0.41	17.91	nr	19.70
13 amp; two gang	4.78	2.50	4.90	0.43	-	14.68	0.41	19.99	nr	21.99
Flush switched socket outlets with RCD (residual current device) protected at 30 mAmp										
13 amp; two gang	51.55	2.50	52.84	0.43	-	14.68	0.41	67.93	nr	74.72
Flush fused connection units										
13 amp; one gang; switched; flexible outlet	4.54	2.50	4.66	0.50	-	17.07	0.41	22.13	nr	24.35
13 amp; one gang; switched; flexible outlet; pilot lamp	6.37	2.50	6.53	0.50	-	17.07	0.41	24.00	nr	26.40
Accessories, metalclad, with boxes, fixing to masonry with screws; plugging										
Surface plate switches										
5 amp; one gang; two way; single pole	2.97	2.50	3.04	0.42	-	14.33	0.41	17.79	nr	19.57
5 amp; two gang; two way; single pole	3.44	2.50	3.53	0.43	-	14.68	0.41	18.62	nr	20.48
Surface switched socket outlets										
13 amp; one gang	2.96	2.50	3.03	0.43	-	14.68	0.41	18.12	nr	19.93
13 amp; two gang	3.74	2.50	3.84	0.43	-	14.68	0.41	18.92	nr	20.82
Weatherproof accessories, with boxes, fixing to masonry with screws; plugging										
Surface plate switches										
20 amp; one gang; two way; single pole	4.32	2.50	4.43	0.43	-	14.68	0.41	19.52	nr	21.47
LED strip lamp fittings, mains voltage operations; including LEDs										
Single Batten (excludes ballast and driver for fluorescent tube); replaceable LED Tube;										
1500mm; 24W LED Tube; Cool white, Daylight or White	21.48	-	21.48	1.20	-	40.96	0.82	63.26	nr	69.59
Slimline LED Batten Fittings; 4000k; with diffuser										
600mm; 9w; 910 lumens	13.20	-	13.20	1.00	-	34.13	0.82	48.15	nr	52.97
1200mm; 17w; 1800 lumens	17.58	-	17.58	1.00	-	34.13	0.82	52.54	nr	57.79
1500mm; 22w; 2300 lumens	24.36	-	24.36	1.20	-	40.96	0.82	66.14	nr	72.76
Single LED Batten Fittings; 4000K; with diffuser										
600mm; 10w; 1200 lumens	20.22	-	20.22	1.00	-	34.13	0.82	55.18	nr	60.69
1200mm; 20w; 2300 lumens	23.40	-	23.40	1.00	-	34.13	0.82	58.36	nr	64.19
1500mm; 26w; 1525 lumens	26.82	-	26.82	1.20	-	40.96	0.82	68.60	nr	75.46
1800mm; 30w; 3450 lumens	33.48	-	33.48	1.20	-	40.96	0.82	75.26	nr	82.79
Twin LED Batten Fitting; 4000K; with diffuser										
600mm; 20w; 2200 lumens	26.88	-	26.88	1.00	-	34.13	0.82	61.83	nr	68.02
1200mm; 40w; 4500 lumens	40.08	-	40.08	1.00	-	34.13	0.82	75.04	nr	82.54

Labour hourly rates: (except Specialists) Craft Operatives 34.13 Labourer 15.57 Rates are national average prices. Refer to REGIONAL VARIATIONS for indicative levels of overall pricing in regions	MATERIALS			LABOUR				RATES		
	Del to Site £	Waste %	Material Cost £	Craft Optve Hrs	Lab Hrs	Labour Cost £	Sunds £	Nett Rate £	Unit	Gross rate (10%) £
TERMINAL EQUIPMENT AND FITTINGS (Cont'd)										
LED strip lamp fittings, mains voltage operations; including LEDs (Cont'd)										
Twin LED Batten Fitting; 4000K; with diffuser (Cont'd)										
1500mm; 50w; 5250 lumens	45.18	-	45.18	1.20	-	40.96	0.82	86.96	nr	95.66
1800mm; 60w; 6500 lumens	59.76	-	59.76	1.20	-	40.96	0.82	101.54	nr	111.70
Tri Colour; LED Batten Fittings; 3000k to 6000k; with diffuser										
1200mm; 22w; 2500 to 2800 lumens	28.80	-	28.80	1.00	-	34.13	0.82	63.76	nr	70.13
1500mm); 35w; 3800 to 4200 lumens	34.56	-	34.56	1.20	-	40.96	0.82	76.34	nr	83.98
1800mm; 40w; 4600 to 5000 lumens	41.76	-	41.76	1.20	-	40.96	0.82	83.54	nr	91.90
Tri Colour; High Output; LED Batten Fittings; with diffuser										
1500mm; 60w; 6700 to 7400 lumens	56.82	-	56.82	1.20	-	40.96	0.82	98.60	nr	108.46
1800mm; 67w; 7300 to 7700 lumens	50.40	-	50.40	1.20	-	40.96	0.82	92.18	nr	101.40
Lighting fittings complete with lamps										
Bulkhead; polycarbonate										
12W Round with energy saving LED lamp	17.10	2.50	17.53	0.65	-	22.18	0.41	40.12	nr	44.14
Ceramic Wall Uplighter										
9W energy saving LED lamp	22.04	2.50	22.59	0.75	-	25.60	0.41	48.60	nr	53.46
Ceiling sphere										
150mm, 6W LED lamp	12.50	2.50	12.81	0.65	-	22.18	0.41	35.41	nr	38.95
180mm, 9W LED lamp	13.94	2.50	14.29	0.65	-	22.18	0.41	36.89	nr	40.57
Commercial Down light; recessed										
LED 24w c/w driver	26.09	2.50	26.74	0.65	-	22.18	0.41	49.34	nr	54.27
Lighting track; low Voltage										
1m track, transformer and 3 x 50W halogen lamps	68.73	2.50	70.45	1.20	-	40.96	0.82	112.23	nr	123.45
Plug-in fitting; 50W halogen lamp	12.59	2.50	12.90	0.20	-	6.83	0.41	20.14	nr	22.16
Fan heaters										
3kw unit fan heaters										
for commercial application	140.83	2.50	144.35	1.50	-	51.19	0.82	196.37	nr	216.01
Thermostatic switch units										
with concealed setting	27.48	2.50	28.17	1.00	-	34.13	0.41	62.71	nr	68.98
Tubular heaters										
Less than 150w per metre										
305mm long	16.14	2.50	16.54	1.00	-	34.13	1.24	51.91	nr	57.10
610mm long	18.54	2.50	19.00	1.00	-	34.13	1.24	54.37	nr	59.81
915mm long	21.78	2.50	22.32	1.00	-	34.13	1.65	58.10	nr	63.91
1220mm long	27.72	2.50	28.41	1.25	-	42.66	1.65	72.73	nr	80.00
1830mm long	40.62	2.50	41.64	1.50	-	51.19	2.47	95.31	nr	104.84
Night storage heaters to Lot 20 of ERP Directive; installed complete in new building including wiring										
Plastics insulated and sheathed cabled										
0.5KW	480.78	2.50	494.73	6.10	-	208.19	-	702.93	nr	773.22
0.7KW	513.18	2.50	527.94	6.30	-	215.02	-	742.96	nr	817.26
1KW	565.32	2.50	581.39	6.50	-	221.85	-	803.23	nr	883.56
1.25KW	622.92	2.50	640.43	7.00	-	238.91	-	879.34	nr	967.27
1.5KW	668.28	2.50	686.92	7.50	-	255.98	-	942.90	nr	1037.19
Mineral insulated copper sheathed cables										
0.5KW	567.62	2.50	589.05	10.50	-	358.37	-	947.41	nr	1042.15
0.7KW	600.02	2.50	622.26	11.00	-	375.43	-	997.69	nr	1097.46
1KW	652.16	2.50	675.70	12.00	-	409.56	-	1085.26	nr	1193.79
1.25KW	709.76	2.50	734.74	13.00	-	443.69	-	1178.43	nr	1296.27
1.5KW	755.12	2.50	781.23	14.00	-	477.82	-	1259.05	nr	1384.96
Bell equipment										
Transformers										
4-8-12V	7.80	2.50	7.99	0.40	-	13.65	0.40	22.04	nr	24.25
Bells for transformer operation										
chime 2-note	15.60	2.50	15.99	0.50	-	17.07	0.40	33.45	nr	36.80
76mm domestic type	9.72	2.50	9.96	0.50	-	17.07	0.40	27.42	nr	30.17
180mm round bell type	41.28	2.50	42.31	0.40	-	13.65	0.40	56.36	nr	62.00
Bell pushes										
domestic	2.39	2.50	2.45	0.25	-	8.53	-	10.98	nr	12.08
industrial/weatherproof	7.02	2.50	7.20	0.30	-	10.24	-	17.43	nr	19.18
Immersion heaters and thermostats										
Note: the following prices exclude Plumber's work										
2 or 3KW immersion heaters; without flanges										
305mm; non-withdrawable elements	13.68	2.50	14.02	0.65	-	22.18	7.67	43.88	nr	48.27
457mm; non-withdrawable elements	14.58	2.50	14.94	0.80	-	27.30	7.67	49.92	nr	54.91
686mm; non-withdrawable elements	16.50	2.50	16.91	0.95	-	32.42	7.67	57.01	nr	62.71
Thermostats										
immersion heater	7.98	2.50	8.18	0.50	-	17.07	0.41	25.66	nr	28.22
16 amp a.c. for air heating; without switch	26.58	2.50	27.24	0.40	-	13.65	0.41	41.31	nr	45.44

Labour hourly rates: (except Specialists) Craft Operatives 34.13 Labourer 15.57 Rates are national average prices. Refer to REGIONAL VARIATIONS for indicative levels of overall pricing in regions	MATERIALS			LABOUR				RATES		
	Del to Site £	Waste %	Material Cost £	Craft Optve Hrs	Lab Hrs	Labour Cost £	Sunds £	Nett Rate £	Unit	Gross rate (10%) £
TERMINAL EQUIPMENT AND FITTINGS (Cont'd)										
Water heaters										
Note: the following prices exclude Plumber's work										
Storage type units; oversink, single outlet										
5 liter, 2kW	63.42	-	63.42	1.50	-	51.19	8.50	123.11	nr	135.42
7 litre, 3kW	91.63	-	91.63	1.50	-	51.19	8.50	151.33	nr	166.46
10 litre, 2kW	124.04	-	124.04	1.50	-	51.19	8.50	183.73	nr	202.11
Storage type units; unvented; multi-point										
30 litre, 3kW	277.48	-	277.48	4.00	-	136.52	13.17	427.17	nr	469.89
50 litre, 3kW	299.15	-	299.15	4.50	-	153.59	13.17	465.90	nr	512.49
80 litre, 3kW	365.82	-	365.82	5.25	-	179.18	16.99	561.99	nr	618.19
100 litre, 3kW	381.65	-	381.65	6.00	-	204.78	16.99	603.42	nr	663.77
Shower units										
Note: the following prices exclude Plumber's work										
Instantaneous shower units complete with fittings	112.86	2.50	115.68	4.00	-	136.52	12.75	264.95	nr	291.45
Street lighting columns and set in ground; excavate hole, remove surplus spoil, filling with concrete mix ST4, working around base										
Galvanised steel columns; nominal mounting height										
4.00m										
30w LED post top sphere lantern; Part night photo cell	561.79	5.00	562.36	4.75	9.50	310.03	35.13	907.52	nr	998.28
40w LED lantern; Single arm mounted; Full night photo cell	360.51	5.00	361.09	4.75	9.50	310.03	35.13	706.25	nr	776.88
5.00m										
25w LED post top elegant lantern; Single arm mounted: Part night photo cell	808.77	5.00	809.34	4.75	9.50	310.03	54.65	1174.02	nr	1291.43
2 off 25w LED post top elegant lanterns; Double arm mounted: Part night photo cell	822.59	5.00	823.16	4.75	9.50	310.03	54.65	1187.84	nr	1306.63
6.00m										
40w (5600 lumens) Cobra style LED lantern; Single arm mounted: Part night photo cell	347.06	5.00	347.76	4.75	9.50	310.03	119.06	776.86	nr	854.54
2 off 40w (5600 lumens) Cobra style LED lanterns; Double arm mounted: Part night photo cell	452.42	5.00	453.12	4.75	9.50	310.03	119.06	882.22	nr	970.44
8.00m										
60w (8400 lumens) Cobra style LED lantern; Single arm mounted: Full night photo cell	544.04	5.00	544.87	4.75	9.50	310.03	119.06	973.96	nr	1071.36
2 off 60w (8600 lumens) Cobra style LED lanterns; Double arm mounted: Full night photo cell	663.24	5.00	664.07	4.75	9.50	310.03	119.06	1093.17	nr	1202.48
10.00m										
80w (11200 lumens) Cobra style LED lantern; Single arm mounted: Full night photo cell	726.63	5.00	727.66	4.75	9.50	310.03	119.06	1156.75	nr	1272.43
2 off 80w (11200 lumens) Cobra style LED lanterns; Double arm mounted: Full night photo cell	740.45	5.00	741.48	4.75	9.50	310.03	119.06	1170.57	nr	1287.63
CABLE CONTAINMENT										
Steel trunking										
Lighting trunking 50mm x 50mm; PVC lid										
straight lengths, per m	5.33	5.00	5.60	0.40	-	13.65	0.82	20.07	m	22.08
extra; end cap	1.07	-	1.07	0.08	-	2.73	0.41	4.21	nr	4.63
extra; internal angle	7.87	-	7.87	0.25	-	8.53	0.41	16.82	nr	18.50
extra; external angle	7.76	-	7.76	0.25	-	8.53	0.41	16.71	nr	18.38
extra; tee	8.50	-	8.50	0.25	-	8.53	0.41	17.44	nr	19.19
extra; flat bend	7.76	-	7.76	0.40	-	13.65	0.41	21.82	nr	24.01
extra; trunking suspension fixed to 10mm studding	1.97	-	1.97	0.25	-	8.53	0.82	11.33	nr	12.46
Dado trunking, 150mm x 40mm, two compartment; steel lid										
straight lengths, per m	36.75	5.00	38.59	0.45	-	15.36	0.82	54.77	m	60.25
extra; end cap	9.27	-	9.27	0.08	-	2.73	0.41	12.42	nr	13.66
extra; internal angle	34.64	-	34.64	0.35	-	11.95	0.41	47.00	nr	51.70
extra; external angle	34.64	-	34.64	0.35	-	11.95	0.41	47.00	nr	51.70
extra; single socket plate	17.56	-	17.56	0.16	-	5.46	0.41	23.43	nr	25.78
extra; twin socket plate	17.56	-	17.56	0.16	-	5.46	0.41	23.43	nr	25.78
Dado trunking, 200mm x 40mm, three compartment; steel lid										
straight lengths, per m	50.78	5.00	53.32	0.50	-	17.07	1.24	71.62	m	78.78
extra; end cap	35.22	-	35.22	0.08	-	2.73	0.41	38.37	nr	42.20
extra; internal angle	54.85	-	54.85	0.40	-	13.65	0.41	68.91	nr	75.80
extra; external angle	54.85	-	54.85	0.40	-	13.65	0.41	68.91	nr	75.80
extra; single socket plate	28.47	-	28.47	0.16	-	5.46	0.41	34.34	nr	37.78
extra; twin socket plate	28.47	-	28.47	0.16	-	5.46	0.41	34.34	nr	37.78
Skirting trunking; 200mm x 40mm, three compartment; steel lid										
straight lengths, per m	46.76	5.00	49.10	0.50	-	17.07	1.24	67.40	m	74.14
extra; internal bend	50.92	-	50.92	0.40	-	13.65	0.41	64.99	nr	71.49
extra; external bend	50.92	-	50.92	0.40	-	13.65	0.41	64.99	nr	71.49
extra; single socket plate	20.62	-	20.62	0.16	-	5.46	0.41	26.49	nr	29.14
extra; twin socket plate	20.62	-	20.62	0.16	-	5.46	0.41	26.49	nr	29.14
Underfloor trunking; 150mm x 25mm, two compartments										
straight lengths, per m	19.58	5.00	20.56	0.70	-	23.89	-	44.45	m	48.89
extra; floor junction boxes; four way; adjustable frame and trap	110.98	-	110.98	1.85	-	63.14	-	174.12	nr	191.54
extra; horizontal bend	56.82	-	56.82	0.50	-	17.07	-	73.88	nr	81.27

Labour hourly rates: (except Specialists) Craft Operatives 34.13 Labourer 15.57 Rates are national average prices. Refer to REGIONAL VARIATIONS for indicative levels of overall pricing in regions	MATERIALS			LABOUR				RATES		
	Del to Site £	Waste %	Material Cost £	Craft Optve Hrs	Lab Hrs	Labour Cost £	Sunds £	Nett Rate £	Unit	Gross rate (10%) £
CABLE CONTAINMENT (Cont'd)										
PVC trunking; white										
Straight mini-trunking; clip on lid										
16 x 16mm										
straight lengths, per m	1.38	5.00	1.45	0.20	-	6.83	0.82	9.10	m	10.01
extra; end cap	0.61	-	0.61	0.04	-	1.37	0.21	2.19	nr	2.41
extra; internal bend	0.79	-	0.79	0.08	-	2.73	0.21	3.73	nr	4.11
extra; external bend	0.79	-	0.79	0.08	-	2.73	0.21	3.73	nr	4.11
extra; flat bend	0.79	-	0.79	0.08	-	2.73	0.21	3.73	nr	4.11
extra; equal tee	1.49	-	1.49	0.17	-	5.80	0.21	7.51	nr	8.26
25 x 16mm										
straight lengths, per m	1.48	5.00	1.55	0.20	-	6.83	0.21	8.59	m	9.45
extra; end cap	0.61	-	0.61	0.04	-	1.37	0.21	2.19	nr	2.41
extra; internal bend	0.79	-	0.79	0.08	-	2.73	0.21	3.73	nr	4.11
extra; external bend	0.79	-	0.79	0.08	-	2.73	0.21	3.73	nr	4.11
extra; flat bend	0.79	-	0.79	0.08	-	2.73	0.21	3.73	nr	4.11
extra; equal tee	1.60	-	1.60	0.17	-	5.80	0.21	7.62	nr	8.38
40 x 16mm										
straight lengths, per m	2.80	5.00	2.94	0.25	-	8.53	0.21	11.69	m	12.86
extra; end cap	0.61	-	0.61	0.04	-	1.37	0.21	2.19	nr	2.41
extra; internal bend	1.04	-	1.04	0.08	-	2.73	0.21	3.98	nr	4.38
extra; external bend	1.94	-	1.94	0.08	-	2.73	0.21	4.88	nr	5.37
extra; flat bend	1.19	-	1.19	0.08	-	2.73	0.21	4.13	nr	4.55
extra; equal tee	1.60	-	1.60	0.17	-	5.80	0.21	7.62	nr	8.38
Straight dado trunking, three compartment; clip on lid										
145 x 50mm										
straight lengths, per m	13.99	5.00	14.69	0.40	-	13.65	0.82	29.17	m	32.09
extra; end caps	2.29	-	2.29	0.08	-	2.73	0.41	5.43	nr	5.98
extra; internal bend; adjustable	5.99	-	5.99	0.30	-	10.24	0.41	16.64	nr	18.31
extra; external bend; adjustable	4.99	-	4.99	0.30	-	10.24	0.41	15.64	nr	17.21
extra; tee	39.98	-	39.98	0.40	-	13.65	0.41	54.04	nr	59.45
extra; flat angle	31.98	-	31.98	0.30	-	10.24	0.41	42.63	nr	46.89
extra; straight coupler	2.00	-	2.00	0.20	-	6.83	0.41	9.24	nr	10.16
180 x 57mm curved profile										
straight lengths, per m	21.63	5.00	22.71	0.45	-	15.36	0.82	38.90	m	42.78
extra; end caps	3.50	-	3.50	0.08	-	2.73	0.41	6.64	nr	7.31
extra; internal bend	6.50	-	6.50	0.30	-	10.24	0.41	17.15	nr	18.87
extra; external bend	6.50	-	6.50	0.30	-	10.24	0.41	17.15	nr	18.87
extra; straight coupler	4.29	-	4.29	0.20	-	6.83	0.41	11.53	nr	12.68
Straight skirting trunking, three compartment; clip on lid										
170 x 50mm										
straight lengths, per m	10.87	5.00	11.42	0.35	-	11.95	0.82	24.19	m	26.61
extra; end cap	1.40	-	1.40	0.06	-	2.05	0.41	3.86	nr	4.25
extra; internal corner	3.60	-	3.60	0.25	-	8.53	0.41	12.55	nr	13.80
extra; external corner	3.50	-	3.50	0.25	-	8.53	0.41	12.44	nr	13.69
extra; straight coupler	1.23	-	1.23	0.16	-	5.46	0.41	7.10	nr	7.81
extra; socket adaptor, box one gang	1.55	-	1.55	0.25	-	8.53	0.41	10.49	nr	11.54
extra; socket adaptor box, two gang	1.78	-	1.78	0.25	-	8.53	0.41	10.73	nr	11.80
PVC heavy gauge conduit and fittings; push fit joints; spacer bar saddles at 600mm centres										
Conduits; straight										
20mm diameter; plugging to masonry; to surfaces										
straight lengths, per m	0.50	10.00	0.55	0.17	-	5.80	0.69	7.04	m	7.74
extra; small circular terminal boxes	1.12	2.50	1.14	0.10	-	3.41	0.45	5.00	nr	5.50
extra; small circular angle boxes	1.12	2.50	1.15	0.11	-	3.75	0.45	5.35	nr	5.89
extra; small circular three way boxes	1.12	2.50	1.14	0.13	-	4.44	0.45	6.03	nr	6.63
extra; small circular through way boxes	1.12	2.50	1.14	0.11	-	3.75	0.45	5.34	nr	5.88
25mm diameter; plugging to masonry; to surfaces										
straight lengths, per m	0.76	10.00	0.83	0.18	-	6.14	0.69	7.67	m	8.44
extra; small circular terminal boxes	1.17	2.50	1.20	0.10	-	3.41	0.45	5.05	nr	5.56
extra; small circular angle boxes	1.27	2.50	1.31	0.11	-	3.75	0.45	5.51	nr	6.06
extra; small circular three way boxes	1.30	2.50	1.33	0.13	-	4.44	0.45	6.21	nr	6.84
extra; small circular through way boxes	1.29	2.50	1.32	0.11	-	3.75	0.45	5.52	nr	6.08
20mm diameter; plugging to masonry; in chases										
straight lengths, per m	0.50	10.00	0.55	0.15	-	5.12	0.69	6.36	m	6.99
extra; small circular terminal boxes	1.12	2.50	1.14	0.10	-	3.41	0.45	5.00	nr	5.50
extra; small circular angle boxes	1.12	2.50	1.15	0.11	-	3.75	0.45	5.35	nr	5.89
extra; small circular three way boxes	1.12	2.50	1.14	0.13	-	4.44	0.45	6.03	nr	6.63
extra; small circular through way boxes	1.12	2.50	1.14	0.11	-	3.75	0.45	5.34	nr	5.88
25mm diameter; plugging to masonry; in chases										
straight lengths, per m	0.76	10.00	0.83	0.16	-	5.46	0.45	6.74	m	7.41
extra; small circular terminal boxes	1.17	2.50	1.20	0.10	-	3.41	0.45	5.05	nr	5.56
extra; small circular angle boxes	1.27	2.50	1.31	0.11	-	3.75	0.45	5.51	nr	6.06
extra; small circular three way boxes	1.30	2.50	1.33	0.13	-	4.44	0.45	6.21	nr	6.84
extra; small circular through way boxes	1.29	2.50	1.32	0.11	-	3.75	0.45	5.52	nr	6.08
Oval conduits; straight										
20mm (nominal size); plugging to masonry; in chases	0.45	10.00	0.50	0.15	-	5.12	0.69	6.31	m	6.94
25mm (nominal size); plugging to masonry in chases	0.32	10.00	0.36	0.16	-	5.46	0.69	6.51	m	7.16
20mm (nominal size); fixing to timber	0.45	10.00	0.50	0.13	-	4.44	0.35	5.28	m	5.81
25mm (nominal size); fixing to timber	0.32	10.00	0.36	0.15	-	5.12	0.35	5.82	m	6.40
Steel welded heavy gauge conduits and fittings, screwed joints; spacer bar saddles at 1000mm centres; enamelled black inside and outside by manufacturer										
Conduits; straight										
20mm diameter; plugging to masonry; to surfaces										
straight lengths, per m	2.52	10.00	2.76	0.33	-	11.26	0.45	14.47	m	15.92
extra; small circular terminal boxes	2.27	2.50	2.32	0.13	-	4.44	0.45	7.21	nr	7.93

Labour hourly rates: (except Specialists) Craft Operatives 34.13 Labourer 15.57 Rates are national average prices. Refer to REGIONAL VARIATIONS for indicative levels of overall pricing in regions	MATERIALS			LABOUR				RATES		
	Del to Site £	Waste %	Material Cost £	Craft Optve Hrs	Lab Hrs	Labour Cost £	Sunds £	Nett Rate £	Unit	Gross rate (10%) £
CABLE CONTAINMENT (Cont'd)										
Steel welded heavy gauge conduits and fittings, screwed joints; spacer bar saddles at 1000mm centres; enamelled black inside and outside by manufacturer (Cont'd)										
Conduits; straight (Cont'd)										
20mm diameter; plugging to masonry; to surfaces (Cont'd)										
extra; small circular angle boxes	2.49	2.50	2.55	0.16	-	5.46	0.45	8.45	nr	9.30
extra; small circular three way boxes	2.71	2.50	2.77	0.20	-	6.83	0.45	10.05	nr	11.05
extra; small circular through way boxes	2.63	2.50	2.69	0.16	-	5.46	0.45	8.60	nr	9.46
25mm diameter; plugging to masonry; to surfaces										
straight lengths, per m	3.34	10.00	3.67	0.42	-	14.33	0.45	18.45	m	20.29
extra; small circular terminal boxes	3.05	2.50	3.12	0.13	-	4.44	0.45	8.00	nr	8.81
extra; small circular angle boxes	25.01	2.50	25.63	0.16	-	5.46	0.45	31.54	nr	34.69
extra; small circular three way boxes	3.78	2.50	3.87	0.20	-	6.83	0.45	11.14	nr	12.26
extra; small circular through way boxes	3.57	2.50	3.66	0.16	-	5.46	0.45	9.56	nr	10.52
Steel welded heavy gauge conduits and fittings, screwed joints; spacer bar saddles at 1000mm centres; galvanised inside and outside by manufacturer										
Conduits; straight										
20mm diameter; plugging to masonry; to surfaces										
straight lengths, per m	2.50	10.00	2.74	0.33	-	11.26	0.45	14.45	m	15.89
extra; small circular terminal boxes	2.14	2.50	2.19	0.13	-	4.44	0.45	7.07	nr	7.78
extra; small circular angle boxes	1.91	2.50	1.96	0.16	-	5.46	0.45	7.86	nr	8.65
extra; small circular three way boxes	2.15	2.50	2.20	0.20	-	6.83	0.45	9.47	nr	10.42
extra; small circular through way boxes	1.91	2.50	1.96	0.16	-	5.46	0.45	7.86	nr	8.65
25mm diameter; plugging to masonry; to surfaces										
straight lengths, per m	2.36	10.00	2.58	0.42	-	14.33	0.41	17.33	m	19.06
extra; small circular terminal boxes	2.92	2.50	2.99	0.13	-	4.44	0.45	7.87	nr	8.66
extra; small circular angle boxes	2.02	2.50	2.07	0.16	-	5.46	0.45	7.98	nr	8.77
extra; small circular three way boxes	2.52	2.50	2.58	0.20	-	6.83	0.45	9.85	nr	10.84
extra; small circular through way boxes	2.27	2.50	2.33	0.16	-	5.46	0.45	8.23	nr	9.06
Galvanised standard cable tray and fittings										
Light duty; straight										
50mm tray										
straight lengths, per m	2.50	5.00	2.62	0.25	-	8.53	0.15	11.31	m	12.44
extra; flat bend	10.64	-	10.64	0.20	-	6.83	0.41	17.88	nr	19.67
extra; tee	15.69	-	15.69	0.25	-	8.53	0.41	24.63	nr	27.10
extra; cross piece	12.26	-	12.26	0.40	-	13.65	0.82	26.74	nr	29.41
extra; riser bend	6.26	-	6.26	0.20	-	6.83	0.41	13.50	nr	14.85
100mm tray										
straight lengths, per m	5.01	5.00	5.26	0.33	-	11.26	0.15	16.68	m	18.34
extra; flat bend	10.04	-	10.04	0.23	-	7.85	0.41	18.30	nr	20.13
extra; tee	12.19	-	12.19	0.30	-	10.24	0.41	22.84	nr	25.13
extra; cross piece	17.56	-	17.56	0.41	-	13.99	0.82	32.38	nr	35.62
extra; riser bend	7.02	-	7.02	0.23	-	7.85	0.41	15.28	nr	16.81
extra; reducer 100 to 50mm	12.40	-	12.40	0.23	-	7.85	0.41	20.67	nr	22.73
150mm tray										
straight lengths, per m	6.14	5.00	6.44	0.42	-	14.33	0.15	20.93	m	23.02
extra; flat bend	16.30	-	16.30	0.25	-	8.53	0.41	25.24	nr	27.77
extra; tee	20.67	-	20.67	0.33	-	11.26	0.41	32.35	nr	35.58
extra; cross piece	23.12	-	23.12	0.42	-	14.33	0.82	38.28	nr	42.11
extra; riser bend	8.23	-	8.23	0.25	-	8.53	0.41	17.17	nr	18.89
extra; reducer 150 to 100mm	13.72	-	13.72	0.25	-	8.53	0.41	22.67	nr	24.93
300mm tray										
straight lengths, per m	9.92	5.00	10.42	0.50	-	17.07	0.15	27.63	m	30.40
extra; flat bend	29.05	-	29.05	0.33	-	11.26	0.41	40.73	nr	44.80
extra; tee	31.89	-	31.89	0.50	-	17.07	0.41	49.37	nr	54.30
extra; cross piece	41.84	-	41.84	0.58	-	19.80	0.82	62.46	nr	68.71
extra; riser bend	13.55	-	13.55	0.33	-	11.26	0.41	25.23	nr	27.75
extra; reducer 300 to 150mm	16.65	-	16.65	0.33	-	11.26	0.41	28.32	nr	31.15
450mm tray										
straight lengths, per m	33.79	5.00	35.48	0.58	-	19.80	0.15	55.42	m	60.96
extra; flat bend	46.77	-	46.77	0.50	-	17.07	0.41	64.25	nr	70.67
extra; tee	56.98	-	56.98	0.75	-	25.60	0.41	82.99	nr	91.29
extra; cross piece	71.35	-	71.35	1.00	-	34.13	0.82	106.31	nr	116.94
extra; riser bend	19.08	-	19.08	0.50	-	17.07	0.41	36.56	nr	40.21
extra; reducer 450 to 300mm	24.56	-	24.56	0.50	-	17.07	0.41	42.04	nr	46.24
Medium duty; straight										
75mm tray										
straight lengths, per m	4.16	5.00	4.37	0.26	-	8.87	0.15	13.39	m	14.73
extra; flat bend	11.06	-	11.06	0.21	-	7.17	0.41	18.64	nr	20.50
extra; tee	12.67	-	12.67	0.26	-	8.87	0.41	21.96	nr	24.15
extra; cross piece	19.81	-	19.81	0.42	-	14.33	0.82	34.97	nr	38.47
extra; riser bend	6.92	-	6.92	0.21	-	7.17	0.41	14.50	nr	15.95
100mm tray										
straight lengths, per m	4.53	5.00	4.75	0.34	-	11.60	0.15	16.51	m	18.16
extra; flat bend	10.98	-	10.98	0.24	-	8.19	0.41	19.58	nr	21.54
extra; tee	13.98	-	13.98	0.31	-	10.58	0.41	24.97	nr	27.47
extra; cross piece	19.69	-	19.69	0.43	-	14.68	0.82	35.19	nr	38.71
extra; riser bend	7.02	-	7.02	0.24	-	8.19	0.41	15.62	nr	17.19
extra; reducer 100 to 75mm	11.12	-	11.12	0.24	-	8.19	0.41	19.73	nr	21.70
150mm tray										
straight lengths, per m	4.73	5.00	4.96	0.44	-	15.02	0.15	20.13	m	22.14
extra; flat bend	12.23	-	12.23	0.26	-	8.87	0.41	21.52	nr	23.67
extra; tee	14.78	-	14.78	0.34	-	11.60	0.41	26.80	nr	29.48
extra; cross piece	22.92	-	22.92	0.44	-	15.02	0.82	38.76	nr	42.64
extra; riser bend	8.23	-	8.23	0.26	-	8.87	0.41	17.52	nr	19.27
extra; reducer 150 to 100mm	11.61	-	11.61	0.26	-	8.87	0.41	20.90	nr	22.99

Labour hourly rates: (except Specialists) Craft Operatives 34.13 Labourer 15.57 Rates are national average prices. Refer to REGIONAL VARIATIONS for indicative levels of overall pricing in regions	MATERIALS			LABOUR				RATES		
	Del to Site £	Waste %	Material Cost £	Craft Optve Hrs	Lab Hrs	Labour Cost £	Sunds £	Nett Rate £	Unit	Gross rate (10%) £
CABLE CONTAINMENT (Cont'd)										
Galvanised standard cable tray and fittings (Cont'd)										
Medium duty; straight (Cont'd)										
300mm tray										
straight lengths, per m	12.19	5.00	12.80	0.52	-	17.75	0.15	30.70	m	33.77
extra; flat bend	18.98	-	18.98	0.34	-	11.60	0.41	31.00	nr	34.10
extra; tee	21.43	-	21.43	0.52	-	17.75	0.41	39.59	nr	43.55
extra; cross piece	35.89	-	35.89	0.61	-	20.82	0.82	57.53	nr	63.29
extra; riser bend	13.55	-	13.55	0.34	-	11.60	0.41	25.57	nr	28.12
extra; reducer 300 to 150mm	17.15	-	17.15	0.34	-	11.60	0.41	29.17	nr	32.09
450mm tray										
straight lengths, per m	17.95	5.00	18.85	0.61	-	20.82	0.15	39.82	m	43.80
extra; flat bend	24.97	-	24.97	0.52	-	17.75	0.41	43.13	nr	47.44
extra; tee	29.72	-	29.72	0.78	-	26.62	0.41	56.75	nr	62.43
extra; cross piece	58.83	-	58.83	1.05	-	35.84	0.82	95.49	nr	105.04
extra; riser bend	19.08	-	19.08	0.52	-	17.75	0.41	37.24	nr	40.96
extra; reducer 450 to 300mm	17.74	-	17.74	0.52	-	17.75	0.41	35.90	nr	39.49
Heavy duty; straight										
75mm tray										
straight lengths, per m	5.05	5.00	5.30	0.27	-	9.22	0.15	14.67	m	16.13
extra; flat bend	11.50	-	11.50	0.22	-	7.51	0.41	19.42	nr	21.36
extra; tee	13.11	-	13.11	0.27	-	9.22	0.41	22.74	nr	25.01
extra; cross piece	17.99	-	17.99	0.44	-	15.02	0.82	33.83	nr	37.21
extra; riser bend	8.61	-	8.61	0.22	-	7.51	0.41	16.53	nr	18.18
100mm tray										
straight lengths, per m	5.36	5.00	5.62	0.36	-	12.29	0.15	18.06	m	19.87
extra; flat bend	11.59	-	11.59	0.25	-	8.53	0.41	20.53	nr	22.59
extra; tee	13.20	-	13.20	0.33	-	11.26	0.41	24.88	nr	27.36
extra; cross piece	18.66	-	18.66	0.45	-	15.36	0.82	34.84	nr	38.32
extra; riser bend	9.10	-	9.10	0.25	-	8.53	0.41	18.05	nr	19.85
extra; reducer 100 to 75mm	12.55	-	12.55	0.25	-	8.53	0.41	21.49	nr	23.64
150mm tray										
straight lengths, per m	5.94	5.00	6.24	0.46	-	15.70	0.15	22.09	m	24.30
extra; flat bend	12.70	-	12.70	0.27	-	9.22	0.41	22.33	nr	24.56
extra; tee	19.65	-	19.65	0.36	-	12.29	0.41	32.35	nr	35.58
extra; cross piece	23.51	-	23.51	0.46	-	15.70	0.82	40.03	nr	44.03
extra; riser bend	9.88	-	9.88	0.27	-	9.22	0.41	19.51	nr	21.46
extra; reducer 150 to 100mm	13.11	-	13.11	0.27	-	9.22	0.41	22.74	nr	25.02
300mm tray										
straight lengths, per m	11.99	5.00	12.59	0.55	-	18.77	0.15	31.51	m	34.66
extra; flat bend	16.79	-	16.79	0.36	-	12.29	0.41	29.49	nr	32.44
extra; tee	20.35	-	20.35	0.55	-	18.77	0.41	39.53	nr	43.49
extra; cross piece	46.65	-	46.65	0.64	-	21.84	0.82	69.32	nr	76.25
extra; riser bend	15.62	-	15.62	0.36	-	12.29	0.41	28.32	nr	31.15
extra; reducer 300 to 150mm	17.11	-	17.11	0.36	-	12.29	0.41	29.81	nr	32.79
450mm tray										
straight lengths, per m	30.30	5.00	31.82	0.64	-	21.84	0.15	53.81	m	59.19
extra; flat bend	20.56	-	20.56	0.55	-	18.77	0.41	39.74	nr	43.72
extra; tee	30.43	-	30.43	0.83	-	28.33	0.41	59.17	nr	65.09
extra; cross piece	82.13	-	82.13	1.10	-	37.54	0.41	120.09	nr	132.10
extra; riser bend	49.51	-	49.51	0.55	-	18.77	0.41	68.69	nr	75.56
extra; reducer 450 to 300mm	20.06	-	20.06	0.55	-	18.77	0.41	39.24	nr	43.16
Supports for cable tray										
Cantilever arms; mild steel; hot dip galvanised; fixing to masonry										
100mm wide	5.72	2.50	5.87	0.33	-	11.26	0.41	17.54	nr	19.30
300mm wide	14.80	2.50	15.17	0.33	-	11.26	0.41	26.84	nr	29.53
450mm wide	18.58	2.50	19.04	0.33	-	11.26	0.41	30.71	nr	33.79
Stand-off bracket; mild steel; hot dip galvanised; fixing to masonry										
75mm wide	3.11	2.50	3.18	0.33	-	11.26	0.41	14.86	nr	16.34
100mm wide	3.76	2.50	3.85	0.33	-	11.26	0.41	15.53	nr	17.08
150mm wide	3.84	2.50	3.93	0.33	-	11.26	0.41	15.61	nr	17.17
300mm wide	6.70	2.50	6.87	0.42	-	14.33	0.41	21.61	nr	23.77
450mm wide	7.37	2.50	7.55	0.42	-	14.33	0.41	22.30	nr	24.53
CABLES										
PVC insulated cables; single core; reference 6491X; stranded copper conductors; to BS 6004										
Drawn into conduits or ducts or laid or drawn into trunking										
1.5mm²	0.20	15.00	0.23	0.03	-	1.02	-	1.25	m	1.37
2.5mm²	0.30	15.00	0.34	0.03	-	1.02	-	1.37	m	1.50
4.0mm²	0.49	15.00	0.56	0.04	-	1.37	-	1.93	m	2.12
6.0mm²	0.73	15.00	0.84	0.05	-	1.71	-	2.55	m	2.80
10.0mm²	1.24	15.00	1.42	0.05	-	1.71	-	3.13	m	3.44
16.0mm²	0.02	15.00	0.02	0.08	-	2.56	-	2.58	m	2.84
PVC double insulated cables; single core; reference 6181Y; stranded copper conductors; to BS 6004										
Fixed to timber with clips										
10.0mm²	1.66	15.00	1.90	0.08	-	2.73	-	4.63	m	5.10
16.0mm²	3.00	15.00	3.45	0.10	-	3.41	-	6.86	m	7.55
25.0mm²	3.18	15.00	3.66	0.15	-	5.12	-	8.78	m	9.65
35.0mm²	5.70	15.00	6.55	0.20	-	6.83	-	13.38	m	14.72

Labour hourly rates: (except Specialists) Craft Operatives 34.13 Labourer 15.57 Rates are national average prices. Refer to REGIONAL VARIATIONS for indicative levels of overall pricing in regions	MATERIALS			LABOUR				RATES		
	Del to Site £	Waste %	Material Cost £	Craft Optve Hrs	Lab Hrs	Labour Cost £	Sunds £	Nett Rate £	Unit	Gross rate (10%) £
CABLES (Cont'd)										
PVC insulated and PVC sheathed cables; multicore; copper conductors and bare earth continuity conductor 6242Y; to BS 6004										
Drawn into conduits or ducts or laid or drawn into trunking										
1.0mm²; twin with bare earth	0.38	15.00	0.44	0.05	-	1.71	-	2.15	m	2.36
1.5mm²; twin with bare earth	0.49	15.00	0.57	0.05	-	1.71	-	2.27	m	2.50
2.5mm²; twin with bare earth	0.72	15.00	0.83	0.05	-	1.71	-	2.53	m	2.79
4.0mm²; twin with bare earth	1.27	15.00	1.46	0.06	-	2.05	-	3.51	m	3.86
6.0mm²; twin with bare earth	1.78	15.00	2.05	0.07	-	2.39	-	4.44	m	4.88
Fixed to timber with clips										
1.0mm²; twin with bare earth	0.38	15.00	0.44	0.07	-	2.39	0.10	2.93	m	3.22
1.5mm²; twin with bare earth	0.49	15.00	0.57	0.07	-	2.39	0.10	3.05	m	3.36
2.5mm²; twin with bare earth	0.72	15.00	0.83	0.07	-	2.39	0.12	3.33	m	3.67
4.0mm²; twin with bare earth	1.27	15.00	1.46	0.08	-	2.73	0.13	4.33	m	4.76
6.0mm²; twin with bare earth	1.78	15.00	2.05	0.09	-	3.07	0.13	5.25	m	5.78
PVC insulated SWA armoured and PVC sheathed cables; multicore; copper conductors										
Laid and laced on cable tray										
16mm²; three core	5.33	5.00	5.60	0.17	-	5.80	0.18	11.58	m	12.74
Fixed to masonry with screwed clips at average 300mm centres; plugging										
16mm²; three core	5.33	5.00	5.60	0.25	-	8.53	1.55	15.68	m	17.25
Mineral insulated copper sheathed cables; PVC outer sheath; copper conductors; 600V light duty to BS EN 60702-1										
Fixed to masonry with screwed clips at average 300mm centres; plugging										
1.5mm²; two core	4.28	10.00	4.70	0.17	-	5.80	1.55	12.06	m	13.26
extra; termination including gland, seal and shroud	3.31	2.50	3.39	0.42	-	14.33	-	17.73	nr	19.50
2.5mm²; two core	5.41	10.00	5.95	0.17	-	5.80	1.55	13.30	m	14.63
extra; termination including gland, seal and shroud	3.31	2.50	3.39	0.42	-	14.33	-	17.73	nr	19.50
4.0mm²; two core	8.12	10.00	8.94	0.20	-	6.83	1.55	17.31	m	19.05
extra; termination including gland, seal and shroud	3.31	2.50	3.39	0.50	-	17.07	-	20.46	nr	22.50
FINAL CIRCUITS; DOMESTIC LIGHTING AND POWER (SMALL SCALE)										
Electric wiring										
Note the following approximate prices of various types of installations are dependant on the number and disposition of points; lamps and fittings together with cutting and making good are excluded										
Electric wiring in new building										
Domestic metalclad, 17th Edition, 3rd Amendment, Consumer unit, fixed to masonry with screws; plugging										
2 usable ways 60A DP main Switch	43.38	2.50	44.46	1.10	-	37.54	0.41	82.42	nr	90.66
6 usable ways 100A DP main Switch	53.40	2.50	54.73	2.00	-	68.26	0.41	123.41	nr	135.75
10 usable ways 100A DP main Switch	64.20	2.50	65.81	2.60	-	88.74	0.41	154.96	nr	170.45
14 usable ways 100A DP main Switch	72.60	2.50	74.42	3.50	-	119.46	0.41	194.28	nr	213.71
19 usable ways 100A DP main Switch	81.00	2.50	83.02	5.00	-	170.65	0.41	254.09	nr	279.50
2 usable ways 63A, 30mA RCD main Switch	60.96	2.50	62.48	1.15	-	39.25	0.41	102.15	nr	112.36
6 usable ways 80A, 30mA RCD main Switch	69.36	2.50	71.09	2.05	-	69.97	0.41	141.47	nr	155.62
10 usable ways 80A, 30mA RCD main Switch	80.16	2.50	82.16	2.65	-	90.44	0.41	173.02	nr	190.32
14 usable ways 80A, 30mA RCD main Switch	88.56	2.50	90.77	3.55	-	121.16	0.41	212.35	nr	233.58
19 usable ways 80A, 30mA RCD main Switch	96.96	2.50	99.38	5.05	-	172.36	0.41	272.15	nr	299.37
Domestic weatherproof consumer unit, fixed to masonry with screws; plugging										
4 usable ways 60A DP main Switch	64.50	3.00	66.37	1.90	-	64.85	0.41	131.63	nr	144.80
8 usable ways 100A DP main Switch	85.14	3.00	87.63	2.70	-	92.15	0.41	180.19	nr	198.21
10 usable ways 100A DP main Switch	132.48	3.00	136.39	3.10	-	105.80	0.41	242.60	nr	266.86
22 usable ways 100A DP main Switch	199.50	3.00	205.42	5.50	-	187.72	0.41	393.54	nr	432.90
34 usable ways 100A DP main Switch	268.08	3.00	276.05	7.90	-	269.63	0.41	546.09	nr	600.70
4 usable ways 63A, 30mA RCD main Switch	82.08	3.00	84.39	1.95	-	66.55	0.41	151.36	nr	166.50
8 usable ways 80A, 30mA RCD main Switch	101.10	3.00	103.98	2.75	-	93.86	0.41	198.25	nr	218.08
10 usable ways 80A, 30mA RCD main Switch	148.44	3.00	152.74	3.15	-	107.51	0.41	260.67	nr	286.73
22 usable ways 80A, 30mA RCD main Switch	215.46	3.00	221.77	5.55	-	189.42	0.41	411.61	nr	452.77
34 usable ways 80A, 30mA RCD main Switch	284.04	3.00	292.41	7.95	-	271.33	0.41	564.16	nr	620.57
17th Edition, 3rd Amendment, metalclad consumer unit and accessories, fixed to masonry with screws; plugging										
6 useable ways with main switch and 2 off 63A 30mA RCD and 6 MCBs	79.80	3.00	82.19	2.60	-	88.74	0.41	171.34	nr	188.48
10 useable ways with main switch and 2 off 63A 30mA RCD and 10 MCBs	75.60	2.50	77.49	2.60	-	88.74	0.41	166.64	nr	183.30
15 useable ways with main switch and 2 off 63A 30mA RCD and 12 MCBs	104.40	2.50	107.01	3.80	-	129.69	0.41	237.12	nr	260.83
Switches and Circuit Breakers fitted in above consumer units										
60A Main switch, double pole	12.18	2.50	12.48	0.18	-	6.14	-	18.63	nr	20.49
100A Main switch, double pole	13.80	2.50	14.14	0.19	-	6.48	-	20.63	nr	22.69
32 Amp 30mA RCD, double pole	29.76	3.00	30.65	0.21	-	7.17	-	37.82	nr	41.60
40 Amp 30mA RCD, double pole	29.76	3.00	30.65	0.21	-	7.17	-	37.82	nr	41.60
63 Amp 30mA RCD, double pole	29.76	2.50	30.50	0.22	-	7.34	-	37.84	nr	41.63
80 Amp 30mA RCD, double pole	29.76	2.50	30.50	0.22	-	7.34	-	37.84	nr	41.63
3A to 50A single pole MCB	3.00	2.50	3.07	0.13	-	4.44	-	7.51	nr	8.26
6A to 50A, 30mA single unit RCBO	25.80	2.50	26.44	0.14	-	4.61	-	31.05	nr	34.16

Labour hourly rates: (except Specialists) Craft Operatives 34.13 Labourer 15.57 Rates are national average prices. Refer to REGIONAL VARIATIONS for indicative levels of overall pricing in regions	MATERIALS			LABOUR				RATES		
	Del to Site £	Waste %	Material Cost £	Craft Optve Hrs	Lab Hrs	Labour Cost £	Sunds £	Nett Rate £	Unit	Gross rate (10%) £
FINAL CIRCUITS; DOMESTIC LIGHTING AND POWER (SMALL SCALE) (Cont'd)										
Electric wiring in new building (Cont'd)										
Switches and Circuit Breakers fitted in above consumer units (Cont'd)										
6 to 40 Amp RCBO AFDD Combination	114.93	3.00	118.38	0.22	-	7.51	-	125.89	nr	138.48
Installation with PVC insulated and sheathed cables										
lighting points	14.64	2.50	15.48	3.25	-	110.92	-	126.40	nr	139.04
socket outlets; 5A	15.97	2.50	16.91	4.40	-	150.17	-	167.09	nr	183.80
socket outlets; 13A ring main	12.73	2.50	13.64	3.70	-	126.28	-	139.93	nr	153.92
socket outlets; 13A radial circuit	15.66	2.50	16.83	3.85	-	131.40	-	148.23	nr	163.05
cooker points; 45A	35.49	2.50	38.78	6.30	-	215.02	-	253.79	nr	279.17
immersion heater points	20.38	2.50	21.90	4.60	-	157.00	-	178.90	nr	196.79
shaver sockets (transformer)	36.46	2.50	38.45	1.82	-	62.12	-	100.56	nr	110.62
Installation with black enamel heavy gauge conduit with PVC cables										
lighting points	47.67	2.50	50.89	4.65	-	158.70	-	209.59	nr	230.55
socket outlets; 5A	48.66	2.50	52.21	4.70	-	160.41	-	212.62	nr	233.88
socket outlets; 13A ring main	39.53	2.50	42.26	4.25	-	145.05	-	187.32	nr	206.05
socket outlets; 13A radial circuit	46.56	2.50	50.06	6.00	-	204.78	-	254.84	nr	280.32
cooker points; 45A	82.80	2.50	90.02	9.65	-	329.35	-	419.37	nr	461.31
immersion heater points	56.46	2.50	60.78	7.15	-	244.03	-	304.81	nr	335.29
shaver sockets (transformer)	64.78	2.50	68.43	2.53	-	86.35	-	154.78	nr	170.26
Installation with black enamel heavy gauge conduit with coaxial cable										
TV/FM sockets	57.08	2.50	60.43	5.75	-	196.25	-	256.67	nr	282.34
Installation with black enamel heavy gauge conduit with 2 pair cable										
telephone points	56.31	2.50	59.58	5.45	-	186.01	-	245.59	nr	270.15
Electric wiring in extension to existing building										
Installation with PVC insulated and sheathed cables										
lighting points	14.64	2.50	15.48	3.25	-	110.92	-	126.40	nr	139.04
socket outlets; 5A	15.97	2.50	16.91	4.40	-	150.17	-	167.09	nr	183.80
socket outlets; 13A ring main	12.73	2.50	13.64	3.70	-	126.28	-	139.93	nr	153.92
socket outlets; 13A radial circuit	15.66	2.50	16.83	3.85	-	131.40	-	148.23	nr	163.05
cooker points; 45A	35.49	2.50	38.78	6.30	-	215.02	-	253.79	nr	279.17
immersion heater points	20.38	2.50	21.90	4.60	-	157.00	-	178.90	nr	196.79
shaver sockets (transformer)	36.46	2.50	38.45	1.82	-	62.12	-	100.56	nr	110.62
Installation with mineral insulated copper sheathed cables										
lighting points	46.53	2.50	50.26	6.20	-	211.61	-	261.86	nr	288.05
socket outlets; 5A	56.94	2.50	61.61	4.85	-	165.53	-	227.14	nr	249.85
socket outlets; 13A ring main	42.53	2.50	46.02	4.15	-	141.64	-	187.66	nr	206.43
socket outlets; 13A radial circuit	54.83	2.50	59.45	5.55	-	189.42	-	248.87	nr	273.76
immersion heater points	70.63	2.50	76.45	6.60	-	225.26	-	301.71	nr	331.88
shaver sockets (transformer)	85.96	2.50	92.16	3.30	-	112.63	-	204.79	nr	225.27
Installation with black enamel heavy gauge conduit with PVC cables										
lighting points	47.67	2.50	50.89	4.65	-	158.70	-	209.59	nr	230.55
socket outlets; 5A	48.66	2.50	52.21	4.70	-	160.41	-	212.62	nr	233.88
socket outlets; 13A ring main	39.53	2.50	42.26	4.25	-	145.05	-	187.32	nr	206.05
socket outlets; 13A radial circuit	46.56	2.50	50.06	6.00	-	204.78	-	254.84	nr	280.32
cooker points; 45A	82.80	2.50	90.02	9.65	-	329.35	-	419.37	nr	461.31
immersion heater points	56.46	2.50	60.78	7.15	-	244.03	-	304.81	nr	335.29
shaver sockets (transformer)	64.78	2.50	68.43	2.53	-	86.35	-	154.78	nr	170.26
Installation with black enamel heavy gauge conduit with coaxial cable										
TV/FM sockets	57.08	2.50	60.43	5.75	-	196.25	-	256.67	nr	282.34
Installation with black enamel heavy gauge conduit with 2 pair cable										
telephone points	56.31	2.50	59.58	5.45	-	186.01	-	245.59	nr	270.15
Electric wiring in extending existing installation in existing building										
Installation with PVC insulated and sheathed cables										
lighting points	14.64	2.50	15.48	3.75	-	127.99	-	143.46	nr	157.81
socket outlets; 5A	15.97	2.50	16.91	5.05	-	172.36	-	189.27	nr	208.20
socket outlets; 13A ring main	12.73	2.50	13.64	4.25	-	145.05	-	158.70	nr	174.57
socket outlets; 13A radial circuit	15.66	2.50	16.83	4.45	-	151.88	-	168.71	nr	185.58
cooker points; 45A	35.49	2.50	38.78	7.25	-	247.44	-	286.22	nr	314.84
immersion heater points	20.38	2.50	21.90	5.30	-	180.89	-	202.79	nr	223.07
shaver sockets (transformer)	36.46	2.50	38.45	2.09	-	71.33	-	109.78	nr	120.76
Installation with mineral insulated copper sheathed cables										
lighting points	52.43	2.50	57.11	7.15	-	244.03	-	301.14	nr	331.26
socket outlets; 5A	56.94	2.50	61.61	5.60	-	191.13	-	252.73	nr	278.01
socket outlets; 13A ring main	42.53	2.50	46.02	4.80	-	163.82	-	209.85	nr	230.83
socket outlets; 13A radial circuit	54.83	2.50	59.45	6.40	-	218.43	-	277.88	nr	305.67
immersion heater points	70.63	2.50	76.45	7.60	-	259.39	-	335.84	nr	369.43
shaver sockets (transformer)	85.96	2.50	92.16	3.80	-	129.69	-	221.86	nr	244.04
Installation with black enamel heavy gauge conduit with PVC cables										
lighting points	47.67	2.50	50.89	5.35	-	182.60	-	233.48	nr	256.83
socket outlets; 5A	48.66	2.50	52.21	5.40	-	184.30	-	236.51	nr	260.16
socket outlets; 13A ring main	39.53	2.50	42.26	4.90	-	167.24	-	209.50	nr	230.45

Labour hourly rates: (except Specialists) Craft Operatives 34.13 Labourer 15.57 Rates are national average prices. Refer to REGIONAL VARIATIONS for indicative levels of overall pricing in regions	MATERIALS			LABOUR				RATES		
	Del to Site £	Waste %	Material Cost £	Craft Optve Hrs	Lab Hrs	Labour Cost £	Sunds £	Nett Rate £	Unit	Gross rate (10%) £
FINAL CIRCUITS; DOMESTIC LIGHTING AND POWER (SMALL SCALE) (Cont'd)										
Electric wiring in extending existing installation in existing building (Cont'd)										
Installation with black enamel heavy gauge conduit with PVC cables (Cont'd)										
socket outlets; 13A radial circuit	46.56	2.50	50.06	6.90	-	235.50	-	285.55	nr	314.11
cooker points; 45A	82.80	2.50	90.02	11.10	-	378.84	-	468.86	nr	515.75
immersion heater points	56.46	2.50	60.78	8.25	-	281.57	-	342.35	nr	376.59
shaver sockets (transformer)	64.78	2.50	68.43	2.92	-	99.66	-	168.09	nr	184.90
Installation with black enamel heavy gauge conduit with coaxial cable										
TV/FM sockets	57.08	2.50	60.43	6.60	-	225.26	-	285.68	nr	314.25
Installation with black enamel heavy gauge conduit with 2 pair cable										
telephone points	56.31	2.50	59.58	6.25	-	213.31	-	272.90	nr	300.19
TESTING										
Testing; existing installations										
Point										
from	-	-	-	2.25	-	76.79	-	76.79	nr	84.47
to	-	-	-	3.85	-	131.40	-	131.40	nr	144.54
Complete installation; three bedroom house										
from	-	-	-	11.00	-	375.43	-	375.43	nr	412.97
to	-	-	-	17.50	-	597.28	-	597.28	nr	657.00
FIRE AND LIGHTNING PROTECTION										
Fire detection and alarm; Terminal equipment and fittings										
Fittings and equipment										
fire alarm 2 zone panel with batteries and charger	110.04	2.50	112.79	3.30	-	112.63	0.82	226.24	nr	248.87
fire alarm 4 zone panel with batteries and charger	137.28	2.50	140.71	4.40	-	150.17	0.82	291.71	nr	320.88
fire alarm 8 zone panel with batteries and charger	220.20	2.50	225.71	6.60	-	225.26	0.82	451.79	nr	496.97
Ionisation smoke detector	8.40	2.50	8.61	0.30	-	10.24	0.82	19.67	nr	21.64
Optical smoke detector	13.62	2.50	13.96	0.30	-	10.24	0.82	25.02	nr	27.53
Smoke detector mounting base with sounder	22.92	2.50	23.49	0.75	-	25.60	0.82	49.92	nr	54.91
Manual surface mounted call point	7.68	2.50	7.87	0.75	-	25.60	0.82	34.29	nr	37.72
Emergency lighting										
General purpose 4 watt 180 lm LED fitting for maintained or non maintained operation	18.25	2.50	18.71	1.00	-	34.13	0.82	53.66	nr	59.03
Exit signage affixed to light fitting, excluding the light fitting	1.65	-	1.65	0.15	-	5.12	-	6.77	nr	7.45
Lightning protection; conductors										
Note: the following are indicative average prices										
Air termination rods										
610mm long; in clips, fixing to masonry	-	-	Specialist	-	-	Specialist	-	66.73	nr	73.41
Air termination tape										
fixing to masonry	-	-	Specialist	-	-	Specialist	-	16.08	m	17.69
Copper tape down conductors										
19 x 3mm; in clips, fixing to masonry	-	-	Specialist	-	-	Specialist	-	24.20	m	26.62
25 x 3mm; in clips, fixing to masonry	-	-	Specialist	-	-	Specialist	-	25.89	m	28.48
Test clamps										
with securing bolts	-	-	Specialist	-	-	Specialist	-	37.14	nr	40.86
Copper earth rods; tape connectors										
2438 x 16mm; driving into ground	-	-	Specialist	-	-	Specialist	-	236.38	nr	260.01

This page left blank intentionally

Labour hourly rates: (except Specialists) Craft Operatives 20.87 Labourer 15.57 Rates are national average prices. Refer to REGIONAL VARIATIONS for indicative levels of overall pricing in regions	MATERIALS			LABOUR				RATES		
	Del to Site £	Waste %	Material Cost £	Craft Optve Hrs	Lab Hrs	Labour Cost £	Sunds £	Nett Rate £	Unit	Gross rate (10%) £
LIFTS										
Generally										
Note: the following are average indicative prices										
Light passenger lifts; standard range										
Electro Hydraulic drive; 630 kg, 8 person, 0.63m/s, 3 stop										
basic; primed car and entrances	-	-	Specialist	-	-	Specialist	-	25156.50	nr	27672.15
median; laminate walls, standard carpet floor, painted entrances	-	-	Specialist	-	-	Specialist	-	29538.60	nr	32492.46
ACVF drive; 1000 kg, 13 person, 0.63m/s, 4 stop										
basic; primed car and entrances	-	-	Specialist	-	-	Specialist	-	56155.80	nr	61771.38
median; laminate walls, standard carpet floor, painted entrances	-	-	Specialist	-	-	Specialist	-	58265.70	nr	64092.27
Extras on the above lifts										
800/900mm landing doors in cellulose paint finish	-	-	Specialist	-	-	Specialist	-	243.45	nr	267.80
800/900mm landing doors in brushed stainless steel	-	-	Specialist	-	-	Specialist	-	681.66	nr	749.83
800/900mm landing doors in brushed brass	-	-	Specialist	-	-	Specialist	-	1963.83	nr	2160.21
landing position indicators	-	-	Specialist	-	-	Specialist	-	384.65	nr	423.12
landing direction arrows and gongs	-	-	Specialist	-	-	Specialist	-	227.22	nr	249.94
car preference key switch	-	-	Specialist	-	-	Specialist	-	194.76	nr	214.24
car entrance safety (Progard L)	-	-	Specialist	-	-	Specialist	-	649.20	nr	714.12
fluorescent emergency light	-	-	Specialist	-	-	Specialist	-	603.76	nr	664.13
half height mirror to rear wall	-	-	Specialist	-	-	Specialist	-	681.66	nr	749.83
full height mirror to rear wall	-	-	Specialist	-	-	Specialist	-	990.03	nr	1089.03
vandal resistant buttons; per car/entrance	-	-	Specialist	-	-	Specialist	-	220.73	nr	242.80
car bumper rail	-	-	Specialist	-	-	Specialist	-	1330.86	nr	1463.95
trailing cable for Warden Call System	-	-	Specialist	-	-	Specialist	-	566.43	nr	623.07
car telephone	-	-	Specialist	-	-	Specialist	-	444.70	nr	489.17
General purpose passenger lifts										
ACVF drive; 630 kg, 8 person, 1.0m/s, 4 stop median; laminate walls, standard carpet floor, painted entrances	-	-	Specialist	-	-	Specialist	-	57778.80	nr	63556.68
Variable speed a/c drive; 1000 kg, 13 person, 1.6m/s, 5 stop median; laminate walls, standard carpet floor, painted entrances	-	-	Specialist	-	-	Specialist	-	61998.60	nr	68198.46
Variable speed a/c drive; 1600 kg, 21 person, 1.6m/s, 6 stop median; laminate walls, standard carpet floor, painted entrances	-	-	Specialist	-	-	Specialist	-	149316.00	nr	164247.60
If a high quality architectural finish is required, e.g. veneered panelling walls, marble floors, special ceiling, etc, add to the above prices										
from	-	-	Specialist	-	-	Specialist	-	24345.00	nr	26779.50
to	-	-	Specialist	-	-	Specialist	-	68166.00	nr	74982.60
Bed/Passenger lifts										
Electro Hydraulic drive; 1800 kg, 24 person, 0.63m/s, 3 stop standard specification	-	-	Specialist	-	-	Specialist	-	78228.60	nr	86051.46
Variable speed a/c drive; 2000 kg, 26 person, 1.6m/s, 4 stop standard specification	-	-	Specialist	-	-	Specialist	-	142012.50	nr	156213.80
Goods lifts (direct coupled)										
Electro Hydraulic drive; 1500 kg, 0.4m/s, 3 stop stainless steel car lining with chequer plate floor and galvanised shutters	-	-	Specialist	-	-	Specialist	-	61998.60	nr	68198.46
Electro Hydraulic drive; 2000 kg, 0.4m/s, 3 stop stainless steel car lining with chequer plate floor and galvanised shutters	-	-	Specialist	-	-	Specialist	-	63946.20	nr	70340.82
Service hoists										
Single speed a/c drive; 50 kg, 0.63m/s, 2 stop standard specification	-	-	Specialist	-	-	Specialist	-	8764.20	nr	9640.62
Single speed a/c drive; 250 kg, 0.4m/s, 2 stop standard specification	-	-	Specialist	-	-	Specialist	-	11117.55	nr	12229.31
Extra on the above hoists two hour fire resisting shutters; per landing	-	-	Specialist	-	-	Specialist	-	368.42	nr	405.26
ESCALATORS										
Escalators										
30 degree inclination; 3.00m vertical rise department store specification	-	-	Specialist	-	-	Specialist	-	94134.00	nr	103547.40

TRANSPORTATION

This page left blank intentionally

BUILDERS WORK IN CONNECTION WITH INSTALLATIONS

Labour hourly rates: (except Specialists) Craft Operatives 20.87 Labourer 15.57 Rates are national average prices. Refer to REGIONAL VARIATIONS for indicative levels of overall pricing in regions	MATERIALS			LABOUR				RATES		
	Del to Site £	Waste %	Material Cost £	Craft Optve Hrs	Lab Hrs	Labour Cost £	Sunds £	Nett Rate £	Unit	Gross rate (10%) £
WORK FOR SERVICES INSTALLATIONS IN NEW BUILDINGS; MECHANICAL INSTALLATIONS										
Cutting holes for services										
For ducts through concrete; making good										
rectangular ducts not exceeding 1.00m girth										
150mm thick	-	-	-	1.60	-	33.39	0.76	34.16	nr	37.57
200mm thick	-	-	-	1.90	-	39.65	0.92	40.57	nr	44.62
300mm thick	-	-	-	2.20	-	45.91	1.07	46.98	nr	51.68
rectangular ducts 1.00-2.00m girth										
150mm thick	-	-	-	3.20	-	66.78	1.70	68.48	nr	75.33
200mm thick	-	-	-	3.80	-	79.31	1.85	81.15	nr	89.27
300mm thick	-	-	-	4.40	-	91.83	2.14	93.97	nr	103.37
rectangular ducts 2.00-3.00m girth										
150mm thick	-	-	-	4.00	-	83.48	1.95	85.43	nr	93.97
200mm thick	-	-	-	4.75	-	99.13	2.31	101.44	nr	111.59
300mm thick	-	-	-	5.50	-	114.79	2.64	117.43	nr	129.17
For pipes through concrete; making good										
pipes not exceeding 55mm nominal size										
150mm thick	-	-	-	0.90	-	18.78	0.48	19.26	nr	21.19
200mm thick	-	-	-	1.15	-	24.00	0.62	24.62	nr	27.08
300mm thick	-	-	-	1.45	-	30.26	0.76	31.03	nr	34.13
pipes 55 - 110mm nominal size										
150mm thick	-	-	-	1.12	-	23.37	0.60	23.97	nr	26.37
200mm thick	-	-	-	1.36	-	28.38	0.70	29.09	nr	32.00
300mm thick	-	-	-	1.80	-	37.57	0.96	38.53	nr	42.38
pipes exceeding 110mm nominal size										
150mm thick	-	-	-	1.35	-	28.17	0.68	28.85	nr	31.73
200mm thick	-	-	-	1.72	-	35.90	0.86	36.75	nr	40.43
300mm thick	-	-	-	2.18	-	45.50	1.11	46.61	nr	51.27
For ducts through reinforced concrete; making good										
rectangular ducts not exceeding 1.00m girth										
150mm thick	-	-	-	2.40	-	50.09	1.11	51.20	nr	56.32
200mm thick	-	-	-	2.85	-	59.48	1.30	60.78	nr	66.86
300mm thick	-	-	-	3.30	-	68.87	1.53	70.40	nr	77.44
rectangular ducts 1.00-2.00m girth										
150mm thick	-	-	-	4.80	-	100.18	2.25	102.43	nr	112.67
200mm thick	-	-	-	5.70	-	118.96	2.65	121.61	nr	133.78
300mm thick	-	-	-	6.60	-	137.74	3.09	140.83	nr	154.92
rectangular ducts 2.00-3.00m girth										
150mm thick	-	-	-	6.00	-	125.22	2.79	128.01	nr	140.81
200mm thick	-	-	-	7.00	-	146.09	3.32	149.40	nr	164.35
300mm thick	-	-	-	8.25	-	172.18	3.78	175.96	nr	193.55
For pipes through reinforced concrete; making good										
pipes not exceeding 55mm nominal size										
150mm thick	-	-	-	1.35	-	28.17	0.69	28.86	nr	31.75
200mm thick	-	-	-	1.75	-	36.52	0.90	37.42	nr	41.16
300mm thick	-	-	-	2.20	-	45.91	1.12	47.04	nr	51.74
pipes 55 - 110mm nominal size										
150mm thick	-	-	-	1.70	-	35.48	0.87	36.35	nr	39.98
200mm thick	-	-	-	2.05	-	42.78	1.05	43.83	nr	48.22
300mm thick	-	-	-	2.70	-	56.35	1.38	57.73	nr	63.50
pipes exceeding 110mm nominal size										
150mm thick	-	-	-	2.00	-	41.74	1.02	42.76	nr	47.04
200mm thick	-	-	-	2.60	-	54.26	1.32	55.58	nr	61.14
300mm thick	-	-	-	3.20	-	66.78	1.63	68.42	nr	75.26
For ducts through brickwork; making good										
rectangular ducts not exceeding 1.00m girth										
102.5mm thick	-	-	-	1.20	-	25.04	0.52	25.57	nr	28.13
215mm thick	-	-	-	1.40	-	29.22	0.63	29.85	nr	32.83
327.5mm thick	-	-	-	1.65	-	34.44	0.75	35.19	nr	38.70
rectangular ducts 1.00-2.00m girth										
102.5mm thick	-	-	-	2.40	-	50.09	1.05	51.14	nr	56.25
215mm thick	-	-	-	2.80	-	58.44	1.26	59.70	nr	65.67
327.5mm thick	-	-	-	3.30	-	68.87	1.50	70.37	nr	77.41
rectangular ducts 2.00-3.00m girth										
102.5mm thick	-	-	-	3.00	-	62.61	1.35	63.96	nr	70.36
215mm thick	-	-	-	3.50	-	73.05	1.58	74.62	nr	82.08
327.5mm thick	-	-	-	4.10	-	85.57	1.88	87.44	nr	96.19
For pipes through brickwork; making good										
pipes not exceeding 55mm nominal size										
102.5mm thick	-	-	-	0.40	-	8.35	0.21	8.56	nr	9.41
215mm thick	-	-	-	0.66	-	13.77	0.33	14.10	nr	15.51
327.5mm thick	-	-	-	1.00	-	20.87	0.51	21.38	nr	23.52
pipes 55 - 110mm nominal size										
102.5mm thick	-	-	-	0.53	-	11.06	0.27	11.33	nr	12.46
215mm thick	-	-	-	0.88	-	18.37	0.45	18.82	nr	20.70
327.5mm thick	-	-	-	1.33	-	27.76	0.68	28.43	nr	31.28

Labour hourly rates: (except Specialists) Craft Operatives 20.87 Labourer 15.57 Rates are national average prices. Refer to REGIONAL VARIATIONS for indicative levels of overall pricing in regions	MATERIALS			LABOUR				RATES		
	Del to Site £	Waste %	Material Cost £	Craft Optve Hrs	Lab Hrs	Labour Cost £	Sunds £	Nett Rate £	Unit	Gross rate (10%) £
WORK FOR SERVICES INSTALLATIONS IN NEW BUILDINGS; MECHANICAL INSTALLATIONS (Cont'd)										
Cutting holes for services (Cont'd)										
For pipes through brickwork; making good (Cont'd)										
pipes exceeding 110mm nominal size										
102.5mm thick	-	-	-	0.67	-	13.98	0.34	14.33	nr	15.76
215mm thick	-	-	-	1.10	-	22.96	0.56	23.51	nr	25.86
327.5mm thick	-	-	-	1.67	-	34.85	0.84	35.69	nr	39.26
For ducts through brickwork; making good fair face or facings one side										
rectangular ducts not exceeding 1.00m girth										
102.5mm thick	-	-	-	1.45	-	30.26	0.82	31.09	nr	34.20
215mm thick	-	-	-	1.65	-	34.44	0.98	35.41	nr	38.95
327.5mm thick	-	-	-	1.90	-	39.65	1.05	40.70	nr	44.77
rectangular ducts 1.00-2.00m girth										
102.5mm thick	-	-	-	2.70	-	56.35	1.65	58.00	nr	63.80
215mm thick	-	-	-	3.10	-	64.70	1.95	66.65	nr	73.31
327.5mm thick	-	-	-	3.60	-	75.13	2.10	77.23	nr	84.96
rectangular ducts 2.00-3.00m girth										
102.5mm thick	-	-	-	3.40	-	70.96	2.10	73.06	nr	80.36
215mm thick	-	-	-	3.90	-	81.39	2.47	83.87	nr	92.25
327.5mm thick	-	-	-	4.50	-	93.92	2.62	96.54	nr	106.19
For pipes through brickwork; making good fair face or facings one side										
pipes not exceeding 55mm nominal size										
102.5mm thick	-	-	-	0.50	-	10.44	0.27	10.71	nr	11.78
215mm thick	-	-	-	0.76	-	15.86	0.39	16.25	nr	17.88
327.5mm thick	-	-	-	1.10	-	22.96	0.56	23.51	nr	25.86
pipes 55 - 110mm nominal size										
102.5mm thick	-	-	-	0.68	-	14.19	0.33	14.52	nr	15.97
215mm thick	-	-	-	1.03	-	21.50	0.50	21.99	nr	24.19
327.5mm thick	-	-	-	1.48	-	30.89	0.74	31.62	nr	34.78
pipes exceeding 110mm nominal size										
102.5mm thick	-	-	-	0.87	-	18.16	0.41	18.56	nr	20.42
215mm thick	-	-	-	1.30	-	27.13	0.60	27.73	nr	30.50
327.5mm thick	-	-	-	1.87	-	39.03	0.88	39.91	nr	43.90
For ducts through blockwork; making good										
rectangular ducts not exceeding 1.00m girth										
100mm thick	-	-	-	0.90	-	18.78	0.52	19.31	nr	21.24
140mm thick	-	-	-	1.00	-	20.87	0.63	21.50	nr	23.65
190mm thick	-	-	-	1.10	-	22.96	0.75	23.71	nr	26.08
rectangular ducts 1.00-2.00m girth										
100mm thick	-	-	-	1.80	-	37.57	1.05	38.62	nr	42.48
140mm thick	-	-	-	1.95	-	40.70	1.26	41.96	nr	46.15
190mm thick	-	-	-	2.10	-	43.83	1.50	45.33	nr	49.86
rectangular ducts 2.00-3.00m girth										
100mm thick	-	-	-	2.25	-	46.96	1.35	48.31	nr	53.14
140mm thick	-	-	-	2.45	-	51.13	1.58	52.71	nr	57.98
190mm thick	-	-	-	2.65	-	55.31	1.88	57.18	nr	62.90
For pipes through blockwork; making good										
pipes not exceeding 55mm nominal size										
100mm thick	-	-	-	0.30	-	6.26	0.19	6.46	nr	7.10
140mm thick	-	-	-	0.40	-	8.35	0.31	8.66	nr	9.53
190mm thick	-	-	-	0.50	-	10.44	0.48	10.91	nr	12.01
pipes 55 - 110mm nominal size										
100mm thick	-	-	-	0.40	-	8.35	0.25	8.60	nr	9.46
140mm thick	-	-	-	0.53	-	11.06	0.42	11.48	nr	12.63
190mm thick	-	-	-	0.66	-	13.77	0.64	14.42	nr	15.86
pipes exceeding 110mm nominal size										
100mm thick	-	-	-	0.50	-	10.44	0.33	10.77	nr	11.84
140mm thick	-	-	-	0.68	-	14.19	0.52	14.72	nr	16.19
190mm thick	-	-	-	0.83	-	17.32	0.81	18.13	nr	19.95
For ducts through existing brickwork with plaster finish; making good each side										
rectangular ducts not exceeding 1.00m girth										
102.5mm thick	-	-	-	1.95	-	40.70	0.90	41.60	nr	45.76
215mm thick	-	-	-	2.25	-	46.96	1.12	48.08	nr	52.89
327.5mm thick	-	-	-	2.55	-	53.22	1.27	54.49	nr	59.94
rectangular ducts 1.00-2.00m girth										
102.5mm thick	-	-	-	3.60	-	75.13	1.80	76.93	nr	84.63
215mm thick	-	-	-	4.20	-	87.65	2.25	89.90	nr	98.89
327.5mm thick	-	-	-	4.80	-	100.18	2.55	102.73	nr	113.00
rectangular ducts 2.00-3.00m girth										
102.5mm thick	-	-	-	4.50	-	93.92	2.70	96.62	nr	106.28
215mm thick	-	-	-	5.25	-	109.57	3.38	112.94	nr	124.24
327.5mm thick	-	-	-	6.05	-	126.26	3.83	130.09	nr	143.10
For ducts through existing brickwork with plaster finish; making good one side										
rectangular ducts not exceeding 1.00m girth										
102.5mm thick	-	-	-	1.75	-	36.52	0.81	37.33	nr	41.07
215mm thick	-	-	-	2.05	-	42.78	1.02	43.80	nr	48.18
327.5mm thick	-	-	-	2.30	-	48.00	1.14	49.14	nr	54.06
rectangular ducts 1.00-2.00m girth										
102.5mm thick	-	-	-	3.25	-	67.83	1.62	69.45	nr	76.39
215mm thick	-	-	-	3.80	-	79.31	2.03	81.33	nr	89.46
327.5mm thick	-	-	-	4.35	-	90.78	2.33	93.11	nr	102.42
rectangular ducts 2.00-3.00m girth										
102.5mm thick	-	-	-	4.05	-	84.52	2.40	86.92	nr	95.62

Labour hourly rates: (except Specialists) Craft Operatives 20.87 Labourer 15.57 Rates are national average prices. Refer to REGIONAL VARIATIONS for indicative levels of overall pricing in regions	MATERIALS			LABOUR				RATES		
	Del to Site £	Waste %	Material Cost £	Craft Optve Hrs	Lab Hrs	Labour Cost £	Sunds £	Nett Rate £	Unit	Gross rate (10%) £
WORK FOR SERVICES INSTALLATIONS IN NEW BUILDINGS; MECHANICAL INSTALLATIONS (Cont'd)										
Cutting holes for services (Cont'd)										
For ducts through existing brickwork with plaster finish; making good one side (Cont'd)										
rectangular ducts 2.00-3.00m girth (Cont'd)										
215mm thick	-	-	-	4.75	-	99.13	3.00	102.13	nr	112.35
327.5mm thick	-	-	-	5.45	-	113.74	3.45	117.19	nr	128.91
For pipes through existing brickwork with plaster finish; making good each side										
pipes not exceeding 55mm nominal size										
102.5mm thick	-	-	-	0.65	-	13.57	0.33	13.90	nr	15.29
215mm thick	-	-	-	1.00	-	20.87	0.47	21.34	nr	23.47
327.5mm thick	-	-	-	1.45	-	30.26	0.66	30.92	nr	34.01
pipes 55 - 110mm nominal size										
102.5mm thick	-	-	-	0.95	-	19.83	0.39	20.22	nr	22.24
215mm thick	-	-	-	1.35	-	28.17	0.60	28.77	nr	31.65
327.5mm thick	-	-	-	1.95	-	40.70	0.88	41.58	nr	45.74
pipes exceeding 110mm nominal size										
102.5mm thick	-	-	-	1.20	-	25.04	0.48	25.52	nr	28.08
215mm thick	-	-	-	1.75	-	36.52	0.72	37.24	nr	40.97
327.5mm thick	-	-	-	2.50	-	52.18	1.07	53.24	nr	58.56
For pipes through existing brickwork with plaster finish; making good one side										
pipes not exceeding 55mm nominal size										
102.5mm thick	-	-	-	0.60	-	12.52	0.27	12.79	nr	14.07
215mm thick	-	-	-	0.90	-	18.78	0.39	19.17	nr	21.09
327.5mm thick	-	-	-	1.30	-	27.13	0.56	27.69	nr	30.45
pipes 55 - 110mm nominal size										
102.5mm thick	-	-	-	0.85	-	17.74	0.33	18.07	nr	19.88
215mm thick	-	-	-	1.20	-	25.04	0.50	25.54	nr	28.09
327.5mm thick	-	-	-	1.75	-	36.52	0.74	37.26	nr	40.98
pipes exceeding 110mm nominal size										
102.5mm thick	-	-	-	1.10	-	22.96	0.41	23.36	nr	25.70
215mm thick	-	-	-	1.60	-	33.39	0.60	33.99	nr	37.39
327.5mm thick	-	-	-	2.25	-	46.96	0.81	47.77	nr	52.54
For pipes through softwood										
pipes not exceeding 55mm nominal size										
19mm thick	-	-	-	0.10	-	2.09	-	2.09	nr	2.30
50mm thick	-	-	-	0.13	-	2.71	-	2.71	nr	2.98
pipes 55 - 110mm nominal size										
19mm thick	-	-	-	0.15	-	3.13	-	3.13	nr	3.44
50mm thick	-	-	-	0.20	-	4.17	-	4.17	nr	4.59
For pipes through plywood										
pipes not exceeding 55mm nominal size										
13mm thick	-	-	-	0.10	-	2.09	-	2.09	nr	2.30
19mm thick	-	-	-	0.13	-	2.71	-	2.71	nr	2.98
pipes 55 - 110mm nominal size										
13mm thick	-	-	-	0.15	-	3.13	-	3.13	nr	3.44
19mm thick	-	-	-	0.20	-	4.17	-	4.17	nr	4.59
For pipes through existing plasterboard with skim finish; making good one side										
pipes not exceeding 55mm nominal size										
13mm thick	-	-	-	0.20	-	4.17	-	4.17	nr	4.59
pipes 55 - 110mm nominal size										
13mm thick	-	-	-	0.30	-	6.26	-	6.26	nr	6.89
Cutting chases for services										
In concrete; making good										
15mm nominal size pipes -1	-	-	-	0.30	-	6.26	-	6.26	m	6.89
22mm nominal size pipes -1	-	-	-	0.35	-	7.30	-	7.30	m	8.03
In brickwork										
15mm nominal size pipes -1	-	-	-	0.25	-	5.22	-	5.22	m	5.74
22mm nominal size pipes -1	-	-	-	0.30	-	6.26	-	6.26	m	6.89
In brickwork; making good fair face or facings										
15mm nominal size pipes -1	-	-	-	0.30	-	6.26	0.17	6.43	m	7.07
22mm nominal size pipes -1	-	-	-	0.35	-	7.30	0.25	7.56	m	8.32
In existing brickwork with plaster finish; making good										
15mm nominal size pipes -1	-	-	-	0.40	-	8.35	0.33	8.68	m	9.55
22mm nominal size pipes -1	-	-	-	0.50	-	10.44	0.51	10.95	m	12.04
In blockwork; making good										
15mm nominal size pipes -1	-	-	-	0.20	-	4.17	-	4.17	m	4.59
22mm nominal size pipes -1	-	-	-	0.25	-	5.22	-	5.22	m	5.74
Pipe and duct sleeves										
Steel pipes BS 1387 Table 2; casting into concrete; making good										
100mm long; to the following nominal size steel pipes										
15mm	0.85	5.00	0.89	0.12	0.06	3.44	-	4.33	nr	4.77
20mm	0.94	5.00	0.99	0.14	0.07	4.01	-	5.00	nr	5.50
25mm	1.15	5.00	1.21	0.15	0.08	4.38	-	5.59	nr	6.15
32mm	1.35	5.00	1.42	0.16	0.08	4.58	-	6.01	nr	6.61
40mm	1.56	5.00	1.64	0.18	0.09	5.16	-	6.80	nr	7.48
50mm	1.97	5.00	2.07	0.22	0.11	6.30	-	8.37	nr	9.21
150mm long; to the following nominal size steel pipes										
15mm	1.05	5.00	1.10	0.14	0.07	4.01	-	5.11	nr	5.63

Labour hourly rates: (except Specialists) Craft Operatives 20.87 Labourer 15.57 Rates are national average prices. Refer to REGIONAL VARIATIONS for indicative levels of overall pricing in regions	MATERIALS			LABOUR				RATES		
	Del to Site	Waste	Material Cost	Craft Optve	Lab	Labour Cost	Sunds	Nett Rate		Gross rate (10%)
	£	%	£	Hrs	Hrs	£	£	£	Unit	£
WORK FOR SERVICES INSTALLATIONS IN NEW BUILDINGS; MECHANICAL INSTALLATIONS (Cont'd)										
Pipe and duct sleeves (Cont'd)										
Steel pipes BS 1387 Table 2; casting into concrete; making good (Cont'd)										
150mm long; to the following nominal size steel pipes (Cont'd)										
20mm	1.18	5.00	1.24	0.16	0.08	4.58	-	5.82	nr	6.40
25mm	1.47	5.00	1.54	0.17	0.09	4.95	-	6.49	nr	7.14
32mm	1.73	5.00	1.81	0.18	0.09	5.16	-	6.97	nr	7.67
40mm	1.97	5.00	2.07	0.19	0.10	5.52	-	7.59	nr	8.35
50mm	2.57	5.00	2.69	0.23	0.12	6.67	-	9.36	nr	10.30
200mm long; to the following nominal size steel pipes										
15mm	1.24	5.00	1.30	0.15	0.08	4.38	-	5.67	nr	6.24
20mm	1.39	5.00	1.46	0.17	0.09	4.95	-	6.41	nr	7.05
25mm	1.76	5.00	1.85	0.18	0.09	5.16	-	7.01	nr	7.71
32mm	2.10	5.00	2.20	0.19	0.10	5.52	-	7.73	nr	8.50
40mm	2.40	5.00	2.52	0.20	0.10	5.73	-	8.25	nr	9.08
50mm	3.16	5.00	3.32	0.24	0.12	6.88	-	10.20	nr	11.22
250mm long; to the following nominal size steel pipes										
15mm	1.43	5.00	1.51	0.15	0.08	4.38	-	5.88	nr	6.47
20mm	1.61	5.00	1.69	0.19	0.10	5.52	-	7.21	nr	7.93
25mm	2.07	5.00	2.17	0.20	0.10	5.73	-	7.90	nr	8.69
32mm	2.48	5.00	2.61	0.21	0.11	6.10	-	8.70	nr	9.58
40mm	2.84	5.00	2.98	0.22	0.11	6.30	-	9.28	nr	10.21
50mm	3.77	5.00	3.96	0.26	0.13	7.45	-	11.41	nr	12.55
100mm long; to the following nominal size copper pipes										
15mm	0.94	5.00	0.99	0.12	0.06	3.44	-	4.43	nr	4.87
22mm	1.04	5.00	1.09	0.14	0.07	4.01	-	5.10	nr	5.61
28mm	1.28	5.00	1.35	0.15	0.08	4.38	-	5.72	nr	6.30
32mm	1.49	5.00	1.57	0.16	0.08	4.58	-	6.15	nr	6.77
45mm	1.72	5.00	1.80	0.18	0.09	5.16	-	6.96	nr	7.65
54mm	2.18	5.00	2.29	0.22	0.11	6.30	-	8.59	nr	9.45
150mm long; to the following nominal size copper pipes										
15mm	1.15	5.00	1.21	0.14	0.07	4.01	-	5.22	nr	5.75
22mm	1.29	5.00	1.36	0.16	0.08	4.58	-	5.94	nr	6.54
28mm	1.62	5.00	1.70	0.17	0.09	4.95	-	6.65	nr	7.32
32mm	1.90	5.00	2.00	0.18	0.09	5.16	-	7.15	nr	7.87
45mm	2.18	5.00	2.29	0.19	0.10	5.52	-	7.81	nr	8.59
54mm	2.82	5.00	2.96	0.23	0.12	6.67	-	9.63	nr	10.60
200mm long; to the following nominal size copper pipes										
15mm	1.35	5.00	1.42	0.15	0.08	4.38	-	5.80	nr	6.38
22mm	1.53	5.00	1.60	0.17	0.09	4.95	-	6.55	nr	7.21
28mm	1.92	5.00	2.02	0.18	0.09	5.16	-	7.18	nr	7.90
32mm	2.31	5.00	2.43	0.19	0.10	5.52	-	7.95	nr	8.74
45mm	2.66	5.00	2.79	0.20	0.10	5.73	-	8.52	nr	9.38
54mm	3.49	5.00	3.66	0.24	0.12	6.88	-	10.54	nr	11.59
250mm long; to the following nominal size copper pipes										
15mm	1.52	5.00	1.59	0.17	0.09	4.95	-	6.54	nr	7.20
22mm	1.76	5.00	1.85	0.19	0.10	5.52	-	7.37	nr	8.11
28mm	2.28	5.00	2.39	0.20	0.10	5.73	-	8.12	nr	8.93
32mm	2.73	5.00	2.87	0.21	0.11	6.10	-	8.96	nr	9.86
45mm	3.10	5.00	3.26	0.22	0.11	6.30	-	9.56	nr	10.52
54mm	4.14	5.00	4.35	0.26	0.13	7.45	-	11.80	nr	12.98
Steel pipes BS 1387 Table 2; building into blockwork; bedding and pointing in cement mortar (1:3); making good										
100mm long; to the following nominal size steel pipes										
15mm	0.85	5.00	0.89	0.17	0.09	4.95	-	5.84	nr	6.43
20mm	0.94	5.00	0.99	0.18	0.09	5.16	-	6.15	nr	6.77
25mm	1.15	5.00	1.21	0.19	0.10	5.52	-	6.74	nr	7.41
32mm	1.35	5.00	1.42	0.20	0.10	5.73	-	7.15	nr	7.87
40mm	1.56	5.00	1.64	0.21	0.11	6.10	-	7.74	nr	8.51
50mm	1.97	5.00	2.07	0.22	0.11	6.30	-	8.37	nr	9.21
140mm long; to the following nominal size steel pipes										
15mm	1.00	5.00	1.05	0.19	0.10	5.52	-	6.58	nr	7.23
20mm	1.13	5.00	1.19	0.20	0.10	5.73	-	6.92	nr	7.61
25mm	1.40	5.00	1.47	0.21	0.11	6.10	-	7.57	nr	8.32
32mm	1.66	5.00	1.74	0.22	0.11	6.30	-	8.04	nr	8.85
40mm	1.90	5.00	2.00	0.23	0.12	6.67	-	8.66	nr	9.53
50mm	2.45	5.00	2.57	0.24	0.12	6.88	-	9.45	nr	10.39
190mm long; to the following nominal size steel pipes										
15mm	1.20	5.00	1.26	0.21	0.11	6.10	-	7.36	nr	8.09
20mm	1.34	5.00	1.41	0.22	0.11	6.30	-	7.71	nr	8.48
25mm	1.72	5.00	1.80	0.23	0.12	6.67	-	8.47	nr	9.32
32mm	2.04	5.00	2.14	0.24	0.12	6.88	-	9.02	nr	9.92
40mm	2.31	5.00	2.43	0.25	0.13	7.24	-	9.67	nr	10.63
50mm	3.05	5.00	3.20	0.26	0.13	7.45	-	10.65	nr	11.71
215mm long; to the following nominal size steel pipes										
15mm	1.29	5.00	1.36	0.22	0.11	6.30	-	7.66	nr	8.43
20mm	1.45	5.00	1.52	0.23	0.12	6.67	-	8.19	nr	9.01
25mm	1.87	5.00	1.96	0.24	0.12	6.88	-	8.84	nr	9.72
32mm	2.23	5.00	2.34	0.25	0.13	7.24	-	9.58	nr	10.54
40mm	2.53	5.00	2.66	0.26	0.13	7.45	-	10.11	nr	11.12
50mm	3.35	5.00	3.52	0.27	0.14	7.81	-	11.33	nr	12.46
100mm long; to the following nominal size copper pipes										
15mm	0.94	5.00	0.99	0.17	0.09	4.95	-	5.94	nr	6.54
22mm	1.01	5.00	1.07	0.18	0.09	5.16	-	6.22	nr	6.85
28mm	1.28	5.00	1.35	0.19	0.10	5.52	-	6.87	nr	7.56
32mm	1.49	5.00	1.57	0.20	0.10	5.73	-	7.30	nr	8.03
45mm	1.56	5.00	1.64	0.21	0.11	6.10	-	7.74	nr	8.51
54mm	2.18	5.00	2.29	0.22	0.11	6.30	-	8.59	nr	9.45

Labour hourly rates: (except Specialists) Craft Operatives 20.87 Labourer 15.57 Rates are national average prices. Refer to REGIONAL VARIATIONS for indicative levels of overall pricing in regions	MATERIALS			LABOUR				RATES		
	Del to Site £	Waste %	Material Cost £	Craft Optve Hrs	Lab Hrs	Labour Cost £	Sunds £	Nett Rate £	Unit	Gross rate (10%) £
WORK FOR SERVICES INSTALLATIONS IN NEW BUILDINGS; MECHANICAL INSTALLATIONS (Cont'd)										
Pipe and duct sleeves (Cont'd)										
Steel pipes BS 1387 Table 2; building into blockwork; bedding and pointing in cement mortar (1:3); making good (Cont'd)										
140mm long; to the following nominal size copper pipes										
15mm	1.11	5.00	1.16	0.19	0.10	5.52	-	6.69	nr	7.35
22mm	1.24	5.00	1.30	0.20	0.10	5.73	-	7.03	nr	7.73
28mm	1.56	5.00	1.64	0.21	0.11	6.10	-	7.74	nr	8.51
32mm	1.82	5.00	1.91	0.22	0.11	6.30	-	8.22	nr	9.04
45mm	2.09	5.00	2.19	0.23	0.12	6.67	-	8.86	nr	9.75
54mm	2.71	5.00	2.84	0.24	0.12	6.88	-	9.72	nr	10.69
190mm long; to the following nominal size copper pipes										
15mm	1.33	5.00	1.40	0.21	0.11	6.10	-	7.49	nr	8.24
22mm	1.48	5.00	1.56	0.22	0.11	6.30	-	7.86	nr	8.65
28mm	1.88	5.00	1.97	0.23	0.12	6.67	-	8.64	nr	9.50
32mm	2.24	5.00	2.35	0.24	0.12	6.88	-	9.23	nr	10.15
45mm	2.54	5.00	2.67	0.25	0.13	7.24	-	9.91	nr	10.90
54mm	3.35	5.00	3.52	0.26	0.13	7.45	-	10.97	nr	12.06
215mm long; to the following nominal size copper pipes										
15mm	1.42	5.00	1.49	0.23	0.12	6.67	-	8.16	nr	8.98
22mm	1.59	5.00	1.67	0.24	0.12	6.88	-	8.54	nr	9.40
28mm	2.05	5.00	2.16	0.25	0.13	7.24	-	9.40	nr	10.34
32mm	2.44	5.00	2.56	0.26	0.13	7.45	-	10.01	nr	11.01
45mm	2.78	5.00	2.91	0.27	0.14	7.81	-	10.73	nr	11.80
54mm	3.69	5.00	3.87	0.28	0.14	8.02	-	11.89	nr	13.08
Trench covers and frames										
Duct covers in cast iron, coated; continuous covers in 610mm lengths; steel bearers										
22mm deep, for pedestrian traffic; bedding frames to concrete in cement mortar (1:3); nominal width										
150mm	278.67	-	278.67	0.50	0.50	18.22	1.02	297.91	m	327.70
225mm	313.00	-	313.00	0.55	0.55	20.04	1.02	334.06	m	367.47
300mm	331.76	-	331.76	0.65	0.65	23.69	1.02	356.46	m	392.11
375mm	392.24	-	392.24	0.70	0.70	25.51	1.02	418.77	m	460.65
450mm	442.43	-	442.43	0.75	0.75	27.33	1.02	470.78	m	517.86
Alumasc Interior Building Products Ltd., Pendock FDT floor ducting profiles; galvanised mild steel tray section with 12mm plywood cover board; fixing tray section to masonry with nails; fixing cover board with screws, countersinking										
For 50mm screeds										
reference FDT 100/50, 100mm wide										
straight lengths	10.66	2.50	10.93	0.35	-	7.30	0.15	18.39	m	20.22
extra; stop end	3.10	2.50	3.18	0.10	-	2.09	-	5.26	nr	5.79
extra; corner	16.50	2.50	16.91	0.25	-	5.22	0.22	22.35	nr	24.59
extra; tee	16.50	2.50	16.91	0.30	-	6.26	0.22	23.40	nr	25.74
reference FDT 150/50, 150mm wide										
straight lengths	13.54	2.50	13.88	0.40	-	8.35	0.15	22.38	m	24.61
extra; stop end	3.10	2.50	3.18	0.12	-	2.50	-	5.68	nr	6.25
extra; corner	16.50	2.50	16.91	0.30	-	6.26	0.22	23.40	nr	25.74
extra; tee	16.50	2.50	16.91	0.35	-	7.30	0.22	24.44	nr	26.89
reference FDT 200/50, 200mm wide										
straight lengths	13.67	2.50	14.01	0.50	-	10.44	0.15	24.60	m	27.06
extra; stop end	3.15	2.50	3.23	0.15	-	3.13	-	6.36	nr	7.00
extra; corner	22.42	2.50	22.98	0.35	-	7.30	0.22	30.51	nr	33.56
extra; tee	22.42	2.50	22.98	0.40	-	8.35	0.22	31.55	nr	34.71
For 70mm screeds										
reference FDT 100/70, 100mm wide										
straight lengths	11.60	2.50	11.89	0.35	-	7.30	0.15	19.34	m	21.27
extra; stop end	3.10	2.50	3.18	0.10	-	2.09	-	5.26	nr	5.79
extra; corner	14.93	2.50	15.30	0.25	-	5.22	0.22	20.75	nr	22.82
extra; tee	14.93	2.50	15.30	0.30	-	6.26	0.22	21.79	nr	23.97
reference FDT 150/70, 150mm wide										
straight lengths	14.58	2.50	14.95	0.40	-	8.35	0.15	23.45	m	25.79
extra; stop end	3.10	2.50	3.18	0.12	-	2.50	-	5.68	nr	6.25
extra; corner	14.93	2.50	15.30	0.30	-	6.26	0.22	21.79	nr	23.97
extra; tee	14.93	2.50	15.30	0.35	-	7.30	0.22	22.83	nr	25.12
reference FDT 200/70, 200mm wide										
straight lengths	14.28	2.50	14.64	0.50	-	10.44	0.15	25.22	m	27.74
extra; stop end	3.15	2.50	3.23	0.15	-	3.13	-	6.36	nr	7.00
extra; corner	22.42	2.50	22.98	0.35	-	7.30	0.22	30.51	nr	33.56
extra; tee	22.42	2.50	22.98	0.40	-	8.35	0.22	31.55	nr	34.71
Ends of supports for equipment, fittings, appliances and ancillaries										
Fix only; casting into concrete; making good										
holderbat or bracket	-	-	-	0.25	-	5.22	0.42	5.64	nr	6.20
Fix only; building into brickwork										
holderbat or bracket	-	-	-	0.10	-	2.09	-	2.09	nr	2.30
Fix only; cutting and pinning to brickwork; making good										
holderbat or bracket	-	-	-	0.12	-	2.50	0.14	2.64	nr	2.90
Fix only; cutting and pinning to brickwork; making good fair face or facings one side										
holderbat or bracket	-	-	-	0.15	-	3.13	0.19	3.33	nr	3.66

Labour hourly rates: (except Specialists) Craft Operatives 20.87 Labourer 15.57 Rates are national average prices. Refer to REGIONAL VARIATIONS for indicative levels of overall pricing in regions	MATERIALS			LABOUR				RATES		
	Del to Site £	Waste %	Material Cost £	Craft Optve Hrs	Lab Hrs	Labour Cost £	Sunds £	Nett Rate £	Unit	Gross rate (10%) £
WORK FOR SERVICES INSTALLATIONS IN NEW BUILDINGS; MECHANICAL INSTALLATIONS (Cont'd)										
Cavity fixings for ends of supports for pipes and ducts										
Rawlnut Multi-purpose fixings, plated pan head screws; The Rawlplug Co. Ltd; fixing to soft building board, drilling										
M4 with 32mm long screw; product code 09 - 130 (RNT-M4x30)										
at 300mm centres	0.37	5.00	0.39	0.17	-	3.55	-	3.94	m	4.33
at 450mm centres	0.25	5.00	0.26	0.11	-	2.30	-	2.55	m	2.81
isolated	0.11	5.00	0.12	0.05	-	1.04	-	1.16	nr	1.28
M5 with 32mm long screw; product code 09 - 235 (RNT-M5x30)										
at 300mm centres	0.33	5.00	0.35	0.20	-	4.17	-	4.52	m	4.98
at 450mm centres	0.22	5.00	0.23	0.13	-	2.71	-	2.95	m	3.24
isolated	0.10	5.00	0.10	0.06	-	1.25	-	1.36	nr	1.49
M5 with 52mm long screw; product code 09 - 317 (RNT-M5x50)										
at 300mm centres	0.51	5.00	0.54	0.20	-	4.17	-	4.71	m	5.18
at 450mm centres	0.34	5.00	0.36	0.13	-	2.71	-	3.07	m	3.38
isolated	0.15	5.00	0.16	0.06	-	1.25	-	1.41	nr	1.56
Rawlnut Multi-purpose fixings, plated pan head screws; The Rawlplug Co. Ltd; fixing to sheet metal, drilling										
M4 with 32mm long screw; product code 09 - 130 (RNT-M4x30)										
at 300mm centres	0.37	5.00	0.39	0.33	-	6.89	-	7.28	m	8.00
at 450mm centres	0.25	5.00	0.26	0.22	-	4.59	-	4.85	m	5.34
isolated	0.11	5.00	0.12	0.10	-	2.09	-	2.20	nr	2.42
M5 with 32mm long screw; product code 09 - 235 (RNT-M5x30)										
at 300mm centres	0.33	5.00	0.35	0.40	-	8.35	-	8.70	m	9.57
at 450mm centres	0.22	5.00	0.23	0.27	-	5.63	-	5.87	m	6.46
isolated	0.10	5.00	0.10	0.12	-	2.50	-	2.61	nr	2.87
M5 with 52mm long screw; product code 09 - 317 (RNT-M5x50)										
at 300mm centres	0.51	5.00	0.54	0.40	-	8.35	-	8.89	m	9.78
at 450mm centres	0.34	5.00	0.36	0.27	-	5.63	-	5.99	m	6.59
isolated	0.15	5.00	0.16	0.12	-	2.50	-	2.67	nr	2.93
Interset high performance cavity fixings, plated pan head screws; The Rawlplug Co. Ltd; fixing to soft building board, drilling										
M4 with 40mm long screw; product code 41 - 622										
at 300mm centres	0.32	5.00	0.34	0.17	-	3.55	-	3.89	m	4.28
at 450mm centres	0.22	5.00	0.23	0.11	-	2.30	-	2.52	m	2.77
isolated	0.10	5.00	0.10	0.05	-	1.04	-	1.15	nr	1.26
M5 with 40mm long screw; product code 41 - 638										
at 300mm centres	0.45	5.00	0.48	0.20	-	4.17	-	4.65	m	5.11
at 450mm centres	0.30	5.00	0.32	0.13	-	2.71	-	3.03	m	3.33
isolated	0.14	5.00	0.14	0.06	-	1.25	-	1.40	nr	1.53
M5 with 65mm long screw; product code 41 - 654										
at 300mm centres	0.60	5.00	0.63	0.20	-	4.17	-	4.80	m	5.28
at 450mm centres	0.40	5.00	0.42	0.13	-	2.71	-	3.13	m	3.45
isolated	0.18	5.00	0.19	0.06	-	1.25	-	1.44	nr	1.59
Spring toggles plated pan head screws; The Rawlplug Co. Ltd; fixing to soft building board, drilling										
M5 with 80mm long screw; product code 94 - 439										
at 300mm centres	1.23	5.00	1.29	0.20	-	4.17	-	5.47	m	6.02
at 450mm centres	0.82	5.00	0.86	0.13	-	2.71	-	3.58	m	3.93
isolated	0.37	5.00	0.39	0.06	-	1.25	-	1.64	nr	1.80
M6 with 60mm long screw; product code 94 - 442										
at 300mm centres	0.71	5.00	0.75	0.20	-	4.17	-	4.92	m	5.42
at 450mm centres	0.48	5.00	0.50	0.13	-	2.71	-	3.21	m	3.53
isolated	0.21	5.00	0.22	0.06	-	1.25	-	1.48	nr	1.62
M6 with 80mm long screw; product code 94 - 464										
at 300mm centres	1.60	5.00	1.68	0.20	-	4.17	-	5.85	m	6.44
at 450mm centres	1.07	5.00	1.12	0.13	-	2.71	-	3.83	m	4.22
isolated	0.48	5.00	0.50	0.06	-	1.25	-	1.76	nr	1.93
Casings, bearers and supports for equipment										
Softwood, sawn										
25mm boarded platforms	12.70	10.00	13.98	1.10	0.14	25.14	0.22	39.34	m²	43.27
50 x 50mm bearers	0.98	10.00	1.08	0.16	0.02	3.65	0.03	4.76	m	5.24
50 x 75mm bearers	1.44	10.00	1.59	0.19	0.02	4.28	0.03	5.90	m	6.48
50 x 100mm bearers	2.02	10.00	2.22	0.23	0.03	5.27	0.05	7.54	m	8.29
38 x 50mm bearers; framed	0.75	10.00	0.83	0.25	0.03	5.68	0.05	6.56	m	7.21
Softwood, wrought										
25mm boarded platforms; tongued and grooved	14.44	10.00	15.88	1.20	0.15	27.38	0.25	43.52	m²	47.87
19mm boarded sides; tongued and grooved	9.82	10.00	10.80	1.10	0.14	25.14	0.22	36.16	m²	39.78
extra for holes for pipes not exceeding 55mm nominal size	-	-	-	0.25	-	5.22	-	5.22	nr	5.74
19mm boarded cover; tongued and grooved; ledged; sectional	18.09	10.00	19.90	1.20	0.15	27.38	0.25	47.53	m²	52.28
Fibreboard										
12.5mm sides	5.03	10.00	5.54	2.10	0.26	47.88	0.44	53.85	m²	59.23
extra for holes for pipes not exceeding 55mm nominal size	-	-	-	0.20	-	4.17	-	4.17	nr	4.59
Slag wool insulation										
packing around tank	26.00	10.00	28.60	6.00	0.75	136.90	-	165.50	m³	182.05
WORK FOR SERVICES INSTALLATIONS IN NEW BUILDINGS; WORK FOR ELECTRICAL INSTALLATIONS										
Cutting or forming holes, mortices, sinkings and chases										
Concealed steel conduits; making good										
luminaire points	-	-	-	0.70	0.35	20.06	0.52	20.58	nr	22.64
socket outlet points	-	-	-	0.60	0.30	17.19	0.45	17.64	nr	19.41
fitting outlet points	-	-	-	0.60	0.30	17.19	0.45	17.64	nr	19.41
equipment and control gear points	-	-	-	0.80	0.40	22.92	0.62	23.54	nr	25.89

Labour hourly rates: (except Specialists) Craft Operatives 20.87 Labourer 15.57 Rates are national average prices. Refer to REGIONAL VARIATIONS for indicative levels of overall pricing in regions	MATERIALS			LABOUR				RATES		
	Del to Site £	Waste %	Material Cost £	Craft Optve Hrs	Lab Hrs	Labour Cost £	Sunds £	Nett Rate £	Unit	Gross rate (10%) £
WORK FOR SERVICES INSTALLATIONS IN NEW BUILDINGS; WORK FOR ELECTRICAL INSTALLATIONS (Cont'd)										
Cutting or forming holes, mortices, sinkings and chases (Cont'd)										
Exposed p.v.c. conduits; making good										
luminaire points	-	-	-	0.25	0.13	7.24	0.18	7.42	nr	8.16
socket outlet points	-	-	-	0.20	0.10	5.73	0.15	5.88	nr	6.47
fitting outlet points	-	-	-	0.20	0.10	5.73	0.15	5.88	nr	6.47
equipment and control gear points	-	-	-	0.30	0.15	8.60	0.21	8.81	nr	9.69
WORK FOR SERVICES INSTALLATIONS IN EXISTING BUILDINGS										
Cutting on in-situ concrete										
Cutting chases										
depth not exceeding 50mm	-	-	-	-	0.19	2.96	-	2.96	m	3.25
Cutting chases; making good										
depth not exceeding 50mm	-	-	-	-	0.22	3.43	0.41	3.84	m	4.22
Cutting mortices										
50 x 50mm; depth not exceeding 100mm	-	-	-	-	0.50	7.78	-	7.78	nr	8.56
75 x 75mm; depth not exceeding 100mm	-	-	-	-	0.55	8.56	-	8.56	nr	9.42
100 x 100mm; depth 100 - 200mm	-	-	-	-	0.66	10.28	-	10.28	nr	11.30
38mm diameter; depth not exceeding 100mm	-	-	-	-	0.39	6.07	-	6.07	nr	6.68
Cutting holes										
225 x 150mm; depth not exceeding 100mm	-	-	-	-	1.32	20.55	0.56	21.11	nr	23.22
300 x 150mm; depth not exceeding 100mm	-	-	-	-	1.45	22.58	0.63	23.20	nr	25.52
300 x 300mm; depth not exceeding 100mm	-	-	-	-	1.60	24.91	0.63	25.54	nr	28.09
225 x 150mm; depth 100 - 200mm	-	-	-	-	1.89	29.43	0.79	30.22	nr	33.24
300 x 150mm; depth 100 - 200mm	-	-	-	-	2.11	32.85	0.89	33.74	nr	37.12
300 x 300mm; depth 100 - 200mm	-	-	-	-	2.32	36.12	0.89	37.01	nr	40.71
225 x 150mm; depth 200 - 300mm	-	-	-	-	2.20	34.25	0.92	35.18	nr	38.70
300 x 150mm; depth 200 - 300mm	-	-	-	-	2.43	37.84	1.01	38.84	nr	42.73
300 x 300mm; depth 200 - 300mm	-	-	-	-	2.65	41.26	1.01	42.27	nr	46.49
50mm diameter; depth not exceeding 100mm	-	-	-	-	0.85	13.23	0.33	13.56	nr	14.92
100mm diameter; depth not exceeding 100mm	-	-	-	-	0.94	14.64	0.43	15.06	nr	16.57
150mm diameter; depth not exceeding 100mm	-	-	-	-	1.03	16.04	0.43	16.47	nr	18.11
50mm diameter; depth 100 - 200mm	-	-	-	-	1.37	21.33	0.54	21.88	nr	24.06
100mm diameter; depth 100 - 200mm	-	-	-	-	1.51	23.51	0.63	24.14	nr	26.55
150mm diameter; depth 100 - 200mm	-	-	-	-	1.62	25.22	0.63	25.85	nr	28.44
50mm diameter; depth 200 - 300mm	-	-	-	-	1.63	25.38	0.71	26.09	nr	28.70
100mm diameter; depth 200 - 300mm	-	-	-	-	1.79	27.87	0.76	28.63	nr	31.49
150mm diameter; depth 200 - 300mm	-	-	-	-	1.97	30.67	0.76	31.43	nr	34.58
Grouting into mortices with cement mortar (1:1); around steel										
50 x 50mm; depth not exceeding 100mm	-	-	-	-	0.12	1.87	0.84	2.71	nr	2.98
75 x 75mm; depth not exceeding 100mm	-	-	-	-	0.13	2.02	0.84	2.87	nr	3.15
100 x 100mm; depth 100 - 200mm	-	-	-	-	0.17	2.65	1.07	3.72	nr	4.09
38mm diameter; depth not exceeding 100mm	-	-	-	-	0.09	1.40	0.61	2.01	nr	2.21
Cutting holes on reinforced in-situ concrete										
Cutting holes										
225 x 150mm; depth not exceeding 100mm	-	-	-	-	1.64	25.53	0.71	26.24	nr	28.87
300 x 150mm; depth not exceeding 100mm	-	-	-	-	1.81	28.18	0.76	28.94	nr	31.83
300 x 300mm; depth not exceeding 100mm	-	-	-	-	1.99	30.98	0.76	31.74	nr	34.92
225 x 150mm; depth 100 - 200mm	-	-	-	-	2.39	37.21	1.04	38.25	nr	42.08
300 x 150mm; depth 100 - 200mm	-	-	-	-	2.63	40.95	1.09	42.04	nr	46.24
300 x 300mm; depth 100 - 200mm	-	-	-	-	2.89	45.00	1.09	46.09	nr	50.69
225 x 150mm; depth 200 - 300mm	-	-	-	-	2.78	43.28	1.17	44.46	nr	48.90
300 x 150mm; depth 200 - 300mm	-	-	-	-	3.06	47.64	1.29	48.93	nr	53.82
300 x 300mm; depth 200 - 300mm	-	-	-	-	3.33	51.85	1.29	53.14	nr	58.45
50mm diameter; depth not exceeding 100mm	-	-	-	-	1.05	16.35	0.45	16.79	nr	18.47
100mm diameter; depth not exceeding 100mm	-	-	-	-	1.18	18.37	0.51	18.88	nr	20.77
150mm diameter; depth not exceeding 100mm	-	-	-	-	1.30	20.24	0.51	20.75	nr	22.83
50mm diameter; depth 100 - 200mm	-	-	-	-	1.72	26.78	0.73	27.51	nr	30.26
100mm diameter; depth 100 - 200mm	-	-	-	-	1.89	29.43	0.78	30.20	nr	33.22
150mm diameter; depth 100 - 200mm	-	-	-	-	2.02	31.45	0.78	32.23	nr	35.45
50mm diameter; depth 200 - 300mm	-	-	-	-	2.04	31.76	0.86	32.62	nr	35.88
100mm diameter; depth 200 - 300mm	-	-	-	-	2.24	34.88	0.96	35.83	nr	39.42
150mm diameter; depth 200 - 300mm	-	-	-	-	2.46	38.30	0.96	39.26	nr	43.19
Cutting mortices, sinking and the like for services										
In existing concrete; making good										
75 x 75 x 35mm	-	-	-	0.45	0.13	11.42	0.75	12.17	nr	13.38
150 x 75 x 35mm	-	-	-	0.60	0.15	14.86	1.12	15.98	nr	17.58
In existing brickwork										
75 x 75 x 35mm	-	-	-	0.25	0.10	6.77	0.45	7.22	nr	7.95
150 x 75 x 35mm	-	-	-	0.40	0.13	10.37	0.68	11.05	nr	12.15
In existing brickwork with plaster finish; making good										
75 x 75 x 35mm	-	-	-	0.30	0.18	9.06	0.75	9.81	nr	10.79
150 x 75 x 35mm	-	-	-	0.45	0.20	12.51	1.05	13.56	nr	14.91
In existing blockwork; making good										
75 x 75 x 35mm	-	-	-	0.25	0.08	6.46	0.50	6.96	nr	7.65
150 x 75 x 35mm	-	-	-	0.35	0.10	8.86	0.54	9.40	nr	10.34
In existing blockwork with plaster finish; making good										
75 x 75 x 35mm	-	-	-	0.40	0.13	10.37	0.68	11.05	nr	12.15
150 x 75 x 35mm	-	-	-	0.46	0.15	11.94	0.60	12.54	nr	13.79

Labour hourly rates: (except Specialists) Craft Operatives 20.87 Labourer 15.57 Rates are national average prices. Refer to REGIONAL VARIATIONS for indicative levels of overall pricing in regions	MATERIALS			LABOUR				RATES		
	Del to Site £	Waste %	Material Cost £	Craft Optve Hrs	Lab Hrs	Labour Cost £	Sunds £	Nett Rate £	Unit	Gross rate (10%) £
WORK FOR SERVICES INSTALLATIONS IN EXISTING BUILDINGS (Cont'd)										
Cutting chases for services										
In existing concrete; making good										
20mm nominal size conduits -1	-	-	-	0.40	0.20	11.46	0.52	11.99	m	13.19
20mm nominal size conduits -3	-	-	-	0.50	0.25	14.33	0.62	14.94	m	16.44
20mm nominal size conduits -6	-	-	-	0.60	0.30	17.19	0.70	17.90	m	19.69
In existing brickwork										
20mm nominal size conduits -1	-	-	-	0.30	0.15	8.60	0.52	9.12	m	10.03
20mm nominal size conduits -3	-	-	-	0.40	0.20	11.46	0.62	12.08	m	13.28
20mm nominal size conduits -6	-	-	-	0.50	0.25	14.33	0.70	15.03	m	16.54
In existing brickwork with plaster finish; making good										
20mm nominal size conduits -1	-	-	-	0.45	0.23	12.97	0.69	13.66	m	15.03
20mm nominal size conduits -3	-	-	-	0.55	0.28	15.84	0.78	16.62	m	18.28
20mm nominal size conduits -6	-	-	-	0.65	0.33	18.70	0.87	19.57	m	21.53
In existing blockwork										
20mm nominal size conduits -1	-	-	-	0.23	0.12	6.67	0.52	7.19	m	7.91
20mm nominal size conduits -3	-	-	-	0.30	0.15	8.60	0.62	9.21	m	10.13
20mm nominal size conduits -6	-	-	-	0.38	0.19	10.89	0.70	11.59	m	12.75
In existing blockwork with plaster finish; making good										
20mm nominal size conduits -1	-	-	-	0.38	0.19	10.89	0.69	11.58	m	12.74
20mm nominal size conduits -3	-	-	-	0.45	0.23	12.97	0.78	13.75	m	15.13
20mm nominal size conduits -6	-	-	-	0.53	0.27	15.27	0.87	16.14	m	17.75
Lifting and replacing floorboards										
For cables or conduits										
in groups 1 - 3	-	-	-	0.16	0.08	4.58	0.15	4.73	m	5.21
in groups 3 - 6	-	-	-	0.20	0.10	5.73	0.17	5.90	m	6.49
in groups exceeding 6	-	-	-	0.25	0.13	7.24	0.18	7.42	m	8.16

This section continues on the next page

Labour hourly rates: (except Specialists) Craft Operatives 20.87 Labourer 15.57 Rates are national average prices. Refer to REGIONAL VARIATIONS for indicative levels of overall pricing in regions	PLANT AND TRANSPORT			LABOUR				RATES		
	Plant Cost £	Trans Cost £	P and T Cost £	Craft Optve Hrs	Lab Hrs	Labour Cost £	Sunds £	Nett Rate £	Unit	Gross rate (10%) £
WORK FOR EXTERNAL SERVICES INSTALLATIONS										
Underground service runs; excavating trenches to receive services not exceeding 200mm nominal size - by machine										
Note:										
Notwithstanding the requirements of NRM2 ducts are not included with items of excavation and the appropriate ducts must be added to to the rates as noted below										
Excavations commencing from natural ground level; compacting; backfilling with excavated material										
not exceeding 1m deep; average 750mm deep	3.18	1.14	4.32	-	0.25	3.89	3.45	11.66	m	12.83
not exceeding 1m deep; average 750mm deep; next to roadways	3.42	1.14	4.57	-	0.25	3.89	5.46	13.92	m	15.31
Excavations commencing from existing ground level; levelling and grading backfilling to receive turf										
not exceeding 1m deep; average 750mm deep	3.42	1.14	4.57	-	0.25	3.89	5.51	13.97	m	15.37
Extra over service runs										
Extra over excavating trenches irrespective of depth; breaking out existing hard pavings										
concrete 150mm thick	3.59	-	3.59	-	-	-	-	3.59	m²	3.95
reinforced concrete 200mm thick	7.45	-	7.45	-	-	-	-	7.45	m²	8.19
concrete 150mm thick; reinstating	4.36	-	4.36	-	-	-	19.59	23.95	m²	26.35
macadam paving 75mm thick	0.64	-	0.64	-	-	-	-	0.64	m²	0.71
macadam paving 75mm thick; reinstating	0.64	-	0.64	-	-	-	25.05	25.69	m²	28.26
concrete flag paving 50mm thick	-	-	-	-	0.26	4.05	-	4.05	m²	4.45
concrete flag paving 50mm thick; re-instating	-	-	-	0.50	0.76	22.27	16.45	38.72	m²	42.60
Lifting turf for preservation										
stacking on site average 50 metres distance for immediate use; watering	0.01	-	0.01	-	0.60	9.34	-	9.35	m²	10.28
Re-laying turf										
taking from stack average 50 metres distance, laying on prepared bed, watering, maintaining	0.01	-	0.01	-	0.60	9.34	-	9.35	m²	10.28
Extra over excavating trenches irrespective of depth; breaking out existing materials										
hard rock	28.24	-	28.24	-	-	-	-	28.24	m³	31.07
concrete	23.11	-	23.11	-	-	-	-	23.11	m³	25.42
reinforced concrete	34.66	-	34.66	-	-	-	-	34.66	m³	38.13
brickwork, blockwork or stonework	15.41	-	15.41	-	-	-	-	15.41	m³	16.95
Extra over excavating trenches irrespective of depth; excavating next to existing services										
electricity services -1	-	-	-	-	5.00	77.85	-	77.85	m	85.64
gas services -1	-	-	-	-	5.00	77.85	-	77.85	m	85.64
water services -1	-	-	-	-	5.00	77.85	-	77.85	m	85.64
Extra over excavating trenches irrespective of depth; excavating around existing services crossing trench										
electricity services; cables crossing -1	-	-	-	-	7.50	116.77	-	116.77	nr	128.45
gas services services crossing -1	-	-	-	-	7.50	116.77	-	116.77	nr	128.45
water services services crossing -1	-	-	-	-	7.50	116.77	-	116.77	nr	128.45
Underground service runs; excavating trenches to receive services not exceeding 200mm nominal size - by hand										
Note:										
Notwithstanding the requirements of NRM2 ducts are not included with items of excavation and the appropriate ducts must be added to to the rates as noted below										
Excavations commencing from natural ground level; compacting; backfilling with excavated material										
not exceeding 1m deep; average 750mm deep	-	-	-	-	1.20	18.68	11.20	29.89	m	32.88
not exceeding 1m deep; average 750mm deep; next to roadways	-	-	-	-	1.20	18.68	12.74	31.42	m	34.56
Excavations commencing from existing ground level; levelling and grading backfilling to receive turf										
not exceeding 1m deep; average 750mm deep	-	-	-	-	1.20	18.68	13.07	31.75	m	34.93
Extra over service runs										
Extra over excavating trenches irrespective of depth; breaking out existing hard pavings										
concrete 150mm thick	-	-	-	-	1.50	23.35	-	23.35	m²	25.69
reinforced concrete 150mm thick	-	-	-	-	3.00	46.71	-	46.71	m²	51.38
concrete 150mm thick; reinstating	-	-	-	-	3.00	46.71	21.73	68.44	m²	75.28
macadam paving 75mm thick	-	-	-	-	0.25	3.89	-	3.89	m²	4.28
macadam paving 75mm thick; reinstating	-	-	-	-	0.25	3.89	27.56	31.45	m²	34.59
concrete flag paving 50mm thick	-	-	-	-	0.26	4.05	-	4.05	m²	4.45
concrete flag paving 50mm thick; re-instating	-	-	-	-	0.76	11.83	18.36	30.20	m²	33.22
Extra over excavating trenches irrespective of depth; breaking out existing materials										
hard rock	-	-	-	-	13.35	207.86	-	207.86	m³	228.65
concrete	-	-	-	-	10.00	155.70	-	155.70	m³	171.27
reinforced concrete	-	-	-	-	15.00	233.55	-	233.55	m³	256.90
brickwork, blockwork or stonework	-	-	-	-	7.00	108.99	-	108.99	m³	119.89

Labour hourly rates: (except Specialists) Craft Operatives 20.87 Labourer 15.57 Rates are national average prices. Refer to REGIONAL VARIATIONS for indicative levels of overall pricing in regions	PLANT AND TRANSPORT			LABOUR				RATES		
	Plant Cost £	Trans Cost £	P and T Cost £	Craft Optve Hrs	Lab Hrs	Labour Cost £	Sunds £	Nett Rate £	Unit	Gross rate (10%) £
WORK FOR EXTERNAL SERVICES INSTALLATIONS (Cont'd)										
Extra over service runs (Cont'd)										
Extra over excavating trenches irrespective of depth; excavating next existing services										
electricity services -1	-	-	-	-	5.00	77.85	-	77.85	m	85.64
gas services -1	-	-	-	-	5.00	77.85	-	77.85	m	85.64
water services -1	-	-	-	-	5.00	77.85	-	77.85	m	85.64
Extra over excavating trenches irrespective of depth; excavating around existing services crossing trench										
electricity services; cables crossing -1	-	-	-	-	7.50	116.77	-	116.77	nr	128.45
gas services services crossing -1	-	-	-	-	7.50	116.77	-	116.77	nr	128.45
water services services crossing -1	-	-	-	-	7.50	116.77	-	116.77	nr	128.45

This section continues
on the next page

Labour hourly rates: (except Specialists) Craft Operatives 20.87 Labourer 15.57 Rates are national average prices. Refer to REGIONAL VARIATIONS for indicative levels of overall pricing in regions	MATERIALS			LABOUR				RATES		
	Del to Site £	Waste %	Material Cost £	Craft Optve Hrs	Lab Hrs	Labour Cost £	Sunds £	Nett Rate £	Unit	Gross rate (10%) £
WORK FOR EXTERNAL SERVICES INSTALLATIONS (Cont'd)										
Underground ducts; vitrified clayware, BS 65 extra strength; flexible joints										
Straight										
100mm nominal size single way duct; laid in position in trench	21.07	5.00	22.12	0.16	0.02	3.65	-	25.77	m	28.35
100mm nominal size bonded to form 2 way duct; laid in position in trench	42.13	5.00	44.24	0.25	0.03	5.68	-	49.93	m	54.92
100mm nominal size bonded to form 4 way duct; laid in position in trench	84.27	5.00	88.48	0.35	0.04	7.93	-	96.41	m	106.05
100mm nominal size bonded to form 6 way duct; laid in position in trench	126.40	5.00	132.72	0.45	0.06	10.33	-	143.05	m	157.35
extra; providing and laying in position nylon draw wire	0.37	10.00	0.40	0.02	-	0.42	-	0.82	m	0.90
Cast iron surface boxes and covers, coated to BS EN 10300; bedding in cement mortar (1:3)										
Surface boxes, BS 5834 Part 2 marked S.V.										
hinged lid; 150 x 150mm overall top size, 75mm deep	20.42	15.00	20.64	0.75	0.38	21.57	0.33	42.54	nr	46.79
Surface boxes, BS 750, marked 'FIRE HYDRANT'										
heavy grade; minimum clear opening 230 x 380mm, minimum depth 125mm	47.51	15.00	47.94	1.25	0.63	35.90	1.63	85.47	nr	94.02
Surface boxes, BS 5834 Part 2 marked 'W' or WATER										
medium grade; double triangular cover; minimum clear opening 300 x 300mm, minimum depth 100mm	65.76	15.00	66.19	1.50	0.75	42.98	1.62	110.79	nr	121.87
Stop cock pits, valve chambers and the like										
Stop cock pits; half brick thick sides of common bricks, BS EN 772, Category M, 215 x 102.5 x 65mm, compressive strength 20.5 N/mm², in cement mortar (1:3); 100mm thick base and top of plain in-situ concrete, BS 8500, ordinary prescribed mix ST4, 20mm aggregate, formwork; including all excavation, backfilling, disposal of surplus excavated material, earthwork support and compaction of ground										
600mm deep in clear; (surface boxes included elsewhere)										
internal size 225 x 225mm	207.18	5.00	208.91	1.50	1.50	54.66	0.08	269.37	nr	296.31
internal size 338 x 338mm	273.97	5.00	277.97	2.25	2.25	81.99	0.13	368.86	nr	405.75
aggregate, formwork										
750mm deep in clear; (surface boxes included elsewhere)										
150mm diameter	221.25	5.00	222.73	1.15	1.15	41.91	0.10	270.45	nr	297.49
Stop cock keys										
tee	3.76	-	3.76	-	-	-	-	3.76	nr	4.14

BASIC PRICES OF MATERIALS

This section gives basic prices of materials delivered to site. Prices are exclusive of Value Added Tax.

Excavation and Earthwork

Filling

Broken brick or stone filling.	43.20 m^3
MOT type 1 filling	46.08 m^3
MOT type 2 filling	46.08 m^3
Imported topsoil	32.64 m^3
Sand	29.76 m^3

Gravel

Coarse gravel	43.78 m^3
Blinding gravel	54.97 m^3

Earthwork support

Earthwork support timber	308.94 m^3

Concrete Work

Materials for site mixed concrete	
40mm Aggregate	50.02 m^3
20mm Aggregate	50.02 m^3
10mm Aggregate	50.02 m^3
Portland Cement	163.60 t
White Portland Cement	387.60 t
Sharp sand	58.08 m^3
White silver sand	80.00 m^3
Ready mixed concrete, prescribed mix	
ST1 - 40mm aggregate - 7.5% waste	98.28 m^3
ST3 - 20mm aggregate - 7.5% waste	101.40 m^3
ST4 - 20mm aggregate - 7.5% waste	105.04 m^3
ST5 - 20mm aggregate - 7.5% waste	110.24 m^3
Ready mixed concrete, design mix	
C 12/15 - 15 N/mm² - 20mm - 2.5% waste	93.60 m^3
C 16/20 - 20 N/mm² - 20mm - 2.5% waste	97.76 m^3
C 20/25 - 25 N/mm² - 20mm - 2.5% waste	101.92 m^3
C 25/30 - 30 N/mm² - 20mm - 2.5% waste	106.08 m^3
Site mixed concretes, mortars, various mixes	
1:6, all in aggregate	144.57 m^3
1:8, all in aggregate	136.60 m^3
1:12, all in aggregate	131.67 m^3
Lightweight concrete	
20.5 N/mm²; vibrated	149.06 m^3
26.0 N/mm²; vibrated	153.83 m^3
41.5 N/mm²; vibrated	157.08 m^3
Mild steel rod reinforcement	
32mm diameter	1,107.97 t
25mm diameter	1,175.89 t
20mm diameter	1,211.11 t
16mm diameter	1,269.23 t
12mm diameter	1,266.67 t
10mm diameter	1,497.73 t
8mm diameter	1,630.77 t
6mm diameter	1,731.03 t
High yield rod reinforcement	
32mm diameter	918.64 t
25mm diameter	919.85 t
20mm diameter	1,187.65 t
16mm diameter	1,253.14 t
12mm diameter	1,420.51 t
10mm diameter	1,428.10 t
8mm diameter	1,623.08 t
6mm diameter	1,630.14 t
Stainless steel rod reinforcement	
25mm diameter	4,340.63 t
20mm diameter	4,525.61 t
16mm diameter	4,429.63 t
12mm diameter	4,545.46 t
10mm diameter	4,506.02 t
8mm diameter	4,800.00 t
Fabric reinforcement, BS Ref 4483	
A393	10.91 m^2
A252	6.81 m^2
A193	5.29 m^2
A142	3.78 m^2
A98	3.79 m^2
B1131	20.29 m^2
B785	15.42 m^2
B503	11.04 m^2
B385	9.54 m^2
B283	6.98 m^2
B196	6.17 m^2
C785	13.94 m^2
C636	11.81 m^2
C503	9.04 m^2
C385	8.08 m^2
C283	6.68 m^2
D98	5.34 m^2
D49	6.93 m^2

Formwork

Basic finish	
Sides of foundations	
height exceeding 1.00m.	5.15 m^2
height not exceeding 250mm	1.60 m
Sides of ground beams and edges of beds	
height exceeding 1.00m.	5.15 m^2
height not exceeding 250mm	1.60 m
Edges of suspended slabs	
height not exceeding 250mm	1.93 m
height 250 - 500mm	3.60 m
Sides of upstands	
height not exceeding 250mm	2.29 m
height 250 - 500mm	2.68 m
Soffits of slabs	
horizontal slab thickness not exceeding 200mm	15.58 m^2
horizontal slab thickness 200 - 300mm	17.14 m^2
sloping not exceeding 15 degrees slab thickness not exceeding 200mm - 15% waste	17.16 m^2
sloping exceeding 15 degrees slab thickness not exceeding 200mm - 15% waste	17.95 m^2
Walls	
plain	12.61 m^2
plain; height exceeding 3.00m above floor level	11.63 m^2
Beams	
attached to slabs	10.88 m^2
with 50mm wide chamfers	11.08 m^2
isolated	11.41 m^2
isolated with 50mm wide chamfers	11.63 m^2
Columns	
attached to walls	7.56 m^2
attached to walls, height exceeding 3.00m above floor level	6.89 m^2
Wall kickers	
straight	1.50 m
curved 2m radius	3.68 m
curved 10m radius	2.24 m
Stairflights	
1000mm wide; 155mm thick waist; 178mm risers	23.25 m
1500mm wide; 180mm thick waist; 178mm risers	29.10 m
1000mm wide; 155mm thick waist; 178mm undercut risers	23.25 m
1500mm wide; 180mm thick waist; 178mm undercut risers	29.08 m
Claymaster expanded polystyrene permanent formwork	
2400 x 1200 by	
75mm thick	6.49 m^2
100mm thick	9.48 m^2
150mm thick	13.81 m^2

Damp proofing

Liquid damp proof applications	
Synthaprufe bituminous emulsion	5.71 l
Bituminous emulsion	2.67 l
R.I.W. liquid asphaltic composition	9.15 l
Flexible sheet damp proof membranes	
Polythene sheeting, 125mu	0.45 m^2
Polythene sheeting, 250mu (1000g)	0.30 m^2
Polythene sheeting, 300mu (1200g)	0.31 m^2
Waterproof building paper to BS 1521	
Visqueen 300mu damp proof membrane	0.39 m^2

Prestressed precast lintels

100 x 65mm	
900mm long	5.23 nr
1200mm long	6.96 nr
1500mm long	8.58 nr
1800mm long	10.29 nr
2100mm long	12.04 nr
2400mm long	13.76 nr
2700mm long	15.47 nr
3000mm long	17.21 nr
140 x 65mm	
1200mm long	11.45 nr
1800mm long	16.50 nr
3000mm long	27.14 nr
215 x 65mm	
1200mm long	17.20 nr
1800mm long	25.28 nr
3000mm long	43.90 nr
255 x 65mm	
1200mm long	23.50 nr
1800mm long	35.22 nr
3000mm long	58.72 nr
215 x 100mm	
1800mm long	49.46 nr
3000mm long	84.02 nr
100 x 140mm	
1200mm long	16.04 nr
3000mm long	42.56 nr
215 x 140mm	
1200mm long	41.41 nr
1800mm long	62.12 nr

Precast concrete sills

figure 2 or figure 4; splayed and grooved	
50 x 150mm	
300mm long	73.33 nr
700mm long	73.33 nr
1300mm long	102.67 nr
stooled end	15.83 nr
100 x 150mm	
300mm long	66.00 nr
700mm long	66.00 nr
1300mm long	115.50 nr
stooled end	22.00 nr

Concrete Work (Cont'd)

Precast concrete copings; figure 1

75 x 200mm
splayed; rebated joints ... 29.52 m
extra; stopped ends........ 2.95 nr
100 x 300mm
splayed; rebated joints ... 45.83 m
extra; stopped ends........ 4.58 nr
75 x 200mm
saddleback; rebated joints .... 28.47 m
extra; hipped ends.......... 2.85 nr
100 x 300mm
saddleback; rebated joints .... 37.15 m
extra; hipped ends.......... 3.71 nr

Precast concrete padstones

215 x 215 x 102mm .... 15.26 nr
215 x 215 x 140mm .... 17.81 nr
330 x 215 x 102mm .... 27.74 nr
440 x 215 x 140mm .... 23.73 nr
440 x 440 x 140mm .... 47.46 nr
600 x 140 x 102mm .... 21.45 nr

Brickwork and Blockwork

Bricks

Common bricks
plain................................ 311.88 1000
Selected
regraded bricks............... 320.00 1000
Second hard stock
bricks............................... 620.00 1000
Engineering bricks
class A............................ 1,055.72 1000
class B............................ 390.00 1000
Staffordshire Blue Brindle
wirecut bricks Ibstock
A2221A........................... 980.00 1000
pressed bricks................. 1,900.00 1000

Special bricks

Claydon Red Multi............. 690.00 1000
Tudors.............................. 742.38 1000
Milton Buff Ridgefaced....... 970.00 1000
Heathers........................... 742.38 1000
Brecken Grey.................... 850.00 1000
Leicester Red Stock.......... 832.60 1000
West Hoathly Medium
multi-stock 1,080.00 1000
Himley Dark Brown Rustic.. 1,091.77 1000

Miscellaneous materials for brickwork and blockwork

Cement lime mortar (1:1:6) 317.03 m³
Hydrated Lime .... 366.00 t

Cavity wall insulation

Glass fibre slabs 50mm
(Dritherm 37) .... 2.35 m²
Glass fibre slabs 75mm
(Dritherm 37) .... 3.03 m²
Glass fibre slabs 100mm
(Dritherm 37) .... 3.37 m²
Glass fibre slabs 75mm
(Dritherm 32) .... 7.01 m²
Glass fibre slabs 100mm
(Dritherm 32) .... 8.86 m²
insulation board 50mm
(Celotex)........................... 8.87 m²
insulation board 75mm
(Celotex)........................... 13.09 m²
insulation board 100mm
(Celotex)........................... 16.76 m²

Wall Ties

Stainless steel
200mm Housing type 4 ... 67.50 250
250mm Housing type 4 ... 45.00 250
Staifix RT2 200mm........... 46.28 250
Staifix RT2 250mm 60.68 250
ST1 250mm Heavy duty
type 1 .... 429.68 1000
ST1 300mm Heavy duty
type 1 .... 523.52 1000
Vertical twisted
203 x 19 x 3mm 484.00 1000

Extension Profiles

Catnic Stronghold 60-
250mm ref SWC................ 4.41 m
Simpson C2K Crocodile
Wall Starter Stainless Steel 3.00 m

Thermabate insulated cavity closers for fixing to masonry with PVCU ties at 225mm centres

Thermabate 50.................. 5.19 m
Thermabate 75.................. 5.67 m
Thermabate 100................ 5.95 m
Thermabate 125................ 8.22 m

Blockwork

Thermalite Shield blocks
75mm thick blocks........... 11.80 m²
100mm thick blocks......... 13.10 m²
140mm thick blocks......... 25.15 m²
150mm thick blocks......... 24.10 m²
Thermalite Turbo blocks
100mm thick blocks......... 14.00 m²
215mm thick blocks......... 26.20 m²
265mm thick blocks......... 38.67 m²
Thermalite Party Wall blocks
215mm thick blocks......... 31.60 m²
Thermalite Hi-Strength blocks
100mm thick blocks......... 20.40 m²
140mm thick blocks......... 27.90 m²
Thermalite Trench blocks
300mm thick blocks......... 44.00 m²
355mm thick blocks......... 61.70 m²
Lignacite blocks solid Fair Face 7.0 N/mm²
100mm thick blocks......... 16.42 m²
140mm thick blocks......... 23.85 m²
190mm thick blocks......... 51.66 m²
Toplite solid '7' blocks 7.0 N/mm²
100mm thick blocks......... 14.00 m²
140mm thick blocks......... 35.44 m²
190mm thick blocks......... 47.69 m²
215mm thick blocks......... 53.68 m²
Hemelite solid Standard blocks 3.5 N/mm²
100mm thick blocks......... 11.10 m²
140mm thick blocks......... 16.18 m²
Hemelite solid Standard blocks 7.0 N/mm²
100mm thick blocks......... 14.40 m²
140mm thick blocks......... 15.00 m²
Tarmac Topcrete cellular blocks
100mm thick.................... 10.25 m²
140mm thick.................... 12.75 m²
Hollow glass blocks, white, cross ribbed
190 x 190 x 80mm blocks. 2.25 nr
240 x 240 x 80mm blocks. 6.50 nr

Damp proof course

Hyload "Original", pitch
polymer............................ 6.18 m²
BS 6515 Polythene DPC .... 0.72 m²
Synthaprufe bituminous
latex emulsion................... 3.22 l
Bituminous emulsion.......... 4.68 l
Slates 400mm x 250mm..... 1,020.00 1000

Cavity trays and closers

Type G Cavitray without lead
900mm long cavitray .... 9.83 nr
220 x 332mm external
angle............................... 5.39 nr
230 x 117mm internal
angle............................... 5.39 nr
Type X Cavitray with lead, 40 degree pitch
Intermediate tray; short..... 7.28 nr
Ridge tray........................ 14.24 nr
Catchment tray; long .... 9.70 nr
Corner catchment angle
tray.................................. 14.87 nr
Type W
Cavity weep ventilator ...... 0.64 nr
Extension duct................. 1.13 nr
Fire rated cavity closers by Cavity Trays Ltd
Cavi Type V; Cavicloser
vertical .... 6.94 m
Cavi Type V; Cavicloser
horizontal .... 6.94 m
Cavi 240 type CFIS;
Cavicheck vertical........... 3.68 m
Cavi 240 type CFIS;
Cavicheck horizontal....... 3.68 m
Cavi 240 type PWIB;
Party wall integrity barrier
vertical sleeved............... 9.48 m
Cavi 240 type PWIB;
Party wall integrity barrier
horizontal........................ 9.48 m
Stainless steel mesh reinforcement
65mm mesh..................... 1.11 m
115mm mesh................... 2.93 m
175mm mesh................... 2.84 m
225mm mesh................... 4.80 m
305mm mesh................... 4.75 m
Brickforce stainless steel joint reinforcement
60mm wide ref
SBF30W60...................... 1.54 m
60mm wide ref
SBF50W60...................... 5.04 m
175mm wide ref
SBF30W175.................... 1.95 m
175mm wide ref
SBF50W175.................... 5.35 m
100mm wide ref
SBF30W100.................... 1.68 m
100mm wide ref
SBF50W100.................... 5.13 m

Air Bricks

Terra cotta, red or buff, square hole
215 x 140mm.................. 6.18 nr
215 x 215mm.................. 14.53 nr
215 x 140 Cavity liner 200
long .... 4.21 nr
215 x 215 Cavity liner 200
long .... 19.55 nr
Iron, light
225 x 75mm.................... 14.17 nr
225 x 150mm.................. 25.83 nr
Plastic
225 x 75mm.................... 1.01 nr
225 x 150mm.................. 2.02 nr
225 x 225mm.................. 3.03 nr

Arch bars

30 x 6mm flat.................... 5.05 m
50 x 6mm flat.................... 6.00 m
50 x 50 x 6mm angle .... 9.89 m
75 x 50 x 6mm angle .... 17.33 m

Yorkshire Limestone

Random stones 500mm
thick .... 59.70 m²
Squared rubble face
stones, irregular coursed,
100 - 150mm on bed
scappled or axed face........ 73.50 m²

Portland stone, plain and rubbed one side

50mm thick dressing.......... 191.10 m²
75mm thick dressing.......... 259.90 m²
100mm thick dressing........ 343.98 m²

Simulated Dorset limestone

100mm thick, plain and
rubbed one side.............. 100.33 m²
200 x 100mm lintels......... 51.50 m
200 x 75mm sills.............. 58.98 m
200 x 75mm sills extra;
stoolings .... 10.51 nr
175 x 75mm jamb stones. 45.52 m
225 x 125mm band
courses........................... 45.52 m

Roofing

Profile 3 sheeting fibre cement

Standard grey colour
coverings......................... 18.64 m²
eaves filler pieces;
Polyethylene.................... 2.25 m
two piece plain angular
adjustable ridge tiles .... 17.03 m
standard barge boards..... 11.35 m
apron flashings .... 24.64 m
standard ridge cap finials. 18.57 nr

Roofing (Cont'd)

Profile 6 sheeting

Standard coloured
- coverings .... 12.79 m^2
- eaves filler pieces .... 2.25 m
- two piece plain angular adjustable ridge tiles .... 17.90 m
- standard barge boards .... 16.90 m
- apron flashings .... 16.87 m
- standard ridge cap finials .... 21.90 nr

Treated softwood roofing battens
- 25 x 19mm .... 1.07 m
- 32 x 19mm .... 1.07 m
- 32 x 25mm .... 1.07 m
- 38 x 19mm .... 0.78 m
- 50 x 19mm .... 1.80 m
- 50 x 25mm .... 1.35 m

Roofing underfelts, reinforced bitumen
- Underlay; twin-ply; 145gsm with polypropylene .... 0.68 m^2

Tiles

Clay tiles

Machine made
- Plain tiles; 268 x 165mm. 490.00 1000
- Eaves tiles .... 0.49 nr
- Tile and a half .... 0.98 nr
- Ridge tiles, half round; 300mm long .... 5.78 nr
- Hip tiles; arris .... 5.78 nr
- Hip tiles; bonnet .... 5.78 nr
- Hip irons .... 1.02 nr

Hand made
- Clay tiles .... 1.31 nr
- Eaves tiles .... 1.31 nr
- Clay tile and a half .... 2.64 nr
- Ridge tiles, half round; 300mm long .... 7.93 nr
- Hip tiles; bonnet pattern .. 13.45 nr
- Valley tiles; angular .... 7.93 nr
- Vertical angle tile .... 8.48 nr

Redland Plain tiles, 268 x 165mm

Concrete granular faced
- Tiles 420.00 1000
- Tile and a half 83.00 100

Heathland
- Standard 511.22 1000
- Tile and a half 101.00 100

Concrete granular faced
- Half round ridge or hip tile 450mm long .... 8.01 nr

Slates

Fibre cement slates
- 600 x 300mm 960.00 1000
- 500 x 250mm 1,050.00 1000
- 400 x 200mm 830.00 1000
- Ridges or hips .... 22.76 m

Welsh Blue/grey slates, 6.5mm thick
- 600 x 300mm 12,450.00 1000
- 500 x 250mm 5,190.00 1000
- 400 x 200mm 2,610.00 1000

Redland Cambrian interlocking slates
- 300 x 336mm 2,300.00 1000
- Slate and a half slates to match 300 x 336mm 4,650.00 1000
- 150 x 6mm fibre cement undercloak .... 2.05 m
- Stainless steel eaves clip to each slate .... 0.35 nr
- Redland third round ridge or hip .... 14.07 nr
- Redland half round ridge or hip .... 4.57 nr
- Redland universal angle ridge or hip .... 10.11 m
- Redland Dry Ridge system with half round ridge tiles .... 26.93 m
- Redland Dry Ridge system with universal angle ridge tiles .... 26.93 m
- Monoridge filler units .... 30.86 m
- Universal valley troughs 3.00m long .... 25.31 nr

Timloc uPVC ventilators
- Soffit ventilators; reference 1137 .... 1.02 m
- Over-fascia ventilators; reference 3011 10mm airflow .... 2.68 m

Tiles

Redland single lap tiles
- 430 x 380mm 5,657.27 1000
- 418 x 332mm 1,173.75 1000
- 381 x 227mm 840.00 1000
- 418 x 330mm 1,080.88 1000

Timber shingling
- Western Red Cedar Shingles; best grade; bundle (2.28m^2) .... 104.17 nr

Felt or similar

Roofing Felt BS 13707
- Perforated glass fibre underlay 2mm .... 2.76 m^2
- Sanded underlay 4mm .... 3.58 m^2
- Mineral surface top sheet 4mm .... 6.01 m^2
- Sand surfaced glassfibre underlay - 1.8 Kg/m^2 .... 1.78 m^2
- Top sheet green mineral surface - 3.8 kg/m^2 .... 4.41 m^2
- Hot bitumen bonding compound .... 1.49 kg

Insulating boards for felt roofing
- 50mm Kingspan Thermaroof TR27 .... 14.79 m^2
- 100mm Kingspan Thermaroof TR27 .... 32.66 m^2
- 120mm Kingspan Thermaroof TR27 .... 40.25 m^2
- 70mm Xtratherm Flat Roof FR-MG .... 19.69 m^2
- 100mm Xtratherm Flat Roof FR-MG .... 30.13 m^2
- 150mm Xtratherm Flat Roof FR-MG .... 68.91 m^2

Lead sheet
- Code 3 .... 36.00 m^2
- Code 4 .... 49.00 m^2
- Code 5 .... 61.00 m^2

Aluminium roofing
- 0.6 mm thick sheets .... 19.23 m^2
- 150 mm girth flashings .... 2.88 m
- 180 mm girth flashings .... 3.46 m
- 240 mm girth flashings .... 4.62 m
- 300 mm girth flashings .... 5.77 m
- 450 mm girth flashings .... 8.65 m
- 180 x 180 mm soakers .... 3.46 nr
- 180 x 300 mm soakers .... 5.77 nr
- 360mm girth gutter linings 6.92 m
- 420mm girth gutter linings 8.08 m

Copper roofing
- 0.55 mm thick sheets .... 102.00 m^2
- 0.70 mm thick sheets .... 124.00 m^2

Zinc roofing - 0.80mm thick
- 0.80 mm thick sheets .... 65.00 m^2
- 150 mm girth flashings .... 9.75 m
- 180 mm girth flashings .... 11.70 m
- 240 mm girth flashings .... 15.60 m
- 300 mm girth flashings .... 19.50 m
- 180 x 180 mm soakers .... 2.11 nr
- 180 x 300 mm soakers .... 3.51 nr
- 450 x 450 mm soakers .... 13.16 nr

Woodwork

Sawn Softwood

General Structural Grade C16

25mm
- by 50mm .... 0.71 m
- by 100mm .... 1.01 m
- by 150mm .... 2.12 m
- by 200mm .... 2.83 m
- by 225mm .... 3.18 m

32mm
- by 100mm .... 2.20 m
- by 125mm .... 2.76 m
- by 150mm .... 3.22 m
- by 175mm .... 3.76 m
- by 200mm .... 4.30 m
- by 225mm .... 4.84 m
- by 250mm .... 8.64 m
- by 300mm .... 10.03 m

38mm
- by 38mm .... 0.84 m
- by 100mm .... 2.20 m
- by 125mm .... 2.76 m
- by 150mm .... 3.22 m
- by 175mm .... 3.76 m
- by 200mm .... 4.30 m
- by 225mm .... 4.84 m
- by 250mm .... 8.64 m
- by 300mm .... 10.03 m

44mm
- by 100mm .... 2.59 m
- by 125mm .... 3.24 m
- by 150mm .... 3.88 m
- by 175mm .... 4.53 m
- by 200mm .... 5.18 m
- by 225mm .... 5.83 m
- by 250mm .... 9.87 m
- by 300mm .... 11.63 m

50mm
- by 50mm .... 1.31 m
- by 75mm .... 1.97 m
- by 100mm .... 2.59 m
- by 125mm .... 3.24 m
- by 150mm .... 3.88 m
- by 175mm .... 4.53 m
- by 200mm .... 5.18 m
- by 225mm .... 5.83 m
- by 250mm .... 9.87 m
- by 300mm .... 11.63 m

63mm
- by 63mm .... 3.18 m
- by 75mm .... 3.18 m
- by 100mm .... 4.19 m
- by 125mm .... 6.20 m
- by 150mm .... 6.20 m
- by 175mm .... 7.23 m
- by 200mm .... 8.27 m
- by 225mm .... 9.30 m
- by 250mm .... 15.75 m
- by 300mm .... 18.56 m

75mm
- by 75mm .... 3.18 m
- by 100mm .... 4.19 m
- by 125mm .... 6.20 m
- by 150mm .... 6.20 m
- by 175mm .... 7.23 m
- by 200mm .... 8.27 m
- by 225mm .... 9.30 m
- by 250mm .... 15.75 m
- by 300mm .... 18.56 m

100mm
- by 100mm .... 9.00 m
- by 200mm .... 16.24 m
- by 250mm .... 21.00 m
- by 300mm .... 24.75 m

150mm
- by 150mm .... 17.78 m
- by 250mm .... 34.42 m
- by 300mm .... 37.13 m

200mm
- by 200mm .... 10.88 m

250mm
- by 250mm .... 56.10 m

300mm
- by 300mm .... 81.60 m

General Structural Grade C24 Pressure impregnated

32mm
- by 125mm .... 3.28 m
- by 150mm .... 3.51 m
- by 175mm .... 4.09 m
- by 200mm .... 4.68 m
- by 225mm .... 5.27 m
- by 250mm .... 10.09 m
- by 300mm .... 11.65 m

38mm
- by 125mm .... 3.28 m
- by 150mm .... 3.51 m
- by 175mm .... 4.09 m
- by 200mm .... 4.68 m

Woodwork (Cont'd)

Sawn Softwood (Cont'd)

General Structural Grade C24 Pressure impregnated (Cont'd)

38mm (Cont'd)

by 225mm	5.27 m
by 250mm	10.28 m
by 300mm	12.00 m

44mm

by 125mm	3.76 m
by 150mm	4.23 m
by 175mm	4.94 m
by 200mm	5.65 m
by 225mm	6.36 m
by 250mm	10.46 m
by 300mm	12.34 m

50mm

by 50mm	1.43 m
by 63mm	2.31 m
by 75mm	2.15 m
by 100mm	2.83 m
by 125mm	3.76 m
by 150mm	4.23 m
by 175mm	4.94 m
by 200mm	5.65 m
by 225mm	6.36 m
by 250mm	10.46 m
by 300mm	12.34 m

63mm

by 63mm	3.46 m
by 75mm	3.46 m
by 100mm	4.57 m
by 125mm	4.11 m
by 150mm	6.76 m
by 175mm	8.40 m
by 200mm	10.14 m
by 225mm	10.14 m
by 250mm	16.69 m
by 300mm	19.68 m

75mm

by 75mm	3.46 m
by 100mm	4.57 m
by 125mm	4.92 m
by 150mm	6.76 m
by 175mm	7.89 m
by 200mm	9.02 m
by 225mm	10.14 m
by 250mm	16.69 m
by 300mm	19.68 m

100mm

by 100mm	5.25 m
by 150mm	12.93 m
by 225mm	19.40 m

150mm

by 150mm	12.15 m
by 225mm	25.50 m
by 250mm	35.70 m
by 300mm	39.38 m

200mm

by 200mm	22.40 m

250mm

by 250mm	59.50 m

Softwood boarding, wrot, impregnated

19mm thick	13.89 m²
25mm thick	17.51 m²

Plywood BB/CC Far Eastern H/W

18mm thick	14.04 m²
25mm thick	19.67 m²

Wrought softwood SW PAR

6mm

by 38mm	0.26 m

12mm

by 38mm	0.53 m

16mm

by 25mm	0.53 m

19mm

by 38mm	0.64 m

25mm

by 50mm	0.83 m

38mm

by 125mm	3.03 m
by 150mm	3.63 m
by 50mm	1.24 m

50mm

by 50mm	1.61 m
by 75mm	2.42 m
by 100mm	3.15 m
by 150mm	4.73 m
by 200mm	6.35 m
by 300mm	10.88 m

75mm

by 75mm	3.63 m
by 100mm	4.87 m
by 150mm	7.09 m

100mm

by 100mm	9.20 m
by 150mm	12.75 m

150mm

by 150mm	19.04 m

Pressure Impregnated Softwood Boarding

25 x 200mm	3.44 m
25 x 225mm	3.95 m

Softwood window components

19mm splayed glazing bead	0.99 nr

Boarded flooring

Softwood, wrought

19 x 75mm, square edge	12.93 m²
25 x 125mm, square edge	16.83 m²
32 x 150mm, square edge	24.20 m²
19 x 75mm, tongued and grooved joint	13.09 m²
25 x 125mm, tongued and grooved joint	18.36 m²

Wall and ceiling boarding

Western Red Cedar, wrought, tongued, grooved and veed joints

19mm thick, 100mm wide	101.74 m²
25mm thick, 100mm wide	138.37 m²

Knotty Pine, wrought, selected for transparent finish

19mm thick, 100mm wide	44.25 m²
25mm thick, 100mm wide	64.09 m²

Sapele, wrought, selected for transparent finish, tongued, grooved and veed joints

19mm thick, 100mm wide	114.27 m²
25mm thick, 100mm wide	154.70 m²

Timber for First and Second Fixings

Ash	2,550.00 m³
Iroko	2,642.00 m³
Idigbo	3,688.00 m³
Mahogany	6,035.19 m³
American Walnut	7,736.00 m³
Beech	1,890.00 m³
American Oak White	4,444.00 m³
Sapele	2,200.00 m³
British Columbian Pine (Douglas Fir)	2,158.00 m³
Teak	18,866.00 m³

Blockboard

Birch faced

16mm	16.47 m²
18mm	9.72 m²
25mm	32.12 m²

Oak faced

18mm	24.83 m²

Sapele faced

18mm	36.96 m²

Beech faced

18mm	40.59 m²

Plywood

Douglas Fir T&G, unsanded select sheathing quality, WBP bonded

15mm thick	18.67 m²
18mm thick	15.75 m²

Birch faced T&G, BB quality, WBP bonded

12mm thick	13.46 m²
15mm thick	15.60 m²
18mm thick	18.29 m²

Wood particle board (chipboard) BS EN 312

P4 load bearing boards, square edge

18mm thick	6.85 m²
22mm thick	8.69 m²

P5 load bearing moisture resistant boards, square edge

18mm thick	6.08 m²
22mm thick	7.50 m²

P4 T&G load bearing boards

18mm thick	6.08 m²
22mm thick	7.50 m²

P2 Furniture Grade Chipboard, moisture resisting

18mm thick	4.92 m²
12mm thick	3.66 m²

P5 T&G load bearing moisture resistant boards

18mm thick	8.33 m²
22mm thick	11.11 m²

Hardboard

Standard, type SHA; butt joints

3.2mm thick linings	1.57 m²
4.8mm thick linings	5.52 m²
6.4mm thick linings	7.37 m²

Tempered, Type THE; butt joints

3.2mm thick linings	3.43 m²
4.8mm thick linings	4.83 m²
6.4mm thick linings	6.81 m²

Medium density fibreboard (MDF)

Type MDF; linings to walls, butt joints

9mm thick	4.46 m²
12mm thick	5.79 m²
18mm thick	9.66 m²
25mm thick	10.22 m²

Linings; butt joints; Pine veneered

6mm thick	20.30 m²
19mm thick	23.49 m²

Linings; butt joints; Oak veneered

6mm thick	11.49 m²
13mm thick	13.41 m²
19mm thick	14.60 m²

Linings; Maple veneered

19mm thick	28.52 m²

Insulating board

Softboard, type SBN butt joints

13mm thick thick linings	2.92 m²

Fire resisting boards

Masterboard Class O; butt joints

6mm thick linings	19.84 m²
9mm thick linings	39.15 m²
12mm thick linings	51.65 m²

Supalux, Sanded; butt joints

6mm thick linings	26.33 m²
9mm thick linings	34.78 m²
12mm thick linings	45.20 m²
15mm thick linings	66.51 m²

Promatect L500; butt joints

20mm thick casings	67.01 m²
30mm thick casings	106.77 m²
40mm thick casings	164.77 m²
50mm thick casings	227.15 m²

Vermiculite fire board; butt joints

20mm thick casings	95.56 m²
25mm thick casings	49.16 m²
30mm thick casings	81.97 m²

PVC Fascia and bargeboards

Fascia; 22mm thick; white; bullnose with soffit groove

150mm wide	7.70 m
200mm wide	10.80 m
250mm wide	13.00 m

Fascia; 10mm thick; white; square edge flat board

100mm wide	2.22 m
150mm wide	3.11 m
225mm wide	4.77 m

Soffit board; pre vented 9mm thick; white

150mm wide	4.15 m
225mm wide	5.15 m
300mm wide	6.60 m
100mm wide	2.22 m
175mm wide	3.45 m
300mm wide	6.21 m

Woodwork (Cont'd)

Skirtings, picture rails, architraves and the like

Softwood wrought
19 x 100mm .... 1.24 m
19 x 150mm .... 1.86 m
25 x 100mm .... 1.61 m
25 x 150mm .... 2.33 m
splays -1
19 x 50mm .... 0.68 m
19 x 75mm .... 1.02 m
19 x 100mm .... 1.24 m
32 x 100mm .... 3.50 m

Oak
19 x 95mm .... 6.90 m
19 x 145mm .... 10.46 m
25 x 100mm .... 10.49 m
25 x 150mm .... 13.88 m

MDF
chamfered
18 x 44mm .... 1.33 m
chamfered
18 x 94mm .... 2.37 m
moulded
18 x 44mm .... 1.33 m
moulded
18 x 144mm .... 3.56 m

Cover fillets, stops, trims, beads, nosings and the like

MDF
Dado rail
18 x 58mm .... 1.85 m
25 x 70mm .... 2.74 m

Cappings

Softwood, wrought
level; rebates -1; mouldings -1
25 x 50mm .... 2.55 m
50 x 75mm .... 5.74 m
50 x 100mm .... 8.74 m

Window boards

Softwood wrought
mouldings -1
25 x 150mm .... 6.94 m
32 x 150mm .... 8.91 m
rounded edges -1
25 x 150mm .... 6.94 m
32 x 150mm .... 8.91 m

MDF
nosed and tongued
25 x 200mm .... 7.86 m
25 x 244mm .... 9.58 m

Windows

Jeld-Wen Ltd. Stormsure windows; factory glazed 24mm low E glass
630 x 900mm overall
LEW109C.................. 261.93 nr
1200 x 750mm overall
LEW207CC .... 422.12 nr
1200 x 900mm overall
LEW209CC .... 443.95 nr
1200 x 1050mm overall
LEW210CC .... 466.71 nr
1200 x 1200mm overall
LEW212CC .... 379.28 nr
1200 x 1350mm overall
LEW213CC .... 529.36 nr
1770 x 750mm overall
LEW307CC .... 537.84 nr
1770 x 900mm overall
LEW309CC .... 431.60 nr
1770 x 1050mm overall
LEW310CC .... 464.31 nr
1770 x 1200mm overall
LEW312CC .... 462.75 nr
2339 x 900mm overall
LEW409CMC .... 688.91 nr
2339 x 1050mm overall
LEW410CMC .... 727.01 nr
2339 x 1200mm overall
LEW412CMC .... 766.78 nr
2339 x 1350mm overall
LEW413CMC .... 820.33 nr

Purpose made windows in softwood, wrought; 68 x 75mm frame; 72 x 64mm casement
38mm moulded casements or fanlights
divided into panes.......... 306.51 m²
50mm moulded casements or fanlights
divided into panes.......... 367.81 m²

Purpose made windows in Sapele, wrought
38mm moulded casements or fanlights
divided into panes.......... 300.80 m²
50mm moulded casements or fanlights
divided into panes.......... 360.96 m²

Skylights

Velux roof windows GGL/GPL 3066 Pine Range, factory triple glazed sealed unit
550 x 980mm overall
CK04 GGL Centre Pivot. 310.59 nr
660 x 1180mm overall
FK06 GGL Centre Pivot . 342.01 nr
940 x 1600mm overall
PK10 GGL Centre Pivot. 439.83 nr
660 x 1180mm overall
FK06 GPL Top Hung ..... 426.98 nr
780 x 1400mm overall
MK08 GPL Top Hung..... 478.38 nr

Windows, UPVC

Windows uPVC white; fixed light, factory glazed 28mm double glazed units
600 x 600mm.................. 71.23 nr
600 x 1200mm.................. 82.68 nr
750 x 1050mm.................. 85.53 nr
900 x 1050mm.................. 89.83 nr
1200 x 1200mm.............. 104.13 nr

Windows uPVC white; 2 fixed lights, factory glazed 28mm double glazed units
750 x 1350mm.................. 128.43 nr
900 x 1350mm.................. 132.73 nr
1200 x 1350mm.............. 145.60 nr
1200 x 1500mm
toughened glass .... 180.12 nr

Windows uPVC white; overall, tilt/turn, factory glazed 28mm double glazed units
600 x 900mm.................. 187.61 nr
600 x 1200mm.................. 167.52 nr
750 x 650mm.................. 140.98 nr
750 x 900mm.................. 161.93 nr
750 x 1200mm.................. 174.50 nr
900 x 900mm.................. 178.69 nr
900 x 1200mm.................. 192.66 nr
900 x 1500mm toughened
glass.............................. 248.07 nr

Windows uPVC white; 1 fixed light; 1 opening top light; factory glazed 40mm triple glazed units
600 x 900mm.................. 273.78 nr
600 x 1400mm.................. 334.98 nr
800 x 900mm.................. 311.42 nr
900 x 900mm.................. 330.24 nr
1200 x 900mm.................. 403.53 nr
1200 x 1500mm
toughened glass .... 583.96 nr

Rooflights

Rooflights, 'Thermadome' from the National Domelight Company; triple skin; UV protected polycarbonate domes
600 x 600mm.................. 208.33 nr
1200 x 1200mm.............. 455.00 nr

Rooflights, 'Thermadome' from the National Domelight Company; triple skin; UV protected polycarbonate domes; manually controlled rotating vents
600 x 600mm.................. 230.83 nr
900 x 900mm.................. 345.83 nr
1200 x 1200mm.............. 480.00 nr

Rooflights, 'Thermadome' from the National Domelight Company; triple skin; UV protected polycarbonate domes; manually hinged opening
600 x 600mm.................. 292.50 nr
900 x 900mm.................. 420.00 nr
1200 x 1200mm.............. 565.00 nr

Doors

Doors in softwood, wrought, Magnet Trade

Internal panelled doors
SA; pine; glazed with toughened bevelled glass; 762 x 1981 x 34mm............................ 107.40 nr

Doors in softwood, wrought, preservative treated
Ext. ledged and braced doors
L & B 838 x 1981 x 44mm............................ 53.00 nr
Ext. framed, ledged and braced doors
YX; 838 x 1981 x 44mm . 72.30 nr
Ext. panelled doors
KXT CDS; 762 x 1981 x 44mm............................ 121.90 nr
2XG; 762 x 1981 x 44mm............................ 100.70 nr
2XG; 838 x 1981 x 44mm............................ 100.70 nr
Garage doors
MFL, pair, side hung; 2134 x 2134 x 44mm...... 279.16 nr
301, pair, pre-glazed obscure, side hung; 2134 x 2134 x 44mm............... 316.66 nr

Doors in Hardwood (solid, laminated or veneered), wrought, Magnet Trade
Ext. panelled doors
Carolina M & T, unglazed; 813 x 2032 x 44mm............................ 180.10 nr
Carolina M & T, pre-glazed; 813 x 2032 x 44mm............................ 258.30 nr
Colonial 6 panel meranti veneer; 762 x 1981 x 44mm............................ 180.10 nr
Int. panelled doors
Regency 6 panel; prefinished oak; 762 x 1981 x 35mm .... 150.25 nr
Regency 6 panel; prefinished oak; FD30 fire door; 762 x 1981 x 44mm............................ 244.90 nr
Mexicana unfinished oak; 762 x 1981 x 35mm 117.20 nr

Hollowcore doors with moulded panel facings; Magnet Trade
Int. panelled doors
6 Panel Smooth; 610 x 1981 x 35mm .... 43.80 nr
6 Panel Smooth; 838 x 1981 x 35mm .... 43.80 nr

Flush doors, Magnet Trade
Int. Magnaseal; smooth; unlipped
610 x 1981 x 35mm........ 34.90 nr
762 x 1981 x 35mm........ 34.90 nr
838 x 1981 x 35mm........ 34.90 nr
Int. veneered paintgrade facings
381 x 1981 x 35mm........ 42.40 nr
610 x 1981 x 35mm........ 42.40 nr
762 x 1981 x 35mm........ 42.40 nr
838 x 1981 x 35mm........ 42.40 nr
Int. Ash; prefinished
686 x 1981 x 35mm........ 106.20 nr
838 x 1981 x 35mm........ 106.20 nr
Ext. veneered paintgrade facings; FD 30
838 x 1981 x 44mm........ 87.00 nr
Int. fire resisting
4 Panel Smooth; FD30; 838 x 1981 x 44mm........ 96.40 nr
veneered paintgrade facings; FD30; 838 x 1981 x 44mm .... 60.70 nr
Ext. fire resisting
veneered paintgrade facings; FD30; 838 x 1981 x 44mm .... 87.00 nr
Hardwood lipped; solid core; FD60; 838 x 1981 x 44mm............................ 145.90 nr

Patio doors in uPVC
1500 x 2020mm overall.... 530.18 nr
2390 x 2090mm overall.... 613.68 nr

Staircases

Straight flight softwod staircase and balustrade 22mm MDF treads and risers; 32mm strings; 75 x 75mm newels; square balusters; 38 x 75mm hardwood handrail
855mm wide x 2600mm rise overall .... 584.58 nr
Isolated softwood balustrades
41 x 41mm balusters at 150mm centres
914mm high .... 10.40 m
41 x 41mm square balusters at 150mm centres, moulded rails
914mm high .... 24.07 m
Handrails
in softwood, wrought
44mm mopstick............. 4.75 m
94 x 34mm Pigs Ear....... 6.18 m

Furniture and fixings

Wall rack RAJA Workplace; oak
8 hooks; 1800 long reference 787-021.......... 62.95 nr
Hat and coat hooks
RAJA Workplace; steel coloured reference 456-122.......... 4.20 nr
Kitchen units; melamine finish; self assembly; high gloss white finish doors
wall units
500 x 330 x 700mm........ 47.68 nr
1000 x 330 x 700mm...... 68.79 nr
floor units without drawers
500 x 600 x 900mm........ 52.08 nr
1000 x 600 x 900mm...... 73.24 nr
floor units with three drawers
600 x 600 x 900mm........ 109.40 nr
store cupboards with two doors
600 x 600 x 2120mm...... 144.92 nr

Fixings

Nails, Oval brads, 50mm; galvanised .... 2.87 kg
Nails, Lost Head Oval brads 50mm; bright steel.... 1.82 kg
Nails, Round wire, plain head, 50mm....................... 1.74 kg
Nails, cut clasp, 50mm....... 3.99 kg
Nails, galvanised clout, 50mm .... 2.26 kg
25mm masonry nails.......... 1.50 100
40mm masonry nails.......... 2.20 100
50mm masonry nails.......... 2.60 100
60mm masonry nails.......... 3.20 100
75mm masonry nails.......... 4.50 100
80mm masonry nails.......... 5.20 100
100mm masonry nails........ 6.60 100
Screws 3.5 x 20mm Pozidrive............................ 1.00 100
Screws 3.5 x 25mm Pozidrive............................ 1.10 100
Screws 3.5 x 30mm Pozidrive............................ 1.40 100
Screws 3.5 x 40mm Pozidrive............................ 1.80 100
Screws 4 x 50mm Pozidrive............................ 2.50 100
Screws 4 x 70mm Pozidrive............................ 4.10 100
Screws 5 x 100mm Pozidrive............................ 7.70 100
5 mm plastic plug.............. 0.50 100
6 mm plastic plug.............. 0.60 100
7 mm plastic plug.............. 0.80 100
8 x 40mm plastic plug 3.50 100
10 x 80mm plastic plug ...... 0.24 nr

Hardware

butt hinges
38mm; steel .... 0.15 nr
63mm; steel .... 0.24 nr
75mm; steel .... 0.10 nr
100mm; steel .... 0.25 nr
100mm; steel; strong...... 0.74 nr
38mm; brass, brass pin.. 1.13 nr
63mm; brass, brass pin.. 1.25 nr
75mm; brass, brass pin.. 0.28 nr
100mm; brass, brass pin 0.70 nr
rising hinges
75mm; steel.................... 1.57 nr
100mm; steel.................. 1.99 nr
tee hinges
300mm; japanned; light .. 1.35 nr
230mm; galvanised .... 2.73 nr
450mm; galvanised .... 6.85 nr
mortice latches; tubular stamped steel case; 75mm............................ 0.80 nr
cylinder rim night latches
Legge' 707; silver grey finish; brass bolt .... 23.88 nr
Union' 1022; silver case, chromium plated cylinder 23.01 nr
Yale' 88; grey case, chromium plated cylinder 17.89 nr
cupboard locks
4 lever; brass; 63mm ...... 22.05 nr
rim dead lock
japanned case; 102 x 76mm............................ 6.25 nr
mortice locks
three levers .... 5.55 nr
five levers .... 8.65 nr
hasps and locks; 'Squire' Stronghold restricted profile; 150mm overall width; HLS50S; hardened steel; Electrophoretic finish ...... 102.22 nr
barrel bolts
150mm; japanned, steel barrel; medium .... 1.48 nr
300mm; japanned, steel barrel; heavy .... 11.54 nr

Insulation quilts

Glass fibre 100mm thick ... 1.43 m²
Glass fibre 200mm thick ... 3.61 m²
Glass fibre 400mm thick ... 7.22 m²
Sheeps wool insulation 200mm thick..................... 15.75 m²
Knauf 'Earthwool Loftroll 44' 200mm thick .... 3.61 m²
Rockwool Rollbatts 100mm thick..................... 7.17 m²
Rockwool Rollbatts 150mm thick..................... 11.38 m²
Insulation boards
Glass fibre medium density 50mm thick........... 2.35 m²
Glass fibre medium density 75mm thick........... 3.03 m²
Celotex GA4050 - 50mm thick .... 7.39 m²
Celotex GA4100 - 100mm thick .... 13.08 m²
Insulation sheets
Expanded polystyrene sheeting 20mm thick......... 2.00 m²
Expanded polystyrene sheeting 50mm thick......... 5.00 m²

Structural Steelwork

Universal beams (S355J)
914 x 305 x 201............... 1,150.00 t
914 x 305 x 253............... 1,150.00 t
838 x 292 x 176............... 1,270.00 t
838 x 292 x 226............... 1,270.00 t
762 x 267 x 134............... 1,190.00 t
762 x 267 x 173............... 1,190.00 t
762 x 267 x 197............... 1,190.00 t
686 x 254 x 125............... 1,190.00 t
686 x 254 x 152............... 1,190.00 t
686 x 254 x 170............... 1,190.00 t
610 x 305 x 179............... 1,150.00 t
610 x 305 x 149............... 1,150.00 t
610 x 229 x 125............... 1,130.00 t
610 x 229 x 113............... 1,190.00 t
610 x 229 x 101............... 1,190.00 t
533 x 210 x 122............... 1,150.00 t
533 x 210 x 101............... 1,190.00 t
533 x 210 x 92................. 1,100.00 t
533 x 210 x 82................. 1,200.00 t
457 x 191 x 98................. 1,190.00 t
457 x 191 x 82................. 1,200.00 t
457 x 191 x 67................. 1,260.00 t
457 x 152 x 82................. 1,220.00 t
457 x 152 x 67................. 1,260.00 t
457 x 152 x 52................. 1,260.00 t
406 x 178 x 74................. 1,220.00 t
406 x 178 x 60................. 1,220.00 t
406 x 178 x 54................. 1,260.00 t
406 x 140 x 46................. 1,260.00 t
406 x 140 x 39................. 1,300.00 t
356 x 171 x 67................. 1,100.00 t
356 x 171 x 51................. 1,100.00 t
356 x 171 x 45................. 1,100.00 t
356 x 127 x 39................. 1,100.00 t
356 x 127 x 33................. 1,100.00 t
305 x 165 x 54................. 1,080.00 t
305 x 165 x 40................. 1,080.00 t
305 x 127 x 48................. 1,080.00 t
305 x 127 x 37................. 1,160.00 t
305 x 102 x 33................. 1,160.00 t
305 x 102 x 25................. 1,160.00 t
254 x 102 x 28................. 1,120.00 t
254 x 102 x 22................. 1,120.00 t
Universal Columns (S355J)
356 x 406 x 467............... 1,150.00 t
356 x 406 x 393............... 1,150.00 t
356 x 406 x 287............... 1,150.00 t
356 x 406 x 235............... 1,150.00 t
356 x 368 x 202............... 1,150.00 t
356 x 368 x 153............... 1,150.00 t
356 x 368 x 129............... 1,150.00 t
305 x 305 x 283............... 1,100.00 t
305 x 305 x 198............... 1,060.00 t
305 x 305 x 158............... 1,060.00 t
305 x 305 x 118............... 1,060.00 t
305 x 305 x 97................. 1,040.00 t
254 x 254 x 167............... 1,040.00 t
254 x 254 x 107............... 1,050.00 t
254 x 254 x 89................. 1,050.00 t
254 x 254 x 73................. 1,050.00 t
203 x 203 x 86................. 1,050.00 t
203 x 203 x 60................. 1,080.00 t
203 x 203 x 52................. 1,080.00 t
203 x 203 x 46................. 1,080.00 t
152 x 152 x 37................. 1,080.00 t
152 x 152 x 23................. 1,080.00 t
Quantity extras
Under 5 tonnes to 2 tonnes .... 80.00 t
Under 2 tonnes to 1 tonne 96.00 t
Parallel flange channels
430 x 100 x 64................. 1,360.00 t
380 x 100 x 54................. 1,330.00 t
300 x 100 x 46................. 1,300.00 t
300 x 90 x 41................... 1,300.00 t
260 x 90 x 35................... 1,350.00 t
230 x 90 x 32................... 1,350.00 t
200 x 90 x 30................... 1,300.00 t
150 x 90 x 24................... 1,300.00 t
Extra; Parallel flange channels, non-standard sizes............................... 180.00 t
Equal and unequal angles
200 x 150 x 12................. 1,400.00 t
200 x 100 x 15................. 1,300.00 t
200 x 100 x 10................. 1,310.00 t
200 x 200 x 16................. 1,200.00 t
150 x 90 x 15................... 1,300.00 t
150 x 90 x 10................... 1,240.00 t
150 x 150 x 12................. 1,210.00 t
150 x 150 x 10................. 1,200.00 t
150 x 75 x 10................... 1,210.00 t
120 x 120 x 12................. 1,000.00 t
120 x 120 x 8................... 1,000.00 t
125 x 75 x 8..................... 1,040.00 t
100 x 75 x 8..................... 1,030.00 t
100 x 65 x 7..................... 1,080.00 t
100 x 100 x 10................. 950.00 t
100 x 100 x 8................... 980.00 t
90 x 90 x 8....................... 1,000.00 t
90 x 90 x 6....................... 1,070.00 t
Extra; angles non-standard sizes .... 110.00 t
Cold rolled zed purlins and cladding rails, Metsec purlin sleeved system ref: 14214; 3.03 kg/m....... 31.68 m

Structural Steelwork (Cont'd)

Cold rolled zed purlins and cladding rails, Metsec purlin sleeved system (Cont'd)

ref: 14216; 3.47 kg/m	35.76 m
ref: 17214; 3.66 kg/m	37.47 m
ref: 17216; 4.11 kg/m	42.59 m
ref: 20216; 4.49 kg/m	46.49 m
ref: 20218; 5.03 kg/m	52.45 m
ref: 20220; 5.57 kg/m	57.81 m
ref: 23218; 5.73 kg/m	59.51 m
ref: 23220; 6.34 kg/m	66.00 m

Cold rolled zed purlins and cladding rails, Metsec galvanised purlin cleats

ref: 142 for 142mm deep purlins	10.74 nr
ref: 172 for 172mm deep purlins	12.69 nr
ref: 202 for 202mm deep purlins	13.35 nr
ref: 232 for 232mm deep purlins	14.70 nr
ref: 262 for 262mm deep purlins	16.08 nr

Cold rolled zed purlins and cladding rails, Metsec Round Lok anti-sag rods

1150mm centres	10.83 nr
1350mm centres	12.56 nr
1550mm centres	14.19 nr
1700mm centres	16.00 nr
1950mm centres	16.48 nr

Cold rolled zed purlins and cladding rails, Metsec side rail sleeved/single span system

ref: 14214; 3.03 kg/m	30.75 m
ref: 14216; 3.47 kg/m	34.72 m
ref: 17215; 3.85 kg/m	36.37 m
ref: 17216; 4.11 kg/m	41.35 m
ref: 20216; 4.49 kg/m	45.14 m
ref: 20218; 5.03 kg/m	50.92 m
ref: 20220; 5.57 kg/m	56.13 m
ref: 23218; 5.73 kg/m	57.78 m
ref: 23223; 7.26 kg/m	64.08 m

Cold rolled zed purlins and cladding rails, Metsec side rail cleats

ref: 142 for 142mm rails	10.74 nr
ref: 172 for 172mm rails	12.69 nr
ref: 202 for 202mm rails	13.35 nr
ref: 232 for 232mm rails	14.70 nr

Cold rolled zed purlins and cladding rails, Metsec galvanised side rail suports, 122-262 series

rail 1000mm long	31.61 nr
rail 1400mm long	34.49 nr
rail 1600mm long	38.25 nr
rail 1800mm long	46.06 nr

Cold rolled zed purlins and cladding rails, Metsec diagonal tie wire supports

1700mm long	61.66 nr
2200mm long	68.99 nr
2600mm long	76.32 nr
3600mm long	94.24 nr

Steel short span lattice joists primed at works

200mm deep, 8.2 kg/m	30.97 m
250mm deep, 8.5 kg/m	30.97 m
300mm deep, 10.7 kg/m	34.06 m
350mm deep, 11.6 kg/m	37.16 m
350mm deep, 12.8 kg/m	52.64 m

Steel long span lattice joists primed at works

700mm deep, 39.2 kg/m	114.57 m
800mm deep, 44.1 kg/m	117.67 m
900mm deep, 45.3 kg/m	148.64 m
1000mm deep, 46.1 kg/m	151.74 m
1500mm deep, 54.2 kg/m	161.02 m

Metalwork

Steel; galvanised - 27.5 x 2.5mm standard strapping

600mm long	1.36 nr
800mm long	1.94 nr
1000mm long	2.24 nr
1200mm long	2.29 nr
1600mm long	3.86 nr

Truss clips

for 38mm thick members	0.31 nr
for 50mm thick members	0.40 nr

Joist hangers; BAT Building Products Ltd

SPH type S

for 75 x 100mm joist	3.20 nr
for 75 x 150mm joist	3.74 nr
for 75 x 200mm joist	3.76 nr
for 75 x 250mm joist	4.28 nr
for 100 x 100mm joist	4.33 nr
for 100 x 150mm joist	4.77 nr
for 100 x 200mm joist	4.97 nr
for 100 x 250mm joist	5.56 nr

SPH type R

for 50 x 100mm joist	6.46 nr
for 50 x 150mm joist	6.43 nr
for 50 x 200mm joist	8.13 nr
for 50 x 250mm joist	10.57 nr
for 63 x 100mm joist	9.53 nr
for 63 x 150mm joist	10.20 nr
for 63 x 200mm joist	10.72 nr
for 63 x 250mm joist	12.19 nr

Steel; galvanised - truss plates and framing anchors

51 x 114mm	0.36 nr
76 x 254mm	1.24 nr
114 x 152mm	1.00 nr
114 x 254mm	1.82 nr
152 x 152mm	1.21 nr

Expanding bolts; bolt projecting Rawlbolts, ref

44505 (M6 10P)	0.40 nr
44510 (M6 25P)	0.48 nr
44605 (M10 15P)	0.96 nr
44610 (M10 30P)	0.99 nr
44615 (M10 60P)	1.05 nr
44660 (M12 30P)	2.03 nr
44710 (M16 35P)	3.70 nr
44760 (M20 30P)	12.65 nr

Chemical anchors; Kemfix capsules and standard studs

capsule reference 60-428; stud reference 60-708; with nuts and washers (M8 x 110mm)	0.95 nr
capsule reference 60-432; stud reference 60-712; with nuts and washers (M12 x 160mm)	1.48 nr

Steel Lintels

Galvanised steel lintels; SUPERGALV (BIRTLEY) lintels reference CB 50

125 x 750mm	20.49 nr
125 x 1200mm	31.76 nr
125 x 1500mm	41.68 nr
125 x 1650mm	48.03 nr
165 x 1800mm	51.42 nr
165 x 2100mm	59.06 nr
165 x 2250mm	68.42 nr
165 x 2400mm	71.58 nr
215 x 2550mm	81.57 nr
215 x 3000mm	117.08 nr
215 x 3300mm	136.46 nr
215 x 3600mm	154.68 nr
215 x 3900mm	190.81 nr

Galvanised steel lintels; SUPERGALV (BIRTLEY) lintels reference AT 50

165 x 750mm	34.36 nr
165 x 1050mm	47.67 nr
165 x 1200mm	54.88 nr
165 x 1500mm	67.36 nr
215 x 1650mm	76.75 nr
215 x 1800mm	84.20 nr
215 x 2100mm	99.55 nr
215 x 2400mm	119.45 nr
215 x 2550mm	126.92 nr
215 x 3000mm	144.79 nr

Galvanised steel lintels; SUPERGALV (BIRTLEY) lintels reference CB 70

120 x 750mm	19.85 nr
120 x 1200mm	31.54 nr
120 x 1500mm	41.15 nr
160 x 1800mm	50.61 nr
215 x 2400mm	72.36 nr
215 x 3000mm	118.02 nr
215 x 3900mm	183.15 nr

Galvanised steel lintels; SUPERGALV (BIRTLEY) lintels reference AT 70

160 x 750mm	32.22 nr
160 x 1200mm	50.17 nr
160 x 1500mm	65.76 nr
215 x 1800mm	77.79 nr
215 x 2400mm	114.57 nr
215 x 3000mm	146.47 nr

Galvanised steel lintels; SUPERGALV (BIRTLEY) lintels reference CB 50/130

120 x 750mm	20.58 nr
120 x 1200mm	32.71 nr
120 x 1500mm	41.45 nr
165 x 1800mm	51.94 nr
165 x 2400mm	75.70 nr
215 x 3900mm	225.21 nr

Galvanised steel lintels; SUPERGALV (BIRTLEY) lintels reference HS 50

160 x 750mm	34.74 nr
160 x 1200mm	55.38 nr
160 x 1500mm	68.68 nr
215 x 1800mm	79.19 nr
215 x 2400mm	116.50 nr
215 x 3300mm	178.18 nr

Galvanised steel lintels; SUPERGALV (BIRTLEY) lintels reference CB 70/130

115 x 750mm	24.91 nr
115 x 1200mm	41.04 nr
115 x 1500mm	51.82 nr
155 x 1800mm	71.29 nr
155 x 2400mm	118.46 nr
210 x 3300mm	215.06 nr

Galvanised steel lintels; SUPERGALV (BIRTLEY) lintels reference CB 90

750mm long	21.15 nr
1200mm long	32.78 nr
1500mm long	40.87 nr
1800mm long	50.36 nr
2400mm long	78.40 nr
3000mm long	117.36 nr

Galvanised steel lintels; SUPERGALV (BIRTLEY) lintels reference CB 110

750mm long	25.31 nr
1500mm long	50.65 nr
1800mm long	71.20 nr
2400mm long	152.48 nr
3000mm long	190.60 nr

Galvanised steel lintels; SUPERGALV (BIRTLEY) lintels reference CB 125

750mm long	36.73 nr
1200mm long	58.31 nr
1500mm long	72.73 nr
1800mm long	87.10 nr
2400mm long	138.69 nr
3000mm long	188.77 nr

Galvanised steel lintels; SUPERGALV (BIRTLEY) lintels reference TF 50

750mm long	9.01 nr
1200mm long	14.36 nr
1800mm long	24.84 nr
2400mm long	41.34 nr
3000mm long	68.04 nr

Galvanised steel lintels; SUPERGALV (BIRTLEY) lintels reference SB 100

75 x 750mm	13.64 nr
75 x 1200mm	20.97 nr
140 x 1800mm	40.18 nr
140 x 2400mm	56.29 nr
215 x 3000mm	103.49 nr

Galvanised steel lintels; SUPERGALV (BIRTLEY) lintels reference SB 140

140 x 750mm	17.24 nr
140 x 1200mm	28.05 nr
140 x 1800mm	47.18 nr
140 x 2400mm	67.31 nr
215 x 3000mm	113.96 nr

Galvanised steel lintels; SUPERGALV (BIRTLEY) lintels reference SBL 200

142 x 750mm	23.84 nr
142 x 1200mm	40.30 nr
142 x 1800mm	61.13 nr
142 x 2400mm	86.19 nr
218 x 3000mm	140.82 nr

Metalwork (Cont'd)

Steel Lintels (Cont'd)

Galvanised steel lintels; SUPERGALV (BIRTLEY) internal door lintels reference INT 100	
100 x 900mm	5.05 nr
100 x 1050mm	5.79 nr
100 x 1200mm	6.52 nr

Mechanical Installations

Red Primer steel pipes, BS EN 10255 Table 2; steel fittings BS EN 10241	
15mm	
pipes	5.08 m
fittings; one end	0.68 nr
fittings; two ends	0.79 nr
fittings; three ends	1.16 nr
20mm	
pipes	5.69 m
fittings; one end	0.69 nr
fittings; two ends	0.99 nr
fittings; three ends	1.35 nr
25mm	
pipes	8.28 m
fittings; one end	0.82 nr
fittings; two ends	1.42 nr
fittings; three ends	2.07 nr
32mm	
pipes	9.12 m
fittings; one end	1.57 nr
fittings; two ends	2.59 nr
fittings; three ends	3.45 nr
40mm	
pipes	10.81 m
fittings; one end	1.67 nr
fittings; two ends	4.34 nr
fittings; three ends	4.63 nr
50mm	
pipes	15.58 m
fittings; one end	2.45 nr
fittings; two ends	5.79 nr
fittings; three ends	6.99 nr
Black steel pipe brackets	
15mm malleable iron	1.03 nr
20mm malleable iron	1.17 nr
25mm malleable iron	1.38 nr
32mm malleable iron	1.80 nr
40mm malleable iron	2.43 nr
50mm malleable iron	4.40 nr
Galvanised steel pipes, BS EN 10255 Table 2; steel fittings BS EN 10241	
15mm	
pipes	5.08 m
pipe connectors	0.83 nr
fittings; one end	0.68 nr
fittings; two ends	0.79 nr
fittings; three ends	1.16 nr
20mm	
pipes	5.69 m
pipe connectors	0.94 nr
fittings; one end	0.69 nr
fittings; two ends	0.99 nr
fittings; three ends	1.35 nr
25mm	
pipes	8.28 m
pipe connectors	1.16 nr
fittings; one end	0.82 nr
fittings; two ends	1.42 nr
fittings; three ends	2.07 nr
32mm	
pipes	9.12 m
pipe connectors	1.69 nr
fittings; one end	1.57 nr
fittings; two ends	2.59 nr
fittings; three ends	3.45 nr
40mm	
pipes	10.81 m
pipe connectors	2.40 nr
fittings; one end	1.67 nr
fittings; two ends	4.34 nr
fittings; three ends	4.63 nr
50mm	
pipes	15.58 m
pipe connectors	3.59 nr
fittings; one end	2.45 nr
fittings; two ends	5.79 nr
fittings; three ends	6.99 nr
Galvanised steel pipe brackets	
15mm malleable iron	1.03 nr
20mm malleable iron	1.17 nr
25mm malleable iron	1.38 nr
32mm malleable iron	1.80 nr
40mm malleable iron	2.43 nr
50mm malleable iron	4.40 m
Stainless steel pipes, BS EN 10312-2002	
15mm pipes	12.07 m
22mm pipes	11.47 m
28mm pipes	18.17 m
35mm pipes	20.26 m
42mm pipes	24.71 m
Copper pipes, BS EN 1057	
15mm pipes	2.82 m
22mm pipes	5.65 m
28mm pipes	8.93 m
35mm pipes	16.29 m
42mm pipes	19.69 m
54mm pipes	26.07 m
67mm pipes	24.60 m
76mm pipes	33.26 m
108mm pipes	54.89 m
Copper pipes, BS EN 1057 2871 Part 1 Table Y	
15mm pipes	6.19 m
22mm pipes	11.21 m
28mm pipes	14.46 m
42mm pipes	22.40 m
Copper coil pipes,EN 1057 R220 (Annealed) Table Y plastic coated	
15mm pipes	8.39 m
22mm pipes	14.82 m
Capillary fittings for copper pipes	
15mm	
fittings; one end	0.11 nr
fittings; two ends	0.15 nr
fittings; three ends	0.30 nr
22mm	
fittings; one end	0.28 nr
fittings; two ends	0.42 nr
fittings; three ends	0.79 nr
28mm	
fittings; one end	0.75 nr
fittings; two ends	1.32 nr
fittings; three ends	2.03 nr
35mm	
fittings; one end	1.44 nr
fittings; two ends	3.22 nr
fittings; three ends	5.65 nr
42mm	
fittings; one end	2.29 nr
fittings; two ends	4.93 nr
fittings; three ends	8.34 nr
54mm	
fittings; one end	4.20 nr
fittings; two ends	7.84 nr
fittings; three ends	14.25 nr
Compression fittings type A for copper pipes	
15mm	
fittings; one end	0.49 nr
fittings; two ends	0.74 nr
fittings; three ends	1.05 nr
22mm	
fittings; one end	0.87 nr
fittings; two ends	1.34 nr
fittings; three ends	1.72 nr
28mm	
fittings; one end	2.28 nr
fittings; two ends	4.13 nr
fittings; three ends	6.03 nr
35mm	
fittings; one end	4.00 nr
fittings; two ends	8.64 nr
fittings; three ends	11.22 nr
42mm	
fittings; one end	5.64 nr
fittings; two ends	11.69 nr
fittings; three ends	14.80 nr
54mm	
fittings; one end	9.18 nr
fittings; two ends	19.42 nr
fittings; three ends	24.10 nr
Wavin Hep2O polybutylene pipes	
15mm pipes	1.64 m
22mm pipes	3.47 m
28mm pipes	6.08 m
Blue polythene pipes MDPE, BS EN 12201	
20mm pipes	0.54 m
25mm pipes	0.70 m
32mm pipes	1.20 m
50mm pipes	3.13 m
63mm pipes	4.91 m
PVC-U pipes, BS EN 1452 Class E	
3/8" - 17.1mm diameter pipes	6.43 m
1/2" - 21.5mm diameter pipes	0.89 m
3/4" - 26.7mm diameter pipes	1.28 m
1" - 33.4mm diameter pipes	1.71 m
1 1/4" - 42.2mm diameter pipes	2.10 m
1 1/2" - 48.3mm diameter pipes	2.70 m
PVC-U pipes self coloured white	
1/2" - 21.5mm diameter pipes	0.50 m
Ductile iron pipes	
100mm pipes	21.96 m
150mm pipes	43.20 m
Brass stopcocks	
Crutch head; DZR; joints to polythene	
22mm	7.68 nr
Crutch head; compression joints to copper (Type A)	
15mm	4.03 nr
22mm	5.67 nr
28mm	11.00 nr
Crutch head; DZR; compression joints to copper (Type A)	
15mm	6.62 nr
22mm	9.57 nr
28mm	16.56 nr
35mm	40.75 nr
42mm	50.05 nr
54mm	83.47 nr
Polybutylene stopcocks	
Fitted with Hep2O ends	
15mm	8.23 nr
22mm	9.83 nr
Brass gate valves	
BS 5154 series B; compression joints to copper (Type A)	
15mm	4.91 nr
22mm	5.61 nr
28mm	10.23 nr
35mm	18.07 nr
42mm	27.77 nr
54mm	51.66 nr
DZR; fitted with Hep2O ends	
15mm	6.29 nr
22mm	9.16 nr
Lever ball valves	
Screwed and PTFE joints	
15mm	3.10 nr
22mm	4.41 nr
28mm	8.12 nr
35mm	15.85 nr
42mm	22.87 nr
54mm	36.25 nr
Brass ball valves	
For low pressure; BS 1212	
13mm; part 1; copper float	14.46 nr
13mm; part 2; copper float	14.46 nr
13mm; part 1; plastics float	7.46 nr
13mm; part 2; plastics float	7.46 nr
For high pressure; BS 1212	
13mm; part 1; copper float	14.46 nr
13mm; part 2; copper float	13.04 nr

Mechanical Installations (Cont'd)

Brass ball valves (Cont'd)

For high pressure; BS 1212 (Cont'd)

19mm; part 1; copper float	20.16 nr
25mm; part 1; copper float	54.23 nr
13mm; part 1; plastics float	7.46 nr
13mm; part 2; plastics float	6.04 nr
19mm; part 1; plastics float	11.02 nr
25mm; part 1; plastics float	34.60 nr

One piece GRP water storage tanks including cover

Pre insulated

90 litre	264.00 nr
160 litre	302.00 nr
225 litre	338.00 nr
250 litre	377.00 nr
340 litre	442.00 nr
500 litre	522.00 nr
750 litre	682.00 nr
1000 litre	722.00 nr
1500 litre	1,066.00 nr
2500 litre	1,524.00 nr
5000 litre	2,375.00 nr

Plastics water storage cisterns

With sealed lid / Byelaw 30 thick

18 litres	30.53 nr
114 litres	89.14 nr
190 litres	139.21 nr
227 litres	146.53 nr

Direct Hot water cylinder; copper

Four bosses; pre-insulated

120 litres	156.49 nr
144 litres	179.09 nr
166 litres	283.24 nr

Indirect Hot water cylinder; copper

Double feed; four bosses; pre-insulated

114 litres	176.76 nr
117 litres	176.15 nr
140 litres	200.11 nr
162 litres	292.55 nr

Rainwater pipes and fittings

Cast iron rainwater pipes and fittings, BS 460 Type A sockets; dry joints

75mm

pipes	57.85 m
shoes	43.72 nr
bends	37.49 nr
offset bends 150mm projection	47.22 nr
offset bends 230mm projection	54.91 nr
offset bends 305mm projection	64.37 nr
angled branches	65.62 nr

100mm

pipes	78.92 m
shoes	58.87 nr
bends	53.05 nr
offset bends 75mm projection	89.09 nr
offset bends 150mm projection	89.09 nr
offset bends 230mm projection	107.90 nr
offset bends 305mm projection	107.90 nr
angled branches	77.91 nr

Cast iron rainwater pipes and fittings, BS 460 Type A sockets; ears cast on; dry joints

65mm

pipes	61.76 m
shoes	50.44 nr
bends	30.86 nr

75mm

pipes	61.76 m
shoes	50.44 nr
bends	37.49 nr

100mm

pipes	82.90 m
shoes	65.62 nr
bends	53.05 nr

PVC-U rainwater pipes and fittings, BS EN 607; push fit joints; self coloured

68mm

pipes	3.81 m
pipe brackets	2.29 nr
shoes	5.41 nr
bends	5.03 nr

Cast iron half round gutters and fittings, BS 460

100mm

gutters	31.74 m
gutter brackets	6.67 nr
stopped ends	5.57 nr
running outlets	23.94 nr
stopped ends with outlet	23.94 nr
angles	23.94 nr

115mm

gutters	33.02 m
gutter brackets	6.67 nr
stopped ends	7.13 nr
running outlets	25.50 nr
stopped ends with outlet	25.50 nr
angles	25.50 nr

125mm

gutters	38.58 m
gutter brackets	7.21 nr
stopped ends	7.71 nr
running outlets	29.77 nr
stopped ends with outlet	29.77 nr
angles	29.77 nr

150mm

gutters	58.79 m
gutter brackets	8.24 nr
stopped ends	8.81 nr
running outlets	48.44 nr
stopped ends with outlet	48.44 nr
angles	48.44 nr
gutter brackets	8.14 nr

Cast aluminium half round gutters and fittings, BS EN 612 Section A

100mm

gutters	23.14 m
gutter brackets	3.56 nr
stopped ends	6.04 nr
running outlets	14.65 nr
angles	15.57 nr

125mm

gutters	27.17 m
gutter brackets	5.62 nr
stopped ends	6.72 nr
running outlets	16.79 nr
angles	17.03 nr

PVC-U half round gutters and fittings, BS 4576, Part 1; push fit connector joints; self coloured grey

112mm

gutters	2.73 nr
Union	3.37 m
gutter brackets	2.29 nr
stopped ends	3.49 nr
running outlets	5.34 nr
angles	7.44 nr

Soil and Waste pipes and fittings

Cast iron soil and waste pipes and fittings, BS 416

75mm

pipes	52.55 m
pipe couplings	26.44 nr

100mm

pipes	69.87 m
pipe couplings	27.97 nr

50mm

pipes	48.86 m
pipe couplings	25.06 nr

MuPVC waste pipes and fittings, BS EN 1329-1 Section Three; solvent welded joints

32mm

pipes	2.43 m
pipe couplings	0.72 nr
pipe brackets	0.21 nr
fittings; three ends	0.76 nr

40mm

pipes	2.90 m
pipe couplings	0.73 nr
pipe brackets	0.21 nr
fittings; three ends	0.76 nr

50mm

pipes	3.67 m
pipe couplings	1.05 nr
pipe brackets	0.35 nr
fittings; three ends	1.40 nr

Polypropylene waste pipes and fittings; butyl ring joints

32mm

pipes	0.73 m
pipe couplings	0.88 nr
fittings; three ends	1.15 nr

40mm

pipes	0.88 m
pipe couplings	0.88 nr
pipe brackets	0.50 nr
fittings; three ends	1.23 nr

PVC-U soil and vent pipes and fittings, BS 4514; rubber ring joints; self coloured grey

82mm

pipes	10.20 m
pipe couplings	11.52 nr

110mm

pipes	3.88 m
pipe couplings	4.69 nr
short radius bends	7.50 nr
single angled branches	15.79 nr
straight wc connectors	11.42 nr
Air admittance valve push fit	15.36 nr

160mm

pipes	11.82 m
pipe couplings	9.44 nr

PVC-U soil and vent pipes, solvent joints; self coloured grey

110mm

pipes	5.77 m
pipe couplings	4.24 nr
short radius bends	7.42 nr
single angled branches	8.79 nr
straight wc connectors	12.10 nr
Air admittance valve solvent joint	12.58 nr

Pipe supports for PVC-U soil and vent pipes

for building in

for 82mm pipes	4.94 nr
for 110mm pipes	6.15 nr

for fixing to timber

for 82mm pipes	3.95 nr
for 110mm pipes	5.82 nr
for 160mm pipes	9.33 nr

PVC Vent Terminal

50mm pipes	2.78 nr
82mm pipes	5.67 nr
110mm pipes	3.38 nr

Plastic traps

Two piece, 75mm seal, Inlet with coupling nut, outlet with seal ring socket

32mm outlet, P	6.07 nr
40mm outlet, P	6.72 nr
32mm outlet, S	7.06 nr
40mm outlet, S	7.44 nr
40mm outlet, P, with flexible polypropylene pipe for overflow connection	8.62 nr

Copper traps

Two piece, 75mm seal, inlet with coupling nut, compression outlet

35mm outlet, P	39.36 nr
42mm outlet, P	40.94 nr
54mm outlet, P	481.07 nr
35mm outlet, S	121.17 nr
42mm outlet, S	145.02 nr
54mm outlet, S	508.11 nr
42mm outlet, bath set, including overflow connection	230.35 nr

Mechanical Installations (Cont'd)

Boilers

High efficiency gas boilers

Item	Price
Wall mounted; regular; output rating 15 KW	877.48 nr
Wall mounted; regular; output rating 24 KW	985.82 nr
Wall mounted; regular; output rating 30 KW	953.32 nr
Wall mounted; combination; output rating 24 KW	671.40 nr
Wall mounted; combination; output rating 35 KW	854.97 nr

Central heating

Pressed steel radiators; double panel with single convector; air cock, plain plug

Item	Price
300 x 600mm long	25.32 nr
300 x 800mm long	27.49 nr
500 x 600mm long	35.65 nr
500 x 800mm long	47.90 nr
500 x 1200mm long	81.65 nr
600 x 600mm long	42.40 nr
600 x 900mm long	71.32 nr
600 x 1200mm long	64.15 nr
600 x 1600mm long	108.66 nr
600 x 2400mm long	249.00 nr
700 x 700mm long	47.91 nr
700 x 1200mm long	74.41 nr

Plumbing Sanitary fittings and sundries

Bath Panel

Item	Price
Plastic front	12.50 nr
Plastic end	10.00 nr

Electrical Installations

Lighting columns

Galvanised steel column; nominal mounting height

Item	Price
3.00m	139.00 nr
4.00m	132.05 nr
5.00m	153.70 nr
5.00m mid-hinged	347.20 nr
6.00m	176.90 nr
8.00m	371.25 nr
10.0m	524.70 nr

Optional extras

Item	Price
Single arm mounting bracket	39.80 nr
Double arm mounting bracket	53.62 nr
Photo cell	10.99 nr
Part night photo cell	24.75 nr
Blanking plug (no photo cell)	5.75 nr

Lanterns; Amenity/Decorative

Item	Price
40w LED; Regency or Modern	166.16 nr
60w LED; Regency or Modern	180.16 nr
25w LED post top elegant lantern	579.00 nr
30w LED post top sphere	393.47 nr
35w LED post top stylish amenity lantern	339.25 nr

LED Street light; Cobra style head; Up to 140lm/W; 5yr warranty

Item	Price
20W (2,800 lumens)	73.06 nr
30W (4,200 lumens)	82.00 nr
40W (5,600 lumens)	91.54 nr
50W (7,000 lumens)	102.19 nr
60W (8,400 lumens)	105.38 nr
70W (9,800 lumens)	117.42 nr
80W (11,200 lumens)	130.66 nr
90W (12,600 lumens)	145.23 nr
100W (14,000 lumens)	243.85 nr
120W (16,800 lumens)	282.94 nr
150W (21.800 lumens	320.17 nr

Trunking

Steel lighting trunking; PVC lid

50 x 50mm

Item	Price
straight body	13.05 3m
straight Lid	2.94 3m
end cap	1.07 nr
internal angle	7.87 nr
external angle	7.76 nr
tee	8.50 nr
flat bend	7.76 nr
trunking suspension (for 10mm studding)	1.97 nr

Steel dado trunking, two compartment; steel lid

150 x 40mm

Item	Price
straight body	37.19 2m
straight lid	36.31 2m
end cap	9.27 nr
internal angle body	16.49 nr
internal angle lid	18.16 nr
external angle body	16.49 nr
external angle lid	18.16 nr
single socket plate	17.56 nr
twin socket plate	17.56 nr

Steel dado trunking, three compartment; steel lid

200 x 40mm

Item	Price
straight body	44.75 2m
straight lid	56.81 2m
end cap	35.22 nr
internal angle body	17.66 nr
internal angle lid	37.19 nr
external angle body	17.66 nr
external angle lid	37.19 nr
single socket plate	28.47 nr
twin socket plate	28.47 nr

Steel skirting trunking; three compartments; steel lid

200 x 40mm

Item	Price
straight body	44.75 2m
straight lid	48.77 2m
internal angle body	17.66 nr
internal angle lid	33.26 nr
external angle body	17.66 nr
external angle lid	33.26 nr
single socket plate	20.62 nr
twin socket plate	20.62 nr

Steel underfloor trunking; two compartments

150 x 25mm

Item	Price
straight	39.15 2m
floor junction boxes, four way; adjustable frame and trap	110.98 nr
horizontal bend	56.82 nr

PVC trunking; white mini-trunking; clip on lid

16 x 16mm

Item	Price
straight	4.14 3m
end cap	0.61 nr
internal bend	0.79 nr
external bend	0.79 nr
flat bend	0.79 nr
equal tee	1.49 nr

25 x 16mm

Item	Price
straight	4.44 3m
end cap	0.61 nr
internal bend	0.79 nr
external bend	0.79 nr
flat bend	0.79 nr
equal tee	1.60 nr

40 x 16

Item	Price
straight	8.40 3m
end cap	0.61 nr
internal bend	1.04 nr
external bend	1.94 nr
flat bend	1.19 nr
equal tee	1.60 nr

PVC trunking; white dado trunking, three compartment; clip on lid

145 x 50mm

Item	Price
straight	41.98 3m
end caps	2.29 nr
internal bend; adjustable	5.99 nr
external bend; adjustable	4.99 nr
fabricated flat tee	39.98 nr
fabricated flat elbow	31.98 nr
straight coupler	2.00 nr

180 x 57mm curved profile

Item	Price
straight	64.89 3m
end caps	3.50 nr
internal bend	6.50 nr
external bend	6.50 nr
straight coupler	4.29 nr

PVC trunking; white skirting trunking, three compartment; clip on lid

170 x 50 mm

Item	Price
straight	32.62 3m
end cap	1.40 nr
internal corner	3.60 nr
external corner	3.50 nr
straight coupler	1.23 nr
socket adaptor box, one gang	1.55 nr
socket adaptor box, two gang	1.78 nr

Conduit

PVC conduits, PVC boxes are inclusive of lid, gasket and screws; small circular boxes with lid, gasket and screws

20mm diameter

Item	Price
straight tube, light guage	2.35 3m
straight tube, heavy guage	0.99 2m
terminal boxes	1.12 nr
angle boxes	1.13 nr
three way boxes	1.12 nr
through way boxes	1.12 nr

25mm diameter

Item	Price
straight tube, heavy guage	1.52 2m
terminal boxes	1.17 nr
angle boxes	1.27 nr
three way boxes	1.30 nr
through way boxes	1.29 nr
Repalcement replacment PVC lid for Circular box..	0.42 nr
rubber gasket for PVC or steel circular box	0.27 nr
cover screws (need 2 per box)	4.80 100

PVC oval conduits

Item	Price
16mm (nominal size) straight tube	0.75 2m
20mm (nominal size) straight tube	0.90 2m
25mm (nominal size) straight tube	0.97 3m

Steel welded black enamelled heavy gauge conduits, circular boxes are exclusive of lid, gasket and screws; small circular boxes without lid, gasket or screws

20mm diameter

Item	Price
straight tube	7.19 3m
terminal boxes	1.54 nr
angle boxes	1.54 nr
three way boxes	1.54 nr
through way boxes	1.68 nr
inspection bends	3.79 nr
inspection elbow	3.12 nr
couplers	0.49 nr
saddle spacer bar	0.22 nr

25mm diameter

Item	Price
straight tube	9.60 3m
terminal boxes	2.29 nr
angle boxes	24.00 nr
three way boxes	2.52 nr
through way boxes	2.56 nr
inspection bends	4.35 nr
inspection elbow	3.75 nr
couplers	0.54 nr
saddle spacer bar	0.25 nr
steel lid for circular box (see above for gasket and screws)	0.14 nr

Steel welded galvanised heavy gauge conduits, circular boxes are exclusive of lid, gasket and screws; small circular boxes without lid, gasket or screws

20mm diameter

Item	Price
straight tube	7.12 3m
terminal boxes	1.54 nr
angle boxes	1.09 nr
three way boxes	1.11 nr
through way boxes	1.09 nr

25mm diameter

Item	Price
straight tube	8.30 3.75m
terminal boxes	2.29 nr

Electrical Installations (Cont'd)

Conduit (Cont'd)

Steel welded galvanised heavy gauge conduits, circular boxes are exclusive of lid, gasket and screws; small circular boxes without lid, gasket or screws (Cont'd)

25mm diameter (Cont'd)

angle boxes	1.39 nr
three way boxes	1.39 nr
through way boxes	1.39 nr
steel lid for circular box (see above for gasket and screws)	0.12 10

Cable Tray

Galvanised light duty

50mm	
straight tray	7.50 3m
flat bend	10.64 nr
tee	15.69 nr
cross piece	12.26 nr
riser bend	6.26 nr
100mm	
straight tray	15.04 3m
flat bend	10.04 nr
tee	12.19 nr
cross piece	17.56 nr
riser bend	7.02 nr
reducer 100 to 50mm	12.40 nr
150mm	
straight tray	18.41 3m
flat bend	16.30 nr
tee	20.67 nr
cross piece	23.12 nr
riser bend	8.23 nr
reducer 150 to 100mm	13.72 nr
300mm	
straight tray	29.77 3m
flat bend	29.05 nr
tee	31.89 nr
cross piece	41.84 nr
riser bend	13.55 nr
reducer 300 to 150mm	16.65 nr
450mm	
straight tray	101.36 3m
flat bend	46.77 nr
tee	56.98 nr
cross piece	71.35 nr
riser bend	19.08 nr
reducer 450 to 300mm	24.56 nr

Galvanised medium duty

75mm	
straight tray	12.49 3m
flat bend	11.06 nr
tee	12.67 nr
cross piece	19.81 nr
riser bend	6.92 nr
100mm	
straight tray	13.58 3m
flat bend	10.98 nr
tee	13.98 nr
cross piece	19.69 nr
riser bend	7.02 nr
reducer 100 to 75mm	11.13 nr
150mm	
straight tray	14.18 3m
flat bend	12.23 nr
tee	14.78 nr
cross piece	22.92 nr
riser bend	8.23 nr
reducer 150 to 100mm	11.61 nr
300mm	
straight tray	36.58 3m
flat bend	18.98 nr
tee	21.43 nr
cross piece	35.89 nr
riser bend	13.55 nr
reducer 300 to 150mm	17.15 nr
450mm	
straight tray	53.85 3m
flat bend	24.97 nr
tee	29.72 nr
cross piece	58.83 nr
riser bend	19.08 nr
reducer 450 to 300mm	17.74 nr

Galvanised heavy duty

75mm	
straight tray	15.15 3m
flat bend	11.50 nr
tee	13.11 nr
cross piece	17.99 nr
riser bend	8.61 nr
100mm	
straight tray	16.07 3m
flat bend	11.59 nr
tee	13.20 nr
cross piece	18.66 nr
riser bend	9.10 nr
reducer 100 to 75mm	12.55 nr
150mm	
straight tray	17.83 3m
flat bend	12.70 nr
tee	19.65 nr
cross piece	23.51 nr
riser bend	9.88 nr
reducer 150 to 100mm	13.11 nr
300mm	
straight tray	35.98 3m
flat bend	16.79 nr
tee	20.35 nr
cross piece	46.65 nr
riser bend	15.62 nr
reducer 300 to 150mm	17.11 nr
450mm	
straight tray	90.90 3m
flat bend	20.56 nr
tee	30.43 nr
cross piece	82.13 nr
riser bend	49.51 nr
reducer 450 to 300mm	20.06 nr

Supports for cable tray; ms; galv

100mm cantilever arms	5.72 nr
300mm cantilever arms	14.80 nr
450mm cantilever arms	18.58 nr
75mm stand-off bracket	3.11 nr
100mm stand-off bracket	3.76 nr
150mm stand-off bracket	3.84 nr
300mm stand-off bracket	6.70 nr
450mm stand-off bracket	7.37 nr

Steel Basket; bright zink plated

Straight	
100 x 35mm	8.04 3m
150 x 35mm	9.60 3m
200 x 35mm	11.34 3m
300 x 35mm	15.12 3m
Accesories for 35mm Basket Tray	
Coupler set (of 2)	1.01 nr
Suspension Bracket	2.89 nr

Cable

PVC insulated cables; single core; reference 6491X; stranded copper conductors; to BS 6004

1.5mm²	19.62 100m
2.5mm²	29.76 100m
4.0mm²	48.84 100m
6.0mm²	73.20 100m
10.0mm²	123.60 100m
16.0mm²	1.93 100m

PVC double insulated cables; single core; reference 6181Y; stranded copper conductors; to BS 6004

16.0mm² meter tails	150.00 50m
25.0mm² meter tails	159.00 50m
35.0mm² meter tails	285.00 50m

PVC insulated and PVC sheathed cables; multicore; copper conductors and bare earth continuity conductor 6242Y; to BS 6004

1.00mm²; twin and earth	38.40 100m
1.50mm²; twin and earth	49.20 100m
2.5mm²; twin and earth	71.94 100m
4.00mm²; twin and earth	127.20 100m
6.00mm²; twin and earth	178.20 100m

PVC insulated SWA armoured and LSF sheathed cables; multicore; copper conductors to BS 6724

16mm²; 3 core (per m)	5.33 m

PVC Sheathed, polyethylene insulated cables

Co-axial, braid screened, copper conductor 75 ohm (per m)	19.74 100m

Telephone cables

4 core (per m)	10.68 100m

Mineral insulated copper sheathed cables; PVC outer sheath; copper conductors; 600V light duty to BS EN 60702-1

1.5mm²; two core cable (per m)	4.28 m
1.5mm²; termination including gland and seal	24.60 10
2.5mm²; two core cable (per m)	5.41 m
2.5mm²; termination including gland and seal	24.60 10
4.0mm²; two core cable (per m)	8.13 m
4.0mm²; termination including gland and seal	24.60 10
Shroud for terminations	0.85 nr

FP200 gold, fire rated cable, red outer

1.5mm; 2 core + E (per m)	80.75 100m

CAT5E cable

LSZH rated (per m)	59.98 305m

Switchgear and Distribution boards (Three phase)

Switch fuse, mild steel enclosure, TP & N

32 Amp	148.98 nr

Distribution boards TP & N, IP41 protection

8 x 3 Way TP&N Distribution Board 125A Max Incomer	138.00 nr
16 x 3 Way TP&N Distribution Board 125A Max Incomer	126.00 nr

Accessories for distribution boards

125 Amp TP Switch Disconnector	22.20 nr
Incommer connection kit	21.56 nr
Type B, single pole MCB 10KA	4.62 nr
Type B, triple pole MCB 10KA	19.62 nr
Type C, single pole MCB 10KA	4.62 nr
Type C, triple pole MCB 10KA	19.62 nr

Accessories and fittings

White plastics, without boxes

Plate switches 10 amp; one gang; one way; single pole	1.05 nr
Plate switches 10 amp; two gang; two way; single pole	2.01 nr
Plate switches 20amp; double pole with neon	4.03 nr
Ceiling switches 6 amp; one gang; one way; single pole	2.77 nr
Switched socket outlets 13 amp; one gang	1.90 nr
Switched socket outlets 13 amp; two gang	3.14 nr
Switched socket outlets with RCD (residual current device) protected at 30 mAmp 13 amp; two gang	51.08 nr
Fused connection units 13 amp; one gang; switched; flexible outlet	4.18 nr
Fused connection units 13 amp; one gang; switched; flexible outlet; pilot lamp	6.00 nr
Batten lampholder; shockguard	4.09 nr
Ceiling rose and pendant	1.88 nr
Cooker point 45A (with neon, no socket)	7.86 nr
Shaver socket (transformer)	19.50 nr
TV/FM Socket	2.88 nr
Telephone point, slave	3.20 nr
Socket outlet 5 Amp	5.24 nr

BASIC PRICES OF MATERIALS

Electrical Installations (Cont'd)

Accessories and fittings (Cont'd)

White plastics boxes for surface fitting
- 1G 16mm deep ... 0.73 nr
- 1G 30mm deep ... 0.85 nr
- 2G 30mm deep ... 1.64 nr

Galvanised boxes for flush fitting
- Plaster depth box, 1G 16mm deep ... 0.26 nr
- 1G 35mm deep ... 0.37 nr
- 2G 35mm deep ... 0.47 nr

Metalclad, with boxes
- Surface plate switches 5 amp; one gang; two way; single pole ... 2.97 nr
- Surface plate switches 5 amp; two gang; two way; single pole ... 3.44 nr
- Surface switched socket outlets 13 amp; one gang. ... 2.96 nr
- Surface switched socket outlets 13 amp; two gang. ... 3.74 nr

Weatherproof accessories, with boxes
- Surface plate switches 20 amp; one gang; two way; single pole ... 4.32 nr

Bell equipment
- Transformers; 4-8-12v ... 7.80 nr
- Bells for transformer operation
  - Chime 2-note ... 15.60 nr
  - 73mm domestic type ... 9.72 nr
  - 180 mm commercial ... 41.28 nr
- Bell pushes
  - Domestic ... 2.39 nr
  - Industrial/weatherproof ... 7.02 nr

Extras
- Draw wire, 20m length, reusable ... 8.39 20
- Grommets ... 1.83 100

Domestic consumer units

17th Edition, 3rd Amendment, consumer unit
- 10 useable ways and main switch and 2 off 63A 30mA RCDs and 10 MCBs ... 75.60 nr
- 15 useable ways and main switch and 2 off 63A 30mA RCDs and 12 MCBs ... 104.40 nr

Accessories for consumer units
- 63 Amp 30mA RCD double pole ... 29.76 nr
- 80 Amp 30mA RCD double pole ... 29.76 nr
- 3 to 45 Amp single pole MCB ... 3.00 nr
- 6 to 50 Amp 30mA RCBO (single unit) ... 25.80 nr
- 6 to 40 Amp RCBO AFDD Combination ... 114.93 nr

Lighting; Accessories and fittings

LED strip lamp fittings, mains voltage operations
- 5ft Single Batten
  - Single T8 LED Ready (No LED tube and no balast or driver for fluorescent tube) ... 11.52 nr
  - 24w LED Tube; Cool white, Daylight or White.. ... 9.96 nr

Slimline LED Batten Fittings; 4000k; with diffuser
- 2ft (605mm); 9w; 910 lumens ... 13.20 nr
- 4ft (1200mm); 17w; 1800 lumens ... 17.58 nr
- 5ft (1500mm); 22w; 2300 lumens ... 24.36 nr

Single LED Batten Fittings; 4000K; with diffuser
- 2ft (605mm); 10w; 1200 lumens ... 20.22 nr
- 4ft (1200mm); 20w; 2300 lumens ... 23.40 nr
- 5ft (1500mm); 26w; 1525 lumens ... 26.82 nr
- 6ft (1800mm); 30w; 3450 lumens ... 33.48 nr

Twin LED Batten Fitting; 4000K; with diffuser
- 2ft (605mm); 20w; 2200 lumens ... 26.88 nr
- 4ft (1200mm); 40w; 4500 lumens ... 40.08 nr
- 5ft (1500mm); 50w; 5250 lumens ... 45.18 nr
- 6ft (1800mm); 60w; 6500 lumens ... 59.76 nr

Tri Colour; LED Batten Fittings; 3000k to 6000k; with diffuser
- 4ft (1200mm); 22w; 2500 to 2800 lumens ... 28.80 nr
- 5ft (1500mm); 35w; 3800 to 4200 lumens ... 34.56 nr
- 6ft (1800mm); 40w; 4600 to 5000 lumens ... 41.76 nr

Tri Colour; High Output; LED Batten Fittings; with diffuser
- 5ft (1500mm); 60w; 6700 to 7400 lumens ... 56.82 nr
- 6ft (1800mm); 67w; 7300 to 7700 lumens ... 50.40 nr

Lighting fittings complete with lamps
- Bulkhead; Polycarbonate
  - 12W Round energy saving LED lamp ... 17.10 nr
- Ceramic Wall Uplighter
  - 9W LED lamp ... 22.04 nr
- Ceiling sphere
  - 150mm, 6W LED lamp ... 12.50 nr
  - 180mm, 9W LED lamp ... 13.94 nr
- Commercial Down light; recessed
  - LED 24w c/w driver ... 26.09 nr
- Lighting track; low Voltage
  - 1m track, transformer and 3 x 50W halogen lamps ... 68.73 nr
  - Plug-in fitting; 50W halogen lamp ... 12.59 nr

Heating

Fan heaters
- 3kW unit fan heaters for commercial application ... 140.83 nr
- Thermostatic switch units with concealed setting ... 27.48 nr

Turbular heaters (including 2 way brackets, excluding wire guards), less than 150w per metre loading
- 305mm long, 45w ... 16.14 nr
- 610mm long, 80w ... 18.54 nr
- 915mm long, 135w ... 21.78 nr
- 1220mm long, 180w ... 27.72 nr
- 1830mm long, 270w ... 40.62 nr

Night storage heaters (Lot 20)
- 0.5KW heater ... 412.20 nr
- 0.7KW heater ... 444.60 nr
- 1KW heater ... 496.74 nr
- 1.25KW heater ... 554.34 nr
- 1.5KW heater ... 599.70 nr

Immersion heaters and thermostats; 2 or 3kW non-withdrawable elements
- Without flanges 305mm ... 13.68 nr
- Without flanges 457mm ... 14.58 nr
- Without flanges 686mm ... 16.50 nr

Thermostats
- immersion heater ... 7.98 nr
- 16 amp a.c. for air heating; without switch ... 26.58 nr

Water heaters; Storage type units
- Oversink, single outlet, 5L, 2kW ... 63.42 nr
- Oversink, single outlet, 7L, 3kW ... 91.63 nr
- Oversink, single outlet, 10L, 2kW ... 124.04 nr
- Unvented, multipoint, 30L, 3kW ... 277.48 nr
- Unvented, multipoint, 50L, 3kW ... 299.15 nr
- Unvented, multipoint, 80L, 3kW ... 365.82 nr

Shower units; Instantaneous
- Complete with fittings ... 112.86 nr

Extract fans, window or wall mounted; with incorporated shutter
- 105mm diameter; ref DX100PC ... 24.72 nr
- 257mm diameter; ref GX9 ... 162.48 nr
- 324mm diameter; ref GX12 ... 209.99 nr
- Wall duct kit for GX9 ... 24.00 nr
- Wall duct kit for GX12 ... 20.79 nr
- 290 x 321mm; ref WX6 ... 74.96 nr
- 409 x 433mm; ref WX9 ... 313.20 nr
- 473 x 476mm; ref WX12 .. 354.00 nr
- PIR fan controller ... 64.02 nr

Floor Wall and Ceiling Finishes

Screeds and toppings
- Cement and sand (1:3) ... 142.61 m^3

Surface hardener for paving
- Epoxy resin based sealer. ... 23.33 l
- Polyurethane ... 16.09 l

Latex Flooring
- One coat levelling screeds ... 0.49 kg

Gypsum plasterboard
- 9.5mm handiboard ... 4.10 m^2
- 12.5mm handiboard ... 9.41 m^2
- 9.5mm square edge wallboard ... 2.05 m^2
- 12.5mm square edge wallboard ... 2.08 m^2
- 15mm square edge wallboard ... 3.54 m^2
- 12.5mm tapered edge moisture resistant wallboard ... 4.67 m^2
- 15mm tapered edge moisture resistant wallboard ... 5.45 m^2
- 12.5mm tapered edge Fireline wallboard ... 3.25 m^2
- 15mm tapered edge Fireline wallboard ... 5.05 m^2
- 12.5mm tapered edge Soundbloc wallboard ... 3.38 m^2
- 15mm tapered edge Soundbloc wallboard ... 4.82 m^2

Rendering and the like
- Pea shingle for pebbledash ... 43.50 t

Plasters
- Board finish ... 221.67 t
- Hardwall ... 342.00 t
- Multi finish ... 238.40 t
- Universal one coat ... 256.00 t
- Thistle browning ... 390.14 t
- Thistle bonding ... 321.20 t
- Thistle tough coat ... 440.00 t

Plaster beads and stops
- Angle, standard ... 0.41 m
- Angle, thin ct 3mm ... 0.43 m
- Angle, thin ct 6mm ... 0.43 m
- Stop, thin ct 3mm ... 0.66 m
- Stop, thin ct 6mm ... 0.72 m
- Stop, 10mm ... 0.64 m
- Stop, 13mm ... 0.64 m
- Stop, 16mm ... 0.77 m
- Stop, 19mm ... 0.77 m
- Plasterboard edging, 10mm ... 0.84 m
- Plasterboard edging, 13mm ... 0.84 m

Bonding fluid
- Bonding fluid ... 3.40 l

Metal lathing
- Expanded metal lath (galv)
  - 9mm mesh x 0.89 kg/m^2. ... 6.49 m^2
  - 9mm mesh x 1.11 kg/m^2. ... 8.90 m^2
  - 9mm mesh x 1.61 kg/m^2. ... 12.91 m^2

Floor Wall and Ceiling Finishes (Cont'd)

Item	Price
Metal lathing (Cont'd)	
Rib-Lath	
0.300mm thick x 1.16 kg/m^2	9.78 m^2
0.500mm thick x 1.86 kg/m^2	12.34 m^2
Stainless steel Rib-Lath	
1.48 kg/m^2	15.65 m^2
Expanded metal lath (stainless steel)	
1.11 kg/m^2	13.42 m^2
Red-rib lath	
0.500mm thick x 1.91 kg/m^2	49.61 m^2
Galvanised arch formers	
Arch corners (2 pieces)	
372mm radius	12.31 nr
452mm radius	13.43 nr
602mm radius	16.22 nr
752mm radius	21.91 nr
Plasterboard coving	
cove 100mm girth	1.42 m
Gyproc cove 127mm girth.	1.65 m
Coving Adhesive	0.95 kg
Plaster ventilators	
Plain 229 x 79mm	1.00 nr
Plain 229 x 152mm	1.50 nr
Plain 229 x 229mm	2.06 nr
Clay floor quarry tiles - terracotta	
150 x 150 x 12.5mm	558.43 1000
150 x 150 x 20mm	805.39 1000
225 x 225 x 25mm	936.66 1000
Terrazzo tiles	
300 x 300 x 28mm units	71.20 m^2
305 x 165 x 28mm units	23.75 m
Terrazzo	
Terrazzo mix 1:2	1,281.73 m^3
Wood block flooring, tongued and grooved, 70 x 230 x 20mm units	
Maple wood blocks	46.00 m^2
Merbau wood blocks	40.00 m^2
Oak wood blocks	31.66 m^2
PVC flooring	
300 x 300 x 2mm tiles	6.95 m^2
300 x 300 x 3.2mm tiles	10.80 m^2
610 x 610 x 2mm heavy duty tiles	8.95 m^2
610 x 610 x 2.5mm heavy duty tiles	12.50 m^2
Linoleum flooring - BSEN ISO 24011	
330 x 330 x 2mm tiles	15.95 m^2
2.5mm sheet flooring	15.80 m^2
3.2mm sheet flooring	17.80 m^2
Adhesive for linoleum flooring	4.96 l
Carpet tiling, 500 x 500mm tiles	
loop pile general contract.	16.60 m^2
twist cut pile heavy contract	18.80 m^2
Carpet sheeting	
Fibre bonded heavy contract	11.45 m^2
Ribbed fibre bonded heavy contract	12.00 m^2
Adhesive for carpeting	5.82 l
Edge fixed carpeting	
Tredaire underlay; Brio 8mm	1.90 m^2
Tufted wool/nylon	26.60 m^2
Axminster wool/nylon	45.00 m^2
Gyproc Thermaline BASIC grade plasterboard	
22mm	7.16 m^2
30mm	9.84 m^2
40mm	9.61 m^2
50mm	21.39 m^2
60mm	24.29 m^2
70mm	27.25 m^2
Gypsum laminated partitions plasterboard components	
25 x 38mm softwood battens	0.95 m
Metal stud partitions	
48mm studs	1.61 m
50mm floor and ceiling channels	2.57 m
Suspended ceiling tiles, mineral fibre, bevelled, grooved and rebated	
1200 x 600 x 15.8mm	6.81 m^2
600 x 600 x 15.8mm	6.60 m^2

Glazing

Item	Price
Float glass	
4mm GG quality	31.51 m^2
6mm GG quality	51.86 m^2
10mm GG quality	88.00 m^2
Rough cast glass	
6mm	49.46 m^2
Pyroshield glass	
6mm clear	100.18 m^2
6mm safety clear	117.56 m^2
7mm texture	47.93 m^2
7mm safety texture	61.57 m^2
Patterned glass	
4mm white	37.40 m^2
6mm white	68.20 m^2
4mm tinted	44.00 m^2
6mm tinted	78.65 m^2
Thick float glass	
10mm GG quality	122.76 m^2
12mm GG quality	171.60 m^2
15mm GG quality	226.80 m^2
19mm GG quality	307.32 m^2
25mm GG quality	482.20 m^2
Toughened safety glass	
4mm clear float glasses	44.00 m^2
5mm clear float glasses	56.55 m^2
6mm clear float glasses	66.00 m^2
10mm clear float glasses	78.00 m^2
12mm clear float glasses	85.00 m^2
4mm white	67.10 m^2
6mm white	84.70 m^2
Clear laminated glass - float quality	
6.4mm safety glass	56.00 m^2
8.8mm safety glass	114.00 m^2
10.8mm safety glass	123.00 m^2
9.5mm anti-bandit glass	155.00 m^2
13.5mm anti-bandit glass	180.00 m^2
13.5mm anti-bandit glass, large panes	20.74 m^2
Georgian wired glass	
7mm standard	72.60 m^2
7mm safety	88.00 m^2
7mm polished	118.80 m^2
7mm polished safety	136.00 m^2
Sundries	
linseed oil putty	43.75 25kg
metal casement putty	43.75 25kg
washleather strip, 3mm glass	0.13 m
washleather strip, 6mm glass	0.27 m
butyl rubber glazing strip, 3mm glass	0.40 m
butyl rubber glazing strip, 6mm glass	0.79 m

Mirrors; 6mm clear float; copper plastic safety backing

Item	Price
with polished edges, 6mm diameter holes	
254 x 400mm	48.92 nr
460 x 900mm	72.15 nr
600 x 900mm	82.42 nr

Painting and Decorating

Item	Price
Creosote	273.17 200l
Wood preservative	33.29 5l
Emulsion paint	
matt brilliant white	8.53 5l
matt colours	15.40 5l
silk brilliant white	11.45 5l
silk colours	27.46 5l
Priming, paint	
wood primer	44.75 5l
primer sealer	79.96 5l
aluminium sealer and wood primer	66.45 5l
alkali-resisting primer	44.12 5l
universal primer	54.96 5l
red oxide primer	54.96 5l
zinc phosphate primer	44.96 5l
acrylic primer	24.12 5l
Undercoat paint	
Alkyd based - brilliant white	26.24 5l
Alkyd based - colours	45.41 5l
Water based - brilliant white	49.99 5l
Gloss paint	
Alkyd based - brilliant white	31.66 5l
Alkyd based - colours	45.41 5l
Water based - brilliant white	48.74 5l
Eggshell paint	
Oil based - brilliant white	37.08 5l
Oil based - colours	51.66 5l
Plastic finish	
coating compound	33.33 25kg
Waterproof cement paint	
cream or white	24.12 5l
colours	33.29 5l
sealer	44.57 5l
Textured masonry paint	
white	55.82 10l
colours	70.82 10l
Stabilising solution	79.84 20l
Multicolour painting	
primer	44.57 5l
basecoat	33.29 5l
finish	33.29 5l
Metallic paint	
aluminium or silver	65.41 5l
gold or bronze	99.73 5l
Bituminous paint	
Bituminous paint	19.16 5l
Polyurethane lacquer	
clear (varnish)	34.57 5l
Linseed oil	
raw	32.49 5l
boiled	32.49 5l
Fire retardant paints and varnishes	
fire retardant paint	105.00 5l
fire retardant varnish	140.62 5l
overcoat varnish	87.05 5l
French polishing	
white polish	21.53 l
button polish	23.87 l
garnet polish	16.50 l
methylated spirit	4.70 l

Road marking materials

Item	Price
solvent based paint chlorinated rubber	137.80 20kg
50mm wide non-reflective self adhesive tape	6.26 5m
100mm wide non-reflective self adhesive tape	6.26 5m
50mm wide reflective self adhesive tape	10.59 5m
100mm wide reflective self adhesive tape	8.00 5m
road marking primer	320.00 25kg

Surface treatments

Item	Price
silicone based water repellent	17.46 5l
fungicide	9.57 2.5l

Drainage

Vitrified Clay pipes and fittings

Item	Price
Drains; normal; flexible mechanical joints	
375mm pipes	233.20 m
375mm bend	582.02 nr
450mm pipes	771.25 m
450mm bend	866.89 nr
Drains; sleeve joints, push-fit polypropylene standard ring flexible couplings; Hepworth Supersleve	
100mm pipes	10.33 m
100mm pipe couplings	11.09 nr
100mm bends	14.03 nr
100mm branches	30.30 nr

Drainage (Cont'd)

Vitrified Clay pipes and fittings (Cont'd)

Drains; sleeve joints, push-fit polypropylene standard ring flexible couplings; Hepworth Supersleve (Cont'd)

150mm pipes	22.15 m
150mm pipe couplings	15.58 nr
150mm bends	32.31 nr
150mm branches	44.34 nr

Sleeve joints, push-fit polypropylene neoprene ring flexible couplings; Hepworth Supersleve/Densleve

100mm pipes	10.60 m
100mm pipe couplings	0.75 nr
150mm pipes	25.41 m
150mm pipe couplings	1.78 nr

Drains; normal; cement mortar (1:3)

100mm pipes	12.69 m
100mm double collars	17.68 nr
100mm bends	17.61 nr
100mm rest bends	48.13 nr
100mm branches	43.85 nr
150mm pipes	30.57 m
150mm double collars	32.16 nr
150mm bends	44.56 nr
150mm rest bends	51.82 nr
150mm branches	59.24 nr
225mm pipes	70.63 m
225mm double collars	29.32 nr
300mm pipes	102.22 m

PVC-U pipes and Fittings

Drains; ring seal joints

110mm pipes	8.85 3m
110mm pipe couplings	3.77 nr
110mm connections to cast iron and clay sockets	19.10 nr
110mm 45 degree bends	11.75 nr
110mm branches	22.24 nr
110mm connections cast iron and clay spigot	16.59 nr
160mm pipes	41.40 3m
160mm pipe couplings	14.32 nr
160mm connections to cast iron and clay sockets	30.90 nr
160mm 45 degree bends	45.72 nr
160mm branches	92.40 nr
160mm connections to cast iron and clay spigot	41.38 nr

Solid wall concentric external rib-reinforced Wavin "Ultra-Rib"

150mm pipes 6UR043	134.80 6m
150mm pipe couplings	23.21 nr
150mm bends 6UR563	31.05 nr
150mm branches 6UR213	162.14 nr
150mm connections to clayware pipe ends 6UR129	132.29 nr
225mm 9UR043 pipes	211.50 3m
225mm pipe couplings	125.69 nr
225mm bends 9UR563	282.05 nr
225mm branches 9UR213	562.42 nr
300mm 12UR043 pipes	146.84 3m
300mm pipe couplings	219.87 nr
300mm bends 12UR563	434.08 nr
300mm branches 12UR213	1,101.32 nr
300mm connections to clayware pipe ends 12UR112	612.30 nr
Reducers 40/32mm	1.73 nr
32mm Pipe brackets - Metal	2.40 nr
40mm Pipe brackets - Metal	3.31 nr

Concrete pipes and fittings (BS 5911)

Unreinforced, Class H, flexible joints

300mm pipes	76.08 2.5m
300mm bends	271.73 nr
300mm, 100mm branches	238.71 nr
300mm, 150mm branches	238.71 nr
300mm, 225mm branches	420.18 nr
300mm, 300mm branches	482.63 nr
375mm pipes	94.17 2.5m
375mm bends	336.33 nr
375mm, 100mm branches	279.27 nr
375mm, 150mm branches	279.27 nr
375mm, 225mm branches	438.72 nr
375mm, 300mm branches	499.23 nr
375mm, 375mm branches	559.73 nr
450mm pipes	111.20 2.5m
450mm bends	397.16 nr
450mm, 100mm branches	422.26 nr
450mm, 150mm branches	422.26 nr
450mm, 225mm branches	562.76 nr
450mm, 300mm branches	635.38 nr
450mm, 375mm branches	708.00 nr
450mm, 450mm branches	835.07 nr
525mm pipes	145.89 2.5m
525mm bends	521.03 nr
525mm, 100mm branches	518.36 nr
525mm, 150mm branches	518.36 nr
525mm, 225mm branches	608.31 nr
525mm, 300mm branches	684.35 nr
525mm, 375mm branches	760.40 nr
525mm, 450mm branches	893.46 nr
600mm pipes	111.20 2.5m
600mm bends	654.01 nr
600mm, 100mm branches	651.08 nr
600mm, 150mm branches	651.08 nr
600mm, 225mm branches	609.97 nr
600mm, 300mm branches	682.59 nr
600mm, 375mm branches	755.19 nr
600mm, 450mm branches	882.27 nr

Reinforced, Class H, flexible joints

450mm pipes	59.72 m
450mm bends	922.94 nr
450mm, 100mm branches	257.56 nr
450mm, 150mm branches	263.39 nr
450mm, 225mm branches	272.24 nr
450mm, 300mm branches	331.16 nr
450mm, 375mm branches	375.37 nr
450mm, 450mm branches	434.31 nr
525mm pipes	52.10 m
525mm bends	1,128.05 nr
525mm, 100mm branches	290.19 nr
525mm, 150mm branches	296.09 nr
525mm, 225mm branches	304.92 nr
525mm, 300mm branches	349.12 nr
525mm, 375mm branches	408.06 nr
525mm, 450mm branches	467.00 nr
600mm pipes	65.40 m
600mm bends	1,230.57 nr
600mm, 100mm branches	263.08 nr
600mm, 150mm branches	327.92 nr
600mm, 225mm branches	336.75 nr
600mm, 300mm branches	380.95 nr
600mm, 375mm branches	439.89 nr
600mm, 450mm branches	498.83 nr

Metal pipes and fittings

Cast iron, BS 437, coated; bolted cast iron coupling and synthetic rubber gasket joints

100mm pipes	21.96 m
100mm pipe couplings	12.48 nr
100mm connectors, large socket for clayware	38.47 nr
100mm bends	27.73 nr
100mm branches	26.33 nr
150mm pipes	43.20 m
150mm pipe couplings	24.43 nr
150mm connectors, large socket for clayware	73.47 nr
150mm diminishing pieces, reducing to 100mm	40.25 nr
150mm bends	60.67 nr
150mm branches	63.28 nr

Stainless steel, Blucher UK Ltd; ring seal push fit joints (AISI 316)

75mm pipes	24.17 m
75mm pipe couplings	14.58 nr
75mm bends	20.83 nr
75mm branches	51.67 nr
110mm pipes	31.25 m
110mm pipe couplings	18.75 nr
110mm diminishing pieces, reducing to 75mm	41.67 nr
110mm bends	24.58 nr
110mm branches	61.67 nr

Gullies, Channels, Gratings etc

Concrete gullies; BS 5911; with stopper

375mm diameter x 750mm deep internally	62.10 nr
375mm diameter x 900mm deep internally	64.05 nr
450mm diameter x 750mm deep internally	65.10 nr
450mm diameter x 900mm deep internally	66.15 nr

Cast iron accesories, painted black

gratings

140mm diameter	12.07 nr
197mm diameter	18.43 nr
150 x 150mm	11.53 nr
225 x 225mm	35.88 nr

Alloy accessories

gratings

140mm diameter	12.07 nr
197mm diameter	18.43 nr
150 x 150mm	11.53 nr
225 x 225mm	35.88 nr

Cast iron accesories, painted black

gratings and frames, Watergate C250

370 x 305mm	279.88 nr
370 x 430mm	336.00 nr

Channels; vitrified clay, BS 65, normal, glazed

100mm, half section straight

600mm effective length	11.39 nr
1000mm effective length	15.93 nr

150mm, half section, straight

1000mm effective length	28.00 nr

Inspection chambers and Manholes

Precast circular concrete inspection chambers; standard or stock pattern units; BS 5911

250mm high, 900mm internal diameter	46.11 nr
500mm high, 900mm internal diameter	69.16 nr
750mm high, 900mm internal diameter	69.16 nr
1000mm high, 900mm internal diameter	92.22 nr
250mm high, 1050mm internal diameter	58.42 nr
500mm high, 1050mm internal diameter	92.81 nr
750mm high, 1050mm internal diameter	103.21 nr
1000mm high, 1050mm internal diameter	130.00 nr
250mm high, 1200mm internal diameter	68.90 nr
500mm high, 1200mm internal diameter	108.60 nr
750mm high, 1200mm internal diameter	119.00 nr
1000mm high, 1200mm internal diameter	149.94 nr

Galvanised malleable cast iron steps

step irons BS EN 13101	15.94 nr

Cover slabs, heavy duty, min. 125mm thick, for chamber sections

2400mm internal diameter	972.40 nr
2700mm internal diameter	1,496.74 nr
3000mm internal diameter	1,921.40 nr

Precast rectangular concrete inspection chambers; standard or stock pattern units; BS 5911

150mm high, internal size 1200 x 750mm	42.60 nr
225mm high, internal size 1200 x 750mm	57.25 nr

Polypropylene shallow inspection chamber with preformed benching. Light duty single sealed cover and frame ref. 4D.961

300mm diameter; for 100mm diameter pipes ref. 4D960, depth to invert 600mm	105.45 nr

Polypropylene universal inspection chamber; 475mm diameter

Drainage (Cont'd)

Inspection chambers and Manholes (Cont'd)

Polypropylene universal inspection chamber; 475mm diameter (Cont'd)

preformed chamber base benching; for 100mm pipes, ref. 4D922	97.20 nr
chamber shaft 185mm effective length, ref. 4D925	27.74 nr
cast iron cover and frame; single seal light duty to suit, ref. 4D942	84.44 nr
Polypropylene sealed cover and frame, ref. 4D969	49.87 nr
Cast iron inspection chambers	
100mm diameter straight with one branch	307.03 nr
150 x 100mm diameter straight with one branch	397.69 nr
150mm diameter straight with one branch	504.84 nr
Manhole step irons; figure 1 general purpose pattern	
110mm tail	4.97 nr
225mm tail	6.83 nr
Manhole covers, A15 light duty, Single Seal, ductile iron	
Solid top Circular 450mm dia	18.33 nr
Solid top 450mm x 450mm	29.77 nr
Solid top 600mm x 450mm	31.75 nr
Solid top 600mm x 600mm	35.76 nr
Recessed top 600mm x 450mm	52.62 nr
Recessed top 600mm x 600mm	63.25 nr
Recessed top 750mm x 600mm	119.79 nr
Manhole covers, A15 light duty, Double Seal	
Solid top 450mm x 450mm	24.90 nr
Solid top 600mm x 450mm	23.27 nr
Solid top 600mm x 600mm	36.48 nr
A15 light duty, lifting keys	5.90 nr
Manhole covers, B125 medium duty	
450mm diameter	36.79 nr
600 x 450 x 75mm	58.31 nr
600 x 600 x 75mm	81.07 nr
750 x 600 x 75mm	103.26 nr
B125 medium duty, lifting keys	5.26 nr
Manhole covers, cast iron, D400 heavy duty	
600mm diameter	132.27 nr
600 x 600 x 100mm	149.35 nr
750 x 750 x 100mm	230.34 nr
D400 heavy duty, lifting keys	6.96 nr
Clayware land drain pipes, BS 1196; butt joints	
75mm	11.60 m
100mm	19.73 m
150mm	28.77 m
Plastic land drain pipe	
80mm	56.53 50m
100mm	118.58 100m
160mm	117.56 50m

Fencing

Strained wire fencing - concrete posts

900mm intermediate post	12.75 nr
900mm end/angle post	17.02 nr
900mm strutt	12.73 nr
900mm stretcher bar	9.41 nr
1050mm intermediate post	16.07 nr
1050mm end/angle post	20.18 nr
1050mm strutt	13.28 nr
1050mm stretcher bar	10.40 nr
Ratchet winders	2.42 nr
2.5mm Stirrup wire	49.95 651
4mm galvanised line wire	33.15 254m

Chain link fencing

900mm - concrete posts - plastic coated mesh	
intermediate post	12.75 nr
end straining post	17.02 nr
strutt	12.73 nr
stretcher bar	9.41 nr
chain link (3.15 gauge)	98.33 25m
1200mm - concrete posts - plastic coated mesh	
intermediate post	16.07 nr
end straining post	20.18 nr
strutt	13.28 nr
stretcher bar	10.40 nr
chain link (3.15 gauge)	132.00 25m
1500mm - concrete posts - plastic coated mesh	
intermediate post	22.03 nr
end straining post	24.42 nr
strutt	18.45 nr
stretcher bar	11.81 nr
chain link (3.15 gauge)	161.60 25m
1800mm - concrete posts - plastic coated mesh	
intermediate post	23.68 nr
end straining post	29.30 nr
strutt	20.75 nr
stretcher bar	14.85 nr
chain link (3.15 gauge)	191.84 25m
Sundries	
Ratchet winders	2.42 nr
Stirrup wire (3.55/2.5mm)	49.95 575
Line wire (4/3mm)	4.99 450m
Ring fasteners	11.95 1000
900mm - steel posts - plastic coated mesh	
intermediate post PLS (heavy)	12.85 nr
end post with strutts	45.32 nr
angle post with strutts	53.37 nr
chain link	98.33 25m
1200mm - steel posts - plastic coated mesh	
intermediate post PLS (heavy)	14.98 nr
end post with strutts	54.24 nr
angle post with strutts	74.12 nr
chain link	132.00 25m
1500mm - steel posts - plastic coated mesh	
intermediate post PLS (heavy)	16.38 nr
end post with strutts	59.21 nr
angle post with strutts	81.37 nr
chain link	161.60 25m
1800mm - steel posts - plastic coated mesh	
intermediate post PLS (heavy)	19.23 nr
end post with strutts	71.35 nr
angle post with strutts	97.63 nr
chain link	191.84 25m

Wooden fencing

Chestnut	
900mm high fencing - 2 wire	58.80 9.5m
900mm intermediate post	3.95 nr
900mm end/angle post	12.76 nr
900mm strutts	2.85 nr
1200mm high fencing - 3 wire	74.70 9.5m
1200mm intermediate post	4.30 nr
1200mm end/angle post	12.76 nr
1200mm strutts	4.20 nr
1500mm high fencing - 3 wire	56.35 4.5m
1500mm intermediate post	7.15 nr
1500mm end/angle post	14.56 nr
1500mm strutts	4.95 nr
Close boarded fencing	
1200mm posts	17.91 nr
1200mm pales	1.20 nr
1500mm posts	21.33 nr
1500mm pales	1.58 nr
1800mm posts	24.09 nr
1800mm pales	1.89 nr
Rails	2.82 m
Gravel boards 150x22	3.16 m
Centre stumps	2.18 nr
50mm nails (galv)	2.15 kg
75mm nails (galv)	2.03 kg
Wooden palisade fencing	
1050mm posts	15.10 nr
1050mm pales	1.50 nr
1200mm posts	17.95 nr
1200mm pales	1.80 nr

Railings

Ornamental steel railings; Cannock Gates (UK) Ltd; 914mm high x 1829mm wide gap	
Marlborough	128.00 nr
Royale	291.20 nr
Royale Talisman	493.40 nr
Clifton	125.00 nr
Winchester	105.60 nr
Aluminium guard rail of tubing to BS EN 10255; medium grade with Kee Klamp fittings and intersections	
42mm diameter	15.53 m
flanged end - wall fixing No.61-7	7.55 nr
bend No.15-7	8.68 nr
three-way No.20-7	13.09 nr
three-way No.25-7	12.50 nr
four-way No.21-7	10.23 nr
four-way No.26-7	9.66 nr
five-way No.35-7	13.98 nr
five-way No.40-7	20.81 nr
floor plate No.62-7	11.06 nr

Fencing extras

Precast concrete posts	
Fence posts 100 x 100mm tapering intermediate post 1570mm long	14.14 nr
Fence posts 100 x 100mm square strainer post (end or intermediate) 1570mm long	16.60 nr

Gates

Timber gates	
Feather edge gate 1200 x 900mm	50.00 nr
Feather edge gate 1500 x 900mm	59.00 nr
Ornamental steel gates; Cannock Gates (UK) Ltd	
Clifton, 914mm high single gate, for 762 mm wide opening	73.00 nr
Clifton, 914mm high double gate, for 2591 mm wide opening	186.00 nr
Clifton, 1829mm high single gate, for 1067 mm wide opening	142.00 nr
Clifton, 1829mm high double gate, for 2286 mm wide opening	318.00 nr
Winchester, 914mm high single gate, for 762 mm wide opening	73.35 nr
Winchester, 914mm high double gate, for 2438 mm wide opening	196.70 nr
Marlborough, 914mm high single gate, for 762 mm wide opening	80.00 nr
Marlborough, 1829mm high single gate, for 762 mm wide opening	119.00 nr
Marlborough, 1829mm high single gate, for 1067 mm wide opening	154.00 nr
Royale Talisman, 1219mm high single gate, for 914mm wide opening	266.70 nr

Fencing (Cont'd)

Gates (Cont'd)

Ornamental steel gates; Cannock Gates (UK) Ltd (Cont'd)

Royale Talisman, 1829mm high arched double gate, for 4267mm wide opening.................... 1,446.70 nr

Gates in chain link fencing

1000 x 1800mm; plastic coated mesh.................... 355.83 nr

External works and landscaping

Precast concrete kerbs

125 x 255 x 915mm.......... 6.00 nr

125 x 255 x 915mm; curved 6.00m radius......... 10.35 nr

150 x 305 x 915mm......... 19.75 nr

150 x 305 x 915mm; curved 10.00m radius....... 27.62 nr

Precast concrete edgings

50 x 150 x 915mm........... 2.73 m

50 x 200 x 915mm........... 4.92 m

50 x 250 x 915mm........... 7.66 m

Granite edge kerb

150 x 300mm .... 51.10 m

200 x 300mm .... 70.05 m

Yorkstone paving

50mm thick....................... 104.63 m²

75mm thick....................... 146.30 m²

Precast concrete flags, BS EN 1339, natural finish

600 x 450 x 50mm .... 3.98 nr

600 x 600 x 50mm .... 4.49 nr

600 x 900 x 50mm .... 5.63 nr

600 x 450 x 63mm .... 7.69 nr

Granite sett paving

100mm thick; new........... 93.00 m²

150mm thick; new........... 100.00 m²

Precast concrete perforated slabs - Grassguard

100mm thick units........... 52.95 m²

COMPOSITE PRICES FOR APPROXIMATE ESTIMATING

The purpose of this section is to provide an easy reference to costs of "composite" items of work which would usually be measured for Approximate Estimates. Rates for items, which are not included here, may be found by reference to the preceding pages of this volume. Allowance has been made in the rates for the cost of works incidental to and forming part of the described item although not described therein, i.e. the cost of formwork to edges of slabs have been allowed in the rates for slabs; the cost of finishings to reveals has been allowed in the rates for finishings to walls.

The rates are based on rates contained in the preceding Works section of the book and include the cost of materials, labour fixing or laying and allow 10% for overheads and profit: Preliminaries are not included within the rates. The rates are related to a housing or simple commercial building contract. For contracts of higher or lower values, rates should be adjusted by the percentage adjustments given in Essential Information at the beginning of this volume. Landfill tax is included for inert waste.

The following cost plans are priced as examples on how to construct an Elemental Cost Plan, for information and to demonstrate how to use the Approximate Estimating Section.

COST PLAN FOR AN OFFICE DEVELOPMENT

The Cost Plan that follows gives an example of an Approximate Estimate for an office building as the attached sketch drawings. The estimate can be amended by using the examples of Composite Prices following or the prices included within the preceding pages. Details of the specification used are indicated within the elements. The cost plan is based on a fully measured bill of quantities priced using the detailed rates within this current edition of Laxton's. Preliminaries are shown separately.

Floor area 932 m²

Description	Item	Qty		Rate	Item Total	Cost per m²	Total
1.0 SUBSTRUCTURE							
Note: Rates allow for excavation by machine							
1.1 Foundations (271 m²)							
Clear site vegetation; excavate 150 topsoil and remove spoil	Site clearance	288	m²	1.79	516.69	0.55	
300 x 600 reinforced concrete perimeter ground beams with attached 180 x 300 toes; damp proof membrane 50 concrete blinding; 102.5 thick common and facing bricks from toe to top of ground beam; 100 cavity filled with plain concrete; cavity weeps; damp proof courses (excavation included in ground slab excavation)	Ground beam	81	m	299.06	24,223.56	25.99	
600 x 450 reinforced concrete internal ground beams, mix C30; 50 thick concrete blinding; formwork; 100 GA4000 insulation (excavation included in ground slab excavation)	Ground beam	34	m	251.37	8,546.47	9.17	
1900 x 1900 x 1150 lift pit; excavate; level and compact bottoms; working space; earthwork support; 50 concrete blinding; damp proof membrane; 200 reinforced concrete slab, 200 reinforced concrete walls, formwork; Bituthene tanking and protection board	Lift pit	1	nr	3,268.42	3,268.42	3.51	
1500 x 1500 x 1000 stanchion bases; excavate; level and compact bottoms; earthwork support; reinforced concrete foundations; 102.5 bricks from top of foundation to ground slab level	Stanchion base	13	nr	1,179.29	15,330.73	16.45	51,885.88
(Element unit rate = £ 191.46 m²)					51,885.88	55.67	
1.4 Ground floor construction (271 m²)							
Excavate to reduce levels; level and compact bottoms; remove from site; 400 thick hardcore filling, blinded; damp proof membrane; 100 Celotex GA4000 insulation; 150 thick reinforced concrete ground slab with 2 layers A252 fabric reinforcement; tamped finish	Ground floor slab	271	m²	142.68	38,667.32	41.49	38,667.32
(Element unit rate = £ 142.68 m²)					38,667.32	41.49	
2.0 SUPERSTRUCTURE							
2.1 Frame (932 m²)							
Excavate to reduce levels; level and compact bottoms; remove from site; 400 thick hardcore filling, blinded; damp proof membrane; 100 Celotex GA4000 insulation; 150 thick reinforced concrete ground slab with 2 layers A252 fabric reinforcement; tamped finish	Columns	111	m	142.82	15,852.67	17.01	
29.5m girth x 1.0m high steel frame to support roof over high level louvres	Frame	1	nr	8,980.66	8,980.66	9.64	
300 x 550 reinforced concrete beams; formwork	Beams	61	m	202.38	12,344.96	13.25	37,178.30
(Element unit rate = £ 39.89 m²)					37,178.30	39.89	
2.2 Upper floors (614 m²)							
275 reinforced concrete floor slab; formwork	Floor slab	614	m²	172.59	105,968.51	113.70	
300 x 400: 675 x 175 : 300 x 150 reinforced concrete attached beams; formwork	Attached beams	273	m	156.37	42,688.51	45.80	148,657.02
(Element unit rate = £ 242.11 m²)					148,657.02	159.50	

COST PLAN FOR AN OFFICE DEVELOPMENT (Cont'd)

Description	Item	Qty		Rate	Item Total	Cost per m²	Total
2.0 SUPERSTRUCTURE (Cont'd)							
2.3 Roof (403 m² on plan)							
2.3.1 Roof structure							
Pitched roof trusses, wall plates; 400 thick insulation and net support	Roof structure	403	m²	64.81	26,119.84	28.03	
100 thick blockwork walls in roof space	Blockwork	27	m²	45.18	1,219.77	1.31	
Lift shaft capping internal size 1900 x 1900; 200 thick blockwork walls and 150 reinforced concrete slab	Lift shaft	1	nr	985.23	985.23	1.06	
2.3.2 Roof coverings							
Concrete interlocking roof tiles, underlay and battens	Roof finish	465	m²	61.60	28,644.00	30.73	
Ridge	Ridge	22	m	24.22	532.84	0.57	
Hip	Hip	50	m	24.85	1,242.43	1.33	
Valley	Valley	6	m	86.92	521.52	0.56	
Abutments to cavity walls, lead flashings and cavity tray damp proof courses	Abutments	9	m	120.62	1,085.60	1.16	
Eaves framing, 25 x 225 softwood fascia, 950 wide soffit and ventilator; eaves tile ventilator and decoration; 164 x 127 pressed Aluminium gutters and fittings	Eaves	102	m	308.86	31,504.02	33.80	
2.3.4 Roof drainage							
100 x 100 Aluminium rainwater pipes and rainwater heads and hopper heads	Rain water pipes	58	m	99.31	5,760.26	6.18	97,615.51
(Element unit rate = £ 242.22 m²)					97,615.51	104.74	
2.4 Stairs and ramps							
Reinforced in-situ concrete staircase; blockwork support walls screed and vinyl floor finishes; plaster and paint to soffits; to wall							
3nr 1200 wide flights, 1nr half landing and 1nr quarter landing; 3100 rise; handrail one side	Stairs	1	nr	6,264.46	6,264.46	6.72	
4nr 1200 wide flights, 2nr half landings 6200 rise; plastics coated steel balustrade one side and handrail one side	Stairs	1	nr	20,236.17	20,236.17	21.71	
4nr 1200 wide flights, 2nr half landings mix; 6200 rise; plastics coated steel and glass in fill panels balustrade one side and handrail one side	Stairs	1	nr	19,801.79	19,801.79	21.25	46,302.43
					46,302.43	49.68	
2.5 External walls (614 m²)							
Cavity walls, 102.5 thick facing bricks (PC £500 per 1000), 100 wide insulated cavity, 140 thick lightweight concrete blockwork	Facing brick wall	455	m²	183.84	83,647.20	89.75	
Cavity walls, 102.5 thick facing bricks (PC £500 per 1000), built against concrete beams and columns	Facing brick wall	159	m²	136.78	21,748.75	23.34	
880 x 725 x 150 cast stonework pier cappings	Stonework	9	nr	137.16	1,234.45	1.32	
780 x 1300 x 250 cast stonework spandrels	Stonework	9	nr	274.34	2,469.07	2.65	
6500 x 2500 attached main entrance canopy	Canopy	1	nr	12,047.37	12,047.37	12.93	
Milled lead sheet on impregnated softwood boarding and framing, and building paper	Lead sheet	4	m²	451.74	1,806.97	1.94	
Expansion joint in facing brickwork	Expansion joint	118	m	20.76	2,449.78	2.63	125,403.59
(Element unit rate = £ 204.24 m²)					125,403.59	134.55	
2.6 Windows and external doors (214 m²)							
2.6.1 External windows (190 m²)							
Polyester powder coated Aluminium vertical pivot double glazed windows	Windows	190	m²	741.28	140,842.52	151.12	
Polyester powder coated Aluminium fixed louvre panels	Louvres	35	m²	309.82	10,843.60	11.63	
Heads 150 x 150 x 10 stainless steel angle bolted to concrete beam, cavity damp proof course, weep vents, plaster and decoration	Heads	98	m	109.73	10,754.01	11.54	
Reveals closing cavity with facing bricks, damp proof course, plaster and decoration	Reveals	99	m	43.40	4,296.95	4.61	
Works to reveals of openings comprising closing cavity with facing bricks, damp proof course, 13 thick cement and sand render with angle beads, and ceramic tile finish	Reveals	27	m	64.53	1,742.38	1.87	
Sills closing cavity with blockwork, damp proof course, and 25 x 200 decorated MDF window boards	Sills	8	m	51.00	407.99	0.44	
Sills 230 x 150 cast stonework sills and damp proof course	Sills	36	m	79.16	2,849.82	3.06	
Sills 250 x 75 cast stonework sills, damp proof course, and 25 x 200 decorated MDF window boards	Sills	36	m	430.67	15,504.19	16.64	
Sills closing cavity with blockwork, damp proof course, and ceramic tile sill finish	Sills	9	m	61.39	552.50	0.59	
Cavity wall lintels	Lintels	15	m	43.21	648.08	0.70	
Surrounds to 900 diameter circular openings; stainless steel radius lintels, 102.5 x 102.5 facing brick on edge surround, 13 thick plaster, and eggshell decoration	Lintels	8	m	237.99	1,903.92	2.04	

COST PLAN FOR AN OFFICE DEVELOPMENT (Cont'd)

Description	Item	Qty		Rate	Item Total	Cost per m²	Total
2.0 SUPERSTRUCTURE (Cont'd)							
2.6 Windows and external doors (214 m²) (Cont'd)							
2.6.1 External windows (190 m²) (Cont'd)							
300 x 100 cast stonework surrounds to openings	Stonework	20	m	86.85	1,736.98	1.86	
2.6.2 External doors (24 m²)							
Polyester powder coated Aluminium double glazed doors and any integral screens	External doors	24	m²	697.39	16,737.41	17.96	
Cavity wall lintels	Lintels	3	m	43.21	129.62	0.14	208,949.95
(Element unit rate = £ 976.40 m²)					208,949.95	224.20	
2.7 Internal walls and partitions (481 m²)							
100 thick blockwork walls	Block walls	231	m²	52.04	12,021.79	12.90	
200 thick blockwork walls	Block walls	113	m²	93.27	10,540.03	11.31	
215 thick common brickwork walls	Brick walls	84	m²	139.20	11,692.53	12.55	
Demountable partitions	Partitions	42	m²	45.90	1,927.97	2.07	
Extra over demountable partitions for single doors	Partitions	2	nr	44.16	88.31	0.09	
Extra over demountable partitions for double doors	Partitions	1	nr	53.00	53.00	0.06	
WC Cubicles	Cubicles	9	nr	212.67	1,914.00	2.05	
Screens in softwood glazed with 6 thick GWPP glass	Screens	11	m²	515.38	5,669.21	6.08	
Duct panels in Formica Beautyboard and 50 x 75 softwood framework	Ducts	27	m²	91.61	2,473.59	2.65	
Duct panels in veneered MDF board and 50 x 75 softwood framework	Ducts	26	m²	80.98	2,105.47	2.26	48,485.91
(Element unit rate = £ 100.80 m²)					48,485.91	52.02	
2.8 Internal doors (84 m²)							
900 x 2100 half hour fire resistant single doorsets comprising doors, softwood frames, ironmongery and decoration	Doors	45	m²	368.04	16,561.89	17.77	
900 x 2100 one hour fire resistance single doorsets comprising doors, softwood frames, ironmongery and decoration	Doors	9	m²	571.12	5,140.06	5.52	
900 x 2100 half hour fire resistance single doorsets comprising doors with 2nr vision panels, softwood frames, ironmongery and decoration	Doors	11	m²	466.89	5,135.82	5.51	
1500 x 2100 half hour fire resistance double doorsets comprising Ash veneered doors with 2nr vision panels, Ash frames, ironmongery and decoration	Doors	19	m²	416.21	7,907.98	8.48	
100 wide lintels	Lintels	41	m	24.72	1,013.55	1.09	
215 wide lintels	Lintels	7	m	78.75	551.25	0.59	36,310.56
(Element unit rate = £ 432.27 m²)					36,310.56	38.96	
3.0 INTERNAL FINISHES							
3.1 Wall finishes (1,086 m²)							
13 thick plaster to blockwork walls with eggshell paint finish	Plaster work	703	m²	27.44	19,290.95	20.70	
13 thick plaster to blockwork walls with lining paper and vinyl wall paper finish	Plaster work	124	m²	27.42	3,400.45	3.65	
10 thick plaster to concrete walls with eggshell paint finish	Plaster work	75	m²	39.53	2,965.04	3.18	
13 thick cement and sand render to blockwork walls with 150 x 150mm ceramic tiles finish (tiles pc £15.00/m²)	Tiling	184	m²	65.86	12,118.24	13.00	37,774.68
(Element unit rate = £ 34.78 m²)					37,774.68	40.53	
3.2 Floor finishes (779 m²)							
50 thick sand and cement screed with 300 x 300 x 3.2 vinyl tile finish	Vinyl tiling	19	m²	49.31	936.85	1.01	
50 thick sand and cement screed with 2 thick sheet vinyl finish	Sheet vinyl	108	m²	44.19	4,772.15	5.12	
50 thick sand and cement screed with 250 x 250 x 6 carpet tile finish	Carpet tiling	587	m²	48.70	28,588.66	30.67	
50 thick sand and cement screed with carpet finish	Carpeting	17	m²	71.22	1,210.76	1.30	
50 thick sand and cement screed with 150 x 150mm ceramic tile finish (tiles pc £20.00/m²)	Ceramic tiling	46	m²	75.61	3,477.83	3.73	
Entrance mats comprising brass Matt frame, 60 thick cement and sand screed and matting	Matting	2	m²	332.30	664.59	0.71	
150 high x 2.5 thick vinyl skirting	Skirting	45	m	9.65	434.25	0.47	
100 high x 2 thick sheet vinyl skirtings with 19 x 38 lacquered softwood cover fillet	Skirting	116	m	29.40	3,409.95	3.66	
25 x 150 Softwood skirtings with lacquer finish	Skirting	214	m	17.54	3,753.13	4.03	
150 x 150mm ceramic tile skirtings on 13 thick sand and cement render	Skirting	74	m	15.02	1,111.78	1.19	48,359.96
(Element unit rate = £ 62.08 m²)					48,359.96	51.89	
3.3 Ceiling finishes (809 m²)							
Suspended ceiling systems to offices	Suspended	587	m²	45.91	26,949.17	28.92	

COST PLAN FOR AN OFFICE DEVELOPMENT (Cont'd)

Description	Item	Qty		Rate	Item Total	Cost per m²	Total
3.0 INTERNAL FINISHES (Cont'd)							
3.3 Ceiling finishes (809 m²) (Cont'd)							
Suspended ceiling systems to toilets	Suspended	46	m²	52.21	2,401.75	2.58	
Suspended ceiling systems to reception area	Suspended	18	m²	52.61	947.00	1.02	
Suspended ceiling plain edge trims and 25 x 38 painted softwood shadow battens	Edge trim	300	m	20.52	6,157.50	6.61	
Gyproc MF suspended ceiling system with eggshell paint finish	Suspended	127	m²	45.79	5,815.00	6.24	
12.5 Gyproc Square edge plaster board and skim on softwood supports with eggshell paint finish	Plastering	29	m²	61.87	1,794.15	1.93	
10 thick plaster to concrete with eggshell paint finish	Plastering	2	m²	98.48	196.95	0.21	
Plaster coving	Cove	234	m	9.23	2,160.21	2.32	46,421.73
(Element unit rate = £ 57.38 m²)					46,421.73	49.81	
4.0 FITTINGS AND FURNISHINGS AND EQUIPMENT							
4.1 General fittings, furnishings and equipment							
2100 x 500 x 900 reception counter in softwood	Counter	1	nr	1,703.57	1,703.57	1.83	
2700 x 500 x 900 vanity units in Formica faced chipboard	Units	6	nr	1,106.27	6,637.65	7.12	
600x 400 x 6 thick mirrors	Mirror	15	nr	105.05	1,575.75	1.69	
Vertical fabric blinds	Blinds	161	m²	83.32	13,413.72	14.39	
900 x 250 x 19 blockboard lipped shelves on spur support system	Shelves	12	nr	46.95	563.40	0.60	
1200 x 600 x 900 sink base units in melamine finished particle board	Sink base unit	3	nr	297.19	891.57	0.96	24,785.66
					24,785.66	26.59	
5.0 SERVICES							
5.1 Sanitary appliances							
965 x 500 stainless steel sink units with pillar taps	Sink	3	nr	178.43	535.29	0.57	
White glazed fireclay cleaners sink units with pillar taps	Cleaners sink	3	nr	397.18	1,191.54	1.28	
Vitreous china vanity basins with pillar taps	Vanity basins	12	nr	385.58	4,626.96	4.96	
Vitreous china wash hand basins and pedestal with pillar taps	Wash hand basin	1	nr	197.63	197.63	0.21	
Vitreous china wash hand basin with pillar taps	Wash hand basin	1	nr	245.87	245.87	0.26	
Vitreous china disabled wash hand basin with pillar taps	Wash hand basin	1	nr	208.25	208.25	0.22	
Close coupled vitreous china WC suites	WC suite	11	nr	328.26	3,610.86	3.87	
Showers comprising shower tray, mixer valve and fittings, and corner shower cubicle	Shower	1	nr	950.90	950.90	1.02	
Vitreous china urinals with automatic cistern	Urinals	3	nr	247.49	742.47	0.80	
Disabled grab rails set	Grab rails	1	nr	662.45	662.45	0.71	
Toilet roll holders	Accessories	11	nr	25.59	281.52	0.30	
Paper towel dispensers	Accessories	8	nr	42.07	336.53	0.36	
Paper towel waste bins	Accessories	8	nr	64.01	512.09	0.55	
Sanitary towel disposal units	Accessories	3	nr	1,207.11	3,621.32	3.89	
Hand dryers	Accessories	8	nr	420.73	3,365.87	3.61	21,089.56
					21,089.56	22.63	
5.2 Services equipment							
Allowance for kitchenette fittings		1	nr	3,518.52	3,518.52	2.15	3,518.52
5.3 Disposal installations							
Upvc waste pipes and fittings to internal drainage	Internal Drainage	37	nr	155.40	5,749.96	6.17	5,749.96
5.4 Water installations							
Hot and cold water supplies		37	nr	346.03	12,803.04	13.74	12,803.04
5.5 Heat source							
Gas boiler for radiators and hot water from indirect storage tank		1	nr	135,335.16	135,335.16	145.21	135,335.16
5.6 Space heating and air conditioning							
Low temperature hot water heating by radiators		1	nr	4,501.10	4,501.10	4.83	4,501.10
5.7 Ventilating Systems							
Extractor fan to toilet and kitchen areas		9	nr	1,107.74	9,969.64	10.70	9,969.64
5.8 Electrical installations							
Lighting & Power		1	nr	164,825.13	164,825.13	176.85	164,825.13
5.9 Gas and other fuel installations							
To boiler room		1	nr	3,522.60	3,522.60	3.78	3,522.60
5.10 Lift and conveyor installations							
8 person 3 stop hydraulic lift		1	nr	38,316.02	38,316.02	41.11	38,316.02

COST PLAN FOR AN OFFICE DEVELOPMENT (Cont'd)

Description	Item	Qty		Rate	Item Total	Cost per m²	Total
5.0 SERVICES (Cont'd)							
5.12 Communication, security and control systems							
Burglar Alarm System		1	nr	10,991.83	10,991.83	11.79	
Cabling for telephones		1	nr	14,721.21	14,721.21	15.80	
Door entry to receptions on all floors		1	nr	2,431.47	2,431.47	2.61	28,144.52
					28,144.52	30.20	
5.14 Builders' work in connection with services							
Builders work in connection with plumbing, mechanical and electrical installations		1	nr	9,252.07	9,252.07	9.93	
Builders Profit and Attendance on Services		1	nr	1,759.26	1,759.26	1.89	11,011.33
					11,011.33	11.81	
8.0 EXTERNAL WORKS							
8.1 Site preparation works							
Clearing site vegetation, filling root voids with excavated material	Site clearance	1716	m²	1.17	2,007.72	2.15	
Excavated topsoil 150 deep and preserve on site	Clear topsoil	214	m³	12.47	2,668.90	2.86	
Dispose of surplus topsoil off site	Disposal	70	m³	41.94	2,935.80	3.15	7,612.42
					7,612.42	8.17	
8.2 Roads, paths and pavings							
Excavated to reduce levels 400 deep; dispose of excavated material on site; level and compact bottoms; herbicide; 250 thick granular material filling, levelled, compacted and blinded; 70 thick two coat coated macadam pavings; white road lines and markings	Pavings	719	m²	62.79	45,144.31	48.44	
Excavate to reduce levels 400 deep; dispose of excavated material off site; level and compact bottoms; herbicide; 150 thick granular material filling, levelled compacted, and blinded; 200 x 100 x 65 thick clay paviors	Pavings	40	m²	103.22	4,128.72	4.43	
Excavate to reduce levels 400 deep; dispose of excavated material off site; level and compact bottoms; herbicide; 150 thick granular material filling, levelled, compacted and blinded; 900 x 600 x 50 thick concrete paving flags	Pavings	149	m²	56.63	8,437.80	9.05	
125 x 255 precast concrete road kerbs and foundations	Kerbs	265	m	42.71	11,319.21	12.15	
50 x 150 precast concrete edgings and foundations	Kerbs	48	m	25.17	1,208.16	1.30	70,238.19
					70,238.19	75.36	
8.3 Planting							
Excavate to reduce levels 400 deep; dispose of excavated material off site; prepare sub-soil; herbicide; 150 thick preserved topsoil filling; rotavate; turf	Landscaping	55	m²	42.74	2,350.55	2.52	
Excavate to reduce levels 400 deep; dispose of excavated material off site; prepare sub-soil; herbicide; 450 thick preserved topsoil filling; cultivate; plant 450 - 600 size herbaceous plants - 3/m², and 3m high trees - 1nr per 22m²; fertiliser; 25 thick peat mulch	Planting	397	m²	63.76	25,312.92	27.16	27,663.47
					27,663.47	29.68	
8.4 Fencing, railings and walls							
Palisade fencing	Fencing	62	m	64.19	3,979.78	4.27	
1800 high fencing	Fencing	96	m	43.80	4,205.20	4.51	
Extra for 1000 x 1800 gate	Gate	1	nr	549.84	549.84	0.59	8,734.82
					8,734.82	9.37	
8.6 External drainage							
Excavate trench 250 - 500 deep; lay 100 diameter vitrified clay pipe and fittings bedded and surrounded in granular material	Pipes in trenches	44	m	73.82	3,247.86	3.48	
Excavate trench 500 - 750 deep; lay 100 diameter vitrified clay pipe and fittings bedded and surrounded in granular material	Pipes in trenches	59	m	78.23	4,615.30	4.95	
Excavate trench 750 - 1000 deep; lay 100 diameter vitrified clay pipe and fittings bedded and surrounded in granular material	Pipes in trenches	49	m	81.61	3,998.82	4.29	
Excavate trench 1000 - 1250 deep; lay 100 diameter vitrified clay pipe and fittings bedded and surrounded in granular material	Pipes in trenches	4	m	83.59	334.36	0.36	
Excavate trench 250 - 500 deep; lay 100 diameter vitrified clay pipe and fittings bedded and surrounded in in-situ concrete	Pipes in trenches	8	m	81.02	648.16	0.70	
Excavate trench 1000 - 1250 deep; lay 150 diameter vitrified clay pipe and fittings bedded and surrounded in in-situ concrete	Pipes in trenches	23	m	121.55	2,795.55	3.00	

COST PLAN FOR AN OFFICE DEVELOPMENT (Cont'd)

Description	Item	Qty		Rate	Item Total	Cost per m²	Total
8.0 EXTERNAL WORKS (Cont'd)							
8.6 External drainage (Cont'd)							
Excavate trench 1500 - 1750 deep; lay 150 diameter vitrified clay pipe and fittings bedded and surrounded in in-situ concrete	Pipes in trenches	10	m	134.46	1,344.60	1.44	
100 diameter vertical vitrified clay pipe and fittings cased in in-situ concrete	Pipes in trenches	3	m	172.27	516.81	0.55	
100 outlet vitrified clay yard gully with cast iron grating, surrounded in in-situ concrete	Gully	1	nr	266.16	266.16	0.29	
100 outlet vitrified clay road gully with brick kerb and cast iron grating, surrounded in in-situ concrete	Gully	7	nr	504.06	3,528.42	3.79	
Inspection chambers 600 x 900 x 600 deep internally comprising excavation works, in-situ concrete bases, suspended slabs and benchings, engineering brick walls and kerbs, clay channels, galvanised iron step irons and grade A access covers and frames	Insp. chamber	4	nr	1,096.93	4,387.71	4.71	
Inspection chambers 600 x 900 x 600 deep internally comprising excavation works, in-situ concrete bases, suspended slabs and benchings, engineering brick walls and kerbs, clay channels, galvanised iron step irons and grade B access covers and frames	Insp. chamber	3	nr	1,087.02	3,261.05	3.50	28,944.81
					28,944.81	31.06	
8.7 External services							
Excavate trench for 4nr ducts; lay 4nr 100 diameter UPVC ducts and fittings; lay warning tape; backfill trench		20	m	132.89	2,657.88	2.85	
Sewer connection charges		1	nr	8,796.30	8,796.30	9.44	
Gas main and meter charges		1	nr	7,037.03	7,037.03	7.55	
Electricity main and meter charges		1	nr	7,037.03	7,037.03	7.55	
Water main and meter charges		1	nr	5,277.78	5,277.78	5.66	30,806.01
					30,806.01	33.05	
10 MAIN CONTRACTOR'S PRELIMINARIES							
Site staff, accommodation, lighting, water safety health and welfare, rubbish disposal, cleaning, drying, protection, security, plant, transport, temporary works and scaffolding with a contract period of 38 weeks		item		179,482.20	179,482.20	192.58	179,482.20
				Total			**1,789,066.99**
				Cost per m²		**1,919.60**	

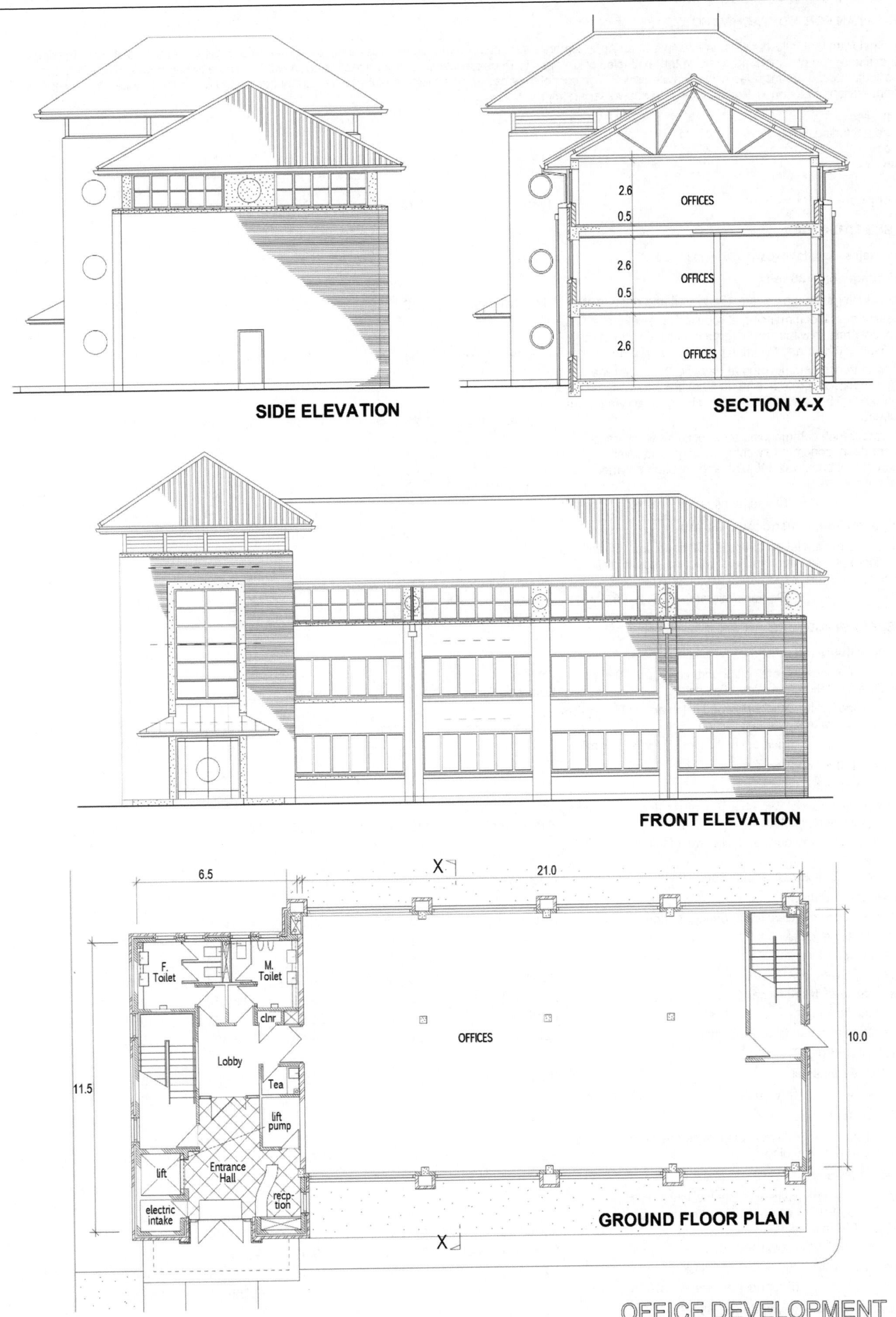
SIDE ELEVATION
SECTION X-X
2.6
0.5
OFFICES
FRONT ELEVATION
6.5
21.0
X
F. Toilet
M. Toilet
clnr
Lobby
Tea
lift pump
lift
Entrance Hall
recp-tion
electric intake
11.5
10.0
GROUND FLOOR PLAN
OFFICE DEVELOPMENT

COST PLAN FOR A DETACHED HOUSE

The Cost Plan that follows gives an example of an Approximate Estimate for a detached house with garage and porch as the attached sketch drawings. The estimate can be amended by using the examples of Composite Prices following or the prices included within the preceding pages. Details of the specification used are included within the elements. The cost plan is based on a fully measured bill of quantities priced using the detailed rates within this current edition of Laxton's. Preliminaries are shown separately.

Floor area

House (Including porch 5 m²)	120 m²
Garage	22 m²
Total	**142 m²**

Description	Item	Qty		Rate	Item Total	Cost per m²	Total
1.0 SUBSTRUCTURE							
Note: Rates allow for excavation by machine							
1.1 Foundations (86 m²)							
Clear site vegetation excavate 150 topsoil and remove spoil	Site clearance	113	m²	8.22	928.97	6.54	
Excavate trench commencing at reduced level, average 800 deep, concrete to within 150 of ground level, construct cavity brick wall 300 high and lay pitch polymer damp proof course	Strip foundation	33	m	223.43	7,373.09	51.92	
Excavate trench commencing at reduced level, average 800mm deep, concrete to within 150 of ground level, construct 103 brick wall 300 high and lay pitch polymer damp proof course	Strip foundation	26	m	179.26	4,660.88	32.82	
Excavate trench commencing at reduced level, average 800mm deep, concrete to within 150 of ground level, construct 215 brick wall 300 high and lay pitch polymer damp proof course	Strip foundation	2	m	385.16	770.32	5.42	13,733.26
(Element unit rate = £ 159.69 m²)					13,733.26	96.71	
1.4 Ground floor construction (86 m²)							
Excavate to reduce levels average 250 deep, lay 150mm bed of hardcore blinded, dpm and 150 concrete ground slab reinforced with Ref. A193 Fabric reinforcement	Ground floor slab	86	m²	101.03	8,688.96	61.19	8,688.96
(Element unit rate = £ 101.03 m²)					8,688.96	61.19	
2.0 SUPERSTRUCTURE							
2.2 Upper floors (55 m²)							
175 deep floor joists with 22 chipboard finish and 100mm glass fibre insulation with supporting netting	Softwood floor	49	m²	63.08	3,091.10	21.77	
175 deep floor joists with 22 plywood finish and 100mm glass fibre insulation with supporting netting	Softwood floor	6	m²	76.42	458.51	3.23	3,549.61
(Element unit rate = £ 64.54 m²)					3,549.61	25.00	
2.3 Roof (110 m² on plan)							
2.3.1 Roof structure							
35 degree pitched roof with 50 x 100 rafters and ceiling joists, 400mm glass fibre insulation	Pitched roof	110	m²	91.05	10,015.48	70.53	
Gable end 302 cavity brick and blockwork facings PC £600/1000	Gable wall	29	m²	155.59	4,512.21	31.78	
Gable end 102 brick wall facings £600/1000	Gable wall	8	m²	111.39	891.14	6.28	
2.3.2 Roof coverings							
Interlocking concrete tiles, felt underlay, battens	Roof tiling	143	m²	30.80	4,404.40	31.02	
Verge, 150 under cloak	Verge	38	m	27.20	1,033.60	7.28	
Ridge, half round	Ridge	14	m	24.17	338.38	2.38	
Valley trough tiles	Valley	2	m	86.92	173.84	1.22	
Abutments, lead flashings cavity trays	Abutment	11	m	168.71	1,855.78	13.07	
Sheet lead cladding	Lead roof	2	m²	759.66	1,519.32	10.70	
Eaves soffit, fascia and 100 PVC gutter	Eaves	29	m	74.03	2,146.90	15.12	
2.3.4 Roof drainage							
68 PVCU rainwater pipe.	Rainwater pipe	24	m	33.79	811.01	5.71	27,702.06
(Element unit rate = £ 251.84 m²)					27,702.06	195.08	
2.4 Stairs (1nr)							
Softwood staircase 2600 rise, balustrade one side, 855 wide two flights with half landing	Stairs	1	nr	2,317.01	2,317.01	16.32	2,317.01
2.5 External walls (152 m²)							
Brick and blockwork cavity wall, light weight blocks, facing bricks PC £600/1000, wall ties and 100mm CavityTherm Thin-R CT/PIR insulation	Hollow wall	127	m²	184.68	23,454.98	165.18	
Facing brick wall PC £600/1000 102 thick	1/2B Facing wall	25	m²	109.07	2,726.72	19.20	
Facing brick wall PC £600/1000 215 thick	1B Facing wall	3	m²	192.46	577.38	4.07	26,759.08
(Element unit rate = £ 176.05 m²)					26,759.08	188.44	
2.6 Windows and external doors (35 m²)							
2.6.1 External windows (16 m²)							
Hardwood double glazed casement windows	HW windows	16	m²	1,162.50	18,599.94	130.99	
Galvanised steel lintel, dpc, brick soldier course	Lintels	16	m	60.60	969.61	6.83	

COST PLAN FOR A DETACHED HOUSE (Cont'd)

Description	Item	Qty		Rate	Item Total	Cost per m²	Total
2.0 SUPERSTRUCTURE (Cont'd)							
2.6 Windows and external doors (35 m²) (Cont'd)							
2.6.1 External windows (16 m²) (Cont'd)							
Softwood window board, dpc close cavity	Window board	15	m	9.49	142.35	1.00	
Close cavity at jamb, dpc facings to reveal	Jamb	32	m	17.50	559.92	3.94	
2.6.2 External Doors (19 m²)							
Hardwood glazed doors, frames, cills, ironmongery	Hardwood doors	6	m²	885.69	5,314.14	37.42	
Aluminium, oak finish patio doors	Patio doors	9	m²	858.02	7,722.15	54.38	
Galvanised steel garage door	Garage door	4	m²	262.60	1,050.39	7.40	
Galvanised steel lintel, dpc, brick soldier course	Lintels	12	m	57.80	693.62	4.88	
Close cavity at jamb, dpc, facings to reveal	Jamb	4	m	17.48	69.92	0.49	35,122.04
(Element unit rate = £ 1,003.49 m²)					35,122.04	247.34	
2.7 Internal walls and partitions (153 m²)							
Lightweight concrete block 100 thick	Block walls	104	m²	51.63	5,369.99	37.82	
75 timber stud partition plasterboard, insulation and skim both sides	Stud partitions	53	m²	83.25	4,412.51	31.07	9,782.50
(Element unit rate = £ 63.94 m²)					9,782.50	68.89	
2.8 Internal doors (40 m²)							
12 hardboard embossed panel door, linings ironmongery PC £20.00	Flush doors	18	m²	303.20	5,457.63	38.43	
3 softwood 2XG glazed door, linings ironmongery PC £20.00	Glazed doors	6	m²	313.84	1,883.06	13.26	
6 Plywood faced door, linings, ironmongery PC £20.00	Flush doors	12	m²	288.42	3,461.07	24.37	
1 plywood faced half hour fire check flush door, frame, ironmongery PC £60.00	Fire doors	2	m²	246.37	492.75	3.47	
Insulated white plastic ceiling hatch	Hatch	1	nr	143.23	143.23	1.01	
Precast concrete lintels	Lintels	10	m	26.94	269.38	1.90	11,707.12
(Element unit rate = £ 292.68 m²)					11,707.12	82.44	
3.0 INTERNAL FINISHES							
3.1 Wall finishes (264 m²)							
15 plasterboard, dot and dabbed	Plasterboard	264	m²	30.23	7,980.51	56.20	
13 light weight plaster	Plaster work	264	m²	25.59	6,755.07	47.57	
150 x 150mm ceramic wall tiling PC £15.00	Tiling	13	m²	51.47	669.11	4.71	15,404.69
(Element unit rate = £ 58.35 m²)					15,404.69	108.48	
3.2 Floor finishes (63 m²)							
22 Chipboard,100 GA4000 insulation	Board flooring	63	m²	27.54	1,734.74	12.22	
3 PVC sheet flooring	Sheet vinyl	18	m²	20.40	367.20	2.59	
25 x 125 softwood skirting	Skirting	131	m	13.61	1,782.91	12.56	3,884.85
(Element unit rate = £ 61.66 m²)					3,884.85	27.36	
3.3 Ceiling Finishes (115 m²)							
12.5 Plasterboard and set	Plasterboard	109	m²	32.00	3,488.00	24.56	
Plywood finish	Plywood	6	m²	61.25	367.50	2.59	3,855.50
(Element unit rate = £ 33.53 m²)					3,855.50	27.15	
4.0 FITTINGS AND FURNISHINGS AND EQUIPMENT							
4.1 General fittings, furnishings and equipment							
Kitchen units :-							
600 base unit		2	nr	142.04	284.08	2.00	
1000 base unit		6	nr	178.53	1,071.18	7.54	
500 broom cupboard		1	nr	147.28	147.28	1.04	
600 wall unit		3	nr	114.22	342.66	2.41	
1000 wall unit		2	nr	151.75	303.50	2.14	
Work tops		10	m	64.06	640.60	4.51	
Gas fire surround		1	nr	647.96	647.96	4.56	3,437.26
					3,437.26	24.21	
5.0 SERVICES							
5.1 Sanitary appliances							
Lavatory basin with pedestal		3	nr	197.63	592.89	4.18	
Bath with front panel and plinth		1	nr	360.89	360.89	2.54	
WC suite		3	nr	321.46	964.38	6.79	
Stainless steel sink and drainer (500)		1	nr	178.43	178.43	1.26	
Stainless steel sink and drainer (600)		1	nr	211.74	211.74	1.49	
Shower		1	nr	713.86	713.86	5.03	3,022.19
					3,022.19	21.28	

COST PLAN FOR A DETACHED HOUSE (Cont'd)

Description	Item	Qty		Rate	Item Total	Cost per m²	Total
5.0 SERVICES (Cont'd)							
5.2 Services Equipment							
Electric oven built in		1	nr	915.55	915.55	6.45	
Gas hob built in		1	nr	480.66	480.66	3.38	
Kitchen extract unit		1	nr	337.61	337.61	2.38	
Gas fire with balanced flue		1	nr	457.78	457.78	3.22	2,191.60
					2,191.60	15.43	
5.3 Disposal Installations							
Upvc soil and vent pipe		15	m	110.45	1,656.75	11.67	
Air admittance valve		3	nr	31.75	95.25	0.67	1,752.00
					1,752.00	12.34	
5.4 Water Installations							
Cold water, tanks, 9 draw off points		item		1,489.28	1,489.28	10.49	
Hot water cylinder, 7 draw off points		item		1,136.41	1,136.41	8.00	2,625.70
					2,625.70	18.49	
5.5 Heat Source							
Boiler, pump, weather compensator and time and temperature zone controls		item		1,628.83	1,628.83	11.47	1,628.83
5.6 Space heating and air conditioning							
Low temperature hot water radiator system		item		5,460.49	5,460.49	38.45	5,460.49
5.7 Ventilating Systems							
Extract fan units		3	nr	82.48	247.43	1.74	247.43
5.8 Electrical Installations							
Electrical Installation comprising: 16 Nr lighting, 30 Nr outlet, cooker, immersion heater and 9 Nr fittings points to include smoke alarms, bells, telephone and aerial installation		item		6,896.65	6,896.65	48.57	6,896.65
5.9 Gas and other fuel installations							
Installation for boiler, hob and fire		item		685.60	685.60	4.83	685.60
5.14 Builders' work in connection with services							
Building work for service installation		item		2,344.83	2,344.83	16.51	2,344.83
8.0 EXTERNAL WORKS							
8.1 Site preparation works							
Clear site vegetation excavate 150 topsoil and remove spoil	Site clearance	479	m²	8.22	3,937.86	27.73	3,937.86
8.2 Roads, paths and pavings							
Excavate and lay 50 precast concrete flag paving on hardcore	Paving	120	m²	107.36	12,883.20	90.73	12,883.20
8.3 Planting							
Turfed Areas	Landscaping	103	m²	61.33	6,316.56	44.48	6,316.56
8.4 Fencing, railings and walls							
Brick wall, excavation 600 deep, concrete foundation, 215 brickwork facing. PC £600/1000, damp proof course, brick on edge coping PC £500/1000, 900 high	Garden wall	13	m	176.39	2,293.10	16.15	
Plastic coated chain link fencing 900 high on angle iron posts	Fencing	92	m	66.16	6,087.09	42.87	8,380.19
					8,380.19	59.02	
8.6 External drainage							
100 diameter clay pipes, excavation, 150 bed and surround, pea shingle, backfill 750 deep		85	m	94.13	8,001.15	56.35	
Polypropylene universal inspection chamber;; 475 diameter, 185mm deep for 100mm pipe; cast iron cover and frame; single seal A15 light duty to suit		6	nr	251.31	1,507.86	10.62	9,509.01
					9,509.01	66.96	
8.7 External services							
100 diameter clay duct, excavation backfill, polythene warning tape, 500 deep		38	m	39.79	1,511.85	10.65	
Provisional sums for External Services Gas, electric, water, telephone		item		4,829.42	4,829.42	34.01	6,341.27
					6,341.27	44.66	
10 MAIN CONTRACTOR'S PRELIMINARIES							
Site staff, accommodation, lighting, water, safety and health and welfare, rubbish disposal cleaning, drying, protection, security, plant, transport, temporary works and scaffolding with a contract period of 28 weeks				18,167.42	18,167.42	127.94	18,167.42
				Total			**258,334.76**
				Cost per m²		**1,819.26**	

REAR ELEVATION

SIDE ELEVATION

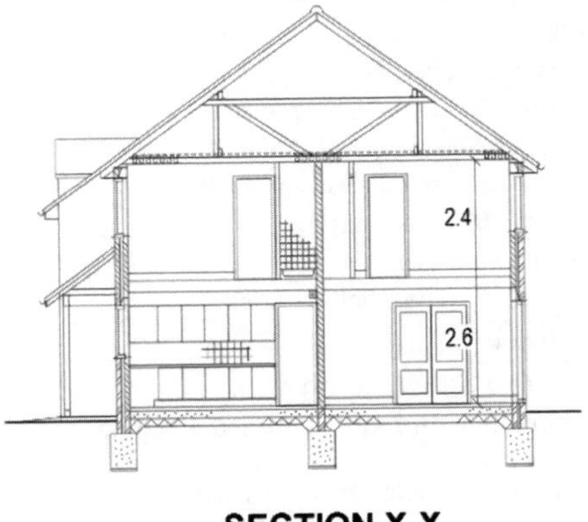

SECTION X-X

FRONT ELEVATION

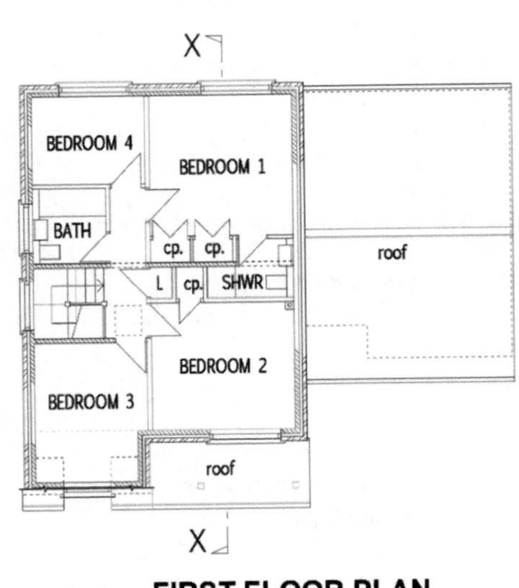

FIRST FLOOR PLAN

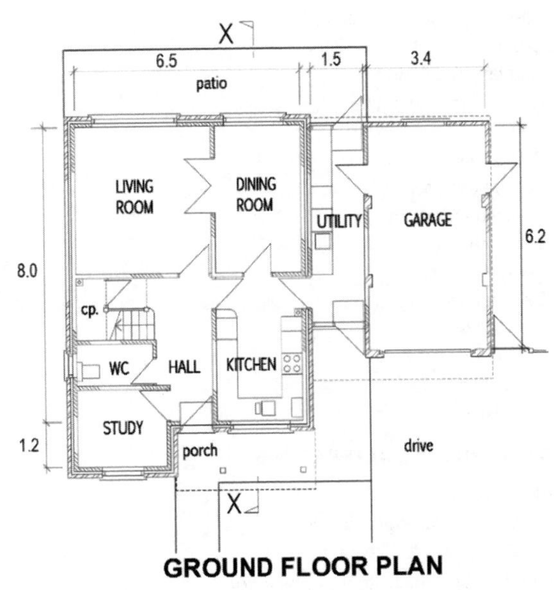

GROUND FLOOR PLAN

4 - BEDROOM DETACHED HOUSE

COMPOSITE PRICES

The following composite prices are based on the detailed rates herein and may be used to amend the previous example cost plans or to create new approximate budget estimates.

The composite prices can be further extended and amended by reference to the various sections.

Allowances should be made for location factors, tender values and price changes.

PRELIMINARIES

		£
The following preliminary items need to be added to the composite prices that follow.		
A calculation can be made by reference to the preliminaries section.		
Management and staff - average each		
Site accommodation		
Power and lighting		
add setup and remove		
Heating		
Water		
add setup and remove		
Telephone		
Safety, health and welfare		
Rubbish disposal and cleaning site		
Final clean		
Drying out building		
Security		
Small plant and tools		
Insurance of works		
Travelling time and fares		
Rates on temporary buildings		
Signboards and notices		
Glass breakage		
Sample panels		
Testing		
Attendance; chainman etc (on clerk of works etc)		
Setting out equipment, pegs		
Provision for winter working		
Defects		
Sureties and bonds		
Special conditions of contract		
Attendance on subcontractors		
Cranes - mobile tower		
Cranes - static tower		
Cranes - mobile crane		
Hoist		
Pumping		
On-site transport		
Transport for plant		
Temporary roads		
Temporary access		
External access scaffold		
Mobile tower		
Support scaffold		
Internal scaffold		
Hoardings		

DEMOLITIONS AND ALTERATIONS

Demolition		
Demolish timber outbuilding		
2.50 x 2.00 x 3.00 high	nr	281.73
Demolish brick lean-to and make good		
1.50 x 1.00 x 2.00 high	nr	364.19
Demolishing parts of structures		
Substructures		
incl. Excavation and removal by hand		
break out brickwork	m³	250.53
break out concrete	m³	305.60
break out reinforced concrete	m³	397.38
break up concrete bed		
100 thick	m²	30.56
150 thick	m²	45.84
200 thick	m²	61.11
break up reinforced concrete bed		
100 thick	m²	39.74
150 thick	m²	59.61
200 thick	m²	73.38
Walls		
brick internal		
102 thick	m²	21.58
215 thick	m²	44.43
327 thick	m²	68.08
brick external		
102 thick	m²	16.24
250 thick cavity wall	m²	33.75
Floors		
concrete reinforced; screed		
150 thick; 50 screed	m²	74.63
200 thick; 50 screed	m²	93.38
timber boarded on joists		
225 x 50 joists; floor boards	m²	17.25
Roofs		
timber flat roofs		
150 x 50 joists, 25 boards; felt	m²	18.07
timber pitched roof		
100 x 50 rafters; joists; plain tile	m²	22.45
100 x 50 rafters; joists; interlocking tiles	m²	19.53
100 x 50 rafters; joists; slates	m²	22.39
Alterations		
Includes make good finishes		
Cut opening through reinforced concrete floor		
150 thick x 900 x 2134 for staircase	nr	1,233.64
Cut opening through block wall		
100 thick x 838 x 2032 for doorway	nr	783.83
Cut opening through brick wall		
215 thick x 914 x 2082 for doorway	nr	1,148.62
275 thick cavity wall x 900 x 900 for window	nr	736.12
Cut opening through stud partition		
100 thick x 838 x 2032 for doorway	nr	560.76
Fill opening in block wall		
100 thick x 838 x 2032; door removed	nr	539.51
Fill opening in brick wall		
102 thick x 838 x 2032; door removed	nr	659.73
215 thick x 914 x 2082; external door removed	nr	1,053.97
275 thick cavity wall x 914 x 2082; external door removed	nr	969.90
Fill opening in stud partition		
100 thick x 838 x 2032; door removed	nr	507.03
Removal		
Remove window		
1486 x 923 metal	nr	30.66
1225 x 1070 wood casement; frame	nr	33.99
915 x 1525 cased frame; sashes	nr	50.75
Remove door and frame		
single internal	nr	24.44
single external	nr	27.02
Remove roof coverings		
3 layer felt	m²	5.83
asphalt	m²	7.29
slates	m²	16.46
tiles	m²	16.52

COMPOSITE PRICES (Cont'd)		£
SUBSTRUCTURE		
Note: Rates allow for excavation by machine.		
Strip Foundations		
Excavating, 225 x 450 concrete, brickwork, dpc, common bricks		
800 deep for 103 wall	m	96.70
1000 deep for 103 wall	m	117.04
1200 deep for 103 wall	m	152.54
800 deep for 215 wall	m	143.96
1000 deep for 215 wall	m	177.20
1200 deep for 215 wall	m	210.06
800 deep for 300 wall	m	176.42
1000 deep for 300 wall	m	222.12
1200 deep for 300 wall	m	262.33
Extra 100mm depth concrete foundation; excavation; concrete	m	12.15
Extra 100mm depth 103 brick wall in foundation; excavation; brickwork	m	10.31
Extra 100mm depth 215 brick wall in foundation; excavation; brickwork	m	16.58
Extra 100mm depth 300 brick wall in foundation; excavation; brickwork	m	18.52
Extra for four courses facing bricks P.C. £400.00 per 1000	m	5.06
Excavating, 225 x 600 concrete, brickwork, dpc, common bricks		
800 deep for 300 wall	m	180.30
1000 deep for 300 wall	m	240.59
1200 deep for 300 wall	m	279.69
Extra 100mm depth 300 brick wall in foundation; excavation; brickwork	m	18.81
Extra for four courses facing bricks P.C. £400.00 per 1000	m	5.06
Excavating, 225 x 450 concrete, brickwork, dpc, Engineering bricks Class B		
800 deep for 215 wall	m	156.50
1000 deep for 215 wall	m	193.18
1200 deep for 215 wall	m	229.48
800 deep for 300 wall	m	195.14
1000 deep for 300 wall	m	247.23
1200 deep for 300 wall	m	293.83
Extra 100mm depth concrete foundation; excavation; concrete	m	12.15
Extra 100mm depth 103 brick wall in	m	11.23
Extra 100mm depth 215 brick wall in foundation; excavation; brickwork	m	18.29
Extra 100mm depth 300 brick wall in foundation; excavation; brickwork	m	20.35
Extra for four courses facing bricks P.C. £400.00 per 1000	m	2.32
Excavating, 225 x 450 concrete, blockwork, dpc, Concrete blocks		
800 deep for 100 wall	m	82.70
1000 deep for 100 wall	m	88.62
1200 deep for 100 wall	m	102.85
Extra 100mm depth concrete foundation; excavation; concrete	m	12.15
Extra 100mm depth 100 block wall in foundation; excavation; blockwork	m	7.26
800 deep for 140 wall	m	91.11
1000 deep for 140 wall	m	109.90
1200 deep for 140 wall	m	128.70
Extra 100mm depth concrete foundation; excavation; concrete	m	12.15
Extra 100mm depth 140 block wall in foundation; excavation; blockwork	m	9.50
Excavating, 225 x 600 concrete, blockwork, dpc, Thermalite Trenchblocks		
800 deep for 305 wall	m	138.91
1000 deep for 305 wall	m	168.42
1200 deep for 305 wall	m	197.56
Extra 100mm depth concrete foundation; excavation; concrete	m	12.15
Extra 100mm depth 305 block wall in foundation; excavation; blockwork	m	14.58
Fabric reinforcement ref. A193 (no allowance for working space or formwork)		
350 wide	m	2.31
600 wide	m	3.95
750 wide	m	5.61
Trench Fill Foundations		
Excavating 450 wide concrete fill to 150 of ground level, brickwork, dpc, Common bricks		
800 deep for 102 wall	m	102.25
1000 deep for 102 wall	m	124.31
1200 deep for 102 wall	m	146.37
800 deep for 215 wall	m	119.90
1000 deep for 215 wall	m	141.96
1200 deep for 215 wall	m	164.03
800 deep for 300 wall	m	132.65
1000 deep for 300 wall	m	154.71
1200 deep for 300 wall	m	176.78
Extra 100mm depth concrete foundation; excavation; concrete;	m	12.15
Extra for four courses facing bricks PC £400 per 1000	m	5.06
Column bases		
Excavating, 450 concrete		
1000 x 1000 x 1000 deep	nr	136.24
1000 x 1000 x 1200 deep	nr	153.54
1000 x 1000 x 1500 deep	nr	169.89
1200 x 1200 x 1000 deep	nr	191.55
1200 x 1200 x 1200 deep	nr	214.17
1200 x 1200 x 1500 deep	nr	235.99
1500 x 1500 x 1000 deep	nr	292.05
1500 x 1500 x 1200 deep	nr	323.82
1500 x 1500 x 1500 deep	nr	355.21
2000 x 2000 x 1000 deep	nr	506.33
2000 x 2000 x 1200 deep	nr	556.45
2000 x 2000 x 1500 deep	nr	607.45
Excavating, 750 concrete		
1000 x 1000 x 1000 deep	nr	194.70
1000 x 1000 x 1200 deep	nr	212.00
1000 x 1000 x 1500 deep	nr	228.35
1000 x 1000 x 2000 deep	nr	255.61
1200 x 1200 x 1000 deep	nr	275.73
1200 x 1200 x 1200 deep	nr	298.35
1200 x 1200 x 1500 deep	nr	320.17
1200 x 1200 x 2000 deep	nr	356.54
1500 x 1500 x 1000 deep	nr	423.59
1500 x 1500 x 1200 deep	nr	455.36
1500 x 1500 x 1500 deep	nr	486.75
1500 x 1500 x 2000 deep	nr	539.07
2000 x 2000 x 1000 deep	nr	740.17
2000 x 2000 x 1200 deep	nr	790.29
2000 x 2000 x 1500 deep	nr	841.29
2000 x 2000 x 2000 deep	nr	926.29
3000 x 3000 x 1000 deep	nr	1,636.40
3000 x 3000 x 1200 deep	nr	1,734.88
3000 x 3000 x 1500 deep	nr	1,838.81
3000 x 3000 x 2000 deep	nr	2,012.03
Excavating, 1000 concrete		
1000 x 1000 x 1000 deep	nr	243.42
1000 x 1000 x 1200 deep	nr	260.71
1000 x 1000 x 1500 deep	nr	277.07
1000 x 1000 x 2000 deep	nr	304.33
1200 x 1200 x 1000 deep	nr	345.89
1200 x 1200 x 1200 deep	nr	368.50
1200 x 1200 x 1500 deep	nr	390.33
1200 x 1200 x 2000 deep	nr	426.70

COMPOSITE PRICES (Cont'd)

SUBSTRUCTURE (Cont'd)

Column bases (Cont'd)

		£
Excavating, 1000 concrete (Cont'd)		
1500 x 1500 x 1000 deep	nr	533.20
1500 x 1500 x 1200 deep	nr	564.97
1500 x 1500 x 1500 deep	nr	596.36
1500 x 1500 x 2000 deep	nr	648.68
2000 x 2000 x 1000 deep	nr	935.04
2000 x 2000 x 1200 deep	nr	985.16
2000 x 2000 x 1500 deep	nr	1,036.16
2000 x 2000 x 2000 deep	nr	1,121.16
3000 x 3000 x 1000 deep	nr	2,074.86
3000 x 3000 x 1200 deep	nr	2,173.34
3000 x 3000 x 1500 deep	nr	2,277.27
3000 x 3000 x 2000 deep	nr	2,450.49
Excavating, 1500 concrete		
1000 x 1000 x 1500 deep	nr	374.50
1000 x 1000 x 2000 deep	nr	401.76
1500 x 1500 x 1500 deep	nr	815.59
1500 x 1500 x 2000 deep	nr	867.91
2000 x 2000 x 1500 deep	nr	1,425.90
2000 x 2000 x 2000 deep	nr	1,510.90
3000 x 3000 x 1500 deep	nr	3,154.18
3000 x 3000 x 2000 deep	nr	3,327.40
Excavating, 450 reinforced concrete		
1000 x 1000 x 1000 deep	nr	397.28
1000 x 1000 x 1200 deep	nr	431.37
1000 x 1000 x 1500 deep	nr	470.39
1000 x 1000 x 2000 deep	nr	535.43
1200 x 1200 x 1000 deep	nr	539.63
1200 x 1200 x 1200 deep	nr	580.38
1200 x 1200 x 1500 deep	nr	629.41
1200 x 1200 x 2000 deep	nr	711.11
Excavating, 750 reinforced concrete		
1000 x 1000 x 1000 deep	nr	654.92
1000 x 1000 x 1200 deep	nr	687.32
1000 x 1000 x 1500 deep	nr	726.35
1000 x 1000 x 2000 deep	nr	791.39
1200 x 1200 x 1000 deep	nr	882.68
1200 x 1200 x 1200 deep	nr	923.44
1200 x 1200 x 1500 deep	nr	972.46
1200 x 1200 x 2000 deep	nr	1,054.16

Ground beams

Excavation, blinding, reinforced concrete		
300 x 450	m	132.19
300 x 600	m	199.26
450 x 450	m	183.26
450 x 600	m	264.39

Ground slabs

Excavation, 150 hardcore, blinding, concrete		
150 ground slab	m²	61.88
200 ground slab	m²	69.81
225 ground slab	m²	75.15
Extra: 50 blinding	m²	11.76
Extra: Fabric reinforcement A142	m²	5.38
Extra: Fabric reinforcement A193	m²	6.59
Slab thickening 450 wide x 150 thick	m²	14.42
Damp proof membrane		
250mu Polythene sheeting	m²	1.88
2 coats Bitumen emulsion	m²	16.70
Extra: 50mm Expanded polystyrene insulation	m²	6.47
Extra: 50mm Concrete thickness	m²	8.43
Extra: 100mm Reduced level excavation	m²	4.50
Extra: 100mm hardcore filling	m²	5.43

Beam and block floors

(excludes excavation, blinding etc.)		
155mm beam floor span 3.9m	m²	50.14
Extra: 150mm Reduced level excavation; 50 concrete blinding	m²	15.60

Piling

On/off site charge	nr	9,955.41
450 bored cast piles n/e 6m deep	m	58.30
610 bored cast piles n/e 6m deep	m	88.19
Cutting off tops of piles	nr	19.98

INSIDE EXISTING BUILDING

Note: rates allow for excavation by hand.

Strip foundations

Excavating, 225 concrete, brickwork, dpc Common bricks		
800 deep for 103 wall	m	124.23
1000 deep for 103 wall	m	150.41
1200 deep for 103 wall	m	215.45
800 deep for 215 wall	m	173.91
1000 deep for 215 wall	m	214.24
1200 deep for 215 wall	m	264.27
Extra 100mm depth concrete foundation; excavation; concrete	m	17.00

Trench Fill Foundations

Excavating 450 wide concrete fill to 150 of ground level, brickwork, dpc Common bricks		
800 deep for 102 wall	m	136.45
1000 deep for 102 wall	m	167.27
800 deep for 215 wall	m	154.11
1000 deep for 215 wall	m	160.71
Extra 100mm depth concrete foundation; excavation; concrete	m	17.00

Ground slabs

Excavation, 150 hardcore, blinding, concrete		
150 ground slab	m²	93.17
200 ground slab	m²	109.20
Slab thickening 450 wide x 150 thick	m	21.65
Damp proof membrane		
250 mu polythene sheeting	m²	1.88
2 coats bitumen emulsion	m²	16.70

FRAME

Reinforced concrete

200 x 200 column	m	78.52
225 x 225 column	m	88.33
300 x 300 column	m	130.33
200 x 200 attached beam	m	79.32
225 x 250 attached beam	m	98.79
300 x 450 attached beam	m	180.28
400 x 650 attached beam	m	289.75
Casing to 152 x 152 steel column	m	63.24
Casing to 203 x 203 steel column	m	81.93
Casing to 146 x 254 steel beam	m	81.35
Casing to 165 x 305 steel beam	m	95.80
Extra: wrought formwork	m²	5.84

Steel

Columns and beams	tonne	1,240.86
Roof trusses	tonne	2,227.56
Purlins and cladding rails	tonne	1,818.36
Small sections	tonne	726.00
Two coats primer at works	tonne	277.38
Prime, undercoat and gloss paint	m²	12.39

Glued laminated softwood beams

65 x 150 x 4000 long	nr	67.04
65 x 250 x 4000 long	nr	116.88
65 x 300 x 6000 long	nr	188.54
65 x 325 x 8000 long	nr	360.51
90 x 200 x 4000 long	nr	125.16
90 x 325 x 8000 long	nr	482.05
90 x 400 x 10000 long	nr	722.46
90 x 450 x 12000 long	nr	956.23

COMPOSITE PRICES (Cont'd)

FRAME (Cont'd)

		£
Glued laminated softwood beams (Cont'd)		
115 x 250 x 4000 long	nr	192.72
115 x 300 x 4000 long	nr	226.74
115 x 350 x 8000 long	nr	651.66
115 x 425 x 12000 long	nr	1,138.31
115 x 450 x 8000 long	nr	831.69
115 x 500 x 14000 long	nr	1,543.10
140 x 350 x 8000 long	nr	782.68
140 x 450 x 12000 long	nr	1,452.27
165 x 450 x 12000 long	nr	1,699.30
190 x 475 x 14000 long	nr	2,376.55

UPPER FLOORS

		£
Concrete		
In-situ reinforced concrete		
150 thick	m^2	102.90
200 thick	m^2	111.80
225 thick	m^2	121.76
In-situ reinforced concrete with permanent Expamet		
Hy-rib formwork ref 2411 and A142 mesh reinforcement		
100 thick	m^2	106.89
125 thick	m^2	112.35
150 thick	m^2	117.94
Hollow prestressed concrete		
125 thick	m^2	78.24
150 thick	m^2	85.65
200 thick	m^2	93.45
Beam and block		
150 thick	m^2	50.14
Timber		
Softwood joist including acoustic insulation		
100 thick	m^2	40.24
150 thick	m^2	44.60
175 thick	m^2	44.46
200 thick	m^2	49.27
225 thick	m^2	52.44
250 thick	m^2	61.73
Floor boarding		
19 square edge softwood	m^2	27.13
25 square edge softwood	m^2	28.38
19 tongued and grooved softwood	m^2	30.97
25 tongued and grooved softwood	m^2	32.09
18 tongued and grooved chipboard	m^2	14.97
22 tongued and grooved chipboard	m^2	17.14
15 tongued and grooved plywood, Douglas Fir unsanded	m^2	28.03
18 tongued and grooved plywood, Douglas Fir unsanded	m^2	21.36
15 tongued and grooved plywood, Birch Faced BB quality	m^2	25.10
18 tongued and grooved plywood, Birch Faced BB quality	m^2	28.50
Extra: machine sanding	m^2	12.29
Extra: prepare, prime and seal	m^2	4.13

ROOF

		£
Roof structure		
Reinforced in-situ concrete		
100 thick	m^2	85.63
150 thick	m^2	99.91
200 thick	m^2	103.25
50 lightweight screed to falls	m^2	32.45
50 cement sand screed to falls	m^2	19.94
50 vermiculite screed to falls	m^2	26.78
75 flat glass fibre insulation board	m^2	13.63
Extra for vapour barrier	m^2	3.43
Softwood flat roof joists		
50 x 100 joists @ 400 centres	m^2	33.40
50 x 175 joists @ 400 centres	m^2	35.48
50 x 200 joists @ 400 centres	m^2	41.07
50 x 225 joists @ 400 centres	m^2	44.46
50 x 100 joists @ 600 centres	m^2	23.90
50 x 175 joists @ 600 centres	m^2	27.00
50 x 200 joists @ 600 centres	m^2	28.93
50 x 225 joists @ 600 centres	m^2	31.22
Boarding		
18 chipboard	m^2	17.72
25 softwood tongued grooved	m^2	21.36
18 plywood decking	m^2	21.17
24 plywood decking	m^2	25.02
Pitched roof with 50 x 100 rafters and ceiling joists at 400 centres	m^2	53.08
Pitched roof with trussed rafters at 600 centres	m^2	26.64
Roof coverings		
Bitumen felt roofing		
Three layer fibre based felt	m^2	36.67
Three layer high performance felt	m^2	73.76
Mastic asphalt		
20 two coat mastic asphalt	m^2	51.07
Screeds		
50 lightweight screed to falls	m^2	32.45
50 cement sand screed to falls	m^2	19.94
60 Vermiculite screed to falls	m^2	31.34
75 flat glass fibre insulation board	m^2	13.63
Extra for vapour barrier	m^2	3.43
Sheets (on slope)		
Profile 3 fibre cement sheeting	m^2	33.05
Profile 6 fibre cement sheeting	m^2	23.06
Colour coated galvanised steel sheeting	m^2	24.58
Tiles and slates (on slope)		
381 x 227 concrete interlocking tiles	m^2	38.79
268 x 165 plain concrete tiles	m^2	56.19
268 x 165 machine made clay tiles	m^2	60.33
265 x 165 handmade tiles	m^2	29.23
400 x 200 fibre cement slates	m^2	56.99
500 x 250 fibre cement slates	m^2	48.99
600 x 300 fibre cement slates	m^2	36.73
400 x 200 natural slates	m^2	115.45
500 x 250 natural slates	m^2	127.29
600 x 300 natural slates	m^2	173.71
Insulation (horizontal)		
100 Fibreglass insulation quilt	m^2	3.90
100 Rockwool insulation quilt	m^2	11.47
150 Rockwool insulation quilt	m^2	13.91
300 Rockwool insulation quilt	m^2	26.31
400 Rockwool insulation quilt	m^2	37.11
Eaves, soffits, fascia's and gutters		
Eaves soffit, fascia, gutter and decoration		
225 x 150, 112 pvc-u	m	58.08
225 x 150, 100 half round Cast Iron gutter	m	102.74
225 x 150, 114 half round Cast Iron gutter	m	105.41
225 x 150, 125 half round Cast Iron gutter	m	115.53
225 x 150, 150 half round Cast Iron gutter	m	152.83
225 x 150, 100 OG Cast Iron gutter	m	104.64
225 x 150, 114 OG Cast Iron gutter	m	109.63
225 x 150, 125 OG Cast Iron gutter	m	116.04
400 x 200, 112 pvc-u	m	68.00
400 x 200, 100 half round Cast Iron gutter	m	112.66
400 x 200, 114 half round Cast Iron gutter	m	115.33
400 x 200, 125 half round Cast Iron gutter	m	125.45
400 x 200, 150 half round Cast Iron gutter	m	162.75
400 x 200, 100 OG Cast Iron gutter	m	114.56
400 x 200, 114 OG Cast Iron gutter	m	119.55
400 x 200, 125 OG Cast Iron gutter	m	125.96

COMPOSITE PRICES (Cont'd)

ROOF (Cont'd)

		£
Eaves, soffits, fascia's and gutters (Cont'd)		
Eaves soffit, fascia, gutter and decoration (Cont'd)		
400 x 200, 102 half round cast aluminium gutter	m	107.92
400 x 200, 127 half round cast aluminium gutter	m	116.42
Verges, hips, ridges and valleys		
Verge undercloak, barge board and decoration		
225 x 25	m	39.51
Hip rafter and capping		
225 x 50, concrete capping tiles	m	45.58
225 x 50, clay machine made capping tiles	m	45.83
225 x 50, clay handmade capping tiles	m	49.95
225 x 50, concrete bonnet hip tiles	m	119.86
225 x 50, clay machine made bonnet hip tiles	m	73.12
225 x 50, clay handmade bonnet hip tiles	m	119.86
Ridge board and capping		
175 x 32, concrete capping tile	m	40.33
175 x 32, machine made clay tile	m	40.58
175 x 32, handmade clay tile	m	44.70
Valley rafter and tile		
225 x 32, concrete angular valley tile	m	69.31
225 x 32, concrete valley trough	m	37.49
225 x 32, machine made clay valley tile	m	69.48
225 x 32, handmade clay valley tile	m	79.97
Valley rafter, sole boards and leadwork		
225 x 32, code 4 lead	m	139.40
225 x 32, code 5 lead	m	151.82
Rain water pipes		
Rainwater pipe		
68 pvc-u pipe	m	27.98
63 cast iron pipe and decoration	m	123.68
75 cast iron pipe and decoration	m	138.86
100 cast iron pipe and decoration	m	181.72
63 cast aluminium pipe	m	73.15
75 cast aluminium pipe	m	87.65
100 cast aluminium pipe	m	119.42

STAIRS

Concrete		
Reinforced concrete 2670 rise, mild steel balustrade one side, straight flight		
1000 wide granolithic finish	nr	3,404.64
1500 wide granolithic finish	nr	4,759.12
1000 wide pvc sheet finish non-slip nosings	nr	3,964.61
1500 wide pvc sheet finish non-slip nosings	nr	4,469.21
1000 wide terrazzo finish	nr	4,643.61
1500 wide terrazzo finish	nr	5,329.34
Reinforced concrete 2670 rise, mild steel balustrade one side in two flights with half landing		
1000 wide granolithic finish	nr	4,055.73
1500 wide granolithic finish	nr	4,670.90
1000 wide pvc sheet finish non-slip nosings	nr	4,647.89
1500 wide pvc sheet finish non-slip nosings	nr	5,095.25
1000 wide terrazzo finish	nr	5,363.20
1500 wide terrazzo finish	nr	6,764.77
Timber		
Softwood staircase 2600 rise, balustrade one side.		
855 wide straight flight	nr	1,606.31
855 wide 1 flight with 3 winders at bottom	nr	1,976.67
855 wide 1 flight with 3 winders at top	nr	1,976.67
Steel		
Mild steel staircase 2600 rise, balustrade both sides.		
920 wide straight flight	nr	3,883.26
920 wide 2 flights with quarter landing	nr	7,229.11
920 wide 2 flights with half landing	nr	8,754.68
Spiral steel staircase, balustrade,		
1600 diameter 2640 rise, domestic, powder coated	nr	2,641.10
1600 diameter 3000 rise, external, galvanised, decorated	nr	3,084.55

EXTERNAL WALLS

Brickwork		
Common bricks		
102 wall	m²	75.30
215 wall	m²	134.15
327 wall	m²	179.03
Hollow wall with stainless steel ties		
275 common bricks both skins	m²	155.26
275 facings one side P.C. £600/1000	m²	165.31
Fully filled cavity wall with galvanised ties, 100mm CavityTherm Thin-R CT/PIR insulation		
300 facings one side P.C. £400/1000	m²	208.48
300 facings one side P.C. £500/1000	m²	211.88
300 facings one side P.C. £600/1000	m²	215.29
300 facings one side P.C. £700/1000	m²	218.70
300 facings one side P.C. £800/1000	m²	225.51
300 facings one side P.C. £900/1000	m²	232.33
Engineering bricks Class B		
102 wall	m²	84.42
215 wall	m²	151.33
327 wall	m²	202.33
Engineering bricks Class A		
102 wall	m²	124.62
215 wall	m²	232.42
327 wall	m²	324.31
Facing bricks		
102 wall P.C. £400 per 1000	m²	81.95
102 wall P.C. £500 per 1000	m²	85.35
102 wall P.C. £600 per 1000	m²	88.76
102 wall P.C. £700 per 1000	m²	92.17
102 wall P.C. £800 per 1000	m²	98.98
102 wall P.C. £900 per 1000	m²	105.80
215 wall P.C. £400 per 1000	m²	137.33
215 wall P.C. £500 per 1000	m²	144.20
215 wall P.C. £600 per 1000	m²	151.07
215 wall P.C. £700 per 1000	m²	157.94
215 wall P.C. £800 per 1000	m²	171.69
215 wall P.C. £900 per 1000	m²	185.43
Blockwork		
Aerated concrete block 7.0n/mm²		
100 wall	m²	52.83
140 wall	m²	67.91
215 wall	m²	89.63
Dense concrete block 7.0n/mm²		
100 wall	m²	64.74
140 wall	m²	90.72
190 wall	m²	108.69
215 wall	m²	119.46
Fair face concrete block		
100 wall	m²	56.43
140 wall	m²	67.89
190 wall	m²	92.81
Composite		
Hollow wall in light weight blocks with stainless steel ties.		
300 facings one side P.C. £600/1000	m²	127.94

COMPOSITE PRICES (Cont'd)

EXTERNAL WALLS (Cont'd)

Composite (Cont'd)

		£
Fully filled light weight block cavity wall with galvanised ties, 100mm CavityTherm Thin-R CT/PIR insulation		
300 facings one side P.C. £400/1000	m²	177.92
300 facings one side P.C. £500/1000	m²	181.32
300 facings one side P.C. £600/1000	m²	184.73
300 facings one side P.C. £700/1000	m²	188.14
300 facings one side P.C. £800/1000	m²	194.95
300 facings one side P.C. £900/1000	m²	201.77
Extra for:		
13 mm two coat plain render painted	m²	14.39
15 mm pebbled dash render	m²	28.95

WINDOWS AND EXTERNAL DOORS

Windows

		£
Softwood double glazed, prefinished casement window		
630 x 750	nr	393.39
630 x 1050	nr	469.01
1200 x 750	nr	581.68
1200 x 1200	nr	735.72
1770 x 900	nr	951.64
1770 x 1200	nr	1,040.39
average cost	m²	553.94
purpose made in panes 0.10-0.50m²	m²	507.69
Hardwood double glazed, prefinished standard casement windows		
630 x 750	nr	622.25
630 x 1200	nr	869.03
915 x 1050	nr	1,005.08
average cost	m²	1,109.81
Sapele double glazed casement windows		
purpose made in panes 0.l0-0.50m²	m²	561.42
European Oak double glazed casement windows		
purpose made in panes 0.10-0.50m²	m²	645.41
Softwood double glazed, tensioned balances; prefinished sliding sash window		
855 x 1045	nr	1,280.64
855 x 1345	nr	1,428.88
1080 x 1345	nr	1,675.90
average cost	m²	708.80
Softwood double glazed, corded sash window 50 thick; cased frames; oak cills; sash cords		
1050 x 1200	nr	1,660.44
1200 x 1500	nr	2,164.23
1200 x 1800	nr	2,562.17
1500 x 1800	nr	3,109.32
average cost	m²	649.12
Galvanised steel windows;4mm glass		
279 x 923	nr	200.30
508 x 1067	nr	256.60
997 x 628	nr	293.80
997 x 1067	nr	556.49
997 x 1218	nr	533.81
1486 x 923	nr	695.27
1486 x 1067	nr	747.07
1486 x 1218	nr	709.53
1994 x 923	nr	792.22
1994 x 1218	nr	897.19
average cost	m²	310.52
Aluminium double glazed; vertical sliders; cill		
600 x 800	nr	726.08
600 x 1200	nr	970.93
800 x 800	nr	1,191.41
800 x 1200	nr	1,528.52
1200 x 800	nr	2,369.92
1200 x 1200	nr	2,729.27
Aluminium double glazed; horizontal sliders; cill		
1200 x 800	nr	729.63
1200 x 1400	nr	858.08
1400 x 800	nr	777.57
1400 x 1400	nr	910.63
1600 x 800	nr	832.49
1600 x 1600	nr	1,020.75
Upvc windows; opening/fixed lights; factory double glazed		
600 x 1000	nr	254.92
750 x 1350	nr	271.52
900 x 1350	nr	285.08
1200 x 1350	nr	315.17
Upvc windows tilt / turn factory double glazed		
600 x 650	nr	226.65
600 x 1050	nr	284.15
750 x 1050	nr	300.73
900 x 1200	nr	344.40
900 x 1500; toughened glass	nr	416.63
Upvc windows tilt / turn; fixed side light; factory double glazed		
1800 x 1050	nr	469.35
1800 x 1350; toughened glass	nr	597.17
Upvc windows tilt / turn; fixed centre light; factory double glazed		
2400 x 1200	nr	677.88
2400 x 1350	nr	709.42

Doors

		£
44 External ledged and braced door, 50 x 100 softwood frame, ironmongery P.C. £50.00 per leaf and decorate		
762 x 1981	nr	374.41
838 x 1981	nr	385.48
1372 x 1981; pair	nr	606.52
44 External framed, ledged and braced door, 50 x 100 softwood frame, ironmongery P.C. £50.00 per leaf and decorate		
762 x 1981	nr	392.34
838 x 1981	nr	403.41
1372 x 1981; pair	nr	642.38
44 External plywood flush door, 50 x 100 SW frame, architrave one side, ironmongery P.C. £50.00 per leaf and decorate		
762 x 1981	nr	443.95
838 x 1981	nr	453.83
1372 x 1981; pair	nr	650.00
44 Softwood external panel door glazed panels, 50 x 100 softwood frame, architrave one side, ironmongery P.C. £50.00 decorated.		
762 x 1981; type 2XG	nr	541.96
838 x 1981; type 2XG	nr	478.13
762 x 1981; type KXT	nr	487.65
44 Hardwood Magnet Carolina door, clear glass 50 x 100 hardwood frame architrave one side, ironmongery P.C. £50.00 decorated.		
838 x 1981	nr	669.66
813 x 2032	nr	676.28
44 Hardwood Magnet Malton door, clear glass 50 x 100 hardwood frame architrave one side, ironmongery P.C. £50.00 decorated.		
762 x 1981	nr	677.99
838 x 1981	nr	689.59

COMPOSITE PRICES (Cont'd)		£
WINDOWS AND EXTERNAL DOORS (Cont'd)		
Garage doors		
Galvanised steel garage door		
2135 x 1980	nr	1,232.26
4265 x 1980	nr	2,230.91
Western Red Cedar garage door		
2135 x 1980 side hung pair	nr	1,281.46
2135 x 1980 up and over	nr	1,511.87
Opening in cavity wall		
Galvanised steel lintel, DPC, brick soldier course	m	127.55
Softwood window board, DPC, close cavity	m	29.50
Close cavity at jamb, DPC, facings to reveal	m	18.24
INTERNAL WALLS		
Brickwork		
Common bricks		
102 wall	m²	75.30
215 wall	m²	134.15
327 wall	m²	179.03
Engineering bricks		
102 wall	m²	84.42
215 wall	m²	151.33
327 wall	m²	202.33
Blockwork		
Light weight concrete block 4.0 n/m²		
75 wall	m²	38.81
100 wall	m²	44.74
140 wall	m²	65.68
Dense concrete block 7.0 n/m²		
90 wall	m²	70.69
100 wall	m²	64.74
140 wall	m²	90.72
190 wall	m²	108.69
215 wall	m²	119.46
Hollow glass blocks		
80 wall - 190 x 190 blocks	m²	259.84
80 wall - 240 x 240 blocks	m²	292.85
Partitions		
Timber stud partition with plasterboard both sides		
75 partition, direct decoration	m²	95.29
100 partition direct decoration	m²	100.82
75 partition with skim coat plaster and decorate	m²	112.75
100 partition with skim coat plaster and decorate	m²	118.28
Extra for 100 insulation	m²	5.05
Metal stud partition with one layer plasterboard each side		
75 partition direct decoration	m²	80.50
75 partition with skim coat plaster and decorate	m²	97.96
Metal stud partition with two layers plasterboard each side		
100 partition direct decoration	m²	105.77
100 partition with skim coat plaster and decorate	m²	123.23
INTERNAL DOORS		
Panel doors		
34 softwood panelled type SA door; glazed, 38 x 150 lining, stop, architrave both sides, ironmongery PC £20.00 per leaf; decorated		
762 x 1981	nr	425.48
34 Magnet Oak veneered hardwood panelled door; 38 x 150 lining, stop, architrave both sides, ironmongery PC £20.00 per leaf; decorated		
762 x 1981	nr	480.34
44 softwood panelled pattern 2G door; glazed, 38 x 150 lining, stop, architrave both sides, ironmongery PC £20.00 per leaf; decorated		
762 x 1981	nr	435.27
35 oak veneered pattern 10 door; toughened glass; 38 x 150 lining, stop, architrave both sides, ironmongery PC £20.00 per leaf; decorated		
762 x 1981	nr	470.91
Softwood panelled door 38 x 150 lining, stop, architrave both sides, ironmongery PC £20.00 per leaf; decorated		
35 x 762 x 1981 two panel	nr	445.01
35 x 762 x 1981 four panel	nr	450.80
35 x 762 x 1981 six panel	nr	456.58
44 x 838 x 1981 six panel	nr	612.89
Oak panelled door 38 x 150 swd lining, stop, architrave both sides, ironmongery PC £20.00 per leaf; decorated		
35 x 762 x 1981 two panel	nr	1,196.03
35 x 762 x 1981 four panel	nr	1,254.64
35 x 762 x 1981 six panel	nr	1,313.17
44 x 838 x 1981 six panel	nr	1,410.91
Flush doors		
34 flush door 38 x 150 lining, stop, architrave both sides, ironmongery PC £20.00 per leaf, decorated		
762 x 1981 hardboard faced	nr	349.08
838 x 1981 hardboard faced	nr	364.41
1372 x 1981 pair hardboard faced	nr	515.78
762 x 1981 plywood faced	nr	350.12
838 x 1981 plywood faced	nr	363.05
1372 x 1981 pair plywood faced	nr	518.20
762 x 1981 Ash faced	nr	353.63
838 x 1981 Ash faced	nr	356.60
1372 x 1981 pair Ash faced	nr	526.65
44 half hour fire check flush door 50 x 100 frame, architrave both sides, ironmongery PC £60.00 per leaf, decorated.		
762 x 1981 plywood faced	nr	350.41
838 x 1981 plywood faced	nr	392.06
1372 x 1981 pair plywood faced	nr	598.81
44 half hour fire check flush door, polished wired glass panel, 50 x 100 frame, architrave both sides, ironmongery PC £60.00 per leaf, decorated.		
762 x 1981 plywood faced	nr	481.24
838 x 1981 plywood faced	nr	523.05
44 one hour fire check flush door 50 x 100 frame, architrave both sides, ironmongery PC £60.00 per leaf, decorated.		
762 x 1981 plywood faced	nr	380.51
838 x 1981 plywood faced	nr	388.12
Lintels		
Precast prestressed concrete lintels		
100 x 65 x 900	nr	13.35
100 x 65 x 1200	nr	17.17
100 x 65 x 1800	nr	24.29
100 x 65 x 2400	nr	31.35
100 x 65 x 3000	nr	38.21
140 x 65 x 1200	nr	21.56
140 x 65 x 3000	nr	48.61
215 x 65 x 1200	nr	30.75
215 x 65 x 3000	nr	71.89
215 x 65 x 1200	nr	33.13
215 x 65 x 3000	nr	78.49
100 x 140 x 1800	nr	39.63

COMPOSITE PRICES (Cont'd)

INTERNAL DOORS (Cont'd)

		£
Lintels (Cont'd)		
Precast prestressed concrete lintels (Cont'd)		
100 x 140 x 3000	nr	64.05
Galvanized steel lintels - Birtley		
ref INT100; 100 x 900	nr	19.84
ref INT100; 100 x 1050	nr	22.04
ref INT100; 100 x 1200	nr	23.70
ref SB100; 75 x 1200	nr	52.01
ref SB100; 140 x 1800	nr	80.72
ref SB100; 215 x 3000	nr	180.53
ref SB140; 140 x 1200	nr	59.96
ref SB140; 140 x 1800	nr	90.48
ref SB140; 215 x 3000	nr	195.10
ref SBL200; 142 x 1200	nr	74.45
ref SBL200; 142 x 1800	nr	112.47
ref SBL200; 218 x 3000	nr	231.38
ref HS50; 225 x 3900	nr	292.09

WALL FINISHES

Plaster		
Hardwall plaster in two coats		
13 thick	m²	17.96
13 thick, emulsion	m²	22.78
13 thick, oil paint	m²	27.59
13 thick textured plastic coating, stipple	m²	23.58
Lightweight plaster in two coats		
13 thick	m²	15.46
13 thick, emulsion	m²	20.28
13 thick, oil paint	m²	25.09
13 thick textured plastic coating, stipple	m²	21.08
Plasterboard		
Plasterboard for direct decoration		
9.5 thick	m²	15.73
9.5 thick, emulsion	m²	20.55
9.5 thick, oil paint	m²	25.36
9.5 thick textured plastic coating, stipple	m²	21.35
12.5 thick	m²	23.03
12.5 thick, emulsion	m²	27.85
12.5 thick, oil paint	m²	32.66
12.5 thick textured plastic coating, stipple	m²	28.65
15 thick	m²	22.59
15 thick, emulsion	m²	27.41
15 thick, oil paint	m²	32.22
15 thick textured plastic coating, stipple	m²	28.21
two layer 9.5 thick total 19mm thick	m²	28.42
two layer 9.5 + 12.5; total 22mm thick	m²	35.73
two layer 12.5; total 25mm thick	m²	43.03
Plasterboard with 3 plaster skim coat finish		
9.5 thick plasterboard; skim	m²	20.28
9.5 thick plasterboard; skim, emulsion	m²	25.10
9.5 thick plasterboard; skim, oil paint	m²	29.91
9.5 thick plasterboard; skim, textured plastic coating, stipple	m²	17.17
12.5 thick plasterboard and skim	m²	22.14
12.5 thick plasterboard and skim, emulsion	m²	26.96
12.5 thick plasterboard and skim, oil paint	m²	31.77
12.5 thick plasterboard and skim, textured plastic coating; stipple	m²	27.76
15 thick plasterboard and skim	m²	28.38
15 thick plasterboard and skim, emulsion	m²	33.20
15 thick plasterboard and skim, oil paint	m²	38.01
15 thick plasterboard and skim, textured plastic coating; stipple	m²	34.00
two layer 9.5 thick total 21mm thick including skim	m²	32.35
two layer 9.5 + 12.5; total 25mm thick including skim	m²	33.98
two layer 12.5; total 28mm thick including skim	m²	35.45
Gyproc plaster cove		
100 girth	m	8.76
127 girth	m	9.00
Extra		
lining paper PC £1.00/roll	m²	3.79
wall paper PC £6.00/roll	m²	7.39
vinyl coated wall paper PC £7.00/roll	m²	7.66
embossed paper PC £6.00/roll	m²	12.55
wall tiling 100 x 100mm PC £15.00/m²	m²	60.77
wall tiling 150 x 150mm PC £15.00/m²	m²	51.47
wall tiling 150 x 150mm PC £25.00/m²	m²	63.02
Redecorations		
Stripping existing paper and lining with paper PC £1.00 per roll	m²	9.19
Two coats emulsion paint on existing	m²	6.86
One undercoat; one gloss paint on existing	m²	8.89
One undercoat; one eggshell paint on existing	m²	8.96
Textured plastic coating on existing painted plaster	m²	8.90

FLOOR FINISHES

Cement; sand bed		
25 thick	m²	12.83
32 thick	m²	14.96
38 thick	m²	16.55
50 thick	m²	19.94
Cement; sand bed and GA4000 insulation		
25 thick bed and 50 insulation	m²	22.66
32 thick bed and 50 insulation	m²	24.79
38 thick bed and 50 insulation	m²	26.38
50 thick bed and 50 insulation	m²	29.77
25 thick bed and 100 insulation	m²	29.72
32 thick bed and 100 insulation	m²	31.85
38 thick bed and 100 insulation	m²	33.44
50 thick bed and 100 insulation	m²	36.83
Cement, sand bed, 100 insulation and flooring		
25 bed, insulation and quarry tile paving	m²	86.13
32 bed, insulation and quarry tile paving	m²	88.26
38 bed, insulation and quarry tile paving	m²	89.85
50 bed, insulation and quarry tile paving	m²	93.24
25 bed, insulation and 3 pvc sheet	m²	58.10
32 bed, insulation and 3 pvc sheet	m²	60.23
38 bed, insulation and 3 pvc sheet	m²	61.82
50 bed, insulation and 3 pvc sheet	m²	65.21
25 bed, insulation and 2.5 pvc tile	m²	58.10
32 bed, insulation and 2.5 pvc tile	m²	60.23
38 bed, insulation and 2.5 pvc tile	m²	61.82
50 bed, insulation and 2.5 pvc tile	m²	65.21
25 bed, insulation and 20 oak wood block	m²	125.44
32 bed, insulation and 20 oak wood block	m²	127.57
38 bed, insulation and 20 oak wood block	m²	129.16
50 bed, insulation and 20 oak wood block	m²	132.55
25 bed, insulation and 20 maple wood block	m²	137.47
32 bed, insulation and 20 maple wood block	m²	139.60
38 bed, insulation and 20 maple wood block	m²	141.19
50 bed, insulation and 20 maple wood block	m²	144.58
25 bed, insulation and 20 Merbau wood block	m²	134.11
32 bed, insulation and 20 Merbau wood block	m²	136.24
38 bed, insulation and 20 Merbau wood block	m²	137.83
50 bed, insulation and 20 Merbau wood block	m²	141.22
Cement; sand bed; 100 insulation, carpet and underlay		
25 bed, insulation and carpet PC £35/m²	m²	73.27
32 bed, insulation and carpet PC £35/m²	m²	75.40
38 bed, insulation and carpet PC £35/m²	m²	76.99
50 bed, insulation and carpet PC £35/m²	m²	80.38

COMPOSITE PRICES (Cont'd)

		£
FLOOR FINISHES (Cont'd)		
Granolithic pavings		
25 thick	m²	17.76
32 thick	m²	20.10
38 thick	m²	22.08
50 thick	m²	26.20
Granolithic skirtings		
19 thick x 150 high	m	19.54
25 thick x 150 high	m	21.06
32 thick x 150 high	m	22.37
Levelling screed		
Latex levelling screed; one coat		
3 thick average to concrete	m²	12.31
Terrazzo		
300x300x28 tiles; 40 bed; polished	m²	124.46
16 thick laid insitu in bays	m²	92.22
6 thick skirtings laid insitu 75 high	m	31.75
16 thick skirtings laid insitu 150 high	m	46.07
PVC sheet flooring		
2 thick	m²	20.40
3.2 thick	m²	22.71
PVC coved skirting		
100 high set in	m	9.49
100 high sit on	m	9.65
Softwood flooring		
Floor boarding and insulation to concrete		
22 tongued and grooved chipboard and 50 insulation board	m²	24.85
22 tongued and grooved chipboard and 100 insulation board	m²	31.91
Softwood skirting decorated		
19 x 50 chamfered and rounded	m	13.35
19 x 63 chamfered and rounded	m	14.21
32 x 100 chamfered and rounded	m	17.72
19 x 100 square	m	12.89
19 x 150 square	m	14.21
25 x 100 square	m	13.61
25 x 150 square	m	15.29
15 x 100 moulded	m	13.96
19 x 125 moulded	m	13.92
CEILING FINISHES		
Plaster		
Hardwall plaster in two coats		
13 thick	m²	19.98
13 thick, emulsion	m²	23.71
13 thick, oil paint	m²	30.31
13 thick textured plastic coatings, stipple	m²	27.58
Lightweight plaster in two coats		
10 thick	m²	17.19
10 thick, emulsion	m²	20.92
10 thick, oil paint	m²	27.52
10 thick textured plastic coatings, stipple	m²	24.79
Plasterboard		
Plasterboard for direct decoration		
9.5 thick	m²	16.95
9.5 thick, emulsion	m²	20.68
9.5 thick, oil paint	m²	27.28
9.5 thick textured plastic coatings, stipple	m²	24.55
12.5 thick	m²	17.01
12.5 thick, emulsion	m²	20.74
12.5 thick, oil paint	m²	27.34
12.5 thick textured plastic coating, stipple	m²	24.61
two layer 9.5 thick total 19mm thick	m²	30.68
two layer 9.5 + 12.5; total 22mm thick	m²	38.29
two layer 12.5; total 25mm thick	m²	45.74
Plasterboard with 3 plaster skim coat finish		
9.5 thick plasterboard and skim	m²	22.74
9.5 thick plasterboard and skim, emulsion	m²	26.47
9.5 thick plasterboard and skim, oil paint	m²	33.07
9.5 thick plasterboard; skim, textured plastic coating, stipple	m²	30.34
12.5 thick plasterboard and skim	m²	24.82
12.5 thick plasterboard and skim, emulsion	m²	28.55
12.5 thick plasterboard and skim, oil paint	m²	35.15
12.5 thick plasterboard; skim, textured plastic coating, stipple	m²	32.42
two layer 9.5 thick total 21mm thick including skim	m²	36.15
two layer 9.5 + 12.5; total 25mm thick including skim	m²	38.01
two layer 12.5; total 28mm thick including skim	m²	39.70
Suspended ceilings		
300 x 300 x 15.8 plain mineral fibre tile	m²	30.24
300 x 300 x 15.8 textured mineral fibre tile	m²	36.02
300 x 300 patterned tile P.C. £15.00	m²	45.64
600 x 600 x 15.8 plain mineral fibre tile	m²	30.23
600 x 600 x 15.8 drilled mineral fibre tile	m²	36.85
600 x 600 patterned tile P.C. £15.00	m²	45.91
FITTINGS AND FURNISHINGS		
Mirrors		
6mm bevelled edges; silvered; copper backing		
250 x 400	nr	72.43
460 x 600	nr	105.05
600 x 900	nr	147.84
Venetian blinds		
25mm slat; plain colours		
1000 wide x 1200 drop	nr	55.35
2000 wide x 1200 drop	nr	88.11
3000 wide x 1200 drop	nr	116.23
50mm slat; plain colours		
1000 wide x 1200 drop	nr	78.00
2000 wide x 1200 drop	nr	136.52
3000 wide x 1200 drop	nr	186.81
Roller blinds		
self acting roller		
1000 wide x 1200 drop	nr	78.25
2000 wide x 1200 drop	nr	109.18
3000 wide x 1200 drop	nr	150.06
Vertical louvre blinds		
89mm wide louvres		
1000 wide x 1200 drop	nr	61.72
2000 wide x 1200 drop	nr	94.54
3000 wide x 1200 drop	nr	126.40
127mm wide louvres		
1000 wide x 1200 drop	nr	63.01
2000 wide x 1200 drop	nr	95.84
3000 wide x 1200 drop	nr	127.54
Kitchen units		
Pre-assembled domestic kitchen units		
400 floor unit	nr	118.84
500 floor unit	nr	125.17
600 floor unit	nr	142.04
1000 floor unit	nr	178.53
1200 floor unit	nr	168.90
1000 sink unit	nr	178.53
600 floor four drawer unit	nr	208.45
500 wall unit	nr	111.93
600 wall unit	nr	114.22
1200 wall unit	nr	151.75
1200 wall unit	nr	162.67
600 tall store unit with no doors	nr	147.28

COMPOSITE PRICES (Cont'd) £

FITTINGS AND FURNISHINGS (Cont'd)

Kitchen units (Cont'd)

Pre-assembled domestic kitchen units (Cont'd)

600 tall store unit with two doors	nr	276.10
38 work top	m	64.06
plinth	m	16.03
cornice	m	17.07
pelmet	m	17.07

SANITARY APPLIANCES

Sanitary appliance with allowance for waste fittings, traps, overflows, taps and builder's work

Domestic building, with plastic wastes

lavatory basin	nr	260.45
lavatory basin with pedestal	nr	212.21
bath with panels to front and one end	nr	423.79
low level w.c. suite	nr	306.94
stainless steel sink and drainer	nr	193.53
shower	nr	393.42

Commercial building, with copper wastes

lavatory basin	nr	391.33
low level w.c. suite	nr	306.94
bowl type urinal	nr	297.76
stainless steel sink	nr	228.70
drinking fountain	nr	732.70
shower	nr	377.02

DISPOSAL INSTALLATIONS

Soil and vent pipe for ground and first floor

plastic wastes and SVP	nr	334.35
copper wastes and cast iron SVP	nr	1,908.84

WATER INSTALLATIONS

Hot and cold water services domestic building	nr	2,292.60
Gas instantaneous sink water heater	nr	1,191.29
Electric instantaneous sink water heater	nr	1,078.28
Undersink electric water heater	nr	1,170.75
Electric shower unit	nr	372.01

HEATING INSTALLATIONS

Boiler, radiators, pipework, controls and pumps

Domestic building

100m², solid fuel	m²	65.93
100m², gas	m²	60.34
100m², oil	m²	75.22
150m², solid fuel	m²	58.84
150m², gas	m²	52.93
150m², oil	m²	65.78

Commercial building

500m², gas	m²	87.93
500m², oil	m²	102.33
1000m², gas	m²	104.31
1000m², oil	m²	123.71
1500m², gas	m²	121.26
1500m², oil	m²	142.10
2000m², gas	m²	131.75
2000m², oil	m²	155.48
Underfloor heating with polymer pipework and insulation - excludes screed.	m²	45.60

ELECTRICAL INSTALLATIONS

Concealed installation with lighting, power, and ancillary cooker, immersion heater etc. circuit.

100m² domestic building

PVC insulated and sheathed cables	m²	73.68
MICS cables	m²	101.30
steel conduit	m²	118.03

150m² domestic building,

PVC insulated and sheathed cables	m²	66.12
MICS cables	m²	89.47
steel conduit	m²	103.27

500m² commercial building incl light fittings

steel conduit	m²	147.54

1000m² commercial building incl light fittings

steel conduit	m²	156.75

1500m² commercial building incl light fittings

steel conduit	m²	165.97

2000m² commercial building incl light fittings

steel conduit	m²	175.18

LIFT AND ESCALATOR INSTALLATIONS

Light passenger lift, laminate walls, stainless steel doors

3 stop, 8 person	nr	36,693.37
4 stop, 13 person	nr	68,517.06

General purpose passenger lift, laminate walls, stainless steel doors

4 stop, 8 person	nr	67,996.98
5 stop, 13 person	nr	73,643.31
6 stop, 21 person	nr	168,049.96

Service hoist

2 stop, 50 kg	nr	11,029.50

Escalator 30 degree inclination department store specification

3.00m rise	nr	100,548.80

SITE WORK

Kerbs, edgings channels

Precast concrete kerb and foundation

125 x 255 kerb	m	49.89
150 x 305 kerb	m	68.77

Precast concrete edging and foundation

50 x 150 edging	m	34.27
50 x 200 edging	m	40.82
50 x 250 edging	m	47.77

Precast concrete channel and foundation

255 x 125 channel	m	49.22

Granite kerb on edge and foundation

150 x 300 kerb	m	79.62
200 x 300 kerb	m	96.72

Granite kerb laid flat and foundation

300 x 150 kerb	m	83.08
300 x 200 kerb	m	98.53

Pavings

Concrete; 250 excavation, 150 hardcore

150 concrete road tamped	m²	65.15
200 concrete road tamped	m²	73.45
150 concrete and 70 bitumen macadam	m²	84.96
200 concrete and 70 bitumen macadam	m²	93.26
Extra for Ref. A252 fabric reinforcement	m²	8.12
Extra for Ref. C636 fabric reinforcement	m²	12.23

Gravel; 250 excavation; 100 hardcore; 75 clinker;

75 course gravel; 38 blinding gravel	m²	42.90

Gravel; 150 excavation; 100 hardcore;

50 blinding gravel	m²	21.20

Gravel; 150 excavation; 100 hardcore; 50 clinker;

38 blinding gravel	m²	24.84

York Stone; 200 excavation, 150 hardcore

50 paving	m²	157.17
75 paving	m²	209.20

Precast concrete; 200 excavation, 150 hardcore

600 x 450 x 50 slabs	m²	50.34
600 x 600 x 50 slabs	m²	46.47
600 x 750 x 50 slabs	m²	49.52
600 x 900 x 50 slabs	m²	46.88
600 x 450 x 63 slabs	m²	64.55

COMPOSITE PRICES (Cont'd) £

SITE WORK (Cont'd)

Pavings (Cont'd)

Precast concrete; 200 excavation, 150 hardcore (Cont'd)		
600 x 600 x 63 slabs	m²	56.14
600 x 750 x 63 slabs	m²	59.66
600 x 900 x 63 slabs	m²	55.03
50 thick crazy paving	m²	50.27
Precast concrete; 200 excavation, 150 hardcore		
200 x 100 x 50 Blocks on 50 sand	m²	83.56
Granite Sets; 300 excavation, 100 hardcore		
150 thick on 100 concrete	m²	238.39
Cobbles; 200 excavation, 150 hardcore		
Cobbles set in 100 concrete	m²	129.09

Seeding/Turfing

Seeding; Cultivating;digging over one spit deep; removing debris; weeding; weedkiller; Grass seed; fertilizer; maintain	m²	9.59
Seeding; 150 excavation; 150 topsoil; weedkiller; Grass seed; fertilizer; maintain	m²	19.81
Turfing; Cultivating;digging over one spit deep; removing debris; weeding; weedkiller; Turf; maintain	m²	13.42
Turfing; 150 excavation; 150 topsoil; weedkiller; Turf; maintain	m²	23.64

Walls

Brick wall, excavation 600 deep concrete foundation, 215 wall with piers at 3m centres in facings PC £300/1000, damp proof course.		
900 high brick on edge coping	m	246.40
1800 high brick on edge coping	m	394.69
900 high 300 x 75 PCC coping	m	289.85
1800 high 300 x 75 PCC coping	m	438.14

Fences

Plastic coated chain link fencing, posts at 2743 centres.		
900 high 38 x 38 angle iron posts, two line wires	m	23.61
1200 high 38 x 38 angle iron posts, two line wires	m	26.97
1500 high 38 x 38 angle iron posts, three line wires	m	29.61
1800 high 38 x 38 angle iron posts, three line wires	m	34.96
900 high concrete posts two line wires	m	29.44
1200 high concrete posts two line wires	m	33.38
1500 high concrete posts three line wires	m	40.61
1800 high concrete posts three line wires	m	44.83
Gates; chain link; posts		
1000 x 1800	nr	797.22
Close boarded fencing, 100 x 100 posts at 2743 centres 25 x 100 pales, 25 x 150 gravel boards, creosote, post holes filled with concrete		
1200 high two arris rails	m	68.25
1500 high three arris rails	m	81.55
1800 high three arris rails	m	88.80
Gates; timber		
900 x 1200	nr	177.19
900 x 1500	nr	184.87

DRAINAGE

Drains

Vitrified clay sleeve joint drain, excavation and backfill.		
100 diameter 500 deep	m	38.80
100 diameter 750 deep	m	43.47
100 diameter 1000 deep	m	48.00
100 diameter 1500 deep	m	58.19
150 diameter 500 deep	m	58.48
150 diameter 750 deep	m	63.23
150 diameter 1000 deep	m	67.84
150 diameter 1500 deep	m	78.19
Vitrified clay sleeve joint drain, excavation 150 bed and surround pea shingle and backfill.		
100 diameter 500 deep	m	64.44
100 diameter 750 deep	m	69.11
100 diameter 1000 deep	m	73.64
100 diameter 1500 deep	m	83.83
150 diameter 500 deep	m	89.58
150 diameter 750 deep	m	94.33
150 diameter 1000 deep	m	98.94
150 diameter 1500 deep	m	109.29
Vitrified clay sleeve joint drain, excavation 150 bed and haunch concrete and backfill.		
100 diameter 500 deep	m	61.61
100 diameter 750 deep	m	66.28
100 diameter 1000 deep	m	70.81
100 diameter 1500 deep	m	81.47
150 diameter 500 deep	m	81.52
150 diameter 750 deep	m	86.26
150 diameter 1000 deep	m	90.87
150 diameter 1500 deep	m	101.22
Vitrified clay sleeve joint drain, excavation 150 bed and surround concrete and back fill.		
100 diameter 500 deep	m	78.98
100 diameter 750 deep	m	83.65
100 diameter 1000 deep	m	88.18
100 diameter 1500 deep	m	98.37
150 diameter 500 deep	m	99.83
150 diameter 750 deep	m	104.58
150 diameter 1000 deep	m	109.19
150 diameter 1500 deep	m	119.54
Upvc drain, excavation 50 mm bed sand and backfill.		
110 diameter 500 deep	m	26.26
110 diameter 750 deep	m	30.93
110 diameter 1000 deep	m	35.46
110 diameter 1500 deep	m	45.65
160 diameter 500 deep	m	41.73
160 diameter 750 deep	m	46.48
160 diameter 1000 deep	m	51.09
160 diameter 1500 deep	m	61.44
Upvc drain, excavation bed, and surround pea shingle and back fill.		
110 diameter 500 deep	m	36.66
110 diameter 750 deep	m	41.33
110 diameter 1000 deep	m	45.86
110 diameter 1500 deep	m	56.05
160 diameter 500 deep	m	53.65
160 diameter 750 deep	m	58.40
160 diameter 1000 deep	m	63.01
160 diameter 1500 deep	m	73.36
Upvc drain, excavation bed and haunch concrete and back fill.		
110 diameter 500 deep	m	61.45
110 diameter 750 deep	m	66.12
110 diameter 1000 deep	m	70.65
110 diameter 1500 deep	m	80.84
160 diameter 500 deep	m	63.16
160 diameter 750 deep	m	67.91
160 diameter 1000 deep	m	72.52
160 diameter 1500 deep	m	82.86
Upvc drain, excavation bed and surround concrete and back fill.		
110 diameter 500 deep	m	64.21
110 diameter 750 deep	m	68.88
110 diameter 1000 deep	m	73.41
110 diameter 1500 deep	m	83.60
160 diameter 500 deep	m	89.11

COMPOSITE PRICES (Cont'd)

DRAINAGE (Cont'd)

Drains (Cont'd)

		£
Upvc drain, excavation bed and surround concrete and back fill. (Cont'd)		
160 diameter 750 deep	m	93.86
160 diameter 1000 deep	m	98.47
160 diameter 1500 deep	m	108.82
Cast iron drain, excavation and back fill.		
100 diameter 500 deep	m	77.01
100 diameter 750 deep	m	81.68
100 diameter 1000 deep	m	86.21
100 diameter 1500 deep	m	96.40
150 diameter 500 deep	m	122.22
150 diameter 750 deep	m	126.97
150 diameter 1000 deep	m	131.58
150 diameter 1500 deep	m	141.93
Cast iron drain, excavation, bed and haunch concrete and back fill.		
100 diameter 500 deep	m	114.34
100 diameter 750 deep	m	119.01
100 diameter 1000 deep	m	123.54
100 diameter 1500 deep	m	133.73
150 diameter 500 deep	m	146.07
150 diameter 750 deep	m	150.82
150 diameter 1000 deep	m	155.43
150 diameter 1500 deep	m	165.78
Cast iron drain, excavation, bed and surround concrete and back fill.		
100 diameter 500 deep	m	117.19
100 diameter 750 deep	m	121.86
100 diameter 1000 deep	m	126.39
100 diameter 1500 deep	m	136.58
150 diameter 500 deep	m	172.22
150 diameter 750 deep	m	176.97
150 diameter 1000 deep	m	181.58
150 diameter 1500 deep	m	191.93

Brick manhole

Excavation; 150 concrete bed; 215 class B engineering brick walls; 100 clayware main channel; concrete benching; step irons and cast iron manhole cover		
600 x 450, two branches 750 deep	nr	763.76
600 x 450, two branches 1500 deep	nr	1,302.00
750 x 450, three branches 750 deep	nr	1,136.61
750 x 450, three branches 1000 deep	nr	1,346.38
750 x 450, three branches 1500 deep	nr	1,707.38
900 x 600, five branches 750 deep	nr	1,305.63
900 x 600, five branches 1000 deep	nr	1,545.88
900 x 600, five branches 1500 deep	nr	1,976.84

Concrete circular manhole

Excavation; 150 concrete bed; manhole rings; cover slab; 100 clayware main channel; concrete benching; step irons; cast iron manhole cover		
900 dia., two branches 750 deep	nr	1,135.25
900 dia., two branches 1000 deep	nr	1,415.05
900 dia., two branches 1500 deep	nr	1,755.09
1050 dia., three branches 750 deep	nr	1,351.73
1050 dia., three branches 1000 deep	nr	1,615.72
1050 dia., three branches 1500 deep	nr	2,090.59
1200 dia., five branches 750 deep	nr	1,582.35
1200 dia., five branches 1000 deep	nr	1,861.10
1200 dia., five branches 1500 deep	nr	2,312.15

Concrete rectangular manhole

Excavation; concrete bed; manhole sections; base unit; cover slab with integral cover		
610 x 457 x 500 deep	nr	437.17
610 x 457 x 750 deep	nr	589.24
610 x 457 x 1000 deep	nr	704.48

Polypropolene Inspection chamber

Excavation; Polypropolene Inspection chamber cast iron manhole cover		
250 diameter, 600 deep	nr	216.03
450 diameter, 600 deep	nr	426.49
450 diameter, 1000 deep	nr	589.30

Concrete gullies

Excavation; concrete bed; gully; bricks; cast iron road grating		
375 diameter x 750 deep	nr	819.83
375 diameter x 900 deep	nr	865.70
450 diameter x 750 deep	nr	639.22
450 diameter x 900 deep	nr	683.96

Vitrified clay gullies

Excavation; concrete bed; gully; grating		
trapped round; 100 outlet	nr	673.32

Pvc-u gullies

Excavation; concrete bed; bottle gully; grating		
200 diameter top; trapped round	nr	172.74

This page left blank intentionally

STANDARD RATES OF WAGES

WAGES

Note: Wage agreements and amendments to the following made after the end of October 2021 and notified to us prior to publication will be noted within the Preliminaries section or as noted herein.

NATIONAL MINIMUM WAGE

The hourly rate for the minimum wage must apply and depends on age or status as an apprentice.

National Living Wage and the National Minimum Wage

	25 +	21 to 24	18 to 20	Under18	Apprentice
1st April 2021	£8.91	£8.36	£6.56	£4.62	£4.30
1st April 2022	£9.50	£9.18	£6.83	£4.81	£4.81

Apprentices are entitled to the apprentice rate if they're either aged under 19 or aged 19 or over and in the first year of their apprenticeship.

Apprentices are entitled to the minimum wage for their age if they are aged 19 or over and have completed the first year of their apprenticeship

CONSTRUCTION - ENGLAND, SCOTLAND AND WALES

Following negotiations between the parties to the Construction Industry Joint Council, the Council typically adopt recommendations for a one-year agreement on pay and conditions.

With effect on and from Monday, 28th June 2021 the following basic rates of pay, allowances and additional payments were adopted.

Note: The rates shown below are weekly rates. The hourly equivalents for a 39 hour week are shown in brackets.

1 ENTITLEMENT TO BASIC AND ADDITIONAL RATES -WR.1

28th June 2021	per week £	per hour £
Craft Operative	506.61	(12.99)
Skill Rate - 1	482.04	(12.36)
- 2	464.49	(11.91)
- 3	434.46	(11.14)
- 4	410.67	(10.53)
General Operative	381.03	(9.77)

Apprentice Rates – WR. 1.4.2

28th June 2021	per week £	per hour £
Year – 1	227.76	(5.84)
Year – 2	271.83	(6.97)
Year - 3 Without NVQ 2	317.07	(8.13)
Year - 3 with NVQ 2	405.60	(10.40)
Year - 3 with NVQ 3	506.61	(12.99)
On completion of apprenticeship with NVQ 2	506.61	(12.99)

2. BONUS - WR.2

It shall be open to employers and operatives on any job to agree a bonus scheme based on measured output and productivity for any operation or operations on that particular job.

3. DAILY FARE AND TRAVEL ALLOWANCES – WR.5

The taxed and non-taxed daily travel allowance increased and qualifying conditions and allowances are calculated per mile.

4. STORAGE OF TOOLS - WR.12

Employers maximum liability is £750.00 per annum

5. SUBSISTENCE ALLOWANCE - WR.15

£ 41.66 per night (approved by HMRC and is subject to the operative completing the relevant applications)

6. HOLIDAYS WITH PAY – WR 18.3 and 19.2

Annual Holidays – WR 18.3

Operative's pay does not vary with work done WR 18.3.1
A week's pay is the normal weekly wage as defined by the contract of employment.

Operative's pay varies with work done WR 18.3.2
A week's pay is calculated from the average of the immediate previous 12 weeks, from earnings during the normal working week as defined by the contract of employment. Weeks the operative is absent due to sickness are excluded.

Public/Bank Holidays – WR 19.2
Calculated all as Annual Holidays, WR 18.3.

7. SICK PAY - WR.20

Effective on and from 28th June 2021 employers whose terms and conditions of employment incorporate the Working Rule Agreement of the CIJC should make a payment to operatives, who are absent from work due to sickness or injury, of £138.38 per week in addition to Statutory Sick Pay.

8. BENEFIT SCHEMES WR 21

Death benefit – WR 21.1
The operative is entitled to insurance cover for £40,000. Such benefit to be doubled to £80,000 if death occurs either at work or travelling to and from work (effective from 1st January 2019).

EasyBuild pension contributions – WR 21.2
The minimum employer contribution shall be £5.00 per week. Where the operative contributes between £5.01 and £10.00 per week the employer shall increase the minimum contribution to match that of the operative up to a maximum of £10.00 per week.

The EasyBuild pension is now closed and since 1st September 2017 all employees have been transferred to the Peoples Pension.

The Pension Regulator - Workplace Pension
Employers must provide a workplace pension for eligible staff through automatic enrolment. Eligible staff are those who ordinarily work in the UK, are aged between 22 and state pension age, with earnings in excess of £6,240.

Minimum contribution rates of qualifying earnings:

Prior to 5th April 2018	Employer 1% : Total 2%
6th April 2018 to 5th April 2019	Employer 2% : Total 5%
From 6th April 2019	Employer 3% : Total 8%

Note: Contributions will be based on an employee's qualifying earnings, currently between £6,240 and £50,270 per annum before tax.

WAGES (Cont'd)
CONSTRUCTITON - ENGLAND, SCOTLAND AND WALES (Cont'd)

The following tables give the weekly rate of wages since 2000 (based on 39 hours).

	Craft Operative	Skilled Operative Rate: 1	2	3	4	General Building Operative
June 26th 2000	247.65	235.95	227.37	212.94	200.85	186.42
June 25th 2001	261.30	248.82	239.85	224.64	211.77	196.56
June 24th 2002	284.70	271.05	261.30	244.53	230.49	214.11
June 30th 2003	299.13	284.70	274.56	257.01	242.19	225.03
June 28th 2004	320.38	305.37	294.06	273.34	259.35	241.02
June 27th 2005	351.00	334.62	322.14	301.47	284.31	264.03
June 26th 2006	363.48	346.32	333.45	312.00	294.45	273.39
June 25th 2007	379.08	361.53	347.88	325.65	306.93	285.09
June 30th 2008	401.70	382.98	368.94	345.15	325.65	302.25
September 5th 2011	407.94	388.83	374.40	350.22	330.72	306.93
January 7th 2013	416.13	396.63	381.81	357.24	337.35	313.17
June 30th 2014	429.00	408.72	393.12	367.77	347.49	322.53
June 30th 2015	441.87	420.81	405.21	379.08	358.02	332.28
July 25th 2016	452.79	431.34	415.35	388.44	366.99	340.47
June 26th 2017	465.27	443.04	426.66	399.36	377.13	349.83
June 25th 2018	480.09	457.08	440.31	412.23	398.22	361.14
June 24th 2019	494.13	470.34	453.18	423.93	400.53	371.67
June 22nd 2020	494.13	470.34	453.18	423.93	400.53	371.67
June 28th 2021	506.61	482.04	464.49	434.46	410.67	381.03

CONSTRUCITON - NORTHERN IRELAND

The Joint Council for the Building and Civil Engineering Industry in Northern Ireland has agreed wage awards for the Building and Civil Engineering Industry (Northern Ireland). For information on current rates contact:-

Construction Employers Federation (Northern Ireland), 143 Malone Road, Belfast, BT9 6SX
Tel: 028 9087 7143 Email: mail@cefni.co.uk Website: www.cefni.co.uk

HOLIDAYS WITH PAY

From 31st July 2000, holiday pay was equivalent to basic wages to comply with the Working Time Regulations.

The total number of days holiday from 23 June 2016 was 29 days and this increased to 30 days for the 2018 leave year.

HEATING, VENTILATING, AIR CONDITIONING, PIPING AND DOMESTIC ENGINEERING CONTRACTS

Rates agreed between the Building and Engineering Services Association (formerly HVCA) and Unite.

RATES OF WAGES

All districts of the United Kingdom

Wage agreements effective from 7th October 2019. Note: a pay freeze occurred in 2020

RATES AND ALLOWANCES	From 7th October 2019	From 4th October 2021	From 3rd October 2022
Hourly Rate			
	£	£	£
Building Services Engineering Supervisor	21.59	22.02	22.46
Team Leader (formerly Foreman)	17.70	18.05	18.41
Senior Craftsman (+ Supervisory Responsibility and 2 Units of Responsibility Allowance)	16.94	17.28	17.62
Senior Craftsman (+ Supervisory Responsibility and 1 Unit of Responsibility Allowance)	16.37	16.69	17.02
Senior Craftsman (+ Supervisory Responsibility)	15.79	16.11	16.42
Senior Craftsman (+ 2 Units of Responsibility Allowance)	15.79	16.11	16.42
Senior Craftsman (+ 1 Unit of Responsibility Allowance)	15.21	15.51	15.82
Senior Craftsman	14.63	14.92	15.22
Craftsman (+ 3 Units of Responsibility Allowance)	15.21	15.51	15.82
Craftsman (+ 2 Units of Responsibility Allowance)	14.63	14.92	15.22
Craftsman(+ 1 Unit of Responsibility Allowance)	14.05	14.33	14.62
Craftsman	13.47	13.74	14.02
Installer	12.16	12.40	12.65
Adult Trainee	10.25	10.46	10.67
Mate (18 and over)	10.25	10.46	10.67
Modern Apprentices			
Senior	12.16	12.40	12.65
Intermediate	9.43	9.62	9.81
Junior	6.65	6.78	6.92
Responsibility Allowances (Senior Craftsmen) per hour			
Second welding skill	0.58	0.59	0.58
Gas responsibility	0.58	0.59	0.60
Supervisory responsibility	1.16	1.18	1.20
Responsibility Allowance (Craftsmen) per hour			
Second welding skill	0.58	0.59	0.60
Gas responsibility	0.58	0.59	0.60
Supervisory responsibility	1.16	1.18	1.20
DAILY ABNORMAL CONDITIONS MONEY £ per day	3.45	3.52	3.59
LODGING ALLOWANCE - £ per night	41.70	Awaiting agreement	Awaiting agreement

DAILY TRAVELLING ALLOWANCE - Scale 1

C = Craftsmen including installers
M & A = Mates, Apprentices, Adult Trainees.

Direct distance from centre to job in miles	From 7 Oct 2019		From 4 Oct 2021		From 3 Oct 2022	
	C	M & A	C	M & A	C	M & A
Over-Not exceeding	£	£	£	£	£	£
0 - 15	7.69	7.69	7.84	7.84	8.00	8.00
15 - 20	10.51	10.11	10.72	10.31	10.93	10.52
20 - 30	14.93	13.95	15.23	14.23	15.54	14.52
30 - 40	18.10	16.71	18.46	17.05	18.83	17.40
40 - 50	21.39	19.44	21.82	19.82	22.26	20.23

DAILY TRAVELLING ALLOWANCE - Scale 2 – (Outside M25)

C = Craftsmen including installers
M & A = Mates, Apprentices, Adult Trainees.

Direct distance from centre to job in miles	From 7 Oct 2019		From 4 Oct 2021		From 3 Oct 2022	
	C	M & A	C	M & A	C	M & A
Over-Not exceeding	£	£	£	£	£	£
15 - 20	2.82	2.41	2.88	2.46	2.94	2.51
20 - 30	7.23	6.26	7.38	6.39	7.53	6.52
30 - 40	10.41	9.00	10.62	9.18	10.84	9.37
40 - 50	13.72	11.72	14.00	11.96	14.28	12.20

Note: Ductwork Erection Operatives, are entitled to the same rates and allowances as the parallel fitter grades shown.

HEATING, VENTILATING AND DOMESTIC ENGINEERING CONTRACTS (Cont'd)

WEEKLY HOLIDAY CREDIT VALUES

An industry holiday scheme is no longer centrally operated.

WELFARE CONTRIBUTIONS

The employer must make the following Weekly Welfare Contribution to ensure compliance through Welplan.

WELFARE CONTRIBUTION	From 7th October 2019	From 4th October 2021	From 3rd October 2022
	£	£	£
Weekly Rate – All Operatives	9.65	9.98	10.07

WEEKLY PENSION CONTRIBUTIONS – EMPLOYERS' AND EMPLOYEE CONTRIBUTIONS

National Agreement Grade and Allowance(s)		*From 4 October 2021*			*From 3 October 2022*		
Pension Contribution Rate – Percentage of pre-tax basic pay (hourly rate x 37½):	**Employer** **Employee**	**5 %** ***4 %***			**5 %** ***4 %***		
	Credit Value Category	Employer Contribution £	Employee Contribution £	Total Contribution £	Employer Contribution £	Employee Contribution £	Total Contribution £
Building Services Engineering Supervisor	y	41.31	33.05	74.36	42.11	33.69	72.88
Team Leader (formerly Foreman)	a	33.86	27.09	60.95	34.54	27.63	62.17
Senior Craftsman (+ Supervisory Responsibility and 2 Units of Responsibility Allowance)	z	32.42	25.94	58.36	33.06	26.45	59.51
Senior Craftsman (+ Supervisory Responsibility and 1 Unit of Responsibility Allowance)	b	31.31	25.05	56.36	31.93	25.55	57.46
Senior Craftsman (+ Supervisory Responsibility)	c	30.21	24.17	54.38	30.81	24.65	55.46
Senior Craftsman (+ 2 units of Responsibility Allowance)	c	30.21	24.17	54.38	30.81	24.65	55.46
Senior Craftsman (+ 1 unit of Responsibility Allowance)	d	29.10	23.28	52.38	29.68	23.75	53.43
Senior Craftsman	e	27.99	22.40	50.39	28.56	22.82	51.41
Craftsman (+ 3 units of Responsibility Allowance)	d	29.08	23.27	52.35	29.68	23.75	53.43
Craftsman (+ 2 units of Responsibility Allowance)	e	27.98	22.38	50.36	29.64	23.72	53.36
Craftsman (+ 1 unit of Responsibility Allowance)	F	26.87	21.50	48.37	28.52	22.82	51.34
Craftsman	g	25.76	20.61	46.37	27.39	21.92	49.31
Installer	h	23.27	18.62	41.89	23.72	18.98	42.70
Adult Trainee	i	19.61	15.69	35.30	19.85	16.00	35.85
Mate (18 and over)	i	19.61	15.69	35.30	19.85	16.00	35.85
Senior **Modern Apprentice**	h	23.27	18.62	41.89	23.74	18.99	42.73
Intermediate **Modern Apprentice**	j	18.01	14.43	32.47	18.39	14.72	33.11
Junior **Modern Apprentice**	k	12.73	10.19	22.92	12.98	10.38	23.36

Pension contributions rates:

5th February 2018 - Employer = 5 % and Employee = 2.25 %
1st October 2018 - Employer = 5 % and Employee = 3 %
1st April 2019 - Employer = 5 % and Employee = 4 %
7th October 2019 - Employer = 5 % and Employee = 4 %

For premium rates explanations, overtime payments, fuller details and general conditions the reader is advised to obtain a copy of the National Working Rule Agreement available from:

Building and Engineering Services Association
(BESA) Publications Department,
Rotherwick House, 3 Thomas More St,
London, E1W 1YZ.
Email: contact@thebesa.com
Tel: 020 7313 4900;
www.thebesa.com

JOINT INDUSTRY BOARD FOR THE ELECTRICAL CONTRACTING INDUSTRY

JIB INDUSTRIAL DETERMINATION 2017 - 2020

Promulgated by the JIB National Board to be effective from the dates shown. Note: A pay freeze occurred in 2021 and no rates were set

WAGE RATES

There are different wage rates applied to JIB Graded operatives working on site, depending on whether the employer transports them to site or whether they provide their own transport. The two categories are:

Job Employed (Transport Provided)
Payable to operatives who are transported to and from the job by their employer. Operatives shall also be entitled to payment of a Mileage Rate, when travelling in their own time, as detailed in the appropriate scale.

Job Employed (Own Transport)
Payable to operatives who travel by their own means to and from the job. Operatives under this category shall be entitled to payment of a Mileage Allowance and when travelling in their own time to a Mileage Rate, as detailed in the appropriate scale.

There are separate rates to accommodate a) London workers and b) those few operatives who are employed permanently at the shop and who do not work on site. These rates are shown in the appropriate table.

WAGES 2022

From and including **3rd January 2022,** the JIB hourly rates for Job Employed operatives, are shown below.

(i) National Standard Rates

Grade	Transport Provided	Own Transport	Shop Employed
Electrical / Site Technician Mechanical Technician Cable Installation Supervisor (or equivalent specialist grade)	£18.97	£19.94	£17.75
Approved Electrician Advanced Craftsperson Cable Foreman Approved Jointer (or equivalent specialist grade)	£16.78	£17.70	£15.54
Electrician Craftsperson Leading Cable Hand Jointer (or equivalent specialist grade)	£15.36	£16.32	£14.16
ECS Experienced Worker Cardholder ECS Mature Candidate Assessment Cardholder Trainee Electrician (Stage 3) Mechanical Trainee (Stage 3)	£14.62	£15.51	£13.46
Trainee Electrician (Stage 2) Mechanical Trainee (Stage 2) Senior Graded Electrical Trainee Electrical Improver	£13.81	£14.71	£12.77
Trainee Electrician (Stage 1) Mechanical Trainee (Stage 1) Adult Trainee Labourer	£12.20	£13.10	£10.94

(ii) London Rate

for Operatives engaged upon work falling within the terms of JIB National Working Rule 6.2 will be:

Grade	Transport Provided	Own Transport	Shop Employed
Electrical / Site Technician Mechanical Technician Cable Installation Supervisor (or equivalent specialist grade)	£21.27	£22.31	£19.87
Approved Electrician Advanced Craftsperson Cable Foreman Approved Jointer (or equivalent specialist grade)	£18.78	£19.82	£17.40
Electrician Craftsperson Leading Cable Hand Jointer (or equivalent specialist grade)	£17.20	£18.29	£15.87
ECS Experienced Worker Cardholder ECS Mature Candidate Assessment Cardholder Trainee Electrician (Stage 3) Mechanical Trainee (Stage 3)	£16.33	£17.38	£15.08
Trainee Electrician (Stage 2) Mechanical Trainee (Stage 2) Senior Graded Electrical Trainee Electrical Improver	£15.47	£16.47	£14.50
Trainee Electrician (Stage 1) Mechanical Trainee (Stage 1) Adult Trainee Labourer	£13.68	£14.68	£12.26

Apprentices registered on or after 7th January 2013

There are 2 different rates of pay for apprentices determined by whether the apprentice is at work, or, at college or the equivalent.

(i) National Standard Rates

	At College	At Work
Apprentice (Stage 4)	£11.02	£12.15
Apprentice (Stage 3)	£10.35	£11.31
Apprentice (Stage 2)	£ 7.10	£ 7.89
Apprentice (Stage 1)	£ 4.92	£ 5.59

ii) London Rate

	At College	At Work
Apprentice (Stage 4)	£12.36	£13.62
Apprentice (Stage 3)	£11.59	£12.66
Apprentice (Stage 2)	£ 8.02	£ 8.86
Apprentice (Stage 1)	£ 5.51	£ 6.26

JOINT INDUSTRY BOARD FOR THE ELECTRICAL CONTRACTING INDUSTRY (Cont'd)

WAGES 2023

From and including **2nd January 2023,** the JIB hourly rates for Job Employed operatives, shall be:

(i) National Standard Rates

Grade	Transport Provided	Own Transport	Shop Employed
Electrical / Site Technician Mechanical Technician Cable Installation Supervisor (or equivalent specialist grade)	£19.44	£20.44	£18.19
Approved Electrician Advanced Craftsperson Cable Foreman Approved Jointer (or equivalent specialist grade)	£17.20	£18.14	£15.93
Electrician Craftsperson Leading Cable Hand Jointer (or equivalent specialist grade)	£15.74	£16.73	£14.51
ECS Experienced Worker Cardholder ECS Mature Candidate Assessment Cardholder Trainee Electrician (Stage 3) Mechanical Trainee (Stage 3)	£14.99	£15.90	£13.80
Trainee Electrician (Stage 2) Mechanical Trainee (Stage 2) Senior Graded Electrical Trainee Electrical Improver	£14.16	£15.08	£13.09
Trainee Electrician (Stage 1) Mechanical Trainee (Stage 1) Adult Trainee Labourer	£12.50	£13.43	£11.21

(ii) London Rate

for Operatives engaged upon work falling within the terms of JIB National Working Rule 6.2 will be:

Grade	Transport Provided	Own Transport	Shop Employed
Electrical / Site Technician Mechanical Technician Cable Installation Supervisor (or equivalent specialist grade)	£21.80	£22.87	£20.37
Approved Electrician Advanced Craftsperson Cable Foreman Approved Jointer (or equivalent specialist grade)	£19.25	£20.32	£17.84
Electrician Craftsperson Leading Cable Hand Jointer (or equivalent specialist grade)	£17.63	£18.75	£16.27
ECS Experienced Worker Cardholder ECS Mature Candidate Assessment Cardholder Trainee Electrician (Stage 3) Mechanical Trainee (Stage 3)	£16.74	£17.81	£15.46
Trainee Electrician (Stage 2) Mechanical Trainee (Stage 2) Senior Graded Electrical Trainee Electrical Improver	£15.86	£16.88	£14.86
Trainee Electrician (Stage 1) Mechanical Trainee (Stage 1) Adult Trainee Labourer	£14.02	£15.05	£12.57

Apprentices registered on or after 7th January 2013

There are 2 different rates of pay for apprentices determined by whether the apprentice is at work, or, at college or the equivalent.

(i) National Standard Rates

	At College	At Work
Apprentice (Stage 4)	£11.30	£12.45
Apprentice (Stage 3)	£10.61	£11.59
Apprentice (Stage 2)	£ 7.28	£ 8.09
Apprentice (Stage 1)	£ 5.04	£ 5.73

ii) London Rate

	At College	At Work
Apprentice (Stage 4)	£12.66	£13.96
Apprentice (Stage 3)	£11.88	£12.98
Apprentice (Stage 2)	£ 8.22	£ 9.08
Apprentice (Stage 1)	£ 5.65	£ 6.42

Further details of the wage agreement, allowances and working rules may be obtained on written application to the Joint Industry Board for the Electrical Contracting Industry, Kingswood House, 47/51 Sidcup Hill, Sidcup, Kent DA14 6HP. Email: administration@jib.org.uk

THE NATIONAL JOINT COUNCIL FOR THE LAYING SIDE OF THE MASTIC ASPHALT INDUSTRY

Operative Date	Spreaders	Mixermen	Potman	Classified Labourers
25th June 2018	10.91	10.09	10.09	10.09
24th June 2019	11.24	10.39	10.39	10.39
28th June 2021	11.52	10.65	10.65	10.65

The basic working week is 39 hours, work executed after 39 hours is at an agreed rate. For further information as approved by the National Joint Council for the Laying Side of the Mastic Asphalt Industry contact:-

Mastic Asphalt Council Ltd, 27 Greenways Crescent, Shoreham by Sea, Sussex, BN43 6HR.
Tel: 01273 242778 : Email: info@masticasphaltcouncil.co.uk : www.masticasphaltcouncil.co.uk

THE JOINT INDUSTRY BOARD FOR PLUMBING MECHANICAL ENGINEERING SERVICES IN ENGLAND AND WALES

At the time of writing no rates have been agreed for 2021 and it is thought a pay freeze will be announced.

Basic hourly rates of pay inclusive of tool allowance

		From 6th January 2020	From 3rd January 2022	From 2nd January 2023
(a)	**Operatives**			
	Technical Plumber & Gas Service Technician	£17.71	£18.06	£18.60
	Advanced Plumber & Gas Service Engineer	£15.94	£16.26	£16.75
	Plumber & Gas Service Fitter	£13.69	£13.96	£14.38
(b)	**Apprentices**			
	4th year of training............................	£10.55	£10.76	£11.08
	3rd year of training............................	£ 8.58	£ 8.75	£ 9.01
	2nd year of training............................	£ 7.61	£ 7.76	£ 7.99
	1st year of training............................	£ 6.62	£ 6.75	£ 6.95
(c)	**Adult Trainees**			
	3rd - 6 months of employment	£11.92	£11.92	£11.92
	2nd - 6 months of employment	£11.45	£11.45	£11.45
	1st - 6 months of employment	£10.68	£10.68	£10.68

- Notes
- Operative covers Plumbers, Gas Service Fitters, Mechanical Pipe Fitters and Heating Fitters

Working Hours and Overtime

The normal working week shall be 37.5 hours

Overtime:- Each week, 37.5 hours at normal rates are to be worked (Monday to Friday) before overtime rates shall apply
Rate:- Overtime hours worked Monday to Friday shall be paid at time and a half up to 8.00pm and double time after 8pm.

Responsibility/Incentive Pay allowance

Employers may, in consultation with the employees concerned, enhance the basic graded rates of pay by the payment of an additional amount, as per the bands shown below, where it is agreed that their work involves extra responsibility, productivity or flexibility.

		From 6th Jan 2020
Band 1	additional hourly rate of	up to £0.32
Band 2	an additional rate of	up to £0.54
Band 3	an additional rate of	up to £0.80
Band 4	an additional rate of	up to £1.05

This allowance forms part of an operative's basic rate of pay and shall be used to calculate premium payments. It is payable EITHER on a contract-by-contract basis OR on an annual review basis

Major Projects Agreement

When a job is designated a Major Project additional supplements apply dependent on Operative type and location.

ANNUAL HOLIDAY PAY

The total holiday entitlement was increased to 32 days annual leave from the 6th January 2020 inclusive of Public holidays.

PENSION SCHEME

The Plumbing Pension scheme has been closed.

From 1st July 2019, plumbing employers should enrol all operatives within their employment, who are under state pension age, in an 'auto-enrolment' or 'qualifying' pension scheme. The minimum rates are in addition to their hourly rates of pay and are set out below.

From 1st July 2019
Employee @ 3.75%   Employer @ 7.5%

The JIB-PMES has nominated 'The People's Pension' as the preferred pension scheme provider. This isn't compulsory but the employer must register their scheme with the Plumbing Joint Industry Board.

Further information can be obtained from:

The Joint Industry Board for Plumbing Mechanical Engineering Services in England and Wales,
Lovell House, Sandpiper Court,
Phoenix Business Park, Eaton Socon,
St Neots, Cambridgeshire PE19 8EP

Tel: 01480 476925 : Fax: 01480 403081
Email: info@jib-pmes.rog.uk

NATIONAL INSURANCES

Employers Contribution:

April 2010	12.8% of employee's earnings above the earnings threshold where exceeding £110.00 per week
April 2011	13.8% of employee's earnings above the earnings threshold where exceeding £136.00 per week
April 2012	13.8% of employee's earnings above the earnings threshold where exceeding £144.00 per week
April 2013	13.8% of employee's earnings above the earnings threshold where exceeding £148.00 per week
April 2014	13.8% of employee's earnings above the earnings threshold where exceeding £153.00 per week
April 2015/2016	13.8% of employee's earnings above the earnings threshold where exceeding £156.00 per week
April 2017	13.8% of employee's earnings above the earnings threshold where exceeding £157.00 per week
April 2018	13.8% of employee's earnings above the earnings threshold where exceeding £162.00 per week
April 2019	13.8% of employee's earnings above the earnings threshold where exceeding £166.00 per week
April 2020	13.8% of employee's earnings above the earnings threshold where exceeding £169.00 per week
April 2021	13.8% of employee's earnings above the earnings threshold where exceeding £170.00 per week

Note: If employer is under 21, or an apprentice under 25, employers contributions may only be due when earnings threshold exceeds £967.00 per week.

CITB LEVY

The CITB levies applicable following The Industrial Training Levy (Construction Board) orders are as follows:

The Industrial Training Levy (Construction Industry Training Board) Order 2012

Date came into force	Payroll	Labour only
28th March 2012	0.5%	1.5%
6th April 2015 (2016 Levy)	0.5%	1.25%
6th April 2016 (2017 Levy)	0.35%	1.25%
6th April 2021 (2020 Levy)	0.175%	0.625%
6th April 2022 (2021 Levy	0.35%	1.25%

Note: Labour only rate applies to CIS Subcontractors to whom CIS tax is deducted

Exemption for small businesses – Applies if an organisation total wage bill (PAYE and net CIS) is under £80,000. This is increased to £120,000 for the 2020 Levy.

Reduction for small businesses – 50% reduction applies if an organisation total wage bill (PAYE and net CIS) is between £80,000 and £399,999. Note this is increased to between £120,000 and £399,99 for the 2020 Levy.

Further information can be found at www.citb.co.uk including details of Small Business Levy Exemption and Reduction.

Mechanical Plant

The following rates are inclusive of operator as noted, fuel, consumables, reparis and maintenance, but excludes transport.

	£	
Excavators including Driver and Banksman		
Hydraulic, full circle slew, crawler mounted with single equipment (shovel)		
0.70 m³	59.05	hr
1.00 m³	59.05	hr
1.50 m³	62.65	hr
Hydraulic, offset or centre post, half circle slew, wheeled, dual purpose (back loader)		
0.60 m³	63.82	hr
0.80 m³	64.38	hr
1.00 m³	69.18	hr
1.20 m³	70.65	hr
Mini excavators, full circle slew, crawler mounted with single equipment (back actor)		
1.4 tonne capacity	73.43	hr
2.4 tonne capacity	74.92	hr
3.6 tonne capacity	78.25	hr
Compactor including operator		
Vibrating plate		
90kg	19.39	hr
120kg	19.58	hr
176kg	19.68	hr
310kg	19.85	hr
Rollers including operator		
Road roller dead-weight		
2.54 tonnes	23.36	hr
6.10 tonnes	24.66	hr
8.13 tonnes	26.28	hr
10.20 tonnes	30.20	hr
Vibratory pedestrian operated		
Single roller 550kg	19.52	hr
Single roller 680kg	20.74	hr
Twin roller 650kg	22.63	hr
Twin roller 950kg	23.58	hr
Twin roller 1300kg	24.25	hr
Self propelled vibratory tandem roller		
1.07 tonne	25.47	hr
2.03 tonne	26.82	hr
3.05 tonne	28.17	hr
6.10 tonne	29.52	hr
Pumps including attendant quarter time		
Single diaphragm (excluding hoses)		
51mm	5.85	hr
75mm	7.54	hr
102mm	10.07	hr
Double diaphragm (excluding hoses)		
51mm	5.85	hr
76mm	7.54	hr
102mm	10.87	hr
Suction or delivery hose, flexible, including coupling, valve and strainer, per 7.62m length		
51mm	0.73	hr
76mm	0.80	hr
102mm	1.27	hr
Compressors including driver quarter time		
Portable, normal delivery of free air at 7kg/cm³		
2.0m³/min	8.87	hr
Compressor tools with 15.3m hose (excluding operator)		
Breaker including steels	1.63	hr
Light pick including steels	2.80	hr
Clay spade including blade	2.80	hr
Compressor tool sundries		
Muffler	0.30	hr
Concrete Mixers Including Driver		
Closed drum		
0.20/0.15m³	18.04	hr
0.30/0.20m³	18.23	hr
Closed drum with swing batch weighing gear		
0.40/0.30m³	20.63	hr
Mixer with batch weighing gear and power loading shovel		
0.30/0.20m³	20.47	hr
0.40/0.30m³	20.85	hr
Mortar Mixers Including Driver		
Mortar Mixer		
0.15/0.10m³	17.53	hr
Concrete Equipment including Driver/Operator		
Concrete pump, skid mounted, exclusive of piping		
20/26m³	53.98	hr
30/45m³	56.85	hr
46/54m³	59.73	hr
Piping per 3.05m length		
102mm diameter	0.61	hr
127mm diameter	0.67	hr
152mm diameter	0.73	hr
Vibrator poker		
Petrol	18.72	hr
Diesel	18.72	hr
Electric	18.66	hr
Air	19.20	hr
Vibrator, external type, clamp on		
Small	21.42	hr
Medium	21.82	hr
Large	22.09	hr
Lorries including Driver		
Ordinary of the following plated gross vehicle weights		
3.56 tonnes	41.15	hr
5.69 tonnes	73.15	hr
8.74 tonnes	84.82	hr
10.16 tonnes	106.38	hr
Tipper of the following plated gross vehicle weights		
6.60 tonnes	83.82	hr
8.74 tonnes	95.49	hr
9.65 tonnes	108.82	hr
Vans, including driver, carrying capacity		
0.4 tonnes	30.82	hr
1.0 tonnes	31.55	hr
1.25 tonnes	33.15	hr
Dumpers including Driver		
Manual gravity tipping 2 wheel drive		
750kg	25.25	hr
1000kg	24.40	hr
2 tonnes	25.97	hr
3 tonnes	28.37	hr

Mechanical Plant (Cont'd)

	£	
Hydraulic tipping 4 wheel drive		
2 tonnes	25.91	hr
3 tonnes	24.99	hr
4 tonnes	26.75	hr
5 tonnes	26.75	hr

Hoists

Scaffold type hoist excluding operator		
250 kg	142.40	week
Ladder type hoist excluding operator		
150 kg electric	231.00	week
Goods type hoist up to 10m height including operator, excluding erecting and dismantling		
Mobile type 500 kg	868.75	week
Tied-in type 750 kg	974.14	week

CHARGES FOR HIRE

The following Trade List Prices have been provided by HSS Hire Shops, to whom acknowledgement is hereby given. All hire charges are per week, day rates available on application. Guide prices only and subject to alteration without notice. All carriage to and from site charged extra.

Builders' Ladders

		£
Extension ladder (push up)		
3 part, up to 6.0m	each	39.60
Glass fibre ladder - up to 2.9m	each	54.00
Combination ladder – up to 1.9m	each	36.00
Roof ladder - double, up to 4.6m	each	40.00
Ladder safety foot	each	20.00

Adjustable Steel Trestles

	closed		extended		
no 1	0.5m	to	0.8m	each	9.00
no 2	0.8m	to	1.2m	each	9.00
no 3	1.1m	to	1.6m	each	9.00

Low Level Access

Pop up access platform		
Working height of 3.0m	each	148.80
Self-propelled low level platforms		
Working height of 4.5m	each	275.00
Power tower	each	170.00
MiTower Plus – one person quick build tower		87.40
Superboard staging		
2.4m	each	50.00

Non-conductive systems

Podium platform	each	111.00
Narrow width tower – 0.85 x 1.8 x 4.2m	each	172.00
Full width tower – 1.45 x 1.8 x 4.2m	each	172.00
Additional metre	each	42.00

Scissor Lifts Electric

Narrow Aisle (2.44 x 0.81 x 2.44m) up to 10m... (includes extension lead and transformer)	296.00

PURCHASE PRICES

RAMSAY LADDERS

The following Trade Prices have been provided by Ramsay Ladders, Forfar, Angus, DD8 1BH, www.ramsayladders.co.uk, to whom acknowledgement is hereby given. Prices may be subject to delivery charges. Some sizes made to order only.

Aluminium Ladders

Single (parallel sides)

Serrated round rungs fitted at 250mm centres. Ends of stiles fitted with rubber feet.

	length (m)	rungs	weight (kg)	£
SA2.0MK	2.05	8	4	41.40
SA3.0MK	3.05	12	6	58.20
SA4.0MK	4.05	16	8	75.60
SA5.0ML	5.05	20	12	103.80
SA6.0MF	6.05	24	18	153.00
SA8.0MF	8.05	32	32	311.20
SA10.0MJ	10.05	40	40	354.00

Large D shaped rungs with twist proof joint fitted at 300mm centres. Ends of stiles fitted with rubber feet.

	length (m)	rungs	weight (kg)	£
TDS20	1.85	6	4.5	36.00
TDS30	3.05	10	7	55.20
TDS40	4.00	13	10	70.20
TDS50	5.15	17	14	100.20
TDS55	5.75	19	15	117.60

Double extending (push up type)

Serrated round rungs fitted at 250mm centres. Ends of stiles fitted with rubber feet.

	closed height (m)	extended height (m)	rungs	approx. weight (kg)	£
DE3.0ML	3.05	5.55	24	13	155.35
DE4.0MF	4.05	7.55	32	27	262.50
DE5.0MF	5.05	9.30	40	33	309.40
DE6.0MJ	6.05	11.05	47	52	528.43
DE7.0MJ	7.05	12.75	57	63	605.80

Ropes and pulleys - per double ladder £ 52.80

Large D shaped rungs with twist proof joint fitted at 300mm centres. Ends of stiles fitted with rubber feet

	closed height (m)	extended height (m)	rungs	approx. weight (kg)	£
TDD20	1.85	3.03	12	9.5	83.85
TDD30	3.05	5.44	20	13.5	126.75
TDD40	4.00	7.28	26	20	176.80
TDD55	5.75	10.40	38	30	261.95

Triple extending (push up type)

Serrated round rungs fitted at 250mm centres. Ends of stiles fitted with rubber feet.

	closed height (m)	extended height (m)	rungs	approx. weight (kg)	£
TE3.0MF	3.05	7.30	35	32	362.05
TE4.0MF	4.05	10.30	47	42	448.50
TE5.0MF	5.05	13.30	59	52	549.25

Ropes and pulleys - Per triple Ladder £ 88.00

PURCHASE PRICES (Cont'd)

RAMSAY LADDERS (Cont'd)

GRP ladders

Glass fibre ladders, channel stiles fitted with square rungs, ends of stiles fitted with rubber feet.

	length (m)	rungs	weight (kg)	£
Single section				
AFL09	2.35	9	7	166.40
AFL12	3.05	12	9	187.20
AFL14	3.55	14	11	209.04
AFL16	4.10	16	14	225.68
Double section				
AFD09	2.35	18	14	352.00
AFD12	3.05	24	17	389.00
AFD14	3.55	28	22	435.00

Aluminium heavy-duty platform steps

Platform measures 406mm x 305mm, 89mm deep treads. Fitted with rubber feet front and rear.

	height to platform (m)	treads	weight (kg)	£
AFS7	1.66	7	15	157.20
AFS9	2.13	9	17	180.60
AFS11	2.60	11	19	204.00
AFS13	3.07	13	22	286.80
AFS15	3.54	15	31	346.20
AFS20	4.72	20	45	516.00
AFS24	5.66	24	54	660.00

GRP platform steps

Platform measures 255mm x 435mm, stiles fitted with 85mm deep treads. Ends of channels have rubber feet.

	height to platform (m)	treads	weight (kg)	£
AFPS05	1.18	5	11	225.00
AFPS07	1.68	7	15	244.00
AFPS09	2.18	9	19	276.00
AFPS10	3.05	10	21.5	295.00

Loft ladders

Complete with one handrail, operating pole and fixings; excludes trap door.

		£
AL1	2.29m to 2.54m	236.80
AL2	2.57m to 2.82m	247.20
AL3	2.84m to 3.10m	257.20
AL4	3.12m to 3.38m	268.00
AL5	3.40m to 3.66m	320.80

Additional safety handrail per ladder varies

Telescopic loft ladder

Fully assembled, cradle 105mm deep, 520mm width of ladder/springs, 150kg rated.

		£
TEL01	2.45m maximum	165.00

Aluminium fixed industrial platform steps (no handrails)

Platform measures 405mm x 610mm, 89mm deep treads. Handrails can be fitted.

	height (m)	weight (kg)	£
Single Sided			
DPS 01	0.240	6	86.10
DPS 02	0.475	7	107.80
DPS 03	0.710	9	129.50
DPS 04	0.945	10	152.60
DPS 06	1.415	12	197.40
DPS 07	1.645	14	219.80
DPS 08	1.880	15	227.50
Fixed pair of wheels			32.80
Double Sided			
DPD 02	0.475	8	163.80
DPD 03	0.710	10	179.20
DPD 04	0.945	12	195.30
DPD 05	1.180	15	211.40
DPD 06	1.415	17	227.50
DPD 07	1.645	19	243.60
DPD 08	1.88	23	268.10
Fixed pair of wheels			26.00

GUIDE PRICES TO BUILDING TYPES PER SQUARE METRE

The prices throughout this section are ranged over the most commonly occurring average building prices and are based upon the total floor area of all storeys measured inside external walls and over internal walls and partitions. They exclude contingencies, external works, furniture, fittings and equipment, professional fees and VAT.

Building prices are influenced significantly by location, market, local conditions, size and specification. The prices given are intended only as an indicative guide to representative building types in a U.K. location and must be used with caution, professional skill, and judgement. Prices considerably outside the ranges stated can, of course, be encountered when meeting specific requirements.

New Build..........................

Industrial Buildings............	per m2 £
Agricultural Shed...................	600-1250
Factory, light industrial for letting	
incoming mains only........	550-1250
including lighting and power, toilets and basic office accommodation...	750-1550
for owner occupation	
including all services and basic accommodation...	700-1700
high tech: with controlled environment..................	850-2200
Garage/Showroom................	1100-1550
Workshop............................	900-1500
Warehouse/Store..................	600-1200

Administrative Buildings

Council Offices......................	2000-2800
Magistrates Court.................	2200-3100
Offices, Low rise (for letting)	
non air conditioned..........	1400-2200
air conditioned................	1600-2250
Offices, High rise (for owner occupation)	
air conditioned................	2100-2400
Bank (branch)........................	2450-2800
Shops	900-2000
Retail Warehouse..................	750-1000
Shopping Centre	
air-conditioned.................	1100-1700
Police Station	2050-2600
Ambulance Station.	1250-1600
Fire Station........................	2450-3100

Health and Welfare Buildings

General Hospital.................	2750-4100
Private Hospital..................	2900-4100
Day Hospital	2100-2600
Health Centre......................	1950-2900
Hospice..............................	2150-2600
Day Centre	2100-2500
Home for Mental Health......	1600-2200
Children's Home	2300-2950
Home for the Elderly	1500-2150

Refreshment, Entertainment and Recreation Buildings

Restaurant..........................	2000-2600
Public House.......................	2200-2700
Kitchen with equipment.......	2500-4000
Theatres	3000-3800
Community Centre.............	1750-2600
Swimming Pool (covered)...	2750-3700
Sports Centre......................	1500-2000
Squash Courts....................	1200-1800
Sports Pavilion....................	1700-2650
Golf Club House	1650-3000

Religious Buildings

Church...............................	1850-3100
Church Hall.........................	2000-2500
Crematoria	1900-2900

Educational, Cultural and Scientific Buildings

Nursery School	2150-3000
Primary School	2100-2900
Middle School.....................	1900-2600
Secondary School..............	1900-2550
Special School.....................	2200-2800
Universities........................	2500-2800
College	1650-2350
Training Centre..................	1800-2500
Laboratory Building............	2250-4400
Computer Building	2100-3750
Libraries.............................	2400-3050

Residential Buildings

Local Authority and Housing Association Schemes	
low rise flats..................	1250-1700
4/5 person two storey houses	1150-1450
Private Developments	
low rise flats..................	1300-1750
4/5 person two storey houses	1150-1500
Private Houses, detached...	1650-2750
Sheltered Housing	
Bungalows	1600-2100
low rise..........................	1450-1900
flats with lifts and Warden's accommodation, etc.....	1400-1750
Student's Residence...........	1800-2250
Hotel	1800-2800

Refurbishment

Factories	300-850
Offices (basic refurbishment)	750-1500
Offices (high quality including air conditioning)..................	1150-1600
Banks................................	11000-1650
Shops	500-1800
Hospitals............................	1650-3300
Public Houses.....................	1000-1400
Theatres.............................	1500-2400
Churches	500-1900
Schools..............................	700-1600
Housing & Flats..................	850-1950
Hotels	1550-2100

CAPITAL ALLOWANCES

It is important to recognise that construction tax advice is a complex area because the variables that need to be considered are many and dependent on particular circumstances. This section is therefore intended only as a guide.

The Act

This is the Capital Allowances Act 2001. Any updates are issued through the Finance Act annually or other relevant Acts or Regulations.

Regular updates include guidance on withdrawal of allowances on sports grounds, business premises renovation allowances, hotel allowances etc and updates or new schemes for energy saving plant and machinery, flat conversion allowances, structures and building allowances etc. The Housing and Regeneration Transfer Schemes (Tax Consequences) Regulations 2015 included guidance on the disposal value of plant, machinery and fixtures.

Plant and Machinery

Sections 21-22 of the 2001 Act set out details of those assets which are specifically excluded from qualifying as plant and machinery under all circumstances. Section 23 gives a list of those items within a building which may qualify as expenditure on plant and machinery. This does not mean that the items listed automatically qualify as this will depend on the nature of the trade carried on in the building.

Case law governs the interpretation of the items listed in Section 23 and the circumstances required to confirm qualification in each separate situation. For example, the provision of a swimming pool in a hotel would be regarded as plant and machinery whereas it would not be in an office block. Relevant case law goes back as far as 1887 and there are "landmark" cases identified, on which the HM Customs and Revenue heavily rely.

Solar panels, which include photovoltaic varieties, which generate electricity; and solar thermal systems, which provide hot water; are classed as plant and machinery capital expenditure and are specifically designated as special rate. Effective from 1 April 2012 for corporation tax and 6 April 2012 for income tax.

Annual Investment Allowance (AIA)

This allows the full cost of plant and machinery to be deducted from profits before tax in most cases. The AIA has changed several times and increased from £200,000 to £1,000,000 on the 1st January 2019. This is due to end on 31st December 2021 when it will revert to £200,000.

Rate of Allowances

Writing Down Allowance

If the AIA is not appropriate for all or part of the item, then writing down allowances are used instead. These items are put in a general pool and a writing down allowance of 18% per annum on a reducing balance basis is used.

Special Rate Allowance

Some items are placed in a special rate pool of plant and machinery expenditure with a writing down allowance of 6% per annum (reduced from 8% in April 2019). These items include integral parts of the building (e.g. lifts, air-conditioning, electrical systems, etc), items with a long life, safety measures at sports grounds, thermal insulation of buildings, and cars with CO^2 emissions of more than 130g/km.

Note: The actual buildings and structures do not qualify for this capital allowance.

Long Life Assets

A long-life asset is defined as plant and machinery that can reasonably be expected to have a useful economic life of at least 25 years. A reduced writing down allowance of 6% per annum should be used for the long-life items with a total value of over £100,000 in a single accounting period. The depreciation policy for accounting purposes or the client's design requirements may help to determine the useful economic life.

Solar panels have been treated as long-life assets since April 2012

The Enhanced Capital Allowance Scheme

Enhanced Capital Allowances (ECAs) enabled a business to claim 100% first-year capital allowances on their spending on qualifying plant and machinery. This included energy-saving plant and machinery; low carbon dioxide emission cars and natural gas and hydrogen refuelling infrastructure; and water conservation plant and machinery.

The products must be new or unused plant and machinery with claims made based on actual cost.

The ECA scheme ended in April 2020.

Building Refurbishment and Alterations

Section 25 of the Act allows that where capital expenditure is incurred that is incidental to the installation of plant and machinery it can be treated as part of the expenditure on the item. This means that in an existing building, elements of structure and the like can be allowed whereas in a new building they would not be allowable. An example is a lift shaft, where inserted into an existing building would be allowable whereas a lift shaft in a new building is deemed to be structure and non allowable.

Elements in a refurbishment project may be a mixture of capital and revenue expenditure. A repair or a "like for like" replacement of part of an asset would be a revenue expense and this would enable the whole amount to be deducted from the taxable profit in the accounts covering the year of expenditure.

Electric Vehicle Charging Points Allowance

A business can claim a 100% first-year allowance on qualifying electric vehicle charging points. This was first introduced in the Finance (no 2) Act 2017 and extended in the Finance Bill 2018-19. The measure included for expenditure incurred on or after 23rd November 2016 and will expire on 5th April 2023 (Income tax) and 31st March 2023 (Corporation tax).

CAPITAL ALLOWANCES (Cont'd)

Contaminated Land Remediation Tax Relief

Land remediation of contaminated or derelict land became available on expenditure incurred on or after 11th May 2001 and the provisions were included in the 2001 Finance Act updated in April 2009. It enables companies to claim relief on capital and revenue expenditure on qualifying land remediation expenditure including establishing the level of contamination, and the cost of removal or containing it. It is important to note that this is relief from corporation tax; individuals and partnerships are not eligible for this relief and a company cannot claim where they caused the contamination.

Relief is given at the rate of 100% plus 50% for qualifying expenditure on the actual amount incurred and should be claimed within two years of the year in which the expenditure is incurred.

Structures and Buildings Allowance

This tax relief became available for construction contracts signed on or after 29th October 2018 on qualifying costs for new non-residential structures and buildings which are used for qualifying activities.

The rate of Structures and Buildings Allowance was set at 2% per year and increased to 3% per year from 5th April 2020, on qualifying costs. The allowance period is 33 and one third years from the start date, which can be the date the expenditure was incurred or the date the building first used for a non-residential purpose.

Research and Development Allowances (R&D)

The Finance Act 2000 provided for Corporation Tax relief for small and medium companies (SMEs) undertaking qualifying R&D activities. For work to qualify for R&D relief it must be part of a specific project to make an advance in science or technology. To get the relief the project must look for an advance in the field, overcome uncertainty and show that the solution couldn't be worked out by a professional in the field.

The Finance Act 2007 extended the support available under the SME scheme to companies with fewer than 500 employees which have an annual turnover not exceeding €100 million and/or who have an annual balance sheet total not exceeding €86 million.

The SME R&D relief currently allows companies to:

- Make a total deduction of 230% from their yearly profit (an extra 130%)
- Claim a tax credit of up to 14.5% of the company is making a loss.

Large companies can claim a Research and Development Tax Credit of 13% of qualifying R&D expenditure from 1st April 2020. The rate of relief was 11% up to 31st December 2017, 12% from 1st January 2018 and 13% from 1st April 2020.

EXPIRED CAPITAL ALLOWANCES

Agricultural Building Allowances

This allowance ceased in 2011.

Business Premises Renovation Allowance (BPRA)

Capital expenditure on the renovation of business premises in certain 'disadvantaged areas' may qualify for the Business Premises Renovation Allowance if they have been unused for at least a year.

The BPRA scheme took effect from 11 April 2007 and ended on 31st March 2017 (Income tax) and 5th April 2017 (corporation tax). It covered expenditure on the conversion or renovation of unused business premises that brought them back into business use.

Flats Conversion Allowance

Flat conversion allowances were withdrawn on 6th April 2013.

Hotel Allowances

This allowance ceased in 2011.

Industrial Building Allowances

This allowance ceased in 2011.

SUMMARY

In order to maximise the tax relief available in claiming capital allowances, it is important to seek expert professional advice at an early date.

HOMES ENGLAND

The new national agency – Homes England - was launched in January 2018 to replace the previous Homes and Communities Agency. Affordable Housing, as defined by the National Planning Policy Framework, is housing for sale or rent for those whose needs are not met by the market, and is delivered through the Affordable Homes Programme from 2012-2026.

Capital Funding Guide 2016, updated October 2021

The Capital Funding Guide 2016 replaced the Affordable Housing Capital Funding Guide 2015-18 and has been updated several times since.

The Guide contains the rules and procedures for all providers delivering affordable housing under one of the Home England's affordable homes programmes.

Scope and Format

The Guide is organised into a number of chapters:

GENERAL

1. Shared Ownership
2. Rent to Buy
3. Specialist Homes
4. Housing for Rent
5. Department of Health and Social Care Programmes
6. Programme Management
7. Grant Recovery – Registered Provider
8. Grant Recovery – Unregistered Bodies
9. Procurement and Scheme Issues
10. Finance
11. Right to Acquire
12. Social HomeBuy
13. Voluntary Right to Buy Pilot
14. Strategic Partnerships
15. Capital Funding Guide Library and Updates
16. Glossary

1) SHARED OWNERSHIP

This covers all properties developed with grant funding specifically for sale on shared ownership terms from January 2016. The model was updated for the Affordable Homes Programme on 1st April 2021.

Help to Buy: Shared Ownership is largely the same as other shared ownership products. In all of these products, the dwellings are part-rent /part-buy (i.e. the property title and equity are split between the leaseholder (the shared ownership purchaser) and the landlord (the shared ownership provider) and are provided using the standard model shared ownership lease. The term 'shared ownership' has a legal meaning and is used in this context.

Help to Buy: Shared Ownership is aimed at helping people in housing need who are unable to afford to purchase a property on the open market. Applicants are subject to applicant eligibility and affordability requirements.

The minimum initial equity share that can be purchased was 25% up to April 2021 when it was reduced to 10%; the maximum initial equity share is 75% based on the full market value of the property. Further shares can be purchased at a later date and purchasers are encouraged to buy the maximum share they can afford and sustain from the outset. It is anticipated that applicants purchase a share in a property using savings and a mortgage from a qualifying institution. Staircasing has been introduced allowing shares to be purchased in 1% increments for the first 15 years, and larger shares can still be purchased with the minimum lowered to 5%.

From April 2021 the landlord is responsible for maintenance and repairs for the first 10 years instead of the shared owner.

The scheme is extended with the following variations which may be provided using grants:-

- Home Ownership for people with a long-term disability
- Older Persons Shared Ownership
- Rural Schemes
- Designated Protected Area schemes
- Self Build

2) RENT TO BUY

This scheme allows working households to rent a home at Intermediate Rent providing them the opportunity to save for a deposit to then go on and purchase their first home.

The scheme will enable Registered Providers to build housing that will be let at Intermediate Rent but with the ultimate aim to sell the home to the tenant after they have been able to save for the deposit required.

Main features of the scheme are:

- Homes let to working householders who are intending to buy their own home in the future.
- The homes will be let at an Intermediate Rent for a minimum of five years while the tenants save for a deposit.
- After the initial letting period the property can continue to be Rent to Buy, sold or converted to another form of affordable rent. Rent to Buy homes are sold at current market value.
- Intermediate Rents are offered above social rents but below market levels and must not exceed 80% of the current market rent with maximum annual rent increases.
- The maximum annual rent increases is the CPI (Consumer Price Index) plus 1%.

3) SPECIALIST HOMES

Within the Shared Ownership and Affordable Homes Programme (SOAHP) 2016 to 2021, the Affordable Homes Programme (AHP) 2021 to 2026 and the Rough Sleeping Accommodation Programme (RSAP) there is a separate funding stream for specialist rental accommodation. This should not be interpreted as the only funding available for specialist housing. Specialist housing may also be funded, as appropriate, through the Help to Buy: Shared Ownership and Rent to Buy funding streams.

These programmes are intended to meet a diverse range of housing needs. These include supported housing and designated housing where access to support is provided where needed and ensures specialist homes for older people, those classed as disabled and/or vulnerable as well as housing for Gypsies and Travellers.

Capital Funding Guide 2016, updated Oct 2021 (Cont'd)
3) SPECIALIST HOMES (Cont'd)

Housing covered by SOAHP 2016 to 2021, AHP 2021 to 2026 and RSAP may include, but is not limited to:

- Sheltered housing
- Extra care housing
- Retirement villages
- Move-on housing
- Domestic violence refuges
- Hostels
- Housing intended for Gypsies and Travellers
- Traveller pitches

4) HOUSING FOR RENT

Affordable Rent and Social Rent are forms of low cost rental social housing.

Affordable Rent property is made available for rent up to a maximum of 80% of gross market rent (inclusive of service charges). Tenancies may be either long term periodic assured or secure tenancies, or they may be for a fixed term (for a period no less than five years).

Social Rent is low cost rental social housing that is made available at rent levels that are set in accordance with the regulator's Rent Standard.

5) DEPARTMENT OF HEALTH AND SOCIAL CARE PROGRAMMES

This chapter sets out the requirements and procedures which must be followed when developing affordable housing funded through the Department of Health and Social Care's, Care and Support Specialised Housing Fund, the Homelessness Change fund and the Platform for Life fund – all delivered by Homes England.

Care and Support Specialised Housing Fund - supports and accelerates the development of the specialised housing market for older people and adults with disabilities, in order to stimulate the market, for both affordable and private homes

Homelessness Change Fund - provides tailored hostel accommodation and improved facilities for the provision of healthcare, training or education for rough sleepers, and other non-statutory homeless people, with the aim of helping them off the streets and transforming their lives.

Platform for Life Fund - provides stable, transitional, shared accommodation for young people who are homeless or in insecure housing that provides a positive environment from which they can engage with work, training and education and progress towards full independence.

6) PROGRAMME MANAGEMENT

This chapter sets out the Agency's requirements in relation to management of a provider's approved allocation funded through one of the Agency's affordable homes programmes.

7) GRANT RECOVERY – REGISTERED PROVIDER

Capital grant is subject to recovery by Homes England. This chapter sets out grant recovery requirements for Registered Providers only. The Recovery of Capital Grants and Recycled Capital Grant Fund General Determination 2017 makes provision for the recycling of grants by all classes of Registered Provider regardless of whether they are non-profit or profit making providers.

8) GRANT RECOVERY – UNREGISTERED BODIES

This section extends the previous section to cover all unregistered bodies.

9) PROCUREMENT AND SCHEME ISSUES

This section encourages more efficient and effective ways of procuring affordable housing. The scheme types and associated topics are discussed.

10) FINANCE

This chapter sets out the conditions and procedural requirements which aim to ensure that the public subsidy is used correctly and in accordance with general fiscal legislation, accounted for accurately and administered in line with the correct procedures.

11) RIGHT TO ACQUIRE

The Right to Acquire is a statutory scheme which offers eligible tenants in eligible properties the opportunity to purchase the home they currently rent at a discount. The landlord of an eligible property will be a housing association or housing company registered with Homes England. The discount is a fixed sum of money which varies geographically. Eligible tenants can receive the full funding if they have never received any form of public subsidy to purchase a property before, other tenants remain eligible but the funding will be reduced by the amount they have previously received.

12) SOCIAL HOMEBUY

Social HomeBuy allows eligible tenants of Registered Providers who participate in the scheme and who occupy eligible properties to purchase their social or affordable rented housing at discount either outright or on shared ownership terms. Social HomeBuy can only be used to purchase self-contained property for rent. There are eligibility criteria for both properties and tenants.

13) VOLUNTARY RIGHT TO BUY PILOT

This is a pilot programme for tenanted homes based in the Midlands only. The pilot is a voluntary scheme and is not a Homes England programme. Landlords will receive compensation from Homes England if they follow the relevant requirements.

14) STRATEGIC PARTNERSHIPS

Introduced in 2018 to set out the requirements that apply to 'not for profit' housing associations to deliver affordable supply under the principles of the Shared Ownership and Affordable Homes Programme (SOAHP) 2016 to 2021 with different contractual terms. Each grant recipient has a separate grant funding agreement for the delivery of additional grant funded homes, outside of any existing SOAHP contract.

FURTHER INFORMATION

For further information visit the Homes England website at:

www.gov.uk/government/organisations/homes-england

Homes England, 50 Victoria Street, London, SW1H 0TL

Email: enquiries@homesengland.gov.uk

Telephone: 0300 1234 5000

NATIONAL WORKING RULE AGREEMENT

The following are extracts from the Working Rule Agreement for the Construction Industry as approved by the Construction Industry Joint Council (Revised 1st August 2018)

WR.1 ENTITLEMENT TO BASIC RATES OF PAY

Operatives employed to carry out work in the Building and Civil Engineering Industry are entitled to basic pay in accordance with this Working Rule (WR. 1). Rates of pay are set out in a separate schedule, published periodically by the Council.

Classification of basic and additional pay rates of operatives:

General Operative
Skilled Operative Rate: 4
Skilled Operative Rate: 3
Skilled Operative Rate: 2
Skilled Operative Rate: 1
Craft Operative

1.1 General Operatives

1.1.1 General Operatives employed to carry out general building and/or civil engineering work are entitled to receive the General Operatives Basic Rate of Pay.

Payment for Occasional Skilled Work

1.1.2 General Operatives, employed as such, who are required to carry out building and/or civil engineering work defined in Schedule 1, on an occasional basis, are entitled to receive the General Operative Basic Rate of Pay increased to the rate of pay specified in Schedule 1 for the hours they are engaged to carry out the defined work.

1.2 Skilled Operatives

1.2.1 Skilled Operatives engaged and employed whole time as such, who are required to carry out skilled building and/or civil engineering work defined in Schedule 1, on a continuous basis, are entitled to the Basic Rate of Pay specified in Schedule 1.

1.3 Craft Operatives

Craft Operatives employed to carry out craft building and/or civil engineering work are entitled to receive the Craft Operative Basic Rate of Pay.

1.4 Conditions of Employment of Apprentices.

1.4.1 Conditions

An apprentice who has entered into a training service agreement is subject to the same conditions of employment as other operatives employed under the Working Rule Agreement except as provided in WR.1.4.2 to 1.4.6.

1.4.2 Wages

Rates of pay are set out in a separate schedule, published periodically by the Council *(See Standard Rates of Wages section)*. Payment under the schedule is due from the date of entry into employment as an apprentice, whether the apprentice is working on site or undergoing full-time training on an approved course, subject to the provisions of WR.1.4.3. Payment under the scale is due from the beginning of the pay week during which the specified period starts.

1.4.3 Payment During Off-the-Job Training

Apprentices are entitled to be paid during normal working hours to attend approved courses off-the-job training in accordance with the requirement of their apprenticeship. Payment during such attendance shall be at their normal rate of pay, but the employer may withhold payment for hours during which an apprentice, without authorisation, fails to attend the course.

1.4.4 Overtime

The working of overtime by apprentices under 18 years of age shall not be permitted. Where an apprentice age 18 or over is required to work overtime payment shall be in accordance with the provisions of WR.4.

1.4.5 Daily Fare and Travel Allowances

The apprentice shall be entitled to fare and travel allowances in accordance with WR.5.

1.4.6 Absence and Sick Pay

The employer must be notified at the earliest practical time during the first day of any absence and no later than midday. The first seven days may be covered by self certification. Thereafter absence must be covered by a certificate or certificates given by a registered medical practitioner. The apprentice shall be entitled to Statutory Sick Pay (SSP) plus Industry sick pay in accordance with WR.20 save the aggregate amount of SSP plus Industry sick pay shall not exceed a normal week's pay in accordance with WR.1.4.2.

1.4.7 Other Terms and Conditions of Engagement

The apprentice shall be subject to all other provisions and entitlements contained within the Working Rule Agreement.

Note: Normal hourly rate
The expression 'normal hourly rate' in this agreement means the craft, skilled or general operatives' weekly basic rate of pay as above, divided by the hours defined in WR.3 "Working Hours". Additional payments for occasional skilled or bonus payments are not taken into account for calculating the "normal hourly rate".

WR.2 BONUS

It shall be open to employers and employees on any job to agree a bonus scheme based on measured output and productivity for any operation or operations on that particular job.

WR.3 WORKING HOURS

The normal working hours shall be:

Monday to Thursday	8 hours per day
Friday	7 hours per day
Total	39 hours per week

except for operatives working shifts whose working hours shall continue to be 8 hours per weekday and 40 hours per week.

The expression "normal working hours" means the number of hours prescribed above for any day (or night) when work is actually undertaken reckoned from the starting time fixed by the employer.

WR.3 WORKING HOURS (Cont'd)

3.1 Rest/Meal Breaks

3.1.1. Meal/Refreshment Breaks

At each site or job there shall be a break or breaks for rest and/or refreshment at times to be fixed by the employer. The breaks, which shall not exceed one hour per day on aggregate, shall include a meal break of not less than half an hour.

3.1.2. Daily/Weekly Rest Breaks

Where there are objective or technical reasons concerning the organisation of work the application of the Working Time Regulations 1998 – Regulations 10(1) Daily Rest Period – 11(1) and 11(2) Weekly Rest Period is excluded.

3.2. Average Weekly Working Hours

Where there are objective or technical reasons concerning the organisation of work, average weekly working hours will be calculated by reference to a 12 month period subject to the employer complying with the general principles relating to the protection of Health and Safety of workers and providing equivalent compensatory rest periods or, in exceptional cases where it is not possible for objective reasons to grant such periods, ensuring appropriate protection for the operatives concerned.

WR.4 OVERTIME RATES

The employer may require overtime to be worked and the operative may not unreasonably refuse to work overtime.

Overtime will be calculated on a daily basis, but overtime premium rates will not be payable until the normal hours (39 hours-WR.3) have been worked in the pay week unless the short time is authorised by the employer on compassionate or other grounds or is a certified absence due to sickness or injury.

Note: The number of hours worked in excess of normal hours will be reduced by the number of hours of unauthorised absence before the overtime premium is calculated.

Overtime shall be calculated as follows:

Monday to Friday
For the first four hours after completion of the normal working hours of the day at the rate of time and a half; thereafter at the rate of double time until starting time the following day.

Saturday
Time and a half, until completion of the first four hours, and thereafter at double time.

Sunday
At the rate of double time, until starting time on Monday morning.

When an operative is called out after completing the normal working hours of the day or night, he shall be paid at overtime rates for the additional time worked as if he had worked continuously. Any intervening period shall count to determine the rate, but shall not be paid.

Overtime shall be calculated on the normal hourly rate. Additional payments for intermittent skill, responsibility or adverse conditions and bonus shall not be included when calculating overtime payments.

In no case shall payment exceed double time.

WR.5 DAILY FARE AND TRAVEL ALLOWANCES

5.1 Extent of Payment

Operatives are entitled to a daily fare and travel allowance, measured one way from their home to the job/site. The allowances will be paid in accordance with the table published periodically by the Council. There is no entitlement to allowances under this Rule for operatives who report, at normal starting time, to a fixed establishment, such as the employers yard, shop or permanent depot. The distance travelled will be calculated by reference to WR.5.2. There is no entitlement under this Rule to allowances for distances less than 9 miles. Having due regard for Health and Safety an operative may be required to travel distances beyond the published scale; in which case payment for each additional kilometre should be made based on the difference between the rate for the 49th and 50th mile.

5.2 Measurement of Distance

All distances shall be measured utilising the AA, RAC, or similar, Route Planner using the post codes of the operative's home and place of work based on the most direct route.

An operative's home is the address at which the operative is living while employed on the work to which travelled.

In the event that there is no post code for the operative's home and/or place of work the closest post code should be used.

5.3 Transport Provided Free by the Employer

Where the employer provides free transport, the operative shall not be entitled to fare allowance. However, operatives who travel to the pick up point for transport provided free by the employer are entitled to fare allowance for that part of the journey, in accordance with the table.

5.4 Transfer during Working Day

An operative transferred to another place of work during work hours shall, on the day of the transfer only, be paid any fares actually incurred:

(a) in the transfer, and

(b) in travelling home from the place where he finishes work if this differs from the place where he reported for work at starting time, subject to deduction of half the daily fare allowance.

5.5 Emergency Work

An operative called from the home (or temporary place of residence) outside normal working hours to carry out emergency work shall be paid travelling expenses and his normal hourly rate for the time spent travelling to and from the job.

WR.6 SHIFT WORKING

6.1 Shift working means a situation in which more than one shift of not less than eight hours is worked on a job in a 24 hour period and such shifts do not overlap.

On all work which is carried out on two or more shifts in a 24 hour period the following provisions shall apply:

The first shift in the week shall be the first shift that ends after midnight on Sunday

The normal hours of a shift shall be eight hours, excluding meal breaks, notwithstanding which, the hours to be worked on any particular shift shall be established by the employer.

WR.6 SHIFT WORKING (Cont'd)

The rate payable for the normal hours of the shift shall be the operative's normal hourly rate plus, in the case of an operative completing a shift, a shift allowance of 14% of the normal rate.

An operative required to work continuously for over eight hours on a shift or shifts shall be paid at the rate of time and a half, plus a shift allowance of 14% of his normal hourly rate, for the first four hours beyond eight and thereafter at double time but such double time payment shall not be enhanced by the 14% shift allowance (i.e. the maximum rate in any circumstance shall be double the normal hourly rate).

After having worked five complete scheduled shifts in a week an operative shall on the first shift thereafter be paid at the rate of time and a half of normal rate plus 12.5% shift allowance for the first eight hours of the shift and thereafter and on any subsequent shift in that week at the rate of double time but with no shift allowance.

Where the nature of the work is such as to require an operative to remain at his workplace and remain available for work during mealtimes a shift allowance of 20% shall apply instead of the 14% or 12.5% otherwise referred to in this rule.

Where the work so requires, an operative shall be responsible for taking over from and handing over to his counterpart at commencement and on completion of duty unless otherwise instructed by his employer.

6.2 Employers and operatives may agree alternative shift working arrangements and rates of pay where, at any job or site, flexibility is essential to effect completion of the work.

Under this rule the first five complete shifts worked by an operative shall count as meeting the requirements of the Guaranteed Minimum Weekly Earnings Rule (WR. 17).

The shift allowance shall be regarded as a conditions payment and shall not be included when calculating overtime payments.

This Rule does not apply to operatives employed under the Continuous Working, Night Work, or Tunnel Work Rules.

WR.7 NIGHT WORK (see WR 29.1 for definition)

7.1 Night Work Allowance and Overtime

Where work is carried out at night by a separate gang of operatives from those working during daytime, operatives so working shall be paid at their normal hourly rate plus an allowance of 25% of the normal hourly rate.

Overtime shall be calculated on the normal hourly rate provided that in no case shall the total rate exceed double the normal hourly rate. Overtime shall therefore be paid as follows:

Monday to Friday
After completion of the normal working hours at the rate of time and a half plus the night work allowance (i.e. time and a half plus 25% of normal hourly rate) for the next four working hours and thereafter at double time.

Weekends
All hours worked on Saturday or Sunday night at double time until the start of working hours on Monday.

This rule does not apply to operatives employed on shift work, tunnel work or continuous working.

7.2 Health Assessments

Under the terms of this agreement night workers shall be provided with a free confidential health assessment before starting night work and repeated on a regular basis. The frequency of repeat assessments will vary between individuals according to factors such as type of night work, its duration and the age and health of the individual worker.

WR.8 CONTINUOUS WORKING

8.1 An operative whose normal duties are such as to require him to be available for work during mealtimes and consequently has no regular mealtime, shall be deemed a "continuous worker" and shall be responsible for taking over from and handing over to a work colleague at commencement and completion of duty unless otherwise instructed by his employer.

8.2 Continuous working payment will be calculated as follows:

(a) All times but excluding those in point (b)
The rate of pay will be at the normal hourly rate plus 20% for the number of hours on duty on the job.

(b) Saturday 10 p.m. to Sunday 10 p.m.
The rate of pay will be at time and a half plus 20% of the normal hourly rate.
If work between 10 p.m. Saturday to 10 p.m. Sunday is not within the normal cycle of operations for the particular job, then no continuous working allowance shall be paid but the rate of payment shall be double the normal hourly rate.

The continuous working allowance shall be regarded as a conditions payment and shall not be included when calculating overtime payments.

This rule does not apply to operatives on night-work, shift work or tunnel work.

WR.9 TIDE WORK

9.1 Where work governed by tidal conditions is carried out during part only of the normal working hours, and an operative is employed on other work for the remainder of the normal working hours, the normal hourly rate shall be paid during the normal working hours and thereafter shall be in accordance with the Rule on Overtime Rates.

9.2 Where work governed by tidal conditions necessitates operatives turning out for each tide and they are not employed on other work, they shall be paid a minimum for each tide of six hours pay at normal hourly rates, provided they do not work more than eight hours in the two tides. Payment for hours worked beyond a total of eight on two tides shall be calculated proportionately i.e. those hours worked in excess of eight multiplied by the total hours worked and the result divided by eight, to give the number of hours to be paid in addition to the twelve paid hours (six for each tide) provided for above.

Work done on Saturday after 4 p.m. and all Sunday shall be paid at the rate of double time. Operatives shall be guaranteed eight hours at ordinary rate for time work between 4 p.m. and midnight on Saturday and 16 hours at ordinary rates for two tides work on Sunday.

The rule on Overtime Rates does not apply to this paragraph 9.2.

9.3 See full rules for table showing how hours of overtime are calculated.

WR.10 TUNNEL WORK

The long-standing custom of the industry that tunnel work is normally carried out by day and by night is reaffirmed. Where shifts are being worked within and in connection with the construction of tunnels the first period of a shift equivalent to the normal working hours specified in the Working Hours rule for that day shall be deemed to be the ordinary working day. Thereafter the next four working hours shall be paid at time and a half and thereafter at double time provided that:

(a) In the case of shifts worked on Saturday the first four hours shall be paid at time and a half and thereafter at double time.

(b) In the case of shifts worked wholly on Sunday, payment shall be made for all hours worked at double time.

(c) In the case of shifts commencing on Saturday but continuing into Sunday, payment shall be made for all hours worked at double time.

(d) In case of shifts commencing on Sunday but continuing into Monday, hours worked before midnight shall be paid at double time and thereafter four working hours calculated from midnight shall be at time and a half and thereafter at double time.

This rule does not apply to an operative employed under the Continuous Working or Shift Working Rules.

WR.11 REFUELLING, SERVICING, MAINTENANCE AND REPAIRS

Operators of mechanical plant, such as excavators, cranes, generators, compressors or concrete mixers shall, if required, work and be paid at their normal hourly rate for half an hour before and half an hour after the working hours prescribed by the employer for preparatory or finishing work such as refuelling, oiling, greasing, getting out, starting up, checking over, cleaning out and parking and securing the machine or equipment.

Refuelling, Servicing, Maintenance and Repair work carried out on Saturday and Sunday shall be paid in accordance with the Rule on Overtime Rates.

WR.12 STORAGE OF TOOLS

When practicable and reasonable on a site, job or in a workshop the employer shall provide an adequate lock-up or lock-up boxes, where the operative's tools can be securely stored. The operative shall comply with the employer's requirements as regards the storage of tools. At all times an operative shall take good care of his tools and personal property and act in a responsible manner to ensure their reasonable safety.

The employer shall accept liability for such tools up to a maximum amount specified by the Council for any loss caused by fire or theft of tools which have been properly secured by an operative in such lock-up facilities or lock-up boxes. The employer does not have liability for loss in excess of the specified amount or loss caused other than by fire or theft.

WR.13 HIGHWAYS MAINTENANCE.

Where an operative is engaged in highways maintenance work the requirements of the job/contract may require that the operatives working arrangements vary from the normal provisions of this agreement. This may require, by way of example, a 12 hour working day rotating by day and night.

Such variations should be agreed in advance and the employer should advise the operative in writing of all such variations within one month.

This rule is designed to clarify how variations maybe approached.

It is open to employers and operatives to agree alternative arrangements, subject to the principles of WR.13.

13.1 Shift Working

Where an operative is required to work a shift pattern, other than five days each week, the following entitlements will need to be adjusted.

13.1.1 **Statutory and Industry Sick Pay**

The qualifying days and waiting days for both SSP and ISP may need to be adjusted in order not to disadvantage the operative and to take account of the shift pattern being worked.

13.1.2 **Payment for Absence**

The daily rate of payment for both SSP and ISP, following the first three waiting days (as per WR13.1.1), shall be based on the weekly entitlement for both SSP and ISP divided by the number of days the operative would have worked in the next seven days.

13.1.3 **Annual Holiday Entitlement (both Public & Bank)**

Where an operative is required to work a shift pattern, other than five days each week, the annual holiday entitlement and its accrual will need to be adjusted. Hours, shift patterns and working week need to be taken into account.

13.1.4 **Call out and Standby**

Where an operative is required to be available (standby) for "call out" it is open to the employer and operatives to agree appropriate working and payment arrangements.

WR.14 TRANSFER ARRANGEMENTS

14.1 At any time during the period of employment, the operative may, at the discretion of the employer be transferred from one job to another.

14.2 The employer shall have the right to transfer an operative to any site within daily travelling distance of where the operative is living. A site is within daily travelling distance if:

(a) when transport is provided free by the employer the operative can normally get from where he is living to the pickup point designated by the employer within one hour, using public transport if necessary or

(b) in any other case the operative, by using the available public transport on the most direct surface route, can normally get to the site within two hours.

14.3 Transfer to a job which requires the operative to live away from home shall be by mutual consent. The consent shall not be necessary where the operative has been in receipt of subsistence allowance in accordance with the Subsistence Allowance Rule from the same employer at any time within the preceding 12 months.

WR.15 SUBSISTENCE ALLOWANCE

When an operative is recruited on the job or site and employment commences on arrival at job or site he shall not be entitled to payment of subsistence allowance. An operative necessarily living away from the place in which he normally resides shall be entitled to a subsistence allowance of an amount specified by the Council.

Subsistence allowance shall not be paid in respect of any day on which an operative is absent from work except when that absence is due to sickness or industrial injury and he continues to live in the temporary accommodation and meets the industry sick pay requirements.

Alternatively, the employer may make suitable arrangements for a sick or injured operative to return home, the cost of which shall be met in full by the employer.

An operative in receipt of subsistence allowance shall only be entitled to daily fare and travel allowances under WR.5 between his accommodation and the job if he satisfies the employer that he is living as near to the job as there is accommodation available.

WR.16 PERIODIC LEAVE

16.1 Entitlement

When an operative is recruited on the job or site and employment commences on arrival at the job or site he shall not be entitled to the periodic leave allowances in this Rule. In other cases when an operative is recruited or a sent to a job which necessitates his living away from the place in which he normally resides, he shall he entitled to payment of his fares or conveyance in transport provided by the employer as follows:-

(a) from a convenient centre to the job at commencement

(b) to the convenient centre and back to the job at the following periodic leave intervals

(i) for jobs up to 80 miles from the convenient centre (measured utilising the AA, RAC or similar Route Planner on the shortest direct route), every four weeks

(ii) for jobs over 80 miles from the convenient centre (measured utilising the RAC Route Planner or similar on the shortest distance route) at an interval fixed by mutual arrangement between the employer and operative before he goes to the job.

(c) from the job to the convenient centre at completion.

16.2 Payment of Fares and Time Travelling

Where an employer does not exercise the option to provide free transport, the obligation to pay fares may at the employer's option be discharged by the provision of a free railway or bus ticket, or travel voucher or the rail fare.

Payment for the time spent travelling between the convenient centre and the job is as follows:

(a) On commencement of his employment at the job, the time travelling from the convenient centre to the job, provided that an operative shall not be entitled to such payment if within one month from the date of commencement of his employment on the job he discharges himself voluntarily or is discharged for misconduct.

(b) When returning to the job (i.e. one way only) after periodic leave, provided that he returns to the job at the time specified by the employer and provided also that an operative shall not be entitled to such payment if, within one month from the date of his return to the jobs, he discharges himself voluntarily or is discharged for misconduct.

(c) On termination of his employment on the job by his employer, the time spent travelling from the job to the convenient centre, provided that he is not discharged for misconduct.

(d) Time spent in periodic travelling is not to be reckoned as part of the normal working hours; periodic travelling time payments shall in all cases be at the operative's normal hourly rate to the nearest quarter of an hour and shall not exceed payment for eight hours per journey.

16.3 Convenient centre

The convenient centre shall be a railway station, bus station or other similar suitable place in the area in which the operative normally resides.

WR.17 GUARANTEED MINIMUM WEEKLY EARNINGS

An operative, who has been available for work for the week, whether or not work has been provided by the employer, shall be entitled to guaranteed minimum weekly earnings as defined in WR.1.

17.1 Loss of Guarantee

There shall be no entitlement to guaranteed minimum weekly earnings where the employer is unable to provide continuity of work due to industrial action.

17.2 Proportional Reduction

Where an operative is absent for part of normal working hours due to certified sickness or injury or for one or more days of annual or recognised public holiday, the requirement for the operative to be available for work will be deemed to be met and the payment of Guaranteed Minimum Weekly Earnings will be proportionately reduced. The proportionate reduction will not apply where the employer authorises the absence on compassionate or other grounds.

17.3 Availability for Work

An operative has satisfied the requirements to remain available for work during normal working hours if he complies with the following conditions:

(a) That, unless otherwise instructed by the employer, he has presented himself for work at the starting time and location prescribed by the employer and has remained available for work during normal working hours.

(b) Carries out satisfactorily the work for which he was engaged or suitable alternative work if instructed by the employer and

(c) He complies with the instructions of the employer as to when, during normal working hours, work is to be carried out, interrupted or resumed.

17.4 Temporary Lay-off

17.4.1 Where work is temporarily stopped or is not provided by the employer the operative may be temporarily laid off. The operative shall, subject to the provisions of WR.17.4.2 be paid his normal rate of pay for the day on which he is notified of the lay-off and one fifth of "Guaranteed Minimum Weekly Earnings" as defined in WR.17 for each of the first five days of temporary lay-off. While the stoppage of work continues and the operative is prevented from actually working, the operative will be required by the employer to register as available for work at the operative's local job centre.

WR.17 GUARANTEED MINIMUM EARNINGS (Cont'd)

17.4 **Temporary Lay-off (cont'd)**

17.4.2 The payment described in WR.17.4.1 will be made provided that, in the three months prior to any lay-off, there has not been a previous period or periods of lay-off in respect of which a guaranteed payment was made for five consecutive days or five days cumulative, excluding the day or days of notification or lay-off. In any such case the operative will not be entitled to a further guaranteed payment until a total of three months has elapsed from the last day of the period covered by the previous payment. Thereafter and for so long as the stoppage lasts, the operative shall be entitled to a further guaranteed payment of up to five days.

17.4.3 The temporary lay-off provisions may only be used when the employer has a reasonable expectation of being able to provide work within a reasonable time.

In this context, an example of an employer who has a reasonable expectation to be able to provide work maybe where a tender has been accepted but commencement has been delayed, where work is temporarily stopped due to weather conditions or for some other reason outside the employer's control. Reasonable time is not legally defined, however, an operative who has been temporarily laid off for four or more consecutive weeks (excluding the first week when the operative received full basic pay) or six weeks cumulative in any 13-week period may resign and claim a redundancy payment.

17.4.4 In no circumstances may the temporary lay-off rule be used where a genuine redundancy situation exists or to evade statutory obligations.

17.4.5 An operative who is temporarily laid off is entitled to normal payment for the day of notification of lay-off and one fifth of his guaranteed minimum earnings for each of the first days of the lay-off subject to the limitation in WR.17.4.2.

17.5 **Disputes**

A dispute arising under this Agreement concerning guaranteed minimum payment due may, at the option of the claimant, be referred to ACAS and/or an employment tribunal in the event of no decision by the Council.

WR.18 ANNUAL HOLIDAYS

The holiday year runs from the 1st January for each year with an annual (52 weeks) entitlement of 22 days of industry plus 8 days of Public / Bank holidays. Total paid holiday entitlement accrues at the rate of 0.577 days per week of service in the relevant holiday year.

This is an absolute entitlement that cannot be replaced by rolling it up into basic pay, bonus or any other allowance which would result in the operative not receiving their full holiday pay when taking annual leave.

Under the provisions of the EU Working Time Directive the entitlement to paid holidays continues to accrue during employment, notwithstanding that the operative may be absent due to sickness, paternity/maternity leave etc.

18.1 **The Winter Holiday** shall be seven working days taken in conjunction with Christmas Day, Boxing Day and New Year's Day, to give a Winter Holiday of two calendar weeks. The Council shall publish the dates of each Winter Holiday. It shall be open to employers and operatives to agree that all or some of the Winter Holiday will be taken on alternative dates. Those days of Winter Holiday that fall into the next calendar year are normally allocated to days of holiday earned in the previous year.

18.2 **Other Holidays**. The remaining 15 days of Industry Holiday may be taken at any time by agreement with the employer. An operative requesting to take paid holiday must give the employer reasonable written notice and, as a minimum, equivalent to twice the duration of holiday requested (ie. two weeks written notice to take a one week holiday) and the employer can either accept or reject the request, not later than the period equivalent to the period of holiday requested.

18.3 **Payment for Annual Holiday (22 day's each full year)**

Payment for annual holiday, which shall be made on the last pay-day preceding the commencement of each holiday period, shall be made as follows:

18.3.1 **Calculation of pay for Annual Holiday**
A weeks' pay is the average of the previous 52 complete weeks including overtime in accordance with WR.4, taxable travel allowance in accordance with WR.5.1, bonus in accordance with WR.2 and regular allowances in accordance with WR's 6, 7, 8, 9, 10, 11 & 13. Weeks during which the operative is absent due to sickness are to be excluded.

18.3.2 One day's pay is calculated by dividing a week's pay as defined by WR.18.3.1 by the contractual hours in the normal working week and multiplying by the contractual hours in the particular day.

18.4 **Leavers**

18.4.1 Operatives who leave the employment of the employer during a leave year are entitled to a compensatory payment calculated as follows:

(A÷52) x 30 - B

Where;

A is the number of complete weeks of service in the leave year.

B is the number of days leave taken by the operative in the leave year including public / bank holidays.

18.4.2 Where the number of days leave taken exceeds the operative's entitlement the employer has the right to make a deduction from payment made to the operative leaving the employment of the employer in respect of any overpayment of holiday pay. Such deduction will be calculated in accordance with WR.18.6.

18.5 **Amount of the Compensatory Payment**

The operative is entitled to a compensatory payment for each day, or part of a day, of entitlement calculated by reference to the hourly rate of pay under WR.18.4 multiplied by the normal contractual working hours.

18.6 **General Provisions related to Annual Holiday**

Where employment commences after the start of the leave year the operatives will be entitled to the proportion of the 30 days Annual Holiday equivalent to the proportion of the leave year calculated from the first week of employment to the last week of the leave year.

An operative has no entitlement to payment for holidays not taken during the holiday leave year or to carry forward entitlement to holiday from one holiday year to the subsequent holiday year.

WR.19 PUBLIC HOLIDAYS

19.1 The following are recognised as public holiday for the purpose of this agreement:

(a) **England and Wales**
Christmas Day, Boxing Day, New Year's Day, Good Friday, Easter Monday, the May Day Bank Holiday, the Spring Bank Holiday and the Summer Bank Holiday shall be recognised as public holidays, provided that such days are generally recognised as holidays in the locality in which the work is being done.

(b) **Scotland**
Christmas Day, Boxing Day, New Year's Day, Easter Monday, the first Monday in May, the Friday immediately preceding the Annual Summer Local Trades Holiday and the Friday and Monday at the Autumn Holiday, as fixed by the competent Local Authority.

(c) **Local Variations**
Where, in any locality, any of the above public holidays is generally worked and another day is recognised instead as a general holiday, such other day shall be recognised as the alternative holiday.

(d) **Alternative Days**
When Christmas Day, Boxing Day or New Year's Day falls on a Saturday or Sunday an alternative day or days of public holiday will be promulgated. Any reference in this Rule to Christmas Day, Boxing Day or New Year's Day shall be taken to apply to the alternative day so fixed.

19.2 **Payment in respect of Public Holidays**

Payment for days of public holiday recognised under this rule shall be made by the employer to an operative in his employment at the time of each such holiday on the pay day in respect of the pay week in which such holiday occurs, except that payment for Christmas Day, Boxing Day and New Year's Day shall be made on the last pay day before the Winter Holiday. The amount of payment for each day of public holiday shall be in accordance with either:

19.2.1 **Where the operatives pay does not vary with the amount of work done**
A weeks pay is simply the normal weekly wage for the contractual weekly hours as defined by the contract of employment, including, where appropriate, any fixed bonus and regular payments and/or allowances made under WR's 6, 7, 8, 9, 10, 11 & 13 but ***excluding*** overtime in accordance with WR.4.

19.2.2 **Where the operatives pay varies with the amount of work done**
Where earnings vary because of piecework or productivity bonus arrangements, then a week's pay is arrived at by calculating the earnings during the normal working week as defined by the contract of employment, averaged over the 52 complete weeks worked immediately prior to the holiday week, including, where appropriate, any fixed bonus and regular payments and/or allowances made under WR's 2, 6, 7, 8, 9, 10, 11 & 13 but ***excluding*** overtime in accordance with WR.4. Weeks during which the operative is absent due to sickness are to be ***excluded.***

19.2.3
One day's pay is calculated by dividing a week's pay as defined by either WR.19.2.1 or 19.2.2 by the contractual hours in the normal working week and multiplying by the contractual hours in the particular day.

19.2.4 **Calculation of holiday entitlement for an operative who either leaves or joins during the year**
See the Construction Industry Joint Council, Holiday Entitlement 2021 briefing note for further details .

19.3 **General Provisions Related to Payment for Public Holidays**

An operative who is required to work on a public holiday has the option, by arrangement with the employer, of an alternative day of holiday as soon thereafter as its mutually convenient, in which case the payment prescribed by this Rule shall be made in the respect of such alternative day instead of the public holiday. When the employment is terminated before such alternative day occurs, the operative shall receive such payment on the termination of employment.

19.4 **Payment for Work on a Public Holiday**

All hours worked on a day designated as a public holiday shall be paid for at double time.

WR.20 PAYMENT OF INDUSTRY SICK PAY

20.1 **Relationship of Industry Sick Pay with Statutory Sick Pay (SSP)**

Under existing legislation there is an entitlement to statutory sick pay. Any payment due under this rule shall be increased by an amount equivalent to any Statutory Sick Pay that may be payable in respect of the same day of incapacity for work under the Regulations made under that Act. These are referred to elsewhere in this Rule as "SSP Regulations".

20.2 **Limit of weekly payment**

The aggregate amount of SSP plus industry Sick Pay shall not exceed a normal weeks pay in accordance with WR.1.

20.3 **Qualifying Days**

For the purpose of both this Rule and the SSP Regulations, the Qualifying Days that shall generally apply in the industry are Monday to Friday in each week.

While the Qualifying Days referred to above shall generally be the same five days as those which form the normal week of guaranteed employment under this agreement, it is accepted that there might be certain exceptions, e.g. where the particular circumstances of the workplace require continuous six or seven day working. In these situations, it is in order, where there is mutual agreement, for other days to be regarded as 'Qualifying Days' for the purpose of this Rule and SSP.

20.4 **Amount and Duration of Payment**

(a) An operative who during employment with an employer is absent from work on account of sickness or injury shall, subject to satisfying all the conditions set out in this Rule be paid the appropriate proportion of a weekly amount specified by the Council for each qualifying day of incapacity for work. For this purpose, the appropriate proportion due for a day shall be the weekly rate divided by the number of Qualifying Days specified under WR.20.3 above.

(b) During the first four continuous weeks of employment with a new employer the Operative shall be entitled to Statutory Sick Pay for absence which the employer is satisfied is due to genuine sickness or injury.

(c) After four continuous weeks of employment the Operative shall be entitled to a total of four weeks Industry Sick Pay in addition to SSP in respect of absence that starts after these four weeks.

WR.20 PAYMENT OF INDUSTRY SICK PAY (cont'd)

20.4 Amount and Duration of Payment (cont'd)

(d) After 15 continuous weeks of employment the Operative shall be entitled to a total of seven weeks Industry Sick Pay in addition to SSP (inclusive of any ISP received in the previous 12 months) in respect of absence that starts after these 15 weeks.

(e) After 26 continuous weeks of employment the Operative shall be entitled to a total of 13 weeks Industry Sick Pay in addition to SSP (inclusive of any ISP received in the previous 12 months) in respect of absence that starts after these 26 weeks.

(f) This entitlement is based on a rolling 12 month period or single period of absence, whichever is the longer.

20.5 Notification of Incapacity for Work

An operative shall not be entitled to payment under this Rule unless, during the first Qualifying Day in the period of incapacity, his employer is notified that he is unable to work due to sickness or injury and when the incapacity for work started. Thereafter, the operative shall, at intervals not exceeding one week throughout the whole period of absence, keep the employer informed of his continuing incapacity for work. Where the employer is notified later than this Rule requires, he may nevertheless make payment under the Rule if satisfied that there was good cause for the delay.

20.6 Certification of Incapacity for Work

The whole period of absence from work shall be covered by a certificate or certificates of incapacity for work to the satisfaction of the employer. For the first seven consecutive days of sickness absence, including weekends and public holidays, a self certificate will normally suffice for this purpose. Any additional days of the same period of absence must be covered by a certificate or certificates given by a registered medical practitioner.

NOTE: For the purpose of this paragraph a self certificate means a signed statement made by the operative in a form that is approved by the employer, that he has been unable to work due to sickness/injury for the whole period specified in the statement.

20.7 Qualifying Conditions for Payment

An operative shall not be entitled to the payment prescribed in this Rule unless the following conditions are satisfied:

(a) That incapacity has been notified to the employer in accordance with WR.20.5 above

(b) That the requirements of WR.20.6 above to supply certificate(s) of incapacity for work have been complied with.

(c) That the first three Qualifying Days (for which no payment shall be due) have elapsed in each period of absence – subject to the SSP linking provisions.

(d) That none of the Qualifying Days concerned is a day of annual or public holiday granted in accordance with the provisions of this Working Rule Agreement.

(e) That the incapacity does not arise directly or indirectly from insurrection or war, attempted suicide or self-inflicted injury, the operative's own misconduct, any gainful occupation outside working hours or participation as a professional in sports or games.

(f) That the limit of payment has not been reached.

20.8 Record of Absence

The employer shall be responsible for keeping records of absence and payments made to operatives under this Rule.

WR.21 BENEFIT SCHEMES

21.1 Accident and Death Benefit

An operative is entitled to and the employer will provide insurance cover for:

(a) accidental injury in accordance with the table below as a result of an injury sustained as a result of an accident at the place of work or an accident while travelling to or from work.

Claim Type	Cover
Loss of Sight in both eyes	£30,000
Loss of Sight in one eye	£12,000
Loss of hearing in one ear	£3,600
Loss of hearing in both ears	£12,000
Loss of hand or foot	£30,000
Loss of arm or leg	£30,000
Loss of big toe	£1,600
Loss of any other toe	£700
Loss of thumb or index finger	£4,800
Loss of any other finger	£1,000
Total Disablement:	
12 Months (or more)	£3,000
24 Months (or more)	£3,000
Permanent	£15,000*

*Less any payment previously made in respect of the total disablement

(b) Death benefit, of £40,000.00 is provided on a 24/7 basis with cover doubled to £80,000 if death occurs either at the place of work or travelling to or from work. Death Benefit also covers operatives who have been continuously absent from any work since the cover ceased for a period of 2 years if unemployed or 3 years if incapacitated. The death benefit payable reduces depending on the period of absence.

(c) Employers must provide cover from the first day of employment, which includes all of the above features. Both Employee Accident Cover and Employee Life Cover are available from B&CE Benefits Schemes who can be contacted on 01293 586666.

(d) The above entitlements will be the subject of periodic review.

21.2 Pension Arrangements

Under the provisions of the Pensions Act 2011 the government is progressively introducing new, statutory pensions requirements. Stage 2 was triggered on 6th April 2018 and Stage 3 came into force on 6th April 2019. CIJC employers comply fully with the requirements.

CIJC has nominated B&CE "The People's Pension" as the preferred pension scheme for operatives employed under CIJC terms. An industry wide scheme is important because of the transient nature of employment and the aim to reduce the number of pension pots held by individuals. However, CIJC recognises that it is ultimately for the employer to decide on a pension provider and in the event that an employer utilises an alternative to B&CE the contribution levels and general arrangements in respect of pension provision shall be no less favourable than the following:

WR.21 BENEFIT SCHEMES (Cont'd)

21.2 Pension Arrangements (Cont'd)

(a) Operatives within the age range 22 up to State Pension Age who earn at least the auto-enrolment earnings trigger (as defined by Department of Work and Pensions) to be auto-enrolled. Those who fall outside of this range to be given the opportunity to enrol if they wish.

(b) The existing £5.00 per week employer contribution to be maintained during Phase Two with employers making a higher level of contribution if required as a result of the operatives' level of earnings. Operatives to make a minimum £5.00 per week contribution during Phase Two and a higher level of contribution if required as a result of the operatives' level of earnings.

(c) Contribution to be based on banded earnings as determined by Department of Work and Pensions.

(d) Operatives who currently receive a £5.00 per week employer contribution but make no personal contribution and decide to opt-out and therefore do not make a personal contribution of at least £5.00 per week shall continue to receive the existing £5.00 per week employer contribution.

(e) Operatives who currently neither receive an employer contribution nor make a personal contribution and decide to opt-out shall not be eligible to receive any employer contributions.

(f) Operatives who currently make a voluntary personal contribution of between £5.01 and £10.00 per week and while they continue to do so shall receive a matching employer contribution.

(g) An operative who has opted-out of the new pension arrangements may, at any time decide to enrol and providing such operative makes a minimum £5.00 per week personal contribution will receive a matched contribution from the employer up to a maximum of £10 per week.

(h) An operative may, at any time, decide to increase their personal weekly contribution from £5.00 up to £10.00 per week in which event such operative will receive a matching contribution from the employer.

(i) An operative may choose to make a personal contribution of any amount above £10.00 per week. In such circumstances the employer's contribution will be limited to £10.00 per week or that required as a result of the operatives' level of earnings.

(j) As an objective newly employed eligible operatives should be auto-enrolled within 6 weeks of commencing employment.

(k) Under the regulations an operative may choose to opt-out at any time in the future in which case such operative shall not be entitled to receive any employer contributions.

Nothing within the above shall diminish or detract from the operative's statutory entitlements.

The above arrangements shall apply during Phase Two of the new regulations. April 2019 will see the introduction of Stage Three of the regulations and new arrangements will then apply.

WR.22 GRIEVANCE PROCEDURE

22.1 Procedure

Grievances are concerns, problems or complaints that operatives raise with their employers. Any issue which may give rise to or has given rise to a grievance (including issues relating to discipline) affecting the employer's workplace and operatives employed by that employer at that workplace shall be dealt with in accordance with the following procedure.

Operatives should aim to resolve most grievances informally with their line manager. This has advantages for all work places, particularly where there might be a close working relationship between a manager and operative. It also allows for problems to be resolved quickly.

If appropriate the employer should give consideration to the use of mediation to assist in resolving the matter.

If a grievance cannot be settled informally, or the matter is considered sufficiently serious, the following procedure should be followed:

Step 1

The operative must write to the employer setting out the details of the grievance or complaint.

Step 2

The employer must investigate the allegations detailed in writing by the operative and arrange a meeting with the operative at the earliest practical opportunity.

The employer shall arrange a meeting and advise the operative of the right to be accompanied at the meeting by either a trade union representative or work colleague (WR.22.3)

Where possible, the employer should allow a companion to have a say in the date and time of the hearing. If the companion cannot attend on a proposed date, the operative can suggest an alternative time and date so long it is reasonable and it is not more than five working days after the original date.

Step 3

Following the meeting the employer shall write to the operative with a decision on their grievance and notify the operative of the right of appeal against that decision if the operative is not satisfied with it.

22.2 Appeals

Step 1

If the operative wishes to appeal against the employer's decision then the operative must write to the employer within five working days of the operative receiving the employer's written decision.

Step 2

The employer shall arrange a meeting at a time, date and place convenient to the operative and advise the operative of the right to be accompanied at the meeting by either a trade union representative or work colleague (WR.22.3). As far as is reasonably practicable the appeal should be with the must senior appropriate manager/director who has not previously been involved in the matter.

Step 3

Following the meeting the employer shall write to the operative with a decision on the grievance, which shall be regarded as the final stage of the grievance procedure.

WR.22 GRIEVANCE PROCEDURE (Cont'd)

22.3 The Accompanying Person (The Companion)

Accompanying an operative at a grievance hearing is a serious responsibility and the companion is entitled to a reasonable amount of paid time off to fulfil this responsibility. The time off should not only cover the hearing but also allow a reasonable amount of time to become familiar with the case and confer with the operative before the hearing. The operative must inform the employer in advance of the hearing of the identity of the proposed companion.

Companions have an important role to play in supporting the operative and should be allowed to participate as fully as possible in the hearing in order to:

- Put the operative's case
- Sum up the operative's case
- Respond on the operative's behalf to any view expressed at the hearing.

The companion may confer privately with the operative either in the hearing room or outside. The companion has no right to answer questions on the operative's behalf.

22.4 Raising a Grievance

Setting out a grievance in writing is not easy – especially for those operatives whose first language is not English or have difficultly expressing themselves on paper. In these circumstances the operative should be encouraged to seek help for example from a work colleague or a trade union representative. Under the Disciplinary Discrimination Act 1995 employers are required to make reasonable adjustments which may include assisting operatives to formulate a written grievance if they are unable to do so themselves because of a disability.

22.5 Collective Grievances or Disputes

Any issue which may give rise to or has given rise to a written grievance involving more than one operative or interpretation of the Working Rule Agreement affecting the employer's workplace and operatives employed at that workplace shall be dealt with in accordance with the following procedure.

There shall be no stoppage of work, either partial or general, including a 'go slow', strike, lock out or any other kind of disruption or restriction in output or departure from normal working, in relation to any grievance unless the grievance procedure has been fully used and exhausted at all levels.

Every effort should be made by all concerned to resolve any issue at the earliest stage. To assist in the speedy resolution of a collective grievance the matter should be referred to a steward, if appointed, or a full-time union representative where no steward is appointed.

A written record shall be kept of meetings held and conclusions reached, or decisions taken. The appropriate management or trade union representative should indicate at each stage of the procedure when a response to questions arising is likely to be given, which should be as quickly as practicable.

Stage 1

If the matter then remains unresolved, and, has not already been referred to a full time union representative, the steward shall report the matter to the appropriate full time trade union representative who shall, if he considers it appropriate, pursue any outstanding issue with the employer or his nominee. The employer should be advised him in writing of the issues(s).

Stage 2

Failing resolution of the issue at stage 1, and within 28 day, or such further period as may be agreed between the parties, the full time local union representative shall report the matter up to the appropriate senior full time representative and to an appropriate representative of the employer. Such senior trade union representative, if there are good grounds for so doing, shall pursue the issue with the appropriate representative of the employer.

Where a collective grievance reaches this stage it would be appropriate for each party to notify the appropriate CIJC joint secretary of the grievance.

Stage 3

Failing resolution of the issue at stage 2, and within 28 days, or such further period as may be agreed between the parties, the senior union representative concerned shall, if it is decided to pursue the matter further, put the issue in writing to the employer and it is the duty of such representative and / or the employer to submit the matter, as quickly as practical, to the Construction Industry Joint Council for settlement.

The decisions of the Construction Industry Joint Council shall be accepted and implemented by all concerned.

WR.23 DISCIPLINARY PROCEDURE

It is recognised that, in order to maintain high standards of efficiency, safety, quality and good morale, the employer has the right to discipline any operative:

- who fails to perform his or her duties and responsibilities competently and in accordance with the instructions of the employer; and/or
- whose behaviour is unsatisfactory; and/or
- who fails to make appropriate use of the disputes procedure for the resolution of questions arising without recourse to strike or other industrial action.

It is equally recognised that the employer must exercise this right with fairness and care.

Cases of minor misconduct or unsatisfactory performance are usually best dealt with informally. A quiet word is often all that is required to improve an operative's conduct or performance. The informal approach may be particularly helpful in small firms, where problems can be dealt with quickly and confidentially. There will, however, be situations where matters are more serious or where an informal approach has been tried and isn't working.

If informal action doesn't bring about an improvement, or the misconduct or unsatisfactory performance is considered to be too serious to be classed as minor, the employer should provide the operative with a clear signal of their dissatisfaction by taking formal action as follows:-

Note: The employer will not take any disciplinary action before carrying out a full investigation into the matter for which the disciplinary hearing is to be held.

If appropriate the employer should give consideration to the use of mediation to assist in resolving the matter.

Where there is cause to take disciplinary action, the employer will give the operative adequate written notice of the date, time and place of the disciplinary hearing. The notice must contain details of the complaint against the operative and advise of the right to be accompanied at the hearing or appeal stage by either a trade union representative or a work colleague. (WR.23.7). Prior to the disciplinary hearing the operative should be given copies of any documents that will be produced at the hearing.

WR.23 DISCIPLINARY PROCEDURE (Cont'd)

Where possible, the employer should allow a companion to have a say in the date and time of the hearing. If the companion can't attend on a proposed date, the operative can suggest an alternative time and date so long as it is reasonable and it is not more than five working days after the original date.

Discipline shall be applied in accordance with the following procedure:

23.1 Disciplinary Action and Stages

Disciplinary action will comprise the following stages unless WR.23.4 is applicable:

(a) A written warning

(b) A final written warning

(c) Dismissal

(d) Following each of the above stages the employer will notify the operative of the decision in writing including the right of appeal under WR.23.3.

(e) The employer shall deal with disciplinary matters without undue delay.

(f) Where an operative has been accompanied at a disciplinary or appeal hearing by a trade union representative the employer shall provide the representative or the trade union with a copy of any letter of warning or dismissal providing the operative gives express permission.

23.2 **Duration of Warnings**

Warnings will normally be discarded after 6 months in the case of a written warning and 12 months in the case of a final warning.

23.3 **Right of Appeal**

The operative shall be advised of the right to appeal at every stage of the procedure. Where the employer's organisation structure allows, the appeal should be heard by a senior manager / director of the employer who has not been involved in the disciplinary procedure. The request for an appeal must be made in writing within five working days of the date of the disciplinary decision. The employer will inform the operative of the final decision in writing.

23.4 **Serious Misconduct**

In exceptional circumstances and if the matter is sufficiently serious, a final written warning may be issued in the first instance.

23.5 Gross Misconduct

23.5.1 In certain circumstances the conduct may be so serious as to be referred to as gross misconduct. In such circumstances the first two stages of the disciplinary procedure, written warning, and final warning, may be omitted and the operative may be summarily dismissed without notice or pay in lieu of notice, but only after following a fair disciplinary process in line with the ACAS Code of Practice. The employer will notify the operative of the alleged gross misconduct in writing and invite them to a disciplinary hearing advising them of their right to be accompanied at the disciplinary hearing or appeal stage by either a trade union representative or a work colleague (WR.23.7).

Set out below is a list, although not exhaustive, of behaviour, which will be considered by the employer to be gross misconduct:

- Being under the influence of alcohol or other stimulants or illicit drugs during working hours,
- Physical violence – actual or threatened,
- Violent, disorderly or indecent conduct.
- Deliberate damage to property,
- Theft, fraud or falsification of company records, documents or time sheets,
- Serious breach of confidence (subject to the Public Interest Disclosure legislation)
- Removal from company sites or other premises of property belonging to the company, fellow operative, client, sub-contractor, supplier or other without the approval of the employer,
- Serious breach of the employer's safety policy, rules or regulations,
- Bringing the employer into serious disrepute,
- Acts of incitement to or actual acts of discrimination on grounds of sex, race, religion, belief, colour, ethnic origin, disability, age or sexual orientation.
- Serious bullying or harassment,
- Serious carelessness resulting in loss or damage – or potential loss or damage,
- Serious insubordination,
- Misuse of the employers or clients property or name.

23.5.3 Summary dismissal means termination of employment without notice or pay in lieu of notice. In circumstances where a gross misconduct is alleged to have occurred the operative will be suspended on full pay whilst an investigation is carried out prior to a disciplinary hearing.

23.6 **Shop Stewards**

Where it is proposed to take disciplinary action against a duly appointed Shop Steward, or other trade union official, then before doing so, the employer shall notify the appropriate full time official of the trade union concerned.

23.7 **The Accompanying Person (The Companion)**

Accompanying an operative at a disciplinary hearing is a serious responsibility and the companion is entitled to a reasonable amount of paid time off to fulfil this responsibility all as item WR 22.2.

Companions have an important role to play in supporting the operative and should be allowed to participate as fully as possible the hearing in order to:

- Put the operative's case
- Sum up the operative's case
- Respond on the operative's behalf to any view expressed at the hearing

The companion may confer privately with the operative, either in the hearing room or outside. The companion has no right to answer questions on the operative's behalf.

WR.24 TERMINATION OF EMPLOYMENT

24.1 Employer Notice to Operative

The employment may be terminated at any time by mutual consent which should preferably be expressed in writing.

All outstanding wages including holiday pay are to be paid at the expiration of the period of notice and the employee advised of his entitlement to PAYE certificates or, in lieu thereof, a written statement that they will be forwarded as soon as possible.

The minimum period of notice of termination of employment that an employer shall give to an employee is:-

(a) During the first month	One day's notice
(b) After one months' continuous employment but less than two years	One week's notice
(c) After two years' continuous employment but less than twelve years	One weeks notice for each full year of continuous employment.
(d) Twelve years' continuous employment or more	Twelve weeks' notice

24.2 Operative Notice to Employer

The minimum period of notice of termination of employment that an employee shall give an employer is:

(a) During the first month -	one day's notice
(b) After one month's' continuous employment -	one week's notice.

WR.25 TRADE UNIONS

25.1 The Employers' Organisations recognises the Signatory Trade Unions within the Construction Industry Joint Council for the purposes of collective bargaining. Both parties are fully committed to the Working Rule Agreement and strongly urge employers to:

(a) recognise the trade unions who are signatories to the Agreement;

(b) ensure that all operatives are in the direct employment of the company or its sub contractors and are engaged under the terms and conditions of the Working Rule Agreement.

25.2 Deduction of Union Subscriptions

When requested by a Signatory Trade Union, employers should provide facilities for the deduction of union subscriptions (check-off) from the pay of trade union members.

25.3 Full Time Trade Union Officials

A full time official of a trade union which is party to the Agreement shall be entitled, by prior arrangement with the employer's site manager or other senior representative in charge and on presenting his credentials, to visit a workplace to carry out trade union duties and to see that the Working Rule Agreement is being properly observed.

25.4 Trade Union Shop Steward

An operative is eligible for appointment as a Steward on completion of not less than four weeks continuous work in the employment of the employer. Where an operative has been properly appointed as a Steward in accordance with the rules of his trade union (being a trade union signatory to the Agreement) and issued with written credentials by the trade union concerned, the trade union shall notify the employer's site manager or other senior representative of the appointment, for formal recognition by the employer of the Steward. On completion of this procedure the employer will recognise the Steward, unless the employer has any objection to granting recognition, in which case he shall immediately notify the trade union with a view to resolving the question.

An employer shall not be required to recognise for the purposes of representation more than one officially accredited Steward for each trade or union at any one site or workplace.

25.5 Convenor Stewards

Where it is jointly agreed by the employer and the trade unions, having regard to the number of operatives employed by the employer at the workplace and/or the size of the workplace, the recognised trade unions may appoint a Convenor Steward, who should normally be in the employment of the main contractor, from among the Stewards and such appointment shall be confirmed in writing by the Operatives' side. On completion of this procedure the employer will recognise the Convenor Steward, unless the employer has any objection to granting recognition in which case he shall immediately notify the trade union with a view to resolving the question.

25.6 Duties and Responsibilities of Stewards and Convenor Stewards.

25.6.1 Duties of the Shop Stewards shall be:

(a) To represent the members of their trade union engaged on the site/factory/depot,

(b) to ensure that the Working Rule Agreement is observed,

(c) to recruit members on the site / factory / depot into a signatory trade union,

(d) to participate in the Grievance Procedure at the appropriate stage under WR. 22,

(e) to assist in the resolution of disputes in accordance with the Working Rule Agreement.

25.6.2 Duties of the Convenor Steward, in addition to those set out in WR 25.6.1 shall be:

(a) to represent the operatives on matters concerning members of more than one trade union,

(b) to co-operate with management and to assist individual Shop Stewards

(c) to ensure that disputes are resolved by negotiation in accordance with the Working Rule Agreement.

25.6.3 No Steward or Convenor Steward shall leave their place of work to conduct trade union business without prior permission of their immediate supervisor. Such permission should not be unreasonably withheld but should only be given where such business is urgent and relevant to the site, factory or shop.

WR.25 TRADE UNIONS (Cont'd)

25.7 **Steward Training**

To assist them in carrying out their functions, Shop Stewards will be allowed reasonable release to attend training courses approved by their trade union.

25.8 **Stewards Facilities**

Management shall give recognised trade union officials and/or convenor stewards reasonable facilities for exercising their proper duties and functions. These facilities, which must not be unreasonably withheld, must not be abused. The facilities should include use of a meeting room, access to a telephone and the use of a notice board on site. If the Convenor Steward so requests, the employer shall provide him regularly with the names of operatives newly engaged by that contractor for work on that site, factory or depot.

25.9 **Meetings**

Meetings of operatives, stewards or convenor stewards may be held during working hours only with the prior consent of Management.

25.10 Blacklisting

The CIJC does not condone any form of blacklisting of any worker.

WR.26 SCAFFOLDERS

The following provisions are to be read in conjunction with the provisions of the Construction Industry Scaffolders' Record Scheme (CISRS) General Information publication. It should be noted that if a scaffolder or trainee scaffolder is not in possession of a valid CISRS card at the time of engagement, the new employer should make an application immediately. Any difficulties should be referred to the Joint Secretaries for action in accordance with the Scheme.

26.1 Scaffolders employed whole time as such come under one of the categories outlined below:

Trainee Scaffolder: an operative who can produce a current, valid CISRS Trainee Scaffolder card

Scaffolder: an operative who can produce a current, valid CISRS Scaffolders card

Advanced Scaffolder: an operative who can produce a current, valid CISRS Advanced Scaffolders card.

Operatives holding expired CISRS Scaffolder or Advanced Scaffolder Cards will be paid at the Trainee rate (see WR.26.4) until their card is renewed.

CISRS have introduced a new category of card, **Basic Access System Erector** (BASE) for non scaffolding operatives. This will allow an operative upon completion of the appropriate CISRS course to erect some specified simple scaffolding structures using prefabricated systems scaffold, which will be restricted by height, structure and work environment. See www.cisrs.org.uk for further information.

Note: operatives carrying the BASE card are not fully qualified scaffolders and must not carry out any works in tube and fittings, also they must not carry out any works in prefabricated systems which exceed the scope of their training.

26.2 No operative other than a Scaffolder or Advanced Scaffolder, as defined above, may be employed on scaffolding operations and no operative other than an Advanced Scaffolder may be employed on advanced scaffolding operations (see schedule WR 26.6 and 26.7) unless working together and under the direct supervision of a qualified CISRS Scaffolder or Advanced Scaffolder

26.3 The onus of proof of training and experience required under this Rule is on the operative concerned and the onus on checking the proof submitted is on the employer.

26.4 Employers will fund the CPD course fee and reasonable associated costs of attendance, including wages, for scaffolders in their direct employment as at the date of CISRS Scaffolder and CISRS Advanced Scaffolder card renewal. As with other employer funded training, such funding may be linked to Training Agreements. Any training Agreements shall not be financially onerous on the operative.

26.5 Scaffolders covered by WR 26.1 are entitled to the Skilled Operative Basic Rate of Pay 4,3,2,1 or Craft Rate as follows:

	Rate
CISRS Labourer	General Operative Rate
CISRS BASE (Basic Access Systems Erector)	4
CISRS Trainee	4
CISRS Scaffolder	Craft Rate
CISRS Advanced	Craft Rate

26.6 **Approved List of Scaffolding Operations**,

Erecting, adapting and dismantling:
Independent, putlog and birdcage scaffolds, static and mobile towers.
Beams to form gantries and openings, correctly braced.
Hoist frameworks
Protective fans.
Stack scaffolds.
Roof scaffolds
Scaffolds to form truss out scaffolds
Simple cantilevers
Edge protection
Proprietary systems (see rear of card to verify product training)
Fixing sheeting/netting to scaffold framework
Interpreting simple design layout drawing for scaffolding detailed above.
Applying knowledge of Construction
Regulations / Legislation / Industry best practice and guidance to operations listed above.

Note: CISRS Scaffolders are sufficiently qualified and deemed competent for onsite supervision for all of the operations listed above.

26.7 **Advanced List**

All work in list of Scaffolding operations plus:

Erecting, adapting or dismantling
Suspended scaffolds
Raking or flying shores.
Other forms of designed structures, e.g. complex design drawings, larger truss-outs, cantilevers, lifting structures, ramps, footbridges and temporary roofs.
Scaffolding or standard props (including all bracing) to form a dead shore, including adjustable bases and fork heads.
Scaffolding and proprietary systems (including levelling to within reasonable tolerances) to support formwork as laid out in engineering scaffold drawings (see rear of card to verify product training)
Interpreting scaffold design drawings.

GENERAL INFORMATION

WR.26 SCAFFOLDERS (Cont'd)

26.7 **Advanced List (Cont'd)**

Applying knowledge of Construction Regulations / Legislation / Industry best practice and guidance to operations listed above.

Note: Only CISRS Advanced Scaffolders are sufficiently qualified and deemed competent for onsite supervision for all of the operations listed above.

Note: See the CISRS website www.cisrs.org.uk for further information

WR.27 HEALTH SAFETY AND WELFARE

27.1 The Employers and Operatives Organisation who are signatories to the Working Rule Agreement are committed to operating construction sites that provide a working environment which is both safe and free from hazards for everybody within the construction industry and for members of the public. All workers, whether operatives or management, comply with the requirement of legislation dealing with health, safety and welfare.

27.2 **Trade Union Safety Representatives**

Legislation provides that recognised trade unions may appoint safety representatives to represent operatives. Provision is also made for the establishment of safety committees where a formal request, in writing, is made to an employer by at least two safety representatives who have been appointed in accordance with legislation.

Trade union safety representatives are an appropriate means of consulting with those workers who are represented by a trade union, however not all workers will be represented by the appointed person and they need an alternative method of consultation.

27.3 **Site Induction**

Everyone working on site will go through a health and safety induction process before they are allowed to commence work on site. This induction training will concentrate on site specific health and safety factors and will be given by appropriate personnel nominated by the employer.

27.4 **Consultation with the Workforce**

Employers' and Operatives' Organisations wish to create an industry where everyone is valued, all views are listened to and a safe and healthy working environment is the norm. Employers are committed to worker consultation on health, safety and welfare issues. Consultation mechanisms, such as toolbox talks, notice boards and other appropriate means determined by the employer, will be made known to all workers on site and details will be included in the construction phase health and safety plan.

WR. 28 REFERENCE PERIOD

28.1 For the purpose of compliance with the Working Rule Agreement, statutory definitions, entitlements and calculations the reference period shall, subject to the requirements of WR.3.2 - "Average Weekly Working Hours" - be 12 months, in accordance with the Working Time Regulations 1998.

WR.29 LENGTH OF NIGHT WORK WR.6-10, 13

29.1 Night Worker

A 'night worker' is defined as a worker who works at least 3 hours of his daily working time between the hours of 11.00pm and 6.00am on the majority of days worked.

29.2 Length of Night Work

The parties to this agreement recognise that working patterns occasionally arising within the construction industry require recognition in order that operations comply with the Working Time Regulations 1998. In the light of this the parties have agreed that in accordance with Regulation 23(a) of that act and any amendments or modifications thereof, the following Regulations are excluded in relation to work undertaken under the provisions of the above Working Rules:

(a) Regulation 6(1) - eight hour average limit on length of night work;

(b) Regulation 6(2) - application of average eight hour limit to night workers;

(c) Regulation 6(3) - 17-week reference period; and

(d) Regulation 6(7) - eight hour absolute limit on the length of night work in the case of work involving special hazards or heavy physical or mental strain.

Whilst establishing the ability to work night shifts of longer than 8 hours, nothing in this rule places any obligation on any worker to work a night shift of longer than 8 hours.

WR.30 SUPPLEMENTARY AGREEMENTS

When it is agreed between the employer(s) and operative(s) that at any particular workplace it would be appropriate to enter into an agreement specifically for that workplace, any such agreement shall be supplementary to and not in conflict with this Working Rule Agreement. Where any dispute arises in this respect the Working Rule Agreement takes precedence.

WR.31 DURATION OF AGREEMENT

This Agreement shall continue in force and the parties to it agree to honour its terms until the expiration of three calendar month's notice to withdraw from it, given by either the Employers' side or the Operatives' side.

NOTES

Joint Secretaries Guidance Notes on the Working Rule Agreement of the Construction Industry Joint Council.

Introduction

These Guidance Notes, whilst not forming part of the Working Rules, are intended to assist employers and operatives to understand and implement the Working Rule Agreement.

It is the intent of all parties to this Agreement that operatives employed in the building and civil engineering industry are engaged under the terms and conditions of the CIJC Working Rule Agreement.

Requests for definitions, clarification or resolution of disputes in relation to this Agreement should be addressed to the appropriate adherent body.

WR.1 Entitlement to Basic Rates of Pay

WR.1 sets out the entitlement to the basic rate of pay, additional payments for skilled work and occasional skilled work.

There are six basic rates of pay and rates for Apprentices under this Agreement; a General Operative rate, four rates for Skilled Operatives, a rate for a Craft Operative and rates for Apprentices.

WR.1 Entitlement to Basic Rates of Pay (Cont'd)

Payment for Occasional Skilled Work

WR.1.1.2 deals with the payment for occasional skilled work and provides that general operatives who are required to carry out work defined in Schedule 1 on an occasional basis should receive an increased rate of pay commensurate with the work they are carrying out for the period such work is undertaken. This sets out the flexibility to enable enhanced payment to be made to general operatives undertaking skilled work for a limited amount of time but should not be used where the operative is engaged whole time on skilled work.

Skilled Operatives

WR.1.2.1 sets out a permanent rate of pay for skilled operatives who are engaged whole time on the skilled activity and does not permit the operative engaged on whole time skilled work to have his pay reduced to the General Operative basic rate when occasional alternative work is undertaken.

WR.3.2 Average Weekly Working Hours.

Working Rules 3.2 and 7.2 provide, where there are objective or technical reasons, for the calculation of average weekly working hours by reference to a period of twelve months.

Whilst it is open to employers and employees to agree to work additional hours over the "normal working hours," Rule 3.2 does not give the employer the unilateral right to introduce excessive hours on a job or site. The 12 month averaging period referred to may only be applied where, for objective reasons, it is necessary to ensure completion of the work efficiently and effectively or where there are technical reasons that require additional hours to be worked.

Examples of objective and/or technical reasons which may require average weekly working hours to be calculated using a twelve month reference period are set out below. The list is not exhaustive other objective or technical reasons may apply.

Objective Reasons:

Work on infrastructure, roads, bridges, tunnels and tide work etc.

Client requirements for work to be completed within a tightly defined period, work undertaken for exhibitions, schools, retail outlets, shopfitting and banks etc.

Emergency work, glazing and structural safety etc.

Technical Reasons;

Work requiring a continuous concrete pour, surfacing and coating work, tunnelling etc.

Note Any disputes regarding the validity of objective and/or technical reasons may be referred to the National Conciliation Panel of the Construction Industry Joint Council.

WR. 4 Overtime Rates

Where an operative who has worked overtime fails without authorisation to be available for work during normal weekly working hours he may suffer a reduction in or may not be entitled to premium payments in respect of overtime worked.

To calculate the number of hours paid at premium rate (overtime) you subtract the number of hours of unauthorised absence from the total number of hours overtime worked. This is in effect using a part of the hours of overtime worked to make the hours paid at the normal hourly rate up to 39 hours per week, the balance of overtime is paid at the appropriate premium rate.

N.B. For full details of the conciliation dispute machinery please see the Constitution and Rules of the CIJC.
Any question relating to Working Rules not covered by the notes of guidance should be referred to the appropriate adherent body

EXAMPLES

Example 1.

An operative works three hours overtime on Monday, Tuesday and Wednesday; works normal hours on Thursday and is unavailable for work on Friday due to unauthorised absence. In these circumstances overtime premia will be calculated as follows:

	Normal Hours	Overtime Hours
Monday	8	3
Tuesday	8	3
Wednesday	8	3
Thursday	8	-
Friday	-	-
Total hours worked	(A) 32	(B) 9

Normal weekly working hours	(C)	39
Less total normal hours worked	(A)	32
Hours required to make up to 39	(D)	7
Total overtime hours	(B)	9
Less	(D)	7
Hours to be paid at premium rate	(E)	2

The operative is therefore, entitled to be paid:

(A+D)	39	Hours at "Normal Hourly Rate"
(E)	2	Hours at premium rate (time and a half)
Total	41	Hours

EXAMPLE

Example 2

An operative works four hours overtime on a Monday, three hours on Tuesday, five hours (one hour double time) on Wednesday, no overtime on either Thursday or Friday and absents himself from work on Friday at 12 noon without authorisation and then works six hours on Saturday. This calculation would be as follows:

	Normal Hours	Overtime Hours	
Monday	8	4	
Tuesday	8	3	
Wednesday	8	5	(1hour double time)
Thursday	8	-	
Friday	3 ½	-	
Saturday	-	6	(2hours double time)
Total Hours worked	(A) 35½	(B) 18	

Normal weekly working hours	(C)	39
Less total normal hours worked	(A)	35 ½
Hours required to make up to 39	(D)	3 ½
Total overtime hours	(B)	18
Less	(D)	3 ½
Hours to be paid at premium rate	(E)	14 ½

The operative is, therefore, entitled to be paid:

(A+D)	39	Hours at "Normal Hourly Rate"
(E)	14 ½	Hours at premium rate (time and a half)
Total	53 ½	Hours

The entitlement to 3 hours pay at double time is extinguished in this example by the hours of unauthorised absence. If the number of hours worked at double time exceeds the number of hours of unauthorised absence the balance must be paid at the rate of double time.

Note There shall be no reduction in overtime premium payments for operatives who are absent from work with the permission of the employer or who are absent due to sickness or injury

SCHEDULE 1

Specified Work Establishing Entitlement to the Skilled Operative Pay Rate 4, 3, 2, 1 or Craft Rate

	Basic Rate of Pay
BAR BENDERS AND REINFORCEMENT FIXERS	
Bender and fixer of Concrete Reinforcement capable of reading and understanding drawings and bending schedules and able to set out work	Craft Rate
CONCRETE	
Concrete Leveller or Vibrator Operator	4
Screeder and Concrete Surface Finisher working from datum such as road-form, edge beam or wire	4
Operative required to use trowel or float (hand or powered) to produce high quality finished concrete	3
DRILLING AND BLASTING	
Drills, rotary or percussive: mobile rigs, operator of	3
Operative attending drill rig	4
Shotfirer, operative in control of and responsible for explosives, including placing, connecting and detonating charges	3
Operatives attending on shotfirer including stemming	4
DRYLINERS	
Operatives undergoing approved training in drylining	4
Operatives who can produce a certificate of training achievement indicating satisfactory completion of at least one unit of approved drylining training	3
Dryliners who have successfully completed their training in drylining fixing and finishing	Craft Rate
FORMWORK CARPENTERS	
1st year trainee	4
2nd year trainee	3
Formwork Carpenters	Craft Rate
GANGERS AND TRADE CHARGEHANDS	
(Higher Grade payments may be made at the employer's discretion)	2
GAS NETWORK OPERATIONS	
Operatives who have successfully completed approved training to the standard of:	
GNO Trainee	4
GNO Assistant	3
Team Leader - Services	2
Team Leader - Mains	1
Team Leader - Main and Services	1
HIGHWAYS MAINTENANCE	
Lead safety fence installer: Holder of appropriate qualification in vehicle restraint systems. Team leader, erector, installer and maintenance of vehicle safety fencing.	Craft
Safety fence installer: Holder of appropriate qualification in vehicle restraint systems. Erector, installer and maintenance of vehicle safety fencing.	3
Traffic management operative: Installing, maintaining and removal of traffic management systems.	3
Trainee traffic management operative: Assist in Installing, maintaining and removal of traffic management systems.	4
Lead traffic management operative (TMF equivalent): Holder of appropriate qualification in installation, maintenance and removal of traffic management systems.	Craft

	Basic Rates of Pay
Highways Maintenance operative: Undertake routine and cyclical maintenance duties and secondary response. To include; lighting, structures and other general highways duties.	3
Highways Incident Response Operative: Holder of appropriate qualification in incident response. Routine and cyclical maintenance and incident response.	2
LINESMEN - ERECTORS	
1st Grade (Skilled in all works associated with the assembly, erection, maintenance of Overhead Lines Transmission Lines on Steel Towers; concrete or Wood Poles; including all overhead lines construction elements.)	2
2nd Grade (As above but lesser degree of skill - or competent and fully skilled to carry out some of the elements of construction listed above.)	3
Linesmen-erector's mate (Semi-skilled in works specified above and a general helper)	4
MASON PAVIORS	
Operative assisting a Mason Pavior undertaking kerb laying, block and sett paving, flag laying, in natural stone and precast products	4
Operative engaged in stone pitching or dry stone walling	3
MECHANICS	
Maintenance Mechanic capable of carrying out field service duties, maintenance activities and minor repairs	2
Plant Mechanic capable of carrying out major repairs and overhauls including welding work, operating metal turning lathe or similar machine and using electronic diagnostic equipment	1
Maintenance/Plant Mechanics' Mate on site or in depot	4
Tyre Fitter, heavy equipment tyres	2
MECHANICAL PLANT DRIVERS AND OPERATORS	
Backhoe Loaders (with rear excavator bucket and front shovel and additional equipment such as blades, hydraulic hammers, and patch planers)	
Backhoe, up to and including 50kW net engine power; driver of	4
Backhoe, over 50kW up to and including 100kW net engine power; driver of	3
Backhoe, over 100kW net engine power; driver of	2
Compressors and Generators	
Air compressor or generators over 10 KW: operator of	4
Concrete Mixers	
Operative responsible for operating a concrete mixer or mortar pan up to and including 400 litres drum capacity	4
Operative responsible for operating a concrete mixer over 400 litres and up to and including 1,500 litres drum capacity	3
Operative responsible for operating a concrete mixer over 1,500 litres drum capacity	2
Operative responsible for operating a mobile self-loading and batching concrete mixer up to 2,500 litres drum capacity	2
Operative responsible for a operating a mechanical drag-shovel	4

GENERAL INFORMATION

SCHEDULE 1 (Cont'd) | **Basic Rates of Pay**

MECHANICAL PLANT DRIVERS AND OPERATORS (cont'd)

Concrete Placing Equipment

Trailer mounted or static concrete pumps; self-propelled concrete placers; concrete placing booms; operator of | 3

Self-propelled Mobile Concrete Pump, with or without boom, mounted on lorry or lorry chassis; driver/operator of | 2

Mobile Cranes

Self-propelled Mobile Crane on road wheels, rough terrain wheels or caterpillar tracks including lorry mounted:

Max. lifting capacity at min. radius, up to and including 5 Tonne; driver of | 4

Max. lifting capacity at min. radius, over 5 Tonne and up to and including 10 Tonne; driver of | 3

Max. lifting capacity at min. radius, over 10 Tonne | Craft Rate

Where grabs are attached to Cranes the next higher skill rate of pay applies except over 10 tonne where the rate is at the employer's discretion.

Tower Cranes (including static or travelling: standard trolley or luffing jib)

Up to and including 2 Tonne max. lifting capacity at min. radius; driver of | 4

Over 2 Tonne up to and including 10 Tonne max. lifting capacity at min. radius; driver of | 3

Over 10 Tonne up to and including 20 Tonne max. lifting capacity at min. radius; driver of | 2

Over 20 Tonne max. lifting capacity at min. radius; driver of | Craft Rate

Miscellaneous Cranes and Hoists

Overhead bridge crane or gantry crane up to and including 10 Tonne capacity; driver of | 3

Overhead bridge crane or gantry crane over 10 Tonne capacity up to and including 20 Tonne capacity; driver of | 2

Power driven hoist or jib crane; driver of | 4

Slinger / Signaller appointed to attend Crane or hoist to be responsible for fastening or slinging loads and generally to direct lifting operations | 3

Dozers

Crawler dozer with standard operating weight up to and including 10 Tonne; driver of | 3

Crawler dozer with standard operating weight over 10 Tonne and up to and including 50 Tonne; driver of | 2

Crawler dozer with standard operating weight over 50 Tonne; driver of | 1

Dumpers and Dump Trucks

Up to and including 10 tonne rated payload; driver of | 4

Over 10 Tonne and up to and including 20 Tonne rated payload; driver of | 3

Over 20 Tonne and up to and including 50 Tonne rated payload; driver of | 2

Over 50 Tonne and up to and including 100 Tonne rated payload; driver of | 1

Over 100 Tonne rated payload; driver of | Craft Rate

Excavators (360 degree slewing)

Excavators with standard operating weight up to and including 10 Tonne; driver of | 3

Excavator with standard operating weight over 10 Tonne and up to and including 50 Tonne; driver of | 2

Excavator with standard operating weight over 50 Tonne; driver of | 1

Banksman appointed to attend excavator or responsible for positioning vehicles during loading of tipping | 3

Basic Rates of Pay

Fork-Lifts Trucks and Telehandlers

Smooth or rough terrain fork lift trucks (including side loaders) and telehandlers up to and including 3 Tonne lift capacity; driver of | 3

Over 3 Tonne lift capacity; driver of | 2

Motor Graders; driver of | 2

Motorised Scrapers; driver of | 2

Motor Vehicles (Road Licensed Vehicles) Driver and Vehicle Licensing Agency (DVLA)

Vehicles requiring a driving licence of category C1; driver of | 4

(Goods vehicle with maximum authorised mass (mam) exceeding 3.5 Tonne but not exceeding 7.5 Tonne and including such a vehicle drawing a trailer with a mam not over 750kg)

Vehicles requiring a driving licence of category C; driver of | 2

(Goods vehicle with a maximum authorised mass (mam) exceeding 3.5 Tonne and including such a vehicle drawing a trailer with mam not over 750kg)

Vehicles requiring a driving licence of category C plus E; driver of | 1

(Combination of a vehicle in category C and a trailer with maximum authorised mass over 750kg)

Power Driven Tools

Operatives using power-driven tools such as breakers, percussive drills, picks and spades, rammers and tamping machines. | 4

Power Rollers

Roller, up to and including 4 tonne operating weight; driver of | 4

Roller, over 4 Tonne operating weight and upwards; driver of | 3

Pumps

Power-driven pump(s); attendant of | 4

Shovel Loaders (wheeled or tracked, including skid steer)

Up to and including 2 cubic metre shovel capacity; driver of | 4

Over 2 cubic metre and up to and including 5 cubic metre shovel capacity; driver of | 3

Over 5 cubic metre shovel capacity; driver of | 2

Tractors (wheeled or tracked)

Tractor, when used to tow trailer and/or with mounted compressor up to and including 100kW rated engine power; driver of | 4

Tractor, ditto, over 100KW up to and including 250kW rated engine power; driver of | 3

Tractor, ditto, over 250kW rated engine power; driver of | 2

Trenchers (type wheel, chain or saw)

Trenching Machine, up to and including 50kW gross engine power; driver of | 4

Trenching Machine, over 50kW and up to and including 100kW gross engine power; driver of | 3

Trenching Machine, 100kW gross engine power; driver of | 2

Winches, Power driven winch, driver of | 4

SCHEDULE 1 (Cont'd)

Basic Rates of Pay

PILING

	Basic Rates of Pay
General Skilled Piling Operative	4
Piling Chargehand/Ganger	3
Pile Tripod Frame Winch Driver	3
CFA or Rotary or Driven Mobile Piling Rig Driver	2
Concrete Pump Operator	3

PIPE JOINTERS

Jointers, pipes up to and including 300mm diameter	4
Jointers, pipes over 300mm diameter and up to 900mm diameter	3
Jointers, pipes over 900mm diameter	2
except in HDPE mains when experienced in butt fusion and/or electrofusion jointing operations	2

PIPELAYERS

Operative preparing the bed and laying pipes up to and including 300 mm diameter	4
Operative preparing the bed and laying pipes over 300 mm diameter and up to and including 900mm diameter.	3
Operative preparing the bed and laying pipes over 900mm diameter	2

PRE-STRESSING CONCRETE

Operative in control of and responsible for hydraulic jack and other tensioning devices engaged in post-tensioning and/or pre-tensioning concrete elements	3

RAIL

Plate layer (Not labourer in a gang)	3

ROAD SURFACING WORK (includes rolled asphalt, dense bitumen macadam and surface dressings)

Operatives employed in this category of work to be paid as follows:

Chipper	4
Gritter Operator	4
Raker	3
Paver Operator	3
Leveller on Paver	3
Road Planer Operator	3
Road Roller Driver, 4 Tonne and upwards	3
Spray Bar Operator	4

SCAFFOLDERS See WR. 26 above

STEELWORK CONSTRUCTION

Basic Rates of Pay

A skilled steel erector engaged in the assembly erection and fixing of steel-framed buildings and structures	1
Operative capable of and engaged in fixing simple steelwork components such as beams, girders and metal decking	3

TIMBERMAN

Timberman, installing timber supports	3
Highly skilled timberman working on complex supports using timbers of size 250mm by 125mm and above	2
Operative attending	4

TUNNELS

Operative working below ground on the construction of tunnels underground spaces or sinking shafts:

Tunnel Boring Machine operator	2
Tunnel Miner (skilled operative working at the face)	3
Tunnel Miner's assistants (operative who assists the tunnel miner).	4
Other operatives engaged in driving headings, in connection with cable and pipe laying	4
Operative driving loco	4

WELDERS

Grade 4 (Fabrication Assistant) Welder able to tack weld using SMAW or MIG welding processes in accordance with verbal instructions and including mechanical preparation such as cutting and grinding	3
Grade 3 (Basic Skill Level) Welder able to weld carbon and stainless steel using at least one of the following processes SMAW, GTAW, GMAW for plate-plate fillet welding in all major welding positions, including mechanical preparation and complying with fabrication drawings	2
Grade 2 (Intermediate Skill Level) Welder able to weld carbon and stainless steel using manual SMAW, GTAW, semi-automatic MIG or MAG, and FCAW welding processes including mechanical preparation, and complying with welding procedures, specifications and fabrication drawings.	1
Grade 1 (Highest Skill Level) Welder able to weld carbon and stainless steel using manual SMAW, GTAW, semi-automatic GMAW or MIG or MAG, and FCAW welding processes in all modes and directions in accordance with BSEN 287-1 and/or 287-2 Aluminium Fabrications including mechanical preparation and complying with welding procedures, specifications and fabrication drawings.	Craft Rate

YOUNG WORKERS

Operatives below 18 years of age will receive payment of 60% of the General Operative Basic Rate

At 18 years of age or over the payment is 100% of the relevant rate.

PRIME COST OF DAYWORK CARRIED OUT UNDER A BUILDING CONTRACT

The Royal Institution of Chartered Surveyors and The Construction Confederation released the third edition of the Definition in June 2007.

The third edition is easy to follow and provides two options for dealing with the cost of labour; either to use the traditional Percentage Addition method or to use All-inclusive Rates.

The example calculations for a typical Standard Hourly Rate have been updated for a Craft Operative and for a General Operative, and to include for a work place pension in accordance with the Pensions Act 2011.

The Definition states that it is provided 'for convenience and for use by people who choose to use it'. Provision for dayworks is generally included on all Projects and all specifiers should ensure that their documentation follows and refers to the Definition and agreement should be reached on the definition of daywork prior to ordering daywork.

The percentage addition method is calculated on the labour rates current at the time the works are carried out, whilst the all-inclusive rates will be at the rates stated at the time of tender although these could be adjusted by reference to a suitable index.

The composition of Daywork includes for labour, materials and plant with incidental costs, overheads and profit being added as a percentage, except in the case of the labour all-inclusive rates where these are deemed to be included.

A summary of the requirements of the Definition follows, users should refer to the full document to calculate the applicable rate, view model documentation and examples and to understand the limitations and inclusions of the Definition:

LABOUR

Option A - The percentage addition rate provides for:

- Guaranteed minimum weekly earnings (e.g. Standard Basic Rate of Wages, Joint Board Supplement and Guaranteed Minimum Bonus Payment in the case of NJCBI rules).
- All other guaranteed minimum payments (unless included with incidental costs, overheads and profit).
- Differentials or extra payments in respect of skill, responsibility, discomfort, inconvenience or risk (excluding those in respect of supervisory responsibility).
- Payments in respect of public holidays.
- Any amounts which may become payable by the Contractor to or in respect of operatives arising from the operation of the rules referred to.
- Employer's contributions to annual holidays
- Employer's contributions to benefit schemes
- Employer's National Insurance contributions
- Any contribution, levy or tax imposed by statute, payable by the Contractor in his capacity as an employer.

Differentials or extra payments in respect of supervisory responsibility are excluded from the annual prime cost. The time of supervisory staff, principals, foremen, gangers, leading hands and similar categories, when working manually, is admissible under this Section at the appropriate rates.

Option B - The all-inclusive rate provides for:

- Items as listed above pre-calculated by the tenderer inclusive of costs associated with employing the labour
- All rates deemed to be fixed for the length of the contract unless the contract specifies different

MATERIALS AND GOODS

- The Prime cost of materials obtained for daywork is the invoice cost after discounts over 5%
- The Prime cost of materials supplied from stock for daywork is the current market price after discounts over 5%

PLANT

- Where hired for the daywork it is the invoice cost after discounts over 5%
- Where not hired for the daywork it is calculated in accordance with the RICS Schedule of Basic Plant Charges.
- Includes for transport, erection, dismantling and qualified operators.

CONTRACT WORK

DEFINITION OF PRIME COST OF DAYWORK CARRIED OUT UNDER A BUILDING CONTRACT

The Second Edition is reproduced by permission of the Royal Institution of Chartered Surveyors.

This Definition of Prime Cost is published by The Royal Institution of Chartered Surveyors and the National Federation of Building Trades Employers, for convenience and for use by people who choose to use it. Members of the National Federation of Building Trades Employers are not in any way debarred from defining Prime Cost and rendering their accounts for work carried out on that basis in any way they choose. Building owners are advised to reach agreement with contractors on the Definition of Prime Cost to be used prior to issuing instructions.

SECTION 1

Application

1.1 This definition provides a basis for the valuation of daywork executed under such building contracts as provide for its use (e.g. contracts embodying the Standard Forms issued by the Joint Contracts Tribunal).

1.2 It is not applicable in any other circumstances, such as jobbing or other work carried out as a separate or main contract nor in the case of daywork executed during the Defects Liability Period of contracts embodying the above mentioned Standard Forms.

CONTRACT WORK (Cont'd)
DEFINITION OF PRIME COST OF DAYWORK CARRIED OUT UNDER A BUILDING CONTRACT (Cont'd)

SECTION 2

Composition of total charges

2.1 The prime cost of daywork comprises the sum of the following costs:

(a) Labour as defined in Section 3.

(b) Materials and goods as defined in Section 4.

(c) Plant as defined in Section 5.

2.2 Incidental costs, overheads and profit as defined in Section 6, as provided in the building contract and expressed therein as percentage adjustments, are applicable to each of 2.1 (a)-(c).

SECTION 3

Labour

3.1 The standard wage rates, emoluments and expenses referred to below and the standard working hours referred to in 3.2 are those laid down for the time being in the rules or decisions of the National Joint Council for the Building Industry and the terms of the Building and Civil Engineering Annual and Public Holiday Agreements applicable to the works, or the rules or decisions or agreements of such body, other than the National Joint Council for the Building Industry, as may be applicable relating to the class of labour concerned at the time when and in the area where the daywork is executed.

3.2 Hourly base rates for labour are computed by dividing the annual prime cost of labour, based upon standard working hours and as defined in 3.4 (a)-(i), by the number of standard working hours per annum (see examples)

3.3 The hourly rates computed in accordance with 3.2 shall be applied in respect of the time spent by operatives directly engaged on daywork, including those operating mechanical plant and transport and erecting and dismantling other plant (unless otherwise expressly provided in the building contract).

3.4 The annual prime cost of labour comprises the following:

(a) Guaranteed minimum weekly earnings (e.g. Standard Basic Rate of Wages, Joint Board Supplement and Guaranteed Minimum Bonus Payment in the case of NJCBI rules).

(b) All other guaranteed minimum payments (unless included in Section 6).

(c) Differentials or extra payments in respect of skill, responsibility, discomfort, inconvenience or risk (excluding those in respect of supervisory responsibility - see 3.5).

(d) Payments in respect of public holidays.

(e) Any amounts which may become payable by the Contractor to or in respect of operatives arising from the operation of the rules referred to in 3.1 which are not provided for in 3.4 (a)-(d) or in Section 6.

(f) Employer's National Insurance contributions applicable to 3.4 (a)-(e).

(g) Employer's contributions to annual holiday credits.

(h) Employer's contributions to death benefit scheme.

(i) Any contribution, levy or tax imposed by statute, payable by the Contractor in his capacity as an employer.

3.5 Note:

Differentials or extra payments in respect of supervisory responsibility are excluded from the annual prime cost (see Section 6). The time of principals, foremen, gangers, leading hands and similar categories, when working manually, is admissible under this Section at the appropriate rates for the trades concerned.

SECTION 4

Materials and Goods

4.1 The prime cost of materials and goods obtained from stockists or manufacturers is the invoice cost after deduction of all trade discounts but including cash discounts not exceeding 5 per cent and includes the cost of delivery to site

4.2 The prime cost of materials and goods supplied from the Contractor's stock is based upon the current market prices plus any appropriate handling charges.

4.3 Any Value Added Tax which is treated, or is capable of being treated, as input tax (as defined in the Finance Act, 1972) by the Contractor is excluded.

SECTION 5

Plant

5.1 The rates for plant shall be as provided in the building contract.

5.2 The costs included in this Section comprise the following:

(a) Use of mechanical plant and transport for the time employed on daywork.

(b) Use of non-mechanical plant (excluding non-mechanical hand tools) for the time employed on daywork.

5.3 Note: The use of non-mechanical hand tools and of erected scaffolding, staging, trestles or the like is excluded (see Section 6).

SECTION 6

Incidental Costs, Overheads and Profit

6.1 The percentage adjustments provided in the building contract, which are applicable to each of the totals of Sections 3, 4 and 5, comprise the following:

(a) Head Office charges

(b) Site staff including site supervision.

(c) The additional cost of overtime (other than that referred to in 6.2).

(d) Time lost due to inclement weather.

(e) The additional cost of bonuses and all other incentive payments in excess of any guaranteed minimum included in 3.4 (a).

(f) Apprentices study time.

(g) Subsistence and periodic allowances.

(h) Fares and travelling allowances.

(i) Sick pay or insurance in respect thereof.

(j) Third party and employer's liability insurance.

(k) Liability in respect of redundancy payments to employees.

(l) Employer's National Insurance contributions not included in Section 3.4

CONTRACT WORK (Cont'd)
DEFINITION OF PRIME COST OF DAYWORK CARRIED OUT UNDER A BUILDING CONTRACT (Cont'd)
SECTION 6.1 (Cont'd)

(m) Tool allowances.

(n) Use, repair and sharpening of non-mechanical hand tools.

(o) Use of erected scaffolding, staging, trestles or the like.

(p) Use of tarpaulins, protective clothing, artificial lighting, safety and welfare facilities, storage and the like that may be available on the site.

(q) Any variation to basic rates required by the Contractor in cases where the building contract provides for the use of a specified schedule of basic plant charges (to the extent that no other provision is made for such variation).

(r) All other liabilities and obligations whatsoever not specifically referred to in this Section nor chargeable under any other section.

(s) Any variation in welfare/pension payments from industry standard.

(t) Profit.

Note: The additional cost of overtime, where specifically ordered by the Architect/Supervising Officer, shall only be chargeable in the terms of prior written agreement between the parties to the building contract.

Example of calculation of typical standard hourly base rate (as defined in Section 3) for NJCBI building craft operative and labour in Grade A areas **based upon rates ruling at 1st July 1975.**

		Rate £	Craft Operative £	Rate £	Labourer £
Guaranteed minimum weekly earnings					
Standard Basic Rate	49 wks	37.00	1813.00	31.40	1538.60
Joint Board Supplement	49 wks	5.00	245.00	4.20	205.80
Guaranteed Minimum Bonus	49 wks	4.00	196.00	3.60	176.40
			2254.00		1920.80
Employer's National Insurance Contribution at 8.5%			191.59		63.27
			2445.59		2084.07
Employer's Contributions to: CITB annual levy			15.00		3.00
Annual holiday credits	49 wks	2.80	137.20	2.80	137.20
Public holidays (included in guaranteed minimum weekly earnings above)			-		-
Death benefit scheme	49 wks	0.10	4.90	0.10	4.90
Annual labour cost as defined in Section 3		£	2602.69	£	2229.17

	Craft Operative	Labourer
Hourly base rates as defined in Section 3, clause 3.2	£ 2602.69 / 1904 = **£ 1.37**	£2229.17 / 1904 = **£ 1.17**

Note: (1) Standard working hours per annum calculated as follows:

	52 weeks at 40 hours	=		2080
Less	3 weeks holiday at 40hours	=	120	
	7 days public holidays at 8 hours	=	56	176
				1904 hours

(2) It should be noted that all labour costs incurred by the Contractor in his capacity as an employer, other than those contained in the hourly base rate, are to be taken into account under Section 6.

(3) The above example is for the convenience of users only and does not form part of the Definition; all the basic costs are subject to re-examination according to the time when and in the area where the daywork is executed.

CONTRACT WORK (Cont'd)
DEFINITION OF PRIME COST OF DAYWORK CARRIED OUT UNDER A BUILDING CONTRACT (Cont'd)

BUILD UP OF STANDARD HOURLY BASE RATES - RATES APPLICABLE AT 22nd JUNE 2020

Under the JCT Standard Form, dayworks are calculated in accordance with the Definition of the Prime Cost of Dayworks carried out under a Building Contract published by the RICS and the NFBTE. The following build-up has been calculated from information provided by the Building Cost Information Service (BCIS) in liaison with the NFBTE. The example is for the calculation of the standard hourly base rates and is for convenience only and does not form part of the Definition; all basic rates are subject to re-examination according to when and where the dayworks are executed. From January 2017, the holiday year runs from the 1st January for each year with an annual entitlement of 22 days of industry plus 8 days of Public / Bank holidays.

Standard working hours per annum 52 weeks at 39 hours		2028 hours
Less - 22 days annual holiday:		
17 days at 8 hours	136	
5 days at 7 hours	35	
8 days public holiday		
7 days at 8 hours	56	
1 day at 7 hours	7	234 hours
		1794 hours

Guaranteed Minimum weekly earnings	Craft Rate £	General Operative £
Standard basic rate (39 hour week)	494.13	371.67
Hourly Rate	12.67	9.53

Hourly Base Rate	Rate £	Craftsman £	Rate £	General Operative £
Guaranteed minimum weekly earnings – 1794 hours at	12.67	22,729.98	9.53	17,096.82
Extra payments for skill, responsibility, discomfort, inconvenience or risk*	-	-	-	-
Holidays with Pay – 234 Hours	12.67	2,964.78	9.53	2,230.02
Employer's National Insurance Contribution** - 13.8% of	16,906.24	2,333.06	10,538.32	1,454.29
*** CITB Annual Levy - 0.35% of	25,694.76	89.93	19,326.84	67.64
Retirement benefit – 3% of	25,694.76	770.84	19,326.84	579.81
Death benefit – 52 weeks at £1.49		77.48		77.48
Public holidays (included with Holidays with Pay above).		-		-
		£28,966.07		£21,506.06
Hourly Base Rate : Divide by 1794 hours		**£ 16.15**		**£ 11.99**

Notes

* Only included in hourly base rate for operatives receiving such payments.

** National Insurance Contribution based on 13.8% above the Earnings Threshold for 52 weeks at £169.01 (£8,788.52).

*** From 1st April 2018 the CITB levy is calculated at 0.35% of the PAYE payroll of each employee plus 1.25% of payments made under a labour only agreement (CIS subcontractors). Building contractors having a combined payroll of £80,000 (2016 assessment) or less are exempt. The levy is included in the daywork rate of each working operative, the remainder being a constituent part of the overheads percentage.

Holidays – The winter holiday is 2 calendar weeks taken in conjunction with Christmas, Boxing and New Years Day.
The remaining 15 days of holiday may be taken at any time in agreement with the Employer and with reasonable written notice.

DAYWORK, OVERHEADS AND PROFIT

Fixed percentage additions to cover overheads and profit no longer form part of the published Daywork schedules issued by the Royal Institution of Chartered Surveyors and Contractors are usually asked to state the percentages they require as part of their tender. These will vary from firm to firm and before adding a percentage, the list of items included in Section 6 of the above Schedule should be studied and the cost of each item assessed and the percentage overall additions worked out.

As a guide, the following percentages are extracted from recent tenders for Contract Work:

On Labour costs	80-200%
On Material costs	10-20%
On Plant costs	5-30%

Much higher percentages may occur on small projects or where the amount of daywork envisaged is low.

JOBBING WORK

DEFINITION OF PRIME COST OF BUILDING WORKS OF A JOBBING OR MAINTENANCE CHARACTER

Reproduced by permission of the Royal Institution of Chartered Surveyors.

This Definition of Prime Cost is published by the Royal Institution of Chartered Surveyors and the National Federation of Building Trades Employers for convenience and for use by people who choose to use it. Members of the National Federation of Building Trades Employers are not in any way debarred from defining prime cost and rendering their accounts for work carried out on that basis in any way they choose.

Building owners are advised to reach agreement with contractors on the Definition of Prime Cost to be used prior to issuing instructions.

SECTION 1

Application

1.1 This definition provides a basis for the valuation of work of a jobbing or maintenance character executed under such building contracts as provide for its use.

1.2 It is not applicable in any other circumstances such as daywork executed under or incidental to a building contract.

SECTION 2

Composition of Total Charges

2.1.1 The prime cost of jobbing work comprises the sum of the following costs:

(a) Labour as defined in Section 3.

(b) Materials and goods as defined in Section 4.

(c) Plant, consumable stores and services as defined in Section 5.

(d) Sub-contracts as defined in Section 6.

2.2 Incidental costs, overhead and profit as defined in Section 7 and expressed as percentage adjustments are applicable to each of 2.1 (a)-(d).

SECTION 3

Labour

3.1 Labour costs comprise all payments made to or in respect of all persons directly engaged upon the work, whether on or off the site, except those included in Section 7.

3.2 Such payments are based upon the standard wage rates, emoluments and expenses as laid down for the time being in the rules or decisions of the National Joint Council for the Building Industry and the terms of the Building and Civil Engineering Annual and Public Holiday Agreements applying to the works, or the rules or decisions or agreements of such other body as may relate to the class of labour concerned, at the time when and in the area where the work is executed, together with the Contractor's statutory obligations, including:

(a) Guaranteed minimum weekly earnings (e.g. Standard Basic Rate of Wages and Guaranteed Minimum Bonus Payment in the case of NJCBI rules).

(b) All other guaranteed minimum payments (unless included in Section 7).

(c) Payments in respect of incentive schemes or productivity agreements applicable to the works.

(d) Payments in respect of overtime normally worked; or necessitated by the particular circumstances of the work; or as otherwise agreed between parties.

(e) Differential or extra payments in respect of skill responsibility, discomfort, inconvenience or risk.

(f) Tool allowance.

(g) Subsistence and periodic allowances.

(h) Fares, travelling and lodging allowances.

(j) Employer's contributions to annual holiday credits.

(k) Employer's contributions to death benefit schemes.

(l) Any amounts which may become payable by the Contractor to or in respect of operatives arising from the operation of the rules referred to in 3.2 which are not provided for in 3.2 (a)-(k) or in Section 7.

(m) Employer's National Insurance contributions and any contributions, levy or tax imposed by statute, payable by the Contractor in his capacity as employer.

Note: Any payments normally made by the Contractor which are of a similar character to those described in 3.2 (a)-(c) but which are not within the terms of the rules and decisions referred to above are applicable subject to the prior agreement of the parties, as an alternative to 3.2(a)-(c).

3.3 The wages or salaries of supervisory staff, timekeepers, storekeepers, and the like, employed on or regularly visiting site, where the standard wage rates etc. are not applicable, are those normally paid by the Contractor together with any incidental payments of a similar character to 3.2 (c)-(k).

3.4 Where principals are working manually their time is chargeable, in respect of the trades practised, in accordance with 3.2.

SECTION 4

Materials and Goods

4.1 The prime cost of materials and goods obtained by the Contractor from stockists or manufacturers is the invoice cost after deduction of all trade discounts but including cash discounts not exceeding 5 per cent, and includes the cost of delivery to site.

4.2 The prime cost of materials and goods supplied from the Contractor's stock is based upon the current market prices plus any appropriate handling charges.

4.3 The prime cost under 4.1 and 4.2 also includes any costs of:

(a) non-returnable crates or other packaging.

(b) returning crates and other packaging less any credit obtainable.

4.4 Any Value Added Tax which is treated, or is capable of being treated, as input tax (as defined in the Finance Act, 1972 or any re-enactment thereof) by the Contractor is excluded.

JOBBING WORK (Cont'd)

DEFINITION OF PRIME COST OF BUILDING WORKS OF A JOBBING OR MAINTENANCE CHARACTER (Cont'd)

SECTION 5

Plant, Consumable Stores and Services

5.1 The prime cost of plant and consumable stores as listed below is the cost at hire rates agreed between the parties or in the absence of prior agreement at rates not exceeding those normally applied in the locality at the time when the works are carried out, or on a use and waste basis where applicable:

(a) Machinery in workshops.

(b) Mechanical plant and power-operated tools.

(c) Scaffolding and scaffold boards.

(d) Non-Mechanical plant excluding hand tools.

(e) Transport including collection and disposal of rubbish.

(f) Tarpaulins and dust sheets.

(g) Temporary roadways, shoring, planking and strutting, hoarding, centering, formwork, temporary fans, partitions or the like.

(h) Fuel and consumable stores for plant and power-operated tools unless included in 5.1 (a), (b), (d) or (e) above.

(i) Fuel and equipment for drying out the works and fuel for testing mechanical services.

5.2 The prime cost also includes the net cost incurred by the Contractor of the following services, excluding any such cost included under Sections 3, 4 or 7:

(a) Charges for temporary water supply including the use of temporary plumbing and storage

(b) Charges for temporary electricity or other power and lighting including the use of temporary installations.

(c) Charges arising from work carried out by local authorities or public undertakings.

(d) Fee, royalties and similar charges.

(e) Testing of materials

(f) The use of temporary buildings including rates and telephone and including heating and lighting not charged under (b) above.

(g) The use of canteens, sanitary accommodation, protective clothing and other provision for the welfare of persons engaged in the work in accordance with the current Working Rule Agreement and any Act of Parliament, statutory instrument, rule, order, regulation

(h) The provision of safety measures necessary to comply with any Act of Parliament.

(j) Premiums or charges for any performance bonds or insurances which are required by the Building Owner and which are not referred to elsewhere in this Definition. or bye-law.

SECTION 6

Sub-Contracts

6.1 The prime cost of work executed by sub-contractors, whether nominated by the Building Owner or appointed by the Contractor is the amount which is due from the Contractor to the sub-contractors in accordance with the terms of the sub-contracts after deduction of all discounts except any cash discount offered by any sub-contractor to the Contractor not exceeding 2 1/2 per cent.

SECTION 7

Incidental Costs, Overheads and Profit

7.1 The percentages adjustments provided in the building contract, which are applicable to each of the totals of Sections 3-6, provide for the following:-

(a) Head Office Charges.

(b) Off-site staff including supervisory and other administrative staff in the Contractor's workshops and yard.

(c) Payments in respect of public holidays.

(d) Payments in respect of apprentices' study time.

(e) Sick pay or insurance in respect thereof.

(f) Third Party and employer's liability insurance.

(g) Liability in respect of redundancy payments made to employees.

(h) Use, repair and sharpening of non-mechanical hand tools.

(j) Any variation to basic rates required by the Contractor in cases where the building contract provides for the use of a specified schedule of basic plant charges (to the extent that no other provision is made for such variation).

(k) All other liabilities and obligations whatsoever not specifically referred to in this Section nor chargeable under any other section.

(l) Profit.

SPECIMEN ACCOUNT FORMAT

If this Definition of Prime Cost is followed the Contractor's account could be in the following format:-

	£
Labour (as defined in Section 3)	
Add % (see Section 7)	
Materials and goods (as defined in Section 4)	
Add % (see Section 7)	
Plant, consumable stores and services (as defined in Section 5)	
Add % (see Section 7)	
Sub-contracts (as defined in Section 6)	
Add % (see Section 7)	
	£

VAT to be added if applicable

SCHEDULE OF BASIC PLANT CHARGES

The RICS has now published the 2010 edition of the Schedule of Basic Plant Charges and which came into effect from the 1st July 2010. The Schedule includes rates for of plant covering the following sections:

- Pumps
- Concrete Equipment
- Scaffolding, Shoring, Fencing
- Testing Equipment
- Lighting Appliances and Conveyors
- Site Accommodation
- Construction Vehicles
- Temporary Services
- Excavators and Loaders
- Site Equipment
- Compaction Equipment
- Small Tools

For information the explanatory notes for use in connection with Dayworks under a Building Contract (Fifth revision - 1st May 2001) stated;-

1. The rates in the Schedule are intended to apply solely to daywork carried out under and incidental to a Building Contract. They are NOT intended to apply to:-
(i) Jobbing or any other work carried out as a main or separate contract; or
(ii) Work carried out after the date of commencement of the Defects Liability Period.
2. The rates apply only to plant and machinery already on site, whether hired or owned by the Contractor.
3. The rates, unless otherwise stated, include the cost of fuel and power of every description, lubricating oils, grease, maintenance, sharpening of tools, replacement of spare parts, all consumable stores and for licences and insurances applicable to items of plant.
4. The rates, unless otherwise stated, do not include the cost of drivers and attendants.
5. The rates are base costs and may be subject to the overall adjustment for price movement, overheads and profit, quoted by the Contractor prior to the placing of the Contract.
6. The rates should be applied to the time during which the plant is actually engaged in daywork.
7. Whether or not plant is chargeable on daywork depends on the daywork agreement in use and the inclusion of an item of plant in this schedule does not necessarily indicate that that item is chargeable.
8. Rates for plant not included in the Schedule or which is not on site and is specifically provided or hired for daywork shall be settled at prices which are reasonably related to the rates in the Schedule having regard to any overall adjustment quoted by the Contractor in the Conditions of Contract.

ELECTRICAL CONTRACTORS

A "Definition of Prime Cost of Daywork carried out under an Electrical Contract" agreed between the Royal Institution of Chartered Surveyors and the Electrical Contractors Associations can be obtained from the RICS, 12 Great George Street, London SW1P 3AD, Tel. 024 7686 8555

Example of calculation of typical standard hourly base rate (as defined in Section 3) for JIB Electrical Contracting Industry Approved Electrician and Electrician based upon rates applicable at 6th January 2020, National Insurance from 6th April 2020.

		Rate	Approved Electrician	Rate	Electrician
		£	£	£	£
Basic Wages:	1717.5 hours	17.27	29,661.23	15.92	27,342.60
Public Holidays:	60 hours	17.27	1,036.20	15.92	955.20
Holidays with Pay:	172.5 hours	17.27	2,979.08	15.92	2,746.20
Extra Payments:	where applicable				
Sub Total:			£ 33,676.51		£ 31,044.00
National Insurance 13.80% Contribution on		£ 24,887.98	3,434.54	£ 22,255.48	3,071.26
Welfare Stamps :	52 stamps at	£ 15.50	806.00	£ 15.50	806.00
Industry Pension :	3%		1,010.30		931.32
Annual Labour Cost :			£ 38,927.35		£ 35,852.58
Hourly Base Rate :	**Divide by 1717.5 hours**		**£ 22.67**		**£ 20.87**

Note:

Standard working hours per annum calculated as follows

52 weeks at 37.5 hours	1950
Less	
hours annual holiday	172.50
hours public holiday	60
Standard working hours per year	1717.50

GENERAL INFORMATION

TERRAZZO, MARBLE AND MOSAIC SPECIALISTS

Daywork rates for terrazzo, marble, mosaic and the like for:

Terrazzo Marble or Mosaic Craftsman
General Operatives

All travelling, waiting time and fares to be paid.
Non-productive overtime or overtime premiums

Floor grinding machines (single head)
Dry sanding machines
Multi-head floor polishing machines,
Fuel, abrasive stones and discs.
Delivery and collection of materials/plant not included

Full details can be obtained from:

The National Federation of Terrazzo Marble & Mosaic Specialists, 4 The Oval, Broxbourne, EN10 6DQ.
Tel: 01992 445090. www.nftmms.co.uk

HEATING, VENTILATING, AIR CONDITIONING, REFRIGERATION, PIPEWORK AND/OR DOMESTIC ENGINEERING CONTRACTS

A "Definition of Prime Cost of Daywork carried out under a heating, ventilating and air conditioning, refrigeration, pipework and/or domestic engineering contract" agreed between the Royal Institution of Chartered Surveyors and the Heating and Ventilating Contractors' Association can be obtained from:

RICS, 12 Great George Street, London SW1P 3AD.
Tel. 024 7686 8555 Email: contactrics@rics.org

THE CIVIL ENGINEERING CONTRACTORS ASSOCIATION

CECA Schedules of Daywork Carried Out Incidental to Contract Work 2011

These Schedules are the Schedules referred to in the I.C.E. Conditions of Contract and have been prepared for use in connection with Dayworks carried out incidental to contract work where no other rates have been agreed. They are not intended to be applicable for Dayworks ordered to be carried out after the contract works have been substantially completed or to a contract to be carried out wholly on a daywork basis. The circumstances of such works vary so widely that the rates applicable call for special consideration and agreement between contractor and employing authority.

Contents

The schedules may be obtained from the ICE Bookshop or other relevant booksellers.

ICE Publishing, 8 Storey's Gate, London, SW1P 3AT.
Tel: 01235 465577, Email: orders@icepublishing

ROYAL INSTITUTE OF BRITISH ARCHITECTS (RIBA)

There is no fixed fee scale in the UK, so an architect will charge a fee taking into account the requirements of the project, his or her skills, experience, overheads, the resources needed to undertake the work, profit and competition. In 2010 RIBA issued a Fees Toolkit available for architects, to help the profession combat harmful low fee bids. The Toolkit comprises the new RIBA Fees Calculator alongside the RIBA Benchmarking service.

The following may assist in calculating likely fees for budget purposes and are extracts from 'A guide to RIBA Standard Forms of Appointment 1999 and other Architect's Appointments', 'Standard Form of Agreement for the Appointment of an Architect (SFA/99) (Updated April 2000)', 'A Client's Guide to Engaging an Architect including guidance on fees' and 'Conditions of Engagement for the appointment of an Architect (CE/99)' are printed by permission of the Royal Institute of British Architects, 66 Portland Place, London, W1N 4AD from whom full copies can be obtained.

Note: The RIBA Agreements 2010 (2012 revision) replace the 'Standard Form of Agreement for the Appointment of an Architect (SFA/99) (Updated April 2004) and should be referred to for details. These are currently being revised and 2018 versions are expected in the near future. The information below is historic and the current versions should be used where appropriate.

A guide to RIBA Standard Forms of Appointment 1999 and other Architect's Appointments

The guide provides Architects with advice on the application and completion of the RIBA Forms of Appointment1999 and their various supplements, with worked examples.

Clients may also find the guide useful to understand the Architect's role and the responsibilities of the parties.

RIBA Forms of Appointment 1999

SFA/99 - Standard Form of Agreement for the appointment of an Architect

The core document from which all other forms are derived. It is suitable for use where an Architect is to provide services for a fully designed building project in a wide range of sizes or complexity and/or to provide other professional services. It is used with Articles of Agreement and includes notes on completion and an optional Services Supplement

CE/99 - Conditions of Engagement for the Appointment of an Architect

Suitable for use where an architect is to provide services for a fully designed building project and/or to provide other professional services where a letter of Appointment is preferred to the Articles of Agreement in SFA/99.It includes notes on completion, a draft Model Letter and an optional (modified) Services Supplement.

SW/99 - Small Works

Suitable for use where an architect is to provide services of a relatively straightforward nature where the cost of construction works is not expected to exceed £150,000 and use of the JCT Agreement for Minor Works is appropriate. It is used with a Letter of Appointment and includes notes on completion a draft Model Letter and an optional Schedule of Services for Small Works

SC/99 - Form of appointment as Sub-consultant

Suitable for use where a consultant wishes another consultant (sub-consultant) to perform a part of his or her responsibility but not for use where the intention is for the client to appoint consultants directly. It is used With Articles of Agreement and includes notes on completion and a draft form of Warranty to the Client

DB1/99 - Employers Requirements

An amendment for SFA/99 and CE/99 where an architect is appointed by the employer client to prepare Employer's requirements for a design and build contract. It includes a replacement Services Supplement and notes on completion for initial appointment where a change to design and build occurs later or where 'consultant switch' or 'Novation' is contemplated

DB2/99 - Contractors proposals

An amendment for SFA/99 where an architect is appointed by the contractor client to prepare Contractor's Proposals under a design and build contract. (Use with CE/99 is not recommended.) It includes replacement Articles, Appendix and Services Supplement and notes on completion for initial appointment and for 'consultant switch' and 'Novation'.

PS/99 - Form of Appointment as Planning Supervisor

Used for the appointment as planning supervisor under the CDM Regulations l994 of suitably qualified construction professionals. An appointment as planning supervisor is distinct from the provisions of architectural services under other RIBA Forms of Appointment It is used with Articles of Agreement and includes notes on completion. Advice on use with a Letter of Appointment is given in this Guide

PM/99 - Form of Appointment as Project Manager

Suitable for a Wide range of projects where the client wishes to appoint a Project Manager to provide a management service and/or other professional services. Does not duplicate or conflict with an architect's services under other RIBA Forms. It is used with Articles of Agreement and includes notes on completion. Not yet published, at the time of going to press.

STANDARD FORM OF AGREEMENT
For the appointment of an Architect (SFA/99)

The Standard Form of Agreement for the appointment of an Architect (SFA/99) has been issued to replace the previous Architects Appointment (1992).

The Standard Form of Agreement for the Appointment of an Architect (SFA/99) consists of:-

Articles of Agreement

Schedule One:	- Project Description
Schedule Two:	- Services
Schedule Three:	- Fees and Expenses
Schedule Four:	- Other Appointments - made under separate Agreements by the Client).
Services Supplement	- Optional
Notes for Architects	on the use and completion of SFA/99

Conditions of Engagement

STANDARD FORM OF AGREEMENT (Cont'd)
For the appointment of an Architect (SFA/99) (Cont'd)

Conditions of Engagement - Extracts

CONDITIONS

1 General

Interpretation 1.1 The headings and notes to these conditions are for convenience only and do not affect the interpretation of the conditions.

1.2 Words denoting the masculine gender include the feminine gender and words denoting natural persons include corporations and firms and shall be construed interchangeably in that manner.

Applicable law 1.3 The law applicable to this Agreement shall be that stated in the letter of Appointment and, if not so stated, shall be the law of England and Wales.

Communications 1.4 Communications, between the Client and the Architect, including any notice or other document required under the Agreement, shall be in writing and given or served by any effective means. Communications that are not in writing shall be of no effect unless and until confirmed in writing by the sender or the other party. Communications shall take effect when received at an agreed address of the recipient. Communications sent by recorded or registered fist-class post shall be presumed to have arrived at the address to which they are posted on the second day after posting.

Public Holidays 1.5 Where under this Agreement an action is required within a specific period of days, that period shall exclude any day which is a Public Holiday.

Services Variation 1.6 In relation to the Services, either party shall advise the other upon becoming aware of:

.1 a need to vary the Services, the Project Timetable and/or the fees and/or any other part of the Agreement;
.2 any incompatibility in or between any of the Client's requirements in the Brief, any Client's instruction, the Construction Cost, the Timetable and/or the approved design; or any need to vary any part of them;
.3 any issues affecting or likely to affect the progress, quality or cost of the Project;
.4 any information or decisions required from the Client or others in connection with performance of the Services;

and the parties shall agree how to deal with the matter.

2 Obligations & authority of the Architect

Duty of care 2.1 The Architect shall in performing the Services and discharging all the obligations under this part 2 of these Conditions, exercise reasonable skill and care in conformity with the normal standards of the Architect's profession.

Architect's authority 2.2 The Architect shall act on behalf of the Client in the matters set out or necessarily implied in the Agreement.

2.3 In relation to the Services, the Architect shall obtain the authority of the Client before proceeding with the Services or initiating any Work Stage. The Architect shall confirm such authority in writing.

Appointment of Consultants or other persons 2.4 The Architect shall advise the Client on the appointment of Consultants or other persons, other than those named in Schedule 4, to design and/or carry out certain parts of the Works or to provide specialists advice if required in connection with the Project.

Appointment of Site Inspectors 2.5 The Architect shall advise the Client on the appointment of full- or part-time Site Inspectors, other than those named in Schedule 4, under separate agreements where the Architect considers that the execution of the Works warrants such appointment.

Co-operation etc 2.6 The Architect in performing the Services shall when reasonably required by any of the persons identified in Schedule 4:

.1 Co-operate with them as reasonably necessary for carrying out their services;
.2 provide them with information concerning the Services for carrying out their services;
.3 consider and where appropriate comment on their work so that they may consider making any necessary changes to their work;
.4 integrate into his work relevant information provided by them.

No alteration to Services or design 2.7 The Architect shall make no material alteration or addition to or omission from the Services or the approved design without the knowledge and consent of the Client, which consent shall be confirmed in writing by the Architect. In an emergency the Architect may make such alteration, addition or omission without the knowledge and consent of the Client but shall inform the Client without delay and subsequently confirm such action.

Visits to the Works 2.8 The Architect shall in providing the Services make such visits to the Works as the Architect at the date of the appointment reasonably expected to be necessary.

3 Obligations and authority of the Client

Client's representative 3.1 The Client shall name the person who shall exercise the powers of the Client under the Agreement and through whom all instructions shall be given.

Information, decisions, approvals and instructions 3.2 The Client shall supply, free of charge, accurate information as necessary for the proper and timely performance of the Services and to comply with CDM Regulation 11.

3.3 The Client, when requested by the Architect, shall give decisions and approvals as necessary for the proper and timely performance of the Services.

3.4 The Client shall advise the Architect of the relative priorities of the Brief, the Construction Cost and the Timetable.

STANDARD FORM OF AGREEMENT
For the appointment of an Architect (SFA/99) (Cont'd)
Conditions of Engagement (Cont'd)
Obligations & authority of the Client (Cont'd)

3.5 The Client shall have authority to issue instructions to the Architect, subject to the Architect's right of reasonable objection. Such instructions and all instructions to any Consultants or Contractors or other persons providing services in connection with the project shall be issued through the Lead Consultant.

Statutory and other consents required

3.6 The Client shall instruct the making of applications for consents under planning legislation, building acts, regulations or other statutory requirements and by freeholders and others having an interest in the Project. The Client shall pay any statutory charges and any fees, expenses and disbursements in respect of such applications.

CDM Regulations

3.7 The Client Shall, *where required by CDM Regulations:*

.1 comply with his obligations under the CDM Regulations and in any conflict between the obligations under the Regulations and this Agreement, the former shall take precedence;

.2 appoint a competent planning Supervisor;

.3 appoint a competent Principal Contractor.

Appointments and payment others

3.8 Where it is agreed Consultants, or other persons, are to be appointed, the Client shall appoint and pay them under separate agreements and shall confirm in writing to the Architect the services to be performed by such persons so appointed.

Nominations

3.9 Either the Client or the Architect may propose the appointment of such Consultants or other persons, at any time, subject to acceptance by each party.

Site Inspectors

3.10 Where it is agreed Site inspectors shall be appointed they shall be under the direction of the Lead Consultant and the Client shall appoint and pay them under separate agreements and shall confirm in writing to the Architect the services to be performed, their disciplines and the expected duration of their employment.

Responsibilities of others

3.11 The Client, in respect of any work or services in connection with the Project performed or to be performed by any person other than the Architect, shall:

.1 hold such person responsible for the competence and performance of his services and for visits to the site in connection with the work undertaken by him;

.2 ensure that such person shall co-operate with the Architect and provide to the Architect drawings and information reasonably needed for the proper and timely performance of the Services;

.3 ensure that such person shall, when requested by the Architect, consider and comment on work of the Architect in relation to their own work so that the Architect may consider making any necessary change to his work.

3.12 The client shall hold the Principle Contractor and/or other contractors appointed to undertake construction works and not the Architect responsible for their management and operational methods, for the proper carrying out and completion of the Works in compliance with the building contract and for health and safety provisions on the Site.

Legal advice

3.13 The Client shall procure such legal advice and provide such information and evidence as required for the resolution of any dispute between the Client and any parties providing services in connection with the Project.

4 Assignment and sub-letting

Assignment

4.1 Neither the Architect nor the Client shall assign the whole or any part of the Agreement without the consent of the other in writing.

Sub-letting

4.2 The Architect shall not appoint and Sub-Consultants to perform any part of the Services without the consent of the Client, which consent shall not be unreasonably withheld. The Architect shall confirm such consent in writing.

5 Payment

Fees for performance of the Services

5.1 The Fees for performance of the Services, including the anticipated Visits to the Works, shall be calculated and charged as set out in Schedule 3.
Works Stage Fees shall be:

.1 as a percentage of the Construction Costs calculated in accordance with clause 5.2.2; or

.2 as lumps sums in accordance with clause 5.3; or

.3 as time charges in accordance with clause 5.4; or

.4 other agreed method.

Percentage fees

5.2 .1 Percentage fees shall be in accordance with clause 5.2.2 or 5.3.1 as stated in Schedule 3.

.2 Where this clause 5.2.2 is stated to apply in Schedule 3 the percentage or percentages stated therein shall be applied to the Construction Costs. Until the final Construction Cost has been ascertained interim fee calculations shall be based on:

(a) before tenders have been obtained - the lowest acceptable estimate of the Construction Cost;

(b) after tenders have been obtained - the lowest acceptable tender;

(c) after the contract is let either the certified value or the anticipated final account.

The final fee shall be calculated on the ascertained gross final cost of all Works included in the Construction Cost, excluding any adjustment for loss and/or expense payable to or liquidated damages recoverable from a contractor by the Client.
Where the Client is the Contractor, the final cost shall include an allowance for the Contractor's profit and overheads.

STANDARD FORM OF AGREEMENT
For the appointment of an Architect (SFA/99) (Cont'd)
Conditions of Engagement (Cont'd)
Payment (Cont'd)

Lump sums

5.3 A lump sum fee or fees shall be in accordance with clause 5.3.1 or 5.3.2 as stated in Schedule 3 and subject to clause 5.5. Such fee or fees shall be:

.1 calculated by applying the percentage stated in Schedule 3, to be in accordance with this clause 5.3.1, to create:

(a) a lump sum or sums based on the Construction Cost approved by the Client at the end of Work Stage D; or

(b) separate lump sums for each Work Stages based on the Construction Cost approved by the Client at the end of the previous stage; or

.2 a fixed lump sum or sums stated in Schedule 3 to be in accordance with this clause 5.3.2, which shall be adjusted in accordance with clause 5.6 if substantial amendments are made to the Brief and/or the Construction Cost and/or the Timetable.

Time charges

5.4 A time based fee shall be ascertained by multiplying the time reasonably spent in the performance of the Services by the relevant hourly rate set out in Schedule 3. Time 'reasonably spent' shall include the time spent in connection with performance of the Services in travelling from and returning to the Architect's office.

Revision of lump sums and time charge and other rates

5.5 Lump sums complying with clause 5.3.1a or 5.3.2, rates for time charges mileage and printing carried out in the Architect 's office shall be revised every 12 months in accordance with changes in the Retail Price Index*. Each 12-month period shall commence on the anniversary of the Effective Date of the Agreement, or the date of calculation of lump sums complying with clause 5.3.1a, whichever is the later.

**Retail Price Index is set out in Table 6.1 (All items) to 'Labour Market trends' published by the Office for National Statistics.*

Additional Fees

5.6 If the Architect, for reasons beyond his control is involved in extra work or incurs extra expense, for which he will not otherwise be remunerated, the Architect shall be entitled to additional fees calculated on a time basis unless otherwise agreed. Reasons for such entitlement include, but shall not be limited to:

.1 the scope of the Services or the Timetable or the period specified for any work stage is varied by the Client;

.2 the nature of the Project requires that substantial parts of the design can not be completed or must be specified provisionally or approximately before construction commences;

.3 the Architect is required to vary any item of work commenced or completed pursuant to the Agreement or to provide a new design after the Client has authorised the Architect to develop an approved design;

.4 delay or disruption by others;

.5 prolongation of any building contract(s) relating to the Project;

.6 the Architect consents to enter into any third party agreement the form or beneficiary of which had not been agreed by the Architect at the date of the Agreement;

.7 the cost of any work designed by the Architect or the cost of special equipment is excluded from the Construction Cost.

This clause 5.6 shall not apply where the extra work and/or expense to which it refers is due to a breach of the Agreement by the Architect.

5.7 Where for any reason the Architect completed provides only part of the Services specified in Schedule 2, the Architect shall be entitled to fees calculated as follows:

.1 for completed Services, as described for those Services in Schedule 3;

.2 for completed Work Stages, as apportioned for those Work Stages in Schedule 3;

.3 for services or Work Stages not completed, a fee proportionate to that described or apportioned in Schedule 3 based on the Architect's estimate of the percentage of completion.

Expenses and disbursements

5.8 The Client shall reimburse at net cost plus the handling charge stated in Schedule 3:

.1 expenses specified in Schedule 3;

.2 expenses other than those specified and incurred with the prior authorisation of the Client;

.3 any disbursements made on the Client's behalf.

Maintain records

5.9 If the Architect is entitled to reimbursement of time spent on Services performed on a time basis, and of expenses and disbursements, the Architect shall maintain records and shall make these available to the Client on reasonable request.

Payments

5.10 Payments under the Agreement shall become due to the Architect on issue of the Architect's accounts. The final date for such payments by the Client shall be 30 days from the date of issue of an account.

The Architect's account shall be issued at intervals of not less than one month and shall include any additional fees, expenses or disbursements and state the basis of calculation of the amounts due.

Instalments of the fees shall be calculated on the basis of the Architect's estimate of the percentage of completion of the Work Stage or other Services or such other method specified in Schedule 3.

5.11 The Client may not withhold payment of any part of an account for a sum or sums due to the Architect under the Agreement by reason of claims or alleged claims against the Architect unless the amount to be withheld has been agreed by the Architect as due to the Client, or has been awarded in adjudication, arbitration or litigation in favour of the Client and arises out of or under the Agreement. Save as aforesaid, all rights of set-off at common law or in equity which the Client would otherwise be entitled to exercise are hereby expressly excluded.

STANDARD FORM OF AGREEMENT
For the appointment of an Architect (SFA/99) (Cont'd)
Conditions of Engagement (Cont'd)
Payment (Cont'd)

Payment notices

5.12 A written notice from the Client to the Architect:
.1 may be given within 5 days of the date of issue of an account specifying the amount the Client proposes to pay and the basis of calculation of that amount; and/or
.2 shall be given not later than 5 days before the final date for payment of any amount due to the Architect if the Client intends to withhold payment of any part of that amount stating the amount proposed to be withheld and the ground for doing so or, if there is more than one ground, each ground and the amount attributable to it.

If no such notices are given the amount due shall be the amount stated as due in the account. The Client shall not delay payment of any undisputed part of an account.

Late payment

5.13 Any sums due and remaining unpaid at the expiry of 30 days after the date of issue of an account from the Architect shall bear interest. Interest shall be payable at 8% over Bank of England base rate current at the date of issue of the account.

For the avoidance of doubt the Architect's entitlement to interest at the expiry of 30 days after the date of issue of an account shall also apply to any amount which an Adjudicator decides should be paid to the Architect.

Payment on suspension or determination

5.15 If the Client or the Architect suspends or determines performance of the Services, the Architect shall be entitled to payment of any part of the fee or other amounts due at the date of suspension or determination on issue of the Architect's account in accordance with clause 5.10.

5.16 Where the performance of the Services is suspended or determined by the Client, or suspended or determined by the Architect because of breach of the Agreement by the Client, the Architect shall be entitled to payment of all expenses and other costs necessarily incurred as a result of any suspension and any resumption or determination. On issue of the Architect's account in accordance with clause 5.10.

VAT

5.17 Fees, expenses and disbursements arising under the Agreement do not include Value Added Tax. The Client shall pay any Value Added Tax chargeable on the net value of the Architect's fees and expenses.

6 Copyright

Copyright

6.1 The Architect owns the copyright on the work produced by him in performing the Services and generally asserts the right to be identified as the author of the artistic work/work of architecture comprising the Project.

Licence

6.2 The Client shall have a licence to copy and use and allow other Consultants and contractors providing services to the Project to use and copy drawings, documents and bespoke software produced by the Architect, in performing the Services hereinafter called 'the Material', but only for purposes related to the Project on the Site or part of the Site to which the design relates.

Such purposes shall include its operation, maintenance, repairs, reinstatement, alteration, extending, promotion, leasing and/or sale, but shall exclude the reproduction of the Architect's design for any part of any extension of the Project and/or for any other project unless a licence fee in respect of any identified part of the Architect's design stated in Schedule 3.

Provided that:
.1 the Architect shall not be liable if the Material is modified other than by or with the consent of the Architect, or used for any purpose other than that for which it was prepared; or used for any unauthorised purpose;

.2 in the event of any permitted use occurring after the date of the last Service performed under the Agreement and prior to practical completion of the completion of the construction of the project, the Client shall:
(a) where the Architect has not completed Detailed Proposals (Work Stage D), obtain the Architect's consent, which consent shall not be unreasonably withheld; and/or
(b) pay to the Architect a reasonable licence fee where no licence fee is specified in Schedule 3;

.3 in the event of the Client being in default of payment of any fees or other amounts due, the Architect may suspend further use of the licence on giving 7 day's notice of the intention of doing so. Use of the licence maybe resumed on receipt of outstanding amounts.

7 Liabilities and Insurance

Limitation of warranty by Architect

7.1 Subject always to the provisions of clause 2.1, the Architect does not warrant:
.1 that the Services will be completed in accordance with the Timetable;
.2 that planning permission and other statutory approvals will be granted;
.3 the performance, work or the products of others;
.4 the solvency of any other appointed body whether or not such appointment was made on the advice of the Architect.

Time limit for action or proceeding

7.2 No action or proceedings whatsoever for any breach of this Agreement or arising out of or in connection with this Agreement whether in contract, negligence, tort or howsoever shall be commenced against the Architect after the expiry of the period stated in the Letter of Appointment from the date of the Last Services performed under the Agreement or (if earlier) practical completion of the construction of the project.

STANDARD FORM OF AGREEMENT
For the appointment of an Architect (SFA/99) (Cont'd)
Conditions of Engagement (Cont'd)
Liabilities and Insurance (Cont'd)

Architect's liability

7.3 In any action or proceedings brought against the Architect under or in connection with the Agreement whether in contract, negligence, tort or howsoever the Architect's liability for loss or damage in respect of any one occurrence or series of occurrences arising out of one event shall be limited to whichever is the lesser of the sum:

.1 stated in the Appendix; or

.2 such sum as it is just and equitable for the Architect to pay having regard to the extent of his responsibility for the loss and/or damage in question when compared with the responsibilities of contractors, sub-contractors, Consultants and other persons for that loss and/or damage. Such sums to be assessed on the basis that such persons are deemed to have provided contractual undertakings to the Client no less onerous than those of the Architect under the Agreement and had paid to the Client such sums as it would be just and equitable for them to pay having regard to the extent of their responsibility for that loss and/or damage.

Professional Indemnity Insurance

7.4 The Architect shall maintain Professional Indemnity Insurance cover in the amount stated in the Appendix for any one occurrence or series of occurrences arising out of any one event until at least the expiry of the period stated in the Appendix from the date of the Last Services, performed under the Agreement or (if earlier) practical completion of the construction of the Project provided such insurance is available at commercially reasonable rates and generally available in the insurance market to the Architect.

The Architect when requested by the Client, shall produce for inspection documentary evidence that the Professional Indemnity Insurance required under the Agreement is being maintained.

The Architect shall inform the Client if such insurance ceases to be available at commercially reasonable rates in order that the Architect and Client can discuss the best means of protecting their respective positions in respect of the project in the absence if such insurance.

Third Party Agreements

7.5 Where the Client has notified, prior to the signing of this Agreement, that he will require the Architect to enter into an agreement with a third party or third parties, the terms of which and the names or categories of other parties who will sign similar agreements are set out in an annex to this Agreement, then the Architect shall enter such agreement or agreements within a reasonable period of being requested to do so by the Client.

Rights of Third Parties

7.6 For the avoidance of doubt nothing in this Agreement shall confer or purport to confer on any third party any benefit or the right to enforce any term of this Agreement.

8 Suspension and determination

Suspension

8.1 The Client may suspend the performance of any or all of the Services by giving at least 7-days' notice to the Architect. The notice shall specify the Services affected.

8.2 The Architect may suspend performance of the Services and his obligations under the Agreement on giving at least 7-days' notice to the Client of his intention and the grounds for doing so in the event that the Client:

Is in default of any fees or other amounts due; or

Fails to comply with the requirements of the CDM Regulations.

The Architect shall resume performance of his obligations on receipt of the outstanding amounts.

8.3 If any period of suspension arising from a valid notice given under clause 8.1 or clause 8.2 exceeds 6 months the Architect shall request the Client to issue instructions. If written instructions have not been received within 30 days of the date of such request the Architect shall have the right to treat performance of any Service or his obligations affected as determined.

8.4 Any period of suspension arising from a valid notice given under clause 8.1 or clause 8.2 shall be disregarded in computing any contractual date for completion of the Services.

Determination

8.5 The Client or the Architect may by giving 14-days' notice in writing to the other determine performance of any or all of the Services and the Architect's obligations under Part 2 of these conditions stating the grounds for doing so and the Services and obligations affected.

8.6 Performance of the Services and the Architect's obligations under Part 2 of these Conditions may be determined immediately by notice from either party in the event of:

.1 insolvency of the Client or the Architect; or

.2 the Architect becoming unable to provide the Services through death or incapacity.

8.7 On determination on performance of the Services or the Architect's obligations under Part 2 of these conditions, a copy of the Material referred to in clause 6.2 shall be delivered on demand to the Client by the Architect, subject to the terms of the licence under clause 6.2 and payment of the Architect's reasonable copying charges.

8.8 Determination of the performance of the Services or the Architect's obligations shall be without prejudice to the accrued rights and remedies of either party.

9 Dispute resolution*

Negotiation or conciliation

9.1 In the event of any dispute or difference arising under the Agreement, the Client and the Architect may attempt to settle such dispute or difference by negotiation or in accordance with the RIBA Conciliation Procedure.

STANDARD FORM OF AGREEMENT
For the appointment of an Architect (SFA/99) (Cont'd)
Conditions of Engagement (Cont'd)
Dispute resolution (Cont'd)

Adjudication: England and Wales

9.2 Where the law of England and Wales is England the applicable law, any dispute or difference arising out of this Agreement may be referred to adjudication by the Client or the Architect at any time. The adjudication procedures and the Agreement for the Appointment of an Adjudicator shall be as set out in the "Model Adjudication Procedures" published by the *Construction Industry Council* current at the date of the reference. Clause 28 of the 'Model Adjudication Procedures' shall be deleted and replaced as follows: 'The adjudicator may in his discretion direct the payment of legal costs and expenses of one party by another as part of his decision. The adjudicator may determine the amount of costs to be paid or may delegate the task to an independent costs draftsman.

Adjudication: Scotland

9.3 .1 Where the law of Scotland is the applicable law, any dispute or difference touching or concerning any matter or thing arising out of this Agreement (other than with regard to the meaning or construction of this Agreement) may be referred to some independent and fit persons within 7 days of the application of the Client or the Architect and any fees which may become payable to the persons so appointed shall be within the award of that person.

.2 Any such Adjudicator appointed in terms of clause 9.3.1 hereof shall have 28 days from the date of referral within which to reach a decision on the dispute, or such longer period as is agreed between the parties after the dispute has been referred but without prejudice, to the foregoing the Adjudicator shall be permitted to extend the said period of 28 days by up to 14 days, with the consent of the party by whom the dispute was referred.

The Adjudicator shall act impartially and shall be entitled to take the initiative in ascertaining the facts and the law relating to the dispute. The decision of the Adjudicator shall be binding on both parties until the dispute is finally determined by arbitration pursuant to clause 9.5 hereof.

The Adjudicator shall not be liable for anything done or omitted in the discharge or purported discharge of his functions as Adjudicator unless the act or omission is in bad faith, and all employees or agents of the Adjudicator are similarly protected from liability subject to the same proviso.

Naming or nomination of an Adjudicator

9.4 Where no Adjudicator is named in the Agreement and the parties are unable to agree on a person to act as Adjudicator, the Adjudicator shall be a person to be nominated at the request of either party by the nominator identified in the Letter of Appointment.

Arbitration

9.5 When in accordance with the Letter of Appointment either the Client or the Architect require any dispute or difference to be referred to Arbitration the requiring party shall give notice to the other to such effect and the dispute or difference shall or referred to the arbitration and final decision of a person to be agreed between the parties or, failing agreement within 14 days of the date of the notice, the Appointor shall be the person identified in the Appendix.

Provided that where the law of England and Wales is applicable to the Agreement:

.1 the Client or the Architect may litigate any claim for a pecuniary remedy which does not exceed £5,000 or such other sum as is provided by statute pursuant to section 91 of the Arbitration Act 1996;

.2 the Client or the Architect may litigate the enforcement of any decision of an Adjudicator;

.3 where and to the extent that the claimant in any dispute which is referred to arbitration is the Architect, the arbitrator shall not have the power referred to in Section 38(3) of the Arbitration Act 1996.

Costs

9.6 The Client shall indemnify the Architect in respect of his legal and other costs in any action or proceedings, together with a reasonable sum in respect of his time spent in connection with such action or proceedings or any part thereof, if:

.1 the Architect obtains a judgement of the court or an Arbitrator's award on his favour for the recovery of fees and/or expenses under the Agreement; or

.2 the Client fails to obtain a judgement of the court or an Arbitrator's award in the Client's favour for any claim or any part of any claim against the Architect.

Architects are subject to the disciplinary sanction of the Architects Registration Board in relation to complaints of unacceptable professional conduct or serious professional incompetence.

STANDARD FORM OF AGREEMENT
For the appointment of an Architect (SFA/99) (Cont'd)

Schedule Two **Services**

The Architect shall:

1. Perform the Services as designer, design leader, lead consultant during pre-construction and construction Work Stages.
2. Perform the Services for the Work Stages indicated below and in accordance with the Services Supplement.
3. Make visits to the Works in accordance with clause 2.8.
4. Perform any other Services identified below.

Feasibility	**A** Appraisal	**B** Strategic Brief
Pre-Construction	**C** Outline Proposals **D** Detailed Proposals **E** Final Proposals	**F** Production Information **G** Tender Documentation **H** Tender Action
Construction	**J** Mobilisation **K** To Practical Completion	**L** After Practical Completion

Other Services *If identifying any other services the description should be sufficient to identify its scope.*

Other Activities

These activities do not form part of the services unless identified under 'Other Services'

Performance of any of these activities will attract additional fees in accordance with clause 5.6.

Activities - *These may be required in connection with:*

Sites and Buildings

- o Selection of Consultants
- o Options approval
- o Compiling, revising and editing:
  - (a) strategic brief
  - (b) detailed (written) brief
  - (c) room data sheets
- o Selection of site and/or buildings
- o Outline planning submission
- o Environmental studies
- o Surveys, inspection or specialist investigations
- o Party wall matters
- o Two-stage tendering
- o Negotiating a price with a contractor (in-lieu tendering)
- o Use of energy in new or existing buildings
- o Value management services
- o Compiling maintenance and operational manuals
- o Specially prepared drawings of a building as built
- o Submission of plans for proposed works for approval of landlords, founders, freeholders, tenants etc
- o Applications or negotiations for statutory and other grants

Design Skills

- o Interior design services
- o Selection of furniture and fittings
- o Design of furniture and fittings
- o Landscape design services
- o Special drawings, photographs, models or technical information produced at the Client's request

Historic Buildings and Conservation

- o Detailed inspection and report
- o Historical research and archaeological records
- o Listed building consent
- o Conservation area consents
- o Grant aided works

Special Activities - These may be required in connection with:

- o Exceptional negotiations with planning or other statutory authorities
- o Revision of documents to
  - (a) comply with requirements of planning or statutory authorities, or landlords, etc
  - (b) comply with changes in interpretation or enactment or revisions to laws or statutory regulations
  - (c) make corrections not arising from any failure of the Architect
- o Ascertainment of contractor's claims
- o Investigations and instructions relating to work not in accordance with the building contract
- o Assessment of alternative designs, materials or products proposed by the contractor
- o Dispute resolution services on behalf of the Client
- o Damage to or destruction of a building in construction or to existing buildings
  - o Determination of any contract or agreement with any other party providing services to the project
  - o Insolvency of any other party providing services to the project
  - o Valuations for mortgage or other purposes
  - o Easements or other legal agreements
  - o Investigation of building failures
- o Feed Back – post-completion evaluation

STANDARD FORM OF AGREEMENT
For the appointment of an Architect (SFA/99) (Cont'd)

Services Supplement: Design and Management.

Architect's design services

All Commissions

1.1 Receive Client's instructions

1.2 Advise Client on the need to obtain statutory approvals and of the duties of the Client under the CDM Regulations

1.3 Receive information about the site from the Client (CDM 11)

1.4 Where applicable, co-operate with and pass information to the Planning Supervisor

1.5 Visit the site and carry out an initial appraisal

A Appraisal

1 Carry out studies to determine the feasibility of the Client's Requirements

2A Review with Client alternative design and construction approaches and the cost implications, *or*

2B Provide information for report on cost implications

B Strategic Brief

1 (Strategic Brief prepared by or for the Client)

C Outline Proposals

1 Receive Strategic Brief and Commence development into Project Brief

2 Prepare Outline Proposals

3A Prepare an approximation of construction cost, *or*

3B Provide information for cost planning

4 Submit to Client Outline Proposals and approximate construction cost

D Detailed Proposals

1 Complete development of Project Brief

2 Develop the Detailed Proposals from approved Outline Proposals

3A Prepare a cost estimate, *or*

3B Provide information for preparation of cost estimate

4 Consult statutory authorities

5 Submit to Client the Detailed Proposals, showing spatial arrangements, materials and appearance, and a cost estimate

6 Prepare and submit application for full planning permission

E Final Proposals

1 Develop Final Proposals from approved Detailed Proposals

2A Revise cost estimate, *or*

2B Provide information for revision of cost estimate

3 Consult statutory authorities on developed design proposals

4 Submit to Client type of construction, quality of materials, standard of workmanship and revised cost estimate

5 Advise on consequences of any subsequent changes on cost and programme

F Production Information

1 Prepare production information for tender purposes

2A Prepare schedules of rates and/or quantities and/or schedules of works for tendering purposes and revise cost estimate, *or*

2B Provide information for preparation of tender pricing documents and revision of cost estimate

3A Prepare and make submissions under building acts and/or regulations or other statutory requirements, *or*

3B Prepare and give building notice under building acts and/or regulations*
**Not applicable in Scotland*

3 Prepare further production information for construction purposes

G Tender Documentation

1 Prepare and collate tender documents in sufficient detail to enable a tender or tenders to be obtained

2 Where applicable pass final information to Planning Supervisor for pre-tender Health and Safety Plan

3A Prepare pre-tender cost estimate, *or*

3B Provide information for preparation of pre-tender cost estimate

H Tender Action

1 Contribute to appraisal and report on tenders/ negotiations

2 If instructed, revise production information to meet adjustments in the tender sum

J Mobilisation

1 Provide production information as required for the building contract and for construction

K Construction to Practical Completion

1 Make Visits to the Works in connection with the Architect's design

2 Provide further information reasonably required for construction

3 Review design information from contractors or specialists

4 Provide drawings showing the building and main lines of drainage and other information for the Health and Safety File

4 Give general advice on operation and maintenance of the building

L After Practical Completion

1 Identify defects and make final inspections

2A Settle Final Account, *or*

2B Provide information required by others for settling final account

If the Architect is to provide cost advice Alternative **A** applies

If a Quantity Surveyor is appointed Alternative **B** applies

STANDARD FORM OF AGREEMENT
For the appointment of an Architect (SFA/99) (Cont'd)
Services Supplement (Cont'd)

Architect's Management Services

As Design Leader

The Architect has authority and responsibility for:

1 directing the design process;

2 co-ordinating design of all constructional elements, including work by any Consultants, specialists or suppliers;

3 establishing the form and content of design outputs, their interfaces and a verification procedure;

5 communicating with the Client on significant design issues.

As Lead Consultant (pre-construction)

The Architect has authority and responsibility in the pre-construction Work Stages for:

1 co-ordinating and monitoring design work;

2 communications between the Client and the Consultants; except that communications on significant design matters are dealt with as design leader;

3 advising on the need for and the scope of services by Consultants, specialists, sub-contractors or suppliers;

4 advising on methods of procuring construction;

5 receiving regular status reports from each Consultant, including the design leader;

6 developing and managing change control procedures, making or obtaining decisions necessary for time and cost control;

7 reporting to the Client as appropriate.

As Lead Consultant and Contract Administrator

The Architect has authority and responsibility in the tender and construction Work Stages A-G for:

1 inviting and appraising a tender or tenders, including:
- considering with the Client a tenderer or a list of tenderers for the Works;
- considering with the Client appointment of a contractor, and the responsibilities of the parties and the Architect/Contract Administrator under the building contract;
- preparing the building contract and arranging for signatures;

2 administering the building contract, including:
- monitoring the progress of the Works against the Contractor's programme;
- issuing information, instructions, etc;
- preparing and certifying valuations of work carried out or completed and preparing financial reports for the Client; or
- certifying valuations of work prepared by others, and presenting financial reports prepared by others to the Client;
- collating record information including the Health and Safety File;

3 co-ordinating and monitoring the work of Consultants and Site Inspectors, if any, to the extent required for the administration of the building contract, including:
- receiving reports from such Consultants and Site Inspectors to enable decisions to be made in respect of the administration of the building contract;
- consulting any Consultant or other person whose design or specification may be affected by a Client instruction relating to the construction contract, obtaining any information required and issuing any necessary instructions to the Contractor;
- managing change control procedures and making or obtaining decisions as necessary for cost control during the construction period;
- providing information obtained during the administration of the building contract to the Consultants and Site Inspectors;

4 communications between the Client and the Consultants;

5 reporting to the Client as appropriate.

ROYAL INSTITUTE OF BRITISH ARCHITECTS

A Client's guide to Engaging an Architect including guidance on fees

The Royal Institute of British Architects Guide provides guidance for Clients on engaging an Architect, and on professional services, conditions of engagement and fees, together with information on :-

Architect's Services
Other services
Appointment
RIBA Standard Forms
Design and Build
Historic buildings
CDM Regulations

The Client – Architect Agreement
The architect
The client
Statutory requirements
Other appointments
Copyright
Liability and insurance
Suspension and determination
Dispute Resolution

Architect's Fees and Expenses
Percentage basis
Lump sums
Time basis
Expenses
Payment

Architect's Fees and Expenses

RIBA forms of appointment provide a number of options for the calculation of the architect's fee, i.e.:

- a quoted percentage of the final cost of the building work;
- a fixed or calculated lump sum or sums;
- time charge; or
- an other agreed basis.

There is no 'standard' or 'recommended' basis for calculation of the fee, but the relative cost usually incurred in providing architects' normal services is indicated in the tables below. The tables recognise that the additional complexity of the work in alterations or extensions or to historic buildings may justify a higher fee than for new work. Figures 1 and 2 show indicative percentage rates in relation to construction cost for new works and works to existing buildings respectively for five classes of building (Fig 5). Figure 6 and 7 provide similar information for historic buildings.

Before fees can be agreed, client and architect should establish the requirements, the services to be provided, the approximate construction cost and the timetable. It is usually helpful to identify the proportion of the fee for each work Stage (Fig 3) and any other fees payable for additional services such as a survey.

In proposing a fee the architect will take account of the requirement that a client must be '*reasonably satisfied*' that designers will allocate adequate resources for the purposes of CDM Regulations.

Percentage basis

The architect's fees for normal services are expressed as a percentage of the final construction cost executed under the architect's direction. This method is best used for clearly defined building projects. Figures 1 and 2 may be a helpful point of reference in selecting the percentage(s).

Lump sums

Fixed lump sums – may be suitable where the parameters of the services, i.e. the requirements, time and cost, can be clearly defined from the outset. Then, if these are varied by more than a stated amount the lump sum itself may be varied.

Calculated lump sums – with this option the lump sums for the Work Stages are calculated by applying quoted percentages to the latest approved cost either, when the design and estimated cost have been settled at the end of Stage D or at the commencement of each stage. This method will be particularly appropriate where the project parameters cannot be pre-determined with the necessary accuracy or there are inflationary or deflationary pressures in the market place.

Time basis

This basis is best used where the scope of the work cannot be reasonably foreseen or where services do not relate to the cost of construction, for example, for:

- varied or additional services to an otherwise basic service;
- open-ended exploration work, particularly for repair and conservation work;
- feasibility studies;
- protracted planning negotiations;
- party wall services, etc.

The time spent on such services by principals and technical staff is charged at agreed rates, usually expressed as hourly rates, which may be revised at 12-monthly intervals. A range of indicative values is given in Figure 4. Time spent in travelling in conjunction with the time-charged services is chargeable, but the time of secretarial and administrative staff is usually excluded.

Expenses

In addition to the fees, expenses identified in the Agreement or Letter of Appointment for reimbursement may include:

- the cost of copies of drawings and other documents;
- the purchase of maps and printed contract documentation;
- the cost of photography;
- postage and fax charges;
- travel costs and accommodation where relevant.

Additionally, the relevant fee must accompany applications for building regulations or planning approval. If the architect agrees to make such payments on behalf of the client, these disbursements will also be chargeable, perhaps with a handling charge.

Payment

Under RIBA forms of appointment accounts for instalments of the fees and expenses will normally be issued monthly for payment within 30 days. If required, regular payments can be budgeted over a period with review at completion of say the pre-construction Work Stages. Alternatively, fees may be paid at the completion of each Work Stage.

The agreed arrangements will be set out in the Agreement or Letter of Appointment, showing the basis on which the fee is calculated and the rates that are to apply. Statutory provision apply to the payment terms.

Architects will keep and make available for inspection records of expenditure on expenses and disbursements and time spent on services carried out on a time-charged basis. Where applicable, VAT is due on architects' fees and expenses at the appropriate rate.

A Clients guide to Engaging an Architect (cont'd.)
Architect's Fees and Expenses (Cont'd)

Indicative Percentage Fee Scales – Normal Services

Figure 1
New Works

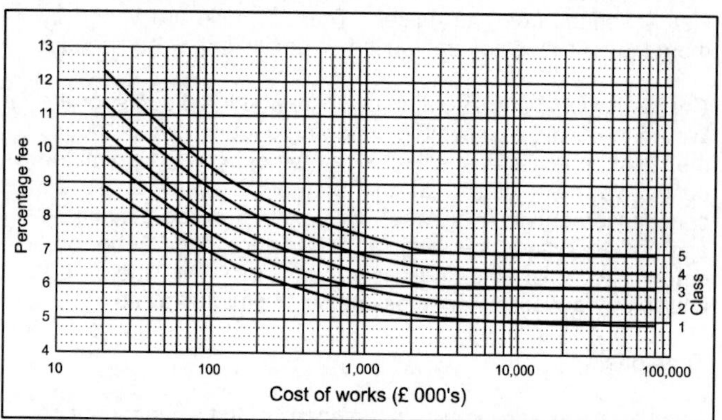

Figure 2
Works to existing buildings

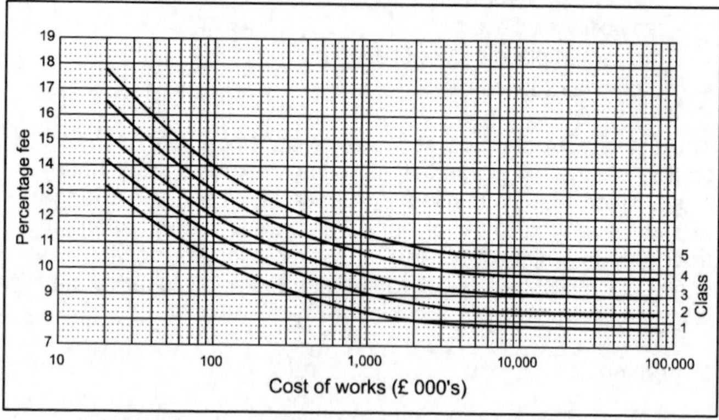

Figure 6
Historic Buildings

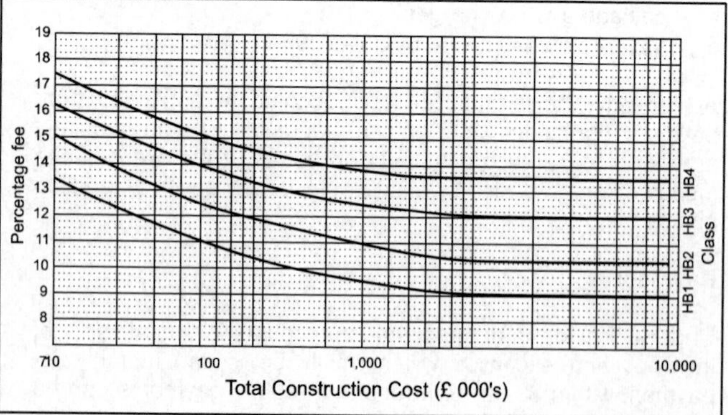

Figure 3

Proportion of fee by Work stage

Proportion of fee			%
Work stage	C	Outline proposals	20
	D	Detailed Proposals	20
	E	Final Proposals	15
	F	Production Information	20
	G	Tender Documentation	2
	H	Tender Action	1
	J	Mobilisation	1
	K	Construction to Practical Completion	20
	L	After Practical Completion	1
			100%

Stages A and B. Appraisal and strategic brief, are normally carried out on a time-charged basis and are therefore not included above.

Figure 4

Indicative hourly rates (June 1999)

Type of work	*General*	*Complex*	*Specialist*
Partner/director Or equivalent	£95	£140	£180
Senior Architect	£75	£105	£140
Architect	£55	£75	£95

Rates are purely indicative and may be negotiated above or below the figures suggested to reflect the nature of the work.

Figure 7

Classification of work to Historic Buildings

Class HB1	Work of a straight forward nature where one repair element predominates (eg large areas of re-roofing).
Class HB2	Work of general repair not including a great deal; of internal alteration.
Class HB3	Work of general repair and alteration, including substantial alteration work. Repair work where the services installations are to be renewed or replaced.
Class HB4	Work including specialist conservation work, requiring an exceptional amount of detailed specification and inspection.

A Clients guide to Engaging an Architect (cont'd.)

Figure 5 **Classification by building type**

Type	Class 1	Class 2	Class 3	Class 4	Class 5
Industrial	• Storage sheds	• Speculative factories and warehouse • Assembly and machine workshops • Transport garages	• Purpose-built factories and warehouses		
Agricultural	• Barns and sheds	• Stables	• Animal breeding units		
Commercial	• Speculative shops • Surface car parks	• Multi-storey and underground car parks	• Supermarkets • Banks • Purpose-built shops • Office developments • Retail warehouses • Garages/ showrooms	• Department stores • Shopping centres • Food processing units • Breweries • Telecommunications and computer buildings • Restaurants • Public houses	• High risk research and production buildings • Research and development laboratories • Radio, TV and recording studios
Community		• Community halls	• Community centres • Branch libraries • Ambulance and fire stations • Bus stations • Railway stations • Airports • Police stations • Prisons • Postal Buildings • Broadcasting	• Civic centres • Churches and crematoria • Specialist libraries • Museums and art galleries • Magistrates/ County Courts	• Theatres • Opera houses • Concert halls • Cinemas • Crown Courts
Residential		• Dormitory hostels	• Estates housing and flats • Barracks • Sheltered housing • Housing for single people • Student housing	• Parsonages/ manses • Apartment blocks • Hotels • Housing for the handicapped • Housing for the frail elderly	• Houses and flats for individual clients
Education			• Primary/ nursery/ first schools	• Other schools including middle and secondary • University complexes	• University laboratories
Recreation			• Sports halls • Squash courts	• Swimming pools • Leisure complexes	• Leisure pools • Specialised complexes
Medical/Social services			• Clinics	• Health Centres • General hospitals • Nursing homes • Surgeries	• Teaching hospitals • Hospital laboratories • Dental surgeries

CONDITIONS OF ENGAGEMENT FOR THE APPOINTMENT OF AN ARCHITECT (CE/99)

The RIBA *Conditions of Engagement for the Appointment of an Architect (CE/99)* is suitable for use where an architect is to provide services for fully designed building project in a wide range of sizes or complexity and/or to provide other professional services. It is fully compliant with the requirements of the Housing Grants, Construction and Regeneration Act 1996.

The Agreement is completed by the exchange of a Letter of Appointment to which a copy of the form is attached, after completion of the Schedules.

'Notes for Architects' and a draft Model letter is included in CE/99 and may assist in identifying those matters which will affect the scope and terms of the Agreement.

It should be noted that the appointment of an architect as Planning Supervisor, where required by the CDM Regulations 1994, is separate from the provision of architectural services under CE/99 and should be made using the RIBA *Form of Appointment as Planning Supervisor (PS/99)*

A series of guides addressed directly to Clients is also published on topics associated with the appointment of an Architect, which Architects may wish to send to their Clients as appropriate and also refer to themselves. The guides can be obtained from RIBA Publications by mail order (020) 7251 0791 or from RIBA bookshops in London and the regions.

THE ROYAL INSTITUTION OF CHARTERED SURVEYORS

Consultant's appointment form

The RICS consultant's appointment forms include a full and short form of appointment, with coordinated scopes of services for:

- Building surveyors
- CDM co-ordinators
- Employer's agents
- Project managers
- Project monitors
- Quantity surveyors

Standard form

The standard form of consultant's appointment is suitable for use in relation to projects of any size or value. However, it is most likely to be used for projects where clients and consultants have experience of development projects of relatively high value. Where the services and project are more straightforward, the short form of consultant's appointment may be more appropriate.

Short form

The short form of consultant's appointment is appropriate where the project and services are more straightforward. More complex projects should use the RICS standard form of consultant's appointment.

Explanatory notes

Explanatory notes for the RICS consultant's appointment forms are also available

Appointing a Quantity Surveyor

The Scales of Professional Charges for Quantity Surveying Services have been withdrawn as has the replacement 'Appointing a Quantity Surveyor: A guide for Clients and Surveyors'. The document gives no indication of the level of fees to be anticipated although a Form of Enquiry, Schedule of Services, Fee Offer, Form of Agreement and Terms of Appointment are included. The view being that consultants are now appointed less often by reputation and recommendation and more often after a process of competition. To assist employers, quantity surveyors and those procuring professional services and where consultants are being appointed by reputation or recommendation the following will assist in assessing the reasonableness of any fee proposal.

Extracts from 'Appointing a Quantity Surveyor: A guide for Clients and Surveyors' includes

Scales of Professional Charges
Example of calculation of fees for lump sum and % basis as clause 5.6 of the guide
Anticipated Percentage fees by project and value based on calculations as example.

The following extracts are for information and the full document should be referred to for further advice.

Contents

RICS Guidance Notes

SECTION 1

Selection and Appointment Advice

This Section outlines for Clients and Surveyors when and how to select and appoint a Quantity Surveyor

1. Introduction

1.1 The Royal Institution of Chartered Surveyors ('the RICS') has published this Guide to assist Clients when they wish to appoint a chartered Quantity Surveyor. The contents of the Guide should also assist Quantity Surveyors when concluding an agreement with their Client.

THE ROYAL INSTITUTION OF CHARTERED SURVEYORS
Appointing a Quantity Surveyor (Cont'd)
Selection and Appointment Advice (Cont'd)

1.2 Over the last few years changes have taken place in the market place for professional services. Consultants are now appointed less often by reputation and recommendation and more often after a process of competition. Competition takes place in the private and public sectors and is supported by European Union requirements and UK Compulsory Competitive Tendering legislation.

1.3 This Guide is applicable to a range of situations - whether details of the services required are proposed to or by the Quantity Surveyor; or whether appointment is of a single Quantity Surveyor or following selection from a limited list. The Guide sets out principles to be considered and applied rather than a detailed step-by-step procedure. Details often vary from project to project depending on the type of Client and the nature of the project. A detailed procedure that attempts to cover all projects is not therefore considered appropriate.

1.4 Quantity Surveyors may be appointed directly by a Client or as part of a multidisciplinary team. The RICS recommends that the quantity surveying appointment is made directly by a Client so as to ensure that independent financial advice is made directly to that Client by the Quantity Surveyor

1.5 The Guide provides a basis for the appointment of a Quantity Surveyor so that those concerned are clear about:

- the services being requested and/or offered
- the terms and conditions of the contract
- the fee payable and the method of payment.

A Client and his Quantity Surveyor should set out clearly their requirements in their agreement so that the services to be provided and the conditions of engagement are certain. It is necessary for a Client to set out his requirements with the same clarity as when seeking tenders from contractors on construction projects. It is now compulsory for Members of the RICS to provide written notification to their Client of the terms and conditions of the appointment. This documentation is intended to form a good basis upon which this certainty can be achieved and is recommended for use between the Client and his Quantity Surveyor.

2. Notes on use and completion of documents

2.1 **Form of Enquiry**
The Form of Enquiry sets out the details of the services a Client wishes a Quantity Surveyor to provide and should be attached to the Form of Agreement and identified as belonging to it.

2.2 **Form of Agreement and Terms of Appointment**
The Form of Agreement should be completed and signed only when the services, fees and expenses have been agreed between a Client and his Quantity Surveyor. The Form of Agreement states the names of the parties, their intentions and their arrangement.

The names and addresses of the parties should be inserted, a brief description of the project given and any site identified. If the Form of Agreement is to made as a simple contract it should be signed by both parties and the date entered. If it is to be executed as a Deed the alternative version should be used. See notes *1 and *2.

3. When to appoint a Quantity Surveyor

In order that maximum benefit can be gained from his skills a Quantity Surveyor should be appointed by a Client as soon as possible in the life of a project, preferably at the inception of a scheme, so that advice can be provided on:

- the costs of the project so that a realistic budget can be set at inception and cost management can be applied throughout
- the procurement method best suited to the requirements of the Client
- the implications of the appointment of other consultants and contractors.

It is recommended that a Client and his prospective Quantity Surveyor should meet and discuss the appointment before an agreement is reached, unless the services of the Quantity Surveyor are to be restricted only to some of those from the range available and shown in the Form of Enquiry.

4. How to select and appoint a Quantity Surveyor

4.1 Detailed guidance on the selection and appointment of Chartered Surveyors is given in the RICS publication A Guide to Securing the Services of a Chartered Surveyor. Chapters 2, 3 and 4 also provide useful information on preparing a brief for a Client's requirements, producing tender and contract documentation, organising competitions and evaluating offers.

4.2 Methods of selecting a Quantity Surveyor include:-

Selection based on existing knowledge
A Client may select and then appoint a Quantity Surveyor using existing knowledge of that Quantity Surveyor's performance and reputation. This knowledge may arise from a previous working relationship or be based on the recommendation of others

Selection from a panel maintained by a Client
A Client may maintain a panel of Quantity Surveyors. He will have records of their experience which will enable him to make his selection and appointment

Selection from an ad hoc list produced by a Client
If a Client is unable to make an appointment based on knowledge or reputation or by selection from a standing panel it may be more appropriate for an ad hoc list to be prepared.

4.3 Whichever of the above methods of selection is used it is important for the selection criteria to include the following:

- the financial standing of the Quantity Surveyor under consideration
- the experience, competence and reputation of each Quantity Surveyor in the area of the project/skill being considered so that selection is made using comparable standards between firms.
- the ability of each Quantity Surveyor to provide the required service at the relevant time.

There is no one correct way to use competitive tendering as a basis for appointment and no single way of complying with legislation. It is important, however, that the procedure is always fair and open. Where legislation means that competition is compulsory, reference should be made to Clause 4.8 below and any other guidance available.

THE ROYAL INSTITUTION OF CHARTERED SURVEYORS
Appointing a Quantity Surveyor (Cont'd)
Selection and Appointment Advice (Cont'd)

4.4 If competition is to be used in the selection process the following should be borne in mind:

- a Client should choose between the various methods of competition from either open, selective or restrictive lists, or single- or two-stage tenders, according to the complexity of the project which is to be the subject of competition
- the basis of selection can be on quality, competence or price, or a combination of all three. Whichever basis is chosen it must be clearly stated in the documentation inviting interest in the commission
- it is recommended that price is never regarded in isolation, as will be clear from the detailed guidance set out below.

4.5 To ensure that any competition is well organised the key ingredients required are that:

- specification of the service required is clear
- definition of the skills and competencies required to deliver the services is clear
- criteria on which offers will be evaluated will be made available with the tender documents
- any weighting to be applied to skills, competencies and price is made available with the tender documents
- each stage of the tender process is documented and the procedures for selection and invitation to tender match the requirements of the commission.

4.6 Every effort should be made to ensure that contract documentation is complete. If circumstances change to the extent that criteria are altered all tenderers should immediately be advised and given the opportunity to respond and confirm a willingness to continue.

4.7 **Private contracts**
In the case of private contracts there is no upper or lower limit to the number of private sector firms that may be invited to tender, nor formal rules as to their selection. Nevertheless, the RICS recommends that not less than 3 and not more than 6 firms are invited to submit proposals.

4.8 **Public contracts**
In the case of public sector contracts Compulsory Competitive Tendering rules and European Union rules, together with relevant Treasury regulations and DETR guidance, need to be followed. More information is available in the RICS publication A Guide to Securing the Services of a Chartered Surveyor. Chapter 2, pages 3 to 6, provides details on regulations but it is emphasised that current requirements should always be verified before seeking public sector offers.

5. **Specifying the quantity surveying service and determining the fee options and expense costs**

5.1 It is emphasised that the fee for a project can either be negotiated, sought as a sole offer or sought in competition. The following considerations may apply to any of the methods of selecting a Quantity Surveyor and determining his fee in relation to the services to be provided.

5.2 When fee quotations are to be sought from more than one Quantity Surveyor it is of paramount importance that the enquiry and/or the submissions relate precisely to the same details of service(s) required. Proper use of the Form of Enquiry should ensure that this is achieved. In particular, the services required should be specified in detail, by using the Schedule of Services provided and/or by adding or deleting any special services not listed or required in that Schedule.

5.3 Information provided by a Client in an offer document should include, as a minimum:

- the complete scope of the project
- a full and precise description of the quantity surveying services to be provided
- the terms and conditions which will apply, preferably the Form of Agreement and Terms of Appointment contained in this Guide, together with any further requirements that will apply
- the anticipated time scales that will apply, both for the quantity surveying service and for the project
- information on the inclusion or exclusion of expense costs
- the basis of the fee upon which the offer is being invited or offered including:
  - where a fee submission is to deal separately with different components of the service, the way in which any components will be evaluated in order to give comparable totals for selection purposes; and
  - wherever a percentage is to be quoted by a Quantity Surveyor; the definition of the total construction cost to which that percentage is to be applied
- provisions for stage or instalment payments
- where the nature, size, scope, time or value of the project or of the quantity surveying service(s) are likely to vary, the method(s) of appropriately adjusting the fee.

5.4 In determining the basis of the services and the fees required the following should be considered:

- where quantity surveying services are incapable of precise definition at the time of appointment, or where they could change substantially, enough information should be contained in an agreement to enable possible variations in those services to be negotiated
- where services are likely to be executed over a particularly long period, or where the service and/or the project might be delayed or postponed, the method and timing of any increase(s) in the fees should be stated
- the basis of the fees to be offered might be one of, or a combination of:
  - a single percentage encompassing all the described services
  - separate percentages for individually defined components of services
  - a single lump sum encompassing all the described services
  - separate lump sums for individually defined components of services
  - a time charge with either hourly rates quoted or a multiplier or adjustment factor to be applied to a specified definition of hourly cost.

5.5 Where the nature or scale of the project warrants it Quantity Surveyors may be invited to:

- explain in outline their proposed method of operation for the project, and/or
- demonstrate their ability to provide the services required from their own resources, and/or
- state the extent of partner/director involvement, and/or
- name the key personnel to be allocated to the project with details of relevant experience.

THE ROYAL INSTITUTION OF CHARTERED SURVEYORS
Appointing a Quantity Surveyor (Cont'd)
Selection and Appointment Advice (Cont'd)

5.6 **Fee options**

Before offering any fee proposal a Quantity Surveyor will need to evaluate the costs of carrying out the service being offered. Options for charging fees are given below and may be used alone or in combination.

5.6.1 Percentage fees

This method of charging fees is appropriate when a construction project is reasonably straightforward and the quantity surveying service can be clearly defined but the exact amount of the total construction cost cannot be determined with much certainty

In determining a fee, judgements need to be made by the Quantity Surveyor on the size of the project, its complexity, degree of repetition, method of procurement and contract arrangements. This method may be seen as a 'broad brush' way of assessment which sometimes may be vulnerable to market forces and their influence on contractors' tenders.

Fees are expressed as a percentage of a sum, which is invariably the total construction cost, for the provision of a defined service. This sum will generally be calculated from the value of all construction contracts and other items of work carried out directly by a Client on a project.

It is advisable to have a definition of total construction cost agreed between a Client and his Quantity Surveyor Exclusions from the total construction cost should also be defined.

5.6.2 Lump sum fee

This method of charging fees is appropriate when a construction project is reasonably certain in programme time, project size and construction cost and the quantity surveying service can be clearly defined. A total fee is agreed for providing a defined service or amount of work. If appropriate, percentage-based or time-based fees may be converted to a lump sum fee once a project has become sufficiently defined.

If time, size, cost or circumstances of the project are significantly varied by more than specified amounts the lump sum fee may be varied, perhaps according to a formula contained in the Agreement. Otherwise the fee remains fixed. It should be borne in mind that a lump sum fee, whilst giving certainty to both parties at the start of a commission, may not always be appropriate unless the circumstances of the project remain significantly as stated at the time that the Agreement was signed.

5.6.3 Time charge fees

This method of charging fees is appropriate where the scope and/or the extent of the services to be provided cannot reasonably be foreseen and/or cannot reasonably be related to the cost of construction. It is often appropriate where open-ended services are required on feasibility studies, negotiation, claims consultancy etc. It is also a method that allows for additional or varied services to be provided, in addition to the provision of basic services quoted for in a fee agreement.

Fees are calculated from all the time expended on a project by partners/directors and staff and charged at rates previously agreed. The rates may be increased periodically to allow for the effects of inflation.

It is advisable to have previously agreed rates for grades of staff and partners/directors and methods of revising those rates periodically to reflect subsequent changes in salaries and costs. The inclusion of overhead allowances, generally including secretarial and administrative staff, within the rates needs careful calculation by the Quantity Surveyor Principles for the reimbursement of the time involved also need to have been agreed in advance. Sometimes this method may appear to be open ended, perhaps with little incentive for working efficiently. Periodic review of the charges is important so that progress is monitored against budgets.

5.6.4 Target cost fees

This method is appropriate where time charge fees are the basis for the Agreement but a Client wishes to have a guaranteed maximum target for fees.
Fees are recovered on a time charge basis but a 'capped' or guaranteed target cost is agreed between the parties before the work is carried out by the Quantity Surveyor If the target cost is exceeded then the Quantity Surveyor may not receive all of his costs, for instance part of his overhead allowances. If alternatively the total amount of the time charges falls below the budget cost then the Quantity Surveyor may receive an additional payment, a 'bonus' to reflect or share in the 'saving' to his Client. A formula for this should be agreed at the outset.

5.7 **Expense costs**

Expense costs are the costs to a firm such as the provision of cars, mileage-based payments to staff for travel, other travel costs, hotels, subsistence, meals, reproduction of documents, photocopying, postage and phone/fax charges, purchase costs of items bought specifically for a project, expenses in connection with appointing and engaging site-based staff, exceptional time spent by staff in travelling outside of usual hours and/or beyond usual distances etc.

In any agreement on fees it is advisable to be clear about the inclusion or exclusion of any category of expense costs within the fee charges, to identify which expenses are chargeable and to have a machinery for adjustment where necessary.

5.7.1 Recovering expense costs in fee arrangements.

Expense costs in fee bids and fee arrangements may be dealt with in a number of ways. Tender enquiries may prescribe the way required or there may be flexibility in how expense costs are included within the fee figures or shown separately from them. Three options exist for the recovery of expense costs in fee arrangements:

- **Expense costs may be included within a lump sum fee**
  Expense costs of any variety can be assessed and included within a fee and not shown separately. The fee offer thus includes a lump sum for all expense costs. This is often referred to as a 'rolled-up' offer in that the costs have not been shown separately in the bid. Although expense costs have been so included it is often necessary to consider how any adjustment to those costs may be made if changed circumstances require. For instance, if travel costs have been included in a 'rolled-up' fee and much more travel becomes necessary, it may then be required to demonstrate the basis of travel expenses that had been included in the fee offer in order to agree an adjustment

THE ROYAL INSTITUTION OF CHARTERED SURVEYORS
Appointing a Quantity Surveyor (Cont'd)
Selection and Appointment Advice (Cont'd)

- **Expense costs may be converted to a percentage of the total construction cost of the project**
  An assessment is made of the likely expense costs that may be incurred and the amount is then converted into a percentage of the total construction cost. This percentage may be added to the percentage shown as a fee offer for the quantity surveying service or it may be shown separately. The relationship between construction costs, to which a percentage fee would be applied, and the amount of expense costs that will be incurred is often tenuous and this method should only be entered into after careful consideration by a Client and his Quantity Surveyor

- **Expense costs may be paid as a separate lump sum**
  A lump sum can be calculated for expense costs and shown separately from any other lump sum, percentage-based or time charge fee for the project. Whilst this method will give a Client certainty at the outset, provision should be made for adjustment by the parties if circumstances change.

5.7.2 Constituents of expense costs and payment considerations
If expense costs are not to be included in a lump sum, percentage-based or time charge fee they may be recovered by the Quantity Surveyor on the submission of the cost records. If this method is used it is important to establish how expense costs will be calculated and reimbursed to a Quantity Surveyor by his Client. There are three methods for this:

- **Recovery of actual expense costs of disbursements incurred by a Quantity Surveyor with the authority of his Client**
  This category of cost would normally include items such as public transport costs, hotels and subsistence, and sundry expenses incurred, for instance, in obtaining financial reports on companies when considering prospective tender lists, or in establishing a site office

- **Recovery of expense costs for in-house resources provided by an organisation**
  This would include, for example, photocopying and the reproduction of tender and contract documentation. The amounts due under this category of costs are not always as clearly demonstrable as the costs referred to in the previous category. It may be helpful to set up an agreement between the parties that allows the Quantity Surveyor to recover an amount in addition to the actual material costs incurred so that some staff and overhead costs can be recovered in addition to the basic costs

- **Recovery of expense costs at market rates**
  This category is for resources provided by an organisation from its in-house facilities, for example photocopying or drawing reproduction, travel carried out by personnel using company cars etc. These costs would be recovered at what is agreed to be the market rate for the service provided.

5.8 **Implication of termination or suspension**
If a project is terminated or suspended it may become necessary to consider the implications on fees and on expenses, for instance for staff, offices, cars, rented accommodation or leased equipment taken on especially for a project. It may be that some of these costs cannot readily be avoided if termination or suspension occurs and a fee agreement should contain provisions to allow adjustments to be made, particularly to lump sum, 'rolled-up' or percentage fees.

6. Submission and comparison of fee offers and selection and notification of results

6.1 **Submission**

6.1.1 Clients are advised to invite fee offers only from firms of comparable capability and to make a selection taking into account value as well as the fee bid.

6.1.2 Where competitive offers have been sought, instructions on the submission of offers should be clear; giving the date, time and place for their delivery. Offers should all be opened at the same time and treated as confidential until notification of results is possible.

6.2 **Comparison and selection**

6.2.1 Competitive offers should be analysed and compared (including where there are different components of a fee evaluation, as referred to above). Comparison of offers should be on a basis which incorporates all the component parts of an offer in order to indicate the lowest offer and its relationship with other offers.

6.2.2 If two or more submissions give identical or very close results then it may be appropriate to apply a sensitivity test, namely to check the impact of possible or probable changes in the scope, size or value of the project on the fee bids.

6.2.3 In comparing offers it is advisable to weigh quality criteria against the offer price. Further detailed guidance is given in Appendix 10 of the RICS publication A Guide to Securing the Services of a Chartered Surveyor. It is usual to weigh quality of service criteria at a minimum of 60 per cent relative to price criteria at a maximum of 40 per cent.

6.3 **Notification**

6.3.1 Once a decision has been taken to appoint a Quantity Surveyor; the successful firm should be notified. Unsuccessful firms should also be notified of the decision and given information on the bids received (where appropriate this can be by the use of 'indices' which do not link the names of each firm to its offer). All notifications should be made in writing and be sent as soon as possible after the decision to appoint has been made.

THE ROYAL INSTITUTION OF CHARTERED SURVEYORS
Appointing a Quantity Surveyor (Cont'd)
Selection and Appointment Advice (Cont'd)

7. **Confirmation of the Agreement between the Client and the Quantity Surveyor**

7.1 The Agreement between a Client and his Quantity Surveyor should be effected by either:

- using the Form of Agreement and Terms of Appointment contained in this Guide, with cross-reference to the Form of Enquiry, Schedule of Services and Fee Offer
- using a separate form of agreement, terms and conditions, with cross reference to the services to be provided and to the fee offer
- a simple exchange of letters incorporating the information given above, making reference to the fee offer.

The 1996 Housing Grants, Construction and Regeneration Act ('the HGCR Act') introduced a right to refer any dispute to adjudication and certain provisions relating to payment. This documentation complies with the HGCR Act and includes the necessary adjudication and payment provisions. Other forms of agreement will need to comply with the HGCR Act or the adjudication and payment provisions of the Statutory Scheme for Construction Contracts will apply. An exchange of letters is unlikely to comply and the Scheme will therefore also apply to these.

8. **Complaints handling and disputes resolution**

8.1 Quantity Surveyors who are partners or directors in firms providing surveying services must operate an internal complaints handling procedure, which applies to disputes less than £50,000, under the RICS Bye-Laws. The RICS also sets a minimum standard of complaints handling, as laid out in its Professional Conduct – Rules of Conduct and Disciplinary Procedures. If the complaint cannot be resolved internally by the firm then the matter must go to final resolution by a third party. A reference to adjudication under the HGCR Act would be sufficient for the purposes of satisfying RICS regulations, pending any final resolution of the dispute at the end of the contract period. See also Clause 11 of the Terms of Appointment.

8.2 The HGCR Act introduced a compulsory scheme of third party neutral dispute resolution – which can occur at any time during the construction process – called adjudication. Any party may refer any dispute to an adjudicator at any time.

SECTION 2
Form of Enquiry
Schedule of Services

1. **Category One: General services**

The following services may be provided on any project, whatever its nature and whatever the method of procurement adopted.

☐ The following services shall, where relevant, also apply to environmental engineering service (mechanical and electrical engineering) if indicated by placing a cross in this box.

1.1 Inception and feasibility

1.1.1 ☐ Liaise with Client and other consultants to determine Client's initial requirements and subsequent development of the full brief

1.1.2 ☐ Advise on selection of other consultants if not already appointed

1.1.3 ☐ Advise on implications of proposed project and liase with other experts in developing such advice

1.1.4 ☐ Advise on feasibility of procurement options

1.1.5 ☐ Establish Client's order of priorities for quality, time and cost

1.1.6 ☐ Prepare initial budget estimate from feasibility proposals

1.1.7 ☐ Prepare overall project cost calculation and cash flow projections

1.2 Pre-contract cost control

1.2.1. ☐ Prepare and develop preliminary cost plan

1.2.2 ☐ Advise on cost of design team's proposals, including effects of site usage, shape of buildings, alternative forms of design and construction as design develops

1.2.3 ☐ Monitor cost implications during detailed design stage

1.2.4 ☐ Maintain and develop cost plan, and prepare periodic reports and updated cash flow forecasts

1.3 Tender and contractual documentation

1.3.1 ☐ Advise on tendering and contractual arrangements taking into account the Client's priorities and information available from designers

1.3.2 ☐ Advise on insurance responsibilities and liase with Client's insurance adviser

1.3.3 ☐ Advise on warranties

1.3.4 ☐ Advise on bonds for performance and other purposes

1.3.5 ☐ Prepare tender and contract documentation in conjunction with the Client and members of the design team

1.3.6 ☐ Provide copies of documentation as agreed

1.3.7 ☐ Advise on use and/or amendment of standard forms of contract or contribute to drafting of particular requirements in association with Client's legal advisers

THE ROYAL INSTITUTION OF CHARTERED SURVEYORS
Appointing a Quantity Surveyor (Cont'd)
Schedule of Services (Cont'd)
Category One: General services (Cont'd)

1.3.8 ☐ Draw up forms of contract, obtain contract drawings from members of design team and prepare and deliver to both parties contract copies of all documents

1.4 Tender selection and appraisal

1.4.1 ☐ Advise on short listing prospective tenderers

1.4.2 ☐ Investigate prospective tenderers and advise Client on financial status and experience

1.4.3 ☐ Attend interviews with tenderers

1.4.4 ☐ Arrange delivery of documents to selected tenderers

1.4.5 ☐ Check tender submissions for accuracy, level of pricing, pricing policy etc.

1.4.6 ☐ Advise on errors and qualifications and, if necessary, negotiate thereon

1.4.7 ☐ Advise on submission of programme of work and method statement

1.4.8 ☐ Prepare appropriate documentation, if required, to adjust the tender received to an acceptable contract sum

1.4.9 ☐ Review financial budget in view of tenders received and prepare revised cash flow

1.4.10 ☐ Prepare report on tenders with appropriate recommendations

1.4.11 ☐ Advise on letters of intent and issue in conjunction with Client's advisers

1.5 Interim valuations

1.5.1 ☐ Prepare recommendations for interim payments to contractors, subcontractors and suppliers in accordance with contract requirements

1.6 Post-contract cost control

1.6.1 ☐ Value designers' draft instructions for varying the project before issue

1.6.2 ☐ Prepare periodic cost reports in agreed format at specified intervals including any allocations of cost and/or copies as requested by third parties

1.7 Final account

1.7.1 ☐ Prepare the final account

1.8 Attendance at meetings

1.8.1 ☐ Attend meetings as provided for under this Agreement

1.9 Provision of printing/reproduction/copying of documents and the like

1.9.1 ☐ Provide copies of documentation as provided for under this Agreement

2. Category Two: Services particular to non-traditional methods of procurement

These services relate to particular methods of procurement and contract arrangement and should be incorporated into the Agreement as required in conjunction with services from Categories One and Three of the Schedule.

2.1 Services particular to prime cost and management or construction management contracts

2.1.1 ☐ Obtain agreement of a contractor to the amount of the approximate estimate and confirm the amount of the fee for the contract

2.1.2 ☐ Prepare recommendations for interim payments to contractor based on contractor's prime costs

2.1.3 ☐ Adjust the approximate estimate to take account of variations and price fluctuations

2.1.4 ☐ Check the final amounts due to contractors, subcontractors and suppliers

2.2 Services particular to management and construction management contracts

The terms 'management contracting' and 'construction management' mean contractual arrangements where a firm is employed for a fee to manage, organise, supervise and secure the carrying out of the work by other contractors.

2.2.1 ☐ If required, assist in drafting special forms of contract

2.2.2 ☐ Prepare tender documents for the appointment of a management contractor or construction manager

2.2.3 ☐ Attend interviews of prospective contractors or managers

2.2.4 ☐ Obtain manager's agreement to contract cost plan and confirm amount of manager's fee

2.2.5 ☐ Assist in allocation of cost plan into work packages

2.2.6 ☐ Assist in preparation of tender and contract documents

2.2.7 ☐ Price tender documents to provide an estimate comparable with tenders

2.2.8 ☐ Review cost plan as tenders are obtained and prepare revised forecasts of cash flow

THE ROYAL INSTITUTION OF CHARTERED SURVEYORS
Appointing a Quantity Surveyor (Cont'd)
Schedule of Services (Cont'd)
Category Two: Services particular to non-traditional methods of procurement (Cont'd)

2.2.9 ☐ Prepare periodic cost reports to show effect of variations, tenders let and prime costs

2.2.10 ☐ Check the final amounts due to managers, contractors, subcontractors or works contractors and suppliers

2.3 Services particular to design and build contracts - services available to a Client

2.3.1 ☐ Draft the Client's brief, in association with the Client and his designers

2.3.2 ☐ Prepare tender documents incorporating the Client's requirements

2.3.3 ☐ Prepare contract documentation, taking into account any changes arising from the contractor's proposals

2.3.4 ☐ Prepare recommendations for interim and final payments to the contractor; including compliance with statutory requirements of the 1996 Housing Grants, Construction and Regeneration Act

2.3.5 ☐ Assist in agreement of settlement of the contractor's final account

2.4 Services particular to design and build contracts - services available to a contractor

2.4.1 ☐ Prepare bills of quantities to assist in the preparation of a contractor's tender

2.4.2 ☐ Prepare alternative cost studies to assist in determining the optimum scheme for a contractor's submission

2.4.3 ☐ Draft specifications forming the contractor's proposals

2.4.4 ☐ Assist with specialist enquiries in compiling the contractor's tender

2.4.5 ☐ Measure and price variations for submission to the Client's representative

2.4.6 ☐ Prepare applications for interim payments

2.4.7 ☐ Agree final account with Client's representative

2.5 Services particular to measured term contracts

2.5.1 ☐ Take measurements, price from agreed schedule of rates and agree totals with contractor

2.5.2 ☐ Check final amounts due to contractor(s)

3. Category Three: Services not always required in Categories One and Two

These services should be incorporated into the Agreement in conjunction with services from Categories One and Two of the Schedule as required. Where points are left blank, the Client and/or the Quantity Surveyor should specify their own service as required.

3.1 Bill of quantities

3.1.1 ☐ Provide bills of quantities for mechanical and engineering services

3.1.2 ☐ Price bills of quantities to provide an estimate comparable with tenders

3.2 Cost analysis

3.2.1 ☐ Prepare cost analysis based on agreed format or special requirement

3.3 Advise on financial implications as follows:

3.3.1 ☐ Cost options of developing different sites

3.3.2 ☐ Preparation of development appraisals

3.3.3 ☐ Cost implications of alternative development programmes

3.3.4 ☐ Effect of capital and revenue expenditure

3.3.5 ☐ Life cycle cost studies and estimate of annual running costs

3.3.6 ☐ Availability of grants

3.3.7 ☐ Assist in applications for grants and documentation for these

3.3.8 ☐ Evaluation of items for capital allowances, grant payments or other such matters

3.4 Advice on use of areas and provide:

3.4.1 ☐ Measurement of gross floor areas

3.4.2 ☐ Measurement of net lettable floor areas

3.5 Provide advice on contractual matters affecting the following:

3.5.1 ☐ Entitlement to liquidated and ascertained damages

3.5.2 ☐ Final assessment of VAT

3.5.3 ☐ Opinion on delays and/or disruptions and requests for extensions of time

3.5.4 ☐ Consequences of acceleration

3.5.5 ☐ Assessment of the amount of loss and expense or other such matters and if instructed carrying out negotiations with contractors to reach a settlement

THE ROYAL INSTITUTION OF CHARTERED SURVEYORS
Appointing a Quantity Surveyor (Cont'd)
Schedule of Services (Cont'd)
Category Three: Services not always required (Cont'd)

3.6 Provide value management and value engineering services as follows:

3.6.1 ☐
(state)______________________________

3.6.2 ☐
(state)______________________________

3.7 Provide risk assessment and management services as follows:

3.7.1 ☐
(state)______________________________

3.7.2 ☐
(state)______________________________

3.8 Adjudication services

3.8.1 ☐ Provide services acting as an adjudicator in construction disputes

3.8.2 ☐ Provide services in connection with advising the Client in relation to active or threatened adjudication proceedings

3.9 Provide services in connection with arbitration and/or litigation as follows:

3.9.1 ☐
(state)______________________________

3.9.2 ☐
(state)______________________________

3.10 Provide services arising from fire or other damage to buildings including preparing and negotiating claims with loss adjusters as follows:

3.10.1 ☐
(state)______________________________

3.10.2 ☐
(state)______________________________

3.11 Provide services to a contractor in connection with negotiation of claims as follows:

3.11.1 ☐
(state)______________________________

3.11.2 ☐
(state)______________________________

3.12 Project Management

Project management services are available from Quantity Surveyors and are set out in detail (together with a Form of Agreement and Guidance Notes) in the RICS publication Project Management Agreement and Conditions of Engagement.

Clients are referred to the Project Management Agreement if the service is mainly for project management. This section is intended to be used if ancillary project management is required to a mainly quantity surveying service.

Provide project management services as follows:

3.12.1 ☐
(state)______________________________

3.12.2 ☐
(state)______________________________

3.13 Provide programme co-ordination and monitoring services as follows:

3.13.1 ☐
(state)______________________________

3.13.2 ☐
(state)______________________________

3.14 Provide planning supervisor services as follows:

3.14.1 ☐
(state)______________________________

3.14.2 ☐
(state)______________________________

3.15 Provide information for use in future management and / or maintenance of the building as follows:

3.15.1 ☐
(state)______________________________

3.15.2 ☐
(state)______________________________

3.16 Any other services not listed elsewhere in the Form of Enquiry:

3.16.1 ☐
(state)______________________________

3.16.2 ☐
(state)______________________________

3.16.3 ☐
(state)______________________________

Other Quantity Surveying Services

Other services required or provided by quantity surveyors include:-

- Planning Supervisor duties
- Cost Estimating
- Preparation of tender documents
- Contractors Services
  - Measurement / Pricing
  - Procurement advice
  - Post Contract services
- Whole life Costings
- Adjudication
- Mediation / Arbitration
- Expert Witness

FEE CALCULATION

The following is an example of the calculations necessary to establish the level of fee required for a specific project. The reader should adjust the rates as appropriate to a level based on in-house costs and the complexity, duration and scope of the project and as noted below.

Example - Quantity Surveying Fee Calculation (see clause 5.6 of Guide)

Example - Complex Project Resource Schedule

Project Value £1,500,000 (Including alteration works value £150,000)

	Hours	Rate	Cost
1. COST PLANNING			
Client Liaison	18	30.00	540.00
Attendance at meetings	18	30.00	540.00
Pre tender cost planning	60	25.00	1,500.00
			2,580.00
2. BILLS OF QUANTITIES			
Client Liaison	12	30.00	360.00
Attendance at meetings	20	30.00	600.00
Demolitions & Alterations	28	20.00	560.00
Substructures	20	20.00	400.00
Frame	12	20.00	240.00
Upper floors	10	20.00	200.00
Roof	14	20.00	280.00
Stairs	8	20.00	160.00
External walls	14	20.00	280.00
Windows & Doors	26	20.00	520.00
Internal Doors	12	20.00	240.00
Wall Finishes	12	20.00	240.00
Floor Finishes	9	20.00	180.00
Ceiling Finishes	8	20.00	160.00
Fittings & Furnishings	6	20.00	120.00
Sanitary appliances	6	20.00	120.00
Services equipment	6	20.00	120.00
Disposal installations	10	20.00	200.00
Water installations	6	20.00	120.00
Heat source	6	20.00	120.00
Space heating & air treatment	6	20.00	120.00
Ventilation installations	6	20.00	120.00
Electrical installations	18	20.00	360.00
Gas Installations	6	20.00	120.00
Lift installations	6	20.00	120.00
Protective installations	6	20.00	120.00
Communication installations	6	20.00	120.00
Special installations	6	20.00	120.00
Builders work in connection	19	20.00	380.00
External works	36	20.00	720.00
Drainage	12	20.00	240.00
External services	6	20.00	120.00
Preliminaries & Preambles	20	20.00	400.00
Pre-tender estimates	20	20.00	400.00
Tender report & Cost Analysis	12	20.00	240.00
Contract documentation	8	25.00	200.00
			9,120.00
3. POST CONTRACT			
Client liaison	20	30.00	600.00
Attendance at meetings	80	22.00	1,760.00
Valuations	66	22.00	1,452.00
Cost Reports	60	22.00	1,320.00
Pre Estimate Instructions	30	22.00	660.00
Final Account	60	22.00	1,320.00
			7,112.00
Total estimated cost			18,812.00
Add overheads		60 %	11,287.20
			30,099.20
Add profit		25 %	7,524.80
			£37,624.00

Cost Planning only

Estimated Cost		2,580.00
Add Overheads	60 %	1,548.00
		4,128.00
Add Profit	25 %	1,032.00
		5,160.00

Bills of Quantities only

Estimated Cost		9,120.00
Add Overheads	60%	5,472.00
		14,592.00
Add Profit	25%	3,648.00
		18,240.00

Post Contract only

Estimated Cost		7,112.00
Add Overheads	60%	4,267.20
		11,379.20
Add Profit	25%	2,844.80
		14,224.00

Total £37,624.00

The above example excludes all disbursements – travel, reproduction of documents, forms of contracts and the like.

The rates indicated equate to:

Partner	cost rate £30.00	Charge Rate £60.00
Senior Surveyor	cost rate £25.00	Charge Rate £50.00
Taker off	cost rate £20.00	Charge Rate £40.00
Post Contract Surveyor	cost rate £22.00	Charge Rate £44.00

The hours indicated and rates used should be adjusted as appropriate to suit each individual project and the costs, overheads and profit requirements of the practice bidding for work.

Other factors that should be considered when calculating fees include timescale, workload, relationship with client and other consultants, prestige, locality of project, likely ongoing programme of work, availability of labour.

Typical Quantity Surveying fees

Typical fees calculated as above for provision of basic services

	Cost Planning	Bills of Quantities	Post Contract services
Complex Works with little repetition			
Work Value			
50,000	280	1,240	790
150,000	730	3,210	2,140
300,000	1,410	5,520	3,830
600,000	2,810	9,120	7,090
1,500,000	5,180	18,240	14,980
3,000,000	9,230	30,400	27,000
6,000,000	16,300	52,600	49,300
10,000,000	24,200	79,200	76,300
Less Complex work with some repetition			
Work Value			
50,000	280	1,130	790
150,000	730	3,040	2,140
300,000	1,400	5,010	3,830
600,000	2,800	8,000	6,800
1,500,000	5,100	14,700	13,500
3,000,000	9,200	24,700	23,600
6,000,000	16,300	43,000	41,800
10,000,000	24,200	64,600	63,500

Example - Quantity Surveying Fee Calculation (Cont'd)
Example - Complex Project Resource Schedule (Cont'd)

Typical fees calculated as above for provision of basic services

	Cost Planning	Bills of Quantities	Post Contract services
Simple works or works with a substantial amount of repetition			
Work Value			
50,000	230	1,010	680
150,000	560	2,700	1,800
300,000	1,130	4,500	3,260
600,000	2,020	6,860	6,080
1,500,000	3,800	12,200	12,700
3,000,000	6,800	20,300	21,800
6,000,000	11,900	34,500	38,000
10,000,000	17,300	50,600	56,900

Alteration Works – Additional Fee on value of alteration works

Work Value	
50,000	340
150,000	1,010

Decoration Works – Additional Fee on value of alteration works

Work Value	
50,000	510
150,000	1,520

Where Provisional Sums, Prime Cost Sums, Subcontracts, Dayworks or contingencies form a substantial part of the project the above figures may require adjustment accordingly.

Mechanical and Electrical Services – Additional Fee for provision of Bills of Quantities

Value of M & E work	Bills of Quantities	Post Contract services
120,000	2,020	1,690
240,000	3,850	2,900
600,000	8,400	5,900
1,000,000	12,300	9,200
4,000,000	35,600	29,500
6,000,000	51,200	50,000

Negotiating Tenders – Additional Fee

Work Value	
150,000	500
600,000	1,400
1,200,000	2,200
3,000,000	3,400

THE ROYAL INSTITUTION OF CHARTERED SURVEYORS

The following Scales of Professional Charges printed by permission of The Royal Institution of Chartered Surveyors, 12 Great George Street, Westminster, London SW1P 3AD, are now obsolete and are reproduced for information only.

SCALE NO. 36

INCLUSIVE SCALE OF PROFESSIONAL CHARGES FOR QUANTITY SURVEYING SERVICES FOR BUILDING WORKS

(Effective from 29th July, 1988)

This Scale has been determined by the Fees Committee appointed by the Quantity Surveyors Divisional Council of The Royal Institution of Chartered Surveyors. The Scale is for guidance and is not mandatory.

1.0 GENERALLY

1.1 This scale is for use when an inclusive scale of professional charges is considered to be appropriate by mutual agreement between the employer and the quantity surveyor.

1.2 This scale does not apply to civil engineering works, housing schemes financed by local authorities and the Housing Corporation and housing improvement work for which separate scales of fees have been published.

1.3 The fees cover quantity surveying services as may be required in connection with a building project irrespective of the type of contract from initial appointment to final certification of the contractor's account such as:

(a) Budget estimating; cost planning and advice on tendering procedures and contract arrangements.

(b) Preparing tendering documents for main contract and specialist sub-contracts; examining tenders received and reporting thereon or negotiating tenders and pricing with a selected contractor and/or sub-contractors.

(c) Preparing recommendations for interim payments on account to the contractor; preparing periodic assessments of anticipated final cost and reporting thereon; measuring work and adjusting variations in accordance with the terms of the contract and preparing final account, pricing same and agreeing totals with the contractor.

(d) Providing a reasonable number of copies of bills of quantities and other documents; normal travelling and other expenses. Additional copies of documents, abnormal travelling and other expenses (e.g. in remote areas or overseas) and the provision of checkers on site shall be charged in addition by prior arrangement with the employer.

1.4 If any of the materials used in the works are supplied by the employer or charged at a preferential rate, then the actual or estimated market value thereof shall be included in the amounts upon which fees are to be calculated.

1.5 If the quantity surveyor incurs additional costs due to exceptional delays in building operations or any other cause beyond the control of the quantity surveyor then the fees shall be adjusted by agreement between the employer and the quantity surveyor to cover the reimbursement of these additional costs.

1.6 The fees and charges are in all cases exclusive of value added tax which will be applied in accordance with legislation.

1.7 Copyright in bills of quantities and other documents prepared by the quantity surveyor is reserved to the quantity surveyor.

THE ROYAL INSTITUTION OF CHARTERED SURVEYORS (Cont'd)
SCALE NO. 36 (Cont'd)

2.0 INCLUSIVE SCALE

2.1 The fees for the services outlined in paragraph 1.3, subject to the provision of paragraph 2.2, shall be as follows:

(a) CATEGORY A. Relatively complex works and/or works with little or no repetition.

Examples:
Ambulance and fire stations; banks; cinemas; clubs; computer buildings; council offices; crematoria; fitting out of existing buildings; homes for the elderly; hospitals and nursing homes; laboratories; law courts; libraries; 'one off' houses; petrol stations; places of religious worship; police stations; public houses, licensed premises; restaurants; sheltered housing; sports pavilions; theatres; town halls; universities, polytechnics and colleges of further education (other than halls of residence and hostels); and the like.

Value of Work			Category A Fee	
		£	£	£
Up to		150,000	380 + 6.0% (Minimum Fee £3,380)	
150,000	-	300,000	9,380 + 5.0% on balance over	150,000
300,000	-	600,000	16,880 + 4.3% on balance over	300,000
600,000	-	1,500,000	29,780 + 3.4% on balance over	600,000
1,500,000	-	3,000,000	60,380 + 3.0% on balance over	1,500,000
3,000,000	-	6,000,000	105,380 + 2.8% on balance over	3,000,000
Over		6,000,000	189,380 + 2.4% on balance over	6,000,000

(b) CATEGORY B. Less complex works and/or works with some element of repetition.

Examples:
Adult education facilities; canteens; church halls; community centres; departmental stores; enclosed sports stadia and swimming baths; halls of residence; hostels; motels; offices other than those included in Categories A and C; railway stations; recreation and leisure centres; residential hotels; schools; self-contained flats and maisonettes; shops and shopping centres; supermarkets and hypermarkets; telephone exchanges; and the like.

Value of Work			Category B Fee	
		£	£	£
Up to		150,000	360 + 5.8% (Minimum Fee £3,260)	
150,000	-	300,000	9,060 + 4.7% on balance over	150,000
300,000	-	600,000	16,110 + 3.9% on balance over	300,000
600,000	-	1,500,000	27,810 + 2.8% on balance over	600,000
1,500,000	-	3,000,000	53,010 + 2.6% on balance over	1,500,000
3,000,000	-	6,000,000	92,010 + 2.4% on balance over	3,000,000
Over		6,000,000	164,010 + 2.0% on balance over	6,000,000

(c) CATEGORY C. Simple works and/or works with a substantial element of repetition.

Examples:
Factories; garages; multi-storey car parks; open-air sports stadia; structural shell offices not fitted out; warehouses; workshops; and the like.

Value of Work			Category C Fee	
		£	£	£
Up to		150,000	300 + 4.9% (Minimum Fee £2,750)	
150,000	-	300,000	7,650 + 4.1% on balance over	150,000
300,000	-	600,000	13,800 + 3.3% on balance over	300,000
600,000	-	1,500,000	23,700 + 2.5% on balance over	600,000
1,500,000	-	3,000,000	46,200 + 2.2% on balance over	1,500,000
3,000,000	-	6,000,000	79,200 + 2.0% on balance over	3,000,000
Over		6,000,000	139,200 + 1.6% on balance over	6,000,000

THE ROYAL INSTITUTION OF CHARTERED SURVEYORS (Cont'd)
SCALE NO. 36 (Cont'd)
INCLUSIVE SCALE (Cont'd)

2.1 (d) Fees shall be calculated upon the total of the final account for the whole of the work including all nominated sub-contractors' and nominated suppliers' accounts. When work normally included in a building contract is the subject of a separate contract for which the quantity surveyor has not been paid fees under any other clause hereof, the value of such work shall be included in the amount upon which fees are charged.

(e) When a contract comprises buildings which fall into more than one category, the fee shall be calculated as follows:

(i) The amount upon which fees are chargeable shall be allocated to the categories of work applicable and the amounts so allocated expressed as percentages of the total amount upon which fees are chargeable.

(ii) Fees shall then be calculated for each category on the total amount upon which fees are chargeable.

(iii) The fee chargeable shall then be calculated by applying the percentages of work in each category to the appropriate total fee and adding the resultant amounts.

(iv) A consolidated percentage fee applicable to the total value of the work may be charged by prior agreement between the employer and the quantity surveyor. Such a percentage shall be based on this scale and on the estimated cost of the various categories of work and calculated in accordance with the principles stated above.

(f) When a project is the subject of a number of contracts then, for the purpose of calculating fees, the values of such contracts shall not be aggregated but each contract shall be taken separately and the scale of charges (paragraphs 2.1 (a) to (e)) applied as appropriate.

2.2 Air Conditioning, Heating, Ventilating and Electrical Services

(a) When the services outlined in paragraph 1.3 are provided by the quantity surveyor for the air conditioning, heating, ventilating and electrical services there shall be a fee for these services in addition to the fee calculated in accordance with paragraph 2.1 as follows:

Value of Work			Additional Fee	
£		£	£	£
Up to		120,000	5.0%	
120,000	-	240,000	6,000 + 4.7% on balance over	120,000
240,000	-	480,000	11,640 + 4.0% on balance over	240,000
480,000	-	750,000	21,240 + 3.6% on balance over	480,000
750,000	-	1,000,000	30,960 + 3.0% on balance over	750,000
1,000,000	-	4,000,000	38,460 + 2.7% on balance over	1,000,000
Over		4,000,000	119,460 + 2.4% on balance over	4,000,000

(b) The value of such services, whether the subject of separate tenders or not, shall be aggregated and the total value of work so obtained used for the purpose of calculating the additional fee chargeable in accordance with paragraph (a). (Except that when more than one firm of consulting engineers is engaged on the design of these services, the separate values for which each such firm is responsible shall be aggregated and the additional fees charged shall be calculated independently on each such total value so obtained.)

(c) Fees shall be calculated upon the basis of the account for the whole of the air conditioning, heating, ventilating and electrical services for which bills of quantities and final accounts have been prepared by the quantity surveyor.

2.3 Works of Alteration

On works of alteration or repair, or on those sections of the work which are mainly works of alteration or repair, there shall be a fee of 1.0% in addition to the fee calculated in accordance with paragraphs 2.1 and 2.2.

2.4 Works of Redecoration and Associated Minor Repairs

On works of redecoration and associated minor repairs, there shall be a fee of 1.5% in addition to the fee calculated in accordance with paragraphs 2.1 and 2.2.

2.5 Generally

If the works are substantially varied at any stage or if the quantity surveyor is involved in an excessive amount of abortive work, then the fees shall be adjusted by agreement between the employer and the quantity surveyor.

THE ROYAL INSTITUTION OF CHARTERED SURVEYORS (Cont'd)
SCALE NO. 36 (Cont'd)
INCLUSIVE SCALE (Cont'd)

3.0 ADDITIONAL SERVICES

3.1 For additional services not normally necessary, such as those arising as a result of the termination of a contract before completion, liquidation, fire damage to the buildings, services in connection with arbitration, litigation and investigation of the validity of contractors' claims, services in connection with taxation matters and all similar services where the employer specifically instructs the quantity surveyor, the charges shall be in accordance with paragraph 4.0 below.

4.0 TIME CHARGES

4.1 (a) For consultancy and other services performed by a principal, a fee by arrangement according to the circumstances including the professional status and qualifications of the quantity surveyor.

(b) When a principal does work which would normally be done by a member of staff, the charge shall be calculated as paragraph 4.2 below.

4.2 (a) For services by a member of staff, the charges for which are to be based on the time involved, such charges shall be calculated on the hourly cost of the individual involved plus 145%.

4.2 (b) A member of staff shall include a principal doing work normally done by an employee (as paragraph 4.1 (b) above), technical and supporting staff, but shall exclude secretarial staff or staff engaged upon general administration.

(c) For the purpose of paragraph 4.2 (b) above, a principal's time shall be taken at the rate applicable to a senior assistant in the firm.

(d) The supervisory duties of a principal shall be deemed to be included in the addition of 145% as paragraph 4.2 (a) above and shall not be charged separately.

(e) The hourly cost to the employer shall be calculated by taking the sum of the annual cost of the member of staff of:

(i) Salary and bonus but excluding expenses;
(ii) Employer's contributions payable under any Pension and Life Assurance Schemes;
(iii) Employer's contributions made under the National Insurance Acts, the Redundancy Payments Act and any other payments made in respect of the employee by virtue of any statutory requirements; and
(iv) Any other payments or benefits made or granted by the employer in pursuance of the terms of employment of the member of staff; and dividing by 1650.

5.0 INSTALMENT PAYMENTS

5.1 In the absence of agreement to the contrary, fees shall be paid by instalments as follows:

(a) Upon acceptance by the employer of a tender for the works, one half of the fee calculated on the amount of the accepted tender.

(b) The balance by instalments at intervals to be agreed between the date of the first certificate and one month after final certification of the contractor's account.

5.2 (a) In the event of no tender being accepted, one half of the fee shall be paid within three months of completion of the tender documents. The fee shall be calculated upon the basis of the lowest original bona fide tender received. In the event of no tender being received, the fee shall be calculated upon a reasonable valuation of the works based upon the tender documents.
Note: In the foregoing context "bona fide tender" shall be deemed to mean a tender submitted in good faith without major errors of computation and not subsequently withdrawn by the tenderer.

(b) In the event of the project being abandoned at any stage other than those covered by the foregoing, the proportion of the fee payable shall be by agreement between the employer and the quantity surveyor.

SCALE NO. 37

ITEMISED SCALE OF PROFESSIONAL CHARGES FOR QUANTITY SURVEYING SERVICES FOR BUILDING WORKS
(29th July, 1988)

This Scale has been determined by the Fees Committee appointed by the Quantity Surveyors Divisional Council of The Royal Institution of Chartered Surveyors. The Scale is for guidance and is not mandatory.

1.0 GENERALLY

1.1 The fees are in all cases exclusive of travelling and other expenses (for which the actual disbursement is recoverable unless there is some prior arrangement for such charges) and of the cost of reproduction of bills of quantities and other documents, which are chargeable in addition at net cost.

1.2 The fees are in all cases exclusive of services in connection with the allocation of the cost of the works for purposes of calculating value added tax for which there shall be an additional fee based on the time involved (see paragraphs 19.1 and 19.2)

1.3 If any of the materials used in the works are supplied by the employer or charged at a preferential rate, then the actual or estimated market value thereof shall be included in the amounts upon which fees are to be calculated.

1.4 The fees are in all cases exclusive of preparing a specification of the materials to be used and the works to be done, but the fees for preparing bills of quantities and similar documents do include for incorporating preamble clauses describing the materials and workmanship (from instructions given by the architect and/or consulting engineer).

THE ROYAL INSTITUTION OF CHARTERED SURVEYORS (Cont'd)
SCALE NO. 37 (Cont'd)

1.5 If the quantity surveyor incurs additional costs due to exceptional delays in building operations or any other cause beyond the control of the quantity surveyor then the fees may be adjusted by agreement between the employer and the quantity surveyor to cover the reimbursement of these additional costs.

1.6 The fees and charges are in all cases exclusive of value added tax which will be applied in accordance with legislation.

1.7 Copyright in bills of quantities and other documents prepared by the quantity surveyor is reserved to the quantity surveyor.

2.0 BILLS OF QUANTITIES

2.1 Basic Scale: For preparing bills of quantities and examining tenders received and reporting thereon.

2.1 (a) CATEGORY A: Relatively complex works and/or works with little or no repetition.

Examples:

Ambulance and fire stations; banks; cinemas; clubs; computer buildings; council offices; crematoria; fitting out of existing buildings; homes for the elderly; hospitals and nursing homes; laboratories; law courts; libraries; 'one off' houses; petrol stations; places of religious worship; police stations; public houses, licensed premises; restaurants; sheltered housing; sports pavilions; theatres; town halls; universities, polytechnics and colleges of further education (other than halls of residence and hostels); and the like.

Value of Work			Category A Fee	
£			£	£
Up to 150,000			230 + 3.0% (minimum fee £1,730)	
150,000	-	300,000	4,730 + 2.3% on balance over	150,000
300,000	-	600,000	8,180 + 1.8% on balance over	300,000
600,000	-	1,500,000	13,580 + 1.5% on balance over	600,000
1,500,000	-	3,000,000	27,080 + 1.2% on balance over	1,500,000
3,000,000	-	6,000,000	45,080 + 1.1% on balance over	3,000,000
Over	-	6,000,000	78,080 + 1.0% on balance over	6,000,000

2.1 (b) CATEGORY B: Less complex works and/or works with some element of repetition.

Examples:

Adult education facilities; canteens; church halls; community centres; departmental stores; enclosed sports stadia and swimming baths; halls of residence; hostels; motels; offices other than those included in Categories A and C; railway stations; recreation and leisure centres; residential hotels; schools; self-contained flats and maisonettes; shops and shopping centres; supermarkets and hypermarkets; telephone exchanges; and the like.

Value of Work			Category B Fee	
£			£	£
Up to150,000			210 + 2.8% (minimum fee £1610)	
150,000	-	300,000	4,410 + 2.0% on balance over	150,000
300,000	-	600,000	7,410 + 1.5% on balance over	300,000
600,000	-	1,500,000	11,910 + 1.1% on balance over	600,000
1,500,000	-	3,000,000	21,810 + 1.0% on balance over	1,500,000
3,000,000	-	6,000,000	36,810 + 0.9% on balance over	3,000,000
Over		6,000,000	63,810 + 0.8% on balance over	6,000,000

(c) CATEGORY C: Simple works and/or works with a substantial element of repetition.

Examples:

Factories; garages; multi-storey car parks; open-air sports stadia; structural shell offices not fitted out; warehouses; workshops; and the like.

Value of Work			Category C Fee	
£			£	£
Up to 150,000			180 + 2.5% (minimum fee £1,430)	
150,000	-	300,000	3,930 + 1.8% on balance over	150,000
300,000	-	600,000	6,630 + 1.2% on balance over	300,000
600,000	-	1,500,000	10,230 + 0.9% on balance over	600,000
1,500,000	-	3,000,000	18,330 + 0.8% on balance over	1,500,000
3,000,000	-	6,000,000	30,330 + 0.7% on balance over	3,000,000
Over		6,000,000	51,330 + 0.6% on balance over	6,000,000

THE ROYAL INSTITUTION OF CHARTERED SURVEYORS (Cont'd)
SCALE NO. 37 (Cont'd)
BILLS OF QUANTITIES (Cont'd)

2.1 (d) The scales of fees for preparing bills of quantities (paragraphs 2.1 (a) to (c)) are overall scales based upon the inclusion of all provisional and prime cost items, subject to the provision of paragraph 2.1 (g). When work normally included in a building contract is the subject of a separate contract for which the quantity surveyor has not been paid fees under any other clause hereof, the value of such work shall be included in the amount upon which fees are charged.

(e) Fees shall be calculated upon the accepted tender for the whole of the work subject to the provisions of paragraph 2.6. In the event of no tender being accepted, fees shall be calculated upon the basis of the lowest original bona fide tender received. In the even of no such tender being received, the fees shall be calculated upon a reasonable valuation of the works based upon the original bills of quantities.

Note: In the foregoing context "bona fide tender" shall be deemed to mean a tender submitted in good faith without major errors of computation and not subsequently withdrawn by the tenderer.

(f) In calculating the amount upon which fees are charged the total of any credits and the totals of any alternative bills shall be aggregated and added to the amount described above. The value of any omission or addition forming part of an alternative bill shall not be added unless measurement or abstraction from the original dimension sheets was necessary.

(g) Where the value of the air conditioning, heating, ventilating and electrical services included in the tender documents together exceeds 25% of the amount calculated as described in paragraphs 2.1 (d) and (e), then, subject to the provisions of paragraph 2.2, no fee is chargeable on the amount by which the value of these services exceeds the said 25% in this context the term "value" excludes general contractor's profit, attendance, builder's work in connection with the services, preliminaries and any similar additions.

(h) When a contract comprises buildings which fall into more than one category, the fee shall be calculated as follows:

(i) The amount upon which fees are chargeable shall be allocated to the categories of work applicable and the amounts so allocated expressed as percentages of the total amount upon which fees are chargeable.
(ii) Fees shall then be calculated for each category on the total amount upon which fees are chargeable.
(iii) The fee chargeable shall then be calculated by applying the percentages of work in each category to the appropriate total fee and adding the resultant amounts.

(j) When a project is the subject of a number of contracts then, for the purpose of calculating fees, the values of such contracts shall not be aggregated but each contract shall be taken separately and the scale of charges (paragraphs 2.1 (a) to (h)) applied as appropriate.

(k) Where the quantity surveyor is specifically instructed to provide cost planning services the fee calculated in accordance with paragraphs 2.1 (a) to (j) shall be increased by a sum calculated in accordance with the following table and based upon the same value of work as that upon which the aforementioned fee has been calculated:

2.1 (k) CATEGORIES A & B: (as defined in paragraphs 2.1 (a) and (b)).

Value of Work		Fee		
	£	£		£
Up to	600,000		0.7%	
600,000	- 3,000,000	4,200 + 0.4%	on balance over	600,000
3,000,000	- 6,000,000	13,800 + 0.35%	on balance over	3,000,000
Over	6,000,000	24,300 + 0.3%	on balance over	6,000,000

CATEGORY C: (as defined in paragraph 2.1 (c)).

Value of Work		Fee		
	£	£		£
Up to	600,000		0.5%	
600,000	- 3,000,000	3,000 + 0.3%	on balance over	600,000
3,000,000	- 6,000,000	10,200 + 0.25%	on balance over	3,000,000
Over	6,000,000	17,700 + 0.2%	on balance over	6,000,000

THE ROYAL INSTITUTION OF CHARTERED SURVEYORS (Cont'd)
SCALE NO. 37 (Cont'd)
BILLS OF QUANTITIES (Cont'd)

2.2 Air Conditioning, Heating, Ventilating and Electrical Services

(a) Where bills of quantities are prepared by the quantity surveyor for the air conditioning, heating, ventilating and electrical services there shall be a fee for these services (which shall include examining tenders received and reporting thereon), in addition to the fee calculated in accordance with paragraph 2.1 as follows:

Value of Work			Additional Fee	
		£	£	£
Up to		120,000	2.5%	
120,000	-	240,000	3,000 + 2.25% on balance over	120,000
240,000	-	480,000	5,700 + 2.0% on balance over	240,000
480,000	-	750,000	10,500 + 1.75% on balance over	480,000
750,000	-	1,000,000	15,225 + 1.25% on balance over	750,000
Over		1,000,000	18,350 + 1.15% on balance over	1,000,000

(b) The values of such services, whether the subject of separate tenders or not, shall be aggregated and the total value of work so obtained used for the purpose of calculating the additional fee chargeable in accordance with paragraph (a).

(Except that when more than one firm of consulting engineers is engaged on the design of these services, the separate values for which each such firm is responsible shall be aggregated and the additional fees charged shall be calculated independently on each such total value so obtained).

(c) Fees shall be calculated upon the accepted tender for the whole of the air conditioning, heating, ventilating and electrical services for which bills of quantities have been prepared by the quantity surveyor. In the event of no tender being accepted, fees shall be calculated upon the basis of the lowest original bona fide tender received. In the event of no such tender being received, the fees shall be calculated upon a reasonable valuation of the services based upon the original bills of quantities.

Note: In the foregoing context "bona fide tender" shall be deemed to mean a tender submitted in good faith without major errors of computation and not subsequently withdrawn by the tenderer.

(d) When cost planning services are provided by the quantity surveyor for air conditioning, heating, ventilating and electrical services (or for any part of such services) there shall be an additional fee based on the time involved (see paragraphs 19.1 and 19.2). Alternatively the fee may be on a lump sum or percentage basis agreed between the employer and the quantity surveyor.

Note: The incorporation of figures for air conditioning, heating, ventilating and electrical services provided by the consulting engineer is deemed to be included in the quantity surveyor's services under paragraph 2.1.

2.3 Works of Alteration

On works of alteration or repair, or on those sections of the works which are mainly works of alteration or repair, there shall be a fee of 1.0% in addition to the fee calculated in accordance with paragraphs 2.1 and 2.2.

2.4 Works of Redecoration and Associated Minor Repairs On works of redecoration and associated minor repairs, there shall be a fee of 1.5% in addition to the fee calculated in accordance with paragraphs 2.1 and 2.2.

2.5 Bills of Quantities Prepared in Special Forms

Fees calculated in accordance with paragraphs 2.1, 2.2, 2.3 and 2.4 include for the preparation of bills of quantities on a normal trade basis. If the employer requires additional information to be provided in the bills of quantities or the bills to be prepared in an elemental, operational or similar form, then the fee may be adjusted by agreement between the employer and the quantity surveyor.

2.6 Action of Tenders

(a) When cost planning services have been provided by the quantity surveyor and a tender, when received, is reduced before acceptance and if the reductions are not necessitated by amended instructions of the employer or by the inclusion in the bills of quantities of items which the quantity surveyor has indicated could not be contained within the approved estimate, then in such a case no charge shall be made by the quantity surveyor for the preparation of bills of reductions and the fee for the preparation of the bills of quantities shall be based on the amount of the reduced tender.

(b) When cost planning services have not been provided by the quantity surveyor and if a tender, when received, is reduced before acceptance, fees are to be calculated upon the amount of the unreduced tender. When the preparation of bills of reductions is required, a fee is chargeable for preparing such bills of reductions as follows:

(i) 2.0% upon the gross amount of all omissions requiring measurement or abstraction from original dimension sheets.

(ii) 3.0% upon the gross amount of all additions requiring measurement.

(iii) 0.5% upon the gross amount of all remaining additions.

Note: The above scale for the preparation of bills of reductions applies to work in all categories.

2.7 Generally

If the works are substantially varied at any stage or if the quantity surveyor is involved in an excessive amount of abortive work, then the fees shall be adjusted by agreement between the employer and the quantity surveyor.

GENERAL INFORMATION

THE ROYAL INSTITUTION OF CHARTERED SURVEYORS (Cont'd)
SCALE NO. 37 (Cont'd)

3.0 NEGOTIATING TENDERS

3.1 (a) For negotiating and agreeing prices with a contractor:

Value of Work		Fee	
	£	£	£
Up to	150,000	0.5%	
150,000	- 600,000	750 + 0.3% on balance over	150,000
600,000	- 1,200,000	2,100 + 0.2% on balance over	600,000
Over	1,200,000	3,300 + 0.1% on balance over	1,200,000

3.1 (b) The fee shall be calculated on the total value of the works as defined in paragraphs 2.1 (d), (e), (f), (g) and (j).

(c) For negotiating and agreeing prices with a contractor for air conditioning, heating, ventilating and electrical services there shall be an additional fee as paragraph 3.1 (a) calculated on the total value of such services as defined in paragraph 2.2 (b).

4.0 CONSULTATIVE SERVICES AND PRICING BILLS OF QUANTITIES

4.1 Consultative Services

Where the quantity surveyor is appointed to prepare approximate estimates, feasibility studies or submissions for the approval of financial grants or similar services, then the fee shall be based on the time involved (see paragraphs 19.1 and 19.2) or, alternatively, on a lump sum or percentage basis agreed between the employer and the quantity surveyor.

4.2 Pricing Bills of Quantities

(a) For pricing bills of quantities, if instructed, to provide an estimate comparable with tenders, the fee shall be one-third (33 1/3%) of the fee for negotiating and agreeing prices with a contractor, calculated in accordance with paragraphs 3.1 (a) and (b).

(b) For pricing bills of quantities, if instructed, to provide an estimate comparable with tenders for air conditioning, heating, ventilating and electrical services the fee shall be one-third (33 1/3%) of the fee calculated in accordance with paragraph 3.1 (c).

CONTRACTS BASED ON BILLS OF QUANTITIES: POST-CONTRACT SERVICES

Alternative Scales (I and II) for post-contract services are set out below to be used at the quantity surveyor's discretion by prior agreement with the employer.

ALTERNATIVE 1

5.0 OVERALL SCALE OF CHARGES FOR POST-CONTRACT SERVICES

5.1 If the quantity surveyor appointed to carry out the post-contract services did not prepare the bills of quantities then the fees in paragraphs 5.2 and 5.3 shall be increased to cover the additional services undertaken by the quantity surveyor.

5.2 Basic Scale: For taking particulars and reporting valuations for interim certificates for payments on account to the contractor, preparing periodic assessments of anticipated final cost and reporting thereon, measuring and making up bills of variations including pricing and agreeing totals with the contractor, and adjusting fluctuations in the cost of labour and materials if required by the contract.

(a) CATEGORY A: Relatively complex works and/or works with little or no repetition.

Examples:
Ambulance and fire stations; banks; cinemas; clubs; computer buildings; council offices; crematoria; fitting out of existing buildings; homes for the elderly; hospitals and nursing homes; laboratories; law courts; libraries; 'one-off' houses; petrol stations; places of religious worship; police stations; public houses, licensed premises; restaurants; sheltered housing; sports pavilions; theatres; town halls; universities, polytechnics and colleges of further education (other than halls of residence and hostels); and the like.

Value of Work		Category A Fee	
£		£	£
Up to 150,000		150 + 2.0% (minimum fee £1,150)	
150,000	- 300,000	3,150 + 1.7% on balance over	150,000
300,000	- 600,000	5,700 + 1.6% on balance over	300,000
600,000	- 1,500,000	10,500 + 1.3% on balance over	600,000
1,500,000	- 3,000,000	22,200 + 1.2% on balance over	1,500,000
3,000,000	- 6,000,000	40,200 + 1.1% on balance over	3,000,000
Over	6,000,000	73,200 + 1.0% on balance over	6,000,000

THE ROYAL INSTITUTION OF CHARTERED SURVEYORS (Cont'd)
SCALE NO. 37 (Cont'd)
CONTRACTS BASED ON BILLS OF QUANTITIES: POST-CONTRACT SERVICES (Cont'd)
ALTERNATIVE 1 (Cont'd)
OVERALL SCALE OF CHARGES FOR POST-CONTRACT SERVICES (Cont'd)

(b) CATEGORY B: Less complex works and/or works with some element of repetition.

Examples:
Adult education facilities; canteens; church halls; community centres; departmental stores; enclosed sports stadia and swimming baths; halls of residence; hostels; motels; offices other than those included in Categories A and C; railway stations; recreation and leisure centres; residential hotels; schools; self-contained flats and maisonettes; shops and shopping centres; supermarkets and hypermarkets; telephone exchanges; and the like.

Value of Work			Category B Fee	
£			£	£
Up to150,000			150 + 2.0% (minimum fee £1150)	
150,000	-	300,000	3,150 + 1.7% on balance over	150,000
300,000	-	600,000	5,700 + 1.5% on balance over	300,000
600,000	-	1,500,000	10,200 + 1.1% on balance over	600,000
1,500,000	-	3,000,000	20,100 + 1.0% on balance over	1,500,000
3,000,000	-	6,000,000	35,100 + 0.9% on balance over	3,000,000
Over		6,000,000	62,100 + 0.8% on balance over	6,000,000

(c) CATEGORY C: Simple works and/or works with a substantial element of repetition.

Examples:
Factories; garages; multi-storey car parks; open-air sports stadia; structural shell offices not fitted out; warehouses; workshops; and the like.

Value of Work			Category C Fee	
£			£	£
Up to 150,000			120 + 1.6% (minimum fee £920)	
150,000	-	300000	2,520 + 1.5% on balance over	150,000
300,000	-	600,000	4,770 + 1.4% on balance over	300,000
600,000	-	1,500,000	8,970 + 1.1% on balance over	600,000
1,500,000	-	3,000,000	18,870 + 0.9% on balance over	1,500,000
3,000,000	-	6,000,000	32,370 + 0.8% on balance over	3,000,000
Over		6,000,000	56,370 + 0.7% on balance over	6,000,000

(d) The scales of fees for post-contract services (paragraphs 5.2 (a) and (c) are overall scales, based upon the inclusion of all nominated sub-contractors' and nominated suppliers' accounts, subject to the provision of paragraph 5.2 (g). When work normally included in a building contract is the subject of a separate contract for which the quantity surveyor has not been paid fees under any other clause hereof, the value of such work shall be included in the amount on which fees are charged.

(e) Fees shall be calculated upon the basis of the account for the whole of the work, subject to the provisions of paragraph 5.3.

(f) In calculating the amount on which fees are charged the total of any credits is to be added to the amount described above.

(g) Where the value of air conditioning, heating, ventilating and electrical services included in the tender documents together exceeds 25% of the amount calculated as described in paragraphs 5.2 (d) and (e) above, then, subject to the provisions of paragraph 5.3, no fee is chargeable on the amount by which the value of these services exceeds the said 25%. In this context the term "value" excludes general contractor's profit, attendance, builders work in connection with the services, preliminaries and any other similar additions.

(h) When a contract comprises buildings which fall into more than one category, the fee shall be calculated as follows:

(i) The amount upon which fees are chargeable shall be allocated to the categories of work applicable and the amounts so allocated expressed as percentages of the total amount upon which fees are chargeable.

(ii) Fees shall then be calculated for each category on the total amount upon which fees are chargeable.

(iii) The fee chargeable shall then be calculated by applying the percentages of work in each category to the appropriate total fee and adding the resultant amounts.

(j) When a project is the subject of a number of contracts then, for the purposes of calculating fees, the values of such contracts shall not be aggregated but each contract shall be taken separately and the scale of charges (paragraphs 5.2 (a) to (h)) applied as appropriate.

(k) When the quantity surveyor is required to prepare valuations of materials or goods off site, an additional fee shall be charged based on the time involved (see paragraphs 19.1 and 19.2).

THE ROYAL INSTITUTION OF CHARTERED SURVEYORS (Cont'd)
SCALE NO. 37 (Cont'd)
OVERALL SCALE OF CHARGES FOR POST-CONTRACT SERVICES (Cont'd)
Air Conditioning, Heating, Ventilating and Electrical Services (Cont'd)

(l) The basic scale for post-contract services includes for a simple routine of periodically estimating final costs. When the employer specifically requests a cost monitoring service which involves the quantity surveyor in additional or abortive measurement an additional fee shall be charged based on the time involved (see paragraphs 19.1 and 19.2), or alternatively on a lump sum or percentage basis agreed between the employer and the quantity surveyor.

(m) The above overall scales of charges for post contract services assume normal conditions when the bills of quantities are based on drawings accurately depicting the building work the employer requires. If the works are materially varied to the extent that substantial remeasurement is necessary then the fee for post-contract services shall be adjusted by agreement between the employer and the quantity surveyor.

5.3 Air Conditioning, Heating, Ventilating and Electrical Services

(a) Where final accounts are prepared by the quantity surveyor for the air conditioning, heating, ventilating and electrical services there shall be a fee for these services, in addition to the fee calculated in accordance with paragraph 5.2, as follows:

Value of Work			Additional Fee		
		£	£		£
Up to		120,000		2.0%	
120,000	-	240,000	2,400 + 1.6%	on balance over	120,000
240,000	-	1,000,000	4,320 + 1.25%	on balance over	240,000
1,000,000	-	4,000,000	13,820 + 1.0%	on balance over	1,000,000
Over		4,000,000	43,820 + 0.9%	on balance over	4,000,000

(b) The values of such services, whether the subject of separate tenders or not, shall be aggregated and the total value of work so obtained used for the purpose of calculating the additional fee chargeable in accordance with paragraph (a).

(Except that when more than one firm of consulting engineers is engaged on the design of these services the separate values for which each such firm is responsible shall be aggregated and the additional fee charged shall be calculated independently on each such total value so obtained).

(c) The scope of the services to be provided by the quantity surveyor under paragraph (a) above shall be deemed to be equivalent to those described for the basic scale for post-contract services.

(d) When the quantity surveyor is required to prepare periodic valuations of materials or goods off site, an additional fee shall be charged based on the time involved (see paragraphs 19.1 and 19.2).

(e) The basic scale for post-contract services includes for a simple routine of periodically estimating final costs. When the employer specifically requests a cost monitoring service which involves the quantity surveyor in additional or abortive measurement an additional fee shall be charged based on the time involved (see paragraph 19.1 and 19.2), or alternatively on a lump sum or percentage basis agreed between the employer and the quantity surveyor.

(f) Fees shall be calculated upon the basis of the account for the whole of the air conditioning, heating, ventilating and electrical services for which final accounts have been prepared by the quantity surveyor.

Scale 37 Alternative II; - Separate Stages of Post Contract Services and Scales 38 - 47 are not reproduced here.

BUILDING CONTROL CHARGES

Notes

Before you build, extend or convert, you or your agent must advise your local authority either by submitting Full Plans or a Building Notice. The fee payable depends on the type of work. The number of dwellings in a building and the total floor area. The following tables may be used in conjunction with the Fees Regulations as a guide to calculating the fees, however different authorities charge different fees and advise should be taken from the local authority(ies) involved.

Should you submit Full Plans, the full planning application fee could be split into a plan fee at the time of submission to cover their passing or rejection and an inspection fee covering all necessary site visits, will be payable following the first inspection.

Should you submit a Building Notice, the appropriate Building Notice fee is payable at the time of submission and covers all necessary checks and site visits. The Building Notice fee is equivalent to the sum of the relevant plan fee and inspection fee.

Total estimated cost means an estimate accepted by the local authority of a reasonable cost that would be charged by a person in business to carry out the work shown or described in the application excluding VAT and any fees paid to an architect, engineer or surveyor etc. and also excluding land acquisition costs.

A supplementary charge will apply if electrical works, that are controlled under part P of the regulations, are not carried out by a competent person to self certify the work.

For further advice and to check current fees consult your local authority.

FULL PLAN AND INSPECTION CHARGES

Notes: Guide fees only as some charges vary dependent on Local Authority and other factors
Regularisation charge is fee for retrospective approval of unauthorised works.

Table 1 – New Dwellings (new build and conversions)

No. of dwellings	Full Planning Application	Building Notice	Regularisation Charge
Description	£	£	£
Creation of 1 new dwelling.	462.00	840.00	870.00
Creation of 2 new dwellings.	924.00	1,140.00	1,210.00
Creation of 3 new dwellings.	1,386.00	1,440.00	1,545.00
Creation of 4 new dwellings.	1,848.00	1,740.00	1,885.00
Creation of 5 new dwellings.	2,310.00	1,920.00	2,224.00
Over 5 dwellings.	Subject to an individually determined charge		
Conversion of dwelling into 2 flats	924.00	1,140.00	1,210.00
Conversion of dwelling into 3 flats	1,386.00	1,440.00	1,545.00
Over 3 flats	Subject to an individually determined charge		

New dwellings over 300m² subject to an individually determined charge
Subject to VAT at 20%
Regularisation Charge not subject to VAT
For further information consult the Charges Scheme

Table 2 – Domestic Extensions and Alterations

Domestic extensions, garages and non-exempt outbuildings

Description	Full Plans: Plan Charge £	Full Plans: Inspection Charge £	Building Notice Charge £	Regularisation Charge £
Extension internal floor area under 40m²	200.00	360.00	560.00	636.48
Extension over 40m² and under 60m²	200.00	540.00	740.00	919.36
Extensions where the total floor area exceeds 60m²	Subject to an individually determined charge			
Loft conversion not including a dormer	200.00	360.00	560.00	636.48
Loft conversion including a dormer	200.00	540.00	740.00	919.36
Loft conversion where the total floor area exceeds 100m²	Subject to an individually determined charge			
Carport, attached garage, detached garage and outbuildings under 40m²	200.00	100.00	300.00	300.00
Garage, conversion	200.00	100.00	340.00	360.00

Certain garages, carport (and conservatories) under 30m² may be exempt buildings
'Extension' includes attached garages and non-exempt conservatories
Subject to VAT at 20%
Regularisation charges are not subject to VAT
For further information contact the local authority planning and building control

BUILDING CONTROL CHARGES (Cont'd)

FULL PLAN AND INSPECTION CHARGES (Cont'd)

Table 2 – Domestic Extensions and Alterations (Cont'd)

Domestic alterations

Description	Full Plans £	Building Notice Charge £	Regularisation Charge £
Alterations (including chimney breast removal) up to £5,000 estimated cost of work	250.00	250.00	285.00
Alterations over £5,000 and up to £10,000 estimated cost of work	470.00	540.00	345.00
Alterations over £10,000 estimated cost of work	Subject to an individually determined charge		
Installation of replacement windows or external doors (up to 6 on one site)	200.00	200.00	200.00
Electrical works up to £10,000 estimated cost of work		100.00	290.00
Installation of solar panels (up to 6 panels)		100.00	150.00
Installation of a solid fuel stove		80.00	250.00
Installation of a gas fired boiler			350.00
Installation of an oil fired boiler.			450.00
Subject to VAT at 20% Regularisation Charge not subject to VAT For further information consult the charges scheme			

Table 3 – Non-domestic Extensions and Alterations

Description	Full plans		Building Notice £	Regularisation Charge £
	Plan Charge £	Inspection Charge £		
Extension under $40m^2$	234.00	388.00	625.00	875.00
Extension over $40m^2$ and under $100m^2$	200.00	462.00	850.00	1025.00
Extensions over 100 m^2	Subject to an individually determined charge			
Internal alterations up to £5,000 estimated cost of work	200.00	62.00	300.00	350.00
Internal alterations over £5,000 and up to £10,000 estimated cost of work	200.00	130.00	675.00	750.00
Installation of mezzanine floor up to $100m^2$	200.00	160.00	500.00	600.00

PLANNING APPLICATION FEES

The following is extracted from **A Guide to the Fees for Planning Applications in England** available from on the Planning Portal.

All outline applications		
£462 per 0.1 hectare for sites up to and including 2.5 hectares	Not more than 2.5 hectares	£462 per 0.1 hectare
£11,432 + £138 for each 0.1 in excess of 2.5 hectares to a maximum of £150,000	More than 2.5 hectares	£11,432 + £138 per 0.1 hectare

Householder applications		
Alterations/extensions to a **single dwellinghouse,** including works within boundary	Single dwellinghouse	£206

Full Applications (and First Submissions of Reserved Matters)		
Alterations/extensions to **two or more dwellinghouses**, including works within boundaries	Two or more dwellinghouses (or two or more flats)	£407
New dwellinghouses (up to and including 50)	New dwellinghouses (not more than 50)	£462 per dwellinghouse
New dwellinghouses (for *more* than 50) £22,859 + £138 per additional dwellinghouse in excess of 50 up to a maximum fee of £300,000	New dwellinghouses (more than 50)	£22,859 + £138 per additional dwellinghouse

Details are available for other types of development on the Planning Portal website
If unsure of fees applicable contact the local planning authority

GENERAL INFORMATION

This page left blank intentionally

CONSTRUCTION (DESIGN AND MANAGEMENT) REGULATIONS 2015

CONSTRUCTION (DESIGN AND MANAGEMENT) REGULATIONS 2015

The Construction (Design and Management) Regulations 2015 came into force on 6th April 2015. The CDM Regulations and Amendments provide a framework in health and safety terms for the design, construction, maintenance and demolition of a structure. The Building Safety Bill is due to be published which will have an impact on the CDM Regulations.

If you have not followed the relevant provisions of the Regulations you may be prosecuted for breach of health and safety law.

The following is an outline of the requirements of the Regulations. No attempt has been made to cover all the detail and readers are advised to study the Regulations and Guidance in full.

CDM 2015 is divided into five parts:

- Part 1 deals with the application of CDM 2015 and definitions
- Part 2 covers the duties of clients for all construction projects. These duties apply in full for commercial clients.
- Part 3 covers the health and safety duties and roles of other dutyholders including designers, principal designers, principal contractors and contractors
- Part 4 contains general requirements for all construction sites
- Part 5 contains transitional arrangements and revocations

The regulations place duties upon clients, client's agents, principal designers, designers, principal contractors, contractors and subcontractors so that health and safety is taken into account and then co-ordinated and managed effectively throughout all stages of a construction project; from conception to execution of works on site and subsequent maintenance and repair and demolitions.

Key Elements

Key elements to securing construction health and safety include:

a) managing the risks by applying the general principles of prevention;
b) appointing the right people and organisations at the right time;
c) making sure everyone has the information, instruction, training and supervision they need to carry out their jobs in a way that secures health and safety;
d) dutyholders cooperating and communicating with each other and coordinating their work
e) consulting workers and engaging with them to promote and develop effective measures to secure health, safety and welfare.

General Principles of Prevention

These set out the principles dutyholders should use in their approach to identifying the measures they should take to control the risks to health and safety in a particular project

a) avoid risks where possible;
b) evaluate those risks that cannot be avoided
c) put in place measures that control them at source.
d) adapt the work to the individual and technical progress
e) replace the dangerous by the non or less-dangerous
f) give appropriate instructions to employees.

Due regard must be made of

- The Health and Safety at Work etc Act 1974,
- Construction (Design and Management) Regulations 2015
- The Construction (Health, Safety and Welfare) Regulations 1996
- Lifting Operations and Lifting Equipment Regulations 1998
- Health and Safety (Consultation with Employees) Regulations 1996
- Control of Substances Hazardous to Health Regulations 2002
- Electricity at Work Regulations 1989
- Regulatory Reform (Fire Safety) Order 2005
- Control of Noise at Work Regulations 2005
- The Control of Asbestos Regulations 2012,
- Management of Health and Safety at Work Regulations 1999
- The Workplace (Health, Safety and Welfare) Regulations 1992
- Control of Vibration at Work Regulations 2005,
- The Work at Height Regulations 2005,
- Provision and Use of Work Equipment Regulations 1998,
- Building Regulations 2010,
- The Occupiers' Liability Acts 1957 and 1984

Notifiable and Non-notifiable Projects

A project is notifiable that lasts more than 30 days and have more than 20 workers at any point in the project or will involve more than 500 person days, other projects are non-notifiable and do not require the appointment of a project co-ordinator. For such non-notifiable projects clients, designers and contractors will still have responsibilities and duties.
The client must submit the notice as soon as practicable before the construction phase begins, the client may request someone else do this. The notice must be displayed in the site office
The requirements of CDM 2015 also apply whether or not the project is notifiable.
The regulations do not impose duties on householders having construction work carried out on their own home however designers and contractors still have duties and domestic clients will have duties if they control the way in which construction work is carried out .

DUTIES AND DUTY HOLDERS

General Duties

A designer or contractor must have the skills, knowledge, experience and organisational capability necessary to fulfil the role that they undertake in a manner that secures the health and safety of any person affected by the project.
A person who is responsible for appointing a designer or contractor to carry out work on a project must take reasonable steps to satisfy themselves that the designer or contractor fulfils the above conditions
A person with a duty or function under these Regulations must cooperate with any other person working on or in relation to a project to enable any person with a duty or function to fulfil that duty or function
A person working on a project under the control of another must report to that person anything they are aware of in relation to the project which is likely to endanger their own health or safety or that of others.
Anyone with a duty under CDM 2015 to provide health and safety information or instructions to anyone else must ensure that it is easy to understand

CONSTRUCTION (DESIGN AND MANAGEMENT) REGULATIONS 2015 (Cont'd)
DUTIES AND DUTY HOLDERS (Cont'd)

THE CLIENT
Organisations or individuals for whom a construction project is carried out.

Duties

Project Management
Make arrangements for managing a project to include:-
a) assembling the project team – appointing designers and contractors.
b) ensuring the roles, functions and responsibilities of the project team are clear;
c) ensuring sufficient resources and time are allocated for each stage of the project – from concept to completion;
d) ensuring effective mechanisms are in place for members of the project team to communicate and cooperate with each other and coordinate their activities;
e) reasonable steps to ensure that the principal designer and principal contractor comply with their separate duties. This could take place at project progress meetings or via written updates;
f) setting out the means to ensure that the health and safety performance of designers and contractors is maintained throughout;
g) ensuring that workers are provided with suitable welfare facilities for the duration of construction work.

Client's Brief
Clients should prepare a clear 'client's brief' as a way of setting out the arrangements which;-
a) sets out the main function and operational requirements of the finished project;
b) outlines how the project is expected to be managed including its health and safety risks;
c) sets a realistic timeframe and budget; and
d) covers other relevant matters, such as establishing design direction and a single point of contact in the client's organisation.

Risks
Where risks involved in the work warrants, the management arrangements should also include:
a) the expected standards of health and safety, including safe working practices,
b) what is expected from the design team in terms of the steps they should reasonably take to ensure their designs help manage foreseeable risks during the construction phase and when maintaining and using the building once it is built;
c) the arrangements for commissioning the new building and a well-planned handover procedure to the new user.

The principal designer should be in a position to help in making these arrangements. Clients could also draw on the advice of a competent person under the Management of Health and Safety at Work Regulations 1999

Pre-construction Information
Pre-construction information is information already in the client's possession.
The client has the main duty for providing pre-construction information. This must be provided as soon as practicable to each designer and contractor

The Construction Phase Plan
The client must ensure that a construction phase plan for the project is prepared before the construction phase begins. The plan outlines the health and safety arrangements, site rules and specific measures concerning any work involving the particular risks

The Health and Safety File
A health and safety file is only required for projects involving more than one contractor.
The client must ensure that the principal designer prepares a health and safety file for their project. Its purpose is to ensure that, at the end of the project, the client has information that anyone carrying out subsequent construction work on the building will need to know about in order to be able to plan and carry out the work safely and without risks to health

DOMESTIC CLIENTS
People who have construction work carried out on their own home, or the home of a family member that is not done as part of a business, whether for profit or not.

Duties
Domestic clients are within the scope of CDM 2015, but their duties as a client are normally transferred to:
- the contractor, on a single contractor project; or;
- the principal contractor, on a project involving more than one contractor.

However, the domestic client can choose to have a written agreement with the principal designer to carry out the client duties.

DESIGNERS
An organisation or individual, who:
(a) prepares or modifies a design for a construction project or
(b) arranges for, or instructs someone else to do so.

The term 'design' includes drawings, design details, specifications, bills of quantity and calculations prepared for the purpose of a design. Designers include architects, architectural technologists, consulting engineers, quantity surveyors, interior designers, temporary work engineers, chartered surveyors, technicians or anyone who specifies or alters a design. They can include others if they carry out design work, such as principal contractors, specialist contractors and commercial clients.

Duties
A designer must not commence work in relation to a project unless satisfied that the client is aware of the duties owed by the client under these Regulations.
When preparing or modifying a design the designer must take into account the general principles of prevention and any pre-construction information to eliminate foreseeable risks to the health or safety of any person—
(a) carrying out or liable to be affected by construction work;
(b) maintaining or cleaning a structure; or
(c) using a structure designed as a workplace
If it is not possible to eliminate these risks, the designer must, so far as is reasonably practicable—
(a) take steps to reduce or, if that is not possible, control the risks through the subsequent design process;
(b) provide information about those risks to the principal designer
(c) ensure appropriate information is included in the health and safety file.
A designer must take steps to provide, with the design, sufficient information about the design, construction or maintenance of the structure, to assist the client, other designers and contractors to comply with these Regulations.
The designer should agree with the principal designer the arrangements for sharing information to avoid omissions or duplicated effort.
Liaise with any others so that work can be coordinated to establish how different aspects of designs interact and influence health and safety. This includes temporary and permanent works designers, contractors and principal contractors so that their knowledge and experience is taken into account.

Working for Domestic Clients
A designer's role on a project for a domestic client is no different to the role undertaken for commercial clients.

CONSTRUCTION (DESIGN AND MANAGEMENT) REGULATIONS 2015 (Cont'd)
DUTIES AND DUTY HOLDERS (Cont'd)

PRINCIPAL DESIGNER

Designers appointed by the client in projects involving more than one contractor. They can be an organisation or an individual with sufficient knowledge, experience and ability to carry out the role.
Principal designers may have separate duties as designers
Principal designers are not a direct replacement for CDM co-ordinators. The range of duties they carry out is different to those undertaken by CDM co-ordinators

Duties

Pre-construction Phase

Plan, manage, monitor and coordinate health and safety. This includes:

- identifying, eliminating or controlling foreseeable risks;
- ensuring designers carry out their duties.
- take into account the general principles of prevention and, the content of any construction phase plan and health and safety file.
- ensure that all persons working in relation to the pre-construction phase cooperate with the client, the principal designer and each other.
- assist the client in the provision of the pre-construction information
- Prepare and provide relevant information to other dutyholders.
- Provide relevant information to the principal contractor to help them plan, manage, monitor and coordinate health and safety in the construction phase.

A principal designer's role on a project for a domestic client is no different to the role undertaken for commercial clients.

Construction Phase Plan, and, Health and Safety File

The principal designer must assist the principal contractor in preparing the construction phase plan by providing to the principal contractor all information the principal designer holds that is relevant to the construction phase plan including;-

a) pre-construction information obtained from the client;
b) any information obtained from designers

During the pre-construction phase, the principal designer must prepare a health and safety file appropriate to the characteristics of the project which must contain information relating to the project which is likely to be needed during any subsequent project to ensure the health and safety of any person
If the principal designer's appointment concludes before the end of the project, the principal designer must pass the health and safety file to the principal contractor.
The health and safety file is only required for projects involving more than one contractor

Construction Phase

The principal designer must ensure that the health and safety file is appropriately reviewed, updated and revised from time to time to take account of the work and any changes that have occurred
At the end of the project, the principal designer, or where there is no principal designer the principal contractor, must pass the health and safety file to the client.

PRINCIPAL CONTRACTOR

Contractors appointed by the client before the construction phase begins to coordinate the construction phase of a project where it involves more than one contractor.
Contractors must not carry out any construction work on a project unless they are satisfied that the client is aware of the duties the client has under CDM 2015.

Duties

Planning, Managing and Monitoring Construction Work

Plan, manage, monitor and coordinate health and safety in the construction phase of a project. This includes:

- liaising with the client and principal designer;
- preparing the construction phase plan;
- organising cooperation between contractors and coordinating their work.
- Ensure: suitable site inductions are provided;
- steps are taken to prevent unauthorised access;
- workers are consulted and engaged in securing their health and safety
- welfare facilities are provided.
- ensure anyone they appoint has the skills, knowledge, and experience and, where they are an organisation, the organisational capability to carry out the work in a way that secures health and safety

A systematic approach to managing should be taken to ensure workers understand:

a) the risks and control measures on the project;
b) who has responsibility for health and safety;
c) that consistent standards apply throughout the project and will be checked frequently;
d) where they can locate health and safety information which is understandable, organised and relevant to the site;
e) that incidents will be investigated and lessons learned.

Special consideration will be required for sites that have:

a) rights of way through them;
b) other work areas next to them
c) occupied houses next to them
d) children or vulnerable people nearby.

Providing Welfare Facilities

The principal contractor must ensure that suitable and sufficient welfare facilities are provided and maintained throughout the construction phase. Facilities must be made available before any construction work starts and should be maintained until the end of the project.
The principal contractor should liaise with other contractors involved with the project to ensure appropriate welfare facilities are provided. Such liaison should continue for the duration of the construction phase and take account of any changes in the nature of the site.

Liaising with the Principal Designer

The principal contractor must liaise with the principal designer for the duration of the project. The early appointment of a principal contractor by the client will allow their construction expertise to be used from the earliest stages of designing and planning a project. They should also liaise with the principal designer throughout the construction phase on matters such as changes to the designs and the implications these changes may have for managing the health and safety risks.
Liaison should cover drawing together information the principal designer will need:

a) to prepare the health and safety file; or
b) that may affect the planning and management of the pre-construction phase. The pre-construction information is important for planning and managing this phase and the subsequent development of the construction phase plan

A principal contractor's role on a project for a domestic client is no different to the role undertaken for commercial clients.

Consult and Engage with Workers

The principal contractor must;-

a) make and maintain arrangements which will enable the principal contractor and workers engaged in construction work to cooperate in developing, promoting and checking the effectiveness of measures to ensure the health, safety and welfare of the workers;
b) consult those workers or their representatives in good time on matters connected with the project which may affect their health, safety or welfare,

CONSTRUCTION (DESIGN AND MANAGEMENT) REGULATIONS 2015 (Cont'd)
DUTIES AND DUTY HOLDERS (Cont'd)
PRINCIPAL CONTRACTOR (Cont'd)
Duties - Consult and Engage with Workers (Cont'd)

c) ensure that those workers or their representatives can inspect and take copies of any information which the principal contractor has, or which these Regulations require to be provided to the principal contractor, which relate to the health, safety or welfare of workers at the site, except any information

i) the disclosure of which would be against national security;

ii) which the principal contractor could not disclose without contravening a prohibition imposed by or under an enactment;

iii) relating specifically to an individual, unless that individual has consented to its being disclosed;

iv) the disclosure of which would, for reasons other than its effect on health, safety or welfare at work, cause substantial injury to the principal contractor's undertaking or, where the information was supplied to the principal contractor by another person, to the undertaking of that other person;

v) obtained by the principal contractor for the purpose of bringing, prosecuting or defending any legal proceedings.

Construction Phase Plan

During the pre-construction phase, and before setting up a construction site, the principal contractor must draw up a construction phase plan or make arrangements for a construction phase plan to be drawn up.

Throughout the project the principal contractor must ensure that the construction phase plan is appropriately reviewed, updated and revised from time to time so that it continues to be sufficient to ensure that construction work is carried out, so far as is reasonably practicable, without risks to health or safety.

The construction phase plan must set out the arrangements for securing health and safety during the period construction work is carried out. These arrangements include site rules and any specific measures put in place where work involves one or more of listed risks

Health and Safety File

During the project, the principal contractor must provide the principal designer with any information in the principal contractor's possession relevant to the health and safety file, for inclusion in the health and safety file.

Where the health and safety file is passed to the principal contractor, the principal contractor must ensure that the health and safety file is reviewed, updated and revised to take account of the work and any changes that have occurred.

At the end of the project where there is no principal designer the principal contractor, must pass the health and safety file to the client.

CONTRACTORS

Those who do the actual construction work and can be either an individual or a company.

Anyone who directly employs or engages construction workers or manages construction is a contractor. Contractors include sub-contractors, any individual, sole trader, self-employed worker, or business that carries out, manages or controls construction work. This also includes companies that use their own workforce to do construction work on their own premises. The duties on contractors apply whether the workers under their control are employees, self-employed or agency workers.

Where contractors are involved in design work, including for temporary works, they also have duties as designers

Contractors must not carry out any construction work on a project unless they are satisfied that the client is aware of their duties under CDM 2015.

Duties

Plan, manage and monitor construction work under their control so that it is carried out without risks to health and safety.

For projects involving more than one contractor, coordinate their activities with others in the project team – comply with principal designer or principal contractor directions.

For single-contractor projects, prepare a construction phase plan.

Planning, Managing and Monitoring Construction Work

Contractors are required to plan, manage and monitor the construction work under their control so that it is carried out in a way that controls the risks to health and safety.

On projects involving more than one contractor, this will involve the contractor coordinating the planning, management and monitoring of their own work with that of the principal contractor, other contractors and the principal designer.

For single contractor projects, the arrangements to plan, manage and monitor the construction phase will normally be simpler.

Planning

In planning the work, the contractor must take into account the risks to those who may be affected.

On projects involving more than one contractor, each contractor must plan their own work so it is consistent with the project-wide arrangements.

On single contractor projects, the contractor is responsible for planning the construction phase and for drawing up the construction phase plan before setting up the construction site.

Managing

The arrangements for managing construction work must take into account the same issues as for principal contractors

Monitoring

The contractor should monitor their work to ensure that the health and safety precautions are appropriate, remain in place and are followed in practice.

On projects involving more than one contractor the contractor should provide the principal contractor with any relevant information that stems from their own monitoring.

Complying with directions and the construction phase plan

For projects involving more than one contractor, the contractor is required to comply with any directions to secure health and safety given to them by the principal designer or principal contractor.

Drawing up a construction phase plan

For single contractor projects, the contractor must ensure a construction phase plan is drawn up as soon as practicable before the construction site is set up.

Appointing and Employing Workers
Appointing Workers

When a contractor employs or appoints an individual to work on a construction site, they should make enquiries to make sure the individual: has the skills, knowledge, training and experience to carry out the work they will be employed to do in a way that secures health and safety for anyone working on the site or is in the process of obtaining them.

Sole reliance should not be placed on industry certification cards or similar being presented to them as evidence that a worker has the right qualities. Nationally recognised qualifications can provide contractors with assurance that the holder has the skills, knowledge, training and experience to carry out the task(s)

Newly trained individuals need to be supervised and given the opportunity to gain positive experience of working in a range of conditions.

When appointing individuals who may be skilled but who do not have any formal qualifications, contractors may need to assess them in the working environment.

Training workers

Establish whether training is necessary for any worker.

This assessment should take account of the training required by other health and safety legislation as well as that needed to meet the requirements of CDM 2015.

Assessing training needs should be an ongoing process throughout the project.

CONSTRUCTION (DESIGN AND MANAGEMENT) REGULATIONS 2015 (Cont'd)
DUTIES AND DUTY HOLDERS (Cont'd)
CONTRACTORS (Cont'd)

Providing Supervision
A contractor who employs or manages workers under their control must ensure that appropriate supervision is provided. The level of supervision provided will depend on the risks to health and safety involved, and the skills, knowledge, training and experience of the workers concerned.

Providing Information and Instructions
Contractors should provide employees and workers under their control with the information and instructions they need to carry out their work without risk to health and safety to include:

a) suitable site induction where this has not been provided by the principal contractor.
b) the procedures to be followed in the event of serious and imminent danger to health and safety.
c) take account of the relevant requirements which set out provisions relating to emergency procedures, emergency routes and exits and fire detection and fire-fighting;
d) information on the hazards on site relevant to their work, the risks associated with those hazards and the control measures put in place.

Preventing Unauthorised Access to the Site
A contractor must not begin work on a construction site unless steps have been taken to prevent unauthorised access to the site.

Providing Welfare Facilities
Contractors are required to provide welfare facilities as far as is reasonably practicable. This duty only extends to the provision of welfare facilities for the contractor's own employees who are working on a construction site or anyone else working under their control. Facilities must be made available before any construction work starts and should be maintained until the end of the project.

Working for Domestic Clients
A contractor's role on a project for a domestic client is no different to the role undertaken for commercial clients.

WORKERS
The people who work for or under the control of contractors on a construction site.

Duties
They must: be consulted about matters which affect their health, safety and welfare;
take care of their own health and safety and others who may be affected by their actions;
report anything they see which is likely to endanger either their own or others' health and safety;
cooperate with their employer, fellow workers, contractors and other dutyholders.

PRE-CONSTRUCTION INFORMATION
Pre-construction information must include proportionate information about:

(a) the project, such as the client brief and key dates of the construction phase;
(b) the planning and management of the project such as the resources and time being allocated to each stage of the project and the arrangements to ensure there is cooperation between dutyholders and the work is coordinated;
(c) the health and safety hazards of the site, including design and construction hazards and how they will be addressed;
(d) any relevant information in an existing health and safety file.

CONSTRUCTION PHASE PLAN
During the pre-construction phase the principal contractor must draw up a construction phase plan. For single contractor projects the contractor must draw up a construction phase plan
The construction phase plan must set out the health and safety arrangements and site rules for the project during the period construction work is carried out
The principal designer must assist the principal contractor in preparing the construction phase plan to include pre-construction information obtained from the client and information obtained from designers.
Throughout the project the principal contractor must ensure that the construction phase plan is appropriately reviewed, updated and revised.
The construction phase plan must record the:

a) health and safety arrangements for the construction phase;
b) site rules;
c) Any specific measures concerning listed work

Information included should be:

a) is relevant to the project;
b) has sufficient detail to set out the arrangements, site rules and special measures needed to manage the construction phase;
c) proportionate to the scale and complexity of the project and the risks involved.

HEALTH AND SAFETY FILE
The health and safety file is only required for projects involving more than one contractor.
During the pre-construction phase, the principal designer must prepare a health and safety file which must contain information relating to the project which is likely to be needed during any subsequent project to ensure the health and safety of any person.
The principal designer must ensure that the health and safety file is appropriately reviewed, updated and revised from time to time to take account of the work and any changes that have occurred.
During the project, the principal contractor must provide the principal designer with any information in the principal contractor's possession relevant to the health and safety file, for inclusion in the health and safety file.
If the principal designer's appointment concludes before the end of the project, the principal designer must pass the health and safety file to the principal contractor.
Where the health and safety file is passed to the principal contractor the principal contractor must ensure that the health and safety file is appropriately reviewed, updated and revised from time to time to take account of the work and any changes that have occurred.
At the end of the project the health and safety file must be passed to the client.
The file must contain information about the current project likely to be needed to ensure health and safety during any subsequent work, such as maintenance, cleaning, refurbishment or demolition. When preparing the health and safety file, information on the following should be considered for inclusion:

(a) a brief description of the work carried out;
(b) any hazards that have not been eliminated through the design and construction processes, and how they have been addressed;
(c) key structural principles and safe working loads for floors and roofs;
(d) hazardous materials used;
(e) information regarding the removal or dismantling of installed plant and equipment;
(f) health and safety information about equipment provided for cleaning or maintaining the structure;
(g) the nature, location and markings of significant services, including underground cables; gas supply equipment; fire-fighting services etc;
(h) information and as-built drawings of the building, its plant and equipment

CONSTRUCTION (DESIGN AND MANAGEMENT) REGULATIONS 2015 (Cont'd)

GENERAL REQUIREMENTS FOR ALL CONSTRUCTION SITES

Safe Places of Construction Work

There must, so far as is reasonably practicable, be suitable and sufficient safe access and egress from every construction site or place construction work is being carried out to every other place provided for the use of any person whilst at work or have access to within a construction site;

A construction site must be, so far as is reasonably practicable, made and kept safe for, and without risks to, the health of any person at work there.

A construction site must, so far as is reasonably practicable, have sufficient working space and be arranged so that it is suitable for any person who is working or who is likely to work there, taking account of any necessary work equipment likely to be used.

Good Order and Site Security

Each part of a construction site must, so far as is reasonably practicable, be kept in good order and those parts in which construction work is being carried out must be kept in a reasonable state of cleanliness

Where necessary in the interests of health and safety, a construction site must, so far as is reasonably practicable, have its perimeter identified by suitable signs and be arranged so that its extent is readily identifiable; or be fenced off.

No timber or other material with projecting nails (or similar sharp object) must be used in any construction work; or be allowed to remain in any place, if the nails (or similar sharp object) may be a source of danger to any person.

Stability of Structures

1) All practicable steps must be taken, where necessary to prevent danger to any person, to ensure that any new or existing structure does not collapse if, due to the carrying out of construction work, it may become unstable; or is in a temporary state of weakness or instability.

2) Any buttress, temporary support or temporary structure must be of such design and installed and maintained so as to withstand any foreseeable loads which may be imposed on it; and only be used for the purposes for which it was designed, and installed and is maintained.

3) A structure must not be so loaded as to render it unsafe to any person.

Demolition or Dismantling

1) The demolition or dismantling of a structure must be planned and carried out in such a manner as to prevent danger or, where it is not practicable to prevent it, to reduce danger to as low a level as is reasonably practicable.

2) The arrangements for carrying out such demolition or dismantling must be recorded in writing before the demolition or dismantling work begins.

Excavations

All practicable steps must be taken to prevent danger to any person including, where necessary, the provision of supports or battering.

Construction work must not be carried out in an excavation where any supports or battering have been provided unless the excavation and any work equipment and materials which may affect its safety have been inspected by a competent person

Reports of Inspections

Where a person who carries out an inspection is not satisfied that construction work can be carried out safely at the place inspected, that person must inform the person on whose behalf the inspection was carried out and prepare and provide the report

Acknowledgement

Excerpts reproduced from HSE publications –

- further details from www.hse.gov.uk

The Construction (Design and Management) Regulations 2015 covers the following topics.

Introduction

CONSTRUCTION PROCUREMENT GUIDE

Introduction

There are numerous issues that need to be considered when deciding upon the means of procurement of a building project, and which will determine the Form of Contract to define the obligations and responsibilities between the Parties.

Procurement is the term used to enable the process of creating a contractual relationship. There are four essential elements:

1) Offer
2) Acceptance
3) Consideration (payment)
4) The intention to create a legal relationship

Factors which influence the procurement process include:

- the experience of client and the business case for the project including any particular requirements that the client and his funders, if separate, may have
- the client's desired programme for development, including the timing of the start and finish dates
- the nature, size and complexity of the project
- the state and completeness of the designs
- the degree of cost certainty, or conversely the requirement for risk aversion
- the need for competitive prices
- the apportionment of risk between client and contractor

There are eight main recognised procurement routes:

a) traditional *(bills of quantities; schedules of work; specification and drawings; and the like)*
b) target cost
c) design and build; and target cost design and build
d) design, manage and construct
e) management contracting
f) construction management
g) engineer, procure & construct (turnkey) - not dealt with here
h) partnering (also a process – see below)

Further specialised routes used by public authorities are PFI – the private finance initiative; and PRIME contracting. In the latter case variants of PRIME contracting have been adopted by the NHS, Defence Estates and several 'blue chip' private sector organisations. PFI and PRIME are not dealt with here.

For the HM Treasury definition of PFI see: www.hm-treasury.gov.uk/hmt/documents/public_private_partnerships/ppp_index.cfm

For a definition of PRIME contracting see: www.contracts.mod.uk/dc/pdfs/Prime_Contracting.pdf

With the exception of partnering, all of the above routes can be used with:

- a single stage process (tendered or negotiated)
- a two-stage process
- as a process to define a GMP – guaranteed maximum price

Partnering – as a route and a process
Partnering is both a procurement route and a tendering process. Although now well defined and much written about, it is still misunderstood by many professionals and contractors alike, who consider that they have been *'partnering'* with their clients long before Egan, having had longstanding and 'ongoing' relationships with clients for a considerable number of years. However, in many cases this is not partnering in the style championed in 1998 by The Egan Report, "Rethinking Construction".

Partnering seeks to create open relationships between members of the whole project team including the client, design team, contractor(s) and the underlying supply chain. This creates a framework to deliver demonstrable (through KPIs) and continuing economies over time from: better design and construction; lower risk; less waste (time, material, etc); and as a result avoid disputes. Partnering workshops provide for better knowledge, communication, sharing, education and team building to create a much more purposeful relationship than merely continuing to work together with a client.! Egan's Partnering is discussed more fully later.

Single Stage – as a process
The single stage process is in many cases the conventional process of procurement. Tenders are sought based upon one of the routes set out herein and bids are considered and a contractor selected and then appointed based upon chosen criteria defined to suit the project. In most cases the 'choice criteria' involved in the contractor selection will be based upon the most economic cost, but can also be based upon programme, quality of design solution (in the case of a Design and Construct Tender) or a mixture of these criteria.

Two Stage – as a process
In the case of a two-stage process, the selection of a contractor is made by means of a first-stage tender early in the project programme before the design is well advanced. With the exception of partnering this process can be used in connection with most of the routes listed above

Normally, the first-stage is by means of a competitive tender based on limited elements of the work, for example:

- a schedule of unitary rates provisionally prepared from the design drawings as prepared at the time of the stage-one tender. *
- preliminaries costs (site staffing, plant, site setup, scaffolding, craneage, insurances, etc);
- the percentage required for overheads and profit;
- the percentages required on Dayworks;
- additions required on the sub-contract work which is to be sub-let;
- submission of CV's for proposed site and head office staff; and
- method statements - so that the contractor's understanding of the project can be assessed by the design team and the client.

* If time and design information is available, measurements might be made of selected major work elements (for example demolitions) and Bills of Approximate Quantities (or a Schedule of Works) can then be included for fuller pricing in the first-stage documents.

Contractor selection at stage-one, is made on the limited information available from the stage-one bids. If sufficient information is available further evaluation may be made on the basis of a notionally calculated contract cost generated by the Quantity Surveyor from his most up to date estimate at the time of the decision being made; together with:

- interviews and assessments of the contractor's proposed staff;
- project understanding and proposed method statements; and
- the contractor's willingness to enter into the second-stage negotiations.

Construction Procurement Guide (Cont'd)
Introduction (Cont'd)
Two Stage – as a process (Cont'd)

At the second-stage, a Bill of Quantities/Schedule of Work or a more fully detailed Schedule of Rates or a mixture of both, is generally prepared by the Quantity Surveyor and is priced with the chosen contractor by means of 'open book' negotiation in order to calculate the contract sum.

As referred to above, a two-stage tender process can overlay any of the 'traditional' procurement routes and can bring an additional set of advantages and disadvantages to the chosen means of tendering. Set alone, two-stage procurement can provide:

- Early appointment of contractor and access to his experience of programming and buildability.
- An earlier start on site than with a single stage process, because the works can proceed, if required, before a contract sum has been negotiated and fixed.

However two-stage procurement does not establish a firm contract sum at the time when the contractor is initially appointed as this is calculated later. It is therefore most appropriate for projects where an early start on site is required and where a project is reasonably well defined, in terms of the scope of work; and for which management or construction management are not considered appropriate.

Guaranteed Maximum Price (GMP) – as a process

A GMP can be tendered at outset, but more often a previously tendered lump sum contract (excluding Target type contracts) is converted to a GMP following a traditional single or two-stage tender process utilising:

- Bills of Quantity (either Firm or Approximate); or
- a Schedule of Works; or
- Specification and Drawings

Thus the definition of a GMP can occur, either before commencing the works or during the course of the works. The GMP is negotiated with the chosen contractor and his sub-contractor(s) on a basis that includes for the contractor's future design development of the scheme, albeit in many cases the initial tender methodology may not have included design.

The Contractor therefore assume a larger element of risk that with other contract relationships and takes responsibility for matters that would normally cause extensions of time and potentially additional payment(s).

There are no generally available standard Forms of Contract for a GMP, it will require bespoke contracts or a standard contract modified by a bespoke addendum agreement.
The advantages of a GMP are that it:

- Gives cost certainty similar to that of a design and build contract whilst the client employs and retains control of the design team.
- Provides the client often with a more appropriately detailed building than might be the case if let as a design and build contract, because the client's design team retain control of detailing.
- Potentially means that the design needs to be completed to a greater degree than normal in order to let contract as a GMP, because after the GMP is agreed all variations that cause change, will attract cost and programme alterations. Therefore the design team will want to avoid such 'change'

However, it is also important to note that a GMP contract has the potential to provide 'rich' grounds for disputes; particularly in respect of whether varied work has resulted from design detailing and therefore included in the GMP, or whether it is a variation caused by client change, which is an addition to the contract sum.

Very few contractors have experience of GMP contracts and those that do have had mixed experiences. Particularly because the financial and programme risk for unforeseen circumstances is entirely borne by the contractor.

The creation of a GMP creates certainty for both parties. However, a GMP can mean that the contractor can take a heavy fall if things go wrong! Examples of GMP style contracts are those for Cardiff Arms Park and the new Wembley Stadiums.

With the exception of a GMP, the eight routes noted are served by a plethora of standard forms of contract, sub-contract, supply agreements, warranties, etc. Such forms are widely available, with versions for use in England and Wales, and Scotland, where the law relating to contract differs from English law.

The success of any procurement route and process will depend largely on the ability and experience of both the chosen designers and contractor(s).

In all cases it is to be recommended that pre-tender interviews take place at the time of Tender, it is therefore very important that care is exercised in the selection of tendering contractors. In all cases it is to be recommended that pre-tender interviews take place with the potential tenderers to confirm their suitability for the work in advance; followed by both mid-tender review meetings and post-tender interviews to assess the understanding of the project, the calibre of staff and other resourcing that each prospective contractor will provide. This is particularly important where the proposed project is complex, fast-track, or involves 'business as usual' working.

The sections following this Introduction provide an overview of some of the main procurement methods in use in the UK today. It is by not intended to cover every type of procurement route or all the issues and should be considered as a guide only.

Bills of Quantities

Basis

Often referred to as "traditional Bills of Quantities".

A lump sum tender price based upon the priced Bills of Quantities is normally tendered in competition by a pre-selected list of between three and six contractors.

Selection of a contractor is made on the basis of the tenderer pricing measured Bills of Quantities, prepared to standard rules of measurement, for example:

- SMM7 (the rules of measurement upon which Laxton's SMM is based)
- NRM – RICS New Rules of Measurement – (the rules of measurement upon which Laxton's NRM is based)
- POMI – Principles of Measurement International
- ARM – Agreed Rules of Measurement (in the Republic of Ireland)
- CESMM – Civil Engineering Standard Method of Measurement

Bills of Quantities include definitive measurements of the major elements of the building. Where design is not complete, 'provisional' and/or 'approximate' quantities can be included.

Additionally Provisional Sum allowances for undefined and defined works can also be included, together with provisional sum allowances for works to be carried out by 'named' specialist sub-contractors; which, if required, can be tendered separately – although this is relatively uncommon today and it is more likely that such work will be part of the main contractor's tender by means of selection from list of 'preferred sub-contractors', to then be employed as 'Domestic sub-contractors'.

Construction Procurement Guide (Cont'd)
Bills of Quantities (Cont'd)

This method of procurement is the oldest methodology in the UK. It is not now as popular as it was in the first 85 years of the 20th century, but is still often preferred by Public sector clients.

Advantages

- Cost certainty is generally high but depends on the degree of completeness of design at the time when the Bills of Quantity are prepared.
- Gives excellent comparison of tender bids because all tenders are based on the same measured information.
- Creates a low risk tendering environment allowing tenderers to give their most competitive price because the risk for the contractor is well understood and defined.
- This is a procurement process which is widely understood.
- Gives a good basis for measurement and valuation of variations and for the calculation of interim valuations and the eventual final account.
- Needs the design team to have prepared and developed the building design before the Bills of Quantity can be prepared and so through reduction of design risk often leads to a much greater level of programme certainty and thus the date for completion.
- Can incorporate Design and Build and Performance Specified works if required

Disadvantages

- For the level of cost certainty expected by this procurement methodology to be delivered, the design must have evolved before preparation of the Bills of Quantity is started.
- Pre-contract phase of procurement is lengthy compared to other procurement methods and so often leads to a later start on site.

Suitability

More appropriate for projects where time is available for design work to largely be completed so that detailed measurements can be made before the tenders are sought.

Bills of Quantity can be used on any size project but are particularly suitable for those which are extremely large and complex and where the design time required would mean a long lead-in period.

Bills of Approximate Quantities

Basis

Bills of Approximate Quantities are an alternative form of Bills of Quantities (see above) and are prepared early in the design process before a firm design is available.

The contractor is selected, normally by competition from a pre-selected list of between three and six contractors. Contractors prepare a tender bid based on pricing a Bill of Approximate Quantities. This is essentially a traditional Bill of Quantities but with the quantities assessed from professional experience by the Quantity Surveyor rather than firmly measured, as would be the case with "Bills of Quantities".

Advantages

- Allows early appointment of a contractor and access to experience in terms of his programming and buildability skills.
- Enables an earlier start on site to be made than with Traditional Bills of Quantities.
- Can incorporate Design and Build and Performance Specified works if required

Disadvantages

Approximate Bills of Quantities do not establish a firm cost for the work at the time the contractor is appointed, thus there is less price certainty. This is because the actual cost of the works is calculated only when the design is available and detailed re-measurements have been made.

- The client proceeds to the construction stage at greater risk, despite a check being made at the tender stage by means of bids being submitted by the tendering contractors.

Suitability

More appropriate for projects for which an early start on site is required or where the design is reasonably well defined or alternatively where the work is of a repetitive nature following on from other similar projects (allowing assessments to be made of the quantity of works from previous experience), but where time is not available for full Bills of Quantities to be prepared.

Schedules of Work

Basis

A Schedule of Works document lists all of the main sections and heads of work to be undertaken by the contractor.
A lump sum tender price based upon the priced Schedule of Works and associated documents are normally tendered in competition by a pre-selected list of between three and six contractors.

The Schedule of Works must be read in conjunction with the specification and the drawings and is required to be priced by the tenderer on a lump sum basis. Normally if given, quantities of work are for guidance only and the contractor is required to make his own measurements in order to prepare his tender bid.

Often in addition to the Schedule of Works, the contractor is requested to price a 'unitary' schedule of rates relating to the principal items of material, etc to be carried out. This can assist in the valuation of variations that may be later instructed. Provisional sum items in the Schedule of Works can be included where these can be defined. Additionally and as with Bills of Quantity, Provisional allowances for undefined and defined works can be included and if required. Also allowances for works to be carried out by 'named' specialist sub-contractors can be included and if required can then be tendered separately – although this is relatively uncommon today and it is more likely that such work will be part of the main contractor's tender by means of his selection from list of 'preferred sub-contractors' to be employed as 'Domestic sub-contractors'.

However, it is important to note that because a Schedule of Works does not refer to a set of Measurement Rules, the documents must set out the basis (or rules) upon which Provisional Sums are included. Additionally and similarly definitions for General Attendances and Special Attendances to be included in connection with specialist sub-contractors must also be defined in the tender/contract documents.

This method of procurement became popular after the introduction of the JCT Intermediate Form of Contract in 1984 and continues to be popular today.

Advantages

- The lump sum price is firm, subject only to variations which may be instructed during the course of the contract works.
- Client risk tends to be avoided because the contractor prepares his own measurements and quantities.
- Can incorporate Design and Build and Performance Specified works if required

Construction Procurement Guide (Cont'd)
Schedules of Work (Cont'd)

Disadvantages

- The design must be reasonably well advanced (like Bills of Quantity) in order that tender documentation can be prepared.
- When variations occur, the valuation of changes can be more difficult to agree with the contractor than if firm Bills of Quantities exist, because individual prices for items of work do not exist unless a 'unitary' schedule of rates has been requested as part of the Tender.
- Tenders are not as easily comparable to each other as is possible with Bills of Quantity, because the tendering contractors may interpret and price risk in the tender of document in different ways.

Suitability

More appropriate for use on small to medium sized projects. Tenderers need to carry out their own measurements and produce their own quantities.

The use of Schedules of Works is not particularly appropriate where change can be foreseen post-contract.

Specification and Drawings

Basis

A contractor is selected and appointed on the basis of a lump sum bid provided in response to a detailed Specification document, which when read in conjunction with the drawings, defines the scope of work to be carried out as the contract works.

The Specification can also include provisional allowances for unforeseen or undesigned work; and also allowances can be included for specialist works yet to be tendered. Measurements and quantities are prepared by the tenderers to enable them to price the work. Like Schedules of Work, the use and meaning of these provisional sums needs to be described and defined in the documents.

Normally, tendering is in competition with a pre-selected list of approximately five contractors.

Advantages

- The lump sum price is firm, subject only to variations which may be instructed during the course of the contract works.
- Client risk tends to be avoided because the contractor prepares his own measurements and quantities.
- Can incorporate Design and Build and Performance Specified works if required

Disadvantages

- The design must be well advanced in order to prepare the detailed Specification documents. This procurement route can therefore mean a later site start than with alternative procurement routes.
- Give less control of cost when variations are instructed than firm Bills of Quantities because of the lack of a defined system of measurement of the building elements.
- Tenders are not as easily comparable to each other as is possible with Bills of Quantities, because the tendering contractors may interpret and price risk in the tender document in different ways.

Suitability

Specification and Drawings are Appropriate to smaller projects such as house extensions and renovations; partly because all tenderers need to produce their own quantities and partly because of the time involved in achieving a sufficiency of the designs to enable the Specification tender documents to be prepared.

Like Schedules of Work, the use this form of procurement is not particularly appropriate where it is likely that change will be required by the client after the contract has been started.

Target Cost Contracts

Basis

A contractor is appointed, either in competition or by negotiation, on the basis of pricing of simplified Bills of Quantities or a Schedule of Works. The tender price forms the Target Cost but the contractor is paid the actual costs for executing the work, as audited by the quantity surveyor, so long as this is less than the tendered Target Cost.

The Target Cost is, in effect, a 'Guaranteed Maximum'. Any saving on the Target Cost is split, normally 50/50 (but can be varied) between the contractor and the client

Advantages

- Enables an early start to be made on site as the tender documents can be prepared and a contractor appointed before the full design is completed.
- Establishes the client's maximum financial commitment (subject to client variations). If the contractor's costs exceed the Target Cost, only the Target Cost sum is paid.
- Gives the opportunity for the client to benefit from any savings made by the contractor. It is particularly useful in cases where risks may be priced in the tender, as under this system if those risks do not materialise the saving is shared.
- Leads to a less adversarial attitude between contractor and client with both benefiting from savings made.
- Can give early warning of future financial problems as the auditing quantity surveyor has complete access to the contractor's actual costs.
- Can incorporate Design and Build and Performance Specified works if required

Disadvantages

- The contractor and design team need to fully understand the Target Cost process.
- Can prove marginally more expensive than a more traditional contract where more risk is taken by the contractor.

Suitability

More appropriate for projects where an early start is required on site, and where the client wants to establish a maximum financial commitment, together with a less adversarial relationship.

Management Contracting

Basis

The philosophy of Management Contracting differs from that of other more traditional procurement methods in that the management contractor is appointed to manage the construction of the project rather than build it.

The contractor is selected, normally in competition, early in the programme based on a response to a tender enquiry document. This requires the contractor to tender a fee for pre-commencement services and construction services during and after the project as well as a lump sum or guaranteed maximum for site staffing and facilities, etc. As well as price, the required performance of the management contractor is a major factor in the selection process.

For the actual building process the works are divided into separate trade packages which are tendered by trade contractors. The selected trade-contractors are taken on by the management contractor who is responsible for managing them and meet quality and programme targets.

Construction Procurement Guide (Cont'd)
Management Contracting (Cont'd)

Advantages

- Enables an early start to be made on site before design is well advanced.
- Allows flexibility for change as the works are tendered progressively. There is a reduced likelihood of claims affecting other packages in the event that major changes are made.
- Lends itself well to complex construction projects as construction can commence before design work is completed. It is important, however, that the design of each trade package is complete at the time of tendering that package.
- Leads to a less adversarial relationship between management contractor and client.
- Can incorporate Design and Build and Performance Specified works if required

Disadvantages

- Can lead to duplication of resources between trade-contractors and the management contractor and therefore higher tenders than would be the case under a more traditional route.
- As no contract sum is established, the client relies upon the Quantity Surveyor's estimate. This is, however, endorsed by the management contractor initially and subsequently firm costs are established progressively during the course of the works.
- The client accepts a greater degree of risk because he has financial responsibility for the default of sub-contractors.

Suitability

More appropriate for large, complex projects where an earlier start is required than can be made by proceeding with the full design process and tendering by a more traditional route. This is achieved by overlapping design, preparation of tender documents and construction.

Design and Build

Basis

A contractor is selected, normally in competition, to Design and Build the project. Tenders are invited on the basis of an "Employer's Requirements" document prepared normally by the client or his consultants. The Employers Requirements set out the project needs in terms specification, function and performance of the building required and if applicable will also define planning and any other restrictions.

The contractor responds with a set of "Contractor's Proposals" upon which the tender bids are assessed. Assuming the Contractors Proposals fulfil the employer's requirements, the lowest bid is often accepted, but this may not be the case because subjective consideration of the overall design and quality of the proposals may be important than cost alone.

Once appointed the contractor employs and is therefore responsible for the design team. In this connection, it should be noted that under a JCT form of Design and Build contract, the Employer, unless he/she appoints somebody else, becomes the "Employer's Agent". In the JCT contract this person is assumed to be non-technical and could be the only named party apart from the Contractor – there is normally no quantity surveyor. In most cases the client would be advised to retain the services of his own consultants including a quantity surveyor to protect his interests and act on his behalf.

In many cases nowadays and particularly where the project is of a complex nature or facing difficult town planning procedures, the client often appoints a design team to negotiate planning, prepare preliminary designs and specifications and a detailed design brief before seeking Design and Build proposals from contractors – this is referred to by clients as "Develop then Design and Build", or by contractors colloquially as "Design and Dump".

Develop then Design and Build ensures that the client gets a design that works for him and the risk of the final design and construction works is assumed by the contractor. In some instances, and where the employer agrees or requires it, the initial design team can be novated to the contractor.

Advantages

- Establishes a fixed lump sum price, subject only to client's required changes
- Leaves responsibility with the contractor for organising and programming the design team's activities. The client is therefore not responsible for extensions of time in the event that design information is not produced on time.
- Variations (known as Changes) are normally pre-agreed and the client has the opportunity to instruct or otherwise, knowing the full consequences in terms of cost and time.
- The risk for unforeseen circumstances lies with the contractor.
- Gives single point responsibility.

Disadvantages

- Provides the client with arguably a less sophisticated building in terms of design detailing than would be the case with other forms of procurement.
- Gives less control over the work in total and of the costs of any variations required.
- Can be difficult in certain instances to precisely define the standards and quality of design required.
- Depending on the risks imposed on the contractor at tender stage can result in a higher contract value than would otherwise be the case.

Suitability

More appropriate where the client requires a firm lump sum price and where the required standards and quality can be easily defined before tenders are sought.

For more control over quality and cost, this procurement route can be used in a "Develop then Design and Build" form where the client's design team initially negotiates and obtains planning permission, prepares outline designs, specifications and a detailed brief for the Employer's Requirements, particularly where more complex buildings are required under this procurement method. In some cases the employer's design team is required to be novated to the contractor after obtaining planning permission.

Target Cost Design and Build

Basis

As with traditional Design and Build, a contractor is selected, normally in competition, to Design and Build the building. Tenders are invited based on "Employer's Requirements" which sets out the specification of the building required and defines the planning and other restrictions. The contractor is responsible for the design team, although the client should retain the services of consultants to protect his interests and act on his behalf.

The contractor's costs are audited by the Quantity Surveyor and the contractor is paid the actual cost of the work so long as it is less than the tendered Target Cost. In addition, any saving (or loss) on the Target Cost Design and Build tender sum is split, at agreed percentages e.g. 50/50, 40/60, or over a range dependant on profit, between the contractor and the client.

Like Design and Build, Target Cost Design and Build is possible. However because of the inherent sharing of savings the potential for such economies being made is reduced and unlikely to be as attractive to the contractor.

Construction Procurement Guide (Cont'd)
Target Cost Design and Build (Cont'd)

Advantages

- Establishes the client's maximum financial commitment (subject to client variations). If the contractor's costs exceed the Target Cost, only the Target Cost sum is paid.
- Leaves responsibility with the contractor for organising and programming the design team's activities. The client is therefore not responsible for extensions of time in the event that design information is not produced on time.
- Variations are normally pre-agreed and the client has the opportunity to instruct or otherwise knowing the consequences in terms of cost and time.
- Gives single point responsibility.
- Leads to a less adversarial attitude between contractor and client as both benefit from savings.
- Can give prior warning of future financial problems as the Quantity Surveyor has complete access to the contractor's actual costs.
- The risk for unforeseen circumstances is shared more equitably between the client and the contractor.

Disadvantages

- Provides the client with arguably a less sophisticated building in terms of design detailing then would be the case with other forms of procurement.
- Gives less control over the work in total and of the costs of any variations required.
- Can be difficult in certain instances to precisely define the standards and quality of design required.

Suitability

More appropriate for contracts where the client requires a firm lump sum price but where risks are likely to be priced by the contractor in the tender. Probably appropriate for less sophisticated buildings where the standards and quality can be easily defined.

Design, Manage and Construct

Basis

The Design, Manage and Construct route is a hybrid route between Design and Build and Management Contracting.
Like Management Contracting, the Design, Manage and Construct contractor is appointed to manage the construction of the project through a series of trade-contracts. It differs, in that the contractor is also given responsibility for programming and procuring the design information, so that the design consultants are employed by the 'design and manage' contractor, rather than the client.

The Design, Manage and Construct contractor is selected, usually in competition, early in the programme on the basis of a response to a set of tender enquiry documents which requires the contractor to tender a fee for:

- pre-commencement services;
- construction services during and after the project;
- a lump sum for site staffing and facilities, etc

As well as price, the required performance of the design and manage contractor is a major factor in the selection process.
For the actual building process, the works are divided into separate trade packages, for which tenders are sought from trade-contractors by means of a variety of tender routes, vut by preference on a lump sum basis. The selected trade-contractors are taken on by the design and manage contractor.

Advantages

- Gives single point responsibility.
- Enables an early start to be made on site before the design is completed.
- Creates a flexible tendering environment. Allows for ongoing change because works are tendered progressively. In turn this reduces the ongoing likelihood of claims being made by the trade-contractors, should significant changes be made.
- The 'Design, Manage and Construct' method lends itself well to complex or fast track construction because construction work is able to be started before the design is finished.
- Leads to a less confrontational relationship between the Design and Manage contractor and the client.
- Management of the design information production by the design and manage contractor has the potential to lead to fewer delays arising from lack of information.
- In most cases the Design and Manage contractor adopts overall financial responsibility for the default of sub-contractors.

Disadvantages

- Can lead to duplication of resources between trade-contractors and the Design and Manage contractor and therefore can also lead to a higher level of tenders.
- No contract sum is established. Therefore the client relies upon the Quantity Surveyor's estimate, endorsed by the Design and Manage contractor initially and then progressively firmed up as tendering progresses during the course of works.
- There is an 'arms-length' relationship between the client and the contractor's design team, which can potentially lead to lower client satisfaction with the final design.

Suitability

More appropriate for large, complex projects or fast track projects where potentially an early start is required and where the client wishes to have a single point responsibility.

Construction Management

Basis

The original philosophy of Construction Management was that the client would organise the management of the construction activities in-house. As with Management Contracting, the actual works are divided into separate trade packages that are tendered by trade contractors. However, the major difference from management contracting is that the client employs the selected trade contractors direct. Because of the criticism of Management Contracting that has arisen over the past few years, the Construction Management approach has become more widely applied. Not all clients have the facility to manage their own construction work in-house and it is now normal for an outside construction manager to be appointed - either an independent consultant, or a contractor. In these cases the trade contracts are still direct with the client.

Advantages

- Enables an early start to be made on site before design is well advanced.
- Allows flexibility for change as the works are tendered progressively. There is a reduced likelihood of claims affecting other packages in the event that major changes are made.
- Lends itself well to complex construction projects as construction can commence before design work is completed.
- Direct contracts between the works contractors and the client should result in stronger relationships and potentially a less adversarial situation.
- Trade Packages can include design where specialist works are required and are let on a Design and Build basis.
- The client has a greater degree of control over the works contractors.
- Can incorporate Design and Build and Performance Specified works if required

Construction Procurement Guide (Cont'd)
Construction Management (Cont'd)

Disadvantages

- As no contract sum is established, the client relies upon the Quantity Surveyor's estimate. This is, however, endorsed by the construction manager initially and firm costs are established progressively during the course of the works.
- Organisation costs such as site accommodation, telephones, copying etc., are likely to be paid on a prime cost basis. This gives the client less cost certainty.
- The client accepts a greater degree of risk because he has financial responsibility for the default of the works contractors.
- The client takes on the burden of dealing with additional correspondence, multiple payments and possibly adjudication on disputes and extensions of time, etc., for all individual trade contractors.

Suitability

More appropriate for large, complex projects where the client is experienced in the construction process, wishes to have a "hands on" approach and where an earlier start is required than can be made by proceeding with the full design process and tendering in a more traditional way. This is achieved by overlapping design, preparation of tender documents and construction.

Measured Term Maintenance Contract

Basis

A method of contracting is used where there is much repetition of work, for example in the case of regular or planned preventive maintenance work is required, e.g. Housing, Schools, etc.

Tenders are sought on the basis of a Schedule of Rates, chosen for their applicability to the proposed work. Tenderers quote either their price for each work item, or where the Schedule of rates are a standard priced document, on the basis of a 'plus or minus' rate in each case. Additionally, the tenderer will likely be asked to quote his minimum charge, or call out rate.

Contracts are generally let on a 'Framework' basis, generally for a period of between 2 and 3 years, although longer periods can be agreed and the contract often incorporates a means by which the contract can be extended for a further period of time, perhaps one or two years as an incentive for the contractor to perform. In this respect clients often define KPI's (Key Performance Indicators) as part of the contract in order to provide measurement of the performance of the contractor.
After the contract commences, the Contractor measures the works carried out and raises invoices against the Schedule of Rates for each separate job. Applications for payment are based upon a monthly schedule and application for payment.

Invoices are generally payable on completion of the service and monthly in arrears. There can also be an additional annual sum per property for reactive repairs; and a further schedule of rates for renewals rather than repairs as applicable.

Payments for the reactive repairs element can be allowed to be adjusted down for any system down time or unavailability during the contract period.

Often used for repairs, maintenance, renewals and minor works by councils and other public authorities with major estate portfolios.

Advantages

- Creates a long-term integrated multi-party partnering approach between the client's estate management team and the chosen contractor, to provide better communication and response.
- Allows the development of more open pricing over the life of the term programme
- Allows proactive change and risk management, including use of a risk register.
- Creates a supply chain partnering environment whereby problem solving and alternative dispute resolution can thrive.
- Provides process for continuous improvement by allowing the measurement of improvement and related incentives which may be incorporated into the contract terms
- Certainty of cost for each work task and can be verified and easily audited.
- Can incorporate Design and Build and Performance Specified works if required

Disadvantages

- Some clients believe that an open book agreement with a contractor may be a more economic way to proceed.
- Minimum charges can cause a feeling of mistrust between the client and contractor, where an apparently large number of 'small' charge jobs are carried out.
- A change in personnel may bring conflict and when things go wrong, there can be a serious breakdown between the parties

Suitability

Works well where there is a high degree of repetition in the works, for example the renewal of locks, painting, replacement of glazing, plant repairs, which can be reasonably foreseen.

Cost Reimbursable or Prime Cost

Basis

The contractor is appointed, possibly in competition, but on many occasions by negotiation, to carry out the works on the basis that he is paid his actual costs. He also receives a fixed fee or percentage for overheads and profit, which if competitive tendering is possible, can form the basis of the tender.

Some practitioners argue that this procurement method can be likened to being on a time and materials basis, or otherwise 'Daywork'; albeit with modified terms.

Advantages

- Enables an incredibly early start to be made on site, but at the expense of cost certainty.

Disadvantages

- Overall cost control can be difficult because the contractor does not have any great incentive to work efficiently. Although interim assessments can be made, the total cost is not known until the work is largely completed.
- There is often no means to ensure that errors and bad workmanship are borne by the contractor and sub-contracted works, particularly if all works are let on a prime cost 'style' basis. It is for this reason that in many cases sub-contract packages are let on a competitive lump sum basis in order to maintain an element of cost control. Additionally, it may be a term of the tender that a reduction in the costs is made to cover abortive work. Similarly, it is normal to restrict head office staff costs so that a proportion of these are included in the fixed fee; and to agree a schedule of Head office staff and site establishment costs with the tender in order to create a greater level of cost certainty.
- Risk for unforeseen circumstances is borne by the client.

Construction Procurement Guide (Cont'd)
Cost Reimbursable or Prime Cost (Cont'd)

Suitability

Probably a last resort method of procurement in view of the uncertainty of total cost inherent in the process. Really only suitable for projects where an immediate start on site is required, for example where fire damage or terrorist damage has occurred, or perhaps with difficult refurbishments where the scope of work cannot be established until the work progresses.

Partnering

Basis

"*Effective partnering should allow formal contracts to be dispensed with*"- Sir John Egan.

The partnering approach creates a trust relationship, fairness and dedication between all the parties to the contract which involves the client, the design team, the contractor(s) and sub-contractor(s) working to identified common goals.

A suite of contracts now provides the necessary framework to enable Partnering and the most popular, known as PPC2000 is published by the Association of Consultant Architects (ACA).

Partnering often allows projects to start on site many months earlier than would have been the case if a more traditional procurement method had been used. However, whilst PPC 2000 is a sound foundation for partnering it is up to the project team to deliver the benefits. It is therefore important for the project team to be aware that "PPC 2000 cannot assist partnering teams who do not give serious thought to the best way in which its provisions are to put into effect".

The management of risk is an important element of partnering and demands a structured approach to establish and actively maintain a project risk register.

The client can appoint a Partnering Advisor to record and document the project team relationships, the commitments made by each party and their expectations. He is an honest broker who has no affiliation to any party.

PPC 2000 is not alone as a contractual solution; other standard forms exist, for example:

- ECC (NEC 2 and 3)
- JCT 2016 suite with the JCT "Non-Binding Partnering Charter" – refer to JCT 2016 Practice Note 4 – Partnering.
- Be Collaborative Contract
- Perform21 (PSPC + Local Government Practice toolkit)
- TPC2005 (PPC2000 for term contracts)

Taking the PPC2000 as an example, the documents would be as follows:

- The Project Partnering Agreement - sets out and governs the activities of all the partnering team members during the pre-construction phase and is signed as far in advance of the start on site as is possible.
- The Partnering Terms – will include The partnering terms, the project brief, the project proposal, known costs, provisional KPI's, preliminaries (site overheads) and a partnering charter. A budget at this stage is not required.
- Any Joining Agreements – this replaces sub-contract forms. Partners can join at any time.
- Any Pre Possession Agreement – the purpose of this document is to provide the ability to undertake work on or off site prior to approval to commence on site. For example: surveys and investigations, planning and building regulations approvals, Insurances and Bonds and Health and Safety plan (pre-possession only), and the like.
- The Commencement Agreement – the document includes the document includes express confirmation by all the partnering team members that to the best of their knowledge the project is ready to commence on site. It will include an 'agreed maximum price' (note not guaranteed), the project drawings, supply chain packages and associated drawings, the project timetable, KPI/Incentives, Surveys and other investigations, Planning and Building regulations, funding, H&S plan, Bond, Insurances, etc.
- The Partnering Charter – an agreed statement of the values, goals and priorities of the Partnering team members and interested parties
- The Project Brief
- The Project Proposals
- The Price Framework
- The Consultant Service Schedule
- The Consultant Payment Terms
- The KPI's – to measure and judge performance and service quality; to assess strengths and weaknesses and to act as an aid to continuous improvement; to create a financial incentive to perform well in key areas; to indicate the local social and economic impact of the construction phase of a project; and for benchmarking purposes

Advantages

- Increased client satisfaction
- Creates better value for money
- Projects benefit from the inherent consistency of the design / construction teams
- Improved predictability of out-turn costs and time - in most cases partnering projects are completed on time and within target cost and moreover handed over defect free.
- Better resource planning with a faster start on site
- Better design and whole life value
- Higher quality construction with fewer defects
- More effective procurement and administrative procedures
- Fewer disputes and more respect for people
- Reduced accidents
- Better use of resources, including Improved supply chain management
- Using construction work to gain social and economic benefit
- Can incorporate Design and Build and Performance Specified works if required

The following list notes some problems that have been encountered by partnering teams:

- The client must stay interested and actively involved as a partnering team member, otherwise the lack of interest and support has a tendency to encourage cynicism and apathy in team members; and a belief that ideas for innovation or early warnings will not reach the client
- Partnering team members must be committed to changing their way of working – partnering is a major departure from familiar ways of working and an uncommitted attitude is likely to undermine effective partnering and furthermore create the problems that partnering is intended to prevent. Complete buy in from top management down is required.
- Failure to complete the partnering timetable – means that there is a serious risk that pre-construction activities will be delayed; particularly if members cannot rely on each other to meet deadlines and in turn relationships may suffer.
- Failure to clarify and integrate the Project Brief, Brief Proposals and the consultant services schedule – this creates a risk of gaps in agreed activities and potential later disputes; and duplication in agreed activities wasting money and causing confusion
- KPI's and incentives not agreed early – KPI's must be firmed up not later than the date of the commencement agreement. If KPI's are neglected or targets/incentives not agreed this will reduce the motivation of the partnering team members
- Joint risk management is neglected – meaning that Risks will be transferred to constructor and priced rather than managed. This means that the opportunity to consider who is best to take the risk is missed

Construction Procurement Guide (Cont'd)
Partnering (Cont'd)
Disadvantages/problems recorded (Cont'd)

- Failure to appoint an independent or suitably experienced partnering adviser – This affects understanding, focus and driving forward the partnering process. A lack of an independent adviser can undermine team confidence
- Failure to read PPC 2000 – this obviously affects understanding and may lead to traditional adversarial alternatives being put into practice

Suitability

Partnering is a major departure from familiar ways of working. It is a new way of working to many of us
Professionals and constructors need to be:

- Enthusiastic
- Working to the same goal
- Co–operative and effective communicators
- Flexible
- Willing to manage the process

Partnering is about being fair and challenging, and about value and performance, it is not just about being friendly.

The design professionals are required be proactive and assertive during the project. A strong, determined, value/performance driven and professional stance is essential.

The constructor only has guaranteed work provided value for money; quality and performance are being achieved. Underperformance must be tackled by an assertive, (not an aggressive) approach.

The NEC/ECC Contract

It is appropriate here to also mention the New Engineering Contract (referred to above), which was introduced in 1993. Published by the Institute of Civil Engineers it was intended to respond to:

- Client dissatisfaction with existing forms - too many, too adversarial
- The inflexibility of existing contracts
- Disputes - too many, too expensive, too long to settle
- Management of contracts seen as more important than legal niceties
- UK as a member of Europe – national distinctions disappearing
- Clients looking to seek alternative procurement strategies

The Latham report of 1994 recommended that the NEC contract should become a national standard contract across the whole of the construction industry. In response, the ICE introduced various changes as recommended in the Report, creating the second edition in 1995, re-named as "The Engineering and Construction Contract" (ECC). It requires the parties to work "in a spirit of mutual trust and co-operation".

The ECC was followed by the Construction Act and as a combination then sought to reduce confrontation and to encourage all concerned to "get on with the job". The NEC contracts have subsequently been improved by third editions in 2005 and fourth editions (NEC4) in 2017.

As a contract it:

- Is intended to be suitable for all the needs of the construction industry and allows a wide range of tender procurement methods
- Provides for a variety of approaches to risk allocation.
- Can be Adapted for partial design, full design or no design responsibility, and for all current contract options including target, management and cost reimbursable contracts.
- Creates a stimulus for good management

There are six main methods for seeking tendered works under a ECC partnering contract:

- A Lump sum with activity schedule
- Priced contract with Bill of Quantities (Note - the bill is used only for interim payments, not for valuation of compensation events).
- Target contract with activity schedule (lump sum quoted by tenderer as target)
- Target contract with Bill of Quantities (subject to remeasurement)
- Cost reimbursable contract
- Management contract (by involvement of a management contractor).

In addition, Construction Management can also be used. It is therefore extremely flexible. Indeed, it provides a contract to enable good management and a broad set of contract procurement guides which goes well beyond the scope of this section.

CONCLUSION

The choice of a procurement route and tendering process is a complex matter. This section has attempted to set out the main features of the principal procurement routes and processes available.

It is intended as a broad guide to assist in understanding the main issues, advantages and disadvantages. In order to make a full assessment of what can be a set of complex issues, before entering into a contract/agreement you are strongly advised to seek professional advice.

This page left blank intentionally

AVERAGE COVERAGE OF PAINTS

The following information has been provided by the British Decorators Association, whose permission to publish is hereby acknowledged.

In this revision a range of spreading capacities is given. Figures are in square metres per litre, except for oil-bound water paint and cement-based paint which are in square metres per kilogram.

For comparative purposes, figures are given for a single coat, but users are recommended to follow manufactures' recommendations as to when to use single or multicoat systems.

It is emphasised that the figures quoted in the schedule are practical figures for brush application, achieved in big scale painting work and losses and wastage must be considered. They are not optima figures based upon ideal conditions of surface, nor minima figures reflecting the reverses of these conditions.

There will be instances when the figures indicated by paint manufacturers in their literature will be higher than those shown in the schedule. The Committee realise that under ideal conditions of application, and depending on such factors as the skill of the applicator, type and quality of the product, substantially better covering figures can be achieved.

The figures given below are for application by brush and to appropriate systems on each surface. They are given for guidance and are qualified to allow for variation depending on certain factors.

SCHEDULE OF AVERAGE COVERAGE OF PAINTS IN SQUARE METRES (M^2) PER LITRE

Coating per litre	Finishing plaster	Wood floated rendering	Smooth concrete/ cement	Fair faced brick-work	Block work -	Roughcast pebble dash -	Hardboard	Soft fibre insulating board
Water thinned primer/undercoat								
as primer	13-15	-	-	-	-	-	10-12	7-10
as undercoat	-	-	-	-	-	-	-	10-12
Plaster primer (including building board)	9-11	8-12	9-11	7-9	5-7	2-4	8-10	7-9
Alkali resistant primer	7-11	6-8	7-11	6-8	4-6	2-4	-	-
External wall primer sealer	6-8	6-7	6-8	5-7	4-6	2-4	-	-
Undercoat	11-14	7-9	7-9	6-8	6-8	3-4	11-14	10-12
Oil based thixotropic finish		Figures should be obtained from individual manufacturers						
Eggshell/semi-gloss finish (oil based)	11-14	9-11	11-14	8-10	7-9	-	10-13	10-12
Acrylic eggshell	11-14	10-12	11-14	8-11	7-10	-	11-14	10-12
Emulsion paint								
standard	12-15	8-12	11-14	8-12	6-10	2-4	12-15	8-10
contract	10-12	7-11	10-12	7-10	5-9	2-4	10-12	7-9
Glossy emulsion		Figures should be obtained from individual manufacturers						
Heavy textured coating	2-4	2-4	2-4	2-4	2-4	-	2-4	2-4
Masonry paint	5-7	4-6	5-7	4-6	3-5	2-4	-	-
Coating per kilogram								
Oil bound water paint	7-9	6-8	7-9	6-8	5-7	-	-	-
Cement based paint	-	4-6	6-7	3-6	3-6	2-3	-	-

Coating per litre	Fire retardent fibre insulating board	Smooth paper faced board	Hard asbestos sheet **	Structural steel work	Metal sheeting	Joinery	Smooth primed surfaces	Smooth under-coated surfaces
Wood primer (oil based)	-	-	-	-	-	8-11	-	-
Water thinned primer/undercoat								
as primer	-	8-11	**	-	-	10-14	-	-
as undercoat.	-	10-12	-	-	-	12-15	12-15	-
Aluminium sealer +								
spirit based	-	-	-	-	-	7-9	-	-
oil based	-	-	-	-	9-13	9-13	-	-

AVERAGE COVERAGE OF PAINTS (Cont'd)

SCHEDULE OF AVERAGE COVERAGE OF PAINTS IN SQUARE METRES PER LITRE (Cont'd)

Coating per litre	Fire retardant fibre insulating board	Smooth paper faced board	Hard asbestos sheet **	Structural steel work	Metal sheeting	Joinery	Smooth primed surfaces	Smooth under-coated surfaces
Metal primer								
conventional	-	-	-	7-10	10-13	-	-	-
Specialised		Figures should be obtained from individual manufacturers						
Plaster primer (including building board)	8-10	10-12	10-12	-	-	-	-	-
Alkali resistant primer	-	-	8-10	-	-	-	-	-
External wall primer sealer		-	6-8	-	-	-	-	-
Undercoat	10-12	11-14	10-12	10-12	10-12	10-12	11-14	-
Gloss finish	10-12	11-14	10-12	10-12	10-12	10-12	11-14	11-14
Eggshell/semi-gloss finish (oil based)	10-12	11-14	10-12	10-12	10-12	10-12	11-14	11-14
Acrylic eggshell	10-12	11-14	-	-	11-14	11-13	11-14	-
Emulsion paint								
standard	8-10	12-15	10-12	-	-	10-12	12-15	12-15
contract	-	10-12	8-10	-		10-12	10-12	10-12
Heavy textured coating	2-4	2-4	2-4	2-4	2-4	2-4	2-4	2-4
Masonry paint	-	-	5-7		-	-	6-8	6-8
Coating per kilogram								
Oil bound water paint	-	-	7-9	-	-	-	-	-
Cement based paint	-	-	4-6	-	-	-	-	-
Glossy emulsion		Figures should be obtained from individual manufacturers						

+ Aluminium primer / sealer is normally used over "bitumen" painted surfaces.

* On some roughcast / pebbledash surfaces appreciably lower coverage may be obtained.

In many instances the coverages achieved will be affected by the suction and texture to the backing; for example the suction and texture of brickwork can vary to such an extent that coverages outside those quoted may on occasions be obtained.

It is necessary to take these factors into account when using this table.

** Owing to legislation (COSHH) further advice regarding the encapsulation of asbestos should be sought.

STANDARD WIRE GAUGE (SWG)

in millimetres and inches

SWG	mm	inches	SWG	mm	inches	SWG	mm	inches
1	7.62	0.300	11	2.95	0.116	21	0.813	0.032
2	7.00	0.276	12	2.64	0.104	22	0.711	0.028
3	6.40	0.252	13	2.34	0.092	23	0.610	0.024
4	5.89	0.232	14	2.03	0.080	24	0.559	0.022
5	5.38	0.212	15	1.83	0.072	25	0.508	0.020
6	4.88	0.192	16	1.63	0.064	26	0.457	0.018
7	4.47	0.176	17	1.42	0.056	27	0.417	0.016
8	4.06	0.160	18	1.22	0.048	28	0.376	0.015
9	3.66	0.144	19	1.02	0.040	29	0.345	0.014
10	3.25	0.128	20	0.914	0.036	30	0.315	0.012

WEIGHTS OF VARIOUS METALS

in kilogrammes per square metre

		Steel		Wt. iron		Cast iron		Brass		Copper		Cast Lead	
mm	in	kg/m²	lb/m²	kg/m²	lb/m²	kg/m²	lb/m²	kg/m²	lb/m²	kg/m²	lb/m²	kg/m²	lb/m²
1.59	1/16	12.45	2.55	12.21	2.50	11.47	2.35	13.43	2.75	14.11	2.89	18.07	3.70
3.18	1/8	24.90	5.10	24.41	5.00	22.90	4.69	26.76	5.48	28.22	5.78	36.08	7.39
6.35	1/4	49.80	10.20	48.82	10.00	45.75	9.37	53.41	10.94	56.44	11.56	72.16	14.78
9.53	3/8	74.70	15.30	73.24	15.00	68.65	14.06	80.17	16.42	84.66	17.34	108.24	22.17
12.70	1/2	99.60	20.40	97.65	20.00	91.55	18.75	106.83	21.88	112.88	23.12	144.32	29.56
15.88	5/8	124.50	25.50	122.06	25.00	114.44	23.44	133.49	27.34	141.54	28.99	180.41	36.95
19.05	3/4	149.40	30.60	146.47	30.00	137.29	28.12	160.19	32.81	169.32	36.68	216.49	44.34
22.23	7/8	174.30	35.70	170.88	35.00	160.19	32.81	186.95	38.29	197.54	40.46	252.57	51.73
25.40	1	199.20	40.80	195.30	40.00	183.09	37.50	213.65	43.76	225.76	46.24	288.65	59.12

WEIGHTS OF MATERIALS

in kilogrammes per metre cubed (see end of section for lb per cubed/square foot)

Material	kg/m³
Aerated concrete	800-960
Aluminium	
cast	2550
rolled	2700
Asphalt	
natural	1000
paving	2080
Ballast, loose, graded	1600
Beech	700
Birch	
American	640
yellow	700
Brass	
cast	8330
rolled	8570
Bricks (common burnt clay)	
stacked	1600-1920
sand cement	1840
sand lime	2080
ballast	1200
brickwork	1920
Cement	
bags	1280
bulk	1281-1442
casks	960
Concrete (cement, plain)	
brick aggregate	1840
clinker	1440
stone ballast	2240
Concrete (cement, reinforced)	
1% steel	2370
2% steel	2420
5% steel	2580
Copper	
cast	8760
drawn or sheet	8940
Cork	130-240
Deal, yellow	430
Ebony	1180-1330
Elm	
American	670
Dutch	580
English	580
Wych	690
Fir	
Douglas	530
Silver	480
Flint	2560
Foam slag	700
Freestone	2243-4280
masonry, dressed	2400
rubble	2240
Glass	
bottle	2720
flint, best	3080
flint, heavy	5000-6000
plate	2800
Granolithic	2240
Hardcore	1920
Hoggin	1760
Iroko	600
Iron	
cast	7200
malleable cast	7370-7500
wrought	7690
Lead	
cast or rolled	11300
Lime	
acetate or, bags	1280
blue lias, ground	850
carbonate of, barrels	1280
chloride of, lead-lined cases	450
grey chalk, lump	700
grey stone, lump	800
hydrate, bags	510

Material	kg/m³
Macadam	2100
Mahogany	
African	560
Honduras	540
Spanish	690
Marble	2590-2830
Mortar	
cement, set	1920-2080
lime, set	1600-1760
Oak	
African	960
American red	720
English	800-880
Padouk	780
Paint	
aluminium	1200
bituminous emulsion	1120
red lead	3120
white lead	2800
zinc	2400
Pine	
American red	530
British Columbian	530
Christina	690
Oregon	530
Pitch	650
Plywood	480-640
Polyvinyl chloride acetate	1200-1350
Poplar	450
Portland cement	
loose	1200-1360
bags	1120-1280
drums	1200
Redwood	
American	530
Baltic	500
non-graded	430
Rhodesian	910
Slate	
Welsh	2800
Westmorland	3000
Steel	7830
Stone	
Ancaster	2500
Bath	2080
Darley Dale	2370
Forest of Dean	2430
Granite	2640
Hopton Wood	2530
Kentish rag	2670
Mansfield	2260
Portland	2240
Purbeck	2700
York	2240
Tarmacadam	2080
Teak	
Burma, African	650
Walnut	660
Water	
fresh	1001
salt	1009-1201
Whitewood	460
Zinc	
cast	6840
rolled	7190
sheets, packed	900

WEIGHTS OF ROUND AND SQUARE STEEL BARS

length	Round		Square	
mm	kg/m	lb/ft	kg/m	lb/ft
6	0.222	0.149	0.283	0.190
8	0.395	0.265	0.503	0.338
10	0.616	0.414	0.784	0.527
12	0.888	0.597	1.130	0.759
16	1.579	1.061	2.010	1.351
20	2.466	1.657	3.139	2.110
25	3.854	2.590	4.905	3.296
32	6.313	4.243	8.035	5.400
40	9.864	6.629	12.554	8.437
50	15.413	10.358	19.617	13.183

WEIGHTS OF FLAT STEEL BARS

in kilogrammes per linear metre (see end of section for lb per linear foot)

Width		Thickness in millimetres and inches									
		3.18 (1/8 in)	6.35 (1/4 in)	7.94 (5/16 in)	9.53 (3/8 in)	11.11 (7/16 in)	12.70 (1/2 in)	15.88 (5/8 in)	19.05 (3/4 in)	22.23 (7/8 in)	25.40 (1 in)
mm	in										
25.40	1	0.64	1.27	1.58	1.91	2.22	2.53	3.17	3.80	4.44	5.06
28.58	1 1/8	0.71	1.43	1.79	2.13	2.49	2.84	3.56	4.27	4.99	5.70
31.75	1 1/4	0.79	1.58	1.98	2.37	2.77	3.17	3.96	4.75	5.54	6.33
34.93	1 3/8	0.86	1.74	2.17	2.60	3.05	3.48	4.35	5.22	6.09	6.97
38.10	1 1/2	0.95	1.91	2.37	2.84	3.32	3.80	4.75	5.70	6.64	7.59
41.28	1 5/8	1.03	2.05	2.58	3.08	3.60	4.11	5.13	6.16	7.19	8.23
44.45	1 3/4	1.10	2.22	2.77	3.32	3.87	4.44	5.54	6.64	7.75	8.86
50.80	2	1.27	2.53	3.17	3.80	4.44	5.06	6.33	7.59	8.86	10.12
57.15	2 1/4	1.44	2.84	3.56	4.27	4.99	5.70	7.11	8.54	9.96	11.39
63.50	2 1/2	1.58	3.17	3.96	4.75	5.54	6.33	7.90	9.50	11.07	12.68
69.85	2 3/4	1.74	3.48	4.35	5.22	6.09	6.97	8.69	10.43	12.17	13.92
76.20	3	1.91	3.80	4.75	5.70	6.64	7.59	9.50	11.39	13.29	15.18
82.55	3 1/4	2.05	4.11	5.13	6.16	7.19	8.23	10.28	12.34	14.39	16.44
88.90	3 1/2	2.22	4.44	5.54	6.64	7.75	8.86	11.07	13.29	15.49	17.71
95.25	3 3/8	2.37	4.75	5.92	7.11	8.30	9.50	11.86	14.23	16.61	18.97
101.60	4	2.53	5.06	6.33	7.59	8.86	10.12	12.65	15.18	17.71	20.24
107.95	4 1/4	2.69	5.37	6.73	8.07	9.41	10.76	13.44	16.13	18.81	21.50
114.30	4 1/2	2.84	5.70	7.11	8.54	9.96	11.39	14.23	17.08	19.93	22.77
120.65	4 3/4	3.01	6.01	7.52	9.02	10.52	12.02	15.02	18.02	21.03	24.03
127.00	5	3.17	6.33	7.90	9.50	11.07	12.65	15.82	18.97	22.14	25.30
139.70	5 1/2	3.48	6.97	8.69	10.43	12.17	13.92	17.40	20.88	24.35	27.83
152.40	6	3.80	7.59	9.50	11.39	13.29	15.18	18.97	22.77	26.56	30.36
165.10	6 1.2	4.11	8.23	10.28	12.34	14.39	16.44	20.55	24.67	28.78	32.89
177.80	7	4.44	8.86	11.07	13.29	15.49	17.71	22.14	26.56	31.00	35.42
190.50	7 1/2	4.75	9.50	11.86	14.23	16.61	18.97	23.72	28.47	33.20	37.95
203.20	8	5.06	10.12	12.65	15.18	17.71	20.24	25.30	30.36	35.42	40.48
228.60	9	5.70	11.39	14.23	17.08	19.93	22.77	28.47	34.15	39.85	45.54
254.00	10	6.73	12.65	15.82	18.97	22.14	25.30	31.62	37.95	44.27	50.50
279.40	11	6.97	13.92	17.40	20.88	24.35	27.83	34.79	41.74	48.71	55.66
304.80	12	7.59	15.18	18.97	22.77	26.56	30.36	37.95	45.54	53.13	60.72

WEIGHTS OF STEEL JOISTS TO BS 4: PART 1: 1980

Size		Weight	
inches	millimetres	lb/ft	kg/m
10 x 8	254 x 203	55.0	81.85
10 x 4.5	254 x 114	25.0	37.20
8 x 6	203 x 152	35.0	52.09
6 x 5	152 x 127	25.0	37.20
5 x 4.5	127 x 114	20.0	29.76
5 x 4.5	127 x 114	18.0	26.79
4.5 x 4.5	114 x 114	18.0	26.79
4 x 4	102 x 102	15.5	23.07
3.5 x 3.5	89 x 89	13.0	19.35
3 x 3	76 x 76	8.5	12.65

WEIGHTS OF STEEL CHANNELS TO BS 4: PART 1: 1980

Size of channel		Weight	
in	mm	lb/ft	kg/m
17 x 4	432 x 102	44	65.54
15 x 4	381 x 102	37	55.10
12 x 4	305 x 102	31	46.18
12 x 3.5	305 x 89	28	41.69
10 x 3.5	254 x 89	24	35.74
10 x 3	254 x 76	19	28.29
9 x 3.5	229 x 89	22	32.76
9 x 3	229 x 76	17.5	26.06
8 x 3.5	203 x 89	20	29.78
8 x 3	203 x 76	16	23.82
7 x 3.5	178 x 89	18	26.81
7 x 3	178 x 76	14	20.84
6 x 3.5	152 x 89	16	23.84
6 x 3	152 x 76	12	17.88
5 x 2.5	127 x 64	10	14.90

WEIGHTS OF STRUCTURAL STEEL TEE BARS SPLIT FROM UNIVERSAL COLUMNS

Size of Tee		Weight	
in	mm	lb/ft	kg/m
12 x 6	305 x 152	53.0	79
12 x 6	305 x 152	32.5	49
10 x 5	254 x 127	44.5	66
10 x 5	254 x 127	24.5	37
8 x 4	203 x 102	29.0	43
8 x 4	203 x 102	15.5	23
6 x 3	152 x 76	12.5	19
6 x 3	152 x 76	7.85	12

WEIGHTS OF STRUCTURAL STEEL TEE BARS SPLIT FROM UNIVERSAL BEAMS

Size of Tee Inch	mm	Weight lb/ft	kg/m	Size of Tee Inch	mm	Weight lb/ft	kg/m
12 x 12	305 x 305	60.0	90	7 x 8	178 x 203	18.0	27
10 x 13.5	254 x 343	42.0	63	5.5 x 8	140 x 203	15.5	23
9 x 12	229 x 305	47.0	70	6.75 x 7	171 x 178	22.5	34
9 x 12	229 x 305	34.0	51	6.75 x 7	171 x 178	15.0	23
8.25 x 10.5	210 x 267	41.0	61	5 x 7	127 x 178	13.0	20
8.25 x 10.5	210 x 267	27.5	41	6.5 x 6	165 x 152	18.0	27
7 x 9	191 x 229	33.0	49	5 x 6	127 x 152	16.0	24
7 x 9	191 x 229	22.5	34	4 x 6	102 x 152	11.0	17
6 x 9	152 x 229	27.5	41	5.75 x 5	146 x 127	14.5	22
6 x 9	152 x 229	17.5	26	4 x 5	102 x 127	9.5	14
7 x 8	178 x 203	25.0	37	5.25 x 4	133 x 102	10.0	15

WEIGHTS OF STEEL EQUAL ANGLES TO B.S. 4848 PART 4: 1972

Size mm	Thickness mm	Weight kg/m
250 x 250	35	128.0
	32	118.0
	28	104.0
	25	93.6
200 x 200	24	71.1
	20	59.9
	18	54.2
	16	48.5
150 x 150	18	40.1
	15	33.8
	12	27.3
150 x 150	10	23.0
130 x 130	16	30.8
	12	23.5
	10	19.8
	8	16.0
120 x 120	15	26.6
	12	21.6
	10	18.2
	8	14.7
110 x 110	16	25.8
110 x 110	12	19.8
	10	16.7
	8	13.5
100 x 100	15	21.9
	12	17.8
	10	15.0
	8	12.2
90 x 90	12	15.9
	10	13.4
	8	10.9
	6	8.3

WEIGHTS OF STEEL UNEQUAL ANGLES TO B.S. 4848 PART 4: 1972 (except where marked *)

Size mm	Thickness mm	Weight kg/m
200 x 150	18	47.1
	15	39.6
	12	32.0
200 x 100	15	33.7
	12	27.3
	10	23.0
150 x 90	15	26.6
	12	21.6
	10	18.2
150 x 75	15	24.8
	12	20.2
	10	17.0
*137 x 102	9.5	17.3
	7.9	14.5
	6.4	11.7
125 x 75	12	17.8
	10	15.0
	8	12.2
	6.5	9.98
100 x 75	12	15.4
	10	13.0
	8	10.6
100 x 65	10	12.3
	8	9.94
	7	8.77

WEIGHTS OF UNIVERSAL COLUMNS TO B.S. 4 PART 1: 1980

Size in	mm	Weight lb/ft	kg/m
14 x 16	356 x 406	426	634
		370	551
		314	467
		264	393
		228	340
		193	287
		158	235
12 x 12	305 x 305	109	283
		161	240
		133	198
		106	158
		92	137
		79	118
		65	97
8 x 8	203 x 203	58	86
		48	71
		40	60
		35	52
		31	46
14 x 14.5	356 x 368	136	202
		119	177
		103	153
		87	129
10 x 10	254 x 254	112	167
		89	132
		72	107
		60	89
		49	73
6 x 6	152 x 152	25	37
		20	30
		15.7	23

WEIGHTS OF UNIVERSAL BEAMS TO B.S. 4 PART 1: 1980

Size in	mm	Weight lb/ft	kg/m
36 x 16.5	914 x 419	260	388
		230	343
36 x 12	914 x 305	194	289
		170	253
		150	224
		135	201
33 x 11.5	838 x 292	152	226
		130	194
		118	176
30 x 10.5	762 x 267	132	197
		116	173
		99	147
27 x 10	686 x 254	114	170
		102	152
		94	140
		84	125
24 x 12	610 x 305	160	238
		120	179
		100	149
24 x 9	610 x 229	94	140
		84	125
		76	113
		68	101
21 x 8.25	533 x 210	82	122
		73	109
		68	101
		62	92
		55	82
18 x 7.5	457 x 191	66	98
		60	89
		55	82
		50	74
		45	67

Size in	mm	Weight lb/ft	kg/m
18 x 6	457 x 152	55	82
		50	74
		45	67
		40	60
		35	52
16 x 7	406 x 178	50	74
		45	67
		40	60
		36	54
16 x 5.5	406 x 140	31	46
		26	39
14 x 6.75	356 x 171	45	67
		38	57
		34	51
		30	45
14 x 5	356 x 127	26	39
		22	33
12 x 6.5	305 x 165	35	54
		31	46
		27	40
12 x 5	305 x 127	32	48
		28	42
		25	37
12 x 4	305 x 102	22	33
		19	28
		16.5	25
10 x 5.75	254 x 146	29	43
		25	37
		21	31
10 x 4	254 x 102	19	28
		17	25
		15	22
8 x 5.25	203 x 133	20	30
		17	25

WEIGHTS OF STEEL ROUND AND SQUARE BARS IN LB PER LINEAR FOOT

Inches	Round	Square
1/8	0.042	0.053
3/16	0.094	0.120
1/4	0.167	0.213
5/16	0.261	0.332
3/8	0.376	0.478
7/16	0.511	0.651
1/2	0.668	0.849
9/16	0.845	1.076
5/8	1.043	1.328
11/16	1.262	1.607
3/4	1.502	1.912
13/16	1.763	2.245

Inches	Round	Square
7/8	2.044	2.603
15/16	2.347	2.988
1	2.670	3.400
1 1/8	3.380	4.303
1 1/4	4.172	5.312
1 3/8	5.049	6.428
1 1/2	6.008	7.650
1 5/8	7.051	8.978
1 3/4	8.178	10.412
1 7/8	9.388	11.953
2	10.681	13.600
2 1/8	12.06	15.35
2 1/4	13.52	17.21

Inches	Round	Square
2 3/8	15.06	19.18
2 1/2	16.69	21.25
2 5/8	18.40	23.43
2 3/4	20.19	25.71
2 7/8	22.07	28.10
3	24.03	30.60
3 1/4	28.21	35.91
3 1/2	32.71	41.65
3 3/4	37.55	47.81
4	42.73	54.40
4 1/4	48.23	61.41
4 1/2	54.07	68.85
4 3/4	60.25	76.71

Inches	Round	Square
5	66.76	85.00
5 1/4	73.60	93.71
5 1/2	80.78	102.85
5 3/4	88.29	112.41
6	96.13	122.40
6 1/4	104.31	138.81
6 1/2	112.82	143.65
6 3/4	121.67	154.88
7	130.85	-
7 1/2	150.21	-
8	170.90	-
9	216.00	-
10	267.00	-

WEIGHTS OF STEEL FLAT BAR IN LB PER LINEAR FOOT

Width Inches	Thickness 1/8	1/4	5/16	3/8	7/16	1/2	5/8	3/4	7/8	1
1	0.43	0.85	1.06	1.28	1.49	1.70	2.13	2.55	2.98	3.40
1 1/8	0.48	0.96	1.20	1.43	1.67	1.91	2.39	2.87	3.35	3.83
1 1/4	0.53	1.06	1.33	1.59	1.86	2.13	2.66	3.19	3.72	4.25
1 3/8	0.58	1.17	1.46	1.75	2.05	2.34	2.92	3.51	4.09	4.68
1 1/2	0.64	1.28	1.59	1.91	2.23	2.55	3.19	3.83	4.46	5.10
1 5/8	0.69	1.38	1.73	2.07	2.42	2.76	3.45	4.14	4.83	5.53
1 3/4	0.74	1.49	1.86	2.23	2.60	2.98	3.72	4.46	5.21	5.95
1 7/8	0.80	1.59	1.99	2.39	2.79	3.19	3.98	4.78	5.58	6.38
2	0.85	1.70	2.13	2.55	2.98	3.40	4.25	5.10	5.95	6.80
2 1/4	0.96	1.91	2.39	2.87	3.35	3.83	4.78	5.74	6.69	7.65
2 1/2	1.06	2.13	2.66	3.19	3.72	4.25	5.31	6.38	7.44	8.50
2 3/4	1.17	2.34	2.92	3.51	4.09	4.68	5.84	7.01	8.18	9.35
3	1.28	2.55	3.19	3.83	4.46	5.10	6.38	7.65	8.93	10.20
3 1/4	1.38	2.76	3.45	4.14	4.83	5.53	6.91	8.29	9.67	11.05
3 1/2	1.49	2.98	3.72	4.46	5.21	5.95	7.44	8.93	10.41	11.90
3 3/4	1.59	3.19	3.98	4.78	5.58	6.38	7.97	9.56	11.16	12.75
4	1.70	3.40	4.25	5.10	5.95	6.80	8.50	10.20	11.90	13.60
4 1/4	1.81	3.61	4.52	5.42	6.32	7.23	9.03	10.84	12.64	14.45
4 1/2	1.91	3.83	4.78	5.74	6.69	7.65	9.56	11.48	13.39	15.30
4 3/4	2.02	4.04	5.05	6.06	7.07	8.08	10.09	12.11	14.13	16.15
5	2.13	4.25	5.31	6.38	7.44	8.50	10.63	12.75	14.88	17.00
5 1/2	2.34	4.68	5.84	7.01	8.18	9.35	11.69	14.03	16.36	18.70
6	2.55	5.10	6.38	7.56	8.93	10.20	12.75	15.30	17.85	20.40
6 1/2	2.76	5.53	6.91	8.29	9.67	11.05	13.81	16.58	19.34	22.10
7	2.98	5.95	7.44	8.93	10.41	11.90	14.88	17.85	20.83	23.80
7 1/2	3.19	6.38	7.97	9.56	11.16	12.75	15.94	19.13	22.31	25.50
8	3.40	6.80	8.50	10.20	11.90	13.60	17.00	20.40	23.80	27.20
9	3.83	7.65	9.56	11.48	13.39	15.30	19.13	22.95	26.78	30.60
10	4.25	8.50	10.63	12.75	14.88	17.00	21.25	25.50	29.75	34.00
11	4.68	9.35	11.69	14.03	16.36	18.70	23.38	28.05	32.73	37.40
12	5.10	10.20	12.75	15.30	17.85	20.40	25.50	30.60	35.70	40.80

APPROXIMATE WEIGHT OF SUNDRY MATERIALS - IMPERIAL

Material	lb per ft²	lb per ft³
Asbestos-cement sheeting		
1/4 in corrugated	3 1/4	-
1/4 in flat	2 1/4	-
Asbestos-cement slating		
Diamond	3	-
Rectangular	4	-
Asphalt 1 in thick	12	-
Ballast, river	-	120
Bituminous felt roofing	1	-
Brickwork, Commons	-	113
Cement, Portland	-	90
Cement screeding (1:3) 1/2 in	6	-
Concrete, cement		
Ballast	-	140
Brick	-	115
Clinker	-	95
Pumice	-	70
Reinforced (about 2% steel).		150
Cork slabs 1 in thick	1	-
Fibre boards		
1/2 in thick	3/4	-
Compressed 1/4 in thick.	2/3	-
Fibrous plaster 5/8 in thick	3	-
Flooring		
1/4 in Rubber	2 3/4	-
1 in (Nominal) softwood	2 1/4	-
1 in (Nominal) pitchpine	3	-
1 in (Nominal) hardwood	3 1/4	-
Glass, 1/4 in plate	3 1/2	-
Gravel	-	115
Lime, chalk	-	44
Partition slabs (solid)		
2 in Coke breeze or pumice	11 1/2	-
2 in Clinker	15	-
2 in Terrazzo	25	-
Partition slabs (hollow)		
2 in Coke breeze or pumice	9 1/4	-
2 in Clinker	11 1/2	-
2 in Moler	2 1/2	-
Reconstructed stone	-	145

Material	lb per ft²	lb per ft³
Plastering		
3/4 in Lime or gypsum	7 1/2	-
on lathing	8 3/4	-
Roof boarding, 1 in	2 1/2	-
Sand, pit	-	90
river	-	120
Shingle	-	90
Slag wool	-	17
Slate 1 in slab	15	-
Slating, 3 in lap		
Cornish (medium)	7 1/2	-
Welsh (medium)	8 1/2	-
Westmorland (medium)	11 1/2	-
Westmorland (thin)	9	-
Terrazzo pavings 5/8 in	7	-
Tiling, roof		
Machine made 4 in gauge.	13	-
Hand made 4 in gauge	14	-
Tiling floor (1/2 in)	5 3/4	-
wall (3/8 in)	4	-
Timber, seasoned		
Elm	-	39
Baltic Fir	-	35-38
Red Pine	-	40
Yellow Pine	-	28
Douglas Fir	-	33
Canadian Spruce	-	29
White Pine	-	27
Yellow Birch	-	44
Canadian Maple	-	47
Honduras Mahogany	-	34
Spanish Mahogany	-	44
English Oak	-	45
American Oak	-	47
Baltic Oak	-	46
Indian Teak	-	41
African Teak	-	60
Blackbean	-	40-47
Water	-	62 1/2
rain	-	62 1/2
sea	-	64

This page left blank intentionally

METRIC & IMPERIAL SYSTEMS

SYMBOLS USED

Length	m =	linear metre
	cm =	linear centimetre
	mm =	linear millimetre
Area	m^2 =	square metre
	cm^2 =	square centimetre
	mm^2 =	square millimetre
Volume	m^3 =	cubic metre
	cm^3 =	cubic centimetre
	mm^3 =	cubic millimetre
Mass	kg =	kilogramme
	g =	gram
Pressure	N/m^2 =	Newton per square metre
Density	kg/m =	kilogrammes per linear metre
	kg/m^3 =	kilogrammes per cubic metre

METRIC SYSTEM – WEIGHTS & MEASURES

LENGTH

1000 picometres	= 1 nanometre
1000 nanometres	= 1 micrometre
1000 micrometres	= 1 millimetre
10 millimetres	= 1 centimetre
10 centimetres	= 1 decimetre
1000 millimetres	= 1 metre
100 centimetres	= 1 metre
100 metres	= 1 hectometre
1000 metres	= 1 kilometre
1000 kilometres	= 1 megametre
1852 nautical metres	= 1 international nautical mile

AREA

100 sq millimetres	= 1 sq centimetre
100 sq centimetres	= 1 sq decimetre
10000 sq centimetres	= 1 sq metre
100 sq metres	= 1 are
10 ares	= 1 dekare
10000 sq metres	= 1 hectare
100 hectares	= 1 sq kilometre

VOLUME AND CAPACITY

1000 cu millimetres	= 1 cu centimetre
1000 cu centimetres	= 1 cu decimetre
1000 cu decimetres	= 1 cu metre
1000 cu metres	= 1 cu dekametre
1000 cu dekametres	= 1 cu hectometre
1000 cu hectometre	= 1 cu kilometre
1000 microlitres	= 1 millilitres (1cc)
10 millilitres	= 1 centilitre
10 centilitres	= 1 decilitre
1000 millilitres	= 1 litre
100 centilitres	= 1 litre
1000 litres	= 1 kilolitre
1000 litres	= 1 cu metre

MASS

1000 nanograms	= 1 microgram
1000 micrograms	= 1 milligram
200 milligrams	= 1 metric carat
1000 milligrams	= 1 gram
25 grams	= 1 metric ounce
100 grams	= 1 hectogram
1000 grams	= 1 kilogram
100 kilograms	= 1 quintal
1000 kilograms	= 1 megagram

FORCE

10 micronewtons	= 1 dyne
1000 micronewtons	= 1 millinewton
10 millinewtons	= 1 centinewton
1000 millinewtons	= 1 newton
1000 newtons	= 1 kilonewton
1000 kilonewtons	= 1 meganewton

VELOCITY

36 km/hour	= 1 metre/second
3600 km/hour	= 1 km/second

ENERGY (WORK AND HEAT)

10000 ergs	= 1 millijoule
1000 millijoules	= 1 joule
1000 joules	= 1 kilojoule
1000 kilojoules	= 1 megajoule
3.6 megajoules	= 1 kilowatt hour
1000 megajoules	= 1 gigajoule
1000 gigajoules	= 1 terajoule

POWER

1000 microwatts	= 1 milliwatt
1000 milliwatts	= 1 watt
1000 watts	= 1 kilowatt
1000 kilowatts	= 1 megawatt
1000 gigawatts	= 1 terawatt

PRESSURE AND STRESS

1000 micropascals	= 1 millipascal
100 millipascals	= 1 microbar
1000 millipascals	= 1 pascal
100 pascals	= 1 millibar
1000 pascals	= 1 kilopascal
1000 millibars	= 1 bar
1000 kilopascals	= 1 megapascal
1000 bars	= 1 kilobar
1000 megapascals	= 1 gigapascal

ELECTRICITY AND MAGNETISM

1000 picoamperes	= 1 nanoampere
1000 nanoamperes	= 1 microampere
1000 microamperes	= 1 milliampere
1000 milliamperes	= 1 ampere
1000 amperes	= 1 kiloampere
1000 millicoulombs	= 1 coulomb
1000 coulombs	= 1 kilocoulomb
1000 microvolts	= 1 millivolt
1000 millivolts	= 1 volt
1000 volts	= 1 kilovolt
1000 kilovolts	= 1 megavolt
1000 microhms	= 1 milliohm
1000 milliohms	= 1 ohm
1000 ohms	= 1 kilohms
1000 kilohms	= 1 megaohm
1000 millisiemens	= 1 siemen
1000 millihenrys	= 1 henry
1000 milliteslas	= 1 tesla

FREQUENCY

1000 hertz	= 1 kilohertz
1000 kilohertz	= 1 megahertz
1000 megahertz	= 1 gigahertz
1000 gigahertz	= 1 terahertz
1000 terahertz	= 1 petahertz
1000 petahertz	= 1 exahertz

IMPERIAL SYSTEM – WEIGHTS AND MEASURES

LINEAL MEASURE

225 in	= 1 nail
3 in	= 1 palm
4 in	= 1 hand
9 in or 4 nails	= span, or 1/4 yd
12 in	= 1 ft
3 ft or 4 quarters	= 1 yd
5 quarters of yd	= 1 ell
6 ft or 2 yd	= 1 fathom
16 ft 6 in or 55 yd	= 1 rod, pole or perch
4 poles or 22 yd	= 1 chain
220 yd or 40 poles	= 1 furlong
1760 yd or 8 furlongs	= 1 mile or 5280 ft
792 in	= 1 link
100 links or 66 ft	= 1 chain
10 chains	= 1 furlong
80 chains	= 1 mile
3 miles	= 1 league
2027 yd	= 1 Admiralty knot
60755 ft	= 1 nautical mile
The Cheshire pole	= 8 yd
6904 miles	= 1 degree of latitude
6916 miles	= 1 degree of longitude at Equator
4308 miles	= 1 degree of longitude at London

SQUARE MEASURE

144 in^2	= 1 ft^2
10 square chains	= 1 acre
9 ft^2	= 1 yd^2
30 acres	= 1 yard land
100 ft^2	= 1 square
100 acres	= 1 hide
27225 ft^2	= 1 rod, pole or perch
460 acres	= 1 square mile
3025 yd^2	= 1 rod, pole or perch
40 square rods	= 1 rood
7840 yd^2	= 1 Irish acre
43560 ft^2	= 1 acre
6084 yd^2	= 1 Scotch acre
677264 in^2	= 1 square link
4 roods or 4840 yd^2	= 1 acre
1 mile by 1 chain	= 8 acres
1 mile by 80 chains	= 1 square mile
10000 square links	= 1 square chain

SOLID OR CUBIC MEASURE

1728 in^3	= 1 ft^3
327 ft^3	= 1 yd^3
42 ft^3 of timber	= 1 shipping ton
108 ft^3	= 1 stack of wood
165 ft^3	= 1 standard of wood
128 ft^3	= 1 cord of wood

IMPERIAL SYSTEM – WEIGHTS AND MEASURES (Cont'd)

AVOIRDUPOIS WEIGHT

16 drachms	= 1 ounce
20 cwt	= 1 ton
16 ounces	= 1 lb
7000 grains	= 1 lb avoirdupois
28 lb	= 1 qr cwt
4375 grains	= 1 oz avoirdupois
112 lb	= 1 cwt

TROY WEIGHT

24 grains	= 1 dwt
5760 grains	= 1 lb troy
20 dwts	= 1 ounce
480 grains	= 1 oz troy
12 ounces	= 1 lb

DRY MEASURE

2 gal	= 1 peck
6232 gal	= 1 ft^3
8 gal	= 1 bushel
168264 gal	= 1 yd^3
64 gal	= 1 quarter
4893 gal	= 1 cyl ft

LIQUID MEASURE

8665 in^2	= 1 gill
4 gills	= 1 pint
2 pints	= 1 quart
4 quarts	= 1 gal
1 gal	= 27725 in^3 or 016 ft^3
1 ft^3	= 6232 gal
1 cwt water	= 18 ft^3
1 bushel	= 128 ft
38 gal	= 1 bushel

An imperial gallon of water weighs 10 lb at 62 degrees F

CONVERSION FACTORS

To convert items priced in Imperial units into Metric or vice versa, multiply by the following conversion factors.

Priced units	£ Factor
Linear feet to linear metres	3.281
Linear yards to linear metres	1.094
Square feet to square metres	10.764
Square yards to square metres	1.196
Cubic feet to cubic metres	35.315
Cubic yards to cubic metres	1.308
Pounds to kilogrammes	2.2046
Cwts (hundredweight) to kilogrammes	0.0196
Cwts to tonnes	19.684
Tons to tonnes	0.9842
Gallons to litres	0.22

Priced units	£ Factor
Linear metres to linear feet	0.3048
Linear metres to linear yards	0.9144
Square metres to square feet	0.0929
Square metres to square yards	0.8361
Cubic metres to cubic feet	0.028
Cubic metres to cubic yards	0.7645
Kilogrammes to pounds	0.454
Kilogrammes to cwts	50.802
Tonnes to cwts	0.051
Tonnes to tons	1.0161
Litres to gallons	4.54

To convert Imperial weights and measures into Metric or vice versa, multiply by the following conversion factors.

	Factor
Length	
Inches to millimetres (mm)	25.4
Feet to metres (m)	0.3048
Yards to metres (m)	0.9144
Area	
Square feet to square metres (m^2)	0.0929
Square yards to ditto	0.8361
Volume	
Cubic feet to cubic metres (m^3)	0.0283
Cubic yards to ditto	0.7645
Mass	
Tons (2240 lbs) to tonnes	1.0161
Cwts to kilogrammes	50.802
Pounds to kilogrammes (kg)	0.454
Ounces to grammes (g)	28.35
Pressure	
Pounds per square inch to Newtons per square metre (N/mm2)	6894.8
Density	
Pounds per linear foot to kilogrammes per linear metre (kg/m)	1.488
Pounds per square foot to kilogrammes per metre (k/m2)	4.882
Pounds per square yard to ditto	0.542
Pounds per cubic foot to kilogrammes per cubic metre (kg/m3)	16.019
Capacity	
Gallons to litres	4.546

	Factor
Length	
Millimetres to inches	0.0394
Metres to feet	3.281
Metres to yards	1.094
Area	
Square metres to square feet	10.764
Ditto to square yards	1.196
Volume	
Cubic metres to cubic feet	35.315
Ditto to cubic yards	1.308
Mass	
Tonnes (1000 kg) to tons	0.9842
Kilogrammes to cwts	0.0196
Kilogrammes to pounds	2.205
Grammes to ounces	0.0353
Pressure	
Newtons per square metre to pounds per square inch	0.000145
Density	
Kilogrammes per linear metre to Pounds per linear foot	0.672
Kilogrammes per square metre to Pounds per square foot	0.2048
Ditto to pounds per square yard	1.845
Kilogrammes per cubic metre to Pounds per cubic foot	0.0624
Capacity	
Litres to gallons	0.22

CONVERSION FACTORS (Cont'd)

METRIC EQUIVALENTS

Linear inches to linear millimetres — 1 inch = 25.4 millimetres

Inches	0	1	2	3	4	5	6	7	8	9	10	11
0		25.40	50.80	76.20	101.60	127.00	152.40	177.80	203.20	228.60	154.00	279.40
1/32	0.79	26.19	51.59	76.99	102.39	127.79	153.19	178.59	203.99	229.39	254.79	280.19
1/16	1.59	26.99	52.39	77.79	103.19	128.59	153.99	179.39	204.79	230.19	255.59	280.99
3/32	2.38	27.78	53.18	78.58	103.98	129.38	154.78	180.18	205.58	230.98	256.38	281.78
1/8	3.18	28.58	53.98	79.38	104.78	130.18	155.58	180.98	206.38	231.78	257.18	282.58
5/32	3.97	29.37	54.77	80.17	105.57	130.97	156.37	181.77	207.17	232.57	257.97	283.37
3/16	4.76	30.16	55.56	80.96	106.36	131.76	157.16	182.56	207.96	233.36	258.76	284.16
7/32	5.56	30.96	56.36	81.76	107.16	132.56	157.96	183.36	208.76	234.16	259.56	284.96
1/4	6.35	31.75	57.15	82.55	107.95	133.35	158.75	184.15	209.55	234.95	260.35	285.75
3/8	9.53	34.93	60.33	85.73	111.13	136.53	161.93	187.33	212.73	238.13	263.53	288.93
1/2	12.70	38.10	63.50	88.90	114.30	139.70	165.10	190.50	215.90	241.30	266.70	292.10
5/8	15.88	41.28	66.68	92.08	117.48	142.88	168.28	193.68	219.08	244.48	269.88	295.28
3/4	19.05	44.45	69.85	95.25	120.65	146.05	171.45	196.85	222.25	247.65	273.05	298.45
7/8	22.23	47.63	98.43	98.43	123.83	149.23	174.63	200.03	225.43	150.83	276.23	301.63

Linear feet and inches to linear millimetres — 1 foot = 304.80 millimetres

Feet	1	2	3	4	5	6	7	8	9	10	11	12
0 in	304.8	609.6	914.4	1219.2	1524.0	1828.8	2133.6	2438.4	2743.2	3048.0	3352.8	3657.6
1 in	330.2	635.0	939.8	1244.6	1549.4	1854.2	2159.0	2463.8	2768.6	3073.4	3378.2	2683.0
2 in	355.6	660.4	965.2	1270.0	1574.8	1879.6	2184.4	2489.2	2794.0	3098.8	3403.6	3708.4
3 in	381.0	385.8	990.6	1295.4	1600.2	1905.0	2209.8	2514.6	2819.4	3124.2	3429.0	3733.8
4 in	406.4	711.2	1016.0	1320.8	1625.6	1930.4	2235.2	2540.0	2844.8	3149.6	3454.4	3759.2
5 in	431.8	736.6	1041.4	1346.4	1651.0	1955.8	2260.6	2565.4	2870.2	3175.0	3479.8	3784.6
6 in	457.2	762.0	1066.8	1371.6	1676.4	1981.2	2286.0	2590.8	2895.6	3200.4	3505.2	3810.0
7 in	482.6	787.4	1092.2	1397.0	1701.8	2006.6	2311.4	2616.2	2921.0	3225.8	3530.6	3835.4
8 in	508.0	812.8	1117.6	1422.4	1727.2	2032.0	2336.8	2641.6	2946.4	3251.2	3556.0	3860.8
9 in	533.4	838.2	1143.0	1447.8	1752.6	2057.4	2362.2	2667.0	2971.8	3276.6	3581.4	3886.2
10 in	558.8	863.6	1168.4	1473.2	1778.0	2082.8	2387.6	2692.4	2997.2	3302.0	3606.8	3911.6
11 in	584.2	889.0	1193.8	1498.6	1803.4	2108.2	2413.0	2717.8	3022.6	3327.4	3632.2	3937.0

IMPERIAL EQUIVALENTS

Linear millimetres to linear inches — 1 millimetre = 0.03937 inches

mm	0	10	20	30	40	50	60	70	80	90	100
0		0.394"	0.787"	1.181"	1.575"	1.969"	2.362"	2.756"	3.15"	3.543"	3.937"
1	0.039"	0.433"	0.827"	1.22"	1.614"	2.008"	2.402"	2.795"	3.189"	3.583"	3.976"
2	0.079"	0.472"	0.866"	1.26"	1.654"	2.047"	2.441"	2.835"	3.228"	3.622"	4.016"
3	0.118"	0.512"	0.906"	1.299"	1.693"	2.087"	2.48"	2.874"	3.268"	3.661"	4.055"
4	0.157"	0.551"	0.945"	1.339"	1.732"	2.126"	2.52"	2.913"	3.307"	3.701"	4.094"
5	0.197"	0.591"	0.984"	1.378"	1.772"	2.165"	2.559"	2.953"	3.346"	3.74"	4.134"
6	0.236"	0.63"	1.024"	1.417"	1.811"	2.205"	2.598"	2.992"	3.386"	3.78"	4.173"
7	0.276"	0.669"	1.063"	1.457"	1.85"	2.244"	2.638"	3.031"	3.425"	3.819"	4.213"
8	0.315"	0.709"	1.102"	1.496"	1.89"	2.283"	2.677"	3.071"	3.465"	3.858"	4.252"
9	0.354"	0.748"	1.142"	1.535"	1.929"	2.323"	2.717"	3.11"	3.504"	3.898"	4.291"

Linear metres to linear feet and inches — 1 metre = 3 feet and 3.37 inches

m	0	1	2	3	4	5	6	7	8	9	10
0.0		3' 3.4"	6' 6.7"	9' 10.1"	13' 1.5"	16' 4.9"	19' 8.2"	22' 11.6"	26' 3"	29' 6.3"	32' 9.7"
0.1	3.9"	3' 7.3"	6' 10.7"	10' 2"	13' 5.4"	16' 8.8"	20' 0.2"	23' 3.5"	26' 6.9"	29' 10.3"	33' 1.6"
0.2	7.9"	3' 11.2"	7' 2.6"	10' 6"	13' 9.4"	17' 0.7"	20' 4.1"	23' 7.5"	26' 10.8"	30' 2.2"	33' 5.6"
0.3	11.8"	4' 3.2"	7' 6.6"	10' 9.9"	14' 1.3"	17' 4.7"	20' 8"	23' 11.4"	27' 2.8"	30' 6.1"	33' 9.5"
0.4	1' 3.7"	4' 7.1"	7' 10.5"	11' 1.9"	14' 5.2"	17' 8.6"	20' 12"	24' 3.3"	27' 6.7"	30' 10.1"	34' 1.4"
0.5	1' 7.7"	4' 11.1"	8' 2.4"	11' 5.8"	14' 9.2"	18' 0.5"	21' 3.9"	24' 7.3"	27' 10.6"	31' 2"	34' 5.4"
0.6	1' 11.6"	5' 3"	8' 6.4"	11' 9.7"	15' 1.1"	18' 4.5"	21' 7.8"	24' 11.2"	28' 2.6"	31' 6"	34' 9.3"
0.7	2' 3.6"	5' 6.9"	8' 10.3"	12' 1.7"	15' 5"	18' 8.4"	21' 11.8"	25' 3.1"	28' 6.5"	31' 9.9"	35' 1.3"
0.8	2' 7.5"	5' 10.9"	9' 2.2"	12' 5.6"	15' 9"	19' 0.3"	22' 3.7"	25' 7.1"	28' 10.5"	32' 1.8"	35' 5.2"
0.9	2' 11.4"	6' 2.8"	9' 6.2"	12' 9.5"	16' 0.9"	19' 4.3"	22' 7.7"	25' 11"	29' 2.4"	32' 5.8"	35' 9.1"

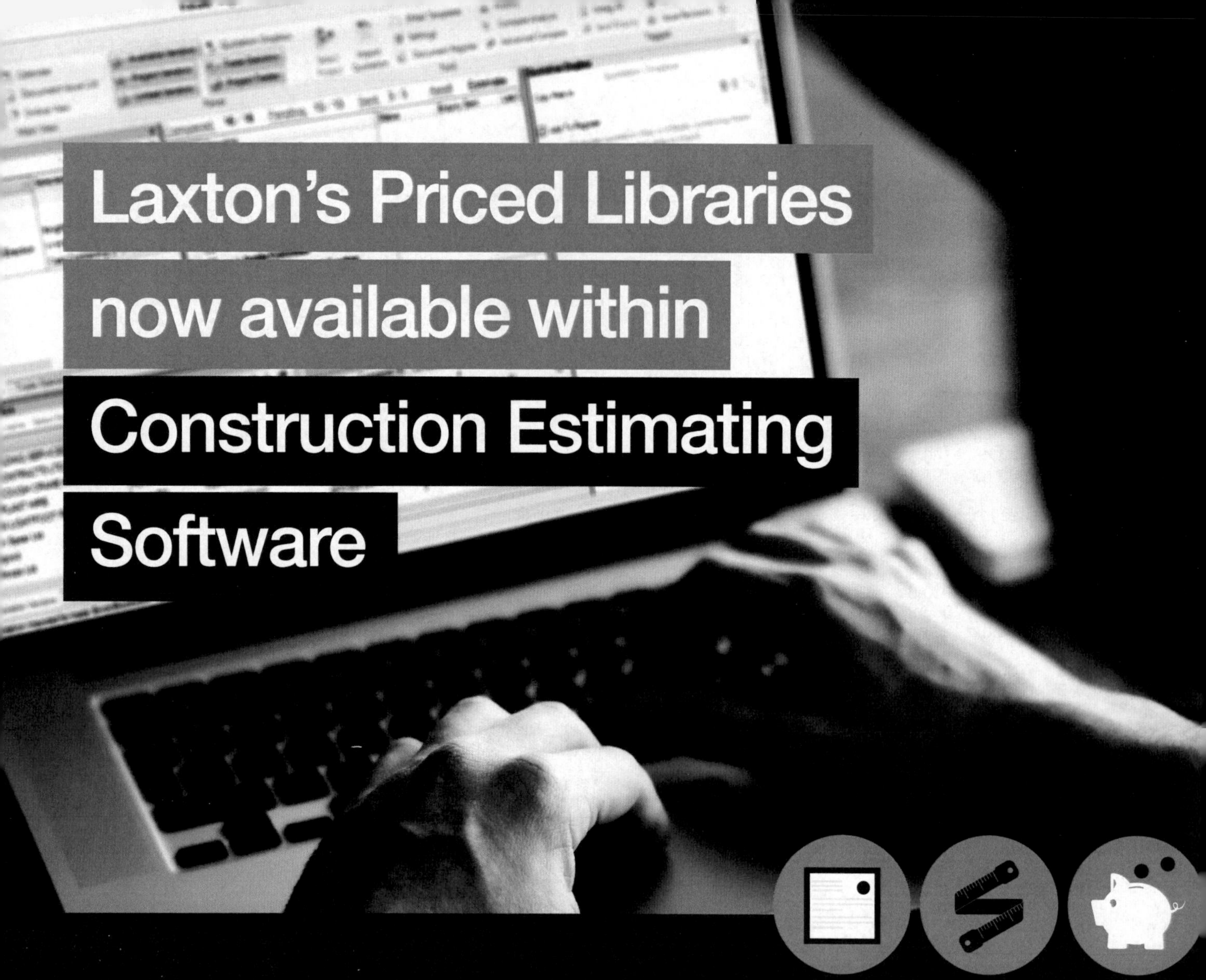

BRANDS AND TRADE NAMES

7 - Interclad (UK) Ltd
202 - Sapa Building Systems (monarch and glostal)
238 - Chalmit Lighting
325 - Sapa Building Systems (monarch and glostal)
(IPAF Training) - Turner Access Ltd
(PASMA Training) - Turner Access Ltd
'Airtec Stone' by Alsecco - Telling Architectural Ltd
>B< Range : >B< ACR, >B< Oyster, >B< Press, >B< Press Carbon Steel, >B< Press Gas, >B< Press Inox, >B< Press Solar, >B< Press Tools, >B< Push - Conex Universal Limited
0.35 Loft Match - Polypipe Building Products
100 High - Hudevad Britain
1581 Silicone - Dunbrik (Yorks) Ltd
1890's (GA) - Barber Wilsons & Co Ltd
20/20 Interlocking clay plain (tile) - Sandtoft Roof Tiles Ltd
25/40/56 Series - Albany Standard Pumps
3 Step Mat - Dycem Ltd
316 Range - James Gibbons Format Ltd
3230 Classic Fibre Bonded Carpet - Burmatex Ltd
3500 Range - EcoWater Systems Ltd
3BoxStack™ - Straight Ltd
3D Range - Twyford Bathrooms
3Dlockers - 3d Storage Systems (UK) LTD
3G Synthetic Turf - Charles Lawrence Surfaces Ltd
3M - Kenyon Paints Limited
3M Commercial Graphics - Northgate Solar Controls
4000 home lift - Gartec Ltd
4200 Sidewalk fibre bonded carpet - Burmatex Ltd
425 Range - Horstmann Controls Ltd
4250 Alarm Confirmation - ADT Fire and Security Plc
4400 Broadway fibre bonded carpet - Burmatex Ltd
500 Series - Opella Ltd
6000 home lift - Gartec Ltd
7000 Flexi - Gartec Ltd
7000 platform lift - Gartec Ltd
7000XT - Gartec Ltd
800 Series conventional call systems - C-TEC (Computionics) Ltd
900 Series - Weir Pumps Ltd
9000 cabin lift - Gartec Ltd
9235 Waterproof membrane - Laticrete International Inc. UK

A

A + K - Anders + Kern UK Ltd
A Division of Castle House Joinery - Orchard Street Furniture
A F Jones Stonemasons - A. F Jones (Stonemasons)
A1 Concrete Flue Liners - Dunbrik (Yorks) Ltd
Aaztec - Aaztec Cubicles
Aaztec Associates Limited - Aaztec Cubicles
Aaztec Health - Aaztec Cubicles
Abacus - Smart F & G (Shopfittings)Ltd
Abacus Lighting Ltd - Abacus Lighting Ltd
Abacus, Aeon, Alien, Arat, Atilla - Pitacs Ltd
Abanaki - TEAM INDUSTRIAL SERVICES (UK) LIMITED
Abbeydale - Chiltern Invadex
Abbotsford - Brintons Ltd
ABFT - Fire Industry Association
ABG - Ingersoll-Rand European Sales Ltd
ABK - Arnull Bernard J & Co Ltd
Abloy - ASSA ABLOY Limited
Abloy Disklock Pro - Abloy UK
Abloy Exec - Abloy UK
Abloy High Profile - Abloy UK
Abloy Protec - Abloy UK
Aborslot - Jones of Oswestry Ltd
ABS Floors - Maxit UK
ABS Pumps - Sulzer Pumps Wastewater UK Ltd
AbSence/ PreSense - Philips Lighting Solutions
Absolute - Johnson Tiles
Abtex - ABG Ltd
AC - Howden Buffalo
AC 2000 - CEM Systems Ltd
AC 2000 Airport - CEM Systems Ltd
AC 2000 Lite - CEM Systems Ltd
Academy Bedrooms - Moores Furniture Group Ltd
Acare - ArjoHuntleigh UK
ACAS - Advisory, Conciliation and Arbitration Service
AccentHansen - HansenFacades
Accents (noticeboards) - Spaceright Europe Limited
Access - Gradus Ltd
Access Ramp - Sportsmark Group Ltd
Access Steps - Sportsmark Group Ltd
Acclaim - Chalmit Lighting
Acclaim - Dudley Thomas Ltd
Acclaim - Sidhil Care
Accoflex - DLW Flooring
Accolade - Gledhill Water Storage Ltd
Accolade - Heatrae Sadia Heating Ltd
Accord - Stocksigns Ltd
Accorroni - May William (Ashton) Ltd
Accuro - Draeger Safety UK Ltd
Accu-Tune - IAC Acoustic Company UK Ltd
Acczent - Tarkett Ltd
ACE - Association for Consultancy and Engineering (ACE)
ACF DuraLED - Whitecroft Lighting Limited
ACH - Acoustic Ceiling Hangers - Christie & Grey Ltd
Ackermann Spider - Ackermann Ltd
Acklaim - Ackermann Ltd
Acknowledge - Ackermann Ltd
Ackwire - Ackermann Ltd
ACO Building Drainage - ACO Technologies plc
ACO Commercial Gully - ACO Technologies plc
ACO FreeDeck - ACO Technologies plc
ACO HexDrain® - ACO Technologies plc
ACO KerbDrain - ACO Technologies plc
ACO Modular 125 - ACO Technologies plc
ACO MultiDrain™ - ACO Technologies plc
ACO RainDrain® - ACO Technologies plc
ACO StormBrixx - ACO Technologies plc
ACO Water Management - ACO Technologies plc
Acorn - Oakdale (Contracts) Ltd
Acorn, Axis - TBS Amwell Ltd
Acoustic Vents - Simon R W Ltd
Acousticel - Bicester Products Ltd
Acousticel M20AD - Sound Service (Oxford) Ltd
Acousticel R10 - Sound Service (Oxford) Ltd
Acousticurtain - Acousticabs Industrial Noise Control Ltd
Acoustifoam - Acousticabs Industrial Noise Control Ltd
Acoustilay - Sound Reduction Systems Ltd
Acoustilouvre - Acousticabs Industrial Noise Control Ltd
ACOVA - Zehnder Group UK Ltd
ACP - ACP (Concrete) Ltd
Acrylacote - Dacrylate Paints Ltd
Acrylic 2 - Dufaylite Developments Ltd
ACT - Artur Fischer (UK) Ltd
Actimatic - Wade International Ltd
Actionair - Swegon Air Management Ltd
Activ - Pilkington Birmingham
ActiV conventional fire detectors - C-TEC (Computionics) Ltd
Activa - Full Spectrum Fluorescent Tubes - FEILO SYLVANIA EUROPE LIMITED
Active 8 - Gas Measurement Instruments Ltd
Activent - Fläkt Woods Ltd
Activity Floor - British Harlequin Plc
Activ-Ox - Feedwater Ltd
AD11 - Tapworks Water Softeners
Adam Equipment - Phoenix Scales Ltd
Adams Rite - ASSA ABLOY Limited
Adaptalok - Adaptaflex Ltd
Adaptaring - Adaptaflex Ltd
Adaptaseal - Adaptaflex Ltd
Adaptasteel - Adaptaflex Ltd
Adash - Cil Retail Solutions Ltd
Adcor - GCP APPLIED TECHNOLOGIES (UK) LIMITED
Addabound - Addagrip Terraco Ltd
Addaflor - Addagrip Terraco Ltd
Addagrip1000 System - Addagrip Terraco Ltd
Addalevel - Addagrip Terraco Ltd
Addaprime - Addagrip Terraco Ltd
Addaset - Addagrip Terraco Ltd
Addastone, Addastone TP - Addagrip Terraco Ltd
Addinox - Venator
Adhesin - Henkel Ltd
Adhesives Toolkit - TWI Ltd
Adjusta Kitchens - Moores Furniture Group Ltd
Adjustable Support Pedestals - Buzon UK
Adjustable Support Pedestals and accessories - Buzon UK
Admatic - Potter & Soar Ltd
Adorn - Valor
ADPRO - Xtralis
Adria Perla - Armstrong World Industries Ltd
Adroit - Airflow Developments Ltd
ADS - Schueco UK
ADT - Tyco Fire and Integrated Solutions
Adva - GCP APPLIED TECHNOLOGIES (UK) LIMITED
Advance - Nilfisk Advance Ltd
Advance - Tata Steel Europe Limited
Advance Matt Gaffa - Advance Tapes International Ltd
Advance Premier Closure Plate Tape - Advance Tapes International Ltd
Advantage - Dixon Turner Wallcoverings
Advantage - Saint-Gobain Ecophon Ltd
Advantage Respirators - MSA (Britain) Ltd
AEG - Electrolux Domestic Appliances
AELtherm Packaged Plate Heat Exchangers - AEL
Aercon - Aercon Consultants Ltd
Aerodyne cowl - Brewer Metalcraft
AET - AET.gb Ltd
AF29 Anti-Fracture for tile and stone - Carter-Dal International
Afasil - Illbruck Sealant Systems UK Ltd
Affinity - Hille Educational Products Ltd
Affinity Disposable Respirtiors - MSA (Britain) Ltd
Afghan - Carpets of Worth Ltd
A-Frame Picnic Suite - Branson Leisure Ltd
Agabekov - Crescent Lighting
Agastat - ABB Installation Products Ltd
Agglio Conglomerate Marble - Reed Harris - Reed Harris
Agglosimplex Conglomerate Marble - Marble Flooring Spec. Ltd
Agito - HAGS SMP
Agrement certificates - British Board of Agrément
Agri Drain - Naylor Drainage Ltd
Aida-DENCO - DencoHappel UK Ltd
Aidalarm - Hoyles Electronic Developments Ltd
Ainsworth OSB - Wood International Agency Ltd
Ainsworth Pourform 107 - Wood International Agency Ltd
Ainsworth Pourform H00 - Wood International Agency Ltd
Air Minder - Vent-Axia
Air Safety Ltd - GVS Filter Technology UK
Air Sentry - S & B Ltd
Airack - Clenaware Systems Ltd
Aircare 2000 series - Aircare Europe Ltd
Aircool® - Passivent Ltd
AirCore®, AirLiner® - Rytons Building Products Ltd
Airdale - Airedale International Air Conditioning Ltd
Airdale Service - Airedale International Air Conditioning Ltd
Airdor - S & P Coil Products Ltd
AirDuct - Airflow (Nicoll Ventilators) Ltd
Airetronix - Airedale International Air Conditioning Ltd
Airfix - Flamco UK Ltd
Airguard - Aquastat Ltd
Airmaster ventilation - SAV United Kingdom Ltd
Airscoop® - Passivent Ltd
Airseal - Fillcrete Ltd
Airspeed - Warner Howard Group Ltd
Airsprung Beds Ltd - Airsprung Beds Ltd
Airstract® - Passivent Ltd
Airstream - PHS Group plc
Airstrip - Simon R W Ltd
Airtec Glass Walling - Telling Architectural Ltd
Airworld - Warner Howard Group Ltd
Aitersall - Deva Tap Co Ltd
AJ - Architects Journal - EMAP
Akademy Classroom System - Portakabin Ltd
Akord - DW Windsor Lighting
Aktivated Showers - Hansgrohe
AkzoNobel - Dulux Trade
AL 50 - SG System Products Ltd
Alag Aggregate - Lafarge Aluminates Ltd
Alarm-a-fence® - Jackson H S & Son (Fencing) Ltd
Alarmline - Linear Heat Detection - Kidde Fire Protection Ltd
AlarmSense - Apollo Fire Detectors Ltd
ALB Difutec Underfloor heating - SAV United Kingdom Ltd
Albany Paints, Wallcoverings, Brushes, Paint rollers - Brewer C & Sons Ltd
Albany Plus - MK (MK Electric Ltd)
Albi-Grips - Albion Manufacturing Ltd
Albion - Swedecor
Albi-Slings - Albion Manufacturing Ltd
Albi-Traps - Albion Manufacturing Ltd
Alclad - Solair Ltd
Alco Controls - Emerson Climate Technologies
Alcona Range - Twyford Bathrooms
ALD - ALD Lighting Solutions
Aldwark - York Handmade Brick Co Ltd
Alfacryl - Illbruck Sealant Systems UK Ltd
Alfapower - M.J. Electronic Services (International) Ltd
Alfas - Illbruck Sealant Systems UK Ltd
Alfas Bond FR - Compriband Ltd
Alfix - Baj System Design Ltd
Aligator - Alutec
Aligator ® - Marley Plumbing and Drainage
Alimaster Shelving - Bedford Shelving Ltd
Alimat - Watts Industries UK Ltd
Aline - Cil Retail Solutions Ltd
Alitherm - Smart Systems Ltd
ALKORBRIGHT - RENOLIT Cramlington Limited
ALKORDESIGN - RENOLIT Cramlington Limited
ALKORGREEN - RENOLIT Cramlington Limited
ALKORPLAN - RENOLIT Cramlington Limited
ALKORPLUS - RENOLIT Cramlington Limited
ALKORSOLAR - RENOLIT Cramlington Limited
ALKORTOP - RENOLIT Cramlington Limited
Alkysil - Dacrylate Paints Ltd
All in one sealer - Sealocrete PLA Ltd
All Range - Twyford Bathrooms
Allart Deco - Allart, Frank, & Co Ltd
AllClear - Lakes Bathrooms Limited
Allegra - Hansgrohe
Allegro - Erlau AG
Allen Bradley - Electrix International Ltd
Allergi Guard - GVS Filter Technology UK Ltd
Allgood Hardware - Allgood plc
Allgood Secure - Allgood plc
Allied Kingswood - Waterline Limited
alligator entrance matting - Jaymart Rubber & Plastics Ltd
Allmat - Allmat (East Surrey) Ltd
AL-OR - Harbro Supplies Ltd
Alpha - Titan Pollution Control - Part of The Kingspan Group
Alpha 24 Secure - Premdor
Alpha Cool - Airedale International Air Conditioning Ltd
Alpha Design 24 - Premdor
Alpha scan - Milliken Carpet
Alpha, Alpha Flow, Alpha Kerb, Alpha Antique - Brett Landscaping
Alphaline - ABG Ltd
Alpolic - Euroclad Ltd
ALPOLIC®/fr - Booth Muirie
Altholz - LSA Projects Ltd
Althon - Althon Ltd
Althon-Lite - Althon Ltd
Altitude - Dunhams of Norwich
Alto - Ideal-Standard Ltd
Altro PU - Altro Ltd
Altroscreed Quartz - Altro Ltd
Altrosmooth - Altro Ltd
Altrotimber - Altro Ltd
Alu - Aluline Precision Engineering Ltd
ALU - Osram Ltd
Alu Combi, Alu Dano, Alu Intro, Alu Rapid, Alu Rapid Junior, Alu Rapid Super and Alu Top staging - CPS Manufacturing Co
Alucobond® - Booth Muirie
Aluglas - Clow Group Ltd
Aluglaze - Panel Systems Ltd
Alu-Lift portable aluminium gantry crane - Metreel Ltd
Aluma - Sapphire Balustrades
Alumatilt - Caldwell Hardware (UK) Ltd
Aluminex - HW Architectural Ltd
Aluminium Systems - Barlow Group
aluminium/hybrid curtain walling, windows and doors - Senior Aluminium Systems plc
Alutec - Marley Plumbing and Drainage
AluTrap - Aluline Precision Engineering Ltd
Aluzinc - SSAB Swedish Steel Ltd
AluZorb - Aluline Precision Engineering Ltd
Aluzyme - Aluline Precision Engineering Ltd
Alwitra - ICB (International Construction Bureau) Ltd
Ama Drainer - KSB Ltd
Amadeus-equipment - Amadeus
Ama-Drainer Box - KSB Ltd
Ama-porter - KSB Ltd
Ama-Porter ICS - KSB Ltd
Amarex - KSB Ltd
Amazon - Potter & Soar Ltd
Amazon Filters - Barr & Wray Ltd
Ambi-deck - Redman Fisher Engineering
Ambi-Rad - AmbiRad Ltd
Amdega - Amdega Ltd
Amercoat - Kenyon Group Ltd
Amercoat - PPG Protective and Marine Coatings
Amerlock - Kenyon Group Ltd
Ameron - Andrews Coatings Ltd
AMF - Knauf AMF Ceilings Ltd
Amida - Genie Europe
Amie - Tunstal Healthcare (UK) Ltd
AmiLake Solutions - Amilake Southern Ltd
AMIRAN Anti-Reflective Glass - SCHOTT UK Ltd
AML Connections Ltd - Keyline Civils Specialist Ltd
Amore - Brockway Carpets Ltd
AMP - Tyco Fire and Integrated Solutions
Amphistoma - Adams- Hydraulics Ltd
Amtico - The Amtico Company
Ancestry - Ibstock Brick Ltd
Ancon - Ancon Limited
AnconOptima - Ancon Limited
Anda-Crib - PHI Group Ltd
Anders & Kern - Anders + Kern UK Ltd
Anderton - Grange Fencing Limited
Anderton interloc - Anderton Concrete Products Ltd
Andrews - Andrews Sykes Hire Ltd
Andrews Air Conditioning - Andrews Sykes Hire Ltd
Andrews Heat for Hire - Andrews Sykes Hire Ltd
Andromeda, APC - Schneider Electric Ltd
Andura - Andura Coatings Ltd
Anglepoise - Anglepoise Lighting Ltd
Angletie - Redifix Ltd
Anglian - Invicta Window Films Ltd
Anglo - Quiligotti Terrazzo Tiles Limited
Ankalok Revetment - Ruthin Precast Concrete Ltd
Anki - Sparkes K & L
Annabelle Classique - Brintons Ltd
Anolight - Gooding Aluminium
Anstone® (Stone Walling) - Forticrete Walling Stone
Antel - Andrews Coatings Ltd
Anti Climb - Andura Coatings Ltd
Anti fatigue mat - Dycem Ltd
Antique - Samuel Heath & Sons plc
Anti-Social Stud - Sportsmark Group Ltd
AP Acoustic Absorption Panel - Salex Acoustics Limited
Apa plywood - Wood International Agency Ltd
Apache - Ellis Patents
apachestat soft foot - Jaymart Rubber & Plastics Ltd
Aperture - BriggsAmasco
Apex Concrete Garages - Liget Compton
Apex heritage - Alumasc Exterior Building Products Ltd
Apex range - Dixon Turner Wallcoverings
APF International Forestry Exhibition - Confor: Promoting forestry and wood
APHC - Association of Plumbing and Heating Contractors

A (con't)

Apollo incinerators - Combustion Linings Ltd
Apollo Windows - HW Architectural Ltd
APP Liner - Acousticabs Industrial Noise Control Ltd
Apropos - Apropos Conservatories Ltd
APS Masonry Ltd - APS Masonry Ltd
APT Barriers - APT Controls Ltd
APT Bollards (Hydraulic) - APT Controls Ltd
Apton Partitions - Adex Interiors for industry Ltd
APW Ltd - Mevaco Ltd
Aqua - Clear - Aldous & Stamp (Services) Ltd
Aqua Blue Designs - Aqua-Blue Designs
Aqua Tackseal - Tarmac - Specialist Products
AquaBarrier - Mat.Works Flooring Solutions
Aquaboost - Stuart Turner Ltd
AquaCal - HRS Hevac Ltd
Aquachill - J & E Hall Ltd
Aquaflex - Richard Hose Ltd
Aquaflow - Formpave Ltd
Aquaflow ML - Formpave Ltd
Aquaflow® - Forterra Building Products Ltd
Aquafun - Hansgrohe
Aquagrip - Bostik Ltd
Aquagrip - Viking Johnson
Aquaguard - Aquastat Ltd
Aquaheat and Aquaheat SS - Santon
Aquahib - Aquastat Ltd
Aquair, AquaTec - Johnson & Starley
Aqualine - Alumasc Exterior Building Products Ltd
Aqualine - Rangemaster
Aqualine - Santon
Aqualine Range - TBS Amwell Ltd
Aqualock - FIBO UK LTD
Aqualock Surface DPM - Isocrete Floor Screeds Ltd
Aquamac - Schlegel UK (2006) Ltd
Aquamaster - ABB Instrumentation Ltd
Aquaminder - Mode Lighting
Aquamix - Watts Industries UK Ltd
Aquamixa - Aqualisa Products
Aquamodule DHW generator - HRS Hevac Ltd
Aquapanel - Knauf UK
AquaPiv - HRS Hevac Ltd
Aquaprobe - ABB Instrumentation Ltd
Aquarian - Aqualisa Products
Aquarius - Santon
Aquasave - HRS Hevac Ltd
Aquasentry - Aquasentry
Aquasil - Aldous & Stamp (Services) Ltd
Aquaslab - Formpave Ltd
Aquaslot, Aquadish, Aquadrain - Jones of Oswestry Ltd
Aquasol - Conren Ltd
Aquastore - CST Industries, Inc. - UK
Aquastream - Aqualisa Products
Aquastyle - Aqualisa Products
Aquasystems - George Fischer Sales Ltd
Aquatek - Grace De Neef UK
Aquatique - Aqualisa Products
Aquator - Jacopa Limited
Aquavalve - Aqualisa Products
AquaWorks - Mat.Works Flooring Solutions
AR - The Architectural Review - EMAP
Arbo - Adshead Ratcliffe & Co Ltd
Arbocrylic - Adshead Ratcliffe & Co Ltd
Arbofoam - Adshead Ratcliffe & Co Ltd
Arbokol - Adshead Ratcliffe & Co Ltd
Arbomast - Adshead Ratcliffe & Co Ltd
Arboseal - Adshead Ratcliffe & Co Ltd
Arbosil - Adshead Ratcliffe & Co Ltd
Arbothane - Adshead Ratcliffe & Co Ltd
Arc - Illuma Lighting
ARCA - Asbestos Removal Contractors' Association
Arcade - Shackerley (Holdings) Group Ltd incorporating Designer ceramics
Arcadia Pantile - Sandtoft Roof Tiles Ltd
Arcadian - Haddonstone Ltd
Arcadian garden features - Haddonstone Ltd
Arcelik - Beko plc
Archco-Rigidon - Winn & Coales (Denso) Ltd
Archform - Helmsman
Architectural - Protim Solignum Ltd
Architectural Concrete Ltd - Marble Mosaic Co Ltd, The
Architectural Facing Masonry - Lignacite Ltd
Architectural Vinyls - Architectural Textiles Ltd
Architectural Wallcoverings - Architectural Textiles Ltd
Architectural Window Films - Northgate Solar Controls
Architen Landrell Associates Ltd - Architen Landrell Associates Ltd
Archmaster® - Simpson Strong-Tie®
Archtec - Cintec International Ltd
Arcitectural Textiles - Architectural Textiles Ltd
Arcus - Erlau AG
Arcus - Laidlaw Ltd
Ardesia - EBC UK Ltd
Ardex - Ardex UK Ltd
Ardex - R J Stokes & Co Limited
Ardex DPM - Ardex UK Ltd
Ardex Feather Finish - Ardex UK Ltd
Ardex UK Ltd - Ardex UK Ltd
Ardex-flex - Ardex UK Ltd
Arditex - Ardex UK Ltd
Arena - HAGS SMP
arena stadia seating - Metalliform Products Plc
Arena Walsall - Legrand Electric Ltd
ARES - Commercial Lighting Systems
Arezzo-25, Alto and Demi Alto - Lang+Fulton
Argelith - Ancorite Surface Protection Ltd
Argenta - Imperial Machine Co Ltd
ArGeton - Telling Architectural Ltd
Argo - TSE Brownson
Argo-Braze™ - Johnson Matthey PLC - Metal Joining
Ariane Spiral - Loft Centre Products
Aries - Fitzgerald Lighting Ltd
Aritco - Gartec Ltd
Arlon - DLW Flooring
Armabuild - Elwell Buildings Ltd
Armadillo Range - Wybone Ltd
Armaflex - Davant Products Ltd
Armaseam - Alumasc Exterior Building Products Ltd
Armbond - Armstrong (Concrete Blocks), Thomas, Ltd
Armordon - Attwater & Sons Ltd
Armorflex - Armortec
Armorloc - Armortec
Armortec - Armortec
Armourcast - Gillespie (UK) Ltd
armourclad - HMG Paints
Armourguard - HAG Shutters & Grilles Ltd
Armstead - Brewer C & Sons Ltd
Armstead - Dulux Trade
Armstead Trade - AkzoNobel Decorative Paints UK
Armstrong - Kitsons Insulation Products Ltd
Armstrong - Nevill Long
Armstrong - New Forest Ceilings Ltd
Armstrong DLW - Armstrong Floor Products UK Ltd
Armtage - Olby H E & Co Ltd
Aro Pumps - Ingersoll-Rand European Sales Ltd
Arpa - Deralam Laminates Ltd
Arpax - Leigh's Paints
Arpeggio - Rawson Carpets Ltd
Arresta Rail - Unistrut Limited
Arriaga Stone - Stone & Fire
Arroclip - Barlow Group
Arrogard - Barlow Group
Arrolok - Barlow Group
Arrone - HOPPE (UK) Ltd
Arrow - Walls & Ceilings International Ltd
Arstyl - NMC (UK) Ltd
Art Deco Suite - Brass Art Ltd
Artalu - Baj System Design Ltd
Arteco - British Gypsum Ltd
Artemis - Stocksigns Ltd
Artesit - Erlau AG
Artificial Grass - Sportsmark Group Ltd
Artikula - Anglepoise Lighting Ltd
Artile - Johnson Tiles
Artoleum - Forbo Flooring
Arunhithe - Falco UK Ltd
AS Aqua Seal - Consult Lighting Ltd
ASA - Association of Sealant Applicators Ltd (ASA)
Ascari - Dimplex UK Limited
Asco - ASCO Extinguishers Co. Ltd
ASFP - Association of Specialist Fire Protection (ASFP)
Ashbury - Paragon by Heckmondwike
AshDeck™ Structural decking - Ash & Lacy Building Products Ltd
AshFab™ Specialist fabrications - Ash & Lacy Building Products Ltd
AshFix™ Fasteners - Ash & Lacy Building Products Ltd
AshFlow™ Rainwater amangement systems - Ash & Lacy Building Products Ltd
AshGrid™ Spacer support system - Ash & Lacy Building Products Ltd
AshJack™ Lightweight over roof conversion system - Ash & Lacy Building Products Ltd
Ashley - Hager Ltd
Ashmount (cigarette bins) - Glasdon UK Limited
Ashphaltic Roofing Supplies - SIG Roofing
AshScreen™ Solid, perforated and expanded screens - Ash & Lacy Building Products Ltd
AshTech™ Rainscreen cladding - Ash & Lacy Building Products Ltd
AshTray™ Structural trays - Ash & Lacy Building Products Ltd
Ashworth Speedy tester - Protimeter, GE Thermometrics (UK) Ltd
Ashworth Weyrite - Phoenix Scales Ltd
AshZip™ Standing seam roofing system - Ash & Lacy Building Products Ltd
ASIM - Xtralis
ASIS-Y - Optelma Lighting Ltd
Aspect - Dunhams of Norwich
Aspiromatic - Docherty New Vent Chimney Group
Aspirotor - Brewer Metalcraft
Aspirotor - Marflex Chimney Systems
ASR 683 - Monowa Manufacturing (UK) Ltd
ASR, Architectural System Ramps, AeroLight, Accesscentre - Enable Access
Assa Abloy - Mul-T-Lock
Asset seating - CPS Manufacturing Co
Associated Metal - Pland Stainless Ltd
Assure - Tata Steel Colors
Assured Data Sheets - British Board of Agrément
Astera Lighting - LSA Projects Ltd
Astoria - Muraspec
Astra - UTC Fire & Securites
Astra Micra - UTC Fire & Securites
Astralite (minor surgical lamps) - Brandon Medical
Astro - Zellweger Analytic Ltd, Sieger Division
ASX - Hochiki Europe (UK) Ltd
AT ™ - Pressure Coolers Ltd T/A Maestro Pressure Coolers
Atea - Kermi (UK) Ltd
Atelier Sedap - Optelma Lighting Ltd
Athletics – Non Porous Prefabricated System - Charles Lawrence Surfaces Ltd
Athletics - Porous Spray System - Charles Lawrence Surfaces Ltd
Athletics- Non Porous Sandwich System - Charles Lawrence Surfaces Ltd
Athmer - Strand Hardware Ltd
Atlantic - Signs & Labels Ltd
Atlantis - Lotus Water Garden Products Ltd
Atlas - Ellis Patents
Atlas (medical equipment pendants) - Brandon Medical
Atlas (Smart & Brown) - Bernlite Ltd
Atlas Buildings - Severfield (Design & Build) Ltd
Atlas Concorde - Swedecor
Atlas Fire - Tyco Fire and Integrated Solutions
Atox - Aldous & Stamp (Services) Ltd
Audiopath' Voice Alarm Systems - PEL Services Limited
Aura - Eaton Electric Limited
Aura, Aura Kerb - Brett Landscaping
Authentic Collection - Masterframe Windows Ltd
Auto M - Nederman Filtration Ltd
Auto Pile - Skanska UK Plc
Autodor - Garador Ltd
Auto-Freway - Tuke & Bell Ltd
Autoglide - Cardale Garage Doors
Autoglide - Silent Gliss Ltd
AutoKote - GCP APPLIED TECHNOLOGIES (UK) LIMITED
Automat - Dyniq UK Ltd
Automax - Flowserve Flow Control
Autopa - Autopa Ltd
AutoStamp™ Franking & Weighing System - Neopost Ltd
Autostic - Minkon Ltd
Autowalk - Kone Escalators Ltd
Avalon Glass Tiles - Kirkstone
Avance 500 stove - Dunsley Heat Ltd
Avanta - Broag Ltd
Avanti Partitions - Logic Office Contracts
Avanza Benching System - Envopak Group Ltd
Avaya - Connaught Communications Systems Ltd
Avenue - Neptune Outdoor Furniture Ltd
Avenue Dot - Whitecroft Lighting Limited
Avipoint, Avishock - P+L Systems Ltd
avon gutter system - Dales Fabrications Ltd
Avon Industrial Doors Ltd - Avon Industrial Doors Ltd
AWS - Schueco UK
Axa - Hansgrohe
Axcess - Rackline Systems Storage Ltd
Axiom - Armstrong World Industries Ltd
Axis - Dixon Turner Wallcoverings
Axis Digital - Aqualisa Products
Axjet - Howden Buffalo
Axor - Hansgrohe
Axor Citterio - Hansgrohe
Axpet - Amari Plastics Plc
Axxo - Rivermeade Signs Ltd
Axxys - Benlowe Stairs
Azimex - Azimex Fabrications Ltd
Aztec Boilers - TR Engineering Ltd
Aztec Europe Ltd - Flexel International Ltd

B

B&ES - Building & Engineering Services Association
B&F - BF Bassett & Findley
BA Systems - Brass Age Ltd
Baby Ben - General Time Europe
BACS - British Association for Chemical Specialities
Bacticell - GVS Filter Technology UK Ltd
Bacti-clean - Liquid Technology Ltd
Bacticoat - GVS Filter Technology UK Ltd
Bacti-coat floor coating - Liquid Technology Ltd
Bacti-coat wall / ceiling coating - Liquid Technology Ltd
Bactiguard - GVS Filter Technology UK Ltd
Bactiguard - Liquid Technology Ltd
Badu - Golden Coast Ltd
Baggeridge - Baggeridge Brick PLC
Bal - Admix AD1/GT1 - Building Adhesives Ltd
Bal - Easypoxy - Building Adhesives Ltd
Bal - Floor Epoxy - Building Adhesives Ltd
Bal - Grout - Building Adhesives Ltd
Bal - Pourable Thick Bed - Building Adhesives Ltd
Bal - Rapidset - Building Adhesives Ltd
Bal - Superflex Wall & Wide Joint Grouts - Building Adhesives Ltd
Bal - Wall Green/Blue/White Star - Building Adhesives Ltd
Bal Gold Star - Building Adhesives Ltd
Bal Microseal - Building Adhesives Ltd
Bal Supergrout - Building Adhesives Ltd
Bal- Wide Joint Grout - Building Adhesives Ltd
Baldocer - R J Stokes & Co Limited
Balley Birkett - The BSS Group
Balmoral - Davant Products Ltd
Balmoral - Loft Centre Products
Balmoral - Sandtoft Roof Tiles Ltd
Balmoral bunded tanks - Balmoral Tanks
Balmoral spaceformer modular buildings - Balmoral Tanks
Balmoral superfill - Balmoral Tanks
Baltic - Neptune Outdoor Furniture Ltd
Baltimore - Townscape Products Ltd
Balzaro - Girsberger London
Bamboo,Banio, Bolero, Bombe, Bosporos, Buckingham - Pitacs Ltd
Barbican - Carpets of Worth Ltd
Barbican® - Jackson H S & Son (Fencing) Ltd
Barclay Kellett - Albany Standard Pumps
Barcooler - Imperial Machine Co Ltd
Bardoline - Onduline Building Products Ltd
Barduct - Eaton Electric Ltd
Bare Plate Heat Exchangers - AEL
Barent - Neptune Outdoor Furniture Ltd
Barkeller - Imperial Machine Co Ltd
Barkers engineering Ltd - Chestnut Products Limited
Barkwith engineering - Ermine Engineering Co. Ltd
Barley Twist - Benlowe Stairs
Barlow metal fabrications - Barlow Group
Barnwood - Barnwood Ltd
Barrier Foil - Thatching Advisory Services Ltd
Barrikade - Minkon Ltd
Bartender - Imperial Machine Co Ltd
Bartoline - Bartoline Ltd
Barwil - Barber Wilsons & Co Ltd
BASA - British Adhesives and Sealants Association
Basalton Revetment - Ruthin Precast Concrete Ltd
Basepak - Flamco UK Ltd
BASF - Licensed applicators for BASF Resin Products - Ancorite Surface Protection Ltd
Basis - Flexiform Business Furniture Ltd
Bat - Allmat (East Surrey) Ltd
Bat - Expamet Building Products
Batchmatic - BSA Machine Tools Ltd
Bathrooms - Ellis J T & Co Ltd
Bathscreens by Coram - Coram Showers Ltd
Battleship - Heckmondwicke FB
Bauclad - Omnis
Baufix - Pump Technical Services Ltd
Baxall - Vidionics Security Systems Ltd
Bayferrox - LANXESS Inorganic Pigments Group
BBA - British Board of Agrément
BCA - MPA Cement
BCC - British Ceramic Confederation
BCF - British Coatings Federation Ltd
BCIA - The Federation of Environmental Trade Association (FETA)
BCIS - Royal Institution of Chartered Surveyors (RICS)
BCIS Online - BCIS
BCMA - The Carpet Foundation
B-Comm - Kaba Ltd
BDR Thermea - Santon
Beach Glass Mosaics - Kirkstone
Beam seating, Bench seating - CPS Manufacturing Co
BEAMA - British Electrotechnical and Allied Manufacturers Association
Beamform - Rom Ltd
Beany Block - Marshalls Mono Ltd
Bearl Sandstone - Dunhouse Quarry Co Ltd
Beaufont - Benlowe Group Limited
Beaufort - BF Bassett & Findley
Beaufort - Neptune Outdoor Furniture Ltd
Beaumont Chimneys - Beaumont Ltd F E
Beaver - Hipkiss, H, & Co Ltd
BEBO® - Asset International Ltd
Beco Wallform - Beco Products Ltd
Bedale - Oakdale (Contracts) Ltd
Beehive Grit Bin - Sportsmark Group Ltd
Beeline - Ciret Limited
Beemul - Emusol Products (LEICS) Ltd
Bekaert - Betafence Limited
Bekaert fencing - Chestnut Products Limited
Bekaert Fencing 10 yr guarantee system - SJ McBride Ltd T/A Warefence
Bekassure - Termstall Limited
Beko - Beko plc
Belair - Draeger Safety UK Ltd
Belcor - May William (Ashton) Ltd
Belgravia - S & P Coil Products Ltd
BELL - British Electric Lamps Ltd
Bell Bollard - Furnitubes International Ltd
Bell Fireplaces - Bell & Co Ltd
Bell fires - Bell & Co Ltd
Bell Twist - Brintons Ltd
Belle - Chippindale Plant Ltd
Belzona 3131 WG Membrane - Belzona PolymericLtd
Belzona 4111 Magma Quartz - Belzona PolymericLtd
Belzona 4131 Magma Screed - Belzona PolymericLtd
Belzona 4141 Magma Build - Belzona PolymericLtd
Belzona 4311 CRI Chemical Barrier - Belzona PolymericLtd
Belzona 441 Granogrip - Belzona PolymericLtd
Belzona 5122 Clear Cladding Concentrate - Belzona PolymericLtd
Belzona 5231 SG Laminate - Belzona PolymericLtd
Belzona 5811 Immersion Grade - Belzona PolymericLtd
Belzona 8111 Mouldable Wood - Belzona PolymericLtd
Bendix - Electrolux Domestic Appliances
Bendywood - The Angle Ring Company Ltd
Benga W - Jotun Henry Clark Ltd Decorative Division
BentoJect, Bentorub, Bentosteel, Bentostic - Grace De Neef UK
Benton - Guardian Lock & Engineering Co. Ltd
Berber Twist Forte - Brockway Carpets Ltd
Bergen - Loft Centre Products
Berger Lahr - Schneider Electric Ltd
Berkeley - Carpets of Worth Ltd
Berkeley - Crittall Steel Windows Ltd
Berkeley Variations - Carpets of Worth Ltd
Berriedale - Chiltern Invadex
Berry - Dimplex UK Limited
Berry - Seagoe Technologies Ltd
Berry Beam - Berry Systems
Besaplast - Movement Joints (UK)
Beta De Luxe - Naco
Beta Naco - Naco
Beta Tower - Turner Access Ltd
Beta, Beta Flow - Brett Landscaping
Betoatlas - Grass Concrete Ltd
Betoconcept - Grass Concrete Ltd
Betokem - Maxit UK
Betonap - Grass Concrete Ltd
Betotitan - Grass Concrete Ltd
Bewater - Vidionics Security Systems Ltd
BFCMA - British Flue & Chimney Manufacterers Association
BFCMA - The Federation of Environmental Trade Association (FETA)
BFPSA - Fire Industry Association
BFRC - British Fenestration Rating Council

B (con't)

BFT gate automation and barriers - Parsons Brothers Gates

BGL - Benlowe Stairs

BiDi Safe - Safetell Ltd

Bidston Door - AS Newbould Ltd

Bifjet - Howden Buffalo

Biflo - Grohe Ltd

Big Ben - General Time Europe

Big Bertha - Kair Ventilation Ltd

Bigbond - bigHead Bonding Fasteners Ltd

Bighead ® - bigHead Bonding Fasteners Ltd

Bigrings - bigHead Bonding Fasteners Ltd

Bigstrip - bigHead Bonding Fasteners Ltd

Bigwood Stokers - Hodgkinson Bennis Ltd

Bilco - Bilco UK Ltd

Bimagrip - Clare R S & Co Ltd

Binnlock Mesh Fencing - Binns Fencing Ltd

Binwall - Grass Concrete Ltd

Bioclip - Delabie UK Ltd

Biofil - Delabie UK Ltd

Biogard - Leigh's Paints

Biogaurd - Armstrong World Industries Ltd

Biogene - Corroless Corrosion Control

Biomass Grease Traps - Progressive Product Developments Ltd

Biometric - FC Frost Ltd

Biopure - Veoila Water Technologies UKElga Ltd

Biostat - Tuke & Bell Ltd

Biotec - Titan Pollution Control - Part of The Kingspan Group

Birch Interiors - Designer Radiators Direct

Birco - Marshalls Mono Ltd

BIS - Walraven Ltd

Bisley - Bisley Office Equipment

Bison - Forterra Building Products Ltd

Bison Beams - ACP (Concrete) Ltd

Bitubond - SCP Concrete Sealing Technology Ltd

Bituflex - SCP Concrete Sealing Technology Ltd

Bitufor - Bekaert Building Products

Bitusheet - SCP Concrete Sealing Technology Ltd

Bituthene - GCP APPLIED TECHNOLOGIES (UK) LIMITED

Bitutint - Procter Johnson & Co Ltd

BK - Imperial Machine Co Ltd

BL Bollard - Consult Lighting Ltd

Black Beauty - Valor

Blackbox Domestic Safe - Chubb Safe Equipment Company

Blackfriar - Blackfriar Paints Ltd

Blackheat ® - Combat Heating Solutions

Blackjack Square Spiral - Loft Centre Products

Blade - Cil Retail Solutions Ltd

Blairs Aluminium Systems - Saveheat Group

Blairs PVCu - Saveheat Group

Blairs Timber Windows - Saveheat Group

Blairs Windows Limited - Blairs Windows Limited

Blake - Tuke & Bell Ltd

Blakley - Blakley Electrics Ltd

Blanc de Bierges - Blanc de Bierges

Blast Coolers - Turnbull & Scott (Engineers) Ltd

Blaw-Knox - Ingersoll-Rand European Sales Ltd

Blaxter Sandstone - Dunhouse Quarry Co Ltd

Blazex - Britannia Fire

Blenheim - Adam Carpets Ltd

Blenheim - BF Bassett & Findley

Blenheim - Race Furniture Ltd

Blink - Shackerley (Holdings) Group Ltd incorporating Designer ceramics

Blockleys - Michelmersh Brick Holdings PLC

Bloomberg - Beko plc

Bloomsbury - Hamilton R & Co Ltd

BluBat - Junckers Limited

Blue 92 - Laticrete International Inc. UK

Blue Circle - LaFarge Cement UK

Bluesense - Ves Andover Ltd

Blueshield Pmb - Pitchmastic PmB Ltd

Bluesil - Bluestar Silicones

BM TRADA - TRADA Bookshop

BM TRADA Certification - BM TRADA

BMA - Bathroom Manufacturers Association, The

BMF - Builders Merchants Federation

BMI - BCIS

BML - Booth Muirie

Bn - Wilo Samson Pumps Ltd

BOB Stevensons - BOB Stevenson Ltd

Bobi Mail Boxes - JB Architectural Ltd

Boiler noise Silencer F2, Superconcentrate Boiler Noise Silencer F2, Boiler Noise Silencer F2 Express - Fernox

Boilermate - Gledhill Water Storage Ltd

Bolderaja - Boardcraft Ltd

Boldroll - Britmet Tileform Limited

Bolton Wood Yorkstone - Hard York Quarries Ltd

Bomag - Chippindale Plant Ltd

Bond It - Avocet Hardware Ltd

Bondax - Carpets of Worth Ltd

Bondel - Boardcraft Ltd

Bondite - Trade Sealants Ltd

Bondmaster - National Starch & Chemical Ltd

Bondwave - Flexible Reinforcements Ltd

Bookman - Sidhil Care

Booths - Tyco Waterworks - Samuel Booth

Bordalok - Rawson Fillings Ltd

Bosch - Robert Bosch Ltd

BoSS - Youngman Group Limited

Boss White - The BSS Group

Boston Home Care, Bradshaw - Sidhil Care

Boulevard - Fitzgerald Lighting Ltd

Boulevard - Gradus Ltd

Boulevard - Marshalls Mono Ltd

Bowater - Veka Plc

BowTie - Helifix

BPF - British Plastics Federation, The

BPMA - British Pump Manufacturers Association

BPT - Vidionics Security Systems Ltd

BRA - The Federation of Environmental Trade Association (FETA)

BrackettGreen - Jacopa Limited

Bradbury Security - Bradbury Group Ltd

Brade Engineering - Ormandy Rycroft Engineering

Bradley Washroom Products - Relcross Ltd

Bradstone Paving - B & M Fencing Limited

Bradstone slabs - B & M Fencing Limited

Braeburn - Ulster Carpet Mills Ltd

Braemar suite - Armitage Shanks Ltd

Brailliant Touch - Signs & Labels Ltd

Bramah - Bramah Security Equipment Ltd

Brand Energy & Infrastructure Services UK, Ltd - SGB, a Brand Company

Brand-seal - Naylor Drainage Ltd

Brandy Crag - Burlington Slate Ltd

Brathay Blue/Black Slate - Kirkstone

Bray - Chromalox (UK) Ltd

Brazed Plate Heat Exchangers - AEL

Brazilian Pinc plywood - Wood International Agency Ltd

BRC - BRC Reinforcement

BRE - Building Research Establishment

Breathalyzer - Draeger Safety UK Ltd

Brecon - Sashless Window Co Ltd

Breeam - BRE

Breeza - London Fan Company Ltd

Breezair - Radiant Services Ltd

Breezax - London Fan Company Ltd

Breeze - Ormandy Rycroft Engineering

Brett Landscaping and Building Products - B & M Fencing Limited

Brewer - Brewer Metalcraft

Brick & Stone - Maxit UK

Brickfill - Fillcrete Ltd

Brickforce - Masonry Reinforcement - Bekaert Building Products

Brickforce® - BRC Special Products - Bekaert Ltd

Bricklifter - Benton Co Ltd Edward

Bricklifter - Edward Benton & Co Ltd

Brickseal - Fillcrete Ltd

BrickTie - Masonry Reinforcement - Bekaert Building Products

Bricktie® - BRC Special Products - Bekaert Ltd

Bricktor - Masonry Reinforcement - Bekaert Building Products

Bricktor® - BRC Special Products - Bekaert Ltd

Bridge - Townscape Products Ltd

Bridgestone - Braithwaite Engineers Ltd

Bridgman Doors - Bridgman IBC Ltd

Bridgwater - Sandtoft Roof Tiles Ltd

Brigadier - Richard Hose Ltd

Brillite - Witham Oil & Paint Ltd

Brimar Tanks - Brimar Plastics Ltd

Bristan - Olby H E & Co Ltd

Bristlex - Exitex Ltd

Bristol Maid - Hospital Metalcraft Ltd

Brit Clips - Kem Edwards Ltd

Britannia - Marflow Eng Ltd

Britannia Garden Products - Grange Fencing Limited

Britclips® - Walraven Ltd

Britelux - Metal Halide Lamps - FEILO SYLVANIA EUROPE LIMITED

British Electric Lamps Ltd - British Electric Lamps Ltd

British Glass - British Glass Manufacturers Confederation

British Gypsum - Hatmet Limited

British Gypsum - Kitsons Insulation Products Ltd

British Gypsum - Nevill Long

British Monorail - Konecranes UK

British Nova - Cleenol Group Ltd

British Standards Online - British Standards Institution

Britlock - Sandtoft Roof Tiles Ltd

Briton - Allegion (UK) Ltd

Briton - Laidlaw Ltd

Britstream - Britannia Kitchen Ventilation Ltd

BRIX - Federation of Master Builders

Briza 12 & 22 (Fan coil) - Jaga UK

BRK Brands Europe Ltd - BRK Brands Europe Ltd

Broadmead - Broadmead Cast Stone

Broadrib - Heckmondwicke FB

Broadsword - TROAX UK Ltd

Broadway - Race Furniture Ltd

Broag-Remeha - Broag Ltd

Brodclad - Roles Broderick Roofing Ltd

Brodeck - Roles Broderick Roofing Ltd

Brodform - Roles Broderick Roofing Ltd

Brodscrean - Roles Broderick Roofing Ltd

Brodseam - Roles Broderick Roofing Ltd

Broflame - Bollom Fire Protection Ltd

Bromgard - Feedwater Ltd

Brookes - Dynniq UK Ltd

Brooking - Clement Steel Windows

Brooking Collection - Brass Art Ltd

Brooks Roof Units - Matthews & Yates Ltd

Brosteel - Bollom Fire Protection Ltd

Broughton Controls - Geoquip Worldwide

Broughton Moor - Burlington Slate Ltd

Brown Rustic /Drag - Carlton Main Brickworks Ltd

Broxap ® - Broxap Ltd

BRUCK - Optelma Lighting Ltd

Bruynzeel - Construction Group UK Ltd

BSA - BSA Machine Tools Ltd

BSI British Standards - British Standards Institution

BSI Business Solution - British Standards Institution

BSI Information - British Standards Institution

BSI Inspectorate - British Standards Institution

BSI Management System - British Standards Institution

BSI Product Services - British Standards Institution

BSIA - British Security Industry Association

BSSA - British Stainless Steel Association

BSWA - British Structural Waterproofing Association, The

BTA PrintMachine Eazimark™ Laserprint Management - Neopost Ltd

Bticino - Legrand Electric Ltd

Buchanan - ABB Installation Products Ltd

Buckingham - Triton PLC

BUFCA - British Urethane Foam Contractors Association

Buff Rustic/ Dragwire - Carlton Main Brickworks Ltd

Buggie - Manitou (Site Lift) Ltd

Buggiescopic - Manitou (Site Lift) Ltd

Builders Guild - Guild of Builders & Contractors, The

Buildex - ITW Spit

Building Adhesives - R J Stokes & Co Limited

Building Bookshop - The Building Centre Group Ltd

Building Centre - The Building Centre Group Ltd

Building Cost Information Service - BCIS

Building Systems UK - Tata Steel Europe Limited

Bulb-Tite Rivet - SFS Intec LTD

BulkTec - CST Industries, Inc. - UK

bullnose fascia soffit - Dales Fabrications Ltd

Bunnie Dryers - Wandsworth Elecrtical Ltd

Bunzl - Lockhart Catering Equipment

Buroflex - Metalliform Products Plc

Bursting Stone - Burlington Slate Ltd

Bush Circulators - Pumps & Motors UK Ltd

Butler MR24 Standing seam roofing systems - CA Group Ltd - MR-24 Division

Butterley - Forterra Building Products Ltd

Butterley - Hanson Building Products

Butzbach - Envirodoor Markus Ltd

Buy A Digger - www.buyadigger.com - HE Services (Plant Hire) Ltd

BVC - Bivac - Barloworld Vacuum Technology Plc

Bvent Universal Gas Vent - Rite-Vent Ltd

BWF - British Woodworking Federation

BWPDA - The Property Care Association

BX2000 - Horstmann Controls Ltd

Bygone Collection - Masterframe Windows Ltd

Byland - York Handmade Brick Co Ltd

Byron - Ellis J T & Co Ltd

C

C & R - Leofric Building Systems Ltd

C.A.T - Radiodetection Ltd

C.F.P - Westpile Ltd

C+/C plywood - Wood International Agency Ltd

C4000 Combination - Elster Metering Ltd

C6L - McMullen Facades

CA Profiles - CA Group Ltd - MR-24 Division

CAA is a trade association that does not market any products - Cement Admixtures Association

Caberdek - Norbord

Caberfloor - Norbord

Caberfloor P5 - Norbord

Cable Tidy - Tower Manufacturing

Cablelink-Rapide - Ackermann Ltd

Cablemann - Ackermann Ltd

Cablofil - Legrand Electric Ltd

CABU Limited - Cowley Timber & Partners Limited

Cada - Kermi (UK) Ltd

Cadenza - Laird Security Hardware

Cadet seating - CPS Manufacturing Co

Cadiz - Dimplex UK Limited

Cadweld ® - Erico Europa (GB) Ltd

Cafco - Firebarrier International Ltd T/A Firebarrier Services Ltd

Cafco - Promat UK Ltd

Caimi - Lesco Products Ltd

Caithness Stone - Caithness Flagstone Limited

Calder - Calder Industrial Materials Ltd

Calderdale - Sandtoft Roof Tiles Ltd

Caldy Door - AS Newbould Ltd

Caledonian - Caledonian Modular

Caleffi - Altecnic Ltd

Calibre - BRE

Calor Autogas - Calor Gas Ltd

Calor Gas - Calor Gas Ltd

Calypso - Eltron Chromalox

Calypso Range - Evergreens Uk

Camargue - Carpets of Worth Ltd

Cambourne, Clarendon - Sidhil Care

Cambrian slates - Monier Redland Limited

Camlok - Camlok Lifting Clamps Ltd

Camouflage™ - Venator

Can-Corp - Bush Nelson PLC

Candy - British Ceramic Tile Ltd

Canexel - Vulcan Cladding Systems

Canigo' - Harbro Supplies Ltd

Cannon Consumables - Cannon Hygiene Ltd

Cannon Horticulture - Cannon Hygiene Ltd

Cannon Pest Control - Cannon Hygiene Ltd

Cannon Textile CARE - Cannon Hygiene Ltd

Canply Cofi plywood - Wood International Agency Ltd

Canterbury, Chaucer, Classico - Brett Landscaping

Canti-Bolt - Hi-Store Ltd

Canti-Clad - Hi-Store Ltd

Canti-Frame - Hi-Store Ltd

Canti-Guide - Hi-Store Ltd

Canti-Lec - Hi-Store Ltd

Canti-Lock - Hi-Store Ltd

Canti-Track - Hi-Store Ltd

Canti-Weld - Hi-Store Ltd

Capco - Capco Test Equipment, A division of Castlebroom Engineering Ltd

Cape - Firebarrier International Ltd T/A Firebarrier Services Ltd

Cape Boards - Kitsons Insulation Products Ltd

Capella - Ward Insulated Panels Ltd

Capex - Exitex Ltd

Capital Bollard - Furnitubes International Ltd

Caplock - Ibstock Building Products Ltd

Cappadocia, Cat Ladder, Cengiz, Chelmsford, Clipper, Coffer, Combe, Compact4, Compact 6 - Pitacs Ltd

Cappair - Swish Building Products

Cappit - Swish Building Products

Carbital SB - Imerys Minerals Ltd

Carboline - Nullifire Ltd

Cardale - Cardale Garage Doors

Cardale - Chiltern Invadex

Cardale - Moffett Thallon & Co Ltd

Cardale, Cedar - Acorn Garage Doors Ltd

Cardax - Vidionics Security Systems Ltd

Care LST - Hudevad Britain

Carefree Buffable - Johnson Wax Professional

Carefree Emulsion - Johnson Wax Professional

Carefree Eternum - Johnson Wax Professional

Carefree Gloss Restorer - Johnson Wax Professional

Carefree Maintainer - Johnson Wax Professional

Carefree Satin - Johnson Wax Professional

Carefree Speed Stripper - Johnson Wax Professional

Carefree Stride 1000 - Johnson Wax Professional

Carefree Stride 2000 - Johnson Wax Professional

Carefree Stride 3000 - Johnson Wax Professional

Carefree Stripper - Johnson Wax Professional

Carefree Undercoat - Johnson Wax Professional

Caremix - Altecnic Ltd

Carerscreen - Contour Showers Ltd

Caribe - Holophane Europe Ltd

Caribe ® - Combat Heating Solutions

Carina Quality Agent Assessment System - Computertel Ltd

Carina Quality Dashboard - Real Time Display - Computertel Ltd

Carina range of recording solutions - Computertel Ltd

Carlton - Triton PLC

Carlton - Tuke & Bell Ltd

Carlton Brick - Carlton Main Brickworks Ltd

Carousel - Heatrae Sadia Heating Ltd

Carrier air - Toshiba Carrier UK

Carron Phoenix - Carron Phoenix Ltd

CarStop - Rediweld Rubber & Plastics Ltd

Carter Coldstores - Carter Retail Equipment Ltd

Carter Refridgeration Display - Carter Retail Equipment Ltd

Carter Refridgeration Services - Carter Retail Equipment Ltd

Carter-Dal - Carter-Dal International

Cascade - Calomax Ltd

Cascade - Potter & Soar Ltd

Cascade - Whitecroft Lighting Limited

Cascade Wallwash Luminaire - ITAB Prolight UK Limited

Cascamite - Wessex Resins & Adhesives Ltd

Cascamite (see Extramite) - Humbrol

Cascofil - Humbrol

Cascophen - Humbrol

Cascophen - Wessex Resins & Adhesives Ltd

Cascorez - Humbrol

Casco-Tape - Wessex Resins & Adhesives Ltd

Casella CEL - Casella UK

Casella ET - Casella UK

Casella Monitor - Casella UK

Cashflow - Masterbill Micro Systems Ltd

CasoLine - British Gypsum Ltd

CASTALDI - Optelma Lighting Ltd

Castalia cistern - Opella Ltd

Castalia Filter Clear - Opella Ltd

Castalia Tap Range - Opella Ltd

Castelco - Omeg Ltd

Castell - Castell Safety International

Castell 150 - Lok - Castell Safety International

Castelli - Haworth UK Ltd

Castle Multicem - Castle Cement Ltd

Castlemead Twist - Adam Carpets Ltd

Cataphos Paint - Sportsmark Group Ltd

Cataphos CR Paint - Sportsmark Group Ltd

Catcastle Sandstone - Dunhouse Quarry Co Ltd

Category Grid systems - SIG Interiors

Caterclad - Interclad (UK) Ltd

Caterpillar - Briggs Industrial Footwear Ltd t/a Briggs Safety Wear

Catnic - Catnic

Catnic - Tata Steel Europe Limited

Catnic - Wade Building Services Ltd

Catnic Classic - Catnic

Catnic Unique - Garador Ltd

Catseye - Reflecting Roadstuds Ltd

Cavicloser - Cavity Trays Ltd

Caviflash - Cavity Trays Ltd

Caviroll - Cavity Trays Ltd

Cavitray - Cavity Trays Ltd

Cavity stop - Polypipe Building Products

Cavity Trays of Yeovil - Cavity Trays Ltd

Cavity Wall Batts - Rockwool Ltd

Cavivent - Cavity Trays Ltd

Caviweep - Cavity Trays Ltd

CAYONO, CONODUO - Kaldewei

Caysbriggs quarry pebbles and cobbles - Tarmac Trading Limited (Aggregates)

CBA - Concrete Block Association

Cbi - Worcester Heat Systems Ltd

CCF - Keyline Civils Specialist Ltd

CDI - Worcester Heat Systems Ltd

CDX - Hochiki Europe (UK) Ltd

CECA - Civil Engineering Contractors Association

Cedagravel - CED Ltd

Cedec footpath gravel - CED Ltd

CeeJay - Simpson Strong-Tie®

Cefndy Healthcare - Cefndy Healthcare

Cego - Laird Security Hardware

Ceillex - Salex Acoustics Limited

Celafelt - Davant Products Ltd

Celeste - Ubbink (UK) Ltd

Cellarcote - Sealocrete PLA Ltd

Cellarguard - Trade Sealants Ltd

Cellcore - Jablite Ltd

Cellcore HX, Cellform HX, Cellvent HX - Cordek Ltd

Cellio - Armstrong World Industries Ltd

Celmac - Wirquin Ltd

C (con't)

Celmac Wirquin - Wirquin Ltd
Celotex - Celotex Ltd
Celsi - BFM Europe Limited
Celsius - Tata Steel Europe Limited
Celuform - Celuform Building Products
Celuform - FGF Ltd
Celutex - Celuform Building Products
Cembrit PB - Cembrit Ltd
Cementation - Skanska UK Plc
Cementitious Coating 851 - Flexcrete Technologies Limited
Cementone - Bostik Ltd
Cempatch - Don Construction Products Ltd
Cemprotec E. Floor - Flexcrete Technologies Limited
Cemprotec E942 - Flexcrete Technologies Limited
Cemprotec Elastic - Flexcrete Technologies Limited
Cemrok - Tarmac Building Products Ltd
Cemset - Skanska UK Plc
CemTie - Helifix
Centaur Plus - Horstmann Controls Ltd
Centaurstat - Horstmann Controls Ltd
Centerline - Crane Fluid Systems
Centra - Veolia Water Technologies UKElga Ltd
CentrAlert - Heras
CentralScotland Plumbers - Ogilvie Construction Ltd
Centrel - Emergi-Lite Safety Systems
Centro - Hille Educational Products Ltd
Centurion - Laidlaw Ltd
Centurion - Shackerley (Holdings) Group Ltd incorporating Designer ceramics
Centurion® (Low Pitch Roof Tile) - Forticrete Roofing
Century - Yale Security Products Ltd
Cepac - Emusol Products (LEICS) Ltd
Ceram - Lucideon
Cerrad - R J Stokes & Co Limited
Certificates of Conformity - British Board of Agrément
Certikin - Certikin International Ltd
Certikin, Crystal - Golden Coast Ltd
Cerus - Tidmarsh & Sons
Cesi - Arnull Bernard J & Co Ltd
Cetol - Akzo Noble Coatings Ltd
CFP AlarmSense 2-wire fire panels - C-TEC (Computionics) Ltd
CFP conventional fire panels - C-TEC (Computionics) Ltd
CGL - CGL Facades
CGL Totalwall - CGL Facades
Challenge Fencing Ltd - Challenge Fencing Ltd
Challenger - Abacus Lighting Ltd
Challenger - En-tout-cas Tennis Courts Ltd
Challenger - Flamco UK Ltd
Chamelneon - Oldham Lighting Ltd
Champion - Rawson Carpets Ltd
Chancery - Muraspec
Channel Plus - Horstmann Controls Ltd
Charisma - Laird Security Hardware
Charles Yorke - Symphony Group PLC, The
Charlotte Space Saver Spiral - Loft Centre Products
Charlton Gates - B & M Fencing Limited
Charnwood - Michelmersh Brick Holdings PLC
Chartered Institution of Waste Management - Chartered Institute of Wastes Management
Chartres - Formpave Ltd
Chase - Chase Equipment Ltd
Chateau - Muraspec
Chem-crete - Cross-Guard International Ltd
Chemflo - CPV Ltd
Cheriton - Hamilton R & Co Ltd
Cheshire Heritage - Maxit UK
Chesil - Hamworthy Heating Limited & ACV UK
Chess - Flexiform Business Furniture Ltd
Chesterfoil Vapour Barrier - Chesterfelt Ltd
Chestertorch - Chesterfelt Ltd
Chevlol Walling - Ruthin Precast Concrete Ltd
Chichester Stoneworks Ltd - Chichester Stoneworks Limited
Childers - Kingspan Industrial Ins. Ltd
Chilstone Architectural Stonework - Chilstone
Chilstone Garden Ornaments - Chilstone
Chiltern - Macemain + Amstad Ltd
Chiltern Dynamics - BM TRADA
Chiltern International Fire - BM TRADA
Chimaster MF - Docherty New Vent Chimney Group
Chimflex LW/SB - Rite-Vent Ltd
Chimliner - Marflex Chimney Systems
Chimney Capper - Brewer Metalcraft
C-Hitlite - BLV Licht-und Vakuumtecnik
Chromalox - Chromalox (UK) Ltd
Chrome Plus - MK (MK Electric Ltd)
Chubb - ASSA ABLOY Limited
Chubb - Olby H E & Co Ltd
Chubb Locks - Mul-T-Lock
Chubbsafes - Gunnebo UK Limited
Churchill - BSA Machine Tools Ltd
Churchill - Gunnebo UK Limited
Churchill - Longden
Churchill - Northcot Brick Ltd
Chuted - The Safety Letterbox Company Ltd
CIArb - Chartered Institute of Arbitrators
CIBSE - Chartered Institution of Building Services Engineers (CIBSE)
CIBSE Certification - Chartered Institution of Building Services Engineers (CIBSE)
CIBSE Services - Chartered Institution of Building Services Engineers (CIBSE)
Cilplan - Cil Retail Solutions Ltd
Cimberio Valves - SAV United Kingdom Ltd
Ciment Fondu Lafarge - Lafarge Aluminates Ltd
CINCA Mosaic & Tiles - Reed Harris
Cintec - Cintec International Ltd
CIP - Construction Industry Publications
CIPEC JEP Asphaltic plug joints - Pitchmastic PmB Ltd
CIRIA - Construction Industry Research & Information Association
Cirkit - Metalliform Products Plc
CIS - Crack Inducing System - Compriband Ltd
CISA - Allegion (UK) Ltd
Cissell Dryers - Warner Howard Group Ltd
Cistermiser - Cistermiser Ltd
Citadel - SG System Products Ltd
Citadel - WF Senate
Citadel, Carleton, Consul - Glasdon U.K. Limited
Citax - Henkel Ltd
CITB - Construction Industry Training Board
Citizen - Townscape Products Ltd
City Plumbing Supplies - Keyline Civils Specialist Ltd
Citycabin - Wernick Group Ltd
Cityflor - Axter Ltd
Cityspace - Kone PLC
civic Multi - Carlton Main Brickworks Ltd
CK Station - KSB Ltd
CL - Clever - Staverton (UK) Ltd
Clairsol™ - Petrochem Carless
Clarice Range - Twyford Bathrooms
Clarity - Girsberger London
Clarke - Nilfisk Limited
Clarke "C" spray - Clarke UK Ltd
Clarus Immersive 3d Screens - Harkness Screens
Clarus XC - Harkness Screens
Class I Chimney Systems - Dunbrik (Yorks) Ltd
Classic - Airdri Ltd
Classic - Kompan Ltd
Classic - Rangemaster
Classic - Rivermeade Signs Ltd
Classic - Vicaima Ltd
Classic 25 - Altro Ltd
Classic 62 - Spectus Systems
Classic Bathrooms - Silverdale Bathrooms
Classic Coarse and Fine Texture - Andura Coatings Ltd
Classic Collection - Lakes Bathrooms Limited
Classic Collection - Masterframe Windows Ltd
Classic Communal Entrance Doors - Bradbury Group Ltd
Classic Trolleys - Envopak Group Ltd
Classic, Concept - Kermi (UK) Ltd
Classic+ MkII - Airdri Ltd
Classica - Matki plc
Classicair louvres - Grille Diffuser & Louvre Co Ltd The
Classical - Saint-Gobain PAM UK
Classical plus - Saint-Gobain PAM UK
Classics - Muraspec
Classidur - Blackfriar Paints Ltd
Classmate - Rawson Carpets Ltd
Claudgen - Consort Equipment Products Ltd
Clayboard - Dufaylite Developments Ltd
Claymaster - Jablite Ltd
Claypenny - Oakdale (Contracts) Ltd
Clayslate - Sandtoft Roof Tiles Ltd
Clean steam - Fulton Boiler Works (Great Britain) Ltd
Cleaneo Akustik (Apertura) - Knauf UK
Cleaner F3, Superconcentrate Cleaner F3, Cleaner F3 Express, Powerflushing Cleaner F5, DS40 System cleaner, System Neutraliser, HVAC Protector F3, DS-10 Dryside Cleaner - Fernox
Cleanflow - Johnson & Starley
Clean-Flow Silencers - IAC Acoustic Company UK Ltd
CleanPipe - Radius Systems Ltd
Cleanshield ™ - Accent Hansen
Clear Erase - Tektura Plc
Clearfire 2000 - McKenzie-Martin Ltd
Clearstor Shelving - Moresecure Ltd
Clearview Glazed Overhead Doors - Avon Industrial Doors Ltd
Cleenol - Cleenol Group Ltd
Cleenzyme - Cleenol Group Ltd
Clenaglass - Clenaware Systems Ltd
Cleveland - Sashless Window Co Ltd
Clic - Signs & Labels Ltd
Clifton - Formpave Ltd
Clifton - Macemain + Amstad Ltd
Climaflex - Davant Products Ltd
Climaflex - NMC (UK) Ltd
ClimEight - Benlowe Group Limited
Climmy - LTI Advanced Systems Technology Ltd
Clinicall - Tunstal Healthcare (UK) Ltd
Clino21 - Ackermann Ltd
ClinoOpt 99 - Ackermann Ltd
Clipclad Panel Management - Grant Westfield Ltd
Clip-In - PFP Electrical Products Ltd
Clipper - Calomax Ltd
Clipper - Norton Diamond Products
Clipsal - Schneider Electric Ltd
Clip-Top - Gradus Ltd
Clivet porducts - Clivet UK Ltd
Clorocote - Witham Oil & Paint Ltd
Club - Lappset UK Ltd
CME Sanitary Systems - Wirquin Ltd
CMF - Cast Metals Federation
CMIX - ITW Construction Products
CN - Construction News - EMAP
CO2 Monitor - Gas Measurement Instruments Ltd
CoachStop - Rediweld Rubber & Plastics Ltd
Coalmaster - Docherty New Vent Chimney Group
Coastline Collection - Lakes Bathrooms Limited
Cobden, Contour, Curzon - Samuel Heath & Sons plc
Cobra - Allmat (East Surrey) Ltd
Cobra - MSA (Britain) Ltd
Codelock - Exidor Limited
Coem - Arnull Bernard J & Co Ltd
Cofast adhesive - Combustion Linings Ltd
Cofax castables - Combustion Linings Ltd
Cofax cements - Combustion Linings Ltd
Colaquex - Emusol Products (LEICS) Ltd
Cold Cathode - Oldham Lighting Ltd
Coldblocker - Space - Ray UK
Coldmaster - Clark Door Ltd
Coldseal - SCP Concrete Sealing Technology Ltd
Colflex - Bostik Ltd
Colflex HN - Grace De Neef UK
Colonade - Matki plc
Colonial - Intersolar Group Ltd
Colorail - Rothley Limited
Colorcoat - Tata Steel Colors
Colorcoat - Tata Steel Europe Limited
Colorcoat Celestia - Tata Steel Colors
Colorcoat HBS200 - Tata Steel Colors
Colorcoat Urban - Tata Steel Europe Limited
Colorduct 2 - Hotchkiss Air Supply
Colorfarm - Tata Steel Colors
Colorlite - BLV Licht-und Vakuumtecnik
Colorsteels - Tata Steel Europe Limited
Colortone - Armstrong World Industries Ltd
Colortread - EMS Entrance Matting Systems Ltd
Colosseum - Metalliform Products Plc
Colour dimensions - AkzoNobel Decorative Paints UK
Colour Express - Milliken Carpet
Colour Index - Muraspec
Colour Palette - AkzoNobel Decorative Paints UK
Colour Range - Ibstock Brick Ltd
Colour Select Glazed Bricks - Ibstock Brick Ltd
Colourcast - Procter Bros Limited
Colourfan - Ves Andover Ltd
Colourfast - EJOT UK Limited
Colouroute - Clare R S & Co Ltd
Colourpave - Clare R S & Co Ltd
Colourplex™ - Venator
Colourseal - Movement Joints (UK)
Colourtex S - LaFarge Cement UK
Colson - Avocet Hardware Ltd
Colt Houses - W.H Colt Son & Co Ltd
Coltage - Loft Centre Products
Coltlite - Colt International
Column System - S & B Ltd
Combat - Range Cylinders
Combat ® - Combat Heating Solutions
Combi LNHI - Babcock Wanson Uk Ltd
Combiflex - Sika Ltd
Combihatch - Howe Green Ltd
Combimate - Cistermiser Ltd
Combo-Line - Hunter Douglas Architectural Ltd
Come Back to Carpit - The Carpet Foundation
Comet - Laird Security Hardware
Cometec - CGL Facades
Comflor - Tata Steel Europe Limited
Comfo Tube - Zehnder Group UK Ltd
Comfort Plus - Milliken Carpet
Comforto - Haworth UK Ltd
Command Elite, Command, Command Connect, Command Plus and Command Fast Link controls - Whitecroft Lighting Limited
Commander - ABB Instrumentation Ltd
Commando - Richard Hose Ltd
Communicall - Tunstal Healthcare (UK) Ltd
Compac - Ormandy Rycroft Engineering
Compact - Calomax Ltd
Compact - Dewhurst plc
Compact - The Safety Letterbox Company Ltd
Compact & Origin Switches - Ensto Briticent Ltd
Compact grade - Bridgman IBC Ltd
Compas Sort Units - Envopak Group Ltd
COMPLi7 - Lumitron Ltd
Compriband - Compriband Ltd
Compriband - Illbruck Sealant Systems UK Ltd
Comprisil - Compriband Ltd
Compton - Bambi Air Compressors Ltd.
Conbextra - Fosroc Ltd
Conbloc - Forterra Building Products Ltd
Concept - Ideal-Standard Ltd
Concept 2000 bath - Chiltern Invadex
Concept Suite - Armitage Shanks Ltd
Concepta - Illuma Lighting
Concertainer gabions and mattresses - BRC Reinforcement
Concrete Cleaner - Tank Storage & Services Ltd
Concrex - Watco UK Ltd
Condensor - Poujoulat (UK) Ltd
Conductite - Laybond Products Ltd
Cone Crushers - Parker Plant Ltd
Conex Range : Conex Compression, Conex Compression Chrome Plated, Conex Compression Manifolds, Conex Valves, Conex Waste Traps - Conex Universal Limited
Confidex - Tata Steel Colors
Congress - Project Office Furniture PLC
Congrip - Conren Ltd
Conic Flow Silencers - IAC Acoustic Company UK Ltd
Conision - Potter & Soar Ltd
Connect - Metalliform Products Plc
Connect grid - Saint-Gobain Ecophon Ltd
Conservation Rooflights - The Rooflight company
Consort - Consort Equipment Products Ltd
Consort - Marflow Eng Ltd
Consort - Vantrunk Engineering Ltd
Constable suite - Brass Art Ltd
Constant Force™ - Latchways plc

Construction Books - Professional Books Limited
Constructionline - Chestnut Products Limited
Constructionline - Constructionline
Constructor - Construction Group UK Ltd
Contact - Girsberger London
Contact Telecoms - Designer Radiators Direct
Contain-It - George Fischer Sales Ltd
Contemporary (Q) - Barber Wilsons & Co Ltd
Contemporary Bathrooms - Silverdale Bathrooms
Contemporary Tile Effect - FIBO UK LTD
Contigym - Continental Sports Ltd
Contimat - Continental Sports Ltd
Continental Range - Pedley Furniture International Ltd
Contitramp - Continental Sports Ltd
Contour - Airdri Ltd
Contour - Hambleside Danelaw Ltd
Contour - Levolux A.T. Limited
Contour - Valor
Contour 2 - Armitage Shanks Ltd
Contour Cisterns - Dudley Thomas Ltd
Contour EAGLE - Contour Showers Ltd
Contour ECO-DEC - Contour Showers Ltd
Contour Factor 20 - Hambleside Danelaw Ltd
Contour FALCON - Contour Showers Ltd
Contour OTT - Hambleside Danelaw Ltd
Contour Primo - Contour Showers Ltd
Contour SNIFT - Contour Showers Ltd
Contour Stepsafe - Hambleside Danelaw Ltd
Contract 'E' - Eltron Chromalox
Contract Journal - Contract Journal
Control Packs - Horstmann Controls Ltd
CONTURAN Display Enhancement Glass - SCHOTT UK Ltd
Cool-fit - George Fischer Sales Ltd
Coolfit - Low voltage Halogen Lamps - FEILO SYLVANIA EUROPE LIMITED
Coolflow - Biddle Air Systems Ltd
Coolguard - Feedwater Ltd
Coolkote - Bonwyke Ltd
Coolkote - Invicta Window Films Ltd
COOL-PHASE® - Monodraught Ltd
Coolplex - Feedwater Ltd
CoolView (examination lamps) - Brandon Medical
coopers-uk.com - Cooper Group Ltd
Coopertiva D'imola - Arnull Bernard J & Co Ltd
Coo-Var ® - Coo-Var Ltd
Coo-Var ® - Teal & Mackrill Ltd
Cop Crag Sandstone - Dunhouse Quarry Co Ltd
Copa® - Jacopa Limited
Copar 700 - Monowa Manufacturing (UK) Ltd
CopaSac® - Jacopa Limited
Copeland Brand Products - Emerson Climate Technologies
Copenhagen - Loft Centre Products
Copley Decor - Copley Decor Ltd
Copon - Andrews Coatings Ltd
Coppa Gutter - Metal Gutta
Copperad - The BSS Group
Copperfield - Swintex Ltd
Copper-Fin - Lochinvar Limited
Copper-Flo™ - Johnson Matthey PLC - Metal Joining
Copydex - Henkel Consumer Adhesives
CoRayVac ® - Combat Heating Solutions
Corbin - Mul-T-Lock
CORGI - Corgi Technical Devices
Corian - DuPont Corian
Corium - Baggeridge Brick PLC
Cork Essence - Amorim Cork Flooring
Cork Pure - Amorim Cork Flooring
Corkfast - Western Cork Ltd
Corklok - Gradient Insulations (UK) Ltd
Corniche - Geberit Ltd
Cornish - Formpave Ltd
Corofil - Firebarrier International Ltd T/A Firebarrier Services Ltd
Corogrid - Omnis
Coroline - Ariel Plastics Ltd
Corotherm - Ariel Plastics Ltd
Corporate W20 - Crittall Steel Windows Ltd
Corporate 2000 - Crittall Steel Windows Ltd
Corporate W20 - Crittall Steel Windows Ltd
Correx, Corgrid, Corbreak, Sideform - Cordek Ltd
Corridor - Saint-Gobain Ecophon Ltd
Corroban - Feedwater Ltd
Corrocure - Corroless Corrosion Control
Corrocure - Kenyon Group Ltd
Corrocure - Kenyon Paints Limited
Corrogiene - Corroless Corrosion Control
Corroguard - Corroless Corrosion Control
Corroless - Corroless Corrosion Control
corroless® - Kenyon Paints Limited
Corroshield - Corroless Corrosion Control
Corrosion Control Services Limited - Freyssinet Ltd
Corrosperse - Feedwater Ltd
Corruspan - Compriband Ltd
Corruspan - Illbruck Sealant Systems UK Ltd
Corsehill Sandstone - Dunhouse Quarry Co Ltd
Cortal - Haworth UK Ltd
Cost planner - Masterbill Micro Systems Ltd
Costmodelling Software - Johnson VB LLP
Cosybug - Harton Heating Appliances
Cotswold - Carl F Groupco Limited
Coubro & Scrutton - PCT Group
Cougar - Catnic
Countershield - Safetell Ltd
County Concrete Ditch Channels - Sportsmark Group Ltd
County pantile - Sandtoft Roof Tiles Ltd
Couplerbox - RFA-Tech Ltd
Courtrai - Smithbrook Building Products Ltd
Coustifoam - Sound Reduction Systems Ltd
Covent Garden Litter Bins - Furnitubes International Ltd
Coverlife - EBC UK Ltd
Cowley Timber & Partners Limited - CABU Limited
Coxdome Skytube - Cox Building Products Ltd
Coxdome T.P.X - Cox Building Products Ltd
Coxdome Trade - Cox Building Products Ltd
Coxdone 2000 - Cox Building Products Ltd
Coxdone Mark 5 - Cox Building Products Ltd
Coxspan Baselock - Cox Building Products Ltd

C (con't)

Coxspan GlassPlank - Cox Building Products Ltd
Coxspan Modular roof glazing - Cox Building Products Ltd
CoxwindowsScape - Cox Building Products Ltd
CP Canopy - Consult Lighting Ltd
CPA - Construction Plant-hire Association
CPSA - Concrete Pipeline Systems Association
Cpv - df - CPV Ltd
CPV-Safeflo - CPV Ltd
CPV-Zurn - CPV Ltd
CrackBond - Helifix
Cractie - Redifix Ltd
Cradley - Forterra Building Products Ltd
Craftsman Elite - Brockway Carpets Ltd
Craftwork - Benlowe Group Limited
Cranham, Cranham Picnic Suite - Branson Leisure Ltd
Craven - Konecranes UK
Create - Ideal-Standard Ltd
Creative Glass - Creative Glass
Credifon® Remote Postage Meter Recrediting System - Neopost Ltd
Credo, Credo-Uno - Kermi (UK) Ltd
Crendon - Crendon Timber Engineering Ltd
Crescent - Crescent Lighting
Crescent - Geberit Ltd
Cresfinex - Exitex Ltd
Cresset - Adams- Hydraulics Ltd
Cresta - Brockway Carpets Ltd
Cresta - MSA (Britain) Ltd
Cresta Supreme - Brockway Carpets Ltd
Cresta Supreme Heathers - Brockway Carpets Ltd
Creteangle - Benton Co Ltd Edward
Creteangle - Edward Benton & Co Ltd
Cricket Gas Detectors - MSA (Britain) Ltd
Cristal - Johnson Tiles
Critic - Surge Protection Products - Erico Europa (GB) Ltd
Crittall Composite - Crittall Steel Windows Ltd
Crocodile - Simpson Strong-Tie®
Croda - Andrews Coatings Ltd
Cromleigh - Chameleon Stone Ltd
Cromleigh S.V.K - Chameleon Stone Ltd
Crompton - ERA Home Security Ltd
Crosinox - Strand Hardware Ltd
Crosland Hill Hard Yorkstone - Johnsons Wellfield Quarries Ltd
Crosland Hill Multi - Johnsons Wellfield Quarries Ltd
Cross-cote - Cross-Guard International Ltd
Crossgrip - Plastic Extruders Ltd
Crossvent - Howden Buffalo
Croston Plumbing and Heating - Designer Radiators Direct
Crown - Albany Standard Pumps
Crown - Brewer C & Sons Ltd
Crown Trade - Crown Paints Ltd
Crown Wool - Knauf Insulation Ltd
CRT - Range Cylinders
Cryotherme - Firebarrier International Ltd T/A Firebarrier Services Ltd
Crystal - Sapphire Balustrades
Crystal Tanks - Water Technology Engineering Ltd
crystic - SIG Roofing
CU PHOSCO - CU Phosco Lighting
Cube wall - Grant Westfield Ltd
Cubes Range - Pedley Furniture International Ltd
Cubo enclosures - Ensto Briticent Ltd
Culina - Vianen KVS BV
Cullamix Tyrolean - Weber Building Solutions
Cullen - Allmat (East Surrey) Ltd
Cummins - Cummins Power Generation Ltd
Cummins Power Generation - Cummins Power Generation Ltd
Cupola - Hughes Safety Showers Limited
Cuprinol - Dulux Trade
Cuprofit, Pushfit - Conex Universal Limited
Cupropight 70 - Righton Ltd
Cupropight 90 - Righton Ltd
Curve - Ellis J T & Co Ltd
Curvetech - Stocksigns Ltd
Cushion Coil - Kleen-Tex Industries Ltd
Cutan - Deb Group Limited
Cutler-Hammer - Eaton Electric Ltd
Cwt y Bugail - Welsh Slate Limited
Cyclone - Colt International

D

d Line - Allgood plc
D + H Mechantronic - Dyer Environmental Controls
D.F.D. - (Dudley Factory Doors Ltd.) - Shutter Door Repair & Maintenance Ltd
D.F.D.-(Dudley Factory Doors Ltd.) - Priory Shutter & Door Co Ltd
D50N - Movement Joints (UK)
Dac Chlor - Dacrylate Paints Ltd
Dac Crete - Dacrylate Paints Ltd
Dac flex - Dacrylate Paints Ltd
Dac Roc - Dacrylate Paints Ltd
Dac Shield - Dacrylate Paints Ltd
Dacatie - Quantum Profile Systems Ltd
Dacpol - Dacrylate Paints Ltd
Dacrylate paints - Kenyon Paints Limited
Daikin - Purified Air Ltd
Dalamatic - Donaldson Filtration (GB) Ltd
DalChoc - Dalhaus Ltd
Dales Decor - Copley Decor Ltd
Dalesauna - Dalesauna Ltd
Dalhem Panel - LSA Projects Ltd
DALI - Helvar Ltd
DalLastic - Dalhaus Ltd
DalMagnetic - Dalhaus Ltd
DalOmni - Dalhaus Ltd
DalRollazzo - Dalhaus Ltd
DalRollo - Dalhaus Ltd
DalRollo Satin - Dalhaus Ltd
DalUni - Dalhaus Ltd
DalWerk - Dalhaus Ltd
DalZone - Dalhaus Ltd
Damcor - Polypipe Building Products
DamRyt® - Rytons Building Products Ltd
Danelaw - Hambleside Danelaw Ltd
Danesmoor - Worcester Heat Systems Ltd
Danfoss - Danfoss Ltd
Danfoss Heat Interface Units and DPCVs - SAV United Kingdom Ltd
Danish Oil - Anglo Building Products Ltd
Darkroom safelights - Encapsulite International Ltd
Daryl - Kohler UK
Datacall Aquarius - Blick Communication Systems Ltd
Datacall Gemini - Blick Communication Systems Ltd
Datacall Minder - Blick Communication Systems Ltd
Dataworks - MK (MK Electric Ltd)
Davenset - Dynniq UK Ltd
David Ball Test Sands - DB Group (Holdings) Ltd
Davis - Legrand Electric Ltd
Day-Lite - Emergi-Lite Safety Systems
Daylux - Mode Lighting
dBan - Interfloor Limited
D-Bus - Eaton Electric Limited
DCE - Donaldson Filtration (GB) Ltd
DCE10000 - Donaldson Filtration (GB) Ltd
Dea Madore Range - Brass Art Ltd
Deaf Alerter - Deaf Alerter plc
Deanlite - Deans Blinds & Awnings (UK) Ltd
Deanmaster - Deans Blinds & Awnings (UK) Ltd
Deanox - Elementis Pigments
Deans - Deans Blinds & Awnings (UK) Ltd
Deans signs - Deans Blinds & Awnings (UK) Ltd
Deb Stoko®, Deb InstantFOAM®, Deb® InstantGel - Deb Group Limited
Deben Systems - Phoenix Scales Ltd
Deborah Services - Actavo (UK) Ltd
Debotec Torch-On - Chesterfelt Ltd
Debut - Ness Furniture Ltd
Decaflex - Sika Liquid Plastics Limited
Decamel - Formica Ltd
Decathlon - Hodkin Jones (Sheffield) Ltd
Decimetric - GEC Anderson Ltd
Deck drain - ABG Ltd
Deckmaster - Resdev Ltd
Deckshield - Flowcrete Plc
Deckspan - Richard Lees Decking Limited
Decoline - Deceuninck Ltd
Decolite - The Window Film Company UK Ltd
Decomatic - Goelst
Deconyl - Plascoat Systems Ltd
Deconyl - Plastic Coatings Ltd
Decoquick - Sika Liquid Plastics Limited
Decor - Deceuninck Ltd
Décor Profile - Sarnafil Ltd
Decoroc - Deceuninck Ltd
Decorscreed - Conren Ltd
Decostar - Osram Ltd
Decothane, Decothane Balcons, Decothane Ultra - Sika Liquid Plastics Limited
Decotherm - Sika Liquid Plastics Limited
Dedicated Micro's - Vidionics Security Systems Ltd
Deep lane Yorkstone - Hard York Quarries Ltd
Deepflow - Marley Plumbing and Drainage
Deeplas - Deceuninck Ltd
Deepstor - Construction Group UK Ltd
Defender - Glasdon U.K. Limited
Defendor - Gilgen Door Systems UK Ltd
Defensor - Heras
Deflector - Chesterfelt Ltd
Deflex - Movement Joints (UK)
Deha - Halfen Ltd
Dekguard - Fosroc Ltd
Dekordor ® - Vicaima Ltd
Dektite - ITW Construction Products
DEL - Golden Coast Ltd
Delabole - The Delabole Slate Co. Ltd
Delabole Slate - The Delabole Slate Co. Ltd
Delamere - Delta Balustrades
Delbraze, Delcop End Feed - Conex Universal Limited
Delchem - Opella Ltd
Delight - Glamox Electric (UK) Ltd
Delmag - Schwing Stetter (UK) Ltd
Delphis Glass Mosaics - Kirkstone
Delta - Gilgen Door Systems UK Ltd
Delta - Harbro Supplies Ltd
Delta - Sika Liquid Plastics Limited
delta gutter system - Dales Fabrications Ltd
DeltaBox, DeltaFoil, DeltaWing, DeltaBox Cladding and Screening and DeltaWing Cladding and Screening - Lang+Fulton
Deltadeck - Turner Access Ltd
Deltapox, Deneblock, Denepox, DenePur, DeneSteel - Grace De Neef UK
Deltascreen - Quartet-GBC UK Ltd/ ACCO UK Ltd
Deltos - Charles Lightfoot Ltd
DeLuxe - Hansgrohe
Deluxe Concrete Garages - Liget Compton
Demarcation Stud - Sportsmark Group Ltd
Demidekk - Jotun Henry Clark Ltd Decorative Division
Deminpac - Feedwater Ltd
Denby - Rawson Carpets Ltd
DencoHappel Service - DencoHappel UK Ltd
Denka Lifts - Denka International
Denlok - Naylor Drainage Ltd
Densleeve - Naylor Drainage Ltd
Denso - Winn & Coales (Denso) Ltd
Densostrip - Winn & Coales (Denso) Ltd
Derablok - Deralam Laminates Ltd
Deralam - Deralam Laminates Ltd
Derawood - Deralam Laminates Ltd
Derbigum - Alumasc Exterior Building Products Ltd
Derbyshire Peakstone - Tarmac Trading Limited (Aggregates)
Design Council - Design Council
Design-5 - Benlowe Group Limited
Designer - Clark Door Ltd
Designer 2000 - BF Bassett & Findley
Designer Collection - Brintons Ltd
Designer Partitions - Avanti Systems
Designer Slimline Showertrays by Coram - Coram Showers Ltd
Designerlite - Lumitron Ltd
DesignLine - AudiocomPendax Ltd
Desimpel - Hanson Building Products
Desktop - Forbo Flooring
DespatchLink™ Despatch Management Software - Neopost Ltd
Desso - Armstrong Floor Products UK Ltd
Detan - Halfen Ltd
Devweld structural - Kenyon Group Ltd
Dexlux - Chalmit Lighting
DF.D- (Dudley Factory Doors Ltd.) - Neway Doors Ltd
Di Lusso - Stone & Fire
Dialock - Hafele UK Ltd
DIAlux - Glamox Luxo Lighting Limited
Diamard - Emusol Products (LEICS) Ltd
Diamond - Cembrit Ltd
Diamond - Heckmondwicke FB
Diamond - Tank Storage & Services Ltd
Diamond Access Floor - Stone Raised Access Floor - Chelsea Artisans Ltd
Diamond Décor - Impact Resistant Decorative Glass - Chelsea Artisans Ltd
Diamond Glaze - AkzoNobel Decorative Paints UK
Diamond Mirror - Impact Resistant Safety Mirror - Chelsea Artisans Ltd
Diamond Optic® - DW Windsor Lighting
Diamond Ultralite Internal/External - Chelsea Artisans Ltd
Dibond ® - Righton Ltd
Dicon Safety Products (Europe) Ltd - BRK Brands Europe Ltd
Dictator - Coburn Sliding Systems Ltd
Dielectric - Radiodetection Ltd
Diga - Kermi (UK) Ltd
Digidim - Helvar Ltd
Digifort - Tektura Plc
Digital Mercury - Hamilton R & Co Ltd
Digital Screen: Modeller, Checker, Archiver, Calculator - Harkness Screens
Dimplex - Dimplex UK Limited
Diplomat - Dudley Thomas Ltd
Directflow - Johnson & Starley Ltd
Direx - Universal Components Ltd
Discovery - Apollo Fire Detectors Ltd
Diva - Black Cat Music
Dixell Controld - Emerson Climate Technologies
DK - Harbro Supplies Ltd
DM - Schiedel Chimney Systems Ltd
DMP Bonder - Isocrete Floor Screeds Ltd
DNA - Bernlite Ltd
Dobel - SSAB Swedish Steel Ltd
Dobelshield - SSAB Swedish Steel Ltd
DOCM Packs - Armitage Shanks Ltd
Doherty - Sidhil Care
DoMarKit - Safety Works & Solutions Ltd
Dome - Ves Andover Ltd
Dominator - Crane Fluid Systems
Domo - Dalesauna Ltd
DoMoGuard - Safety Works & Solutions Ltd
Domostyl - NMC (UK) Ltd
Domus - Domus Ventilation
Domus Radial - Domus Ventilation
Domus Thermal - Domus Ventilation
Domus Ventilation - Polypipe Ventilation Ltd
Don - Gazco Ltd
Donaldson filter components - Encon Air Systems Ltd
Doncrete Dense Concrete Blocks - Broome Bros (Doncaster) Ltd
Doncrete Paintgrade Blocks - Broome Bros (Doncaster) Ltd
Donio - Dalesauna Ltd
Donlite Building Blocks - Broome Bros (Doncaster) Ltd
Donlite Foundation Blocks - Broome Bros (Doncaster) Ltd
Donlite light weight concrete blocks - Broome Bros (Doncaster) Ltd
Donlite Paintgrade Blocks - Broome Bros (Doncaster) Ltd
Donn - Knauf AMF Ceilings Ltd
Doorfit - Doorfit Products Ltd
doorline, connectplatform - Enable Access
Doors 4 Net Floors - Contour Showers Ltd
DoorsByDesign - Bridgman IBC Ltd
Doorseal - Exidor Limited
Doosan Babcock - Doosan Power Systems Ltd
Doosan Lentjes - Doosan Power Systems Ltd
Doosan Power Systems - Doosan Power Systems Ltd
Dorchester - Hamworthy Heating Limited & ACV UK
Dorfab - Premdor
Dorma ED800 - Dorma Door Services Ltd
Dorma Huppe - Style Door Systems Ltd
Dorothea ® - Broxap Ltd
Dorothea Restorations® - Wallis Conservation Limited trading as Dorothea Restorations
Dorus - Henkel Ltd
Double Roman - Russell Roof Tiles Ltd
dove gutter system - Dales Fabrications Ltd
Dovedale - Chiltern Invadex
Dovre - Gazco
Dow Corning - Geocel Ltd
DowCorning - Dow Corning Europe S.A
Downflo - Donaldson Filtration (GB) Ltd
DPn - Wilo Samson Pumps Ltd
Dr Martens - Briggs Industrial Footwear Ltd t/a Briggs Safety Wear
Draeger-Tubes - Draeger Safety UK Ltd
Dragon - Fulton Boiler Works (Great Britain) Ltd
Dragon HLO - Elan-Dragonair
Dragon HNG - Elan-Dragonair
Drainmaster - Pump Technical Services Ltd
Drakon and Mesa Concrete Bench Seats - Furnitubes International Ltd
Dramix - Steel Wire Fibres - Bekaert Building Products
Draper - Kem Edwards Ltd
Draper - Unifix Ltd
Draught Buster - Airflow (Nicoll Ventilators) Ltd
Draughtbuster - Timloc Expamet Building Products
Dravo - Johnson & Starley Ltd
Dreadnought - Heckmondwicke FB
Dreadnought Tiles - Hinton Perry & Davenhill Ltd
Dream Fireslide - Valor
Dreamfold - Coburn Sliding Systems Ltd
Dremel - Robert Bosch Ltd
Dricon - Arch Timber Protection
Dri-Marker - Magiboards Ltd
Dritherm - Knauf Insulation Ltd
Driva - ITW Construction Products
Driveaway Domestic Car Turntable - British Turntable Ltd
Drum Form - Scapa Tapes UK Ltd
Dry Fix - Repair care International
Dry Flex - Repair care International
Dry Seal - Repair care International
Dry Shield - Repair care International
Drybase liquid-applied DPM - Safeguard Europe Ltd
DryFix - Helifix
Dryflo - Donaldson Filtration (GB) Ltd
Dryflow - Johnson & Starley
Dryseal - Hambleside Danelaw Ltd
Drywall Acadamy - British Gypsum Ltd
drywall thermotek - Peter Cox Ltd
Dryzone DPC injection cream for rising damp - Safeguard Europe Ltd
DS System - Lewes Design Contracts Ltd
DSA - Drilling & Sawing Association, The
DSL - Actavo (UK) Ltd
DSMA - Door and Hardware Federation
D-stain - Milliken Carpet
DTFA and DTFN Elite - Whitecroft Lighting Limited
DTX - UTC Fire & Securites
Dual seal - SCP Concrete Sealing Technology Ltd
DualAir ® - Combat Heating Solutions
Dual-Care - Heckmondwicke FB
Dualcase - Universal Components Ltd
Dualframe - Sapa Building Systems (monarch and glostal)
Dualinox - Poujoulat (UK) Ltd
Dualstrip - Dufaylite Developments Ltd
Dublo - Range Cylinders
Duck Tapes - Henkel Consumer Adhesives
Ductex - Rega Ductex Ltd
Ductex - Ubbink (UK) Ltd
Ductube® - BRC Special Products - Bekaert Ltd
Duette® Shades - Luxaflex®
Duke - Iles Waste Systems
Dulux - Brewer C & Sons Ltd
Dulux - Olby H E & Co Ltd
Dulux Diamond Glaze - ICI Woodcare
Dulux Polyurethane Varnish - ICI Woodcare
Dulux Quick Dry Varnish - ICI Woodcare
Dulux Trade Ecosure - AkzoNobel Decorative Paints UK
Dulux Trade High Performance Floor Paint - AkzoNobel Decorative Paints UK
Dulux Trade Natural Wood Finishes - AkzoNobel Decorative Paints UK
Dulux Trade, Dulux Trade Gloss, Dulux Trade Emulsions - AkzoNobel Decorative Paints UK
Dunabout - ITW Construction Products
Dune Supreme Premier - Armstrong World Industries Ltd
Dunham Strip - Dunham Bush Ltd
Dunhouse Sandstone - Dunhouse Quarry Co Ltd
Dunseal - Dunbrik (Yorks) Ltd
Dunton - Michelmersh Brick Holdings PLC
Dunvent Ridge Vent Terminal - Dunbrik (Yorks) Ltd
Duo - Delta Balustrades
DUO – Panel and Slab formwork - PERI Ltd
Duo-Fast - Paslode
DuoGas - Poujoulat (UK) Ltd
DuoHeat - Dimplex UK Limited
Duotherm - Smart Systems Ltd
Dupar - Dewhurst plc
Duplex - Airsprung Beds Ltd
Duplex - Fillcrete Ltd
Duplex Building System - Portakabin Ltd
Duplex Coating - Jones of Oswestry Ltd
Duplexvent - Airflow Developments Ltd
Duplo - Becker (SLIDING PARTITIONS) Ltd
Dupox - Andrews Coatings Ltd
Durabase - Duraflex Limited
Durable - Durable Ltd
Durabuild - Duraflex Limited
DuraDeco - Knauf UK
Duraflex Diamond Suite - Duraflex Limited
Duraflon - Plastic Coatings Ltd
Durafort - Dixon Turner Wallcoverings
Duraframe - Duraflex Limited
Duragalv - Jones of Oswestry Ltd
Duraglas - Amari Plastics Plc
Duraglas - Flexitallic Ltd
Duraglass - Duraflex Limited
Duraglass - Leigh's Paints
Duragreen - Duraflex Limited
Duraguard - Plastic Coatings Ltd
Duralay - Interfloor Limited

D (con't)

Duralife Polyester Powder Coat - Crittall Steel Windows Ltd
Duralite - Pryorsign
Duralock Performance Fencing - Duralock (UK) Ltd
Duralok - Duraflex Limited
Durama X - Quartet-GBC UK Ltd/ ACCO UK Ltd
DuraPine - The Outdoor Deck Company
Duraroof - Duraflex Limited
Duraroom - Duraflex Limited
Durashape - Duraflex Limited
Duraspring - Airsprung Beds Ltd
Durasteel - Promat UK Ltd
Duratech - Golden Coast Ltd
Duravent - Duraflex Limited
Duravit - Olby H E & Co Ltd
DureDeck - The Outdoor Deck Company
Duropal - Deralam Laminates Ltd
Durotan Limited - Durotan Ltd
Durox - Tarmac Building Products Ltd
Durox - Tarmac Trading Limited (Blocks)
Dušo sport shower column - Horne Engineering Ltd
Dustguard - Conren Ltd
Dycel Revetment - Ruthin Precast Concrete Ltd
Dycem Clean-Zone - Dycem Ltd
Dycem Protectamat - Dycem Ltd
Dycem Work - Zone - Dycem Ltd
Dyform - Navtec
DYKA - John Davidson (Pipes) Ltd
Dyke- Roof Solar - Dyke Chemicals Ltd
Dyke-Aluminium - Dyke Chemicals Ltd
Dyke-Flashing - Dyke Chemicals Ltd
Dyke-Glass - Dyke Chemicals Ltd
Dyke-Mastic - Dyke Chemicals Ltd
Dyke-Roof - Dyke Chemicals Ltd
Dyke-Roof universal primer - Dyke Chemicals Ltd
Dyke-Seal - Dyke Chemicals Ltd
Dyke-Sil - Dyke Chemicals Ltd
Dyke-Silver - Dyke Chemicals Ltd
DYNA - Kaldewei
Dyna Quell Waterstop - BRC Reinforcement
Dyno Plumbers - Dyno-Rod PLC
Dyno-locks - Dyno Rod PLC
Dyno-plumbing - Dyno Rod PLC
Dyno-rod - Dyno Rod PLC
Dyno-Rod - Dyno-Rod PLC
Dyno-Rod Commercial - Dyno-Rod PLC
Dyno-Rod Drains - Dyno-Rod PLC
Dynotile - Rockwell Sheet Sales Ltd
Dytap Revetment - Ruthin Precast Concrete Ltd

E

E Range - James Gibbons Format Ltd
E&T Magazine - The Institution of Engineering and Technology
E. F.S - Fulton Boiler Works (Great Britain) Ltd
E7BX - Horstmann Controls Ltd
EAC - Harbro Supplies Ltd
Earth square - Milliken Carpet
Earthstone - Wilsonart Ltd
Easby - Oakdale (Contracts) Ltd
Easi joist - Wyckham Blackwell Ltd
Easiclamp - Viking Johnson
Easicollar - Viking Johnson
EasiCool - Airedale International Air Conditioning Ltd
Easi-Fit - Vicaima Ltd
Easifoam - Vita Liquid Polymers Ltd
Easipipe - Domus Ventilation
Easitap - Viking Johnson
Easitee - Viking Johnson
Easivent - SCS Group
Easy Change - Tapworks Water Softeners
Easy•Q - Repair care International
Easyarch - Simpson Strong-Tie®
Easybolt - Eliza Tinsley Ltd
Easyclad - Advanced Hygienic Contracting Ltd
Easyfix - Eliza Tinsley Ltd
Easy-Flo™ - Johnson Matthey PLC - Metal Joining
EasyFlue - Alpha Therm Ltd
Easy-flush - Cistermiser Ltd
Easyguard - Safety Works & Solutions Ltd
easySwitch - Helvar Ltd
Easyway - Sapa Building Systems (monarch and glostal)
Eaton - Eaton Electric Ltd
Eauzone - Matki plc
Eazimark™ OMR Coding Software - Neopost Ltd
Eazistrip - reinforcement continuity system - BRC Reinforcement
EB - Clement Steel Windows
EB Handietch - Eyre & Baxter Limited
EBC UK Ltd - EBC UK Ltd
Ebmena Concrete Paving - Alfresco Floors
Ebm-Papst - Air Control Industries Ltd
EC Power CHP - SAV United Kingdom Ltd
ECB - Donaldson Filtration (GB) Ltd
Echelon (cycle shelters) - Glasdon UK Limited
Echosorba - Soundsorba Ltd
Echosorption - Bicester Products Ltd
Eclipse - Chalmit Lighting
Eclipse - Eclipse Blind Systems Ltd
Eclipse - Fitzgerald Lighting Ltd
Eclipse - Hawker Siddley Switchgear
Eclipse - Safetell Ltd
Eclipse - Spear & Jackson
Eclipse - Veka Plc
Eclipse CS - CSSP (Construction Software Services Partnership)
Eclipse Premium - Tarkett Ltd
Eclipse Sliding Glazed Doors - Avanti Systems
Eclipse Spiralux - Spear & Jackson
Eclipse - GCP APPLIED TECHNOLOGIES (UK) LIMITED
ECO - Kair Ventilation Ltd
Eco - Townscape Products Ltd
Eco Collection - Solus Ceramics Ltd
ECO Lift - Phoenix Lifting Systems Ltd
Eco Parking (Grass Paver & Soil Stabilisation) - EBP Building Products Ltd
Ecoarc - Improved Retrofit for Mercury Vapour Lamp - FEILO SYLVANIA EUROPE LIMITED
EcoCaddy™ - Straight Ltd
Ecodisc - Kone PLC
Ecofibre - Gilmour Ecometal
Ecoflex - Uponor Ltd
Ecoflex/Ecoline - Axter Ltd
EcoGard - Lonsdale Metal Company
Ecoheat - IPPEC Systems Ltd
Ecohome - Gilmour Ecometal
Ecojoist - ITW Consutruction Products
Ecomax Reduc - Trim Acoustics
Ecomax Soundslab - Trim Acoustics
EcoMembrane - Visqueen Building Products
Ecometal - George Gilmour (Metals) Ltd
Ecometal - Gilmour Ecometal
ECOMIN - Knauf AMF Ceilings Ltd
Econet - Fläkt Woods Ltd
Econoboost - Stokvis Industrial Boilers (International) Limited
Econoloc - Arvin Motion Control Ltd
Economaire, ElJan - Johnson & Starley
Economatic - Stokvis Industrial Boilers (International) Limited
Economix - Delabie UK Ltd
Economy 7 QTZ - Horstmann Controls Ltd
Econoplate - Stokvis Industrial Boilers (International) Limited
Econopress - Stokvis Industrial Boilers (International) Limited
Econospan - Gilmour Ecometal
Ecopack - Airedale International Air Conditioning Ltd
Ecopanel - Gilmour Ecometal
Ecophon - Nevill Long
Ecophon - New Forest Ceilings Ltd
Eco-rail, Ectasy, Elixir - Pitacs Ltd
EcoShield, EcoForce, EcoKnight - Lochinvar Limited
EcoSort® - Straight Ltd
Ecospan - Gilmour Ecometal
Ecostock - Forterra Building Products Ltd
Ecostream - Britannia Kitchen Ventilation Ltd
Ecotel - Airedale International Air Conditioning Ltd
ecotile - Ecotile Flooring Ltd
Ecotray - Gilmour Ecometal
Ecotube - Stokvis Industrial Boilers (International) Limited
Ecovent - Ves Andover Ltd
Ecowall - Gilmour Ecometal
Ecozip - Gilmour Ecometal
ECS - Electrotechnical Certification Scheme - Joint Industry Board for the Electrical Contracting Industry
ECS epoxy floor coating - Safeguard Europe Ltd
ECS Reset - Philips Lighting Solutions
Edale - Chiltern Invadex
Edelman Leather (Europe) - Edelman Leather
Eden - Rawson Carpets Ltd
EDENAIRE® - Eaton-Williams Group Limited
Edge - Cil Retail Solutions Ltd
Edge - Ellis J T & Co Ltd
Edge - MK (MK Electric Ltd)
Edge leathers - Edelman Leather
Edwin clarke stairways - Ermine Engineering Co. Ltd
EEKO - Electric Elements Co, The
Eeto - Davant Products Ltd
Eetofoam - Davant Products Ltd
EF Series Paint - Ennis-Flint
EF Series RFT - Ennis-Flint
E-fix - Artur Fischer (UK) Ltd
Egcobox® - BRC Special Products - Bekaert Ltd
Egger - Meyer Timber Limited
EGGER Advanced Structural Flooring - Egger (UK) Ltd
EGGER Decorative Protect K20 and + K20 - Egger (UK) Ltd
EGGER Decorative Protect Loft Panels K20 - Egger (UK) Ltd
EGGER DHF K20 - Egger (UK) Ltd
EGGER Eurospan - Egger (UK) Ltd
EGGER OSB K20 - Egger (UK) Ltd
EGGER P5 K20 - Egger (UK) Ltd
EGGER Peel Clean Xtra K20 - Egger (UK) Ltd
EGGER Protect K20 - Egger (UK) Ltd
Eiffelgres - Arnull Bernard J & Co Ltd
ElMeter - EnergyICT Ltd
Eisotech Services - Geoquip Worldwide
EJ - Zon International
ejotherm - EJOT UK Limited
Elasto - Fillcrete Ltd
Elastopak, Epicol T - Grace De Neef UK
Elau AG - Schneider Electric Ltd
Eleco - Bell & Webster Concrete Ltd
Electrak - Electrak International Ltd
Electramate - Gledhill Water Storage Ltd
Electrisaver - Horstmann Controls Ltd
Electrix - Electrix International Ltd
electro+ - Peter Cox Ltd
Electro-Fence - Advanced Perimeter Systems Ltd
Electrofusion - Radius Systems Ltd
Electrolux - Electrolux Domestic Appliances
Electrolux - Electrolux Laundry Systems
Electrolux proffessional service - Electrolux Foodservice
Electromatic - Tuke & Bell Ltd
Electronic 7 - Horstmann Controls Ltd
Electropack - Fulton Boiler Works (Great Britain) Ltd
Electrospot - Illuma Lighting
ElectroWire - Heras
Eleganza - Matki plc
Element - RB UK Ltd
Elementis - Venator
Elementis Pigments - Elementis Pigments
Elementix® (Concrete Rainscreen Cladding System) - Forticrete Masonry
Elements Seating Range - Furnitubes International Ltd
Elequant Cost Modelling Software - Johnson VB LLP
Elequip - Dynniq UK Ltd
Elesse Luxury Home Lift - Wessex Lift Co Ltd
Elga, Elga Labwater - Veolia Water Technologies UKElga Ltd
Elica Handrail - Lewes Design Contracts Ltd
Eliminodor - Purified Air Ltd
Elite - Airdri Ltd
Elite - Cardale Garage Doors
Elite - Dudley Thomas Ltd
Elite - Ellis Patents
Elite - Fitzgerald Lighting Ltd
Elite - Gradus Ltd
Elite - Shackerley (Holdings) Group Ltd incorporating Designer ceramics
Elite Single Point Glazing System - Avanti Systems
Elixir - Matki plc
Eliza Tinley gate fittings - B & M Fencing Limited
Elliott Lucas - Spear & Jackson
Elliptipar - Crescent Lighting
Elster - EnergyICT Ltd
Elterwater - Burlington Slate Ltd
Eltron - Chromalox (UK) Ltd
Eltron (London) Limited - Chromalox (UK) Ltd
Embedded Retaining Walls - Westpile Ltd
EMEA - Ennis-Flint
emerald intelligent touchscreen terminal - CEM Systems Ltd
Emergi - Man - Emergi-Lite Safety Systems
Emergi-Lite - ABB Installation Products Ltd
Emir - Emmerich (Berlon) Ltd
Emit - Allgood plc
Emperor - Ellis Patents
Ems - Envirodoor Markus Ltd
Enable Access, Exitmaster - Enable Access
ENACTO™ - EnergyICT Ltd
Enamelcoat - Conren Ltd
Endura seating - CPS Manufacturing Co
Energy Focus - Crescent Lighting
Energy Range - Twyford Bathrooms
Engineered Wall - ITW Consutruction Products
EnOcean - Helvar Ltd
Ensign - Saint-Gobain PAM UK
Ensign EEZI-FIT - Saint-Gobain PAM UK
Ensto - Ensto Briticent Ltd
Enterprise - ArjoHuntleigh UK
Enterprise - Leofric Building Systems Ltd
Enterprise coal fire - Dunsley Heat Ltd
Envirofast - Envirodoor Markus Ltd
Envirogard - Leigh's Paints
Envirograf - Firebarrier International Ltd T/A Firebarrier Services Ltd
Envirolite - Envirodoor Markus Ltd
Enviromat - Linatex Ltd
Enviropave - Linatex Ltd
Enviroplast - Envirodoor Markus Ltd
Enviva - Durable Ltd
Enyiroseal - Mann McGowan Group
EP203 automatic extinguisher fire panels - C-TEC (Computionics) Ltd
EPB Drain (Channel Drainage Systems) - EBP Building Products Ltd
Epcon/ Epobar - ITW Construction Products
Epidek - Leigh's Paints
Epidox - Witham Oil & Paint Ltd
Epigrip - Leigh's Paints
E-Plex - Kaba Ltd
Epocem - Sika Ltd
Epomax - ITW Construction Products
Epoxy Verti-Patch - Anglo Building Products Ltd
Epoxy Wall Shield - Anglo Building Products Ltd
Epwin Group - Windowbuild
eQ Master Air Handling Units - Fläkt Woods Ltd
eQ Prime Air Handling Units - Fläkt Woods Ltd
Equator - Marley Plumbing and Drainage
Equity Cutpile Carpet Tiles - Burmatex Ltd
ERA - ERA Home Security Ltd
Era - Olby H E & Co Ltd
ERA - Schlegel UK (2006) Ltd
Erdu - Hughes Safety Showers Limited
Ergonomic Kitchens - Moores Furniture Group Ltd
Erico - Kem Edwards Ltd
Erico-caddy ® - Erico Europa (GB) Ltd
Ericson - Sunrite Blinds Ltd
Eriflex®, Eriflex® Flexibar - Erico Europa (GB) Ltd
Erik Joergensen - Zon International
Eritech - Ground Rods - Erico Europa (GB) Ltd
Ermine engineering - Ermine Engineering Co. Ltd
Erosamat - ABG Ltd
Erskines - Newton John & Co Ltd
Esam - Barloworld Vacuum Technology Plc
Esavian - 1200 - Jewers Doors Ltd
Esavian - 126 - Jewers Doors Ltd
Esavian - 127 - Jewers Doors Ltd
Esavian - 128 - Jewers Doors Ltd
Escalator SafetyStrip - Kleeneze Sealtech Ltd
ESCO - Pre-finished Flooring - OSMO UK
E-Screen - Mermet U.K
ESM - EcoWater Systems Ltd
ESM11 - EcoWater Systems Ltd
ESM15 - EcoWater Systems Ltd
ESM9 - EcoWater Systems Ltd
ESP - Hochiki Europe (UK) Ltd
Esplanade - Gradus Ltd
Esprit - Whitecroft Lighting Limited
Essar Aquacoat SP - Smith & Rodger Ltd
Essar Aquacoat Xtra - Smith & Rodger Ltd
Essar Bar Top Lacquer - Smith & Rodger Ltd
Essar French Polish - Smith & Rodger Ltd
Essar Precatalysed Lacquers - Smith & Rodger Ltd
Essar Woodshield - Smith & Rodger Ltd
Essential - Vicaima Ltd
Essential Collection - Solus Ceramics Ltd
Essentials & EVA - Golden Coast Ltd
Esterol®, Estesol® FX™ - Deb Group Limited
Esthetique - Veka Plc
Estudio - Ellis J T & Co Ltd
Eternal - Coburn Sliding Systems Ltd
Eternit - FGF Ltd
Eternit-Promat - Firebarrier International Ltd T/A Firebarrier Services Ltd
Euracom - Ackermann Ltd
Eurisol - Mineral Wool Insulation Manufacturers Association
Euro Lift - Phoenix Lifting Systems Ltd
Euro Shelving - Moresecure Ltd
Eurobar - Imperial Machine Co Ltd
Eurobench - Q.M.P
Eurobox - The Safety Letterbox Company Ltd
Eurocord 2000 - Rawson Carpets Ltd
Eurocoustic - British Gypsum Ltd
Eurodek Raised Access Floors - SIG Interiors
Euroflex - Pitchmastic PmB Ltd
Euroflow - Johnson & Starley Ltd
Euroglas - Clow Group Ltd
Eurograde - Securikey Ltd
Euro-Guard® - Jackson H S & Son (Fencing) Ltd
Euroline - Rangemaster
Euroline - S & B Ltd
Euroll UK - Acorn Garage Doors Ltd
Euro-meridian - Pyronix
Euronox - Wellman Robey Ltd
Europack - Fulton Boiler Works (Great Britain) Ltd
European - Wellman Robey Ltd
European Technical Approvals - British Board of Agrément
EuroPipe - Blucher UK LTD
Eurosafe - Chubb Safe Equipment Company
Euroslide - Q.M.P
Eurostar - BLV Licht-und Vakuumtecnik
Eurostar Boilers - TR Engineering Ltd
Eurotherm - Watts Industries UK Ltd
EV2008 and EV2008 No Touch - Santon
Evac+Chair - Evac+Chair International Ltd
Evacast facing masonary - Hanson Concrete Products
Evalast - Hanson Building Products UK
Evalast Blocks - Hanson Concrete Products
Evalastic - ICB (International Construction Bureau) Ltd
Evalon - ICB (International Construction Bureau) Ltd

Evamatic - KSB Ltd
Evamatic Box - KSB Ltd
Evans - Evans Vanodine International PLC
Evans Pourform - Wood International Agency Ltd
Evaporative Coolers - Radiant Services Ltd
Evelite - Amari Plastics Plc
Everbind, Everblock - Everlac (GB) Ltd
Evercoat - Everlac (GB) Ltd
Everdry - Timloc Expamet Building Products
Everflex - Everlac (GB) Ltd
Everlac - Everlac (GB) Ltd
Everlast Paint grade Masonary - Hanson Concrete Products
Everlite Facing Masonary - Hanson Concrete Products
Everply - Everlac (GB) Ltd
Eversan - Everlac (GB) Ltd
Everseal - Everlac (GB) Ltd
Evertaut - Evertaut Ltd
Evertex - Everlac (GB) Ltd
Everthane - Everlac (GB) Ltd

eVision Supercars - www.evrent.co.uk - HE Services (Plant Hire) Ltd
Evo - Hyperion Wall Furniture Ltd
Evoke - Alutec
Evolution - Carter Retail Equipment Ltd
Evolution - Chalmit Lighting
Evolution - En-tout-cas Tennis Courts Ltd
Evolution - Mode Lighting (UK) Ltd
Evolution - T B S Fabrications
Evolution radiant strip - Dunham Bush Ltd
Evolve - Alutec
evolve - Bushboard Limited
Evolve - Flexiform Business Furniture Ltd
Evo-Stik - Evode Ltd
EWS® - Eaton-Williams Group Limited
EWT - Dimplex UK Limited
Excalibar - A Kenrick & Sons
Excalibur - TROAX UK Ltd
Excalibur - UTC Fire & Securites
Excel - Axter Ltd
Excel - James Gibbons Format Ltd
Excel - Kleeneze Sealtech Ltd
Excel 5000 - Honeywell Control Systems Ltd
Excel Life Safety - Honeywell Control Systems Ltd
Excel Pro - Marlow Ropes Ltd
Excel Security Manager - Honeywell Control Systems Ltd
Excelastic - Geosynthetic Technology Ltd
Exceliner - Geosynthetic Technology Ltd
Excelsior - ADT Fire and Security Plc
Excil - LPA Group PLC
ExcluDoor - Sunray Engineering Ltd
Exclusive - Vicaima Ltd
ExecDoor - Sunray Engineering Ltd

E (con't)

Exhausterl blowers - Quirepace Ltd
Exide - M.J. Electronic Services (International) Ltd
Exit Box - Fitzgerald Lighting Ltd
Exit:Way guidance - Hoyles Electronic Developments Ltd
Exitguard - Hoyles Electronic Developments Ltd
Exmet - Expamet Building Products
Exodraft - Poujoulat (UK) Ltd
EXOS - Franke Sissons Ltd
Exos - Kaba Ltd
Expamet - Allmat (East Surrey) Ltd
Expamet - Expamet Building Products
Expamet fencing - Chestnut Products Limited
Expandafoam - Fosroc Ltd
Expansionthene - SCP Concrete Sealing Technology Ltd
Expelex, Exi-Fire and Exi-Sound - Exitex Ltd
Exposit - Erlau AG
Expowall - Deceuninck Ltd
Express - Heatrae Sadia Heating Ltd
Extaseal - SCP Concrete Sealing Technology Ltd
Extralyte Low Density Blocks - Broome Bros (Doncaster) Ltd
Extraproof - BriggsAmasco
Eye2Eye - Safetell Ltd
Eyeball – Self Testing and Remote Monitoring Systems - SCS Group
E-Z Rect - E-Z Rect Ltd
Ezi - lift - Didsbury Engineering Co Ltd

F

F Shield - Bollom Fire Protection Ltd
F.S.B - Hafele UK Ltd
F'Light - Glamox Electric (UK) Ltd
F2P - Artur Fischer (UK) Ltd
F2P-G - Artur Fischer (UK) Ltd
Fab&Fix - Schlegel UK (2006) Ltd
Fablok - SFS Intec LTD
Fabresa - R J Stokes & Co Limited
Fabrex - Tuke & Bell Ltd
Façade System - Paroc Panel Systems Uk Ltd
Facet - Zon International
Facette® Shades - Luxaflex®
Factor 4 - Interface Europe Ltd
Fagley Yorkstone - Hard York Quarries Ltd
Fairfield - Samuel Heath & Sons plc
Falco - Falco UK Ltd
Falcon - James Gibbons Format Ltd
Falcon - Swintex Ltd
Falcon - Water Technology Engineering Ltd
Fallguard vertical fall arrest ladder system - Metreel Ltd
Fanaire - Fantasia Distribution Ltd
Fantasia - Lappset UK Ltd
Fantasia ceiling fans - Fantasia Distribution Ltd
FAR Manifolds and Components - SAV United Kingdom Ltd
FARAL ALBA Aluminium Radiators - AEL
FARAL Alliance Aluminium Radiators - AEL
FARAL Tropical Aluminium Radiators - AEL
Farmington - Farmington Masonry LLP
Farr 3D/3D - Camfil Farr Ltd
Fascinating finishes - Kingstonian Paint Ltd
Fascinations - Carpets of Worth Ltd
Fast Air Handling Units - Thermal Technology Sales Ltd
Fast build barriers - Bell & Webster Concrete Ltd
fast build platforms - Bell & Webster Concrete Ltd
Fast build rooms - Bell & Webster Concrete Ltd
fast build rooms - Bell & Webster Concrete Ltd
Fast build tendering - Bell & Webster Concrete Ltd
fast build walls - Bell & Webster Concrete Ltd
Fast fit - Panel & Louvre Co Ltd
Fast Gate - APT Controls Ltd
Fast rack - Legrand Electric Ltd
FastArch - EHSmith
Fastcall - Tunstal Healthcare (UK) Ltd
FastClad - EHSmith
Fastel - P4 Limited
Fastel Care - P4 Limited
Fastel SRM - P4 Limited
Fastel Wireless - P4 Limited
Fastel Within - P4 Limited
Fastelink - P4 Limited
Fastelwatch - P4 Limited
Fastfill - Flexcrete Technologies Limited
Fastfloor Beam and Block Flooring System - Tarmac Trading Limited (Blocks)
Fastie - Redifix Ltd
FastTrack™ Folder-Inserter System - Neopost Ltd
Fastwall - Fastwall Ltd
FaTec - Artur Fischer (UK) Ltd
Favourite - Valor
FCA member - Chestnut Products Limited
FEB - Strand Hardware Ltd
Fecon Filters - Vianen KVS BV
Felix Dance Floor - Felix Design Ltd
Felix Riser Stage - Felix Design Ltd
Felix Staging - Felix Design Ltd
Feltex - Rawson Fillings Ltd
Fence Decor - Jotun Henry Clark Ltd Decorative Division
Fence Mate - Danbury Fencing Limited
Fencetone - Protim Solignum Ltd
Fenlite - Hanson Building Products UK
Fenlite Blocks - Hanson Concrete Products
Fentox - Aldous & Stamp (Services) Ltd
Fep 'O' rings - Ashton Seals Ltd
Fermacell (K10) - Fermacell
Fermacell Powerpanel H20 (H30) - Fermacell
Fermacell Powerpanel HD (H30) - Fermacell
Ferndale - Chiltern Invadex
Feron - Weyland incorporating Clayton Munroe
Ferramenta - Weyland incorporating Clayton Munroe
FETA - Fire Industry Association
Ffestiniog - Welsh Slate Limited
FG Contracts - Laytrad Contract Furniture Ltd
Fibercill - Fibercill
Fiberskirt - Fibercill
Fibertrave - Fibercill
Fibo - Lignacite (North London) Ltd
Fibo Lightweight Insulation Blocks - Stowell Concrete Ltd
FibreFlex - Radius Systems Ltd
Fibrethatch - Africa Roofing Uk
Fibrocem - LaFarge Cement UK
Fibrotrace ® - Pressure Coolers Ltd T/A Maestro Pressure Coolers
Fife Alarms - Fife Fire Engineers & Consultants Ltd
Fife Fire - Fife Fire Engineers & Consultants Ltd
Fiji 2 - Rangemaster
Filcor EPS - Cordek Ltd
Fildek - Don Construction Products Ltd
Filestation, Filetrack, Filing Heaven - Rackline Systems Storage Ltd
Filia XP - Kermi (UK) Ltd
Fillaboard - Fillcrete Ltd
Fillcrete - Fillcrete Ltd
Filmatic - Watts Industries UK Ltd
Filon - Filon Products Ltd
Filon Citadel - Filon Products Ltd
Filon DR - Filon Products Ltd
Filon Fixsafe - Filon Products Ltd
Filon Monarch-F Barrel Vault Rooflights - Filon Products Ltd
Filon mpGRP - Filon Products Ltd
Filon Multiclad-F - Filon Products Ltd
Filon Over-roofing with Profix Spacer System - Filon Products Ltd
Filon SupaSafe - Filon Products Ltd
Filon V-Flow Valley Gutters - Filon Products Ltd
Filter Pod - Water Technology Engineering Ltd
Filterball - Marflow Eng Ltd
Filtermate - Marflow Eng Ltd
Filto-Bench - Horizon International Ltd
Fimap - Barloworld Vacuum Technology Plc
Fin Cycle Stand - Furnitubes International Ltd
Find A Builder - Federation of Master Builders
Fine Uplands Twist - Adam Carpets Ltd
Fine Worcester Twist - Adam Carpets Ltd
Fineline - Fastwall Ltd
Fineline - Matki plc
Finesse - ABG Ltd
Finger Protector - Safety Assured Ltd
FingerSafe - Dorma Door Services Ltd
Finned Tube - Turnbull & Scott (Engineers) Ltd
Finned Tube Radiators - Turnbull & Scott (Engineers) Ltd
Finno - Lappset UK Ltd
Finsa - Boardcraft Ltd
Finsa - Meyer Timber Limited
Finvector - Dunham Bush Ltd
Firaqua - Firwood Paints Ltd
Fire Curtain - Colt International
Fire Curtain- Fibreroll E120 - Bolton Gate Company Ltd
Fire Curtain- Fibreroll EW120 - Bolton Gate Company Ltd
Fire Curtain- Fibreroll S Smoketight/ fire Curtain - Bolton Gate Company Ltd
Fire Flexmaster - Docherty New Vent Chimney Group
Fire Path - Colt International
Fire Protection Prducts - Smith & Rodger Ltd
Fire Rated - The Safety Letterbox Company Ltd
Fire Safe - Kingspan Ltd
Fire secur - Ide T & W Ltd
Fire Shutter - Fireroll E60 - Bolton Gate Company Ltd
Fire Shutter- Fireroll Acoustic E120 - Bolton Gate Company Ltd
Fire Shutter- Fireroll E120 - Bolton Gate Company Ltd
Fireact - Rea Metal Windows Ltd
Fireblock - Dufaylite Developments Ltd
Firebrand - Hart Door Systems Ltd
Firebrand - Minkon Ltd
Firebreak - Rea Metal Windows Ltd
Firechef - Profab Access Ltd
Firecom' Fire Telephone Systems - PEL Services Limited
Firecryl FR - Thatching Advisory Services Ltd
Fired Earth - Fired Earth
Fired Earth H2O (The Miracle of Water) - Fired Earth
Firedex - Cooper Lighting
Firedex 3302 - Cooper Lighting
Firedex Biwire - Cooper Lighting
FireFace Plus - Sealmaster
FireFoam - Sealmaster
Fireframe - Sapa Building Systems (monarch and glostal)
FireGlaze - Sealmaster
Fireguard - TCW Services (Control) Ltd
Firelite - Valor
FireLock - Sunray Engineering Ltd
Firelok Cladding Panel - Gradient Insulations (UK) Ltd
Firelok Deck - Gradient Insulations (UK) Ltd
Firemac 2000 - McKenzie-Martin Ltd
Fireman - Clark Door Ltd
FireMaster - Cooper Group Ltd
Firemaster - Docherty New Vent Chimney Group
Firemaster - Firemaster Extinguisher Ltd
Firemaster - Premdor
Fireplan - Internal Partitions Systems
FirePlugs - Sealmaster
Firepoint - Hoyles Electronic Developments Ltd
Fireshield - Bollom Fire Protection Ltd
Fireshield - Premdor
Fireshield Partitions - Avanti Systems
Fireshield ™ - Accent Hansen
Firesleeve - Dufaylite Developments Ltd
FireSmart - Icopal Limited
Firestile - Mann McGowan Group
Firestone RubberCover (EPDM single ply roofing membranes) - EBP Building Products Ltd
Firestop - Dow Corning Europe S.A
Firestop - George Fischer Sales Ltd
Firestore - Franklin Hodge Industries Ltd
Firetainer - Franklin Hodge Industries Ltd
Firetech - Knauf Insulation Ltd
Firetex - Gilgen Door Systems UK Ltd
Firetex - Leigh's Paints
Firewarn' Fire Alarm Systems - PEL Services Limited
Firewatch - TCW Services (Control) Ltd
Firglo - Firwood Paints Ltd
Firlene - Firwood Paints Ltd
Firlex - Firwood Paints Ltd
Firpavar - Firwood Paints Ltd
First Alert - BRK Brands Europe Ltd
First class - Lappset UK Ltd
First-Rol - Reflex-Rol (UK)
Firsyn - Firwood Paints Ltd
Firth Carpets - Interface Europe Ltd
Firwood - Firwood Paints Ltd
Fischer - Artur Fischer (UK) Ltd
Fischer - Kem Edwards Ltd
Fitex - Airsprung Beds Ltd
Fitt box - PFP Electrical Products Ltd
Fitter & Poulton - PFP Electrical Products Ltd
Five Brazilian Slates - Kirkstone
Fix - Grorud Industries Ltd
Fix=r - SIG Roofing
FL Façade - Consult Lighting Ltd
Flagmaster - Zephyr The Visual Communicators
Flame Bar - Fire Protection Ltd
Flamecheck - Arch Timber Protection
Flameguard - Bollom Fire Protection Ltd
FlameShield - Spaceright Europe Limited
Flametex - Airsprung Beds Ltd
Flamlac - Bollom Fire Protection Ltd
Flammtex - Vita Liquid Polymers Ltd
Flamrad - Infraglo Limited
Flaplock - The Safety Letterbox Company Ltd
Flashpoint infra red - Emergi-Lite Safety Systems
Flavel - Beko plc
Flavel - BFM Europe Limited
Flaviker - Arnull Bernard J & Co Ltd
Flaviker Tiles - Reed Harris
Flex - Harbro Supplies Ltd
Flex - seal - Flex-Seal Couplings Ltd
Flexbond - Rawson Fillings Ltd
Flexcase - Universal Components Ltd
Flexcon - Flamco UK Ltd
Flexconpak - Flamco UK Ltd
FlexDrum - Flexelec(UK) Ltd
Flexfelt - Rawson Fillings Ltd
Flexfiller - Flamco UK Ltd
FlexFloor - Flexelec(UK) Ltd
Flexible Window Foil - Illbruck Sealant Systems UK Ltd
Flexi-bollard - Berry Systems
Flexibuild Sort Units - Envopak Group Ltd
Flexiburo - Flexiform Business Furniture Ltd
Flexideck - Safety Works & Solutions Ltd
Flexidoor - Envirodoor Markus Ltd
Flexiglas - Coburn Sliding Systems Ltd
Flexiglaze - Safetell Ltd
Flexiglide - Flexiform Business Furniture Ltd
Flexiguard - Advanced Perimeter Systems Ltd
Flexiline - Ennis-Flint
Fleximetric - Flexiform Business Furniture Ltd
Flexiphalte - BriggsAmasco
Flexi-post - Berry Systems
Flexistor - Flexiform Business Furniture Ltd
Flexiwall acrylic wall coating - Altro Ltd
FlexKit - Flexelec(UK) Ltd
Flexlock - Viking Johnson
FlexMat - Flexelec(UK) Ltd
Flex-net - Metway Electrical Industries Ltd
Flex-net II - Metway Electrical Industries Ltd
Flexocel - Lanxess Urethanes UK Ltd
FlexTrace - Flexelec(UK) Ltd
Flexvent - Flamco UK Ltd
Flipflap - Envirodoor Markus Ltd
Floating Solar Fountain - Intersolar Group Ltd
Flocke - Mermet U.K
FloCon Commissioning Modules - SAV United Kingdom Ltd
FloDrain Channel Drainage - FloPlast Ltd
FloFit Hot and Cold Plumbing Systems - FloPlast Ltd
FloGuard - FloPlast Ltd
Flo-jo ® - Pressure Coolers Ltd T/A Maestro Pressure Coolers
Floodline - Illuma Lighting
FloodSax® - Straight Ltd
Floor Muffle - Polypipe Building Products
Floorcote - Coo-Var Ltd
Floor-fast - Lindapter International
Flooritall - Spaceway South Ltd
Floormaker - Western Cork Ltd
Floormaster - Interfloor Limited
Floorshield - Springvale E P S
Floorworks - Interfloor Limited
Flopast - Allmat (East Surrey) Ltd
Floralsilk - Floralsilk Ltd
Florence - Whitecroft Lighting Limited
Florette - Carpets of Worth Ltd
FloSaver - FloPlast Ltd
Floway - CPV Ltd
Flowchem - Flowcrete Plc
Flowcrete - Flowcrete Plc
Flowdeck - Redman Fisher Engineering
Flowfast - Flowcrete Plc
Flowforge® - Redman Fisher Engineering
Flowfresh - Flowcrete Plc
Flowgrid - Redman Fisher Engineering
FlowGRiP TM - Redman Fisher Engineering
Flowguard - Pentair Thermal Management
Flowlok - Redman Fisher Engineering
Flowmax - Range Cylinders
FlowRyt® - Rytons Building Products Ltd
Flowseal - Movement Joints (UK)
FlowSmart - Alpha Therm Ltd
Flowtop - Watco UK Ltd
Flowtread - Redman Fisher Engineering
Fluemaster - Docherty New Vent Chimney Group
Fluidair Economy drive system - Fluidair Ltd
Fluidair rotary - Fluidair Ltd
Flush - T B S Fabrications
Flush glazing - Clestra Limited
Flushplan - Internal Partitions Systems
Flushslide - Coburn Sliding Systems Ltd
Fluxite, Fernox - Fernox
FLX Floodlight - Consult Lighting Ltd
FMB - Federation of Master Builders
FMB Masterbond - Federation of Master Builders
Foamalux ® - Righton Ltd
FOAMGLAS - Pittsburgh Corning (United Kingdom) Limited
Foamtex - Exitex Ltd
Foam-Tite - Schlegel UK (2006) Ltd
Focal Point - Brintons Ltd
Focus - Ellis J T & Co Ltd
Focus - James Gibbons Format Ltd
Focus - Saint-Gobain Ecophon Ltd
Foil IP44, Foiul Single Optic and Foil Twin Optic - Whitecroft Lighting Limited
Foldaside - Coburn Sliding Systems Ltd
Foldaway - Tilley International Ltd
Folio - Girsberger London
Fondu - Lafarge Aluminates Ltd
Football Goals - Sportsmark Group Ltd
Footlights - Paragon by Heckmondwike
Footprint - Footprint Sheffield Ltd
Force Dalle - Axter Ltd
Force Line - Axter Ltd
Forceflow - Biddle Air Systems Ltd
Forest - Lappset UK Ltd
Forest-Saver - Earth Anchors Ltd
Forma D400 - Althon Ltd
Format - James Gibbons Format Ltd
Format 50 - James Gibbons Format Ltd
Formica - Formica Ltd
Formica Spawall - Formica Ltd
Formica Cubewall - Formica Ltd
Formica Firewall - Formica Ltd
Formica Lifeseal - Formica Ltd
Formica Prima - Formica Ltd
Formica Unipanel - Formica Ltd
Formost - Flexiform Business Furniture Ltd
Formpave - Forterra Building Products Ltd
Forterra - Bison Precast
Fortic - Range Cylinders
Fospro - Hellermann Tyton
Foulmaster - Pump Technical Services Ltd
Foxtrot Underlay - Panel Agency Limited
Foxxx swimming pool kits - Fox Pool (UK) Ltd
FP McCann - Bell & Webster Concrete Ltd
fpdc - Federation of Plastering and Drywall Contractors
FPS - Federation of Piling Specialists
Framelights - Illuma Lighting
Frametherm - Davant Products Ltd
Frameworks - Mat.Works Flooring Solutions
Frami Panel System - Mabey Hire Ltd
Franch - Zon International
Francis Pegler - Pegler Ltd
Franke Eco System - Franke UK Ltd
Franke Kitchen Systems - Franke UK Ltd
Franke Sinks - Franke UK Ltd
Franke Taps - Franke UK Ltd
Franke Triflow - Franke UK Ltd
Franki - Skanska UK Plc
FreeFlush - Cistermiser Ltd
Freespace - Project Office Furniture PLC
Freestyle - Swedecor
Freeway - Cistermiser Ltd
Freeway - Rawson Carpets Ltd
Freeway - Vantrunk Engineering Ltd
FreeWeigh™ In-Motion Electronic Weighing System - Neopost Ltd
Fresfield Lane - Michelmersh Brick Holdings PLC
Fresh Touch - Floralsilk Ltd
Freyssibar - Freyssinet Ltd
Freyssinet Makers - Freyssinet Ltd
Fridgewatch - J & E Hall Ltd
Friedland - Friedland Ltd
Frimeda - Halfen Ltd
Fritztile Resilient Terrazzo - Marble Flooring Spec. Ltd
Frontrunner - Plastic Extruders Ltd
Frost - FC Frost Ltd
Frostar - Imperial Machine Co Ltd
Frostguard - Pentair Thermal Management
Froth-pak - Dow Building Solutions
FRX (Fluidair rotary Screw) - Fluidair Ltd
FS Screed - Conren Ltd
FSB - Allgood plc
FSB Door Furniture - JB Architectural Ltd
FST (Flexible Security Topping) - Binns Fencing Ltd
FT Gearing Landscape Services Ltd - Gearing F T Landscape Services Ltd
FTPG Olympic Anti-Stain Grout - Carter-Dal International
Fuel bank bunded storage units - Cookson and Zinn (PTL) Ltd
Fufil - Springvale E P S
FUHR - Carl F Groupco Limited
Fujitsu - Purified Air Ltd
Fullflow - Fullflow Group Ltd
Fulton-Series J - Fulton Boiler Works (Great Britain) Ltd
Fundermax - Telling Architectural Ltd

F (con't)

Fungishield - Glixtone Ltd
Funtheme - Design & Display Structures Ltd
Furfix Wall Profiles - Simpson Strong-Tie®
Furmanite Flange Covers - TEAM INDUSTRIAL SERVICES (UK) LIMITED
Furmanite Sheet/Jointing Compound - TEAM INDUSTRIAL SERVICES (UK) LIMITED
Furmanite Tube Plug - TEAM INDUSTRIAL SERVICES (UK) LIMITED
Fuseal - George Fischer Sales Ltd
Fusion - Quiligotti Terrazzo Tiles Limited
Fusite - Emerson Climate Technologies
Futura - T B S Fabrications
Futurewall - Optima
FW 50 - Schueco UK
FW 60 - Schueco UK
fwd products - Rivermeade Signs Ltd
Fyrebag 240 - Mann McGowan Group
Fyrex - Iles Waste Systems

G

G3000 - Girsberger London
G3300 - Girsberger London
Gabions - PHI Group Ltd
GAI - Guild of Architectural Ironmongers
Galaxy - Kompan Ltd
Galaxy spring operated cable reels - Metreel Ltd
Galaxy Ultra (operating theatre lamps) - Brandon Medical
Galena Spencer Ltd - Kidde Fire Protection Services Ltd
Galerie & Galerie Optimise Ranges - Twyford Bathrooms
Galleria - Brintons Ltd
Galloway - Russell Roof Tiles Ltd
Galparket - Deralam Laminates Ltd
Galtee - Meyer Timber Limited
Galtres - York Handmade Brick Co Ltd
Galvalloy - Tata Steel Colors
Gamma - Sika Liquid Plastics Limited
Gang-Nail Connectors - ITW Consutruction Products
Garaclad - Liget Compton
Garador - Acorn Garage Doors Ltd
Garador - Garador Ltd
Garbina - Unicorn Containers Ltd
Garfa - Zon International
Garrison, Genesis, Glasdon Jubilee - Glasdon U.K. Limited
Gartec Dumb Waiter - Gartec Ltd
Gartec Goods Lift - Gartec Ltd
Gartec Home lifts - Gartec Ltd
Gas 210 ECO - Broag Ltd
Gas 310 ECO - Broag Ltd
Gas 610 ECO - Broag Ltd
Gas zips - Power Plastics Ltd
Gascogne Limestone - Kirkstone
Gascool - Birdsall Services Ltd
Gascoseeker - Gas Measurement Instruments Ltd
Gasgard - MSA (Britain) Ltd
Gasgard gas detector - MSA (Britain) Ltd
GasSaver - Alpha Therm Ltd
Gastech - Birdsall Services Ltd
Gastyle II Ridge Terminal - Dunbrik (Yorks) Ltd
Gasurveyor - Gas Measurement Instruments Ltd
Gates - Harling Security Solutions Limited
Gateway - Gunnebo UK Limited
Gatic Access Covers - Gatic
Gatic Drainage Gratings - Gatic
Gatic Fibrelite - Gatic
Gatic Slotdrain - Gatic
Gatic Streetwise - Gatic
Gatorband - Simplex Signs Limited
Gayton Door - AS Newbould Ltd
GEA - Garage Equipment Association Ltd
GEC Anderson - GEC Anderson Ltd
Gedina - Saint-Gobain Ecophon Ltd
Geepee - Swish Building Products
GeGe - Kaba Ltd
Gelacryl - Grace De Neef UK
Gem - Crane Fluid Systems
Gem - Tunstal Healthcare (UK) Ltd
Gemini - Hoyles Electronic Developments Ltd
Gemini - Rangemaster
Gemini® (Twin Interlocking Plain Tile) - Forticrete Roofing
General Combustion - Beverley Environmental Ltd
Genesis - Dixon Turner Wallcoverings
Genesis - Eltron Chromalox
Genesis - T B S Fabrications
Genie - Genie Europe
Genny range - Radiodetection Ltd
Genoa, and HS Grating - Lang+Fulton
Genovent - Gebhardt Kiloheat
Genpac - Sandhurst Manufacturing Co Ltd
Gent - Gent Limited
Gent Services - Gent Limited
Geocel - Geocel Ltd
GeoGard - Firestone Building Products
Geologica - R J Stokes & Co Limited
George Fischer - The BSS Group
Georgian - Samuel Heath & Sons plc
Georgian & Victorian Brass - Eaton Electric Limited
Geotextile - Pitchmastic PmB Ltd
Gerbergraphix - GB Sign Solutions Limited
Gerni - Nilfisk Advance Ltd
Geryon - Gilgen Door Systems UK Ltd
Geschwender - LSA Projects Ltd
Gestra - Flowserve Flow Control
GET - Schneider Electric Ltd
Gethal FSC Certiply - Wood International Agency Ltd
Getinge - ArjoHuntleigh UK
Geze - Hafele UK Ltd
GIAS - ITAB Prolight UK Limited
GIFAfloor - Knauf UK
Gifcrete - Don Construction Products Ltd
Gillair smoke vent products - Matthews & Yates Ltd
Gilt - Baggeridge Brick PLC
Girdlestone - Weir Pumps Ltd
GL Globe - Consult Lighting Ltd
Glade - SC Johnson Wax
Glamox - Glamox Electric (UK) Ltd
Glamox - Glamox Luxo Lighting Limited
Glamur - Jotun Henry Clark Ltd Decorative Division
Glasbord - Crane Composites
Glasdon Jubilee (litter bins) - Glasdon UK Limited
Glasroc - British Gypsum Ltd
Glass Blocks - Swedecor
Glass chalkboards - Charles Lightfoot Ltd
Glass fibre Manufacturors - Aden Hynes Sculpture Studios
Glass Shower Panels by Coram - Coram Showers Ltd
Glass Technology Services - British Glass Manufacturers Confederation
Glassgard - Bonwyke Ltd
Glasswhite - Cardale Garage Doors
Glasswood - Cardale Garage Doors
Glasurit - HMG Paints
GlazaTherm - Lonsdale Metal Company
Glazed Bricks - Ibstock Hathernware Ltd
Glazing Accessories - Simon R W Ltd
Glen - Dimplex UK Limited
Glendyne Slate - Cembrit Ltd
Glenfield - Benlowe Group Limited
Gleno - Coverworld UK Limited
Glidetrak - Rackline Systems Storage Ltd
Global - BFM Europe Limited
Global 2 - EBC UK Ltd
Glocote - Coo-Var Ltd
Glo-dac - Dacrylate Paints Ltd
Glostal - Sapa Building Systems (monarch and glostal)
Glostal - Technal UK
Glover Series 2000 Extinguishers - Fife Fire Engineers & Consultants Ltd
Glow-Worm - Hepworth Heating Ltd
Gloy - Henkel Consumer Adhesives
Gluegunsdirect - Kenyon Performance Adhesives
Glulam Beams - Kingston Craftsmen Structural Timber Engineers Ltd
Glynn-Johnson Door Controls - Relcross Ltd
Go Green - ABG Ltd
Godwin Pumps - Goodwin HJ Ltd
Gold - Wilo Samson Pumps Ltd
Goldstar - Wilo Samson Pumps Ltd
Golf Range - Helmsman
Good Directions - Metal Gutta
Goodsmaster - Stannah Lifts Ltd
Gordon Russell - Steelcase Strafor Plc
Goxhill Plain Tile - Sandtoft Roof Tiles Ltd
Grad Decking System - Alfresco Floors
GRAD Decking System - The Outdoor Deck Company
Grada - Panel & Louvre Co Ltd
Gradus - Gradus Ltd
Grafati Re-Gard - Andura Coatings Ltd
Grafik Eye - Tidmarsh & Sons
Grafix - Dunhams of Norwich
G-Rail 4100 - Goelst
G-Rail 5100 - Goelst
Grampian - Russell Roof Tiles Ltd
Grampian - Sashless Window Co Ltd
Granclene - Harbro Supplies Ltd
Grando UK - Buckingham Swimming Pools Ltd
Grange Wilton - Ulster Carpet Mills Ltd
Granit Multisafe - Tarkett Ltd
Granit SafeT - Tarkett Ltd
Granito™ (Etched Blocks) - Forticrete Masonry
Graphic Inlay - Kleen-Tex Industries Ltd
Grass Flow - Brett Landscaping
Grassblock - Grass Concrete Ltd
Grasscel Cellular Paving - Ruthin Precast Concrete Ltd
Grasscrete - Grass Concrete Ltd
Grasshopper - Charles Lawrence Surfaces Ltd
Grasskerb - Grass Concrete Ltd
Grasspave - ABG Ltd
Grassroad - Grass Concrete Ltd
Grate-fast - Lindapter International
Gravelsafe - CED Ltd
Graviner - Explosion Protection Systems - Kidde Fire Protection Ltd
Grease Bugs - Progressive Product Developments Ltd
Grease Shield - Vianen KVS BV
Great-stuf - Dow Building Solutions
Green Basalt - Tarmac Trading Limited (Aggregates)
Green Genie - Lotus Water Garden Products Ltd
Green Help App - Institute of Specialist Surveyors and Engineers
Green2Clean - Lotus Water Garden Products Ltd
Greenstar HE - Worcester Heat Systems Ltd
greenteQ - VBH (GB) Ltd
Greenwich - Branson Leisure Ltd
Greenwood - Carl F Groupco Limited
Greenwood Airvac - Zehnder Group UK Ltd
Grid Liner - Sportsmark Group Ltd
Grid Plus - MK (MK Electric Ltd)
Gridframe - Sapa Building Systems (monarch and glostal)
Grid-it - Hamilton R & Co Ltd
Grid-lok - Vantrunk Engineering Ltd
Gridmaster - Mat.Works Flooring Solutions
Gridpart - Gridpart Interiors Ltd
Griffin - Eliza Tinsley Ltd
Griffin Fire - Griffin and General Fire Services Ltd
grime grabber entrance matting - Jaymart Rubber & Plastics Ltd
Grinnell Firekill - Tyco Fire and Integrated Solutions
Gripfalt SMA - Breedon Aggregates
Gripfill - Laybond Products Ltd
Gripline - Enable Access
Grippa - Tyco Water Works
Gripper handlamps - Ensto Briticent Ltd
Gripperrods - Interfloor Limited
Gripple - Kem Edwards Ltd
Griptight Plus Woodscrews - UK Fasteners Ltd
Griptop - Don Construction Products Ltd
Groheart - Grohe Ltd
Grohedal - Grohe Ltd
Grohetec - Grohe Ltd
Grohetec special fittings - Grohe Ltd
Gro-Lux - Plant House /Greenhouse & Aquarium Lamps - FEILO SYLVANIA EUROPE LIMITED
Ground Engineering - EMAP
Groundform - Cordek Ltd
GRP 4 - Group Four Glassfibre Ltd
GRP System - Intergrated Polymer Systems (UK) Ltd
Grundfos - The BSS Group
GT Trolleys - Envopak Group Ltd
GTEC Acoustic Homespan - Siniat Ltd
GTEC Aqua Board - Siniat Ltd
GTEC db Board - Siniat Ltd
GTEC Drywall Fixings - Siniat Ltd
GTEC Fire Board - Siniat Ltd
GTEC Joint Compounds - Siniat Ltd
GTEC LaDura Board - Siniat Ltd
GTEC Megadeco - Siniat Ltd
GTEC Moisture Board - Siniat Ltd
GTEC Thermal Board - Siniat Ltd
Guard - Dixon Turner Wallcoverings
Guardian - Alumasc Exterior Building Products Ltd
Guardian - Guardian Lock & Engineering Co. Ltd
Guardian - Intersolar Group Ltd
Guardian - The Safety Letterbox Company Ltd
Guardian LST - Jaga UK
Guardmaster - Docherty New Vent Chimney Group
Guardstation - UTC Fire & Securites
Guardwire - Heras
Gulfstream - Gledhill Water Storage Ltd
Gummers - Bristan Group
Gummybins® - Straight Ltd
Gunnebo - Gunnebo UK Limited
Gun-point - Gun-Point Ltd
Gustafs - LSA Projects Ltd
GutterBrush Leaf Protection System - FloPlast Ltd
GVR Recloser - Hawker Siddley Switchgear
GVS Sectionaliser - Hawker Siddley Switchgear
GW Axial - Matthews & Yates Ltd
Gwent Weighing Systems - Phoenix Scales Ltd
GWF - Switch2 Energy Solutions Ltd
GX Geomembrane, GX Flexi, GX Barrier Membrane - Visqueen Building Products
Gypframe - Metsec Ltd
Gyproc, Gyptone, Gyprex, GypFloor, Gypframe, GypWall, GypLyner - British Gypsum Ltd
Gyvlon - Isocrete Floor Screeds Ltd

H

H & R Johnson - R J Stokes & Co Limited
H & S Whelan - Stamford Products Limited
H&V News - Heating and Ventilation News - EMAP
H.S.M - Tony Team Ltd
H4000 Helix - Elster Metering Ltd
HA CUT AF/HA FLEX AF - Grace De Neef UK
Habitus - Ulster Carpet Mills Ltd
Haddon - Tecstone - Haddonstone Ltd
Haddoncraft - Haddonstone Ltd
Haddonstone - Haddonstone Ltd
Hadrian Toilet Cubicles - Relcross Ltd
Haffele UK Ltd - Hafele UK Ltd
HAG - HAG Shutters & Grilles Ltd
Hager - Hager Ltd
Hairfelt - Davant Products Ltd
Halcyon - Rixonway Kitchens Ltd
Hale Hamilton Ltd - Hale Hamilton Valves Ltd
Halfen - Halfen Ltd
Hall Clips - BLM British Lead
Halla - ALD Lighting Solutions
Hallamshire - Phoenix Scales Ltd
Hallclip - SIG Roofing
Hallmark - J & E Hall Ltd
Hallmark - Marcrist International Ltd
Hallscrew - J & E Hall Ltd
Halo - Veka Plc
Halolux - Cooper Lighting
Halopar - Osram Ltd
Hambleton - Sashless Window Co Ltd
Hambleton - York Handmade Brick Co Ltd
Hamilton Litestat - Hamilton R & Co Ltd
Hammerite - Dulux Trade
Hammersmith Bollard, Post & Rail - Furnitubes International Ltd
Handi-Access - Profab Access Ltd
Handiclamp - Viking Johnson
Handitap - Viking Johnson
Handsafe - Tank Storage & Services Ltd
Handy Angle - Link 51 (Storage Products)
Handy Tube - Link 51 (Storage Products)
Hangmann - Ackermann Ltd
Hanovia UV - Barr & Wray Ltd
Hansen Millennium - HansenFacades
Hansen UnitAl - HansenFacades
HansenFacades - HansenFacades
HansenGroup - HansenFacades
Hansgrohe - Hansgrohe
Hansgrome - Olby H E & Co Ltd
Hanson Aquaflow - Visqueen Building Products
Harbex - Harris & Bailey Ltd
Harcostar® - Straight Ltd
Hard Hat - Andrews Coatings Ltd
Hardall - Hardall International Ltd
Harden Red Gravel - Tarmac Trading Limited (Aggregates)
Hardrive - Westpile Ltd
Hardrow® (Slates) - Forticrete Roofing
Hardwood Flooring Imports - Atkinson & Kirby Ltd
Hardyhemp - Marlow Ropes Ltd
Harland Fire Extinguishers - Nu-Swift International Ltd
Harmer - Alumasc Exterior Building Products Ltd
Harmonica-in-vinyl - Becker (SLIDING PARTITIONS) Ltd
Harmonika-on-wood - Becker (SLIDING PARTITIONS) Ltd
Harmonise - Paragon by Heckmondwike
Harrow - Ellis J T & Co Ltd
Hart - Hart Door Systems Ltd
Hart - High Sensitivity Smoke Detection - Kidde Fire Protection Ltd
Hart Door Systems - Hart Door Systems Ltd
Hart Doors - Hart Door Systems Ltd
Hartland - Hamilton R & Co Ltd
Hartley & Sugden - Ormandy Rycroft Engineering
Hartleybotanic - Apropos Conservatories Ltd
Harton and Harco Pak - Harton Heating Appliances
Harton Boost - Harton Heating Appliances
Harvestore - CST Industries, Inc. - UK
HAS seal - Hotchkiss Air Supply
Hasflex - Hotchkiss Air Supply
Hatcrete - Hatfield Ltd, Roy
Hathern Terra Cotta - Michelmersh Brick Holdings PLC
Hathernware - Ibstock Brick Ltd
Hathernware architectural faience - Ibstock Hathernware Ltd
Hathernware architectural terracotta - Ibstock Hathernware Ltd
Hathernware faience - Ibstock Hathernware Ltd
Hathernware terracotta - Ibstock Hathernware Ltd
Hattersley - The BSS Group
Hatz - Chippindale Plant Ltd
Hawa - Hafele UK Ltd
Hawk White - Fernox
Haworth - Haworth UK Ltd
Hazguard - Thurston Building Systems
HBS flagpoles - Harrision Flagpoles
HC Slingsby PLC - HC Slingsby PLC
HCI - Osram Ltd
HCS (HOPPE Compact System) - HOPPE (UK) Ltd
HDPE - Geberit Ltd
HE Transport Services - www.hetransportservices.co.uk - HE Services (Plant Hire) Ltd
Healthguard® - Earth Anchors Ltd
Heartbeat - Valor
HeartFelt - Hunter Douglas Architectural Ltd
Heartfelt Baffles - Hunter Douglas Architectural Ltd
Heartfelt Linear - Hunter Douglas Architectural Ltd
HeatFlex - Radius Systems Ltd
Heathland - Monier Redland Limited
Heathland - Neptune Outdoor Furniture Ltd
Heating & Ventilating Contractors Association - Building & Engineering Services Association
Heatkeeper Homes - Walker Timber Ltd
Heatline - Ves Andover Ltd
Heatovent - Seagoe Technologies Ltd
Heat-Rad - Horizon International Ltd
Heatrae Industrial - Ormandy Rycroft Engineering
Heatrae Sadia - Baxi Heating UK Ltd
Heat-Saver - Horizon International Ltd
Heatslave - Worcester Heat Systems Ltd
Heatwave - Jaga UK
Heaveguard - Cordek Ltd
Heavy V - Raised Floor Systems Ltd
Heavyside - Oakdale (Contracts) Ltd
Hebefix - Pump Technical Services Ltd
Hebel - Xella Aircrete Systems UK
Hedgehog Ditch Liner - Sportsmark Group Ltd
Hedin - Chromalox (UK) Ltd
HeiTel - Xtralis
Helagrip - Hellermann Tyton
Helatemp - Hellermann Tyton
Heldite - Heldite Ltd
HeliBar, HeliBond - Helifix
Helit - Lesco Products Ltd
Hellerman - Hellermann Tyton
Hellermann - Kem Edwards Ltd
Hellermark - Hellermann Tyton
Helmsman - Helmsman
Helsyn - Hellermann Tyton
Helvar - Bernlite Ltd
Helvin - Hellermann Tyton
Hemelite - Tarmac Building Products Ltd
Hemelite - Tarmac Trading Limited (Blocks)
Hemera external roller blind - Hallmark Blinds Ltd
Henderson, Horman - Acorn Garage Doors Ltd
Henslowe & Fox - Commodore Kitchens Ltd
Hentage Collection - Masterframe Windows Ltd
Hep2O - Hepworth Building Products Ltd
Hep3O - Hepworth Building Products Ltd
HepBio - Hepworth Building Products Ltd
Hepflow - Hepworth Building Products Ltd
Hepseal - Hepworth Building Products Ltd
Hepsleve - Hepworth Building Products Ltd
Hepsure - Hepworth Building Products Ltd
HepvO - Hepworth Building Products Ltd
Hepworth - Sibelco UK Ltd
Heradesign - Skanda Acoustics Limited
Heraklith - Nevill Long
Heraklith - Skanda Acoustics
Heraklith - Skanda Acoustics Limited
Herakustic star - Skanda Acoustics
Herakustik - Skanda Acoustics
Herakustik - Skanda Acoustics Limited
HERALD - Iles Waste Systems
Heraldesign - Knauf AMF Ceilings Ltd
Heraperm - Isocrete Floor Screeds Ltd
Heratekta - Skanda Acoustics

BRANDS AND TRADE NAMES

H (con't)

Herbert - BSA Machine Tools Ltd
Herbol - HMG Paints
Hercal - Range Cylinders
Hercules - Berry Systems
Heritage - Alumasc Exterior Building Products Ltd
Heritage - Benlowe Group Limited
Heritage - K. V. Radiators
Heritage - Marshalls Mono Ltd
Heritage Bathrooms - Bristan Group
Heritage Brass - Marcus M Ltd
Heritage Range - Pedley Furniture International Ltd
Heritage Tip-Up Seating System - Race Furniture Ltd
Hermit - Glasdon U.K. Limited
Hessian 51 - Muraspec
Heswell Door - AS Newbould Ltd
Heuga - Interface Europe Ltd
HEVAC - Heating Ventilating and Air Conditioning Manufacturers Association (HEVAC)
HEVAC - The Federation of Environmental Trade Association (FETA)
Hevilifts - Hydratight Sweeney Limited
Hewetson Floors - Kingspan Access Floors Ltd
HEWI - HEWI UK Ltd
Heydal - Britannia Kitchen Ventilation Ltd
Heyes - PFP Electrical Products Ltd
HFB - Motorised Air Products Ltd
Hi Grip Excel Decking - CTS Bridges Ltd
Hi Grip Plus Decking - CTS Bridges Ltd
Hi Grip Standard Decking - CTS Bridges Ltd
HI Hibay - Consult Lighting Ltd
Hi Load Masonry - Simpson Strong-Tie®
Hi Spot - Mains Voltage Halogen Lamps - FEILO SYLVANIA EUROPE LIMITED
Hi Watt Batteries - J.F. Poynter Ltd
HiBuild - Delta Balustrades
Hi-Cap Rainwater System - FloPlast Ltd
Hideaway - Coburn Sliding Systems Ltd
Hi-Deck - Hi-Store Ltd
Hi-Frame - Hi-Store Ltd
High Performance 2 Kitchens - Moores Furniture Group Ltd
High Performance Kitchens - Moores Furniture Group Ltd
High Performance Sports 2-part Aqueous Lacquer - Junckers Limited
high street entrance matting - Jaymart Rubber & Plastics Ltd
Highbeam Refractor - DW Windsor Lighting
Highlander - Richard Hose Ltd
Highlander and Highlander Solo stoves - Dunsley Heat Ltd
Highlux - Illuma Lighting
Highplow - Worcester Heat Systems Ltd
Highways Agency Products - International Protective Coatings
HiJan, Hispec - Johnson & Starley
Hiline - CPV Ltd
HiLiner Concrete Garages - Liget Compton
Hill & Knowles - CrowsonFabrics Ltd
Hill Top Sections - Hadley Industries Plc
Hilltop - Welsh Slate Limited
Hilmor - Hilmor
Hilo - MSA (Britain) Ltd
Hiltons Italian Plaster Coving - Hilton Banks Ltd
Hilume AAA - Stocksigns Ltd
Himalayan - Briggs Industrial Footwear Ltd t/a Briggs Safety Wear
Himalayan Iconic - Briggs Industrial Footwear Ltd t/a Briggs Safety Wear
HiMet - Delta Balustrades
Hiper Bar - Exitex Ltd
Hiperlan - Nexans UK Ltd
Hiperlan-E - Nexans UK Ltd
Hiperlink - Nexans UK Ltd
Hipernet - Nexans UK Ltd
Hiperway - Nexans UK Ltd
Hippo - Heckmondwicke FB
Hippo - Horizon International Ltd
HIR Acoustic Absorption Panel - Salex Acoustics Limited
Hi-Slim - Oldham Lighting Ltd
Hit - BLV Licht-und Vakuumtecnik
Hitherm - Kingspan Industrial Ins. Ltd
Hit-Lite - BLV Licht-und Vakuumtecnik
Hi-Trolley - Hi-Store Ltd
Hi-way - Vantrunk Engineering Ltd
Hodge Close - Burlington Slate Ltd
Hodgkinson Bennis Stokers - Hodgkinson Bennis Ltd
Hodgkisson - TSE Brownson
Holec - Eaton Electric Ltd
Hollo-bolt - Lindapter International
Holorib - Richard Lees Decking Limited
Home 'n' dry - Johnson & Starley
Homefit - Doorfit Products Ltd
Homeguard - The Safety Letterbox Company Ltd
Homelight - Crittall Steel Windows Ltd
Home-Loc 6000 - Timloc Expamet Building Products
Homelux - Homelux Nenplas
Homeqest - RB UK Ltd
Homeworks - Tidmarsh & Sons
Honeywell - The BSS Group
Hoppe - Carl F Groupco Limited
Hoppe (UK) LTD - Moffett Thallon & Co Ltd
Hoppings decking products - B & M Fencing Limited
Hopton Wood Limestone - Kirkstone
Horizon - Hawker Siddley Switchgear
Horizon - Hudevad Britain
Hormann - Hörmann (UK) Ltd
Horne - Horne Engineering Ltd
Horne 15 - Horne Engineering Ltd
Horne 15 4th Connection - Horne Engineering Ltd
Horne 20 - Horne Engineering Ltd
Horne ILTDU (In-line Thermal Disinfection Unit) - Horne Engineering Ltd
Hospital (HEC) - Barber Wilsons & Co Ltd
Hospital (HFC) - Barber Wilsons & Co Ltd
Hospital (NC) - Barber Wilsons & Co Ltd
Hotflo - Heatrae Sadia Heating Ltd
Hotfoil - Pentair Thermal Management
Hotlinee - Sportsmark Group Ltd
Houair Systems - British Turntable Ltd
Housesafe - Securikey Ltd
How Fire - Tyco Fire and Integrated Solutions
Howard Bird - Deva Tap Co Ltd
Hoylake Door - AS Newbould Ltd
HPA - The Federation of Environmental Trade Association (FETA)
HPI, HPL, HPS - High Pressure Series - Grosvenor Pumps Ltd
HPT Carrier - Hemsec Panel Technologies
HPT Clean - Hemsec Panel Technologies
HPT Control - Hemsec Panel Technologies
HPT Control 30 - Hemsec Panel Technologies
HPT Control 60 - Hemsec Panel Technologies
HPT External - Hemsec Panel Technologies
HPT Internal - Hemsec Panel Technologies
HQI - Osram Ltd
HRV - Kair Ventilation Ltd
HSS Hire - Weld - HSS Hire Service Group
HSS Lift & Shift - HSS Hire Service Group
HSS One call - HSS Hire Service Group
HSS Safe & Sure - HSS Hire Service Group
HSS Workshops - HSS Hire Service Group
HSV and HSK - Lochinvar Limited
HT Range - Ormandy Rycroft Engineering
HTH Door Systems - Carter Retail Equipment Ltd
HTK/TKR - EJOT UK Limited
HTV - Babcock Wanson Uk Ltd
Hufcor - Gilgen Door Systems UK Ltd
Hughes & Lancaster - Satec Service Ltd
Humber Plain Tile - Sandtoft Roof Tiles Ltd
HumidiSMART - Zehnder Group UK Ltd
Humidity Vents - Simon R W Ltd
Humidvent - Airflow Developments Ltd
Hünnebeck, a Brand company - SGB, a Brand Company
HunterDouglas - Hunter Douglas Architectural Ltd
Hush Acoustic Battens - Hush Acoustics
Hush Acoustic Flooring - Hush Acoustics
Hush Joist Strips - Hush Acoustics
Hush Panel 28 - Hush Acoustics
Hush Slab 100 - Hush Acoustics
Hush Systems - Hush Acoustics
Huwil - RB UK Ltd
HVCA - Building & Engineering Services Association
Hyarain - KSB Ltd
Hybox - Tata Steel Europe Limited
Hyclean - Potter & Soar Ltd
Hycor System 3000/F - Polypipe Building Products
Hyde - Hyde Brian Ltd
Hydome - Axter Ltd
Hydrakerb Barrier - APT Controls Ltd
Hydrasenta - Kohler UK
Hydroban ® - TRC (Midlands) Ltd
Hydrocol - LANXESS Inorganic Pigments Group
Hydrocol - W. Hawley & Son Ltd
Hydrocork - Amorim Cork Flooring
Hydrocure - Tarmac Trading Limited (Mortars)
Hydroduct - GCP APPLIED TECHNOLOGIES (UK) LIMITED
Hydroferrox - W. Hawley & Son Ltd
Hydrophilic Joint Seals - Tarmac - Specialist Products
Hydrophilic Sealant - Tarmac - Specialist Products
Hydrostal Pumps - Barr & Wray Ltd
HydroTec - CST Industries, Inc. - UK
Hydrotech - Alumasc Exterior Building Products Ltd
Hydrothane - Conren Ltd
Hydrotite - Laybond Products Ltd
Hydrotite - Tarmac - Specialist Products
Hydulignum - Permali Deho Ltd
Hye Oak - Hye Oak
Hyflex - BriggsAmasco
Hyflex 10 - Hyflex Roofing
Hyflex 10 Plus - Hyflex Roofing
Hyflex 15 - Hyflex Roofing
Hyflex 15 Plus - Hyflex Roofing
Hyflex 5 - Hyflex Roofing
Hyflex Exemplar Car Park System - Hyflex Roofing
Hyflex Exemplar PMMA - Hyflex Roofing
Hyflex Exemplar PU - Hyflex Roofing
Hyflex Exemplar Balcony System - Hyflex Roofing
Hyflex Exemplar Polyester - Hyflex Roofing
Hyflex Profile - Hyflex Roofing
Hygiene - Saint-Gobain Ecophon Ltd
Hygiene Safe - Kingspan Ltd
Hyload Structural Waterproofing - IKO PLC
Hyranger - Axter Ltd
Hy-rib - Expamet Building Products
Hytex - Potter & Soar Ltd
Hyweld - Potter & Soar Ltd

I

I - Worcester Heat Systems Ltd
IAT - Institute of Ashphalt Technology, the
IBC - Bridgman IBC Ltd
Ibex- Transeat - Evac+Chair International Ltd
Ibiza 2000 - Kermi (UK) Ltd
Ibstock Hathernware - Ibstock Building Products Ltd
Ibstock Scottish brick - Ibstock Building Products Ltd
Ibstock Scottish Stone - Ibstock Scotish Brick
ICAM - Xtralis
ICEL - Lighting Industry Association, The
Icelert - Findlay Irvine Ltd
Icepac - CSSP (Construction Software Services Partnership)
ICID Plus - Schiedel Chimney Systems Ltd
iCON - Airflow Developments Ltd
Icon - Valor
IcoScaff - Icopal Limited
ICS - Schiedel Chimney Systems Ltd
ICS chimney system - Rite-Vent Ltd
ICS5000 chimney system - Rite-Vent Ltd
ICT - The Institute of Concrete Technology
ID Inspiration - Tarkett Ltd
Ideal - The BSS Group
Ideal - Tuke & Bell Ltd
Idenden - Bostik Ltd
IDEX Blagdon Pumps - Barr & Wray Ltd
iDim - Helvar Ltd
IDM - Kone PLC
IET - The Institution of Engineering and Technology
IET Electrical Standards Plus - The Institution of Engineering and Technology
IET Membership - The Institution of Engineering and Technology
IET Venues - The Institution of Engineering and Technology
IET Wiring Regulations Bookshop - Professional Books Limited
IET.tv - The Institution of Engineering and Technology
IG - IG Limited
Iguana - Jaga UK
IKO Single Ply - IKO PLC
Illbruk - Tremco Illbruck Ltd
Illusion - Matki plc
Image - Interface Europe Ltd
Imagine - Helvar Ltd
iMEV Local and Total - Passivent Ltd
Imit - Altecnic Ltd
Imola - Arnull Bernard J & Co Ltd
Impact - TBS Amwell Ltd
Impact Crusher - Parker Plant Ltd
Impactafoam - Sound Reduction Systems Ltd
Impactor - Heras
Impactor - Imperial Machine Co Ltd
Imperial - Miele Co Ltd
Imperial - Smart Systems Ltd
Impetus - Lochinvar Limited
Impex - Construction Group UK Ltd
Impressionist II - Altro Ltd
Impulse - ITW Construction Products
Impulse - Mode Lighting (UK) Ltd
Index of Quality Names - The Carpet Foundation
Ind-Oil-Taper - Olley & Sons Ltd, C
Inducool - LTI Advanced Systems Technology Ltd
Indul - LTI Advanced Systems Technology Ltd
Industrial Range : Industrial Air Vent Valves, Industrial Balancing Valves, Industrial Butterfly Valves, Industrial Check Valves, Industrial Expansion Joint, Industrial Gate Valves, Industrial Y Strainer Valves - Conex Universal Limited
Inergen - ADT Fire and Security Plc
Infiltra Stop, IP - Grace De Neef UK
Infiniti - Levolux A.T. Limited
Infinity - Shackerley (Holdings) Group Ltd incorporating Designer ceramics
Infinity - Tapworks Water Softeners
Influences - Muraspec
infopanel - Stocksigns Ltd
Inforail ® - Broxap Ltd
Infrapod - Mode Lighting
ingenius entrance matting - Jaymart Rubber & Plastics Ltd
Ingeny - Interphone Limited
Ingersoll - Yale Security Products Ltd
Ingersoll Security - Mul-T-Lock
Ingersol-Rand - Ingersoll-Rand European Sales Ltd
Initial Electronic Security Systems Ltd - Chubb Systems Ltd
Initial Sherrock Monitoring - Initial Electronic Security Systems Ltd
Initial Sherrork Surveilance - Initial Electronic Security Systems Ltd
Initial Shorrock Fire - Initial Electronic Security Systems Ltd
Initial Shorrock Monitoring - Ingersoll-Rand European Sales Ltd
Initial Shorrock Security - Initial Electronic Security Systems Ltd
Initial Shorrock Surveillance - Ingersoll-Rand European Sales Ltd
Initial Shorrock Systems - Initial Electronic Security Systems Ltd
Initial Shorrrock - Chubb Systems Ltd
Injection Plastics - Hines & Sons, P E, Ltd
Inlay Range - Pedley Furniture International Ltd
INMP/ NDF - Babcock Wanson Uk Ltd
Innov8, Independence Versa, Inspiration - Sidhil Care
Innova - Premdor
Innovair - Biddle Air Systems Ltd
Innovation - Rawson Carpets Ltd
Innovators in Clay - Ibstock Brick Ltd
In-Oil-Board - Olley & Sons Ltd, C
Inova Interactive Seating - CPS Manufacturing Co
Inperim - Polypipe Building Products
Inpro - Gradus Ltd
insectacoat - Peter Cox Ltd
Insect-O-Cutor - P+L Systems Ltd
Inserdor - Coburn Sliding Systems Ltd
InSkew - Helifix
Inspec - The Institution of Engineering and Technology
Insta Wall - Spaceright Europe Limited
Instacoustic - InstaGroup Ltd
Instafibre - InstaGroup Ltd
Instaflex - George Fischer Sales Ltd
Install Plus - Tata Steel Europe Limited
Instant Adhesive - Loctite UK Ltd
Insta-stik - Dow Building Solutions
Insugard - Gilgen Door Systems UK Ltd
Insuglaze - Panel Systems Ltd
INSULATH™ - Hadley Industries Plc
Insulator - Hambleside Danelaw Ltd
Insulight - Pilkington Plyglass
Insuloid - Hellermann Tyton
Insul-Quilt specialist film studio acoustic liner - Salex Acoustics Limited
Insul-Sheet - NMC (UK) Ltd
Insultube - Davant Products Ltd
Insul-Tube - NMC (UK) Ltd
Insupex - IPPEC Systems Ltd
InTec - Alpha Therm Ltd
Integra - Durable Ltd
Integra - Fitzgerald Lighting Ltd
Integra - LANXESS Inorganic Pigments Group
integra - W. Hawley & Son Ltd
Intejan - Johnson & Starley
Inteli-Fin - Lochinvar Limited
Intelligent Brick Work - Ibstock Brick Ltd
Intelligent Glass - Pro Display TM Limited
Intelock - Vantrunk Engineering Ltd
Interact - Ackermann Ltd
Interbond FP thin film intumescent coating - International Protective Coatings
Intercell - Interface Europe Ltd
Intercure rapid curing epoxies - International Protective Coatings
Interface - Interface Europe Ltd
Interface Fabrics - Interface Europe Ltd
Interfine 629 iso cyonate free finishes - International Protective Coatings
Interfine Polysiloxane - International Protective Coatings
Interfloor Ltd - Interfloor Limited
Interglaze - Exitex Ltd
Interior Contracting - Parthos UK Ltd
Interline Tank linings - International Protective Coatings
Interlock - Interclad (UK) Ltd
Interlock - Interface Europe Ltd
International Forestry Exhibition - Confor: Promoting forestry and wood
Interphone - Interphone Limited
Interplan - Internal Partitions Systems
Interplan maintanance Painting - International Protective Coatings
Interplus Surface Tolerant - International Protective Coatings
Interpretations - Paragon by Heckmondwike
Interscreen - Safetell Ltd
Interspan - Compriband Ltd
Interspan All Metal - Compriband Ltd
Interstrip - Shackerley (Holdings) Group Ltd incorporating Designer ceramics
Intertspan - Illbruck Sealant Systems UK Ltd
Interzinc 72 epoxy zinc rich - International Protective Coatings
Interzone high solid expoxies - International Protective Coatings
Intrad - Fixatrad Ltd
Intravent - Gebhardt Kiloheat
Intuclear - Bollom Fire Protection Ltd
Intulac - Bollom Fire Protection Ltd
Intumescent Compound - Sealmaster
Intusteel WB - Bollom Fire Protection Ltd
Invadex - Chiltern Invadex
Invaflo Shower Drain - Chiltern Invadex
Invicta - Invicta Plastics Ltd
Invikta - Grosvenor Pumps Ltd
Invincible bucket - Airflow (Nicoll Ventilators) Ltd
Invisidor - Biddle Air Systems Ltd
Invisirung vertical fall arrest ladder system - Metreel Ltd
Ipe - Wilo Samson Pumps Ltd
Ipn - Wilo Samson Pumps Ltd
IPS washroom systems - Armitage Shanks Ltd
IQ - Trend Control Systems Ltd
Iq Locker - T B S Fabrications
iQ Ranges - Tarkett Ltd
Irby Door - AS Newbould Ltd
IRC - Osram Ltd
Irius - SFS Intec LTD
Iron Duke - Heckmondwicke FB
Iron-Horse - Kleen-Tex Industries Ltd
IRT - Pentair Thermal Management
IRTS - Institute of Specialist Surveyors and Engineers
Isis suite - Brass Art Ltd
ISO 95+ GL Polyiso roof insulation boards - Firestone Building Products
Isoconex - Conex Universal Limited
Isocrete - Flowcrete Plc
Isocrete Self Level - Isocrete Floor Screeds Ltd
Isofast - SFS Intec LTD
Isoflex - Isolated Systems Ltd
Isofoam - Lanxess Urethanes UK Ltd
Isogran - Isocrete Floor Screeds Ltd
Isokern - Schiedel Chimney Systems Ltd
Isokoat - Schiedel Chimney Systems Ltd
Isola Marble & Granite - Reed Harris
Isolan - Ancon Limited
Isolgomma - Sound Service (Oxford) Ltd
Isoline - Onduline Building Products Ltd
Isotape - Pentair Thermal Management
Isotherm - Biddle Air Systems Ltd
Isothin - Isocrete Floor Screeds Ltd
Isoval - Clivet UK Ltd
Isowarm - Flowcrete Plc
Ispotherm - Alumasc Exterior Building Products Ltd
ISSE - Institute of Specialist Surveyors and Engineers
Ista - Switch2 Energy Solutions Ltd
Italia Collection - Lakes Bathrooms Limited
Italia-80, Italia-100, Italia-80 Cladding and Screening and Italia-100 Cladding and Screening - Lang+Fulton

I (con't)

Italian Travertines - Kirkstone
Itconi - Lewes Design Contracts Ltd
iTrack - Whitecroft Lighting Limited
Iviring & Sellers - IJK Timber Group Ltd

J

J D Interiors - Shaylor Group Plc
Jabcore - Jablite Ltd
Jabfloor - Jablite Ltd
Jablite - Jablite Ltd
Jabroc - Permali Deho Ltd
Jabroof Board - Jablite Ltd
Jabroof Panel - Jablite Ltd
Jabroof Slimfix - Jablite Ltd
Jabsqueeze - Jablite Ltd
Jabtherm - Jablite Ltd
Jacksons fencing® - Jackson H S & Son (Fencing) Ltd
Jacksons finefencing® - Jackson H S & Son (Fencing) Ltd
Jacuzzi® - Jacuzzi® Spa and Bath Ltd
Jakcure® - Jackson H S & Son (Fencing) Ltd
Jakob Rope Systems - MMA Architectural Systems Ltd
Jaktop® - Jackson H S & Son (Fencing) Ltd
JALI - Jali Ltd
Janitol - Deb Group Limited
Janus - Johnson & Starley
Jasper - Project Office Furniture PLC
Jasper Morrison - Ideal-Standard Ltd
Jasper - Sapphire Balustrades
JB Kind Doors - JB Kind Ltd
JCB - J C Bamford (Excavators) Ltd
Jebron - Exidor Limited
Jenny Twin - Owen Slate Services Ltd
Jenny Twin - Owens Slate Services Ltd
Jet Print - Kleen-Tex Industries Ltd
Jet stream - Vianen KVS BV
Jetdye Digital Printing - Zephyr The Visual Communicators
Jetfloor - Hanson Concrete Products Ltd
Jet-rite - Flamco UK Ltd
Jetslab - Hanson Concrete Products Ltd
Jetstream Ventilation Fan - Colt International
Jet-Thrust Fans - Fläkt Woods Ltd
Jewel - Metalliform Products Plc
J-Fix - Unifix Ltd
JFS - Fulton Boiler Works (Great Britain) Ltd
JIB - Joint Industry Board for the Electrical Contracting Industry
JM Aerofoil - Fläkt Woods Ltd
JM Landscaping - Jack Moody Ltd
JMix - Jack Moody Ltd
Jobomulch - ABG Ltd
John Watson & Carter - Johnson VB LLP
Johnson - Johnson Tiles
Johnson Controls - Johnson Controls Building Efficiency UK Ltd
Johnson Tiles - Johnson Tiles
Johnstones - Brewer C & Sons Ltd
Johnstones Paints - Manders Paint Ltd
Johnstone's Paints - Kalon Decorative Products
Johnstones Performance Coatings - Kalon Decorative Products
Johnstone's Woodworks - Kalon Decorative Products
Joltec - Ronacrete Ltd
Jomy - Baj System Design Ltd
Jones+Attwood - Jacopa Limited
Joseph Bramah - Bramah Security Equipment Ltd
Jotalakk - Jotun Henry Clark Ltd Decorative Division
Jotaplast - Jotun Henry Clark Ltd Decorative Division
Jotapro - Jotun Henry Clark Ltd Decorative Division
Jotawall - Jotun Henry Clark Ltd Decorative Division
Joy - Zon International
JPA Furniture - John Pulsford Associates Ltd
Jubilee - Clenaware Systems Ltd
Jubilee - Cooper Lighting
Jubilee - Wade International Ltd
Juggenaut Poles - Harrision Flagpoles
Juliette Spiral - Loft Centre Products
Jumbo - Swish Building Products
Jumbotec - Swish Building Products
Jumbovent - Swish Building Products
Jung - Pump Technical Services Ltd
Jung Pumpen - Pump Technical Services Ltd
Jupiter - Fabrikat (Nottingham) Ltd
Jupiter - Samuel Heath & Sons plc
Jupiter - Ubbink (UK) Ltd
Jupiter - UTC Fire & Securites
Jupiter spring / motor operated cable reels - Metreel Ltd
Just Shelving - Moresecure Ltd
Jutland - Cembrit Ltd
JVC - Vidionics Security Systems Ltd
JW Green Swimming Pools Ltd - J W Green Swimming Pools Ltd

K

K Bead - Kilwaughter Chemical Co Ltd
K Dash - Kilwaughter Chemical Co Ltd
K Lime - Kilwaughter Chemical Co Ltd
K Mix - Kilwaughter Chemical Co Ltd
K Post - Kilwaughter Chemical Co Ltd
K Rend - Kilwaughter Chemical Co Ltd
K Screed - Isocrete Floor Screeds Ltd
K40 - Gilgen Door Systems UK Ltd
K65 - Conex Universal Limited
K7 - Komfort Workspace PLC
Kaba - Kaba Ltd
Kair - Kair Ventilation Ltd
Kalahari - Architen Landrell Associates Ltd
Kaloric - Kaloric Heater Co Ltd
Kameleon - Colt International
Kameo - Komfort Workspace PLC
Kamstrup - Switch2 Energy Solutions Ltd
Kana - Ciret Limited
Kappa - Rockwell Sheet Sales Ltd
Kappa Curvo - Rockwell Sheet Sales Ltd
Kaptan, Kare, Karnak, Kensington, Klon, Kupka - Pitacs Ltd
Kara - Neptune Outdoor Furniture Ltd
Karibia - Kompan Ltd
Kasbah Twist - Adam Carpets Ltd
kato - Ellis J T & Co Ltd
K-Bond - Kenyon Group Ltd
K-Bond - Kenyon Performance Adhesives
Kederflex - Icopal Limited
Kee Anchor® - Kee Klamp Ltd
Kee Guard ® - Kee Klamp Ltd
Kee Klamp ® - Kee Klamp Ltd
Kee Koat® - Kee Klamp Ltd
Kee Line ® - Kee Klamp Ltd
Kee Lite® - Kee Klamp Ltd
Kee Mark™ - Kee Klamp Ltd
Kee nect ™ - Kee Klamp Ltd
Keep Kool - Airedale International Air Conditioning Ltd
Keim Concretal Lasur - Keim Mineral Paints Ltd
Keim Ecosil - Keim Mineral Paints Ltd
Keim Granital - Keim Mineral Paints Ltd
Keim Lotexan - Keim Mineral Paints Ltd
Keim Optil - Keim Mineral Paints Ltd
Keim Restauro - Keim Mineral Paints Ltd
Keim Royalan - Keim Mineral Paints Ltd
Keim Soldalit - Keim Mineral Paints Ltd
Keim Universal Render - Keim Mineral Paints Ltd
Keizer Venesta - IJK Timber Group Ltd
Keller Foundations - Keller Ground Engineering
Kemira - Andrews Coatings Ltd
Kemlite - Crane Composites
Kempergro Green Roof - Kemper System Ltd
Kemperol 1K-PUR - Kemper System Ltd
Kemperol 2K-PUR - Kemper System Ltd
Kemperol V210 - Kemper System Ltd
Kemperspeed AC - Kemper System Ltd
Kempertherm Insulation - Kemper System Ltd
Kempston - Hanson Building Products
Kenco - The Kenco Coffee Company
Kenco In-Cup - The Kenco Coffee Company
Kenco Singles - The Kenco Coffee Company
Kencot Linking Chair - Race Furniture Ltd
Kenngott international - Ermine Engineering Co. Ltd
Kenrick - A Kenrick & Sons
Kenrick - Carl F Groupco Limited
KensalFlame - Gazco Ltd
Kensington - Branson Leisure Ltd
Kenstack - McKenzie-Martin Ltd
Kentish Range - Hye Oak
Kenyon floor paint - Kenyon Group Ltd
Keps - Springvale E P S
Kerastar - Johnson Tiles
Keratint - Procter Johnson & Co Ltd
Kerbmaster - Benton Co Ltd Edward
Kerbmaster - Edward Benton & Co Ltd
Kernal - Range Cylinders
Kerridge Stone - Kerridge Stone Ltd
Kew - Nilfisk Limited
Keybak - Securikey Ltd
Keyblok - Marshalls Mono Ltd
Keyguard - Hoyles Electronic Developments Ltd
Keylex Digital Locks - Relcross Ltd
Keylite - Allmat (East Surrey) Ltd
Keymer - Wienerberger Ltd (Keymer Handmade Clay Plain Tiles)
Keymer Clayton - Wienerberger Ltd (Keymer Handmade Clay Plain Tiles)
Keymer Ditchling - Wienerberger Ltd (Keymer Handmade Clay Plain Tiles)
Keymer Inline Ventilation System - Wienerberger Ltd (Keymer Handmade Clay Plain Tiles)
Keymer Shire - Wienerberger Ltd (Keymer Handmade Clay Plain Tiles)
Keymer Traditional - Wienerberger Ltd (Keymer Handmade Clay Plain Tiles)
Keypac - Wernick Group Ltd
Keystone - Allmat (East Surrey) Ltd
K-Flex - Pentair Thermal Management
K-HRV150 - Kair Ventilation Ltd
K-HRVF100 - Kair Ventilation Ltd
KiddEx - Explosion Suppression agent - Kidde Fire Protection Ltd
Killaspray - Hozelock Ltd
Kimpton - Branson Leisure Ltd
Kinder - BFM Europe Limited
Kinder - Dunhams of Norwich
kinetics rubber floorings - Jaymart Rubber & Plastics Ltd
King hoists and trollys - PCT Group
King Sliding Door Gear - Lakeside Group
Kingfisher - William Hopkins & Sons Ltd
Kingley - Flowflex Components Ltd
Kings Fund - Sidhil Care
KingShield - Green Brook
Kingspan - FGF Ltd
Kingspan Environmental Service - Kingspan Environmental Ltd
Kingspan Klargester - Kingspan Environmental
Kingspan Water - Kingspan Environmental
Kingspan Water - Kingspan Environmental Ltd
Kingstonian - Kingstonian Paint Ltd
Kingswood - Waterline Limited
Kirkby - Burlington Slate Ltd
Kirkstone Volcanic Stone - Kirkstone
Kitchen Confidence - Symphony Group PLC, The
Kitchens - Ellis J T & Co Ltd
Kito Bitumen Emultions - Colas Ltd
Klargester - Kingspan Environmental Ltd
Klassic - Komfort Workspace PLC
Klaxon Signals - Texecom Limited
Kleen Thru Plus - Kleen-Tex Industries Ltd
Kleenscrape - Kleen-Tex Industries Ltd
Kleen-Stat - Kleen-Tex Industries Ltd
Kleertred - Exitex Ltd
Klemm - Ingersoll-Rand European Sales Ltd
Klensorb - B & D Clays & Chemicals Ltd
Klik - Hager Ltd
Klimavent - Motorised Air Products Ltd
Kliplok - Unifix Ltd
KM 3 - Komfort Workspace PLC
Knauf - Firebarrier International Ltd T/A Firebarrier Services Ltd
Knauf - Kitsons Insulation Products Ltd
Knauf - Nevill Long
Knauf AMF - Nevill Long
Knauf Insulation Polyfoam - Knauf Insulation Ltd
Knight - Iles Waste Systems
Knobs Range - Pedley Furniture International Ltd
Knorr - The Kenco Coffee Company
Kofferlite - IKM Systems Ltd
Kohlangax - BFM Europe Limited
Kohler - Kohler UK
Kolorband - Kronospan Ltd
Kolorcourt - Emusol Products (LEICS) Ltd
Kolourseal Roofing System - Kingfisher Building Products Ltd
Kombimetall - Knauf AMF Ceilings Ltd
Kombivol - Skanda Acoustics Limited
Komfire - Komfort Workspace PLC
Komfort - New Forest Ceilings Ltd
Komfort CX - Komfort Workspace PLC
Kompan - Kompan Ltd
Konaflex - (Above ground drainage systems) - Servomac Limited
Kone Eco3000 - Kone PLC
Konexion - Kone PLC
Kontrakt - Pedley Furniture International Ltd
KoolDuct - Kingspan Industrial Ins. Ltd
Koolshade - Cooper Group Ltd
Kooltherm - Kingspan Industrial Ins. Ltd
Kooltherm - Kingspan Insulation Ltd
Kooltherm - Kitsons Insulation Products Ltd
Kopex - Kem Edwards Ltd
Korean plywood - Wood International Agency Ltd
Korifit - Adaptaflex Ltd
Koverflor - Witham Oil & Paint Ltd
Kraftex - Package Products Ltd
Kresto® - Deb Group Limited
Kriblok Crb Walling - Ruthin Precast Concrete Ltd
Krion - Porcelanosa Group Ltd
Kromax - Tyco Waterworks - Samuel Booth
Krono Country - Kronospan Ltd
Krono LAQ - Kronospan Ltd
Kronofix - Kronospan Ltd
Kronofloor - Kronospan Ltd
Kronoplus - Kronospan Ltd
Kronosilent - Kronospan Ltd
Kronospan - Boardcraft Ltd
Kronospan - Meyer Timber Limited
Kryptonite - Allegion (UK) Ltd
KS1000 - Kingspan Ltd
K-Seal patio range - Kingfisher Building Products Ltd
KT3 - Marlow Ropes Ltd
Kudos - Calomax Ltd
Kuterlex - Yorkshire Copper Tube
Kuterlex plus - Yorkshire Copper Tube
Kuterlon - Yorkshire Copper Tube
Kvent - Rite-Vent Ltd
Kwikastrip - BRC Reinforcement
Kwikastrip - Halfen Ltd
kwikfix fascia soffit system - Dales Fabrications Ltd
Kwikpoint - Kingfisher Building Products Ltd
Kwikroll - Gilgen Door Systems UK Ltd
Kwikstage - Mabey Hire Ltd
KX10 wood stains - Kingfisher Building Products Ltd
Kynar 500 - Arkema France
Kynar Aquatec - Arkema France

L

La Linea - Lumitron Ltd
Labren, Lanner, Linear, Lokum, Lunar, Lstrad - Pitacs Ltd
Lacdor - Vicaima Ltd
Lachat - Zellweger Analytic Ltd, Sieger Division
Ladder Up Safety Post - Bilco UK Ltd
LadderLatch™ - Latchways plc
Laddermatic - Clow Group Ltd
Laguna - Kompan Ltd
Lakeside Group - Lakeside Group
Lakeside Lifestyle.com - Lakeside Group
Lakeside Sercurity - Lakeside Group
Lami - Lami Doors UK Ltd
Lamina - FGF Ltd
Lamina Filtertrap - Progressive Product Developments Ltd
Laminated Supplies Ltd - Halmark Panels Ltd
Lampro Systems - Crane Composites
Lamson - Barloworld Vacuum Technology Plc
Lamwood - Lilleheden Ltd
Lancashire Interiors - Designer Radiators Direct
Lancaster - BF Bassett & Findley
Landcoil - Polypipe Civils
Landis & Gyr - Switch2 Energy Solutions Ltd
Landmark (Slate, Double Pantile & Double Roman) - Monier Redland Limited
Landsurveyor - Gas Measurement Instruments Ltd
Langley By Shavrin - Shavrin Levatap Co Ltd
Lanka - Swedecor
LANmark - Nexans UK Ltd
Lantana - Brockway Carpets Ltd
Lapidolith - Conren Ltd
Laser - Flexiform Business Furniture Ltd
Laser Gold 20 Year & Laser Torch 15 Year - Chesterfelt Ltd
Latapoxy - Laticrete International Inc. UK
Lateral Restraint Tie (LRT.) - Redifix Ltd
Latham Clad - James Latham plc
Laticrete - Laticrete International Inc. UK
Laumans - Smithbrook Building Products Ltd
Laura Ashley - British Ceramic Tile Ltd
Lavanda - Saint-Gobain Ecophon Ltd
Lawapan ceiling and wall panels - Salex Acoustics Limited
Laxton's - Laxton's Publishing Ltd
Laxton's - V B Johnson LLP
Laxtons's Building Price Book - Johnson VB LLP
Laybond adhesives - Laybond Products Ltd
Laytrad contract furnishers - Laytrad Contract Furniture Ltd
LB lighting - ALD Lighting Solutions
Lbofall - Leofric Building Systems Ltd
LC-35 Barrier - APT Controls Ltd
LCN Door Closers - Relcross Ltd
LD Barrier - APT Controls Ltd
Lead Pointing Sealant - BLM British Lead
Lead T-Pren - BLM British Lead
Lead T-Pren Plus - BLM British Lead
Lead-Cote - BLM British Lead
LeaderFlush Shapland - Moffett Thallon & Co Ltd
Leaf - Metalliform Products Plc
Leak Sealer F4, Superconcentrate Leak Sealer F4, Leak Sealer F4 Express - Fernox
Leakguard - Pentair Thermal Management
Leakmaster - Tarmac - Specialist Products
Legge - Allegion (UK) Ltd
Legge - Laidlaw Ltd
Legno Partitions - Avanti Systems
Legrand - Legrand Electric Ltd
LEIA - Lift and Escalator Industry Association,The
Leisure - Beko plc
Leisure Sinks - Rangemaster
Lentex - Dixon Turner Wallcoverings
Lenton ® - Erico Europa (GB) Ltd
Lenton reinforcing bar couplers - BRC Reinforcement
Leromur - Grass Concrete Ltd
Les Actuels de Lucien Gau - Myddleton Hall Lighting, Division of Peerless Design Ltd
Lesco - Lesco Products Ltd
Lessman - Hyde Brian Ltd
Letterboxes @ Signs of the times - Signs Of The Times Ltd
Levelay HO - Conren Ltd
Levelmaster - Stannah Lifts Ltd
Levit - Glamox Luxo Lighting Limited
Levolux - Levolux A.T. Limited
Lexin - Rangemaster
Leyland - Brewer C & Sons Ltd
Leyland Paints - Kalon Decorative Products
Leyland Paints - Manders Paint Ltd
LFH - Hellermann Tyton
LHC Kitchens - Moores Furniture Group Ltd
LIA Laboratories Ltd - Lighting Industry Association, The
LIA Quality Assurance - Lighting Industry Association, The
Liberator - Allart, Frank, & Co Ltd
Liberty 3 - Wessex Lift Co Ltd
Liberty Open - Wessex Lift Co Ltd
Liddle Doors - Bradbury Group Ltd
Lieutenant - Neptune Outdoor Furniture Ltd
Lifeguard - ArjoHuntleigh UK
Lifestyle Elite, Luxe, Delight, Lawn, Multi, City - Artificial Grass Ltd
Lifestyle Showers - Hansgrohe
LifeSystem - HEWI UK Ltd
Li-Flat - Aremco Products
Lift 'n' Lock - Airsprung Beds Ltd
Liftingclamps.com - Camlok Lifting Clamps Ltd
Lift-Slab - Hydratight Sweeney Limited
Light Coffers - Saint-Gobain Ecophon Ltd
Light Fantastic - Intersolar Group Ltd
Lighting Industry Academy - Lighting Industry Association, The
Lighting Systems UK - CU Phosco Lighting
Lightmanager - Philips Lighting Solutions
Lightmaster - Philips Lighting Solutions
Lightmatic - Optex (Europe) Ltd
Lightning NDC - Hawker Siddley Switchgear
Lightpack - Fitzgerald Lighting Ltd
Lightrak - Electrak International Ltd
Lightseal - Illuma Lighting
Lightspan - Duplus Architectural Systems Ltd
Lignacite - Lignacite (North London) Ltd
Lignacite - Lignacite Ltd
Lignacrete - Lignacite (North London) Ltd
Lignacrete - Lignacite Ltd
Lignastone Architectural Dressings - Lignacite Ltd
Lilliput Nursery - Portakabin Ltd
Lime Heritage Pointing Mortar - Limelite - Tarmac Building Products Ltd
Limebacker cable ramps - Lewden Electrical Industries
Limelite - Limelite - Tarmac Building Products Ltd
Limelite Easy Bond - Limelite - Tarmac Building Products Ltd
Limelite Heritage Lime Mortar - Limelite - Tarmac Building Products Ltd
Limelite High Impact Finishing Plaster - Limelite - Tarmac Building Products Ltd
Limelite Renovating Plaster - Limelite - Tarmac Building Products Ltd
Limelite St Pauls Heritage Grout - Limelite - Tarmac Building Products Ltd
Limelite St. Pancras Heritage Grout - Limelite - Tarmac Building Products Ltd
Limelite Whitewall One Coat Plaster - Limelite - Tarmac Building Products Ltd
Limelite Winchester Heritage Grout - Limelite - Tarmac Building Products Ltd

L (con't)

Limescale Remover DS-3, Superconcentrate Limescale Preventer - Fernox

Limpet BD6 self setting composition - Thermica Ltd

Limpetite Rubber Coatings - Bristol Metal Spraying & Protective Coatings Ltd

Lindapter - Kem Edwards Ltd

Linden Homes - GallifordTry

Lindiclip - Lindapter International

Lindum - York Handmade Brick Co Ltd

Linea - Hamilton R & Co Ltd

Linea Duo - Hamilton R & Co Ltd

Linea, Minima - TBS Amwell Ltd

Linear - Rangemaster

Linear Closed - Hunter Douglas Architectural Ltd

Linear Open - Hunter Douglas Architectural Ltd

Linect - Glamox Luxo Lighting Limited

Liner Hydratow Fast Tow Concrete Mixer - Multi Marque Production Engineering Ltd

Liner Major Concrete Mixers - Multi Marque Production Engineering Ltd

Liner Rolpanit Pan Mixers - Multi Marque Production Engineering Ltd

Liner Roughrider Dumpers - Multi Marque Production Engineering Ltd

Linergrip - Viking Johnson

Linesman - MSA (Britain) Ltd

Linflex Fin and Narrow Filter Drain - Polypipe Civils

Linido - Amilake Southern Ltd

Link 51 - Libraco

Lintie - Redifix Ltd

Linx Range; Bollards, Railing System, Cycle stands - Furnitubes International Ltd

Lion - Boardcraft Ltd

Lion Brand - Cottam Brush Ltd

LION: LION Floor™, LION Softboards, LION Oil tempered™, LION Roofing™, LION Superior™, LION General™, LION Protect™, LION HD Panel™, LION Superior™, LION Perforated™, LION Furniture Painted™ - Finnish Fibreboard (UK) Ltd

Liquistore - Franklin Hodge Industries Ltd

Liquitainer - Franklin Hodge Industries Ltd

Lisbon - Swedecor

Lister-Petter - Chippindale Plant Ltd

Liteglaze - Ariel Plastics Ltd

Litelink LSC - Eaton Electric Limited

Liteminder - Mode Lighting

Litetile - Catnic

Litevent - Passivent Ltd

Litex - Lawton Tube Co Ltd, The

Little Acorns and Little Rainbows - Spaceright Europe Limited

Little crown - Kompan Ltd

Livewire Shelving - Bedford Shelving Ltd

Living Stone - Armortec

LivLoc - Atkinson & Kirby Ltd

LO Lobay - Consult Lighting Ltd

Load Pro - Nico Manufacturing Ltd

Load Release System - Goelst

Loadbank - Dorman Smith Switchgear

Loadframe - Dorman Smith Switchgear

Loadlimiter - Dorman Smith Switchgear

Loadline - Dorman Smith Switchgear

Loadmaster - Cooke Brothers Ltd

Loadswitch - Dorman Smith Switchgear

LOC Strip - Marble Flooring Spec. Ltd

Locate - Universal Components Ltd

LocFold - Omnis

Lochrin ® - Wm. Bain Fencing Ltd

Lochrin Classic Rivetless Palisade - Wm. Bain Fencing Ltd

Lochrin® Bain - Wm. Bain Fencing Ltd

Lockhart Project services - Lockhart Catering Equipment

Lockstone - PHI Group Ltd

Loctite - Henkel Consumer Adhesives

Loctite - Loctite UK Ltd

Logic Plus - MK (MK Electric Ltd)

Logicwall Cupboard Storage - Logic Office Contracts

LokFacade - Omnis

Lokfix - Fosroc Ltd

Lokmesh - Potter & Soar Ltd

LokRoll - Omnis

London - Hanson Building Products

Longlife - Nicholson Plastics Ltd

Longline - Nevill Long

Longspan - Link 51 (Storage Products)

Longspan Shelving - Moresecure Ltd

Loo-Clean - Tank Storage & Services Ltd

LookRyt® - Rytons Building Products Ltd

Loovent - Airflow Developments Ltd

Lord's - Scotts of Thrapston Ltd

Lorient - Humphrey & Stretton PLC

Lothian - Russell Roof Tiles Ltd

Lotrak geotextiles - Don & Low Ltd

Lotrak pavelay - Don & Low Ltd

Lotus - Gazco

Lotus - Lotus Water Garden Products Ltd

Louver-Lite Ltd - Louver-Lite Ltd

Louvolite - Louver-Lite Ltd

Louvrestyle - Hallmark Blinds Ltd

Low Energy Lighting Systems - Connect Lighting Systems (UK) Ltd

Lowara Pumps - Barr & Wray Ltd

Lozaron - Schlegel UK (2006) Ltd

LPA - LPA Group PLC

LPS – Light Protection Screen - PERI Ltd

LR Platform Lift - Wessex Lift Co Ltd

LR800 - Wessex Lift Co Ltd

LR900 - Wessex Lift Co Ltd

LS Longden - Longden

LT - Staverton (UK) Ltd

LTG - Motorised Air Products Ltd

Lucas Furniture Systems - Carleton Furniture Group Ltd

Lumaseal - Illuma Lighting

Lumax - light shelf blind - Hallmark Blinds Ltd

Lumicom - Lighting Industry Association, The

Lumilux - Osram Ltd

Lumisty - Northgate Solar Controls

Lutron - Tidmarsh & Sons

Lux Classic - Kronospan Ltd

Lux Lok - Kronospan Ltd

Luxaclair - Pilkington Plyglass

Luxaflex ® - Luxaflex®

Luxcrete - Luxcrete Ltd

Luxe - Rangemaster

Luxflex - IKM Systems Ltd

Luxfloor - Kronospan Ltd

Luxline Plus - Triphosphor Fluorescent Tubes - FEILO SYLVANIA EUROPE LIMITED

Luxo - Glamox Luxo Lighting Limited

Luxury Feature Panels - FIBO UK LTD

Lynx - Compact Fluorescent Lamps - FEILO SYLVANIA EUROPE LIMITED

Lysander - Brockway Carpets Ltd

Lytag - CEMEX

Lytag - Lytag Ltd

M

M & C Energy group, Merlin Gerin, Modicon, Mita - Schneider Electric Ltd

M E Duffells - Duffells Limited

M+P Labs - Lucideon

M2 - UTC Fire & Securites

M2M Steel Doors - Bradbury Group Ltd

Mab Door Closers - JB Architectural Ltd

MAC - Pressure Coolers Ltd T/A Maestro Pressure Coolers

Macalloy - MacAlloy Limited

Macaw - Paragon by Heckmondwike

Macclex - Exitex Ltd

Macdee Wirquin - Wirquin Ltd

Mach Engineering & Fabrications - Metal Gutta

Machin - Amdega Ltd

Mackay Engineering - Mackay Engineering

Mackridge - McKenzie-Martin Ltd

MacMount - MacLellan Rubber Ltd

MACO - Carl F Groupco Limited

Macpherson - Akzo Noble Coatings Ltd

Macphersons - Crown Paints Ltd

Macromelt - Henkel Ltd

Mactac - Northgate Solar Controls

Mactie - Redifix Ltd

Macvent - MacLellan Rubber Ltd

Maddalena Water Meters - SAV United Kingdom Ltd

Madico - Invicta Window Films Ltd

Madico - Northgate Solar Controls

Madico - The Window Film Company UK Ltd

Madonna, Marion, Maze, Meridien, Mystic - Pitacs Ltd

Maestro - Lewden Electrical Industries

Maestro - Vianen KVS BV

Maestro ® - Pressure Coolers Ltd T/A Maestro Pressure Coolers

Maestroflo ® - Pressure Coolers Ltd T/A Maestro Pressure Coolers

Maestropac ® - Pressure Coolers Ltd T/A Maestro Pressure Coolers

Mag Master - ABB Instrumentation Ltd

Magiboards - Magiboards Ltd

MagiCAD - Glamox Luxo Lighting Limited

MagiRail - Magiboards Ltd

Magis - Laytrad Contract Furniture Ltd

Magnapleat - Camfil Farr Ltd

Magnaseal - Magnet Ltd

Magnastar - Magnet Ltd

Magnastorm - Magnet Ltd

Magnetek - Bernlite Ltd

Magnetic accessories - Clestra Limited

Magnum Firechests - Schiedel Chimney Systems Ltd

Mahtal - James Latham plc

Mailbox - Stamford Products Limited

Mailforce - The Safety Letterbox Company Ltd

MailManager™ Mail Management Software - Neopost Ltd

Main - Myson

Mainsboost - Stuart Turner Ltd

Majestic - Brintons Ltd

Majestic - Majestic Shower Co Ltd

Majestic - Triton PLC

Makrolon - Amari Plastics Plc

Makroswing - Envirodoor Markus Ltd

Malindi - Hyperion Wall Furniture Ltd

Malvern Beam Mounted Seating System - Race Furniture Ltd

Mammoth hoists - PCT Group

Mamoreete - DLW Flooring

Manade - Lesco Products Ltd

Managed Garment range - Helmsman

Managers Decorating Sundries - Kalon Decorative Products

Manders Paints - Manders Paint Ltd

Mangers - Davant Products Ltd

Manhattan - Cooper Lighting

Manhattan - DW Windsor Lighting

Manhattan - Laird Security Hardware

Manhattan Furniture - Dennis & Robinson Ltd

Maniaccess - Manitou (Site Lift) Ltd

Manifestation - Optima

Manifix - Manitou (Site Lift) Ltd

Manireach - Manitou (Site Lift) Ltd

Maniscopic - Manitou (Site Lift) Ltd

Manitransit - Manitou (Site Lift) Ltd

Mann+Hummel - Vokes Air

Mannesmann - Cento Engineering Company Ltd

Manntech - Cento Engineering Company Ltd

Mansafe - Unistrut Limited

ManSafe® - Latchways plc

Manuvic jacks - PCT Group

MAOF - Schlegel UK (2006) Ltd

Mapress - Geberit Ltd

Marblex - Swish Building Products

Marchrist - Marcrist International Ltd

Mardome - Ariel Plastics Ltd

Margard - Dacrylate Paints Ltd

Marghestone Assimilated Granite - Marble Flooring Spec. Ltd

Marine - Richard Hose Ltd

Marineflex - Trade Sealants Ltd

Marineseal - Trade Sealants Ltd

Markar Hinges - Relcross Ltd

Markus - Envirodoor Markus Ltd

Marlborough - Adam Carpets Ltd

Marley - DC Plastic Handrails Ltd

Marley Ltd - Marley Ltd

Marley Roof Tiles - Marley Ltd

Marley Solartile - Marley Ltd

Marley Waterproofing - IKO PLC

Marleyrail - Brighton (Handrails), W

Marlux ® - Marlux Medical Ltd

Marmoleum - Forbo Flooring

Marmolit - Harbro Supplies Ltd

Marquis - Brintons Ltd

Marrakesh - Brintons Ltd

Marshalite - Marshalls Mono Ltd

Marstair - TEV Limited

Marstron - Marlow Ropes Ltd

Martin Roberts - Bradbury Group Ltd

Marutex Magnum stainless drilling screws - UK Fasteners Ltd

Marxco - Marcrist International Ltd

MAS - Optelma Lighting Ltd

Masco - Bristan Group

Masco OneStep Installation Services - Moores Furniture Group Ltd

Masonite - Boardcraft Ltd

Masonite - Premdor

Masonite beams - Panel Agency Limited

Masons Timber Products - Mason FW & Sons Ltd

Masq - Ciret Limited

Massey Ferguson - AGCO Ltd

Master - Securikey Ltd

Master Craftsman Forte - Brockway Carpets Ltd

Master Life, MasterMatrix - BASF plc, Construction Chemicals

Master X-Seed - BASF plc, Construction Chemicals

MasterAir, MasterCast, MasterCell - BASF plc, Construction Chemicals

Masterbill - Masterbill Micro Systems Ltd

Masterbill Elite - Masterbill Micro Systems Ltd

Masterboard - Promat UK Ltd

Mastercraft (MC) - Barber Wilsons & Co Ltd

MasterEmaco - BASF plc, Construction Chemicals

MasterFinish, MasterFlow - BASF plc, Construction Chemicals

MasterGlenium, MasterKure - BASF plc, Construction Chemicals

Masterhitch - www.masterhitch.co.uk - HE Services (Plant Hire) Ltd

MasterPel, MasterPolyheed, MasterPozzolith, MasterProtect - BASF plc, Construction Chemicals

MasterRheobuild, MasterRoc - BASF plc, Construction Chemicals

Masterseal - MK (MK Electric Ltd)

Masterseal - Sealmaster

MasterSeal, MasterSet - BASF plc, Construction Chemicals

Mastersolve - Tank Storage & Services Ltd

Match® - Vicaima Ltd

Matchplay - En-tout-cas Tennis Courts Ltd

Material Lab - Johnson Tiles

Mather & Platt - Tyco Fire and Integrated Solutions

Mathys - Andrews Coatings Ltd

Matki - Matki plc

Matrex - Terrapin Ltd

Matrix - Dixon Turner Wallcoverings

Matrix - Levolux A.T. Limited

Matrix - Lumitron Ltd

Matterson Cranes - PCT Group

Matthews & Yates Centrifugal Fans - Matthews & Yates Ltd

Maurice Hill - BriggsAmasco

Mawrob ® - Broxap Ltd

Max - Jotun Henry Clark Ltd Decorative Division

Max - Ves Andover Ltd

Max ST - Max Appliances Ltd

Max-Econ - Horizon International Ltd

Maxi - Construction Group UK Ltd

Maxi - Isolated Systems Ltd

Maxi 60 Ceiling Systems - Sound Reduction Systems Ltd

Maxi LST - Jaga UK

Maxi Sky - ArjoHuntleigh UK

Maxiboard - Sound Reduction Systems Ltd

Maxifit - Viking Johnson

Maxilift - Stannah Lifts Ltd

Maxim - J.F. Poynter Ltd

Maxim - Laird Security Hardware

Maxima - Fastwall Ltd

Maximair - McKenzie-Martin Ltd

Maximin - Max Appliances Ltd

Maximiser - Ormandy Rycroft Engineering

Maxi-Mixer - Cardale Garage Doors

MAXIMO – Panel Wall formwork - PERI Ltd

Maxinex - Chalmit Lighting

Maxivent - Airflow Developments Ltd

Maxmatic 1000 - Max Appliances Ltd

Maxmatic 1500 - Max Appliances Ltd

Maxmatic 2000 - Max Appliances Ltd

Maxmatic 3000 - Max Appliances Ltd

Maxmatic 4000 - Max Appliances Ltd

Maxmatic 5000 - Max Appliances Ltd

Maxol 12D - Burco Maxol

Maxol M10D - Burco Maxol

Maxol M15 - Burco Maxol

Maxol Microturbo - Burco Maxol

Maxol Mirage - Burco Maxol

Maxol Montana - Burco Maxol

Maxol Morocco - Burco Maxol

Maxum R ™ - Dezurik International Ltd

Maxum V ™ - Dezurik International Ltd

Maxwell House - The Kenco Coffee Company

Maybeguard - Mabey Hire Ltd

Mayfair - Gower Furniture Ltd

Mayfair - Kaloric Heater Co Ltd

Mayfield Brol - Kingstonian Paint Ltd

MBCad - Masterbill Micro Systems Ltd

M-Bond - Isocrete Floor Screeds Ltd

M-Bond Xtra - Isocrete Floor Screeds Ltd

MBR Technology - Jacopa Limited

MC - Howden Buffalo

McPherson - Brewer C & Sons Ltd

MCR Barrier - APT Controls Ltd

MCR Recycling - Jack Moody Ltd

MCS Barrier - APT Controls Ltd

mctavishramsay - Bridgman IBC Ltd

Mc-Wall - Smart Systems Ltd

MDA Scientific - Zellweger Analytic Ltd, Sieger Division

Meadrain - Mea UK Ltd

Meagard - Mea UK Ltd

Meagard S - Mea UK Ltd

Meakerb - Mea UK Ltd

Mealine - Mea UK Ltd

Meaplas - Mea UK Ltd

Mearin - Mea UK Ltd

Mecury - Fabrikat (Nottingham) Ltd

medeco - Mul-T-Lock

Medica - Veoila Water Technologies UKElga Ltd

Medical Gas - Conex Universal Limited

Mediclad - Interclad (UK) Ltd

Medicool (bedhead lamps) - Brandon Medical

Medilog - ArjoHuntleigh UK

Medisan - Cleenol Group Ltd

Medite - Boardcraft Ltd

Medite - Meyer Timber Limited

Medstor - Stamford Products Limited

Medway - Potter & Soar Ltd

Meg - Abet Ltd

Megaduct - Domus Ventilation

Megafilm, Megatac, Megaboard - Visqueen Building Products

Megafit - Viking Johnson

Megaflo, MegaLife - Heatrae Sadia Heating Ltd

Megasys - Advanced Perimeter Systems Ltd

Melbury - Hamworthy Heating Limited & ACV UK

Meleto - Panel Systems Ltd

meltaway - Uponor Ltd

MEM - Eaton Electric Ltd

Memera 2000 - Eaton Electric Limited

Memera 2000 AD - Eaton Electric Limited

Memlite BC3 - Eaton Electric Limited

Memstyle - Eaton Electric Limited

Menvier - Cooper Safety

Menvier Security - Eaton's Security Business

Meols Door - AS Newbould Ltd

Mepla - Geberit Ltd

Merchant Hardware - Avocet Hardware Ltd

Mercury - Eltron Chromalox

Mercury - S & B Ltd

Mercury - Triton PLC

Merlin - Swintex Ltd

Merlin Network (Scotland) - Saveheat Group

Mermaid Panels - Mermaid Panels Ltd

Mermet - Mermet U.K

Mervene - Firwood Paints Ltd

Meshtec - Cadisch MDA

Meshtrack - Bekaert Building Products

Message Manager - Deaf Alerter plc

Metagard - Leigh's Paints

Metal Gutta - Metal Gutta

Metal Halide Lamps - FEILO SYLVANIA EUROPE LIMITED

Metalarc - Metal Halide Lamps - FEILO SYLVANIA EUROPE LIMITED

Metalclad Plus - MK (MK Electric Ltd)

Metalliform - Metalliform Products Plc

Metalphoto - Pryorsign

Metalset - Loctite UK Ltd

Metasys - Johnson Controls Building Efficiency UK Ltd

Meteon - Trespa UK Ltd

Meters Direct - Switch2 Energy Solutions Ltd

Metframe - Metsec Ltd

Metlex - Triton PLC

Metpost - Expamet Building Products

Metpost - Grange Fencing Limited

Metpost products - B & M Fencing Limited

Metro - Harton Heating Appliances

Metro - Townscape Products Ltd

Metro Therm - Harton Heating Appliances

Metrobond - Britmet Tileform Limited

MetroDrain - Naylor Drainage Ltd

MetroDuct - Naylor Drainage Ltd

Metropole - Silent Gliss Ltd

Metsec - Metsec Lattice Beams Ltd

Metsec - Metsec Ltd

Metsec floor beams - Metsec Lattice Beams Ltd

Metsec lattice joists - Metsec Lattice Beams Ltd

Metsec lattice trusses - Metsec Lattice Beams Ltd

Metsec Zed purlins - Metsec Ltd

Metspan - Metsec Ltd

Metstrut - Metsec Ltd

Met-Track enclosed track system - Metreel Ltd

Metway - Metway Electrical Industries Ltd

Meva Screens - Adams- Hydraulics Ltd

Meyer - Commercial Lighting Systems

Meynell - Kohler Mira Ltd

Mezzo - Kermi (UK) Ltd

MGE Office Protection Systems - Eaton Electric Ltd

Michelmersh - Michelmersh Brick Holdings PLC

Micrex - Stamford Products Limited

Microbore - Wednesbury Tube

Microcard Readers - Time and Data Systems International Ltd (TDSI)

Microdek® - Metalfloor UK Ltd

Microflon - Plastic Coatings Ltd

M (con't)

Microfloor 600® - Workspace Technology Ltd
Microlift - Stannah Lifts Ltd
Microlock Systems - Time and Data Systems International Ltd (TDSI)
Micronex - Chalmit Lighting
MicroPac - Draeger Safety UK Ltd
MicroPoint - Paragon by Heckmondwike
Micropol - Stamford Products Limited
Microvent - Watts Industries UK Ltd
Midlift - Stannah Lifts Ltd
Miele - Miele Co Ltd
MIENA MEISTERSTUCK - Kaldewei
Mightyflex - Airflow (Nicoll Ventilators) Ltd
Milano - Symphony Group PLC, The
Millenium - Stocksigns Ltd
Miller by Honeywell - Honeywell Safety Products
Millhouse (early years furniture) - Spaceright Europe Limited
Milliken Colours - Milliken Carpet
Milltown Blend - Carlton Main Brickworks Ltd
Millwood - Project Office Furniture PLC
Milner - Chubb Safe Equipment Company
Milnrow Sandstone - Kerridge Stone Ltd
Minerva MX - ADT Fire and Security Plc
MinGardi - Dyer Environmental Controls
Mini (Wall and Freestanding) - Jaga UK
Mini Canal - Jaga UK
Mini Clearflow Gas Flue Blocks - Dunbrik (Yorks) Ltd
Mini Compack - Fulton Boiler Works (Great Britain) Ltd
Mini Glaze - Pearce Security Systems
Mini Locker - Helmsman
Minibore - Yorkshire Copper Tube
Mini-compacta - KSB Ltd
Miniflo Rainwater System - FloPlast Ltd
Minilift - Didsbury Engineering Co Ltd
Mini-Lynx - Compact Fluorescent Lamps - FEILO SYLVANIA EUROPE LIMITED
Minima - Fastwall Ltd
Minislate® (Roof Tiles) - Forticrete Roofing
Minispace - Kone PLC
Miniwarn - Draeger Safety UK Ltd
Minster - Minsterstone Ltd
Minton Hollins - Johnson Tiles
Miodox - Witham Oil & Paint Ltd
Mipolam - Brighton (Handrails), W
Mipolam - DC Plastic Handrails Ltd
Mipolam EL - Gerflor Ltd
Mipolam Esprit 500 - Gerflor Ltd
Mira - Kohler Mira Ltd
Miraclean - AudiocomPendax Ltd
Miraflex - Knauf Insulation Ltd
Mirage - Dudley Thomas Ltd
Mirage - Komfort Workspace PLC
Mirage - Matki plc
Mirage - Mode Lighting (UK) Ltd
Mirage - Muraspec
Mirage - Shackerley (Holdings) Group Ltd incorporating Designer ceramics
Mirage - Whitecroft Lighting Limited
MIRANIT - Franke Sissons Ltd
MIRO - Alanod Ltd
MIROGARD Anti-Reflective Glass - SCHOTT UK Ltd
Mirrorvision - Pro Display TM Limited
Mistral - Airedale International Air Conditioning Ltd
Mistral - Imperial Machine Co Ltd
Mistral - Optima
Mita - Schneider Electric Ltd
Mitsubishi - Deralam Laminates Ltd
Mitsubishi - Purified Air Ltd
Mixcal - Altecnic Ltd
MJC - Nederman Filtration Ltd
MJX - Nederman Filtration Ltd
MK - MK (MK Electric Ltd)
MMAXGrip™ - Ennis-Flint
MMS - Kone PLC
Mobile 2000 - Lappset UK Ltd
Mobilier International - Haworth UK Ltd
Mobility Kerb - Brett Landscaping
Mod 4 - Leofric Building Systems Ltd
Moda Range - Twyford Bathrooms
Mode - Allgood plc
Mode - Bernlite Ltd
Moderna, Metro and Micro - Lang+Fulton
Modric - Allgood plc
MODUCEL® - Eaton-Williams Group Limited
Modul - Glamox Luxo Lighting Limited
Modulair - Biddle Air Systems Ltd
Modular - Helmsman
Modular Glazing - HW Architectural Ltd
Modulight - Mermet U.K
Moduline - IAC Acoustic Company UK Ltd
Modupak - Stokvis Industrial Boilers (International) Limited
Modus - Glasdon U.K. Limited
Moeller - Eaton Electric Ltd
Moeller Electric - Electrix International Ltd
Molosil - Notcutt Ltd
Monaframe - Sapa Building Systems (monarch and glostal)
Monaframe - Technal UK
Monaperm 700 - Icopal Limited
Monarch - Sapa Building Systems (monarch and glostal)
Monarch - Technal UK
Monarflex - Icopal Limited
Monarsound - Icopal Limited
Mondéco - Flowcrete Plc
Mondo Sportflex - Altro Ltd
Mondo Sportflex Athletic Surface - Bernhards Landscapes Ltd
Mondopave - Altro Ltd
Monnex - Britannia Fire
Mono - Delta Balustrades
Mono - Parthos UK Ltd
Mono Comtrol - Tidmarsh & Sons
monocoque support system - Dales Fabrications Ltd
Monodec - Flowcrete Plc
Monoglass - Aardvark Transatlantic Ltd
Monoglass - Becker (SLIDING PARTITIONS) Ltd
Monolevel - Flexcrete Technologies Limited
Monolite - Flexcrete Technologies Limited
Monomix - Flexcrete Technologies Limited
Monoplan - Becker (SLIDING PARTITIONS) Ltd
Monopour - Flexcrete Technologies Limited
Monoprufe - Ronacrete Ltd
Monoscape - Marshalls Mono Ltd
Monoshake - Don Construction Products Ltd
Monospace - Kone PLC
MonoSpace® - Kone
Monostrip - Dufaylite Developments Ltd
Monotrak, Multitrak - Rackline Systems Storage Ltd
Monowall5oo - Monowa Manufacturing (UK) Ltd
Monroe Sign Family - GB Sign Solutions Limited
Monsoon - Stuart Turner Ltd
Montage - Heckmondwicke FB
Montana - Armitage Shanks Ltd
Montanna - Libraco
Monument - Monument Tools Ltd
Monza - Laird Security Hardware
Moonlight Marker - Intersolar Group Ltd
Moorland - Cembrit Ltd
Morcton Door - AS Newbould Ltd
Morion - Moravia (UK) Ltd
Morris - Konecranes UK
Morris and Co - Sanderson
Morrison Construction - GallifordTry
Mosaic Collection - Solus Ceramics Ltd
Mosaiq - Kompan Ltd
Motala™ - Kone
Motor Up staging - CPS Manufacturing Co
mould clear - Peter Cox Ltd
Mould Making - Aden Hynes Sculpture Studios
Mouldguard - Trade Sealants Ltd
Mouldshield - AkzoNobel Decorative Paints UK
Moventi - Zon International
Moveo - Style Door Systems Ltd
Mozaico - Resdev Ltd
MP Acoustic Control (vibration and acoustic control) - Mansfield Pollard & Co Ltd
MP Air Handling (air handling units) - Mansfield Pollard & Co Ltd
MP Kitchen Ventilation (kitchen canopies) - Mansfield Pollard & Co Ltd
MP Total Solutions (general ventilation) - Mansfield Pollard & Co Ltd
M-Screen - Mermet U.K
MSR Columns - Consult Lighting Ltd
MT70 IP67 waterproof fitting - Encapsulite International Ltd
MTX Engineering - Multitex GRP LLP
MudularUK - Caledonian Modular
Muhlhauser - Schwing Stetter (UK) Ltd
Multi - Glamox Electric (UK) Ltd
Multibeam - Ward Insulated Panels Ltd
Multibond - Loctite UK Ltd
Multibond Gold - Laybond Products Ltd
Multibrace - Mabey Hire Ltd
Multichannel - Ward Insulated Panels Ltd
Multicryl - Laybond Products Ltd
Multideck - Ward Insulated Panels Ltd
Multi-DENCO - DencoHappel UK Ltd
Multiduct - Ward Insulated Panels Ltd
Multifix Airbrick® - Rytons Building Products Ltd
Multiflex - Marflex Chimney Systems
Multiflex - Multikwik Ltd
Multiflush - Multikwik Ltd
Multiguard - Hoyles Electronic Developments Ltd
Multikwik - Multikwik Ltd
Multilab laboratory furniture - Grant Westfield Ltd
Multilock - Nico Manufacturing Ltd
Multipanel Shower Panels - Grant Westfield Ltd
Multi-Plate - Asset International Ltd
Multipoint - Heatrae Sadia Heating Ltd
Multipor - Xella Aircrete Systems UK
Multipot - TSE Brownson
MULTIPROP- Propping and Shoring Tower - PERI Ltd
Multishield ™ - Accent Hansen
Multi-system Less-abled Products - Armitage Shanks Ltd
Multitack - Laybond Products Ltd
Multitex - Multitex GRP LLP
Multivap - Ubbink (UK) Ltd
Multivent - Ubbink (UK) Ltd
Multivent - Vent-Axia
Multiwarn - Draeger Safety UK Ltd
MUL-T-LOCK - ASSA ABLOY Limited
Muncher - Mono Pumps Ltd
Munchpump - Mono Pumps Ltd
Municiple - Fitzgerald Lighting Ltd
Muralon - Muraspec
Murek - Muraspec
Murfor - Masonry Reinforcement - Bekaert Building Products
Mutrator - Mono Pumps Ltd
Mvi - Wilo Samson Pumps Ltd
MW Motorway - Consult Lighting Ltd
MWD - Waterline Limited
Myrtha - Barr & Wray Ltd
Myson - The BSS Group

N

Nailor - Advanced Air (UK) Ltd
Nano - Delabie UK Ltd
Nanu - Girsberger London
Nappigon - Imperial Machine Co Ltd
Nappychanger - LSA Projects Ltd
NAS - National Association of Shopfitters
NASC - National Access & Scaffolding Confederation (NASC)
National - Kenyon Performance Adhesives
National bondmaster - Kenyon Group Ltd
National Register of Warranted Builders - Federation of Master Builders
Natte - Mermet U.K
Natural Choice Axminster - Ulster Carpet Mills Ltd
Natural Collection - Solus Ceramics Ltd
Natural Ventilation Solutions - SE Controls
Naturdor® - Vicaima Ltd
Nature Play - HAGS SMP
Nautilus - Aldous & Stamp (Services) Ltd
Navigator - Project Office Furniture PLC
NBS - NBS
NBS - RIBA Enterprises
NBS Building - NBS
NBS Building Regulations - NBS
NBS Create - NBS
NBS Engineering Services - NBS
NBS Landscape - NBS
NBS Plus - Knauf AMF Ceilings Ltd
nce - New Civil Engineer - EMAP
nDura - Delta Balustrades
Neaco - Norton Engineering Alloys Co Ltd
Neaco Support Systems - Norton Engineering Alloys Co Ltd
Neatdek 2 - Norton Engineering Alloys Co Ltd
Neatedge - Enable Access
Neatgrille - Norton Engineering Alloys Co Ltd
Neatmat - Norton Engineering Alloys Co Ltd
NeatraZone - PHS Group plc
Nelson - Marlow Ropes Ltd
Nemef - Mul-T-Lock
Neo Pantile - Sandtoft Roof Tiles Ltd
Neopolitan - Glasdon U.K. Limited
Neopost™ Mailroom Equipment and Supplies - Neopost Ltd
Neotran - Mode Lighting (UK) Ltd
Neotronics - Zellweger Analytic Ltd, Sieger Division
Neptune - Neptune Outdoor Furniture Ltd
NET LED Lighting - NET LED Limited
Net Play - HAGS SMP
NetComms - ADT Fire and Security Plc
Network bird management - P+L Systems Ltd
Net-works - Metway Electrical Industries Ltd
New c3m/p5. Moisture Resistant Carcase - Rixonway Kitchens Ltd
New Era - Benlowe Group Limited
New Ultomat - Project Office Furniture PLC
Neway - Neway Doors Ltd
Neway - (Neway Doors Ltd.) - Shutter Door Repair & Maintenance Ltd
Neway-(Neway Doors Ltd) - Priory Shutter & Door Co Ltd
Newdawn - Newdawn & Sun Ltd
Newdome (Rooflights) - Novaglaze Limited
Newlath - Newton John & Co Ltd
Newline - Tunstal Healthcare (UK) Ltd
Newspack - Leofric Building Systems Ltd
Newteam - NewTeam Ltd
Newton Door - AS Newbould Ltd
Newton Security Doors - Bradbury Group Ltd
NEXSYS - Kaldewei
Nexus - HAGS SMP
Nexus 100 (recycling Bins) - Glasdon UK Limited
Nexxus - Chalmit Lighting
NFC Specialist Products - GVS Filter Technology UK
NFDC - National Federation of Demolition Contractors
NFRC - National Federation of Roofing Contractors Ltd., The
NHBC - National House Building Council
Niagara Rainwater system - FloPlast Ltd
Nic-cool - Nicholson Plastics Ltd
NICEIC - National Inspection Council for Electrical Installation Contracting
Nickleby - Swintex Ltd
Nico - Nico Manufacturing Ltd
Nicobond - Nicholls & Clarke Ltd
Nico-O-Grout - Nicholls & Clarke Ltd
Night Cradle - Deaf Alerter plc
Nilfisk Advance - Nilfisk Limited
Nilfisk CFM - Nilfisk Limited
Nilfisk-ALTO - Nilfisk Limited
Nilflam - Kingspan Industrial Ins. Ltd
Nimbus® - ArjoHuntleigh UK
Nite Site - Leigh's Paints
Nitobond - Fosroc Ltd
Nitofil - Fosroc Ltd
Nitoflor - Fosroc Ltd
Nitoseal - Fosroc Ltd
Nitriflex - Movement Joints (UK)
Nitromors - Henkel Consumer Adhesives
No Skidding - Kenyon Paints Limited
Noise Lock - IAC Acoustic Company UK Ltd
NoiseStopSystems - The Sound Solution
Noishield Acoustic Louvres - IAC Acoustic Company UK Ltd
Nomafoam - NMC (UK) Ltd
Nomapack - NMC (UK) Ltd
Nomastyl - NMC (UK) Ltd
Non Com X - Arch Timber Protection
Non-slip Bench Mat - Dycem Ltd
Norbo - Booth Muirie
Norbro - Flowserve Flow Control
nordic light - ITAB Prolight UK Limited
Nordica - Deceuninck Ltd
Nordpeis - Gazco
Nordyl - Dixon Turner Wallcoverings
Nori - Marshalls Mono Ltd
Norlyn - Smart F & G (Shopfittings)Ltd
Normbau - Allegion (UK) Ltd
Nor-Ray-Vac - Continuous radiant tube heating - AmbiRad Ltd
Norseman Swageless - Navtec
Norslo - Green Brook
North Star - Tapworks Water Softeners
Northern Hardwood - IJK Timber Group Ltd
NOS - Strand Hardware Ltd
Notifier Fire Detection - Fife Fire Engineers & Consultants Ltd
Nova - Rawson Fillings Ltd
Nova - The Window Film Company UK Ltd
Nova - Zon International
Nova Brand - Cleenol Group Ltd
Novaglaze - Swedecor
Novalin - Dixon Turner Wallcoverings
Novara-25 and Novara-34 - Lang+Fulton
Nova-Seal - Schlegel UK (2006) Ltd
Novastone - Swedecor
Noviasol - Dalesauna Ltd
Novis - Samuel Heath & Sons plc
Novoferm - Envirodoor Markus Ltd
Novoferm UK - Novoferm Europe Ltd
Novoferm, Nrg Automation - Acorn Garage Doors Ltd
NOVOLA - Kaldewei
Novolit - Skanda Acoustics Limited
Novomatic - Novoferm Europe Ltd
NovoPort - Novoferm Europe Ltd
NovoShield - Novoferm Europe Ltd
NP100 Slurry - Imerys Minerals Ltd
NRG - HAGS SMP
NRWB - Federation of Master Builders
NSC4OUD1 - Tapworks Water Softeners
nuance - Bushboard Limited
Nuastyle taps - Armitage Shanks Ltd
Nucana - Ward's Flexible Rod Company Ltd
Nufins - Hines & Sons, P E, Ltd
Nuflex - Ward's Flexible Rod Company Ltd
Nu-klad - Kenyon Group Ltd
Nulfire - Tremco Illbruck Ltd
Nullifire - Firebarrier International Ltd T/A Firebarrier Services Ltd
Nullifire - Nullifire Ltd
Nutristore - CST Industries, Inc. - UK
NVS (Natural Ventilation Solutions) - SE Controls

O

Oasis - Architen Landrell Associates Ltd
Oasis - Kompan Ltd
Oasis - Water Technology Engineering Ltd
Oberflex - Abet Ltd
Oboin - Mermet U.K
Ocala - Ellis J T & Co Ltd
Ocean - Signs & Labels Ltd
Octadoor - Righton Ltd
Octanorm - RTD Systems Ltd
OCTO 250 - Turner Access Ltd
Octoflex - Mat.Works Flooring Solutions
Ocula - SIG Interiors
Odex, OxyBAC® - Deb Group Limited
Odoni - Elwell Buildings Ltd
OfficeCool - DencoHappel UK Ltd
Ogilive Sealants - Ogilvie Construction Ltd
Ogilvie Construction Ltd - Ogilvie Construction Ltd
Oilmaster - Docherty New Vent Chimney Group
Old Clamp - York Handmade Brick Co Ltd
Old English pantile - Sandtoft Roof Tiles Ltd
Oldroyd Gtx geotextile cavity drainage membrane - Safeguard Europe Ltd
Oldroyd XP plaster membrane - Safeguard Europe Ltd
Oldroyd Xv cavity drainage membrane - Safeguard Europe Ltd
Oldstock Autique - Carlton Main Brickworks Ltd
Ollevibe - Olley & Sons Ltd, C
Olympia - Erlau AG
Olympic - Swedecor
Olympus - Carpets of Worth Ltd
OMA - Harbro Supplies Ltd
Omeg - Omeg Ltd
omega - Bushboard Limited
Omega - Sika Liquid Plastics Limited
Omega 4 - Cooper Lighting
Omega®, Omega Pencil Edge, Omega Flow - Brett Landscaping
Omegadeck - Turner Access Ltd
Omniclay - En-tout-cas Tennis Courts Ltd
Omnipex Horticulture - IPF Omnipex
Omnitek - Grace De Neef UK
Onduline - Onduline Building Products Ltd
Ondutiss - Onduline Building Products Ltd
Onduvilla - Onduline Building Products Ltd
One Step - Tank Storage & Services Ltd
Onyx - Pland Stainless Ltd
Onyx - Project Office Furniture PLC
Onyx - Sapphire Balustrades
OP 763 Waterstop - Carter-Dal International
Opal - Sapphire Balustrades
Opalux - Northgate Solar Controls
Open Options - Project Office Furniture PLC
Open Spaces - Ulster Carpet Mills Ltd
Openlok - Unifix Ltd
Opertis - HEWI UK Ltd
Opiocolour Mosaics - Reed Harris
OPT539 Waterproof membrane - Carter-Dal International
Optelma - Optelma Lighting Ltd
OptiDome - CST Industries, Inc. - UK
Optiflame - Dimplex UK Limited
Optiflex - Anglepoise Lighting Ltd
Optiflex - Hughes Safety Showers Limited
Optifloat - Pilkington Birmingham
Optilam - Pilkington Birmingham
Optima - Cardale Garage Doors
Optima - DW Windsor Lighting
Optima - Optima
Optima - Paslode
Optima by Coram - Coram Showers Ltd
Optimirror - Pilkington Birmingham
Option Range - Twyford Bathrooms
options - Bushboard Limited
Options - Hands of Wycombe

BRANDS AND TRADE NAMES

O (con't)

Options - Sanderson
Options Toilet Cubicles - Grant Westfield Ltd
Optitherm - Pilkington Birmingham
Optitherm thermostatic tap - Horne Engineering Ltd
Optivision - The Window Film Company UK Ltd
Optiwin - Glamox Luxo Lighting Limited
Opto - Stamford Products Limited
Opto Thermo - Aqualisa Products
Opus - Booth Muirie
OPV 2000 - Colt International
Orator - Gent Limited
Oratorio carpet tiles cut pile - Burmatex Ltd
Orbik - Bernlite Ltd
Orbis - Apollo Fire Detectors Ltd
Orbis - Delta Balustrades
Orbis - Laidlaw Ltd
Orbit - Cil Retail Solutions Ltd
Orca - Rediweld Rubber & Plastics Ltd
Orcal Infusions - Armstrong World Industries Ltd
Orchestra - Vianen KVS BV
Orcon - Fillcrete Ltd
Original - C - Paroc Panel Systems Uk Ltd
Original - E - Paroc Panel Systems Uk Ltd
Original - I - Paroc Panel Systems Uk Ltd
Original No Butts - The No Butts Bin Company (NBB), Trading as NBB Outdoor Shelters
Origins - Baggeridge Brick PLC
Orion - Ubbink (UK) Ltd
Orsogril - Squires Metal Fabrications Ltd
Ortega - Lumitron Ltd
Ortho Mat - Interface Europe Ltd
Ortronics - Legrand Electric Ltd
OS2 - SE Controls
OSID - Xtralis
Osma - Wavin Ltd
Osma DeepLine - Wavin Ltd
Osma RoofLine - Wavin Ltd
Osma Roundline - Wavin Ltd
Osma Squareline - Wavin Ltd
Osma Stormline - Wavin Ltd
Osma SuperLine - Wavin Ltd
Osma UltraRib - Wavin Ltd
OsmaDrain - Wavin Ltd
OsmaGold - Wavin Ltd
OsmaSoil - Wavin Ltd
OsmaWeld - Wavin Ltd
OSMO - Wood Finishes - OSMO UK
Osprey - Swintex Ltd
Osram - Bernlite Ltd
Osram Dulux - Osram Ltd
OT Medipower (isolated power systems) - Brandon Medical
Ovalgrip - Hellermann Tyton
OWA - OWA UK Ltd
OWAconstruct - OWA UK Ltd
OWAcoustic - OWA UK Ltd
OWAcoustic Janus - OWA UK Ltd
OWAcoustic smart - OWA UK Ltd
OWAdeco - OWA UK Ltd
OWAlux - OWA UK Ltd
OWALux Clean - OWA UK Ltd
OWAspectra - OWA UK Ltd
OWAtecta - OWA UK Ltd
OWAtecta Perfora - OWA UK Ltd
Owens Corning - Kitsons Insulation Products Ltd
Oxan WP - Jotun Henry Clark Ltd Decorative Division
Oxygen - Jaga UK
Oxypic - Dunsley Heat Ltd

P

P. S. Fan units - Elan-Dragonair
P.P.P - Wade International Ltd
P+L Systems Washroom - P+L Systems Ltd
P2000 - Johnson Controls Building Efficiency UK Ltd
P5 - Hudevad Britain
P50 - Britannia Fire
P5K - Hudevad Britain
PAC - Vidionics Security Systems Ltd
Pace - Caldwell Hardware (UK) Ltd
Pacemaker - Portakabin Ltd
Pacific - Deceuninck Ltd
Pacifyre® - Walraven Ltd
Pactan - Tremco Illbruck Ltd
PaintSpec Finder™ - Crown Paints Ltd
Palace - Parthos UK Ltd
Palace Switches - Wandsworth Elecrtrical Ltd
Palazzoli - Lewden Electrical Industries
Palermo and Pastica - Lang+Fulton
Pallas - Architectural Textiles Ltd
Palletstor - Moresecure Ltd
Pamec - Schwing Stetter (UK) Ltd
Panacea, Pegasus, Petit, Planal, Planet Moon, Poplar, Portofino, Porte - Pitacs Ltd
Panasonic - Connaught Communications Systems Ltd
Panasonic - Vidionics Security Systems Ltd
Panatrim - Universal Components Ltd
Panda - Horizon International Ltd
Panel Glide - Silent Gliss Ltd
Panel&Frame - TBS Amwell Ltd
Panelam® - Panel Agency Limited
Paneline - Panel Agency Limited
Panelmaster - Timeguard Ltd
Panelvent® - Panel Agency Limited
Panic Hardware - Dorma Door Services Ltd
Pan-L-Trim - Gooding Aluminium
Panorama - Muraspec
Panther - Simpson Strong-Tie®
Pantile 2000 - Britmet Tileform Limited
Paptrim Aluminium - Pitchmastic PmB Ltd
Paptrim Roof Edge Trime - Pitchmastic PmB Ltd
Parade - Iles Waste Systems
Paradyz - R J Stokes & Co Limited
Parafon - CoolZone - Armstrong World Industries Ltd
Paragon - Macemain + Amstad Ltd
Paragon AV - Macemain + Amstad Ltd
Paraline - Marlow Ropes Ltd
Paramount - Macemain + Amstad Ltd
Parat C - Draeger Safety UK Ltd
Parflu - May William (Ashton) Ltd
Pargon - Fitzgerald Lighting Ltd
Parigi - Altecnic Ltd
Parinox - Altecnic Ltd
Park Home Coatings - Everlac (GB) Ltd
Par-Ker - Porcelanosa Group Ltd
Parker Bath - ArjoHuntleigh UK
Parkiflex - Western Cork Ltd
Parkray - Hepworth Heating Ltd
Parmet - May William (Ashton) Ltd
Paroc - Knauf Insulation Ltd
Parocs Structural - Paroc Panel Systems Uk Ltd
Parri - Laytrad Contract Furniture Ltd
Partnerships & Regeneration - GallifordTry
Pasa XP - Kermi (UK) Ltd
Paslode - ITW Construction Products
Paslode - ITW Spit
Passivent Tricklevents - Passivent Ltd
Patay Pumps - Pump International Ltd
Patchfast - Conren Ltd
Patented energy control - Fluidair Ltd
Patex - Henkel Ltd
Pathfinder - Intersolar Group Ltd
Patina - Shadbolt F R & Sons Ltd
Patination Oil - BLM British Lead
Patio - Rawson Carpets Ltd
Pavia Toscana - Kirkstone
PCA - The Property Care Association
PCE - PCE Instruments UK Ltd
PDA Range of induction loop systems - C-TEC (Computionics) Ltd
Peabody Water Services - Satec Service Ltd
Peakstone - CEMEX
Pearce Homes - Pearce Construction (Barnstaple) Limited
Pearce Property Services - Pearce Construction (Barnstaple) Limited
Pearpoint - Radiodetection Ltd
Pecafil® - BRC Special Products - Bekaert Ltd
Pedalo - Erlau AG
Pegler - Olby H E & Co Ltd
Pegler - Pegler Ltd
Pelham Picnic Suite - Branson Leisure Ltd
Pelican - Amilake Southern Ltd
Pelican - Tuke & Bell Ltd
Pel-Job - Chippindale Plant Ltd
PEMKO - ASSA ABLOY Limited
Pemko Seals and Thresholds - Relcross Ltd
Pendock Casings and Enclosures - Alumasc Interior Building Products Limited
Pendock profiles - Alumasc Interior Building Products Limited
Pennine - Laidlaw Ltd
Pennine - Russell Roof Tiles Ltd
Pennine Stone - Haddonstone Ltd
Penrhyn - Welsh Slate Limited
Pensby Door - AS Newbould Ltd
Pent Concrete Garages - Liget Compton
Pent Mansard Concrete Garages - Liget Compton
People Flow™ - Kone
Pepex Pipes - Uponor Ltd
Pepperpot Stool - Hille Educational Products Ltd
Perfect Fit - Tidmarsh & Sons
Perfector - Crane Fluid Systems
PerfoLight - Enable Access
Performa - Pegler Ltd
Performing Art - Brintons Ltd
Perftec - Cadisch MDA
Pergola - Panel & Louvre Co Ltd
PERI UP - System scaffolding - PERI Ltd
Perimate DI-A - Dow Building Solutions
Perinsul - Pittsburgh Corning (United Kingdom) Limited
Period suite - Brass Art Ltd
Periscope® - Rytons Building Products Ltd
Perko, Perkomatic, Powermatic - Samuel Heath & Sons plc
Perlux Digital 2D/3D Screens - Harkness Screens
Permaban - BRC Reinforcement
Permabond - Kenyon Group Ltd
Permacrib - PHI Group Ltd
Permafoam - Isocrete Floor Screeds Ltd
Permagard - Andura Coatings Ltd
Permagold - Deva Tap Co Ltd
Permakote - Wessex Resins & Adhesives Ltd
Permali - Permali Deho Ltd
Permalux - Lumitron Ltd
Permanite - IKO PLC
permaramp, swift ramp system - Enable Access
PermaRend - PermaRock Products Ltd
PermaRock - PermaRock Products Ltd
Permascreed - DPC Screeding Ltd
Permasint - Plastic Coatings Ltd
Permastrip - BLM British Lead
Permatred - Permali Deho Ltd
Permavoid - Polypipe Civils
Permawood - Permali Deho Ltd
Permoglaze - Akzo Noble Coatings Ltd
Permoglaze - Brewer C & Sons Ltd
Permoglaze - Crown Paints Ltd
Personal Surveyor - Gas Measurement Instruments Ltd
Perspectives - Gradus Ltd
Pest-Stop - P+L Systems Ltd
Petrel - PFP Electrical Products Ltd
Petrelux - PFP Electrical Products Ltd
Petro fast modular forecourt systems - Cookson and Zinn (PTL) Ltd
Petrochem - SSAB Swedish Steel Ltd
PetroTec - CST Industries, Inc. - UK
Pexapipe - IPPEC Systems Ltd
Pexatherm - IPPEC Systems Ltd
PFI Group - GB Sign Solutions Limited
Pfliederer - Deralam Laminates Ltd
Phantom - Dudley Thomas Ltd
Pharo - Hansgrohe
Phenblox® - Walraven Ltd
Phenomenon - Paragon by Heckmondwike
Phillip Jeffries - Architectural Textiles Ltd
Phillips - Bernlite Ltd
Phlexicare - Nicholls & Clarke Ltd
Phoenix - Cooke Brothers Ltd
Phoenix - Glasdon U.K. Limited
Phoenix - Intersolar Group Ltd
Phoenix - Swintex Ltd
Phoenix - Kingfisher - Jewers Doors Ltd
Phoenix - Osprey - Jewers Doors Ltd
Phoenix - Swift - Jewers Doors Ltd
Phoenix (seating) - Glasdon UK Limited
Phoenix Fire Doors - Benlowe Group Limited
Phonic - Parthos UK Ltd
Phosco - CU Phosco Lighting
Photosorption - Bicester Products Ltd
Piazza - Erlau AG
Piccola - Draeger Safety UK Ltd
Piccolo - Stannah Lifts Ltd
PICDOR - TORMAX United Kingdom Ltd
Pickering Europe Ltd - Pickerings Ltd
Pickwick - Swintex Ltd
Picture Perf perforated metal Pictures/Logos - Graepels Perforators Ltd
Pieri - GCP APPLIED TECHNOLOGIES (UK) LIMITED
Piggyback - Safety Assured Ltd
Pikes - Pike Signals Ltd
Piling Accessories - Cordek Ltd
Pilkington Acoustic Laminate - Pilkington UK Ltd
Pilkington Insulight - Pilkington UK Ltd
Pilkington K Glass - Pilkington UK Ltd
Pilkington 'K' Glass - Pilkington Birmingham
Pilkington Optifloat - Pilkington UK Ltd
Pilkington Optimirror Plus - Pilkington UK Ltd
Pilkington Planar Structural Glazing - Pilkington UK Ltd
Pilkington Planarclad - Pilkington UK Ltd
Pilkington Pyrodur - Pilkington UK Ltd
Pilkington Pyroshield Safety - Pilkington UK Ltd
Pilkington Pyrostop - Pilkington UK Ltd
Pilkington Satin - Pilkington UK Ltd
Pilkington Suncool - Pilkington UK Ltd
Pin Panelz - Spaceright Europe Limited
Pinoleum - Tidmarsh & Sons
Pinpoint - Stocksigns Ltd
Pinsulator - bigHead Bonding Fasteners Ltd
Pioneer Mr Kitchens - Moores Furniture Group Ltd
Pipeflex - Armortec
Pipegard - Leigh's Paints
Piper Lifeline - Tunstal Healthcare (UK) Ltd
Pirelli - Kem Edwards Ltd
Pirouette - Rackline Systems Storage Ltd
Pirthane 0 - Modern Plan Insulation Ltd
PivotSafe - Dorma Door Services Ltd
Pladek - En-tout-cas Tennis Courts Ltd
Plain - Russell Roof Tiles Ltd
Plan - Hudevad Britain
Planar - Ide T & W Ltd
Planar - Pilkington Birmingham
Planet - Pland Stainless Ltd
Planrad Strong Steel Radiators - AEL
Plant Managers Journal & Plant Spec & Dealer Guide - Contract Journal
Planta - Erlau AG
Plascoat - Plastic Coatings Ltd
Plasflow - Fullflow Group Ltd
Plasgard - Lonsdale Metal Company
Plasinter - Plastic Coatings Ltd
Plassim - Brett Martin Ltd
Plastalux - Clare R S & Co Ltd
Plastex - Plastic Extruders Ltd
Plasti Drain - Hepworth Building Products Ltd
Plastic Padding - Henkel Consumer Adhesives
Plastic padding - Loctite UK Ltd
Plastilac - Trimite Ltd
Plastimetal - EBC UK Ltd
Plaswood - Visqueen Building Products
Platinum Care - Heckmondwicke FB
platinum Floorshield - Springvale E P S
Platinum Fulfil - Springvale E P S
Platinum Wallshield - Springvale E P S
Platinum Warm shark - Springvale E P S
Platinum Warm Squeez - Springvale E P S
Platoon Brush - Mat.Works Flooring Solutions
Platoon Premier - Mat.Works Flooring Solutions
Playa - Ideal-Standard Ltd
Playtime - TBS Amwell Ltd
Playtime® - Jackson H S & Son (Fencing) Ltd
Playtop 3D Range - Playtop Licensing Limited
Playtop Safer Surfacing - Playtop Licensing Limited
Playtop Spheres - Playtop Licensing Limited
Playtop Walkways - Playtop Licensing Limited
Playtop with Nike Grind - Playtop Licensing Limited
Plaza (litter bins) - Glasdon UK Limited
Plaza Range - Pedley Furniture International Ltd
Plexiglas - Amari Plastics Plc
Plise Shades - Luxaflex®
PLS - Topcon GB Ltd
Plumbers bits - Traps & wc connectors - Hunter Plastics Ltd
Plumbfit - Brett Martin Ltd
Plumbfit - Davant Products Ltd
Plumbing-flexi hoses - Guest (Speedfit) Ltd, John
Plus Clips - Tower Manufacturing
Plycorapid - Laybond Products Ltd
Plyload - SCP Concrete Sealing Technology Ltd
Plylok Deck - Gradient Insulations (UK) Ltd
Plymovent Limited - Encon Air Systems Ltd
Plywood & Panels - PERI Ltd
PM2000 - Gas Measurement Instruments Ltd
PmB : Waterproofing - Pitchmastic PmB Ltd
Pmb waterproofing Systmes - Pitchmastic PmB Ltd
PNC 3 Vision - Tunstal Healthcare (UK) Ltd
Podium - Barlow Group
Podium Steps - Turner Access Ltd
Polar - Komfort Workspace PLC
Polaris™ - Kone
Polcarb 40 S - Imerys Minerals Ltd
Polcarb 45 Slurry - Imerys Minerals Ltd
Polcarb 60 (S) - Imerys Minerals Ltd
Polcarb 60 Slurry - Imerys Minerals Ltd
Polcarb 90 - Imerys Minerals Ltd
Polcarb SB - Imerys Minerals Ltd
Policor C.C - Polypipe Building Products
Polo - Swish Building Products
Poly-Bond - Schlegel UK (2006) Ltd
Polycell - Dulux Trade
Polycote - Cross-Guard International Ltd
Polycup - Rockwell Sheet Sales Ltd
Polyduct, Polysewer, Polystorm - Polypipe Civils
Polyflex - Polyflor Ltd
Polyflor - Polyflor Ltd
Polyfoam - Knauf Insulation Ltd
PolyLay - Junckers Limited
Polymatic - CPV Ltd
Polymer Modified Bitumen Emultions and cutbacks - Colas Ltd
Polymetron - Zellweger Analytic Ltd, Sieger Division
Polyplumb - Polypipe Building Products Ltd
PolyPlus - Helifix
Polyrail - Brighton (Handrails), W
Polysafe - Polyflor Ltd
Polyscreed - Cross-Guard International Ltd
Polyshield - Anglo Building Products Ltd
Polyshield - Feedwater Ltd
Polysil - Modern Plan Insulation Ltd
Polystar - Rockwell Sheet Sales Ltd
Polystyrene - FGF Ltd
Polytan - Feedwater Ltd
Polytek - Notcutt Ltd
Polytherm - Smart Systems Ltd
Polytred - Polyflor Ltd
Polytron - Draeger Safety UK Ltd
Polyu - Rockwell Sheet Sales Ltd
PondGard - Firestone Building Products
Pool Collection - Solus Ceramics Ltd
Poplar - Branson Leisure Ltd
Popstar - BLV Licht-und Vakuumtecnik
Pop-up - Ackermann Ltd
Porcelain paving - Alfresco Floors
Porcupine - Armortec
Porotherm - Wienerberger Ltd
Portadec - Hughes Safety Showers Limited
Portaflex - Hughes Safety Showers Limited
Portaheater - Hughes Safety Showers Limited
Portaro® - Vicaima Ltd
Portasilo - Portasilo Ltd
Portaspray - Bambi Air Compressors Ltd.
Portway - BFM Europe Limited
Posicote - Cross-Guard International Ltd
Posilok - Exitex Ltd
Posi-Strut - MiTek Industries Ltd
Posi-Web - MiTek Industries Ltd
Posners - Tutto Parquet Limited
Possi - Pitchmastic PmB Ltd
Pottelberg - Smithbrook Building Products Ltd
Potterton - Baxi Heating UK Ltd
Pouliot - Floralsilk Ltd
Powa glide - Moresecure Ltd
Powdermark - Marcrist International Ltd
Power - Kenyon Performance Adhesives
Power hotmelts - Kenyon Group Ltd
Powerball - Osram Ltd
Powerbond - Gilmour Ecometal
PowerBreaker - Green Brook
Powercyl - Gledhill Water Storage Ltd
Power-Fin - Lochinvar Limited
Powerform 25 - Dorman Smith Switchgear
Powerform 63 - Dorman Smith Switchgear
Powerframe - Sapa Building Systems (monarch and glostal)
Powerlab 8 - S & B Ltd
Powerlink Plus - MK (MK Electric Ltd)
Powerman - Schneider Electric Ltd
PowerPack - Santon
PowerPlas 520 - Power Plastics Ltd
PowerPlas 541 - Power Plastics Ltd
Powerrac - Dezurik International Ltd
Powerstar - Osram Ltd
Powerstock - Hamworthy Heating Limited & ACV UK
Powertrack - Legrand Electric Ltd
Powertrak - Rackline Systems Storage Ltd
Powertrak plastic drag chains & carriers - Metreel Ltd
Powervent - Watts Industries UK Ltd
Powerware - Eaton Electric Ltd
Powrmatic - The BSS Group
Pozament (Specialist mortars - pozament.co.uk/product-family/mortar) - Tarmac Trading Limited (Mortars)
Pozidrain - ABG Ltd
Pozidry - Vent-Axia
PPA 571 - Plascoat Systems Ltd
PPC - Brighton (Handrails), W
PPG High Performance Coatings - PPG Protective and Marine Coatings
PPG Protective & Marine Coatings - Kenyon Paints Limited
PR - Pure - Staverton (UK) Ltd
PRA - PRA
Precedence - Paragon by Heckmondwike
Precious Gems - Carpets of Worth Ltd
PRELAQ - SSAB Swedish Steel Ltd
Prelasti - AAC Waterproofing Ltd
Premier - Dixon Turner Wallcoverings
Premier - Fitzgerald Lighting Ltd
Premier - Securikey Ltd
Premier - Xpelair Ltd

P (con't)

Premier by Coram - Coram Showers Ltd
Premier Fire Extinguishers - Nu-Swift International Ltd
Premier Frameless by Coram - Coram Showers Ltd
Premier hoists - PCT Group
Premier Interlink Waco UK Limited - Waco UK Limnited
Premier Plus - Heatrae Sadia Heating Ltd
Premier Service - Flexiform Business Furniture Ltd
PremierPlus and PremierPlus Solar - Santon
Premix - Delabie UK Ltd
Premseal - BRC Reinforcement
Prep - Ciret Limited
Prepakt - Westpile Ltd
Preprufe - GCP APPLIED TECHNOLOGIES (UK) LIMITED
Presbury - Race Furniture Ltd
Prescor - Flamco UK Ltd
PreSense/ AbSence - Philips Lighting Solutions
President - Deans Blinds & Awnings (UK) Ltd
President - Parthos UK Ltd
Pressalit - Amilake Southern Ltd
Presspak - Flamco UK Ltd
Prestex - Pegler Ltd
Prestige - Gent Limited
Prestige - Stocksigns Ltd
Prestige Plus - MK (MK Electric Ltd)
Presto - Girsberger London
Preston Refrigeration - Johnson Controls Building Efficiency UK Ltd
prialpas rubber floorings - Jaymart Rubber & Plastics Ltd
Price Guides Direct - Professional Books Limited
Prima - Cardale Garage Doors
Prima - Prima Security & Fencing Products
Prima - Sampson & Partners Fencing
Prima Axal - Armstrong World Industries Ltd
Prima 2 Gas Vent - Rite-Vent Ltd
Prima Plus - Schiedel Chimney Systems Ltd
Prima Plus Single Wall System - Rite-Vent Ltd
Prima SW Single Wall System - Rite-Vent Ltd
Primacalc - Fullflow Group Ltd
Primaflow - Fullflow Group Ltd
Primary Options - Project Office Furniture PLC
Primatic - Range Cylinders
Primofit - George Fischer Sales Ltd
Primus Washers/ Ironers - Warner Howard Group Ltd
Princess suite - Brass Art Ltd
Prinmuls Lite LMP90K Polymer Emultion - Colas Ltd
Prinmuls Mac H.A.U.C. Binder - Colas Ltd
Prinmuls MP90X Polymer Emultion - Colas Ltd
Print HPL - Abet Ltd
PrintMachine™ Laserprinting Management Software - Neopost Ltd
Priory - CEMEX
Priory - Priory Shutter & Door Co Ltd
Priory - (The Priory Shutter & Door Co. Ltd.) - Shutter Door Repair & Maintenance Ltd
Priory Mixture - Carlton Main Brickworks Ltd
Priory Mixtures - Carlton Main Brickworks Ltd
Priory-(The Priory Shutter & Door Co. Ltd.) - Neway Doors Ltd
Prisma - Quiligotti Terrazzo Tiles Limited
Prismafit - Johnson Tiles
Prismatics - Johnson Tiles
Prismo - Ennis-Flint
Pritt - Henkel Consumer Adhesives
Pro - Net Contractor - Termstall Limited
Pro Clear - Andura Coatings Ltd
Pro Display - Pro Display TM Limited
Pro Flex - Andura Coatings Ltd
Pro-Balance - Crane Fluid Systems
Procast - Procter Bros Limited
Procor - GCP APPLIED TECHNOLOGIES (UK) LIMITED
procter cast stone - Newlay Cast Stone Limited t/as Procter Cast Stone
Proctor Johnson Colour - Procter Johnson & Co Ltd
Prodigy - Oldham Lighting Ltd
Profil - Fillcrete Ltd
Profile - Samuel Heath & Sons plc
Profile - VBH (GB) Ltd
Profile 22 - Plastal (SBP Ltd)
Profile 49 - Britmet Tileform Limited
Profile, Proform - Rackline Systems Storage Ltd
Profiled Screen - Acousticabs Industrial Noise Control Ltd
Pro-flite Suspended Aerofoil - ITAB Prolight UK Limited
Proforce - Briggs Industrial Footwear Ltd t/a Briggs Safety Wear
Proframe - Sapa Building Systems (monarch and glostal)
ProFuse® - Radius Systems Ltd
Progef - George Fischer Sales Ltd
Programastat - Timeguard Ltd
Progress - Parthos UK Ltd
Prolift hoists and winches - PCT Group
Proline - Rangemaster
Pro-Line - Moravia (UK) Ltd
Promat - FGF Ltd
Promat - Kitsons Insulation Products Ltd
Promat, Promatect, Promo seal, Promafour, Promina - Promat UK Ltd
Promenade - Lappset UK Ltd
Promesh - Procter Bros Limited
Pronto - Girsberger London
Proofex - Fosroc Ltd
Propex Concrete Systems - Sika Ltd
Proplene - CPV Ltd
Propulsion - Golden Coast Ltd
Proseal - Illuma Lighting
Proseal - Sika Ltd
Pro-Set - Wessex Resins & Adhesives Ltd
Prospex - Terrapin Ltd
Protal - Winn & Coales (Denso) Ltd
Protecsol - Gerflor Ltd
Protect and Protect OD - Tank Storage & Services Ltd
Protecta - Chalmit Lighting
Protecta - Unifix Ltd
Protector - Securikey Ltd
Protector F1, Superconcentrate Protector F1, Protector F1 Express, Protector MB-1, Antifreeze Protector Alphi-11, HVAC Protector F1 - Fernox
Pro-Tee - Crane Fluid Systems
Protega Paints - Kenyon Paints Limited
Protim - Protim Solignum Ltd
Protim- Prevac - Protim Solignum Ltd
Protimeter Hygromaster - Protimeter, GE Thermometrics (UK) Ltd
Protimeter Mini - Protimeter, GE Thermometrics (UK) Ltd
Protimeter MMS - Protimeter, GE Thermometrics (UK) Ltd
Protimeter Surveymaster - Protimeter, GE Thermometrics (UK) Ltd
Protimeter Timbermaster - Protimeter, GE Thermometrics (UK) Ltd
PS Concrete Repair System - DB Group (Holdings) Ltd
PS Gel Retarder - DB Group (Holdings) Ltd
PS HDBR Adhesive - DB Group (Holdings) Ltd
PS Hi-Flow Grouting Mortar - DB Group (Holdings) Ltd
PS Liquid Retarder - DB Group (Holdings) Ltd
PS Primer Latex - DB Group (Holdings) Ltd
PS Swell Mastic - DB Group (Holdings) Ltd
PS2000 - Gas Measurement Instruments Ltd
Psicon - Heras
PSM - Elster Metering Ltd
Public - Macemain + Amstad Ltd
Pudlo - DB Group (Holdings) Ltd
Pudlo CWP Waterproofer - DB Group (Holdings) Ltd
Puf - Macemain + Amstad Ltd
Pullman - Portakabin Ltd
Pulsa - ITW Construction Products
Pulsacoil - Gledhill Water Storage Ltd
pulse secure electric fencing - Chestnut Products Limited
Puma - Mode Lighting (UK) Ltd
Puma - Resdev Ltd
Pumadur - Resdev Ltd
Pumaflor - Resdev Ltd
Pumathane - Resdev Ltd
Pumpen - Pump Technical Services Ltd
PUR - Gerflor Ltd
Puraflex VOC Membrane - Cordek Ltd
Purbeck Limestone - J Suttle Swanage Quarries Ltd
Pure - Isolated Systems Ltd
Pure Air - Consort Equipment Products Ltd
Purelab, Purelab Chorus - Veolia Water Technologies UKElga Ltd
Purewater - Veolia Water Technologies UKElga Ltd
Purewell - Hamworthy Heating Limited & ACV UK
Purilan - Ubbink (UK) Ltd
Puriton® - Radius Systems Ltd
Purmelt - Henkel Ltd
Purmo Radiators - Purmo-UK
Purmo Underfloor Heating - Purmo-UK
PURO, PUROSET - Kaldewei
Purogene - Hertel Services
Purogene - Verna Ltd
Push & Lock® - Rytons Building Products Ltd
Pushfit - Tyco Water Works
PushLock™ - Latchways plc
PV Low Profile - Domus Ventilation
PX Control Panel - UTC Fire & Securites
Pygme - Grosvenor Pumps Ltd
PYRAN S Fire-Resistant Glass - SCHOTT UK Ltd
PYRANOVA Insulated Fire-resistant Glass - SCHOTT UK Ltd
Pyratox - Aldous & Stamp (Services) Ltd
Pyrocoil - Mann McGowan Group
Pyrodur - Ide T & W Ltd
Pyrodur - Pilkington Birmingham
Pyrodur plus - Ide T & W Ltd
Pyroglaze - Mann McGowan Group
Pyrogrille - Mann McGowan Group
Pyroguard El - Pyroguard UK Ltd
Pyroguard EW - Pyroguard UK Ltd
Pyroguard T - Pyroguard UK Ltd
Pyromas - Mann McGowan Group
Pyroshield - Pilkington Birmingham
Pyrosleeve - Mann McGowan Group
Pyrospan - Mann McGowan Group
Pyrostem - Pyroguard UK Ltd
Pyrostop - Ide T & W Ltd
Pyrostop - Pilkington Birmingham
Pyrostrip - Mann McGowan Group
Pyrovista - Mann McGowan Group
Pyxel - Grosvenor Pumps Ltd

Q

Q Doors - HAG Shutters & Grilles Ltd
Q Lean Solutions - Quantum Profile Systems Ltd
Q screed - Carter-Dal International
QD 90 - Blackfriar Paints Ltd
QHG - Motorised Air Products Ltd
Q-Lon - Schlegel UK (2006) Ltd
Q-Rail 2000 - Quartet-GBC UK Ltd/ ACCO UK Ltd
QSBIM - Masterbill Micro Systems Ltd
QSCad - Masterbill Micro Systems Ltd
QUAD - Optelma Lighting Ltd
Quadro - Franke Sissons Ltd
Quality Mark - The Carpet Foundation
Qualube - Witham Oil & Paint Ltd
Quantec - Johnson & Starley
Quantec addressable call systems - C-TEC (Computionics) Ltd
Quantum - Calomax Ltd
Quantum - Marley Plumbing and Drainage
Quantum - Rackline Systems Storage Ltd
Quantum - Valor
Quantum Flooring Solutions - Quantum Profile Systems Ltd
Quarter 2 - Litex Design Ltd
Quartermaster Shelving - Bedford Shelving Ltd
Quartz - TEV Limited
Quartz Digital - Aqualisa Products
Quartzstone Quartz Tiles - Marble Flooring Spec. Ltd
Quasar - Fitzgerald Lighting Ltd
Quasilan - Lanxess Urethanes UK Ltd
Quatro and DemiQuattro - Lang+Fulton
Queensfil 240 - Imerys Minerals Ltd
Queensfil 25 - Imerys Minerals Ltd
Queensfil 300 - Imerys Minerals Ltd
Quelfire - Firebarrier International Ltd T/A Firebarrier Services Ltd
Quick Clip - Junckers Limited
Quickbridge - Mabey Hire Ltd
Quickfit - Vantrunk Engineering Ltd
Quickfit - Viking Johnson
Quickflex - Sealocrete PLA Ltd
Quickframe - IPPEC Systems Ltd
Quickheat - IPPEC Systems Ltd
Quickmast - Don Construction Products Ltd
Quickpost - Catnic
Quickscreed - Laticrete International Inc. UK
Quickslate - BLM British Lead
Quickstrip - Laybond Products Ltd
Quicktronic - Osram Ltd
Quiclean - Hansgrohe
QuietBoard - Bicester Products Ltd
Quietboard - Sound Service (Oxford) Ltd
Quiet-Duct Silencers - IAC Acoustic Company UK Ltd
QuietFloor - Bicester Products Ltd
Quietfloor - Sound Service (Oxford) Ltd
Quikaboard - QK Honeycomb Products Ltd
Quil-nazzo - Quiligotti Terrazzo Tiles Limited
Quinta - Broag Ltd
Quintesse - Matki plc
QVC - Motorised Air Products Ltd
Q-Vent - Johnson & Starley
Qwood - Quantum Profile Systems Ltd
QX Control Panel - UTC Fire & Securites

R

R Accommodation - Rollalong Ltd
R Defence - Rollalong Ltd
R Healthcare - Rollalong Ltd
R Modular - Rollalong Ltd
R Schools - Rollalong Ltd
R Units - Santon
R.A.M - RAMGROUP (UK) Ltd
R.C.C - Roofing Contractors (Cambridge) Ltd
rac - Refrigeration & Air Conditioning - EMAP
Rada - Kohler Mira Ltd
Radcrete - Radflex Contract Services Ltd
Radflex 125 - Radflex Contract Services Ltd
Radflex Expantion Joints - Radflex Contract Services Ltd
Radflex FP - Radflex Contract Services Ltd
Radflex S100 - Radflex Contract Services Ltd
Radflex S150 - Radflex Contract Services Ltd
Radflex S200 - Radflex Contract Services Ltd
Radflex WF - Radflex Contract Services Ltd
RadiAL Windows & Louvres - Midland Alloy Ltd
Radiance - Matki plc
Radipex - Uponor Ltd
Radius - Hudevad Britain
Radjoint - Radflex Contract Services Ltd
Radon Aquis Double Defence System - ProTen Services
Radroof - Radflex Contract Services Ltd
Radson Radiators - Purmo-UK
Rafid - Heras
Rail Master - Youngman Group Limited
Rail Track Specialists - Southern Zone - GJ Durafencing Limited
RailRoad Range; Seating, Planters, Tables - Furnitubes International Ltd
Railtrack Propducts - International Protective Coatings
Rainbox - John Davidson (Pipes) Ltd
Raindance - Hansgrohe
Raindance Allrounder - Hansgrohe
Raindance Puro Air - Hansgrohe
Raindance Unica - Hansgrohe
Rainsaver® - Straight Ltd
Rainspan - Booth Muirie
Rallisil - Trade Sealants Ltd
Ram Pumps - Barr & Wray Ltd
Ramesis - Oldham Lighting Ltd
Rampcentre, rollouttrackway, rampkit - Enable Access
Ramsay Access - Ramsay & Sons (Forfar) Ltd
Ramsay Ladders - Ramsay & Sons (Forfar) Ltd
Ramset - ITW Construction Products
Ramset - ITW Spit
Randi-line - Laidlaw Ltd
Rangemaster - Rangemaster
Ranger - GfA UK Ltd
Rangewood - Vulcan Cladding Systems
Rapid - Fillcrete Ltd
Rapidac - Dacrylate Paints Ltd
Rapide - Clark Door Ltd
Rapide - Project Office Furniture PLC
Rapidflow - Geberit Ltd
Rapidobad - BRC Reinforcement
Rapidplan - Wernick Group Ltd
RapidRail® - Walraven Ltd
RapidSTACK - MCL Composites Ltd
RapidStrut® - Walraven Ltd
Rapier - A Kenrick & Sons
Rapier rising screen - Pearce Security Systems
Raumluft - Motorised Air Products Ltd
Ravenna - Paragon by Heckmondwike
Rawlplug - Kem Edwards Ltd
Raya - Kermi (UK) Ltd
RB Horizontal - Fulton Boiler Works (Great Britain) Ltd
RBC - Fulton Boiler Works (Great Britain) Ltd
RD Road - Consult Lighting Ltd
RD series locators and detectors - Radiodetection Ltd
Rea frame - Rea Metal Windows Ltd
Rea W20 - Rea Metal Windows Ltd
Rea W40 - Rea Metal Windows Ltd
Ready span - CEMEX
Readymix, Ready floor, Ready block, Ready Pave - CEMEX
Rebound Signmaster - Glasdon U.K. Limited
ReCooler HP - Fläkt Woods Ltd
Rectaleen - Flexible Reinforcements Ltd
Recupovent - Thermal Technology Sales Ltd
Red Bank - Forterra Building Products Ltd
Red Engineering Type - Carlton Main Brickworks Ltd
Red Rustic/ Dragwire - Carlton Main Brickworks Ltd
Reddicord - Reddiglaze Ltd
Reddifoam - Reddiglaze Ltd
Reddihinges - Reddiglaze Ltd
Reddilock - Reddiglaze Ltd
Reddipile - Reddiglaze Ltd
Reddiprene - Reddiglaze Ltd
Redfyre - Gazco Ltd
Redfyre Cookers - TR Engineering Ltd
Redhall - Booth Industries Ltd
Rediguard - Hoyles Electronic Developments Ltd
RediKerb - Rediweld Rubber & Plastics Ltd
Redipress - Hoyles Electronic Developments Ltd
Redi-Resin - Redifix Ltd
RedLine - Monier Redland Limited
Redman™ - Radius Systems Ltd
Redufix - Watts Industries UK Ltd
Redupress - Watts Industries UK Ltd
RedVent - Monier Redland Limited
Reemat Premium - Sika Liquid Plastics Limited
Reflections - Ideal-Standard Ltd
Reflect™ - Venator
RefleKto - BLV Licht-und Vakuumtecnik
Reflex - Altecnic Ltd
Reflex-Rol - Mermet U.K
Reflex-Rol - Reflex-Rol (UK)
Refresh - Britannia Kitchen Ventilation Ltd
Refresh Range - Twyford Bathrooms
Refresh™ - Deb Group Limited
Regaflex S - Rega Ductex Ltd
Regaflex W - Rega Ductex Ltd
Regency Ashlar & Regency Textured Ashlar Blocks & Quoins - Forticrete Cast Stone
Regency Swimming Pools - J W Green Swimming Pools Ltd
Regent - Cooper Lighting
Regent (R) - Barber Wilsons & Co Ltd
Registered Specialists - The Carpet Foundation
Rehau - Architectural Plastics (Handrail) Ltd
Rehau - Brighton (Handrails), W
Rehau - DC Plastic Handrails Ltd
Reid Span - Reid John & Sons (Strucsteel) Ltd
Rei-Lux - Valmont Stainton
Reinforced Earth™ TerraBlock - Freyssinet Ltd
Relite - Fantasia Distribution Ltd
RELUX - ALD Lighting Solutions
Relux - Glamox Luxo Lighting Limited
Relux - ITAB Prolight UK Limited
Remix - SIG Roofing
Rendalath® - BRC Special Products - Bekaert Ltd
Rendalite® - BRC Special Products - Bekaert Ltd
Rendcomse - Race Furniture Ltd
Renderoc - Fosroc Ltd
Renno - Lumitron Ltd
Renovent - Ubbink (UK) Ltd
Renovisions - Interface Europe Ltd
Repair Care Mini-Profi - Repair care International
Repair Care Sander - Repair care International
Repair Care Scraper - Repair care International
Repcoat - Don Construction Products Ltd
Repertiore - Tata Steel Colors
Resiblock 22 - Resiblock Ltd
Resiblock ER - Resiblock Ltd
Resiblock F.R.I - Resiblock Ltd
Resiblock OR - Resiblock Ltd
Resiblock Superior - Resiblock Ltd
Resiblock Ultra - Resiblock Ltd
Resiblock Ultra Matt - Resiblock Ltd
Resiclean - Resiblock Ltd
Resicure - Benlowe Group Limited
Resiecco - Resiblock Ltd
Resistex - Leigh's Paints
ResiTie - Helifix
Resotec - Richard Lees Decking Limited
Restol - Arch Timber Protection
RESTOVER restoration glass - SCHOTT UK Ltd
Restwall - Architectural Textiles Ltd
RETINO - Lumitron Ltd
Retriever 35 (dog waste bins) - Glasdon UK Limited
retroflect - HMG Paints
Retrofloor - Redman Fisher Engineering
RetroTie - Helifix
Retrotread - Redman Fisher Engineering
Rettig - Myson
Rettig - Purmo-UK
Revelation - Spectus Systems
Revolution - Optima
Reynobond 33 - Amari Plastics Plc
RFS - Raised Floor Systems Ltd
RFS Heavy 4x4 - Raised Floor Systems Ltd
RFS Meduim 4x4 - Raised Floor Systems Ltd
RFS Meduim V - Raised Floor Systems Ltd

R (con't)

RH 'U' Tube Heater - Radiant Services Ltd
RHD Double Linear Heater - Radiant Services Ltd
Rhino Flex - DLW Flooring
Rhino Quartz - DLW Flooring
Rhino Tex - DLW Flooring
Rhino Tough - Wybone Ltd
RHL Linear Heater - Radiant Services Ltd
Rhodius - Hyde Brian Ltd
Rhodorsil - Bluestar Silicones
Rhomax Engineering - Tyco Fire and Integrated Solutions
RIAS Bookshops - Royal Incorporation of Architects in Scotland
RIAS Competitions - Royal Incorporation of Architects in Scotland
RIAS Consultancy - Royal Incorporation of Architects in Scotland
RIAS CPD - Royal Incorporation of Architects in Scotland
RIAS Gallery - Royal Incorporation of Architects in Scotland
RIAS Insurance Services - Royal Incorporation of Architects in Scotland
RIAS Practice Services - Royal Incorporation of Architects in Scotland
RIBA Appointments - RIBA Enterprises
RIBA Bookshops - RIBA Enterprises
RIBA Insight - RIBA Enterprises
RIBA Journal - RIBA Enterprises
RIBA Product Selector - NBS
RIBA Publishing - RIBA Enterprises
Ribblelite - Richard Hose Ltd
Ribdeck - Richard Lees Decking Limited
Richardson - Amdega Ltd
Richter System - Knauf UK
RICS Data Products - BCIS
RIDBA - Rural & Industrial Design & Building Association
Ridgicoil - Polypipe Civils
Ridgidrain Surface water Drainage System - Polypipe Civils
Ridgiduct Power HV - Polypipe Civils
Ridgiduct, Ridgigully, Ridgisewer - Polypipe Civils
Ridgistorm-XL Large Diameter Piping System - Polypipe Civils
Ridgitreat - Polypipe Civils
Rigaflo - Camfil Farr Ltd
Righton PQ - Righton Ltd
Rigidal Lokrol - Rigidal
Rigidal Thermocore - Rigidal
Rigidal Thermowall - Rigidal
Rigidal Trocaldek - Rigidal
Rigidal Ziplok - Rigidal
Rigid-Cor/F - Polypipe Building Products
Rigidur, Rigitone - British Gypsum Ltd
Rilass V - Camfil Farr Ltd
Rior - Ward's Flexible Rod Company Ltd
Ripac - CSSP (Construction Software Services Partnership)
Riposeal - Shackerley (Holdings) Group Ltd incorporating Designer ceramics
Riser Showertrays by Coram - Coram Showers Ltd
Rite-Vent - Schiedel Chimney Systems Ltd
Ritz - New Haden Pumps Ltd
rla - Robinson Lloyds Architecture
RMC Concrete Products - CEMEX
Roadline - Leigh's Paints
Roadside - Macemain + Amstad Ltd
Robec - Tuke & Bell Ltd
Robertshaw - SK Environmental Ltd
Robette - Tuke & Bell Ltd
Robey - Wellman Robey Ltd
Robocal - Altecnic Ltd
Robofil - Altecnic Ltd
Robokit - Altecnic Ltd
Robolink - Altecnic Ltd
Robust Detail Socket Box - Sound Reduction Systems Ltd
Rocal - Gazco
Rockclad - FGF Ltd
RockDelta Acoustic Barriers - Ruthin Precast Concrete Ltd
Rockfon - Nevill Long
Rockfon - New Forest Ceilings Ltd
Rockliner - Cryotherm Insulation Ltd
Rockranger Primary Crushing Outfits - Parker Plant Ltd
Rocksil - Knauf Insulation Ltd
Rockwell - Rockwell Sheet Sales Ltd
Rockwood - Rockwell Sheet Sales Ltd
Rockwool - FGF Ltd
Rockwool - Firebarrier International Ltd T/A Firebarrier Services Ltd
Rockwool - Rockwool Ltd
Rocwall Walling/Cladding - Ruthin Precast Concrete Ltd
Rodan - Franke Sissons Ltd
Rogada - Knauf AMF Ceilings Ltd
Rola - Bramah Security Equipment Ltd
Rolfe King - Legrand Electric Ltd
Roll-A-Door - Rolflex Doors Ltd
Rollaplay - En-tout-cas Tennis Courts Ltd
Rollatape - Advance Tapes International Ltd
Rolled Lead Sheet & Flashings - BLM British Lead
Rollercash - Safetell Ltd
Rollerseal - Kleeneze Sealtech Ltd
Roll-fix ridge - Klober Ltd
Rolls Rotary - Tuke & Bell Ltd
Rolux - Ubbink (UK) Ltd
Roma Transport - Phoenix Scales Ltd
Roma-3 and Roma-4 - Lang+Fulton
Romney Roof Tiles - Tudor Roof Tile Co Ltd
RonaBond - Ronacrete Ltd
RonaDeck Resin Bonded Surfacing - Ronacrete Ltd
RonaDeck Resin Bound Surfacing - Ronacrete Ltd
Ronafix - Ronacrete Ltd
RonaFloor - Ronacrete Ltd
RonaRoad - Ronacrete Ltd
RonaScreed - Ronacrete Ltd
RonaStreet - Ronacrete Ltd
Rondo - Franke Sissons Ltd
RONDO - Kaldewei
RONDOR - TORMAX United Kingdom Ltd
Roof ventilation - Airflow (Nicoll Ventilators) Ltd
Roofdek - Tata Steel Europe Limited
Roofdex - Flexcrete Technologies Limited
Roofite - Watco UK Ltd
Roofline - Celuform Building Products
Roofmate SL-A - Dow Building Solutions
Roofmax - Knauf Insulation Ltd
RoofShop - SIG Roofing
Rooftex - Conren Ltd
Room Service - Brintons Ltd
Roomstat - Horstmann Controls Ltd
Rootbox - Jones of Oswestry Ltd
Rootfast® - Earth Anchors Ltd
Rope Descent - Baj System Design Ltd
Rosemary Clay - Monier Redland Limited
Rosengrens - Gunnebo UK Limited
Rossetti - Symphony Group PLC, The
Rota - Ciret Limited
Rota Guard - Heras
Rota spike® - Jackson H S & Son (Fencing) Ltd
Rotaflow - Gebhardt Kiloheat
Rotapak - Fluidair Ltd
Rotasoc - Electrak International Ltd
Rotastar - Fluidair Ltd
Rotavent - Gebhardt Kiloheat
Rotaworm - Ward's Flexible Rod Company Ltd
Rothwell - Deva Tap Co Ltd
Roto - Carl F Groupco Limited
Roto - Roto Frank Ltd
Roto - SIG Roofing
RotoLatch™ - Latchways plc
Rougeite - CED Ltd
Rough at the edges - Weyland incorporating Clayton Munroe
Rovacabin - Wernick Group Ltd
Royal Forest - Formpave Ltd
Royalux - Cooper Lighting
Royce - Konecranes UK
Royde & Tucker HI-LOAD hinges - Bridgman IBC Ltd
RS Rotary screw compressor - Fluidair Ltd
RubberCover EPDM - Firestone Building Products
Rubberfuse - Intergrated Polymer Systems (UK) Ltd
RubberGard EPDM - Firestone Building Products
Rubberline - Dudley Thomas Ltd
Rubberwell - Dudley Thomas Ltd
Rubboseal - Trade Sealants Ltd
Ruberoid Building Products - IKO PLC
Rubit - Hansgrohe
Rudgwick - Baggeridge Brick PLC
Rugby - CEMEX
RUNDFLEX - Circular wall formwork - PERI Ltd
Runtal - Arteplano, Jet, LST & RX - Zehnder Group UK Ltd
Rustins - Rustins Ltd
Rustique - Veka Plc
Rustiver - Mermet U.K
Rustoleum - Andrews Coatings Ltd
Rustoleum - Kenyon Group Ltd
Rutland Range - Evergreens Uk
RV Active Inra Red Beams - Heras
Rycroft - Ormandy Rycroft Engineering
Rylstone - GB Architectural Cladding Products Ltd
RytDuct®, RytHose®, Rytweep® - Rytons Building Products Ltd
Ryterna - Acorn Garage Doors Ltd
Rytons Retro Weep Vent® - Rytons Building Products Ltd

S

S.D.R.M.-(Shutter & Door Repare & Maintenance Ltd) - Shutter Door Repair & Maintenance Ltd
S.D.R.M.-(Shutter Door Repair & Maintenance Ltd.) - Priory Shutter & Door Co Ltd
S.V.K. Cromleigh - Chameleon Stone Ltd
S2000 CSJ - Elster Metering Ltd
S3040 Portable Reader - CEM Systems Ltd
S610 intelligent card reader - CEM Systems Ltd
Sabre - TROAX UK Ltd
Sabroe - Johnson Controls Building Efficiency UK Ltd
Sadolin Fencing Wood Stain - Sadolin UK Ltd
Sadolin High Performance Varnish - Sadolin UK Ltd
Sadolin Prestige - Sadolin UK Ltd
Sadolin Supercoat - Sadolin UK Ltd
Safe Call - Raidio-Based Nurse Call System - Wandsworth Elecrtrical Ltd
Safe Glaze - Tank Storage & Services Ltd
Safe guard - DLW Flooring
Safe 'n' Sound - Premdor
Safe T Epoxy - Anglo Building Products Ltd
SafeDeck - Graepels Perforators Ltd
safe-deko vinyl floorings - Jaymart Rubber & Plastics Ltd
Safedrive® - GfA UK Ltd
Safeguard - Securikey Ltd
SafeGuard - Resident Monitoring/Patient Tagging - Wandsworth Elecrtrical Ltd
SafePay - Gunnebo UK Limited
Safetred Ranges - Tarkett Ltd
Safety Deck (fall prevention system and lightweight access platform) - Tarmac Building Products Ltd - SafetyDeck
Sahara - Architen Landrell Associates Ltd
Salamandre - Legrand Electric Ltd
Salex Acoustic Products - Salex Acoustics Limited
Salmen's - Fine H & Son Ltd
Salter, Salter Brecknell, Salter Abbey - Phoenix Scales Ltd
SAM - Optelma Lighting Ltd
SaMontec - Artur Fischer (UK) Ltd
Sampson and Partners Fencing - Prima Security & Fencing Products
Samsumo TM Safety Access Systems - Redman Fisher Engineering
Samsung - Connaught Communications Systems Ltd
Samuel Booth collection - Tyco Waterworks - Samuel Booth
SanCeram - Bushboard Washrooms
Sand Drain - ABG Ltd
Sand Dressed Turf - Charles Lawrence Surfaces Ltd
Sandene - Intergrated Polymer Systems (UK) Ltd
Sanderson - Sanderson
Sandfilled Turf - Charles Lawrence Surfaces Ltd
Sandler Seating - Sandler Seating Ltd
Sandringham - Loft Centre Products
Sandringham suite - Armitage Shanks Ltd
Sandtex - Akzo Noble Coatings Ltd
Sandtex - Brewer C & Sons Ltd
Sandtex - Crown Paints Ltd
Sandtoft - Wienerberger Ltd
Sandwell - Chiltern Invadex
Sangwin Educational Furniture - Sangwin Group
Sangwin group - Sangwin Concrete Products Ltd
Sangwin Machine Moving - Sangwin Group
Sangwin Plant hire - Sangwin Group
Sangwin Surfacing - Sangwin Group
Sanicat - B & D Clays & Chemicals Ltd
Sani-fem - Unicorn Containers Ltd
SANIFORM, SANILUX, SILENIO - Kaldewei
Sanistrel - Imperial Machine Co Ltd
Sanitop - Mat.Works Flooring Solutions
Sanosol - Gerflor Ltd
Santak - Eaton Electric Ltd
Santon - Baxi Heating UK Ltd
Santric - Pland Stainless Ltd
Saphir - EJOT UK Limited
Saracen - Laird Security Hardware
Sarel, Serk Controls, Square D - Schneider Electric Ltd
Sarina rubber floorings - Jaymart Rubber & Plastics Ltd
Sarnafast - Sarnafil Ltd
Sarnafil - Sarnafil Ltd
Sarnalite - Sarnafil Ltd
Sarnatherm - Sarnafil Ltd
Sarnatred - Sarnafil Ltd
Sartorius - Phoenix Scales Ltd
Sasmox - Panel Agency Limited
Satalico - Satec Service Ltd
Satime 5500 - Mermet U.K
Saturn - Fabrikat (Nottingham) Ltd
Saturn - S & B Ltd
Saunier Duval - Hepworth Heating Ltd
Savanna - En-tout-cas Tennis Courts Ltd
Saveheat Glass - Saveheat Group
Saveheat Group - Blairs Windows Limited
Saver CF - Draeger Safety UK Ltd
Saver PP - Draeger Safety UK Ltd
SaverDoor - Sunray Engineering Ltd
Savolit - Skanda Acoustics
Savolit - Skanda Acoustics Limited
Savotherm - Skanda Acoustics
Savotherm - Skanda Acoustics Limited
Sawco - The Saw Centre Group
Sawcut - The Saw Centre Group
Saxon - Monier Redland Limited
SB - Wilo Samson Pumps Ltd
SBM5 Soundproofing Mat - Sound Service (Oxford) Ltd
SBP 646 - Specialist Building Products
SC - Hudevad Britain
SCA - Sprayed Concrete Association
Scaffband - Icopal Limited
Scala - DLW Flooring
Scan Pumps - Sulzer Pumps Wastewater UK Ltd
Scanco - McMullen Facades
Scandinavian Tile Effect - FIBO UK LTD
Scan-Q - Zon International
Scantronic - Eaton's Security Business
Scenario - Mode Lighting (UK) Ltd
Scenestyle - Mode Lighting (UK) Ltd
Schindler - Schindler Ltd
Schlage Locks - Relcross Ltd
Schluter - R J Stokes & Co Limited
Schoema - Schwing Stetter (UK) Ltd
SCHOTT TERMOFROST Cold Room Doors - SCHOTT UK Ltd
Schwan - Hyde Brian Ltd
Schwarzwald - Erlau AG
Schwing - Schwing Stetter (UK) Ltd
Scimitar - TROAX UK Ltd
Scotchshield - Durable Ltd
Scotchtint - Durable Ltd
Scottish Brick - Ibstock Brick Ltd
Scottish Range - Forticrete Cast Stone
SCP - SCP Concrete Sealing Technology Ltd
Screedmaster - Laybond Products Ltd
Screening Outfits - Parker Plant Ltd
Screenmaster - ABB Instrumentation Ltd
Screensorption - Bicester Products Ltd
Screwlok - Camlok Lifting Clamps Ltd
Scroll - Emerson Climate Technologies
Sculpture Products - Aden Hynes Sculpture Studios
Sculpture Services - Aden Hynes Sculpture Studios
SD.RM- (Shutter Door Repair & Maintenance Ltd.) - Neway Doors Ltd
SDR - Stoves PLC
SE Ergonomic chair - Hille Educational Products Ltd
SE Stool - Hille Educational Products Ltd
Seagull - Gledhill Water Storage Ltd
Sealdeck - Laybond Products Ltd
Sealmaster - Sealmaster
Sealobond - Sealocrete PLA Ltd
Seal-O-Cork - Olley & Sons Ltd, C
Sealocrete - Olby H E & Co Ltd
Sealoflash - Sealocrete PLA Ltd
Sealofoam - Sealocrete PLA Ltd
Sealomix - Sealocrete PLA Ltd
Sealopol - Sealocrete PLA Ltd
Sealoproof - Sealocrete PLA Ltd
Sealoshield Asbestos - Sealocrete PLA Ltd
Sealotone - Sealocrete PLA Ltd
Sealtite - Movement Joints (UK)
Secar Cements - Lafarge Aluminates Ltd
Secritron Magnets - Relcross Ltd
Sector - WF Senate
Secure-Mix - FC Frost Ltd
Secureshield ™ - Accent Hansen
Securiglass - Promat UK Ltd
Securiguard Security Rolling Shutters - Bolton Gate Company Ltd
securistyle - ASSA ABLOY Limited
Securitherm - Delabie UK Ltd
Security Plus® - Nico Manufacturing Ltd
SecurityLine - Briggs Industrial Footwear Ltd t/a Briggs Safety Wear
SED - The National Event For Construction - Contract Journal
Sedia - Erlau AG
Seefire - Colt International
Seepex Pumps - Barr & Wray Ltd
Segga - Metalliform Products Plc
Sela - SFS Intec LTD
Seldex - Haworth UK Ltd
Select Range - Pedley Furniture International Ltd
Selectarail - Rothley Limited
Selectascreen - Pearce Security Systems
Self Serve - Unicorn Containers Ltd
Sellite - Sellite Blocks Ltd
Sembla - Allgood plc
Semiautomatic Palace - Parthos UK Ltd
Senator - Chubb Safe Equipment Company
Senator - Deans Blinds & Awnings (UK) Ltd
Senator - Dudley Thomas Ltd
Senator® (Pantiles) - Forticrete Roofing
Sensalux - Mode Lighting
Sensor Coil 600 - Heras
Sensor flow & electronic taps - Armitage Shanks Ltd
Sensor Systems - Kingspan Environmental Ltd
Sentinal ATM enclosure - Pearce Security Systems
Sentinel - Fitzgerald Lighting Ltd
Sentinel - Shackerley (Holdings) Group Ltd incorporating Designer ceramics
Sentrilock - A Kenrick & Sons
Sentry - MK (MK Electric Ltd)
Sentry® - Jackson H S & Son (Fencing) Ltd
Sequentia - Crane Composites
SerckAudio - Flowserve Flow Control
Serenade, Softrest - Sidhil Care
Series 2100 - James Gibbons Format Ltd
Series 3000 and Series 8000 - Conex Universal Limited
Series 65 - Apollo Fire Detectors Ltd
Series 90 Heavy Duty Benching - Envopak Group Ltd
Series AM - Dunham Bush Ltd
Series BM - Dunham Bush Ltd
Series CM - Dunham Bush Ltd
Series E - Hille Educational Products Ltd
Series F - Dunham Bush Ltd
Series J - Fulton Boiler Works (Great Britain) Ltd
Series UH - Dunham Bush Ltd
Serina - DW Windsor Lighting
Serpo RG - Maxit UK
Serpo Rock - Maxit UK
Serristrap - GCP APPLIED TECHNOLOGIES (UK) LIMITED
SERVERCOOL® - Eaton-Williams Group Limited
Servery - Cooper Group Ltd
ServiCare - Evac+Chair International Ltd
Servicised - GCP APPLIED TECHNOLOGIES (UK) LIMITED
Serviflex® - Radius Systems Ltd
Serviseal - GCP APPLIED TECHNOLOGIES (UK) LIMITED
Servitherm - Morgan Hope Industries Ltd
Servowarm - Servowarm
SES - Shepherd Engineering Services Ltd
Sesame - Profab Access Ltd
Seth Thomas - General Time Europe
Setlite - Mode Lighting
Seventh Heaven - Interfloor Limited
severn gutter system - Dales Fabrications Ltd
Sewer Drain - Hepworth Building Products Ltd
SFS-Masterflash - SFS Intec LTD
SGB, a Brand company - SGB, a Brand Company
SGG Bioclean - Glassolutions Saint-Gobain Ltd
SGG Cool-Lite - Glassolutions Saint-Gobain Ltd
SGG Diamant - Glassolutions Saint-Gobain Ltd
SGG Emalit Evolution - Glassolutions Saint-Gobain Ltd
SGG Planiclear - Glassolutions Saint-Gobain Ltd
SGG Planitherm - Glassolutions Saint-Gobain Ltd
SGG Priva-Lite - Glassolutions Saint-Gobain Ltd
SGG Seralit - Glassolutions Saint-Gobain Ltd
SGG Stadip range - Glassolutions Saint-Gobain Ltd
SGG Viewclear - Glassolutions Saint-Gobain Ltd
SGT - Illbruck Sealant Systems UK Ltd
Shadacrete - W. Hawley & Son Ltd
Shadeacrete - LANXESS Inorganic Pigments Group
Shadeplay - Architen Landrell Associates Ltd
shadex shading system - Dales Fabrications Ltd
Shadflam - Shadbolt F R & Sons Ltd
Shadmaster - Shadbolt F R & Sons Ltd
Shadoglass Glass louvre - Colt International
ShaftBrace, Super Shaftbrace, Supershaft Plus - Mabey Hire Ltd
Shaftwall - Knauf UK

S (con't)

Shaker - Illuma Lighting
Shallovent - Thermal Technology Sales Ltd
Shapphire, Streamline - Heatrae Sadia Heating Ltd
Shavrin - Shavrin Levatap Co Ltd
Shavrin Bijoux - Shavrin Levatap Co Ltd
Shavrin Levamixa - Shavrin Levatap Co Ltd
Shavrin Levatap - Shavrin Levatap Co Ltd
Shavrin Modesta - Shavrin Levatap Co Ltd
Shaws glazed bricks - Ibstock Building Products Ltd
Shearail® - BRC Special Products - Bekaert Ltd
Shearfix - Ancon Limited
Shearstone® (Stone Walling) - Forticrete Walling Stone
Sheartech - RFA-Tech Ltd
Sheartech Grid - RFA-Tech Ltd
Sheer - Hamilton R & Co Ltd
SheetGuard - Mabey Hire Ltd
Sheffield - Gilgen Door Systems UK Ltd
Shell Tixophalte - Chesterfelt Ltd
Shepherd - A Kenrick & Sons
Sherrill - Vermeer United Kingdom
SHEVTEC - SE Controls
Shield - Stocksigns Ltd
Shield LST - Hudevad Britain
Shiluvit by Oranit - LSA Projects Ltd
Shire Clocks - Metal Gutta
Shopline - Smart Systems Ltd
Shoresafe - Mabey Hire Ltd
Shoreseal - Shackerley (Holdings) Group Ltd incorporating Designer ceramics
Show 'N' Tell Boards - Spaceright Europe Limited
Shower Accessories by Coram - Coram Showers Ltd
Shower DEC - Contour Showers Ltd
Shower Panels - Hansgrohe
Shower Temples - Hansgrohe
Showercyl - Gledhill Water Storage Ltd
Showerforce - NewTeam Ltd
Showermate - Stuart Turner Ltd
Showermax - Range Cylinders
Showerpannel - Hansgrohe
Showerpipe - Hansgrohe
Shutters - Harling Security Solutions Limited
Si - Worcester Heat Systems Ltd
Sichenia - Arnull Bernard J & Co Ltd
Sidetrak - Rackline Systems Storage Ltd
Sidewinder - Clarke UK Ltd
Siegenia - Carl F Groupco Limited
Sieger - Zellweger Analytic Ltd, Sieger Division
Siena and Siena Sport - Lang+Fulton
Sierra - Sierra Windows
Siesta - Erlau AG
SIG - SIG Roofing
SIG UK Exteriors - SIG Roofing
Sightline 70 - Spectus Systems
Sigma - Andrews Coatings Ltd
Sigma - Brett Landscaping
Sigma - Delta Balustrades
Sigma Coatings - PPG Protective and Marine Coatings
Sigmadeck - Turner Access Ltd
Signal - Shadbolt F R & Sons Ltd
Signature Collection - FIBO UK LTD
SignEdge - Rivermeade Signs Ltd
Signet - George Fischer Sales Ltd
Signicolour - Amari Plastics Plc
Signmaster (bollards) - Glasdon UK Limited
Signscape modular systems - GB Sign Solutions Limited
SigTEL disabled refuge systems - C-TEC (Computionics) Ltd
Sika - Sika Fibres Limited
Sika-1 - Sika Ltd
SikaBond, SikaDur - Sika Ltd
Sikaflex - Sika Ltd
SikaFloor - Sika Ltd
Sikaplan - Sika Ltd
Sikatop - Sika Ltd
Sikkens - Akzo Noble Coatings Ltd
Sikkens - Brewer C & Sons Ltd
Sikkens - Dulux Trade
Silavent - Domus Ventilation
Silavent - Polypipe Ventilation Ltd
Silbione - Bluestar Silicones
Silbralloy™ - Johnson Matthey PLC - Metal Joining
Silent Gliss - Silent Gliss Ltd
SilentMAX - Marcrist International Ltd
Silfos™ - Johnson Matthey PLC - Metal Joining
Silhouette® Shades - Luxaflex®
Silicone 4 - Dufaylite Developments Ltd
Silk Machines - TEAM INDUSTRIAL SERVICES (UK) LIMITED
Silka - Xella Aircrete Systems UK
Silkalastic 625 for Metal/Asbestos Cement roofs - Sika Liquid Plastics Limited
Silktrim - James Donaldson Timber
Silver-Flo™ - Johnson Matthey PLC - Metal Joining
Silverline - Britannia Kitchen Ventilation Ltd
Simon Fiesta - Simon R W Ltd
Simpak compactors - Randalls Fabrications Ltd
Simplex - Kaba Ltd
Simply Elegant - Hodkin Jones (Sheffield) Ltd
SimplyU - Ideal-Standard Ltd
Simpson Strong-Tie® - Simpson Strong-Tie®
Single Point Gas Alarm - Gas Measurement Instruments Ltd
Sintamatic - Donaldson Filtration (GB) Ltd
Sintesi - Laytrad Contract Furniture Ltd
Sirius - Valor
Sirocco - Paragon by Heckmondwike
Sirrus - Bristan Group
Sissons - Franke Sissons Ltd
SITE BOOK - British Gypsum Ltd
SiteCop - Rediweld Rubber & Plastics Ltd
Sitesealer Membrane - Cavity Trays Ltd
Sivoia - Tidmarsh & Sons
Six hundred 600 Series - Komfort Workspace PLC
SKI - Komfort Workspace PLC
Skil - Robert Bosch Ltd
SKIL - SK Environmental Ltd
Skoda Power - Doosan Power Systems Ltd
SKYDECK - Aluminum panel slab formwork - PERI Ltd
Skye, Style Moderne - Samuel Heath & Sons plc
Skyfold - Style Door Systems Ltd
Skygard - Lonsdale Metal Company
Skyline - Alumasc Exterior Building Products Ltd
Skypod - Ves Andover Ltd
Skyvane - Levolux A.T. Limited
Slab Stress - Freyssinet Ltd
Slate2000 - Britmet Tileform Limited
Slide Safe - Safety Assured Ltd
Slik Bar - TEAM INDUSTRIAL SERVICES (UK) LIMITED
Slim Vent® - Rytons Building Products Ltd
Slimline - Cooke Brothers Ltd
Slimline - Dudley Thomas Ltd
Slimline - T B S Fabrications
Slimshield Acoustic Louvres - IAC Acoustic Company UK Ltd
Slimstyle - Hallmark Blinds Ltd
Slimstyle Groundfloor Treatments - HW Architectural Ltd
Slingsby - HC Slingsby PLC
Sloan & Davidson - Longbottom J & J W Ltd
Slot 20 - Air Diffusion Ltd
Slot 25 - Air Diffusion Ltd
Slotz - Winther Browne & co Ltd
Slurrystore - CST Industries, Inc. - UK
Slyde - Coburn Sliding Systems Ltd
SM Range - Becker (SLIDING PARTITIONS) Ltd
Smart - S & B Ltd
Smart Air Curtain - Vianen KVS BV
Smart Drive 1101 - TORMAX United Kingdom Ltd
Smartank Duplux Pump Sets - Metcraft Ltd
Smartank Overfill Alarm Unit - Metcraft Ltd
Smartank Pump Control Panels - Metcraft Ltd
SmartPly - Meyer Timber Limited
Smartroof - Wyckham Blackwell Ltd
SmartSash - Veka Plc
Smartscreen - Smart Systems Ltd
smartsigns - Stocksigns Ltd
SmartSystem - Vulcan Cladding Systems
Smiths - Timeguard Ltd
Smog-Eater - Horizon International Ltd
Smog-Mobile - Horizon International Ltd
Smog-Rambler - Horizon International Ltd
Smoke Control Services Ltd - SCS Group
Smoke Curtain- D120 Smokebarrier - Bolton Gate Company Ltd
Smoke Ventilation Louvres - Matthews & Yates Ltd
Smokeguard - Pyroguard UK Ltd
Smokemaster curtain - Colt International
Smokescreen - The No Butts Bin Company (NBB), Trading as NBB Outdoor Shelters
SmokeStop - Cooper Group Ltd
Smooth - On - Notcutt Ltd
Smooth 600 - E - Paroc Panel Systems Uk Ltd
Smoothline - Rega Ductex Ltd
Smoothline - WP Metals Ltd
Snake Way - Marshall-Tufflex Ltd
Snaptyte - Newdawn & Sun Ltd
snipef - Scottish & Northern Ireland Plumbing Employers' Federation
SnoMelt - Spiral Construction Ltd
Sobrano (Natural Roofing Slates) - EBP Building Products Ltd
Sofco ® - Broxap Ltd
Softgrip Tools - Tower Manufacturing
Softmood - Ideal-Standard Ltd
Soil nails - PHI Group Ltd
Soil Panel - PHI Group Ltd
Soilcrete - Keller Ground Engineering
Soilfrac - Keller Ground Engineering
soilmaster entrance matting - Jaymart Rubber & Plastics Ltd
Sokkia - Topcon GB Ltd
SOLA-BOOST® - Monodraught Ltd
Solair - Solair Ltd
Solaplex® - Venator
Solar Bronze - The Window Film Company UK Ltd
Solar C Brise soleil - Colt International
Solar Knight - Intersolar Group Ltd
Solar Moler - Intersolar Group Ltd
Solar Pumpkit - Intersolar Group Ltd
Solar PV - Axter Ltd
Solar PV Tiles - Monier Redland Limited
Solare Frameless Glazed Partitions - Avanti Systems
Solarfin - Colt International
Solarglaze - National Domelight Company
Solaris - Shackerley (Holdings) Group Ltd incorporating Designer ceramics
SolarSmart - Alpha Therm Ltd
Solarvent - Intersolar Group Ltd
Solarvent Turbo - Intersolar Group Ltd
Solatherm - IPPEC Systems Ltd
SOLA-VENT® - Monodraught Ltd
Solenium - Interface Europe Ltd
Solga - Harbro Supplies Ltd
Solignum - Protim Solignum Ltd
Solite - Sidhil Care
Solitex Plus - Fillcrete Ltd
Solitex Wa - Fillcrete Ltd
Solo - Köttermann Ltd
Soloblock - Jones of Oswestry Ltd
Solomat - Zellweger Analytic Ltd, Sieger Division
Solopol®, Stokoderm®, Stokolan® - Deb Group Limited
Solosun - Ubbink (UK) Ltd
Solray - Comyn Ching & Co (Solray) Ltd
Solutions - Hands of Wycombe
Solvite - Henkel Consumer Adhesives
Sombra - Saint-Gobain Ecophon Ltd
Somdrain - Geosynthetic Technology Ltd
Somtube - Geosynthetic Technology Ltd
Sonacoustic seamless acoustic ceiling - Salex Acoustics Limited
Sonae - Boardcraft Ltd
Sonae - Deralam Laminates Ltd
Sonaroll Acoustic Rolling shutter - Bolton Gate Company Ltd
Sonata - Quartet-GBC UK Ltd/ ACCO UK Ltd
Sondes - Radiodetection Ltd
Sonicaid - ArjoHuntleigh UK
Sony - Vidionics Security Systems Ltd
Sorbent - B & D Clays & Chemicals Ltd
SOS - Pressure Coolers Ltd T/A Maestro Pressure Coolers
Soss Invisible Hinges - Notcutt Ltd
SOTERIA - Apollo Fire Detectors Ltd
Sound Control Ear Muffs - MSA (Britain) Ltd
Sound Reduction Systems Ltd Acoustilay - Trim Acoustics
Sound secure - Premdor
Sound Sentinel - AET.gb Ltd
SoundBar 53 - Sound Reduction Systems Ltd
SoundBlocker - Bicester Products Ltd
SoundBlocker - Sound Reduction Systems Ltd
Soundmaster - Monowa Manufacturing (UK) Ltd
Soundpac - Hotchkiss Air Supply
Soundsafe - Emergi-Lite Safety Systems
Soundscoop® - Passivent Ltd
Soundseal - Sound Reduction Systems Ltd
Soundshield - Knauf UK
Soundshield ™ - Accent Hansen
Soundsorba - Soundsorba Ltd
SoundStop - Sound Reduction Systems Ltd
Soundtube wall panels - Salex Acoustics Limited
Soundvision - Pro Display TM Limited
Southampton - Neptune Outdoor Furniture Ltd
Sovereign - Baggeridge Brick PLC
Sovereign - Clenaware Systems Ltd
Sovereign - Commercial Lighting Systems
Sovereign Doors - Jeld-Wen UK Ltd
Sovereign Paving - Thakeham Tiles Ltd
Sovereign Windows - Jeld-Wen UK Ltd
SP Panel - Acousticabs Industrial Noise Control Ltd
SP Step Lift - Wessex Lift Co Ltd
SP10 Street Scape Mortar - Carter-Dal International
SP100 - Laticrete International Inc. UK
SPAC - Brighton (Handrails), W
Space -Ray - Space - Ray UK
Spacebuild - Wernick Group Ltd
Spacemaster Bollard - Dee-Organ Ltd
Spacepac - Wernick Group Ltd
Spaceright and Space/Dividers - Spaceright Europe Limited
Spacers - Parthos UK Ltd
Spacesaver Bollard - Dee-Organ Ltd
Spacestopper Major - Dee-Organ Ltd
Spae - DC Plastic Handrails Ltd
Spalex - Vita Liquid Polymers Ltd
Spandex - Invicta Window Films Ltd
Spandex Modular System - GB Sign Solutions Limited
Spangard - Lonsdale Metal Company
Spania - Marshalls Mono Ltd
Spanseal - Compriband Ltd
Spanwall - McMullen Facades
Sparclean - Gerflor Ltd
Spartacus - Metalliform Products Plc
Sparyfilm - Promat UK Ltd
Spawall wall lining - Grant Westfield Ltd
SPC - TEAM INDUSTRIAL SERVICES (UK) LIMITED
Spear & Jackson - Spear & Jackson
Spechra - T B S Fabrications
Specialist Formwork 3D - Cordek Ltd
Specifinder.com - The Building Centre Group Ltd
Specify it (online service) - IHS
Speck - Golden Coast Ltd
Specktralock non stain grout - Laticrete International Inc. UK
Spectator seating - CPS Manufacturing Co
Spector Lumenex - Tyco Fire and Integrated Solutions
Spectral Passive 3D - Harkness Screens
Spectrum - Norton Engineering Alloys Co Ltd
Spectrum Paint - Sanderson
Specula - Shadbolt F R & Sons Ltd
Spedec - SFS Intec LTD
Spediboil - Santon
Speed Bumps - Sportsmark Group Ltd
Speed Patch - Anglo Building Products Ltd
Speed Screed - Anglo Building Products Ltd
Speed Set - Premdor
Speedal ® - Righton Ltd
Speedbolt® - Nico Manufacturing Ltd
Speededge formwork - BRC Reinforcement
speedfab - Speedfab Midlands
Speedfit - Guest (Speedfit) Ltd, John
Speedframe - Construction Group UK Ltd
Speedlock - Construction Group UK Ltd
Speedmaster - Bostik Ltd
Speedor - Hart Door Systems Ltd
Speedturn - BSA Machine Tools Ltd
Speedwall, Speedfit - Bridgman IBC Ltd
Speedway - Vantrunk Engineering Ltd
SPF - Prima Security & Fencing Products
Spike - SFS Intec LTD
Spiked Grid Liner - Sportsmark Group Ltd
Spikemaster - Rawson Carpets Ltd
Spiral construction - In Steel (Blacksmiths & Fabricators) Ltd
Spiral Stairs - In Steel (Blacksmiths & Fabricators) Ltd
Spiralift - Caldwell Hardware (UK) Ltd
Spiralite - Cryotherm Insulation Ltd
Spirex - Caldwell Hardware (UK) Ltd
Spirotred - Pedley Furniture International Ltd
Spirtech - Monier Redland Limited
Spit - ITW Construction Products
Spit - ITW Spit
SPL - Stamford Products Limited
Splash, Sylan - TBS Amwell Ltd
Splitline - Lewden Electrical Industries
Sport M - Gerflor Ltd
Sporturf - En-tout-cas Tennis Courts Ltd
SPRA - Single Ply Roofing Association
Sprayed Limpet Mineral Wool-GP - Thermica Ltd
Sprayed Limpet Mineral Wool-HT - Thermica Ltd
Sprayed Limpet Vermiculite-external - Thermica Ltd
Sprayed Limpet Vermiculite-Internal - Thermica Ltd
Spraymark - Marking Machines International
Spring steel buffer - Berry Systems
Springflex - Rawson Fillings Ltd
Springlok - Rawson Fillings Ltd
Sprint Truss Equipment - ITW Consutruction Products
SPS Screen - Acousticabs Industrial Noise Control Ltd
Spur Shelving - Storage Solutions Ltd
Spyder - Mode Lighting
Squire - Henry Squire & Sons Ltd
Squire - Iles Waste Systems
Squire - Lochinvar Limited
SRD - Stamford Products Limited
SRS acoustic floating floor - Christie & Grey Ltd
SSI Schaefer Noell - SSI Schaefer Ltd
SSI Schaefer Peem - SSI Schaefer Ltd
SSI 1000 - SSL Access
SSL A300 - SSL Access
SSL Melody - SSL Access
St James - Marflow Eng Ltd
STA - Solar Trade Association, The
Stabila - Hyde Brian Ltd
StackFast - EHSmith
Stadium - Flambeau
Staifix - Ancon Limited
Stainless Gutta - Metal Gutta
Stainless Steel - Swift & Sure - Arvin Motion Control Ltd
Stainton Metal - Valmont Stainton
Stairiser - Stannah Lifts Ltd
Sta-Lok Rigging - Scotia Handling Services
Standard Dimensions Wall Chart - Sportsmark Group Ltd
Standard Patent Glazing - Standard Patent Glazing Co Ltd
Stanford - Glasdon U.K. Limited
Stanhope - Albany Standard Pumps
Stanley - Ciret Limited
Stanley Hinges - Relcross Ltd
Stanton - Saint-Gobain PAM UK
Stanway High Density Stacking Chair - Race Furniture Ltd
Stanwin - Albany Standard Pumps
Star spring operated cable reels - Metreel Ltd
Starcoat - Axter Ltd
Stardome - National Domelight Company
StarFix - Star Uretech Ltd
Starflex - Poujoulat (UK) Ltd
Stargard - SG System Products Ltd
Starglaze - National Domelight Company
Starline - Deceuninck Ltd
StarPolymers - Star Uretech Ltd
Starquest - Rawson Carpets Ltd
StarScape - Star Uretech Ltd
Starsystem - Watco UK Ltd
Startabox - RFA-Tech Ltd
Statements of Conformity - British Board of Agrément
Statesman - Magnet Ltd
Statesman - Project Office Furniture PLC
Stayflex - Adaptaflex Ltd
Steamline - Geberit Ltd
Steden - Laidlaw Ltd
Steel Doors - Harling Security Solutions Limited
Steel monoblock - Clestra Limited
Steelcase Strafor - Steelcase Strafor Plc
Steelcoat - Winn & Coales (Denso) Ltd
Steelite - Marlow Ropes Ltd
Steelkane - Ward's Flexible Rod Company Ltd
Steel-line - Cardale Garage Doors
Steelplan - Elliott Ltd
Steelybin® - Straight Ltd
Steicoflex - Steico
Steicojoist - Steico
Steicolvl - Steico
Stent - Stent Foundations Ltd
Stereo and Stretto - Lang+Fulton
Steristeel - Pland
Sterling - Chalmit Lighting
Sterling - Marlow Ropes Ltd
Sterling OSB - Norbord
Sterling range of cable management systems - Marshall-Tufflex Ltd
Sterox, LP Sterox - Fernox
Sterreberg - Smithbrook Building Products Ltd
Stetter - Schwing Stetter (UK) Ltd
Stewart Film Screen - Anders + Kern UK Ltd
Stick-Lite - Encapsulite International Ltd
Sticks and Stones - Mat.Works Flooring Solutions
Stik - Iles Waste Systems
Stilpro - Althon Ltd
Stimsonite - Ennis-Flint
Sto Rend - STO Ltd
Sto Silent - STO Ltd
Sto Therm Classic - STO Ltd
Sto Therm Mineral - STO Ltd
Sto Therm Protect - STO Ltd
Sto Therm Vario - STO Ltd
Sto Ventec Glass - STO Ltd
Stockmaster Shelving - Bedford Shelving Ltd
Stockrax - Link 51 (Storage Products)
Stomor Shelving - Link 51 (Storage Products)

S (con't)

Stone Collection - Solus Ceramics Ltd
Stone Italiana - Diespeker Marble & Terrazzo Ltd
Stonebound - Addagrip Terraco Ltd
Stonecor - Polypipe Building Products
Stoneguard LTD - Stoneguard (London) Ltd
Ston-Ker - Porcelanosa Group Ltd
Stopdust - Don Construction Products Ltd
Stopgap - Ball F & Co Ltd
Stoplite - Cryotherm Insulation Ltd
Storbox - Moresecure Ltd
Storemaster - Airedale International Air Conditioning Ltd
Storm - English Braids
Stormdry masonry protection cream - Safeguard Europe Ltd
Stormflo Rainwater Sytems - Hunter Plastics Ltd
Stormframe - Sapa Building Systems (monarch and glostal)
Stormgard - Corroless Corrosion Control
Stormor Euro - Link 51 (Storage Products)
Stormor XL Pallet - Link 51 (Storage Products)
Stormproof - Premdor
StormSaver Rainwater Harvesting System - FloPlast Ltd
Stortech - Rothley Limited
Stovax - Gazco
Stoves - Stoves PLC
Stoves Newhome - Stoves PLC
Stowlite Medium Blocks - Stowell Concrete Ltd
Stra - Maxit UK
Strada - Jaga UK
Strading - SG System Products Ltd
Straightaway - Coburn Sliding Systems Ltd
Straightpoint - Phoenix Scales Ltd
Strand - Carl F Groupco Limited
Strand - DW Windsor Lighting
Strand FEB - Strand Hardware Ltd
Strate-Grip - Andura Coatings Ltd
Stratex Warm Roof - Kemper System Ltd
Stratos - Franke Sissons Ltd
Stratpord Tip-Up Seating System - Race Furniture Ltd
Stratton - Hamworthy Heating Limited & ACV UK
Stratus Lighting - WF Senate
Streamline - Wade International Ltd
street king entrance matting - Jaymart Rubber & Plastics Ltd
Streetcrete ™ - Broxap Ltd
Streetiron ™ - Broxap Ltd
Streetscene ® - Broxap Ltd
Stremaform® - BRC Special Products - Bekaert Ltd
Stren-Cor - Asset International Ltd
Stretch Acoustic - Acousticabs Industrial Noise Control Ltd
Stretch Metal - Hunter Douglas Architectural Ltd
Strip Form - Scapa Tapes UK Ltd
Stroke - Bernhards Landscapes Ltd
Strong Water Based Lacquer - Junckers Limited
Strongbond - Chesterfelt Ltd
Strongbox - Tata Steel Europe Limited
Stronghold - Catnic
Stronghold - SG System Products Ltd
Strongoat - Don Construction Products Ltd
Structural Soils (Northern) Ltd - Structural Soils Ltd
Strypit - Rustins Ltd
Stuart - Stuart Turner Ltd
Stucanet - Metal Mesh Lathing for Plaster & Render - Bekaert Building Products
Studflex vibration isolation mat - Christie & Grey Ltd
Studio - Ideal-Standard Ltd
Studio 3 - Eaton Electric Limited
Studio 5 - Eaton Electric Limited
Studio Sanderson - Sanderson
Studrail system acoustic floating floor - Christie & Grey Ltd
Sturdee - Marlow Ropes Ltd
Styccobond - Ball F & Co Ltd
Stylefold - Style Door Systems Ltd
S-type, Seren, Serhad, Serif, Sesriem, Siesta, Smyrna, Sofi, Sovran, Speira, Stanza, Stargate, Stria, Sumela, Supra - Pitacs Ltd
Styrene - Ariel Plastics Ltd
Styroclad - Panel Systems Ltd
Styrodur - Kingspan Insulation Ltd
Styrofloor - Panel Systems Ltd
Styrofoam-A - Dow Building Solutions
Styroglaze - Panel Systems Ltd
Styroliner - Panel Systems Ltd
SubPrimo - Sound Reduction Systems Ltd
Succah - NuLite Ltd
Suffolk - Dixon Turner Wallcoverings
Suhner - Harbro Supplies Ltd
Sumo - Pump Technical Services Ltd
Sumo can crushers - Randalls Fabrications Ltd
Sumpmaster - Pump Technical Services Ltd
SUNCATCHER® - Monodraught Ltd
Suncell - CPV Ltd
Suncool - Pilkington Birmingham
Suncuva - Architen Landrell Associates Ltd
Sundeala K Grade - Sundeala Ltd
Sundeala FRB Flame Retardant Board - Sundeala Ltd
Sunfold - Becker (SLIDING PARTITIONS) Ltd
Sungard - Bonwyke Ltd
Sungard - Invicta Window Films Ltd
Sun-Guard: White-Out, Black-Out and Frost Matte - The Window Film Company UK Ltd
SUNPIPE® - Monodraught Ltd
Sunray - Sunray Engineering Ltd
Sunrite - Sunrite Blinds Ltd
Sunscreen - Mermet U.K
Sunstar - Space - Ray UK
Sunstract® - Passivent Ltd
Suntech - Deans Blinds & Awnings (UK) Ltd
Suntech systems - Deans Blinds & Awnings (UK) Ltd
Sunvizor - Levolux A.T. Limited
Supa Glide - Moresecure Ltd
Supabore - Outokumpu Stainless Ltd
Supacord - Heckmondwicke FB
Supafil - Knauf Insulation Ltd
Supalux - FGF Ltd
Supalux - Promat UK Ltd
Supapac - Ormandy Rycroft Engineering
Supastor - Flamco UK Ltd
Supatube - Outokumpu Stainless Ltd
Super Saphir - EJOT UK Limited
Super Seal - Hepworth Building Products Ltd
Superbolt - TEAM INDUSTRIAL SERVICES (UK) LIMITED
Superbond - Interclad (UK) Ltd
Supercal - Range Cylinders
Supercast - Fosroc Ltd
Superchill - Heatrae Sadia Heating Ltd
Supercoil - Airsprung Beds Ltd
Supercomfort - Dunham Bush Ltd
Supercote - Witham Oil & Paint Ltd
Supercut - Unifix Ltd
Superdeck Insulated Composite System - Intergrated Polymer Systems (UK) Ltd
Superdeluxe - Premdor
Superfoot - Bernhards Landscapes Ltd
Superfoot plus - Bernhards Landscapes Ltd
SuperG - Saint-Gobain Ecophon Ltd
Supergalv Lintels - Birtley Group
Supergres - Arnull Bernard J & Co Ltd
Superib - Richard Lees Decking Limited
Superior - Beacon Machine Tools Ltd
Superline - BLV Licht-und Vakuumtecnik
Superline - Marlow Ropes Ltd
Superlintels - Jones of Oswestry Ltd
Superlite Blocks - Hanson Concrete Products
Superlite masonary - Hanson Concrete Products
Supermat - Kleen-Tex Industries Ltd
Supermix - Marlow Ropes Ltd
Supermix products - B & M Fencing Limited
Supersaver gas burners - Infraglo Limited
Superseal - Kleeneze Sealtech Ltd
Superseal - Unifix Ltd
Superseal-pipe insert - Guest (Speedfit) Ltd, John
Supersleve House Drain - Hepworth Building Products Ltd
Superspan - Compriband Ltd
Superspan - Illbruck Sealant Systems UK Ltd
Superswitch - Friedland Ltd
Supertube - Domus Ventilation
Supervisor - Gent Limited
Supplymaster - Timeguard Ltd
SupraBlock, SupraDrain - Jones of Oswestry Ltd
Supreme Boiling Water Products - Heatrae Sadia Heating Ltd
Sure Ballistics - Specialist Building Products
Sure GRP Finishes - Specialist Building Products
Sure Rend - Specialist Building Products
Surefire - Thurston Building Systems
Surefire Adhesive - Advance Tapes International Ltd
Surefit Rainwater Sytems - Hunter Plastics Ltd
suregrip - Ecotile Flooring Ltd
Suregrip - Wincro Metal Industries Ltd
Suregrip ® - Coo-Var Ltd
Suregrip ® - Teal & Mackrill Ltd
Sureguard - Thurston Building Systems
Surell - Formica Ltd
Surelock - Laird Security Hardware
Sureloo - Thurston Building Systems
Surespace - Thurston Building Systems
Surespan - Thurston Building Systems
Suresport - Thurston Building Systems
Surface Mounted Road Blockers - APT Controls Ltd
Sussex Broadware - Focus SB Ltd
S-Vap 5000E SA vapour control layer - Sika Liquid Plastics Limited
SWA - Steel Window Association
Swaledale - Oakdale (Contracts) Ltd
Swan - Boardcraft Ltd
Swarfega, Swarfega Orange, Swarfega Power, S C Johnson Professional - Deb Group Limited
Swedeglaze - Swedecor
Swedsign - Signs & Labels Ltd
Swellseal - Grace De Neef UK
Swift Signs - Metal Gutta
Swift-and-Sure - Arvin Motion Control Ltd
Swiftplan - Wernick Group Ltd
Swiftrack - Legrand Electric Ltd
Swifts - Legrand Electric Ltd
Swiftsafe - Clark Door Ltd
Swiftshop - Stamford Products Limited
Swimmer - Golden Coast Ltd
Swing-Boom - Horizon International Ltd
Swish - FGF Ltd
Swisslab/therm/pan/tech/rail - Alumasc Exterior Building Products Ltd
Swisspearl® - Omnis
SX Environmental - P+L Systems Ltd
Sygef - George Fischer Sales Ltd
Sygnette - Wellman Robey Ltd
Sykes Pumps - Andrews Sykes Hire Ltd
SylvaFoam - Junckers Limited
SylvaKet - Junckers Limited
SylvaRed - Junckers Limited
SylvaSport Club - Junckers Limited
SylvaSport Premium - Junckers Limited
SylvaSquash - Junckers Limited
SylvaThene - Junckers Limited
Synergetic flylights - P+L Systems Ltd
Synergy - Legrand Electric Ltd
Synergy - Valspar Powder Coatings Ltd
Syntha Pulvin - Valspar Powder Coatings Ltd
Synthascreed - DPC Screeding Ltd
Synthatec - Valspar Powder Coatings Ltd
Synthtec Metallics - Valspar Powder Coatings Ltd
Syntropal - ICB (International Construction Bureau) Ltd
System 100 - Domus Ventilation
System 160, Superprop - Mabey Hire Ltd
System 2000 - NMC (UK) Ltd
System 3 - CBS (Curtain and Blind Specialists Ltd)
System 4 - Simplex Signs Limited
System 500 - Newton John & Co Ltd
System 6 - CBS (Curtain and Blind Specialists Ltd)
System 8 - CBS (Curtain and Blind Specialists Ltd)
System 9000 - Timloc Expamet Building Products
System Access - Saint-Gobain Ecophon Ltd
System J - Nullifire Ltd
System S - Nullifire Ltd
System W - Nullifire Ltd
System10 - Veka Plc
System2000 range - Helmsman
Systemate - Gledhill Water Storage Ltd
SystemFit - Santon
Systemlabor - Köttermann Ltd
SystemLogic - Range Cylinders
SystemRoMedic - Amilake Southern Ltd
Syston doors - Syston Rolling Shutters Ltd
Syvac - Donaldson Filtration (GB) Ltd

T

T line counters - Platonoff & Harris Ltd
T.I.P.S - Hellermann Tyton
T14 storage wall - Gifford Grant Ltd
T2 - Flexiform Business Furniture Ltd
T5 Lighting - Encapsulite International Ltd
TAC, Telemecanique, Thorsman, Tower - Schneider Electric Ltd
Tactual - Stocksigns Ltd
TakPave - Rediweld Rubber & Plastics Ltd
Talisman - Tilley International Ltd
Tanalith - Arch Timber Protection
Tanalith Extra - Arch Timber Protection
Tanatone - Arch Timber Protection
Tangent - Marflow Eng Ltd
Tango - Litex Design Ltd
Tangye Pumps - Satec Service Ltd
Taperell Taylor - Michelmersh Brick Holdings PLC
Tapes4 Builders - Advance Tapes International Ltd
Tapetex - Architectural Textiles Ltd
Tapiflex Collections - Tarkett Ltd
Taplon - ITW Construction Products
Tappex - Uponor Ltd
Tapworks - Tapworks Water Softeners
Tapworks - Northstar - EcoWater Systems Ltd
Tapworks Domestic - AD11 - EcoWater Systems Ltd
Tapworks Domestic - AD15 - EcoWater Systems Ltd
Tapworks Domestic - NSC40 UDI - EcoWater Systems Ltd
Tapworks Domestic - Ultra 9 - EcoWater Systems Ltd
Taraflex - Gerflor Ltd
Tarasafe - Gerflor Ltd
Tarmac Flowing (40N) Concrete - Tarmac - Specialist Products (Packed Highway Products)
Tarmac High Strength 40N Concrete - Tarmac - Specialist Products (Packed Highway Products)
Tarmac Lime Sand Mortars - Tarmac Trading Limited (Mortars)
Tarmac Postmix Concrete - Tarmac - Specialist Products (Packed Highway Products)
Tarmac Quick Set 40N Concrete - Tarmac - Specialist Products (Packed Highway Products)
TAS100 - Thatch Fibreboard - Thatching Advisory Services Ltd
TAS-33 Thatch Alert - Thatching Advisory Services Ltd
Taskmaster - Taskmaster Doors Ltd
Taskmaster - Titan Door Systems Ltd
Taskmaster S series - Taskmaster Doors Ltd
Taskmaster T series - Taskmaster Doors Ltd
Taskworthy - Taskworthy Ltd
Tate Access Floors - Kingspan Access Floors Ltd
Tate Automation - Tate Fencing
Tate Floors - Hatmet Limited
TATOO - Optelma Lighting Ltd
Tayler tools - Hyde Brian Ltd
TB professional staple gun and staples for stainless steel wire - Thatching Advisory Services Ltd
T-Bar, Tardis, Tilbrook, TimeCables, Tora, Truva, Trojan, Tubo, Tudor, Twister - Pitacs Ltd
TBS Baffle - Acousticabs Industrial Noise Control Ltd
TBS Panels - Acousticabs Industrial Noise Control Ltd
TD - Donaldson Filtration (GB) Ltd
TD50 - Clenaware Systems Ltd
Teamac - Teal & Mackrill Ltd
TEBRAX - Tebrax Ltd
Tecbond - Kenyon Performance Adhesives
TecCast, TecLite, TecStone - Haddonstone Ltd
Tech Eco Slate - SIG Roofing
Techdek - Norton Engineering Alloys Co Ltd
Technal - Cantifix of London Limited
Technics - Interfloor Limited
Technishield - Optima
Technomelt - Henkel Ltd
TechSpan® - Freyssinet Ltd
Techtonic rooflight blinds - Hallmark Blinds Ltd
TecnoFlex - Schiedel Chimney Systems Ltd
Tectrix Fins - Hallmark Blinds Ltd
Tectum Abuse Resistant Panel - Salex Acoustics Limited
Tee Gee - Swish Building Products
Teetector Golf - Evergreens Uk
Tegola - Matthew Hebden
Tegometall - RB UK Ltd
Tegometall - Smart F & G (Shopfittings)Ltd
Tegula - Marshalls Mono Ltd
Tehalit - Hager Ltd
Tektalan - Skanda Acoustics
Tektalan - Skanda Acoustics Limited
Tektura - Tektura Plc
Teleblock - Jones of Oswestry Ltd
Tele-Call - bedside TV/Telephone system - Wandsworth Elecrtrical Ltd
Teleguard - Youngman Group Limited
Telelight - Sandhurst Manufacturing Co Ltd
Telford Flip-Chart - Magiboards Ltd
Telling GFRC - Telling Architectural Ltd
Tema - Optelma Lighting Ltd
Temcem - Minkon Ltd
Tem-Energy - May William (Ashton) Ltd
Tempo LST - Jaga UK
Tempomatic - Delabie UK Ltd
Tempomix - Delabie UK Ltd
Tempostop - Delabie UK Ltd
Tempsoft - Delabie UK Ltd
Tempus - Zon International
Ten Brazilian Granites - Kirkstone
Ten Plus - Kompan Ltd
Tenniturf - En-tout-cas Tennis Courts Ltd
Tenon Flexplus, Fire & Sound, Ovation, Vitrage, Vitrage (db), Scion - SIG Interiors
Tenon Operable Walls, Wasllstore - SIG Interiors
Tenon Pace - SIG Interiors
Tenon Washrooms - SIG Interiors
Tensabarrier® - Tensator Ltd
Tensaguide® - Tensator Ltd
Tensar - Tensar International Ltd
Tensator® - Tensator Ltd
Terca - Wienerberger Ltd
Terminator - Marflow Eng Ltd
Termodeck - Tarmac Building Products Ltd
Terodem - Henkel Ltd
Terokal - Henkel Ltd
Terophon - Henkel Ltd
Teroson - Henkel Ltd
Terostat - Henkel Ltd
Terra-34, Torino and Verona - Lang+Fulton
Terrabase Rustic - Addagrip Terraco Ltd
Terrabound - Addagrip Terraco Ltd
TerraClass™ - Freyssinet Ltd
Terraen - Ulster Carpet Mills Ltd
Terraforce - Keller Ground Engineering
Terraglass - Diespeker Marble & Terrazzo Ltd
Terrain - Geberit Ltd
Terrain Blocker - APT Controls Ltd
Terrapin - Terrapin Ltd
TerraTrel™ - Freyssinet Ltd
Terrex - ABG Ltd
Terrier - Pegler Ltd
Terrings - Compriband Ltd
Terry's - The Kenco Coffee Company
Tesa - Beiersdorf (UK) Ltd
TESS100 to TESS600 series - Guthrie Douglas
Texaa Panels - LSA Projects Ltd
Texitone ECO - Brett Landscaping
Texsol - Trade Sealants Ltd
Textomur - Keller Ground Engineering
Textura - Gradus Ltd
Texture - Pilkington Birmingham
TF1 Total Filter, TF1 Omega Filter and TF1 Sigma Filter - Fernox
Thatchbatt - Thatching Advisory Services Ltd
The Carpet Foundation - The Carpet Foundation
The Carpet Foundation Quality Mark - The Carpet Foundation
The CAST Rooflight - Clement Steel Windows
The Construction Information Service - NBS
The Design Archives - CrowsonFrabrics Ltd
The Diamond System - Chelsea Artisans Ltd
The Executive Range - Security Doors Direct
The Finishing Touch - www.ubendwemend.co.uk - HE Services (Plant Hire) Ltd
The Gallery - Symphony Group PLC, The
The Invisible Lightswitch - Forbes & Lomax Ltd
The Painting and Decorating Association - Painting & Decorating Association
The Part System - S & B Ltd
The Pyramid - The Rooflight company
The Rapid Range - Monier Redland Limited
The Resin Flooring Association - FeRFA
The Rutland Press - Royal Incorporation of Architects in Scotland
The Stationary Office - tso shop
Theben - Timeguard Ltd
Therapeutic Support Systems™ - ArjoHuntleigh UK
Therma - Kingspan Industrial Ins. Ltd
Thermac - McKenzie-Martin Ltd
Thermachem - Naylor Drainage Ltd
Thermadome - National Domelight Company
Thermafibre - Davant Products Ltd
Thermafloor - Kingspan Insulation Ltd
Thermafold Insulated Folding doors - Bolton Gate Company Ltd
Thermaglide - Cardale Garage Doors
Thermal Safe - Kingspan Ltd
Thermalight - National Domelight Company
Thermaline - Harton Heating Appliances
Thermaliner - Kingspan Insulation Ltd
Thermalite - Forterra Building Products Ltd
Thermalsave Heat Re-circulators - Turnbull & Scott (Engineers) Ltd
Thermapave - Forterra Building Products Ltd
Thermapitch - Kingspan Insulation Ltd
Thermaroof - Kingspan Insulation Ltd
Thermashield - Glixtone Ltd
Thermataper - Kingspan Insulation Ltd
Thermatex - Knauf AMF Ceilings Ltd
Thermatic - Watts Industries UK Ltd
Thermawall - Kingspan Insulation Ltd
Thermax - Birdsall Services Ltd
Thermgard - Lonsdale Metal Company
THERMIC - K. V. Radiators
THERMIC Zana-line - K. V. Radiators
Therminox - Poujoulat (UK) Ltd

T (con't)

Thermo Guard - Kenyon Paints Limited
Thermocor C.C - Polypipe Building Products
Thermoflue - Marflex Chimney Systems
ThermoKote Anti Condensation Paint - ProTen Services
Thermolier unit heaters - Turnbull & Scott (Engineers) Ltd
Thermoliner - The Rooflight company
Thermomax Refrigeration - Kingspan Environmental Ltd
Thermonda - Rockwell Sheet Sales Ltd
thermosave - Peter Cox Ltd
Thermoscreens - Thermoscreens Ltd
thermotek drywall - Peter Cox Ltd
Thioflex - Fosroc Ltd
Thirkleby - York Handmade Brick Co Ltd
Thistle - British Gypsum Ltd
Tholoflow - Fullflow Group Ltd
Thomas Dudley - Olby H E & Co Ltd
Thomas Lowe Joinery - Benlowe Stairs
Thor - Thor Hammer Co Ltd
Thorace - Thor Hammer Co Ltd
Thorex - Thor Hammer Co Ltd
Thorlite - Thor Hammer Co Ltd
Thormajoint - Ennis-Flint
Thorn Security - Tyco Fire and Integrated Solutions
Threshex - Exitex Ltd
Thrii handwash unit - Wallgate Ltd
Thunderbolt - Unifix Ltd
Thwaites - Chippindale Plant Ltd
Tibmix - Don Construction Products Ltd
TICA - Thermal Insulation Contractors Association
Tico - Tiflex Ltd
Tidy Bin - Unicorn Containers Ltd
Tiefoam - Modern Plan Insulation Ltd
Tie-Sleeve - Redifix Ltd
Tiger - Mode Lighting (UK) Ltd
Tikkurila - Andrews Coatings Ltd
Tikkurila - Valtti ltd
Tile Association - The Tile Association
Tile-A-Door - Howe Green Ltd
Tileflex - Compriband Ltd
Tilley Lamp-Kerosene - Tilley International Ltd
Timbacrib - Keller Ground Engineering
Timbalok Crib Walling - Ruthin Precast Concrete Ltd
Timbasol™ - Venator
Timb-a-Tilt - Caldwell Hardware (UK) Ltd
Timber Resin Splice - ProTen Services
Timber Shade - Tidmarsh & Sons
timberline - DLW Flooring
TimberLine - Premdor
Timbertie - Redifix Ltd
Timbertone - Protim Solignum Ltd
Timbridge - Panel Agency Limited
Timeless Collection - FIBO UK LTD
Timesaver - Saint-Gobain PAM UK
Timloc - Allmat (East Surrey) Ltd
Timonox - Crown Paints Ltd
Tintersol® - Venator
Titan - Fabrikat (Nottingham) Ltd
Titan - Ingersoll-Rand European Sales Ltd
Titan - Osram Ltd
Titan - PHI Group Ltd
Titan - Titan Ladders Ltd
Titan Environmental - Kingspan Environmental Ltd
Tivoli 21 carpet tiles loop pile - Burmatex Ltd
TKV - LTI Advanced Systems Technology Ltd
TL Board, TLFR Board, TD Board - Promat UK Ltd
T-line 120 - Ves Andover Ltd
TMC Fine Texture - Andura Coatings Ltd
Toby Dustbins - Iles Waste Systems
Toesavers - Briggs Industrial Footwear Ltd t/a Briggs Safety Wear
Toledo - Townscape Products Ltd
Tomkinson - Jacopa Limited
Tonon Fan Coil Units - Thermal Technology Sales Ltd
Tony Team - Tony Team Ltd
ToolShield - Green Brook
TOP FOLDOR - TORMAX United Kingdom Ltd
Top Star Rooflights - Klober Ltd
Top Vent - Klober Ltd
Topcon - Topcon GB Ltd
Topcrete - Tarmac Building Products Ltd
Topcrete - Tarmac Trading Limited (Blocks)
Topdek - Ward Insulated Panels Ltd
Topflex - Topseal Systems Ltd
Topflood - BLV Licht-und Vakuumtecnik
Topflow (Self compacting concrete) - Tarmac Trading Limited (Readymix Concrete & Screed)
Topforce (Fibre reinforced concrete) - Tarmac Trading Limited (Readymix Concrete & Screed)
TopForm - SFS Intec LTD
Topguard 10 Year - Chesterfelt Ltd
Toplab Base - Trespa UK Ltd
Toplab Plus - Trespa UK Ltd
Toplab Vertical - Trespa UK Ltd
Topliflow Screed A (Flowing, Anhydrite Self Levelling Screed) - Tarmac Trading Limited (Readymix Concrete & Screed)
Topline - Hunter Douglas Architectural Ltd
Topline wall panels - Salex Acoustics Limited
Toplite - Tarmac Building Products Ltd
Toplite - Tarmac Trading Limited (Blocks)
Toplite C - Tarmac Trading Limited (Readymix Concrete & Screed)
Topmix Permeable [Permeable concrete for improved drainage] - Tarmac Trading Limited (Readymix Concrete & Screed)
Topproof (Waterproof concrete) - Tarmac Trading Limited (Readymix Concrete & Screed)
Toprail - Toprail Systems Ltd
Toproc (High strength and abrasion resisting concrete) - Tarmac Trading Limited (Readymix Concrete & Screed)
Toproc Rapid (rapid setting and high early strength) - Tarmac Trading Limited (Readymix Concrete & Screed)
Topscape - Topscape/Topsport - Tarmac Trading Limited
Topseal - Topseal Systems Ltd
Topsport - Topscape/Topsport - Tarmac Trading Limited
Topsport Equisand - Topscape/Topsport - Tarmac Trading Limited
Topspot - BLV Licht-und Vakuumtecnik
Topsy 2000 (litter bins) - Glasdon UK Limited
Toptek - Barlow Group
Toptint (Coloured and Decorative Concretes) - Tarmac Trading Limited (Readymix Concrete & Screed)
Torbeck - Opella Ltd
Torbeck Variflush - Opella Ltd
Toreador carpet tiles loop pile - Burmatex Ltd
Torit - Donaldson Filtration (GB) Ltd
TORMAX - TORMAX United Kingdom Ltd
Toro - Hille Educational Products Ltd
Torrent - Gledhill Water Storage Ltd
Torso - Caldwell Hardware (UK) Ltd
Toscana - Marshalls Mono Ltd
Toscana - Paragon by Heckmondwike
Toshiba - Purified Air Ltd
Toshiba air conditioning - Toshiba Carrier UK
Total Care - Heckmondwicke FB
Totem - Directional Data Systems Ltd
Tough-Cote™ High Build Texture - Glixtone Ltd
Towerfill - Tower Manufacturing
Towerfire - Tower Manufacturing
Towerfoam - Tower Manufacturing
Towergrip - Tower Manufacturing
Towerpak - Tower Manufacturing
Towerseal - Tower Manufacturing
TP Plumbing & Heating - Keyline Civils Specialist Ltd
TPC LN/B - Babcock Wanson Uk Ltd
T-Pren - Matthew Hebden
TR Freeman - Kershaw Mechanical Services Ltd
Trackmaster - Rawson Carpets Ltd
Trackranger Crawler Primary Crushing Outfits - Parker Plant Ltd
TRADA Technology - BM TRADA
Trade Range - Cox Building Products Ltd
Trademark - Marcrist International Ltd
Tradesman - Ibstock Brick Ltd
Traditional - Northcot Brick Ltd
Traffic - Kompan Ltd
Trafficline - Moravia (UK) Ltd
TrafiCop - Rediweld Rubber & Plastics Ltd
TRAKA - ASSA ABLOY Limited
Trakelast - Tiflex Ltd
Trakway - Eve Trakway
Trammel fin drain - Don & Low Ltd
Transaction - Rackline Systems Storage Ltd
Transfastener™ - Latchways plc
Transforma - Youngman Group Limited
TransitMaster™ - Kone
Transmit - Tunstal Healthcare (UK) Ltd
Transpalace - Parthos UK Ltd
Transvario - Kone Escalators Ltd
Trashmaster - Pump Technical Services Ltd
Travabon - Deb Group Limited
TravelLED - Glamox Luxo Lighting Limited
TravelMaster™ - Kone
Travertin - Skanda Acoustics
Travertin - Skanda Acoustics Limited
Travis Perkins Trading Company - Keyline Civils Specialist Ltd
Tread Safe - Anglo Building Products Ltd
TreadGUARD - Visqueen Building Products
Treadmaster - Tiflex Ltd
Treadspire - In Steel (Blacksmiths & Fabricators) Ltd
Trebitt - Jotun Henry Clark Ltd Decorative Division
Trebitt Opaque - Jotun Henry Clark Ltd Decorative Division
Tredaire - Interfloor Limited
Trellidor - Harling Security Solutions Limited
Tremco - Tremco Illbruck Ltd
Trench Heating - Turnbull & Scott (Engineers) Ltd
trent gutter system - Dales Fabrications Ltd
Trentobond - Tremco Illbruck Ltd
Trentocrete - Tremco Illbruck Ltd
Trentodel - Tremco Illbruck Ltd
Trentoflex - Tremco Illbruck Ltd
Trentoshield - Tremco Illbruck Ltd
Trentothane - Tremco Illbruck Ltd
Trespa - Amari Plastics Plc
Trespa - FGF Ltd
Trespa - Trespa UK Ltd
Trevi Showers - Armitage Shanks Ltd
Trevira CS - Silent Gliss Ltd
Triaqua - Multikwik Ltd
Tricity - Electrolux Domestic Appliances
Trident - Marflow Eng Ltd
Tridonic - Bernlite Ltd
Triflo Solder Ring - Conex Universal Limited
Tri-Gas Gas Membrane - Cordek Ltd
Trigon - Hamworthy Heating Limited & ACV UK
Tri-Guard® - Jackson H S & Son (Fencing) Ltd
Trilax - Girsberger London
Triline - Smart Systems Ltd
Tri-lock - Grass Concrete Ltd
Trim Acoustic Cradle System - Trim Acoustics
Trim Defender Door Bars - Trim Acoustics
Trim Defender Wall - Trim Acoustics
Trimalac - Trimite Ltd
TRIMEC - ASSA ABLOY Limited
Trimite - Andrews Coatings Ltd
Trimite - Trimite Ltd
Trimtop - Swish Building Products
Triniti - Levolux A.T. Limited
Trio - Panel & Louvre Co Ltd
TRIO - Panel wall formwork - PERI Ltd
Triogen & Tylo - Golden Coast Ltd
Triple Seven - Dunbrik (Yorks) Ltd
Tri-Plugs - Tower Manufacturing
Tri-Shell - Dudley Thomas Ltd
Tritainer - Franklin Hodge Industries Ltd
Triton - Albany Standard Pumps
Triton - Triton PLC
Trixene - Lanxess Urethanes UK Ltd
Trizone - Airsprung Beds Ltd
Trojan - Crane Fluid Systems
Trojan - Hallmark Blinds Ltd
Trojan - Shackerley (Holdings) Group Ltd incorporating Designer ceramics
Troldtekt - Skanda Acoustics
Troldtekt - Skanda Acoustics Limited
Trolleylift - Stannah Lifts Ltd
Tropicano - Xpelair Ltd
Trough & Waffle Moulds - Cordek Ltd
Trubed - Tarmac Trading Limited (Mortars)
Trubed Eco - Tarmac Trading Limited (Mortars)
Trubed Utility - Tarmac Trading Limited (Mortars)
Trubert - Watts Industries UK Ltd
TruckStop - Rediweld Rubber & Plastics Ltd
Trueflue - Marflex Chimney Systems
Trugrain - Laird Security Hardware
Truline - Simpson Strong-Tie®
Trulok Prelude - Armstrong World Industries Ltd
Truspread dry silo mortar - Tarmac Trading Limited (Mortars)
Truspread Mortar (Factory produced mortar with added lime) - Tarmac Trading Limited (Mortars)
Truth - Caldwell Hardware (UK) Ltd
Truth Hardware - Schlegel UK (2006) Ltd
Trutone Coloured Mortar - Tarmac Trading Limited (Mortars)
T-Screen - Mermet U.K
TSV1 surface mounted shower panel - Horne Engineering Ltd
TT - Lochinvar Limited
TT - Optelma Lighting Ltd
TT - Technology Tower - Staverton (UK) Ltd
T-T controls - T-T Pumps & T-T controls
TTA - The Tile Association
TTF - Simon R W Ltd
TTF - Timber Trade Federation
Tubarad Steel Column Radiators - AEL
Tubeclamps - Tubeclamps Ltd
Tubela - Tubela Engineering Co Ltd
Tube-U-Fit Hanging Rail & Supports - Daro UK Ltd
Tudor - Branson Leisure Ltd
Tudor Roof Tiles - Tudor Roof Tile Co Ltd
Tufcon 80 - Conren Ltd
TuffBin™ - Straight Ltd
Tufftrak - Mabey Hire Ltd
Tuftex - Vita Liquid Polymers Ltd
Tung Oil - Chestnut Products
Turbocast 800 (winter gritting machines) - Glasdon UK Limited
TurboCharger - Lochinvar Limited
TurboFast - Helifix
Turbo-Flo - MSA (Britain) Ltd
Turbolite - Marcrist International Ltd
TurboSyphons - Dudley Thomas Ltd
Turkish room - Dalesauna Ltd
Turney Turbines - Pumps & Motors UK Ltd
Turnquest - HEWI UK Ltd
Tusc - Unistrut Limited
Tuscany - Lotus Water Garden Products Ltd
Tuscany - Muraspec
TVSS - Eaton Electric Limited
Tweeny - The Haigh Tweeny Co Ltd
Twenty-one Limestones - Kirkstone
Twiclad - Ide T & W Ltd
Twilfix - Betafence Limited
Twilweld - United Wire Ltd
Twin & Big Twin - Helmsman
Twinarc - Two Arc Tube High Pressure Sodium Lamps - FEILO SYLVANIA EUROPE LIMITED
Twindisk - bigHead Bonding Fasteners Ltd
Twinfix - Amari Plastics Plc
Twinfold Fine Twist - Brockway Carpets Ltd
Twinlok® - Walraven Ltd
Twinlux - Illuma Lighting
TwinSash - Veka Plc
Twisco - Manitou (Site Lift) Ltd
Twist® Roller Blinds - Luxaflex®
Twyford Range - Twyford Bathrooms
Tycho - Kronospan Ltd
Tyglas - Fothergill Engineered Fabrics Ltd
Type E - Cavity Trays Ltd
Type seating - CPS Manufacturing Co
Type X - Cavity Trays Ltd
Typhoo - The Kenco Coffee Company
Tyre Tile - Mat.Works Flooring Solutions
Tyrolean Rendadash - LaFarge Cement UK
Tyton - Hellermann Tyton
Tyveks - Klober Ltd
Tyzack - Spear & Jackson

U

U.S.G Donn - New Forest Ceilings Ltd
U45 Insulated Sectional Doors - Avon Industrial Doors Ltd
UbiSoil - Ubbink (UK) Ltd
Ubivent - Ubbink (UK) Ltd
Ucrete - BASF plc, Construction Chemicals
UESA - High efficiency condensing warm air heaters - AmbiRad Ltd
Uginox Roll On - Aperam Stainless Services & Solutions UK Limited
Uginox Bright - Aperam Stainless Services & Solutions UK Limited
Uginox Leather, Uginox Linen, Uginox Lozenge - Aperam Stainless Services & Solutions UK Limited
Uginox Mat - Aperam Stainless Services & Solutions UK Limited
Uginox Patina K44 - Aperam Stainless Services & Solutions UK Limited
Uginox Sand, Uginox Square - Aperam Stainless Services & Solutions UK Limited
Uginox Top, Uginox Touch - Aperam Stainless Services & Solutions UK Limited
UL-M - Breedon Aggregates
Ulster Velvet - Ulster Carpet Mills Ltd
Ulta-pals Packless Silencers - IAC Acoustic Company UK Ltd
Ultibed Bedding Mortar - Tarmac - Specialist Products (Packed Highway Products)
Ultibed Concrete - Tarmac - Specialist Products (Packed Highway Products)
Ultibed Flowing Concrete - Tarmac - Specialist Products (Packed Highway Products)
Ulticolour/ Ulticolour Porous (Coloured asphalt/ Coloured Porous Asphalt) - Tarmac Trading Limited (Asphalt)
Ultidrive/ Ultidrive Porous (Asphalts for driveways) - Tarmac Trading Limited (Asphalt)
Ultifastpath (Asphalt for Footpaths) - Tarmac Trading Limited (Asphalt)
Ultiflow (Sustainable Drainage Aggregates) - Tarmac Trading Limited (Aggregates)
Ultigrip (Skid resisting asphalt for high risk locations) - Tarmac Trading Limited (Asphalt)
Ultilayer (Crack resisting asphalt for roads) - Tarmac Trading Limited (Asphalt)
Ultilow (Warm mix asphalt with lower carbon emissions) - Tarmac Trading Limited (Asphalt)
Ultima - Airedale International Air Conditioning Ltd
Ultima - Armstrong World Industries Ltd
Ultima - Laird Security Hardware
Ultima - Wincro Metal Industries Ltd
Ultima - For the less abled - Rixonway Kitchens Ltd
Ultimate Collection - Ball William Ltd
Ultimate flue outlet - Brewer Metalcraft
Ultimate Range - Valor
Ultipatch Footway (Asphalt for footpath repair) - Tarmac - Specialist Products (Packed Highway Products)
Ultipatch Pothole (Asphalt for Pothole repair) - Tarmac - Specialist Products (Packed Highway Products)
ULTIPATCH Viafix Quick (Rapid all-weather pothole repair) - Tarmac - Specialist Products (Packed Highway Products)
Ultipave (Asphalt for Highways) - Tarmac Trading Limited (Asphalt)
Ultiplay/ Ultiplay Porous (Asphalts for Playgrounds) - Tarmac Trading Limited (Asphalt)
Ultisport Tennis/ Ultisport MUGA (Asphalts for Outdoor Tennis Courts/ Sports Pitches) - Tarmac Trading Limited (Asphalt)
Ultra - Eaton Electric Limited
ULTRA - Lakes Bathrooms Limited
Ultra 9 - Tapworks Water Softeners
Ultra Bar - Sections & Profiles Ltd
Ultra Fence - Sections & Profiles Ltd
Ultra Post - Sections & Profiles Ltd
Ultra Rail - Sections & Profiles Ltd
Ultra Sheet - Sections & Profiles Ltd
Ultracal - Range Cylinders
Ultra-DENCO - DencoHappel UK Ltd
Ultraflex - Dyer Environmental Controls
Ultraframe - Ultraframe PLC
Ultragard Software - Time and Data Systems International Ltd (TDSI)
Ultragard Vision-ID - Time and Data Systems International Ltd (TDSI)
Ultragrain ® - Righton Ltd
UltraGRID™ - Hadley Industries Plc
UltraLATH™ - Hadley Industries Plc
Ultralife - BLV Licht-und Vakuumtecnik
Ultralift - Caldwell Hardware (UK) Ltd
ultralight, utilityramp - Enable Access
Ultralite 500 - Ultraframe PLC
Ultralite Blocks - Hanson Concrete Products
UltraMEZZ™ - Hadley Industries Plc
Ultramix - Watts Industries UK Ltd
UltraPALE™ - Hadley Industries Plc
UltraPly TPO - Firestone Building Products
Ultra-Rib - Brett Martin Ltd
UltraSHEET™ - Hadley Industries Plc
UltraSTEEL™ - Hadley Industries Plc
Ultrastream - Britannia Kitchen Ventilation Ltd
UltraSTRUT™ - Hadley Industries Plc
Ultratile - Britmet Tileform Limited
Ultraturn - Righton Ltd
Unbreakable - Briggs Industrial Footwear Ltd t/a Briggs Safety Wear
Uni- Ecoloc - CEMEX
Unibond - Henkel Consumer Adhesives
Unibond No More Nails - Henkel Consumer Adhesives
Unibond No More Sealent Guns - Henkel Consumer Adhesives
Unibond Unifilla - Henkel Consumer Adhesives
Unica - Hansgrohe
Unicell - Donaldson Filtration (GB) Ltd
Unidare - Dimplex UK Limited
Unidare - Seagoe Technologies Ltd
Unidox - Witham Oil & Paint Ltd
Unieck - DLW Flooring
Unifit - NewTeam Ltd
Unifloor Flooring System - Hanson Concrete Products
UniForce – Mechanical Smoke Ventilation System - SCS Group
Uniframe - Hanson Concrete Products
Unify - Connaught Communications Systems Ltd

U (con't)

Unigas - GP Burners (CIB) Ltd
Unijet - Carpark Ventilation System - SCS Group
Unikrame - Hanson Concrete Products
Unilight - Universal Components Ltd
Unilin - Meyer Timber Limited
Uniline - Rangemaster
Unimaster - Donaldson Filtration (GB) Ltd
Unimate - Quartet-GBC UK Ltd/ ACCO UK Ltd
UniMini - HAGS SMP
UNINEP - TORMAX United Kingdom Ltd
Union - ASSA ABLOY Limited
Union - Mul-T-Lock
Union - Olby H E & Co Ltd
Union Jack Label Fittings - Daro Uk Ltd Partners to both Blum & Hafele
Uniperf - United Wire Ltd
Unipipe - Uponor Ltd
Uniplant - Witham Oil & Paint Ltd
UniPlay - HAGS SMP
Unislate - BLM British Lead
Unistrut - Kem Edwards Ltd
Unistrut - Unistrut Limited
Unit Swimming Pools - J W Green Swimming Pools Ltd
Unitas - Witham Oil & Paint Ltd
Uni-Trex - Terrapin Ltd
Unity Expandable Aluminium Door & Glazing Frames - Avanti Systems
UniVent – Natural Smoke Control System - SCS Group
Universal - Matki plc
Universal Louvre - Colt International
Universal range of rainwater products - Marshall-Tufflex Ltd
Uniwall - Hanson Concrete Products
Uno - Becker (SLIDING PARTITIONS) Ltd
Upat - Artur Fischer (UK) Ltd
UPE - Tyco Water Works
UPM - Meyer Timber Limited
Upton - Hamworthy Heating Limited & ACV UK
Upton Door - AS Newbould Ltd
Uraflex - SCP Concrete Sealing Technology Ltd
Urban - TBS Amwell Ltd
Uretek - Uretek (UK) Ltd
USDA - High Efficiency warm air heaters - AmbiRad Ltd
uSee - Helvar Ltd
USVR - Watts Industries UK Ltd
Utiform - Schwing Stetter (UK) Ltd
Utility Elite Lift - Phoenix Lifting Systems Ltd
Utility Lift - Phoenix Lifting Systems Ltd
UV Dermagard - Bonwyke Ltd
UV Free Lighting - Encapsulite International Ltd

V

V B Johnson - V B Johnson LLP
V Gard Vapour Control Layer - Firestone Building Products
V100 PSM - Elster Metering Ltd
V2® (Re-Roofing Tiles) - Forticrete Roofing
V200 - Elster Metering Ltd
V210 - Elster Metering Ltd
V300 Master - Elster Metering Ltd
Vac Vac - Arch Timber Protection
Vacsol - Arch Timber Protection
Vacurain - John Davidson (Pipes) Ltd
VAIO - Kaldewei
Valiant - Laird Security Hardware
Valley - Iles Waste Systems
Valspar - Akzo Noble Coatings Ltd
Valtek - Flowserve Flow Control
Valtti - Valtti ltd
Valves - Horstmann Controls Ltd
Vandalene ® - Coo-Var Ltd
Vandex BB75 - Safeguard Europe Ltd - Safeguard Europe Ltd
Vandex Super - Safeguard Europe Ltd - Safeguard Europe Ltd
Vandex Unimortar - Safeguard Europe Ltd - Safeguard Europe Ltd
Vandgard® - Anti-Climb Guards Ltd
Vanera (bedhead lamps) - Brandon Medical
Vanguard - Benlowe Group Limited
Vanities Range - TBS Amwell Ltd
Vanodine - Evans Vanodine International PLC
Vanquisher - Heckmondwicke FB
VAPAC® - Eaton-Williams Group Limited
Vapourguard - Trade Sealants Ltd
Varde - Gazco
Vari-Ceat - Ellis Patents
Varicool Spectra - LTI Advanced Systems Technology Ltd
Variflow - Grosvenor Pumps Ltd
Varihi - Emmerich (Berlon) Ltd
Vari-Level - Wade International Ltd
Varilift - Arvin Motion Control Ltd
Vario - Kompan Ltd
Vario - RTD Systems Ltd
VARIO - Wall formwork - PERI Ltd
Vario seating, Venue seating - CPS Manufacturing Co
Vari-Purpose - FC Frost Ltd
Varitone - IAC Acoustic Company UK Ltd
Varitrans - Style Door Systems Ltd
Varmax - Hamworthy Heating Limited & ACV UK
Vasura - Erlau AG
VCD - Naco
V-CHR - K. V. Radiators
V-Clix Light Fittings - Vianen KVS BV
VDC - Motorised Air Products Ltd
VE Enclosed Home Lift - Wessex Lift Co Ltd
VEA - Vitreous Enamel Association, The
VECTOR - Vantrunk Engineering Ltd
Vedette - Helmsman
Vedette Specialized range - Helmsman
Vee - Project Office Furniture PLC
VeeBee Filtration - Barr & Wray Ltd
Vega - UTC Fire & Securites
VELFAC - DOVISTA UK LTD
Velocity - Komfort Workspace PLC
Velopa - Autopa Ltd
Velour carpet tiles fibre bonded - Burmatex Ltd
Velux - Tidmarsh & Sons
Velux - VELUX Co Ltd, The
Venetian - Symphony Group PLC, The
Veneto xf2 - Tarkett Ltd
Vent A Matic - Simon R W Ltd
VENTATEC - Knauf AMF Ceilings Ltd
Ventform - Cordek Ltd
Ventform - Jablite Ltd
Venti Seal - Trelleborg Sealing Profiles Germany GmbH
Ventmaster AG - Docherty New Vent Chimney Group
Ventrolla - Durable Ltd
Ventrolla Perimeter Sealing System - Ventrolla Ltd
Ventrolla Sash Removal System - Ventrolla Ltd
VENTSAIR - Monodraught Ltd
Ventuno - Ideal-Standard Ltd
Ventura - McKenzie-Martin Ltd
Venture Parry - Bernlite Ltd
Venvaer - SE Controls
Verco - Verco Office Furniture Ltd
Verena - Deceuninck Ltd
Verges - Zon International
Verine - BFM Europe Limited
Vermeer - Vermeer United Kingdom
Vermiculux - Promat UK Ltd
Vermont - Deceuninck Ltd
Vernacare - Verna Ltd
Vernagene - Verna Ltd
Veronastone Assimilated Limestone - Marble Flooring Spec. Ltd
Versaline - Lewden Electrical Industries
Versalite - Black Cat Music
Versalite - Righton Ltd
Versalux - Cooper Lighting
VersaTank - CST Industries, Inc. - UK
Versatemp - Clivet UK Ltd
Versiplan - Becker (SLIDING PARTITIONS) Ltd
Verti-Frame - Hi-Store Ltd
Vescent - Ulster Carpet Mills Ltd
VESDA - Xtralis
Vesselpak - Flamco UK Ltd
Vestos - Arch Timber Protection
Vetcare™ - Steel Line Ltd
Vetec - Vianen KVS BV
Vetex - Tata Steel Europe Limited
Vetter UK - Vetter UK
Vex - UTC Fire & Securites
V-Gard - MSA (Britain) Ltd
Viajoint 'D' Expansion Ioint - Pitchmastic PmB Ltd
Vianergy - Vianen KVS BV
Vibro - Keller Ground Engineering
Victaulic - Midland Tube and Fabrications
Victaulic - Victaulic Systems
Victoria - Vianen KVS BV
Victoriana Cast Iron Radiators - AEL
Victory - PCT Group
Vicuclad - Promat UK Ltd
Viewpoint - Pryorsign
Vigilante - Blick Communication Systems Ltd
Vigilon - Gent Limited
Viking - Girbau UK ltd
Villa - Kompan Ltd
Village Stone - CEMEX
Vilter - Emerson Climate Technologies
Vinadac - Dacrylate Paints Ltd
Vintage Collection - Masterframe Windows Ltd
Vinyllon - Dixon Turner Wallcoverings
Viper spike® - Jackson H S & Son (Fencing) Ltd
Viroc - FGF Ltd
Visage - Valor
Viscacid - Kenyon Group Ltd
Viscount Cast Iron Radiators - AEL
Visedge - Howe Green Ltd
Vision Series - Radianr rube heaters - AmbiRad Ltd
Visit Range - Twyford Bathrooms
Visofold - Smart Systems Ltd
Visoglide - Smart Systems Ltd
Visoline - Smart Systems Ltd
Visqueen - Visqueen Building Products
vista - Bushboard Limited
Vista - Delta Balustrades
Vista - Dunhams of Norwich
Vista - Fabrikat (Nottingham) Ltd
Vista - Stocksigns Ltd
Vista modular systems - GB Sign Solutions Limited
Vista-Fix - Vista Engineering Ltd
Vistalux - Ariel Plastics Ltd
Vista-Plas - Vista Engineering Ltd
Visual Surveillance Systems - Vador Security Systems Ltd
Visualdirect - The Visual Systems Healthcare
Vitachem - Vita Liquid Polymers Ltd
Vitaplas - Vita Liquid Polymers Ltd
Vitopan Steel Clean - Kleen-Tex Industries Ltd
Vitra - R J Stokes & Co Limited
Vitra - Swedecor
Vitra - Vitra (UK) Ltd
Vitram - Evans Concrete Products Ltd
Vitramesh - Cadisch MDA
Vitrogres - Arnull Bernard J & Co Ltd
Vittera - Switch2 Energy Solutions Ltd
Vivak - Amari Plastics Plc
VKH - Motorised Air Products Ltd
V-Kool - Northgate Solar Controls
VLT ® - Danfoss Ltd
VM Open Home Lift - Wessex Lift Co Ltd
Vmag - Hawker Siddley Switchgear
Voidak - Dunham Bush Ltd
Vokes - Vokes Air
Voltan - Townscape Products Ltd
Volumeter - Gebhardt Kiloheat
Volute - Benlowe Stairs
Volvo Compact Equipment - Chippindale Plant Ltd
Von Duprin Exit Devices - Relcross Ltd
Vormatic - RB UK Ltd
Vortax - Axial - Howden Buffalo
Vor-Tec™ - Lotus Water Garden Products Ltd
Vortex - Unifix Ltd
Vortex - Water Technology Engineering Ltd
Vortibreak® - Franklin Hodge Industries Ltd
VortX - Saint-Gobain PAM UK
Vossloh Schwabe - Bernlite Ltd
VPX LN/RR - Babcock Wanson Uk Ltd
VR90 Timber Repair - Ventrolla Ltd
VSoL® - Asset International Ltd
VSS - Vador Security Systems Ltd
Vtech - Vantrunk Engineering Ltd
Vulcaboard - Vulcan Cladding Systems
Vulcalap - Vulcan Cladding Systems
Vulcalucent - Vulcan Cladding Systems
Vulcan - Ellis Patents
Vulcan - Tuke & Bell Ltd
Vulcan Tank - CST Industries, Inc. - UK
Vulcascot Floor Laid Flexible Cable Protectors - Vulcascot Cable Protectors Ltd
Vulcatuf - Vulcan Cladding Systems
Vyflex - Plastic Coatings Ltd
Vylon Plus - Tarkett Ltd

W

W/A formwork plywood - Wood International Agency Ltd
W/A pine doors - Wood International Agency Ltd
W20 - Clement Steel Windows
W20 Range Steel Windows - Monk Metal Windows Ltd
W40 - Clement Steel Windows
W40 Range Steel Windows - Monk Metal Windows Ltd
Wachenfeld - Spiral Construction Ltd
Wacker Silicones - Notcutt Ltd
Wade - Wade International Ltd
Waldor - Howe Green Ltd
wales and wales - Wales & Wales
Walker Timber Frame - Walker Timber Ltd
Walksafe - McKenzie-Martin Ltd
WalkSafe® - Latchways plc
Wall panels - Saint-Gobain Ecophon Ltd
Wall Shield - Springvale E P S
Wall Tile Collection - Solus Ceramics Ltd
Wallmate - Dow Building Solutions
Wallsorba - Soundsorba Ltd
Wallsorption - Bicester Products Ltd
Walltalker - Tektura Plc
Walraven - Kem Edwards Ltd
Walther - Barloworld Vacuum Technology Plc
Wamsler - Gazco
WAP - Nilfisk Limited
Warm Air Cabinet Heaters - Radiant Services Ltd
Warm Air Unit Heaters - Radiant Services Ltd
Warm Squeez - Springvale E P S
Warm Touch - HEWI UK Ltd
Warmafloor - Warmafloor (GB) Ltd
WarmCair - Johnson & Starley
warmerwall - Peter Cox Ltd
Warmsafe LST - Dunham Bush Ltd
Warmskark - Springvale E P S
Warren G-V - Radiodetection Ltd
Warrior - Glasdon U.K. Limited
Warwick - Benlowe Stairs
Wascator - Electrolux Laundry Systems
Wash-Horse - Kleen-Tex Industries Ltd
Washroom Control - Cistermiser Ltd
Wasteflo - Stuart Turner Ltd
Wastematic Bench Mounted - Max Appliances Ltd
Wastematic Free Standing - Max Appliances Ltd
Wastematic Sink Mounted - Max Appliances Ltd
Watchman - Kingspan Environmental Ltd
Waterco - Golden Coast Ltd
Watercolours - Ulster Carpet Mills Ltd
Watergem - Franke Sissons Ltd
Water-Horse - Kleen-Tex Industries Ltd
Waterless Urinals - Relcross Ltd
Waterseal - Sealocrete PLA Ltd
Watertight - Laticrete International Inc. UK
Watrous - FC Frost Ltd
Wauderer-Castle care-tech - Pyronix
Wavespan - Flexible Reinforcements Ltd
Wavetec - Cadisch MDA
Waylite 800 - Cooper Lighting
WBB Minerals - Sibelco UK Ltd
Weather Safe - Kronospan Ltd
Weather Ten - Exitex Ltd
Weatherbeta - Naco
Weatherbeta 24 - Naco
Weathercor/F - Polypipe Building Products
Weatherfin - Ventrolla Ltd
Weathershield - AkzoNobel Decorative Paints UK
Weathershield - The No Butts Bin Company (NBB), Trading as NBB Outdoor Shelters
WeatherTone - Vulcan Cladding Systems
Weatherwhite - Cardale Garage Doors
Weatherwood - Cardale Garage Doors
Weavespread - Flexible Reinforcements Ltd
Weavetop - Flexible Reinforcements Ltd
Web wall - ABG Ltd
Weber Building solutions - Weber Building Solutions
Weber cem - Weber Building Solutions
Weber certite - Weber Building Solutions
Weber cote - Weber Building Solutions
Weber fix - Weber Building Solutions
Weber Joint - Weber Building Solutions
Weber mulsifix - Weber Building Solutions
Weber Pral - Weber Building Solutions
Weber rent - Weber Building Solutions
Weber Set - Weber Building Solutions
Weber tec - Weber Building Solutions
WebRTU - EnergyICT Ltd
Weep - Airflow (Nicoll Ventilators) Ltd
Weger Air Handling Units - Thermal Technology Sales Ltd
WEHA - Harbro Supplies Ltd
Weigh-tronix - Phoenix Scales Ltd
Welcome - Enable Access
Weldmesh - Betafence Limited
Wellington - BF Bassett & Findley
Welmade - Q.M.P
Wenger V-Room - Black Cat Music
Wensleydale - Carpets of Worth Ltd
Wernick - Wernick Group Ltd
Wessex - Multitex GRP LLP
Wessex ModuMax - Hamworthy Heating Limited & ACV UK
Wessex, Woodrite - Acorn Garage Doors Ltd
West Pennine Gritstone - Johnsons Wellfield Quarries Ltd
West System - Wessex Resins & Adhesives Ltd
West System Epoxy - Wessex Resins & Adhesives Ltd
Westbrick - Ibstock Brick Ltd
Westclox - General Time Europe
Westdale - Chiltern Invadex
Westerland - Cembrit Ltd
Westman Systems - M.J. Electronic Services (International) Ltd
Westminster - Branson Leisure Ltd
Weston Fencing - Grange Fencing Limited
WF - Westbury Filters Limited
WF1 - Westbury Filters Limited
WFB - Westbury Filters Limited
WFC - Westbury Filters Limited
WFF - Westbury Filters Limited
WFG - Westbury Filters Limited
WFH HEPA - Westbury Filters Limited
WFK - Westbury Filters Limited
WFR - Movement Joints (UK)
WFV - Westbury Filters Limited
Whirlwind - Envirodoor Markus Ltd
Whispair - Xpelair Ltd
WHITE BOOK - British Gypsum Ltd
Whitehill - Whitehill Spindle Tools Ltd
Whiterock Doors - Altro Ltd
Whiterock PVC Ceiling system - Altro Ltd
Whiterock PVC Sport Cladding - Altro Ltd
Whitestar - BLV Licht-und Vakuumtecnik
WHS - Spear & Jackson
Wicanders - Amorim Cork Flooring
Widra - Metal Wire Plaster & Render Beads - Bekaert Building Products
Wilclo - Clow Group Ltd
Wildgoose - Derby Timber Supplies
Wilka Locks & Cylinders - JB Architectural Ltd
Wilkinson's Furniture - Carleton Furniture Group Ltd
Williams Lea Group - tso shop
Williams Lea Tag - tso shop
Wilo SE - Wilo Samson Pumps Ltd
Wilo Top E - Wilo Samson Pumps Ltd
Wilo Top S - Wilo Samson Pumps Ltd
Wilo Top SD - Wilo Samson Pumps Ltd
Wilotekt-Plus - Axter Ltd
Wilson & Garden - Spaceright Europe Limited
Wilsonart - Wilsonart Ltd
Win Drive - TORMAX United Kingdom Ltd
Winchester - BSA Machine Tools Ltd
Winchester - Sidhil Care
Wincro - Wincro Metal Industries Ltd
WINDCATCHER® - Monodraught Ltd
Windoline - Celuform Building Products
Window and Door Security Systems - Rolflex Doors Ltd
Window Care Systems - Repair care International
Windowgard - Gilgen Door Systems UK Ltd
Windowmaster Screws - UK Fasteners Ltd
Windsor - DW Windsor Lighting
Windsor Water Fittings - Deva Tap Co Ltd
Wing - Illuma Lighting
Wings - Bisley Office Equipment
Winther Browne & Co Ltd - Winther Browne & co Ltd
Wiremaster - Philips Lighting Solutions
Wiring Regulations - The Institution of Engineering and Technology
Wiring Regulations Bookshop - Professional Books Limited
WirralRange - AS Newbould Ltd
Wisa-Deck - Schauman (UK) Ltd
Wise by Amorim - Amorim Cork Flooring
Wise Cork - Amorim Cork Flooring
Wise Wood - Amorim Cork Flooring
Wispa Hoist - Chiltern Invadex
WMA - Wallcovering Manufacturers Association (now part of the British Coatings Federation)
WMS - Avocet Hardware Ltd
Woco - Witham Oil & Paint Ltd
Wolfin - Pitchmastic PmB Ltd
Wonderex - Optex (Europe) Ltd
Wondertrack - Optex (Europe) Ltd
Wonderwall - Hanson Building Products
Wood Symetra - Knauf AMF Ceilings Ltd
Wooden Lockers - Helmsman
Woodgrip - Pedley Furniture International Ltd
Woodhead Natural York Stone - Johnsons Wellfield Quarries Ltd
Woodland - Neptune Outdoor Furniture Ltd
Woodman Twist - Brockway Carpets Ltd
Woodro - Hille Educational Products Ltd
Woods - Hamilton R & Co Ltd
Woodscape - Woodscape Ltd
Woodsorption - Bicester Products Ltd
Woodstock Accent - Adam Carpets Ltd
Woodstock Classic - Adam Carpets Ltd
Woodworks - Interfloor Limited
Worcester - The BSS Group

W (con't)

Work-Safe-Matting - Olley & Sons Ltd, C
Workspace - Paragon by Heckmondwike
World hand dryers - Warner Howard Group Ltd
Worldspan - Clow Group Ltd
Wormald Ansul - Tyco Fire and Integrated Solutions
Worrall - Guardian Lock & Engineering Co. Ltd
Woven - Cadisch MDA
WP Wallpack - Consult Lighting Ltd
WPIF - Wood Panels Industries Federation
WSC - Wallcovering Sector Council - see - Wallcovering Manufacturers Association (now part of the British Coatings Federation)
WSG Donn Floors - Hatmet Limited
WTIF - Wall Tie Installers Federation
WW - Workwalls - Staverton (UK) Ltd
www.constructionjobsuk.com - Contract Journal
www.contractjournal.com - Contract Journal
www.electrolux.com/laundrysystems - Electrolux Laundry Systems
Wyre Forest - Adam Carpets Ltd
Wyvern Fireplaces - Wyvern Marlborough Ltd

X

XC - Harkness Screens
Xena - Marflow Eng Ltd
Xenex - CEMEX
Xenex - Gent Limited
Xenon, Xira - Samuel Heath & Sons plc
Xerra - Girsberger London
Xetex - Electrix International Ltd
XFP addressable fire panels - C-TEC (Computionics) Ltd
X-Frame Picnic Suite - Branson Leisure Ltd
Xinox - Franke Sissons Ltd
XLight - Porcelanosa Group Ltd
X-Line - AudiocomPendax Ltd
XLnt - Hunter Douglas Architectural Ltd
Xodus - Xpelair Ltd
XP95 - Apollo Fire Detectors Ltd
XP95 Intrinsically safe - Apollo Fire Detectors Ltd
Xtraflex - Adaptaflex Ltd
Xtraflo Rainwater System - FloPlast Ltd
Xtralift - Stannah Lifts Ltd
Xtralis - Xtralis
Xtreme - Harkness Screens
XXL Sliding Wall - Parthos UK Ltd

Y

Yale - ASSA ABLOY Limited
Yale - Carl F Groupco Limited
Yale - Olby H E & Co Ltd
Yale - Yale Security Products Ltd
YBS - Allmat (East Surrey) Ltd
Yeoman - Gazco
Yeoman Custom mouldings - Harrison Thompson & Co Ltd
Yeoman Formula One seating - Harrison Thompson & Co Ltd
Yeoman Rainguard - Harrison Thompson & Co Ltd
Yeoman Shield total surface protection - Harrison Thompson & Co Ltd
YeomanShield Total Surface Protection - Moffett Thallon & Co Ltd
Ygnette - Wellman Robey Ltd
Ygnis - Wellman Robey Ltd
Ykrlin Automobile Car Turntable - British Turntable Ltd
Yoke System - S & B Ltd
York - Architectural Textiles Ltd
York - Johnson Controls Building Efficiency UK Ltd
York Wilton - Ulster Carpet Mills Ltd
Yorkex - Yorkshire Copper Tube
Yorkshire - The BSS Group
Yorkshire - Yorkshire Copper Tube
Yorkshire stove - Dunsley Heat Ltd
Youngman - Youngman Group Limited
Ytong - Xella Aircrete Systems UK

Z

Zampano - Girsberger London
Zannussi - Electrolux Domestic Appliances
Zaun fencing - Chestnut Products Limited
ZD - Staverton (UK) Ltd
Zedex - Visqueen Building Products
Zeeland - Cembrit Ltd
Zehnder - Alumline, Carboline, Multicolumn, Radiavector, ZFP & ZIP - Zehnder Group UK Ltd
Zenith Club Class - Brintons Ltd
Zenith Range; Bollard, Seat, Litter Bin & Ash Waste Bin, Cycle Stand, Signage - Furnitubes International Ltd
Zerodec - Gillespie (UK) Ltd
Zeta - Zon International
Zeta II - Cooper Lighting
Zeta Lock - Brett Landscaping
ZFP addressable fire panels - C-TEC (Computionics) Ltd
Zig Zag - Zarges (UK) Ltd
Zinco - Alumasc Exterior Building Products Ltd
Zingo - HAGS SMP
Zink Gutta - Metal Gutta
Zone: 1 - Youngman Group Limited
Zoneguard - Hoyles Electronic Developments Ltd
Zsolnay - LSA Projects Ltd
Zuccini - Legrand Electric Ltd
ZV1 - K. V. Radiators
ZV2 - K. V. Radiators
Zwick Mail Boxes - JB Architectural Ltd
Zykon - Artur Fischer (UK) Ltd

COMPANY INFORMATION

3d Storage Systems (UK) LTD - Suite 1, 30 Station Road, Ossett, Wakefield, West Yorkshire. WF5 8AD tel:(01924) 240291, fax:(01924) 261677. sales@3dlockers.co.uk, http://www.3dlockers.co.uk

3M - 3M Centre, Cain Road, Bracknell. RG12 8HT tel:(08705) 360036. commcareuk@mmm.com, www.3m.co.uk

A

A & G Structures Ltd - Unit 38, Longshot Lane Industrial Estate, Bracknell, Berkshire. RG12 1RL tel:(01344) 485085, fax:(01344) 411359. enquiries@aandgstructures.co.uk, www.aandgstructures.co.uk

A Kenrick & Sons - Union Street, West Bromwich, W. Midlands. B70 6BD tel:(0121) 500 3266, fax:(0121) 500 6332. sales@kenricks.co.uk, www.kenricks.co.uk

A. F Jones (Stonemasons) - 33, Bedford Road, Reading, Berkshire. RG1 7EX tel:(0118) 957 3537. info@afjones.co.uk, www.afjones.co.uk

AAC Waterproofing Ltd - Industrial Estate, Gaerwen, Anglesey, North Wales. LL60 6HR tel:(01248) 421 955. info@aacwaterproofing.co.uk, www.aacwaterproofing.co.uk

Aardee Security Shutters Ltd - 5 Dalsholm Ave, Dawsholm Industrial Estate, Glasgow. G20 0TS tel:(0141) 810 3444. sales@aardee.co.uk, www.aardee.co.uk

Aardvark Transatlantic Ltd - 106 New Road, Ascot. SL5 8QH tel:(01344) 882 314, fax:(01334) 884 506. sweeks7956@aol.com, www.srindustrial.co.uk

Aaztec Cubicles - Becklands Close, Bar Lane, Roecliffe, Boroughbridge, N. Yorks. YO51 9NR tel:(01423) 326400, fax:(01423) 325115. sales@aaztec.com, www.aaztec.com

Abacus Lighting Ltd - Oddicroft Lane, Sutton-in-Ashfield, Notts. NG17 5FT tel:(01623) 511111, fax:(01623) 552133. sales@abacuslighting.com, www.abacuslighting.com

ABB Installation Products Ltd - Bruntcliffe Lane, Morley, Leeds, W. Yorks. LS27 9LL tel:(0113) 281 0600. enquiryuk@tnb.com, https://new.abb.com/low-voltage/products/lighting-emergency-lighting/emergency-lighting/emergi-lite

ABB Instrumentation Ltd - Howard Road, Eaton Socon, St. Neots, Huntingdon. PE19 3EU tel:(0808) 258 2000. info@gb.abb.com, www.abb.com

Abbey Nameplates - Beech Court, 127 Haslemere Road, Liphook, Hampshire. GU30 7BX tel:(0800) 092 3317, fax:(0800) 056 1362. abbeynameplates@gmail.com, www.abbeynameplates.co.uk

Abel Alarm Co Ltd - Detection House, 4 Vaughan Way, Leicester. LE1 4ST tel:(0116) 265 4200. info@abelalarm.co.uk, www.abelalarm.co.uk

Abet Ltd - 70 Roding Road, London Industrial Park, London. E6 6LS tel:(020) 7473 6910. sales@abet.ltd.uk, https://uk.abetlaminati.com

ABG Ltd - Unit E7, Meltham Mills, Meltham Mills Road, Meltham, W. Yorks. HD9 4DS tel:(01484) 852096. enquiries@abgltd.com, www.abg-geosynthetics.com

Abloy UK - Portobello Works, School Street, Willenhall, West Midlands. WV13 3PW tel:(01902) 364500, fax:(01902) 364501. info@abloy.co.uk, www.abloy.co.uk

Accent Hansen - Cedar House, Sandbrook Business Park, Rochdale, Gt Man. OL11 1LQ tel:(0161) 284 4100, fax:(0161) 655 3119. sales@accenthansen.com, www.accenthansen.com

Access Industries Group Ltd - Edgeworth House, 20 High Street, Northchurch, Berkhampstead, Herts. HP4 3LS tel:(01442) 87 45 34, fax:(01442) 878525. sales@accessequipment.net, www.accessequipment.net

Ackermann Ltd - The Arnold Centre, Paycocke Road, Basildon, Essex. SS14 3EA tel:(01268) 563252, fax:(01268) 563437. ackermann.enquiries@honeywell.com, www.ackermann.co.uk

ACO Technologies plc - ACO Business Park, Hitchin Road, Shefford, Beds. SG17 5TE tel:(01462) 816666, fax:(01462) 815895. technologies@aco.co.uk, www.aco.co.uk

Acorn Garage Doors Ltd - Beckley Four Oaks, Near Rye, East Sussex. TN31 6RG tel:(01797) 260243, fax:(01797) 260504. contact@acorngaragedoorsltd.co.uk, www.acorngaragedoorsltd.co.uk

Acorn Powell Ltd - 5 Brearley Court, Baird Road Waterwells Business Park, Quedgeley, Gloucester, Gloucestershire. GL2 2AF tel:(01452) 721211, fax:(01452) 721231. sales@acornpowell.co.uk, www.acornpowell.co.uk

Acousticabs Industrial Noise Control Ltd - Unit 52, Heyford Road, Pocklington Ind Estate, Pocklington, York. YO42 1NR tel:(01759) 305266, fax:(01759) 305268. info@acousticabs.com, www.acousticabs.com

ACP (Concrete) Ltd - Risehow Industrial Estate, Firmby, Maryprot, Cumbria. CA15 8PD tel:(01900) 814659, fax:(01900) 816200. sales@acp-concrete.co.uk, www.acp-concrete.co.uk

ACP Concrete Limited - Wood Lane Business Centre, Wood Lane, Uttoxeter, Staffordshire. ST14 8JR tel:(01889) 598660, fax:(01889) 568160. sales@acp-concrete.co.uk, www.acp-concrete.co.uk

Actavo (UK) Ltd - Unit C, Cedar Court Office Park, Denby Dale Road, Calder Grove, Wakefield, West Yorkshire. WF4 3QZ tel:(01924) 416000, fax:(01924) 366250. info@actavo.com, www.actavo.com

Active Carbon Filters Ltd - Unit 4, Vickers Industrial Estate, Mellishaw Lane, Morecambe, Lancs. LA3 3EN tel:(01524) 383200, fax:(01524) 389438. info@activecarbonfilters.com, www.fengroup.com

Adam Carpets Ltd - Greenhill Works, Birmingham Road, Kidderminster, Worcs. DY10 2SH tel:(01562) 829966, fax:(01562) 751741. eprescott@adamcarpets.com, www.adamcarpets.com

Adams- Hydraulics Ltd - Unit B & E Spitfire House, Aviator Court, York, North Yorkshire. YO30 4UZ tel:(01782) 202300, fax:(01782) 203649. marketing@hambakergroup.com, www.adamshydraulics.co.uk

Adaptaflex Ltd - Station Road, Coleshill, Birmingham. B46 1HT tel:(01675) 468200, fax:(01675) 464930. www.adaptaflex.com

Addagrip Terraco Ltd - Addagrip House, Bell Lane Industrial Estate, Uckfield, Sussex. TN22 1QL tel:(01825) 761333. sales@addagrip.co.uk, www.addagrip.co.uk

Aden Hynes Sculpture Studios - Unit 3F Harvey Road, Nevendon Industrial Estate, Basildon, Essex. SS13 1DA tel:(01268) 726470. aden.hynes@hotmail.com, www.sculpturestudios.co.uk

Adex Interiors for industry Ltd - 5 Avebury Court, Mark Road, Hemel Hempstead, Herts. HP2 7TA tel:(01442) 232327. info@adex.co.uk, www.Adex.co.uk

Adshead Ratcliffe & Co Ltd - Derby Road, Belper, Derbyshire. DE5 1WJ tel:(01773) 826661, fax:(01773) 821215. arbo@arbo.co.uk, www.arbo.co.uk

ADT Fire and Security Plc - Security House, The Summmitt, Hanworth Road, Sunbury-on-Thames, Middx. TW16 5DB tel:(0344) 800 1999, fax:(01932) 743155. www.adt.co.uk

Advance Tapes International Ltd - Westmoreland, Thurmaston, Leics. LE4 8PH tel:(0116) 251 0191. sales@advancetapes.com, www.advancetapes.com

Advanced Air (UK) Ltd - Burell Way, Thetford, Norfolk. IP24 3QU tel:(01842) 762032. info@advancedair.co.uk, www.advancedair.co.uk

Advanced Hygienic Contracting Ltd - Unit A1 Greengate, Cardale Park, Harrogate, N. Yorks. HG3 1GY tel:(0330) 100 0313. sales@bioclad.com, www.cladding.co.uk

Advanced Interior Solutions Ltd - St Paul's House, Warwick Lane, London. EC4 7BP tel:(020) 7101 1177. enquiries@aisworkplace.com, https://www.ais-interiors.com/

Advanced Perimeter Systems Ltd - 16 Cunningham Road, Springkerse Ind Est, Stirling. FK7 7TP tel:(01786) 479862, fax:(01786) 470331. admin@apsltd.net, www.apsltd.net

Advisory, Conciliation and Arbitration Service - Euston Tower, 286 Euston Road, London. NW1 3DP tel:(08457) 474747. www.acas.org.uk

AEL - 4 Berkeley Court, Manor Park, Runcorn, Cheshire. WA7 1TQ tel:(01928) 579068, fax:(01928) 579523. sales@aelheating.com, www.aelheating.com

Aercon Consultants Ltd - 47 Anvil Terrace, Bexley Park, Dartford, Kent. DA2 7WR tel:(01268) 418822, fax:(01268) 418822. enquiries@aercon.com, www.aercon.com

AET.gb Ltd - 82 Basepoint, Andersons Road, Southampton, Hants. SO14 5FE tel:(08453) 700400. sales@aet.gb.com, www.aet.co.uk

Africa Roofing Uk - Sunnyhills Road, Barnfields, Staffordshire. ST13 5RJ tel:(01538) 398488, fax:(01538) 398456. sales@africaroofinguk.co.uk, www.africaroofinguk.co.uk

AGC Glass UK Ltd - Lumonics House, Valiant Office Suits, Valley Drive, Rugby, Warwickshire. CV21 1TQ tel:(01788) 535353, fax:(01788) 560853. andrea.marston@eu.agc.com, www.agc-yourglass.com

AGCO Ltd - Abbey Park, Stoneleigh, Kenilworth. CV8 2TQ tel:(024) 76 852 164, fax:(024) 76 851 172. shop@masseyferguson.com, www.agcocorp.com

Air Control Industries Ltd - Weycroft Avenue, Millwey Rise Industrial Estate, Axminister, Devon. EX13 5HU tel:(01297) 529 242, fax:(01297) 529 241. sales@aircontrolindustries.com, www.aircontrolindustries.com

Air Diffusion Ltd - Stourbridge Road, Bridgnorth, Shropshire. WV15 5BB tel:(01746) 761921, fax:(01746) 760127. sales@air-diffusion.co.uk, www.air-diffusion.co.uk

Aircare Europe Ltd - GVS Filter Technology UK, NFC House, Vickers Industrial Estate, Lancashire. LA3 3EN tel:(08707) 445588, fax:(01925) 850325. gvsuk@gvs.com, www.aircareeurope.com

Airdri Ltd - Technology House, Oakfield Industrial Est, Eynsham, Oxford. OX29 4AQ tel:(01865) 882330, fax:(01865) 881647. sales@airdri.com, www.airdri.com

Airedale International Air Conditioning Ltd - Leeds Road, Rawdon, Leeds. LS19 6JY tel:(0113) 239 1000, fax:(0113) 250 7219. connect@airedale.com, www.Airedale.com

Airflow (Nicoll Ventilators) Ltd - 15 Queen's Lane, Stem Lane Industrial Estate, New Milton, Hampshire. BH25 5NN tel:(01425) 611547. sales@airflow-vent.co.uk, www.airflow-vent.co.uk

Airflow Developments Ltd - Lancaster Road, Cressex Business Park, High Wycombe, Bucks. HP12 3QP tel:(01494) 525252. info@airflow.co.uk, www.airflow.co.uk

Airsprung Beds Ltd - Ladydown Industrial Estate, Canal Road, Trowbridge, Wilts. BA14 8RQ tel:(01225) 754411. contracts@airsprungbeds.co.uk, www.airsprungbeds.co.uk

Akzo Noble Coatings Ltd - Wexham Road, Slough, Berkshire. SL5 5DS tel:(01753) 550000. sikkens.advice@akzonobel.com, www.akzonobel.com

AkzoNobel Decorative Paints UK - Wexham Road, Slough, Berks. SL2 5DS tel:(01753) 691690, fax:(01753) 530336. john.ashford@akzonobel.com, www.duluxtrade.co.uk

Alanod Ltd - Chippenham Drive, Kingston, Milton Keynes. MK10 0AN tel:(01908) 282044. info@alanod.co.uk, www.alanod.co.uk

Albany Engineering Co Ltd - Church Road, Lydney, Glos. GL15 5EQ tel:(01594) 842275, fax:(01594) 842574. sales@albany-pumps.co.uk, www.albany.pumps.co.uk

Albany Standard Pumps - Richter Works, Garnett Street, Bradford, W. Yorks. BD3 9HB tel:(01274) 725351, fax:(01274) 742467. sales@albany-pumps.co.uk, www.albany-pumps.co.uk

Albion Manufacturing Ltd - Units 16 & 17 Turing Park, Potash Lane, Hethel, Norfolk. NR14 8QR tel:(01953) 605983, fax:(01953) 606764. sales@albionmanufacturing.com, www.albionmanufacturing.com

ALD Lighting Solutions - Unit 6E, Southbourne Business Park, Courtlands Road, Eastbourne, East Sussex. BN22 8UY tel:(01323) 729337, fax:(01323) 732356. sales@aldlighting.com, www.aldlighting.com

Aldous & Stamp (Services) Ltd - 86-90 Avenue Road, Beckenham, Kent. BR3 4SA tel:(020) 8659 1833, fax:(020) 8676 9679. sales@aldous-stamp.co.uk, www.aldous-stamp.co.uk

Alfresco Floors - Unit 6, Teddington Business Park, Station Road, Teddington. TW11 9BQ tel:(020) 8977 0904, fax:(020) 8977 0825. info@alfrescofloors.co.uk, www.alfrescofloors.co.uk

Alitex Ltd - Torbery Farm, South Harting, Petersfield. GU31 5RG tel:(01730) 826900, fax:(01730) 826901. enquiries@alitex.co.uk, www.alitex.co.uk

Allart, Frank, & Co Ltd - 15-35 Great Tindal Street, Ladywood, Birmingham. B16 8DR tel:(0121) 410 6000, fax:(0121) 410 6066. sales@frankallart.co.uk, www.allart.co.uk

Allaway Acoustics Ltd - 1 Queens Road, Hertford. SG14 1EN tel:(01992) 550825. enquiries@allawayacoustics.co.uk, www.allawayacoustics.co.uk

Allegion (UK) Ltd - 35 Rocky Lane, Aston, Birmingham, West Midlands. B6 5RQ tel:(0121) 3802454, fax:(0191) 335 2020. info@allegion.com, www.allegion.co.uk

Allen (Concrete) Ltd - 38 Willow Lane, Micham, Surrey. CR4 4NA tel:(020) 86872222. sales@allenconcrete.co.uk, www.allenconcrete.co.uk

Allen (Fencing) Ltd - Birch Walk, West Byfleet, Surrey. KT14 6EJ tel:(01932) 349607, fax:(01932) 354868. info@allenstps.com, www.allenstps.com

Allgood plc - 18 Holborn, London. EC1N 2LE tel:(020) 7387 9951. info@allgood.co.uk, www.allgood.co.uk

Allmat (East Surrey) Ltd - Kenley Treatment Works, Godstone Road, Kenley, Surrey. CR8 5AE tel:(020) 8668 6666, fax:(020) 8763 2110. info@allmat.co.uk, www.allmat.co.uk

Allsebrook Pump and Electrical Services Limited - Allsebrook Pumps, 5 Chesterholm, Bancroft, Milton Keynes, Bucks. MK13 0PG tel:(01491) 680628, fax:(01491) 682318. sales@allsebrookpumps.co.uk, www.allsebrookpump.co.uk

Alltype Fencing Specialists - Ye Wentes Wayes, High Road, Langdon Hills, Basildon, Essex. SS16 6HY tel:(01268) 545192. sales@alltypefencing.com, www.alltypefencing.com

Alpha Mosaic & Terrazzo Ltd - Unit 3, Munro Drive, Cline Road, London. N11 2LZ tel:(020) 8368 2230, fax:(020) 8368 2301. sales@romamarble.co.uk, www.romamarble.co.uk

Alpha Therm Ltd - Nepicar House, London Road, Wrotham Heath, Sevenoaks, Kent. TN15 7RS tel:(0344) 871 8760. info@alpha-innovation.co.uk, www.alpha-innovation.co.uk

Altecnic Ltd - Mustang Drive, Stafford, Staffordshire. ST16 1GW tel:(01785) 218200. sales@altecnic.co.uk, www.altecnic.co.uk

Althon Ltd - MAG Group Building, Vulcan Road South, Norwich, Norfolk. NR6 6AF tel:(01603) 488700, fax:(01603) 488598. sales@althon.co.uk, www.althon.co.uk

Altro Ltd - Head Office, Works Road, Letchworth, Herts. SG6 1NW tel:(01462) 489 516. enquiries@altro.co.uk, www.altro.co.uk

Aluline Precision Engineering Ltd - 60-62 Brindley Road, Astmoor, Runcorn, Cheshire. WA7 1PF tel:(01928) 563 532, fax:(01928) 582 224. enquiry@alulinegroup.com, www.alulinegms.com

Alumasc Exterior Building Products Ltd - White House Works, Bold Road, Sutton, St. Helens, Merseyside. WA9 4JG tel:(01744) 648400, fax:(01744) 648401. info@alumasc-exteriors.co.uk, www.alumasc-exteriors.co.uk

Alumasc Interior Building Products Limited - Halesfield 19, Telford, Shropshire. TF7 4QT tel:(01952) 580590, fax:(01952) 587805. sales@pendock.co.uk, www.pendock.co.uk

Alutec - Unit 1 (G-H), Elms Farm Industrial Estate, Bedford, Bedfordshire. MK41 0LZ tel:(01234) 359438. projects@marleyalutec.co.uk, www.marleyalutec.co.uk

Amadeus - Vantage Point, North Trade Road, Battle, East Sussex. TN33 9QU tel:(01424) 775867. info@amadeus-equipment.co.uk, http://www.amadeus-equipment.co.uk/

Amari Plastics Plc - Holmes House, 24-30 Baker Street, Weybridge, Surrey. KT13 8AU tel:(01932) 835000, fax:(01932) 835002. sales@amariplastics.com, www.amariplastics.com

Ambec Fencing - Hall Lane, Farnworth, Bolton, Lancashire. BL4 7QF tel:(01204) 574 011, fax:(01204) 861 653. sales@ambecfencing.co.uk, http://ambecfencing.co.uk/

Amberol Ltd - The Plantation, King Street, Alfreton, Derbys. DE55 7TT tel:(01773) 830930, fax:(01773) 834191. sales@amberol.co.uk, www.amberol.co.uk

AmbiRad Ltd - Fens Pool Avenue, Wallows Industrial Estate, Brierley Hill, W. Midlands. DY5 1QA tel:(01384) 489700, fax:(01384) 489707. www.reznor.eu

Amdega Ltd - Unit 7, North Orbital Commercial Park, St Albans. AL1 1XB tel:(0800) 652 7590, fax:(01325) 489209. info@amdega.co.uk, www.amegda.com

Amilake Southern Ltd - Penrose Road, Ferndown, Dorset. BH22 9FJ tel:(07857) 603031, fax:(01202) 891 716. info@amilakesouthern.co.uk, www.amilakesouthern.co.uk

AMK Fence-In Limited - Wallace Road, Parkwood Springs, Sheffield, Yorks. S3 9SR tel:(0114) 2739372, fax:(0114) 2739373. amkfencein@aol.com, www.amkfence-in.co.uk

Amorim Cork Flooring - R.Ribeirinho 202, 4536-907, Portugal. tel:+351 227475791. geral.ar@amorim.com, www.amorim.com

Ancon Limited - President Way, President Park, Sheffield, S. Yorks. S4 7UR tel:(0114) 275 5224, fax:(0114) 276 8543. info@ancon.co.uk, www.ancon.co.uk

Ancorite Surface Protection Ltd - Millbuck Way, Ettiley Heath, Sandbach, Cheshire. CW11 3AB tel:(01270) 761720, fax:(01270) 761697. david.clegg@ancorite.co.uk, www.ancorite.co.uk

A (con't)

Anders + Kern UK Ltd - Norderstedt House, James Carter Road, Mildenhall, Suffolk. IP28 7RQ tel:(01638) 510900. sales@anders-kern.co.uk, www.anders-kern.co.uk

Anderton Concrete Products Ltd - Anderton Wharf, Soot Hill, Anderton, Northwich, Cheshire. CW9 6AA tel:(0333) 234 3434. sales@andertonconcrete.co.uk, www.andertonconcrete.co.uk

Andrew Moor Associates - 14 Chamberlain Street, London. NW1 8XB tel:(020) 7586 8181, fax:(020) 7586 8484. andrew@andrewmoor.co.uk, www.andrewmoor.com

Andrews Coatings Ltd - Carver Building, Littles Lane, Wolverhampton, W. Midlands. WV1 1JY tel:(01902) 429190. info@andrewscoatings.co.uk, www.antigraffiti.co.uk

Andrews Sykes Hire Ltd - Premier House, Darlington Street, Wolverhampton, W. Midlands. WV1 4JJ tel:(01902) 328700, fax:(01902) 422466. info@andrews-sykes.com, www.andrew-sykes.com

Andrews Sykes Hire Ltd - St David's Court, Union Street, Wolverhampton, W. Midlands. WV1 3JE tel:(0800) 211 611. info@andrews-sykes.com, www.andrews-sykes.com

Andura Coatings Ltd - 20 Murdock Road, Bicester, Oxon. OX26 4PP tel:(01869) 240374, fax:(01869) 240375. info@andura.co.uk, www.andura.com

Andy Thornton Ltd - Rosemount, Huddersfield Road, Elland, West Yorkshire. HX5 0EE tel:(01422) 376000, fax:(01422) 376060. marketing@andythornton.com, www.andythornton.com

Anglepoise Lighting Ltd - Unit 51, Enfield Industrial Area, Redditch, Worcs. B97 6DR tel:(01527) 63771, fax:(01527) 61232. hello@anglepoise.com, www.anglepoise.com

Anglian Building Products - 59 Hurricane Way, Norwich, Norfolk. NR6 6JB tel:(01603) 428455, fax:(01603) 420500. contact@angliangroup.com, www.anglianhome.co.uk

Anglo Building Products Ltd - Branksome House, Filmer Grove, Godalming, Surrey. GU7 3AB tel:(01483) 427777. r.nivison@rust-oleum.eu, https://www.rust-oleum.eu/products/by-brand/anglo-building-products/

Angus Fire - Haddenham Business Park, Pegasus Way, Haddenham - Aylesbury, Buckinghamshire. HP17 8LB tel:(01844) 293600, fax:(01844) 293664. general.enquiries@angusuk.co.uk, www.angusfire.co.uk

Anixter (UK) Ltd - 1 York Road, Uxbridge, Middx. UB8 1RN tel:(01895) 818138. contact.europe@anixter.com, www.anixter.co.uk

Anti-Climb Guards Ltd - PO Box 127, Winchelsea, East Sussex. TN8 6WY tel:(01797) 229872, fax:(01797) 229872. Exec@vanDGard.co.uk, www.vandgard.co.uk

APA - Youlditch Barns, Peter Tavy, Tavistock, Devon. PL19 9LY tel:(01822) 810187/8, fax:(01822) 810189. sales@alanpow.co.uk, www.alanpow.co.uk

Aperam Stainless Services & Solutions UK Limited - 9 Midland Way, Barlborough Links, Barlborough, Derbyshire. S43 4XA tel:(01246) 571660. david.barker@aperam.com, www.aperam.com

Apollo Fire Detectors Ltd - 36 Brookside Road, Havant, Hants. PO9 1JR tel:(023) 92492412, fax:(023) 9249 2754. enquiries@apollo-fire.co.uk, www.apollo-fire.co.uk

Applied Felts Ltd - Castle Bank Mills, Portobello Road, Wakefied, W. Yorks. WF1 5PS tel:(01924) 200535, fax:(01924) 366951. sales@appliedfelts.co.uk, www.appliedfelts.com

Apropos Conservatories Ltd - Greenside House, Richmond Street, Ashton-under-Lyne, Lancs. OL6 7ES tel:(0800) 328 0033. info@aproposuk.com, https://aproposconservatories.co.uk/

APS Masonry Ltd - APS Masonry, Osney Mead, Oxford, Oxfordshire. OX2 0EQ tel:(01865) 254600. enquiries@apsmasonry.com, www.apsmasonry.com

APT Controls Ltd - Unit 1 Maxted Corner, Maxted Road, Hemel Hempstead. HP2 7RA tel:(020) 8421 2411, fax:(020) 8421 3951. webenquiries@aptcontrols.co.uk, www.aptcontrols.co.uk

Aqua-Blue Designs - The Studio, 47 Flexford Close, Chandlers Ford, Hampshire. SO53 5RY tel:(02380) 260888. mc@aquabluedesigns.net, www.aquabluedesigns.net

Aqualisa Products - The Flyer's Way, Westerham, Kent. TN16 1DE tel:(01959) 560000, fax:(01959) 560030. sales.admin@aqualisa.co.uk, www.aqualisa.co.uk

Aquasentry - Unit 2 Britannia Mills, Gelderd Road, Birstall, West Yorkshire. WF17 9QD tel:(01924) 284900, fax:(01924) 284911. info@aquasentry.co.uk, www.aquasentry.co.uk

Aquastat Ltd - Unit N, The Old Parlour, Purn House Farm, Bleadon, Weston-Super-Mare, North Somerset. BS24 0QE tel:(01934) 811264. enquiries@aquastat.co.uk, www.aquastat.co.uk

Arch Timber Protection - Wheldon Road, Castleford, W. Yorks. WF10 2JT tel:(01977) 71400, fax:(01977) 714001. advice@archchemicals.com, www.archtp.com

Architectural Association - 36 Bedford Square, London. WCIB 3ES tel:(0207) 8874090. development1@aaschool.ac.uk, www.aaschool.ac.uk

Architectural Plastics (Handrail) Ltd - Unit One, Saint Roberts Mews, Harrogate, N. Yorks. HG1 1HR tel:(01423) 561852. info@architecturalplastics.co.uk, www.architecturalplastics.co.uk

Architectural Textiles Ltd - Kemp House, City Road, London. EC1V 2NX tel:(020) 7079 4329. sales@architecturaltextiles.co.uk, www.architecturaltextiles.co.uk

Architen Landrell Associates Ltd - Station Road, Chepstow, Monmouthshire. NP16 5PF tel:(01291) 638200, fax:(01291) 621991. mail@architen.com, www.architen.com

Ardex UK Ltd - Homefield Road, Haverhill, Suffolk. CB9 8QP tel:(01440) 714939, fax:(01440) 716640. info@ardex.co.uk, www.ardex.co.uk

Aremco Products - Units 1 & 2 Penn Industrial Estate, Providence Street, Cradley Heath, W. Midlands. B64 5DJ tel:(01384) 566222, fax:(01384) 412209. sales@aremco-products.co.uk, www.aremcobarriers.co.uk

Ariel Plastics Ltd - Speedwell Ind. Est, Staveley, Derbys. S34 3JP tel:(01246) 281111, fax:(01246) 561111. info@arielplastics.com, www.arielplastics.com

ArjoHuntleigh UK - ArjoHuntleigh House, Houghton Hall Business Park, Houghton Regis, Bedfordshire. LU5 5XF tel:(01582) 413104. sales.admin@ArjoHuntleigh.com, www.ArjoHuntleigh.co.uk

Arkema France - 429 rue d'Estienne d'Orves, 92705 Colombes Cedex. FRANCE tel:(0121) 7434811, fax:(0121) 7434811. ken.griffiths@arkema.com, www.arkema.com

Arkinstall Galvanizing Ltd - Barn Street, Birmingham, W. Midlands. B5 5QD tel:(0121) 522 0500. info@galvanizing.co.uk, www.galvanizing.co.uk

Armes, Williams, Ltd - Armes Trading Estate, Cronard Road, Sudbury, Suffolk. CO10 6XB tel:(01787) 372988. sales@william-armes.co.uk

Armitage Shanks Ltd - The Bathroom Works, National Avenue, Kinston Upon Hull. HU5 4HS tel:(01543) 413204. productinfo@idealspec.co.uk, www.idealspec.co.uk

Armortec - Quarryfields, Ruthin, Denbighshire. LL15 2UG tel:(01824) 709102, fax:(01824) 709 105. info@armortec.co.uk, www.armortec.co.uk

Armstrong (Concrete Blocks), Thomas, Ltd - Whinfield Industrial Estate, Rowlands Gill, Tyne & Wear. NA39 1EH tel:(01207) 544214, fax:(01207) 542761. blocks@thomasarmstrong.co.uk, www.xlomasarmstrong.co.uk

Armstrong (Timber), Thomas, Ltd - Workington Road, Flimby, Maryport, Cumbria. CA15 8RY tel:(01900) 68211, fax:(01900) 602672. timber@thomasarmstrong.co.uk, www.thomasarmstrong.co.uk

Armstrong Floor Products UK Ltd - Hitching Court, Abingdon Business Park, Abingdon, Oxon. OX14 1RB tel:(01235) 554 848, fax:(01235) 553 583. sales-support@armstrong.com, www.armstrong-europe.com

Armstrong Integrated Ltd - Wenlock Way, Manchester. M12 5JL tel:(0161) 223 2223, fax:(0161) 220 9660. salesuk@armlink.com, www.armstrongpumps.com

Armstrong World Industries Ltd - Harman House 2nd Floor, George Street, Uxbridge, Middlesex. UB8 1QQ tel:(0800) 371849, fax:(01895) 274287. sales_support@armstrong.com, www.armstrong-ceilings.co.uk

Arnold Wragg Ltd - Unit 2, parkway, Parkway Drive, Sheffield, S. Yorks. S9 4WU tel:(0114) 2519050, fax:(0114) 2446635. sales@arnold-wragg.com, www.stag-aerospace.com

Arnull Bernard J & Co Ltd - The Paddock, Reigate Road, Ewell, Epsom, Surrey. KT17 3BZ tel:(01932) 341078. info@bernardarnull.com, www.bernardarnull.co.uk

Artex Ltd - Artex Ltd Head Office, Pasture Lane, Ruddington, Nottingham. NG11 6AE tel:(0800) 0326345. artexcustomerservice@saint-gobain.com, www.artexltd.com

Artificial Grass Ltd - Tavistock Works, Glasson Industrial Estate, Maryport, Cumbria. CA15 8NT tel:(01900) 811970, fax:(01900) 817605. sales@artificial-grass.com, www.artificial-grass.com

Artistic Plastercraft Ltd - 4 Lyndhurst Mews, Oldfield Park, Bath, Avon. BA2 3FZ tel:(01225) 315404. artisticplastercraft@outlook.com, www.artisticplastercraft.co.uk

Arts Council England - The Hive, 49 Lever Street, Manchester. M1 1FN tel:(0845) 300 6200. foi@artscouncil.org.uk, www.artscouncil.org.uk

Artur Fischer (UK) Ltd - Whiteley Road, Hithercroft Trading Est, Willingford, Oxon. OX10 9AT tel:(01491) 827900, fax:(01491) 827953. info@fischer.co.uk, www.fischer.co.uk

Arundel Stoneworks Ltd - Norfolk Estate Saw Mill, London Road, Arundel, West Sussex. BN18 9AU tel:(01903) 885016. info@arundelstoneworksltd.co.uk, www.arundelstoneworksltd.co.uk

Arvin Motion Control Ltd - 15 New Star Road, Leicester, Leics. LE4 9JD tel:(0116) 274 3600, fax:(0116) 274 3620. enquiries@camloc.com, www.camloc.com

AS Newbould Ltd - 19 Tarran Way West, Tarran Way Industrial Estate, Moreton, Wirral. CH46 4TT tel:(0151) 677 6906, fax:(0151) 678 0680. sales@newbould-joinery.co.uk, www.newbould-joinery.co.uk

Asbestos Removal Contractors' Association - Arca House, 237 Branston Road, Burton-on-Trent, Staffs. DE13 0BY tel:(01283) 566467, fax:(01283) 505770. info@arca.org.uk, www.arca.org.uk

ASCO Extinguishers Co. Ltd - Unit 1, 1 Festival Court, Brand Place, Glasgow. G51 1DJ tel:(0141) 427 1144. web.enquiry@asco.uk.com, www.asco.uk.com

Ascot Doors Ltd - Brittania Way Industrial Park, Union Road, Bolton, Greater Manchester. BL2 2HE tel:(01204) 545801, fax:(01204) 545800. sales@ascotdoors.co.uk, www.ascotdoors.co.uk

Ash & Lacy Building Products Ltd - Bromford Lane, West Bromwich, West Midlands. B70 7JJ tel:(0121) 525 1444, fax:(0121) 524 3444. info@ashandlacy.com, www.ashandlacy.com

Ashton Seals Ltd - Speedwell Works, Cortonwood Drive, Cortonwood Business Park, Brampton, S. Yorks. S73 0UF tel:(01226) 273700, fax:(01226) 756774. ask@ashton-group.co.uk, www.ashton-group.co.uk

ASSA ABLOY Limited - School Street, Willenhall, W. Midlands. WV13 3PW tel:(01902) 364500, fax:(01902) 364501. info@uniononline.co.uk, www.assaabloy.co.uk

ASSA ABLOY Ltd - School Street, Willenhall, West Midlands. WV13 3PW tel:(0845) 070 6713. customerservices@assaabloy.co.uk, www.assaabloyopeningsolutions.co.uk

Asset International Ltd - Stephenson Street, Newport, S. Wales. NP19 4XH tel:(01633) 637505. info@multiplate.co.uk, www.assetint.co.uk

Association for Consultancy and Engineering (ACE) - Alliance House, 12 Caxton Street, London. SW1H 0QL tel:(020) 7222 6557. consult@acenet.co.uk, www.acenet.co.uk

Association of Concrete Industrial Flooring Contractors (ACIFC) - 6-8 Bonhill Street, London. EC2A 4BX tel:(0844) 2499176, fax:(0844) 2499177. info@acifc.org, www.acifc.org

Association of Cost Engineers - Administrative Office, Lea House, 5 Middlewich Road, Sandbach, Cheshire. CW11 1XL tel:(01270) 764798, fax:(01270) 766180. enquiries@ACostE.org.uk, www.acoste.org.uk

Association of Interior Specialists (AIS) - Olton Bridge, 245 Warwick Road, Solihull, W. Midlands. B92 7AH tel:(0121) 707 0077, fax:(0121) 706 1949. info@ais-interiors.org.uk, www.ais-interiors.org.uk

Association of Plumbing and Heating Contractors - 12 The Pavilions, Cranmore Drive, Solihull. B90 4SB tel:(0121) 711 5030, fax:(0121) 705 7871. info@aphc.co.uk, www.aphc.co.uk

Association of Sealant Applicators Ltd (ASA) - 8 Westwood Road, Canvey Island, Essex. SS8 0ED tel:(07557) 650625, fax:(01268) 511247. arichardson.asa@hotmail.co.uk, www.associationofsealantapplicators.org

Association of Specialist Fire Protection (ASFP) - Kingsley House, Ganders Business Park, Kingsley, Bordon, Hampshire. GU35 9LU tel:(01420) 471612, fax:(01420) 471611. info@asfp.org.uk, www.asfp.org.uk

Association of Technical Lightning & Access Specialists (ATLAS) - The Building Centre, 26 Store Street, London. WC1E 7BT tel:(0844) 249 0026, fax:(0844) 249 0027. info@atlas.org.uk, www.atlas.org.uk/

Astro Lighting Ltd - 21 River Way, Mead Ind Park, Harlow, Essex. CM20 2SE tel:(01279) 427001, fax:(01279) 427002. sales@astrolighting.co.uk, www.astrolighting.co.uk

Astrofade Ltd - Kyle Road, Gateshead, Tyne & Wear. NE8 2YE tel:(0191) 420 0515, fax:(0191) 460 4185. info@astrofade.com, www.astrofade.co.uk

Atkinson & Kirby Ltd - Archwood House, Kingsfield Court, Chester. CH4 9RE tel:(01695) 573234. sales@akirby.co.uk, www.akirby.co.uk

Attwater & Sons Ltd - Hopwood Street Mills, Preston, Lancs. PR1 1TH tel:(01772) 258245, fax:(01772) 203361. info@attwater.com, www.attwater.com

AudiocomPendax Ltd - 57 Suttons Park Avenue, Reading, Berkshire. RG6 1AZ tel:(0118) 966 8383, fax:(0118) 966 8895. info@aupx.com, ww.audicompendax.com

Aura - Unit 3.3 Central Point, Kirpal Road, Portsmouth, Hampshire. PO3 6FH tel:(02392) 001322. info@auracustom.com, www.auracanopies.com

Autobar Vending Services Limited - Apollo House, Odyssey Business Park, West End Road, Ruislip, Middlesex. HA4 6QD tel:(020) 3697 0620. enquiries@bunzlvend.com, www.autobar.co.uk

Autopa Ltd - Cottage Leap, Off Butlers Leap, Rugby, Warwicks. CV21 3XP tel:(01788) 550 556, fax:(01788) 550 265. info@autopa.co.uk, www.autopa.co.uk

Avanti Systems - Avanti House, Albert Drive, Burgess Hill, W. Sussex. RH15 9DN tel:(01444) 247360, fax:(01444) 258 137. enquiries@avantisystems.co.uk, www.avantisystems.co.uk

Avocet Hardware Ltd - Brookfoot Mills, Elland Road, Brighouse, W. Yorks. HD6 2RW tel:(01484) 711700, fax:(01484) 720124. enquiries@avocet-hardware.co.uk, www.avocet-hardware.co.uk

Avon Industrial Doors Ltd - Armstrong Way, Yate, Bristol, Avon. BS37 5NG tel:(01454) 273110, fax:(01454) 323224. sales@avondoors.co.uk, www.avondoors.co.uk

Avonside Roofing Group T/A Letchworth Roofing - Unit 2 Business Centre East, Avenue One, Letchworth Garden City, Hertfordshire. SG6 2HB tel:(01462) 755755, fax:(01462) 755750. letchworthsales@avonsidegroup.co.uk, www.letchworthroofing.co.uk

Axter Ltd - West Road, Ransomes Europark, Ipswich, Suffolk. IP3 9SX tel:(01473) 724056. info@axterltd.co.uk, www.axter.co.uk

Azimex Fabrications Ltd - Cartwright House, 44 Cartwright Road, Northampton, Northants. NN2 6HF tel:(01604) 717712, fax:(01604) 791087. azimex@outlook.com, www.azimex.co.uk

B

B & D Clays & Chemicals Ltd - 10 Wandle Way, Willow Lane Trading Estate, Mitcham, Surrey. CR4 4NB tel:(020) 8640 9221. sales@bdclays.co.uk

B & M Fencing Limited - Reading Road, Hook, Basingstoke, Hants. RG27 9DB tel:(01256) 762739, fax:(01256) 766891. enquiries@bmfencing.co.uk, www.bmfencing.co.uk

Babcock Wanson Uk Ltd - 7 Elstree Way, Borehamwood, Herts. WD6 1SA tel:(020) 8953 7111, fax:(020) 8207 5177. info@babcock-wanson.co.uk, www.babcock-wanson.co.uk

Bacon Group - Unit 7 West Station Business Park, Spital Road, Maldom, Essex. CM9 6FF tel:(01621) 230100. sales@bacongroup.co.uk, www.bacongroup.co.uk

Baggeridge Brick PLC - Fir Street, Sedgley, Dudley, W. Midlands. DY3 4AA tel:(01902) 880555, fax:(01902) 880432. office@wienerberger.co.uk, www.baggeridge.co.uk

Bainbridge Engineering Ltd - East Farm, Cold Kirby, Thirsk, North Yorkshire. YO7 2HL tel:(01845) 597655, fax:(01845) 597528. info@bainbridge-engineering.com, www.bainbridge-engineering.com

Baj System Design Ltd - Unit 45A-C, Hartlebury Trading Estate, Kidderminster. DY10 4JB tel:(01299) 250052, fax:(01299) 251153. info@jomy.be, www.jomy.co.uk

Ball F & Co Ltd - Churnetside Business Park, Station Road, Cheddleton, Leek, Staffs. ST13 7RS tel:(01538) 361633, fax:(01538) 361622. mail@f-ball.co.uk, www.f-ball.co.uk

Ball William Ltd - Ultimate House, London Road, Grays, Essex. RM20 4WB tel:(01375) 375151, fax:(01375) 393355. sales@terenceballkitchens.co.uk, www.wball.co.uk

Ballantine Castings - Links Road, Bo'ness, Scotland. EH51 9PW tel:(01506) 822721, fax:(01506) 827326. sales@ballantineboness.co.uk, ballantinecastings.co.uk

Balmoral Tanks - Balmoral Park, Loirston, Aberdeen. AB12 3GY tel:(01224) 859100, fax:(01224) 859123. tanks@balmoral.co.uk, www.balmoraltanks.com

Bambi Air Compressors Ltd. - 152 Thimble Mill Lane, Heartlands, Birmingham. B7 5HT tel:(0121) 3222299, fax:(0121) 3222297. enquiries@bambi-air.co.uk, www.bambi-air.co.uk

Barber Wilsons & Co Ltd - Crawley Road, Wood Green, London. N22 6AH tel:(020) 8888 3461, fax:(020) 88882041. sales@barwil.co.uk, www.barwil.co.uk

Barbour Enquiry Service - New Lodge, Drift Road, Windsor. SL4 4RQ tel:(01344) 884999, fax:(01344) 899377. enquiries@barbourehs.com, www.barbour-index.co.uk

Barker & Geary Limited - The Yard, Romsey Road, Kings Somborne, Nr Stockbridge, Hants. SO20 6PW tel:(01794) 388205, fax:(01794) 388205. info@barkerandgeary.co.uk, www.barkerandgeary.co.uk

Barlow Group - 136 London Road, Sheffield, S. Yorks. S2 4NX tel:(0114) 280 3000, fax:(0114) 280 3001. info@barlowgroup.co.uk, www.barlowgroup.co.uk

Barlow Tyrie Ltd - Braintree, Essex. CM7 2RN tel:(01376) 557600, fax:(01376) 557610. sales@teak.com, www.teak.com

Barloworld Vacuum Technology Plc - Harbour Road, Gosport, Hants. PO12 1BG tel:(0870) 0106929, fax:(0870) 0106916. marketing@bvc.co.uk, www.barloworldvt.com

Barnwood Ltd - 203 Barnwood Road, Gloucester. GL4 3HS tel:(01452) 614124, fax:(01452) 372933. mail@barnwood.co.uk, www.barnwood.co.uk

Barr & Wray Ltd - 1 Buccleuch Avenue, Hillington Park, Glasgow. G52 4NR tel:(0141) 882 9991, fax:(0141) 882 3690. sales@barrandwray.com, www.barrandwray.com/

Bartoline Ltd - Barmston Close, Beverley, E. Yorks. HU17 0LW tel:(01482) 678710, fax:(01482) 872606. info@bartoline.co.uk, www.bartoline.co.uk

B (con't)

Barton Engineering - Rose Street, Bradley, Bilston, W.Midlands. WV14 8TS tel:(01902) 407199, fax:(01902) 495106. bartonsales@barton-engineering.co.uk, www.hublebas.co.uk

BASF plc, Construction Chemicals - Earl Road, Cheadle Hulme, Cheadle, Cheshire. SK8 6QG tel:(0161) 485 6222, fax:(0161) 488 5220. info@master-builders-solutions.basf.co.uk, www.master-builders-solutions.basf.co.uk

Bassaire Ltd - Duncan Road, Park Gate, Southampton. SO31 1ZS tel:(01489) 885111, fax:(01489) 885211. sales@bassaire.co.uk, www.bassaire.co.uk

Bathroom Manufacturers Association, The - Innovation Centre 1, Keele University Science & Business Park, Newcastle-under-Lyme. ST5 5NB tel:(01782) 631619, fax:(01782) 630155. info@bathroom-association.org.uk, www.bathroom-association.org

Bathstore - PO Box 21, Boroughbridge Road, Ripon, North Yorkshire. HG4 1SL tel:(08000) 23 23 23. customerservices@wolseley.co.uk, www.bathstore.com

Bauder Limited - 70 Landseer Road, Ipswich, Suffolk. IP3 0DH tel:(01473) 257671, fax:(01473) 230761. info@bauder.co.uk, www.bauder.co.uk

Bauer Renewables Ltd - 4-6 Swaby's Yard, Walkergate, Beverley, East Yorkshire. HU17 9BZ tel:(01279) 715492. info@bauerinnercity.co.uk, www.bauer-renewables.co.uk

Baxi Heating UK Ltd - Brooks House, Coventry Road, Warwick. CV34 4LL tel:(0844) 8711525. info@baxi.co.uk, www.baxi.co.uk

Baz-Roll Products Ltd - Porte Marsh Road, Calne, Wiltshire. SN11 9BW tel:(01249) 822222, fax:(01249) 822300. sales@bilgroup.eu, www.bilgroup.eu

BCIS - Parliament Square, London. SW1P 3AD tel:(024) 7686 8555. contactbcis@bcis.co.uk, www.bcis.co.uk

Beacon Machine Tools Ltd - 24 Ireland Green Road, West Bromwich, W. Midlands. B70 8QS tel:(0121) 553 5203. amyzhang@beacon-machine.com, http://www.beacon-machine.com/

Beama Ltd - Westminster Tower, 3 Albert Embankment, London. SE1 7SL tel:(020) 7793 3000, fax:(020) 7793 3003. info@beama.org.uk, www.beama.org.uk

Beaumont Ltd F E - Woodlands Road, Mere, Wilts. BA12 6BT tel:(01747) 860481, fax:(01747) 861076. sales@beaumont-chimneys.co.uk, www.beaumont-chimneys.co.uk

Becker (SLIDING PARTITIONS) Ltd - Wemco House, 477 Whippendell Road, Watford, Herts. WD1 7PS tel:(01923) 236906, fax:(01923) 230149. sales@becker.uk.com, www.becker.uk.com

Beco Products Ltd - Albert Street, Brigg, North Lincolnshire. DN20 8HQ tel:(01652) 653 844. info@becowallform.co.uk, www.becowallform.co.uk

Bedford Fencing Co. Limited - Unit 8 Sargeant Turner Ind. Estate, Bromley Street , Lye, Stourbridge, W. Midlands. DY9 8HZ tel:(01384) 422688, fax:(01384) 422688. bedfordfencing@btconnect.com, www.bedfordfencing.org.uk

Bedford Shelving Ltd - Springvale Works, Elland Road, Brighouse. HD6 2RN tel:(01525) 852121, fax:(01525) 851666. sales@bedfordshelf.com, www.bedfordshelf.co.uk

Beehive Coils Ltd - Studlands Park Avenue, Newmarket, Suffolk. CB8 7AU tel:(01638) 664134, fax:(01638) 561542. info@beehivecoils.co.uk, www.beehivecoils.co.uk

Begetube UK Ltd - 8 Carsegate Road South, Inverness. IV3 8LL tel:(01463) 246600, fax:(01463) 246624. info@begetube.co.uk, www.begetube.co.uk

Beiersdorf (UK) Ltd - tesa Division, Yeomans Drive, Blakelands, Milton Keynes, Bucks. MK14 5LS tel:(01908) 211333, fax:(01908) 211555. consumer.relations.uk@beiersdorf.com, www.beiersdorf.co.uk

Bekaert Building Products - Park House Road, Low Moor, Bradford, West Yorkshire. BD12 0PX tel:(0114) 2427485, fax:(0114) 2427490. building.uk@bekaert.com, www.bekaert.com/building

Beko plc - Beko House, 1 Greenhill Crescent, Watford, Herts. WD18 8QU tel:(0845) 600 4904, fax:(0845) 600 4925. www.beko.co.uk

Bell & Co Ltd - Kingsthorpe Road, Northampton. NN2 6LT tel:(01604) 777500, fax:(01604) 777501. sales@abell.co.uk, www.abell.co.uk

Bell & Webster Concrete Ltd - Alma Park Road, Grantham, Lincsonshire. NG31 9SE tel:(01476) 562277, fax:(01476) 562944. bellandwebster@eleco.com, www.bellandwebster.co.uk

Belzona PolymericLtd - Claro Road, Harrogate, N. Yorks. HG1 4AY tel:(01423) 567641, fax:(01423) 505967. belzona@belzona.co.uk, www.belzona.com

Be-Modern Ltd - Western Approach, 19/34 Bedesway, Jarrow, Tyne & Wear. NE22 3HQ tel:(0191) 428 0444. info@bemodern.com, www.bemodern.com

Benlowe Group Limited - Benlowe Windows And Doors, Park Road, Ratby, Leicestershire. LE6 0JL tel:(0116) 2395353, fax:(0116) 2387295. info@benlowe.co.uk, www.benlowe.co.uk

Benlowe Stairs - Coppice Side Industrial Estate, Engine Lane, Brownhills, West Midlands. WS8 7ES tel:(0116) 2395353, fax:(01543) 375300. info@benlowe.co.uk, www.benlowe.co.uk

Benton Co Ltd Edward - Creteangle Works, Brook Lane, Ferring, Worthing, W. Sussex. BN12 5LP tel:(01903) 241349, fax:(01903) 700213. sales@creteangle.com, www.creteangle.com

Be-Plas Marketing Ltd - Unit 2, Junction 8 Business Park, Ellesmere Port, Wirral. CH65 3AS tel:(0800) 413 758. sales@beplas.com, www.beplas.com

Bernhards Landscapes Ltd - Bilton Road, Rugby, Warwicks. CV22 7DT tel:(01788) 811500, fax:(01788) 816803. bernhards@btconnect.com, www.bernhards.co.uk

Bernlite Ltd - 3 Brookside, Colne Way, Watford, Herts. WD24 7QJ tel:(01923) 200160, fax:(01923) 246057. sales@bernlite.co.uk, www.bernlite.co.uk

Berry Systems - A Memberof Hill & Smith Infrastructure Group, Springvale Business and Ind. Park, Bilston, Wolverhampton, W. Midlands. WV14 0QL tel:(01902) 491100, fax:(01902) 494080. sales@berrysystems.co.uk, www.berrysystems.co.uk

Bertrams - 1, Broadland Business Park, Norwich, Norfolk. NR7 0WF tel:(01603) 648400, fax:(0871) 803 6709. books@bertrams.com, www.bertrams.com

Best & Lloyd Ltd - 9 Zeal House, 8 Deer Park Road, London. SW19 3UU tel:(0207) 6109191, fax:(0207) 6109193. info@bestandlloyd.com, www.bestandlloyd.com

Betafence Limited - PO Box 119, Shepcote Lane, Sheffield, S. Yorks. S9 1TY tel:(0870) 120 3252, fax:(0870) 120 3242. sales.sheffield@betafence.com, www.betafence.co.uk

Bevan Funnell Group Limited - Norton Road, Newhaven, Sussex. BN9 0BZ tel:(01273) 616100, fax:(01273) 611167. sales@bevan-funnell.co.uk, www.bevan-funnell.co.uk

Beverley Environmental Ltd - Unit 49, Bolney Grange Industrial Park, Haywards Heath, West Sussex. RH17 5PB tel:(01444) 248 930. info@beverley-environmental.co.uk, www.beverley-environmental.co.uk

BF Bassett & Findley - Talbot Road North, Wellingborough, Northants. NN8 1QS tel:(01933) 224898, fax:(01933) 227731. info@bassettandfindley.co.uk, www.bassettandfindley.co.uk

BFM Europe Limited - Trentham Lakes, Stoke-on-Trent, Staffordshire. ST4 4TJ tel:(01782) 339000, fax:(01782) 339009. info@bfm-europe.com, www.bfm-europe.com

BFRC Services Ltd - 177 Bagnall Road, Basford, Nottingham, Notts. NG6 8SJ tel:(0115) 942 4200, fax:(0115) 942 4488. enquiries@bfrc.org, www.roofinguk.com

Bicester Products Ltd - 7 Crawley Mill, Dry Lane, Witney, Oxon. OX29 9TJ tel:(01993) 704810, fax:(01993) 779569. bicpro@soundservice.co.uk, www.bicpro.co.uk

Biddle Air Systems Ltd - St Mary's Road, Nuneaton, Warwicks. CV11 5AU tel:(024) 76 384233, fax:(024) 76 373621. sales@biddle-air.co.uk, www.biddle.air.co.uk

bigHead Bonding Fasteners Ltd - Unit 1, Black Moor Business Park, 36A Black Moor Road, Ebblake Industrial Estate, Dorset. BH31 6BB tel:(01202) 574601, fax:(01202) 578300. info@bighead.co.uk, www.bighead.co.uk

Bilco UK Ltd - Park Farm Business Centre, Fornham St Genevieve, Bury St Edmunds, Suffolk. IP28 6TS tel:(01284) 701696, fax:(01284) 702531. bilcouk@bilco.com, www.bilcouk.co.uk

Bill Switchgear - Reddings Lane, Birmingham. B11 3EZ tel:(0121) 685 2080, fax:(0121) 685 2184. uksystorders@eaton.com, www.bill-switchgear.com

Billericay Fencing Ltd - Morbec Farm, Arterial Road, Wickford, Essex. SS12 9JF tel:(01268) 727712, fax:(01268) 590225. sales@billericayfencing.co.uk, www.billericay-fencing.co.uk

Binder - Old Ipswich Road, Claydon, Ipswich. IP6 0AG tel:(01473) 830582, fax:(01473) 832175. info@binder.co.uk, www.binder.co.uk

Binns Fencing Ltd - Harvest House, Cranborne Road, Potters Bar, Herts. EN6 3JF tel:(01707) 855555, fax:(01707) 857565. contracts@binns-fencing.com, www.binns-fencing.com

Birdsall Services Ltd - 6 Frogmore Road, Hemel Hempstead, Herts. HP3 9RW tel:(01442) 212501, fax:(01442) 248989. sales@birdsall.co.uk, www.birdsall.co.uk

Birtley Group - Mary Avenue, Birtley, Co. Durham. DH3 1JF tel:(0191) 410 6631, fax:(0191) 410 0650. info@birtley-building.co.uk, www.birtley-building.co.uk

BIS Door Systems Ltd - 13 Hodgson Court, Hodgson Way, Wickford, Essex. SS11 8XR tel:(01268) 767566, fax:(01268) 560284. sales@bis-doors.co.uk, www.bis-doors.co.uk

Bisley Office Equipment - Queens Road, Bisley, Woking, Surrey. GU24 9BJ tel:(01483) 474577, fax:(01483) 489962. marketing@bisley.com, www.bisley.com

Bison Precast - Forterra Building Products, Tetron Point, William Nadin Way, Swadlincote, Derbyshire. DE11 0BB tel:(01283) 817500, fax:(01283) 220563. concrete@bison.co.uk, www.bison.co.uk

Black Cat Music - Festival House, 4 Chapman Way, Tunbridge Wells, Kent. TN2 3EF tel:(01732) 371555, fax:(01732) 371556. sales@blackcatmusic.co.uk, www.blackcatmusic.co.uk

Blackfriar Paints Ltd - Portobello Industrial Estate, Bitley, Chester-le-Street, County Durham. DH3 2RE tel:(0191) 411 3146, fax:(0191) 492 0125. blackfriar@tor-coatings.com, www.blackfriar.co.uk

Blagg & Johnson Ltd - Newark Business Park, Brunel Drive, Newark, Notts. NG24 2EG tel:(01636) 703137, fax:(01636) 701914. sales@blaggs.co.uk, www.blaggs.co.uk

Blairs Windows Limited - 9 Baker Street, Greenock, Inverclyde. PA15 4TU tel:(01475) 721256, fax:(01475) 729313. sales@blairswindows.co.uk, www.blairswindows.co.uk

Blakell Europlacer Ltd - 30 Factory Road, Upton Industrial Estate, Poole, Dorset. BH16 5SL tel:(01202) 266500, fax:(01202) 266599. sales@europlacer.co.uk, www.europlacer.com

Blakley Electrics Ltd - 1 Thomas Road, Optima Park, Crayford, Kent. DA1 4GA tel:(0845) 074 0084, fax:(0845) 074 0085. sales@blakley.co.uk, www.blakley.co.uk

Blanc de Bierges - Pye Bridge Industrial Estate, Main Road, Pie Bridge, Near Alfreton, Derbyshire. DE55 4NX tel:(01733) 202566, fax:(01733) 205405. info@blancdebierges.com, http://blancdebierges.com/

Blaze Signs Ltd - 5 Patricia Way, Pysons Road, Broadstairs, Kent. CT10 2XZ tel:(01843) 601 075, fax:(01843) 867 924. info@blazesigns.co.uk, www.blaze-signs.com

Blick Communication Systems Ltd - Blick House, Bramble Road, Swindon, Wilts. SN2 8ER tel:(01793) 692401, fax:(01793) 615848. info@stanleysecuritysolutions.co.uk, www.blick.co.uk

BLM British Lead - Peartree Lane, Welwyn Garden City, Herts. AL7 3UB tel:(01707) 324595, fax:(01707) 328941. sales@britishlead.co.uk, www.britishlead.co.uk

Blount Shutters Ltd - Unit B, 734 London Road, West Thurrock, Essex. RM20 3NL tel:(08456) 860000, fax:(01708) 861272. sales@blountshutters.co.uk, www.blountshutters.co.uk

Blucher UK LTD - Station Road Industrial Estate, Tadcaster, North Yorkshire. LS24 9SG tel:(01937) 838000, fax:(01937) 832 454. mailuk@blucher.co.uk, www.blucher.co.uk

Bluestar Silicones - Wolfe Mead, Farnham Road, Bordon, Hampshire. GU35 0NH tel:(01420) 477000, fax:0483200. webmaster.silicones@bluestarsilicones.com, www.bluestarsilicones.com

BLV Licht-und Vakuumtecnik - Units 25 & 26, Rabans Close, Rabans Lane Industrial Estate, Aylesbury, Bucks. HP19 3RS tel:(01296) 399334, fax:(01296) 393422. info@blv.co.uk, www.blv.co.uk

BM TRADA - Chiltern House, Stocking Lane, Hughenden Valley, High Wycombe, Bucks. HP14 4ND tel:(01494) 569750, fax:(01494) 564895. info.highwycombe@bmtrada.com, www.bmtrada.com

Boardcraft Ltd - Howard Road, Eaton Socon, St Neots, Huntingdon, Cambs. PE19 3ET tel:(01480) 213266, fax:(01480) 219095. info@boardcraft.co.uk, www.boardcraft.co.uk

BOB Stevenson Ltd - 5 Coleman Street, Derby, Derbys. DE24 8NN tel:(01332) 574112, fax:(01332) 757286. sales@bobstevenson.co.uk, www.bobstevenson.co.uk

Bodycote Metallurgical Coatings Ltd - Tyherington Business Park, Macclesfield, Cheshire. SK10 2XF tel:(01625) 505300, fax:(01625) 505320. Phil.Adams@bodycote.com, www.bodycotemetallurgicalcoatings.com

Bollom Fire Protection Ltd - Croydon Road, Elmers End, Beckenham, Kent. BR3 4BL tel:(020) 8658 2299, fax:(020) 8658 8672. enquiries@tor-coatings.com, www.bollom.com

Bolton Gate Company Ltd - Waterloo Street, Bolton. BL1 2SP tel:(01204) 871021. sales@boltongate.co.uk, www.boltongate.co.uk

Bonwyke Ltd - Bonwyke House, 41-43 Redlands Lane, Fareham, Hants. PO14 1HL tel:(01329) 289621, fax:(01329) 822768. sales@bonwyke.co.uk, www.bonwyke.demon.co.uk

Booth Industries Ltd - PO Box 50, Nelson Street, Bolton, Lancashire. BL3 2RW tel:(01204) 366333, fax:(01204) 380888. marketing@booth-industries.co.uk, www.booth-industries.co.uk

Booth Muirie - South Caldeen Road, Coadbridge, North Lanarkshire. ML5 4EG tel:(01236) 354 500, fax:(01236) 345 515. enquiries@boothmuirie.co.uk, www.boothmuirie.co.uk

Border Concrete Products Ltd - Jedburgh Road, Kelso, Roxburghshire. TD5 8-JG tel:(01573) 224393, fax:(01573) 226360. sales@borderconcrete.co.uk, www.borderconcrete.co.uk

Bostik Ltd - Ulverscroft Road, Leicester. LE4 6BW tel:(01785) 272727, fax:(0116) 2513943. technical.service@bostik.com, www.bostik.co.uk

Bowden Fencing Ltd - Leicester Lane, Great Bowden, Market Harborough, Leics. LE16 7HA tel:(01858) 410660, fax:(01858) 433957. info@bowdenfencing.co.uk, www.bowdenfencing.co.uk

BPT Automation Ltd - Unit 16, Sovereign Park, Cleveland Way, Hemel Hempstead, Herts. HP2 7DA tel:(01442) 235355, fax:(01442) 244729. sales@bpt.co.uk, www.bptautomation.co.uk

Bradbury Group Ltd - 6 Atkinsons Way, Foxhills Industrial Estate, Scunthorpe, North Lincolnshire. DN15 8QJ tel:(01724) 271999, fax:(01724) 271888. enquiries@bradburyuk.com, www.bradburyuk.com

Braithwaite Engineers Ltd - Units A & B, Leeway House, Leeway Industrial Estate, Newport. NP19 4SL tel:(01633) 262141, fax:(01633) 250631. tanks@braithwaite.co.uk, www.braithwaite.co.uk

Bramah Security Equipment Ltd - 7 Goodge Place, Fitzrovia, London. W1T 4SF tel:(020) 7637 8500 option 3, fax:(020) 7636 5598. lock.sales@bramah.co.uk, www.bramah.co.uk

Brandon Hire PLC - 72-75 Feeder Road, St Philips, Bristol. BS2 0TQ tel:(0117) 9413 550, fax:(0117) 9540 972. info@brandonhire.co.uk, www.brandontoolhire.co.uk

Brandon Medical - Holme Well Road, Leeds, W. Yorks. LS10 4TQ tel:(0113) 2777393, fax:(0113) 2728844. enquiries@brandon-medical.com, www.brandon-medical.com

Brannan S & Sons Ltd - Leconfield Ind Est, Cleator Moor, Cumbria. CA25 5QE tel:(01946) 816600, fax:(01946) 816625. sales@brannan.co.uk, www.brannan.co.uk

Brannan Thermometers & Gauges - Leconfield Industrial Estate, Cleator Moor, Cumbria. CA25 5QE tel:(01946) 816624, fax:(01946) 816625. sales@brannan.co.uk, www.brannan.co.uk

Branson Leisure Ltd - Fosters Croft, Foster Street, Harlow, Essex. CM17 9HS tel:(01279) 432151, fax:(01279) 432151. sales@bransonleisure.co.uk, www.bransonleisure.co.uk

Brass Age Ltd - 22 Bidwell Rd, Rackheath Industrial Estate, Norwich. NR13 6PT tel:(01603) 722330. sales@basystems.co.uk

Brass Art Ltd - Regent Works, Attwood Street, Lye, Stourbridge, W. Midlands. DY9 8RY tel:(01384) 894814, fax:(01384) 423824. sales@brassart.com, www.brassart.co.uk

BRC Reinforcement - Brierley Park Close, Stanton Hill, Sutton-in-Ashfield, Nottinghamshire. NG17 3FW tel:(01623) 555111, fax:(01623) 440932. sales@midlands.brc.ltd.uk, www.brc.ltd.uk

BRC Special Products - Bekaert Ltd - Park House Road, Low Moor, Bradford, West Yorkshire. BD12 0PX tel:(01142) 427 480, fax:(01142) 427 490. infobuilding@bekaert.com, www.brc-special-products.co.uk

BRE - Bucknalls Lane, Garston, Watford, Herts. WD25 9XX tel:(01923) 664000, fax:(01923) 664010. enquiries@bre.co.uk, www.bre.co.uk

Breedon Aggregates - Breedon Quarry, Breedon on the Hill, Derby. DE73 8AP tel:(01332) 862254, fax:(01332) 864320. sales@breedonaggregates.com, www.breedonaggregates.com

Brett Aggregates - Brett House, Bysing Wood Road, Faversham, Kent. ME13 7UD tel:(01795) 594000. aggsalesenquiries@brett.co.uk, www.brett.co.uk/aggregates

Brett Landscaping - Sileby Road, Barrow upon Soar, Leicestershire. LE12 8LX tel:(0845) 60 80 570, fax:(0845) 60 80 575. sales@brettpaving.co.uk, www.brettpaving.co.uk

Brett Martin Ltd - Speedwell Industrial Estate, Staveley, Chesterfield, Derbys. S43 3JP tel:(01246) 280000, fax:(01246) 280001. mail@brettmartin.com, www.brettmartin.co.uk

Brewer C & Sons Ltd - Albany House, Ashford Road, Eastbourne, Sussex. BN21 3TR tel:(01323) 411080, fax:(01323) 721435. enquiries@brewers.co.uk, www.brewers.co.uk

Brewer Metalcraft - W. Sussex. BN18 0DF tel:(01243) 539639, fax:(01243) 533184. sales@brewercowls.co.uk, www.brewercowls.co.uk

Brick Development Association - The Building Centre, 26 Store Street, London. WC1E 7BT tel:(020) 7323 7030, fax:(020) 7580 3795. brick@brick.org.uk, www.brick.org.uk

Bridgman & Bridgman LLP

26 Cambridge Street, Wolverton, Milton Keynes. MK12 5AJ tel:(01908) 579080. info@bridgmanlandscapes.co.uk, www.gardensinthesky.co.uk

---

Bridgman IBC Ltd - Grealtham Street, Longhill Industrial Estate (North), Hartlepool, Cleveland. TS25 1PU tel:(01429) 221111, fax:(01429) 274035. sales@bridgman-ibc.com, www.bridgman-ibc.com

Briggs Industrial Footwear Ltd t/a Briggs Safety Wear - Briggs House, 430 Thurmaston Boulevard, Leicester, Leics. LE4 9LE tel:(01162) 444700, fax:(01162) 444744. sales@briggsfootwear.co.uk, www.briggsfootwear.co.uk

BriggsAmasco - Amasco House, 101 Powke Lane, Cradley Heath, West Midlands. B64 5PX tel:(0121) 502 9600, fax:(0121) 502 9601. enquiries@briggsamasco.co.uk, www.briggsamasco.co.uk

B (con't)

Brighton (Handrails), W - 55 Quarry Hill, Tamworth, Staffs. B77 5BW tel:(01827) 284488, fax:(01827) 250907. wbrightonhandrails@ntlworld.com, www.wbrightonhandrails.com

Brimar Plastics Ltd - 18 Dixon Road, Brislington, Bristol. BS4 5QW tel:(0117) 971 5976, fax:(0117) 971 6839. sales@brimarplastics.co.uk, www.brimarplastics.co.uk

Brintons Ltd - PO Box 16, Exchange Street, Kidderminster, Worcs. DY10 1AG tel:(01562) 820000, fax:(01562) 515597. solutions@brintons.co.uk, www.brintons.net

brissco signs & graphics - Block 9, 25 Cater Road, Bishopsworth, Bristol, Avon. BS13 7TX tel:(0117) 311 3777, fax:(0117) 311 6777. sales@brissco.co.uk, www.brissco.com/

Bristan Group - Pooley Hall Drive, Birch Coppice Business Park, Dordon, Tamworth. B78 1SG tel:(0330) 026 6273. enquire@bristan.com, www.bristan.com

Bristol Metal Spraying & Protective Coatings Ltd - Paynes Shipyard, Coronation Road, Bristol. BS3 1RP tel:(0117) 966 2206, fax:(0117) 966 1158. sales@bmspc.co.uk, www.bmspc.co.uk

Britannia Fire - Ashwellthorpe Industrial Estate, Ashwellthorpe, Norwich, Norfolk. NR16 1ER tel:(01508) 488416, fax:(01508) 481753. sales@britannia-fire.co.uk, www.britannia-fire.co.uk

Britannia Kitchen Ventilation Ltd - AGA Rangemaster, C/O Britannia Kitchen Ventilation, Clarence Street, Leamington Spa, Warwickshire. CB31 2AD tel:(01926) 675420, fax:(Fax:) 1926463541. sales@kitchen-ventilation.co.uk, www.kitchen-ventilation.co.uk

British Adhesives and Sealants Association - 24 Laurel Close, Mepal, Ely, Cambridgeshire. CB6 2BN tel:(0330) 22 33 290, fax:(0330) 22 33 408. secretary@basa.uk.com, http://www.basa.uk.com

British Association for Chemical Specialities - Simpson House, Windsor Court, Clarence Drive, Harrowgate. HG1 2PE tel:(01423) 700249, fax:(01423) 520297. enquiries@bacsnet.org, www.bacsnet.org

British Association of Landscape Industries - Landscape House, Stoneleigh Park, National Agricultural Centre, Warwickshire. CV8 2LG tel:(024) 7669 0333, fax:(024) 7669 0077. contact@bali.org.uk, www.bali.org.uk

British Blind and Shutter Association (BBSA) - PO Box 232, Stowmarket, Suffolk. IP14 9AR tel:(01449) 780444, fax:(01449) 780444. info@bbsa.org.uk, www.bbsa.org.uk

British Board of Agrément - Bucknalls Lane, Garston, Watford, Herts. WD25 9BA tel:(01923) 665300, fax:(01923) 665301. clientservices@bbacerts.co.uk, www.bbacerts.co.uk

British Ceramic Confederation - Federation House, Station Road, Stoke-on-Trent. ST4 2SA tel:(01782) 744631, fax:(01782) 744102. bcc@ceramfed.co.uk, www.ceramfed.co.uk

British Ceramic Tile Ltd - Heathfield, Newton Abbot, Devon. TQ12 6RF tel:(01626) 834774. www.britishceramictile.com

British Coatings Federation Ltd - Spectra House, Westwood Way, Westwood Business Park, Coventry. CV4 8HS tel:(0247) 693 5390. info@bcf.co.uk, www.coatings.org.uk

British Constructional Steelwork Association Ltd - 4 Whitehall Court, Westminster, London. SW1A 2ES tel:(020) 7839 8566, fax:(020) 7976 1634. postroom@steelconstruction.org, www.steelconstruction.org

British Drilling Association (BDA) - Wayside, London End, Upper Boddington, Daventry, Northamptonshire. NN11 6DP tel:(01327) 264622, fax:(01327) 264623. office@britishdrillingassociation.co.uk, www.britishdrillingassociation.co.uk

British Electric Lamps Ltd - Spencer Hill Road, London. SW19 4EN tel:(01924) 893380, fax:(01924) 894320. sales@belllighting.co.uk, www.belllighting.co.uk

British Electrotechnical and Allied Manufacturers Association - Westminster Tower, 3 Albert Embankment, London. SE1 7SL tel:(020) 7793 3000, fax:(020) 7793 3003. info@beama.org.uk, www.beama.org.uk

British Fenestration Rating Council - Newspaper House, 40 Rushworth Street, London. SE1 0RB tel:(020) 7403 9200, fax:(08700) 278 493. enquiries@bfrc.org, www.bfrc.org

British Flue & Chimney Manufacterers Association - FETA, 2 Waltham Court, Milley Lane, Hare Hatch, Reading, Berks. RG10 9TH tel:(0118) 9403416, fax:(0118) 9406258. info@feta.co.uk, www.feta.co.uk/associations/bfcma

British Glass Manufacturers Confederation - 9 Churchill Road, Chapeltown, Sheffield. S35 2PY tel:(0114) 290 1850, fax:(0114) 290 1851. info@britglass.co.uk, www.britglass.org.uk

British Gypsum Ltd - Head Office, East Leake, Loughborough, Leicestershire. LE12 6HX tel:(0115) 9451000, fax:(0115) 9451901. bgtechnical.enquiries@bpb.com, www.british-gypsum.com

British Harlequin Plc - Festival House, Chapman Way, Tunbridge Wells, Kent. TN2 3EF tel:(01892) 514888. enquiries@harlequinfloors.com, www.harlequinfloors.com

British Library – Business & Intellectual Property Centre - The British Library, 96 Euston Road, London. NW1 2DB tel:(020) 7412 7454. bipc@bl.uk, www.bl.uk/business-and-ip-centre

British Plastics Federation, The - 5-6 Bath Place, Rivington Street, London. EC2A 3JE tel:(020) 7457 5000, fax:(020) 7457 5045. reception@bpf.co.uk, www.bpf.co.uk

British Precast Concrete Federation - The Old Rectory, Main Street, Leicester, Leics. LE3 8DG tel:(0116) 253 6161, fax:(0116) 251 4568. info@britishprecast.org, www.britishprecast.org

British Precast Flooring Federation - The Old Rectory, Main Street, Glenfield, Leics. LE3 8DG tel:(0116) 232 5170. info@britishprecast.org, www.precastfloors.info

British Pump Manufacturers Association - The National Metalforming Centre, 47 Birmingham Road, West Bromwich. B70 6PY tel:(0121) 200 1299, fax:(0121) 200 1306. enquiry@bpma.org.uk, www.bpma.org.uk

British Refrigeration Association (BRA) - 2 Waltham Court, Milley Lane, Hare Hatch, Reading, Berkshire. RG10 9TH tel:(01189) 403416, fax:(01189) 406258. bra@feta.co.uk, www.feta.co.uk

British Security Industry Association - Anbrian House, 1 The Tything, Worcester. WR1 1HD tel:(01905) 342020. info@bsia.co.uk, www.bsia.co.uk

British Slate Association - Channel Business Centre, Ingles Manor, Castle Hill Avenue, Folkestone, Kent. CT20 2RD tel:(01303) 856123, fax:(01303) 221095. enquiries@stone-federationgb.org.uk, www.stone-federationgb.org.uk

British Spirals & Castings - Peak Building, El=ccles Road, Chapel-en-le-Firth, High Peak. SK23 9RG tel:(01663) 750716, fax:(01663) 751093. sales@britishsc.co.uk, www.britishsc.co.uk

British Stainless Steel Association - Regus, Blades Enterprise Centre, John Street, Sheffield. S2 4SW tel:(0114) 292 2636, fax:(0114) 292 2633. admin@bssa.org.uk, www.bssa.org.uk

British Standards Institution - 389 Chiswick High Road, London. W4 4AL tel:(020) 8996 9000, fax:(020) 8996 7001. orders@bsi-global.com, www.bsi-global.com

British Structural Waterproofing Association, The - Westcott House, Catlins Lane, Pinner, Middx. HA5 2EZ tel:(020) 8866 8339, fax:(020) 8868 9971. enquiries@bswa.org.uk, www.bswa.org.uk

British Turntable Ltd - Emblem Street, Bolton. BL3 5BW tel:(01252) 319922, fax:(01252) 341872. info@movetechuk.com, www.hovair.co.uk

British Urethane Foam Contractors Association - P O Box 12, Haslemere, Surrey. GU27 3AH tel:(01428) 870150. info@bufca.co.uk, www.bufca.co.uk

British Water - 1 Queen Anne's Gate, London. SW1H 9BT tel:(020) 7957 4554, fax:(020) 7957 4565. info@britishwater.co.uk, www.britishwater.co.uk

British Woodworking Federation - The Building Centre, 26 Store Street, London. WC1E 7BT tel:(0844) 209 2610, fax:(0844) 458 6949. bwf@bwf.org.uk, www.bwf.org.uk

Britmet Tileform Limited - Spital Farm, Thorpe Mead, Banbury, Oxon. OX16 4RZ tel:(01295) 250998, fax:(01295) 271068. BritmetTileform@hotmail.com, www.britmet.co.uk

BRK Brands Europe Ltd - Carter Court, Unit 6 Davy Way, Gloucester. GL2 2DE tel:(01452) 887570. info@brk.co.uk, www.brk.co.uk

Broadbent - Droppingstone Farm, New Lane, Harthill, Chester. CH3 9LG tel:(01829) 782822, fax:(01829) 782820. enquiries@sbal.co.uk, www.sbal.co.uk

Broadcrown Ltd - Alliance Works, Airfield Industrial Estate, Hixon, Stafford, Staffs. ST18 0PF tel:(08794) 122200, fax:(01889) 272220. info@broadcrown.co.uk, www.broadcrown.com

Broadmead Cast Stone - Broadmead Works, Hart Street, Maidstone, Kent. ME16 8RE tel:(01622) 690960, fax:(01622) 765484. info@topbond.co.uk, www.kier.co.uk

Broag Ltd - Remeha House, Molly Millars Lane, Wokingham, Berks. RG41 2QP tel:(0118) 978 3434, fax:(0118) 978 6977. boilers@broag-remeha.com, www.uk.remeha.com

Brockway Carpets Ltd - Hoobrook, Kidderminster, Worcs. DY10 1XW tel:(01562) 824737, fax:(01562) 752010. sales@brockway.co.uk

Broen-Lab Ltd - Unit 7 Clecton Street Business Park, Clecton Street, Tipton, W. Midlands. DY4 7TR tel:(0121) 522 4515, fax:(0121) 522 4535. broen@broen.co.uk, www.broen.co.uk

Broome Bros (Doncaster) Ltd - Lineside, Cheswold Lane, Doncaster, S. Yorks. DN5 8AR tel:(01302) 361733, fax:(01302) 328536. jeff@broomebros.co.uk

Broxap Ltd - Rowhurst Industrial Estate, Chesteron, Newcastle-under-Lyme, Staffs. ST5 6BD tel:(01782) 564411, fax:(01782) 565357. dave.challinor@broxap.com, www.broxap.com

BSA Machine Tools Ltd - Mackadown Lane, Kitts Green, Birmingham. B33 0LE tel:(0121) 783 4071, fax:(0121) 784 5921. ch&ceo@bsatools.co.uk, www.bsamachinetools.co.uk

Buckingham Swimming Pools Ltd - Dalehouse Lane, Kenilworth, Warwicks. CV8 2EB tel:(01926) 852351, fax:(01926) 512387. info@buckinghampools.com, www.buckinghampools.com

Builders Merchants Federation - 1180 Elliott Court, Coventry Business Park, Herald Avenue, Coventry. CV5 6UB tel:(02476) 854980, fax:(02476) 854981. info@bmf.org.uk, www.bmf.org.uk

Building & Engineering Services Association - Esca House, 34 Palace Court, London. W2 4JG tel:(020) 7313 4900, fax:(020) 7727 9268. contact@b-es.org.uk, www.b-es.org.uk

Building Additions Ltd - Unit C1, Southgate Commerce Park, Frome, Somerset. BA11 2RY tel:(01373) 454577, fax:(01373) 454578. sales@buildingadditions.co.uk, www.buildingadditions.co.uk

Building Adhesives Ltd - Longton Road, Trentham, Stoke-on-Trent. ST4 8JB tel:(01782) 591100, fax:(01782) 591101. info@building-adhesives.com, www.building-adhesives.com

Building Controls Industry Association (BCIA) - FETA, 2 Waltham Court, Milley Lane, Hare Hatch, Reading, Berkshire. RG10 9TH tel:(01189) 403416. rogerb@feta.co.uk, www.bcia.co.uk

Building Research Establishment - BRE, Bucknalls Lane, Watford, Herts. WD25 9XX tel:(01923) 664000. enquiries@bre.co.uk, www.bre.co.uk

Bunting Magnetics Europe Limited - Northbridge Road, Berkhampstead, Hertfordshire. HP4 1EH tel:(01442) 875081, fax:(01442) 875009. sales@buntingeurope.com, www.buntingeurope.com

Burco Maxol - Rosegrove, Burnley, Lancs. BB12 6AL tel:(0844) 8153755, fax:(0844) 8153748. sales@burco.co.uk, www.burco.co.uk

Burlington Slate Ltd - Cavendish House, Kirkby in Furness, Cumbria. LA17 7UN tel:(01229) 889661, fax:(01229) 889466. sales@burlingtonstone.co.uk, www.burlingtonstone.co.uk

Burmatex Ltd - Victoria Mills, The Green, Ossett, W. Yorks. WF5 0AN tel:(01924) 262525, fax:(01924) 280033. projects@burmatex.co.uk, www.burmatex.co.uk

Burn Fencing Limited - West End Farm, West End Lane, Balne, Goole, E. Yorks. DN14 0EH tel:(01302) 708706, fax:(01302) 707377. richard@burnfencing.co.uk, www.burnfencing.co.uk

Bush Nelson PLC - Stephenson Way, Three Bridges, Crawley, W. Sussex. RH10 1TN tel:(01293) 547361, fax:(01293) 531432. sales@bnthermic.co.uk, www.bush-nelson.com

Bushboard Limited - 9-29 Rixon Road, Wellingborough, Northamptonshire. NN8 4BA tel:(01933) 232272. worktops@bushboard.co.uk, www.bushboard.co.uk

Bushboard Washrooms - Unit 1400 1st Floor Montagu Court, Kettering Parkway, Kettering Venture Park, Kettering, Northamptonshire. NN15 6XR tel:(01536) 533620. washrooms@bushboard-washrooms.co.uk, https://bushboard-washrooms.co.uk/

Butterworth-Heinemann - The Boulevard, Langford Lane, Kidlington, Oxford. OX5 1GB tel:(01865) 844640, fax:(01865) 843912. andrew.davis@elsevier.com, www.elsevier.com

Buzon UK - Unit 6, Teddington Business Park, Station Road, Teddington. TW11 9BQ tel:(020) 8614 0874, fax:(020) 8977 0825. sales@buzonuk.com, www.buzonuk.com

C

C & W Fencing Ltd - The Steelworks, Bradfield Road, Wix, Manningtree, Essex. CO11 2SG tel:(01255) 871300, fax:(01255) 871309. Sales@cw-fencing.co.uk, www.cw-fencing.co.uk

C.R. Longley & Co. Ltd - Ravensthorpe Road, Thornhill Lees, Dewsbury, W. Yorks. WF12 9EF tel:(01924) 464283, fax:(01924) 459183. sales@longley.uk.com, www.longley.uk.com

CA Group Ltd - MR-24 Division - No 1 The Parade, Lodge Drive, Culcheth, Cheshire. WA3 4ES tel:(01925) 764335, fax:(01925) 763445. info@cagroup.ltd.uk, www.cagroupltd.co.uk

CABU Limited - 20a Northburgh Street, London. EC1V 0EA tel:(020) 3019 1970. mail@cabu.co.uk, Website: www.cabu.co.uk

Cadisch MDA - Unit 2, The IO Centre, Hearle Way, Hatfield, Hertfordshire. AL10 9EW tel:(020) 8492 7622. info@cadisch.com, www.cadischmda.com

Caithness Flagstone Limited - 4, The Shore, Wick, Caithness. KW1 4JX tel:(01847) 841239, fax:(01847) 841321. lyndsay@caithnessflagstone.co.uk, www.caithnessflagstone.co.uk

Calder Industrial Materials Ltd - Elder House, Park West, Jupiter Drive, Chester. CH1 4RL tel:(01244) 393708, fax:(01244) 393740. Info@caldergroup.co.uk, www.caldergroup.co.uk

Caldwell Hardware (UK) Ltd - Herald Way, Binley Industrial Estate, Coventry, Warwicks. CV3 2RQ tel:(024) 7643 7900, fax:(024) 7643 7969. sales@caldwell.co.uk, www.caldwell.co.uk

Caledonian Modular - Carlton Works, Carlton-on-Trent, Newark, Nottinghamshire. NG23 6NT tel:(01636) 821645, fax:(01636) 821261. sales@caledonianmodular.com, www.caledonianmodular.com

Calomax Ltd - Lupton Avenue, Leeds, W. Yorks. LS9 7DD tel:(0113) 249 6681, fax:(0113) 235 0358. sales@calomax.co.uk, www.calomax.co.uk

Calor Gas Ltd - Athena Drive, Tachbrook Park, Warwick. CV34 6RL tel:(0800) 216659, fax:(0870) 4006904. enquiries@calor.co.uk, www.calor.co.uk

Calpeda Limited - Wedgwood Road Industrial Estate, Bicester, Oxon. OX26 4UL tel:(01869) 241441, fax:(01869) 240681. pumps@calpeda.co.uk, www.calpeda.co.uk

Camfil Farr Ltd - Knowsley Park Way, Haslingden, Lancs. BB4 4RS tel:(01706) 238000, fax:(01706) 226736. dustcollectors@camfil.co.uk, www.farrapc.com

Camlok Lifting Clamps Ltd - Knutsford Way, Sealand Industrial Estate, Chester, Cheshire. CH14NZ tel:(01244) 375375, fax:(01244) 377403. sales.uk@cmco.eu, www.camlok.co.uk

Cannock Gates UK Ltd - Martindale Industrial Estate, Hawks Green, Connock, Staffs. WS11 7XT tel:(01543) 462500, fax:(01543) 506237. sales@cannockgates.co.uk, www.cannockgates.co.uk

Cannon Hygiene Ltd - Northgate, White Lund Industrial Estate, Morecambe, Lancs. LA3 3BJ tel:(0870) 444 1988, fax:(0807) 444 3938. hygiene@citronhygiene.com, www.citronhygiene.com

Canopy Products Ltd - Paradise Works, Paradise Street, Ramsbottom. BL0 9BS tel:(01706) 822665, fax:(01706) 823333. sales@canopyproducts.co.uk, www.canopyproducts.co.uk

Cantifix of London Limited - Unit 9, Garrick Industrial Centre, Irving Way, London. NW9 6AQ tel:(020) 8203 6203, fax:(020) 8203 6454. webenquiries@cantifix.co.uk, www.cantifix.co.uk

Capco Test Equipment, A division of Castlebroom Engineering Ltd - Unit 10, Farthing Road, Ipswich, Suffolk. IP1 5AP tel:(01473) 748144, fax:(01473) 748179. sales@capco.co.uk, www.capco.co.uk

Capel Fencing Contractors Ltd - 22 Sychem Lane, Five Oak Green, Tonbridge, Kent. TNI2 6TR tel:(01892) 836036, fax:(01892) 834844. info@capelfencing.co.uk, www.capelfencing.co.uk

Cardale Garage Doors - Unit 5-9, North Luton Industrial Estate, Sedgewick Road, Luton, Beds. LU4 9DT tel:(01582) 563777, fax:(01582) 568801. customerservice@novoferm.co.uk, www.cardale.com

Carl F Groupco Limited - 130 Culley Court, Orton Southgate, Peterborough, Cambs. PE2 6WA tel:(01733) 393 330, fax:(01733) 393 336. sales@carlfgroupco.co.uk, www.carlfgroupco.co.uk

Carleton Furniture Group Ltd - Mill Dam Lane, Monkill, Pontefract, W. Yorks. WF8 2NS tel:(01977) 700770, fax:(01977) 708740. sales@carletonfurniture.com, www.carletonfurniture.com

Carlton Main Brickworks Ltd - Grimethorpe, Barnsley, S. Yorks. S72 7BG tel:(01226) 711521, fax:(01226) 780417. sales@carltonbrick.co.uk, www.carltonbrick.co.uk

Caroflow Ltd - Edgebarn, 11 Market Hill, Royston. SG8 9JN tel:(01763) 244446, fax:(01763) 244111. info@caro.co.uk, www.caro.co.uk

Carpets of Worth Ltd - Townshed Works, Puxton Lane, Kidederminster, Worcs. DY11 5DF tel:(01562) 745000, fax:(01562) 732827. sales@carpetsofworth.co.uk, www.carpetsofworth.co.uk

Carron Phoenix Ltd - Stenhouse Road, Carron, Falkirk, Stirlingshire. FK2 8DW tel:(01324) 638321, fax:(01324) 620978. sales@carron.com, www.carron.com

Carter Concrete Ltd - Stonehill Way, Holt Road, Cromer, Norfolk. NR27 9JW tel:(01263) 516919, fax:(01263) 512399. mail@carter-concrete.co.uk, www.carter-concrete.co.uk

Carter Environmental Engineers Ltd - Hamilton House, 2 Lawley, Midleway, Birmingham. B4 7XL tel:(0121) 250 1415, fax:(0121) 250 1400. sales@cee.co.uk, www.cee.co.uk

Carter Retail Equipment Ltd - Redhill Road, Birmingham. B25 8EY tel:(0121) 250 1000, fax:(0121) 250 1005. info@cre-ltd.co.uk, www.cre-ltd.co.uk

Carter-Dal International - New Broad Street House, New Broad Street House, London. EC2M 1NH tel:(0207) 030 3395. info@carter-dal.com, www.Carter-Dal.com

Casella UK - Regent House, Wolseley Road, Kempston, Bedford, Beds. MK42 7JY tel:(01234) 844100, fax:(01234) 844150. info@casellasolutions.com, www.casellasolutions.com

Cast Metals Federation - The National Metal Forming Centre, 47 Birmingham Road, West Bromwich, W. Midlands. B70 6PY tel:(0121) 601 6397, fax:(0121) 601 6391. admin@cmfed.co.uk, www.castmetalsfederation.com

Castell Safety International - The Castell Building, 217 Kingsbury Road, Kingsbury, London. NW9 9PQ tel:(020) 8200 1200, fax:(020) 8205 0055. sales@castell.com, www.castell.com

Castle Cement Ltd - Park Square, 3160 Solihull Parkway, Brimingham Business Park, Birmingham, W. Midlands. B37 7YN tel:(0121) 779 7771, fax:(0121) 779 7609. enquiries@hanson.com, www.castlecement.co.uk

C (con't)

Castle Composites Ltd - Nisbet Way, Ravenstruther, Lanark. ML11 7SF tel:(01555) 870 003, fax:(01555) 870 040. sales@castlecomposites.co.uk, www.castlecomposites.co.uk

Caswell & Co Ltd - 6 Princewood Road, Earlstrees Ind. Estate, Corby, Northants. NN17 4AP tel:(01536) 464800, fax:(01536) 464801. sales@caswell-adhesives.co.uk, www.caswell-adhesives.co.uk

Catering Equipment Suppliers Association - 235/237 Vauxhall Bridge Road, London. SW1V 1EJ tel:(020) 7233 7724, fax:(020) 7828 0667. enquiries@cesa.org.uk, www.cesa.org.uk

Catnic - Pontypandy Industrial Estate, Caerphilly, M. Glam. CF83 3GL tel:(029) 20337900, fax:(029) 20867796. catnic.technical@tatasteel.com, www.catnic.com

Caunton Engineering Ltd - Moorgreen Industrial Park, Moorgreen, Nottingham, Notts. NG16 3QU tel:(01773) 531111, fax:(01773) 532020. sales@caunton.co.uk, www.caunton.co.uk

Cave Tab Ltd - 1 Sovereign Court, South Portway Close, Round Spinney, Northampton, Northants. NN3 8RH tel:(01604) 798500, fax:(01604) 798505. info@civica.co.uk, www.cavetab.co.uk

Cavity Trays Ltd - Administration Centre, Boundary Avenue, Yeovil, Somerset. BA22 8HU tel:(01935) 474769, fax:(01935) 428223. sales@cavitytrays.co.uk, www.cavitytrays.com

CB Arts Ltd - Low Mill Business Park, Morecambe Road, Ulverston. LA12 9EE tel:(01229) 588580. enquiries@cb-arts.co.uk, www.cb-arts.co.uk

CBS (Curtain and Blind Specialists Ltd) - 1 Fellgate, White Lund Industrial Estate, Morecambe. LA3 3PE tel:(01524) 383000, fax:(01524) 383111. sales@cbseurope.com, www.cbseurope.com

CED Ltd - 728 London Road, West Thurrock, Grays, Essex. RM20 3LU tel:(01708) 867237, fax:(01708) 867230. sales@ced.ltd.uk, www.ced.ltd.uk

Cefndy Healthcare - Cefndy Road, Rhyl, Denbighshire. LL18 2HG tel:(01745) 343877, fax:(01745) 355806. cefndy.sales@denbighshire.gov.uk, www.cefndy.com

Celotex Ltd - Lady Lane Industrial Estate, Hadleigh, Ipswich, Suffolk. IP7 6BA tel:(01473) 822093, fax:(01473) 820880. info@celotex.co.uk, www.celotex.co.uk

Celuform Building Products - Billet Lane, Normanby Enterprise Park, Normanby Road, Scunthorpe, North Lincolnshire. DN15 9YH tel:(08705) 920930, fax:(08700) 720930. info@celuform.co.uk, www.celuform.co.uk

CEM Systems Ltd - 195 Airport Road West, Belfast. BT3 9ED tel:(028) 90 456767, fax:(028) 90 454535. cem.sales@tycoint.com, www.cemsys.com

Cembrit Ltd - Studio 39, Thames Innovation Centre, 2 Veridion Way, Erith, Kent. DA18 4AL tel:(020) 3372 2300. sales@cembrit.co.uk, www.cembrit.co.uk

Cement Admixtures Association - C/o Hillier Hopkins LLP, Radius House, 51 Clarendon Road, Watfotd, Herts. WD17 1HP tel:(07702) 635231. info@admixtures.org.uk, www.admixtures.org.uk

CEMEX - CEMEX House, Coldharbour Lane, Thorpe, Egham, Surrey. TW20 8TD tel:(01788) 517000. sales@cemex.com, www.cemex.co.uk

Cento Engineering Company Ltd - Unit 6, Baddow Park, West Hanningfield, Chelmsford, Essex. CM2 7SY tel:(01245) 477708, fax:(01245) 477748. info@cento.co.uk, www.cento.co.uk

Certikin International Ltd - Unit 9, Witan Park, Avenue 2, Station Lane Industrial Estate, Witney, Oxon. OX28 4FJ tel:(01993) 778855, fax:(01993) 778620. info@certikin.co.uk, www.certikin.co.uk

CFS Carpets - Arrow Valley, Claybrook Drive, Redditch, Worcestershire. B98 0FY tel:(01527) 511860, fax:(01527) 511864. sales@cfscarpets.co.uk, www.cfscarpets.co.uk

CGL Facades - 2 Young Place, Kelvin Industrial Estate, East Kilbridge, Lanarkshire. G75 0TD tel:(01355) 235561, fax:(01355) 247189. sales@cglfacades.co.uk, www.cglfacades.co.uk

Challenge Fencing Ltd - Downside Road, Cobham, Surrey. KT11 3LY tel:(01932) 866555, fax:(01932) 866445. cobhamsales@challengefencing.com, www.challengefencing.com

Chalmit Lighting - 388 Hillington Road, Glasgow, Lanarkshire. G52 4BL tel:(0141) 882 5555, fax:(0141) 883 3704. info@chalmit.com, www.chalmit.com

Chameleon Stone Ltd - Unit 3 Longton Industrial Estate, Winterstoke Road, Weston-Super-Mare, N. Somerset. BS23 3YB tel:(01934) 616275. chameleonstone@live.co.uk, www.tilesofnaturalstone.co.uk

Channel Safety Systems Ltd - 9 Petersfield Business Park, Bedford Road, Petersfield, Hants. GU32 3QA tel:(0870) 243 0931, fax:(0870) 243 0932. sales@channelsafety.co.uk, www.channelsafety.co.uk

Chapel Studio - Bridge Road, Hunton Bridge, Kings Langley, Herts. WD4 8RE tel:(01923) 226386, fax:(01923) 269707. customer@chapelstudio.co.uk, www.btinternet.com/~chapelstudio

Charles Lawrence Surfaces Ltd - Brunel House, Jessop Way, Newark, Notts. NG24 2ER tel:(01636) 615866, fax:(01636) 615867. sales@charleslawrencesurfaces.co.uk, www.charleslawrencesurfaces.co.uk

Charles Lightfoot Ltd - Orchard House, Heywood Road, Sale. M33 3WB tel:(0161) 973 6565. info@charleslightfoot.co.uk, www.charleslightfoot.co.uk

Charnwood Fencing Limited - Beveridge Lane, Bardon Hill, Leicester, Leics. LE67 1TB tel:(01530) 835835, fax:(01530) 814545. darren@charnwoodfencing.com, www.charnwoodfencing.com

Chartered Building Company Scheme - Englemere, Kings Ride, Ascot, Berks. SL5 7TB tel:(01344) 630 743, fax:(01344) 630777. cbcinfo@ciob.org.uk, www.cbcscheme.org.uk

Chartered Building Consultancy Scheme - Englemere, Kings Ride, Ascot, Berks. SL5 7TB tel:(01344) 630700, fax:(01344) 630777. cbcinfo@ciob.org.uk, www.cbcscheme.org.uk

Chartered Institute of Arbitrators - International Arbitration Centre, 12 Bloomsbury Square, London. WC1A 2LP tel:(020) 7421 7444, fax:(020) 7404 4023. info@ciarb.org, www.arbitrators.org

Chartered Institute of Building - 1 Arlington Square, Downshire Way, Bracknell, Berkshire. RG12 1WA tel:(01344) 630 700, fax:(01344) 306 430. info@ciob-mail.org.uk, www.ciob.org

Chartered Institute of Plumbing & Heating Engineering - 64 Station Lane, Hornchurch, Essex. RM12 6NB tel:(01708) 472791, fax:(01708) 448987. info@ciphe.org.uk, www.ciphe.org.uk

Chartered Institute of Wastes Management - 9 Saxon Court, St Peters Gardens, Northampton, Northants. NN1 1SX tel:(01604) 620426, fax:(01604) 621339. ciwm@ciwm.co.uk, www.ciwm.co.uk

Chartered Institution of Building Services Engineers (CIBSE) - Delta House, 222 Balham High Road, London. SW12 9BS tel:(020) 8675 5211, fax:(020) 8675 5449. www.cibse.org

Chase Equipment Ltd - Wellington House, Sangwin Road, Coseley, Bilston, West Midlands. WV14 9EE tel:(01902) 675835, fax:(01902) 674998. sales@chaseequipment.com, www.chaseequipment.com

Chelsea Artisans Ltd - Units 1-2 Pylon Way, Beddington Farm Road, Croydon. CR0 4XX tel:(0208) 665 0558, fax:(0208) 689 6288. info@chelsea-fusion.com, www.chelsea-fusion.com

Chesterfelt Ltd - Foxwood Way, Sheepbridge, Chesterfield, Derbys. S41 9RA tel:(01246) 268000, fax:(01246) 268001. general@chesterfelt.co.uk, www.chesterfelt.co.uk

Chestnut Products - PO Box 260, Stowmarket. IP14 9BX tel:(01473) 890118, fax:(01473) 206522. mailroom@chestnutproducts.co.uk, www.chestnutproducts.co.uk

Chestnut Products Limited - Unit 15, Gaza Trading Estate, Hildenborough, Tonbridge, Kent. TN11 8PL tel:(01732) 463 777, fax:(01732) 454 636. sales@chestnut-products.co.uk, www.chestnut-products.co.uk

Chichester Stoneworks Limited - Chichester Stoneworks Limited, Terminus Road, Chichester, West Sussex. PO19 8TX tel:(01243) 784225, fax:(01243) 785616. info@csworks.co.uk, www.chichesterstoneworks.co.uk

Chilstone - Victoria Park, Fordcombe Road, Langton Green, Tunbridge Wells, Kent. TN3 0RD tel:(01892) 740 866, fax:(01892) 740 785. office@chilstone.com, www.chilstone.com

Chiltern Concrete and Stone - 21, Murdock Road, Bedford, Bedfordshire. MK41 7PE tel:(01246) 856 497, fax:(01234) 35 25 75. sales@chilternconcreteandstone.co.uk, www.chilternconcreteandstone.co.uk

Chiltern Invadex - Chiltern House, 6 Wedgewood Road, Bichester, Oxon. OX26 4UL tel:(01869) 246470, fax:(01869) 247214. sales@chilterninvadex.co.uk, www.chilterninvadex.co.uk

Chiorino UK Ltd - Phoenix Avenue, Green Lane Industrial Park, Featherstone, West Yorkshire. WF7 6EP tel:(01977) 691880, fax:(01977) 791 547. sales@chiorino.co.uk, www.chiorino.co.uk

Chippindale Plant Ltd - Prima House, Lower Wortley Ring Road, Leeds, W. Yorks. LS12 5PX tel:(0113) 263 2344, fax:(0113) 279 1710. sales@chippindale-plant.co.uk, www.chippindale-plant.co.uk

Christie & Grey Ltd - Morley Road, Tonbridge, Kent. TN9 1RA tel:(01732) 371100, fax:(01732) 359666. sales@christiegrey.com, www.christiegrey.com

Chromalox (UK) Ltd - Amp House, 2nd Floor, Dingwall Road, Croydon, Surrey. CR0 2LX tel:(0208) 6658900, fax:(0208) 6890571. uksales@chromalox.com, www.chromalox.co.uk

Chubb Safe Equipment Company - PO Box 61, Wednesfield Road, Wolverhampton. WV10 0EW tel:(01902) 455111, fax:(01902) 351961. marketing.uk@gunnebo.com, www.chubb-safes.com

Chubb Systems Ltd - Number One @ The Beehive Shadsworth Business Park, Lions Drive, Blackburn, Lancashire. BB1 2QS tel:(01254) 688583, fax:(01254) 667663. systems-sales@chubb.co.uk, www.chubbsystems.co.uk

Cil Retail Solutions Ltd - Unit 8, Temple House Estate, 7 West Road, Harlow, Essex. CM20 2DU tel:(01279) 444448. info@cil.co.uk, www.cil.co.uk

Cintec International Ltd - Cintec House, 11 Gold Tops, Newport, S. Wales. NP20 4PH tel:(01633) 246614, fax:(01633) 246110. hqcintec@cintec.com, www.cintec.com

Ciret Limited - FulFlood Road, Havant, Hampshire. PO9 5AX tel:(02392) 457450, fax:(02392) 457451. enquiries@ciret.co.uk, www.ciret.co.uk

Cistermiser Ltd - Unit 1, Woodley Park Estate, 59-69 Reading Raod, Woodley, Reading. RG5 3AN tel:(0118) 969 1611. sales@cistermiser.co.uk, www.cistermiser.co.uk

Civil Engineering Contractors Association - 1 Birdcage Walk, London. SW1H 9JJ tel:(0207) 340 0450. lauraellis@ceca.co.uk, www.ceca.co.uk

Clare R S & Co Ltd - Stanhope Street, Liverpool, Merseyside. L8 5RQ tel:(0151) 709 2902. info@rsclare.co.uk , www.rsclare.com

Clark Door Ltd - Unit F, Central Kingmoor Park, Carlisle, Cumbria. CA6 4SD tel:(01228) 522321, fax:(01228) 401854. mail@clarkdoor.com, www.clarkdoor.com

Clarke UK Ltd - Grange Works, Lomond Road, Coatbridge, Lanarkshire. ML5 2NN tel:(0123) 6707560, fax:(0123) 6427274. dmurray@clarkefire.com, www.clarkefire.com

Clarksteel Ltd - Station Works, Station Road, Yaxley, Peterborough. PE7 3EQ tel:(01733) 765 317. sales@clarksteel.com, www.clarksteel.com

Clay Pipe Development Association Ltd - Copsham House, 53 Broad Street, Chesham, Bucks. HP5 3EA tel:(01494) 791456, fax:(01494) 792378. cpda@aol.com, www.cpda.co.uk

Cleenol Group Ltd - Beaumont Road, Banbury, Oxon. OX16 1RB tel:(01295) 251721, fax:(01295) 269561. sales@cleenol.co.uk, www.cleenol.co.uk

Clement Steel Windows - Clement House, Weydown Industrial Estate, Haslemere, Surrey. GU27 1HR tel:(01428) 643 393, fax:(01428) 644 436. info@clementwg.co.uk, www.clementwindows.co.uk

Clenaware Systems Ltd - 44 Huxley Close, Park Farm Industrial Estate, Wellingborough, Northamptonshire. NN8 6AB tel:(01933) 666244. info@clenaware.co.uk, www.clenaware.co.uk

Clestra Limited - 1st Floor, Kent House, 27-33 Upper Mulgrave Road, Cheam, Surrey. SM2 7AY tel:(020) 8773 2121. uksales@clestra.com, www.clestra.com

Clifford Partitioning Co Ltd - 433, Kingston Road, Ewell, Surrey. KT19 0DB tel:(0208) 7861974. admin@clifford56.com, www.cliffordpartitioning.co.uk

Climate Center - The Wolseley Center, Harrison Way, Spa Park, Royal Leamington Spa. CV31 3HH tel:(01282) 834498. customerservices@wolseley.co.uk, www.climatecenter.co.uk

Clivet UK Ltd - 4 Kingdom Close, Segensworth East, Hants. PO15 5TJ tel:(01489) 572238, fax:(01489) 573033. l.joy@clivet-uk.co.uk, www.clivet.com

Clow Group Ltd - Diamond Ladder Factory, 562-584 Lea Bridge Road, Leyton, London. E10 7DW tel:(020) 8558 0300, fax:(020) 8558 0301. clow@ladders-direct.co.uk, www.ladders-direct.co.uk

Coblands Landscapes Ltd - South Farm Barn, South Farm Lane, Langton Green, Tunbridge Wells, Kent. TN3 9JN tel:(01892) 863535, fax:(01892) 863778. info@coblandslandscapes.co.uk, www.coblandslandscapes.co.uk

Coburn Sliding Systems Ltd - Unit 1, Cardinal West, Cardinal Distribution Park, Cardinal Way, Godmanchester, Huntingdon, Cambridgeshire. PE29 2XN tel:(020) 8545 6700, fax:(020) 8545 6720. sales@coburn.co.uk, www.coburn.co.uk

Colas Ltd - Cakemore Road, Rowley Regis, Warley, W. Midlands. B65 0QU tel:(0121) 561 4332, fax:(0121) 559 5217. info@colas.co.uk, www.colas.co.uk

Colebrand Ltd - 162-168, Regent Street, London. W1B 5TD tel:(020) 7439 1000, fax:(020) 7734 3358. enquiries@colebrand.com, www.colebrand.com

Coleford Brick & Tile Co Ltd - The Royal Forest of Dean Brickworks, Hawkwell Green, Cinderford, Glos. GL14 3JJ tel:(01594) 822160, fax:(01594) 826655. sales@colefordbrick.co.uk, www.colefordbrick.co.uk

Collier W H Ltd - Church Lane, Marks Tey, Colchester, Essex. CO6 1LN tel:(01206) 210301, fax:(01206) 212540. sales@whcollier.co.uk, www.whcollier.co.uk

Collins Walker Ltd, Elec Steam & Hot Water Boilers - 78, College Street, Kempston, Bedford. MK42 8LU tel:(01234) 34 00 44, fax:(01234) 34 00 65. enquiries@collins-walker.co.uk, www.collins-walker.co.uk

Colt International - Unit 3 Kenwood Business Park, New Lane, Havant, Hants. PO9 2LY tel:(023) 92451111, fax:(023) 92454220. info@coltgroup.com, www.coltinfo.co.uk

Coltman Precast Concrete Ltd - London Road, Canwell, Sutton Coldfield, W. Midlands. B75 5SX tel:(01543) 480482, fax:(01543) 481587. enquiries@coltman.co.uk, www.coltman.co.uk

Comar Architectural Aluminium Systems - Unit 5, The Willow Centre, 17 Willow Lane, Mitcham, Surrey. CR4 4NX tel:(020) 8685 9685, fax:(020) 8646 5096. sales@parksidegrp.co.uk, www.comar-alu.co.uk

Combat Heating Solutions - Unit 20, Red Mill Trading Estate, Rigby St, Wednesbury. WS10 0NP tel:(0121) 506 7700. uksales@combat.co.uk, www.combat.co.uk

Comber Models - 17, London Lane, London. E8 3PR tel:(01622) 355 850. info@combermodels.com, www.combermodels.com

Combustion Linings Ltd - Jacaidem Works, Walley Street, Burslem, Stoke-on-Trent. ST6 2AH tel:(01782) 822712, fax:(01782) 823920. jeff.hurst@combustionlinings.com, www.combustionlinings.com

Commercial Lighting Systems - Units 16 &17, Chandlers Way, Swanick, Southampton. SO31 1FQ tel:(01489) 581002, fax:(01489) 576262. sales@commercial-lighting.co.uk, www.commercial-lighting.co.uk

Commodore Kitchens Ltd - Acorn House, Gumley Road, Grays, Essex. RM20 4XP tel:(01375) 382323, fax:(01375) 394955. info@commodorekitchens.co.uk, www.commodorekitchens.co.uk

Company name: Britannia Metalwork Services Ltd - Units N1-N4 Andoversford Link, Andoversford Industrial Estate, Cheltenham, Gloucestershire. GL54 4LB tel:(01242) 820 037. info@britannia.uk.com, www.britannia.uk.com

Component Developments - Halesfield 10, Telford, Shropshire. TF7 4QP tel:(01952) 588488. sales@componentdevelopments.com, www.componentdevelopments.com

Composite Panel Services Ltd - CPS House, Clay Street, Hull, N. Humberside. HU8 8HA tel:(01482) 620277, fax:(01482) 587121. info@cps-hull.co.uk, www.cps-hull.co.uk

Compriband Ltd - Bentall Business Park, Glover, District II, Washington, Tyne & Wear. NE37 3JD tel:(0191) 4196860, fax:(0191) 4196861. uk.sales@tremco-illbruck.com, www.compribrand.co.uk

Computertel Ltd - CTL House, 52 Bath Street, Gravesend, Kent. DA11 0DF tel:(01474) 561111, fax:(01474) 561122. sales@computertel.co.uk, www.computertel.co.uk

Comyn Ching & Co (Solray) Ltd - Garngoch Ind. Est, Phoenix Way, Gorseinon, Swansea. SA4 9WF tel:(01792) 892211, fax:(01792) 898855. sales@solray.co.uk, www.solray.co.uk

Concept Sign & Display Ltd - 22 Gas Street, Birmingham, West Midlands. B1 2JT tel:(0121) 693 0005, fax:(0121) 747 3602. signs@conceptsigns.co.uk, www.conceptsigns.co.uk

Concrete Block Association - 60 Charles Street, Leicester. LE1 1FB tel:(0116) 222 1507, fax:(0116) 251 4568. is@britishprecast.org, www.cba-blocks.org.uk

Concrete Pipeline Systems Association - The Old Rectory, Main Street, Glenfield, Leicestershite. LE3 8DG tel:(0116) 232 5170, fax:(0116) 232 5197. email@concretepipes.co.uk, www.concretepipes.co.uk

Concrete Repairs Ltd - Cathite House, 23a Willow Lane, Mitcham, Surrey. CR4 4TU tel:(020) 8288 4848, fax:(020) 8288 4847. contact@crl.eu.com, www.crl.uk.com

Condair Plc - Artex Avenue, Rustington, Littlehampton, West Sussex. BN16 3LN tel:(01903) 850200, fax:(01903) 850345. uk.sales@condair.com, www.condair.co.uk

Conex Universal Limited - Global House, 95 Vantage Point, The Pensnett Estate, Kingswinford, West Midlands. DY6 7FT tel:(0121) 557 2831 2955, fax:(0121) 520 8778. salesuk@ibpgroup.com, www.conexbanninger.com

Confederation of British Metalforming - The National Metalforming Centre, 47 Birmingham Road, West Bromwich, West Midlands. B70 6PY tel:(0121) 601 6350, fax:(0121) 601 6373. crsa@crsauk.com, www.crsauk.com

Confor: Promoting forestry and wood - 59 George Street (3rd Floor), Edinburgh. EH2 2JG tel:(0131) 240 1410, fax:(0131) 240 1411. mail@confor.org.uk, www.confor.org.uk

Connaught Communications Systems Ltd - Systems House, Reddicap Estate, Sutton Coalfield, Birmingham. B75 7BU tel:(0121) 311 1010, fax:(0121) 311 1890. info@connaughtltd.co.uk, www.connaughtltd.co.uk

Connect Lighting Systems (UK) Ltd - 1B Wessex Gate, Portsmouth Road, Horndean, Hants. PO8 9LP tel:(023) 9257 0098, fax:(023) 9257 0097. sales@connectlighting.co.uk, www.connectlighting.co.uk

Conren Ltd - Unit 1 The Bridge Business Centre Ash Road South, Wrexham Industrial Estate, Wrexham. LL13 9UG tel:(01978) 661 991, fax:(01978) 664 664. info@conren.com, www.conren.com

Consort Equipment Products Ltd - Thornton Industrial Estate, Milford Haven, Pembs. SA73 2RT tel:(01646) 692172, fax:(01646) 695195. enquiries@consortepl.com, www.consortepl.com

Constant Air Systems Ltd - Unit L Castle Estate, Turnpike Way, Cressex Business Park, High Wycombe, Bucks. HP12 3TF tel:(01494) 469529. admin@constantair.co.uk, www.constantair.co.uk

Construction Employers Federation - 143 Malone Road, Belfast. BT9 6SU tel:(028) 90 877143, fax:(028) 90 877155. mail@cefni.co.uk, www.cefni.co.uk

C (con't)

Construction Group UK Ltd - Dexion Comino Ltd, Murdock Road, Dorcan, Swindon, Wiltshire. SN3 5HY tel:(0870) 224 0220 , fax:(0870) 224 0221. enquiries@dexion.co.uk, www.dexion.co.uk

Construction Industry Publications - C/o Knowledgepoint LTD, C2 Eksdale Road, Winnersh Triangle, Wokingham. RG41 5TS tel:(0870) 078 4400. sales@cip-books.com, www.cip-books.com

Construction Industry Research & Information Association - Griffin Court, 15 Long Lane, London. EC1A 9PN tel:(020) 7549 3300, fax:(020) 7549 3349. enquiries@ciria.org, www.ciria.org

Construction Industry Training Board - CITB, Bircham Newton, Kings Lynn, Norfolk. PE31 6RH tel:(01485) 577577, fax:(01485) 577793. press.office@citb.co.uk, www.citb.org.uk

Construction Plant-hire Association - 27/28 Newbury Street, Barbican, London. EC1A 7HU tel:(020) 7796 3366, fax:(020) 7796 3399. enquiries@cpa.uk.net, www.cpa.uk.net

Constructionline - PO Box 6441, Basingstoke, Hants. RG21 7FN tel:(0844) 892 0312, fax:(0844) 892 0315. constructionline@capita.co.uk, www.constructionline.co.uk

Consult Lighting Ltd - 92 Grange Lane (rear Of), Barnsley, S. Yorks. S71 5QQ tel:(01226) 956820. john@consultlighting.co.uk, www.consultlighting.co.uk

Contactum Ltd - Edgware Road, London. NW2 6LF tel:(020) 8452 6366, fax:(020) 8208 3340. enquiries@contactum.co.uk, www.contactum.co.uk

Continental Sports Ltd - Hill Top Road, Paddock, Huddersfield. HD1 4SD tel:(01484) 542051, fax:(01484) 539148. sales@contisports.co.uk, www.contisports.co.uk

Contour Showers Ltd - Siddorn Street, Winsford, Cheshire. CW7 2BA tel:(01606) 592586, fax:(01606) 861260. sales@contour-shower.co.uk, www.contour-showers.co.uk

Contract Flooring Association - Unit 23 Eldon Business Park, Eldon road, Chilwell, Nottingham. NG9 6DZ tel:(0115) 941 1126, fax:(0115) 941 2238. info@cfa.org.uk, www.cfa.org.uk

Contract Journal - Reed Business Information, Quadrant House, The Quadrant, Sutton, Surrey. SM2 5AS tel:(020) 8652 4805, fax:(020) 8652 4804. contract.journale@rbi.co.uk, www.contractjournal.com

Cooke Brothers Ltd - Northgate, Aldridge, Walsall, W. Midlands. WS9 8TL tel:(01922) 740001, fax:(01922) 456227. sales@cookebrothers.co.uk, www.cookebrothers.co.uk

Cookson and Zinn (PTL) Ltd - Station Road Works, Hadleigh, Ipswich, Suffolk. IP7 5PN tel:(01473) 825200, fax:(01473) 824164. info@czltd.com, www.czltd.com

Cooper & Turner - Sheffield Road, Sheffield. S9 1RS tel:(0114) 256 0057, fax:(0114) 244 5529. sales@cooperandturner.co.uk, www.cooperandturner.co.uk

Cooper Group Ltd - Unit 18, The Tanneries, Brockhampton Lane, Havant, Hants. PO9 1JB tel:(02392) 454405, fax:(02392) 492732. info@coopersfire.com, www.coopersblinds.co.uk

Cooper Lighting - Wheatley Hall Road, Doncaster, S. Yorks. DN2 4NB tel:(01302) 303303, fax:(01302) 367155. sales@cooper-ls.com, www.jsb-electrical.com

Cooper Safety - Jephson Court, Tancred Close, Royal Leamington Spa, Warwickshire. CV31 3RZ tel:(01926) 439200, fax:(01926) 439240. sales@cooper-ls.com, www.cooper-safety.com

Coo-Var Ltd - Elenshaw Works, Lockwood Street, Hull. HU2 0HN tel:(01482) 328053, fax:(01482) 219266. info@coo-var.co.uk, www.coo-var.co.uk

Copley Decor Ltd - Unit 1 Leyburn Business Park, Leyburn, N. Yorks. DL8 -5QA tel:(01969) 623410, fax:(01969) 624398. mouldings@copleydecor.co.uk, www.copleydecor.com

Coram Showers Ltd - Stanmore Industrial Estate, Bridgnorth, Shropshire. WV15 5HP tel:(01746) 766466, fax:(01746) 764140. sales@coram.co.uk, www.coram.co.uk

Corbett & Co (Galvanising) W Ltd - New Alexandra Works, Haledane, Halesfield 1, Telford, Shropshire. TF7 4QQ tel:(01952) 412777, fax:(01952) 412888. sales@wcorbett.co.uk, www.wcorbett.co.uk

Cordek Ltd - Spring Copse Business Park, Slinfold, W. Sussex. RH13 0SZ tel:(01403) 799601, fax:(01403) 791718. info@cordek.com, www.cordek.com

Corgi Technical Dervices - Unit 8, The Park Centre, Easter Park, Benyon Road, Silchester, Berkshire. RG7 2PQ tel:(01256) 548 040, fax:(01256) 548055. Enquiries@trustcorgi.org, www.corgitechnical.com

Corroless Corrosion Control - Kelvin Way, West Bromwich, W. Midlands. B70 7JZ tel:(0121) 524 2235, fax:(0121) 553 2787. info-corroless@axalta.com, www.corroless.com

Cottam & Preedy Ltd - Bishopsgate Works, 68 Lower City Road, Oldbury, W. Midlands. B69 2HF tel:(0121) 552 5281, fax:(0121) 552 6895. enquiries@cottamandpreedy.co.uk, www.cottamandpreedy.co.uk

Cottam Brush Ltd - Monkton Business Park, North Hebburn. NE31 2JZ sales@cottambrush.com, www.cottambrush.com

Cottam Brush Ltd - Unit 7, Monkton Business Park North, Hebburn. NE31 2JZ tel:(0845) 4348436, fax:(0845) 4348437. info@cottambrush.com, www.cottambrush.com

Council for Aluminium in Building - River View House, Bond's Mill, Stonehouse, Glos. GL10 3RF tel:(01453) 828851, fax:(01453) 828861. enquiries@c-a-b.org.uk, www.c-a-b.org.uk

Covers Timber & Builders Merchants - Sussex House, Quarry Lane, Chichester, West Sussex. PO19 8PE tel:(01243) 785141, fax:(01243) 531151. enquiries@coversmerchants.co.uk, www.coversmerchants.co.uk

Coverscreen UK LLP - Unit 192, 19 - 21 Crawford Street, London. W1H 1PJ tel:(0845) 680 0409 . sales@brass-grilles.co.uk, www.brass-grilles.co.uk

Coverworld UK Limited - Mansfield Road, Bramley Vale, Chesterfield, Derbyshire. S44 5GA tel:(01246) 858222, fax:(01246) 858223. sales@coverworld.co.uk, www.coverworld.co.uk

Cowley Timber & Partners Limited - Unit 13 Abbotts Way, Newark Business Park, Newark, Notts. NG24 2EL tel:(01522) 720022. mail@cowleytimber.co.uk, www.cowleytimber.co.uk

Cox Building Products Ltd - Unit 1, Shaw Road, Bushbury, Wolverhampton, W. Midlands. WV10 9LA tel:(01902) 371800, fax:(01902) 371810. sales@coxdome.co.uk, www.coxbp.com

Cox Long Ltd - Airfield Industrial Estate, Hixon, Stafford, Staffs. ST18 0PA tel:(01889) 270166, fax:(01889) 271041. info@coxlong.com

CPS Manufacturing Co - Brunel House, Brunel Close, Harworth, Doncaster. DN11 8QA tel:(01302) 741888, fax:(01302) 741999. sales@cpsmanufacturingco.com, www.cpsmanufacturingco.com

CPV Ltd - Woodington Mill, East Wellow, Romsey, Hampshire. SO51 6DQ tel:(01794) 322884, fax:(01794) 322885. enquiries@cpv.co.uk, www.cpv.co.uk

Craft Guild of Chefs - 1 Victoria Parade, by 331 Sandycombe Road, Richmond, Surrey. TW9 3NB tel:(020) 8948 3870. enquiries@craftguildofchefs.org, www.craftguildofchefs.org

Cranborne Stone Limited - Butts Pond, Sturminster Newton, Dorset. DT10 1AZ tel:(01258) 472685. team@cranbornestone.com, www.cranbornestone.co.uk

Crane Composites - 25 Caker Stream Road, Mill Lane Industry Estate, Alton, Hampshire. GU34 2QF tel:(01420) 593270, fax:(01420) 541124. sales@cranecomposites.com, www.cranecomposites.com

Crane Fluid Systems - Crane House, Epsilon Terrace, West Road, Ipswich, Suffolk. IP3 9FJ tel:(01473) 277 300, fax:(01473) 277 301. enquiries@cranefs.com, www.cranefs.com

Creative Glass - Design House, 20-22 Lustrum Avenue, Portrack Lane, Stockton-on-Tees. TS18 2RB tel:(01642) 603545, fax:(01642) 604667. info@creativeglass.co.uk, www.creativeglass.co.uk

Crendon Timber Engineering Ltd - Drakes Drive, Long Crendon, Aylesbury, Bucks. HP18 9BA tel:(01844) 201020, fax:(01844) 201625. sales@crendon.co.uk, www.crendon.co.uk

Crescent Lighting - Unit H2 Raceview Business Centre, Hambridge Road, Newbury, Berkshire. RG14 5SA tel:(01635) 899 616. info@crescent.co.uk, www.crescent.co.uk

Crittall Steel Windows Ltd - Francis House, Freebournes Road, Witham, Essex. CM8 3UN tel:(01376) 530 800. hq@crittall-windows.co.uk, www.crittall-windows.co.uk

Crittall Steel Windows Ltd - Springwood Drive, Braintree, Essex. CM7 2YN tel:(01376) 324106, fax:(01376) 349662. hq@crittall-windows.co.uk, www.crittall-windows.co.uk

Cross-Guard International Ltd - Bridge House, Severn Bridge Riverside North, Bewdley, Worcs. DY12 1AB tel:(01299) 406022, fax:(01299) 406023. info@cross-guard.co.uk, www.cross-guard.co.uk

Crown Paints Ltd - Crown House, P O Box 37, Hollins Road, Darwen, Lancashire. BB3 0BG tel:(0330) 0240310. info@crownpaintspec.co.uk, www.crownpaintspec.co.uk

CrowsonFabrics Ltd - Crowson House, Bolton Close, Bellbrook Ind Est, Uckfield, Sussex. TN22 1QZ tel:(01202) 753277, fax:(01202) 762582. sales@crowsonfabrics.com, www.monkwell.com

Crowthorne Fencing - Englemere Sawmill, London Road, Ascot, Berks. SL5 8DG tel:(01344) 885451, fax:(01344) 893101. ascot@crowthornefencing.co.uk, www.crowthorneascot.co.uk

Cryotherm Insulation Ltd - Hirst Wood Works, Hirst Wood Road, Shipley, W. Yorks. BD18 4BU tel:(01274) 589175, fax:(01274) 531 969. enquiries@cryotherm.co.uk, www.cryotherm.co.uk

CSSP (Construction Software Services Partnership) - Regus Bromley South, 1 Elmfield Park, Bromley, Kent. BR1 1LU tel:(020) 3900 2515. enq@cssp.co.uk, www.cssp.co.uk

CST Industries, Inc. - UK - Cotes Park Lane, Cotes Park Industrial Estate, Alfreton, Derbyshire. DE55 4NJ tel:(01773) 835321, fax:(01773) 836578. europe@cstindustries.com, www.cstindustries.com

C-TEC (Computionics) Ltd - Challenge Way, Martland Park, Wigan, Lancs. WN5 0LD tel:(01942) 322744, fax:(01942) 829867. sales@c-tec.co.uk, www.c-tec.co.uk

CTS Bridges Ltd - Abbey Road, Shepley, Huddersfield, W. Yorks. HD8 8BX tel:(01484) 606 416, fax:(01484) 608 763. enquiries@ctsbridges.co.uk, www.ctsbridges.co.uk

CU Lighting Ltd - Great Amwell, Ware, Herts. SG12 9AT tel:(01920) 462272, fax:(01920) 461370. sales@cuphosco.co.uk, www.cuphosco.com

CU Phosco Lighting - Charles House, Lower Road, Great Amwell, Ware, Herts. SG12 9TA tel:(01920) 860600, fax:(01920) 485915. sales@cuphosco.co.uk, www.cuphosco.com

Cumberland Construction - Orchard Court, 4 Station Square, Gidea Park, Romford, Essex. RM2 6AT tel:(01708) 766 369, fax:(01708) 520231. contracts@cumberlandgroup.co.uk, www.cumberland-construction.co.uk

Cummins Power Generation Ltd - Manston Park, Columbus Avenue, Manston, Ramsgate, Kent. CT12 5BF tel:(01843) 255000, fax:(01843) 255913. cpg.uk@cummins.com, www.cumminspower.com

Cutting R C & Co - 12/10/2019, Arcadia Avenue, Finchley, London. N3 2JU tel:(020) 8371 0001, fax:(020) 8371 0003. info@rccutting.co.uk, www.rccutting.co.uk

D

Dacrylate Paints Ltd - Lime Street, Kirkby in Ashfield, Nottingham, Notts. NG17 8AL tel:(01623) 753845, fax:(01623) 757151. sales@dacrylate.co.uk, www.dacrylate.co.uk

Daikin Airconditioning UK Ltd - The Heights, Brooklands, Weybridge, Surrey. KT13 0NY tel:(0845) 6419000, fax:(0845) 6419009. marketing@daikin.co.uk, www.daikin.co.uk

Dalair Ltd - Southern Way, Wednesbury, W. Midlands. WS10 7BU tel:(0121) 556 9944, fax:(0121) 502 3124. sales@dalair.co.uk, www.dalair.co.uk

Dales Fabrications Ltd - Crompton Road Industrial Estate, Ilkeston, Derbys. DE7 4BG tel:(0115) 930 1521, fax:(0115) 930 7625. sales@dales-eaves.co.uk, www.dales-eaves.co.uk

Dalesauna Ltd - Grombald Crag Close, St James Business Park, Knaresborought, N. Yorks. HG5 8PJ tel:(01423) 798630, fax:(01423) 798670. sales@dalesauna.co.uk, www.dalesauna.co.uk

Dalhaus Ltd - Showground Road, Bridgwater, Somerset. TA6 6AJ tel:(01278) 727727, fax:(01278) 727766. info@dalhaus.co.uk, www.dalhaus.co.uk

Dampcoursing Limited - 10-12 Dorset Road, Tottenham, London. N15 5AJ tel:(020) 8802 2233, fax:(020) 8809 1839. info@dampcoursing.com, www.dampcoursing.com

Danbury Fencing Limited - Olivers Farm, Maldon Road, Witham, Essex. CM8 3HY tel:(01376) 502020, fax:(01376) 520500. sales@danburyfencing.com, www.danburyfencing.com

Dandy Booksellers - 15 Hoopers Yard, Kimberley Road, London. NW6 7EJ tel:(020) 7624 2993, fax:(020) 7624 5049. enquiries@dandybooksellers.com, www.dandybooksellers.com

Danfoss Ltd - Capswood, Oxford Road, Denham, Bucks. UB9 4LH tel:(0870) 241 7030, fax:(0870) 241 7035. com, www.danfoss.co.uk

Danfoss Ltd - Capswood, Oxford Road, Denham, Bucks. UB9 4LH tel:(01895) 617000. customerservice.uk@danfoss.com, www.heating.danfoss.co.uk

Daniel Platt Ltd - Canal Lane, Tunstall, Stoke-on-Trent, Staffs. ST6 4NY tel:(01782) 577187, fax:(01782) 577877. sales@danielplatt.co.uk, www.danielplatt.co.uk

Dantherm Ltd - Hither Green, Clevedon, Avon. BS21 6XT tel:(01275) 876851, fax:(01275) 343086. ikf.ltd.uk@dantherm.com

Darfen Durafencing - Unit 12 Smallford Works, Smallford Lane, St. Albans, Herts. AL4 0SA tel:(01727) 828290, fax:(01727) 828299. enquiries@darfen.co.uk, www.darfen.co.uk

Darfen Durafencing, Scottish Region - Units 7-8, Rochsolloch Road Industrial Estate, Airdrie, Scotland. ML6 9BG tel:(01236) 755001, fax:(01236) 747012. scottish@darfen.co.uk, www.darfen.co.uk

Daro UK Ltd - 34-36 Eastbury Road, London. E6 6LW tel:(020) 8510 4000, fax:(020) 8510 4001. sales@daro.com, www.daro.com

Daro Uk Ltd Partners to both Blum & Hafele - 34-36 Eastbury Road, London. E6 6LW tel:(020) 8510 4000. sales@daro.com, www.daro.com

Dart Valley Systems Ltd - Kemmings Close, Long Road, Paignton, Devon . TQ4 7TW tel:(01803) 592021, fax:(01803) 559016. sales@dartvalley.co.uk, www.dartvalley.co.uk

Dartford Portable Buildings Ltd - 389-397 Princes Road, Dartford, Kent. DA1 1JU tel:(01322) 229521, fax:(01322) 221948. info@dpbl.co.uk, www.dpbl.co.uk

Davant Products Ltd - Davant House, Jugs Green Business Park, Jugs Green, Staplow, nr Ledbury, Herefordshire. HR8 1NR tel:(01531) 640880, fax:(01531) 640827. info@davant.co.uk, www.davant.co.uk

Davicon - The Wallows Industrial Estate, Dudley Road, Brierley Hill. DY5 1QA tel:(01384) 572 851, fax:(01384) 265 098. sales@davicon.com, www.davicon.com

DB Group (Holdings) Ltd - Wellington Way, Bourn Airfield, Cambridge. CB23 2TQ tel:(01954) 780687, fax:(01954) 782912. sales@dbgholdings.com, www.dbgholdings.com

DC Plastic Handrails Ltd - Unit 3 TVB Factory, Whickham Industrial Estate, Swalwell, Newcastle Upon Tyne, Tyne & Wear. NE16 3DA tel:(0191) 488 1112, fax:(0191) 488 1112. sales@dcplastics.co.uk, www.dcplastics.co.uk

De Longhi Limited - 1 Kenwood Business Park, 1-2 New Lane, Havant, Hampshire. PO9 2NH tel:(0845) 600 6845. www.delonghi.com/en-gb

Deaf Alerter plc - Enfield House, 303 Burton Road, Derby. DE23 6AG tel:(01332) 363981, fax:(01332) 293267. info@deaf-alerter.com, www.deaf-alerter.com

Deans Blinds & Awnings (UK) Ltd - Unit 7 Kimpton Trade & Business Centre, Minden Road, Sutton, Surrey. SM3 9PF tel:(020) 8947 8931, fax:(020) 8947 8336. www.deansblinds.com

Deb Group Limited - Denby Hall Way, Denby, Derbys. DE5 8JZ tel:(01773) 855 100, fax:(01773) 855 107. talktous@debgroup.com, www.debgroup.com

Deceuninck Ltd - Unit 2, Stanier Road, Porte Marsh Industrial Estate, Calne, Wilts. SN11 9PX tel:(01249) 816969, fax:(01249) 815234. deceuninck.ltd@deceuninck.com, www.deceuninck.com

Dee-Organ Ltd - 5 Sandyford Road, Paisley, Renfrewshire. PA3 4HP tel:(0141) 889 7000, fax:(0141) 889 7764. signs@dee-organ.co.uk

Deepdale Engineering Co Ltd - Pedmore Road, Dudley, W. Midlands. DY2 0RD tel:(01384) 480022, fax:(01384) 480489. sales@deepdale-eng.co.uk, www.deepdale-eng.co.uk

Delabie UK Ltd - Henderson House, Hithercroft Road, Wallingford, Oxon. OX10 9DG tel:(01491) 824449, fax:(01491) 825729. sales@delabie.co.uk, www.delabie.co.uk

Delta Balustrades - Millbuck Way, Sandbach, Cheshire. CW11 3JA tel:(01270) 753383, fax:(01270) 753207. info@deltabalustrades.com, www.deltabalustrades.com

Delta Fire - 8 Mission Road, Rackheath Business Estate, Norwich. NR13 6PL tel:(01603) 735000, fax:(01603) 735009. sales@deltafire.co.uk, www.deltafire.co.uk

DencoHappel UK Ltd - Dolphin House, Moreton Business Park, Moreton-on-Lugg, Hereford. HR4 8DS tel:(01432) 277277, fax:(01432) 268005. sales.enquiry@dencohappel.com, www.dencohappel.com/en-gb

Denka International - Red Roofs, Chinnor Road, Thame, Oxon. OX9 3RF tel:(01844) 216754, fax:(01844) 216141. info@denka.nl

Dennis & Robinson Ltd - Blenheim Road, Churchill Industrial Estate, Lancing, W. Sussex. BN15 8HU tel:(01903) 524300, fax:(01903) 750679. manhattan@manhattan.co.uk, www.manhattan.co.uk

Department for Business, Innovation & Skills - 1 Victoria Street, London. SW1H 0ET tel:(020) 7215 5000, fax:(020) 7215 6740. www.bis.gov.uk

Deralam Laminates Ltd - West Coast Park, Bradley Lane, Standish Wigan, Lancs. WN6 OYR tel:(01257) 478540, fax:(01257) 478550. sales@deralam.co.uk

Derby Timber Supplies - 3 John Street, Derby, Derbys. DE1 2LU tel:(01332) 348340, fax:(01332) 385573. info@derbytimbersupplies.co.uk, www.derbytimbersupplies.co.uk

Design & Display Structures Ltd - Unit 2, 158 Yateley Street, Westminster Industrial Estate, London. SE18 5TA tel:(0844) 736 5995, fax:(0844) 736 5992. grp@design-and-display.co.uk, www.design-and-display.co.uk

Design Council - Eagle House, 167 City Road, London. EC1V 1AW tel:(020) 7420 5200. info@designcouncil.org.uk, www.designcouncil.org.uk

Designer Radiators Direct - Unit 15, Matrix Way, Buckshaw Village, Preston. PR7 7ND tel:(01257) 442911, fax:(01772) 314516. enquiries@designerradiatorsdirect.co.uk, www.designerradiatorsdirect.co.uk

Designplan Lighting Ltd - 16 Kimpton Park Way, Kimpton Business Park, Sutton, Surrey. SM3 9QS tel:(020) 8254 2020. sales@designplan.co.uk, www.designplan.co.uk

Deva Composites - A Division of Cope Engineering (Rollmakers) Limited - Sion Street Works, Radcliffe, Manchester. M26 3SF tel:(01617) 060 522. info@devacomposites.com, www.devacomposites.com

Deva Tap Co Ltd - Brooklands Mill, English Street, Leigh, Lancs. WN7 3EH tel:(01942) 680177, fax:(01942) 680190. sales@uk.methven.com, www.devatap.co.uk

Devar Premier Flooring - Spiersbridge Business Park, Thornliebank, Glasgow. G46 8NL tel:(0141) 638 2203, fax:(0141) 620 0207. enquiries@devarflooring.com, www.devargroup.com

D (con't)

Dewey Waters Ltd - Heritage Works, Winterstoke Road, Weston-Super-Mare, N. Somerset. BS24 9AN tel:(01934) 421477, fax:(01934) 421488. sales@deweywaters.co.uk, www.deweywaters.co.uk

Dewhurst plc - Inverness Road, Hounslow, Middx. TW3 3LT tel:(020) 8607 7300, fax:(020) 8572 5986. info@dewhurst.co.uk, www.dewhurst.co.uk

Dezurik International Ltd - Unit 15, Orton Way, Hayward Industrial Estate, Castle Bromich, Birmingham. B35 7BT tel:(0121) 748 6111, fax:(0121) 747 4324. sales@industrialvalve.co.uk, www.industrialvalve.co.uk

Didsbury Engineering Co Ltd - Lower Meadow Road, Brooke Park, Handforth, Wilmslow, Cheshire. SK9 3LP tel:(0161) 486 2200, fax:(0161) 486 2211. sales@didsbury.com, www.didsbury.com

Diespeker Marble & Terrazzo Ltd - 132-136 Ormside Street, Peckham, London. SE15 1TF tel:(020) 7358 0160, fax:(020) 7358 2897. sales@diespeker.co.uk, www.diespeker.co.uk

Dimplex UK Limited - Millbrook House, Grange Drive, Hedge End, Southampton. SO30 2DF tel:(0870) 077 7117, fax:(0870) 727 0109. presales@dimplex.co.uk, www.dimplex.co.uk

Dinnington Fencing Co. Limited - North Hill, Dinnington, Newcastle-upon-Tyne. NE13 7LG tel:(01661) 824046, fax:(01661) 872234. info@dinningtonfencing.co.uk, www.dinningtonfencing.co.uk

Directional Data Systems Ltd - 5, Dalsholm Avenue, Dawsholm Industrial Estate, Glasgow. G20 0TS tel:(0141) 945 4243, fax:(0141) 810 3777. sales@directionaldata.co.uk, www.directionaldata.co.uk

Dixon International Group Ltd - Brewery Road, Pampisford, Cambs. CB22 3HG tel:(01223) 832 851. info@dig.co.uk, www.dig.co.uk

Dixon Turner Wallcoverings - Brecon Works, Henfaes Lane, Welshpool, Powys. SY21 7BE tel:(0870) 606 1237, fax:(0870) 606 1239. enquiries@dixon-turner.co.uk, www.dixon-turner.co.uk

DIY Doctor - The Workshop, Newbury Works, Coleford, Somerset. BA3 5RX tel:(0845) 634 2179. www.diydoctor.org.uk

DLW Flooring - St Centurion Court, Milton Park, Addington, Oxon. OX14 4RY tel:(01642) 763224, fax:(01642) 750213. sales@dlw.co.uk, www.dlw.co.uk

Docherty New Vent Chimney Group - Unit 3, Sawmill Road, Redshute Hill Indusrial Estate, Hermitage, Newbury, Berks. RG18 9QL tel:(01635) 200145, fax:(01635) 201737. sales@docherty.co.uk

Domus Tiles Ltd - Cantebury Court, Brixton Road, Battersea, London. SW9 6TA tel:(020) 7223 5555, fax:(020) 7924 2556. service@domustiles.com, www.domustiles.co.uk

Domus Ventilation - Cambria House, Block C, Van Court, Van Road, Caerphilly Business Park, Caerphilly. CF83 3ED tel:(03443) 715523, fax:(03443) 715524. vent.info@domusventilation.co.uk, www.domusventilation.co.uk

Don & Low Ltd - Newfordpark House, Glamis Road, Forfar, Angus. DD8 IFR tel:(01307) 452200, fax:(01307) 452300. lotrak@donlow.co.uk, www.donlow.co.uk

Don Construction Products Ltd - Churnetside Business Park, Station Road, Cheddleton, Leek, Staffs. ST13 7RS tel:(01538) 361799, fax:(01538) 361899. info@donconstruction.co.uk, www.donconstruction.co.uk

Donaldson Filtration (GB) Ltd - Humberstone Lane, Thumaston, Leicester, Leics. LE4 8HP tel:(0116) 269 6161, fax:(0116) 269 3028. IAF-uk@donaldson.com, www2.donaldson.com/toritdce

Door and Hardware Federation - 42 Heath Street, Tamworth, Staffs. B79 7JH tel:(01827) 52337, fax:(01827) 310827. info@dhfonline.org.uk, www.dhfonline.org.uk

Door Panels by Design - Unit 27 Moorland Mills, Moorland Industrial Est, Law Street, Cleckheaton, Bradford. BD19 3QR tel:(01274) 852488, fax:(01274) 851819. lee.harding@dpbd.co.uk, www.dpbd.co.uk

Doorfit Products Ltd - Icknield House, Heaton Street, Hockley, Birmingham, W. Midlands. B18 5BA tel:(0121) 523 4171, fax:(0121) 554 3859. enquiries@doorfit.co.uk, www.doorfit.co.uk

Doosan Power Systems Ltd - Porterfield Road, Renfrew. PA4 8DJ tel:(0141) 886 4141, fax:+44 0 141 885 3338. dps.info@doosan.com, www.doosanpowersystems.com

Dorma Door Services Ltd - Wilbury Way, Hitchen, Herts. SG4 0AB tel:(01462) 477600, fax:(01462) 477601. info@dorma-uk.co.uk, www.dorma-uk.co.uk

DORMA UK Ltd - Wilbury Way, Hitchin, Herts. SG4 0AB tel:(01462) 477600, fax:(01462) 477601. info@dorma-uk.co.uk, www.dorma-uk.co.uk

Dorman Smith Switchgear - 1 Nile Close, Nelson Court Business Centre, Ashton-on-Ribble, Preston, Lancs. PR2 2XU tel:(01772) 325389, fax:(01772) 726276. sales@dormansmith.co.uk, www.dormansmithswitchgear.com/

Dover Trussed Roof Co Ltd - Shelvin Manor, Shelvin, Canterbury, Kent. CT4 6RL tel:(01303) 844303, fax:(01303) 844342. sales@dovertruss.co.uk, www.dovertruss.co.uk

DOVISTA UK LTD - The Forum, Ground Floor, Lancaster Way, Ermine Business Park, Huntingdon. PE29 6XU tel:(01480) 759510. enquiries@dovista.com, www.velfac.co.uk

Dow Building Solutions - Diamond House, Lotus Park, Kingsbury Crescent, Staines, Middlesex. TW18 3AG tel:(015530) 692100, fax:(020) 8917 5413. FKLMAIL@dow.com, www.dow.com

Dow Corning Europe S.A - Parc Industriel Zone C, Rue Jules Bordet, B-7180 Seneffe, Belgium. tel:+32 64 88 80 00, fax:+32 64 88 84 01. eutech.info@dowcorning.com, www.dowcorning.com

DP Sercurity - Ryecroft Buildings, Cireon Street Green Road, Longfield, Kent. DA2 8DX tel:(01322) 278178, fax:(01322) 284315. davidpaul120@hotmail.com, www.dpsecurity.co.uk

DPC Screeding Ltd - Brunswick Industrial Estate, Brunswick Village, Newcastle-upon-Tyne. NE13 7BA tel:(0191) 236 4226, fax:(0191) 236 2242. dpcscreeding@btconnect.com

Draeger Safety UK Ltd - Blyth Riverside Business Park, Ullswater Close, Blyth, Northumberland. NE24 4RG tel:(01670) 352 891, fax:(01670) 356 266. michaela.wetter@draeger.com, http://www.draeger.com/sites/en_uk/Pages/Applications/Advisor.aspx?navID=1875

Drain Center - The Wolseley Center, Harrison Way, Spa Park, Royal Leamington Spa. CV31 3HH tel:(0870) 16 22557. customerservices@wolseley.co.uk, www.draincenter.co.uk

Drawn Metal Ltd - Swinnow Lane, Leeds, W. Yorks. LS13 4NE tel:(0113) 256 5661, fax:(0113) 239 3194. systems@drawnmetal.co.uk, www.dmlas.co.uk

Drilling & Sawing Association, The - Suite 5.0 North Mill, Bridge Foot, Belper, Derbyshire. DE56 1YD tel:(01773) 820000, fax:(01773) 821284. dsa@drillandsaw.org.uk, www.drillandsaw.org.uk

Drugasar Ltd - Deans Road, Swinton, Manchester. M27 0JH tel:(0161) 793 8700, fax:(0161) 727 8057. info@drufire.co.uk, www.drugasar.co.uk

Dry Stone Walling Association of Great Britain - Lane Farm, Crooklands, Milnthorpe, Cumbria. LA7 7NH tel:(015395) 67953. information@dswa.org.uk, www.dswa.org.uk

DSM UK Ltd - DSM House, Papermill Drive, Redditch, Worcs. B98 8QJ tel:(01527) 590590, fax:(01527) 590555. marketing.dnpe@dsm.com, www.dsm.com

Du Pont (UK) Ltd - 4th Floor, Kings Court, London Road, Stevenage, Herts. SG1 2NG tel:(01438) 734 000. www.dupont.co.uk

Dudley Thomas Ltd - PO Box 28, Birmingham New Road, Dudley. DY1 4SN tel:(0121) 557 5411, fax:(0121) 557 5345. info@thomasdudley.co.uk

Dufaylite Developments Ltd - Cromwell Road, St Neots, Huntingdon, Cambs. PE19 1QW tel:(01480) 215000, fax:(01480) 405526. enquiries@dufaylite.com, www.dufaylite.com

Duffells Limited - 3 Commerce Park, 19 Commerce Way, Croydon, London. CR0 4YL tel:(020) 8662 4010, fax:(020) 8662 4039. enquiries@duffells.co.uk, http://www.duffells.com/

Dulux Trade - AkzoNobel, Wexham Road, Slough. SL2 5DS tel:(0333) 222 70 70. duluxtrade.advice@akzonobel.com, www.duluxtrade.co.uk

Dunbrik (Yorks) Ltd - Ferry Lane, Stanley Ferry, Wakefield, W. Yorks. WF3 4LT tel:(01924) 373694, fax:(01924) 383459. Flues@dunbrik.co.uk, www.dunbrik.co.uk

Dunham Bush Ltd - European Headquaters, Downley Road, Havant, Hants. PO9 2JD tel:(02392) 477700, fax:(02392) 450396. info@dunham-bush.co.uk

Dunhams of Norwich - t/a Dunhams Washroom Systems, The Granary, School Road, Neatishead, Norwich. NR12 8BU tel:(01603) 424855, fax:(01603) 413336. info@dunhamsofnorwich.co.uk, www.dunhamsofnorwich.co.uk

Dunhouse Quarry Co Ltd - Dunhouse Quarry Works, Staindrop, Darlington. DL2 3QU tel:(01833) 660208, fax:(01833) 660748. paul@dunhouse.co.uk, www.dunhouse.co.uk

Dunlop Adhesives - Building Adhesives, Longton Road, Trentham, Stoke-on-Trent. ST4 8JB tel:(01782) 591100, fax:(01782) 591101. info@building-adhesives.com, www.dunlop-adhesives.co.uk

Dunphy Combustion Ltd - Queensway, Rochdale, Lancs. OL11 2SL tel:(01706) 649217, fax:(01706) 655512. sharon.kuligowski@dunphy.co.uk, www.dunphy.co.uk

Dunsley Heat Ltd - Bridge Mills, Huddersfield Road, Holmfirth. HD9 3TW tel:(01484) 682635, fax:(01484) 688428. sales@dunsleyheat.co.uk, www.dunsleyheat.co.uk

Duplus Architectural Systems Ltd - 370 Melton Road, Leicester, Leics. LE4 7SL tel:(0116) 261 0710, fax:(0116) 261 0539. sales@duplus.co.uk, www.duplus.co.uk

Duplus Architectural Systems Ltd - 370 Melton Road, Leicester. LE4 7SL tel:(0116) 2610710, fax:(0116) 2610539. sales@duplus.co.uk, www.duplus.co.uk

DuPont Corian - McD Marketing Ltd, 10 Quarry Court, Pitstone Green Business Park, Pitstone. LU7 9GW tel:(01296) 663555, fax:(01296) 663599. info@corian.co.uk, www.corian.co.uk

Dupré Minerals - Spencroft Road, Newcastle-under-Lyme, Staffs. ST5 9JE tel:(01782) 383000, fax:(01782) 383101. info@dupreminerals.com, www.dupreminerals.com

Durable Contracts (Roofing) Ltd - Durable House, Crabtree Manorway, Belvedere, Kent. DA17 6AB tel:(020) 8311 1211, fax:(020) 8310 7893. sales@durable-online.com, www.durable-online.com

Durable Ltd - Unit 1, 498 Reading Road, Winnersh, Reading, Berkshire. RG41 5EX tel:(0118) 989 5200, fax:(0118) 989 5209. mail@durable.co.uk, www.durable.co.uk

Duraflex Limited - Severn Drive, Tewkesbury Business Park, Tewkesbury, Glos. GL20 8SF tel:(08705) 351351, fax:(01684) 852701. info@duraflex.co.uk, www.duraflex.co.uk

Dural UK Ltd - Unit 6a, Wakefield Business Centre, Denby Dale Road, Wakefield. WF2 7AZ tel:(01924) 360110, fax:(01924) 360660. welcome@dural.de, www.dural.com

Duralock (UK) Ltd - 6A Enstone Business Park, Enstone, Chipping Norton. OX7 4NP tel:(01608) 678238, fax:(01608) 677170. info@duralock.com, www.duralock.com

Durey Casting Ltd - Hawley Road, Dartford, Kent. DA1 1PU tel:(01322) 272424, fax:(01322) 288073. sales@dureycastings.co.uk, www.dureycastings.co.uk

Durotan Ltd - West House, 20 West Street, Buckingham. MK18 1HE tel:(01280) 814048, fax:(01280) 817842. sales@durotan.ltd.uk, www.durotan.ltd.uk

Duroy Fibreglass Mouldings Ltd - Mercury Yacht Harbour, Satchell Lane, Hamble, Southampton. SO31 4HQ tel:(023) 80453781, fax:(023) 80455538. duroygrp@aol.com

DW Windsor Lighting - Pindar Road, Hoddesdon, Herts. EN11 0DX tel:(01992) 474600, fax:(01992) 474601. info@dwwindsor.co.uk, www.dwwindsor.co.uk

Dycem Ltd - Ashley Trading Estate, Bristol. BS2 9BB tel:(0117) 955 9921, fax:(0117) 954 1194. uk@dycem.com, www.dycem.com

Dyer Environmental Controls - Unit 10, Lawnhurst Trading Est, Cheadle Heath, Stockport. SK3 0SD tel:(0161) 491 4840, fax:(0161) 491 4841. enquiry@dyerenvironmental.co.uk, www.dyerenvironmental.co.uk

Dyke Chemicals Ltd - PO Box 381, Cobham. KT11 9EF tel:(01932) 866096, fax:(01932) 866097. info@dykechemicals.co.uk, www.dykechemicals.co.uk

Dynniq UK Ltd - Hazlewood House, Lime Tree Way, Chineham Business Park, Basingstoke, Hants. RG24 8WZ tel:(01256) 891800, fax:(01256) 891870. info@dynniq.co.uk, www.dynniq.com

Dyno Rod PLC - Millstream, Maidenhead Road, Windsor. SL4 5GD tel:(020) 8481 2200, fax:(020) 8481 2288. DynoOnlineBookings@britishgas.co.uk, www.dyno.com

Dyno-Rod PLC - Swan House, The Causeway, Staines, Middlesex. TW18 3BF tel:(0333) 305 6020. www.dyno.com

E

Eagles, William, Ltd - Units B/c, North Stage Business Park, 88 Broadway, Salford, Mamchester. M50 2UW tel:(0161) 8761560, fax:(0161) 745 7765. sales@william-eagles.co.uk, www.william-eagles.co.uk

Earth Anchors Ltd - 15 Campbell Road, Croydon, Surrey. CR0 2SQ tel:(020) 8684 9601, fax:(020) 8684 2230. info@earth-anchors.com, www.earth-anchors.com

Eaton Electric Limited - Grimshaw Lane, Middleton, Manchester. M23 1GQ tel:(0161) 655 8900, fax:(08700) 507 525. ukresiorders@eaton.com, www.mem250.com

Eaton Electric Ltd - Grimshaw Lane, Middleton, Manchester. M24 1GQ tel:(0161) 655 8900, fax:(08700) 540 333. ukcommorders@eaton.com, www.eaton.uk.com

Eaton's Security Business - Security House, Vantage Point Business Village, Mitcheldean, Glos. GL17 0SZ tel:(01594) 545400, fax:(01594) 545401. enquiries@coopersecurity.co.uk, www.coopersecurity.co.uk

Eaton-Williams Group Limited - Fircroft Way, Edenbridge, Kent. TN8 6EZ tel:(01782) 599995, fax:(01782) 599220. info@eaton-williams.com, www.eaton-williams.com

EBC UK Ltd - Kirkes Orchard, Church Street, East Markham, Newark, Notts. NG22 0QW tel:(01777) 871134, fax:(01777) 871134. rob@ebcuk.f9.co.uk, www.e-b-c-uk.com

Ebor Concrete Ltd - PO Box 4, Ure Bank Top, Ripon, North Yorkshire. HG4 1JE tel:(01765) 604351, fax:(01765) 690065. sales@eborconcrete.co.uk, www.eborconcrete.co.uk

EBP Building Products Ltd - Blackamoor Road, Blackburn, Lancs. BB1 2LQ tel:(01254) 52244, fax:(01254) 682371. team@ebpbuilding.com, www.ebpbuilding.com

Eclipse Blind Systems Ltd - Inchinnan Business Park, 10 Founain Cress, Inchinnan, Renfrew. PA4 9RE tel:(0141) 812 3322, fax:(0141) 812 5253. www.eclipseblinds.co.uk

Eclipse Sprayers Ltd - 120 Beakes Road, Smethwick, W. Midlands. B67 5AB tel:(0121) 420 2494, fax:(0121) 429 1668. eclipsesales@btconnect.com, www.eclipsesprayers.co.uk

Ecolec - Sharrocks Street, Wolverhampton, West Midlands. WV1 3RP tel:(01902) 457575, fax:(01902) 457797. info@ecolec.co.uk, www.ecolec.co.uk

Ecotherm Insulation (UK) Ltd - Harvey Road, Burnt Mills Industrial Estate, Basildon, Essex. SS13 1QJ tel:(01268) 591155, fax:(01268) 597242. info@ecotherm.co.uk, www.ecotherm.co.uk

Ecotile Flooring Ltd - Unit 15 North Luton Industrial Estate, Sedgewick Road, Luton. LU4 9DT tel:(01582) 788232, fax:(020) 8929 9150. info@ecotileflooring.com, www.ecotileflooring.com

EcoWater Systems Ltd - Solar House, Mercury Park, Wooburn Green, Buckinghamshire. HP10 0HH tel:(01494) 484000, fax:(01494) 484312. info@ecowater.co.uk, www.ecowater.co.uk

Edelman Leather - 2/11 Centre Dome, Design Centre Chelsea Harbour, London. SW10 0XE tel:(0207) 351 7305, fax:(0207) 349 0515. hughk@edelmanleather.com, www.edelmanleather.com

Eden Springs (UK) Ltd - 3 Livingstone Boulevard, Blantyre, St Neots, Glasgow, Lanarkshire. G72 0BP tel:(0845) 5280975. sales@uk.edensprings.com, www.edensprings.co.uk

Edmonds A & Co Ltd - 91 Constitution Hill, Birmingham. B19 3JY tel:(0121) 236 8351, fax:(0121) 236 4793. enquiries@edmonds.uk.com, www.edmonds.co.uk

Edward Benton & Co Ltd - Creteangle Works, Brook Lane, Ferring, Worthing, W. Sussex. BN12 5LP tel:(01903) 241349, fax:(01903) 700213. sales@creteangle.com, www.creteangle.com

EFG Office Furniture Ltd - 3 Clearwater, Lingley Mere Business Park, Lingley Green Avenue, Warrington. WA5 3UZ tel:(0845) 608 4100, fax:(0845) 604 1924. sales@efgoffice.co.uk, www.efgoffice.co.uk

EGE Carpets Ltd - Suite 1, Ground Floor, Conway House, Chorley, Lancs. PR7 1NY tel:(01257) 239000, fax:(01257) 239001. UK@egecarpet.com, www.egecarpet.com/uk

Egger (UK) Ltd - Anick Grange Road, Hexham, Northumberland. NE46 4JS tel:(0845) 602 4444, fax:(01434) 613302. building.uk@egger.com, www.egger.co.uk

Eglo UK - Unit 12 Cirrus Park, Lower Farm Road, Moulton Park, Northampton. NN3 6UR tel:(01604) 790986, fax:(01604) 670282. info-greatbritain@eglo.com, www.elgo.com

EHSmith - Westhaven House, Arleston Way, Shirley, West Midlands. B90 4LH tel:(0121) 713 7100. enquiries@ehsmith.co.uk, www.ehsmith.co.uk

EJOT UK Limited - Hurricane Close, Sherburn Enterprise Park, Sherburn-in-Elmet, Leeds. LS25 6PB tel:(01977) 68 70 40, fax:(01977) 68 70 41. sales@ejot.co.uk, www.ejot.co.uk

Elan-Dragonair - Units 7-8, Dragon Industrial Centre, Fitzherbert Road, Farlington, Portsmouth. PO6 1SQ tel:(023) 92376451, fax:(023) 92370411. david@elan-dragonair.co.uk, www.elan-dragonair.co.uk

Electrak International Ltd - Unit 12, No.1 Industrial Estate, Medomsley Road, Consett, Co. Durham. DH8 6SR tel:(01207) 503400, fax:(01207) 501799. sales@electrak.co.uk, www.electrak.co.uk

Electric Center - The Wolseley Center, Harrison Way, Spa Park, Royal Leamington Spa. CV31 3HH tel:(01926) 705000, fax:(0870) 410 3933. customerservices@wolseley.co.uk, www.electric-center.co.uk

Electric Elements Co, The - Electric Elements Company Ltd, Greens Lane, Kimberley, Nottingham. NG16 2PB tel:(0115) 9459944, fax:(0115) 9384909. info@elelco.co.uk, www.elelco.co.uk

Electrical Contractors' Association (ECA) - ECA Court, 24-26 South Park, Sevenoaks, Kent. TN13 1DU tel:(020) 7313 4800. info@eca.co.uk, www.eca.co.uk

Electrical Review - Quadrant House, The Quadrant, Sutton. SM2 tel:(020) 8652 3492. johns@stjohnpatrick.com, www.electricalreview.co.uk

Electrical Times - The Old School House, St Stephen's Street, Tonbridge, Kent. TN9 2AD tel:(01732) 371 579, fax:(01732) 371 571. lisa.peake@purplems.com, www.electricaltimes.co.uk

Electrix International Ltd - Dovecot Hill, South Church Enterprise Park, Bishop Auckland, Co. Durham. DL14 6XP tel:(01388) 774455, fax:(01388) 777359. info@electrixinternational.com, www.electrixinternational.com

Electrolux Domestic Appliances - PO Box 545, 55-57 High Street, Slough, Berks. SL1 9BG tel:(01753) 872500, fax:(01753) 872381. elsinfo@electrolux.co.uk, www.electrolux.co.uk

Electrolux Foodservice - Crystal Court, Aston Cross Business Park, Rocky Lane, Aston, Birmingham, W. Midlands. B6 5RQ tel:(0121) 220 2800, fax:(0121) 220 2801. professional@electrolux.com, www.foodservice.electrolux.com

E (con't)

Electrolux Laundry Systems - Unit 3A, Humphrys Road, Woodside Estate, Dunstable, Beds. LU5 4TP tel:(0870) 0604118, fax:(0870) 0604113. els.info@electrolux.co.uk, www.electrolux-wascator.co.uk

Electrosonic Ltd - Hawley Mill, Hawley Road, Dartford, Kent. DA2 7SY tel:(01322) 222211, fax:(01322) 282282. info@electrosonic.com, www.electrosonic.co.uk

Elementis Pigments - Liliput Road, Bracksmills Industrial Estate, Northampton. NN4 7DT tel:(01604) 827403, fax:(01604) 827400. pigmentsinfo.eu@elementis.com, www.elementis.com

Elite Trade & Contract Kitchens Ltd - 90 Willesden Lane, Kiburn, London. NW6 7TA tel:(020) 7328 1243, fax:(020) 7328 1243. sales@elitekitchens.co.uk, www.elitekitchens.co.uk

Eliza Tinsley Ltd - Potters Lane, Wednesbury, West Midlands. WS10 0AS tel:(0121) 502 0055, fax:(0121) 502 7348. orders@elizatinsley.co.uk, www.elizatinsley.co.uk

Elliott Ltd - Manor Drive, Peterborough. PE4 7AP tel:(01733) 298700, fax:(01733) 298749. info@elliottuk.com, www.elliottuk.com

Ellis J T & Co Ltd - Kilner Bank Industrial Esatae, Silver Street, Huddersfield, W. Yorks. HD5 9BA tel:(01484) 514212, fax:(01484) 456433/533454. Sales@jtellis.co.uk, www.jtellis.co.uk

Ellis Patents - High Street, Rillington, Malton, N. Yorks. YO17 8LA tel:(01944) 758395, fax:(01944) 758808. sales@ellispatents.co.uk, www.ellispatents.co.uk

Elster Metering Ltd - 130 Camford Way, Luton, Beds. LU3 3AN tel:(01582) 846400, fax:(01582) 564728. metering-water-uk7m@honeywell.com, www.elstermetering.com

Elta Fans Ltd - 17 Barnes Wallis Road, Segensworth East Industrial Estate, Fareham, Hants. PO15 5ST tel:(01489) 566 500, fax:(01489) 566555. at@eltafans.co.uk, www.eltafans.com

Eltron Chromalox - Eltron House, 28 Whitehorse Road, Croydon, Surrey. CR0 2JA tel:(020) 8665 8900, fax:(020) 8689 0571. uksales@chromalox.com, www.chromalox.co.uk

Elwell Buildings Ltd - Capital Works, Garratts Lane, Cradley Heath. B64 5RE tel:(0121) 561 5656, fax:(0121) 559 0505. paul.clews@elwells.co.uk, www.elwells.co.uk

Elwell Buildings Ltd - Unit 5 Excelsior Industrial Estate, Cakemore Road, Blackheath, W. Midlands. B65 0QT tel:(01495) 273 795. sales@odoni-elwells.com, www.elwells.co.uk

EMAP - 7th Floor, Vantage London, Great West Road, Brentford. TW8 9AG tel:(020) 3033 2600. telephonehouse.reception@emap.com, www.emap.com

Emergi-Lite Safety Systems - (Thomas & Betts Ltd), Bruntcliffe Lane, Morley, Leeds, W. Yorks. LS27 9LL tel:(0113) 2810600, fax:(0113) 2810601. emergi-lite_sales@tnb.com, www.emergi-lite.co.uk

Emerson Climate Technologies - 1 Harvest Avenue, D2 Business Park, Dyce, Aberdeen. AB21 0BQ tel:(01224) 776200. sales@climate-emerson.com, www.climate-emerson.com/en-gb/

Emmerich (Berlon) Ltd - Kingsnorth Industrial Estate, Wotton Road, Ashford, Kent. TN23 6JY tel:(01233) 622684, fax:(01233) 645801. enquiries@emir.co.uk, www.emir.co.uk

EMS Entrance Matting Systems Ltd - Freiston Business Park, Priory Road, Freiston, Boston, Lincolnshire. PE22 0JZ tel:(01205) 761757, fax:(01205) 761811. info@entrance-matting.com, www.entrance-matting.com

Emusol Products (LEICS) Ltd - Unit 1, Trowel Lane, Loughborough, Leics. LE12 5RW tel:(01509) 857880, fax:(01509) 857881. info@emusolproducts.com, www.emusolproducts.com

Enable Access - Marshmoor Works, Great North Road, North Mymms, Hatfield, Herts. AL9 5SD tel:(020) 8275 0375, fax:(0208) 4490326. sales@enable-access.com, www.enable-access.com

Encapsulite International Ltd - 17 Chartwell Business Park, Chartmoor Road, Leighton Buzzard, Beds. LU7 4WG tel:(01525) 376974, fax:(01525) 850306. reply@encapsulite.co.uk, www.encapsulite.co.uk

Encon Air Systems Ltd - 31 Quarry Park Close, Charter Gate, Moulton Park Industrial Estate, Northampton. NN3 6QB tel:(01604) 494187, fax:(01604) 645848. sales@encon-air.co.uk, www.encon-air.co.uk

Encon Insulation Limited - 1 Deighton Close, Wetherby, W. Yorks. LS22 7GZ tel:(01937) 524200, fax:(01937) 524222. info@encon.co.uk, www.encon.co.uk

EnergyICT Ltd - Tollgate Business Park, Paton Drive, Beaconside, Stafford. ST16 3EF tel:(01785) 275200, fax:(01785) 275300. info-uk@energyict.com, www.energyict.co.uk

Enfield Speciality Doors - Alexandra Road, The Ride, Enfield, Middx. EN3 7EH tel:(020) 8805 6662, fax:(020) 8443 1290. sales@enfielddoors.co.uk, www.enfielddoors.co.uk

English Architectural Glazing Ltd - Chiskwick Avenue, Mildenhall, Suffolk. IP28 7AY tel:(01638) 510000, fax:(01638) 510400. sales@eag.uk.com, www.eag.uk.com

English Braids - Spring Lane, Malvern Link, Worcestershire. WR14 1AL tel:(01684) 89222, fax:(01684) 892111. info@englishbraids.com, www.englishbraids.com

Ennis-Flint - 5 Drumhead Road, Chorley North Industrial Park, Chorley, Lancs. PR6 7BX tel:(01302) 309335, fax:(013020) 309342. info@ennisflint.com, www.ennisflintemea.com

Ensto Briticent Ltd - Unit 6, Priory Industrial park, Airspeed Road, Christchurch, Dorset. BH23 4HD tel:(01425) 283300, fax:(01425) 280480. salesuk@ensto.com, www.ensto.com

En-tout-cas Tennis Courts Ltd - 20 Nene Valley Business Park, Oundle, Peterborough. PE8 4HN tel:(01832) 274199. info@tenniscourtsuk.co.uk, www.tenniscourtsuk.co.uk

Envair Ltd - York Avenue, Haslingden, Rossendale, Lancs. BB4 4HX tel:(01706) 228416, fax:(01706) 242205. info@envair.co.uk, www.envair.co.uk

Envirodoor Markus Ltd - Viking Close, Willerby, Hull, E. Yorks. HU10 6BS tel:(01482) 659375, fax:(01482) 655131. sales@envirodoor.com, www.envirodoor.com

Envirotech Ltd - Desborough Park Road, High Wycombe. HP12 3BX tel:(01494) 525342. freshthinking@envirotec.co.uk, www.envirotec.co.uk

Envopak Group Ltd - Edgington Way, Sidcup, Kent. DA14 5EF tel:(020) 8308 8000, fax:(020) 8300 3832. sales@envopak.co.uk, www.envopak.com

---

Eque2 Limited

Nicholsons House, Nicholson Walk, Maidenhead. SL6 1LD tel:(0161) 939 0111. construction@eque2.com, www.eque2-evaluate.co.uk

---

ERA Home Security Ltd - Valiant Way (i54), Wolverhampton. WV9 5GB tel:(01922) 490000, fax:(01922) 490044. info@erahomesecurity.com, www.erahomesecurity.com

Erico Europa (GB) Ltd - 52 Milford Road, Reading, Berkshire. RG1 8LJ tel:(0808) 2344 670, fax:(0808) 2344 676. info@erico.com, www.erico.com

Erlau AG - UK Sales Office, 42 Macclesfield Road, Hazel Grove, Stockport. SK7 6BE tel:(01625) 877277, fax:(01625) 850242. erlau@zuppinger.u-net.com, www.erlau.de

Ermine Engineering Co. Ltd - Freancis House, Silver Birch Park, Great Northern Terrace, Lincoln, Lincolnshire. LN5 8LG tel:(01522) 510977. info@ermineengineering.co.uk, www.ermineengineering.co.uk

Eurobrick Systems Ltd - Unit 7, Wilverley Trading Estates, Bath Road, Brislington, Bristol. BS4 5NL tel:(0117) 971 7117, fax:(0117) 971 7217. richard@eurobrick.co.uk, www.eurobrick.co.uk

Euroclad Ltd - Wentloog Corperate Park, Wentloog Road, Cardiff. CF3 2ER tel:(029) 2079 0722, fax:(029) 2079 3149. sales@euroclad.com, www.euroclad.com

European Lamp Group - Allenby House, Knowles Lane, Wakfield Road, Bradford, W. Yorks. BD4 9AB tel:(01274) 473 400, fax:(01274) 680157. info@elg-solutions.com, www.elg-solutions.com

European Lead Sheet Industry Association - Bravington House, 2 Bravingtons Walk, London. N1 9AF tel:(020) 7833 8090, fax:(020) 7833 1611. davidson@ila-lead.org, www.elsia.org

Evac+Chair International Ltd - ParAid House, Weston Lane, Birmingham. B11 3RS tel:(0121) 706 6744, fax:(0121) 706 6746. info@evacchair.co.uk, www.evacchair.co.uk

Evans Concrete Products Ltd - Pye Bridge Industrial Estate, Main Road, Pye Bridge, Near Alfreton, Derbyshire. DE55 4NX tel:(01773) 529200, fax:(01773) 529217. sales@evansconcrete.co.uk, www.evansconcrete.co.uk

Evans Howard Roofing Ltd - Tyburn Road, Erdington, Birmingham. B24 8NB tel:(0121) 327 1336, fax:(0121) 327 3423. info@howardevansroofingandcladding.co.uk, www.howardevansroofingandcladding.co.uk

Evans Vanodine International PLC - Brierley Road, Walton Summit Centre, Bamber Bridge, Preston. PR5 8AH tel:(01772) 322200, fax:(01772) 626000. sales@evansvanodine.co.uk, www.evansvanodine.co.uk

Eve Trakway - Bramley Vale, Chesterfield, Derbys. S44 5GA tel:(08700) 767676, fax:(08700) 737373. mail@evetrakway.co.uk, www.evetrakway.co.uk

Evergreens Uk - No. 2 Extons Units, MKT overton Ind. Est., Market Overton, Nr. Oakham, Leics. LE15 7PP tel:(01572) 768208, fax:(01572) 768261. sales@evergreensuk.com, www.evergreensuk.com

Everlac (GB) Ltd - Hawthorn House, Helions Bumpstead Road, Haverhill, Suffolk. CB9 7AA tel:(01440) 766360, fax:(01440) 768897. enquiries@everlac.co.uk, www.everlac.co.uk

Evertaut Ltd - Lions Drive, Shadsworth Business Park, Blackburn, Lancs. BB1 2QS tel:(01254) 297 880, fax:(01254) 274 859. sales@evertaut.co.uk, www.evertaut.co.uk

Evode Ltd - Common Road, Stafford. ST16 3EH tel:(01785) 257755, fax:(01785) 252337. technical.service@bostik.com, www.evode.co.uk

Exidor Limited - Progress Drive, Cannock, Staffordshire. WS11 0JE tel:(01543) 460030, fax:(01543) 573534. info@exidor.co.uk, www.exidor.co.uk

Exitex Ltd - Dundalk. Ireland tel:+353 4293 71244, fax:+353 4293 71221. info@exitex.com, www.exitex.xom

Expamet Building Products - Greatham Street, Longhill Industrial Estate (North), Hartlepool. TS25 1PR tel:(0191) 410 6631, fax:(0191) 410 0650. info@birtleygroup.co.uk, www.expamet.co.uk

Expanded Piling Ltd - Cheapside Works, Waltham, Grimsby, Lincs. DN37 0JD tel:(01472) 822552, fax:(01472) 220675. info@expandedpiling.com, www.expandedpiling.com

Eyre & Baxter Limited - 229 Derbyshire Lane, Sheffield. S8 8SD tel:(0114) 250 0153, fax:(0114) 258 0856. enquiries@eyreandbaxter.co.uk, www.eryeandbaxter.co.uk

E-Z Rect Ltd - Unit 8c, Witan Park, Avenue 2, Station Lane, Witney. OX28 4FH tel:(01993) 779494, fax:(01993) 704111. sales@ezrshelving.com, www.ezrshelving.com

F

Fabrikat (Nottingham) Ltd - Hamilton Road, Sutton-in-Ashfield, Nottingham, Notts. NG17 5LN tel:(01623) 442200, fax:(01623) 442233. sales@fabrikat.co.uk, www.fabrikat.co.uk

Fagerhult Lighting - 33-34 Dolben Street, London. SE1 0UQ tel:(020) 7403 4123, fax:(020) 7378 0906. light@fagerhult.co.uk, www.fagerhult.co.uk

Fairfield Displays & Lighting Ltd - 127 Albert Street, Fleet, Hants. GU51 3SN tel:(01252) 812211, fax:(01252) 812123. info@fairfielddisplays.co.uk, www.fairfielddisplays.co.uk

Fairport Construction Equipment - Blagden Street, Sheffield. S2 5QS tel:(01142) 767921, fax:(01142) 720965. sales@fairport.uk.com, www.fairport.uk.com

Falco UK Ltd - Unit 8, Leekbrook Way, Leekbrook, Staffs. ST13 7AP tel:(01538) 380080, fax:(01538) 386421. sales@falco.co.uk, www.falco.co.uk

Fantasia Distribution Ltd - Unit B, The Flyers Way, Westerham, Kent. TN16 1DE tel:(01959) 564440, fax:(01959) 564829. info@fantasiaceilingfans.com, www.fantasiaceilingfans.com

Farefence (NW) Ltd - Pinfold House, Pinfold Road, Worsley, Manchester. M28 5DZ tel:(0161) 799 4925, fax:(0161) 703 8542. info@farefence.co.uk, www.farefence.co.uk

Farmington Masonry LLP - Farmington Quarry, Northleach, Cheltenham, Glos. GL54 3NZ tel:(01451) 860280, fax:(01451) 860115. info@farmington.co.uk, www.farmington.co.uk

Fastclean Blinds Ltd - 45 Townhill Road, Hamilton Road. ML63 9RH tel:(01698) 538392. gordonmichael18@yahoo.co.uk, www.fastcleanblindshamilton.co.uk

Fastwall Ltd - Units 3/10, Overfield, Thorpe Way Ind Estate, Banbury, Oxon. OX16 4XR tel:(01295) 25 25 88, fax:(01295) 25 25 84. keri@fastwall.com, www.fastwall.com

FC Frost Ltd - Bankside Works, Benfield Way, Braintree, Essex. CM7 3YS tel:(01376) 329 111, fax:(01376) 347 002. info@fcfrost.com, www.fcfrost.com

Federation of Master Builders - David Croft House, 25 Ely Place, London. EC1N 6TD tel:(020) 7025 2900, fax:(020) 7025 2929. jaynerunacres@fmb.org.uk, www.fmb.org.uk

Federation of Piling Specialists - Forum Court, 83 Copers Cope Road, Beckenham, Kent. BR3 1NR tel:(020) 8663 0947, fax:(020) 8663 0949. fps@fps.org.uk, www.fps.org.uk

Federation of Plastering and Drywall Contractors - Unit 4, Olton Bridge, 245 Warwick Road, Solihill, West Midlands. B92 7AH tel:(0121) 707 0077. info@thefis.org, www.thefis.org

Feedwater Ltd - Tarran Way, Moreton, Wirral. L46 4TP tel:(0151) 606 0808, fax:(0151) 678 5459. enquiries@feedwater.co.uk, www.feedwater.co.uk

FEILO SYLVANIA EUROPE LIMITED - Avis Way, Newhaven, East Sussex. BN9 0ED tel:(0800) 440 2478. info.uk@havells-sylvania.com, www.sylvania-lighting.com

Felix Design Ltd - Unit 15, Tiverton Way, Tiverton Business Park, Tiverton, Devon. EX16 6SR tel:(01884) 255420, fax:(01884) 242613. sales@felixstaging.co.uk, www.felixstaging.co.uk

Fencelines Ltd - Unit 16, Westbrook Road, Trafford Park, Manchester. M17 1AY tel:(0161) 848 8311, fax:(0161) 872 9643. sell@fencelines.co.uk, www.fencelines.co.uk

Fenlock-Hansen Ltd - Heworth House, William Street, Felling, Gateshead, Tyne & Wear. NE10 0JP tel:(0191) 438 3222, fax:(0191) 438 1686. sales@fendorhansen.co.uk, www.hansongroup.biz

FeRFA - The Resin Flooring Association, 16 Edward Road, Farnham, Surrey. GU9 8NP tel:(07484) 075 254, fax:(01252) 739140. lisa@ferfa.org.uk, www.ferfa.org.uk

Fermacell - Unit 2, The Courtyard, Reddicap Trading Estate, Sutton Coldfield, West Midlands. B75 7BU tel:(0870) 609 0306, fax:(0870) 240 2948. fermacell-uk@xella.com, www.fermacell.co.uk

Fernden Construction (Winchester) Ltd - Barfield Close, Winchester, Hants. SO23 9SQ tel:(01962) 866400, fax:(01962) 864139. sales@ferndenwin.co.uk, www.ferndenwin.co.uk

Fernox - 2 Genesis Business Park, Albert Drive, Sheerwater, Woking, Surrey. GU21 5RW tel:(0330) 100 7750, fax:(0330) 100 7751. sales@fernox.com, www.fernox.com

Ferrograph Limited - New York Way, New York Industrial Park, Newcastle-upon-Tyne. NE27 0QF tel:(0191) 280 8800, fax:(0191) 280 8810. info@ferrograph.com, www.ferrograph.com

Ferroli Ltd - Lichfield Road, Branston Industrial Estate, Burton-on-Trent. DE14 3HD tel:(0870) 728 2882, fax:(0870) 728 2883. sales@ferroli.co.uk, www.ferroli.co.uk

FGF Ltd - Shadwell House, Shadwell Street, Birmingham. B4 6LJ tel:(0121) 233 1144, fax:(0121) 212 2539. info@fgflimited.co.uk, www.fgflimited.co.uk

Fibaform Products Ltd - Unit 22, Lansil Industrial Estate, Caton Road, Lancaster. LA1 3PQ tel:(01524) 60182, fax:(01524) 389829. info@fibaform.co.uk, www.fibaform.co.uk

Fibercill - The Moorings, Hurst Business Park, Brierley Hill, W. Midlands. DY5 1UX tel:(01384) 482221, fax:(01384) 482212. mail@fibercill.com, www.fibercill.com

FIBO UK LTD - Water Meadow House, Watermeadow, Chesham, Buckinghamshire. HP5 1LF tel:(01494) 771242. sales@fibo.co.uk, www.fibo.co.uk

Fife Fire Engineers & Consultants Ltd - Waverley Road, Mitchelston Industrial Estate, Kirkcaldy, Fife. KY1 3NH tel:(01592) 653661, fax:(01592) 653990. a.tasker@ffec.co.uk, www.ffec.co.uk

Fighting Films - PO BOX 2405, Bristol. BS1 9BA tel:(0845) 408 5836, fax:(0845) 929 4540. info@fightingfilms.com, www.fightingfilms.com

Fillcrete Ltd - Maple House, 5 Over Minnis, New Ash Green, Kent. DA3 8JA tel:(01474) 872444, fax:(01474) 872426. sales@fillcrete.com, www.fillcrete.com

Filon Products Ltd - Unit 3 Ring Road, Zone 2, Burntwood Business Park, Burntwood, Staffordshire. WS7 3JQ tel:(01543) 687300, fax:(01543) 687303. sales@filon.co.uk, www.filon.co.uk

Findlay Irvine Ltd - Bog Road, Penicuik, Midlothian. EH26 9BU tel:(01968) 671200, fax:(01968) 671237. sales@findlayirvine.com, www.findlayirvine.com

Fine H & Son Ltd - Victoria House, 93 Manor Farm Road, Wembley, Middx. HA0 1XB tel:(020) 8997 5055, fax:(020) 8997 8410. sales@hfine.co.uk, www.hfine.co.uk

Finnish Fibreboard (UK) Ltd - 146 New London Road, Chelmsford, Essex. CM2 0AW tel:+358 20 110 3343. sales@finfib.fi, www.finnishfibreboard.com

Firco Ltd - Unit 3, Beckley Hill Industrial Estate, Lowwer Higham, Kent. ME3 7HX tel:(01474) 824338. info@firco.co.uk, www.firco.co.uk

Fire Industry Association - Tudor House, Kingsway Business Park, Oldfield Road, Hampton, Middlesex. TW12 2HD tel:(020) 3166 5002. info@fia.uk.com, www.fia.uk.com

Fire Protection Ltd - Millars 3, Southmill Road, Bishop's Stortford, Herts. CM23 3DH tel:(01279) 467077, fax:(01279) 466994. fire.protection@btinternet.com

Fire Security (Sprinkler Installations) Ltd - Homefield Road, Haverhill, Suffolk. CB9 8QP tel:(01440) 705815, fax:(01440) 704352. info@firesecurity.co.uk, www.firesecurity.co.uk

Firebarrier International Ltd T/A Firebarrier Services Ltd - 1 Lowman Way, Hilton Business Park, Hilton, Derby. DE65 5LJ tel:(01803) 291185, fax:(01803) 290026. sales@firebarrier.co.uk, www.firebarrier.co.uk

Fired Earth - Twyford Mill, Oxford Road, Adderbury, Oxon. OX17 3HP tel:(01295) 812088, fax:(01295) 810832. enquiries@firedearth.com, www.firedearth.com

Firemaster Extinguisher Ltd - Firex House, 174-176 Hither Green Lane, London. SE13 6QB tel:(020) 8852 8585, fax:(020) 8297 8020. sales@firemaster.co.uk, www.firemaster.co.uk

Firestone Building Products - Premier Park, Road One, Winsford Industrial Estate, Winsford, Cheshire. CW7 3PH tel:(01606) 552026. info@fbpl.co.uk, www.firestonebpe.co.uk

Firetecnics Systems Ltd - Southbank House, Black Prince Road, London. SE1 7SJ tel:(020) 7587 1493, fax:(020) 7582 3496. info@firetecnics.co.uk, www.firetecnics.com

Firwood Paints Ltd - Victoria Works, Oakenbottom Road, Bolton, Lancs. BL2 6DP tel:(01204) 525231, fax:(01204) 362522. sales@firwood.co.uk, www.firwood.co.uk

Fisher Scientific (UK) Ltd - Bishop Meadow Road, Loughborough, Leics. LE11 5RG tel:(01509) 231166, fax:(01509) 231893. fsuk.sales@thermofisher.com, www.fisher.co.uk

Fitzgerald Lighting Ltd - Normandy Way, Bodmin, Cornwall. PL31 1HH tel:(01208) 795 24, fax:(01208) 728 32. info@powerlite.net, www.powerlitefitz.co.uk

F (con't)

Fixatrad Ltd - Unit 7, Stadium Way, Reading, Berks. RG30 6BX tel:(0118) 921 2100, fax:(0118) 921 0634. sales@intrad.com, www.intrad.com

Fläkt Woods Ltd - Axial Way, Colchester, Essex. CO4 5ZD tel:(01206) 222555, fax:(01206) 222777. info.uk@flaktwoods.com, www.flaktwoods.co.uk

Flambeau - Manston Road, Ramsgate, Kent. CT12 6HW tel:(01843) 854000. eusales@flambeau.com, www.flambeau.co.uk

Flamco UK Ltd - Unit 4, St Micheals Road, Lea Green Industrial Estate, St. Helens, Merseyside. WA9 4WZ tel:(01744) 818100, fax:(01744) 830400. info@flamco.co.uk, www.flamco.co.uk

Fleming Buildings Ltd - 23 Auchinloch Road, Lenzie, Dunbartonshire. G66 5ET tel:(0141) 776 1181, fax:(0141) 775 1394. office@fleming-buildings.co.uk, www.fleming-buildings.co.uk

Fleming Homes Ltd - Coldstream Road, Duns, Berwickshire. TD11 3HS tel:(01361) 883785, fax:(01361) 883898. enquiries@fleminghomes.co.uk, www.fleminghomes.co.uk

Flexcrete Technologies Limited - Tomlinson Road, Leyland, Lancs. PR25 2DY tel:(0845) 260 7005, fax:(0845) 260 7006. info@flexcrete.com, www.flexcrete.com

Flexel International Ltd - Telford Road, Glenrothes, Fife. KY7 4NX tel:(01592) 760 928, fax:(01592) 760 929. sales@flexel.co.uk, www.flexel.co.uk

Flexelec(UK) Ltd - Unit 11, Kings Park Industrial Estate, Primrose Hill, Kings Langley, Herts. WD4 8ST tel:(01923) 274477, fax:(01923) 270264. sales@omerin.co.uk, www.flexelec.com

Flexible Reinforcements Ltd - Queensway House, Queensway, Clitheroe, Lancs. BB7 1AU tel:(01200) 442266, fax:(01200) 452010. sales@flexr.co.uk, www.flexr.co.uk

Flexiform Business Furniture Ltd - The Business Furniture Centre, 1392 Leeds Road, Bradford, W. Yorks. BD3 7AE tel:(01274) 706206, fax:(01274) 660867. info@flexiform.co.uk, www.flexiform.co.uk

Flexitallic Ltd - Marsh Works, Dewsbury Rd, Cleckheaton, W. Yorks. BD19 5BT tel:(01274) 851273, fax:(01274) 851386. sales@flexitallic.com, www.flexitallic.com

Flex-Seal Couplings Ltd - Endeavour Works, Newlands Way, Valley Park, Wombwell, Barnsley, S. Yorks. S73 OUW tel:(01226) 340888, fax:(01226) 340999. sales@flexseal.co.uk, www.flexseal.co.uk

Float Glass Industries - Float Glass House, Floats Road, Roundthorn, Manchester. M23 9QA tel:(0161) 946 8000, fax:(0161) 946 8092. salesorders@floatglass.co.uk, www.floatglass.co.uk

FloPlast Ltd - Eurolink Business Park, Castle Road, Sittingbourne, Kent. ME10 3FP tel:(01795) 431731, fax:(01795) 431188. sales@floplast.co.uk, www.floplast.co.uk

Floralsilk Ltd - Meadow Drove Business Park, Meadow Drove, Bourne. PE10 0BE tel:(01778) 425 205, fax:(01778) 420 457. sales@floralsilk.co.uk, www.floralsilk.co.uk

Flowcrete Plc - The Flooring Technology Centre, Booth Lane, Moston, Sandbach, Cheshire. CW11 3QF tel:(01270) 753000, fax:(01270) 753333. ukweb@flowcrete.com, www.flowcrete.co.uk

Flowflex Components Ltd - Samuel Blaser Works, Tounge Lane Industrial Estate, Buxton, Derbys. SK17 7LR tel:(01298) 77211, fax:(01298) 72362. hello@flowflex.com, www.flowflex.com

Flowserve Flow Control - Burrell Road, Haywards Heath, W. Sussex. RH16 1TL tel:(01444) 314400, fax:(01444) 314401. wvukinfo@flowserve.com, www.flowserve.com

Fluidair Ltd - Unit 4 Vale Works, Vale Street, Bolton, Lancashire. BL2 6QF tel:(01204) 559955, fax:(01204) 559966. enquiries@fluidair.co.uk, www.fluidair.co.uk

Fluorel Ltd - Suite F Spa House, 69 Southend Road, Hockley, Essex. SS5 4PZ tel:(020) 8504 9691, fax:(020) 8506 1792. sales@fluorel.co.uk, www.fluorel.co.uk

Foamseal Ltd - Market Square House, Petworth, W. Sussex. GU28 0AH tel:(01798) 345400. info@foamseal-insulation.co.uk, www.foamseal.co.uk

Focal Signs Ltd - 12 Wandle Way, Mitcham, Surrey. CR4 4NB tel:(020) 8687 5300, fax:(020) 8687 5301. sales@safetyshop.com, www.focalsigns.co.uk

Focus SB Ltd - Napier Road, Castleham Industrial Estate, St. Leonards-on-Sea, Sussex. TN38 9NY tel:(01424) 858060, fax:(01424) 853862. sales@focus-sb.co.uk, www.focus-sb.co.uk

Footprint Sheffield Ltd - Admiral Works, Sedgley Road, Sheffield, S. Yorks. S6 2AH tel:(01142) 327080, fax:(01142) 327089. sales@footprint-tools.co.uk, www.footprint-tools.co.uk

Forbes & Lomax Ltd - 205a St John's Hill, London. SW11 1TH tel:(020) 7738 0202, fax:(020) 7738 9224. sales@forbesandlomax.co.uk, www.forbesandlomax.co.uk

Forbo Flooring - PO Box 1, Den Road, Kirkcaldy, Fife. KY1 2SB tel:(01592) 643777, fax:(01592) 643999. info.uk@forbo.com, www.forbo-flooring.co.uk

Forest of Dean Stone Firms Ltd - Bixslade Stone Works, Parkend, Nr Lydney, Glos. GL15 4JS tel:(01594) 562304, fax:(01594) 564184. info@fodstone.co.uk, www.fodstone.co.uk

Formica Ltd - 11 Silver Fox Way, Cobalt Business Park, Newcastle Upon Tyne. NE27 0QJ tel:(0191) 2593100, fax:(0191) 2592648. formica.limited@formica.com, www.Formica.eu/uk

Formpave Ltd - Tufthorne Avenue, Coleford, Glos. GL16 8PR tel:(01594) 836999, fax:(01594) 810577. sales@formpave.co.uk, www.formpave.co.uk

Forterra Building Products Ltd - 5 Grange Park Court, Roman Way, Northampton. NN4 5EA tel:(01604) 707600. forterramail@forterra.co.uk, www.forterra.co.uk

Forticrete Cast Stone - Anstone Works, Kiveton Park, Sheffield. S26 6NP tel:(01909) 775000. caststone@forticrete.com, www.forticrete.co.uk

Forticrete Masonry - Anstone Works, Kiveton Park, Sheffield. S26 6NP tel:(01909) 775000. masonry@forticrete.com, www.forticrete.co.uk

Forticrete Roofing - Boss Avenue, Leighton Buzzard. LU7 4SD tel:(01525) 244900. roofing@forticrete.com, www.forticrete.co.uk

Forticrete Walling Stone - Kiveton Park Station, Kiveton Park, Sheffield. S26 6NP tel:(01909) 775000. walling@forticrete.com, www.forticrete.com

Fosroc Ltd - Drayton Manor Business Park, Coleshill Road, Tamworth, Staffordshire. B78 3TL tel:(01827) 262222, fax:(01827) 262444. enquiryuk@fosroc.com, www.fosroc.com

Fothergill Engineered Fabrics Ltd - PO Box 1, Summit, Littleborough, Lancs. OL15 OLU tel:(01706) 372414, fax:(01706) 376422. sales@fothergill.co.uk, www.fothergill.co.uk

Fountains Direct Ltd - The Office, 41 Dartnell Park, West Byfleet, Surrey. KT14 6PR tel:(01259) 722628, fax:(01259) 722732. gordon@fountains-direct.co.uk, www.fountains-direct.co.uk

Fox Pool (UK) Ltd - Mere House, Stow, Lincoln, Lincs. LN1 2BZ tel:(01427) 788662, fax:(01427) 788526. sales@grayfoxswimmingpools.co.uk, www.fox-pool.co.uk

Francis Frith Collection - Frith's Barn, Teffont, Salisbury, Wilts. SP3 5QP tel:(01722) 716376, fax:(01722) 716 881. sales@francisfrith.com, www.francisfrith.com

Franke Sissons Ltd - 14 Napier Court, Gander Lane, Barlborough Link Business Park, Barlborough, Derbyshire. S43 4PZ tel:(01246) 450 255, fax:(01246) 451 276. ws-info.uk@franke.com, www.franke.co.uk

Franke UK Ltd - West Park, Manchester Int'l Office Centre, Styal Road, Manchester, Gt Man. M22 5WB tel:(0161) 436 6280, fax:(0161) 436 2180. info.uk@franke.com, www.franke.co.uk

Franklin Hodge Industries Ltd - Jubilee Building, Faraday Raod, Westfield Trading Estate, Hereford, Herefordshire. HR4 9NS tel:(01432) 269605, fax:(01432) 277454. sales@franklinhodge.co.uk, www.franklinhodge.com

Fray Design Ltd - Ghyll Way, Airedale Business Centre, Keighley Road, Skipton. BD23 2TZ tel:(01756) 704040, fax:(01756) 704041. sales@fraydesign.co.uk, www.fraydesign.co.uk

Freyssinet Ltd - Innovation House, Euston Way, Town Centre, Telford, Shropshire. TF3 4LT tel:(01952) 201901, fax:(01952) 201753. info@freyssinet.co.uk, www.freyssinet.co.uk

Friedland Ltd - The Arnold Centre, Parcocke Road, Basildon, Essex. SS14 3EA tel:(01268) 563000, fax:(01268) 563538. friedlandorderenquiries@honeywell.com, www.friedland.co.uk

Friends of the Earth - 26 Underwood Street, London. N1 7JQ tel:(020) 7490 1555, fax:(020) 7490 0881. info@foe.co.uk, www.foe.co.uk

Frosts Landscape Construction Ltd - Liscombe Central, Liscombe Park, Soulbury, Leighton Buzzard. LU7 0JL tel:(0845) 021 9001, fax:(0845) 299 1893. info@frostslandscapes.com, www.frostsgroup.com

Fuchs Lubricants (UK) PLC - New Century Street, Hanley, Stoke-On-Trent. ST1 5HU tel:(08701) 200400, fax:(01782) 203775. ukwebsite@fuchs-oil.com, www.fuchslubricants.com

Fujichem Sonneborn Ltd - Jaxa Works, 91-95 Peregrine Road, Hainault, Ilford. IG6 3XH tel:(020) 8500 0251, fax:(020) 8500 3696. info@fcsonneborn.com, www.fcsonneborn.com/en/

Fullflow Group Ltd - Fullflow House, Holbrook Avenue, Holbrook, Sheffield, S. Yorks. S20 3FF tel:(0114) 247 3655, fax:(0114) 247 7805. info@uk.fullflow.com, www.fullflow.com

Fulton Boiler Works (Great Britain) Ltd - Fernhurst Road, Bristol. BS5 7FG tel:(0117) 972 3322, fax:(0117) 972 3358. enquiries@fulton.com, www.fulton.com

Furnitubes International Ltd - 3rd Floor, Meridian House, Royal Hill, Greenwich, London. SE10 8RD tel:(020) 8378 3200, fax:(020) 8378 3250. sales@furnitubes.com, www.furnitubes.com

Furse - Wilford Road, Nottingham, Notts. NG2 1EB tel:(0115) 964 3700, fax:(0115) 986 0538. enquiry@furse.com, www.furse.com

G

G Miccoli & Sons Limited - 5 Vulcan Way, New Addington, Croydon, Surrey. CR0 9UG tel:(0208) 684 3816, fax:(020) 8689 6514. info@stonebymiccoli.co.uk, www.stonebymiccoli.co.uk

GallifordTry - Cowley Business Park, Cowley, Uxbridge, Middlesex. UB8 2AL tel:(01895) 855001. info@gallifordtry.co.uk, http://www.gallifordtry.co.uk

Galvanizers Association - Wrens Court, 56 Victoria Road, Sutton Coldfield, W. Midlands. B72 1SY tel:(0121) 355 8838, fax:(0121) 355 8727. ga@hdg.org.uk, www.galvanizing.org.uk

Garador Ltd - Bunford Lane, Yeovil, Somerset. BA20 2YA tel:(01935) 443700, fax:(01935) 443744. enquiries@garador.co.uk, www.garador.co.uk

Garage Equipment Association Ltd - 2-3 Church Walk, Daventry. NN11 4BL tel:(01327) 312616, fax:(01327) 312606. info@gea.co.uk, www.gea.co.uk

Gardners Books - 1, Whittle Drive, Eastbourne, East Sussex. BN23 6QH tel:(01323) 521 555. sales@gardners.com, www.gardners.com

Garran Lockers Ltd - Garran House, Nantgarw Road, Caerphilly. CF83 1AQ tel:(0845) 658 8600, fax:(0845) 6588601. info@garran-lockers.co.uk, www.garran-lockers.ltd.uk

Gartec Ltd - Midshires Business Park, Smeaton Close, Aylesbury, Bucks. HP19 8HL tel:(01296) 768977, fax:(01296) 397600. sales@gartec.com, www.gartec.com

Gas Measurement Instruments Ltd - Inchinnan Business Park, Renfrew, Renfrewshire. PA4 9RG tel:(0141) 812 3211, fax:(0141) 812 7820. sales@gmiuk.com, www.gmiuk.com

Gatic - Poulton Close, Dover, Kent. CT17 0UF tel:(01304) 203545, fax:(01304) 215001. info@gaticdover.co.uk, www.gatic.com

Gazco - Osprey Road, Sowton Industrial Estate, Exeter, Devon. EX2 7JG tel:(01392) 474000, fax:(01392) 219932. info@gazco.com, www.gazco.com

Gazco Ltd - Osprey Road, Sowton Industrial Estate, Exeter, Devon. EX2 7JG tel:(01392) 216999, fax:(01392) 444148. info@gazco.com, www.gazco.com

GB Architectural Cladding Products Ltd - Spen Valley Works, Carr Street, Liversedge, West Yorkshire. WF15 6EE tel:(01924) 404045, fax:(01924) 401070. jim.gorst@artstone.co.uk, www.artstone-gbgroup.co.uk/

GB Sign Solutions Limited - Unit 5, Orion Trading Estate, Tenax Road, Trafford Park, Manchester. M17 1JT tel:(0161) 741 7270, fax:(0161) 741 7272. sales@greensigns.co.uk, www.greensigns.co.uk

GBG Fences Limited - 25 Barns Lane, Rushall, Walsall, Staffs. WS4 1HQ tel:(01922) 623207, fax:(01922) 722110. enquiries@gbgfences.co.uk

GCP APPLIED TECHNOLOGIES (UK) LIMITED - 580-581 Ipswich Road, Slough, Berks. SL1 4EQ tel:(01753) 490000, fax:(01753) 490001. uksales@grace.com, www.graceconstruction.com

GE Lighting Ltd - Lincoln Road, Enfield, Surrey. EN1 1SB tel:(020) 8626 8500, fax:(020) 8626 8501. englishsupport@tungsram.com, www.gelighting.com

Gearing F T Landscape Services Ltd - Crompton Road Depot, Stevenage, Herts. SG1 2EE tel:(01438) 369321, fax:(01483) 353039. Sales@ft-gearing.co.uk, www.ft-gearing.co.uk

Geberit Ltd - Geberit House, Acadamy Drive, Warwick, Warwickshire. CV34 6QZ tel:(0800) 077 8365, fax:(0844) 800 6604. enquiries@geberit.co.uk, www.geberit.co.uk

Geberit Ltd - Geberit House, Edgehill Drive, Warwick, Warwickshire. CV34 6NH tel:(01926) 516800, fax:(01926) 400101. sales.gb@geberit.co.uk, www.geberit.co.uk

Gebhardt Kiloheat - Kiloheat House, Enterprise Way, Edenbridge, Kent. TN8 6HF tel:(01732) 866000, fax:(01732) 866370. sales@nicotra.co.uk, www.nicotra-gebhardt.com

GEC Anderson Ltd - Oakengrove, Shire Lane, Hastoe, Tring, Herts. HP23 6LY tel:(01442) 826999, fax:(01442) 825999. webinfo@gecanderson.co.uk, www.gecanderson.co.uk

Geemat - 1 Triangle houseq, 2 Broomhill Road, Wandsworth, London. SW18 4HX tel:(020) 8877 1441, fax:(020) 8874 8590. info@fightingfilms.com, www.fightingfilms.com

General Time Europe - 8 Heathcote Way, Warwick. CV34 6TE tel:(01926) 885400, fax:(01926) 885723. naomi@nylholdings.com, www.westclox.co.uk

Genie Europe - The Maltings, Wharf Road, Grantham, Lincs. NG31 6BH tel:(01476) 584333, fax:(01476) 584334. infoeurope@genieind.com, www.genieindustries.com

Gent Limited - 140 Waterside Road, Hamilton Industrial Park, Leicester, Leics. LE5 1TN tel:(0116) 246 2000, fax:(0116) 246 2300. gent_enquiry@gent.co.uk, www.gent.co.uk

Geocel Ltd - Sherwin-Williams Diversified Brands Ltd, Thorncliffe Park, Chapeltown, Sheffield. S35 2YP tel:(01752) 202060, fax:(01752) 334384. info@geocel.co.uk, www.geocel.co.uk

Geoquip Worldwide - 33 Stakehill Industrial Estate, Middleton, Manchester. M24 2RW tel:(0161) 655 1020, fax:(0161) 655 1021. info@geoquip.com, www.geoquip.com

George Fischer Sales Ltd - Paradise Way, Coventry, W. Midlands. CV2 2ST tel:(024) 765 35535, fax:(024) 765 30450. uk.ps@georgfischer.com, ww.gfps.com

George Gilmour (Metals) Ltd - 245 Govan Road, Glasgow. G51 2SQ tel:(0141) 427 1264, fax:(0141) 427 2205. info@gilmour-ecometal.co.uk, www.gilmour-ecometal.com

Geosynthetic Technology Ltd - Nags Corner, Wiston Road, Nayland, Colchester, Essex. CO6 4LT tel:(01206) 262676, fax:(01206) 262998. sales@geosynthetic.co.uk, www.geosynthetic.co.uk

Gerflor Ltd - Wedgnock House, Wedgnock Lane, Warwick, Warwicks. CV34 5AP tel:(01926) 622612, fax:(01926) 401647. gerflorebayuk@gerflor.com, www.gerflor.co.uk

GEZE UK - Blenheim Way, Fradley Park, Lichfield, Staffs. WS13 8SY tel:(01543) 443000, fax:(01543) 443001. info.uk@geze.com, www.geze.co.uk

GfA UK Ltd - Unit 1 Titan Business Centre, Spartan Close, Warwick. CV34 6RR tel:(01926) 452452. sales@gfa-elektromaten.co.uk, www.gfa-elektromaten.co.uk

Gifford Grant Ltd - 20 Wrecclesham Hill, Farnham, Surrey. GU10 4JW tel:(01252) 816188. Enquiries@gifford-grant.com, http://www.gifford-grant.com

Gilgen Door Systems UK Ltd - Crow House, Crow Arch Lane, Ringwood, Hampshire. BH24 1PD tel:(01425) 46200, fax:(0870) 000 5299. info@gilgendoorsystems.co.uk, www.gilgendoorsystems.com

Gillespie (UK) Ltd - Alma House, 38 Crimea Road, Aldershot, Hants. GU11 1UD tel:(01252) 323311, fax:(01252) 336836. michaelt@gillespieuk.co.uk, www.gillespieuk.co.uk

Gilmour Ecometal - 245 Govan Road, Glasgow. G51 2SQ tel:(0141) 427 7000, fax:(0141) 427 5345. info@gilmour-ecometal.co.uk, www.gilmour-ecometal.com

Girbau UK ltd - Girbau House, Trust Industrial Estate, Wilbury Way, Hitchin, Herts. SG4 0UZ tel:(01462) 427780, fax:(01462) 427799. sales@girbau.co.uk, www.girbau.co.uk

Girsberger London - 140 Old Street, London. EC1V 9BJ tel:(020) 7490 3223, fax:(020) 7490 5665. info@girsberger.com, www.girsberger.com

GJ Durafencing Limited - Silverlands Park Nursery, Holloway Hill, Chertsey, Surrey. KT16 0AE tel:(01932) 568727, fax:(01932) 567799. sales@theplantationnursery.co.uk, www.gavinjones.co.uk

Glamox Electric (UK) Ltd - 5 College Street, Mews, Northampton. NN1 2QF tel:(01604) 635611, fax:(01604) 630131. info.uk@glamox.com, www.glamox.com

Glamox Luxo Lighting Limited - Unit 3, Capital Business Park, Mannor Way, Borehamwood, Hertfordshire. WD6 1GW tel:(0208) 9530540, fax:(0208) 9539580. ukoffice@glamoxluxo.com, www.glamoxluxo.co.uk

Glasdon U.K. Limited - Preston New Road, Blackpool, Lancs. FY4 4UL tel:(01253) 600410, fax:(01253) 792558. sales@glasdon-uk.co.uk, www.glasdon.com

Glasdon UK Limited - Preston New Road, Blackpool, Lancashire. FY4 4UL tel:(01253) 600410, fax:(01253) 792558. sales@glasdon-uk.co.uk, www.glasdon.com

Glass and Glazing Federation - 54 Ayres Street, London. SE1 1EU tel:(020) 7939 9100, fax:(0870) 042 4266. info@ggf.org.uk, www.ggf.org.uk

Glassolutions Saint-Gobain Ltd - Herald Way, Binley, Coventry. CV3 2ZG tel:(024) 7654 7400, fax:(024) 7654 7799. enquiries@glassolutions.co.uk, www.glassolutions.co.uk

Gledhill Water Storage Ltd - Sycamore Trading Estate, Squires Gate Lane, Blackpool, Lancs. FY4 3RL tel:(01253) 474444, fax:(01253) 474445. sales@gledhill.net, www.gledhill.net

Glenigan Ltd - 41-47 Seabourne Road, Bournemouth, Dorset. BH5 2HU tel:(0800) 373771, fax:(01202) 431204. info@glenigan.com, www.glenigan.com

Glixtone Ltd - Westminster Works, Alvechurch Road, West Heath, Birmingham. B31 3PG tel:(0121) 243 1122, fax:(0121) 243 1123. info@carrscoatings.com, www.carrspaints.com

godfrey syrett ltd - Godfrey Syrett Ltd, Planet Place, Killingworth, Newcastle Upon Tyne. NE12 6DY tel:(0191) 640 3840, fax:(0191) 268 3134. sales@godfreysyrett.co.uk, www.godfreysyrett.co.uk

Goelst - Crimple Court, Hornbeam Park, Harrogate. HG2 8PB tel:(01423) 873002, fax:(01423) 874006. info@goelstuk.com, www.goelst.nl

Gold & Wassall (Hinges) Ltd - Castle Works, Linchfield Road, Tamworth, Staffs. B79 7TH tel:(01827) 63391, fax:(01827) 310819. enquiries@goldwassallhinges.co.uk, www.goldwassallhinges.co.uk

Golden Coast Ltd - Fishleigh Road, Roundswell Commercial Park West, Barnstaple, Devon. EX31 3UA tel:(01271) 378100, fax:(01271) 371699. swimmer@goldenc.com, www.goldenc.com

Goodacres Fencing - Shoby Lodge Farm, Loughborough Road, Melton Mowbray, Leics. LE14 3PF tel:(01664) 813989, fax:(01664) 813989. kgoodacre1@aol.com

Gooding Aluminium - 1 British Wharf, Landmann Way, London. SE14 5RS tel:(020) 8692 2255, fax:(020) 8469 0031. sales@goodingalum.com, www.goodingalum.com

G (con't)

Goodwin HJ Ltd - Quenington, nr Cirencester, Glos. GL7 5BX tel:(01285) 750271, fax:(01285) 750352. sales@godwinpumps.co.uk, www.godwinpumps.com/

Goodwin Tanks Ltd - Pontefract Street, Derby. DE24 8JD tel:(01332) 363112, fax:(01332) 294 683. info@goodwintanks.co.uk, www.goodwintanks.co.uk

Gower Furniture Ltd - Holmfield Industrial Estate, Holmefield, Halifax, W. Yorks. HX2 9TN tel:(01422) 232200, fax:(01422) 249624. enquiries@gower-furniture.co.uk, www.gower-furniture.co.uk

GP Burners (CIB) Ltd - 2d Hargreaves Road, Groundwell Industrial Estate, Swindon, Wilts. SN25 5AZ tel:(01793) 709050, fax:(01793) 709060. info@gpburners.co.uk, www.gpburners.co.uk

Grace De Neef UK - 830 Birchwood Boulevard, Birchwood, Warrington, Cheshire. CH41 3PE tel:(01925) 855 335, fax:(01925) 855 350. amanda.browne@deneef.com, www.deneef.com

Gradient Insulations (UK) Ltd - Station Road, Four Ashes, Wolverhampton, W. Midlands. WV10 7DB tel:(01902) 791888, fax:(01902) 791886. sales@gradientuk.com, www.gradientuk.com

Gradus Ltd - Park Green, Macclesfield, Cheshire. SK11 7LZ tel:(01625) 428922, fax:(01625) 433949. imail@gradus.com, www.gradus.com

Gradwood Ltd - Landsdowne House, 85 BuxtonRoad, Stockport, Cheshire. SK2 6LR tel:(0161) 480 9629, fax:(0161) 474 7433. tonydavies@gradwood.co.uk, www.gradwood.co.uk

Graepels Perforators Ltd - Unit 5, Burtonwood Industial Centre, Burtonwood, Warrington, Cheshire. WA5 4HX tel:(01925) 229809, fax:(01925) 228069. sales@graepels.com, www.graepels.co.uk

Grando (UK) Ltd - Dalehouse Lane, Kenilworth, Warwicks. CV8 2EB tel:(01926) 854977, fax:(01926) 856772. info@grando.uk.com, www.grando.uk.com

Grange Fencing Limited - Capital House, Hadley Park East, Telford, Shropshire. TF1 6QJ tel:(01952) 586 460, fax:(01952) 581 522. sales@grangefen.co.uk, www.grangefen.co.uk

Grant Westfield Ltd - Westfield Avenue, Edinburgh, Lothian. EH11 2QH tel:(0131) 337 6262, fax:(0131) 337 2859. sales@grantwestfield.co.uk, www.grantwestfield.co.uk

Grass Concrete Ltd - Duncan House, 142 Thornes Lane, Wakefield, W. Yorks. WF2 7RE tel:(01924) 379443, fax:(01924) 290289. info@grasscrete.com, www.grasscrete.com

Gravesend Fencing Limited - Lower Range Road, Denton, Gravesend, Kent. DA12 2QL tel:(01474) 326016, fax:(01474) 324562. gravesendfencing@btconnect.com, www.gravesendfencing.co.uk

Great British Lighting - 1 Denham Way, Fleetwood. FY7 6PR tel:(01253) 873 503. info@greatbritishlighting.co.uk, www.greatbritishlighting.co.uk

Green Brook - West Road, Harlow, Essex. CM20 2BG tel:(01279) 772 772, fax:(01279) 422 007. gbe@greenbrook.co.uk, www.greenbrook.co.uk

Greif UK Ltd - Merseyside Works, Ellesmere Port, Cheshire. CH65 4EZ tel:(0151) 373 2000, fax:(0151) 373 2072. info.uk@greif.com, www.greif.com

Gridpart Interiors Ltd - 159, Stamford Street Central, Ashton-Under-Lyne, Lancashire. OL6 6XW tel:(0161) 883 2111. mail@gridpart.co.uk, www.gridpart.co.uk

Griff Chains Ltd - Quarry Road, Dudley Wood, Dudley, W. Midlands. DY2 0ED tel:(01384) 569415, fax:(01384) 410580. sales@griffchains.co.uk, www.griffchairs.co.uk

Griffin and General Fire Services Ltd - Unit F, 7 Willow Street, London. EC2A 4BH tel:(020) 7251 9379, fax:(020) 7729 5652. headoffice@griffinfire.co.uk, www.griffinfire.co.uk

Grille Diffuser & Louvre Co Ltd The - Air Diffusion Works, Woolley Bridge Road, Hollingworth, Hyde, Cheshire. SK14 7BW tel:(01457) 861538, fax:(01457) 866010. sales@grille.co.uk, www.grille.co.uk

Gripperrods Ltd - Wyrley Brook Park, Walkmill Lane, Bridgtown, Cannock, Staffs. WS11 3RX tel:(01922) 417777, fax:(01922) 419411. sales@interfloor.com, www.interfloor.com

Grohe Ltd - 1 River Road, Barking, Essex. IG11 0HD tel:(020) 8594 7292, fax:(020) 8594 8898. info-uk@grohe.com, www.grohe.co.uk

Grorud Industries Ltd - Castleside Industrial Estate, Consett, Co. Durham. DH8 8HG tel:(01207) 581485, fax:(01207) 580036. enquiries@grorud.com, www.grorud.com

Grosvenor Pumps Ltd - Trevoole, Praze, Camborne, Cornwall. TR14 0PJ tel:(01209) 831500, fax:(01209) 831939. sales@grosvenorpumps.com, www.grosvenorpumps.com

Group Four Glassfibre Ltd - Church Road Business Centre, Murston, Sittingbourne, Kent. ME10 3RS tel:(01795) 429424, fax:(01795) 476248. info@groupfourglassfibre.co.uk, www.groupfourglassfibre.co.uk

Grundfos Pumps Ltd - Groveberry Road, Leighton Buzzard, Beds. LU7 4TL tel:(01525) 850000, fax:(01525) 850011. grundfos-uk@sale.grundfos.com, uk.grundfos.com

Guardian Lock & Engineering Co. Ltd - Imperial Works, Wednesfield Road, Willenhall, W. Midlands. WV13 1AL tel:(01902) 635964, fax:(01902) 630675. sales@imperiallocks.co.uk, www.imperiallocks.co.uk

Guardian Wire Ltd - Guardian Works, Stock Lane, Chadderton, Lancs. OL9 9EY tel:(0161) 624 6020, fax:(0161) 620 2880. sales@guardianwire.co.uk, www.guardianwire.co.uk/

Guest (Speedfit) Ltd, John - Horton Road, West Drayton, Middx. UB7 8JL tel:(01895) 449233, fax:(01895) 420321. info@johnguest.co.uk, www.johnguest.co.uk

Guild of Architectural Ironmongers - BPF House, 6 Bath Place, Rivington Street, London. EC2A 3JE tel:(020) 7033 2480. info@gai.org.uk, www.gai.org.uk

Guild of Builders & Contractors, The - Crest House, 102-104 Church Road, Teddington, Middx. TW11 8PY tel:(020) 8977 1105, fax:(020) 8943 3151. info@buildersguild.co.uk, www.buildersguild.co.uk

Gunnebo UK Limited - Fairfax House, Pendeford Business Park, Wobaston Road, Wolverhampton, West Midlands. WV9 5HA tel:(01902) 455111, fax:(01902) 351961. info.uk@gunnebo.com, www.gunnebo.co.uk

Gun-Point Ltd - Thavies Inn House, 3-4 Holborn Circus, London. EC1N 2PL tel:(020) 7353 1759, fax:(020) 7583 7259. enquiries@gun-pointltd.com, www.gunpointlimited.co.uk

Guthrie Douglas - 12 Heathcote Way, Heathcote Industrial Estate, Warwick, Warwickshire. CV34 6TE tel:(01926) 310850. projects@guthriedouglas.com, www.guthriedouglas.com

Guttercrest - Victoria Road, Oswestry, Shropshire. SY11 2HX tel:(01691) 663300, fax:(01691) 663311. info@guttercrest.co.uk, www.guttercrest.co.uk

GVS Filter Technology UK - NFC House, Vickers Ind. Est, Morecambe, Lancs. LA3 3EN tel:(01524) 847600, fax:(01524) 847800. gvsuk@gvs.com, www.airsafetymedical.com

GVS Filter Technology UK - NFC House, Vickges Industrial Estate, Mellishaw Lane, Morecambe, Lancs. LA3 3EN tel:(01524) 847600, fax:(01524) 847800. gvsuk@gvs.com, www.fengroup.com

GVS Filter Technology UK Ltd - NFC House, Vickers Industrial Estate, Mellishaw Lane, Morecambe, Lancashire. LA3 3EN tel:(01524) 847600, fax:(01524) 847800. gvsuk@gvs.com, www.gvs.com

H

H Pickup Mechanical & Electrical Services Ltd - Durham House, Lower Clark Street, Scarborough, N. Yorks. YO12 7PW tel:(01723) 369191, fax:(01723) 362044. pickup@hpickup.co.uk, www.hpickup.co.uk/

Haddonstone Ltd - The Forge House, Church Lane, East Haddon, Northampton. NN6 8DB tel:(01604) 770711, fax:(01604) 770027. info@haddonstone.co.uk, www.haddonstone.com

Hadley Industries Plc - PO Box 92, Downing Street, Smethwick, W. Midlands. B66 2PA tel:(0121) 555 1300, fax:(0121) 555 1301. sales@hadleygroup.co.uk, www.hadleygroup.co.uk

Hafele UK Ltd - Swift Valley Industrial Estate, Rugby, Warwicks. CV21 1RD tel:(01788) 542020, fax:(01788) 544440. info@hafele.co.uk, www.hafele.co.uk

HAG Shutters & Grilles Ltd - Unit 1, Oak Lane, Fishponds Trading Estate, Fishponds, Bristol. BS5 7UY tel:(0117) 9654888, fax:(0117) 9657773. info@hag.co.uk, www.hag.co.uk

Hager Ltd - Hortonwood 50, Telford, Shropshire. TF1 7FT tel:(01952) 675675. sales@hager.co.uk, www.hager.co.uk

HAGS SMP - Clockhouse Nurseries, Clockhouse Lane East, Egham, Surrey. TW20 8PG tel:(01784) 489100, fax:(01784) 431079. sales@hags-smp.co.uk, www.hags.co.uk

Hale Hamilton Valves Ltd - Frays Mills Works, Cowley Road, Uxbridge, Middlesex. UB8 2AF tel:(01895) 236525, fax:(01895) 231407. _HHVWebEnquiries@circor.com, www.halehamilton.com

Halfen Ltd - A1/A2 Portland Close, Houghton Regis, Beds. LU5 5AW tel:(01582) 470300, fax:(01582) 470304. info@halfen.co.uk, www.halfen.co.uk

Hallidays UK Ltd - 3a Queen Street, Dorchester On Thames, Oxon. OX10 7HR tel:(01865) 340028. info@hallidays.com, www.hallidays.com

Hallmark Blinds Ltd - Hallmark House, 173 Caladonian Road, Islington, London. N1 0SL tel:(020) 7837 0964. info@hallmarkblinds.co.uk, www.hallmarkblinds.co.uk

Halmark Panels Ltd - Valletta House, Valletta Street, Hedon Road, Hull. HU9 5NP tel:(01482) 703222, fax:(01482) 701185. sales@hallmarkpanels.com, www.hallmarkpanels.com

Hambleside Danelaw Ltd - Long March, Long March Industrial Estate, Daventry, Northamptonshire. NN11 4NR tel:(01327) 701900, fax:(01327) 701909. marketing@hambleside-danelaw.co.uk, www.hambleside-danelaw.co.uk

Hamilton Acorn Ltd - Halford Road, Attleborough, Norfolk. N17 2HZ tel:(01953) 453201, fax:(01953) 454943. info@hamilton-acorn.co.uk, www.hamilton-acorn.co.uk

Hamilton R & Co Ltd - Unit G, Quarry Industrial Estate, Mere, Wilts. BA12 6LA tel:(01747) 860088, fax:(01747) 861032. info@hamilton-litestat.com, www.hamilton-litestat.com

Hammonds - New Home Division - Fleming Road, Harrowbrook Industrial Estate, Hinckley, Leics. LE10 3DT tel:(01455) 251451, fax:(01455) 633981. correspondence@hammonds-uk.com, www.hammonds-uk.com

Hamworthy Heating Limited & ACV UK - Wessex House, Newfields Business Park, Stinsford Road, Poole, Dorset. BH17 0NF tel:(01202) 662510, fax:(01202) 662544. marketing@hamworthy-heating.com, www.hamworthy-heating.com

Hands of Wycombe - 36 Dashwood Avenue, High Wycombe, Bucks. HP12 3DX tel:(01494) 524222, fax:(01494) 526508. info@hands.co.uk, www.hands.co.uk

Hanovia Ltd - 145 Farnham Road, Slough, Berks. SL1 4XB tel:(01753) 515300, fax:(01753) 534277. sales@aquionics.com, www.hanovia.co.uk

HansenFacades - Unit 2.08 Hollinwood Business Centre, Albert Street, Oldham. OL8 3QL tel:(0161) 284 4109. sales@hansenfacades.com, www.hansenfacades.com

Hansgrohe - Unit D1-2, Sandown Park Trading Estate, Royal Mills, Esher, Surrey. KT10 8BL tel:(0870) 7701972, fax:(0870) 7701973. enquiries@hansgrohe.co.uk, www.hansgrohe.co.uk

Hansgrohe - Units D1 & D2, Sandown Park Trading Estate, Royal Mills, Esher, Surrey. KT10 8BL tel:(0870) 7701972, fax:(0870) 7701973. enquiries@hansgrohe.co.uk, www.hansgrohe.co.uk

Hanson Building Products - Sales Office, 222 Peterborough Road, Whittlesey, Peterborough. PE7 1PD tel:(0330) 123 1017, fax:(01733) 206040. bricks@hanson.com, www.ask-hanson.com

Hanson Building Products - Stewartby, Bedford. MK43 9LZ tel:(01773) 514011, fax:(01773) 514044. info@hansonbp.com, www.hanson.biz

Hanson Building Products - Stewartby, Bedford. MK43 9LZ tel:(08705) 258258, fax:(01234) 762040. info@hansonbrick.com, www.hansonbrick.com

Hanson Building Products UK - 222 Peterborough Road, Whittlesey, Peterborough. PE7 1PD tel:(0330) 123 1015, fax:(01733) 206170. enquiries@hanson.com, www.hanson.co.uk

Hanson Concrete Products - Alfreton Road, Derby. DE21 4BN tel:(01332) 364314, fax:(01332) 372208. info@lehighhanson.com, www.hanson.biz

Hanson Concrete Products - PO Box 14, Appleford Road, Sutton Courtenay, Abbingdon, Oxon. OX14 4UB tel:(01235) 848877, fax:(01235) 848767. sales@hansonconcreteproducts.com, www.hansonplc.com

Hanson Concrete Products Ltd - Hoveringham, Nottingham, Notts. NG14 7JX tel:(01636) 832000, fax:(01636) 832020. concrete@hanson.com, www.heidelbergcement.com

Harbro Supplies Ltd - Morland Street, Bishop Auckland, Co. Durham. DL14 6JQ tel:(01388) 605363, fax:(01388) 603263. harbrosupplies@hotmail.com, www.habrosupplies.com

Hard York Quarries Ltd - Fagley Lane, Eccleshill, Bradford, W. Yorks. BD2 3NT tel:(01274) 637307, fax:(01274) 626146. sales@hardyorkquarries.co.uk, www.hardyorkquarries.co.uk

Hardall International Ltd - Hardall House, Ludun Close, Dunstable, Beds. LU5 4PN tel:(01582) 500860, fax:(01582) 690975. service@hardalluk.com, www.hardall.co.uk

Harewood Products Ltd (Adboards) - Unit 1, Union Road, The Valley, Bolton. BL2 2DT tel:(01204) 395730, fax:(01204) 388018. sales@adboards.com, www.adboards.com

Hargreaves Group GB Ltd - Westleigh House, Wakefield Road, Denby Dale, Huddersfield. HD8 8QJ tel:(01484) 866634, fax:(01484) 865268. dawn.hedley@hsgplc.co.uk, www.hsgplc.co.uk

Harkness Screens - Unit A, Norton Road, Stevenage, Herts. SG1 2BB tel:(01438) 725 200, fax:(01438) 344 400. Sales@harkness-screens.com, www.harkness-screens.com

Harling Security Solutions Limited - Regent House, Queens Road, Barnet, Herts. EN6 4DN tel:(0845) 177 0540, fax:(0845) 177 0541. sales@harlingsecurity.com

Harris & Bailey Ltd - 50 Hastings Road, Croydon, Surrey. CR9 6BR tel:(020) 8654 3181, fax:(020) 8656 9369. mail@harris-bailey.co.uk, www.harris-bailey.co.uk

Harrision Flagpoles - Borough Road, Darlington, Co. Durham. DL1 1SW tel:(01325) 355433, fax:(01325) 461726. sales@harrisoneds.com, www.flagpoles.co.uk

Harrison Thompson & Co Ltd - Yeoman House, Whitehall Estate, Whitehall Road, Leeds. LS12 5JB tel:(0113) 279 5854, fax:(0113) 231 0406. info@yeomanshield.com, www.yeomanshield.com

Hart Door Systems Ltd - Redburn Road, Westerhope Industrial Estate, Newcastle-upon-Tyne, Tyne & Wear. NE5 1PJ tel:(0191) 214 0404, fax:(0191) 271 1611. response@speedor.com, www.speedor.com

Hartley Botanic Ltd - Wellington Road, Greenfield, Oldham, Lancs. OL3 7AG tel:(01457) 873244. info@hartleybotanic.co.uk, www.hartley-botanic.co.uk

Harton Heating Appliances - Unit 6, Thustlebrook Industrial Est, Eynsham Drive, Abbey Wood. SE2 9RB tel:(020) 8310 0421, fax:(020) 8310 6785. info@hartons.globalnet.co.uk, www.hartons.co.uk

Harvey Steel Lintels Limited - Commerce Way, Whitehall Industrial Estate, Colchester, Essex. CO2 8HH tel:(01206) 792001, fax:(01206) 792022. harvey@lintels.co.uk, www.lintels.co.uk

Harviglass-Fibre Ltd - Alexandra Street, Hyde, Cheshire. SK14 1DX tel:(0161) 3682398, fax:(0161) 3681508. info@harviglass.com, www.harviglass.com

Hatfield Ltd, Roy - Fullerton Road, Rotherham, S. Yorks. S60 1DL tel:(01709) 820855, fax:(01709) 374062. info@royhatfield.com, www.royhatfield.com

Hatmet Limited - No. 3 The Courtyard, Lynton Road, Crouch End, London. N8 8SL tel:(020) 8341 0200, fax:(020) 8341 9878. trevorh@hatmet.co.uk, www.hatmet.co.uk

Hattersley - P O Box 719, Ipswich, Suffolk. IP1 9DU tel:(01744) 458670, fax:(01744) 458671. uksales@hattersley.com, www.hattersley.com

Havering Fencing Co - 237 Chase Cross Road, Collier Row, Romford, Essex. RM5 3XS tel:(01708) 747855, fax:(01708) 721010. enquiries@haveringfencing.com, www.haveringfencing.com

Hawker Siddley Switchgear - Unit 3, Blackwood Business Park, Newport Road, Blackwood, South Wales. NP12 2XH tel:(01495) 223001, fax:(01495) 225674. sales@hss-ltd.com, www.hss-ltd.com

Hawkesworth Appliance Testing - Guidance House, York Road, Thirsk. YO7 3BT tel:(01845) 524498, fax:(01845) 526884. sales@hawktest.co.uk, www.hawktest.co.uk

Hawkins Insulation Ltd - Central House, 101Central Park, Petherton Road, Hengrave, Bristol, Avon. BS14 9BZ tel:(01275) 839500, fax:(01275) 835555. enquiries@hawkinsulation.co.uk, www.hawkinsulation.co.uk

Haworth UK Ltd - Cannon Court, Brewhouse Yard, St. John Street, Clerkenwell, London. EC1V 4JQ tel:(020) 7324 1360, fax:(020) 7490 1513. info.uk@haworth.com, www.haworthuk.com/en

Hayes Cladding Systems - Brindley Road, (off Hadfield Road), Cardiff. CF11 8TL tel:(029) 2038 9954, fax:(029) 2039 0127. sales@hayescladding.co.uk, www.hayescladding.co.uk

Haysom (Purbeck Stone) Ltd - Lander's Quarry, Kingston Road, Langton Matravers, Swanage, Dorset. BH19 3JP tel:(01929) 439205, fax:(01929) 439268. haysom@purbeckstone.co.uk, www.purbeckstone.co.uk

Hazard Safety Products Ltd - 55-57 Bristol Road, Edgbaston, Birmingham. B5 7TU tel:(0121) 446 4433, fax:(0121) 446 4230. sales@hazard.co.uk, www.hazard.co.uk

HC Slingsby PLC - Otley Road, Baildon, Shipley, W. Yorks. BD17 7LW tel:(0800) 294 4440, fax:(0800) 294 4442. sales@slingsby.com, www.slingsby.com

HCL Contracts Ltd - Bridge House, Commerce Road, Brentford, Middx. TW8 8LQ tel:(0800) 212867, fax:(020) 8847 9003. info@hclsafety.com, www.hclgroup.co.uk

HCL Devizes - Hopton Park, Devizes, Wiltshire. SN10 2JP tel:(0845) 600 0086, fax:(0121) 285 1671. info@hclsafety.com, www.hclsafety.com

HE Services (Plant Hire) Ltd - Whitewall Road, Strood, Kent. ME2 4DZ tel:(0208) 804 2000, fax:(0871) 534437. nhc@heservices.co.uk, www.heservices.co.uk

Heat Merchants - Moydrum Road, Athlone, Westmeath, Ireland. tel:+353 90 6424000, fax:+353 90 6424067. customerservices@wolseley.co.uk, www.heatmerchants.ie

Heat Pump Association (HPA) - 2 Waltham Court, Milley Lane, Hare Hatch, Reading, Berkshire. RG10 9TH tel:(01189) 403416, fax:(01189) 406258. info@feta.co.uk, www.feta.co.uk

Heath Samuel & Sons PLC - Cobden Works, Leopold Street, Birmingham. B12 0UJ tel:(0121) 766 4200, fax:(0121) 772 3334. info@samuel-heath.com, www.samuel-heath.co.uk

Heating Ventilating and Air Conditioning Manufacturers Association (HEVAC) - 2 Waltham Court, Milley Lane, Hare Hatch, Reading, Berkshire. RG10 9TH tel:(01189) 403416, fax:(01189) 406258. info@feta.co.uk, www.feta.co.uk

HeatProfile Ltd - Unit 1, Walnut Tree Park, Walnut Tree Close, Guildford, Surrey. GU1 4TR tel:(01483) 537000, fax:(01483) 537500. sales@heatprofile.co.uk, www.heatprofile.co.uk

Heatrae Sadia Heating Ltd - Hurricane Way, Norwich. NR6 6EA tel:(01603) 420220, fax:(01603) 420149. sales@heatraesadia.com, www.heatraesadia.com

Heckmondwicke FB - PO Box 7, Wellington Mills, Liversedge, West Yorkshire. WF15 7XA tel:(01924) 406161, fax:(0800) 136769. sales@heckmondwike-fb.co.uk, www.heckmondwike-fb.co.uk

Heldite Ltd - Heldite Centre Bristow Road, Hounslow, Middx. TW3 1UP tel:(020) 8577 9157/9257, fax:(020) 8577 9057. sales@heldite.com, www.heldite.com

H (con't)

Helifix - The Mille, 1000 Great West Road, Brentford, London. TW8 9DW tel:(020) 8735 5200, fax:(020) 8735 5201. sales@helifix.co.uk, www.helifix.co.uk

Hellermann Tyton - Sharston Green Buisness Park , 1 Robeson Way, Altrincham Road, Wythenshawe, Manchester. M22 4TY tel:(0161) 945 4181, fax:(0161) 954 3708. ric.kynnersley@hellermanntyton.co.uk, www.hellermanntyton.co.uk

Helmsman - Northern Way, Bury St Edmunds, Suffolk. IP32 6NH tel:(01284) 727600, fax:(01284) 727601. sales@helmsman.co.uk, www.helmsman.co.uk

Helvar Ltd - Hawley Mill, Hawley Road, Dartford, Kent. DA2 7SY tel:(01322) 617 200, fax:(01322) 617 229. uksystemsales@helvar.com, www.helvar.com

Hemsec Panel Technologies - Stoney Lane, Rainhill, Prescot, Merseyside. L35 9LL tel:(0151) 426 7171, fax:(0151) 493 1331. sales@hemsec.com, www.hpt-panels.com

Henkel Consumer Adhesives - Road 5, Winsford Ind Est, Winsford, Cheshire. CW7 3QY tel:(020) 8804 3343, fax:(020) 8443 4321. technical.services@henkel.co.uk, www.henkel.com

Henkel Ltd - Wood Lane End, Hemel Hempstead, Hertfordshire. HP2 4RQ tel:(01442) 27 8000, fax:(01442) 278071. info@henkel.co.uk, www.henkel.co.uk

Henry Squire & Sons Ltd - Hilton Cross Business Park, Cannock Road, Featherstone, Wolverhampton. WV10 7QZ tel:(01902) 308050, fax:(01902) 308051. info@henry-squire.co.uk, www.squirelocks.co.uk

Hepworth Building Products Ltd - Hazlehead, Crow Edge, Sheffield, S. Yorks. S36 4HG tel:(01226) 763561, fax:(01226) 764827. customerservices@wavin.co.uk, www.hepworthbp.co.uk

Hepworth Heating Ltd - Nottingham Road, Belper, Derbys. DE56 1JT tel:(01773) 824141, fax:(01773) 820569. info@glow-worm.co.uk, www.glow-worm.co.uk

Heras - Units 3 & 4, Duffield Road, Little Eaton, Derbyshire. DE21 5DR tel:(01629) 824891, fax:(01629) 824896. info@heras.com, www.heras.co.uk

Herga Electric Ltd - Northern Way, Bury St Edmunds, Suffolk. IP32 6NN tel:(01284) 701422, fax:(01284) 753112. sales@herga.com, www.herga.com

Hertel Services - Alton House, Alton Business Park, Alton Road, Ross-on-Wye, Herefordshire. HR9 5BP tel:(0845) 604 6729. www.hsltd.com

Herz Valves UK Ltd - Progress House, Moorfield Point, Moorfield Road, Slyfield Industrial Estate, Guildford, Surrey. GU1 1RU tel:(01483) 502211, fax:(01483) 502025. sales@herzvalves.com, www.herzvalves.com

Hettich UK Ltd - Unit 200, Metroplex Business Park, Broadway, Salford, Manchester. M50 2UE tel:(0161) 872 9552, fax:(0161) 848 7605. info@uk.hettich.com, www.hettich.com

HEWI UK Ltd - Holm Oak Barn, Beluncle Halt, Stoke Road, Hoo, Rochester, Kent. ME3 9NT tel:(01634) 258200, fax:(01634) 250099. info@hewi.co.uk, www.hewi.co.uk

Higginson Staircases Ltd - Unit 17 Atlas Business Centre, Oxgate Lane, London. NW2 7HJ tel:(020) 8200 4848, fax:(020) 8200 8249. sales@higginson.co.uk, www.higginson.co.uk

Higginson Staircases Ltd - Unit 17, Atlas Business Centre, London. NW2 7HJ tel:(020) 8200 4848. sales@higginson.co.uk, www.higginson.co.uk

Hill and Smith - Springvale Business & Industrial Park, Bilston, Wolverhampton. WV14 0QL tel:(01902) 499400. sales@hill-smith.co.uk, www.hill-smith.co.uk

Hille Educational Products Ltd - Unit 27, Rassau Industrial Estate, Ebbw Vale, Gwent. NP23 5SD tel:(01495) 352187, fax:(01495) 306646. info@hille.co.uk, www.hille.co.uk

Hilmor - Caxton Way, Stevenage, Herts. SG1 2DQ tel:(01438) 312466, fax:(01438) 728327. uksales@irwin.co.uk, www.hilmar.co.uk

Hilti (Great Britain) Ltd - 1 Trafford Wharf Road, Manchester. M17 1BY tel:(0800) 886100, fax:(0800) 886200. gbsales@hilti.co.uk, www.hilti.co.uk

Hilton Banks Ltd - 74 Oldfield Road, Hampton, Middx. TW12 2HR tel:(08452) 300 404, fax:(020) 8779 8294. hiltonbanks@btinternet.com

Hines & Sons, P E, Ltd - Whitbridge Lane, Stone, Staffs. ST15 8LU tel:(01785) 814921, fax:(01785) 818808. sales@hines.co.uk, www.hines.co.uk

Hinton Perry & Davenhill Ltd - Dreadnought Works, Pensnett, Brierley Hill, Staffs. DY5 4TH tel:(01384) 77405, fax:(01384) 74553. sales@dreadnought-tiles.co.uk, www.dreadnought-tiles.co.uk

Hipkiss, H, & Co Ltd - Park House, Clapgate Lane, Woodgate, Birmingham. B32 3BL tel:(0121) 421 5777, fax:(0121) 421 5333. info@hipkiss.co.uk, www.hipkiss.co.uk

Hi-Store Ltd - Station Approach, Four Marks, Alton, Hants. GU34 5HN tel:(01420) 562522, fax:(01420) 564420. sales@hi-store.com, www.hi-store.com

Historic England - 4th Floor, Cannon Bridge House, 25 Dowgate Hill, London. EC4R 2YA tel:(020) 7973 3700, fax:(020) 7973 3001. customers@HistoricEngland.org.uk, https://historicengland.org.uk/

HMG Paints - Riverside Works, Collyhurst Road, Manchester, Gt Man. M40 7RU tel:(0161) 205 7631, fax:(0161) 205 4829. sales@hmgpaint.com, www.hmgpaint.com

HMSO Publications Office - Parliamentary Press, Mandela Way, London. SE1 tel:(020) 7394 4200. book.orders@tso.co.uk, www.legislation.gov.uk

Hoben International Ltd - Brassington Works, Manystones Lane, Matlock, Derbyshire. DE4 4HF tel:(01629) 540201, fax:(01629) 540205. sales@hobeninternational.com, www.hobeninternational.com

Hochiki Europe (UK) Ltd - Grosvenor Road, Gillingham Business Park, Gillingham, Kent. ME8 0SA tel:(01634) 260133, fax:(01634) 260132. sales@hochikieurope.com, www.hochikieurope.com

Hodgkinson Bennis Ltd - Unit 7A, Highfield Road, Little Hulton, Worsley, Manchester. M38 9SS tel:(0161) 790 4411, fax:(0161) 703 8505. enquiries@hbcombustion.com, www.hbcombustion.co.uk

Hodkin Jones (Sheffield) Ltd - Callywhite Lane, Dronfield, Sheffield. S18 2XP tel:(01246) 290890, fax:(01246) 290292. info@hodkin-jones.co.uk, www.hodkin-jones.co.uk

Holophane Europe Ltd - Bond Avenue, Bletchley, Milton Keynes. MK1 1JG tel:(01908) 649292, fax:(01908) 367618. info@holophane.co.uk, www.holophane.co.uk

Homelux Nenplas - Airfield Industrial, Airfield Industrial Estate, Ashbourne, Derbys. DE6 1HA tel:(01335) 347300, fax:(01335) 340333. enquiries@nenplas.co.uk, www.homeluxnenplas.com

Honeywell Control Systems Ltd - Honeywell House, Arlington Business Park, Bracknell, Berks. RG12 1EB tel:(01344) 656000, fax:(01344) 656240. uk.infocentre@honeywell.com, www.honeywell.com/uk

Honeywell Safety Products - Edison Road, Basingstoke. RG21 6QD tel:(01256) 693200, fax:(01256) 693300. info-uk.hsp@honeywell.com, www.honeywellsafety.com

HOPPE (UK) Ltd - Gailey Park, Gravelly Way, Standeford, Wolverhampton, W. Midlands. WV10 7GW tel:(01902) 484400, fax:(01902) 484406. info.uk@hoppe.com, www.hoppe.co.uk

Horizon International Ltd - Willment Way, Avonmouth, Bristol, Avon. BS11 8DJ tel:(0117) 982 1415, fax:(0117) 982 0630. sales@horizon-int.com, www.horizon-int.com

Hörmann (UK) Ltd - Gee Road Coalville, Coalville, Leicestershire. LE67 4JW tel:(01530) 513000, fax:(01530) 513001. info@hormann.co.uk, www.hormann.co.uk

Horne Engineering Ltd - PO Box 7, Rankine Street, Johnstone, Renfrewshire. PA5 8BD tel:(01505) 321455, fax:(01505) 336287. sales@horne.co.uk, www.horne.co.uk

Horstmann Controls Ltd - South Bristol Business Park, Roman Farm Road, Bristol. BS4 1UP tel:(0117) 978 8700, fax:(0117) 978 8701. sales@horstmann.co.uk, www.horstmann.co.uk

Hospital Metalcraft Ltd - Blandford Heights, Blandford Forum, Dorset. DT11 7TG tel:(01258) 451338, fax:(01258) 455056. sales@bristolmaid.com, www.bristolmaid.com

Hotchkiss Air Supply - Heath Mill Road, Wombourne, Wolverhampton, W. Midlands. WV5 8AP tel:(01903) 895161, fax:(01903) 892045. sales@hotchkissairsupply.co.uk, www.hotchkissairsupply.co.uk

Hoval Ltd - Northgate, Newark-on-Trent, Notts. NG24 1JN tel:(01636) 72711, fax:(01636) 73532. boilersales@hoval.co.uk, www.hoval.co.uk

Howard Bros Joinery Ltd - Station Approach, Battle, Sussex. TN33 0DE tel:(01424) 773272, fax:(01424) 773836. sales@howard-bros-joinery.com, www.howard-bros-Joinery.com

Howard Evans Roofing and Cladding Ltd - C/O SPV Group, Westgate, Aldridge Walsall, West Midlands. WS9 8EX tel:(0121) 327 1336, fax:(01922) 749 515. info@howardevansroofingandcladding.co.uk, www.howardevansroofingandcladding.co.uk

Howden Buffalo - Old Govan Road, Renfrew, Renfrewshire. PA4 8XJ tel:(0141) 885 7500, fax:(0141) 885 7555. sales@howdenbuffalo.com, www.howden.com

Howe Fencing & Sectional Buildings - Horse Cross, Standon Road, Standon, Nr Ware, Herts. SG11 2PU tel:(01920) 822055, fax:(01920) 822871. bps@avsfencing.co.uk, www.howefencing.co.uk

Howe Green Ltd - Marsh Lane, Ware, Herts. SG12 9QQ tel:(01920) 463 230, fax:(01920) 463 231. info@howegreen.co.uk, www.howegreen.com

Hoyles Electronic Developments Ltd - Sandwash Close, Rainford Industrial Estate, Rainford, St. Helens, Merseyside. WA11 8LY tel:(01744) 886600, fax:(01744) 886607. info@hoyles.com, www.hoyles.com

Hozelock Ltd - Midpoint Park, Minworth, Birmingham, W. Midlands. B76 1AB tel:(0121) 313 4242. support@hozelock.zendesk.com, www.hozelock.com

HRS Hevac Ltd - 10-12 Caxton Way, Watford Business Park, Watford, Herts. WD18 8JY tel:(01923) 232335, fax:(01923) 230266. mail@hrs.co.uk, www.hrshevac.co.uk

HSS Hire Service Group - 25 Willow Lane, Mitcham, Surrey. CR4 4TS tel:(020) 8260 3100, fax:(020) 8687 5005. hire@hss.co.uk, www.hss.co.uk

Hudevad Britain - Hudevad House, Walton Lodge, Bridge Street, Walton-on-Thames, Surrey. KT12 1BT tel:(01932) 247835, fax:(01932) 247694. sales@hudevad.co.uk, www.hudevad.co.uk

Hughes Safety Showers Limited - Whitefield Road, Bredbury, Stockport, Cheshire. SK6 2SS tel:(0161) 430 6618, fax:(0161) 4307928. sales@hughes-safety-showers.co.uk, www.hughes-safety-showers.co.uk

Humbrol - Hornby Hobbies LTD, 3rd Flr, Thegate Way, Innovation Way, Discovery Park, Sandwich, Kent. CT13 9FF tel:(01843) 233525. internetsales@hornby.com, www.humbrol.com

Humphrey & Stretton PLC - Pindar Road Industrial Estate, Hoddesdon, Herts. EN11 0EU tel:(01992) 462965, fax:(01992) 463996. enquiries@humphreystretton.com, www.humphreystretton.com/

Hunter Douglas Architectural Ltd - Suite 2, Newton House, Northampton Science Park, Kings Park Road, Moulton Park Industrial Estate, Northampton. NN3 6LG tel:(01604) 648 229, fax:(01604) 212863. info@hunterdouglas.co.uk, www.hunterdouglas.co.uk

Hunter Douglas Ltd (Wood Division) - Kingswick House, Kingswick Drive, Sunninghill, Berkshire. SL5 7BH tel:(01344) 292293, fax:(01344) 292214. hswood@compuserve.com

Hunter Douglas UK Ltd (Window Fashions Division) - Mersey Industrial Estate, Heaton Mersey, Stockport, Cheshire. SK4 3EQ tel:(0161) 442 9500, fax:(0161) 431 5087. russell.malley@luxaflex-sunway.co.uk, www.luxalon.com

Hunter Plastics Ltd - Nathan Way, London. SE28 0AE tel:(020) 8855 9851, fax:(020) 8317 7764. info@multikwik.com, www.hunterplastics.co.uk

Huntree Fencing Ltd - Cosy Corner, Great North Road, Little Paxton, Cambs. PE19 6EH tel:(01234) 870864, fax:(01480) 471082. karen@huntreefencing.co.uk, www.huntreefencing.co.uk

Hush Acoustics - 44 Canal Street, Bootle, Liverpool. L20 8QU tel:(0151) 9332026, fax:(0151) 9441146. info@hushacoustics.co.uk, www.hushacoustics.co.uk

HW Architectural Ltd - Birds Royd Lane, Brighouse, W. Yorks. HD6 1NG tel:(01484) 717677, fax:(01484) 400148. enquiry@hwa.co.uk, www.hwa.co.uk

Hyde Brian Ltd - Stirling Road, Shirley, Solihull, W. Midlands. B90 4LZ tel:(0121) 705 7987, fax:(0121) 711 2465. sales@brianhyde.co.uk, www.brianhyde.co.uk

Hydraseeders Ltd - Coxbench, Derby, Derbys. DE21 5BH tel:(01332) 880364, fax:(01332) 883241. hydraseeders1@btconnect.com, www.hydraseeders.uk.com

Hydratight Sweeney Limited - Bently Road South, Darlaston, W. Midlands. WS10 8LQ tel:(0121) 5050 600, fax:(0121) 5050 800. enquiry@hydratight.com, www.hevilifts.com

Hydrovane Compressor Co Ltd - Claybrook Drive, Washford Industrial Estate, Redditch. B98 0DS tel:(01527) 525522, fax:(01527) 521140. hydrovane.red@gardnerdenver.com, www.hydrovane.co.uk

Hye Oak - Denton Wharf, Gravesend, Kent. DA12 2QB tel:(01474) 332291, fax:(01474) 564491. enquiries@hyeoak.co.uk, www.hyeoak.co.uk

Hyflex Roofing - Amasco House, 101 Powke Lane, Cradley Heath, West Midlands. B64 5PX tel:(0121) 502 9580, fax:(0121) 502 9581. enquiries@hyflex.co.uk, www.hyflex.co.uk

Hymo Ltd - 35 Cornwell Business Park, Salthouse Road, Brackmills, Northampton, Northants. NN4 7EX tel:(01604) 661601, fax:(01604) 660166. info@hymo.ltd.uk, www.hymo.com

Hyperion Wall Furniture Ltd - Business Park 7, Brook Way, Leatherhead, Surrey. KT22 7NA tel:(01932) 844783, fax:(01372) 362004. enquiries@hyperion-furniture.co.uk, http://hyperion-furniture.co.uk

Hy-Ten Ltd - 12 The Green, Richmond, Surrey. TW9 1PX tel:(020) 8940 7578, fax:(020) 8332 1757. admin@hy-ten.co.uk, www.hy-ten.co.uk

I

IAC Acoustic Company UK Ltd - IAC House, Electron Way, Chandlers Ford, Hampshire. SO53 4SE tel:(01962) 873 000. info@iacl-uk.com, www.iac-noisecontrol.com

IBL Lighting Limited - 1 Farnham Road, Guildford, Surrey. GU2 4RG tel:(0844) 822 5210, fax:(0844) 822 5211. info@ibl.co.uk, www.ibl.co.uk

Ibstock Brick Ltd - Leicester Road, Ibstock, Leics. LE67 6HS tel:(01530) 261999, fax:(01530) 261888. marketing@ibstock.co.uk, www.ibstock.co.uk

Ibstock Building Products Ltd - Anstone Office, Kiveton Park Station, Kiveton Park, Sheffield, S. Yorks. S26 6NP tel:(01909) 771122, fax:(01909) 515281. marketing@ibstock.co.uk, www.ibstock.com/

Ibstock Hathernware Ltd - Station Works, Rempstone Road, Normanton on Soar, Loughborough, Leics. LE12 5EW tel:(01509) 842273, fax:(01509) 843629. enquiries@ibstock.co.uk, www.hathernware.co.uk

Ibstock Scotish Brick - Tannochside Works, Old Edingburgh Road, Tanockside, Uddingston, Strathclyde. G71 6HL tel:(01698) 810686, fax:(01698) 812364. enquiries@ibstock.co.uk, www.ibstock.co.uk

ICB (International Construction Bureau) Ltd - Unit 9, Elliott Road, West Howe Industrial Estate, Bournemouth, Dorset. BH11 8JX tel:(01202) 579208, fax:(01202) 581748. info@icb.uk.com, www.icb.uk.com

ICI Woodcare - ICI Paints plc, Wexham Road, Slough. SL2 5DS tel:(0870) 242 1100, fax:(01753) 556938. duluxtrade.advice@ici.com, www.duluxtrade.co.uk

Icopal Limited - Barton Dock Road, Stretford, Manchester. M32 0YL tel:(0161) 865 4444, fax:(0161) 864 2616. info.uk@icopal.com, www.icopal.co.uk

Icopal Limited - Barton Rock Rd, Stretford, Manchester. M32 0YC tel:(0161) 865 4444, fax:(0161) 864 2616. info.uk@icopal.com, www.monarflex.co.uk

Ide T & W Ltd - 5 Sovereign Close, Wapping, London. E1W 3HW tel:(020) 7790 2333, fax:(020) 7790 0201. contracting@idecon.co.uk, www.twigroup.co.uk

Ideal Building Systems Ltd - Lancaster Road, Carnaby Industrial Estate, Bridlington, E. Yorks. YO15 3QY tel:(01262) 606750, fax:(01262) 671960. sales@idealbuildingsystems.co.uk, www.idealbuildingsystems.co.uk

Ideal-Standard Ltd - The Bathroom Works, National Avenue, Kingston Upon Hull. HU5 4HS tel:(01482) 346461, fax:(01482) 445886. UKCustcare@idealstandard.com, www.ideal-standard.co.uk

IG Limited - Avondale Road, Cwmbran, Gwent. NP44 1XY tel:(01633) 486486, fax:(01633) 486465. info@igltd.co.uk, www.igltd.co.uk

IHS - Viewpoint One Willoughby Road, Bracknell, Berks. RG12 8FB tel:(01344) 426311, fax:(01344) 424971. systems@ihs.com, www.ihs.com

IJK Timber Group Ltd - 24-28 Duncrue Street, Belfast. BT3 9AR tel:(028) 9035 1224, fax:(028) 9035 1527. sales@ijktimber.co.uk, www.ijktimbergroup.co.uk

IKM Systems Ltd - Unit7A, The Seedbed Business Centre, Vangaurd Way, Shoeburyness, Southend-on-Sea, Essex. SS3 9QX tel:(01702) 382321, fax:(01702) 382323. ikmsystems@btopenworld.com, www.ikmsystems.co.uk

IKO PLC - Appley Lane North, Appley Bridge, Wigan, Lancashire. WN6 9AB tel:(01257) 256097. sales@ikogroup.co.uk, www.ikogroup.co.uk

Iles Waste Systems - Valley Mills, Valley Road, Bradford, W. Yorks. BD1 4RU tel:(01274) 728837, fax:(01274) 734351. wastesystems@trevoriles.co.uk, www.ileswastesystems.co.uk

Illbruck Sealant Systems UK Ltd - Bentall Business Park, Glover, District 11, Washington, Tyne & Wear. NE37 3JD tel:(0191) 4190505, fax:(0191) 4192200. uk.info@tremco-illbruck.com, www.illbruck.com

Illuma Lighting - Sills Road, Willow Farm Business Park, Castle Donington, Derbyshire. DE74 2US tel:(01332) 818200, fax:(01332) 818222. info@illuma.co.uk, www.illuma.co.uk

Imerys Minerals Ltd - Westwood, Beverley, N. Humberside. HU17 8RQ tel:(01482) 881234, fax:(01482) 872301. perfmins@imerys.com, www.imerys.com

Imperial Machine Co Ltd - Harvey Road, Croxley Green, Herts. WD3 3AX tel:(01923) 718000, fax:(01923) 777273. sales@imco.co.uk, www.imco.co.uk

IMS UK - Arley Road, Saltley, Birmingham. B8 1BB tel:(0121) 326 3100, fax:(0121) 326 3105. a.uk@abraservice.com, www.abraservice.com/uk

In Steel (Blacksmiths & Fabricators) Ltd - United Downs Industrial Park, St. Day, Redruth, Cornwall. TR16 5HY tel:(01209) 822233, fax:(01209) 822596. enquiries@spiralstairs.uk.com, www.spiralstairs.uk.com

Industrial Brushware Ltd - Ibex House, 76-77 Malt Mill Lane, Halesowen, West Midlands. B62 8JJ tel:(0121) 559 3862, fax:(0121) 559 9404. sales@industrialbrushware.co.uk, www.industrialbrushware.co.uk

Infraglo Limited - Dannemora Drive, Greenland Road Industrial Park, Sheffield, South Yorks. S9 5DF tel:(0114) 249 5445, fax:(0114) 249 5066. info@infraglo.com, www.infraglo.com

Ingersoll-Rand European Sales Ltd - PO Box 2, Chorley New Road, Horwich, Bolton. BL6 6JN tel:(01204) 690690, fax:(01204) 690388. hibon@eu.irco.com, www.ingersollrand.com

Initial Electronic Security Systems Ltd - Shadsworth Road, Blackburn. BB1 2PR tel:(01254) 688688, fax:(01254) 662571. citsales@chubb.co.uk, www.chubbsystems.co.uk

Insituform Technologies® Ltd - 24-27 Brunel Close, Park Farm Industrial Estate, Wellingborough, Northamptonshire. NN8 6QX tel:(01933) 678 266, fax:(01933) 678 637. uksales@insituform.com, www.insituform.co.uk

I (con't)

InstaGroup Ltd - Insta House, Ivanhoe Road, Hogwood Business Park, Finchampstead, Wokingham, Berks. RG40 4PZ tel:(0118) 932 8811, fax:(0118) 932 8314. info@instagroup.co.uk, www.instagroup.co.uk

Institute of Ashphalt Technology, the - PO Box 15690, Bathgate. EH48 9BT tel:(0131) 3333 953. info@instituteofasphalt.org, www.instituteofasphalt.org

Institute of Historic Building Conservation - Jubilee House, High Street, Tisbury, Wiltshire. SP3 6HA tel:(01747) 873133, fax:(01747) 871718. admin@ihbc.org.uk, www.ihbc.org.uk

Institute of Quarrying - 8a Regan Way, Chetwynd Business Park, Chilwell, Nottingham. NG9 6RZ tel:(0115) 972 9995. mail@quarrying.org, www.quarrying.org

Institute of Specialist Surveyors and Engineers - Amity House, 156 Ecclesfield Road, Chapeltown, Shefield. S35 1TE tel:(0800) 915 6363. enquiries@isse.org.uk, www.isse.co.uk

Institution of Civil Engineers - One Great George Street, London. SW1P 3AA tel:(020) 7222 7722, fax:(020) 7222 7500. communications@ice.org.uk, www.ice.org.uk

Institution of Engineering and Technology - Savoy Place, London. WC2R OBL tel:(020) 7240 1871, fax:(020) 7240 7735. postmaster@theiet.org, www.theiet.org

Institution of Mechanical Engineers - 1 Birdcage Walk, Westminster, London. SW1H 9JJ tel:(020) 7222 7899, fax:(020) 7222 4557. enquiries@imeche.org.uk, www.imeche.org.uk

Institution of Structural Engineers - 47-58 Bastwick Street, London. EC1V 3PS tel:(020) 7235 4535, fax:(020) 7235 4294. pr@istructe.org, www.istructe.org

Insulated Render & Cladding Association - PO Box 12, Haslemere, Surrey. GU27 3AH tel:(01428) 654011, fax:(01428) 651401. info@inca-ltd.org.uk, www.inca-ltd.org.uk

Insulated Render & Cladding Assocation (INCA) - PO Box 12, Haslemere, Surrey. GU27 3AH tel:(01428) 654011, fax:(01428) 651401. info@inca-ltd.org.uk, www.inca-ltd.org.uk

Interclad (UK) Ltd - 173 Main Road, Biggin Hill, Kent. TN16 3JR tel:(01959) 572447, fax:(01959) 576974. sales@interclad.co.uk, www.interclad.co.uk

Interface Europe Ltd - Shelf Mills, Shelf, Halifax, W. Yorks. HX3 7PA tel:(01274) 690690, fax:(01274) 694095. enquiries@eu.interfaceinc.com, www.interfaceeurope.com

Interfloor Limited - Edinburgh Road, Heathhall, Dumfries. DG1 1QA tel:(01387) 253111, fax:(01387) 255726. sales@interfloor.com, www.interfloor.com

Interframe Ltd - Aspen Way, Yalberton Industrial Estate, Paignton, Devon. TQ4 7QR tel:(01803) 666633, fax:(01803) 663030. mail.interframe@btconnect.com, www.interframe.co.uk

Intergrated Polymer Systems (UK) Ltd - Allen House, Harmby Road, Leyburn, N. Yorks. DL8 5QA tel:(01969) 625000, fax:(01969) 623000. info@ipsroofing.co.uk, www.ipsroofing.co.uk

Internal Partitions Systems - Interplan House, Dunmow Industrial Estate, Chelmsford Road, Great Dunmow, Essex. CM6 1HD tel:(01371) 874241, fax:(01371) 873848. contact@ips-interiors.co.uk, www.ips-interiors.co.uk

International Protective Coatings - Stoneygate Lane, Felling on Tyne, Tyne & Wear. NE10 0JY tel:(0191) 469 6111, fax:(0191) 495 0676. protectivecoatings@akzonobel.com, www.international-pc.com

Interpave - The Old Rectory, Main Street, Glenfield, Leicestershire. LE3 8DG tel:(01162) 325170, fax:(01162) 325197. info@paving.org.uk, www.paving.org.uk

Interphone Limited - Interphone House, 12-22 Herga Road, Wealdstone, Middx. HA3 5AS tel:(020) 8621 6000, fax:(020) 8621 6100. sales@interphone.co.uk, www.interphone.co.uk

Intersolar Group Ltd - Magdalen Center, The Oxford Science Park, Oxford, Oxon. OX4 4GA tel:(01865) 784670, fax:(01865) 784681. intersolar@intersolar.com, www.intersolar.com

Intime Fire and Security - Nimax House, 20 Ullswater Crescent, Coulsdon, Surrey. CR5 2HR tel:(020) 8763 8800, fax:(020) 8763 9996. lee.james@intimefireandsecurity.co.uk, www.intimefireandsecurity.co.uk

Intrad Architectural Systems - PJP plc, St. Albans Road West, Hatfield, Herts. AL10 0TF tel:(0170) 7266 726, fax:(01707) 263614. sales@intrad.com, http://www.intrad.com/

Invicita Plastics Ltd - Harborough Road, Oadby, Leics. LE2 4LB tel:(0116) 272 0555, fax:(0116) 272 0626. sales@invictagroup.co.uk, www.invictagroup.co.uk

Invicta Window Films Ltd - Unit 25, Salbrook Road Industrial Estate, Salfords, Redhill, Surrey. RH1 5GJ tel:(01293) 786079, fax:(01293) 784 061. invictafilms@btconnect.com, www.invicawindowfilms.com

IPF Omnipex - Upshire House, Hungerford Hill, Lambourn, Berkshire. RG17 7LE tel:(01488) 71614. info@plants4business.com, www.plants4business.com

IPPEC Systems Ltd - 21 Buntsford Drive, Buntsford Gate Business Park, Worcestershire. B60 3AJ tel:(01527) 579705, fax:(01527) 574109. info@ippec.co.uk, www.ippec.co.uk

Irish Shell Ld - Embassy House, Herbert Park Lane, Ballsbridge, Dublin, Ireland. DO4 H6YO tel:+353 9 727100, fax:+353 1 767489. shell@shs-sales.ie, www.shell.com/

ISGUS UK Limited - 5 Stirling Road, South Marston Industrial Estate, Swindon, Wiltshire. SN3 4YH tel:(01793) 766211. sales@uk.isgus.com, www.isgus-uk.com

Isocrete Floor Screeds Ltd - Flowcrete Business Park, Booth Lane, Moston, Sandbach, Cheshire. CW11 3QF tel:(01270) 753753, fax:(01270) 753333. ukweb@flowcrete.com, www.flowcrete.co.uk

Isolated Systems Ltd - Adams Close, Heanor Gate Industrial Estate, Heanor, Derbys. DE75 7SW tel:(01773) 761226, fax:(01773) 760408. sales@isolatedsystems.com, www.isolatedsystems.com

ITAB Prolight UK Limited - 4, 5 & 6 Raynham Road, Bishop's Stortford, Herts. CM23 5PB tel:(01279) 757595, fax:(01279) 755599. enquiries@itabprolight.co.uk, www.itabprolight.co.uk

ITM Communications LtdLtd - 41 Alston Drive, Bradwell Abbey, Milton Keynes. MK13 9HA tel:(01908) 318844, fax:(01908) 318833. enquiries@itm.uk.com, www.itm.uk.com

ITT Flygt Ltd - Colwick, Nottingham. NG4 2AN tel:(0115) 940 0111, fax:(0115) 940 0444. flygtgb@flygt.com, www.flygt.com

ITW Construction Products - Fleming Way, Crawley, W.Sussex. RH10 9DP tel:(01293) 523372, fax:(01293) 515186. generalenquiry@itwcp.co.uk, www.itwcp.co.uk

ITW Consutruction Products - 3rd Floor, Westmead House, Farnborough, Hampshire. GU14 7LP tel:(01252) 551960, fax:(01252) 543436. gangnail@itw-industry.com, www.itw-industry.com

ITW Spit - Fleming Way, Crawley, W. Sussex. RH10 2QR tel:(01293) 523372, fax:(01293) 515186. gmason@itwcp.co.uk, www.itwcp.co.uk

J

J & E Hall Ltd - Questor House, Hawley Road, Dartford, Kent. DA1 1PU tel:(01322) 394 420, fax:(01322) 394 421. helpline@jehall.co.uk, www.jehall.co.uk

J & M Fencing Services - Unit Q, Wrexham Road, Laindon, Basildon, Essex. SS15 6PX tel:(01268) 415233, fax:(01268) 417357. m.cottage@btconnect.com, www.jandmfencingservices.co.uk

J C Bamford (Excavators) Ltd - Rocester, Staffs. ST14 5JP tel:(01889) 590312, fax:(01889) 590588. enquiries@jcb.co.uk, www.jcb.com

J Pugh-Lewis Limited - The Old Sawmills, Moreton Road, Pilsley, Chesterfield. S45 8EE tel:(01773) 872362, fax:(01773) 874763. info@pugh-lewis.co.uk, www.pugh-lewis.co.uk

J Suttle Swanage Quarries Ltd - California Quarry, Panorama Road, Swanage, Dorset. BH19 2QS tel:(01929) 423576, fax:(01929) 427656. nick.crocker@btconnect.com; cjs@stone.uk.com, www.stone.uk.com

J W Gray Lightning Protection Ltd - Unit 1, Swanbridge Industrial Park, Black Croft Road, Witham, Essex. CM8 3YN tel:(01376) 503330, fax:(01376) 503337. enquiries@jwgray.com, www.jwgray.com

J W Green Swimming Pools Ltd - The Coach House Office, 11 Regis Road, Tettenhall, Wolverhampton, West Midlands. WV6 8RU tel:(01902) 757 757. info@jwgswimming.co.uk, www.jwgswimming.co.uk

J. B. Corrie & Co Limited - Frenchmans Road, Petersfield, Hants. GU32 3AP tel:(01730) 237100, fax:(01730) 264915. sales@jbcorrie.co.uk, www.jbcorrie.co.uk

J.F. Poynter Ltd - Maxim Lamps, Unit E Consort Way, Victoria Industrial Estate, Burgess Hill. RH15 9TJ tel:(01444) 239223, fax:(01444) 245366. sales@maximlamps.co.uk, www.maxinlamps.co.uk

Jablite Ltd - Infinity House, Anderson Way, Belvedere, Kent. DA17 6BG tel:(020) 83209100, fax:(020) 83209110. sales@jablite.co.uk, www.jablite.co.uk

Jack Brunsdon & Son - The Old Mill, Blenheim Palace Sawmills, Swan Lane, Combe, Oxon. OX29 8ET tel:(01993) 885080. enquiries@jackbrunsdon.co.uk, www.jackbrunsdon.com

Jack Moody Ltd - Hollybush Farm, Warstone Road, Shareshill, Wolverhampton, West Midlands. WV10 7LX tel:(01922) 417648, fax:(01922) 413420. sales@jackmoodylimited.co.uk, www.jackmoodyltd.co.uk

Jackson H S & Son (Fencing) Ltd - Stowting Common, Ashford, Kent. TN25 6BN tel:(01233) 750393, fax:(01233) 750403. sales@jacksons-fencing.co.uk, www.jacksons-fencing.co.uk

Jacopa Limited - Cornwallis Road, Millard Industrial Estate, West Bromwich, West Midlands. B70 7JF tel:(0121) 511 2400, fax:(0121) 511 2401. info@jacopa.com, www.jacopa.com

Jacuzzi® Spa and Bath Ltd - Old Mill Lane, Low Road, Hunslet, Leeds. LS10 1RB tel:(0113) 2727430, fax:(0113) 2727445. retailersales@jacuzziemea.com, www.jacuzziuk.co.uk

Jaga UK - Jaga House, Orchard Business Park, Bromyard Road, Ledbury, Herefordshire. HR8 1LG tel:(01531) 631533, fax:(01531) 631534. jaga@jaga.co.uk, www.jaga.co.uk

Jali Ltd - Albion Works, Church Lane, Barham, Canterbury, Kent. CT4 6QS tel:(01227) 833333, fax:(01227) 831950. sales@jali.co.uk, www.jali.co.uk

JAMAK Fabrication Europe - 52 & 53 Oakhill Industrial Estate, Devonshire Rd, Worsley, Manchester. M28 3PT tel:(01204) 794554, fax:(01204) 574521. sales@jamak.co.uk, www.jamak.co.uk

James Donaldson Timber - Elm Park Sawmills, Leven, Fife. KY8 4PS tel:(01333) 422 222, fax:(01333) 429 469. elmpark@donaldson-timber.co.uk, www.don-timber.co.uk

James Gibbons Format Ltd - Neachells Lane, Wednesfield, Wolverhampton, W. Midlands. WV11 3PU tel:(01902) 303230, fax:(01902) 303239. enquiries@jgf.co.uk, www.jgf.co.uk

James Latham plc - Unit 2, Swallow Park, Finley Road, Hemel Hampstead, Herts. HP2 7QU tel:(020) 8806 3333, fax:(020) 8806 7249. marketing@lathams.co.uk, www.lathamtimber.co.uk

James Lever 1856 Ltd - Unit 26 Morris Green Business Park, Prescott Street, Bolton, Lancs. BL3 3PE tel:(01204) 61121, fax:(01204) 658154. sales@jameslever.co.uk, www.jameslever.co.uk

James Walker & Co Ltd - 1 Millennium Gate, Westmere Drive, Crewe, Cheshire. CW1 6AY tel:+44 0 1270 536000, fax:+44 0 1270 536100. csc@jameswalker.biz, www.jameswalker.biz

Jaymart Rubber & Plastics Ltd - Roman Way, Crusader Park, Warminster. BA12 8SP tel:(01985) 218994, fax:(01985) 217417. matting@jaymart.co.uk, www.jaymart.net

JB Architectural Ltd - Unit C, Rich Industrial Estate, Avis Way, Newhaven, East Sussex. BN9 0DU tel:(01273) 514961, fax:(01273) 516764. sales@jbai.co.uk, https://www.jbai.co.uk/

JB Kind Ltd - Portal Place, Astron Business Park, Hearthcote Road, Swadlincote, Derbyshire. DE11 9DW tel:(01283) 554197, fax:(01283) 554182. info@jbkind.com, www.jbkind.com

Jeld-Wen UK Ltd - Retford Road, Woodhouse Mill, Sheffield, S. Yorks. S13 9WH tel:(0845) 122 2890, fax:(01302) 787383. marketing@jeld-wen.co.uk, www.jeld-wen.co.uk

Jewers Doors Ltd - Stratton Business Park, Normandy Lane, Biggleswade, Beds. SG18 8QB tel:(01767) 317090, fax:(01767) 312305. postroom@jewersdoors.co.uk, www.jewersdoors.co.uk

Jewson Ltd - High Street, Brasted, Westerham, Kent. TN16 1NG tel:(01959) 563856, fax:(01959) 564666. customer.feedback@jewson.co.uk, www.jewson.co.uk

John Davidson (Pipes) Ltd - Townfoot Industrial Estate, Longtown, Carlisle, Cumbria. CA6 5LY tel:(01228) 791503, fax:(01228) 792051. headoffice@jdpipes.co.uk, www.jdpipes.co.uk

John Pulsford Associates Ltd - Sphere Industrial Estate, Campfield Road, St. Albans, Herts. AL1 5HT tel:(01727) 840800, fax:(01727) 840083. info@jpa-furniture.com, www.jpa-furniture.com

John Watson & Carter

Suite 2, Studio 700, Princess Street, Hull. HU2 8BJ tel:(01482) 492191, fax:(03332) 407363. hull@johnwatsonandcarter.co.uk, www.vbjohnson.co.uk

Johnson & Starley - Rhosili Road, Brackmills, Northampton, Northants. NN4 7LZ tel:(01604) 762881, fax:(01604) 767408. marketing@johnsonandstarley.co.uk, www.johnsonandstarley.co.uk

Johnson & Starley Ltd - Dravo Division, Rhosili Road, Brackmills, Northampton. NN4 7LZ tel:(01604) 707022, fax:(01604) 706467. Dravo@johnsonandstarley.co.uk, www.dravo.co.uk

Johnson Controls Building Efficiency UK Ltd - 9-10 The Briars, Waterberry Drive, Waterlooville, Hampshire. PO7 7YH tel:(0845) 108 0001, fax:(01236) 738937. serviceinfo.uki@jci.com, www.johnsoncontrols.com

Johnson Matthey PLC - Metal Joining - York Way, Royston, Herts. SG8 5HJ tel:(01763) 253200, fax:(01763) 253168. mj@matthey.com, www.jm-metaljoining.com

Johnson Tiles - Harewood Street, Tunstall, Stoke-on-Trent. ST6 5JZ tel:(01782) 575575, fax:(01782) 524138. sales@johnson-tiles.com, www.johnson-tiles.com

Johnson VB LLP

St John's House, 304-310 St Albans Road, Watford, Herts. WD24 6PW tel:(01923) 227236, fax:(03332) 407363. watford@vbjohnson.co.uk, www.vbjohnson.co.uk

Johnson Wax Professional - Frimley Green, Camberley, Surrey. GU16 7AJ tel:(01276) 852852, fax:(01276) 852800. ask.uk@scj.com, www.scjohnson.co.uk

Johnsons Wellfield Quarries Ltd - Crosland Hill, Huddersfield, W. Yorkshire. HD4 7AB tel:(01484) 652 311, fax:(01484) 460007. sales@johnsons-wellfield.co.uk, www.myersgroup.co.uk/jwq/

Joint Council For The Building & Civil Engineering Industry (N. Ireland) - 143 Marlone Road, Belfast. BT9 6SU tel:(028) 90 877143, fax:(028) 90 877155. mail@cefni.co.uk, www.cefni.co.uk

Joint Industry Board for the Electrical Contracting Industry - Kingswood House, 47/51 Sidcup Hill, Sidcup, Kent. DA14 6HP tel:(020) 8302 0031, fax:(020) 8309 1103. administration@jib.org.uk, www.jib.org.uk

Jolec Electrical Supplies - Unit 2, The Empire Centre, Imperial Way, Watford, Herts. WD24 4YH tel:(01923) 375 178. sales@jolec.co.uk, www.jolecelectricalsupplies.co.uk

Jones of Oswestry Ltd - Haselfield 18, Telford, Shropshire. TF7 4JS tel:(01691) 653251, fax:(01691) 658222. sales@jonesofoswestry.com, www.jonesofoswestry.co.uk

Joseph Ash Ltd - The Alcora Building 2, Mucklow Hill, Halesowen. B62 8DG tel:(0121) 5042560. sales@josephash.co.uk, www.josephash.co.uk

Jotun Henry Clark Ltd Decorative Division - Stather Road, Flixborough, Lincs. DN15 8RR tel:(01724) 400123, fax:(01724) 400100. deco.uk@jotun.co.uk, www.jotun.com

Junckers Limited - Unit A, 1 Wheaton Road, Witham, Essex. CM8 3UJ tel:(01376) 534700, fax:(01376) 514401. brochures@junckers.co.uk, www.junckers.co.uk

K

K. V. Radiators - 6 Postle Close, Kilsby, Rugby, Warwickshire. CV23 8YG tel:(01788) 823286, fax:(01788) 823002. solutions@kvradiators.com, www.kvradiators.com

KAB Seating Ltd - Round Spinney, Northampton. NN3 8RS tel:(01604) 790500, fax:(01604) 790155. infouk@cvgrp.com, www.kabseating.com

Kaba Ltd - Lower Moor Way, Tiverton Business Park, Tiverton, Devon. EX16 6SS tel:(0870) 000 5625, fax:(0870) 000 5397. info@kaba.co.uk, www.kaba.co.uk

KAC Alarm Company Ltd - KAC House, Thornhill Road, North Moons Moat, Redditch, Worcs. B98 9ND tel:(01527) 406655, fax:(01527) 406677. marketing@kac.co.uk, www.kac.co.uk

Kair Ventilation Ltd - 9a Sidcup High Street, Sidcup, Kent. DA14 6EN tel:(08451) 662240, fax:(08451) 662250. info@kair.co.uk, www.kair.co.uk

Kaldewei - Kings Hall, St Ives Business Park, Parsons Green, St Ives, Cambridgeshire. PE27 4WY tel:(01480) 498053, fax:(01480) 493046. sales-uk@kaldewei.com, www.kaldewei.com

Kalon Decorative Products - Huddersfield Road, Birstall, Batley, W. Yorks. WF17 9XA tel:(01924) 354000, fax:(01924) 354001. paint247.acuk@ppg.com, www.kalon.co.uk

Kaloric Heater Co Ltd - 31-33 Beethoven Street, London. W10 4LJ tel:(020) 8969 1367, fax:(020) 8968 8913. admin@kaloricheater.co.uk, www.kaloricheaters.co.uk

Kawneer UK Ltd - Astmoor Road, Astmoor Industrial Estate, Runcorn, Cheshire. WA7 1QQ tel:(01928) 502500, fax:(01928) 502501. kuk.kawneer@alcoa.com, www.kawneer.co.uk

Kaye Aluminium plc - Shaw Lane Industrial Estate, Ogden Road, Wheatley Hills, Doncaster, S. Yorks. DN2 4SG tel:(01302) 762500, fax:(01302) 360307. design@kayealu.co.uk, www.kayealuminium.co.uk

KCW Comercial Windows Ltd - 25A Shuttleworth Road, Goldington, Bedford, Beds. MK41 0HS tel:(01234) 269911, fax:(01234) 325034. sales@kcwwindows.com, www.kcwwindows.com

Kee Klamp Ltd - Unit A2 Cradley Business Park, Overend Road, Cradley Heath, West Midlands. B64 7DW tel:(01384) 632188, fax:(01384) 632192. sales@keesafety.co.uk, www.keesafety.co.uk

Keim Mineral Paints Ltd - Santok Building, Deer Park Way, Telford. TF2 7NA tel:(01952) 231250, fax:(01952) 231251. sales@keimpaints.co.uk, www.keimpaints.co.uk

Keller Ground Engineering - Oxford Road, Ryton-on-Dunsmore, Coventry. CV8 3EG tel:(024) 76 511266, fax:(024) 76 305230. foundations@keller.co.uk, www.keller-uk.com

Kem Edwards Ltd - Longwood Business Park, Fordbridge Road, Sunbury-on-Thames, Middx. TW16 6AZ tel:(01932) 754700, fax:(01932) 754754. sales@kemedwards.co.uk, www.kemedwards.co.uk

Kemper System Ltd - Kemper House, 30 Kingsland Grange, Woolston, Warrington, Cheshire. WA1 4RW tel:(01925) 445532, fax:(01925) 575096. enquiries@kempersystem.co.uk, www.kempersystem.co.uk

Kensal CMS - Kensal House, President Way, Luton, Beds. LU2 9NR tel:(01582) 425777, fax:(01582) 425776. sales@kensal.co.uk, www.kensal.co.uk

Kenyon Group Ltd - Regent House, Regent Street, Oldham, Lancs. OL1 3TZ tel:(0161) 633 6328, fax:(0161) 627 5072. sales@kenyon-group.co.uk, www.kenyon-group.co.uk

Kenyon Paints Limited - Regent Street, Oldham. OL1 3TZ tel:(0161) 624 4942. sales@kenyonpaints.co.uk, www.kenyonpaints.co.uk

K (con't)

Kenyon Performance Adhesives - Regent House, Regent Street, Oldham, Lancs. OL1 3TZ tel:(0161) 633 6328, fax:(0161) 627 5072. sales@kenyon-group.co.uk, www.4adhesives.com

Kermi (UK) Ltd - 7, Brunel Road, Earlstrees Industrial Estate, Corby, Northants. NN17 4JW tel:(01536) 400004, fax:(01536) 446614. info@kermi.co.uk, www.kermi.co.uk

Kerridge Stone Ltd - Endon Quarry, Windmill Lane, Kerridge, Cheshire. SK10 5AZ tel:(01625) 575722. www.kerridgestone.co.uk

Kershaw Mechanical Services Ltd - Edward Leonard House, Pembroke Ave, Denny End Rd, Waterbeach, Cambridge. CB25 9QR tel:(01223) 715800, fax:(01223) 411061. sales@kershaw-grp.co.uk, www.kershawmechanical.co.uk/

Ketley Brick Co Ltd , The - Dreadnought Road, Pensnett, Brierley Hill, W. Midlands. DY5 4TH tel:(01384) 77405, fax:(01384) 74553. sales@ketley-brick.co.uk, www.ketley-brick.co.uk

Keyline Civils Specialist Ltd - 50 Mauchline Street, Glasgow. G5 8HQ tel:(0844) 892 2548. customerservice@keyline.co.uk, www.keyline.co.uk

Kidde Fire Protection Ltd - Belvue Road, Northolt, Middx. UB5 5QW tel:(020) 8839 0700, fax:(020) 8845 4304. general.enquiries@kiddeuk.co.uk, www.kfp.co.uk

Kidde Fire Protection Services Ltd - 400 Dallows Road, Luton, Beds. LU1 1UR tel:(01582) 413694, fax:(01582) 402339. general.enquiries@kiddeuk.co.uk, www.kfp.co.uk

Kier Limited - Tempsford Hall, Sandy, Bedfordshire. SG19 2BD tel:(01767) 355000, fax:(01767) 355633. info@kier.co.uk, www.kier.co.uk

Kilwaughter Chemical Co Ltd - Kilwaughter Chemical Co Ltd, 9 Starbog Road, Larne, Co. Antrim. BT40 2JT tel:(028) 2826 0766, fax:(028) 2826 0136. sales@K-Rend.co.uk, www.K-Rend.co.uk

Kimberly-Clark Ltd - 1 Tower View, Kings Hill, West Malling, Kent. ME19 4HA tel:(01732) 594 000, fax:(01732) 594 001. consumeruk@kcc.com, www.kcprofessional.co.uk

Kinder-Janes Engineering Ltd - Porters Wood, St. Albans, Hertfordshire. AL3 6HU tel:(01727) 844441, fax:(01727) 844247. info@kinder-janes.co.uk, www.kinder-janes.co.uk

Kinetico Water Softeners - 11 The Maltings, Thorney, Peterborough, Cambs. PE6 0QF tel:(01733) 270463. enquiries@harvey.co.uk, www.kineticoltd.co.uk

Kingfisher Building Products Ltd - Cooper Lane, Bardsea, Ulverston, Cumbria. LA12 9RA tel:(01229) 869100, fax:(01229) 869101. sales@kingfisheruk.com, www.kingfisheruk.com

Kingscourt Country Manor Bricks - Unit 26, Airways Industrial Estate, Santry, Dublin 17. Ireland tel:+353 1836 6901, fax:+353 1855 4743. sales@cmb.ie, www.cmb.ie

Kingsforth Security Fencing Limited - Mangham Way, Barbot Hall Industrial Estate, Rotherham, S. Yorks. S61 4RL tel:(01709) 378 977, fax:(01709) 838992. info@kingsforthfencing.co.uk, www.securityfencingyorkshire.co.uk/

Kingspan Ltd - Greenfield Business Park 2, Greenfield, Holywell, Flintshire. CH8 7GJ tel:(01352) 716100, fax:(01352) 710616. info@kingspanpanels.com, www.kingspanpanels.com

Kingspan Access Floors Ltd - Burma Drive, Marfleet, Hull. HU9 5SG tel:(01482) 781701, fax:(01482) 799276. info@kingspanaccessfloors.co.uk, www.kingspanaccessfloors.co.uk

Kingspan Environmental - College Road North, Aston Clinton, Aylesbury, Buckinghamshire. HP22 5EW tel:(01296) 633000, fax:(01296) 633001. online@kingspan.com, www.kingspanenviro.com

Kingspan Environmental - College Road North, Aston Clinton, Aylesbury, Bucks. HP22 5EW tel:(01296) 633000, fax:(01296) 633001. online@kingspan.com, www.kingspanenviro.com

Kingspan Environmental Ltd - 180 Gilford Road, Portadown, Co Armagh, Northern Ireland. BT63 5LF tel:02838364400, fax:02838364445. enquiry@kingspanenv.com, www.kingspanenv.com

Kingspan Industrial Ins. Ltd - PO Box 3, Charlestown, Glossop, Derbys. SK13 8LE tel:(01457) 861611, fax:(01457) 852319. info@kingspaninsulation.co.uk, www.kingspan.kooltherm.co.uk

Kingspan Insulation Ltd - Pembridge, Leominster, Herefordshire. HR6 9LA tel:(0870) 8508555, fax:(0870) 8508666. info@kingspaninsulation.co.uk, www.insulation.kingspan.com

Kingston Craftsmen Structural Timber Engineers Ltd - Cannon Street, Hull, East Yorkshire. HU2 0AD tel:(01482) 225171, fax:(01482) 217032. sales@kingston-craftsmen.co.uk, www.kingston-craftsmen.co.uk

Kingstonian Paint Ltd - Mayfield House, Sculcoates Lane, Hull, E. Yorks. HU5 1DR tel:(01482) 342216, fax:(01482) 493096. info@kpaints.co.uk, www.kpaints.co.uk

Kirkpatrick Ltd - Frederick Street, Walsall, Staffs. WS2 9NF tel:(01922) 620026, fax:(01922) 722525. enquiries@kirkpatrick.co.uk, www.kirkpatrick.co.uk

Kirkstone - Skelwith Bridge, Ambleside, Cumbria. LA22 9NN tel:(01539) 433296, fax:(01539) 434006. sales@kirkstone.com, www.kirkstone.com

Kitsons Insulation Products Ltd - Kitsons House, Centurion Way, Meridian Business Park, Leicester, Leics. LE3 2WH tel:(0116) 201 4499, fax:(0116) 201 4498. leicester@kitsonsthermal.co.uk, www.kitsonsthermal.co.uk

Kleeneze Sealtech Ltd - Ansteys Road, Hanham, Bristol, Avon. BS15 3SS tel:(0117) 958 2450, fax:(0117) 960 0141. sales@ksl.uk.com, www.ksltd.com

Kleen-Tex Industries Ltd - Emlyn Street, Bolton, Lancashire. BL4 7EB tel:(01204) 70 50 70, fax:(01204) 861 016. info@kleen-tex.co.uk, www.kleentexuk.co.UK

Klick Technology Ltd - Claverton Road, Wythenshawe, Manchester. M23 9FT tel:(0161) 998 9726, fax:(0161) 946 0419. webcontact@klicktechnology.co.uk, www.klicktechnology.co.uk

Klober Ltd - Ingleberry Road, Shepshed, Loughborough. LE12 9DE tel:(0800) 7833216, fax:(011509) 505535. support@klober.co.uk, www.klober.co.uk

Knauf AMF Ceilings Ltd - Thames House, 6 Church Street, Twickenham, Middlesex. TW1 3NJ tel:(020) 8892 3216, fax:(020) 8892 6866. sales@amfceilings.co.uk, www.amfceilings.co.uk

Knauf Drywall - PO Box 133, Sittingbourne, Kent. ME10 3HW tel:(01795) 424499, fax:(01795) 428651. info@knauf.co.uk, www.knaufdrywall.co.uk

Knauf Insulation Ltd - Hunter House Industrial Estate, Brenda Road, Hartlepool, Cleveland. TS25 2BE tel:(01429) 855100, fax:(01429) 855138. sales@knaufinsulation.com, www.knaufinsulation.co.uk

Knauf Insulation Ltd - PO Box 10, Stafford Road, St. Helens, Merseyside. WA10 3NS tel:(01270) 824024, fax:(01270) 824025. sales.uk@knaufinsulation.com, www.knaufinsulation.co.uk

Knauf UK - Kemsley Fields Business Park, Sittingbourne, Kent. ME9 8SR tel:(01795) 424499. cservice@knauf.co.uk, www.knauf.co.uk

Knightbridge Furniture Productions Ltd - 191 Thornton Road, Bradford, W. Yorks. BD1 2JT tel:(01274) 731442, fax:(01274) 736641. enquiries@knightsbridge-furniture.co.uk, www.knightsbridge-furniture.co.uk

Knowles W T & Sons Ltd - Ash Grove Sanitary Works, Elland, W. Yorks. HX5 9JA tel:(01422) 372833, fax:(01422) 370900. sales@wtknowles.co.uk, www.wtknowles.co.uk

Kobi Ltd - Unit 19 Seax Court, Southfields Industrail Estate, Laindon, Essex. SS15 6SL tel:(01268) 416335, fax:(01268) 542148. cradles@kobi.co.uk, www.kobi.co.uk

Kohler Mira Ltd - Cromwell Road, Cheltenham, Glos. GL52 5EP tel:+0014040, fax:(01242) 221925. askus@mirashowers.com, www.mirashowers.com

Kohler UK - Cromwell Road, Cheltenahm, Gloucestershire. GL52 5EP tel:(0844) 571 0048, fax:(0844) 571 1001. info@kohler.co.uk, www.kohler.co.uk

Komfort Workspace PLC - Unit 1-10, Whittle Way, Crawley, W. Sussex. RH10 9RT tel:(01293) 592500, fax:(01293) 553271. general@komfort.com, www.komfort.com

Kommerling UK Ltd - Unit 27, Riverside Way, Uxbridge, Middx. UB8 2YF tel:(01895) 465600, fax:(01895) 465617. enquiries@profine-group.com

Kompan Ltd - 20 Denbigh Hall, Bletchley, Milton Keynes, Bucks. MK3 7QT tel:(01908) 642466, fax:(01908) 270137. KOMPAN.uk@KOMPAN.com, www.kompan.com

Kone - Global House Station Place, Fox Lane North, Chertsey, Surrey. KT16 9HW tel:(08451) 999 999. sales.marketinguk@kone.com, www.kone.co.uk

Kone Escalators Ltd - Worth Bridge Road, Keighley, W. Yorks. BD21 4YA tel:(01535) 662841, fax:(01535) 680498. sales.marketinguk@kone.com, www.kone.com

Kone PLC - Global House, Station Place, Fox Lane North, Chertsey, Surrey. KT16 9HW tel:(0845) 1 999 999, fax:(0870) 774 8347. sales.marketinguk@kone.com, www.kone.co.uk

Konecranes UK - Unit 1 Charter Point Way, Coalfield Way, Ashby Business Park, Ashby De La Zouch, Leics. LE65 1NF tel:(08443) 246599. ukparts.sales@konecranes.com, www.konecranes.co.uk

Köttermann Ltd - Unit 8, The Courtyard, Furlong Road, Bourne End, Bucks. SL8 5AU tel:(01628) 532211, fax:(01628) 532233. systemlabor.uk@koettermann.com, www.kottermann.com

Kronospan Ltd - Chirk, Wrexham. LL14 5NT tel:(01691) 773361, fax:(01691) 773292. sales@kronospan.co.uk, www.kronospan.co.uk

KSB Ltd - 2 Cotton Way, Loughborough, Leics. LE11 5TF tel:(01509) 231872, fax:(01509) 215228. sales@kgnpillinger.com, www.ksbuk.com

Kush UK Ltd - 48/50 St Johns Street, London. EC1M 4DG tel:(01684) 850787, fax:(01684) 850758. info-uk@kusch.com, www.kusch.de

L

Lab Systems Furniture Ltd - Rotary House, Bontoft Avenue, Hull, Yorks. HU5 4HF tel:(01482) 444650, fax:(01482) 444730. office@lab-systems.co.uk, www.labsystemsfurniture.co.uk

Lafarge Aluminates Ltd - 730 London Road, Grays, Essex. RM20 3NJ tel:(01708) 863333, fax:(01708) 861033. www.lafarge.com

LaFarge Cement UK - Manor Court, Chiltern, Oxon. OX11 0RN tel:(0870) 6000203. info@lafargecement.co.uk, www.lafargecement.co.uk

Laidlaw Ltd - 344 – 354 Grays Inn Road, London. WC1E 7BT tel:(020) 7436 0779, fax:(020) 7436 0740. info.london@laidlaw.net, www.laidlaw.net

Laird Security Hardware - Western Road, Silver End, Witham, Essex. CM8 3QB tel:(0121) 224 6000, fax:(0121) 520 1039. sales@lairdsecurity.co.uk, www.lairdsecurity.co.uk

Lakes Bathrooms Limited - Alexandra Way, Ashchurch, Tewkesbury, Gloucestershire. GL20 8NB tel:(01242) 620061, fax:(01684) 850912. info@lakesbathrooms.co.uk, www.lakesbathrooms.co.uk

Lakeside Group - Bruce Grove, Forest Fach Industrial Estate, Swansea, Swansea. SA5 4HS tel:(01792) 561117, fax:(01792) 587046. sales@lakesidesecurity.co.uk, www.lakesidesercurity.co.uk

Lami Doors UK Ltd - Station House, Stamford New Road, Altrincham, Cheshire. WA14 1EP tel:(0161) 9242217, fax:(0161) 9242218. lamidoors@lamidoors.com, www.lamidoors.com

Lampost Construction Co Ltd - Greenore, Co. Louth. Ireland tel:+353 42 93 73554, fax:+353 42 93 73378. lampost@iol.ie

Lancashire Fittings Ltd - The Science Village, Claro Road, Harrogate, N. Yorks. HG1 4AF tel:(01423) 522355, fax:(01423) 506111. kenidle@lancashirefittings.com, www.lancashirefittings.com

Landscape Institute - Charles Darwin House, 12 Roger Street, London. WC1N2JU tel:(020) 7685 2640. mail@landscapeinstitute.org, www.landscapeinstitute.org

Lane Roofing Contractors Ltd - Walsall House, 165-167 Walsall Road, Perry Barr, Birmingham. B42 1TX tel:(08450) 0667000, fax:(0121) 344 3782. info@laneroofing.co.uk, www.laneroofing.co.uk

Lang+Fulton - Unit 2b, Newbridge Industrial Estate, Edinburgh. EH28 8PJ tel:(0131) 441 1255, fax:(0131) 441 4161. sales@langandfulton.co.uk, www.langandfulton.co.uk

LANXESS Inorganic Pigments Group - Colour Works, Lichfield Road, Branston, Staffs. DE14 3WH tel:(01283) 714200, fax:(01283) 714210. simon.kentesber@lanxess.com, www.bayferrox.com

Lanxess Urethanes UK Ltd - Paragon Works, Baxenden, Accrington, Lancs. BB5 2SL tel:(01254) 302 412. orders.apac@chemtura.com, http://ure.lanxess.com

Lappset UK Ltd - Lappset House, Henson Way, Telford Industrial Estate, Kettering, Northants. NN16 8PX tel:(01536) 412612, fax:(01536) 521703. uk@lappset.com, www.lappset.co.uk

Latchways plc - Hopton Park, Devizes, Wilts. SN10 2JP tel:(01380) 732700, fax:(01380) 732701. info@latchways.com, www.latchways.com

Laticrete International Inc. UK - Hamilton House, Mabledon Place, London. WC1H 9BB tel:+44 0871 284 5959, fax:+44 0 208 886 2880. ukinfo@laticrete.com, www.laticrete.com

Laurier M & Sons - Unit 10, Triumph Trading Estate, Tariff Road, Tottenham, London. N17 0EB tel:(0208) 365 9000, fax:(020) 8365 9005. info@laurier.co.uk, www.laurier.co.uk

Lawton Tube Co Ltd, The - Torrington Avenue, Coventry. CV4 9AB tel:(024) 7646 6203, fax:(024) 7669 4183. sales@lawtontubes.co.uk, www.lawtontubes.co.uk

Laxton's Publishing Ltd

8 Ruslands Circus, Emerson Valley, Milton Keynes, Buckinghamshire. MK4 2LL tel:(01908) 859035, fax:(03332) 407363. info@laxton-s.co.uk, www.laxton-s.co.uk

Laybond Products Ltd - Riverside, Saltney, Chester. CH4 8RS tel:(01244) 674774, fax:(01244) 680215. technical.service@bostik.com, www.laybond.com

Laytrad Contract Furniture Ltd - Unit 3 Millennia Park, Wakefield, West Yorkshire. WF2 8PW tel:(01924) 377 300. info@laytrad.com, www.laytrad.com

Leaflike - Olympic House, Collett, Southmead Park, Didcot. OX11 7WB tel:(01235) 515050. info@leaflike.co.uk

Leander Architectural - Fletcher Foundry, Hallsteads Close, Dove Holes, Buxton, Derbys. SK17 8BP tel:(01298) 814941, fax:(01298) 814970. sales@leanderarchitectural.co.uk, www.leanderarchitectural.co.uk

Leatherhead Food Research Association - Randalls Road, Leatherhead, Surrey. KT22 7RY tel:(01372) 376761, fax:(01372) 386228. help@lfra.co.uk, www.leatherheadfood.com

Ledlite Glass (Southend) Ltd - 168 London Road, Southend on Sea, Essex. SS1 1PH tel:(01702) 345893, fax:(01702) 435099. ledliteglass@gmail.com, www.ledliteglass.co.uk

Legrand Electric Ltd - Dial Lane, West Bromwich, W. Midlands. B70 0EB tel:(0845) 6054333, fax:(0845) 605 4334. legrand.sales@legrand.co.uk, www.legrand.co.uk

Legrand Electric Ltd - Great King Street North, Birmingham. B19 2LF tel:(0121) 515 0515, fax:(0121) 515 0516. legrand.sales@legrand.co.uk, www.legrand.co.uk

Legrand Power Centre - Brookside, Wednesbury, W. Midlands. WS10 0QF tel:(0121) 506 4506, fax:(0121) 506 4507. legrand.sales@legrand.co.uk, www.legrand.co.uk

LEIA - 33 Devonshire Street, London. W1G 6PY tel:(020) 7935 3013, fax:(020) 7935 3321. enquiries@leia.co.uk, www.leia.co.uk

Leigh's Paints - Tower Works, Kestor Street, Bolton, Lancs. BL2 2AL tel:(01204) 521771, fax:(01204) 382115. enquiries@leighspaints.com, www.leighspaints.co.uk

Leofric Building Systems Ltd - Hillside House, Stratford Road, Mickleton, Glos. GL55 6SR tel:(01386) 430121, fax:(01386) 438135. sales@leofricbuildings.co.uk, www.leofricbuildings.co.uk

Lesco Products Ltd - Wincheap Industrial Estate, Canterbury, Kent. CT1 3RH tel:(01227) 763637, fax:(01227) 762239. sales@lesco.co.uk, www.lesco.co.uk

Levolux A.T. Limited - 24 Easville Close Eastern Avenue, Gloucester. GL4 3SJ tel:(01452) 500007, fax:(01452) 527496. info@levolux.co.uk, www.levolux.com

Lewden Electrical Industries - Argall Avenue, Leyton, London. E10 7QD tel:(020) 8539 0237, fax:(020) 8558 2718. sales@lewden.co.uk, www.lewden.net

Lewes Design Contracts Ltd - The Mill, Glynde, Lewes, Sussex. BN8 6SS tel:(01273) 858341, fax:(01273) 858200. info@spiralstairs.co.uk, www.spiralstairs.co.uk

Leyland Paint Company, The - Huddersfield Road, Birstall, Batley, W. Yorks. WF17 9XA tel:(01924) 354354, fax:(01924) 354001. leylandtrade.acuk@ppg.com, www.leyland-paints.co.uk

LHC - Royal House, 4th Floor, 2-4 Vine Street, Uxbridge, Middx. UB8 1QE tel:(01895) 274800. mail@lhc.gov.uk, www.lhc.gov.uk

Libraco - The Cowbarn, Filston Farm, Shoreham, Stevenoaks, Kent. TN14 5JU tel:(01959) 524074, fax:(01959) 525218. libraco@btconnect.com, www.libraco.uk.com

Library Furnishing Consultants - Grange House, Geddings Road, Hoddesdon, Hertfordshire. EN11 0NT tel:(01992) 454545, fax:(0800) 616629. enquiries@gresswell.co.uk, www.lfcdespatchline.co.uk

Lift and Escalator Industry Association,The - 33/34 devonshire Street, London. W1G 6PY tel:(020) 7935 3013, fax:(020) 7935 3321. enquiries@leia.co.uk, www.leia.co.uk

Liget Compton - Albion Drive, Lidget Lane Industrial Estate, Thurnscoe, Rotherham. S63 0BA tel:(01709) 881 844. sales@lidget.co.uk, www.lidget.co.uk

Light (Multiforms), H A - Woods Lane, Cradley Heath, Warley, W. Midlands. B64 7AL tel:(01384) 569283, fax:(01384) 633712. enquiry@multiforms.co.uk, www.multiforms.co.uk

Lighting Industry Association, The - Stafford Park 7, Telford, Shropshire. TF3 3BQ tel:(01952) 290905, fax:(01952) 290906. info@thelia.org.uk, www.thelia.org.uk

Lignacite (North London) Ltd - Meadgate Works, Nazeing, Waltham Abbey, Essex. EN9 2PD tel:(01992) 464661, fax:(01992) 445713. info@lignacite.co.uk, www.lignacite.co.uk

Lignacite Ltd - Norfolk House, High Street, Brandon, Suffolk. IP27 0AX tel:(01842) 810678, fax:(01842) 814602. info@lignacite.co.uk, www.lignacite.co.uk

Lilleheden Ltd - Digital Media Centre, County Way, Barnsley. S70 2JW tel:+44 1226 720 760, fax:+44 1226 720 701. mailuk@lilleheden.com, www.lilleheden.dk/uk

Limelite - Tarmac Building Products Ltd - Swains Park Industrial Estate, Park Road, Swadlincote, Derbyshire. DE12 6JT tel:(03444) 630 046. limelite@tarmacbp.co.uk, www.tarmac.com

Linatex Ltd - Wilkinson House, Galway Road, Blackbush Business Park, Yateley, Hants. GU46 6GE tel:(01252) 743000, fax:(01252) 743030. sales.uk@weirminerals.com, www.linatex.net

Lindapter International - Lindsay House, Brackenbeck Road, Bradford, W. Yorks. BD7 2NF tel:(01274) 521444, fax:(01274) 521130. enquiries@lindapter.com, www.lindapter.com

Link 51 (Storage Products) - Link House, Halesfield 6, Telford, Shropshire. TF7 4LN tel:(0800) 1695151, fax:(01384) 472599. sales@link51.co.uk, www.link51.co.uk

L (con't)

Liquid Technology Ltd - Unit 27, Tatton Court, Kingsland Grange, Woolston, Warrington, Cheshire. WA1 4RR tel:(01925) 850324, fax:(01925) 850325. info@liquidtechnologyltd.com, www.fengroup.com

Litex Design Ltd - 3 The Metro Centre, Dwight Road, Watford, Herts. WD18 9HG tel:(01923) 247254, fax:(01923) 226772. john@litexgroup.co.uk, www.litexuk.com

LMOB Electrical Contractors Ltd - Unit 28, Balfour Business Centre, Balfour Road, Southall, Middx. UB2 5BD tel:(020) 8574 6464, fax:(020) 8573 1189. sales@lmob.co.uk, www.lmob.co.uk

Lochinvar Limited - 7 Lombard Way, The MXL Centre, Banbury, Oxon. OX16 4TJ tel:(01295) 269981, fax:(01295) 271640. info@lochinvar.ltd.uk, www.lochinvar.ltd.uk

Lockhart Catering Equipment - Lockhart House, Brunel Road, Theale, Reading, Berks. RG7 4XE tel:(0118) 930 3900, fax:(0118) 930 0757. bceweb@bunzl.co.uk, www.lockhartcatering.co.uk

Loctite UK Ltd - Watchmead, Welwyn Garden City, Herts. AL7 1JB tel:(01707) 358800, fax:(01707) 358900. kieran.bowden@loctite-europe.com, www.loctite.co.uk

Loft Centre Products - Thicket Lane, Halnaker nr. Chichester, W. Sussex. PO18 OQS tel:(01243) 785246/785229, fax:(01243) 533184. sales@loftcentre.co.uk, www.loftcentreproducts.co.uk

Logic Office Contracts - Vestry Estate, Otford Road, Sevenoaks, Kent. TN14 5EL tel:(01732) 457636, fax:(01732) 740706. contracts.admin@logic-office.co.uk, www.logic-office.co.uk

London Concrete Ltd - London House, 77 Boston Manor Road, Brentford, Middlesex. TW8 9JQ tel:(0208) 380 7300, fax:(0208) 380 7301. london.concrete@aggregate.com, www.aggregate.com

London Fan Company Ltd - 75-81 Stirling Road, Acton, London. W3 8DJ tel:(020) 8992 6923, fax:(020) 8992 6928. sales@londonfan.co.uk, www.londonfan.co.uk

London Shopfitters Ltd - Unit 6, Blackwater Close, Fairview Ind. Est, Marsh Way, Rainham, Essex. RM13 8UA tel:(01708) 552225, fax:(01708) 557567. sales@londonshopfitters.co.uk, www.londonshopfitters.co.uk

Longbottom J & J W Ltd - Bridge Foundry, Holmfirth, Huddersfield, W. Yorks. HD9 7AW tel:(01484) 682141, fax:(01484) 681513. www.longbottomfoundry.co.uk

Longden - 55 Parkwood Road, Sheffield, South Yorkshire. S3 8AH tel:(0114) 2706330. enquiries@longdendoors.co.uk, www.lslongden.co.uk

Lonsdale Metal Company - Unit 40 Millmead Industrial Centre, Mill Mead Road, London. N17 9QU tel:(020) 8801 4221, fax:(020) 8801 1287. info@lonsdalemetal.co.uk, www.lonsdalemetal.co.uk

Lord Isaac Ltd - Desborough Road, High Wycombe, Bucks. HP11 2QN tel:(01494) 459191, fax:(01494) 461376. info@isaaclord.co.uk, www.isaaclord.co.uk

Lotus Water Garden Products Ltd - Lotus House, Deer Park Industrial Estate, Knowle Lane, Fair Oak, Eastleigh, Hampshire. SO50 7DZ tel:(023) 8060 2602, fax:(023) 8060 2603. info@lotuswgp.com, www.lotuswatergardenproducts.com

Louver-Lite Ltd - Ashton Road, Hyde, Cheshire. SK14 4BG tel:(0161) 882 5000, fax:(0161) 882 5009. janet.dunn@louvolite.com, www.louvolite.com

Lowe & Fletcher Ltd - Moorcroft Drive, Wednesbury, W. Midlands. WS10 7DE tel:(0121) 5050400, fax:(0121) 5050420. sales@lowe-and-fletcher.co.uk, www.lowe-and-fletcher.co.uk

LPA Group PLC - Tudor Works, Debden Road, Saffron Walden, Essex. CB11 4AN tel:(01779) 512800, fax:(01779) 512826. enquiries@lpa-group.com, www.lpa-group.com

LSA Projects Ltd - The Barn, White Horse Lane, Witham, Essex. CM8 2BU tel:(01376) 501199, fax:(01376) 502027. sales@lsaprojects.co.uk, www.lsaprojects.co.uk

LTI Advanced Systems Technology Ltd - 3 Kinsbourne Court, 96-100 Luton Road, Harpenden, Herts. AL5 3BL tel:(01582) 469 769, fax:(01582) 469 789. sales@lti-ast.co.uk, www.lti-ast.co.uk

Lucideon - Queens Road, Penkhull, Stoke-on-Trent, Staffordshire. ST4 7LQ tel:(01782) 764428, fax:(01782) 412331. enquiries@lucideon.com, www.lucideon.com

Lucideon - Queens Road, Penkhull, Stoke-on-Trent. ST4 7LQ tel:(01782) 764428, fax:(01782) 412331. enquiries@lucideon.com, www.lucideon.com

Lumitron Ltd - Unit 31, The Metro Centre Tolpits Lane, Watford, Herts. WD18 9UD tel:(01923) 226222, fax:(01923) 211300. sales@lumitron.co.uk, www.lumitron.co.uk

Luxaflex® - Hunter Douglas Ltd, Battersea Road, Heaton Mersey Industrial Estate, Stockport, Cheshire. SK4 3EQ tel:(0161) 442 9500, fax:(0161) 432 3200. info@luxaflex.co.uk, www.luxaflex.co.uk

Luxcrete Ltd - Unit 2, Firbank Industrial Estate, Dallow Road, Luton. LU1 1TW tel:(01582) 488767, fax:(01582) 724607. enquiries@luxcrete.co.uk, www.luxcrete.co.uk

Lytag Ltd - Second Floor (front), 75/77 Margaret Street, London. W1W 8SY tel:(0207) 4995242. sales@lytag.com, www.lytag.com

M

M.J. Electronic Services (International) Ltd - 5 Castle Street, Bridgewater, Somerset. TA6 3DD tel:(01278) 422882, fax:(01278) 453331. www.m-mes.com

Mabey Hire Ltd - 1 Railway Street, Scout Hill, Ravensthorpe, Dewsbury, W. Yorks. WF13 3EJ tel:(01924) 589377, fax:(01924) 457932. info@mabeyhire.co.uk, www.mabeyhire.co.uk

MacAlloy Limited - PO Box 71, Hawke Street, Sheffield. S9 2LN tel:(0114) 242 6704, fax:(0114) 243 1324. sales@macalloy.com, www.macalloy.com

Macemain + Amstad Ltd - Boyle Road, Willowbrook Industrial Estate, Corby, Northants. NN17 5XU tel:(01536) 401331, fax:(01536) 401298. sales@macemainamstad.com, www.macemainamstad.com

Mackay Engineering - Unit 2 Mackay Business Park, 120 Church End, Cherry Hinton, Cambridge, Cambs. CB1 3LB tel:(01223) 508222, fax:(01223) 510222. engineering@mackay.co.uk, www.mackay.co.uk

Mackwell Electronics Ltd - Virgo Place, Aldridge, W. Midlands. WS9 8UG tel:(01922) 58255, fax:(01922) 51263. sales@mackwell.com, www.mackwell.com

MacLellan Rubber Ltd - Unit 16, Planetary Road Industrial Estate, Wednesfield, Wolverhampton. WV13 3XA tel:(01902) 307711, fax:(0151) 946 5222. sales@maclellanrubber.com, www.maclellanrubber.com

MacMarney Refrigeration & Air Conditioning Ltd - The Old Forge, Stone Street, Crowfield, Ipswich, Suffolk. IP6 9SZ tel:(01449) 760560, fax:(01449) 760590. sales@macmarney.co.uk, www.macmarney.co.uk

Maco Door & Window Hardware (UK) Ltd - Eurolink Ind. Centre, Castle Road, Sittingbourne, Kent. ME10 3LY tel:(01795) 433900, fax:(01795) 433901. enquiry@macouk.net, www.maco-europe.com

Macpuarsa (UK) Ltd - 13 14 Charlton Business Centre, 15 The Avenue, Bromley, Kent. BR1 2BS tel:(01932) 223161, fax:(01932) 223181. hc@mpcorporacion.com, www.macpuarsa.es

Magiboards Ltd - Unit B3, Stafford Park 11, Telford, Shropshire. TF3 3AY tel:(01952) 292111, fax:(01952) 292280. sales@magiboards.com, www.magiboards.com

Magiglo Ltd - Lysander Close, Broadstairs, Kent. CT10 2YJ tel:(01843) 602863, fax:(01843) 860108. info@magiglo.co.uk, www.magiglo.co.uk

Magnet Ltd - Allington Way, Yarm Road Ind. Estate, Darlington, Co. Durham. DR1 4XT tel:(01325) 744093. www.magnet.co.uk

Magnum Ltd T/A Magnum Scaffolding - Yard Brook Estate, Stockwood Vale, Keynsham, Bristol, Avon. BS31 2AL tel:(0117) 986 0123, fax:(0117) 986 2123. chris@magnumltd.co.uk, www.magnumltd.co.uk

Magpie Furniture - Blundell Harling Ltd, 9 Albany Road, Granby Industrial Estate, Weymouth, Dorset. DT4 9TH tel:(01305) 206000, fax:(01305) 760598. www.magpiefurniture.com

Magrini Ltd - Unit 5, Maybrook Industrial Estate, Brownhills, Walsall, W. Midlands. WS8 7DG tel:(01543) 375311, fax:(01543) 361172. sales@magrini.co.uk, www.magrini.co.uk

Majestic Shower Co Ltd - 1 North Place, Edinburgh Way, Harlow, Essex. CM20 2SL tel:(01279) 443644, fax:(01279) 635074. info@majesticshowers.com, www.majesticshowers.com

Maldon Fencing Co - Burnham Road, Latchingdon, Nr Chelmsford, Essex. CM3 6HA tel:(01621) 740415, fax:(01621) 740769. maldonfencing@btconnect.com, www.maldonfencing.com

Manders Paint Ltd - 5-11 St Georges Street, Northampton, Northamptonshire. NN1 2TN tel:(01604) 639 898, fax:(01604) 629 590. richard@mandersconstruction.co.uk, www.manderspaints.co.uk

Manitou (Site Lift) Ltd - Ebblake Industrial Estate, Verwood, Wimborne, Dorset. BH31 6BB tel:(01202) 825331, fax:(01202) 813027. www.manitou.com

Mann McGowan Group - Unit 4 Brook Trading Estate, Deadbrook Lane, Aldershot, Hants. GU12 4XB tel:(01252) 333601, fax:(01252) 322724. sales@mannmcgowan.co.uk, www.mannmcgowan.co.uk

Mansfield Pollard & Co Ltd - Edward House, Parry Lane, Bradford. BD4 8TL tel:(01274) 774050, fax:(01274) 77 54 24. salesteam@mansfieldpollard.co.uk, www.mansfieldpollard.co.uk

Mansfield Sand Co Ltd (Brick Division) - Crown Farm Way, Forest Town, Mansfield, Notts. NG19 0FT tel:(01623) 416861, fax:(01623) 420904. sales@mansfield-brick.co.uk, www.mansfield-sand.co.uk

MANTAIR Ltd - Suite 3, Connaught Mews, 118-120 Connaught Avenue, Frinton-on-Sea, Essex. CO13 9AD tel:(01255) 853 890. info@mantair.com, www.mantair.com

Marble Flooring Spec. Ltd - Verona house, Filwood Road, Bristol. BS16 3RY tel:(0117) 9656565, fax:(0117) 9656573. maryford@marbleflooring.co.uk, www.marbleflooring.co.uk

Marble Mosaic Co Ltd, The - Winterstoke Road, Weston-Super-Mare, N. Somerset. BS23 3YE tel:(01934) 419941, fax:(01934) 625479. sales@marble-mosaic.co.uk, www.marble-mosaic.co.uk

Marcrist International Ltd - Marcrist House, Kirk Sandall Industrial Estate, Doncaster, S. Yorks. DN3 1QR tel:(01302) 890888, fax:(01302) 883864. info@marcrist.com, www.marcrist.co.uk

Marcus M Ltd - Unit 7 Narrowboat Way, Peartree Lane, Dudley, W. Midlands. DY2 0XW tel:(01384) 457900, fax:(01384) 457903. info@m-marcus.com, www.m-marcus.com

Mardale Pipes Plus Ltd - PO BOX 86, Davy Road, Astmoor Industrial Estate, Runcorn, Cheshire. WA7 1PX tel:(01928) 580555, fax:(01928) 591033. sales@ippgrp.com, www.mardale-pipes.com

Marflex Chimney Systems - Unit 40, Vale Business Park, Cowbridge, S. Glams. CF71 7PF tel:(01446) 775551, fax:(01446) 772468. sales@pd-edenhall.co.uk, www.pd-edenhall.co.uk

Marflow Eng Ltd - Britannia House, Austin Way, Hamstead Industrial Estate, Birmingham. B42 1DU tel:(0121) 358 1555, fax:(0121) 358 1444. sales@marflow.co.uk, www.marflow.co.uk

Margolis Office Interiors Ltd - 341 Euston Road, London. NW1 3AD tel:(020) 7387 8217, fax:(020) 7388 0625. info@margolisfurniture.co.uk, www.margolisfurniture.co.uk

Marking Machines International - Hartshill Nursery, Thong Lane, Shorne, Gravesend. DA12 4AD tel:(01635) 867537, fax:(01635) 864588. sales@sportsmark.net, www.sportsmark.net

Marleton Cross Ltd - Unit 2 Alpha Close, Delta Drive, Tewkesbury Industrial Estate, Tewkesbury, Glos. GL20 8JF tel:(01684) 293311, fax:(01684) 293900. enquiries@mx-group.com, www.mx-group.com

Marley Ltd - Litchfield Road, Branston, Burton On Trent, Staffs. DE14 3HD tel:(01283) 722588. info@marley.co.uk, www.marley.co.uk

Marley Plumbing and Drainage - Dickley Lane, Lenham, Maidstone, Kent. ME17 2DE tel:(01622) 858888, fax:(01622) 858725. marketing@marleypd.com, www.marley.co.uk

Marlow Ropes Ltd - Diplocks Way, Hailsham, Sussex. BN27 3JS tel:(01323) 847234, fax:(01323) 440093. industrial@marlowropes.com, www.marlowropes.com

Marlux Medical Ltd - Unit 15, Roman Way, Coleshill, Birmingham. B46 1HG tel:(0121) 783 5777. sales@marluxmedical.com, www.marluxmedical.com

Marshalls Mono Ltd - Southowram, Halifax, Yorks. HX3 9SY tel:(01422) 306000, fax:(01422) 330185. customeradvice@marshalls.co.uk, www.marshalls.co.uk

Marshall-Tufflex Ltd - Churchfields Ind.Estate, Hastings, Sussex. TN38 9PU tel:(0870) 2403200, fax:(0870) 2403201. sales@marshall-tufflex.com, www.marshall-tufflex.com

Martello Plastics Ltd - Unit 11, Ross Way, Shorncliffe Industrial Estate, Folkestone, Kent. CT20 3UJ tel:(01303) 256848, fax:(01303) 246301. mail@martelloplastics.co.uk, www.martelloplastics.co.uk

Martin & Co Ltd - 160 Dollman Street, Duddeston, Birmingham. B7 4RS tel:(0121) 233 2111, fax:(0121) 236 0488. sales@armacmartin.co.uk, www.armacmartin.co.uk

Martin Childs Limited - 1 Green Way, Swaffham, Norfolk. PE37 7FD tel:(01760) 722 275. enquiries@martinchilds.com, www.martinchilds.com

Mason FW & Sons Ltd - Colwick Industrial Estate, Colwick, Nottingham, Notts. NG4 2EQ tel:(0115) 911 3500, fax:(0115) 911 35444. enquiries@masons-timber.co.uk, www.masons-timber.co.uk

Masonry Cleaning Services - 1A Alpines Road, Calow. S44 5AU tel:(01246) 209926, fax:(01246) 221620. maxblastuk@btinternet.com

Masson Seeley & Co Ltd - Howdale, Downham Market, Norfolk. PE38 9AL tel:(01366) 388000, fax:(01366) 385222. admin@masson-seeley.co.uk, www.masson-seeley.co.uk

Masterbill Micro Systems Ltd - 5b Cedar Court, Porters Wood, St. Albans, Herts. AL3 6PA tel:(01727) 855563, fax:(01727) 854626. sales@masterbill.com, www.masterbill.com

Masterframe Windows Ltd - 4 Crittall Road, Witham, Essex. CM8 3DR tel:(01376) 510410, fax:(01376) 510400. sales@masterframe.co.uk, www.masterframe.co.uk

Mastic Asphalt Council - 27 Greenways Crescent, Shoreham By Sea, Sussex. BN43 6HR tel:(01273) 242 778. info@masticasphaltcouncil.co.uk, www.masticasphaltcouncil.co.uk

Mat.Works Flooring Solutions - A Division of National Floorcoverings Ltd, Farfield Park, Manvers, Wath on Dearne. S63 5DB tel:(01709) 763839, fax:(01709) 763813. sales@mat-works.co.uk, www.mat-works.co.uk

Matki plc - Churchward Road, Yate, Bristol, S. Glos. BS37 5PL tel:(01454) 322888, fax:(01454) 315284. helpline@matki.co.uk, www.matki.co.uk

Mattersons Cranes - 45 Regent Street, Rochdale, Lancs. OL12 0HQ tel:(01706) 649321, fax:(01706) 657452. matterson@pctgroup.co.uk, www.mattersoncranes.co.uk

Matthew Hebden - 54 Blacka Moor Road, Sheffield. S17 3GJ tel:(0114) 236 8122. sales@matthewhebden.co.uk, www.matthewhebden.co.uk

Matthews & Yates Ltd - Peartree Road, Stanway, Colchester, Essex. CO3 0LD tel:(01206) 543311, fax:(01206) 760497. info@systemair.co.uk, www.matthewyates.co.uk

Mawdsleys Ber Ltd - Unit 2C, Kingsland Trading Estate, St. Philips Road, Bristol. BS2 0JZ tel:(0117) 955 2481, fax:(0117) 955 2483. enquiries@mawdsleysber.co.uk, www.mawdsleysber.co.uk

Max Appliances Ltd - Wheel Park Farm Ins Est, Wheel Lane, Hastings, Sussex. TN35 4SE tel:(01424) 854 444, fax:(01424) 853862. sales@max-appliances.co.uk, www.max-appliances.co.uk

Maxit UK - The Heath, Runcorn, Cheshire. WA7 4QX tel:(01928) 515656. sales@maxit.com, www.maxit.com

May William (Ashton) Ltd - Cavendish Street, Ashton-under-Lyne, Lancs. OL6 7BR tel:(0161) 330 3838/4879, fax:(0161) 339 1097. sales@william-may.com, www.william-may.com

Mayplas Ltd - Building 1, Peel Mills, Chamberhall Street, Bury, Lancs. BL9 0JU tel:(0161) 447 8320, fax:(Fax:) 1614478333. sales@mayplas.co.uk, www.mayplas.co.uk

McAlpine & Co Ltd - Hillington Industrial Estate, Glasgow. G52 4LF tel:(0141) 6389 123. www.mcalpineplumbing.com

McCarthy & Stone Construction Services - 4th Floor, Holdenhurst Road, Bournemouth, Dorset. BH88AQ tel:(01202) 292480, fax:(01202) 557261. info@homelife.co.uk, www.mccarthyandstone.co.uk

McKenzie-Martin Ltd - Eton Hill Works, Eton Hill Road, Radcliffe, Gt Man. M26 2US tel:(0161) 723 2234, fax:(0161) 725 9531. hilda@mckenziemartin.co.uk, www.mckenziemartin.co.uk

MCL Composites Ltd - New Street, Biddulph Moor, Stoke-on-Trent, Staffs. ST8 7NL tel:(01782) 375450. sales@mcl-grp.co.uk, www.mcl-grp.co.uk

McMullen Facades - 66 Lurgan Road, Moira, Craigavon, Co. Armagh. BT67 0LX tel:(028) 9261 9688, fax:(028) 9261 9711. enquiries@mcmullenfacades.com, www.mcmullenfacades.com

Mea UK Ltd - Rectors Lane, Pentre, Deeside, Flintshire. CH5 2DH tel:(01244) 534455, fax:(01244) 534477. uk.technical@mea.de, www.mea.uk.com

Mells Roofing Ltd - Beehive Works, Beehive Lane, Chelmsford, Essex. CM2 9JY tel:(01245) 262621, fax:(01245) 260060. info@mellsroofing.co.uk, www.mellsroofing.co.uk

Mentha & Hessal (Shopfitters) Ltd - 95a Linaker Street, Southport, Merseyside. PR8 5BU tel:(01704) 530800, fax:(01704) 500601. paulmentha@mentha-halsall.com, www.mentha-halsall.com/

Mercian Industrial Doors - Pearsall Drive, Oldbury, West Midlands. B69 2RA tel:(0121) 544 6124, fax:(0121) 552 6793. info@merciandoors.co.uk, www.merciandoors.co.uk

Mermaid Panels Ltd - DBC House, Laceby Business Park, Grimsby, Humb. DN37 7DP tel:(01472) 279940, fax:(01472) 752575. sales@mermaidpanels.com, www.mermaidpanels.com

Mermet U.K - Ryeford Hall, Ryeford, Nr Ross on Wye, Herefordshire. HR9 7PU tel:(01989) 750910, fax:(01989) 750768. info@mermet.co.uk, www.mermet.co.uk

Merronbrook Ltd - Hazeley Bottom, Hartley Wintney, Hook, Hants. RG27 8LX tel:(01252) 844747, fax:(01252) 845304. sales@merronbrook.co.uk

Metal Gutta - (part Of Good Directions Ltd Group Of Companies), Time House, Hillsons Road, Botley, Southampton, Hants. SO30 2DY tel:(01489) 797774, fax:(01489) 796700. enquiries@coppagutta.co.uk, www.metal-guttering.co.uk

Metal Technology Ltd - Steeple Road Industrial Estate, Steeple Road, Antrim. BT41 1AB tel:(028) 94487777, fax:(028) 94487878. sales@metaltechnology.com, www.metaltechnology.com

Metalcraft (Tottenham) Ltd - 6-40 Durnford Street, Seven Sisters Road, Tottenham, London. N15 5NQ tel:(020) 8802 1715, fax:(020) 8802 1258. sales@makingmetalwork.com, www.makingmetalwork.com

Metalfloor UK Ltd - Unit 103, Ringtail Road, Merlin Park, Burscough, Lancashire. L40 8JY tel:(01704) 896061, fax:(01704) 897293. sales@metalfloor.co.uk, www.metalfloor.co.uk

Metalliform Products Plc - Chambers Road, Hoyland, Barnsley, S. Yorks. S74 0EZ tel:(01226) 350555, fax:(01226) 350112. sales@metalliform.co.uk, www.metalliform.co.uk

M (con't)

Metalline Signs Ltd - Unit 18, Barton Hill Trading Estate, Bristol, Avon. BS5 9TE tel:(01179) 555291, fax:(01179) 557518. info@metalline-signs.co.uk, www.metalline-signs.co.uk
Metalwood Fencing (Contracts) Limited - Hutton House, Soothouse Spring, Valley Road Industrial Estate, St. Albans, Herts. AL3 6PG tel:(01727) 861141/2, fax:(01727) 846018. info@metalwoodfencing.com, www.metalwoodfencing.com
Metcraft Ltd - Harwood Industrial Estate, Harwood Road, Littlehampton, Sussex. BN17 7BB tel:(01903) 714226, fax:(01903) 723206. www.metcraft.co.uk
Metreel Ltd - Cossall Industrial Estate, Coronation Road, Ilkeston, Derbys. DE7 5UA tel:(0115) 932 7010, fax:(0115) 930 6263. sales@metreel.co.uk, www.metreel.co.uk
Metsä Wood - Old Golf Course, Fishtoft Road, Boston, Lincs. PE21 OBJ tel:(0800) 00 44 44, fax:(01205) 354488. uk@metsagroup.com, www.metsawood.com
Metsa Wood UK Ltd - Old Golf Course, Fishtoft Road, Boston, Lincolnshire. PE21 0BJ tel:(0800) 004444. uk@metsagroup.com, www.metsawood.com
Metsec Lattice Beams Ltd - Units 10 & 11 Rolls Royce Estate, Spring Road, Etingshall, Wolverhampton. WV4 6JX tel:(01902) 408011, fax:(01902) 490440. Sales@mlb-steel.com, www.mlb-steel.com
Metsec Ltd - Broadwell Road, Oldbury, Warley, W. Midlands. B69 4HF tel:(0121) 601 6000, fax:(0121) 601 6109. metsecplc@metsec.com, www.metsec.com
Metway Electrical Industries Ltd - Barrie House, 18 North Street, Portslade, Brighton. BN41 1DG tel:(01273) 431600, fax:(01273) 439288. sales@metway.co.uk, www.metway.co.uk
Mevaco Ltd - Unit 5 Riverbank Business Park, Old Grantham Road, Whatton, Nottingham. NG13 9FX tel:(01925) 438 104. contact@mevaco.co.uk, www.mevaco.co.uk
Meyer Timber Limited - Meyer House, Hadleigh Park, Grindley Lane, Blythe Bridge, Stoke on Trent. ST11 9LW tel:(0845) 873 5000, fax:(0845) 873 5005. sales.stoke@meyertimber.com, www.meyertimber.com
Michelmersh Brick Holdings PLC - Freshfield Lane, Danehill, Sussex. RH17 7HH tel:(0844) 931 0022, fax:(01794) 368845. sales@mbhplc.co.uk, www.mbhplc.co.uk
Midland Alloy Ltd - Stafford Park 17, Telford, Shropshire. TF3 3DG tel:(01952) 290961, fax:(01952) 290441. sales@midlandalloy.com, www.midlandalloy.com
Midland Tube and Fabrications - Corngreave Works, Unit 4, Corngreave Road, Cradley Heath, Warley, W. Midlands. B64 7DA tel:(01384) 566364, fax:(01384) 566365. Keithcadman@btconnect.com
Midland Wire Cordage Co Ltd - Wire Rope House, Eagle Rd, North Moons Moat, Redditch, Worcs. B98 9HF tel:(01527) 594150, fax:(01527) 64322. info@ormiston-wire.co.uk, www.midlandwirecordage.co.uk
Miele Co Ltd - Fairacres, Marcham Road, Abingdon, Oxon. OX14 1TW tel:(01235) 554455, fax:(01235) 554477. info@miele.co.uk, www.miele.co.uk
Miles Stone - Quarry Yard, Woodside Avenue, Boyattwood Industrial Estate, Eastleigh, Hants. SO50 9ES tel:(023) 80613178. info@milesstone.com, www.milesstone.co.uk
Milestone Reclaim and Landscaping Ltd - 732 London Road, Grays, West Thurrock, Essex. RM20 3NL tel:(0844) 826 3252. sales@milestonesupplies.co.uk, https://milestonesupplies.co.uk/
Milliken Carpet - Beech Hill Plant, Gidlow Lane, Wigan, Lancs. WN6 8RN tel:(01942) 612783, fax:(01942) 826570. carpetenquiries@milliken.com, www.millikencarpeteurope.com
Mineral Wool Insulation Manufacturers Association - 16 Old Queen Street, London. SW1H 9HP tel:(020) 7293 0870. admin@mima.info, http://www.mima.info/
Minkon Ltd - Tofts Farm Industrial Estate, Brenda Road, Hartlepool. TS25 2BS tel:(01429) 273252. fortafix@minkon.co.uk, www.fortafix.com
Minsterstone Ltd - Unit 4, Canal Wharf Industrial Units, Harts Close, Ilminster, TA19 9DJ. TA17 8SU tel:(01460) 52277, fax:(01460) 57865. varyl@minsterstone.ltd.uk, www.minsterstone.ltd.uk
MiTek Industries Ltd - MiTek House, Grazebrook Industrial Park, Pear Tree Lane, Dudley, W. Midlands. DY2 OXW tel:(01384) 451400, fax:(01384) 451411. info@mitek.co.uk, www.mitek.co.uk
MK (MK Electric Ltd) - The Arnold Centre, Paycocke Road, Basildon, Essex. SS14 3EA tel:(01268) 563000, fax:(01268) 563563. mkorderenquiries@honeywell.com, www.mkelectric.co.uk
MMA Architectural Systems Ltd - 35c Fourth Avenue, Westfield Industrial Estate, Midsomer Norton, Somerset. BA3 4XE tel:(01761) 419427. sales@mma-architectural.co.uk, www.jakob.co.uk
Mockridge Labels & Nameplates Ltd - Cavendish Street, Ashton-under-Lyne, Lancs. OL6 7QL tel:(0161) 308 2331, fax:(0161) 343 1958. sales@mockridge.com, www.mockridge.com
Mode Lighting - The Maltings, 63 High Street, Ware, Herts. SG12 9AD tel:(01920) 462121, fax:(01920) 466881. sales@modelighting.com, www.modelighting.com
Mode Lighting (UK) Ltd - The Maltings, 63 High Street, Ware, Herts. SG12 9AD tel:(01920) 462121, fax:(01920) 466881. sales@modelighting.com, www.modelighting.com
Modelscape - Adams House, Dickerage Lane, New Malden, Surrey. KT3 3SF tel:(020) 8949 9286, fax:(020) 8949 7418. ian@ianmorton.me.uk, www.modelscape.co.uk
Modern Plan Insulation Ltd - Church Street, Westhoughton, Bolton. BL5 3QW tel:(01942) 811839, fax:(01942) 812310. mpinsulations@btconnect.com, www.mpinsulations.co.uk
Moffat Ltd, E & R - Seabegs Road, Bonnybridge, Stirlingshire. FK4 2BS tel:(01324) 812272, fax:(01324) 814107. sales@ermoffat.co.uk, www.ermoffat.co.uk
Moffett Thallon & Co Ltd - 143 Northumberland Street, Belfast. BT13 2JF tel:(028) 90 322802, fax:(028) 90 241428. info@moffett-thallon.co.uk, www.moffett-thallon.co.uk
Monier Redland Limited - Sussex Manor Business Park, Gatwick Road, Crawley, West Sussex. RH10 9NZ tel:(08705) 601000, fax:(08705) 642742. sales.redland@monier.com, www.redland.co.uk
Monk Metal Windows Ltd - Hansons Bridge Road, Erdington, Birmingham, W. Midlands. B24 0QP tel:(0121) 351 4411, fax:(0121) 351 3673. bromilow.d@monkmetal.co.uk, www.monkmetalwindows.co.uk
Mono Pumps Ltd - Martin Street, Audenshaw, Manchester, Gt Man. M34 5JA tel:(0161) 339 9000, fax:(0161) 344 0727. info-web@nov.com, www.mono-pumps.com
Monodraught Ltd - Halifax House, Cressex Business Park, High Wycombe, Bucks. HP12 3SE tel:(01494) 897700, fax:(01494) 532465. info@monodraught.com, www.monodraught.com
Monowa Manufacturing (UK) Ltd - Unit 6 Llyn-yr-Eos, Parc Menter, Cross Hands Industrial Estate, Llanelli, Carmarthenshire. SA14 6RA tel:(01269) 845554, fax:(01269) 845515. sales@accordial.co.uk, www.monowa.com
Montrose Fasteners - Montrose House, Lancaster Road, High Wycombe, Bucks. HP12 3PY tel:(01494) 451227, fax:(01494) 436270. sales@themontrosegroup.com, www.themontrosegroup.com
Monument Tools Ltd - Restmor Way, Hackbridge Road, Hackbridge, Wallington, Surrey. SM6 7AH tel:(020) 8288 1100, fax:(020) 8288 1108. info@monument-tools.com, www.monument-tools.com
Moores Furniture Group Ltd - Thorp Arch Trading Estate, Wetherby, W. Yorks. LS23 7DD tel:(01937) 842394, fax:(01937) 845396. marketing@moores.co.uk, www.moores.co.uk
Moravia (UK) Ltd - Unit A-C Stonedale Road, Oldends Industrial Estate, Stonehouse, Glos. GL10 3SA tel:(01453) 852620, fax:(01453) 852625. sales@moravia.co.uk, www.moravia.co.uk
Moresecure Ltd - Haldane House, Halesfield 1, Telford. TF7 4EH tel:(01952) 683900, fax:(01952) 683982. sales@moresecure.co.uk, www.moresecure.co.uk
Morgan Hope Industries Ltd - Units 5 and 6 Blowick Industrial Park, Crowland Street, Southport, Merseyside. PR9 7RU tel:(01704) 512000, fax:(01704) 542632. info@morganhope.com, www.morganhope.com
Morrison Chemicals Ltd - Bedford Place, Derby Road, Liverpool. L20 8LQ tel:(0151) 933 0044. enquiries@morrisonsgrp.co.uk, www.morrisonsgrp.co.uk
Mortar Industry Association - Gillingham House, 38-44 Gillingham Street, London. SW1V 1HU tel:(020) 7963 8000, fax:(020) 7963 8001. brian.james@mineralproducts.org, www.mortar.org.uk
Moseley GRP Product (Division of Moseley Rubber Co Ltd) - Hoyle Street, Mancunian Way, Manchester, Gt Man. M12 6HL tel:(0161) 273 3341, fax:(0161) 274 3743. sales@moseleyrubber.com, www.moseleyrubber.com
Moss WM & Sons (Stove Anamellers Ripon) Ltd - Unit 5, Mooring Close, Lower Hollin Bank Street, Blackburn, Lancs. BB2 4AH tel:(01765) 604351, fax:(01765) 690065. info@moseleyrubber.com, www.moseleyrubber.com
Motorised Air Products Ltd - Unit 5a, Sopwith Crescent, Wickford Business Park, Wickford, Essex. SS11 8YU tel:(01268) 574442, fax:(01268) 574443. info@mapuk.com, www.mapuk.com
Mountford Rubber & Plastics Ltd - 44 Bracebridge Street, Aston, Birmingham. B6 4PE tel:(0121) 359 0135, fax:(0121) 333 3204. sales@mrp.uk.net, http://www.mrp.uk.net/page6.html
Movement Joints (UK) - Unit 3, 57 Thorby Avenue, March, Cambs. PE15 0AR tel:(01354) 607960, fax:(01354) 607833. info@mjuk.co.uk, www.mjuk.co.uk
MPA Cement - Riverside House, 4 Meadows Business Park, Station Approach, Blackwater, Camberly, Surrey. GU17 9AB tel:(01276) 608700, fax:(01276) 608701. mpacement@mineralproducts.org, www.mineralproducts.org
MSA (Britain) Ltd - Unit 2 Waller Road, Hopton Park, Devizes, Wiltshire. SN10 2JP tel:(0800) 066 2222, fax:(01698) 740141. info.gb@msasafety.com, www.msabritain.co.uk/msa
Mueller Europe - Oxford Street, Bilston, W. Midlands. WV14 7DS tel:(01902) 499700, fax:(01902) 405838. sales@muellereurope.com, www.muellereurope.com
Multi Marque Production Engineering Ltd - 33 Monkton Road Industrial Estate, Wakefield, W. Yorks. WF2 7AL tel:(01924) 290231, fax:(01924) 382241. enquiries@multi-marque.co.uk, www.multi-marque.co.uk
Multi Mesh Ltd - Eurolink House, Lea Green Industrial Estate, St. Helens, Merseyside. WA9 4QU tel:(01744) 820 666, fax:(01744) 821 417. enquiries@multimesh.co.uk, www.multimesh.co.uk
Multibeton Ltd - 15 Oban Court, Wickford Business Park, Wickford, Essex. SS11 8YB tel:(01268) 561688, fax:(01268) 561690. multibeton@btconnect.com
Multikwik Ltd - Dickley Lane, Lenham, Maidstone, Kent. ME17 2DE tel:(01622) 852654, fax:(01622) 852723. info@multikwik.com, www.multikwik.com
Multitex GRP LLP - Unit 5, Dolphin Industrial Estate, Southampton Road, Salisbury, Wilts. SP1 2NB tel:(01722) 332139, fax:(01722) 338458. sales@wessexbps.co.uk, www.multitex.co.uk
Mul-T-Lock - Portobello Works, Wood Street, Willenhall, W. Midlands. WV13 3PW tel:(01902) 364 200, fax:(01902) 364 201. enquiries@mul-t-lock.co.uk, www.mul-t-lock.co.uk
Muraspec - 74-78 Wood Lane End, Hemel Hempstead, Herts. HP2 4RF tel:(08705) 117118, fax:(08705) 329020. customerservices@muraspec.com, www.muraspec.com
Muswell Manufacturing Co Ltd - UNIT 4, Mill River Trading Estate, Brimsdown, Enfield. EN3 7QF tel:(020) 8443 2711, fax:(020) 3417 2827. sales@muswell.co.uk, www.muswell.co.uk
Myddleton Hall Lighting, Division of Peerless Design Ltd - Unit 9, Brunswick Industrial Park, Brunswick Way, London. N11 1JL tel:(020) 8362 8500, fax:(020) 8362 8525. enquiries@peerlessdesigns.com, www.peerlessdisplay.com
Myson - Rettig UK Ltd, Eastern Avenue, Team Valley, Gateshead, Tyne & Wear. NE11 0PG tel:(0845) 402 34 34, fax:(0191) 491 7568. sales@myson.co.uk, www.myson.co.uk

N

N R Burnett Ltd - West Carr Lane, Hull, Humb. HU7 0AW tel:(01482) 830870, fax:(01482) 830887. kevinprowse@nrburnett.co.uk, www.nrburnett.co.uk
Naco - Swegon Air Management, Stourbridge Road, Bridgenorth, Shropshire. WV15 5BB tel:(01746) 761921, fax:(01746) 766450. sales@naco.co.uk, www.naco.co.uk
National Access & Scaffolding Confederation (NASC) - 4th Floor, 12 Bridewell Place, London. EC4V 6AP tel:(0207) 822 7400, fax:(0207) 822 7401. enquiries@nasc.org.uk, www.nasc.org.uk
National Association of Shopfitters - NAS House, 411 Limpsfield Road, Warlingham, Surrey. CR6 9HA tel:(01883) 624961, fax:(01883) 626841. enquiries@shopfitters.org, www.shopfitters.org
National Council of Master Thatchers Associations - Foxhill, Hillside, South Brent, Devon. TQ10 9AU tel:(07000) 781909. gandewakley@btinternet.com, www.ncmta.co.uk
National Domelight Company - Pyramid House, 52 Guildford Road, Lightwater, Surrey. GU18 5SD tel:(01276) 451555, fax:(01276) 450 610. info@nationaldomes.com, www.nationaldomelightcompany.co.uk
National Federation of Builders - B & CE Building, Manor Royal, Crawley, West Sussex. RH10 9QP tel:(08450) 578 160, fax:(08450) 578 161. national@builders.org.uk, www.builders.org.uk
National Federation of Demolition Contractors - Resurgam House, Paradise, Hemel Hempstead, Hertfordshire. HP2 4TF tel:(01442) 217144, fax:(01442) 218268. info@demolition-nfdc.com, www.demolition-nfdc.com
National Federation of Roofing Contractors Ltd., The - Roofing House, 31 Worship Street, London. EC2A 2DY tel:(020) 7638 7663, fax:(020) 7256 2125. info@nfrc.co.uk, www.nfrc.co.uk
National House Building Council - NHBC House, Davy Avenue, Knowlhill, Milton Keynes, Bucks. MK5 8FP tel:(0844) 633 1000, fax:(0908) 747 255. cssupport@nhbc.co.uk, www.nhbc.co.uk
National Inspection Council for Electrical Installation Contracting - Warwick House, Houghton Hall Park, Houghton Regis, Dunstable. LU5 5ZX tel:(0870) 013 0382, fax:(01582) 539090. enquiries@niceic.com, www.niceic.org.uk
National Insulation Association Ltd - 3 Vimy Court, Vimy Road, Leighton Buzzard, Bedfordshire. LU7 1FG tel:(08451) 636363, fax:(01525) 854918. info@nia-uk.org, www.nia-uk.org
National Starch & Chemical Ltd - Wexham Road, Slough, Berks. SL2 5DS tel:(01753) 533494, fax:(01753) 501241. Joyce.Corbett@nstarch.com, www.nationalstarch.com
Nationwide Premixed Ltd - 22 Thorne Way, Woolsbridge Industrial Park, Three Legged Cross, Wimborne, Dorset. BH21 6SP tel:(01202) 824700, fax:(01202) 827757. sales@nationwidedirect.uk.com, www.nationwidepremixed.com
Navtec - Southmoor Lane, Havent, Hants. PO9 1JJ tel:(023) 9248 5777, fax:(023) 92485770. navnor@navtec.net, www.navtec.net
Naylor Drainage Ltd - Clough Green, Cawthorne, Nr Barnsley, S. Yorks. S75 4AD tel:(01226) 790591, fax:(01226) 790531. info@naylor.co.uk, www.naylor.co.uk
NBS - The Old Post Office, St. Nicholas Street, Newcastle-upon-Tyne. NE1 1RH tel:(0191) 244 5500, fax:(0191) 232 5714. info@thenbs.com, www.thenbs.com
Nederman Filtration Ltd - Limewood Approach, Seacroft, Leeds. LS14 1NG tel:(0113) 273 9400, fax:(0113) 265 0735. info@dantherm.com, www.dantherm.com
Nederman UK - PO Box 503, 91 Walton Summit, Bamber Bridge, Preston. PR5 8AF tel:(01772) 334721, fax:(01772) 315273. info@nederman.co.uk, www.nederman.co.uk
Nendle Acoustic Company Ltd - Tacitus House, 153 High Street, Aldershot, Hants. GU11 1TT tel:(01252) 344222, fax:(01252) 333782. sales@nendle.co.uk, www.nendle.co.uk
Nenplas - Airfield Industrial Estate, Ashbourne, Derbys. DE6 1HA tel:(01335) 347300, fax:(01335) 340271. enquiries@nenplas.co.uk, www.nenplas.co.uk
Neopost Ltd - Neopost House, South Street, Romford, Essex. RM1 2AR tel:(01708) 746000, fax:(01708) 714050. www.neopost.co.uk
Neptune Outdoor Furniture Ltd - Thompsons Lane, Marwell, Nr Winchester, Hants. SO21 1JH tel:(01962) 777799, fax:(01962) 777723. sales@nofl.co.uk, www.nofl.co.uk
Neslo Interiors - 10 Woodway Court, Thursby Road, Wirral International Business Park, Bromborough, Wirral, Merseyside. CH62 3PR tel:(0151) 334 9326, fax:(0151) 334 0668. steve.lamb@neslointeriors.co.uk, www.neslopartitioning.co.uk
Ness Furniture Ltd - Croxdale, Durham. DH6 5HT tel:(01388) 816109, fax:(01388) 812416. sales@nessfurniture.co.uk, www.nessfurniture.co.uk
NET LED Limited - 18-21 Evolution Business Park, Milton Road, Impington, Cambridge. CB24 9NG tel:(01223) 851505, fax:(01223) 851506. jack@netled.co.uk, www.netled.co.uk
Nevill Long - Brunswick House, 1 Deighton Close, Wetherby, West Yorkshire. LS22 7GZ tel:(0116) 2570670, fax:(0116) 2570044. info@nevilllong.co.uk, www.nevilllong.co.uk
New Forest Ceilings Ltd - 61-65 High Street, Totton, Southampton. SO40 9HL tel:(023) 80869510, fax:(023) 80862244. nfcl@btconnect.com, www.newforestceilings.co.uk
New Haden Pumps Ltd - Draycott Cross Road, Cheadle, Stoke on Trent, Staffs. ST10 2NW tel:(01538) 757900, fax:(01538) 757999. info@nhpumps.com, www.nhpumps.com
Neway Doors Ltd - 89-91 Rolfe Street, Smethwick, Warley, W. Midlands. B66 2AY tel:(0121) 558 6406, fax:(0121) 558 7140. sales@priory-group.co.uk, www.priory-group.co.uk
Newdawn & Sun Ltd - Springfield Business Park, Arden Forest Inustrial Estate, Alcester, Warwicks. B49 6EY tel:(01789) 764444, fax:(01789) 400164. sales@livingspaceltd.co.uk, www.newdawn-sun.co.uk
Newey Ceilings - 1-4, South Uxbridge St, Burton-on-Trent, Staffs. DE14 3LD tel:(01865) 337200, fax:(01865) 337201. info@neweyceilings.co.uk, www.neweyceilings.co.uk
Newlay Cast Stone Limited t/as Procter Cast Stone - Isabella Road, Garforth, Leeds, Yorks. LS25 8DY tel:(01132) 863 329. james.mcvicar@proctercaststone.co.uk, www.proctercaststone.co.uk
NewTeam Ltd - Brunel Road, Earlstrees Industrial Estate, Corby, Northants. NN17 4JW tel:(01536) 409222, fax:(01536) 400144. cjennings@bristan.com, www.newteamshowers.com
Newton & Frost Fencing Ltd - Downsview Yard, North Corner, Horam, Heathfield, East Sussex. TN21 9HJ tel:(01435) 813 535, fax:(01435) 813 687. enquiries@nffltd.co.uk, www.nffltd.co.uk
Newton John & Co Ltd - Newton House, 17-20 Sovereign Way, Tonbridge. TN9 1RH tel:(01732) 360 095. info@newton-membranes.co.uk, www.newton-membranes.co.uk
Nexans UK Ltd - Nexans House, Chesney Wold, Bleak Hall, Milton Keynes, Buckinghamshire. MK6 1LA tel:(01908) 250848, fax:(01908) 250851. wholesale.uk@nexans.com, www.nexans.co.uk
Nicholls & Clarke Ltd - Niclar House, Shoreditch High Street, London. E1 6PE tel:(020) 7247 5432, fax:(020) 7247 7738. info@nichollsandclarke.com, www.nichollsandclarke.com/
Nicholson Plastics Ltd - Riverside Road, Kirkfieldbank, Lanarkshire. ML11 9JS tel:(01555) 664316, fax:(01555) 663056. sales@nicholsonplastics.co.uk, www.nicholsonplastics.co.uk
Nico Manufacturing Ltd - 109 Oxford Road, Clacton on Sea, Essex. CO15 3TJ tel:(01255) 422333, fax:(01255) 432909. sales@nico.co.uk, www.nico.co.uk

N (con't)

Nilfisk Advance Ltd - Nilfisk House, Bowerbank Way, Gilwilly Ind Est, Penrith, Cumbria. IP33 3SR tel:(01768) 868995, fax:(01768) 864713. mail.uk@nilfisk.com, www.nilfisk.co.uk

Nilfisk Limited - Bowerbank Way, Gilwilly Industrial Estate, Penrith, Cumbria. CA11 9BN tel:(01768) 868995, fax:(01768) 864713. mail.uk@nilfisk.com, www.nilfisk.co.uk

Nimlok Ltd - Booth Drive, Park Farm, Wellingborough, Northants. NN8 6NL tel:(01933) 409409, fax:(01933) 409451. info@nimlok.co.uk, www.nimlok.co.uk

Nittan (UK) Ltd - Hipley Street, Old Woking, Surrey. GU22 9LQ tel:(01483) 769555, fax:(01483) 756686. sales@nittan.co.uk, www.nittan.co.uk

NMC (UK) Ltd - Unit B, Tafarnaubach Industrial Estate, Tredegar, S. Wales. NP22 3AA tel:(01495) 713266, fax:(01495) 713277. enquiries@nmc-uk.com, www.nmc-uk.com

Norbord - Station Road, Cowie, Sterlingshire. FK7 7BQ tel:(01786) 812921, fax:(01786) 817143. info@norbord.com, www.norbord.com

North Herts Asphalte (Roofing) Ltd - 70 Hawthorn Hill, Letchworth Garden City, Herts. SG6 4HQ tel:(01462) 434 877, fax:(01462) 421539. nhasphalte@gmail.com, www.northherts-asphalteroofing.co.uk

Northcot Brick Ltd - Blockley, Nr Moreton in Marsh, Glos. GL56 9LH tel:(01386) 700551, fax:(01386) 700852. info@northcotbrick.co.uk, www.northcotbrick.co.uk

Northern Joinery Ltd - Daniel Street, Whitworth, Rochdale, Lancs. OL12 8DA tel:(01706) 852345, fax:(01706) 853114. office@northernjoinery.co.uk, www.northernjoinery.co.uk

Northgate Solar Controls - PO Box 200, Barnet, Herts. EN4 9EW tel:(020) 8441 4545, fax:(020) 8441 4888. enquiries@northgateuk.com, www.northgateuk.com

Northwest Pre-cast Ltd - Holmefield Works, Garstang Road, Pilling, Preston. PR3 6AN tel:(01253) 790444, fax:(01253) 790085. nwprecast@talk21.com, https://nwprecast.com/

Norton Diamond Products - Unit 2, Meridian West, Meridian Business Park, Leicester, Leics. LE3 2WX tel:(0116) 263 2302, fax:(0116) 282 7292. sales.nlx@saint-gobain.com, www.norton-diamond.com

Norton Engineering Alloys Co Ltd - Norton Grove Industrial Estate, Norton, Malton, N. Yorks. YO17 9HQ tel:(01653) 695721, fax:(01653) 600418. sales@neaco.co.uk, www.neaco.co.uk

Norwegian Log Buildings Ltd - 230 London Road, Reading, Berks. RG6 1AH tel:(0118) 9669236, fax:(0118) 9660456. sales@norwegianlog.co.uk, www.norwegianlog.co.uk

Notcutt Ltd - Homeward Farm, Newark Lane, Ripley, Surrey. GU23 6DJ tel:(020) 8977 2252, fax:(020) 8977 6423. sales@notcutt.com, www.notcutt.com

Nova Group Ltd - Norman Road, Board Heath, Altrincham, Cheshire. WA14 4EN tel:(0161) 6139600, fax:(0161) 926 8405. sales@novagroup.co.uk, www.windows-conservatories.co.uk

Novaglaze Limited - Queens Mill Road, Lockwood, Huddersfield, W. Yorks. HD1 3PG tel:(01484) 517 010, fax:(01484) 517 050. sales@novaglaze.co.uk, www.novaglaze.co.uk

Novoferm Europe Ltd - Unit 5-9 North Luton Industrial Estate, Sedgewick Road, Luton, GB. LU4 9DT tel:(0800) 656 96 66, fax:(01582) 344833. info@novoferm.co.uk, http://novoferm.co.uk/

NRG Fabrications - Harlestone Firs, Harlestone Road, Northampton, Northants. NN5 6UJ tel:(01604) 580022, fax:(01604) 580033. sales@thewildegroup.co.uk, www.thewildegroup.co.uk

NuAir Ltd - Western Industrial Estate, Caerphilly, M. Glam. CF83 1NA tel:(029) 20 858200, fax:(029) 20 887033. info@nuairegroup.com, www.nuaire.co.uk

NuLite Ltd - Unit 51 Hutton Close, Crownther Industrial Estate, District 3, Washington, Tyne & Wear. NE38 0AH tel:(0191) 419 1111, fax:(0191) 419 1123. sales@nulite-ltd.co.uk, www.nulite-ltd.co.uk

Nullifire Ltd - Torrington Avenue, Coventry. CV4 9TJ tel:(024) 7685 5000, fax:(024) 7646 9547. protect@nullifire.com, www.nullifire.com

Nu-Swift International Ltd - Elland, W. Yorks. HX5 9DS tel:(01422) 372852, fax:(01422) 379569. customer.service@nuswift.co.uk, www.nu-swift.co.uk

Nu-Way Ltd - Ten Acres, Berry Hill Industrial Estate, Droitwich, Worcestershire. WR9 9AQ tel:(01905) 794331, fax:(01905) 794017. info@nu-way.co.uk, www.nu-way.co.uk/

O

Oakdale (Contracts) Ltd - Walkerville Industrial Estate, Catterick Garrison, N. Yorks. DL9 4SA tel:(01748) 834184, fax:(01748) 833003. sales@oakdalecontracts.co.uk, www.oakdalecontracts.co.uk

Oakleaf Reproductions Ltd - Unit A Melbourn Mills, Chesham Street, Keighley, W. Yorks. BD21 4LG tel:(01535) 663274, fax:(01535) 661951. sales@oakleaf.co.uk, www.oakleaf.co.uk

Oakwood Property Solutions

34 Dulverton Drive, Furzton, Milton Keynes, Buckinghamshire. MK4 1DF tel:(07879) 417 061. info@oakwoodps.co.uk, www.oakwoodps.co.uk

O'Connor Fencing Limited - Whitehaven Commercial Park, Moresby Parks, Whitehaven, Cumbria. CA28 8YD tel:(01946) 693983, fax:(01946) 693984. enquiries@oconorfencing.co.uk, http://oconnorfencing.co.uk

Ogilvie Construction Ltd - Pirnhall Works, 200 Glasgow Road, Whins of Milton, Stirling, Stirlingshire. FK7 8ES tel:(01786) 812273, fax:(01786) 816287. enq@ogilvie.co.uk

Ogley Bros Ltd - Allen Street, Smithfield, Sheffield. S3 7AS tel:(0114) 276 8948, fax:(0114) 275 8948. ogleybrothers@btconnnect.com, https://www.ogleybrothers.co.uk/

Olby H E & Co Ltd - 229-313 Lewisham High Street, London. SE13 6NW tel:(020) 8690 3401, fax:(020) 8690 1408. mark@heolby.co.uk

Oldham Lighting Ltd - 41 Church Street, Birmingham. B3 2RT tel:(0131) 452 2024. info@oldhamlighting.co.uk, www.oldhamlighting.com

Olley & Sons Ltd, C - Iberia House, 36, Southgate Avenue, Mildenhall, Suffolk. IP28 7AT tel:(01638) 712076, fax:(01638) 717304. olley-cork@btconnect.com, www.olleycork.co.uk

Omeg Ltd - Imberhorne Industrial Estate, East Grinstead, W. Sussex. RH19 1RJ tel:(01342) 410420, fax:(01342) 316253. sales@omeg.co.uk, www.omeg.co.uk

Omnis - Unit 62, Blackpole Trading Estate Wes, Worcester. WR3 8JZ tel:(01905) 750500. enquiries@omnisexteriors.com, www.omnisexteriors.com

Onduline Building Products Ltd - Dawson House, 5 Jewry Street, London. EC3N 2EX tel:(020) 7727 0533, fax:(020) 7792 1390. enquiries@onduline.net, www.onduline.co.uk

Opella Ltd - Twyford Road, Rotherwas Industrial Estate, Hereford, Herefordshire. HR2 6JR tel:(01432) 357331, fax:(01432) 264014. sales@opella.co.uk, www.opella.co.uk

Optelma Lighting Ltd - 14 Napier Court, The Science Park, Abingdon, Oxon. OX14 3NB tel:(01235) 553769, fax:(01235) 523005. sales@optelma.co.uk, www.optelma.co.uk

Optex (Europe) Ltd - Clivemont Road, Cordwallis Park, Maidenhead, Berks. SL6 7BU tel:(01628) 631000, fax:(01628) 636311. sales@optex-europe.com, www.optex-europe.com/

Optima - Courtyard House, West End Road, High Wycombe, Buckinghamshire. HP11 2QB tel:(01494) 492600, fax:(01494) 492800. info@optimasystems.com, www.optimasystems.com

Opus 4 Ltd - Orchard House, Orchard Business Centre, North Farm Road, Tunbridge Wells, Kent. TN2 3DY tel:(01892) 515157, fax:(01892) 515417. hello@opus-4.com, www.opus-4.com

Orbik Electrics Ltd - Orbik House, Northgate Way, Aldridge, Walsall. WS9 8TX tel:(01922) 743515, fax:(01922) 743173. uksales@orbik.co.uk, www.orbik.co.uk

Orchard Street Furniture - 119 The Street, Crowmarsh & Gifford, Nr. Waringford, Oxon. OX10 8EF tel:(01491) 642123, fax:(01491) 642126. sales@orchardstreet.co.uk, www.orchardstreet.co.uk

Ordnance Survey - Explorer House, Adanac Drive, Southampton. SO16 0AS tel:(03456) 050505, fax:(03450) 990494. customerservices@ordnancesurvey.co.uk, www.ordnancesurvey.co.uk

Ormandy Rycroft Engineering - Duncombe Road, Bradford, W. Yorks. BD8 9TB tel:(01274) 490911, fax:(01274) 498580. sales@ormandygroup.com, https://ormandygroup.com

OSF Ltd - Unit 6, The Four Ashes Industrial Estate, Station Road, Four Ashes, Wolverhampton, W. Midlands. WV10 7DB tel:(01902) 798080, fax:(01902) 794750. sales@osfltd.com, www.osfltd.com

OSMO UK - Unit 24, Anglo Business Park, Smeaton Close, Aylesbury, Bucks. HP19 8UP tel:(01296) 481220, fax:(01296) 424090. info@osmouk.com, www.osmouk.com

Osram Ltd - Customer Service Centre, Neills Road, Bold Industrial Park, St. Helens. WA9 4XG tel:(01744) 812221, fax:(01744) 831900. csc@osram.co.uk, www.osram.co.uk

Outokumpu - Europa Link, Sheffield, S. Yorks. S9 1TZ tel:(01142) 613701, fax:(0114) 243 1277. PSCSales.Sheffield@outokumpu.com, www.outokumpu.com

Outokumpu Stainless Ltd - PO Box 161, Europa Link, Sheffield, Yorkshire. S9 1TZ tel:(0114) 261 5210. sales.bar@outokumpu.com, www.outokumpu.com

OWA UK Ltd - 10 Perth Trading Estate, Perth Avenue, Slough, Berkshire. SL1 4XX tel:(01753) 552489. sales@owa-ceilings.co.uk, www.owa-ceilings.co.uk

Owen Slate Services Ltd - 2 Tanysgrafell, Coed y Parc, Bethesda, Gwynedd. LL57 4AJ tel:(01248) 605575, fax:(01248) 605574. Sales@owens-slate.com, www.owens-slate.com

Owens Slate Services Ltd - 2 Tanysgrafell, Coed y Parc, Bethesda, Gwynedd. LL57 4AJ tel:(01248) 605575, fax:(01248) 605574. sales@owens-slate.com, www.owens-slate.com

P

P+L Systems Ltd - Sterling House, Grimbald Crag Close, Knaresborough, N. Yorks. HG5 9PJ tel:(0800) 988 5359, fax:(01423) 863497. info@pandlsystems.com, www.pandlsystems.com

P4 Limited - 1 Wymans Way, Fakenham, Norfolk. NR21 8NT tel:(01328) 850 555, fax:(01328) 850 559. info@p4fastel.co.uk, www.p4fastel.co.uk

Pac International Ltd - 1 Park Gate Close, Bredbury, Stockport, Gt Man. SK6 2SZ tel:(0161) 494 1331, fax:(0161) 430 9658. customerservices@stanleysecurityproducts.com, www.pac.co.uk

Package Products Ltd - Little Green Works, Collyhurst Road, Manchester. M40 7RT tel:(0161) 205 4181, fax:(0161) 203 4678. sales@packagingproducts.co.uk, www.packagingproducts.co.uk

Painting & Decorating Association - 32 Coton Road, Nuneaton, Warwicks. CV11 5TW tel:(024) 7635 3776, fax:(024) 7635 4513. info@paintingdecoratingassociation.co.uk, www.paintingdecoratingassociation.co.uk

PAL Extrusions - Darlaston Road, Wednesbury, W. Midlands. WS10 7TN tel:(0121) 526 4048, fax:(0121) 526 4658. sales@palextrusions.co.uk, www.palextrusions.co.uk

Palladio Stone - Station House, Station Road, Tisbury, Salisbury. SP3 6JT tel:(01747) 871546, fax:(01747) 871547. admin@palladiostone.com, www.palladiostone.com

Panasonic UK Ltd - Maxis 2, Western Rd, Bracknell, Berks. RG12 1RT tel:(01344) 862444, fax:(01344) 853704. www.panasonic.co.uk

Panel & Louvre Co Ltd - 49-61 Jodrell Street, Nuneaton, Warwickshire. CV11 5EG tel:(024) 7518 7518, fax:(01933) 228580. info@palcouk.com, www.palcouk.com

Panel Agency Limited - Maple House, 5 Over Minnis, New Ash Green, Kent. DA3 8JA tel:(01474) 872578, fax:(01474) 872426. sales@panelagency.com, www.panelagency.com

Panel Systems Ltd - 3-9 Welland Close, Parkwood Industrial Estate, Rutland Road, Sheffield, S. Yorks. S3 9QY tel:(0114) 275 2881, fax:(0114) 278 6840. sales@panelsystems.co.uk, www.panelsystems.co.uk

Paragon by Heckmondwike - Farfield Park, Manvers, Wath-Upon-Dearne, Rotherham. S63 5DB tel:(0845) 601 0431, fax:(0800) 731 4521. sales@paragon-carpets.co.uk, www.pbyh.co.uk

Parker Plant Ltd - PO Box 146, Canon Street, Leicester. LE4 6HD tel:(0116) 266 5999, fax:(0116) 268 1254. sales@parkerplant.com, www.parkerplant.com

Parklines Building Ltd - Gala House, 3 Raglan Road, Edgbaston, Birmingham. B5 7RA tel:(0121) 446 6030, fax:(0121) 446 5991. sales@parklines.co.uk, www.parklines.co.uk

Paroc Panel Systems Uk Ltd - Stoney Lane, Rainhill, Prescot, Merseyside. L35 9LL tel:(0151) 4266555, fax:(0151) 426 6622. technical.insulation@paroc.com, www.paroc.com

Parsons Brothers Gates - 5 Prior Wharf, Harris Business Park, Bromsgrove, W. Midlands. B60 4FG tel:(01527) 576355, fax:(01527) 579419. gates@parsonsbrothers.com, www.parsonsbrothers.com

Parthos UK Ltd - 1 The Quadrant, Howarth Road, Maidenhead, Berks. SL6 1AP tel:(01628) 773 353, fax:(01628) 773 363. info@parthos.co.uk, www.parthos.co.uk

Parts Centre - The Wolseley Center, Harrison Way, Spa Park, Royal Leamington Spa. CV31 3HH tel:(01282) 834400. customerservices@wolseley.co.uk, www.partscenter.co.uk

Paslode - Diamond Point, Fleming Way, Crawley, West Sussex. RH10 9DP tel:(0800) 652 9260. technical@itwcp.co.uk, www.paslode.co.uk

Passivent Ltd - North Frith Oasts, Ashes Lane, Hadlow, Kent. TN11 9QU tel:(01732) 850 770, fax:(01732) 850 949. projects@passivent.com, www.passivent.com

PCE Instruments UK Ltd - Units 11 South Point, Ensign Way, Southampton, Hampshire. SO31 4RF tel:(02380) 987030, fax:(02380) 987039. info@industrial-needs.com, www.pce-instruments.com/english/

PCT Group - 37 Dalsetter Avenue, Glasgow. G15 8TE tel:(0141) 944 4000, fax:(0141) 944 9000. sales@pctgroup.co.uk, www.pctgroup.co.uk

Pearce Construction (Barnstaple) Limited - Pearce House, Brannam Crescent, Roundswell Business Park, Barnstaple, Devon. EX31 3TD tel:(01271) 345261, fax:(01271) 852134. buildit@pearceconstruction.co.uk, www.pearcebarnstaple.co.uk

Pearce Security Systems - Ensign House, Green Lane, Felling, Gateshead, Tyne & Wear. NE10 0QH tel:(0191) 438 1177, fax:(0191) 495 0227. sales@ensig.co.uk, www.ensig.co.uk

Pearce Signs Ltd - Unit 28, Regent Trade Park, Barnwell Lane, Gosport, Hampshire. PO13 0EQ tel:(01329) 238015. info@pearcesigns.com, www.pearcegroup.com

Pearman Fencing - Greystone Yard, Notting Hill Way, Lower Weare, Axbridge, Somerset. BS26 2JU tel:(01934) 733380, fax:(01934) 733398. pearmanfencing@btconnect.com, www.premier-pearman.co.uk

Pedley Furniture International Ltd - Shirehill Works, Saffron Walden, Essex. CB11 3AL tel:(01799) 522461, fax:(01799) 513403. sales@pedley.com, www.pedley.com

Pegler Ltd - St Cathrines Avenue, Doncaster, S. Yorks. DN4 8DF tel:(01302) 560560, fax:(01302) 367661. uk.sales@pegleryorkshire.co.uk, www.pegler.co.uk

Pegson Ltd - 200 Coalisland, Dungannon, Co. Tyrone. BT71 4DR tel:+44 2887718500. sales@bl-pegson.com, www.powerscreen.com/en

PEL Services Limited - Belvue Business Centre, Belvue Road, Northolt, Middx. UB5 5QQ tel:(020) 8839 2100, fax:(020) 8841 1948. pel@pel.co.uk, www.pel.co.uk

Pembury Fencing Ltd - Unit 2 Church Farm, Collier Street, Marden, Tonbridge, Kent. TN12 9RT tel:(0870) 242 3707. sonia@pemburygroup.co.uk, www.pemburygroup.co.uk

Pentair Thermal Management - 3 Rutherford Road, Stephenson Industrial Estate, Washington, Tyne & Wear. NE37 3HX tel:(0800) 969013, fax:(0800) 968624. sales@pentairthermal.co.uk, www.pentairthermal.co.uk

PERI Ltd - Market Harborough Road, Clifton Upon Dunsmore, Rugby, Warwicks. CV23 0AN tel:(01788) 861646. info@peri.ltd.uk, www.peri.ltd.uk

Permali Deho Ltd - Unit 4, Permali Park, Bristol Road, Gloucester, Glos. GL1 5SR tel:(01452) 411 607, fax:(01452) 411 617. sales@permalideho.co.uk, www.permalideho.co.uk

Perman Briggs Ltd - 224 Cheltenham Road, Longlevens, Gloucester. GL2 0JW tel:(01452) 524192, fax:(01452) 309879. sales@pearmanbriggs.co.uk, www.pearmanbriggs.co.uk

Permanoid Ltd - Hulme Hall Road, Manchester. M40 8HH tel:(0161) 205 6161, fax:(0161) 205 9325. sales@permanoid.co.uk, www.permanoid.co.uk

PermaRock Products Ltd - Jubilee Drive, Loughborough, Leicestershire. LE11 5TW tel:(01509) 262924, fax:(01509) 230063. permarock@permarock.com, www.permarock.com

Petal Postforming Limited - Gibbs House, Kennel Ride, Ascot, Berkshire. SL5 7NT tel:(01344) 893990, fax:(01344) 893 930. info@petal.co.uk, www.petal.co.uk

Peter Cox Ltd - Aniseed Park, Broadway Business Park, Chadderton, Manchester. OI9 9XA tel:(0800) 030 4701, fax:(020) 8642 0677. headoffice@petercox.com, www.petercox.com

Petrochem Carless - Cedar Court, Guildford Road, Leatherhead, Surrey. KT22 9RX tel:(01372) 360 000, fax:(01372) 380 400. de@h-c-s-group.com, www.petrochemcarless.com

PFC Corofil - Units 3 & 4 King George Trading Estate, Davis Road, Chessington, Surrey. KT9 1TT tel:(0208) 391 0533, fax:(0208) 391 2723. sales@pfc-corofil.com, www.pfc-corofil.com

PFP Electrical Products Ltd - Fortnum Close, Mackadown Lane, Kitts Green, Birmingham. B33 0LB tel:(0121) 783 7161, fax:(0121) 783 5717. sales@petrel-ex.co.uk, www.pfp-elec.co.uk

PHI Group Ltd - Montis Court, Bouncers Lane, Cheltenham, Glos. GL52 8JG tel:(01242) 707600. southern@phigroup.co.uk, www.phigroup.co.uk

Philips Lighting - Philips Centre, Guildford Business Park, Guildford, Surrey. GU2 8XH tel:(08706) 010 101, fax:(01483) 575534. signify_press_office@signify.com, www.lighting.philips.com

Philips Lighting Solutions - Philips Centre, Guildford Business Park, Guildford, Surrey. GU2 8XH tel:(020) 8751 6514, fax:(020) 8890 438. signify_press_office@signify.com, www.lighting.philips.co.uk

Phoenix Engineering Co Ltd, The - Phoenix Works, Combe Street, Chard, Somerset. TA20 1JE tel:(01460) 63531, fax:(01460) 67388. sales@phoenixeng.co.uk, www.phoenixeng.co.uk

Phoenix Lifting Systems Ltd - Unit 5B/C Castlegate Business Park, Old Sarum, Salisbury, Wiltshire. SP4 6QX tel:(01722) 410144, fax:(01722) 331814. sales@phoenix.co.uk, www.phoenixlifts.co.uk

Phoenix Scales Ltd - 34 Oldbury Road, West Bromwich, West Midlands. B70 9ED tel:(0845) 601 7464, fax:(0845) 602 4205. sales@phoenixscales.co.uk, www.phoenixscales.co.uk

Photofabrication Limited - 14 Cromwell Road, St Neots, Cambs. PE19 2HP tel:(01480) 226 699, fax:(01480) 475801. sales@photofab.co.uk, www.photofab.co.uk

PHS Group plc - Block B, Western Industrial Estate, Caerphilly. CF83 1XH tel:(02920) 851 000, fax:(02920) 863 288. Enquiries@phs.co.uk, www.phs.co.uk

P (con't)

Pickerings Ltd - Globe Elevator Works, PO Box 19, Stoke-on-Tees, Cleveland. TS20 2AD tel:(01642) 607161, fax:(01642) 677638. info@pickeringslifts.co.uk, www.pickerings.co.uk

Pike Signals Ltd - Equipment Works, Alma Street, Birmingham, W. Midlands. B19 2RS tel:(0121) 359 4034, fax:(0121) 333 3167. enquiries@pikesignals.com, www.pikesignals.com

Pilkington Birmingham - Nechells Park Road, Nechells, Birmingham. B7 5NQ tel:(0121) 326 5300, fax:(0121) 328 4277. pilkington@respond.uk.com, www.Pilkington.com

Pilkington Plyglass - Cotes Park, Somercotes, Derbys. DE55 4PL tel:(01773) 520000, fax:(01773) 520052. pilkington@respond.uk.com, www.pilkington.com

Pilkington UK Ltd - Prescot Road, St. Helens, Merseyside. WA10 3TT tel:(01744) 692000, fax:(01744) 613049. pilkington@respond.uk.com, www.pilkington.co.uk

Pims Pumps Ltd - 22 Invincible Rd Ind Est, Farnborough, Hants. GU14 7QU tel:(01252) 513366, fax:(01252) 516404. sales@pimsgroup.co.uk, www.pimsgroup.co.uk

Pipe Centre - The Wolseley Center, Harrison Way, Spa Park, Royal Leamington Spa. CV31 3HH tel:(08701) 600909. customerservices@wolseley.co.uk, www.pipecenter.co.uk

Pitacs Ltd - Bradbourne Point, Bradbourne Drive, Tillbrook, Milton Keynes, Buckinghamshire. MK7 8AT tel:(01908) 271155, fax:(01908) 640017. info@pitacs.com, www.pitacs.com

Pitchmastic PmB Ltd - Panama House, 184 Attercliffe Road, Sheffield, S. Yorks. S4 7WZ tel:(0114) 270 0100, fax:(0114) 276 8782. info@pitchmasticpmb.co.uk, www.pitchmasticpmb.co.uk

Pittsburgh Corning (United Kingdom) Limited - 31-35 Kirby Street, Hatton Garden, London. EC1N 8TE tel:(020) 7492 1731, fax:(020) 7492 1730. info@foamglas.co.uk, www.foamglas.co.uk

Pland - Lower Wortley Ring Road, Leeds. LS12 6AA tel:(0113) 263 4184, fax:(0113) 231 0560. sales@plandstainless.co.uk, www.plandstainless.co.uk

Pland Stainless Ltd - Lower Wortley Ring Road, Leeds, W. Yorks. LS12 6AA tel:(0113) 263 4184, fax:(0113) 231 0560. sales@plandstainless.co.uk, www.plandstainless.co.uk

Plansee Tizit (UK) Ltd - 3 Lidstone Court,george Green, Slough. SL3 6AG tel:(01753) 576 959, fax:(01753) 577 591. uk@plansee.com, www.plansee.com

Plascoat Systems Ltd - Trading Estate, Farnham, Surrey. GU90 0NY tel:(01252) 733777, fax:(01252) 721250. sales@plascoat.com, www.plascoat.com

Plasmor - PO Box 44, Womersley Road, Knottingley, W. Yorks. WF11 0DN tel:(01977) 673221, fax:(01977) 607071. knott@plasmor.co.uk, www.plasmor.co.uk

Plastal (SBP Ltd) - Unit D1-D4, 4 Stafford Park, Telford, Shropshire. TF3 3BA tel:(01952) 205000, fax:(01952) 290956. estimating@plastal.co.uk, www.plastal.co.uk

Plastic Coatings Ltd - Woodbridge Meadow, Guildford, Surrey. GU1 1BG tel:(01483) 531155, fax:(01483) 533534. enquiries@plastic-coatings.com, www.plasticcoatings.co.uk

Plastic Extruders Ltd - Russell Gardens, Wickford, Essex. SS11 8DN tel:(01268) 735231, fax:(01268) 560027. sales@plastex.co.uk, www.plastex.co.uk

Platform Lift Company Ltd, The - Millside House, Anton Business Park, Andover, Hampshire. SP10 2RW tel:(01256) 896000. info@platformliftco.co.uk, www.platformliftco.co.uk/

Platonoff & Harris Ltd - Ambler View, Marsh Lane, Stanstead Abbotts, Ware, Herts. SG12 8HH tel:(01920) 449449. info@platonoffharris.co.uk, www.platonoffharris.co.uk

Playtop Licensing Limited - Brunel House, Jessop Way, Newark, Notts. NG24 2ER tel:(01636) 642461, fax:(01636) 642478. sales@playtop.com, www.playtop.com

PLC Hunwick Ltd - The Foundry, Factory Road, Sandycroft, Chester. CH52QJ tel:(01244) 521 860, fax:(Fax:) 1244 521 862. sales@durablecast.com, www.lightning-crushers.co.uk

Plumb Centre - The Wolseley Center, Harrison Way, Spa Park, Royal Leamington Spa. CV31 3HH tel:(0870) 16 22557. customerservices@wolseley.co.uk, www.plumbcenter.co.uk

Polyflor Ltd - PO Box 3, Radcliffe New Road, Whitefield, Gt Man. M45 7NR tel:(0161) 767 1122, fax:(0161) 767 1128. info@polyflor.com, www.polyflor.com

Polypipe Building Products - Broomhouse Lane, Edlington, Doncaster. DN12 1ES tel:(01709) 770 000, fax:(01709) 770 001. info@polypipe.com, www.polypipe.com/building-products

Polypipe Building Products Ltd - Broomhouse Lane, Edlington, Doncaster, S. Yorks. DN12 1ES tel:(01709) 770000, fax:(01709) 770001. info@polypipe.com, www.polypipe.com

Polypipe Civils - Unit 1A, Charnwood Business Park, North Road, Loughborough, Leics. LE11 1LE tel:(01509) 615100, fax:(01509) 610215. civils@polypipe.com, www.polypipe.com/civils

Polypipe Terrain Ltd - College Road, Aylesford, Maidstone, Kent. ME20 7PJ tel:(01622) 795200, fax:(01622) 716796. commercialenquiries@polypipe.com, www.polypipe.com

Polypipe Ventilation Ltd - Polypipe, Broomhouse Lane, Doncaster, South Yorkshire. DN12 1ES tel:(01709) 770 000, fax:(01709) 770 001. vent.info@domusventilation.co.uk, http://www.polypipe.com/ventilation

Porcelanosa Group Ltd - Unit 1 – 6, Otterspool Way, Watford, Hertfordshire. WD25 8HL tel:(01923) 831 867, fax:(01923) 691 600. group@porcelanosa.com, www.porcelanosa.co.uk

Portakabin Ltd - Huntington, York. YO32 9PT tel:(01904) 611655, fax:(01904) 611644. solutions@portakabin.com, www.portakabin.com

Portasilo Ltd - New Lane, Huntington, York. YO32 9PR tel:(01904) 624872, fax:(01904) 611760. bulk@portasilo.co.uk, www.portasilo.co.uk

Potter & Soar Ltd - Beaumont Road, Banbury, Oxon. OX16 1SD tel:(01295) 253344, fax:(01295) 272132. potter.soar@btinternet.com, www.wiremesh.co.uk

Poujoulat (UK) Ltd - Unit 1 Quadrum Park, Old Portsmouth Road, Guildford. GU3 1LU tel:(01483) 461 700, fax:(01483) 533 435. sales@poujoulat.co.uk, www.poujoulat.co.uk

Power Plastics Ltd - Station Road, Thirsk, Yorks. YO7 1PZ tel:(01845) 525503, fax:(01845) 525485. info@powerplastics.co.uk, www.powerplastics.com

PPG Protective and Marine Coatings - PPG Architectural Coatings UK Limited, Huddersfield Road, Birstall, Batley, West Yorkshire. WF17 9XA tel:(01924) 354000. pmcsalesuk@ppg.com, www.ppgpmc.com

PRA - Pera Business Park, Nottingham Road, Melton Mowbray, Leicester. LE13 0PB tel:(01664) 501 212. coatings@pra-world.com, www.pra-world.com

Precolor Sales Ltd - Newport Road, Market Drayton, Shropshire. TF9 2AA tel:(01630) 657281, fax:(01630) 655545. enquiries@precolortankdivision.co.uk, www.precolor.co.uk

Premdor - Birthwaite Business Park, Huddersfield Road, Darton, Barnsley, South Yorkshire. S75 5JS tel:(0844) 209 0008, fax:(0844) 371 5333. enquiries@premdor.com, www.premdor.co.uk

Premdor - Birthwaite Business Park, Huddersfield Road, Darton, Barnsley. S75 5JS tel:(0844) 209 0008, fax:(0844) 371 5333. ukmarketing@premdor.com, www.premdor.co.uk

PRE-MET Ltd - Studley Road, Redditch, Worcs. B98 7HJ tel:(01527) 510535, fax:(01527) 500868. sales@pre-met.com, www.lewis-spring.com

President Blinds Ltd - Unit 13 Forest Hill Business Centre, Clyde Vale, Forest Hill, London. SE23 3JF tel:(020) 8699 8885. info@presidentblinds.co.uk, www.presidentblinds.com

Pressalit Care - 100 Longwater Avenue, Green Park, Reading, Berkshire. RG2 6GP tel:(0844) 8806950, fax:(0844) 8806951. uk@pressalit.com, www.pressalitcare.com

Pressmain - 130 Princess Road, Manchester. M16 7BY tel:(01422) 349560, fax:(01274) 483459. info@aquatechpressmain.co.uk, www.aquatechpressmain.co.uk

Pressure Coolers Ltd T/A Maestro Pressure Coolers - 67-69 Nathan Way, London. SE28 0BQ tel:(020) 8302 4035, fax:(020) 8302 8933. sales@maestrointl.co.uk, www.pressurecoolers.co.uk

Presto Engineers Cutting Tools Ltd - Newton Chambers Road, Thorncliffe Park Estate, Chapeltown, Sheffield. S35 2PH tel:(0114) 2578 932, fax:(0114) 2347 446. sales@presto-tools.com, www.presto-tools.co.uk

Preston & Thomas Ltd - 1a Crabtree Close, Gravesend Road, Wrotham, Sevenoaks, Kent. TN15 7JL tel:(01372) 727424. prestonandthomas@hotmail.co.uk, www.prestonandthomas.co.uk

Prestressed Concrete Association - 60 Charles Street, Leicester, Leics. LE1 1FB tel:(0116) 253 6161, fax:(0116) 251 4568. pca@britishprecast.org, www.bridgebeams.org.uk

Prima Security & Fencing Products - Redwell Wood Farm, Ridge Hill, Potters Bar, Herts. EN6 3NA tel:(01707) 663 400, fax:(01707) 661112. sales@sampsonfencing.co.uk, www.sampsonfencing.co.uk

Prima Systems (South East) Ltd - The Old Malt House, Easole Street, Nonington, Dover, Kent. CT15 4HF tel:(01304) 842888, fax:(01304) 842840. halfpennyd@primasystems.co.uk, www.primasystems.co.uk

Priory Castor & Engineering Co Ltd - Aston Hall Road, Aston, Birmingham. B6 7LA tel:(0121) 327 0832, fax:(0121) 322 2123. enquiries@priorycastor.co.uk, www.priorycastor.co.uk

Priory Shutter & Door Co Ltd - 89-91 Rolfe Street, Smethwick, Warley, W. Midlands. B66 2AY tel:(0121) 558 6406, fax:(0121) 558 7140. enquiries@sis-group.co.uk, www.sis-group.co.uk/priory-roller-shutters

Pro Display TM Limited - Unit 5 Shortwood Business Park, Hoyland, Barnsley, South Yorkshire. S74 9LH tel:(0870) 766 8438, fax:(0870) 766 8437. sales@prodisplay.co.uk, www.prodisplay.com

Procter Bros Limited - 4 Beaconsfield Court, Garfirth, Leeds, W. Yorks. LS25 1QH tel:(0113) 287 2777, fax:(0113) 287 1177. enquiries@procterfencing.co.uk, www.fencing-systems.co.uk

Procter Johnson & Co Ltd - Excelsior Works, Castle Park, Evans Street, Flint, Flintshire. CH6 5NT tel:(01352) 732157, fax:(01352) 735530. info@pjcolours.com, www.pjcolours.com

Profab Access Ltd - Riversdale House, Unit C & D Riversdale Road, Carlyon Road Ind Est, Atherstone, Warwicks. CV9 1FA tel:(01827) 718222, fax:(01827) 721092. sales@profabaccess.com, www.profabaccess.com

Pro-Fence (Midlands) - Heathmill Industrial Estate, Heathmill Road, Wolverhampton, W. Midlands. WV5 8AP tel:(01902) 894747. info@pro-fence.co.uk, www.pro-fence.co.uk

Professional Books Limited - Winkworth House, 4 Market Place, Devizes, Wiltshire. SN10 1HT tel:(01380) 820003, fax:(01380) 730218. customerservice@professionalbooks.co.uk, www.professionalbooks.co.uk

Profile 22 Systems Ltd - Stafford Park 6, Telford, Shropshire. TF3 3AT tel:(01952) 290910, fax:(01952) 290460. mail@profile22.co.uk, www.profile22.co.uk

Progress Work Place Solutions - Ground Floor, Taunton House, Waterside Court, Neptune Way, Medway City Estate, Rochester, Kent. ME2 4NZ tel:(01634) 290988, fax:(01634) 291028. info@progressfurnishing.co.uk, www.progressfurnishing.co.uk

Progressive Product Developments Ltd - Unit 21, Algernon Industrial Estate, New York Road, Newcastle Upon Tyne. NE27 0NB tel:(03300) 585633, fax:(08456) 123 334. sales@ppd-ltd.com, www.ppd-ltd.com

Project Aluminium Ltd - 418-420 Limpsfield Road, Warlington, Surrey. CR6 9LA tel:(01883) 624004, fax:(01883) 627201. lesley@projects.co.uk, http://www.projectali.co.uk/

Project Office Furniture PLC - 103 High Street, Waltham Cross, Herts. EN8 7AN tel:(01440) 705411, fax:(01440) 703376. enquiries@project.co.uk, www.project.co.uk

Promat UK Ltd - The Sterling Centre, Eastern Road, Bracknell, Berks. RG12 2TD tel:(01344) 381300, fax:(01344) 381301. salesuk@promat.co.uk, www.promat.co.uk

Protecter Lamp & Lighting Co Ltd - Lansdowne Road, Eccles, Gt Man. M30 9PH tel:(0161) 789 5680, fax:(0161) 787 8257. dmather@protectorlamp.com, www.protectorlamp.com

ProTen Services - Unit 10, Progress Business Park, Progress Road, Leigh-on-Sea, Essex. SS9 5PR tel:(01702) 471666, fax:(01702) 471927. info@protenservices.co.uk, www.protenservices.co.uk

Proteus Switchgear - Pipers Road, Park Farm Industrial Estate, Redditch, Worcs. B98 0HU tel:(01527) 517 117, fax:(01527) 526873. cons@proteusswitchgear.co.uk, www.proteusswitchgear.co.uk

Protim Solignum Ltd - Fieldhouse Lane, Marlow, Bucks. SL7 1LS tel:(01628) 486644, fax:(01628) 476757. info@osmose.co.uk, www.solignum.com

Protimeter, GE Thermometrics (UK) Ltd - Crown Industrial Estate, Priorswood Road, Taunton, Somerset. TA2 8QY tel:(01823) 335 200, fax:(01823) 332 637. Taunton.cc@ge.com, www.protimeter.com

Pryorsign - Field View, Brinsworth Lane, Brinsworth, Rotherham, S. Yorks. S60 5DG tel:(01709) 839559, fax:(01709) 837659. phil@pryorsign.com, www.buyersguide.co.uk/document/pryor-sign/

PTS Plumbing Trade Supplies - PTS House, Eldon Way, Crick, Northamptonshire. NN6 7SL tel:(01788) 527700, fax:(01788) 527799. ptsplumbing@ptsplumbing.co.uk, www.ptsplumbing.co.uk

Pump International Ltd - Trevoole Praze, Camborne, Cornwall. TR14 0PJ tel:(01209) 831937, fax:(01209) 831939. sales@pumpinternational.com, www.pumpinternational.com

Pump Technical Services Ltd - Beco Works, Cricket Lane, off Kent House Lane, Beckenham, Kent. BR3 1LA tel:(020) 8778 4271, fax:(020) 8659 3576. sales@ptsjung.co.uk, www.pts-jung.co.uk

Pumps & Motors UK Ltd - Units 3-4, Abbey Grange Works, 52 Hertford Road, Barking, Essex. IG11 8BL tel:(020) 8507 2288, fax:(020) 8591 7757. sales@pumpsmotors.co.uk, www.pumpsmotors.co.uk

Purewell Timber Buildings Limited - Unit 4, Lea Green Farm, Christchurch Road, Lymington, Hants. SO41 0LA tel:(01590) 644 477, fax:(01202) 490151. mail@purewelltimber.co.uk, www.purewelltimber.co.uk

Purified Air Ltd - Lyon House, Lyon Road, Romford, Essex. RM1 2BG tel:(01708) 755414, fax:(01708) 721488. enq@purifiedair.com, www.purifiedair.com/

Purmo-UK - Rettig Park, Drum Lane, Birtley, County Durham. DH2 1AB tel:(0191) 492 1700, fax:(0191) 492 9484. uk@purmo.co.uk, www.purmo.com/en

Pyramid Plastics UK Ltd - Unit 22 Corringham Road Industrial Estate, Corringham Road, Gainsborough, Linconshire. DN21 1QB tel:(01427) 677990, fax:(01427) 612204. website@pyramid-plastics.co.uk, www.pyramid-plastics.co.uk

Pyroguard UK Ltd - International House, Millford Lane, Haydock, Merseyside. WA11 9GA tel:(01942) 710720, fax:(01942) 710730. info@pyroguard.eu, www.pyroguard.eu

Pyronix - Secure House, Braithwell Way, Hellaby, Rotherham. S66 9QY tel:(01709) 535230. sales@pyronix.com, www.pyronix.com/uk/

Q

Q.M.P - Timmis Road, Lye, Stourbridge, W. Midlands. DY9 7BQ tel:(01384) 899 800, fax:(01384) 899 801. sales@qmp.uk.com, www.qmp.uk.com

QK Honeycomb Products Ltd - Creeting Road, Stowmarket, Suffolk. IP14 5AS tel:(01449) 612145, fax:(01449) 677604. sales@qkhoneycomb.co.uk, www.qkhoneycomb.co.uk

Quantum Profile Systems Ltd - Salmon Fields, Royton, Oldham, Lancs. OL2 6JG tel:(0161) 627 4222, fax:(0161) 627 4333. info@quantum-ps.co.uk, www.quantumprofilesystems.com

Quarry Products Association - Gillingham House, 38-44 Gillingham Street, London. SW1W 1HU tel:(020) 7730 8194, fax:(020) 7730 4355. info@qpa.org, www.qpa.org

Quartet-GBC UK Ltd/ ACCO UK Ltd - Oxford House, Oxford Road, Aylesbury, Bucks. HP21 8SZ tel:(01256) 842828, fax:(01256) 476001. www.quartet.com/ www.gbceurope.com

Quelfire Limited - Unit 3, Millbuck Way, Springvale Industrial Estate, Sandbach. CW11 3HT tel:(0161) 928 7308, fax:(0161) 924 1340. sales@quelfire.co.uk, www.quelfire.co.uk

Quiligotti Terrazzo Tiles Limited - PO Box 4, Clifton Junction, Manchester. M27 8LJ tel:(0161) 727 9798, fax:(0161) 727 0457. sales@quiligotti.co.uk, www.quiligotti.co.uk

Quirepace Ltd - Quirepace House, 6 Pennant Park, Fareham, Hampshire. PO16 8XU tel:(023) 92584281, fax:(023) 92504648. marketing@quirepace.co.uk, www.quirepace.co.uk

R

R J Stokes & Co Limited - Holbrook Industrial Estate, Rother Valley Way, Sheffield, South Yorkshire. S20 3RW tel:(0114) 2512680, fax:(01142) 512 661. info@stokestiles.co.uk, www.stokestiles.co.uk

R. C. Cutting & Company Ltd - 10-12 Arcadia Avenue, Finchley Central, London. N3 2JU tel:(020) 8371 0001, fax:(020) 8371 0003. info@rccutting.co.uk, www.rccutting.co.uk

R.M. Easdale & Co Ltd - 67 Washington Street, Glasgow. G3 8BB tel:(0141) 204 2708, fax:(0141) 204 3159. david@rmeasdale.com, www.rmeasdale.com

Race Furniture Ltd - Bourton Industrial Park, Bourton-on-the-Water, Glos. GL54 2HQ tel:(01451) 821446, fax:(01451) 821686. sales@racefurniture.com, www.racefurniture.com

Rackline Systems Storage Ltd - Oaktree Lane, Talke, Newcastle-under-Lyme, Staffs. ST7 1RX tel:(01782) 777666, fax:(01782) 777444. now@rackline.com, www.rackline.com

Radflex Contract Services Ltd - Unit 35, Wilks Avenue, Questor, Dartford, Kent. DA1 1JS tel:(01322) 276363, fax:(01322) 270606. expjoint@radflex.co.uk, www.radflex.co.uk

Radiant Services Ltd - Barrett House, 111 Millfields Road, Ettingshall, Wolverhampton, W. Midlands. WV4 6JQ tel:(01902) 494266, fax:(01902) 494153. radser@btconnect.com, www.radiantservices.co.uk

Radiodetection Ltd - Western Drive, Bristol. BS14 0AF tel:(0117) 976 7776, fax:(0117) 976 7775. rd.sales.uk@spx.com, www.spx.com/en/radiodetection

Radius Systems Ltd - Radius House, Berristow Lane, South Normanton, Alfreton, Derbys. DE55 2JJ tel:(01773) 811112, fax:(01773) 812432. sales@radius-systems.com, www.radius-systems.com

Railex Systems Ltd, Elite Division - Elite Works, Station Road, Manningtree, Essex. CO11 1DZ tel:(01206) 392171, fax:(01206) 391465. info@railex.co.uk, www.railexstorage.co.uk

Rainham Steel Co Ltd - Kathryn House, Manor Way, Rainham, Essex. RM13 8RE tel:(01708) 522311, fax:(01708) 559024. sales@rainhamsteel.co.uk, www.rainhamsteel.co.uk

Raised Floor Systems Ltd - Unit 3-4, Henlow Industrial Estate, Henlow, Bedfordshire. SG16 6DS tel:(01462) 685898. enquiries@raisedfloorsystems.co.uk, www.raisedfloorsystems.co.uk

RAJA Workplace - Innovation Centre, 1 Devon Way, Longbridge Technology Park, Birmingham. B31 2TS tel:(0800) 954 9001, fax:(0845) 688 8900. sales@welco.co.uk, www.welco.co.uk

R (con't)

RAMGROUP (UK) Ltd - 1A Levens Road, Hazel Grove, Stockport, Cheshire. SK7 5DL tel:(0161) 477 4001, fax:(0161) 477 1007. sales@ramgroupuk.com, https://rampost.co.uk/

Ramsay & Sons (Forfar) Ltd - 61 West High Street, Forfar, Angus. DD8 1BG tel:(01307) 462255, fax:(01307) 466956. enquiries@ramsayladders.co.uk, www.ramsayladders.co.uk

Randalls Fabrications Ltd - Hoyle Mill Road, Kinsley, Pontefract, W. Yorks. WF9 5JB tel:(01977) 615132, fax:(01977) 610059. sales@randallsfabrications.co.uk, www.randallsfabrications.co.uk

Range Cylinders - Tadman Street, Wakefield, W. Yorks. WF1 5QU tel:(01924) 376026, fax:(01924) 385015. sales@range-cylinders.co.uk, www.range-cylinders.co.uk

Rangemaster - Meadow Lane, Long Eaton, Notts. NG10 2AT tel:(0115) 946 4000, fax:(0115) 946 0374. sales@rangemaster.co.uk, www.rangemaster.co.uk

Rawson Carpets Ltd - Castle Bank Mills, Portobello Road, Wakefield, W. Yorks. WF1 5PS tel:(01924) 382860, fax:(01924) 366204. sales@rawsoncarpets.co.uk, www.rawsoncarpets.co.uk

Rawson Fillings Ltd - Castle Bank Mills, Portobello Road, Wakefield, W. Yorks. WF1 5PS tel:(01924) 373421, fax:(01924) 290334. sales@rawsonfillings.co.uk

RB UK Ltd - Element House, Napier Road, Bedford, Beds. MK41 0QS tel:(01234) 272717, fax:(01234) 270202. customerservices@rbuk.co.uk, www.rbuk.co.uk

Rea Metal Windows Ltd - 126-136 Green Lane, Liverpool. L13 7ED tel:(0151) 228 6373, fax:(0151) 254 1828. all@reametal.co.uk, www.reametal.co.uk

Record Electrical - Unit C1 Longford Trading Estate, Thomas Street, Stretford, Manchester. M32 0JT tel:(0161) 937 5331, fax:(0161) 926 9750. info@reauk.com, www.reauk.com

Red Bank Manufacturing Co Ltd - Atherstone Road, Measham, Swandlincote, Derbys. DE12 7EL tel:(01530) 270333, fax:(01530) 273667. meashamsalesuk@hanson.biz, www.forterra.co.uk

Reddiglaze Ltd - The Furlong, Droitwich, Worcs. WR9 9BG tel:(01905) 795432, fax:(01905) 795757. sales@reddiplex.com, www.reddiglaze.co.uk

Redifix Ltd - Queenslie Industrial Estate, 44 Coltness Lane, Glasgow. G33 4DR tel:(0141) 774 2020, fax:(0141) 774 3080. sales@redifix.co.uk, www.redifix.co.uk

Rediweld Rubber & Plastics Ltd - 6-10 Newman Lane, Alton, Hants. GU34 2QR tel:(01420) 543007, fax:(01420) 546740. info@rediweld.co.uk, www.rediweldtraffic.co.uk

Redman Fisher Engineering - Birmingham New Road, Tipton, W. Midlands. DY4 9AA tel:(01902) 880880, fax:(01902) 880446. flooring@redmanfisher.co.uk, www.redmanfisher.co.uk

Reed Harris - Unit 10 The Talina Centre, 23a Bagleys Lane, London. SW6 2BW tel:(020) 7736 7511, fax:(020) 7736 2988. architectural@reed-harris.co.uk, www/reedharris.co.uk

Reflecting Roadstuds Ltd - Boothtown, Halifax, W. Yorks. HX3 6TR tel:(01422) 360208, fax:(01422) 349075. info@percyshawcatseyes.com, www.percyshawcatseyes.com

Reflex-Rol (UK) - Ryeford Hall, Ryeford, Nr Ross-on-Wye, Herefordshire. HR9 7PU tel:(01989) 750704, fax:(01989) 750768. info@reflex-rol.co.uk, www.reflex-rol.co.uk

Rega Ductex Ltd - 21 Elton Way, Biggleswade, Beds. SG18 8NH tel:(01767) 600499, fax:(01767) 692451. sales@rega-uk.com, www.regaductex.co.uk

REHAU Ltd - Hill Court, Walford, Ross-on-Wye, Herefordshire. HR9 5QN tel:(01989) 762600, fax:(01989) 762601. enquiries@rehau.com, www.rehau.co.uk

Reid John & Sons (Strucsteel) Ltd - Strucsteel House, 264-266 Reid Street, Christchurch, Dorset. BH23 2BT tel:(01202) 483333, fax:(01202) 470103. sales@reidsteel.co.uk, www.reidsteel.com

Relcross Ltd - Hambleton Avenue, Devizes, Wilts. SN10 2RT tel:(01380) 729600, fax:(013080) 729888. sales@relcross.co.uk, www.relcross.co.uk

Remploy Ltd - Unit 2, Brocastle Avenue, Waterton Industrial Estate, Bridgend, Bridgend. CF31 3YN tel:(01656) 653982, fax:(01656) 767499. info@remploy.co.uk, www.remploy.co.uk

Renderplas Ltd - Number 2, 70-72 High Street, Bewdley, Worcs. DY12 2DJ tel:(01299) 888333, fax:(01299) 888234. info@renderplas.co.uk, www.renderplas.co.uk

RENOLIT Cramlington Limited - Station Road, Cramlington, Northumberland. NE23 8AQ tel:(01670) 718283, fax:(01670) 590096. renolit.cramlington@renolit.com, www.renolit.com/waterproofing-roofing/en/

Rentokil Property Care Services - Riverbank, Meadows Business Park, Camberley, Surrey. GU17 9AB tel:(0808) 250 1133. rsh-info-uk@rentokil-initial.com, www.rentokil.co.uk

Rentokil Specialist Hygiene - 139-140 Southbank House, Lambeth, London. SE1 7SJ tel:(020) 3733 1578. rsh-info-uk@rentokil-initial.com, www.rentokil-hygiene.co.uk

Rentokil Specialist Hygiene - 2nd Floor, Riverbank Meadows Business Park, Camberley. GU17 9AB tel:(0800) 028 0839, fax:(01342) 326229. rsh-info-uk@rentokil-initial.com, www.rentokil-hygiene.co.uk

Repair care International - Unit 19, Darwell Park, Mica Close, Amington, Tamworth, Staffordshire. PE28 5GQ tel:(01827) 302 517. salesuk@repair-care.com, uk.repair-care.com

Resdev Ltd - Pumaflor House, Ainleys Industrial Estate, Elland, W. Yorks. HX5 9JP tel:(01422) 379131, fax:(01422) 370943. info@resdev.co.uk, www.resdev.co.uk

Resiblock Ltd - Resiblock House, Archers Fields Close, Basildon, Essex. SS13 1DW tel:(01268) 273344, fax:(01268) 273355. mail@resiblock.com, www.resiblock.com

Resin Flooring Association (FeRFA) - 16 Edward Road, Farnham, Surrey. GU9 8NP tel:(07484) 075 254, fax:(01252) 714250. lisa@ferfa.org.uk, www.ferfa.org.uk

Revol Products Ltd - Samson Close, Killingworth, Newcastle-upon-Tyne. NE12 6DZ tel:(0191) 268 4555, fax:(0191) 216 0004. sales@revol.co.uk, www.revol.co.uk

RFA-Tech Ltd - Eastern Avenue, Trent Valley, Lichfield, Staffordshire. WS13 6RN tel:(0870) 011 2881, fax:(0870) 011 2882. sales@rfa-tech.co.uk, www.rfa-tech.co.uk

Rheinzink UK - Building 3, Riverside Way, Camberley, Surrey. GU15 3YL tel:(01276) 686725, fax:(01276) 64480. info@rheinzink.co.uk, www.rheinzink.co.uk

Rhodar Limited - Astra Park, Parkside Lane, Leeds. LS11 5SZ tel:(0113) 270 0775, fax:(0113) 270 4124. info@rhodar.co.uk, www.Rhodar.co.uk

RIBA Enterprises - The Old Post Office, St Nicholas Street, Newcastle Upon Tyne. NE1 1RH tel:(0191) 244 5500. info@ribaenterprises.com, www.ribaenterprises.com

Richard Hose Ltd - Unit 7, Roman Way Centre, Longridge Road, Ribbleton, Preston, Lancs. PR2 5BB tel:(01772) 651550, fax:(01772) 651325. richards.fire@btinternet.com, www.richardsfire.co.uk

Richard Lees Decking Limited - Brandlesholme House, Brandlesholme Road, Bury, Greater Manchester. BL8 1JJ tel:(0161) 609 0455. sales@richardlees.co.uk, www.richardlees.co.uk

Richards H S Ltd - King Street, Smethwick, Warley, W. Midlands. B66 2JW tel:(0121) 558 2261, fax:(0121) 558 3607. info@richards-paints.co.uk, www.richards-paints.co.uk

RICS Book Shop - 12, Great George Street, London. SW1P 3AD tel:(024) 7686 8555, fax:(020) 7334 3811. contactrics@rics.org, www.rics.org/uk/shop/

Righton Ltd - Righton House, Brookvale Road, Witton, Birmingham. B6 7EY tel:(0121) 356 1141, fax:(0121) 331 1347. marketing@righton.co.uk, www.righton.co.uk

Rigidal - Blackpole Trading Estate West, Worcester. WR3 8ZJ tel:(01905) 750500, fax:(01905) 750555. enquiries@omnisexteriors.com, w.rigisystems.org

Rite-Vent Ltd - Crowther Estate, Washington, Tyne & Wear. NE38 0AQ tel:(0191) 416 1150, fax:(0191) 415 1263. sales@rite-vent.co.uk, www.rite-vent.co.uk

Ritherdon & Co Ltd - Lorne Street, Darwen, Lancs. BB3 1QW tel:(01254) 819100, fax:(01254) 819101. sales@ritherdon.co.uk, www.ritherdon.co.uk

Rivermeade Signs Ltd - Roslin Road, South Acton Industrial Estate, London. W3 8BW tel:(020) 8896 6900, fax:(020) 8752 1691. salesw@rivermeade.com, www.rivermeade.com

Rixonway Kitchens Ltd - Shaw Cross Busness Park, Dewsbury, W. Yorks. WF12 7RD tel:(01924) 431300, fax:(01924) 431301. info@rixonway.co.uk, www.rixonway.co.uk

RMIG Ltd - Units 1-7, Adlington Court, Risley Road, Birchwood, Warrington, Cheshire. WA3 6PL tel:(01925) 839607. info.uk@rmig.com, www.rmig.com

Robert Bosch Ltd - PO Box 98, Broadwater Park, North Orbital Road, Denham, Uxbridge, Middx. UB9 5HJ tel:(0344) 892 0115. www.bosch.co.uk

Robinson Lloyds Architecture - Keepers Lodge Farm, Corby Road, Gretton, Northamptonshire. NN17 3BW tel:(01536) 772555. projects@robinson-lloyd.com, www.robinson-lloyd.com

Rock & Alluvium Ltd - SBC House, Restmor Way, Wallington, Surrey. SM6 7AH tel:(020) 8255 2088, fax:(020) 82416934. Enquiries@rockal.com, www.rockal.com

Rockwell Sheet Sales Ltd - Rockwell House, Birmingham Road, Millisons Wood, Coventry. CV5 9AZ tel:(01676) 523386, fax:(01676) 523630. info@rockwellsheet.com, www.rockwellsheet.com

Rockwool Ltd - Pencoed, Bridgend, M. Glam. CF35 6NY tel:(01656) 862621, fax:(01656) 862302. info@rockwool.co.uk, www.rockwool.co.uk

Roles Broderick Roofing Ltd - 4 High Street, Woking, Surrey. GU24 8AA tel:(01276) 856604. info@rolesbroderick.com

Rolflex Doors Ltd - 86 Melchett Road, Kings Norton, Birmingham. B30 3HX tel:(01384) 401555, fax:(01384) 401556. sales@rolflex.co.uk, www.rolflex.co.uk

Rollalong Ltd - Woolsbridge Industrial Estate, Three Legged Cross, Wimborne, Dorset. BH21 6SF tel:(01202) 824541, fax:(01202) 812584. enquiries@rollalong.co.uk, www.rollalong.co.uk

Rollins & Sons (London) Ltd - Rollins House, 1 Parkway, Harlow. CM19 5QF tel:(01279) 401570, fax:(01279) 401580. sales@rollins.co.uk, www.rollins.co.uk

Rom Ltd - Eastern Avenue, Trent Valley, Lichfield, Staffs. WS13 6RN tel:(01543) 414111, fax:(01543) 421672. sales@rom.co.uk, www.rom.co.uk

Ronacrete Ltd - Ronac House, Flex Meadow, Harlow, Essex. CM19 5TD tel:(020) 8593 7621, fax:(020) 8595 6969. sales@ronacrete.co.uk, www.ronacrete.co.uk

Roofing Contractors (Cambridge) Ltd - 5 Winship Road, Milton, Cambridge, Cambs. CB24 6BQ tel:(01223) 423059. info@rcc-cambridge.co.uk, www.rcc-cambridge.co.uk

RoofRite - 164 Meadow Rise, Brynna, Mid Glamorgan. CF72 9TJ tel:(01443) 227840. dennis@roofs4u.co.uk, www.roofs4u.co.uk

RoofRite Stirling Scotland - 4 Riverside Drive, Riverside, Stirling. FK8 1LR tel:(01786) 464395. info@roofrite.co.uk, www.roofrite.co.uk

Rotafix Resins - Rotafix House, Abercraf, Swansea. SA9 1UR tel:(01639) 730481, fax:(01639) 730858. rotafixltd@aol.com, www.rotafix.co.uk

Rothley Limited - 2 Discovery park, Wobaston Road, Wolverhampton, W. Midlands. WV10 6QJ tel:(01902) 756461, fax:(01902) 745554. sales@rothley.com, www.rothley.co.uk

Roto Frank Ltd - Swift Point, Rugby, Warwicks. CV21 1QH tel:(01788) 558600, fax:(01788) 558605. uk-sales@roto-frank.com, www.roto-frank.co.uk

Royal Incorporation of Architects in Scotland - 15 Rutland Square, Edinburgh. EH1 2BE tel:(0131) 229 7545, fax:(0131) 228 2188. info@rias.org.uk, www.rias.org.uk

Royal Institute of British Architects (RIBA) - 66 Portland Place, London. W1B 1AD tel:(020) 7580 5533, fax:(020) 7255 1541. info@riba.org, www.architecture.com

Royal Institution of Chartered Surveyors (RICS) - 12 Great George Street, Parliament Square, London. SW1P 3AD tel:(024) 7686 8555. contactrics@rics.org, www.rics.org

Royal Town Planning Institute - 41 Botolph Lane, London. EC3R 8DL tel:(020) 7929 9494, fax:(020) 7929 9490. online@rtpi.org.uk, www.rtpi.org.uk

Royde & Tucker - Bilton Road, Cadwell Lane, Hitchen. SG4 0SB tel:(01462) 444444, fax:(01462) 444433. sales@ratman.co.uk, www.ratman.co.uk

Royston Lead Ltd - Pogmoor Works, Stocks Lane, Barnsley, S. Yorks. S75 2DS tel:(01226) 770110, fax:(01226) 730359. info@roystonlead.co.uk, www.roystonlead.co.uk

RTD Systems Ltd - Unit 10 Mole Business Park, Randalls Road, Leatherhead, Surrey. KT22 7BA tel:(020) 8545 2945, fax:(020) 8545 2955. solutions@octanorm.co.uk, www.octanorm.co.uk

Ruabon Sales Limited - Hafod Tileries, Ruabon, Wrexham, Clwyd. LL14 6ET tel:(01978) 843484, fax:(01978) 843276. sales@ruabonsales.co.uk, www.ruabonsales.co.uk

Rubert & Co Ltd - Acru Works, Demmings Road, Cheadle, Cheshire. SK8 2PG tel:(0161) 428 6058, fax:(0161) 428 1146. info@rubert.co.uk, www.rubert.co.uk

Rundum Meir (UK) Ltd - 1 Troutbeck Road, Liverpool. L18 3LF tel:(0151) 280 6626, fax:(0151) 737 2504. info@rundum.co.uk, www.rundum.co.uk

Rural & Industrial Design & Building Association - The Building Centre, 26 Store Street, Bloomsbury, London. WC1E 7BT tel:(0844) 249 0043. admin@ridba.org.uk, www.ridba.org.uk

Rural & Industrial Design and Building Association (RIDBA) - The Building Centre, 26 Store Street, Bloomsbury, London. WC1E 7BT tel:(0844) 249 0043. admin@ridba.org.uk, www.ridba.org.uk

Russell Roof Tiles Ltd - Nicolson Way, Wellington Road, Burton-on-trent, Staffordshire. DE14 2AW tel:(01283) 517070, fax:(01283) 516290. james.pendleton@russellrooftiles.co.uk, www.russellrooftiles.co.uk

Rustins Ltd - Waterloo Road, Cricklewood, London. NW2 7TX tel:(020) 8450 4666, fax:(020) 8452 2008. rustins@rustins.co.uk, www.rustins.co.uk

Ruthin Precast Concrete Ltd - 1st. Floor, 11 Paul Street, Taunton, Somerset. TA1 3PF tel:(01823) 274232, fax:(01823) 274231. enquiries@rpcltd.co.uk, www.rpcltd.co.uk

Ryall & Edwards Limited - Green Lane Sawmills, Outwood, Redhill, Surrey. RH1 5QP tel:(01342) 842288, fax:(01342) 843312. enquiries@ryall-edwards.co.uk, www.ryall-edwards.co.uk

Rytons Building Products Ltd - Design House, Orion Way, Kettering Business Park, Kettering, Northants. NN15 6NL tel:(01536) 511874, fax:(01536) 310455. admin@rytons.com, www.vents.co.uk

S

S & B Ltd - Labtec Street, Swinton, Gt Man. M27 8SE tel:(0161) 793 9333, fax:(0161) 728 2233. sales@splusb.co.uk, www.splusb.info

S & P Coil Products Ltd - SPC House, Evington Valley Road, Leicester. LE5 5LU tel:(0116) 2490044, fax:(0116) 2490033. spc@spcoils.co.uk, www.spcoils.co.uk

Saacke Combustion Services Ltd - Langstone Technology Park, Langstone Road, Havant, Hants. PO9 1SA tel:(023) 9233 3900, fax:(023) 9233 3901. ukservice@saacke.com, www.saacke.com

Sadolin UK Ltd - PO Box 37, Crown House, Hollins Road, Darwin, Lancashire. BB3 0BG tel:(0330) 0240310. info@crownpaintspec.co.uk, www.crownpaintspec.co.uk

Safeguard Europe Ltd - Redkiln Close, Horsham, West Sussex. RH13 5QL tel:(01403) 210204, fax:(01403) 217529. info@safeguardeurope.com, www.safeguardeurope.com

Safetell Ltd - Unit 46, Fawkes Avenue, Dartford, Kent. DA1 1JQ tel:(01322) 223233, fax:(01322) 277751. sales@safetell.co.uk, www.safetell.co.uk

Safety Assured Ltd - Home Farm Estate, Fen Lane, North Ockendon, Essex. RM14 3RD tel:(01708) 855 777, fax:(01708) 855 125. info@safetyassured.com, www.safetyassured.com

Safety Works & Solutions Ltd - Unit 6, Earith Business Park, Meadow Drove, Earith. Huntingdon, Cambs. PE28 3QF tel:(01487) 841 400, fax:(01487) 841 100. marco@safetyworksandsolutions.co.uk, www.safetyworksandsolutions.co.uk

Saint-Gobain Abrasives - Doxey Road, Stafford. ST16 1EA tel:(01785) 222000, fax:(01785) 213487. enquiries.sgauk@saint-gobain.com, ww.saint-gobain-abrasives.com

Saint-Gobain Ecophon Ltd - Old Brick Kiln, Ramsdell, Tadley, Hants. RG26 5PP tel:(01256) 850977, fax:(01256) 850600. info@ecophon.co.uk, www.ecophon.co.uk

Saint-Gobain Glass UK Ltd - Saint-Gobain House, East Leake, Loughborough, Leicestershire. LE12 6JU tel:(02476) 438400. sgukinfo@saint-gobain.com, www.saint-gobain.co.uk

Saint-Gobain PAM UK - Lows Lane, Stanton-By-Dale, Ilkeston, Derbys. DE7 4QU tel:(0115) 930 0781, fax:(0115) 932 9513. sales.uk.pam@saint-gobain.com, www.pamline.co.uk

Salex Acoustics Limited - 8 London Road, Woolmer Green, Hertfordshire. SG3 6JS tel:(01438) 545772, fax:(08700) 941918. info@salexacoustics.com, www.salexacoustics.com

Sampson & Partners Fencing - Redwell Wood Farm, Ridgehill, Potters Bar, Herts. EN6 3NA tel:(01707) 663400, fax:(01707) 661112. sales@sampsonfencing.co.uk, www.sampsonandpartners.com

Sampson Windows Ltd - Maitland Road, Lion Barn Business Park, Needham Market, Ipswich, Suffolk. IP6 8NZ tel:(01449) 722922, fax:(01449) 722911. info@nordan.co.uk, www.sampsonwindows.co.uk

Samuel Heath & Sons plc - Cobden Works, Leopold Street, Birmingham. B12 0UJ tel:(0121) 766 4200. info@samuel-heath.com, www.samuel-heath.co.uk

Sanderson - Sanderson House, Oxford Road, Denham, Bucks. UB9 4DX tel:(01895) 830000, fax:(01895) 830031. info@stylelibrarycontract.com, www.sanderson-uk.com

Sandhurst Manufacturing Co Ltd - Belchmire Lane, Gosberton, Spaling, Lincolnshire. PE11 4HG tel:(01775) 840020, fax:(01775) 843063. enqs@sandhurst.co.uk, www.sandhurst-mfg.com

Sandler Seating Ltd - 1A Fountayne Road, London. N15 4QL tel:(020) 7799 3000, fax:(020) 7729 2843. sales@sandlerseating.com, www.sandlerseating.com

Sandtoft Roof Tiles Ltd - Belton Road, Sandtoft, Doncaster, S. Yorks. DN8 5SY tel:(01427) 871200, fax:(01427) 871222. info@sandtoft.co.uk, www.sandtoft.com

Sangwin Concrete Products Ltd - Sangwin Group Of Companies, Dansome Lane, South Hull. HU8 7LN tel:(01482) 329 921, fax:(01482) 215 353. sales@sangwin.co.uk, www.sangwin.co.uk

Sangwin Group - Dansom Lane South, Hull. HU8 7LN tel:(01482) 329921, fax:(01482) 215353. sales@sangwin.co.uk, www.sangwin.co.uk

Santon - Hurricane Way, Norwich, Norfolk. NR6 6EA tel:(01603) 420100, fax:(01603) 420229. specifier@santon.co.uk, www.santon.co.uk

Sapa Building Systems (monarch and glostal) - Alexandra Way, Ashchurch, Tewkesbury, Glos. GL20 8NB tel:(01684) 297073, fax:(01684) 293904. info.buildingsystems.uk@sapagroup.com, www.sapagroup.com/uk/buildingsystems

Sapphire Balustrades - 11 Arkwright Road, Reading. RG2 0LU tel:(0844) 8800553, fax:(0844) 8800530. sales@sapphirebalustrades.com, www.sapphirebalustrades.com

Sarnafil Ltd - Robberds Way, Bowthorpe Industrial Estate, Norwich, Norfolk. NR5 9JF tel:(01603) 748985, fax:(01603) 743054. roofing@sarnafil.co.uk, www.sarnafill.co.uk

S (con't)

Sashless Window Co Ltd - Standard Way, Northallerton, N. Yorks. DL6 2XA tel:(01609) 780202, fax:(01609) 779820. alastair@sashless.com, www.sashless.com

Satec Service Ltd - Unit 5 Wokingham Commercial Centre, Molly Millars Lane, Wokingham, Berkshire. RG41 2RF tel:(01189) 649006, fax:(01189) 640074. info@satec.co.uk, www.satec.co.uk

SAV United Kingdom Ltd - Scandia House, Boundary Road, Woking, Surrey. GU21 5BX tel:(01483) 771 910, fax:(01483) 227 519. info@sav-systems.com, www.sav-systems.com

Saveheat Group - 9 Baker Street, Greenock, Scotland. PA15 4TU tel:(01475) 601960. enquiries@saveheatgroup.co.uk, www.saveheatgroup.co.uk

Sawyer & Fisher - Rosebery House, 61A East Street, Epsom, Surrey. KT17 1BP tel:(01372) 742815, fax:(01372) 729710. qs@sawyerfisher.co.uk

SC Johnson Wax - Frimley Green, Camberley, Surrey. GU16 5AJ tel:(01276) 852000, fax:(01276) 852308. www.scjohnson.co.uk

Scandanavian Timber - 73 Queens Road, Cheltenham, Gloucestershire. GL50 2NH tel:(01242) 694352. enquiries@scandinaviantimber.com, www.scandinaviantimber.com

Scapa Tapes UK Ltd - Gordleton Industrial Park, Hannah Way, Lymington, Hants. SO41 8JD tel:(01590) 684400, fax:(01590) 683728. technical.services@henkel.co.uk, www.sellotape.co.uk

Schauman (UK) Ltd - Stags End House, Gaddesden Row, Hemel Hempstead, Herts. HP2 6HN tel:(01582) 794661, fax:(01582) 794661. media@upm.com, http://www.upm.com

Schiedel Chimney Systems Ltd - Units 8 & 9 Block A, Holton Road, Holton Heath Industrial Estate, Poole, Dorset. BH16 6LG tel:(01202) 861650, fax:(01202) 861632. info@schiedel.co.uk, www.schiedel.co.uk

Schindler Ltd - 400 Dashwood Lang Road, Bourne Business Park, Addlestone. KT15 2HJ tel:(01932) 758100, fax:(01932) 758258. info@gb.schindler.com, www.schindlerlifts.co.uk

Schlegel UK (2006) Ltd - Henlow Industrial Estate, Henlow Camp, Bedfordshire. SG16 6DS tel:(01462) 815 500, fax:(01462) 811 963. schlegeluk@schlegel.com, www.schlegel.com/eu/en/

Schmidlin (UK) Ltd - White Lion Court, Swan Street, Old Isleworth, Middx. TW7 6RN tel:(020) 8560 9944, fax:(020) 8568 7081. info@lindner-group.com, www.lindner-schmidlin.com

Schneider Electric - Stafford Park 5, Telford, Shropshire. TF3 3BL tel:(0870) 6088608, fax:(01753) 611001. gb-customerservices@gb.schneider-electric.com, www.schneider-electric.com

Schneider Electric Ltd - Stafford Park 5, Telford, Shropshire. TF3 3BL tel:(01952) 290029, fax:(01952) 290534. gb-orders@schneider-electric.com, www.schneider-electric.co.uk

SCHOTT UK Ltd - Sales Office, Drummond Road, Stafford. ST16 3EL tel:(01785) 223166, fax:(01785) 223522. info.uk@schott.com, www.schott.com/uk

Schueco UK - Whitehall Avenue, Kingston, Milton Keynes. MK10 0AL tel:(01908) 282111, fax:(01908) 282124. mkinfobox@schueco.com, www.schueco.co.uk

Schwing Stetter (UK) Ltd - Unit 11, Perivale Industrial Park, Horsenden Lane South, Greenford, Middx. UB6 7RL tel:(020) 8997 1515, fax:(020) 8998 3517. info@schwing-stetter.co.uk, www.schwing-stetter.co.uk

Scotia Handling Services - 68 Bridge Street, Linwood, Paisley, Renfrewshire. PA3 3DR tel:(01505) 321127, fax:(01505) 321333. enquiries@scotia-handling-rigging.co.uk, http://scotiahandling.co.uk/

Scott Fencing Limited - Brunswick Industrial Estate, Newcastle-upon-Tyne, Tyne & Wear. NE13 7BA tel:(0191) 236 5314, fax:(0191) 217 0193. admin@scottfencing.ltd.uk

Scottish & Northern Ireland Plumbing Employers' Federation - Bellevue House, 22 Hopetoun Street, Edinburgh. EH7 4GH tel:(0131) 556 0600, fax:(0131) 557 8409. info@snipef.org, www.snipef.org

Scottish Building Federation - Carrongrange House, Carrongrange Avenue, Stenhousemuir, Larbert. FK5 3BQ tel:(0131) 556 8866. info@scottish-building.co.uk, www.scottish-building.co.uk

Scotts of Thrapston Ltd - Bridge Street, Thrapston, Northants. NN14 4LR tel:(01832) 732366. info@scottsofthrapston.co.uk, www.scottsofthrapston.co.uk

SCP Concrete Sealing Technology Ltd - 500 Avebury Boulevard, Milton Keynes, Bucks. MK9 2BE tel:(01908) 540660, fax:(07973) 907063. info@scpwaterproofing.com, www.scpwaterproofing.com

SCS Group - T2 Capital Business Park, Parkway, Cardiff. CF3 2PZ tel:(0300) 303 4104, fax:(02921) 510 058. info@groupscs.co.uk, www.groupscs.co.uk

SE Controls - Lancaster House, Wellington Crescent, Fradley Park, Lichfield, Staffs. WS13 8RZ tel:(01543) 443060, fax:(01543) 443070. sales@secontrols.co.uk, www.secontrols.com

Seagoe Technologies Ltd - Church Road, Portadown, Co. Armagh. BT63 5HU tel:(028) 38333131, fax:(028) 38333042. enquiries@glendimplex.com, www.glendimplexireland.com

Sealmaster - Brewery Road, Pampisford, Cambridge, Cambs. CB22 3HG tel:(01223) 832851, fax:(01223) 837215. sales@sealmaster.co.uk, www.sealmaster.co.uk

Sealocrete PLA Ltd - Greenfield Lane, Rochdale. OL11 2LD tel:(01706) 352255, fax:(01706) 860880. technical.service@bostik.com, www.sealocrete.co.uk

Sections & Profiles Ltd - Gaitskell Way, Dartmouth Road, Smethwick, W. Midlands. B66 1BF tel:(0121) 555 1400, fax:(0121) 555 1431. ask.hadley@hadleygroup.co.uk, www.hadleygroup.co.uk

Securikey Ltd - PO Box 18, Aldershot, Hants. GU12 4SL tel:(01252) 311888, fax:(01252) 343950. enquires@securikey.co.uk, www.securikey.co.uk

Security Doors Direct - 313 Old Birmingham Road, Marlbrook, Bromsgrove, Worcestershire. B60 1HQ tel:(01214) 682 063. sales@steeldoorssecurity.co.uk, www.steeldoorssecurity.co.uk

---

Select Aerial Photography

Milton Keynes, Buckinghamshire. tel:(07917) 344132. info@sesmk.co.uk, www.selectaerialphotography.co.uk

---

Sellite Blocks Ltd - Old Quarry, Long Lane, Great Heck, N. Yorks. DN14 0BT tel:(01977) 661631, fax:(01977) 662155. sales@sellite.co.uk, www.sellite.co.uk

Senior Aluminium Systems plc - Eland Road, Denaby Main, Doncaster, S. Yorkshire. DN12 4HA tel:(01709) 772600, fax:(01709) 772601. enquiry@senioraluminium.co.uk, www.senioraluminium.co.uk

Servomac Limited - Meadows Drive, Ireland Industrial Estate, Staveley, Chesterfield. S43 3LH tel:(01246) 472631, fax:(01246) 470259. info@servomac.com, www.servomac.com

Servowarm - Unit 9, The Gateway Centre, Coronation Road, High Wycombe, Bucks. HP12 3SU tel:(01494) 474474, fax:(01494) 472906. newbusiness@npower.com, www.servowarm.co.uk

Severfield (Design & Build) Ltd - Severs House Dalton Airfield Industrial Estate, Dalton, Thirsk, N. Yorks. YO7 3JN tel:(01845) 577896, fax:(01845) 577411. www.severfield.com

SFC (Midlands) Ltd - Unit 35, Hayhill Industrial Estate, Barrow Upon Soar, Loughborough, Leics. LE12 8LD tel:(01509) 816700. dansleeman@sfcmidlands.co.uk, www.sfcmidlands.co.uk

SFS Intec LTD - 153 Kirkstall Road, Leeds, W. Yorks. LS4 2AT tel:(0113) 2085 500, fax:(0133) 2085573. gb.leeds@sfsintec.biz, www.sfsintec.biz/uk

SG System Products Ltd - Unit 22, Wharfedale Road, Ipswich, Suffolk. IP1 4JP tel:(01473) 240055, fax:(01473) 461616. Sales@sgsystems.co.uk, www.handrailsuk.co.uk

SGB, a Brand Company - Regent Park, 299 Kingston Road, Leatherhead, Surrey. KT22 7SG tel:(01372) 569 100. ukinfo@beis.com, www.sgb.co.uk

Shackerley (Holdings) Group Ltd incorporating Designer ceramics - Ceramics House, 139 Wigan Road, Euxton, Chorley, Lancs. PR7 6JH tel:(01257) 273114, fax:(01257) 262386. info@shackerley.com, www.shackerley.com

Shadbolt F R & Sons Ltd - North Circular Road, South Chingford, London. E4 8PZ tel:(020) 8527 6441, fax:(020) 8523 2774. sales@shadbolt.co.uk, www.shadbolt.co.uk

Sharman Fencing Ltd - Robinswood Farm, Bere Regis, Wareham, Dorset. BH20 7JJ tel:(01929) 472181, fax:(01929) 472182. info@sharmanfencing.co.uk, www.sharmanfencing.co.uk

Shavrin Levatap Co Ltd - 32 Waterside, Kings Langley, Herts. WD4 8HH tel:(01923) 267678, fax:(01923) 265050. info@shavrinlevatap.co.uk, www.shavrinlevatap.co.uk/top menu.htm

Shaws of Darwen - Waterside, Darwen, Lancs. BB3 3NX tel:(01254) 775111, fax:(01254) 873462. sales@shawsofdarwen.com, www.shawsofdarwen.com

Shaylor Group Plc - Frederick James House, 52 Wharf Approach, Anchor Brook Business Park, Aldridge, West Midlands. WS9 8BX tel:(01922) 741570, fax:(01922) 745604. enquiries@shaylorgroup.com, www.shaylorgroup.com

Shell Bitumen - Shell House, Beach Hill, Clonskeagh, Dublin 4. Ireland tel:+353 1819 7030, fax:+353 1808 8250. shell-bitumen@shell.com, www.shell.com

Shellcast Security Shutters - Hornby Road, Claughton, Lancaster. LA2 9LA tel:(01524) 772 425. shellcast@btconnect.com, www.shellcast-shutters.co.uk

Shepherd Engineering Services Ltd - Mill Mount, York, N. Yorks. YO24 1GH tel:(01904) 629151, fax:(01904) 610175. mfaxon@ses-ltd.co.uk, www.ses-ltd.co.uk

Showerlux UK - 140 Wolvey Rd, Burbage, Leicestershire. LE10 2JJ tel:(024) 76 639400, fax:(024) 76 305457. sales@showerlux.co.uk, www.showerlux.uk.com

Shutter Door Repair & Maintenance Ltd - 89-91 Rolfe Street, Smethwick, Warley, W. Midlands. B66 2AY tel:(0121) 558 6406, fax:(0121) 558 7140. enquiries@sis-group.co.uk, www.sis-group.co.uk

Sibelco UK Ltd - Brookside Hall, Sandbach, Cheshire. CW11 4TF tel:(01270) 752 752, fax:(01270) 752753. info@sibelco.co.uk, www.sibelco.com

Sidhil Care - Sidhil Business Park, Holmfield, Halifax, West Yorkshire. HX2 9NT tel:(01422) 363447, fax:(01422) 344270. sales@sidhil.com, www.sidhil.com

Siemens Building Technologies - Brunel House, Sir William Siemens Square, Frimley, Camberley, Surrey. GU16 8QD tel:(01784) 461616, fax:(01784) 464646. support.industry@siemens.com, www.siemens.co.uk/buildingtechnologies

Sierra Windows - Alders Way, Yalberton Industrial Estate, Paignton, Devon. TQ4 7QE tel:(01803) 697000, fax:(01803) 697071. info@sierrawindows.co.uk, www.sierrawindows.co.uk

SIG Interiors - Adsetts House, 16 Europa View, Sheffield Business Park, Sheffield. S9 1XH tel:(0114) 2318030, fax:(0114) 2318031. info@sigplc.com, www.sigplc.co.uk

SIG Roofing - Harding Way, St Ives, Cambridgeshire. PE27 3YJ tel:(01480) 466777, fax:(01480) 300269. info@sigroofing.co.uk, www.sigroofing.co.uk

Sign Industries - Gardyn, Forfar, Angus. DD8 2SQ tel:(01241) 828694, fax:(01241) 828331. info@signindustries.com, www.signindustries.com

Signs & Labels Ltd - Douglas Bruce House, Corrie Way, Stockport, Cheshire. SK6 2RR tel:(0800) 132323, fax:(0161) 430 8514. sales@signsandlabels.co.uk, www.safetyshop.com

Signs Of The Times Ltd - Wingfield Road, Tebworth, Leighton Buzzard, Beds. LU7 9QG tel:(01525) 874185, fax:(01525) 875746. enquiries@sott.co.uk, www.sott.co.uk

Sika Fibres Limited - Propex House, 9 Royal Court, Basil Close, Chesterfield, Derbyshire. S41 7SL tel:(01707) 394444. concrete@uk.sika.com, www.fibermesh.com

Sika Liquid Plastics Limited - Sika House, Miller Street, Preston, Lancashire. PR1 1EA tel:(01772) 259781, fax:(01772) 255672. info@liquidplastics.co.uk, http://gbr.liquidplastics.sika.com

Sika Ltd - Watchmead, Welwyn Garden City, Herts. AL7 1BQ tel:(01707) 394444, fax:(01707) 329129. sales@uk.sika.com, www.sika.co.uk

Silent Gliss Ltd - Pyramid Business Park, Poorhole Lane, Broadstairs, Kent. CT10 2PT tel:(01843) 863571, fax:(01843) 864503. info@silentgliss.co.uk, www.silentgliss.co.uk

Silverdale Bathrooms - 293, Silverdale Road, Newcastle Under Lyme, Staffordshire. ST5 6EH tel:(01782) 717 175, fax:(01782) 717 166. sales@silverdalebathrooms.co.uk, www.silverdalebathrooms.co.uk

Simflex Grilles and Closures Ltd - 9 Woburn Street, Ampthill, Beds. NK45 2HP tel:(01525) 841100, fax:(01525) 405561. sales@simflex.co.uk, www.simflex.co.uk

Simon Moore Water Services - Unit 2, Poundbury West Industrial Estate, Dorchester. DT1 2BG tel:(01305) 251551, fax:(01305) 257107. info@simon-moore.com, www.simon-moore.com

Simon R W Ltd - System Works, Hatchmoor Industrial Estate, Torrington, Devon. EX38 7HP tel:(01805) 623721, fax:(01805) 624578. info@rwsimon.co.uk, www.rwsimon.co.uk

Simplex Signs Limited - Unit C, Peter Road, Lancing Business Park, Lancing, W. Sussex. BN15 8TH tel:(01903) 750333, fax:(01903) 750444. sales@simplexltd.com, www.simplexltd.com

Simplylabs Limited - 4 Aerodrome Close, Loughborough, Leicestershire. LE11 5RJ tel:(01509) 611322, fax:(01509) 611416. sales@simplylabs.co.uk, www.simplylabs.co.uk

Simpson Strong-Tie® - Winchester Road, Cardinal Point, Tamworth, Staffs. B78 3HG tel:(01827) 255600, fax:(01827) 255616. info@strongtie.com, www.strongtie.com

Single Ply Roofing Association - Roofing House, 31 Worship Street, London. EC2A 2DY tel:(0845) 154 7188. enquiries@spra.co.uk, www.spra.co.uk

Siniat Ltd - Redland Avenue, Easton-in-Gordano, Bristol. BS20 0FB tel:(01275) 377773, fax:(01275) 379037. marketing@etexbp.co.uk, www.siniat.co.uk

Sinotech Limited - Unit B1Sovereign Court, Lathkill Street, Market Harborough, Leics. LE16 9EG tel:(01858) 433 067, fax:(01858) 410 205. sales@sinotechltd.co.uk, www.coldform.co.uk

SJ McBride Ltd T/A Warefence - Unit H, Ventura Park, Broadshires Way, Carterton, Oxon. OX18 1AD tel:(01993) 845279, fax:(01993) 840551. info@warefence.co.uk, www.warefence.co.uk

SK Environmental Ltd - 28 Moss Lane, Hesketh Bank, Preston. PR4 6AB tel:(01695) 714600. sales@skenvironmental.com, www.skenvironmental.com

Skanda Acoustics - 67 Clywedog Road North, Wrexham Industrial Estate, Wrexham. LL13 9XN tel:(01978) 664255, fax:(01978) 661427. info@skanda-uk.com, www.savolit.co.uk

Skanda Acoustics Limited - 67 Clywedog Road North, Wrexham Industrial Estate, Wrexham. LL13 9XN tel:(01978) 664255, fax:(01978) 661427. sales@skanda-uk.com, www.skanda-uk.com

Skanska UK Plc - Maple Cross House, Denham Way, Maple Cross, Rickmansworth, Herts. WD3 9SW tel:(01923) 776666, fax:(01923) 423681. srw.enquiries@skanska.co.uk, www.skanska.co.uk

SLE Cladding Ltd - Tilstock Lane, Prees Heath, Whitchurch, Shropshire. SY13 3JP tel:(01948) 666321, fax:(01948) 665532. enquiries@excelclad.co.uk, www.slecladding.co.uk/

Slipstop - P.O. Box 7404, Coalville. LE67 4ZS tel:(01530) 813 500, fax:(01530) 813 400. info@slipstop.co.uk, www.slipstop.co.uk

Smart F & G (Shopfittings)Ltd - Unit 1, Beecham Close, Aldridge, Walsall. WS9 8UZ tel:(0121) 772 5634. info@smartsshopfittings.co.uk, www.smartsshopfittings.co.uk

Smart Systems Ltd - Arnolds Way, Yatton, N. Somerset. BS49 4QN tel:(01934) 876100, fax:(01934) 835169. sales@smartsystems.co.uk, www.smartsystems.co.uk

Smith & Choyce Ltd - 280 Barton Street, Gloucester, Glos. GL1 4JJ tel:(01452) 523531, fax:(01452) 310032. martin@smithandchoyce.co.uk

Smith & Rodger Ltd - 24-36 Elliot Street, Glasgow. G3 8EA tel:(0141) 248 6341, fax:(0141) 248 6475. info@smithandrodger.co.uk, www.frenchpolishes.com

Smithbrook Building Products Ltd - PO Box 2133, Shoreham-by-Sea. BN43 9BD tel:(01273) 573811, fax:(01273) 689021. info@smithbrookproducts.com, www.smithbrookproducts.com

Society for the Protection of Ancient Buildings (SPAB) - 37 Spital Square, London. E1 6DY tel:(020) 7377 1644, fax:(020) 7247 5296. info@spab.org.uk, www.spab.org.uk

Solair Ltd - Pennington Close, Albion Road, West Bromwich, W. Midlands. B70 8BA tel:(0121) 525 2722, fax:(0121) 525 6786. sales@solair.co.uk, www.solair.co.uk

Solair GRP Architectural Products - Smeaton Road, Churchfields Industrial Estate, Sailsbury, Wilts. SP2 7NQ tel:(01722) 323036, fax:(01722) 337546. sales@solair.co.uk, www.solair.co.uk

Solar Trade Association, The - The National Energy Centre, Davy Avenue, Knowlhill, Milton Keynes. MK5 8NG tel:(01908) 442290, fax:(01908) 665577. enquiries@solar-trade.org.uk, www.solartradeassociation.org.uk

Solus Ceramics Ltd - Unit 1, Cole River Park, 285 Warwick Road, Birmingham. B11 2QX tel:(0121) 753 0777, fax:(0121) 753 0888. specify@solusceramics.com, www.solusceramics.com

Sommerfeld Flexboard Ltd - New Works Lane, Arleston Hill, Wellington,Telford, Shropshire. TF1 2JY tel:(07770) 822973. info@sommerfeld.co.uk, www.sommerfeld.co.uk

Sound Reduction Systems Ltd - Adam Street, Off Lever Street, Bolton. BL3 2AP tel:(01204) 380074, fax:(01204) 380957. info@soundreduction.co.uk, www.soundreduction.co.uk

Sound Service (Oxford) Ltd - 55 West End, Witney, Oxon. OX28 1NJ tel:(08707) 203093, fax:(01993) 779569. soundservice@btconnect.com, www.soundservice.co.uk

Soundsorba Ltd - Shaftesbury Street, High Wycombe, Bucks. HP11 2NA tel:(01494) 536888, fax:(01494) 536818. info@soundsorba.com, www.soundsorba.com

South Durham Structures Limited - Dovecot Hill, South Church Enterprise Park, Bishop Auckland, Co. Durham. DL14 6XR tel:(01388) 777350, fax:(01388) 775225. info@southdurhamstructures.co.uk, www.south-durham-structures.co.uk/

South East Bird Control - SVS House, Oliver Grove, London. SE25 6EJ tel:(0800) 612 2842. info@southeastbirdcontrol.com, www.southeastbirdcontrol.com

Sovereign Chemicals Limited - 14 Spring Road, Park Road, Barrow In Furness, Cumbria. LA14 4EQ tel:(01229) 870 800, fax:(0121) 525 1740. sales@sovchem.co.uk, www.sovchem.co.uk

Space - Ray UK - Chapel Lane, Claydon, Ipswich, Suffolk. IP6 0JL tel:(01473) 830551, fax:(01473) 832055. info@spaceray.co.uk, www.spaceray.co.uk

Spaceright Europe Limited - 38 Tollpark Road, Wardpark East, Cumbernauld. G68 0LW tel:(01236) 853120, fax:(01236) 853123. info@spacerighteurope.com, www.spacerighteurope.com

Spaceway South Ltd - Premier House, Abbey Park Industrail Estate, Romsey, Hants. SO51 9DG tel:(01794) 835600, fax:(01794) 835601. sales@spaceway.co.uk, www.spaceway.co.uk

S (con't)

Sparkes K & L - The Forge, Claverdon, Nr Warwick, Warwicks. CV35 8P tel:(01926) 842545, fax:(01926) 842559. info@sparkesstoves.co.uk, www.sparkesstoves.co.uk

Spear & Jackson - Atlas Way, Atlas North, Sheffield, S. Yorks. S4 7QQ tel:(0114) 281 4242, fax:(0114) 281 4252. sales@spear-and-jackson.com, www.spear-and-jackson.com

Spear & Jackson Interntional Ltd - Atlas Way, Atlasnorth, Sheffield. S4 -7QQ tel:(0114) 256 1133, fax:(0114) 243 1360. sales@neill-tools.co.uk, www.spear-and-jackson.com

Specialist Access Engineering and Maintenance Association (SAEMA) - Afford Bond, 31 Wellington Road, Nantwich, Cheshire. CW5 7ED tel:(01948) 838 616. info@saema.org, www.saema.org

Specialist Building Products - Suite: 4, 571 Finchley Road, Hampstead, London. NW3 7BN tel:(020) 8458 8212, fax:(020) 8458 4116. specialistbuildingproducts@yahoo.co.uk

Spectra Glaze Services - Unit 3, Ensign House, Woodmansterne Lane, Carshalton, Surrey. RH2 7QL tel:(020) 8647 1545, fax:(020) 8647 8070. sales@spectraglaze.co.uk, www.spectraglaze.co.uk

Spectus Systems - Snape Road, Macclesfield, Cheshire. SK10 2NZ tel:(01625) 420400, fax:(01625) 433946. contacting@spectus.co.uk, www.spectussystems.com

Speedfab Midlands - Unit 10, Credenda Road, West Bromwich, West Midlands. B70 7JE tel:(0121) 541 1761, fax:(0121) 544 0028. Sales@speedfab.com, www.speedfab.com

Sperrin Metal Products Ltd - Cahore Road, Draperstown, Co. Derry. BT45 7AP tel:(028) 79628362, fax:(028) 79628972. sales@sperrin-metal.com, www.sperrin-metal.com

Spindlewood - 8 Edward Street, Bridgewater, Somerset. TA6 5ET tel:(01278) 453665, fax:(01278) 453666. info@spindlewoodturning.co.uk, www.spindlewoodturning.co.uk

Spiral Construction Ltd - Helston, Cornwall. TR13 0LW tel:(0330) 123 2447, fax:(01326) 574760. info@spiral.uk.com, www.spiral.uk.com

Spontex Ltd - Berkley Business Park, Wainwright Road, Worcester. WR4 9ZS tel:(01305) 450300, fax:(01905) 450350. webmail.spontexuk@newellco.com, www.spontex.co.uk

Sports and Play Construction Association - Federation House, Stoneleigh Park, Kenilworth, Warwickshire. CV8 2RF tel:(024) 7641 6316, fax:(024) 7641 4773. info@sapca.org.uk, www.sapca.org.uk

Sportsmark Group Ltd - Hartshill Nursery, Thong Lane, Shorne, Gravesend. DA12 4AD tel:(01635) 867537 . sales@sportsmark.net, www.sportsmark.net

Sportsmark Group Ltd - Hartshill Nursery, Thong Lane, Shorne, Gravesend. DA12 4AD tel:(01635) 867537, fax:(01635) 864588. sales@sportsmark.net, www.sportsmark.net

Sprayed Concrete Association - Kingsley House, Ganders Business Park, Kingsley, Bordon, Hampshire. GU35 9LU tel:(01420) 471622, fax:(01420) 471611. admin@sca.org.uk, www.sca.org.uk

Springvale E P S - 75 Springvale Road, Ballyclare, Co. Antrim. BT39 0SS tel:(028) 93340203, fax:(028) 93341159. sales@springvale.com, www.springvale.com

SPX Flow Technology Crawley Ltd - Building A, Compasss House, Manor Royal, Crawley, W. Sussex. RH10 9PY tel:(01293) 527777, fax:(01293) 552640. apvwebsite@apv.com, www.apv.com

Squires Metal Fabrications Ltd - 6 Burgess Road, Ivyhouse Lane industrial Estate, Hastings, Sussex. TN35 4NR tel:(01424) 428794, fax:(01424) 431567. squiresmetal@tiscali.co.uk, www.squiresmetal.co.uk

SSAB Swedish Steel Ltd - Narrow Boat Way, Hurst Business Park, Brierley Hill, West Midlands. DY5 1UF tel:(01384) 74660, fax:(01384) 77575. sales@dobel.co.uk, https://www.ssab.com

SSI Schaefer Ltd - 83-84 Livingstone Road, Walworth Industrial Estate, Andover, Hants. SP10 5QZ tel:(01264) 386600, fax:(01264) 386611. solutions@ssi-schaefer.co.uk, www.ssi-schaefer.co.uk

SSL Access - Arrol House, 9 Arroy Road, Glasgow. G40 3DQ tel:(0141) 551 0807, fax:(0141) 554 7803. sales@sslaccess.co.uk, www.sslaccess.co.uk

Stamford Products Limited - Bayley Street, Stalybridge, Cheshire. SK15 1QQ tel:(0161) 330 6511, fax:(0161) 330 5576. enquiry@stamford-products.co.uk, www.stamford-products.co.uk

Stancliffe Stone - Grangemill, Matloc, Derbyshire. DE4 4BW tel:(01629) 653 000, fax:(01629) 650 996. info@stancliffe.com, www.stancliffe.com

Standard Patent Glazing Co Ltd - Flagship House, Forge Lane, Dewsbury, W. Yorks. WF12 9EL tel:(01924) 461213, fax:(01924) 458083. sales@patent-glazing.com, www.patent-glazing.com

Stanley Security Solutions - Bramble Road, Swindon, Whiltshire. SN2 8ER tel:(01793) 692 401, fax:(01793) 615848. info@stanleysecuritysolutions.co.uk, www.stanleysecuritysolutions.co.uk

Stannah Lifts Ltd - Anton Mill, Andover, Hants. SP10 2NX tel:(01264) 339090, fax:(01264) 337942. contact@stannah.co.uk, www.stannahlifts.co.uk

Star Uretech Ltd - Enterprise House, Hollin Bridge Street, Blackburn, Lancashire. BB2 4AY tel:(01254) 663444, fax:(01254) 681886. info@star-uretech.com, www.star-uretech.com

Staverton (UK) Ltd - Micklebring Way, Rotherham, South Yorkshire. S66 8QD tel:(0844) 225 7474. info@staverton.co.uk, www.staverton.co.uk/

Staytite Ltd - Staylite House, Halifax Road, Cressex Business Park, High Wycombe, Herts. HP12 3SN tel:(01494) 462322, fax:(01494) 464747. fasteners@staytite.com, www.staytite.com

Steel Line Ltd - Unit 27B, Orgreave Drive, Sheffield. S13 9NR tel:(0114) 288 0622. enquiries@steelline.co.uk, www.steelline.co.uk

Steel Window Association - Steel Window Association, Unit 2 Temple Place, 247 The Broadway, London. SW19 1SD tel:(0844) 249 1355, fax:(0844) 249 1356. info@steel-window-association.co.uk, www.steel-window-association.co.uk

Steelcase Strafor Plc - 183 Eversholt Street, London. NW1 1BU chessie@mediahouse.co.uk, www.steelcase.com

Steelway Fensecure Ltd - Queensgate Works, Bilston Road, Wolverhampton, W. Midlands. WV2 2NJ tel:(01902) 451733, fax:(01902) 452256. sales@steelway.co.uk, www.steelway.co.uk

Steico - 3 Eden Brae Business Park, Dunstable Road, Caddington, Bedfordshire. LU1 4FF tel:(01727) 515 120, fax:(01582) 391355. a.moore@steico.com, www.steico.co.uk

Steinel (UK) Ltd - 25 Manasty Road, Axis Park, Orton Southgate, Peterborough. PE2 6UP tel:(01733) 366700, fax:(01733) 238270. steinel@steinel.co.uk, www.steinel.co.uk

Stent Foundations Ltd - The Square, Basing View, Basingstoke. RG21 4EB tel:(01256) 637837. foundations@stent.co.uk, www.stent.co.uk

Stevenson & Cheyne (1983) - Unit 7, Butlerfield Industrial Estate, Bonnyrigg, Midlothian. EH19 3JQ tel:(01875) 822822, fax:(01875) 823723. farser-s-smith@btconnect.com, www.platerolling.co.uk

Stiebel Eltron Ltd - Lyveden Road, Brackmills, Northampton, Northants. NN4 7ED tel:(01604) 766421, fax:(01604) 765283. info@stiebel-eltron.co.uk, www.Stiebel-eltron.co.uk

STO Ltd - Unit 700, Catesby Park, Kings Norton, Birmingham. B38 8SE tel:(0141) 892 8000. info.uk@sto.com, www.sto.co.uk

Stocksigns Ltd - 43 Ormside Way, Redhill, Surrey. RH1 2-LG tel:(01737) 764764, fax:(01737) 763763. info@stocksigns.co.uk, www.stocksigns.co.uk

Stokvis Industrial Boilers (International) Limited - Unit 34 Central Park Estate, 34 Central Avenue, West Molesey, Surrey. KT8 2QZ tel:(020) 8783 3050, fax:(020) 8783 3051. info@stokvisboilers.com, www.stokvisboilers.com

Stone & Fire - The Gas Fireplace, 215 High Street, Beckenham, Kent. BR3 1BN tel:(0208) 663 3223. www.stoneandfire.co.uk

Stone Fasteners Ltd - Woolwich Road, London. SE7 8SL tel:(020) 8293 5080, fax:(020) 8293 4935. sales@stonefasteners.com, www.stonefasteners.com

Stone Federation Great Britain - Channel Business Centre, Ingles Manor, Castle Hill Avenue, Folkstone, Kent. CT20 2RD tel:(01303) 856123, fax:(01303) 221095. enquiries@stone-federationgb.org.uk, www.stone-federationgb.org.uk

Stoneguard (London) Ltd - Unit 46 Hallmark Trading Centre, Fourth Way, Wembley, London. HA9 0LB tel:(020) 8450 9933. sales@stoneguard.co.uk, www.stoneguard.co.uk

Stoneham PLc - Powerscroft Road, Foots Cray, Sidcup, Kent. DA14 5DZ tel:(020) 83008181, fax:(020) 8300 8183. kitchens@stoneham.plc.uk, www.stoneham-kitchens.co.uk/

Stonewest Ltd - 4 Dean Stanley Street, London. SW1P 3JH tel:(020) 8684 6646, fax:(020) 8684 9323. info@stonewest.co.uk, www.stonewest.co.uk

Storage Solutions Ltd - Linden Close, Great Torrington, Devon. EX38 7AL tel:(01367) 711800. www.storagesolutions.co.uk

Stoves PLC - Stoney Lane, Prescot, Liverpool, Merseyside. L35 2XW tel:(0151) 426 6551, fax:(0151) 426 3261. productsales@gdha.com, www.stoves.co.uk

Stowell Concrete Ltd - Arnolds Way, Yatton, N. Somerset. BS49 4QN tel:(01934) 834000, fax:(01934) 835474. sales@stowellconcrete.co.uk, www.stowellconcrete.co.uk

Strada London - Unit 2C Kimberley Business Park, Blackness Lane, Keston, Kent. BR2 6HL tel:(0808) 1786007, fax:(0808) 1789007. sales@strada.uk.com, www.strada.uk.com

Straight Ltd - No 1 Whitehall Riverside, Leeds. LS1 4BN tel:(0113) 245 2244, fax:(0843) 557 0011. info@straight.co.uk, www.straight.co.uk

Strand Hardware Ltd - Strand House, Premier Business Park, Long Street, Walsall, W. Midlands. WS2 9DY tel:(01922) 639111, fax:(01922) 626025. info@strandhardware.co.uk, www.strandhardware.co.uk

Streamtec Limited - 2 Kirkgate House, Baden-Powell Road, Arbroath, Angus. DD11 3LS tel:(01241) 436862, fax:(01241) 436787. info@streamtec.com, www.streamtec.com

Structural Soils Ltd - The Old School, Stillhouse Lane, Bedminster, Bristol. BS3 4EB tel:(0117) 947 1000, fax:(0117) 947 1004. admin@soils.co.uk, www.soils.co.uk

Stuart Turner Ltd - Market Place, Henley-on-Thames, Oxfordshire. RG9 2AD tel:(01491) 572655, fax:(01491) 573704. pumps@stuart-turner.co.uk, www.stuart-turner.co.uk

Stuarts Industrial Flooring Ltd - Stuart House, Trinity Road, Kingsbury Link, Tamworth. B78 2EX tel:(01827) 871140, fax:(01827) 871144. chris.henderson@stuarts-flooring.co.uk, www.stuarts-flooring.co.uk

Style Door Systems Ltd - The Old Stables, 42a Chorley New Road, Bolton, Lancashire. BL1 4NX tel:(01204) 845590, fax:(01204) 849065. north@style-partitions.co.uk, www.style-partitions.co.uk

Sulzer Pumps Wastewater UK Ltd - 5th Floor, Astral Towers, Betts Way, London Road, Crawley, W. Sussex. RH10 9UY tel:(01293) 558 140. www.sulzer.com

Sundeala Ltd - Middle Mill, Cam, Dursley, Glos. GL11 5LQ tel:(01453) 542286, fax:(01453) 549085. sales@sundeala.co.uk, www.sundeala.co.uk

Sunflex Ltd - Keys Park Road, Hednesford, Cannock, Staffs. WS12 2FR tel:(01543) 271421, fax:(01543) 279505. info@sunflex.co.uk, www.sunflex.co.uk

Sunray Engineering Ltd - Kingsnorth Industrial Estate, Wotton Road, Ashford, Kent. TN23 6LL tel:(01233) 639039, fax:(01233) 625137. sales@sunraydoors.co.uk, www.sunraydoors.co.uk

Sunrite Blinds Ltd - 4 Newhailes Ind Estate, Musselburgh. EH21 6SY tel:(0131) 669 2345, fax:(0131) 657 3595. info@sunrite.co.uk, www.sunrite.co.uk

Surespan Ltd - PO Box 52, Walsal, W. Midlands. WS2 7PL tel:(01922) 711185, fax:(01822) 497943. sales@surespancovers.com, www.surespancovers.com

Swedecor - First Floor, Rotterdam Road, Hull, E. Yorks. HU7 0XU tel:(01482) 329691, fax:(01482) 212988. info@swedecor.com, www.swedecor.com

Swegon Air Management Ltd - Wilson Industrial Estate, South Street, Whistable, Kent. CT5 3DU tel:(01227) 276100. sales@actionair.co.uk, www.actionair.co.uk

Swintex Ltd - Derby Works, Manchester Road, Bury, Lancs. BL9 9NX tel:(0161) 761 4933, fax:(0161) 797 1146. alan.armitage@swintex.co.uk, www.swintex.com

Swish Building Products - Pioneer House, Lichfield Rd Industrial Estate, Mariner, Tamworth, Staffs. B79 7TF tel:(01827) 317200, fax:(01827) 317201. marketing@swishbp.co.uk, www.swishbp.co.uk

Switch2 Energy Solutions Ltd - High Mill, Cullingworth, Bradford, W. Yorks. BD13 5HA tel:(0870) 9996030, fax:(0870) 9996031. sales@switch2.com, www.switch2.com

Symphony Group PLC, The - Gelderd Lane, Leeds. LS12 6AL tel:(0113) 230 8000, fax:(0113) 230 8134. enquiries@symphony-group.co.uk, www.symphonygroup.co.uk

System Building Products - Brookfield Road, Hinkley, Leics. LE10 2LL tel:(01455) 618787, fax:(01455) 251061. enquiries@systembuildingproducts.com, www.systembuildingproducts.com

Systemair Ltd - Unit 28, Gravelly Industrial Park, Birmingham. B24 8HZ tel:(01634) 735 020, fax:(01634) 735 019. info@systemair.co.uk, www.systemair.com

Syston Rolling Shutters Ltd - 33 Albert Street, Syston, Leicester, Leics. LE7 2JB tel:(0116) 2608841, fax:(0116) 2640846. sales@syston.com, www.syston.com

Szerelmey Ltd - 369 Kennington Lane, Vauxhall, London. SE11 5QY tel:(020) 7735 9995, fax:(020) 7793 9800. info@szerelmey.com, www.szerelmey.com

T

T B S Fabrications - Martens Road, Northbank Ind. Estate, Irlam, Manchester, Gt Man. M44 5AX tel:(0161) 775 7915, fax:(0161) 775 8929. contact@tbs-amwell.co.uk, www.abp-tbswashrooms.co.uk

TA Lucas Sails - Porchester House, Hospital Lane, Portchester, Hants. PO16 9QP tel:(02392) 373699, fax:(02392) 373656. info@lucas-sails.com, www.lucas-sails.com

Tank Storage & Services Ltd - Lilley Farm, Thurlow Road, Withersfield, Suffolk. CB9 7SA tel:(01440) 712614, fax:(01440) 712615. tom@tankstorage.co.uk, www.tankstorage.co.uk

Tapworks Water Softeners - Solar House, Mercury Park, Wooburn Green, Buckinghamshire. HP10 0HH tel:(01494) 480621, fax:(01494) 484312. info@tapworks.co.uk, www.tapworks.co.uk

Tarkett Ltd - Floor 4 Connect 38, 1 Dover Place, Ashford, Kent. TN23 1FB tel:(0800) 328 2115. salesuk@tarkett.com, www.tarkett.co.uk

Tarmac - Specialist Products - Park Road, Swadlincote, Derbyshire. DE12 6JT specialistproducts@tarmacbp.co.uk, www.tarmac.com

Tarmac - Specialist Products (Packed Highway Products) - Swains Park Industrial Estate, Park Road, Swadlincote, Derbyshire. DE12 6JT specialistproducts@tarmacbp.co.uk, www.tarmac.com

Tarmac Building Products Ltd - Millfields Road, Ettingshall, Wolverhampton, W. Midlands. WV4 6JP tel:(01902) 353 522, fax:(01902) 382219. enquiries@tarmac.co.uk, www.tarmacbuildingproducts.co.uk

Tarmac Building Products Ltd - SafetyDeck - Tunstead House, Buxton, Derbyshire. tel:(03456) 007 702. safetydeck@tarmacbp.co.uk, www.tarmac.com

Tarmac Trading Limited (Aggregates) - Tarmac Central Regional Office, Wood Lane, Quorn, Loughborough, Leicestershire. LE12 8GE tel:(0116) 264 8540. centralwestsales@tarmac.com, www.tarmac.com

Tarmac Trading Limited (Aggregates) - Tarmac London & South Regional Office, Holborough House, Holborough Road, Snodland, Kent. ME6 5PJ tel:(0208) 896 5760. londonandsesales@tarmac.com, www.tarmac.com

Tarmac Trading Limited (Aggregates) - Tarmac North Of England & Scotland, PO Box 5, Fellbank, Chester Le Street, Birtley, County Durham. DH3 2ST tel:(0191) 492 4000. birtley.reception@tarmac.com, www.tarmac.com

Tarmac Trading Limited (Asphalt) - Tarmac Central Regional Office, Wood Lane, Quorn, Loughborough, Leicestershire. LE12 8GE tel:(0116) 264 8540. centralwestsales@tarmac.com, www.tarmac.com

Tarmac Trading Limited (Asphalt) - Tarmac London & South Regional Office, Holborough House, Holborough Road, Snodland, Kent. ME6 5PJ tel:(0208) 896 5760. londonandsesales@tarmac.com, www.tarmac.com

Tarmac Trading Limited (Asphalt) - Tarmac North Of England & Scotland, PO Box 5, Fellbank, Chester Le Street, Birtley, County Durham. DH3 2ST tel:(0191) 492 4000. birtley.reception@tarmac.com, www.tarmac.com

Tarmac Trading Limited (Blocks) - Hilton Industrial Estate, Cannock Road, Featherstone, Wolverhampton. WV10 7HP tel:(0345) 013 3592 aircrete blocks 0345 606 2468 aggregate blocks. aircretetechnical@tarmacbp.co.uk (aircrete blocks) technical.services@tarmacbp.co.uk (aggregate blocks), www.tarmac.com

Tarmac Trading Limited (Mortars) - Tunstead House, Wormhill, Buxton, Derbyshire. SK17 8TG tel:(03701) 116 116. mortar.internalsales@tarmacbp.co.uk; pozament@tarmacbp.co.uk (Pozament Pressure Pointing Mortar), www.tarmac.com

Tarmac Trading Limited (Readymix Concrete & Screed) - Tarmac Central Regional Office, Wood Lane, Quorn, Loughborough, Leicestershire. LE12 8GE tel:(0116) 264 8540. centralwestsales@tarmac.com, www.tarmac.com

Tarmac Trading Limited (Readymix Concrete & Screed) - Tarmac London &South Regional Office, Holborough House, Holborough Road, Snodland, Kent. ME6 5PJ tel:(0208) 896 5760. londonandsesales@tarmac.com, www.tarmac.com

Tarmac Trading Limited (Readymix Concrete & Screed) - Tarmac North Of England & Scotland, PO Box 5, Fellbank, Chester Le Street, Birtley, County Durham. DH3 2ST tel:(0191) 492 4000. birtley.reception@tarmac.com, www.tarmac.com

Taskmaster Doors Ltd - Unit 5 Parkway Ind Estate, Heneage Street, Birmingham. B7 4LY tel:(0121) 351 5276. sales@taskmaster.co.uk, www.taskmaster.co.uk

Taskworthy Ltd - 1 Stainiers Way, Hereford, Herefordshire. HR1 1JT tel:(01432) 376000, fax:(0432) 376001. sales@taskworthy.co.uk, www.taskworthy.co.uk

Tata Steel Colors - Tata Steel, 30 Millbank, London. SW1P 4WY tel:(0207) 7174444, fax:(0207) 7174455. feedback@tatasteel.com, www.colorcoat-online.com

Tata Steel Europe Limited - Tata Steel, 30 Millbank, London. SW1P 4WY tel:(020) 7717 4444, fax:(020) 7717 4455. technicalmarketing@tatasteel.com, www.tatasteelconstruction.com

Tate Fencing - Yellowcoat Sawmill, Hastings Road, Flimwell, Sussex. TN5 7PR tel:(01580) 879900, fax:(01580) 879677. sales@tate-fencing.co.uk, www.tate-fencing.co.uk

TBA Sealing Materials Ltd - PO Box 21, Rochdale, Lancs. OL12 7EQ tel:(01706) 715000, fax:(01706) 42284. info@tbaecp.co.uk, www.tbaecp.co.uk

TBS Amwell Ltd - Ground Floor, Suite 2, Middlesex House, Meadway Corporate Centre, Stevenage, Hertfordshire. SG21 2EF tel:(01763) 276200. contact@tbs-amwell.com, www.tbs-amwell.co.uk

TBS Fabrications Ltd - Martens Road, Northbank Industrial Park, Irlam, Manchester. M44 5AX tel:(0161) 775 1971, fax:(0161) 775 8929. contact@tbs-amwell.co.uk, www.abp-tbswashrooms.co.uk

T (con't)

TCW Services (Control) Ltd - 293 New Mill Road, Brockholes, Huddersfield, West Yorkshire. HD9 7AL tel:(01484) 662865, fax:(01484) 667574. sales@tcw-services.co.uk, www.tcw-services.co.uk

Teal & Mackrill Ltd - Ellenshaw Works, Lockwood Street, Hull, E. Yorks. HU2 0HN tel:(01482) 320194, fax:(01482) 219266. info@teamac.co.uk, www.teamac.co.uk

TEAM INDUSTRIAL SERVICES (UK) LIMITED - Furman House, Shap Road, Kendal, Cumbria. LA9 6RU tel:(01539) 729009, fax:(01539) 729359. www.furmanite.com

Tebrax Ltd - International House, Cray Avenue, Orpington, Kent. BR5 3RY tel:(01689) 897766, fax:(01689) 896789. brackets@tebrax.co.uk, www.tebrax.co.uk

Technal UK - Severn Drive, Tewkesbury, Gloucestershire. GL20 8SF tel:(01684) 853500, fax:(01684) 851850. info.uk@technal.com, www.technal.com

Technical Control Systems Ltd - Treefield Industrial Estate, Gildersome, Leeds. LS27 7JU tel:(0113) 252 5977, fax:(0113) 238 0095. sales@tcspanels.co.uk, www.tcspanels.co.uk

Techrete (UK) Ltd - Feldspar Close, Warren Park Way, Enderby, Leicester. LE19 4SD tel:(01162) 865 965, fax:(01162) 750 778. info@techrete.com, http://techrete.com

Teddington Controls Ltd - Daniels Lane, Holmbush, St Austell, Cornwall. PL25 3HG tel:(01726) 74400, fax:(01726) 67953. info@tedcon.com, www.tedcon.com

Tefcote Surface Systems - Central House, 4 Christchurch Road, Bournemouth, Dorset. BH1 3LT tel:(01202) 551212, fax:(01202) 559090. office@tefcote.co.uk, www.tefcote.co.uk

Tektura Plc - Customer Services, 34 Harbour Exchange Square, London. E14 9GE tel:(020) 7536 3300, fax:(020) 7536 3322. enquiries@tektura.com, www.tektura.com

Telling Architectural Ltd - Unit 4E Station Road, Four Ashes, Wolverhampton, West Midlands. WV10 7DF tel:(01902) 797 700, fax:(01902) 797 720. info@telling.co.uk, www.telling.co.uk

Tensar International Ltd - New Wellington Street, Blackburn, Lancs. BB2 4PJ tel:(01254) 262431, fax:(01254) 266868. info@tensar.co.uk, www.tensar.co.uk

Tensator Ltd - Danbury Court, Linford Wood, Milton Keynes. MK14 6TS tel:(01908) 684600, fax:(01582) 684700. info@tensator.com, www.tensator.com

Terex Construction - Central Boulevard, ProLogis Park, Keresley End, Coventry. CV6 4BX tel:(02476) 339400, fax:(02476) 339500. customercare@terex.com, www.terexcompactequipment.com

Terminix Property Services - Oakhurst Drive, Cheadle Heath, Stockport, Cheshire. SK3 0XT tel:(0161) 491 3181, fax:(0161) 428 8138. headoffice@petercox.com, www.petercox.com

Termstall Limited - 50 Burman Street, Droylsden, Gt Man. M43 6TE tel:(0161) 370 2835, fax:(0161) 370 9264. enquiries@termstallltd.co.uk, www.termstallfencing.co.uk

Terrapin Ltd - Bond Avenue, Bletchley, Milton Keynes. MK1 1JJ tel:(01908) 270900, fax:(01908) 270052. info@terrapin-ltd.co.uk, www.terrapin-ltd.co.uk

Terry of Redditch Ltd - 19 Oxleaslow Rd, East Moons Moat, Redditch, Worcs. B98 0RE tel:(01527) 517100. info.uk@normagroup.com, www.normagroup.com

TEV Limited - Armytage Road, Brighouse, West Yorks. HD6 1QF tel:(01484) 405600, fax:(01484) 405620. sales@tevlimited.com, www.tevlimited.com

Tex Engineering Ltd - Unit 35, Claydon Ind Park, Gipping Road, Great Blakenham, Ipswich, Suffolk. IP6 0NL tel:(01870) 751 3977, fax:(0870) 751 3978. info@bitmen.co.uk, www.tex-engineering.co.uk

Texecom Limited - Bradwood Court, St. Crispin Way, Haslingden, Lancashire. BB4 4PW tel:(01706) 234800. pharries@texe.com, www.texe.com

TH Kenyon & Sons Ltd - Kenyon House, 14a Hockerill Street, Bishop's Stortford, Herts. CM23 2DW tel:(01279) 661800, fax:(01279) 661807. enquiries@kenyonplc.com, www.kenyonplc.com

Thakeham Tiles Ltd - Rock Road, Heath Common, Storrington, W. Sussex. RH20 3AD tel:(01903) 742381, fax:(01903) 746341. support@thakeham.co.uk, www.Thakeham.co.uk

Thatching Advisory Services Ltd - 8-10 QueenStreet, Seaton, Devon. EX12 2NY tel:(08455) 20 40 60, fax:(01297) 624177. info@thatchingadvisoryservices.co.uk, http://thatchingadvisoryservices.co.uk

The Access Panel Company Ltd - Unit 5 Atkinsons Way, Foxhills Industrial Estate, Scunthorpe, N. Lincolnshire. DN15 8QJ tel:(01724) 853 090, fax:(01724) 848 030. sales@accesspanels.co.uk, www.accesspanels.co.uk

The Amtico Company - Solar Park Southside, Solihull, West Midlands. B90 4SH tel:(0121) 745 0800. info@amtico.com, www.amtico.com

The Angle Ring Company Ltd - Bloomfield Road, Tipton, W. Midlands. DY4 9EH tel:(0121) 557 7241, fax:(0121) 522 4555. sales@anglering.com, www.anglering.com

The Association of Technical Lighting & Access Specialists - 4c St. Mary's Place, The Lace Market, Nottingham. NG1 1PH tel:(01159) 558818, fax:(01159) 412238. info@atlas.org.uk, www.atlas-1.org.uk

The Benbow Group - 1 Minerva Way, Brunel Industrial Estate, Newton Abbott, Devon. TQ12 4PJ tel:(01626) 883400. mail@benbowgroup.co.uk, www.benbowgroup.co.uk

The Book Depository Ltd - 1 Principal Place, Worship Street, London. EC2A 2FA help@support.bookdepository.com, www.bookdepository.com

The BSS Group - 7 Barton Close, Leicester. LE19 1SJ tel:(0116) 245 5500. reception@bssgroup.com, www.bssgroup.co.uk

The Building Centre Group Ltd - 26 Store Street, Camden, London. WC1E 7BT tel:(020) 7692 4000, fax:(020) 7580 9641. information@buildingcentre.co.uk, www.buildingcentre.co.uk

The Carpet Foundation - MCF Complex, 60 New Road, P. O. Box 1155, Kidderminster, Worcs. DY10 1AQ tel:(01562) 755568, fax:(01562) 865405. info@carpetfoundation.com, www.carpetfoundation.com

The Concrete Society - Riverside House, 4 Meadows Business Park, Station Approach, Blackwater, Camberley, Surrey. GU17 9AB tel:(01276) 607140, fax:(01276) 607141. j.luckey@concrete.org.uk, www.concrete.org.uk

The Cotswold Casement Company - Cotswold Business Village, London Road, Moreton-on-Marsh, Glos. GL56 0JQ tel:(01608) 650568, fax:(01608) 651699. info@cotswold-casements.co.uk, www.cotswold-casements.co.uk

The David Sharp Studio Ltd - 201A Nottinham Road, Summercoats, Alfreton. DE55 4JG tel:(01773) 606066, fax:(01773) 540737. info@david-sharp.co.uk, www.david-sharp.co.uk

The Delabole Slate Co. Ltd - Delabole Slate Quarry, Pengelly, Delabole, Cornwall. PL33 9AZ tel:(01840) 212242, fax:(01840) 212948. sales@delaboleslate.co.uk, www.delaboleslate.co.uk

The Federation of Environmental Trade Association (FETA) - 2 Waltham Court, Milley Lane, Hare Hatch, Reading, Berkshire. RG10 9TH tel:(01189) 403416, fax:(01189) 406258. info@feta.co.uk, www.feta.co.uk

The Filter Business Ltd - Unit 8 Ardley Works, London Road, Billericay, Essex. CM12 9HP tel:(01277) 634637, fax:(01277) 632655. info@thefilterbusiness.com, www.thefilterbusiness.com

The Flyscreen Company Ltd - Unit 4, Warren Business Park, Knockdown, Tetbury. GL8 8QY tel:(01454) 238288, fax:(01454) 238988. sales@flyscreen.com, www.flyscreen.com

The Fountain Company - Etherow House, Woolley Bridge Road, Glossop, Derbyshire. SK13 2NS tel:(01457) 866088, fax:(01457) 865588. fountain.co@btconnect.com, www.thefountaincompany.co.uk

The Haigh Tweeny Co Ltd - Haigh Industrial Estate, Alton Road, Ross-on-Wye, Herefordshire. HR9 5LA tel:(01989) 566222, fax:(01989) 767498. sales@tweeny.co.uk, www.tweeny.co.uk

The Institute of Concrete Technology - Riverside House, 4 Meadows Business Park, Station Approach, Blackwater, Camberley, Surrey. GU17 9AB tel:(01276) 607140, fax:(01276) 607141. ict@concrete.org.uk, http://ict.concrete.org.uk/

The Institution of Engineering and Technology - Michael Farady House, Six Hills Way, Stevenage, Hertfordshire. SG1 2AY tel:(01438) 313 311, fax:(01438) 765 526. postmaster@theiet.org, www.theiet.org.uk

The Kenco Coffee Company - St. Georges House, Bayshill Road, Cheltenham, Glos. GL50 3AE tel:(0800) 242000, fax:(01295) 264602. orders.kenco@krafteurope.com, www.kencocoffeecompany.co.uk

The Kitchen Bathroom Bedroom Specialists Association - Unit L4A Mill 3, Pleasley Vale Business Park, Mansfield, Notts. NG19 8RL tel:(01623) 818808, fax:(01623) 818808. info@kbsa.org.uk, www.kbsa.org.uk

The No Butts Bin Company (NBB), Trading as NBB Outdoor Shelters - Unit 5, Sterte Road Industrial Estate, 145 Sterte Road, Poole, Dorset. BH15 2AF tel:(0800) 1777 052, fax:(0800) 1777 053. sales@nobutts.co.uk, www.nobutts.co.uk

The Outdoor Deck Company - Unit 6, Teddington Business Park, Station Road, Teddington. TW11 9BQ tel:(020) 8977 0820, fax:(020) 8977 0825. sales@outdoordeck.co.uk, www.outdoordeck.co.uk

The Pavement Light Company - 46 Westside, Dogget Street, Leighton Buzzard. LU7 1BE tel:(Tel:) 1525 377513. Enquiries@thepavementlightcompany.com, https://thepavementlightcompany.com/

The Property Care Association - 11 Ramsay Court, Kingfisher Way, Hinchingbrooke Business Park, Huntingdon, Cambs. PE29 6FY tel:(01480) 400 000, fax:(01480) 417587. pca@property-care.org, www.property-care.org

The Rooflight company - Unit 8, Wychwood Business Centre, Milton Road, Shipton-under-Wychwood, Chipping Norton, Oxon. OX7 6XU tel:(01993) 833108, fax:(01993) 831066. info@therooflightcompany.co.uk, www.therooflightingcompany.co.uk

The Safety Letterbox Company Ltd - Unit B, Milland Industrial Estate, Milland Road, Neath, West Glamorgan. SA11 1NJ tel:(01639) 633 525, fax:(01639) 646 359. sales@safetyletterbox.com, www.safetyletterbox.com

The Saw Centre Group - 650 Eglinton Street, Glasgow. G5 9RP tel:(0141) 429 4444, fax:(0141) 429 5609. sales@thesawcentre.co.uk, www.thesawcentre.co.uk

The Senator Group - Altham Business Park, Sykeside Drive, Accrington, Lancs. BB5 5YE tel:(01282) 725000, fax:(01254) 673793. contact@senator.co.uk, www.thesenatorgroup.co.uk

The Silk Forest - Main Street, Bagworth, Leics. LE67 1DW tel:(01530) 231241, fax:(01530) 231240. info@thesilkforest.com, www.thesilkforest.com

The Sound Solution - Unit 2 Carr House Farm, Nun Monkton, Pool Lane, York. YO26 8EH tel:(01423) 339 163. info@noisestopsystems.co.uk, www.noisestopsystems.co.uk

The Tile Association - The Mount, 43 Stafford Road, Stone, Staffordshire. ST15 0HG tel:(020) 8663 0946, fax:(020) 8663 0949. info@tiles.org.uk, www.tiles.org.uk

The Visual Systems Healthcare - Penine Court, Standback Way, Station Raod Technology Park, Skelmanthorpe, Huddersfield, West Yorkshire. HD8 9GA tel:(01484) 865786, fax:(01484) 865788. sales@visualsystemsltd.co.uk, www.visualsystemshealthcare.co.uk

The Window Film Company UK Ltd - Unit 5 Power House, Higham Mead, Chesham, Buckinghamshire. HP5 2AH tel:(01494) 797800, fax:(01494) 794488. info@windowfilms.co.uk, www.windowfilms.co.uk

The Wykamol Group - Knowsley Road Industrial Estate, Haslingden, Rossendale, Lancs. BB4 4RX tel:(01706) 831223, fax:(01706) 214998. sales@lectros.com, www.wykamol.com

Thermal Insulation Contractors Association - TICA House, Allington Way, Yarm Road Business Park, Darlington, Co. Durham. DL1 4QB tel:(01325) 466704, fax:(01325) 487691. ralphbradley@tica-acad.co.uk, www.tica-acad.com/tica.htm

Thermal Technology Sales Ltd - Bridge House, Station Road, Westbury, Wilts. BA13 4HR tel:(01373) 865454, fax:(01373) 864425. sales@thermaltechnology.co.uk, www.thermaltechnology.co.uk

Thermica Ltd - Cleveland House, 1-10 Sitwell Street, Hull. HU8 7BE tel:(01482) 348771. info@thermica.co.uk, www.thermica.co.uk

Thermoscreens Ltd - St. Mary's Road, Nuneaton, Warwickshire. CV11 5AU tel:(02476) 384646, fax:(02476) 388578. sales@thermoscreens.com, www.thermoscreens.com

Thomas Sanderson - Waterberry Drive, Waterlooville, Hants. PO7 7UW tel:(02392) 232600, fax:(02392) 232700. customerservices@thomas-sanderson.co.uk, www.thomas-sanderson.co.uk

Thor Hammer Co Ltd - Highlands Road, Shirley, Birmingham. B90 4NJ tel:(0121) 705 4695, fax:(0121) 705 4727. info@thorhammer.com, www.thorhammer.com

Thorlux Lighting - Merse Road, North Moons Moat, Redditch, Worcs. B98 9HH tel:(01527) 583200, fax:(01527) 584177. thorlux@thorlux.co.uk, www.thorlux.com

Thorn Lighting - ZG Lighting (UK) Limited, Durhamgate, Spennymoor, Co Durham. DL16 6HL tel:(01388) 420042. www.thornlighting.co.uk

Thurston Building Systems - Quarry Hill Industrial Estate, Hawkingcroft Road, Horbury, Wakefield, W. Yorks. WF4 6AJ tel:(01924) 265461, fax:(01924) 280246. sales@thurstongroup.co.uk, www.thurstongroup.co.uk

ThyssenKrupp Encasa, A Division of ThyssenKrupp Access Ltd - Unit E3 Eagle Court, Preston Farm Industrial Estate, Stockton -On-Tees, Cleveland. TS18 3TB tel:(0800) 783 9551. enquiries@tkencasa.co.uk, www.tkencasa.co.uk

Tidmarsh & Sons - Pleshey Lodge Farm, Pump Lane, Chelmsford, Essex. CM3 1HF tel:(01245) 237288. info@tidmarsh.co.uk, www.tidmarsh.co.uk

Tiflex Ltd - Tiflex House, Liskeard, Cornwall. PL14 4NB tel:(01579) 320808, fax:(01579) 320802. sales@tiflex.co.uk, www.tiflex.co.uk

Till & Whitehead Ltd - Eadon House, 2 Lonsdale Road, Heaton, Bolton, Lancs. BL1 4PW tel:(01204) 493000, fax:(01204) 493888. bolton@tillwite.com, www.tillwite.com

Tilley International Ltd - 30-32 High Street, Frimley, Surrey. GU16 5JD tel:(01276) 691996, fax:(01276) 27282. tilleyuk@globalnet.co.uk, www.tilleylamp.co.uk

Tillicoutry Quarries Ltd - Tulliallan Quarry, Kincardine, Fife. FK10 4DT tel:(01259) 730481, fax:(01259) 731201. sales@tillicoultryquarries.com, www.tillicoultryquarries.com

Timber Components (UK) Ltd - Wood Street, Grangemouth, Stirlingshire. FK3 8LH tel:(01324) 666222, fax:(01324) 666322. info@tcuk.co.uk, www.tcuk.co.uk

Timber Trade Federation - The Building Centre, 26 Store Street, London. WC1E 7BT tel:(020) 3205 0067, fax:(020) 7291 5379. ttf@ttf.co.uk, www.ttf.co.uk

Timberwise (UK) Ltd - 1 Drake Mews, Gadbrook Park, Cheshire. CW9 7XF tel:(01606) 33 36 36, fax:(01606) 33 46 64. hq@timberwise.co.uk, www.timberwise.co.uk

Timbmet Ltd - Kemp House, Chawley Works, Cumnor Hill, Oxford. OX2 9PH tel:(01865) 862223, fax:(01865) 864367. marketing@timbmet.com, www.timbmet.com

Time and Data Systems International Ltd (TDSI) - Sentinel House, Nuffield Road, Poole, Dorset. BH17 0RE tel:(01202) 666222, fax:(01202) 679730. sales@tdsi.co.uk, www.tdsi.co.uk

Timeguard Ltd - Apsley Way, London. NW2 7UR tel:(020) 8450 8944, fax:(020) 8452 5143. csc@timeguard.com, www.timeguard.com

Timloc Expamet Building Products - Rawcliffe Road, Goole, E. Yorks. DN14 6UQ tel:(01405) 765567, fax:(01405) 720479. sales@timloc.co.uk, www.timloc.co.uk

Titan Door Systems Ltd - Units 115-119 Fort Dunlop Building, Fort Parkway, Birmingham. B24 9FE tel:(0121) 352 2359. SALES@TITANDOORS.CO.UK, www.titandoors.co.uk

Titan Ladders Ltd - 191-201 Mendip Road, Yatton, Bristol, Avon. BS19 4ET tel:(01934) 832161, fax:(01934) 876180. sales@titanladders.co.uk, www.titanladders.co.uk

Titan Pollution Control - Part of The Kingspan Group - Unit 21 Slader Business Park, Witney Road, Poole, Dorset. BH17 0GP tel:(0800) 160 1130. mtmcivils@gmail.com, www.mtmdrains.co.uk

TLC Southern Ltd - Unit 10, Chelsea Fields Industrial Estate, 278 Western Road, Merton, London. SW19 2QA tel:(020) 8646 6866, fax:(020) 8646 6750. sales@tlc-direct.co.uk, www.tlc-direct.co.uk

Today Interiors Ltd - Unit 5, Orchard Park, Isaac Newton Way, Grantham, Lincs. NG31 9RT tel:(01476) 574401, fax:(01476) 590208. info@today-interiors.co.uk, www.todayinteriors.com

Tonbridge Fencing Limited - Court Lane Farm, Court Lane, Hadlow, Tonbridge, Kent. TN11 0DP tel:(01732) 852596, fax:(01732) 852593. geoff.wallace@tonbridgefencing.co.uk

Tony Team Ltd - Unit 6, Station Road, Bakewell, Derbys. DE45 1GE tel:(01629) 813859, fax:(01629) 814334. sales@tonyteam.co.uk, www.tonyteam.co.uk

Topcon GB Ltd - Topcon House, Kennet Side, Bone Lane, Newbury, Berks. RG14 5PX tel:(01635) 551120, fax:(01635) 551170. info@topconsokkia.co.uk, www.topcon-positioning.eu

Toprail Systems Ltd - Unit 17, Shepperton Business Park, Govett Avenue, Shepperton. TW17 8BA tel:(0870) 777 5557, fax:(0870) 777 5556. sales@toprail.com, www.toprail.com

Topscape/Topsport - Tarmac Trading Limited - Tunstead House, Wormhill, Buxton, Derbyshire. SK17 8TG tel:(0345) 600 7704. topsport@tarmacbp.co.uk, www.tarmac.com

Topseal Systems Ltd - Unit 4, Saltergate Business Park, Burley Bank Road, Harrogate. HG3 2BX tel:(01423) 886495, fax:(01423) 889550. enquiries@topseal.co.uk, www.topseal.co.uk

TORMAX United Kingdom Ltd - Unit1, Shepperton Business Park, Govett Avenue, Sheperton, Middlesex. TW17 8BA tel:(01932) 238040, fax:(01932) 238055. sales@tormax.co.uk, www.tomax.co.uk

Tormo Ltd - Unit 7, Devonshire Business Park, 4 Chester Road, Borehamwood, Herts. WD6 1NA tel:(020) 8205 5533, fax:(020) 8201 3656. sales@tormo.co.uk, www.tormo.co.uk

Toshiba Carrier UK - United Technologies House, Guildford Road, Leatherhead, Surrey. KT22 9UT tel:(01372) 220240, fax:(01372) 220241. general.enquiries@toshiba-ac.com, www.toshiba-aircon.co.uk

Tower Flue Components Ltd - Tower House, Vale Rise, Tonbridge, Kent. TN9 1TB tel:(01732) 351680. sales@tfc.uk.com, www.tfc-group.co.uk

Tower Manufacturing - Navigation Road, Worcester, Worcs. WR5 3DE tel:(01905) 763012, fax:(01905) 763610. clips@towerman.co.uk, www.towerman.co.uk

Town and Country Planning Association - 17 Carlton House Terrace, London. SW1Y 5AS tel:(020) 7930 8903, fax:(020) 7930 3280. tcpa@tcpa.org.uk, www.tcpa.org.uk

Townscape Products Ltd - Fulwood Road South, Sutton in Ashfield, Notts. NG17 2JZ tel:(01623) 513355, fax:(01623) 440267. sales@townscape-products.co.uk, www.townscapeproducts.co.uk

TR Engineering Ltd - Thorncliffe, Chapeltown, Sheffield, S. Yorks. S35 2PZ tel:(0114) 257 2300, fax:(0114) 257 1419. info@trianco.co.uk, www.trianco.co.uk

TRADA Bookshop - Bookshop, BM TRADA, Stocking Lane, Hughenden Valley, High Wycombe. HP14 4ND tel:(01494) 569602. bookshop@bmtrada.com, http://bookshop.bmtrada.com

TRADA Technology Ltd - Stocking Lane, Hughenden Valley, High Wycombe. HP14 4ND tel:(01494) 569642, fax:(01494) 565487. information@trada.co.uk, www.tradatechnology.co.uk

T (con't)

Trade Sealants Ltd - 34 Aston Road, Waterlooville, Hampshire. PO7 7XQ tel:(02392) 251321, fax:(023) 92264307. marinemastics@gmail.com, www.marinemastics.com

Travis Perkins (Southern) - 149 Harrow Road, London. W2 6NA tel:(020) 7262 6602, fax:(020) 7724 7485. paul.lonsdale@travisperkins.co.uk, www.tradmate.co.uk

TRC (Midlands) Ltd - 1 Mount Pleasant Street, West Bromwich, W. Midlands. B70 7DL tel:(0121) 5006181, fax:(0121) 5005075. info@totalroofcontrol.co.uk, www.totalroofcontrol.co.uk

Trelleborg Ltd - Trelleborg Building Systems UK Ltd, Maybrook Rd, Castle Vale Ind. Estate, Minworth, Sutton Coldfield, W. Midlands. B76 1AX tel:(0121) 352 3800, fax:(0121) 352 3899. tssuk@trelleborg.com, www.trelleborg.com

Trelleborg Sealing Profiles Germany GmbH - Auweg 27, 63920 Großheubach, Bayern, Germany. tel:(07867) 391381. john.connor@trelleborg.com, www.trelleborg.com/sealsandprofiles

Tremco Illbruck Ltd - Coupland Road, Hindley Green, Wigan. WN2 4HT tel:(01942) 251400, fax:(01942) 251410. uk.info@tremco-illbruck.com, www.tremco-illbruck.co.uk

Trend Control Systems Ltd - St Mark's Court, North Street, Horsham, West Sussex. RH12 1BW tel:(01403) 211888. marketing@trendcontrols.com, www.trendcontrols.com

Trespa UK Ltd - 35 Calthorpe Road, Edgbaston, Birmingham. B15 1TS tel:(0808) 234 02 68, fax:(0808) 234 13 77. info.uk@trespa.com, www.trespa.com

Trico V.E. Ltd (Signage Division) - 76 Windmill Hill, Colley Gate, Halesowen, West Midlands. B63 2BZ tel:(01384) 569555, fax:(01384) 565777. info@trico-ve.co.uk, www.trico-ve.co.uk

Trim Acoustics - Unit 4, Leaside Industrial Estate, Stockingswater Lane, Enfield, London. EN3 7PH tel:(020) 8443 0099, fax:(020) 8443 1919. sales@trimacoustics.co.uk, www.trimacoustics.co.uk

Trimite Ltd - Arundel Road, Uxbridge, Middx. UB8 2SD tel:(01895) 951234, fax:(01895) 256789. info@trimite.com, www.trimite.com

Trimite Scotland Ltd - 38 Welbeck Road, Darnley Industrial Estate, Glasgow. G53 7RG tel:(0141) 881 9595, fax:(0141) 881 9333. sales@tslpaints.com, www.tslpaints.com

Triton PLC - Shepperton Park, Caldwell Road, Nuneaton, Warwicks. CV11 4NR tel:(024) 76 344441, fax:(024) 76 324424. serviceenquiries@tritonshowers.co.uk, www.tritonshowers.co.uk

TROAX UK Ltd - Enterprise House, Murdock Road, Dorcan, Swindon, Wilts. SN3 5HY tel:(01793) 520000, fax:(01793) 618784. info@troax.com, www.troax.com

TROX (UK) Ltd - Caxton Way, Thetford, Norfolk. IP24 3SQ tel:(01842) 754545, fax:(01842) 763051. trox@troxuk.co.uk, www.troxuk.co.uk

TSE Brownson - Sacksville Street, Skipton, N. Yorks. BD23 2PR tel:(01756) 797744, fax:(01756) 796644. info@rewardtrolleys.com, www.rewardmanufacturing.com

tso shop - TSO Customer Services, PO Box 29, Norwich. NR3 1GN tel:(0333) 200 5070, fax:(0333) 202 5080. customer.services@tso.co.uk, www.tsoshop.co.uk

T-T Pumps & T-T controls - Onneley Works, Newcastle Road, Woore. CW3 9RU tel:(01630) 647200, fax:(01630) 642100. response@ttpumps.com, www.ttpumps.com

Tubeclamps Ltd - PO Box 41, Petford Street, Cradley Heath, Warley, W. Midlands. B64 6EJ tel:(01384) 565241, fax:(01384) 410490. sales@tubeclamps.co.uk, www.tubeclamps.co.uk

Tubela Engineering Co Ltd - 11 A/B Hoblongs Ind Estate, Chelmsford Road, Gt Dunmow, Essex. CM6 1JA tel:(01371) 859100, fax:(01371) 859101. tubebending@tubela.com, www.tubela.com

Tubs & Tiles - Moydrum Road, Athlone, Westmeath, Ireland. tel:+353 90 6424000, fax:+353 90 6424050. customerservices@wolseley.co.uk, www.tubstiles.ie

Tudor Roof Tile Co Ltd - Denge Marsh Road, Lydd, Kent. TN29 9JH tel:(01797) 320202, fax:(01797) 320700. info@tudorrooftiles.co.uk, www.tudorrooftiles.co.uk

Tuke & Bell Ltd - Lombard house, No 1 Cross Keys, Lichfield, Staffs. WS13 6DN tel:(01543) 414161, fax:(01543) 250462. sales@tukeandbell.co.uk, www.tukeandbell.co.uk

Tunstal Healthcare (UK) Ltd - Whitley Lodge, Whitley Bridge, N. Yorks. DN14 0HR tel:(01977) 661234, fax:(01977) 661993. sales@tunstall.co.uk, www.tunstallgroup.com

Turnbull & Scott (Engineers) Ltd - Unit 1a, Burnfoot Industrial Estate, Hawick, Scottish Borders. TD9 8SL tel:(01450) 372 053, fax:(01450) 377 800. info@turnbull-scott.co.uk, www.turnbull-scott.co.uk

Turner Access Ltd - 65 Craigton Road, Glasgow. G51 3EQ tel:(0141) 309 5555, fax:(0141) 309 5436. enquiries@turner-access.co.uk, www.turner-access.co.uk

Tuscan Foundry Products Ltd - Cowfold, W. Sussex. RH13 8AZ tel:(0800) 174093, fax:(0845) 3450215. info@tuscanfoundry.co.uk, www.tuscanfoundry.co.uk

Tutto Parquet Limited - Unit 6/7 Arrow Business Centre, 19/21 Aintree Road, Perivale, Greenford. UB6 7LA tel:(0207) 435 8282. info@tuttoparquet.co.uk, www.tuttoparquet.co.uk

TWI - Abington Hall, Abington, Cambridge. CB21 6AL tel:(01223) 891162, fax:(01223) 892588. twi@twi.co.uk, www.twi.co.uk

TWI Ltd - Granta Park, Great Abington, Cambridge. CB21 6AL tel:(01223) 891162. adhesivestoolkit@twi.co.uk, www.twi-global.com

Twyford Bathrooms - Lawton Road, Alsager, Stoke-on-Trent. ST7 2DF tel:(01270) 879777, fax:(01270) 873864. enquiries@geberit.co.uk, www.twyfordbathrooms.com

Tyco Fire and Integrated Solutions - Tyco Park, Grimshaw Lane, Newton Heath, Manchester. M40 2WL tel:(0161) 455 4400. tfis.marketing.uk@tycoint.com, www.tycofis.co.uk

Tyco Water Works - Nobel Road, Eley Trading Estate, Edmonton, London. N18 3DW tel:(020) 8884 4388, fax:(020) 8884 4766. enquiries@talis-group.com, www.tycowaterworks.com

Tyco Waterworks - Samuel Booth - Samuel Booth Works, Warstock Road, Kings Heath, Birmingham. B14 4RT tel:(0121) 772 2717, fax:(0121) 766 6962. tfis.marketing.uk@tycoint.com, www.tycowaterworks.com/sbooth

U

Ubbink (UK) Ltd - Borough Road, Brackley, Northants. NN13 7TB tel:(01280) 700211, fax:(01280) 705332. info@ubbink.co.uk, www.ubbink.co.uk

UK Fasteners Ltd - C1 Liddington Trading Estate, Leckhampton Road, Cheltenham, Glos. GL53 0DL tel:(01242) 577077, fax:(01242) 577078. sales@ukfasteners.co.uk, www.ukfasteners.co.uk

UK Lift Co Ltd - Westminster Wks, Sandown Road, Watford, Herts. WD24 7UB tel:(01923) 656200. info@uk-lift.co.uk, www.uk-lift.co.uk

Ulster Carpet Mills Ltd - Castleisland Factory, Craigavon, Co. Armagh. BT62 1EE tel:(028) 38334433, fax:(028) 38333142. marketing@ulstercarpets.com, www.ulstercarpets.com

Ultraframe PLC - Salthill Road, Clitheroe, Lancs. BB7 1PE tel:(0500) 822340, fax:(01200) 425455. info@ultraframe.co.uk, www.ultraframe.co.uk/ultra

Unicorn Containers Ltd - 5 Ferguson Drive, Knockmore Hill Industrial Park, Lisburn, Antrim. BT28 2EX tel:(02892) 667264, fax:(02892) 625616. info@unicorn-containers.com, www.unicorn-containers.com

Unifix Ltd - Hexstone, Opal Way, Stone Business Park, Stone, Staffordshire. ST15 0SW tel:(0800) 808 7172, fax:(0800) 731 3579. sales@unifix.co.uk, www.unifix.co.uk

UNION Locks and Hardware - School Street, Willenhall, W. Midlands. WV13 3PW info@uniononline.co.uk, www.uniononline.co.uk

Unistrut Limited - Unistrut House, Delta Point Greets Green Road, West Bromwich. B70 9PL tel:(0121) 580 6300, fax:(0121) 580 6370. www.unistrut.co.uk

United Flexibles (A Division of Senior Flex) - Abercanaid, Merthyr Tydfil, M. Glam. CF48 1UX tel:(01685) 385641, fax:(01685) 389683. sales@amnitec.co.uk, www.amnitec.co.uk

United Wire Ltd - Granton Park Avenue, Edinburgh. EH5 1HT tel:(0131) 552 6241, fax:(0131) 552 8462. info@unitedwire.com, www.unitedwire.com

Universal Components Ltd - Universal House, Pennywell Road, Bristol, Avon. BS5 0ER tel:(0117) 955 9091, fax:(0117) 955 6091. sales@universal-aluminium.co.uk, www.universal-aluminium.co.uk

Uponor Ltd - The Pavilion, Blackmoor Lane, Watford, Hertfordshire. WD18 8GA tel:(01923) 927000, fax:(01923) 223760. enquiries.uk@uponor.com, www.uponor.co.uk

Urban Planters - PO Box 24, Skipton, North Yorkshire. BD23 9AN tel:(01274) 579331, fax:(01274) 521150. sales@urbanplanters.co.uk, www.urbanplanters.co.uk

Urbis Schreder Ltd - Sapphire House, Lime Tree Way, Hampshire Int Business Park, Chineham. RG24 8GG tel:(01256) 679 860. sales@urbislighting.com, www.urbislighting.com

Uretek (UK) Ltd - Mere One, Mere Grange, Elton Head Road, St Helens, Lancashire. WA9 5GG tel:(01695) 50525, fax:(01695) 555212. sales@uretek.co.uk, www.uretek.co.uk

UTC Fire & Securites - 8 Newmarket Court, Chippenham Drive, Milton Keynes. MK10 0AQ tel:(01908) 281981. customerservice.uk@fs.utc.com, www.uk.firesecurityproducts.com

V

V B Johnson LLP

9-11 Castleford Road, Normanton, W. Yorks. WF6 2DP tel:(01924) 897373, fax:(03332) 407363. wakefield@vbjohnson.co.uk, www.vbjohnson.co.uk

V B Johnson LLP

St John's House, 304-310 St Albans Road, Watford, Herts. WD24 6PW tel:(01923) 227236. watford@vbjohnson.co.uk, www.vbjohnson.co.uk

Vador Security Systems Ltd - 52 Lowdown, Pudsey, West Yorkshire. LS28 7AA tel:(0800) 037 5365, fax:(0870) 766 4025. info@vadorsecurity.co.uk, www.vadorsecurity.co.uk

Valmont Stainton - Teeside Industrial Estate, Thornaby, Cleveland. TS17 9LT tel:(01642) 766242, fax:(01642) 765509. stainton@valmont.com, www.stainton-metal.co.uk

Valor - Wood Lane, Erdington, Birmingham. B24 9QP tel:(0121) 373 8111, fax:(0121) 373 8181. marketing@valor.co.uk, www.valor.co.uk

Valspar Powder Coatings Ltd - 177 Argyle Street, Nechells, Birmingham. B7 5TE tel:(0121) 328 5227. industrialfinishes@valspar.com, www.valspar.com

Valspar UK Corporation Ltd - Avenue One, Station Lane, Witney, Oxon. OX28 4XR tel:(01993) 707400, fax:(01993) 775579. packaging@valspareurope.com, www.valspareurope.com/

Valtti ltd - 27 Marnin Way, West Edingburgh Business Park, Edinburgh. EH12 9GD tel:(0131) 334 4999, fax:(0131) 334 3987. enquiries@valtti.co.uk, https://www.tikkurila.co.uk/decorative_paints

Vantrunk Engineering Ltd - Goodard Road, Astmoor, Runcorn, Cheshire. WA7 1QF tel:(01928) 564211, fax:(01928) 580157. sales@vantrunk.co.uk, www.Vantrunk.com

Varley & Gulliver Ltd - 57-70 Alfred Street, Sparkbrook, Birmingham. B12 8JR tel:(0121) 773 2441, fax:(0121) 776 6875. sales@v-and-g.co.uk, www.v-and-g.co.uk

VBH (GB) Ltd - VBH House, Bailey Drive, Gillingham Business Park, Gillingham, Kent. ME8 0WG tel:(01634) 263 263, fax:(01634) 263 300. sales@vbhgb.com, www.vbhgb.com

Veka PLC - Farrington Road, Rossendale Road Indstrial Estate, Burnley, Lancs. BB11 5DA tel:(01282) 416611, fax:(01282) 439260. salesenquiry@veka.com, www.vekauk.com

Veka Plc - Farrington Road, Rossendale Road Industrial Estate, Burnley. BB11 5DA tel:(01282) 716611, fax:(01282) 725257. salesenquiry@veka.com, www.veka.com

VELUX Co Ltd, The - Woodside Way, Glenrothes, E. Fife. KY7 4ND tel:(01592) 772211, fax:(01592) 771839. sales@velux.co.uk, www.velux.co.uk

Venator - Liverpool Road East, Kidsgrove, Stoke-on-Trent, Staffordshire. ST7 3AA tel:(01782) 794400, fax:(01782) 787338. info@venatorcorp.com, www.venatorcorp.com

Vent-Axia - Flemming Way, Crawley, W. Sussex. RH10 9YX tel:(0844) 856 0590, fax:(01293) 565169. info@vent-axia.com, www.vent-axia.com

Ventrolla Ltd - Crimple Court, Hornbeam Business Park, Harrogate, N. Yorks. HG2 8PB tel:(01423) 859323, fax:(01423) 859321. info@ventrolla.co.uk, www.ventrolla.co.uk

Veolia Water Technologies UKElga Ltd - Unit 10 Lane End Industrial Park, Lane End, High Wycombe, Bucks. HP14 3BY tel:(0203) 567 7300, fax:(0203) 567 7205. sales.uk@veolia.com, www.elgalabwater.com

Verco Office Furniture Ltd - Chapel lane, Sands, High Wycombe, Bucks. HP12 4BG tel:(01494) 448000, fax:(01494) 464216. info@verco.co.uk, www.verco.co.uk

Vermeer United Kingdom - 45-51 Rixon Road, Wellingborough, Northants. NN8 4BA tel:(01933) 274400, fax:(01933) 274403. sales@vermeeruk.co.uk, http://vermeer-uk.co.uk/

Verna Ltd - Folds Road, Bolton, Lancs. BL1 2TX tel:(01204) 529494, fax:(01204) 521862. vcorders@vernagroup.com, www.vernagroup.com

Ves Andover Ltd - Eagle Close, Chandlers Ford Industrial Estate, Eastleigh, Hampshire. SO53 4NF tel:(08448) 15 60 60, fax:(02360) 261 204. info@ves.co.uk, www.ves.co.uk

Vescom UK Limited - Unit 3 Canada Close, Banbury, Oxfordshire. OX16 2RT tel:(01295) 273644, fax:(01295) 273646. uk@vescom.com, www.vescom.com

Vetter UK - City Gate 2, Cross Street, Sale, Manchester. M33 7JR tel:(01322) 736 507. enquiries@vetteruk.com, www.vetteruk.com

Vianen KVS BV - Finse Golf 18, 3446 CK Woerden, The Netherlands. tel:+31 348 416 300, fax:+31 348 421 595. sales@vianenkvs.com, www.vianenkvs.com

Vicaima Ltd - Marlowe Avenue, Greenbridge Industrial Estate, Swindon, Wilts. SN3 3JF tel:(01793) 532333, fax:(01793) 530193. info@vicaima.com, www.vicaima.com

Vicon Industries Ltd - Brunel Way, Fareham, Hants. PO15 5TX tel:(01489) 566300, fax:(01489) 566322. sales@vicon.co.uk, www.vicon-cctv.com

Victaulic Systems - 46-48 Wibury Way, Hitchin, Herts. SG4 0UD tel:(01462) 443322, fax:(01462) 443148. info@victaulic.co.uk, www.victaulic.co.uk

Vidionics Security Systems Ltd - Systems House, Desborough Industrial Park, Desborough Park Road, High Wycombe, Bucks. HP12 3BG tel:(01494) 459606, fax:(01494) 461936. sales@vidionics.co.uk, www.vidionics.co.uk

Viking Johnson - 46-48 Wilbury Way, Hichen, Herts. SG4 0UD tel:(0121) 700 1000, fax:(0121) 700 1001. info@vikingjohnson.com, www.glynwedpipesystems-uk.com

Vink Plastics Ltd - 27 Long Wood Road, Trafford Park, Manchester. M17 1PZ tel:(01618) 737080, fax:(01618) 737079. info@vink.com, www.vinkplastics.co.uk

Visqueen Building Products - Heanor Gate, Heanor, Derbyshire. DE75 7RG tel:(0845) 302 4758, fax:(0845) 017 8663. enquiries@visqueenbuilding.co.uk, www.visqueenbuilding.co.uk

Vista Engineering Ltd - Carr Brook Works, Shallcross Mill Road, Whaley Bridge, High Peak. SK23 7JL tel:(01663) 736700, fax:(01663) 736710. sales@vistaeng.co.uk, www.vistaeng.co.uk

Vista Plan International PLC - High March, Daventry, Northants. NN11 4QE tel:(01327) 704767, fax:(01327) 300243. sales@vistaplan.com, www.vistaplan.com

Vita Liquid Polymers Ltd - Harling Road, Wythenshawe, Manchester. M22 4SZ tel:(0161) 998 3226, fax:(0161) 946 0118. info@vita-liquid.co.uk, www.vita-liquid.co.uk

Vitra (UK) Ltd - Park 34, Collet Way, Didcot, Oxon. OX11 7WB tel:(01235) 750990, fax:(01235) 750980. info@vitra.co.uk, www.vitrauk.com

Vitra UK Ltd - 30 Clerkenwell Road, London. EC1M 5PG tel:(020) 7608 6200, fax:(020) 7608 6201. info-uk@vitra.com, www.vitra.com

Vitreous Enamel Association, The - Belfield House, Firs Lane, Appleton, Warrington. WA4 5LE tel:(0755) 55 96164. info@vea.org.uk, www.vea.org.uk

Vokes Air - Farrington Road, Farrington Road, Burnley, Lancs. BB11 5SY tel:(01282) 413131, fax:(01282) 686200. vokes@btinc.com, www.vokesair.com

Vola - Unit 12, Ampthill Business Park, Station Road, Ampthill, Beds. MK45 2QW tel:(01525) 841155, fax:(01525) 841177. sales@vola.co.uk, www.vola.com

Volex Group PLC - Dornoch House, Kelvin Close, Birchwood, Warrington. WA3 7JX tel:(01925) 830101, fax:(01925) 830141. sales@volex.com, www.volex.com

Vortice Ltd - Beeches House, Eastern Avenue, Burton-on-Trent, Staffs. DE13 0BB tel:(01283) 492949, fax:(01283) 544121. sales@vortice.ltd.uk, www.vortice.ltd.uk

Vulcan Cladding Systems - 4 Imperial Way, Croydon. CR0 4RR tel:(020) 8681 0617, fax:(020) 8256 5977. sales@vulcansystems.co.uk, www.vulcansystems.co.uk

Vulcascot Cable Protectors Ltd - Unit 12, Norman-D-Gate, Bedford Road, Northampton. NN1 5NT tel:(0800) 0352842, fax:(01604) 632344. sales@vulcascotcableprotectors.co.uk, www.vulcascotcableprotectors.co.uk

W

W. Hawley & Son Ltd - Colour Works, Lichfield Road, Branston, Burton-on-Trent, Staffs. DE14 3WH tel:(01283) 714200, fax:(01283) 714201. info@concos.co.uk, www.hawley.co.uk

W.H Colt Son & Co Ltd - Unit 4 Counter Buildings, Brook Street, Woodchurch, Kent. TN26 3SP tel:(01233) 812919. mail@colthouses.co.uk, www.colthouses.co.uk

W.L. West & Sons Ltd - Selham, Petworth, W. Sussex. GU28 0PJ tel:(01798) 861611, fax:(01798) 861633. sales@wlwest.co.uk, www.wlwest.co.uk

Waco UK Limnited - Catfoss Lane, Brandsburton, Nr Driffield, E. Yorks. YO25 8EJ tel:(0800) 3160888, fax:(01964) 545001. sales@waco.co.uk, www.waco.co.uk

Wade Building Services Ltd - Groveland Road, Tipton, W. Midlands. DY4 7TN tel:(0121) 520 8121, fax:(0121) 557 7061. sales@wade-bs.co.uk, www.wade-bs.co.uk

Wade Ceramics Ltd - Bessemer Drive, Stoke-on-Trent, Staffordshire. ST1 5GR tel:(01782) 577321, fax:(01782) 575195. enquiries@wade.co.uk, www.wade.co.uk

Wade International Ltd - Third Avenue, Halstead, Essex. CO9 2SX tel:(01787) 475151, fax:(01787) 475579. tech@wadedrainage.co.uk, www.wadedrainage.co.uk

Wales & Wales - The Long Barn Workshop, Muddles Green, Chiddingly, Lewes, Sussex. BN8 6HW tel:(01825) 872764, fax:(01825) 873197. info@walesandwales.com, www.walesandwales.com

Walker Timber Ltd - Carriden Sawmills, Bo'ness, W. Lothian. EH51 9SQ tel:(01506) 823331, fax:(01506) 822590. mail@walkertimber.com

Wall Tie Installers Federation - Heald House, Heald Street, Liverpool. L19 2LY tel:(0151) 494 2503. admin@wtif.org.uk, www.wtif.org.uk

W (con't)

Wallace & Tiernan - Office 12, Dana Estate, Transfesa Road, Paddock Wood, Kent. TN12 6UT tel:(0300) 124 0500. info.uk@evoqua.com, www.wallace-tiernan.com

Wallbank - P.O. Box 317, Wilmslow, Cheshire. SK9 5WA tel:(0161) 439 0908, fax:(0161) 439 0908. john@wallbank-lfc.co.uk, www.wallbank-lfc.co.uk

Wallcovering Manufacturers Association (now part of the British Coatings Federation) - Riverbridge House, Guildford Road, Leatherhead, Surrey. KT22 9AD tel:(01372) 365989. info@bcf.co.uk, www.coatings.org.uk

Wallgate Ltd - Crow Lane, Wilton, Salisbury, Wiltshire. SP2 0HB tel:(01722) 744594, fax:(01722) 742096. sales@wallgate.com, www.wallgate.com

Wallis Conservation Limited trading as Dorothea Restorations - Unit 4, William Street, Bristol. BS2 0RG tel:(0117) 979 8397 , fax:(0117) 977 1677. john@dorothearestorations.com, www.dorothearestorations.com

Walls & Ceilings International Ltd - Tything Road, Arden Forest Industrial Estate, Alcester, Warwicks. B49 6EP tel:(01789) 763727, fax:(01789) 400312. sales@walls-and-ceilings.co.uk, www.walls-and-ceilings.co.uk

Walney UK Ltd - The Keys, Latchford Mews, Wheathampstead, Hertfordshire. AL4 8BB tel:(0870) 733 0011, fax:(0870) 733 0016. sales@walneyuk.com, www.walneyuk.com

Walraven Ltd - Thorpe Way, Banbury, Oxon. OX16 4UU tel:(01295) 75 34 00, fax:(01295) 75 34 28. sales.banbury@walraven.com, www.walraven.com/gb/en/

Wandsworth Elecrtrical Ltd - Albert Drive, Sheerwater, Woking, Surrey. GU21 5SE tel:(01483) 740740, fax:(01483) 740384. info@wandsworthgroup.com, www.wandsworth-electrical.com

Ward & Co (Letters) Ltd - Maze House, Maze Street, Barton Hill, Bristol. BS5 9TE tel:(0117) 955 5292, fax:(0117) 955 7518. info@ward-signs.co.uk, www.ward-signs.co.uk

Ward Insulated Panels Ltd - Sherburn, Malton, N. Yorks. YO17 8PQ tel:(01944) 710591, fax:(01944) 710555. wbc@wards.co.uk, www.wards.co.uk

Wardle Storeys - Grove Mill, Earby via Colne, Lancs. BB18 6UT tel:(01282) 842511, fax:(01282) 843170. sales@wardlestoreys.com, www.wardlestoreys.com

Ward's Flexible Rod Company Ltd - 22 James Carter Road, Mildenhall, Suffolk. IP28 7DE tel:(01638) 713800, fax:(01638) 716863. sales@wardsflex.co.uk, www.wardsflex.co.uk

Warmafloor (GB) Ltd - Onyx, 12 Little Park Farm Road, Segensworth West, Fareham, Hampshire. PO15 5TD tel:(01489) 581787, fax:(01489) 57644. sales@warmafloor.co.uk, www.warmafloor.co.uk

Warner Howard Group Ltd - Warner Howard House, 2 Woodgrange Avenue, Harrow, Middx. HA3 0XD tel:(020) 8206 2900, fax:(020) 8206 1313. info@warnerhoward.co.uk, www.warnerhoward.w.uk

Watco UK Ltd - Watco House, Filmer Grove, Godalming, Surrey. GU7 3AL tel:(01483) 427373, fax:(01483) 428888. sales@watco.co.uk, www.watco.co.uk

Water Technology Engineering Ltd - Unit 2, Bolton Lane, York, Yorkshire. YO41 5QX tel:(01759) 369915. info@wte-ltd.co.uk, www.wte-ltd.co.uk

Waterline Limited - Crown House, North Crawley Road, Newport Pagnell, Bucks. MK16 9TG tel:(03330) 149149, fax:(0800) 585 531. sales@waterline.co.uk, www.waterline.co.uk

Waterstones - 203/206 Piccadilly, London. W1J 9HD tel:(0808) 118 8787. support@waterstones.com, www.waterstones.com

Watts Industries UK Ltd - Colmworth Business Park, St Neots. PE19 8YX tel:(01480) 407074. wattsuk@wattswater.com, www.wattsindustries.co.uk

Wavin Ltd - Parsonage Way, Chippenham, Wilts. SN15 5PN tel:(01249) 766600, fax:(01249) 443286. info@wavin.co.uk, www.wavin.co.uk

Weatherley Fencing Contractors Limited - The Orchard, 135 North Cray Road, Sidcup, Kent. DA14 5HE tel:(020) 8300 6421, fax:(020) 8308 1317. weatherleyfence@btconnect.com, www.weatherleyfencing.co.uk/

Weber Building Solutions - Dickens House, Enterprise Way, Flitwick, Beds. MK45 5BY tel:(08703) 330070, fax:(01525) 718988. mail@weberbuildingsolutions.co.uk, www.weberbuildingsolutions.co.uk

Wednesbury Tube - Oxford Street, Bilston, W. Midlands. WV14 7DS tel:(01902) 491133, fax:(01902) 405838. sales@muellereurope.com, www.muellereurope.com

Weir Group - The Weir Group PLC, 1 West Regent Street, Glasgow. G2 1RW tel:(0141) 637 7111, fax:(0141) 221 9789. contact-us@mail.weir, www.weir.co.uk

Weir Pumps Ltd - 149 Newlands Road, Cathcart, Glasgow. G44 4EX tel:(01416) 377141, fax:(01416) 377358. weirspmaberdeen@weirspm.com, www.weirclearliquid.com

Wellman Robey Ltd - Newfield Road, off Dudley Road East, Oldbury, Warley, W. Midlands. B69 3ET tel:(0121) 552 3311, fax:(0121) 552 4571. sales@wellmanrobey.com, www.wellmanrobey.com

Welsh Slate Limited - Penrhyn Quarry, Bethesda, Bangor, Gwynedd. LL57 4YG tel:(01248) 600656, fax:(01248) 601171. enquiries@welshslate.com, www.welshslate.com

Wentworth Sawmills Ltd - Barrowfield Lane, Wentworth, Nr. Rotherham, S. Yorks. S62 7TP tel:(01226) 742206, fax:(01226) 742484. victoria.earnshaw@jobearnshaw.co.uk, www.jobearnshaw.co.uk/

Wernick Group Ltd - Molineux House, Russell Gardens, Wickford, Essex. SS11 8BL tel:(01268) 735544, fax:(01268) 560026. sales@wernick.co.uk, www.wernick.co.uk

Wessex Lift Co Ltd - Budds Lane, Romsey, Hants. SO51 0HA tel:(01794) 830303, fax:(01794) 512621. info@wessexlifts.co.uk, www.wessexlifts.co.uk

Wessex Resins & Adhesives Ltd - Cuperham House, Cuperham Lane, Romsey, Hants. SO51 7LF tel:(01794) 521111, fax:(01794) 521271. info@wessex-resins.com, www.wessex-resins.com

Wesson Fencing - 48 High Street, Knaphill, Woking, Surrey. GU21 2PY tel:(01483) 472124, fax:(01483) 472115. wesson-fencing@hotmail.co.uk, www.wesson-fencing.co.uk

West London Security - 22-36 Paxton Place, London. SE27 9SS tel:(020) 8676 4300, fax:(020) 8676 4301. info@westlondonsecurity.com, www.westlondonsecurity.com

Westbury Filters Limited - Hall Farm Estate, Gadbrook Road, Betchworth, Surrey. RH3 7AH tel:(01306) 611611, fax:(01306) 611613. sales@westburyfiltermation.com, www.westburyfilters.co.uk

Western Cork Ltd - Penarth Road, Cardiff. CF11 8YN tel:(029) 20 376700, fax:(029) 20 383573. customerservices@westcodiy.co.uk, www.westcofloors.co.uk

Westpile Ltd - Dolphin Bridge House, Rockingham Road, Uxbridge, Middx. UB8 2UB tel:(01895) 258266, fax:(01895) 271805. estimating@westpile.co.uk, www.westpile.co.uk

Weyland incorporating Clayton Munroe - Unit C, Chancel Close, Gloucester. GL4 3SN tel:(01452) 313051. sales@claytonmunroe.com, www.claytonmunroe.com

WF Senate - 313-333 Rainham Road South, Dagenham, Essex. RM10 8SX tel:(0208) 984 2000, fax:(0121) 567 2638. info@rexelsenate.co.uk, www.wfsenate.co.uk

Which Building Contract - 96, Rutland Road, Forest Gate, London. E7 8PH tel:(0203) 002 0034. malcolmb@goeshere.co.uk, www.whichbuildingcontract.co.uk

Whitecroft Lighting Limited - Burlington Street, Ashton-under-Lyne, Lancs. OL7 0AX tel:(0870) 5087087, fax:(0870) 5084210. email@whitecroftlight.com, www.whitecroftlighting.com

Whitehill Spindle Tools Ltd - 2-8 Bolton Road, Luton, Beds. LU1 3HR tel:(01582) 736881, fax:(01582) 488987. sales@whitehill-tools.com, www.whitehill-tools.com

Whitmore's Timber Co Ltd - Main Road, Claybrooke Magna, Lutterworth, Leics. LE17 5AQ tel:(01455) 209121, fax:(01455) 209041. esales@whitmores.co.uk, www.whitmores.co.uk/

Wienerberger Ltd - Wienerberger House, Brooks Drive, Cheadle Royal Business Park, Cheadle, Cheshire. SK8 3SA tel:(0161) 491 8200, fax:(0161) 491 1270. office@wienerberger.co.uk, www.wienerberger.co.uk

Wienerberger Ltd (Keymer Handmade Clay Plain Tiles) - Ewhurst Works, Wallis Wood, Ockley, Surrey. RH5 5QH tel:(01444) 232931, fax:(01444) 871852. info@keymer.co.uk, www.keymer.co.uk

William Hopkins & Sons Ltd - Gardine House, 147-147 Dollman Street, Nechells, Birmingham. B7 4RS tel:(0121) 333 3577, fax:(0121) 333 3480. info@william-hopkins.co.uk, www.william-hopkins.co.uk

William Wilson Ltd - SCO 14691 Registered office, Hareness Road, Altens Industrial Estate, Aberdeen. AB12 3QA tel:(01224) 877522, fax:(01224) 879650. marketing@williamwilson.co.uk, www.williamwilson.co.uk

Williamson T & R Ltd - 36 Stonebridge Gate, Ripon, N. Yorks. HG4 1TP tel:(01765) 607711, fax:(01765) 607908. enquiries@trwilliamson.co.uk, www.trwilliamson.co.uk

Wilo Samson Pumps Ltd - 2ND Avenue, Centrum 100, Burton-on-Trent, Staffs. DE14 2WJ tel:(01332) 385181, fax:(01332) 344423. sales@wilo.co.uk, www.wilo.co.uk

Wilsonart Ltd - Lambton Street Industrial Estate, Shildon, County Durham. DL4 1PX tel:+44 0 1388 774661, fax:+44 0 1388 774861. customerservices@wilsonart.co.uk, www.wilsonart.co.uk

Wincro Metal Industries Ltd - Fife Street, Wincobank, Sheffield, S. Yorks. S9 1NJ tel:(0114) 242 2171, fax:(0114) 243 4306. sales@wincro.com, www.wincro.com

Windowbuild - 55-56 Lewis Road, East Moors, Cardiff. CF24 5EB tel:(029) 20 307 200, fax:(029) 20 480 030. info@windowbuild.co.uk, www.windowbuild.co.uk

Winn & Coales (Denso) Ltd - Denso House, Chapel Road, London. SE27 0TR tel:(020) 8670 7511, fax:(020) 8761 2456. mail@denso.net, www.denso.net

Winther Browne & co Ltd - 75 Bilton Way, Enfield, London. EN3 7ER tel:(020) 8884 6000, fax:(020) 8884 6001. sales@wintherbrowne.co.uk, www.wintherbrowne.co.uk

Wirquin Ltd - Unit 3 Alpha Court, Capitol Park, Thorne. DN8 5TZ tel:(03332) 224488, fax:(01302) 312251. sales@wirquin.co.uk, www.wirquin.co.uk

Witham Oil & Paint Ltd - Stanley Road, Oulton Broad, Lowestoft, Suffolk. NR33 9ND tel:(01502) 563434, fax:(01502) 500010. enquiries@withamgroup.co.uk, www.withamoil.co.uk

Wm. Bain Fencing Ltd - Lochrin Works, 7 Limekilns Road, Blairlinn Ind. Est, Cumbernauld. G67 2RN tel:(01236) 457333. sales@lochrin-bain.co.uk, www.lochrin-bain.co.uk

Wolseley UK - The Wolseley Center, Harrison Way, Spa Park, Royal Leamington Spa. CV31 3HH tel:(01923) 705 000. customerservices@wolseley.co.uk, www.wolseley.co.uk

Wood International Agency Ltd - Wood House, 16 King Edward Road, Brentwood, Essex. CM14 4HL tel:(01277) 232991, fax:(01277) 222108. woodia@msn.com, www.ourworld.compuserve.com/homepages/wood_international_agency

Wood Panels Industries Federation - Autumn Park Business Centre, Dysart Road, Grantham, Lincolnshire. NG31 7EU tel:(01476) 512381. enquiries@wpif.org.uk, www.wpif.org.uk

Woodburn Engineering Ltd - Rosganna Works, Trailcock Road, Carrickfergus, Co. Antrim. BT38 7NU tel:(028) 93366404, fax:(028) 93367539. rose@woodburnengineeringltd.co.uk

Woodscape Ltd - 1 Sett End Road West, Shadsworth Business Park, Blackburn, Lancashire. BB1 2QJ tel:(01254) 685185. sales@woodscape.co.uk, www.woodscape.co.uk

Worcester Heat Systems Ltd - Cotswold Way, Warndon, Worcester, Worcs. WR4 9SW tel:(01905) 754624, fax:(01905) 754619. sales.mailbox@uk.bosch.com, www.worcester-bosch.co.uk

Workspace Technology Ltd - Unit 10, Reddicap Trading Estate, Sutton Coldfield, West Midlands. B75 7BU tel:(0121) 354 4894, fax:(0121) 354 6447. sales@workspace-technology.com, www.workspace-technology.com

WP Metals Ltd - Westgate, Aldridge, W. Midlands. WS9 8DJ tel:(01922) 743111, fax:(01922) 743344. info@wpmetals.co.uk

WT Henley Ltd - Crete Hall Road, Gravesend, Kent. DA11 9DA tel:(01474) 564466, fax:(01474) 566703. sales@wt-henley.com, www.wt-henley.com

Wybone Ltd - Mason Way, Platts Common Industrial Estate, Hoyland, Nr Barnsley, S. Yorks. S74 9TF tel:(01226) 744010, fax:(01226) 350105. sales@wybone.co.uk, www.wybone.co.uk

Wyckham Blackwell Ltd - Old Station Road, Hampton in Arden, Solihull, W. Midlands. B92 0HB tel:(01675) 442233, fax:(01675) 442227. enquiries@wyckhamblackwell.co.uk, www.wyckham-blackwell.co.uk

Wylex Ltd - Wylex Works, Wythenshaw, Manchester. M22 4RA tel:(0161) 998 5454, fax:(0161) 945 1587. wylex.sales@electrium.co.uk, www.electrium.co.uk/wylex.htm

Wymark Ltd - Runnings Road Industrial Estate, Cheltenham, Glos. G51 9NQ tel:(01242) 520966, fax:(01242) 519925. info@wymark.co.uk, www.wymark.co.uk

Wyvern Marlborough Ltd - Grove Trading Estate, Dorchester, Dorset. DT1 1SU tel:(01305) 264716, fax:(01305) 264717. mailto:info@wyvernfireplaces.com, www.wyvernfireplaces.com

X

Xella Aircrete Systems UK - PO Box 10028, Sutton Coldfield. B75 7ZF tel:(08432) 909 080, fax:(08432) 909 081. hebel-uk@xella.com, www.xella.co.uk

Xpelair Ltd - PO Box 279, Morley Way, Peterborough. PE2 9JJ tel:(01733) 456789, fax:(01733) 310606. info@redring.co.uk, www.xpelair.co.uk

Xtralis - Peoplebuilding, Ground Floor, Maylands Avenue, Hemel Hempstead, Herts. HP2 4NW tel:(01442) 242330, fax:(01442) 240327. sales@xtralis.com, http://xtralis.com

Y

Yale Security Products Ltd - Wood Street, Willenhall, W. Midlands. WV13 1LA tel:(01902) 366911, fax:(01902) 368535. info@yale.co.uk, www.yale.co.uk

York Handmade Brick Co Ltd - Winchester House, Forest Lane, Alne, York, N. Yorks. Y061 1TU tel:(01347) 838881, fax:(01347) 830065. sales@yorkhandmade.co.uk, www.yorkhandmade.co.uk

Yorkon Ltd - New Lane, Huntington, York, Yorks. YO32 9PT tel:(01904) 610990, fax:(01904) 610880. contact@yorkon.com, www.yorkon.com

Yorkshire Copper Tube - East Lancashire Road, Kirkby, Liverpool. L33 7TU tel:(0151) 545 5079, fax:(0151) 549 2139. sales@yct.com, www.yct.com

Yorkstone Supplies Ltd - Unit 14, Phoenix House, Littlemeads Industrial Estate, Alfold Road, Cranleigh. GU6 8ND tel:(01483) 930 104. sales@yorkstonesupplies.co.uk, www.yorkstonesupplies.co.uk

Youngman Group Limited - The Causeway, Maldon, Essex. CM9 4LJ tel:(01621) 745900. uk.customercare@wernerco.com, www.youngmangroup.com

Youngs Doors Ltd - City Road Works, Norwich, Norfolk. NR1 3AN tel:(01603) 629889, fax:(01603) 764650. mail@youngs-doors.co.uk, www.youngs-doors.co.uk

Z

Zarges (UK) Ltd - 8 Holdom Avenue, Saxon Park Industrial Estate, Bletchley, Milton Keynes. MK1 1QU tel:(01908) 641118, fax:(01908) 648176. sales@zarges.co.uk, www.zargesuk.co.uk

Zehnder Group UK Ltd - Concept House, Watchmoor Point, Camberley, Surrey. GU15 3AD tel:(01276) 605800. sales@zehnder.co.uk, www.zehnder.co.uk

Zellweger Analytic Ltd, Sieger Division - Hatch Pond House, 4 Stinsford Road, Poole, Dorset. BH17 0RZ tel:(01202) 676161, fax:(01202) 678 011. consumer@honeywell.com, www.zelana.com

Zephyr The Visual Communicators - Midland Road, Thrapston, Northants. NN14 4LX tel:(01832) 734 484, fax:(01832) 733 064. sales@zephyr-tvc.com, www.zephyr-tvc.com

Zon International - PO Box 329, Edgware, Middx. HA8 6NH tel:(020) 8381 1222, fax:(020) 8381 1333. sales@zon.co.uk, www.zon.co.uk

This page left blank intentionally

A1 fire rated ducting kits - Rytons Building Products Ltd

A01 Institutions/ Associations/ Trade Organisations

Accrediting body and learned society - Chartered Institution of Building Services Engineers (CIBSE)
Aluminium window association - Council for Aluminium in Building
Architectural aluminium association - Council for Aluminium in Building
Asbestos training courses for management and operatives - Asbestos Removal Contractors' Association
Association - Resin Flooring Association (FeRFA)
Association and institution - Joint Council For The Building & Civil Engineering Industry (N. Ireland)
Association of concrete technologists - The Institute of Concrete Technology
Association of Concrete Industrial Flooring Contractors - Association of Concrete Industrial Flooring Contractors (ACIFC)
BCIS Dayworks Rates Online - BCIS
BCIS Online - BCIS
BCIS Rebuild Online - BCIS
BCIS Review Online - BCIS
Bookshops - Royal Incorporation of Architects in Scotland
Brick information service - Brick Development Association
Builders and Master Wrights Association, Scotland - Scottish Building Federation
Builders federation - Federation of Master Builders
Builders federation - National Federation of Builders
Building & Engineering Services Association - Building & Engineering Services Association
Building Cost Information Service - BCIS
CAA - Cement Admixtures Association
Campaigns in Britain and abroad - Society for the Protection of Ancient Buildings (SPAB)
Carpet manufacturers trade association - The Carpet Foundation
Carpet Industry Trade Association - The Carpet Foundation
Carpet promotion - The Carpet Foundation
Casework to save old buildings at risk from damage or demolition - Society for the Protection of Ancient Buildings (SPAB)
Ceramic Research Association (formerly Ceram) - Lucideon
Clay pipe trade asssociation - Clay Pipe Development Association Ltd
Client services and advice - Royal Incorporation of Architects in Scotland
Concrete Society - The Institute of Concrete Technology
Conferences and events - Royal Incorporation of Architects in Scotland
Construction employers federation - Construction Employers Federation
Construction information on CD-Rom - IHS
Construction information service online - IHS
Consultancy on Timber - TRADA Technology Ltd
Consultancy services on procurement - Royal Incorporation of Architects in Scotland
Contract flooring journal - Contract Flooring Association
Cost engineers' association - Association of Cost Engineers
Damp control - The Property Care Association
Decorators trade association - Painting & Decorating Association
Design competitions administration - Royal Incorporation of Architects in Scotland
Distributor of the Arts' share of the National Lottery - Arts Council England
Dry stone walling association - Dry Stone Walling Association of Great Britain
Education and training for building professionals - Brick Development Association
Electrical association - Electrical Contractors' Association (ECA)
Estimators - John Watson & Carter
Estimators - V B Johnson LLP
Event organizing/book seller/information provider - Chartered Institution of Building Services Engineers (CIBSE)
Events including lectures and regional group visits - Society for the Protection of Ancient Buildings (SPAB)
Fire Safety Industry - Fire Industry Association
Flood Protection - The Property Care Association
Flood remediation - The Property Care Association
Forestry - Confor: Promoting forestry and wood
Free technical advice on the maintenance of old buildings - Society for the Protection of Ancient Buildings (SPAB)
Gallery - Royal Incorporation of Architects in Scotland
Galvanizers trade association - Galvanizers Association
Gas safety consultants - Corgi Technical Dervices
Glazing trade association - Glass and Glazing Federation
Heating and ventilating trade association - Building & Engineering Services Association
Imlementation of working rules & wage rates for the industry - Joint Industry Board for the Electrical Contracting Industry
Information & advice on craft of dry stone walling - Dry Stone Walling Association of Great Britain
Information service to businesses - British Library – Business & Intellectual Property Centre
Institution of Incorporated Engineers in electronic, electrical and mechanical engineering (IIE) - The Institution of Engineering and Technology
Institutions and association - Architectural Association
Institutions and association - Asbestos Removal Contractors' Association
Institutions and association - Association of Interior Specialists (AIS)
Institutions and association - British Precast Concrete Federation
Institutions and association - British Standards Institution
Institutions and association - Catering Equipment Suppliers Association
Institutions and association - Craft Guild of Chefs
Institutions and association - Friends of the Earth
Institutions and association - Historic England
Institutions and association - HMSO Publications Office
Institutions and association - Institution of Engineering and Technology
Institutions and association - Institution of Mechanical Engineers
Institutions and association - Institution of Structural Engineers
Institutions and association - Mortar Industry Association
Institutions and association - Ordnance Survey
Institutions and association - Royal Institute of British Architects (RIBA)
Institutions and association - Royal Town Planning Institute
Institutions and associations - Association of Technical Lightning & Access Specialists (ATLAS)
Institutions and associations - British Association for Chemical Specialities
Institutions and associations - British Association of Landscape Industries
Institutions and associations - British Precast Flooring Federation
Institutions and associations - British Refrigeration Association (BRA)
Institutions and Associations - Building Controls Industry Association (BCIA)
Institutions and Associations - Confederation of British Metalforming
Institutions and associations - European Lead Sheet Industry Association
Institutions and associations - Institution of Civil Engineers
Institutions and associations - Interpave
Institutions and associations - Prestressed Concrete Association
Institutions and associations - Quarry Products Association
Institutions and associations - Society for the Protection of Ancient Buildings (SPAB)
Institutions and associations - The Concrete Society
Institutions and associations - The Kitchen Bathroom Bedroom Specialists Association
Institutions/ Associations/ Trade Organisations - Design Council
Institutions/Associations - British Slate Association
Institutions/Associations - FeRFA
Institutions/Associations - Institute of Quarrying
Institutions/Associations - Leatherhead Food Research Association
Institutions/Associations - Sprayed Concrete Association
Institutions/Associations - Stone Federation Great Britain
Institutions/Associations/Trade Organisations - Be-Plas Marketing Ltd
Insulated Render & Cladding Association Ltd - Insulated Render & Cladding Association
Insulation association - National Insulation Association Ltd
Invasive weed control - The Property Care Association
Journals - Contract Journal
LIA - Lighting Industry Association, The
Lift and Escalator Industry Association - LEIA
Lighting Industry Association - Lighting Industry Association, The
Lucideon - Ceramic Research - Lucideon
Manholes - Concrete Pipeline Systems Association
National Access & Scaffolding Confederation Ltd (NASC) - National Access & Scaffolding Confederation (NASC)
National funding body for arts in England - Arts Council England
National organisation for the steel construction industry - British Constructional Steelwork Association Ltd
Nurseries - Confor: Promoting forestry and wood
Painting contractors trade association - Painting & Decorating Association
Patent glazing contractors association - Council for Aluminium in Building
Pipes - Concrete Pipeline Systems Association
Plant Managers' Journal - Contract Journal
Product and material information and literature - The Building Centre Group Ltd
Professional body - Chartered Institute of Building
Professional Body - Royal Institution of Chartered Surveyors (RICS)
Professional body registered as an educational charity - Chartered Institute of Plumbing & Heating Engineering
Professional institution - Chartered Building Company Scheme
Professional institution - Chartered Building Consultancy Scheme
Professional membership organisation for the resources and waste management sector - Chartered Institute of Wastes Management
Professional recognition and development for Incorporated Engineers and Engineering Technicians in electronic, electrical and mechanical engineering - The Institution of Engineering and Technology
Publications on care and repair of old buildings - Society for the Protection of Ancient Buildings (SPAB)
Publications: contract flooring association members handbook - Contract Flooring Association
Publishing house (rutland press), guides etc - Royal Incorporation of Architects in Scotland
Registration of apprentice electricians - Joint Industry Board for the Electrical Contracting Industry
Represent RIBA in Scotland - Royal Incorporation of Architects in Scotland
Scottish architectural trade association - Royal Incorporation of Architects in Scotland
Sealant Applicators Trade Organisation - Association of Sealant Applicators Ltd (ASA)
SED - The National Event For Construction - Contract Journal
Separate mills section - Society for the Protection of Ancient Buildings (SPAB)
Services to architects including PI insurance - Royal Incorporation of Architects in Scotland
Special events run by SPAB in Scotland - Society for the Protection of Ancient Buildings (SPAB)
Steel window association - Steel Window Association
Structural repair - The Property Care Association
Structural Waterproofing - The Property Care Association
TCPA Publications - Town and Country Planning Association
Technical Consultancy - British Glass Manufacturers Confederation
Telephone enquiry point - British Library – Business & Intellectual Property Centre
Telephone help line for building professionals - Barbour Enquiry Service
Testing, certification and technical approval - British Board of Agrément
Thatched roof advice, training and insurance - Thatching Advisory Services Ltd
The construction information service - NBS
The Institution of Engineering and Technology - The Institution of Engineering and Technology
The Lighting Industry Association - Lighting Industry Association, The
The welding institute - TWI
Timber preservation - The Property Care Association
Town and Country Planing Journal - Town and Country Planning Association
Trade Association - Association of Specialist Fire Protection (ASFP)
Trade association - Brick Development Association
Trade Association - British Blind and Shutter Association (BBSA)
Trade Association - British Coatings Federation Ltd
Trade association - British Constructional Steelwork Association Ltd
Trade Association - British Electrotechnical and Allied Manufacturers Association
Trade Association - British Fenestration Rating Council
Trade Association - British Flue & Chimney Manufacturers Association
Trade Association - British Glass Manufacturers Confederation
Trade Association - British Plastics Federation, The
Trade Association - British Pump Manufacturers Association
Trade Association - British Security Industry Association
Trade Association - British Stainless Steel Association
Trade Association - British Structural Waterproofing Association, The
Trade Association - British Woodworking Federation
Trade Association - Builders Merchants Federation
Trade Association - Building Research Establishment
Trade Association - Chartered Institute of Arbitrators
Trade Association - Civil Engineering Contractors Association
Trade Association - Concrete Block Association
Trade Association - Construction Industry Research & Information Association
Trade Association - Construction Industry Training Board
Trade Association - Construction Plant-hire Association
Trade Association - Constructionline
Trade Association - Door and Hardware Federation
Trade Association - Drilling & Sawing Association, The
Trade Association - Federation of Piling Specialists
Trade Association - Federation of Plastering and Drywall Contractors
Trade Association - Garage Equipment Association Ltd
Trade Association - Guild of Architectural Ironmongers
Trade Association - Guild of Builders & Contractors, The
Trade Association - Heating Ventilating and Air Conditioning Manufacturers Association (HEVAC)
Trade Association - Institute of Ashphalt Technology, the
Trade Association - Institute of Specialist Surveyors and Engineers
Trade Association - Joint Industry Board for the Electrical Contracting Industry
Trade Association - Lift and Escalator Industry Association,The
Trade Association - Mineral Wool Insulation Manufacturers Association
Trade Association - National Association of Shopfitters
Trade Association - National Federation of Demolition Contractors
Trade Association - National Federation of Roofing Contractors Ltd., The
Trade Association - National House Building Council
Trade Association - National Inspection Council for Electrical Installation Contracting
Trade Association - Painting & Decorating Association
Trade Association - PRA
Trade association - Quarry Products Association
Trade Association - Rural & Industrial Design & Building Association
Trade Association - Scottish & Northern Ireland Plumbing Employers' Federation
Trade Association - Single Ply Roofing Association
Trade Association - Solar Trade Association, The
Trade Association - The Tile Association
Trade Association - Thermal Insulation Contractors Association
Trade Association - Timber Trade Federation
Trade Association - Vitreous Enamel Association, The
Trade Association - Wall Tie Installers Federation
Trade Association - Wallcovering Manufacturers Association (now part of the British Coatings Federation)
Trade association for the ceramic tile industry - The Tile Association
Trade association for the factory produced mortar industry - Mortar Industry Association
Trade association for the lift & escalator industry - LEIA
Trade Association Service - Mastic Asphalt Council
Trade associations of electrical and electronics sector - Beama Ltd
Trade Body - British Adhesives and Sealants Association
Trade Organisation - Advisory, Conciliation and Arbitration Service
Trade Organisation - Association for Consultancy and Engineering (ACE)
Trade Organisation - Association of Plumbing and Heating Contractors
Trade Organisation - Bathroom Manufacturers Association, The
Trade Organisation - British Ceramic Confederation
Trade Organisation - MPA Cement
Training programs and courses for professionals, craftsmen and owners - Society for the Protection of Ancient Buildings (SPAB)
Urethane foam industry trade association - British Urethane Foam Contractors Association
Water and Wastewater Association - British Water
Wood - Confor: Promoting forestry and wood
Wood Panels - Wood Panels Industries Federation

A02 Building contractors

Asbestos removal - Rhodar Limited
Association of Concrete Industrial Flooring Contractors - Association of Concrete Industrial Flooring Contractors (ACIFC)
Bespoke joinery - Pearce Construction (Barnstaple) Limited
Builders - Ogilvie Construction Ltd
Building and development - Pearce Construction (Barnstaple) Limited
Building contractor - TH Kenyon & Sons Ltd
Building contractor incorporating partnering, guaranteed max price, PFI, lease back, facilities management, site finding - GallifordTry
Building contractors - Advanced Interior Solutions Ltd
Building Contractors - Clifford Partitioning Co Ltd
Civil engineering - Freyssinet Ltd
Construction - Kier Limited
Electrical services Contractor - Kershaw Mechanical Services Ltd
Fencing contractors - Burn Fencing Limited
Housing - Kier Limited
Housing - Pearce Construction (Barnstaple) Limited
Interior contractors - Gifford Grant Ltd
Landscape contractors - Gearing F T Landscape Services Ltd
Mechcanical services Contractor - Kershaw Mechanical Services Ltd
Minor civil engineering - Chestnut Products Limited
Plumbers - Ogilvie Construction Ltd
Property development - Kier Limited
Refurbishment and Building contractors - Shaylor Group Plc
Roofing contractor - Evans Howard Roofing Ltd
Sports field contractor - Bernhards Landscapes Ltd
Sports ground construction - AMK Fence-In Limited
Structural enhancement - Freyssinet Ltd

A10 Project particulars

Architectural and Exhibition model makers - Modelscape
Architectural presentation planning design - Comber Models
ATM enclosures - Pearce Security Systems
Business to Business Listings - Glenigan Ltd
Capital Allowance Assessors - Johnson VB LLP
Chartered quantity surveyors - John Watson & Carter
Chartered quantity surveyors - Sawyer & Fisher
Chartered quantity surveyors - V B Johnson LLP
Construction related Sector - Glenigan Ltd
Consultancy - Carter Retail Equipment Ltd
Cost Engineers - Johnson VB LLP
Design an Procurement - Robinson Lloyds Architecture
Education services design and procurement - Robinson Lloyds Architecture
Electrical services - H Pickup Mechanical & Electrical Services Ltd

Energy Performance Certificates
Oakwood Property Solutions

Estimators - Johnson VB LLP
General engineering - Turnbull & Scott (Engineers) Ltd
Health services design and procurement - Robinson Lloyds Architecture
Mechanical services - H Pickup Mechanical & Electrical Services Ltd
Mechanical, electrical and process services engineers - Shepherd Engineering Services Ltd
Models - Comber Models
Modular cash rooms - Pearce Security Systems
On Line Home improvements support - DIY Doctor
Project management - Carter Retail Equipment Ltd
Project Managers - Johnson VB LLP
Project particulars - Advanced Interior Solutions Ltd
Project particulars - British Standards Institution
Quantity Surveyors - Johnson VB LLP
Rising armour screens - Pearce Security Systems
Rotary transfer units - Pearce Security Systems
Sales Leads - Glenigan Ltd

SAP Calculations
Oakwood Property Solutions

Security lobbies - Pearce Security Systems
Social care services design and procurement - Robinson Lloyds Architecture
Stats & Rankings Lists - Glenigan Ltd
Trade Association - Cast Metals Federation

Water Calculations
Oakwood Property Solutions

A12 The site/ Existing buildings

Drone Surveys
Select Aerial Photography

A20 The Contract/ Sub-contract

Advice given to Contractors - National Federation of Builders
Expert witness - British Glass Manufacturers Confederation
Guide to sustainable procurement in the water industry - British Water

A30 Tendering/ Subletting/ Supply

Building Price Book - Laxton's Publishing Ltd

A31 Provision, content and use of documents

Books - Town and Country Planning Association
CPD seminars - DW Windsor Lighting
NBS Building - NBS
NBS Create - NBS
Online bookshop - BRE

A32 Management of the Works

Building regulations approved documents England & Wales - NBS
Management of the Works - Advanced Interior Solutions Ltd
Project management - DW Windsor Lighting
Publishers of the National Building Specification - NBS
Sub Contract Engineers - Multi Marque Production Engineering Ltd
Windows based estimating and contract cost control system - CSSP (Construction Software Services Partnership)

A33 Quality standards/ control

Administration of electrotechnical certification scheme in affiliation with CSCS - Joint Industry Board for the Electrical Contracting Industry
Alarm monitoring & routine maintenance - ADT Fire and Security Plc
Analysis & Testing - British Glass Manufacturers Confederation
ATaC asbestos testing and consulting - a division of Arca - Asbestos Removal Contractors' Association
Carpet quality control - The Carpet Foundation
Civil engineering test equipment - Capco Test Equipment, A division of Castlebroom Engineering Ltd
Drone Surveys - Select Aerial Photography
Environmental services - British Glass Manufacturers Confederation
Fracture & failure - British Glass Manufacturers Confederation
In-house laboratory - DW Windsor Lighting
Methodologies within the water industry - British Water
Product & Perfomance - British Glass Manufacturers Confederation
Quality standards/control - British Standards Institution
SAP Calculations - Oakwood Property Solutions
Service & Inspection Schemes for mechanical Plant - Multi Marque Production Engineering Ltd
Stock testing - British Glass Manufacturers Confederation
Technical support & customer service - Hilmor
Water Calculations - Oakwood Property Solutions

A34 Security/ Safety/ Protection

Access - Magnum Ltd T/A Magnum Scaffolding
Access and Fall Arrest Systems - Safety Works & Solutions Ltd
Access control - Allegion (UK) Ltd
Access systems - Clow Group Ltd
Anti bandit & bullet resistant counters - Pearce Security Systems
Asbestos Removal - Kitsons Insulation Products Ltd
Automatic / Self-Testing Emergency Lighting - P4 Limited
Battery operated smoke & fire alarms - BRK Brands Europe Ltd
Bullet resistant gazing, windows, doors, screens - Pearce Security Systems
Cable fall arrest system - Latchways plc
Carbon monoxide - detectors - BRK Brands Europe Ltd
Cash Handling & Recycling - Gunnebo UK Limited
Door and window Locks - Securikey Ltd
Energy conservation in built environment - BRE
External Mirrors - Moravia (UK) Ltd
Fall arrest and safety - Bacon Group
Fall arrest systems - Latchways plc
Fencing Security - Darfen Durafencing
Fire research/consultancy - BRE
Fire training - Griffin and General Fire Services Ltd
Floor protection - PHS Group plc
Footwear - industrial - Briggs Industrial Footwear Ltd t/a Briggs Safety Wear
Fragile roof and rooflight covers - Latchways plc
Gaseous extinguishing - ADT Fire and Security Plc
Hardwire smoke & fire alarms - BRK Brands Europe Ltd
High security locking systems - Chubb Safe Equipment Company
Industrial footwear - Briggs Industrial Footwear Ltd t/a Briggs Safety Wear
Ladder safety systems - Latchways plc
Manufacturers of Fast Tow Mixers - Multi Marque Production Engineering Ltd
Marking Tapes - Moravia (UK) Ltd
Natural gas alarms - BRK Brands Europe Ltd
Passive fire protection, Resistance fire testing, Reaction to fire testing - BM TRADA
Pedestrian barrier - Wade Building Services Ltd
Personal Protective Equipment - Briggs Industrial Footwear Ltd t/a Briggs Safety Wear
Personal Protective Equipment - Kem Edwards Ltd
Planning Supervisors - Johnson VB LLP
Portable Security - Allegion (UK) Ltd
Protection sheets - Cordek Ltd
Respiratory protection and safety helmets - MSA (Britain) Ltd
Roof safety systems - Latchways plc
Safe Deposit Lockers - Gunnebo UK Limited
Safes - Chubb Safe Equipment Company
Safes & Vaults - Gunnebo UK Limited
Safety access systems - Kobi Ltd
Safety Equipment - HSS Hire Service Group
Safety eyebolts - Latchways plc
Safety systems - Unistrut Limited
Safety/ security/ protection - Pilkington UK Ltd
Security / safety protection - Specialist Building Products
Security units - Parklines Building Ltd
Security/ Safety/ Protection - Abloy UK
Security/ Safety/ Protection - Harling Security Solutions Limited
Security/ Safety/ Protection - Tarmac Building Products Ltd - SafetyDeck
Security/safety - Intersolar Group Ltd
Security/safety/protection - BPT Automation Ltd
Site Safety Equipment - Sportsmark Group Ltd
Steel Hoard Site Hoarding - Darfen Durafencing
Steel security units - Ideal Building Systems Ltd
Strongrooms - Chubb Safe Equipment Company
Superbolt - TEAM INDUSTRIAL SERVICES (UK) LIMITED
Temporary security fences - Wade Building Services Ltd
Temporary site hoarding - Wade Building Services Ltd
Vaults - Chubb Safe Equipment Company
Workwear - Briggs Industrial Footwear Ltd t/a Briggs Safety Wear

A36 Facilities/ Temporary works/ services

Bespoke esign services - Camlok Lifting Clamps Ltd
Builders bags - Hilton Banks Ltd
Cabins, site accommodation and event toilets - Rollalong Ltd
Demountable Flood Defense Systems - Bauer Renewables Ltd
Emergency Lighting - P4 Limited
Facilities/temporary works/services - Interface Europe Ltd
Non-mechanical access and building equipment (hire and sales) - Actavo (UK) Ltd
Palletwrap - Hilton Banks Ltd
Repairs and service of industrial doors - Avon Industrial Doors Ltd
Spill Kits - TEAM INDUSTRIAL SERVICES (UK) LIMITED
Tarpaulins - Hilton Banks Ltd
Temporary fencing and site guard panels - Guardian Wire Ltd
Temporary roadways - Eve Trakway
Temporary works - Frosts Landscape Construction Ltd
Trench Cover - MCL Composites Ltd

A37 Operation/ Maintenance of the finished building

Anti-finger trap devices - Dorma Door Services Ltd
BCIS Building Running Costs Online - BCIS
Door safety products - Dorma Door Services Ltd
Engineers tools - Spear & Jackson
Garage door repairs - Acorn Garage Doors Ltd
Hand tools - Hilmor
Lift & Escalator Maintenance / Repair / Service - Schindler Ltd
Maintenance and service - Cooper Group Ltd
Maintenance and Service of environmental systems - Kingspan Environmental Ltd
On Line Home improvements support - DIY Doctor
Operation/ Maintenance of the finished building - Advanced Interior Solutions Ltd
Operation/ Maintenance of the finished building - Johnson Controls Building Efficiency UK Ltd
Operational and maintenance contracts and technical advice - Doosan Power Systems Ltd
Repair of Garage doors - Acorn Garage Doors Ltd
Service - GP Burners (CIB) Ltd
Structural repairs - ProTen Services

A40 Management and staff

Training - Airedale International Air Conditioning Ltd

A41 Site accommodation

Modular buildings - Wernick Group Ltd
Modular buildings hire - Waco UK Limnited
Modular buildings sale - Waco UK Limnited
Schools, Key Worker & Student Accomadation - Rollalong Ltd
Secure accommodation - Waco UK Limnited
Site accommodation - Waco UK Limnited
Site Accomodation - Caledonian Modular
Site Accomodation - Thurston Building Systems

A42 Services and facilities

24 hour service - Servowarm
24 hour service call out - Chubb Safe Equipment Company
Abrasives tungsten carbide burs - PCT Group
Access Equipment hire - HSS Hire Service Group
Air qulity monitoring - Zellweger Analytic Ltd, Sieger Division
Air tightness testing, Acoustic testing, Mechanical testing, Passive fire protection, Structural testing, Timber testing, Third party certification - BM TRADA
Alloy tower and aerial platform training - Turner Access Ltd
Aluminium towers, aerial platforms, scissors and booms - Turner Access Ltd
Annual Services - Servowarm
Application Tooling - Hellermann Tyton
Asbestos abatement and consultancy services - Rhodar Limited
Automative tools - Spear & Jackson
Bonded abrasives - Marcrist International Ltd
Bookshop - The Building Centre Group Ltd
Breakdown repairs - Servowarm
Bricklifter handlifting tools (bricks) - Edward Benton & Co Ltd
Buckets - Airflow (Nicoll Ventilators) Ltd
Builders tools - Spear & Jackson
Building Project Information - The Building Centre Group Ltd
Bulk handling systems - Portasilo Ltd
Caddies - Airflow (Nicoll Ventilators) Ltd
Cartridge tools - ITW Spit
Conference & Seminar Facilities - The Building Centre Group Ltd
Conferences and seminars - Town and Country Planning Association
Construction equipment - Schwing Stetter (UK) Ltd
Construction research and development - BRE
Construction tools - Ingersoll-Rand European Sales Ltd
Core drills - Norton Diamond Products
Cutting machines - Norton Diamond Products
Decontamination units - Rollalong Ltd
Decorators Tools - Ciret Limited
Diamond blades - Norton Diamond Products
Disabled access door operators - Dorma Door Services Ltd
Drainage industry and plumbers tools - Monument Tools Ltd
Electric Tools - ITW Spit
Electrical and Mechanical Services Contractor - Kershaw Mechanical Services Ltd
Engineering and production tools - Spear & Jackson
Engineering Stockist - A & G Structures Ltd
Exhibitions - building materials and products - The Building Centre Group Ltd
Exhibitions, conferences, and meeting rooms - The Building Centre Group Ltd
Flexible tubs - Airflow (Nicoll Ventilators) Ltd
Guideline - The Building Centre Group Ltd
Hand & power tools - Kem Edwards Ltd
Hand and garden tools - Spear & Jackson
Hand tools - Footprint Sheffield Ltd
Hand tools, power tool accessories and abrasives - Hyde Brian Ltd
Hot dip galvanising - Jones of Oswestry Ltd
Installation - Servowarm
Kermaster handlifting tools (Kerbs) - Edward Benton & Co Ltd
Lifting Equipment hire - HSS Hire Service Group
Local engineers (corgi registered) - Servowarm
Lubricants - Witham Oil & Paint Ltd
Market & research schemes - The Building Centre Group Ltd
Masking tape - Ciret Limited
Metal cutting tools - Spear & Jackson
Mop Buckets - Airflow (Nicoll Ventilators) Ltd
Office Equipment - Cave Tab Ltd
Open and enclosed skips, cargo containers and custom built units - Randalls Fabrications Ltd
Organisational Tools - Cave Tab Ltd
Pipe tools - Hilmor
Plant - Linatex Ltd
Power tools-pneumatic/electric/hydraulic - PCT Group
Publications - Butterworth-Heinemann
Publications and technical information on timber - TRADA Technology Ltd
Scaffold hire - HSS Hire Service Group
Services and facilities - Advanced Interior Solutions Ltd
Services and Facilities - B & D Clays & Chemicals Ltd
Services and facilities - Barlow Group
Services and facilities - Frosts Landscape Construction Ltd
Services and facilities - Tarmac Building Products Ltd - SafetyDeck
Servocare economic insurance - Servowarm
Servocare priority insurance - Servowarm
Site services - Magnum Ltd T/A Magnum Scaffolding
Skin care products - Deb Group Limited
Soft faced hammers and mallets - Thor Hammer Co Ltd
Spindle tooling - Whitehill Spindle Tools Ltd
Suppliers of Bituminous Binders Road Surface Dressing Contractors - Colas Ltd
Support Services - Kier Limited
Surveying Equipment - HSS Hire Service Group

A42 Services and facilities (con't)

Timber merchants, Importers, Oak specialist - W.L. West & Sons Ltd
Tool & Equipment Repair - HSS Hire Service Group
Tool hire - HSS Hire Service Group
Tools - Eliza Tinsley Ltd
Tools - Footprint Sheffield Ltd
Tools - Walls & Ceilings International Ltd
Transportation of Brituminous Products, Liquid and Oils - Colas Ltd
Upgrade to existing system - Servowarm
Wall protection - Moffett Thallon & Co Ltd
Wall tie condition surveys - HCL Contracts Ltd
Wallpaper pasting machines - Ciret Limited

A43 Mechanical plant

Access platforms - Manitou (Site Lift) Ltd
Attachments/Accessories - HE Services (Plant Hire) Ltd
Backhoe Loaders, Dumpers, Excavators, and Rollers - HE Services (Plant Hire) Ltd
Boring machines, boring tools and trenchers - Vermeer United Kingdom
C-hooks/coil hooks - Camlok Lifting Clamps Ltd
Compressor crankcase heaters - Flexelec(UK) Ltd
Construction equipment - Schwing Stetter (UK) Ltd
Construction equipment, compressors, rock drills and accessories, compaction and paving equipment - Ingersoll-Rand European Sales Ltd
Core drills - Harbro Supplies Ltd
Crane forks - Camlok Lifting Clamps Ltd
Creteangle bulkbag systems - Edward Benton & Co Ltd
Creteangle hopper vibratory feeder systems - Edward Benton & Co Ltd
Creteangle moulds for precast concrete products - Edward Benton & Co Ltd
Creteangle pan type mixers - Edward Benton & Co Ltd
Diesel power generators - Sandhurst Manufacturing Co Ltd
Directional drill rigs - Vermeer United Kingdom
Double vacuum impregnation plant - Protim Solignum Ltd
Drill bits - Artur Fischer (UK) Ltd
Drum handling Equipment - Camlok Lifting Clamps Ltd
Electric tools - ITW Construction Products
Excavating and earth moving plant - J C Bamford (Excavators) Ltd
Forklift truck attachments - Camlok Lifting Clamps Ltd
Gas nailers - ITW Construction Products
Gas power tools - ITW Spit
General Site Equipment - Kem Edwards Ltd
Grinding machines, surface and double ended grinders - Beacon Machine Tools Ltd
Hire of Mechanical Plant - HE Services (Plant Hire) Ltd
Horizontal grinders - Vermeer United Kingdom
Horticultural and agricultural tools - Spear & Jackson
Lifting clamps and grabs - Camlok Lifting Clamps Ltd
Machine tools for the manufacture of building products - BSA Machine Tools Ltd
Machinery - The Saw Centre Group
Manual and powered hoists, winches and jacks - PCT Group
Manufacturer of Conveyors - Multi Marque Production Engineering Ltd
Manufacturers of Roller Mixer - Multi Marque Production Engineering Ltd
Material handling equipment - Harbro Supplies Ltd
Mechanical Plant - Access Industries Group Ltd
Mechanical plant - Johnson Controls Building Efficiency UK Ltd
Mechcanical services Contractor - Kershaw Mechanical Services Ltd
Mini excavators, dumper trucks, rollers and cement mixers - Chippindale Plant Ltd
Mobile site lighting - Sandhurst Manufacturing Co Ltd
Moles - Vermeer United Kingdom
Pan type mixing machinery - Benton Co Ltd Edward
Plant Body Shop - HE Services (Plant Hire) Ltd
Plant hire - HSS Hire Service Group
Plate compactors - Chippindale Plant Ltd
Pneumatic nailers - ITW Construction Products
Power actuated tools - ITW Construction Products
Power tools and accessories - Robert Bosch Ltd
Rail handling Equipment - Camlok Lifting Clamps Ltd
Road Maintenance Equipment - Phoenix Engineering Co Ltd, The
Rough terrain forklifts - Manitou (Site Lift) Ltd
Sand blast equipment - Harbro Supplies Ltd
Screwlok beam clamps - Camlok Lifting Clamps Ltd
Scrubber driers - Quirepace Ltd
Site dumpers, concrete and mortar mixers, sawbenches and telescopic handlers - Multi Marque Production Engineering Ltd
Snow Clearance - HE Services (Plant Hire) Ltd
Sorbents - TEAM INDUSTRIAL SERVICES (UK) LIMITED
Special rigging structures - Scotia Handling Services
Stone processing machinery - Harbro Supplies Ltd
Telehandlers - Chippindale Plant Ltd
Telehandlers - HE Services (Plant Hire) Ltd
Telescopic loaders - Manitou (Site Lift) Ltd
Tipping skips - Woodburn Engineering Ltd
Tools - Duffells Limited
Transport Services - HE Services (Plant Hire) Ltd
Tree equipment, woodchippers, stump cutters and tub grinders - Vermeer United Kingdom
Trenchers - Vermeer United Kingdom
Truck mounted forklift - Manitou (Site Lift) Ltd
Tube Bending Machines - Tubela Engineering Co Ltd
Vehicle turntables - British Turntable Ltd
Welding and Brazing equipment \\ consumables - Johnson Matthey PLC - Metal Joining
Welding Equipment - HSS Hire Service Group
Welding equipment - PCT Group

A44 Temporary works

Abnormal lead support - Eve Trakway
Access platforms - Chippindale Plant Ltd
Access towers - SGB, a Brand Company
Adhesive, solid, metallic, plastic tapes - Marking Machines International
All forms of line (sports and commercial) marking machines - Marking Machines International
Aluminium towers - Youngman Group Limited
Anchor testing & installation - HCL Contracts Ltd
Bridge jacking and monitoring - Mabey Hire Ltd
Bridges - Eve Trakway
Cable grips - Albion Manufacturing Ltd
Contract scaffolding - Magnum Ltd T/A Magnum Scaffolding
Ground protection - Eve Trakway
Industrial scaffolding - Industrial Solutions - Actavo (UK) Ltd
Ladders - Titan Ladders Ltd
Ladders - Youngman Group Limited
Ladders & steps - Youngman Group Limited
Loftladders - Titan Ladders Ltd
Measuring tapes and equipment - Marking Machines International
Modular buildings - Elliott Ltd
Pest control - humane live catch and trap - Albion Manufacturing Ltd
Safety Deck Systems – Hire and Sales - Actavo (UK) Ltd
Scaffold sheeting - Icopal Limited
Scaffold towers - Titan Ladders Ltd
Scaffolding - Howard Evans Roofing and Cladding Ltd
Scaffolding - Schauman (UK) Ltd
Scaffolding - SGB, a Brand Company
Scaffolding - Wade Building Services Ltd
Scaffolding restraints - HCL Contracts Ltd
Scaffolding Systems - Turner Access Ltd
Site buildings - Elliott Ltd
Staging - CPS Manufacturing Co
Stagings - Clow Group Ltd
Steps - Titan Ladders Ltd
Temporary fencing - Rom Ltd
Temporary fencing and barriers - Elliott Ltd
Temporary Road Markings - Sportsmark Group Ltd
Temporary roadway - Sommerfeld Flexboard Ltd
Temporary roadways and bridging - Mabey Hire Ltd
Temporary works - Freyssinet Ltd
Towers - Clow Group Ltd

A45 Computer software and software licenses

Construction Software - Eque2 Limited

A55 Dayworks

BCIS Dayworks Online - BCIS
Building Price Book - Laxton's Publishing Ltd

A61 Preliminaries/ General conditions for investigation/ survey contract

Drone Surveys - Select Aerial Photography
Energy Performance Certificates - Oakwood Property Solutions

A63 Preliminaries/ General conditions for landscape contract

Drone Surveys - Select Aerial Photography

A70 General specification requirements for work package

BCIS Schedule of Rates - BCIS
Book Sales - Gardners Books
Book sales - Professional Books Limited
Book sales - RIBA Enterprises
Book Sales - TRADA Bookshop
Book sales - TRADA Technology Ltd
Book sales - tso shop
Book Sales - Waterstones
Book Sales - Which Building Contract
Book sellers - Construction Industry Publications
Book sellers - Dandy Booksellers
Book Sellers - RICS Book Shop
Business to Business Publications - EMAP
Online Book Suppliers - The Book Depository Ltd
RICS publications - Dandy Booksellers
Specialist Book Sellers - RICS Book Shop
Wholsale booksellers - Bertrams

B10 Prefabricated buildings/ structures

Architectural fabrications - Clow Group Ltd
Barns - Purewell Timber Buildings Limited
Battery Garages - concrete - Liget Compton
Bespoke aluminum structures - Apropos Conservatories Ltd
Bike Shelters - Glasdon U.K. Limited
Bridges in timber or steel, boardwalks, decking, ramps, steps and bespoke structures - CTS Bridges Ltd
Builders merchant - Jewson Ltd
Builders merchant - Nicholls & Clarke Ltd
Building systems to buy or hire, self contained buildings and modular buildings - Portakabin Ltd
Buildings - Glasdon U.K. Limited
Buildings and Housings - Glasdon UK Limited
Cantilever and pigeon hole racking - Hi-Store Ltd
Chemical stores - Parklines Building Ltd
Complete buildings - Elliott Ltd
Concrete Garages - Parklines Building Ltd
Concrete garages, sheds, workshops, garden rooms - Liget Compton
Conservatories - Alitex Ltd
Conservatories - Duraflex Limited
Conservatories - Saveheat Group
Conservatories - Solair Ltd
Conservatories - Spectra Glaze Services
Conservatories, garden buildings - Amdega Ltd
Corrugated structural steel plate bridges - Asset International Ltd
Covered Walkways - Fibaform Products Ltd
Cycle Shelter - The No Butts Bin Company (NBB), Trading as NBB Outdoor Shelters
Environmental trade products - TEAM INDUSTRIAL SERVICES (UK) LIMITED
Equestrian buildings - Scotts of Thrapston Ltd
Export Buildings - Wernick Group Ltd
Extruded conservatories - Smart Systems Ltd
Field Shelters - Newton & Frost Fencing Ltd
Flat Pack Buildings - Wernick Group Ltd
Garages - concrete - Liget Compton
Garden buildings - Weatherley Fencing Contractors Limited
Garden rooms - concrete - Liget Compton
Garden structures - Pergolas, Arbours, Arches, Gazebos - Grange Fencing Limited
Gatehouses - Fibaform Products Ltd
Grp modular buildings - Dewey Waters Ltd
Hire of buildings - Wernick Group Ltd
Industrial housings - Fibaform Products Ltd
Kennels - Weatherley Fencing Contractors Limited
Log cabins - Newton & Frost Fencing Ltd
Log Cabins - Purewell Timber Buildings Limited
Log stores - Purewell Timber Buildings Limited
Magnum firechests - Schiedel Chimney Systems Ltd
Mechcanical services - Kershaw Mechanical Services Ltd
Modular and volumetric buildings - Rollalong Ltd
Modular buildings - Bell & Webster Concrete Ltd
Modular buildings - Terrapin Ltd
Modular buildings - Wernick Group Ltd
Modular portable and prefabricated buildings - Ideal Building Systems Ltd
Module based buildings - Thurston Building Systems
Outbuildings, garages, stables and accessories - Scotts of Thrapston Ltd
Outdoor Shelter - The No Butts Bin Company (NBB), Trading as NBB Outdoor Shelters
Play Houses - Purewell Timber Buildings Limited
Play houses - Weatherley Fencing Contractors Limited
Pre engineered buildings - Terrapin Ltd
Pre engineered metal buildings - Severfield (Design & Build) Ltd
Pre fabricated buildings - Brimar Plastics Ltd
Prefabricated buildings - Elwell Buildings Ltd
Prefabricated Buildings - Fibaform Products Ltd
Prefabricated buildings - Parklines Building Ltd
Prefabricated buildings - Waco UK Limnited
Prefabricated buildings / structures - Caledonian Modular
Prefabricated buildings /structures - Rom Ltd
Prefabricated Buildings/Structures - Dartford Portable Buildings Ltd
Prefabricated Log Buildings - Norwegian Log Buildings Ltd
Prefabricated metal buildings - Elwell Buildings Ltd
Proprietary buildings - Leander Architectural
PVCu & Aluminium Conservatories - KCW Comercial Windows Ltd
Security Kiosks - Glasdon U.K. Limited
Sheds - Purewell Timber Buildings Limited
Sheds - Weatherley Fencing Contractors Limited
Sheds - concrete - Liget Compton
sheds and workshops - Newton & Frost Fencing Ltd
Sheds, Timber Buildings - Tate Fencing
Silos - CST Industries, Inc. - UK
Single storey luxury timber cabins, two Storey timber Barnhouses - CABU Limited
Single storey luxury timber cabins, two Storey timber Barnhouses - Cowley Timber & Partners Limited
Smartroof panels - Wyckham Blackwell Ltd
Smoking Shelter - The No Butts Bin Company (NBB), Trading as NBB Outdoor Shelters
Smoking shelters - Fibaform Products Ltd
Smoking Shelters - Glasdon U.K. Limited
Stables - Newton & Frost Fencing Ltd
Steel frame buildings - Terrapin Ltd
Steel framed buildings - Yorkon Ltd
Steel portal frame buildings - Leofric Building Systems Ltd
Summer Houses - Purewell Timber Buildings Limited
Summer houses - Weatherley Fencing Contractors Limited
Summerhouses, Clubhouses, Pavilions, Gazebos and Garden Buildings - Scotts of Thrapston Ltd
System Buildings - Wernick Group Ltd
Technical consultancy - BFRC Services Ltd
Timber framed buildings - Wyckham Blackwell Ltd
Timber framed houses and structures - W.H Colt Son & Co Ltd
Timber Storage Buildings - Parklines Building Ltd
Tool Stores - Purewell Timber Buildings Limited
Units available for hire - Fibaform Products Ltd
Waiting Shelter - The No Butts Bin Company (NBB), Trading as NBB Outdoor Shelters
Weather shelters - NuLite Ltd
Workshops - Purewell Timber Buildings Limited
Workshops - concrete - Liget Compton
Workshops (Garden) - Weatherley Fencing Contractors Limited

B11 Prefabricated building units

Bathroom pods - Caledonian Modular
Boarding kennel & cattery maufacturers - Broxap Ltd
Cleanrooms - Hemsec Panel Technologies
Conservatories - Ultraframe PLC
Dock Leveller Pits - Ebor Concrete Ltd
Enclosures and cabinets - Glasdon UK Limited
Factory Prefabricated Boiler Plant Rooms - Fulton Boiler Works (Great Britain) Ltd
Glazed Extensions - Ultraframe PLC
Horizontal panel concrete buildings - Leofric Building Systems Ltd
Hotels, Timber or Steel Framed Buildings - Rollalong Ltd
Housing - Glasdon U.K. Limited
Loggia - Ultraframe PLC
Modular building units - Caledonian Modular
Modular Buildings – Building Solutions - Actavo (UK) Ltd
Orangeries - Ultraframe PLC
Pre fabricated building units - Brimar Plastics Ltd
Prefabricated building units - Ideal Building Systems Ltd
Smoking shelters - Elwell Buildings Ltd
Stadium Terracing - Ebor Concrete Ltd
Temporary buildings - Waco UK Limnited
Vertical panel concrete buildings - Leofric Building Systems Ltd

C10 Site survey

Asbestos removal - Hawkins Insulation Ltd
Disability access audits - Peter Cox Ltd
Drone Surveys - Select Aerial Photography
Site survey - Landscape Institute
Site surveys - Focal Signs Ltd
Survey anchors and markers - Earth Anchors Ltd

C11 Ground investigation

Geotechnical consultancy and contamination assessment - Structural Soils Ltd
Ground improvement - Keller Ground Engineering
Groundworks - Rom Ltd
Site investigation,soils and material testing - Structural Soils Ltd
Surveying instruments - Topcon GB Ltd

C12 Underground services survey

Cable locator - Radiodetection Ltd
Leak detection - Radiodetection Ltd
Pipe locator - Radiodetection Ltd
Underground services survey - Radiodetection Ltd

C13 Building fabric survey

Building fabric survey - Colebrand Ltd
Building Fabric Survey - Concrete Repairs Ltd
Consultancy and building survey, schedules of work - Stonewest Ltd
Drone Surveys - Select Aerial Photography
Glass assessment surveys - Durable Ltd
Large-scale structural testing, On-site testing and consultancy, Testing to standard or bespoke requirements, Dynamic wind loading and uplift testing, Hygrothermal performance testing - Lucideon
Toxic mould detection - Peter Cox Ltd

C14 Building services survey

Energy Performance Certificates - Oakwood Property Solutions
Preparation of boilers for insurance inspection - Hodgkinson Bennis Ltd
Preparation of boilers for ultrsonic testing - Hodgkinson Bennis Ltd
Structural testing and consultancy for masonry/steel/concrete/timber - Lucideon

C20 Demolition

Demolition - Parker Plant Ltd
Demolition Attachments and Accessories - HE Services (Plant Hire) Ltd
Office refurbishment - Cumberland Construction

C21 Toxic/ Hazardous material removal

Asbestos removal - Industrial Solutions - Actavo (UK) Ltd
Toxic / Hazardous material removal - Hertel Services

C30 Shoring/ Facade retention

Ground Support System - Hire and Sales - Actavo (UK) Ltd
Proping and needling - Mabey Hire Ltd
Shoring/Façade retention - PERI Ltd
Trench strutting equipment - Mabey Hire Ltd

C40 Cleaning masonry/ concrete

Brick and stone cleaning - Gun-Point Ltd
Brick replacement - Gun-Point Ltd
Cleaning &restoration of building facades - Szerelmey Ltd
Cleaning &restoration of building stonework - Szerelmey Ltd
Cleaning masonary/concrete - TH Kenyon & Sons Ltd

C40 Cleaning masonry/ concrete (con't)

Cleaning masonry/ concrete - Chichester Stoneworks Limited
Cleaning masonry/ concrete - Colebrand Ltd
Concrete cleaner - Tank Storage & Services Ltd
Concrete maintenance and repair products - HMG Paints
Concrete repair mortars - Hines & Sons, P E, Ltd
Designed grout anchoring system - Cintec International Ltd
Epoxy resin repairs - Gun-Point Ltd
Grouting - Gun-Point Ltd
Physical dpc insertion - Dampcoursing Limited
Pressure pointing - Gun-Point Ltd
Remedial pointing - Kingfisher Building Products Ltd
Repairing concrete/ brick/ block/ stone - Concrete Repairs Ltd
Repairs and restorations - Alpha Mosaic & Terrazzo Ltd
Repointing brickwall and stonework - Gun-Point Ltd
Restoration of facades in stone, brick & terracotta - Stonewest Ltd
Wall tie replacement - Timberwise (UK) Ltd

C41 Repairing/ Renovating/Conserving masonry

Chemical DPC and remedial treatments - Protim Solignum Ltd
Chemical dpc installers - Dampcoursing Limited
Chemicals - Lanxess Urethanes UK Ltd
Conservation works - Szerelmey Ltd
Damp-proofing - Timberwise (UK) Ltd
External refurbishment works - Szerelmey Ltd
Faience blocks - Shaws of Darwen
Isokoat - Schiedel Chimney Systems Ltd
Lightweight Concrete Repair Materials - Belzona PolymericLtd
Lintel replacement - HCL Contracts Ltd
On-site sampling and structural testing - Lucideon
Polyurethane and acylic resins - Lanxess Urethanes UK Ltd
Remedial wall ties - Peter Cox Ltd
Repairing masonry - Flexcrete Technologies Limited
Repairing/ renovating conserving masonry - Colebrand Ltd
Repairing/ Renovating/Conserving masonry - Chichester Stoneworks Limited
Repairing/ Renovating/Conserving masonry - Limelite - Tarmac Building Products Ltd
Repairing/Renovating/Conserving masonry - DB Group (Holdings) Ltd
Repairing/renovating/conserving masonry - G Miccoli & Sons Limited
Repairing/Renovating/Conserving masonry - Safeguard Europe Ltd
Restoration of facades in stone, brick & terracotta - Stonewest Ltd
Stainless steel remedial wall ties - Helifix
Structural repairs - Szerelmey Ltd
Technical publications and publication brick bulletin - Brick Development Association
Terracotta blocks - Shaws of Darwen
Underground Waterproffing - Sika Ltd

C42 Repairing/ Renovating/Conserving concrete

Commercial Conncrete repair - HCL Contracts Ltd
Concrete repair - BASF plc, Construction Chemicals
Concrete repair - Sealocrete PLA Ltd
Concrete repair mortars - Fosroc Ltd
Concrete repair products - Flexcrete Technologies Limited
Concrete repairs - Freyssinet Ltd
On-site sampling and structural testing - Lucideon
Protective coatings - Fosroc Ltd
Repair Mortars, Corrosion inhibitor, Anti-carbonation/waterproof/elastomeric coatings - Ronacrete Ltd
Repairing concrete - Don Construction Products Ltd
Repairing/ renovating conserving Concrete - Colebrand Ltd
Repairing/renovating concrete - Anglo Building Products Ltd
Repairing/Renovating/Conserving Concrete - Concrete Repairs Ltd
Repairing/Renovating/Conserving concrete - DB Group (Holdings) Ltd
Repairing/renovating/conserving concrete - TH Kenyon & Sons Ltd
Resinboard Concrete Repair Materials - Belzona PolymericLtd
Sprayed concrete - Freyssinet Ltd

C45 Damp proof course renewal/ insertion

Chemical dpcs to existing walls - Peter Cox Ltd
Damp proof course renewal/ insertion - Terminix Property Services
Damp proof course renewal/insertion - Safeguard Europe Ltd

C50 Repairing/ Renovating/Conserving metal

Rail infrastructure coatings - Corroless Corrosion Control
Repairing/ renovating conserving Metal - Colebrand Ltd
Restoration work in metal - Ballantine Castings

C51 Repairing/ Renovating/Conserving timber

Condition surveys, Historic Buildings - BM TRADA
Repairing/ renewing/ conserving timber - Terminix Property Services
Solvent based and water based preservatives - Protim Solignum Ltd
Timber Repair Product - Belzona PolymericLtd
Timber Resin Repairs - ProTen Services
Timber resin repairs - Timberwise (UK) Ltd
Timber treatment and dry rot eradication - Dampcoursing Limited
Window repair - Repair care International
Wood decay repair products - Repair care International

C52 Fungus/ Beetle eradication

Fungus and beetle eradication - Peter Cox Ltd
Fungus/ beetle eradication - Terminix Property Services
Fungus/beetle eradication - Specialist Building Products
Timber treatment - Timberwise (UK) Ltd

C90 Alterations - spot items

Refurbishments & replicas - DW Windsor Lighting
Sash renovation - Durable Ltd

D11 Soil stabilisation

Armortec concrete erosion - Armortec
CFA Piling - Stent Foundations Ltd
Chemicals - Lanxess Urethanes UK Ltd
Civil engineering systems - Sarnafil Ltd
Dynamic Compaction - Bauer Renewables Ltd
Eco Parking - EBP Building Products Ltd
Erosion control mats - ABG Ltd
Geopolymer Injection - Uretek (UK) Ltd
Geotextiles - Don & Low Ltd
Green roof systems - ABG Ltd
Ground improvement - Keller Ground Engineering
Ground movement products - Cordek Ltd
Lime columns - Stent Foundations Ltd
Load bearing anchors - Earth Anchors Ltd
Retaining walls - ABG Ltd
Retaining walls - PHI Group Ltd
Soil stabilisation - Skanska UK Plc
Soil stabilization - Grass Concrete Ltd
Soil stabilization - Jablite Ltd
Soil stabilization - Tensar International Ltd
Soil stabilization/ ground anchors - Freyssinet Ltd
Vibro and dynamic compaction - Bauer Renewables Ltd
Vibro Concrete Columns - Bauer Renewables Ltd
Vibro Stone Columns - Bauer Renewables Ltd

D12 Site dewatering

De watering - Keller Ground Engineering
Flood Barriers - Lakeside Group
Flood Protection - Lakeside Group
Pumping systems for ground water control - Andrews Sykes Hire Ltd
Water drainage geocomposites - Geosynthetic Technology Ltd

D20 Excavating and filling

Excavating and Filling - HE Services (Plant Hire) Ltd
Excavating and filling - Jablite Ltd
Excavators, all sizes - Mini, Midi Large - HE Services (Plant Hire) Ltd
Land reclamation - Bernhards Landscapes Ltd
Structural Fill - Cordek Ltd

D21 Ground gas venting

Gas barrier membranes - SCP Concrete Sealing Technology Ltd
Gas drainage geocomposites - Geosynthetic Technology Ltd
Gas venting - Cordek Ltd
ground gas venting - Jablite Ltd
Ground gas venting - Keller Ground Engineering
Methane gas venting - ABG Ltd
Radon Barriers - BRC Reinforcement
Radon membranes - Visqueen Building Products

D30 Cast in place concrete piling

Bored Piling - Stent Foundations Ltd
Cased flight auger piling - Westpile Ltd
Cast in place concrete piling - Bauer Renewables Ltd
Cast in place concrete piling - Expanded Piling Ltd
Cast in place concrete piling - Freyssinet Ltd
Cast in place concrete piling - Skanska UK Plc
Cast in place concrete piling - Stent Foundations Ltd
Composite Sheet Pile Wall System - Asset International Ltd
Continuous flight auger bored piling - Westpile Ltd
Ductile Piling - Bauer Renewables Ltd
Ground engineering, Piling - Keller Ground Engineering
Large diameter bored piling - Westpile Ltd
Piling - Bauer Renewables Ltd
Piling Accessories - Cordek Ltd
Piling and ground engineering - Stent Foundations Ltd
Rotary bored piling - Westpile Ltd
Tripod bored piling - Westpile Ltd

D31 Preformed concrete piling

Bored, CFA, driven precast piling - Stent Foundations Ltd
Driven precast - Westpile Ltd
Ground engineering, piling - Keller Ground Engineering
Preformed concrete piling - Expanded Piling Ltd
Preformed concrete piling - Skanska UK Plc
Preformed concrete piling - Stent Foundations Ltd

D32 Steel piling

Composite Sheet Pile Wall System - Asset International Ltd
Driven Tube Piling - Westpile Ltd
Ground engineering, piling - Keller Ground Engineering
Pipe piling - Asset International Ltd
Steel piling - Deepdale Engineering Co Ltd
Steel piling - Stent Foundations Ltd
Trench strutting equipment - Mabey Hire Ltd

D40 Embedded retaining walls

Diaphragm walling - Keller Ground Engineering
Diaphragm walling - Skanska UK Plc
Diaphragm Walling - Stent Foundations Ltd
Embedded retaining walls - Expanded Piling Ltd
Hydrophilk waterstop - SCP Concrete Sealing Technology Ltd
P.V.C. Waterstop - SCP Concrete Sealing Technology Ltd
Prestressed concrete retaining wall units - ACP Concrete Limited
Structural retaining walls and bridge abutments - Asset International Ltd

D41 Crib walls/ Gabions/ Reinforced earth

Armortec control products - Armortec
Crib walls/ Gabions/ Reinforced earth supplies - Johnsons Wellfield Quarries Ltd
Crib walls/Gabions/Reinforced earth - RFA-Tech Ltd
Crib walls/Gabions/Reinforced earth - Skanska UK Plc
Crib walls/Gabions/Reinforced earth - Phi Group - Keller Ground Engineering
Cribwalls/Gabions/Reinforced Earth - Grass Concrete Ltd
Geotextiles - Don & Low Ltd
Ground engineering - PHI Group Ltd
Ground stabilization - PHI Group Ltd
Precast concrete products - Ruthin Precast Concrete Ltd
Reinforced earth - Tensar International Ltd
Reinforced earth retaining walls/ bridge abutments/precast arch system - Freyssinet Ltd
Retaining walls - ABG Ltd
Tee walls - Bell & Webster Concrete Ltd

E05 In situ concrete construction generally

Association of Concrete Industrial Flooring Contractors - Association of Concrete Industrial Flooring Contractors (ACIFC)
Castle brickbond SR cement - Castle Cement Ltd
Castle high alumina cement - Castle Cement Ltd
Castle hydrated lime - Castle Cement Ltd
Castle natural hydraulic lime - Castle Cement Ltd
Castle OPC cement - Castle Cement Ltd
Castle rapid hardening portland cement - Castle Cement Ltd
Castle sulfate-resisting portland cement - Castle Cement Ltd
Castle white portland cement - Castle Cement Ltd
In situ concrete construction generally - PERI Ltd
In-situ concrete - The Concrete Society
Insulated concrete formwork system - Beco Products Ltd
Lightweight aggregate - Lytag Ltd
Synthetic ironoxide colouring agents - LANXESS Inorganic Pigments Group

E10 Mixing/ Casting/ Curing in situ concrete

Admixtures - Sealocrete PLA Ltd
Aggregate suppliers - Kerridge Stone Ltd
Bagged Aggregates - Hye Oak
Cavity fill - Knauf Insulation Ltd
Cement, high alumina cement, calcium aluminate cement - Lafarge Aluminates Ltd
Colours for concrete - Procter Johnson & Co Ltd
Columns - Broadmead Cast Stone
Concrete chemicals - GCP APPLIED TECHNOLOGIES (UK) LIMITED
Concrete plasticizers - Sika Ltd
Concrete repair materials - Maxit UK
Mixing/ Casting/ Curing in situ concrete - Tarmac Trading Limited (Readymix Concrete & Screed)
Pier caps - Broadmead Cast Stone
Porticos - Broadmead Cast Stone
Ready Mix - London Concrete Ltd
Readymix - Tillicoutry Quarries Ltd
Structural concrete - Lytag Ltd

E11 Sprayed in situ concrete

Institutions/Associations - Sprayed Concrete Association
Shotcrete systems - Clarke UK Ltd
Sprayed insitu concrete - Colebrand Ltd
Tunnel concrete pumps - Clarke UK Ltd

E20 Formwork for in situ concrete

Adjustible steel pipes - Wade Building Services Ltd
Concrete formwork plywood - Wood International Agency Ltd
Film faced formwork ply - Wood International Agency Ltd
Formwork - Jablite Ltd
Formwork and Scaffolding - PERI Ltd
Formwork board - Dufaylite Developments Ltd
Formwork coatings - Hines & Sons, P E, Ltd
Formwork equipment - Mabey Hire Ltd
Formwork for in situ concrete - Rom Ltd
Hy-rib permanent formwork - Expamet Building Products
Insulated concrete formwork system - Beco Products Ltd
Metal deck flooring - Caunton Engineering Ltd
Permanent Formwork - BRC Special Products - Bekaert Ltd
Permanent shuttering - Cordek Ltd
Pneumatic void former - BRC Special Products - Bekaert Ltd
Specialist formwork 3D - Cordek Ltd
Trough moulds - Cordek Ltd
Void formers & formwork - Cordek Ltd

E30 Reinforcement for in situ concrete

Contractor Detailing Services - BRC Reinforcement
Prefabrication - BRC Reinforcement
Punching Shear Reinforcement - BRC Special Products - Bekaert Ltd
Re-bar coating - Plastic Coatings Ltd
Reinforcement - Expamet Building Products
Reinforcement accessories - Rom Ltd
Reinforcement accessories and spacers - Hines & Sons, P E, Ltd
Reinforcement for insitu concrete - Freyssinet Ltd
Reinforcement for Insitu Concrete - Halfen Ltd
Reinforcement mesh and bar - BRC Reinforcement
Reinforcing accessories - Rainham Steel Co Ltd
Reinforcing bar and mesh - Hy-Ten Ltd
Reinforcing Bar Couplers - Ancon Limited
Reinforcing mesh - Rainham Steel Co Ltd
Stainless steel reinforcement - Helifix
Stainless steel reinforcing rods - Helifix
Steel reinforcement, fibre, mesh and industrial wire - Rom Ltd
Steel wire fibres for concrete reinforcement - Bekaert Building Products

E31 Post tensioned reinforcement for insitu concrete

Post-tensioned floor slabs - Freyssinet Ltd
Steel wire, cables, rods and bars - MacAlloy Limited

E40 Designed joints in insitu concrete

Concrete balcony insulated connection system - BRC Special Products - Bekaert Ltd
Concrete floor jointing system - Compriband Ltd
Designed joints in insitu concrete (Hydrophilic joint seals) - Tarmac - Specialist Products
Permanent joining formwork - BRC Special Products - Bekaert Ltd
Seals - Trelleborg Sealing Profiles Germany GmbH
Shear load connectors - Ancon Limited
Structural expansion joints - Radflex Contract Services Ltd
Waterstops - RFA-Tech Ltd

E41 Worked finishes/ Cutting into in situ concrete

Anti slip surfacing - Addagrip Terraco Ltd
Concrete airfield pavement protection - Addagrip Terraco Ltd
Floor ventilators - Airflow (Nicoll Ventilators) Ltd
Worked finishes/Cutting into in situ concrete - Safeguard Europe Ltd

E42 Accessories cast into insitu concrete

Accessories - RFA-Tech Ltd
Accessories cast into in-situ concrete - PERI Ltd
Accessories cast into insitu concrete (Hydrophilic joint seals) - Tarmac - Specialist Products
Concrete related accessories - BRC Reinforcement
Corner protection - Fixatrad Ltd
Precast Accessories - BRC Special Products - Bekaert Ltd
Reinforcement couplers - Halfen Ltd
Tying wire, spacers and chemicals for concrete - Hy-Ten Ltd

E50 Precast concrete frame structures

Architectural precast cladding - Marble Mosaic Co Ltd, The
Bespoke concrete products - Bell & Webster Concrete Ltd
Bespoke concrete products - Hanson Concrete Products
Concrete Arch Bridge System - Asset International Ltd
Concrete products - Bell & Webster Concrete Ltd
Engineering castings - Ballantine Castings
Ground Beams - Border Concrete Products Ltd
Ground Beams - Ebor Concrete Ltd
Jointing strips for precast concrete units - Winn & Coales (Denso) Ltd
Platform walls - Bell & Webster Concrete Ltd
Precast concrete fixings - Halfen Ltd
Precast concrete floor beams, staircases, sills and lintols - ACP (Concrete) Ltd

E50 Precast concrete frame structures (con't)

Precast concrete joists - supply & fix or supply only - C.R. Longley & Co. Ltd
Precast concrete lifting - Halfen Ltd
Precast concrete products - Ruthin Precast Concrete Ltd
Precast Concrete Stairs & Landings - Ebor Concrete Ltd
Precast concrete structural components - Hanson Concrete Products
Precast concrete units - Evans Concrete Products Ltd
Prestressed concrete retaining wall units - ACP Concrete Limited
Retaining Walls - Ebor Concrete Ltd
Retaining walls, tee walls - Bell & Webster Concrete Ltd
Stadia components - Bell & Webster Concrete Ltd
Structural frames - Bison Precast
Synthetic iron oxide pigments and coloured pigments - Elementis Pigments
Timberframed multi storey modular buildings - Leofric Building Systems Ltd

E60 Precast/ Composite concrete decking

Concrete flooring - Hanson Concrete Products
Concrete Floors - CEMEX
Floor beams - Stowell Concrete Ltd
Ground beams - Bell & Webster Concrete Ltd
Hollowcore Floors - Bison Precast
Interior flooring - Blanc de Bierges
Precast composite concrete decking - ACP (Concrete) Ltd
Precast composite concrete decking - ACP Concrete Limited
Precast concrete flooring - Marshalls Mono Ltd
Precast concrete units - Caunton Engineering Ltd
Precast concrete; stairs, terraced seating, lintols etc - Border Concrete Products Ltd
Prestressed flooring slabs - Coltman Precast Concrete Ltd
Prestressed floors - Carter Concrete Ltd
Solid Composite Floors - Bison Precast
Staircases, stadium terraces, columns, wall and ground beams - Coltman Precast Concrete Ltd

F10 Brick/ Block walling

Aircrete Blocks - Tarmac Building Products Ltd
Aircrete Blocks - Tarmac Trading Limited (Blocks)
Architectural facing masonry, medium and dense concrete blocks - Lignacite Ltd
Architectural masonry - Broadmead Cast Stone
Berry Machine Made Bricks - Collier W H Ltd
Brick Slips - Hye Oak
Brick specials - Michelmersh Brick Holdings PLC
Brick trade association - Brick Development Association
Brick/ block walling - Collier W H Ltd
Brick/ Block walling - Tarmac Trading Limited (Mortars)
Brick/block walling - Broome Bros (Doncaster) Ltd
Brick/block walling - Mansfield Sand Co Ltd (Brick Division)
Bricks - Baggeridge Brick PLC
Bricks - Carlton Main Brickworks Ltd
Bricks - Hye Oak
Bricks - Ibstock Scotish Brick
Bricks - Kingscourt Country Manor Bricks
Bricks - Wienerberger Ltd
Bricks - York Handmade Brick Co Ltd
Bricks & Blocks - Hanson Building Products
Buff Clay - Carlton Main Brickworks Ltd
Burnished Blocks - Forticrete Masonry
Calcium silicate facing bricks - Hye Oak
Chimney systems - Marflex Chimney Systems
Chimney systems - Poujoulat (UK) Ltd
Clay commons, facing bricks and engineering bricks - Hanson Building Products
Clay facing bricks - Ibstock Brick Ltd
Clay facing bricks - Ibstock Building Products Ltd
Commodity Blocks - Forticrete Masonry
Commons - Northcot Brick Ltd
Concrete blocks - CEMEX
Concrete blocks - Hanson Concrete Products
Concrete blocks - Sellite Blocks Ltd
Concrete blocks - Stowell Concrete Ltd
Concrete building blocks - Lignacite (North London) Ltd
Concrete Drainage System - Hepworth Building Products Ltd
Coping stones - Chiltern Concrete and Stone
Dense, lightweight, insulating solid, cellular and hollow concrete Blocks - Armstrong (Concrete Blocks), Thomas, Ltd
Engineering and facing bricks - Carlton Main Brickworks Ltd
Engineering bricks - Hye Oak
Engineering bricks - Northcot Brick Ltd
Extruded Brick Slips - Ketley Brick Co Ltd , The
Facing Brick - Carlton Main Brickworks Ltd
Facing bricks - Baggeridge Brick PLC
Facing Bricks - Hanson Building Products
Faience - Ibstock Building Products Ltd
Faience blocks - Shaws of Darwen
Fair face blocks - Thakeham Tiles Ltd
Fairfaced Concrete Blocks - Forticrete Masonry
Fireplace briquettes - Michelmersh Brick Holdings PLC
Freeze/thaw testing, Compressive/shear testing, Water absorption, Dimensional tolerances - Lucideon
Glazed Blocks - Forticrete Masonry
Glazed Bricks - Hye Oak
Glazed bricks - Smithbrook Building Products Ltd
Glazed terracotta wall facings - Smithbrook Building Products Ltd
Hand Made Bricks - Coleford Brick & Tile Co Ltd
Hand Made Bricks - Collier W H Ltd
Handmade facing bricks - Michelmersh Brick Holdings PLC
Handmade facing bricks - Northcot Brick Ltd
Insulated concrete formwork block - Beco Products Ltd
Insulation - Polypipe Building Products
Isokern DM block chimney systems & Isokern pumice flue linings - Schiedel Chimney Systems Ltd
Large format blocks - Tarmac Building Products Ltd
Large format blocks - Tarmac Trading Limited (Blocks)
Linear Brick - Forticrete Masonry
Machine made bricks - Michelmersh Brick Holdings PLC
Polished Blocks - Forticrete Masonry
Precast Concrete Specials - Forticrete Masonry
Reclaimed bricks - Maxit UK
reclaimed facing bricks - Northcot Brick Ltd
Red Clay - Carlton Main Brickworks Ltd
Refractory brickwork - Ancorite Surface Protection Ltd
Rustic wirecut facing bricks - Northcot Brick Ltd
Shot-blasted Blocks - Forticrete Masonry
Special shaped bricks - Baggeridge Brick PLC
Special Shaped Bricks - Carlton Main Brickworks Ltd
Specials - Northcot Brick Ltd
Splitface Blocks - Forticrete Masonry
staffordshire clay engineering bricks - Ketley Brick Co Ltd , The
Staffordshire clay facing bricks - Ketley Brick Co Ltd , The
Synthetic ironoxide colouring agents - LANXESS Inorganic Pigments Group
Terracotta - Ibstock Building Products Ltd
Terracotta blocks - Shaws of Darwen
traditional & thin joint systems - Tarmac Building Products Ltd
Traditional & thin joint systems - Tarmac Trading Limited (Blocks)

F11 Glass block walling

Glass blocks - Shackerley (Holdings) Group Ltd incorporating Designer ceramics
Polycarbonate clip blocks - Rockwell Sheet Sales Ltd

F20 Natural stone rubble walling

Architectural masonry - Farmington Masonry LLP
Building stone - J Suttle Swanage Quarries Ltd
Customised sheet metal in all metals - Azimex Fabrications Ltd
Dressed stone - Forest of Dean Stone Firms Ltd
Drystone walling - Dunhouse Quarry Co Ltd
Natural stone - Brett Aggregates
Natural stone - Miles Stone
Natural stone rubble walling - Chichester Stoneworks Limited
Natural stone rubble walling - Limelite - Tarmac Building Products Ltd
Natural stone rubble walling - Stonewest Ltd
Natural stone rubble walling - Tarmac Trading Limited (Mortars)
Natural stone rubble walling supplies - Johnsons Wellfield Quarries Ltd
Natural stone suppliers - A. F Jones (Stonemasons)
Natural stone suppliers - APS Masonry Ltd
Natural stone suppliers - Chichester Stoneworks Limited
Natural stone suppliers - Dunhouse Quarry Co Ltd
Natural stone suppliers - Stancliffe Stone
Natural stone suppliers - Stoneguard (London) Ltd
Paving and walling stone - The Delabole Slate Co. Ltd
Rock face walling - Thakeham Tiles Ltd
Sandstone - Dunhouse Quarry Co Ltd
Stone suppliers - Kerridge Stone Ltd

F21 Natural stone ashlar walling/ dressings

Architectural Mouldings - Arundel Stoneworks Ltd
Architectural Mouldings - The David Sharp Studio Ltd
Architectural terracotta and faience - Ibstock Hathernware Ltd
Cleft stone and screen walling - Thakeham Tiles Ltd
Facades in stone, brick & terracotta - Stonewest Ltd
Granite and marble - design, procurement - Szerelmey Ltd
Monumental - Forest of Dean Stone Firms Ltd
Natural stone - Miles Stone
Natural stone ashlar walling/ dressings - Chichester Stoneworks Limited
Natural stone ashlar walling/ dressings - Limelite - Tarmac Building Products Ltd
Natural stone ashlar walling/dressing - G Miccoli & Sons Limited
Rapid Set Carter-Dal FTSB spot bond - Carter-Dal International
Rapid Set Façade StopBonds - 6 min - Laticrete International Inc. UK
Sandstone - Dunhouse Quarry Co Ltd
Stone suppliers - Kerridge Stone Ltd

F22 Cast stone walling/ dressings

Architectural precast cladding - Marble Mosaic Co Ltd, The
Architectural Stonework - Blanc de Bierges
Architectural Stonework - Cranborne Stone Limited
Architectural stonework - Haddonstone Ltd
Artificial stone - Allen (Concrete) Ltd
Artificial stone units - Northwest Pre-cast Ltd
Bespoke Cast Stone - Forticrete Cast Stone
Blocks & Quoins - Forticrete Cast Stone
Cast stone - Border Concrete Products Ltd
Cast stone - Ibstock Building Products Ltd
Cast stone - Lignacite Ltd
Cast Stone - Newlay Cast Stone Limited t/as Procter Cast Stone
Cast stone - Procter Bros Limited
Cast stone walling - Chiltern Concrete and Stone
Cast stone walling/ dressings - Chilstone
Cast stone walling/ dressings - GB Architectural Cladding Products Ltd
Cast stone walling/ dressings - Ruthin Precast Concrete Ltd
Cast stone walling/ dressings - Stonewest Ltd
Cast stone; sills, lintols, copings, features etc - Border Concrete Products Ltd
Cock & Hen Capping Stones - Forticrete Walling Stone
Copings, Pier Caps, Spheres & Finial Sets - Forticrete Cast Stone
Door Surrounds & Porticos - Forticrete Cast Stone
Fencing - Procter Bros Limited
Precast concrete and cast stone products - Sangwin Concrete Products Ltd
Precast walling - Oakdale (Contracts) Ltd
Reconstructed cast stone architectural units - Broadmead Cast Stone
Stone - Ibstock Scotish Brick
Stone walling - reconstructed - Forticrete Walling Stone
Window Heads, Cills & Surrounds - Forticrete Cast Stone

F30 Accessories/ Sundry items for brick/ block/ stone walling

Abrasive discs and blocks - Harbro Supplies Ltd
Accessories/ Sundry items for stone walling - Johnsons Wellfield Quarries Ltd
Accessories/sundry items for brick/ block/stone - Mansfield Sand Co Ltd (Brick Division)
Accessories/sundry items for brick/block/stone - Haddonstone Ltd
Acoustic ventilators - Rytons Building Products Ltd
Air Bricks - Forterra Building Products Ltd
Air bricks (cast iron) - Longbottom J & J W Ltd
Arch lintels - Catnic
Arches - Cavity Trays Ltd
Arches - Northcot Brick Ltd
Blocks - Forterra Building Products Ltd
Brick reinforcement - RFA-Tech Ltd
Bricks - Forterra Building Products Ltd
Brickties and windposts - Halfen Ltd
Brickwork reinforcement - BRC Special Products - Bekaert Ltd
Brickwork support - Halfen Ltd
Building products - cavity closers - Quantum Profile Systems Ltd
Cast stone, sills, lintels, copings, features etc - Border Concrete Products Ltd
Cavity and through wall ventilators - Rytons Building Products Ltd
Cavity fixings - Artur Fischer (UK) Ltd
Cavity trays - Cavity Trays Ltd
Cavity trays - IG Limited
Cavity Trays - SCP Concrete Sealing Technology Ltd
Cavity trays, hight performance dpc - Timloc Expamet Building Products
Cavity wall tie installation - ProTen Services
Chimney bird guards - Dunbrik (Yorks) Ltd
Chimney flues and linings - Rite-Vent Ltd
Chimney open fire - Dunbrik (Yorks) Ltd
Chimney pots & terminals - Dunbrik (Yorks) Ltd
Chimney stove connection - Dunbrik (Yorks) Ltd
Chimney systems - Marflex Chimney Systems
Chimney technical services - Dunbrik (Yorks) Ltd
Chimney twin wall flue pipes - Dunbrik (Yorks) Ltd
Chimneys, Roofing and Flues - Forterra Building Products Ltd
Clay Chimney Pots - Knowles W T & Sons Ltd
Closers - Cavity Trays Ltd
Copings and cills - Burlington Slate Ltd
Diamond blades - Harbro Supplies Ltd
Diamond Blades - Marcrist International Ltd
Diamond core drills - Marcrist International Ltd
Enforce - composite strengthening - Weber Building Solutions
Expension joint fillers - SCP Concrete Sealing Technology Ltd
Faience blocks - Shaws of Darwen
Fireplaces - Farmington Masonry LLP
Flue liners - Forterra Building Products Ltd
Flue linings - Dunbrik (Yorks) Ltd
Flues and chimneys - Docherty New Vent Chimney Group
Gas flue blocks - Dunbrik (Yorks) Ltd
Gold leaf - Harbro Supplies Ltd
High performance DPC and cavity trays - Visqueen Building Products
Insulated Concrete Formwork - Beco Products Ltd
Insulating cavity closers and insulated DPC - Polypipe Building Products
Insulation fixings - Artur Fischer (UK) Ltd
Internal room ventilators - Airflow (Nicoll Ventilators) Ltd
Isokern pumic flue linings - Schiedel Chimney Systems Ltd
Isolation Sleves Remedial - Redifix Ltd
Lateral restraint - HCL Contracts Ltd
Lintels - Ancon Limited
Lintels - Cavity Trays Ltd
Lintels - CEMEX
Lintels - Stainless steel lintels - Wincro Metal Industries Ltd
Lintels and other hand made shapes - Lignacite Ltd
Lintels, cils and padstones - Chiltern Concrete and Stone
Manor firechests - Schiedel Chimney Systems Ltd
Masonry coatings - Jotun Henry Clark Ltd Decorative Division
Masonry reinforcement - Bekaert Building Products
Masonry support systems - Ancon Limited
Masonry support systems - Stainless steel brickwork support systems - Wincro Metal Industries Ltd
Masonry to masonry connectors - Simpson Strong-Tie®
Masonry tools - tungsten tipped chisels - Harbro Supplies Ltd
Movement joint - Shackerley (Holdings) Group Ltd incorporating Designer ceramics
Movement joints - Allmat (East Surrey) Ltd
Movement Joints - Illbruck Sealant Systems UK Ltd
Movement Joints - Movement Joints (UK)
Natural stone fixing - Halfen Ltd
Non standard precast units in special finishes - Chiltern Concrete and Stone
Polythene damp-proof courses - Visqueen Building Products
Power tools - Harbro Supplies Ltd
Pumice stone chimney systems - Sparkes K & L
Remedial wall ties - Redifix Ltd
Roof ventilation, underfloor ventilation, through the wall ventilation - Timloc Expamet Building Products
Special Shaped Bricks - Forterra Building Products Ltd
Special shaped clay bricks - Ibstock Brick Ltd
Specialist waterproofing materials, admixtures & grouts - DB Group (Holdings) Ltd
Stainless steel remedial wall ties - Helifix
Steel lintels - Catnic
Steel lintels - Expamet Building Products
Steel Lintels - Harvey Steel Lintels Limited
Steel lintels - IG Limited
Steel lintels - Wade Building Services Ltd
Steel wall connectors - Allmat (East Surrey) Ltd
Straps - Expamet Building Products
Structural Frames - Beco Products Ltd
Terracotta blocks - Shaws of Darwen
Through wall ventilators - Airflow (Nicoll Ventilators) Ltd
Timber to masonry connectors - Simpson Strong-Tie®
Twinwall flue pipe - Dunbrik (Yorks) Ltd
Ventilators - Cavity Trays Ltd
Wall connectors - Catnic
Wall insulation - Dow Building Solutions
Wall starters - Expamet Building Products
Wall tie replacement - HCL Contracts Ltd
Wall ties - Catnic
Wall ties - Vista Engineering Ltd
Wall ties and restraint fixings - Ancon Limited
Wall ties and restraint fixings - Stainless steel building components - Wincro Metal Industries Ltd
Windposts Masonry support systems reinforcement for masonry - Vista Engineering Ltd

F31 Precast concrete sills/ lintels/ copings/ features

3-point bending, Rebar corrosion, Shear testing - Lucideon
Architectural Stonework - Blanc de Bierges
Balustrades - The David Sharp Studio Ltd
Bespoke - Allen (Concrete) Ltd
Cast stone, sills, lintels, copings, features etc - Border Concrete Products Ltd
Chimney systems - Marflex Chimney Systems
Cills - Allen (Concrete) Ltd
Copings - Allen (Concrete) Ltd
Copings Lintels - Stowell Concrete Ltd
Lintels - Allen (Concrete) Ltd
Lintels - Allmat (East Surrey) Ltd
Lintels - Newlay Cast Stone Limited t/as Procter Cast Stone
Precast - Northwest Pre-cast Ltd
Precast Concrete - Bison Precast
Precast concrete - Border Concrete Products Ltd
Precast Concrete - Forterra Building Products Ltd
Precast concrete and cast stone products - Sangwin Concrete Products Ltd
Precast concrete products - Allen (Concrete) Ltd
Precast concrete sills/ lintels/ copings/ features - Chilstone
Precast concrete sills/ lintels/ copings/ features - Evans Concrete Products Ltd
Precast concrete sills/lintels/copings/features - Broadmead Cast Stone
Precast concrete sills/lintels/copings/features - Haddonstone Ltd
Precast Concrete Stairs, Beams, Cills Etc - Carter Concrete Ltd
Precast lintels and prestressed lintels - Procter Bros Limited
Precast sills/lintels/ coping and features - Chiltern Concrete and Stone
Prestressed wide slab flooring - ACP (Concrete) Ltd
Prestressed wide slab flooring, precast lintels - ACP Concrete Limited
Reconstituted Artstone - GB Architectural Cladding Products Ltd
Retaining walls - Armortec
Shutters and Lintels - Shellcast Security Shutters
Steel cavity fixings - Lindapter International
Structural Precast concrete - Ebor Concrete Ltd
Supergalv steel lintels - Birtley Group

G10 Structural steel framing

Aluminium and steel fabricators - Ramsay & Sons (Forfar) Ltd
Aluminium fabrications - Midland Alloy Ltd
Architectural & General Metalwork - A & G Structures Ltd
Blasting - Bristol Metal Spraying & Protective Coatings Ltd
Cast iron metalwork - Company name: Britannia Metalwork Services Ltd
Coated steel - SSAB Swedish Steel Ltd
Cold rolled purlins and rails - Ward Insulated Panels Ltd
Cold rolled steel sections - Hadley Industries Plc
Collled rolled sections - Walls & Ceilings International Ltd
Copper wire and rods - United Wire Ltd
C-sections - Hayes Cladding Systems
Domestic and industrial tongue and grooved flooring - Egger (UK) Ltd
Eaves beams - Hayes Cladding Systems
Flat to pitch conversions - Alumasc Exterior Building Products Ltd
Footbridges in steel, boardwalks decking and bespoke landscape structures - CTS Bridges Ltd
Gypframe (steel framed houses) - Metsec Ltd
Heavy duty protective coatings - International Protective Coatings
Industrial Coating Specialists - Bristol Metal Spraying & Protective Coatings Ltd
Laser Welded Sections - Sections & Profiles Ltd
Meshes - Cadisch MDA
Metal Framing - British Gypsum Ltd
Metal framing - Unistrut Limited
Metsec framing - panelised light steel buildings - Metsec Ltd
Mezanine floor structures - Hadley Industries Plc
Mezzanine floor channels and CEE section floor bea - Metsec Ltd
Mezzanine Floors - Spaceway South Ltd
Open grill flooring - Norton Engineering Alloys Co Ltd
Rail fixings - Lindapter International
Roof and soffit ventilators - Rytons Building Products Ltd
Roof truss system - MiTek Industries Ltd
Spacejoist V webs - ITW Consutruction Products
Stainless steel fabrications - Midland Alloy Ltd
Steel - Tata Steel Europe Limited
Steel fabrication - Woodburn Engineering Ltd
Steel framed buildings complete with fixtures, fittings and cladding - Reid John & Sons (Strucsteel) Ltd
Steel framing - Hadley Industries Plc
Steel framing - Vantrunk Engineering Ltd
Steel tube stockholders, fabrications, welding and fittings - Midland Tube and Fabrications
Steel wires, cables, rods and bars - Light (Multiforms), H A
Structural frames - Bison Precast
Structural hollow sections - Rainham Steel Co Ltd
Structural steel - Hy-Ten Ltd
Structural steel - Woodburn Engineering Ltd
Structural steel framing - Caunton Engineering Ltd
Structural steel framing - The Angle Ring Company Ltd
Structural steel towers - Franklin Hodge Industries Ltd
Structural steelwork - Ermine Engineering Co. Ltd
Structural steelwork - Severfield (Design & Build) Ltd
Structural steelwork - South Durham Structures Limited
Support systems - Lindapter International
Universal beams & Columns - Rainham Steel Co Ltd
Wire rope assemblies and fittings - Midland Wire Cordage Co Ltd
Zed and CEE purlins - Metsec Ltd
Z-purlins - Hayes Cladding Systems

G11 Structural aluminium framing

Aluminium fabrications - Midland Alloy Ltd
Curved canopies, barrel vaults and fabrications - Midland Alloy Ltd
Glasshouses - Manufacturers of Aluminium
Glasshouses and Greenhouses - Hartley Botanic Ltd
Greenhouses: Large, Small, Bespoke, Made to measure, made to order - Manufacturers of Aluminium
Glasshouses and Greenhouses - Hartley Botanic Ltd
Ground floor framing - Comar Architectural Aluminium Systems
Orangeries - Manufacturers of Aluminium Glasshouses and Greenhouses - Hartley Botanic Ltd
Structural Steel Framing - Blagg & Johnson Ltd

G12 Isolated structural metal members

Aluminium Architectural Products - Gooding Aluminium
Blasting - Bristol Metal Spraying & Protective Coatings Ltd
Cold roll sections/forming - Metsec Lattice Beams Ltd
Cold roll sections/forming - Metsec Ltd
Curved steel sections, tubes, roof and cambered beams - The Angle Ring Company Ltd
Industrial Coating Specialists - Bristol Metal Spraying & Protective Coatings Ltd
Isolated structural members - Hy-Ten Ltd
Lattice joist and trusses - Metsec Lattice Beams Ltd
Lattice joist and trusses - Metsec Ltd
Metal post supports/shoes - Canopy Products Ltd
Metal web floor beams - Wyckham Blackwell Ltd
Steel chimneys and associated structural steelwork - Beaumont Ltd F E
Subcontract fabrication - Mackay Engineering
Subcontract machining - Mackay Engineering
Tension systems - Ancon Limited
Tubes, fittings & flanges - The BSS Group
Welding and fabrication work - Griff Chains Ltd

G20 Carpentry/ Timber framing/ First fixing

Aluminuim Fascia / Soffit - Guttercrest
Bespoke joinery - Howard Bros Joinery Ltd
Carpenters Metalwork - Allmat (East Surrey) Ltd
Carpentry/ Timber framing/ First fixing - Polypipe Building Products
Chimney systems - Poujoulat (UK) Ltd
Cladding Insect Mesh - The Flyscreen Company Ltd
Construction & joniery softwoods - Cox Long Ltd
Door Kits - Premdor
Engineered Floor Systems - Scotts of Thrapston Ltd
Engineered I beams - IJK Timber Group Ltd
Engineered Timber Edge Bonders - Panel Agency Limited
Fixings to trusses - MiTek Industries Ltd
Flooring - Metsä Wood
Footbridges in timber, boardwalks, decking and bespoke landscape structures - CTS Bridges Ltd
Glue Laminated Timber - Panel Agency Limited
Glulam beams - Lilleheden Ltd
Hardwood - IJK Timber Group Ltd
Hardwood - James Latham plc
Hardwood - Metsä Wood
I Beams - Steico
Industrial pre-treatment preservatives for timber - Protim Solignum Ltd
Intumescent coatings for timber - Quelfire Limited
Joist hangers - Expamet Building Products
Laminated Timber Beams - Kingston Craftsmen Structural Timber Engineers Ltd
Laminated Timber Columns - Kingston Craftsmen Structural Timber Engineers Ltd
Lightweight lattice joists and trusses - Metsec Lattice Beams Ltd
Load bearing and non LB site fixed panels - Metsec Ltd
Nail plates - ITW Consutruction Products
Planed and sawn timber - Mason FW & Sons Ltd
Portal frames and cranked beams - Lilleheden Ltd
Re-sawn carcassing - James Donaldson Timber
Roof trusses - Armstrong (Timber), Thomas, Ltd
Roof trusses - Crendon Timber Engineering Ltd
Roof trusses - Merronbrook Ltd
Roof trusses - Scotts of Thrapston Ltd
Roofing contractor - Evans Howard Roofing Ltd
Saw millers and timber merchants - Whitmore's Timber Co Ltd
Softwood - Metsä Wood
Softwood - Panel Agency Limited
Spruce Glulam Beams, Larch Glulam Beams, Oak Glulam Beams, Insulated timber floor panels, insulated timber wall panels, insulated timber roof panels - Cowley Timber & Partners Limited
Stainless steel timber to masonry fixings - Helifix
Stainless steel warm roof fixings - Helifix
Stress grading - Cox Long Ltd
Structural timber - James Donaldson Timber
Structural timber engineers - Kingston Craftsmen Structural Timber Engineers Ltd
Timber - Covers Timber & Builders Merchants
Timber - IJK Timber Group Ltd
Timber Floor Beams - Steico
Timber frame buildings - Fleming Buildings Ltd
Timber frame design supply & fix - Cox Long Ltd
Timber frame housing - Fleming Homes Ltd
Timber frames and roof trusses - Walker Timber Ltd
Timber framing - BM TRADA
Timber I Beams - Panel Agency Limited
Timber importers & sawmillers - Walker Timber Ltd
Timber merchants - Derby Timber Supplies
Timber merchants - Timbmet Ltd
Timber panels - Challenge Fencing Ltd
Timber Portal Frames - Kingston Craftsmen Structural Timber Engineers Ltd
Timber preservative treatments - Kingfisher Building Products Ltd
Timber roof trusses - Dover Trussed Roof Co Ltd
Timber Roof Trusses - Kingston Craftsmen Structural Timber Engineers Ltd
Timber strength grading - Walker Timber Ltd
Timber to masonry connectors - Simpson Strong-Tie®
Timber to timber connectors - Simpson Strong-Tie®
Trussed rafter design & manufacture - Cox Long Ltd
Trussed rafters - Crendon Timber Engineering Ltd
Trussed rafters - Wyckham Blackwell Ltd

G30 Metal profiled sheet decking

Cold Roll Forming - Blagg & Johnson Ltd
Composite decking - Roles Broderick Roofing Ltd
Damping for footfall vibration for steel deck construction - Richard Lees Decking Limited
Decking - Tata Steel Europe Limited
Footfall vibration damping for steel deck construction - Richard Lees Decking Limited
Insulated Roof & Wall Systems - Kingspan Ltd
Metal profile sheet decking - BriggsAmasco
Profiled metal floor decking - Ward Insulated Panels Ltd
Steel Decking - Richard Lees Decking Limited
Structural Metal Decking - Omnis

G31 Prefabricated timber unit decking

Sheet materials - Metsä Wood
Timber Decking - The Outdoor Deck Company
Timber frame kits - Merronbrook Ltd

G32 Edge supported/ Reinforced woodwool/rock fibre decking

Wood wool boards - Skanda Acoustics Limited

H10 Patent glazing

Aluminium and lead clothed steel patent glazing systems - Standard Patent Glazing Co Ltd
Aluminium conservatory roofs - Technal UK
aluminium/hybrid curtain walling, windows and doors - Senior Aluminium Systems plc
Anti-vandal glazing - Amari Plastics Plc
Cladding/ covering - Pilkington UK Ltd
Conservatory components - Exitex Ltd
Curtain walling - Astrofade Ltd
Curtain Walling - Duplus Architectural Systems Ltd
Curtain walling - HW Architectural Ltd
Curved Glass - Novaglaze Limited
Patent glazing - Cantifix of London Limited
Patent glazing - Duplus Architectural Systems Ltd
Patent glazing - Glassolutions Saint-Gobain Ltd
Patent Glazing - HansenFacades
Patent glazing - Ide T & W Ltd
Patent glazing - Lonsdale Metal Company
Rooflights, lantern lights and pyramid lights - Standard Patent Glazing Co Ltd

H11 Curtain walling

Aluminium curtain walling - Technal UK
aluminium/hybrid curtain walling, windows and doors - Senior Aluminium Systems plc
Curtain wall systems - Comar Architectural Aluminium Systems
Curtain walling - Barlow Group
Curtain walling - Cantifix of London Limited
Curtain walling - Colt International
Curtain walling - Crittall Steel Windows Ltd
Curtain walling - Deceuninck Ltd
Curtain walling - Duplus Architectural Systems Ltd
Curtain walling - English Architectural Glazing Ltd
Curtain walling - Glassolutions Saint-Gobain Ltd
Curtain walling - Ide T & W Ltd
Curtain Walling - McMullen Facades
Curtain Walling - Metal Technology Ltd
Curtain walling - Panel Systems Ltd
Curtain Walling - Sapa Building Systems (monarch and glostal)
Curtain Walling - Schueco UK
Curtain walling and cladding - Schmidlin (UK) Ltd
Extruded curtain walling - Smart Systems Ltd
Facades, architectural and construction solutions - Porcelanosa Group Ltd
Fire Resistant glass - SCHOTT UK Ltd
Glazing and Curtain walling - Howard Evans Roofing and Cladding Ltd
Non- combustible roofing and cladding systems - Gilmour Ecometal
Patent glazing - Astrofade Ltd
Patent Glazing - Duplus Architectural Systems Ltd
Patent glazing - HW Architectural Ltd
Rainscreen - Gilmour Ecometal
Stainless Steel Cladding - Aperam Stainless Services & Solutions UK Limited
Structural wall solutions - CGL Facades
Terracotta Cladding Systems - Telling Architectural Ltd
Terracotta Curtain Walling - Telling Architectural Ltd
Timber and Timber aluminium - Scandanavian Timber
Unitised curtain walling - English Architectural Glazing Ltd
Unitised Windows and Curtain Walling - HansenFacades

H12 Plastic glazed vaulting/ walling

Opaque chemical resistant cladding - Filon Products Ltd
Plastic glazed vaulting - Duplus Architectural Systems Ltd
Plastic glazed vaulting/ walling - Astrofade Ltd
Plastic glazed vaulting/walling - Amari Plastics Plc
Polycarbonate glazing for flat and industrial roofs - Cox Building Products Ltd

H13 Structural glass assemblies

Architectural Glass - Creative Glass
Atria Glazing - Fenlock-Hansen Ltd
Barrelvaults, ridgelights, pyramids in glass or polycarbonate - Cox Building Products Ltd
Canopies - Glassolutions Saint-Gobain Ltd
Glass Walling - Telling Architectural Ltd
Steel wire, cables, rods and bars - MacAlloy Limited
Structural glass assemblies - Astrofade Ltd
Structural glass assemblies - Cantifix of London Limited
Structural glass assemblies - Colt International
Structural glass assemblies - Pilkington UK Ltd
Structural Glass Assemblies - Schueco UK
Structural Glazing - Ide T & W Ltd

H14 Concrete rooflights/ pavement lights

Floor lights - Luxcrete Ltd
Glass arches - Luxcrete Ltd
Hygienic GRP Wall Cladding - Crane Composites
Pavement lights - Longbottom J & J W Ltd
Pavement lights - Luxcrete Ltd
Police cell windows and observation units - Luxcrete Ltd
Roof lights - Luxcrete Ltd
smoke outlets - Luxcrete Ltd

H20 Rigid sheet cladding

B.R.E. Structural Render Panels - Gradient Insulations (UK) Ltd
Balcony panels - Trespa UK Ltd
Building boards - Finnish Fibreboard (UK) Ltd
Cladding - Burlington Slate Ltd
Cladding - James Donaldson Timber
Cladding - wall and ceiling - Flexitallic Ltd
Cladding and Fascias - Howard Evans Roofing and Cladding Ltd
Cladding panels - Blaze Signs Ltd
Composite panels - EBC UK Ltd
Composite panels - Gradient Insulations (UK) Ltd
Exterior cladding panels - Trespa UK Ltd
Exterior grade high pressure laminate - Abet Ltd
Exterior systems - Knauf UK
Glass reinforced polyester profiled and flat sheeting - Filon Products Ltd
Gypsum Rienforced Fibreboard - Panel Agency Limited
High performance building panel - Trespa UK Ltd
High performance claddings and Fire Protection Boards - Cembrit Ltd
Hygenic wall + ceiling services - Altro Ltd
Hygienic cladding - Amari Plastics Plc
Hygrothermal performance testing, Water penetration, Pull testing, Impact testing, Dynamic wind loading and uplift testing - Lucideon
Kerto LVL (laminated veneer lumber) - Metsä Wood
L.P.C.B Roof systems - Gradient Insulations (UK) Ltd
L.P.C.B Wall panels - Gradient Insulations (UK) Ltd
Laminated Boards - Steico
Metal Façade Systems - Omnis
Metal roofing and cladding - Ash & Lacy Building Products Ltd
PVC claddings and fascias - Rockwell Sheet Sales Ltd
Rainscreen cladding - Omnis
Rigid sheet cladding - FGF Ltd
Rigid sheet cladding - Panel Systems Ltd
Rigid sheet cladding for kitchens and walls - FIBO UK LTD
Sheet materials - Mason FW & Sons Ltd
Stainless Steel cladding - Aperam Stainless Services & Solutions UK Limited
Structural Insulated Panels - EBC UK Ltd
Wall cladding - Dunhams of Norwich
Wall cladding, roof cladding, insulated wall and roof cladding - Kingspan Ltd
Wall lining systems - Formica Ltd
Wood wool boards - Skanda Acoustics

H21 Timber weatherboarding

Cladding - James Donaldson Timber
Cladding Insect Mesh - The Flyscreen Company Ltd
Exterior systems - Knauf UK
Larch Timber Cladding, Spruce Timber Cladding, Douglas Fir Timber Cladding – Cowley Timber & Partners Limited - Cowley Timber & Partners Limited
Timber cladding - LSA Projects Ltd
Timber cladding - OSMO UK
Timber weatherboarding - Challenge Fencing Ltd
Timber weatherboarding - Vulcan Cladding Systems
Timber weatherboarding suppliers - W.L. West & Sons Ltd

H30 Fibre cement profiled sheet cladding/ covering/siding

External Wall Cladding - Caithness Flagstone Limited
External Wall Cladding - Hanson Building Products
External Wall Cladding - Paroc Panel Systems Uk Ltd
Fastenings - Cooper & Turner
Fibre cement - FGF Ltd
Fibre cement profiled sheet cladding / covering - TRC (Midlands) Ltd
Fibre cement profiled sheet cladding/ covering/siding - SLE Cladding Ltd
Fibre cement sheeting - Coverworld UK Limited
Fundermax cladding - Telling Architectural Ltd
Profiled Sheets - Cembrit Ltd

H31 Metal profiled/ flat sheet cladding/ covering/ siding

Aluminium cladding and roofing - Rigidal
CA Profiles - CA Group Ltd - MR-24 Division
Cladding - FGF Ltd
Cladding - Tata Steel Europe Limited
Cladding Systems - Cadisch MDA
Column Cladding - Cadisch MDA
Composite aluminium and steel flat cladding systems - Booth Muirie
Composite aluminium and steel rain screens - Booth Muirie
Composite panels - Composite Panel Services Ltd
Corrugated & Cladding Sheets - Sections & Profiles Ltd
Expanded Mesh - Cadisch MDA
Fastenings - Cooper & Turner
Galvanised Corrugated sheet - Rainham Steel Co Ltd
Industrial and commercial roofing, Cladding and Sheeting - Avonside Roofing Group T/A Letchworth Roofing
Insulated Roof & Wall Systems - Kingspan Ltd
Insulated roof panels - Composite Panel Services Ltd
Insulated wall and roof panels and cladding sheets - Ward Insulated Panels Ltd

H31 Metal profiled/ flat sheet cladding/ covering/ siding (con't)

Lightweight sheet and panel roofing systems - Britmet Tileform Limited
Metal cladding - LSA Projects Ltd
Metal Cladding Systems - Euroclad Ltd
Metal Façade Systems - Omnis
Metal profiled / flat sheet cladding / covering - TRC (Midlands) Ltd
Metal profiled and flat sheet cladding, covering and siding - Hayes Cladding Systems
Metal profiled/ flat sheet cladding/ covering - Hadley Industries Plc
Metal profiled/ flat sheet cladding/ covering - Reid John & Sons (Strucsteel) Ltd
Metal profiled/ flat sheet cladding/ covering/ siding - SLE Cladding Ltd
Metal profiled/ flat sheet cladding/ covering/ siding - Vulcan Cladding Systems
Metal profiled/flat sheet cladding/covering - Amari Plastics Plc
Metal Profiled/flat sheet cladding/covering - Britmet Tileform Limited
Metal roof tiles - Catnic
Metal roofing and cladding - Ash & Lacy Building Products Ltd
Metal roofing and cladding - BriggsAmasco
Metal screens and louvres - Lang+Fulton
Metal tiles - EBC UK Ltd
Perforated Sheet - Cadisch MDA
Pre Crimp Meshes - Cadisch MDA
Prebonded claddding - Roles Broderick Roofing Ltd
Prefabricated bathroom structures - IPPEC Systems Ltd
Profiled metal sheeting - Coverworld UK Limited
Rainscreen cladding systems - Booth Muirie
Sheet Metal Work - A & G Structures Ltd
Single ply flat roof system - Intergrated Polymer Systems (UK) Ltd
Standing Seam Roof Decking - Gradient Insulations (UK) Ltd
Traditional flat roofing systems - IKO PLC
Waterproofing (inc. standing seam roofing) - Alumasc Exterior Building Products Ltd
Woven Wire Mesh - Cadisch MDA

H32 Plastic profiled sheet cladding/ covering/ siding

Cellular PVC fascias and soffits - Celuform Building Products
Cellular Pvc fascias, soffits, barge boards and claddings - Swish Building Products
Corotherm Clickfit - Ariel Plastics Ltd
Corrugated or flat PVC and polycarbonate clear or coloured plastic sheets - Rockwell Sheet Sales Ltd
Covers for new and existing pools of almost any shape - Grando (UK) Ltd
Decorative internal cladding system - Swish Building Products
Fascia, soffit and cladding systems - FloPlast Ltd
Fastenings - Cooper & Turner
Flat roof outlets - Hunter Plastics Ltd
Glass reinforced polyesther profiled and flat sheeting - Filon Products Ltd
GRP/APC roof lights and cladding products - Hambleside Danelaw Ltd
Internal & external cladding - Amari Plastics Plc
Multiwall polycarbonate sheets - Rockwell Sheet Sales Ltd
Over-roofing - Filon Products Ltd
Plastic coated steel flashings - Azimex Fabrications Ltd
Plastic mouldings - Invicita Plastics Ltd
Plastic profiled sheet cladding /covering - TRC (Midlands) Ltd
Plastic profiled sheet cladding and roofing - Ariel Plastics Ltd
Plastic profiled sheet cladding, facias, soffits, interior wall and ceiling panelling - Deceuninck Ltd
Plastic profiled sheet cladding/ covering/ siding - SLE Cladding Ltd
PVCu sills, trims, cladding and roof line products - Duraflex Limited
PVC-V facia & Soffit - Allmat (East Surrey) Ltd
Roof sheets - profiled and structured in GRP, PVC and polycarbonate - Brett Martin Ltd
Rooflights - Hayes Cladding Systems
Soffits and fascias - Spectra Glaze Services
Translucent profiled sheeting - Coverworld UK Limited
Vinyl cladding system for fascias soffits and full elevations - Cox Building Products Ltd

H33 Bitumen & fibre profile sheet cladding/ covering

Bitumen & fibre profile sheet cladding/ covering - SLE Cladding Ltd
Bitumen & fibre profile sheet cladding/ covering - Onduline Building Products Ltd
Bitumen saturate organic fibre profiled sheet roofing - Ariel Plastics Ltd
Bitumious felt roofing systems - IKO PLC

H40 Glassfibre reinforced cement panel cladding/ features

Cladding systems - BRC Special Products - Bekaert Ltd
Exterior systems - Knauf UK
Glassfibre reinforced cement panel cladding - Telling Architectural Ltd
Glassfibre reinforced cement panel cladding/ features - SLE Cladding Ltd
Glassfibre reinforced cement panel cladding/ features - Vetter UK
Glassfibre reinforced cement panel cladding/features - Aden Hynes Sculpture Studios
Hygrothermal performance testing, Water penetration, Pull testing, Impact testing, Dynamic wind loading and uplift testing - Lucideon
TecLite GRC based stone - Haddonstone Ltd

H41 Glassfibre reinforced plastics panel cladding/ features

Architectural Moldings GRP - Halmark Panels Ltd
Bespoke architectural mouldings and features in GRP - Design & Display Structures Ltd
Columns, canopies, cornices, porticos, bay canopies - Solair GRP Architectural Products
Dormer windows - Solair GRP Architectural Products
G. R. P . Porches - Solair Ltd
Glass fibre reinforced cladding - Brimar Plastics Ltd
Glass fibre reinforced plastics cladding features - Amari Plastics Plc
Glass reinforced polyester profiled and flat sheeting - Filon Products Ltd
Glassfibre plastics reinforced cladding/features - Martello Plastics Ltd
Glassfibre reinforced plastics cladding/architectural features - Duroy Fibreglass Mouldings Ltd
Glassfibre reinforced plastics panel cladding/ features - SLE Cladding Ltd
Glassfibre reinforced plastics panel cladding/ features - Vulcan Cladding Systems
Glassfibre reinforced plastics panel cladding/features - Aden Hynes Sculpture Studios
GRG internal cladding - Multitex GRP LLP
GRP - Hodkin Jones (Sheffield) Ltd
GRP (Glass Reinforced Polyester) - Gillespie (UK) Ltd
GRP canopies - Halmark Panels Ltd
GRP cladding - Adams- Hydraulics Ltd
GRP cladding, specialist moulding, door canopies and columns - Multitex GRP LLP
GRP conservatory roofs - Halmark Panels Ltd
GRP flashings - Hambleside Danelaw Ltd
GRP housings - Precolor Sales Ltd
GRP Mouldings - Harviglass-Fibre Ltd
GRP porches - Halmark Panels Ltd
GRP roofing systems - Hambleside Danelaw Ltd
GRP structures & plant rooms - APA
GRP/APC roof lights and cladding products - Hambleside Danelaw Ltd
Interior and exterior laminated glassfibre components - Pyramid Plastics UK Ltd
Plastic profiled sheet cladding and roofing - Ariel Plastics Ltd
Quickfix Dormers - Multitex GRP LLP
Quickstack Chimneys - Multitex GRP LLP
RSJ Cladding Beams - Oakleaf Reproductions Ltd

H42 Precast concrete panel cladding/ features

Architectural precast cladding - Marble Mosaic Co Ltd, The
Architectural Precast concrete cladding - Techrete (UK) Ltd
Precast & prestressed concrete panels - ACP Concrete Limited
Precast concrete and cast stone products - Sangwin Concrete Products Ltd
Precast concrete panel cladding/ features - SLE Cladding Ltd
Precast concrete panel cladding/ features - Vetter UK
Precast Concrete Panel/ Cladding - Carter Concrete Ltd
TecStone precast concrete - Haddonstone Ltd

H43 Metal Panel Cladding/ features

Façade Systems - Rheinzink UK
Metal Cladding Pannel - McMullen Facades
Metal Panel Cladding/ features - SLE Cladding Ltd
Profiled Sheet Cladding - Tata Steel Colors
Vitreous Enamal Cladding - Trico V.E. Ltd (Signage Division)
Vitreous Enamel Panels - Trico V.E. Ltd (Signage Division)

H50 Precast concrete slab cladding/ features

Architectural precast cladding - Marble Mosaic Co Ltd, The
Brick Cladding Systems - Eurobrick Systems Ltd
Precast concrete slab cladding/ features - Evans Concrete Products Ltd
Precast concrete slab cladding/ features - Vetter UK
Precast Slab Cladding - Carter Concrete Ltd
Prestressed concrete wall panels - ACP (Concrete) Ltd
Prestressed concrete wall panels - ACP Concrete Limited
Retaining walls - Grass Concrete Ltd

H51 Natural stone slab cladding/ features

Airtec Stone - Telling Architectural Ltd
External Wall Cladding - Johnsons Wellfield Quarries Ltd
Glazed terracotta rain screen cladding - Smithbrook Building Products Ltd
Natural stone cladding - Kirkstone
Natural Stone Cladding - Palladio Stone
Natural Stone Slab Cladding - Carter Concrete Ltd
Natural stone slab cladding/ features - Chichester Stoneworks Limited
Natural stone slab cladding/ features - Stonewest Ltd
Natural stone slab cladding/ features - Vetter UK
Natural stone slab cladding/features - G Miccoli & Sons Limited
Sandstone - Dunhouse Quarry Co Ltd
Stone faced precast cladding - Marble Mosaic Co Ltd, The
Stonework - design, procurement and installation of - Szerelmey Ltd
Yorkstone - Hard York Quarries Ltd

H52 Cast stone slab cladding/ features

Architectural precast cladding - Marble Mosaic Co Ltd, The
Architectural Stonework - Cranborne Stone Limited
Bespoke cast stone features - GB Architectural Cladding Products Ltd
Brick & stone insulated cladding systems - Eurobrick Systems Ltd
Cast stone cladding/ features - GB Architectural Cladding Products Ltd
Cast stone cladding/features - G Miccoli & Sons Limited
Cast stone slab cladding /features - Haddonstone Ltd
Cast stone slab cladding/ features - Chilstone
Cast stone slab/ cladding/ features - Evans Concrete Products Ltd
Cladding - Blanc de Bierges
Mullion windows, quoins, cornices and doorways - Minsterstone Ltd

H60 Plain roof tiling

Acrylic glass tiles - Klober Ltd
Classic Handformed Tiles - Hinton Perry & Davenhill Ltd
Clay and concrete tiles - Sandtoft Roof Tiles Ltd
Clay hanging tiles - clayton - Wienerberger Ltd (Keymer Handmade Clay Plain Tiles)
Clay peg tiles - traditional handmade - Wienerberger Ltd (Keymer Handmade Clay Plain Tiles)
Clay plain tiles - traditional handmade - Wienerberger Ltd (Keymer Handmade Clay Plain Tiles)
Clay roof tiles - Hinton Perry & Davenhill Ltd
Clay Roof Tiles - Marley Ltd
Clay roofing tiles - Michelmersh Brick Holdings PLC
Concrete roof tiles - Forticrete Roofing
Concrete Roof Tiles - Marley Ltd
Finials - Hinton Perry & Davenhill Ltd
Glazed clay roof tiles - Smithbrook Building Products Ltd
Glazed roof tiles - Hye Oak
Handmade Clay, roof tiles plus under tile vent - Tudor Roof Tile Co Ltd
Ornamental Ridges - Hinton Perry & Davenhill Ltd
Ornamental Tiles and Fittings - Hinton Perry & Davenhill Ltd
Plain Clay Roof Tiles - Hinton Perry & Davenhill Ltd
Plain Roof Tiling - Britmet Tileform Limited
Plain roof tiling - Mells Roofing Ltd
Plain roof tiling - SIG Roofing
Plain tiles - Monier Redland Limited
Ridge Tiles - Forterra Building Products Ltd
Roof Coverings - Howard Evans Roofing and Cladding Ltd
Roof space ventilating tiles - Klober Ltd
Roof Tiles - Russell Roof Tiles Ltd
Roof ventilation - Hambleside Danelaw Ltd
Roofing - InstaGroup Ltd
Roofing Accessories - Monier Redland Limited
Roofing claywork - Red Bank Manufacturing Co Ltd
Roofing fittings - Monier Redland Limited
Roofing underlay felt - Newton John & Co Ltd
Technical Solutions - Monier Redland Limited
Terracotta ridges and finals - Wienerberger Ltd (Keymer Handmade Clay Plain Tiles)
Tileline Ventilation Products - Hinton Perry & Davenhill Ltd
Tiling - Avonside Roofing Group T/A Letchworth Roofing
Tiling - Durable Contracts (Roofing) Ltd
Ventilated ridge system - Klober Ltd
Ventilation system - Wienerberger Ltd (Keymer Handmade Clay Plain Tiles)

H61 Fibre cement slating

Fibre cement slating - Mells Roofing Ltd
Fibre cement slating - SIG Roofing
Roof space ventilating slates - Klober Ltd
Roof ventilation - Hambleside Danelaw Ltd
Roofing - Avonside Roofing Group T/A Letchworth Roofing
Roofing slate - Chameleon Stone Ltd
Roofing slates, ventilation products - Cembrit Ltd
Slating - Durable Contracts (Roofing) Ltd
Synthetic Slates and Tiles - EBC UK Ltd

H62 Natural slating

Copings and sills - Kirkstone
Flooring Slate - Chameleon Stone Ltd
Natural Roofing Slates - EBP Building Products Ltd
Natural slate cladding - Welsh Slate Limited
Natural slate copings - Welsh Slate Limited
Natural slate counters - Welsh Slate Limited
Natural slate flooring - Welsh Slate Limited
Natural slate landscaping - Welsh Slate Limited
Natural slate roofing - Burlington Slate Ltd
Natural slate roofing - Welsh Slate Limited
Natural slate sills - Welsh Slate Limited
Natural slate walling - Welsh Slate Limited
Natural slate worktops - Welsh Slate Limited
Natural Slates - IJK Timber Group Ltd
Natural slating - Mells Roofing Ltd
Natural slating - SIG Roofing
Polythene under slating sheet - Visqueen Building Products
Roof Tiles & Slates - Caithness Flagstone Limited
Roof ventilation - Hambleside Danelaw Ltd
Roofing Natural Tiles - Milestone Reclaim and Landscaping Ltd
Roofing slate - Chameleon Stone Ltd
Roofing slate - The Delabole Slate Co. Ltd
Slate Repair Clips - Owens Slate Services Ltd
Slate Repair Fixings - Owen Slate Services Ltd
Slating - Avonside Roofing Group T/A Letchworth Roofing
Welsh, Spanish Brazilian and Canadian slates - Cembrit Ltd

H63 Reconstructed stone slating/ tiling

Concrete slates - Forticrete Roofing
Green roofs - Alumasc Exterior Building Products Ltd
Recon: stone - Chiltern Concrete and Stone
Reconstructed stone slating/ tiling - SIG Roofing
Slates - Monier Redland Limited
Slates - Sandtoft Roof Tiles Ltd
Tiles and specialist works - conglomerate marble, limestone & assimilated granite - Marble Flooring Spec. Ltd

H64 Timber shingling

Cedar shingles - Cembrit Ltd
K20 Timber Boarding etc - Challenge Fencing Ltd
Timber shingling - SIG Roofing
Timber shingling suppliers - W.L. West & Sons Ltd

H65 Single lap roof tiling

Concrete Roof Tiles - Marley Ltd
Profile tiles - Monier Redland Limited
Roofing - Avonside Roofing Group T/A Letchworth Roofing
Roofing Systems - Sandtoft Roof Tiles Ltd
Single lap roof tiling - Mells Roofing Ltd
Single lap roof tiling - Sandtoft Roof Tiles Ltd
Single lap roof tiling - SIG Roofing
Thatching, thatching materials and fire retardants - Thatching Advisory Services Ltd

H66 Bituminous felt shingling

Bitumen felt shingles - Cembrit Ltd
Bituminous felt shingling - Mells Roofing Ltd
Bituminous felt shingling - Onduline Building Products Ltd
Bituminous felt shingling - SIG Roofing
Tegola asphalt shingles - Matthew Hebden

H70 Malleable metal sheet prebonded covering/ cladding

Fully supported roofing and cladding - Roles Broderick Roofing Ltd
Malleable metal sheet prebonded covering/ cladding - Reid John & Sons (Strucsteel) Ltd
Metal cladding coatings - Jotun Henry Clark Ltd Decorative Division
Metal roofing - Omnis

H71 Lead sheet coverings/ flashings

Aluminium flashing - George Gilmour (Metals) Ltd
Cloaks - Cavity Trays Ltd
Flashings - Cavity Trays Ltd
Hyclad matt finish - Outokumpu
Lead and sheet flashings - Royston Lead Ltd
Lead sheet - R.M. Easdale & Co Ltd
Lead sheet and flashing - Calder Industrial Materials Ltd
Lead sheet covering and flashings - Roles Broderick Roofing Ltd
Lead Sheet Coverings/ Flashings - BLM British Lead
Lead sheet coverings/ flashings - Harris & Bailey Ltd
Low reflective satin finish - Outokumpu
Ternie coated lead finish - Outokumpu

H72 Aluminium strip/ sheet coverings/ flashings

Aluminium covers - Franklin Hodge Industries Ltd
Aluminium & Steel Composite Roof & Wall Cladding - Rigidal
Aluminium coping - WP Metals Ltd
Aluminium coping systems - Dales Fabrications Ltd
Aluminium Facia and Soffit systems - Alutec
Aluminium flashings - WP Metals Ltd
Aluminium flashings and trims - Azimex Fabrications Ltd
Aluminium glazing sheet coverings/flashings - Exitex Ltd
Aluminium roof outlets - Marley Plumbing and Drainage
Aluminium roofing and cladding sheets - Gilmour Ecometal
Aluminium sheet coverings/ flashings - HW Architectural Ltd
Aluminium sheet coverings/ flashings - Reid John & Sons (Strucsteel) Ltd
Aluminum sheet covering and flashings - Roles Broderick Roofing Ltd
Anodised Aluminium sheet - Alanod Ltd
Insulated Roof & Wall Systems - Kingspan Ltd
Metal facia systems - Alumasc Exterior Building Products Ltd
Metal roofing and cladding - Ash & Lacy Building Products Ltd
Perforated panels in aluminium - Winther Browne & co Ltd
Powder coated aluminium - Dales Fabrications Ltd

H73 Copper strip/ sheet coverings/ flashings

Copper flashings and trims - Azimex Fabrications Ltd

H73 Copper strip/ sheet coverings/ flashings (con't)

Copper sheet coverings and flashings - Roles Broderick Roofing Ltd

H74 Zinc strip/ sheet coverings/ flashings

Zinc flashings and trims - Azimex Fabrications Ltd
Zinc roofing - Rheinzink UK
Zinc sheet coverings and flashings - Roles Broderick Roofing Ltd

H75 Stainless steel strip/ sheet coverings/ flashings

Insulated Roof & Wall Systems - Kingspan Ltd
Profiled Sheet Roofing - Tata Steel Colors
Stainless steel flashings and trims - Azimex Fabrications Ltd
Stainless Steel Roofing Sheet - Aperam Stainless Services & Solutions UK Limited
Stainless steel strip/ sheet coverings/ fashings - Barlow Group
Stainless steel strip/ sheet coverings/ flashings - Aluline Precision Engineering Ltd
Stainless steel strip/sheet coverings and flashings - Roles Broderick Roofing Ltd
Stainless steel strip/sheet coverings/flashings - Britmet Tileform Limited
Stainless steel traditional longstrip roofing and cladding material - Outokumpu

H76 Fibre bitumen thermoplastic sheet coverings/ flashings

Roofing membranes - EBC UK Ltd
Roofing Membranes - Sika Ltd

H90 Tensile fabric coverings

Architectural Fabric Structures - TA Lucas Sails
Banners - TA Lucas Sails
Breathable membranes - Fillcrete Ltd
Covers - TA Lucas Sails
Fabric Canopies - Aura
Fabric Ceilings - Architen Landrell Associates Ltd
Rigging - TA Lucas Sails
Sails - TA Lucas Sails
Tensile structure material - Mermet U.K
Tensile Structures - Architen Landrell Associates Ltd
Vapour barriers - Fillcrete Ltd

H91 Thatch roofing

Stainless steel wire - Thatching Advisory Services Ltd
Staple gun and staples for stainless steel wire - Thatching Advisory Services Ltd
Thatch Roof Tiles - Africa Roofing Uk
Thatch roofing materials - Thatching Advisory Services Ltd

H92 Rainscreen cladding

Bespoke profiled GRP FRP fibreglass rainscreen feature cladding - Design & Display Structures Ltd
Cellular PVC cladding - Celuform Building Products
Ceramic Rainscreens - Telling Architectural Ltd
Cladding - Blanc de Bierges
Cladding - Tata Steel Europe Limited
Concrete Rainscreen Cladding System - Forticrete Masonry
External decorative claddings - Cembrit Ltd
Faience blocks - Shaws of Darwen
Hygrothermal performance testing, Water penetration, Pull testing, Impact testing, Dynamic wind loading and uplift testing - Lucideon
Metal roofing and cladding - Ash & Lacy Building Products Ltd
PVC Sheeting - Power Plastics Ltd
Rainscreed Cladding stone - Johnsons Wellfield Quarries Ltd
Rainscreen - Howard Evans Roofing and Cladding Ltd
Rainscreen cladding - Baggeridge Brick PLC
Rainscreen cladding - English Architectural Glazing Ltd
Rainscreen cladding - FGF Ltd
Rainscreen Cladding - McMullen Facades
Rainscreen cladding - Panel Systems Ltd
Rainscreen Cladding - Schueco UK
Rainscreen cladding - STO Ltd
Rainscreen cladding - Vetter UK
Rainscreen cladding - Vulcan Cladding Systems
Rainscreen facade systems - CGL Facades
Rainscreen Panels - Rheinzink UK
Screening - Power Plastics Ltd
Terracotta and faience - design, procurement and installation of - Szerelmey Ltd
Terracotta blocks - Shaws of Darwen
Terracotta Cladding - Telling Architectural Ltd

J10 Specialist waterproof rendering

Basement tanking - Safeguard Europe Ltd
Cementitious and dry line membrane tanking - Dampcoursing Limited
Cementitious waterproof systems - Kingfisher Building Products Ltd
External rendering systems - PermaRock Products Ltd
External Wall Coatings - Belzona PolymericLtd
Institutions/Associations - Sprayed Concrete Association
Polymer modified renders - Ronacrete Ltd
renders Carter-Dal Micro Coat 701 (45) colours - Carter-Dal International
Sealants for waterproofing and damp proofing - Ancorite Surface Protection Ltd
Silicone waterproofing - Bluestar Silicones
Specialist waterproof render - Flexcrete Technologies Limited
Specialist waterproof rendering - Concrete Repairs Ltd
Specialist waterproof rendering - Don Construction Products Ltd
Specialist waterproof rendering - Peter Cox Ltd
Specialist waterproof rendering - Specialist Building Products
Waterproof renders(30 colours) - Laticrete International Inc. UK
Waterproofing - BASF plc, Construction Chemicals
Waterproofing products - IKO PLC
Waterproofing Products - Sealocrete PLA Ltd
Waterproofing systems - Grace De Neef UK

J20 Mastic asphalt tanking/ damp proofing

Asphalt - Tillicoutry Quarries Ltd
Damp proof membranes - Icopal Limited
Mastic asphalt tanking / damp proof membranes - Durable Contracts (Roofing) Ltd
Mastic asphalt tanking/ damp proofing - North Herts Asphalte (Roofing) Ltd
Tanking - Dyke Chemicals Ltd
Tanking - Newton John & Co Ltd
Tanking - Roofing Contractors (Cambridge) Ltd
Tanking and damp proof membranes - BriggsAmasco
Waterproofing membranes - Fosroc Ltd

J21 Mastic asphalt roofing/ insulation/ finishes

Colours for Asphalt - Procter Johnson & Co Ltd
Emergency Repair Compounds - Dyke Chemicals Ltd

GRP and aluminium roof edge trims and flashings - Pitchmastic PmB Ltd
Insulation - Rockwool Ltd
Mastic asphalt roofing and car parks - BriggsAmasco
Mastic asphalt roofing/ insulation/ finishes - BFRC Services Ltd
Movement Joints - Movement Joints (UK)
Recycled glass tiles - Spear & Jackson Interntional Ltd
Roof insulation - North Herts Asphalte (Roofing) Ltd
Roof Waterproofing Systems - Topseal Systems Ltd
Roof waterproofing systems, colour solar reflective roof finishes - Dyke Chemicals Ltd
Roofing - North Herts Asphalte (Roofing) Ltd
Roofing - Roofing Contractors (Cambridge) Ltd
Roofing contractors - Durable Contracts (Roofing) Ltd
Roofing insulation boards - Firestone Building Products
Tarpauling - Power Plastics Ltd
Tarpaulins - Icopal Limited
Urethane foam industry trade association - British Urethane Foam Contractors Association

J22 Proprietary roof decking with asphalt finish

Colours for Asphalt - Procter Johnson & Co Ltd
Flat roof decking - Isocrete Floor Screeds Ltd
Proprietary roof decking with asphalt finish - Durable Contracts (Roofing) Ltd
Proprietary roof decking with asphalt finish - Onduline Building Products Ltd
Roof decking with asphalt finish - BriggsAmasco
Roof tile underlays - Icopal Limited
Roofing contractor - Evans Howard Roofing Ltd
Torch on roofing - IKO PLC

J30 Liquid applied tanking/ damp proofing

Adhesives - Carter-Dal International
Adhesives - Laticrete International Inc. UK
Balcony waterproofing - Sika Liquid Plastics Limited
Basement tanking - Safeguard Europe Ltd
Basement water proofing - Timberwise (UK) Ltd
Basement waterproofing - ProTen Services
Damp proof membrane - Ardex UK Ltd
Damp Proofing - ProTen Services
Damp proofing - RFA-Tech Ltd
DPC tanking systems - IKO PLC
Flashings - Dyke Chemicals Ltd
Heldite Jointing Compound - Heldite Ltd
Liquid applied coating - StarFix TANKING - Star Uretech Ltd
Liquid applied damp proof membranes - Kingfisher Building Products Ltd
Liquid Applied Tanking Materials - Belzona PolymericLtd
Liquid applied tanking/ damp proof membrane - Colebrand Ltd
Liquid applied tanking/ damp proof membranes - Cross-Guard International Ltd
Liquid applied tanking/ damp proof membranes - Don Construction Products Ltd
Liquid applied tanking/ damp proof membranes - Specialist Building Products
Liquid applied tanking/ damp proofing - Flexcrete Technologies Limited
Liquid applied tanking/ damp proofing - Tremco Illbruck Ltd
Liquid applied tanking/damp proof membranes - Trade Sealants Ltd
Polymer modified coatings - Ronacrete Ltd
Structural waterproofing - Alumasc Exterior Building Products Ltd
Structural waterproofing - GCP APPLIED TECHNOLOGIES (UK) LIMITED
Tanking - RFA-Tech Ltd
Waterproof membranes - Carter-Dal International
Waterproof membranes - Laticrete International Inc. UK
Waterproofing membranes - Kenyon Group Ltd

J31 Liquid applied waterproof roof coatings

Asbsetos roof coatings - Sika Liquid Plastics Limited
Bituminous roofing - TRC (Midlands) Ltd
Coatings - Bostik Ltd
Cold Bonded Built-up Roofs - Sika Liquid Plastics Limited
Damp-proof membranes - Dyke Chemicals Ltd
Epoxy Resins & Adhesives - Wessex Resins & Adhesives Ltd
Green roofs - Sika Liquid Plastics Limited
High performance roof coatings - Intergrated Polymer Systems (UK) Ltd
Inverted Roofs - Sika Liquid Plastics Limited
Liquid applied roof waterproof coatings - Flexcrete Technologies Limited
Liquid applied waterproof coating - Brimar Plastics Ltd
Liquid applied waterproof coatings - BFRC Services Ltd
Liquid applied waterproof coatings - Brewer C & Sons Ltd
Liquid applied waterproof coatings - BriggsAmasco
Liquid applied waterproof coatings - Colebrand Ltd
Liquid applied waterproof coatings - Concrete Repairs Ltd
Liquid applied waterproof coatings - Cross-Guard International Ltd
Liquid applied waterproof coatings - Don Construction Products Ltd
Liquid applied waterproof coatings - Precolor Sales Ltd
liquid applied waterproof coatings - Trade Sealants Ltd
Liquid applied waterproof roof coatings - Hyflex Roofing
Liquid applied waterproof roof coatings - Mells Roofing Ltd
Liquid applied waterproof roof coatings - Sika Liquid Plastics Limited
Liuquid Applied Roof Waterproofing - Belzona PolymericLtd
Mechanically Fixed Insulation with Cold Bonded Built-up Roofs - Sika Liquid Plastics Limited
PmB Structural Waterproofing Systems - Pitchmastic PmB Ltd
Roof Renovation Paints - Kingfisher Building Products Ltd
Roof repair and protection - Sealocrete PLA Ltd
Roof repair membranes - Kingfisher Building Products Ltd
Roof repair systems - Williamson T & R Ltd
Roof Waterproofing systems - Axter Ltd
Roofing - Avonside Roofing Group T/A Letchworth Roofing
Root resistant cold liquid applied green roof coating - Sika Liquid Plastics Limited
Structural roof waterproofing - Alumasc Exterior Building Products Ltd
Ultraflex Liquid Waterproofing System - EBP Building Products Ltd
Waterproofing membranes - Conren Ltd
Waterproofing Membranes - Kemper System Ltd

J32 Sprayed vapour control layers

Radon and methane gas barriers - Icopal Limited
Sprayer vapour barriers - Trade Sealants Ltd
Vapour barriers and breather membranes - Icopal Limited

J33 In situ glassfibre reinforced plastics

Fibertex geotextiles - Tex Engineering Ltd
In situ glass reinforced plastic - Specialist Building Products
In situ GRP - Precolor Sales Ltd
In-situ glass reinforced plastics - Brimar Plastics Ltd
In-situ GRP - BriggsAmasco

J40 Flexible sheet tanking/ damp proofing

Basement tanking - Safeguard Europe Ltd
Basement waterproofing - ProTen Services
Condensation control - Peter Cox Ltd
Damp proof courses - Cavity Trays Ltd
Damp proof membranes - Bostik Ltd
Damp proof membranes - Isocrete Floor Screeds Ltd
Damp proofing - ProTen Services
Damp proofing - RFA-Tech Ltd
Dampproof membranes - Newton John & Co Ltd
Flexible sheet tanking / damp proof membranes - Durable Contracts (Roofing) Ltd
Flexible sheet tanking, damp proof membanes - Terminix Property Services
Flexible sheet tanking/ damp proof membranes - BFRC Services Ltd
Flexible sheet tanking/ damp proof membranes - John Davidson (Pipes) Ltd
Flexible sheet tanking/ damp proof membranes - Specialist Building Products
Flexible Sheet Tanking/Waterproofing - Peter Cox Ltd
Gas barrier membranes - Visqueen Building Products
Gas barrier membranes and pond liners - Geosynthetic Technology Ltd
Membranes - Cavity Trays Ltd
Polythene Building Films and DPC - EBP Building Products Ltd
Polythene dampproof membranes - Visqueen Building Products
Roofing Membranes - Sarnafil Ltd
Single Ply Roofing Systems - Sarnafil Ltd
Tanking - RFA-Tech Ltd
Waterproof expansion joints - Radflex Contract Services Ltd
Waterproof membranes - GCP APPLIED TECHNOLOGIES (UK) LIMITED
Waterproofing membranes - SCP Concrete Sealing Technology Ltd
Waterproofing sheets - ABG Ltd
Waterproofing: Breather Membranes - Icopal Limited
Waterstops - Fosroc Ltd

J41 Built up felt roof coverings

Built up felt roof covering - Brewer C & Sons Ltd
Built up felt roof coverings - Durable Contracts (Roofing) Ltd
Built up felt roof coverings - TRC (Midlands) Ltd
Built up felt roofing - BriggsAmasco
Built Up Felt Roofing - North Herts Asphalte (Roofing) Ltd
Built up felt roofing - Roofing Contractors (Cambridge) Ltd
Built-up felt roof coverings - Mells Roofing Ltd
Felting and single ply - Avonside Roofing Group T/A Letchworth Roofing
Flat roofing built up felt roofing - Chesterfelt Ltd
High performance roofing - Alumasc Exterior Building Products Ltd
Membrane waterproofing - BFRC Services Ltd
Movement Joints - Movement Joints (UK)
Roof coverings - Howard Evans Roofing and Cladding Ltd
Roof Waterproofing membranes - Axter Ltd
Roofing Accessories - Ubbink (UK) Ltd
Roofing compound - Bartoline Ltd
Roofing contractor - Evans Howard Roofing Ltd
Roofing Felt - Milestone Reclaim and Landscaping Ltd
Roofing products - Cavity Trays Ltd
Roofing products - Klober Ltd
Structural Protection Membranes - StarFix TANKING - Star Uretech Ltd
Vapour membranes - Klober Ltd
Weather protection sheeting and sheeting - Power Plastics Ltd

J42 Single layer polymeric roof coverings

Conservatory roof systems, vents and glazing bars - Newdawn & Sun Ltd
Firestone RubberCover (EPDM) - EBP Building Products Ltd
Grren Roof Systems - AAC Waterproofing Ltd
Roof Membranes - AAC Waterproofing Ltd
Roofing - Avonside Roofing Group T/A Letchworth Roofing
Single layer plastic roof coverings - BFRC Services Ltd
Single layer polymeric roof coverings - Durable Contracts (Roofing) Ltd
Single Layer Polymeric Sheet Roof Coverings - Safeguard Europe Ltd
Single Layer Polymetric roof coverings - Mells Roofing Ltd
Single layer PVC and CPE membrane roofing systems - RENOLIT Cramlington Limited
Single ply polymetric membranes - Roofing Contractors (Cambridge) Ltd
Single ply PVC roof waterproofing - Axter Ltd
Single ply roofing - Firestone Building Products
Single ply roofing - ICB (International Construction Bureau) Ltd
Single Ply Roofing - Sika Ltd
Single ply systems - BriggsAmasco
Water repellent solutions - Dyke Chemicals Ltd

J43 Proprietary roof decking with felt finish

Proprietary roof decking with felt finish - Durable Contracts (Roofing) Ltd
Roll panel - Airflow (Nicoll Ventilators) Ltd
Roof decking with felt finish - BriggsAmasco
Roofing - Avonside Roofing Group T/A Letchworth Roofing
Roofing centilators - Airflow (Nicoll Ventilators) Ltd

J44 Sheet linings for pools/ lakes/waterways

Gas barrier membranes and pond liners - Geosynthetic Technology Ltd
Pond / landfill lining systems - ABG Ltd
Pool liners - Firestone Building Products
Single Ply Roofing Systems - Sarnafil Ltd

K10 Plasterboard dry linings/ partitions/ceilings

Access panels ceilings - Panel & Louvre Co Ltd
Building Boards - Cembrit Ltd
Ceilings - Hunter Douglas Architectural Ltd
Ceilings - Plasterboard, Suspended - Gridpart Interiors Ltd
Clean Room Partitioning - TROAX UK Ltd
Dry Lining - Covers Timber & Builders Merchants
Dry lining systems - British Gypsum Ltd
Dry Linings - Skanda Acoustics Limited

K10 Plasterboard dry linings/ partitions/ceilings (con't)

Dry wall partitions - Optima
Drywall systems - Knauf UK
Drywall systems - Siniat Ltd
Fire resistant panels - Promat UK Ltd
Fire stopping and barriers - Firebarrier International Ltd T/A Firebarrier Services Ltd
Full fit out, refurbishment and partitioning service - Neslo Interiors
GRG (glass reinforced gypsum) products - design, manufacture and installation - Gillespie (UK) Ltd
Interior wall linings - Trespa UK Ltd
Linings - FGF Ltd
Moveable walls - Becker (SLIDING PARTITIONS) Ltd
Partitioning - Hatmet Limited
Partitioning - RAJA Workplace
Partitions - Fastwall Ltd
Partitions - Glazed, Metal stud, Aluminium, Fire barriers - Gridpart Interiors Ltd
Plasterboard - British Gypsum Ltd
Plasterboard accessories - British Gypsum Ltd
Plasterboard acoustic wall products - Trim Acoustics
Plasterboard dry lining - Harris & Bailey Ltd
Plasterboard dry lining/ partitions/ ceilings - Logic Office Contracts
Plasterboards and drywall Accessories - Knauf Drywall
Steel Partition - TROAX UK Ltd
Supplier of Ceilings, Partitioning, Dry lining and Interior Building products - Nevill Long
Trade Association - Association of Specialist Fire Protection (ASFP)

K11 Rigid sheet flooring/ sheathing/ decking/sarking/ linings/casings

Access flooring - Nevill Long
Acoustic Insulation - Hush Acoustics
Blockboard - Wood International Agency Ltd
Building boards - Finnish Fibreboard (UK) Ltd
Cladding - James Donaldson Timber
Column and beam encasement systems - Knauf Drywall
Column Cladding Systems - Jali Ltd
Cutting, drilling and machining - Boardcraft Ltd
Drylining material - Avanti Systems
Drywall systems - Knauf UK
Film Faced plywood - Wood International Agency Ltd
Fire resistant panels - Promat UK Ltd
Flooring accessories - Atkinson & Kirby Ltd
Flooring systems - Knauf UK
Fsc certified plywood - Wood International Agency Ltd
Glass partitions - Style Door Systems Ltd
Hardboard - Panel Agency Limited
Hardboard - Wood International Agency Ltd
Hardwood and softwood - Boardcraft Ltd
Hardwood plywood - Wood International Agency Ltd
Insulating laminates - Knauf Drywall
Insulation Boards - Skanda Acoustics Limited
Internal Walls & Partitions - Avanti Systems
Laminates and MDF's - Kronospan Ltd
Lightweight composite boards and panels - QK Honeycomb Products Ltd
Linigs and castings - Cox Long Ltd
Medium Density Fibrboard (MDF) - Meyer Timber Limited
Mezanine floors - Adex Interiors for industry Ltd
Moveable internal walls and partitions - Style Door Systems Ltd
Oriented Strand Board (OSB) - Meyer Timber Limited
OSB - Kronospan Ltd
OSB - Wood International Agency Ltd
Panel products - James Latham plc
Perforated MDF - Mevaco Ltd
Perforated Perforations - Mevaco Ltd
Perforated Products - RMIG Ltd
Pipe and column casings - Alumasc Interior Building Products Limited
Plain and melamine faced chipboard - Kronospan Ltd
Plain and melamine faced flooring - Kronospan Ltd
Plain, melamine faced and lacquered MDF - Kronospan Ltd
Plywood-structure + non-structure - Meyer Timber Limited
Polyisocyanurate insulation board manufacture - Celotex Ltd
rigid sheet flooring, sheathing, decking, sarking - Cox Long Ltd
Rigid sheet flooring/ sheathing/ decking/sarking/ linings/casings - Cembrit Ltd
Rigid sheet flooring/ sheathing/ decking/sarking/ linings/casings - Skanda Acoustics
Semi finished plastics and building products - Amari Plastics Plc
Sheet materials - Cox Long Ltd
Sheet Materials - Walker Timber Ltd
Softwood plywood - Wood International Agency Ltd
Sprays fire proof - Firebarrier International Ltd T/A Firebarrier Services Ltd
Stainless Steel Chequered plate - Aperam Stainless Services & Solutions UK Limited
Stainless steel flooring - Wincro Metal Industries Ltd
Thermal insulated panels - Panel Systems Ltd
Undercarrige Systems - Atkinson & Kirby Ltd
Underlay - Atkinson & Kirby Ltd
Veneered Boards - Meyer Timber Limited
Wet wall and showerwall panels, wet area wall lining and ceiling panels - Mermaid Panels Ltd
Wood Partical Board - Meyer Timber Limited
Woodbased panels - Egger (UK) Ltd
Woodfibre Underlays - Panel Agency Limited

K12 Under purlin/ Inside rail panel linings

Plywood, hard, fibre, chip and particle boards - Boardcraft Ltd
Under Purlin Linings - Skanda Acoustics Limited
Under purlin/Inside rail panel linings - Skanda Acoustics

K13 Rigid sheet fine linings/ panelling

Access panels walls - Panel & Louvre Co Ltd
Acoustic Baffles, Barriers, Ceiling Panels, Curtains, Attenuators, Enclosures, Panels, Louvers and Wall Panels - including perforated timber/metal - Acousticabs Industrial Noise Control Ltd
Acoustic Ceiling & wall panels - Skanda Acoustics Limited
Acoustic flooring and acoustic wall products - Trim Acoustics
Acoustic wall panels - Skanda Acoustics
Aquapanel Tile Backing Board - Knauf Drywall
Bespoke infil panels - Halmark Panels Ltd
Bespoke joinery - Howard Bros Joinery Ltd
Broadcast and Audio Studios - IAC Acoustic Company UK Ltd
Carved cornice, frieze and embellishments - Oakleaf Reproductions Ltd
Cladding panel - Panel Systems Ltd
Composite infil pannels - VBH (GB) Ltd
Cubicle systems - Formica Ltd
Facing laminates - Wilsonart Ltd
Faux book spines, mirrors and frames - Oakleaf Reproductions Ltd
Full fit out, refurbishment and partitioning service - Neslo Interiors
High pressure decorative laminates - Abet Ltd
Hygienic and railway arch lining materials - Rockwell Sheet Sales Ltd
Hygienic Wall & Ceiling Linings - Interclad (UK) Ltd
Hygienic wall linings - Filon Products Ltd
Hygienic walls and ceiling cladding systems - Advanced Hygienic Contracting Ltd
Impact resistant Acoustic Wall Panels - Knauf AMF Ceilings Ltd
Laminates - Meyer Timber Limited
Linenfold wall panelling, riven oak wall panelling - Oakleaf Reproductions Ltd
Melamine faced chipboard - Deralam Laminates Ltd
Metal + melamine laminates - Deralam Laminates Ltd
Multi-wall roofing products - Amari Plastics Plc
Panel Products - Panel Agency Limited
Panelled interiors - Hallidays UK Ltd
Partitions - Optima
Plywood, hard, fibre, chip and particle boards - Boardcraft Ltd
Purpose made Wall Panelling - Platonoff & Harris Ltd
Real wood veneer laminates - Deralam Laminates Ltd
Rigid sheet fine linings/ panelling - Cembrit Ltd
Sheet materials - IJK Timber Group Ltd
Slat board - Smart F & G (Shopfittings)Ltd
Softwood - James Latham plc
Structural wall panels - Marshalls Mono Ltd
Timber decorative wall panels - Vicaima Ltd
Veneered boards - Atkinson & Kirby Ltd
Wall Access Panels - The Access Panel Company Ltd
Wall lining systems - Knauf Drywall
Wall Panels and Hygienic Wall Linings - Aaztec Cubicles
Wet wall and showerwall panels, wet area wall lining and ceiling panels - Mermaid Panels Ltd
Wood Based Panel Products - Meyer Timber Limited

K20 Timber board flooring/ decking/sarking/linings/casings

Acoustic Baffles, Barriers, Ceiling Panels, Curtains, Attenuators, Enclosures, Panels, Louvers and Wall Panels - including perforated timber/metal - Acousticabs Industrial Noise Control Ltd
Acoustic suspended ceilings - Skanda Acoustics Limited
Building boards - Finnish Fibreboard (UK) Ltd
Cane woven panels - Winther Browne & co Ltd
Decking - James Donaldson Timber
Decorative laminated flooring - Egger (UK) Ltd
Densified wood and industrial flooring - Permali Deho Ltd
Duct walling - LSA Projects Ltd
Fire protection boards - Knauf Drywall
Floor ducting - Alumasc Interior Building Products Limited
Flooring Panels - Norbord
Full fit out, refurbishment and partitioning service - Neslo Interiors
Hardwood flooring - W.L. West & Sons Ltd
MDF - Metsä Wood
Mezzanine Flooring - Sperrin Metal Products Ltd
Non-slip/Anti-slip Decking in hardwood or softwood - CTS Bridges Ltd
Perimeter casing - Alumasc Interior Building Products Limited
Pipe boxing - Alumasc Interior Building Products Limited
Plywood, hard, fibre, chip and particle boards - Boardcraft Ltd
Roofing Boards - Norbord
Sanding and Sealing wood floors - Sportsmark Group Ltd
Softboard - Panel Agency Limited
Timber board flooring - Atkinson & Kirby Ltd
Timber board flooring/decking - Magnet Ltd
Timber Boarding etc - Challenge Fencing Ltd
Timber Boards - Norbord
Timber cladding, mouldings and flooring - James Latham plc
Timber decking - Wyckham Blackwell Ltd
Timber Suppliers - Crowthorne Fencing

K21 Timber strip/ board fine flooring/ linings

Dance floor - Felix Design Ltd
Hardwood flooring - Atkinson & Kirby Ltd
Laminates - Egger (UK) Ltd
Movement Joints - Movement Joints (UK)
Panel products - IJK Timber Group Ltd
Perforated panels in hardboard and MDF - Winther Browne & co Ltd
Solid hardwood flooring - Junckers Limited
Timber decorative wall panels - Vicaima Ltd
Timber strip/board flooring/lining - Magnet Ltd
Timber strips/ board fine flooring / linings - Barlow Group
Timber Suppliers - Crowthorne Fencing

K30 Panel partitions

Acoustic folding partitions - Parthos UK Ltd
Acoustic Movable Walls - Coburn Sliding Systems Ltd
Acoustic movable walls - Parthos UK Ltd
Brushstrip sealing for cable management - Kleeneze Sealtech Ltd
Changing cubicles - unframed - Helmsman
Concertina Partitions - Coburn Sliding Systems Ltd
Demountable partitioning - Internal Partitions Systems
Demountable partitions - Komfort Workspace PLC
Demountable partitions and associated electrical works - Opus 4 Ltd
Drywall systems - Knauf UK
Duct panelling and frames - TBS Amwell Ltd
Duct Panels - Aaztec Cubicles
Fire rated partitions - Avanti Systems
Fire resistant panels - Promat UK Ltd
Firewalls - Composite Panel Services Ltd
Frameless glazed partitions - Avanti Systems
Full fit out, refurbishment and partitioning service - Neslo Interiors
Insulated wall panels - Composite Panel Services Ltd
Interior contractors - Gifford Grant Ltd
Internal Panels - Paroc Panel Systems Uk Ltd
IPS Systems - Aaztec Cubicles
Laminate wall claddings - T B S Fabrications
Office partitioning - Construction Group UK Ltd
Operable wall systems - Monowa Manufacturing (UK) Ltd
Panel partitions - Logic Office Contracts
Panel partitions - Optima
Partitioning - Hatmet Limited
Partitioning - New Forest Ceilings Ltd
Partitioning - Newey Ceilings
Partitioning - Optima
Partitioning and wall storage systems - Fastwall Ltd
Partitioning systems - Knauf Drywall
Partitioning systems - Nevill Long
Partitions - Adex Interiors for industry Ltd
Partitions - Firco Ltd
Partitions - Shaylor Group Plc
Partitions - SIG Interiors
Partitions - Glazed, Metal stud, Aluminium, Fire barriers - Gridpart Interiors Ltd
Plywood, hard, fibre, chip and particle boards - Boardcraft Ltd
Relocatable partitioning - Clestra Limited
Relocateable partitions - Fastwall Ltd
Sliding folding partition manufacturer - Building Additions Ltd
Sliding partitions - Becker (SLIDING PARTITIONS) Ltd
Steel caging/ partitioning - Bradbury Group Ltd

K32 Panel cubicles

Changing cubicles - framed - Helmsman
Cubicle systems - Panel Systems Ltd
Cubicles - Bushboard Washrooms
Cubicles - Nevill Long
Cubicles, Duct Panels and Vanity Units - Aaztec Cubicles
Cubicles/lockers - Trespa UK Ltd
Duct panelling and frames - TBS Amwell Ltd
Framed panel cubicles - T B S Fabrications
Full fit out, refurbishment and partitioning service - Neslo Interiors
Panel cubicals - Mermaid Panels Ltd
Panel cubicles - FGF Ltd
Panel Cubicles - Grant Westfield Ltd
Plywood, hard, fibre, chip and particle boards - Boardcraft Ltd
Purpose made doors, toilet cubicles and washroom systems - Moffett Thallon & Co Ltd
Steel caging/ partitioning - Bradbury Group Ltd
Toilet cubicle Systems - Bushboard Washrooms
Toilet, Shower, Washroom and Changing cubicles - Aaztec Cubicles
Toilet/Shower/Changing Cubicles - Dunhams of Norwich
Washroom cubicle systems - Bushboard Washrooms
WC cubicles and washroom systems - Bridgman IBC Ltd

K33 Concrete/ Terrazzo partitions

Specialist contractors in mosaic and terrazzo - Alpha Mosaic & Terrazzo Ltd

K40 Demountable suspended ceilings

Acoustic ceilings - STO Ltd
Ceiling Access Panels - Howe Green Ltd
Ceiling grid systems - Hadley Industries Plc
Ceiling systems - Knauf AMF Ceilings Ltd
Ceiling systems - OWA UK Ltd
Ceilings - Adex Interiors for industry Ltd
Ceilings - Hunter Douglas Architectural Ltd
Ceilings - Plasterboard, Suspended - Gridpart Interiors Ltd
Ceilings (suspended) - Firco Ltd
Demountable suspended ceilings - STO Ltd
Designer ceiling range systems - Knauf AMF Ceilings Ltd
Fire rated ceiling systems - Fire Protection Ltd
Fire resistant ceilings - Knauf AMF Ceilings Ltd
Full fit out, refurbishment and partitioning service - Neslo Interiors
Grid, Mineral, metal, wood and soft fibre suspended ceilings - Armstrong World Industries Ltd
Kitchen extraction systems - Britannia Kitchen Ventilation Ltd
Metal and 3D ceiling systems - Knauf AMF Ceilings Ltd
Metal ceiling products - OWA UK Ltd
Metal panels/tiles - System Building Products
Mineral wool ceiling products - OWA UK Ltd
Performance ceilings - OWA UK Ltd
Plasterboard dry linings/partitions/ceilings - Skanda Acoustics
Specialist designer ceilings - OWA UK Ltd
Suspended ceiling brackets and accessories - PRE-MET Ltd
Suspended ceilings - Hatmet Limited
Suspended ceilings - Internal Partitions Systems
Suspended Ceilings - Knauf UK
Suspended ceilings - Nevill Long
Suspended ceilings - New Forest Ceilings Ltd
Suspended ceilings - Newey Ceilings
Suspended ceilings - Opus 4 Ltd
Suspended ceilings - Shaylor Group Plc
Suspended Ceilings - Skanda Acoustics Limited
Suspended ceilings - Walls & Ceilings International Ltd
Suspended ceilings, shaftwall Systems - Knauf Drywall

K41 Raised access floors

Access flooring - Moseley GRP Product (Division of Moseley Rubber Co Ltd)
Access Flooring Products - Metalfloor UK Ltd
Access panels floors - Panel & Louvre Co Ltd
Access Ramps - Enable Access
Adhesives for access flooring - StarFix &: Ultra High Performance – StarFix PED-ULTRA, High Performance – StarFix PED-PRO, General Purpose – StarFix PED, Acoustic – StarFix ACOUSTIC - Star Uretech Ltd
Adjustable Support Pedestals and accessories - Buzon UK
Cable management - Interface Europe Ltd
Flooring and access - Wincro Metal Industries Ltd
Full fit out, refurbishment and partitioning service - Neslo Interiors
Mezzanine Floors - Davicon
Panel and pedestal testing, Air plenum testing, On-site and laboratory testing - Lucideon
Plywood, hard, fibre, chip and particle boards - Boardcraft Ltd
Raised Access Flooring - SIG Interiors
Raised access flooring systems - Knauf UK
Raised access floors - Adex Interiors for industry Ltd
Raised access floors - Devar Premier Flooring
Raised Access Floors - Hatmet Limited
Raised access floors - Interface Europe Ltd
Raised access floors - Kingspan Access Floors Ltd
Raised access floors - New Forest Ceilings Ltd
Raised access floors - Raised Floor Systems Ltd
Raised access floors - Redman Fisher Engineering
Raised Access Floors - Shaylor Group Plc
Raised access floors - Trim Acoustics
Raised access floors - Workspace Technology Ltd
Raised Flooring and accessories - Metalfloor UK Ltd
Secondary Flooring - Safety Works & Solutions Ltd
Secondary Floors - Ecotile Flooring Ltd

L10 Windows/ Rooflights/ Screens/ Louvres

Acoustic Louvres and Screens - Acousticabs Industrial Noise Control Ltd
Acoustic Louvres, Acoustic Windows - IAC Acoustic Company UK Ltd
Aluminium - Technal UK
Aluminium clad timber wibdows - Benlowe Group Limited
Aluminium louvres - WP Metals Ltd
Aluminium windows - Comar Architectural Aluminium Systems
Aluminium windows - KCW Comercial Windows Ltd
Aluminium windows - Midland Alloy Ltd
Aluminium windows - Prima Systems (South East) Ltd
Aluminium windows - Technal UK
aluminium/hybrid curtain walling, windows and doors - Senior Aluminium Systems plc
Anit-shatter films for bomb-blast applications - Northgate Solar Controls
Anti-Reflective Glass - SCHOTT UK Ltd
Armour plate door assemblies - Ide T & W Ltd
Atria - Lonsdale Metal Company
Atrium - Apropos Conservatories Ltd
Automatic opening roof vents - National Domelight Company
Bespoke joinery - AS Newbould Ltd
Bespoke joinery - Howard Bros Joinery Ltd
Bespoke Timber Windows - Scotts of Thrapston Ltd
Bird screen - Timberwise (UK) Ltd
Blind Systems - Silent Gliss Ltd

L10 Windows/ Rooflights/ Screens/ Louvres (con't)

Blinds - Luxaflex®
Blinds and Curtain Track Systems - Goelst
Brise Soleil & Security - Lang+Fulton
Brush strip window seals - Kleeneze Sealtech Ltd
Building hinges - Nico Manufacturing Ltd
Capping bars - Exitex Ltd
Commercial windows - KCW Comercial Windows Ltd
Composite aluminium windows - Scandanavian Timber
Composite aluminum/wood windows & doors - DOVISTA UK LTD
Composite windows - Crittall Steel Windows Ltd
Conservatories - Smith & Choyce Ltd
Conservatory roofing, atria, canopies and rooflights - Ultraframe PLC
Domes and Pyramids - National Domelight Company
Door Canopies - Canopy Products Ltd
Dormer Windows/Louvres - Duroy Fibreglass Mouldings Ltd
Double glazed roof windows - Klober Ltd
Double glazed units - Ledlite Glass (Southend) Ltd
Double Swing Windows - Blairs Windows Limited
Enhanced Casement Windows - Blairs Windows Limited
Entrance Canopies - Duroy Fibreglass Mouldings Ltd
Extruded aluminium composite windows - Smart Systems Ltd
Extruded aluminum windows - Smart Systems Ltd
Extruded shopfronts and entrance screens - Smart Systems Ltd
Extruded UPVC windows - Smart Systems Ltd
Extruded UPVC windows - Veka Plc
Filters/Screening - Mevaco Ltd
Fire resistant glazing systems - Promat UK Ltd
Fly Screens - Graepels Perforators Ltd
G. R. P. Canopies - Solair Ltd
Glass & window supplies - Spectra Glaze Services
Glazed malls - Lonsdale Metal Company
Grillers/Panels - Mevaco Ltd
Grilles, Registers & Diffusers - Air Diffusion Ltd
GRP louvers - APA
High performance windows - Sashless Window Co Ltd
Historic Rooflights - Clement Steel Windows
Industrial and Commercial Insect Screens - The Flyscreen Company Ltd
Industrial grade plastic framed roof windows for slate/tile roofs - Cox Building Products Ltd
Insect screens - President Blinds Ltd
Insect Screens - The Flyscreen Company Ltd
Lantern lights - Lonsdale Metal Company
Louvre blind material - Mermet U.K
Louvres - Hallmark Blinds Ltd
Louvres - McKenzie-Martin Ltd
Low Pitch Roof Window System - Forticrete Roofing
Made to measure windows - Jeld-Wen UK Ltd
Mess Screens - Cadisch MDA
Metal and glass louvers grilles, diffusers and dampers - Naco
Metal framed double glazed windows - Nova Group Ltd
Metal Windows - A & G Structures Ltd
Metal windows - Anglian Building Products
Metal windows - The Cotswold Casement Company
Metal windows/ rooflights/ screens/ louvers - HW Architectural Ltd
Metal windows/ rooflights/ screens/ louvres - Reid John & Sons (Strucsteel) Ltd
North lights - Lonsdale Metal Company
Perforated Metal - Mevaco Ltd
Perforated Products - Mevaco Ltd
Plastic framed double glazed windows - Nova Group Ltd
Plastic profiled sheet cladding and roofing - Ariel Plastics Ltd
Plastic windows - Anglian Building Products
Profiled Acoustic Screens - Acousticabs Industrial Noise Control Ltd
Purpose made windows & security windows - Platonoff & Harris Ltd
PVC extrusions - Nenplas
PVC window profiles - Profile 22 Systems Ltd
PVC windows - Prima Systems (South East) Ltd
PVCU extrusions for window systems - Spectus Systems
PVC-U vertical sliding windows - Masterframe Windows Ltd
PVCu windows - Interframe Ltd
PVCu windows - KCW Comercial Windows Ltd
PVCu windows - Plastal (SBP Ltd)
PVC-U Windows - Magnet Ltd
Replacement window service - Spectra Glaze Services
Roller blind material - Mermet U.K
Roof lights - Lonsdale Metal Company
Roof vents, ventilators - Lonsdale Metal Company
Roof windows - SIG Roofing
Roof windows - VELUX Co Ltd, The
Rooflights - Apropos Conservatories Ltd
Rooflights - Astrofade Ltd
Rooflights - Axter Ltd
Rooflights - Duplus Architectural Systems Ltd
Rooflights - McKenzie-Martin Ltd
Rooflights - National Domelight Company
Rooflights - NuLite Ltd
Rooflights - Ubbink (UK) Ltd
Rooflights - profiled and structured in GRP, PVC and polycarbonate - Brett Martin Ltd
Rooflights (Newdome) - Novaglaze Limited
Rooflights, skylights, covered walkways, barrel vaults, deadlights, aluminium windows - Duplus Architectural Systems Ltd
Rooftop Acoustic Screens - Acousticabs Industrial Noise Control Ltd
Room Darkening Systems - CBS (Curtain and Blind Specialists Ltd)
Ropes and sashcords - Marlow Ropes Ltd
Sarnalite rooflights - Sarnafil Ltd
Sash & Case Windows - Blairs Windows Limited
Sash balances - Garador Ltd
Sash Window Renovation - Ventrolla Ltd
Sash windows - Masterframe Windows Ltd
Screening Pannels - Winther Browne & co Ltd
Screens - Enfield Speciality Doors
Screens - Komfort Workspace PLC
Screens - Project Aluminium Ltd
Screens/louvers - Allaway Acoustics Ltd
Screens/louvers - Levolux A.T. Limited
Security Grilles - HAG Shutters & Grilles Ltd
Security Grills - O'Connor Fencing Limited
Security grills - Squires Metal Fabrications Ltd
Security Solutions - Harling Security Solutions Limited
Shades - Luxaflex®
Shading solutions - Guthrie Douglas
Shading System - CBS (Curtain and Blind Specialists Ltd)
Shaped Aluminium Windows - Midland Alloy Ltd
Shaped Louvres - Midland Alloy Ltd
Shelters and Canopies - Elwell Buildings Ltd
Shopfront systems - Aardee Security Shutters Ltd
Shopfronts - BF Bassett & Findley
Shopfronts & Entrance Screens - Metal Technology Ltd
Shopfrontsand Entrance Screens - Sapa Building Systems (monarch and glostal)
SOLA-BOOST® Solar assisted natural ventilation systems - Monodraught Ltd
Solar blinds material - Reflex-Rol (UK)
Solar control window films - The Window Film Company UK Ltd
Solar, safety, security, UV control, aesthetic and architectural films - Northgate Solar Controls
SOLA-VENT® Natural daylight and solar powered extract ventilation systems - Monodraught Ltd
Steal rooflights - The Rooflight company
Steel caging - Bradbury Group Ltd
Steel window association - Steel Window Association
Steel windows - Crittall Steel Windows Ltd
Steel windows - Monk Metal Windows Ltd
Steel windows and doors - Clement Steel Windows
Steel Windows Installation + glazing - Rea Metal Windows Ltd
Steel Windows Manufacture - Rea Metal Windows Ltd
Sun tunnels - NuLite Ltd
SUNCATCHER® Natural ventilation and daylight systems - Monodraught Ltd
SUNPIPE® Natural daylight systems - Monodraught Ltd
Suntubes - Duplus Architectural Systems Ltd
Suspended glass smoke screens - Fenlock-Hansen Ltd
Tensioned Fabric Shading - Guthrie Douglas
Tilt and Turn Windows - Blairs Windows Limited
Timber framed double glazed windows - Nova Group Ltd
Timber windows - Anglian Building Products
Timber windows - Benlowe Group Limited
Timber windows - Jeld-Wen UK Ltd
Timber Windows - Magnet Ltd
Timber windows - Premdor
Timber windows - Sampson Windows Ltd
Timber windows - Scandanavian Timber
Timber windows - Timber Components (UK) Ltd
Timber windows - Walker Timber Ltd
Timber windows mauufacture - Blairs Windows Limited
Translucent rooflights - Filon Products Ltd
Unique view control films - Northgate Solar Controls
UPVC conservatories - Windowbuild
UPVC double glazed windows - Sierra Windows
UPVC window casements - Windowbuild
UPVC window systems - REHAU Ltd
Ventilated roof lights - Passivent Ltd
VENTSAIR Louvres and penthouse louvres - Monodraught Ltd
Walkways, Porches, Entrance Canopies - Falco UK Ltd
Window Grilles, Window Screens - Bradbury Group Ltd
Window hinges - Nico Manufacturing Ltd
Window Protector - Hilton Banks Ltd
Window repair - Repair care International
Window systems - Deceuninck Ltd
Window tinting - Durable Ltd
Window ventilator manufactures - Simon R W Ltd
Window/ rooflights/ screens/ Lorrles - McMullen Facades
Windows - English Architectural Glazing Ltd
Windows - Glassolutions Saint-Gobain Ltd
Windows - HansenFacades
Windows - Moores Furniture Group Ltd
Windows - Smith & Choyce Ltd
Windows - Solair Ltd
Windows - PVCu, Aluminium and Timber - Saveheat Group
Windows (alum) - Duplus Architectural Systems Ltd
windows /rooflight/ screens/ louvres - Universal Components Ltd
Windows/ rooflights/ screens/ louvers - Colt International
Windows/ Rooflights/ Screens/ Louvres - Schueco UK
Windows/ Rooflights/ Screens/ Louvres - Till & Whitehead Ltd
Windows/ Rooflights/ Screens/Luvres - Harling Security Solutions Limited
Windows/rooflights/ screens/louvers - Cantifix of London Limited
Windows/Rooflights/Screens/Louvers - Novaglaze Limited
Windows/rooflights/screens/louvres - SCS Group
Windows: Aluminium - Metal Technology Ltd

L20 Doors/ Shutters/hatches

Acoustic Doors - Amadeus
Acoustic doors - Clark Door Ltd
Acoustic doors - Jewers Doors Ltd
Acoustic Doors, Acoustic Glazed screens, Acoustic windows - IAC Acoustic Company UK Ltd
Acoustic Doorsets - Humphrey & Stretton PLC
Acoustic seals - Sealmaster
Aircraft hangar doors - Jewers Doors Ltd
Aluminium - Project Aluminium Ltd
Aluminium Entrances and patio doors - KCW Comercial Windows Ltd
Aluminium doors - Comar Architectural Aluminium Systems
Aluminium doors - Duplus Architectural Systems Ltd
Aluminium doors - Prima Systems (South East) Ltd
Aluminium doors - Sapa Building Systems (monarch and glostal)
Aluminium doors - Technal UK
aluminium/hybrid curtain walling, windows and doors - Senior Aluminium Systems plc
Apartment Entrance Doors - Vicaima Ltd
Automatic & manual door repair & maintenance - Dorma Door Services Ltd
Automatic door operating equipment - GfA UK Ltd
Automatic Doors - DORMA UK Ltd
Automatic doors - Kone
Automatic Doors - Kone PLC
Automatic Doors - TORMAX United Kingdom Ltd
Automatic doors - swing, slide and folding - Gilgen Door Systems UK Ltd
Ballistic doors - Jewers Doors Ltd
Bespoke joinery - AS Newbould Ltd
Bespoke joinery - Howard Bros Joinery Ltd
Blast doors - Jewers Doors Ltd
Brush strip door seals - Kleeneze Sealtech Ltd
Bullet Proof Doorsets - Humphrey & Stretton PLC
Bullet resistant doors and frames - Cumberland Construction
Ceiling Access Panels - The Access Panel Company Ltd
Clean room doors - Clark Door Ltd
Clossures - Simflex Grilles and Closures Ltd
Cold store doors - Ascot Doors Ltd
Coldstore doors - Clark Door Ltd
Collapsible Gate Shutters - Mercian Industrial Doors
Commercial and public doors - Titan Door Systems Ltd
Commercial Doors - London Shopfitters Ltd
Commercial steel doors - Sunray Engineering Ltd
Composite doors - Jeld-Wen UK Ltd
Composite doors - Halmark Panels Ltd
Composite doors - Laird Security Hardware
Composite doors - Spectra Glaze Services
Conservatories - Solair Ltd
Corrosion Resistant Sliding and Folding Door Gear - Coburn Sliding Systems Ltd
Cottage doors - AS Newbould Ltd
Custom made doors and doorsets - Bridgman IBC Ltd
Decorative doors - Foil faced, Inlay, Veneered - Vicaima Ltd
Door - purpose made flush - Humphrey & Stretton PLC
Door & window control equipment - GEZE UK
Door damping Solutions - Coburn Sliding Systems Ltd
Door frames - Enfield Speciality Doors
Door Hardware and accessories - Strada London
Door kits - Vicaima Ltd
Door manufactures - Edmonds A & Co Ltd
Door panels - Door Panels by Design
Door panels - Halmark Panels Ltd
Door protection - Moffett Thallon & Co Ltd
Door systems - Deceuninck Ltd
Doors - Altro Ltd
Doors - Cantifix of London Limited
Doors - Glassolutions Saint-Gobain Ltd
Doors - HansenFacades
Doors - IJK Timber Group Ltd
Doors - Komfort Workspace PLC
Doors - Magnet Ltd
DOORS - McMullen Facades
Doors - Metsä Wood
Doors - Project Aluminium Ltd
Doors - Scotts of Thrapston Ltd
Doors - Smith & Choyce Ltd
Doors - Walker Timber Ltd
Doors - PVCu, Aluminium and Timber - Saveheat Group
Doors & sets - Cox Long Ltd
Doors (alum) - Duplus Architectural Systems Ltd
Doors and entrances - BF Bassett & Findley
Doors architectural - Timbmet Ltd
Doors/ Shutters/ hatches - Harling Security Solutions Limited
Doors/ Shutters/ Hatches - Schueco UK
Doors/ Windows/ Stairs - Covers Timber & Builders Merchants
Doors/hatches - Allaway Acoustics Ltd
Doors/shutters/hatches - Hadley Industries Plc
Doors/shutters/hatches - Hart Door Systems Ltd
Doors; Commercial & Public Amenities - BIS Door Systems Ltd
Doorsets - Vicaima Ltd
Electric openers/ spare parts - Cardale Garage Doors
Entrance systems - Taskmaster Doors Ltd
External Doors - Premdor
External doorsets - Blairs Windows Limited
Extruded aluminium composite doors - Smart Systems Ltd
Extruded aluminium doors - Smart Systems Ltd
Extruded UPVC doors - Smart Systems Ltd
Extruded UPVC doors - Veka Plc
Fast action doors - Neway Doors Ltd
Fibre composite residential doors - Birtley Group
Fibreglass doors - Premdor
Fire and security doors - Tyco Fire and Integrated Solutions
Fire door certification schemes, Mechanical testing - BM TRADA
Fire doors - Enfield Speciality Doors
Fire doors - Scotts of Thrapston Ltd
Fire Doors - Sunray Engineering Ltd
Fire doors - Vicaima Ltd
Fire doors and door sets - Shadbolt F R & Sons Ltd
Fire rated door sets - Lami Doors UK Ltd
Fire rated doors - Clark Door Ltd
Fire Resistant glass - SCHOTT UK Ltd
fire resistant Glazed screens and doors - Fenlock-Hansen Ltd
Fire resistant glazing systems, fire resistant panels - Promat UK Ltd
Fire resisting doors - Mann McGowan Group
Fire shutters - Ascot Doors Ltd
Fire Shutters - Blount Shutters Ltd
Flush and feature doors - Vicaima Ltd
Flush doors - Enfield Speciality Doors
Folding doors and partitions - Parthos UK Ltd
Folding Grilles - Simflex Grilles and Closures Ltd
Food industry doors - Ascot Doors Ltd
Frames and covers - Bilco UK Ltd
Freezer doors - Clark Door Ltd
G. R. P. Porches - Solair Ltd
Garage and industrial doors - Hörmann (UK) Ltd
Garage doors - Doorfit Products Ltd
Garage Doors - Rundum Meir (UK) Ltd
Garage Doors - Electric Operated - Avon Industrial Doors Ltd
Garage doors - Roller - Moffett Thallon & Co Ltd
Garage doors - Sectional - Moffett Thallon & Co Ltd
Garage doors - Up and Over - Moffett Thallon & Co Ltd
Garage Roller Shutter Doors - Rolflex Doors Ltd
Garrage Doors: Supply, Instalation, Repair - Acorn Garage Doors Ltd
Gates and barriers - automatic doors - Hart Door Systems Ltd
Glass Door Fitting - DORMA UK Ltd
Glass doors - Style Door Systems Ltd
Glazing maintenance - Spectra Glaze Services
Glazing trade association - Glass and Glazing Federation
Grilles - Bradbury Group Ltd
GRP door sets - Lami Doors UK Ltd
GRP doors - Benlowe Group Limited
GRP hatches - Group Four Glassfibre Ltd
Hatches - metal - McKenzie-Martin Ltd
High integrity doors windows blast and fire protection systems - Booth Industries Ltd
High performance doors - Sashless Window Co Ltd
High speed doors - Clark Door Ltd
Hinged access panels for ceilings and walls - Profab Access Ltd
Hinged steel dorrs - Clark Door Ltd
Hinged, pivoting and sliding doors - Optima
Industrial and cold storage strip curtain systems - Flexible Reinforcements Ltd
Industrial & commercial doors, shutters, grilles and partitions - Gilgen Door Systems UK Ltd
Industrial & commercial security & fire resisting metal doors & shutters - Bolton Gate Company Ltd
Industrial and Commercial Insect Screens - The Flyscreen Company Ltd
Industrial Doors - BIS Door Systems Ltd
Industrial Doors - Blount Shutters Ltd
Industrial Doors - HAG Shutters & Grilles Ltd
Industrial Doors - Kone
Industrial doors - Sunray Engineering Ltd
Industrial doors and loading bay equipment - Envirodoor Markus Ltd
Industrial doors, roller, folding and insulated - Avon Industrial Doors Ltd
Industrial Roller Shutter Doors - Rolflex Doors Ltd
Industrial Sliding and Folding Door Gear - Coburn Sliding Systems Ltd
Insect Screens - The Flyscreen Company Ltd
Installation of Garage doors - Acorn Garage Doors Ltd
Insulated bifolding doors - Jewers Doors Ltd
insulated doors - AS Newbould Ltd
Insulated Roller Shutter Doors - Rolflex Doors Ltd
Insulated sliding doors - Jewers Doors Ltd
Insulated sliding folding doors - Jewers Doors Ltd
Internal Doors - Premdor
Laminate doors - Vicaima Ltd
Laminated Door sets - T B S Fabrications
Loft access doors - Timloc Expamet Building Products
Made to measure doors - Jeld-Wen UK Ltd
Maintenance of industrial doors, shutters and shopfronts - Shutter Door Repair & Maintenance Ltd
Metal doors - The Cotswold Casement Company
Metal doors/ shutters/ hatches - HW Architectural Ltd
Metal doors/ shutters/ hatches - Reid John & Sons (Strucsteel) Ltd
Metal meter boxes and replacement architrave units - Ritherdon & Co Ltd

L20 Doors/ Shutters/hatches (con't)

Moveable internal walls and partitions - Style Door Systems Ltd
Operable walls - Avanti Systems
Oversized doors - Clark Door Ltd
Panel tracks - Goelst
Partitioning Systems - DORMA UK Ltd
Patio Doors - Solair Ltd
Pine doors - Wood International Agency Ltd
Pine furniture doors - Mason FW & Sons Ltd
Plant Room Doors - Avon Industrial Doors Ltd
Purpose made flush timber doors - Youngs Doors Ltd
Purpose made internal & external doorsets - Platonoff & Harris Ltd
Purpose made panel doors - Youngs Doors Ltd
Purpose made timber fire doors & frames - Platonoff & Harris Ltd
PVC and Rubber Curtains - Mercian Industrial Doors
PVC crash and strip doors - Avon Industrial Doors Ltd
PVC door profiles - Profile 22 Systems Ltd
PVC doors - Prima Systems (South East) Ltd
PVCu doors - Interframe Ltd
PVCu doors - Plastal (SBP Ltd)
PVCu Entrances and patio doors - KCW Comercial Windows Ltd
PVCU extrusions for door systems - Spectus Systems
Rapid roll doors - Ascot Doors Ltd
Repair of Garage doors - Acorn Garage Doors Ltd
Repairs - Syston Rolling Shutters Ltd
Residential garage doors - Garador Ltd
Revolving doors - Gilgen Door Systems UK Ltd
Revolving doors - LMOB Electrical Contractors Ltd
Roller doors/ side-hinged doors - Cardale Garage Doors
Roller Shutter Doors - BIS Door Systems Ltd
Roller shutter doors, fast action doors - Priory Shutter & Door Co Ltd
Roller shutters - Ascot Doors Ltd
Roller Shutters - Blount Shutters Ltd
Roller shutters - Lakeside Group
Rolling Shutters - Simflex Grilles and Closures Ltd
Rolling shutters and individual doors in steel, aluminum and timber. Service and maintenance available nationwide - Syston Rolling Shutters Ltd
Roof Access Hatches - The Access Panel Company Ltd
Ropes and sashcords - Marlow Ropes Ltd
Rubber and PVC flexible crash doors, PVC strip curtains - Neway Doors Ltd
Sectional overhead doors - Ascot Doors Ltd
Sectional Overhead Doors - Novoferm Europe Ltd
Security door systems - Bridgman IBC Ltd
Security door systems - Vicaima Ltd
Security Doors - ASSA ABLOY Limited
Security doors - Gilgen Door Systems UK Ltd
Security doors - Jewers Doors Ltd
Security Doorsets - Humphrey & Stretton PLC
Security Grills - O'Connor Fencing Limited
Security grills - Squires Metal Fabrications Ltd
Security metal doors and shutters - Ascot Doors Ltd
Security roller shutters - Lakeside Group
Security shutters - Aardee Security Shutters Ltd
Security Shutters - HAG Shutters & Grilles Ltd
Security shutters - Hart Door Systems Ltd
Security Solutions - Harling Security Solutions Limited
Self Storage Doors - Rolflex Doors Ltd
Shopfronts and Entrance Screens - London Shopfitters Ltd
Shutters - Luxaflex®
Side hung and double action door sets - Lami Doors UK Ltd
Sliding and folding partitions - Building Additions Ltd
Sliding door operating equipment - GfA UK Ltd
Sliding door sets - Lami Doors UK Ltd
Sliding Door Systems - Schueco UK
Sliding doors - Clark Door Ltd
Sliding folding doors - Ascot Doors Ltd
Special timber flush doors and door sets - Bridgman IBC Ltd
Specialist dooors - Clark Door Ltd
Specialist steel doorsets - Accent Hansen
Specialized timber doors - AS Newbould Ltd
Stable doors - AS Newbould Ltd
Stable Doors - Scotts of Thrapston Ltd
Steel Commercial and Industrial doors - Mercian Industrial Doors
Steel Door Frames - Coburn Sliding Systems Ltd
Steel Door Installation +glazing - Rea Metal Windows Ltd
Steel Door Manufacture - Rea Metal Windows Ltd
Steel door sets - Ascot Doors Ltd
Steel doors - Bradbury Group Ltd
Steel doors - Crittall Steel Windows Ltd
Steel doors - Gilgen Door Systems UK Ltd
Steel Doors - Jeld-Wen UK Ltd
Steel doors - Monk Metal Windows Ltd
Steel doors - Premdor
Steel doors, frames and entrance systems - Taskmaster Doors Ltd
Steel faced doors - Benlowe Group Limited
Steel Firescreen Installation + glazing - Rea Metal Windows Ltd
Steel Firescreen Manufacture - Rea Metal Windows Ltd
Steel hinged Doorsets - Accent Hansen
Steel louvred doorsets - Sunray Engineering Ltd
Steel Paneled Doors - Longden
Steel pedestrian doors - Hart Door Systems Ltd
Steel residential doors - Birtley Group
Steel Security Doors - Rolflex Doors Ltd
Steel Security Doors - Security Doors Direct
Steel security doorsets - Sunray Engineering Ltd
Steel shutters (Mall, Shop front, Bar/Counter) - Mercian Industrial Doors
Steel window association - Steel Window Association
Steel windows and doors - Clement Steel Windows
Straight Sliding Door Gear, Folding Door Gear and Hideaway Pocket Door Kits - Coburn Sliding Systems Ltd
Supply of Garage doors - Acorn Garage Doors Ltd
Synthetic rubber moulding components and ironmongery - Notcutt Ltd
Syston doors - Syston Rolling Shutters Ltd
Timber doors - Benlowe Group Limited
Timber doors - JB Kind Ltd
Timber doors - Jeld-Wen UK Ltd
Timber Doors - Longden
Timber doors - Premdor
Traditional oak doors - W.L. West & Sons Ltd
Train and Platform door systems - Gilgen Door Systems UK Ltd
Transformer chamber doorsets - Sunray Engineering Ltd
Turnstiles - full and half height - Gilgen Door Systems UK Ltd
Turnstiles for access and flow control of people - Kone
Up and over doors/ sectional doors - Cardale Garage Doors
UPVC doors - Spectra Glaze Services
UPVC french doors - Windowbuild
Vision see-through security shutters - Cooper Group Ltd
Wall access hatches - Howe Green Ltd
Wardrobe and Cupboard Sliding and Folding Door Gear - Coburn Sliding Systems Ltd
X-ray Doorsets - Humphrey & Stretton PLC

L30 Stairs/ Walkways/Balustrades

Access & Escape Ladders - Baj System Design Ltd
Access Ladders - Surespan Ltd
Acrylic, glass, steel and timber stairs - Lewes Design Contracts Ltd
Aluminium Bridge parapets - Varley & Gulliver Ltd
Aluminium floor outlets - Marley Plumbing and Drainage
Aluminium handrails/balustrades - Norton Engineering Alloys Co Ltd
Aluminium ladders and step ladders - Ramsay & Sons (Forfar) Ltd
Aluminium staircase fire escapes - Baj System Design Ltd
Aluminium stairways - Zarges (UK) Ltd
Architectural Glass - Creative Glass
Balconies - Squires Metal Fabrications Ltd
Balcony ladder - Baj System Design Ltd
Balconys - Woodburn Engineering Ltd
Ballstrades - Strand Hardware Ltd
Ballustrading - Challenge Fencing Ltd
Balustrade & Barrier Systems - Brass Age Ltd
Balustrade & Handrail Systems - Delta Balustrades
Balustrade and handrail coating - Plastic Coatings Ltd
Balustrade and Handrails - Safety Works & Solutions Ltd
Balustrades - Ermine Engineering Co. Ltd
Balustrades - Glassolutions Saint-Gobain Ltd
Balustrades - Lang+Fulton
Balustrades - Squires Metal Fabrications Ltd
Balustrades - Steel Line Ltd
Balustrades and wallrails - HEWI UK Ltd
Bespoke joinery - AS Newbould Ltd
Bespoke Timber Staircases - Platonoff & Harris Ltd
Cast Spiral Stairs - British Spirals & Castings
Curved wooden handrails - The Angle Ring Company Ltd
Customs staircases in steel, stainless steel, waxed steel, wrought iron, wood or concrete with options for glass treads/balustrades - In Steel (Blacksmiths & Fabricators) Ltd
Decking - B & M Fencing Limited
Domestic and comercial - Loft Centre Products
Drainpipe ladders - Baj System Design Ltd
Escape and electric stairway ladders, roof exit systems, spiral, spacesaver and traditional stairs - Loft Centre Products
Fabricators of open metal flooring, handrails and standards - OSF Ltd
Fibreglass ladders and step ladders - Ramsay & Sons (Forfar) Ltd
Fire escapes - In Steel (Blacksmiths & Fabricators) Ltd
Fire escapes - Squires Metal Fabrications Ltd
Fire escapes, gates, railings, balustrades, guardrails and spiral staircases - Metalcraft (Tottenham) Ltd
Flooring - Lang+Fulton
Folding escape ladders - Baj System Design Ltd
Glass Balustrade - SG System Products Ltd
GRP Handrails - Brighton (Handrails), W
Guardrail - Kee Klamp Ltd
Hand rails - RB UK Ltd
Hand rails - Squires Metal Fabrications Ltd
Handrail and Balustrade Systems - Sapphire Balustrades
Handrail Covers - DC Plastic Handrails Ltd
Handrailing - Steel Line Ltd
Handrails/balustrades - stainless - Norton Engineering Alloys Co Ltd
Hooped/caged ladder - Baj System Design Ltd
In floor telescopic ladder - Baj System Design Ltd
Industrial flooring, handrailing systems and stairtreads - Redman Fisher Engineering
Insulated Door panels - Ward Insulated Panels Ltd
Ladders, walkways and hand railing - Moseley GRP Product (Division of Moseley Rubber Co Ltd)
Mechanical testing - BM TRADA
Metal railings - Varley & Gulliver Ltd
Metal stairs - British Spirals & Castings
Metal stairs / walkways / balustrades - Steelway Fensecure Ltd
Metal stairs/balustrades - NRG Fabrications
Pedstrian walkways - Eve Trakway
Perforated sheets and balustrading - Mevaco Ltd
Plywood, hard, fibre, chip and particle boards - Boardcraft Ltd
Pre-Cast Terrazzo Staircases - Quiligotti Terrazzo Tiles Limited
PVC handrails - Architectural Plastics (Handrail) Ltd
PVC handrails - Brighton (Handrails), W
Railing systems - Brass Age Ltd
Roof walkway/ fall arrest system - McKenzie-Martin Ltd
Ropes and sashcords - Marlow Ropes Ltd
Spiral and helical p.c. stairs - In Steel (Blacksmiths & Fabricators) Ltd
Spiral and straight staircases - Mackay Engineering
Spiral Staircase Systems - Lewes Design Contracts Ltd
Spiral Staircases - Spiral Construction Ltd
Spiral Staircases - Titan Ladders Ltd
Spiral staircases and special precast stairs - In Steel (Blacksmiths & Fabricators) Ltd
Spiral stairs - Pedley Furniture International Ltd
Spiral stairways - Blanc de Bierges
Stainless Steel Balustrade Infills - Navtec
Stainless steel flooring - Ancon Limited
Stainless steel Stairs/walkways - Wincro Metal Industries Ltd
Stainless steel, aluminium, PVC covered, galvanized and brass balustrades - SG System Products Ltd
Stair edgings - Gradus Ltd
Stair/ walkways - Redman Fisher Engineering
Staircases - Company name: Britannia Metalwork Services Ltd
Staircases - Higginson Staircases Ltd
Staircases - Metalcraft (Tottenham) Ltd
Stairs - Blanc de Bierges
Stairs - Kirkstone
Stairs - Magnet Ltd
Stairs - Smith & Choyce Ltd
Stairs - Squires Metal Fabrications Ltd
Stairs manufactured to order - Higginson Staircases Ltd
Stairs walkways and Balustrades - Midland Wire Cordage Co Ltd
Stairs/ walkways - Steelway Fensecure Ltd
Stairs/ walkways/ balustrades - Broxap Ltd
Stairs/ Walkways/ Balustrades - Chilstone
Stairs/ walkways/ balustrades - Quantum Profile Systems Ltd
Stairs/walkways - Ancon Limited
Stairs/Walkways/ Balusters - Andy Thornton Ltd
Stairs/walkways/ balustrades - Cantifix of London Limited
Steel bridge parapets - Varley & Gulliver Ltd
Steel fabrication railings, gates, fire escapes - SFC (Midlands) Ltd
Steel Hand Rails - The Angle Ring Company Ltd
Steel Spiral Staircases - Graepels Perforators Ltd
Steel spiral stairs - Higginson Staircases Ltd
Steel staircases - Ermine Engineering Co. Ltd
Steel, Stainless steel and aluminium - Speedfab Midlands
Steps - Blanc de Bierges
Straight Flights - British Spirals & Castings
Straight helical and spiral stairs - Lewes Design Contracts Ltd
Straight, Winder & geometric timber stairs - Higginson Staircases Ltd
Timber loft and escape ladders, roof exit systems, spiral, spacesaver and traditional stairs - Loft Centre Products
Timber Spiral Stairs - British Spirals & Castings
Timber spiral stairs - Higginson Staircases Ltd
Timber staircases - Benlowe Stairs
Timber staircases - Jeld-Wen UK Ltd
Timber staircases - Northern Joinery Ltd
Timber stairs - British Spirals & Castings
Timber stairs/balustrades - Timber Components (UK) Ltd
Walkways - Clow Group Ltd
Walkways and platforms - Woodburn Engineering Ltd
Walkways/balustrades - Levolux A.T. Limited
Wall corner & Door Protection - Gradus Ltd
Wallrails and balustrades - HEWI UK Ltd
Wooden ladders and step ladders - Ramsay & Sons (Forfar) Ltd
Woodturning - Spindlewood

L40 General glazing

aluminium/hybrid curtain walling, windows and doors - Senior Aluminium Systems plc
Architectural aluminium systems for glazing - Universal Components Ltd
Architectural Glass - Creative Glass
Architectural glass - Komfort Workspace PLC
Architectural glass and glazing - Avanti Systems
Atrium glazing - English Architectural Glazing Ltd
Canopies - Apropos Conservatories Ltd
Display Enhancement Glass - SCHOTT UK Ltd
Double glazed units - Ledlite Glass (Southend) Ltd
Dry glazing systems and ventilated glazing beads etc - Exitex Ltd
Etched and sand blasted glass - Charles Lightfoot Ltd
Films for glass - Northgate Solar Controls
Films: Solar control, Tinted, Reflective, Anti-UV, Anti-Grafiti, Anti-Fog - The Window Film Company UK Ltd
Fire rated glazing - English Architectural Glazing Ltd
Fire resistant glazing - Ide T & W Ltd
Fire resistant glazing - Mann McGowan Group
Fire resistant glazing systems - Promat UK Ltd
Fire resistant safety glasses - Pyroguard UK Ltd
General glazing - AGC Glass UK Ltd
General glazing - Glassolutions Saint-Gobain Ltd
General glazing - Pilkington UK Ltd
General glazing - Saint-Gobain Glass UK Ltd
Glass - Fenlock-Hansen Ltd
Glass - Glassolutions Saint-Gobain Ltd
Glass - Pilkington Birmingham
Glass & Glazing - Clement Steel Windows
Glass melting - British Glass Manufacturers Confederation
Glass Technology Services - British Glass Manufacturers Confederation
Glazed canopies - Lonsdale Metal Company
Glaziers and glassmerchants - Ledlite Glass (Southend) Ltd
Glazing - Ide T & W Ltd
Glazing Accessories - Reddiglaze Ltd
Glazing Accessories - Simon R W Ltd
Glazing bars for glass sealed units - Newdawn & Sun Ltd
Glazing bars for timber roofs - Newdawn & Sun Ltd
Glazing gaskets to windows, doors and facades - Trelleborg Sealing Profiles Germany GmbH
Glazing maintenance - Spectra Glaze Services
Glazing trade association - Glass and Glazing Federation
High performance window films - The Window Film Company UK Ltd
Insulated Fire Resistant Glass - SCHOTT UK Ltd
Insulated Glazing - Saveheat Group
Laminated - Pilkington Birmingham
Laminated glass - Float Glass Industries
Low - emissivity - Pilkington Birmingham
Manifestation graphics - Invicta Window Films Ltd
Manifestation marking of glass - Northgate Solar Controls
Opaque bullet resistant glass - Attwater & Sons Ltd
Patterned - Pilkington Birmingham
Patterned glass - Float Glass Industries
Plastic profiled sheet cladding and roofing - Ariel Plastics Ltd
Polycarbonate glazing - Cox Building Products Ltd
Privacy window films - Invicta Window Films Ltd
Putty - Adshead Ratcliffe & Co Ltd
Restoration Glass - SCHOTT UK Ltd
Roof glazing - English Architectural Glazing Ltd
Safety and security window films - Durable Ltd
Secondary glazing manufactures - Simon R W Ltd
Security/ safety window films - Invicta Window Films Ltd
Self support glazing beams - Newdawn & Sun Ltd
Selfcleaning - Pilkington Birmingham
Shopfronts - Comar Architectural Aluminium Systems
Silvered - Pilkington Birmingham
Smart Film - Switchable between clear and frosted - Pro Display TM Limited
Smart Glass - Switchable between clear and frosted - Pro Display TM Limited
Solar control glass - Float Glass Industries
Solar control window films - Invicta Window Films Ltd
Stock glass - Float Glass Industries
Structural bolted glazing - English Architectural Glazing Ltd
Tinted - Pilkington Birmingham
Toughened - Pilkington Birmingham
Toughened glass - Float Glass Industries
Toughened, laminate, ceramic, acoustic glass and screen printing on glass - Pilkington Plyglass
Welded Wire Mesh - Multi Mesh Ltd
Window Films - 3M
Window films - Bonwyke Ltd

L41 Lead light glazing

Architectural Glass - Creative Glass
Glazing maintenance - Spectra Glaze Services
Glazing trade association - Glass and Glazing Federation
Impact resistant safety mirrors and glass - Chelsea Artisans Ltd
Leaded lights - Charles Lightfoot Ltd
Leaded lights - Ledlite Glass (Southend) Ltd
Leaded lights - The Cotswold Casement Company
Restoration/ conservation/ design and production of stained glass - Chapel Studio
Specialist glazing - Charles Lightfoot Ltd
Stained glass - Charles Lightfoot Ltd
Stained glass windows - Ide T & W Ltd

L42 Infill panels/ sheets

Architectural Glass - Creative Glass
Clear heat control films - Northgate Solar Controls
Glazing maintenance - Spectra Glaze Services
Glazing trade association - Glass and Glazing Federation
Infill panels/sheets - Panel Systems Ltd
Mirrors - Float Glass Industries
Privacy, patterned, decorative and manifestation films - Northgate Solar Controls
Screens - Glassolutions Saint-Gobain Ltd

M10 Cement: sand/ Concrete screeds/ toppings

Association of Concrete Industrial Flooring Contractors - Association of Concrete Industrial Flooring Contractors (ACIFC)
Calcium carbonate - Imerys Minerals Ltd
Cement based screeds - Flowcrete Plc
Cement: sand/ concrete screeds/ toppings - Flexcrete Technologies Limited
Cement: sand/ Concrete screeds/ toppings - Vetter UK
Cements - LaFarge Cement UK

M10 Cement: sand/ Concrete screeds/ toppings (con't)

Chemical resistant screed - Addagrip Terraco Ltd
Colours for cement - Procter Johnson & Co Ltd
Concrete topping - Ardex UK Ltd
Cristobalite flour - Sibelco UK Ltd
Cristobalite sand - Sibelco UK Ltd
Floor screed - Lytag Ltd
Floor screeds and roof screeds - Isocrete Floor Screeds Ltd
Flooring - BASF plc, Construction Chemicals
Flooring - Hanson Concrete Products Ltd
Industrial flooring - Stuarts Industrial Flooring Ltd
Movement Joints - Movement Joints (UK)
Permascreed - DPC Screeding Ltd
Polymer modified/ rapid drying screeds - Ronacrete Ltd
Polymer/cementitions screeds - Conren Ltd
Repair mortars - Conren Ltd
Sand & balast - Milestone Reclaim and Landscaping Ltd
Sand cement/ Concrete/ Granolithic screeds/ flooring - Don Construction Products Ltd
Screeds and floor coatings - Addagrip Terraco Ltd
Silica Flour - Sibelco UK Ltd
Silica Sand - Sibelco UK Ltd
Specialist screeds - Carter-Dal International
Specialist screeds - Laticrete International Inc. UK
Steel framed multi storey volumetric buildings - Leofric Building Systems Ltd
Subfloor preparation products - Ardex UK Ltd
Wilsonart solid surfacing - Wilsonart Ltd

M11 Mastic asphalt flooring/ floor underlays

Colours for Asphalt - Procter Johnson & Co Ltd
Mastic asphalt flooring - North Herts Asphalte (Roofing) Ltd
Paving and flooring - Roofing Contractors (Cambridge) Ltd
Tiling accessories - Dural UK Ltd

M12 Trowelled bitumen/ resin/ rubber-latex flooring

Anti slip surfacing - Addagrip Terraco Ltd
Car Park Decking - Sika Ltd
Celicote resin coatings - Ancorite Surface Protection Ltd
Colours for Asphalt - Procter Johnson & Co Ltd
Epoxy flooring systems - Cross-Guard International Ltd
Epoxy resin coatings for floors - Watco UK Ltd
Epoxy resin repair materials - Anglo Building Products Ltd
Floor coatings - Jotun Henry Clark Ltd Decorative Division
Flooring systems - Cross-Guard International Ltd
Industrial Flooring - Sika Ltd
Resin based floor & wall finishes - Flowcrete Plc
Resin Flooring - Altro Ltd
Resinbased Floor Coatingss - Belzona PolymericLtd
Self Leveling Moread Beds Latex - Carter-Dal International
Self Leveling Moread Beds Latex - Laticrete International Inc. UK
Trowelled bitumen/ resins/ rubber latex flooring - Don Construction Products Ltd
Urethame screeds - Cross-Guard International Ltd

M13 Calcium sulphate based screeds

Architectural Mouldings - Hodkin Jones (Sheffield) Ltd
Association - Resin Flooring Association (FeRFA)
Calcium sulphate based screeds - Flowcrete Plc
Synthascreed - DPC Screeding Ltd

M20 Plastered/ Rendered/ Roughcast coatings

Building plasters - British Gypsum Ltd
Ceiling Refurbishment - Great British Lighting
Cement based floor screeds, external render systems - Maxit UK
Coil mesh - Catnic
Coloured limestone, dolomite and white sand internal and external renders - Kilwaughter Chemical Co Ltd
Drywall decorating products - Siniat Ltd
Drywall finishing systems - Siniat Ltd
Drywall Joint & Flex Tapes - Siniat Ltd
Epoxy resin coatings for walls - Watco UK Ltd
High performance building boards - Knauf Drywall
Metal lath - Catnic
Mineral renders - Keim Mineral Paints Ltd
Movement Joints - Movement Joints (UK)
Plaster - Knauf Drywall
Plaster beads - Walls & Ceilings International Ltd
Plasterboard accessories - Walls & Ceilings International Ltd
Plastered / Rendered / Roughcast Coatings - Kilwaughter Chemical Co Ltd
Plastered / Rendered / Roughcast Coatings - Safeguard Europe Ltd
Plastered / Rendered / Roughcast coatings - STO Ltd
Plastered/ Rendered/ Roughcast coatings - Limelite - Tarmac Building Products Ltd
Plastered/ Rendered/ Roughcast coatings - Skanda Acoustics
Plastered/Rendered/Roughcast fittings - PermaRock Products Ltd
Plasterers beads - Vista Engineering Ltd
Plasterers bends - Catnic
plastic rendering plaster and dry wall beads - Nenplas
Polymer modified renders - Ronacrete Ltd
Premix Renders - LaFarge Cement UK
Render systems - BRC Special Products - Bekaert Ltd
Renders - Weber Building Solutions
Roughcast coatings - Andrews Coatings Ltd
Silicone Renders - Kilwaughter Chemical Co Ltd
Sprayed Vermiculite - Thermica Ltd
Synthetic resin renders - STO Ltd
Textured coatings & grout - Ciret Limited

M21 Insulation with rendered finish

Expanded polystyrene insulation - Jablite Ltd
External wall insulation - STO Ltd
External wall insulation systems - Skanda Acoustics
Foamglas Cellular glass insulation for wall - Pittsburgh Corning (United Kingdom) Limited
Insulated external render - Maxit UK
Insulated external renders/systems - Alumasc Exterior Building Products Ltd
Insulation - Rockwool Ltd
Insulation - Skanda Acoustics Limited
Insulation with rendered finish - Concrete Repairs Ltd
Insulation with rendered finish - Insulated Render & Cladding Association
Insulation with rendered finish - PermaRock Products Ltd
Insulation with rendered finish - STO Ltd
Sprayed Vermiculite - Thermica Ltd
Trade Association - Association of Specialist Fire Protection (ASFP)

M22 Sprayed monolithic coatings

Grout pumps - Clarke UK Ltd
Intimescent paint - Firebarrier International Ltd T/A Firebarrier Services Ltd
Specialist coatings - Valtti ltd
Sprayed & trowelled on resin coatings - Ancorite Surface Protection Ltd
Sprayed monolithic coatings - Specialist Building Products
Spray-On Insulation - Aardvark Transatlantic Ltd
Trade Association - Association of Specialist Fire Protection (ASFP)

M23 Resin bound mineral coatings

Anti skid surfacing products - Clare R S & Co Ltd
Association - Resin Flooring Association (FeRFA)
Coloured sufacing products - Clare R S & Co Ltd
Decorative bound/bonded surfacing resin – StarScape ULTRA &: Professional - StarScape PRO, Flexible – StarScape FLEXIBLE, Summer – StarScape THERMAL - Star Uretech Ltd
Epoxy coatings - Cross-Guard International Ltd
Epoxy Floor Paint - Everlac (GB) Ltd
Industrial Flooring Products - Ardex UK Ltd
Manufacture of Industrial Resin Flooring in Polyurethane or Epoxy materials - Resdev Ltd
Polymer caotings - Cross-Guard International Ltd
Resin bound mineral coatings - Addagrip Terraco Ltd
Resin bound mineral coatings - Aden Hynes Sculpture Studios
Resin bound mineral coatings - Don Construction Products Ltd
Resins - DSM UK Ltd
Seamless resin floors - Ancorite Surface Protection Ltd
Specialist coatings - Valtti ltd
Trade Association - Association of Specialist Fire Protection (ASFP)
Urethame coatings - Cross-Guard International Ltd

M30 Metal mesh lathing/ Anchored reinforcement for plastered coatings

Arch formers - Catnic
Arch formers - Expamet Building Products
Cladding systems - BRC Special Products - Bekaert Ltd
Mesh arches - Allmat (East Surrey) Ltd
Metal lathing - Expamet Building Products
Metal beads - Expamet Building Products
Metal lathing and mesh - Simpson Strong-Tie®
Metal mesh lathing - Bekaert Building Products
Metal mesh lathing/ Anchored reinforcement for plastered coatings - Skanda Acoustics
Metal wire plaster & render beads - Bekaert Building Products
PVCu plasters beads for drylining, plastering and rendering - Renderplas Ltd
Resin bound mineral coatings - Specialist Building Products
Stainless Steel Reinforcement Mesh - Multi Mesh Ltd
Stainless steel surface protection - Component Developments
Welded Wire Mesh - Multi Mesh Ltd

M31 Fibrous plaster

Decorative mouldings, cornices, dados, ceiling roses and coving - Copley Decor Ltd
Decorative plaster coving and ceiling roses - Hilton Banks Ltd
Plaster cornices and archways - Artistic Plastercraft Ltd

M40 Stone/ Concrete/ Quarry/ Ceramic tiling/ Mosaic

Acid resistant brickwork and Vibration tile system - Ancorite Surface Protection Ltd
Air tools - Marcrist International Ltd
Anit-Fracture Membranes for Natural Stone - Carter-Dal International
Anit-Fracture Membranes for Natural Stone - Laticrete International Inc. UK
Architectural Tiles - Solus Ceramics Ltd
Association of Concrete Industrial Flooring Contractors - Association of Concrete Industrial Flooring Contractors (ACIFC)
Bespoke glazed wall tiles and terracotta floor tiles - Smithbrook Building Products Ltd
Ceramic fiber products - Combustion Linings Ltd
Ceramic floor and wall tiles - R J Stokes & Co Limited
Ceramic marble and granite tiles - Reed Harris
Ceramic tile and stone installation system - Carter-Dal International
Ceramic tile and stone installation systems - Laticrete International Inc. UK
Ceramic tiles - Bell & Co Ltd
Ceramic tiles - British Ceramic Tile Ltd
Ceramic Tiles - Porcelanosa Group Ltd
Ceramic tiles - Swedecor
Ceramic, marble and glass mosaics, swimming pool tiles and porcelain stoneware - Domus Tiles Ltd
Ceramic, marble, granite tiles - Reed Harris
Ceramic, porcelain and mosaic tiles - Arnull Bernard J & Co Ltd
Ceramics - Wade Ceramics Ltd
Ceramics and mosaics - Shackerley (Holdings) Group Ltd incorporating Designer ceramics
Cladding tiles - porcelain - Johnson Tiles
Diamond Sawn -Yorkstone - Hard York Quarries Ltd
Digital transfer decoration - wall tiles - Johnson Tiles
Faience blocks - Shaws of Darwen
Floor and wall tiles - Porcelanosa Group Ltd
Floor slabs and floor tiles - The Delabole Slate Co. Ltd
Floor systems - MiTek Industries Ltd
Floor tile separators - Compriband Ltd
Floor tiles - ceramic - Johnson Tiles
Floor tiles - porcelain - Johnson Tiles
Floor tiling - Fired Earth
Flooring - Burlington Slate Ltd
Flooring - Farmington Masonry LLP
Flooring - Kirkstone
Flooring Marble and granite - Diespeker Marble & Terrazzo Ltd
Glass mosaic -sandstone - Reed Harris
Grouts - Fosroc Ltd
Industrial floor tiles - Swedecor
Internal Paving - Caithness Flagstone Limited
Internal Paving - Johnsons Wellfield Quarries Ltd
Internal Paving; Limwstone and Sandstone - J Suttle Swanage Quarries Ltd
Keope Tiles - Italian Porecellian - Ruabon Sales Limited
Limestone Flooring - Chameleon Stone Ltd
Limestone quarry tiles - Reed Harris
Marble Flooring - Chameleon Stone Ltd
Marble, granite, slate, limestone & terrazzo - Diespeker Marble & Terrazzo Ltd
Mosaic tiles - Chameleon Stone Ltd
Mosaics - Porcelanosa Group Ltd
Movement Joints - Movement Joints (UK)
Natural Stone paving - Palladio Stone
Natural stone tiles - R J Stokes & Co Limited
Natural stones like marble, slate - Porcelanosa Group Ltd
New Staining Silicon Joint for String Work - Carter-Dal International
New Staining Silicon Joint for String Work - Laticrete International Inc. UK
Promenade Tiles - Castle Composites Ltd
Purbeck Limestone - Haysom (Purbeck Stone) Ltd
Quality tile adhesives - Ardex UK Ltd
Quality Tile Grout - Ardex UK Ltd
Quarry tiling - Ruabon Sales Limited
Quartz - Diespeker Marble & Terrazzo Ltd
Quartzite Flooring - Chameleon Stone Ltd
Slate - Reed Harris
Slate Flooring - Chameleon Stone Ltd
Specialist contractors in marble and granite mosaics - Alpha Mosaic & Terrazzo Ltd
Sphinx Ttiles - Glazed Wall and Floor - Ruabon Sales Limited
Split face wall tiles - Chameleon Stone Ltd
Stone Quarries & Sandstone - Johnsons Wellfield Quarries Ltd
Stone Quarries: Sandstone - Caithness Flagstone Limited
Stone tiles - Kirkstone
Stone/ Concrete/ Quarry/ Ceramic tiling/ Mosaic - Haddonstone Ltd
Stone/ Concrete/ Quarry/ Ceramic tiling/ Mosaic - Stonewest Ltd
Stone/ Concrete/ Quarry/ Ceramic tiling/ Mosaic - Vetter UK
Stone/concrete/quarry/ceramic tiling/mosaic - Chilstone
Stone/concrete/quarry/ceramic tiling/mosaic - G Miccoli & Sons Limited
Surface Preparation Equipment - Marcrist International Ltd
Swimming pool tiles - Swedecor
Swimmingpool tiles - ceramic - Johnson Tiles
Terracotta - Reed Harris
Terracotta blocks - Shaws of Darwen
Terrazzo - Reed Harris
Tile cleaners - Tank Storage & Services Ltd
Tiling accessories - Dural UK Ltd
Tiling Products - Sealocrete PLA Ltd
Travertine Limestone Flooring - Chameleon Stone Ltd
Vessel & tank linings - Ancorite Surface Protection Ltd
Wall tile fittings - ceramic - Johnson Tiles
Wall tiles - Fired Earth
Wall tiles - ceramic - Johnson Tiles
Water jet cut murals - wall & floor tiles - Johnson Tiles
Wire Brushes - Marcrist International Ltd

M41 Terrazzo tiling/ In situ terrazzo

Association - Resin Flooring Association (FeRFA)
Bespoke Terrazzo Tiling - Quiligotti Terrazzo Tiles Limited
Customised Terrazzo Tiling - Quiligotti Terrazzo Tiles Limited
Finished Laid Terrazzo - Quiligotti Terrazzo Tiles Limited
Specialist contractors in terrazzo - Alpha Mosaic & Terrazzo Ltd
Stainless Grout - Carter-Dal International
Stainless Grout - Laticrete International Inc. UK
Terracotta floor tiles - York Handmade Brick Co Ltd
Terrazzo flooring - Diespeker Marble & Terrazzo Ltd
Terrazzo polishing and grinding - Ancorite Surface Protection Ltd
Terrazzo Tiling - Quiligotti Terrazzo Tiles Limited
Terrazzo tiling/ In situ terrazzo - Stonewest Ltd
Terrazzo tiling/ In situ terrazzo - Vetter UK
Tiling accessories - Dural UK Ltd

M42 Wood block/ Composition block/ Parquet flooring

Ceramic Parquet - Porcelanosa Group Ltd
Dance floor - Felix Design Ltd
ESCO flooring pre-finished with Polyx®-Oil - OSMO UK
Flooring - Deralam Laminates Ltd
Flooring (leather) - Edelman Leather
Hardwood - Porcelanosa Group Ltd
HPL flooring - Abet Ltd
Laminated flooring - Kronospan Ltd
Parquet and laminate flooring - Western Cork Ltd
Solid & engineered parquet - Western Cork Ltd
Solid wood flooring - Fired Earth
Sprung Floor Systems - British Harlequin Plc
Wood Flooring - Tutto Parquet Limited

M50 Rubber/ Plastics/ Cork/ Lino/ Carpet tiling/ sheeting

Accessories - Interfloor Limited
Aluminium edge trim for vinyl flooring - Howe Green Ltd
Anti Slip Products - 3M
Anti-Fatique Matting - Kleen-Tex Industries Ltd
Anti-slip surfaces - Redman Fisher Engineering
Bonded tiles - Carpets of Worth Ltd
Carpet - Armstrong Floor Products UK Ltd
Carpet and tiles - Adam Carpets Ltd
Carpet fitting tools and accessories - Interfloor Limited
Carpet Protector - Hilton Banks Ltd
Carpet Tiles - Armstrong Floor Products UK Ltd
Carpet tiles - Brintons Ltd
Carpet tiles - Milliken Carpet
Carpet tiles - Rawson Carpets Ltd
Carpet Tiling and Sheeting - Mat.Works Flooring Solutions
Carpet, cork and vinyl tiles and laminate flooring - Western Cork Ltd
Carpet, Vinyl and Laminate flooring - Tutto Parquet Limited
Carpets - CFS Carpets
Carpets - Opus 4 Ltd
Contamination control flooring - Dycem Ltd
Contamination control mats - Dycem Ltd
Contract carpet and carpet tile manufacturer - Burmatex Ltd
Cork - Olley & Sons Ltd, C
Cork flooring - Amorim Cork Flooring
Cork Rubber and Non slip Surfaces - Tiflex Ltd
Custom mixing - Interfloor Limited
Desk chair mats - Jaymart Rubber & Plastics Ltd
Discipative matting soloutions - Kleen-Tex Industries Ltd
Duckboard matting - Jaymart Rubber & Plastics Ltd
Dust control matting soloutions - Kleen-Tex Industries Ltd
Edging - Egger (UK) Ltd
Electrical Safety Matting - Jaymart Rubber & Plastics Ltd
Electrical Safety Matting - MacLellan Rubber Ltd
Entrance barrier systems - Kleen-Tex Industries Ltd
Entrance Matting - 3M
Entrance matting - Gradus Ltd
entrance matting systems - Jaymart Rubber & Plastics Ltd
Entrance matting, flooring and roof walkway matting - Plastic Extruders Ltd
Flameproof sheeting - Icopal Limited
Flexible sheets and Tiles - Forbo Flooring
Floor protection coatings - Glixtone Ltd
Floor smoothing underlay - Ball F & Co Ltd
Floor trims - Gradus Ltd
Floorcoverings - Interface Europe Ltd
Flooring accessories, stair nosings and PVC accessories - Quantum Profile Systems Ltd
Flooring adhesives - Ball F & Co Ltd
Flooring coatings - Williamson T & R Ltd
Flooring products - Weber Building Solutions
Garage floor tiles - Rockwell Sheet Sales Ltd
Handrail Covers - DC Plastic Handrails Ltd
Heavy duty carpet tiles - Paragon by Heckmondwike
Heavy duty impact protection rubber sheeting - MacLellan Rubber Ltd
High pressure decorative laminates - Abet Ltd
Hygiene matting - Kleen-Tex Industries Ltd
Interlocking tiles - Jaymart Rubber & Plastics Ltd
Leather floor and wall tiles - Edelman Leather
Lettered & logo mats - Jaymart Rubber & Plastics Ltd

M50 Rubber/ Plastics/ Cork/ Lino/ Carpet tiling/ sheeting (con't)

Linoleum - Armstrong Floor Products UK Ltd
Luxury Vinyl Tiles - Armstrong Floor Products UK Ltd
Natural floor covering - Fired Earth
Non-slip floor coatings - Andura Coatings Ltd
Non-slip matting soloutions - Kleen-Tex Industries Ltd
Nylon reinfoced PVC sheeting - Flexible Reinforcements Ltd
Plastic coatings - Plastic Coatings Ltd
Plastic roofing, cladding, and glazing - Amari Plastics Plc
Polyurethane re-bond underlays - Interfloor Limited
PTFE coatings - Plastic Coatings Ltd
Publications: contract flooring association guide to contract flooring - Contract Flooring Association
PVC floorcoverings and accessories - Polyflor Ltd
PVC safety floor coverings - Polyflor Ltd
PVC sheeting - Flexible Reinforcements Ltd
Realwood HPL Decorative Laminates - Abet Ltd
Recycled flooring products - Jaymart Rubber & Plastics Ltd
Room Improvement Products - NMC (UK) Ltd
Rubber flooring - Altro Ltd
Rubber flooring systems - Jaymart Rubber & Plastics Ltd
Rubber for floors and other surfaces in a huge range of colours and textures - Dalhaus Ltd
Rubber linings - Ancorite Surface Protection Ltd
Rubber sheeting and expansion joints & bellows - MacLellan Rubber Ltd
Rubber sheeting and flooring - Linatex Ltd
Rubber stud tiles - Polyflor Ltd
Rugs - Brintons Ltd
Safety Flooring - Armstrong Floor Products UK Ltd
Safety floorings - Jaymart Rubber & Plastics Ltd
Sheeting and matting - Interfloor Limited
Slip resistant flooring - Altro Ltd
Smooth vinyl flooring - Altro Ltd
Specialised flooring materials, nosing and adhesives - Tiflex Ltd
Sponge rubber underlays (carpets/wood & laminate) - Interfloor Limited
Sports flooring - Jaymart Rubber & Plastics Ltd
Sports Surfaces - Altro Ltd
Underlay and flooring - Interfloor Limited
Vinyl - Armstrong Floor Products UK Ltd
Vinyl floorcovering sheets, tiles and accessories - Tarkett Ltd
Vinyl sheet and tile flooring - DLW Flooring
Vinyl, safety and sports flooring - Gerflor Ltd
Wall and Furniture Linoleum - Forbo Flooring
Wall furnishings - Vescom UK Limited

M51 Edge fixed carpeting

Carpet - EGE Carpets Ltd
Carpet (office/Domestic) - Evergreens Uk
Carpet for domestic and contract use - Carpets of Worth Ltd
Carpeting - Shaylor Group Plc
Carpets - CFS Carpets
Carpets - Ulster Carpet Mills Ltd
Carpets and Matting - Heckmondwicke FB
Carpets and Matting - Mat.Works Flooring Solutions
Contract flooring manufacturers - Rawson Carpets Ltd
Custom carpets - Ulster Carpet Mills Ltd
Domestic and contract locations - Adam Carpets Ltd
Edge fixed carpeting - Brockway Carpets Ltd
Edge fixed carpeting - Quantum Profile Systems Ltd
Edge fixed floorcoverings - Interface Europe Ltd
Entrance Matting - Heckmondwicke FB
Fibre bonded floor coverings - Rawson Carpets Ltd
Fitted Carpets - Tutto Parquet Limited
Floorcovering accessories - Gripperrods Ltd
Heavy duty carpets - Paragon by Heckmondwike
Surface membranes and release systems for carpet - Laybond Products Ltd
Wool-rich Natural products - Ulster Carpet Mills Ltd
Woven and tufted carpet - Brintons Ltd
Woven axminster carpets - Ulster Carpet Mills Ltd
Woven wilton carpets - Ulster Carpet Mills Ltd

M52 Decorative papers/ fabrics

130cm wide fabric backed vinyls - Dixon Turner Wallcoverings
135cm wide fabric backed vinyls - Dixon Turner Wallcoverings
53cm x 10m paper backed vinyls - Dixon Turner Wallcoverings
Acrylic coatd paper - Package Products Ltd
Authentic tribal rugs - Fired Earth
Contract wall coverings - Muraspec
Contract wallcoverings - Dixon Turner Wallcoverings
Decorative finishes - Glixtone Ltd
Decorative finishes - Weber Building Solutions
Decorative papers/ fabrics - Brewer C & Sons Ltd
Decorative wallcoverings, fabrics and borders - Dixon Turner Wallcoverings
Fabric backed wall coverings - Muraspec
Fabrics - Tektura Plc
Fabrics and papers - Interface Europe Ltd
Fabrics and wall papers - Today Interiors Ltd
Fabrics and wallpapers - Sanderson
Flexible sheets and Tiles - Forbo Flooring
Glass fibre - Muraspec
Hessian - Muraspec
Interior finishes - Muraspec
Metallic finishes - Muraspec
Notice board material - Forbo Flooring
Paint alternatives - Muraspec
Paint stripper, wall paper stripping machines - Ciret Limited
Paints and wallcoverings - Kalon Decorative Products
Paperbacked wall coverings - Muraspec
Primers - Tektura Plc
PVC coated fabrics - Flexible Reinforcements Ltd
Textile wallcoverings - Dixon Turner Wallcoverings
Textiles - Muraspec
Textured coatings - Glixtone Ltd
Timeless fabrics - Fired Earth
Wall coverings - Porcelanosa Group Ltd
Wallcoverings - Muraspec
Wallcoverings - Tektura Plc
Wallcoverings and adhesives - Architectural Textiles Ltd
Wholesalers of furnishing fabrics & wallpapers - CrowsonFabrics Ltd

M60 Painting/ Clear finishing

Agricultural paints - Teal & Mackrill Ltd
Anit graffiti - Kingstonian Paint Ltd
Anti - static coatings - Kenyon Group Ltd
Anti Climb, Anti Fly Poster, Anti Graffiti, paints and coatings - Kenyon Paints Limited
Anti Condensation Paints - Witham Oil & Paint Ltd
Anti condensation - Kingstonian Paint Ltd
Anti corrosion coatings - Corroless Corrosion Control
Anti corrosion coatings - Kenyon Group Ltd
Anticlimb paint - Coo-Var Ltd
Antifouling paints - Teal & Mackrill Ltd
Antigraffiti coatings - Coo-Var Ltd
Blasting - Bristol Metal Spraying & Protective Coatings Ltd
Cadmium pigments - Venator
Chrome oxide green pigments - Venator
Cladding paint - Kingstonian Paint Ltd
Cleaners for paving - Resiblock Ltd
Cleaning Chemicals - Tank Storage & Services Ltd
Coatings - Fujichem Sonneborn Ltd
Coatings - PPG Protective and Marine Coatings
Coatings for concrete floors - Everlac (GB) Ltd
Colour Schemes - Kalon Decorative Products
Complex inorganic pigments - Venator
Decorating - Shaylor Group Plc
Decorating materials - Brewer C & Sons Ltd
Decorative ancillary products - Bartoline Ltd
Decorative coatings for timber - Protim Solignum Ltd
Decorative Finishes - ICI Woodcare
Decorative paints - Akzo Noble Coatings Ltd
Decorative paints, opaque and translucent wood stains - Jotun Henry Clark Ltd Decorative Division
Decorative Sundries - Kalon Decorative Products
Decorative surface enhancer – StarScape RESTORE - Star Uretech Ltd
Decorative Walls - Altro Ltd
Elastomeric, anticarbonation coatings - Andura Coatings Ltd
Electroplating, powder coating and painting - Ritherdon & Co Ltd
Epoxy floor/wall coatings - Conren Ltd
Epoxy paints - Trade Sealants Ltd
Epoxy resin coatings - Anglo Building Products Ltd
Epoxy resins - Addagrip Terraco Ltd
Epoxy systems - Teal & Mackrill Ltd
Exterior woodcare - Blackfriar Paints Ltd
External Decorative Finishes - ICI Woodcare
Fillers - Sadolin UK Ltd
Fine and coarse textured coatings - Andura Coatings Ltd
First for finishes - Chestnut Products
Flame retardant lacquers - Bollom Fire Protection Ltd
Flame retardant paints - Bollom Fire Protection Ltd
Flame retardant varnishes - Bollom Fire Protection Ltd
Floor and line paint - Coo-Var Ltd
Floor coating systems - Corroless Corrosion Control
Floor coatings - Firwood Paints Ltd
Floor coatings, self levellers - Kenyon Group Ltd
Floor paints - Kingstonian Paint Ltd
Floor paints - Teal & Mackrill Ltd
Floor Paints - Witham Oil & Paint Ltd
Floor seals - Evans Vanodine International PLC
Fluorescent Systems - Witham Oil & Paint Ltd
Glass flake reinforced coatings - Corroless Corrosion Control
High performance coatings - Leigh's Paints
Hygiene coatings - Kenyon Group Ltd
Hygienic coatings - Corroless Corrosion Control
Hygienic coatings for walls & ceilings - Tefcote Surface Systems
Industrial Coating Specialists - Bristol Metal Spraying & Protective Coatings Ltd
Industrial paints - Firwood Paints Ltd
Industrial paits - Teal & Mackrill Ltd
Interior coatings - Jotun Henry Clark Ltd Decorative Division
Interior varnishes - Sadolin UK Ltd
Internal Special Effects - Dulux Trade
Internal/External Decorative Finishes - Dulux Trade
Intumescent coatings - Bollom Fire Protection Ltd
Lacquers and seals - Junckers Limited
Long life exterior wall coating - Everlac (GB) Ltd
Luminous & fluorescent paints - Coo-Var Ltd
Maintanance Painting service - International Protective Coatings
Maintenance & Protective Coatings - ICI Woodcare
Maintenance paints - Firwood Paints Ltd
Marine & antifouling coatings - Coo-Var Ltd
Marine paints - Witham Oil & Paint Ltd
Marine paints and coatings - Teal & Mackrill Ltd
Masonry paint - STO Ltd
Metal - Bristol Metal Spraying & Protective Coatings Ltd
Mineral Paints - Keim Mineral Paints Ltd
Natural Oil Woodstain - OSMO UK
Opaque finishes - Sadolin UK Ltd
Opaque ironoxide pigments - Venator
Paint - Fired Earth
Paint - Sanderson
Paint brushes, rollers and decorating tools - Hamilton Acorn Ltd
Paint effects - Kingstonian Paint Ltd
Paint spraying equipment - Bambi Air Compressors Ltd.
Painting / Clear Finishing - Safeguard Europe Ltd
Painting / Clear finishing - STO Ltd
Painting /Clear Finishing - Wessex Resins & Adhesives Ltd
Painting and decorating materials - Covers Timber & Builders Merchants
Painting/ Clear finishing - Andura Coatings Ltd
Painting/ Clear finishing - Arkema France
Painting/ clear finishing - Concrete Repairs Ltd
Painting/ clear finishing - Coo-Var Ltd
Painting/ Clear finishing - Don Construction Products Ltd
Painting/ clear finishing - Liquid Technology Ltd
Painting/clear finishes - TH Kenyon & Sons Ltd
Painting/Clear Finishing - International Protective Coatings
Painting/clear finishing - Tefcote Surface Systems
Paints - AkzoNobel Decorative Paints UK
Paints - Crown Paints Ltd
Paints - Emusol Products (LEICS) Ltd
Paints - HMG Paints
Paints - Manders Paint Ltd
Paints - PPG Protective and Marine Coatings
Paints - Weber Building Solutions
Paints and coatings for tennis courts and other sports surfaces - Everlac (GB) Ltd
Paints and high temperature resistant coatings - Minkon Ltd
Paints and surface coatings - Dacrylate Paints Ltd
Paints primers and specialized coatings - Coo-Var Ltd
Partnering - Kalon Decorative Products
Pigments for the surface coatings - Venator
Polish and sealers - Cleenol Group Ltd
Polyx®-Oil - OSMO UK
Powder and ready mixed fillers - Ciret Limited
Preparation products - Blackfriar Paints Ltd
Primers - ICI Woodcare
Protective and decorative masonry coatings - Andura Coatings Ltd
Protective coating for steelwork - International Protective Coatings
Protective coatings - Andrews Coatings Ltd
Protective Coatings - Dulux Trade
Protective maintenance coatings - Corroless Corrosion Control
Rust stabilising primers - Corroless Corrosion Control
Seals and coatings for wood floors - Everlac (GB) Ltd
Silicone waterproofing - Bluestar Silicones
Slurry Granules - LANXESS Inorganic Pigments Group
Solvent bourne coatings - Sadolin UK Ltd
Specialised paints - Teal & Mackrill Ltd
Specialist Coatings - Valtti ltd
Specialist paint systems - Williamson T & R Ltd
Specialist Paints Varnishes and Woodcare Products - Blackfriar Paints Ltd
Specialist Primers - Witham Oil & Paint Ltd
Specialist Water Based Coattings - Witham Oil & Paint Ltd
Standard, paint quality and fair face finishes - Tarmac Building Products Ltd
Structural painting and spraying - Masonry Cleaning Services
Surface dressings - Decorating products - Sealocrete PLA Ltd
Swimming Pool Paints - Witham Oil & Paint Ltd
Technical Specifications - Kalon Decorative Products
Tennis court spraying - Sportsmark Group Ltd
Tile transfers - Homelux Nenplas
Timber preservatives, fire retardants - decorative finishes - Arch Timber Protection
Trade Paints and coatings - Kenyon Paints Limited
Translucent finishes - Sadolin UK Ltd
Transparent ironoxide pigments - Venator
Twin Pack Paints - Witham Oil & Paint Ltd
Two Pack Floor Paints - Coo-Var Ltd
UV-Protection Oil - OSMO UK
Vapour corrosion inhibitors - Corroless Corrosion Control
Wall and floor coatings - Sealocrete PLA Ltd
Waterbourne coatings - Sadolin UK Ltd
Wet paint - Plastic Coatings Ltd
Wood Finishes - Dulux Trade
Wood Finishes - ICI Woodcare
Wood finishes, speciality paints, paint removers and decorating sundries - Rustins Ltd
Wood protection products - Sadolin UK Ltd
Wood Stains - Akzo Noble Coatings Ltd
Wood Wax Finish - OSMO UK
Woodfinishes - Smith & Rodger Ltd
woodworm, rot and damp treatment - Rentokil Property Care Services

M61 Intumescent coatings for fire protection of steelwork

Fire Retart and Coatings - Bristol Metal Spraying & Protective Coatings Ltd
High temperature coatings - Kenyon Paints Limited
Hyclad matt finish - Outokumpu
Industrial Coating Specialists - Bristol Metal Spraying & Protective Coatings Ltd
Intermescant coatings for fire protection of steelwork - International Protective Coatings
Intumescant coatings - Andrews Coatings Ltd
Intumescent coating, protecting steel from fire - Smith & Rodger Ltd
Intumescent Coatings - Brewer C & Sons Ltd
Intumescent coatings - PPG Protective and Marine Coatings
Intumescent coatings for steel - Quelfire Limited
Nullifire intumescent range - Nullifire Ltd
Passive fire protection products - Leigh's Paints
Structural steel fire protection - GCP APPLIED TECHNOLOGIES (UK) LIMITED
Structural steel protection - Promat UK Ltd
Trade Association - Association of Specialist Fire Protection (ASFP)

N10 General fixtures/ furnishings/ equipment

100% waterproof bathroom panels - Bushboard Limited
Acoustic telephone enclosure - System Building Products
All types of window blinds - Northgate Solar Controls
Aluminium Shelving - Bedford Shelving Ltd
Aluminum shelving - RB UK Ltd
Anti fatigue mats - Dycem Ltd
Anti-Ligature Furniture - Aaztec Cubicles
Architectural antiques and Furniture - Andy Thornton Ltd
Archive research - Sanderson
Awnings - Luxaflex®
Awnings - Tidmarsh & Sons
Bamer Carpeting/Matting - PHS Group plc
Banks of post boxes - Signs Of The Times Ltd
Basket units - Smart F & G (Shopfittings)Ltd
Bathroom cabinets and tube fittings - William Hopkins & Sons Ltd
Bathroom Surfaces: Acrylic and Laminate - Bushboard Limited
Bathroom wall panels and vanity surfaces - Bushboard Limited
Baulstrading - Spindlewood
Bedroom & home study furniture - Ball William Ltd
Bedroom furniture - Magnet Ltd
Bedrooms - Moores Furniture Group Ltd
Bedspreads - Sanderson
Benching - Aaztec Cubicles
Benching - Envopak Group Ltd
Bencing - Libraco
Bespoke furniture - Hyperion Wall Furniture Ltd
Bespoke Furniture Design - Branson Leisure Ltd
Bespoke Furniture Manufacturers - Branson Leisure Ltd
Bespoke museum display cases - The Benbow Group
BioCote - The Senator Group
Blackout blinds - Tidmarsh & Sons
Blind and awning fabrics - Flexible Reinforcements Ltd
Blinds - Durable Ltd
Blinds - Eclipse Blind Systems Ltd
Blinds - Hallmark Blinds Ltd
Blinds - Invicta Window Films Ltd
Blinds - Opus 4 Ltd
Blinds - VELUX Co Ltd, The
Blinds in sealed units - Pilkington Plyglass
Blinds, curtains, tracks - Sunrite Blinds Ltd
Block & sheet polyester, bonded products - Rawson Fillings Ltd
Boards for furniture, whiteboards, chaklboards advertising - Finnish Fibreboard (UK) Ltd
Boltless Shelving - Sperrin Metal Products Ltd
Bookcase Systems - Jali Ltd
Bracketry - Vantrunk Engineering Ltd
Broadcast and audio visual products & services - Streamtec Limited
Brush strip cable management - Kleeneze Sealtech Ltd
Brushes - Industrial Brushware Ltd
Cabinet Hinge Manufacturers - Daro UK Ltd
Caravan security boxes - Ritherdon & Co Ltd
Card/ magazine racks - Smart F & G (Shopfittings)Ltd
Carpet Tile - PHS Group plc
Carved stone - Caithness Flagstone Limited
Cash and security boxes - Securikey Ltd
Cast aliminium mail boxes - Signs Of The Times Ltd
Changing room furniture - Helmsman
Choir risers - Felix Design Ltd
Chrome Plated Steel Shelving - Bedford Shelving Ltd
Chrome shelving - RB UK Ltd
Coal and log effect gas fires - BFM Europe Limited
Coir matting & logo - PHS Group plc
Conservatory Blinds - Amdega Ltd
Conservatory blinds - Tidmarsh & Sons
Contract fruniture - Taskworthy Ltd
Contract furnishers - John Pulsford Associates Ltd
Contract furniture - Metalliform Products Plc
Contract furniture - Ness Furniture Ltd
Contract office and leisure furniture - Zon International
Contract Residential Furniture - Ellis J T & Co Ltd
Contract seating - Laytrad Contract Furniture Ltd
Contract seating & tables - Knightbridge Furniture Productions Ltd
Contract tables - Laytrad Contract Furniture Ltd
Cord drawn tracks - Goelst
Cotton & wool felt - Rawson Fillings Ltd
Curtain fabrics - Eclipse Blind Systems Ltd
Curtain poles - Rothley Limited
Curtain poles - Silent Gliss Ltd

N10 General fixtures/ furnishings/ equipment (con't)

Curtain tracks, antibacterial curtains and blinds - Marlux Medical Ltd
Curtain tracks, cubicle rails and window blinds - electric & manual operation - Silent Gliss Ltd
Curtains - Sanderson
Custom design staging - Felix Design Ltd
Custom mouldings - Harrison Thompson & Co Ltd
Customer guidence and queue management systems - Tensator Ltd
Customised metal trims in all metals - Azimex Fabrications Ltd
Customized panel work - Ritherdon & Co Ltd
Decorative melamine faced chipboard - Egger (UK) Ltd
Designers for Working, Learning and Living Spaces - John Pulsford Associates Ltd
Desk lighting - Anglepoise Lighting Ltd
Desks and furniture in metalwork, glass, marble and granite - Howard Bros Joinery Ltd
Display Panels - Harewood Products Ltd (Adboards)
Domestic bedroom furniture - Ball William Ltd
Door Closers - DORMA UK Ltd
Drop down grab rails - Cefndy Healthcare
Electronic fly killers - P+L Systems Ltd
Entrance Matting - EMS Entrance Matting Systems Ltd
Entrance matting - Norton Engineering Alloys Co Ltd
Entrance matting - Shackerley (Holdings) Group Ltd incorporating Designer ceramics
EOS roller blinds - Guthrie Douglas
Equestrian Arenas and Track PVC-u Fencing and Barriers - Duralock (UK) Ltd
External Ashtray - The No Butts Bin Company (NBB), Trading as NBB Outdoor Shelters
External blinds - Tidmarsh & Sons
External Litter Bins - The No Butts Bin Company (NBB), Trading as NBB Outdoor Shelters
Filing and storage cabinets - Railex Systems Ltd, Elite Division
Fine surfaced furniture chip board - Egger (UK) Ltd
Finger posts - Signs Of The Times Ltd
Fire Blankets - BRK Brands Europe Ltd
Fire extinguishers - ASCO Extinguishers Co. Ltd
Fire extinguishers - BRK Brands Europe Ltd
Fire extinguishers - Fife Fire Engineers & Consultants Ltd
Fire extinguishers - Firetecnics Systems Ltd
Fire extinguishers - Griffin and General Fire Services Ltd
Fire extinguishers - Kidde Fire Protection Services Ltd
Fire extinguishers - Richard Hose Ltd
Fire fighting equipment - Eagles, William, Ltd
Fire rated mailboxes - The Safety Letterbox Company Ltd
Fire resistant fabrics - Mermet U.K
Fireplaces - Wyvern Marlborough Ltd
Fireplaces and fires - Bell & Co Ltd
Fireplaces, surrounds, suites and hearths - Winther Browne & co Ltd
Fitted Bedrooms - Hammonds - New Home Division
Fitted Bedrooms - Symphony Group PLC, The
Fitting & Installation - Sanderson
Fittings - Kee Klamp Ltd
Flags, flagstaffs, banners and bunting - Zephyr The Visual Communicators
Flat end grab rails - Cefndy Healthcare
Flooring solutions - Mat.Works Flooring Solutions
Fragrance dispensers - P+L Systems Ltd
Frames Historical Photographs - Francis Frith Collection
Freestanding mailboxes - The Safety Letterbox Company Ltd
Furniture - Bevan Funnell Group Limited
Furniture - Fired Earth
Furniture - Moores Furniture Group Ltd
Furniture - RAJA Workplace
Furniture - Sanderson
Furniture - Bedroom, Office and School - Aaztec Cubicles
Furniture fittings - Nico Manufacturing Ltd
Furniture fittings and accessories - Hafele UK Ltd
Furniture for restuarants and catering facilities - Sandler Seating Ltd
Furniture lifting device - Interface Europe Ltd
Furniture Repairs & Restoration - Branson Leisure Ltd
Furniture, fittings and hardware - manufacturers and importers - Daro UK Ltd
Garment rails/shoe fittings - Smart F & G (Shopfittings)Ltd
Geeral fixture/ furnishings and equipment - Hipkiss, H, & Co Ltd
General Equipment - Cottam Brush Ltd
General fixtures - Anders + Kern UK Ltd
General Fixtures and Fittings - Coverscreen UK LLP
General fixtures and furnishings - Be-Modern Ltd
General fixtures and furnishings - Elite Trade & Contract Kitchens Ltd
General fixtures/ furnishings/ equipment - Artex Ltd
General fixtures/ furnishings/ equipment - Barlow Group
General fixtures/ furnishings/ equipment - Covers Timber & Builders Merchants
General fixtures/ furnishings/ Equipment - Laidlaw Ltd
General fixtures/ furnishings/ equipment - Libraco
General furniture - Ellis J T & Co Ltd
General purpose fittings and furnishings - Hettich UK Ltd
Glass fibre UPVC fabrics - Mermet U.K
Greenhouse accessories for Hartley Greenhouses - Hartley Botanic Ltd
GRP enclosures and kiosks - Dewey Waters Ltd
hand drawn tracks - Goelst
Handling equipment - RAJA Workplace
Handmade Fireplace Briquettes - Collier W H Ltd
Hardwood worktops & bartops - W.L. West & Sons Ltd
Hinges - Cooke Brothers Ltd
Home furniture - Vitra UK Ltd
Hotel bedroom Furniture - Ellis J T & Co Ltd
Hotel bedroom furniture and contract furniture - Pedley Furniture International Ltd
Hotel furniture - Laytrad Contract Furniture Ltd
Hotel security boxes - Ritherdon & Co Ltd
Illuminated Mirrors - Astro Lighting Ltd
Import furniture - Kush UK Ltd
Insect Screens - The Flyscreen Company Ltd
Installation Services - Moores Furniture Group Ltd
Instrument cabinet - Ruthin Precast Concrete Ltd
Interior and exterior blinds and awnings - Deans Blinds & Awnings (UK) Ltd
Iso-design venetian blinds - Eclipse Blind Systems Ltd
Key filing, security cabinets and safes - Securikey Ltd
Kiosks - Fibaform Products Ltd
Kitchen Surfaces: Acrylic, Laminate and Compact laminate - Bushboard Limited
Kitchen worksurfaces, splashbacks and upstands - Bushboard Limited
Leaflet holders - Smart F & G (Shopfittings)Ltd
Leather for walling/upholstry - Edelman Leather
Letter Boxes - Signs Of The Times Ltd
Lifestyle user friendly shelving kits - RB UK Ltd
Litter bins and recycling containers - Glasdon UK Limited
Lockers - School, Sport, Office, Healthcare, MoD, Police etc - 3d Storage Systems (UK) LTD
Lockers and cubicles - Shackerley (Holdings) Group Ltd incorporating Designer ceramics
Made-to-measure furnishings - Sanderson
Magnetic picture hooks and coat hooks - Bunting Magnetics Europe Limited
Mailboxes - The Safety Letterbox Company Ltd
Mailing systems - The Safety Letterbox Company Ltd
Manufacturers of display & exhibition systems - Nimlok Ltd
Material handling equipment - Moresecure Ltd
Mats and matting - PHS Group plc
Matwell frames - PHS Group plc
Mechanical extract units - Zehnder Group UK Ltd
Mirrors - Charles Lightfoot Ltd
Mirrors - Ledlite Glass (Southend) Ltd
Mobile Folding Furniture - Spaceright Europe Limited
Moulded grab rails - Cefndy Healthcare
Music Suite Equipment - Black Cat Music
Nameplates and fireplaces - The Delabole Slate Co. Ltd
Natural & polyester fillings for bedding & upholstery - Rawson Fillings Ltd
Natural ventilation products - Zehnder Group UK Ltd
Non slip bench mat - Dycem Ltd
Nostalgic gift products - Francis Frith Collection
Notice Boards - Harewood Products Ltd (Adboards)
Nylon Coated Steel Shelving - Bedford Shelving Ltd
Odour control products - P+L Systems Ltd
P.O.S support - Eclipse Blind Systems Ltd
Pallet racking, shelving systems and lockers - Sperrin Metal Products Ltd
Panel Blinds - Louver-Lite Ltd
Panel glides - Silent Gliss Ltd
Parafin pressure lamp - Tilley International Ltd
Perfect Fit Blinds - Louver-Lite Ltd
Perforated hardboard - Finnish Fibreboard (UK) Ltd
Pine beds, bunk beds and headboards - Airsprung Beds Ltd
Pine room paneling, bookcases and display cupboards - Hallidays UK Ltd
Plastic injection moulding for custom furnishing, fittings and parts - Hille Educational Products Ltd
Portable auditorium seating - Sandler Seating Ltd
Portable gas cookers - Tilley International Ltd
Press tooling - Cooke Brothers Ltd
Pressings - Cooke Brothers Ltd
Product finishing - Cooke Brothers Ltd
Public area bins, ashtrays and fire safe bins - Lesco Products Ltd
Purpose made joinery - Platonoff & Harris Ltd
Radiator casings - T B S Fabrications
Ready made curtain - Eclipse Blind Systems Ltd
Reconstructed stone fireplaces - Minsterstone Ltd
Recycled Plastic Outdoor Furniture (Picknic Tables, Benches, Seating) - The No Butts Bin Company (NBB), Trading as NBB Outdoor Shelters
Refuse sack holders and fire retardant bins - Unicorn Containers Ltd
Roller blind systems - Goelst
Roller blinds - Reflex-Rol (UK)
Roller blinds - Tidmarsh & Sons
Roller/roman/venetian/vertical blinds - Silent Gliss Ltd
Roman blinds - Goelst
Room Darkening Systems - CBS (Curtain and Blind Specialists Ltd)
Rose end grab rails - Cefndy Healthcare
Safety films - The Window Film Company UK Ltd
Satallite TV - West London Security
School blinds - CBS (Curtain and Blind Specialists Ltd)
School Fit Out - West London Security
Screens & decorative panels - Jali Ltd
Sculptures - Aden Hynes Sculpture Studios
Sealer units - Pilkington Plyglass
Seating - CPS Manufacturing Co
Seating and tables for schools, waiting areas, train stations, airports, ferry terminals, hospitals and surgeries - Hille Educational Products Ltd
Seating systems - Harrison Thompson & Co Ltd
Seating: Lecture theatre, Theater and Stadium - Evertaut Ltd
Security mirrors - Securikey Ltd
Self retracting key reels - Securikey Ltd
Service desking - Grant Westfield Ltd
Shading System - CBS (Curtain and Blind Specialists Ltd)
Shatterproof safety mirrors - Deralam Laminates Ltd
Sheet metal enclosures - Ritherdon & Co Ltd
Shelving - RB UK Ltd
Shelving - Smart F & G (Shopfittings)Ltd
Shelving systems - E-Z Rect Ltd
Shelving systems - Moresecure Ltd
Shoot bolt Locking Mechanisms - A Kenrick & Sons
Showroom design - Eclipse Blind Systems Ltd
Slotted angle plastic containers and boxes - Moresecure Ltd
Slotvents - Zehnder Group UK Ltd
Soft fabrics - Eclipse Blind Systems Ltd
Solar blinds material - Reflex-Rol (UK)
Solar reflective fabrics - Mermet U.K
Solar shading - Levolux A.T. Limited
Solid surface fabrication - Grant Westfield Ltd
Special Stainless Fabrications - Pland Stainless Ltd
Sprung mattresses, divan bases, pillows and accessories - Airsprung Beds Ltd
Square tube construction systems - Moresecure Ltd
Stainless steel general fixings - Pland
Stainless steel post boxes - Signs Of The Times Ltd
Stainless steel, aluminium, PVC covered, galvanized and brass handrails - SG System Products Ltd
Statement splashbacks - Bushboard Limited
Steel shelving uprights and brackets - RB UK Ltd
Steel Storage Fittings - TROAX UK Ltd
Steel tube and fittings - Rothley Limited
Storage - Rothley Limited
Storage cabinets - Richard Hose Ltd
Storage walls - Avanti Systems
Study, lounge, bedroom, fitted furniture - Hyperion Wall Furniture Ltd
Sun blinds - Tidmarsh & Sons
Sunbeds, lockers and cubicles - Dalesauna Ltd
Support rails and systems - Amilake Southern Ltd
Synthetic grass for display - Artificial Grass Ltd
Tables - Libraco
TESS - Guthrie Douglas
Themed features (any material) - Design & Display Structures Ltd
Tiered floor structures - Evertaut Ltd
Trolley - Unicorn Containers Ltd
Vandal resistant blinds for public buildings - CBS (Curtain and Blind Specialists Ltd)
Vending machines - Unicorn Containers Ltd
Venetian blinds - Komfort Workspace PLC
Venetian blinds - Tidmarsh & Sons
Vertical and horizontal carousels - Construction Group UK Ltd
Vertical Blind System - Goelst
Vertical blinds - Marlux Medical Ltd
Vertical Blinds - Tidmarsh & Sons
Wall mounted mailboxes - The Safety Letterbox Company Ltd
Wall Murals - Francis Frith Collection
Wall rails - Fixatrad Ltd
Weighing scales and weigh bridges - Phoenix Scales Ltd
Window blind systems, fabrics - vertical, roller, venetian, pleated, woven wood, contract/perofrmance - Louver-Lite Ltd
Wooden venetian blinds - Eclipse Blind Systems Ltd
Wooden venetian blinds, timbershades - Tidmarsh & Sons
Work benches - Fine H & Son Ltd
Work benches and cupboards - Emmerich (Berlon) Ltd
Worktops - The Delabole Slate Co. Ltd
Worktops and vanity units - Domus Tiles Ltd
Woven fabrics - Mermet U.K
Write-on, wipe-off products - Tektura Plc
Writing boards and notice boards - AudiocomPendax Ltd
Zinc Plated Steel Shelving - Bedford Shelving Ltd

N11 Domestic kitchen fittings

Appliances - Beko plc
Basin traps and wastes - Wirquin Ltd
Built -in cookers - Stoves PLC
Built-in dishwashers - Stoves PLC
Built-in ovens and hobs - Rangemaster
Built-in refrigerators - Stoves PLC
Cookers - Stoves PLC
Cookers and electrical appliances - Electrolux Domestic Appliances
Customised work tops: stainless steel - Azimex Fabrications Ltd
Domestic kitchen appliances - De Longhi Limited
Domestic kitchen fittings - Be-Modern Ltd
Domestic kitchen fittings - Commodore Kitchens Ltd
Domestic kitchen fittings - Covers Timber & Builders Merchants
Domestic kitchen fittings - Elite Trade & Contract Kitchens Ltd
Domestic kitchen fittings - Hipkiss, H, & Co Ltd
Domestic kitchen fittings, Lever action - Shavrin Levatap Co Ltd
Domestic kitchen furniture - Ball William Ltd
Domestic kitchen sinks, taps and accessories - Carron Phoenix Ltd
Fitted kitchens - Miele Co Ltd
Free standing cookers - Stoves PLC
Kitchen and bathroom furniture - Dennis & Robinson Ltd
Kitchen Appliances - Waterline Limited
Kitchen fittings - Magnet Ltd
Kitchen fittings - Symphony Group PLC, The
Kitchen furniture - Ellis J T & Co Ltd
Kitchen furniture - Gower Furniture Ltd
Kitchen furniture - Waterline Limited
Kitchen sinks - Kohler UK
Kitchen Surfaces: Laminate, Compact laminate and Solid - Bushboard Limited
Kitchen units - Ball William Ltd
Kitchen worksurfaces, splashbacks and upstands - Bushboard Limited
Kitchen worktops - Kronospan Ltd
Kitchens - Bell & Co Ltd
Kitchens - Moores Furniture Group Ltd
Kitchens - Smith & Choyce Ltd
Kitchens - Taskworthy Ltd
Kitchens, kitchen furniture, taps - Porcelanosa Group Ltd
Laminated + Solid Hardwood Worktops - Meyer Timber Limited
Oil stoves - Gazco Ltd
Range Cookers - Gazco Ltd
Range cookers - Rangemaster
Shelving - Bedford Shelving Ltd
Solid hardwood worktops - Junckers Limited
Solid wood + melamine worktops - Deralam Laminates Ltd
Statement splashbacks - Bushboard Limited
Takeaway Kitchens - Jewson Ltd
Taps - kitchen - Hansgrohe
Traditional kitchen taps and Mixers - Shavrin Levatap Co Ltd
Vanitories worktops - Burlington Slate Ltd
Work surfaces - Kirkstone
Worktops - Formica Ltd

N12 Catering Equipment

Automatic fill water boilers - Calomax Ltd
Bacteria Grease traps - Progressive Product Developments Ltd
Bar Tender Sinks - Pland Stainless Ltd
Bars - Smith & Choyce Ltd
Canteen tables and chairs - Q.M.P
Cast iron multifuel stoves - Valor
Catering - RAJA Workplace
Catering and culinary fittings - DuPont Corian
Catering equipment - Barlow Group
Catering equipment - Electrolux Foodservice
Catering equipment - Franke Sissons Ltd
Catering equipment - Miele Co Ltd
Catering Equipment - Stamford Products Limited
Catering sinks and tables - Pland Stainless Ltd
Catering water boilers - Calomax Ltd
Coffee Machines - Pressure Coolers Ltd T/A Maestro Pressure Coolers
Coffee percolators - TSE Brownson
Commercial catering and bar equipment - Imperial Machine Co Ltd
Commercial catering facilities - design, supply, and installation UK wide - Lockhart Catering Equipment
Counter top water boilers - Calomax Ltd
Deep fat fryers - Preston & Thomas Ltd
Dishwashers - Clenaware Systems Ltd
Display carts - TSE Brownson
Domestic and commercial waste disposal units - Max Appliances Ltd
Domestic kitchen foodwaste disposers - The Haigh Tweeny Co Ltd
Filtered water dispensers - PHS Group plc
Fish and chip frying ranges - Preston & Thomas Ltd
Food processing - Hemsec Panel Technologies
Food waste bins - Glasdon UK Limited
Freezers - Hemsec Panel Technologies
Gas stoves - Valor
Glass dryers - Clenaware Systems Ltd
Glasswashers - Clenaware Systems Ltd
Grease traps, oil and grease water separators - Progressive Product Developments Ltd
Grease treatment plants - Progressive Product Developments Ltd
Heater service counter tops - TSE Brownson
High performance kitchen furniture - Rixonway Kitchens Ltd
Insulated Urns - TSE Brownson
Kitchen equipment - Magnet Ltd
Milk heaters - TSE Brownson
Show cases - TSE Brownson
Stainless Steel Cabinets - GEC Anderson Ltd
Stainless steel catering equipment - Moffat Ltd, E & R
Stainless steel catering equipment - Pland
Stainless Steel Shelving - GEC Anderson Ltd
Stainless steel shelving systems for kitchens and coldrooms - Bedford Shelving Ltd
Stainless Steel Sinks - GEC Anderson Ltd
Stainless Steel Worktops - GEC Anderson Ltd
Steel, Stainless steel and aluminium - Speedfab Midlands
Tray/plate dispensers - TSE Brownson
Trolleys - TSE Brownson
Undersink Chillers - Pressure Coolers Ltd T/A Maestro Pressure Coolers
Vending machines - Autobar Vending Services Limited
Vending systems - The Kenco Coffee Company
Ventilated ceiling system for commercial cooking areas - Britannia Kitchen Ventilation Ltd
Ventilation / gas interlocks - TCW Services (Control) Ltd
Wall kettles - Calomax Ltd
Waste disposal equipment, balers, shredders, drinks can crushers - Tony Team Ltd
Waste disposal units and catering cupboards - Pland Stainless Ltd

N12 Catering Equipment (con't)

Water calcium treatment - Clenaware Systems Ltd
Water softeners - Clenaware Systems Ltd

N13 Sanitary appliances/ fittings

Accessories - Deva Tap Co Ltd
Accessories - Ideal-Standard Ltd
Acrylic baths - Vitra (UK) Ltd
Aluminium Shower outlets - Alutec
Aluminium shower outlets - Marley Plumbing and Drainage
Anti-ligature system for hospital cubicle/shower curtain tracks - President Blinds Ltd
Anti-ligature tracks - Marlux Medical Ltd
Anti-vandal showers - Shavrin Levatap Co Ltd
Architechtural hardware - Samuel Heath & Sons plc
Architectural Glass - Creative Glass
Bath and kitchen seals - Homelux Nenplas
Bath Screens - Lakes Bathrooms Limited
Bath screens - Majestic Shower Co Ltd
Bathing equipment for elderly and disabled - Chiltern Invadex
Bathroom accessories - HEWI UK Ltd
Bathroom Accessories - Marflow Eng Ltd
Bathroom accessories - Samuel Heath & Sons plc
Bathroom accessories - Triton PLC
Bathroom accessories - Vitra (UK) Ltd
Bathroom and shower accessories - Marleton Cross Ltd
Bathroom and showering equipment - Amilake Southern Ltd
Bathroom fittings - Rothley Limited
Bathroom fittings - Silverdale Bathrooms
Bathroom fittings - William Hopkins & Sons Ltd
Bathroom furniture - Ellis J T & Co Ltd
Bathroom furniture - Kohler UK
Bathroom furniture - Vitra (UK) Ltd
Bathroom suites - Kohler UK
Bathroom systems - Multikwik Ltd
Bathrooms - Bell & Co Ltd
Bathrooms - Fired Earth
Bathrooms - Vitra (UK) Ltd
Bathrooms, bathroom accessories and furniture, Sanitary ware, taps - Porcelanosa Group Ltd
Baths - Ideal-Standard Ltd
Baths and Bathroom suites - Silverdale Bathrooms
Baths, special shaped baths - Kaldewei
Bedroom furniture - Bell & Co Ltd
Bidets - Kohler UK
Brassware for bathrooms - Silverdale Bathrooms
Brassware, showers and accessories - Hansgrohe
Cabinet furniture - HEWI UK Ltd
Ceramic and acrylic sanitaryware - Armitage Shanks Ltd
Childrens Washrooms - TBS Amwell Ltd
Chrome bathroom accessories - William Hopkins & Sons Ltd
Cisterns - Multikwik Ltd
Cisterns - Wirquin Ltd
Cubicle tracks - Marlux Medical Ltd
Curved glass bathroom bowls - Novaglaze Limited
Domestic showering products - Kohler Mira Ltd
Drinking fountains and water coolers - Pressure Coolers Ltd T/A Maestro Pressure Coolers
Duct Panelling - TBS Amwell Ltd
Duct panels - Dunhams of Norwich
Dušo sport shower column - Horne Engineering Ltd
Electric mixer and power showers, hand wash units and water heaters - Triton PLC
Electric showers - Heatrae Sadia Heating Ltd
Electric towel rails - Ecolec
Enclosures - Ideal-Standard Ltd
Fill valves - Multikwik Ltd
Fitted Bathrooms - Symphony Group PLC, The
Fittings for disabled and aged - HEWI UK Ltd
Flexible plumbing fittings - Multikwik Ltd
Flushing systems - Wirquin Ltd
Flushvalves - Multikwik Ltd
Grab rails - Rothley Limited
Grabrails - William Hopkins & Sons Ltd
Group thermostatic valves - Delabie UK Ltd
Hand dryers - Warner Howard Group Ltd
Handwash units and Sanitaryware - Wallgate Ltd
Hygiene equipment - Imperial Machine Co Ltd
Hygiene equipment - P+L Systems Ltd
In Wall Frames - Wirquin Ltd
Incinerators - Combustion Linings Ltd
Intumescent mastics - Bollom Fire Protection Ltd
Jacuzzi®, Whirlpool Baths - Jacuzzi® Spa and Bath Ltd
Kick Space electric heaters - Ecolec
Kits - Ideal-Standard Ltd
Lead Sheet Coverings/ Flashings - BLM British Lead
Modern bathroom taps and mixers - Shavrin Levatap Co Ltd
Nappy changing units - Magrini Ltd
Optitherm thermostatic tap - Horne Engineering Ltd
Outdoor Hot tubs - Jacuzzi® Spa and Bath Ltd
Pan connectors - Multikwik Ltd
Pillar taps - Tyco Waterworks - Samuel Booth
Plumbing fittings - Flowflex Components Ltd
Power, mixer valve and electric showers - NewTeam Ltd
Ready Plumbed Modules - Bushboard Washrooms
Safety accessories for bathrooms (seats, handles, supports) - Lakes Bathrooms Limited
Sanitary appliances - ArjoHuntleigh UK
Sanitary appliances - Bathstore
Sanitary appliances & fittings - Olby H E & Co Ltd
Sanitary appliances and accessories - **Secure Sanitaryware, Toilets, Basins, Showers, Vanity units and Washroom accessories** - Aaztec Cubicles
Sanitary appliances and fittings - Bristan Group
Sanitary appliances and fittings - Cefndy Healthcare
Sanitary appliances and fittings - Guest (Speedfit) Ltd, John
Sanitary appliances/ fittings - Covers Timber & Builders Merchants
Sanitary appliances/ fittings - Geberit Ltd
Sanitary appliances/ fittings - Harris & Bailey Ltd
Sanitary appliances/fittings - Allgood plc
Sanitary appliances/fittings - FC Frost Ltd
Sanitary appliances/fittings - The Haigh Tweeny Co Ltd
Sanitary Appliances/Fittings - Wybone Ltd
Sanitary bins - Unicorn Containers Ltd
Sanitary disposal units, washroom and baby room products - Cannon Hygiene Ltd
Sanitary equipment and accessories - Ideal-Standard Ltd
Sanitary Fittings - Acorn Powell Ltd
Sanitary Fittings - Dart Valley Systems Ltd
Sanitary fittings - DuPont Corian
Sanitary fittings - Franke Sissons Ltd
Sanitary Fittings - Wallgate Ltd
Sanitary fittings - Wirquin Ltd
Sanitary fixings - Artur Fischer (UK) Ltd
Sanitary towel incinerator and towel rails - Consort Equipment Products Ltd
Sanitary ware and fittings - Twyford Bathrooms
Sanitory units - Max Appliances Ltd
Sauna - Golden Coast Ltd
Saunas, steam rooms and spa baths - Dalesauna Ltd
Seats for bathrooms - Lakes Bathrooms Limited
Shower accessories - Bristan Group
Shower accessories - Delabie UK Ltd
Shower accessories - NewTeam Ltd
Shower Doors - Lakes Bathrooms Limited
Shower doors - Majestic Shower Co Ltd
Shower doors and carer screens - Norton Engineering Alloys Co Ltd
Shower doors, enclosures, bath screen and shower trays - Kohler UK
Shower doors, trays bath screens and shower mixers - Matki plc
Shower enclosers - Majestic Shower Co Ltd
Shower enclosures - Contour Showers Ltd
Shower Enclosures - Lakes Bathrooms Limited
Shower enclosures and towel rails - Kermi (UK) Ltd
Shower grilles - Norton Engineering Alloys Co Ltd
Shower products - Aqualisa Products
Shower pumps - NewTeam Ltd
Shower screens - Majestic Shower Co Ltd
Shower trays, cubicles and bath screens - Coram Showers Ltd
Shower valves - Ideal-Standard Ltd
Showering systems - Kohler UK
Showers - Samuel Heath & Sons plc
Showers - Silverdale Bathrooms
Showers and Baths - Hansgrohe
Showers and shower trays - Kaldewei
Sinks - Franke UK Ltd
Spa & Wellness - Kaldewei
Specialist sanitaryware - Wallgate Ltd
Stainless Steel Basins - GEC Anderson Ltd
Stainless Steel Faucets - Vola
Stainless Steel Sanitaryware - GEC Anderson Ltd
Stainless steel sanitaryware - Pland Stainless Ltd
Stainless steel sanitaryware and washroom equipment - Pland
Stainless Steel Sluices - GEC Anderson Ltd
Stainless Steel Urinals - GEC Anderson Ltd
Stainless Steel W.C.s - GEC Anderson Ltd
Stainless Steel Washing Troughs - GEC Anderson Ltd
Stainless steel, ceramic, synthetic sinks and shower cubicles - Rangemaster
Taps - Deva Tap Co Ltd
Taps - Franke UK Ltd
Taps - Samuel Heath & Sons plc
Taps - Shavrin Levatap Co Ltd
Taps and mixers - Ideal-Standard Ltd
Taps and valves - Opella Ltd
Taps for the disabled and elderly - Shavrin Levatap Co Ltd
Taps, mixers, and showers - Pegler Ltd
Taps, showers and thermostatic mixers - Grohe Ltd
Thermostatic mixing valves - Delabie UK Ltd
Thermostatic Mixing Valves - Horne Engineering Ltd
Thermostatic shower controls - Delabie UK Ltd
Thermostatic shower panels - Horne Engineering Ltd
Thermostatic shower valves - Shavrin Levatap Co Ltd
Time flow shower controls - Delabie UK Ltd
Toilet cubicles - Grant Westfield Ltd
Toilet Cubicles - Relcross Ltd
Toilet Cubicles - TBS Amwell Ltd
Toilet cubicles and washroom systems - Moffett Thallon & Co Ltd
Toilet seats - Pressalit Care
Toilet Seats - Wirquin Ltd
Toilet, shower and changing cubicles - Dunhams of Norwich
Tool hire - Jewson Ltd
Towel and soap dispensers - Kimberly-Clark Ltd
Trays - Ideal-Standard Ltd
Urinal controls - Delabie UK Ltd
Urinal filters - Cistermiser Ltd
Urinal flush controls - Cistermiser Ltd
Vanity units - Dunhams of Norwich
Vitreous china ceramic sanitaryware and brassware - Vitra (UK) Ltd
Vitrious Sanitryware - Relcross Ltd
W. C.'s - Ideal-Standard Ltd
Walk-in Shower Enclosures - Lakes Bathrooms Limited
Warm air hand and face dryers - Airdri Ltd
Warm air hand dryers - Wandsworth Elecrtrical Ltd
Wash basins - Ideal-Standard Ltd
Washbasins - Kaldewei
Washbasins - Kohler UK
Washroom control systems - Cistermiser Ltd
Washroom Equipment - Relcross Ltd
Washroom Services - PHS Group plc
Washroom system - DuPont Corian
Washrooms - SIG Interiors
Washrooms and washroom cubicles - TBS Amwell Ltd
Wastes - Deva Tap Co Ltd
Water saving taps - Delabie UK Ltd
Water taps and mixers - Barber Wilsons & Co Ltd
Waterless Urinals - Relcross Ltd
WC flush controls - Delabie UK Ltd
WC flush valves - Cistermiser Ltd
WC suites - Kohler UK
Wetrooms - Wirquin Ltd
Whirlpool Baths - Jacuzzi® Spa and Bath Ltd
Whirlpools, steam showers - Hansgrohe

N15 Signs/ Notices

3D. Domed labels - Mockridge Labels & Nameplates Ltd
All health & safety signs - Masson Seeley & Co Ltd
Anit-vandal signage - Trico V.E. Ltd (Signage Division)
Anodised aluminium labels - Mockridge Labels & Nameplates Ltd
Architectural aluminium systems for signs - Universal Components Ltd
Architectural signage - Signs & Labels Ltd
Automatic / Self-Testing Emergency Lighting - P4 Limited
Badges - Mockridge Labels & Nameplates Ltd
Banners - GB Sign Solutions Limited
Bespoke Signage - Concept Sign & Display Ltd
Bespoke Signs - The Delabole Slate Co. Ltd
Braille signs - Signs & Labels Ltd
Canvas prints - Francis Frith Collection
Carved stone - Caithness Flagstone Limited
Cast polyester resin molded letters - Metalline Signs Ltd
Cast signs - Signs Of The Times Ltd
CCTV mandatory sinage - Hoyles Electronic Developments Ltd
Chemical Etching - Mockridge Labels & Nameplates Ltd
Coats of arms - Signs Of The Times Ltd
Commemorative plaques, coats of arms and architectural lettering in cast bronze & cast aluminum - Metalline Signs Ltd
Commercial signs - Dee-Organ Ltd
Company logos - Signs Of The Times Ltd
Contract enameling - Trico V.E. Ltd (Signage Division)
Corporate signs - Pryorsign
Custom Made signage - Stocksigns Ltd
Decorative etching - Mockridge Labels & Nameplates Ltd
Design service - Pryorsign
Digital Signage - Concept Sign & Display Ltd
Direction signs - Simplex Signs Limited
Directory systems - Simplex Signs Limited
Doors - Pearce Security Systems
Electric, illuminated and neon signs - Pearce Signs Ltd
Enameling cladding panels - Trico V.E. Ltd (Signage Division)
Engraved metals - Signs Of The Times Ltd
Engraved signs - Signs & Labels Ltd
Engraved slate - Signs Of The Times Ltd
Engravers - Abbey Nameplates
Fabricated signs - Simplex Signs Limited
Financial services signs & structures - Pryorsign
Fingerposts - GB Sign Solutions Limited
GRP structures - Pryorsign
Health and Safety Signage - Stocksigns Ltd
Heritage and conservation signs - Pryorsign
Housesigns - The Delabole Slate Co. Ltd
Illuminated signs - Signs & Labels Ltd
Instrumentation panels - Pryorsign
Large format digital printing - Signs & Labels Ltd
Large format printing - Zephyr The Visual Communicators
LED signs - Pearce Signs Ltd
Marking inks and products - Eyre & Baxter Limited
Metal lettering - Simplex Signs Limited
Nameplates - Eyre & Baxter Limited
Nameplates - Mockridge Labels & Nameplates Ltd
Nameplates & Memorial Tablets in Metal & Plastic - Abbey Nameplates
Notice board material - Forbo Flooring
Notice panels - Stamford Products Limited
Noticeboards, pinboards - Magiboards Ltd
Personnel equipment - RAJA Workplace
Pinboards - Sundeala Ltd
Plaques - GB Sign Solutions Limited
Plaques - stainless steel, brass, engraved - Mockridge Labels & Nameplates Ltd
Poster displays - Fairfield Displays & Lighting Ltd
Printed banner material - Mermet U.K
Road traffic signs - Dee-Organ Ltd
Safety signs - ASCO Extinguishers Co. Ltd
Safety signs - Eyre & Baxter Limited
Safety signs - Fife Fire Engineers & Consultants Ltd
Sign manufacturers - Blaze Signs Ltd
Sign posts - Fabrikat (Nottingham) Ltd
Sign Solutions - Concept Sign & Display Ltd
Sign systems - Signs & Labels Ltd
Signage - Fairfield Displays & Lighting Ltd
Signage - Furnitubes International Ltd
Signage - Mockridge Labels & Nameplates Ltd
Signage & graphics - Komfort Workspace PLC
Signboards - Duroy Fibreglass Mouldings Ltd
Signing Systems - Concept Sign & Display Ltd
Signing Systems - Ward & Co (Letters) Ltd
Signs - Allgood plc
Signs - Dee-Organ Ltd
Signs - Doorfit Products Ltd
Signs - GB Sign Solutions Limited
Signs - Hoyles Electronic Developments Ltd
Signs - design - Masson Seeley & Co Ltd
Signs - manufacture - Masson Seeley & Co Ltd
Signs - site surveying - Masson Seeley & Co Ltd
Signs and Notices - brissco signs & graphics
Signs and notices - Focal Signs Ltd
Signs and notices - Trico V.E. Ltd (Signage Division)
Signs and Plaques - Sign Industries
Signs and sign systems - Simplex Signs Limited
Signs installation - Masson Seeley & Co Ltd
Signs/ notices - Laidlaw Ltd
Signs/ Notices - Leander Architectural
Signs/ notices - Stocksigns Ltd
Signs/notices - Duroy Fibreglass Mouldings Ltd
Signs/notices - Rivermeade Signs Ltd
Stencils - Eyre & Baxter Limited
Traffic management systems - Marshalls Mono Ltd
uv Stable Signage - Trico V.E. Ltd (Signage Division)
Viewpoint window display signs - Pryorsign
Vinyl signs - Invicta Window Films Ltd
Visual communication equipment - Spaceright Europe Limited
Vitreous Enamal Signs - Trico V.E. Ltd (Signage Division)
Waterproof, vandal resistant illuminated, health and safety and shop signs, nameplates and fascias labels - Pryorsign
Wayfinding schemes - Masson Seeley & Co Ltd
Whiteboards - Magiboards Ltd

N16 Bird/ Vermin control

Bait boxes - P+L Systems Ltd
Bird control - South East Bird Control
Bird Nets - P+L Systems Ltd
Bird Spikes - P+L Systems Ltd
Bird/ vermin control - Terminix Property Services
Brushstrip for pest and bird control - Kleeneze Sealtech Ltd
Cladding Insect Mesh - The Flyscreen Company Ltd
Flyscreens - P+L Systems Ltd
Industrial and Commercial Insect Screens - The Flyscreen Company Ltd
Insect Screens - The Flyscreen Company Ltd
Pest Control Services - Rentokil Specialist Hygiene

N20 Safety Equipment

Anti slip metal flooring - Graepels Perforators Ltd
Anti-slip sighting bars - Redman Fisher Engineering
Barriers - Q.M.P
Breathing apparatus - Draeger Safety UK Ltd
Burglary resistant equipment - Chubb Safe Equipment Company
Carbon monoxide detectors - Firemaster Extinguisher Ltd
Confined Space access Equipment - Didsbury Engineering Co Ltd
Confined space equipment - MSA (Britain) Ltd
Davits - Didsbury Engineering Co Ltd
Disabled toilet alarms - Hoyles Electronic Developments Ltd
Domestic safes - Chubb Safe Equipment Company
Domestic smoke alarms - Firemaster Extinguisher Ltd
Emergency evacuation equipment for the mobility impaired - Evac+Chair International Ltd
Emergency Lighting Exit Signs - P4 Limited
Emergency safety showers and eye and face wash units - Pressure Coolers Ltd T/A Maestro Pressure Coolers
Environemental monitoring & measurement equipment - Casella UK
Evacuation Equipment - Enable Access
Explosion containment tubes - Attwater & Sons Ltd
Fall arrest systems and Cable fall arrest systems - Latchways plc
Fire & Burglary Resistant Equipment - Gunnebo UK Limited
Fire blankets - Firemaster Extinguisher Ltd
Fire hose reels - Kidde Fire Protection Services Ltd
Firemaster powder, water, AFFF foam, and carbon dioxide fire extinguishers - Firemaster Extinguisher Ltd
Footwear - industrial - Briggs Industrial Footwear Ltd t/a Briggs Safety Wear
Fragile roof and rooflight covers - Latchways plc
Gas detection equipment - Draeger Safety UK Ltd
Gas detection systems - Blakell Europlacer Ltd
Harnesses, lanyards and fall arrest blocks - **Miller by Honeywell** - Honeywell Safety Products
Hoists - Didsbury Engineering Co Ltd
Industrial footwear - Briggs Industrial Footwear Ltd t/a Briggs Safety Wear
Ladder safety post - Bilco UK Ltd
Ladders and safety cages - Redman Fisher Engineering
Personal Protective Equipment - Briggs Industrial Footwear Ltd t/a Briggs Safety Wear
Personal Protective equipment - MSA (Britain) Ltd
Respiratory filter masks - Draeger Safety UK Ltd
Ropes and sashcords - Marlow Ropes Ltd
Safety & Security - HC Slingsby PLC
Safety and Security Equipment - RAJA Workplace
Safety equipment - Focal Signs Ltd
Safety equipment - Hoyles Electronic Developments Ltd
Safety equipment - Interface Europe Ltd
Safety equipment - Kee Klamp Ltd
Safety equipment - Metreel Ltd
Safety equipment - MSA (Britain) Ltd
Safety equipment - Radiodetection Ltd

N20 Safety Equipment (con't)

Safety eyebolts - Latchways plc
Safety interlocking systems - Castell Safety International
Safety, drench, decontamination, emergency showers and eyebaths - Hughes Safety Showers Limited
Safty systems for Ladder and Roof - Latchways plc
Special purpose safety equipment - Hazard Safety Products Ltd
Sports Markings - Sportsmark Group Ltd
Steel security doorsets - Sunray Engineering Ltd
Vertical access fall safe access ladders - Miller by Honeywell - Honeywell Safety Products
Welding curtains and hangers - Nederman UK
Workwear - Briggs Industrial Footwear Ltd t/a Briggs Safety Wear

N21 Storage Equipment

Adjustable pallet racking - Link 51 (Storage Products)
Aluminium shelving brackets - Tebrax Ltd
Archive storage - Construction Group UK Ltd
Bespoke/Musical instrument storage - Amadeus
Cantilever Racking - Sperrin Metal Products Ltd
Coldstores - Carter Retail Equipment Ltd
Construction products - Link 51 (Storage Products)
Cupboards, lockers - Q.M.P
Desk-side storage units - Rackline Systems Storage Ltd
Document storage shelving systems - Link 51 (Storage Products)
Drum storage - Q.M.P
Filing systems - Construction Group UK Ltd
Heavy duty shelving systems - Link 51 (Storage Products)
Library shelving - Sperrin Metal Products Ltd
Lockers - Aaztec Cubicles
Lockers - Grant Westfield Ltd
Lockers - electronic lock - Helmsman
Lockers - laminate - Helmsman
Lockers - mild steel - Helmsman
Lockers - wooden - Helmsman
Lockers and cubicles - LSA Projects Ltd
Lockers and personal storage - Moresecure Ltd
Lockers, Cloakroom equipment, Cabinets - 3d Storage Systems (UK) LTD
Megyanine Floors - Hi-Store Ltd
Mobile and static shelving equipment - Railex Systems Ltd, Elite Division
Mobile shelving - Construction Group UK Ltd
Mobile shelving - Link 51 (Storage Products)
Moblie shelving systems - Moresecure Ltd
Pallet parking systems - Moresecure Ltd
Pallet Racking - Construction Group UK Ltd
Picking systems - Construction Group UK Ltd
Safes and Key cabinets - Duffells Limited
Shelving - Bedford Shelving Ltd
Shelving - Lesco Products Ltd
Shelving / Racking - Smart F & G (Shopfittings)Ltd
Shelving and storage racking - Construction Group UK Ltd
Shelving Solutions - Storage Solutions Ltd
Small parts storage - Link 51 (Storage Products)
Small storage - Moresecure Ltd
Specialist Joinery - Taskworthy Ltd
Stainless steel cabinets IP65 - Kensal CMS
Storage - Rothley Limited
Storage & shelving equipment - Broxap Ltd
Storage cabinets - Unicorn Containers Ltd
storage equipment - Emmerich (Berlon) Ltd
Storage equipment - Envopak Group Ltd
Storage equipment - Garran Lockers Ltd
Storage Equipment - Hi-Store Ltd
Storage equipment - Kee Klamp Ltd
Storage equipment - Libraco
Storage equipment - Logic Office Contracts
Storage equipment - Project Office Furniture PLC
Storage equipment - Rackline Systems Storage Ltd
Storage equipment - RAJA Workplace
Storage Equipment - SSI Schaefer Ltd
Storage Equipment - Wybone Ltd
Storage furniture - John Pulsford Associates Ltd
Storage systems - Komfort Workspace PLC
Storage systems - Moresecure Ltd
Task lighting - Anglepoise Lighting Ltd
Vanity units - LSA Projects Ltd
Wallstorage systems - Fastwall Ltd
Waste containment - Randalls Fabrications Ltd

N22 Office Equipment

Audiovisual Presentation Systems - AudiocomPendax Ltd
Binders - Quartet-GBC UK Ltd/ ACCO UK Ltd
Church seating & accessories - Knightbridge Furniture Productions Ltd
Computer document paper handling systems - Neopost Ltd
Conference and training room systems - track based - Magiboards Ltd
Desk top products - Lesco Products Ltd
Domestic and commercial office furniture - Ball William Ltd
Education and Office Storage - Stamford Products Limited
Electronic file tracking - Rackline Systems Storage Ltd
Ergonomic products - Lesco Products Ltd
Fire & Burglary Resistant Equipment - Gunnebo UK Limited
Fire resistant cabinets for media and document protection - Chubb Safe Equipment Company
Flipcharts - Magiboards Ltd
Folder-inserter systems - Neopost Ltd
Franking machines - Neopost Ltd
Home office to the housebuilder market - Hammonds - New Home Division
Home Offices - Moores Furniture Group Ltd
Interactive whiteboards - Quartet-GBC UK Ltd/ ACCO UK Ltd
Laminators - Quartet-GBC UK Ltd/ ACCO UK Ltd
Letter openers & extractors - Neopost Ltd
Litter bins and recycling containers - Glasdon UK Limited
Lockers, Cloakroom equipment, Cabinets - 3d Storage Systems (UK) LTD
Magnetic white boards, hooks and drawing pins - Bunting Magnetics Europe Limited
Mailing systems - Neopost Ltd
Mailroom & packaging - HC Slingsby PLC
Mailroom equipment & supplies - Neopost Ltd
Mobile Shelving - Sperrin Metal Products Ltd
Office - RAJA Workplace
Office chairs - KAB Seating Ltd
Office equipment - Carleton Furniture Group Ltd
Office equipment - EFG Office Furniture Ltd
Office equipment - Envopak Group Ltd
Office equipment - HC Slingsby PLC
Office equipment - Libraco
Office Equipment - SSI Schaefer Ltd
Office equipment - Vista Plan International PLC
Office fit out - Staverton (UK) Ltd
Office Fit Out - West London Security
Office furinture - Vitra UK Ltd
Office furniture - Fray Design Ltd
Office furniture - Girsberger London
Office furniture - Haworth UK Ltd
Office furniture - John Pulsford Associates Ltd
Office furniture - Komfort Workspace PLC
Office furniture - Laytrad Contract Furniture Ltd
Office furniture - Progress Work Place Solutions
Office furniture - Project Office Furniture PLC
Office furniture - Staverton (UK) Ltd
Office furniture and accessories - Lesco Products Ltd
Office furniture including storage cabinets and desks - Flexiform Business Furniture Ltd
Office furniture, desking, storage, boardroom and conference furniture - Hands of Wycombe
Office furniture, seating and board room tables - Steelcase Strafor Plc
Office racking, storage cabinets, mobile shelving and filing systems - Rackline Systems Storage Ltd
Office seating - Evertaut Ltd
Office seating - Laytrad Contract Furniture Ltd
Office seating and desking - Metalliform Products Plc
Office storage equipment and desking - Bisley Office Equipment
Offices - Taskworthy Ltd
Pigeon Holes - Jali Ltd
Planning boards - Magiboards Ltd
Post room furniture - Lesco Products Ltd
Postroom equipment & supplies - Neopost Ltd
Printroom equipment - Envopak Group Ltd
PVC printers - Zephyr The Visual Communicators
Rail presentation systems - Quartet-GBC UK Ltd/ ACCO UK Ltd
Reception - Evertaut Ltd
Reception desks/counters - Smith & Choyce Ltd
Residential furniture - Carleton Furniture Group Ltd
Rubber stamps - Eyre & Baxter Limited
Scales, electronic postal - Neopost Ltd
Seating and executive furniture - Verco Office Furniture Ltd
Seating and tables for schools, waiting areas, train stations, airports, ferry terminals, hospitals and surgeries - Hille Educational Products Ltd
Seating equipment - Evertaut Ltd
Shelving - Bedford Shelving Ltd
Shredders - Quartet-GBC UK Ltd/ ACCO UK Ltd
Side-opening tambour cabinets - Rackline Systems Storage Ltd
Software, laserprinting management - Neopost Ltd
Software, mail & despatch management - Neopost Ltd
Staff locators - Magiboards Ltd
Storage and shelving - HC Slingsby PLC
System desking & sorage - Verco Office Furniture Ltd
Tables - offices - Verco Office Furniture Ltd
Task lights - Lesco Products Ltd
Visual display products - Lesco Products Ltd
Work stations & work benches - Moresecure Ltd
Writing boards, Rollerboards, Notice boards, Rail systems - Spaceright Europe Limited

N23 Special purpose fixtures/ furnishings/equipment

Auditorium, theatre, multi purpose, public area and courtroom seating - Race Furniture Ltd
Automatic / Self-Testing Emergency Lighting - P4 Limited
Bar Stools - Sandler Seating Ltd
Barstool systems - Laytrad Contract Furniture Ltd
Bespoke joinery/ counters & desks - Libraco
Binders - Quartet-GBC UK Ltd/ ACCO UK Ltd
Broadcast and audio visual products & services - Streamtec Limited
Canteen Furniture - Sandler Seating Ltd
Classroom furniture and equipment - Metalliform Products Plc
Computer furniture (education) - Klick Technology Ltd
Conference - Evertaut Ltd
Conference and training room systems - track based - Magiboards Ltd
Corporate seating & tables - Knightbridge Furniture Productions Ltd
Dance floor - Felix Design Ltd
Dining tables for schools etc - Metalliform Products Plc
Domestic car turntables - British Turntable Ltd
Education equipment - Evertaut Ltd
Educational equipment - Invicita Plastics Ltd
Educational furniture - Ellis J T & Co Ltd
Educational furniture for science and technology - S & B Ltd
Educational seating and desking - Metalliform Products Plc
Educational workshop equipment - Emmerich (Berlon) Ltd
Exhibition and display - Spaceright Europe Limited
Exhibition, Retail, Graphic and Presentation Systems - RTD Systems Ltd
Flood protection - Straight Ltd
Food technology furniture (education) - Klick Technology Ltd
Furniture design and production - Wales & Wales
Greenhouse accessories for Hartley Greenhouses - Hartley Botanic Ltd
In-Line Thermal Disinfection Unit (ILTDU) - Horne Engineering Ltd
Interactive whiteboards - Quartet-GBC UK Ltd/ ACCO UK Ltd
Laboratory tables - Metalliform Products Plc
Laminators - Quartet-GBC UK Ltd/ ACCO UK Ltd
Library furniture - Metalliform Products Plc
Nursery furniture and equipment - Metalliform Products Plc
Optitherm thermostatic tap - Horne Engineering Ltd
Padlocks and Chain - Duffells Limited
Public area seating - Evertaut Ltd
Rail presentation systems - Quartet-GBC UK Ltd/ ACCO UK Ltd
Raised slating rostra - Felix Design Ltd
Recycling bins, boxes and containers - Straight Ltd
Restaurant Furniture - Sandler Seating Ltd
Sanctuary stages - Felix Design Ltd
Screen printing on whiteboards - Magiboards Ltd
Seating - auditorium, theater, lecture theater, courtroom, conference - Race Furniture Ltd
Seating and tables for schools, waiting areas, train stations, airports, ferry terminals, hospitals and surgeries - Hille Educational Products Ltd
Shelving & Display - Libraco
Special Equipment (mixing Machines for wet-pour Rubber Crumb) - Edward Benton & Co Ltd
Special purpose equipment - Baz-Roll Products Ltd
Special Purpose Fixtures - Harling Security Solutions Limited
Special purpose storage systems - Stamford Products Limited
Stacking chairs - Laytrad Contract Furniture Ltd
Staging - carpet, hard deck, custom build, raised seating - Felix Design Ltd
Staging rostra - Felix Design Ltd
Stainless steel Welded Wire Products and Welded Wire Mesh - Multi Mesh Ltd
Technology furniture (education) - Klick Technology Ltd
Thermostatic mixing valves - Horne Engineering Ltd
Toys & games - Invicita Plastics Ltd
Whiteboard accessories - Magiboards Ltd

N24 Shopfitting

Ambient shelving - Carter Retail Equipment Ltd
Architectural Glass - Creative Glass
Bar railing - William Hopkins & Sons Ltd
Bespoke display cases - The Benbow Group
Bespoke shopfitting - Pearce Security Systems
Boards for shopfitting - Finnish Fibreboard (UK) Ltd
Cash Management systems and lobby shutters - Safetell Ltd
Checkouts - Carter Retail Equipment Ltd
Commercial shelving - Construction Group UK Ltd
Contour showcases - Stamford Products Limited
Counters and showcases - Smart F & G (Shopfittings)Ltd
Decorative tube & fittings - William Hopkins & Sons Ltd
Entrances - Comar Architectural Aluminium Systems
Extrusions - Stamford Products Limited
Fabrics - Mermet U.K
Fast security screen counters - Safetell Ltd
Grabrails - William Hopkins & Sons Ltd
Interior Contracting - Parthos UK Ltd
Maintenance of industrial doors, shutters and shopfronts - Shutter Door Repair & Maintenance Ltd
Passive fire protection - BM TRADA
Point-of-sale, promotional and incentive products - Invicita Plastics Ltd
Premises equipment - HC Slingsby PLC
Refridgerated cabinets - Carter Retail Equipment Ltd
Retail and display fittings - DuPont Corian
Retractable glazed screen counters and secure access systems - Safetell Ltd
Rotary filing cabinets - Rackline Systems Storage Ltd
Screens - Pearce Security Systems
Shelving brackets - Tebrax Ltd
Shelving Solutions - Storage Solutions Ltd
Shop fittings - Stamford Products Limited
Shopfitters - Cumberland Construction
Shopfitting - Blaze Signs Ltd
Shopfitting - Carter Retail Equipment Ltd
Shopfitting - Cil Retail Solutions Ltd
Shopfitting - Kee Klamp Ltd
Shopfitting - Smart F & G (Shopfittings)Ltd
Shopfitting - Steel Line Ltd
Shopfitting - Taskworthy Ltd
Shopfitting - The Benbow Group
Shopfitting and specialist joinery - Barlow Group
Shopfitting and specialist joinery - Barnwood Ltd
Shopfitting products and accessories - RB UK Ltd
Shopfronts - Comar Architectural Aluminium Systems
Shopfronts - Project Aluminium Ltd
Shopfronts and showrooms - Glassolutions Saint-Gobain Ltd
Tube connectors - Stamford Products Limited

N25 Hospital/ Health Equipment

250 Series Mini Sound Shelter - IAC Acoustic Company UK Ltd
350 Series Maxi Sound Shelter - IAC Acoustic Company UK Ltd
Anechoic Rooms - IAC Acoustic Company UK Ltd
Audiology Rooms - IAC Acoustic Company UK Ltd
Bariatric Products - Sidhil Care
Beds - Sidhil Care
Clean rooms and Containment Suites - Envair Ltd
Conduit systems - Marshall-Tufflex Ltd
Couches, Plinths & Treatment Chairs - Sidhil Care
Data management systems - Marshall-Tufflex Ltd
Disabled and elderly equipment - Nicholls & Clarke Ltd
Disposable Antibacterial Hospital Curtains - Marlux Medical Ltd
Disposable hospital products - Verna Ltd
Environmental and waste equipment - RAJA Workplace
First Aid & Treatment Room - Sidhil Care
Flipcharts, hanging rail systems and visual aids - The Visual Systems Healthcare
Floor graphics - The Visual Systems Healthcare
Grabrails - William Hopkins & Sons Ltd
Healthcare - Komfort Workspace PLC
Healthcare fittings - DuPont Corian
Hospital and health equipment - Brandon Medical
Hospital and laboratory equipment - Pland
Hospital Equipment, Elbow control - Shavrin Levatap Co Ltd
Hospital furniture, accessories - Sidhil Care
Hospital Sinks - Pland Stainless Ltd
Hospital/ Health Equipment - Amilake Southern Ltd
Hospital/ health equipment - ArjoHuntleigh UK
Hospital/ Health Equipment - Franke Sissons Ltd
Hospital/ Health Equipment - The Kenco Coffee Company
Hospital/ Health furniture - Klick Technology Ltd
Hospital/health equipment - FC Frost Ltd
Hospital/health equipment - Miele Co Ltd
Hospital/Health Equipment - Wybone Ltd
Hospitol Health equipment - Hospital Metalcraft Ltd
Hotel & Leisure seating & tables - Knightbridge Furniture Productions Ltd
HTM71 medical cabinets - Klick Technology Ltd
Lifting, moving and handling products for disabled - Chiltern Invadex
Living aids, commodes - Sidhil Care
Lockable and Confidential notice boards - The Visual Systems Healthcare
Lockers, Cloakroom equipment, Cabinets - 3d Storage Systems (UK) LTD
Magnetic indicators and symbols - The Visual Systems Healthcare
Mattresses - Sidhil Care
Medical and first aid furniture - Hospital Metalcraft Ltd
Medical examination lamps - Wandsworth Elecrtrical Ltd
Medical storage systems - Stamford Products Limited
Medical supplies - Kimberly-Clark Ltd
Nursing Chairs, Lifting aids - Sidhil Care
Overbed tables - Sidhil Care
Pedal bins - Unicorn Containers Ltd
Roller boards - The Visual Systems Healthcare
Seating and tables for schools, waiting areas, train stations, airports, ferry terminals, hospitals and surgeries - Hille Educational Products Ltd
Shower enclosures & Shower - Contour Showers Ltd
Slophers - Pland Stainless Ltd
Sprung mattresses, divan bases, pillows and accessories - Airsprung Beds Ltd
Stainless steel shelving systems for sterile areas - Bedford Shelving Ltd
Steel Trunking systems - Marshall-Tufflex Ltd
Support systems for elderly/disabled - Norton Engineering Alloys Co Ltd
Supportive bathroom products for disabled people - Pressalit Care
Surgeons scrub up trough - Pland Stainless Ltd
Swivel and fixed frame boards - The Visual Systems Healthcare
Trolleys - Sidhil Care
Water taps and mixers - Barber Wilsons & Co Ltd
White boards - The Visual Systems Healthcare
X-ray door sets - Lami Doors UK Ltd
X-ray Doorsets - Humphrey & Stretton PLC

N26 Gymnastic/ Sport/ Play Equipment

Activity Nets - HAGS SMP
Automatic slatted pvc swimming pool covers - Grando (UK) Ltd
Changing room equipment - Broxap Ltd
Cloakroom rails - HEWI UK Ltd
Dojo Matting - Fighting Films
Dojo matting - Geemat
Drama staging - Felix Design Ltd
Furniture, leisure - The Senator Group
Goals, Groundmans Supplies, Nets and Sports Equipment - Sportsmark Group Ltd
Golf tee mats & frames - Evergreens Uk
GRP and plaster castings and molds - J W Green Swimming Pools Ltd
Gymnastic matting - Continental Sports Ltd
Gymnastic/sport/play equipment - Kee Klamp Ltd
Hydrotherapy pools - Aqua-Blue Designs
Judo Matts - Fighting Films
Judo matts - Geemat

N26 Gymnastic/ Sport/ Play Equipment (con't)

Lockers, Cloakroom equipment, Cabinets - 3d Storage Systems (UK) LTD
Maintenance service - Continental Sports Ltd
Multi-Use Games Areas and Multi-Play units - HAGS SMP
Nappy changers - LSA Projects Ltd
Outdoor Fitness equipment - HAGS SMP
Panel pool kits - Golden Coast Ltd
Physical education equipment - Continental Sports Ltd
Playground equipment - HAGS SMP
Playground equipment - Lappset UK Ltd
Playground equipment and associated works - Kompan Ltd
Saunas, steam rooms and jacazzi spa pools - Aqua-Blue Designs
Seating - cinema, public area - Race Furniture Ltd
Spare parts - Continental Sports Ltd
Sports Arena/Grounds PVC-u Fencing and Barriers - Duralock (UK) Ltd
Sports Covers - Power Plastics Ltd
Sports equipment - Continental Sports Ltd
Stadia and auditorium seating - Metalliform Products Plc
Swimming Pool Designs - Aqua-Blue Designs
Swimming pools and equipment - Golden Coast Ltd
Trampoline equipment - Continental Sports Ltd
Vanity units - Helmsman

N27 Cleaning Equipment

Brooms - Cottam Brush Ltd
Carpet cleaning machines - Nilfisk Limited
Cleaning & Waste - HC Slingsby PLC
Cleaning equipment - ArjoHuntleigh UK
Cleaning equipment - Donaldson Filtration (GB) Ltd
Cleaning equipment - Interface Europe Ltd
Cleaning equipment - Monument Tools Ltd
Cleaning maintenance equipment - Cento Engineering Company Ltd
Cleaning materials suppliers - Spontex Ltd
Cleaning Products - SC Johnson Wax
Floor polishers & burnishers - Nilfisk Limited
Hand cleaner - Ciret Limited
Industrial and commercial scrubbers, vacuum cleaners and floor maintenance equipment - Nilfisk Advance Ltd
Industrial and commercial vacuum cleaners - Quirepace Ltd
Maintenance, polish and cleaning chemicals - Cleenol Group Ltd
Portable vacuum cleaners - Barloworld Vacuum Technology Plc
Power washers - Nilfisk Limited
Pressure washers - Industrial - Nilfisk Limited
Scrubber driers - Nilfisk Limited
Specialist brushes - Cottam Brush Ltd
Sweepers - Nilfisk Limited
Vacuum cleaners - Commercial & industrial - Nilfisk Limited
Wire Brushes - Cottam Brush Ltd

N28 Laboratory furniture/ equipment

Bench top extraction - Nederman UK
Ceramic and acrylic sanitaryware - Armitage Shanks Ltd
Creteangle vibrating tables - Edward Benton & Co Ltd
Design, manufacture and installation of laboratory furniture and fume cupboards - Lab Systems Furniture Ltd
Gas isolation and detection - TCW Services (Control) Ltd
Industrial laboratory furniture - S & B Ltd
Lab Furniture - Köttermann Ltd
Laboratory design and build project management - Fisher Scientific (UK) Ltd
Laboratory Equipment - Edward Benton & Co Ltd
Laboratory furniture - Grant Westfield Ltd
Laboratory furniture - John Pulsford Associates Ltd
Laboratory Furniture - Simplylabs Limited
Laboratory furniture - Trespa UK Ltd
Laboratory furniture (education) - Klick Technology Ltd
Laboratory furniture/ equipment - Benton Co Ltd Edward
Laboratory furniture/equipment - FC Frost Ltd
Laboratory furniture/equipment - Franke Sissons Ltd
Laboratory furniture/equipment - Miele Co Ltd
Laboratory Sinks - Pland Stainless Ltd
Primary & Secondary Pharaceutical Solutions - Envair Ltd
Reprographic room equipment - Envopak Group Ltd
Shelving - Bedford Shelving Ltd

N29 Industrial Equipment

Access equipment - HC Slingsby PLC
Aero-Engine Test Control System - IAC Acoustic Company UK Ltd
Bowl Pressings - Pland Stainless Ltd
Commercial and industrial equipment - HC Slingsby PLC
Handling & lifting - HC Slingsby PLC
Hopper feeder systems - Benton Co Ltd Edward
Industrial equipment - Benton Co Ltd Edward
Industrial equipment - Edward Benton & Co Ltd
Industrial Equipment - Emmerich (Berlon) Ltd
Industrial Equipment - Harling Security Solutions Limited
Industrial equipment - Kee Klamp Ltd
Industrial equipment - Monument Tools Ltd
Industrial equipment - bins - Unicorn Containers Ltd
Industrial instrumentation - ABB Instrumentation Ltd
Industrial shelving - Construction Group UK Ltd
Industrial turntables - British Turntable Ltd
Industrial workbenches and storage drawer cabinets - Q.M.P
Key Blanks and Machines - Duffells Limited
Magnetic holding etc - Bunting Magnetics Europe Limited
Maintenance of industrial doors, shutters and shopfronts - Shutter Door Repair & Maintenance Ltd
Manual handling equipment - Hymo Ltd
Packaging - RAJA Workplace
Paint brushes, rollers and brooms - Cottam Brush Ltd
Power plant noise control systems - IAC Acoustic Company UK Ltd
Ropes and sashcords - Marlow Ropes Ltd
Specialist brushes - Cottam Brush Ltd
Surveying instruments - Topcon GB Ltd
Trolleys and trucks - Q.M.P
Ultra violet chambers, lamps and control panels - Hanovia Ltd
Vehicle livery - Signs & Labels Ltd
Vibratory equipment and moulds - Benton Co Ltd Edward
Workshop equipment - HC Slingsby PLC
X-ray door sets - Lami Doors UK Ltd

N30 Laundry Equipment

Clothes lines - James Lever 1856 Ltd
Domestic appliances - Miele Co Ltd
Finishing equipment - Electrolux Laundry Systems
Hydro extractors - Electrolux Laundry Systems
Ironing tables - Electrolux Laundry Systems
Laundry equipment - Girbau UK ltd
Linen chutes - Hardall International Ltd
Roller ironers - Electrolux Laundry Systems
Tumble dryers - Electrolux Laundry Systems
Washers, dryers and ironers - Warner Howard Group Ltd
Washing machines - Electrolux Laundry Systems

N31 Entertainment/ Auditorium equipment

Acoustic Doorsets - Humphrey & Stretton PLC
Architectural dimming systems - Mode Lighting (UK) Ltd
AV Screens - Harkness Screens
Conference Equipment - Spaceright Europe Limited
Entertainment/ Auditorium Equipment - Harkness Screens
Exhibition, Retail, Graphic and Presentation Systems - RTD Systems Ltd
Seating: Auditorium, Lecture theatre, Theater and Stadium - Evertaut Ltd

P10 Sundry insulation/ proofing work/ fire stops

Acoustic design - Sound Reduction Systems Ltd
Acoustic door seals - AET.gb Ltd
Acoustic Doors - Amadeus
Acoustic flooring - Interfloor Limited
Acoustic insulation - InstaGroup Ltd
Acoustic insulation - Knauf Insulation Ltd
Acoustic insulation - The Sound Solution
Acoustic panels - AET.gb Ltd
Acoustic Treatment - Amadeus
Automatic fire barrier-curtains - Cooper Group Ltd
Automatic fire shutters - Cooper Group Ltd
Bitumen building papers, film/paper laminated papers - Package Products Ltd
Ceilings, floors and roofs - Promat UK Ltd
cold seal paper - Package Products Ltd
Expanded polystyrene insulation - Jablite Ltd
Expanded polystyrene insulation - Springvale E P S
External Wall Insulations - Skanda Acoustics Limited
Extruded polystyrene insulation - Dow Building Solutions
Fiberglass fabrics - Fothergill Engineered Fabrics Ltd
Fibreglass loft insulation - Davant Products Ltd
Fire Barriers - Gridpart Interiors Ltd
Fire collars - FloPlast Ltd
Fire doors and doorsets - Bridgman IBC Ltd
Fire proof cladding - Firebarrier International Ltd T/A Firebarrier Services Ltd
Fire proof panels - Hemsec Panel Technologies
Fire proofing board - Dufaylite Developments Ltd
Fire Protection - Knauf Insulation Ltd
Fire protection casings - Cryotherm Insulation Ltd
Fire protection for ductwork, seals and joints - Promat UK Ltd
Fire resisting partitions - Mann McGowan Group
Fire sound and thermal soloutions - Siniat Ltd
Fire stopping systems - Cryotherm Insulation Ltd
Fire stops - FGF Ltd
Fire stops - Fire Protection Ltd
Fire stops - Quelfire Limited
Fire stops around pipes - Walraven Ltd
Fire stops for cables pipes and ductwork - Quelfire Limited
Fire stops for joints - Quelfire Limited
Fire walls - Gilmour Ecometal
Fire walls and barriers - Cryotherm Insulation Ltd
Firestopping materials - PFC Corofil
Flame Retardant Boards - Meyer Timber Limited
Flat roof insulation - Isocrete Floor Screeds Ltd
Floor insulation - Springvale E P S
Foamglas Cellular glass insulation for cut to falls roof systems - Pittsburgh Corning (United Kingdom) Limited
Foamglas Cellular glass internal and external insulation for roof, wall, floor, below ground conditions and foundations - Pittsburgh Corning (United Kingdom) Limited
Full-Fire Certificate - Firebarrier International Ltd T/A Firebarrier Services Ltd
Hot and cold water cylinder jackets - Davant Products Ltd
Insuation panels - Cryotherm Insulation Ltd
Insulaion for Heating and Ventilation - Kingspan Industrial Ins. Ltd
Insulation - British Gypsum Ltd
Insulation - Covers Timber & Builders Merchants
Insulation - Nevill Long
Insulation - Rockwool Ltd
Insulation - Steico
Insulation - Industrial Solutions - Actavo (UK) Ltd
Insulation for Process industries - Kingspan Industrial Ins. Ltd
Insulation Products - Allmat (East Surrey) Ltd
Insulation, fire protection and fire stopping - Kitsons Insulation Products Ltd
Intermescant fire and smoke seals - Mann McGowan Group
Intumescent fire seals - Humphrey & Stretton PLC
Intumescent Firestop - Dow Corning Europe S.A
Nullifire fire stopping range - Nullifire Ltd
paritions and external walls - Promat UK Ltd
PIR Fire rated panels - Hemsec Panel Technologies
PIR insulated panels - Hemsec Panel Technologies
Polyethylene and PVC pipe insulation - Davant Products Ltd
Polythene vapor barrier - Visqueen Building Products
Rigid insulation boards - Kingspan Insulation Ltd
Rigid thermal board - National Insulation Association Ltd
Roof insulation - Dow Building Solutions
Roof insulation - Springvale E P S
Seals - Mann McGowan Group
Self sealing test plugs - Walraven Ltd
Seperating Floors - Sound Service (Oxford) Ltd
Servery fire curtain-industrial/commercial/residential - Cooper Group Ltd
Solid wall insulation - National Insulation Association Ltd
Sound absorbtion panels - Henkel Ltd
Sound insulation - Sound Service (Oxford) Ltd
Sound insulation systems/containers - Mansfield Pollard & Co Ltd
Sound proof Acoustic Rooms - Amadeus
Sound Proofing - InstaGroup Ltd
Sound proofing - The Sound Solution
soundproofing materials - Bicester Products Ltd
Spray Foam Insulation - Foamseal Ltd
Sprayed Vermiculite - Thermica Ltd
Standard corkboard - Gradient Insulations (UK) Ltd
Sundry Insulation - Strand Hardware Ltd
Sundry insulation/ proofing work/ fire Stops - Polypipe Building Products
Sundry insulation/proofing work/ fire stops - Knauf Insulation Ltd
Tapered Rockwool - Gradient Insulations (UK) Ltd
Tapered, corkboard, cork/PUR composite, polystyrene and PUR - Gradient Insulations (UK) Ltd
Thatch Firewall Membrane - Thatching Advisory Services Ltd
Thermal dry lining - National Insulation Association Ltd
Thermal insulation boards & quilts - Skanda Acoustics
Trade Association - Association of Specialist Fire Protection (ASFP)
Urethane foam industry trade association - British Urethane Foam Contractors Association
Vessel,Tank and Pipe insulation - NMC (UK) Ltd
Wall insulation - Springvale E P S
Wax coated paper - Package Products Ltd

P11 Foamed/ Fibre/ Bead cavity wall insulation

Bead cavity wall insulation - National Insulation Association Ltd
British wall cavity insulation - Kleeneze Sealtech Ltd
Cavity wall insulation and loft insulation - InstaGroup Ltd
Expanded polystyrene insulation - Jablite Ltd
External wall insulation - Weber Building Solutions
Extruded polystyrene - Knauf Insulation Ltd
Fibre cavity wall insulation - Knauf Insulation Ltd
Foamed/ Fibre/ Bead cavity wall insulation - Polypipe Building Products
Insulation - FGF Ltd
Insulation Products - Allmat (East Surrey) Ltd
Mineral wool cavity wall insulation - National Insulation Association Ltd
Polyisocyanurate insulation board manufacture - Celotex Ltd
Sprayed Vermiculite - Thermica Ltd
Urethane foam industry trade association - British Urethane Foam Contractors Association

P20 Unframed isolated trims/ skirtings/ sundry items

Architectural and decorative mouldings - Mason FW & Sons Ltd
Architectural trims - Rockwell Sheet Sales Ltd
Architraue - Enfield Speciality Doors
Bath and Kitchen Trims - Homelux Nenplas
Cellular PVC window trims, skirtings & architraves - celuform - Celuform Building Products
Finger Guards - Safety Assured Ltd
Fixings for fall arrest and safety - Bacon Group
Hardwood - Panel Agency Limited
Hardwood mouldings - Atkinson & Kirby Ltd
Hardwoods - James Donaldson Timber
MDF moldings - Fibercill
MDF Mouldings (Silktrim) - James Donaldson Timber
Metal Trims - Homelux Nenplas
Perimeter Casing Systems - Jali Ltd
Plastic and Foam Components - NMC (UK) Ltd
Plastic handrails - Brighton (Handrails), W
Protection rails and corner angles - Harrison Thompson & Co Ltd
PVC trims, angles & edges - Homelux Nenplas
Rope and harness - Baj System Design Ltd
Simulated wood mouldings, reproduction oak beams - Oakleaf Reproductions Ltd
Skirting - Enfield Speciality Doors
Softwoods: Mouldings, CLS, Clear softwoods - James Donaldson Timber
Trims/ skirtings - Jali Ltd
UPVC Plaster Beading & Trims - Homelux Nenplas
Veneered MDF Mouldings - James Donaldson Timber

P21 Door/ Window ironmongery

Architectural door furniture and security hardware - Allgood plc
Architectural Hardware - Allegion (UK) Ltd
Architectural Hardware - Duffells Limited
Architectural hardware - Laidlaw Ltd
Architectural hardware including hinges, locks, levers, flush bolts and other ancilliary items including ceiling fans - James Gibbons Format Ltd
Architectural hinges, door closers and thresholds - Relcross Ltd
Architectural ironmomgery - Samuel Heath & Sons plc
Architectural ironmongerers - Moffett Thallon & Co Ltd
Architectural ironmongery - Doorfit Products Ltd
Architectural ironmongery - Hafele UK Ltd
Architectural ironmongery, cabinet hardware and fittings - Lord Isaac Ltd
Bespoke Ironmongery Package Provision - Strada London
Black Antique Ironmongery - Kirkpatrick Ltd
Brass furniture fittings - Martin & Co Ltd
Brass hardware - Marcus M Ltd
Brass, bronze door and window hardware - Allart, Frank, & Co Ltd
Brush strip door and window seals - Kleeneze Sealtech Ltd
Brushstrip door and letterbox seals - Kleeneze Sealtech Ltd
Butt hinges - Caldwell Hardware (UK) Ltd
Catches & bolts - Caldwell Hardware (UK) Ltd
Closers and Panic Hardware - Duffells Limited
Concealed door closers - Samuel Heath & Sons plc
Cotton twine - James Lever 1856 Ltd
Cupboard fittings - Samuel Heath & Sons plc
Door & window control equipment - GEZE UK
Door & window ironmongery - Olby H E & Co Ltd
Door / window ironmongery - Brass Art Ltd
Door closers - Exidor Limited
Door entry equipment - The Safety Letterbox Company Ltd
Door furniture - ASSA ABLOY Ltd
Door furniture - HEWI UK Ltd
Door furniture - Samuel Heath & Sons plc
Door hardware - ASSA ABLOY Limited
Door hardware - ASSA ABLOY Ltd
Door ironmongery - Dorma Door Services Ltd
Door Locks - Bramah Security Equipment Ltd
Door Operators/Closers & Accessories - Abloy UK
Door/ Window ironmongery - Schlegel UK (2006) Ltd
Door/ Window ironmongery - Till & Whitehead Ltd
door/window iironmongery - UK Fasteners Ltd
Door/Window Ironmongery - Crowthorne Fencing
Door/Window Ironmongery - Daro UK Ltd
Door/window ironmongery - Hart Door Systems Ltd
Door/window ironmongery - Magnet Ltd
Door/Window ironmongery - Roto Frank Ltd
Dor plates - Fixatrad Ltd
Draught, weather, intumescent, fire and smoke seals - Sealmaster
Draught/Acoustic Seal - Dixon International Group Ltd
Duncombe - Exidor Limited
Electric Door Operator - Relcross Ltd
Emergency exit door hardware - Exidor Limited
Emergency exit hardware - VBH (GB) Ltd
Espagnolette locking systems - Nico Manufacturing Ltd
Fire door motors and controls - GfA UK Ltd
Fire door operating equipment - GfA UK Ltd
Flyscreens - P+L Systems Ltd
Folding openers - Caldwell Hardware (UK) Ltd
Furniture castors and hardware - A Kenrick & Sons
Gas springs - Arvin Motion Control Ltd
Glazing trade association - Glass and Glazing Federation
Gloro door furniture - Focus SB Ltd
Hardware - Reddiglaze Ltd
Hardware for windows and doors - Avocet Hardware Ltd
Hardware for windows and doors - Roto Frank Ltd
High security locks and locking systems - Abloy UK
Hinges - Cooke Brothers Ltd
Hotel locking - Allegion (UK) Ltd
Industrial locks - ASSA ABLOY Ltd
Intumescent fire stopping products - Sealmaster
Ironmongery - Allegion (UK) Ltd
Ironmongery - Caldwell Hardware (UK) Ltd
Ironmongery - Carl F Groupco Limited
Ironmongery - Challenge Fencing Ltd
Ironmongery - Covers Timber & Builders Merchants
Ironmongery - Eliza Tinsley Ltd

P21 Door/ Window ironmongery (con't)

Ironmongery - Grorud Industries Ltd
Ironmongery - Harris & Bailey Ltd
Ironmongery - Hipkiss, H, & Co Ltd
Ironmongery - Maco Door & Window Hardware (UK) Ltd
Ironmongery - Strand Hardware Ltd
Ironmongery - Weyland incorporating Clayton Munroe
Leading manufacturer for door and window furnitures - HOPPE (UK) Ltd
Locks - Aardee Security Shutters Ltd
Locks - Guardian Lock & Engineering Co. Ltd
Locks - Lowe & Fletcher Ltd
Locks and Security - Duffells Limited
Locks, Door number plates - 3d Storage Systems (UK) LTD
Locksmiths - Doorfit Products Ltd
Magnetic door stops and catches - Bunting Magnetics Europe Limited
Mail boxes, door closers, door furniture, door locks and cylinders - JB Architectural Ltd
Manual and electrical systems for opening windows - Dyer Environmental Controls
Multipoints and UPVC - Duffells Limited
Padlocks - Bramah Security Equipment Ltd
Padlocks - Securikey Ltd
Padlocks security products, cyclelocks and motorcycle locks - Henry Squire & Sons Ltd
Panic Exit Hardware - Abloy UK
Panic hardware - ASSA ABLOY Ltd
Patio hardware - Caldwell Hardware (UK) Ltd
Pivot hinges - Caldwell Hardware (UK) Ltd
Profile cylinder master keying service - VBH (GB) Ltd
Push button and combination locks - Relcross Ltd
Restrictors - Caldwell Hardware (UK) Ltd
Rim, mortice, padlocks, cylinders and panic escape locks - Yale Security Products Ltd
Roller shutter motors and controls - GfA UK Ltd
Rolling Fire Shutters - Avon Industrial Doors Ltd
Roof windows and ventilators - NuLite Ltd
Ropes and sashcords - Marlow Ropes Ltd
Sah window hardware and accessories - Garador Ltd
Sash balances - Caldwell Hardware (UK) Ltd
Sash cord - James Lever 1856 Ltd
Sash Window Locks - Bramah Security Equipment Ltd
Sectional door motors and controls - GfA UK Ltd
Secure Letterboxes - The Safety Letterbox Company Ltd
Security Door Hardware - Exidor Limited
Security Equipment - Gunnebo UK Limited
Security Grills - O'Connor Fencing Limited
Security products - Marcus M Ltd
Security products, black ironmongery and hardware - ERA Home Security Ltd
Shelving brackets - decorative - Winther Browne & co Ltd
Shootbolt Locking Systems - Nico Manufacturing Ltd
Sliding door gear - Avon Industrial Doors Ltd
Sliding Door Gear - Lakeside Group
Smoke ventilation systems - Dyer Environmental Controls
Specialist ironmongery - The Cotswold Casement Company
Steel Hinged Doors for Fire Exits - Avon Industrial Doors Ltd
Trickle Ventilations - Rytons Building Products Ltd
Weatherstriping joinery seal, roof cappings, glazing bars and ridge systems - Exitex Ltd
Weatherstripping - Reddiglaze Ltd
Window and door hardware - PVCu, timber and aluminum - VBH (GB) Ltd
Window and door ironmongery - Laird Security Hardware
Window furniture - Samuel Heath & Sons plc
Window Locks - Bramah Security Equipment Ltd

P22 Sealant joints

Acoustic seals - Mann McGowan Group
Adhesives - Geocel Ltd
Bath and kitchen seals - Homelux Nenplas
Building chemicals - Geocel Ltd
Expansion joints - Fillcrete Ltd
Expansion Joints - Movement Joints (UK)
Expansion joints - Pitchmastic PmB Ltd
Fire resistant expansion joint seals - Mann McGowan Group
Joint fillers - Fosroc Ltd
Joint sealants - Fosroc Ltd
Joint sealants - SCP Concrete Sealing Technology Ltd
Jointing & tooling - The BSS Group
Jointing compounds - The BSS Group
Jointing compounds, quick repair products and solder & flux - Fernox
Jointing materials - TEAM INDUSTRIAL SERVICES (UK) LIMITED
Mechanical movement joints and fire rated sealants - Compriband Ltd
Profiled sealants - Henkel Ltd
Sealant joints - Firebarrier International Ltd T/A Firebarrier Services Ltd
Sealants - Geocel Ltd
Sealants, solvents, wood preservatives and creosote - Bartoline Ltd
Seals and Caulking Profiles - Trelleborg Sealing Profiles Germany GmbH
Seals for doors, windows, glazing - Schlegel UK (2006) Ltd
Silicone sealants - Bluestar Silicones
Weather draft seals - Mann McGowan Group

P30 Trenches/ Pipeways/Pits for buried engineering services

Chambers - Tyco Water Works
Hydroelectric Energy/Power pipe - Radius Systems Ltd
Meter Boxes - Tyco Water Works
Pipeways - Polypipe Civils
Plastic Drainage System - Hepworth Building Products Ltd
Trench Cover - MCL Composites Ltd
Underground chambers - MCL Composites Ltd

P31 Holes/ Chases/ Covers/ Supports for services

Access covers - Bilco UK Ltd
Access Covers and Panels - Surespan Ltd
Access floor service outlet boxes and grommet outlets - Electrak International Ltd
Aluminium and brass recessed floor access covers - Howe Green Ltd
Builders cast iron products - Dudley Thomas Ltd
Cabinets - Glasdon U.K. Limited
Channel Supports - Kem Edwards Ltd
Electrical fixings - Walraven Ltd
Enclosures - Glasdon U.K. Limited
Inlet cabinets - Delta Fire
Manhole covers - MCL Composites Ltd
Mechanical Pipe Supports - Kem Edwards Ltd
Micro Trenching Compound – StarPolymers TRENCH - Star Uretech Ltd
Pipe support componants - Walraven Ltd
Radiator cabinets / covers - Winther Browne & co Ltd
Roll grooving machine - Hilmor
Stainless steel access covers - Howe Green Ltd

Q10 Kerbs/ Edgings/Channels/Paving accessories

Car Park Marking - Sportsmark Group Ltd
Cast Pavament Lights - The Pavement Light Company
Channel Drainage System - EBP Building Products Ltd
Channels - Polypipe Civils
Cills, lintols, steps - Forest of Dean Stone Firms Ltd
Combined kerb/drainage units, Grease traps, Protective skirting - ACO Technologies plc
Edgings and copings - Oakdale (Contracts) Ltd
Floor & Line markings - Kenyon Paints Limited
Garden edgings - York Handmade Brick Co Ltd
Granite kerbs - CED Ltd
Grass concrete blocks - Armortec
GRC surface water channels - Althon Ltd
Handcut & Masoned - Yorkstone - Hard York Quarries Ltd
Kerbing - Rediweld Rubber & Plastics Ltd
Kerbing & Paving - Gearing F T Landscape Services Ltd
Kerbing, drainage, brickwork, road planing and white lining - AMK Fence-In Limited
Kerbs - Harris & Bailey Ltd
Kerbs / Edgings / Channels / Paving Accessories - Formpave Ltd
Kerbs and accessories - Brett Landscaping
Kerbs edgings - Stowell Concrete Ltd
Kerbs, edgings, Channels, Paving accessavial - Grass Concrete Ltd
Kerbs/ Edgings/Channels/Paving accessories - Vetter UK
Kerbs/ Edgings/Channels/Paving accessories, Bowling ditch channels and athletics kerbs - Sportsmark Group Ltd
Kerbs/ Edgings/Channels/Paving stone accessories - Johnsons Wellfield Quarries Ltd
Kerbs/Edgings/channels/pavind accessories - Townscape Products Ltd
Landscape Suppliers - Crowthorne Fencing
Leaks to Pavement lights Repairs - The Pavement Light Company
Lens Repairs to Pavement lights - The Pavement Light Company
Living stone paving - Armortec
Marking - Moravia (UK) Ltd
Natural Stone Kerbs - Palladio Stone
Pavement Lights, Supply and Installation - The Pavement Light Company
Pavers - Baggeridge Brick PLC
Paving slab supports - Compriband Ltd
Precast concrete products - Ruthin Precast Concrete Ltd
Precast concrete surface water channels - Althon Ltd
Reclaimed Kerbs - Milestone Reclaim and Landscaping Ltd
Repairs to Pavement Lights - The Pavement Light Company
Reseals to Pavement Lights - The Pavement Light Company
Road Blockers - Darfen Durafencing
Road Stud - Sportsmark Group Ltd
Sidewalk prisms, Supply and Installation - The Pavement Light Company
Sleeping Policemen - Sportsmark Group Ltd
Specialist Kerbs - Brett Landscaping
Stone suppliers - Kerridge Stone Ltd
Synthetic ironoxide colouring agents - LANXESS Inorganic Pigments Group
Traffic Calmings - Moravia (UK) Ltd
Traffic Regulations - Moravia (UK) Ltd
Vault Lights, Supply and Installation - The Pavement Light Company
White Lining - Sportsmark Group Ltd

Q20 Granular sub-bases to roads/ pavings

Clay Pavers - Hanson Building Products
Crushed & graded stone - Aggregates - Hard York Quarries Ltd

Q21 Insitu concrete roads/ pavings/ bases

Insitu concrete roads/ pavings/ bases (Concrete repair) - Tarmac - Specialist Products (Packed Highway Products)
Insitu concrete roads/ pavings/ bases (Permeable concrete) - Tarmac Trading Limited (Readymix Concrete & Screed)
Insitu concrete roads/pavings/bases - Grass Concrete Ltd
Movement Joints - Movement Joints (UK)
Resin bonded surfacing, Resin bound surfacing, Repair mortars - Ronacrete Ltd

Q22 Coated macadam/ Asphalt roads/ pavings

Anti Slip Surface - Sportsmark Group Ltd
Ashphalt road reinforcement - Bekaert Building Products
Asphalt Roads - Gearing F T Landscape Services Ltd
Asphalt, tar macadam roads/ pavings - AMK Fence-In Limited
Bitumen macadam, hot rolled asphalt, and sub base aggregates - Breedon Aggregates
Bituminous Binders Road Surface Dressing - Colas Ltd
Coated macadam/ Asphalt roads/ pavings (Asphalt repair) - Tarmac - Specialist Products (Packed Highway Products)
Colours for Asphalt - Procter Johnson & Co Ltd
Ironwork installation: Bedding and Locking – StarPolymers IRONBED, IRONLOCK - Star Uretech Ltd
Mastic Asphalt roads/ pavings - North Herts Asphalte (Roofing) Ltd
Movement Joints - Movement Joints (UK)
Paver hire - Breedon Aggregates
Permanent Pothole Repair – StarPolymers POTHOLE System - Star Uretech Ltd
Red macadam - Breedon Aggregates
Reflective tarffic markings - Reflecting Roadstuds Ltd
Resin bonded surfacing, Resin bound surfacing, Pot hole repair - Ronacrete Ltd
Synthetic ironoxide colouring agents - LANXESS Inorganic Pigments Group

Q23 Gravel/ Hoggin/ Woodchip roads/ pavings

Bark - Milestone Reclaim and Landscaping Ltd
Decorative Aggregates - Brett Landscaping
Decorative aggregates - CED Ltd
Footpath gravels & hoggin - CED Ltd
Gravel/ Hoggin/ pavings - Tarmac Trading Limited (Aggregates)
Gravel/ Hoggin/ Woodchip roads/ pavings - Topscape/Topsport - Tarmac Trading Limited
Living stone decorative aggregates - Armortec
Loose aggregates - B & M Fencing Limited
Slate chippings - The Delabole Slate Co. Ltd

Q24 Interlocking brick/ block roads/ pavings

Block Paving - B & M Fencing Limited
Block paving - Thakeham Tiles Ltd
Block pavings - AMK Fence-In Limited
Blockpaving contractors - Gearing F T Landscape Services Ltd
Clay block paving - Oakdale (Contracts) Ltd
Clay pavers - Ibstock Brick Ltd
Clay pavers - Marshalls Mono Ltd
Concrete Block Kerbs - Brett Landscaping
Concrete block paving - CEMEX
Concrete Block Permeable Paving - Brett Landscaping
Interlocking block pavings - Formpave Ltd
Interlocking brick/ block roads/ pavings - Grass Concrete Ltd
Pavers - Baggeridge Brick PLC
Pavers - Ibstock Building Products Ltd
Pavers - York Handmade Brick Co Ltd
Paving - Townscape Products Ltd
Paving - block - Brett Landscaping
Paving/ hard landscaping - Blanc de Bierges
Pavings - Ennis-Flint
Pavings - York Handmade Brick Co Ltd
Porcelain paving - Alfresco Floors
Q24 Concrete Block Paving - Brett Landscaping
Staffordshire Clay paving - Ketley Brick Co Ltd , The
Synthetic ironoxide colouring agents - LANXESS Inorganic Pigments Group

Q25 Slab/ Brick/ Sett/ Cobble pavings

Armorflex concrete mattresses - Armortec
Boulders, cobbles and pebbles - CED Ltd
Clay pavers - Hanson Building Products
Clay Pavers - Ruabon Sales Limited
Cobbles - York Handmade Brick Co Ltd
Concrete Flag Paving - Brett Landscaping
Concrete paving - Ebema - Alfresco Floors
Concrete slab, block paving - Marshalls Mono Ltd
Decorative precast paving - Oakdale (Contracts) Ltd
Granite paving - CED Ltd
Granite setts - CED Ltd
Grass reinforcement systems - Grass Concrete Ltd
Heavyside paving - Oakdale (Contracts) Ltd
Landscape Suppliers - Crowthorne Fencing
Landscaping - J Suttle Swanage Quarries Ltd
Limestone paving - CED Ltd
Municipal Paving - Hye Oak
Natural Stone Cobbles & Setts - Palladio Stone
Natural Stone Paving - Brett Landscaping
Natural stone paving - Marshalls Mono Ltd
Pavers - Baggeridge Brick PLC
Paving - Burlington Slate Ltd
Paving - Forest of Dean Stone Firms Ltd
Paving - Forterra Building Products Ltd
Paving - sett - Brett Landscaping
Paving slabs - Stowell Concrete Ltd
Paving, Gravels, Aggregates, Steps, Circles, Pebbles, Cobbles & Setts - Milestone Reclaim and Landscaping Ltd
Pavings - Ennis-Flint
Pavings - Ruthin Precast Concrete Ltd
Paviors - Kingscourt Country Manor Bricks
Porphyry setts and edging - CED Ltd
Promenade Tiling - North Herts Asphalte (Roofing) Ltd
Reclaimed Paving, Setts & Cobbles - Milestone Reclaim and Landscaping Ltd
Regency paving and flagstone paving - Thakeham Tiles Ltd
Roadstone - Hard York Quarries Ltd
Sett/ Cobble pavings - Tarmac Trading Limited (Aggregates)
Slab / Brick / Sett / Cobble pavings - Formpave Ltd
Slab / brick/ sett/ cobble pavings - Harris & Bailey Ltd
Slab/ Brick/ Sett/ Cobble pavings - Chichester Stoneworks Limited
Slab/ brick/ sett/ cobble pavings - Chilstone
Slab/ Brick/ Sett/ Cobble pavings - Vetter UK
Slab/ Brick/stett/cobble pavings - Townscape Products Ltd
Slab/ Sett Stone pavings - Johnsons Wellfield Quarries Ltd
Slabs - B & M Fencing Limited
Staffordshire Patterned Paving - Ketley Brick Co Ltd , The
Stone suppliers - Kerridge Stone Ltd
Synthetic ironoxide colouring agents - LANXESS Inorganic Pigments Group
Yorkstone paving - CED Ltd

Q26 Special surfacings/ pavings for sport/general amenity

Anti skid surfacing products - Clare R S & Co Ltd
Anti slip metal flooring - Graepels Perforators Ltd
Anti slip surfacing - Addagrip Terraco Ltd
Antiskid surfaces - Colas Ltd
Artifical sports surfaces - En-tout-cas Tennis Courts Ltd
Artificial Grass - Evergreens Uk
Athletic tracks and synthetic grass sports pitches - Bernhards Landscapes Ltd
Bowling green equipment, channels and Sports court marking - Sportsmark Group Ltd
Bridge Joints & Crack Repairs - Ennis-Flint
Clay pavers - Michelmersh Brick Holdings PLC
Coloured sufacing products - Clare R S & Co Ltd
Construction, refurbishing and all types of tennis courts - En-tout-cas Tennis Courts Ltd
Decorative bound/bonded surfacing resin - StarScape ULTRA &: Professional - StarScape PRO, Flexible – StarScape FLEXIBLE , Summer – StarScape THERMAL, High Friction / Anti-skid road coating – StarPolymers HFS - Star Uretech Ltd
Decorative Surfacing - Ennis-Flint
Exterior Pitch Markings - Sportsmark Group Ltd
Floor & Line markings - Kenyon Paints Limited
Games area surfaces - Playtop Licensing Limited
Gauged arches - Michelmersh Brick Holdings PLC
Grass Honeycomb Rubber Matting - MacLellan Rubber Ltd
Hardwood decking - W.L. West & Sons Ltd
High Friction Surfacing - Ennis-Flint
Indoor/outdoor wet areas - Evergreens Uk
Marking products and materials - Marking Machines International
Mulit-Use Games Areas (fencing and artificial surfaces) - En-tout-cas Tennis Courts Ltd
Outdoor matting soloutions - Kleen-Tex Industries Ltd
Permeable paving - CEMEX
Play area surfaces - Playtop Licensing Limited
Playground surfacing - HAGS SMP
Poolsurrounds - Evergreens Uk
Resin bonded surface dressing - Addagrip Terraco Ltd
Resin bonded surfacing, Resin bound surfacing - Ronacrete Ltd
Resin bound porous surfacing - Addagrip Terraco Ltd
Road Carpet - Howard Evans Roofing and Cladding Ltd
Road markings - Ennis-Flint
Road studs - Ennis-Flint
Rubber paving - Linatex Ltd
Safety surfaces - Playtop Licensing Limited
Seeding Turfing - Jack Moody Ltd
Special surfacings/ pavings for sport/general amenity - Tarmac Trading Limited (Aggregates)
Special surfacings/ pavings for sport/general amenity - Topscape/Topsport - Tarmac Trading Limited
Special surfacings/ pavings for sport/general amenity (Asphalt repair) - Tarmac - Specialist Products (Packed Highway Products)
Special surfacings/pavings for span/general amenity - Grass Concrete Ltd
Specialist surfaces for raods - Conren Ltd
Sports ground construction - AMK Fence-In Limited
Sports Hall Markings - Sportsmark Group Ltd

Q26 Special surfacings/ pavings for sport/general amenity (con't)

Sports Surfaces - Evergreens Uk
Sports surfacing and pavings - Charles Lawrence Surfaces Ltd
Synthetic grass for residential use - Artificial Grass Ltd
Synthetic grass for sport - Artificial Grass Ltd
Tactile surfaces for visually impaired - Rediweld Rubber & Plastics Ltd

Q30 Seeding/ Turfing

External planting - Jack Moody Ltd
Grass seed and turf - Sportsmark Group Ltd
Hydraulic seedings - Hydraseeders Ltd
Landscapes - Ogilvie Construction Ltd
Seeding/ turfing - Coblands Landscapes Ltd
Seeding/ turfing - Frosts Landscape Construction Ltd
Seeding/ Turfing - Topscape/Topsport - Tarmac Trading Limited
Seeding/Turfing - Gearing F T Landscape Services Ltd
Soft landscaping - AMK Fence-In Limited

Q31 External planting

External planting - Landscape Institute
External planting - Topscape/Topsport - Tarmac Trading Limited
External planting - Urban Planters
External planting - Wybone Ltd
General exterior works contractors - Gearing F T Landscape Services Ltd
Interiorscapes - Leaflike
Landscape contractors - Gearing F T Landscape Services Ltd
Landscape mulcher - ABG Ltd
Landscape ornaments - Haddonstone Ltd
Landscapes - Ogilvie Construction Ltd
Plant trellis - Lang+Fulton
Planting - Bernhards Landscapes Ltd
Planting - Coblands Landscapes Ltd
Planting - Frosts Landscape Construction Ltd
Soft landscaping - AMK Fence-In Limited
Topsoil - Milestone Reclaim and Landscaping Ltd

Q32 Internal planting

Aftercare - IPF Omnipex
Artificial plants and trees - Floralsilk Ltd
Bespoke design service - IPF Omnipex
Containers - IPF Omnipex
In house horticulture - IPF Omnipex
Interior planting - Urban Planters
Interiorscapes - IPF Omnipex
Interiorscapes - Leaflike
Internal planting - Frosts Landscape Construction Ltd
Internal planting - Landscape Institute
Internal planting - Topscape/Topsport - Tarmac Trading Limited
Mail order range - Leaflike
Professional interior landscaping - Leaflike
Rental - IPF Omnipex
Rental & maintenance schemes - Leaflike
Replica, living & preserved displays (interior & exterior) - Leaflike
Sale - IPF Omnipex
Thermoplastic road marking - Clare R S & Co Ltd

Q35 Landscape maintenance

Boulders, Rockery & Feature Stones - Milestone Reclaim and Landscaping Ltd
Full landscaping installation and maintenance - Sportsmark Group Ltd
Garden edgings and sleepers - Grange Fencing Limited
Garden timbers - Metsä Wood
Landscape featurestone - The Delabole Slate Co. Ltd
Landscape Maintenance - Chilstone
Landscape maintenance - Coblands Landscapes Ltd
Landscape maintenance - Frosts Landscape Construction Ltd
Landscape maintenance - Gearing F T Landscape Services Ltd
Landscape maintenance - Landscape Institute
Landscape maitenance - Jack Moody Ltd
Landscaping - Bernhards Landscapes Ltd

Manufacturer of artificial trees and plant displays - The Silk Forest
Special surfaces etc - Jack Moody Ltd
Sports/Play Sands and Rootzones - Sibelco UK Ltd
Top dressings - Sibelco UK Ltd
Tree soils - Sibelco UK Ltd
Tree surrounds - Jones of Oswestry Ltd
Walling and rockery - Forest of Dean Stone Firms Ltd
Wood pole protectors - Anti-Climb Guards Ltd

Q37 Green Roof

Green Roof - Mells Roofing Ltd
Green Roofing - Kemper System Ltd
Waterproofing & green roof covering - Axter Ltd

Q40 Fencing

Agricultural fencing - Chestnut Products Limited
Alarm fencing - Allen (Fencing) Ltd
All Types - Havering Fencing Co
All types of fencing - Dinnington Fencing Co. Limited
Agricultural & Equestrian - Metalwood Fencing (Contracts) Limited
Automated & manual gates - Metalwood Fencing (Contracts) Limited
Automated gates - Dinnington Fencing Co. Limited
Automatic Gates - Tate Fencing
Barbed wire - Anti-Climb Guards Ltd
Barbican steel fencing - Jackson H S & Son (Fencing) Ltd
BFS Pro-net Licensed - Burn Fencing Limited
Bollards, cable covers, troughs and bespoke products - Anderton Concrete Products Ltd
Bowtop fencing - Jackson H S & Son (Fencing) Ltd
BS1722 parts 1-16 inclusive - Burn Fencing Limited
Chain - open linked for fencing or lifting - Griff Chains Ltd
Chain Link - Alltype Fencing Specialists
Chainlink - B & M Fencing Limited
Chainlink fencing - Hy-Ten Ltd
Chestnut steel palisade, chain link, railings, weld mesh, barbed and razor wire - Guardian Wire Ltd
Closeboard - B & M Fencing Limited
Closeboard - Danbury Fencing Limited
Closeboard fencing - SJ McBride Ltd T/A Warefence
Commercial fencing and gates - Tonbridge Fencing Limited
Concrete, wire fencing and gates - Challenge Fencing Ltd
Diamond trellis - Danbury Fencing Limited
Domestic - Metalwood Fencing (Contracts) Limited
Domestic fencing and gates - Tonbridge Fencing Limited
Enclosures - Fibaform Products Ltd
Environmental barrier/ acoustic fencing - Newton & Frost Fencing Ltd
Erectors for private, domestic and commercial - Danbury Fencing Limited
Euroguard mesh fencing - Jackson H S & Son (Fencing) Ltd
Fence panel manufacturers - Derby Timber Supplies
Fencepost Support System - Catnic
Fencing - Allen (Concrete) Ltd
Fencing - Alltype Fencing Specialists
Fencing - Ambec Fencing
Fencing - AMK Fence-In Limited
Fencing - B & M Fencing Limited
Fencing - Barker & Geary Limited
Fencing - Bedford Fencing Co. Limited
Fencing - Berry Systems
Fencing - Betafence Limited
Fencing - Bowden Fencing Ltd
Fencing - Burn Fencing Limited
Fencing - Capel Fencing Contractors Ltd
Fencing - Challenge Fencing Ltd
Fencing - Chestnut Products Limited
Fencing - Covers Timber & Builders Merchants
Fencing - Danbury Fencing Limited
Fencing - Dinnington Fencing Co. Limited
Fencing - Ebor Concrete Ltd
Fencing - Eve Trakway
Fencing - Fabrikat (Nottingham) Ltd
Fencing - Fernden Construction (Winchester) Ltd
Fencing - Frosts Landscape Construction Ltd
Fencing - GBG Fences Limited
Fencing - GJ Durafencing Limited
Fencing - Goodacres Fencing
Fencing - Gravesend Fencing Limited
Fencing - Hadley Industries Plc
Fencing - HAGS SMP
Fencing - Harling Security Solutions Limited
Fencing - Havering Fencing Co
Fencing - Huntree Fencing Ltd
Fencing - J Pugh-Lewis Limited
Fencing - J. B. Corrie & Co Limited
Fencing - Jack Moody Ltd
Fencing - Kingsforth Security Fencing Limited
Fencing - Maldon Fencing Co
Fencing - Metalwood Fencing (Contracts) Limited
Fencing - Newton & Frost Fencing Ltd
Fencing - Pearman Fencing
Fencing - Pembury Fencing Ltd
Fencing - Pro-Fence (Midlands)
Fencing - Ryall & Edwards Limited
Fencing - Scott Fencing Limited
Fencing - SFC (Midlands) Ltd
Fencing - SJ McBride Ltd T/A Warefence
Fencing - Squires Metal Fabrications Ltd
Fencing - Termstall Limited
Fencing - W.L. West & Sons Ltd
Fencing - Wallbank
Fencing - Weatherley Fencing Contractors Limited
Fencing - Wentworth Sawmills Ltd
Fencing - Wesson Fencing
Fencing - all types - Anti-Climb Guards Ltd
Fencing (industrial) - Darfen Durafencing
Fencing and gates - Farefence (NW) Ltd
Fencing and gates, security fencing - Binns Fencing Ltd
Fencing and Sectional Buildings - Howe Fencing & Sectional Buildings
Fencing and security fencing - Jackson H S & Son (Fencing) Ltd
Fencing contractors - Gearing F T Landscape Services Ltd
Fencing contractors - Grange Fencing Limited
Fencing including steel palisade, power operated gates and metal railings - Charnwood Fencing Limited
Fencing suppliers - Crowthorne Fencing
Fencing Supply - Havering Fencing Co
Fencing, gates, automatic gates and barriers - Tate Fencing
Fencing, gates, railings, pedestrian guard rail and crash barrier - Billericay Fencing Ltd
Fencino (metal) - Steelway Fensecure Ltd
Flow plates - Autopa Ltd
Games area fencing - En-tout-cas Tennis Courts Ltd
Gate automation - Kingsforth Security Fencing Limited
Gates - Alltype Fencing Specialists
Gates - Cannock Gates UK Ltd
Gates - Lang+Fulton
Gates and access control - Chestnut Products Limited
Gates, barriers, shutters, fencing and parking post - DP Sercurity
Gates, coloured concrete posts, ornamental, vertical bar and bow top railings - Procter Bros Limited
Grating fencing - Lang+Fulton
Guard rail and barrier fencing - Valmont Stainton
Heavy duty gates and railings - Ermine Engineering Co. Ltd
High Security - Alltype Fencing Specialists
Highway safety fencing - Chestnut Products Limited
Hinged poles - Valmont Stainton
Jakcure treated timber fencing - Jackson H S & Son (Fencing) Ltd
Lintels - Anderton Concrete Products Ltd
Local authority suppliers of PVC-u fencing - Duralock (UK) Ltd
Lochrin classic rivetless palisade - Wm. Bain Fencing Ltd
Mesh - Darfen Durafencing
NRG fabrications - NRG Fabrications
On site welding - C & W Fencing Ltd
Paladin - Alltype Fencing Specialists
Palisade - Alltype Fencing Specialists
Palisade fencing and gates - Wm. Bain Fencing Ltd
Panels and posts - B & M Fencing Limited
Perimeter Protection - UTC Fire & Securites
Perimeter security - Heras
Plastic battens and fencing - Rockwell Sheet Sales Ltd
Post & Rail - B & M Fencing Limited
Post and rail fencing - SJ McBride Ltd T/A Warefence
Power fencing - Allen (Fencing) Ltd
Precast concrete fencing - Anderton Concrete Products Ltd
Precast concrete panels - Anderton Concrete Products Ltd
Railings - Alltype Fencing Specialists
Recycling green waste - Jack Moody Ltd
Rotating anti climb guards - Anti-Climb Guards Ltd
Safety fencing - Newton & Frost Fencing Ltd
Security - Metalwood Fencing (Contracts) Limited
Security and industrial fencing - Sampson & Partners Fencing
Security barriers - Bell & Webster Concrete Ltd
Security fencing - Allen (Fencing) Ltd
Security fencing - C & W Fencing Ltd
Security fencing - Chestnut Products Limited
Security fencing - Dinnington Fencing Co. Limited
Security Fencing - Sharman Fencing Ltd
Security fencing and gates - SJ McBride Ltd T/A Warefence
Security fencing, gates and access systems - O'Connor Fencing Limited
Security palisade fencing - GJ Durafencing Limited
Security steel palisade fencing and gates - Prima Security & Fencing Products
Security, industrial fencing, railings, crash barriers, gates, palisade, posts and rails - J & M Fencing Services
Security, industrial, commercial new housing and highways - Ambec Fencing
Sentry bar steel fencing - Jackson H S & Son (Fencing) Ltd
Speed ramps - Autopa Ltd
Sports - Metalwood Fencing (Contracts) Limited
Sports pitch fencing - Chestnut Products Limited
Steel fencing and gates - C & W Fencing Ltd
Steel Gates - Simflex Grilles and Closures Ltd
Steel mesh system fences - SJ McBride Ltd T/A Warefence
Steel Palisade - Darfen Durafencing
Steel palisading, welded mesh, chainlink fencing - Fencelines Ltd
Supply & Fix - Havering Fencing Co
Tennis court fencing - En-tout-cas Tennis Courts Ltd
Timber fencing and gates - Tonbridge Fencing Limited
Timber garden products - OSMO UK
Timber palisade - Danbury Fencing Limited
Timber Panels - Huntree Fencing Ltd
Timber, chainlink and weldmesh fencing systems - Prima Security & Fencing Products
Trellis - Danbury Fencing Limited
Tubular construction, barriers and rials - Tubeclamps Ltd
Ultra bar (adaptable ranking fence) - Sections & Profiles Ltd
Ultra Fence (Palisade Fence) - Sections & Profiles Ltd
Vertical tube fencing - Lang+Fulton
Waney Lap - Danbury Fencing Limited
Weld mesh - Alltype Fencing Specialists
Welded Mesh - Kingsforth Security Fencing Limited
Wire - Betafence Limited
Wire mesh - Betafence Limited
Wood - Alltype Fencing Specialists

Q41 Barriers/ Guard-rails

Acoustic barriers - Chestnut Products Limited
Anti-Ram Perimeter protection - RAMGROUP (UK) Ltd
Architectural railings - Chestnut Products Limited
Automated gates and barriers - Sampson & Partners Fencing
Automated traffic barriers - Dinnington Fencing Co. Limited
Automatic Barriers - Kone PLC
Balustrade & Barrier Systems - Brass Age Ltd
Barriers - Autopa Ltd
Barriers - Metalwood Fencing (Contracts) Limited
Barriers - Moravia (UK) Ltd
Barriers - Rediweld Rubber & Plastics Ltd
Barriers and guard rails - Havering Fencing Co
Barriers and guardrails - Hart Door Systems Ltd
Barriers and guardrails - J. B. Corrie & Co Limited
Barriers Guardrails - Steelway Fensecure Ltd
Barriers/ Guard-rails - O'Connor Fencing Limited
Barriers/Gaurdrails - Crowthorne Fencing
Barriers/guard rails - Challenge Fencing Ltd
Barriers/Guard Rails - Gearing F T Landscape Services Ltd
Barriers/guard rails - NRG Fabrications
Barriers/guardrails - Metalcraft (Tottenham) Ltd
Barriers/guard-rails - Berry Systems
Barriers/guard-rails - BPT Automation Ltd
Barriers/Guard-rails - Pembury Fencing Ltd
Barriers/sGuard-rails - Newton & Frost Fencing Ltd
Cantilever gates - Jackson H S & Son (Fencing) Ltd
Domestic PVC-u fencing for housing projects - Duralock (UK) Ltd
Electrically operated barriers - O'Connor Fencing Limited
Endless cords - James Lever 1856 Ltd
Fencing - Lang+Fulton
Garden twines - James Lever 1856 Ltd
Gates and barriers - Hart Door Systems Ltd
Guardrails/ Barriers - Harling Security Solutions Limited
Handrail - Kee Klamp Ltd
Handrail Covers - DC Plastic Handrails Ltd
Hazard Warning & Protection - Moravia (UK) Ltd
Hoop Barriers - RAMGROUP (UK) Ltd
Industrial and Commercial - Metalwood Fencing (Contracts) Limited
Industrial gates - Guardian Wire Ltd
Pedguard rail - Jackson H S & Son (Fencing) Ltd
Perimeter protection - APT Controls Ltd
Post & Rail - Furnitubes International Ltd
Precast concrete products - Ruthin Precast Concrete Ltd
Racecourse rails and PVC-u equestrian fencing - Duralock (UK) Ltd
Railing systems - Brass Age Ltd
Railings - Darfen Durafencing
Railings and gates - installers - GJ Durafencing Limited
Ropes and sashcords - Marlow Ropes Ltd
Safe,strong PVC-u fencing for Schools and Education Facilities - Duralock (UK) Ltd
Security barriers - APT Controls Ltd
Security equipment - Anti-Climb Guards Ltd
Security fencing and gates - Tonbridge Fencing Limited
Steel security palisade fencing and gates - Wm. Bain Fencing Ltd
Steel, Stainless steel and aluminium - Speedfab Midlands
Swing gates - Jackson H S & Son (Fencing) Ltd
Timber gate manufacturers - W.L. West & Sons Ltd
Traffic Barriers and Gates - Kone
Turnstiles - Kone

Q50 Site/ Street furniture/ equipment

Access covers and frames - Jones of Oswestry Ltd
Aggregate Blocks - Hanson Building Products UK
Architectural Artwork - Broadbent
Architectural Glass - Creative Glass
Automated gates - West London Security
Automatic Bollards - APT Controls Ltd
Automatic gates and barriers - BPT Automation Ltd
Automatic Sliding and Hinged Gates - Geoquip Worldwide
Balustrade - Kee Klamp Ltd
Barrier posts - Aremco Products
Bench seating - LSA Projects Ltd
Benches - Dee-Organ Ltd
Benches - Erlau AG
Bespoke planters - Design & Display Structures Ltd
Bi - foloding Gates - APT Controls Ltd
Bicycle Racks - Moravia (UK) Ltd
Bins - Cigarette & Litter - Glasdon U.K. Limited
Bollards - Autopa Ltd
Bollards - Dee-Organ Ltd
Bollards - Erlau AG
Bollards - Furnitubes International Ltd
Bollards - Glasdon U.K. Limited
Bollards - Orchard Street Furniture
Bollards - RAMGROUP (UK) Ltd
Bollards - Rediweld Rubber & Plastics Ltd
Bollards and airlock doors - Geoquip Worldwide
Bollards and verge marker posts - Glasdon UK Limited
Bridges, boardwalks, decking and pergolas - CTS Bridges Ltd
Bus & rail shelters - Abacus Lighting Ltd
Bus and glazed shelters - Midland Alloy Ltd
Car Park Posts - Furnitubes International Ltd
Car park/Forecourt boundary PVC-u fencing - Duralock (UK) Ltd
Carved stone - Caithness Flagstone Limited
Cigarette ash bins - Swintex Ltd
Covered walkways - Q.M.P
Cycle & Motorcycle parking - Furnitubes International Ltd

Q50 Site/ Street furniture/ equipment (con't)

Cycle Lockers - Autopa Ltd
Cycle parking - Q.M.P
Cycle parking equipment - Broxap Ltd
Cycle shelters - Dee-Organ Ltd
Cycle Shelters - Fibaform Products Ltd
Cycle Shelters - Parklines Building Ltd
Cycle stands - Dee-Organ Ltd
Cycle stands - Erlau AG
Cycle stands - HAGS SMP
Cycle stands - Rediweld Rubber & Plastics Ltd
Cycle stands and shelters - Autopa Ltd
Cycle storage systems - Elwell Buildings Ltd
Demarcation studs - brass, aluminum, stainless steel - Reflecting Roadstuds Ltd
Dog bins - Neptune Outdoor Furniture Ltd
Dog waste bins - Glasdon UK Limited
Drainage gratings - Jones of Oswestry Ltd
Electrical termination/ service pillar - Ritherdon & Co Ltd
Electrically operated gates - SJ McBride Ltd T/A Warefence
Entrance Gates, Turnstiles - Gunnebo UK Limited
Exterior lighting - Abacus Lighting Ltd
Furniture - Barlow Tyrie Ltd
Garden and Entrance Gates - Danbury Fencing Limited
Garden furniture - Grange Fencing Limited
Gates - Squires Metal Fabrications Ltd
Gates timber & metal - B & M Fencing Limited
Glass fibre and aluminium flag poles - Harrision Flagpoles
Grit bins - Amberol Ltd
Grit bins and spreaders - Glasdon UK Limited
Grit/ salt bins - Balmoral Tanks
Ground and wall mounted banner poles - Harrision Flagpoles
Landscape components and street furniture - Woodscape Ltd
Landscape furniture, seatings, shelters, bridges, litter bins, and trim trails - Lappset UK Ltd
Landscape Suppliers - Crowthorne Fencing
Letter bins - Iles Waste Systems
Litter bins - Amberol Ltd
Litter bins - Erlau AG
Litter Bins - Furnitubes International Ltd
Litter bins - Swintex Ltd
Litter Bins and Ashtrays - The No Butts Bin Company (NBB), Trading as NBB Outdoor Shelters
Litter bins and Recycling containers - Glasdon UK Limited
Loungers - Erlau AG
Manufacturers - Autopa Ltd
Natural Stone Fountains & Features - Palladio Stone
Outdoor litter bins - Unicorn Containers Ltd
Parking posts - Autopa Ltd
Parking posts - Rediweld Rubber & Plastics Ltd
PAS 68 crash rated products - Geoquip Worldwide
Pavior infill covers and frames - Jones of Oswestry Ltd
Pedestrian guard rails - Fabrikat (Nottingham) Ltd
Pedestrian Turnstiles & Gates - Geoquip Worldwide
Picnic tables - HAGS SMP
Planters - Erlau AG
Play area rubber animals and spheres - Playtop Licensing Limited
Posts, Chains, Stands, Bollards - Moravia (UK) Ltd
Public seats, litter bins, benches, bollards, picnic tables and planters - Neptune Outdoor Furniture Ltd
Purpose made furniture - Orchard Street Furniture
Reconstructed stone balustrading, paving, garden ornaments and architectural dressings - Minsterstone Ltd
Recycled Plastic Outdoor Furniture (Picknic Tables, Benches, Seating) - The No Butts Bin Company (NBB), Trading as NBB Outdoor Shelters
Recycling bins - Amberol Ltd
Recycling bins - Iles Waste Systems
Recycling bins, boxes and containers - Straight Ltd
Recycling units & liter bins - Broxap Ltd
Restaurant chairs - Laytrad Contract Furniture Ltd
Retractable Posts - RAMGROUP (UK) Ltd
Rising Arm Barriers - Darfen Durafencing
Road Blockers - APT Controls Ltd
Road Blockers - Geoquip Worldwide
Rockery stone - The Delabole Slate Co. Ltd
Scaffolding protectors - Anti-Climb Guards Ltd
Seating - Erlau AG
Seating - Glasdon U.K. Limited
Seating and tables for schools, waiting areas, train stations, airports, ferry terminals, hospitals and surgeries - Hille Educational Products Ltd
Seating, Benches - Furnitubes International Ltd
Seats - HAGS SMP
Seats and benches - Glasdon UK Limited
Security bolders - Kerridge Stone Ltd
Self watering baskets - Amberol Ltd
Self watering Precinct planters - decorative planters - Amberol Ltd
Self watering window boxes and barrier baskets - Amberol Ltd
Shelters - Broxap Ltd
Shelters (Smoking, Cycle, Waiting) - The No Butts Bin Company (NBB), Trading as NBB Outdoor Shelters
Sign posts - Valmont Stainton
Site Equipment - Bainbridge Engineering Ltd
Site equipment - Frosts Landscape Construction Ltd
Site furniture, car park furniture and equipment - APT Controls Ltd
Site furniture/ equipment - Broxap Ltd
Site/ Street furniture/ equipment - 3d Storage Systems (UK) LTD
Site/ street furniture/ equipment - Chilstone
Site/ street furniture/ equipment - Haddonstone Ltd
Site/ Street furniture/ equipment - Leander Architectural
Site/Street funiture/ Equipment - Berry Systems
Site/Street furniture/Equipment - Pembury Fencing Ltd
Site/Street Furniture/Equipment - Wybone Ltd
Sleeping policemen - Rediweld Rubber & Plastics Ltd
Sliding Gates - Darfen Durafencing
Smoking shelters - Autopa Ltd
Smoking shelters - Q.M.P
Speed ramp - Swintex Ltd
Speed ramps - Berry Systems
Steel Storage Buildings - Parklines Building Ltd
Steel, Stainless steel and aluminium - Speedfab Midlands
Stone street furniture - CED Ltd
Storage Systems - Toprail Systems Ltd
Street furniture - Abacus Lighting Ltd
Street furniture - Ballantine Castings
Street furniture - Blanc de Bierges
Street furniture - Broxap Ltd
Street Furniture - CU Phosco Lighting
Street furniture - Dee-Organ Ltd
Street furniture - DW Windsor Lighting
Street furniture - Earth Anchors Ltd
Street Furniture - Ebor Concrete Ltd
Street Furniture - Falco UK Ltd
Street Furniture - Furnitubes International Ltd
Street Furniture - Harling Security Solutions Limited
Street furniture - Marshalls Mono Ltd
Street Furniture - Townscape Products Ltd
Street furniture - Urbis Schreder Ltd
Street furniture - Wales & Wales
Street Furniture Installation Services - Branson Leisure Ltd
Street Furniture Manufacturers - Branson Leisure Ltd
Street furniture, lighting, equipment installation - AMK Fence-In Limited
Street furniture, shelters and walkways - design and manufacture - Macemain + Amstad Ltd
Tables - Erlau AG
Tables - Furnitubes International Ltd
Tactile bars, Road studs, Demarcation Studs and Anti skate studs - Sportsmark Group Ltd
Talking bin - Amberol Ltd
Teen shelters - HAGS SMP
Temporary flood defence systems - Bauer Renewables Ltd
Timber, steel, cast iron street and garden furniture - Orchard Street Furniture
Tower protectors - Anti-Climb Guards Ltd
Traffic calming products - Rediweld Rubber & Plastics Ltd
Traffic products - Swintex Ltd
Tree grilles and guards - Furnitubes International Ltd
Turnstyles - Darfen Durafencing
Vehicle Barriers - Geoquip Worldwide
Wase and recycling bins - Straight Ltd
Waste containers and systems - Iles Waste Systems
Water gardens and water features - Lotus Water Garden Products Ltd

R10 Rainwater pipework/ gutters

Aluminium flashings - Gilmour Ecometal
Aluminium gutter and rainwater pipe products - Marley Plumbing and Drainage
Aluminium gutters - George Gilmour (Metals) Ltd
Aluminium gutters - Gilmour Ecometal
Aluminium rainwater goods - WP Metals Ltd
Aluminium Roof Outlets - Alutec
Aluminuim Gutters, Downpipes and Hoppers - Alutec
Aluminuim rainwater goods - Guttercrest
Building Products incl window & guttering systems - Marshall-Tufflex Ltd
Building Rainwater Disposals - Geberit Ltd
Cast iron rainwater and soil goods - Longbottom J & J W Ltd
Cast iron Rainwater gutter systems to BS 460 - Saint-Gobain PAM UK
Cast iron roof outlets to BS EN 1253 - Saint-Gobain PAM UK
Cast iron soil, vent and waste and rainwater pipes to BS EN 877 - Saint-Gobain PAM UK
Channel Drainage - Wavin Ltd
Clay, Plastic and concrete drainage systems - Hepworth Building Products Ltd
Copper pipework - Servomac Limited
Copper rainwater system - Klober Ltd
Copper Rainwater Systems - Metal Gutta
Custom fabricated in metals - Azimex Fabrications Ltd
Downpipe - Round & Square - Metal Gutta
Fascia and soffit systems in powder coated aluminium and steel - Dales Fabrications Ltd
Galvanised steel pipework - Servomac Limited
GRP valley troughs - Timloc Expamet Building Products
Gutter heating - Findlay Irvine Ltd
Gutter leaf protection system - FloPlast Ltd
Guttering - Avonside Roofing Group T/A Letchworth Roofing
Guttering - 1/2 Round, Box & Ogee - Metal Gutta
Insulated gutters - CGL Facades
Pipes and fittings - Geberit Ltd
Plastic drainage systems - Hunter Plastics Ltd
PVCu rainwater systems - Marley Plumbing and Drainage
Rain water management systems - Fullflow Group Ltd
Rainwater diverter and systems - FloPlast Ltd
Rainwater Goods - Rheinzink UK
Rainwater goods - Rockwell Sheet Sales Ltd
Rainwater goods - Roles Broderick Roofing Ltd
Rainwater outlets/ gutters - McKenzie-Martin Ltd
Rainwater pipework & gutters - Olby H E & Co Ltd
Rainwater pipework and gutters - Geberit Ltd
Rainwater pipework/ gutters - Harris & Bailey Ltd
Rainwater pipework/ gutters - John Davidson (Pipes) Ltd
Rainwater recirculation systems - Kingspan Environmental
Rainwater systems - Allmat (East Surrey) Ltd
Rainwater systems - Harrison Thompson & Co Ltd
Rainwater systems in powder coated aluminium and steel - Dales Fabrications Ltd
Rainwater systems, sacias and soffits - Alumasc Exterior Building Products Ltd
Rainwater, soil and wate systems - Brett Martin Ltd
Roof Drainage Outlets - Caroflow Ltd
Roof outlets - ACO Technologies plc
Stainless Steel Drainage systems - Aperam Stainless Services & Solutions UK Limited
Stainless Steel Guttering - Metal Gutta
Stainless steel pipework - Blucher UK LTD
Stainless steel pipework - Servomac Limited
Surface water drainage - Hodkin Jones (Sheffield) Ltd
Syphonic drainage systems - Fullflow Group Ltd
Syphonic roof drainage - Fullflow Group Ltd
T-Pren-gutter expansion material - Matthew Hebden
Water storage containers and accessories - Straight Ltd
Zinc Guttering - Metal Gutta

R11 Foul drainage above ground

Above ground drainage - Ballantine Castings
Above ground drainage - FloPlast Ltd
Air admittance valves - FloPlast Ltd
Cast iron above ground system to BS 416 - Saint-Gobain PAM UK
Cast iron floor and shower gullies, gratings and accessories to BS EN 1253 - Saint-Gobain PAM UK
Cast iron sanitary pipework system to BS EN 877 - Saint-Gobain PAM UK
Connectors - Wirquin Ltd
Drainage above ground - Brett Martin Ltd
Drainage systems - Alumasc Exterior Building Products Ltd
Foul Drainage above ground - Aluline Precision Engineering Ltd
Foul drainage above ground - Durey Casting Ltd
Foul drainage above ground - FC Frost Ltd
Foul drainage above ground - Wavin Ltd
Gutters, drainage pipes and fittings - Longbottom J & J W Ltd
Metal pipework - Copper, Galvanised steel and Stainless steel - Servomac Limited
MUPVC waste system - Davant Products Ltd
Plastic drainage systems - Hunter Plastics Ltd
PVCu soil and waste systems - Marley Plumbing and Drainage
Retro fit above ground & built in submerged covers - Grando (UK) Ltd
Seamless cold drawn copper tube - Lawton Tube Co Ltd, The
Soil and vent terminals - Klober Ltd
Stainless steel drainage channels, gratings and gullies - Component Developments
Stainless Steel Drainage systems - Aperam Stainless Services & Solutions UK Limited
Stainless Steel Pipes - ACO Technologies plc
Stainless steel pipework - Blucher UK LTD
Traps and waste fittings - Opella Ltd
Waste Traps - FloPlast Ltd
Wastes - Wirquin Ltd

R12 Drainage below ground

Access covers and frames linear surface water drainage system and special fabrication - Clarksteel Ltd
Bacteria Grease traps - Progressive Product Developments Ltd
Barrier pipe for contaminated land - Wavin Ltd
Below ground drainage and maholes - Ballantine Castings
Cast iron Below ground system to BS 437 - Saint-Gobain PAM UK
Cast iron, below ground system to BS EN 877 - Saint-Gobain PAM UK
Cesspools and septic tanks - Kingspan Environmental
Channel grating - Shackerley (Holdings) Group Ltd incorporating Designer ceramics
Clay Drainage - Knowles W T & Sons Ltd
Commercial Gullies, gratings, channels and traps - ACO Technologies plc
Concrete drainage systems - Hanson Concrete Products
Cop - SUDS - British Water
Cover slabs - Chiltern Concrete and Stone
Drain and pipework cleaning - Dyno Rod PLC
Drain and pipework inspection - Dyno Rod PLC
Drain and pipework installation - Dyno Rod PLC
Drain and pipework repairs - Dyno Rod PLC
Drain cleaning - Dyno-Rod PLC
Drainage - Marshalls Mono Ltd
Drainage - Polypipe Civils
Drainage below ground - Aluline Precision Engineering Ltd
Drainage below ground - CPV Ltd
Drainage below ground - FC Frost Ltd
Drainage below ground - Formpave Ltd
Drainage Below Ground - Gatic
Drainage below ground - Geberit Ltd
Drainage below ground - Harris & Bailey Ltd
Drainage below ground - John Davidson (Pipes) Ltd
Drainage Below Ground - Safeguard Europe Ltd
Drainage below ground - Wavin Ltd
Drainage media - Lytag Ltd
Drainage membranes - SCP Concrete Sealing Technology Ltd
Flexible couplings - Flex-Seal Couplings Ltd
Floor Drainage Outlets - Caroflow Ltd
Floor gullies, roof outlets, access covers, grease converters and linear drainage - Wade International Ltd
Gravity drain systems - Radius Systems Ltd
Grease traps, oil and grease water separators - Progressive Product Developments Ltd
Grease treatment plants - Progressive Product Developments Ltd
GRP Kiosks - Adams- Hydraulics Ltd
Installation services - Radius Systems Ltd
Jetters cold and hot, winches, rods and accessories - Ward's Flexible Rod Company Ltd
Manhole covers and gratings - Durey Casting Ltd
Manhole covers and reservoir lid - Ruthin Precast Concrete Ltd
Non entry inspection chambers - Wavin Ltd
Package sewage pumping stations - KSB Ltd
Plastic drainage systems - Hunter Plastics Ltd
Pump stations - Kingspan Environmental
Pumping stations for storm water/Foul Water - Pims Pumps Ltd
PVCu underground drainage systems - Marley Plumbing and Drainage
Rainwater Harvesting System & Underground Drainage - FloPlast Ltd
Rainwater harvesting systems - Kingspan Environmental Ltd
Septic tank conversion unit - MANTAIR Ltd
Septic tanks - Balmoral Tanks
Sewer systems - Radius Systems Ltd
Stainless steel manhole covers - Component Developments
Stainless steel pipework - Blucher UK LTD
StormWater Management - Wavin Ltd
Surface water drainage systems - Mea UK Ltd
Terracotta - Hepworth Building Products Ltd
Underground drainage - Naylor Drainage Ltd
Underground drainage systems (PVC) - Brett Martin Ltd

R13 Land drainage

Cast Iron gratings and grills - Company name: Britannia Metalwork Services Ltd
Clay Drainage System - Hepworth Building Products Ltd
Inspection chambers - Hunter Plastics Ltd
Land drainage - Durey Casting Ltd
Land drainage - Flex-Seal Couplings Ltd
Land drainage - J Pugh-Lewis Limited
Land drainage - John Davidson (Pipes) Ltd
Land Drainage - Naylor Drainage Ltd
Land drainage - Polypipe Civils
Land Drainage - T-T Pumps & T-T controls
Paving Support & Drainage - Caroflow Ltd
Plumbing and Drainage - Wavin Ltd
Preformed sheets, cavity and channel drainage - ABG Ltd
PVCu quantum highway and sewer drainage - Marley Plumbing and Drainage
Rainwater harvesting - MANTAIR Ltd
Vertical Band Drains - Bauer Renewables Ltd

R14 Laboratory/ Industrial waste drainage

Bacteria Grease traps - Progressive Product Developments Ltd
Grease traps, oil and grease water separators - Progressive Product Developments Ltd
Grease treatment plants - Progressive Product Developments Ltd
Laboratory drainage systems - CPV Ltd
Laboratory Ind Waste - George Fischer Sales Ltd
Laboratory/ Industrial Waste - Naylor Drainage Ltd
Laboratory/industrial waste drainage - Satec Service Ltd
Stainless steel drainage systems - ACO Technologies plc
Stainless Steel Drainage systems - Aperam Stainless Services & Solutions UK Limited
Stainless steel pipework - Blucher UK LTD
Thermoplastic pipes - CPV Ltd
Underground storage tanks - Kingspan Environmental Ltd

R20 Sewage pumping

Centrifugal pumps - Calpeda Limited
Drainage and sewage package systems - Pump Technical Services Ltd
Maintenance and repair of pumping equipment - Pims Pumps Ltd
Package pump stations - Tuke & Bell Ltd
Pumps and ejectors - Tuke & Bell Ltd
Sewage pumping - Adams- Hydraulics Ltd
Sewage Pumping - Binder
Sewage Pumping - Mono Pumps Ltd
Sewage pumping - Satec Service Ltd
Sewage Pumping - T-T Pumps & T-T controls
Sewage pumps and pumping systems - New Haden Pumps Ltd
Sewage, drainage, pumps and systems - KSB Ltd

R21 Sewage treatment/ sterilisation

Cesspools and septic tanks - Kingspan Environmental
Cop - Flows & Loads - British Water
Fuel water seperators - Kingspan Environmental
Grease removal system - Tuke & Bell Ltd
Grease traps - Kingspan Environmental
Grit removal systems - Tuke & Bell Ltd
GRP Equipment - Adams- Hydraulics Ltd

R21 Sewage treatment/ sterilisation (con't)

Package sewage treatment plants - Kingspan Environmental
Package sewage treatment plants - Tuke & Bell Ltd
Packaged Sewage Treatment Plant - MANTAIR Ltd
Packaged Sewage Treatment Plant - Titan Pollution Control - Part of The Kingspan Group
Pump stations - Kingspan Environmental
Rotating biological contactors - Tuke & Bell Ltd
Sample chambers - Kingspan Environmental
Separators - Kingspan Environmental
Settling tank scrapers - Tuke & Bell Ltd
Sewage purification equipment - Tuke & Bell Ltd
Sewage storage tanks - Franklin Hodge Industries Ltd
Sewage treatment - Balmoral Tanks
Sewage treatment equipment - Adams- Hydraulics Ltd
Sewage treatment systems - Kingspan Environmental Ltd
Sewage treatment/ sterilisation - Aldous & Stamp (Services) Ltd
Sewage treatment/sterilization - Satec Service Ltd
Supply of electric Sewage Treatment Plants - Water Technology Engineering Ltd
Supply of Non-electric Sewage Treatment Plants - Water Technology Engineering Ltd
Surface aerators - Tuke & Bell Ltd
Trickling filter distributors - Tuke & Bell Ltd
Ultra violet chambers, lamps and control panels - Hanovia Ltd

R30 Centralised vacuum cleaning

Central Vacuum Systems - Barloworld Vacuum Technology Plc
Centralised vacuum cleaning - Donaldson Filtration (GB) Ltd
Centralised vacuum systems - Nilfisk Limited
Centralized vacuum cleaning systems - Quirepace Ltd

R31 Refuse chutes

Refuse chutes - Aluline Precision Engineering Ltd
Waste Disposal Systems - Hardall International Ltd

R32 Compactors/ Macerators

Bag compactors - Tony Team Ltd
Bin compactors - Tony Team Ltd
Compactors/ Macerators - Mono Pumps Ltd
Demountable compactors - Randalls Fabrications Ltd
Domestic lifting stations - Stuart Turner Ltd
Harpac Compactors - Hardall International Ltd
Shower Waste Pumps - Stuart Turner Ltd
Sluiceroom macerators - Verna Ltd
Static & portable compaction units - Randalls Fabrications Ltd
Waste management equipment, compactors/ macerators - Imperial Machine Co Ltd
WC Macerators - Stuart Turner Ltd

S10 Cold Water

Booster sets - Stokvis Industrial Boilers (International) Limited
Cold Water - British Water
Cold Water - George Fischer Sales Ltd
Cold water - John Davidson (Pipes) Ltd
Copper tube for water - Yorkshire Copper Tube
Distribution Mains - Durotan Ltd
Ductwork clearing - Aquastat Ltd
External Mains - Durotan Ltd
Manufacturer & supplier of materials & liners for cured-in-place pipe rehabilitation - Applied Felts Ltd
MDPE pipe and fittings - FloPlast Ltd
MDPE water pipes and fittings - Brett Martin Ltd
Non potable water systems - Radius Systems Ltd
Packaged Cold Water Storage/Pump - Harton Heating Appliances
Pipe bending equipment - Hilmor
Pipe cleaning - Dyno-Rod PLC
Pipe freezing kits - Hilmor
Piped supply systems cold water - Precolor Sales Ltd
Piping systems - George Fischer Sales Ltd
Plumbing systems - Hepworth Building Products Ltd
Polyethylene systems - Radius Systems Ltd
Potable water pipe fittings - Radius Systems Ltd
Seamless cold drawn copper tube - Lawton Tube Co Ltd, The
Threading equipment - Hilmor
Valves - Delta Fire
Water Calculations - Oakwood Property Solutions
Water fittings and controls - Flamco UK Ltd
Water meters - SAV United Kingdom Ltd
Water meters - Switch2 Energy Solutions Ltd
Water meters and oil meters - Elster Metering Ltd

S11 Hot Water

Boiling water products - Heatrae Sadia Heating Ltd
Cistern & Cistern - Opella Ltd
Cistern & Cistern Fittings - Opella Ltd
Commercial Water Heating - Heatrae Sadia Heating Ltd
Copper tube for water - Yorkshire Copper Tube
Dual fired boilers - Stokvis Industrial Boilers (International) Limited
Heat exchangers - Stokvis Industrial Boilers (International) Limited
Heated towel rails - electric - Pitacs Ltd
Hot Water - George Fischer Sales Ltd
Hot Water and Pressurized Water (S13) - Chromalox (UK) Ltd
Industrial boilers - Stokvis Industrial Boilers (International) Limited
Pre-commisson clearing of heating & chilled water systems - Aquastat Ltd
Pre-insulated Pipework supply and installation - Durotan Ltd
Pre-insulated Pipework Supply only - Durotan Ltd
Premix boilers - Stokvis Industrial Boilers (International) Limited
Solar collector systems - Stokvis Industrial Boilers (International) Limited
Temperature blending valves - Deva Tap Co Ltd
Thermal Stores and storage vessels - Lochinvar Limited
Unvented Combination Units with Unvented Hot Water Storage & Boilers - Harton Heating Appliances
Water heaters - Stokvis Industrial Boilers (International) Limited

S12 Hot & cold water (self-contained specification)

Cable Duct - Hepworth Building Products Ltd
Commercial water control systems - Kohler Mira Ltd
Copper tube for water - Yorkshire Copper Tube
Copper Unvented Units - Harton Heating Appliances
Cylinder Packs With Integral Controls - Harton Heating Appliances
Direct Electric Boilers - Dimplex UK Limited
Drinking Water System - Tapworks Water Softeners
Drinking water systems - EcoWater Systems Ltd
Electric Showers - Deva Tap Co Ltd
Enamelled Steel Unvented Units - Harton Heating Appliances
Filtration equipment - EcoWater Systems Ltd
Fittings - Pegler Ltd
Flexible plastic plumbing - IPPEC Systems Ltd
FloFit plumbing system - FloPlast Ltd
Hot & Cold Water - George Fischer Sales Ltd
Hot & cold water - Hertel Services
Hot and cold water - Guest (Speedfit) Ltd, John
Hot and cold water and central heating, polybutylene pipework - Brett Martin Ltd
Hot and cold water cylinder jackets - Davant Products Ltd
Hot and cold water systems - Equator PEX - Marley Plumbing and Drainage
Manifold Plumbing Systems - Davant Products Ltd
Mixers - Marflow Eng Ltd
Packaged boiler houses - Stokvis Industrial Boilers (International) Limited
Plumbing - Marflow Eng Ltd
Plumbing accessories - PTS Plumbing Trade Supplies
Plumbing systems - REHAU Ltd
Pre- insulated pipes - IPPEC Systems Ltd
Prefabricated Plumbing Units - Harton Heating Appliances
Presurised hot and chilled water units - Stokvis Industrial Boilers (International) Limited
Sealed system equipment - Flamco UK Ltd
Shower Valves - Marflow Eng Ltd
Showers - Deva Tap Co Ltd
Stainless Steel Pipes - ACO Technologies plc
Swivel ferrule straps, stop taps, leadpacks and boundary boxes - Tyco Waterworks - Samuel Booth
Taps - Marflow Eng Ltd
Tube Plugs - TEAM INDUSTRIAL SERVICES (UK) LIMITED
Water pumps - Stuart Turner Ltd
Water purifiers - EcoWater Systems Ltd
Water Purifiers - Tapworks Water Softeners
Water saving products - Deva Tap Co Ltd
Water softeners - EcoWater Systems Ltd
Water softeners - tapworks water softeners - Tapworks Water Softeners

S13 Pressurised water

Expansion vessels for portable water - Flamco UK Ltd
Pressure booster pumps - Stuart Turner Ltd
Pressure boosting systems - Armstrong Integrated Ltd
Pressure sets - Stuart Turner Ltd
Pressure sprayers - Hozelock Ltd
Pressure units - Pressmain
Pressurised water - Armstrong Integrated Ltd
Pressurised water - Danfoss Ltd
Pressurized Water - British Water
Pressurized water - Calpeda Limited
Pressurized water - John Davidson (Pipes) Ltd
Pressurized water - New Haden Pumps Ltd
Rainwater utilization pump systems - KSB Ltd
Shower booster pumps - Stuart Turner Ltd
Shower pumps - Deva Tap Co Ltd
Valves for high pressure pneumatic and hydraulic appliances - Hale Hamilton Valves Ltd
Water Booster - Pressmain
Water management - Verna Ltd
Water Supply Pipe - Hepworth Building Products Ltd

S14 Irrigation

Irrigation - Calpeda Limited

S15 Fountains/ Water features

Architectural Glass - Creative Glass
Fountain and Water Display Equipment - Simon Moore Water Services
Fountains and Water Displays - Fountains Direct Ltd
Fountains/ Water Features - Chilstone
Fountains/ Water features - Haddonstone Ltd
Internal Fountains - The Fountain Company
Millstone & Boulder Fountains - Fountains Direct Ltd
Stainless Steel Pipes - ACO Technologies plc
Water gardens, pumps, filters, fountains - Lotus Water Garden Products Ltd
Water storage containers and accessories - Straight Ltd

S20 Treated/ Deionised/ Distilled water

Cooling tower water treatment, cleaning and refurb - Aquastat Ltd
Filteration Equipment - Tapworks Water Softeners
Flexible tubes - United Flexibles (A Division of Senior Flex)
Treated/ Deionised/ Distilled water - Aldous & Stamp (Services) Ltd
Treated/ deionized/distilled water - Satec Service Ltd
Treated/Deionised/Distilled Water - British Water
Treated/Deionised/Distilled water - Hertel Services
Ultra violet chambers, lamps and control panels - Hanovia Ltd
Water conditioners - Cistermiser Ltd
Water filtration and treatment - Barr & Wray Ltd
Water filtration equipment - Eden Springs (UK) Ltd
Water filtration media - Lytag Ltd
Water purification systems - Veolia Water Technologies UKElga Ltd
Water treatment - Feedwater Ltd

S21 Swimming pool water treatment

Automatic chemical control and dosing - Golden Coast Ltd
Pool covers - Amdega Ltd
Spas - Barr & Wray Ltd
Stainless Steel Pipes, Commercial Gullies, Stainless Steel hygienic channels - ACO Technologies plc
Swimming pool installations - Barr & Wray Ltd
Swimming pool kits and accessories-domestic - Fox Pool (UK) Ltd
Swimming pool water treatment - Aldous & Stamp (Services) Ltd
Swimming pool water treatment - British Water
Swimming pool water treatment - Precolor Sales Ltd
Swimming pools and accessories - Aqua-Blue Designs
Swimming pools and equipment, spas, heat pumps, water features and chemicals - Certikin International Ltd
Swimming pools, spa baths, sauna and steam rooms - Buckingham Swimming Pools Ltd
Swimming pools, spas, saunas, steam rooms, baptisteries and mosaic murals - J W Green Swimming Pools Ltd
Ultra violet chambers, lamps and control panels - Hanovia Ltd
Water features - Aqua-Blue Designs
Watertank refurbishment - Aquastat Ltd

S30 Compressed air

Compressed air - Danfoss Ltd
Compressed air - Guest (Speedfit) Ltd, John
Compressed air - Hertel Services
Compressed air supply systems - Fluidair Ltd
Compressors - Chippindale Plant Ltd
Hand and actuated valves - George Fischer Sales Ltd
Oil free air compressors, vacuum pumps and gas circulators - Bambi Air Compressors Ltd.
Pipework and Installation - Fluidair Ltd
Valves and controls for presurised gas - Hale Hamilton Valves Ltd

S31 Instrument air

Valves and controls for presurised gas - Hale Hamilton Valves Ltd

S32 Natural gas

Gas and sanitation applications - Yorkshire Copper Tube
Gas Detection Equipment - TCW Services (Control) Ltd
Gas detection systems - Blakell Europlacer Ltd
Gas fires - natural - Valor
Gas isolation devices - TCW Services (Control) Ltd
Gas Isolation Equipment - TCW Services (Control) Ltd
Gas meters - Switch2 Energy Solutions Ltd
Gas pipe fittings - Radius Systems Ltd
Natural gas - John Davidson (Pipes) Ltd
Natural Gas - Saacke Combustion Services Ltd
Seamless cold drawn copper tube - Lawton Tube Co Ltd, The
Valves and controls for presurised gas - Hale Hamilton Valves Ltd

S33 Liquefied petroleum gas

Calor gas - Bell & Co Ltd
Cylinder & bulk LPG - Calor Gas Ltd
Gas Detection Equipment - TCW Services (Control) Ltd
Gas Isolation Equipment - TCW Services (Control) Ltd
Heating appliances - Bell & Co Ltd
LPG gas fires - Valor
LPG vessels - Flamco UK Ltd
Portable gas heaters - Valor
Valves and controls for presurised gas - Hale Hamilton Valves Ltd

S34 Medical/ Laboratory gas

Stainless Steel Pipes - ACO Technologies plc
Valves and controls for presurised gas - Hale Hamilton Valves Ltd

S40 Petrol/ Diesel storage/distribution

Bulk liquid/ chemical storage tanks - Balmoral Tanks
Fill Point cabinets - Metcraft Ltd
Fuel tanks - Balmoral Tanks
Insulation for Petrochemical Industries - Kingspan Industrial Ins. Ltd
Oil pollution monitoring and control systems - design, manufacture, installation and commissioning of - Aquasentry

S41 Fuel oil storage/ distribution

Adblue storage and dispensing Tanks - Kingspan Environmental Ltd
Bunded storage tanks - Cookson and Zinn (PTL) Ltd
Fuel oil storage/ distribution - John Davidson (Pipes) Ltd
Fuel oil storage/ distribution - Metcraft Ltd
Liquid storage tanks - Franklin Hodge Industries Ltd
Oil and Fuel Tanks - Kingspan Environmental Ltd
Oil meters - Switch2 Energy Solutions Ltd
Oil pollution monitoring and control systems - design, manufacture, installation and commissioning of - Aquasentry
Oil refinery - Petrochem Carless
Oil storage tanks - Davant Products Ltd
Refurbishment of tanks - Franklin Hodge Industries Ltd
Tank level monitoring Domestic and Commercial - Kingspan Environmental Ltd

S50 Vacuum

Vacuum - Barloworld Vacuum Technology Plc
Vacuum controls - Danfoss Ltd

S51 Steam

Steam - Golden Coast Ltd
Steam Boilerhouse Equipment - Thermal Technology Sales Ltd
Steam design plate heat exhanger packages - AEL
Steam meters - Switch2 Energy Solutions Ltd
Steam Traps - Flowserve Flow Control

S60 Fire hose reels

Fire fighting hoses, nozzles, adaptors and standpipes - Richard Hose Ltd
Fire Hose Reel - Angus Fire
Fire hose reels - Armstrong Integrated Ltd
Fire hose reels - Fire Security (Sprinkler Installations) Ltd
Fire hose reels - Nu-Swift International Ltd
Firefighting equipment - The BSS Group

S61 Dry risers

Dry riser - Eagles, William, Ltd
Dry riser equipment - Delta Fire
Dry riser equipment - Kidde Fire Protection Services Ltd
Dry Risers - Armstrong Integrated Ltd
Dry risers - Firetecnics Systems Ltd
Flooring Installation - Tiflex Ltd
Hose reels for fire fighting - Richard Hose Ltd
Metal pipework - Copper, Galvanised steel and Stainless steel - Servomac Limited
Safety and Fire resistant flooring - Tiflex Ltd
Sprinkler Systems - Kidde Fire Protection Services Ltd

S62 Wet risers

Metal pipework - Copper, Galvanised steel and Stainless steel - Servomac Limited
Wet Risers - Armstrong Integrated Ltd

S63 Sprinklers

Fire sprinkler tanks - Franklin Hodge Industries Ltd
GRP sprinkler and pump suction tanks - Dewey Waters Ltd
Sprinkler systems - Firetecnics Systems Ltd
Sprinklers - Fire Security (Sprinkler Installations) Ltd
Sprinklers - Richard Hose Ltd

S64 Deluge

Deluge - Fire Security (Sprinkler Installations) Ltd
Fire hydrant valves including dry riser equipment - Richard Hose Ltd

S65 Fire hydrants

Fire extinguishers supply and maintenance - Nu-Swift International Ltd
Fire Hydrants - Angus Fire

S70 Gas fire fighting

Explosion suppression systems - Kidde Fire Protection Ltd
Fire extinguishers - Britannia Fire
Fire extinguishers supply and maintenance - Nu-Swift International Ltd
Fire suppression equipment - Kidde Fire Protection Ltd
Gas detection equipment - MSA (Britain) Ltd
Gas detection equipment - Zellweger Analytic Ltd, Sieger Division
Gas detection systems - Blakell Europlacer Ltd
Marine fire protection systems - Kidde Fire Protection Ltd
Rail fire protection systems - Kidde Fire Protection Ltd

S70 Gas fire fighting (con't)

Vehicle fire protection systems - Kidde Fire Protection Ltd

S71 Foam fire fighting

Extinguishers - Channel Safety Systems Ltd
Fire extinguisher systems - Fife Fire Engineers & Consultants Ltd
Fire extinguishers - Britannia Fire
Fire extinguishers - Richard Hose Ltd
Fire extinguishers supply and maintenance - Nu-Swift International Ltd
Foam equipment - Eagles, William, Ltd
Foam Fire Fighting - Angus Fire
Foam fire fighting - Fire Security (Sprinkler Installations) Ltd
Hose assemblies for fire fighting, industrial and drinking purposes - Richard Hose Ltd

T10 Gas/ Oil fired boilers

Biomass boilers - Broag Ltd
Boiler maintenance - H Pickup Mechanical & Electrical Services Ltd
Boiler Paint Instrumentation - SK Environmental Ltd
Boilers - Alpha Therm Ltd
Boilers - Ferroli Ltd
Combustion equipment - Nu-Way Ltd
Condensing boilers (domestic & commercial) - Broag Ltd
Electric Boilers - Baxi Heating UK Ltd
Floor standing condensing boilers - Upton, Purewell VariHeat, Varmax - Hamworthy Heating Limited & ACV UK
Floor standing condensing vertical modular boilers - Upton and Wessex ModuMax - Hamworthy Heating Limited & ACV UK
Floor standing high efficiency steel boiler - Melbury - Hamworthy Heating Limited & ACV UK
Flue and chimney systems - Flamco UK Ltd
Flue and chimney systems - Poujoulat (UK) Ltd
Flue systems - Marflex Chimney Systems
Flue terminals - Tower Flue Components Ltd
Gas and solid fuel heating appliances - Hepworth Heating Ltd
Gas boilers - AEL
Gas central heating boilers - Burco Maxol
Gas fired boilers - Fulton Boiler Works (Great Britain) Ltd
Gas flue systems - Ubbink (UK) Ltd
Gas, oil fired boilers - Broag Ltd
Gas, oil, dual fuel - GP Burners (CIB) Ltd
Gas/oil fired boilers - Docherty New Vent Chimney Group
Gas/Oil Fired Boilers - service maintenance - Hodgkinson Bennis Ltd
Gas/oil fired burners - Worcester Heat Systems Ltd
Heat transfer thermal fluid systems and heaters - Babcock Wanson Uk Ltd
Heating - Dantherm Ltd
Heating controls - Danfoss Ltd
Heating products - The BSS Group
High Efficiency Boilers - Baxi Heating UK Ltd
High Efficiency Water Heaters and Boilers - Lochinvar Limited
Metal pipework - Copper, Galvanised steel and Stainless steel - Servomac Limited
Prefabricated boilers and cylinder sets - IPPEC Systems Ltd
Quantec LPG HR28C - High efficiency Boiler Range, Passive Flue Gas Heat Recovery - Johnson & Starley
Refractory boiler linings, bricks, castables, ceramic fibre products & incinerators - Combustion Linings Ltd
Service Terminals - Ubbink (UK) Ltd
Skid mounted Boiler Plant - Fulton Boiler Works (Great Britain) Ltd
Spare parts for burners - Nu-Way Ltd
Spares - GP Burners (CIB) Ltd
Steam and hot water boilers and pressure vessels - Wellman Robey Ltd
Steam generators & fire tube boilers - Babcock Wanson Uk Ltd
TecnoFlex flexible liner - Schiedel Chimney Systems Ltd
Thermal fluid heaters, thermal oxidizers for solids, liquids & gaseous waste - Beverley Environmental Ltd
Wall hung, condensing modular boilers - Stratton - Hamworthy Heating Limited & ACV UK
Water boilers - TSE Brownson

T11 Coal fired boilers

Coal fired boilers - Docherty New Vent Chimney Group
Coal fired boilers repair and maintenance - Doosan Power Systems Ltd
Combustion equipment - Saacke Combustion Services Ltd
Flue and chimney systems - Poujoulat (UK) Ltd
Flue systems - Marflex Chimney Systems
Refractory boiler linings, bricks, castables, ceramic fibre products & incinerators - Combustion Linings Ltd
Solid fuel central HT boiler - Dunsley Heat Ltd
Steam and hot water boilers and pressure vessels - Wellman Robey Ltd
Stokers and associated equipment - service and maintenance - Hodgkinson Bennis Ltd
TecnoFlex flexible liner - Schiedel Chimney Systems Ltd

T12 Electrode/ Direct electric boilers

Electric boilers - Eltron Chromalox
Electric boilers - Fulton Boiler Works (Great Britain) Ltd
Electric boilers - Technical Control Systems Ltd
Electric calorifiers - Eltron Chromalox
Electrical boilers:Aztec Boilers 2-12KW - TR Engineering Ltd
Electrode Boilers - Dimplex UK Limited
Electrode/ Direct electric boilers - Chromalox (UK) Ltd
Electrode/direct electric boilers - Collins Walker Ltd, Elec Steam & Hot Water Boilers
Flue systems - Marflex Chimney Systems
Hot Water - Dimplex UK Limited
Refractory boiler linings, bricks, castables, ceramic fibre products & incinerators - Combustion Linings Ltd

T13 Packaged steam generators

Bird/vermin control - Cannon Hygiene Ltd
Packaged steam generators - Collins Walker Ltd, Elec Steam & Hot Water Boilers
Packaged steam generators - Ormandy Rycroft Engineering
Packaged steam generators and Steam heating (T33) - Chromalox (UK) Ltd
Packaged steam turbines and generator equipment - Doosan Power Systems Ltd
Steam and hot water boilers and pressure vessels - Wellman Robey Ltd
Steam boilers - Fulton Boiler Works (Great Britain) Ltd

T14 Heat pumps

Air Source Heat Pump - Lochinvar Limited
Ground Source Heat Pumps - H Pickup Mechanical & Electrical Services Ltd
Heat pumps - MacMarney Refrigeration & Air Conditioning Ltd
Heat pumps - Ormandy Rycroft Engineering
Heat Pumps - Stiebel Eltron Ltd
Jaga's Dynamic Boost Effect (DBE) range of radiators are the perfect partners for heat pumps and other renewable energy sources - Jaga UK
Water chillers - Thermal Technology Sales Ltd

T15 Solar collectors

Boiler controls and accessories - Alpha Therm Ltd
Renewable Energy Solutions - Schueco UK
Solar - Stiebel Eltron Ltd
Solar collectors - Aqua-Blue Designs
Solar collectors - Solar Trade Association, The
Solar collectors - Ubbink (UK) Ltd
Solar collectors, solar electric powered products - Intersolar Group Ltd
Solar hot water systems - Trigon - Hamworthy Heating Limited & ACV UK
Solar panels - CPV Ltd
Solar panelsand cylinders - IPPEC Systems Ltd
Solar PV - Schueco UK
Solar slats - Grando (UK) Ltd
Solar Thermal - Schueco UK
Solar thermal and photo voltaic installation - H Pickup Mechanical & Electrical Services Ltd
Solar thermal hot water - Lochinvar Limited
Solar water heating - Alpha Therm Ltd
Trigon solar hot water systems - Hamworthy Heating Limited & ACV UK

T16 Alternative fuel boilers

Biomass, Energy from Waste - Doosan Power Systems Ltd
Boiler stoves - Gazco
Combustion burners - GP Burners (CIB) Ltd
Energy meters - Switch2 Energy Solutions Ltd
Energy saving equipment - Saacke Combustion Services Ltd
Flue and chimney systems - Poujoulat (UK) Ltd
Flue systems - Marflex Chimney Systems
ICS System Chimneys - Schiedel Chimney Systems Ltd
Multi fuel Stoves - Dunsley Heat Ltd
Multi fuel/wood burning stoves - TR Engineering Ltd
Neutralizer for multi boiler applications - Dunsley Heat Ltd
Refractory boiler linings, bricks, castables, ceramic fibre products & incinerators - Combustion Linings Ltd
Solid fuel boilers - TR Engineering Ltd
Spares - GP Burners (CIB) Ltd
Wood Pellet and Wood Chip Boilers - H Pickup Mechanical & Electrical Services Ltd

T20 Primary heat distribution

Custom made fires - Valor
Drum heaters - Flexelec(UK) Ltd
Flue systems - Marflex Chimney Systems
Heater cables - Flexelec(UK) Ltd
Heater mats - Flexelec(UK) Ltd
Heating - Birdsall Services Ltd
Heating - PTS Plumbing Trade Supplies
Industrial and commercial heating systems - AmbiRad Ltd
Industrial heating equipment Manufacturers - Turnbull & Scott (Engineers) Ltd
Primary heat distribution - Chromalox (UK) Ltd
Primary Heat distribution - Saacke Combustion Services Ltd
Temperature controls - Flexelec(UK) Ltd
Thermal fluid heaters - Fulton Boiler Works (Great Britain) Ltd

T30 Medium temperature hot water heating

Control equipment - The BSS Group
Decorative heating - Bristan Group
Drinking water heaters - Santon
Heating - Dunham Bush Ltd
Heating and Plumbing Design & Installation - H Pickup Mechanical & Electrical Services Ltd
Hot Water Heating, Medium Temperature, Low Temperature (T31), Low Temperature Self-Contained Specification (T32) - Chromalox (UK) Ltd
Hot water steel panel radiators - Pitacs Ltd
Immersion heaters and thermostats - Heatrae Sadia Heating Ltd
LST Radiators - Myson
MTHW Heating - Ormandy Rycroft Engineering
Radiators - Designer Radiators Direct
Thermostats - Danfoss Ltd
Valves - The BSS Group

T31 Low temperature hot water heating

Boiler and calorifier descaling - Aquastat Ltd
Buffer and storage vessels - Flamco UK Ltd
Butterfly valves - Watts Industries UK Ltd
Cast Iron radiators - Designer Radiators Direct
Central heating - Walney UK Ltd
Central heating equipment - Hudevad Britain
Central heating programmers, water heating controllers, motorised valves, room stats and thermostats - Horstmann Controls Ltd
Cistern fed water heaters - Heatrae Sadia Heating Ltd
Cylinder Stats - Horstmann Controls Ltd
Domestic and commercial central heating controls - Danfoss Ltd
Gas convector heaters - Burco Maxol
Gate valves - Watts Industries UK Ltd
Heating - Dunham Bush Ltd
Heating - Myson
Heating - PTS Plumbing Trade Supplies
Heating & Cooling Systems - Durotan Ltd
Heating Controls - Myson
Heating to pool areas - Buckingham Swimming Pools Ltd
Hot water heating - Jaga UK
Large unvented water heaters - Heatrae Sadia Heating Ltd
Low surface temperature radiators - Jaga UK
Low water content heating solutions - Jaga UK
LPHW - Turnbull & Scott (Engineers) Ltd
LTHW Heating - Ormandy Rycroft Engineering
LTHW Heating - SAV United Kingdom Ltd
Manifolds - Watts Industries UK Ltd
Panel Radiators - Myson
Point of use water heaters - Heatrae Sadia Heating Ltd
Pressure reducing valves - Watts Industries UK Ltd
Radiant Ceiling Panels - Zehnder Group UK Ltd
Radiator gaurds (low surface temperature) - Alumasc Interior Building Products Limited
Radiator thermostats - Danfoss Ltd
Radiator valves - Watts Industries UK Ltd
Radiators - Designer Radiators Direct
Radiators - Zehnder Group UK Ltd
Solar heating - Solar Trade Association, The
Stainless steel designer radiators - Pitacs Ltd
Steam and hot water boilers and pressure vessels - Wellman Robey Ltd
Swing check valves - Watts Industries UK Ltd
Thermostatic mixinet valves - Watts Industries UK Ltd
Towel Rails - Designer Radiators Direct
Underfloor central heating - Polypipe Building Products Ltd
Underfloor heating - Myson
Underfloor Heating - Wavin Ltd
Underfloor, ceiling and wall heating cooling - Warmafloor (GB) Ltd
Valves - Designer Radiators Direct
Valves - Watts Industries UK Ltd
Warm water underfloor heating - IPPEC Systems Ltd
Water Heating - Stiebel Eltron Ltd

T32 Low temperature hot water heating (self-contained specification)

Aluminum radiators - AEL
Cast Iron Radiators - AEL
Commissioning Valves - Marflow Eng Ltd
Decorative Radiators - Myson
Gas Central Heating - Servowarm
Heating - Beehive Coils Ltd
Heating - Morgan Hope Industries Ltd
Heating systems - Marflow Eng Ltd
Low surface temperature radiator gaurds - Alumasc Interior Building Products Limited
Low temperature hot water heating - Multibeton Ltd
LTHW Heating (self contained) - Ormandy Rycroft Engineering
Manifolds - Marflow Eng Ltd
Panel radiators - Pitacs Ltd
Radiator valves - AEL
Radiator valves - Pegler Ltd
Radiators - K. V. Radiators
Radiators - Kermi (UK) Ltd
Small unvented water heaters - Heatrae Sadia Heating Ltd
Steel Panel Radiators - AEL
Steel Tubular Column Radiators - AEL
Storage water heating - Johnson & Starley
Underfloor heating - Multibeton Ltd
Water Heaters - Baxi Heating UK Ltd
Water heaters - Johnson & Starley Ltd
Water Heaters - Santon
Water treatment of heating and chilled water systems - Aquastat Ltd

T33 Steam heating

Air conditioning - Dunham Bush Ltd
Clean steam boilers - Fulton Boiler Works (Great Britain) Ltd
Controls - Danfoss Ltd
Metal pipework - Copper, Galvanised steel and Stainless steel - Servomac Limited
Radiators - Designer Radiators Direct
Steam - Turnbull & Scott (Engineers) Ltd
Steam heating - Ormandy Rycroft Engineering
Stream heating - Saacke Combustion Services Ltd

T40 Warm air heating

Air conditioning - Dunham Bush Ltd
Air warmers - Seagoe Technologies Ltd
Electric warm air heating - Kaloric Heater Co Ltd
Fan convectors - S & P Coil Products Ltd
Finned tubing & trench heaters - Turnbull & Scott (Engineers) Ltd
Gas-fired warm aire unit heaters - Radiant Services Ltd
Heat exchangers gasketted plate - HRS Hevac Ltd
Heating - Encon Air Systems Ltd
Heating equipment - NuAir Ltd
HPHW - Turnbull & Scott (Engineers) Ltd
Industrial & commercial, gas or oil indirect fired warm air heating systems - Elan-Dragonair
Industrial and commercial heating systems - AmbiRad Ltd
Industrial heating - Hoval Ltd
Radiant ceiling panels - S & P Coil Products Ltd
Thermal Fluid - Turnbull & Scott (Engineers) Ltd
Timers - Danfoss Ltd
Trench Heating - S & P Coil Products Ltd
Unit heater - Johnson & Starley Ltd
Warm air heaters - Saacke Combustion Services Ltd
Warm air heating - Combat Heating Solutions
Warm air heating - Consort Equipment Products Ltd
Warm air heating - Docherty New Vent Chimney Group
Warm air heating - May William (Ashton) Ltd
Warm Air heating - Nu-Way Ltd

T41 Warm air heating (self-contained specification)

Basket fires - Valor
Controls - Systemair Ltd
Convectors - Systemair Ltd
Electric warm air heating - Kaloric Heater Co Ltd
Heating - Systemair Ltd
Natural and fan assisted floor convectors - Multibeton Ltd
Oil & gas fired warm air cabinet - Radiant Services Ltd
Oil fired warm air unit heaters - Radiant Services Ltd
Unit Heaters - Turnbull & Scott (Engineers) Ltd
Warm air heating - Dimplex UK Limited
Warm Air Heating - Vortice Ltd
Warm air heating (small scale) - Consort Equipment Products Ltd
Warm air heating (small scale) - May William (Ashton) Ltd

T42 Local heating units

Anti condensation heaters - Eltron Chromalox
Central heating equipment - Hudevad Britain
Ceramic gas burners - Infraglo Limited
Convector heaters - De Longhi Limited
Custom gas burners - Infraglo Limited
Decorative gas fires & stoves - Magiglo Ltd
Electric fires - Gazco Ltd
Electric fires - Valor
Electric fuel effect fires - BFM Europe Limited
Electric radiant heater panel - Morgan Hope Industries Ltd
Electric radiators and heating - Myson
Electric water heating - Kaloric Heater Co Ltd
Fires and fireplaces - Gazco
Flameproof heaters, radiant panel heaters - Seagoe Technologies Ltd
Gas burners - Infraglo Limited
Gas fired radiant heating equipment - Horizon International Ltd
Gas fired space heating - domestic/commercial - Johnson & Starley
Gas fires - Gazco Ltd
Gas stoves - Gazco Ltd
Gas wall heaters - Valor
Gas-fired radiant tube heater - Radiant Services Ltd
Heating - Andrews Sykes Hire Ltd
Heating products - Pressmain
Local heating units - Consort Equipment Products Ltd
Local Heating Units and Local Electric Heating Units (V51) - Chromalox (UK) Ltd
Metal fibre gas burners - Infraglo Limited
Mobile radiant gas heaters - Infraglo Limited
Portable heating - Andrews Sykes Hire Ltd
Premix gas burneres - Infraglo Limited
Products for commercial and industrial applications - Bush Nelson PLC
Radiant gas heaters - Infraglo Limited
Radiant infra-red plaque gas heaters - Space - Ray UK
Radiant infra-red poultry gas brooders - Space - Ray UK
Radiant infra-red tube gas heaters - Space - Ray UK
Radiant tube and radiant heaters - Radiant Services Ltd
Radiators - Purmo-UK
Radiators (oil filled electric) - De Longhi Limited
Refractory boiler linings, bricks, castables, ceramic fibre products & incinerators - Combustion Linings Ltd
Solid Fuel Suites - Winther Browne & co Ltd
Space Heating - Stiebel Eltron Ltd

T42 Local heating units (con't)

- **Storage and panel heaters** - Seagoe Technologies Ltd
- **Storage gas water heaters, focal point fan convector** - Burco Maxol
- **Stoves** - Gazco
- **Stoves, wood burning and multifuel** - BFM Europe Limited
- **Unit heaters** - Biddle Air Systems Ltd

T50 Heat recovery

- **Brazed plate heat exchangers** - HRS Hevac Ltd
- **Heat meters** - Switch2 Energy Solutions Ltd
- **Heat pipes** - S & P Coil Products Ltd
- **Heat recovery** - Aqua-Blue Designs
- **Heat recovery** - Dantherm Ltd
- **Heat recovery** - Domus Ventilation
- **Heat recovery** - Flambeau
- **Heat recovery** - Kair Ventilation Ltd
- **Heat recovery** - May William (Ashton) Ltd
- **Heat recovery** - Ormandy Rycroft Engineering
- **Heat Recovery** - Ubbink (UK) Ltd
- **Heat Recovery** - Vent-Axia
- **Heat recovery** - Zehnder Group UK Ltd
- **Heat Recovery and Heat Exchangers (Y22)** - Chromalox (UK) Ltd
- **Heat recovery units** - Thermal Technology Sales Ltd
- **Heat recovery ventilation units** - Ves Andover Ltd
- **Heating and heat recovery equipment thermal wheels** - AEL
- **Home 'n' Dry units** - Johnson & Starley
- **Passive Stack Ventilation** - Johnson & Starley
- **Q-Vent** - Johnson & Starley
- **Run around coils** - S & P Coil Products Ltd
- **Steam and hot water boilers and pressure vessels** - Wellman Robey Ltd

T60 Central refrigeration plant

- **Air conditioning** - Clivet UK Ltd
- **Central refrigeration plant** - Johnson Controls Building Efficiency UK Ltd
- **Central refrigeration plant** - MacMarney Refrigeration & Air Conditioning Ltd
- **Industrial refridgeration equipment and systems** - J & E Hall Ltd
- **Refrigerant dryers** - Fluidair Ltd
- **Refrigeration** - Birdsall Services Ltd
- **Refrigeration Controllers and Data loggers** - Kingspan Environmental Ltd
- **Refrigeration plant** - Emerson Climate Technologies
- **Refrigeration systems** - Tyco Fire and Integrated Solutions

T61 Chilled water

- **Chilled water** - J & E Hall Ltd
- **Chilled water** - Johnson Controls Building Efficiency UK Ltd
- **Chilled water** - Ormandy Rycroft Engineering
- **Chilled water** - TEV Limited
- **Data centre cooling** - Eaton-Williams Group Limited
- **Stainless Steel Pipes** - ACO Technologies plc

T70 Local cooling units

- **Absorption chillers** - Birdsall Services Ltd
- **Close cooling units** - Clivet UK Ltd
- **Cooling Units** - Carter Environmental Engineers Ltd
- **Heating & Cooling Systems** - Durotan Ltd
- **Local Cooling Units** - Climate Center
- **multi service chilled beam** - TROX (UK) Ltd
- **Portable coolers** - London Fan Company Ltd
- **Portable heating** - Andrews Sykes Hire Ltd

T71 Cold rooms

- **Cold rooms** - J & E Hall Ltd
- **Cold rooms** - MacMarney Refrigeration & Air Conditioning Ltd
- **Cold rooms** - SCHOTT UK Ltd
- **Cold rooms** - TEV Limited
- **Commercial freezer environments** - Hemsec Panel Technologies

T72 Ice pads

- **Ice pads** - J & E Hall Ltd

U10 General ventilation

- **Access doors** - Hotchkiss Air Supply
- **Air conditioners, dampers, air ductline** - Advanced Air (UK) Ltd
- **Air conditioning** - Birdsall Services Ltd
- **Air conditioning** - Purified Air Ltd
- **Air conditioning** - TROX (UK) Ltd
- **Air Distribution Products** - Systemair Ltd
- **Air flow cooling and heating** - Passivent Ltd
- **Air Handing Units** - Fläkt Woods Ltd
- **Air seperators** - Watts Industries UK Ltd
- **Air transfer grilles** - Mann McGowan Group
- **Air-conditioning** - Andrews Sykes Hire Ltd
- **Anti-condensation for motors heater tapes** - Flexelec(UK) Ltd
- **Domestic ventilation systems** - Airflow (Nicoll Ventilators) Ltd
- **Exhauster blowers** - Quirepace Ltd
- **Fan convectors** - Biddle Air Systems Ltd
- **Flanging systems** - Hotchkiss Air Supply
- **Flatoval tube** - Hotchkiss Air Supply
- **Flexible ducting** - Hotchkiss Air Supply
- **Flue systems** - Marflex Chimney Systems
- **Full freshair systems** - Dantherm Ltd
- **General supply/ extract** - Donaldson Filtration (GB) Ltd
- **General ventilation** - Colt International
- **General Ventilation** - Constant Air Systems Ltd
- **General ventilation** - Dyer Environmental Controls
- **General ventilation** - Flambeau
- **General ventilation** - GVS Filter Technology UK
- **General ventilation** - Intersolar Group Ltd
- **General ventilation** - London Fan Company Ltd
- **General ventilation** - May William (Ashton) Ltd
- **Industrial air filtration** - GVS Filter Technology UK
- **Mechanical extract terminals** - Klober Ltd
- **Modular ventilation ducting** - Domus Ventilation
- **Moisture removal** - Passivent Ltd
- **Natural ventalation Systems** - Passivent Ltd
- **Natural Ventilation Systems** - Dyer Environmental Controls
- **Oxygen is our energy efficient, intelligent, fully programmable and modular heating and ventilation solution which improves Indoor Air Quality (IAQ) in classrooms and buildings** - Jaga UK
- **Roof Ventilation** - Forticrete Roofing
- **Roof ventilators - (ridge & slope mounted)** - McKenzie-Martin Ltd
- **Sealed system equipment and air separation and dirt removal equipment** - Flamco UK Ltd
- **Smoke and natural ventilation systems** - SE Controls
- **SOLA-BOOST®** - Monodraught Ltd
- **Spiral tube** - Hotchkiss Air Supply
- **Splits, VRF, Packaged & Chillers** - Toshiba Carrier UK
- **Support systems** - Hotchkiss Air Supply
- **Trade suppliers of commercial and decorative ceiling fans** - Fantasia Distribution Ltd
- **Underfloor ventilators** - Rytons Building Products Ltd
- **Ventelated Ceilings** - Vianen KVS BV
- **Ventilation** - Encon Air Systems Ltd
- **Ventilation** - Johnson & Starley Ltd
- **Ventilation** - NuAir Ltd
- **Ventilation** - Systemair Ltd
- **Ventilation** - Thermal Technology Sales Ltd
- **Ventilation** - Ubbink (UK) Ltd
- **Ventilation - domestic, commercial and industrial** - Vent-Axia
- **Ventilation equipment** - Johnson & Starley
- **Ventilation of pool areas** - Buckingham Swimming Pools Ltd
- **Ventilation products** - VBH (GB) Ltd
- **Ventilation systems** - Mansfield Pollard & Co Ltd
- **Ventilation systems** - Polypipe Ventilation Ltd
- **Ventilation Systems for roofing** - Forticrete Roofing
- **Ventilators** - Kair Ventilation Ltd
- **WINDCATCHER® Natural ventilation systems** - Monodraught Ltd
- **Window ventilator manufactures** - Simon R W Ltd
- **Window Ventilators** - Passivent Ltd

U11 Toilet ventilation

- **Domestic extractor fans** - Domus Ventilation
- **Toilet ventilation** - Flambeau
- **Toilet ventilation** - Kair Ventilation Ltd

U12 Kitchen ventilation

- **Design, Supply and Installation of Commercial Kitchen Ventelation** - Vianen KVS BV
- **Domestic extractor fans** - Domus Ventilation
- **Ducting and fans** - Waterline Limited
- **Extract fan units** - Ves Andover Ltd
- **Extraction systems and odour control** - Purified Air Ltd
- **Grease eliminators** - GVS Filter Technology UK Ltd
- **Grease filters** - Camfil Farr Ltd
- **Grease filters** - Westbury Filters Limited
- **Kitchen extract** - Fire Protection Ltd
- **Kitchen extraction systems** - Britannia Kitchen Ventilation Ltd
- **Kitchen ventilation** - Flambeau
- **Kitchen ventilation** - Kair Ventilation Ltd
- **Kitchen ventilation** - London Fan Company Ltd
- **Kitchen ventilation** - Rytons Building Products Ltd
- **Kitchen Ventiliation Canopies and Ceilings** - Vianen KVS BV
- **Ventilation - domestic, commercial and industrial** - Vent-Axia

U13 Car park ventilation

- **Air Handing Units** - Fläkt Woods Ltd
- **Car park extract** - Fire Protection Ltd
- **Car park Ventilation** - Lang+Fulton
- **car park ventilation** - SCS Group
- **Carpark ventilation** - London Fan Company Ltd

U14 Smoke extract/ Smoke control

- **Air filtration units** - PHS Group plc
- **Air Handing Units** - Fläkt Woods Ltd
- **Ancillaries** - Advanced Air (UK) Ltd
- **Automatic smoke barrier-curtains / blinds** - Cooper Group Ltd
- **Birdguards** - Brewer Metalcraft
- **Chimney cappers** - Brewer Metalcraft
- **Chimney cowls** - Brewer Metalcraft
- **Chimneys and flues** - Metcraft Ltd
- **Emission monitors** - SK Environmental Ltd
- **Exhaust gas cleaning** - Saacke Combustion Services Ltd
- **Fire safety** - Systemair Ltd
- **Floor, fire vents, Smoke vents and roof hatches** - Bilco UK Ltd
- **Industrial exhaust ventilation** - Horizon International Ltd
- **Industrial fume extractors** - Horizon International Ltd
- **Powered cowls** - Brewer Metalcraft
- **Rain caps** - Brewer Metalcraft
- **Smoke and natural ventilation systems** - SE Controls
- **Smoke control systems** - SCS Group
- **Smoke extract** - Consort Equipment Products Ltd
- **Smoke extract** - McKenzie-Martin Ltd
- **Smoke extract fans** - London Fan Company Ltd
- **Smoke extract/ smoke control** - Active Carbon Filters Ltd
- **Smoke extract/ smoke control** - Colt International
- **Smoke extract/ smoke control** - Fire Protection Ltd
- **Smoke extract/control** - TROX (UK) Ltd
- **Smoke management systems** - Advanced Air (UK) Ltd
- **Spark arrestors** - Brewer Metalcraft
- **Specials** - Brewer Metalcraft
- **Spinning cowls** - Brewer Metalcraft
- **Terminals** - Brewer Metalcraft
- **Vehicle exhaust extraction** - Nederman UK
- **Ventilation - domestic, commercial and industrial** - Vent-Axia

U15 Safety cabinet/ Fume cupboard extract

- **Domestic and commercial flue and ventilation products** - Rega Ductex Ltd
- **Downflow Booths** - Envair Ltd
- **Fume cupboards** - S & B Ltd
- **Fume Cupboards** - Simplylabs Limited
- **Fume Extraction** - Simplylabs Limited
- **Laminar Flow Cabinets** - Envair Ltd
- **Pharmaceutical Isolators** - Envair Ltd
- **Safety cabinet / fume cupboards** - Envair Ltd
- **Safety cabinet/fume cupboard** - TROX (UK) Ltd
- **Safety extract/ smoke control** - Fire Protection Ltd

U16 Fume extract

- **Air pollution control equipment and technical advice** - Doosan Power Systems Ltd
- **Boiler Flue** - Alpha Therm Ltd
- **Dust and fume extraction** - Encon Air Systems Ltd
- **Extractor fans** - Tower Flue Components Ltd
- **Flue systems** - Marflex Chimney Systems
- **Fume extract** - Donaldson Filtration (GB) Ltd
- **Fume extract** - TROX (UK) Ltd
- **Fume extraction** - London Fan Company Ltd
- **Fume extraction** - Nederman UK
- **Fume extraction** - PCT Group
- **Industrial fume extractors** - Horizon International Ltd
- **Portable heating** - Andrews Sykes Hire Ltd

U17 Anaesthetic gas extract

- **Anaesthetic gas extract** - Active Carbon Filters Ltd

U20 Dust collection

- **Clean Rooms** - DencoHappel UK Ltd
- **Dust Collection** - Barloworld Vacuum Technology Plc
- **Dust collection** - Camfil Farr Ltd
- **Dust collection** - Donaldson Filtration (GB) Ltd
- **Dust collection** - Encon Air Systems Ltd
- **Dust collection** - Quirepace Ltd
- **Dust control equipment** - Nederman Filtration Ltd
- **Dust extraction** - Nederman UK
- **Dust extractors** - Horizon International Ltd
- **Industrial health & safety vacuums** - Nilfisk Limited
- **Industrial vacuums with power tool extraction** - Nilfisk Limited

U30 Low velocity air conditioning

- **Air conditioning** - Airedale International Air Conditioning Ltd
- **Air conditioning** - Dalair Ltd
- **Air conditioning** - Johnson & Starley Ltd
- **Air conditioning** - Toshiba Carrier UK
- **Air conditioning accessories** - Johnson Matthey PLC - Metal Joining
- **Air conditioning supply and servicing** - Aircare Europe Ltd
- **Air conditioning systems** - Mansfield Pollard & Co Ltd
- **Air handling units** - Eaton-Williams Group Limited
- **Comfort** - Airedale International Air Conditioning Ltd
- **Condensing units** - Ves Andover Ltd
- **Domestic and commercial flue and ventilation products** - Rega Ductex Ltd
- **HVAC service and maintenance providers** - Eaton-Williams Group Limited
- **Low velocity air conditioning** - MacMarney Refrigeration & Air Conditioning Ltd
- **Portable heating** - Andrews Sykes Hire Ltd
- **Spares** - Airedale International Air Conditioning Ltd

U31 VAV air conditioning

- **Air Handing Units** - Fläkt Woods Ltd
- **VAV air conditioning** - Andrews Sykes Hire Ltd
- **VAV air conditioning** - MacMarney Refrigeration & Air Conditioning Ltd
- **VAV air conditioning** - May William (Ashton) Ltd
- **VAV Air conditioning** - TROX (UK) Ltd
- **VAV terminal units** - Advanced Air (UK) Ltd

U32 Dual-duct air conditioning

- **Dual-duct air conditioning** - Advanced Air (UK) Ltd
- **Dual-duct air conditioning** - MacMarney Refrigeration & Air Conditioning Ltd

U33 Multi-zone air conditioning

- **Multi-zone air conditioning** - Andrews Sykes Hire Ltd
- **Multi-zone air conditioning** - MacMarney Refrigeration & Air Conditioning Ltd

U41 Fan-coil air conditioning

- **Air conditioning** - Encon Air Systems Ltd
- **Air Handing Units** - Fläkt Woods Ltd
- **Dampers** - Swegon Air Management Ltd
- **Data centre cooling solutions** - Eaton-Williams Group Limited
- **Fan coil air conditioning** - Colt International
- **Fan coil air conditioning** - TROX (UK) Ltd
- **Fan coil heater casings** - Alumasc Interior Building Products Limited
- **Fan Coil Induction Units** - Motorised Air Products Ltd
- **Fan coil units** - Thermal Technology Sales Ltd
- **Fan coil valves** - Watts Industries UK Ltd
- **Fan coils units** - Biddle Air Systems Ltd
- **Fan-coil air conditioning** - Advanced Air (UK) Ltd
- **Fan-coil air conditioning** - Andrews Sykes Hire Ltd
- **Fan-coil air conditioning** - DencoHappel UK Ltd
- **Fan-coil air conditioning** - MacMarney Refrigeration & Air Conditioning Ltd
- **Fan-coil air conditioning** - TEV Limited
- **Legionella prevention and control** - Aquastat Ltd
- **Refrigeration equipment** - Dunham Bush Ltd
- **Service** - Airedale International Air Conditioning Ltd
- **Split unit air conditioning** - Emerson Climate Technologies

U42 Terminal re-heat air conditioning

- **Heat exchangers gasketted plate** - HRS Hevac Ltd
- **Terminal re-heat air conditioning** - Advanced Air (UK) Ltd

U43 Terminal heat pump air conditioning

- **Air conditioning** - Clivet UK Ltd
- **Chillers / Heat Pumps** - DencoHappel UK Ltd
- **Terminal heat pump air conditioning** - MacMarney Refrigeration & Air Conditioning Ltd

U50 Hybrid system air conditioning

- **COOL-PHASE® Low energy cooling and ventilation systems** - Monodraught Ltd
- **Heat recovery** - Eaton-Williams Group Limited
- **Hybrid system air conditioning** - TEV Limited
- **Integrated air conditioning and HVAC systems** - Tyco Fire and Integrated Solutions

U60 Air conditioning units

- **Air Conditioning** - Climate Center
- **Air Conditioning** - Daikin Airconditioning UK Ltd
- **Air conditioning** - Systemair Ltd
- **Air Conditioning Systems** - LTI Advanced Systems Technology Ltd
- **Air conditioning units** - Andrews Sykes Hire Ltd
- **Air conditioning units** - Colt International
- **Air conditioning Units** - Constant Air Systems Ltd
- **Air conditioning units** - DencoHappel UK Ltd
- **Air conditioning units** - Emerson Climate Technologies
- **Air conditioning units** - Encon Air Systems Ltd
- **Air conditioning units** - Johnson Controls Building Efficiency UK Ltd
- **Air conditioning units** - MacMarney Refrigeration & Air Conditioning Ltd
- **Air conditioning units** - Mansfield Pollard & Co Ltd
- **Air conditioning units** - TEV Limited
- **Air conditioning units** - Toshiba Carrier UK
- **Air Cooled Condensers** - Thermal Technology Sales Ltd
- **Air Handing Units** - Fläkt Woods Ltd
- **Chillers** - Daikin Airconditioning UK Ltd
- **Condensing units** - Airedale International Air Conditioning Ltd
- **Portable air conditioners** - Thermoscreens Ltd
- **Portable heating** - Andrews Sykes Hire Ltd
- **Refrigeration equipment** - Dunham Bush Ltd

U70 Air curtains

- **Air curtains** - Biddle Air Systems Ltd
- **Air curtains** - DencoHappel UK Ltd
- **Air Curtains** - Envirotech Ltd
- **Air curtains** - Systemair Ltd
- **Air curtains** - Thermoscreens Ltd
- **Air curtains / Convectors** - S & P Coil Products Ltd
- **Aircurtains** - AmbiRad Ltd

V10 Electricity generation plant

- **Automatic start generators** - Cummins Power Generation Ltd
- **Automatic synchronising generators** - Cummins Power Generation Ltd
- **Baseload diesel generator** - Broadcrown Ltd
- **Central battery systems** - Channel Safety Systems Ltd
- **General electrical products** - WF Senate
- **General electrical products - wholesale** - Jolec Electrical Supplies
- **Generation plant** - Broadcrown Ltd
- **generators** - Chippindale Plant Ltd
- **Mobile generators** - Cummins Power Generation Ltd
- **Peak loppingd diesel generators** - Broadcrown Ltd
- **Power generators** - Cummins Power Generation Ltd
- **Power plants** - Cummins Power Generation Ltd
- **Silenced generators** - Cummins Power Generation Ltd
- **Standby diesel generators** - Broadcrown Ltd
- **Super silenced generators** - Cummins Power Generation Ltd

PRODUCTS AND SERVICES

V10 Electricity generation plant (con't)

Transformers and packaged substations - Schneider Electric Ltd
Ventilation Products - Allmat (East Surrey) Ltd

V11 HV supply/ distribution/ public utility supply

Accessories for electrical services - Lewden Electrical Industries
Electrical distribution - Schneider Electric Ltd
Extra high voltage - Schneider Electric Ltd
HV Supply/Distribution/Public Utility Supply - Dynniq UK Ltd
Public distribution - Schneider Electric Ltd
Substation kiosks - MCL Composites Ltd

V12 LV supply/ public utility supply

Electricity meters - Switch2 Energy Solutions Ltd
Final distribution - Schneider Electric Ltd
LV Supply/Public Utility Supply - Dynniq UK Ltd
Retail Lighting - Fitzgerald Lighting Ltd

V20 LV distribution

2V Distribuition - Eaton Electric Limited
Accessories for electrical services - Lewden Electrical Industries
Cable Reel - Metreel Ltd
Circuit protection and control - Bill Switchgear
Electricity meter boxes - MCL Composites Ltd
Festoon Systems - Metreel Ltd
Low voltage distribution - Schneider Electric Ltd
LV Distribution - Dynniq UK Ltd
Modular desk & Screen Power, Telecom & Data Units - Electrak International Ltd
Permanent Power Distribution - 110v to 400v - Blakley Electrics Ltd
Protected sockets - Blakley Electrics Ltd
Safe Supply Units - Blakley Electrics Ltd
Small power distribution - Ackermann Ltd
Surge protection systems - Erico Europa (GB) Ltd
Temporary power Distribution - 110v to 400v - Blakley Electrics Ltd
Tranformers 100VA to 250kVA, 12v to 3300v - Blakley Electrics Ltd

V21 General lighting

Access panels to ceiling void - Saint-Gobain Ecophon Ltd
Accessories for electrical services - Lewden Electrical Industries
Acoustic suspended ceiling systems - Saint-Gobain Ecophon Ltd
Aisle and step lighting - Gradus Ltd
Architectural lighting - Optelma Lighting Ltd
Asymmetric lighting - Crescent Lighting
Ballasts: magnetic and electronic - Helvar Ltd
Bathroom Lighting - Astro Lighting Ltd
Bespoke Lighting - ALD Lighting Solutions
Cabinet and display lighting - Crescent Lighting
Cold cathode - Oldham Lighting Ltd
Commercial Lighting - Illuma Lighting
Commercial wiring systems - Metway Electrical Industries Ltd
Compact Fluorecent Downlights - ITAB Prolight UK Limited
Decorative and display lighting - Myddleton Hall Lighting, Division of Peerless Design Ltd
Design, supply and install - Oldham Lighting Ltd
Display lighting - FEILO SYLVANIA EUROPE LIMITED
Display Lighting - Fitzgerald Lighting Ltd
Domestic lighting - FEILO SYLVANIA EUROPE LIMITED
Downlights - Illuma Lighting
Electrical Accessories - Focus SB Ltd
Emergency batteries - Bernlite Ltd
Emergency modules - Bernlite Ltd
Energy saving lighting - Anglepoise Lighting Ltd
Energy saving lighting - FEILO SYLVANIA EUROPE LIMITED
Exterior lighting - DW Windsor Lighting
Exterior lighting - Fagerhult Lighting
Feature Lighting - Illuma Lighting
Fibre optic systems - ALD Lighting Solutions
Fibreoptic lighting - Crescent Lighting
Genaral Lighting - Commercial Lighting Systems
Genaral Lighting - Best & Lloyd Ltd
General lighting - Brandon Medical
General Lighting - Consult Lighting Ltd
General Lighting - Designplan Lighting Ltd
General Lighting - Dynniq UK Ltd
General lighting - European Lamp Group
General lighting - FEILO SYLVANIA EUROPE LIMITED
General lighting - Glamox Electric (UK) Ltd
General lighting - Glamox Luxo Lighting Limited
General lighting - IBL Lighting Limited
General lighting - IKM Systems Ltd
General Lighting - Morgan Hope Industries Ltd
General lighting - Oldham Lighting Ltd
General lighting and bulbs - GE Lighting Ltd
General lighting products - Whitecroft Lighting Limited
General, modular, compact Fluorescent - Lumitron Ltd
Gimbal spots - ITAB Prolight UK Limited
Green (Low enegry) Lighting - Blakley Electrics Ltd
Handlamps - Ensto Briticent Ltd
Hazardous area lighting - Glamox Electric (UK) Ltd
Hazardous area lighting - PFP Electrical Products Ltd
Healthcare lighting - Glamox Luxo Lighting Limited
High Bay Lighting - Mode Lighting
High frequency electronic ballasts - Bernlite Ltd
Hospital lighting - Thorlux Lighting
Ignitors - Bernlite Ltd
Industrial Lighting - Fitzgerald Lighting Ltd
Interior and exterior lighting - Andy Thornton Ltd
Kitchen lighting - Waterline Limited
Lamps - Philips Lighting
Lamps - ceramic - BLV Licht-und Vakuumtecnik
LED Drivers/Modules - Helvar Ltd
LED lighting - Glamox Luxo Lighting Limited
LED lighting - ITAB Prolight UK Limited
LED Lighting - NET LED Limited
LED lighting for pool installations - Golden Coast Ltd
LED luminaires - ALD Lighting Solutions
LED luminaires - Crescent Lighting
LED replacement flourescent tubes - Crescent Lighting
LED retrofit lighting - Crescent Lighting
Light bulbs, tungsten halogen and metal halide - BLV Licht-und Vakuumtecnik
Light fittings - ITAB Prolight UK Limited
Light fittings - Thorn Lighting
Lighting - Eglo UK
Lighting - Litex Design Ltd
Lighting - Optelma Lighting Ltd
Lighting - Shaylor Group Plc
Lighting control equipment - Philips Lighting Solutions
Lighting control gear inc. ballasts, chokes - Bernlite Ltd
Lighting Control Products - Eaton Electric Limited
Lighting control systems - Hamilton R & Co Ltd
Lighting controllers, sensors, relay units, interfaces, input devices and enclosures - Helvar Ltd
Lighting Controls - Fitzgerald Lighting Ltd
Lighting Controls - Mode Lighting
Lighting controls - Philips Lighting
Lighting equipment - Thorlux Lighting
Lighting Manufacturer and supply - Whitecroft Lighting Limited
Lighting products - Friedland Ltd
Lighting support systems - Vantrunk Engineering Ltd
Low energy lighting systems - Connect Lighting Systems (UK) Ltd
Low voltage - ITAB Prolight UK Limited
Low-voltage lighting - Fairfield Displays & Lighting Ltd
Luminaires - Philips Lighting
Luminaires - office, retail, industrial, amenity, pharmaceutical, hospital etc - Whitecroft Lighting Limited
Mains voltage halogen lighting - FEILO SYLVANIA EUROPE LIMITED
Marine lighting - Chalmit Lighting
Marshalling Boxes - Mode Lighting
Office lighting - FEILO SYLVANIA EUROPE LIMITED
PowerX, Lighting, Timers, Chimes, Wiring Accessories, Ventilation - KingShield - Green Brook
Purpose made luminaires - ALD Lighting Solutions
Recessed Lighting - Fitzgerald Lighting Ltd
Recessed and Surface LG3 Luminaires - ITAB Prolight UK Limited
Retail and Display Lighting - Illuma Lighting
Retail Display Luminaires - ITAB Prolight UK Limited
Security PIR lighting - Timeguard Ltd
Self-learning lighting control solutions - Helvar Ltd
Site Lighting 110v Lighting - Blakley Electrics Ltd
Specialist Lighting - LPA Group PLC
Specials - ITAB Prolight UK Limited
Spotlights - Illuma Lighting
Standalone solutions - Helvar Ltd
Suspended ceiling luminaires - System Building Products
Task Lighting - Glamox Luxo Lighting Limited
Track - Illuma Lighting

V22 General LV power

Dimmers, switches, sockets, on plates of brass, bronze,steel, chrome, wood polycarbonate - Hamilton R & Co Ltd
Electrical Engineering Services (Mains Distribution, Single and Three Phase Power) - H Pickup Mechanical & Electrical Services Ltd
Power - Shaylor Group Plc
Power cables - Pitacs Ltd

V30 Extra low voltage supply

Accessories for electrical services - Lewden Electrical Industries
Entry sound communoication products - Friedland Ltd
Exrta low voltage supply - Brandon Medical
General electrical products - WF Senate
General electrical products - wholesale - Jolec Electrical Supplies
LED Lighting - NET LED Limited
Miniature precision switches, push button and cord pull etc - Omeg Ltd
Transformers for low voltage lighting - Mode Lighting (UK) Ltd

V31 DC supply

Accessories for electrical services - Lewden Electrical Industries
Batteries - M.J. Electronic Services (International) Ltd
Battery chargers - M.J. Electronic Services (International) Ltd
DC Supplies - Dynniq UK Ltd
Direct current supply - Brandon Medical

V32 Uninterruptible power supply

Central battery systems - Emergi-Lite Safety Systems
Electrical accessories - Electrak International Ltd
Power electronic repair and service - M.J. Electronic Services (International) Ltd
Uninterruptible power supply - ITM Communications LtdLtd
Uninterupted Power Supply - Eaton Electric Limited
Uniterupted power supply - Channel Safety Systems Ltd
UPS services - M.J. Electronic Services (International) Ltd
UPS Systems - Dynniq UK Ltd
UPS systems and inverters - M.J. Electronic Services (International) Ltd

V40 Emergency lighting

Automatic / Self-Testing Emergency Lighting - P4 Limited
Emergency lighting - ADT Fire and Security Plc
Emergency lighting - ALD Lighting Solutions
Emergency lighting - Channel Safety Systems Ltd
Emergency lighting - Connect Lighting Systems (UK) Ltd
Emergency lighting - Cooper Safety
Emergency lighting - Designplan Lighting Ltd
Emergency lighting - Emergi-Lite Safety Systems
Emergency lighting - Fagerhult Lighting
Emergency Lighting - Fitzgerald Lighting Ltd
Emergency lighting - Gent Limited
Emergency lighting - Glamox Electric (UK) Ltd
Emergency Lighting - Illuma Lighting
Emergency lighting - M.J. Electronic Services (International) Ltd
Emergency lighting - Metway Electrical Industries Ltd
Emergency Lighting - Morgan Hope Industries Ltd
Emergency lighting - Orbik Electrics Ltd
Emergency lighting - PFP Electrical Products Ltd
Emergency lighting - Thorlux Lighting
Emergency lighting systems - Cooper Safety
Emergency lighting systems - Mackwell Electronics Ltd
Emergency lighting testing systems - Emergi-Lite Safety Systems
Emergency lighting, switch tripping and battery chargers - Dynniq UK Ltd
Emergency lighting/exit lights - ABB Installation Products Ltd
Emergency lights - Firetecnics Systems Ltd
Emergency Lights - Whitecroft Lighting Limited
General electrical products - WF Senate
General electrical products - wholesale - Jolec Electrical Supplies
Hazardous area lighting - Chalmit Lighting
Integral emergency lighting - Lumitron Ltd
LED Emergency Lighting - NET LED Limited
Light fittings - Thorn Lighting
Powdered way guidance - Hoyles Electronic Developments Ltd
Security lighting - ASCO Extinguishers Co. Ltd

V41 Street/ Area/ Flood lighting

Amenity & area lighting - DW Windsor Lighting
Amenity Lighting - Fitzgerald Lighting Ltd
Architectural interior lighting for commercial applications - Fagerhult Lighting
Architectural lighting - Thorlux Lighting
Area/street lighting, floodlights - CU Phosco Lighting
Coloured metal hacide floodlamps - BLV Licht-und Vakuumtecnik
Emergency lighting - Chalmit Lighting
Exterior uplighters - Lumitron Ltd
External Lighting - UTC Fire & Securites
Flood Lighting - Blakley Electrics Ltd
Flood Lighting - Fitzgerald Lighting Ltd
Floodlighting - Thorlux Lighting
Floodlighting poles - Valmont Stainton
Hazardous area lighting - Thorlux Lighting
High Mast Lighting - CU Phosco Lighting
LED Flood Lighting - NET LED Limited
LED street lighting - Glamox Luxo Lighting Limited
Light Towers - Genie Europe
Outdoor lighting - Holophane Europe Ltd
Outdorr Lights - Astro Lighting Ltd
Street lighting - DW Windsor Lighting
Street lighting - Urbis Schreder Ltd
Street lighting columns and accessories - Lampost Construction Co Ltd
Street lighting columns and high masts - Valmont Stainton
Street lighting columns and sign posts - Fabrikat (Nottingham) Ltd
Street/ area & flood lighting - FEILO SYLVANIA EUROPE LIMITED
Street/ Area/ Flood lighting - Consult Lighting Ltd
Street/ area/ flood lighting - Designplan Lighting Ltd
Street/ Area/ Flood lighting - Glamox Luxo Lighting Limited
Street/Area/Flood Lighting - Commercial Lighting Systems
Street/Area/Flood Lighting - Whitecroft Lighting Limited
Tunnel and underpass lighting - Thorlux Lighting

V42 Studio/ Auditorium/ Arena lighting

Dimming Systems - Mode Lighting
DLCMS Lighting control system - Mode Lighting
Emergency Lighting - P4 Limited
Industrial lighting - Chalmit Lighting
Industrial lighting - Glamox Electric (UK) Ltd
Lamps - capsule - BLV Licht-und Vakuumtecnik
Lamps - dichroic - BLV Licht-und Vakuumtecnik
LED Tube and Panel Lighting - NET LED Limited
Lighting project design - DW Windsor Lighting
Scene Setting - Mode Lighting
Sports arera lighting - En-tout-cas Tennis Courts Ltd
Studio/ Auditorium/ Arena Lighting - Consult Lighting Ltd
Studio/ auditorium/ arena lighting - FEILO SYLVANIA EUROPE LIMITED
Studio/Auditorium/Arena Lighting - Dynniq UK Ltd
Tennis court lighting - En-tout-cas Tennis Courts Ltd
Theatrical lighting - Multitex GRP LLP

V50 Electric underfloor/ ceiling heating

Ceiling electric heating - Flexel International Ltd
Electric underfloor heating - Bush Nelson PLC
Electric underfloor/ ceiling heating - Dimplex UK Limited
Electric underfloor/ceiling heating - Flexel International Ltd
Ramp heating - Findlay Irvine Ltd
Undefloor Heating - Begetube UK Ltd
Underfloor electric heating - Flexel International Ltd
Underfloor heating - H Pickup Mechanical & Electrical Services Ltd
Underfloor heating - Purmo-UK
Underfloor heating - Uponor Ltd
Underfloor heating controls - Danfoss Ltd
Underfloor heating systems - REHAU Ltd

V51 Local electric heating units

Ceiling heaters - Ecolec
Electric air duct heaters - Eltron Chromalox
Electric cartridge heaters - Eltron Chromalox
Electric convector heaters - Eltron Chromalox
Electric fan heaters - Eltron Chromalox
Electric fire manufacturer - Dimplex UK Limited
Electric Fires - Winther Browne & co Ltd
Electric heater batteries - Ves Andover Ltd
Electric heaters - Eltron Chromalox
Electric heating - Kaloric Heater Co Ltd
Electric panel heaters - Valor
Electric Stoves - Gazco Ltd
Electric stripring heaters - Eltron Chromalox
Electrical heating units - Consort Equipment Products Ltd
Fan heaters - Ecolec
General electrical products - WF Senate
General electrical products - wholesale - Jolec Electrical Supplies
Glass radiators - Ecolec
Heated towel rails - hot water - Pitacs Ltd
Local electric heating units - Bush Nelson PLC
Local electric heating units - Dimplex UK Limited
Local electrical heating units - Flexel International Ltd
Local heating units - Dimplex UK Limited
Local Heating Units - Morgan Hope Industries Ltd
Low energy electric panel heaters - Ecolec
Mirror radiators - Ecolec
Radiators - Designer Radiators Direct
Towel rails - Ecolec

V90 Electrical installation (self-contained spec)

Accessories for electrical services - Lewden Electrical Industries
Design of electrical services - Aercon Consultants Ltd
Domestic wiring accessories and circuit protection equipment - Contactum Ltd
Electrcity supply: switches & accessories - Hamilton R & Co Ltd
Electrical accessories - Marcus M Ltd
Electrical distribution blocks - Erico Europa (GB) Ltd
Electrical Installation - West London Security
Electrical installation equipment - Legrand Power Centre
Electrical installation products - Barton Engineering
Electrical Instillation - Barton Engineering
Electrical wiring accessories - Eaton Electric Limited
Electrical works - Shaylor Group Plc
Electrically operated tracks - Goelst
Floor laid flexible cable protectors for every application - Vulcascot Cable Protectors Ltd
General electrical products - WF Senate
General electrical products - wholesale - Jolec Electrical Supplies
Mains lighting - Cooper Lighting
Ropes and sashcords - Marlow Ropes Ltd
Specialsist electrical connectors - LPA Group PLC
Wire accessories - Hellermann Tyton
Workplace systems - Ackermann Ltd

W10 Telecommunications

Cables - Nexans UK Ltd
Communications - Ackermann Ltd
Communications - Ogilvie Construction Ltd
Hospital communications systems - Tunstal Healthcare (UK) Ltd
Telecommunications - Connaught Communications Systems Ltd
Telecommunications - ITM Communications LtdLtd
Telephone enclosures - Midland Alloy Ltd
TV/ Telephone systems for hospitals - Wandsworth Elecrtical Ltd
Voice recording, processing and training enhancement software - Computertel Ltd

PRODUCTS AND SERVICES

W11 Paging/ Emergency call

Care communications - ADT Fire and Security Plc
Data paging systems - Channel Safety Systems Ltd
Deaf emergency alerter - Deaf Alerter plc
Doctor call systems - Channel Safety Systems Ltd
Intercoms - PEL Services Limited
Nurse call and on-site paging systems - Blick Communication Systems Ltd
Nurse call systems - Channel Safety Systems Ltd
Paging - Wandsworth Elecrtrical Ltd
Paging/ Emergency call - C-TEC (Computionics) Ltd
Signalling and warning equipment - Pyronix

W12 Public address/ Conference audio facilities

Background music - PEL Services Limited
Broadcast and audio visual products & services - Streamtec Limited
Conference equipment - Anders + Kern UK Ltd
Public address - Blick Communication Systems Ltd
Public address - PEL Services Limited
Public address system - AET.gb Ltd
Sound masking systems - AET.gb Ltd

W20 Radio/ TV/ CCTV

advanced digital video recording - Xtralis
Audio visual - Anders + Kern UK Ltd
Broadcast and audio visual products & services - Streamtec Limited
C.C.T.V - Sampson & Partners Fencing
CCTV - Abel Alarm Co Ltd
CCTV - ADT Fire and Security Plc
CCTV - Allen (Fencing) Ltd
CCTV - Allgood plc
CCTV - Connaught Communications Systems Ltd
CCTV - PEL Services Limited
CCTV - Prima Security & Fencing Products
CCTV - UTC Fire & Securites
CCTV - Ward's Flexible Rod Company Ltd
CCTV - West London Security
CCTV systems - Interphone Limited
CCTV's - Chubb Systems Ltd
CCTV's - Initial Electronic Security Systems Ltd
Closed circuit television - Vicon Industries Ltd
Closed circuit television - Vidionics Security Systems Ltd
Design, manufacture and installation of audio visual systems - Spaceright Europe Limited
Design, Supply & Installation - Vidionics Security Systems Ltd
Ethernet video surveillance - Vidionics Security Systems Ltd
Home Automation & AV - West London Security
Plasma/LCD Systems - Spaceright Europe Limited
Presentation and conference equipment - Anders + Kern UK Ltd
Radio / TV / CCTV - ITM Communications LtdLtd
Radio telemetry - Eaton's Security Business
remote video transmition - Xtralis
Social care alarms - Eaton's Security Business
Transmission poles - Valmont Stainton
TV distribution - Blick Communication Systems Ltd
Visual communications systems - Quartet-GBC UK Ltd/ ACCO UK Ltd

W21 Projection

Big screens (indoor/outdoor) - Pro Display TM Limited
Electronic displays - Pro Display TM Limited
Plasma monitors/TVs - Pro Display TM Limited
Projection equipment - Spaceright Europe Limited
Projection Screen Systems - Harkness Screens
Projection screens - Magiboards Ltd
Projectors and projection screens - Pro Display TM Limited
Simulation display projection screens floor standing and moving platform versions - Design & Display Structures Ltd
Touch screens - Pro Display TM Limited
TV feature walls - Gridpart Interiors Ltd
Video walls - Pro Display TM Limited

W22 Information/ Advertising display

Broadcast and audio visual products & services - Streamtec Limited
Information cases - GB Sign Solutions Limited
Information kiosks - Pryorsign
Information/ advertising display - Focal Signs Ltd
Information/ advertizing display - Stocksigns Ltd
Interpretation Boards - GB Sign Solutions Limited
Light boxes - Simplex Signs Limited
Poster/ menu cases/cabinets - Simplex Signs Limited
Showcases - Fairfield Displays & Lighting Ltd
Suspend display systems - Fairfield Displays & Lighting Ltd
TV feature walls - Gridpart Interiors Ltd

W23 Clocks

Clock towers - Scotts of Thrapston Ltd
Clocks - General Time Europe
Clocks - Lesco Products Ltd
Time Recording Equipment - ISGUS UK Limited
Timer switches for central heating and controls for central heating - Tower Flue Components Ltd

W30 Data transmission

Cables - Nexans UK Ltd
Data cabling - Shaylor Group Plc
Data transmission - C-TEC (Computionics) Ltd
Data Transmission - ITM Communications LtdLtd
Datacoms - MK (MK Electric Ltd)
Electric information systems - Ferrograph Limited
Software for the construction industry - Masterbill Micro Systems Ltd

W40 Access control

Access - Doorfit Products Ltd
Access control - Abel Alarm Co Ltd
Access control - ADT Fire and Security Plc
Access control - Allen (Fencing) Ltd
Access control - Allgood plc
Access control - BPT Automation Ltd
Access control - Chubb Systems Ltd
Access Control - Connaught Communications Systems Ltd
Access control - Dinnington Fencing Co. Limited
Access Control - Directional Data Systems Ltd
Access control - Dorma Door Services Ltd
Access Control - Duffells Limited
Access Control - Eaton's Security Business
Access Control - Focus SB Ltd
Access control - GfA UK Ltd
Access control - Honeywell Control Systems Ltd
Access control - Hoyles Electronic Developments Ltd
Access control - Initial Electronic Security Systems Ltd
Access control - ITM Communications LtdLtd
Access control - Laidlaw Ltd
Access control - PEL Services Limited
Access Control - Pike Signals Ltd
Access control - Siemens Building Technologies
Access Control - Tate Fencing
Access control - Trend Control Systems Ltd
Access Control - UTC Fire & Securites
Access control - Vidionics Security Systems Ltd
Access control equipment - Hafele UK Ltd
Access control products - ASSA ABLOY Limited
Access control products - ASSA ABLOY Ltd
Access control systems - CEM Systems Ltd
Access control systems - Interphone Limited
Access control systems - Pac International Ltd
Access control systems - Sampson & Partners Fencing
Access control systems - Securikey Ltd
Access control systems - Time and Data Systems International Ltd (TDSI)
Access control systems - Wandsworth Elecrtrical Ltd
Access control systems - Yale Security Products Ltd
Access control systems / equipment - APT Controls Ltd
Access control systems, ID and access card production and registered key systems - Kaba Ltd
Access Control, Biometric Access Systems, Door Entry Systems - West London Security
Access control, exit devices, electromagnetic locks and electric strikes - Relcross Ltd
Auto sliding gates - Allen (Fencing) Ltd
Automatic gates, barriers and railings - Parsons Brothers Gates
Automatic Rising Bollards - BPT Automation Ltd
Barriers and fully automated equipment - Prima Security & Fencing Products
Bird control - Timberwise (UK) Ltd
Call systems - Wandsworth Elecrtrical Ltd
Card readers - CEM Systems Ltd
Door & window control equipment - GEZE UK
Door entry systems - Aardee Security Shutters Ltd
Electric openers/ spare parts - Cardale Garage Doors
Electrical garage door accessories - Garador Ltd
ID badging systems - CEM Systems Ltd
Intercom - Wandsworth Elecrtrical Ltd
Mechanical and electrical locks - ASSA ABLOY Limited
Mechanical and electrical locks - ASSA ABLOY Ltd
Security access and control - Hart Door Systems Ltd
Security detection and alarm control equipment - Pyronix
Sliding Door gear - Hafele UK Ltd
Standalone Access control panels - Abloy UK
Turnstiles - Allen (Fencing) Ltd
Vehicle access control - Autopa Ltd
Video Entry systems - Tate Fencing

W41 Security detection and alarm

Access Control - Vador Security Systems Ltd
Access Control Systems - Intime Fire and Security
Anti-terrorist devices - Pyronix
Automated gates and barriers - Vador Security Systems Ltd
Burglar alarms - Chubb Systems Ltd
Burglar alarms - Initial Electronic Security Systems Ltd
CCTV Systems - Intime Fire and Security
Digital image recorders - Optex (Europe) Ltd
Disabled toilet alarm systems - Channel Safety Systems Ltd
Door security locks - Hafele UK Ltd
Electric fence system for commercial & industrial sites - Advanced Perimeter Systems Ltd
Electronic security services, Intruder Alarms - West London Security
Fence Intrusion Detection System - Advanced Perimeter Systems Ltd
Gates and barriers - high speed - Hart Door Systems Ltd
Integrated security systems - Vidionics Security Systems Ltd
Intruder alarm and CCTV - PEL Services Limited
Intruder alarms - ADT Fire and Security Plc
Intruder alarms - Eaton's Security Business
Intruder Alarms - Intime Fire and Security
Intruder Detection - UTC Fire & Securites
passive infared detectors - Xtralis
Passive infra red detectors and photoelectric beams - Optex (Europe) Ltd
PC based security control and monitoring system - Advanced Perimeter Systems Ltd
Perimeter protection - Vidionics Security Systems Ltd
Personal security system - Wandsworth Elecrtrical Ltd
Security systems - Pac International Ltd
security and surveillance systemas - Xtralis
Security detection - Friedland Ltd
Security detection - Honeywell Control Systems Ltd
Security detection & alarms - Siemens Building Technologies
Security detection and alarm - Johnson Controls Building Efficiency UK Ltd
Security detection and alarm - Tower Manufacturing
Security detection and alarm control equipment - Pyronix
Security detection and alarm systems - Abel Alarm Co Ltd
Security detection and alarm systems - Interphone Limited
Security detection and alarms - Heras
Security detection equipment - Hoyles Electronic Developments Ltd
Security detection screening - Specialist Building Products
Security doors - Jewers Doors Ltd
Security equipment and alarms - ADT Fire and Security Plc
Security equipment and alarms - Advanced Perimeter Systems Ltd
Security fencing - C & W Fencing Ltd
Security management systems and high security locks - Relcross Ltd
Security mirrors - Smart F & G (Shopfittings)Ltd
Security Systems - Cooper Lighting
Security, CCTV - WF Senate
Sounders and strobes - KAC Alarm Company Ltd
Vibration sensors - Optex (Europe) Ltd
video intrusion detection - Xtralis
Voice alarms - PEL Services Limited
Warehouse intrusion detection system - Advanced Perimeter Systems Ltd

W50 Fire detection and alarm

Battery & Mains Heat Alarms - BRK Brands Europe Ltd
Break glass and call points - KAC Alarm Company Ltd
Emergency Lighting - P4 Limited
Fire alarm equipment - Hoyles Electronic Developments Ltd
Fire Alarm Systems - Intime Fire and Security
Fire alarms - Chubb Systems Ltd
Fire alarms - Fife Fire Engineers & Consultants Ltd
Fire alarms - Griffin and General Fire Services Ltd
Fire alarms - Initial Electronic Security Systems Ltd
Fire alarms and smoke detectors - ASCO Extinguishers Co. Ltd
Fire Alarms, Data Wiring, Call Systems - H Pickup Mechanical & Electrical Services Ltd
Fire and gas control systems - Zellweger Analytic Ltd, Sieger Division
Fire detection - ABB Installation Products Ltd
Fire detection - Abel Alarm Co Ltd
Fire detection - ADT Fire and Security Plc
Fire detection - Honeywell Control Systems Ltd
Fire detection - Kidde Fire Protection Ltd
Fire detection and alarm - Johnson Controls Building Efficiency UK Ltd
Fire detection and alarm - PEL Services Limited
Fire detection and alarm systems - Blick Communication Systems Ltd
Fire detection and alarm systems - BRK Brands Europe Ltd
Fire detection and alarm systems - Channel Safety Systems Ltd
Fire detection and alarm systems - Firetecnics Systems Ltd
Fire detection and alarm systems - Gent Limited
Fire detection and alarm systems - Hochiki Europe (UK) Ltd
Fire detection and alarm systems - Interphone Limited
Fire detection and alarm systems - Kidde Fire Protection Services Ltd
Fire detection and alarms - C-TEC (Computionics) Ltd
Fire detection and suppression - Tyco Fire and Integrated Solutions
Fire detection equipment - Nittan (UK) Ltd
Fire detection Systems - Cooper Lighting
Fire detection systems - Cooper Safety
Fire detection systems - Emergi-Lite Safety Systems
Fire protection and alarm - Siemens Building Technologies
Fire protection products for doors and building openings - Moffett Thallon & Co Ltd
Fire systems - West London Security
Gas detection - Gas Measurement Instruments Ltd
Gates and barriers - Hart Door Systems Ltd
Lifts - SCS Group
Radio fire alarm systems - Channel Safety Systems Ltd
Smoke and heat detectors - Apollo Fire Detectors Ltd
Vesda aspirating smoke detection equipment - Xtralis

W51 Earthing and bonding

Earth rods and earthing systems - Erico Europa (GB) Ltd
Earthing & Bonding - Tower Manufacturing
Earthing and bonding - Cutting R C & Co
Earthing systems - Furse
Lighting protection engineers - J W Gray Lightning Protection Ltd

W52 Lightning protection

Earthing & bonding installations - J W Gray Lightning Protection Ltd
Lightning conductor systems - Erico Europa (GB) Ltd
Lightning protection - Cutting R C & Co
Lightning protection - Furse
Lightning Protection - R. C. Cutting & Company Ltd
Lightning protection, earthing and electronic protection - Bacon Group
Transient overvoltage protection - Furse

W53 Electromagnetic screening

Patient tagging system - Wandsworth Elecrtrical Ltd

W54 Liquid detection alarm

Gas detection and alarm - Tyco Fire and Integrated Solutions
Liquid detection alarm - Specialist Building Products
Oil pollution monitoring and control systems - design, manufacture, installation and commissioning of - Aquasentry
Water leak detection equipment - Aquasentry

W60 Central control/ Building management

Access Control - Allegion (UK) Ltd
Automatic / Self-Testing Emergency Lighting - P4 Limited
Automation and control - Schneider Electric Ltd
Broadcast and audio visual products & services - Streamtec Limited
Building and energy management - ADT Fire and Security Plc
Building control and management systems - Siemens Building Technologies
Building management systems - Honeywell Control Systems Ltd
Building management systems - Trend Control Systems Ltd
CCTV - Vador Security Systems Ltd
Central control systems - Honeywell Control Systems Ltd
Central control/ Building management - C-TEC (Computionics) Ltd
Central control/ Building management - Johnson Controls Building Efficiency UK Ltd
Central control/Building management - SCS Group
Community care alarm and monitering equipment - Tunstal Healthcare (UK) Ltd
Control equipment - George Fischer Sales Ltd
Control systems - Eltron Chromalox
Control systems - Technical Control Systems Ltd
Energy management systems - EnergyICT Ltd
Energy monitoring & targeting - Trend Control Systems Ltd
Home control products - Friedland Ltd
Indicator panels - Hoyles Electronic Developments Ltd
Instrumentation for boiler plant, incinerators and furnaces - SK Environmental Ltd
Integrated security management systems (SMS) - CEM Systems Ltd
Led's & colour mixing - Mode Lighting (UK) Ltd
Lighting control systems - Electrak International Ltd
Lighting control systems - Whitecroft Lighting Limited
Monitoring - Chubb Systems Ltd
Monitoring - Initial Electronic Security Systems Ltd
Remote management and monitoring - UTC Fire & Securites
Safety control systems - Tyco Fire and Integrated Solutions
Voice recording, processing and training enhancement software - Computertel Ltd

X10 Lifts

Access Lifts - Phoenix Lifting Systems Ltd
Access wheelchair platforms lifts - Stannah Lifts Ltd
Access, hydraulic and towable lifts - Denka International
Brush sealing for lifts and glass doors - Kleeneze Sealtech Ltd
Disabled access lifts - Hymo Ltd
Disabled access lifts and ramps - Chase Equipment Ltd
Dissabld Access Lifts - ThyssenKrupp Encasa, A Division of ThyssenKrupp Access Ltd
Dumb waiter - Platform Lift Company Ltd, The
dumb waiters - Gartec Ltd
Elevators - Kone
Good lifts - Stannah Lifts Ltd
goods lifts - Gartec Ltd
Goods lifts - Hymo Ltd
Goods lifts - Platform Lift Company Ltd, The
home lifts - Gartec Ltd
Home lifts - Wessex Lift Co Ltd
Hydraulic lifting equipment - Hymo Ltd
Hydraulic passenger lifts - Stannah Lifts Ltd

X10 Lifts (con't)

Lift manufacturers, installers service and maintenance - Pickerings Ltd
Lifting equipment - Hymo Ltd
Lifting platforms - Wessex Lift Co Ltd
Lifts - Gartec Ltd
Lifts - Kone PLC
Lifts - Schindler Ltd
Lifts - SSL Access
Lifts, ramps and loading bay equipment - specialist manufacturer - Chase Equipment Ltd
Lifts: Passenger, Platform, Goods and Vehicle - Kone
maintenance of lifts - Gartec Ltd
Mechanical Screw Lifts - Hymo Ltd
Mobile scissors lifts - Hymo Ltd
Pallet lifts - Hymo Ltd
Passenger lifts - Platform Lift Company Ltd, The
platform lifts - Gartec Ltd
Platform lifts - Platform Lift Company Ltd, The
Platform lifts - ThyssenKrupp Encasa, A Division of ThyssenKrupp Access Ltd
Pool lifts - Platform Lift Company Ltd, The
Portable material lifts - Genie Europe
Portable personal lifts - Genie Europe
Public access wheelchair - ThyssenKrupp Encasa, A Division of ThyssenKrupp Access Ltd
Pushbuttons and controls for lifts - Dewhurst plc
Scissor lift tables - Hymo Ltd
Scissor lifts - Platform Lift Company Ltd, The
Scissors lifts - Hymo Ltd
Service lifts - Gartec Ltd
servicing and maintenance of lifts - Gartec Ltd
Stair lifts - Stannah Lifts Ltd
Step lifts - Wessex Lift Co Ltd
Stretcher lifts - Gartec Ltd
Trolley lifts - Gartec Ltd
Wheelchair lifts - Stannah Lifts Ltd

X11 Escalators

Brush deflection for escalators - Kleeneze Sealtech Ltd
Escalators - Kone
Escalators - Kone PLC
Escalators - Schindler Ltd
Escalators and passenger conveyers, service and maintenance - Kone Escalators Ltd

X12 Moving pavements

Moving pavements - Schindler Ltd
Moving walkways and autowalks - Kone
Passenger conveyors - Kone PLC

X13 Powered stairlifts

Domestic stairlifts - ThyssenKrupp Encasa, A Division of ThyssenKrupp Access Ltd
Stairlifts - ThyssenKrupp Encasa, A Division of ThyssenKrupp Access Ltd

X14 Fire escape chutes/ slings

Fire escape chutes/slings - NRG Fabrications
Ropes and sashcords - Marlow Ropes Ltd

X20 Hoists

Access lifting equipment - Genie Europe
Access platforms - Kobi Ltd
Confined Space access Equipment - Didsbury Engineering Co Ltd
Davits - Didsbury Engineering Co Ltd
Hoists - Didsbury Engineering Co Ltd
Hoists - Konecranes UK
Hoists - Metreel Ltd
Hoists & handling equipment - Randalls Fabrications Ltd
Hoists and trolleys - PCT Group
Hydraulic movement systems - Hydratight Sweeney Limited
Manhole cover lifter - Didsbury Engineering Co Ltd
Permanent access cradles - Kobi Ltd
Personnel and material transport hoists - SGB, a Brand Company
Ropes and sashcords - Marlow Ropes Ltd
Telehanders - Genie Europe
Tripods - Didsbury Engineering Co Ltd
Wheelchair Platform Lifts - ThyssenKrupp Encasa, A Division of ThyssenKrupp Access Ltd
Woven lifting slings - Albion Manufacturing Ltd

X21 Cranes

Boom lifts (Telescopic articulating) - Genie Europe
Crane support - Eve Trakway
Cranes - Konecranes UK
Cranes - Metreel Ltd
Cranes - PCT Group
Grade 8 chain slings - PCT Group
Webbing slings - PCT Group

X22 Travelling cradles/ gantries/ladders

Access cradles - Cento Engineering Company Ltd
Access ladders - Clow Group Ltd
Cradle runways - Cento Engineering Company Ltd
Cradles - Clow Group Ltd
Façade access equipment - Cento Engineering Company Ltd
Façade hoists - Cento Engineering Company Ltd
Gantries - Clow Group Ltd
Gantry - Cento Engineering Company Ltd
Glazing trade association - Glass and Glazing Federation
Hoists and trolleys - PCT Group
Latchways - Cento Engineering Company Ltd
Steps - Clow Group Ltd
Suspended access equipment - Cento Engineering Company Ltd
Travelling Cradles/ Gantrie/ Ladders - Metreel Ltd
Travelling gantries - Kobi Ltd
Travelling ladders - Cento Engineering Company Ltd
Travelling ladders - Kobi Ltd
Trestles - Clow Group Ltd
Window cleaning cradles - Cento Engineering Company Ltd

X23 Goods distribution/ Mechanised warehousing

Dock levelers - Chase Equipment Ltd
Dock shelters - Chase Equipment Ltd
Mechanised Warehousing - Chiorino UK Ltd
Mobile food conveyors - TSE Brownson
Mobile yard ramps - Chase Equipment Ltd
Modular loading dock - Chase Equipment Ltd
Road haulage - Eve Trakway
Scissor lifts - Genie Europe
Steel conyor plates for sugar industry - manufacturer - Wm. Bain Fencing Ltd

X30 Mechanical document conveying

Despatch equipment - Envopak Group Ltd

X31 Pneumatic document conveying

Air tube conveying systems - Barloworld Vacuum Technology Plc
Mailroom equipment - Envopak Group Ltd
Pneumatic air tube conveying systems:- cash, sample, hospital and document - Barloworld Vacuum Technology Plc
Pneumatic conveying systems - Quirepace Ltd
Transport systems - Hardall International Ltd

X32 Automatic document filing and retrieval

Sorting equipment - Envopak Group Ltd

Y10 Pipelines

Cost Forecasting and Reporting - Procurement - British Water
DuraFuse - Viking Johnson
Durapipe ABS - Viking Johnson
Friatherm - Viking Johnson
GRE GRP pipes, tubes and fabrications - Deva Composites - A Division of Cope Engineering (Rollmakers) Limited
Mechanical joints - Victaulic Systems
Metal pipework - Copper, Galvanised steel and Stainless steel - Servomac Limited
Philmac - Viking Johnson
Pipe clips - Unifix Ltd
Pipe couplings - Viking Johnson
Pipelines - CPV Ltd
Pipelines - Deepdale Engineering Co Ltd
Pipelines - Insituform Technologies® Ltd
Pipelines - John Davidson (Pipes) Ltd
Pipelines - Polypipe Civils
Pipelines - Tata Steel Europe Limited
Pipelines - Yorkshire Copper Tube
Pipework - Woodburn Engineering Ltd
Pipework Fabrication - Turnbull & Scott (Engineers) Ltd
Plastic pipelines - IPPEC Systems Ltd
Plumbing accessories - PTS Plumbing Trade Supplies
Polybutylene pipe and fittings - Davant Products Ltd
Polyethylene plastic pipes - Uponor Ltd
Posiflex - Viking Johnson
Preinsulated Piping - Uponor Ltd
Pressure Pipes - Wavin Ltd
Proctect-line - Viking Johnson
Service fittings - Tyco Water Works
Spiral weld steel tube - Tex Engineering Ltd
Stainless steel fittings, flanges and fabrications - Lancashire Fittings Ltd
Stainless steel tubes and sections - Outokumpu Stainless Ltd
Stainless steel valves - Lancashire Fittings Ltd
Victaulic - Viking Johnson
Wask - Viking Johnson

Y11 Pipeline ancillaries

Accessories - Tyco Water Works
Air release valves - Delta Fire
Balancing valves - Crane Fluid Systems
Balancing valves - Static, DPCV, PICV - Hattersley
Ball valves - Crane Fluid Systems
Boiler House Equipment - Flowserve Flow Control
Butterfly valves - Crane Fluid Systems
Check valves - Crane Fluid Systems
Check Valves - Flowserve Flow Control
Control Valves - Flowserve Flow Control
Diverters - Deva Tap Co Ltd
Fire and gas safety valves - Teddington Controls Ltd
Fitttings, valves and tanks - CPV Ltd
Gate valves - Crane Fluid Systems
Gate valves - Delta Fire
Globe valves - Crane Fluid Systems
Hand- Hydraulic -Electric - Tube & Pipe Manuipulation Service - Tubela Engineering Co Ltd
Heating manifolds - SAV United Kingdom Ltd
Hydrant valves and pressure valves - Eagles, William, Ltd
Industrial Flow Control Equipment - Flowserve Flow Control
Inlet breeching - Delta Fire
In-Line Thermal Disinfection Unit (ILTDU) - Horne Engineering Ltd
Isolation Ball Valves - Flowserve Flow Control
Isolation valves and expansion vessels - SAV United Kingdom Ltd
Main Fittings - Tyco Water Works
Malleable iron pipe fittings - Crane Fluid Systems
Mixer valves - Bristan Group
Pipe fixings - Ellis Patents
Pipeline ancillaries - Deepdale Engineering Co Ltd
Pipeline ancillaries - Flex-Seal Couplings Ltd
Pipeline ancillaries - Isolated Systems Ltd
Pipeline ancillaries - John Davidson (Pipes) Ltd
Pipeline ancillaries - Polypipe Civils
Plug valves, control valves, gate valves, butterfly valves, check valves and consistency transmitters - Dezurik International Ltd
Plumbing accessories - PTS Plumbing Trade Supplies
Plumbing products and pipe fixings - Conex Universal Limited
Pushfit systems - Davant Products Ltd
Radiator valves - Crane Fluid Systems
Relief valves - Crane Fluid Systems
Sealed system equipment, air vents, pressure reducers, mixing valves, flow switches etc - Altecnic Ltd
Strainers - Crane Fluid Systems
Temperature control valves - Horne Engineering Ltd
Thermostatic and manual shower controls - Bristan Group
Valves - Pegler Ltd
Valves - Ball, Butterfly, Check, Gate, Press-Fit and Strainers - Hattersley
Welding and Brazing equipment \\ consumables - Johnson Matthey PLC - Metal Joining

Y20 Pumps

AP1610 - Weir Pumps Ltd
Centrifugal pumps - Weir Pumps Ltd
Diaphragm hand pumps - Pump International Ltd
Fixing systems for building services - Erico Europa (GB) Ltd
Gear and centrifugal pumps - Albany Standard Pumps
Grout pumps - Clarke UK Ltd
GRP packaged pumping stations - Pims Pumps Ltd
H.V Pumps - Pressmain
Industrial, chemical, oil & gas, and petrochemical pumps - Weir Pumps Ltd
Mixers - Hansgrohe
Oil pollution monitoring and control systems - design, manufacture, installation and commissioning of - Aquasentry
Packaged pump sets - Armstrong Integrated Ltd
Process pumps - Clarke UK Ltd
Pump repair - Pumps & Motors UK Ltd
Pumps - Albany Engineering Co Ltd
Pumps - Andrews Sykes Hire Ltd
Pumps - Armstrong Integrated Ltd
Pumps - Barr & Wray Ltd
Pumps - Calpeda Limited
Pumps - Goodwin HJ Ltd
Pumps - Grosvenor Pumps Ltd
Pumps - Ingersoll-Rand European Sales Ltd
Pumps - Mono Pumps Ltd
Pumps - New Haden Pumps Ltd
Pumps - Polypipe Civils
Pumps - Pumps & Motors UK Ltd
Pumps - The BSS Group
Pumps - T-T Pumps & T-T controls
Pumps - Wilo Samson Pumps Ltd
Pumps and Pump stations - Kingspan Environmental Ltd
Pumps, mixers and aerators - Sulzer Pumps Wastewater UK Ltd
Submersible electric pumps and mixers - ITT Flygt Ltd
Submersible pumps, servicing, maintenance and technical back up - Pump Technical Services Ltd
Sump drainage pumps - Stuart Turner Ltd
Trays for the elderly & special needs - Contour Showers Ltd
Tunnel concrete pumps - Clarke UK Ltd
Variable pumpdrives - Armstrong Integrated Ltd
Water leak detection equipment - Aquasentry
Water pumps - Stuart Turner Ltd

Y21 Water tanks/ cisterns

Carbon and stainless steel storage tanks - Cookson and Zinn (PTL) Ltd
Cold watertank upgrading, refurbishment & replacement Y21 - Nicholson Plastics Ltd
Custom moulded GRP products - Nicholson Plastics Ltd
Epoxy Tanks - CST Industries, Inc. - UK
G R P Tanks - Pressmain
Glass-Fused-to-Steel-Tanks - CST Industries, Inc. - UK
GRP one piece and sectional water storage tanks - Dewey Waters Ltd
GRP storage cisterns - Precolor Sales Ltd
GRP storage tanks - APA
GRP tank housings - Group Four Glassfibre Ltd
GRP water storage tanks - Group Four Glassfibre Ltd
Hot water cylinders and tanks - Gledhill Water Storage Ltd
Liquid Storage Tanks - CST Industries, Inc. - UK
Plastic cisterns - Dudley Thomas Ltd
Rainwater harvesting - Kingspan Environmental
Refurbishment of tanks - Franklin Hodge Industries Ltd
Rust stabilisation coatings - Corroless Corrosion Control
Sectional and one piece GRP cold water tanks - Nicholson Plastics Ltd
Sectional Steel Tanks and foundations - Goodwin Tanks Ltd
Silage storage tanks - Kingspan Environmental
Silage Storage tanks - Kingspan Environmental
Sprinkler Tanks - CST Industries, Inc. - UK
Storage tanks - Franklin Hodge Industries Ltd
Storage tanks and vessels - Metcraft Ltd
Tanks - Balmoral Tanks
Tanks - Braithwaite Engineers Ltd
Tanks - Fibaform Products Ltd
Water storage containers and accessories - Straight Ltd
Water storage tanks - Balmoral Tanks
Water storage tanks - Brimar Plastics Ltd
Water storage tanks - CST Industries, Inc. - UK
Water tanks - Harris & Bailey Ltd

Y22 Heat exchangers

Coil heat exchangers - S & P Coil Products Ltd
Corrugated shell and tube heat exchanger - HRS Hevac Ltd
Heat exchangers - Armstrong Integrated Ltd
Heat exchangers - Ormandy Rycroft Engineering
Heat Exchangers - SAV United Kingdom Ltd
Heat exchangers - Turnbull & Scott (Engineers) Ltd
Manufacturer of heating elements - Electric Elements Co, The
Plate heat exchangers - AEL
Plate heat exchangers Brazed - AEL

Y23 Storage cylinders/ Calorifiers

Calorifiers and Storage Tanks - Powerstock - Hamworthy Heating Limited & ACV UK
Carbon and stainless steel pressure vessels - Cookson and Zinn (PTL) Ltd
Cold water storage cisterns - Davant Products Ltd
Corrugated shell and tube heat exchanger - HRS Hevac Ltd
Mains pressure thermal storage - Gledhill Water Storage Ltd
Powerstock Calorifiers and Storage Tanks - Hamworthy Heating Limited & ACV UK
Storage cylinders/ calorifiers - Harris & Bailey Ltd
Storage cylinders/ Calorifiers - Ormandy Rycroft Engineering
Vented hot water storage cylinders - Range Cylinders
Water heaters/calorifiers - Flamco UK Ltd

Y24 Trace heating

Electric space heating - Bush Nelson PLC
Electric surface heating systems manufacturer - Pentair Thermal Management
Heating jackets and panels manufacturer - Pentair Thermal Management
Resistance heating equipment manufacturer - Pentair Thermal Management
Self- regulating cut-to-length heater tapes - Flexelec(UK) Ltd
Trace heating - Chromalox (UK) Ltd
Trace heating - Flexel International Ltd
Zone parallel constant wattage heater tapes - Flexelec(UK) Ltd

Y25 Cleaning and chemical treatment

Central heating system corrosion protectors, cleaners and leak sealers - Fernox
Chemical photo etchings - Photofabrication Limited
Chemicals - DSM UK Ltd
Chemicals - Lanxess Urethanes UK Ltd
Chlorination of water services - Aquastat Ltd
Cleaners and descalers - Tank Storage & Services Ltd
Cleaning & chemical treatment - Precolor Sales Ltd
Cleaning and chemical treatment - Frosts Landscape Construction Ltd
Cleaning and chemical treatment - Hertel Services
Cleaning and chemical treatments - Deb Group Limited
Cleaning materials - Evans Vanodine International PLC
Construction chemicals - Artur Fischer (UK) Ltd
Detergents - Evans Vanodine International PLC
Detergents & Disinfectants - Deb Group Limited
Disinfectants - Evans Vanodine International PLC
Grit blasting, chemical cleaning, high pressure water jetting - Masonry Cleaning Services
Jointing compounds, quick repair products and solder & flux - Fernox
Leak stopper and inhibitor for central heating systems - Dunsley Heat Ltd
Limescale remedies - Fernox
On site services - flue cleaning, pipework and fabrications - Hodgkinson Bennis Ltd
Polishes - Evans Vanodine International PLC
Polishes and floor cleaners - Johnson Wax Professional
Solvent Degreasers - Deb Group Limited
Specialist cleaning services - Rentokil Specialist Hygiene
Specialist pigments : artist colours - W. Hawley & Son Ltd
Specialist pigments : asphalt - W. Hawley & Son Ltd
Specialist pigments : concrete paving - W. Hawley & Son Ltd
Specialist pigments : concrete roofing - W. Hawley & Son Ltd
Specialist pigments : concrete walling - W. Hawley & Son Ltd
Specialist pigments : mortar - W. Hawley & Son Ltd
Specialist pigments : paint - W. Hawley & Son Ltd
Specialist pigments : plastic - W. Hawley & Son Ltd
Vehicle Cleaners - Deb Group Limited
Water treatment chemicals - Tower Flue Components Ltd
Water treatment products and services - Aldous & Stamp (Services) Ltd

Y30 Air ductlines/ Ancillaries

Air ductlines/Ancillaries - Isolated Systems Ltd
Connection and sleeves for air ducts - Westbury Filters Limited
Ducting - Alumasc Interior Building Products Limited
Ducting - MacLellan Rubber Ltd
Ductwork cleaning - GVS Filter Technology UK Ltd
Fire rated ductwork - Mansfield Pollard & Co Ltd
Fire rated ductwork systems - Fire Protection Ltd
Rubber mouldings and elastomeric bearings - MacLellan Rubber Ltd

Y40 Air handling units

Air conditioning - Dantherm Ltd
Air Handling Units - Aqua-Blue Designs
Air handling units - Colt International
Air handling units - Domus Ventilation
Air handling units - Dunham Bush Ltd
Air handling units - May William (Ashton) Ltd
Air handling units - Thermal Technology Sales Ltd
Air handling units - Ves Andover Ltd
Air Handling Units and Warm Air Heating (T40) and Self-Contained Specification (T41) - Chromalox (UK) Ltd
Air Handling Units, with heat recovery - SAV United Kingdom Ltd
Connect grid and air handling - Saint-Gobain Ecophon Ltd
Curve and coffers - Saint-Gobain Ecophon Ltd
Hybrid system air conditioning - Eaton-Williams Group Limited

Y41 Fans

Axial Fan - Air Control Industries Ltd
Axial, centrifugal, mixed flow fans and dust extraction units - Howden Buffalo
Axial, roof extract and centrifugal fans - Matthews & Yates Ltd
Backward Curve Fan - Air Control Industries Ltd
Chimney extractor fans - Poujoulat (UK) Ltd
Crossflow fans - Consort Equipment Products Ltd
Diagonal Fans - Air Control Industries Ltd
Domestic and commercial and industrial fans - Xpelair Ltd
Domestic and industrial fans - Airflow Developments Ltd
Dust and fume extraction - Horizon International Ltd
EC Fans - Air Control Industries Ltd
Fans - BOB Stevenson Ltd
Fans - Colt International
Fans - Domus Ventilation
Fans - Elta Fans Ltd
Fans - Gebhardt Kiloheat
Fans - Hotchkiss Air Supply
Fans - Mawdsleys Ber Ltd
Fans - McKenzie-Martin Ltd
fans - SCS Group
Fans - Vortice Ltd
Forward Curve Fan - Air Control Industries Ltd
Industrial axial fans and impellers - London Fan Company Ltd
Jet tunnel fans - Matthews & Yates Ltd
Mixed Flow Fans - Air Control Industries Ltd
PowerX, Lighting, Timers, Chimes, Wiring Accessories, Ventilation - KingShield - Green Brook
Road fans - Matthews & Yates Ltd
Road tunnel fans - Matthews & Yates Ltd
Tangential Fans - Air Control Industries Ltd
Twin fans - Ves Andover Ltd

Y42 Air filtration

10 Year guarantees - Fluidair Ltd
Air ailtration - Bassaire Ltd
Air cleaners - Warner Howard Group Ltd
Air cleaning equipment - Horizon International Ltd
Air filters - GVS Filter Technology UK Ltd
Air filters - The Filter Business Ltd
Air filters - Vokes Air
Air filtration - Camfil Farr Ltd
Air filtration - Donaldson Filtration (GB) Ltd
Air filtration - GVS Filter Technology UK
Air Filtration - Vortice Ltd
Air filtration (aircleaners) - Aircare Europe Ltd
Air Purifiers - De Longhi Limited
Air purifiers - Purified Air Ltd
Air quality consultancy - GVS Filter Technology UK Ltd
Air quality testing - Westbury Filters Limited
Antimicrobial filters - GVS Filter Technology UK Ltd
Carbon filters - GVS Filter Technology UK Ltd
Carbon filters - Westbury Filters Limited
Dust and fume extraction - Horizon International Ltd
Equipment filters - GVS Filter Technology UK
Face masks - GVS Filter Technology UK
Filter loss gauges - Westbury Filters Limited
Filtration - Fluidair Ltd
Filtration - TROX (UK) Ltd
Fit & disposal service - GVS Filter Technology UK Ltd
Health air filters - GVS Filter Technology UK
Industrial air filtration - GVS Filter Technology UK
Medical air filters - GVS Filter Technology UK
Odour control - Britannia Kitchen Ventilation Ltd
Panel filters - Westbury Filters Limited
Pleateed filters - Westbury Filters Limited
Replacement elements - Fluidair Ltd
Roll filters - Westbury Filters Limited
Rotary screw - Fluidair Ltd
Rotary sliding vane - Fluidair Ltd
Slimline filters - Westbury Filters Limited
Washable filters - Westbury Filters Limited

Y43 Heating/ Cooling coils

Chillers - Airedale International Air Conditioning Ltd
Condensers - Airedale International Air Conditioning Ltd
Fan Coils Units - Swegon Air Management Ltd
Heat exchangers gasketted plate - HRS Hevac Ltd
Heating and cooling coils - S & P Coil Products Ltd
Heating and cooling radiant panel manufacturer - Comyn Ching & Co (Solray) Ltd
Heating/ Cooling coils - Chromalox (UK) Ltd
Heating/Cooling coils - Andrews Sykes Hire Ltd

Y44 Air treatment

Air cleaners - GVS Filter Technology UK Ltd
Air dryers - Fluidair Ltd
Air treatment - Consort Equipment Products Ltd
Air treatment - Danfoss Ltd
Air treatment - Hertel Services
Condensate treatment - Fluidair Ltd
Condensation control - ProTen Services
Dehumidifiers - De Longhi Limited
Dehumidifiers - S & P Coil Products Ltd
Dehumification - Dantherm Ltd
Disinfection system - Britannia Kitchen Ventilation Ltd
Dust and fume extraction - Horizon International Ltd
Humidifiers - Eaton-Williams Group Limited
Local cooling units - Eaton-Williams Group Limited
Radon control - ProTen Services
Roof extract units - Ves Andover Ltd
Ultra violet chambers, lamps and control panels - Hanovia Ltd

Y45 Silencers/ Acoustic treatment

Abuse resistant panels - Salex Acoustics Limited
Accoustic flooring - Icopal Limited
Acoustic Baffles, Barriers, Ceiling Panels, Curtains, Attenuators, Enclosures, Panels, Louvers and Wall Panels - including perforated timber/metal - Acousticabs Industrial Noise Control Ltd
Acoustic Barriers - IAC Acoustic Company UK Ltd
Acoustic ceilings - Knauf AMF Ceilings Ltd
Acoustic cladding and lining products - Gilmour Ecometal
Acoustic Flooring Products - Coburn Sliding Systems Ltd
Acoustic inserts - Hotchkiss Air Supply
Acoustic products - Nendle Acoustic Company Ltd
Acoustic Walling Products - Coburn Sliding Systems Ltd
Attenuators/ silencers - Allaway Acoustics Ltd
Boiler Noise Silencer - Fernox
Building regs. Part E compliances - Sound Reduction Systems Ltd
Ceiling panels - Salex Acoustics Limited
Ductwork, silencers, acoustic products - Isolated Systems Ltd
Fabric wrapped panels - Salex Acoustics Limited
Impact resistant Acoustic Wall Panels - Knauf AMF Ceilings Ltd
Noise absorbing panels - Salex Acoustics Limited
Noise Limiters - AET.gb Ltd
Seamless ceilings - Salex Acoustics Limited
Silencers - Hotchkiss Air Supply
Silencers - Ves Andover Ltd
Silencers - Acoustic - Sound Service (Oxford) Ltd
Silencers/ Acoustic treatment - Domus Ventilation
Sound masking systems - AET.gb Ltd
Studio lining - Salex Acoustics Limited
Timber veneered panels - Salex Acoustics Limited
Wall panels - Salex Acoustics Limited

Y46 Grilles/ Diffusers/Louvres

Acoustic products - Nendle Acoustic Company Ltd
Anodised Aluminium coils - Alanod Ltd
Design and CAD support - Saint-Gobain Ecophon Ltd
Diffusion accessories - Panel & Louvre Co Ltd
Flange Covers - TEAM INDUSTRIAL SERVICES (UK) LIMITED
Grilles - Panel & Louvre Co Ltd
Grilles & diffusers - Hotchkiss Air Supply
Grilles and diffusers - TROX (UK) Ltd
Grilles, diffusers and louvres - Grille Diffuser & Louvre Co Ltd The
Grilles/ Diffusers/ Louvres - Aluline Precision Engineering Ltd
Grilles/ Diffusers/Louvres - Domus Ventilation
Grilles/Diffusers/Louvres - Isolated Systems Ltd
Grills /diffusers/ louvres - SCS Group
Integrated lighting systems - Saint-Gobain Ecophon Ltd
Louvers - McKenzie-Martin Ltd
Louvre, hit and miss ventilators - Rytons Building Products Ltd
Security grilles - Cooper Group Ltd
Smoke ventilation louvres - Matthews & Yates Ltd
Solar shading systems - Dales Fabrications Ltd

Y50 Thermal insulation

Acoustic Insulation - Sound Reduction Systems Ltd
Acoustic Insulation - Soundsorba Ltd
Aluzink insulated jacketing - SSAB Swedish Steel Ltd
Cork/ rubber - Olley & Sons Ltd, C
Dobelshield - SSAB Swedish Steel Ltd
Draught proofing/ loft insulation - National Insulation Association Ltd
Energy services - BM TRADA
Expanded polystyrene insulation - Jablite Ltd
Floor insulation - Springvale E P S
Foamglas Cellular glass insulation for cut to falls roof systems - Pittsburgh Corning (United Kingdom) Limited
Foamglas Cellular glass internal and external insulation for roof, wall, floor, below ground conditions and foundations - Pittsburgh Corning (United Kingdom) Limited
Garden Products - NMC (UK) Ltd
Insulation - Rockwool Ltd
Insulation - Skanda Acoustics Limited
Insulation cork - Olley & Sons Ltd, C
Insulation materials - Gradient Insulations (UK) Ltd
Pre-insulated pipework - CPV Ltd
Roof insulation - Springvale E P S
Sarnatherm insulation - Sarnafil Ltd
Sprayed Vermiculite - Thermica Ltd
Thermal Insulation - Aqua-Blue Designs
Thermal insulation - Domus Ventilation
Thermal insulation - Firebarrier International Ltd T/A Firebarrier Services Ltd
Thermal Insulation - Hawkins Insulation Ltd
Thermal insulation - Hertel Services
Thermal Insulation - Insulated Render & Cladding Association
Thermal Insulation - Isolated Systems Ltd
Thermal Insulation - Knauf Insulation Ltd
Thermal Insulation - Modern Plan Insulation Ltd
Thermal Insulation - National Insulation Association Ltd
Trade Association - Association of Specialist Fire Protection (ASFP)
Urethane foam industry trade association - British Urethane Foam Contractors Association
Wall insulation - Springvale E P S

Y51 Testing and commissioning of mechanical services

Acoustic testing, Air tightness testing, Secured by design, durability and weather tightness testing - BM TRADA
Equipment for measuring, testing and commissioning of mechanical services - PCE Instruments UK Ltd
Installation & Commissioning - GP Burners (CIB) Ltd
Testing and commissioning of mechanical services - Domus Ventilation
Testing and maintenance for fall arrest and safety - Bacon Group
Testing facilities for GRP tanks - APA

Y52 Vibration isolation mountings

Acoustic products - Nendle Acoustic Company Ltd
Anti - vibration mountings - MacLellan Rubber Ltd
Anti Vibration mountings and hangers - Salex Acoustics Limited
Anti vibration products - Nendle Acoustic Company Ltd
Anti-vibration mounts - Isolated Systems Ltd
Anti-vibration pads - Olley & Sons Ltd, C
Building vibration control products - Salex Acoustics Limited
Machine Mounting Anti Vibration Materials, Structural and sliding bearings and resilient - Tiflex Ltd
Structural. Bridge & Seismic Bearings - Tiflex Ltd
Vibration control equipment/containers - Mansfield Pollard & Co Ltd
Vibration isolation - Allaway Acoustics Ltd
Vibration Isolation - Sound Service (Oxford) Ltd
Vibration isolation mountings - Christie & Grey Ltd

Y53 Control components - mechanical

Boiler controls and accessories - Alpha Therm Ltd
Close Control - Airedale International Air Conditioning Ltd
Control - Airedale International Air Conditioning Ltd
Control - T-T Pumps & T-T controls
Control components - Danfoss Ltd
Control equipment, timers and relays - ABB Installation Products Ltd
Control Systems - Air Control Industries Ltd
Control systems - SK Environmental Ltd
Controls - Ves Andover Ltd
Embeded control systems - M.J. Electronic Services (International) Ltd
Hazardous area control gear - PFP Electrical Products Ltd
Heating controls - SAV United Kingdom Ltd
Heating programmers - Timeguard Ltd
Lighting controls - Thorlux Lighting
Moisture meters, hygrometers - Protimeter, GE Thermometrics (UK) Ltd
Pump selection software - Armstrong Integrated Ltd
Thermometers, hygrometers, hydrometers, pressure and altitude gauges - Brannan S & Sons Ltd
Thermometers, pressure gauges and associated instruments - Brannan Thermometers & Gauges
Thermostats - Teddington Controls Ltd
Valve Actuators - Flowserve Flow Control
Valve Refurbishment - Hodgkinson Bennis Ltd
Water Controls - Mode Lighting

Y59 Sundry common mechanical items

Air receivers - Flamco UK Ltd
Exterior surface heating - Uponor Ltd
Flexible plumbing - Uponor Ltd
Gaskets - Olley & Sons Ltd, C
Gaskets and Sealing Products - MacLellan Rubber Ltd
GRP Kiosks & modular enclosures - Group Four Glassfibre Ltd
Machines for Plastic Pipe Joinings - George Fischer Sales Ltd
Manufacturers of: Metal Cutting Circular Saws - Spear & Jackson Interntional Ltd
O Rings, bonded seals, grease guns, grease nipples and bucket pumps - Ashton Seals Ltd
Pipe cutting machines - George Fischer Sales Ltd
Pulley lines - James Lever 1856 Ltd
Resharpners of Circular saw blades - Spear & Jackson Interntional Ltd
Seals - Atkinson & Kirby Ltd
Smoke and natural ventilation systems - SE Controls
System 21 - the latest in enrgy efficiency - Servowarm
Welding and Brazing equipment \\ consumables - Johnson Matthey PLC - Metal Joining

Y60 Conduit and Cable trunking

Adaptable boxes - Vantrunk Engineering Ltd
All insulated plastic enclosures - Ensto Briticent Ltd
Aluminium Trunking Systems - Marshall-Tufflex Ltd
Cable management - Ackermann Ltd
Cable management - Hager Ltd
Cable management - Kem Edwards Ltd
Cable management systems - MK (MK Electric Ltd)
Cable management systems - REHAU Ltd
Cable management/Termination and Fixing accessories - Norslo - Green Brook
Cable routing - Hellermann Tyton
Cable tray - Legrand Electric Ltd
Cable trunking - Legrand Electric Ltd
Conduit and Cable Trunking - Barton Engineering
Conduit and ductwork - Polypipe Civils
Electrical cable management systems - Marshall-Tufflex Ltd
Electrical Conduit & Accessories - Kem Edwards Ltd
Flexible conduit systems - Adaptaflex Ltd
Floor laid flexible cable protectors for every application - Vulcascot Cable Protectors Ltd
Flooring systems - Legrand Electric Ltd
G R P systems - Marshall-Tufflex Ltd
L.S.F. Conduit - Aercon Consultants Ltd
Ladder rack - Legrand Electric Ltd
Lighting trunking - Legrand Electric Ltd
Metal cable trunking - Legrand Power Centre
Pipe supports - Unistrut Limited
Pre wired PVC conduit - Aercon Consultants Ltd
Specialised Applications - Marshall-Tufflex Ltd
Stainless steel conduit - Kensal CMS
Stainless Steel Enclosures - Electrix International Ltd
Stainless Steel Trunking and Conduit - Electrix International Ltd
Stainless Steel Wire Basket Tray - Electrix International Ltd
Steel and stainless steel enclosures - Ensto Briticent Ltd
Steel Cable Support System - Marshall-Tufflex Ltd
Trunking - Vantrunk Engineering Ltd

Y61 HV/ LV cables and wiring

Cable protection - Hellermann Tyton
Cables - Nexans UK Ltd
Cables and wiring accessories - Ellis Patents
Electrical cables - Pitacs Ltd
Electrical Insulation Blankets - MacLellan Rubber Ltd
HV/ LV cables & wiring - Metway Electrical Industries Ltd
HV/ LV cables and wiring - Anixter (UK) Ltd
Wiring accessories - MK (MK Electric Ltd)

Y62 Busbar trunking

Busbar - Marshall-Tufflex Ltd
Busbar power distribution systems - Electrak International Ltd
Busbar trunking - Legrand Electric Ltd
Busbar, cable management systems for floors - Legrand Power Centre
Inceiling busbar trunking - Electrak International Ltd
Stainless steel enclosures IP65 - Kensal CMS
Stainless steel trunking - Kensal CMS
Underfloor busbar trunking - Electrak International Ltd

Y63 Support components-cables

Cable ladders - Vantrunk Engineering Ltd
Cable management/Termination and Fixing accessories - Norslo - Green Brook
Cable routing - Hellermann Tyton
Cable support systems - Hadley Industries Plc
Cable supports - Unistrut Limited
Cable ties and cable clips - Unifix Ltd
Cable tray - Vantrunk Engineering Ltd
Cable tray/ladder - Unistrut Limited
Cleats and cable ties - Vantrunk Engineering Ltd
Office power, data and cable management system - Staverton (UK) Ltd
Pipe and cable suppoers - LPA Group PLC
Stainless Steel Cabinets - Electrix International Ltd
Stainless Steel Cable Tray - Electrix International Ltd
Stainless steel cable tray - Kensal CMS
Stainless Steel Supports & Fasteners - Electrix International Ltd
Support Components Cables - Ellis Patents
Support systems - Legrand Electric Ltd
Wire basket cable tray - Vantrunk Engineering Ltd

Y70 HV switchgear

HV Switchgear - Dynniq UK Ltd
HV switchgear - Hager Ltd
Switchboards - Technical Control Systems Ltd
Switchgear - Hawker Siddley Switchgear

Y71 LV switchgear and distribution boards

Circuit protection - MK (MK Electric Ltd)
Domestic switch gear - Eaton Electric Limited
Earth leakage electrical protection equipment - Paslode
Earth monitoring - Paslode
Electrical switchgear - Dorman Smith Switchgear
Enclosed isolators - Ensto Briticent Ltd
LV switchgear - T-T Pumps & T-T controls
LV Switchgear & Distribution Boards - Dynniq UK Ltd
LV switchgear and distribution boards - Eaton Electric Ltd
LV switchgear and distribution boards - Hager Ltd
Mains Distribution Assemblies 100A to 3000 A, 110v to 400v - Blakley Electrics Ltd
potentiometers - Omeg Ltd
RCDs - PowerBreaker - Green Brook
Residual current circuit breakers - Paslode
Residual current monitors - Paslode
Switches - Ensto Briticent Ltd
Switchgear - Green Brook
Switchgear - Hawker Siddley Switchgear

Y72 Contactors and starters

Contactors and starters - Eaton Electric Ltd
Contracts and starters - Danfoss Ltd

Y73 Luminaires and lamps

Associated accessories - Bernlite Ltd
Cable management systems - Vantrunk Engineering Ltd
Ceiling Lights - Astro Lighting Ltd
Coloured and clear covers for fluorescent lamps and fittings - Encapsulite International Ltd
Columns and brackets - DW Windsor Lighting
Converters for cold cathode - Mode Lighting (UK) Ltd
Direct and indirect luminaires - Lumitron Ltd
Downlights - Astro Lighting Ltd
Flameproof EExd fluorescents - PFP Electrical Products Ltd
Fluorescent and discharge lighting - Fitzgerald Lighting Ltd
General fluorescent lighting - Fluorel Ltd
Incandesant light bulbs and other domestic lighting - J.F. Poynter Ltd
Increased safety fluorescents - PFP Electrical Products Ltd
Lampholders - Bernlite Ltd
Lamps and electronic control gear - Osram Ltd
Light bulbs and fittings - British Electric Lamps Ltd
Light sensors - Timeguard Ltd
Lighting designers - Thorlux Lighting
Low voltage spots - Lumitron Ltd
Luminaire & Lamp - Andy Thornton Ltd
Luminaires - Ensto Briticent Ltd
Luminaires and lamps - Brandon Medical
Luminaires and lamps - Connect Lighting Systems (UK) Ltd
Luminaires and Lamps - Consult Lighting Ltd
Luminaires and lamps - Designplan Lighting Ltd
Luminaires and lamps - Eaton Electric Ltd
Luminaires and lamps - Focal Signs Ltd
Luminares & Lamps - Glamox Electric (UK) Ltd
Project management services - Saint-Gobain Ecophon Ltd
Spotlights - Astro Lighting Ltd
Stair components - Spindlewood
Wall Lights - Astro Lighting Ltd
Zone 1 Bulkheads - PFP Electrical Products Ltd
Zone 1 floodlights - PFP Electrical Products Ltd
Zone 1 wellglasses - PFP Electrical Products Ltd

Y74 Accessories for electrical services

Accessories for electrical services - Anixter (UK) Ltd
Accessories for electrical services - Brass Art Ltd
Accessories for electrical services - Tower Manufacturing
Dimming switches - Mode Lighting (UK) Ltd
Din-rail time switches and surge protectors - Timeguard Ltd
Domestic electrical accessories and dry cell batteries and torches - J.F. Poynter Ltd
Electrical Accessories - Legrand Electric Ltd
Electrical fittings and wire accessories - Legrand Electric Ltd
Electrical products - Panasonic UK Ltd
Electrical swithces - Wandsworth Elecrtical Ltd
General Electrical Products - WF Senate
General electrical products - wholesale - Jolec Electrical Supplies
Invisible light switches and sockets - Forbes & Lomax Ltd
Light switches - Proteus Switchgear
Modular wiring systems - Thorlux Lighting
Painted, nickel silver, brass and frosted acrylic stainless steel switches and sockets - Forbes & Lomax Ltd
Pipeline Gaskets & Seals WRAS Approved - MacLellan Rubber Ltd
Residual current protected skt outlets - Paslode
Secure connection systems - Hager Ltd
Switch and socket boxes - Legrand Power Centre
Switches - Teddington Controls Ltd
Time controllers, security light switches and RCD switched sockets - Timeguard Ltd
Track Support Materials - Tiflex Ltd
Ultrasonic sensors - ABB Installation Products Ltd
Wire accessories - Hellermann Tyton
Wiring accessories - Eaton Electric Ltd
Wiring accessories - Hager Ltd

Y80 Earthing and bonding components

Earth leakage electrical protection equipment - Paslode
Earth monitoring - Paslode
Earth Monitoring Equipment - Blakley Electrics Ltd

Y81 Testing & commissioning of electrical services

Appliance Testing - Hawkesworth Appliance Testing
Emergency Lighting - P4 Limited
Equipment for measuring, testing & commissioning of electrical services - PCE Instruments UK Ltd
Hygrometers - Protimeter, GE Thermometrics (UK) Ltd
Moisture meters - Protimeter, GE Thermometrics (UK) Ltd
Super Rod, Tools - ToolShield - Green Brook
Testing & commissioning of electrical services - Eaton Electric Ltd
Testing and maintenance of lightning protection - Bacon Group

Y82 Identification - electrical

Breezair Evaporative Coolers - Radiant Services Ltd
Cable identification - Hellermann Tyton
Identification labels - Mockridge Labels & Nameplates Ltd
Street/Area/Flood Lighting - CU Phosco Lighting

Y89 Sundry common electrical items

Automatic Pool covers - Golden Coast Ltd
Clip in conduit fittings - PFP Electrical Products Ltd
Custom build control panels - Golden Coast Ltd
Electrical Distribution Equipment - WT Henley Ltd
Electronic accessories - VELUX Co Ltd, The
Filter and poulton - PFP Electrical Products Ltd
MV primary and secondary products - Schneider Electric Ltd
Stainless steel isolators - Kensal CMS
Sundry common electrical items - Metway Electrical Industries Ltd
Sundry common electrical items - Tower Manufacturing

Y90 Fixing to building fabric

Cable tie and fixing assemblies - Hellermann Tyton
Fixings and fastenings - Tower Manufacturing
Frame cramps, restraint straps, sliding anchor stems - Vista Engineering Ltd
Nails - Stone Fasteners Ltd
Remedial fixing systems - Redifix Ltd
Rotary impact and masonry drills - Unifix Ltd
Stainless steel building components - Wincro Metal Industries Ltd
Wall ties - remedial - Redifix Ltd
Wood, coach, self tapping, fastbrolley screws, frame anchors, hammer and expansion plugs - Unifix Ltd

Y91 Off-site painting/ Anti-corrosion treatments

Anti-corrosion and sealing systems - Winn & Coales (Denso) Ltd
Corrosion Inhibitors - Kenyon Paints Limited
Hot dip galvanizing - Arkinstall Galvanizing Ltd
Hot dip galvinizing - Joseph Ash Ltd
Inks and metal coatings - Valspar UK Corporation Ltd
Off-site painting/ Anti-corrosion treatments - Aluline Precision Engineering Ltd
Paint and powder coatings - Trimite Ltd
Potable water coatings - Corroless Corrosion Control
Primers Rust Stabilising - Kenyon Paints Limited
Printing solutions - Hellermann Tyton
Thermoplastic coating powders - Plascoat Systems Ltd

Y92 Motor drives - electric

Automatic gates - Jackson H S & Son (Fencing) Ltd
Door motors - GfA UK Ltd
Drive Systems - Air Control Industries Ltd
Electric motor repairs - Pumps & Motors UK Ltd
Electrical motors - Eaton Electric Ltd
Motor drives (electric) - T-T Pumps & T-T controls
Motor drives-electric - Danfoss Ltd

Z10 Purpose made joinery

Architectural joinery manufacturers - Edmonds A & Co Ltd
Bespoke - Evertaut Ltd
Bespoke joinery - Howard Bros Joinery Ltd
Bespoke Joinery - Taskworthy Ltd
Bespoke joinery products - Alumasc Interior Building Products Limited
Bespoke laminated components - T B S Fabrications
Bespoke museum display cases - The Benbow Group
Bespoke Study, lounge, bedroom, fitted furniture - Hyperion Wall Furniture Ltd
Bespoke Window and External Door Manufacturers - Blairs Windows Limited
Bespoke windows and doors - Saveheat Group
Decorative wood moulding and carvings, cornice, picture rail, dado rail, skirting, architrave and pediments, radiator cabinet grilles - Winther Browne & co Ltd
Door joinery manufacturer - Humphrey & Stretton PLC
Hardwood mouldings - W.L. West & Sons Ltd
High class joinery - Platonoff & Harris Ltd
Joinery - Firco Ltd
Joinery solutions - Taskworthy Ltd
Machined softwood and machined MDF mouldings - Metsä Wood
Pine room paneling, bookcases and display cupboards - Hallidays UK Ltd
Propose Made Jointery - AS Newbould Ltd
Purpose made joinery - The Benbow Group
Purpose made Joinery - Canopy Products Ltd
Purpose made joinery - Enfield Speciality Doors
purpose made joinery - Jali Ltd
Purpose made joinery - Jeld-Wen UK Ltd
Purpose made joinery - Smith & Choyce Ltd
Purpose made joinery - Spindlewood
Purpose made timber bedroom joinery - Platonoff & Harris Ltd
Purpose made timber kitchen joinery - Platonoff & Harris Ltd
Purpose made timber vanity joinery - Platonoff & Harris Ltd
Radiator cabinets - Jali Ltd
Specialist joinery - Barlow Group
Specialist joinery - Barnwood Ltd
Specialist joinery - Cumberland Construction
Timber engineering services - Wyckham Blackwell Ltd
Timber specialist - Challenge Fencing Ltd
Window Manufacture - HansenFacades

Z11 Purpose made metalwork

Aluminium and steel fabricators - Ramsay & Sons (Forfar) Ltd
Aluminium extrusions, powder coating, anodising and fabrication - Kaye Aluminium plc
Aluminium fabrication - Panel Systems Ltd
Aluminum and steel standing seam roofing system - CA Group Ltd - MR-24 Division
Architectural metalwork - Broxap Ltd
Architectural metalwork - Andy Thornton Ltd
Architectural Metalwork - CB Arts Ltd
architectural metalwork - Ermine Engineering Co. Ltd
Architectural metalwork - Mackay Engineering
Architectural metalwork - Multitex GRP LLP
Architectural Metalwork - Wallis Conservation Limited trading as Dorothea Restorations
Architectural metalwork - Woodburn Engineering Ltd
Architectural metalworkers - Edmonds A & Co Ltd
Bespoke metal products - Alumasc Interior Building Products Limited
Bespoke museum display cases - The Benbow Group
Brass and bronze heritage products - Brass Art Ltd
Brick bond grilles - Priory Shutter & Door Co Ltd
Cast iron fittings and finishings - Company name: Britannia Metalwork Services Ltd
Ceiling tiles & Systems - British Gypsum Ltd
CNC milling and turning of specialist ports in metal and plastic - Griff Chains Ltd
Copper tubing - Wednesbury Tube
Custom sheet metal - Azimex Fabrications Ltd
Decorative castings - Andy Thornton Ltd
Engineering castings - Ballantine Castings
Galvanising Services - Birtley Group
GRP, aluminum, mild and stainless steel - Redman Fisher Engineering
Hot dip galvanizing - Corbett & Co (Galvanising) W Ltd
Lead ingots - R.M. Easdale & Co Ltd
Marine Craft - A & G Structures Ltd
Mesh Screens - Cadisch MDA
Metal fabrications - Squires Metal Fabrications Ltd
Metal framing - Unistrut Limited
Metal roofing and cladding - Ash & Lacy Building Products Ltd
Metal Spraying - A & G Structures Ltd
Metalwork - Doorfit Products Ltd
On site welding - C & W Fencing Ltd
Perforated sheet metal (mild steel, galvanised, aluminium, stainless steel and special alloys) - Multi Mesh Ltd
Purpose made joinery - Barlow Group
Purpose made metal work - Metalcraft (Tottenham) Ltd
Purpose made metalwork - Aluline Precision Engineering Ltd
Purpose Made Metalwork - BLM British Lead
Purpose made metalwork - Canopy Products Ltd
Purpose made metalwork - Consort Equipment Products Ltd
Purpose Made Metalwork - Deepdale Engineering Co Ltd
Purpose made metalwork - Hipkiss, H, & Co Ltd
Purpose made metalwork - Leander Architectural
Purpose made metalwork - NRG Fabrications
Purpose made metalwork - The Benbow Group
Purpose Made Metalworks - Blagg & Johnson Ltd
S.F.S. building systems (Metframe - Metsec Ltd
Seamless cold drawn copper tube - Lawton Tube Co Ltd, The
Security Grilles and Shutters - London Shopfitters Ltd
Special arichitectural metalwork - BF Bassett & Findley
Special castings in brass and bronze - Brass Art Ltd
Stainless steel and sheet metal - Kensal CMS
Stainless steel brackets - Kensal CMS
Stainless steel cleaning products - Kleen-Tex Industries Ltd
Stainless steel columns - Valmont Stainton
Stainless steel custom fabrication - Kensal CMS
Stainless steel fabrications - Component Developments
Stainless Steel Mesh - MMA Architectural Systems Ltd
Stainless Steel Rods - MMA Architectural Systems Ltd
Stainless steel wire mesh - Multi Mesh Ltd
Stainless Steel Wire products - MMA Architectural Systems Ltd
Stainless steel, angles, beams, tees, channels, flats and bar - IMS UK
Steel Cables - MMA Architectural Systems Ltd
Steel fabrication, plate bending & rolling, welding, drilling, turning, milling etc - Stevenson & Cheyne (1983)
Steel lintels - Jones of Oswestry Ltd
Steel plates, angles, RSJ's, Flats - Rainham Steel Co Ltd
Steel, Stainless steel and aluminium fabrications - Speedfab Midlands
Structural fixings - Expamet Building Products
Structures - Kee Klamp Ltd
Welding and Brazing equipment \\ consumables - Johnson Matthey PLC - Metal Joining
Welding engineers - Woodburn Engineering Ltd
Wirecloth, screens, filters, vent mesh and welded mesh - United Wire Ltd
Woven wirecloth, welded wiremesh, perforated metal, quarry screening, wire products - Potter & Soar Ltd

Z12 Preservative/ Fire retardant treatments for timber

Passive fire protection - Industrial Solutions - Actavo (UK) Ltd
Preservation - Cox Long Ltd
Preservative / fire retardent treatment - Brewer C & Sons Ltd
Preservative and fire retardant treatments for timber - Dover Trussed Roof Co Ltd
Preservative/Fire retardant treatments for timber - BM TRADA
Preservative/fire retardent treatments - Arch Timber Protection
Preservative/Fireretardant treatments for timber - Smith & Rodger Ltd
Timber treatment - ProTen Services
Timber treatment - Walker Timber Ltd
Trade Association - Association of Specialist Fire Protection (ASFP)

Z20 Fixings/ Adhesives

Adhesive - Loctite UK Ltd
Adhesive - Tremco Illbruck Ltd
Adhesive for access flooring/Laminating/Panel: Ultra High Performance – StarFix PED-ULTRA, High Performance – StarFix PED-PRO, Acoustic – StarFix ACOUSTIC, Laminating / Panel adhesive – StarFix PANEL-PRO - Star Uretech Ltd
Adhesive products - Henkel Consumer Adhesives
Adhesive Tape - Bostik Ltd
Adhesive tapes - Advance Tapes International Ltd
Adhesive Tapes - Hilton Banks Ltd
Adhesives - Atkinson & Kirby Ltd
Adhesives - Bostik Ltd
Adhesives - Building Adhesives Ltd
Adhesives - Dunlop Adhesives
Adhesives - Evode Ltd
Adhesives - Henkel Ltd
Adhesives - Kenyon Group Ltd
Adhesives - Kenyon Performance Adhesives
Adhesives - Sealocrete PLA Ltd
Adhesives - Tarkett Ltd
Adhesives - Tektura Plc
Adhesives - manufacturer - National Starch & Chemical Ltd
Adhesives and grouts - Shackerley (Holdings) Group Ltd incorporating Designer ceramics
Adhesives Design Toolkit - TWI Ltd
Adhesives for wall covering and wood - Ciret Limited
Adhesives selector - TWI Ltd
Adhesives, wood filler and glue - Humbrol
Admixtures - BASF plc, Construction Chemicals
Ahesives - Combustion Linings Ltd
Airtight adhesives and tapes - Fillcrete Ltd
Blue Polypropylene Ropes - James Lever 1856 Ltd
Cable clips - Artur Fischer (UK) Ltd
Cast-in fixing channel - Halfen Ltd
Chemical anchors - ITW Spit
Connectors - Simpson Strong-Tie®
Cyanoacrylate adhesives - Kenyon Group Ltd
Cyanoarylate adhesives - Kenyon Performance Adhesives
Elastic Bonding - Sika Ltd
Epoxy resins - Hatfield Ltd, Roy
Fastener systems for the roofing, cladding and construction industry - EJOT UK Limited
Fasteners - UK Fasteners Ltd
Fixing and adhesives - BASF plc, Construction Chemicals
Fixing for masonry - Vista Engineering Ltd
Fixing systems - remedial - Redifix Ltd
Fixings - British Gypsum Ltd
Fixings - Broen-Lab Ltd
Fixings - Canopy Products Ltd
Fixings - Hipkiss, H, & Co Ltd
Fixings - ITW Construction Products
Fixings - ITW Spit
Fixings - Power Plastics Ltd
Fixings - RFA-Tech Ltd
Fixings & adhesives - Olby H E & Co Ltd
Fixings / Adhesives - Interface Europe Ltd
Fixings and adhesives - Caswell & Co Ltd
Fixings and fastenings - Kem Edwards Ltd
Fixings/ Adhesives - Till & Whitehead Ltd
Fixings/ Adhesives - Tower Manufacturing
Fixings/Adhesives - Crowthorne Fencing
Flat roofing fasteners - SFS Intec LTD
Floor Covering Adhesives - Ardex UK Ltd
Flooring adhesives - Ball F & Co Ltd

Z20 Fixings/ Adhesives (con't)

Flooring adhesives, smoothing compounds - Laybond Products Ltd
Foill Tape - Bostik Ltd
For Flat roofing built up felt roofing - Chesterfelt Ltd
Frame fixings - Artur Fischer (UK) Ltd
Freyssinet Asphaltic plug joints - Pitchmastic PmB Ltd
General fixings - Artur Fischer (UK) Ltd
Glue guns - Kenyon Performance Adhesives
Glues, cleaners for PVCu window construction - VBH (GB) Ltd
Heavy Duty fixings - Artur Fischer (UK) Ltd
High Temperature Adhesives - Minkon Ltd
Hot melt adhesives - Kenyon Group Ltd
Hot melt ahesives - Kenyon Performance Adhesives
Hot melt guns - Kenyon Performance Adhesives
Industrial fasterners & raw materials - Montrose Fasteners
Large perforated headed, steel and stainless steel anchorages - bigHead Bonding Fasteners Ltd
Lateral Restraint Fixings - Redifix Ltd
Light & heavyduty anchors - ITW Construction Products
Lightweight fixings - Artur Fischer (UK) Ltd
Lintel Reinforcing - Redifix Ltd
Metal roofing and cladding - Ash & Lacy Building Products Ltd
Nailing Machines and Nails - Atkinson & Kirby Ltd
Packaging and security fasteners - Hellermann Tyton
Polyurethane adhesives - Dow Building Solutions
Polyurethane foam sealant - Dow Building Solutions
Polyurethane foam spray systems - Dow Building Solutions
Rayon Twines - James Lever 1856 Ltd
Resin Bonded Steel Female Sockets - Redifix Ltd
Resins and grouts - Helifix
Screned anchors - ITW Construction Products
Screws and frame fixings - VBH (GB) Ltd
Sealants - Kenyon Performance Adhesives
Self drilling fastener - SFS Intec LTD
Self tapping fasteners - SFS Intec LTD
Sisal Twines - James Lever 1856 Ltd
Special length studs BZP and S/Steel - Redifix Ltd
Stainless steel channel bolts & screws fixings etc - Ancon Limited
Stainless steel channel bolts & screws fixings etc -
Stainless steel fixings/fasteners - Wincro Metal Industries Ltd
Stainless steel fasteners - SFS Intec LTD
Stainless steel fixings/fasteners - Wincro Metal Industries Ltd
Stainless steel timber to masonry fixings - Helifix
Stainless steel warm roof fixings - Helifix
Steelwork fixings - Lindapter International
Structural adhesives - Kenyon Group Ltd
Structural steel connectors - Unistrut Limited
Styreen Free Resin - Redifix Ltd
Surface Mount Adhesives - bigHead Bonding Fasteners Ltd
Technical adhesive tapes - Beiersdorf (UK) Ltd
Threaded fasteners - Arnold Wragg Ltd
Tile adhesives - IKO PLC
Tiling adhesives and grout - Weber Building Solutions
Tying wire, spacers and chemicals for concrete - Hy-Ten Ltd
Valves - Cottam & Preedy Ltd
Various types of metal and plastic fasteners - Righton Ltd
Wall Paper Paste - Ciret Limited
Wallpaper Adhesives - Bartoline Ltd
Water based adhesives - Kenyon Group Ltd
Wood glue and resins - Wessex Resins & Adhesives Ltd

Z21 Mortars

Admixtures - Building Adhesives Ltd
Admixtures - Fosroc Ltd
Building solutions and compounds - IKO PLC
Cement - Combustion Linings Ltd
Cement admixtures - IKO PLC
Colour hardeners - Hatfield Ltd, Roy
Colouring admixtures - Hatfield Ltd, Roy
Grouts and resins - Helifix
High Temperature Cements - Minkon Ltd
Industrial hardeners - Hatfield Ltd, Roy
Manufacturers of mortars & Resin systems - Ancorite Surface Protection Ltd
Mortars - BASF plc, Construction Chemicals
Mortars - Flexcrete Technologies Limited
Mortars - LaFarge Cement UK
Mortars - Limelite - Tarmac Building Products Ltd
Powder - LANXESS Inorganic Pigments Group
Ready mixed fillers - Bartoline Ltd
Thin bed mortars, Repair Mortars - Ronacrete Ltd

Z22 Sealants

Block and patio sealers - Kingfisher Building Products Ltd
Butyl sealants and foam fillers - Scapa Tapes UK Ltd
Ceramic tiling tools & accessories - Building Adhesives Ltd
Chemical fixings - ITW Construction Products
Concrete products - SFS Intec LTD
Concrete Repair - Sika Ltd
Façade Sealants - Sika Ltd
Fillers - Loctite UK Ltd
Fire rated sealants - Compriband Ltd
Floor fixings - Lindapter International
Grouts - BASF plc, Construction Chemicals
Grouts - Building Adhesives Ltd
Heldite Jointing Compound - Heldite Ltd
High Temperature Sealants - Minkon Ltd
Impregnated foam sealants - Compriband Ltd
Insulating Glass Silicone Sealant - Dow Corning Europe S.A
Intumescent sealant - Mann McGowan Group
Mastic sealant - Trade Sealants Ltd
Metal roofing and cladding - Ash & Lacy Building Products Ltd
Movement joint materials - Building Adhesives Ltd
Natural stone & facade sealant - Dow Corning Europe S.A
Plaster Accessories - British Gypsum Ltd
Polyurathane sealers - Hatfield Ltd, Roy
Sealant - Olby H E & Co Ltd
Sealants - Adshead Ratcliffe & Co Ltd
Sealants - Amari Plastics Plc
Sealants - BASF plc, Construction Chemicals
Sealants - Brewer C & Sons Ltd
Sealants - Evode Ltd
Sealants - Exitex Ltd
Sealants - Firebarrier International Ltd T/A Firebarrier Services Ltd
Sealants - Fosroc Ltd
Sealants - Henkel Ltd
Sealants - IKO PLC
Sealants - Loctite UK Ltd
Sealants - Ogilvie Construction Ltd
Sealants - Sealocrete PLA Ltd
Sealants - Smith & Rodger Ltd
Sealants - Till & Whitehead Ltd
Sealants - Tower Manufacturing
Sealants - Tremco Illbruck Ltd
Sealants & Adhesives - Illbruck Sealant Systems UK Ltd
Sealants & Primers - Ciret Limited
Sealants, adhesives and building chemicals - Kalon Decorative Products
Sealers - Hatfield Ltd, Roy
Sealers for paving-Resiblock Ltd - Resiblock Ltd
Sealing systems - silicones and impregnated tape - VBH (GB) Ltd
Self-smoothing compounds & surface treatments - Building Adhesives Ltd
Silicone - Unifix Ltd
Silicone products - JAMAK Fabrication Europe
Silicone sealants - Compriband Ltd
Silicone weatherseal sealant - Dow Corning Europe S.A
Structural Glazing Silicone Sealant - Dow Corning Europe S.A
Waterproof expansion joints - Radflex Contract Services Ltd
Weatherproofing silicone sealant - Dow Corning Europe S.A

Z31 Powder coatings

aluminium/hybrid curtain walling, windows and doors - Senior Aluminium Systems plc
Powder coating - Consort Equipment Products Ltd
Powder coatings - Aluline Precision Engineering Ltd
Powder coatings - Arkema France
Powder coatings - Plastic Coatings Ltd
Powder coatings - Valspar Powder Coatings Ltd

Z32 Liquid coatings

Anti-carbonation coatings - Glixtone Ltd
Anti-graffiti coatings - Andura Coatings Ltd
Anti-graffiti coatings - Glixtone Ltd
Anti-microbial liquid coatings - Liquid Technology Ltd
Automotive lubricants and industrial paints - Witham Oil & Paint Ltd
Chemical stains - Hatfield Ltd, Roy
Clear protective coatings - Andura Coatings Ltd
Fungicidal coatings - Glixtone Ltd
Hi-tech Paint Finishes - Bristol Metal Spraying & Protective Coatings Ltd
Liquid coatings - Andrews Coatings Ltd
Liquid coatings - Arkema France
Liquid coatings - Conren Ltd
Liquid coatings - Flexcrete Technologies Limited
Liquid coatings - Smith & Rodger Ltd
Liquid Coatings - Wessex Resins & Adhesives Ltd
Liquide coatings - Mells Roofing Ltd
Nylon coating - Plastic Coatings Ltd
Paint - Fired Earth
Polymer modified coatings - Ronacrete Ltd
Protective coating - Industrial Solutions - Actavo (UK) Ltd
Specialist decorative protective surface paints and coatings - Glixtone Ltd

Z33 Anodising

Anodised metal - Alanod Ltd

PRODUCTS AND SERVICES WORKS SECTIONS INDEX

A

B

C

C (cont'd)

D

E

F

R (cont'd)

S

T